University Casebook Series

December, 1984

ACCOUNTING AND THE LAW, Fourth Edition (1978), with Problems Pamphlet (Successor to Dohr, Phillips, Thompson & Warren)

George C. Thompson, Professor, Columbia University Graduate School of Business.
Robert Whitman, Professor of Law, University of Connecticut.
Ellis L. Phillips, Jr., Member of the New York Bar.
William C. Warren, Professor of Law Emeritus, Columbia University.

ACCOUNTING FOR LAWYERS, MATERIALS ON (1980)

David R. Herwitz, Professor of Law, Harvard University.

ADMINISTRATIVE LAW, Seventh Edition (1979), with 1983 Problems Supplement (Supplement edited in association with Paul R. Verkuil, Dean and Professor of Law, Tulane University)

Walter Gellhorn, University Professor Emeritus, Columbia University.
Clark Byse, Professor of Law, Harvard University.
Peter L. Strauss, Professor of Law, Columbia University.

ADMIRALTY, Second Edition (1978), with Statute and Rule Supplement

Jo Desha Lucas, Professor of Law, University of Chicago.

ADVOCACY, see also Lawyering Process

AGENCY, see also Enterprise Organization

AGENCY—PARTNERSHIPS, Third Edition (1982)

Abridgement from Conard, Knauss & Siegel's Enterprise Organization, Third Edition.

ANTITRUST: FREE ENTERPRISE AND ECONOMIC ORGANIZATION, Sixth Edition (1983), with Problems in Antitrust Supplement

Louis B. Schwartz, Professor of Law, University of Pennsylvania.
John J. Flynn, Professor of Law, University of Utah.
Harry First, Professor of Law, New York University.

ANTITRUST SUPPLEMENT—SELECTED STATUTES AND RELATED MATERIALS (1977)

John J. Flynn, Professor of Law, University of Utah.

BUSINESS ORGANIZATION, see also Enterprise Organization

BUSINESS PLANNING, Temporary Second Edition (1984)

David R. Herwitz, Professor of Law, Harvard University.

BUSINESS TORTS (1972)

Milton Handler, Professor of Law Emeritus, Columbia University.

CHILDREN IN THE LEGAL SYSTEM (1983)

Walter Wadlington, Professor of Law, University of Virginia.
Charles H. Whitebread, Professor of Law, University of Southern California.
Samuel Davis, Professor of Law, University of Georgia.

CIVIL PROCEDURE, see Procedure

CLINIC, see also Lawyering Process

COMMERCIAL LAW (1983)

Robert L. Jordan, Professor of Law, University of California, Los Angeles.
William D. Warren, Professor of Law, University of California, Los Angeles.

COMMERCIAL LAW, CASES & MATERIALS ON, Fourth Edition (1985)

E. Allan Farnsworth, Professor of Law, Columbia University.
John Honnold, Professor of Law, University of Pennsylvania.

COMMERCIAL PAPER, Third Edition (1984)

E. Allan Farnsworth, Professor of Law, Columbia University.

COMMERCIAL PAPER (1983) (Reprinted from COMMERCIAL LAW)

Robert L. Jordan, Professor of Law, University of California, Los Angeles.
William D. Warren, Professor of Law, University of California, Los Angeles.

COMMERCIAL PAPER AND BANK DEPOSITS AND COLLECTIONS (1967), with Statutory Supplement

William D. Hawkland, Professor of Law, University of Illinois.

COMMERCIAL TRANSACTIONS—Principles and Policies (1982)

Alan Schwartz, Professor of Law, University of Southern California.
Robert E. Scott, Professor of Law, University of Virginia.

COMPARATIVE LAW, Fourth Edition (1980)

Rudolf B. Schlesinger, Professor of Law, Hastings College of the Law.

COMPETITIVE PROCESS, LEGAL REGULATION OF THE, Second Edition (1979), with 1984 Statutory Supplement and 1984 Case Supplement

Edmund W. Kitch, Professor of Law, University of Chicago.
Harvey S. Perlman, Professor of Law, University of Virginia.

CONFLICT OF LAWS, Eighth Edition (1984)

Willis L. M. Reese, Professor of Law, Columbia University,
Maurice Rosenberg, Professor of Law, Columbia University.

CONSTITUTIONAL LAW, Sixth Edition (1981), with 1984 Supplement

Edward L. Barrett, Jr., Professor of Law, University of California, Davis.
William Cohen, Professor of Law, Stanford University.

CONSTITUTIONAL LAW: THE STRUCTURE OF GOVERNMENT (Reprinted from CONSTITUTIONAL LAW, Sixth Edition), with 1984 Supplement

Edward L. Barrett, Jr., Professor of Law, University of California, Davis.
William Cohen, Professor of Law, Stanford University.

CONSTITUTIONAL LAW, CIVIL LIBERTY AND INDIVIDUAL RIGHTS, Second Edition (1982), with 1983 Supplement

William Cohen, Professor of Law, Stanford University.
John Kaplan, Professor of Law, Stanford University.

CONSTITUTIONAL LAW, Tenth Edition (1980), with 1984 Supplement (Supplement edited in association with Frederick F. Schauer, Professor of Law, College of William and Mary)

Gerald Gunther, Professor of Law, Stanford University.

CONSTITUTIONAL LAW, INDIVIDUAL RIGHTS IN, Third Edition (1981) (Reprinted from CONSTITUTIONAL LAW, Tenth Edition), with 1984 Supplement (Supplement edited in association with Frederick F. Schauer, Professor of Law, College of William and Mary)

Gerald Gunther, Professor of Law, Stanford University.

CONSUMER TRANSACTIONS (1983), with Selected Statutes and Regulations Supplement

Michael M. Greenfield, Professor of Law, Washington University.

CONTRACT LAW AND ITS APPLICATION, Third Edition (1983)

The late Addison Mueller, Professor of Law, University of California, Los Angeles.
Arthur I. Rosett, Professor of Law, University of California, Los Angeles.
Gerald P. Lopez, Professor of Law, University of California, Los Angeles.

CONTRACT LAW, STUDIES IN, Third Edition (1984)

Edward J. Murphy, Professor of Law, University of Notre Dame.
Richard E. Speidel, Professor of Law, Northwestern University.

CONTRACTS, Fourth Edition (1982)

John P. Dawson, Professor of Law Emeritus, Harvard University.
William Burnett Harvey, Professor of Law and Political Science, Boston University.
Stanley D. Henderson, Professor of Law, University of Virginia.

CONTRACTS, Third Edition (1980), with Statutory Supplement

E. Allan Farnsworth, Professor of Law, Columbia University.
William F. Young, Professor of Law, Columbia University.

CONTRACTS, Second Edition (1978), with Statutory and Administrative Law Supplement (1978)

Ian R. Macneil, Professor of Law, Cornell University.

COPYRIGHT, PATENTS AND TRADEMARKS, see also Competitive Process

COPYRIGHT, PATENT, TRADEMARK AND RELATED STATE DOCTRINES, Second Edition (1981), with Problem Supplement and Statutory Supplement

Paul Goldstein, Professor of Law, Stanford University.

COPYRIGHT, Unfair Competition, and Other Topics Bearing on the Protection of Literary, Musical, and Artistic Works, Third Edition (1978)

Benjamin Kaplan, Professor of Law Emeritus, Harvard University,
Ralph S. Brown, Jr., Professor of Law, Yale University.

CORPORATE FINANCE, Second Edition (1979), with 1984 Supplement

Victor Brudney, Professor of Law, Harvard University.
Marvin A. Chirelstein, Member of New York Bar.

CORPORATE READJUSTMENTS AND REORGANIZATIONS (1976)

Walter J. Blum, Professor of Law, University of Chicago.
Stanley A. Kaplan, Professor of Law, University of Chicago.

CORPORATION LAW, BASIC, Second Edition (1979), with 1983 Case and Documentary Supplement

Detlev F. Vagts, Professor of Law, Harvard University.

CORPORATIONS, see also Enterprise Organization

CORPORATIONS, Fifth Edition—Unabridged (1980), with 1984 Supplement

The late William L. Cary, Professor of Law, Columbia University.
Melvin Aron Eisenberg, Professor of Law, University of California, Berkeley.

CORPORATIONS, Fifth Edition—Abridged (1980), with 1984 Supplement

The late William L. Cary, Professor of Law, Columbia University.
Melvin Aron Eisenberg, Professor of Law, University of California, Berkeley.

CORPORATIONS, Second Edition (1982), with 1982 Corporation and Partnership Statutes, Rules and Forms

Alfred F. Conard, Professor of Law, University of Michigan.
Robert N. Knauss, Dean of the Law School, University of Houston.
Stanley Siegel, Professor of Law, University of California, Los Angeles.

CORPORATIONS COURSE GAME PLAN (1975)

David R. Herwitz, Professor of Law, Harvard University.

CORRECTIONS, SEE SENTENCING

CREDIT TRANSACTIONS AND CONSUMER PROTECTION (1976)

John Honnold, Professor of Law, University of Pennsylvania.

CREDITORS' RIGHTS, see also Debtor-Creditor Law

CRIMINAL JUSTICE ADMINISTRATION, Second Edition (1982), with 1984 Supplement

Frank W. Miller, Professor of Law, Washington University.
Robert O. Dawson, Professor of Law, University of Texas.
George E. Dix, Professor of Law, University of Texas.
Raymond I. Parnas, Professor of Law, University of California, Davis.

CRIMINAL LAW, Third Edition (1983)

Fred E. Inbau, Professor of Law Emeritus, Northwestern University.
James R. Thompson, Professor of Law Emeritus, Northwestern University.
Andre A. Moenssens, Professor of Law, University of Richmond.

CRIMINAL LAW (1982), with 1983 Supplement

Peter W. Low, Professor of Law, University of Virginia.
John C. Jeffries, Jr., Professor of Law, University of Virginia.
Richard C. Bonnie, Professor of Law, University of Virginia.

CRIMINAL LAW, Third Edition (1980)

Lloyd L. Weinreb, Professor of Law, Harvard University.

CRIMINAL LAW AND PROCEDURE, Sixth Edition (1984)

Rollin M. Perkins, Professor of Law Emeritus, University of California, Hastings College of the Law.
Ronald N. Boyce, Professor of Law, University of Utah.

UNIVERSITY CASEBOOK SERIES—Continued

CRIMINAL PROCEDURE, Second Edition (1980), with 1984 Supplement

Fred E. Inbau, Professor of Law Emeritus, Northwestern University.
James R. Thompson, Professor of Law Emeritus, Northwestern University.
James B. Haddad, Professor of Law, Northwestern University.
James B. Zagel, Chief, Criminal Justice Division, Office of Attorney General of Illinois.
Gary L. Starkman, Assistant U. S. Attorney, Northern District of Illinois.

CRIMINAL PROCESS, Third Edition (1978), with 1984 Supplement

Lloyd L. Weinreb, Professor of Law, Harvard University.

DAMAGES, Second Edition (1952)

Charles T. McCormick, late Professor of Law, University of Texas.
William F. Fritz, late Professor of Law, University of Texas.

DEBTOR–CREDITOR LAW (1984)

Theodore Eisenberg, Professor of Law, Cornell University.

DEBTOR–CREDITOR LAW, Second Edition (1981), with Statutory Supplement

William D. Warren, Dean of the School of Law, University of California, Los Angeles.
William E. Hogan, Professor of Law, New York University.

DECEDENTS' ESTATES (1971)

Max Rheinstein, late Professor of Law Emeritus, University of Chicago.
Mary Ann Glendon, Professor of Law, Boston College.

DECEDENTS' ESTATES AND TRUSTS, Sixth Edition (1982)

John Ritchie, Emeritus Dean and Wigmore Professor of Law, Northwestern University.
Neill H. Alford, Jr., Professor of Law, University of Virginia.
Richard W. Effland, Professor of Law, Arizona State University.

DOMESTIC RELATIONS, see also Family Law

DOMESTIC RELATIONS, Successor Edition (1984)

Walter Wadlington, Professor of Law, University of Virginia.

ELECTRONIC MASS MEDIA, Second Edition (1979)

William K. Jones, Professor of Law, Columbia University.

EMPLOYMENT DISCRIMINATION (1983)

Joel W. Friedman, Professor of Law, Tulane University.
George M. Strickler, Professor of Law, Tulane University.

ENERGY LAW (1983)

Donald N. Zillman, Professor of Law, University of Utah.
Laurence Lattman, Dean of Mines and Engineering, University of Utah.

ENTERPRISE ORGANIZATION, Third Edition (1982), with 1982 Corporation and Partnership Statutes, Rules and Forms Supplement

Alfred F. Conard, Professor of Law, University of Michigan.
Robert L. Knauss, Dean of the Law School, University of Houston.
Stanley Siegel, Professor of Law, University of California, Los Angeles.

ENVIRONMENTAL POLICY LAW, 1985 Edition

Thomas J. Schoenbaum, Professor of Law, Tulane University.

EQUITY, see also Remedies

EQUITY, RESTITUTION AND DAMAGES, Second Edition (1974)

Robert Childres, late Professor of Law, Northwestern University.
William F. Johnson, Jr., Professor of Law, New York University.

ESTATE PLANNING, Second Edition (1982), with 1985 Case, Text and Documentary Supplement

David Westfall, Professor of Law, Harvard University.

ETHICS, see Legal Profession, and Professional Responsibility

ETHICS AND PROFESSIONAL RESPONSIBILITY (1981) (Reprinted from THE LAWYERING PROCESS)

Gary Bellow, Professor of Law, Harvard University.
Bea Moulton, Legal Services Corporation.

EVIDENCE, Fifth Edition (1984)

John Kaplan, Professor of Law, Stanford University.
Jon R. Waltz, Professor of Law, Northwestern University.

EVIDENCE, Seventh Edition (1983), with Rules and Statute Supplement (1984)

Jack B. Weinstein, Chief Judge, United States District Court.
John H. Mansfield, Professor of Law, Harvard University.
Norman Abrams, Professor of Law, University of California, Los Angeles.
Margaret Berger, Professor of Law, Brooklyn Law School.

FAMILY LAW, see also Domestic Relations

FAMILY LAW (1978), with 1983 Supplement

Judith C. Areen, Professor of Law, Georgetown University.

FAMILY LAW AND CHILDREN IN THE LEGAL SYSTEM, STATUTORY MATERIALS (1981)

Walter Wadlington, Professor of Law, University of Virginia.

FEDERAL COURTS, Seventh Edition (1982), with 1984 Supplement

Charles T. McCormick, late Professor of Law, University of Texas.
James H. Chadbourn, late Professor of Law, Harvard University.
Charles Alan Wright, Professor of Law, University of Texas.

FEDERAL COURTS AND THE FEDERAL SYSTEM, Hart and Wechsler's Second Edition (1973), with 1981 Supplement

Paul M. Bator, Professor of Law, Harvard University.
Paul J. Mishkin, Professor of Law, University of California, Berkeley.
David L. Shapiro, Professor of Law, Harvard University.
Herbert Wechsler, Professor of Law, Columbia University.

FEDERAL PUBLIC LAND AND RESOURCES LAW (1981), with 1983 Case Supplement and 1984 Statutory Supplement

George C. Coggins, Professor of Law, University of Kansas.
Charles F. Wilkinson, Professor of Law, University of Oregon.

FEDERAL RULES OF CIVIL PROCEDURE, 1984 Edition

FEDERAL TAXATION, see Taxation

FOOD AND DRUG LAW (1980), with Statutory Supplement

Richard A. Merrill, Dean of the School of Law, University of Virginia.
Peter Barton Hutt, Esq.

FUTURE INTERESTS (1958)

Philip Mechem, late Professor of Law Emeritus, University of Pennsylvania.

FUTURE INTERESTS (1970)

Howard R. Williams, Professor of Law, Stanford University.

FUTURE INTERESTS AND ESTATE PLANNING (1961), with 1962 Supplement

W. Barton Leach, late Professor of Law, Harvard University.
James K. Logan, formerly Dean of the Law School, University of Kansas.

GOVERNMENT CONTRACTS, FEDERAL, Successor Edition (1985)

John W. Whelan, Professor of Law, Hastings College of the Law.

INJUNCTIONS, Second Edition (1984)

Owen M. Fiss, Professor of Law, Yale University.
Doug Rendleman, Professor of Law, College of William and Mary.

INSTITUTIONAL INVESTORS, 1978

David L. Ratner, Professor of Law, Cornell University.

INSURANCE (1971)

William F. Young, Professor of Law, Columbia University.

INTERNATIONAL LAW, see also Transnational Legal Problems and United Nations Law

INTERNATIONAL LAW IN CONTEMPORARY PERSPECTIVE (1981), with Essay Supplement

Myres S. McDougal, Professor of Law, Yale University.
W. Michael Reisman, Professor of Law, Yale University.

INTERNATIONAL LEGAL SYSTEM, Second Edition (1981), with Documentary Supplement

Joseph Modeste Sweeney, Professor of Law, Tulane University.
Covey T. Oliver, Professor of Law, University of Pennsylvania.
Noyes E. Leech, Professor of Law, University of Pennsylvania.

INTRODUCTION TO LAW, see also Legal Method, On Law in Courts, and Dynamics of American Law

INTRODUCTION TO THE STUDY OF LAW (1970)

E. Wayne Thode, late Professor of Law, University of Utah.
Leon Lebowitz, Professor of Law, University of Texas.
Lester J. Mazor, Professor of Law, University of Utah.

JUDICIAL CODE and Rules of Procedure in the Federal Courts with Excerpts from the Criminal Code, 1984 Edition

Henry M. Hart, Jr., late Professor of Law, Harvard University.
Herbert Wechsler, Professor of Law, Columbia University.

JURISPRUDENCE (Temporary Edition Hardbound) (1949)

Lon L. Fuller, Professor of Law Emeritus, Harvard University.

JUVENILE, see also Children

UNIVERSITY CASEBOOK SERIES—Continued

JUVENILE JUSTICE PROCESS, Second Edition (1976), with 1980 Supplement

Frank W. Miller, Professor of Law, Washington University.
Robert O. Dawson, Professor of Law, University of Texas.
George E. Dix, Professor of Law, University of Texas.
Raymond I. Parnas, Professor of Law, University of California, Davis.

LABOR LAW, Ninth Edition (1981), with 1983 Case Supplement and 1977 Statutory Supplement

Archibald Cox, Professor of Law, Harvard University.
Derek C. Bok, President, Harvard University.
Robert A. Gorman, Professor of Law, University of Pennsylvania.

LABOR LAW, Second Edition (1982), with Statutory Supplement

Clyde W. Summers, Professor of Law, University of Pennsylvania.
Harry H. Wellington, Dean of the Law School, Yale University.
Alan Hyde, Professor of Law, Rutgers University.

LAND FINANCING, Third Edition (1985)

The late Norman Penney, Professor of Law, Cornell University.
Richard F. Broude, Member of the California Bar.
Roger Cunningham, Professor of Law, University of Michigan.

LAW AND MEDICINE (1980)

Walter Wadlington, Professor of Law and Professor of Legal Medicine, University of Virginia.
Jon R. Waltz, Professor of Law, Northwestern University.
Roger B. Dworkin, Professor of Law, Indiana University, and Professor of Biomedical History, University of Washington.

LAW, LANGUAGE AND ETHICS (1972)

William R. Bishin, Professor of Law, University of Southern California.
Christopher D. Stone, Professor of Law, University of Southern California.

LAW, SCIENCE AND MEDICINE (1984)

Judith C. Areen, Professor of Law, Georgetown University.
Patricia A. King, Professor of Law, Georgetown University.
Steven P. Goldberg, Professor of Law, Georgetown University.
Alexander M. Capron, Professor of Law, Georgetown University.

LAWYERING PROCESS (1978), with Civil Problem Supplement and Criminal Problem Supplement

Gary Bellow, Professor of Law, Harvard University.
Bea Moulton, Professor of Law, Arizona State University.

LEGAL METHOD (1980)

Harry W. Jones, Professor of Law Emeritus, Columbia University.
John M. Kernochan, Professor of Law, Columbia University.
Arthur W. Murphy, Professor of Law, Columbia University.

LEGAL METHODS (1969)

Robert N. Covington, Professor of Law, Vanderbilt University.
E. Blythe Stason, late Professor of Law, Vanderbilt University.
John W. Wade, Professor of Law, Vanderbilt University.
Elliott E. Cheatham, late Professor of Law, Vanderbilt University.
Theodore A. Smedley, Professor of Law, Vanderbilt University.

UNIVERSITY CASEBOOK SERIES—Continued

LEGAL PROFESSION (1970)

Samuel D. Thurman, Dean of the College of Law, University of Utah.
Ellis L. Phillips, Jr., Professor of Law, Columbia University.
Elliott E. Cheatham, late Professor of Law, Vanderbilt University.

LEGAL PROFESSION, THE, Responsibility and Regulation (1985)

Geoffrey C. Hazard, Jr., Professor of Law, Yale University.
Deborah L. Rhode, Professor of Law, Stanford University.

LEGISLATION, Fourth Edition (1982) (by Fordham)

Horace E. Read, late Vice President, Dalhousie University.
John W. MacDonald, Professor of Law Emeritus, Cornell Law School.
Jefferson B. Fordham, Professor of Law, University of Utah.
William J. Pierce, Professor of Law, University of Michigan.

LEGISLATIVE AND ADMINISTRATIVE PROCESSES, Second Edition (1981)

Hans A. Linde, Judge, Supreme Court of Oregon.
George Bunn, Professor of Law, University of Wisconsin.
Fredericka Paff, Professor of Law, University of Wisconsin.
W. Lawrence Church, Professor of Law, University of Wisconsin.

LOCAL GOVERNMENT LAW, Revised Edition (1975)

Jefferson B. Fordham, Professor of Law, University of Utah.

MASS MEDIA LAW, Second Edition (1982) with 1985 Supplement

Marc A. Franklin, Professor of Law, Stanford University.

MENTAL HEALTH PROCESS, Second Edition (1976), with 1981 Supplement

Frank W. Miller, Professor of Law, Washington University.
Robert O. Dawson, Professor of Law, University of Texas.
George E. Dix, Professor of Law, University of Texas.
Raymond I. Parnas, Professor of Law, University of California, Davis.

MUNICIPAL CORPORATIONS, see Local Government Law

NEGOTIABLE INSTRUMENTS, see Commercial Paper

NEGOTIATION (1981) (Reprinted from THE LAWYERING PROCESS)

Gary Bellow, Professor of Law, Harvard Law School.
Bea Moulton, Legal Services Corporation.

NEW YORK PRACTICE, Fourth Edition (1978)

Herbert Peterfreund, Professor of Law, New York University.
Joseph M. McLaughlin, Dean of the Law School, Fordham University.

OIL AND GAS, Fourth Edition (1979)

Howard R. Williams, Professor of Law, Stanford University.
Richard C. Maxwell, Professor of Law, University of California, Los Angeles.
Charles J. Meyers, Dean of the Law School, Stanford University.

ON LAW IN COURTS (1965)

Paul J. Mishkin, Professor of Law, University of California, Berkeley.
Clarence Morris, Professor of Law Emeritus, University of Pennsylvania.

PATENTS AND ANTITRUST (Pamphlet) (1983)

Milton Handler, Professor of Law Emeritus, Columbia University.
Harlan M. Blake, Professor of Law, Columbia University.
Robert Pitofsky, Professor of Law, Georgetown University.
Harvey J. Goldschmid, Professor of Law, Columbia University.

PERSPECTIVES ON THE LAWYER AS PLANNER (Reprint of Chapters One through Five of Planning by Lawyers) (1978)

Louis M. Brown, Professor of Law, University of Southern California.
Edward A. Dauer, Professor of Law, Yale University.

PLANNING BY LAWYERS, MATERIALS ON A NONADVERSARIAL LEGAL PROCESS (1978)

Louis M. Brown, Professor of Law, University of Southern California.
Edward A. Dauer, Professor of Law, Yale University.

PLEADING AND PROCEDURE, see Procedure, Civil

POLICE FUNCTION, Third Edition (1982), with 1984 Supplement

Reprint of Chapters 1–10 of Miller, Dawson, Dix and Parnas's CRIMINAL JUSTICE ADMINISTRATION, Second Edition.

PREPARING AND PRESENTING THE CASE (1981) (Reprinted from THE LAWYERING PROCESS)

Gary Bellow, Professor of Law, Harvard Law School.
Bea Moulton, Legal Services Corporation.

PREVENTIVE LAW, see also Planning by Lawyers

PROCEDURE—CIVIL PROCEDURE, Second Edition (1974), with 1979 Supplement

The late James H. Chadbourn, Professor of Law, Harvard University.
A. Leo Levin, Professor of Law, University of Pennsylvania.
Philip Shuchman, Professor of Law, Cornell University.

PROCEDURE—CIVIL PROCEDURE, Fifth Edition (1984)

Richard H. Field, late Professor of Law, Harvard University.
Benjamin Kaplan, Professor of Law Emeritus, Harvard University.
Kevin M. Clermont, Professor of Law, Cornell University.

PROCEDURE—CIVIL PROCEDURE, Third Edition (1976), with 1982 Supplement

Maurice Rosenberg, Professor of Law, Columbia University.
Jack B. Weinstein, Professor of Law, Columbia University.
Hans Smit, Professor of Law, Columbia University.
Harold L. Korn, Professor of Law, Columbia University.

PROCEDURE—PLEADING AND PROCEDURE: State and Federal, Fifth Edition (1983)

David W. Louisell, late Professor of Law, University of California, Berkeley.
Geoffrey C. Hazard, Jr., Professor of Law, Yale University.
Colin C. Tait, Professor of Law, University of Connecticut.

PROCEDURE—FEDERAL RULES OF CIVIL PROCEDURE, 1983 Edition

PRODUCTS LIABILITY (1980)

Marshall S. Shapo, Professor of Law, Northwestern University.

PRODUCTS LIABILITY AND SAFETY (1980), with 1983 Case and Documentary Supplement

W. Page Keeton, Professor of Law, University of Texas.
David G. Owen, Professor of Law, University of South Carolina.
John E. Montgomery, Professor of Law, University of South Carolina.

PROFESSIONAL RESPONSIBILITY, Third Edition (1984), with 1985 Selected National Standards Supplement

Thomas D. Morgan, Dean of the Law School, Emory University.
Ronald D. Rotunda, Professor of Law, University of Illinois.

PROPERTY, Fifth Edition (1984)

John E. Cribbet, Dean of the Law School, University of Illinois.
Corwin W. Johnson, Professor of Law, University of Texas.

PROPERTY—PERSONAL (1953)

S. Kenneth Skolfield, late Professor of Law Emeritus, Boston University.

PROPERTY—PERSONAL, Third Edition (1954)

Everett Fraser, late Dean of the Law School Emeritus, University of Minnesota.
Third Edition by Charles W. Taintor, late Professor of Law, University of Pittsburgh.

PROPERTY—INTRODUCTION, TO REAL PROPERTY, Third Edition (1954)

Everett Fraser, late Dean of the Law School Emeritus, University of Minnesota.

PROPERTY—REAL AND PERSONAL, Combined Edition (1954)

Everett Fraser, late Dean of the Law School Emeritus, University of Minnesota.
Third Edition of Personal Property by Charles W. Taintor, late Professor of Law, University of Pittsburgh.

PROPERTY—FUNDAMENTALS OF MODERN REAL PROPERTY, Second Edition (1982)

Edward H. Rabin, Professor of Law, University of California, Davis.

PROPERTY—PROBLEMS IN REAL PROPERTY (Pamphlet) (1969)

Edward H. Rabin, Professor of Law, University of California, Davis.

PROPERTY, REAL (1984)

Paul Goldstein, Professor of Law, Stanford University.

PROSECUTION AND ADJUDICATION, Second Edition (1982), with 1984 Supplement

Reprint of Chapters 11–26 of Miller, Dawson, Dix and Parnas's CRIMINAL JUSTICE ADMINISTRATION, Second Edition.

PUBLIC REGULATION OF DANGEROUS PRODUCTS (paperback) (1980)

Marshall S. Shapo, Professor of Law, Northwestern University.

PUBLIC UTILITY LAW, see Free Enterprise, also Regulated Industries

REAL ESTATE PLANNING (1980), with 1980 Problems, Statutes and New Materials Supplement

Norton L. Steuben, Professor of Law, University of Colorado.

REAL ESTATE TRANSACTIONS (1980), with Statute, Form and Problem Supplement

Paul Goldstein, Professor of Law, Stanford University.

RECEIVERSHIP AND CORPORATE REORGANIZATION, see Creditors' Rights

REGULATED INDUSTRIES, Second Edition, 1976

William K. Jones, Professor of Law, Columbia University.

REMEDIES (1982) with 1984 Case Supplement

Edward D. Re, Chief Judge, U. S. Court of International Trade.

RESTITUTION, Second Edition (1966)

John W. Wade, Professor of Law, Vanderbilt University.

SALES (1980)

Marion W. Benfield, Jr., Professor of Law, University of Illinois.
William D. Hawkland, Chancellor, Louisiana State University Law Center.

SALES AND SALES FINANCING, Fifth Edition (1984)

John Honnold, Professor of Law, University of Pennsylvania.

SALES LAW AND THE CONTRACTING PROCESS (1982)

Reprint of Chapters 1–10 of Schwartz and Scott's Commercial Transactions.

SECURED INTERESTS IN PERSONAL PROPERTY (1984)

Douglas G. Baird, Professor of Law, University of Chicago.
Thomas H. Jackson, Professor of Law, Stanford University.

SECURED TRANSACTIONS IN PERSONAL PROPERTY (1983) (Reprinted from COMMERCIAL LAW)

Robert L. Jordan, Professor of Law, University of California, Los Angeles.
William D. Warren, Professor of Law, University of California, Los Angeles.

SECURITIES REGULATION, Fifth Edition (1982), with 1984 Cases and Releases Supplement and 1984 Selected Statutes, Rules and Forms Supplement

Richard W. Jennings, Professor of Law, University of California, Berkeley.
Harold Marsh, Jr., Member of the California Bar.

SECURITIES REGULATION (1982), with 1983 Supplement

Larry D. Soderquist, Professor of Law, Vanderbilt University.

SECURITY INTERESTS IN PERSONAL PROPERTY (1985) (Reprinted from Sales and Sales Financing, Fifth Edition)

John Honnold, Professor of Law, University of Pennsylvania.

SENTENCING AND THE CORRECTIONAL PROCESS, Second Edition (1976)

Frank W. Miller, Professor of Law, Washington University.
Robert O. Dawson, Professor of Law, University of Texas.
George E. Dix, Professor of Law, University of Texas.
Raymond I. Parnas, Professor of Law, University of California, Davis.

SOCIAL SCIENCE IN LAW, Cases and Materials (1985)

John Monahan, Professor of Law, University of Virginia.
Laurens Walker, Professor of Law, University of Virginia.

SOCIAL WELFARE AND THE INDIVIDUAL (1971)

Robert J. Levy, Professor of Law, University of Minnesota.
Thomas P. Lewis, Dean of the College of Law, University of Kentucky.
Peter W. Martin, Professor of Law, Cornell University.

TAX, POLICY ANALYSIS OF THE FEDERAL INCOME (1976)

William A. Klein, Professor of Law, University of California, Los Angeles.

TAXATION, FEDERAL INCOME (1976), with 1983 Supplement

Erwin N. Griswold, Dean Emeritus, Harvard Law School.
Michael J. Graetz, Professor of Law, University of Virginia.

TAXATION, FEDERAL INCOME, Fourth Edition (1982)

James J. Freeland, Professor of Law, University of Florida.
Stephen A. Lind, Professor of Law, University of Florida.
Richard B. Stephens, Professor of Law Emeritus, University of Florida.

TAXATION, FEDERAL INCOME, Volume I, Personal Income Taxation (1972), with 1983 Case Supplement; Volume II, Taxation of Partnerships and Corporations, Second Edition (1980), with 1983 Legislative Supplement

Stanley S. Surrey, Professor of Law, Harvard University.
William C. Warren, Professor of Law Emeritus, Columbia University.
Paul R. McDaniel, Professor of Law, Boston College Law School.
Hugh J. Ault, Professor of Law, Boston College Law School.

TAXATION, FEDERAL WEALTH TRANSFER, Second Edition (1982)

Stanley S. Surrey, Professor of Law, Harvard University.
William C. Warren, Professor of Law Emeritus, Columbia University.
Paul R. McDaniel, Professor of Law, Boston College Law School.
Harry L. Gutman, Instructor, Harvard Law School and Boston College Law School.

TAXATION OF INDIVIDUALS, PARTNERSHIPS AND CORPORATIONS, PROBLEMS in the (1978)

Norton L. Steuben, Professor of Law, University of Colorado.
William J. Turnier, Professor of Law, University of North Carolina.

TAXATION, FUNDAMENTALS OF PARTNERSHIP, Cases and Materials (1985)

Stephen A. Lind, Professor of Law, University of California, Hastings.
Stephen Schwarz, Professor of Law, University of California, Hastings.
Daniel J. Lathrope, Professor of Law, University of California, Hastings.
Joshua Rosenberg, Professor of Law, University of San Francisco.

TAXES AND FINANCE—STATE AND LOCAL (1974)

Oliver Oldman, Professor of Law, Harvard University.
Ferdinand P. Schoettle, Professor of Law, University of Minnesota.

TORT LAW AND ALTERNATIVES, Third Edition (1983)

Marc A. Franklin, Professor of Law, Stanford University.
Robert L. Rabin, Professor of Law, Stanford University.

TORTS, Seventh Edition (1982)

William L. Prosser, late Professor of Law, University of California, Hastings College.
John W. Wade, Professor of Law, Vanderbilt University.
Victor E. Schwartz, Professor of Law, American University.

TORTS, Third Edition (1976)

Harry Shulman, late Dean of the Law School, Yale University.
Fleming James, Jr., Professor of Law Emeritus, Yale University.
Oscar S. Gray, Professor of Law, University of Maryland.

TRADE REGULATION, Second Edition (1983)

Milton Handler, Professor of Law Emeritus, Columbia University.
Harlan M. Blake, Professor of Law, Columbia University.
Robert Pitofsky, Professor of Law, Georgetown University.
Harvey J. Goldschmid, Professor of Law, Columbia University.

TRADE REGULATION, see Antitrust

TRANSNATIONAL LEGAL PROBLEMS, Second Edition (1976) with 1982 Case and Documentary Supplement

Henry J. Steiner, Professor of Law, Harvard University.
Detlev F. Vagts, Professor of Law, Harvard University.

TRIAL, see also Evidence, Making the Record, Lawyering Process and Preparing and Presenting the Case

TRIAL ADVOCACY (1968)

A. Leo Levin, Professor of Law, University of Pennsylvania.
Harold Cramer, of the Pennsylvania Bar.
Maurice Rosenberg, Professor of Law, Columbia University, Consultant.

TRUSTS, Fifth Edition (1978)

George G. Bogert, late Professor of Law Emeritus, University of Chicago.
Dallin H. Oaks, President, Brigham Young University.

TRUSTS AND SUCCESSION (Palmer's), Fourth Edition (1983)

Richard V. Wellman, Professor of Law, University of Georgia.
Lawrence W. Waggoner, Professor of Law, University of Michigan.
Olin L. Browder, Jr., Professor of Law, University of Michigan.

UNFAIR COMPETITION, see Competitive Process and Business Torts

UNITED NATIONS LAW, Second Edition (1967), with Documentary Supplement (1968)

Louis B. Sohn, Professor of Law, Harvard University.

WATER RESOURCE MANAGEMENT, Second Edition (1980), with 1983 Supplement

Charles J. Meyers, Dean of the Law School, Stanford University.
A. Dan Tarlock, Professor of Law, Indiana Unversity.

WILLS AND ADMINISTRATION, Fifth Edition (1961)

Philip Mechem, late Professor of Law, University of Pennsylvania.
Thomas E. Atkinson, late Professor of Law, New York University.

WORLD LAW, see United Nations Law

*

University Casebook Series

CONSTITUTIONAL LAW

CASES AND MATERIALS

By

EDWARD L. BARRETT, Jr.
Professor of Law, University of California, Davis

WILLIAM COHEN
C. Wendell and Edith M. Carlsmith
Professor of Law, Stanford University

SEVENTH EDITION

Mineola, New York
THE FOUNDATION PRESS, INC.
1985

Library of Congress Cataloging in Publication Data

Barrett, Edward L.
  Constitutional law.

  (University casebook series)
  Includes index.
  1. United States—Constitutional law—Cases.
I. Cohen, William. II. Title. III. Series.
KF4549.B3 1985   342.73   84–29979
ISBN 0–88277–224–4   347.302

For Beth and Nancy

*

PREFACE

Some long-time users of this book may notice a change on page one. The bold-faced legend beginning that page has read, from the time of the first edition in 1959, "CASES ON CONSTITUTIONAL LAW." In this seventh edition, it reads "CONSTITUTIONAL LAW CASES AND MATERIALS." We want to reassure users that this change simply marks a belated stab at consistency [1]—to make the first page coincide with the book's title. [2] This book's philosophy remains as it has been from the beginning. We described it in the preface to the sixth edition as a book that attempts to be "at the same time intellectually challenging and flexible enough to be used by law teachers with widely varying approaches." Our experience has suggested, too, that most of the major reorganization accomplished in the sixth edition has worked, and we have resisted the temptation to start over merely to innovate. The preface to the sixth edition, reproduced below, explains much of the organization of this seventh edition.

Still, each new edition of this book has had to be more than a melding of a fat supplement into the previous edition. [3] Moreover, our own teaching has shown that some of the last edition's organization either did not teach as well as we thought it would or that it could be improved. The largest organizational change this time has been a return to the organization of the fifth edition for the substantive due process and equal protection cases, considering each concept in a separate chapter. Other changes have been the consequence of further developments in the case law since the last edition. They include reorganization, usually with increased internal outlining, of: the materials on standing in Chapter 3; Chapter 5 on the scope of state regulatory power; Chapter 8 on separation of powers; the state action cases in Chapter 13; and Chapter 15 on time, place, and manner regulation of speech. [4]

While we held the manuscript open through the end of January, 1985, no relevant Supreme Court cases in the 1984–1985 Term came down before our

---

1. We confess that none of the editors of this book had ever noticed the discrepancy. It was discovered, just as the manuscript was being sent off, by our eagle-eyed friend, Professor Gerald Gunther.

2. The reasons for the discrepancy are even more puzzling than our failure to notice it in twenty-five years. Our speculation is that the first edition was among the pioneers using the now-ubiquitous "cases and materials" title, but that the first page was composed using the then-universal "cases on" title.

3. While this edition is nearly 100 pages shorter than the last edition, that is the result of the new type face. Had our previous type style, unfortunately no longer available, been used, there would have been a slight increase in length. We apologize, as we do each time, for the increase, but it is considerably less than the 474 pages in the last supplement to the sixth edition.

4. Special thanks are due to Professor Marc Rohr of Nova University for his extensive and perceptive suggestions for re-doing the case and controversy section in Chapter 3 and for useful suggestions at other places in the book.

cut-off date. Decisions in that term will be covered in a supplement available in August 1985.

EDWARD L. BARRETT, JR.
WILLIAM COHEN

Davis, California
Stanford, California
February, 1985

PREFACE TO THE SIXTH EDITION

Although it follows on the heels of major revisions in the fourth and fifth editions, the sixth edition of the book is a more ambitious restructuring. We could attribute much of the change to the usual outpouring of major constitutional decisions of the Supreme Court in the four years since the last edition. However, while the number of new pages in the United States Reports involving the topics we cover seems to increase geometrically each year, this is the first time that the membership of the Court has remained constant between editions of this book. It would overstate the case considerably to describe the interval between editions as marked by major new approaches to constitutional adjudication. Rather, it has been a period of continued elaboration by an eclectic, and often divided, Court.

Obviously, the occasion for major revision has been the addition of a new co-editor to this volume. We can report that it has been a true collaboration. While each of us took primary responsibility for about half of the book, we have spent considerable time critiquing each other's outlines, organization, editing and drafts. There are few chapters that either of us can identify as primarily our own work product. This book represents the distillation of our experience in teaching constitutional law, which combines to total more than fifty years in the classroom.[1]

Our approaches were occasionally sharply different, requiring us to spend considerable time in redrafting to produce a finished product both of us could use comfortably in our teaching. We did begin, however, with clear agreement on the basic goal—to produce a book which was at the same time intellectually challenging and flexible enough to be used by law teachers with widely varying approaches to the material. To the extent that it is possible to do so, we have relied on the raw materials—cases, constitutional provisions, and statutes—allowing teachers maximum freedom to pursue their own teaching strategies and requiring students to create their own generalizations from the materials. Unfortunately, the great bulk of relevant material has required more compromise than previous editions. There are more brief forms of cases, and more textual notes. Still, we have tried to keep notes lucid and impartial, and have avoided the temptation to use them as vehicles for expressing our views on or our approaches to controversial questions. We have also attempted to minimize questions and problems which interest us, but may impede the use of the book by others. In short, the book is intended as a teaching tool for a wide variety of approaches, and not as a text, research aid, or forum for our own conclusions. (As was said in the preface to the previous edition, we respect the judgment of those whose works follow a different strategy. Particularly, we have often learned much from Gerald Gunther's brilliant book, Cases and Materials on Constitutional Law [10th ed. 1980].)

This edition continues the trend of the previous edition, increasing the use of internal outlining within chapters. Also, most chapters and many

---

1. The implications of the statistic contained in the last clause of this sentence comes as a shock to both of us. It is particularly disturbing that solutions to the basic mysteries of constitutional law seem more elusive to us now than when we first entered the classroom.

sections begin with introductory notes explaining the scope of their coverage, and the rationale for their organization and selection of materials. Many of the cases appearing both here and in the fifth edition or supplement have been re-edited. While the result has usually been to shorten the printed excerpt, the reports of some cases have been expanded.

Coverage of this edition. Part I of this edition examines the institution of judicial review. A brief historical note was added to the text of the Constitution in Chapter 1, dealing with the history of its adoption. Text dealing with the history of the adoption of the Bill of Rights and the Civil War amendments was also moved here from other sections of the book. In Chapter 2, we have returned to the organization of some earlier editions, adding the material on Congressional control of federal court jurisdiction to the discussion of Marbury v. Madison. Chapter 3, which deals with issues of federal jurisdiction, has major changes. The changes are modest in section 3 of that chapter, which covers issues of case and controversy. Sections 1 and 2 however, are almost entirely new. Section 1 covers the process of Supreme Court review of state court decisions, and section 2 deals with constitutional adjudication begun in federal courts. Basic themes of both sections concern the friction created by the final responsibility of state courts to declare state law and federal courts to declare federal law, and the actual or potential concurrent jurisdiction of the two court systems in constitutional litigation. The increased use of text notes should make it possible to assign all, or portions, of these sections as outside reading. (Our experience has been that time has been too short to do justice to these problems in class but, nevertheless, students need some grounding in basic federal jurisdiction to understand many constitutional decisions.) Still, the materials are structured to provide opportunity for lively classroom discussion of those topics suggested by an individual instructor's available time, or interest.

Part II looks at the allocation of governmental powers—between the nation and the states and among the President, Congress, and the courts. Chapter 4 on the scope of national power contains much of the material included in a separate historical chapter in the previous edition. The principal changes have involved the use of more textual notes to reduce the space allocated to the interesting and useful historical development and some minor internal reorganization. Chapter 5 on the scope of state regulatory power is a substantial revision of Chapter 6 of the fifth edition. Many of the older cases have been shortened in order to make room for the series of recent cases in which the Court has been taking a new look at old doctrines. The production and trade cases have been reorganized into three major groups—those restricting the importation of goods, those restricting exportation, and those restricting entry of out-of-state businesses—but can easily be reorganized to fit the inclinations of individual teachers. Of the fourteen principal cases in this chapter, all but four have been decided since the printing of the fifth edition.

Chapter 6 is a total restructuring of the materials relating to state taxation and it is hoped the new format will tempt teachers to restore the subject to their classes. An elaborate introductory note summarizes the historical development and emphasizes the interrelationships between the regulation and the taxation cases. The remainder of the chapter takes advantage of the fact that the Court in the past few years has reexamined its approach to taxation cases and moved substantially toward simpler doctrines emphasizing the realities of the burdens on commerce and abandoning many of the purely formal distinctions which characterized the earlier cases. Seven cases, the earliest decided in 1976, constitute the substance of the chapter.

The organization of Chapter 7, dealing with intergovernmental relationships, remains much as it was in the last edition. A major change has been the elimination of much of the text in the previous edition, and the use of a few principal cases as the content of this chapter. The lively nature of the issues of state immunity and autonomy is demonstrated by the fact that most of the principal cases have been decided in the last five years. The major change in Chapter 8 on separation of powers has been to limit the focus of that chapter to conflicts between the President and Congress.

The fifth edition's Part III—Government and the Individual—has now been subdivided into two parts with the current Part III covering due process and equal protection, and Part IV covering the first amendment.

Chapter 9 which opens Part III presents the historical materials relating to the interrelationship of the Bill of Rights and the Civil War amendments. It is a reorganization of the materials presented in Chapters 10 and 11 of the fifth edition, omitting the historical materials which have been transferred to Chapter 1. Chapter 10 discusses the various constitutional doctrines which limit government in enacting economic regulatory legislation. Section 1 covers the due process cases, with some shortening of the previous historical coverage. Section 2 features two recent contract clause cases and asks the question whether that clause imposes restrictions beyond those of due process. Section 3 is a substantial revision of the materials arising under the just compensation clause. Substantially all of the material from earlier editions has been replaced by three recent cases which explore the range of problems. Section 4 discusses the equal protection limitation in the economic area. It also introduces the students to the analytical problems presented by equal protection which carry over into the materials in Chapters 11 and 12.

Chapter 11 brings together the due process and equal protection cases relating to legislation which burdens fundamental personal interests. The chapter is organized in terms of the interest at stake rather than the constitutional clause being applied. Section 1 deals with privacy, personal autonomy, and family relationships; section 2 with voting and elections; section 3 with travel and interstate migration; and section 4 with provision of essential governmental services. This organization is intended to highlight the process by which the Court determines those interests which are subjected to special protection and to permit comparison of the way due process and equal protection are used for that purpose. Again the materials can easily be reordered if it is thought desirable to discuss separately the due process and equal protection cases. Chapter 12 brings together the equal protection cases where the classifying factor is the basis for heightened judicial scrutiny—the suspect classification cases. The first six sections represent minor changes in the materials in the previous edition. Section 7 brings together the race and gender cases on the requirement of showing a discriminatory purpose in addition to discriminatory impact. Section 8 introduces the problems underlying affirmative action—"benign" discrimination—with the gender cases and follows with the three major race cases—*Bakke, Weber* and *Klutznick*. The demands of publishing schedules have forced us to allocate major amounts of space to these important cases even though cases before the Court during the 1980 term (which will be incorporated in a 1981 Supplement) may render one or more of them less important.

Chapter 13 is new. It builds on materials on procedural due process contained in a section in the fifth edition but represents a major change in emphasis. The chapter is not designed to teach the basic coverage of the procedural aspect of due process. Instead, it uses the procedure cases to focus on the substantive coverage of due process—what is the "liberty" and "property" which is protected—and to explore the interrelationships of the substantive and procedural guarantees. The "conclusive presumption" cases are included in this chapter because they raise the related question whether due process constrains the legislature from proceeding by classification rather than by individualized hearings.

Chapter 14, which covers the state action concept and explores the scope of Congressional power to enforce the Civil War amendments, is much changed from the equivalent chapter in the last edition. We decided to begin, as in earlier editions, with the Civil Rights Cases, and to structure the rest of the chapter to ask the question how far that case's narrow reading of the amendments, and concomitant narrow construction of federal enforcement power, represent current constitutional law. Generally, there has been, along with reorganization, a substantial replacement of some cases with text, and considerable expansion of the material dealing with Congressional power. The order of presenting the state action cases in section 2 is considerably different from the previous edition, which organized the cases chronologically. We have separated, in distinct subsections, those cases whose principal theme is public function or state enforcement of private action, with the third subsection focusing on the remainder of the significant state action cases. Section 3 contains the relevant Reconstruction and contemporary civil rights laws. Text covers the fate of Reconstruction laws after decision of the Civil Rights Cases, and some of the non-constitutional issues of interpretation which have been resolved since re-discovery of those laws in the last four decades. The issue of Congressional power to outlaw private discrimination has been subdivided into two sections, dealing respectively with the thirteenth and fourteenth amendments. Section 4, on the thirteenth amendment power, consists entirely of principal cases beginning with the 1968 decision in Jones v. Alfred H. Mayer Co. These cases illustrate both the sweeping nature of the Court's construction of remaining fragments of the 1866 Civil Rights Act, and the impact of that construction on constitutional issues surrounding the enforcement power under the thirteenth amendment. Section 5, dealing with the scope of fourteenth amendment power to prohibit private discrimination, in contrast to the previous section consists entirely of text.

It has been our experience that teaching this material through cases, given the available time and the difficulty of separating the constitutional kernel from very technical chaff of statutory construction, has not been satisfactory. Section 6, which is considerably enlarged, deals with the general issue of Congressional power to expand or restrict the scope of constitutionally protected liberty through exercise of the enforcement power. Separate subsections consider the power to provide "remedies" and potential Congressional power to "interpret" the Constitution.

Part IV covers the first amendment. The three chapters of the previous edition covering the speech and press clauses have been expanded to four chapters, and completely re-organized. Those four chapters attempt to consider separately the issues surrounding control of speech content, control of time, place and manner of speech, defining the penumbral rights associated with speech, and issues of freedom for the printed media. As in the previous edition, the fifth chapter in this Part completes the analysis with the religion clauses.

Chapter 15 combines most of the diverse areas where the court has grappled with the control of speech because of content. It begins, as did previous editions, with an exploration of basic first amendment theory as applied to seditious speech. The first section concludes with some basic questions about first amendment theory and the judicial process. After a digression in section 2, which deals with overbreadth and prior restraint theory, section 3 examines the other major doctrinal areas concerning control of speech content—defamation and privacy, obscenity, offensive speech, and commercial speech.

The organization of Chapter 16 is similar to that of the first part of the similar chapter in the last edition. Section 1 provides an initial look at the intellectual problem of controls which combine concern with content with time or place restrictions (a pervasive theme), and the possible application of equal protection analysis to discriminatory speech restrictions. Section 2 deals with the traditional public forum—the use of parks and streets. Succeeding sections deal with less traditional forums which are publicly owned, and restrictions designed either to protect users of private property or control them. New in this edition is a subsection dealing with application of first amendment theory to government speech in the context of controlling government property whose primary function is speech. Throughout this chapter, many changes were necessitated by cases decided since publication of the previous edition.

Chapter 17 is new, and groups together all instances of indirect restriction of speech, and penumbral rights associated with speech. Most of the material included here, however, was in the previous edition, although located elsewhere. The specific topics covered are symbolic expression, compelled affirmation of belief, freedom to associate and not to associate (including restrictions on political campaigns), compelled disclosure of belief and association, speech and association rights of government employees, and restrictions on speech and association as a condition of granting other government benefits.

Chapter 18 deals with the press. The organizing philosophy of the equivalent chapter in the previous edition was to group materials dealing with problems which impact primarily on the press. This chapter concentrates on a narrower inquiry whether there is anything special about the media, and whether the press clause provides protection beyond that provided by general conceptions of freedom of speech. (Accordingly, material dealing with defamation and privacy, obscenity, and commercial advertising have been moved to Chapter 15, as part of the general issue of defining constitutionally protected speech). Specific topics covered here are: control of publication of state secrets and information prejudicing fair trials; private rights of access to the privately owned media; press access to government information; government access to confidential press information; and the special problem of the electronic media.

Chapter 19, which deals with religion, is the least changed of the chapters in this part. Beyond taking account of cases decided since publication of the last edition, and some expansion in the editing of a few cases, the most noticeable changes are a minor reorganization of the free exercise section and elimination of the note on litigation over church property.

. . .

Suggestions for course coverage. We would not expect any user of this book to assign it from cover to cover, without deletions or changes in order. There are too many ways to structure a constitutional law course for any book to reflect them all. One reason for the bloated size of major constitutional law casebooks is the obligation to provide materials sufficient for a wide range of courses. Internal outlining within chapters has increased again, making it still easier for each instructor to reduce coverage and change the order of presentation.

We can report that the two co-editors plan to assign materials from this book in very different ways. One of us begins, after *Marbury*, with coverage of due process, equal protection, and the first amendment; turns then to federalism issues of the extent of federal power (including Chapter 14 on power to enforce the Civil War amendments) and state power; and saves issues of case, controversy and judiciability for last (including there some selected issues of separation of powers) after students have had a thorough grounding in substantive constitutional law concepts. The other editor presents materials, with significant omissions, more nearly in the order in which the chapters appear. One of us treats issues of taxation of multi-state enterprise, while the other avoids them as he would avoid contagious disease. Each of us prefers his own order of approach. Without the device of a dissenting preface, we have been unable to agree to a coherent structure for suggested omissions or the preferable order of assigning materials to recommend to others. This time, we offer no suggestions for course coverage, despite the subtitle which precedes this part of the preface.

. . .

Style. The restatement of facts of principal cases are indicated by square brackets. Citations to briefs and records, internal cross references in opinions and footnotes of the Court, have been omitted without specific indication. Footnotes which have been retained have not been renumbered. Footnotes to cases added by the editors are indicated by letters.

Acknowledgments. We have learned most of what we know from conversations with former and present colleagues, and the extensive literature of constitutional law. If our intellectual debts are too numerous to acknowledge, we can acknowledge our more finite debt for the research assistance provided by Andrew Morrow of the Stanford Law School class of 1980, John Osterhaus of the Stanford Law School class of 1981, and for the extensive secretarial services of Mrs. Jean Castle of the Stanford Law School and the "Second Floor Secretariat" at U.C. Davis Law School, in the preparation of this edition.

Finally, we acknowledge a debt to Paul Bruton, co-editor of the first four editions, and John Honnold, co-editor of the first three. While they have not participated in preparation of the last two editions, their imprint is still upon the book and upon our own education in constitutional law.

EDWARD L. BARRETT, JR.
WILLIAM COHEN

Davis, California
Stanford, California
March, 1981

*

SUMMARY OF CONTENTS

Page

PREFACE _____ xxi

TABLE OF CASES _____ lxiii

PART I. THE CONSTITUTION AND THE COURTS: THE JUDICIAL FUNCTION IN CONSTITUTIONAL CASES

Chapter 1. The Constitution _____ 2

Section
1. The Constitution of the United States of America _____ 2
2. History of the Adoption of the Constitution and Its Most Significant Amendments _____ 15
   A. The Articles of Confederation and the Original Constitution _____ 15
   B. The Bill of Rights _____ 16
   C. The Adoption of the Civil War Amendments_____ 19

Chapter 2. Judicial Review _____ 23

Section
1. The Legitimacy of Judicial Review _____ 23
2. Congressional Control of Judicial Review by the Federal Courts _____ 36

Chapter 3. The Jurisdiction of Federal Courts in Constitutional Cases _____ 43

Section
1. Supreme Court Review of State Court Decisions _____ 43
   A. History and Structure _____ 43
   B. Issues of State Law in the Supreme Court: The Adequate and Independent State Ground_____ 48
   C. The Distinction Between Obligatory and Discretionary Jurisdiction _____ 56
2. Constitutional Litigation Initiated in the Federal Courts _____ 63
   A. Jurisdiction of the Federal Courts in Cases Involving Federal Law Issues_____ 64
   B. Enforcement of Federal Rights in Suits Against State Officers: The Eleventh Amendment _____ 66
   C. Non-Constitutional Restrictions on Federal Court Injunctions Against Unconstitutional State Laws_____ 79
3. Cases and Controversies and Justiciability _____ 87
   A. In General_____ 87
   B. Standing_____ 90
      1. "Conventional" Standing_____ 90
      2. Standing to Assert the Rights of Third Parties _____ 103
      3. Taxpayer and Citizen Standing _____ 106
   C. Mootness _____ 115

Page

Chapter 3. The Jurisdiction of Federal Courts in Constitutional Cases—Continued

D. Ripeness _____ 121

E. Political Questions _____ 132

PART II. ALLOCATION OF GOVERNMENTAL POWERS: THE NATION AND THE STATES; THE PRESIDENT, THE CONGRESS, AND THE COURTS

Page

Chapter 4. The Scope of National Power _____ 150

Section

1. The Constitutional Convention and the Establishment of a National Government _____ 150

2. Sources of National Power: Early Developments _____ 158

   A. The Marshall Court's View _____ 158

   B. Power of Congress to Regulate Interstate Commerce—Exclusive or Concurrent _____ 176

   C. The Attempt to Develop Judicially Enforceable Limits on the Power of Congress to Regulate Transportation and the Economy _____ 184

   D. The Abandonment of the Attempt to Restrain Congressional Power to Regulate the Economy _____ 201

3. The Scope of National Power Today _____ 208

   A. The Commerce Power _____ 208

   B. The Taxing Power _____ 223

   C. The Spending Power _____ 226

   D. War and Treaty Powers _____ 230

   E. The Property Power _____ 240

   F. Other Federal Powers _____ 242

      1. Fiscal Powers _____ 242

      2. Naturalization _____ 244

      3. Regulation of Aliens _____ 244

      4. The Admiralty Power _____ 245

Chapter 5. The Scope of State Power—Regulation _____ 247

Section

1. Implied Restrictions of the Commerce Clause—Transportation 248

2. Implied Restrictions of the Commerce Clause—Production and Trade _____ 268

   A. Restricting Importation and Insulating In-State Business From Out-of-State Competition _____ 268

   B. Requiring Business Operations to Be Performed in the Home State _____ 280

   C. Preserving Resources for In-State Consumption _____ 282

   D. Preserving State-Owned Resources for In-State Use _____ 295

   E. Limits on Business Entry _____ 308

   F. Interstate Mobility of Persons _____ 315

Page

Chapter 5.   The Scope of State Power—Regulation—Continued
Section

3.   Effect of Other Constitutional Provisions on State Regulatory
     Power _____ 317
     A.   The Privileges and Immunities Clause of Article IV, Sec-
          tion 2 _____ 317
     B.   The Twenty-First Amendment _____ 323
4.   Preemption of State Legislation by Federal Legislation—The
     Impact of the Supremacy Clause _____ 330

Chapter 6.   The Scope of State Power—Taxation _____ 340
Section

1.   Introduction _____ 340
2.   The General Scope of the Limitations Imposed on State Taxa-
     tion of Interstate and Foreign Commerce by the Commerce
     and Import-Export Clauses _____ 344
3.   Jurisdiction to Tax and Apportionment _____ 372
     A.   Income Taxes _____ 372
     B.   Sales and Use Taxes _____ 387

**Chapter 7.   Intergovernmental Relationships Within the Federal
               System** _____ 391
Section

1.   Intergovernmental Tax Immunity _____ 391
     A.   Federal Immunity _____ 391
     B.   State Immunity _____ 398
2.   Intergovernmental Regulatory Immunity _____ 404
     A.   Federal Immunity _____ 404
     B.   State Immunity _____ 407
3.   Governmental Relationships Among the States _____ 433

Chapter 8.   Separation of Powers _____ 436
Section

1.   The President's Power to Determine National Policy_____ 436
     A.   In General_____ 436
     B.   International Relations _____ 443
     C.   War and National Defense _____ 447
2.   Congressional Interference With Presidential Prerogatives___ 451
     A.   The Legislative Veto _____ 451
     B.   Appointment of "Officers of the United States" _____ 464
     C.   Impeachment _____ 467
3.   Presidential and Congressional Immunities _____ 468

PART III.   GOVERNMENT AND THE INDIVIDUAL: THE PROTECTION OF LIBERTY AND PROPERTY UNDER THE DUE PROCESS AND EQUAL PROTECTION CLAUSES

**Chapter 9.   The Bill of Rights, The Civil War Amendments, and
               Their Interrelationship**_____ 477
Section

1.   The Pre-Civil War Background _____ 477
     A.   The Contract Clause and the Privileges and Immunities
          Clause of Article IV—Early Interpretations _____ 477
     B.   The Bill of Rights _____ 479

Page

Chapter 9. The Bill of Rights, The Civil War Amendments, and Their Interrelationship—Continued

Section

2. The Initial Interpretation of the Civil War Amendments 483
3. The Fourteenth Amendment and Citizenship _____ 495
4. Application of the Bill of Rights to the States _____ 498

Chapter 10. The Due Process, Contract, and Just Compensation Clauses and the Review of the Reasonableness of Legislation _____ 520

Section

1. Economic Regulatory Legislation _____ 520
   A. The Rise and Fall of Due Process _____ 520
   B. The Contract Clause—What Does It Add to the Due Process Limitation? _____ 543
   C. The Just Compensation Clause of the Fifth Amendment— What Does It Add to Due Process? _____ 559
2. Protection of Personal Liberties _____ 577
   A. Introduction _____ 577
   B. Personal Autonomy _____ 584
   C. Family Relationships _____ 617
   D. Rights of Persons Confined in State Institutions _____ 623
   E. Provision of Essential Governmental Benefits and Services to the Poor _____ 624

Chapter 11. The Equal Protection Clause and The Review of The Reasonableness of Legislation _____ 629

Section

1. Introduction—The Scope of Equal Protection _____ 629
2. Socal and Economic Regulatory Legislation _____ 635
3. Suspect Classification _____ 653
   A. Classifications Disadvantaging Racial Minorities _____ 653
   B. Racial Segregation in Schools and Other Public Facilities 663
   C. Classifications Disadvantaging Aliens _____ 690
   D. Classifications Disadvantaging Non-marital Children 699
   E. Classifications Based on Gender _____ 708
   F. Are There Other Suspect Classifications? _____ 744
   G. The Requirement of a Discriminating Purpose—The Relevance of Discriminatory Impact _____ 751
   H. "Benign" Discrimination: Affirmative Action, Quotas, Preferences Based on Gender or Race _____ 776
      1. Classifications Advantaging Females _____ 776
      2. Classifications Advantaging Racial Minorities _____ 786
4. Protection of Personal Liberties _____ 836
   A. Equal Protection and Rights Secured by Other Constitutional Provisions _____ 836
   B. Voting and Elections _____ 843
      1. Introduction _____ 843
      2. Legislative Districting _____ 844
      3. Qualifications of Voters _____ 870
   C. Travel and Interstate Migration _____ 877
   D. Welfare _____ 895
   E. Education _____ 911

Page

Chapter 12. Defining the Scope of "Liberty" and "Property" Protected by the Due Process Clause—The Procedural Due Process Cases _____ 932

Section

1. What Constitutes a Deprivation of Liberty or Property Which Mandates the Provision of a Hearing? _____ 933
2. Procedural Due Process and Irrebuttable Presumptions _____ 950

Chapter 13. Application of the Post Civil War Amendments to Private Conduct: Congressional Power to Enforce the Amendments _____ 960

Section

1. Early Interpretation _____ 960
2. Application of the Constitution to Private Conduct _____ 960
    A. Private Performance of "Government" Functions _____ 967
    B. Governmental Enforcement of "Private" Decisions _____ 974
    C. Government Financing, Regulation and Authorization of Private Conduct _____ 983
        1. Private Activity on Government Property _____ 983
        2. Government Financial Assistance to Private Activities 986
        3. Government Regulation of Private Activity _____ 988
        4. Government Approval of Private Activity _____ 997
3. Federal Civil Rights Legislation _____ 1003
    A. The Reconstruction Legacy _____ 1003
    B. Contemporary Federal Civil Rights Legislation _____ 1006
4. Federal Power to Regulate Private Conduct Under the Thirteenth Amendment _____ 1008
5. Federal Power to Regulate Private Conduct Under the Fourteenth Amendment _____ 1015
6. The Scope of Congressional Power to Redefine the Amendments _____ 1020
    A. "Remedial" Power _____ 1020
    B. "Interpretative" Power _____ 1031

PART IV. CONSTITUTIONAL PROTECTION OF EXPRESSION AND CONSCIENCE

Chapter 14. Governmental Control of the Content of Expression _____ 1046

Section

1. An Introduction to Problems of Content Control of Speech 1046
    A. Historical Introduction—The Status of Free Speech Up to the 1920's _____ 1046
        1. The English Background _____ 1046
        2. The Adoption of the First Amendment and the Controversy Over the Alien and Sedition Laws _____ 1050
        3. Freedom of Speech and Press in the Nineteenth Century _____ 1051
    B. World War I and the Post-War Years: Penalizing the Advocacy of the Overthrow of Government by Force or Violence _____ 1053

Page

Chapter 14. Governmental Control of the Content of Expression—Continued

Section

    C. The Post World War II Cold War Era: Prosecution of Communists Under the Smith Act_____1067

    D. The Current Status of the Clear and Present Danger Test—The "Brandenburg Concerto"_____1078

  2. Intermezzo: An Introduction to the Concepts of Vagueness, Overbreadth and Prior Restaint_____1087

    A. Vagueness and Overbreadth _____1087

    B. Prior Restraint _____1097

  3. Speech Conflicting With Other Community Values: Government Control of the Content of Speech_____1105

    A. Protection of Individual Reputation and Privacy_____1106

    B. Control of Obscenity _____1126

      1. The Rationale for Prohibiting Obscenity_____1126

      2. The Problem of Definition_____1131

    C. Control of "Fighting Words" and Offensive Speech _____1138

    D. Regulation of Commercial Advertising_____1153

Chapter 15. Restrictions on Time, Place, or Manner of Expression _____1170

Section

  1. Discriminatory Regulations_____1170

  2. The Traditional Public Forum: Speech Activities in Streets and Parks_____1177

    A. The Considerations Justifying Denial of the Use of Streets and Parks for Speech Activities_____1177

    B. The Hostile Audience _____1183

  3. The Non-traditional Forum _____1187

    A. Speech Activities in Public Property Other Than Parks and Streets_____1187

    B. The Government Forum and Government Subsidies to Speech _____1209

  4. Speech on Private Premises _____1235

  5. Labor Picketing_____1255

Chapter 16. Protection of Penumbral First Amendment Rights _____1260

Section

  1. Symbolic Speech _____1260

  2. Compelled Affirmation of Belief _____1271

  3. Freedom of Association_____1273

    A. The Right to Associate_____1273

    B. The Right Not to Associate_____1289

    C. Political Association_____1293

      1. Choosing and Electing Candidates for Public Office 1293

      2. Political Fundraising and Expenditures_____1298

  4. Compelled Disclosure of Beliefs and Associations _____1311

    A. Registration and Reporting Requirements_____1311

    B. Legislative Investigations_____1318

    C. Information Requests as a Condition of Issuance of a License to Practice a Profession _____1324

Page

Chapter 16. Protection of Penumbral First Amendment
          —Continued
Section
5. Speech and Association Rights of Government Employees ___1331
   A. Conditioning Government Employment on Speech and
       Political Activity _____1331
   B. Loyalty Programs _____1344
       1. Protection of the Bill of Attainder Clauses _____1345
       2. Protection of the First Amendment_____1349
       3. Loyalty Oaths _____1351
       4. The Privilege Against Self-Incrimination and Procedu-
          ral Due Process _____1354
Chapter 17. Freedom of the Press _____1356
Section
1. Introduction _____1356
   A. Relationship Between the Speech and Press Clauses ____1356
   B. Regulation of the Business of Publishing _____1358
2. Restraints on Editorial Judgment_____1363
3. Prohibition of Publication of Government Information_____1368
4. Government Demands for Confidential Press Information____1382
5. Press Access to Government Information _____1388
6. Special Problems of the Electronic Media_____1399
Chapter 18. Religion and the Constitution _____1412
Section
1. The Establishment Clause _____1412
   A. Introduction_____1412
   B. Religion in Public Schools_____1417
   C. Financial Aid to Church-Related Schools _____1427
       1. Elementary and Secondary Schools _____1427
       2. Higher Education _____1444
   D. Other Government Practices _____1451
2. The Free Exercise of Religion_____1461
   A. Belief, Expression and Conduct_____1461
   B. Regulation of Conduct Compelled by Religious Belief___1467

Appendix _____1483

Index _____1493

*

TABLE OF CONTENTS

(Italic Indicates Principal Cases)

	Page
PREFACE	xxi
TABLE OF CASES	lxiii

PART I. THE CONSTITUTION AND THE COURTS: THE JUDICIAL FUNCTION IN CONSTITUTIONAL CASES

CHAPTER 1. THE CONSTITUTION 2

Section 1. The Constitution of the United States of America 2

Section 2. History of the Adoption of the Constitution and Its Most Significant Amendments 15

  A. The Articles of Confederation and the Original Constitution 15

  B. The Bill of Rights 16

    Note: Protection of Freedom in the Constitution of 1787 ... 16

    Note: The Bill of Rights 17

  C. The Adoption of the Civil War Amendments 19

    Note: Slavery and the Thirteenth Amendment 19

    Note: The 1866 Civil Rights Acts and the Fourteenth and Fifteenth Amendments 20

CHAPTER 2. JUDICIAL REVIEW 23

Section 1. The Legitimacy of Judicial Review 23

    Note: The Constitutional Convention 23

    Marbury v. Madison 24

    Notes: Legitimacy of Judicial Review: Some Comments 31

    Notes: Effect of a Declaration of Unconstitutionality ... 35

Section 2. Congressional Control of Judicial Review by the Federal Courts 36

    Note: The Scope of Congressional Power Over the Jurisdiction of Lower Federal Courts 36

    Ex Parte McCardle 37

    United States v. Klein 39

    Notes: The Scope of Congressional Power Over Supreme Court Jurisdiction Under the Exceptions Clause 40

CHAPTER 3. THE JURISDICTION OF FEDERAL COURTS IN CONSTITUTIONAL CASES 43

Section 1. Supreme Court Review of State Court Decisions 43

  A. History and Structure 43

    Note: Article III of the Constitution and Section 25 of the Judiciary Act of 1789 43

    Martin v. Hunter's Lessee 44

    Note: State Court Resistance to Supreme Court Orders 47

    Note: The Current Jurisdiction of the Supreme Court to Review State Court Decisions 48

Page

Section 1. Supreme Court Review of State Court Decisions—
    Continued

B. Issues of State Law in the Supreme Court: The Adequate
    and Independent State Ground_____ 48

Note: Review of Issues of State Law in Cases Involving
    Federal Questions: The Adequate and Indepen-
    dent State Ground_____ 48

Note: Supreme Court Review of State Court Decisions
    Upholding Claims of Federal Constitutional
    Right_____ 50

Michigan v. Long _____ 51

C. The Distinction Between Obligatory and Discretionary Ju-
    risdiction _____ 56

Note: The Distinction Between Appeal and Certiorari in
    Review of State Court Decisions _____ 56

Note: The Court's Process in Screening Cases_____ 58

Hicks v. Miranda _____ 59

Note: The Precedential Effect of Summary Dispositions
    in the Supreme Court_____ 60

Colorado Springs Amusements, Ltd. v. Rizzo _____ 60

Naim v. Naim _____ 62

Note: Discretionary Dismissal of Appeals_____ 63

Section 2. Constitutional Litigation Initiated in the Federal
    Courts _____ 63

Introduction. Justice Black for the Court in Atlantic
    Coast Line R.R. Co. v. Engineers _____ 63

A. Jurisdiction of the Federal Courts in Cases Involving
    Federal Law Issues_____ 64

Note: Jurisdiction of Lower Court Federal Courts to
    Enforce Federal Rights_____ 64

B. Enforcement of Federal Rights in Suits Against State
    Officers: The Eleventh Amendment _____ 66

*Pennhurst State School & Hospital v. Halderman*_____ 66

Note: Application of the Eleventh Amendment in Suits
    for Damages_____ 75

Fitzpatrick v. Bitzer _____ 76

Note: Congressional Power to Eliminate State Sovereign
    Immunity_____ 78

C. Non-Constitutional Restrictions on Federal Court Injunc-
    tions Against Unconstitutional State Laws_____ 79

Note: Abstention to Allow State Courts to Construe Am-
    biguous State Law _____ 79

Note: Exhaustion of State Administrative Remedies_____ 80

Note: Exhaustion of State Judicial Remedies_____ 81

Note: Enjoining State Judicial Proceedings: The Anti-
    Injunction Act_____ 82

Note: Enjoining State Enforcement Proceedings: Young-
    er v. Harris and "Our Federalism" _____ 82

Trainor v. Hernandez _____ 83

		Page
Section 3.	Cases and Controversies and Justiciability	87
A.	In General	87
	Note: Advisory Opinions	87
	Note: The Flast v. Cohen Summary	88
	Notes: Justiciability and the Form of Litigation—Raising Constitutional Issues	89
B.	Standing	90
	1. "Conventional" Standing	90
	Warth v. Seldin	90
	Village of Arlington Heights v. Metropolitan Housing Development Corp.	99
	Note: Standing and the Requirement of "Injury in Fact"	101
	2. Standing to Assert the Rights of Third Parties	103
	Craig v. Boren	103
	3. Taxpayer and Citizen Standing	106
	Valley Forge Christian College v. Americans United for Separation of Church and State, Inc.	106
C.	Mootness	115
	DeFunis v. Odegaard	115
	Note: Capable of Repetition Yet Evading Review	118
	Note: Case and Controversy Requirements as Applied to Constitutional Litigation Arising in State and Federal Courts	119
D.	Ripeness	121
	United Public Workers v. Mitchell	121
	Adler v. Board of Education	122
	Notes on Mitchell and Adler	123
	Poe v. Ullman	123
	Epperson v. Arkansas	124
	Younger v. Harris	124
	Note: Ripeness and Criminal Prosecutions	125
	City of Los Angeles v. Lyons	125
E.	Political Questions	132
	Note: John Marshall on Political Questions	132
	Baker v. Carr	133
	Powell v. McCormack	135
	Gilligan v. Morgan	138
	Goldwater v. Carter	139
	Notes: Political Questions	144
	Note: The Amendment Process—A Digression	144

PART II. ALLOCATION OF GOVERNMENTAL POWERS: THE NATION AND THE STATES: THE PRESIDENT, THE CONGRESS AND THE COURTS

Page

CHAPTER 4. THE SCOPE OF NATIONAL POWER _____ 150
Section 1. The Constitutional Convention and the Establishment of
    a National Government _____ 150
    Notes: Proceedings in the Federal Convention _____ 150
    Note: Report of the Committee on Detail _____ 154
    Note: Proceedings in the Federal Convention _____ 155
    Note _____ 157
Section 2. Sources of National Power: Early Developments _____ 158
  A. The Marshall Court's View _____ 158
    Note: The Bank of the United States _____ 158
    McCulloch v. Maryland _____ 159
    Notes: *McCulloch* and the Scope of Federal Power _____ 166
    Note: Federal Power to Build Roads and Canals _____ 166
    Note: Madison's Veto of the Internal Improvement Bill
        (1817) _____ 167
    Gibbons v. Ogden _____ 168
    Note _____ 175
    Willson v. Black Bird Creek Marsh Co. _____ 175
  B. Power of Congress to Regulate Interstate Commerce—
    Exclusive or Concurrent _____ 176
    The License Cases _____ 176
    Cooley v. Board of Wardens of the Port of Philadelphia 178
    Questions _____ 181
    Note: Sustaining State Power to Regulate by Defining
        Commerce as Intrastate _____ 182
    Paul v. Virginia _____ 182
    Coe v. Town of Errol _____ 182
    Kidd v. Pearson _____ 183
    Note: Power of Congress to Consent to State Regulation
        of Interstate Commerce _____ 183
  C. The Attempt to Develop Judicially Enforceable Limits on
    the Power of Congress to Regulate Transportation and
    the Economy _____ 184
    United States v. E.C. Knight Co. _____ 186
    Note: The Sherman Act After *E.C. Knight* _____ 187
    Houston, E. & W. Ry. Co. v. United States [The Shreve-
        port Rate Case] _____ 187
    Railroad Comm'n of Wisconsin v. Chicago, B. & Q. R.R.
        Co. _____ 190
    Hammer v. Dagenhart _____ 190
    Note: The Current of Commerce Cases _____ 192
    Note: The Depression and the New Deal _____ 192
    Schechter Poultry Corp v. United States _____ 193
    Note: Impact of Schechter _____ 195

TABLE OF CONTENTS

Page

Section 2. Sources of National Power: Early Developments—
            Continued
            Carter v. Carter Coal Co. _____ 195
            United States v. Butler _____ 197
            Note: The Roosevelt Court Plan _____ 200
     D. The Abandonment of the Attempt to Restrain Congres-
            sional Power to Regulate the Economy _____ 201
         NLRB v. Jones & Laughlin Steel Co. _____ 201
         Note _____ 203
         NLRB v. Fainblatt _____ 203
         United States v. Darby _____ 204
         Note _____ 207
Section 3. The Scope of National Power Today _____ 208
     A. The Commerce Power _____ 208
         Wickard v. Filburn _____ 208
         United States v. South-Eastern Underwriters Ass'n _____ 210
         Heart of Atlanta Motel v. United States _____ 211
         Katzenbach v. McClung _____ 214
         Note: Use of the Commerce Power to Combat Crime __ 216
         Perez v. United States _____ 217
         Note: The Implications of Perez _____ 220
         United States v. Enmons _____ 220
         Note: The Role of the Courts, if Any, in Limiting the
                Regulatory Power of Congress Under the Com-
                merce Clause _____ 221
     B. The Taxing Power _____ 223
         Sonzinsky v. United States _____ 223
         United States v. Ptasynski _____ 225
     C. The Spending Power _____ 226
         Steward Machine Co. v. Davis _____ 226
         Helvering v. Davis _____ 228
         Note: The Impact of Federal Grants to the States _____ 229
         Buckley v. Valeo _____ 229
         Note _____ 230
     D. War and Treaty Powers _____ 230
         Note: The Sources of National Power _____ 230
         United States v. Curtiss-Wright Export Corp. _____ 231
         Woods v. Cloyd W. Miller Co. _____ 232
         Note: International Agreements _____ 234
         Hauenstein v. Lynham _____ 234
         Note: Congressional Legislation Inconsistent With a
                Treaty _____ 234
         Missouri v. Holland _____ 235
         United States v. Belmont _____ 237
         United States v. Pink _____ 238
         Reid v. Covert _____ 238
         Note: The United Nations and the Treaty Power _____ 239
     E. The Property Power _____ 240
         Kleppe v. New Mexico _____ 240

Page

Section 3. The Scope of National Power Today—Continued
 F. Other Federal Powers _____ 242
   1. Fiscal Powers _____ 242
     Norman v. Baltimore & Ohio R.R. _____ 242
   2. Naturalization _____ 244
   3. Regulation of Aliens _____ 244
     Kleindienst v. Mandel _____ 244
   4. The Admiralty Power _____ 245
CHAPTER 5. THE SCOPE OF STATE POWER—REGULATION _____ 247
Section 1. Implied Restrictions of the Commerce Clause—Transportation _____ 248
   Note: State Economic Regulation of Transportation Businesses _____ 248
   Buck v. Kuykendall _____ 248
   Note: State Safety Regulations and Interstate Transportation _____ 250
   Bradley v. Public Utilities Comm'n _____ 251
   South Carolina State Highway Dept. v. Barnwell Bros. 251
   Southern Pacific Co. v. Arizona _____ 253
   Bibb v. Navajo Freight Lines, Inc. _____ 255
   Kassel v. Consolidated Freightways Corp. _____ 257
   Note: Federal Regulation of Truck Sizes _____ 268
Section 2. Implied Restrictions of the Commerce Clause—Production and Trade _____ 268
 A. Restricting Importation and Insulating In-State Business From Out-of-State Competition _____ 268
   Note: State Quarantine and Inspection Laws _____ 268
   Mintz v. Baldwin _____ 269
   Baldwin v. G.A.F. Seelig, Inc. _____ 269
   Dean Milk Co. v. City of Madison _____ 270
   Hunt v. Washington State Apple Advertising Comm'n 274
   Minnesota v. Clover Leaf Creamery Co. _____ 277
 B. Requiring Business Operations to Be Performed in the Home State _____ 280
   Minnesota v. Barber _____ 280
   Foster-Fountain Packing Co. v. Haydel _____ 281
   Pike v. Bruce Church, Inc. _____ 281
 C. Preserving Resources for In-State Consumption _____ 282
   Pennsylvania v. West Virginia _____ 282
   H.P. Hood & Sons v. Du Mond _____ 283
   Philadelphia v. New Jersey _____ 286
   Hughes v. Oklahoma _____ 289
   New England Power Co. v. New Hampshire _____ 292
   Sporhase v. Nebraska _____ 293
 D. Preserving State-Owned Resources for In-State Use _____ 295
   Reeves, Inc. v. Stake _____ 295
   White v. Massachusetts Council of Construction Employers _____ 300
   South Central Timber Development v. Wunnicke _____ 302

Section 2. Implied Restrictions of the Commerce Clause—Pro-
duction and Trade—Continued
E. Limits on Business Entry _____ 308
Lewis v. BT Investment Managers, Inc. _____ 308
Edgar v. MITE Corp. _____ 314
F. Interstate Mobility of Persons _____ 315
Section 3. Effect of Other Constitutional Provisions on State
Regulatory Power _____ 317
A. The Privileges and Immunities Clause of Article IV, Sec-
tion 2_____ 317
*United Building and Construction Trades Council of
Camden County and Vicinity v. Mayor and Council
of the City of Camden* _____ 318
B. The Twenty-First Amendment _____ 323
Bacchus Imports, Ltd. v. Dias _____ 324
Capital Cities Cable, Inc. v. Crisp _____ 327
Section 4. Preemption of State Legislation by Federal Legisla-
tion—The Impact of the Supremacy Clause _____ 330
Ray v. Atlantic Richfield Co. _____ 331

CHAPTER 6. THE SCOPE OF STATE POWER—TAXATION _____ 340
Section 1. Introduction_____ 340
Note: Scope of Immunity of Interstate and Foreign Com-
merce From State Taxation_____ 340
Note: Limits on the Power of States to Tax Property and
Activities Outside Their Borders_____ 342
Section 2. The General Scope of the Limitations Imposed on State
Taxation of Interstate and Foreign Commerce by the
Commerce and Import-Export Clauses _____ 344
Armco, Inc. v. Hardesty _____ 344
Note: The Twenty-First Amendment and Discriminatory
State Taxes _____ 346
Bacchus Imports, Ltd. v. Dias _____ 346
Note: Other Constitutional Limitations on Discriminatory
Taxation—Privileges and Immunities and Equal
Protection _____ 346
Austin v. New Hampshire _____ 346
Western and Southern Life Insurance Co. v. State Board
of Equalization _____ 347
Note _____ 348
Complete Auto Transit, Inc. v. Brady _____ 349
Commonwealth Edison Co. v. Montana _____ 354
*Department of Revenue of Washington v. Association of
Washington Stevedoring Companies* _____ 360
Note _____ 366
Japan Line, Ltd. v. County of Los Angeles _____ 366

Page

Section 3. Jurisdiction to Tax and Apportionment _____ 372
  A. Income Taxes _____ 372
      Note: The Federal Statutory Limitation _____ 372
      Note: The Multistate Compact _____ 372
      Moorman Mfg. Co. v. Bair _____ 373
      *Container Corporation of America v. Franchise Tax
          Board* _____ 378
      Note _____ 387
  B. Sales and Use Taxes _____ 387
      *National Geographic Soc'y v. California Bd. of Equali-
          zation* _____ 387

CHAPTER 7. INTERGOVERNMENTAL RELATIONSHIPS WITHIN THE
              FEDERAL SYSTEM _____ 391
Section 1. Intergovernmental Tax Immunity _____ 391
  A. Federal Immunity _____ 391
      McCulloch v. Maryland _____ 391
      United States v. New Mexico _____ 391
      Note: Congressional Power to Broaden or Constrict Fed-
              eral Immunity From State Taxation _____ 398
  B. State Immunity_____ 398
      Massachusetts v. United States _____ 398
Section 2. Intergovernmental Regulatory Immunity _____ 404
  A. Federal Immunity _____ 404
      Miller v. Arkansas _____ 404
      Public Utilities Commission of California v. United States 405
      Hancock v. Train _____ 406
  B. State Immunity_____ 407
      Note: State Immunity From Federal Regulation—1936–
              1976 _____ 407
      National League of Cities v. Usery _____ 408
      United Transportation Union v. Long Island R.R. Co. ___ 416
      *Equal Employment Opportunity Commission v. Wyo-
          ming* _____ 416
      Hodel v. Virginia Surface Mining & Reclamation Associa-
          tion, Inc. _____ 424
      Federal Energy Regulatory Commission v. Mississippi 425
Section 3. Government Relationships Among the States _____ 433
      Note: Interstate Compacts _____ 433
      Note: Other Intergovernmental Relationships Among
              States_____ 434

CHAPTER 8. SEPARATION OF POWERS_____ 436
Section 1. The President's Power to Determine National Poli-
              cy_____ 436
  A. In General_____ 436
      Youngstown Sheet & Tube Co. v. Sawyer _____ 437
  B. International Relations _____ 443
      Note: International Agreements_____ 444
      Dames & Moore v. Regan_____ 444

Page

Section 1. The President's Power to Determine National Policy—Continued

C. War and National Defense 447

The Prize Cases 447

Mora v. McNamara 449

Note: The Court and the Vietnam Controversy 450

Section 2. Congressional Interference With Presidential Prerogatives 451

A. The Legislative Veto 451

Immigration and Naturalization Service v. Chadha ... 451

B. Appointment of "Officers of the United States" 464

Buckley v. Valeo 464

C. Impeachment 467

Section 3. Presidential and Congressional Immunities 468

United States v. Nixon 468

Nixon v. Administrator of General Services 472

Nixon v. Fitzgerald 474

Note: The Speech or Debate Clause 475

PART III. GOVERNMENT AND THE INDIVIDUAL:
THE PROTECTION OF LIBERTY AND PROPERTY
UNDER THE DUE PROCESS AND EQUAL
PROTECTION CLAUSES

CHAPTER 9. THE BILL OF RIGHTS, THE CIVIL WAR AMENDMENTS, AND THEIR INTERRELATIONSHIP 477

Section 1. The Pre-Civil War Background 477

A. The Contract Clause and the Privileges and Immunities Clause of Article IV—Early Interpretations 477

Note: The Contract Clause 477

Note: The Privileges and Immunities Clause of Article IV 478

Corfield v. Coryell 478

Paul v. Virginia 479

B. The Bill of Rights 479

Barron v. Mayor and City Council of Baltimore 479

Note: Pre-Civil War Interpretations of the Bill of Rights 481

Section 2. The Initial Interpretation of the Civil War Amendments 483

Slaughter-House Cases 483

Note: The Privileges and Immunities Clause of the Fourteenth Amendment 494

Note: Due Process and Jurisdiction 494

Note: Due Process and Fair Procedure 495

Section 3. The Fourteenth Amendment and Citizenship 495

Vance v. Terrazas 497

Page

Section 4. Application of the Bill of Rights to the States _____ 498

Note: The Incorporation Doctrine _____ 499

*Palko v. Connecticut*_____ 499

Adamson v. California_____ 502

Note: The Historical Debate_____ 507

Duncan v. Louisiana _____ 508

Note: Incorporation and the Jury Trial Cases _____ 516

Note: Due Process as a Limitation on Procedures Not
Forbidden by the Bill of Rights _____ 517

In re Winship_____ 517

Notes: "Incorporation"—Its Current Scope _____ 518

CHAPTER 10. THE DUE PROCESS, CONTRACT, AND JUST COMPENSA-
TION CLAUSES AND THE REVIEW OF THE REASON-
ABLENESS OF LEGISLATION _____ 520

Section 1. Economic Regulatory Legislation _____ 520

A. The Rise and Fall of Due Process _____ 520

Note: Due Process as a Restraint on the Substance of
Legislation _____ 520

Note: The Flowering of Economic Due Process _____ 521

Allgeyer v. Louisiana _____ 522

*Lochner v. New York*_____ 523

Note: The Post-*Lochner* Developments_____ 528

*Nebbia v. New York*_____ 530

Note: The Overturning of Adkins v. Children's Hospital 532

*United States v. Carolene Products Co.*_____ 532

Note: The Demise of Liberty of Contract _____ 535

*Williamson v. Lee Optical of Oklahoma*_____ 535

Ferguson v. Skrupa _____ 538

Note: Does the Due Process Clause Today Impose Any
Limitations on the Substance of Economic Regulatory Legislation?_____ 539

Pension Benefit Guaranty Corp. v. R.A. Gray and Co. __ 540

Note: State Courts and Business Regulations _____ 542

B. The Contract Clause—What Does it Add to the Due Process Limitation? _____ 543

*United States Trust Co. of New York v. New Jersey*___ 543

Allied Structural Steel Co. v. Spannaus _____ 550

Energy Reserves Group, Inc. v. Kansas Power and Light
Co._____ 556

Exxon Corp. v. Eagerton_____ 559

C. The Just Compensation Clause of the Fifth Amendment—
What Does it Add to Due Process? _____ 559

*Penn Central Transp. Co. v. City of New York*_____ 559

PruneYard Shopping Center v. Robins_____ 569

Webb's Fabulous Pharmacies, Inc. v. Beckwith _____ 570

Loretto v. Teleprompter Manhattan CATV Corp. _____ 570

Ruckelshaus v. Monsanto Co. _____ 571

San Diego Gas & Electric Co. v. City of San Diego _____ 576

Note: Just Compensation_____ 577

Page

Section 2. Protection of Personal Liberties _____ 577
    A. Introduction _____ 577
        Griswold v. Connecticut _____ 578
        Note: Privacy as Autonomy Versus Privacy as Freedom
               From Intrusion and Disclosure _____ 584
    B. Personal Autonomy _____ 584
        Eisenstadt v. Baird _____ 584
        Roe v. Wade _____ 585
        Note: Requirement of Consent of Spouse to Abortion__ 596
        Note: Limitation on the Access of Minors to Abortions
               and Contraceptives _____ 597
        H.L. v. Matheson _____ 599
        Parham v. J.R. _____ 599
        Note: Restrictions on Private Consensual Sexual Behav-
               ior_____ 601
        Akron v. Akron Center for Reproductive Health, Inc. 602
        Planned Parenthood Ass'n of Kansas City v. Ashcroft__ 616
        Simopoulos v. Virginia_____ 617
    C. Family Relationships _____ 617
        Moore v. City of East Cleveland _____ 617
    D. Rights of Persons Confined in State Institutions_____ 623
        Youngberg v. Romeo _____ 623
    E. Provision of Essential Governmental Benefits and Ser-
        vices to the Poor _____ 624
        Note: The Rights of the Poor Defendant in the Criminal
               Justice System _____ 625
        Note: Access of the Poor to the Courts in Civil Cases 626
        Boddie v. Connecticut_____ 626
        United States v. Kras _____ 626
        Ortwein v. Schwab_____ 628
        Little v. Streater_____ 628
        Lassiter v. Department of Social Services_____ 628

CHAPTER 11. THE EQUAL PROTECTION CLAUSE AND THE REVIEW OF
             THE REASONABLENESS OF LEGISLATION _____ 629
Section 1. Introduction—The Scope of Equal Protection _____ 629
        Note: The Original Understanding _____ 629
        Gulf, C. & S. R. Co. v. Ellis _____ 630
        Note: The Doctrine of Reasonable Classification _____ 630
        Note: Application of the Equal Protection Limitation to
               the Federal Government Through the Due Pro-
               cess Clause of the Fifth Amendment_____ 632
        Note: The Standard of Review _____ 633
Section 2. Social and Economic Regulatory Legislation _____ 635
        *Railway Express Agency v. New York*_____ 635
        Williamson v. Lee Optical of Oklahoma _____ 637
        Morey v. Doud _____ 638
        *New Orleans v. Dukes*_____ 638
        United States Railroad Retirement Bd. v. Fritz _____ 640
        Schweiker v. Wilson_____ 648

TABLE OF CONTENTS

Page

Section 2. Social and Economic Regulatory Legislation—Continued
  Logan v. Zimmerman Brush Co. 650
  Note: Scope and Legitimacy of Judicial Review of the Rationality of Legislation Under Equal Protection 652
Section 3. Suspect Classifications 653
 A. Classifications Disadvantaging Racial Minorities 653
  Loving v. Virginia 653
  Palmor v. Sidoti 657
  Note: The Japanese Curfew and Evacuation Cases 659
  Hirabayashi v. United States 660
  Korematsu v. United States 660
  Ex Parte Endo 661
  Note: What Groups Are Specially Protected Against Discrimination? 662
  Note: Ascertaining the Existence of a Racial Classification 662
 B. Racial Segregation in Schools and Other Public Facilities 663
  Plessy v. Ferguson 663
  Brown v. Board of Educ. of Topeka 666
  Bolling v. Sharpe 669
  Note: *Brown* and the Relevance of Social Science and Historical Materials 670
  Note: Segregation in Public Facilities Other Than Schools 671
  Brown v. Board of Educ. of Topeka 671
  Notes: School Segregation From *Brown* to *Swann* 672
  Swann v. Charlotte-Mecklenburg Board of Educ. 673
  Keyes v. School District No. 1, Denver 680
  Note: May Courts Compel Maintenance of Racial Balance Once Desegregation Has Been Achieved? 684
  Note: Finding De Jure Segregation in Northern Schools 684
  Note: May School Desegregation Orders Extend Beyond School District Lines? 685
  Milliken v. Bradley (Milliken I) 685
  Milliken v. Bradley (Milliken II) 689
 C. Classifications Disadvantaging Aliens 690
  Graham v. Richardson 690
  Bernal v. Fainter 692
  Mathews v. Diaz 696
 D. Classifications Disadvantaging Non-marital Children 699
  Note: The Standard of Review for Legitmacy Classification 699
  Lalli v. Lalli 700
  Pickett v. Brown 705
  Note: Parental Rights of Fathers of Illegitimate Children 706

l

TABLE OF CONTENTS

		Page
Section 3.	Suspect Classifications—Continued	
E.	Classifications Based on Gender	708
	Reed v. Reed	708
	Frontiero v. Richardson	709
	Craig v. Boren	713
	Note: Classifications Advantaging Females	720
	Note: What Constitutes Discrimination Based on Gender?	720
	City of Los Angeles, Dept. of Water and Power v. Manhart	722
	Arizona Governing Committee v. Norris	725
	Michael M. v. Superior Court	725
	Rostker v. Goldberg	733
	Mississippi University for Women v. Hogan	739
	Note: Who Are Discriminated Against—Males or Females?	739
	Wengler v. Druggists Mutual Ins. Co.	740
	Note: Equal Rights Amendment Proposed	744
F.	Are There Other Suspect Classifications?	744
	Massachusetts Bd. of Retirement v. Murgia	744
	Note: Wealth Classifications	750
G.	The Requirement of a Discriminatory Purpose—The Relevance of Discriminatory Impact	751
	Washington v. Davis	751
	Village of Arlington Heights v. Metropolitan Housing Development Corp.	758
	Personnel Administrator of Massachusetts v. Feeney	761
	Columbus Board of Education v. Penick	763
	Rogers v. Lodge	764
	Note	771
	City of Memphis v. Greene	772
	Castaneda v. Partida	773
H.	"Benign" Discrimination: Affirmative Action, Quotas, Preferences Based on Gender or Race	776
	1. Classifications Advantaging Females	776
	Kahn v. Shevin	776
	Califano v. Webster	779
	Orr v. Orr	780
	Mississippi University for Women v. Hogan	781
	2. Classifications Advantaging Racial Minorities	786
	Regents of Univ. of California v. Bakke	786
	Fullilove v. Klutznick	815
Section 4.	Protection of Personal Liberties	836
A.	Equal Protection and Rights Secured by Other Constitutional Provisions	836
	Zablocki v. Redhail	836
	Note: Does Equal Protection Add Anything?	843

TABLE OF CONTENTS

Page

Section 4. Protection of Personal Liberties—Continued
B. Voting and Elections _____ 843
  1. Introduction _____ 843
    Notes: The Constitution and the Franchise _____ 843
    Note: The Equal Protection Clause as the Source of a
        Right to Vote and Run for Elective Office 844
  2. Legislative Districting _____ 844
    Reynolds v. Sims _____ 844
    Note: *Reynolds* and the First Round of Reapportion-
        ment _____ 849
    Note: The 1970 Census and the Second Round of
        Reapportionment _____ 849
    Mahan v. Howell _____ 850
    Gaffney v. Cummings _____ 851
    Karcher v. Daggett _____ 855
    Brown v. Thomson _____ 865
    Note: *Reynolds* and Local Government Units_____ 865
    Note: The Equal Protection Clause and the Require-
        ment of Super-Majorities _____ 869
  3. Qualifications of Voters _____ 870
    Harper v. Virginia State Board of Elections _____ 870
    Dunn v. Blumstein _____ 873
    Marston v. Lewis _____ 874
    Hill v. Stone _____ 874
    Note_____ 875
    Note: The First Amendment as a Limitation on State
        Power to Fix Qualifications for Voters_____ 876
    Note: Access to the Ballot and Other Election Laws 876
    Bullock v. Carter_____ 876
    Lubin v. Panish_____ 877
    Clements v. Fashing _____ 877
C. Travel and Interstate Migration _____ 877
  Shapiro v. Thompson _____ 877
  Dunn v. Blumstein_____ 882
  *Memorial Hospital v. Maricopa County*_____ 883
  Sosna v. Iowa _____ 887
  McCarthy v. Philadelphia Civil Serv. Comm'n_____ 889
  Jones v. Helms_____ 890
  *Zobel v. Williams*_____ *890*
  Martinez v. Bynum _____ 895
D. Welfare_____ 895
  Note: Welfare as a Fundamental Right Calling for Strict
        Scrutiny_____ 895
  *Dandridge v. Williams*_____ 895
  Harris v. McRae _____ 899
E. Education _____ 911
  *San Antonio Independent School Dist. v. Rodriguez*___ 911
  Plyler v. Doe _____ 920
  *Martinez v. Bynum*_____ 929

Page

CHAPTER 12. DEFINING THE SCOPE OF "LIBERTY" AND "PROPERTY" PROTECTED BY THE DUE PROCESS CLAUSE—THE PROCEDURAL DUE PROCESS CASES _____ 932

Section 1. What Constitutes a Deprivation of Liberty or Property Which Mandates the Provision of a Hearing? _____ 933

    Board of Regents of State Colleges v. Roth _____ 933

    Bishop v. Wood _____ 937

    Vitek v. Jones _____ 941

    Hewitt v. Helms _____ 945

    Olim v. Wakinekona _____ 945

    Parratt v. Taylor _____ 945

    Hudson v. Palmer _____ 948

    Logan v. Zimmerman Brush Co. _____ 948

    Note: The Interrelationships of Substantive and Procedural Due Process _____ 949

Section 2. Procedural Due Process and Irrebuttable Presumptions _____ 950

    Vlandis v. Kline _____ 951

    Cleveland Board of Educ. v. LaFleur _____ 953

    Weinberger v. Salfi _____ 956

    Usery v. Turner Elkhorn Mining Co. _____ 959

CHAPTER 13. APPLICATON OF THE POST CIVIL WAR AMENDMENTS TO PRIVATE CONDUCT: CONGRESSIONAL POWER TO ENFORCE THE AMENDMENTS _____ 960

Section 1. Early Interpretation _____ 960

    Civil Rights Cases _____ 960

    Note: The Relationship Between Congressional Power to Enforce the Constitution and Self-Enforcing Provisions of the Constitution _____ 965

Section 2. Application of the Constitution to Private Conduct ____ 966

    Note: Introduction to the State Action Concept _____ 966

  A. Private Performance of "Government" Functions _____ 967

    Note: The White Primary Cases _____ 967

    Steele v. Louisville and Nashville R.R. _____ 968

    Note: Access to Company Towns and Shopping Centers 968

    Evans v. Newton _____ 969

    Flagg Brothers, Inc. v. Brooks _____ 970

  B. Government Enforcement of "Private" Decisions _____ 974

    Shelley v. Kraemer _____ 974

    Note: Restrictive Covenants _____ 979

    Barrows v. Jackson _____ 979

    Note: Prosecution of "Sit-In" Demonstrators in the 1960s _____ 980

    Pennsylvania v. Board of City Trusts _____ 981

    Note: State Enforcement of Charitable Trusts _____ 982

    Evans v. Abney _____ 982

Page

Section 2. Application of the Constitution to Private Conduct—Continued

C. Government Financing, Regulation and Authorization of Private Conduct _____ 983

1. Private Activity on Government Property _____ 983

Burton v. Wilmington Parking Authority _____ 983

Note: Reality v. Appearance of State Action _____ 985

Gilmore v. Montgomery _____ 985

2. Government Financial Assistance to Private Activities 986

Norwood v. Harrison _____ 986

Blum v. Yaretsky _____ 987

Rendell-Baker v. Kohn _____ 988

3. Government Regulation of Private Activity _____ 988

Moose Lodge v. Irvis _____ 988

Jackson v. Metropolitan Edison Co. _____ 993

4. Government Approval of Private Activity _____ 997

Reitman v. Mulkey _____ 997

Note: Precursors and Successors to Reitman v. Mulkey _____ 1001

Section 3. Federal Civil Rights Legislation _____ 1003

A. The Reconstruction Legacy _____ 1003

Notes: Remaining Reconstruction—Era Federal Civil Rights Statutes _____ 1004

Note: Enforcing and Interpreting the Civil Rights Statutes _____ 1005

B. Contemporary Federal Civil Rights Legislation _____ 1006

Note: The Civil Rights Acts of 1957 and 1960 _____ 1006

Note: The Civil Rights Act of 1964 _____ 1007

Note: The Voting Rights Act of 1965 (as amended and extended in 1970, 1975, and 1982) _____ 1007

Note: The Civil Rights Act of April 11, 1968 _____ 1008

Section 4. Federal Power to Regulate Private Conduct Under the Thirteenth Amendment _____ 1008

Jones v. Alfred H. Mayer Co. _____ 1009

Notes: Other Interpretations of Reconstruction-Era Civil Rights Legislation Premised on the Thirteenth Amendment _____ 1012

Section 5. Federal Power to Regulate Private Conduct Under the Fourteenth Amendment _____ 1015

Note: Civil Rights Legislation and the Commerce and Spending Powers _____ 1015

Note: Privileges of National Citizenship _____ 1016

Note: Denial of Fourteenth Amendment Rights Under Color of Law or Custom _____ 1017

Note: Private Interference With Fourteenth Amendment Rights _____ 1018

Page

Section 6. The Scope of Congressional Power to Redefine the
Amendments --1020
A. "Remedial" Power---1020
City of Rome v. United States ----------------------------------1020
Fullilove v. Klutznick --1030
B. "Interpretive" Power---1031
Katzenbach v. Morgan--1031
Oregon v. Mitchell ---1036
Note: The Vitality of Katzenbach v. Morgan as Prece-
dent --1039
Note: Congressional Expansion of Due Process and
Equal Protection ---1040
*Equal Employment Opportunity Commission v. Wyo-
ming* ---1040
Mississippi University for Women v. Hogan ---------------1040
Note: Congressional Power to Dilute Constitutional
Rights--1040
Note: Federalism and Congressional Consent to Uncon-
stitutional State Laws---1043

PART IV. CONSTITUTIONAL PROTECTION OF EXPRESSION AND CONSCIENCE

CHAPTER 14. GOVERNMENT CONTROL OF THE CONTENT OF EXPRES-
SION --1046
Section 1. An Introduction to Problems of Content Control of
Speech ---1046
A. Historical Introduction—The Status of Free Speech up to
the 1920's--1046
1. The English Background -----------------------------------1046
2. The Adoption of the First Amendment and the Contro-
versy Over the Alien and Sedition Laws-------------1050
3. Freedom of Speech and Press in the Nineteenth Centu-
ry--1051
B. World War I and the Post-War Years: Penalizing the
Advocacy of the Overthrow of Government by Force or
Violence ---1053
Note: The Concern for Radical Speech in the First Quar-
ter of the Twentieth Century-------------------------------1053
Masses Publishing Co. v. Patten---------------------------------1054
Schenck v. United States---------------------------------------1055
Abrams v. United States --------------------------------------1056
Note: Hand's "Advocacy" Test v. Holmes' "Clear and
Present" Test --1058
Gitlow v. New York --1059
Whitney v. California ---1063
Note: The Basis of the Brandeis Concurrence in the
Whitney Case ---1065
De Jonge v. Oregon---1065

Page

Section 1. An Introduction to Problems of Content Control of
      Speech—Continued
   C. The Post World War II Cold War Era: Prosecution of
      Communists Under the Smith Act..............................1067
      Note: The Smith Act 1067
      Dennis v. United States 1067
      Note: Clear and Present Danger as a Test for the Validi-
         ty of Legislation 1071
      Yates v. United States 1071
      Scales v. United States 1074
      Note: Aftermath of the *Yates, Scales* and *Noto* Cases 1078
   D. The Current Status of the Clear and Present Danger
      Test—The "Brandenburg Concerto"......................1078
      Brandenburg v. Ohio 1078
      Notes: The Constitutional Law Implications of the
         Court's Smith Act Interpretation 1082
      Notes: The Clear and Present Danger Debate—Some
         General Considerations 1084
Section 2. Intermezzo: An Introduction to the Concepts of Vague-
      ness, Overbreadth and Prior Restraint 1087
   A. Vagueness and Overbreadth 1087
      Herndon v. Lowry 1087
      Coates v. Cincinnati 1088
      Broadrick v. Oklahoma.......................................1091
      Note: Substantial Overbreadth...........................1093
      Secretary of State of Maryland v. Joseph H. Munson Co. 1094
      Notes: Federal Court Injunctions Against Vague and
         Overbroad Statutes 1094
   B. Prior Restraint 1097
      Near v. Minnesota 1098
      Vance v. Universal Amusement Co. 1101
      Note: Injunctions and Prior Restraint 1105
Section 3. Speech Conflicting With Other Community Values:
      Government Control of the Content of Speech.........1105
   A. Protection of Individual Reputation and Privacy.............1106
      Beauharnais v. Illinois...1106
      New York Times Co. v. Sullivan 1107
      Note: New York Times and "The Central Meaning of the
         First Amendment".....................................1111
      Gertz v. Robert Welch, Inc. 1112
      Time, Inc. v. Firestone......................................1120
      Walston v. Reader's Digest Ass'n 1120
      Hutchinson v. Proxmire......................................1121
      Note: Jury Instructions, Directed Verdicts, Summary
         Judgments, and Appellate Review 1121
      Cox Broadcasting Corp. v. Cohn 1122
      Zacchini v. Scrips-Howard Broadcasting Co. 1125

Section 3. Speech Conflicting With Other Community Values: Government Control of the Content of Speech— Continued

B. Control of Obscenity 1126
   1. The Rationale for Prohibiting Obscenity 1126
      Paris Adult Theatre I v. Slayton 1126
      New York v. Ferber 1131
   2. The Problem of Definition 1131
      Miller v. California 1131
      Jenkins v. Georgia 1136
C. Control of "Fighting Words" and Offensive Speech 1138
   Cantwell v. Connecticut 1138
   Chaplinsky v. New Hampshire 1138
   Cohen v. California 1139
   Lewis v. New Orleans 1141
   Federal Communications Commission v. Pacifica Foundation 1143
D. Regulation of Commercial Advertising 1153
   Virginia State Board of Pharmacy v. Virginia Citizens Consumer Council, Inc. 1153
   Note: Time, Place, and Manner Regulation of Commercial Speech 1159
   Note: Attorney Advertising 1159
   Linmark Associates v. Township of Willingboro 1160
   Friedman v. Rogers 1161
   Note: Overbreadth and Commercial Speech 1161
   Central Hudson Gas & Electric Corp. v. Public Service Commission 1162
   Note: The Definition of Commercial Speech 1169

CHAPTER 15. RESTRICTIONS ON TIME, PLACE, OR MANNER OF EXPRESSION 1170
Section 1. Discriminatory Regulations 1170
   Carey v. Brown 1170
   Note: Equal Protection or First Amendment? 1176
Section 2. The Traditional Public Forum: Speech Activities in Streets and Parks 1177
A. The Considerations Justifying Denial of the Use of Streets and Parks for Speech Activities 1177
   Schneider v. New Jersey (Town of Irvington) 1177
   Note: Minimum Access v. Equal Access to the Public Forum 1178
   Kovacs v. Cooper 1178
   Cox v. Louisiana (Cox I) 1179
   Cox v. Louisiana (Cox II) 1180
   United States v. Grace 1180
   Grayned v. Rockford 1181
   Note: Parade and Demonstration Permit Systems 1181

Page

Section 2. The Traditional Public Forum: Speech Activities in Streets and Parks—Continued
  B. The Hostile Audience _____1183
      Feiner v. New York _____1183
      Edwards v. South Carolina _____1184
      Cox v. Louisiana (Cox I) _____1185
Section 3. The Non-traditional Forum _____1187
  A. Speech Activities in Public Property Other Than Parks and Streets_____1187
      *Adderley v. Florida*_____1187
      Tinker v. Des Moines School Dist. _____1189
      Greer v. Spock _____1192
      Heffron v. International Society for Krishna Consciousness, Inc. _____1193
      United States Postal Service v. Council of Greenburgh Civic Associations _____1193
      Perry Education Association v. Perry Local Educators' Association _____1194
      Los Angeles v. Taxpayers for Vincent _____1200
  B. The Government Forum and Government Subsidies to Speech _____1209
      Notes: The Government as Speaker _____1210
      Board of Education v. Pico _____1212
      Federal Communications Commission v. League of Women Voters _____1223
Section 4. Speech on Private Premises_____1235
      *Young v. American Mini Theatres, Inc.*_____1235
      Schad v. Borough of Mount Ephraim _____1239
      Consolidated Edison Co. v. Public Service Commission 1244
      *Village of Schaumburg v. Citizens for a Better Environment*_____1249
      Secretary of State of Maryland v. Joseph H. Munson Co. 1255
Section 5. Labor Picketing _____1255
      International Brotherhood of Teamsters v. Vogt, Inc. 1255

CHAPTER 16. PROTECTION OF PENUMBRAL FIRST AMENDMENT RIGHTS _____1260
Section 1. Symbolic Speech _____1260
      *United States v. O'Brien*_____1260
      Spence v. Washington _____1263
      Clark v. Community for Creative Non-Violence _____1266
Section 2. Compelled Affirmation of Belief _____1271
      West Virginia State Board of Education v. Barnette ____1271
      Wooley v. Maynard_____1272
      Prune Yard Shopping Center v. Robins _____1273

Page

Section 3. Freedom of Association _____1273
   A. The Right Associate _____1273
      NAACP v. Alabama _____1273
      Note: Speech and Non-Speech Association _____1275
      NAACP v. Claiborne Hardware Co. _____1275
      Roberts v. United States Jaycees _____1280
   B. The Right Not to Associate _____1289
      Abood v. Detroit Board of Education _____1289
      Consolidated Edison Co. v. New York Public Service
        Commission _____1293
   C. Political Association _____1293
      1. Chosing and Electing Candidates for Public Office __1293
         Note: Political Association and Selection of Dele-
            gates to Major National Party Conventions1293
         Storer v. Brown _____1294
         Anderson v. Celebrezze_____1298
      2. Political Fundraising and Expenditures_____1298
         Buckley v. Valeo _____1298
         Note: Contributions to Ballot Measure Campaigns__1303
         Note: Political Action Committees _____1303
         First National Bank of Boston v. Bellotti _____1304
         Federal Election Commission v. National Right to
           Work Committee _____1310
Section 4. Compelled Disclosure of Beliefs and Associations_____1311
   A. Registration and Reporting Requirements _____1311
      NAACP v. Alabama _____1311
      Note _____1311
      Notes: Anti-Communist Legislation of the Fifties_____1311
      Communist Party v. Subversive Activities Control Bd.___1312
      Note: The Sequel_____1313
      *Buckley v. Valeo*_____1314
      Brown v. Socialist Workers '74 Campaign Committee ____1317
   B. Legislative Investigations_____1318
      Watkins v. United States_____1319
      *Barenblatt v. United States*_____1320
      Gibson v. Florida Legislative Investigating Committee___1324
   C. Information Requests as a Condition of Issuance of a
      License to Practice a Profession _____1324
      Baird v. Arizona _____1325
      In re Stolar_____1327
      *Law Students Research Council v. Wadmond*_____1328
Section 5. Speech and Association Rights of Government Employ-
      ees _____1331
   A. Conditioning Government Employment on Speech and Po-
      litical Activity_____1331
      *Connick v. Myers*_____1331
      United States Civil Service Commission v. National
        *Association of Letter Carriers*_____1338
      Branti v. Finkel _____1340

Page

Section 5. Speech and Association Rights of Government Em-
                ployees—Continued

  B. Loyalty Programs _____1344

      1. Protection of the Bill of Attainder Clauses _____1345

         Note: The Early Cases: Cummings and Garland ____1345

         United States v. Lovett _____1346

         United States v. Brown _____1346

      2. Protection of the First Amendment _____1349

         Note: Federal Loyalty Security Executive Orders ___1349

         Adler v. Board of Education _____1350

         Konigsberg v. State Bar of California _____1350

         Keyishian v. Board of Regents _____1350

         United States v. Robel _____1351

      3. Loyalty Oaths _____1351

         Elfbrandt v. Russell _____1352

         Cole v. Richardson _____1353

      4. The Privilege Against Self-Incrimination and Procedu-
                    ral Due Process _____1354

         Lefkowitz v. Turley _____1354

         Note: Procedural Due Process and Loyalty Inquiries 1355

CHAPTER 17. FREEDOM OF THE PRESS _____1356

Section 1. Introduction _____1356

  A. Relationship Between the Speech and Press Clauses _____1356

  B. Regulation of the Business of Publishing _____1358

    *Minneapolis Star and Tribune Co. v. Minnesota Commis-
          sioner of Revenue* _____1358

    Calder v. Jones _____1363

Section 2. Restraints on Editorial Judgment _____1363

    *Pittsburgh Press Co. v. Pittsburgh Commission on
          Human Relations* _____1363

    Miami Herald Publishing Co. v. Tornillo _____1365

Section 3. Prohibition of Publication of Government Informa-
                tion _____1368

    New York Times v. United States _____1368

    Note: Protection of the Courts Against Criticism _____1374

    Nebraska Press Association v. Stuart _____1375

    Cox Broadcasting Corp. v. Cohn _____1380

    Landmark Communications, Inc. v. Virginia _____1380

    Smith v. Daily Mail Publishing Co. _____1381

    Seattle Times Co. v. Rhinehart _____1382

Section 4. Government Demands for Confidential Press Informa-
                tion _____1382

    Branzburg v. Hayes _____1382

    Zurcher v. Stanford Daily _____1387

    Herbert v. Lando _____1387

Page

Section 5. Press Access to Government Information _____1388
    Note: Press Access Decisons Prior to 1980 _____1388
    *Richmond Newspapers, Inc. v. Virginia*_____1389
    Note: Press Access Decisions Since Richmond Newspapers, Inc. v. Virginia _____1398
Section 6. Special Problems of the Electronic Media _____1399
    Columbia Broadcasting System, Inc. v. Democratic National Committee _____1399
    Federal Communications Commission v. Pacifica Foundation _____1409
    Federal Communications Commission v. WNCN Listeners Guild_____1409
    CBS, Inc. v. Federal Communications Commission_____1409
    Federal Communications Commission v. League of Women Voters _____1411

CHAPTER 18. RELIGION AND THE CONSTITUTION _____1412
Section 1. The Establishment Clause _____1412
    A. Introduction _____1412
        Everson v. Board of Education _____1413
        Note: Denominational Preferences_____1417
    B. Religion in Public Schools _____1417
        *Zorach v. Clauson*_____1417
        Engel v. Vitale _____1420
        Note: The Bible Reading Cases _____1423
        Widmar v. Vincent_____1425
        Epperson v. Arkansas _____1425
        Note: Religious Motivation and the Establishment Clause 1426
    C. Financial Aid to Church-Related Schools _____1427
        1. Elementary and Secondary Schools _____1427
            Walz v. Tax Commission_____1427
            Lemon v. Kurtzman_____1428
            Committee for Public Education and Religious Liberty v. Nyquist _____1429
            Sloan v. Lemon _____1429
            Levitt v. Committee for Public Education and Religious Liberty _____1429
            *Wolman v. Walter*_____1429
            Committee for Public Education and Religious Liberty v. Regan_____1440
            Mueller v. Allen _____1441
        2. Higher Education _____1444
            Tilton v. Richardson _____1444
            Hunt v. McNair_____1445
            Roemer v. Board of Public Works _____1445
    D. Other Government Practices _____1451
        *Lynch v. Donnelly*_____1451

TABLE OF CONTENTS

Page

Section 2. The Free Exercise of Religion _____1461
   A. Belief, Expression and Conduct_____1461
      Note: The Mormon Polygamy Cases _____1462
      Note: The Flag Salute Cases_____1462
      Cantwell v. Connecticut _____1463
      McDaniel v. Paty _____1463
   B. Regulation of Conduct Compelled by Religious Belief____1467
      Note: The Sunday Closing Decisions _____1467
      Sherbert v. Verner _____1470
      Thomas v. Review Board of the Indiana Employment
        Security Division_____1474
      Note: When Is Objection to War Religiously Conscien-
           tious? The Seeger and Welsh Cases_____1475
      Gillette v. United States _____1476
      Wisconsin v. Yoder _____1477
      United States v. Lee _____1481
      Bob Jones University v. United States _____1482

Appendix_____1483
Index _____1493

TABLE OF CASES

The principal cases are in italic type. Cases cited or discussed are in roman type. References are to pages.

Abington School Dist. v. Schempp, 42, 1423
Abood v. Detroit Board of Education, 1289
Abrams v. United States, 1056, 1058, 1059, 1067, 1085, 1097
Adair v. United States, 528
Adamson v. California, 502, 507
Adderley v. Florida, 1187
Addyston Pipe & Steel Co. v. United States, 187
Adickes v. Kress & Co., 1018
Adkins v. Children's Hosp., 35, 528, 532
Adler v. Board of Education, 120, 122, 123, 1350
Arkon v. Akron Center for Reproductive Health, Inc., 602
Alabama Public Serv. Comm'n v. Southern Ry. Co., 82
Albertson v. Subversive Activities Control Board, 1314
Alexander v. Louisiana, 518
Allen v. Wright, 102
Allgeyer v. Louisiana, 522
Allied Structural Steel Co. v. Spannaus, 478, 550
Amalgamated Food Employees Union v. Logan Valley Plaza, Inc., 966, 969
Anderson v. Celebrezze, 1298
Anderson v. Dunn, 1318
Apodaca v. Oregon, 516
Aptheker v. Secretary of State, 1313
Arizona Governing Committee v. Norris, 725
Arkansas Elec. Coop. Corp. v. Arkansas Public Serv. Comm'n, 248
Arlington Heights, Village of v. Metropolitan Housing Development Corp., 99, 758
Armco, Inc. v. Hardesty, 340, 344
Arnett v. Kennedy, 950
Ashe v. Swenson, 518
Atlantic Coast Line R.R. Co. v. Engineers, 63
Austin v. New Hampshire, 346, 494

Babbitt v. United Farm Workers, 1096
Bacchus Imports, Limited v. Dias, 324, 340, 346
Bacon v. Rutland R.R. Co., 81
Baggett v. Bullitt, 80, 1095
Bailey v. Richardson, 1355

Baird v. Arizona, 1325
Baker v. Carr, 133, 144
Baldwin v. G.A.F. Seelig, Inc., 269, 316, 1043
Baldwin v. Hale, 494, 495
Ballew v. Georgia, 516
Baltimore Radio Show, Inc. v. State, 1084
Bank of Augusta v. Earle, 318
Barbier v. Connolly, 629
Barenblatt v. United States, 1086, 1320
Barron v. Baltimore, 19, 481, 507
Barron v. Mayor and City Council of Baltimore, 479
Barrows v. Jackson, 979
Bates v. State Bar of Arizona, 1159, 1161
Beauharnais v. Illinois, 1106
Beilan v. Board of Education, 1354
Bell v. Maryland, 980
Bellotti v. Baird, 598, 599
Belmont, United States v., 237, 239, 444
Benton v. Maryland, 518
Bernal v. Fainter, 692
Bibb v. Navajo Freight Lines, Inc., 255
Bishop v. Wood, 937
Bivens v. Six Unknown Named Agents of the Fed. Bureau of Narcotics, 65, 1042
Blum v. Yaretsky, 987
Board of Education v. Allen, 1427
Board of Education v. Pico, 1212, 1426
Board of Regents of State Colleges v. Roth, 933, 1345
Bob Jones University v. United States, 1482
Boddie v. Connecticut, 626
Bolger v. Young's Drug Products, 1169
Bolling v. Sharpe, 632, 669
Borden's Farm Products Co. v. Ten Eyck, 634
Bose Corp. v. Consumer's Union, 1121
Boston, City of v. Anderson, 1211
Bouie v. City of Columbia, 980
Bradley v. Public Utilities Commission, 251
Brandenburg v. Ohio, 1078, 1082, 1345
Branti v. Finkel, 1340
Branzburg v. Hayes, 1382
Braunfeld v. Brown, 1467, 1468, 1469
Brewster, United States v., 475
Bridges v. California, 1084, 1375
Broadrick v. Oklahoma, 1091
Brooks v. United States, 216

TABLE OF CASES

Brotherhood of R.R. Trainmen v. Virginia, 1275

Brown v. Board of Education of Topeka, 33, 632, *666*, 670, *671*, 684, 685

Brown v. Maryland, 90, 340

Brown v. Socialist Workers '74 Campaign Committee, 1317

Brown v. Thomson, 865

Brown, United States v., 1346

Buck v. Kuykendall, 248, 250

Buckley v. Valeo, 229, *464*, 1210, *1298*, 1303, *1314*

Bullock v. Carter, 876

Bunting v. Oregon, 528, 529

Burch v. Louisiana, 517

Burford v. Sun Oil Co., 81

Burton v. Wilmington Parking Authority, 983, 985

Butler, United States v., 197, 227

Caban v. Mohammed, 706, 707

Cafeteria Workers v. McElroy, 1355

Calder v. Jones, 1363

Califano v. Goldfarb, 739

Califano v. Webster, 779

California v. Byers, 518

California v. Taylor, 407

California, United States v., 407

California Medical Association v. Federal Election Commission, 1303

Caminetti v. United States, 216

Cantwell v. Connecticut, 1138, 1463

Capital Cities Cable, Inc. v. Crisp, 327

Carey v. Brown, 843, 1097, *1170*, 1177

Carey v. Population Services International, 584, 598, 601

Carolene Products Co., United States v., 532

Carroll v. President and Comm'rs of Princess Anne, 1182

Carter v. Carter Coal Co., 195, 200

Case v. Bowles, 407

Castaneda v. Partida, 773

Causby, United States v., 90

Central Hudson Gas & Electric Corp. v. Public Service Commission, 1162, 1169

Chaplinsky v. New Hampshire, 1105, 1106, 1138

Chicago, Burlington & Quincy Ry. Co. v. Chicago, 518

Chicago, Burlington & Quincy Ry. Co. v. Iowa, 185

Chicago, Milwaukee & St. Paul v. Ackly, 185

Chicago, Milwaukee & St. Paul R. Co. v. Minnesota, 522

Chicot County Drainage Dist. v. Baxter State Bank, 35

Chirac v. Chirac, 244

Cipriano v. Houma, 36

Citizens Against Rent Control/Coalition for Fair Housing v. Berkeley, 1303

City Bank Farmers Trust Co. v. Schnader, 81

City of (see name of city)

Civil Rights Cases, 960

Clark v. Community for Creative Non-Violence, 1266

Clark Distilling Co. v. Western Maryland R.R. Co., 184

Classic, United States v., 1016

Clements v. Fashing, 877

Cleveland Board of Education v. La-Fleur, 953

Coates v. Cincinnati, 1088, 1094

Codd v. Velger, 950

Coe v. Town of Errol, 182, 186

Cohen v. California, 1086, *1139*

Cohen v. Hurley, 1354

Cohens v. Virginia, 47

Cole v. Arkansas, 519

Cole v. Richardson, 1353

Cole v. Young, 1350

Coleman v. Miller, 148

Colgrove v. Battin, 516

Collins v. Hardyman, 1013

Colorado Springs Amusements, Limited v. Rizzo, 60

Columbia Broadcasting System, Inc. v. Democratic National Committee, 1210, 1211, *1399*

Columbia Broadcasting System, Inc. v. Federal Communications Commission, 1409

Columbus Board of Education v. Penick, 684, 763

Committee for Public Education & Religious Liberty v. Nyquist, 1429

Committee for Public Education and Religious Liberty v. Regan, 1440

Common Cause v. Schmitt, 1303

Commonwealth Edison Co. v. Montana, 354

Communist Party v. Subversive Activities Control Board, 1312, 1313

Complete Auto Transit, Inc. v. Brady, 349

Connick v. Myers, 1331, 1345

Consolidated Edison Co. v. New York Public Service Commission, 1244, 1293

Container Corporation of America v. Franchise Tax Board, 343, *378*, 387

Cooley v. Board of Wardens of the Port of Philadelphia, 158, *178*, 181, 183, 186, 247

Cooper v. Aaron, 33

Coppage v. Kansas, 528, 535

Corfield v. Coryell, 317, 318, 478

Cox v. Louisiana (Cox I), 1179, *1185*

Cox v. Louisiana (Cox II), 1180
Cox v. New Hampshire, 1181, 1182
Cox Broadcasting Corp. v. Cohn, 48, *1122,* 1380
Craig v. Boren, 103, 713, 720
Craig v. Harney, 1084, 1375
Crandall v. Nevada, 316
Crawford v. Los Angeles Board of Education, 1003
Cruikshank, United States v., 1005, 1016
Crutcher v. Kentucky, 248
Cummings v. Missouri, 1345, 1346
Curtiss-Wright Export Corp., United States v., 231, 443

Da Costa v. Laird, 451
Dahnke-Walker Milling Co. v. Bondurant, 57
Dames & Moore v. Regan, 444
Damico v. California, 80, 81
Dandridge v. Williams, 895
Daniel v. Family Sec. Life Ins. Co., 535
Daniel Ball, The, 181
Darby, United States v., 192, *204,* 207, 407, 535
Davidson v. New Orleans, 520
Davis v. Beason, 1462
Davis v. Passman, 475
Davis v. Wechsler, 49
Davis, Helvering v., 228
Day-Brite Lighting v. Missouri, 542
Dayton Board of Educ. v. Brinkman, 684, 685
De Jonge v. Oregon, 1065
Dean Milk Co. v. City of Madison, 270
DeFunis v. Odegaard, 115, 118, 119, 120
Delaware v. Prouse, 50
Dennis v. United States, 1067, 1071, 1078, 1082, 1084, 1085
Department of Revenue v. James Beam Distilling Co., 346
Department of Revenue of Washington v. Association of Washington Stevedoring Companies, 360
Deposit Guar. Nat'l Bank v. Roper, 119
Detroit Bank v. United States, 632
Detroit Trust Co. v. The Barlum, 245
Dillon v. Gloss, 147
Doe v. Commonwealth's Attorney, 601
Dombrowski v. Pfister, 1095, 1096
Doran v. Salem Inn, Inc., 83, 1096
Doremus v. Board of Educ., 119, 120
Douglas v. California, 625
Draper v. Washington, 625
Dred Scott v. Sanford, 483, 496, 507, 520
Dugan v. Rank, 75
Duke Power Co. v. Carolina Environmental Study Group, 101
Duncan v. Louisiana, 508, 516, 519
Dunn v. Blumstein, 118, 119, 873, 882

E.C. Knight Co., United States v., 186, 187
Eakin v. Raub, 31
Eastland v. United States Servicemen's Fund, 475
Edelman v. Jordan, 60, 76
Edgar v. Mite Corp., 314, 1043
Edwards v. California, 316, 518
Edwards v. South Carolina, 1184
Eisenstadt v. Baird, 584
Elfbrandt v. Russell, 1082, *1352*
Endo, Ex parte, 661
Energy Reserves Group, Inc. v. Kansas Power & Light Co., 556
Engel v. Vitale, 42, *1420*
Enmons, United States v., 220
Epperson v. Arkansas, 124, 1211, 1425, 1426
Equal Employment Opportunity Commission v. Wyoming, 416, 1040
Erb v. Morasch, 247, 250
Estes v. Texas, 519
Evans v. Abney, 966, 982, 985
Evans v. Newton, 966, 969, 982, 985, 1001
Everson v. Board of Education, 518, 1412, *1413,* 1417, 1423, 1427, 1429
Ex parte (see name of party)
Exxon Corp. v. Eagerton, 559
Exxon Corp. v. Governor of Maryland, 540
Exxon Corp. v. Wisconsin Dept. of Revenue, 343

Fairfax's Devisee v. Hunter's Lessee, 49
Fay v. Noia, 90
Federal Communications Commission v. League of Women Voters, 1223, 1411
Federal Communications Commission v. Pacifica Foundation, 1143, 1409
Federal Communications Commission v. WNCN Listeners Guild, 1409
Federal Election Commission v. National Right to Work Committee, 1310
Federal Energy Regulatory Commission v. Mississippi, 425
Feiner v. New York, 1183
Ferguson v. Skrupa, 538, 539
Fiallo v. Bell, 496
First National Bank of Boston v. Bellotti, 1211, *1304,* 1357
Fitzpatrick v. Bitzer, 76
Flagg Brothers, Inc. v. Brooks, 970
Flast v. Cohen, 88, 101
Fletcher v. Peck, 477
Foster-Fountain Packing Co. v. Haydel, 281
Freedman v. Maryland, 1097, 1182
Freeman v. Hewit, 342
Friedman v. Rogers, 1161
Frontiero v. Richardson, 709, 721, 739
Fry v. United States, 407
Fuentes v. Shevin, 949

Fujii v. State, 239
Fullilove v. Klutznick, 230, *815*, 1030
Furman v. Georgia, 519

Gaffney v. Cummings, 851
Gallagher v. Crown Kosher Super Market, 1467, 1469
Galvan v. Press, 495
Gannett Co. v. DePasquale, 1389
Gardner v. Broderick, 1354
Garlad, Ex parte, 1346
Garnett, In re, 245
Garrity v. New Jersey, 1354
Gault, In re, 519
Gayle v. Browder, 671
Geduldig v. Aiello, 720, 721
General Elec. Co. v. Gilbert, 721
General Trading Co. v. State Tax Comm'n, 343
Gertz v. Robert Welch, Inc., 1112
Gibbons v. Ogden, 89, 158, *168*, 176, 186, 222, 330
Giboney v. Empire Storage and Ice Co., 1086
Gibson v. Florida Legislative Investigating Committee, 1324
Gideon v. Wainwright, 519
Gillette v. United States, 1476
Gilligan v. Morgan, 138
Gilmore v. Montgomery, 985
Girard College Trusteeship, In re, 982
Gitlow v. New York, 498, *1059*, 1067, 1071, 1082
Glidden v. Zdanok, 40
Globe Newspapers Co. v. Superior Court, 1398
Goldwater v. Carter, 139
Gomez v. Perez, 699
Gordon v. Lance, 869
Gosa v. Mayden, 36
Grace, United States v., 1180
Graham v. Richardson, 635, *690*
Gravel v. United States, 475
Grayned v. Rockford, 1181
Greene v. McElroy, 1355
Greer v. Spock, 1192
Griffin v. Breckenridge, 1013, 1017
Griffin v. California, 518
Griffin v. Illinois, 625
Griffin v. Maryland, 980
Griswold v. Connecticut, 578, 584, 1260
Grovey v. Townsend, 967
Guest, United States v., 1016, 1017, 1018, 1019, 1020
Guillory v. Adm'r, Tulane Ed. Fund, 982
Guinn v. United States, 663
Gulf, Colorado & Santa Fe Railroad Co. v. Ellis, 630

H.L. v. Matheson, 599
H.P. Hood & Sons v. Du Mond, 283
Hadley v. Junior College Dist., 865, 868
Hagar v. Reclamation District, 495
Hague v. C.I.O., 1178
Hamm v. City of Rock Hill, 980
Hammer v. Dagenhart, 190, 192
Hampton v. Mow Sun Wong, 633
Hampton & Co. v. United States, 436
Hancock v. Train, 406
Hannibal & St. Joseph R.R. Co. v. Husen, 181, 268
Harisiades v. Shaughnessy, 495
Harper v. Virginia State Board of Elections, 870
Harris v. McRae, 899, 1426
Harris, United States v., 1005, 1016, 1020
Hauenstein v. Lynham, 234
Hawke v. Smith, 147
Heart of Atlanta Motel v. United States, 211, 1015
Heckler v. Mathews, 103
Heffron v. International Society for Krishna Consciousness, Inc., 1193
Heimgaertner v. Benjamin Elec. Mfg. Co., 542
Helstoski, United States v., 475
Helvering v. _____ (see opposing party)
Henry v. Mississippi and the Adequate State Ground, 49, 50, 51
Herb v. Pitcairn, 49
Herbert v. Lando, 1387
Hernandez v. Texas, 662
Herndon v. Lowry, 1087, 1094
Hess v. Indiana, 1082
Hewitt v. Helms, 945
Hicks v. Miranda, 59, 83, 1096
Hill v. Stone, 874
Hirabayashi v. United States, 660
Hodel v. Indiana, 222
Hodel v. Virginia Surface Mining & Reclamation Association, Inc., 222, 424
Hodges v. United States, 1005
Hollingsworth v. Virginia, 148
Holmes v. Atlanta, 671
Hooven & Allison Co. v. Evatt, 366
Houchins v. KQED, 1388
Houston, East & West Texas Railway Co. v. United States (The Shreveport Rate Case), 187
Hudgens v. NLRB, 969
Hudson v. Palmer, 948
Hudson and Goodwin, United States v., 1051
Hughes v. Oklahoma, 289
Hunt v. McNair, 1445
Hunt v. Washington State Apple Advertising Commission, 274
Hunter v. Erickson, 1002

Hurtado v. California, 495, 518
Hutchinson v. Proxmire, 475, 1121
Hutto v. Finney, 76

Immigration and Naturalization Service v. Chadha, 451
In re (see name of party)
International Brotherhood of Teamsters v. Vogt, Inc., 1255
Ives v. South Buffalo Ry. Co., 50

Jackson v. Metropolitan Edison Co., 993
James v. Valtierra, 1002
James Everard's Breweries v. Day, 208
Japan Line, Limited v. County of Los Angels, 343, 366
Jefferson v. Hackney, 635, 663
Jenkins v. Georgia, 1136
Jimenez v. Weinberger, 699
Johnson v. Eisentrager, 496
Johnson v. New Jersey, 36
Johnson v. Virginia, 671
Jones v. Alfred H. Mayer Co., 1009, 1012, 1013
Jones v. Helms, 890

Kahn v. Shevin, 720, 776
Kahriger, United States v., 90
Kaiser Aetna v. United States, 246
Karcher v. Daggett, 855
Kassel v. Consolidated Freightways Corporation, 257
Katzenbach v. *McClung, 214,* 1007, 1015
Katzenbach v. *Morgan, 1031,* 1039, 1040, 1041, 1042
Kentucky v. Dennison, 434
Kerr v. California, 518
Keyes v. School District No. 1, Denver, 680
Keyishian v. Board of Regents, 1082, 1350
Kidd v. Pearson, 183, 186
Kimmish v. Ball, 269
Klein, United States v., 39, 40
Kleindienst v. Mandel, 244, 496
Kleppe v. New Mexico, 240
Klopfer v. North Carolina, 518
Knauff, United States ex rel. v. Shaughnessy, 496
Konigsberg v. State Bar of California, 1086, 1350
Korematsu v. United States, 660
Kovacs v. Cooper, 1178
Kras, United States v., 626
Kunz v. New York, 1182
Kusper v. Pontikes, 876

Labine v. Vincent, 699
Lalli v. Lalli, 700
Lamont v. Postmaster General, 1314

Landmark Communications, Inc. v. Virginia, 1083, 1380
Landon v. Plasencia, 496
Larson v. Domestic & Foreign Commerce Corp., 75
Larson v. Valente, 1417
Lassiter v. Department of Social Services, 628
Law Students Research Council v. Wadmond, 1082, 1328
Lee, United States v., 1481
Lefkowitz v. Turley, 1354
Lehman v. Shaker Heights, 1211
Lehr v. Robertson, 707
Leisy v. Hardin, 183
Lemon v. Kurtzman, 36, 1428
Lerner v. Casey, 1354
Leser v. Garnett, 147
Levitt v. Committee for Public Education and Religious Liberty, 1429
Levy v. Louisiana, 699
Lewis v. BT Investment Managers, Inc., 308
Lewis v. New Orleans, 1141
License Cases, The, 176
Limbach v. Hooven & Allison Co., 366
Lincoln Fed. Labor Union v. Northwestern Iron & Metal Co., 535
Lindsley v. Natural Carbonic Gas Co., 633
Linkletter v. Walker, 36
Linmark Associates v. Township of Willingboro, 1160
Little v. Streater, 628
Lloyd Corp. v. Tanner, 966, 969
Lochner v. New York, 523, 528, 529, 577
Lockport v. Citizens for Community Action, 867
Logan v. United States, 1016
Logan v. Zimmerman Brush Co., 650, 843, 948
Loretto v. Teleprompter Manhattan CATV Corp., 570
Los Angeles v. Taxpayers for Vincent, 1093, 1200
Los Angeles, City of v. Lyons, 125
Los Angeles Department of Water and Power, City of v. Manhart, 722
Lottery case (Champion v. Ames), 216
Louisville & Jefferson Ferry Co. v. Kentucky, 342, 494
Lovell v. Griffin, 1182
Lovett, United States v., 1346
Loving v. Virginia, 653, 662
Lubin v. Panish, 877
Lucas v. Forty-Fourth General Assembly of Colorado, 849
Lugar v. Edmondson Oil Co., 1018
Lynch v. Donnelly, 1451

McCardle, Ex parte, 37, 40, 41

McCarthy v. Philadelphia Civil Service Commission, 889

McCready v. Virginia, 318

McCulloch v. Maryland, 89, 158, 159, 222, 391, 435

McDaniel v. Paty, 1463, 1467

McDonald v. Santa Fe Trail Transportation Co., 1013, 1014

McGowan v. Maryland, 1423, 1467

McGrain v. Daugherty, 1318

McLeod v. Dilworth Co., 343

McNeese v. Board of Education, 80, 81

M., Michael v. Superior Court, 725

Macintosh, United States v., 244

Mackey v. United States, 36

Madden v. Kentucky, 494

Mahan v. Howell, 850

Maine v. Thiboutot, 81

Malloy v. Hogan, 518

Mapp v. Ohio, 36, 518

Marbury v. Madison, 24, 36, 87, 90, 121, 222

Mirks v. United States, 36

Marsh v. Alabama, 968, 969

Marston v. Lewis, 874

Martin v. Hunter's Lessee, 37, 44, 47, 49

Martinez v. Bynum, 895, 929

Maryland v. Wirtz, 407

Maryland, and Two Guys from Harrison-Allentown v. McGinley, 1467

Massachusetts v. Davis, 1178

Massachusetts v. United States, 398

Massachusetts Board of Retirement v. Murgia, 744

Masses Publishing Co. v. Patten, 1054

Mathews v. Diaz, 696, 1043

Mathews v. Lucas, 699, 722

Matter of (see name of party)

Mayflower Farms, Inc. v. Ten Eyck, 634

Mayor and City Council of Baltimore City v. Dawson, 671

Memorial Hospital v. Maricopa County, 883

Memphis, City of v. Greene, 772, 1013

Metromedia, Inc. v. San Diego, 1169

Meyer v. Nebraska, 577, 578

Miami Herald Publishing Co. v. Tornillo, 1365

Michelin Tire Corp. v. Wages, 366

Michigan v. Long, 51

Michigan v. Payne, 36

Miller v. Arkansas, 404

Miller v. California, 1131

Miller, United States v., 577

Milliken v. Bradley, 685

Milliken v. Bradley (Milliken II), 689

Minersville School Dist. v. Gobitis, 1462

Minneapolis Star and Tribune Co. v. Minnesota Commissioner of Revenue, 1358

Minnesota v. Barber, 280

Minnesota v. Clover Leaf Creamery Co., 277

Minor v. Happersett, 844

Mintz v. Baldwin, 269

Miranda v. Arizona, 42, 1041, 1042

Mississippi University for Women v. Hogan, 739, 781, 1040

Missouri v. Holland, 235

Mitchum v. Foster, 82

Mobil Oil Corp. v. Commissioner of Taxes of Vermont, 343

Mobile v. Bolden, 772

Monell v. New York City Dept. of Social Services, 1006

Monroe v. Pape, 1006, 1017

Moore v. City of East Cleveland, 617

Moorman Mfg. Co. v. Bair, 343, 373

Moose Lodge v. Irvis, 988

Mora v. McNamara, 449, 450

Morehead v. New York ex rel. Tipaldo, 532

Morey v. Doud, 638

Mount Healthy City School District v. Doyle, 75

Mueller v. Allen, 1441

Mugler v. Kansas, 522

Muller v. Oregon, 528, 529

Munn v. Illinois, 185, 521

Murdock v. Memphis, 48

Murray v. Curlett, 42

Murray's Lessee v. Hoboken Land & Improvement Co., 481, 495, 507, 520

NAACP v. Alabama, 1273, 1275, 1311

NAACP v. Button, 1275

NAACP v. Claiborne Hardware Co., 1275

Naim v. Naim, 62, 120

Napier v. Atlantic Coast Line R.R. Co., 330

Nashville, Chattanooga & St. Louis Ry. v. Browning, 348

Nashville Gas Co. v. Satty, 721

National Geographic Society v. California Board of Equalization, 343, 387

National League of Cities v. Usery, 223, 408, 435

Near v. Minnesota, 1098, 1105, 1098

Nebbia v. New York, 529, 530, 532, 540

Nebraska Press Association v. Stuart, 1375

Nelson v. County of Los Angeles, 1354

Nevada v. Hall, 434

New England Power Co. v. New Hampshire, 292

New Hampshire v. Maine, 434

New Jersey Welfare Rights Organization v. Cahill, 699

New Mexico, United States v., 391, 398

New Orleans v. Dukes, 638

New Orleans City Parks Improvement Ass'n v. Detiege, 671

New State Ice Co. v. Liebmann, 529

New York v. Ferber, 1093, 1131

New York v. Miln, 316

New York v. O'Neill, 433, 519

New York v. Uplinger, 601

New York Central R.R. Co. v. White, 51

New York ex rel. Bryant v. Zimmerman, 1311

New York Tel. Co., United States v., 118

New York Times Co. v. Sullivan, 1107, 1111, 1210

New York Times Co. v. United States, 1368

Nishimura Ekiu v. United States, 496

Nixon v. Administrator of General Services, 472

Nixon v. Condon, 967

Nixon v. Fitzgerald, 474

Nixon v. Herndon, 967

Nixon, United States v., 66, 144, 468

NLRB v. Fainblatt, 203

NLRB v. Friedman-Harry Marks Clothing Co., 203

NLRB v. Fruehauf Trailer Co., 203

NLRB v. Jones & Laughlin Steel Corp., 200, 201, 203

Norfolk & Western Ry. Co. v. Missouri State Tax Comm'n, 343

Norman v. Baltimore & Ohio Railroad, 242

North Carolina State Bd. of Ed. v. Swann, 1042

Northern Pipeline Co. v. Marathon Pipeline Co., 36

Northern Securities Co. v. United States, 187

Northwestern States Portland Cement Co. v. Minnesota, 372

Norwood v. Harrison, 986, 1427

Noto v. United States, 1078, 1082, 1094

Nye v. United States, 1051, 1374

O'Brien, United States v., 1260

Ohio v. Wyandotte Chem. Corp., 63

Ohralik v. Ohio State Bar Ass'n, 1159

Oklahoma Packing Co. v. Gas Co., 64

Olim v. Wakinekona, 945

Oliver, In re, 519

Olsen v. Nebraska, 535

Oregon v. Mitchell, 1036, 1039, 1041

Orlando v. Laird, 451

Orr v. Orr, 102, 780

Ortwein v. Schwab, 628

Owen v. City of Independence, 1006

Palko v. Connecticut, 499, 519

Palmor v. Sidoti, 657

Parden v. Terminal Ry., 76, 78, 407

Parham v. Hughes, 707

Parhan v. J.R., 599

Paris Adult Theatre I v. Slaton, 1126

Parker v. Gladden, 519

Parratt v. Taylor, 945

Pasadena City Bd. of Educ. v. Spangler, 684

Patsy v. Florida Board of Regents, 81

Patterson v. Colorado, 1097

Paul v. Virginia, 182, 479

Peik v. Chicago & Northwestern Ry., 185

Pell v. Procunier, 1388

Peltier, United States v., 36

Penn Central Transportation Co. v. City of New York, 518, *559*

Pennekamp v. Florida, 1084, 1375

Pennhurst State School & Hospital v. Halderman, 66, 79, 80, 230

Pennoyer v. Neff, 494, 1043

Pennsylvania v. Board of City Trusts, 981, 985

Pennsylvania v. Brown, 982

Pennsylvania v. West Virginia, 282

Pension Benefit Guaranty Corp. v. R.A. Gray & Co., 540

Perez v. United States, 217, 221

Perry Education Association v. Perry Local Educators' Association, 1194

Personnel Administrator of Massachusetts v. Feeney, 722, 761

Peters v. Hobby, 1355

Phelps Dodge Corp. v. Nat'l Labor Relations Board, 535

Philadelphia v. New Jersey, 286

Philadelphia & Reading Ry. Co. v. Pennsylvania, 341

Pickering v. Board of Education, 1345

Pickett v. Brown, 705

Pierce v. Soc'y of Sisters, 578

Pike v. Bruce Church, Inc., 247, 281

Pink, United States v., 238, 239, 444

Pittman v. Home Owner's Loan Corp., 398

Pittsburgh Press Co. v. Pittsburgh Commission of Human Relations, 1105, *1363*

Planned Parenthood v. Danforth, 596, 597

Planned Parenthood Association of Kansas City v. Ashcroft, 616

Plessy v. Ferguson, 663

Plyler v. Doe, 920, 1043

Poe v. Ullman, 120, 123

Pointer v. Texas, 519

Polk County v. Dodson, 1018

Poulos v. New Hampshire, 1182

Powell v. McCormack, 135

Powelson, United States ex rel. T.V.A. v., 577

Press-Enterprise Co. v. Superior Court, 1398

Price, United States v., 1017, 1019
Primus, In re, 1159
Prize Cases, The, 447
Prudential Ins. Co. v. Benjamin, 1043
Prudential Ins. Co. v. Cheek, 1053
Pruneyard Shopping Center v. Robins, 540, 569, 1273
Ptasynski, United States v., 225
Public Utilities Comm'n v. Attleboro Steam & Elec. Co., 248
Public Utilities Commission of California v. United States, 405

Quaker City Cab Co. v. Pennsylvania, 634
Quarles, In re, 1016
Quern v. Jordan, 1006
Quilloin v. Walcott, 706

R.M.J., Matter of, 1160
R.S., Linda v. Richard D., 101
Rahrer, In re, 184
Railroad Commission of Texas v. Pullman Co., 80
Railroad Comm'n of Wisconsin v. Chicago, Burlington & Quincy R.R. Co., 190
Railroad Retirement Board v. Alton R. Co., 195
Railway Express Agency v. New York, 635
Ray v. Atlantic Richfield Co., 331
Reed v. Reed, 708, 721
Reese, United States v., 1005
Reeves, Inc. v. Stake, 295
Regents of the University of California v. Bakke, 786
Regional Rail Reorganization Act Cases, 125
Reid v. Covert, 238, 240
Reitman v. Mulkey, 997, 1001, 1002
Rendell-Baker v. Kohn, 988
Rescue Army v. Municipal Court, 63, 87, 120
Rex v. _____ (see opposing party)
Reynolds v. Sims, 844, 849, 868
Reynolds v. United States, 1462, 1468
Rice v. Santa Fe Elevator Corp., 330
Richardson v. Ramirez, 875
Richmond Newspapers, Inc. v. Virginia, 1389, 1398
Robel, United States v., 1351
Roberts v. United States Jaycees, 1014, 1280
Robertson, State v., 1085
Robinson v. California, 519
Robinson v. Florida, 980
Roe v. Wade, 115, 118, 119, 584, 585, 601
Roemer v. Board of Public Works, 1445
Rogers v. Lodge, 764, 771
Rome, City of v. United States, 1020, 1039, 1040

Ross v. Moffitt, 625
Rostker v. Goldberg, 733
Roth v. United States, 518
Rowoldt v. Perfetto, 495
Ruckelshaus v. Monsanto Company, 571
Runyon v. McCrary, 81, 1012, 1013, 1014
Ryan, United States v., 1183

Salyer Land Co. v. Tulare Lake Basin Water Storage Dist., 868
San Antonio Independent School Dist. v. Rodriguez, 911
San Diego Gas & Electric Co. v. City of San Diego, 576
San Mateo County v. Southern Pacific R.R. Co., 521
Santa Clara County v. Southern Pacific R.R. Co., 521
Santa Clara Pueblo v. Martinez, 75
Scales v. United States, 1067, 1074, 1078, 1082, 1094
Schad v. Borough of Mount Ephraim, 1239
Schapiro v. Thompson, 635, 877, 1041
Schaumburg, Village of v. Citizens for Better Environment, 1249
Schechter Poultry Corp. v. United States, 193
Schenck v. United States, 1055, 1058, 1059, 1067, 1071, 1085
Scheuer v. Rhodes, 76
Schiro v. Bynum, 671
Schneider v. New Jersey (Town of Irvington), 1177
School Dist. of Abington Twp. v. Schempp, 120
Schweiker v. Wilson, 648
SCRAP, United States v., 102
Screws v. United States, 1006, 1017
Seaboard Air Line Ry. Co. v. Blackwell, 250
Seattle Times Co. v. Rhinehart, 1382
Secretary of State of Maryland v. Joseph H. Munson Co., 1094, 1095, 1255
Seeger, United States v., 1475
Service v. Dulles, 1355
Shafer v. Farmers Grain Co., 247
Shaughnessy, United States ex rel. Knauff v., 496
Sheldon v. Sill, 37
Shelley v. Kraemer, 974, 979, 980, 981
Sherbert v. Verner, 1470, 1475
Shuttlesworth v. Birmingham, 1181, 1182
Sierra Club v. Morton, 101, 102
Siler v. Louisville & Nashville R. R. Co., 79, 80
Simon v. Eastern Kentucky Welfare Rights Organization, 102
Simopoulos v. Virginia, 617
Sinclair v. United States, 1319

Skinner v. Oklahoma, 578
Slaughter-House Cases, 483, 520, 629, 662, 1016
Sloan v. Lemon, 1429
Smith v. Allwright, 967
Smith v. Daily Mail Publishing Co., 1381
Smyth v. Ames, 522
Sonzinsky v. United States, 223
Sosna v. Iowa, 119, *887*
South Carolina State Highway Department v. Barnwell Brothers, 251
South-Central Timber Development v. Wunnicke, 302
Southeastern Promotions v. Conrad, 1182
South-Eastern Underwriters Ass'n, United States v., 210, 1043
Southern Pacific Co. v. Arizona, 253
Southern Ry. Co. v. King, 250
Spector Motor Serv. v. O'Connor, 342, 372
Spence v. Washington, 1263
Spevack v. Klein, 1354
Sporhase v. Nebraska, 293
Sprague, United States v., 147
Stafford v. Wallace, 192
Stanley v. Illinois, 706
State v. _____ (see opposing party)
State Athletic Comm'n v. Dorsey, 671
State Board of Equalization v. Young's Market Co., 346
Steele v. Louisville and Nashville Railroad, 968
Steffel v. Thompson, 83, 1096
Steward Machine Co. v. Davis, 201, 226
Stolar, In re, 1327
Storer v. Brown, 1294
Stovall v. Denno, 36
Strauder v. West Virginia, 629
Stump v. Sparkman, 1006
Sullivan v. Little Hunting Park, 1013, 1014
Swann v. Charlotte-Mecklenburg Board of Education, 672, 673
Swift & Co. v. United States, 192

T.V.A., United States ex rel. v. Powelson, 577
Terry v. Adams, 967
Texas, United States v., 75
Thomas v. Review Board of the Indiana Employment Security Division, 1474, 1475
Thompson v. Louisville, 48
Tilton v. Richardson, 1444
Time, Inc. v. Firestone, 1120, 1121
Times Film Corp. v. City of Chicago, 1097
Tinker v. Des Moines School District, 1189
Toledo Newspaper Co. v. United States, 1052
Trainor v. Hernandez, 79, *83*
Tutchin, Rex v., 1048

Twining v. New Jersey, 498, 1016
Tyson & Brother v. Banton, 529

Union Refrigerator Transit Co. v. Kentucky, 343, 495
United Brotherhood of Carpenters v. Scott, 1015
United Building and Construction Trades Council of Camden County and Vicinity v. Mayor and Council of the City of Camden, 318
United Mine Workers, United States v., 1182
United Public Workers, v. Mitchell, 120, 121, 123
United States v. _____ (see opposing party)
United States Civil Service Comm'n v. Letter Carriers, 123
United States Civil Service Commission v. National Association of Letter Carriers, 1338
United States Glue Co. v. Town of Oak Creek, 341
United States Parole Commission v. Geraghty, 119
United States Postal Service v. Council of Greenburgh Civic Associations, 1193
United States Railroad Retirement Board v. Fritz, 640
United States Steel Corp. v. Multistate Tax Comm'n, 373, 434
United States Trust Co. of New York v. New Jersey, 478, 543
United Transportation Union v. Long Island Railroad Co., 416
University of California v. Bakke, 118
Usery v. Turner Elkhorn Mining Co., 959

Valentine v. Chrestensen, 1106, 1159
Valley Forge Christian College v. Americans United For Separation of Church and State, Inc., 106
Vance v. Bradley, 633, 950
Vance v. Terrazas, 497
Vance v. Universal Amusement Co., 1098, *1101,* 1105
Village of (see name of village)
Virginia State Board of Pharmacy v. Virginia Citizens Consumer Council Inc., 1153, 1159
Vitek v. Jones, 941
Vlandis v. Kline, 951

Wabash, St. Louis and Pac. Ry. v. Illinois, 185, 186
Walker v. Birmingham, 1182, 1183
Walker v. Sauvinet, 519
Walz v. Tax Commission, 1427, 1429
Warth v. Seldin, 90, 101

Washington v. Davis, 751, 1003

Washington v. Seattle School Dist. No. 1, pp. 1002, 1003

Washington v. Texas, 519

Watkins v. United States, 1319

Weaver v. Palmer Bros. Co., 530

Webbs' Fabulous Pharmacies, Inc. v. Beckwith, 570

Weber v. Aetna Cas. and Sur. Co., 699

Weinberger v. Salfi, 956

Weinberger v. Wiesenfeld, 633, 739

Welsh v. United States, 1041, 1475

Welton v. Missouri, 340

Wengler v. Druggists Mutual Insurance Co., 740

West Coast Hotel Co. v. Parrish, 35, 200, 532

West Virginia v. Sims, 49, 433

West Virginia State Board of Education v. Barnette, 518, 1271, 1462, 1468

Western and Southern Life Insurance Co. v. State Board of Equalization, 347

Western Livestock v. Bureau of Revenue, 342

Whalen v. Roe, 584

White v. Massachusetts Council of Construction Employers, 300

White, United States v., 36

Whitney v. California, 1063, 1065, 1067, 1082, 1096

Wickard v. Filburn, 208

Widmar v. Vincent, 1412, 1425

Williams v. Florida, 516, 518

Williams v. Georgia, 50

Williams v. Standard Oil Co., 529

Williamson v. Lee Optical Co. of Oklahoma, 535, 637

Willson v. Black Bird Creek Marsh Co., 175

Winona & St. Peter R.R. v. Blake, 185

Winship, In re, 517

Wisconsin v. Yoder, 1477

Wisniewski v. United States, 63

Wolman v. Walter, 1428, 1429

Wolston v. Reader's Digest Association, 1120

Wong Kim Ark, United States v., 495, 497

Wood v. Georgia, 1084

Wood v. Strickland, 1006

Woods v. Cloyd W. Miller Co., 232

Wooley v. Maynard, 83, 1097, 1272, 1462

Wynehamer v. The People, 482

Yarbrough, Ex parte, 1016

Yates v. United States, 1067, *1071*, 1078, 1082, 1094

Yerger, Ex parte, 41

Yick Wo v. Hopkins, 662

Young v. American Mini Theatres, Inc., 1235

Young, Ex parte, 75, 79

Youngberg v. Romeo, 623

Younger v. Harris, 82, 124, 1096

Youngstown Sheet & Tube Co. v. Sawyer, 66, 437

Zablocki v. Redhail, 836

Zacchini v. Scripps-Howard Broadcasting Co., 1125

Zobel v. Williams, 890

Zorach v. Clauson, 1417

Zurcher v. Stanford Daily, 1387

CONSTITUTIONAL LAW

CASES AND MATERIALS

*

CONSTITUTIONAL LAW

CASES AND MATERIALS

Part I

THE CONSTITUTION AND THE COURTS: THE JUDICIAL FUNCTION IN CONSTITUTIONAL CASES

Prefatory Note

A written constitution interpreted and applied by the courts as the supreme law of the nation is the hallmark of our constitutional system. A vital part of this system is the institution of judicial review, the power and duty of the courts to declare legislative or executive acts invalid insofar as they may conflict with the Constitution. How this judicial power, not explicitly provided for in the Constitution, came to be established, and how it is exercised by courts are the subjects of Part I of this book. The Constitution, along with a brief history of its adoption, is set forth in Chapter 1. Chapter 2 deals with the institution of judicial review, its historic origins, and begins exploration of the institution's purpose. Chapter 2 also discusses Congressional control of judicial review through control of federal court jurisdiction. Chapter 3 presents an introduction to the rules that govern the handling of constitutional litigation.

Chapter 1

THE CONSTITUTION

SECTION 1. THE CONSTITUTION OF THE UNITED STATES OF AMERICA

We the People of the United States, in Order to form a more perfect Union, establish Justice, insure domestic Tranquility, provide for the common defence, promote the general Welfare, and secure the Blessings of Liberty to ourselves and our Posterity, do ordain and establish this Constitution for the United States of America.

ARTICLE I

Section 1. All legislative Powers herein granted shall be vested in a Congress of the United States, which shall consist of a Senate and House of Representatives.

Section 2. [1] The House of Representatives shall be composed of Members chosen every second Year by the People of the several States, and the Electors in each State shall have the Qualifications requisite for Electors of the most numerous Branch of the State Legislature.

[2] No Person shall be a Representative who shall not have attained to the Age of twenty five Years, and been seven Years a Citizen of the United States, and who shall not, when elected, be an Inhabitant of that State in which he shall be chosen.

[3] Representatives and direct Taxes shall be apportioned among the several States which may be included within this Union, according to their respective Numbers, which shall be determined by adding to the whole Number of free Persons, including those bound to Service for a Term of Years, and excluding Indians not taxed, three fifths of all other Persons. The actual Enumeration shall be made within three Years after the first Meeting of the Congress of the United States, and within every subsequent Term of ten Years, in such Manner as they shall by Law direct. The Number of Representatives shall not exceed one for every thirty Thousand, but each State shall have at Least one Representative; and until such enumeration shall be made, the State of New Hampshire shall be entitled to chuse three, Massachusetts eight, Rhode Island and Providence Plantations one, Connecticut five, New York six, New Jersey four, Pennsylvania eight, Delaware one, Maryland six, Virginia ten, North Carolina five, South Carolina five, and Georgia three.

[4] When vacancies happen in the Representation from any State, the Executive Authority thereof shall issue Writs of Election to fill such Vacancies.

[5] The House of Representation shall chuse their Speaker and other Officers; and shall have the sole Power of Impeachment.

Section 3. [1] The Senate of the United States shall be composed of two Senators from each State, chosen by the Legislature thereof, for six Years; and each Senator shall have one Vote.

[2] Immediately after they shall be assembled in Consequence of the first Election, they shall be divided as equally as may be into three Classes. The Seats of the Senators of the first Class shall be vacated at the Expiration of the

Second Year, of the second Class at the Expiration of the fourth Year, and of the third Class at the Expiration of the sixth Year, so that one third may be chosen every second Year; and if Vacancies happen by Resignation, or otherwise, during the Recess of the Legislature of any State, the Executive thereof may make temporary Appointments until the next Meeting of the Legislature, which shall then fill such Vacancies.

[3] No Person shall be a Senator who shall not have attained to the Age of thirty Years, and been nine Years a Citizen of the United States, and who shall not, when elected, be an Inhabitant of that State for which he shall be chosen.

[4] The Vice President of the United States shall be President of the Senate, but shall have no Vote, unless they be equally divided.

[5] The Senate shall chuse their other Officers, and also a President pro tempore, in the Absence of the Vice President, or when he shall exercise the Office of President of the United States.

[6] The Senate shall have the sole Power to try all Impeachments. When sitting for that Purpose, they shall be on Oath or Affirmation. When the President of the United States is tried, the Chief Justice shall preside: And no Person shall be convicted without the Concurrence of two thirds of the Members present.

[7] Judgment in Cases of Impeachment shall not extend further than to removal from Office, and disqualification to hold and enjoy any Office of honor, Trust, or Profit under the United States: but the Party convicted shall nevertheless be liable and subject to Indictment, Trial, Judgment, and Punishment, according to Law.

Section 4. [1] The Times, Places and Manner of holding Elections for Senators and Representatives, shall be prescribed in each State by the Legislature thereof; but the Congress may at any time by Law make or alter such Regulations, except as to the Places of chusing Senators.

[2] The Congress shall assemble at least once in every Year, and such Meeting shall be on the first Monday in December, unless they shall by Law appoint a different Day.

Section 5. [1] Each House shall be the Judge of the Elections, Returns, and Qualifications of its own Members, and a Majority of each shall constitute a Quorum to do Business; but a smaller Number may adjourn from day to day, and may be authorized to compel the Attendance of absent Members, in such Manner, and under such Penalties as each House may provide.

[2] Each House may determine the Rules of its Proceedings, punish its Members for disorderly Behavior, and, with the Concurrence of two thirds, expel a Member.

[3] Each House shall keep a Journal of its Proceedings, and from time to time publish the same, excepting such Parts as may in their Judgment require Secrecy; and the Yeas and Nays of the Members of either House on any question shall, at the Desire of one fifth of those Present, be entered on the Journal.

[4] Neither House, during the Session of Congress, shall, without the Consent of the other, adjourn for more than three days, nor to any other Place than that in which the two Houses shall be sitting.

Section 6. [1] The Senators and Representatives shall receive a Compensation for their Services, to be ascertained by Law, and paid out of the Treasury of the United States. They shall in all Cases, except Treason, Felony and Breach of the Peace, be privileged from Arrest during their Attendance at the Session of their respective Houses, and in going to and returning from the same; and for any Speech or Debate in either House, they shall not be questioned in any other Place.

[2]   No Senator or Representative shall, during the Time for which he was elected, be appointed to any civil Office under the Authority of the United States, which shall have been created, or the Emoluments whereof shall have been encreased during such time; and no Person holding any Office under the United States, shall be a Member of either House during his Continuance in Office.

Section 7. [1]   All Bills for raising Revenue shall originate in the House of Representatives; but the Senate may propose or concur with Amendments as on other Bills.

[2]   Every Bill which shall have passed the House of Representatives and the Senate, shall, before it become a Law, be presented to the President of the United States; If he approve he shall sign it, but if not he shall return it, with his Objections to the House in which it shall have originated, who shall enter the Objections at large on their Journal, and proceed to reconsider it. If after such Reconsideration two thirds of that House shall agree to pass the Bill, it shall be sent together with the Objections, to the other House, by which it shall likewise be reconsidered, and if approved by two thirds of that House, it shall become a Law. But in all such Cases the Votes of both Houses shall be determined by yeas and Nays, and the Names of the Persons voting for and against the Bill shall be entered on the Journal of each House respectively. If any Bill shall not be returned by the President within ten Days (Sundays excepted) after it shall have been presented to him, the Same shall be a Law, in like Manner as if he had signed it, unless the Congress by their Adjournment prevent its Return in which Case it shall not be a Law.

[3]   Every Order, Resolution, or Vote, to Which the Concurrence of the Senate and House of Representatives may be necessary (except on a question of Adjournment) shall be presented to the President of the United States; and before the Same shall take Effect, shall be approved by him, or being disapproved by him, shall be repassed by two thirds of the Senate and House of Representatives, according to the Rules and Limitations prescribed in the Case of a Bill.

Section 8. [1]   The Congress shall have Power To lay and collect Taxes, Duties, Imposts and Excises, to pay the Debts and provide for the common Defence and general Welfare of the United States; but all Duties, Imposts and Excises shall be uniform throughout the United States;

[2]   To borrow money on the credit of the United States;

[3]   To regulate Commerce with foreign Nations, and among the several States, and with the Indian Tribes;

[4]   To establish an uniform Rule of Naturalization, and uniform Laws on the subject of Bankruptcies throughout the United States;

[5]   To coin Money, regulate the Value thereof, and of foreign Coin, and fix the Standard of Weights and Measures;

[6]   To provide for the Punishment of counterfeiting the Securities and current Coin of the United States;

[7]   To Establish Post Offices and Post Roads;

[8]   To promote the Progress of Science and useful Arts, by securing for limited Times to Authors and Inventors the exclusive Right to their respective Writings and Discoveries;

[9]   To constitute Tribunals inferior to the supreme Court;

[10]   To define and punish Piracies and Felonies committed on the high Seas, and Offenses against the Law of Nations;

[11]   To declare War, grant Letters of Marque and Reprisal, and make Rules concerning Captures on Land and Water;

[12] To raise and support Armies, but no Appropriation of Money to that Use shall be for a longer Term than two Years;

[13] To provide and maintain a Navy;

[14] To make Rules for the Government and Regulation of the land and naval Forces;

[15] To provide for calling forth the Militia to execute the Laws of the Union, suppress Insurrections and repel Invasions;

[16] To provide for organizing, arming, and disciplining, the Militia, and for governing such Part of them as may be employed in the Service of the United States, reserving to the States respectively, the Appointment of the Officers, and the Authority of training the Militia according to the discipline prescribed by Congress;

[17] To exercise exclusive Legislation in all Cases whatsoever, over such District (not exceeding ten Miles square) as may, by Cession of particular States, and the Acceptance of Congress, become the Seat of the Government of the United States, and to exercise like Authority over all Places purchased by the Consent of the Legislature of the State in which the Same shall be, for the Erection of Forts, Magazines, Arsenals, dock-Yards, and other needful Buildings;—And

[18] To make all Laws which shall be necessary and proper for carrying into Execution for the foregoing Powers, and all other Powers vested by this Constitution in the Government of the United States, or in any Department or Officer thereof.

Section 9. [1] The Migration or Importation of Such Persons as any of the States now existing shall think proper to admit, shall not be prohibited by the Congress prior to the Year one thousand eight hundred and eight, but a Tax or duty may be imposed on such Importation, not exceeding ten dollars for each Person.

[2] The privilege of the Writ of Habeas Corpus shall not be suspended, unless when in Cases of Rebellion or Invasion the public Safety may require it.

[3] No Bill of Attainder or ex post facto Law shall be passed.

[4] No Capitation, or other direct, Tax shall be laid, unless in Proportion to the Census or Enumeration herein before directed to be taken.

[5] No Tax or Duty shall be laid on Articles exported from any State.

[6] No Preference shall be given by any Regulation of Commerce or Revenue to the Ports of one State over those of another: nor shall Vessels bound to, or from, one State be obliged to enter, clear, or pay Duties in another.

[7] No money shall be drawn from the Treasury, but in Consequence of Appropriations made by Law; and a regular Statement and Account of the Receipts and Expenditures of all public Money shall be published from time to time.

[8] No Title of Nobility shall be granted by the United States: And no Person holding any Office of Profit or Trust under them, shall, without the Consent of the Congress, accept of any present, Emolument, Office or Title, of any kind whatever, from any King, Prince, or foreign State.

Section 10. [1] No State shall enter into any Treaty, Alliance, or Confederation; grant Letters of Marque and Reprisal; coin Money; emit Bills of Credit; make any Thing but gold and silver Coin a Tender in Payment of Debts; pass any Bill of Attainder, ex post facto Law, or Law impairing the Obligation of Contracts, or grant any Title of Nobility.

[2] No State shall, without the Consent of the Congress, lay any Imposts or Duties on Imports or Exports, except what may be absolutely necessary for

executing its inspection Laws: and the net Produce of all Duties and Imposts, laid by any State on Imports or Exports, shall be for the Use of the Treasury of the United States; and all such Laws shall be subject to the Revision and Controul of the Congress.

[3] No State shall, without the Consent of Congress, lay any Duty of Tonnage, keep Troops, or Ships of War in time of Peace, enter into any Agreement or Compact with another State, or with a foreign Power, or engage in War, unless actually invaded, or in such imminent Danger as will not admit of delay.

ARTICLE II

Section 1. [1] The executive Power shall be vested in a President of the United States of America. He shall hold his Office during the Term of four Years, and, together with the Vice President, chosen for the same Term, be elected, as follows:

[2] Each State shall appoint, in such Manner as the Legislature thereof may direct, a Number of Electors, equal to the whole Number of Senators and Representatives to which the State may be entitled in the Congress; but no Senator or Representative, or Person holding an Office of Trust or Profit under the United States, shall be appointed an Elector.

[3] The Electors shall meet in their respective States, and vote by Ballot for two Persons, of whom one at least shall not be an Inhabitant of the same State with themselves. And they shall make a List of all the Persons voted for, and of the Number of Votes for each; which List they shall sign and certify, and transmit sealed to the Seat of the Government of the United States, directed to the President of the Senate. The President of the Senate shall, in the Presence of the Senate and House of Representatives, open all the Certificates, and the Votes shall then be counted. The Person having the greatest Number of Votes shall be the President, if such Number be a Majority of the whole Number of Electors appointed; and if there be more than one who have such Majority, and have an equal Number of Votes, then the House of Representatives shall immediately chuse by Ballot one of them for President; and if no Person have a Majority, then from the five highest on the List the said House shall in like Manner chuse the President. But in chusing the President, the Votes shall be taken by States, the Representation from each State having one Vote; A quorum for this Purpose shall consist of a Member or Members from two thirds of the States, and a Majority of all the States shall be necessary to a Choice. In every Case, after the Choice of the President, the Person having the greater Number of Votes of the Electors shall be the Vice President. But if there should remain two or more who have equal Votes, the Senate shall chuse from them by Ballot the Vice President.

[4] The Congress may determine the Time of chusing the Electors, and the Day on which they shall give their Votes; which Day shall be the same throughout the United States.

[5] No person except a natural born Citizen, or a Citizen of the United States, at the time of the Adoption of this Constitution, shall be eligible to the Office of President; neither shall any Person be eligible to that Office who shall not have attained to the Age of thirty five Years, and been fourteen Years a Resident within the United States.

[6] In case of the removal of the President from Office, or of his Death, Resignation or Inability to discharge the Powers and Duties of the said Office, the Same shall devolve on the Vice President, and the Congress may by Law provide for the Case of Removal, Death, Resignation or Inability, both of the President and Vice President, declaring what Officer shall then act as President,

and such Officer shall act accordingly, until the Disability be removed, or a President shall be elected.

[7] The President shall, at stated Times, receive for his Services, a Compensation, which shall neither be encreased nor diminished during the Period for which he shall have been elected, and he shall not receive within that Period any other Emolument from the United States, or any of them.

[8] Before he enter on the Execution of his Office, he shall take the following Oath or Affirmation: "I do solemnly swear (or affirm) that I will faithfully execute the Office of President of the United States, and will to the best of my Ability, preserve, protect and defend the Constitution of the United States."

Section 2. [1] The President shall be Commander in Chief of the Army and Navy of the United States, and of the militia of the several States, when called into the actual Service of the United States; he may require the Opinion, in writing, of the principal Officer in each of the executive Departments, upon any Subject relating to the Duties of their respective Offices, and he shall have Power to grant Reprieves and Pardons for Offenses against the United States, except in Cases of Impeachment.

[2] He shall have Power, by and with the Advice and Consent of the Senate, to make Treaties, provided two thirds of the Senators present concur; and he shall nominate, and by and with the Advice and Consent of the Senate, shall appoint Ambassadors, other public Ministers and Consuls, Judges of the supreme Court, and all other Officers of the United States, whose Appointments are not herein otherwise provided for, and which shall be established by Law; but the Congress may by Law vest the Appointment of such inferior Officers, as they think proper, in the President alone, in the Courts of Law, or in the Heads of Departments.

[3] The President shall have Power to fill up all Vacancies that may happen during the Recess of the Senate, by granting Commissions which shall expire at the End of their next Session.

Section 3. He shall from time to time give to the Congress Information of the State of the Union, and recommend to their Consideration such Measures as he shall judge necessary and expedient; he may, on extraordinary Occasions, convene both Houses, or either of them, and in Case of Disagreement between them, with Respect to the Time of Adjournment, he may adjourn them to such Time as he shall think proper; he shall receive Ambassadors and other public Ministers; he shall take Care that the Laws be faithfully executed, and shall Commission all the Officers of the United States.

Section 4. The President, Vice President and all civil Officers of the United States, shall be removed from Office on Impeachment for, and Conviction of, Treason, Bribery, or other high Crimes and Misdemeanors.

ARTICLE III

Section 1. The judicial Power of the United States, shall be vested in one supreme Court, and in such inferior Courts as the Congress may from time to time ordain and establish. The Judges, both of the supreme and inferior Courts, shall hold their Offices during good Behaviour, and shall, at stated Times, receive for their Services a Compensation, which shall not be diminished during their Continuance in Office.

Section 2. [1] The judicial Power shall extend to all Cases, in Law and Equity, arising under this Constitution, the Laws of the United States, and Treaties made, or which shall be made, under their Authority;—to all Cases affecting Ambassadors, other public Ministers and Consuls;—to all Cases of admiralty and maritime Jurisdiction,—to Controversies to which the United

States shall be a Party;—to Controversies between two or more States;—between a State and Citizens of another State;—between Citizens of different States;—between Citizens of the same State claiming Lands under the Grants of different States, and between a State, or the Citizens thereof, and foreign States, Citizens or Subjects.

[2] In all Cases affecting Ambassadors, other public Ministers and Consuls, and those in which a State shall be a Party, the supreme Court shall have original Jurisdiction. In all the other Cases before mentioned, the supreme Court shall have appellate Jurisdiction, both as to Law and Fact, with such Exceptions, and under such Regulations as the Congress shall make.

[3] The trial of all Crimes, except in Cases of Impeachment, shall be by Jury; and such Trial shall be held in the State where the said Crimes shall have been committed; but when not committed within any State, the Trial shall be at such Place or Places as the Congress may by Law have directed.

Section 3. [1] Treason against the United States, shall consist only in levying War against them, or, in adhering to their Enemies, giving them Aid and Comfort. No Person shall be convicted of Treason unless on the Testimony of two Witnesses to the same overt Act, or on Confession in open Court.

[2] The Congress shall have Power to declare the Punishment of Treason, but no Attainder of Treason shall work Corruption of Blood, or Forfeiture except during the Life of the Person attainted.

ARTICLE IV

Section 1. Full Faith and Credit shall be given in each State to the public Acts, Records, and judicial Proceedings of every other State. And the Congress may by general Laws prescribe the Manner in which such Acts, Records and Proceedings shall be proved, and the Effect thereof.

Section 2. [1] The Citizens of each State shall be entitled to all Privileges and Immunities of Citizens in the several States.

[2] A Person charged in any State with Treason, Felony, or other Crime, who shall flee from Justice, and be found in another State, shall on demand of the executive Authority of the State from which he fled, be delivered up, to be removed to the State having Jurisdiction of the Crime.

[3] No Person held to Service or Labour in one State, under the Laws thereof, escaping into another, shall, in Consequence of any Law or Regulation therein, be discharged from such Service or Labour, but shall be delivered up on Claim of the Party to whom such Service or Labour may be due.

Section 3. [1] New States may be admitted by the Congress into this Union; but no new State shall be formed or erected within the Jurisdiction of any other State; nor any State be formed by the Junction of two or more States, or Parts of States, without the Consent of the Legislatures of the States concerned as well as of the Congress.

[2] The Congress shall have Power to dispose of and make all needful Rules and Regulations respecting the Territory or other Property belonging to the United States; and nothing in this Constitution shall be so construed as to Prejudice any Claims of the United States, or of any particular State.

Section 4. The United States shall guarantee to every State in this Union a Republican Form of Government, and shall protect each of them against Invasion; and on Application of the Legislature, or of the Executive (when the Legislature cannot be convened) against domestic Violence.

ARTICLE V

The Congress, whenever two thirds of both Houses shall deem it necessary, shall propose Amendments to this Constitution, or, on the Application of the Legislatures of two thirds of the several States, shall call a Convention for proposing Amendments, which, in either Case, shall be valid to all Intents and Purposes, as part of this Constitution, when ratified by the Legislatures of three fourths of the several States, or by Conventions in three fourths thereof, as the one or the other Mode of Ratification may be proposed by the Congress; Provided that no Amendment which may be made prior to the Year One thousand eight hundred and eight shall in any Manner affect the first and fourth Clauses in the Ninth Section of the first Article; and that no State, without its Consent, shall be deprived of its equal Suffrage in the Senate.

ARTICLE VI

[1] All Debts contracted and Engagements entered into, before the Adoption of this Constitution shall be as valid against the United States under this Constitution, as under the Confederation.

[2] This Constitution, and the Laws of the United States which shall be made in Pursuance thereof; and all Treaties made, or which shall be made, under the Authority of the United States, shall be the supreme Law of the Land; and the Judges in every State shall be bound thereby, any Thing in the Constitution or Laws of any State to the Contrary notwithstanding.

[3] The Senators and Representatives before mentioned, and the Members of the several State Legislatures, and all executive and judicial Officers, both of the United States and of the several States, shall be bound by Oath or Affirmation, to support this Constitution; but no religious Test shall ever be required as a Qualification to any Office or public Trust under the United States.

ARTICLE VII

The Ratification of the Conventions of nine States shall be sufficient for the Establishment of this Constitution between the States so ratifying the Same.

ARTICLES IN ADDITION TO, AND AMENDMENT OF, THE CONSTITUTION OF THE UNITED STATES OF AMERICA, PROPOSED BY CONGRESS, AND RATIFIED BY THE LEGISLATURES OF THE SEVERAL STATES PURSUANT TO THE FIFTH ARTICLE OF THE ORIGINAL CONSTITUTION.

AMENDMENT I [1791]

Congress shall make no law respecting an establishment of religion, or prohibiting the free exercise thereof; or abridging the freedom of speech, or of the press; or the right of the people peaceably to assemble, and to petition the Government for a redress of grievances.

AMENDMENT II [1791]

A well regulated Militia, being necessary to the security of a free State, the right of the people to keep and bear Arms, shall not be infringed.

AMENDMENT III [1791]

No Soldier shall, in time of peace be quartered in any house, without the consent of the Owner, nor in time of war, but in a manner to be prescribed by law.

AMENDMENT IV [1791]

The right of the people to be secure in their persons, houses, papers, and effects, against unreasonable searches and seizures, shall not be violated, and no Warrants shall issue, but upon probable cause, supported by Oath or affirmation, and particularly describing the place to be searched, and the persons or things to be seized.

AMENDMENT V [1791]

No person shall be held to answer for a capital, or otherwise infamous crime, unless on a presentment or indictment of a Grand Jury, except in cases arising in the land or naval forces, or in the Militia, when in actual service in time of War or public danger; nor shall any person be subject for the same offence to be twice put in jeopardy of life or limb; nor shall be compelled in any criminal case to be a witness against himself, nor be deprived of life, liberty, or property, without due process of law; nor shall private property be taken for public use, without just compensation.

AMENDMENT VI [1791]

In all criminal prosecutions, the accused shall enjoy the right to a speedy and public trial, by an impartial jury of the State and district wherein the crime shall have been committed, which district shall have been previously ascertained by law, and to be informed of the nature and cause of the accusation; to be confronted with the witnesses against him; to have compulsory process for obtaining witnesses in his favor, and to have the Assistance of Counsel for his defence.

AMENDMENT VII [1791]

In Suits at common law, where the value in controversy shall exceed twenty dollars, the right of trial by jury shall be preserved, and no fact tried by jury, shall be otherwise re-examined in any Court of the United States, than according to the rules of the common law.

AMENDMENT VIII [1791]

Excessive bail shall not be required, nor excessive fines imposed, nor cruel and unusual punishments inflicted.

AMENDMENT IX [1791]

The enumeration in the Constitution, of certain rights, shall not be construed to deny or disparage others retained by the people.

AMENDMENT X [1791]

The powers not delegated to the United States by the Constitution, nor prohibited by it to the States, are reserved to the States respectively, or to the people.

AMENDMENT XI [1798]

The Judicial power of the United States shall not be construed to extend to any suit in law or equity, commenced or prosecuted against one of the United States by Citizens of another State, or by Citizens or Subjects of any Foreign State.

AMENDMENT XII [1804]

The Electors shall meet in their respective states and vote by ballot for President and Vice-President, one of whom, at least, shall not be an inhabitant of the same state with themselves; they shall name in their ballots the person voted for as President, and in distinct ballots the person voted for as Vice-President, and they shall make distinct lists of all persons voted for as President, and of all persons voted for as Vice-President, and of the number of votes for each, which lists they shall sign and certify, and transmit sealed to the seat of the government of the United States, directed to the President of the Senate;—The President of the Senate shall, in the presence of the Senate and House of Representatives, open all the certificates and the votes shall then be counted;— The person having the greatest number of votes for President, shall be the President, if such number be a majority of the whole number of Electors appointed; and if no person have such majority, then from the persons having the highest numbers not exceeding three on the list of those voted for as President, the House of Representatives shall choose immediately, by ballot, the President. But in choosing the President, the votes shall be taken by states, the representation from each state having one vote; a quorum for this purpose shall consist of a member or members from two-thirds of the states, and a majority of all the states shall be necessary to a choice. And if the House of Representatives shall not choose a President whenever the right of choice shall devolve upon them before the fourth day of March next following, then the Vice-President shall act as President, as in the case of the death or other constitutional disability of the President.—The person having the greatest number of votes as Vice-President, shall be the Vice-President, if such number be a majority of the whole number of Electors appointed, and if no person have a majority, then from the two highest numbers on the list, the Senate shall choose the Vice-President; a quorum for the purpose shall consist of two-thirds of the whole number of Senators, and a majority of the whole number shall be necessary to a choice. But no person constitutionally ineligible to the office of President shall be eligible to that of Vice-President of the United States.

AMENDMENT XIII [1865]

Section 1. Neither slavery nor involuntary servitude, except as a punishment for crime whereof the party shall have been duly convicted, shall exist within the United States, or any place subject to their jurisdiction.

Section 2. Congress shall have power to enforce this article by appropriate legislation.

AMENDMENT XIV [1868]

Section 1. All persons born or naturalized in the United States, and subject to the jurisdiction thereof, are citizens of the United States and of the State wherein they reside. No State shall make or enforce any law which shall abridge the privileges or immunities of citizens of the United States; nor shall any State deprive any person of life, liberty, or property, without due process of law; nor deny to any person within its jurisdiction the equal protection of the laws.

Section 2. Representatives shall be apportioned among the several States according to their respective numbers, counting the whole number of persons in each State, excluding Indians not taxed. But when the right to vote at any election for the choice of electors for President and Vice President of the United States, Representatives in Congress, the Executive and Judicial officers of a State, or the members of the Legislature thereof, is denied to any of the male inhabitants of such State, being twenty-one years of age, and citizens of the

United States, or in any way abridged, except for participation in rebellion, or other crime, the basis of representation therein shall be reduced in the proportion which the number of such male citizens shall bear to the whole number of male citizens twenty-one years of age in such State.

Section 3.   No person shall be a Senator or Representative in Congress, or elector of President and Vice President, or hold any office, civil or military, under the United States, or under any State, who having previously taken an oath, as a member of Congress, or as an officer of the United States, or as a member of any State legislature, or as an executive or judicial officer of any State, to support the Constitution of the United States, shall have engaged in insurrection or rebellion against the same, or given aid or comfort to the enemies thereof.   But Congress may by a vote of two-thirds of each House, remove such disability.

Section 4.   The validity of the public debt of the United States, authorized by law, including debts incurred for payment of pensions and bounties for services in suppressing insurrection or rebellion, shall not be questioned.   But neither the United States nor any State shall assume or pay any debt or obligation incurred in aid of insurrection or rebellion against the United States, or any claim for the loss or emancipation of any slave; but all such debts, obligations and claims shall be held illegal and void.

Section 5.   The Congress shall have power to enforce, by appropriate legislation, the provisions of this article.

AMENDMENT XV [1870]

Section 1.   The right of citizens of the United States to vote shall not be denied or abridged by the United States or by any State on account of race, color, or previous condition of servitude.

Section 2.   The Congress shall have power to enforce this article by appropriate legislation.

AMENDMENT XVI [1913]

The Congress shall have power to lay and collect taxes on incomes, from whatever source derived, without apportionment among the several States, and without regard to any census or enumeration.

AMENDMENT XVII [1913]

[1]   The Senate of the United States shall be composed of two Senators from each State, elected by the people thereof, for six years; and each Senator shall have one vote.   The electors in each State shall have the qualifications requisite for electors of the most numerous branch of the State legislatures.

[2]   When vacancies happen in the representation of any State in the Senate, the executive authority of such State shall issue writs of election to fill such vacancies: *Provided,* That the legislature of any State may empower the executive thereof to make temporary appointments until the people fill the vacancies by election as the legislature may direct.

[3]   This amendment shall not be so construed as to affect the election or term of any Senator chosen before it becomes valid as part of the Constitution.

AMENDMENT XVIII [1919]

Section 1.   After one year from the ratification of this article the manufacture, sale, or transportation of intoxicating liquors within, the importation thereof into, or the exportation thereof from the United States and all territory subject to the jurisdiction thereof for beverage purposes is hereby prohibited.

Section 2. The Congress and the several States shall have concu power to enforce this article by appropriate legislation.

Section 3. This article shall be inoperative unless it shall have been ratified as an amendment to the Constitution by the legislatures of the several States, as provided in the Constitution, within seven years from the date of the submission hereof to the States by the Congress.

AMENDMENT XIX [1920]

[1] The right of citizens of the United States to vote shall not be denied or abridged by the United States or by any State on account of sex.

[2] Congress shall have power to enforce this article by appropriate legislation.

AMENDMENT XX [1933]

Section 1. The terms of the President and Vice President shall end at noon on the 20th day of January, and the terms of Senators and Representatives at noon on the 3d day of January, of the years in which such terms would have ended if this article had not been ratified; and the terms of their successors shall then begin.

Section 2. The Congress shall assemble at least once in every year, and such meeting shall begin at noon on the 3d day of January, unless they shall by law appoint a different day.

Section 3. If, at the time fixed for the beginning of the term of the President, the President elect shall have died, the Vice President elect shall become President. If the President shall not have been chosen before the time fixed for the beginning of his term, or if the President elect shall have failed to qualify, then the Vice President elect shall act as President until a President shall have qualified; and the Congress may by law provide for the case wherein neither a President elect nor a Vice President elect shall have qualified, declaring who shall then act as President, or the manner in which one who is to act shall be selected, and such person shall act accordingly until a President or Vice President shall have qualified.

Section 4. The Congress may by law provide for the case of the death of any of the persons from whom the House of Representatives may choose a President whenever the right of choice shall have devolved upon them, and for the case of the death of any of the persons from whom the Senate may choose a Vice President whenever the right of choice shall have devolved upon them.

Section 5. Sections 1 and 2 shall take effect on the 15th day of October following the ratification of this article.

Section 6. This article shall be inoperative unless it shall have been ratified as an amendment to the Constitution by the legislatures of three-fourths of the several States within seven years from the date of its submission.

AMENDMENT XXI [1933]

Section 1. The eighteenth article of amendment to the Constitution of the United States is hereby repealed.

Section 2. The transportation or importation into any State, Territory, or possession of the United States for delivery or use therein of intoxicating liquors, in violation of the laws thereof, is hereby prohibited.

Section 3. This article shall be inoperative unless it shall have been ratified as an amendment to the Constitution by conventions in the several States, as provided in the Constitution, within seven years from the date of the submission hereof to the States by the Congress.

AMENDMENT XXII [1951]

Section 1.   No person shall be elected to the office of the President more than twice, and no person who has held the office of President, or acted as President, for more than two years of a term to which some other person was elected President shall be elected to the office of President more than once. But this Article shall not apply to any person holding the office of President when this Article was proposed by the Congress, and shall not prevent any person who may be holding the office of President, or acting as President, during the term within which this Article becomes operative from holding the office of President or acting as President during the remainder of such term.

Section 2.   This article shall be inoperative unless it shall have been ratified as an amendment to the Constitution by the legislatures of three-fourths of the several States within seven years from the date of its submission to the States by the Congress.

AMENDMENT XXIII [1961]

Section 1.   The District constituting the seat of Government of the United States shall appoint in such manner as the Congress may direct:

A number of electors of President and Vice President equal to the whole number of Senators and Representatives in Congress to which the District would be entitled if it were a State, but in no event more than the least populous state; they shall be in addition to those appointed by the states, but they shall be considered, for the purposes of the election of President and Vice President, to be electors appointed by a state; and they shall meet in the District and perform such duties as provided by the twelfth article of amendment.

Section 2.   The Congress shall have power to enforce this article by appropriate legislation.

AMENDMENT XXIV [1964]

Section 1.   The right of citizens of the United States to vote in any primary or other election for President or Vice President, for electors for President or Vice President, or for Senator or Representative in Congress, shall not be denied or abridged by the United States or any State by reason of failure to pay any poll tax or other tax.

Section 2.   The Congress shall have power to enforce this article by appropriate legislation.

AMENDMENT XXV [1967]

Section 1.   In case of the removal of the President from office or of his death or resignation, the Vice President shall become President.

Section 2.   Whenever there is a vacancy in the office of the Vice President, the President shall nominate a Vice President who shall take office upon confirmation by a majority vote of both Houses of Congress.

Section 3.   Whenever the President transmits to the President pro tempore of the Senate and the Speaker of the House of Representatives his written declaration that he is unable to discharge the powers and duties of his office, and until he transmits to them a written declaration to the contrary, such powers and duties shall be discharged by the Vice President as Acting President.

Section 4.   Whenever the Vice President and a majority of either the principal officers of the executive departments or of such other body as Congress may by law provide, transmit to the President pro tempore of the Senate and the Speaker of the House of Representatives their written declaration that the President is unable to discharge the powers and duties of his office, the Vice President shall immediately assume the powers and duties of the office as Acting President.

Thereafter, when the President transmits to the President pro tempore of the Senate and the Speaker of the House of Representatives his written declaration that no inability exists, he shall resume the powers and duties of his office unless the Vice President and a majority of either the principal officers of the executive departments or of such other body as Congress may by law provide, transmit within four days to the President pro tempore of the Senate and the Speaker of the House of Representatives their written declaration that the President is unable to discharge the powers and duties of his office. Thereupon Congress shall decide the issue, assembling within forty-eight hours for that purpose if not in session. If the Congress, within twenty-one days after receipt of the latter written declaration, or, if Congress is not in session, within twenty-one days after Congress is required to assemble, determines by two-thirds vote of both Houses that the President is unable to discharge the powers and duties of his office, the Vice President shall continue to discharge the same as Acting President; otherwise, the President shall resume the powers and duties of his office.

Amendment XXVI [1971]

Section 1. The right of citizens of the United States, who are eighteen years of age or older, to vote shall not be denied or abridged by the United States or by any State on account of age.

Section 2. The Congress shall have power to enforce this article by appropriate legislation.

SECTION 2. HISTORY OF THE ADOPTION OF THE CONSTITUTION AND ITS MOST SIGNIFICANT AMENDMENTS

A. THE ARTICLES OF CONFEDERATION AND THE ORIGINAL CONSTITUTION

The Constitutional Convention, which met in Philadelphia in May, 1787, resulted from a growing belief that the federal government set up by the Articles of Confederation was inadequate. Under the Confederation, the United States were governed by Congress, a unicameral body in which each state had one vote. Nine votes were required for any significant action, and, more restrictively, "alteration" of the Articles required unanimity. There was no national executive, and no significant federal judiciary. Congress lacked the power to tax and, since states were often delinquent in responding to Congress' requisitions, Congress was perpetually hampered by lack of funds. Congress lacked the power to regulate interstate commerce, leading to commercial wars between the states.[1]

Agreement at the Constitutional Convention that a new federal government should be established, with power to act directly on individuals and not just upon the member states, masked considerable disagreement as to the extent of

---

[1] While a number of the features of the Constitution that emerged from the Convention can be traced to perceived inadequacies in the Articles of Confederation, other provisions reflect provisions contained in the Articles. Under the Articles, Congress controlled war, peace and foreign policy; a number of lesser powers described in Art. I, § 8, of the Constitution appeared in the Articles; the concepts of privileges and immunities of state citizens, extradition of fugitives, and full faith and credit were contained in Article IV of the Articles of Confederation.

the powers of that new government. It took four months of debate and compromise before the final draft of the Constitution was approved on September 17, 1787. To protect free debate, the Convention adopted a secrecy rule, and no contemporary accounts were available of the debates and decisions at the Convention. A sketchy journal was kept by William Jackson, secretary of the Convention. The journal remained in the archives of the Department of State until published in 1818 under the editorship of John Quincy Adams. More comprehensive information about the Convention's deliberations is contained in James Madison's account. Madison's notes, however, were not published until 1840, four years after his death, and more than half a century after ratification.

Ratification of the Constitution by the necessary nine states was completed in 1788. The ratification controversy was intense. The Federalist Papers, produced in the debate over ratification, are an important source of information as to contemporary views of the meaning of the Constitution. They are a series of 85 letters published in the New York papers from October, 1787 to April, 1788, under the pseudonym "Publius." The Federalist Papers were, in fact, written by Alexander Hamilton, James Madison and John Jay. One should keep in mind that the Federalist Papers, despite their high quality and the prominence of their authors, were intended as partisan debate on the side of ratification and not as dispassionate analysis of the meaning of the Constitution. Historical treatments of the Confederation period and of the drafting and ratification of the Constitution include: G. Bancroft, *History of the Formation of the Constitution of the United States of America* (1893); J. Fiske, *The Critical Period of American History* (1888); M. Jensen, *The Articles of Confederation: An Interpretation of the Social-Constitutional History of the American Revolution, 1774–1781* (1940); _____, *The New Nation: A History of the United States during the Confederation, 1781–1789* (1950): _____, *The Making of the American Constitution* (1964); A. McLaughlin, *The Confederation and the Constitution: 1783–1789* (1905); C. Rossiter, *1787: The Grand Convention* (1966); C. Van Doren, *The Great Rehearsal: The Story of the Making and Ratification of the Constitution of the United States* (1948); C. Warren, *The Making of the Constitution* (1928); B. Wright, *Consensus and Continuity, 1776–1787* (1958). The Federalist is available in a number of editions. Documentary collections include: H. Commager (ed.), *Documents of American History* (9th ed. 1973); J. Elliott (ed.), *The Debates of the Several State Conventions on the Adoption of the Federal Constitution* (1836); M. Farrand (ed.), *The Records of the Federal Convention of 1787* (1911, 1937); M. Jensen (ed.), *The Documentary History of the Ratification of the Constitution* (1976, 1978) (A multivolume work, only volumes I–III available).

B. THE BILL OF RIGHTS

PROTECTION OF FREEDOM IN THE CONSTITUTION OF 1787

The emphasis which must be placed upon the Bill of Rights and other amendments to the Constitution, Professor Chafee reminds us, should not lead one to ignore the protections for individual liberty which were built into the original document; perhaps the most important of these is the limitation on suspension by the national government of the writ of *habeas corpus*.[1] Professor Chafee adds:

"Among the affirmative rights in Article I are the immunity of debates in Congress; the Interstate Commerce Clause which, without expressly mentioning any human right, has in fact been invoked to protect freedom of movement

---

[1] Art. I, § 9. Chafee, *How Human Rights Got Into the Constitution* (1952) 51.

across state lines; . . . and the prohibition of bills of attainder and *ex post facto* laws in the nation or the states. . . . Article III on the judiciary obliges criminal cases to be tried by a jury of the neighborhood. It also contains the definition of treason. . . . Finally, the miscellaneous provisions found in Article IV entitle citizens of one state to enjoy in another state 'all the Privileges and Immunities' of its own citizens, and empower the United States to preserve in every state a 'Republican Form of Government' and to protect the right to life 'against domestic violence.' " [2]

Professor Chafee's brief summary does not purport to be complete. For example, the protection of economic (and even intellectual) liberty was possible under the prohibition in Article I, Section 10, against state laws impairing the obligation of contracts. But in spite of the importance of these and other guaranties established by the original document, federal constitutional protection for individual liberty must be derived, for the most part, from two groups of amendments separated in time by almost eighty years: the Bill of Rights and the three post-Civil War amendments. The objectives of these two groups of amendments and the relationship between them raise questions which are as important as they are difficult.

THE BILL OF RIGHTS

The importance of a written declaration of the rights of the individual loomed large in the minds of early Americans. This tradition had grown out of struggles against royal prerogative, and was reflected in written guaranties of Magna Carta (1215),[3] the Petition of Right (1628)[4] and the Bill of Rights (1689).[5]

This tradition was carried to the New World. Many of the early Colonial Charters offered important assurances to the settlers of "all Liberties and Immunities of free and natural Subjects . . . ."[6] But the most direct antecedents of modern guarantees of individual rights appeared in the constitutions that the colonists framed for themselves at the outbreak of the Revolution. In eight state constitutions, these guarantees were gathered into separate provisions called a Bill of Rights or Declaration of Rights; three states wove them into the fabric of the document.[7] Probably the most influential of these early bills of rights was that of Virginia.

[2] Id. at 5–6 (Footnotes omitted.) See also: *The Federalist No. 84* (Hamilton); Story, *Commentaries on the Constitution of the United States* (4th ed. 1873) § 1859.

[3] Magna Carta exacted from King John numerous limitations on his prerogative. Chapter 39 read: "No freeman shall be seized or imprisoned or disseised or outlawed or in any way destroyed nor will we go against him or send against him except by the lawful judgment of his peers, or by the law of the land."

[4] The Petition of Right directed to Charles I contained the prayer that further military commissions for proceedings by martial law should not issue "lest by colour of them any of your majesty's subjects be destroyed or put to death, contrary to the laws and franchise of the land. . . ."

[5] The Bill of Rights was designed to limit the power of William of Orange. It proclaimed ". . . that it is the right of the subjects to petition the king and all commitments and prosecutions for such petitioning are illegal . . . that the subjects which are Protestants may have arms for their defense suitable for their conditions and as allowed by law; that election of members of parliament ought to be free; that the freedom of speech and debates or proceedings in parliament ought not to be impeached or questioned in any court or place out of parliament; that excessive bail ought not to be required, nor excessive fines imposed, nor cruel and unusual punishment inflicted; that jurors ought to be duly impanelled and returned, and jurors which pass upon men in trials for high treason ought to be freeholders. . . ."

[6] Charter of Connecticut, 1662, in 1 Thorpe, *American Charters, Constitutions and Organic Laws,* 529, 533 (1909). Similar provisions occur in other colonial charters. See Chafee, *How Human Rights Got into the Constitution* 36 (1952). Several of the charters also had guarantees of religious freedom. Id. at 40–42. Cf. Rutland, *The Birth of the Bill of Rights* (1955).

[7] Connecticut and Rhode Island retained their colonial charters. Chafee, op. cit. supra, pp. 18–19.

Since the Articles of Confederation (1777) did not grant significant legislative power to the central government, the absence of a bill of rights is understandable. It is more surprising that proposals for a Bill of Rights made in the Constitutional Convention of 1787 were rejected. No single explanation is compelling. There is some evidence of concern lest prohibiting Congress from intruding into enumerated areas of individual rights might suggest that Congress possessed power to invade other rights not specifically protected. Another deterrent appears to have been the fear that disagreement over the definition of individual rights might jeopardize the Convention's completion of the Constitution and the launching of the new government.[8] Finally, there is evidence that the delegates were persuaded to avoid the problem by the supposition that the limited powers of Congress made a Bill of Rights unnecessary.[9]

One of the few records of the debates on this question in the constitutional convention is as follows:[10]

"Mr. Pinkney & Mr. Gerry, moved to insert a declaration 'that the liberty of the Press should be inviolably observed—'

"Mr. Sherman—It is unnecessary—The power of Congress does not extend to the Press. On the question, (it passed in the negative)."

The reasons that impelled the Constitutional Convention to omit a federal bill of rights proved unsatisfactory in crucial state ratification conventions. After relatively smooth sailing in Delaware, Pennsylvania, New Jersey, Georgia and Connecticut, the storm broke in Massachusetts. Opposition was quieted in part by the proposal that ratification be coupled with suggestions for amendments to the Constitution that would protect individual liberty; the Federalists tendered a gentleman's agreement to give them favorable consideration. Many of the subsequent state conventions suggested amendments[11] that included proposals for a bill of rights.[12]

To keep faith with these states, James Madison compiled a set of proposed amendments based on the state bills of rights and the amendments proposed by the state conventions. His conception of the role of a bill of rights is summarized in a letter to Jefferson dated October 17, 1788:[13]

"My own opinion has always been in favor of a bill of rights; providing it be so framed as not to imply powers not meant to be included in the enumeration. At the same time I have never thought the omission a material defect, nor been anxious to supply it even by *subsequent* amendment, for any other reason than that it is anxiously desired by others. I favored it

---

[8] On September 12 a motion for a committee to prepare a bill of rights was defeated by a vote of 10–0; the only recorded objection to the motion was in connection with a proposed guaranty of jury trial in civil cases. "Mr. Gorham. It is not possible to discriminate equity cases from those in which juries are proper. The Representatives of the people may be safely trusted in this matter," 2 Farrand, *Records of the Federal Convention* (1911) 587, 588.

Speaking in the South Carolina House of Representatives, C.C. Pinckney summarized the reasons listed above and added the further point that bills of rights "generally begin with declaring that all men are by nature born free. Now, we should make that declaration with a very bad grace, when a large part of our property consists in men who are actually born slaves." 3 Id. at 256.

[9] This and other arguments against the adoption of a Bill of Rights were reviewed and answered at length by Madison in his proposals to the House of Representatives. 1 *Annals of Congress* 438–439 (1834).

[10] 2 Farrand, op. cit. supra 617–618 (Madison's notes for September 14).

[11] Bloom, *History of the Formation of the Union under the Constitution* (1941) 24–27, 280 et seq.; Hart, *Formation of the Union* (1892) 130–31; 1 Nichols & Nichols, *The Republic of the United States* (1942) 262.

[12] Madison believed that the chief basis of popular opposition to ratification of the Constitution to be its omission of such guarantees, 1 *Annals of Congress* 433 (1834).

[13] *Writings of James Madison* 269, 271–274 (Hunt ed. 1904); see further 1 *Annals of Congress* 436–44 (1834). For Jefferson's prodding of Madison see Bowers, *Jefferson and the Bill of Rights*, 41 Va.L. Rev. 709, 712–714 (1955).

because I have supposed it might be of use, and if properly executed could not be of disservice. I have not viewed it in an important light 1. because I conceive that in a certain degree, though not in the extent argued by Mr. Wilson, the rights in question are reserved by the manner in which the federal powers are granted, 2. because there is great reason to fear that a positive declaration of some of the most essential rights could not be obtained in the requisite latitude . . . 3. because the limited powers of the federal Government and the jealousy of the subordinate Governments, afford a security which has not existed in the case of the State Governments, and exists in no other, 4. because experience proves the inefficacy of a bill of rights on those occasions when its control is most needed. . . . . What use then it may be asked can a bill of rights serve in popular Governments? . . . 1. The political truths declared in that solemn manner acquire by degrees the character of fundamental maxims of free Government, and as they become incorporated with the national sentiment, counteract the impulses of interest and passion. 2. Altho it be generally true . . . that the danger of oppression lies in the interested majorities of the people rather than in usurped acts of the Government, yet there may be occasions on which the evil may spring from the latter source; and on such, a bill of rights will be a good ground for an appeal to the sense of the community. . . . absolute restrictions in cases that are doubtful, or where emergencies may overrule them, ought to be avoided."

In the First Congress, Madison proposed detailed amendments to the text of the Constitution which, after material modification, led to the Bill of Rights.[14]

The original Constitution contained relatively few express limitations on state power. (The most important of these are in Section 10 of Article I, and Sections 1 and 2 of Article IV.) The addition of the Bill of Rights left state power unchanged. Forty-two years after their ratification, Chief Justice Marshall confirmed that the provisions of the Bill of Rights were limitations only on the power of the federal government. Barron v. Baltimore, 7 Pet. 243 (1833). Until after the Civil War, state constitutions—interpreted by state courts—were the source of most constitutional limitations on state government.

C. THE ADOPTION OF THE CIVIL WAR AMENDMENTS

Appomattox marked the end of the struggle over the constitutional issue of secession but it precipitated the country's most serious social problem: the future status of the four million individuals who had been held in slavery. This transition to freedom posed an acute problem of assimilation reflected in grave problems of constitutional law.

Slavery and the Thirteenth Amendment. By language only thinly veiled, the Constitution of 1787 recognized and sanctioned slavery.[1] Thus, although

---

[14] Madison's initial proposals called for amendments which were to be worked into the body of the Constitution, rather than supplements added to the original text. Thus, Madison's proposals included ten new provisions to be added to Article I, Section 9. 1 *Annals of Congress* 434–35 (1834). These correspond, for the most part, to the first ten amendments which finally received approval. Madison's proposals also included the following addition to Article I, Section 10: "No state shall violate the equal rights of conscience, or the freedom of the press, or the trial by jury in criminal cases." 1 Id. at 435. He further proposed to rewrite Article III, Section 2 to require, inter alia, that "in all crimes punishable with loss of life or member, presentment or indictment by a grand jury shall be an essential preliminary . . ." and that "In suits at common law, between man and man, the trial by jury, as one of the best securities to the rights of the people, ought to remain inviolate" Ibid.

[1] Art. I, § 2, ¶ 3; Art. I, § 9, ¶ 1; Art. IV, § 2, ¶ 3.

Lincoln's Emancipation Proclamation [2] declared an end to slavery in the Confederacy, firm legal support for the eradication of slavery required constitutional change. This support was provided in 1865 by the Thirteenth Amendment.[3] The original proposition for the Amendment was introduced in Congress in December, 1863, achieving final passage in January, 1865. It was declared ratified and in force on December 18, 1865.

The 1866 Civil Rights Acts and the Fourteenth and Fifteenth Amendments. The Civil Rights Act of 1866 was before Congress at the same time as the Fourteenth Amendment. In large part, the Amendment was designed to assure the constitutionality of the Act.

The Act was Congress's response to the so-called "Black Codes" enacted in several states. Mississippi enactments of 1865, for example, provided:

". . . Every civil officer shall, and every person may, arrest and carry back to his or her legal employer any freedman, free negro, or mulatto who shall have quit the service of his or her employer before the expiration of his or her term of service without good cause. . . ."

". . . If any freedman, free negro or mulatto, convicted of any of the misdemeanors provided against in this act, shall fail or refuse for the space of five days after conviction, to pay the fine and costs imposed, such person shall be hired out by the sheriff or other officer, at the public outcry, to any white person who will pay said fine and all costs, and take the convict for the shortest time." [4]

Other provisions of some of the Black Codes barred Negroes from any business except "husbandry" without obtaining a special license, or forbade Negroes from renting or leasing land except in towns and cities.[5]

The Civil Rights Act [6] which was introduced in January 1866, passed in March, vetoed by President Johnson, and passed over his veto in early April, was designed to put an end to these laws. The two opening sections provided:

"Sec. 1. . . . all persons born in the United States and not subject to any foreign power, excluding Indians not taxed, are hereby declared to be citizens of the United States; and such citizens, of every race and color, without regard to any previous condition of slavery or involuntary servitude, except as a punishment for crime whereof the party shall have been duly convicted, shall have the same right, in every State and Territory in the United States, to make and enforce contracts, to sue, be parties, and give evidence, to inherit, purchase, lease, sell, hold, and convey real and personal property, and to full and equal benefit of all laws and proceedings for the security of person and property, as is enjoyed by white citizens, and shall be subject to like punishment, pains, and penalties, and to none other, any law, statute, ordinance, regulation, or custom, to the contrary notwithstanding.

"Sec. 2. *And be it further enacted,* That any person who, under color of any law, statute, ordinance, regulation, or custom, shall subject, or cause to be subjected, any inhabitant of any State or Territory to the deprivation of any right secured or protected by this act, or to different punishment, pains, or penalties on account of such person having at any time been held in a

---

[2] 12 Stat. 1268 (1863).

[3] See tenBroek, *Thirteenth Amendment to the Constitution of the United States—Consummation to Abolition and Key to the Fourteenth Amendment,* 39 Calif.L.Rev. 171 (1951).

[4] Laws of Mississippi, 1865, 82, 84, 166–167. See also Laws of Mississippi, 1865, 86–96; Acts of the General Assembly of Louisiana Regulating Labor. Extra Session, 1865, 3 et seq.; 2 Commager, *Documents of American History,* 2–7 (5th ed. 1949).

[5] Stephenson, *Race Distinctions in American Law* 41–43 (1910); Maslow and Robison, *Civil Rights Legislation and the Fight for Equality,* 20 U.Chi.L.Rev. 363, 367 (1953).

[6] Act of April 9, 1866, 14 Stat. 27.

condition of slavery or involuntary servitude, except as a punishment for crime whereof the party shall have been duly convicted, or by reason of his color or race, than is prescribed for the punishment of white persons, shall be deemed guilty of a misdemeanor, and, on conviction, shall be punished by fine not exceeding one thousand dollars, or imprisonment not exceeding one year, or both, in the discretion of the court."

The question arose: was there constitutional support for this Act? Did the racial discrimination in question reach the level of "involuntary servitude" encompassed by the Thirteenth Amendment? If not, where else could constitutional support be found? This difficulty was one of President Johnson's grounds for vetoing the bill. He said: [7]

"Hitherto every subject embraced in the enumeration of rights contained in this bill has been considered as exclusively belonging to the States. They all relate to the internal police and economy of the States. They are matters which in each State concern the domestic condition of its people, varying in each according to its own peculiar circumstances, and the safety and well-being of its own citizens. I do not mean to say that upon all these subjects there are not Federal restraints, as for instance, in the State power of legislation over contracts, there is a Federal limitation that no State shall pass a law impairing the obligations of contracts; and, as to crimes, that no State shall pass an *ex post facto* law; and, as to money that no State shall make anything but gold and silver a legal tender. But where can we find a Federal prohibition against the power of any state to discriminate, as do most of them, between aliens and citizens, between artificial persons called corporations, and natural persons, in the right to hold real estate?

"If it be granted that Congress can repeal all State laws discriminating between whites and blacks in the subjects covered by this bill, why, it may be asked, may not Congress repeal in the same way all State laws discriminating between the two races on the subjects of suffrage and office? If Congress can declare by law who shall hold lands, who shall testify, who shall have capacity to make a contract in a State, then Congress can by law also declare who, without regard to color or race, shall have the right to sit as a juror or as a judge, to hold any office, and, finally, to vote 'in every State and Territory of the United States.' "

Concurrently with the early debates on the Civil Rights Bill Congress was also considering drafts of a constitutional amendment. The Joint Committee on Reconstruction referred to Congress on February 10, 1866 a draft of an amendment designed to grant Congress general power to legislate for the protection of civil rights.[8] The draft was promptly tabled in the Senate. On February 26–28 it was debated in the House but action was postponed and it was never taken up.

Although Congress had overridden the President's veto of the Civil Rights Act, the challenge to the constitutionality was not resolved. So in April the Joint Committee on Reconstruction returned to the problem of constitutional amendment, reporting a new version to Congress on April 28. This version was debated in May and June and finally adopted with amendments on June 13. By March, 1867, the Amendment had been ratified by 20 states and rejected by

---

[7] Cong. Globe, 39th Cong., 1st Sess., 1680 (1866).

[8] Unlike Section 1 of the final draft, these earlier versions of the Fourteenth Amendment were, in form, grants to Congress of a general power to legislate for the protection of civil rights. The first draft reported by the committee considering the amendment read: "Congress shall have power to make all laws necessary and proper to secure to all citizens of the United States, in every State, the same political rights and privileges; and to all persons in every State equal protection in the enjoyment of life, liberty and property." See Fairman, *Does the Fourteenth Amendment Incorporate the Bill of Rights: The Original Understanding,* 2 Stanf.L.Rev. 5, 20–21 (1949); Flack, *The Adoption of the Fourteenth Amendment* (1908).

11. Also in March Congress passed over the President's veto a bill setting the conditions under which the Rebel States would be entitled to representation in Congress. One of those conditions for readmission was that the state should have ratified the Fourteenth Amendment and that the Amendment should have become part of the Constitution. By July, 1868, 9 more states had ratified, including 7 of the southern states seeking readmission pursuant to the 1867 statute, and the Amendment was declared adopted on July 28.[9]

One of the conditions imposed for the readmission of the Rebel States was that their constitutions guarantee the continuance of the suffrage provisions adopted during the period of federal control through the Reconstruction Acts. These constitutions guaranteed Negro suffrage and disenfranchised large elements of the white population. Texas, Mississippi, and Virginia were delayed in readmission because of opposition to the franchise provisions. In 1869 a bargain was struck under which these states were not required to accept the rigor of the original franchise provisions but were required to ratify a constitutional amendment then being proposed to guarantee the franchise to Negroes. The three states complied, were readmitted in early 1870, and the Fifteenth Amendment was finally ratified in March, 1870.

[9] For a modern revival of the contention that the fourteenth amendment was not validly adopted, see Suthon, *The Dubious Origin of the Fourteenth Amendment,* 28 Tulane L.Rev. 22 (1953); Call, *The Fourteenth Amendment and Its Skeptical Background,* 9 La.B.J. 45 (1961); Call, *Unconstitutional Creation of the 14th Amendment,* 13 Baylor L.Rev. 1 (1961).

Chapter 2

JUDICIAL REVIEW

SECTION 1. THE LEGITIMACY OF JUDICIAL REVIEW

THE CONSTITUTIONAL CONVENTION

In the Constitutional Convention of 1787 the Virginia Plan proposed to the Convention by Mr. Randolph (Va.) on May 29 served as the basis for the ensuing discussion and action of the delegates.

The sixth resolution in the Virginia Plan contained the provision that the national legislature be empowered "to negative all laws passed by the several States, contravening in the opinion of the National Legislature the articles of Union. . . ." This provision was ultimately rejected, in part because of the adoption of the Supremacy Clause, Art. VI, cl. 2.

The eighth resolution provided "that the Executive and a convenient number of the National Judiciary, ought to compose a council of revision with authority to examine every act of the National Legislature before it shall operate, & every act of a particular Legislature before a Negative thereon shall be final; and that the dissent of the said Council shall amount to a rejection, unless the Act of the National Legislature be again passed, or that of a particular Legislature be again negatived by _____[a] of the members of each branch." The Convention ultimately rejected the participation of the judiciary in the veto process and adopted the executive veto. Art. I, § 7, cl. 2.

The following excerpts from the debate on the eighth resolution will give a little of the flavor of the discussion which led to its rejection. They are taken from Madison's Notes of the proceedings on July 21, 1787, 2 Farrand, *The Records of the Federal Convention of 1787* (1911) 74, 76, 78:

"Mr. [Madison]—considered the object of the motion as of great importance to the meditated Constitution. It would be useful to the Judiciary departmt. by giving it an additional opportunity of defending itself agst: Legislative encroachments; It would be useful to the Executive, by inspiring additional confidence & firmness in exerting the revisionary power: It would be useful to the Legislature by the valuable assistance it would give in preserving a consistency, conciseness, perspicuity & technical propriety in the laws, qualities peculiarly necessary; & yet shamefully wanting in our republican Codes. It would moreover be useful to the Community at large as an additional check agst. a pursuit of those unwise & unjust measures which constituted so great a portion of our calamities. If any solid objection could be urged agst. the motion, it must be on the supposition that it tended to give too much strength either to the Executive or Judiciary. He did not think there was the least ground for this apprehension. It was much more to be apprehended that notwithstanding this co-operation of the two departments, the Legislature would still be an overmatch for them. Experience in all the States had evinced a powerful tendency in the Legislature to absorb all power into its vortex. This was the real source of danger to the American Constitutions; & suggested the necessity of giving every defensive

---

[a] Blank left in original.

authority to the other departments that was consistent with republican principles. . . .

"Mr. L. Martin. considered the association of the Judges with the Executive as a dangerous innovation; as well as one which, could not produce the particular advantage expected from it. A knowledge of mankind, and of Legislative affairs cannot be presumed to belong in a higher degree to the Judges than to the Legislature. And as to the Constitutionality of laws, that point will come before the Judges in their proper official character. In this character they have a negative on the laws. Join them with the Executive in the Revision and they will have a double negative. It is necessary that the Supreme Judiciary should have the confidence of the people. This will soon be lost, if they are employed in the task of remonstrating agst. popular measures of the Legislature. Besides in what mode & proportion are they to vote in the Council of Revision? . . .

"Col Mason Observed that the defence of the Executive was not the sole object of the Revisionary power. He expected even greater advantages from it. Notwithstanding the precautions taken in the Constitution of the Legislature, it would so much resemble that of the individual States, that it must be expected frequently to pass unjust and pernicious laws. This restraining power was therefore essentially necessary. It would have the effect not only of hindering the final passage of such laws; but would discourage demagogues from attempting to get them passed. It had been said (by Mr. L. Martin) that if the Judges were joined in this check on the laws, they would have a double negative, since in their expository capacity of Judges they would have one negative. He would reply that in this capacity they could impede in one case only, the operation of laws. They could declare an unconstitutional law void. But with regard to every law however unjust oppressive or pernicious, which did not come plainly under this description, they would be under the necessity as Judges to give it a free course. He wished the further use to be made of the Judges, of giving aid in preventing every improper law. Their aid will be the more valuable as they are in the habit and practice of considering laws in their true principles, and in all their consequences."

MARBURY v. MADISON

5 U.S. (1 Cranch) 137, 2 L.Ed. 60 (1803).

[John Marshall was Secretary of State in the Adams administration when he took office as Chief Justice on January 31, 1801. He continued as Acting Secretary of State until the last day of the Adams administration, March 3, 1801. William Marbury was one of a number of persons who were appointed justices of the peace in the District of Columbia and who were confirmed by the Senate on March 3. His commission remained in Marshall's office undelivered when the new administration took over. President Jefferson directed his Secretary of State, James Madison, to withhold several commissions, including that of Marbury. Marbury then brought this suit against Madison, taking the unusual step of starting the action in the Supreme Court, invoking its original jurisdiction.[a]]

[a] For accounts of the background of the case, see Burton, *The Cornerstone of Constitutional Law: The Extraordinary Case of Marbury v. Madison*, 36 A.B.A.J. 805 (1950); Van Alstyne, *A Critical Guide to Marbury v. Madison*, 1969 Duke L.J. 1.

For an interesting discussion of the last minute appointment of judges by President Adams, see Turner, *The Midnight Judges*, 109 U.Pa.L.Rev. 494 (1961).

Mr. Chief Justice Marshall delivered the opinion of the Court.

At the last term on the affidavits then read and filed with the clerk, a rule was granted in this case, requiring the secretary of state to shew cause why a mandamus should not issue, directing him to deliver to William Marbury his commission as a justice of the peace for the county of Washington, in the district of Columbia.

No cause has been shewn, and the present motion is for a mandamus. The peculiar delicacy of this case, the novelty of some of its circumstances, and the real difficulty attending the points which occur in it, require a complete exposition of the principles, on which the opinion to be given by the court, is founded.

These principles have been, on the side of the applicant, very ably argued at the bar. In rendering the opinion of the court, there will be some departure in form, though not in substance, from the points stated in that argument.

In the order in which the court has viewed this subject, the following questions have been considered and decided.

1st. Has the applicant a right to the commission he demands?

2dly. If he has a right, and that right has been violated, do the laws of his country afford him a remedy?

3dly. If they do afford him a remedy, is it a *mandamus* issuing from this court?

The first object of enquiry is,

1st. Has the applicant a right to the commission he demands?

His right originates in an act of congress passed in February 1801, concerning the district of Columbia.

After dividing the district into two counties, the 11th section of this law enacts, "that there shall be appointed in and for each of the said counties, such number of discreet persons to be justices of the peace as the president of the United States shall, from time to time, think expedient, to continue in office for five years."

It appears, from the affidavits, that in compliance with this law, a commission for William Marbury as a justice of peace for the county of Washington, was signed by John Adams, then president of the United States; after which the seal of the United States was affixed to it; but the commission has never reached the person for whom it was made out.

In order to determine whether he is entitled to this commission, it becomes necessary to enquire whether he has been appointed to the office. For if he has been appointed, the law continues him in office for five years, and he is entitled to the possession of those evidences of office, which, being completed, became his property.

The 2d section of the 2d article of the constitution, declares, that, "the president shall nominate, and, by and with the advice and consent of the senate, shall appoint ambassadors, other public ministers and consuls, and all other officers of the United States, whose appointments are not otherwise provided for."

The third section declares, that "he shall commission all the officers of the United States."   .   .   .

It is therefore decidedly the opinion of the court, that when a commission has been signed by the President, the appointment is made; and that the commission is complete, when the seal of the United States has been affixed to it by the secretary of state.   .   .   .

To withhold his commission, therefore, is an act deemed by the court not warranted by law, but violative of a vested legal right.

This brings us to the second enquiry; which is,

2dly. If he has a right, and that right has been violated, do the laws of his country afford him a remedy?

The very essence of civil liberty certainly consists in the right of every individual to claim the protection of the laws, whenever he receives an injury. One of the first duties of government is to afford that protection. In Great Britain the king himself is sued in the respectful form of a petition, and he never fails to comply with the judgment of his court. . . .

The government of the United States has been emphatically termed a government of laws, and not of men. It will certainly cease to deserve this high appellation, if the laws furnish no remedy for the violation of a vested legal right.

If this obloquy is to be cast on the jurisprudence of our country, it must arise from the peculiar character of the case. . . .

It follows then that the question, whether the legality of an act of the head of a department be examinable in a court of justice or not, must always depend on the nature of that act. . . .

By the constitution of the United States, the President is invested with certain important political powers, in the exercise of which he is to use his own discretion, and is accountable only to his country in his political character, and to his own conscience. To aid him in the performance of these duties, he is authorized to appoint certain officers, who act by his authority and in conformity with his orders.

In such cases, their acts are his acts; and whatever opinion may be entertained of the manner in which executive discretion may be used, still there exists, and can exist, no power to control that discretion. The subjects are political. They respect the nation, not individual rights, and being entrusted to the executive, the decision of the executive is conclusive. The application of this remark will be perceived by adverting to the act of congress for establishing the department of foreign affairs. This officer, as his duties were prescribed by that act, is to conform precisely to the will of the President. He is the mere organ by whom that will is communicated. The acts of such an officer, as an officer, can never be examinable by the courts.

But when the legislature proceeds to impose on that officer other duties; when he is directed peremptorily to perform certain acts; when the rights of individuals are dependent on the performance of those acts; he is so far the officer of the law; is amenable to the laws for his conduct; and cannot at his discretion sport away the vested rights of others.

The conclusion from this reasoning is, that where the heads of departments are the political or confidential agents of the executive, merely to execute the will of the President, or rather to act in cases in which the executive possesses a constitutional or legal discretion nothing can be more perfectly clear than that their acts are only politically examinable. But where a specific duty is assigned by law, and individual rights depend upon the performance of that duty, it seems equally clear that the individual who considers himself injured, has a right to resort to the laws of his country for a remedy. . . .

It remains to be enquired whether,

3dly. He is entitled to the remedy for which he applies. This depends on,

1st. The nature of the writ applied for, and,

2dly. The power of this court.

1st. The nature of the writ. . . .

This writ, if awarded, would be directed to an officer of government, and its mandate to him would be, to use the words of Blackstone, "to do a particular thing therein specified, which appertains to his office and duty and which the court has previously determined, or at least supposes, to be consonant to right and justice." Or, in the words of Lord Mansfield, the applicant, in this case, has a right to execute an office of public concern, and is kept out of possession of that right.

These circumstances certainly concur in this case.

Still, to render the mandamus a proper remedy, the officer to whom it is to be directed, must be one to whom, on legal principles, such writ may be directed; and the person applying for it must be without any other specific and legal remedy.

1st. With respect to the officer to whom it would be directed. The intimate political relation, subsisting between the president of the United States and the heads of departments, necessarily renders any legal investigation of the acts of one of those high officers peculiarly irksome, as well as delicate; and excites some hesitation with respect to the propriety of entering into such investigation. Impressions are often received without much reflection or examination, and it is not wonderful that in such a case as this, the assertion, by an individual, of his legal claims in a court of justice, to which claims it is the duty of that court to attend; should at first view be considered by some, as an attempt to intrude into the cabinet, and to intermeddle with the prerogatives of the executive.

It is scarcely necessary for the court to disclaim all pretensions to such a jurisdiction. An extravagance, so absurd and excessive, could not have been entertained for a moment. The province of the court is, solely, to decide on the rights of individuals, not to enquire how the executive, or executive officers, perform duties in which they have a discretion. Questions, in their nature political, or which are, by the constitution and laws, submitted to the executive, can never be made in this court.

But, if this be not such a question; if so far from being an intrusion into the secrets of the cabinet, it respects a paper, which according to law, is upon record, and to a copy of which the law gives a right, on the payment of ten cents; if it be no intermeddling with a subject, over which the executive can be considered as having exercised any control; what is there in the exalted station of the officer, which shall bar a citizen from asserting, in a court of justice, his legal rights, or shall forbid a court to listen to the claim; or to issue a mandamus, directing the performance of a duty, not depending on executive discretion, but on particular acts of congress and the general principles of law?

. . .

This, then, is a plain case for a mandamus, either to deliver the commission, or a copy of it from the record; and it only remains to be enquired,

Whether it can issue from this court.

The act to establish the judicial courts of the United States authorizes the supreme court "to issue writs of mandamus, in cases warranted by the principles and usages of law, to any courts appointed, or persons holding office, under the authority of the United States." [b]

The secretary of the state, being a person holding an office under the authority of the United States, is precisely within the letter of the description; and if this court is not authorized to issue a writ of mandamus to such an officer, it must be because the law is unconstitutional, and therefore absolutely incapable

[b] The full sentence, a part of Section 13 of the Judiciary Act of 1789, read: "The Supreme Court shall also have appellate jurisdiction from the circuit courts and courts of the several states, in the cases herein after specially provided for; and shall have power to issue writs of prohibition to the district courts, when proceeding as courts of admiralty and maritime jurisdiction, and writs of mandamus, in cases warranted by the principles and usages of law, to any courts appointed, or persons holding office, under the authority of the United States."

of conferring the authority, and assigning the duties which its words purport to confer and assign.

The constitution vests the whole judicial power of the United States in one supreme court, and such inferior courts as congress shall, from time to time, ordain and establish. This power is expressly extended to all cases arising under the laws of the United States; and consequently, in some form, may be exercised over the present case; because the right claimed is given by a law of the United States.

In the distribution of this power it is declared that "the supreme court shall have original jurisdiction in all cases affecting ambassadors, other public ministers and consuls, and those in which a state shall be a party. In all other cases, the supreme court shall have appellate jurisdiction."

It has been insisted, at the bar, that as the original grant of jurisdiction to the supreme and inferior courts, is general, and the clause, assigning original jurisdiction to the supreme court, contains no negative or restrictive words; the power remains to the legislature, to assign original jurisdiction to that court in other cases than those specified in the article which has been recited; provided those cases belong to the judicial power of the United States.

If it had been intended to leave it in the discretion of the legislature to apportion the judicial power between the supreme and inferior courts according to the will of that body, it would certainly have been useless to have proceeded further than to have defined the judicial power, and the tribunals in which it should be vested. The subsequent part of the section is mere surplusage, is entirely without meaning, if such is to be the construction. If congress remains at liberty to give this court appellate jurisdiction, where the constitution has declared their jurisdiction shall be original; and original jurisdiction where the constitution has declared it shall be appellate; the distribution of jurisdiction, made in the constitution, is form without substance.

Affirmative words are often, in their operation, negative of other objects than those affirmed; and in this case a negative or exclusive sense must be given to them or they have no operation at all.

It cannot be presumed that any clause in the constitution is intended to be without effect; and therefore such a construction is inadmissible, unless the words require it.

If the solicitude of the convention, respecting our peace with foreign powers, induced a provision that the supreme court should take original jurisdiction in cases which might be supposed to affect them; yet the clause would have proceeded no further than to provide for such cases, if no further restriction on the powers of congress had been intended. That they should have appellate jurisdiction in all other cases, with such exceptions as congress might make, is no restriction; unless the words be deemed exclusive of original jurisdiction.   .   .   .

To enable this court then to issue a mandamus, it must be shewn to be an exercise of appellate jurisdiction, or to be necessary to enable them to exercise appellate jurisdiction.

It has been stated at the bar that the appellate jurisdiction may be exercised in a variety of forms, and that if it be the will of the legislature that a mandamus, should be used for that purpose, that will must be obeyed. This is true, yet the jurisdiction must be appellate, not original.

It is the essential criterion of appellate jurisdiction, that it revises and corrects the proceedings in a cause already instituted, and does not create that cause. Although, therefore, a mandamus may be directed to courts, yet to issue such a writ to an officer for the delivery of a paper, is in effect the same as to sustain an original action for that paper, and therefore seems not to belong to appellate, but to original jurisdiction. Neither is it necessary in such a case as this, to enable the court to exercise its appellate jurisdiction.

The authority, therefore, given to the supreme court by the act establishing the judicial courts of the United States, to issue writs of mandamus to public officers, appears not to be warranted by the constitution; and it becomes necessary to enquire whether a jurisdiction, so conferred, can be exercised.

The question, whether an act, repugnant to the constitution, can become the law of the land, is a question deeply interesting to the United States; but, happily, not of an intricacy proportioned to its interest. It seems only necessary to recognize certain principles, supposed to have been long and well established, to decide it.

That the people have an original right to establish, for their future government, such principles as, in their opinion, shall most conduce to their own happiness, is the basis, on which the whole American fabric has been erected. The exercise of this original right is a very great exertion; nor can it, nor ought it to be frequently repeated. The principles, therefore, so established, are deemed fundamental. And as the authority, from which they proceed, is supreme, and can seldom act, they are designed to be permanent.

This original and supreme will organizes the government, and assigns, to different departments, their respective powers. It may either stop here; or establish certain limits not to be transcended by those departments.

The government of the United States is of the latter description. The powers of the legislature are defined, and limited; and that those limits may not be mistaken, or forgotten, the constitution is written. To what purpose are powers limited, and to what purpose is that limitation committed to writing, if these limits may, at any time, be passed by those intended to be restrained? The distinction, between a government with limited and unlimited powers, is abolished, if those limits do not confine the persons on whom they are imposed, and if acts prohibited and acts allowed, are of equal obligation. It is a proposition too plain to be contested, that the constitution controls any legislative act repugnant to it; or, that the legislature may alter the constitution by an ordinary act.

Between these alternatives there is no middle ground. The constitution is either a superior, paramount law, unchangeable by ordinary means, or it is on a level with ordinary legislative acts, and like other acts, is alterable when the legislature shall please to alter it.

If the former part of the alternative be true, then a legislative act contrary to the constitution is not law: if the latter part be true, then written constitutions are absurd attempts, on the part of the people, to limit a power, in its own nature illimitable.

Certainly all those who have framed written constitutions contemplate them as forming the fundamental and paramount law of the nation, and consequently the theory of every such government must be, that an act of the legislature, repugnant to the constitution, is void.

This theory is essentially attached to a written constitution, and is consequently to be considered, by this court, as one of the fundamental principles of our society. It is not therefore to be lost sight of in the further consideration of this subject.

If an act of the legislature, repugnant to the constitution, is void, does it, notwithstanding its invalidity, bind the courts, and oblige them to give it effect? Or, in other words, though it be not law, does it constitute a rule as operative as if it was a law? This would be to overthrow in fact what was established in theory; and would seem, at first view, an absurdity too gross to be insisted on. It shall, however, receive a more attentive consideration.

It is emphatically the province and duty of the judicial department to say what the law is. Those who apply the rule to particular cases, must of necessity expound and interpret that rule. If two laws conflict with each other, the courts must decide on the operation of each.

So if a law be in opposition to the constitution; if both the law and the constitution apply to a particular case, so that the court must either decide that case conformably to the law disregarding the constitution, or conformably to the constitution disregarding the law; the court must determine which of these conflicting rules governs the case. This is of the very essence of judicial duty.

If then the courts are to regard the constitution, and the constitution is superior to any ordinary act of the legislature, the constitution, and not such ordinary act, must govern the case to which they both apply.

Those then who controvert the principle that the constitution is to be considered, in court, as a paramount law, are reduced to the necessity of maintaining that courts must close their eyes on the constitution, and see only the law.

This doctrine would subvert the very foundation of all written constitutions. It would declare that an act, which, according to the principles and theory of our government, is entirely void, is yet, in practice, completely obligatory. It would declare, that if the legislature shall do what is expressly forbidden, such act, notwithstanding the express prohibition, is in reality effectual. It would be giving to the legislature a practical and real omnipotence, with the same breath which professes to restrict their powers within narrow limits. It is prescribing limits, and declaring that those limits may be passed at pleasure.

That it thus reduces to nothing what we have deemed the greatest improvement on political institutions—a written constitution—would of itself be sufficient, in America, where written constitutions have been viewed with so much reverence, for rejecting the construction. But the peculiar expressions of the constitution of the United States furnish additional arguments in favour of its rejection.

· The judicial power of the United States is extended to all cases arising under the constitution.

Could it be the intention of those who gave this power, to say that, in using it, the constitution should not be looked into? That a case arising under the constitution should be decided without examining the instrument under which it arises?

This is too extravagant to be maintained.

In some cases then, the constitution must be looked into by the judges. And if they can open it at all, what part of it are they forbidden to read, or to obey?

There are many other parts of the constitution which serve to illustrate this subject.

It is declared that "no tax or duty shall be laid on articles exported from any state." Suppose a duty on the export of cotton, of tobacco or of flour; and a suit instituted to recover it. Ought judgment to be rendered in such a case? ought the judges to close their eyes on the constitution, and only see the law?

The constitution declares that "no bill of attainder or *ex post facto* law shall be passed."

If, however such a bill should be passed and a person should be prosecuted under it; must the court condemn to death those victims whom the constitution endeavours to preserve?

"No person," says the constitution, "shall be convicted of treason unless on the testimony of two witnesses to the same overt act, or on confession in open court."

Here the language of the constitution is addressed especially to the courts. It prescribes, directly for them, a rule of evidence not to be departed from. If the legislature should change that rule, and declare one witness, or a confession out of court, sufficient for conviction, must the constitutional principle yield to the legislative act?

From these, and many other selections which might be made, it is apparent, that the framers of the constitution contemplated that instrument, as a rule for the government of courts, as well as of the legislature.

Why otherwise does it direct the judges to take an oath to support it? This oath certainly applies, in an especial manner, to their conduct in their official character. How immoral to impose it on them, if they were to be used as the instruments, and the knowing instruments, for violating what they swear to support!

The oath of office, too, imposed by the legislature, is completely demonstrative of the legislative opinion on this subject. It is in these words, "I do solemnly swear, that I will administer justice without respect to persons, and do equal right to the poor and to the rich; and that I will faithfully and impartially discharge all the duties incumbent on me as _____ according to the best of my abilities and understanding, agreeably to the constitution, and laws of the United States."

Why does a judge swear to discharge his duties agreeably to the constitution of the United States, if that constitution forms no rule for his government? if it is closed upon him, and cannot be inspected by him?

If such be the real state of things, this is worse than solemn mockery. To prescribe, or to take this oath, becomes equally a crime.

It is also not entirely unworthy of observation, that in declaring what shall be the supreme law of the land, the constitution itself is first mentioned; and not the laws of the United States generally, but those only which shall be made in pursuance of the constitution, have that rank.

Thus, the particular phraseology of the constitution of the United States confirms and strengthens the principle, supposed to be essential to all written constitutions, that a law repugnant to the constitution is void; and that courts, as well as other departments, are bound by that instrument.

The rule must be discharged.[c]

LEGITIMACY OF JUDICIAL REVIEW: SOME COMMENTS

(1) Gibson, J., dissenting, in Eakin v. Raub, 12 S. & R. 330, 344–358 (Pa. 1825) considered the question of the legitimacy of judicial review of the constitutionality of legislation. The following excerpts will illustrate the course of his argument:

"The constitution and the *right* of the legislature to pass the act, may be in collision; but is that a legitimate subject for judicial determination? If it be, the judiciary must be a peculiar organ, to revise the proceedings of the legislature, and to correct its mistakes; and in what part of the constitution are we to look

[c] During the tenure of Marshall as Chief Justice, the only other case holding an Act of Congress unconstitutional was the obscure decision in Hodgson v. Bowerbank, 9 U.S. (5 Cranch) 303 (1809). In a brief opinion, Marshall held a provision of the Judiciary Act of 1789 unconstitutional in conferring jurisdiction on federal courts to try suits between aliens. (For a strong argument that Marshall interpreted the statute and did not declare it to be unconstitutional, see Mahoney, *A Historical Note on Hodgson v. Bowerbank,* 49 U.Chi.L.Rev. 725 (1982)). The next Act of Congress to be declared unconstitutional was the Missouri Compromise in Dred Scott v. Sandford, 60 U.S. (19 How.) 393 (1857), overruled by the Civil War. The first Act of Congress of general applicability to be declared unconstitutional was the Legal Tender Act in Hepburn v. Griswold, 75 U.S. (8 Wall.) 603 (1870). This decision was promptly overruled by the Court itself in Knox v. Lee, 75 U.S. (12 Wall.) 457 (1871).

for this proud preeminence? Viewing the matter in the opposite direction, what would be thought of an act of assembly in which it should be declared that the supreme court had in a particular case, put a wrong construction on the constitution of the *United States,* and that the judgment should therefore be reversed? It would, doubtless, be thought a usurpation of judicial power. But it is by no means clear, that to declare a law void, which has been enacted according to the forms prescribed in the constitution, is not a usurpation of legislative power. It is an act of sovereignty; and sovereignty and legislative power are said by Sir William *Blackstone* to be convertible terms. It is the business of the judiciary, to interpret the laws, not scan the authority of the lawgiver; and without the latter, it cannot take cognisance of a collision between a law and the constitution. So that, to affirm that the judiciary has a right to judge of the existence of such collision, is to take for granted the very thing to be proved; and that a very cogent argument may be made in this way, I am not disposed to deny; for no conclusions are so strong as those that are drawn from the *petitio principii.* . . .

"But the judges are sworn to support the constitution, and are they not bound by it as the law of the land? In some respects they are. In the very few cases in which the judiciary, and not the legislature, is the immediate organ to execute its provisions, they are bound by it, in preference to any act of assembly to the contrary; in such cases, the constitution is a rule to the courts. But what I have in view in this inquiry, is, the supposed right of the judiciary, to interfere, in cases where the constitution is to be carried into effect through the instrumentality of the legislature, and where that organ must necessarily first decide on the constitutionality of its own act. The oath to support the constitution is not peculiar to the judges, but is taken indiscriminately by every officer of the government, and is designed rather as a test of the political principles of the man, than to bind the officer in the discharge of his duty: otherwise, it were difficult to determine, what operation it is to have in the case of a recorder of deeds, for instance, who in the execution of his office, has nothing to do with the constitution. But granting it to relate to the official conduct of the judge, as well as every other officer, and not to his political principles, still, it must be understood in reference to supporting the constitution, *only as far as that may be involved in his official duty;* and consequently, if his official duty does not comprehend an inquiry into the authority of the legislature, neither does his oath.

"It is worthy of remark here, that the foundation of every argument in favor of the right of the judiciary, is found, at last, to be an assumption of the whole ground in dispute. Granting that the object of the oath is to secure a support of the constitution in the discharge of official duty, its terms may be satisfied by restraining it to official duty in the exercise of the *ordinary* judicial powers. Thus, the constitution may furnish a rule of construction, where a particular interpretation of a law would conflict with some constitutional principle; and such interpretation, where it may, is always to be avoided. But the oath was more probably designed to secure the powers of each of the different branches from being usurped by any of the rest; for instance, to prevent the house of representatives from erecting itself into a court of judicature, or the supreme court from attempting to control the legislature; and in this view, the oath furnishes an argument equally plausible *against* the right of the judiciary. But if it require a support of the constitution in anything beside official duty, it is, in fact, an oath of allegiance to a particular form of government; and considered as such, it is not easy to see, why it should not be taken by the citizens at large, as well as by the officers of the government. It has never been thought, that an officer is under greater restraint as to measures which have for their avowed end a total change of the constitution, than a citizen who has taken no oath at all.

The official oath, then, relates only to the official conduct of the officer, and does not prove that he ought to stray from the path of his ordinary business, to search for violations of duty in the business of others; nor does it, as supposed, define the powers of the officer.

"But do not the judges do a *positive* act in violation of the constitution, when they give effect to an unconstitutional law? Not if the law has been passed according to the forms established in the constitution. The fallacy of the question is, in supposing that the judiciary adopts the acts of the legislature as its own; whereas, the enactment of a law and the interpretation of it are not concurrent acts, and as the judiciary is not required to concur in the enactment, neither is it in the breach of the constitution which may be the consequence of the enactment; the fault is imputable to the legislature, and on it the responsibility exclusively rests. . . . ."

For a modern assessment see Murray, *Chief Justice Gibson of the Pennsylvania Supreme Court and Judicial Review,* 32 U.Pitt.L.R. 127 (1970).

(2) Abraham Lincoln, First Inaugural Address, March 4, 1861, in 4 Basler, *The Collected Works of Abraham Lincoln* 262, 268 (1953): "I do not forget the position assumed by some, that constitutional questions are to be decided by the Supreme Court; nor do I deny that such decisions must be binding in any case, upon the parties to a suit, as to the object of that suit, while they are also entitled to very high respect and consideration, in all parallel cases by all other departments of the government. And while it is obviously possible that such decision may be erroneous in any given case, still the evil effect following it, being limited to that particular case, with the chance that it may be over-ruled and never become a precedent for other cases, can better be borne than could the evils of a different practice. At the same time the candid citizen must confess that if the policy of the government upon vital questions affecting the whole people, is to be irrevocably fixed by decisions of the Supreme Court, the instant they are made, in ordinary litigation between parties in personal actions, the people will have ceased, to be their own rulers, having, to that extent, practically resigned their government, into the hands of that eminent tribunal. Nor is there, in this view, any assault upon the court, or the judges. It is a duty, from which they may not shrink, to decide cases properly brought before them; and it is no fault of theirs if others seek to turn their decisions to political purposes."

(3) In Cooper v. Aaron, 358 U.S. 1, 17 (1958) the Court made the following statements in answer to an argument that the Governor and the Legislature of Arkansas were not bound by the holding of the Court in the case of Brown v. Board of Educ., 347 U.S. 483 (1954):

"It is necessary only to recall some basic constitutional propositions which are settled doctrine.

"Article VI of the Constitution makes the Constitution the 'supreme Law of the Land'. In 1803, Chief Justice Marshall, speaking for a unanimous Court, referring to the Constitution as 'the fundamental and paramount law of the nation,' declared in the notable case of Marbury v. Madison, 1 Cranch 137, 177, that 'It is emphatically the province and duty of the judicial department to say what the law is.' This decision declared the basic principle that the federal judiciary is supreme in the exposition of the law of the Constitution, and that principle has ever since been respected by this Court and the Country as a permanent and indispensable feature of our constitutional system. It follows that the interpretation of the Fourteenth Amendment enunciated by this Court in the *Brown* case is the supreme law of the land, and Art. VI of the Constitution makes it of binding effect on the States 'any Thing in the Constitution or Laws of any State to the Contrary notwithstanding.' "

(4) For more than a century after Marbury v. Madison, judicial review of legislation was largely an American phenomenon. The Twentieth Century, particularly the years following World War II, has seen an explosion of the concept both on the national and international levels. A comparison of judicial review in the United States and in Western Europe is particularly instructive. Austria, Italy and West Germany have specialized constitutional courts to determine the constitutional validity of legislation. Ordinary courts cannot decide whether laws are constitutional or not, although they can refer those questions for decision to the constitutional courts. This system of "centralized" judicial review is often contrasted with the "decentralized" system represented by Marbury v. Madison. Nearly all of the decisions in this volume are by the Supreme Court of the United States, and most attention centers on the function of judicial review as performed by that court. The theory of *Marbury,* however, requires every court, even the most inferior, to decide whether laws are constitutional. Does it also require that executive officials determine whether their official actions are consistent with the Constitution? Compare the view of President Lincoln, in note 2 above, with that of the Court in Cooper v. Aaron, note 3. For an analysis and description of judicial review systems outside the United States, see Cappelletti and Cohen, *Comparative Constitutional Law: Cases and Materials* 1–196 (1979).

(5) The dispute over the legitimacy of judicial review of legislation has long raged among legal scholars. The following writers, among others, have concluded from the available evidence that the framers of the Constitution intended (or at least did not preclude) judicial review of legislation: Beard, *The Supreme Court and the Constitution* (1912); Warren, *The Making of the Constitution* (1928); Haines, *The American Doctrine of Judicial Supremacy* (2d ed. 1932). Wechsler, *Principles, Politics, and Fundamental Law* (1961). A vigorous attack on the foregoing position will be seen in Boudin, *Government by Judiciary* (1932). For a position sustaining judicial review of state legislation but arguing that it was intended to have only limited operation with reference to acts of Congress, see 2 Crosskey, *Politics and the Constitution in the History of the United States* 1007 (1953). For a position doubting that the framers intended to confer a general power of judicial review but conceding that it was necessary for the Supreme Court to assume at least some power of judicial review, see Hand, *The Bill of Rights* (1958).

Bator, Mishkin, Shapiro and Wechsler, *Hart and Wechsler's The Federal Courts and the Federal System* 9 (2d ed. 1973) [hereinafter cited as Hart and Wechsler, *Federal Courts* (2d ed. 1973)], after a modern reappraisal of the dispute conclude: "The grant of judicial power was to include power, where necessary in the decision of cases, to disregard state or federal statutes found to be unconstitutional. Despite the curiously persisting myth of usurpation, the Convention's understanding on this point emerged from its records with singular clarity." See also Wechsler, *Principles, Politics, and Fundamental Law* 4 (1961): "Let me begin by saying that I have not the slightest doubt respecting the legitimacy of judicial review, whether the action called in question in a case which otherwise is proper for adjudication is legislative or executive, federal or state."

(6) For discussions of the role of the Supreme Court in judicial review, consult Bickel, *The Least Dangerous Branch—The Supreme Court at the Bar of Politics* (1962); Bickel, *The Supreme Court and the Idea of Progress* (1970); Bork, *Neutral Principles and Some First Amendment Problems,* 47 Ind.L.J. 1 (1971); Deutsch, *Neutrality, Legitimacy, and the Supreme Court: Some Intersections Between Law and Political Science,* 20 Stanf.L.Rev. 160 (1968); Gunther, *The Subtle Vices of the "Passive Virtues"—A Comment on Principle and Expediency in Judicial Review,* 64 Colum.L.Rev. 1 (1964); Berger, *Government by Judiciary: The Transformation*

of the Fourteenth Amendment (1977) (debated in *Symposium,* 6 Hast.Con.L.Q. 403–635 (1979); Tribe, *American Constitutional Law* (1978); Tushnet, *Truth, Justice and the American Way: An Interpretation of Public Law Scholarship in the Seventies,* 57 Tex.L.Rev. 1307 (1979); Ely, *Democracy and Distrust: A Theory of Judicial Review* (1980); Choper, *Judicial Review and the National Political Process* (1980); Perry, *The Constitution, The Courts and Human Rights* (1982); Bobbitt, *Constitutional Fate* (1982).

Students interested in the general historical background of judicial review should examine, in addition to the works cited above, 1 *Selected Essays on Constitutional Law* 1–173 (1938), hereinafter cited as *Selected Essays* (1938).

EFFECT OF A DECLARATION OF UNCONSTITUTIONALITY

(1) To what extent does a decision of unconstitutionality nullify the statute in question? For example, could the statute involved in Marbury v. Madison be given any effect after that decision?

(2) In 1923 the Supreme Court in Adkins v. Children's Hosp., 261 U.S. 525, declared the District of Columbia minimum wage law invalid. In 1937 the Court in West Coast Hotel Co. v. Parrish, 300 U.S. 379 (a case involving a state minimum wage law) stated: "Our conclusion is that the case of Adkins v. Children's Hosp., supra, should be, and it is, overruled." On April 3, 1937, the Attorney General of the United States formally advised the President of the United States that the District of Columbia minimum wage law "is now a valid act of the Congress and may be administered in accordance with its terms." He also said: "The decisions are practically in accord in holding that the courts have no power to repeal or abolish a statute, and that notwithstanding a decision holding it unconstitutional a statute continues to remain on the statute books; and that if a statute be declared unconstitutional and the decision so declaring it be subsequently overruled the statute will then be held valid from the date it became effective." 39 *Ops.Atty.Gen.* 22 (1937).

(3) Problems arise from time to time regarding the validity of acts taken in reliance on a statute subsequently declared unconstitutional. Those problems become particularly acute when there has been reliance on an earlier decision declaring the statute valid. In applying the doctrine of res judicata to an unappealed decision applying the Municipal Bankruptcy Act despite a subsequent decision of the Supreme Court in another case holding it invalid, the Court said in Chicot County Drainage Dist. v. Baxter State Bank, 308 U.S. 371, 374 (1940):

"The courts below have proceeded on the theory that the Act of Congress having been found to be unconstitutional, was not a law; that it was inoperative, conferring no rights and imposing no duties, and hence affording no basis for the challenged decree. Norton v. Shelby County, 118 U.S. 425, 442; Chicago, I. & L. Ry. Co. v. Hackett, 228 U.S. 559, 566. It is quite clear, however, that such broad statements as to the effect of a determination of unconstitutionality must be taken with qualifications. The actual existence of a statute, prior to such a determination, is an operative fact and may have consequences which cannot justly be ignored. The past cannot always be erased by a new judicial declaration. The effect of the subsequent ruling as to invalidity may have to be considered in various aspects,—with respect to particular relations, individual and corporate, and particular conduct, private and official. Questions of rights claimed to have become vested, of status, of prior determinations deemed to have finality and acted upon accordingly, of public policy in the light of the nature both of the statute and of its previous application, demand examination. These questions are among the most difficult of those which have engaged the attention of courts, state and federal, and it is manifest from numerous decisions that an all-inclusive statement of a principle of absolute retroactive invalidity cannot be justified."

For a full discussion of the problems, see Field, *The Effect of an Unconstitutional Statute* (1935); Grant, *The Legal Effect of a Ruling that a Law is Unconstitutional,* 1978 Det.Coll.L.Rev. 201.

(4) A related question is whether a new constitutional decision should be given retroactive effect to govern conduct preceding the decision. The theory of judicial review expounded in Marbury v. Madison, coupled with the orthodox theory of the declaratory nature of judicial decisionmaking, requires that decisions of unconstitutionality be applied retroactively. Retroactive decision is still the norm, but in a significant number of cases beginning in 1965, the Supreme Court has applied new rules of constitutional law prospectively only. The major decision was Linkletter v. Walker, 381 U.S. 618 (1965), in which the Court refused to apply the exclusionary rule of Mapp v. Ohio, 367 U.S. 643 (1961) to convictions which had become final prior to the *Mapp* decision. Most of the cases that have followed *Linkletter* have also involved newly-announced rules of constitutional criminal procedure. E.g., Johnson v. New Jersey, 384 U.S. 719 (1966) (*Miranda* doctrine); Stovall v. Denno, 388 U.S. 293 (1967) (rule requiring counsel at post-indictment lineup); United States v. White, 401 U.S. 745 (1971) (application of fourth amendment to electronic eavesdropping); Michigan v. Payne, 412 U.S. 47 (1973) (limits on heavier sentence on retrials after successful appeals); United States v. Peltier, 422 U.S. 531 (1975) (rule invalidating roving warrantless searches by border patrol). There are, however, a significant number of cases of prospective application of new constitutional rules in other areas. E.g., Cipriano v. Houma, 395 U.S. 701 (1969) (rule invalidating property ownership requirements for voting in bond elections); Lemon v. Kurtzman, 411 U.S. 192 (1973) (permitting compensation of church schools for services performed under statute held to violate establishment clause); Gosa v. Mayden, 413 U.S. 665 (1973) (rule forbidding court martial for non-service connected crimes); Marks v. United States, 430 U.S. 188 (1977) (relaxed constitutional standards governing prosecution for obscenity); Northern Pipeline Co. v. Marathon Pipeline Co., 458 U.S. 50 (1982) (bankruptcy court unconstitutional because judges lack tenure during good behavior).

Questions have been raised concerning whether use of prospective constitutional decision making is fundamentally inconsistent with the theory of judicial review expounded in Marbury v. Madison. Mackey v. United States, 401 U.S. 667, 677–681 (1971) (Harlan, J., dissenting). For an earlier statement of a similar point of view, see Mishkin, *The High Court, The Great Writ, and the Due Process of Time and Law,* 79 Harv.L.Rev. 56, 62–66 (1965). Compare Beytagh, *Ten Years of Retroactivity: A Critique and a Proposal,* 61 Va.L.Rev. 1557 (1975). See, generally, Corr, *Retroactivity: A Study in Supreme Court Doctrine "As Applied,"* 61 No.Car.L.Rev. 745 (1983).

SECTION 2. CONGRESSIONAL CONTROL OF JUDICIAL REVIEW BY THE FEDERAL COURTS

THE SCOPE OF CONGRESSIONAL POWER OVER THE JURISDICTION OF LOWER FEDERAL COURTS

While Article III of the Constitution created the Supreme Court, it deliberately gave Congress the option to create "such inferior Courts as the Congress may from time to time ordain and establish." Since inferior federal courts, in theory, exist at the pleasure of Congress, it has always been clear that Article III does not require that any single lower federal court exercise all, or any particular part, of the judicial power described by that Article. Indeed, the current general jurisdiction of the inferior federal courts in civil cases arising under federal law was not conferred until after the Civil War. What has been an issue, however, is whether all of the judicial power must be lodged somewhere in the federal judicial system—either originally in a lower federal court, or on appeal of state court decisions to the Supreme Court.

Justice Story, in dicta in Martin v. Hunter's Lessee, 14 U.S. (1 Wheat.) 304 (1816), stressed the mandatory language of Article III ("The judicial power of the United States shall be vested . . . ." "The judicial power shall extend . . . .") He concluded that Congress had an obligation to vest the entire judicial power somewhere within the federal judicial system. Later, in his writings, he argued that any contrary conclusion would mean that "the judiciary, as a co-ordinate department of the government, may, at the will of Congress, be annihilated, or stripped of all its important jurisdiction." 2 *Commentaries on the Constitution of the United States* 395 (4th ed. 1873). Story's position was authoritatively rejected in Sheldon v. Sill, 49 U.S. (8 How.) 441 (1850). In upholding a restriction on the diversity jurisdiction, the Court concluded that since Congress had the option to create inferior federal courts it also had the power to create them as courts of limited jurisdiction. "[H]aving a right to prescribe, Congress may withhold from any court of its creation jurisdiction of any of the enumerated controversies. Courts created by statute can have no jurisdiction but such as the statute confers." Id. at 449. Notice that the Supreme Court, which was created by the Constitution, has never had power to review state court decisions on the basis that the parties are of diverse citizenship. The result in Sheldon v. Sill was thus to deny all federal courts a portion of the judicial power. If Congress must create a supreme court, must Congress vest in that Court the judicial power not lodged somewhere else in the federal judicial system?

EX PARTE McCARDLE

74 U.S. (7 Wall.) 506, 19 L.Ed. 264 (1868).

Appeal from the Circuit Court for the Southern District of Mississippi.

The case was this:

The Constitution of the United States ordains as follows:

"§ 1. The judicial power of the United States shall be vested *in one Supreme Court,* and in such inferior courts as the Congress may from time to time ordain and establish."

"§ 2. The judicial power shall extend to all cases in law or equity arising *under this Constitution, the laws of the United States,*" &c.

And in these last cases the Constitution ordains that,

"The Supreme Court shall have appellate jurisdiction, both as to law and fact, *with such exceptions, and under such regulations, as the Congress shall make.*"

With these constitutional provisions in existence, Congress, on the 5th February, 1867, by "An act to amend an act to establish the judicial courts of the United States, approved September 24, 1789," provided that the several courts of the United States, and the several justices and judges of such courts, within their respective jurisdiction, in addition to the authority already conferred by law, should have power to grant writs of *habeas corpus* in all cases where any person may be restrained of his or her liberty in violation of the Constitution, or of any treaty or law of the United States. And that, from the final decision of any judge, justice, or court inferior to the Circuit Court, appeal might be taken to the Circuit Court of the United States for the district in which the cause was heard, and *from the judgment of the said Circuit Court to the Supreme Court of the United States.*

This statute being in force, one McCardle, alleging unlawful restraint by military force, preferred a petition in the court below, for the writ of *habeas corpus.*

The writ was issued, and a return was made by the military commander, admitting the restraint, but denying that it was unlawful.

It appeared that the petitioner was not in the military service of the United States, but was held in custody by military authority for trial before a military commission, upon charges founded upon the publication of articles alleged to be incendiary and libellous, in a newspaper of which he was editor. The custody was alleged to be under the authority of certain acts of Congress.

Upon the hearing, the petitioner was remanded to the military custody; but, upon his prayer, an appeal was allowed him to this court, and upon filing the usual appeal-bond, for costs, he was admitted to bail upon recognizance, with sureties, conditioned for his future appearance in the Circuit Court, to abide by and perform the final judgment of this court. The appeal was taken under the above-mentioned act of February 5, 1867.

A motion to dismiss this appeal was made at the last term, and, after argument, was denied.

Subsequently, on the 2d, 3d, 4th, and 9th March, the case was argued very thoroughly and ably upon the merits, and was taken under advisement. While it was thus held, and before conference in regard to the decision proper to be made, an act was passed by Congress, returned with objections by the President, and, on the 27th March, repassed by the constitutional majority, the second section of which was as follows:

"*And be it further enacted,* That so much of the act approved February 5, 1867, entitled 'An act to amend an act to establish the judicial courts of the United States, approved September 24, 1789', as authorized an appeal from the judgment of the Circuit Court to the Supreme Court of the United States, or the exercise of any such jurisdiction by said Supreme Court, on appeals which have been, or may hereafter be taken, be, and the same is hereby repealed."

The attention of the court was directed to this statute at the last term, but counsel having expressed a desire to be heard in argument upon its effect, and the Chief Justice being detained from his place here, by his duties in the Court of Impeachment, the cause was continued under advisement. Argument was now heard upon the effect of the repealing act. . . .

The Chief Justice delivered the opinion of the Court.

The first question necessarily is that of jurisdiction; for, if the act of March, 1868, takes away the jurisdiction defined by the act of February, 1867, it is useless, if not improper, to enter into any discussion of other questions.

It is quite true, as was argued by the counsel for the petitioner, that the appellate jurisdiction of this court is not derived from acts of Congress. It is strictly speaking, conferred by the Constitution. But it is conferred "with such exceptions and under such regulations as Congress shall make."

It is unnecessary to consider whether, if Congress had made no exceptions and no regulations, this court might not have exercised general appellate jurisdiction under rules prescribed by itself. For among the earliest acts of the first Congress, at its first session, was the act of September 24th, 1789, to establish the judicial courts of the United States. That act provided for the organization of this court, and prescribed regulations for the exercise of its jurisdiction.

The source of that jurisdiction, and the limitations of it by the Constitution and by statute, have been on several occasions subjects of consideration here. In the case of Durousseau v. The United States [6 Cranch 312 (1810)], particularly, the whole matter was carefully examined, and the court held, that while "the appellate powers of this court are not given by the judicial act, but are given by the Constitution," they are, nevertheless, "limited and regulated by that act, and by such other acts as have been passed on the subject." The court said, further, that the judicial act was an exercise of the power given by the Constitution to Congress "of making exceptions to the appellate jurisdiction of the Supreme Court." "They have described affirmatively," said the court, "its jurisdiction, and this affirmative description has been understood to imply a negation of the exercise of such appellate power as is not comprehended within it."

The principle that the affirmation of appellate jurisdiction implies the negation of all such jurisdiction not affirmed having been thus established, it was an almost necessary consequence that acts of Congress, providing for the exercise of jurisdiction, should come to be spoken of as acts granting jurisdiction, and not as acts making exceptions to the constitutional grant of it.

The exception to appellate jurisdiction in the case before us, however, is not an inference from the affirmation of other appellate jurisdiction. It is made in terms. The provision of the act of 1867, affirming the appellate jurisdiction of this court in cases of *habeas corpus* is expressly repealed. It is hardly possible to imagine a plainer instance of positive exception.

We are not at liberty to inquire into the motives of the legislature. We can only examine into its power under the Constitution; and the power to make exceptions to the appellate jurisdiction of this court is given by express words.

What, then, is the effect of the repealing act upon the case before us? We cannot doubt as to this. Without jurisdiction the court cannot proceed at all in any cause. Jurisdiction is power to declare the law, and when it ceases to exist, the only function remaining to the court is that of announcing the fact and dismissing the cause. And this is not less clear upon authority than upon principle.

. . .

It is quite clear, therefore, that this court cannot proceed to pronounce judgment in this case, for it has no longer jurisdiction of the appeal; and judicial duty is not less fitly performed by declining ungranted jurisdiction than in exercising firmly that which the Constitution and the laws confer.

Counsel seem to have supposed, if effect be given to the repealing act in question, that the whole appellate power of the court, in cases of *habeas corpus,* is denied. But this is an error. The act of 1868 does not except from that jurisdiction any cases but appeals from Circuit Courts under the act of 1867. It does not affect the jurisdiction which was previously exercised.

The appeal of the petitioner in this case must be dismissed for want of jurisdiction.

UNITED STATES v. KLEIN, 80 U.S. (13 Wall.) 128 (1872). An 1863 statute provided for seizure and sale of captured or abandoned property in areas of rebellion, and for payment of the proceeds into the United States treasury. The statute further provided that loyal owners, upon proof that they had not given aid or comfort to the rebellion, could recover those proceeds by suit in the court of claims. In United States v. Padelford, 76 U.S. (9 Wall.) 531 (1870), the statute was construed to permit recovery by a claimant who had not been loyal in fact, but who had been given a Presidential pardon. Radical

Republicans in Congress were outraged with the Court's decision permitting recovery by participants in the rebellion. Congress promptly passed a statute providing that a claimant under the 1863 Act could not prove loyalty through a presidential pardon. Indeed, a pardon was proof that the claimant had given aid to the rebellion. This 1870 statute provided further that, upon proof of a pardon in either the court of claims or the Supreme Court, "the court shall forthwith dismiss the suit of such claimant." Klein's case was similar to Padelford's. At the time the 1870 Act was passed, the court of claims had given judgment for the claimant, and the government's appeal was pending in the United States Supreme Court. The government moved in the Supreme Court that Klein's suit be dismissed under the Act. The Supreme Court denied the motion, and affirmed the judgment of the court of claims.

Chief Justice Chase's opinion concluded that the 1870 statute was unconstitutional in two respects—in prescribing how a court should decide an issue of fact, and in denying effect to a Presidential pardon. Since the law was unconstitutional, the Court could not constitutionally be required to dismiss Klein's case. "We must think that Congress has inadvertently passed the limit which separates the legislative from the judicial power. . . . Congress has already provided that the Supreme Court shall have jurisdiction of the judgments of the Court of Claims on appeal. Can it prescribe a rule in conformity with which the court must deny to itself its jurisdiction thus conferred, because and only because the decision, in accordance with settled law, must be adverse to the government and favorable to the suitor?"

THE SCOPE OF CONGRESSIONAL POWER OVER
SUPREME COURT JURISDICTION UNDER
THE EXCEPTIONS CLAUSE

(1) Lest students forget that unrestrained political rhetoric has long been used in denunciations of Supreme Court opinions, it is worth recalling the words of one of the counsel for McCardle, Jeremiah S. Black (who formerly had been Chief Justice of Pennsylvania) in commenting on the *McCardle* decision: "The Court stood still to be ravished and did not even hallo while the thing was getting done." He also said that the "whole government is so rotten and dishonest that I can only protest. It is drunk with blood and vomits crime incessantly." Fairman, *History of the Supreme Court of the United States, Reconstruction and Reunion, Part I,* 478 (1971). A newspaper, the Montgomery Mail, referred to the members of the Court as "Ermine clad Crawfishes." Id. at 479.

For full accounts of the background of the *McCardle* case see Fairman, 433–514, and 2 Warren, *Supreme Court in United States History* 464–484 (Rev. ed. 1926).

(2) In his plurality opinion in Glidden v. Zdanok, 370 U.S. 530, 567–568 (1962), Justice Harlan suggested this distinction between the *McCardle* and *Klein* cases: *McCardle* sustained Congressional power to withdraw jurisdiction to proceed with a case then *sub judice; Klein* was an unconstitutional restriction of judicial power because it prescribed an unconstitutional rule of decision in a pending case. (In dissent, Justice Douglas implied that the two cases were inconsistent, and doubted whether the principle of *McCardle* could command a modern majority. Id. at 605, n. 11.) Is it significant that McCardle had lost his case below and Congress directed dismissing his *appeal,* while Klein had won in the court below and Congress directed dismissing his suit? (The Congressional direction to the Supreme Court to dismiss claimants' suits, rather than simply dismiss appeals, was not "inadvertent." Sponsors of the legislation wanted to overturn the results in the cases of claimants who had obtained judgment in the

court of claims where the government's appeal was pending in the Supreme Court.)

(3) The *McCardle* case is the only example of a result-oriented restriction on the Supreme Court's appellate jurisdiction sustained by the Supreme Court. Is it significant that it *was* sustained, even as applied to a case which had been argued and submitted for decision? Less than a year after *McCardle,* another newspaper editor in military custody, who had been denied habeas corpus by a lower federal court, successfully invoked the Supreme Court's jurisdiction to issue an "original" writ of habeas corpus under Section 14 of the Judiciary Act of 1789. Ex parte Yerger, 75 U.S. (8 Wall.) 85 (1869). (The government avoided a constitutional test of the powers of military reconstruction governments by releasing Yerger from military custody, mooting the case.) Can the *McCardle* case then be explained as a narrow decision that one route of Supreme Court review can always be closed so long as another remains open? See Van Alstyne, *A Critical Guide to Ex Parte McCardle,* 15 Ariz.L.Rev. 229, 244–254 (1973).

(4) Some proposals to restrict the jurisdiction of inferior federal courts in constitutional cases would leave undisturbed the appellate jurisdiction of the Supreme Court. Does that kind of legislation present lesser constitutional problems than legislation that closes the door to the Supreme Court? Consider, for example, the "Human Life Statute," introduced in 1981 in both the Senate and House of Representatives.[1] Section 2 [2] provided:

> "Notwithstanding any other provision of law, no inferior Federal court ordained and established by Congress under article III of the Constitution of the United States shall have jurisdiction to issue any restraining order, temporary or permanent injunction, or declaratory judgment in any case involving or arising from any State law or municipal ordinance that (1) protects the rights of human persons between conception and birth, or (2) prohibits, limits, or regulates (a) the performance of abortions, or (b) the provision at public expense of funds, facilities, personnel, or other assistance for the performance of abortions."

Notice that the proposed statute would leave intact the authority of the Supreme Court to review state court decisions, including both abortion convictions and state court actions for injunctions and declaratory judgments. Also undisturbed would be the lower courts' jurisdiction in habeas corpus to review state abortion convictions.

Most troublesome of all are proposals that both deny the lower federal courts' jurisdiction to entertain actions, and the Supreme Court's jurisdiction to review state court decisions, concerning particular constitutional issues. Consider the examples in the next two notes.

(5) The Omnibus Crime Control and Safe Streets Act of 1968 as it was reported to the Senate by the Senate Judiciary Committee contained the following provision which was eliminated on the floor prior to final passage of the bill: "Neither the Supreme Court nor any inferior court ordained and established by Congress under article III of the Constitution of the United States shall have jurisdiction to review or to reverse, vacate, modify, or disturb in any way, a ruling of any trial court of any State in any criminal prosecution admitting in evidence as voluntarily made an admission or confession of an accused if such ruling has been affirmed or otherwise upheld by the highest court of the State having appellate jurisdiction of the cause." See U.S.Code Cong. and Adm.News, 90th Cong.Sec.Sess.1968, p. 2138. This provision was

---

[1] 97th Cong., 1st Sess., H.R. 900 (Hyde and Mazzoli) and S. 158 (Helms and D'Amato).

[2] Section 1 of the Human Life Statute is a substantive provision attempting to change the result in the Supreme Court's abortion decisions by ordinary legislation. See p. 1042, infra.

designed to "revise" the holding in Miranda v. Arizona, 384 U.S. 436 (1966). Would it have been constitutional?

(6) In 1962 and 1963, the Court held that prayers and Bible readings in public schools were unconstitutional, whether or not objecting pupils were excused. Engel v. Vitale, 370 U.S. 421 (1962); Abington School Dist. v. Schempp and Murray v. Curlett, 374 U.S. 203 (1963). (These cases appear infra at pages 1507 and 1510.) Public furor created by the decisions led to proposals for constitutional amendments, on which the House Judiciary Committee held hearings in 1964. The most prominent proposal was the Becker Amendment (H.J.Res. 693, 88th Cong., 1st Sess.), which would have stated that the Constitution did not prohibit public school prayer and Bible reading "if participation therein is on a voluntary basis."

On April 9, 1979, the Senate passed, as a rider to a bill on Supreme Court jurisdiction, an amendment originally proposed by Senator Jesse Helms. (The main bill, s. 450, would have replaced most of the Court's obligatory jurisdiction with discretionary jurisdiction. See p. 57, infra.) The bill was buried in the House Judiciary Committee. The Helms Amendment would have added the following two new sections to 28 U.S.C.:

§ 1259. Notwithstanding the provisions of sections 1253, 1254 and 1257 of this chapter the Supreme Court shall not have jurisdiction to review, by appeal, writ or certiorari, or otherwise, any case arising out of any State statute . . . which relates to voluntary prayers in public school and public buildings.

§ 1364. Notwithstanding any other provision of law, the district courts shall not have jurisdiction of any case or question which the Supreme Court does not have jurisdiction to review under Section 1259. . . .[1]

If the Helms Amendment were to be enacted, and were to be sustained by the federal courts, what would be the impact of the Supreme Court's earlier decisions concerning school prayers when cases were litigated in state courts?

(7) For discussion of the limits of Congressional power to control jurisdiction of the lower federal courts, and a summary of the enormous literature on that question, see Gunther, *Congressional Power to Curtail Federal Court Jurisdiction: An Opinionated Guide to an Ongoing Debate,* 36 Stan.L.Rev. 201 (1984). Two excellent examples in that literature are Sager, *Constitutional Limitations on Congress' Authority to Regulate the Jurisdiction of Federal Courts,* 95 Harv.L.Rev. 17 (1981); Redish, *Limitations on Congressional Power to Control Federal Jurisdiction: A Reaction to Professor Sager,* 77 N.W.U.L.Rev. 143 (1982).

[1] 96th Cong., 1st Sess., 125 Cong.Rec. 4128 (1979).

Chapter 3

THE JURISDICTION OF FEDERAL COURTS IN CONSTITUTIONAL CASES

Introduction. Judicial review can be understood only in the context of constitutional litigation. Minimum familiarity with jurisdictional boundaries and the special rules devised for constitutional cases is necessary to understanding the substantive doctrines. This chapter is designed to present a brief introduction to a very complicated set of doctrines.

The first two sections deal with the complexities introduced into constitutional litigation by the existence of independent state and federal court systems, each with ultimate responsibility for final interpretation of the law originating in its own level of government and with concurrent jurisdiction to adjudicate disputes in which constitutional questions arise. Section 1 covers Supreme Court jurisdiction to review decisions of state courts. Section 2 deals with constitutional litigation originating in the federal courts. Section 3 considers a variety of related doctrines that govern both Supreme Court review and the conduct of the lower federal courts. Those doctrines concern the definition of "cases" and "controversies" and the extent to which issues of constitutional interpretation are justiciable.

SECTION 1. SUPREME COURT REVIEW OF STATE COURT DECISIONS

A. HISTORY AND STRUCTURE

ARTICLE III OF THE CONSTITUTION AND SECTION 25 OF THE JUDICIARY ACT OF 1789

At the Constitutional Convention, there was general agreement that one major weakness of the central government under the Articles of Confederation was the absence of a central court system. Accordingly, there was little discussion of the question whether there should be a federal judicial system with power to act directly on individuals and member states. Article III extends the federal judicial power to cases, among others, "arising under this Constitution, the Laws of the United States, and Treaties made, or which shall be made, under their Authority."

The major dispute at the Convention concerned the nature of the tribunals that would exercise the federal judicial power. Nationalist proposals provided for mandatory establishment of both a supreme court and inferior trial courts. Competing plans provided only for a supreme court. Notice that both sides of the debate conceded the propriety of appellate review over state court decisions, and that a supreme court should be established by the Constitution itself. The controversy concerned whether appeal of state court decisions to a national supreme court was a sufficient mechanism for insuring national authority and the uniformity of application of federal laws. The resulting compromise gave Congress the option to provide for lower federal courts.

The First Congress, in 1789, exercised its option to create lower federal courts. Those courts were given exclusive jurisdiction to try federal crimes and concurrent jurisdiction with the state courts in cases in which the United States was the plaintiff. The lower federal courts were not given general jurisdiction in civil cases arising under federal law. (The most important civil jurisdiction of the lower federal courts was in diversity of citizenship and admiralty cases.) For the most part, the limited number of private federal law rights were entrusted to the state courts, that were required to apply federal law over inconsistent state law by the Supremacy Clause of Article VI of the Constitution.

Appellate review of state court decisions was the primary method for enforcing the Supremacy Clause. Section 25 of the Judiciary Act of 1789 provided that "a final judgment or decree in any suit, in the highest court of law or equity of a State in which a decision in the suit could be had" could be "re-examined and reversed or affirmed in the Supreme Court of the United States upon a writ of error," in three classes of cases: (1) "where is drawn in question the validity of a treaty or statute of, or an authority exercised under the United States, and the decision is against their validity"; (2) "where is drawn in question the validity of a statute of, or an authority exercised under any State, on the ground of their being repugnant to the constitution, treaties or laws of the United States, and the decision is in favour of such of their validity"; (3) "where is drawn in question the construction of any clause of the constitution, or of a treaty, or statute of, or commission held under the United States, and the decision is against the title, right, privilege or exemption . . . claimed by either party, under such clause of the said Constitution, treaty, statute or commission." Notice that all three provisions limited review to those cases where state courts had rejected claims made under the federal Constitution and laws. State court decisions sustaining those claims were not reviewable. (That remained true until 1914. See p. 50, infra.)

For an extensive review of the history of Article III and the Judiciary Act of 1789, and citation to other authority, see Hart and Wechsler, *Federal Courts* 1–36 (2d ed. 1973).

———

MARTIN v. HUNTER'S LESSEE

14 U.S. (1 Wheat.) 304, 4 L.Ed. 97 (1816).

[In 1816 the jurisdiction of the Supreme Court under Section 25 of the Judiciary Act of 1789 was denied by the highest court of Virginia. The Virginia estates of Lord Fairfax (who died in England in 1781) had descended to a relative, Thomas Martin. Virginia claimed to have acquired the estates in 1777 under state legislation confiscating the property of loyalist British subjects and in 1789 had made a conveyance to David Hunter. Hunter's lessee, claiming under this conveyance, brought an action of ejectment. The Fairfax heirs contended that their rights were supported by the treaties of 1783 and 1794 giving protection to British owned property. After years of negotiation and litigation, the Virginia Court of Appeals sustained Hunter's claim. The Supreme Court of the United States reversed and remanded the case, holding that the treaty of 1794 confirmed the title remaining in the Fairfax heirs. Fairfax's Devisee v. Hunter's Lessee, 7 Cranch 603 (1813). The Virginia Court of Appeals, presided over by Judge Spencer Roane,[1] refused to comply with the decision.]

---

[1] Judge Roane was the chief judicial opponent of Chief Justice Marshall's federalist views. It is commonly thought that if the Office of Chief Justice had been vacant when Thomas Jefferson became President, he would have nominated Roane for the position.

Story, J., delivered the opinion of the court:

This is a writ of error from the Court of Appeals of Virginia, founded upon the refusal of that court to obey the mandate of this court, requiring the judgment rendered in this very cause, at February term, 1813, to be carried into due execution. . . .

The government . . . can claim no powers which are not granted to it by the constitution, and the powers actually granted, must be such as are expressly given, or given by necessary implication. On the other hand, this instrument, like every other grant, is to have a reasonable construction, according to the import of its terms; and where a power is expressly given in general terms, it is not to be restrained to particular cases, unless that construction grow out of the context expressly, or by necessary implication. The words are to be taken in their natural and obvious sense, and not in a sense unreasonably restricted or enlarged. . . .[a]

But, even admitting that the language of the constitution is not mandatory, and that Congress may constitutionally omit to vest the judicial power in courts of the United States, it cannot be denied that when it is vested it may be exercised to the utmost constitutional extent.

This leads us to the consideration of the great question as to the nature and extent of the appellate jurisdiction of the United States. We have already seen that appellate jurisdiction is given by the constitution to the Supreme Court in all cases, where it has not original jurisdiction; subject, however, to such exceptions and regulations as Congress may prescribe. It is, therefore, capable of embracing every case enumerated in the constitution, which is not exclusively to be decided by way of original jurisdiction. But the exercise of appellate jurisdiction is far from being limited by the terms of the constitution to the Supreme Court. There can be no doubt that Congress may create a succession of inferior tribunals, in each of which it may vest appellate as well as original jurisdiction. The judicial power is delegated by the constitution in the most general terms, and may, therefore, be exercised by Congress under every variety of form, of appellate or original jurisdiction. And as there is nothing in the constitution which restrains or limits this power, it must, therefore, in all other cases, subsist in the utmost latitude of which, in its own nature, it is susceptible. . . .

It must, therefore, be conceded that the constitution not only contemplated, but meant to provide for cases within the scope of the judicial power of the United States, which might yet depend before state tribunals. It was foreseen that in the exercise of their ordinary jurisdiction, state courts would incidentally take cognizance of cases arising under the constitution, the laws and treaties of the United States. Yet to all these cases the judicial power, by the very terms of the constitution, is to extend. It cannot extend by original jurisdiction if that was already rightfully and exclusively attached in the state courts, which (as has been already shown) may occur; it must, therefore, extend by appellate jurisdiction, or not at all. It would seem to follow that the appellate power of the United States must, in such cases, extend to state tribunals; and if in such cases, there is no reason why it should not equally attach upon all others within the purview of the constitution.

It has been argued that such an appellate jurisdiction over state courts is inconsistent with the genius of our governments, and the spirit of the constitu-

See Warren, *Legislative and Judicial Attacks on the Supreme Court of the United States—A History of the Twenty-Fifth Section of the Judiciary Act,* 47 Am.L.Rev. 1, 3 (1913).

[a] In the omitted portion Story suggested that Congress was constitutionally obligated to create lower federal courts and confer on them the full jurisdiction granted by Article III. See supra p. 37.

tion. That the latter was never designed to act upon state sovereignties, but only upon the people, and that if the power exists, it will materially impair the sovereignty of the states, and the independence of their courts. We cannot yield to the force of this reasoning; it assumes principles which we cannot admit, and draws conclusions to which we do not yield our assent.

It is a mistake that the constitution was not designed to operate upon states, in their corporate capacities. It is crowded with provisions which restrain or annul the sovereignty of the states in some of the highest branches of their prerogatives. The tenth section of the first article contains a long list of disabilities and prohibitions imposed upon the states. Surely, when such essential portions of state sovereignty are taken away, or prohibited to be exercised, it cannot be correctly asserted that the constitution does not act upon the states. The language of the constitution is also imperative upon the states as to the performance of many duties. It is imperative upon the state legislatures to make laws prescribing the time, places, and manner of holding elections for senators and representatives, and for electors of President and Vice-President. And in these, as well as some other cases, Congress have a right to revise, amend, or supersede the laws which may be passed by state legislatures. When, therefore, the states are stripped of some of the highest attributes of sovereignty, and the same are given to the United States; when the legislatures of the states are, in some respects, under the control of Congress, and in every case are, under the constitution, bound by the paramount authority of the United States; it is certainly difficult to support the argument that the appellate power over the decisions of state courts is contrary to the genius of our institutions. The courts of the United States can, without question, revise the proceedings of the executive and legislative authorities of the states, and if they are found to be contrary to the constitution, may declare them to be of no legal validity. Surely the exercise of the same right over judicial tribunals is not a higher or more dangerous act of sovereign power.

Nor can such a right be deemed to impair the independence of state judges.
. . . .

The argument urged from the possibility of the abuse of the revising power is equally unsatisfactory. It is always a doubtful course to argue against the use or existence of a power, from the possibility of its abuse. It is still more difficult, by such an argument, to ingraft upon a general power a restriction which is not to be found in the terms in which it is given. From the very nature of things, the absolute right of decision, in the last resort, must rest some-where—wherever it may be vested it is susceptible of abuse. In all questions of jurisdiction the inferior, or appellate court, must pronounce the final judgment; and common sense, as well as legal reasoning, has conferred it upon the latter.
. . . .

This is not all. A motive of another kind, perfectly compatible with the most sincere respect for state tribunals, might induce the grant of appellate power over their decisions. That motive is the importance, and even necessity of uniformity of decisions throughout the whole United States, upon all subjects within the purview of the constitution. Judges of equal learning and integrity, in different states, might differently interpret a statute, or a treaty of the United States, or even the constitution itself. If there were no revising authority to control these jarring and discordant judgments, and harmonize them into uniformity, the laws, the treaties and the constitution of the United States would be different in different states, and might, perhaps, never have precisely the same construction, obligation, or efficacy, in any two states. The public mischiefs that would attend such a state of things would be truly deplorable; and it cannot be believed that they could have escaped the enlightened convention which formed the constitution. What, indeed, might then have been only prophecy, has now become fact; and the appellate jurisdiction must continue to be the only adequate remedy for such evils. . . .

On the whole, the court are of opinion that the appellate power of the United States does extend to cases pending in the state courts; and that the 25th section of the judiciary act, which authorizes the exercise of this jurisdiction in the specified cases, by a writ of error, is supported by the letter and spirit of the constitution. We find no clause in that instrument which limits this power; and we dare not interpose a limitation where the people have not been disposed to create one. . . .

We have thus gone over all the principal questions in the cause, and we deliver our judgment with entire confidence, that it is consistent with the constitution and laws of the land.

We have not thought it incumbent on us to give any opinion upon the question, whether this court have authority to issue a writ of mandamus to the Court of Appeals to enforce the former judgments, as we do not think it necessarily involved in the decision of this cause.

It is the opinion of the whole court that the judgment of the Court of Appeals of Virginia, rendered on the mandate in this cause, be reversed, and the judgment of the District Court, held at Winchester, be, and the same is hereby affirmed.

Johnson, J. It will be observed in this case, that the court disavows all intention to decide on the right to issue compulsory process to the state courts; thus leaving us, in my opinion, where the constitution and laws place us— supreme over persons and cases as far as our judicial powers extend, but not asserting any compulsory control over the state tribunals.

In this view, I acquiesce in their opinion, but not altogether in the reasoning, or opinion, of my brother who delivered it. Few minds are accustomed to the same habit of thinking, and our conclusions are most satisfactory to ourselves when arrived at in our own way. . . .

STATE COURT RESISTANCE TO SUPREME COURT ORDERS

In Cohens v. Virginia, 19 U.S. (6 Wheat.) 264 (1821) the Court reviewed an appeal from a Virginia state court which involved an alleged conflict between a Virginia criminal statute forbidding the sale of lottery tickets and an Act of Congress. This decision produced even more violent reactions than Martin v. Hunter's Lessee. Judge Roane of Virginia, writing anonymously, said of the decision: "A most monstrous and unexampled decision. It can only be accounted for from that love of power which all history informs us infects and corrupts all who possess it, and from which even the upright and eminent Judges are not exempt." 1 Warren, *Supreme Court in United States History* (1926) 555. See also Note, 66 Harv.L.Rev. 1242 (1953) for an account of the career of Judge Roane.

Since Martin v. Hunter's Lessee there have been many instances of state court resistance to Supreme Court orders. For a discussion of some of the episodes and of the varying techniques used to attempt to compel compliance, see Murphy, *Lower Court Checks on Supreme Court Power,* 53 Am.Pol.Sci.Rev. 1017 (1959); Note, *State Court Evasion of United States Supreme Court Mandates,* 56 Yale L.J. 574 (1947); Note, *Evasion of Supreme Court Mandates in Cases Remanded to State Courts Since 1941,* 67 Harv.L.Rev. 1251 (1954); Beatty, *State*

Court Evasion of United States Supreme Court Mandates During the Last Decade of the Warren Court, 6 Valparaiso L.Rev. 260 (1972).

THE CURRENT JURISDICTION OF THE SUPREME COURT TO REVIEW STATE COURT DECISIONS

The Supreme Court's jurisdiction to review state court decisions has not been modified since 1925.   The current statute provides:

28 U.S.C. § 1257:

"Final judgments or decrees rendered by the highest court of a State in which a decision could be had, may be reviewed by the Supreme Court as follows:

"(1) By appeal, where is drawn in question the validity of a treaty or statute of the United States and the decision is against its validity.

"(2) By appeal, where is drawn in question the validity of a statute of any state on the ground of its being repugnant to the Constitution, treaties or laws of the United States, and the decision is in favor of its validity.

"(3) By writ of certiorari, where the validity of a treaty or statute of the United States is drawn in question or where the validity of a State statute is drawn in question on the ground of its being repugnant to the Constitution, treaties or laws of the United States, or where any title, right, privilege or immunity is specially set up or claimed under the Constitution, treaties or statutes of, or commission held or authority exercised under, the United States."

The requirement that the state court's judgment be "final" has been carried forward from the Judiciary Act of 1789.   The Court's current flexible definition of that requirement is discussed in Cox Broadcasting Corp. v. Cohn, 420 U.S. 469, 476–487 (1975).   The requirement that the decision be of the highest state court "in which a decision could be had" also stems from the Judiciary Act of 1789.   This provision can permit review of decisions of inferior state courts, if further appeals within the state court system are not possible.   For example, Thompson v. Louisville, 362 U.S. 199 (1960), reviewed the decision of a police court.   The distinction between appeal and certiorari stems from legislation in 1916 and 1925.   That distinction will be examined below in Subsection C.

B.   ISSUES OF STATE LAW IN THE SUPREME COURT: THE ADEQUATE AND INDEPENDENT STATE GROUND

REVIEW OF ISSUES OF STATE LAW IN CASES INVOLVING FEDERAL QUESTIONS: THE ADEQUATE AND INDEPENDENT STATE GROUND

The Judiciary Act of 1789 contained a proviso expressly limiting Supreme Court review of state court decisions to the federal questions that provided the basis for its jurisdiction.   That proviso was repealed in 1867, and does not now appear in 28 U.S.C. § 1257.   In a landmark case, the Supreme Court held that repeal of the proviso did not change the basic principle that state court decisions on issues of state law cannot be reviewed by the Supreme Court.   Murdock v.

Memphis, 87 U.S. (20 Wall.) 590 (1875).   State courts are thus the final expositors of the meaning of state law.[1]

Corollary to the finality of state court interpretations of state law is the principle that issues of federal law resolved by state courts will not be reviewed by the Supreme Court if the state court's judgment rests upon an "adequate and independent" state ground.   Thus, if a state court rules against a party on two alternative grounds, one federal and one state, the Supreme Court lacks jurisdiction to inquire into the correctness of the federal law ruling.   The rationale of the adequate and independent state ground rule has been explained as follows.   "Our only power over state judgments is to correct them to the extent that they incorrectly adjudge federal rights.   And our power is to correct wrong judgments, not to revise opinions.   We are not permitted to render an advisory opinion, and if the same judgment would be rendered by the state court after we corrected its views of Federal laws, our review could amount to nothing more than an advisory opinion."   Jackson, J., for the Court in Herb v. Pitcairn, 324 U.S. 117, 125–26 (1945).

The adequate and independent state ground rule has two branches.   The first is procedural.   It arises when the state court has refused or simply failed to rule on the merits of the federal issues because they were not presented to the state court in the manner required by state procedure.   On the one hand, the procedure for raising issues in the state courts—even issues of federal law—is governed by state rules of practice and not by federal law standards.   On the other hand, from the beginning the state courts have been important forums for vindication of federal rights and defenses.   Complete deference to state court rulings refusing to honor federal claims because of state procedure creates possibilities that federal claims will be difficult to enforce, or that state courts will evade the supremacy of federal law.   Justice Holmes said, in a famous dictum: "Whatever springes the State may set for those who are endeavoring to assert rights that the State confers, the assertion of Federal rights, when plainly and reasonably made, is not to be defeated in the name of local practice." Davis v. Wechsler, 263 U.S. 22, 24 (1923).

It is clear that a state court's failure or refusal to decide on federal law issues will not block Supreme Court Review if the procedural decision is not "adequate."   What is less than clear is the standard for judging the "adequacy" of state procedural grounds.   Suppose, for example, that the defendant has been convicted for violating a state criminal statute claimed to violate the United States Constitution.   The highest state court has affirmed the conviction, but has refused to decide whether or not the state statute is constitutional because that issue was not raised at the trial, because it was raised too late, because it was raised in improper form, or the like.   Can the Supreme Court now review the question whether the statute is constitutional?   The Supreme Court's last full-scale discussion of the problem was in Henry v. Mississippi, 379 U.S. 443 (1965).   The Court stated that "in every case" it was necessary to inquire whether "enforcement of a procedural forfeiture" served "a legitimate state

---

[1] There is a limited exception to the principle of state court primacy in construing state law, in cases where a federal right is defined to turn on the meaning of state law.   Martin v. Hunter's Lessee, for example, involved a provision of the Treaty of Peace of 1783, that prevented "future confiscations" of land of British subjects, and the Jay Treaty of 1794, which gave British subjects the rights to grant, sell and devise their estates "as if they were natives."   Decision of the rights granted by the treaties in the particular case required Supreme Court decisions on issues of Virginia law as to who owned the land in 1783.   Fairfax's Devisee v. Hunter's Lessee, 11 U.S. (7 Cranch) 603 (1813).   In the area of constitutional law, similar problems arise where a claim is made that a state has impaired the obligation of a "contract," or denied a person "property" without due process of law, since both the concepts of "contract" and "property" rest, in large part, on state law.   Even within these exceptional areas, decisions of the state courts as to the meaning of state law, will be given considerable deference. See Hart and Wechsler, *Federal Courts* 489–517 (2d ed. 1973).   Another limited exception was established in West Virginia v. Sims, 341 U.S. 22 (1951), discussed infra, page 433.

interest." The *Henry* opinion, however, failed to clarify the standard for judging the adequacy of state procedures. For different assessments of the law prior to *Henry,* and the impact of that decision, see Sandalow, *Henry v. Mississippi and the Adequate State Ground: Proposals for a Revised Doctrine,* 1965 Sup.Ct.Rev. 187 and Hill, *The Inadequate State Ground,* 65 Colum.L.Rev. 943 (1965). A novel and technical ruling on an issue of state procedure may still be judged inadequate either because it is suspected that the state court is evading decision of the federal issue, or because the rule throws unreasonable obstacles in the way of enforcement of federal rights. Williams v. Georgia, 349 U.S. 375, 399 (1955) (Clark, J., dissenting).

There is more certainty, and more deference to state court decisions, in the second branch of the doctrine—where the state ground is substantive. A common situation is one where the state court has held a state statute to be invalid under both the United States and state constitutions. If the state court is one of stature, its disposition of the federal question may have considerable impact in other courts. The application of the independent and adequate state ground rule in that situation is, nevertheless, clear. There is no realistic inquiry into the adequacy of the state ground. The sole issue is whether the state substantive ground is independent—that is, whether, no matter how the federal issue is resolved, the state ground will be dispositive.[2] Thus a state court decision invalidating a state law on both state and federal constitutional grounds cannot be reviewed by the Supreme Court, even if the bulk of the state court's discussion concerned the United States Constitution.

SUPREME COURT REVIEW OF STATE COURT DECISIONS UPHOLDING CLAIMS OF FEDERAL CONSTITUTIONAL RIGHT

Until 1914, the Supreme Court's authority to review state court decisions was limited to cases which denied claims of federal right. Thus, a state court decision that erroneously decided that a state law violated the United States Constitution could not be reviewed in the United States Supreme Court. The 1914 amendment permitting review of state decisions that sustained federal claims and defenses can be traced to a single case. The New York Court of Appeals held that New York's pioneer workers' compensation law was unconstitutional under the fourteenth amendment, on the ground that the employer's liability without fault was a taking of property without due process of law. Ives v. South Buffalo Ry. Co., 201 N.Y. 271, 94 N.E. 431 (1911). The decision could not be reviewed by the United States Supreme Court, because the state court had upheld the claim of federal constitutional right asserted. The decision, which has been described as "the most famous and most bitterly attacked holding of any American court regarding workmen's compensation," (Dodd, *Administration of Workmen's Compensation* 30 [1936]), led to the enactment of a provision permitting Supreme Court review of state court decisions upholding claims of federal right. Act of Dec. 23, 1914, c. 2, 38 Stat. 790. The 1914 provision is now reflected in 28 U.S.C. § 1257(3).

It is both ironic and instructive to note that the 1914 Amendment would not, in fact, have permitted the United States Supreme Court to review the *Ives* decision. The New York Court of Appeals had also struck down the workers' compensation law as a violation of the New York Constitution—an independent

---

[2] Reliance on the state constitution will not preclude Supreme Court review, for example, if the state's constitution has been construed to adopt the United States Supreme Court's construction of the United States Constitution. In that case, if the state court strikes down the state law, the result is compelled by the state court's interpretation of federal law. See Delaware v. Prouse, 440 U.S. 648 (1979).

state ground! New York could—and did—amend its State Constitution to authorize enactment of a workers' compensation law. The New York law was sustained by the Supreme Court in New York Central R.R. Co. v. White, 243 U.S. 188 (1916). For five years, however, proponents of workers' compensation laws throughout the country were confronted with a decision of the most prestigious state court that the basic principle of those laws violated the United States Constitution.

Recent years have seen an increase in the number of state court decisions that have relied on parallel state constitutional provisions, precluding Supreme Court review of decisions that state laws violate the United States Constitution. Falk, *The State Constitution: A More Than "Adequate" Non-federal Ground,* 61 Calif.L.Rev. 273 (1973); Howard, *State Courts and Constitutional Rights in the Day of the Burger Court,* 62 Va.L.Rev. 873 (1976). See also Brennan, *State Constitutions and the Protection of Individual Rights,* 90 Harv.L.Rev. 489 (1977). Where state courts have not relied on state grounds, there has been a significant increase in the number of cases reviewed, and reversed, by the Supreme Court because state courts have read the United States Constitution too expansively. Sager, *Fair Measure: The Legal Status of Underenforced Constitutional Norms,* 91 Harv.L.Rev. 1212, 1243–1247 (1978).

Should the Supreme Court be able to review state decisions holding state laws invalid under the United States Constitution, even when the decision is also based on the state constitution? For an argument that an interest in uniformity of interpretation of the Constitution should permit that review in appropriate cases, see Sandalow, *Henry v. Mississippi and the Adequate State Ground: Proposals for a Revised Doctrine,* 1965 Sup.Ct.Rev. 187, 199–203. On the other hand, should the Supreme Court refuse to review state court decisions holding state laws invalid under the United States Constitution, even when the decision is based entirely on the federal ground? For arguments that the state courts should have some leeway to interpret the United States Constitution more expansively than does the Supreme Court, and that review of those decisions is inappropriate or unwise, see Sager, supra, at 1247–1263, and Tribe, *American Constitutional Law,* 31–33 (1978).

MICHIGAN v. LONG

463 U.S. 1032, 103 S.Ct. 3469, 77 L.Ed.2d 1201 (1983).

Justice O'Connor delivered the opinion of the Court.

In Terry v. Ohio, 392 U.S. 1 (1968), we upheld the validity of a protective search for weapons in the absence of probable cause to arrest because it is unreasonable to deny a police officer the right "to neutralize the threat of physical harm," id., at 24, when he possesses an articulable suspicion that an individual is armed and dangerous. We did not, however, expressly address whether such a protective search for weapons could extend to an area beyond the person in the absence of probable cause to arrest. In the present case, respondent David Long was convicted for possession of marijuana found by police in the passenger compartment and trunk of the automobile that he was driving. The police searched the passenger compartment because they had reason to believe that the vehicle contained weapons potentially dangerous to the officers. We hold that the protective search of the passenger compartment was reasonable under the principles articulated in *Terry* and other decisions of this Court. We also examine Long's argument that the decision below rests upon an adequate and independent state ground, and we decide in favor of our jurisdiction.

I

The Barry County Circuit Court denied Long's motion to suppress the marijuana taken from both the interior of the car and its trunk. He was subsequently convicted of possession of marijuana. The Michigan Court of Appeals affirmed Long's conviction, holding that the search of the passenger compartment was valid as a protective search under *Terry,* supra, and that the search of the trunk was valid as an inventory search under South Dakota v. Opperman, 428 U.S. 364 (1976). See 94 Mich.App. 338, 288 N.W.2d 629 (1979). The Michigan Supreme Court reversed. The court held that "the sole justification of the *Terry* search, protection of the police officers and others nearby, cannot justify the search in this case." 413 Mich., at 472, 320 N.W.2d, at 869. The marijuana found in Long's trunk was considered by the court below to be the "fruit" of the illegal search of the interior, and was also suppressed.

We granted certiorari in this case to consider the important question of the authority of a police officer to protect himself by conducting a *Terry*-type search of the passenger compartment of a motor vehicle during the lawful investigatory stop of the occupant of the vehicle. 429 U.S. 904 (1982).

II

Before reaching the merits, we must consider Long's argument that we are without jurisdiction to decide this case because the decision below rests on an adequate and independent state ground. The court below referred twice to the state constitution in its opinion, but otherwise relied exclusively on federal law. Long argues that the Michigan courts have provided greater protection from searches and seizures under the state constitution than is afforded under the Fourth Amendment, and the references to the state constitution therefore establish an adequate and independent ground for the decision below.

It is, of course, "incumbent upon this Court . . . to ascertain for itself . . . whether the asserted non-federal ground independently and adequately supports the judgment." Abie State Bank v. Bryan, 282 U.S. 765, 773 (1931). Although we have announced a number of principles in order to help us determine whether various forms of references to state law constitute adequate and independent state grounds,[4] we openly admit that we have thus far not developed a satisfying and consistent approach for resolving this vexing issue. In some instances, we have taken the strict view that if the ground of decision was at all unclear, we would dismiss the case. See, e.g., Lynch v. New York, 293 U.S. 52 (1934). In other instances, we have vacated, see, e.g., Minnesota v. National Tea Co., 309 U.S. 551 (1940), or continued a case, see e.g., Herb v. Pitcairn, 324 U.S. 117 (1945), in order to obtain clarification about the

---

[4] For example, we have long recognized that "where the judgment of a state court rests upon two grounds one of which is federal and the other non-federal in character, our jurisdiction fails if the non-federal ground is independent of the federal ground and adequate to support the judgment." Fox Film Corp. v. Muller, 296 U.S. 207, 210 (1935). We may review a state case decided on a federal ground even if it is clear that there was an available state ground for decision on which the state court could properly have relied. Beecher v. Alabama, 389 U.S. 35, 37, n. 3 (1967). Also, if, in our view, the state court " 'felt compelled by what it understood to be federal constitutional considerations to construe . . . its own law in the manner that it did,' " then we will not treat a normally adequate state ground as independent, and there will be no question about our jurisdiction. Delaware v. Prouse, 440 U.S. 648, 653 (1979) (quoting Zacchini v. Scripps-Howard Broadcasting Co., 433 U.S. 562, 568 (1977)). See also South Dakota v. Neville, 459 U.S. 553, 556, n. 5 (1983). Finally, "where the non-federal ground is so interwoven with the [federal ground] as not to be an independent matter, or is not of sufficient breadth to sustain the judgment without any decision of the other, our jurisdiction is plain." Enterprise Irrigation District v. Farmers Mutual Canal Company, 243 U.S. 157, 164 (1917).

nature of a state court decision. See also California v. Krivda, 409 U.S. 33 (1972). In more recent cases, we have ourselves examined state law to determine whether state courts have used federal law to guide their application of state law or to provide the actual basis for the decision that was reached. . . . In Oregon v. Kennedy, 456 U.S. 667, 670–671 (1982), we rejected an invitation to remand to the state court for clarification even when the decision rested in part on a case from the state court, because we determined that the state case itself rested upon federal grounds. We added that "[e]ven if the case admitted of more doubt as to whether federal and state grounds for decision were intermixed, the fact that the state court relied to the extent it did on federal grounds requires us to reach the merits." Id., at 671.

This *ad hoc* method of dealing with cases that involve possible adequate and independent state grounds is antithetical to the doctrinal consistency that is required when sensitive issues of federal-state relations are involved. Moreover, none of the various methods of disposition that we have employed thus far recommends itself as the preferred method that we should apply to the exclusion of others, and we therefore determine that it is appropriate to reexamine our treatment of this jurisdictional issue in order to achieve the consistency that is necessary.

The process of examining state law is unsatisfactory because it requires us to interpret state laws with which we are generally unfamiliar, and which often, as in this case, have not been discussed at length by the parties. Vacation and continuance for clarification have also been unsatisfactory both because of the delay and decrease in efficiency of judicial administration, see Dixon v. Duffy, 344 U.S. 143 (1952), and, more important, because these methods of disposition place significant burdens on state courts to demonstrate the presence or absence of our jurisdiction. See Philadelphia Newspapers, Inc. v. Jerome, 434 U.S. 241, 244 (1978) (Rehnquist, J., dissenting); Department of Motor Vehicles v. Rios, 410 U.S. 425, 427 (1973) (Douglas, J., dissenting). Finally, outright dismissal of cases is clearly not a panacea because it cannot be doubted that there is an important need for uniformity in federal law, and that this need goes unsatisfied when we fail to review an opinion that rests primarily upon federal grounds and where the *independence* of an alleged state ground is not apparent from the four corners of the opinion. We have long recognized that dismissal is inappropriate "where there is strong indication . . . that the federal constitution as judicially construed controlled the decision below." *National Tea Co.,* supra, 309 U.S., at 556 (1940).

Respect for the independence of state courts, as well as avoidance of rendering advisory opinions, have been the cornerstones of this Court's refusal to decide cases where there is an adequate and independent state ground. It is precisely because of this respect for state courts, and this desire to avoid advisory opinions, that we do not wish to continue to decide issues of state law that go beyond the opinion that we review, or to require state courts to reconsider cases to clarify the grounds of their decisions. Accordingly, when, as in this case, a state court decision fairly appears to rest primarily on federal law, or to be interwoven with the federal law, and when the adequacy and independence of any possible state law ground is not clear from the face of the opinion, we will accept as the most reasonable explanation that the state court decided the case the way it did because it believed that federal law required it to do so. If a state court chooses merely to rely on federal precedents as it would on the precedents of all other jurisdictions, then it need only make clear by a plain statement in its judgment or opinion that the federal cases are being used only for the purpose of guidance, and do not themselves compel the result that the court has reached. In this way, both justice and judicial administration will be greatly improved. If the state court decision indicates clearly and expressly that it is alternatively based on bona fide separate, adequate, and independent grounds, we of course, will not undertake to review the decision.

This approach obviates in most instances the need to examine state law in order to decide the nature of the state court decision, and will at the same time avoid the danger of our rendering advisory opinions. It also avoids the unsatisfactory and intrusive practice of requiring state courts to clarify their decisions to the satisfaction of this Court. We believe that such an approach will provide state judges with a clearer opportunity to develop state jurisprudence unimpeded by federal interference, and yet will preserve the integrity of federal law. "It is fundamental that state courts be left free and unfettered by us in interpreting their state constitutions. But it is equally important that ambiguous or obscure adjudications by state courts do not stand as barriers to a determination by this Court of the validity under the federal constitution of state action." *National Tea Co.,* supra, 309 U.S., at 557.

The principle that we will not review judgments of state courts that rest on adequate and independent state grounds is based, in part, on "the limitations of our own jurisdiction." Herb v. Pitcairn, 324 U.S. 117, 125 (1945). The jurisdictional concern is that we not "render an advisory opinion, and if the same judgment would be rendered by the state court after we corrected its views of federal laws, our review could amount to nothing more than an advisory opinion." Id., at 126. Our requirement of a "plain statement" that a decision rests upon adequate and independent state grounds does not in any way authorize the rendering of advisory opinions. Rather, in determining, as we must, whether we have jurisdiction to review a case that is alleged to rest on adequate and independent state grounds, see Abie State Bank v. Bryan, supra, 282 U.S., at 773, we merely assume that there are no such grounds when it is not clear from the opinion itself that the state court relied upon an adequate and independent state ground and when it fairly appears that the state court rested its decision primarily on federal law.[8]

Our review of the decision below under this framework leaves us unconvinced that it rests upon an independent state ground. Apart from its two citations to the state constitution, the court below relied *exclusively* on its understanding of *Terry* and other federal cases. Not a single state case was cited to support the state court's holding that the search of the passenger compartment was unconstitutional. . . .

Rather than dismissing the case, or requiring that the state court reconsider its decision on our behalf solely because of a mere possibility that an adequate and independent ground supports the judgment, we find that we have jurisdiction in the absence of a plain statement that the decision below rested on an adequate and independent state ground. . . .

[8]. . .

In dissent, Justice Stevens proposes the novel view that this Court should never review a state court decision unless the Court wishes to vindicate a federal right that has been endangered. The rationale of the dissent is not restricted to cases where the decision is arguably supported by adequate and independent state grounds. Rather, Justice Stevens appears to believe that even if the decision below rests exclusively on federal grounds, this Court should not review the decision as long as there is no federal right that is endangered.

The state courts handle the vast bulk of all criminal litigation in this country. In 1982, more than twelve million criminal actions (excluding juvenile and traffic charges) were filed in the 50 state court systems and the District of Columbia. See 7 State Court Journal 18 (1983). By comparison, approximately 32,700 criminal suits were filed in federal courts during that same year. See Annual Report of the Director of the Administrative Office of the United States Courts 6 (1982). The state courts are required to apply federal constitutional standards, and they necessarily create a considerable body of "federal law" in the process. It is not surprising that this Court has become more interested in the application and development of federal law by state courts in the light of the recent significant expansion of federally created standards that we have imposed on the States.

.   .   .   .

IV

. . .

V

The decision of the Michigan Supreme Court is reversed, and the case is remanded for further proceedings not inconsistent with this opinion.

It is so ordered.

Justice Blackmun, concurring in part and concurring in the judgment.

. . .

Justice Stevens, dissenting.

The jurisprudential questions presented in this case are far more important than the question whether the Michigan police officer's search of respondent's car violated the Fourth Amendment. The case raises profoundly significant questions concerning the relationship between two sovereigns—the State of Michigan and the United States of America.

. . .

. . . It appears to be common ground that any rule we adopt should show "respect for state courts, and [a] desire to avoid advisory opinions." And I am confident that all members of this Court agree that there is a vital interest in the sound management of scarce federal judicial resources. All of those policies counsel against the exercise of federal jurisdiction. They are fortified by my belief that a policy of judicial restraint—one that allows other decisional bodies to have the last word in legal interpretation until it is truly necessary for this Court to intervene—enables this Court to make its most effective contribution to our federal system of government.

The nature of the case before us hardly compels a departure from tradition. These are not cases in which an American citizen has been deprived of a right secured by the United States Constitution or a federal statute. Rather, they are cases in which a state court has upheld a citizen's assertion of a right, finding the citizen to be protected under both federal and state law. The complaining party is an officer of the state itself, who asks us to rule that the state court interpreted federal rights too broadly and "overprotected" the citizen.

Such cases should not be of inherent concern to this Court. The reason may be illuminated by assuming that the events underlying this case had arisen in another country, perhaps the Republic of Finland. If the Finnish police had arrested a Finnish citizen for possession of marijuana, and the Finnish courts had turned him loose, no American would have standing to object. If instead they had arrested an American citizen and acquitted him, we might have been concerned about the arrest but we surely could not have complained about the acquittal, even if the Finnish Court had based its decision on its understanding of the United States Constitution. That would be true even if we had a treaty with Finland requiring it to respect the rights of American citizens under the United States Constitution. We would only be motivated to intervene if an American citizen were unfairly arrested, tried, and convicted by the foreign tribunal.

In this case the State of Michigan has arrested one of its citizens and the Michigan Supreme Court has decided to turn him loose. The respondent is a United States citizen as well as a Michigan citizen, but since there is no claim that he has been mistreated by the State of Michigan, the final outcome of the state processes offended no federal interest whatever. Michigan simply provided greater protection to one of its citizens than some other State might provide or, indeed, than this Court might require throughout the country.

I believe that in reviewing the decisions of state courts, the primary role of this Court is to make sure that persons who seek to *vindicate* federal rights have been fairly heard.   .   .   .

Until recently we had virtually no interest in cases of this type. Thirty years ago, this Court reviewed only one. Nevada v. Stacher, 346 U.S. 906 (1953). Indeed, that appears to have been the only case during the entire 1952 Term in which a state even sought review of a decision by its own judiciary. Fifteen years ago, we did not review any such cases, although the total number of requests had mounted to three. Some time during the past decade, perhaps about the time of the 5-to-4 decision in Zacchini v. Scripps-Howard Broadcasting Co., 433 U.S. 562 (1977), our priorities shifted. The result is a docket swollen with requests by states to reverse judgments that their courts have rendered in favor of their citizens. I am confident that a future Court will recognize the error of this allocation of resources. When that day comes, I think it likely that the Court will also reconsider the propriety of today's expansion of our jurisdiction.

The Court offers only one reason for asserting authority over cases such as the one presented today: "an important need for uniformity in federal law [that] goes unsatisfied when we fail to review an opinion that rests primarily upon federal grounds and where the independence of an alleged state ground is not apparent from the four corners of the opinion." Of course, the supposed need to "review an opinion" clashes directly with our oft-repeated reminder that "our power is to correct wrong judgments, not to revise opinions." Herb v. Pitcairn, 324 U.S. 117, 126 (1945). The clash is not merely one of form: the "need for uniformity in federal law" is truly an ungovernable engine. That same need is no less present when it is perfectly clear that a state ground is both independent and adequate. In fact, it is equally present if a state prosecutor announces that he believes a certain policy of nonenforcement is commanded by federal law. Yet we have never claimed jurisdiction to correct such errors, no matter how egregious they may be, and no matter how much they may thwart the desires of the state electorate. We do not sit to expound our understanding of the Constitution to interested listeners in the legal community; we sit to resolve disputes. If it is not apparent that our views would affect the outcome of a particular case, we cannot presume to interfere.

.   .   .

I respectfully dissent.[a]

.   .   .

C. THE DISTINCTION BETWEEN OBLIGATORY AND DISCRETIONARY JURISDICTION

THE DISTINCTION BETWEEN APPEAL AND CERTIORARI IN REVIEW OF STATE COURT DECISIONS

The student should consult the text of 28 U.S.C. § 1257 (above, p. 48). Some of the distinctions between obligatory jurisdiction to review state court decisions (appeal), and discretionary appellate jurisdiction (certiorari) are obvious. If a state court holds that a treaty or statute of the United States is unconstitutional, review is by appeal under § 1257(1); if the state court holds the treaty or federal statute valid, review is by certiorari under § 1257(3). If a state court holds that a state statute is invalid on a federal law ground, review is by certiorari under § 1257(3); if the state court holds the state statute valid,

---

[a] A dissent by Justices Brennan and Marshall was not addressed to the adequate and independent state ground issue.

review is by appeal under § 1257(2). Why is there opposite treatment of decisions concerning the validity of federal and state laws?

One distinction between appeal and certiorari under § 1257 is truly technical. Where the validity of a state statute is "drawn in question" and the state court's decision is "in favor of its validity," review is by appeal under § 1257(2). When a "title, right, privilege or immunity" is claimed under the Constitution, review is by certiorari under § 1257(3), no matter which way the question is resolved. Most cases where issues of constitutional law are dispositive in the state courts involve potential conflict between state law and the United States Constitution. If the state court rules against the constitutional claim, review is by appeal or certiorari depending on whether the state court has ruled "in favor of [the] validity" of the state law. At bottom, that issue turns on nothing more than the manner of presenting the question to the state courts. If the losing party has pleaded that a state statute is invalid—even only as applied to a narrow situation—review is by appeal; if the pleading simply claimed a constitutional right or immunity, review is by certiorari. As pointed out by Justice Brandeis, the distinction between appeal and certiorari "will depend, in large classes of cases, not upon the nature of the constitutional question involved, but upon the skill of counsel." Dahnke-Walker Milling Co. v. Bondurant, 257 U.S. 282, 298 (1921) (dissenting opinion).

The most prolific source of potential appeals is § 1257(2), because there are frequent unsuccessful federal constitutional challenges to state laws. (There are few cases under § 1257(1) where state courts have held federal laws invalid.) There have been numerous proposals to eliminate the obligatory review apparently required by § 1257(2), because the Supreme Court is unable, given its current workload, to give full treatment to the hundreds of cases each year framed as appeals under that provision. (See, for example, Federal Judicial Center, Report of the Study Group on the Caseload of the Supreme Court [1972]).[1]

Nevertheless, the provisions of § 1257 have remained substantively unchanged since 1925. Given the Court's workload, and the hypertechnical distinction between appeal and certiorari in many cases where state courts have rejected constitutional arguments, one would expect gradual blurring of the distinction between obligatory and discretionary review. In 1954, Chief Justice Warren candidly stated: "It is only accurate to a degree to say that our jurisdiction in cases on appeal is obligatory as distinguished from discretionary on certiorari." Wiener, *The Supreme Court's New Rules,* 68 Harv.L.Rev. 20, 51 (1954). The following excerpt describes the way the Supreme Court screens appeals and petitions for certiorari. The material in the rest of this Subsection examines the rationale for, and consequences of, summary disposition of appeals.

----

[1] Much more controversial were recommendations of the study group for a National Court of Appeals, below the Supreme Court, to perform the process of screening petitions for certiorari. A different proposal for increasing the capacity for uniform declarations of national law was made in 1975 by the Commission on Revision of the Federal Court Appellate System, which would leave the screening function in the Supreme Court, but permit that Court to refer cases to a National Court of Appeals for decision.

On April 9, 1979, a Bill passed the Senate which would have transformed most of the Court's obligatory appeal jurisdiction into discretionary jurisdiction. S.450, 96th Cong., 1st Sess. All nine Justices supported the bill. Despite wide support, the bill died in the House Judiciary Committee, because of a last-minute attachment of the "Helms Amendment," taking away federal court jurisdiction in school prayer cases. See p. 42, supra.

THE COURT'S PROCESS IN SCREENING CASES

A former law clerk to a Supreme Court Justice has described the internal processes of the Court in screening cases. Alsup, *A Policy Assessment of the National Court of Appeals,* 25 Hast.L.J. 1313, 1315–1318 (1974): [a]

"The present method and practice by which the Supreme Court selects cases for review is a combination of statutory requirement and tradition. In recent years about 3700 applications for review have been filed annually by litigants complaining of adverse judgments rendered in lower federal or state courts. These applications are either by way of appeals which the Court is obliged to decide, or by way of requesting the issuance of a writ of certiorari which the Court may deny in its discretion. Fewer than 200 of these cases are decided on the merits, the rest being denied review without opinion. Nonetheless, the process of choosing the select few is a vital aspect of the justices' work.

"The document filed with the Supreme Court in most instances is called a petition for writ of certiorari. In the relatively rare cases for which Congress has provided for an 'appeal,' the litigant requests the review to which he is entitled by filing a timely 'jurisdictional statement.' When a petition for a writ of certiorari or jurisdictional statement is docketed, the clerk of the Supreme Court gives it a case number and all copies are stamped and then placed for storage in a large room. Usually within the next thirty days the opposing party files a response, arguing that the petition should not be granted or that the appeal should be dismissed. When a response is filed it is coupled with its corresponding petition and both are identified as ripe for circulation to the various chambers. If a respondent or appellee delays too long, the clerk will designate the petition or jurisdictional statement alone as ready for consideration. Each week a bundle of about seventy such cases is distributed by the clerk's staff.

"Once these bundles are received in the various chambers, the method for their screening differs from office to office. The traditional pattern has been for a justice's law clerks to divide the weekly bundle in equal stacks for each clerk to read and summarize with a separate memorandum for each case. Then the week's worth of petitions are delivered to their justice along with the 'cert memos.' After studying their analyses and supplementing their digests by consulting the applications and responses as he believes is necessary, a justice sends to the chief justice an enumeration of those cases which he believes may warrant review by the full Court.

"Some of the present justices do not follow the traditional pattern of asking their law clerks to digest petitions for certiorari and appeals. Justice Brennan, for example, prefers, as did Justice Frankfurter, to scrutinize the applications himself without memoranda from his clerks. In addition, five of the justices (the four most recent appointees and Justice Byron White) have assigned their law clerks to a pooled effort for summarizing petitions. Instead of five separate summaries of each case being prepared, only one memorandum is written, to be shared by all five justices. Regardless of the way in which a justice is exposed to the applications, however, every justice sends to the chief justice a listing of cases which he thinks warrants review.

"Any case which attracts the attention of even one member of the Court is placed by the chief justice on the 'discuss list.' In addition to certiorari cases of interest, all appeals are routinely included on the discuss list even though many of them typically arouse no interest. All cases on the discuss list are mentioned in conference whereas those not on it are denied automatically without further consideration. In recent years about 1100 applications have been discussed in conference annually.

"After the discuss list is transmitted to each of the chambers, the papers and memoranda in all cases contained in the discuss list are gathered together and the remaining items are 'dead listed' and culled. The assembled material is taken by the justice into the conference room during the session in which petitions for certiorari and jurisdictional statements are discussed. Usually this is the Friday conference. Each justice speaks his mind on each application on the agenda and under the traditional Rule of Four a petition is 'granted' and will be scheduled for oral argument when four justices believe it presents a substantial question of national importance. Occasionally a justice who is relatively indifferent on a particular case will join two or three who feel strongly that it should be taken. Precisely what moves the justices to seize upon certain cases and to reject others is something of a mystery and a matter for which one develops a 'feel,' as Justice Harlan put it. Sometimes when further argument would be of little assistance in deciding the merits, a petition is granted and the Court disposes of the merits in the same conference, foregoing oral argument and acting without the benefit of full briefs, provided a majority so votes and fewer than four believe the issue warrants plenary consideration.

"The processing of appeals . . ., is part and parcel of this process. Some important differences remain, however, between the processing of appeals and petitions for certiorari. As noted above, all appeals are mentioned in conference, however briefly, whereas most petitions for certiorari are not. Moreover, by providing for appeals in certain situations, Congress has already decided that the issues raised thereby warrant review—pretermitting the Court's own judgment on the initial question of whether or not to take the case—and the only remaining question is whether plenary or summary review is more appropriate. It has been observed, however, that the two modes of review are gradually being merged for all practical purposes. For example, a great number of appeals are 'dismissed' for lack of a substantial federal question on the theory that the congressional mandate does not require resolution of insubstantial matters. It has been suggested that such dismissals are governed by the same discretionary factors which lead the Court to deny petitions for writ of certiorari, that is, once it is concluded that the issues presented are insubstantial, the application is 'denied' if it is a petition for writ of certiorari and is 'dismissed' or 'affirmed' if it is an appeal. Although there are precedential differences in these dispositions, it is plain that, as Justice Clark acknowledged, the procedures used in reaching them are the same. It is important to remember that most of the discussed items are currently denied review, whether they are appeals or 'certs,' and that about two-thirds of the filings are denied without any discussion." [b]

HICKS v. MIRANDA, 422 U.S. 332 (1975). A three judge district court granted an injunction, in a suit brought by a theatre owner, holding that California's obscenity statute was unconstitutional. While the case was pending in the lower court, the Supreme Court dismissed an appeal from a California decision sustaining the validity of the same statute "for want of a substantial federal question." Miller v. California (Miller II), 418 U.S. 915 (1974). The three judge court concluded that the decision in *Miller II,* since it was a summary disposition, was not binding on it. The Court, in an opinion by Justice Rehnquist, held that summary dispositions were precedents binding lower courts. The Court's opinion said, in part:

[b] For further insight into the Court's screening process, see Linzer, *The Meaning of Certiorari Denials,* 79 Colum.L.Rev. 1227 (1979); Hellman, *The Supreme Court, the National Law, and the Selection of Cases for the Plenary Docket,* 44 U.Pitt.L.Rev. 521 (1983); Hellman, *Error Correction, Lawmaking, and the Supreme Court's Exercise of Discretionary Review,* 44 U.Pitt.L.Rev. 795 (1983).

"We agree with appellants that the District Court was in error in holding that it could disregard the decision in *Miller II*. That case was an appeal from a decision by a state court upholding a state statute against federal constitutional attack. A federal constitutional issue was properly presented, it was within our appellate jurisdiction under 28 U.S.C. § 1257(2), and we had no discretion to refuse adjudication of the case on its merits as would have been true had the case been brought here under our certiorari jurisdiction. We are not obligated to grant the case plenary consideration, and we did not; but we were required to deal with its merits. We did so by concluding that the appeal should be dismissed because the constitutional challenge to the California statute was not a substantial one. The three-judge court was not free to disregard this pronouncement. As Mr. Justice Brennan once observed, '[v]otes to affirm summarily, and to dismiss for want of a substantial federal question, it hardly needs comment, are votes on the merits of a case . . .,' Ohio ex rel. Eaton v. Price, 360 U.S. 246, 247 (1959); cf. R. Stern & E. Gressman, Supreme Court Practice, 197 (4th ed. 1969) ('The Court is, however, deciding a case on the merits, when it dismisses for want of a *substantial* question . . .'); C. Wright, Law of Federal Courts 495 (2d ed. 1970) ('Summary disposition of an appeal, however, either by affirmance or by dismissal for want of a substantial federal question, is a disposition on the merits'). The District Court should have followed the Second Circuit's advice, first, in Port Authority Bondholders Protective Committee v. Port of New York Authority, 387 F.2d 259, 263 n. 3 (1967), that 'unless and until the Supreme Court should instruct otherwise, inferior federal courts had best adhere to the view that if the Court has branded a question as unsubstantial, it remains so except when doctrinal developments indicate otherwise'; and, later, in Doe v. Hodgson, 478 F.2d 537, 539, cert. denied, sub nom. Doe v. Brennan, 414 U.S. 1096 (1973), that the lower courts are bound by summary decisions by this Court 'until such time as the Court informs [them] that [they] are not.' "

THE PRECEDENTIAL EFFECT OF SUMMARY DISPOSITIONS IN THE SUPREME COURT

The Supreme Court is, of course, free as lower courts are not, to overrule its past decisions. Especially in constitutional cases, where the Court feels "less constrained by the principle of stare decisis than . . . in other areas of law," prior summary disposition without argument or opinion is not controlling after the issue is fully briefed and argued in a later case. Edelman v. Jordan, 415 U.S. 651, 670–671 (1974).

COLORADO SPRINGS AMUSEMENTS, LIMITED v. RIZZO

428 U.S. 913, 96 S.Ct. 3228, 49 L.Ed.2d 1222 (1976).

Per Curiam.

The petition for a writ of certiorari is denied.

Mr. Justice Brennan, dissenting.

We depreciate the precedential weight of summary dispositions in our decisional process, expressly holding in Edelman v. Jordan, 415 U.S. 651, 671 (1974), that such dispositions "are not of the same precedential value as would be an opinion of this Court treating the question on the merits." I would not require district courts, courts of appeals, and state courts to ascribe any greater precedential weight to summary dispositions than this Court does. Accordingly, I did not join the holding in Hicks v. Miranda, 422 U.S. 332, 344–345 (1975), that "the lower courts are bound by summary decisions by this Court," which requires state and lower federal courts to treat our summary dispositions of appeals as conclusive precedents regarding constitutional challenges to like state statutes or ordinances.

The Court of Appeals in this case conscientiously followed the procedure mandated by *Hicks.* Faced with a claim that three appeals from state courts that had been dismissed by this Court "for want of a substantial federal question" compelled rejection of petitioners' contentions that the Philadelphia ordinance in question violated the Federal Constitution,[1] the Court of Appeals compared in detail the constitutional issues presented here and those presented in the jurisdictional statements filed in this Court in the three earlier cases. 524 F.2d at 576. *Hicks* makes such analysis obligatory as a condition to reliance on a summary disposition. 422 U.S., at 345 n. 14. Completion of this process satisfied the Court of Appeals that one or more of the earlier jurisdictional statements had presented to this Court constitutional claims addressed to massage parlor ordinances, like those addressed by petitioners to the Philadelphia ordinance, "based upon equal, but reprehensible, treatment of both sexes; an invidiously discriminatory sex-based classification; an irrational exception in the ordinance for massage treatments given under the direction of a medical practitioner; unreasonable abridgement of the right to pursue a legitimate livelihood; and the irrebutable presumption doctrine." 524 F.2d, at 576 (footnotes omitted). Accordingly, the Court of Appeals, without expressing its own views on the merits of the constitutional contentions, but in compliance with the holding of *Hicks,* decided the constitutional questions adversely to petitioners solely and squarely upon the authority of Smith v. Keator, 419 U.S. 1043 (1974), dismissing for want of a substantial federal question 285 N.C. 530, 206 S.E.2d 203; Rubenstein v. Cherry Hill, 417 U.S. 963 (1974) dismissing for want of a substantial federal question No. 10,027 (N.J.Sup.Ct.) (unreported); and Kisley v. City of Falls Church, 409 U.S. 907 (1972); dismissing for want of a substantial federal question 212 Va. 693, 187 S.E.2d 168.

It may be that the Court of Appeals would have reached the same result in a full and reasoned opinion addressed to the merits of the several constitutional contentions. But we do not know, because the Court of Appeals carefully concealed its views on the premise that *Hicks* precluded such expression in holding that state and lower federal courts are conclusively bound by summary dispositions.

. . .

When presented with the contention that our unexplained dispositions are conclusively binding, puzzled state and lower court judges are left to guess as to the meaning and scope of our unexplained dispositions. We ourselves have acknowledged that summary dispositions are "somewhat opaque," Gibson v. Berryhill, 411 U.S. 564, 576 (1973), and we cannot deny that they have sown confusion.

It is no answer that a careful examination of the jurisdictional statements in prior cases—a task required by *Hicks* and fully performed by the Court of Appeals in this case—will resolve the ambiguity. As long as we give no explanation of the grounds supporting our summary disposition, such examination cannot disclose, for example, that there is no rationale accepted by a majority of the Court. Plainly, six Members of the Court may vote to dismiss

---

[1] Although *Hicks* and the instant case involve the precedential effect of dismissals for want of a substantial federal question, the same principles apply to summary affirmances. See Edelman v. Jordan, 415 U.S. 651, 671 (1974). These principles, of course, have no applicability to other forms of summary action, such as dismissals for want of jurisdiction or for want of a properly presented federal question.

or affirm an appeal without any agreement on a rationale. It is precisely in these areas of the law, however, that there probably is the greatest need for this Court to clarify the law.

In addition, there will always be the puzzling problem of how to deal with cases that are similar, but not identical, to some case that has been summarily disposed of in this Court. Courts should, of course, not feel bound to treat a summary disposition as binding beyond those situations in which the issues are the same. Hicks v. Miranda, 422 U.S., at 345 n. 14. But there is a significant risk that some courts may try to resolve the ambiguity inherent in summary dispositions by attaching too much weight to dicta or overbroad language contained in opinions from which appeals were taken and resolved summarily in this Court. The Chief Justice has noted that "[w]hen we summarily affirm, without opinion, the judgment of a three-judge District Court we affirm the judgment but not necessarily the reasoning by which it was reached." Fusari v. Steinberg, 419 U.S. 379, 391 (1975) (concurring opinion). The same principle obviously applies to dismissals for want of a substantial federal question. Moreover, it ought to be clear to state and lower federal courts that principles set forth in full opinions cannot be limited merely by a summary disposition; a summary disposition "settles the issues for the parties, and is not to be read as a renunciation by this Court of doctrines previously announced in our opinions after full argument." Id., at 392. See, also Edelman v. Jordan, 415 U.S., at 671.

. . .

Even if the Court rejects my view that *Hicks* should be modified, at a minimum we have the duty to provide some explanation of the issues presented in the case and the reasons and authorities supporting our summary dispositions. This surely should be the practice in cases presenting novel issues or where there is a disagreement among us as to the grounds of the disposition, and I think it should be the practice in every case. In addition, we ought to distinguish in our dispositions of appeals from state courts between those grounded on the insubstantiality of the federal questions presented and those grounded on agreement with the state court's decision of substantial federal questions. Our own self-interest should counsel these changes in practice. After *Hicks* we necessarily are under pressure to grant plenary review of state and lower federal court decisions . . . that rest exclusively on our unexplained summary dispositions. For since *Hicks* forecloses future plenary review of the issues in the state and lower federal courts, the issues will never have plenary review if not afforded here.

I would grant the petition for certiorari and remand the case to the Court of Appeals for determination of petitioner's constitutional contentions giving appropriate, but not necessarily conclusive, weight to our summary dispositions.

———

NAIM v. NAIM, 350 U.S. 891 (1955), 985 (1956). A suit was begun in the Virginia courts to annul a marriage on the ground that it had been performed in violation of that State's law prohibiting inter-racial marriage. The court found: at the time of the marriage the wife was a resident of Virginia, although the husband was not; that they intended to, and did, reside in Virginia after the marriage; that the marriage had been performed in North Carolina to avoid Virginia's prohibition of inter-racial marriage. The trial court ordered annulment, rejecting a specific contention that Virginia's miscegenation law was unconstitutional. Virginia's Supreme Court of Appeals affirmed. On appeal to the United States Supreme Court, the case was remanded. The Supreme Court's opinion said, in full:

"Per curiam: The inadequacy of the record as to the relationship of the parties to the Commonwealth of Virginia at the time of the marriage in North Carolina and upon their return to Virginia, and the failure of the parties to bring here all questions relevant to the disposition of the case, prevents the constitutional issue of the validity of the Virginia statute on miscegenation tendered here being considered 'in clean cut and concrete form, unclouded' by such problems. Rescue Army v. Municipal Court, 331 U.S. 549, 584. The judgment is vacated and the case remanded to the Supreme Court of Appeals in order that the case may be returned to the Circuit Court of the City of Portsmouth for action not inconsistent with this opinion."

On remand, the Virginia Court of Appeal reinstated the annulment. Its opinion states that the relevant facts had been established at the trial, and no provision of Virginia law permitted the case to be remanded to the trial court for development of other factual issues. 197 Va. 734, 90 S.E.2d 849 (1956).

In the Supreme Court, a motion was made to recall the earlier mandate. The Supreme Court responded as follows:

"The motion to recall the mandate and to set the case down for oral argument upon the merits, or, in the alternative, to recall and amend the mandate is denied. The decision of the Supreme Court of Appeals of Virginia of January 18, 1956, in response to our order of November 14, 1955, leaves the case devoid of a properly presented federal question."

DISCRETIONARY DISMISSAL OF APPEALS

Rescue Army v. Municipal Court, on which the opinion in Naim v. Naim relies, involved first amendment challenges to a complex city ordinance regulating charitable solicitation. *Rescue Army* was an appeal from a state court's denial of a writ of prohibition to restrain a pending criminal prosecution under the ordinance. Justice Rutledge's opinion argued that the manner in which the issues reached the Supreme Court presented serious obstacles to decision of the constitutional questions: it was not clear from the record what charges had been made in the pending criminal case; there were many unclear provisions of the ordinance that had not been construed by the state court; despite the complexity of the ordinance, the constitutional attack was "highly abstract." Notice, also, that dismissal of the *Rescue Army* appeal simply required the litigants to present their constitutional challenges in the pending criminal case. Because none of the preceding factors were present in Naim v. Naim, Professor Bickel argued that *Naim* properly represents a general power to decline the exercise of obligatory jurisdiction for reasons of prudence. Bickel, *The Least Dangerous Branch: The Supreme Court at the Bar of Politics* 126–127, 174 (1962). Professor Bickel's view that discretionary dismissal of appeals is proper has been sharply challenged. Gunther, *The Subtle Vices of the "Passive Virtues"—A Comment on Principle and Expediency in Judicial Review,* 64 Colum.L.Rev. 1 (1964).

Beyond the issue of appeal, there are other examples of situations where the Supreme Court has declined apparently mandatory jurisdiction. E.g., Wisniewski v. United States, 353 U.S. 901 (1957) (certified question by Court of Appeals); Ohio v. Wyandotte Chem. Corp., 401 U.S. 493 (1971) (original jurisdiction).

SECTION 2. CONSTITUTIONAL LITIGATION INITIATED IN THE FEDERAL COURTS

Introduction. Justice Black for the Court in Atlantic Coast Line R.R. Co. v. Engineers, 398 U.S. 281, 285 (1970):

". . . When this Nation was established by the Constitution, each State surrendered only a part of its sovereign power to the national government. But those powers that were not surrendered were retained by the States and unless a State was restrained by 'the supreme Law of the Land' as expressed in the Constitution, laws, or treaties of the United States, it was free to exercise those retained powers as it saw fit. One of the reserved powers was the maintenance of state judicial systems for the decision of legal controversies. Many of the Framers of the Constitution felt that separate federal courts were unnecessary and that the state courts could be entrusted to protect both state and federal rights. Others felt that a complete system of federal courts to take care of federal legal problems should be provided for in the Constitution itself. This dispute resulted in compromise. One 'supreme Court' was created by the Constitution, and Congress was given the power to create other federal courts. In the first Congress this power was exercised and a system of federal trial and appellate courts with limited jurisdiction was created by the Judiciary Act of 1789, 1 Stat. 73.

"While the lower federal courts were given certain powers in the 1789 Act, they were not given any power to review directly cases from state courts, and they have not been given such powers since that time. Only the Supreme Court was authorized to review on direct appeal the decisions of state courts. Thus from the beginning we have had in this country two essentially separate legal systems. Each system proceeds independently of the other with ultimate review in this Court of the federal questions raised in either system. Understandably this dual court system was bound to lead to conflicts and frictions. Litigants who foresaw the possibility of more favorable treatment in one or the other system would predictably hasten to invoke the powers of whichever court it was believed would present the best chance of success. Obviously this dual system could not function if state and federal courts were free to fight each other for control of a particular case. Thus, in order to make the dual system work and 'to prevent needless friction between state and federal courts,' Oklahoma Packing Co. v. Gas Co., 309 U.S. 4, 9 (1940), it was necessary to work out lines of demarcation between the two systems. Some of these limits were spelled out in the 1789 Act. Others have been added by later statutes as well as judicial decisions."

A. JURISDICTION OF THE FEDERAL COURTS IN CASES INVOLVING FEDERAL LAW ISSUES

JURISDICTION OF LOWER FEDERAL COURTS TO ENFORCE FEDERAL RIGHTS

Until after the end of the Civil War, state courts, subject to review by the Supreme Court, were entrusted with litigation to enforce the limited number of private federal rights. The immediate post-Civil War period saw not only an explosion in the creation of federal rights against state governments, but a Congressional decision to use the lower federal courts as the primary mechanism for enforcing those rights.

Section 1 of the Civil Rights Act of 1866 created rights for freed slaves, while Section 2 made it a federal crime for persons to deny those rights under color of state law. After ratification of the Fourteenth Amendment, the Civil Rights Acts of 1870 and 1871 created private rights of action for those who were denied federal rights, and provided for jurisdiction in the lower federal courts to enforce those rights. Section 1 of the 1871 Act is the source of two provisions which are central to modern constitutional litigation. Section 1983 of 42 U.S.C. provides a cause of action for deprivations of federal rights:

> Every person who, under color of any statute, ordinance, regulation, custom, or usage, of any State or Territory or the District of Columbia, subjects, or causes to be subjected, any citizen of the United States or other person within the jurisdiction thereof to the deprivation of any rights, privileges, or immunities secured by the Constitution and laws, shall be liable to the party injured in an action at law, suit in equity, or other proper proceeding for redress.

The corresponding jurisdictional provision is 28 U.S.C. § 1343(a)(3):

> The district courts shall have original jurisdiction of any civil action authorized by law to be commenced by any person: . . . .
>
> (3) to redress the deprivation, under color of any State law, statute, ordinance, regulation, custom or usage, of any right, privilege or immunity secured by the Constitution of the United States or by any Act of Congress providing for equal rights of citizens or of all persons within the jurisdiction of the United States; . . . .

A common form of litigation concerning the constitutionality of state laws is a suit to enjoin the enforcement of those laws, or to obtain a declaratory judgment of their invalidity. Those suits are premised on 42 U.S.C. § 1983. The federal district courts are given jurisdiction over those suits, concurrent with the state courts, by 28 U.S.C. § 1343(3).[1]

No statutory provision, equivalent to 42 U.S.C. § 1983, exists for the denial of constitutional rights by federal officers. The Court has held, however, that those officers may be sued under the Constitution itself. Bivens v. Six Unknown Named Agents of the Fed. Bureau of Narcotics, 403 U.S. 388 (1971). The jurisdictional basis for those suits is 28 U.S.C. § 1331, the general federal question statute, which provides jurisdiction in all cases "arising under the Constitution or laws of the United States." The predecessor of that statute was not enacted until 1875.[2]

Review of decisions of the federal district courts is by the United States Court of Appeals. 18 U.S.C. § 3731; 28 U.S.C. §§ 1291–1292. Appeals to the courts of appeals are a matter of right. Most decisions of the courts of appeals are reviewable in the Supreme Court by certiorari, and are thus

---

[1] In 1910, Congress required that a special three judge court be convened in cases seeking to enjoin the enforcement of state laws on federal constitutional grounds. Direct, and non-discretionary, review of the decision of those courts was by the Supreme Court. Because of the heavy burdens imposed on the lower federal judiciary, and upon the Supreme Court, the three-judge court requirement was substantially repealed in 1975. (Three-judge courts are still required in cases involving apportionment of congressional districts or state legislatures. 28 U.S.C. § 2284.) Prior to its repeal, the three-judge court was a primary source of United States Supreme Court cases concerning the constitutional validity of state laws. A significant number of the cases in this book reached the Court through that route.

[2] A variety of provisions of the Judicial Code (Title 28 of the United States Code) provide for jurisdiction in other cases arising under federal law. Among the more important are, those involving: actions under federal law regulating commerce (§ 1337); admiralty and maritime cases (§ 1333); bankruptcy cases (§ 1334); internal revenue (§ 1340); patents, copyrights, and trademarks (§ 1338); and actions in which the United States is a party (§§ 1345, 1346). Numerous substantive federal statutes contain their own provisions for federal court jurisdiction. Unlike § 1331, the jurisdiction of the federal district court is exclusive under some of these provisions, and not concurrent with the state courts.

Questions of constitutional dimension can, of course, also arise in the course of other cases within the district courts' jurisdiction, such as federal criminal cases and civil cases within the diversity of citizenship jurisdiction, or in the course of review by the courts of appeals of formal orders of federal regulatory agencies. The full complexities surrounding the jurisdiction of federal courts are, of course, beyond the competence of a general course in constitutional law. Students interested in particular federal jurisdictional issues should consult, among other sources, Wright, *Federal Courts* (4th ed. 1983); Hart and Wechsler, *Federal Courts* (2d ed. 1973).

discretionary.[3] 28 U.S.C. § 1254(1). The Supreme Court is empowered to review cases filed "in" a court of appeals prior to that court's judgment, and in rare important cases has done so in the interest of expedition. E.g., Youngstown Sheet & Tube Co. v. Sawyer, 343 U.S. 579 (1952), infra p. 437; United States v. Nixon, 418 U.S. 683 (1974), infra p. 468.

B. ENFORCEMENT OF FEDERAL RIGHTS IN SUITS AGAINST STATE OFFICERS: THE ELEVENTH AMENDMENT

PENNHURST STATE SCHOOL & HOSPITAL v. HALDERMAN

— U.S. —, 104 S.Ct. 900, 79 L.Ed.2d 67 (1984).

Justice Powell delivered the opinion of the Court.

This case presents the question whether a federal court may award injunctive relief against state officials on the basis of state law.

I

This litigation, here for the second time, concerns the conditions of care at petitioner Pennhurst State School and Hospital, a Pennsylvania institution for the care of the mentally retarded. See Pennhurst State School & Hospital v. Halderman, 451 U.S. 1 (1981). . . .

This suit originally was brought in 1974 by respondent Terri Lee Halderman, a resident of Pennhurst, in the District Court for the Eastern District of Pennsylvania. Ultimately, plaintiffs included a class consisting of all persons who were or might become residents of Pennhurst; the Pennsylvania Association for Retarded Citizens (PARC); and the United States. Defendants were Pennhurst and various Pennhurst officials; the Pennsylvania Department of Public Welfare and several of its officials; and various county commissioners, county mental retardation administrators, and other officials of five Pennsylvania counties surrounding Pennhurst. Respondents' amended complaint charged that conditions at Pennhurst violated the class members' rights under the Eighth and Fourteenth Amendments; § 504 of the Rehabilitation Act of 1973, 87 Stat. 394, as amended, 29 U.S.C. § 794 (1976 ed. and Supp. V); the Developmentally Disabled Assistance and Bill of Rights Act, 42 U.S.C. §§ 6001–6081 (1976 ed. and Supp. V); and the Pennsylvania Mental Health and Mental Retardation Act of 1966 (the "MH/MR Act"), Pa.Stat.Ann., Tit. 50, §§ 4101–4704 (Purdon 1969 and Supp.1982). Both damages and injunctive relief were sought.

. . .

The Court of Appeals for the Third Circuit [decided] that respondents had a right to habilitation in the least restrictive environment, but it grounded this right solely on the "bill of rights" provision in the Developmentally Disabled Assistance and Bill of Rights Act, 42 U.S.C. § 6010. See 612 F.2d, at 95–100, 104–107. The court did not consider the constitutional issues or § 504 of the Rehabilitation Act, and while it affirmed the District Court's holding that the MH/MR Act provides a right to adequate habilitation, the court did not decide

---

[3] A decision of a court of appeals that a state statute is invalid is reviewable by appeal in the Supreme Court. 28 U.S.C. § 1254(2). Decisions of any federal court holding a federal law unconstitutional in a case in which the United States or a federal officer is a party are also reviewable on appeal. 28 U.S.C. § 1252. While appeals to the Supreme Court under both these provisions are infrequent, a number of cases in this book reached the Supreme Court through one or the other of these appellate routes.

whether that state right encompassed a right to treatment in the least restrictive setting.

This Court reversed the judgment of the Court of Appeals, finding that 42 U.S.C. § 6010 did not create any substantive rights. 451 U.S. 1 (1981). We remanded the case to the Court of Appeals to determine if the remedial order could be supported on the basis of state law, the Constitution, or § 504 of the Rehabilitation Act. We also remanded for consideration of whether any relief was available under other provisions of the Developmentally Disabled Assistance and Bill of Rights Act. . . .

On remand the Court of Appeals affirmed its prior judgment in its entirety. 673 F.2d 647 (3 Cir.1982) (en banc). It determined that in a recent decision the Supreme Court of Pennsylvania had "spoken definitively" in holding that the MH/MR Act required the State to adopt the "least restrictive environment" approach for the care of the mentally retarded. Id., at 651 (citing In re Schmidt, 494 Pa. 86, 429 A.2d 631 (1981)). The Court of Appeals concluded that this state statute fully supported its prior judgment, and therefore did not reach the remaining issues of federal law. It also rejected petitioners' argument that the Eleventh Amendment barred a federal court from considering this pendent state-law claim. . . .

We granted certiorari, . . . and now reverse and remand.

II

Petitioners raise three challenges to the judgment of the Court of Appeals: (i) the Eleventh Amendment prohibited the District Court from ordering state officials to conform their conduct to state law; (ii) the doctrine of comity prohibited the District Court from issuing its injunctive relief; and (iii) the District Court abused its discretion in appointing two masters to supervise the decisions of state officials in implementing state law. We need not reach the latter two issues, for we find the Eleventh Amendment challenge dispositive.

A

Article III, § 2 of the Constitution provides that the federal judicial power extends, *inter alia,* to controversies "between a State and Citizens of another State." Relying on this language, this Court in 1793 assumed original jurisdiction over a suit brought by a citizen of South Carolina against the State of Georgia. Chisholm v. Georgia, 2 Dall. 419 (1793). The decision "created such a shock of surprise that the Eleventh Amendment was at once proposed and adopted." Monaco v. Mississippi, 292 U.S. 313, 325 (1934). The Amendment provides:

> "The Judicial power of the United States shall not be construed to extend to any suit in law or equity, commenced or prosecuted against one of the United States by Citizens of another State, or by Citizens or Subjects of any Foreign State."

The Amendment's language overruled the particular result in *Chisholm,* but this Court has recognized that its greater significance lies in its affirmation that the fundamental principle of sovereign immunity limits the grant of judicial authority in Art. III. Thus, in Hans v. Louisiana, 134 U.S. 1 (1890), the Court held that, despite the limited terms of the Eleventh Amendment, a federal court could not entertain a suit brought by a citizen against his own State. After reviewing the constitutional debates concerning the scope of Art. III, the Court determined that federal jurisdiction over suits against unconsenting States "was not contemplated by the Constitution when establishing the judicial power of the United States." Id., at 15. See Monaco v. Mississippi, supra, 292 U.S., at

322–323 (1934). In short, the principle of sovereign immunity is a constitutional limitation on the federal judicial power established in Art. III:

"That a State may not be sued without its consent is a fundamental rule of jurisprudence having so important a bearing upon the construction of the Constitution of the United States that it has become established by repeated decisions of this court that *the entire judicial power granted by the Constitution does not embrace authority to entertain a suit brought by private parties against a State without consent given:* not one brought by citizens of another State, or by citizens or subjects of a foreign State, because of the Eleventh Amendment; and not even one brought by its own citizens, because of the fundamental rule of which the Amendment is but an exemplification." Ex parte State of New York No. 1, 256 U.S. 490, 497 (1921) (emphasis added).

A sovereign's immunity may be waived, and the Court consistently has held that a State may consent to suit against it in federal court. See, e.g., Clark v. Barnard, 108 U.S. 436, 447 (1883). We have insisted, however, that the State's consent be unequivocally expressed. See, e.g., Edelman v. Jordan, 415 U.S. 651, 673 (1974). Similarly, although Congress has power with respect to the rights protected by the Fourteenth Amendment to abrogate the Eleventh Amendment immunity, see Fitzpatrick v. Bitker, 427 U.S. 445 (1976), we have required an unequivocal expression of congressional intent to "overturn the constitutionally guaranteed immunity of the several States." Quern v. Jordan, 440 U.S. 332, 342 (1979) (holding that 42 U.S.C. § 1983 does not override States' Eleventh Amendment immunity). Our reluctance to infer that a State's immunity from suit in the federal courts has been negated stems from recognition of the vital role of the doctrine of sovereign immunity in our federal system. A State's constitutional interest in immunity encompasses not merely *whether* it may be sued, but *where* it may be sued. As Justice Marshall well has noted, "[b]ecause of the problems of federalism inherent in making one sovereign appear against its will in the courts of the other, a restriction upon the exercise of the federal judicial power has long been considered to be appropriate in a case such as this." Employees v. Missouri Public Health & Welfare Dep't, 411 U.S. 279, 294 (1973) (Marshall, J., concurring in result). Accordingly, in deciding this case we must be guided by "[t]he principles of federalism that inform Eleventh Amendment doctrine." Hutto v. Finney, 437 U.S. 678, 691 (1978).

B

This Court's decisions thus establish that "an unconsenting State is immune from suits brought in federal courts by her own citizens as well as by citizens of another state." *Employees,* supra, 411 U.S., at 280. There may be a question, however, whether a particular suit in fact is a suit against a State. It is clear, of course, that in the absence of consent a suit in which the State or one of its agencies or departments is named as the defendant is proscribed by the Eleventh Amendment. See, e.g., Florida Department of Health v. Florida Nursing Home Assn., 450 U.S. 147 (1981) (per curiam); Alabama v. Pugh, 438 U.S. 781 (1978) (per curiam). This jurisdictional bar applies regardless of the nature of the relief sought. See, e.g., Missouri v. Fiske, 290 U.S. 18, 27 (1933) ("Expressly applying to suits in equity as well as at law, the Amendment necessarily embraces demands for the enforcement of equitable rights and the prosecution of equitable remedies when these are asserted and prosecuted by an individual against a State").

When the suit is brought only against state officials, a question arises as to whether that suit is a suit against the State itself. Although prior decisions of this Court have not been entirely consistent on this issue, certain principles are well established. The Eleventh Amendment bars a suit against state officials when "the state is the real, substantial party in interest." Ford Motor Co. v. Department of Treasury, 323 U.S. 459, 464 (1945). See, e.g., In re Ayers, 123 U.S. 443, 487–492 (1887); Louisiana v. Jumel, 107 U.S. 711, 720–723, 727–728 (1882). Thus, "[t]he general rule is that relief sought nominally against an officer is in fact against the sovereign if the decree would operate against the latter." Hawaii v. Gordon, 373 U.S. 57, 58 (1963) (per curiam). And, as when the State itself is named as the defendant, a suit against state officials that is in fact a suit against a State is barred regardless of whether it seeks damages or injunctive relief. See Cory v. White, 457 U.S. 85, 91 (1982).

The Court has recognized an important exception to this general rule: a suit challenging the constitutionality of a state official's action is not one against the State. This was the holding in Ex parte Young, 209 U.S. 123 (1908), in which a federal court enjoined the Attorney General of the State of Minnesota from bringing suit to enforce a state statute that allegedly violated the Fourteenth Amendment. This Court held that the Eleventh Amendment did not prohibit issuance of this injunction. The theory of the case was that an unconstitutional enactment is "void" and therefore does not "impart to [the officer] any immunity from responsibility to the supreme authority of the United States." Id., at 160. Since the State could not authorize the action, the officer was "stripped of his official or representative character and [was] subjected to the consequences of his official conduct." Ibid.

While the rule permitting suits alleging conduct contrary to "the supreme authority of the United States" has survived, the theory of *Young* has not been provided an expansive interpretation. Thus, in Edelman v. Jordan, 415 U.S. 651 (1974), the Court emphasized that the Eleventh Amendment bars some forms of injunctive relief against state officials for violation of federal law. Id., at 666–667. In particular, *Edelman* held that when a plaintiff sues a state official alleging a violation of federal law, the federal court may award an injunction that governs the official's future conduct, but not one that awards retroactive monetary relief. Under the theory of *Young,* such a suit would not be one against the State since the federal-law allegation would strip the state officer of his official authority. Nevertheless, retroactive relief was barred by the Eleventh Amendment.

III

With these principles in mind, we now turn to the question whether the claim that petitioners violated *state law* in carrying out their official duties at Pennhurst is one against the State and therefore barred by the Eleventh Amendment. Respondents advance two principal arguments in support of the judgment below. First, they contend that under the doctrine of Edelman v. Jordan, supra, the suit is not against the State because the courts below ordered only prospective injunctive relief. Second, they assert that the state-law claim properly was decided under the doctrine of pendent jurisdiction. Respondents rely on decisions of this Court awarding relief against state officials on the basis of a pendent state-law claim. See, e.g., Siler v. Louisville & Nashville R. Co., 213 U.S. 175, 193 (1909).

A

We first address the contention that respondents' state-law claim is not barred by the Eleventh Amendment because it seeks only prospective relief as defined in Edelman v. Jordan, supra. The Court of Appeals held that if the judgment below rested on federal law, it could be entered against petitioner state officials under the doctrine established in *Edelman* and *Young* even though the prospective financial burden was substantial and ongoing. See 673 F.2d, at 656. The court assumed, and respondents assert, that this reasoning applies as well when the official acts in violation of state law. This argument misconstrues the basis of the doctrine established in *Young* and *Edelman.*

As discussed above, the injunction in *Young* was justified, notwithstanding the obvious impact on the State itself, on the view that sovereign immunity does not apply because an official who acts unconstitutionally is "stripped of his official or representative character," *Young,* 209 U.S., at 160. This rationale, of course, created the "well-recognized irony" that an official's unconstitutional conduct constitutes state action under the Fourteenth Amendment but not the Eleventh Amendment. Florida Department of State v. Treasure Salvors, Inc., 458 U.S. 670, 685 (1982) (opinion of Stevens, J.). Nonetheless, the *Young* doctrine has been accepted as necessary to permit the federal courts to vindicate federal rights and hold state officials responsible to "the supreme authority of the United States." *Young,* 209 U.S., at 160. As Justice Brennan has observed, "Ex parte Young was the culmination of efforts by this Court to harmonize the principles of the Eleventh Amendment with the effective supremacy of rights and powers secured elsewhere in the Constitution." Perez v. Ledesma, 401 U.S. 82, 106 (1971) (Brennan, J., concurring in part and dissenting in part). Our decisions repeatedly have emphasized that the *Young* doctrine rests on the need to promote the vindication of federal rights. See, e.g., Quern v. Jordan, 440 U.S. 332, 337 (1979); Scheuer v. Rhodes, 416 U.S. 232, 237 (1974); Georgia R. & Banking Co. v. Redwine, 342 U.S. 299, 304 (1952).

The Court also has recognized, however, that the need to promote the supremacy of federal law must be accommodated to the constitutional immunity of the States. This is the significance of Edelman v. Jordan, supra. . . . [W]e declined to extend the fiction of *Young* to encompass retroactive relief, for to do so would effectively eliminate the constitutional immunity of the States. Accordingly, we concluded that . . . an award of retroactive relief necessarily " 'fall[s] afoul of the Eleventh Amendment if that basic constitutional provision is to be conceived of as having any present force.' " . . . In sum *Edelman's* distinction between prospective and retroactive relief fulfills the underlying purpose of Ex parte Young while at the same time preserving to an important degree the constitutional immunity of the States.

This need to reconcile competing interests is wholly absent, however, when a plaintiff alleges that a state official has violated *state* law. In such a case the entire basis for the doctrine of *Young* and *Edelman* disappears. A federal court's grant of relief against state officials on the basis of state law, whether prospective or retroactive, does not vindicate the supreme authority of federal law. On the contrary, it is difficult to think of a greater intrusion on state sovereignty than when a federal court instructs state officials on how to conform their conduct to state law. Such a result conflicts directly with the principles of federalism that underlie the Eleventh Amendment. We conclude that *Young* and *Edelman* are inapplicable in a suit against state officials on the basis of state law.

B

The contrary view of Justice Stevens' dissent rests on fiction, is wrong on the law, and, most important, would emasculate the Eleventh Amendment. Under his view, an allegation that official conduct is contrary to a state statute would suffice to override the State's protection under that Amendment. The theory is that such conduct is contrary to the official's "instructions," and thus *ultra vires* his authority. Accordingly, official action based on a reasonable interpretation of any statute might, if the interpretation turned out to be erroneous, provide the basis for injunctive relief against the actors in their official capacities. In this case, where officials of a major state department, clearly acting within the scope of their authority, were found not to have improved conditions in a state institution adequately under state law, the dissent's result would be that the State itself has forfeited its constitutionally provided immunity.

The theory is out of touch with reality. . . . To the extent there was a violation of state law in this case, it is a case of the State itself not fulfilling its legislative promises.

. . .

. . . Under the dissent's view of the *ultra vires* doctrine, the Eleventh Amendment would have force only in the rare case in which a plaintiff foolishly attempts to sue the State in its own name, or where he cannot produce some state statute that has been violated to his asserted injury. Thus, the *ultra vires* doctrine, a narrow and questionable exception, would swallow the general rule that a suit is against the State if the relief will run against it. That result gives the dissent no pause presumably because of its view that the Eleventh Amendment and sovereign immunity " 'undoubtedly ru[n] counter to modern democratic notions of the moral responsibility of the State.' " . . . The dissent totally rejects the Eleventh Amendment's basis in federalism.

C

The reasoning of our recent decisions on sovereign immunity thus leads to the conclusion that a federal suit against state officials on the basis of state law contravenes the Eleventh Amendment when—as here—the relief sought and ordered has an impact directly on the State itself. In reaching a contrary conclusion, the Court of Appeals relied principally on a separate line of cases dealing with pendent jurisdiction. The crucial point for the Court of Appeals was that this Court has granted relief against state officials on the basis of a pendent state-law claim. We therefore must consider the relationship between pendent jurisdiction and the Eleventh Amendment.

This Court long has held generally that when a federal court obtains jurisdiction over a federal claim, it may adjudicate other related claims over which the court otherwise would not have jurisdiction. See, e.g., Mine Workers v. Gibbs, 383 U.S. 715, 726 (1966); Osborn v. Bank of the United States, 9 Wheat. 738, 819–823 (1824). The Court also has held that a federal court may resolve a case solely on the basis of a pendent state-law claim, see Siler [v. Louisville & Nashville R. Co., 213 U.S. 175, at 192–193 (1909)], and that in fact the court usually should do so in order to avoid federal constitutional questions, see id., at 193; Ashwander v. TVA, 297 U.S. 288, 347 (1936) (Brandeis, J., concurring) ("[I]f a case can be decided on either of two grounds, one involving a constitutional question, the other a question of statutory construction or general law, the Court will decide only the latter"). But pendent jurisdiction is a judge-made doctrine inferred from the general language of Art. III. The question presented is whether this doctrine may be viewed as displacing the explicit limitation on federal jurisdiction contained in the Eleventh Amendment.

As the Court of Appeals noted, in *Siler* and subsequent cases concerning pendent jurisdiction, relief was granted against state officials on the basis of state-law claims that were pendent to federal constitutional claims. In none of these cases, however, did the Court so much as mention the Eleventh Amendment in connection with the state-law claim. . . .

These cases thus did not directly confront the question before us. "[W]hen questions of jurisdiction have been passed on in prior decisions *sub silentio,* this Court has never considered itself bound when a subsequent case finally brings the jurisdictional issue before us." Hagans v. Lavine, 415 U.S. 528, 533, n. 5 (1974). We therefore view the question as an open one.

As noted, the implicit view of these cases seems to have been that once jurisdiction is established on the basis of a federal question, no further Eleventh Amendment inquiry is necessary with respect to other claims raised in the case. This is an erroneous view and contrary to the principles established in our Eleventh Amendment decisions. . . .

. . . . The Eleventh Amendment should not be construed to apply with less force to this implied form of jurisdiction than it does to the explicitly granted power to hear federal claims. The history of the adoption and development of the Amendment, confirms that it is an independent limitation on all exercises of Art. III power: "the entire judicial power granted by the Constitution does not embrace authority to entertain suit brought by private parties against a State without consent given," Ex parte State of New York No. 1, 256 U.S. 490, 497 (1921). . . .

. . . .

D

Respondents urge that application of the Eleventh Amendment to pendent state-law claims will have a disruptive effect on litigation against state officials. They argue that the "considerations of judicial economy, convenience, and fairness to litigants" that underlie pendent jurisdiction, see *Gibbs,* supra, 383 U.S., at 726, counsel against a result that may cause litigants to split causes of action between state and federal courts. They also contend that the policy of avoiding unnecessary constitutional decisions will be contravened if plaintiffs choose to forgo their state-law claims and sue only in federal court or, alternatively, that the policy of Ex parte Young will be hindered if plaintiffs choose to forgo their right to a federal forum and bring all of their claims in state court.

It may be that applying the Eleventh Amendment to pendent claims results in federal claims being brought in state court, or in bifurcation of claims. That is not uncommon in this area. Under Edelman v. Jordan, supra, a suit against state officials for retroactive monetary relief, whether based on federal or state law, must be brought in state court. Challenges to the validity of state tax systems under 42 U.S.C. § 1983 also must be brought in state court. Fair Assessment in Real Estate Ass'n v. McNary, 454 U.S. 100 (1981). Under the abstention doctrine, unclear issues of state law commonly are split off and referred to the state courts.

In any case, the answer to respondents' assertions is that such considerations of policy cannot override the constitutional limitation on the authority of the federal judiciary to adjudicate suits against a State. See Missouri v. Fiske, 290 U.S., at 25–26 ("Considerations of convenience open no avenue of escape from the [Amendment's] restriction"). That a litigant's choice of forum is reduced "has long been understood to be a part of the tension inherent in our system of federalism." Employees v. Missouri Public Health & Welfare Dept., 411 U.S. 279, 298 (1973) (Marshall, J., concurring in result).

. . . .

V

The Court of Appeals upheld the judgment of the District Court solely on the basis of Pennsylvania's MH/MR Act. We hold that these federal courts lacked jurisdiction to enjoin petitioner state institutions and state officials on the basis of this state law. The District Court also rested its decision on the Eighth and Fourteenth Amendments and § 504 of the Rehabilitation Act of 1973. On remand the Court of Appeals may consider to what extent, if any, the judgment may be sustained on these bases. The court also may consider whether relief may be granted to respondents under the Developmentally Disabled Assistance and Bill of Rights Act, 42 U.S.C. §§ 6011, 6063. The judgment of the Court of Appeals is reversed, and the case remanded for further proceedings consistent with this opinion.

It is so ordered.

Justice Brennan, dissenting.

I fully agree with Justice Stevens' dissent. Nevertheless, I write separately to explain that in view of my continued belief that the Eleventh Amendment "bars federal court suits against States only by citizens of other States," . . . I would hold that petitioners are not entitled to invoke the protections of that Amendment in this federal court suit by citizens of Pennsylvania. . . . To the extent that such nonconstitutional sovereign immunity may apply to petitioners, I agree with Justice Stevens that since petitioners' conduct was prohibited by state law, the protections of sovereign immunity do not extend to them.

Justice Stevens, with whom Justice Brennan, Justice Marshall, and Justice Blackmun join, dissenting.

. . . In a completely unprecedented holding, today the Court concludes that Pennsylvania's sovereign immunity prevents a federal court from enjoining the conduct that Pennsylvania itself has prohibited. No rational view of the sovereign immunity of the States supports this result. To the contrary, the question whether a federal court may award injunctive relief on the basis of state law has been answered affirmatively by this Court many times in the past. Yet the Court repudiates at least 28 cases, spanning well over a century of this Court's jurisprudence, proclaiming instead that federal courts have no power to enforce the will of the States by enjoining conduct because it violates state law. This new pronouncement will require the federal courts to decide federal constitutional questions despite the availability of state-law grounds for decision, a result inimical to sound principles of judicial restraint. Nothing in the Eleventh Amendment, the conception of state sovereignty it embodies, or the history of this institution, requires or justifies such a perverse result.

. . .

II

The majority proceeds as if this Court has not had previous occasion to consider the Eleventh Amendment argument made by petitioners, and contends that Ex parte Young, 209 U.S. 123 (1908) has no application to a suit seeking injunctive relief on the basis of state law. That is simply not the case. . . .

. . .

. . . Until today the rule has been simple: conduct that exceeds the scope of an official's lawful discretion is not conduct the sovereign has authorized and hence is subject to injunction. Whether that conduct also gives rise to damage liability is an entirely separate question.

III

. . .

The pivotal consideration in *Young* was that it was not conduct of the sovereign that was at issue. The rule that unlawful acts of an officer should not be attributed to the sovereign has deep roots in the history of sovereign immunity and makes *Young* reconcilable with the principles of sovereign immunity found in the Eleventh Amendment, rather than merely an unprincipled accommodation between federal and state interests that ignores the principles contained in the Eleventh Amendment.

. . .

It follows that the basis for the *Young* rule is present when the officer sued has violated the law of the sovereign; in all such cases the conduct is of a type that would not be permitted by the sovereign and hence is not attributable to the sovereign under traditional sovereign immunity principles. In such a case, the sovereign's interest lies with those who seek to enforce its laws, rather than those who have violated them. . . . The majority's position that the Eleventh Amendment does not permit federal courts to enjoin conduct that the sovereign State itself seeks to prohibit thus is inconsistent with both the doctrine of sovereign immunity and the underlying respect for the integrity of State policy which the Eleventh Amendment protects. The issuance of injunctive relief which enforces state laws and policies, if anything, enhances federal courts' respect for the sovereign prerogatives of the States. The majority's approach, which requires federal courts to ignore questions of state law and to rest their decisions on federal bases, will create more rather than less friction between the States and the federal judiciary.

Moreover, the majority's rule has nothing to do with the basic reason the Eleventh Amendment was added to the Constitution. There is general agreement that the Amendment was passed because the States were fearful that federal courts would force them to pay their Revolutionary War debts, leading to their financial ruin. Entertaining a suit for injunctive relief based on state law implicates none of the concerns of the Framers. . . .

. . .

IV

The majority's decision in this case is especially unwise in that it overrules a long line of cases in order to reach a result that is at odds with the usual practices of this Court. In one of the most respected opinions ever written by a Member of this Court, Justice Brandeis wrote:

> "The Court [has] developed, for its own governance in the cases confessedly within its jurisdiction, a series of rules under which it has avoided passing upon a large part of all the constitutional questions pressed upon it for decision. They are:

> . . .

> The Court will not pass upon a constitutional question although properly presented by the record, if there is also present some other ground upon which the case may be disposed of. This rule has found most varied application. Thus, if a case can be decided on either of two grounds, one involving a constitutional question, the other a question of statutory construction or general law, the Court will decide only the latter. Siler v. Louisville & Nashville R. Co., 213 U.S. 175, 191." Ashwander v. Tennessee Valley Authority, 297 U.S. 288, 346–347 (1936) (Brandeis, J., concurring).

The *Siler* case, cited with approval by Justice Brandeis in *Ashwander,* employed a remarkably similar approach to that used by the Court of Appeals in this case. A privately owned railroad corporation brought suit against the members of the railroad commission of Kentucky to enjoin the enforcement of a rate schedule promulgated by the commission. The federal circuit court found that the schedule violated the plaintiff's federal constitutional rights and granted relief. This Court affirmed, but it refused to decide the constitutional question because injunctive relief against the state officials was adequately supported by state law. The Court held that the plaintiff's claim that the schedule violated the Federal Constitution was sufficient to justify the assertion of federal jurisdiction over the case, but then declined to reach the federal question, deciding the case on the basis of state law instead:

> "Where a case in this court can be decided without reference to questions arising under the Federal Constitution, that course is usually pursued and is not departed from without important reasons. In this case we think it much better to decide it with regard to the question of a local nature, involving the construction of the state statute and the authority therein given to the commission to make the order in question, rather than to unnecessarily decide the various constitutional questions appearing in the record." Siler v. Louisville & Nashville R. Co., 213 U.S. 175, 193 (1909).

. . .

Not only does the *Siler* rule have an impressive historical pedigree, but it is also strongly supported by the interest in avoiding duplicative litigation and the unnecessary decision of federal constitutional questions. . . .

In addition, application of the *Siler* rule enhances the decisionmaking autonomy of the States. *Siler* directs the federal court to turn first to state law, which the State is free to modify or repeal. By leaving the policy determinations underlying injunctive relief in the hands of the State, the Court of Appeals' approach gives appropriate deference to established state policies.

In contrast, the rule the majority creates today serves none of the interests of the State. The majority prevents federal courts from implementing State policies through equitable enforcement of State law. Instead, federal courts are required to resolve cases on federal grounds that no State authority can undo. Leaving violations of state law unredressed and ensuring that the decisions of federal courts may never be reexamined by the States hardly comports with the respect for States as sovereign entities commanded by the Eleventh Amendment.

. . .

APPLICATION OF THE ELEVENTH AMENDMENT IN SUITS FOR DAMAGES

Given prior law that the Eleventh Amendment applied to suits by a state's own citizens, and that it applied although only state officers were named parties if the state was the real party in interest, the "stripping doctrine" of Ex parte Young was crucial in permitting private federal court litigation to compel state compliance with the Constitution and federal laws.[1]

The stripping doctrine is not broad enough, however, to permit actions for "retroactive relief" that must be paid from public funds. While a judgment for damages that must be paid only from the state official's personal assets presents

---

[1] The Eleventh Amendment is inapplicable to suits by the federal government against states. United States v. Texas, 143 U.S. 621 (1892). Local political subdivisions, such as cities and counties are not "states" within the meaning of the Eleventh Amendment, and are fully subject to private party suits in the federal courts. Mt. Healthy City Sch. Dist. v. Doyle, 429 U.S. 274 (1977). The Eleventh Amendment is inapplicable, finally, to suits brought in state courts, Nevada v. Hall, 440 U.S. 410 (1979), although state law conceptions of sovereign immunity may bar action in the state courts.

While the Eleventh Amendment has no application to suits against the United States, Indian tribes, or foreign countries, independent conceptions of sovereign immunity do apply. In private actions against federal officials, the stripping doctrine has been applied to determine the extent of federal sovereign immunity. Larson v. Domestic & Foreign Commerce Corp., 337 U.S. 682 (1949); Dugan v. Rank, 372 U.S. 609 (1963); Note, *The Sovereign Immunity Doctrine and Judicial Review of Federal Administrative Action,* 2 U.C.L.A.L.Rev. 382 (1955). In 1976, Public Law 94–574, § 1, 90 Stat. 2721, amended the Administrative Procedure Act (5 U.S.C. §§ 702, 703) to eliminate the defense of sovereign immunity in private suits seeking relief other than money damages against the United States. (Congress had long before consented to suit for money damages for tort and contract claims against the United States.) On the immunity of Indian tribes, see Santa Clara Pueblo v. Martinez, 436 U.S. 49, 58 (1978).

no Eleventh Amendment problem, Scheuer v. Rhodes, 416 U.S. 232 (1974), the Eleventh Amendment is still a serious obstacle if a private plaintiff's suit seeks the payment of state funds for past violations of federal law. That was the situation in Edelman v. Jordan, 415 U.S. 651 (1974), where welfare recipients were seeking reimbursement for past welfare payments withheld by state officials in violation of federal law. The Court held that, while the principle of Ex Parte Young supported the lower federal courts' judgment ordering state welfare officials to pay future benefits, the Eleventh Amendment barred any retroactive relief for benefits withheld in the past.[2]

A second fiction—of state "consent" to suit or "waiver" of sovereign immunity—has been applied to permit private damage actions against states in federal court. In Parden v. Terminal Ry., 377 U.S. 184 (1964), the Court held that an injured railroad worker could sue a state-owned railroad for damages under the Federal Employers' Liability Act. The Court reasoned that ". . . Congress conditioned the right to operate a railroad in interstate commerce upon amenability to suit in federal court as provided by the Act; by thereafter operating a railroad in interstate commerce, Alabama must be taken to have accepted that condition and thus to have consented to suit." Edelman v. Jordan, however, considerably limited the waiver theory. The Court decided that a waiver could not be found whenever a federal statute imposed obligations upon the state, or whenever a state had voluntarily participated in a federal program. It must also be determined "by the most express language or by such overwhelming implications from the text" that Congress intended to abrogate the state's immunity under the Eleventh Amendment.

Does Congress have constitutional power to lift the bar of the Eleventh Amendment, and explicitly authorize damage actions payable from state treasuries for past violations of federal law? The following case deals with that question.

FITZPATRICK v. BITZER

427 U.S. 445, 96 S.Ct. 2666, 49 L.Ed.2d 614 (1976).

Mr. Justice Rehnquist delivered the opinion of the Court.

In the 1972 Amendments to Title VII of the Civil Rights Act of 1964, Congress, acting under § 5 of the Fourteenth Amendment, authorized federal courts to award money damages in favor of a private individual against a state government found to have subjected that person to employment discrimination on the basis of "race, color, religion, sex, or national origin." The principal question presented by these cases is whether, as against the shield of sovereign immunity afforded the State by the Eleventh Amendment, Edelman v. Jordan, 415 U.S. 651 (1974), Congress has the power to authorize federal courts to enter such an award against the State as a means of enforcing the substantive guarantees of the Fourteenth Amendment. The Court of Appeals for the Second Circuit held that the effect of our decision in *Edelman* was to foreclose Congress' power. . . . We reverse.

I.

Petitioners in No. 75–251 sued in the United States District Court for the District of Connecticut on behalf of all present and retired male employees of

---

[2] Where a court's order requires payment of funds from the state treasury, the question is whether the order is ancillary to a "prospective" order, or "retroactive" relief for past disobedience to federal law. In Hutto v. Finney, 437 U.S. 678 (1978), an award of attorney's fees to be paid out of the state treasury for the state's bad faith in complying with a prospective decree was held to be ancillary to the prospective order, and not barred by the Eleventh Amendment.

the State of Connecticut. Their amended complaint asserted, *inter alia,* that certain provisions in the State's statutory retirement benefit plan discriminated against them because of their sex, and therefore contravened Title VII of the Civil Rights Act of 1964, 78 Stat. 253, as amended, 42 U.S.C. § 2000e et seq. (1970 ed., Supp. IV). Title VII, which originally did not include state and local governments, had in the interim been amended to bring the States within its purview.

The District Court held that the Connecticut State Employees Retirement Act violated Title VII's prohibition against sex-based employment discrimination. 390 F.Supp. 278, 285–288 (D.C.1974). It entered prospective injunctive relief in petitioners' favor against respondent state officials. Petitioners also sought an award of retroactive retirement benefits as compensation for losses caused by the State's discrimination, as well as "a reasonable attorney's fee as part of the costs." But the District Court held that both would constitute recovery of money damages from the State's treasury, and were therefore precluded by the Eleventh Amendment and by this Court's decision in Edelman v. Jordan, supra. . . .

On petitioners' appeal, the Court of Appeals affirmed in part and reversed in part. . . .

II.

In *Edelman* this Court held that monetary relief awarded by the District Court to welfare plaintiffs, by reason of wrongful denial of benefits which had occurred previous to the entry of the District Court's determination of their wrongfulness, violated the Eleventh Amendment. . . .

. . .

All parties in the instant litigation agree with the Court of Appeals that the suit for retroactive benefits by these parties is in fact indistinguishable from that sought to be maintained in *Edelman,* since what is sought here is a damage award payable to a private party from the state treasury.

Our analysis begins where *Edelman* ended, for in this Title VII case the "threshold fact of congressional authorization," 415 U.S., at 672, to sue the State as employer is clearly present. This is, of course, the prerequisite found present in *Parden* and wanting in *Employees.* We are aware of the factual differences between the type of state activity involved in *Parden* and that involved in the present case, but we do not think that difference is material for our purposes. The congressional authorization involved in *Parden* was based on the power of Congress under the Commerce Clause; here, however, the Eleventh Amendment defense is asserted in the context of legislation passed pursuant to Congress' authority under § 5 of the Fourteenth Amendment.[9]

. . .

The impact of the Fourteenth Amendment upon the relationship between the Federal Government and the States, and the reach of congressional power under § 5, were examined at length by this Court in Ex parte Virginia, 100 U.S. 339 (1880). . . .

There can be no doubt that this line of cases has sanctioned intrusions by Congress, acting under the Civil War Amendments, into the judicial, executive, and legislative spheres of autonomy previously reserved to the States. The legislation considered in each case was grounded on the expansion of Congress' powers—with the corresponding diminution of state sovereignty—found to be intended by the Framers and made part of the Constitution upon the States'

---

[9] There is no dispute that in enacting the 1972 Amendments to Title VII to extend coverage to the States as employers, Congress exercised its power under § 5 of the Fourteenth Amendment . . . .. Compare National League of Cities v. Usery, 426 U.S. 833 (1976).

ratification of those Amendments, a phenomenon aptly described as a "carv[ing] out" in Ex parte Virginia, 100 U.S., at 346.

It is true that none of these previous cases presented the question of the relationship between the Eleventh Amendment and the enforcement power granted to Congress under § 5 of the Fourteenth Amendment. But we think that the Eleventh Amendment, and the principle of state sovereignty which it embodies, see Hans v. Louisiana, 134 U.S. 1 (1890), are necessarily limited by the enforcement provisions of § 5 of the Fourteenth Amendment. In that section Congress is expressly granted authority to enforce "by appropriate legislation" the substantive provisions of the Fourteenth Amendment, which themselves embody significant limitations on state authority. When Congress acts pursuant to § 5, not only is it exercising legislative authority that is plenary within the terms of the constitutional grant, it is exercising that authority under one section of a constitutional Amendment whose other sections by their own terms embody limitations on state authority. We think that Congress may, in determining what is "appropriate legislation" for the purpose of enforcing the provisions of the Fourteenth Amendment, provide for private suits against States or state officials which are constitutionally impermissible in other contexts.
. . .

III.

. . .

The judgment in No. 75–251 is Reversed.
. . .

Mr. Justice Brennan, concurring in the judgment . . .

Mr. Justice Stevens, concurring.
. . .

———

CONGRESSIONAL POWER TO ELIMINATE
STATE SOVEREIGN IMMUNITY

Is Congress' power to authorize damage awards against the states limited to legislation enforcing the Fourteenth Amendment? What if the obligation imposed on the state was conditioned on state acceptance of federal funds under an appropriation measure? In Parden v. Terminal Ry., 377 U.S. 184 (1964), the Court upheld a provision of the Federal Employers' Liability Act permitting suit by an employee of a state-owned railroad for damages. The Act had been enacted pursuant to Congress' Article I, Section 8, power to regulate interstate commerce; on the other hand, the activity being regulated was a railroad, and not a more traditional state activity such as a school, a court of law, or an administrative agency. For different assessments of the scope of Congress' power to remove the barrier imposed by the Eleventh Amendment, see Nowak, *The Scope of Congressional Power to Create Causes of Action Against State Governments and the History of the Eleventh and Fourteenth Amendments,* 75 Colum.L.Rev. 1413 (1975); Tribe, *Intergovernmental Immunities in Litigation, Taxation, and Regulation: Separation of Powers Issues in Controversies about Federalism,* 89 Harv.L.Rev. 682 (1976); Field, *The Eleventh Amendment and Other Sovereign Immunity Doctrines: Congressional Imposition of Suit Upon the States,* 126 U.Pa.L.Rev. 1203 (1978).

C. NON–CONSTITUTIONAL RESTRICTIONS ON FEDERAL COURT INJUNCTIONS AGAINST UNCONSTITUTIONAL STATE LAWS

Introduction. As the previous subsection demonstrates, the "stripping" doctrine of Ex parte Young has eliminated the possible Eleventh Amendment bar to federal court injunctions against enforcement of state laws violating federal law, or to declaratory judgments of their invalidity. A complex set of statutory restrictions on federal court jurisdiction, combined with judge-made rules of equitable restraint, still serve to control decisions by federal courts that state laws are unconstitutional. A complete assessment of those restrictions and restraints is usually undertaken in specialized courses in federal jurisdiction, and they can only be introduced briefly here. Topics examined include: the problems that arise when the challenged state law is ambiguous, and the ambiguity can only be resolved authoritatively by a state court; whether litigants are required to exhaust state administrative and judicial remedies before going to federal court to enjoin enforcement of a state law; and the applicability of an old federal statute forbidding federal courts to enjoin proceedings in a state court. Trainor v. Hernandez, which concludes this subsection, introduces doctrines of equitable restraint that have been applied when the federal court action is pending at the same time state court proceedings have been brought to enforce the challenged law.

ABSTENTION TO ALLOW STATE COURTS TO CONSTRUE AMBIGUOUS STATE LAW

A complication that arises when a federal court suit is brought to determine the constitutional validity of a state law is that there may be serious questions concerning the proper interpretation of that law—particularly if it was recently enacted.

When the Supreme Court reviews a state court decision concerning the constitutional validity of a state law, the Court can consider only issues of federal law. There has been, however, a decision by a state court, and an opportunity for it to address questions of state law interpretation. (Some of the problems that arise when the state court's opinion does not adequately resolve the possible ambiguities in the challenged law were addressed in Rescue Army v. Municipal Court, discussed above at page 63.)

When suit challenging a state law is brought in a federal court, it must determine, as a court of first instance, the entire controversy under all relevant law. If the constitutionality of the challenged law depends upon its meaning, the federal court must supply an interpretation. If the relevant issues of state law have been decided by a state's highest court, that decision is as binding on the lower federal court as it is in the Supreme Court on appeal. When there is no relevant state court decision, as is often true when the challenged statute was newly enacted, the federal court must predict the resolution of the issue by the state courts.

Until recently, federal courts were required to consider other issues of state law in suits to enjoin state laws alleged to violate the United States Constitution. Siler v. Louisville & Nashville R.R. Co., 213 U.S. 175 (1908), held that the federal court must first decide if the challenged state action violated state law. Even if the constitutional issue could be decided without resolving the ambiguities in state law, a policy of avoiding unnecessary federal constitutional decisions dictated that the court decide first whether the plaintiff could prevail on other issues. The 1984 decision in Pennhurst State School & Hosp. v. Halderman, page 66 supra, holding that relief based on state law is barred by the eleventh amendment, now bars relief against state officers under state law. *Pennhurst* requires that a federal court limit injunctive relief to claims based on federal law.

While the *Siler* doctrine required the federal court to resolve relevant state law issues, state courts were still the authoritative voice on issues of state law. If the issue of state law were important, obvious practical problems arose. The federal court's interpretation of state law might conflict with later state court decisions, or the federal court's injunction might practically foreclose later state court resolution of those issues.

The "*Pullman* doctrine" responded to the problems by allowing or requiring the federal court to withhold action, pending commencement of a state court action to resolve the issues of state law. The doctrine takes its name from Railroad Commission of Texas v. Pullman Co., 312 U.S. 496 (1941). A group of Pullman porters, all of whom were Black, challenged an order of the state regulatory commission assigning work exclusively to conductors, all of whom were White. The Court concluded that the lower federal courts should not have addressed the merits of the federal constitutional attack on the commission's order. There was a question whether the commission had the authority to adopt the order under state law. The Court directed the district court to retain jurisdiction pending a suit brought in state court to resolve the state law issues.

Because of the *Pennhurst* decision, the *Pullman* doctrine is now obsolete when the only unresolved state law issues concern whether the challenged official action violates state law, as in *Pullman* itself. The *Pullman* doctrine is still relevant, however, when the constitutionality of a challenged state law depends upon its meaning.

Bringing a second action in a state court may seriously delay decision by the federal court, however, and maintaining two lawsuits is expensive. The expense and delay may be so serious that the plaintiff will be practically forced to abandon litigating constitutional issues in the federal courts. The opposing advantages and disadvantages of *Pullman* abstention have produced a complex body of decisions. Whether abstention is appropriate in a particular case may depend on arguable conclusions concerning the degree of uncertainty in the state law issues, on the one hand, and the degree of delay and expense involved in seeking guidance from the state courts, on the other. For example, abstention may be inappropriate if there are multiple unsettled questions that cannot be easily resolved in a separate state court proceeding. Baggett v. Bullitt, 377 U.S. 360, 378 (1964).

For a detailed discussion of the *Pullman* doctrine, see Field, *Abstention in Constitutional Cases: The Scope of the Pullman Abstention Doctrine,* 122 U.Pa.L.Rev. 1071 (1974). The special problems posed by the doctrine in free speech cases are discussed below in Chapter 14, at page 1095.

EXHAUSTION OF STATE ADMINISTRATIVE REMEDIES

It used to be the unquestioned rule that a plaintiff seeking a federal court injunction against application of a state law must first exhaust reasonable and available state administrative remedies. Two cases in the 1960's developed an exception to the rule of exhaustion that was so large it virtually swallowed the rule. In McNeese v. Board of Education, 373 U.S. 668 (1963), the Court rejected an argument that plaintiffs challenging a segregated school system should first have used local procedures for reassignment of individual pupils to new schools. In Damico v. California, 389 U.S. 416 (1967), the Court decided that federal court challenges to state denials of welfare benefits did not have to await the resolution of individual administrative proceedings to determine whether benefits were properly denied.

It was possible to argue in both *McNeese* and *Damico* that a requirement of exhaustion of administrative remedies was not practically relevant to decision of the constitutional issues involved. The rationale for decision in both cases, however, was much broader. The Court concluded that cases brought under 42 U.S.C. § 1983 were a categorical exception to the rule requiring exhaustion of administrative remedies. The problem is that 42 U.S.C. § 1983 covers *all* suits against state officials to invalidate state action on the ground that it is in conflict with the United States Constitution or a federal statute. Maine v. Thiboutot, 448 U.S. 1 (1980). Some Justices have argued that the categorical exception should be pared down, and that individual challengers to state action as unconstitutional should be required to exhaust reasonable available state administrative remedies before bringing suit in a federal court. E.g., Runyon v. McCrary, 427 U.S. 160, 186 n * (1976) (Powell, J., concurring). In Patsy v. Florida Board of Regents, 457 U.S. 496 (1982), however, a divided Court reaffirmed its previous rulings that exhaustion of administrative remedies is not required in any § 1983 actions. Thus, barring Congressional action, most constitutional challenges to state legislative or administrative action are not subject to the general rule requiring exhaustion of administrative remedies prior to federal court action.[1]

EXHAUSTION OF STATE JUDICIAL REMEDIES

The exhaustion requirement was never generally applied to require a litigant to exhaust state "judicial" as opposed to "administrative" remedies. Bacon v. Rutland R.R. Co., 232 U.S. 134 (1914); City Bank Farmers Trust Co. v. Schnader, 291 U.S. 24 (1934). Thus, a federal court injunction was not precluded by the existence of an adequate remedy within the state judicial system. Two statutes enacted in the 1930s, however, preclude federal court jurisdiction where "plain, speedy and efficient" remedies are available in state courts.

The Johnson Act, enacted in 1934, and now found in 28 U.S.C. § 1342, reads as follows:

> "The district courts shall not enjoin, suspend or restrain the operation of, or compliance with, any order affecting rates chargeable by a public utility and made by a State administrative agency or a rate-making body of a State political subdivision, where:
>
> "(1) Jurisdiction is based solely on diversity of citizenship or repugnance of the order to the Federal Constitution; and,
>
> "(2) The order does not interfere with interstate commerce; and,
>
> "(3) The order has been made after reasonable notice and hearing; and,
>
> "(4) A plain, speedy and efficient remedy may be had in the courts of such State."

In cases not technically within the terms of the Johnson Act, the Court has relied upon principles of equitable discretion in requiring state court review of state public utility regulatory orders not affecting rates. Burford v. Sun Oil Co., 319 U.S. 315 (1943) (order permitting drilling of new oil well); Alabama

[1] In the Civil Rights of Institutionalized Persons Act, 42 U.S.C. § 1997(e), Congress imposed a limited exhaustion requirement for adult prisoners bringing action under § 1983.

Public Serv. Comm'n v. Southern Ry. Co., 341 U.S. 341 (1951) (order refusing to permit discontinuation of train service).

The Tax Injunction Act, passed in 1937, is now found in 28 U.S.C. § 1341 and reads as follows:

> "The district courts shall not enjoin, suspend or restrain the assessment, levy or collection of any tax under State law where a plain, speedy and efficient remedy may be had in the courts of such State."

ENJOINING STATE JUDICIAL PROCEEDINGS: THE ANTI–INJUNCTION ACT

The Anti-Injunction Act, 28 U.S.C. § 2283, provides that a federal court "may not grant an injunction to stay proceedings in a State Court except as expressly authorized by Act of Congress, or where necessary in aid of its jurisdiction, or to protect or effectuate its judgments." At one time, the statute was significant in precluding federal court action to enjoin enforcement of allegedly unconstitutional state laws if a proceeding to enforce that law was pending against the federal plaintiff in state court. While the statute was inapplicable if the federal suit was brought before the state enforcement proceeding began, the statute was a complete ban on issuing a federal injunction against a pending state proceeding unless one of the exceptions in the statute was applicable. In Mitchum v. Foster, 407 U.S. 225 (1972), the Court held that suits under 42 U.S.C. § 1983 fell within one of those exceptions, as a case where Congress had "expressly authorized" enjoining pending state actions. Since most suits to enjoin enforcement of unconstitutional state action are based on § 1983, the Anti-Injunction Act is no longer a bar to enjoining pending state proceedings in such cases.

ENJOINING STATE ENFORCEMENT PROCEEDINGS: YOUNGER v. HARRIS AND "OUR FEDERALISM"

As previous notes demonstrate, the older judicial doctrine requiring exhaustion of administrative remedies, and the statutory prohibition against enjoining pending state judicial proceedings, are inapplicable to federal court suits to enjoin state officials from enforcing unconstitutional state laws. However, as the Court noted in Mitchum v. Foster, supra, other "principles of equity, comity, and federalism" may still restrain federal courts when there is a pending state criminal action, civil judicial enforcement proceeding, or administrative enforcement proceeding, pending against the plaintiff in the federal court action.

The rules applicable to pending state criminal proceedings have been elaborated in some detail. The seminal decision was Younger v. Harris, 401 U.S. 37 (1971), where the Court held that—in the absence of a clear demonstration that the prosecution was in bad faith—a federal court could not entertain an action by a defendant in a state criminal case alleging that the statute under which he was prosecuted was unconstitutional.[1] Justice Black's opinion for the Court referred to a

> "notion of 'comity,' that is, a proper respect for state functions, a recognition of the fact that the entire country is made up of a Union of separate state governments, and a continuance of the belief that the National Government will fare best if the States and their institutions are left free to perform their

---

[1] The Court also held that a federal court action by persons not threatened with prosecution under the statute was premature. That aspect of the decision is discussed infra, p. 124.

separate functions in their separate ways. This, perhaps for lack of a better and clearer way to describe it, is referred to by many as 'Our Federalism.'"
Justice Black described the pragmatic concerns of "Our Federalism" as the avoidance of unnecessary delay in trying state criminal cases, and preventing what amounted to review of state court decisions by lower federal courts instead of the traditional review by the Supreme Court.

If no prosecution is pending, a person threatened with prosecution is entitled to maintain a suit for declaratory judgment of unconstitutionality (as opposed to an injunction). Steffel v. Thompson, 415 U.S. 452 (1974). The *Younger* doctrine, however, bars an injunction against a later state criminal action, or a declaratory judgment, if the prosecution was begun before "proceedings of substance on the merits" have occurred in the federal action. Hicks v. Miranda, 422 U.S. 332 (1975). (As indicated in the previous note, the Anti-Injunction Act did not apply to bar an injunction against a state criminal enforcement action if the federal court action was begun first.) The federal plaintiff can avoid abatement of the action by later state prosecution (under the rule of Hicks v. Miranda), by obtaining a temporary injunction against prosecution on a sufficient showing of irreparable harm and likely success on the merits. Doran v. Salem Inn, Inc., 422 U.S. 922 (1975). There is some uncertainty whether, if the state statute is declared unconstitutional in the federal action, later state prosecutions under the statute can be enjoined. See Shapiro, *State Courts and Federal Declaratory Judgments,* 80 N.W.U.L.Rev. 759 (1979). The Court has held that a person convicted of violating a statute in the past can sue to enjoin future prosecutions, if the convictions have become final and the requested relief is limited to preventing prosecution in the future. Wooley v. Maynard, 430 U.S. 705 (1977).[2]

Despite the elaborate detail of the post-*Younger* rules, as applied to state criminal prosecutions, there is considerable uncertainty in their application to state civil enforcement proceedings and administrative enforcement proceedings. The question is whether many of the restraints previously imposed by the doctrine of exhaustion of administrative remedies, and the Anti-Injunction Act, will be reintroduced under *Younger* and "Our Federalism." That is one of the issues in Trainor v. Hernandez, which follows.

TRAINOR v. HERNANDEZ

431 U.S. 434, 97 S.Ct. 1911, 52 L.Ed.2d 486 (1977).

Mr. Justice White delivered the opinion of the Court.

The Illinois Department of Public Aid (IDPA) filed a lawsuit in the Circuit Court of Cook County, Ill., on October 30, 1974, against appellees Juan and Maria Hernandez, alleging that they had fraudulently concealed assets while applying for and receiving public assistance. [At the same time, IDPA instituted an attachment proceeding under the Illinois statute applicable to all civil actions, attaching appellees' credit union account. Appellees filed this federal court action, seeking return of the attached money on the ground that the Illinois attachment statute denied procedural due process, in violation of the fourteenth amendment. That suit was eventually certified as a class action, and the district court decided that the attachment statute was unconstitutional, and enjoined IDPA officials from proceeding with the attachment. The district court refused to dismiss the action because of the pending state judicial proceeding, distinguishing the case before it from that in Huffman v. Pursue, Ltd., 420 U.S. 592 (1975). On direct appeal to the Supreme Court, appellants

---

[2] The application of these rules to free speech cases is discussed in Chapter 14, infra, at p. 1096.

argued that the district court should have dismissed the suit without passing on the constitutionality of the Illinois attachment statute.]

. . .

Huffman involved the propriety of a federal injunction against the execution of a judgment entered in a pending state-court suit brought by the State to enforce a nuisance statute. Although the state suit was a civil rather than a criminal proceeding, *Younger* principles were held to require dismissal of the federal suit. Noting that the State was a party to the nuisance proceeding and that the nuisance statute was "in aid of and closely related to criminal statutes," the Court concluded that a federal injunction would be "an offense to the State's interest in the nuisance litigation [which] is likely to be every bit as great as it would be were this a criminal proceeding." 420 U.S., at 604. Thus, while the traditional maxim that equity will not enjoin a criminal prosecution strictly speaking did not apply to the nuisance proceeding in *Huffman,* the " 'more vital consideration' " of comity, id., 420 U.S. at 601, quoting Younger v. Harris, 401 U.S., at 44, counseled restraint as strongly in the context of the pending state civil enforcement action as in the context of a pending criminal proceeding. In these circumstances, it was proper that the federal court stay its hand.

We have recently applied the analysis of *Huffman* to proceedings similar to state civil enforcement actions—judicial contempt proceedings. Juidice v. Vail, 430 U.S. 327 (1977). The Court again stressed the "more vital consideration" of comity underlying the *Younger* doctrine and held that the state interest in vindicating the regular operation of its judicial system through the contempt process—whether that process was labeled civil, criminal, or quasi-criminal—was sufficiently important to preclude federal injunctive relief unless *Younger* standards were met.

These cases control here. An action against appellees was pending in state court when they filed their federal suit. The state action was a suit by the State to recover from appellees welfare payments that allegedly had been fraudulently obtained. The writ of attachment issued as part of that action. The District Court thought that *Younger* policies were irrelevant because suits to recover money and writs of attachment were available to private parties as well as the State; it was only because of the coincidence that the State was a party that the suit was "arguably" in aid of the criminal law. But the fact remains that the State was a party to the suit in its role of administering its public-assistance programs. Both the suit and the accompanying writ of attachment were brought to vindicate important state policies such as safeguarding the fiscal integrity of those programs. The state authorities also had the option of vindicating these policies through criminal prosecutions. Although, as in *Juidice,* the State's interest here is "[p]erhaps . . . not quite as important as is the State's interest in the enforcement of its criminal laws . . . or even its interest in the maintenance of a quasi-criminal proceeding . . .," 430 U.S., at 335, the principles of *Younger* and *Huffman* are broad enough to apply to interference by a federal court with an ongoing civil enforcement action such as this, brought by the State in its sovereign capacity.[8]

For a federal court to proceed with its case rather than to remit appellees to their remedies in a pending state enforcement suit would confront the State with

---

[8] Title 28 U.S.C. § 2283 provides that "[a] court of the United States may not grant an injunction to stay proceedings in a State court except as expressly authorized by Act of Congress, or where necessary in aid of its jurisdiction, or to protect or effectuate its judgments." The section is not applicable here because this 42 U.S.C. § 1983 action is an express statutory exception to its application, Mitchum v. Foster, 407 U.S. 225 (1972); but it is significant for present purposes that the section does not discriminate between civil and criminal proceedings pending in state courts. . . .

As in Juidice v. Vail, 430 U.S. 327, 336 n. 13 (1977), we have no occasion to decide whether *Younger* principles apply to all civil litigation.

a choice of engaging in duplicative litigation, thereby risking a temporary federal injunction, or of interrupting its enforcement proceedings pending decision of the federal court at some unknown time in the future. It would also foreclose the opportunity of the state court to construe the challenged statute in the face of the actual federal constitutional challenges that would also be pending for decision before it, a privilege not wholly shared by the federal courts. Of course, in the case before us the state statute was invalidated and a federal injunction prohibited state officers from using or enforcing the attachment statute for any purpose. The eviscerating impact on many state enforcement actions is readily apparent. This disruption of suits by the State in its sovereign capacity, when combined with the negative reflection on the State's ability to adjudicate federal claims that occurs whenever a federal court enjoins a pending state proceeding, leads us to the conclusion that the interests of comity and federalism on which *Younger* and Samuels v. Mackell primarily rest apply in full force here. The pendency of the state-court action called for restraint by the federal court and for the dismissal of appellees' complaint unless extraordinary circumstances were present warranting federal interference or unless their state remedies were inadequate to litigate their federal due process claim.

No extraordinary circumstances warranting equitable relief were present here. There is no suggestion that the pending state action was brought in bad faith or for the purpose of harassing appellees. It is urged that this case comes within the exception that we said in *Younger* might exist where a state statute is " 'flagrantly and patently violative of express constitutional prohibitions in every clause, sentence and paragraph, and in whatever manner and against whomever an effort might be made to apply it.' " 401 U.S., at 53–54, quoting Watson v. Buck, 313 U.S. 387, 402 (1941). Even if such a finding was made below, which we doubt, it would not have been warranted in light of our cases. Compare North Georgia Finishing, Inc. v. Di-Chem, Inc., 419 U.S. 601 (1975), with Mitchell v. W.T. Grant Co., 416 U.S. 600 (1974).

As for whether appellees could have presented their federal due process challenge to the attachment statute in the pending state proceeding, that question, if presented below, was not addressed by the District Court, which placed its rejection of *Younger* and *Huffman* on broader grounds. The issue is heavily laden with local law, and we do not rule on it here in the first instance.

The grounds on which the District Court refused to apply the principles of *Younger* and *Huffman* were infirm; it was therefore error, on those grounds, to entertain the action on behalf of either the named or the unnamed plaintiffs and to reach the issue of the constitutionality of the Illinois attachment statute.

The judgment is therefore reversed, and the case is remanded to the District Court for further proceedings consistent with this opinion.

It is so ordered.

Mr. Justice Stewart substantially agrees with the views expressed in the dissenting opinions of Mr. Justice Brennan and Mr. Justice Stevens. Accordingly, he respectfully dissents from the opinion and judgment of the Court.

Mr. Justice Blackmun, concurring.

I join the Court's opinion and write only to stress that the substantiality of the State's interest in its proceeding has been an important factor in abstention cases under Younger v. Harris, 401 U.S. 37 (1971), from the beginning.

. . .

. . .

. . . . I, too, find significant the fact that the State was a party in its sovereign capacity to both the state suit and the federal suit. Here, I emphasize the importance of the fact that the state interest in the pending state proceeding was substantial. In my view, the fact that the State had the option of proceeding either civilly or criminally to impose sanctions for a fraudulent concealment of assets while one applies for and receives public assistance demonstrates that the underlying state interest is of the same order of importance as the interests in *Younger* and *Huffman.* The propriety of abstention should not depend on the State's choice to vindicate its interests by a less drastic, and perhaps more lenient, route. In addition, as the Court notes, the state court proceeding played an important role in safeguarding the fiscal integrity of the public assistance programs. Since the benefits of the recovery of fraudulently obtained funds are enjoyed by all the taxpayers of the State, it is reasonable to recognize a distinction between the State's status as creditor and the status of private parties using the same procedures.

For me, the existence of the foregoing factors brings this case squarely within the Court's prior *Younger* abstention rulings.

Mr. Justice Brennan, with whom Mr. Justice Marshall joins, dissenting.

The Court continues on, to me, the wholly improper course of extending *Younger* principles to deny a federal forum to plaintiffs invoking 42 U.S.C. § 1983 for the decision of meritorious federal constitutional claims when a *civil* action that might entertain such claims is pending in a state court. Because I am of the view that the decision patently disregards Congress' purpose in enacting § 1983—to open federal courts to the decision of such claims without regard to the pendency of such state civil actions—and because the decision indefensibly departs from prior decisions of this Court, I respectfully dissent.

. . .

Mr. Justice Stevens, dissenting.

Today the Court adds four new complexities to a doctrine that has bewildered other federal courts for several years. First, the Court finds a meaningful difference between a state procedure which is "patently and flagrantly violative of the Constitution" and one that is "flagrantly and patently violative of express constitutional prohibitions in every clause, sentence and paragraph, and in whatever manner and against whomever an effort might be made to apply it." Second, the Court holds that an unconstitutional collection procedure may be used by a state agency, though not by others, because there is "a distinction between the State's status as creditor and the status of private parties using the same procedures." Third, the Court's application of the abstention doctrine in this case provides even greater protection to a State when it is proceeding as an ordinary creditor than the statutory protection mandated by Congress for the State in its capacity as a tax collector. Fourth, without disagreeing with the District Court's conclusion that the Illinois attachment procedure is unconstitutional, the Court remands in order to enable the District Court to decide whether that invalid procedure provides an adequate remedy for the vindication of appellees' federal rights. . . .

. . .

As I suggested in my separate opinion in Juidice v. Vail, 430 U.S. 339, a principled application of the rationale of Younger v. Harris, 401 U.S. 37, forecloses abstention in cases in which the federal challenge is to the constitutionality of the state procedure itself. Since this federal plaintiff raised a serious question about the fairness of the Illinois attachment procedure, and since that procedure does not afford a plain, speedy, and efficient remedy for his federal claim, it necessarily follows that *Younger* abstention is inappropriate.

Thirty years ago Mr. Justice Rutledge characterized a series of Illinois procedures which effectively foreclosed consideration of the merits of federal constitutional claims as a "procedural labyrinth . . . made up entirely of blind alleys." Marino v. Ragen, 332 U.S. 561, 567. Today Illinois litigants may appropriately apply that characterization to the Court's increasingly Daedalian doctrine of abstention.

I respectfully dissent.

SECTION 3. CASES AND CONTROVERSIES AND JUSTICIABILITY

A. IN GENERAL

Introduction. The limitations explored below arose initially from the Court's early rejection of an advisory opinion role for the federal courts and from the theory of Marbury v. Madison that judicial review is simply a function of deciding ordinary litigation between adverse parties in which it becomes necessary to determine the constitutional validity of legislation to resolve the disputes.

The doctrines involved in this section are characteristically "soft" in the sense that it is difficult to define the rules with precision and in the sense that they do not appear to be consistent in their application. The imprecision and inconsistency result in part from the fact that these doctrines are used by the Court to regulate the extent of its impact. See e.g., the discussion in Rescue Army v. Municipal Court, 331 U.S. 549 (1947). An "activist" Court seeking to expand the application of certain constitutional doctrines is more likely to construe justiciability limitations narrowly in order to reach the merits of cases; a Court interested in "retrenchment and consolidation" is more likely to construe justiciability limitations broadly in order to avoid reaching the merits of cases. For varying points of view concerning the usefulness of these doctrines in regulating the impact of judicial review, see Bickel, *The Least Dangerous Branch*, Ch. 4 (1962); Gunther, *The Subtle Vices of the "Passive Virtues"—A Comment on Principle and Expediency in Judicial Review,* 64 Colum.L.Rev. 1 (1964); Brilmayer, *The Jurisprudence of Article III: Perspectives on the "Case or Controversy" Requirement,* 93 Harv.L.Rev. 297 (1979).

ADVISORY OPINIONS

In 1793 President Washington over the objection of Hamilton, who thought the matter was not within the province of the judiciary, submitted to the Justices 29 questions relating to international law, neutrality, and the construction of the French and British treaties. Secretary of State Jefferson wrote as follows to Chief Justice Jay:

"The war which has taken place among the powers of Europe produces frequent transactions within our ports and limits, on which questions arise of considerable difficulty, and of greater importance to the peace of the United States. These questions depend for their solution on the construction of our treaties, on the laws of nature and nations, and on the law of the land, and are often presented under circumstances which do not give a cognizance of them to the tribunals of the country. Yet their decision is so little analogous to the ordinary functions of the Executive as to occasion much embarrassment and difficulty to them. The President would, therefore, be much relieved if he found himself free to refer questions of this description to the opinions of the Judges of the Supreme Court of the United States, whose knowledge of the subject would secure us as against errors dangerous to the peace of the United States, and their authority ensure the respect of all parties. He has therefore asked the attendance of such of the Judges as could be collected in time for the occasion, to know, in the first place, their opinion, whether the public may, with propriety, be availed of their advice on these questions. And if they may, to present, for their advice, the abstract questions which have already occurred, or may soon occur, from which they will themselves strike out such as any circumstances might, in their opinion, forbid them to pronounce on."

After considering the matter for a few weeks the Justices replied as follows:

"We have considered the previous question stated in a letter written by your direction to us by the Secretary of State, on the 18th of last month regarding the lines of separation, drawn by the Constitution between the three departments of the government. These being in certain respects checks upon each other, and our being Judges of a Court in the last resort, are considerations which afford strong arguments against the propriety of our extra-judicially deciding the questions alluded to, especially as the power given by the Constitution to the President, of calling on the heads of departments for opinions, seems to have been *purposely* as well as expressly united to the *Executive* departments. We exceedingly regret every event that may cause embarrassment to your Administration, but we derive consolation from the reflection that your judgment will discern what is right, and that your usual prudence, decision and firmness will surmount every obstacle to the preservation of the rights, peace, and dignity of the United States."

THE FLAST v. COHEN SUMMARY

Warren, C.J., for the Court in Flast v. Cohen, 392 U.S. 83, 94–97 (1968):

"The jurisdiction of federal courts is defined and limited by Article III of the Constitution. In terms relevant to the question for decision in this case, the judicial power of federal courts is constitutionally restricted to 'cases' and 'controversies.' As is so often the situation in constitutional adjudication, those two words have an iceberg quality, containing beneath their surface simplicity submerged complexities which go to the very heart of our constitutional form of government. Embodied in the words 'cases' and 'controversies' are two complementary but somewhat different limitations. In part those words limit the business of federal courts to questions presented in an adversary context and in a form historically viewed as capable of resolution through the judicial process. And in part those words define the role assigned to the judiciary in a tripartite allocation of power to assure that the federal courts will not intrude into areas committed to the other branches of government. Justiciability is the term of art employed to give expression to this dual limitation placed upon federal courts by the case and controversy doctrine.

"Justiciability is itself a concept of uncertain meaning and scope. Its reach is illustrated by the various grounds upon which questions sought to be adjudicated in federal courts have been held not to be justiciable. Thus, no justiciable controversy is presented when the parties seek adjudication of only a political question, when the parties are asking for an advisory opinion, when the question sought to be adjudicated has been mooted by subsequent developments, and when there is no standing to maintain the action. Yet it remains true that '[j]usticiability is . . . not a legal concept with a fixed content of susceptible or scientific verification. Its utilization is the resultant of many subtle pressures. . . .' Poe v. Ullman, 367 U.S. 497, 508 (1961).

"Part of the difficulty in giving precise meaning and form to the concept of justiciability stems from the uncertain historical antecedents of the case and controversy doctrine. . . . [I]t is quite clear that 'the oldest and most consistent thread in the federal law of justiciability is that federal courts will not give advisory opinions.' Wright, Federal Courts 34 (1963). Thus, the implicit policies embodied in Article III, and not history alone, impose the rule against advisory opinions on federal courts. When the federal judicial power is invoked to pass upon the validity of actions by the Legislative and Executive Branches of the Government, the rule against advisory opinions implements the separation of powers prescribed by the Constitution and confines federal courts to the role assigned them by Article III. . . . However, the rule against advisory opinions also recognizes that such suits often 'are not pressed before the Court with that clear concreteness provided when a question emerges precisely framed and necessary for decision from a clash of adversary argument exploring every aspect of a multifaced situation embracing conflicting and demanding interests.' United States v. Fruehauf, 365 U.S. 146, 157 (1961). Consequently, the Article III prohibition against advisory opinions reflects the complementary constitutional considerations expressed by the justiciability doctrine: Federal judicial power is limited to those disputes which confine federal courts to a role consistent with a system of separated powers and which are traditionally thought to be capable of resolution through the judicial process.

"Additional uncertainty exists in the doctrine of justiciability because that doctrine has become a blend of constitutional requirements and policy considerations. And a policy limitation is 'not always clearly distinguished from the constitutional limitation.' Barrows v. Jackson, 346 U.S. 249, 255 (1953). For example, in his concurring opinion in Ashwander v. Tennessee Valley Authority, 297 U.S. 288, 345–348 (1936), Mr. Justice Brandeis listed seven rules developed by this Court 'for its own governance' to avoid passing prematurely on constitutional questions. Because the rules operate in 'cases confessedly within [the Court's] jurisdiction,' id., at 346, they find their source in policy, rather than purely constitutional, considerations. However, several of the cases cited by Mr. Justice Brandeis in illustrating the rules of self-governance articulated purely constitutional grounds for decision. See, e.g., Massachusetts v. Mellon, 262 U.S. 447 (1923); Fairchild v. Hughes, 258 U.S. 126 (1922); Chicago & Grand Trunk R. Co. v. Wellman, 143 U.S. 339 (1892). The 'many subtle pressures' which cause policy considerations to blend into the constitutional limitations of Article III make the justiciability doctrine one of uncertain and shifting contours."

JUSTICIABILITY AND THE FORM OF THE LITIGATION— RAISING CONSTITUTIONAL ISSUES

(1) **Raising Constitutional Issues.** How do persons go about getting an adjudication concerning the constitutionality of statutes (or other governmental actions) which affect them? In any individual case one or more of the following methods may be available:

(1) If the statute is made the basis of claim or defense in a suit between private individuals, the constitutional issue can be litigated. For an important constitutional law case which arose in this manner, see Gibbons v. Ogden, 22 U.S. (9 Wheat.) 1 (1824), set out infra p. 168.

(2) If the government (federal or state) brings a civil suit based on the statute, the claim of unconstitutionality can be raised in defense. For a leading constitutional case which arose in this matter, see McCulloch v. Maryland, 17 U.S. (4 Wheat.) 316 (1819), set out infra p. 159.

(3) If the government institutes criminal proceedings based on the statute, unconstitutionality of the statute is a defense. For cases in which important issues of state and federal taxing power were raised in this fashion,

see Brown v. Maryland, 25 U.S. (12 Wheat.) 419 (1827); United States v. Kahriger, 345 U.S. 22 (1953).

(4) One damaged by governmental action claimed to be unconstitutional may be able to raise the issue in a suit for damages. For a case where a plaintiff succeeded in such a suit see United States v. Causby, 328 U.S. 256 (1946).

(5) Persons held in official custody may challenge the constitutionality of their detention by writ of habeas corpus (or a statutory substitute for the writ such as 28 U.S.C. § 2255). See, e.g., Fay v. Noia, 372 U.S. 391 (1963).

(6) One may bring a suit seeking an injunction or a declaratory judgment as to the constitutionality of a statute. Frequently such an action is brought in order to challenge constitutionality without taking the risk of civil or criminal liability involved in acting in disregard of the statute. A large portion of constitutional litigation takes this form.

(2) **Relevance of Form of Litigation to Justiciability.** Few issues of justiciability arise where constitutional issues are determined in suits taking the first five forms described above. The litigation involves adverse parties in traditional forms. The constitutional issue is posed in a way quite compatible with the theory of Marbury v. Madison. However, when suits are brought seeking to enjoin the enforcement of statutes on the ground of unconstitutionality or seeking judgments declaring statutes unconstitutional, problems of case and controversy and justiciability frequently arise. The student will notice that most of the cases in this section involve such suits.

B. STANDING

1. "CONVENTIONAL" STANDING

WARTH v. SELDIN

422 U.S. 490, 95 S.Ct. 2197, 45 L.Ed.2d 343 (1975).

Mr. Justice Powell delivered the opinion of the Court.

Petitioners, various organizations and individuals resident in the Rochester, New York, metropolitan area, brought this action in the District Court for the Western District of New York against the Town of Penfield, an incorporated municipality adjacent to Rochester, and against members of Penfield's Zoning, Planning, and Town Boards. Petitioners claimed that the town's zoning ordinance, by its terms and as enforced by the defendant board members, respondents here, effectively excluded persons of low and moderate income from living in the town, in contravention of petitioners' First, Ninth, and Fourteenth Amendment rights and in violation of 42 U.S.C. §§ 1981, 1982, and 1983. The District Court dismissed the complaint and denied a motion by petitioner Rochester Home Builders Association, Inc., for leave to intervene as party-plaintiff. The Court of Appeals for the Second Circuit affirmed, holding that none of the plaintiffs, nor Home Builders Association, had standing to prosecute the action. 495 F.2d 1187 (1974). . . .

. . . .

II

We address first the principles of standing relevant to the claims asserted by the several categories of petitioners in this case. In essence the question of standing is whether the litigant is entitled to have the court decide the merits of the dispute or of particular issues. This inquiry involves both constitutional limitations on federal court jurisdiction and prudential limitations on its exercise. E.g., Barrows v. Jackson, 346 U.S. 249, 255–256 (1953). In both dimensions it is founded in concern about the proper—and properly limited—role of the courts in a democratic society. . . .

In its constitutional dimension, standing imports justiciability: whether the plaintiff has made out a "case or controversy" between himself and the defendant within the meaning of Art. III. This is the threshold question in every federal case, determining the power of the court to entertain the suit. As an aspect of justiciability, the standing question is whether the plaintiff has "alleged such a personal stake in the outcome of the controversy" as to warrant *his* invocation of federal-court jurisdiction and to justify exercise of the court's remedial powers on his behalf. . . . The Art. III judicial power exists only to redress or otherwise to protect against injury to the complaining party, even though the court's judgment may benefit others collaterally. A federal court's jurisdiction therefore can be invoked only when the plaintiff himself has suffered "some threatened or actual injury resulting from the putatively illegal action . . .." Linda R.S. v. Richard D., 410 U.S. 614, 617 (1973). See Data Processing Service v. Camp, 397 U.S. 150, 151–154 (1970).

Apart from this minimum constitutional mandate, this Court has recognized other limits on the class of persons who may invoke the courts' decisional and remedial powers. First, the Court has held that when the asserted harm is a "generalized grievance" shared in substantially equal measure by all or a large class of citizens, that harm alone normally does not warrant exercise of jurisdiction. . . . Second, even when the plaintiff has alleged injury sufficient to meet the "case or controversy" requirement, this Court has held that the plaintiff generally must assert his own legal rights and interests, and cannot rest his claim to relief on the legal rights or interests of third parties. . . . Without such limitations—closely related to Art. III concerns but essentially matters of judicial self-governance—the courts would be called upon to decide abstract questions of wide public significance even though other governmental institutions may be more competent to address the questions and even though judicial intervention may be unnecessary to protect individual rights. . . .

Although standing in no way depends on the merits of the plaintiff's contention that particular conduct is illegal, . . . it often turns on the nature and source of the claim asserted. The actual or threatened injury required by Art. III may exist solely by virtue of "statutes creating legal rights, the invasion of which creates standing . . .." . . . Moreover, the source of the plaintiff's claim to relief assumes critical importance with respect to the prudential rules of standing that, apart from Art. III's minimum requirements, serve to limit the role of the courts in resolving public disputes. Essentially, the standing question in such cases is whether the constitutional or statutory provision on which the claim rests properly can be understood as granting persons in the plaintiff's position a right to judicial relief. In some circumstances, countervailing considerations may outweigh the concerns underlying the usual reluctance to exert judicial power when the plaintiff's claim to relief rests on the legal rights of third parties. . . . In such instances, the Court has found, in effect, that the constitutional or statutory provision in question implies a right of action in the plaintiff. . . . See generally Part IV, *infra.* Moreover, Congress may grant an express right of action to persons who otherwise would be barred by prudential standing rules. Of course, Art. III's requirement remains: the plaintiff still must allege a distinct and palpable injury to himself, even if it is an injury shared by a large class of other possible litigants. . . . But so long as this requirement is satisfied, persons to whom Congress has granted a right of action, either expressly or by clear implication, may have standing to seek relief on the basis of the legal rights and interests of others, and, indeed, may invoke the general public interest in support of their claim. . . .

One further preliminary matter requires discussion. For purposes of ruling on a motion to dismiss for want of standing, both the trial and reviewing courts must accept as true all material allegations of the complaint, and must construe the complaint in favor of the complaining party. . . . At the same time, it is within the trial court's power to allow or to require the plaintiff to supply, by amendment to the complaint or by affidavits, further particularized allegations of fact deemed supportive of plaintiff's standing. If, after this opportunity, the plaintiff's standing does not adequately appear from all materials of record, the complaint must be dismissed.

III

With these general considerations in mind, we turn first to the claims of petitioners Ortiz, Reyes, Sinkler, and Broadnax, each of whom asserts standing as a person of low or moderate income and, coincidentally, as a member of a minority racial or ethnic group. We must assume, taking the allegations of the complaint as true, that Penfield's zoning ordinance and the pattern of enforcement by respondent officials have had the purpose and effect of excluding persons of low and moderate income, many of whom are members of racial or ethnic minority groups. We also assume, for purposes here, that such intentional exclusionary practices, if proved in a proper case, would be adjudged violative of the constitutional and statutory rights of the persons excluded.

But the fact that these petitioners share attributes common to persons who may have been excluded from residence in the town is an insufficient predicate for the conclusion that petitioners themselves have been excluded, or that the respondents' assertedly illegal actions have violated their rights. Petitioners must allege and show that they personally have been injured, not that injury has been suffered by other, unidentified members of the class to which they belong and which they purport to represent. Unless these petitioners can thus demonstrate the requisite case or controversy between themselves personally and respondents, "none may seek relief on behalf of himself or any other member of the class."

In their complaint, petitioners Ortiz, Reyes, Sinkler, and Broadnax alleged in conclusory terms that they are among the persons excluded by respondents' actions. None of them has ever resided in Penfield; each claims at least implicitly that he desires, or has desired, to do so. Each asserts, moreover, that he made some effort, at some time, to locate housing in Penfield that was at once within his means and adequate for his family's needs. Each claims that his efforts proved fruitless. We may assume, as petitioners allege, that respondents' actions have contributed, perhaps substantially, to the cost of housing in Penfield. But there remains the question whether petitioners' inability to locate suitable housing in Penfield reasonably can be said to have resulted, in any concretely demonstrable way, from respondents' alleged constitutional and statutory infractions. Petitioners must allege facts from which it reasonably could be inferred that, absent the respondents' restrictive zoning practices, there is a substantial probability that they would have been able to purchase or lease in Penfield and that, if the court affords the relief requested, the asserted inability of petitioners will be removed. . . .

We find the record devoid of the necessary allegations. As the Court of Appeals noted, none of these petitioners has a present interest in any Penfield property; none is himself subject to the ordinance's strictures; and none has ever been denied a variance or permit by respondent officials. Instead, petitioners claim that respondents' enforcement of the ordinance against third parties—developers, builders, and the like—has had the consequence of precluding the construction of housing suitable to their needs at prices they might be able to afford. The fact that the harm to petitioners may have resulted indirectly does not in itself preclude standing. When a governmental prohibition or restriction imposed on one party causes specific harm to a third party, harm that a constitutional provision or statute was intended to prevent, the indirectness of the injury does not necessarily deprive the person harmed of standing to vindicate his rights. E.g., Roe v. Wade, 410 U.S. 113, 124, 147 (1973). But it may make it substantially more difficult to meet the minimum requirement of Art. III: to establish that, in fact, the asserted injury was the consequence of the defendants' actions, or that prospective relief will remove the harm.

Here, by their own admission, realization of petitioners' desire to live in Penfield always has depended on the efforts and willingness of third parties to build low-and moderate-cost housing. The record specifically refers to only two such efforts: that of Penfield Better Homes Corp., in late 1969, to obtain the rezoning of certain land in Penfield to allow the construction of subsidized cooperative townhouses that could be purchased by persons of moderate income; and a similar effort by O'Brien Homes, Inc., in late 1971. But the record is devoid of any indication that these projects, or other like projects, would have satisfied petitioners' needs at prices they could afford, or that, were the court to remove the obstructions attributable to respondents, such relief would benefit petitioners. Indeed, petitioners' descriptions of their individual financial situations and housing needs suggest precisely the contrary—that their inability to reside in Penfield is the consequence of the economics of the area housing market, rather than of respondents' assertedly illegal acts.[16] In short, the facts alleged fail to support an actionable causal relationship between Penfield's zoning practices and petitioners' asserted injury.

In support of their position, petitioners refer to several decisions in the District Courts and Courts of Appeals, acknowledging standing in low-income, minority-group plaintiffs to challenge exclusionary zoning practices. In those cases, however, the plaintiffs challenged zoning restrictions as applied to particular projects that would supply housing within their means, and of which they were intended residents. The plaintiffs thus were able to demonstrate that unless relief from assertedly illegal actions was forthcoming, their immediate and personal interests would be harmed. Petitioners here assert no like circumstances. Instead, they rely on little more than the remote possibility, unsubstantiated by allegations of fact, that their situation might have been better

[16] Ortiz states in his affidavit that he is now purchasing and resides in a six-bedroom dwelling in Wayland, N.Y.; and that he owns and receives rental income from a house in Rochester. He is concerned with finding a house or apartment large enough for himself, his wife, and seven children, but states that he can afford to spend a maximum of $120 per month for housing. Broadnax seeks a four-bedroom house or apartment for herself and six children, and can spend a maximum of about $120 per month for housing. Sinkler also states that she can spend $120 per month for housing for herself and two children. Thus, at least in the cases of Ortiz and Broadnax, it is doubtful that their stated needs could have been satisfied by the small housing units contemplated in the only moderate-cost projects specifically described in the record. Moreover, there is no indication that any of the petitioners had the resources necessary to acquire the housing available in the projects. The matter is left entirely obscure. The income and housing budget figures supplied in petitioners' affidavits are presumably for the year 1972. The vague description of the proposed O'Brien development strongly suggests that the units, even if adequate for their needs, would have been beyond the means at least of Sinkler and Broadnax. . . . Petitioner Reyes presents a special case: she states that her family has an income of over $14,000 per year, that she can afford $231 per month for housing, and that, in the past and apparently now, she wants to purchase a residence. . . . Penfield Better Homes defined the term ["low and moderate income"] as between $5,000 and $8,000 per year. Since that project was to be subsidized, presumably petitioner Reyes would have been ineligible. There is no indication that in nonsubsidized projects, removal of the challenged zoning restrictions—in 1972—would have reduced the price on new single-family residences to a level that petitioner Reyes thought she could afford.

had respondents acted otherwise, and might improve were the court to afford relief.

. We hold only that a plaintiff who seeks to challenge exclusionary zoning practices must allege specific, concrete facts demonstrating that the challenged practices harm *him,* and that he personally would benefit in a tangible way from the court's intervention.[18]   .   .   .   Schlesinger v. Reservists to Stop the War, 418 U.S., at 221–222.

IV

The petitioners who assert standing on the basis of their status as taxpayers of the city of Rochester present a different set of problems. These "taxpayer-petitioners" claim that they are suffering economic injury consequent to Penfield's allegedly discriminatory and exclusionary zoning practices. Their argument, in brief, is that Penfield's persistent refusal to allow or to facilitate construction of low-and moderate-cost housing forces the city of Rochester to provide more such housing than it otherwise would do; that to provide such housing, Rochester must allow certain tax abatements; and that as the amount of tax-abated property increases, Rochester taxpayers are forced to assume an increased tax burden in order to finance essential public services.

.   .   .

.   .   . In short the claim of these petitioners falls squarely within the prudential standing rule that normally bars litigants from asserting the rights or legal interests of others in order to obtain relief from injury to themselves. As we have observed above, this rule of judicial self-governance is subject to exceptions, the most prominent of which is that Congress may remove it by statute. Here, however, no statute expressly or by clear implication grants a right of action, and thus standing to seek relief, to persons in petitioners' position. In several cases, this Court has allowed standing to litigate the rights of third parties when enforcement of the challenged restriction against the litigant would result indirectly in the violation of third parties' rights.   .   .   . But the taxpayer-petitioners are not themselves subject to Penfield's zoning practices. Nor do they allege that the challenged zoning ordinance and practices preclude or otherwise adversely affect a relationship existing between them and the persons whose rights assertedly are violated.   .   .   .   No relationship, other than an incidental congruity of interest, is alleged to exist between the Rochester taxpayers and persons who have been precluded from living in Penfield. Nor do the taxpayer-petitioners show that their prosecution of the suit is necessary to insure protection of the rights asserted, as there is no indication that persons who in fact have been excluded from Penfield are disabled from asserting their own right in a proper case. In sum, we discern no justification for recognizing in the Rochester taxpayers a right of action on the asserted claim.

V

We turn next to the standing problems presented by the petitioner associations—Metro-Act of Rochester, Inc., one of the original plaintiffs; Housing Council in the Monroe County Area, Inc., which the original plaintiffs sought to

---

[18] This is not to say that the plaintiff who challenges a zoning ordinance or zoning practices must have a present contractual interest in a particular project. A particularized personal interest may be shown in various ways, which we need not undertake to identify in the abstract. But usually the initial focus should be on a particular project. See, e.g., cases cited in n. 17, supra. We also note that zoning laws and their provisions, long considered essential to effective urban planning, are peculiarly within the province of state and local legislative authorities. They are, of course, subject to judicial review in a proper case. But citizens dissatisfied with provisions of such laws need not overlook the availability of the normal democratic process.

join as a party-plaintiff; and Rochester Home Builders Association, Inc., which moved in the District Court for leave to intervene as plaintiff.   There is no question that an association may have standing in its own right to seek judicial relief from injury to itself and to vindicate whatever rights and immunities the association itself may enjoy.   Moreover, in attempting to secure relief from injury to itself the association may assert the rights of its members, at least so long as the challenged infractions adversely affect its members' associational ties. . . .   With the limited exception of Metro-Act, however, none of the associational petitioners here has asserted injury to itself.

Even in the absence of injury to itself, an association may have standing solely as the representative of its members. . . .   The possibility of such representational standing, however, does not eliminate or attenuate the constitutional requirement of a case or controversy. . . .   The association must allege that its members, or any one of them, are suffering immediate or threatened injury as a result of the challenged action of the sort that would make out a justiciable case had the members themselves brought suit. . . .   So long as this can be established, and so long as the nature of the claim and of the relief sought does not make the individual participation of each injured party indispensable to proper resolution of the cause, the association may be an appropriate representative of its members, entitled to invoke the court's jurisdiction.

A

Petitioner Metro-Act's claims to standing on its own behalf as a Rochester taxpayer, and on behalf of its members who are Rochester taxpayers or persons of low or moderate income, are precluded by our holdings in Parts III and IV, supra, as to the individual petitioners, and require no further discussion. Metro-Act . . . alleges . . . that 9% of its membership is composed of present residents of Penfield.   It claims that, as a result of the persistent pattern of exclusionary zoning practiced by respondents and the consequent exclusion of persons of low and moderate income, those of its members who are Penfield residents are deprived of the benefits of living in a racially and ethnically integrated community.   Referring to our decision in Trafficante v. Metropolitan Life Ins. Co., 409 U.S. 205 (1972), Metro-Act argues that such deprivation is a sufficiently palpable injury to satisfy the Art. III case-or-controversy requirement, and that it has standing as the representative of its members to seek redress.

We agree with the Court of Appeals that *Trafficante* is not controlling here. In that case, two residents of an apartment complex alleged that the owner had discriminated against rental applicants on the basis of race, in violation of § 804 of the Civil Rights Act of 1968, 82 Stat. 83, 42 U.S.C. § 3604. . . .   In light of the clear congressional purpose in enacting the 1968 Act, and the broad definition of "person aggrieved" in § 810(a), 42 U.S.C. § 3610(a), we held that petitioners, as "person[s] who claim[ed] to have been injured by a discriminatory housing practice," had standing to litigate violations of the Act. We concluded that Congress had given residents of housing facilities covered by the statute an actionable right to be free from the adverse consequences to them of racially discriminatory practices directed at and immediately harmful to others.   409 U.S., at 212.

Metro-Act does not assert on behalf of its members any right of action under the 1968 Civil Rights Act, nor can the complaint fairly be read to make out any such claim.   In this, we think, lies the critical distinction between *Trafficante* and the situation here.   As we have observed above, Congress may create a statutory right or entitlement the alleged deprivation of which can confer standing to sue even where the plaintiff would have suffered no judicially cognizable injury in the absence of statute. . . .

Even if we assume, *arguendo,* that apart from any statutorily created right the asserted harm to Metro-Act's Penfield members is sufficiently direct and personal to satisfy the case-or-controversy requirement of Art. III, prudential considerations strongly counsel against according them or Metro-Act standing to prosecute this action. We do not understand Metro-Act to argue that Penfield residents themselves have been denied any constitutional rights, affording them a cause of action under 42 U.S.C. § 1983. Instead, their complaint is that they have been harmed indirectly by the exclusion of others. This is an attempt to raise putative rights of third parties, and none of the exceptions that allow such claims is present here. In these circumstances, we conclude that it is inappropriate to allow Metro-Act to invoke the judicial process.

B

Petitioner Home Builders, in its intervenor-complaint, asserted standing to represent its member firms engaged in the development and construction of residential housing in the Rochester area, including Penfield. Home Builders alleged that the Penfield zoning restrictions, together with refusals by the town officials to grant variances and permits for the construction of low-and moderate-cost housing, had deprived some of its members of "substantial business opportunities and profits." Home Builders claimed damages of $750,000 and also joined in the original plaintiffs' prayer for declaratory and injunctive relief.

As noted above, to justify any relief the association must show that it has suffered harm, or that one or more of its members are injured. . . .

Home Builders alleges no monetary injury to itself, nor any assignment of the damages claims of its members. No award therefore can be made to the association as such. Moreover, in the circumstances of this case, the damages claims are not common to the entire membership, nor shared by all in equal degree. To the contrary, whatever injury may have been suffered is peculiar to the individual member concerned, and both the fact and extent of injury would require individualized proof. Thus, to obtain relief in damages, each member of Home Builders who claims injury as a result of respondents' practices must be a party to the suit, and Home Builders has no standing to claim damages on his behalf.

Home Builders' prayer for prospective relief fails for a different reason. It can have standing as the representative of its members only if it has alleged facts sufficient to make out a case or controversy had the members themselves brought suit. No such allegations were made. The complaint refers to no specific project of any of its members that is currently precluded either by the ordinance or by respondents' action in enforcing it. There is no averment that any member has applied to respondents for a building permit or a variance with respect to any current project. Indeed, there is no indication that respondents have delayed or thwarted any project currently proposed by Home Builders' members, or that any of its members has taken advantage of the remedial processes available under the ordinance. In short, insofar as the complaint seeks prospective relief, Home Builders has failed to show the existence of any injury to its members of sufficient immediacy and ripeness to warrant judicial intervention.

A like problem is presented with respect to petitioner Housing Council. The affidavit accompanying the motion to join it as plaintiff states that the Council includes in its membership "at least seventeen" groups that have been, are, or will be involved in the development of low- and moderate-cost housing. But, with one exception, the complaint does not suggest that any of these groups has focused its efforts on Penfield or has any specific plan to do so.

Again with the same exception, neither the complaint nor any materials of record indicate that any member of Housing Council has taken any step toward building housing in Penfield, or has had dealings of any nature with respondents. The exception is the Penfield Better Homes Corp. As we have observed above, it applied to respondents in late 1969 for a zoning variance to allow construction of a housing project designed for persons of moderate income. . . . It is therefore possible that in 1969, or within a reasonable time thereafter, Better Homes itself and possibly Housing Council as its representative would have had standing to seek review of respondents' action. The complaint, however, does not allege that the Penfield Better Homes project remained viable in 1972 when this complaint was filed, or that respondents' actions continued to block a then-current construction project. In short, neither the complaint nor the record supplies any basis from which to infer that the controversy between respondents and Better Homes, however vigorous it may once have been, remained a live, concrete dispute when this complaint was filed.

VI

The rules of standing, whether as aspects of the Art. III case-or-controversy requirement or as reflections of prudential considerations defining and limiting the role of the courts, are threshold determinants of the propriety of judicial intervention. It is the responsibility of the complainant clearly to allege facts demonstrating that he is a proper party to invoke judicial resolution of the dispute and the exercise of the court's remedial powers. We agree with the District Court and the Court of Appeals that none of the petitioners here has met this threshold requirement. Accordingly, the judgment of the Court of Appeals is

Affirmed.

Mr. Justice Douglas, dissenting.

.   .   .

Standing has become a barrier to access to the federal courts, just as "the political question" was in earlier decades. The mounting caseload of federal courts is well known. But cases such as this one reflect festering sores in our society; and the American dream teaches that if one reaches high enough and persists there is a forum where justice is dispensed. I would lower the technical barriers and let the courts serve that ancient need. . . .

.   .   .

. . . I would let the case go to trial and have all the facts brought out. Indeed, it would be better practice to decide the question of standing only when the merits have been developed.

I would reverse the Court of Appeals.

Mr. Justice Brennan, with whom Mr. Justice White and Mr. Justice Marshall join, dissenting.

In this case, a wide range of plaintiffs, alleging various kinds of injuries, claimed to have been affected by the Penfield zoning ordinance, on its face and as applied, and by other practices of the defendant officials of Penfield. Alleging that as a result of these laws and practices low- and moderate-income and minority people have been excluded from Penfield, and that this exclusion is unconstitutional, plaintiffs sought injunctive, declaratory, and monetary relief. The Court today, in an opinion that purports to be a "standing" opinion but that actually, I believe, has overtones of outmoded notions of pleading and of justiciability, refuses to find that any of the variously situated plaintiffs can clear numerous hurdles, some constructed here for the first time, necessary to establish "standing." While the Court gives lip service to the principle, oft repeated in recent years, that "standing in no way depends on the merits of the plaintiff's contention that particular conduct is illegal," in fact the opinion, which tosses out of court almost every conceivable kind of plaintiff who could be injured by the activity claimed to be unconstitutional, can be explained only by an indefensible hostility to the claim on the merits. I can appreciate the Court's reluctance to adjudicate the complex and difficult legal questions involved in determining the constitutionality of practices which assertedly limit residence in a particular municipality to those who are white and relatively well off, and I also understand that the merits of this case could involve grave sociological and political ramifications. But courts cannot refuse to hear a case on the merits merely because they would prefer not to, and it is quite clear, when the record is viewed with dispassion, that at least three of the groups of plaintiffs have made allegations, and supported them with affidavits and documentary evidence, sufficient to survive a motion to dismiss for lack of standing.

. . .

II

Low-income and Minority Plaintiffs

. . .

. . . [T]he Court's real holding is not that these petitioners have not *alleged* an injury resulting from respondents' action, but that they are not to be allowed to prove one, because "realization of petitioners' desire to live in Penfield always has depended on the efforts and willingness of third parties to build low- and moderate-cost housing," and "the record is devoid of any indication that . . . [any] projects, would have satisfied petitioners' needs at prices they could afford."

Certainly, this is not the sort of demonstration that can or should be required of petitioners at this preliminary stage. . . .

Here, the very fact that, as the Court stresses, these petitioners' claim rests in part upon proving the intentions and capabilities of third parties to build in Penfield suitable housing which they can afford, coupled with the exclusionary character of the claim on the merits, makes it particularly inappropriate to assume that these petitioners' lack of specificity reflects a fatal weakness in their theory of causation. Obviously they cannot be expected, prior to discovery and trial, to know the future plans of building companies, the precise details of the housing market in Penfield, or everything which has transpired in 15 years of application of the Penfield zoning ordinance, including every housing plan suggested and refused. To require them to allege such facts is to require them to prove their case on paper in order to get into court at all. . . .

III

Associations Including Building Concerns

. . .

Again, the Court ignores the thrust of the complaints and asks petitioners to allege the impossible. According to the allegations, the building concerns' experience in the past with Penfield officials has shown any plans for low- and moderate-income housing to be futile for, again according to the allegations, the respondents are engaged in a purposeful, conscious scheme to exclude such housing. Particularly with regard to a low- or moderate-income project, the cost of litigating, with respect to any particular project, the legality of a refusal to approve it may well be prohibitive. And the merits of the exclusion of this or that project is not at the heart of the complaint; the claim is that respondents will not approve *any* project which will provide residences for low- and moderate-income people.

When this sort of pattern-and-practice claim is at the heart of the controversy, allegations of past injury, which members of both of these organizations have clearly made, and of a future intent, if the barriers are cleared, again to develop suitable housing for Penfield, should be more than sufficient. The past experiences, if proved at trial, will give credibility and substance to the claim of interest in future building activity in Penfield. These parties, if their allegations are proved, certainly have the requisite personal stake in the outcome of *this* controversy, and the Court's conclusion otherwise is only a conclusion that *this* controversy may not be litigated in a federal court.

I would reverse the judgment of the Court of Appeals.

––––––––

VILLAGE OF ARLINGTON HEIGHTS v. METROPOLITAN HOUSING DEVELOPMENT CORP., 429 U.S. 252 (1977). Metropolitan Housing Development Corporation (MHDC), a builder of low and moderate income housing in the Chicago area, contracted to purchase a 15-acre site in the Village of Arlington Heights. The contract was contingent upon MHDC securing zoning clearances from the Village and federal approval to build a 190-unit project with subsidies under § 236 of the National Housing Act. MHDC submitted detailed plans for the project to the Village which refused to rezone the property to permit the construction of multiple-family housing. MHDC and three Black individuals brought suit in the federal district court seeking an injunction and declaratory relief, alleging that the denial was racially discriminatory. The district court held that the plaintiffs had standing but ruled for the defendants on the merits. The court of appeals reversed on the merits and the defendants petitioned for certiorari. The Supreme Court, in an opinion by Justice Powell (and with no apparent dissent on this point) held that the plaintiffs had standing, saying, in part:

"A.

"Here there can be little doubt that MHDC meets the constitutional standing requirements. The challenged action of the petitioners stands as an absolute barrier to constructing the housing MHDC had contracted to place on the Viatorian site. If MHDC secures the injunctive relief it seeks, that barrier will be removed. An injunction would not, of course, guarantee that Lincoln Green will be built. MHDC would still have to secure financing, qualify for federal subsidies, and carry through with construction. But all housing developments are subject to some extent to similar uncertainties. When a project is as detailed and specific as Lincoln Green, a court is not required to engage in undue speculation as a predicate for finding that the plaintiff has the requisite personal stake in the controversy. MHDC has shown an injury to itself that is 'likely to be redressed by a favorable decision.' . . .

"Petitioners nonetheless appear to argue that MHDC lacks standing because it has suffered no economic injury. MHDC, they point out, is not the owner of the property in question. Its contract of purchase is contingent upon securing rezoning.[8] MHDC owes the owners nothing if rezoning is denied.

––––

[8] Petitioners contend that MHDC lacks standing to pursue its claim here because a contract purchaser whose contract is contingent upon rezoning cannot contest a zoning decision in the Illinois courts. Under the law of Illinois, only the owner of the property has standing to pursue such an action. . . .

State law of standing, however, does not govern such determinations in the federal courts. The constitutional and prudential considerations canvassed at length in Warth v. Seldin, 422 U.S. 490 (1975), respond to concerns that are peculiarly federal in nature. Illinois may choose to close its courts to applicants for rezoning unless they have an interest more direct than MHDC's, but this

"We cannot accept petitioners' argument. In the first place, it is inaccurate to say that MHDC suffers no economic injury from a refusal to rezone, despite the contingency provisions in its contract. MHDC has expended thousands of dollars on the plans for Lincoln Green and on the studies submitted to the Village in support of the petition for rezoning. Unless rezoning is granted, many of these plans and studies will be worthless even if MHDC finds another site at an equally attractive price.

"Petitioners' argument also misconceives our standing requirements. It has long been clear that economic injury is not the only kind of injury that can support a plaintiff's standing. . . . MHDC is a nonprofit corporation. Its interest in building Lincoln Green stems not from a desire for economic gain, but rather from an interest in making suitable low-cost housing available in areas where such housing is scarce. This is not mere abstract concern about a problem of general interest. . . . The specific project MHDC intends to build, whether or not it will generate profits, provides that 'essential dimension of specificity' that informs judicial decisionmaking. . . .

"B.

"Clearly MHDC has met the constitutional requirements and it therefore has standing to assert its own rights. Foremost among them is MHDC's right to be free of arbitrary or irrational zoning actions. . . . [T]he heart of this litigation . . . has been the claim that the Village's refusal to rezone discriminates against racial minorities in violation of the Fourteenth Amendment. As a corporation, MHDC has no racial identity and cannot be the direct target of the petitioners' alleged discrimination. In the ordinary case, a party is denied standing to assert the rights of third persons. Warth v. Seldin, 422 U.S., at 499. But we need not decide whether the circumstances of this case would justify departure from that prudential limitation and permit MHDC to assert the constitutional rights of its prospective minority tenants. . . . For we have at least one individual plaintiff who has demonstrated standing to assert these rights as his own.

"Respondent Ransom, a Negro, works at the Honeywell factory in Arlington Heights and lives approximately 20 miles away in Evanston in a 5-room house with his mother and his son. The complaint alleged that he seeks and would qualify for the housing MHDC wants to build in Arlington Heights. Ransom testified at trial that if Lincoln Green were built he would probably move there, since it is closer to his job.

"The injury Ransom asserts is that his quest for housing nearer his employment has been thwarted by official action that is racially discriminatory. If a court grants the relief he seeks, there is at least a 'substantial probability,' that the Lincoln Green project will materialize, affording Ransom the housing opportunity he desires in Arlington Heights. His is not a generalized grievance. Instead, as we suggested in *Warth*, id., at 507, 508 n. 18, it focuses on a particular project and is not dependent on speculation about the possible actions of third parties not before the court. . . . Unlike the individual plaintiffs in *Warth*, Ransom has adequately averred an 'actionable causal relationship' between Arlington Heights' zoning practices and his asserted injury. Warth v. Seldin, 422 U.S., at 507. We therefore proceed to the merits." [a]

———

choice does not necessarily disqualify MHDC from seeking relief in federal courts for an asserted injury to its federal rights.

[a] For the decision on the merits, see infra p. 758.

STANDING AND THE REQUIREMENT
OF "INJURY IN FACT"

Dicta in Flast v. Cohen, 392 U.S. 83, 102 (1968), stated that to establish standing, plaintiffs must demonstrate not only that they were injured by the challenged legislation but must also show a nexus between that injury and the constitutional violation claimed. The supposed requirement of "nexus" was at issue in Duke Power Co. v. Carolina Environmental Study Group, 438 U.S. 59 (1978). People living near a nuclear power plant under construction brought suit for a declaratory judgment that the Price-Anderson Act was unconstitutional in limiting liability for nuclear accidents in federally licensed private nuclear power plants. The federal district court reached the merits, and held the statute unconstitutional as a violation of the due process clause of the fifth amendment. On direct appeal, the Supreme Court reversed, on the merits.

The Court raised on its own motion, and rejected, the argument that plaintiffs lacked standing to challenge the limitation of liability. The "injury in fact" relied upon by the Court to establish standing, however, was not the possibility that the plaintiffs would be denied adequate compensation in the event of a future nuclear accident. Instead, the relevant injury stemmed from the environmental and esthetic harm that would occur to the plaintiffs by the building of the plant. The statute "caused" the injury only because, without the limitation-of-liability provision, nuclear plants would not be built.

The Court concluded that it was not necessary, to establish standing, that plaintiffs' injuries be caused directly by the alleged unconstitutional feature of the statute—the denial of full compensation in the event of nuclear accident. It was enough to show that without the limitation-of-liability provision the proposed plant would not be built and the environmental injury would not occur. The requirement of nexus was limited to standing in taxpayers' suits.[1]   In conventional lawsuits, a plaintiff need only demonstrate "injury in fact and a substantial likelihood that the judicial relief requested will prevent or redress the claimed injury" in order to establish standing.[2]   Plaintiffs had met that standard.[3]

Consider the following cases dealing with the issue whether plaintiffs had shown the requisite injury in fact to establish standing. Are they consistent? [4]

Linda R.S. v. Richard D., 410 U.S. 614 (1973). The mother of a child born out of wedlock brought suit to compel a state prosecutor to prosecute the child's father for non-support. Plaintiff challenged the constitutionality of a state statute making failure to support children a crime because the state courts had construed it to apply only to the parents of children born in marriage. The Supreme Court concluded plaintiff had no standing. Plaintiff had shown injury from the father's failure to pay support, but it was speculative that the relief requested—jailing the father—would remedy the injury by providing support payments from him.

Sierra Club v. Morton, 405 U.S. 727 (1972). The Court held that an environmental group lacked standing to challenge the construction of a recreation area in a national forest. The fact that the Sierra Club—which did not allege that any of its members were affected by the proposed development—had

---

[1] The problem of standing in taxpayers' suits is examined below in subsection 3.

[2] As in Warth v. Seldin, the Court stated that even when the requisite injury in fact was established, other limits stemming from prudential concerns might apply.

[3] For an argument that *Duke Power* was a departure from traditional standards of standing and ripeness, see Varat, *Variable Justiciability and the Duke Power Case,* 58 Tex.L.Rev. 273 (1980).

[4] For an argument that they are not, unless many other factors beyond the issue of "injury in fact" are considered, see Nichol, *Rethinking Standing,* 72 Cal.L.Rev. 68 (1984).

an interest in the problem of maintaining the environment did not confer standing.

United States v. SCRAP, 412 U.S. 669 (1973). An environmental group had standing to challenge a railroad rate structure of the Interstate Commerce Commission claimed to discourage the shipment, and use, of recycled materials and promote the use of raw materials. Plaintiff alleged that its members (five law students): were caused to pay more for finished products; used the forests, rivers, mountains and other natural resources in the vicinity of Washington, D.C. and those recreational uses had been affected by increased littering; breathed the air in the Washington metropolitan area, which had suffered increased air pollution. All of these effects were alleged to be caused by the ICC rate structure which caused the increased use of raw materials and decreased recycling. (In *Sierra Club* the plaintiff had alleged only a "public interest" and not the injury to its members.)

SCRAP, like *Sierra Club,* was an action based on a provision of the Administrative Procedure Act, conferring standing to sue on persons "adversely affected" or "aggrieved" by an agency's decision. The Court concluded that standing, under that provision, was neither confined to those who suffer economic harm nor denied to many people who suffer the same injury. Otherwise, the most injurious and widespread government actions could be questioned by nobody. (On the merits, the Court reversed the lower court's decision enjoining the Commission's rate structure.)

Simon v. Eastern Kentucky Welfare Rights Organization, 426 U.S. 26 (1976). Indigent persons lacked standing to challenge Internal Revenue Service rulings granting favorable tax treatment to nonprofit hospitals providing inadequate hospital services to indigents. Allegations that the rulings "encouraged" hospitals to deny services were speculative. It was just as plausible that the relevant hospitals would forego favorable tax treatment rather than expend substantial funds for increased hospital services to indigents. Thus, plaintiffs' complaint did not demonstrate a substantial likelihood that declaring the rulings invalid would result in their receiving the hospital services they desire.

Allen v. Wright, 104 S.Ct. 3315 (1984). Parents of black children attending public schools did not have standing to challenge IRS practices concerning denial of tax exemptions to racially discriminatory private schools. Plaintiffs' allegations that the IRS practices inhibited the process of desegregation in their children's public schools did not show injury traceable to the challenged government policy. It was speculative whether denial of tax exemption to any private school would induce it to change its policies and whether children would be transferred to public schools if their private schools were threatened with loss of tax exemption.

Orr v. Orr, 440 U.S. 268 (1979). A divorced husband had standing to challenge the constitutionality of a state statute that required divorced husbands to pay alimony, but did not require payment by similarly-situated wives. It was argued that if the state courts resolved the constitutional problem by extending alimony rights to needy husbands, Mr. Orr would not be relieved of his alimony obligation. (In other words, only a needy husband seeking support from his wife would have standing.) It was, however, possible that the state could respond to a decision that the law was unconstitutional by denying alimony to both needy wives and needy husbands, and that would eliminate Mr. Orr's obligation to pay alimony. Because there was no way to predict what the state court would do, Mr. Orr had standing. (On the merits, the Court held that the statute was unconstitutional.[5] After remand, Mr. Orr lost in the state courts,

[5] For the decision on the merits, see p. 780, infra.

because the unconstitutional distinction was remedied by extending alimony rights to needy husbands.)

Heckler v. Mathews, 104 S.Ct. 1387 (1984). A husband challenged a provision of the Social Security Act providing lower benefits to husbands of female workers than to wives of male workers. A severability clause in the statute provided that if the provision were held invalid, equality should be achieved by denying benefits to wives of male workers. It was argued that plaintiff did not have standing because, if he succeeded, he would not receive the benefits he had been denied; the grant of benefits to wives, which would be invalidated if plaintiff prevailed, did not injure the plaintiff. The Court rejected the argument and reached the merits, sustaining the challenged provision. Plaintiff's injury was to his alleged constitutional right to equal treatment. Denial of that right can cause serious noneconomic injury. Withdrawal of benefits to others would redress that injury.

2. STANDING TO ASSERT THE RIGHTS OF THIRD PARTIES

CRAIG v. BOREN

429 U.S. 190, 97 S.Ct. 451, 50 L.Ed.2d 397 (1976).

Mr. Justice Brennan delivered the opinion of the Court.

This action was brought in the District Court for the Western District of Oklahoma on December 20, 1972, by appellant Craig, a male then between 18 and 21 years of age, and by appellant Whitener, a licensed vendor of 3.2% beer. The complaint sought declaratory and injunctive relief against enforcement of [statutes prohibiting the sale of 3.2% beer to males under age 21 and females under age 18] on the ground that it constituted invidious discrimination against males 18–20 years of age. A three-judge court convened under 28 U.S.C. § 2281 sustained the constitutionality of the statutory differential and dismissed the action. 399 F.Supp. 1304 (1975). . . . We reverse.

I

We first address a preliminary question of standing. Appellant Craig attained the age of 21 after we noted probable jurisdiction. Therefore, since only declaratory and injunctive relief against enforcement of the gender-based differential is sought, the controversy has been rendered moot as to Craig. See, e.g., DeFunis v. Odegaard, 416 U.S. 312 (1974).[2] The question thus arises whether appellant Whitener, the licensed vendor of 3.2% beer, who has a live controversy against enforcement of the statute, may rely upon the equal protection objections of males 18–20 years of age to establish her claim of unconstitutionality of the age-sex differential. We conclude that she may.

Initially, it should be noted that, despite having had the opportunity to do so, appellees never raised before the District Court any objection to Whitener's reliance upon the claimed unequal treatment of 18–20-year-old males as the premise of her equal protection challenge to Oklahoma's 3.2% beer law. Indeed, at oral argument Oklahoma acknowledged that appellees always "presumed" that the vendor, subject to sanctions and loss of license for violation of the statute, was a proper party in interest to object to the enforcement of the sex-based regulatory provision. While such a concession certainly would not be controlling upon the reach of this Court's constitutional authority to exercise jurisdiction under Art. III, . . . our decisions have settled that limitations on a litigant's assertion of *jus tertii* are not constitutionally mandated, but rather stem from a salutary "rule of self-restraint" designed to minimize unwarranted

---

[2] Appellants did not seek class certification of Craig as representative of other similarly situated males 18–20 years of age. See, e.g., Sosna v. Iowa, 419 U.S. 393, 401 (1975).

intervention into controversies where the applicable constitutional questions are ill-defined and speculative. See, e.g., Barrows v. Jackson, 346 U.S. 249 (1953); see also Singleton v. Wulff, 428 U.S. 106, 123–124 (1976) (Powell, J., dissenting). These prudential objectives, thought to be enhanced by restrictions on third-party standing, cannot be furthered here, where the lower court already has entertained the relevant constitutional challenge and the parties have sought—or at least have never resisted—an authoritative constitutional determination. In such circumstances, a decision by us to forgo consideration of the constitutional merits in order to await the initiation of a new challenge to the statute by injured third parties would be impermissibly to foster repetitive and time-consuming litigation under the guise of caution and prudence. Moreover, insofar as the applicable constitutional questions have been and continue to be presented vigorously and "cogently," . . . the denial of *jus tertii* standing in deference to a direct class suit can serve no functional purpose. Our Brother Blackmun's comment is pertinent: "[I]t may be that a class could be assembled, whose fluid membership always included some [males] with live claims. But if the assertion of the right is to be 'representative' to such an extent anyway, there seems little loss in terms of effective advocacy from allowing its assertion by" the present *jus tertii* champion. Singleton v. Wulff, supra, at 117–118.

In any event, we conclude that appellant Whitener has established independently her claim to assert *jus tertii* standing. The operation of §§ 241 and 245 plainly has inflicted "injury in fact" upon appellant sufficient to guarantee her "concrete adverseness," . . . and to satisfy the constitutionally based standing requirements imposed by Art. III. The legal duties created by the statutory sections under challenge are addressed directly to vendors such as appellant. She is obliged either to heed the statutory discrimination, thereby incurring a direct economic injury through the constriction of her buyers' market, or to disobey the statutory command and suffer, in the words of Oklahoma's Assistant Attorney General, "sanctions and perhaps loss of license." This Court repeatedly has recognized that such injuries establish the threshold requirements of a "case or controversy" mandated by Art. III. See, e.g., Singleton v. Wulff, supra, at 113, (doctors who receive payments for their abortion services are "classically adverse" to government as payer); Sullivan v. Little Hunting Park, 396 U.S. 229, 237 (1969); Barrows v. Jackson, supra, 346 U.S., at 255–256.

As a vendor with standing to challenge the lawfulness of §§ 241 and 245, appellant Whitener is entitled to assert those concomitant rights of third parties that would be "diluted or adversely affected" should her constitutional challenge fail and the statutes remain in force. Griswold v. Connecticut, 381 U.S. 479, 481; see Note, Standing to Assert Constitutional Jus Tertii, 88 Harv.L. Rev. 423, 432 (1974). Otherwise, the threatened imposition of governmental sanctions might deter appellant Whitener and other similarly situated vendors from selling 3.2% beer to young males, thereby ensuring that "enforcement of the challenged restriction against the [vendor] would result indirectly in the violation of third parties' rights." Warth v. Seldin, 422 U.S. 490, 510 (1975). Accordingly, vendors and those in like positions have been uniformly permitted to resist efforts at restricting their operations by acting as advocates of the rights of third parties who seek access to their market or function. See, e.g., Eisenstadt v. Baird, 405 U.S. 438 (1972); Sullivan v. Little Hunting Park, supra; Barrows v. Jackson, supra.[4]

---

[4] The standing question presented here is not answered by the principle stated in United States v. Raines, 362 U.S. 17, 21 (1960), that "one to whom application of a statute is constitutional will not be heard to attack the statute on the ground that impliedly it might also be taken as applying to other persons or other situations in which its application might be unconstitutional." In *Raines,* the Court refused to permit certain public officials of Georgia to defend against application of the Civil Rights Act to their official conduct on the ground that the statute also might be construed to encompass the "purely private actions" of others. The *Raines* rule remains germane in such a setting, where the

Indeed, the *jus tertii* question raised here is answered by our disposition of a like argument in Eisenstadt v. Baird, supra. There, as here, a state statute imposed legal duties and disabilities upon the claimant, who was convicted of distributing a package of contraceptive foam to a third party.[5] Since the statute was directed at Baird and penalized his conduct, the Court did not hesitate— again as here—to conclude that the "case or controversy" requirement of Art. III was satisfied. 405 U.S., at 443. In considering Baird's constitutional objections, the Court fully recognized his standing to defend the privacy interests of third parties. Deemed crucial to the decision to permit *jus tertii* standing was the recognition of "the impact of the litigation on the third-party interests." Id., at 445. Just as the defeat of Baird's suit and the "[e]nforcement of the Massachusetts statute will materially impair the ability of single persons to obtain contraceptives," id., at 446, so too the failure of Whitener to prevail in this suit and the continued enforcement of §§ 241 and 245 will "materially impair the ability of" males 18–20 years of age to purchase 3.2% beer despite their classification by an overt gender-based criterion. Similarly, just as the Massachusetts law in *Eisenstadt* "prohibit[ed], not use, but distribution," 405 U.S., at 446, and consequently the least awkward challenger was one in Baird's position who was subject to that proscription, the law challenged here explicitly regulates the sale rather than use of 3.2% beer, thus leaving a vendor as the obvious claimant.

We therefore hold that Whitener has standing to raise relevant equal protection challenges to Oklahoma's gender-based law. We now consider those arguments.

. . .

Mr. Chief Justice Burger, dissenting.

. . .

At the outset I cannot agree that appellant Whitener has standing arising from her status as a saloonkeeper to assert the constitutional rights of her customers. In this Court, "a litigant may only assert his own constitutional rights or immunities." United States v. Raines, 362 U.S. 17, 22 (1960). There are a few, but strictly limited exceptions to that rule; despite the most creative efforts, this case fits within none of them.

This is not Sullivan v. Little Hunting Park, 396 U.S. 229 (1969), or Barrows v. Jackson, 346 U.S. 249 (1953), for there is here no barrier whatever to Oklahoma males 18–20 years of age asserting, in an appropriate forum, any constitutional rights they may claim to purchase 3.2% beer. Craig's successful litigation of this very issue was prevented only by the advent of his 21st birthday. There is thus no danger of interminable dilution of those rights if appellant Whitener is not permitted to litigate them here. . . .

interests of the litigant and the rights of the proposed third parties are in no way mutually interdependent. Thus, a successful suit against Raines did not threaten to impair or diminish the independent private rights of others, and consequently, consideration of those third-party rights properly was deferred until another day.

Of course, the *Raines* principle has also been relaxed where legal action against the claimant threatens to "chill" the First Amendment rights of third parties. See, e.g., Lewis v. New Orleans, 415 U.S. 130 (1974).

[5] The fact that Baird chose to disobey the legal duty imposed upon him by the Massachusetts anticontraception statute, resulting in his criminal conviction, 405 U.S., at 440, does not distinguish the standing inquiry from that pertaining to the anticipatory attack in this case. In both *Eisenstadt* and here, the challenged statutes compel *jus tertii* claimants either to cease their proscribed activities or to suffer appropriate sanctions. The existence of Art. III "injury in fact" and the structure of the claimant's relationship to the third parties are not altered by the litigative posture of the suit. And, certainly, no suggestion will be heard that Whitener's anticipatory challenge offends the normal requirements governing such actions. . . .

Nor is this controlled by Griswold v. Connecticut, 381 U.S. 479 (1965). It borders on the ludicrous to draw a parallel between a vendor of beer and the intimate professional physician-patient relationship which undergirded relaxation of standing rules in that case.

Even in *Eisenstadt*, the Court carefully limited its recognition of third-party standing to cases in which the relationship between the claimant and the relevant third party "was not simply the fortuitous connection between a vendor and potential vendees, but the relationship between one who acted to protect the rights of a minority and the minority itself." 405 U.S., at 445. This is plainly not the case here. . . .

In sum, permitting a vendor to assert the constitutional rights of vendees whenever those rights are arguably infringed introduces a new concept of constitutional standing to which I cannot subscribe.[a]

. . .

3. TAXPAYER AND CITIZEN STANDING

VALLEY FORGE CHRISTIAN COLLEGE v. AMERICANS UNITED FOR SEPARATION OF CHURCH AND STATE, INC.

454 U.S. 464, 102 S.Ct. 752, 70 L.Ed.2d 700 (1982).

Justice Rehnquist delivered the opinion of the Court.

I

Article IV, Section 3, Clause 2 of the Constitution vests Congress with the "Power to dispose of and make all needful Rules and Regulations respecting the . . . Property belonging to the United States." Shortly after the termination of hostilities in the Second World War, Congress enacted the Federal Property and Administrative Services Act of 1949, 63 Stat. 377, 40 U.S.C. § 471 et seq. (1976 ed. and Supp. III). The Act was designed, in part, to provide "an economical and efficient system for . . . the disposal of surplus property." 63 Stat. 378, 40 U.S.C. § 471. . . . Property that has outlived its usefulness to the federal government is declared "surplus" and may be transferred to private or other public entities. See generally 63 Stat. 385, as amended, 40 U.S.C. § 484.

The Act authorizes the Secretary of Health, Education, and Welfare (now the Secretary of Education) to assume responsibility for disposing of surplus real property "for school, classroom, or other educational use." 63 Stat. 387, as amended, 40 U.S.C. § 484(k)(1). Subject to the disapproval of the Administrator of General Services, the Secretary may sell or lease the property to nonprofit, tax exempt educational institutions for consideration that takes into account "any benefit which has accrued or may accrue to the United States" from the transferee's use of the property. 63 Stat. 387, 40 U.S.C. § 484(k)(1) (A), (C). By regulation, the Secretary has provided for the computation of a "public benefit allowance," which discounts the transfer price of the property "on the basis of benefits to the United States from the use of such property for educational purposes." 34 CFR § 12.9(a) (1980).

The property which spawned this litigation was acquired by the Department of the Army in 1942. . . . The Army built on that land the Valley Forge

---

[a] For the opinions on the merits, see page 713, infra. For critiques of the Court's doctrines, and thoughtful discussion, see Rohr, *Fighting for the Rights of Others: The Troubled Law of Third-Party Standing and Mootness in the Federal Courts*, 35 Univ. of Miami L.Rev. 393 (1981); Sedler, *The Assertion of Constitutional Jus Tertii: A Substantive Approach*, 70 Calif.L.Rev. 1308 (1982); Monaghan, *Third Party Standing*, 84 Colum.L.Rev. 277 (1984).

General Hospital, and for 30 years thereafter, that hospital provided medical care for members of the Armed Forces. In April 1973, as part of a plan to reduce the number of military installations in the United States, the Secretary of Defense proposed to close the hospital, and the General Services Administration declared it to be "surplus property."

The Department of Health, Education, and Welfare (HEW) eventually assumed responsibility for disposing of portions of the property, and in August 1976, it conveyed a 77-acre tract to petitioner, the Valley Forge Christian College. The appraised value of the property at the time of conveyance was $577,500. This appraised value was discounted, however, by the Secretary's computation of a 100% public benefit allowance, which permitted petitioner to acquire the property without making any financial payment for it. The deed from HEW . . . required petitioner to use the property for 30 years solely for the educational purposes described in petitioner's application. In that description, petitioner stated its intention to conduct "a program of education . . . meeting the accrediting standards of the State of Pennsylvania, The American Association of Bible Colleges, the Division of Education of the General Council of the Assemblies of God and the Veterans Administration."

Petitioner is a nonprofit educational institution operating under the supervision of a religious order known as the Assemblies of God. By its own description, petitioner's purpose is "to offer systematic training on the collegiate level to men and women for Christian service as either ministers or laymen."

. . .

In September 1976, respondents Americans United for Separation of Church and State, Inc. (Americans United), and four of its employees, learned of the conveyance through a news release. Two months later, they brought suit in the United States District Court for the Eastern District of Pennsylvania to challenge the conveyance on the ground that it violated the Establishment Clause of the First Amendment. In its amended complaint, Americans United described itself as a nonprofit organization composed of 90,000 "taxpayer members." The complaint asserted that each member "would be deprived of the fair and constitutional use of his (her) tax dollar for constitutional purposes in violation of his (her) rights under the First Amendment of the United States Constitution." Respondents sought a declaration that the conveyance was null and void, and an order compelling petitioner to transfer the property back to the United States.

On petitioner's motion, the District Court granted summary judgment and dismissed the complaint. The court found that respondents lacked standing to sue as taxpayers under Flast v. Cohen, 392 U.S. 83 (1968). . . .

. . . [T]he Court of Appeals for the Third Circuit, . . . reversed . . . by a divided vote. All members of the court agreed that respondents lacked standing as taxpayers to challenge the conveyance under Flast v. Cohen, supra, since that case extended standing to taxpayers *qua* taxpayers only to challenge congressional exercises of the power to tax and spend conferred by Art. I, § 8, of the Constitution, and this conveyance was authorized by legislation enacted under the authority of the Property Clause, Art. IV, § 3, cl. 2. Notwithstanding this significant factual difference from *Flast,* the majority of the Court of Appeals found that respondents also had standing merely as "citizens," claiming " 'injury in fact' to their shared individuated right to a government that 'shall make no law respecting the establishment of religion.' "

. . .

. . . . [W]e now reverse.

II

Article III of the Constitution limits the "judicial power" of the United States to the resolution of "cases" and "controversies." . . . The requirements of Art. III are not satisfied merely because a party requests a court of the United States to declare its legal rights, and has couched that request for forms of relief historically associated with courts of law in terms that have a familiar ring to those trained in the legal process. . . .

. . . [T]his . . . Court has always required that a litigant have "standing" to challenge the action sought to be adjudicated in the lawsuit. The term "standing" subsumes a blend of constitutional requirements and prudential considerations, . . . and it has not always been clear in the opinions of this Court whether particular features of the "standing" requirement have been required by Art. III *ex proprio vigore,* or whether they are requirements that the Court itself has erected and which were not compelled by the language of the Constitution. . . .

A recent line of decisions, however, has resolved that ambiguity, at least to the following extent: at an irreducible minimum, Art. III requires the party who invokes the court's authority to "show that he personally has suffered some actual or threatened injury as a result of the putatively illegal conduct of the defendant," Gladstone Realtors v. Village of Bellwood, 441 U.S. 91, 99 (1979), and that the injury "fairly can be traced to the challenged action" and "is likely to be redressed by a favorable decision," Simon v. Eastern Kentucky Welfare Rights Org., 426 U.S. 26, 38, 41 (1976). . . .

. . .

We need not mince words when we say that the concept of "Art. III standing" has not been defined with complete consistency in all of the various cases decided by this Court which have discussed it, nor when we say that this very fact is probably proof that the concept cannot be reduced to a one-sentence or one-paragraph definition. But of one thing we may be sure: Those who do not possess Art. III standing may not litigate as suitors in the courts of the United States. Art. III, which is every bit as important in its circumscription of the judicial power of the United States as in its granting of that power, is not merely a troublesome hurdle to be overcome if possible so as to reach the "merits" of a lawsuit which a party desires to have adjudicated. . . .

III

The injury alleged by respondents in their amended complaint is the "depriv[ation] of the fair and constitutional use of [their] tax dollar." As a result, our discussion must begin with Frothingham v. Mellon, 262 U.S. 447 (1923). In that action a taxpayer brought suit challenging the constitutionality of the Maternity Act of 1921, which provided federal funding to the States for the purpose of improving maternal and infant health. The injury she alleged consisted of the burden of taxation in support of an unconstitutional regime, which she characterized as a deprivation of property without due process. "Looking through forms of words to the substance of [the] complaint," the Court concluded that the only "injury" was the fact "that officials of the executive branch of the government are executing and will execute an act of Congress asserted to be unconstitutional." Any tangible effect of the challenged statute on the plaintiff's tax burden was "remote, fluctuating, and uncertain." In rejecting this as a cognizable injury sufficient to establish standing, the Court admonished:

"The party who invokes the power [of judicial review] must be able to show not only that the statute is invalid but that he has sustained or is immediately in danger of sustaining some direct injury as the result of its enforcement, and not merely that he suffers in some indefinite way in common with people generally. . . . Here the parties plaintiff have no such case."

Following the decision in *Frothingham,* the Court confirmed that the expenditure of public funds in an allegedly unconstitutional manner is not an injury sufficient to confer standing, even though the plaintiff contributes to the public coffers as a taxpayer. In Doremus v. Board of Education, 342 U.S. 429 (1952), plaintiffs brought suit as citizens and taxpayers, claiming that a New Jersey law which authorized public school teachers in the classroom to read passages from the Bible violated the Establishment Clause of the First Amendment. The Court dismissed the appeal for lack of standing: . . . In short, the Court found that plaintiffs' grievance was "not a direct dollars-and-cents injury but is a religious difference." . . .

The Court again visited the problem of taxpayer standing in Flast v. Cohen, 392 U.S. 83 (1968). The taxpayer plaintiffs in *Flast* sought to enjoin the expenditure of federal funds under the Elementary and Secondary Education Act of 1965, which they alleged were being used to support religious schools in violation of the Establishment Clause. The Court developed a two-part test to determine whether the plaintiffs had standing to sue. First, because a taxpayer alleges injury only by virtue of his liability for taxes, the Court held that "a taxpayer will be a proper party to allege the unconstitutionality only of exercises of congressional power under the taxing and spending clause of Art. I, § 8, of the Constitution." Second, the Court required the taxpayer to "show that the challenged enactment exceeds specific constitutional limitations upon the exercise of the taxing and spending power and not simply that the enactment is generally beyond the powers delegated to Congress by Art. I, § 8." The plaintiffs in *Flast* satisfied this test because "[t]heir constitutional challenge [was] made to an exercise by Congress of its power under Art. I, § 8, to spend for the general welfare," and because the Establishment Clause, on which plaintiffs' complaint rested, "operates as a specific constitutional limitation upon the exercise by Congress of the taxing and spending power conferred by Art. I, § 8," id. at 104.

The Court distinguished Frothingham v. Mellon, supra, on the ground that Mrs. Frothingham had relied, not on a specific limitation on the power to tax and spend, but on a more general claim based on the Due Process Clause. Thus, the Court reaffirmed that the "case or controversy" aspect of standing is unsatisfied "where a taxpayer seeks to employ a federal court as a forum in which to air his generalized grievances about the conduct of government or the allocation of power in the Federal System."

Unlike the plaintiffs in *Flast*, respondents fail the first prong of the test for taxpayer standing. Their claim is deficient in two respects. First, the source of their complaint is not a congressional action, but a decision by HEW to transfer a parcel of federal property.[15] *Flast* limited taxpayer standing to challenges directed "only [at] exercises of congressional power." See Schlesinger v. Reservists Committee to Stop the War, 418 U.S. 208, 228 (1974) (denying standing because the taxpayer plaintiffs "did not challenge an enactment under Art. I, § 8, but rather the action of the Executive Branch").

Second, and perhaps redundantly, the property transfer about which respondents complain was not an exercise of authority conferred by the taxing and spending clause of Art. I, § 8. The authorizing legislation, the Federal Property and Administrative Services Act of 1949, was an evident exercise of Congress' power under the Property Clause, Art. IV, § 3, cl. 2. Respondents

---

[15] Respondents do not challenge the constitutionality of the Federal Property and Administrative Services Act itself, but rather a particular Executive branch action arguably authorized by the Act.

do not dispute this conclusion and it is decisive of any claim of taxpayer standing under the *Flast* precedent.[17]

Any doubt that once might have existed concerning the rigor with which the *Flast* exception to the *Frothingham* principle ought to be applied should have been erased by this Court's recent decisions in United States v. Richardson, 418 U.S. 166 (1974), and Schlesinger v. Reservists Committee to Stop the War, 418 U.S. 208 (1974). In *Richardson,* the question was whether the plaintiff had standing as a federal taxpayer to argue that legislation which permitted the Central Intelligence Agency to withhold from the public detailed information about its expenditures violated the Accounts Clause of the Constitution. We rejected plaintiff's claim of standing because "his challenge [was] not addressed to the taxing or spending power, but to the statutes regulating the CIA." The "mere recital" of those claims "demonstrate[d] how far he [fell] short of the standing criteria of *Flast* and how neatly he [fell] within the *Frothingham* holding left undisturbed."

The claim in *Schlesinger* was marred by the same deficiency. Plaintiffs in that case argued that the Incompatibility Clause of Art. I prevented certain Members of Congress from holding commissions in the Armed Forces Reserve. We summarily rejected their assertion of standing as taxpayers because they "did not challenge an enactment under Art. I, § 8, but rather the action of the Executive Branch in permitting Members of Congress to maintain their Reserve status."

Respondents, therefore, are plainly without standing to sue as taxpayers. The Court of Appeals apparently reached the same conclusion. It remains to be seen whether respondents have alleged any other basis for standing to bring this suit.

IV

Although the Court of Appeals properly doubted respondents' ability to establish standing solely on the basis of their taxpayer status, it considered their allegations of taxpayer injury to be "essentially an assumed role." . . . In the court's view, respondents had established standing by virtue of an " 'injury in fact' to their shared individuated right to a government that 'shall make no law respecting the establishment of religion.' " The court distinguished this "injury" from "the question of 'citizen standing' as such." Although citizens generally could not establish standing simply by claiming an interest in governmental observance of the Constitution, respondents had "set forth instead a particular and concrete injury" to a "personal constitutional right."

The Court of Appeals was surely correct in recognizing that the Art. III requirements of standing are not satisfied by "the abstract injury in nonobservance of the Constitution asserted by . . . citizens." Schlesinger v. Reservists Committee to Stop the War, 418 U.S., at 223, n. 13. . . . Such claims amount to little more than attempts "to employ a federal court as a forum in which to air . . . generalized grievances about the conduct of government." Flast v. Cohen, 392 U.S., at 106.

In finding that respondents had alleged something more than "the generalized interest of all citizens in constitutional governance," *Schlesinger,* supra, at 217, the Court of Appeals relied on factual differences which we do not think

[17] Although not necessary to our decision, we note that any connection between the challenged property transfer and respondents' tax burden is at best speculative and at worst nonexistent. . . . In fact, respondents' only objection is that the government did not receive adequate consideration for the transfer, because petitioner's use of the property will not confer a public benefit. Assuming *arguendo* that this proposition is true, an assumption by no means clear, there is no basis for believing that a transfer to a different purchaser would have added to government receipts. As the government argues, "the ultimate purchaser would, in all likelihood, have been another non-profit institution or local school district rather than a purchaser for cash." . . .

amount to legal distinctions. The court decided that respondents' claim differed from those in *Schlesinger* and *Richardson,* which were predicated, respectively, on the Incompatibility and Accounts Clauses, because "it is at the very least arguable that the Establishment Clause creates in each citizen a 'personal constitutional right' to a government that does not establish religion." . . .

. . . To the extent the Court of Appeals relied on a view of standing under which the Art. III burdens diminish as the "importance" of the claim on the merits increases, we reject that notion. The requirement of standing "focuses on the party seeking to get his complaint before a federal court and not on the issues he wishes to have adjudicated." Flast v. Cohen, supra, at 99. Moreover, we know of no principled basis on which to create a hierarchy of constitutional values or a complementary "sliding scale" of standing which might permit respondents to invoke the judicial power of the United States.
. . .

The complaint in this case shares a common deficiency with those in *Schlesinger* and *Richardson.* Although they claim that the Constitution has been violated, they claim nothing else. They fail to identify any personal injury suffered by the plaintiffs *as a consequence* of the alleged constitutional error, other than the psychological consequence presumably produced by observation of conduct with which one disagrees. That is not an injury sufficient to confer standing under Art. III, even though the disagreement is phrased in constitutional terms. It is evident that respondents are firmly committed to the constitutional principle of separation of church and State, but standing is not measured by the intensity of the litigant's interest or the fervor of his advocacy.
. . .

In reaching this conclusion, we do not retreat from our earlier holdings that standing may be predicated on noneconomic injury. See, e.g., United States v. SCRAP, 412 U.S., at 686–688; Data Processing Service v. Camp, 397 U.S., at 153–154. We simply cannot see that respondents have alleged an *injury* of *any* kind, economic or otherwise, sufficient to confer standing. Respondents complain of a transfer of property located in Chester County, Pennsylvania. The named plaintiffs reside in Maryland and Virginia; their organizational headquarters are located in Washington, D.C. They learned of the transfer through a news release. Their claim that the government has violated the Establishment Clause does not provide a special license to roam the country in search of governmental wrongdoing and to reveal their discoveries in federal court. The federal courts were simply not constituted as ombudsmen of the general welfare.

V

The Court of Appeals in this case ignored unambiguous limitations on taxpayer and citizen standing. It appears to have done so out of the conviction that enforcement of the Establishment Clause demands special exceptions from the requirement that a plaintiff allege " 'distinct and palpable injury to himself,' . . . that is likely to be redressed if the requested relief is granted." Gladstone, Realtors v. Village of Bellwood, 441 U.S., at 100 (quoting Warth v. Seldin, 422 U.S., at 501). The court derived precedential comfort from Flast v. Cohen, supra: "The underlying justification for according standing in *Flast* it seems, was the implicit recognition that the Establishment Clause does create in every citizen a personal constitutional right, such that any citizen, including taxpayers, may contest under that clause the constitutionality of federal expenditures." . . .

Implicit in the foregoing is the philosophy that the business of the federal courts is correcting constitutional errors, and that "cases and controversies" are at best merely convenient vehicles for doing so and at worst nuisances that may be dispensed with when they become obstacles to that transcendent endeavor. This philosophy has no place in our constitutional scheme. It does not become more palatable when the underlying merits concern the Establishment Clause. Respondents' claim of standing implicitly rests on the presumption that violations of the Establishment Clause typically will not cause injury sufficient to confer standing under the "traditional" view of Art. III. But "[t]he assumption that if respondents have no standing to sue, no one would have standing, is not a reason to find standing." Schlesinger v. Reservists Committee to Stop the War, 418 U.S., at 227. This view would convert standing into a requirement that must be observed only when satisfied. Moreover, we are unwilling to assume that injured parties are nonexistent simply because they have not joined respondents in their suit. The law of averages is not a substitute for standing.

Were we to accept respondents' claim of standing in this case, there would be no principled basis for confining our exception to litigants relying on the Establishment Clause. Ultimately, that exception derives from the idea that the judicial power requires nothing more for its invocation than important issues and able litigants. The existence of injured parties who might not wish to bring suit becomes irrelevant. Because we are unwilling to countenance such a departure from the limits on judicial power contained in Art. III, the judgment of the Court of Appeals is reversed.

It is so ordered.

Justice Brennan, with whom Justice Marshall and Justice Blackmun join, dissenting.

A plaintiff's standing is a jurisdictional matter for Article III courts, and thus a "threshold question" to be resolved before turning attention to more "substantive" issues. . . . But in consequence there is an impulse to decide difficult questions of substantive law obliquely in the course of opinions purporting to do nothing more than determine what the Court labels "standing"; this accounts for the phenomenon of opinions, such as the one today, that tend merely to obfuscate, rather than inform, our understanding of the meaning of rights under the law. . . .

.   .   .

II

A

Frothingham v. Mellon, 262 U.S. 447 (1923), involved a challenge to the Maternity Act of 1921, 42 Stat. 224, which provided financial grants to states that agreed to cooperate in programs designed to reduce infant and maternal mortality. Appellant contended that Congress, in enacting the program, had exceeded its authority under Article I, and had intruded on authority reserved to the States. . . .

.   .   .

Whatever its provenance, the general rule of *Frothingham* displays sound judgment: Courts must be circumspect in dealing with the taxing power in order to avoid unnecessary intrusion into the functions of the legislative and executive branches. Congress' *purpose* in taxing will not ordinarily affect the validity of the tax. Unless the tax *operates* unconstitutionally, . . . the taxpayer may not object to the use of his funds. Mrs. Frothingham's argument, that the use of tax funds for purposes unauthorized by the Constitution amounted to a violation of due process, did not provide her with the required legal interest because the Due Process Clause of the Fifth Amendment does not protect taxpayers against increases in tax liability. . . . Mrs. Frothingham's claim was thus reduced to an assertion of "the States' interest in their legislative prerogatives," a third-party claim that could properly be barred. But in *Flast* the Court faced a different sort of constitutional claim, and found itself compelled to retreat from the general assertion in *Frothingham* that taxpayers have *no* interest in the disposition of their tax payments. To understand why *Frothingham's* bar necessarily gave way in the face of an Establishment Clause claim, we must examine the right asserted by a taxpayer making such a claim.

B

In 1947, nine Justices of this Court recognized that the Establishment Clause does impose a very definite restriction on the power to tax. The Court held in Everson v. Board of Education, 330 U.S. 1, 15, that the " 'establishment of religion' clause of the First Amendment means at least this:"

> "No tax in any amount, large or small, can be levied to support any religious activities or institutions, whatever they may be called, or whatever form they may adopt, to teach or practice religion." Id., at 16.

.   .   .

.   .   .   [O]ne of the primary purposes of the Establishment Clause was to prevent the use of tax monies for religious purposes. *The taxpayer was the direct and intended beneficiary of the prohibition on financial aid to religion.   .   .   .* Given this view of the issues, could it fairly be doubted that this taxpayer alleged injury in precisely the form that the Establishment Clause sought to make actionable?

C

.   .   .

It is at once apparent that the test of standing formulated by the Court in *Flast* sought to reconcile the developing doctrine of taxpayer "standing" with the Court's historical understanding that the Establishment Clause was intended to prohibit the Federal Government from using tax funds for the advancement of religion, and thus the constitutional imperative of taxpayer standing in certain cases brought pursuant to the Establishment Clause. The two-pronged "nexus" test offered by the Court, despite its general language, is best understood as "a determinant of standing of plaintiffs alleging only injury as taxpayers who challenge alleged violations of the Establishment and Free Exercise Clauses of the First Amendment," and not as a general statement of standing principles. Schlesinger v. Reservists Committee to Stop the War, 418 U.S. 208, 238 (1974) (Brennan, J., dissenting); *Flast,* supra, at 102. The test explains what forms of governmental action may be attacked by someone alleging *only* taxpayer status, and, without ruling out the possibility that history might reveal another similarly founded provision, explains why an Establishment Clause claim is treated differently from any other assertion that the federal government has exceeded the bounds of the law in allocating its largesse.   .   .   .

.   .   .

It may be that Congress can tax for *almost* any reason, or for no reason at all. There is, so far as I have been able to discern, but one constitutionally imposed limit on that authority. Congress cannot use tax money to support a church, or to encourage religion.   .   .   .

A taxpayer cannot be asked to raise his objection to such use of his funds at the time he pays his tax. Apart from the unlikely circumstance in which the Government announced in advance that a particular levy would be used for religious subsidies, taxpayers could hardly assert that they were being injured until the Government actually lent its support to a religious venture. Nor would it be reasonable to require him to address his claim to those officials charged with the collection of federal taxes. Those officials would be without the means to provide appropriate redress—there is no practical way to segregate the complaining taxpayer's money from that being devoted to the religious purpose. Surely, then, a taxpayer must have standing at the time that he learns of the Government's alleged Establishment Clause violation to seek equitable relief in order to halt the continuing and intolerable burden on his pocketbook, his conscience, and his constitutional rights.

III

Blind to history, the Court attempts to distinguish this case from *Flast* by wrenching snippets of language from our opinions, and by perfunctorily applying that language under color of the first prong of *Flast's* two-part nexus test. The tortuous distinctions thus produced are specious, at best: at worst, they are pernicious to our constitutional heritage.

First, the Court finds this case different from *Flast* because here the "source of [plaintiff's] complaint is not a *congressional* action, but a decision by HEW to transfer a parcel of federal property." This attempt at distinction cannot withstand scrutiny. *Flast* involved a challenge to the actions of the Commissioner of Education, and other officials of HEW, in disbursing funds under the Elementary and Secondary Education Act of 1965 to "religious and sectarian" schools. Plaintiffs disclaimed "any intention to challenge all programs under . . . the Act." Rather, they claimed that defendant-administrators' approval of such expenditures was not authorized by the Act, or alternatively, to the extent the expenditure was authorized, the Act was "unconstitutional and void." In the present case, respondents challenge HEW's grant of property pursuant to the Federal Property and Administrative Services Act of 1949, seeking to enjoin HEW "from making a grant of this and other property to the [defendant] so long as such grant will violate the Establishment Clause." It may be that the Court is concerned with the adequacy of respondents' pleading; respondents have not, in so many words, asked for a declaration that the "Federal Property and Administrative Services Act is unconstitutional and void to the extent that it authorizes HEW's actions." I would not construe their complaint so narrowly.

More fundamentally, no clear division can be drawn in this context between actions of the legislative branch and those of the executive branch. To be sure, the First Amendment is phrased as a restriction on Congress' legislative authority; this is only natural since the Constitution assigns the authority to legislate and appropriate only to the Congress. But it is difficult to conceive of an expenditure for which the last governmental actor, either implementing directly the legislative will, or acting within the scope of legislatively delegated authority, is not an Executive Branch official. The First Amendment binds the Government as a whole, regardless of which branch is at work in a particular instance.

The Court's second purported distinction between this case and *Flast* is equally unavailing. The majority finds it "decisive" that the Federal Property and Administrative Services Act of 1949 "was an evident exercise of Congress' power under the Property Clause, Art. IV, § 3, cl. 2," while the government action in *Flast* was taken under the Art. I, § 8. The Court relies on United States v. Richardson, 418 U.S. 166 (1974); and Schlesinger v. Reservists Committee to Stop the War, 418 U.S. 208 (1974), to support the distinction between the two clauses, noting that those cases involved alleged deviations from the requirements of Art. I, § 9, cl. 7, and Art. I, § 6, cl. 2, respectively. The standing defect in each case was *not,* however, the failure to allege a violation of the Spending Clause; rather, the taxpayers in those cases had not complained of the distribution of government largesse, and thus failed to meet the essential requirement of taxpayer standing recognized in *Doremus.*

It can make no constitutional difference in the case before us whether the donation to the defendant here was in the form of a cash grant to build a facility, . . . or in the nature of a gift of property including a facility already built. . . . Whether undertaken pursuant to the Property Clause or the Spending Clause, the breach of the Establishment Clause, and the relationship of the taxpayer to that breach, is precisely the same.

IV

Plainly hostile to the Framers' understanding of the Establishment Clause, and *Flast's* enforcement of that understanding, the Court vents that hostility under the guise of standing, "to slam the courthouse door against plaintiffs who [as the Framers intended] are entitled to full consideration of their [Establishment Clause] claims on the merits." Barlow v. Collins, 397 U.S. 159, 178 (1970) (Brennan, J., concurring in the result and dissenting). Therefore, I dissent.

Justice Stevens, dissenting.

In Parts I, II, and III of his dissenting opinion, Justice Brennan demonstrates that respondent taxpayers have standing to mount an Establishment Clause challenge against the Federal Government's transfer of property worth $1,300,000 to the Assembly of God. For the Court to hold that plaintiffs' standing depends on whether the Government's transfer was an exercise of its power to spend money, on the one hand, or its power to dispose of tangible property, on the other, is to trivialize the standing doctrine.

One cannot read the Court's opinion and the concurring opinions of Justice Stewart and Justice Fortas in Flast v. Cohen, 392 U.S. 83, without forming the firm conclusion that the plaintiffs' invocation of the Establishment Clause was of decisive importance in resolving the standing issue in that case. . . .

. . . With all due respect, I am persuaded that the essential holding of Flast v. Cohen attaches special importance to the Establishment Clause and does not permit the drawing of a tenuous distinction between the Spending Clause and the Property Clause.

For this reason, and for the reasons stated in Parts I, II, and III of Justice Brennan's opinion, I would affirm the judgment of the Court of Appeals.

C.   MOOTNESS

"The usual rule in federal cases is that an actual controversy must exist at stages of appellate or certiorari review, and not simply at the date the action is initiated." Roe v. Wade, 410 U.S. 113, 125 (1973).

DeFUNIS v. ODEGAARD

416 U.S. 312, 94 S.Ct. 1704, 40 L.Ed.2d 164 (1974).

Per Curiam.

In 1971 the petitioner, Marco DeFunis, Jr., applied for admission as a first-year student at the University of Washington Law School, a state-operated institution. The size of the incoming first-year class was to be limited to 150 persons, and the Law School received some 1,600 applications for these 150 places. DeFunis was eventually notified that he had been denied admission. He thereupon commenced this suit in a Washington trial court, contending that the procedures and criteria employed by the Law School Admissions Committee invidiously discriminated against him on account of his race in violation of the Equal Protection Clause of the Fourteenth Amendment to the United States Constitution.

DeFunis brought the suit on behalf of himself alone, and not as the representative of any class, against the various respondents, who are officers,

faculty members, and members of the Board of Regents of the University of
Washington. He asked the trial court to issue a mandatory injunction commanding the respondents to admit him as a member of the first-year class
entering in September of 1971, on the ground that the Law School admissions
policy had resulted in the unconstitutional denial of his application for admission. The trial court agreed with his claim and granted the requested relief.
DeFunis was, accordingly, admitted to the Law School and began his legal
studies there in the fall of 1971. On appeal, the Washington Supreme Court
reversed the judgment of the trial court and held that the Law School admissions
policy did not violate the Constitution. By this time DeFunis was in his second
year at the Law School.

He then petitioned this Court for a writ of certiorari, and Mr. Justice
Douglas, as Circuit Justice, stayed the judgment of the Washington Supreme
Court pending the "final disposition of the case by this Court." By virtue of
this stay, DeFunis has remained in law school, and was in the first term of his
third and final year when this Court first considered his certiorari petition in the
fall of 1973. Because of our concern that DeFunis' third-year standing in the
Law School might have rendered this case moot, we requested the parties to
brief the question of mootness before we acted on the petition. In response,
both sides contended that the case was not moot. The respondents indicated
that, if the decision of the Washington Supreme Court were permitted to stand,
the petitioner could complete the term for which he was then enrolled but
would have to apply to the faculty for permission to continue in the school
before he could register for another term.

We granted the petition for certiorari on November 19, 1973, 414 U.S.
1038. The case was in due course orally argued on February 26, 1974.

In response to questions raised from the bench during the oral argument,
counsel for the petitioner has informed the Court that DeFunis has now
registered "for his final quarter in law school." Counsel for the respondents
have made clear that the Law School will not in any way seek to abrogate this
registration. In light of DeFunis' recent registration for the last quarter of his
final law school year, and the Law School's assurance that his registration is fully
effective, the insistent question again arises whether this case is not moot, and to
that question we now turn.

The starting point for analysis is the familiar proposition that "federal courts
are without power to decide questions that cannot affect the rights of litigants in
this case before them." North Carolina v. Rice, 404 U.S. 244, 246 (1971).
The inability of the federal judiciary "to review moot cases derives from the
requirement of Article III of the Constitution under which the exercise of
judicial power depends upon the existence of a case or controversy." Liner v.
Jafco, Inc., 375 U.S. 301, 306 n. 3 (1964); see also Powell v. McCormack, 395
U.S. 486, 496 n. 7 (1969); Sibron v. New York, 392 U.S. 40, 50 n. 8 (1968).
Although as a matter of Washington state law it appears that this case would be
saved from mootness by "the great public interest in the continuing issues raised
by this appeal," 82 Wash.2d 11, 23 n. 6, 507 P.2d 1169, 1177 n. 6 (1973), the
fact remains that under Art. III "[e]ven in cases arising in the state courts, the
question of mootness is a federal one which a federal court must resolve before
it assumes jurisdiction." North Carolina v. Rice, supra, at 246.

The respondents have represented that, without regard to the ultimate
resolution of the issues in this case, DeFunis will remain a student in the law
school for the duration of any term in which he has already enrolled. Since he
has now registered for his final term, it is evident that he will be given an
opportunity to complete all academic and other requirements for graduation,
and, if he does so, will receive his diploma regardless of any decision this Court
might reach on the merits of this case. In short, all parties agree that DeFunis is

now entitled to complete his legal studies at the University of Washington and to receive his degree from that institution. A determination by this Court of the legal issues tendered by the parties is no longer necessary to compel that result, and could not serve to prevent it. DeFunis did not cast his suit as a class action, and the only remedy he requested was an injunction commanding his admission to the Law School. He was not only accorded that remedy, but he now has also been irrevocably admitted to the final term of the final year of the law school course. The controversy between the parties has thus clearly ceased to be "definite and concrete" and no longer "touch[es] the legal relations of parties having adverse legal interests." Aetna Life Ins. Co. v. Haworth, 300 U.S. 227, 240–241 (1937).

It matters not that these circumstances partially stem from a policy decision on the part of the respondent Law School authorities. The respondents, through their counsel, the Attorney General of the State, have professionally represented that in no event will the status of DeFunis now be affected by any view this Court might express on the merits of this controversy. And it has been the settled practice of the Court in contexts no less significant, fully to accept representations such as these as parameters for decision. . . .

It might also be suggested that this case presents a question that is "capable of repetition, yet evading review," Southern Pacific Terminal Co. v. ICC, 219 U.S. 498, 515 (1911); Roe v. Wade, 410 U.S. 113, 125 (1973), and is thus amenable to federal adjudication even though it might otherwise be considered moot. But DeFunis will never again be required to run the gantlet of the Law School's admission process, and so the question is certainly not "capable of repetition" so far as he is concerned. Moreover, just because this particular case did not reach the Court until the eve of the petitioner's graduation from law school, it hardly follows that the issue he raises will in future evade review. If the admissions procedures of the Law School remain unchanged, there is no reason to suppose that a subsequent case attacking those procedures will not come with relative speed to this Court, now that the Supreme Court of Washington has spoken. This case, therefore, in no way presents the exceptional situation in which the *Southern Pacific Terminal* doctrine might permit a departure from "[t]he usual rule in federal cases . . . that an actual controversy must exist at stages of appellate or certiorari review, and not simply at the date the action is initiated." Roe v. Wade, supra, at 125; United States v. Munsingwear, Inc., 340 U.S. 36 (1950).

Because the petitioner will complete his law school studies at the end of the term for which he has now registered regardless of any decision this Court might reach on the merits of this litigation, we conclude that the Court cannot, consistently with the limitations of Art. III of the Constitution, consider the substantive constitutional issues tendered by the parties. Accordingly, the judgment of the Supreme Court of Washington is vacated, and the cause is remanded for such proceedings as by that Court may be deemed appropriate.

It is so ordered.

Mr. Justice Douglas, dissenting.

I agree with Mr. Justice Brennan that this case is not moot, and because of the significance of the issues raised I think it is important to reach the merits. . . .

· · ·

Mr. Justice Brennan, with whom Mr. Justice Douglas, Mr. Justice White, and Mr. Justice Marshall concur, dissenting

· · ·

Moreover, in endeavoring to dispose of this case as moot, the Court clearly disserves the public interest. The constitutional issues which are avoided today concern vast numbers of people, organizations and colleges and universities, as evidenced by the filing of twenty-six *amici curiae* briefs. Few constitutional questions in recent history have stirred as much debate, and they will not disappear. They must inevitably return to the federal courts and ultimately again to this Court. Cf. Richardson v. Wright, 405 U.S. 208, 212 (1972) (dissenting opinion). Because avoidance of repetitious litigation serves the public interest, that inevitability counsels against mootness determinations, as here, not compelled by the record. . . . Although the Court should, of course, avoid unnecessary decisions of constitutional questions, we should not transform principles of avoidance of constitutional decisions into devices for sidestepping resolution of difficult cases. . . .

On what appears in this case, I would find that there is an extant controversy and decide the merits of the very important constitutional questions presented.

CAPABLE OF REPETITION YET EVADING REVIEW

An exception to the requirement that there be a live controversy at the time of decision exists for those controversies "capable of repetition yet evading review." In its *DeFunis* opinion, the Court concludes that the exception is inapplicable because DeFunis would not be affected by the challenged admission policy in the future and other challengers to the admission procedures could litigate the issues before their claims became moot.[1]

The simplest cases involving the exception are those where the litigated issue will always be mooted by the passage of time in litigation, and the plaintiff will be subject to the challenged action in the future. That was the situation in United States v. New York Tele. Co., 434 U.S. 159 (1977), where a telephone company challenged a federal district court order requiring it to install and use "pen registers" and furnish the Federal Bureau of Investigation with information concerning the use of two telephones. Such orders were issued only for brief periods, and even if an order was stayed pending judicial review, the showing of probable cause that supported the order would become stale before review was completed. Given the telephone company's policy of refusing to comply voluntarily with such orders, it was clear that it would be subjected to similar orders in the future.

More complex are those cases where the plaintiff will not face the litigated issue in the future, but others similarly situated will. That was the situation in Dunn v. Blumstein, 405 U.S. 330 (1972), where plaintiff challenged a state requirement that voters live in the state for one year and the county for three months prior to an election. Plaintiff became eligible to vote long before termination of the litigation. Other new residents would, however, be subject to the durational residency requirement. That was also the situation in Roe v. Wade, 410 U.S. 113 (1973), where a pregnant woman challenged a state abortion statute, asserting her inability to obtain a legal abortion in the state. Plaintiff's 1970 pregnancy had obviously terminated prior to the Court's 1973 decision, and she did not allege that she was affected by the abortion statute with reference to future pregnancies. In both cases, the Court determined that the controversy was capable of repetition, yet evading review. In *Roe*, the Court said:

> "[W]hen . . . pregnancy is a significant fact in the litigation, the normal 266-day gestation period is so short that the pregnancy will come to term

---

[1] The issue mooted in *DeFunis* was decided by the Court four years later in Regents of the University of California v. Bakke, 438 U.S. 265 (1978), infra p. 786. Bakke had been denied admission to medical school, and was not attending the school when his case reached the Supreme Court.

before the usual appellate procedure is complete. If that termination makes a case moot, pregnancy litigation seldom will survive much beyond the trial stage, and appellate review will be effectively denied. Our law should not be that rigid."

Both *Dunn* and *Roe* were class actions. Where litigation is not capable of repetition as to the named plaintiff, later cases have combined concerns about whether the plaintiff's claim is "capable of repetition yet evading review" with questions whether the action to enjoin enforcement of the challenged law has been certified as a class action. In Sosna v. Iowa, 419 U.S. 393 (1975), plaintiffs challenged a state law imposing a durational residency requirement for obtaining a divorce. Sosna had satisfied the residency requirement before the completion of litigation. The Court explained that the case had not become moot because: (1) the case had been certified as a class action, with a class whose members were still subject to the durational residency requirement, *and;* (2) the problem was one capable of repetition yet evading review as to the class.[2] Since *Sosna,* complications have arisen when the claims of the named plaintiff have become moot prior to class certification.[3]

CASE AND CONTROVERSY REQUIREMENTS AS APPLIED TO CONSTITUTIONAL LITIGATION ARISING IN STATE AND FEDERAL COURTS

The *DeFunis* case is the first principal case in this section where the Supreme Court is reviewing the decision of a state court. Standing, mootness and ripeness rules apply both to constitutional litigation arising in the federal courts, and to Supreme Court review of constitutional decisions of state courts. The rules are sometimes different, however, depending on whether the Supreme Court is reviewing a state or federal court decision. One traditional explanation for the difference is that case or controversy limitations represent, in part, rules of self-limitation for the federal courts and as such are irrelevant to Supreme Court review of state decisions. Article III case or controversy requirements, however, bind the Supreme Court, even when it is reviewing the decision of a state court. Under this view, doctrines of standing, ripeness and mootness will not block Supreme Court review of state court decisions unless there is no case or controversy in the sense of Article III. An illustrative case is Doremus v. Board of Educ., 342 U.S. 429 (1952). State taxpayers had attacked the practice of Bible reading in the public schools on federal constitutional grounds. The state court decision ruled against plaintiffs on the merits. The Court's opinion conceded that state courts were not bound by case or controversy limitations, and could even give advisory opinions on constitutional questions. Supreme Court review, however, was bound by the limitations of Article III, making an advisory opinion of a state court unreviewable. The Supreme Court had considered state taxpayers' challenges to state laws in reviewing decisions of state courts, even when the plaintiffs would have been denied standing in a federal court action. Those actions were cases or controversies within Article III. Here, however, the state taxpayers were litigating a "religious difference"

[2] Greenstein, *Bridging the Mootness Gap in Federal Court Class Actions,* 35 Stan.L.Rev. 897, 903 (1983), points out that the combination of two reasons is confusing. "If certification conferred legal status upon the claims of the class and if there were always class members with *current* claims, what did it matter . . . that the claims were 'capable of repetition?' And in what sense were they 'evading review'?"

[3] See Deposit Guar. Nat'l Bank v. Roper, 445 U.S. 326 (1980), and United States Parole Commission v. Geraghty, 445 U.S. 388 (1980). In both cases, the trial court had denied class certification, and the individual plaintiff's claim became moot while the case was on appeal. The Court held that a justiciable controversy remained concerning whether the class should have been certified. For discussion of these cases, see Greenstein, supra note 2.

rather than a "good-faith pocketbook action." Since there was no case or controversy within the meaning of Article III, plaintiffs' appeal was dismissed. Three Justices dissented from the conclusion that there was no Article III case or controversy.[1]

There are two difficulties with the explanation given in *Doremus*. First, it is dubious that the litigation in that case failed to meet the requirements of Article III. (It is likewise dubious that the issue in *DeFunis* was moot "in a constitutional sense.") Moreover, even in apparently mandatory appeals, there is a discretionary element in Supreme Court review of state court decisions.[2] A more complete explanation, then, is that the discretionary, nonconstitutional aspects of standing, mootness and ripeness doctrines apply, but are different for federal court litigation and Supreme Court review of state court decisions. A major reason for the difference may be that a decision by the Supreme Court that there is no case or controversy has a different impact, depending upon whether the case originated in federal or state court. In a federal court case, a decision that a case is not ripe for decision, or that plaintiffs lack standing, requires that the case be sent back to the lower court with directions to dismiss the litigation. The dismissal of the suit removes any formal value of the lower court decisions as precedent. In a case coming from a state court, lack of standing or ripeness requires that the appeal to the Supreme Court be dismissed, leaving the lower court decision in effect. The situation with reference to mootness is similar, but a little more complex.[3]

While cases concerning the requirements of standing and ripeness are often distinguished, according to whether the case arose in a federal or state court,[4] none of the cases involving mootness have drawn that distinction. In other words, if a claim is made that subsequent events have mooted a case pending Supreme Court review, there appears to be a single standard that draws no distinction between federal and state case appeals. Should it have made a difference in *DeFunis* that the Supreme Court was reviewing a state court decision, and not the decision of a federal court?

---

[1] The constitutionality of Bible reading in the public schools, the substantive issue involved in the *Doremus* case, was not resolved for more than a decade. In School Dist. of Abington Twp. v. Schempp, 374 U.S. 203 (1963), the practice was held unconstitutional. One of the two companion cases was a suit for an injunction brought in a federal court; the other was a suit for mandamus in a state court. School children and their parents were held to have standing in both cases. 374 U.S. at 224 n. 9. In *Doremus,* one of the plaintiffs had been the parent of a school child, but the child had graduated from public schools before appeal had been taken to the Supreme Court, mooting that aspect of the plaintiff's standing. 342 U.S. at 432–433.

[2] See the discussion of Naim v. Naim, 350 U.S. 891 (1955), 985 (1956) and Rescue Army v. Municipal Court, 331 U.S. 549 (1947), supra pages 62–63. See also Poe v. Ullman, 367 U.S. 497 (1961), infra p. 123, an avowedly discretionary dismissal of an appeal from a state court on ripeness grounds.

[3] If a federal court decision becomes moot pending Supreme Court review, the decision being reviewed will be "vacated," and the case will be remanded to the trial court with directions that the action be dismissed as moot. If a state court decision becomes moot pending Supreme Court review, standard practice is not to dismiss the appeal, but to vacate and remand to the state's highest court for such proceedings as that court may deem appropriate. Stern and Gressman, *Supreme Court Practice* 897–899 (5th ed. 1978). Arguably, the difference between moot cases and cases that are not ripe or where parties lack standing (where the appeal is dismissed) is that the mootness problem has arisen after the state court decision. Significantly, even though the state court's decision is "vacated" on mootness grounds, the state court remains free to reinstate its opinion if it concludes that the case is not moot by state law standards. On the *DeFunis* remand, the Washington Supreme Court's decision was inconclusive, although a plurality would have reinstated the prior opinion, in part because the issue was of major public importance. 84 Wash.2d 617, 529 P.2d 438 (1974). The Washington Supreme Court's opinion contains an exhaustive treatment of the United States Supreme Court's practice of disposing of moot federal and state appeals.

[4] In addition to the *Doremus* case, supra, see United Public Workers v. Mitchell, 330 U.S. 75 (1947) and Adler v. Board of Educ. 342 U.S. 485 (1952), infra at pp. 121–123.

D. RIPENESS

Criminal prosecutions and suits for damages in tort or contract relate to past conduct. If it is necessary to decide a constitutional issue in order to determine the legal consequences of that conduct, no issues of ripeness or concreteness arise. Such cases present the question of judicial review in the classic Marbury v. Madison form.

Suits for injunctions and declaratory judgments, however, present different problems. Characteristically, they relate to the future. It may not be clear what either the plaintiff or the defendant actually will do. It may not be certain that the conduct alleged to give rise to the constitutional issue will ever take place. The declaratory judgment action, in particular, takes a form suspiciously like that of an advisory opinion. It is in such cases that the Court articulates the doctrines relating to the concreteness of the factual situation and the ripeness of the controversy.

The cases set out below constitute a sample of the Court's approach to the problem. Because of the amorphous nature of the rules being applied, the cases do not fit neatly into rational categories.

For discussions of the problems in this section from differing points of view see Bickel, *The Least Dangerous Branch* 71, 111–98 (1962); 3 Davis, *Administrative Law Treatise,* 116–207 (1958); Scharpf, *Judicial Review and the Political Question: A Functional Analysis,* 75 Yale L.J. 517, 528–533 (1966).

UNITED PUBLIC WORKERS v. MITCHELL, 330 U.S. 75 (1947). The Hatch Act forbade certain classes of federal government employees from taking "any active part in political management or in political campaigns." A group of employees sought an injunction forbidding the Civil Service Commission from enforcing against them this aspect of the Hatch Act as a violation of the Constitution. One group of plaintiffs alleged that they desired to engage in specified acts of political management and political campaigning. One plaintiff (Poole) alleged that he had engaged in forbidden political activity and that proceedings leading to his discharge were under way. The Court held that the first group of plaintiffs could not have their arguments heard in a federal court but that Poole could do so. In discussing its reasons for refusing to hear the first group, the Court said, in part:

"As is well known the federal courts established pursuant to Article III of the Constitution do not render advisory opinions. For adjudication of constitutional issues, 'concrete legal issues, presented in actual cases, not abstractions,' are requisite. This is as true of declaratory judgments as any other field. These appellants seem clearly to seek advisory opinions upon broad claims of rights protected by the First, Fifth, Ninth and Tenth Amendments to the Constitution. As these appellants are classified employees, they have a right superior to the generality of citizens, compare Fairchild v. Hughes, 258 U.S. 126, but the facts of their personal interest in their civil rights, of the general threat of possible interference with those rights by the Civil Service Commission under its rules, if specified things are done by appellants, does not make a justiciable case or controversy. Appellants want to engage in 'political management and political campaigns,' to persuade others to follow appellants' views by discussion, speeches, articles and other acts reasonably designed to secure the selection of appellants' political choices. Such generality of objection is really an attack on the political expediency of the Hatch Act, not the presentation of legal issues. It is beyond the competence of courts to render such a decision. Texas v. Interstate Commerce Commission, 258 U.S. 158, 162.

"The power of courts, and ultimately of this Court to pass upon the constitutionality of acts of Congress arises only when the interests of litigants require the use of this judicial authority for their protection against actual interference. A hypothetical threat is not enough. We can only speculate as to the kinds of political activity the appellants desire to engage in or as to the contents of their proposed public statements or the circumstances of their publication. It would not accord with judicial responsibility to adjudge, in a matter involving constitutionality, between the freedom of the individual and the requirements of public order except when definite rights appear upon the one side and definite prejudicial interferences upon the other.

"The Constitution allots the nation's judicial power to the federal courts. Unless these courts respect the limits of that unique authority, they intrude upon powers vested in the legislative or executive branches. Judicial adherence to the doctrine of the separation of powers preserves the courts for the decision of issues, between litigants, capable of effective determination. Judicial exposition upon political proposals is permissible only when necessary to decide definite issues between litigants. When the courts act continually within these constitutionally imposed boundaries of their power, their ability to perform their function as a balance for the people's protection against abuse of power by other branches of government remains unimpaired. Should the courts seek to expand their power so as to bring under their jurisdiction ill defined controversies over constitutional issues, they would become the organ of political theories. Such abuse of judicial power would properly meet rebuke and restriction from other branches. By these mutual checks and balances by and between the branches of government, democracy undertakes to preserve the liberties of the people from excessive concentrations of authority. No threat of interference by the Commission with rights of these appellants appears beyond that implied by the existence of the law and the regulations. Watson v. Buck, supra, 313 U.S. at page 400. We should not take judicial cognizance of the situation presented on the part of the appellants considered in this subdivision of the opinion. These reasons lead us to conclude that the determination of the trial court, that the individual appellants, other than Poole, could maintain this action, was erroneous."

———

ADLER v. BOARD OF EDUCATION, 342 U.S. 485 (1952). Plaintiffs brought suit in the New York courts seeking a judgment declaring unconstitutional the Feinberg Law, which required the discharge of teachers who belonged to allegedly subversive groups. The plaintiffs moved for a judgment on the pleadings in the trial court, which was granted. The New York Court of Appeals reversed the trial court judgment and the case came to the Supreme Court by appeal. That Court affirmed on the merits without considering issues of ripeness or concreteness. Justice Frankfurter, dissenting, said:

"The allegations in the present action fall short of these found insufficient in the *Mitchell* Case. These teachers do not allege that they have engaged in proscribed conduct or . . . that they have been, or are, deterred from supporting causes or from joining organizations for fear of the Feinberg Law's interdict, except to say generally that the system complained of will have this effect on teachers as a group. They do not assert that they are threatened with action under law, or that steps are imminent whereby they would incur the hazard of punishment for conduct innocent at the time, or under standards too vague to satisfy due process of law. They merely allege that the statutes and Rules permit such action against some teachers. Since we rightly refused in the *Mitchell* Case to hear government employees whose conduct was much more intimately affected by the law there attacked than are the claims of the plaintiffs here, this suit is wanting in the necessary basis for our review."

NOTES ON MITCHELL AND ADLER

1. *Mitchell* and *Adler* suggest that the degree of concreteness required may vary with the nature of the constitutional issue presented. By moving for a judgment on the pleadings the plaintiffs in *Adler* presented the question whether there could be any constitutional applications of the statute—a question that could be decided without reference to the particular conduct of the plaintiffs. See Scharpf, *Judicial Review and the Political Question: A Functional Analysis,* 75 Yale L.J. 517, 531–533 (1966). In United States Civil Service Comm'n. v. Letter Carriers, 413 U.S. 548 (1973) the Court upheld the Hatch Act a second time in a suit brought by plaintiffs who did no more than allege their desire to engage in various political activities—allegations essentially similar to those held inadequate in *Mitchell.* The Court did not discuss the ripeness and concreteness issues. However, this time the Court was considering contentions that the Act was unconstitutional on its face as vague and overbroad—constitutional contentions that do not depend upon the facts of the particular case for resolution.

2. Are *Adler* and *Mitchell* distinguishable on another basis? *Mitchell* arose in a federal court action, and the ripeness issue concerned the standards for granting federal declaratory judgments. In *Adler,* the Court was reviewing a state court decision holding that the challenged statute did not violate the United States Constitution, and the issue of ripeness concerned the appropriate standard for reviewing a state court decision. See note, *Case and Controversy Requirements as Applied to Constitutional Litigation Arising in State and Federal Courts,* supra, p. 119. Contrast Poe v. Ullman, which follows, another case seeking review of a state court declaratory judgment.

POE v. ULLMAN, 367 U.S. 497 (1961). A doctor and his patients brought declaratory judgment actions in the Connecticut courts seeking a determination that a Connecticut statute making it a crime to use birth control devices was unconstitutional. The state courts upheld the validity of the statute. The Supreme Court dismissed the appeals on the ground that there was no real controversy since the Connecticut statute was not enforced and hence there was no real fear of personal liability. In discussing the declaratory judgment problem in the plurality opinion, Mr. Justice Frankfurter said: "For just as the declaratory judgment device does not 'purport to alter the character of the controversies which are the subject of the judicial power under the Constitution,' United States v. State of West Virginia, 295 U.S. 463, 475, . . . it does not permit litigants to invoke the power of this Court to obtain constitutional rulings in advance of necessity. Electric Bond & Share Co. v. Securities and Exchange Comm., 303 U.S. 419, 443. The Court has been on the alert against use of the declaratory judgment device for avoiding the rigorous insistence on exigent adversity as a condition for evoking Court adjudication. This is as true of state court suits for declaratory judgments as of federal. By exercising their jurisdiction, state courts cannot determine the jurisdiction to be exercised by this Court. Tyler v. Judges of the Court of Registration, 179 U.S. 405; Doremus v. Board of Education, 342 U.S. 429. Although we have held that a state declaratory-judgment suit may constitute a case or controversy within our appellate jurisdiction, it is to be reviewed here only 'so long as the case retains the essentials of an adversary proceeding, involving a real, not a hypothetical, controversy, which is finally determined by the judgment below.' Nashville, C. & St. L.R. Co. v. Wallace, 288 U.S. 249, 264. It was with respect to a state-originating declaratory judgment proceeding that we said, in Alabama State Federation of Labor, etc. v. McAdory, 325 U.S. 450, 471, that 'The extent to which the declaratory judgment procedure may be used in the federal courts to control state action lies in the sound discretion of the Court. . . .' Indeed, we have recognized, in such cases, that '. . . the discretionary element characteristic of declaratory jurisdiction, and imported perhaps from equity jurisdiction and practice without the remedial phase, offers a convenient instrument for making . . . effective . . . .' the policy against premature constitutional decision. Rescue Army v. Municipal Court, 331 U.S. 549, 573, note 41."

———

EPPERSON v. ARKANSAS, 393 U.S. 97 (1968). A teacher in a public school brought suit for a declaratory judgment that a state statute prohibiting teaching the theory of evolution in public schools was unconstitutional. Her school adopted a biology textbook containing a chapter on Darwin. The Arkansas Supreme Court upheld the validity of the law. The Supreme Court reversed on the merits. [For the decision, see page 1425, infra.] The Court did not raise any question whether the decision below was reviewable. A concurring opinion by Justice Black, however, expressed doubts whether "there was a genuinely justiciable case or controversy." Justice Black pointed out that the statute had been enacted forty years before, there was no indication it had ever been enforced, and "the pallid, unenthusiastic, even apologetic defense of the Act presented by the State in this Court indicates that the State would make no attempt to enforce the law."

———

YOUNGER v. HARRIS, 401 U.S. 37 (1971). A suit was brought in the federal district court to enjoin the District Attorney of Los Angeles County from prosecuting the plaintiffs under the California Criminal Syndicalism Act. On the question of the concreteness of the controversy the Court said:

"Appellee Harris has been indicted, and was actually being prosecuted by California for a violation of its Criminal Syndicalism Act at the time this suit was filed. He thus has an acute, live controversy with the State and its prosecutor. But none of the other parties plaintiff in the District Court, Dan, Hirsch, or Broslawsky, has such a controversy. None has been indicted, arrested, or even threatened by the prosecutor. About these three the three-judge court said:

" 'Plaintiffs Dan and Hirsch allege that they are members of the Progressive Labor Party, which advocates change in industrial ownership and political change, and that they feel inhibited in advocating the program of their political party through peaceful, nonviolent means, because of the presence of the Act "on the books", and because of the pending criminal prosecution against Harris. Plaintiff Broslawsky is a history instructor, and he alleges that he is uncertain as to whether his normal practice of teaching his students about the doctrines of Karl Marx and reading from the Communist Manifesto and other revolutionary works may subject him to prosecution for violation of the Act.' 281 F.Supp., at 509.

". . . Whatever right Harris, who is being prosecuted under the State Syndicalism law may have, Dan, Hirsch, and Broslawsky cannot share it with him. If these three had alleged that they would be prosecuted for the conduct they planned to engage in, and if the District Court had found this allegation to be true—either on the admission of the State's district attorney or on any other evidence—then a genuine controversy might be said to exist. But here appellees Dan, Hirsch, and Broslawsky do not claim that they have ever been threatened with prosecution, that a prosecution is likely, or even that a prosecution is remotely possible. They claim the right to bring this suit solely because, in the language of their complaint, they 'feel inhibited.' We do not think this allegation even if true, is sufficient to bring the equitable jurisdiction of the federal courts into play to enjoin a pending state prosecution. A federal lawsuit to stop a prosecution in a state court is a serious matter. And persons having no fears of state prosecution except those that are imaginary or speculative, are not to be accepted as appropriate plaintiffs in such cases. See Golden v. Zwickler, 394 U.S. 103 (1969). Since Harris is actually being prosecuted under the challenged laws, however, we proceed with him as a proper party."

RIPENESS AND CRIMINAL PROSECUTIONS

In Regional Rail Reorganization Act Cases, 419 U.S. 102, 143, n. 29 (1974) the Court said: ". . . Because the decision to instigate a criminal prosecution is usually discretionary with the prosecuting authorities, even a person with a settled intention to disobey the law can never be sure that the sanctions of the law will be invoked against him. Further, whether or not the injury will occur is to some extent within the control of the complaining party himself, since he can decide to abandon his intention to disobey the law. For these reasons, the maturity of such disputes for resolution before a prosecution begins is decided on a case-by-case basis, by considering the likelihood that the complainant will disobey the law, the certainty that such disobedience will take a particular form, any present injury occasioned by the threat of prosecution, and the likelihood that a prosecution will actually ensue."

CITY OF LOS ANGELES v. LYONS

461 U.S. 95, 103 S.Ct. 1660, 75 L.Ed.2d 675 (1983).

Justice White delivered the opinion of the Court.

The issue here is whether respondent Lyons satisfied the prerequisites for seeking injunctive relief in the federal district court.

I

This case began on February 7, 1977, when respondent, Adolph Lyons, filed a complaint for damages, injunction, and declaratory relief in the United States District Court for the Central District of California. The defendants were the City of Los Angeles and four of its police officers. The complaint alleged that on October 6, 1976, at 2 a.m., Lyons was stopped by the defendant officers for a traffic or vehicle code violation and that although Lyons offered no resistance or threat whatsoever, the officers, without provocation or justification, seized Lyons and applied a "chokehold"—either the "bar arm control" hold or the "carotid-artery control" hold or both—rendering him unconscious and causing damage to his larynx. Counts I through IV of the complaint sought damages against the officers and the City. Count V, with which we are principally concerned here, sought a preliminary and permanent injunction against the City barring the use of the control holds. That count alleged that the city's police officers, "pursuant to the authorization, instruction and encouragement of defendant City of Los Angeles, regularly and routinely apply these choke holds in innumerable situations where they are not threatened by the use of any deadly force whatsoever," that numerous persons have been injured as the result of the application of the chokeholds, that Lyons and others similarly situated are threatened with irreparable injury in the form of bodily injury and loss of life, and that Lyons "justifiably fears that any contact he has with Los Angeles police officers may result in his being choked and strangled to death without provocation, justification or other legal excuse." Lyons alleged the threatened impairment of rights protected by the First, Fourth, Eighth and Fourteenth Amendments. Injunctive relief was sought against the use of the control holds "except in situations where the proposed victim of said control reasonably appears to be threatening the immediate use of deadly force." Count VI sought declaratory relief against the City, i.e., a judgment that use of the chokeholds absent the threat of immediate use of deadly force is a *per se* violation of various constitutional rights.

The District Court, by order, granted the City's motion for partial judgment on the pleadings and entered judgment for the City on Count V and VI. The Court of Appeals reversed the judgment for the City on Count V and VI, holding over the City's objection that despite our decisions in O'Shea v. Littleton, 414 U.S. 488 (1974), and Rizzo v. Goode, 423 U.S. 362 (1976), Lyons had standing to seek relief against the application of the chokeholds. 615 F.2d 1243. The Court of Appeals held that there was a sufficient likelihood that Lyons would again be stopped and subjected to the unlawful use of force to constitute a case or controversy and to warrant the issuance of an injunction, if the injunction was otherwise authorized. We denied certiorari. 449 U.S. 934.

On remand . . . [a] preliminary injunction was entered enjoining "the use of both the carotid-artery and bar arm holds under circumstances which do not threaten death or serious bodily injury." An improved training program and regular reporting and record keeping were also ordered.[3] The Court of Appeals affirmed in a brief *per curiam* opinion . . . We . . . reverse.

. . .

III

It goes without saying that those who seek to invoke the jurisdiction of the federal courts must satisfy the threshold requirement imposed by Article III of the Constitution by alleging an actual case or controversy. . . .

In O'Shea v. Littleton, 414 U.S. 488 (1974), we dealt with a case brought by a class of plaintiffs claiming that they had been subjected to discriminatory enforcement of the criminal law. Among other things, a county magistrate and judge were accused of discriminatory conduct in various respects, such as sentencing members of plaintiff's class more harshly than other defendants. The Court of Appeals reversed the dismissal of the suit by the District Court, ruling that if the allegations were proved, an appropriate injunction could be entered.

We reversed for failure of the complaint to allege a case or controversy. . . . Although it was claimed in that case that particular members of the plaintiff class had actually suffered from the alleged unconstitutional practices, we observed that "[p]ast exposure to illegal conduct does not in itself show a present case or controversy regarding injunctive relief . . . if unaccompanied by any continuing, present adverse effects." . . . Past wrongs were evidence bearing on "whether there is a real and immediate threat of repeated injury." . . . But the prospect of future injury rested "on the likelihood that [plaintiffs] will again be arrested for and charged with violations of the criminal law and will again be subjected to bond proceedings, trial, or sentencing before petitioners." . . . The most that could be said for plaintiffs' standing was "that *if* [plaintiffs] proceed to violate an unchallenged law and *if* they are charged, held to answer, and tried in any proceedings before petitioners, they will be subjected to the discriminatory practices that petitioners are

---

[3] By its terms, the injunction was to continue in force until the court approved the training program to be presented to it. It is fair to assume that such approval would not be given if the program did not confine the use of the strangleholds to those situations in which their use, in the view of the District Court, would be constitutional. Because of successive stays entered by the Court of Appeals and by this court, the injunction has not gone into effect.

alleged to have followed." . . . . We could not find a case or controversy in those circumstances: the threat to the plaintiffs was not "sufficiently real and immediate to show an existing controversy simply because they anticipate violating lawful criminal statutes and being tried for their offenses. . . . ."
. . . It was to be assumed "that [plaintiffs] will conduct their activities within the law and so avoid prosecution and conviction as well as exposure to the challenged course of conduct said to be followed by petitioners." . . .

We . . . went on to hold that even if the complaint presented an existing case or controversy, an adequate basis for equitable relief against petitioners had not been demonstrated:

> "[Plaintiffs] have failed, moreover, to establish the basic requisites of the issuance of equitable relief in these circumstances—the likelihood of substantial and immediate irreparable injury, and the inadequacy of remedies at law. We have already canvassed the necessarily conjectural nature of the threatened injury to which [plaintiffs] are allegedly subjected. . . . [I]f any of the [plaintiffs] are ever prosecuted and face trial, or if they are illegally sentenced, there are available state and federal procedures which could provide relief from the wrongful conduct alleged." . . .

Another relevant decision for present purposes is Rizzo v. Goode, 423 U.S. 362, 96 S.Ct. 598, 46 L.Ed.2d 561 (1976), a case in which plaintiffs alleged widespread illegal and unconstitutional police conduct aimed at minority citizens and against City residents in general. . . . The claim of injury rested upon "what one or a small, unnamed minority of policemen might do to them in the future because of that unknown policeman's perception" of departmental procedures. . . . This hypothesis was "even more attenuated than those allegations of future injury found insufficient in O'Shea to warrant [the] invocation of federal jurisdiction." . . . The Court also held that plaintiffs' showing at trial of a relatively few instances of violations by individual police officers, without any showing of a deliberate policy on behalf of the named defendants, did not provide a basis for equitable relief.

Golden v. Zwickler, 394 U.S. 103 (1969), a case arising in an analogous situation, is directly apposite. Congressman Zwickler sought a declaratory judgment that a New York statute prohibiting anonymous handbills directly pertaining to election campaigns was unconstitutional. Although Zwickler had once been convicted under the statute, he was no longer a Congressman apt to run for reelection. A unanimous Court held that because it was "most unlikely" that Zwickler would again be subject to the statute, no case or controversy of "sufficient immediacy and reality" was present to allow a declaratory judgment. . . .

. . . .

IV

No extension of *O'Shea* and *Rizzo* is necessary to hold that respondent Lyons has failed to demonstrate a case or controversy with the City that would justify the equitable relief sought. Lyons' standing to seek the injunction requested depended on whether he was likely to suffer future injury from the use of the chokeholds by police officers. Count V of the complaint alleged the traffic stop and choking incident five months before. That Lyons may have been illegally choked by the police on October 6, 1976, while presumably affording Lyons standing to claim damages against the individual officers and perhaps against the City, does nothing to establish a real and immediate threat that he would again be stopped for a traffic violation, or for any other offense, by an officer or officers who would illegally choke him into unconsciousness without any provocation or resistance on his part. The additional allegation in the complaint that the police in Los Angeles routinely apply chokeholds in situations where they are not threatened by the use of deadly force falls far short of the allegations that would be necessary to establish a case or controversy between these parties.

In order to establish an actual controversy in this case, Lyons would have had not only to allege that he would have another encounter with the police but also to make the incredible assertion either, (1) that *all* police officers in Los Angeles *always* choke any citizen with whom they happen to have an encounter, whether for the purpose of arrest, issuing a citation or for questioning or, (2) that the City ordered or authorized police officers to act in such manner.   Although Count V alleged that the City authorized the use of the control holds in situations where deadly force was not threatened, it did not indicate why Lyons might be realistically threatened by police officers who acted within the strictures of the City's policy.   If, for example, chokeholds were authorized to be used only to counter resistance to an arrest by a suspect, or to thwart an effort to escape, any future threat to Lyons from the City's policy or from the conduct of police officers would be no more real than the possibility that he would again have an encounter with the police and that either he would illegally resist arrest or detention or the officers would disobey their instructions and again render him unconscious without any provocation.[7]

Under *O'Shea* and *Rizzo,* these allegations were an insufficient basis to provide a federal court with jurisdiction to entertain Count V of the complaint. . . .   For several reasons—each of them infirm, in our view—the Court of Appeals thought reliance on *O'Shea* and *Rizzo* was misplaced and reversed the District Court.

First, the Court of Appeals thought that Lyons was more immediately threatened than the plaintiffs in those cases since, according to the Court of Appeals, Lyons need only be stopped for a minor traffic violation to be subject to the strangleholds.   But even assuming that Lyons would again be stopped for a traffic or other violation in the reasonably near future, it is untenable to assert, and the complaint made no such allegation, that strangleholds are applied by the Los Angeles police to every citizen who is stopped or arrested regardless of the conduct of the person stopped.   We cannot agree that the "odds" that Lyons would not only again be stopped for a traffic violation but would also be subjected to a chokehold without any provocation whatsoever are sufficient to make out a federal case for equitable relief. . . .

. . .   [I]t is surely no more than speculation to assert either that Lyons himself will again be involved in one of those unfortunate instances, or that he will be arrested in the future and provoke the use of a chokehold by resisting arrest, attempting to escape, or threatening deadly force or serious bodily injury.

---

[7] The centerpiece of Justice Marshall's dissent is that Lyons had standing to challenge the City's policy because to recover damages he would have to prove that what allegedly occurred on October 6, 1976, was pursuant to City authorization.   We agree completely that for Lyons to succeed in his damages action, it would be necessary to prove that what happened to him—that is, as alleged, he was choked without any provocation or legal excuse whatsoever—was pursuant to a City policy. . . .

. . .   [E]ven if the complaint must be read as containing an allegation that officers are authorized to apply the chokeholds where there is no resistance or other provocation, it does not follow that Lyons has standing to seek an injunction against the application of the restraint holds in situations that he has not experienced, as for example, where the suspect resists arrest or tries to escape but does not threaten the use of deadly force.   Yet that is precisely the scope of the injunction that Lyons prayed for in Count B.

. . .   [I]n any event, to have a case or controversy with the City that could sustain Count V, Lyons would have to credibly allege that he faced a realistic threat from the future application of the City's policy.   Justice Marshall nowhere confronts this requirement—the necessity that Lyons demonstrate that he, himself, will not only again be stopped by the police but will be choked without any provocation or legal excuse.   Justice Marshall plainly does not agree with that requirement, and he was in dissent in O'Shea v. Littleton.   We are at issue in that respect.

Second, the Court of Appeals viewed *O'Shea* and *Rizzo* as cases in which the plaintiffs sought "massive structural" relief against the local law enforcement systems and therefore that the holdings in those cases were inapposite to cases such as this where the plaintiff, according to the Court of Appeals, seeks to enjoin only an "established," "sanctioned" police practice assertedly violative of constitutional rights. *O'Shea* and *Rizzo*, however, cannot be so easily confined to their facts. If Lyons has made no showing that he is realistically threatened by a repetition of his experience of October, 1976, then he has not met the requirements for seeking an injunction in a federal court, whether the injunction contemplates intrusive structural relief or the cessation of a discrete practice.

The Court of Appeals also asserted that Lyons "had a live and active claim" against the City "if only for a period of a few seconds" while the stranglehold was being applied to him and that for two reasons the claim had not become moot so as to disentitle Lyons to injunctive relief: First, because under normal rules of equity, a case does not become moot merely because the complained of conduct has ceased; and second, because Lyons' claim is "capable of repetition but evading review" and therefore should be heard. We agree that Lyons had a live controversy with the City. Indeed, he still has a claim for damages against the City that appears to meet all Article III requirements. Nevertheless, the issue here is not whether that claim has become moot but whether Lyons meets the preconditions for asserting an injunctive claim in a federal forum. The equitable doctrine that cessation of the challenged conduct does not bar an injunction is of little help in this respect, for Lyons' lack of standing does not rest on the termination of the police practice but on the speculative nature of his claim that he will again experience injury as the result of that practice even if continued.

.   .   .

V

Lyons fares no better if it be assumed that his pending damages suit affords him Article III standing to seek an injunction as a remedy for the claim arising out of the October 1976 events. .   .   .

.   .   .

Absent a sufficient likelihood that he will again be wronged in a similar way, Lyons is no more entitled to an injunction than any other citizen of Los Angeles; and a federal court may not entertain a claim by any or all citizens who no more than assert that certain practices of law enforcement officers are unconstitutional.

.   .   .

We decline the invitation to slight the preconditions for equitable relief; for as we have held, recognition of the need for a proper balance between state and federal authority counsels restraint in the issuance of injunctions against state officers engaged in the administration of the states' criminal laws in the absence of irreparable injury which is both great and immediate. .   .   .

.   .   .

.   .   . [T]he state courts need not impose the same standing or remedial requirements that govern federal court proceedings. The individual states may permit their courts to use injunctions to oversee the conduct of law enforcement authorities on a continuing basis. But this is not the role of a federal court absent far more justification than Lyons has proffered in this case.

The judgment of the Court of Appeals is accordingly

Reversed.

Justice Marshall, with whom Justice Brennan, Justice Blackmun and Justice Stevens join, dissenting.

The District Court found that the City of Los Angeles authorizes its police officers to apply life-threatening chokeholds to citizens who pose no threat of violence, and that respondent, Adolph Lyons, was subjected to such a chokehold. The Court today holds that a federal court is without power to enjoin the enforcement of the City's policy, no matter how flagrantly unconstitutional it may be. Since no one can show that he will be choked in the future, no one—not even a person who, like Lyons, has almost been choked to death— has standing to challenge the continuation of the policy. The City is free to continue the policy indefinitely as long as it is willing to pay damages for the injuries and deaths that result. I dissent from this unprecedented and unwarranted approach to standing.

II

At the outset it is important to emphasize that Lyons' entitlement to injunctive relief and his entitlement to an award of damages both depend upon whether he can show that the City's chokehold policy violates the Constitution. . . .

III

Since Lyons' claim for damages plainly gives him standing, and since the success of that claim depends upon a demonstration that the City's chokehold policy is unconstitutional, it is beyond dispute that Lyons has properly invoked the District Court's authority to adjudicate the constitutionality of the City's chokehold policy. The dispute concerning the constitutionality of that policy plainly presents a "case or controversy" under Article III. The Court nevertheless holds that a federal court has no power under Article III to adjudicate Lyons' request, in the same lawsuit, for injunctive relief with respect to that very policy. . . .

A

It is simply disingenuous for the Court to assert that its decision requires "[n]o extension" of O'Shea v. Littleton, 414 U.S. 488 (1974), and Rizzo v. Goode, 423 U.S. 362 (1976). In contrast to this case *O'Shea* and *Rizzo* involved disputes focusing solely on the threat of future injury which the plaintiffs in those cases alleged they faced. In *O'Shea* the plaintiffs did not allege past injury and did not seek compensatory relief. In *Rizzo,* the plaintiffs sought only declaratory and injunctive relief and alleged past instances of police misconduct only in an attempt to establish the substantiality of the threat of future injury. . . . was similarly no claim for damages based on past injuries in Ashcroft v. Mattis, 431 U.S. 171 (1977), or Golden v. Zwickler, 394 U.S. 103 (1969), on which the Court also relies.

. . . As the Court recognized in *O'Shea,* standing under Article III is established by an allegation of "threatened or actual injury." Id., 414 U.S., at 493, quoting Linda R.S. v. Richard D., 410 U.S. 614, 617 (1973) (emphasis added). See also 414 U.S., at 493, n. 2. Because the plaintiffs in *O'Shea, Rizzo, Mattis,* and *Zwickler* did not seek to redress past injury, their standing to sue depended entirely on the risk of future injury they faced. Apart from the desire to eliminate the possibility of future injury, the plaintiffs in those cases had no other personal stake in the outcome of the controversies.

By contrast, Lyons' request for prospective relief is coupled with his claim for damages . . . In addition to the risk that he will be subjected to a chokehold in the future, Lyons has suffered past injury. Because he has a live claim for damages, he need not rely solely on the threat of future injury to establish his personal stake in the outcome of the controversy. In the cases relied on by the majority, the Court simply had no occasion to decide whether a plaintiff who has standing to litigate a dispute must clear a separate standing hurdle with respect to each form of relief sought.

. . .

C

By fragmenting the standing inquiry and imposing a separate standing hurdle with respect to each form of relief sought, the decision today departs significantly from this Court's traditional conception of the standing requirement and of the remedial powers of the federal courts. We have never required more than that a plaintiff have standing to litigate a claim. Whether he will be entitled to obtain particular forms of relief should he prevail has never been understood to be an issue of standing. . . .

. . .

IV

Apart from the question of standing, the only remaining question presented in the petition for certiorari is whether the preliminary injunction issued by the District Court must be set aside because it "constitute[s] a substantial interference in the operation of a municipal police department." In my view it does not.

. . .

The principles of federalism simply do not preclude the limited preliminary injunction issued in this case. Unlike the permanent injunction at issue in *Rizzo,* the preliminary injunction involved here entails no federal supervision of the LAPD's activities. The preliminary injunction merely forbids the use of chokeholds absent the threat of deadly force, permitting their continued use where such a threat does exist. This limited ban takes the form of a preventive injunction, which has traditionally been regarded as the least intrusive form of equitable relief. Moreover, the City can remove the ban by obtaining approval of a training plan. Although the preliminary injunction also requires the City to provide records of the uses of chokeholds to respondent and to allow the court access to such records, this requirement is hardly onerous, since the LAPD already maintains records concerning the use of chokeholds.

V

Apparently because it is unwilling to rely solely on its unprecedented rule of standing, the Court goes on to conclude that, even if Lyons has standing, "[t]he equitable remedy is unavailable." . . .

. . .

The District Court concluded, on the basis of the facts before it, that Lyons was choked without provocation pursuant to an unconstitutional City policy. Given the necessarily preliminary nature of its inquiry, there was no way for the District Court to know the precise contours of the City's policy or to ascertain the risk that Lyons, who had alleged that the policy was being applied in a discriminatory manner, might again be subjected to a chokehold. But in view of the Court's conclusion that the unprovoked choking of Lyons was pursuant to a City policy, Lyons has satisfied "the usual basis for injunctive relief, 'that there exists some cognizable danger of recurrent violation.'" . . . The risk of serious injuries and deaths to other citizens also supported the decision to grant a preliminary injunction. Courts of equity have much greater latitude in granting injunctive relief "in furtherance of the public interest . . . than when only private interests are involved." . . . In this case we know that the District Court would have been amply justified in considering the risk to the public, for after the preliminary injunction was stayed, five additional deaths occurred prior to the adoption of a moratorium. Under these circumstances, I do not believe that the District Court abused its discretion.

VI

The Court's decision removes an entire class of constitutional violations from the equitable powers of a federal court. It immunizes from prospective equitable relief any policy that authorizes persistent deprivations of constitutional rights as long as no individual can establish with substantial certainty that he will be injured, or injured again, in the future. . . . Under the view expressed by the majority today, if the police adopt a policy of "shoot to kill," or a policy of shooting one out of ten suspects, the federal courts will be powerless to enjoin its continuation. . . . The federal judicial power is now limited to levying a toll for such a systematic constitutional violation.

E. POLITICAL QUESTIONS

JOHN MARSHALL ON POLITICAL QUESTIONS

"Even before he became a judge, Marshall was aware of a solution to the problem of the political usurpation of judges as evidenced by a speech he made in the House of Representatives.

" 'By extending the judicial power to all *cases in law and equity,* the constitution had never been understood to confer on that department any political power whatever. To come within this department a question must assume a legal form for forensic litigation and judicial decision. There must be parties to come into court, who can be reached by its process, and bound by its power; whose rights admit of ultimate decision by a tribunal to which they are bound to submit.' [38]

"Marshall knew that the court handled political issues; anyone who would deny this is foolish. But Marshall also realized that the handling of such issues by the court is not a political one but a legal one. The question must take on a legal form; it must be argued by real parties; and they are bound by the decision in the case before the bar. The court has no political power at all. What Marshall meant by this was that the court cannot act in a political way. The court can and must handle questions of public policy, political questions; but it cannot handle the question in the way of politics, but in the way of law. The entire question must be changed into a legal question, and the decision on the issue is not a policy decision but a judgment concerning the merits of the two opposing parties who have taken sides on the issue. Granted that the result of this legal decision may have grave effects for public policy and that the judge neither should nor can take his eye off these effects, the judge must always begin and end with the case before him. No matter how far afield his reasoning may take him, he is always forced to return to the case and the parties at bar. Marshall makes here an important distinction which cannot be overlooked by the modern commentators who profess to study the court as if it were an *ad hoc* legislature." Umbanhowar, *Marshall on Judging,* 7 Am.J.Leg.Hist. 210, 224 (1963).

---

[38] Addresss by John Marshall, U.S. House of Representatives, 1794 (on the Resolution of the Honorable Edward Livingston, relative to Thomas Nash, alias Jonathan Robins) 13 (1848).

BAKER v. CARR, 369 U.S. 186 (1962). The Court held that a suit by voters alleging that the apportionment of a state legislature denied to them the equal protection of the laws and seeking reapportionment of that legislature did not involve a nonjusticiable political question. The following discussion of the political questions doctrine in the opinion of the Court by Justice Brennan is significant:

"We have said that 'in determining whether a question falls within [the political question] category, the appropriateness under our system of government of attributing finality to the action of the political departments and also the lack of satisfactory criteria for a judicial determination are dominant considerations.' Coleman v. Miller, 307 U.S. 433, 454–455. The nonjusticiability of a political question is primarily a function of the separation of powers. Much confusion results from the capacity of the 'political question' label to obscure the need for case-by-case inquiry. Deciding whether a matter has in any measure been committed by the Constitution to another branch of government, or whether the action of that branch exceeds whatever authority has been committed, is itself a delicate exercise in constitutional interpretation, and is a responsibility of this Court as ultimate interpreter of the Constitution. To demonstrate this requires no less than to analyze representative cases and to infer from them analytical threads that make up the political question doctrine. We shall then show that none of those threads catches this case.

"*Foreign Relations.* There are sweeping statements to the effect that all questions touching foreign relations are political questions. Not only does resolution of such issues frequently turn on standards that defy judicial application, or involve the exercise of a discretion demonstrably committed to the executive or legislature; but many such questions uniquely demand single-voiced statement of the Government's views. Yet it is error to suppose that every case or controversy which touches foreign relations lies beyond judicial cognizance. Our cases in this field seem invariably to show a discriminating analysis of the particular question posed, in terms of the history of its management by the political branches, of its susceptibility to judicial handling in the light of its nature and posture in the specific case, and of the possible consequences of judicial action. For example, though a court will not ordinarily inquire whether a treaty has been terminated, since on that question 'governmental action   . . .   must be regarded as of controlling importance,' if there has been no conclusive 'governmental action' then a court can construe a treaty and may find it provides the answer. Compare Terlinden v. Ames, 184 U.S. 270, 285, with Society for the Propagation of the Gospel in Foreign Parts v. New Haven, 8 Wheat. 464, 492–495. Though a court will not undertake to construe a treaty in a manner inconsistent with a subsequent federal statute, no similar hesitancy obtains if the asserted clash is with state law. Compare Whitney v. Robertson, 124 U.S. 190, with Kolovrat v. Oregon, 366 U.S. 187.

. . .

"*Dates of Duration of Hostilities.* Though it has been stated broadly that 'the power which declared the necessity is the power to declare its cessation, and what the cessation requires,' Commercial Trust Co. v. Miller, 262 U.S. 51, 57, here too analysis reveals isolable reasons for the presence of political questions, underlying this Court's refusal to review the political departments' determination of when or whether a war has ended. Dominant is the need for finality in the political determination, for emergency's nature demands 'a prompt and unhesitating obedience,' Martin v. Mott, 12 Wheat. 19, 30 (calling up of militia). . . .

"*Validity of Enactments.* In Coleman v. Miller, supra, this Court held that the questions of how long a proposed amendment to the Federal Constitution remained open to ratification and what effect a prior rejection had on a subsequent ratification, were committed to congressional resolution and involved criteria of decision that necessarily escaped the judicial grasp. Similar considerations apply to the enacting process: 'the respect due to coequal and independent departments,' and the need for finality and certainty about the status of a statute contribute to judicial reluctance to inquire whether, as passed, it complied with all requisite formalities. Field v. Clark, 143 U.S. 649, 672, 676–677; see Leser v. Garnett, 258 U.S. 130, 137. But it is not true that courts will never delve into a legislature's records upon such a quest: If the enrolled statute lacks an effective date, a court will not hesitate to seek it in the legislative journals in order to preserve the enactment. Gardner v. Collector, 6 Wall. 499. The political question doctrine, a tool for maintenance of governmental order, will not be so applied as to promote only disorder. . . .

"It is apparent that several formulations which vary slightly according to the settings in which the questions arise may describe a political question, although each has one or more elements which identifies it as essentially a function of the separation of powers. Prominent on the surface of any case held to involve a political question is found a textually demonstrable constitutional commitment of the issue to a coordinate political department; or a lack of judicially discoverable and manageable standards for resolving it; or the impossibility of deciding without an initial policy determination of a kind clearly for nonjudicial discretion; or the impossibility of a court's undertaking independent resolution without expressing lack of the respect due coordinate branches of government; or an unusual need for unquestioning adherence to a political decision already made; or the potentiality of embarrassment from multifarious pronouncements by various departments on one question.

"Unless one of these formulations is inextricable from the case at bar, there should be no dismissal for non-justiciability on the ground of a political question's presence. The doctrine of which we treat is one of 'political questions,' not one of 'political cases.' The courts cannot reject as 'no law suit' a bona fide controversy as to whether some action denominated 'political' exceeds constitutional authority. The cases we have reviewed show the necessity for discriminating inquiry into the precise facts and posture of the particular case, and the impossibility of resolution by any semantic cataloguing.

"But it is argued that this case shares the characteristics of decisions that constitute a category not yet considered, cases concerning the Constitution's guaranty, in Art. IV, § 4, of a republican form of government. A conclusion as to whether the case at bar does present a political question cannot be confidently reached until we have considered those cases with special care. We shall discover that Guaranty Clause claims involve those elements which define a 'political question,' and for that reason and no other, they are nonjusticiable. In particular, we shall discover that the nonjusticiability of such claims has nothing to do with their touching upon matters of state governmental organization.

"*Republican Form of Government.* Luther v. Borden, 7 How. 1, 48 U.S. 1, though in form simply an action for damages for trespass was, as Daniel Webster said in opening the argument for the defense, 'an unusual case.' The defendants, admitting an otherwise tortious breaking and entering, sought to justify their action on the ground that they were agents of the established lawful government of Rhode Island, which State was then under martial law to defend itself from active insurrection; that the plaintiff was engaged in that insurrection; and that they entered under orders to arrest the plaintiff. The case arose 'out of the unfortunate political differences which agitated the people of Rhode Island in 1841 and 1842,' 7 How. at 34, which had resulted in a situation wherein two groups laid competing claims to recognition as the lawful government. The plaintiff's right to recover depended upon which of the two groups was entitled to such recognition; but the lower court's refusal to receive evidence or hear argument on that issue, its charge to the jury that the earlier established or 'charter' government was lawful, and the verdict for the defendants, were affirmed upon appeal to this Court. . . .

"Clearly, several factors were thought by the Court in Luther to make the question there 'political': the commitment to the other branches of the decision as to which is the lawful state government; the unambiguous action by the President, in recognizing the charter government as the lawful authority; the need for finality in the executive's decision; and the lack of criteria by which a court could determine which form of government was republican.[a]"

POWELL v. McCORMACK

395 U.S. 486, 89 S.Ct. 1944, 23 L.Ed.2d 491 (1969).

Mr. Chief Justice Warren delivered the opinion of the Court.

In November 1966, Petitioner Adam Clayton Powell, Jr., was duly elected from the 18th Congressional District of New York to serve in the United States House of Representatives for the 90th Congress. However, pursuant to a House resolution, he was not permitted to take his seat. Powell (and some of the voters of his district) then filed suit in Federal District Court claiming that the House could exclude him only if it found he failed to meet the standing requirements of age, citizenship, and residence contained in Art. I, § 2, of the Constitution—requirements the House specifically found Powell met—and thus had excluded him unconstitutionally. The District Court dismissed petitioners' complaint "for want of jurisdiction of the subject matter." The Court of Appeals affirmed the dismissal, although on somewhat different grounds, each judge filing a separate opinion. We have determined that it was error to dismiss the complaint and that Petitioner Powell is entitled to a declaratory judgment that he was unlawfully excluded from the 90th Congress.

. . .

[At the organization of the 90th Congress in January, 1967, Powell was asked to step aside while the oath was administered to the other members. A Select Committee was then appointed which reported that Powell met the standing qualifications but that he had asserted an unwarranted privilege and immunity from the processes of the courts of New York; that he had wrongfully diverted House funds for the use of others and himself; and that he had made false reports on expenditures of foreign currency to a House committee. After a ruling by the Speaker that only a majority vote would be needed to exclude Powell and declare the seat vacant, the House adopted such a resolution of exclusion. By the time the case got to the Supreme Court Powell had been elected again and was seated in the 91st Congress. The Court held that the case was not moot because Powell had asked for damages. The Court also held that the vote by the House could not be treated as a vote to expel even though the actual vote exceeded a two-thirds majority. The Court's discussion of the political question objection to ruling on the validity of the action of the House follows.]

. . .

---

a Subsequent developments concerning the reapportionment problem are explored in Chapter 11. For a sampling of the articles commenting on Baker v. Carr see Israel, *On Charting a Course Through the Mathematical Quagmire, The Future of Baker v. Carr,* 61 Mich.L.Rev. 107 (1962); McCloskey, *The Reapportionment Case,* 76 Harv.L.Rev. 54 (1962); Neal, *Baker v. Carr: Politics in Search of Law,* 1962 Supreme Court Rev. 252.

See also Elrod v. Burns, 427 U.S. 347 (1976).

B. POLITICAL QUESTION DOCTRINE

1. *Textually Demonstrable Constitutional Commitment*

Respondents maintain that even if this case is otherwise justiciable, it presents only a political question. It is well-established that the federal courts will not adjudicate political questions. See, e.g., Coleman v. Miller, 307 U.S. 433 (1939); Oetjen v. Central Leather Co., 246 U.S. 297 (1918). In Baker v. Carr, supra, we noted that political questions are not justiciable primarily because of the separation of powers within the Federal Government. . . .

Respondents' first contention is that this case presents a political question because under Art. I, § 5, there has been a "textually demonstrable constitutional commitment" to the House of the "adjudicatory power" to determine Powell's qualifications. Thus it is argued that the House, and the House alone, has power to determine who is qualified to be a member.

In order to determine whether there has been a textual commitment to a co-ordinate department of the Government, we must interpret the Constitution. In other words, we must first determine what power the Constitution confers upon the House through Art. I, § 5, before we can determine to what extent, if any, the exercise of that power is subject to judicial review. Respondents maintain that the House has broad power under § 5, and, they argue, the House may determine which are the qualifications necessary for membership. On the other hand, petitioners allege that the Constitution provides that an elected representative may be denied his seat only if the House finds he does not meet one of the standing qualifications expressly prescribed by the Constitution.

If examination of § 5 disclosed that the Constitution gives the House judicially unreviewable power to set qualifications for membership and to judge whether prospective members meet those qualifications, further review of the House determination might well be barred by the political question doctrine. On the other hand, if the Constitution gives the House power to judge only whether elected members possess the three standing qualifications set forth in the Constitution; further consideration would be necessary to determine whether any of the other formulations of the political question doctrine are "inextricable from the case at bar."[42] Baker v. Carr, supra, at 217.

In other words, whether there is a "textually demonstrable constitutional commitment of the issue to a coordinate political department of government" and what is the scope of such commitment are questions we must resolve for the first time in this case. . . .

In order to determine the scope of any "textual commitment" under Art. I, § 5, we necessarily must determine the meaning of the phrase "be the judge of the qualifications of its own members." Petitioners argue that the records of the debates during the Constitutional Convention, available commentary from the post-Convention, pre-ratification period, and early congressional applications of Art. I, § 5, support their construction of the section. Respondents insist, however, that a careful examination of the pre-Convention practices of the English Parliament and American colonial assemblies demonstrates that by 1787, a legislature's power to judge the qualifications of its members was generally understood to encompass exclusion or expulsion on the ground that an individual's character or past conduct rendered him unfit to serve. When the Constitution and the debates over its adoption are thus viewed in historical

---

[42] Consistent with this interpretation, federal courts might still be barred by the political question doctrine from reviewing the House's factual determination that a member did not meet one of the standing qualifications. This is an issue not presented in this case and we express no view as to its resolution.

perspective, argue respondents, it becomes clear that the "qualifications" expressly set forth in the Constitution were not meant to limit the long recognized legislative power to exclude or expel at will, but merely to establish "standing incapacities," which could be altered only by a constitutional amendment. Our examination of the relevant historical materials leads us to the conclusion that petitioners are correct and that the Constitution leaves the House without authority to *exclude* any person, duly elected by his constituents, who meets all the requirements for membership expressly prescribed in the Constitution. [A long review of the historical precedents is omitted.]

Had the intent of the Framers emerged from these materials with less clarity, we would nevertheless have been compelled to resolve any ambiguity in favor of a narrow construction of the scope of Congress' power to exclude members-elect. A fundamental principle of our representative democracy is, in Hamilton's words, "that the people should choose whom they please to govern them." 2 Elliot's Debates 257. As Madison pointed out at the Convention, this principle is undermined as much by limiting whom the people can select as by limiting the franchise itself. In apparent agreement with this basic philosophy, the Convention adopted his suggestion limiting the power to expel. To allow essentially that same power to be exercised under the guise of judging qualifications, would be to ignore Madison's warning, borne out in the *Wilkes* case and some of Congress' own post-Civil War exclusion cases, against "vesting an improper & dangerous power in the Legislature." 2 Farrand 249. Moreover, it would effectively nullify the Convention's decision to require a two-third vote for expulsion. Unquestionably, Congress has an interest in preserving its institutional integrity, but in most cases that interest can be sufficiently safeguarded by the exercise of its power to punish its members for disorderly behavior and, in extreme cases, to expel a member with the concurrence of two-thirds. In short, both the intention of the Framers, to the extent it can be determined, and an examination of the basic principles of our democratic system persuade us that the Constitution does not vest in the Congress a discretionary power to deny membership by a majority vote.

For these reasons, we have concluded that Art. I, § 5, is at most a "textually demonstrable commitment" to Congress to judge only the qualifications expressly set forth in the Constitution. Therefore, the "textual commitment" formulation of the political question doctrine does not bar federal courts from adjudicating petitioners' claims.

2. *Other Considerations*

Respondents' alternate contention is that the case presents a political question because judicial resolution of petitioners' claim would produce a "potentially embarrassing confrontation between coordinate branches" of the Federal Government. But, as our interpretation of Art. I, § 5, discloses, a determination of Petitioner Powell's right to sit would require no more than an interpretation of the Constitution. Such a determination falls within the traditional role accorded courts to interpret the law, and does not involve a "lack of respect due [a] coordinate [branch] of government," nor does it involve an "initial policy determination of a kind clearly for nonjudicial discretion." Baker v. Carr, supra, at 217. Our system of government requires that federal courts on occasion interpret the Constitution in a manner at variance with the construction given the document by another branch. The alleged conflict that such an adjudication may cause cannot justify the courts' avoiding their constitutional responsibility. . . .

Nor are any of the other formulations of a political question "inextricable from the case at bar." Baker v. Carr, supra, at 217. Petitioners seek a determination that the House was without power to exclude Powell from the

90th Congress, which, we have seen, requires an interpretation of the Constitution—a determination for which clearly there are "judicially . . . manageable standards." Finally, a judicial resolution of petitioners' claim will not result in "multifarious pronouncements by various departments on one question." For, as we noted in Baker v. Carr, supra, at 211, it is the responsibility of this Court to act as the ultimate interpreter of the Constitution. Marbury v. Madison, 5 U.S. (1 Cranch) 137 (1803). Thus, we conclude that petitioners' claim is not barred by the political question doctrine, and having determined that the claim is otherwise generally justiciable, we hold that the case is justiciable.

.   .   .

———

GILLIGAN v. MORGAN, 413 U.S. 1 (1973). As an aftermath of the shootings at Kent State University, a group of students brought a suit in the federal district court seeking a declaratory judgment and injunctive relief against the Governor of Ohio and leaders of the National Guard. The district court dismissed the complaint. The appellate court reversed in part, holding that the complaint stated a cause of action with respect to one issue—that the pattern of training, weapons, and orders in the Guard either required or made inevitable the unnecessary use of fatal force in suppressing civilian disorders. The plaintiffs sought as relief on this issue a judicial evaluation of the appropriateness of the training, weapons, and orders of the Guard; a judicial determination establishing standards for such training, weapons, and orders; and continuing judicial surveillance over the Guard to assure compliance with whatever training and operations procedures the court approved. The Supreme Court reversed. Chief Justice Burger, speaking for the Court, referred to Art. I, § 8, cl. 16, vesting in Congress the power to provide for the Militia and reserving to the states the appointment and training of the Militia "according to the discipline prescribed by Congress." He then noted that the relief sought by plaintiffs would require the judge to engage in a process of evaluating procedures in areas outside judicial competence—areas in which trained professionals subject to the day to day control of the responsible civilian authorities must make the judgments. He then concluded as follows:

"It would be difficult to think of a clearer example of the type of governmental action that was intended by the Constitution to be left to the political branches, directly responsible—as the Judicial Branch is not—to the elective process. Moreover, it is difficult to conceive of an area of governmental activity in which the courts have less competence. The complex subtle, and professional decisions as to the composition, training, equipping, and control of a military force are essentially professional military judgments, subject *always* to civilian control of the Legislative and Executive Branches. The ultimate responsibility for these decisions is appropriately vested in branches of the government which are periodically subject to electoral accountability. It is this power of oversight and control of military force by elected representatives and officials which underlies our entire constitutional system; the majority opinion of the Court of Appeals failed to give appropriate weight to this separation of powers.   .   .   .

"In concluding that no justiciable controversy is presented, it should be clear that we neither hold nor imply that the conduct of the National Guard is always beyond judicial review or that there may not be accountability in a judicial forum for violations of law or for specific unlawful conduct by military personnel, whether by way of damages or injunctive relief. We hold only that no such questions are presented in this case. We decline to require a United States district court to involve itself so directly and so intimately in the task assigned that court by the Court of Appeals.   .   .   .   ."

Justices Douglas, Brennan, Stewart, and Marshall, dissented on the ground that the entire controversy should have been dismissed as moot. They did not reach the political questions issue.

GOLDWATER v. CARTER

444 U.S. 996, 100 S.Ct. 533, 62 L.Ed.2d 428 (1979).

ORDER

The petition for a writ of certiorari is granted. The judgment of the Court of Appeals is vacated and the case is remanded to the District Court with directions to dismiss the complaint.

Mr. Justice Marshall concurs in the result.

Mr. Justice Powell concurs in the judgment and has filed a statement.

Mr. Justice Rehnquist concurs in the judgment and has filed a statement in which Mr. Chief Justice Burger, Mr. Justice Stewart, and Mr. Justice Stevens join.

Mr. Justice White and Mr. Justice Blackmun join in the grant of the petition for a writ of certiorari but would set the case for argument and give it plenary consideration. Mr. Justice Blackmun has filed a statement in which Mr. Justice White joins.

Mr. Justice Brennan would grant the petition for certiorari and affirm the judgment of the Court of Appeals and has filed a statement.

Mr. Justice Powell, concurring.

Although I agree with the result reached by the Court, I would dismiss the complaint as not ripe for judicial review.

I.

This Court has recognized that an issue should not be decided if it is not ripe for judicial review. Buckley v. Valeo, 424 U.S. 1, 113–114 (1976) (per curiam). Prudential considerations persuade me that a dispute between Congress and the President is not ready for judicial review unless and until each branch has taken action asserting its constitutional authority. Differences between the President and the Congress are commonplace under our system. The differences should, and almost invariably do, turn on political rather than legal considerations. The Judicial Branch should not decide issues affecting the allocation of power between the President and Congress until the political branches reach a constitutional impasse. Otherwise, we would encourage small groups or even individual Members of Congress to seek judicial resolution of issues before the normal political process has the opportunity to resolve the conflict.

In this case, a few Members of Congress claim that the President's action in terminating the treaty with Taiwan has deprived them of their constitutional role with respect to a change in the supreme law of the land. Congress has taken no official action. In the present posture of this case, we do not know whether there ever will be an actual confrontation between the Legislative and Executive Branches. Although the Senate has considered a resolution declaring that Senate approval is necessary for the termination of any mutual defense treaty, no final vote has been taken on the resolution. Moreover, it is unclear whether the resolution would have retroactive effect. It cannot be said that either the Senate or the House has rejected the President's claim. If the Congress chooses not to confront the President, it is not our task to do so. I therefore concur in the dismissal of this case.

II.

Mr. Justice Rehnquist suggests, however, that the issue presented by this case is a nonjusticiable political question which can never be considered by this Court. I cannot agree. In my view, reliance upon the political-question doctrine is inconsistent with our precedents. As set forth in the seminal case of Baker v. Carr, 369 U.S. 186, 217 (1962), the doctrine incorporates three inquiries: (i) Does the issue involve resolution of questions committed by the text of the Constitution to a coordinate branch of government? (ii) Would resolution of the question demand that a court move beyond areas of judicial expertise? (iii) Do prudential considerations counsel against judicial intervention? In my opinion the answer to each of these inquiries would require us to decide this case if it were ready for review.

First, the existence of "a textually demonstrable constitutional commitment of the issue to a coordinate political branch," ibid., turns on an examination of the constitutional provisions governing the exercise of the power in question. Powell v. McCormack, 395 U.S. 486, 519 (1969). No constitutional provision explicitly confers upon the President the power to terminate treaties. Further, Art. II, § 2 of the Constitution authorizes the President to make treaties with the advice and consent of the Senate. Article VI provides that treaties shall be a part of the supreme law of the land. These provisions add support to the view that the text of the Constitution does not unquestionably commit the power to terminate treaties to the President alone. . . .

Second, there is no "lack of judicially discoverable and manageable standards for resolving" this case; nor is a decision impossible "without an initial policy determination of a kind clearly for nonjudicial discretion." Baker v. Carr, 369 U.S., at 217. We are asked to decide whether the President may terminate a treaty under the Constitution without congressional approval. Resolution of the question may not be easy, but it only requires us to apply normal principles of interpretation to the constitutional provisions at issue. See Powell v. McCormack, 395 U.S., at 548–549. The present case involves neither review of the President's activities as Commander-in-Chief nor impermissible interference in the field of foreign affairs. Such a case would arise if we were asked to decide, for example, whether a treaty required the President to order troops into a foreign country. But "it is error to suppose that every case or controversy which touches foreign relations lies beyond judicial cognizance." Baker v. Carr, supra, 369 U.S., at 211. This case "touches" foreign relations, but the question presented to us concerns only the constitutional division of power between Congress and the President.

A simple hypothetical demonstrates the confusion that I find inherent in Mr. Justice Rehnquist's concurring opinion. Assume that the President signed a mutual defense treaty with a foreign country and announced that it would go into effect despite its rejection by the Senate. Under Mr. Justice Rehnquist's analysis that situation would present a political question even though Art. II, § 2, clearly would resolve the dispute. Although the answer to the hypothetical case seems self-evident because it demands textual rather than interstitial analysis, the nature of the legal issue presented is no different from the issue presented in the case before us. In both cases, the Court would interpret the Constitution to decide whether congressional approval is necessary to give a Presidential decision on the validity of a treaty the force of law. Such an inquiry demands no special competence or information beyond the reach of the judiciary.

Finally, the political-question doctrine rests in part on prudential concerns calling for mutual respect among the three branches of government. Thus, the Judicial Branch should avoid "the potentiality of embarrassment [that would result] from multifarious pronouncements by various departments on one question." Similarly, the doctrine restrains judicial action where there is an "unusual need for unquestioning adherence to a political decision already made." Baker v. Carr, supra, 369 U.S., at 217.

If this case were ripe for judicial review, see Part I supra, none of these prudential considerations would be present. Interpretation of the Constitution does not imply lack of respect for a coordinate branch. Powell v. McCormack, 395 U.S., at 548. If the President and the Congress had reached irreconcilable positions, final disposition of the question presented by this case would eliminate, rather than create, multiple constitutional interpretations. The spectre of the Federal Government brought to a halt because of the mutual intransigence of the President and the Congress would require this Court to provide a resolution pursuant to our duty "to say what the law is." United States v. Nixon, 418 U.S. 683, 703, quoting Marbury v. Madison, 1 Cranch 137, 177 (1803).

III.

In my view, the suggestion that this case presents a political question is incompatible with this Court's willingness on previous occasions to decide whether one branch of our government has impinged upon the power of another. See Buckley v. Valeo, 424 U.S. 1, 138 (1976); United States v. Nixon, 418 U.S. 683, 707 (1974); The Pocket Veto Case, 279 U.S. 655, 676–678 (1929); Myers v. United States, 272 U.S. 52 (1926).[2] Under the criteria enunciated in Baker v. Carr, we have the responsibility to decide whether both the Executive and Legislative Branches have constitutional roles to play in termination of a treaty. If the Congress, by appropriate formal action, had challenged the President's authority to terminate the treaty with Taiwan, the resulting uncertainty could have serious consequences for our country. In that situation, it would be the duty of this Court to resolve the issue.

Mr. Justice Rehnquist, with whom The Chief Justice, Mr. Justice Stewart, and Mr. Justice Stevens join, concurring.

I am of the view that the basic question presented by the petitioners in this case is "political" and therefore nonjusticiable because it involves the authority of the President in the conduct of our country's foreign relations and the extent to which the Senate or the Congress is authorized to negate the action of the President. In Coleman v. Miller, 307 U.S. 433 (1939), a case in which members of the Kansas Legislature brought an action attacking a vote of the State Senate in favor of the ratification of the Child Labor Amendment, Mr.

---

[2] Coleman v. Miller, 307 U.S. 433 (1939), is not relevant here. In that case, the Court was asked to review the legitimacy of a State's ratification of a constitutional amendment. Four Members of the Court stated that Congress has exclusive power over the ratification process. Id., at 456–460 (Black, J., concurring, with whom Roberts, Frankfurter, and Douglas, JJ., joined). Three Members of the Court concluded more narrowly that the Court could not pass upon the efficacy of state ratification. They also found no standards by which the Court could fix a reasonable time for the ratification of a proposed amendment. Id., at 452–454.

The proposed constitutional amendment at issue in *Coleman* would have overruled decisions of this Court. . . . Thus, judicial review of the legitimacy of a State's ratification would have compelled this Court to oversee the very constitutional process used to reverse Supreme Court decisions. In such circumstances it may be entirely appropriate for the Judicial Branch of government to step aside. See Scharpf, Judicial Review and The Political Question: A Functional Analysis, 75 Yale L.J. 517, 589 (1966). The present case involves no similar principle of judicial nonintervention.

Chief Justice Hughes wrote in what is referred to as the "Opinion of the Court":

> "We think that . . . the question of the efficacy of ratifications by state legislatures, in the light of previous rejection or attempted withdrawal, should be regarded as a political question pertaining to the political departments, with the ultimate authority in the Congress in the exercise of its control over the promulgation of the adoption of the Amendment. . . . The precise question as now raised is whether, when the legislature of the State, as we have found, has actually ratified the proposed Amendment, the Court should restrain the State officers from certifying the ratification to the Secretary of State, because of an earlier rejection, and thus prevent the question from coming before the political departments. We find no basis in either Constitution or statute for such judicial action. Article V, speaking solely of ratification, contains no provision as to rejection. . . . " Id., at 450.

Thus, Mr. Chief Justice Hughes' opinion concluded that "Congress in controlling the promulgation of the adoption of a constitutional amendment has the final determination of the question whether by lapse of time its proposal of the amendment had lost its vitality prior to the required ratifications." Id., at 456.

I believe it follows *a fortiori* from *Coleman* that the controversy in the instant case is a nonjusticiable political dispute that should be left for resolution by the Executive and Legislative Branches of the Government. Here, while the Constitution is express as to the manner in which the Senate shall participate in the ratification of a Treaty, it is silent as to that body's participation in the abrogation of a Treaty. In this respect the case is directly analogous to *Coleman,* supra. As stated in Dyer v. Blair, 390 F.Supp. 1291, 1302 (N.D.Ill.1975) (three-judge court):

> "A question that might be answered in different ways for different amendments must surely be controlled by political standards rather than standards easily characterized as judicially manageable."

In light of the absence of any constitutional provision governing the termination of a Treaty, and the fact that different termination procedures may be appropriate for different treaties, the instant case in my view also "must surely be controlled by political standards."

I think that the justifications for concluding that the question here is political in nature are even more compelling than in *Coleman* because it involves foreign relations—specifically a treaty commitment to use military force in the defense of a foreign government if attacked. . . .

The present case differs in several important respects from Youngstown Sheet & Tube Co. v. Sawyer, 343 U.S. 579 (1952), cited by petitioners as authority both for reaching the merits of this dispute and for reversing the Court of Appeals. In *Youngstown* private litigants brought a suit contesting the President's authority under his war powers to seize the Nation's steel industry, an action of profound and demonstrable domestic impact. Here, by contrast, we are asked to settle a dispute between coequal branches of our government, each of which has resources available to protect and assert its interests, resources not available to private litigants outside the judicial forum.[1] Moreover, as in

---

[1] As observed by Judge Wright in his concurring opinion below:

"Congress has initiated the termination of treaties by directing or requiring the President to give notice of termination, without any prior presidential request. Congress has annulled treaties without any presidential notice. It has conferred on the President the power to terminate a particular treaty, and it has enacted statutes practically nullifying the domestic effects of a treaty and thus caused the President to carry out termination. . . . Moreover, Congress has a variety of powerful tools for influencing foreign policy decisions that bear on treaty matters. Under Article I, Section 8 of the Constitution, it can regulate commerce with foreign nations, raise and support

Curtiss-Wright, the effect of this action, as far as we can tell, is "entirely external to the United States, and [falls] within the category of foreign affairs." Finally, as already noted, the situation presented here is closely akin to that presented in *Coleman,* where the Constitution spoke only to the procedure for ratification of an amendment, not to its rejection.

Having decided that the question presented in this action is nonjusticiable, I believe that the appropriate disposition is for this Court to vacate the decision of the Court of Appeals and remand with instructions for the District Court to dismiss the complaint. . . .

Mr. Justice Blackmun, with whom Mr. Justice White joins, dissenting in part.

In my view, the time factor and its importance are illusory; if the President does not have the power to terminate the Treaty (a substantial issue that we should address only after briefing and oral argument), the notice of intention to terminate surely has no legal effect. It is also indefensible, without further study, to pass on the issue of justiciability or on the issues of standing or ripeness. While I therefore join in the grant of the petition for certiorari, I would set the case for oral argument and give it the plenary consideration it so obviously deserves.

Mr. Justice Brennan, dissenting.

I respectfully dissent from the order directing the District Court to dismiss this case, and would affirm the judgment of the Court of Appeals insofar as it rests upon the President's well-established authority to recognize, and withdraw recognition from, foreign governments.

In stating that this case presents a non-justiciable "political question," the plurality, in my view, profoundly misapprehends the political question principle as it applies to matters of foreign relations. Properly understood, the political question doctrine restrains courts from reviewing an exercise of foreign policy judgment by the coordinate political branch to which authority to make that judgment has been "constitutional[ly] commit[ted]." Baker v. Carr, 369 U.S. 186, 211–213, 217 (1962). But the doctrine does not pertain when a court is faced with the *antecedent* question whether a particular branch has been constitutionally designated as the repository of political decisionmaking power. Cf. Powell v. McCormack, 395 U.S. 486, 519–521 (1969). The issue of decisionmaking authority must be resolved as a matter of constitutional law, not political discretion; accordingly, it falls within the competence of the courts.

The constitutional question raised here is prudently answered in narrow terms. Abrogation of the defense treaty with Taiwan was a necessary incident to Executive recognition of the Peking government, because the defense treaty was predicated upon the now-abandoned view that the Taiwan government was the only legitimate political authority in China. Our cases firmly establish that the Constitution commits to the President alone the power to recognize, and withdraw recognition from, foreign regimes. . . . That mandate being clear, our judicial inquiry into the treaty rupture can go no further. . . .

---

armies, and declare war. It has power over the appointment of ambassadors and the funding of embassies and consulates. Congress thus retains a strong influence over the President's conduct in treaty matters. As our political history demonstrates, treaty creation and termination are complex phenomena rooted in the dynamic relationship between the two political branches of our government. We thus should decline the invitation to set in concrete a particular constitutionally acceptable arrangement by which the President and Congress are to share treaty termination."

POLITICAL QUESTIONS

(1) That aspect of the political question doctrine relying on "a textually demonstrable commitment of the issue to a coordinate political department" is, as the Court noted in Baker v. Carr, "primarily a function of the separation of powers." The issue will be raised again in Chapter 8—see especially United States v. Nixon, infra p. 468.

(2) In Baker v. Carr, the Court noted that a case might be held to involve a political question because of "a lack of judicially discoverable and manageable standards for resolving it." The Court held that reapportionment cases did not require "the Court to enter upon policy determinations for which judicially manageable standards are lacking. Judicial standards under the Equal Protection Clause are well developed and familiar, and it has been open to courts since the enactment of the Fourteenth Amendment to determine, if on the particular facts they must, that a discrimination reflects *no* policy, but simply arbitrary and capricious action." When studying the subsequent reapportionment cases infra Chapter 11, the student should ask whether the Court's prediction as to the manageability of the standards proved to be true.

(3) Can the political question doctrine be regarded simply as another device by which the Supreme Court avoids issues it does not wish to decide? Professor Scharpf analyzed the cases and concluded: "The Court has available such a wide variety of procedural and substantive devices for not deciding, and it has in fact decided such a long list of explosive issues, that it appears rather unpersuasive to explain the political question doctrine purely in terms of an opportunistic retreat from 'prickly' cases or issues." Scharpf, *Judicial Review and the Political Question: A Functional Analysis,* 75 Yale L.J. 517 (1966).

(4) Professor Henkin suggests that there is no separate political question doctrine:

> "The thesis I offer for discussion is that there may be no doctrine requiring abstention from judicial review of 'political questions.' The cases which are supposed to have established the political question doctrine required no such extra-ordinary abstention from judicial review; they called only for the ordinary respect by the courts for the political domain. Having reviewed, the Court refused to invalidate the challenged actions because they were within the constitutional authority of President or Congress. In no case did the Court have to use the phrase 'political question' . . . .."

Henkin, *Is There a "Political Question" Doctrine?,* 85 Yale L.J. 597, 600 (1976).

THE AMENDMENT PROCESS—A DIGRESSION

The amendment process as set out in Article V has given rise to a number of questions. Since the Court has indicated that some of these questions are non-justiciable political questions, a general look at the problems relating to Article V seems appropriate at this point.

Proposal of Amendments

Amendments may be proposed either by a two-thirds majority in both Houses of Congress or by a convention called by Congress upon the application of the legislatures of two-thirds of the states. Every proposal made thus far has come from Congress. The process has been generally uncontroversial.

While Article V's alternative mode of proposing amendments by convention has yet to be exercised, it is by no means a dead letter. Well over 300 applications calling for conventions have been sent to Congress by state legislatures to date. Every state has submitted at least one such petition. The applications have ranged from those calling for a general constitutional convention to those calling for conventions to consider such specific topics as slavery, anti-polygamy, and integration of public schools. During the 1960's, in the aftermath of the Supreme Court's decision mandating reapportionment of state legislatures to conform with population distribution, nearly two-thirds of the states submitted applications calling for a convention on the subject of apportionment. Most recently, more than thirty states have requested a convention on the issue of a balanced federal budget.

It is generally agreed that the framers made provision for the proposal of amendments by convention at least in part because they feared that the excesses of the federal government could be most difficult to curtail through amendment if only Congress could initiate constitutional change. While resort to the convention process has not been required to subdue an oppressive Congress, its prospect has operated to prod a reluctant one to action. The raft of applications for a convention to propose popular election of U.S. Senators inspired Congress to propose the Seventeenth Amendment, post haste. Recent applications, such as those addressed to reapportionment and bussing, suggest that the device may be used to apprise Congress of serious dissatisfaction with decisions of the Supreme Court and possibly to directly institute curative amendments.

The treatment in Article V of the convention method of proposing amendments is cryptic indeed, and uncertainty regarding it is the rule rather than the exception. Issues as to the meaning of Article V were widely debated in the aftermath of calls for a convention on apportionment issues in the 1960's,[1] and most recently in the context of calls for a convention on the issue of a balanced budget.[2] Among the more important questions are these:

1. What constitutes a valid application which Congress must count? Is an application valid if it calls for an unlimited convention? if it calls for a convention applicable to a particular subject? if it calls for a convention to vote up or down the text of a particular amendment?

2. How is it to be determined whether two-thirds of the states have applied for a convention? What is the length of time for which applications will be counted? Should applications be counted if they differ with reference to the subject of the proposed convention?

3. If it is decided that there are valid calls for a convention from two-thirds of the states, what are the powers of Congress in calling such a convention? Does Congress have discretion not to call the convention? Can Congress specify the manner of selection of delegates and their numbers? Can Congress specify the procedures to be followed by the Convention? Can Congress limit the subject matter to be considered by the convention?

4. If a convention is called, are Congressional limitations on procedure and subject matter binding on the convention?

5. What is the power of Congress concerning the product of a convention? Can Congress refuse to submit proposed amendments to the states for

[1] E.g., American Bar Association Special Constitutional Convention Study Committee, Amendment of the Constitution by the Convention Method under Article V (1974); Bonfield, *The Dirksen Amendment and the Article V Convention Process,* 66 Mich.L.Rev. 949 (1968); Ervin, *Proposed Legislation to Implement the Convention Method of Amending the Constitution,* 66 Mich.L.Rev. 875 (1968); Black, *Amending The Constitution: A Letter to a Congressman,* 82 Yale L.J. 189 (1972).

[2] E.g., Bator et al., *A Constitutional Convention: How Well Would it Work?* (American Enterprise Institute 1979); Dellinger, *The Recurring Question of the "Limited" Constitutional Convention,* 88 Yale L.J. 1623 (1979); Gunther, *The Convention Method of Amending the United States Constitution,* 14 Ga.L.Rev. 1 (1979); Van Alstyne, *Does Article V Restrict the States to Calling Unlimited Conventions Only?—A Letter to a Colleague,* 1978 Duke L.J. 1295 (1979).

ratification if the convention ignores Congressional directions on voting requirements or limitations on subject matter?

The lack of answers to most of the preceding questions has raised the spectre of a "runaway convention," called for a limited purpose but proposing far-reaching amendments to the Constitution and the Bill of Rights.

Ratification of Amendments

Just as Article V offers two methods for proposal of amendments, it also sets forth alternative modes of ratification: "by the Legislatures of three fourths of the several states, or by Conventions in three fourths thereof, as one or the other Mode of Ratification may be proposed by the Congress . . .." Congress has generally preferred ratification by the state legislatures, invoking the state convention device in only one instance—the Twenty-First Amendment's repeal of national prohibition.

Since amendments to the Constitution have been ratified on seventeen occasions, questions concerning the ratification process are fewer than the untested questions concerning amendments proposed by a constitutional convention. There are questions whose answers are not obvious, however. These concern, among others, the time during which ratification may take place, the extent to which state law controls ratification by state legislatures, and the legal effect of ratification by states that previously, or subsequently, reject an amendment. Two questions that arose in the context of the unsuccessful attempt to ratify the Equal Rights Amendment are instructive.

One question concerns the time limit for ratification. The Eighteenth, Twentieth, Twenty-first and Twenty-second Amendments contain seven year time limits for ratification in their texts. (No time limit for ratification was set in connection with the Nineteenth Amendment.) Time limits for ratification of subsequent amendments were not placed in the amendment text, but in the proposing clause of the resolution submitting the amendment for ratification. The change in practice, designed to avoid "cluttering up" the text of the Constitution with obsolete provisions concerning time limits for ratification, created no legal issues prior to the proposed Equal Rights Amendment, since ratifications occurred well within the seven year limit. The requisite number of states had not ratified the ERA when the time limitation expired on March 22, 1979. In October 1978, Congress extended the time limit to June, 1982. Among the questions raised were whether it was necessary to resubmit the ERA anew, whether the extension measure required a two-thirds vote (it received substantial majorities in both houses, but less than two-thirds), and whether the President's signature was necessary (the President in fact signed the extension measure).[3]

Extension of the time for ratification of ERA exacerbated a second issue. A number of states that had originally ratified acted to rescind their ratifications, and rescission campaigns were pending in other states. One view is that ratification is a final act that can not be withdrawn. The contrary view is that the requisite number of states must agree on ratification at the same time.[4] In

---

[3] On the issue of time for ratification of the ERA see: *Equal Rights Amendment Extension: Hearings on H.J. Res. 638 Before the Subcomm. on Civil and Constitutional Rights of the House Comm. on the Judiciary,* 95th Cong., 1st and 2d Sess. (1977–78); *Equal Rights Amendment Extension: Hearings on S.J. Res. 134 Before the Subcomm. on the Constitution of the Senate Comm. on the Judiciary,* 95th Cong., 2d Sess. (1978); Ginsburg, *Ratification of the Equal Rights Amendment: A Question of Time,* 57 Tex.L.Rev. 919 (1979).

The proposed District of Columbia Representation in Congress Amendment, submitted by Congress for ratification on August 22, 1978, returns to the earlier pattern. The seven year time limit for ratification is contained in the amendment text.

[4] Considerable law review commentary discusses the issue of rescission. E.g., Heckman, *Ratification of a Constitutional Amendment: Can a State Change Its Mind?* 6 Conn.L.Rev. 28 (1973); Elder,

approving extension of the time for ratification, Congress did not resolve this issue.

Congressional Resolution of Constitutional Issues Concerning the Amendment Process

Congress can attempt to determine whether a particular amendment has been ratified by the requisite number of states. In July of 1868, Congress passed a joint resolution declaring that the Fourteenth Amendment had been ratified by the requisite number of states—resolving the question whether states that had previously rejected the Amendment, and states that had rescinded their ratification, should be counted. The Secretary of State's proclamation that the Amendment had been ratified accordingly included both states which had earlier rejected the Amendment, and those that had purported to withdraw their ratifications.[5]

Congress can also attempt to resolve legal issues concerning the amendment process by a general statute not applicable to any particular amendment. Senator Ervin introduced legislation in 1971 and 1973 concerning proposal of amendments by constitutional conventions.[6] An identical "Federal Constitutional Procedures Act" was introduced in 1979 by Senator Helms.[7] Its controversial provisions include requiring state calls for a convention to state the nature of the amendments proposed, requiring a Congressional call for a convention to specify the subject, and authorizing Congress to block submission of amendments on other subjects.

Justiciability

In the absence of a Congressional decision, can any of the questions previously put be answered in litigation? If Congress resolves any of these questions, either in the context of a particular amendment or by general legislation, would those answers be binding on a court? Issues of justiciability are nearly as uncertain as the substantive answers to the constitutional questions.[8]

Prior to 1939, the Supreme Court adjudicated a number of issues concerning the ratification process. (Notice that none of the decisions rejected a contrary resolution of an issue by Congress.) In United States v. Sprague, 282 U.S. 716 (1931), the Supreme Court held that the choice between modes of ratification lies in the sole discretion of Congress. In an earlier Eighteenth Amendment case, Dillon v. Gloss, 256 U.S. 368 (1921), the Court held that Article V implicitly required that ratification be completed within some reasonable time after the proposal of an amendment, and that Congress could fix a definite period for the ratification. Hawke v. Smith, No. 1, 253 U.S. 221 (1920), held that the efficacy of a resolution of Ohio's legislature ratifying the Eighteenth Amendment could not be made subject by the state's constitution to the requirement of approval in a popular referendum. Leser v. Garnett, 258 U.S. 130 (1922), rejected a claim that by virtue of state constitutional constraints,

Article V, Justiciability and the Equal Rights Amendment, 31 Okla.L.Rev. 63 (1978); Ginsburg, supra note 3; Comment, *The Equal Rights Amendment and Article V: A Framework for Analysis of the Extension and Recission Issues,* 127 U.Pa.L.Rev. 494 (1978); Note, *Reversals in the Federal Constitutional Amendment Process: Efficacy of State Ratifications of the Equal Rights Amendment,* 49 Ind.L.J. 147 (1973).

[5] The history of the ratification of the Fourteenth Amendment is contained in Coleman v. Miller, 307 U.S. 433, 448–449 (1939).

[6] S. 215, 92d Cong., 1st Sess., 117 Cong.Rec. 36804–38806 (1971); S. 1272, 93d Cong., 1st Sess., 119 Cong.Rec. 22731–37 (1973).

[7] S. 520, 96th Cong., 1st Sess., 125 Cong.Rec. S. 1935 (1979).

[8] Much of the commentary cited in the previous footnotes discusses issues of justiciability. See also, Orfield, *The Amending of the Federal Constitution* (1942); Scharpf, *Judicial Review and the Political Question: A Functional Analysis,* 75 Yale L.J. 517, 589 (1966).

certain state legislatures were without power to ratify the Nineteenth Amendment. The Court stated that the federal ratification function "transcends any limitations sought to be imposed by the people of a State." (258 U.S. at 137)[9]

In Coleman v. Miller, 307 U.S. 433 (1939), the Court held two questions concerning ratification to be non-justiciable political questions for Congress alone to resolve. Citing the historic precedent of the Fourteenth Amendment, the Court decided that the question of ratification by a state Legislature which had previously rejected an amendment could be decided only by Congress. The question whether, in the absence of Congressional specification of a time limit for ratification, an amendment was open to ratification thirteen years after it had been proposed, was also held to be political. Chief Justice Hughes' opinion emphasized the absence of judicial criteria for determining the length of time which was reasonable. The Court divided evenly on the justiciability of a third question presented by the case—whether the lieutenant governor could cast a tie-breaking ratification vote in the state senate. Moreover, four concurring Justices (Black, Roberts, Frankfurter and Douglas) specifically rejected prior decisions adjudicating issues concerning the amending process, arguing that *all* such issues were political.

[9] See also the National Prohibition Cases, 253 U.S. 350 (1920) (two-thirds vote requirement for proposing amendment means two-thirds of a quorum present and voting); Hollingsworth v. Virginia, 3 Dall. 378 (1878) (Presidential participation not required in proposing an amendment).

Part II

ALLOCATION OF GOVERNMENTAL POWERS: THE NATION AND THE STATES; THE PRESIDENT, THE CONGRESS, AND THE COURTS

A principal concern in the Constitutional Convention was the allocation of governmental powers. Two major issues were before them: (1) The distribution of power among the three branches of the national government—the separation of powers. The aim here was to see that no particular branch was able to achieve an undue concentration of power. (2) The division of powers between the nation and the states. The great objective of the federal system which dominated the thinking of the Framers was a national government with adequate power to handle matters of national interest while the states retained autonomy over local affairs.

One aspect of separation of powers has been introduced in Part I in connection with the discussion of the scope of the judicial power. Other separation of powers issues will appear from time to time in this part of the book, but major discussion, particularly of the relationships between the President and Congress, will be deferred until Chapter 8 at the end of this part.

The major portion of Part II will be devoted to studying the division of powers between the nation and the states. The aim is to give the student a working sense of the principal issues of federalism and the manner in which the Supreme Court addresses them.

Fortunately for our constitutional development, the Convention did not attempt any such detailed specification of national and state powers as is contained in some modern federal constitutions.[1] The Framers were content to give us a rather general enumeration of national powers (principally in Art. I, § 8) plus the principle (made explicit in the Tenth Amendment) that all power not delegated to the national government remains with the states.[2] Thus, provisions delegating power to the national government may be construed in two different contexts: (1) as fixing the scope of national power; and (2) as determining the retained powers of the states. This interrelation of national and state power is explored in Chapters 4 and 5.

With a developing national economy and the search of the states for more revenue, state taxation of multistate business has posed acute problems of federalism which provide the material for Chapter 6.

In Chapter 7 on intergovernmental relationships within the federal system, attention is returned to a dual consideration of national and state power. The questions considered arise when the nation or the states attempt to tax or regulate activities of the other, or when two or more states seek solution to common problems through interstate compacts.

---

[1] See, for example, the 1949 Constitution of India where the division of powers is accomplished by three detailed lists annexed to the Constitution. List I (the "Union List") itemizes the exclusive powers of the central government. List II (the "State List") itemizes the powers given exclusively to the states. List III (the concurrent list) specifies the subjects with which the states may deal in the absence of inconsistent legislation by the Parliament of India. For a general treatise, see Basu, Commentary on the Constitution of India (4th ed. 1961).

[2] The Constitution as originally adopted contains a few explicit limitations on the powers of the states. See Art. I, § 10.

Chapter 4

THE SCOPE OF NATIONAL POWER

SECTION 1. THE CONSTITUTIONAL CONVENTION AND THE ESTABLISHMENT OF A NATIONAL GOVERNMENT

Introduction. The following excerpts from the records of the Constitutional Convention of 1787 are designed to afford an intimate glimpse into the process of deliberation and compromise that produced the Constitution and also to provide a sample of the materials which are available for an examination of the historical setting and meaning of provisions of the Constitution.

A thorough examination of the historical setting and "legislative history" of constitutional provisions requires the weighing of voluminous material; there is room here for only a small sample. But the excerpts that follow can provide a basis for hypotheses, to be checked against the full record, concerning: (1) The weaknesses of the Articles of Confederation which the framers sought to avoid in their new constitution; (2) The choice (or compromise) between conflicting views concerning the power to be given the national government; (3) The nature and scope of the national power over commerce contemplated by the draftsmen.

PROCEEDINGS IN THE FEDERAL CONVENTION:
MAY 29, 1787

Madison's Notes; I Farrand, Records of the Federal Convention of 1787 (1911) 18–19 (hereafter cited as "Farrand")[1]

Mr. Randolph [Va.] opened the main business. He expressed his regret, that it should fall to him, rather than those, who were of longer standing in life and political experience, to open the great subject of their mission. But, as the convention had originated from Virginia, and his colleagues supposed, that some proposition was expected from them, they had imposed this task on him.

He then commented on the difficulty of the crisis, and the necessity of preventing the fulfillment of the prophecies of the American downfall.

He observed that in revising the federal system we ought to inquire (1) into the properties, which such a government ought to possess, (2) the defects of the confederation, (3) the danger of our situation and (4) the remedy.

1. The character of such a governme[nt] ought to secure (1) against foreign invasion: (2) against dissentions between members of the Union, or seditions in particular states: (3) to p[ro]cure to the several states various blessings, of which an isolated situation was i[n] capable: (4) to be able to defend itself against encroachment: and (5) to be paramount to the state constitutions.

2. In speaking of the defects of the confederation he professed a high respect for its authors, and considered them as having done all that patriots could do, in the then infancy of the science, of constitutions, and of confedera-

---

[1] This and the following excerpts are copied by permission of the Yale University Press. [Bracketed references to the states from which the delegates came have been added by the editors.]

cies,—when the inefficiency of requisitions was unknown—no commercial discord had arisen among any states—no rebellion had appeared as in Massachusetts—foreign debts had not become urgent—the havoc of paper money had not been foreseen—treaties had not been violated—and perhaps nothing better could be obtained from the jealousy of the states with regard to their sovereignty.

He then proceeded to enumerate the defects: [a] (1) that the confederation produced no security agai[nst] foreign invasion; congress not being permitted to prevent a war nor to support it by th[eir] own authority—of this he cited many examples; most of whi[ch] tended to show that they could not cause infractions of treaties or of the law of nations, to be punished; that particular states might by their conduct provoke war without control; and that neither militia nor draughts being fit for defense on such occasions, enlistments only could be successful, and these could not be executed without money.

(2) that the foederal government could not check the quarrels between states, nor a rebellion in any not having constitutional power Nor means to interpose according to the exigency:

(3) That there were many advantages, which the U. S. might acquire, which were not attainable under the confederation—such as a productive impost—counteraction of the commercial regulations of other nations—pushing of commerce ad libitum—&c &c.

(4) that the foederal government could not defend itself against the incroachments from the states:

(5) that it was not even paramount to the state constitutions, ratified as it was in may [s. i. c.] of the states.

3.   He next reviewed the danger of our situation appealed to the sense of the best friends of the U. S.—the prospect of anarchy from the laxity of government everywhere; and to other considerations.

4.   He then proceeded to the remedy; the basis of which he said, must be the republican principle.

He proposed as conformable to his ideas the following resolutions, which he explained one by one.

Note.   The "resolutions" to which Randolph referred at the close of this excerpt constituted the "Virginia Plan" which probably had been developed by James Madison.   See Warren, *The Making of the Constitution* (1928) 139–141. These resolutions formed the basis for discussion and action by the Convention in the days which followed.   Thus the proposition debated in the following excerpt from the proceedings of May 31 was the second part of the sixth "resolution" which Randolph proposed.

PROCEEDINGS IN THE FEDERAL CONVENTION:
MAY 31, 1787

Madison's Notes; I Farrand 53

On the proposition for giving "Legislative power in all cases to which the State Legislatures were individually incompetent".

-----

[a] Reasons for the failure of the Articles of Confederation and the need for a stronger national union were eloquently expounded by Alexander Hamilton in The Federalist, Nos. 15 and 22.   See also Kelly & Harbison, *The American Constitution* 108–110 (1970).   On the influence of Hamilton, *see:* Morris, *Alexander Hamilton and the Founding of the Nation* (1957);   Dietze, *Hamilton's Federalist, Treatise for Free Government,* 42 Corn.L.Q. 307, 501 (1957).

Mr. Pinkney [S.Car.] & Mr. Rutledge [S.Car.] objected to the vagueness of the term *incompetent,* and said they could not well decide how to vote until they should see an exact enumeration of the powers comprehended by this definition.

Mr. Butler [S.Car.] repeated his fears that we were running into an extreme in taking away the powers of the States, and called on Mr. Randolph for the extent of his meaning.

Mr. Randolph [Va.] disclaimed any intention to give indefinite powers to the national Legislature, declaring that he was entirely opposed to such an inroad of the State jurisdictions, and that he did not think any considerations whatever could ever change his determination. His opinion was fixed on this point.

Mr. Madison [Va.] said that he had brought with him into the Convention a strong bias in favor of an enumeration and definition of the powers necessary to be exercised by the national Legislature; but had also brought doubts concerning its practicability. His wishes remained unaltered; but his doubts had become stronger. What his opinion might ultimately be he could not yet tell. But he should shrink from nothing which should be found essential to such a form of Govt. as would provide for the safety, liberty and happiness of the Community. This being the end of all our deliberations, all the necessary means for attaining it must, however reluctantly be submitted to.

On the question for giving powers, in cases to which the States are not competent,

Massts. ay. Cont. divd. (Sherman no Ellsworth ay) N.Y. ay. N.J. ay. Pa. ay. Del. ay. Va. ay. N.C. ay. S. Carolina ay. Georgia. ay. [Ayes—9; noes—0; divided—1].

PROCEEDINGS IN THE FEDERAL CONVENTION: JULY 17, 1787

(a) Journal; II Farrant 21

It was moved and seconded to postpone the considn of the second clause of the Sixth resolution [b] reported from the Committee of the whole House in order to take up the following:

"To make laws binding on the People of the United States in all cases which may concern the common interests of the Union: but not to interfere with the government of the individual States in any matters of internal police, which respect the government of such States only, and wherein the general welfare of the United States is not concerned."

which passed in the negative [Ayes—2; noes—8.]

It was moved and seconded to alter the second clause of the 6th resolution so as to read as follows, namely

"and moreover to legislate in all cases for the general interests of the Union, and also in those to which the States are separately incompetent, or in which the harmony of the United States may be interrupted by the exercise of individual legislation."

which passed in the affirmative [Ayes—6; noes—4.]

[b] The Sixth Resolution, based on Randolph's propositions, as adopted by the Committee of the Whole House on May 31, 1787 (see the excerpt from Madison's notes quoted supra), provided in part: "That the national legislature ought to be empowered to enjoy the legislative rights vested in Congress by the Confederation; and moreover To legislate in all cases, to which the separate States are incompetent or in which the harmony of the United States may be interrupted by the exercise of individual legislation." See 1 Farrand 47 (Journal, May 31, 1787).

[To agree to the second clause of the 6. resolution as amended.   Ayes—8; noes—2.]

(b) The same proceedings are reported more fully in Madison's Notes;

II Farrand 25–27

The 6th Resoln. in the Report of the Comm. of the whole relating to the powers, which had been postponed in order to consider the 7 & 8th, relating to the Constitution of the Natl. Legislature, was now resumed—

Mr. Sherman [Conn.] observed that it would be difficult to draw the line between the powers of the Genl. Legislatures, and those to be left with the States; that he did not like the definition contained in the Resolution, and proposed in place of the words "of individual legislation" line 4 inclusive, to insert "to make laws binding on the people of the (United) States in all cases (which may concern the common interests of the Union); but not to interfere with (the Government of the individual States in any matters of internal police which respect the Govt. of such States only, and wherein the General) welfare of the U. States is not concerned."

Mr. Wilson [Pa.] 2ded. the amendment as better expressing the general principle.

Mr. Govr. Morris [Pa.] opposed it.   The internal police, as it would be called & understood by the States ought to be infringed in many cases, as in the case of paper money & other tricks by which Citizens of other states may be affected.

Mr. Sherman, in explanation of his ideas read an enumeration of powers, including the power of levying taxes on trade, but not the power of *direct taxation.*

Mr. Govr. Morris remarked the omission, and inferred that for the deficiencies of taxes on consumption, it must have been the meaning of Mr. Sherman, that the Genl. Govt. should recur to quotas & requisitions, which are subversive of the idea of Govt.

Mr. Sherman acknowledged that his enumeration did not include direct taxation.   Some provision he supposed must be made for supplying the deficiency of other taxation, but he had not formed any.

On Question on Mr. Sherman's motion, (it passed in the negative)

Mas. no. Cont. ay. N.J. no. Pa. no. Del. no. Md. ay. Va. no. N.C. no. S.C. no. Geo. no. [Ayes—2; noes—8].

Mr. Bedford [Del.] moved that the (2d. number of Resolution 6.) be so altered as to read "(and moreover) to legislate in all cases for the general interests of the Union, and also in those to which the States are separately incompetent," (or in which the harmony of the U. States may be interrupted by the exercise of individual Legislation".)

Mr. Govr. Morris 2ds. (the motion.)

Mr. Randolph.   This is a formidable idea indeed.   It involves the power of violating all the laws and constitutions of the States, and of intermeddling with their police.   The last member of the sentence is (also) superfluous, being included in the first.

Mr. Bedford.   It is not more extensive or formidable than the clause as it stands: *no State* being *separately* competent to legislate for the *general interest* of the Union.

On question for agreeing to Mr. Bedford's motion (it passed in the affirmative).

Mas. ay. Cont. no. N.J. ay. Pa. ay. Del. ay. Md. ay. Va. no. N.C. ay. S.C. no. Geo. no. [Ayes—6; noes—4].

On the sentence as amended (it passed in the affirmative).

Mas. ay. Cont. ay. N.J. ay. Pa. ay. Del. ay. Md. ay. Va. ay. N.C. ay. S.C. no. Geo. no. [Ayes—8; noes—2].

REPORT OF THE COMMITTEE OF DETAIL: AUGUST 6, 1787

II Farrand 181–182

[On July 24, 1787, the Convention appointed a Committee of Detail ᶜ "to report a Constitution conformable to the Resolutions passed by the Convention" (II Farrand 106). The Report of the Committee on August 6, 1787 defined as follows the powers of the National Government:]

Art. VII, [erroneously numbered as VI by printer's error].

Sect. I. The Legislature of the United States shall have the power to lay and collect taxes, duties, imposts and excises;

To regulate commerce with foreign nations, and among the several States;

To establish an uniform rule of naturalization throughout the United States;

To coin money;

To regulate the value of foreign coin;

To fix the standard of weights and measures;

To establish Post-offices;

To borrow money, and emit bills on the credit of the United States;

To appoint a Treasurer by ballot;

To constitute tribunals inferior to the Supreme Court;

To make rules concerning captures on land and water;

To declare the law and punishment of piracies and felonies committed on the high seas, and the punishment of counterfeiting the coin of the United States, and of offences against the law of nations;

To subdue a rebellion in any State, on the application of its legislature;

To make war;

To raise armies;

To build and equip fleets;

To call forth the aid of the militia, in order to execute the laws of the Union, enforce treaties, suppress insurrections, and repel invasions;

And to make all laws that shall be necessary and proper for carrying into execution the foregoing powers, and all other powers vested, by this Constitution, in the government of the United States, or in any department or officer thereof.

[The Committee Report on regulation of commerce, as embodied in the second clause, supra, was unanimously approved on August 16, 1787. (II Farrand 308). After this vote, however, strong Southern opposition to this commercial power developed out of fear that commercial regulations in the interest of Northern shipping might restrict free access for Southern staples to foreign shipping and foreign markets. This opposition was in part placated by an agreement by Northern delegates to prohibit the taxation of exports (Art. I, Sec. 9, cl. 1). See II Farrand 305–308 (Aug. 16), 359–363 (Aug. 21), 414–417 (Aug. 25); Warren, *The Making of the Constitution* 567–589 (1928); 2 Curtis, *History of the United States Constitution* 279–308 (1858).

ᶜ The members of the Committee of Detail were John Rutledge (So. Car.), Edmund Randolph (Va.), Nathaniel Gorham (Mass.), Oliver Ellsworth (Conn.), and James Wilson (Pa.).

The reasons for Southern opposition to commercial regulations and the conciliatory effect of the foregoing concessions are shown in the following excerpt.]

PROCEEDINGS IN THE FEDERAL CONVENTION: AUGUST 29, 1787

Madison's Notes; II Farrand 449–453

Mr. Pinkney [S.Car.] moved to postpone the Report [of the Committee of Detail] in favor of the following proposition—"That no act of the Legislature for the purpose of regulating the commerce of the U.S. with foreign powers, or among the several States, shall be passed without the assent of two thirds of the members of each House—"—He remarked that there were five distinct commercial interests—1. the fisheries & W. India trade, which belonged to the N. England States. 2. the interest of N. York lay in a free trade. 3. Wheat & flour the Staples of the two Middle States, (N.J. & Penna.)—4. Tobo. the staple of Maryd. & Virginia (& partly of N. Carolina.) 5. Rice & Indigo, the staples of S. Carolina & Georgia. These different interests would be a source of oppressive regulations if no check to a bare majority should be provided. States pursue their interests with less scruple than individuals. The power of regulating commerce was a pure concession on the part of the S. States. They did not need the protection of the N. States at present.

Mr. Martin [Md.] 2ded. the motion.

Genl. Pinkney said it was the true interest of the S. States to have no regulation of commerce; but considering the loss brought on the commerce of the Eastern States by the revolution, their liberal conduct towards the views * of South Carolina, and the interest the weak Southn. States had in being united with the strong Eastern States, he thought it proper that no fetters should be imposed on the power of making commercial regulations; and that his constituents though prejudiced against the Eastern States, would be reconciled to this liberality—He had himself, he said prejudices agst the Eastern States before he came here, but would acknowledge that he had found them as liberal and candid as any men whatever.

Mr. Clymer [Pa.]. The diversity of commercial interests, of necessity creates difficulties, which ought not to be increased by unnecessary restrictions. The Northern & middle States will be ruined, if not enabled to defend themselves against foreign regulations.

Mr. Sherman [Conn.], alluding to Mr. Pinkney's enumeration of particular interests, as requiring a security agst. abuse of the power; observed that, the diversity was of itself a security, adding that to require more than a majority to decide a question was always embarrassing as had been experienced in cases requiring the votes of nine States in Congress.

Mr. Pinkney replied that his enumeration meant the five minute interests—It still left the two great divisions of Northern & Southern Interests.

Mr. Govr. Morris [Pa.], opposed the object of the motion as highly injurious—Preferences to american ships will multiply them, till they can carry the Southern produce cheaper than it is now carried—A navy was essential to security, particularly of the S. States, and can only be had by a navigation act encouraging american bottoms & seamen—In those points of view then alone, it

---

* He meant the permission to import slaves. [See Art. I, § 9, cl. 1.] An understanding on the two subjects of navigation and slavery, had taken place between those parts of the Union, which explains the vote on the Motion depending, as well as the language of Gen'l Pinkney & others. [Madison's note II Farrand 449.]

is the interest of the S. States that navigation acts should be facilitated. Shipping he said was the worst & most precarious kind of property, and stood in need of public patronage.

Mr. Williamson [N. Car.] was in favor of making two thirds instead of a majority requisite, as more satisfactory to the Southern people. No useful measure he believed had been lost in Congress for want of nine votes. As to the weakness of the Southern States, he was not alarmed on that account. The sickliness of their climate for invaders would prevent their being made an object. He acknowledged that he did not think the motion requiring $\frac{2}{3}$ necessary in itself, because if a majority of Northern States should push their regulations too far, the S. States would build ships for themselves: but he knew the Southern people were apprehensive on this subject and would be pleased with the precaution.

Mr. Spaight [N. Car.] was against the motion. The Southern States could at any time save themselves from oppression, by building ships for their own use.

Mr. Butler [S. Car.] differed from those who considered the rejection of the motion as no concession on the part of the S. States. He considered the interests of these and of the Eastern States, to be as different as the interests of Russia and Turkey. Being notwithstanding desirous of conciliating the affections of the East: States, he should vote agst. requiring $\frac{2}{3}$ instead of a majority.

Col. Mason [Va.]. If the Govt. is to be lasting, it must be founded in the confidence & affections of the people, and must be so constructed as to obtain these. The *Majority* will be governed by their interests. The Southern States are the *minority* in both Houses. Is it to be expected that they will deliver themselves bound hand & foot to the Eastern States, and enable them to exclaim, in the words of Cromwell on a certain occasion—"the lord hath delivered them into our hands."

Mr. Wilson [Pa.] took notice of the several objections and remarked that if every peculiar interest was to be secured, *unanimity* ought to be required. The majority he said would be no more governed by interest than the minority—It was surely better to let the latter be bound hand and foot than the former. Great inconveniences had, he contended, been experienced in Congress from the article of confederation requiring nine votes in certain cases.

Mr. Madison [Va.] went into a pretty full view of the subject. He observed that the disadvantage to the S. States from a navigation act, lay chiefly in a temporary rise of freight, attended however with an increase of Southn. as well as Northern Shipping—with the emigration of Northern seamen & merchants to the Southern States—& with a removal of the existing & injurious retaliations among the States (on each other). The power of foreign nations to obstruct our retaliating measures on them by a corrupt influence would also be less if a majority shd be made competent than if $\frac{2}{3}$ of each House shd. be required to legislative acts in this case. An abuse of the power would be qualified with all these good effects. But he thought an abuse was rendered improbable by the provision of 2 branches—by the independence of the Senate, by the negative of the Executive, by the interest of Connecticut & N. Jersey which were agricultural, not commercial States; by the interior interest which was also agricultural in the most commercial States—by the accession of Western States which wd. be altogether agricultural. He added that the Southern States would derive an essential advantage in the general security afforded by the increase of our maritime strength. He stated the vulnerable situation of them all, and of Virginia in particular. The increase of the Coasting trade, and of seamen, would also be favorable to the S. States, by increasing, the consumption of their produce. If the Wealth of the Eastern should in a still greater proportion be augmented, that wealth wd. contribute the more to the public wants, and be otherwise a national benefit.

Mr. Rutlidge [S. Car.] was agst. the motion of his colleague. It did not follow from a grant of the power to regulate trade, that it would be abused. At the worst a navigation act could bear hard a little while only on the S. States. As we are laying the foundation for a great empire, we ought to take a permanent view of the subject and not look at the present moment only. He reminded the House of the necessity of securing the West India trade to this country. That was the great object, and a navigation Act was necessary for obtaining it.

Mr. Randolph [Va.] said that there were features so odious in the Constitution as it now stands, that he doubted whether he should be able to agree to it. A rejection of the motion would compleat the deformity of the system. He took notice of the argument in favor of giving the power over trade to a majority, drawn from the opportunity foreign powers would have of obstructing retaliating measures, if two thirds were made requisite. He did not think there was weight in that consideration—The difference between a majority & two thirds did not afford room for such an opportunity. Foreign influence would also be more likely to be exerted on the President who could require three fourths by his negative—He did not mean however to enter into the merits. What he had in view was merely to pave the way for a declaration which he might be hereafter obliged to make if an accumulation of obnoxious ingredients should take place, that he could not give his assent to the plan.

Mr. Gorham [Mass.]. If the Government is to be so fettered as to be unable to relieve the Eastern States what motive can they have to join in it, and thereby tie their own hands from measures which they could otherwise take for themselves. The Eastern States were not led to strengthen the Union by fear for their own safety. He deprecated the consequences of disunion, but if it should take place it was the Southern part of the Continent that had the most reason to dread them. He urged the improbability of a combination against the interest of the Southern States, the different situations of the Northern & Middle States being a security against it. It was moreover certain that foreign ships would never be altogether excluded especially those of Nations in treaty with us.

On the question to postpone in order to take up Mr. Pinkney's Motion

N—H. no. Mas. no. Ct. no. N.J. no. Pa. no. Del. no. Md. ay. Va. ay. N.C. ay—S.C. no—Geo. ay, [Ayes—4 noes—7]

The Report of the Committee for striking out sect: 6. requiring two thirds of each House to pass a navigation act was then agreed to, nem: con: [No one contra—Ed.]

NOTE

It is evident from the foregoing excerpts that questions of large import are presented by the shift from a general and loosely-phrased grant of power to the national government, which the Convention initially approved on May 31 and July 17, to the itemized list of national powers embodied in the August 6 report of the Committee of Detail. Consideration should be given to two conflicting interpretations: (a) The enumeration by the Committee of Detail, which the Convention employed as a basis for final action, should be construed to reach towards the same generalized grant of power to the national government which the Convention had earlier approved; (b) The decision to enumerate the powers of Congress reflects a decision sharply to circumscribe national power.[1]

---

[1] See Abel, *The Commerce Clause in the Constitutional Convention and in Contemporary Comment*, 25 Minn.L.Rev. 432 (1941). For general studies, see Warren, *The Making of the Constitution* (1928); Farrand, *The Framing of the Constitution of the United States* (1913). Cf. Brown, *Charles Beard and the Constitution* (1956).

SECTION 2. SOURCES OF NATIONAL POWER: EARLY DEVELOPMENTS

A. THE MARSHALL COURT'S VIEW

Introduction. The allocation of powers between the nation and the states in the Constitution has given rise to three major sets of issues:

(1) What is the scope of the power of the federal government to regulate? Are the specifically granted powers to be construed narrowly or broadly? What is the significance of the clause conferring on Congress the power to make all laws which shall be "necessary and proper" for executing the granted powers?

(2) What are the limits imposed on the powers of the states to regulate and to tax? Does the grant of a power to the federal government imply exclusion of the states from exercising the same power? Does the exercise of a granted power by the federal government imply exclusion of the states from exercising the same power?

(3) Does the Constitution impose any special limitations when the regulations or taxes of the national government impinge on the state governments? To what extent may the states impose regulations or collect taxes from the federal government? In short, what intergovernmental immunities are created by the Constitution?

All three of these issues came before the Court in a set of great cases between 1819 and 1851. The major cases—McCulloch v. Maryland, Gibbons v. Ogden, and Cooley v. Board of Port Wardens—are set out in this section. They provide a useful introduction to the various doctrinal threads which will be pursued in this chapter and in Chapters 5–7. They are also relevant to modern concerns since they are often discussed and applied in current Supreme Court cases.

THE BANK OF THE UNITED STATES

The Bank of the United States moved into the legal arena only after a quarter-century of political controversy. The plan for the Bank was developed by Alexander Hamilton promptly upon the establishment of the new government and led to a bill enacted by Congress in 1791. This First Bank, like the Second Bank which was involved in the McCulloch case, was operated primarily on the basis of privately invested capital and through private control. The national government subscribed to seven millions of the Second Bank's total capitalization of thirty-five millions; the President appointed five of the twenty-five directors. The Act that established the Bank, however, imposed upon it certain public obligations such as providing for free transfer of government deposits and making frequent statements to the Secretary of the Treasury.

Disputes in President Washington's cabinet over the constitutionality of the First Bank shed some light on the issues at stake in the McCulloch case. When in 1791 the bill to establish the bank reached the President, he called upon three members of his cabinet for their opinions. Attorney General Edmund Randolph submitted two opinions one of which was negative and the other noncommittal. Secretary of the Treasury Alexander Hamilton prepared an opinion that Daniel Webster closely followed in his argument for the bank and which in turn was reflected in Marshall's opinion. The opinion of the Secretary of State, Thomas Jefferson, presented a sharply narrower view of the basic powers of the national government.

Washington followed the advice of Hamilton rather than of Jefferson, and signed the bill. During the next twenty years the Bank became unpopular; attempts in 1811 to renew the charter failed. However, the disorganization of the nation's business and fiscal structure during and following the War of 1812 led to support, even among Jefferson's Republican party which then was in power, for a central banking institution to stabilize the economy; in 1816 Congress adopted a plan for a second Bank of the United States which President Madison approved. This new Bank soon encountered hostility from those who believed that its policies were contributing to the financial distress of the state banks. Several states passed legislation to curb the Bank;[1] one of these laws led to the following case.

McCULLOCH v. MARYLAND

17 U.S. (4 Wheat.) 316, 4 L.Ed. 579 (1819)

[The State of Maryland brought an action for debt against McCulloch, cashier of the Baltimore branch of the Bank of the United States. It was admitted that the Bank had issued bank notes which were not on stamped paper as required by the following statute:

"An act to impose a tax on all banks or branches thereof in the state of Maryland, not chartered by the legislature.

"Be it enacted by the General Assembly of Maryland, That if any bank has established, or shall without authority from the State first had and obtained, establish any branch, office of discount and deposit, or office of pay and receipt, in any part of this state, it shall not be lawful for the said branch, office of discount and deposit, or office of pay and receipt, to issue notes in any manner, of any other denomination than five, ten, twenty, fifty, one hundred, five hundred and one thousand dollars, and no note shall be issued except upon stamped paper of the following denominations; that is to say, every five dollar note shall be upon a stamp of ten cents; every ten dollar note upon a stamp of twenty cents; every twenty dollar note, upon a stamp of thirty cents; every fifty dollar note, upon a stamp of fifty cents; every one hundred dollar note, upon a stamp of one dollar; every five hundred dollar note, upon a stamp of ten dollars; and every thousand dollar note, upon a stamp of twenty dollars; which paper shall be furnished by the Treasurer of the Western Shore, under the direction of the Governor and Council, to be paid for upon delivery. Provided always, That any institution of the above description may relieve itself from the operation of the provisions aforesaid, by paying annually, in advance, to the Treasurer of the Western Shore, for the use of the State, the sum of fifteen thousand dollars.

"And be it enacted, That the President, Cashier, each of the Directors and officers of every institution established, or to be established as aforesaid, offending against the provisions aforesaid, shall forfeit a sum of five hundred dollars for each and every offence   . . ."

[1] See Warren, *The Supreme Court in United States History* (Rev.ed.1932) 505–06. The Constitutions of Indiana and Illinois prohibited establishment of banks chartered outside the state. Five states, other than Maryland, resorted to taxation to accomplish the same result; Tennessee and Ohio, $50,000 per branch, North Carolina, $5,000 per branch, and Kentucky, $60,000 per branch. Georgia laid a tax of 31¼% on bank stock employed within the state which on its face appeared nondiscriminatory; the following year the legislature declared that the intent was to tax the Bank of the United States only.

The Court of Appeals of the State of Maryland affirmed a judgment for the plaintiff.]

Mr. Chief Justice Marshall delivered the opinion of the Court:

In the case now to be determined, the defendant, a sovereign state, denies the obligation of a law enacted by the legislature of the Union, and the plaintiff, on his part, contests the validity of an act which has been passed by the legislature of that state. The constitution of our country, in its most interesting and vital parts, is to be considered; the conflicting powers of the government of the Union and of its members, as marked in that constitution, are to be discussed; and an opinion given, which may essentially influence the great operations of the government. No tribunal can approach such a question without a deep sense of its importance, and of the awful responsibility involved in its decision. But it must be decided peacefully, or remain a source of hostile legislation, perhaps of hostility of a still more serious nature; and if it is to be so decided, by this tribunal alone can the decision be made. On the Supreme Court of the United States has the constitution of our country devolved this important duty.

The first question made in the cause is, has Congress power to incorporate a bank? [a]

. . .

The power now contested was exercised by the first Congress elected under the present constitution. The bill for incorporating the bank of the United States did not steal upon an unsuspecting legislature, and pass unobserved. Its principle was completely understood, and was opposed with equal zeal and ability. After being resisted, first in the fair and open field of debate, and afterwards in the executive cabinet, with as much persevering talent as any measure has ever experienced, and being supported by arguments which convinced minds as pure and as intelligent as this country can boast, it became a law. The original act was permitted to expire; but a short experience of the embarrassments to which the refusal to revive it exposed the government, convinced those who were most prejudiced against the measure of its necessity and induced the passage of the present law. It would require no ordinary share of intrepidity to assert that a measure adopted under these circumstances was a bold and plain usurpation, to which the constitution gave no countenance.

These observations belong to the cause; but they are not made under the impression that, were the question entirely new, the law would be found irreconcilable with the constitution.

In discussing this question, the counsel for the state of Maryland have deemed it of some importance, in the construction of the constitution, to consider that instrument not as emanating from the people, but as the act of sovereign and independent states. The powers of the general government, it has been said, are delegated by the states, who alone are truly sovereign; and must be exercised in subordination to the states who alone possess supreme dominion. . . .

The government of the Union, ... (whatever may be the influence of this fact on the case), is, emphatically, and truly, a government of the people. In form and in substance it emanates from them. Its powers are granted by them, and are to be exercised directly on them, and for their benefit.

This government is acknowledged by all to be one of enumerated powers. The principle, that it can exercise only the powers granted to it, would seem too apparent to have required to be enforced by all those arguments which its enlightened friends, while it was depending before the people, found it neces-

---

[a] What is the relationship between the constitutionality of the act of Congress creating the bank and the constitutionality of the Maryland tax?

sary to urge. That principle is now universally admitted. But the question respecting the extent of the powers actually granted, is perpetually arising, and will probably continue to arise, as long as our system shall exist.

In discussing these questions, the conflicting powers of the general and state governments must be brought into view, and the supremacy of their respective laws, when they are in opposition, must be settled.

If any one proposition could command the universal assent of mankind, we might expect it would be this—that the government of the Union, though limited in its powers, is supreme within its sphere of action. This would seem to result necessarily from its nature. It is the government of all; its powers are delegated by all; it represents all, and acts for all. Though any one state may be willing to control its operations, no state is willing to allow others to control them. The nation, on those subjects on which it can act, must necessarily bind its component parts. But this question is not left to mere reason; the people have, in express terms, decided it by saying, "this constitution, and the laws of the United States, which shall be made in pursuance thereof," "shall be the supreme law of the land," and by requiring that the members of the state legislatures, and the officers of the executive and judicial departments of the states shall take the oath of fidelity to it.

The government of the United States, then, though limited in its powers, is supreme; and its laws, when made in pursuance of the constitution, form the supreme law of the land, "anything in the constitution or laws of any state to the contrary notwithstanding."

Among the enumerated powers, we do not find that of establishing a bank or creating a corporation. But there is no phrase in the instrument which, like the articles of confederation, excludes incidental or implied powers,[b] and which requires that everything granted shall be expressly and minutely described. Even the 10th amendment, which was framed for the purpose of quieting the excessive jealousies which had been excited, omits the word "expressly," and declares only that the powers "not delegated to the United States, nor prohibited to the states, are reserved to the states or to the people;" thus leaving the question, whether the particular power which may become the subject of contest has been delegated to the one government, or prohibited to the other, to depend on a fair construction of the whole instrument. The men who drew and adopted this amendment had experienced the embarrassments resulting from the insertion of this word in the articles of confederation, and probably omitted it to avoid those embarrassments. A constitution, to contain an accurate detail of all the subdivisions of which its great powers will admit, and of all the means by which they may be carried into execution, would partake of a prolixity of a legal code, and could scarcely be embraced by the human mind. It would probably never be understood by the public. Its nature, therefore, requires, that only its great outlines should be marked, its important objects designated, and the minor ingredients which compose those objects be deduced from the nature of the objects themselves. That this idea was entertained by the framers of the American constitution, is not only to be inferred from the nature of the instrument but from the language. Why else were some of the limitations, found in the ninth section of the 1st article, introduced? It is also, in some degree, warranted by their having omitted to use any restrictive term which might prevent its receiving a fair and just interpretation. In considering this question, then, we must never forget that it is a constitution we are expounding.

Although, among the enumerated powers of government, we do not find the word "bank" or "incorporation," we find the great powers to lay and collect

---

[b] The Articles of Confederation (1777) provided in Article II: "Each State retains its sovereignty, freedom and independence, and every power, jurisdiction and right, which is not by this confederation expressly delegated to the United States, in Congress assembled."

taxes; to borrow money; to regulate commerce; to declare and conduct a war; and to raise and support armies and navies. The sword and the purse, all the external relations, and no inconsiderable portion of the industry of the nation, are entrusted to its government. It can never be pretended that these vast powers draw after them others of inferior importance, merely because they are inferior. Such an idea can never be advanced. But it may with great reason be contended, that a government, entrusted with such ample powers, on the due execution of which the happiness and prosperity of the nation so vitally depends, must also be entrusted with ample means for their execution. The power being given, it is the interest of the nation to facilitate its execution. It can never be their interest, and cannot be presumed to have been their intention, to clog and embarrass its execution by withholding the most appropriate means. Throughout this vast republic, from the St. Croix to the Gulf of Mexico, from the Atlantic to the Pacific, revenue is to be collected and expended, armies are to be marched and supported. The exigencies of the nation may require that the treasure raised in the north should be transported to the south, that raised in the east conveyed to the west, or that this order should be reversed. Is that construction of the constitution to be preferred which would render these operations difficult, hazardous, and expensive? Can we adopt that construction (unless the words, imperiously require it) which would impute to the framers of that instrument, when granting these powers for the public good, the intention of impeding their exercise by withholding a choice of means? If, indeed, such be the mandate of the constitution, we have only to obey; but that instrument does not profess to enumerate the means by which the powers it confers may be executed; nor does it prohibit the creation of a corporation, if the existence of such a being be essential to the beneficial exercise of those powers. It is, then, the subject of fair inquiry, how far such means may be employed. . . .

But the constitution of the United States has not left the right of Congress to employ the necessary means for the execution of the powers conferred on the government to general reasoning. To its enumeration of powers is added that of making "all laws which shall be necessary and proper, for carrying into execution the foregoing powers, and all other powers vested by this constitution, in the government of the United States, or in any department thereof."

The counsel for the State of Maryland have urged various arguments, to prove that this clause, though in terms a grant of power, is not so in effect; but is really restrictive of the general right, which might otherwise be implied, of selecting means for executing the enumerated powers. . . .

But the argument on which most reliance is placed, is drawn from the peculiar language of this clause. Congress is not empowered by it to make all laws, which may have relation to the powers conferred on the government, but such only as may be "necessary and proper" for carrying them into execution. The word "necessary" is considered as controlling the whole sentence, and as limiting the right to pass laws for the execution of the granted powers, to such as are indispensable, and without which the power would be nugatory. That it excludes the choice of means, and leaves to Congress, in each case, that only which is most direct and simple.

Is it true that this is the sense in which the word "necessary" is always used? Does it always import an absolute physical necessity, so strong that one thing, to which another may be termed necessary, cannot exist without that other? We think it does not. If reference be had to its use, in the common affairs of the world, or in approved authors, we find that it frequently imports no more than that one thing is convenient, or useful, or essential to another. To employ the means necessary to an end, is generally understood as employing any means calculated to produce the end, and not as being confined to those single means, without which the end would be entirely unattainable. Such is the character of human language, that no word conveys to the mind, in all situations, one single definite idea; . . . This word, then, like others, is used in various senses; and, in its construction, the subject, the context, the intention of the person using them, are all to be taken into view.

Let this be done in the case under consideration. The subject is the execution of those great powers on which the welfare of a nation essentially depends. It must have been the intention of those who gave these powers, to insure, as far as human prudence could insure, their beneficial execution. This could not be done by confining the choice of means to such narrow limits as not to leave it in the power of Congress to adopt any which might be appropriate, and which were conducive to the end. This provision is made in a constitution intended to endure for ages to come, and, consequently, to be adapted to the various crises of human affairs. To have prescribed the means by which government should, in all future time, execute its powers, would have been to change, entirely, the character of the instrument, and give it the properties of a legal code. . . .

    . . .

The result of the most careful and attentive consideration bestowed upon this clause is, that if it does not enlarge, it cannot be construed to restrain the powers of Congress, or to impair the right of the legislature to exercise its best judgment in the selection of measures to carry into execution the constitutional powers of the government. If no other motive for its insertion can be suggested, a sufficient one is found in the desire to remove all doubts respecting the right to legislate on that vast mass of incidental powers which must be involved in the constitution, if that instrument be not a splendid bauble.

We admit, as all must admit, that the powers of the government are limited, and that its limits are not to be transcended. But we think the sound construction of the constitution must allow to the national legislature that discretion, with respect to the means by which the powers it confers are to be carried into execution, which will enable that body to perform the high duties assigned to it, in the manner most beneficial to the people. Let the end be legitimate, let it be within the scope of the constitution, and all means which are appropriate, which are plainly adapted to that end, which are not prohibited, but consist with the letter and spirit of the constitution, are constitutional. . . .

If a corporation may be employed indiscriminately with other means to carry into execution the powers of the government, no particular reason can be assigned for excluding the use of a bank, if required for its fiscal operations.
    . . .

But, were its necessity less apparent, none can deny its being an appropriate measure; and if it is, the degree of its necessity, as has been very justly observed, is to be discussed in another place. Should Congress, in the execution of its powers, adopt measures which are prohibited by the constitution; or should Congress, under the pretext of executing its powers, pass laws for the accomplishment of objects not entrusted to the government, it would become the painful duty of this tribunal, should a case requiring such a decision come before it, to say that such an act was not the law of the land. But where the law is not prohibited, and is really calculated to effect any of the objects entrusted to the government, to undertake here to inquire into the degree of its necessity, would be to pass the line which circumscribes the judicial department, and to tread on legislative ground. This court disclaims all pretensions to such a power. . . .

After the most deliberate consideration, it is the unanimous and decided opinion of this court that the act to incorporate the bank of the United States is a law made in pursuance of the constitution, and is a part of the supreme law of the land. . . .

It being the opinion of the court that the act incorporating the bank is constitutional, and that the power of establishing a branch in the state of Maryland might be properly exercised by the bank itself, we proceed to inquire:

2. Whether the state of Maryland may, without violating the constitution, tax that branch?

That the power of taxation is one of vital importance; that it is retained by the states; that it is not abridged by the grant of a similar power to the government of the Union; that it is to be concurrently exercised by the two governments: are truths which have never been denied. But, such is the paramount character of the constitution that its capacity to withdraw any subject from the action of even this power, is admitted. The states are expressly forbidden to lay any duties on imports or exports, except what may be absolutely necessary for executing their inspection laws. If the obligation of this prohibition must be conceded—if it may restrain a state from the exercise of its taxing power on imports and exports—the same paramount character would seem to restrain, as it certainly may restrain, a state from such other exercise of this power, as is in its nature incompatible with, and repugnant to, the constitutional laws of the Union. A law, absolutely repugnant to another, as entirely repeals that other as if express terms of repeal were used.

On this ground the counsel for the bank place its claim to be exempted from the power of a state to tax its operations. There is no express provision for the case, but the claim has been sustained on a principle which so entirely pervades the constitution, is so intermixed with the materials which compose it, so interwoven with its web, so blended with its texture, as to be incapable of being separated from it without rending it into shreds.

This great principle is, that the constitution and the laws made in pursuance thereof are supreme; that they control the constitution and laws of the respective states, and cannot be controlled by them. . . .

. . .

That the power to tax involves the power to destroy; that the power to destroy may defeat and render useless the power to create; that there is a plain repugnance, in conferring on one government a power to control the constitutional measures of another, which other, with respect to those very measures, is declared to be supreme over that which exerts the control, are propositions not to be denied. But all inconsistencies are to be reconciled by the magic of the word CONFIDENCE. Taxation, it is said, does not necessarily and unavoidably destroy. To carry it to the excess of destruction would be an abuse, to presume which, would banish that confidence which is essential to all government.

But is this a case of confidence? Would the people of any one state trust those of another with a power to control the most insignificant operations of their state government? We know they would not. Why, then, should we suppose that the people of any one state should be willing to trust those of another with a power to control the operations of a government to which they have confided the most important and most valuable interests? In the legislature of the Union alone, are all represented. The legislature of the Union alone, therefore, can be trusted by the people with the power of controlling measures which concern all, in the confidence that it will not be abused. This, then, is not a case of confidence, and we must consider it as it really is. . . .

If the states may tax one instrument, employed by the government in the execution of its powers, they may tax any and every other instrument. They may tax the mail; they may tax the mint; they may tax patent-rights; they may tax the papers of the custom-house; they may tax judicial process; they may tax all the means employed by the government, to an excess which would defeat all the ends of government. This was not intended by the American people. They did not design to make their government dependent on the states. . . .

It has also been insisted, that, as the power of taxation in the general and state governments is acknowledged to be concurrent, every argument which would sustain the right of the general government to tax banks chartered by the states, will equally sustain the right of the states to tax banks chartered by the general government.

But the two cases are not on the same reason. The people of all the states have created the general government, and have conferred upon it the general power of taxation. The people of all the states, and the states themselves, are represented in Congress, and, by their representatives, exercise this power. When they tax the chartered institutions of the states, they tax their constituents; and these taxes must be uniform. But, when a state taxes the operations of the government of the United States, it acts upon institutions created, not by their own constituents, but by people over whom they claim no control. It acts upon the measures of a government created by others as well as themselves, for the benefit of others in common with themselves. The difference is that which always exists, and always must exist, between the action of the whole on a part, and the action of a part on the whole—between the laws of a government declared to be supreme, and those of a government which, when in opposition to those laws, is not supreme.

But if the full application of this argument could be admitted, it might bring into question the right of Congress to tax the state banks, and could not prove the right of the states to tax the Bank of the United States.

The court has bestowed on this subject its most deliberate consideration. The result is a conviction that the states have no power, by taxation or otherwise, to retard, impede, burden, or in any manner control the operations of the constitutional laws enacted by Congress to carry into execution the powers vested in the general government. This is, we think, the unavoidable consequence of that supremacy which the constitution has declared.

We are unanimously of opinion that the law passed by the legislature of Maryland, imposing a tax on the Bank of the United States, is unconstitutional and void.

This opinion does not deprive the states of any resources which they originally possessed. It does not extend to a tax paid by the real property of the bank, in common with the other real property within the state, nor to a tax imposed on the interest which the citizens of Maryland may hold in this institution, in common with other property of the same description throughout the state. But this is a tax on the operations of the bank, and is, consequently, a tax on the operation of an instrument employed by the government of the Union to carry its powers into execution. Such a tax must be unconstitutional.

. . . . It is, therefore, adjudged and ordered, that the said judgment of the said Court of Appeals of the state of Maryland in this case, be, and the same hereby is, reversed and annulled. And this court, proceeding to render such judgment as the said Court of Appeals should have rendered; it is further adjudged and ordered, that the judgment of the said Baltimore County Court be reversed and annulled, and that judgment be entered in the said Baltimore County Court for the said James W. M'Culloch.

McCULLOCH AND THE SCOPE OF FEDERAL POWER

(1) Marshall rejected the argument that the powers of the federal government were delegated to it by the sovereign states. The government of the Union, he said, is a government of the people, it "emanates from them. Its powers are granted by them, and are to be exercised directly on them, and for their benefit." What is the significance of this reasoning by Marshall? If powers were granted by the states, could the states insist upon their own interpretation of the powers granted? Could a state legally secede from the Union? These questions assumed importance from the beginning of the country. Examples include the Kentucky-Virginia Resolutions of 1798, the New England resistance to the War of 1812, Calhoun's doctrine of nullification as reflected in the South Carolina Exposition of 1828 and the Statute of Nullification of 1832. The ultimate test took place in the Civil War where the right of secession was rejected on the battlefield. For an account of these early episodes and others, see Reference Note, *Interposition vs. Judicial Power,* 1 Race Rel.L.Rep. 465 (1956). The issue recurred in the middle 1950s when state legislatures passed resolutions seeking to nullify the enforcement of Brown v. Board of Educ., 347 U.S. 483 (1954). The Alabama Resolution, e.g., commenced as follows:

"WHEREAS the Constitution of the United States was formed by the sanction of the several states, given by each in its sovereign capacity; and

"WHEREAS the States, being the parties to the constitutional compact, it follows of necessity that there can be no tribunal above their authority to decide, in the last resort, whether the compact made by them be violated; and, consequently, they must decide themselves, in the last resort, such questions as may be of sufficient magnitude to require their interposition; . . ." Act No. 42, Spec.Sess., 1956, Feb. 2, 1956, set out 1 Race Rel.L. Rptr. 437 (1956). Other resolutions of the time are set out id. 438–447.

The Supreme Court gave its answer to these latter-day nullifiers in Cooper v. Aaron, 358 U.S. 1 (1958).

(2) The Constitution did not contain an express power to create banks. Did Marshall rely primarily upon the "necessary and proper" clause as the basis for inferring such a power from other powers expressly granted? Or is Professor Black correct in suggesting that Marshall "does not place principal reliance on this clause as a ground of decision; that before he reaches it he has already decided, on the basis of far more general implications . . .; that he addresses himself to the . . . clause only in response to counsel's arguing its *restrictive* force; and that he never really commits himself to the proposition that the necessary and proper clause enlarges governmental power . . .." Black, *Structure and Relationship in Constitutional Law* 14 (1969). For an elaborate exegisis of the necessary and proper clause, see Engdahl, *Constitutional Power: Federal and State* 11–65 (1974).

FEDERAL POWER TO BUILD ROADS AND CANALS

The second great issue on the scope of national legislative power grew out of proposals for the building of national roads and canals. A bill appropriating funds for such "internal improvements" was passed in 1817, but was vetoed by President Madison.

MADISON'S VETO OF INTERNAL
IMPROVEMENT BILL (1817)

II Messages and Papers of the Presidents 569, 570 (1897)

I am constrained, by the insuperable difficulty I feel in reconciling the bill with the Constitution of the United States, to return it with that objection, to the House of Representatives, in which it originated.

The legislative powers vested in Congress are specified and enumerated in the 8th section of the first article of the Constitution; and it does not appear that the power proposed to be exercised by the bill is among the enumerated powers; or that it falls, by any just interpretation, within the power to make laws necessary and proper for carrying into execution those or other powers vested by the Constitution in the Government of the United States.

"The power to regulate commerce among the several States," cannot include a power to construct roads and canals, and to improve the navigation of water courses, in order to facilitate, promote, and secure such a commerce, without a latitude of construction departing from the ordinary import of the terms, strengthened by the known inconveniences which doubtless led to the grant of this remedial power to Congress.

To refer the power in question to the clause "to provide for the common defence and general welfare," would be contrary to the established and consistent rules of interpretation, as rendering the special and careful enumeration of powers, which follow the clause, nugatory and improper. Such a view of the Constitution would have the effect of giving to Congress a general power of legislation, instead of the defined and limited one hitherto understood to belong to them, the terms "common defence and general welfare" embracing every object and act within the purview of a legislative trust. It would have the effect of subjecting both the Constitution and laws of the several States, in all cases not specifically exempted, to be superseded by laws of Congress, it being expressly declared "that the Constitution of the United States, and laws made in pursuance thereof, shall be the supreme law of the land, and the judges of every State shall be bound thereby, anything in the Constitution or laws of any State to the contrary notwithstanding." Such a view of the Constitution, finally, would have the effect of excluding the judicial authority of the United States from its participation in guarding the boundary between the legislative powers of the General and the State Governments; inasmuch as questions relating to the general welfare being questions of policy and expediency, are unsusceptible of judicial cognizance and decision.

A restriction of the power "to provide for the common defence and general welfare," to cases which are to be provided for by the expenditure of money, would still leave within the legislative power of Congress all the great and most important measures of Government; money being the ordinary and necessary means of carrying them into execution.

If a general power to construct roads and canals, and to improve the navigation of water-courses, with the train of powers incident thereto, be not possessed by Congress, the assent of the States in the mode provided in the bill cannot confer the power. The only cases in which the consent and cession of particular States can extend the power of Congress, are those specified and provided for in the Constitution. . . .

An appropriation for the preservation and repair of the Cumberland Road was passed in 1822; President Monroe vetoed the bill on constitutional grounds. The President stated that he took the step "with great regret" since he approved the objective of the measure, and suggested that Congress propose an amendment to the Constitution which would authorize this action. The President developed his views on the constitutionality of the measure into a lengthy document (Annals of Cong., 17th Cong. 1809–1863) and sent a copy to each of the Justices. Justice Johnson then sent the President this remarkable reply: [1]

"Judge Johnson has had the Honour to submit the President's argument on the subject of internal improvement to his Brother Judges and is instructed to make the following Report. The Judges are deeply sensible of the mark of confidence bestowed on them in this instance and should be unworthy of that confidence did they attempt to conceal their real opinion. Indeed, to conceal or disavow it would be now impossible as they are all of opinion that the decision on the Bank question completely commits them on the subject of internal improvement, as applied to Postroads and Military Roads. On the other points, it is impossible to resist the lucid and conclusive reasoning contained in the argument. The principle assumed in the case of the Bank is that the granting of the principal power carries with it the grant of all adequate and appropriate means of executing it. That the selection of these means must rest with the General Government, and as to that power and those means the Constitution makes the Government of the U. S. supreme. Judge Johnson would take the liberty of suggesting to the President that it would not be unproductive of good, if the Secretary of State were to have the opinion of this Court on the Bank question, printed and dispersed through the Union."

GIBBONS v. OGDEN

22 U.S. (9 Wheat.) 1, 6 L.Ed. 23 (1824).

[Ogden obtained an injunction from the Court of Chancery of New York ordering Gibbons to stop operating his ferry-boats in the waters of the State of New York. In 1803 the New York legislature had granted to Robert Livingston and Robert Fulton the exclusive right for twenty years to operate ships powered by fire or steam in New York waters; in 1808, on proof that Livingston and Fulton had built a steamboat that could operate at more than four miles per hour, the grant was extended until 1838. Ogden alleged that he held an assignment from these grantees of the exclusive right to run a steamboat between Elizabethtown, New Jersey, and New York City, and that the defendant, Gibbons, was running two boats between these points. Gibbons alleged that his boats, the *Stoudinger* and *Bellana*, had been duly enrolled and licensed under the laws of the United States for carrying on the coasting trade.

Chancellor Kent sustained the injunction prohibiting the operation of Gibbons' boats. 4 Johns.Ch. 150 (1819). The Chancellor rejected the defendant's contention that plaintiff's monopoly was inconsistent with the United States coasting license; Chancellor Kent concluded that the coasting license was designed merely to relieve American ships of the burdens imposed upon foreign shipping. In an earlier case involving the steamboat monopoly the Chancellor had further rejected the contention that this state law, in regulating interstate commerce, fell within an area exclusively reserved to Congress. On the contrary, Chancellor Kent held that the states could regulate interstate commerce unless Congress had enacted inconsistent legislation. Livingston v. Van Ingen, 9 Johns. 507 (1812).

[1] Quoted, 1 Warren, *The Supreme Court in United States History* 596–7 (1926). On the Court's official views concerning advisory opinions, see supra, at 87.

The New York Court for the Correction of Errors affirmed the order sustaining Ogden's injunction.　17 Johns. 488 (1820).]

Mr. Chief Justice Marshall delivered the opinion of the Court, . . .

The appellant contends that this decree is erroneous, because the laws which purport to give the exclusive privilege it sustains, are repugnant to the constitution and laws of the United States.

They are said to be repugnant:

1st.　To that clause in the constitution which authorizes Congress to regulate commerce. . . .

The words are: "Congress shall have power to regulate commerce with foreign nations, and among the several states, and with the Indian tribes."

The subject to be regulated is commerce; and our constitution being, as was aptly said at the bar, one of enumeration, and not of definition, to ascertain the extent of the power it becomes necessary to settle the meaning of the word. The counsel for the appellee would limit it to traffic, to buying and selling, or the interchange of commodities, and do not admit that it comprehends navigation. This would restrict a general term, applicable to many objects, to one of its significations. Commerce, undoubtedly is traffic, but it is something more; it is intercourse. It describes the commercial intercourse between nations, and parts of nations, in all its branches, and is regulated by prescribing rules for carrying on that intercourse. The mind can scarcely conceive a system for regulating commerce between nations, which shall exclude all laws concerning navigation, which shall be silent on the admission of the vessels of the one nation into the ports of the other, and be confined to prescribing rules for the conduct of individuals, in the actual employment of buying and selling, or of barter.

If commerce does not include navigation, the government of the Union has no direct power over that subject, and can make no law prescribing what shall constitute American vessels, or requiring that they shall be navigated by American seamen. Yet this power has been exercised from the commencement of the government, has been exercised with the consent of all, and has been understood by all to be a commercial regulation. All America understands, and has uniformly understood, the word "commerce" to comprehend navigation. It was so understood, and must have been so understood, when the constitution was framed. The power over commerce, including navigation, was one of the primary objects for which the people of America adopted their government, and must have been contemplated in forming it. The convention must have used the word in that sense; because all have understood it in that sense, and the attempt to restrict it comes too late. . . .

The word used in the constitution, then, comprehends, and has been always understood to comprehend, navigation within its meaning; and a power to regulate navigation is as expressly granted as if that term had been added to the word "commerce."

To what commerce does this power extend? The constitution informs us, to commerce "with foreign nations, and among the several states, and with the Indian tribes."

It has, we believe, been universally admitted that these words comprehend every species of commercial intercourse between the United States and foreign nations. No sort of trade can be carried on between this country and any other, to which this power does not extend. It has been truly said, that commerce, as the word is used in the constitution, is a unit, every part of which is indicated by the term.

If this be the admitted meaning of the word, in its application to foreign nations, it must carry the same meaning throughout the sentence, and remain a unit, unless there be some plain intelligible cause which alters it.

The subject to which the power is next applied, is to commerce "among the several states." The word "among" means intermingled with. A thing which is among others, is intermingled with them. Commerce among the states cannot stop at the external boundary line of each state, but may be introduced into the interior.

It is not intended to say that these words comprehend that commerce which is completely internal, which is carried on between man and man in a state, or between different parts of the same state, and which does not extend to or affect other states. Such a power would be inconvenient, and is certainly unnecessary.

Comprehensive as the word "among" is, it may very properly be restricted to that commerce which concerns more states than one. The phrase is not one which would probably have been selected to indicate the completely interior traffic of a state, because it is not an apt phrase for that purpose; and the enumeration of the particular classes of commerce to which the power was to be extended, would not have been made had the intention been to extend the power to every description. The enumeration presupposes something not enumerated; and that something, if we regard the language or the subject of the sentence, must be the exclusively internal commerce of a state. The genius and character of the whole government seem to be, that its action is to be applied to all the external concerns of the nation, and to those internal concerns which affect the states generally; but not to those which are completely within a particular state, which do not affect other states, and with which it is not necessary to interfere, for the purpose of executing some of the general powers of the government. The completely internal commerce of a state, then, may be considered as reserved for the state itself.

But, in regulating commerce with foreign nations, the power of Congress does not stop at the jurisdictional lines of the several states. It would be a very useless power if it could not pass those lines. The commerce of the United States with foreign nations, is that of the whole United States. Every district has a right to participate in it. The deep streams which penetrate our country in every direction, pass through the interior of almost every state in the Union, and furnish the means of exercising this right. If Congress has the power to regulate it, that power must be exercised whenever the subject exists. If it exists within the states, if a foreign voyage may commence or terminate at a port within a state, then the power of Congress may be exercised within a state.

This principle is, if possible, still more clear, when applied to commerce "among the several states." They either join each other, in which case they are separated by a mathematical line, or they are remote from each other, in which case other states lie between them. What is commerce "among" them; and how is it to be conducted? Can a trading expedition between two adjoining states commence and terminate outside of each? And if the trading intercourse be between two states remote from each other, must it not commence in one, terminate in the other, and probably pass through a third? Commerce among the states must, of necessity, be commerce with the states. In the regulation of trade with the Indian tribes, the action of the law, especially when the constitution was made, was chiefly within a state. The power of Congress, then, whatever it may be, must be exercised within the territorial jurisdiction of the several states. The sense of the nation, on this subject, is unequivocally manifested by the provisions made in the laws for transporting goods, by land, between Baltimore and Providence, between New York and Philadelphia, and between Philadelphia and Baltimore.

We are now arrived at the inquiry, What is this power?

It is the power to regulate; that is, to prescribe the rule by which commerce is to be governed. This power, like all others vested in Congress, is complete in itself, may be exercised to its utmost extent, and acknowledges no limitations, other than are prescribed in the constitution. These are expressed in plain terms, and do not affect the questions which arise in this case, or which have been discussed at the bar. If, as has always been understood, the sovereignty of Congress, though limited to specified objects, is plenary as to those objects, the power over commerce with foreign nations, and among the several States, is vested in Congress as absolutely as it would be in a single government, having in its constitution the same restrictions on the exercise of the power as are found in the constitution of the United States. The wisdom and the discretion of Congress, their identity with the people, and the influence which their constituents possess at elections, are, in this, as in many other instances, as that, for example, of declaring war, the sole restraints on which they have relied, to secure them from its abuse. They are the restraints on which the people must often rely solely, in all representative governments. . . .

But it has been urged, with great earnestness, that although the power of Congress to regulate commerce with foreign nations, and among the several states, be co-extensive with the subject itself, and have no other limits than are prescribed in the constitution, yet the states may severally exercise the same power within their respective jurisdictions. In support of this argument, it is said that they possessed it as an inseparable attribute of sovereignty, before the formation of the constitution, and still retain it, except so far as they have surrendered it by that instrument; that this principle results from the nature of the government, and is secured by the tenth amendment; that an affirmative grant of power is not exclusive, unless in its own nature it be such that the continued exercise of it by the former possessor is inconsistent with the grant, and that this is not of that description.

The appellant, conceding these postulates, except the last, contends that full power to regulate a particular subject, implies the whole power, and leaves no residuum; that a grant of the whole is incompatible with the existence of a right in another to any part of it.

Both parties have appealed to the constitution, to legislative acts, and judicial decisions; and have drawn arguments from all these sources to support and illustrate the propositions they respectively maintain.

The grant of the power to lay and collect taxes is, like the power to regulate commerce, made in general terms, and has never been understood to interfere with the exercise of the same power by the states; and hence has been drawn an argument which has been applied to the question under consideration. But the two grants are not, it is conceived, similar in their terms or their nature. Although many of the powers formerly exercised by the states, are transferred to the government of the Union, yet the state governments remain, and constitute a most important part of our system. The power of taxation is indispensable to their existence, and is a power which, in its own nature, is capable of residing in, and being exercised by, different authorities at the same time. We are accustomed to see it placed, for different purposes, in different hands. Taxation is the simple operation of taking small portions from a perpetually accumulating mass, susceptible of almost infinite division; and a power in one to take what is necessary for certain purposes, is not, in its nature, incompatible with a power in another to take what is necessary for other purposes. Congress is authorized to lay and collect taxes, &c., to pay the debts, and provide for the common defence and general welfare of the United States. This does not interfere with the power of the States to tax for the support of their own governments; nor is the exercise of that power by the States, an exercise of any portion of the power that is granted to the United States. In

imposing taxes for State purposes, they are not doing what Congress is empowered to do.   Congress is not empowered to tax for those purposes which are
within the exclusive province of the States.   When, then, each government
exercises the power of taxation, neither is exercising the power of the other.
But, when a State proceeds to regulate commerce with foreign nations, or
among the several States, it is exercising the very power that is granted to
Congress, and is doing the very thing which Congress is authorized to do.
There is no analogy, then, between the power of taxation and the power of
regulating commerce.   .   .   .

But, the inspection laws are said to be regulations of commerce, and are
certainly recognized in the constitution, as being passed in the exercise of a
power remaining with the States.

That inspection laws may have a remote and considerable influence on
commerce, will not be denied; but that a power to regulate commerce is the
source from which the right to pass them is derived, cannot be admitted.   The
object of inspection laws, is to improve the quality of articles produced by the
labour of a country; to fit them for exportation; or, it may be, for domestic use.
They act upon the subject before it becomes an article of foreign commerce, or
of commerce among the States, and prepare it for that purpose.   They form a
portion of that immense mass of legislation, which embraces everything within
the territory of a State, not surrendered to the general government: all which
can be most advantageously exercised by the States themselves.   Inspection
laws, quarantine laws, health laws of every description, as well as laws for
regulating the internal commerce of a State, and those which respect turnpike
roads, ferries, &c., are component parts of this mass.

No direct general power over these objects is granted to Congress; and,
consequently, they remain subject to State legislation.   If the legislative power
of the Union can reach them, it must be for national purposes; it must be where
the power is expressly given for a special purpose, or is clearly incidental to
some power which is expressly given.   It is obvious, that the government of the
Union, in the exercise of its express powers, that, for example, of regulating
commerce with foreign nations and among the States, may use means that may
also be employed by a State, in the exercise of its acknowledged powers; that,
for example, of regulating commerce within the State.   If Congress license
vessels to sail from one port to another, in the same State, the act is supposed to
be, necessarily, incidental to the power expressly granted to Congress, and
implies no claim of a direct power to regulate the purely internal commerce of a
State, or to act directly on its system of police.   So, if a State, in passing laws on
subjects acknowledged to be within its control, and with a view to those
subjects, shall adopt a measure of the same character with one which Congress
may adopt, it does not derive its authority from the particular power which has
been granted, but from some other, which remains with the State, and may be
executed by the same means.   All experience shows, that the same measures, or
measures scarcely distinguishable from each other, may flow from distinct
powers; but this does not prove that the powers themselves are identical.
Although the means used in their execution may sometimes approach each other
so nearly as to be confounded, there are other situations in which they are
sufficiently distinct to establish their individuality.   .   .   .

It has been contended by the counsel for the appellant, that, as the word "to
regulate" implies in its nature full power over the thing to be regulated, it
excludes, necessarily, the action of all others that would perform the same
operation on the same thing.   That regulation is designed for the entire result,
applying to those parts which remain as they were, as well as to those which are
altered.   It produces a uniform whole, which is as much disturbed and deranged

by changing what the regulating power designs to leave untouched, as that on which it has operated.

There is great force in this argument, and the Court is not satisfied that it has been refuted.

Since, however, in exercising the power or regulating their own purely internal affairs, whether of trading or police, the States may sometimes enact laws, the validity of which depends on their interfering with, and being contrary to, an act of Congress passed in pursuance of the constitution, the Court will enter upon the inquiry, whether the laws of New York, as expounded by the highest tribunal of that State, have, in their application to this case, come into collision with an act of Congress, and deprived a citizen of a right to which that act entitles him. Should this collision exist, it will be immaterial whether those laws were passed in virtue of a concurrent power "to regulate commerce with foreign nations and among the several States," or in virtue of a power to regulate their domestic trade and police. In one case and the other, the acts of New York must yield to the law of Congress; and the decision sustaining the privilege they confer, against a right given by a law of the Union, must be erroneous. . . .

But we will proceed briefly to notice those sections which bear more directly on the subject.

The first section declares, that vessels enrolled by virtue of a previous law, and certain other vessels, enrolled as described in that act, and having a license in force, as is by the act required, "and no others, shall be deemed ships or vessels of the United States, entitled to the privileges of ships or vessels employed in the coasting trade."

This section seems to the Court to contain a positive enactment, that the vessels it describes shall be entitled to the privileges of ships or vessels employed in the coasting trade. These privileges cannot be separated from the trade, and cannot be enjoyed, unless the trade may be prosecuted. The grant of the privilege is an idle, empty form, conveying nothing, unless it convey the right to which the privilege is attached, and in the exercise of which its whole value consists. To construe these words otherwise than as entitling the ships or vessels described, to carry on the coasting trade, would be, we think to disregard the apparent intent of the act.

.   .   .   .

But if the license be a permit to carry on the coasting trade, the respondent denies that these boats were engaged in that trade, or that the decree under consideration has restrained them from prosecuting it. The boats of the appellant were, we are told, employed in the transportation of passengers; and this is no part of that commerce which Congress may regulate.

If, as our whole course of legislation on this subject shows, the power of Congress has been universally understood in America, to comprehend navigation, it is a very persuasive, if not a conclusive argument, to prove that the construction is correct; and, if it be correct, no clear distinction is perceived between the power to regulate vessels employed in transporting men for hire, and property for hire. . . .

Powerful and ingenious minds, taking, as postulates, that the powers expressly granted to the government of the Union, are to be contracted by construction, into the narrowest possible compass, and that the original powers of the States are retained, if any possible construction will retain them, may, by a course of well digested, but refined and metaphysical reasoning, founded on these premises, explain away the constitution of our country, and leave it, a magnificent structure, indeed, to look at, but totally unfit for use. They may so entangle and perplex the understanding, as to obscure principles, which were before thought quite plain, and induce doubts where, if the mind were to pursue its own course, none would be perceived. In such a case, it is peculiarly necessary to recur to safe and fundamental principles to sustain those principles, and, when sustained, to make them the tests of the arguments to be examined.

Mr. Justice Johnson.[a] The judgment entered by the Court in this cause, has my entire approbation; but having adopted my conclusions on views of the subject materially different from those of my brethren, I feel it incumbent on me to exhibit those views. I have, also, another inducement: in question of great importance and great delicacy, I feel my duty to the public best discharged, by an effort to maintain my opinions in my own way.

In attempts to construe the constitution, I have never found much benefit resulting from the inquiry, whether the whole, or any part of it, is to be construed strictly, or liberally. The simple, classical, precise, yet comprehensive language, in which it is couched, leaves, at most, but very little latitude for construction; and when its intent and meaning is discovered, nothing remains but to execute the will of those who made it, in the best manner to effect the purposes intended. . . .

. . .

The power of a sovereign state over commerce, . . . amounts to nothing more than a power to limit and restrain it at pleasure. And since the power to prescribe the limits to its freedom, necessarily implies the power to determine what shall remain unrestrained, it follows, that the power must be exclusive; it can reside but in one potentate; hence, the grant of this power carries with it the whole subject, leaving nothing for the State to act upon. . . .

Commerce, in its simplest signification, means an exchange of goods; but in the advancement of society, labour, transportation, intelligence, care, and various mediums of exchange, become commodities, and enter into commerce; the subject, the vehicle, the agent, and their various operations, become the objects of commercial regulation. Ship building, the carrying trade, and propagation of seamen, are such vital agents of commercial prosperity, that the nation which could not legislate over these subjects, would not possess power to regulate commerce.

That such was the understanding of the framers of the constitution is conspicuous from provisions contained in that instrument. . . .

It is impossible, with the views which I entertain of the principle on which the commercial privileges of the people of the United States, among themselves, rests, to concur in the view which this Court takes of the effect of the coasting license in this cause. I do not regard it as the foundation of the right set up in behalf of the appellant. If there was any one object riding over every other in the adoption of the constitution, it was to keep the commercial intercourse among the States free from all invidious and partial restraints. And I cannot overcome the conviction, that if the licensing act was repealed to-morrow, the rights of the appellant to a reversal of the decision complained of, would be as strong as it is under this license. One half the doubts in life arise from the defects of language, and if this instrument had been called an exemption instead of a license, it would have given a better idea of its character. . . .

Decree. . . . [T]his Court is of opinion, that the several licenses to the steam boats, the Stoudinger and the Bellona, to carry on the coasting trade

---

[a] Justice William Johnson, of South Carolina, was appointed to the Supreme Court in 1804 by Jefferson with the hope that the new justice would provide an antidote to Marshall and his Federalism. See Morgan, Justice William Johnson, the First Dissenter (1954). Was this hope realized in the *Gibbons* case? Compare Justice Johnson's letter to President Monroe, quoted, supra, at p. 168.

. . . which were granted under an act of congress, passed in pursuance of the constitution of the United States, gave full authority to those vessels to navigate the waters of the United States, by steam or otherwise, for the purpose of carrying on the coasting trade, any law of the State of New York to the contrary notwithstanding; and that so much of the several laws of the State of New York, as prohibits vessels, licensed according to the laws of the United States, from navigating the waters of the State of New York, by means of fire or steam, is repugnant to the said constitution, and void [Reversed.] b

NOTE

The Chief Justice regarded "inspection laws, quarantine laws, health laws of every description, as well as laws for regulating the internal commerce of a State, and those which respect turnpike roads, ferries, etc." as component parts of "that immense mass of legislation, which embraces everything within the territory of a State, not surrendered to the general government." According to Justice Story, such laws "are not so much regulations of commerce as of police" and the powers exercised in their enactment "are entirely distinct in their nature from that to regulate commerce". Story on the Constitution (1833), § 1066. In what sense these powers, when applied to interstate or foreign commerce, are entirely distinct from the power to regulate such commerce was not made clear, but doctrinal foundations were thus laid which could enable the Court to sustain certain state laws affecting commerce while asserting that the power to regulate such commerce was vested exclusively in the national government. Marshall actually applied the "police power" view in only one case, which follows.

WILLSON v. BLACK BIRD CREEK MARSH CO., 27 U.S. (2 Pet.) 245 (1829). The legislature of Delaware authorized a company owning marshy lands along Black Bird Creek to dam and bank the creek with a view to improving their lands. The creek, which was navigable, flowed into the Delaware, but was described by counsel for the company as "one of those sluggish, reptile streams, that do not run but creep, and which wherever it passes, spreads its venom, and destroys the health of all those who inhabit its marshes." The owners of a sloop, licensed and enrolled under the navigation laws of the United States, broke the dam in order to secure passage for their vessel. The company sued for the resulting damage and defendants claimed that since the dam obstructed navigation, the state law authorizing it was in violation of the commerce clause.

Chief Justice Marshall wrote a brief unanimous opinion for the Court containing the following observations: "The act of assembly by which the plaintiffs were authorized to construct their dam, shows plainly that this is one of those many creeks, passing through a deep, level marsh adjoining the Delaware, up which the tide flows for some distance. The value of the property on its banks must be enhanced by excluding the water from the marsh, and the health of the inhabitants probably improved. Measures calculated to produce these objects, provided they do not come into collision with the powers of the general government, are undoubtedly within those which are reserved to the States.

b The arguments to the Court drove home the fact that the *Gibbons* case involved more than the run between Elizabethtown and New York. In the preceding decade, navigation by steam had developed at a rapid pace. Monopolies for the development of this modern means of travel, similar to that conferred on Fulton by New York, had been granted by New Jersey, Connecticut, Ohio, Massachusetts, New Hampshire, Vermont and Georgia; a particularly significant monopoly by Louisiana covered the mouth of the Mississippi. The legislation of these three states was designed to retaliate against New York. William Wirt's peroration enlarged on the theme that these "three states are almost on the verge of war". 9 Wheat. 184. For popular response to the *Gibbons* decision see: 1 Warren, *The Supreme Court in United States History* 615.

. . . If congress had passed any act which bore upon the case; any act in execution of the power to regulate commerce, the object of which was to control State legislation over those small navigable creeks into which the tide flows, and which abound throughout the lower country of the middle and southern States; we should feel not much difficulty in saying that a state law coming in conflict with such act would be void. But congress has passed no such act. The repugnancy of the law of Delaware to the Constitution is placed entirely on its repugnancy to the power to regulate commerce with foreign nations and among the several States; a power which has not been so exercised as to affect the question. We do not think that the act [authorizing the dam] can, under all the circumstances of the case, be considered as repugnant to the power to regulate commerce in its dormant state, or as being in conflict with any law passed on the subject."

B. POWER OF CONGRESS TO REGULATE INTERSTATE COMMERCE—EXCLUSIVE OR CONCURRENT

For more than half a century after Gibbons v. Ogden, nearly all of the litigation under the commerce clause was concerned with the constitutionality of state rather than national laws. Crucial to the decision of challenges to state legislation was resolution of the issue that Marshall raised but did not decide in *Gibbons*: Was the grant of power to Congress exclusive? If so, a sharp line had to be drawn between the commerce that could be regulated by Congress and that the states could regulate because a determination that one had the power was also a determination that the other did not.

In order to understand the dispute over this issue—that had a substantial impact on early determinations by the Court with respect to the scope of national power—it is necessary at this point to examine some early cases involving the scope of state power to regulate and to tax—subjects that will be pursued in detail in Chapters 5 and 6.

THE LICENSE CASES, 46 U.S. (5 How.) 504 (1847). Roger Taney, who was appointed Chief Justice by President Jackson in 1836, attacked the view, that Marshall appeared to support, that the grant of power to Congress was exclusive. The issue was sharply posed in the license cases. State laws requiring licenses for the sale of intoxicating liquor were challenged by sellers who brought liquor from outside the state. The Court was unanimous in sustaining these laws, but produced six opinions (covering sixty pages) giving differing reasons for the result. Chief Justice Taney summarized his view as follows:

"It is well known that upon this subject a difference of opinion has existed, and still exists, among the members of this court. But with every respect for the opinion of my brethren with whom I do not agree, it appears to me to be very clear, that the mere grant of power to the general government cannot, upon any just principles of construction, be construed to be an absolute prohibition to exercise of any power over the same subject by the States. The controlling and supreme power over commerce with foreign nations and the several States is undoubtedly conferred upon Congress. Yet, in my judgment, the State may nevertheless, for the safety or convenience of trade, or for the protection of the health of its citizens, make regulations of commerce for its own ports and harbours, and for its own territory; and such regulations are valid unless they come in conflict with a law of Congress."

Taney's opinion was vigorously seconded by Mr. Justice Catron, who wrote:

". . . So minute and complicated are the wants of commerce when it reaches its port of destination, that even the State legislatures have been incapable of providing suitable means for its regulation between ship and shore, and therefore charters, granted by the State legislatures, have conferred the power on city corporations.   Owing to situation and climate, every port and place where commerce enters a State must have peculiarity in its regulations; and these it would be exceedingly difficult for Congress to make; nor could it depute the power to corporations, as the States do.   The difficulties standing in the way of Congress are fast increasing with the increase of commerce and the places where it is carried on.   And where it enters States through their inland borders, by land and water, the complication is not less, and especially on the large rivers.   There, too, Congress has the undisputed power to regulate commerce coming from State to State; but as every village would require special legislation, and constant additions as it grew and its commerce increased, to deal with the subject on the part of Congress would be next to impossible in practice.   I admit that this condition of things does not settle the question of contested power; but it satisfactorily shows that Congress cannot do what the States have done, are doing, and must continue to do, from a controlling necessity, even should the exclusive power in Congress be maintained by our decision.   And this state of things was too prominently manifest for the convention to overlook it.

". . . Congress has stood by for nearly sixty years, and seen the States regulate the commerce of the whole country, more or less, at the ports of entry and at their borders, without objection, and for this court now to decide that the power did not exist in the States, and that all they had done in this respect was void from the beginning, would overthrow and annul entire codes of State legislation on the particular subject.   We would by our decision expunge more State laws and city corporate regulations that Congress is likely to make in a century on the same subject, and on no better assumption than that Congress and the State legislatures had been altogether mistaken as to their respective powers for fifty years and more.   If long usage, general acquiescence, and the absence of complaint can settle the interpretation of the clause in question, then it should be deemed as settled in conformity to the usage by the courts."

Mr. Justice McLean apparently felt that he avoided any question of collision with the national commercial power by concluding: "The license acts . . . do not purport to be a regulation of commerce.   They are essentially police laws."   Mr. Justice Grier similarly disposed of the problem: "I do not consider the question of the exclusiveness of the power of Congress to regulate commerce as necessarily connected with the decision of this point;" and quoted with approval the view that "the powers which relate to merely municipal regulations, or what may more properly be called internal police, are not surrendered by the States. . . ."

The divisions of the Court revealed in the License Cases were continued in the Passenger Cases, 48 U.S. (7 How.) 283 (1849).   These cases (Smith v. Turner, Health Commissioner of the Port of New York and Norris v. The City of Boston) involved New York and Massachusetts laws imposing taxes on alien passengers arriving from foreign countries, the proceeds to be used to support a marine hospital (New York) and alien paupers (Massachusetts).   It was argued that the laws were police power measures passed for protection against disease and pauperism from abroad.   The Court held (5 to 4) that the laws were unconstitutional regulations of foreign commerce, but again there was no opinion subscribed to by a majority of the Justices.   Of the dissenters, Taney, C.J., Daniel, J. and Nelson, J., reasserted the general view that the national commerce power is not exclusive.   The fourth dissenter, Woodbury, J., argued that the commerce power was partly exclusive and partly concurrent but he based his vote largely on the ground of state police power.

COOLEY v. BOARD OF WARDENS OF
THE PORT OF PHILADELPHIA

53 U.S. (12 How.) 299, 13 L.Ed. 996 (1851).

[A Pennsylvania statute of 1803 required vessels coming into or leaving the Port of Philadelphia to accept local pilots for pilotage through the Delaware River and upon failure to do so the master, owner or consignee of the vessel was made liable to pay half the pilotage fees as a penalty. Cooley was sued as the consignee of two vessels that sailed from Philadelphia without taking on a local pilot as required by the statute. The court below sustained judgment against Cooley.]

Mr. Justice Curtis [a] delivered the opinion of the court: . . .

That the power to regulate commerce includes the regulation of navigation, we consider settled. And when we look to the nature of the service performed by pilots, to the relations which that service and its compensations bear to navigation between the several States, and between the ports of the United States and foreign countries, we are brought to the conclusion, that the regulation of the qualifications of pilots, of the modes and times of offering and rendering their services, of the responsibilities which shall rest upon them, of the powers they shall possess, of the compensation they may demand, and of the penalties by which their rights and duties may be enforced, do constitute regulations of navigation, and consequently of commerce, within the just meaning of this clause of the Constitution.

The power to regulate navigation is the power to prescribe rules in conformity with which navigation must be carried on. It extends to the persons who conduct it, as well as to the instruments used. Accordingly, the first Congress assembled under the Constitution passed laws, requiring the masters of ships and vessels of the United States to be citizens of the United States, and established many rules for the government and regulation of officers and seamen. 1 Stat. at Large, 55, 131. These have been from time to time added to and changed, and we are not aware that their validity has been questioned.
. . . .

The act of 1789, (1 Stat. at Large, 54,) already referred to, contains a clear legislative exposition of the Constitution by the first Congress, to the effect that the power to regulate pilots was conferred on Congress by the Constitution;
. . . . . And a majority of the court are of opinion, that a regulation of pilots is a regulation of commerce, within the grant to Congress of the commercial power, contained in the third clause of the eighth section of the first article of the Constitution.

It becomes necessary, therefore, to consider whether this law of Pennsylvania, being a regulation of commerce, is valid.

The act of Congress of the 7th of August, 1789, sect. 4, is as follows:

"That all pilots in the bays, inlets, rivers, harbors, and ports of the United States shall continue to be regulated in conformity with the existing laws of the States, respectively, wherein such pilots may be, or with such laws as the States may respectively hereafter enact for the purpose, until further legislative provision shall be made by Congress."

If the law of Pennsylvania, now in question, had been in existence at the date of this act of Congress, we might hold it to have been adopted by Congress, and thus made a law of the United States, and so valid. Because this act does, in effect, give the force of an act of Congress, to the then existing State

---

[a] Justice Curtis had just been appointed to the Court by President Fillmore; he succeeded Justice Woodbury who died in 1851.

laws on this subject, so long as they should continue unrepealed by the State which enacted them.

But the law on which these actions are founded was not enacted till 1803. What effect then can be attributed to so much of the act of 1789, as declares, that pilots shall continue to be regulated in conformity, "with such laws as the States may respectively hereafter enact for the purpose, until further legislative provision shall be made by Congress"?

If the States were divested of the power to legislate on this subject by the grant of the commercial power to Congress, it is plain this act could not confer upon them power thus to legislate. If the Constitution excluded the States from making any law regulating commerce, certainly Congress cannot regrant, or in any manner reconvey to the States that power. And yet this act of 1789 gives its sanction only to laws enacted by the States. This necessarily implies a constitutional power to legislate; for only a rule created by the sovereign power of a State acting in its legislative capacity, can be deemed a law, enacted by a State; and if the State has so limited its sovereign power that it no longer extends to a particular subject, manifestly it cannot, in any proper sense, be said to enact laws thereon. Entertaining these views we are brought directly and unavoidably to the consideration of the question, whether the grant of the commercial power to Congress, did *per se* deprive the States of all power to regulate pilots. This question has never been decided by this court, nor, in our judgment, has any case depending upon all the considerations which must govern this one, come before this court. The grant of commercial power to Congress does not contain any terms which expressly exclude the States from exercising an authority over its subject-matter. If they are excluded it must be because the nature of the power, thus granted to Congress, requires that a similar authority should not exist in the States. If it were conceded on the one side, that the nature of this power, like that to legislate for the District of Columbia, is absolutely and totally repugnant to the existence of similar power in the States, probably no one would deny that the grant of the power to Congress, as effectually and perfectly excludes the States from all future legislation on the subject, as if express words had been used to exclude them. And on the other hand, if it were admitted that the existence of this power in Congress, like the power of taxation, is compatible with the existence of a similar power in the States, then it would be in conformity with the contemporary exposition of the Constitution, (Federalist, No. 32,) and with the judicial construction, given from time to time by this court, after the most deliberate consideration, to hold that the mere grant of such a power to Congress, did not imply a prohibition on the States to exercise the same power; that it is not the mere existence of such a power, but its exercise by Congress, which may be incompatible with the exercise of the same power by the States, and that the States may legislate in the absence of congressional regulations. Sturges v. Crowninshield, 4 Wheat. 193; Moore v. Houston, 5 Wheat. 1; Wilson v. BlackBird Creek Marsh Co., 2 Peters 251.

The diversities of opinion, therefore, which have existed on this subject, have arisen from the different views taken of the nature of this power. But when the nature of a power like this is spoken of, when it is said that the nature of the power requires that it should be exercised exclusively by Congress, it must be intended to refer to the subjects of that power, and to say they are of such a nature as to require exclusive legislation by Congress. Now the power to regulate commerce embraces a vast field, containing not only many, but exceedingly various subjects, quite unlike in their nature; some imperatively demanding a single uniform rule, operating equally on the commerce of the United States in every port; and some, like the subject now in question, as imperatively demanding that diversity, which alone can meet the local necessities of navigation.

Either absolutely to affirm, or deny that the nature of this power requires exclusive legislation by Congress, is to lose sight of the nature of the subjects of this power, and to assert concerning all of them, what is really applicable but to a part. Whatever subjects of this power are in their nature national, or admit only of one uniform system, or plan of regulation, may justly be said to be of such a nature as to require exclusive legislation by Congress. That this cannot be affirmed of laws for the regulation of pilots and pilotage is plain. The act of 1789 contains a clear and authoritative declaration by the first Congress, that the nature of this subject is such, that until Congress should find it necessary to exert its power, it should be left to the legislation of the States; that it is local and not national; that it is likely to be the best provided for, not by one system, or plan of regulations, but by as many as the legislative discretion of the several States should deem applicable to the local peculiarities of the ports within their limits.

Viewed in this light, so much of this act of 1789 as declares that pilots shall continue to be regulated "by such laws as the States may respectively hereafter enact for that purpose," instead of being held to be inoperative, as an attempt to confer on the States a power to legislate, of which the Constitution had deprived them, is allowed an appropriate and important signification. It manifests the understanding of Congress, at the outset of the government, that the nature of this subject is not such as to require its exclusive legislation. The practice of the States, and of the national government, has been in conformity with this declaration, from the origin of the national government to this time; and the nature of the subject when examined is such as to leave no doubt of the superior fitness and propriety, not to say the absolute necessity, of different systems of regulation, drawn from local knowledge and experience, and conformed to local wants. How then can we say, that by the mere grant of power to regulate commerce, the States are deprived of all the power to legislate on this subject, because from the nature of the power the legislation of Congress must be exclusive. This would be to affirm that the nature of the power is in any case, something different from the nature of the subject to which, in such case, the power extends, and that the nature of the power necessarily demands, in all cases exclusive legislation by Congress, while the nature of one of the subjects of that power, not only does not require such exclusive legislation, but may be best provided for by many different systems enacted by the States, in conformity with the circumstances of the ports within their limits. In construing an instrument designed for the formation of a government, and in determining the extent of one of its important grants of power to legislate, we can make no such distinction between the nature of the power and the nature of the subject on which that power was intended practically to operate, nor consider the grant more extensive by affirming of the power, what is not true of its subject now in question.

It is the opinion of a majority of the court that the mere grant to Congress of the power to regulate commerce, did not deprive the States of power to regulate pilots, and that although Congress had legislated on this subject, its legislation manifests an intention, with a single exception, not to regulate this subject, but to leave its regulation to the several States. To these precise questions, which are all we are called on to decide, this opinion must be understood to be confined. It does not extend to the question what other subjects, under the commercial power, are within the exclusive control of Congress, or may be regulated by the States in the absence of all congressional legislation; nor to the general question how far any regulation of a subject by Congress may be deemed to operate as an exclusion of all legislation by the

States upon the same subject. We decide the precise questions before us, upon what we deem sound principles, applicable to this particular subject in the state in which the legislation of Congress has left it. We go no further. . . .

Judgment affirmed.

[McLean and Wayne, JJ., dissented; Daniel, J., concurred for other reasons.]

QUESTIONS

(1) The "rule" of the Cooley case has become famous in constitutional law; we shall meet it repeatedly in subsequent cases. What solution did it offer to the controversy over whether or not the commerce power was exclusive?

(2) The majority of the Court concluded that the pilot regulations did not deal with one of those *"subjects"* of the commerce power which *"are in their nature national, or admit only of one uniform system, or plan of regulation."* Do you see any reason for this conclusion other than the fact that Congress had expressly left the matter to the states? Would the result apparently have been different if Congress had said nothing on the subject?

(3) For an excellent discussion of early commerce clause theory, see Ribble, *State and National Power Over Commerce* (1937).

SUSTAINING STATE POWER TO REGULATE BY DEFINING COMMERCE AS INTRASTATE

Despite the compromise position enunciated in *Cooley,* the Court was still most comfortable with the proposition that the states could regulate and tax commerce which was intrastate and the Congress could regulate that commerce which was interstate. Full acceptance of such a position was made difficult, if not impossible, by the fact that except for water transportation Congress did not attempt to regulate much of either transportation or production and trade prior to the adoption of the Interstate Commerce Act in 1887 and the Sherman Anti-Trust Act in 1890. Railroads spread across the country. Industrialization led to increased commerce and increased concentration of industrial power in a few monopolies. Often the alternative to state regulation was no regulation. Hence, the constant pressure was to find a basis for sustaining the regulations of the states. In the process the Court wrote opinions sustaining state regulations that at the turn of the century were to be used to invalidate federal regulations as Congress began the long trend toward federal regulation of the economy.

A major portion of the Court's attention was given to marking out the boundaries between intrastate and interstate commerce. The easiest way to sustain a state regulation or tax without having to face the doctrinal battles only partially put to rest in *Cooley* was to define the underlying activity either as not constituting commerce or as not being interstate.

The Court early appeared to equate commerce with movement. In Hannibal & St. Joseph R.R. Co. v. Husen, 95 U.S. 465, 470 (1878), the Court, in holding invalid a state regulation forbidding the driving into or through the state of cattle from certain places during several months of the year, said: "Transportation is essential to commerce, or rather it is commerce itself: and every obstacle to it, or burden laid upon it by legislative authority, is regulation."

The determination that movement was essential to interstate commerce led the Court to take a generous view of the power of Congress over water transportation. In The Daniel Ball, 77 U.S. (10 Wall.) 557 (1871), e.g., the Court upheld the power of Congress to license a vessel operating, and capable of operating, only on a river wholly within the state of Michigan because the ship carried goods destined to and brought from points outside the state. But it also led naturally to the conclusion that the insurance business and such activities as farming, manufacturing, and mining were purely local, did not constitute interstate commerce, and hence were subject to state regulation and taxation. The three cases that follow are illustrative of the approach taken by the Court during this period.

PAUL v. VIRGINIA, 75 U.S. (8 Wall.) 168 (1868).   An agent of New York insurance companies was convicted of soliciting business in Virginia without complying with a Virginia statute requiring the agents of out-of-state insurance companies to obtain a license and deposit bonds with the state treasurer.   The Court unanimously sustained the statute.   Mr. Justice Field's opinion disposed of the commerce clause as follows:

"Issuing a policy of insurance is not a transaction of commerce. The policies are simple contracts of indemnity against loss by fire, entered into between the corporations and the assured, for a consideration paid by the latter. These contracts are not articles of commerce in any proper meaning of the word. They are not subjects of trade and barter offered in the market as something having an existence and value independent of the parties to them. They are not commodities to be shipped or forwarded from one State to another, and then put up for sale. They are like other personal contracts between parties which are completed by their signature and the transfer of the consideration. Such contracts are not interstate transactions, though the parties may be domiciled in different States. The policies do not take effect—are not executed contracts— until delivered by the agent in Virginia. They are, then, local transactions, and are governed by the local law. They do not constitute a part of the commerce between the States any more than a contract for the purchase and sale of goods in Virginia by a citizen of New York whilst in Virginia would constitute a portion of such commerce. . . . ."

COE v. TOWN OF ERROL

116 U.S. 517 (1886).

Coe cut logs in the forests of New Hampshire and, in preparation for floating them to Maine by way of the Androscoggin River, placed them on the banks of a stream in the New Hampshire town of Errol. While the logs were in Errol, they were assessed under the town's general property tax. The Court unanimously rejected an attack upon the tax; Justice Bradley wrote:

". . . . It seems to us untenable to hold that a crop or a herd is exempt from taxation merely because it is, by its owner, intended for exportation. If such were the rule in many States there would be nothing but the lands and real estate to bear the taxes. Some of the Western States produce very little except wheat and corn, most of which is intended for export; and so of cotton in the Southern States. Certainly, as long as these products are on the lands which produce them, they are part of the general property of the State. And so we think they continue to be until they have entered upon their final journey for leaving the State and going into another State. It is true, it was said in the case of The Daniel Ball, 10 Wall. 557, 565: 'Whenever a commodity has begun to move as an article of trade from one State to another, commerce in that commodity between the States has commenced.' But this movement does not begin until the articles have been shipped or started for transportation from the one State to the other. The carrying of them in carts or other vehicles, or even floating them, to the depot where the journey is to commence, is no part of that journey. That is all preliminary work, performed for the purpose of putting the property in a state of preparation and readiness for transportation. Until actually launched on its way to another State, or committed to a common carrier for transportation to such State, its destination is not fixed and certain. It may be sold or otherwise disposed of within the State, and never put in course of transportation out of the State. Carrying it from the farm, or the forest, to the depot, is only an interior movement of the property, entirely within the State, for the purpose, it is true, but only for the purpose, of putting it into a course of exportation; it is no part of the exportation itself. Until shipped or started on its final journey out of the State its exportation is a matter altogether in fieri, and not at all a fixed and certain thing. . . ."

KIDD v. PEARSON, 128 U.S. 1 (1888). An Iowa distillery which sold all of its output in other states was confronted with an Iowa statute prohibiting the manufacture of intoxicating beverages. The Court unanimously sustained the law. In answering the contention that this application of the Iowa statute violated the commerce clause, Justice Lamar wrote:

"No distinction is more popular to the common mind, or more clearly expressed in economic and political literature, than that between manufactures and commerce. Manufacture is transformation—the fashioning of raw materials into a change of form for use. The functions of commerce are different. The buying and selling and the transportation incidental thereto constitute commerce; and the regulation of commerce in the constitutional sense embraces the regulation at least of such transportation. The legal definition of the term, as given by this court in County of Mobile v. Kimball, 102 U.S. 691, 702, is as follows: 'Commerce with foreign countries, and among the States, strictly considered, consists in intercourse and traffic, including in these terms navigation, and the transportation and transit of persons and property, as well as the purchase, sale, and exchange of commodities.' If it be held that the term includes the regulation of all such manufactures as are intended to be the subject of commercial transactions in the future, it is impossible to deny that it would also include all productive industries that contemplate the same thing. The result would be that Congress would be invested, to the exclusion of the States, with the power to regulate, not only manufactures, but also agriculture, horticulture, stock raising, domestic fisheries, mining—in short, every branch of human industry. For is there one of them that does not contemplate, more or less clearly, an interstate or foreign market? Does not the wheat grower of the Northwest, and the cotton planter of the South, plant, cultivate, and harvest his crop with an eye on the prices at Liverpool, New York, and Chicago? The power being vested in Congress and denied to the States, it would follow as an inevitable result that the duty would devolve on Congress to regulate all of these delicate, multiform, and vital interests—interests which in their nature are and must be, local in all the details of their successful management."

POWER OF CONGRESS TO CONSENT TO STATE
REGULATION OF INTERSTATE COMMERCE

In *Cooley* it will be remembered, the Court said: "If the Constitution excluded the States from making any law regulating commerce, certainly Congress cannot regrant, or in any manner reconvey to the States that power." By the 1890s, however, the Court had hit upon a theory that would permit Congress to redefine the distribution of power as marked out by the courts. In Leisy v. Hardin, 135 U.S. 100 (1890), the Court in holding that the state could not forbid the sale of liquor brought from another state while in the original package, said:

> "Whenever . . . a particular power of the general government is one which must necessarily be exercised by it, and Congress remains silent, this is not only not a concession that the powers reserved by the States may be exerted as if the specific power had not been elsewhere reposed, but, on the contrary, the only legitimate conclusion is that the general government intended that power should not be affirmatively exercised, and the action of the States cannot be permitted to effect that which would be incompatible with such intention. Hence, inasmuch as interstate commerce, consisting in the transportation, purchase, sale and exchange of commodities, is national in its character, and must be governed by a uniform system, so long as Congress does not pass any law to regulate it, or allowing the States so to do, it thereby indicates its will that such commerce shall be free and untrammelled. . . . Brown v. Houston, 114 U.S. 622, 631; Wabash, St. Louis &c. Railway v. Illinois, 118 U.S. 557. . . ."

Congress took the hint and enacted the Wilson Act (26 Stat. 313) of 1890, providing that all intoxicating liquors transported into any state or remaining therein for use, sale or storage, should "upon arrival in such state" be subject to the state's laws "enacted in the exercise of its police powers," to the same extent as though such liquor had been produced in the state and should "not be exempt therefrom by reason of being introduced therein in original packages or otherwise." The constitutionality of this statute was sustained in In re Rahrer, 140 U.S. 545 (1891), over the objection that as applied to liquor imported and remaining in the original packages it attempted an invalid delegation of the national commerce power to the states. The Court (per Fuller, C.J.) said: "Congress can neither delegate its own powers nor enlarge those of a state," but "Congress has not attempted to delegate the power to regulate commerce, or to exercise any power reserved to the states, or to grant a power not possessed by the states, or to adopt state laws. It has taken its own course and made its own regulation, applying to these subjects of interstate commerce one common rule, whose uniformity is not affected by variations in state laws in dealing with such property." Since the Wilson Act did not authorize state prohibition of importation, but only prohibition of sales after importation, Congress passed the Webb-Kenyon Act (37 Stat. 699) of 1913 forbidding the transportation in interstate commerce of liquor intended to be used contrary to any law of the state of destination. This Act was sustained in Clark Distilling Co. v. Western Maryland R.R. Co., 242 U.S. 311 (1917).

See Bikle, *The Silence of Congress,* 41 Harv.L.Rev. 200 (1927).

C. THE ATTEMPT TO DEVELOP JUDICIALLY ENFORCEABLE LIMITS ON THE POWER OF CONGRESS TO REGULATE TRANSPORTATION AND THE ECONOMY

Introduction. An evil genius choosing a time for a new constitution that would tax its capacity for adaptability could hardly have selected a more trying time than 1789. Some men of vision foresaw that the coastal settlements might expand across the continent, but the framers had no inkling of the impact of the industrial revolution. The power of steam was soon harnessed for steamships and for railroads, which by 1869 spanned the continent. This new source of power also led to undreamed expansion of industrial production. The new Constitution thus was established on the eve of the great transition from an economy based on agriculture and handicraft to an economy based on power, machines and factories. The new forms of production were accompanied by the development of legal devices to organize and concentrate wealth: the business corporation and their combination through "trusts."

State regulation of the railroads in the post Civil War period produced the first test of governmental power to control modern large-scale business enterprise. The issue reached the Supreme Court in the celebrated Granger Cases, so named because they involved laws placed on the state statute books through the influence of the Grange movement which swept the Middle West in the early 1870's. The agricultural areas of that section felt themselves particularly victimized by exorbitant or discriminatory freight rates and clamored for governmental action. On March 1, 1877, the Court held in Munn v. Illinois and companion cases [1] that the states could regulate the rates of railroads and grain elevators operating within their borders. The main thrust of the opinions was to reject the contention that rate regulation deprived the companies of property without due process of law. However, in Wabash, St. Louis and Pac. Ry. v. Illinois, 118 U.S. 557 (1886), the Court held invalid an Illinois statute that imposed a penalty on any railroad that charged more for transporting a passenger or freight any distance in the state than it charged for transportation in the same direction of any passenger or like quantity of freight of the same class over a greater distance of the same road. The statute was designed to avoid discrimination against transportation centers not served by competing railroad lines and was applied to the intrastate portion of an interstate journey. The Court said, in part:

> "It cannot be too strongly insisted upon that the right of continuous transportation from one end of the country to the other is essential in modern times to that freedom of commerce from the restraints which the State might choose to impose upon it, that the commerce clause was intended to secure. This clause, giving to Congress the power to regulate commerce among the States and with foreign nations, as this court has said before, was among the most important of the subjects which prompted the formation of the Constitution. . . . Brown v. Maryland, 12 Wheat. 419, 446. And it would be a very feeble and almost useless provision, but poorly adapted to secure the entire freedom of commerce among the States which was deemed essential to a more perfect union by the framers of the Constitution, if, at every stage of the transportation of goods and chattels through the country, the State within whose limits a part of this transportation must be done could impose regulations concerning the price, compensation, or taxation, or any other restrictive regulation interfering with and seriously embarrassing this commerce."

The decision of the *Wabash* case was taken to mean that the power to regulate interstate railroad rates was vested exclusively in Congress even as to the segment of an interstate journey lying within the borders of the regulating state. 1 Sharfman, *The Interstate Commerce Commission* (1931) 19. Congressional railroad legislation had been the subject of discussion in both Houses for more than a decade, but the *Wabash* decision on October 25, 1886, gave substantial impetus to the passage of the Interstate Commerce Act (24 Stat. 379) on February 4, 1887.[3] The Act created the Interstate Commerce Commission (ICC) with authority to regulate common carriers engaged in the transportation

---

[1] Munn v. Illinois, 94 U.S. 113 (1877) sustained an Illinois statute fixing maximum charges for the storage of grain in grain elevators and public warehouses; Chicago Burlington & Quincy Ry. v. Iowa, 94 U.S. 155 (1877), Peik v. Chicago & Northwestern Ry., 94 U.S. 164 (1877), Chicago, Milwaukee & St. Paul v. Ackly, 94 U.S. 179 (1877), and Winona & St. Peter R. R. v. Blake, 94 U.S. 180 (1877) upheld the validity of laws of Illinois, Wisconsin, Iowa and Minnesota fixing maximum rates for passengers and freight on all railroads operating in those States. For a description of the climate of opinion in which these cases were decided, see 2 Warren, *The Supreme Court in United States History* (Rev. ed. 1926) 574–583.

[3] For a brief but scholarly historical survey of federal regulation of transportation from the enactment of the Act to Regulate Commerce in 1887 to 1952, see Prizer, *Development of the Regulation of Transportation During the Past Seventy-five Years,* 21 I.C.C. Practitioner's Jour. 190 (1953).

of passengers or freight by railroad or partly by rail and partly by water when both were used for continuous carriage or shipment. "Every unjust and unreasonable charge" for service was prohibited and unjustified rate discrimination, such as that involved in the *Wabash* case, was declared unlawful.[4]

The pressure for national regulation of large business enterprise did not stop with the railroads. The Sherman Anti-Trust Act was enacted in 1890; it extended national control into fields of production and trade which theretofore had been regarded as subject only to state regulation.

The fact that the first significant attempts by the national government to regulate business enterprise were launched a century after the adoption of the Constitution had an important effect on the development of constitutional doctrine. During this century practically all of the cases concerning the commerce clause arose from state legislation. Even the leading decisions on national power in *Gibbons,* supra p. 168, and *Cooley,* supra, p. 178, were given in cases involving the validity of state regulations. What precedent value should be given to cases like Kidd v. Pearson, supra p. 183, and Coe v. Errol, supra p. 182, when the real issue became the scope of national power to handle national problems? Was it relevant that new forms of transportation and new forms of business organization that operated across state lines often rendered the states incompetent to regulate effectively?

UNITED STATES v. E. C. KNIGHT CO., 156 U.S. 1 (1895). By stock transfers, the American Sugar Refining Company obtained control of the Knight Company and other sugar refiners with the result that American acquired nearly complete control of the manufacture of refined sugar in the United States. The United States sued to set aside the stock transfers as a violation of the Sherman Act. The Supreme Court affirmed a trial court ruling dismissing the suit.

The Court started by asserting that "the power of a state to protect the lives, health, and property of its citizens, and to preserve good order and the public morals, 'the power to govern men and things within the limits of its dominion,' is a power originally and always belonging to the states, not surrendered by them to the general government, nor directly restrained by the constitution of the United States, and essentially exclusive. . . . On the other hand, the power of congress to regulate commerce among the several states is also exclusive." It then proceeded to analyze the problem before it, as if the choice were between exclusively state or exclusively federal regulation.

Relying on precedents such as Coe v. Errol and Kidd v. Pearson, the Court said that manufacturing was not commerce. "The fact that an article is manufactured for export to another state does not of itself make it an article of commerce, and the intent of the manufacturer does not determine the time when the article or product passes from the control of the state and belongs to commerce."

The Court conceded that monopolization of the refining of sugar would have an effect upon interstate and foreign commerce, "but the restraint would be an indirect result, however inevitable, and whatever its extent . . . .." Then it appeared to reject federal power to regulate such a monopoly because such a holding would mean that the states would have no power to regulate local businesses manufacturing goods for commerce. "Slight reflection will show that, if the national power extends to all contracts and combinations in manufacture, agriculture, mining, and other productive industries, whose ulti-

---

[4] The powers of the Commission were limited and it struggled for years to obtain adequate authority over the national transportation system. The Interstate Commerce Act was repeatedly amended by such legislation as the Hepburn Act of 1906, the Mann-Elkins Act of 1910, the Transportation Act of 1920, the Motor Carrier Act of 1935, and the Transportation Act of 1940.

mate result may affect external commerce, comparatively little of business operations and affairs would be left for state control."

Justice Harlan dissented, contending that the majority view "leaves the public, so far as national power is concerned, entirely at the mercy of combinations which arbitrarily control the prices of articles purchased to be transported from one state to another state."

THE SHERMAN ACT AFTER E. C. KNIGHT

Very soon after the *Knight* case the Court began the process of finding constitutional bases for application of the Sherman Act. In Addyston Pipe & Steel Co. v. United States, 175 U.S. 211 (1899), the Court held that the Act could apply to a conspiracy among companies engaged in the manufacture, sale, and transportation of iron pipe to divide sales territory and arrange for noncompetitive bidding. The Court said that this case differed from *Knight* in that the agreement directly restrained not alone the manufacture but also the purchase, sale or exchange of the manufactured commodity among the states.

In Northern Securities Co. v. United States, 193 U.S. 197 (1904), the Court held that the Act could be applied to break up joint control of competing railroads by a holding company. The Court indicated that this directly embraced interstate commerce. Justice Holmes, who had been appointed to the Court in 1902 by President Theodore Roosevelt in the hope that he would give support to vigorous action against monopolies, wrote an opinion for himself and three other justices dissenting. He referred to the *Knight* holding that mere indirect effect upon commerce was not sufficient for federal power and said that if the logic of the government argument in this case be upheld, "I can see no part of the conduct of life which on similar principle Congress might not interfere." This dissent caused President Roosevelt to erupt: "I could carve out of a banana a judge with more backbone than that." Bowen, *Yankee From Olympus* 370 (1944).

HOUSTON, EAST & WEST TEXAS RAILWAY CO. v. UNITED STATES [THE SHREVEPORT RATE CASE]

234 U.S. 342, 34 S.Ct. 833, 58 L.Ed. 1341 (1914).

[In 1912 the Interstate Commerce Commission issued an order to the Houston E. & W. Texas Ry. Co. and other railroads which operated between Dallas (and other Texas cities) and Shreveport, Louisiana. After hearings, the ICC found that these railroads maintained rates for hauls between points within Texas which were proportionately less than the rates for hauls from Shreveport, Louisiana, into Texas. For example, the freight rate for carrying wagons from Dallas east to Marshall, a distance of 148 miles, was 37 cents, while the rate from Shreveport west to Marshall, Texas a distance of only 42 miles, was 56 cents. The ICC ordered the railroads to end this discrimination.

The railroads brought suit in the Commerce Court[a] to set aside the order. The railroads contended that the ICC had found the interstate rates (in the above example, from Shreveport to Marshall) to be reasonable, and therefore had no power to reduce these rates. Hence, the ICC in substance was ordering the railroads to raise rates for hauls occurring wholly within Texas (e.g., from Dallas to Marshall) which had been set by the Railroad Commission of Texas. The Commerce Court dismissed the railroads' petitions. 205 F. 380, 391.]

---

[a] This specialized court for the review of orders of the ICC was later abolished.

Mr. Justice Hughes delivered the opinion of the Court.

. . .

First. It is unnecessary to repeat what has frequently been said by this court with respect to the complete and paramount character of the power confided to Congress to regulate commerce among the several states. It is of the essence of this power that, where it exists, it dominates. Interstate trade was not left to be destroyed or impeded by the rivalries of local government. The purpose was to make impossible the recurrence of the evils which had overwhelmed the Confederation, and to provide the necessary basis of national unity by insuring "uniformity of regulation against conflicting and discriminating state legislation." By virtue of the comprehensive terms of the grant, the authority of Congress is at all times adequate to meet the varying exigencies that arise, and to protect the national interest by securing the freedom of interstate commercial intercourse from local controls. Gibbons v. Ogden, 9 Wheat. 1, 196, 224; Brown v. Maryland, 12 Wheat. 419; Mobile County v. Kimball, 102 U.S. 691, 696, 697; Smith v. Alabama, 124 U.S. 465; Second Employers' Liability Cases, 223 U.S. 1, 47, 53, 54; Minnesota Rate Cases, 230 U.S. 352, 398, 399.

Congress is empowered to regulate—that is, to provide the law for the government of interstate commerce; to enact "all appropriate legislation" for its "protection and advancement" (The Daniel Ball, 10 Wall. 557, 564); to adopt measures "to promote its growth and insure its safety" (Mobile County v. Kimball, 102 U.S. 691, 696, 697), "to foster, protect, control, and restrain" (Second Employers' Liability Cases, 223 U.S. 1, 47, 53, 54.) Its authority, extending to these interstate carriers as instruments of interstate commerce, necessarily embraces the right to control their operations in all matters having such a close and substantial relation to interstate traffic that the control is essential or appropriate to the security of that traffic, to the efficiency of the interstate service, and to the maintenance of conditions under which interstate commerce may be conducted upon fair terms and without molestation or hindrance. As it is competent for Congress to legislate to these ends, unquestionably it may seek their attainment by requiring that the agencies of interstate commerce shall not be used in such manner as to cripple, retard, or destroy it. The fact that carriers are instruments of intrastate commerce, as well as of interstate commerce, does not derogate from the complete and paramount authority of Congress over the latter, or preclude the Federal power from being exerted to prevent the intrastate operations of such carriers from being made a means of injury to that which has been confided to Federal care. Wherever the interstate and intrastate transactions of carriers are so related that the government of the one involves the control of the other, it is Congress, and not the state, that is entitled to prescribe the final and dominant rule, for otherwise Congress would be denied the exercise of its constitutional authority, and the state, and not the nation, would be supreme within the national field. Baltimore & O. R. Co. v. Interstate Commerce Commission, 221 U.S. 612, 618; Southern R. Co. v. United States, 222 U.S. 20, 26, 27; Second Employers' Liability Cases, 223 U.S. 48, 51; Interstate Commerce Commission v. Goodrich Transit Co., 224 U.S. 194, 205, 213; Minnesota Rate Cases, 230 U.S. 431; Illinois C. R. Co. v. Behrens, 233 U.S. 473.

. . . [I]n Southern R. Co. v. United States, 222 U.S. 20, the question was presented whether the amendment to the safety appliance act (March 2, 1903, 32 Stat. at L. 943, chap. 976) was within the power of Congress in view of the fact that the statute was not confined to vehicles that were used in interstate traffic, but also embraced those used in intrastate traffic. The court answered affirmatively, because there was such a close relation between the two classes of traffic moving over the same railroad as to make it certain that the safety of the interstate traffic and of those employed in its movement would be promoted in a real and substantial sense by applying the requirements of the act to both classes of vehicles. So, in the Second Employers' Liability Cases, supra, it was insisted that while Congress had the authority to regulate the liability of a carrier for injuries sustained by one employee through the negligence of another, where all were engaged in interstate commerce, that power did not embrace instances where the negligent employee was engaged in intrastate commerce. The court said that this was a mistaken theory, as the causal negligence, when operating injuriously upon an employee engaged in interstate commerce, had the same effect with respect to that commerce as if the negligent employee were also engaged therein. . . .

While these decisions sustaining the Federal power relate to measures adopted in the interest of the safety of persons and property, they illustrate the principle that Congress, in the exercise of its paramount power, may prevent the common instrumentalities of interstate and intrastate commercial intercourse from being used in their intrastate operations to the injury of interstate commerce. This is not to say that Congress possesses the authority to regulate the internal commerce of a state, as such, but that it does possess the power to foster and protect interstate commerce, and to take all measures necessary or appropriate to that end, although intrastate transactions of interstate carriers may thereby be controlled.

This principle is applicable here. We find no reason to doubt that Congress is entitled to keep the highways of interstate communication open to interstate traffic upon fair and equal terms. That an unjust discrimination in the rates of a common carrier, by which one person or locality is unduly favored as against another under substantially similar conditions of traffic, constitutes an evil, is undeniable; and where this evil consists in the action of an interstate carrier in unreasonably discriminating against interstate traffic over its line, the authority of Congress to prevent it is equally clear. It is immaterial, so far as the protecting power of Congress is concerned, that the discrimination arises from intrastate rates as compared with interstate rates. The use of the instrument of interstate commerce in a discriminatory manner so as to inflict injury upon that commerce, or some part thereof, furnishes abundant ground for Federal intervention. Nor can the attempted exercise of state authority alter the matter, where Congress has acted, for a state may not authorize the carrier to do that which Congress is entitled to forbid and has forbidden.

. . . It is for Congress to supply the needed correction where the relation between intrastate and interstate rates presents the evil to be corrected, and this it may do completely, by reason of its control over the interstate carrier in all matters having such a close and substantial relation to interstate commerce that it is necessary or appropriate to exercise the control for the effective government of that commerce.

It is also clear that, in removing the injurious discrimination against interstate traffic arising from the relation of intrastate to interstate rates, Congress is not bound to reduce the latter below what it may deem to be a proper standard, fair to the carrier and to the public. Otherwise, it could prevent the injury to interstate commerce only by the sacrifice of its judgment as to interstate rates. Congress is entitled to maintain its own standard as to these rates, and to forbid any discriminatory action by interstate carriers which will obstruct the freedom of movement of interstate traffic over their lines in accordance with the terms it establishes.

Having this power, Congress could provide for its execution through the aid of a subordinate body; and we conclude that the order of the Commission now in question cannot be held invalid upon the ground that it exceeded the authority which Congress could lawfully confer.

Second. The remaining question is with regard to the scope of the power which Congress has granted to the Commission. . . .

[The opinion concluded that the Commission's order was supported by statute.]

Affirmed.

Mr. Justice Lurton and Mr. Justice Pitney dissent.

———————

RAILROAD COMM'N OF WISCONSIN v. CHICAGO, BURLINGTON & QUINCY R.R. CO., 257 U.S. 563 (1922). The ICC, acting under the National Transportation Act of 1920, ordered a 20% increase in interstate passenger rates for a group of railroads including those serving Wisconsin. The Wisconsin Railroad Commission refused to order a corresponding increase in intrastate passenger rates for service within the state, in view of a state statute which prescribed a rate of two cents a mile. The ICC then found under the Transportation Act that the local passenger rates constituted an undue discrimination against persons travelling in interstate commerce and against the system of interstate transportation. In particular, the Commission found that: (1) The carriers involved transported both intrastate and interstate passengers on the same trains. (2) Passengers going to, or coming from, points outside the state found it economical to pay the intrastate fare within Wisconsin and the interstate fare beyond the border. (3) The result was an increase in the yield from intrastate fares and a decrease in that from the interstate fares. The ICC order applied to all intrastate fares charged by carriers engaged in interstate commerce. A three judge district court enjoined state officials from interfering with the application of this order. The Supreme Court affirmed unanimously:

"[ICC orders, such as the one here] as to intrastate traffic are merely incidental to the regulation of interstate commerce and necessary to its efficiency. Effective control of the one must embrace some control over the other in view of the blending of both in actual operation. The same rails and the same cars carry both. The same men conduct them. Commerce is a unit and does not regard state lines, and while, under the Constitution, interstate and intrastate commerce are ordinarily subject to regulation by different sovereignties, yet when they are so mingled together that the supreme authority, the Nation, cannot exercise complete effective control over interstate commerce without incidental regulation of intrastate commerce, such incidental regulation is not an invasion of state authority. . . ."

———————

HAMMER v. DAGENHART, 247 U.S. 251 (1918), arose under the Child Labor Law of 1916 and presented the question: Is it within the authority of Congress in regulating commerce among the states to prohibit the transportation in interstate commerce of manufactured goods, the product of a factory in which, within thirty days prior to their removal therefrom, children of the age of fourteen have been employed, or children between the ages of fourteen and sixteen years have been employed more than eight hours a day, or more than six days in any week, or after 7:00 p.m. or before 6 a.m.?

The Court, in an opinion by Justice Day, answered the question in the negative. The opinion referred first to a series of cases in which the Court had previously upheld prohibitions on interstate shipment of goods. In Champion v. Ames, 188 U.S. 321 (1903) (The Lottery Case) it was held that Congress could prevent the interstate shipment of tickets used in the promotion of lotteries. In Hipolite Egg Co. v. United States, 220 U.S. 45 (1911) the Court upheld the Pure Food and Drug Act which prohibited the introduction into interstate commerce of impure food and drugs. In Hoke v. United States, 227

U.S. 308 (1913) and Caminetti v. United States, 242 U.S. 470 (1917), the Court upheld laws forbidding the transportation of women in interstate commerce for purposes of prostitution and debauchery. And in Clark Distilling Co. v. Western Maryland R.R. Co., 242 U.S. 311 (1917), the Court sustained the power of Congress to prohibit the interstate shipment of intoxicating liquors. The Court distinguished these cases as follows:

"In each of these instances the use of interstate transportation was necessary to the accomplishment of harmful results. In other words, although the power over interstate transportation was to regulate, that could only be accomplished by prohibiting the use of the facilities of interstate commerce to effect the evil intended.

"This element is wanting in the present case. The thing intended to be accomplished by this statute is the denial of the facilities of interstate commerce to those manufacturers in the states who employ children within the prohibited ages. The act in its effect does not regulate transportation among the states, but aims to standardize the ages at which children may be employed in mining and manufacturing within the states. The goods shipped are of themselves harmless. . . ."

It was argued that the act was a valid attempt to protect business in states with high labor standards from unfair interstate competition resulting from production in those states permitting child labor conditions. Replied the Court: "The commerce clause was not intended to give to Congress a general authority to equalize such conditions. In some of the states laws have been passed fixing minimum wages for women, in others the local law regulates the hours of labor of women in various employments. Business done in such states may be at an economic disadvantage when compared with states which have no such regulations; surely this fact does not give Congress the power to deny transportation in interstate commerce to those who carry on business where the hours of labor and the rate of compensation for women have not been fixed by a standard in use in other states and approved by Congress. . . ." The act was held unconstitutional as invading the reserved powers of the states.

Justice Holmes (with McKenna, Brandeis and Clarke, JJ.) dissented, saying:

"The notion that prohibition is any less prohibition when applied to things now thought evil I do not understand. But if there is any matter upon which civilized countries have agreed—far more unanimously than they have with reference to intoxicants . . .—it is the evil of premature and excessive child labor. . . .

"But I had thought that the propriety of the exercise of a power admitted to exist in some cases was for the consideration of Congress alone and that this Court always had disavowed the right to intrude its judgment upon questions of policy or morals. It is not for this Court to pronounce when prohibition is necessary to regulation if it ever may be necessary—to say that it is permissible as against strong drink but not as against the product of ruined lives.

"The Act does not meddle with anything belonging to the States. They may regulate their internal affairs and their domestic commerce as they like. But when they seek to send their products across the State line they are no longer within their rights. If there were no Constitution and no Congress their power to cross the line would depend upon their neighbors. Under the Constitution such commerce belongs not to the States but to Congress to regulate. It may carry out its views of public policy whatever indirect effect they may have upon the activities of the States. . . ." [a]

---

[a] For some of the debate that followed the *Hammer* case, see Powell, *The Child Labor Law, the Tenth Amendment, and the Commerce Clause,* 3 So.L.Q. (now Tul.L.Rev.) 175 (1918), 3 Selected

THE CURRENT OF COMMERCE CASES

During this early restrictive period the Court did open the door to federal regulation of local sales transactions where those sales could be said to be incidental to a flow of commerce into and out of a state. In Swift & Co. v. United States, 196 U.S. 375 (1905), the Court held that the Sherman Act could be applied to price fixing in a livestock market, saying:

"It is said that [the charge] does not set forth a case of commerce among the states. . . . [C]ommerce among the states is not a technical legal conception, but a practical one, drawn from the course of business. When cattle are sent for sale from a place in one State, with the exception that they will end their transit, after purchase, in another, and when in effect they do so, with only the interruption necessary to find a purchaser at the stock yards, and when this is a typical, constantly recurring course, the current thus existing is a current of commerce among the States, and the purchase of the cattle is a part and incident of such commerce. . . ."

In Stafford v. Wallace, 258 U.S. 495 (1922), the Court sustained The Packers and Stockyards Act of 1921 which placed under the administrative control of the Secretary of Agriculture the practices of stockyard owners, dealers, and packers at the large stockyards. The Court said:

". . . The stockyards are but a throat through which the current flows, and the transactions which occur therein are only incident to this current from the West to the East, and from one State to another. Such transactions can not be separated from the movement to which they contribute and necessarily take on its character . . . .

"The application of the commerce clause of the Constitution in the Swift Case was the result of the natural development of interstate commerce under modern conditions. It was the inevitable recognition of the great central fact that such streams of commerce from one part of the country to another which are ever flowing are in their very essence the commerce among the States and with foreign nations which historically it was one of the chief purposes of the Constitution to bring under national protection and control . . . ."

THE DEPRESSION AND THE NEW DEAL

From the great depression of the thirties came constitutional developments of tremendous import. The setting needs to be recalled in reading the cases that follow.

The 1929 crash in the stock market was the prelude for a general economic collapse. Unemployment mounted by 1933 to heights estimated at twelve to fifteen millions. National income fell from 85 billions in 1929 to 37 billions in 1932, and total wages dropped to forty percent of predepression levels. Farmers faced a similar crisis. Farm prices dropped over sixty percent. Ram-

Essays (1938) 314; Green, *The Child Labor Law and the Constitution,* 1 Ill.L.Bull. No. 1:3 (1917), 3 Selected Essays (1938) 336. See United States v. Darby, 312 U.S. 100 (1941), infra. See also Corwin, *The Power of Congress to Prohibit Commerce,* 18 Cornell L.Q. 477 (1933), 3 Selected Essays 103 (1938).

After the decision in *Hammer,* Congress passed a statute imposing a tax of 10% of the net profits of factories and other production enterprises that employed children under circumstances similar to those in *Hammer.* In the Child Labor Tax Case, 259 U.S. 20 (1922), the Court held that statute invalid as being palpably prohibitory and regulatory rather than a tax. "The case before us cannot be distinguished from that of Hammer v. Dagenhart, 247 U.S. 251 (1918). . . . In the case at the bar, Congress in the name of a tax which on the face of the act is a penalty seeks to do the same thing, and the effort be equally futile."

pant farm mortgage foreclosures and business failures led in turn to the failure of over 5,000 banks; a complete banking collapse threatened.

The inauguration of Franklin Roosevelt on March 4, 1933, was followed by a "hundred days" of governmental activity never matched in peacetime. The President immediately ordered all the banks to close in a "bank holiday"; five days later Congress ratified this action, provided for the reopening of liquid banks and ordered gold and gold certificates to be surrendered to the Treasury. At the end of the month, Congress created the Civilian Conservation Corps to put idle manpower to work on government projects. In May Congress devalued the dollar, established the Tennessee Valley Authority, passed the Agriculture Adjustment Act for the reduction of farm production, provided an agency and funds for the refinancing of farm loans, through the Securities Act established requirements of "full disclosure" to purchasers of stocks and bonds, and appropriated 500 million dollars for unemployment relief by grants to the states. During the following month Congress cancelled the promises of the government and private persons to repay debts in gold; passed the National Industrial Recovery Act for the establishment of codes for the general regulation of wages, hours and prices; established the Home Owner's Loan Corporation to refinance home mortgages; and through the Glass-Steagall Banking Act provided extensive regulation of banking practices and machinery for insuring bank deposits.

By the summer of 1933 the legislative pace slackened. But in June 1934 Congress established regulation of security markets through the Securities Exchange Act. In April 1935 Congress established the Works Progress Administration; in July of the same year Congress enacted the National Labor Relations Act and the following month established the social security program for unemployment and old-age benefits.[1]

As we shall see, a substantial portion of this program was the subject of important constitutional litigation. The story of this litigation is told in interesting detail by Robert L. Stern, a participant in the struggle, in *The Commerce Clause and the National Economy, 1933–1946,* 59 Harv.L.Rev. 645, 883 (1946). *Cf.* Stern, *The Scope of the Phrase Interstate Commerce,* 41 A.B.A.J. 823 (1955).

SCHECHTER POULTRY CORP. v. UNITED STATES, 295 U.S. 495 (1935). Perhaps the most widely heralded New Deal measure, designed to stimulate recovery from the Great Depression, was the National Industrial Recovery Act of 1933. An introductory section attempted to lay a constitutional foundation by stating that "a national emergency productive of widespread unemployment and disorganization of industry, which burdens interstate commerce, affects the public welfare, and undermines the standards of living of the American people, is hereby declared to exist." The act authorized the President to approve "codes of fair competition drafted by trade or industrial groups." In the first year of the National Recovery Administration (NRA) over five hundred codes were approved covering twenty-three million workers; the "Blue Eagle", the insignia for compliance with the NRA program, became virtually a national trademark. Typical codes set minimum wages and maximum hours and also implemented Section 7(a) of the act which provided for the right of labor to organize and to engage in collective bargaining. Codes usually prescribed "trade practices" that were deemed to be fair; many prescribed minimum prices. Although monopolies were nominally prohibited, the operation of the anti-trust acts was suspended. The program was greeted with enthusiasm at first, but before long began to run into serious administrative

[1] For fuller background see 2 Morison & Comager, *The Growth of the American Republic* (1950), Ch. 24; Schlesinger, *The Coming of the New Deal* (1959).

difficulties and faced growing opposition. The act was to expire, unless renewed, on June 16, 1935.

The Schechter Poultry Corporation, a Brooklyn wholesale poultry slaughter-house, was convicted of violating the "Live Poultry Code". The indictment included counts which charged violation of code provisions (1) setting minimum wages and maximum hours and (2) prescribing certain "trade practices" which included prohibitions against sales of only certain chickens from a coop and sales of unfit chickens. Schechter's business involved in the case consisted of the slaughtering and wholesale distribution of poultry in New York City, purchases being made at a market or railroad terminal within the City and sales being made to New York dealers who resold to New York consumers. The evidence indicated that ninety-six per cent of the live poultry marketed in New York came from other states.

The act penalized violation of any provision of a code "in any transaction in or affecting foreign or interstate commerce."

In the Supreme Court the conviction was reversed on two grounds: First, the act had attempted an unconstitutional delegation of power to the President. Second, as applied it exceeded the commerce power. Chief Justice Hughes (speaking for a unanimous Court) observed: "Extraordinary conditions do not create or enlarge constitutional power. . . . Such assertions of extraconstitu-tional authority were anticipated and precluded by the explicit terms of the Tenth Amendment. . . ." When the Chief Justice came to the commerce clause point, he elaborated the Court's conclusion that the poultry transactions involved were not "in" interstate commerce because: "The poultry had come to a permanent rest within the State. It was not held, used, or sold by defendants in relation to any further transactions in interstate commerce and was not destined for transportation to other states. Hence, decisions which deal with a stream of interstate commerce—where goods come to rest within a state temporarily and are later to go forward in interstate commerce—and with the regulations of transactions involved in that practical continuity of movement, are not applicable here. See Swift & Co. v. United States, 196 U.S. 375, 387, 388; . . . Stafford v. Wallace, 258 U.S. 495, 519. . . ." Defendant's transac-tions did not "directly 'affect' interstate commerce so as to be subject to federal regulation. . . . In determining how far the federal government may go in controlling intrastate transactions upon the ground that they 'affect' interstate commerce, there is a necessary and well-established distinction between direct and indirect effects. The precise line can be drawn only as individual cases arise, but the distinction is clear in principle. . . . If the commerce clause were construed to reach all enterprises and transactions which could be said to have an indirect effect upon interstate commerce, the federal authority would embrace practically all the activities of the people and the authority of the state over its domestic concerns would exist only by sufferance of the federal government. . . . The distinction between direct and indirect effects has been clearly recognized in the application of the Anti-Trust Act." On this point, the Court made reference to United Mine Workers v. Coronado Coal Co., 259 U.S. 344, 410 (1922) and Local 167 v. United States, 291 U.S. 293 (1934).

In a concurring opinion, Justice Cardozo stated: "The law is not indifferent to considerations of degree. Activities local in their immediacy do not become interstate and national because of distant repercussions. What is near and what is distant may at times be uncertain. . . . There is no penumbra of uncertainty obscuring judgment here. To find immediacy or directness here is to find it almost everywhere. If centrifugal forces are to be isolated to the exclusion of the forces that oppose and counteract them, there will be an end to our federal system."

IMPACT OF SCHECHTER

(1) Attorney General (later Justice) Jackson reported that during the foregoing litigation "hell broke loose" in the lower federal courts. Sixteen hundred injunctions were issued against carrying out Acts of Congress; business flowed to the doors of district judges known to be hostile to the legislation.

(2) If the Court had been convinced that the NRA program was working strongly and effectively to restore business activity, with a substantial increase in the movement of goods in the national market, could the Court have concluded that the relationship between the Codes and interstate commerce was "indirect?" Would it be proper for the judicial arm to be concerned with the effectiveness of economic legislation? In applying a test concerning the degree of effect on interstate commerce can the court escape such questions?

(3) Robert L. Stern reports: "The code structure of the National Recovery Act—which had only three weeks to go unless renewed—collapsed with the Schechter decision. It had proved too cumbersome and unworkable, in part because in seeking to regulate all industry it had attempted to cover too much ground, in part because of the absence of any effective sanction after the original enthusiasm and public support began to fade." (59 Harv.L.Rev. at 663.)[1]

(4) On May 6, 1935, three weeks prior to the Schechter decision, the Court had invalidated the Railroad Retirement Act of 1934 which established a compulsory retirement and pension system for employees of railroads subject to the Interstate Commerce Act. Railroad Retirement Board v. Alton R. Co., 295 U.S. 330 (1935).

CARTER v. CARTER COAL CO.

298 U.S. 238, 56 S.Ct. 855, 80 L.Ed. 1160 (1936).

[Undeterred by the *Schechter* decision, the Roosevelt administration, in the summer of 1935, secured the enactment of new measures of national economic regulation. One of these was the Bituminous Coal Conservation Act (commonly called the Guffey Coal Act), which imposed an excise tax of 15% on the sale of bituminous coal by producers who could obtain a 90% reduction of the tax if they agreed to comply with a code to be formulated by the Bituminous Coal Commission. Such code would establish (a) minimum prices for various mines and areas and (b) minimum wages and maximum hours for workers in the mines. A labor board, to be appointed by the President, was given power to enforce collective bargaining between the mine owners and their employees. Section 1 of the Act declared that the mining and distribution of bituminous coal is of national interest, affecting the health and general welfare of the nation, and detailed certain circumstances thought to justify the conclusion. The Section further declared "that the production and distribution by producers of such coal bear upon and directly affect interstate commerce, and render regulation of production and distribution imperative for the protection of such commerce. . . ."

---

[1] The government's strategy in litigating the *Schechter* case is criticized in Fuchs, *A Postscript—The Schechter Case*, 20 St. Louis L.Rev. 297 (1935), 3 *Selected Essays* (1938) 197. For explanation of the circumstances by which the *Schechter* case was forced on the government, see Stern, 59 Harv.L.Rev. at 657–663.

[Litigation between James Carter and the company of which he was president promptly challenged this Act. The trial court, in the District of Columbia where the suit was brought, found that coal is the nation's greatest and primary source of energy, vital to the public welfare, and that its distribution in interstate commerce should be regular, continuous, and free of obstructions; further that such coal is generally sold f. o. b. mine, and the predominant portion of it shipped outside the state in which it is produced; that the distribution and marketing is predominantly interstate in character, and that the intrastate distribution and sale are so connected that interstate regulation cannot be accomplished effectively unless transactions of intrastate distribution and sale be regulated. The trial court sustained the Act, but pending hearing in the Court of Appeals, the Supreme Court granted certiorari.]

Mr. Justice Sutherland delivered the opinion of the Court. . . .

That the "tax" is in fact a penalty is not seriously in dispute. The position of the government, as we understand it, is that the validity of the exaction does not rest upon the taxing power but upon the power of Congress to regulate interstate commerce; and that if the act in respect of the labor and price-fixing provisions be not upheld, the "tax" must fall with them. With that position we agree and confine our consideration accordingly. . . .

The proposition, often advanced and as often discredited, that the power of the federal government inherently extends to purposes affecting the nation as a whole with which the states severally cannot deal or cannot adequately deal, and the related notion that Congress, entirely apart from those powers delegated by the Constitution, may enact laws to promote the general welfare, have never been accepted but always definitely rejected by this court. . . .

Since the validity of the act depends upon whether it is a regulation of interstate commerce, the nature and extent of the power conferred upon Congress by the commerce clause becomes the determinative question in this branch of the case. . . .

[The Court then cited and quoted from Kidd v. Pearson, 128 U.S. 1, 20; United States v. E.C. Knight, Co., 156 U.S. 1, 12; Coe v. Errol, 116 U.S. 517, 526; and other cases.]

A consideration of the foregoing, and of many cases which might be added to those already cited, renders inescapable the conclusion that the effect of the labor provisions of the act, including those in respect of minimum wages, wage agreements, collective bargaining, and the Labor Board and its powers, primarily falls upon production and not upon commerce; and confirms the further resulting conclusion that production is a purely local activity. It follows that none of these essential antecedents of production constitutes a transaction in or forms any part of interstate commerce. Schechter Corp. v. United States, supra, p. 542 et seq. Everything which moves in interstate commerce has had a local origin. Without local production somewhere, interstate commerce, as now carried on, would practically disappear. Nevertheless, the local character of mining, of manufacturing and of crop growing is a fact, and remains a fact, whatever may be done with the products.

. . . .

Whether the effect of a given activity or condition is direct or indirect is not always easy to determine. The word "direct" implies that the activity or condition invoked or blamed shall operate proximately—not mediately, remotely, or collaterally—to produce the effect. It connotes the absence of an efficient intervening agency or condition. And the extent of the effect bears no logical relation to its character. The distinction between a direct and an indirect effect turns, not upon the magnitude of either the cause or the effect, but entirely upon the manner in which the effect has been brought about. If the production by one man of a single ton of coal intended for interstate sale and shipment, and actually so sold and shipped, affects interstate commerce indirectly, the effect does not become direct by multiplying the tonnage, or increasing the number of men employed, or adding to the expense or complexities of the business, or by all combined. It is quite true that rules of law are sometimes qualified by considerations of degree, as the government argues. But the matter of degree has no bearing upon the question here, since that question is not—What is the *extent* of the local activity or condition, or the *extent* of the effect produced upon interstate commerce? but—What is the *relation* between the activity or condition and the effect? . . .ᵃ

The government's contentions in defense of the labor provisions are really disposed of adversely by our decision in the *Schechter* case, supra. The only perceptible difference between that case and this is that in the *Schechter* case the federal power was asserted with respect to commodities which had come to rest after their interstate transportation; while here, the case deals with commodities at rest before interstate commerce has begun. . . .

[Chief Justice Hughes concurred specially. Justices Cardozo, Brandeis, and Stone dissented.]

———

UNITED STATES v. BUTLER, 297 U.S. 1 (1936). One of the major measures of the "New Deal", in combating the Great Depression, was the Agriculture Adjustment Act of 1933. It was designed to raise farm prices and reduce the farm surplus of certain crops through curtailment of production and a tax upon the first processing of these crops. The Secretary of Agriculture was authorized to enter into agreements with individual farmers to reduce acreage in exchange for benefit payments computed on the basis of the reduction. Funds for the payments were derived from a tax levied upon the processor of the commodity involved, the total revenue from the tax being devoted to crop control and no part of it available for general governmental use. The Secretary entered into agreements for the reduction of acreage devoted to cotton (as well as certain other crops) and a processing tax was imposed upon the processors, including Hoosac Mills for which Butler was receiver. Suit was brought to recover the tax on the ground that it was invalid as an integral part of an unconstitutional program to control agricultural production.

The act did not purport to be a regulation of interstate or foreign commerce and the government did not attempt to uphold it on the basis of the commerce clause. The court of appeals held the tax unconstitutional and the Supreme Court affirmed.

Justice Roberts, speaking for the Court, said:

"The clause thought to authorize the legislation . . . confers upon the Congress power 'to lay and collect taxes, duties, imposts and excises to pay the debts and provide for the common defence and general welfare of the United States'. . . . It is not contended that this provision grants power to regulate agricultural production upon the theory that such legislation would promote the general welfare. . . . The true construction undoubtedly is that the only

---

ᵃ Attention should be given to Justice Sutherland's view that "the relation between the activity or condition and the effect" is not affected "by considerations of degree" or by the magnitude of the cause or effect. Might this approach reflect the thought that courts can more readily establish categories than measure quantity? (Are there overtones here from the law of torts?) Are there considerations of policy implicit in the choice of categories which determine whether an effect is "direct" or "indirect"?

Two weeks after announcing the Carter decision, the Court (over dissent by Chief Justice Hughes and Justices Stone, Brandeis and Cardozo) held that state legislation establishing minimum wages for women was unconstitutional under the due process clause of the Fourteenth Amendment. Morehead v. N.Y. ex rel. Tipaldo, 298 U.S. 587 (1936).

thing granted is the power to tax for the purpose of providing funds for payment of the nation's debts and making provision for the general welfare. . . .

"Since the foundation of the nation, sharp differences of opinion have persisted as to the true interpretation of the phrase [to provide for the general welfare]. Madison asserted it amounted to no more than a reference to the other powers enumerated in the subsequent clauses of the same section; that, as the United States is a government of limited and enumerated powers, the grant of power to tax and spend for the general national welfare must be confined to the enumerated legislative fields committed to the Congress. In this view the phrase is mere tautology, for taxation and appropriation are or may be necessary incidents of the exercise of any of the enumerated legislative powers. Hamilton, on the other hand, maintained the clause confers a power separate and distinct from those later enumerated, is not restricted in meaning by the grant of them, and Congress consequently has a substantive power to tax and to appropriate, limited only by the requirement that it shall be exercised to provide for the general welfare of the United States. Each contention has had the support of those whose views are entitled to weight. This court has noticed the question, but has never found it necessary to decide which is the true construction. Mr. Justice Story, in his Commentaries, espouses the Hamiltonian position. We shall not review the writings of public men and commentators or discuss the legislative practice. Study of all these leads us to conclude that the reading advocated by Mr. Justice Story is the correct one. While, therefore, the power to tax is not unlimited, its confines are set in the clause which confers it, and not in those of section 8 which bestow and define the legislative powers of the Congress. It results that the power of Congress to authorize expenditure of public moneys for public purposes is not limited by the direct grants of legislative power found in the Constitution.

"But the adoption of the broader construction leaves the power to spend subject to limitations. . . .

"We are not now required to ascertain the scope of the phrase 'general welfare of the United States' or to determine whether an appropriation in aid of agriculture falls within it. Wholly apart from that question, another principle embedded in our Constitution prohibits the enforcement of the Agricultural Adjustment Act. The act invades the reserved rights of the states. It is a statutory plan to regulate and control agricultural production, a matter beyond the powers delegated to the federal government. The tax, the appropriation of the funds raised, and the direction for their disbursement, are but parts of the plan. They are but means to an unconstitutional end.

"From the accepted doctrine that the United States is a government of delegated powers, it follows that those not expressly granted, or reasonably to be implied from such as are conferred, are reserved to the states or to the people. To forestall any suggestion to the contrary, the Tenth Amendment was adopted. The same proposition, otherwise stated, is that powers not granted are prohibited. None to regulate agricultural production is given, and therefore legislation by Congress for that purpose is forbidden.

"It is an established principle that the attainment of a prohibited end may not be accomplished under the pretext of the exertion of powers which are granted. . . .

"The power of taxation, which is expressly granted, may, of course, be adopted as a means to carry into operation another power also expressly granted. But resort to the taxing power to effectuate an end which is not legitimate, not within the scope of the Constitution, is obviously inadmissible.
. . .

"In the Child Labor Tax Case, 259 U.S. 20, and in Hill v. Wallace, 259 U.S. 44, this court had before it statutes which purported to be taxing measures. But their purpose was found to be to regulate the conduct of manufacturing and trading, not in interstate commerce, but in the states—matters not within any power conferred upon Congress by the Constitution—and the levy of the tax a means to force compliance. The court held this was not a constitutional use, but an unconstitutional abuse of the power to tax. . . . These decisions demonstrate that Congress could not, under the pretext of raising revenue, lay a tax on processors who refuse to pay a certain price for cotton, and exempt those who agree so to do, with the purpose of benefiting producers.

"If the taxing power may not be used as the instrument to enforce a regulation of matters of state concern with respect to which the Congress has no authority to interfere, may it, as in the present case, be employed to raise the money necessary to purchase a compliance which the Congress is powerless to command? The government asserts that whatever might be said against the validity of the plan if compulsory, it is constitutionally sound because the end is accomplished by voluntary co-operation. There are two sufficient answers to the contention. The regulation is not in fact voluntary. The farmer, of course, may refuse to comply, but the price of such refusal is the loss of benefits. The amount offered is intended to be sufficient to exert pressure on him to agree to the proposed regulation. The power to confer or withhold unlimited benefits is the power to coerce or destroy. . . .

"But if the plan were one for purely voluntary co-operation it would stand no better so far as federal power is concerned. At best, it is a scheme for purchasing with federal funds submission to federal regulation of a subject reserved to the states. . . .

"We are not here concerned with a conditional appropriation of money, nor with a provision that if certain conditions are not complied with the appropriation shall no longer be available. . . . There is an obvious difference between a statute stating the conditions upon which moneys shall be expended and one effective only upon assumption of a contractual obligation to submit to a regulation which otherwise could not be enforced. . . .

"Congress has no power to enforce its commands on the farmer to the ends sought by the Agricultural Adjustment Act. It must follow that it may not indirectly accomplish those ends by taxing and spending to purchase compliance. . . ."

Stone, J. (joined by Brandeis and Cardozo, JJ.) dissented, stating in part:

"The Constitution requires that public funds shall be spent for a defined purpose, the promotion of the general welfare. Their expenditure usually involves payment on terms which will insure use by the selected recipients within the limits of the constitutional purpose. Expenditures would fail of their purpose and thus lose their constitutional sanction if the terms of payment were not such that by their influence on the action of the recipients the permitted end would be attained. The power of Congress to spend is inseparable from persuasion to action over which Congress has no legislative control. Congress may not command that the science of agriculture be taught in state universities. But if it would aid the teaching of that science by grants to state institutions, it is appropriate, if not necessary, that the grant be on the condition, incorporated in the Morrill Act [July 2, 1862], 12 Stat. at L. 503, chap. 130, U.S.C. title 7, § 301, August 30, 1890, 26 Stat. at L. 417, chap. 841, U.S.C. title 7, § 322, that it be used for the intended purpose. Similarly it would seem to be compliance with the Constitution, not violation of it, for the government to take and the university to give a contract that the grant would be so used. It makes no difference that there is a promise to do an act which the condition is calculated to induce. Condition and promise are alike valid since both are in furtherance of the national purpose for which the money is appropriated."

He added: "It is a contradiction in terms to say that there is power to spend for the national welfare, while rejecting the power to impose conditions reasonably adapted to the attainment of the end which alone would justify the expenditure."

THE ROOSEVELT COURT PLAN

The initial New Deal program was shattered by the series of major judicial defeats suffered in the Supreme Court. Stricken down in succession were the Railroad Retirement Act of 1934, the National Industrial Recovery Act of 1933, the Agricultural Adjustment Act of 1933, and the Bituminous Coal Conservation Act of 1935. By the time of the *Carter Coal* decision of May 18, 1936, a feeling was growing within the administration that something had to be done about the Supreme Court. Actual steps awaited the election of November 1936, which returned Roosevelt to the presidency by an overwhelming majority. On February 7, 1937, the President sent to Congress a message calling for legislation to "reorganize the judicial branch"—a proposal commonly known as the court-packing plan. After dealing at some length with other less controversial problems of judicial organization, the message turned to "the question of aged or infirm judges—a subject of delicacy and yet one which requires frank discussion." The message stressed the difficulty for older men to keep up with the work of the courts, and also stated: "A lowered mental or physical vigor leads men to avoid an examination of complicated and changed conditions. Little by little, new facts become blurred through old glasses fitted, as it were, for the needs of another generation; older men, assuming that the scene is the same as it was in the past, cease to explore or inquire into the present or the future." The message then recommended that legislation provide for "the appointment of additional judges, in all Federal Courts, without exception, where there are incumbent judges of retirement age who do not choose to retire or resign." At that time six members of the Supreme Court had passed the voluntary retirement age of 70: Hughes (75), Sutherland (75), Butler (71), Brandeis (81), McReynolds (75), and Van Devanter (78).

The proposal produced a hurricane of controversy which lasted for months.[1] Opposition mounted as it became increasingly clear that the President's object was to change the judicial philosophy of the Supreme Court; on June 14, 1937, the Senate Judiciary Committee recommended rejection of the proposed legislation "as a needless, futile, and utterly dangerous abandonment of constitutional principle," Report No. 711, 75th Cong., 1st Sess. (1937). On July 22, the bill was killed by recommitment to the Judiciary Committee. During this interval, there were before the Supreme Court cases involving the constitutionality of the National Labor Relations Act and the Social Security Act, which had been enacted along with the Bituminous Coal Act in the summer of 1935; NLRB v. Jones & Laughlin Steel Corp., 301 U.S. 1, was argued February 10, 11, 1937,

---

[1] For subsequent developments, and especially the generalship of Chief Justice Hughes in meeting this challenge, see Pusey, *Charles Evans Hughes* (1951). Cf. Robert H. Jackson, *The Struggle for Judicial Supremacy,* 176 et seq. (1941); Leuchtenburg, *The Origins of Franklin D. Roosevelt's "Court-Packing" Plan,* 1966 Supreme Court Review 347 (1966). In answer to the charge that this proposal produced a "switch in time which saved nine", Justice Roberts left a paper with Justice Frankfurter for posthumous publication, which shows that Justice Roberts's vote to sustain state minimum wage legislation in West Coast Hotel Co. v. Parrish, 300 U.S. 379 (1937), although announced on March 29, 1937, reflected a vote taken in conference on December 19, 1936. See Frankfurter, Mr. Justice Roberts, 104 U.Pa.L.Rev. 311, 314, 315 (1955). This memorandum does not deal with the relationship between the *Carter* case, supra, and the *Jones & Laughlin* case, infra. Cf. Stern, 59 Harv. L.Rev. at 681–2.

and decided April 12; Steward Machine Co. v. Davis, 301 U.S. 548, was argued April 8, 9, 1937, and decided May 24.

In both cases the legislation was held valid by votes of 5 to 4.

President Roosevelt lost the battle but won the war. Within four years he was given the opportunity to replace seven members of the Court. In 1937 Justice Van Devanter retired and was succeeded by Senator Hugo Black. The following year Justice Sutherland retired, to be succeeded by Solicitor General Stanley Reed. In 1939, Justice Cardozo was succeeded by Professor Felix Frankfurter, Justice Brandeis by William O. Douglas, Chairman of the Securities and Exchange Commission, and Justice Butler by Attorney General Frank Murphy. In 1941, Justice McReynolds resigned and was succeeded by Senator James Byrnes. Later in 1941, Chief Justice Hughes resigned, Justice Stone was made Chief Justice, and Attorney General Robert H. Jackson was added to the Court.

By 1942 the Court had dramatically reversed itself, sustaining in their broadest applications the National Labor Relations Act, the Fair Labor Standards Act, and the Agricultural Adjustment Act. As we will see in later chapters, the Court also changed its interpretation of the due process and equal protection clauses so as to increase substantially governmental regulatory powers over economic matters.

D. THE ABANDONMENT OF THE ATTEMPT TO RESTRAIN CONGRESSIONAL POWER TO REGULATE THE ECONOMY

NLRB v. JONES & LAUGHLIN STEEL CORP., 301 U.S. 1 (1937). The National Labor Relations Act was enacted in 1935. It created the National Labor Relations Board; set forth the right of employees to self-organization and to bargain collectively; defined "unfair labor practices"; laid down rules as to the representation of employees for the purpose of collective bargaining; and empowered the Board to prevent the described unfair labor practices affecting commerce. In a proceeding under the Act, initiated by a union of steel and tin workers, the NLRB found that Jones & Laughlin had violated the Act by engaging in "unfair labor practices" interfering with the rights of employees to organize and bargain collectively in a plant where iron and steel was manufactured. The Board ordered the corporation to cease and desist from such practices, and when it refused to obey, petitioned the Court of Appeals to enforce the order. That Court held the order to be beyond the range of federal power. The Supreme Court reversed.

Jones & Laughlin argued that the Act could not constitutionally apply to its employees in the manufacturing department because manufacturing is not itself commerce. It relied on cases ranging from Kidd v. Pearson to the *Schechter* and *Carter Coal* cases. The government, emphasizing that the steel company was a large vertically integrated enterprise which owned everything from the mines through the manufacturing plant to the facilities for fabrication and distribution of the product, argued first that the case came within the doctrine of the current of commerce cases—the manufacturing plant was the focal point through which commerce flowed and that industrial strife at that point would cripple the entire movement. Second, the government argued that federal regulation was appropriate because a disruption of the manufacturing process would affect commerce and that under the doctrine of the *Shreveport* case Congress had power to eliminate obstructions to the free flow of commerce.

The Court accepted the government's second argument. The following excerpts give a little of the flavor of the decision on this point:

"We do not find it necessary to determine whether these features of defendant's business dispose of the asserted analogy to the 'stream of commerce' cases. The instances in which that metaphor has been used are but particular, and not exclusive, illustrations of the protective power which the government invokes in support of the present act. The congressional authority to protect interstate commerce from burdens and obstructions is not limited to transactions which can be deemed to be an essential part of a 'flow' of interstate or foreign commerce. Burdens and obstructions may be due to injurious action springing from other sources. The fundamental principle is that the power to regulate commerce is the power to enact 'all appropriate legislation' for its 'protection or advancement' (The Daniel Ball, 10 Wall. 557, 564); to adopt measures 'to promote its growth and insure its safety' (County of Mobile v. Kimball, 102 U.S. 691, 696, 697) 'to foster, protect, control, and restrain.' (Second Employers' Liability Cases, supra, page 47). See Texas & N. O. R. Co. v. Railway & S. S. Clerks, supra. That power is plenary and may be exerted to protect interstate commerce 'no matter what the source of the dangers which threaten it.' Second Employers' Liability Cases, page 51; Schechter Corporation v. United States, supra. Although activities may be intrastate in character when separately considered, if they have such a close and substantial relation to interstate commerce that their control is essential or appropriate to protect that commerce from burdens and obstructions, Congress cannot be denied the power to exercise that control. Schechter Corporation v. United States, supra. Undoubtedly the scope of this power must be considered in the light of our dual system of government and may not be extended so as to embrace effects upon interstate commerce so indirect and remote that to embrace them, in view of our complex society, would effectually obliterate the distinction between what is national and what is local and create a completely centralized government. Id. The question is necessarily one of degree. . . .

"That intrastate activities, by reason of close and intimate relation to interstate commerce, may fall within federal control is demonstrated in the case of carriers who are engaged in both interstate and intrastate transportation. There federal control has been found essential to secure the freedom of interstate traffic from interference or unjust discrimination and to promote the efficiency of the interstate service. The Shreveport Case, 234 U.S. 342, 351, 352; Railroad Commission of Wisconsin v. Chicago, B. & Q. R. Co., 257 U.S. 563, 588. It is manifest that intrastate rates deal *primarily* with a local activity. But in rate making they bear such a close relation to interstate rates that effective control of the one must embrace some control over the other. Id. Under the Transportation Act, 1920, Congress went so far as to authorize the Interstate Commerce Commission to establish a statewide level of intrastate rates in order to prevent an unjust discrimination against interstate commerce. Railroad Commission of Wisconsin v. Chicago, B. & Q. R. Co., supra; Florida v. United States, 282 U.S. 194, 210. Other illustrations are found in the broad requirements of the Safety Appliance Act and the Hours of Service Act. Southern Railway Co. v. United States, 222 U.S. 20; Baltimore & Ohio R. R. Co. v. Interstate Commerce Commission, 221 U.S. 612. It is said that this exercise of federal power has relation to the maintenance of adequate instrumentalities of interstate commerce. But the agency is not superior to the commerce which uses it. The protective power extends to the former because it exists as to the latter.

"The close and intimate effect which brings the subject within the reach of federal power may be due to activities in relation to productive industry although the industry when separately viewed is local. This has been abundantly illustrated in the application of the Federal Anti-Trust Act. . . .

"It is thus apparent that the fact that the employees here concerned were engaged in production is not determinative. The question remains as to the effect upon interstate commerce of the labor practice involved. . . .

". . . Giving full weight to respondent's contention with respect to a break in the complete continuity of the 'stream of commerce' by reason of respondent's manufacturing operations, the fact remains that the stoppage of those operations by industrial strife would have a most serious effect upon interstate commerce. In view of respondent's far-flung activities, it is idle to say that the effect would be indirect or remote. It is obvious that it would be immediate and might be catastrophic. We are asked to shut our eyes to the plainest facts of our national life and to deal with the question of direct and indirect effects in an intellectual vacuum. Because there may be but indirect and remote effects upon interstate commerce in connection with a host of local enterprises throughout the country, it does not follow that other industrial activities do not have such a close and intimate relation to interstate commerce as to make the presence of industrial strife a matter of the most urgent national concern. When industries organize themselves on a national scale making their relation to interstate commerce the dominant factor in their activities, how can it be maintained that their industrial labor relations constitute a forbidden field into which Congress may not enter when it is necessary to protect interstate commerce from the paralyzing consequences of industrial war? We have often said that interstate commerce itself is a practical conception. It is equally true that interferences with that commerce must be appraised by a judgment that does not ignore actual experience."

NOTE

Justice McReynolds, joined by Justices Van Devanter, Sutherland, and Butler, filed a dissenting opinion applicable jointly to the Jones & Laughlin case and to two other cases decided on the same day which sustained applications of the NLRA to other industries. N.L.R.B. v. Fruehauf Trailer Co., 301 U.S. 49 (1937); N.L.R.B. v. Friedman-Harry Marks Clothing Co., 301 U.S. 58 (1937). The latter case involved a clothing manufacturer in Richmond, Virginia, employing eight hundred workers; most of the raw materials came from outside Virginia and most of the finished clothing was marketed in other states.

NLRB v. FAINBLATT, 306 U.S. 601 (1939). After *Jones and Laughlin* the Court sustained the application of the NLRA to a variety of smaller industrial enterprises. In this case the application was to a manufacturer who processed materials into about a thousand dozen garments a month which were shipped in interstate commerce. The Court said that it was not important "that the volume of the commerce here involved though substantial, was relatively small as compared with that in the cases arising under the National Labor Relations Act which have hitherto engaged our attention. The power of Congress to regulate interstate commerce is plenary and extends to all such commerce be it great or small." The Court went on to note that the garment industry was one in which relatively small units contributed in the aggregate to a vast volume of commerce and that strikes in the industry would have a substantial effect on interstate commerce.[1]

---

[1] *Fainblatt* and later cases sustaining the application of the NLRA to quite small business concerns eventually imposed such a burden on the NLRB that it formulated rules for declining to exercise its jurisdiction in particular cases. At first these rules were articulated on a case-to-case basis, but in 1950 the Board announced more general standards in terms of yearly dollar amounts of interstate inflow and outflow. These standards were revised in 1954 and again in 1958 and are summarized in NLRB, *Twenty-Third Annual Report* 8 (1958). In 1959 Congress expressly authorized the Board "by

UNITED STATES v. DARBY

312 U.S. 100, 61 S.Ct. 451, 85 L.Ed. 609 (1941).

[The National Labor Relations Act protected employees' rights to organize and bargain collectively, but did not attempt to regulate hours, wages and other conditions of employment, such as child labor. This was undertaken by the Fair Labor Standards Act of 1938, which prescribed maximum hours and minimum wages. Darby, a Georgia lumber manufacturer, was indicted for violating the Act. He was charged (1) with manufacturing finished lumber with intent to ship it in interstate commerce, (2) with in fact so shipping a large part of the lumber produced, and (3) with employing workmen in his manufacturing operations in violation of the wages and hours provisions of the Act. The district court, on demurrer by Darby, quashed the indictment, ruling that since manufacturing is not interstate commerce, the Act could not constitutionally be applied to Darby's employees. The United States appealed to the Supreme Court.]

Mr. Justice Stone delivered the opinion of the Court. . . .

The two principal questions raised by the record in this case are, first, whether Congress has constitutional power to prohibit the shipment in interstate commerce of lumber manufactured by employees whose wages are less than a prescribed minimum or whose weekly hours of labor at that wage are greater than a prescribed maximum, and, second, whether it has power to prohibit the employment of workmen in the production of goods "for interstate commerce" at other than prescribed wages and hours. . . .

. . .

The Prohibition of Shipment of the Proscribed Goods in Interstate Commerce. Section 15(a)(1) prohibits, and the indictment charges, the shipment in interstate commerce, of goods produced for interstate commerce by employees whose wages and hours of employment do not conform to the requirements of the Act. Since this section is not violated unless the commodity shipped has been produced under labor conditions prohibited by § 6 and § 7, the only question arising under the commerce clause with respect to such shipments is whether Congress has the constitutional power to prohibit them.

While manufacture is not of itself interstate commerce the shipment of manufactured goods interstate is such commerce and the prohibition of such shipment by Congress is indubitably a regulation of the commerce. The power to regulate commerce is the power "to prescribe the rule by which commerce is to be governed." Gibbons v. Ogden, 9 Wheat. 1, 196. It extends not only to those regulations which aid, foster and protect the commerce, but embraces those which prohibit it. . . . It is conceded that the power of Congress to prohibit transportation in interstate commerce includes noxious articles, Lottery Case, supra; Hipolite Egg Co. v. United States, 220 U.S. 45; cf. Hoke v. United States, supra; stolen articles, Brooks v. United States, 267 U.S. 432; kidnapped persons, Gooch v. United States, 297 U.S. 124, and articles such as intoxicating liquor or convict made goods, traffic in which is forbidden or restricted by the laws of the state of destination. Kentucky Whip & Collar Co. v. Illinois Central R. Co., 299 U.S. 334.

But it is said that the present prohibition falls within the scope of none of these categories; that while the prohibition is nominally a regulation of the commerce its motive or purpose is regulation of wages and hours of persons

rule of decision or published rules" to "decline to assert jurisdiction . . . where, in the opinion of the Board, the effect of [the] labor dispute on commerce is not sufficiently substantial to warrant the exercise of its jurisdiction", subject to the limitation that it should not reduce its jurisdictional standards below those in effect in August 1959. 73 Stat. 541, 29 U.S.C. § 164(c)(1).

engaged in manufacture, the control of which has been reserved to the states and upon which Georgia and some of the states of destination have placed no restriction; that the effect of the present statute is not to exclude the prescribed articles from interstate commerce in aid of state regulation as the Kentucky Whip & Collar Co. v. Illinois Central R. Co., supra, but instead, under the guise of a regulation of interstate commerce, it undertakes to regulate wages and hours within the state contrary to the policy of the state which has elected to leave them unregulated. . . .

The motive and purpose of the present regulation are plainly to make effective the Congressional conception of public policy that interstate commerce should not be made the instrument of competition in the distribution of goods produced under substandard labor conditions, which competition is injurious to the commerce and to the states from and to which the commerce flows. The motive and purpose of a regulation of interstate commerce are matters for the legislative judgment upon the exercise of which the Constitution places no restriction and over which the courts are given no control. McCray v. United States, 195 U.S. 27; Sonzinsky v. United States, 300 U.S. 506, 513, and cases cited. "The judicial cannot prescribe to the legislative departments of the government limitations upon the exercise of its acknowledged power". Veazie Bank v. Fenno, 8 Wall. 533, 548. Whatever their motive and purpose, regulations of commerce which do not infringe some constitutional prohibition are within the plenary power conferred on Congress by the Commerce Clause. Subject only to that limitation, presently to be considered, we conclude that the prohibition of the shipment interstate of goods produced under the forbidden substandard labor conditions is within the constitutional authority of Congress.

In the more than a century which has elapsed since the decision of Gibbons v. Ogden, these principles of constitutional interpretation have been so long and repeatedly recognized by this Court as applicable to the Commerce Clause, that there would be little occasion for repeating them now were it not for the decision of this Court twenty-two years ago in Hammer v. Dagenhart, 247 U.S. 251. In that case it was held by a bare majority of the Court over the powerful and now classic dissent of Mr. Justice Holmes setting forth the fundamental issues involved, that Congress was without power to exclude the products of child labor from interstate commerce. The reasoning and conclusion of the Court's opinion there cannot be reconciled with the conclusion which we have reached, that the power of Congress under the Commerce Clause is plenary to exclude any article from interstate commerce subject only to the specific prohibitions of the Constitution.

Hammer v. Dagenhart has not been followed. The distinction on which the decision was rested that Congressional power to prohibit interstate commerce is limited to articles which in themselves have some harmful or deleterious property—a distinction which was novel when made and unsupported by any provision of the Constitution—has long since been abandoned. Brooks v. United States, supra; Kentucky Whip & Collar Co. v. Illinois Central R. Co., supra; Electric Bond & Share Co. v. Securities & Exchange Commission, 303 U.S. 419; Mulford v. Smith, 307 U.S. 38. The thesis of the opinion that the motive of the prohibition or its effect to control in some measure the use or production within the states of the article thus excluded from the commerce can operate to deprive the regulation of its constitutional authority has long since ceased to have force. Reid v. Colorado, supra; Lottery Case, supra; Hipolite Egg Co. v. United States, supra; Seven Cases v. United States, supra, 514; Hamilton v. Kentucky Distilleries & Warehouse Co., supra, 156; United States v. Carolene Products Co., supra, 147. And finally we have declared "The authority of the Federal Government over interstate commerce does not differ in extent or character from that retained by the states over intrastate commerce". United States v. Rock Royal Co-Operative, Inc., 307 U.S. 533, 569.

The conclusion is inescapable that Hammer v. Dagenhart, was a departure from the principles which have prevailed in the interpretation of the commerce clause both before and since the decision and that such vitality, as a precedent, as it then had has long since been exhausted. It should be and now is overruled.

Validity of the wage and hour requirements. Section 15(a)(2) and §§ 6 and 7 require employers to conform to the wage and hour provisions with respect to all employees engaged in the production of goods for interstate commerce. As appellee's employees are not alleged to be "engaged in interstate commerce" the validity of the prohibition turns on the question whether the employment, under other than the prescribed labor standards, of employees engaged in the production of goods for interstate commerce is so related to the commerce and so affects it as to be within the reach of the power of Congress to regulate it.

.   .   .

There remains the question whether such restriction on the production of goods for commerce is a permissible exercise of the commerce power. The power of Congress over interstate commerce is not confined to the regulation of commerce among the states. It extends to those activities intrastate which so affect interstate commerce or the exercise of the power of Congress over it as to make regulation of them appropriate means to the attainment of a legitimate end, the exercise of the granted power of Congress to regulate interstate commerce. See McCulloch v. Maryland, 4 Wheat. 316, 421. Cf. United States v. Ferger, 250 U.S. 199.   .   .   .

Congress, having by the present Act adopted the policy of excluding from interstate commerce all goods produced for the commerce which do not conform to the specified labor standards, it may choose the means reasonably adapted to the attainment of the permitted end, even though they involve control of intrastate activities. Such legislation has often been sustained with respect to powers, other than the commerce power granted to the national government, when the means chosen, although not themselves within the granted power, were nevertheless deemed appropriate aids to the accomplishment of some purpose within an admitted power of the national government. See Ruppert, Inc. v. Caffey, 251 U.S. 264; Everard's Breweries v. Day, 265 U.S. 545, 560; Westfall v. United States, 274 U.S. 256, 259. As to state power under the Fourteenth Amendment, compare Otis v. Parker, 187 U.S. 606, 609; St. John v. New York, 201 U.S. 633; Purity Extract & Tonic Company v. Lynch, 226 U.S. 192, 201, 202. A familiar like exercise of power is the regulation of intrastate transactions which are so commingled with or related to interstate commerce that all must be regulated if the interstate commerce is to be effectively controlled. Shreveport Case, 234 U.S. 342; Wisconsin Railroad Comm. v. Chicago, B. & Q. R. Co., 257 U.S. 563; United States v. New York Central R. R. Co., supra; Currin v. Wallace, 306 U.S. 1; Mulford v. Smith, supra. Similarly Congress may require inspection and preventive treatment of all cattle in a diseased infected area in order to prevent shipment in interstate commerce of some of the cattle without the treatment. Thornton v. United States, 271 U.S. 414. It may prohibit the removal at destination, of labels required by the Pure Food & Drugs Act, to be affixed to articles transported in interstate commerce. McDermott v. Wisconsin, 228 U.S. 115. And we have recently held that Congress in the exercise of its power to require inspection and grading of tobacco shipped in interstate commerce may compel such inspection and grading of all tobacco sold at local auction rooms from which a substantial part but not all of the tobacco sold is shipped in interstate commerce. Currin v. Wallace, supra, and see to the like effect United States v. Rock Royal Co-Op., supra, note 37.

We think also that § 15(a)(2), now under consideration, is sustainable independently of § 15(a)(1), which prohibits shipment or transportation of the proscribed goods. As we have said the evils aimed at by the Act are the spread of substandard labor conditions through the use of the facilities of interstate commerce for competition by the goods so produced with those produced under the prescribed or better labor conditions; and the consequent dislocation of the commerce itself caused by the impairment or destruction of local businesses by competition made effective through interstate commerce. The Act is thus directed at the suppression of a method or kind of competition in interstate commerce which it has in effect condemned as "unfair", as the Clayton Act, 38 Stat. 730, has condemned other "unfair methods of competition" made effective through interstate commerce. . . .

The means adopted by § 15(a)(2) for the protection of interstate commerce by the suppression of the production of the condemned goods for interstate commerce is so related to the commerce and so affects it as to be within the reach of the commerce power. See Currin v. Wallace, supra, 11. Congress, to attain its objective in the suppression of nationwide competition in interstate commerce by goods produced under substandard labor conditions, has made no distinction as to the volume or amount of shipments in the commerce or of production for commerce by any particular shipper or producer. It recognized that in present day industry, competition by a small part may affect the whole and that the total effect of the competition of many small producers may be great. See H.Rept. No. 2182, 75th Cong. 1st Sess., p. 7. The legislation aimed at a whole embraces all its parts. Cf. National Labor Relations Board v. Fainblatt, supra, 606.

So far as Carter v. Carter Coal Co., 298 U.S. 238, is inconsistent with this conclusion, its doctrine is limited in principle by the decisions under the Sherman Act and the National Labor Relations Act, which we have cited and which we follow. . . .

Our conclusion is unaffected by the Tenth Amendment which provides: "The powers not delegated to the United States by the Constitution, nor prohibited by it to the States, are reserved to the States respectively, or to the people". The amendment states but a truism that all is retained which has not been surrendered. There is nothing in the history of its adoption to suggest that it was more than declaratory of the relationship between the national and state governments as it had been established by the Constitution before the amendment or that its purpose was other than to allay fears that the new national government might seek to exercise powers not granted, and that the states might not be able to exercise fully their reserved powers. See e.g., II Elliot's Debates, 123, 131; III id. 450, 464, 600; IV id. 140, 149; I Annals of Congress 432, 761, 767–768; Story, Commentaries on the Constitution, secs. 1907, 1908. . . .

[The opinion also rejected the contention that the establishment of minimum wages and maximum hours violated the due process clause of the Fifth Amendment.]

Reversed.

NOTE

In *Darby* note that the Court sustained not only Section 15(a)(1) which prohibited interstate shipment of goods but also 15(a)(2) which required employers to comply with the wage and hour provisions with respect to all employees engaged in the production of goods for commerce. What was the basis for sustaining the latter provision? What did it add to the former? Note that the Court referred to a line of cases applying a doctrine which has been termed the "penumbra doctrine." Thus in James Everard's Breweries v. Day, 265 U.S. 545 (1924), the Court held that the power given Congress by the 18th Amendment to prevent the sale of intoxicating liquors for beverage purposes extended to legislation prohibiting doctors from prescribing malt liquors for medicinal purposes as a means of preventing clandestine traffic in malt liquors as beverages under the guise of medicines.

SECTION 3. THE SCOPE OF NATIONAL POWER TODAY

A. THE COMMERCE POWER
WICKARD v. FILBURN

317 U.S. 111, 63 S.Ct. 82, 87 L.Ed. 122 (1942).

[Filburn sued Wickard, the Secretary of Agriculture, to enjoin enforcement of the marketing penalty imposed by the Agricultural Adjustment Act of 1938, upon that part of his 1941 wheat crop which was available for marketing in excess of the marketing quota established for his farm. One of his grounds of attack was that the application of the marketing quota to him was beyond the commerce power of Congress. The lower court enjoined enforcement on other grounds and Wickard appealed.]

Mr. Justice Jackson delivered the opinion of the Court. . . .

The appellee for many years past has owned and operated a small farm in Montgomery County, Ohio, maintaining a herd of dairy cattle, selling milk, raising poultry, and selling poultry and eggs. It has been his practice to raise a small acreage of winter wheat, sown in the Fall and harvested in the following July; to sell a portion of the crop; to feed part to poultry and livestock on the farm, some of which is sold; to use some in making flour for home consumption; and to keep the rest for the following seeding. The intended disposition of the crop here involved has not been expressly stated.

In July of 1940, pursuant to the Agricultural Adjustment Act of 1938, as then amended, there were established for the appellee's 1941 crop a wheat acreage allotment of 11.1 acres and a normal yield of 20.1 bushels of wheat an acre. He was given notice of such allotment in July of 1940 before the Fall planting of his 1941 crop of wheat, and again in July of 1941, before it was harvested. He sowed, however, 23 acres, and harvested from his 11.9 acres of excess acreage 239 bushels, which under the terms of the Act as amended on May 26, 1941, constituted farm marketing excess, subject to a penalty of 49 cents a bushel, or $117.11 in all. The appellee has not paid the penalty and he has not postponed or avoided it by storing the excess under regulations of the Secretary of Agriculture, or by delivering it up to the Secretary. The Committee, therefore, refused him a marketing card, which was, under the terms of Regulations promulgated by the Secretary, necessary to protect a buyer from liability to the penalty and upon its protecting lien.

. . .

It is urged that under the Commerce Clause of the Constitution, Article I, § 8, clause 3, Congress does not possess the power it has in this instance sought to exercise. The question would merit little consideration since our decision in United States v. Darby, 312 U.S. 100, sustaining the federal power to regulate production of goods for commerce except for the fact that this Act extends federal regulation to production not intended in any part for commerce but wholly for consumption on the farm. The Act includes a definition of "market" and its derivatives so that as related to wheat in addition to its conventional meaning it also means to dispose of "by feeding (in any form) to poultry or livestock which, or the products of which, are sold, bartered, or exchanged, or to be so disposed of." Hence, marketing quotas not only embrace all that may be sold without penalty but also what may be consumed on the premises. Wheat produced on excess acreage is designated as "available for marketing" as so defined and the penalty is imposed thereon. Penalties do not depend upon whether any part of the wheat either within or without the quota is sold or intended to be sold. The sum of this is that the Federal Government fixes a quota including all that the farmer may harvest for sale or for his own farm needs, and declares that wheat produced on excess acreage may neither be disposed of nor used except upon payment of the penalty or except it is stored as required by the Act or delivered to the Secretary of Agriculture. . . .

[The opinion surveyed the development of national power over commerce and concluded with a quotation from the Shreveport Rate Case.]

The Court's recognition of the relevance of the economic effects in the application of the Commerce Clause exemplified by this statement has made the mechanical application of legal formulas no longer feasible. Once an economic measure of the reach of the power granted to Congress in the Commerce Clause is accepted, questions of federal power cannot be decided simply by finding the activity in question to be "production" nor can consideration of its economic effects be foreclosed by calling them "indirect." . . .

Whether the subject of the regulation in question was "production," "consumption," or "marketing" is, therefore, not material for purposes of deciding the question of federal power before us. That an activity is of local character may help in a doubtful case to determine whether Congress intended to reach it. The same consideration might help in determining whether in the absence of Congressional action it would be permissible for the state to exert its power on the subject matter, even though in so doing it to some degree affected interstate commerce. But even if appellee's activity be local and though it may not be regarded as commerce, it may still, whatever its nature, be reached by Congress if it exerts a substantial economic effect on interstate commerce and this irrespective of whether such effect is what might at some earlier time have been defined as "direct" or "indirect."

The parties have stipulated a summary of the economics of the wheat industry. Commerce among the states in wheat is large and important. Although wheat is raised in every state but one, production in most states is not equal to consumption. Sixteen states on average have had a surplus of wheat above their own requirements for feed, seed, and food. Thirty-two states and the District of Columbia, where production has been below consumption, have looked to these surplus-producing states for their supply as well as for wheat for export and carryover.

The wheat industry has been a problem industry for some years. . . .

. . .

The effect of consumption of homegrown wheat on interstate commerce is due to the fact that it constitutes the most variable factor in the disappearance of the wheat crop. Consumption on the farm where grown appears to vary in an amount greater than 20 per cent of average production. The total amount of wheat consumed as food varies but relatively little, and use as seed is relatively constant.

The maintenance by government regulation of a price for wheat undoubtedly can be accomplished as effectively by sustaining or increasing the demand as by limiting the supply. The effect of the statute before us is to restrict the amount which may be produced for market and the extent as well to which one may forestall resort to the market by producing to meet his own needs. That appellee's own contribution to the demand for wheat may be trivial by itself is not enough to remove him from the scope of federal regulation where, as here, his contribution, taken together with that of many others similarly situated, is far from trivial. National Labor Relations Board v. Fainblatt, 306 U.S. 601, 606, et seq.; United States v. Darby. . . .

It is well established by decisions of this Court that the power to regulate commerce includes the power to regulate the prices at which commodities in that commerce are dealt in and practices affecting such prices. One of the primary purposes of the Act in question was to increase the market price of wheat and to that end to limit the volume thereof that could affect the market. It can hardly be denied that a factor of such volume and variability as home-consumed wheat would have a substantial influence on price and market conditions. This may arise because being in marketable condition such wheat overhangs the market and if induced by rising prices tends to flow into the market and check price increases. But if we assume that it is never marketed, it supplies a need of the man who grew it which would otherwise be reflected by purchases in the open market. Home-grown wheat in this sense competes with wheat in commerce. The stimulation of commerce is a use of the regulatory function quite as definitely as prohibitions or restrictions thereon. This record leaves us in no doubt that Congress may properly have considered that wheat consumed on the farm where grown if wholly outside the scheme of regulation would have a substantial effect in defeating and obstructing its purpose to stimulate trade therein at increased prices.

. . .

[The opinion also rejected contentions based on the due process clause of the Fifth Amendment.]

Reversed.

———

UNITED STATES v. SOUTH–EASTERN UNDERWRITERS ASS'N, 322 U.S. 533 (1944). In 1944, the Supreme Court was presented with the question of the applicability of the Sherman Anti-Trust Act to the insurance business. Indictments under the Act charged that nearly 200 private stock fire insurance companies and the South-Eastern Underwriters Association conspired under Section 1 "in restraint of trade or commerce among the several states . . ." by fixing non-competitive premium rates. The indictment also charged a conspiracy under Section 2 "to monopolize any part of the trade or commerce among the several states . . .". The district court sustained a demurrer to the indictment on the ground, articulated in Paul v. Virginia, 8 Wall. 168 (1868), that "a policy of insurance is not a transaction of commerce" and insurance contracts "are not interstate transactions, although the parties are domiciled in different states".

The Supreme Court reversed. The opinion, by Justice Black, emphasized the size of the insurance business and the extent to which companies located in one part of the country write insurance contracts for persons in other states. The opinion also stated:

"We may grant that a contract of insurance, considered as a thing apart from negotiation and execution, does not itself constitute interstate commerce. Cf. Hall v. Geiger-Jones Co., 242 U.S. 539, 557–558. But it does not follow from this that the Court is powerless to examine the entire transaction, of which that contract is but a part, in order to determine whether there may be a chain of events which becomes interstate commerce. Only by treating the Congressional power over commerce among the states as a 'technical legal conception' rather than as a 'practical one, drawn from the course of business' could such a conclusion be reached. Swift & Co. v. United States, 196 U.S. 375, 398. In short, a nationwide business is not deprived of its interstate character merely because it is built upon sales contracts which are local in nature. Were the rule otherwise, few businesses could be said to be engaged in interstate commerce. . . .

"The power granted Congress is a positive power. It is the power to legislate concerning transactions which, reaching across state boundaries, affect the people of more states than one;—to govern affairs which the individual states, with their limited territorial jurisdictions, are not fully capable of governing."

Chief Justice Stone dissented on the ground that the Sherman Act did not embrace the offenses charged.

Justice Frankfurter joined in the dissenting opinion of the Chief Justice, but added some words apparently designed to show that he was concerned only with the question of statutory construction. Justice Jackson dissented on the ground that an elaborate structure of state regulation had been built on the doctrine of Paul v. Virginia, and that a readjustment of controls should only be made by national legislation addressed to the problem.[a]

HEART OF ATLANTA MOTEL v. UNITED STATES

379 U.S. 241, 85 S.Ct. 348, 13 L.Ed.2d 258 (1964).

[The owner of the Motel brought a declaratory judgment action, attacking the constitutionality of Title II of the Civil Rights Act of 1964. A three-judge court sustained the Act and enjoined its further violation by the Motel. An appeal was taken to the Supreme Court.]

Mr. Justice Clark delivered the opinion of the Court.

. . .

1.　THE FACTUAL BACKGROUND AND CONTENTIONS OF THE PARTIES

. . . Appellant owns and operates the Heart of Atlanta Motel which has 216 rooms available to transient guests. The motel is located on Courtland Street, two blocks from downtown Peachtree Street. It is readily accessible to interstate highways 75 and 85 and state highways 23 and 41. Appellant solicits patronage from outside the State of Georgia through various national advertising media, including magazines of national circulation; it maintains over 50 billboards and highway signs within the State, soliciting patronage for the motel; it accepts convention trade from outside Georgia and approximately 75% of its registered guests are from out of State. Prior to passage of the Act the motel had followed a practice of refusing to rent rooms to Negroes, and it alleged that it intended to continue to do so. In an effort to perpetuate that policy this suit was filed.

. . . .

Since Title II is the only portion under attack here, we confine our consideration to those public accommodation provisions.

---

[a] Following the Southeastern Underwriters decision Congress on March 9, 1945, passed the McCarran Act which, *inter alia,* provided that: "The business of insurance . . . shall be subject to the laws of the several states which relate to the regulation or taxation of such business." In addition, the Act suspended the applicability of the anti-trust acts to the business of insurance until June 30, 1948, and provided that after that date the anti-trust laws "shall be applicable to the business of insurance to the extent that such business is not regulated by state law." 59 Stat. 34, 15 U.S.C. § 1012(a) and (b).

3. TITLE II OF THE ACT

This Title is divided into seven sections beginning with § 201(a) which provides that:

"All persons shall be entitled to the full and equal enjoyment of the goods, services, facilities, privileges, advantages, and accommodations of any place of public accommodation, as defined in this section, without discrimination or segregation on the ground of race, color, religion, or national origin."

There are listed in § 201(b) four classes of business establishments, each of which "serves the public" and "is a place of public accommodation" within the meaning of § 201(a) "if its operations affect commerce, or if discrimination or segregation by it is supported by State action." The covered establishments are:

"(1) any inn, hotel, motel, or other establishment which provides lodging to transient guests, other than an establishment located within a building which contains not more than five rooms for rent or hire and which is actually occupied by the proprietor of such establishment as his residence;

. . . .

Section 201(c) defines the phrase "affect commerce" as applied to the above establishments. It first declares that "any inn, hotel, motel, or other establishment which provides lodging to transient guests" affects commerce *per se.*

. . .

4. APPLICATION OF TITLE II TO HEART OF ATLANTA MOTEL

It is admitted that the operation of the motel brings it within the provisions of § 201(a) of the Act and that appellant refused to provide lodging for transient Negroes because of their race or color and that it intends to continue that policy unless restrained.

The sole question posed is, therefore, the constitutionality of the Civil Rights Act of 1964 as applied to these facts. The legislative history of the Act indicates that Congress based the Act on § 5 and the Equal Protection Clause of the Fourteenth Amendment as well as its power to regulate interstate commerce.

. . .

The Senate Commerce Committee made it quite clear that the fundamental object of Title II was to vindicate "the deprivation of personal dignity that surely accompanies denials of equal access to public establishments." At the same time, however, it noted that such an objective has been and could be readily achieved "by congressional action based on the commerce power of the Constitution." S.Rep. No. 872, supra, at 16–17. Our study of the legislative record, made in the light of prior cases, has brought us to the conclusion that Congress possessed ample power in this regard, and we have therefore not considered the other grounds relied upon. . . .

. . .

6. THE BASIS OF CONGRESSIONAL ACTION

While the Act as adopted carried no congressional findings the record of its passage through each house is replete with evidence of the burdens that discrimination by race or color places upon interstate commerce. . . . This testimony included the fact that our people have become increasingly mobile with millions of people of all races traveling from State to State; that Negroes in particular have been the subject of discrimination in transient accommodations, having to travel great distances to secure the same; that often they have been unable to obtain accommodations and have had to call upon friends to put them up overnight, . . . ; and that these conditions had become so acute as to require the listing of available lodging for Negroes in a special guidebook which was itself "dramatic testimony to the difficulties" Negroes encounter in travel. . . . We shall not burden this opinion with further details since the voluminous testimony presents overwhelming evidence that discrimination by hotels and motels impedes interstate travel.

7. THE POWER OF CONGRESS OVER INTERSTATE TRAVEL

.   .   .

[T]he determinative test of the exercise of power by the Congress under the Commerce Clause is simply whether the activity sought to be regulated is "commerce which concerns more States than one" and has a real and substantial relation to the national interest. Let us now turn to this facet of the problem.

That the "intercourse" of which the Chief Justice [Marshall] spoke included the movement of persons through more States than one was settled as early as 1849. . . . . Nor does it make any difference whether the transportation is commercial in character. . . .

The same interest in protecting interstate commerce which led Congress to deal with segregation in interstate carriers and the white-slave traffic has prompted it to extend the exercise of its power to gambling, Lottery Case, 188 U.S. 321 (1903). . . and to racial discrimination by owners and managers of terminal restaurants, Boynton v. Virginia, 364 U.S. 454 (1960).

That Congress was legislating against moral wrongs in many of these areas rendered its enactments no less valid. In framing Title II of this Act Congress was also dealing with what it considered a moral problem. But that fact does not detract from the overwhelming evidence of the disruptive effect that racial discrimination has had on commercial intercourse. It was this burden which empowered Congress to enact appropriate legislation, and, given this basis for the exercise of its power, Congress was not restricted by the fact that the particular obstruction to interstate commerce with which it was dealing was also deemed a moral and social wrong.

It is said that the operation of the motel here is of a purely local character. But, assuming this to be true, "[i]f it is interstate commerce that feels the pinch, it does not matter how local the operation which applies the squeeze." United States v. Women's Sportswear Mfrs. Assn., 336 U.S. 460, 464 (1949). . . .

.   .   .

We, therefore, conclude that the action of the Congress in the adoption of the Act as applied here to a motel which concededly serves interstate travelers is within the power granted it by the Commerce Clause of the Constitution, as interpreted by this Court for 140 years. . . .

Affirmed.

[Justice Douglas's opinion stated that although he agreed with the Court's opinion, he was reluctant to rest solely on the commerce clause because of his belief that the right of people to be free of state action that discriminates against them because of race "occupies a more protected position in our constitutional system than does the movement of cattle, fruit, steel and coal across state lines." Black and Goldberg, JJ., filed concurring opinions. All of these opinions also applied to the following case.]

KATZENBACH v. McCLUNG

379 U.S. 294, 85 S.Ct. 377, 13 L.Ed.2d 290 (1964).

[This case was argued and decided with Heart of Atlanta Motel v. United States. McClung, as an owner of Ollie's Barbecue restaurant, sued to contest the constitutionality of Title II of the Civil Rights Act of 1964. A three-judge court enjoined Assistant Attorney-General Katzenbach from enforcing the Act against the restaurant and an appeal was taken.]

Mr. Justice Clark delivered the opinion of the Court.

. . .

2. THE FACTS

Ollie's Barbecue is a family-owned restaurant in Birmingham, Alabama, specializing in barbecued meats and homemade pies, with a seating capacity of 220 customers. It is located on a state highway 11 blocks from an interstate one and a somewhat greater distance from railroad and bus stations. The restaurant caters to a family and white-collar trade with a take-out service for Negroes. It employs 36 persons, two-thirds of whom are Negroes.

In the 12 months preceding the passage of the Act, the restaurant purchased locally approximately $150,000 worth of food, $69,783 or 46% of which was meat that it bought from a local supplier who had procured it from outside the State. The District Court expressly found that a substantial portion of the food served in the restaurant had moved in interstate commerce. The restaurant has refused to serve Negroes in its dining accommodations since its original opening in 1927, and since July 2, 1964, it has been operating in violation of the Act. The court below concluded that if it were required to serve Negroes it would lose a substantial amount of business.

. . .

3. THE ACT AS APPLIED

. . . Sections 201(b)(2) and (c) place any "restaurant . . . principally engaged in selling food for consumption on the premises" under the Act "if . . . it serves or offers to serve interstate travelers or a substantial portion of the food which it serves . . . has moved in commerce."

Ollie's Barbecue admits that it is covered by these provisions of the Act. The Government makes no contention that the discrimination at the restaurant was supported by the State of Alabama. There is no claim that interstate travelers frequented the restaurant. The sole question, therefore, narrows down to whether Title II, as applied to a restaurant receiving about $70,000 worth of food which has moved in commerce, is a valid exercise of the power of Congress. The Government has contended that Congress had ample basis upon which to find that racial discrimination at restaurants which receive from out of state a substantial portion of the food served does, in fact, impose commercial burdens of national magnitude upon interstate commerce. The appellees' major argument is directed to this premise. They urge that no such basis existed. It is to that question that we now turn.

4. THE CONGRESSIONAL HEARINGS

As we noted in *Heart of Atlanta Motel* both Houses of Congress conducted prolonged hearings on the Act. . . . The record is replete with testimony of the burdens placed on interstate commerce by racial discrimination in restaurants. . . .

Moreover there was an impressive array of testimony that discrimination in restaurants had a direct and highly restrictive effect upon interstate travel by Negroes.   . . .

We believe that this testimony afforded ample basis for the conclusion that established restaurants in such areas sold less interstate goods because of the discrimination, that interstate travel was obstructed directly by it, that business in general suffered and that many new businesses refrained from establishing there as a result of it.   Hence the District Court was in error in concluding that there was no connection between discrimination and the movement of interstate commerce.   Rather than such connection being outside "common experience," as the court said its conclusion flies in the face of stubborn fact.

It goes without saying that, viewed in isolation, the volume of food purchased by Ollie's Barbecue from sources supplied from out of state was insignificant when compared with the total foodstuffs moving in commerce. But, as our late Brother Jackson said for the Court in Wickard v. Filburn, 317 U.S. 111 (1942): "That appellee's own contribution to the demand for wheat may be trivial by itself is not enough to remove him from the scope of federal regulation where, as here, his contribution, taken together with that of many others similarly situated, is far from trivial."   . . .

. . .

With this situation spreading as the record shows, Congress was not required to await the total dislocation of commerce.   . . .

5.   THE POWER OF CONGRESS TO REGULATE LOCAL ACTIVITIES

. . .   Much is said about a restaurant business being local but "even if appellee's activity be local and though it may not be regarded as commerce, it may still, whatever its nature, be reached by Congress if it exerts a substantial economic effect on interstate commerce . . . ."   . . .

This Court has held time and again that this power extends to activities of retail establishments, including restaurants, which directly or indirectly burden or obstruct interstate commerce.   . . .

Nor are the cases holding that interstate commerce ends when goods come to rest in the state of destination apposite here.   That line of cases has been applied with reference to state taxation or regulation but not in the field of federal regulation.

The appellees contend that Congress has arbitrarily created a conclusive presumption that all restaurants meeting the criteria set out in the Act "affect commerce."   Stated another way, they object to the omission of a provision for a case-by-case determination—judicial or administrative—that racial discrimination in a particular restaurant affects commerce.

But Congress' action in framing this Act was not unprecedented.   In United States v. Darby, 312 U.S. 100 (1941), this Court held constitutional the Fair Labor Standards Act.   . . .

Here, as there, Congress has determined for itself that refusals of service to Negroes have imposed burdens both upon the interstate flow of food and upon the movement of products generally.   Of course, the mere fact that Congress has said when particular activity shall be deemed to affect commerce does not preclude further examination by this Court.   But where we find that the legislators, in light of the facts and testimony before them, have a rational basis for finding a chosen regulatory scheme necessary to the protection of commerce, our investigation is at an end.   The only remaining question—one answered in the affirmative by the court below—is whether the particular restaurant either serves or offers to serve interstate travelers or serves food a substantial portion of which has moved in interstate commerce.

. . .

Confronted as we are with the facts laid before Congress, we must conclude that it had a rational basis for finding that racial discrimination in restaurants had a direct and adverse effect on the free flow of interstate commerce. . . . We think in so doing that Congress acted well within its power to protect and foster commerce in extending the coverage of Title II only to those restaurants offering to serve interstate travelers or serving food, a substantial portion of which has moved in interstate commerce.

The absence of direct evidence connecting discriminatory restaurant service with the flow of interstate food, a factor on which the appellees place much reliance, is not, given the evidence as to the effect of such practices on other aspects of commerce, a crucial matter.

. . . The Civil Rights Act of 1964, as here applied, we find to be plainly appropriate in the resolution of what the Congress found to be a national commercial problem of the first magnitude. We find it in no violation of any express limitations of the Constitution and we therefore declare it valid.

The judgment is therefore reversed.

Reversed.

Justices Black, Douglas, and Goldberg concurred.

USE OF THE COMMERCE POWER TO COMBAT CRIME

The Court had very early upheld the power of Congress to prohibit the transportation in interstate commerce of such things as lottery tickets,[1] stolen vehicles,[2] and women for immoral purposes.[3] During the Kennedy administration these cases were used as precedents for a federal effort to control organized crime. See Pollner, *Attorney General Robert F. Kennedy's Legislative Program to Curb Organized Crime and Racketeering,* 28 Bkln.L.Rev. 37 (1961). The following statute shows the approach used:

18 U.S.C.

"§ 1952. **Interstate and foreign travel or transportation in aid of racketeering enterprises**

"(a) Whoever travels in interstate or foreign commerce or uses any facility in interstate or foreign commerce, including the mail, with intent to—

"(1) distribute the proceeds of any unlawful activity; or

"(2) commit any crime of violence to further any unlawful activity; or

"(3) otherwise promote, manage, establish, carry on, or facilitate the promotion, management, establishment, or carrying on, of any unlawful activity, and thereafter performs or attempts to perform any of the acts specified in subparagraphs (1), (2), and (3), shall be fined not more than $10,000 or imprisoned for not more than five years, or both.

"(b) As used in this section 'unlawful activity' means (1) any business enterprise involving gambling, liquor on which the Federal excise tax has not been paid, narcotics, or prostitution offenses in violation of the laws of the State in which they are committed or of the United States, or (2) extortion, bribery,

---

[1] Lottery Case (Champion v. Ames), 188 U.S. 321 (1903).

[2] Brooks v. United States, 267 U.S. 432 (1925).

[3] Caminetti v. United States, 242 U.S. 470 (1917).

or arson in violation of the laws of the State in which committed or of the United States.

"(c) Investigations of violations under this section involving liquor or narcotics shall be conducted under the supervision of the Secretary of the Treasury. (Added Pub.L. 87–228, § 1(a), Sept. 13, 1961, 75 Stat. 498, amended Pub.L. 89–68, July 7, 1965, 79 Stat. 212."

In 1968 Congress used the 1961 Act as a model for 18 U.S.C. § 2101 making it a crime to travel in interstate commerce or use the facilities of interstate commerce in order to incite or participate in a riot. These provisions have not presented serious constitutional difficulties.

Congress also has used the device of prohibiting interstate shipment or movement as a means of aiding the states in enforcing local laws. For example, 18 U.S.C. § 1073 makes it a federal crime to move in interstate commerce to avoid prosecution or custody after conviction under the laws of the place from which one flees; 18 U.S.C. § 1262 makes it a federal crime to transport intoxicating liquor into a state in which all sales of such liquor are illegal; 18 U.S.C. § 1821 prohibits the transportation of dentures into a state if they have not been manufactured with authorization of a licensed dentist in accordance with the laws of the state. These statutes have not raised substantial constitutional problems.

More recently Congress has gone further to make criminal particular conduct that does not directly affect federal other interests and that is not tied to interstate movement. One such statute was involved in the *Perez* case which follows. See generally, Stern, *The Commerce Clause Revisited—The Federalization of Intrastate Crime,* 15 Ariz.L.Rev. 271 (1973).

PEREZ v. UNITED STATES

402 U.S. 146, 91 S.Ct. 1357, 28 L.Ed.2d 686 (1971).

Mr. Justice Douglas delivered the opinion of the Court.

The question in the case is whether Title II of the Consumer Credit Protection Act, 82 Stat. 159, 18 U.S.C. (Supp. V) § 891 et seq., as construed and applied to petitioner, is a permissible exercise by Congress of its powers under the Commerce Clause of the Constitution. Petitioner's conviction after trial by jury and his sentence were affirmed by the Court of Appeals, one judge dissenting. . . .

Petitioner is one of the species commonly known as "loan sharks" which Congress found are in large part under the control of "organized crime." "Extortionate credit transactions" are defined as those characterized by the use or threat of the use of "violence or other criminal means" in enforcement. There was ample evidence showing petitioner was a "loan shark" who used the threats of violence as a method of collection. He loaned money to one Miranda, owner of a new butcher shop, [demanding repayments which he constantly increased]. Negotiations went on, Miranda finally saying he could only pay $25 a week. Petitioner said that was not enough, that Miranda should steal or sell drugs if necessary to get the money to pay the loan, and that if he went to jail it would be better than going to a hospital with a broken back or legs. He added, "I could have sent you to the hospital, you and your family, any moment I want with my people."

. . . .

The constitutional question is a substantial one.

Two "loan shark" amendments to the bill that became this Act were proposed in the House—one by Congressman Poff of Virginia, 114 Cong.Rec.

pt. 2, pp. 1605–1606—and another one by Congressman McDade of New Jersey. Id., 1609–1610.

. . .

There were objections on constitutional grounds. Congressman Eckhardt of Texas said:

"Should it become law, the amendment would take a long stride by the Federal Government toward occupying the field of general criminal law and toward exercising a general Federal police power; and it would permit prosecution in Federal as well as State courts of a typically State offense.

. . .

"I believe that Alexander Hamilton, though a federalist, would be astonished that such a deep entrenchment on the rights of the States in performing their most fundamental function should come from the more conservative quarter of the House." 114 Cong.Rec. pt. 2, p. 1610.

Senator Proxmire presented to the Senate the Conference Report approving essentially the "loan shark" provision suggested by Congressman McDade, saying:

"Once again these provisions raised serious questions of Federal-State responsibilities. Nonetheless, because of the importance of the problem, the Senate conferees agreed to the House provision. Organized crime operates on a national scale. One of the principal sources of revenue of organized crime comes from loan sharking. If we are to win the battle against organized crime, we must strike at their source of revenue and give the Justice Department additional tools to deal with the problem. The problem simply cannot be solved by the States alone. We must bring into play the full resources of the Federal Government." 114 Cong.Rec. pt. 11, p. 14490.

The Commerce Clause reaches in the main three categories of problems. First, the use of channels of interstate or foreign commerce which Congress deems are being misused, as for example, the shipment of stolen goods (18 U.S.C. §§ 2312–2315) or of persons who have been kidnapped. 18 U.S.C. § 1201. Second, protection of the instrumentalities of interstate commerce, as for example, the destruction of an aircraft (18 U.S.C. § 32), or persons or things in commerce, as for example, thefts from interstate shipments. 18 U.S.C. § 659. Third, those activities affecting commerce. It is with this last category that we are here concerned.

Chief Justice Marshall in Gibbons v. Ogden, 9 Wheat. 1, 195, said:

"The genius and character of the whole government seems to be, that its action is to be applied to all the external concerns of the nation, and to those internal concerns which affect the states generally; but not to those which are completely within a particular state, which do not affect other states, and with which it is not necessary to interfere, for the purpose of executing some of the general powers of the government. The completely internal commerce of a state, then, may be considered as reserved for the state itself."

Decisions which followed departed from that view; but by the time of United States v. Darby, 312 U.S. 100 and Wickard v. Filburn, 317 U.S. 111, 117, the broader view of the Commerce Clause announced by Chief Justice Marshall had been restored. . . .

As pointed out in United States v. Darby, 312 U.S. 100, the decision sustaining an Act of Congress which prohibited the employment of workers in the production of goods "for interstate commerce" at other than prescribed wages and hours—*a class of activities*—was held properly regulated by Congress without proof that the particular intrastate activity against which a sanction was laid had an effect on commerce. . . .

That case is particularly relevant here because it involved a criminal prosecution, a unanimous Court holding that the Act was "sufficiently definite to meet constitutional demands." Id., at 125. Petitioner is clearly *a member of the class* which engages in "extortionate credit transactions" as defined by Congress and the description of that class has the required definiteness.

It was the "class of activities" test which we employed in Heart of Atlanta Motel, Inc. v. United States, 379 U.S. 241 to sustain an Act of Congress requiring hotel or motel accommodations for Negro guests. The Act declared that " 'any inn, hotel, motel, or other establishment which provides lodging to transient guests' affects commerce *per se.*" Id., at 247, 85 S.Ct. at 353. That exercise of power under the Commerce Clause was sustained. . . .

In a companion case, Katzenbach v. McClung, 379 U.S. 294, we ruled on the constitutionality of the restaurant provision of the same Civil Rights Act which regulated the restaurant "if . . . it serves or offers to serve interstate travelers or a substantial portion of the food which it serves . . . has moved in commerce." Id., at 298. Apart from the effect on the flow of food in commerce to restaurants, we spoke of the restrictive effect of the exclusion of Negroes from restaurants on interstate travel by Negroes.

. . . .

In emphasis of our position that it was the *class of activities* regulated that was the measure, we acknowledged that Congress appropriately considered the "total incidence" of the practice on commerce. Id., at 301.

Where the *class of activities* is regulated and that *class* is within the reach of federal power, the courts have no power "to excise, as trivial, individual instances" of the class. Maryland v. Wirtz, 392 U.S. 183, 193.

Extortionate credit transactions, though purely intrastate, may in the judgment of Congress affect interstate commerce. . . .

The findings by Congress are quite adequate on that ground.

. . . .

The essence of all these reports and hearings was summarized and embodied in formal congressional findings. They supplied Congress with the knowledge that the loan shark racket provides organized crime with its second most lucrative source of revenue, exacts millions from the pockets of people, coerces its victims into the commission of crimes against property, and causes the takeover by racketeers of legitimate businesses. See generally 114 Cong.Rec. 14391, 14392, 14395, 14396.

We have mentioned in detail the economic, financial, and social setting of the problem as revealed to Congress. We do so not to infer that Congress need make particularized findings in order to legislate. We relate the history of the Act in detail to answer the impassioned plea of petitioner that all that is involved in loan sharking is a traditionally local activity. It appears instead, that loan sharking in its national setting is one way organized interstate crime holds its guns to the heads of the poor and the rich alike and syphons funds from numerous localities to finance its national operations.

Affirmed.

Mr. Justice Stewart, dissenting.

Congress surely has power under the Commerce Clause to enact criminal laws to protect the instrumentalities of interstate commerce, to prohibit the misuse of the channels or facilities of interstate commerce, and to prohibit or regulate those intrastate activities which have a demonstrably substantial effect on interstate commerce. But under the statute before us a man can be convicted without any proof of interstate movement, of the use of the facilities of interstate commerce, or of facts showing that his conduct affected interstate commerce. I think the Framers of the Constitution never intended that the national Government might define as a crime and prosecute such wholly local activity through the enactment of federal criminal laws.

In order to sustain this law we would, in my view, have to be able at the least to say that Congress could rationally have concluded that loan sharking is an activity with interstate attributes which distinguish it in some substantial respect from other local crime. But it is not enough to say that loan sharking is a national problem, for all crime is a national problem. It is not enough to say that some loan sharking has interstate characteristics, for any crime may have an interstate setting. And the circumstance that loan sharking has an adverse impact on interstate business is not a distinguishing attribute, for interstate business suffers from almost all criminal activity, be it shoplifting or violence in the streets.

Because I am unable to discern any rational distinction between loan sharking and other local crime, I cannot escape the conclusion that this statute was beyond the power of Congress to enact. The definition and prosecution of local, intrastate crime are reserved to the States under the Ninth and Tenth Amendments.

THE IMPLICATIONS OF PEREZ

Stern, *The Commerce Clause Revisited—The Federalization of Intrastate Crime,* 15 Ariz.L.Rev. 271, 279, 280 (1973):

"The significance of *Perez,* therefore, is that it is the first case in which the Court upheld federal regulation of a well-defined but possibly overinclusive class of substantive criminal activity on the grounds that in order to exercise effectively the commerce power over an interstate evil, individual acts unconnected with that evil must also be reached . . . .

"How far can the *Perez* rationale be extended? Can Congress forbid the possession or transfer of all pills, or of all white pills, because of the difficulty of distinguishing dangerous pills from others and because some might move interstate? Could it prohibit all distribution of milk because some might be infected and because it would be difficult to tell the good from the bad and the interstate from the intrastate? Since Congress is unlikely to interject the federal government into local transactions without good reason, such extreme but logical applications of the principle are unlikely to arise."[1]

UNITED STATES v. ENMONS, 410 U.S. 396 (1973). The Hobbs Act (18 U.S.C. § 1951) makes it a federal crime to obstruct interstate commerce by robbery or extortion or physical violence. The Court held the Act inapplicable to violence perpetrated by strikers against their employer in the course of a legal strike. The court indicated its sensitivity to the implications of shifting jurisdiction over the mass of activity now penalized by state law. The Court said:

"The Government's broad concept of extortion—the 'wrongful' use of force to obtain even the legitimate union demands of higher wages—is not easily restricted. It would cover all overtly coercive conduct in the course of an economic strike, obstructing, delaying, or affecting commerce. The worker who threw a punch on a picket line, or the striker who deflated the tires on his employer's truck would be subject to a Hobbs Act prosecution and the possibility of 20 years' imprisonment and a $10,000 fine.

------

[1] Copyright (c) 1970 by the Arizona Board of Regents. Reprinted by permission.

"Even if the language and history of the Act were less clear than we have found them to be, the Act could not properly be expanded as the Government suggests—for two related reasons. First, this being a criminal statute, it must be strictly construed, and any ambiguity must be resolved in favor of lenity. . . . . Secondly, it would require statutory language much more explicit than that before us here to lead to the conclusion that Congress intended to put the Federal Government in the business of policing the orderly conduct of strikes. Neither the language of the Hobbs Act nor its legislative history can justify the conclusion that Congress intended to work such an extraordinary change in federal labor law or such an unprecedented incursion into the criminal jurisdiction of the States. . . .

"As we said last Term:

'[U]nless Congress conveys its purpose clearly, it will not be deemed to have significantly changed the federal-state balance. Congress has traditionally been reluctant to define as a federal crime conduct readily denounced as criminal by the States . . . [W]e will not be quick to assume that Congress has meant to effect a significant change in the sensitive relation between federal and state criminal jurisdiction.' United States v. Bass, 404 U.S. 336, 349 (footnotes omitted).''

THE ROLE OF THE COURTS, IF ANY, IN LIMITING THE REGULATORY POWER OF CONGRESS UNDER THE COMMERCE CLAUSE

After *Perez* are there any judicially enforceable limits on the use of the commerce clause as a basis for federal regulation of local matters? Should there be? Does the Constitution any longer protect the local interests in our federal system? Consider the following:

(1) Professor Wechsler argues: The mere existence of the states as separate sources of authority and organs of administration with general governmental competence unless excluded by the Constitution or valid Act of Congress serves to reinforce local interests. Congress is composed of members who represent essentially local interests. The structure of the Senate clearly reinforces state interests and the members of the House represent the people in their states. The President alone is selected by a national constituency but the mode of his selection and the nature of Congress forces him to be responsive to local values. Hence, "the national political process in the United States—and especially the role of the states in the composition and selection of the central government—is intrinsically well adapted to retarding or restraining new intrusions by the center on the domain of the states." Wechsler, *The Political Safeguards of Federalism,* in *Principles, Politics, and Fundamental Law* 49, 78 (1961).

(2) Robert L. Stern, who participated on the side of government in many of the great cases during the New Deal period, states in *The Commerce Clause Revisited—The Federalization of Intrastate Crime,* 15 Ariz.L.Rev. 271, 284 (1973):

"The commerce clause has come a long way since its nadir in the 1930's when strikes in the coal industry were held to affect interstate commerce only indirectly and not to be subject to congressional regulation. Even a lawyer who fought for a realistic interpretation which would recognize that in commercial matters the United States was one nation finds himself surprised at where we are now—and at how readily the recent expansion is accepted. Perhaps the surprise merely reflects a recollection of what were regarded as great difficulties in the earlier litigation. And yet law students and younger lawyers now probably accept the modern commerce decisions as if they always have been 'the law,' as they accept Marbury v. Madison, McCulloch v. Maryland and Gibbons v. Ogden—which also presented some difficulties in their times.

"The ease with which the public and the judiciary now swallow the federal regulation of what were once deemed exclusively local matters undoubtedly reflects the general integration of the nation, in disregard of state lines. The people recognize that the national government can deal more effectively with problems which do not limit themselves to individual states. This is hardly a novel or radical concept. It underlay the assignment of powers to the federal government at the Constitutional Convention of 1787.[79] There should be no cause for alarm because the same standard is accepted and applied 186 years later." [a]

(3) In Hodel v. Virginia Surface Mining & Reclamation Ass'n, Inc., 452 U.S. 264 (1981), and Hodel v. Indiana, 452 U.S. 314 (1981), the Court unanimously concluded that the Surface Mining Control and Reclamation Act of 1977 fell within the scope of the commerce power. The Act required mine owners, among other things, to restore land after mining is completed. The Court concluded that the commerce power was "broad enough to permit congressional regulation of activities causing air or water pollution, or other environmental hazards that may have effects in more than one State."

Concurring, Justice Rehnquist said in part:

"It is illuminating for purposes of reflection, if not for argument, to note that one of the greatest 'fictions' of our federal system is that the Congress exercises only those powers delegated to it, while the remainder are reserved to the States or to the people. The manner in which this Court has construed the Commerce Clause amply illustrates the extent of this fiction. Although it is clear that the people, through the States, *delegated* authority to Congress to 'regulate Commerce . . . among the several States,' U.S. Const., Art. 1, § 8, cl. 3, one could easily get the sense from this Court's opinions that the federal system exists only at the sufferance of Congress.

. . .

"[I]t would be a mistake to conclude that Congress' power to regulate pursuant to the Commerce Clause is unlimited. Some activities may be so private or local in nature that they simply may not be *in* commerce. Nor is it sufficient that the person or activity reached have *some* nexus with interstate commerce. Our cases have consistently held that the regulated activity must have a *substantial* effect on interstate commerce. E.g., NLRB v. Jones & Laughlin Steel Corp., 301 U.S., at 37 (1937) (local activities may be regulated if they have a 'close and substantial relation to interstate commerce'). Moreover, simply because Congress may conclude that a particular activity substantially affects interstate commerce does not necessarily make it so. Congress' findings must be supported by a 'rational basis' and are reviewable by the courts. Cf. Perez v. United States, 402 U.S. 146 (1971) (Stewart, J., dissenting). In short, unlike the reserved police powers of the States, which are plenary unless challenged as violating some specific provision of the Constitution, the connection with interstate commerce is itself a jurisdictional prerequisite for any substantive legislation by Congress under the Commerce Clause.

"In many ways, the Court's opinions in these cases are consistent with that approach. In both the *Virginia* and *Indiana* cases, the Court exhaustively

---

[79] The Convention had approved the Sixth Randolph Resolution which declared that "the national legislature ought . . . to legislate in all cases for the general interests of the Union, and also in those to which the states are separately incompetent." This was the standard pursuant to which the enumeration of the powers of Congress was drafted. . . .

[a] Copyright (c) 1970 by the Arizona Board of Regents. Reprinted by permission.

analyzes Congress' articulated justifications for the exercise of its power under the Commerce Clause and concludes that Congress' detailed factual findings as to the effect of surface mining on interstate commerce are sufficient to justify the exercise of that power. Though there can be no doubt that Congress in regulating surface mining has stretched its authority to the 'nth degree,' our prior precedents compel me to agree with the Court's conclusion. I therefore concur in the judgments of the Court.

"There is, however, a troublesome difference between what the Court does and what it says. . . . [T]he Court asserts that regulation will be upheld if Congress had a rational basis for finding that the regulated activity affects interstate commerce. The Court takes this statement of the proper 'test' from Heart of Atlanta Motel, Inc. v. United States, 379 U.S. 241, 258 (1964). In my view, the Court misstates the test. As noted above, it has long been established that the commerce power does not reach activity which merely 'affects' interstate commerce. There must instead be a showing that regulated activity has a *substantial effect* on that commerce. See NLRB v. Jones & Laughlin, supra; Shreveport Rate Case, 234 U.S. 342 (1914); Wickard v. Filburn, 317 U.S., at 125 (1942) (local activity may be reached by Congress if 'it exerts a substantial economic effect on interstate commerce'); North American Co. v. SEC, 327 U.S. 686, 705 (1946) (Congress may attack an evil which bears a 'substantial relationship to interstate commerce'). As recently as Maryland v. Wirtz, 392 U.S. 183, 197, n. 27 (1968). Justice Harlan stressed that: '[n]either here nor in *Wickard* has the Court declared that Congress may use a relatively trivial impact on commerce as an excuse for broad general regulation of state or private activities.' Even in *Heart of Atlanta Motel, Inc.,* in the paragraph just prior to the passage relied on by the Court here, the Court emphasized that Congress had the power to regulate local activities 'which might have a substantial and harmful effect upon that commerce.' 379 U.S., at 258.
. . . .

"In sum, my difficulty with some of the recent Commerce Clause jurisprudence is that the Court often seems to forget that legislation enacted by Congress is subject to two different kinds of challenge, while that enacted by the States is subject to only one kind of challenge. Neither Congress nor the States may act in a manner prohibited by any provision of the Constitution. Congress must show that activity it seeks to regulate has a substantial effect on interstate commerce. It is my uncertainty as to whether the Court intends to broaden, by some of its language, this test that leads me to concur only in the judgments."

(4) In 1976 the Supreme Court held that an amendment to the Fair Labor Standards Act making it applicable to employees of states and their local subdivisions was "not within the authority granted Congress" under the commerce clause. National League of Cities v. Usery, 426 U.S. 833 (1976), set out infra p. 408.

B.   THE TAXING POWER

SONZINSKY v. UNITED STATES

300 U.S. 506, 57 S.Ct. 554, 81 L.Ed. 772 (1937).

Mr. Justice Stone delivered the opinion of the Court.

The question for decision is whether § 2 of the National Firearms Act of June 26, 1934, c. 757, 48 Stat. 1236, 26 U.S.C. §§ 1132–1132q, which imposes a $200 annual license tax on dealers in firearms, is a constitutional exercise of the legislative power of Congress.

Petitioner was convicted . . . . on two counts of an indictment, the first charging him with violation of § 2, by dealing in firearms without payment of the tax. On appeal the Court of Appeals set aside the conviction on the second count and affirmed on the first. . . .

Section 2 of the National Firearms Act requires every dealer in firearms to register with the Collector of Internal Revenue in the district where he carries on business, and to pay a special excise tax of $200 a year. Importers or manufacturers are taxed $500 a year. Section 3 imposes a tax of $200 on each transfer of a firearm, payable by the transferor, and § 4 prescribes regulations for the identification of purchasers. The term "firearm" is defined by § 1 as meaning a shotgun or a rifle having a barrel less than eighteen inches in length, or any other weapon, except a pistol or revolver, from which a shot is discharged by an explosive, if capable of being concealed on the person, or a machine gun, and includes a muffler or silencer for any firearm. . . . Petitioner does not deny that Congress may tax his business as a dealer in firearms. He insists that the present levy is not a true tax, but a penalty imposed for the purpose of suppressing traffic in a certain noxious type of firearms, the local regulation of which is reserved to the states because not granted to the national government. To establish its penal and prohibitive character, he relies on the amounts of the tax imposed by § 2 on dealers, manufacturers and importers, and of the tax imposed by § 3 on each transfer of a "firearm," payable by the transferor. The cumulative effect on the distribution of a limited class of firearms, of relatively small value, by the successive imposition of different taxes, one on the business of the importer or manufacturer, another on that of the dealer, and a third on the transfer to a buyer, is said to be prohibitive in effect and to disclose unmistakably the legislative purpose to regulate rather than to tax.

The case is not one where the statute contains regulatory provisions related to a purported tax in such a way as has enabled this Court to say in other cases that the latter is a penalty resorted to as a means of enforcing the regulations. See Child Labor Tax Case, 259 U.S. 20, 35; Hill v. Wallace, 259 U.S. 44; Carter v. Carter Coal Co., 298 U.S. 238. Nor is the subject of the tax described or treated as criminal by the taxing statute. Compare United States v. Constantine,[a] 296 U.S. 287. Here § 2 contains no regulation other than the mere registration provisions, which are obviously supportable as in aid of a revenue purpose. On its face it is only a taxing measure, and we are asked to say that the tax, by virtue of its deterrent effect on the activities taxed, operates as a regulation which is beyond the congressional power.

Every tax is in some measure regulatory. To some extent it interposes an economic impediment to the activity taxed as compared with others not taxed. But a tax is not any the less a tax because it has a regulatory effect, . . .; and it has long been established that an Act of Congress which on its face purports to be an exercise of the taxing power is not any the less so because the tax is burdensome or tends to restrict or suppress the thing taxed. Veazie Bank v. Fenno, 8 Wall. 533, 548; McCray v. United States, 195 U.S. 27, 60–61. . . . .

Inquiry into the hidden motives which may move Congress to exercise a power constitutionally conferred upon it is beyond the competency of courts.

---

[a] In the *Constantine* case (1935) the Court held invalid a federal excise tax of $1000 on liquor dealers "carrying on business . . . contrary to the laws of a State . . . or municipality". The tax was 10 to 50 times greater than the federal tax on dealers operating legally. The Court concluded: "The condition of the imposition is the commission of a crime. This, together with the amount of the tax, is . . . significant of penal and prohibitory intent rather than the gathering of revenue." Cardozo, J., (joined by Brandeis and Stone, JJ.) dissented, saying: "Congress may reasonably have believed in view of the attendant risks, a business carried on illegally and furtively is likely to yield larger profits than one transacted openly by law-abiding men. Not repression, but payment commensurate with the gains is thus the animating motive. . . . . Congress may also have believed that the furtive character of the business would increase the difficulty and expense of the process of tax collection."

Veazie Bank v. Fenno, supra; McCray v. United States, supra, 56–59; United States v. Doremus, supra, 93–94. They will not undertake, by collateral inquiry as to the measure of the regulatory effect of a tax, to ascribe to Congress an attempt, under the guise of taxation, to exercise another power denied by the Federal Constitution. McCray v. United States, supra; cf. Magnano Co. v. Hamilton, supra, 45.

Here the annual tax of $200 is productive of some revenue.[1] We are not free to speculate as to the motives which moved Congress to impose it, or as to the extent to which it may operate to restrict the activities taxed. As it is not attended by an offensive regulation, and since it operates as a tax, it is within the national taxing power. . . .

Affirmed.[b]

UNITED STATES v. PTASYNSKI, 462 U.S. 74 (1983). The Crude Oil Windfall Profit Tax of 1980 imposed a federal tax on oil produced, but contained an exception for "exempt Alaskan oil." The exemption covered about 20% of current Alaskan oil and some oil from offshore northern waters outside of state boundaries. A suit was brought challenging the exemption as a violation of the Uniformity Clause which provides that federal taxes "shall be uniform throughout the United States." The Court, in an opinion by Justice Powell, unanimously upheld the validity of the exemption, saying:

"We do not think that the language of the Clause or this Court's decisions prohibit all geographically defined classifications. . . . [T]he Uniformity Clause requires that an excise tax apply, at the same rate, in all portions of the

---

[1] The $200 tax was paid by 27 dealers in 1934, and by 22 dealers in 1935. Annual Report of the Commissioner of Internal Revenue, Fiscal Year Ended June 30, 1935, pp. 129–131; id., Fiscal Year Ended June 30, 1936, pp. 139–141.

[b] The *McCray-Doremus-Sonzinsky* line of cases was followed in United States v. Sanchez, 340 U.S. 42 (1950), sustaining a federal tax on persons importing or dealing in marihuana.

United States v. Kahriger, 345 U.S. 22 (1953) presented the following situation: As a result of the widely publicized investigations by the Kefauver Crime Committee of the Senate, Congress included in the 1951 Revenue Act provisions requiring persons engaged in the business of accepting wagers to pay an annual tax of $50 plus 10% of the wagers placed. Each person liable for the tax was also required to file a registration statement with the Internal Revenue Service giving his name, residence, place of business and the name and address of each person accepting wagers for him. The lower court held the tax unconstitutional under United States v. Constantine, 296 U.S. 287 (1935). The Supreme Court reversed, pointing out: "The wagering tax with which we are here concerned applies to all persons engaged in the business of receiving wagers regardless of whether such activity violates state law. . . . Appellee would have us say that because there is legislative history indicating a Congressional motive to suppress wagering, this tax is not a proper exercise of such taxing power. . . . It is conceded that a federal excise tax does not cease to be valid merely because it discourages or deters the activities taxed. Nor is the tax invalid because the revenue obtained is negligible. . . . Unless there are provisions extraneous to any tax need, courts are without authority to limit the exercise of the taxing power. All the provisions of this excise are adapted to the collection of a valid tax." Frankfurter, J. (joined by Douglas, J.) dissented, saying: "[W]hen oblique use is made of the taxing power as to matters which substantively are not within the powers delegated to Congress, the Court cannot shut its eyes to what is obviously, because designedly, an attempt to control conduct which the Constitution left to the responsibility of the States, merely because Congress wrapped the legislation in the verbal cellophane of a revenue measure." He believed that "the context of the circumstances which brought forth this enactment—sensationally exploited disclosures regarding gambling in big cities and small, the relation of this gambling to corrupt politics, the impatient public response to these disclosures, the feeling of ineptitude or paralysis on the part of local law-enforcing agencies—emphatically supports . . . that what was formally a means of raising revenue . . . was essentially an effort to check if not to stamp out professional gambling." Black and Douglas, JJ., also dissented on the ground that the reporting provisions of the act required taxpayers to incriminate themselves in violation of the Fifth Amendment. This position was later sustained in Marchetti v. United States, 390 U.S. 39 (1968), which overruled Kahriger on the self-incrimination point. For comment on the *Kahriger* case, see: 67 Harv.L.Rev. 164–7 (1953); 52 Mich.L.Rev. 150 (1953); 101 U.Pa.L.Rev. 877 (1953).

United States where the subject of the tax is found. Where Congress defines
the subject of a tax in nongeographic terms, the Uniformity Clause is satisfied.
. . . . We cannot say that when Congress uses geographic terms to identify
the same subject, the classification is invalidated. The Uniformity Clause gives
Congress wide latitude in deciding what to tax and does not prohibit it from
considering geographically isolated problems. . . . But where Congress does
choose to frame a tax in geographic terms, we will examine the classification
closely to see if there is actual geographic discrimination.

"In this case, we hold that the classification is constitutional. As discussed
above, Congress considered the windfall profit tax a necessary component of its
program to encourage the exploration and production of oil. It perceived that
the decontrol legislation would result—in certain circumstances—in profits
essentially unrelated to the objective of the program, and concluded that these
profits should be taxed. Accordingly, Congress divided oil into various classes
and gave more favorable treatment to those classes that would be responsive to
increased prices.

"Congress clearly viewed 'exempt Alaskan oil' as a unique class of oil that,
consistent with the scheme of the Act, merited favorable treatment. It had
before it ample evidence of the disproportionate costs and difficulties—the
fragile ecology, the harsh environment, and the remote location—associated
with extracting oil from this region. We cannot fault its determination, based
on neutral factors, that this oil required separate treatment. Nor is there any
indication that Congress sought to benefit Alaska for reasons that would offend
the purpose of the Clause. Nothing in the Act's legislative history suggests that
Congress intended to grant Alaska an undue preference at the expense of other
oil-producing States. This is especially clear because the windfall profit tax itself
falls heavily on the State of Alaska."

C. THE SPENDING POWER

Steward Machine Co. v. Davis, 301 U.S. 548 (1937), presented a challenge to Title IX of the Social Security Act of 1935 relating to unemployment
compensation. A tax was imposed on employers of eight or more persons; the
proceeds were not earmarked, but went into the general funds of the Treasury.
If the taxpayer made contributions to a state unemployment compensation fund
created by state law certified by the Social Security Board as meeting certain
minimum standards, he was entitled to credit such contributions against his
federal tax up to 90% of the tax. In order to assure proper administration of
the state compensation system, it was required that contributions to the state
fund be paid over to the Secretary of the Treasury to the credit of the
Unemployment Trust Fund, the Secretary then being required to pay back to
the authorized state agency the sums requisitioned by it. Federal machinery for
the administration of the Social Security Act was quickly provided and most
states immediately enacted legislation making possible their participation in the
program. Steward Machine Company sued Davis, a Collector of Internal
Revenue, to recover payroll taxes paid, claiming that the law, particularly the
90% credit provisions, resulted in "coercion of the states" in violation of the
Tenth Amendment or of restrictions implicit in our federal system.

In a 5–4 decision the Court sustained the statute. In rejecting the coercion
argument, the Court referred to the widespread unemployment during the
Great Depression and continued:

". . . The fact developed quickly that the states were unable to give the
requisite relief. The problem had become national in area and dimensions.
There was need of help from the nation if the people were not to starve. It is
too late today for the argument to be heard with tolerance that in a crisis so
extreme the use of the moneys of the nation to relieve the unemployed and

their dependents is a use for any purpose narrower than the promotion of the general welfare. Cf. United States v. Butler, 297 U.S. 1, 65, 66. . . . . The Social Security Act is an attempt to find a method by which all these public agencies may work together to a common end. Every dollar of the new taxes will continue in all likelihood to be used and needed by the nation as long as states are unwilling, whether through timidity or for other motives, to do what can be done at home. At least the inference is permissible that Congress so believed, though retaining undiminished freedom to spend the money as it pleased. On the other hand, fulfillment of the home duty will be lightened and encouraged by crediting the taxpayer upon his account with the Treasury of the nation to the extent that his contributions under the laws of the locality have simplified or diminished the problem of relief and the probable demand upon the resources of the fisc. . . . The difficulty with the petitioner's contention is that it confuses motive with coercion. 'Every tax is in some measure regulatory. To some extent it interposes an economic impediment to the activity taxed as compared with others not taxed.' Sonzinsky v. United States, 300 U.S. 506. In like manner every rebate from a tax when conditioned upon conduct is in some measure a temptation. But to hold that motive or temptation is equivalent to coercion is to plunge the law in endless difficulties. . . .

"In ruling as we do, we leave many questions open. We do not say that a tax is valid, when imposed by act of Congress, if it is laid upon the condition that a state may escape its operation through the adoption of a statute unrelated in subject-matter to activities fairly within the scope of national policy and power. No such question is before us. In the tender of this credit Congress does not intrude upon fields foreign to its function. The purpose of its intervention, as we have shown, is to safeguard its own treasury and as an incident to that protection to place the states upon a footing of equal opportunity. Drains upon its own resources are to be checked; obstructions to the freedom of the states are to be leveled. It is one thing to impose a tax dependent upon the conduct of the taxpayers, or of the state in which they live, where the conduct to be simulated or discouraged is unrelated to the fiscal need subserved by the tax in its normal operation, or to any other end legitimately national. The Child Labor Tax Case, 259 U.S. 20, and Hill v. Wallace, 259 U.S. 44, were decided in the belief that the statutes there condemned were exposed to that reproach. Cf. United States v. Constantine, 296 U.S. 287. It is quite another thing to say that a tax will be abated upon the doing of an act that will satisfy the fiscal need, the tax and the alternative being approximate equivalents. In such circumstances, if in no others, inducement or persuasion does not go beyond the bounds of power. We do not fix the outermost line. Enough for present purposes that wherever the line may be, this statute is within it. Definition more precise must abide the wisdom of the future. . . .

"United States v. Butler, supra, is cited by petitioner as a decision to the contrary. . . . The decision was by a divided court, a minority taking the view that the objections were untenable. None of them is applicable to the situation here developed.

"(a) The proceeds of the tax in controversy are not earmarked for a special group.

"(b) The unemployment compensation law which is a condition of the credit has had the approval of the state and could not be a law without it.

"(c) The condition is not linked to an irrevocable agreement, for the state at its pleasure may repeal its unemployment law, § 903(a)(6), terminate the credit, and place itself where it was before the credit was accepted.

"(d) The condition is not directed to the attainment of an unlawful end, but to an end, the relief of unemployment, for which nation and state may lawfully cooperate. . . ."

The Court also concluded that the statute did not call "for a surrender by the states of powers essential to their quasi-sovereign existence."

". . . A credit to taxpayers for payments made to a state under a state unemployment law will be manifestly futile in the absence of some assurance that the law leading to the credit is in truth what it professes to be. An unemployment law framed in such a way that the unemployed who look to it will be deprived of reasonable protection is one in name and nothing more. What is basic and essential may be assured by suitable conditions. The terms embodied in these sections are directed to that end. A wide range of judgment is given to the several states as to the particular type of statute to be spread upon their books. . . . What they may not do if they would earn the credit, is to depart from those standards which in the judgment of Congress are to be ranked as fundamental. Even if opinion may differ as to the fundamental quality of one or more of the conditions, the difference will not avail to vitiate the statute. In determining essentials, Congress must have the benefit of a fair margin of discretion. . . ."

Justices McReynolds, Sutherland, Van Devanter and Butler dissented.

Helvering v. Davis, 301 U.S. 619 (1937). This case involved the old age benefit provisions (Titles II and VIII) of the Social Security Act. In meeting the contention that the program for paying old age benefits was not authorized by the general welfare clause, the Court reviewed evidence of the widespread economic plight of the aged and added:

"The problem is plainly national in area and dimensions. Moreover, laws of the separate states cannot deal with it effectively. Congress, at least, had a basis for that belief. States and local governments are often lacking in the resources that are necessary to finance an adequate program of security for the aged. This is brought out with a wealth of illustration in recent studies of the problem. Apart from the failure of resources, states and local governments are at times reluctant to increase so heavily the burden of taxation to be borne by their residents for fear of placing themselves in a position of economic disadvantage as compared with neighbors or competitors.

"We have seen this in our study of the problem of unemployment compensation. Steward Machine Co. v. Davis, supra. A system of old age pensions has special dangers of its own, if put in force in one state and rejected in another. The existence of such a system is a bait to the needy and dependent elsewhere, encouraging them to migrate and seek a haven of repose. Only a power that is national can serve the interests of all.

"Whether wisdom or unwisdom resides in the scheme of benefits set forth in Title II, it is not for us to say. The answer to such inquiries must come from Congress, not the courts. Our concern here, as often, is with power, not with wisdom. Counsel for respondent has recalled to us the virtues of self-reliance and frugality. There is a possibility, he says, that aid from a paternal government may sap those sturdy virtues and breed a race of weaklings. If Massachusetts so believes and shapes her laws in that conviction, must her breed of sons be changed, he asks, because some other philosophy of government finds favor in the halls of Congress? But the answer is not doubtful. One might ask with equal reason whether the system of protective tariffs is to be set aside at will in one state or another whenever local policy prefers the rule of laissez faire. The issue is a closed one. It was fought out long ago. When money is spent to promote the general welfare, the concept of welfare or the opposite is shaped by Congress, not the states. So the concept be not arbitrary, the locality must yield. Constitution, Art. VI, Par. 2. . . ."

THE IMPACT OF FEDERAL GRANTS TO THE STATES

Federal grants to the states have increased rapidly in recent years. Total federal grants-in-aid and shared revenue increased from just under 11 billion dollars in 1965 to an estimated total in excess of 91 billion in 1982. *Statistical Abstract* 1982–83, p. 279. The percentage of state and local government budgets received from the federal government was 9.7% in 1950, 14.5% in 1970, and 18.4% in 1980, *Statistical Abstract* 1982–83, p. 281.

BUCKLEY v. VALEO, 424 U.S. 1 (1976). Subtitle H of the Federal Election Campaign Act, as amended in 1974, establishes a Presidential Election Campaign Fund, financed from general revenues in the aggregate amount designated by individual taxpayers who on their income tax returns may authorize payment to the Fund of one dollar of their tax liability in case of an individual return or two dollars in case of a joint return. The Fund consists of separate accounts to finance party nominating conventions, general election campaigns, and primary campaigns. To the contention that Subtitle H is invalid as contrary to the general welfare clause of Article I, § 8, the Court responded as follows:

"Appellants' 'general welfare' contention erroneously treats the General Welfare Clause as a limitation upon congressional power. It is rather a grant of power, the scope of which is quite expansive, particularly in view of the enlargement of power by the Necessary and Proper Clause. McCulloch v. Maryland, 4 Wheat. 316, 420 (1819). Congress has power to regulate Presidential elections and primaries, United States v. Classic, 313 U.S. 299 (1941); Burroughs v. United States, 290 U.S. 534 (1934); and public financing of Presidential elections as a means to reform the electoral process was clearly a choice within the granted power. It is for Congress to decide which expenditures will promote the general welfare: '[T]he power of Congress to authorize expenditure of public moneys for public purposes is not limited by the direct grants of legislative power found in the Constitution.' United States v. Butler, 297 U.S. 1, 66 (1936). See Helvering v. Davis, 301 U.S. 619, 640–641 (1937). Any limitations upon the exercise of that granted power must be found elsewhere in the Constitution. In this case, Congress was legislating for the 'general welfare'—to reduce the deleterious influence of large contributions on our political process, to facilitate communication by candidates with the electorate, and to free candidates from the rigors of fundraising. See S.Rep. No. 93–689, pp. 1–10 (1974). Whether the chosen means appear 'bad,' 'unwise,' or 'unworkable' to us is irrelevant; Congress has concluded that the means are 'necessary and proper' to promote the general welfare and we thus decline to find this legislation without the grant of power in Art. I, § 8.

"Appellants' challenge to the dollar check-off provision (§ 6096) fails for the same reason. They maintain that Congress is required to permit taxpayers to designate particular candidates or parties as recipients of their money. But the appropriation to the Fund in § 9006 is like any other appropriation from the general revenue except that its amount is determined by reference to the aggregate of the one- and two-dollar authorization on taxpayers' income tax returns. This detail does not constitute the appropriation any less an appropriation by Congress. The fallacy of appellants' argument is therefore apparent; every appropriation made by Congress uses public money in a manner to which some taxpayers object."

NOTE

Are there any limitations on the spending power of Congress?

Read the first three paragraphs of Chief Justice Burger's opinion in Fullilove v. Klutznick, p. 815, infra.

Note also the following language from Justice Rehnquist's opinion for the Court in Pennhurst State Sch. v. Halderman, 451 U.S. 1, 17 (1981):

"Turning to Congress' power to legislate pursuant to the spending power, our cases have long recognized that Congress may fix the terms on which it shall disburse federal money to the States. See, e.g., Oklahoma v. CSC, 330 U.S. 127 (1947); King v. Smith, 392 U.S. 309 (1968); Rosado v. Wyman, 397 U.S. 397 (1970). Unlike legislation enacted under § 5, however, legislation enacted pursuant to the spending power is much in the nature of a contract: in return for federal funds, the States agree to comply with federally imposed conditions. The legitimacy of Congress' power to legislate under the spending power thus rests on whether the State voluntarily and knowingly accepts the terms of the 'contract.' See Steward Machine Co. v. Davis, 301 U.S. 548, 585–598 (1937); Harris v. McRae, 448 U.S. 297 (1980). There can, of course, be no knowing acceptance if a State is unaware of the conditions or is unable to ascertain what is expected of it. Accordingly, if Congress intends to impose a condition on the grant of federal moneys, it must do so unambiguously.[13] . . . By insisting that Congress speak with a clear voice, we enable the States to exercise their choice knowingly, cognizant of the consequences of their participation."

D. WAR AND TREATY POWERS

THE SOURCES OF NATIONAL POWER

Since the primary purpose of the Founding Fathers was "to form a more perfect Union" with a stronger national government, one might suppose that the national powers over foreign affairs would have been quite fully and explicitly stated. But such was not the case. The constitutional provisions dealing expressly with foreign relations, or matters particularly related thereto, are rather sparse and uncorrelated. Most of them appear in the enumeration of executive powers: the President is made "Commander-in-Chief" of the armed forces; he is given the power, with the approval of two-thirds of the Senate, "to make Treaties"; and, with the "advice and consent" of the Senate, he "shall appoint Ambassadors, other public Ministers and Consuls," i.e., our representatives abroad (Art. II, § 2). Also, "he shall receive Ambassadors and other public Ministers" (Art. II, § 3). There are two additional provisions (not referring particularly to foreign affairs) under which the President has extensive undefined power. They provide "the executive power shall be vested in" him (Art. II, § 1) and "he shall take care that the Laws be faithfully executed" (Art. II, § 3).

Aside from Senate participation in the making of treaties, the powers of Congress explicitly relating to foreign affairs or national defense are: the power to regulate commerce with foreign nations; to establish "a uniform rule of naturalization"; to define and punish piracies and felonies committed on the

---

[13] There are limits on the power of Congress to impose conditions on the States pursuant to its spending power, Steward Machine Co. v. Davis, 301 U.S., at 585; Lau v. Nichols, 414 U.S. 563, 569 (1974); Fullilove v. Klutznick, 448 U.S. 448 (1980) (Burger, C.J.); see National League of Cities v. Usery, 426 U.S. 833 (1976). Even the Halderman respondents, like the court below, recognize the "constitutional difficulties" with imposing affirmative obligations on the States pursuant to the spending power. That issue, however, is not now before us.

high seas and offenses against the law of nations; to declare war; to maintain an army and navy; and to make rules for the regulation of the armed forces (Art. I, § 8).

To make clear that some of these powers are exclusively national, a few explicit limitations are imposed on the states; no State shall enter into any treaty, alliance, or confederation; nor, without the consent of Congress, lay any imposts or duties on imports or exports, except what may be necessary for executing state inspection laws; nor, without the consent of Congress, keep "troops or ships of war" in time of peace, or engage in war unless actually invaded or in imminent danger thereof (Art. I, § 10).

———

UNITED STATES v. CURTISS–WRIGHT EXPORT CORP., 299 U.S. 304 (1936). By a Joint Resolution of May 28, 1934, Congress purported to authorize the President to embargo the sale of arms to countries engaged in armed conflict in the Chaco. (Bolivia and Paraguay were so engaged.) The President, by proclamation, immediately imposed an embargo in accordance with the Joint Resolution. Curtiss-Wright contested the validity of the embargo on the ground that the Joint Resolution attempted an unconstitutional delegation of legislative power to the Executive. In rejecting this contention, the Court (per Sutherland, J.) expressed the view that there are fundamental differences between "the powers of the federal government in respect of foreign or external affairs and those in respect of domestic or internal affairs." The opinion continued:

"The two classes of powers are different, both in respect of their origin and their nature. The broad statement that the federal government can exercise no powers except those specifically enumerated in the Constitution, and such implied powers as are necessary and proper to carry into effect the enumerated powers, is categorically true only in respect of our internal affairs. In that field, the primary purpose of the Constitution was to carve from the general mass of legislative powers *then possessed by the states* such portions as it was thought desirable to vest in the federal government, leaving those not included in the enumeration still in the states. Carter v. Carter Coal Co., 298 U.S. 238, 294. That this doctrine applies only to powers which the states had, is self evident. And since the states severally never possessed international powers, such powers could not have been carved from the mass of state powers but obviously were transmitted to the United States from some other source. . . .

"It results that the investment of the federal government with the powers of external sovereignty did not depend upon the affirmative grants of the Constitution. The powers to declare and wage war, to conclude peace, to make treaties, to maintain diplomatic relations with other sovereignties, if they had never been mentioned in the Constitution, would have vested in the federal government as necessary concomitants of nationality. . . . As a member of the family of nations, the right and power of the United States in that field are equal to the right and power of the other members of the international family. Otherwise, the United States is not completely sovereign. The power to acquire territory by discovery and occupation (Jones v. United States, 137 U.S. 202, 212), the power to expel undesirable aliens (Fong Yue Ting v. United States, 149 U.S. 698, 705 et seq.), the power to make such international agreements as do not constitute treaties in the constitutional sense (Altman & Co. v. United States, 224 U.S. 583, 600–601; Crandall, Treaties, Their Making and Enforcement, 2d ed., p. 102 and note 1), none of which is expressly affirmed by the Constitution, nevertheless exist as inherently inseparable from the conception of nationality. This the court recognized, and in each of the cases cited found the warrant for its conclusions not in the provisions of the Constitution, but in the law of nations."[1]

WOODS v. CLOYD W. MILLER CO.

333 U.S. 138, 68 S.Ct. 421, 92 L.Ed. 596 (1948).

Mr. Justice Douglas delivered the opinion of the Court.

The case is here on a direct appeal from a judgment of the District Court holding unconstitutional Title II of the Housing and Rent Act of 1947. 61 Stat. 193, 196.

The Act became effective on July 1, 1947, and the following day the appellee demanded of its tenants increases of 40% and 60% for rental accommodations in the Cleveland Defense-Rental Area, an admitted violation of the Act and regulations adopted pursuant thereto. Appellant thereupon instituted this proceeding under § 206(b) of the Act to enjoin the violations. A preliminary injunction issued. After a hearing it was dissolved and a permanent injunction denied.

The District Court was of the view that the authority of Congress to regulate rents by virtue of the war power (see Bowles v. Willingham, 321 U.S. 503) ended with the Presidential Proclamation terminating hostilities on December 31, 1946, since that proclamation inaugurated "peace-in-fact" though it did not mark termination of the war. . . .

We conclude, in the first place, that the war power sustains this legislation. The Court said in Hamilton v. Kentucky Distilleries Co., 251 U.S. 146, 161, that the war power includes the power "to remedy the evils which have arisen from its rise and progress" and continues for the duration of that emergency. Whatever may be the consequences when war is officially terminated, the war power does not necessarily end with the cessation of hostilities. We recently held that it is adequate to support the preservation of rights created by wartime legislation, Fleming v. Mohawk Wrecking & Lumber Co., 331 U.S. 111. But it has a broader sweep. In Hamilton v. Kentucky Distilleries Co., supra, and Ruppert v. Caffey, 251 U.S. 264, prohibition laws which were enacted after the Armistice in World War I were sustained as exercises of the war power because they conserved manpower and increased efficiency of production in the critical days during the period of demobilization, and helped to husband the supply of grains and cereals depleted by the war effort. Those cases followed the reasoning of Stewart v. Kahn, 11 Wall. 493, which held that Congress had the power to toll the statute of limitations of the States during the period when the process of their courts was not available to litigants due to the conditions obtaining in the Civil War.

The constitutional validity of the present legislation follows *a fortiori* from those cases. The legislative history of the present Act make abundantly clear that there has not yet been eliminated the deficit in housing which in considerable measure was caused by the heavy demobilization of veterans and by the cessation or reduction in residential construction during the period of hostilities due to the allocation of building materials to military projects. Since the war

---

[1] Justice Sutherland's theory of extra-constitutional powers over foreign affairs has been frequently discussed but never resolved. See Henkin, *Foreign Affairs and the Constitution* (1972), Ch. I; Dodd, *Implied Powers and Implied Limitations in Constitutional Law,* 29 Yale L.J. 137 (1919), 1 Selected Essays (1938) 330; Riesenfeld, *The Power of Congress and the President in International Relations,* 25 Calif.L.Rev. 643 (1937). See also Henkin, *The Treaty Makers and the Law Makers,* 107 U.Pa.L.Rev. 903, 922–936 (1959); Perez v. Brownell, 356 U.S. 44, 57 (1958). *Perez* was overruled in Afroyim v. Rusk, 387 U.S. 253 (1967), but not the statement about the extra-constitutional foundations of the power over foreign relations.

effort contributed heavily to that deficit, Congress has the power even after the cessation of hostilities to act to control the forces that a short supply of the needed article created. If that were not true, the Necessary and Proper Clause, Art. I, § 8, cl. 18, would be drastically limited in its application to the several war powers. The Court has declined to follow that course in the past. Hamilton v. Kentucky Distilleries Co., supra, pp. 155, 156; Ruppert v. Caffey, supra, pp. 299, 300. We decline to take it today. The result would be paralyzing. It would render Congress powerless to remedy conditions the creation of which necessarily followed from the mobilization of men and materials for successful prosecution of the war. So to read the Constitution would be to make it self-defeating.

We recognize the force of the argument that the effects of war under modern conditions may be felt in the economy for years and years, and that if the war power can be used in days of peace to treat all the wounds which war inflicts on our society, it may not only swallow up all other powers of Congress but largely obliterate the Ninth and the Tenth Amendments as well. There are no such implications in to-day's decision. We deal here with the consequences of a housing deficit greatly intensified during the period of hostilities by the war effort. Any power, of course, can be abused. But we cannot assume that Congress is not alert to its constitutional responsibilities. And the question whether the war power has been properly employed in cases such as this is open to judicial inquiry. Hamilton v. Kentucky Distilleries Co., supra; Ruppert v. Caffey, supra. . . .

Reversed.

Mr. Justice Frankfurter concurs in this opinion because it decides no more than was decided in Hamilton v. Kentucky Distilleries Co., 251 U.S. 146, and Jacob Ruppert v. Caffey, 251 U.S. 264, and merely applies those decisions to the situation now before the Court.

Mr. Justice Jackson, concurring.

I agree with the result in this case, but the arguments that have been addressed to us lead me to utter more explicit misgivings about war powers than the Court has done. The Government asserts no constitutional basis for this legislation other than this vague, undefined and undefinable "war power."

No one will question that this power is the most dangerous one to free government in the whole catalogue of powers. It usually is invoked in haste and excitement when calm legislative consideration of constitutional limitation is difficult. It is executed in a time of patriotic fervor that makes moderation unpopular. And, worst of all, it is interpreted by judges under the influence of the same passions and pressures. Always, as in this case, the Government urges hasty decision to forestall some emergency or serve some purpose and pleads that paralysis will result if its claims to power are denied or their confirmation delayed.

Particularly when the war power is invoked to do things to the liberties of people, or to their property or economy that only indirectly affect conduct of the war and do not relate to the management of the war itself, the constitutional basis should be scrutinized with care.

I think we can hardly deny that the war power is as valid a ground for federal rent control now as it has been at any time. We still are technically in a state of war. I would not be willing to hold that war powers may be indefinitely prolonged merely by keeping legally alive a state of war that had in fact ended. I cannot accept the argument that war powers last as long as the effects and consequences of war, for if so they are permanent—as permanent as the war debts. But I find no reason to conclude that we could find fairly that the present state of war is merely technical. We have armies abroad exercising our war power and have made no peace terms with our allies, not to mention our principal enemies. I think the conclusion that the war power has been applicable during the lifetime of this legislation is unavoidable.

INTERNATIONAL AGREEMENTS

To what extent may the national government provide the law governing local affairs through entering into international agreements in areas where it is otherwise incompetent to act? This question poses the central issue to be pursued at this point in the materials. The division of authority between the President and Congress with respect to the making of international agreements will be discussed briefly in Chapter 8, Separation of Powers. The international aspects of treaties and executive agreements—the way in which they regulate relationships with other countries and international organizations—is a separate subject reserved for courses in international law and international transactions. For a general study of the problems of federal states in the field of international agreements, see Hendry, *Treaties and Federal Constitutions* (1955). For a penetrating discussion of all of the issues involved here see Henkin, *Foreign Affairs and the Constitution* (1972).

HAUENSTEIN v. LYNHAM, 100 U.S. 483 (1880). Hauenstein died intestate a resident of Richmond, Virginia, where he owned considerable real estate. The proceeds from the sale of this property were claimed by his heirs who were citizens of Switzerland. Their claim was resisted on the ground that the property had escheated to the state because Virginia law provided that aliens were not qualified to inherit property in the state. An 1850 treaty between the United States and Switzerland provided that in this situation the alien-heirs should be permitted to sell the property and withdraw the proceeds. The Virginia courts decided against the heirs.

The Supreme Court reversed and remanded the case, saying:

"That the laws of the State, irrespective of the treaty, would put the fund into her coffers, is no objection to the right or the remedy claimed by the plaintiffs in error. The efficacy of the treaty is declared and guaranteed by the Constitution of the United States. . . . If doubts could exist before the adoption of the present national government, they must be entirely removed by the sixth article of the Constitution, which provides that 'all treaties made or which shall be made under the authority of the United States, shall be *the supreme law of the land,* and the judges in every State shall be bound thereby, any thing in the Constitution or laws of any State to the contrary notwithstanding. . . . A treaty cannot be *the supreme law of the land,* that is, of all the United States, if any act of a State legislature can stand in its way. . . . It must always be borne in mind that the Constitution, laws, and treaties of the United States are as much a part of the law of every State as its own local laws and Constitution. This is a fundamental principle in our system of complex national polity. . . . We have no doubt that this treaty is within the treaty-making power conferred by the Constitution. And it is our duty to give it full effect. We forbear to pursue the topic further. . . ."

CONGRESSIONAL LEGISLATION INCONSISTENT
WITH A TREATY

A treaty which manifests an intention that it become effective as domestic law of the United States supersedes inconsistent provisions of earlier acts of

Congress as well as inconsistent state laws, ALI, *Restatement, Second, (Foreign Relations Law of the United States)* § 141 (1965).[1] However, subsequent Congressional legislation will be given effect even though inconsistent with a prior treaty. See the Chinese Exclusion Cases, 130 U.S. 581 (1889) which sustained legislation excluding the entry of Chinese even though such exclusion was in violation of a treaty with China. The Court said: "The last expression of sovereign will must control." In such a situation, enforcement of the international obligation, if any, must be found in diplomatic negotiations or an international tribunal.

MISSOURI v. HOLLAND

252 U.S. 416, 40 S.Ct. 382, 64 L.Ed. 641 (1920).

Mr. Justice Holmes delivered the opinion of the Court.

This is a bill in equity brought by the State of Missouri to prevent a game warden of the United States from attempting to enforce the Migratory Bird Treaty Act of July 3, 1918, c. 128, 40 Stat. 755, and the regulations made by the Secretary of Agriculture in pursuance of the same. The ground of the bill is that the statute is an unconstitutional interference with the rights reserved to the States by the Tenth Amendment, and that the acts of the defendant done and threatened under that authority invade the sovereign right of the State and contravene its will manifested in statutes. The State also alleges a pecuniary interest, as owner of the wild birds within its borders and otherwise, admitted by the Government to be sufficient, but it is enough that the bill is a reasonable and proper means to assert the alleged quasi sovereign rights of a State. Kansas v. Colorado, 185 U.S. 125, 142 . . . . A motion to dismiss was sustained by the District Court on the ground that the Act of Congress is constitutional. . . . The State appeals.

On December 8, 1916, a treaty between the United States and Great Britain was proclaimed by the President. It recited that many species of birds in their annual migrations traversed many parts of the United States and of Canada, that they were of great value as a source of food and in destroying insects injurious to vegetation, but were in danger of extermination through lack of adequate protection. It therefore provided for specified closed seasons and protection in other forms, and agreed that the two powers would take or propose to their lawmaking bodies the necessary measures for carrying the treaty out. 39 Stat. 1702. The above mentioned act of July 3, 1918, . . . prohibited the killing, capturing or selling any of the migratory birds included in the terms of the treaty except as permitted by regulations compatible with those terms to be made by the Secretary of Agriculture. . . . It is unnecessary to go into any details, because, as we have said, the question raised is the general one whether the treaty and statute are void as an interference with the rights reserved to the States.

To answer this question it is not enough to refer to the Tenth Amendment, reserving the powers not delegated to the United States, because by Article 2, Section 2, the power to make treaties is delegated expressly, and by Article 6 treaties made under the authority of the United States, along with the Constitution and laws of the United States made in pursuance thereof, are declared the supreme law of the land. If the treaty is valid there can be no dispute about the validity of the statute under Article 1, Section 8, as a necessary and proper means to execute the powers of the Government. The language of the

---

[1] There is a distinction between "self-executing" and "non-self-executing" treaties. In general, a non-self-executing treaty is one which, by its terms, requires implementation by legislative or executive action in order to be effective.

Constitution as to the supremacy of treaties being general, the question before us is narrowed to an inquiry into the ground upon which the present supposed exception is placed.

It is said that a treaty cannot be valid if it infringes the Constitution, that there are limits, therefore, to the treaty-making power, and that one such limit is that what an act of Congress could not do unaided, in derogation of the powers reserved to the States, a treaty cannot do. An earlier act of Congress that attempted by itself and not in pursuance of a treaty to regulate the killing of migratory birds within the States had been held bad in the District Court. United States v. Shauver, 214 Fed. 154. United States v. McCullagh, 221 Fed. 288. Those decisions were supported by arguments that migratory birds were owned by the States in their sovereign capacity for the benefit of their people, and that under cases like Geer v. Connecticut, 161 U.S. 519, this control was one that Congress had no power to displace. The same argument is supposed to apply now with equal force.

Whether the two cases cited were decided rightly or not they cannot be accepted as a test of the treaty power. Acts of Congress are the supreme law of the land only when made in pursuance of the Constitution, while treaties are declared to be so when made under the authority of the United States. It is open to question whether the authority of the United States means more than the formal acts prescribed to make the convention. We do not mean to imply that there are no qualifications to the treaty-making power; but they must be ascertained in a different way. It is obvious that there may be matters of the sharpest exigency for the national well being that an act of Congress could not deal with but that a treaty followed by such an act could, and it is not lightly to be assumed that, in matters requiring national action, "a power which must belong to and somewhere reside in every civilized government" is not to be found. . . . We are not yet discussing the particular case before us but only are considering the validity of the test proposed. With regard to that we may add that when we are dealing with words that also are a constituent act, like the Constitution of the United States, we must realize that they have called into life a being the development of which could not have been foreseen completely by the most gifted of its begetters. It was enough for them to realize or to hope that they had created an organism; it has taken a century and has cost their successors much sweat and blood to prove that they created a nation. The case before us must be considered in the light of our whole experience and not merely in that of what was said a hundred years ago. The treaty in question does not contravene any prohibitory words to be found in the Constitution. The only question is whether it is forbidden by some invisible radiation from the general terms of the Tenth Amendment. We must consider what this country has become in deciding what that amendment has reserved.

The State as we have intimated founds its claim of exclusive authority upon an assertion of title to migratory birds, an assertion that is embodied in statute. No doubt it is true that as between a State and its inhabitants the State may regulate the killing and sale of such birds, but it does not follow that its authority is exclusive of paramount powers. To put the claim of the State upon title is to lean upon a slender reed. Wild birds are not in the possession of anyone; and possession is the beginning of ownership. The whole foundation of the State's rights is the presence within their jurisdiction of birds that yesterday had not arrived, tomorrow may be in another State and in a week a thousand miles away. If we are to be accurate we cannot put the case of the State upon higher ground than that the treaty deals with creatures that for the moment are within the state borders, that it must be carried out by officers of the United States within the same territory, and that but for the treaty the State would be free to regulate this subject itself.

As most of the laws of the United States are carried out within the States and as many of them deal with matters which in the silence of such laws the State might regulate, such general grounds are not enough to support Missouri's claim. Valid treaties of course "are as binding within the territorial limits of the States as they are elsewhere throughout the dominion of the United States." Baldwin v. Franks, 120 U.S. 678, 683. No doubt the great body of private relations usually fall within the control of the State, but a treaty may override its power. . . .

Here a national interest of very nearly the first magnitude is involved. It can be protected only by national action in concert with that of another power. The subject matter is only transitorily within the State and has no permanent habitat therein. But for the treaty and the statute there soon might be no birds for any powers to deal with. We see nothing in the Constitution that compels the Government to sit by while a food supply is cut off and the protectors of our forests and our crops are destroyed. It is not sufficient to rely upon the States. The reliance is vain, and were it otherwise, the question is whether the United States is forbidden to act. We are of opinion that the treaty and statute must be upheld.

Decree affirmed.

Mr. Justice Van Devanter and Mr. Justice Pitney dissent.

UNITED STATES v. BELMONT, 301 U.S. 324 (1937). On November 16, 1933 President Roosevelt and Maxim Litvinov executed an agreement whereby the United States first gave recognition to the U.S.S.R. In addition, by this agreement the U.S.S.R. assigned to the United States its claims against Americans who held funds of Russian companies whose assets were confiscated by the Soviets after the revolution.

The United States brought an action based on this agreement to recover money which the Petrograd Metal Works, a Russian corporation, had deposited with the New York banker, August Belmont. The lower federal courts dismissed this action on the ground that recovery of these claims would be contrary to the policy and law of the State of New York which denied effect to decrees of foreign governments purporting to confiscate property in the state. The United States Supreme Court reversed. The opinion by Justice Sutherland included the following:

"We do not pause to inquire whether in fact there was any policy of the State of New York to be infringed, since we are of opinion that no state policy can prevail against the international compact here involved . . . .

"A treaty signifies 'a compact made between two or more independent nations with a view to the public welfare.' Altman & Co. v. United States, 224 U.S. 583, 600. But an international compact, as this was, is not always a treaty which requires the participation of the Senate. There are many such compacts, of which a protocol, a *modus vivendi,* a postal convention, and agreements like that now under consideration are illustrations. See 5 Moore, *Int.Law Digest,* 210–221. . . .

"Plainly, the external powers of the United States are to be exercised without regard to state laws or policies. The supremacy of a treaty in this respect has been recognized from the beginning. . . . And while this rule in respect of treaties is established by the express language of cl. 2, Art. VI, of the Constitution, the same rule would result in the case of all international compacts and agreements from the very fact that complete power over interna-tional affairs is in the national government and is not and cannot be subject to any curtailment or interference on the part of the several states. Compare United States v. Curtiss-Wright Export Corp., 299 U.S. 304, 316, et seq.''

UNITED STATES v. PINK, 315 U.S. 203 (1942). The United States brought a further action on the Roosevelt-Litvinov agreement to recover the funds of the New York branch of a Russian Insurance Company. The New York court dismissed the action because of its rule, mentioned above, barring effect to foreign expropriation decrees. The Supreme Court again reversed. The opinion by Justice Douglas relied upon the above language of the Belmont case, and added:

"A treaty is a 'Law of the Land' under the supremacy clause (Art. 6, Cl. 2) of the Constitution. Such international compacts and agreements as the Litvinov Assignment have a similar dignity. . . .

". . . the action of New York tends to restore some of the precise irritants which had long affected the relations between these two great nations and which the policy of recognition was designed to eliminate.

". . . If state action could defeat or alter our foreign policy, serious consequences might ensue. The nation as a whole would be held to answer if a State created difficulties with a foreign power . . . Certainly, the conditions for 'enduring friendship' between the nations, which the policy of recognition in this instance was designed to effectuate, are not likely to flourish where, contrary to national policy, a lingering atmosphere of hostility is created by state action.''

REID v. COVERT, 354 U.S. 1 (1957). Mrs. Covert, a civilian, killed her husband, a sergeant at a U.S. air base in England where she was residing with him. Her conviction by court-martial was challenged on the ground that it violated the guaranties of indictment and trial by jury as provided by Article III and the Fifth Amendment. A companion case involved a similar conviction of Mrs. Smith for the murder of her husband in Japan. The convictions were reversed and an opinion by Black, J. (joined by Warren C.J., Douglas and Brennan, JJ.) contained the following discussion regarding the constitutional status of international agreements:

"At the time of Mrs. Covert's alleged offense, an executive agreement was in effect between the United States and Great Britain which permitted United States' military courts to exercise exclusive jurisdiction over offenses committed in Great Britain by American servicemen or their dependents. For its part, the United States agreed that these military courts would be willing and able to try and to punish all offenses against the laws of Great Britain by such persons. In all material respects, the same situation existed in Japan when Mrs. Smith killed her husband. Even though a court-martial does not give an accused trial by jury and other Bill of Rights protections, the Government contends that Art. 2(11) of the UCMJ, insofar as it provides for the military trial of dependents accompanying the armed forces in Great Britain and Japan, can be sustained as legislation which is necessary and proper to carry out the United States' obligations under the international agreements made with those countries. The obvious and decisive answer to this, of course, is that no agreement with a foreign nation can confer power on the Congress, or on any other branch of Government, which is free from the restraints of the Constitution.

"Article VI, the Supremacy Clause of the Constitution, declares:

" 'This Constitution, and the Laws of the United States which shall be made in Pursuance thereof; and all Treaties made, or which shall be made, under the Authority of the United States, shall be the supreme Law of the Land; . . . .'

"There is nothing in this language which intimates that treaties and laws enacted pursuant to them do not have to comply with the provisions of the Constitution.   Nor is there anything in the debates which accompanied the drafting and ratification of the Constitution which even suggests such a result. These debates as well as the history that surrounds the adoption of the treaty provision in Article VI make it clear that the reason treaties were not limited to those made in 'pursuance' of the Constitution was so that the agreements made by the United States under the Articles of Confederation, including the important peace treaties which concluded the Revolutionary War, would remain in effect.   It would be manifestly contrary to the objectives of those who created the Constitution, as well as those who were responsible for the Bill of Rights—let alone alien to our entire constitutional history and tradition—to construe Article VI as permitting the United States to exercise power under an international agreement without observing constitutional prohibitions.   In effect, such construction would permit amendment of that document in a manner not sanctioned by Article V.   The prohibitions of the Constitution were designed to apply to all branches of the National Government and they cannot be nullified by the Executive or by the Executive and the Senate combined. . . .

"There is nothing in Missouri v. Holland, 252 U.S. 416, which is contrary to the position taken here.   There the Court carefully noted that the treaty involved was not inconsistent with any specific provision of the Constitution. The Court was concerned with the Tenth Amendment which reserves to the States or the people all power not delegated to the National Government.   To the extent that the United States can validly make treaties, the people and the States have delegated their power to the National Government and the Tenth Amendment is no barrier. . . ."

THE UNITED NATIONS AND THE TREATY POWER

The UN Charter, Art. 55, states that "The United Nations shall promote . . . universal respect for, and observance of, human rights and fundamental freedoms for all without distinction as to race, sex, language, or religion."   By Article 56, all members "pledge themselves to take joint and separate action in cooperation with the Organization for the achievement of the purposes set forth in Article 55."   In Fujii v. State, 217 P.2d 481 (1950), an intermediate court of appeal in California held the state's discriminatory land law invalid on the ground that the UN Charter was self-executing.   The California Supreme Court affirmed the judgment, but on the ground that the state law violated the Fourteenth Amendment, 38 Cal.2d 718, 242 P.2d 617 (1952).

Work in the United Nations toward the drafting of a Covenant on Human Rights [1] and Genocide Convention, and some of the implications of the *Belmont* and *Pink* cases, generated alarm in some quarters over the scope of the power to make treaties and other international agreements.   As a result, various proposals were made to amend the Constitution.   On March 5, 1956, the Senate Judiciary

---

[1] Chafee, *Federal and State Powers and the U.N. Covenant on Human Rights,* 1951 Wis.L.Rev. 389, 623 (1951); Schwelb, *International Conventions on Human Rights,* 9 Int. & Comp.L.Q. 654 (1960).   A striking example of the impact on internal law of the European Convention on Human Rights is reported in Golsong, *The European Convention in a German Court,* 33 Brit.Yearb. of Int.L. 317 (1957) (deportation of person convicted of crime (homosexuality) who had recently married would violate his right under the Convention "to respect for his private and family life").

Committee favorably reported the following proposed constitutional amendment:

"Sec. 1. A provision of a treaty or other international agreement which conflicts with any provision of this Constitution shall not be of any force or effect.

"Sec. 2. On the question of advising and consenting to the ratification of a treaty, the vote shall be determined by yeas and nays, and the names of the persons voting for and against shall be entered on the journal of the Senate."

The next year Senator Bricker proposed a more detailed amendment which included a provision that, "A treaty or other international agreement shall have legislative effect within the United States as a law thereof only through legislation, except to the extent that the Senate shall provide affirmatively, in its resolution advising and consenting to a treaty, that a treaty shall have legislative effect."

None of the proposed amendments received the requisite two-thirds majority vote.[2]

Does the language in Reid v. Covert, supra, show that no amendment was necessary?

E. THE PROPERTY POWER

KLEPPE v. NEW MEXICO

426 U.S. 529, 96 S.Ct. 2285, 49 L.Ed.2d 34 (1976).

Mr. Justice Marshall delivered the opinion of the Court.

At issue in this case is whether Congress exceeded its powers under the Constitution in enacting the Wild Free-Roaming Horses and Burros Act.

I.

The Wild Free-Roaming Horses and Burros Act (the Act), 85 Stat. 649–651, 16 U.S.C. (Supp. IV) §§ 1331–1340, was enacted in 1971 to protect "all unbranded and unclaimed horses and burros on public lands of the United States," § 2(b) of the Act, 16 U.S.C. § 1332(b), from "capture, branding, harassment, or death." § 1 of the Act, 16 U.S.C. § 1331. The Act provides that all such horses and burros on the public lands administered by the Secretary of the Interior through the Bureau of Land Management (BLM) or by the Secretary of Agriculture through the Forest Service are committed to the jurisdiction of the respective Secretaries, who are "directed to protect and manage [the animals] as components of the public lands . . . in a manner that is designed to achieve and maintain a thriving natural ecological balance on the public lands." § 3(a) of the Act, 16 U.S.C. § 1333(a). If protected horses

---

[2] The debate over the proper scope of the treaty power produced voluminous and heated discussion. See e.g. Holman, *Treaty Law-Making; A Blank Check for Writing a New Constitution,* 36 A.B.A.J. 707 (1950). Finch, *The Treaty Clause Amendment: The Case for the Association,* 38 A.B.A.J. 467 (1952); Hatch, *The Treaty Power and the Constitution; The Case for Amendment,* 40 A.B.A.J. 207 (1954); Chafee, *Amending the Constitution to Cripple Treaties,* 12 La.L.Rev. 345 (1952); Sutherland, *Restricting the Treaty Power,* 65 Harv.L.Rev. 1305 (1952); Dean, *Amending the Treaty Power,* 6 Stanford L.Rev. 589 (1954); Nelson, *Subject-Matter Limitation upon the Treaty-Making Power,* 11 J.Pub.L. 122 (1962); Henkin, *Treaty Makers and the Law Makers: The Law of the Land and Foreign Relations,* 107 U. of Pa.L.Rev. 903 (1959); McLaughlin, *Scope of the Treaty Power in the United States,* 43 Minn.L.Rev. 651 (1959). See also Henkin, *Foreign Affairs and the Constitution* (1972) 129–171.

or burros "stray from public lands onto privately owned land, the owners of such land may inform the nearest federal marshall or agent of the Secretary, who shall arrange to have the animals removed." § 4 of the Act, 16 U.S.C. § 1334. . . .

The differences between the [New Mexico] Livestock Board and the Secretaries came to a head in February 1974. On February 1, 1974, a New Mexico rancher, Kelley Stephenson, was informed by BLM that several un- branded burros had been seen near Taylor Well, where Stephenson watered his cattle. Taylor Well is on federal property, and Stephenson had access to it and some 8,000 surrounding acres only through a grazing permit issued pursuant to the Taylor Grazing Act, 48 Stat. 1270, as amended, 43 U.S.C. § 315b. After BLM made it clear to Stephenson that it would not remove the burros and after he personally inspected the Taylor Well area, Stephenson complained to the Livestock Board that the burros were interfering with his livestock operation by molesting his cattle and eating their feed.

Thereupon the Board rounded up and removed 19 unbranded and un- claimed burros pursuant to the New Mexico Estray Law. Each burro was seized on the public lands of the United States and, as the director of the Board conceded, each burro fit the definition of a wild free-roaming burro under § 2(b) of the Act. App. 43. On February 18, 1974, the Livestock Board, pursuant to its usual practice, sold the burros at a public auction. After the sale, BLM asserted jurisdiction under the Act and demanded that the Board recover the animals and return them to the public lands.

On March 4, 1974, appellees filed a complaint in the United States District Court for the District of New Mexico seeking a declaratory judgment that the Wild Free-Roaming Horses and Burros Act is unconstitutional and an injunction against its enforcement. A three-judge court was convened pursuant to 28 U.S.C. § 2282.

Following an evidentiary hearing, the District Court held the Act unconstitu- tional and permanently enjoined the Secretary of the Interior (the Secretary) from enforcing its provisions. . . . We . . . now reverse.

II.

The Property Clause of the Constitution provides that "Congress shall have Power to dispose of and make all needful Rules and Regulations respecting the Territory or other Property belonging to the United States." U.S. Const., Art. IV, § 3, cl. 2. . . .

For these reasons, Congress determined to preserve and protect the wild free-roaming horses and burros on the public lands of the United States. The question under the Property Clause is whether this determination can be sustained as a "needful" regulation "respecting" the public lands. In answering this question, we must remain mindful that, while courts must eventually pass upon them, determinations under the Property Clause are entrusted primarily to the judgment of Congress.

Appellees argue that the Act cannot be supported by the Property Clause. They contend that the Clause grants Congress essentially two kinds of power: (1) the power to dispose of and make incidental rules regarding the use of federal property; and (2) the power to protect federal property. According to appellees, the first power is not broad enough to support legislation protecting wild animals that live on federal property; and the second power is not implicated since the Act is designed to protect the animals, which are not themselves federal property, and not the public lands. As an initial matter, it is far from clear that the Act was not passed in part to protect the public lands of the United States or that Congress cannot assert a property interest in the regulated horses and burros superior to that of the State. But we need not consider whether the Act can be upheld on either of these grounds, for we reject appellees' narrow reading of the Property Clause. . . .

In brief, beyond the dicta [in two cases], appellees have presented no support for their position that the Clause grants Congress only the power to dispose of, to make incidental rules regarding the use of, and to protect federal property. This failure is hardly surprising, for the Clause, in broad terms, gives Congress the power to determine what are "needful" rules "respecting" the public lands. And while the furthest reaches of the power granted by the Property Clause have not yet been definitively resolved, we have repeatedly observed that "[t]he power over the public lands thus entrusted to Congress is without limitations."

The decided cases have supported this expansive reading. It is the Property Clause, for instance, that provides the basis for governing the territories of the United States. Hooven & Allison Co. v. Evatt, 324 U.S. 652, 673–674 (1945). And even over public land within the States, "[t]he general Government doubtless has a power over its own property analogous to the police power of the several States, and the extent to which it may go in the exercise of such power is measured by the exigencies of the particular case." Camfield v. United States, 167 U.S. 518, 525 (1897). We have noted, for example, that the Property Clause gives Congress the power over the public lands "to control their occupancy and use, to protect them from trespass and injury and to prescribe the conditions upon which others may obtain rights in them . . . ." Utah Power & Light Co. v. United States, 243 U.S. 389, 405 (1917). And we have approved legislation respecting the public lands "[i]f it be found necessary for the protection of the public, or of intending settlers [on the public lands]." Camfield v. United States, 167 U.S., at 525. In short, Congress exercises the powers both of a proprietor and of a legislature over the public domain. Alabama v. Texas, 347 U.S., at 273; Sinclair v. United States, 279 U.S. 263, 297 (1929); United States v. Midwest Oil Co., 236 U.S. 459, 474 (1915). Although the Property Clause does not authorize "an exercise of a general control over public policy in a State," it does permit "an exercise of the complete power which Congress has over particular public property entrusted to it." United States v. San Francisco, 310 U.S., at 30 (footnote omitted). In our view, the "complete power" that Congress has over public lands necessarily includes the power to regulate and protect the wildlife living there. . . . .

F. OTHER FEDERAL POWERS

1. FISCAL POWERS

NORMAN v. BALTIMORE & OHIO RAILROAD, 294 U.S. 240 (1935). By the Joint Resolution of June 5, 1933, Congress attempted to nullify the effect of "gold clauses" [a] in contracts for the payment of money. The Resolution (one of a series of measures relating to the currency) provided that such contracts "shall be discharged, dollar for dollar, in any coin or currency which at the time of payment is legal tender for public and private debts". The Court sustained this measure as applied to contracts previously entered into between private parties. On the question of the power of Congress to establish a monetary system, the Court observed:

". . . It is unnecessary to review the historic controversy as to the extent of this power, or again to go over the ground traversed by the Court in reaching

---

[a] A "gold clause" is a provision in a contract entitling the creditor to payment in currency of equivalent value, in terms of gold, to the currency in circulation at the time the contract was made. The purpose is to protect the creditor against devaluation of the currency.

the conclusion that the Congress may make treasury notes legal tender in payment of debts previously contracted, as well as of those subsequently contracted, whether that authority be exercised in course of war or in time of peace.[b] Knox v. Lee, 12 Wall. 457; Juilliard v. Greenman, 110 U.S. 421. We need only consider certain postulates upon which that conclusion rested.

"The Constitution grants to the Congress power 'To coin money, regulate the value thereof, and of foreign coin.' Art. I, § 8, par. 5. But the Court in the legal tender cases did not derive from that express grant alone the full authority of the Congress in relation to the currency. The Court found the source of that authority in all the related powers conferred upon the Congress and appropriate to achieve 'the great objects for which the government was framed,'—'a national government, with sovereign powers.' McCulloch v. Maryland, 4 Wheat. 316, 404–407; Knox v. Lee, supra, pp. 532, 536; Juilliard v. Greenman, supra, p. 438. The broad and comprehensive national authority over the subjects of revenue, finance and currency is derived from the aggregate of the powers granted to the Congress, embracing the powers to lay and collect taxes, to borrow money, to regulate commerce with foreign nations and among the several States, to coin money, regulate the value thereof, and of foreign coin, and fix the standards of weights and measures, and the added express power 'to make all laws which shall be necessary and proper for carrying into execution' the other enumerated powers. Juilliard v. Greenman, supra, pp. 439, 440.

"The Constitution 'was designed to provide the same currency, having a uniform legal value in all the States.' It was for that reason that the power to regulate the value of money was conferred upon the Federal government, while the same power, as well as the power to emit bills of credit, was withdrawn from the States. The States cannot declare what shall be money, or regulate its value. Whatever power there is over the currency is vested in the Congress. Knox v. Lee, supra, p. 545. Another postulate of the decision in that case is that the Congress has power 'to enact that the government's promises to pay money shall be, for the time being, equivalent in value to the representative of value determined by the coinage acts, or to multiples thereof.' Id., p. 553. Or, as was stated in the *Juilliard* case, supra, p. 447, the Congress is empowered 'to issue the obligations of the United States in such form, and to impress upon them such qualities as currency for the purchase of merchandise and the payment of debts, as accord with the usage of sovereign governments.' The authority to impose requirements of uniformity and parity is an essential feature of this control of the currency. The Congress is authorized to provide 'a sound and uniform currency for the country,' and to 'secure the benefit of it to the people by appropriate legislation.' Veazie Bank v. Fenno, 8 Wall. 533, 549.

. . . .

"Dealing with the specific question as to the effect of the legal tender acts upon contracts made before their passage, that is, those for the payment of money generally, the Court, in the legal tender cases, recognized the possible consequences of such enactments in frustrating the expected performance of contracts,—in rendering them 'fruitless or partially fruitless.' The Court pointed out that the exercise of the powers of Congress may affect 'apparent

---

[b] The Legal Tender Acts, passed during the Civil War, made United States notes (greenbacks) legal tender for debts, with certain exceptions. The acts were held invalid as applied to antecedent debts in Hepburn v. Griswold, 8 Wall. 603 (1869). The Court (then composed of eight justices) rendered the decision by a 5 to 3 vote. The Hepburn decision was overruled (5 to 4) in Legal Tender Cases, 12 Wall. 457 (1871), President Grant having appointed two new members of the Court, one of whom (Strong, J.) wrote the opinion. The struggles in the Court over the legal tender issue are described in Fairman, *Mr. Justice Miller and the Supreme Court,* Chap. 7 (1939) and the same author's Reconstruction and Reunion 1864–88, Part I, 677–775 (1971). See also Ratner, *Was the Supreme Court Packed by President Grant?,* 50 Pol.Sci.Q. 343 (1935).

obligations' of contracts in many ways. The Congress may pass bankruptcy acts. The Congress may declare war, or, even in peace, pass non-intercourse acts, or direct an embargo, which may operate seriously upon existing contracts. And the Court reasoned that if the legal tender acts 'were justly chargeable with impairing contract obligations, they would not, for that reason, be forbidden, unless a different rule is to be applied to them from that which has hitherto prevailed in the construction of other powers granted by the fundamental law.' The conclusion was that contracts must be understood as having been made in reference to the possible exercise of the rightful authority of the Government, and that no obligation of a contract 'can extend to the defeat' of that authority. Knox v. Lee, supra, pp. 549–551. . . ."

2. NATURALIZATION

Article I, § 8, Clause 4, provides that Congress shall have power to "establish a uniform Rule of Naturalization." From the beginning the Court said that the power of Naturalization is vested exclusively in Congress to the exclusion of the states. Chirac v. Chirac, 2 Wheat. (15 U.S.) 259, 269 (1817). The Court has also said that "Naturalization is a privilege, to be given, qualified or withheld as Congress may determine, and which the alien may claim as of right only upon compliance with the terms which Congress imposes." United States v. Macintosh, 283 U.S. 605, 615 (1931). ·

The problems of defining citizenship and of expatriation and denaturalization will be considered in Chapter 9, infra.

3. REGULATION OF ALIENS

KLEINDIENST v. MANDEL, 408 U.S. 753 (1972). The Court upheld the action of the Attorney General in refusing to waive a statutory provision excluding aliens who advocate world communism and grant a visa to a person invited to speak to an academic meeting in the United States. The Court noted that "Mandel personally, as an unadmitted and nonresident alien, had no constitutional right of entry to this country as a nonimmigrant or otherwise." In response to the argument that the first amendment rights of persons in this country who wished to hear Mandel were involved, the Court said, in part:

"Recognition that First Amendment rights are implicated, however, is not dispositive of our inquiry here. In accord with ancient principles of the international law of nation-states, the Court in The Chinese Exclusion Case, 130 U.S. 581, 609 (1889), and in Fong Yue Ting v. United States, 149 U.S. 698 (1893), held broadly . . . that the power to exclude aliens is 'inherent in sovereignty, necessary for maintaining normal international relations and defending the country against foreign encroachments and dangers—a power to be exercised exclusively by the political branches of government . . . .' Since that time, the Court's general reaffirmations of this principle have been legion. The Court without exception has sustained Congress' 'plenary power to make rules for the admission of aliens and to exclude those who possess those characteristics which Congress has forbidden.' Boutilier v. Immigration and Naturalization Service, 387 U.S. 118, 123 (1967). '[O]ver no conceivable subject is the legislative power of Congress more complete than it is over' the admission of aliens. Oceanic Navigation Co. v. Stranahan, 214 U.S. 320, 339 (1909). In Lem Moon Sing v. United States, 158 U.S. 538, 547 (1895), the first Mr. Justice Harlan said: 'The power of Congress to exclude aliens altogether from the United States, or to prescribe the terms and conditions upon which they may come to this country, and to have its declared policy in that regard enforced exclusively through executive officers, without judicial intervention, is settled by our previous adjudications.' Mr. Justice Frankfurter ably articulated this history in Galvan v. Press, 347 U.S. 522 (1954), a deportation case, and we can do no better. After suggesting, that 'much could be said for the view' that due process places some limitations on congressional power in this area 'were we writing on a clean slate,' he continued:

'But the slate is not clean. As to the extent of the power of Congress under review, there is not merely "a page of history" . . . but a whole volume. Policies pertaining to the entry of aliens and their right to remain here are peculiarly concerned with the political conduct of government. In the enforcement of these policies, the Executive Branch of the Government must respect the procedural safeguards of due process . . .. But that the formulation of these policies is entrusted exclusively to Congress has become about as firmly embedded in the legislative and judicial tissues of our body politic as any aspect of our government. . . .'

'We are not prepared to deem ourselves wiser or more sensitive to human rights than our predecessors, especially those who have been most zealous in protecting civil liberties under the Constitution, and must therefore under our constitutional system recognize congressional power in dealing with aliens . . . .'

"We are not inclined in the present context to reconsider this line of cases. . . ." a

4. The Admiralty Power

Article III, § 2 provides that "the judicial power shall extend . . . to all cases of admiralty and maritime jurisdiction . . .." Although in form only a grant of jurisdiction to the courts, the admiralty clause early became recognized as a basis for national legislation. "The framers of the Constitution did not contemplate that the maritime law should remain unalterable. The purpose was to place the entire subject, including its substantive as well as its procedural features, under national control. From the beginning the grant was regarded as implicitly investing legislative power for that purpose in the United States. When the Constitution was adopted, the existing maritime law became the law of the United States subject to power in Congress to modify or supplement it as experience or changing conditions might require. But in amending and revising the maritime law, the Congress necessarily acts within a sphere restricted by the concept of the admiralty and maritime jurisdiction." Detroit Trust Co. v. The Barlum, 293 U.S. 21, 43–44 (1934).

This interpretation of the admiralty clause sustained the power of Congress to legislate with respect to events or transactions occurring on navigable waters of the United States (defined as including only those capable in fact of being used for interstate or foreign commerce) whether or not the particular event or transaction occurred in interstate commerce. Thus in In re Garnett, 141 U.S. 1, 12 (1891), the Court upheld the Limited Liability Act as applied to all vessels on inland waters, saying:

"It is unnecessary to invoke the power given to Congress to regulate commerce with foreign nations, and among the several States, in order to find authority to pass the law in question. The Act of Congress which limits the liability of ship owners was passed in amendment of the maritime law of the country, and the power to make such amendments is co-extensive with that law. It is not confined to the boundaries or class of subjects which limit and characterize the power to regulate commerce; but, in maritime matters, it extends to all matters and places to which the maritime law extends."

---

a The constitutional limitations upon the power of Congress to classify aliens who have been admitted to the country and impose special burdens on them is considered in Chapter 11, infra.

For a discussion of the early development, see Note, *From Judicial Grant to Legislative Power: The Admiralty Clause in the Nineteenth Century*, 67 Harv.L.Rev. 1214 (1954).

It may be that this is all ancient history of minimal modern relevance to federal power. It has been suggested that "the conception of the commerce power that now prevails would probably suffice, without reference to any inference from the admiralty judicial power, to validate every statutory enactment in question." Gilmore & Black, *The Law of Admiralty* 47 (2d ed. 1975). This suggestion is reinforced by the recent case of Kaiser Aetna v. United States, 444 U.S. 164, 170–174 (1979), in which the Court said: "Reference to the navigability of a waterway adds little if anything to the breadth of Congress' regulatory power over interstate commerce. It has long been settled that Congress has extensive authority over this Nation's waters under the Commerce Clause." The Court added: "[A] wide spectrum of economic activities 'affect' interstate commerce and thus are susceptible of congressional regulation under the Commerce Clause irrespective of whether navigation, or, indeed, water, is involved. The cases that discuss Congress' paramount authority to regulate waters used in interstate commerce are consequently best understood when viewed in terms of more traditional Commerce Clause analysis than by reference to whether the stream in fact is capable of supporting navigation or may be characterized as 'navigable water of the United States.' " [1]

[1] Congress also has extensive power over American Indians based on its power to regulate commerce "with the Indian Tribes." No attempt is made to look at the work of the Supreme Court in this area. See generally *F. Cohen, Handbook of Federal Indian Law* (1982 ed.)

Chapter 5

THE SCOPE OF STATE POWER—REGULATION

Introduction. In Chapter 4 we explored the early Nineteenth Century dispute in the Supreme Court between those who read the commerce clause as granting to Congress exclusive power to regulate interstate commerce and those who contended that the grant was merely concurrent leaving full power in the states to regulate in the absence of conflicting federal regulation. In Cooley v. Board of Port Wardens, 12 How. 299 (1851), set out supra p. 178, the Court reached a compromise position under which the commerce clause would permit some state regulations of interstate commerce but forbid others even in the absence of federal regulation. Ever since *Cooley* the Court has been struggling to find a formula to determine when state regulations of commerce are permissible.

In *Cooley* the Court attempted to resolve the problem by looking at the subjects being regulated. "Whatever subjects of this power are in their nature national, or admit only of one uniform system, or plan of regulation may justly be said to be of such a nature as to require exclusive legislation by Congress." Other subjects (such as harbor pilots, in that case) are of such a nature "as to leave no doubt of the superior fitness and propriety, not to say the absolute necessity, of different systems of regulation, drawn from local knowledge and experience, and conformed to local wants."

Later cases were more likely to speak in terms of "direct" burdens on commerce being forbidden, "indirect" burdens permitted. Thus in Erb v. Morasch, 177 U.S. 584 (1900) the Court said that a city ordinance regulating the speed of trains was "even as to interstate trains, one only indirectly affecting interstate commerce, and is within the power of the state until at least Congress shall take action in the matter." On the other hand, in Shafer v. Farmers Grain Co., 268 U.S. 189 (1925) the Court held invalid a state regulation of the purchase of wheat for interstate shipment because it constituted a "direct burden" on interstate commerce.

More recently the Court has talked in terms of "balancing" the state interest served by the regulation against the burden imposed on interstate commerce. The Court summarized this approach in the following statement in Pike v. Bruce Church, 397 U.S. 137, 142 (1970), a statement often quoted by the Court in its more recent cases:

"Although the criteria for determining the validity of state statutes affecting interstate commerce have been variously stated, the general rule that emerges can be phrased as follows: Where the statute regulates evenhandedly to effectuate a legitimate local public interest, and its effects on interstate commerce are only incidental, it will be upheld unless the burden imposed on such commerce is clearly excessive in relation to the putative local benefits. Huron Cement Co. v. Detroit, 362 U.S. 440, 443. If a legitimate local purpose is found, then the question becomes one of degree. And the extent of the burden that will be tolerated will of course depend on the nature of the local interest involved, and on whether it could be promoted as well with a lesser impact on interstate activities. Occasionally the Court has candidly undertaken a balancing approach in resolving these issues. Southern Pacific Co. v. Arizona, 325 U.S. 761, but more frequently it has spoken in terms of 'direct' and 'indirect' effects and burdens. See e.g., Shafer v. Farmers Grain Co. . . ."

In Public Utilities Comm'n v. Attleboro Steam & Elec. Co., 273 U.S. 83 (1927), the Court had held that a state could not regulate sales at wholesale by a local electric utility to an out-of-state customer, on the ground that regulation of interstate wholesale sales was a "direct" burden on interstate commerce. In Arkansas Elec. Coop. Corp. v. Arkansas Public Serv. Comm'n, 461 U.S. 375 (1983), the Court overruled *Attleboro,* holding that state regulation of interstate wholesale sales was governed by the balancing approach of Pike v. Bruce Church, Inc. Justice Brennan's opinion for the Court stated:

". . . Bright lines are important and necessary in many areas of the law, including constitutional law . . .

"*Attleboro* and its predecessors are by no means judicial atrocities, plainly wrong at the time they were decided. In the first place, it is not entirely insignificant, . . . that those cases were decided in a day before Congress had already spoken with some breadth on the subject of utility regulation. This Court was in 1927 the sole authority safeguarding federal interests over a wide range of state utility regulation. Under these circumstances, drawing a fairly restrictive bright line may have made considerable sense. . . . Second, the judicial turn of mind apparent in *Attleboro,* although problematic in many respects, can also be a healthy counterweight in many contexts to an otherwise too-easy dilution of guarantees contained in the Constitution. Nevertheless, *Attleboro* can no longer be thought to provide the sole standard by which to decide this case . . . ."

In this chapter the commerce clause cases are divided into two major groups. Section 1 deals with state regulation of transportation. Section 2 considers state regulation of production and trade. Section 3 considers the limitations imposed on state regulation by the privileges and immunities clause of Art. IV and the special rules governing regulation of alcoholic beverages resulting from the twenty-first amendment. Section 4 examines the impact of the supremacy clause.

SECTION 1. IMPLIED RESTRICTIONS OF THE COMMERCE CLAUSE—TRANSPORTATION

STATE ECONOMIC REGULATION OF TRANSPORTATION BUSINESSES

The Supreme Court early took the position that since the right to carry on interstate commerce was conferred by the Constitution, the states had no power to require licenses as conditions of carrying on such commerce. Thus in Crutcher v. Kentucky, 141 U.S. 47 (1891) the Court held invalid a state statute requiring agents of foreign express companies to secure a license that could be secured on payment of a nominal fee and on showing a minimum level of assets. The state argued that the statute was necessary to protect citizens against unreliable and insolvent businesses. The Court responded: "To carry on interstate commerce is not a franchise or a privilege granted by the State; it is a right which every citizen of the United States is entitled to exercise under the Constitution and laws of the United States. . . . We have repeatedly decided that a state law is unconstitutional which requires a party to take out a license for carrying on interstate commerce. . . ." The principal modern application of that rule was in the case which follows:

BUCK v. KUYKENDALL, 267 U.S. 307 (1925), invalidated a statute of the state of Washington requiring all common carriers for hire using highways in the state to obtain certificates of convenience and necessity. The state denied a certificate to a motor carrier operating between Seattle, Washington, and Portland, Oregon on the ground that the route was already adequately served. (No federal regulation of motor carriers was in existence at the time.) The Supreme Court, in an opinion by Justice Brandeis, held the state had no power to require such a license from an interstate carrier:

> "It may be assumed that section 4 of the state statute is consistent with the Fourteenth Amendment; and also, that appropriate state regulations adopted primarily to promote safety upon the highways and conservation in their use are not obnoxious to the commerce clause, where the indirect burden imposed upon interstate commerce is not unreasonable. . . . The provision here in question is of a different character. Its primary purpose is not regulation with a view to safety or to conservation of the highways, but the prohibition of competition. It determines, not the manner of use, but the persons by whom the highways may be used. It prohibits such use to some persons, while permitting it to others for the same purpose and in the same manner. Moreover, it determines whether the prohibition shall be applied by resort, through state officials, to a test which is peculiarly within the province of the federal action—the existence of adequate facilities for conducting interstate commerce. . . .

However, the Court has upheld license requirements in cases where the state has not been asserting the authority to prevent the movement of traffic interstate. In California v. Thompson, 313 U.S. 109 (1941) the Court held valid a California statute requiring agents engaged in selling transportation on the public highways of the state to obtain a license and post a bond. Criminal prosecution was brought against an unlicensed agent who sold interstate transportation in cars not operated as regular carriers; federal regulation of motor carriers which began in 1935 did not apply to such persons. The Court said that the state statute "is not shown to be other than what on its face it appears to be, a measure to safeguard the members of the public desiring to secure transportation by motor vehicle, who are peculiarly unable to protect themselves from fraud and overreaching of those engaged in a business notoriously subject to those abuses. . . . Fraudulent or unconscionable conduct of those so engaged which is injurious to their patrons, is peculiarly a subject of local concern and the appropriate subject of local regulation".

The Court disclaimed any intent to overrule Crutcher v. Kentucky, supra, saying: "The present case is not one of prohibiting interstate commerce or licensing it on conditions which restrict or obstruct it. Cf. Crutcher v. Kentucky, 141 U.S. 47; Dahmke-Walker Co. v. Bondurant, 257 U.S. 282. For here the regulation is applied to one who is not himself engaged in the transportation but who acts only as broker or intermediary in negotiating a transportation contract between the passengers and the carrier. The license required of those engaged in such business is not conditioned upon any control or restriction of the movement of the traffic interstate but only on the good character and responsibility of those engaged locally as transportation brokers."

The federal government now imposes economic regulations on all forms of interstate transportation and communication. Problems such as those involved in *Buck* no longer arise. Thus in 1935 Congress enacted the Federal Motor Carrier Act, which became Part II of the Interstate Commerce Act and gave the Interstate Commerce Commission wide power to regulate common carriers and contract carriers engaged in interstate transportation by motor vehicle. 49 U.S.C. §§ 301–327. It is now the I.C.C. which determines whether licenses to carry on such transportation shall be issued.

STATE SAFETY REGULATIONS AND
INTERSTATE TRANSPORTATION

A much more enduring problem has been that of determining the circumstances under which states may impose regulations on interstate carriers in the interests of safety. Congress was slow to move into the field of safety regulation and hence for a long time the obvious public interest in safety was served only by state regulation. In recent years federal safety regulations have become far more extensive, but the federal government has not purported to assert exclusive authority. As a result there is a continuing docket of litigation involving state safety regulations and the question whether the commerce clause of its own force prohibits them.

Originally, the Court upheld most state safety regulations, but it had difficulty in articulating coherent doctrinal reasons. A common reason given in the early cases for upholding the state regulation was that it only "indirectly" affected interstate commerce. In Erb v. Morasch, 177 U.S. 584 (1900), e.g., the Court held that a city ordinance regulating the speed of trains could be applied to interstate trains because it only "indirectly" affected commerce. The Court was not able, however, to explain why some regulations were direct and others indirect and it soon became apparent that other factors were at work. A principal example of the problem arose in litigation challenging a Georgia statute requiring all trains to check their speed at grade crossings so that they might stop if necessary to avoid hitting persons or vehicles crossing the tracks. Persons injured at grade crossings sued the railroads, seeking to base liability on the failure of the railroad to comply with the statute. In Southern Ry. Co. v. King, 217 U.S. 524 (1910) the Court upheld the sustaining of a demurrer to an answer by the railroad which merely alleged that the statute was in violation of the commerce clause and imposed a direct burden on interstate traffic.

The Court said the averments were mere conclusions. "They set forth no facts which would make the operation of the statute unconstitutional. They do not show the number or location of the crossings at which the railway company would be required to check the speed of its trains, so as to interfere with their successful operation. For aught that appears as allegations of fact in this answer, the crossing at which this injury happened may have been so located and of such dangerous character as to make the slackening of trains at that point necessary to the safety of those using the public highway, and a statute making such requirement only a reasonable police regulation, and not an unlawful attempt to regulate or hinder interstate commerce." In a later case of the same type, Seaboard Air Line Ry. Co. v. Blackwell, 244 U.S. 310 (1917), the railroad's answer alleged that the train involved was running in interstate commerce from Atlanta, Georgia, to other points in Georgia and South Carolina; that in the 123-mile run from Atlanta to the state line there were 124 crossings at which the statute required each train to check its speed; that three minutes would be consumed at each crossing, or about six hours in all, thus increasing the running time between Atlanta and the state line from the scheduled 4½ to a total of 10½ hours. The Court stated that the facts alleged "compel the conclusion that the statute is a direct burden upon interstate commerce, and, being such, is unlawful". Judgment for the plaintiff was reversed.

The Court was even willing to sustain state licensing regulations, at least when they did not totally exclude carriers from interstate commerce, if reasonably necessary to promote safety. The following case, which should be contrasted with Buck v. Kuykendall, supra, is illustrative.

BRADLEY v. PUBLIC UTILITIES COMMISSION, 289 U.S. 92 (1933). The Ohio Public Utilities Commission denied Bradley's application for a certificate of public convenience and necessity to operate a motor carrier service over State Route No. 20 from Cleveland to Flint, Michigan. After a hearing, the Commission determined that Route 20 was so badly congested that adding Bradley's service "would create and maintain an excessive and undue hazard to the safety and security of the traveling public." The Supreme Court unanimously upheld the denial of the certificate. First, the Court noted that the order did not exclude Bradley from operating in interstate commerce. He had failed to apply for an alternate route and had not shown that a feasible route with less congestion was not available.

Second, the Court said:

"It is contended that an order denying to a common carrier by motor a certificate to engage in interstate transportation necessarily violates the Commerce Clause. The argument is that under the rule declared in Buck v. Kuykendall, 267 U.S. 307, . . . an interstate carrier is entitled to a certificate as of right; and that hence the reason for the commission's refusal and its purpose are immaterial. In those cases, safety was doubtless promoted when the certificate was denied, because intensification of traffic was thereby prevented. . . . But there promotion of safety was merely an incident of the denial. Its purpose was to prevent competition deemed undesirable. The test employed was the adequacy of existing transportation facilities; and since the transportation in question was interstate, denial of the certificate invaded the province of Congress. In the case at bar, the purpose of the denial was to promote safety; and the test employed was congestion of the highway. The effect of the denial upon interstate commerce was merely an incident.

"Protection against accidents, as against crime, presents ordinarily a local problem. Regulation to ensure safety is an exercise of the police power. It is primarily a state function, whether the locus be private property or the public highways. Congress has not dealt with the subject. Hence, even where the motorcars are used exclusively in interstate commerce, a state may freely exact registration of the vehicle and an operator's license, Hendrick v. Maryland, 235 U.S. 610, 622 . . .. The state may exclude from the public highways vehicles engaged exclusively in interstate commerce, if of a size deemed dangerous to the public safety, Morris v. Duby, 274 U.S. 135, 144; Sproles v. Binford, 286 U.S. 374, 389–390. Safety may require that no additional vehicle be admitted to the highway. The Commerce Clause is not violated by denial of the certificate to the appellant, if upon adequate evidence denial is deemed necessary to promote the public safety." [a]

The balance of this section will present cases from 1938 to the present involving state safety regulations as applied to interstate transportation. The student should consider whether there is a coherent doctrine which explains the result in these cases.

SOUTH CAROLINA STATE HIGHWAY DEPARTMENT v. BARNWELL BROTHERS, 303 U.S. 177 (1938). A South Carolina statute forbade the use on state highways of motor trucks whose width exceeded 90 inches and whose weight including load exceeded 20,000 pounds. A federal district court weighed conflicting evidence and determined that the width and weight limitations were more restrictive than needed to protect the highways of the state and

[a] For an excellent discussion of the *Buck* and *Bradley* cases as well as state motor carrier regulation prior to the adoption of the Federal Motor Carrier Act in 1935, see Kauper, *State Regulation of Interstate Motor Carriers,* 31 Mich.L.Rev. 920, 1097 (1933). A later brief discussion will be found in Swerer, *State Regulation of Interstate Transportation by Motor Carriers,* 16 Rocky Mt.L.Rev. 1 (1943).

the users of such highways. It also determined that the limitations imposed substantial burdens on interstate commerce since 85 to 90 percent of the trucks used in interstate commerce were 96 inches wide and of a gross weight when loaded in excess of 20,000 pounds.

The Supreme Court reversed in an opinion by Justice Stone, stating:

"While the constitutional grant to Congress of power to regulate interstate commerce has been held to operate of its own force to curtail state power in some measure,[2] it did not forestall all state action affecting interstate commerce.
. . .

"The commerce clause by its own force, prohibits discrimination against interstate commerce, whatever its form or method, and the decisions of this Court have recognized that there is scope for its like operation when state legislation nominally of local concern is in point of fact aimed at interstate commerce, or by its necessary operation is a means of gaining a local benefit by throwing the attendant burdens on those without the state. . . . The commerce clause has also been thought to set its own limitation upon state control of interstate rail carriers so as to preclude the subordination of the efficiency and convenience of interstate traffic to local service requirements.

"But the present case affords no occasion for saying that the bare possession of power by Congress to regulate the interstate traffic forces the states to conform to standards which Congress might, but has not adopted, or curtails their power to take measures to insure the safety and conservation of their highways which may be applied to like traffic moving intrastate. Few subjects of state regulation are so peculiarly of local concern as is the use of state highways. There are few, local regulation of which is so inseparable from a substantial effect on interstate commerce. Unlike the railroads, local highways are built, owned, and maintained by the state or its municipal subdivisions. The state has a primary and immediate concern in their safe and economical administration. The present regulations, or any others of like purpose, if they are to accomplish their end, must be applied alike to interstate and intrastate traffic both moving in large volume over the highways. The fact that they affect alike shippers in interstate and intrastate commerce in large number within as well as without the state is a safeguard against their abuse.
. . .

"Congress, in the exercise of its plenary power to regulate interstate commerce, may determine whether the burdens imposed on it by state regulation, otherwise permissible, are too great, and may, by legislation designed to secure uniformity or in other respects to protect the national interest in the commerce, curtail to some extent the state's regulatory power. But that is a legislative, not a judicial, function, to be performed in the light of the congressional judgment of what is appropriate regulation of interstate commerce, and the extent to which, in that field, state power and local interests should be required to yield to the national authority and interest. In the absence of such legislation the judicial function, under the commerce clause, as well as the Fourteenth Amendment, stops with the inquiry whether the state Legislature in adopting regulations such as the present has acted within its

[2] State regulations affecting interstate commerce, whose purpose or effect is to gain for those within the state an advantage at the expense of those without, or to burden those out of the state without any corresponding advantage to those within, have been thought to impinge upon the constitutional prohibition even though Congress has not acted . . . .

Underlying the stated rule has been the thought, often expressed in judicial opinion, that when the regulation is of such a character that its burden falls principally upon those without the state, legislative action is not likely to be subjected to those political restraints which are normally exerted on legislation where it affects adversely some interests within the state . . . .

province, and whether the means of regulation chosen are reasonably adapted to the end sought. . . .

"Here the first inquiry has already been resolved by our decisions that a state may impose nondiscriminatory restrictions with respect to the character of motor vehicles moving in interstate commerce as a safety measure and as a means of securing the economical use of its highways. In resolving the second, courts do not sit as Legislatures, either state or national. . . . When the action of a Legislature is within the scope of its power, fairly debatable questions as to its reasonableness, wisdom, and propriety are not for the determination of courts, but for the legislative body, on which rests the duty and responsibility of decision. . . . It is not any the less a legislative power committed to the states because it affects interstate commerce, and courts are not any the more entitled, because interstate commerce is affected, to substitute their own for the legislative judgment. . . .

"Since the adoption of one weight or width regulation, rather than another, is a legislative, not a judicial, choice, its constitutionality is not to be determined by weighing in the judicial scales the merits of the legislative choice and rejecting it if the weight of evidence presented in court appears to favor a different standard. . . . Being a legislative judgment it is presumed to be supported by facts known to the Legislature unless facts judicially known or proved preclude that possibility. Hence, in reviewing the present determination, we examine the record, not to see whether the findings of the court below are supported by evidence, but to ascertain upon the whole record whether it is possible to say that the legislative choice is without rational basis. . . . Not only does the record fail to exclude that possibility but it shows affirmatively that there is adequate support for the legislative judgment. . . ."

SOUTHERN PACIFIC CO. v. ARIZONA, 325 U.S. 761 (1945). An Arizona law forbade the operation of railroad trains of more than fourteen passenger or seventy freight cars and authorized the state to recover a monetary penalty for each violation. In 1940 the state brought suit against the railroad in an Arizona state court seeking to recover the statutory penalties for violation of the act. An extended trial was had after which the trial court made detailed findings of fact as to the extent to which the statute burdened commerce and the extent to which it benefited state interests and concluded that the statute was unconstitutional. The Arizona Supreme Court reversed, directing entry of judgment for the state. The Supreme Court in an opinion by Chief Justice Stone, reversed, stating in part:

". . . [E]ver since Gibbons v. Ogden, 9 Wheat. 1, the states have not been deemed to have authority to impede substantially the free flow of commerce from state to state, or to regulate those phases of the national commerce which, because of the need of national uniformity, demand that their regulation, if any, be prescribed by a single authority.[2] Cooley v. Board of Wardens, supra. . . . Whether or not this long recognized distribution of power between the national and the state governments is predicated upon the implications of the commerce clause itself, Minnesota Rate Cases, supra, 399, 400; South Carolina Highway Dept. v. Barnwell Bros., supra, 185 . . . or upon the presumed intention of Congress, where Congress has not spoken, . . . the result is the same.

"In the application of these principles some enactments may be found to be plainly within and others plainly without state power. But between these

---

[2] In applying this rule the Court has often recognized that to the extent that the burden of state regulation falls on interests outside the state, it is unlikely to be alleviated by the operation of those political restraints normally exerted when interests within the state are affected. . . .

extremes lies the infinite variety of cases in which regulation of local matters may also operate as a regulation of commerce, in which reconciliation of the conflicting claims of state and national power is to be attained only by some appraisal and accommodation of the competing demands of the state and national interests involved. . . .

. . .

"Congress has undoubted power to redefine the distribution of power over interstate commerce. It may either permit the states to regulate the commerce in a manner which would otherwise not be permissible, In re Rahrer, supra, 140 U.S. 561, 562, . . . or exclude state regulation even of matters of peculiarly local concern which nevertheless affect interstate commerce. . . .

"But in general Congress has left it to the courts to formulate the rules thus interpreting the commerce clause in its application, doubtless because it has appreciated the destructive consequences to the commerce of the nation if their protection were withdrawn, Gwin, etc., Inc. v. Henneford, supra, 305 U.S. 441, and has been aware that in their application state laws will not be invalidated without the support of relevant factual material which will 'afford a sure basis' for an informed judgment. . . .

"Hence the matters for ultimate determination here are the nature and extent of the burden which the state regulation of interstate trains, adopted as a safety measure, imposes on interstate commerce, and whether the relative weights of the state and national interests involved are such as to make inapplicable the rule, generally observed, that the free flow of interstate commerce and its freedom from local restraints in matters requiring uniformity of regulation are interests safeguarded by the commerce clause from state interference.

"While this Court is not bound by the findings of the state court, and may determine for itself the facts of a case upon which an asserted federal right depends, the facts found by the state trial court showing the nature of the interstate commerce involved, and the effect upon it of the train limit law, are not seriously questioned. Its findings with respect to the need for and effect of the statute as a safety measure, although challenged in some particulars which we do not regard as material to our decision, are likewise supported by evidence. Taken together the findings supply an adequate basis for decision of the constitutional issue.

. . .

"The unchallenged findings leave no doubt that the Arizona Train Limit Law imposes a serious burden on the interstate commerce conducted by appellant. It materially impedes the movement of appellant's interstate trains through that state and interposes a substantial obstruction to the national policy proclaimed by Congress, to promote adequate, economical and efficient railway transportation service. . . . Enforcement of the law in Arizona, while train lengths remain unregulated or are regulated by varying standards in other states, must inevitably result in an impairment of uniformity of efficient railroad operation because the railroads are subjected to regulation which is not uniform in its application. Compliance with a state statute limiting train lengths requires interstate trains of a length lawful in other states to be broken up and reconstituted as they enter each state according as it may impose varying limitations upon train lengths. The alternative is for the carrier to conform to the lowest train limit restriction of any of the states through which its trains pass, whose laws thus control the carriers' operations both within and without the regulating state.

. . .

"The trial court found that the Arizona law had no reasonable relation to safety, and made train operation more dangerous. Examination of the evidence and the detailed findings makes it clear that this conclusion was rested on facts found which indicate that such increased danger of accident and personal injury as may result from the greater length of trains is more than offset by the increase in the number of accidents resulting from the larger number of trains when train lengths are reduced. In considering the effect of the statute as a safety measure, therefore, the factor of controlling significance for present purposes is not whether there is basis for the conclusion of the Arizona Supreme Court that the increase in length of trains beyond the statutory maximum has an adverse effect upon safety of operation. The decisive question is whether in the circumstances the total effect of the law as a safety measure in reducing accidents and casualties is so slight or problematical as not to outweigh the national interest in keeping interstate commerce free from interferences which seriously impede it and subject it to local regulation which does not have a uniform effect on the interstate train journey which it interrupts.

.   .   .

"Here we conclude that the state does go too far. Its regulation of train lengths, admittedly obstructive to interstate train operation, and having a seriously adverse effect on transportation efficiency and economy, passes beyond what is plainly essential for safety since it does not appear that it will lessen rather than increase the danger of accident. Its attempted regulation of the operation of interstate trains cannot establish nation-wide control such as is essential to the maintenance of an efficient transportation system, which Congress alone can prescribe. The state interest cannot be preserved at the expense of the national interest by an enactment which regulates interstate train lengths without securing such control, which is a matter of national concern. To this the interest of the state here asserted is subordinate.

.   .   .

"South Carolina State Highway Dept. v. Barnwell Bros., supra, was concerned with the power of the state to regulate the weight and width of motor cars passing interstate over its highways, a legislative field over which the state has a far more extensive control than over interstate railroads. In that case, .   .   . we were at pains to point out that there are few subjects of state regulation affecting interstate commerce which are so peculiarly of local concern as is the use of the state's highways.   .   .   ."

Justices Black and Douglas dissented. Justice Black stated that the ruling of the Court "makes it necessary for a judge to hear all the evidence offered as to why a legislature passed a law and to make findings of fact as to the validity of those reasons. If under today's ruling a court does make findings, as to a danger contrary to the findings of the legislature, and the evidence heard 'lends support' to those findings, a court can then invalidate the law. In this respect, the Arizona County Court acted, and this Court today is acting, as a 'super-legislature.' "

Justice Douglas said: "My view has been that the courts should intervene only where the state legislation discriminated against interstate commerce or was out of harmony with laws which Congress had enacted."

BIBB v. NAVAJO FREIGHT LINES, INC., 359 U.S. 520 (1959). An Illinois statute required the use of a certain type of rear fender mudguard on trucks and trailers operating on highways in the state. The statute made illegal the use of straight mudflaps which were legal in at least 45 states and required in the state of Arkansas. A federal district court held the statute invalid as placing an undue burden on interstate commerce. The Supreme Court affirmed in an opinion by Justice Douglas.

Justice Douglas commenced his opinion by citing *Barnwell* for the proposition that regulation of highways is peculiarly local and that policy decisions are for the state legislature. "Unless we can conclude on the whole record that the 'total effect of the law as a safety measure in reducing accidents and casualties is so slight or problematic as not to outweigh the national interest in keeping interstate commerce free from interferences which seriously impede it' (Southern Pacific v. Arizona . . .) we must uphold the statute."

Justice Douglas then reviewed the evidence as to the cost of equipping all interstate vehicles with contour mudguards and as to the relative safety of such mudguards and conventional mudflaps. He concluded that review by saying: "If we had here only a question whether the cost of adjusting an interstate operation to these new local safety regulations prescribed by Illinois unduly burdened interstate commerce, we would have to sustain the law. . . . The same result would obtain if we had to resolve the much discussed issues of safety presented in this case."

"This case," he said, "presents a different issue." The equipment here could not pass muster in every state; instead the question is whether one state can prescribe standards which will require shifting cargo to differently designed vehicles at the state border. Because of the practice of "interlining"—transferring loaded trailers between an originating carrier and another carrier—the statute would require carriers who do only a minor amount of their business in Illinois to equip all of their trailers with the contour mudguards.

He then rejected the argument that *Barnwell* stood for the proposition that despite "the rather massive showing of burden on interstate commerce", it was for the state legislature, not the courts, to weigh the relative merits of contour mudguards against any other kind. "The various exercises by the States of their police power stand . . . on an equal footing. All are entitled to the same presumption of validity when challenged under the Due Process Clause. . . . Similarly the various state regulatory statutes are of equal dignity when measured against the Commerce Clause, . . . Local regulation which would pass muster under the Due Process Clause might nonetheless fail to survive other challenges to constitutionality that bring the Supremacy Clause into play. Like any local law that conflicts with federal regulatory measure . . . , state regulations that run afoul of the policy of free trade reflected in the Commerce Clause must also bow.

"This is one of those cases—few in number—where local safety measures that are nondiscriminatory place an unconstitutional burden on interstate commerce. . . . A State which insists on a design out of line with the requirements of almost all the other States may sometimes place a great burden of delay and inconvenience on those interstate motor carriers entering or crossing its territory. Such a new safety device—out of line with the requirements of the other States—may be so compelling that the innovating State need not be the one to give way. The present showing—balanced against the clear burden on commerce—is far too inconclusive to make this mudguard meet that test."

Justice Harlan, joined by Justice Stewart, concurred in the judgment, saying: "The opinion of the Court clearly demonstrates the heavy burden, in terms of cost and interference with 'interlining' which the Illinois statute here involved imposes on interstate commerce. In view of the findings of the District Court . . . to the effect that the contour mudflap 'possesses no advantages' in terms of safety over the conventional flap permitted in all other States, and indeed creates certain safety hazards, this heavy burden cannot be justified on the theory that the Illinois statute is a necessary, appropriate, or helpful safety measure."

KASSEL v. CONSOLIDATED FREIGHTWAYS CORPORATION

450 U.S. 662, 101 S.Ct. 1309, 67 L.Ed.2d 580 (1981).

Justice Powell announced the judgment of the Court and delivered an opinion in which Justice White, Justice Blackmun, and Justice Stevens joined.

The question is whether an Iowa statute that prohibits the use of certain large trucks within the State unconstitutionally burdens interstate commerce.

I

Respondent Consolidated Freightways Corporation of Delaware (Consolidated) is one of the largest common carriers in the country. It offers service in 48 States under a certificate of public convenience and necessity issued by the Interstate Commerce Commission. Among other routes, Consolidated carries commodities through Iowa on Interstate 80, the principal east-west route linking New York, Chicago, and the west coast, and on Interstate 35, a major north-south route.

Consolidated mainly uses two kinds of trucks. One consists of a three-axle tractor pulling a 40-foot two-axle trailer. This unit, commonly called a single, or "semi," is 55 feet in length overall. Such trucks have long been used on the Nation's highways. Consolidated also uses a two-axle tractor pulling a single-axle trailer which, in turn, pulls a single-axle dolly and a second single-axle trailer. This combination, known as a double, or twin, is 65 feet long overall. Many trucking companies, including Consolidated, increasingly prefer to use doubles to ship certain kinds of commodities. Doubles have larger capacities, and the trailers can be detached and routed separately if necessary. Consolidated would like to use 65-foot doubles on many of its trips through Iowa.

The State of Iowa, however, by statute restricts the length of vehicles that may use its highways. Unlike all other States in the West and Midwest, Iowa generally prohibits the use of 65-foot doubles within its borders. Instead, most truck combinations are restricted to 55 feet in length. Doubles, mobile homes, trucks carrying vehicles such as tractors and other farm equipment, and singles hauling livestock, are permitted to be as long as 60 feet. Notwithstanding these restrictions, Iowa's statute permits cities abutting the state line by local ordinance to adopt the length limitations of the adjoining State. Iowa Code § 321.457(7) (1979). Where a city has exercised this option, otherwise oversized trucks are permitted within the city limits and in nearby commercial zones. Ibid.

Iowa also provides for two other relevant exemptions. An Iowa truck manufacturer may obtain a permit to ship trucks that are as large as 70 feet. Iowa Code § 321E.10 (1979). Permits also are available to move oversized mobile homes, provided that the unit is to be moved from a point within Iowa or delivered for an Iowa resident. Id., § 321E.28(5).[7]

---

[7] The parochial restrictions in the mobile home provision were enacted after Governor Ray vetoed a bill that would have permitted the interstate shipment of all mobile homes through Iowa. Governor Ray commented, in his veto message:

"This bill . . . would make Iowa a bridge state as these oversized units are moved into Iowa after being manufactured in another state and sold in a third. None of this activity would be of particular economic benefit to Iowa."

Because of Iowa's statutory scheme, Consolidated cannot use its 65-foot doubles to move commodities through the State. Instead, the company must do one of four things: (i) use 55-foot singles; (ii) use 60-foot doubles; (iii) detach the trailers of a 65-foot double and shuttle each through the State separately; or (iv) divert 65-foot doubles around Iowa.

Dissatisfied with these options, Consolidated filed this suit in the District Court averring that Iowa's statutory scheme unconstitutionally burdens interstate commerce. Iowa defended the law as a reasonable safety measure enacted pursuant to its police power. The State asserted that 65-foot doubles are more dangerous than 55-foot singles and, in any event, that the law promotes safety and reduces road wear within the State by diverting much truck traffic to other States.

In a 14-day trial, both sides adduced evidence on safety, and on the burden on interstate commerce imposed by Iowa's law. On the question of safety, the District Court found that the "evidence clearly establishes that the twin is as safe as the semi." 475 F.Supp. 544, 549 (S.D.Iowa 1979). For that reason,

"there is no valid safety reason for barring twins from Iowa's highways because of their configuration.

"The evidence convincingly, if not overwhelmingly, establishes that the 65 foot twin is as safe as, if not safer than, the 60 foot twin and the 55 foot semi. . . .

. . .

"Twins and semis have different characteristics. Twins are more maneuverable, are less sensitive to wind, and create less splash and spray. However, they are more likely than semis to jackknife or upset. They can be backed only for a short distance. The negative characteristics are not such that they render the twin less safe than semis overall. Semis are more stable but are more likely to 'rear end' another vehicle." Id., at 548–549.

In light of these findings, the District Court applied the standard we enunciated in Raymond Motor Transportation, Inc. v. Rice, 434 U.S. 429 (1978), and concluded that the state law impermissibly burdened interstate commerce:

"[T]he balance here must be struck in favor of the federal interests. The *total effect* of the law as a safety measure in reducing accidents and casualties is so slight and problematical that it does not outweigh the national interest in keeping interstate commerce free from interferences that seriously impede it." 475 F.Supp., at 551 (emphasis in original).

The Court of Appeals for the Eighth Circuit affirmed. 612 F.2d 1064 (1979). It accepted the District Court's finding that 65-foot doubles were as safe as 55-foot singles. Thus, the only apparent safety benefit to Iowa was that resulting from forcing large trucks to detour around the State, thereby reducing overall truck traffic on Iowa's highways. The Court of Appeals noted that this was not a constitutionally permissible interest. It also commented that the several statutory exemptions identified above, such as those applicable to border cities and the shipment of livestock, suggested that the law in effect benefited Iowa residents at the expense of interstate traffic. The combination of these exemptions weakened the presumption of validity normally accorded a state safety regulation. For these reasons, the Court of Appeals agreed with the District Court that the Iowa statute unconstitutionally burdened interstate commerce.

Iowa appealed, and we noted probable jurisdiction. . . . We now affirm.

II

. . .

The Commerce Clause does not, of course, invalidate all state restrictions on commerce. . . . The extent of permissible state regulation is not always easy to measure. It may be said with confidence, however, that a State's power to regulate commerce is never greater than in matters traditionally of local concern. *Washington Apple Advertising Comm.,* supra, at 350. For example, regulations that touch upon safety—especially highway safety—are those that "the Court has been most reluctant to invalidate." *Raymond,* supra, at 443; . . . Indeed, "if safety justifications are not illusory, the court will not second-guess legislative judgment about their importance in comparison with related burdens on interstate commerce." *Raymond,* supra, at 449 (Blackmun, J., concurring). Those who would challenge such bona fide safety regulations must overcome a "strong presumption of validity." Bibb v. Navajo Freight Lines, Inc., 359 U.S. 520, 524 (1959).

But the incantation of a purpose to promote the public health or safety does not insulate a state law from Commerce Clause attack. Regulations designed for that salutary purpose nevertheless may further the purpose so marginally, and interfere with commerce so substantially, as to be invalid under the Commerce Clause. In the Court's recent unanimous decision in *Raymond,* we declined to "accept the State's contention that the inquiry under the Commerce Clause is ended without a weighing of the asserted safety purpose against the degree of interference with interstate commerce." 434 U.S., at 443. This "weighing" by a court requires—and indeed the constitutionality of the state regulation depends on—"a sensitive consideration of the weight and nature of the state regulatory concern in light of the extent of the burden imposed on the course of interstate commerce." . . .

III

Applying these general principles, we conclude that the Iowa truck-length limitations unconstitutionally burden interstate commerce.

In Raymond Motor Transportation, Inc. v. Rice, the Court held that a Wisconsin statute that precluded the use of 65-foot doubles violated the Commerce Clause. This case is *Raymond* revisited. Here, as in *Raymond,* the State failed to present any persuasive evidence that 65-foot doubles are less safe than 55-foot singles. Moreover, Iowa's law is now out of step with the laws of all other Midwestern and Western States. Iowa thus substantially burdens the interstate flow of goods by truck. In the absence of congressional action to set uniform standards, some burdens associated with state safety regulations must be tolerated. But where, as here, the State's safety interest has been found to be illusory, and its regulations impair significantly the federal interest in efficient and safe interstate transportation, the state law cannot be harmonized with the Commerce Clause.

A

Iowa made a more serious effort to support the safety rationale of its law than did Wisconsin in *Raymond,* but its effort was no more persuasive. As noted above, the District Court found that the "evidence clearly establishes that the twin is as safe as the semi." The record supports this finding.

The trial focused on a comparison of the performance of the two kinds of trucks in various safety categories. The evidence showed, and the District Court found, that the 65-foot double was at least the equal of the 55-foot single in the ability to brake, turn, and maneuver. The double, because of its axle placement, produces less splash and spray in wet weather. And, because of its articulation in the middle, the double is less susceptible to dangerous "off-tracking," and to wind.

None of these findings is seriously disputed by Iowa. Indeed, the State points to only three ways in which the 55-foot single is even arguably superior: singles take less time to be passed and to clear intersections; they may back up for longer distances; and they are somewhat less likely to jackknife.

The first two of these characteristics are of limited relevance on modern interstate highways. As the District Court found, the negligible difference in the time required to pass, and to cross intersections, is insignificant on 4-lane divided highways because passing does not require crossing into oncoming traffic lanes, *Raymond,* 434 U.S., at 444, and interstates have few, if any, intersections. The concern over backing capability also is insignificant because it seldom is necessary to back up on an interstate. In any event, no evidence suggested any difference in backing capability between the 60-foot doubles that Iowa permits and the 65-foot doubles that it bans. Similarly, although doubles tend to jackknife somewhat more than singles, 65-foot doubles actually are less likely to jackknife than 60-foot doubles.

Statistical studies supported the view that 65-foot doubles are at least as safe overall as 55-foot singles and 60-foot doubles. One such study, which the District Court credited, reviewed Consolidated's comparative accident experience in 1978 with its own singles and doubles. Each kind of truck was driven 56 million miles on identical routes. The singles were involved in 100 accidents resulting in 27 injuries and one fatality. The 65-foot doubles were involved in 106 accidents resulting in 17 injuries and one fatality. Iowa's expert statistician admitted that this study provided "moderately strong evidence" that singles have a higher injury rate than doubles. Another study, prepared by the Iowa Department of Transportation at the request of the State legislature, concluded that "[s]ixty-five foot twin trailer combinations have *not* been shown by experiences in other states to be less safe than 60-foot twin trailer combinations *or* conventional tractor-semitrailers" (emphasis in original). Numerous insurance company executives, and transportation officials from the Federal Government and various States, testified that 65-foot doubles were at least as safe as 55-foot singles. Iowa concedes that it can produce no study that establishes a statistically significant difference in safety between the 65-foot double and the kinds of vehicles the State permits. Nor, as the District Court noted, did Iowa present a single witness who testified that 65-foot doubles were more dangerous overall than the vehicles permitted under Iowa law. 475 F.Supp., at 549. In sum, although Iowa introduced more evidence on the question of safety than did Wisconsin in *Raymond,* the record as a whole was not more favorable to the State.

B

Consolidated, meanwhile, demonstrated that Iowa's law substantially burdens interstate commerce. Trucking companies that wish to continue to use 65-foot doubles must route them around Iowa or detach the trailers of the doubles and ship them through separately. Alternatively, trucking companies must use the smaller 55-foot singles or 60-foot doubles permitted under Iowa law. Each of these options engenders inefficiency and added expense. The record shows that Iowa's law added about $12.6 million each year to the costs of trucking companies. Consolidated alone incurred about $2 million per year in increased costs.

In addition to increasing the costs of the trucking companies (and, indirectly, of the service to consumers), Iowa's law may aggravate, rather than ameliorate, the problem of highway accidents. Fifty-five foot singles carry less freight than

65-foot doubles. Either more small trucks must be used to carry the same quantity of goods through Iowa, or the same number of larger trucks must drive longer distances to bypass Iowa. In either case, as the District Court noted, the restriction requires more highway miles to be driven to transport the same quantity of goods. Other things being equal, accidents are proportional to distance traveled. Thus, if 65-foot doubles are as safe as 55-foot singles, Iowa's law tends to *increase* the number of accidents, and to shift the incidence of them from Iowa to other States.

IV

Perhaps recognizing the weakness of the evidence supporting its safety argument, and the substantial burden on commerce that its regulations create, Iowa urges the Court simply to "defer" to the safety judgment of the State. It argues that the length of trucks is generally, although perhaps imprecisely, related to safety. The task of drawing a line is one that Iowa contends should be left to its legislature.

The Court normally does accord "special deference" to state highway safety regulations. *Raymond,* 434 U.S., at 444, n. 18. This traditional deference "derives in part from the assumption that where such regulations do not discriminate on their face against interstate commerce, their burden usually falls on local economic interests as well as other States' economic interests, thus insuring that a State's own political processes will serve as a check against unduly burdensome regulations." Ibid. Less deference to the legislative judgment is due, however, where the local regulation bears disproportionately on out-of-state residents and businesses. Such a disproportionate burden is apparent here. Iowa's scheme, although generally banning large doubles from the State, nevertheless has several exemptions that secure to Iowans many of the benefits of large trucks while shunting to neighboring States many of the costs associated with their use.

At the time of trial there were two particularly significant exemptions. First, singles hauling livestock or farm vehicles were permitted to be as long as 60 feet. Iowa Code §§ 321.457(5), 321.457(3) (1979). As the Court of Appeals noted, this provision undoubtedly was helpful to local interests. Cf. *Raymond,* supra, at 434 (exemption in Wisconsin for milk shippers). Second, cities abutting other States were permitted to enact local ordinances adopting the larger length limitation of the neighboring State. Iowa Code § 321.457(7) (1979). This exemption offered the benefits of longer trucks to individuals and businesses in important border cities without burdening Iowa's highways with interstate through traffic. Cf. *Raymond,* supra, at 446–447, and n. 24 (exemption in Wisconsin for shipments from local plants).

The origin of the "border cities exemption" also suggests that Iowa's statute may not have been designed to ban dangerous trucks, but rather to discourage interstate truck traffic. In 1974, the legislature passed a bill that would have permitted 65-foot doubles in the State. Governor Ray vetoed the bill. He said:

> "I find sympathy with those who are doing business in our state and whose enterprises could gain from increased cargo carrying ability by trucks. However, with this bill, the Legislature has pursued a course that would benefit only a few Iowa-based companies while providing a great advantage for out-of-state trucking firms and competitors at the expense of our Iowa citizens."

After the veto, the "border cities exemption" was immediately enacted and signed by the Governor.

B. & C. Cs.Const.Law 7th Ed. UCB—8

It is thus far from clear that Iowa was motivated primarily by a judgment that 65-foot doubles are less safe than 55-foot singles. Rather, Iowa seems to have hoped to limit the use of its highways by deflecting some through traffic. In the District Court and Court of Appeals, the State explicitly attempted to justify the law by its claimed interest in keeping trucks out of Iowa. The Court of Appeals correctly concluded that a State cannot constitutionally promote its own parochial interests by requiring safe vehicles to detour around it. 612 F.2d, at 1070.

V

In sum, the statutory exemptions, their history, and the arguments Iowa has advanced in support of its law in this litigation, all suggest that the deference traditionally accorded a State's safety judgment is not warranted. See *Raymond,* supra, at 444, and n. 18, 446–447. The controlling factors thus are the findings of the District Court, accepted by the Court of Appeals, with respect to the relative safety of the types of trucks at issue, and the substantiality of the burden on interstate commerce.

Because Iowa has imposed this burden without any significant countervailing safety interest, its statute violates the Commerce Clause. The judgment of the Court of Appeals is affirmed.

It is so ordered.

Justice Brennan, with whom Justice Marshall joins, concurring in the judgment.

Iowa's truck-length regulation challenged in this case is nearly identical to the Wisconsin regulation struck down in Raymond Motor Transportation, Inc. v. Rice, 434 U.S. 429 (1978), as in violation of the Commerce Clause. In my view the same Commerce Clause restrictions that dictated that holding also require invalidation of Iowa's regulation insofar as its prohibits 65-foot doubles.

The reasoning bringing me to that conclusion does not require, however, that I engage in the debate between my Brothers Powell and Rehnquist over what the District Court record shows on the question whether 65-foot doubles are more dangerous than shorter trucks. With all respect, my Brothers ask and answer the wrong question.

For me, analysis of Commerce Clause challenges to state regulations must take into account three principles: (1) The courts are not empowered to second-guess the empirical judgments of lawmakers concerning the utility of legislation. (2) The burdens imposed on commerce must be balanced against the local benefits actually sought to be achieved by the State's lawmakers, and not against those suggested after the fact by counsel. (3) Protectionist legislation is unconstitutional under the Commerce Clause, even if the burdens and benefits are related to safety rather than economics.

I

Both the opinion of my Brother Powell and the opinion of my Brother Rehnquist are predicated upon the supposition that the constitutionality of a state regulation is determined by the factual record created by the State's lawyers in trial court. But that supposition cannot be correct, for it would make the constitutionality of state laws and regulations depend on the vagaries of litigation rather than on the judgments made by the State's lawmakers.

In considering a Commerce Clause challenge to a state regulation, the judicial task is to balance the burden imposed on commerce against the local benefits sought to be achieved by the State's *lawmakers.* See Pike v. Bruce Church, Inc., 397 U.S. 137, 142 (1970). In determining those benefits, a court should focus ultimately on the regulatory purposes identified by the lawmakers and on the evidence before or available to them that might have supported their judgment. . . . Since the court must confine its analysis to the purposes the lawmakers had for maintaining the regulation, the only relevant evidence concerns whether the lawmakers could rationally have believed that the challenged regulation would foster those purposes. . . . It is not the function of the court to decide whether *in fact* the regulation promotes its intended purpose, so long as an examination of the evidence before or available to the lawmaker indicates that the regulation is not wholly irrational in light of its purposes.[1]

II

My Brothers Powell and Rehnquist make the mistake of disregarding the intention of Iowa's lawmakers and assuming that resolution of the case must hinge upon the argument offered by Iowa's attorneys: that 65-foot doubles are more dangerous than shorter trucks. They then canvass the factual record and findings of the courts below and reach opposite conclusions as to whether the evidence adequately supports that empirical judgment. I repeat: my Brothers Powell and Rehnquist have asked and answered the wrong question. For although Iowa's lawyers in this litigation have defended the truck-length regulation on the basis of the safety advantages of 55-foot singles and 60-foot doubles over 65-foot doubles, Iowa's actual rationale for maintaining the regulation had nothing to do with these purported differences. Rather, Iowa sought to discourage interstate truck traffic on Iowa's highways. Thus, the safety advantages and disadvantages of the types and lengths of trucks involved in this case are irrelevant to the decision.[3]

My Brother Powell concedes that "[i]t is . . . far from clear that Iowa was motivated primarily by a judgment that 65-foot doubles are less safe than 55-foot singles. Rather, Iowa seems to have hoped to limit the use of its highways by deflecting some through traffic." This conclusion is more than amply supported by the record and the legislative history of the Iowa regulation. The Iowa legislature has consistently taken the position that size, weight, and speed restrictions on interstate traffic should be set in accordance with uniform national standards. The stated purpose was not to further safety but to achieve uniformity with other States. The Act setting the limitations challenged in this case, passed in 1947 and periodically amended since then, is entitled, "An Act *to promote uniformity with other states* in the matter of limitations on the size, weight and speed of motor vehicles. . . ." 1947 Iowa Act, ch. 177 (emphasis

---

[1] Moreover, I would emphasize that in the field of safety—and perhaps in other fields where the decisions of State lawmakers are deserving of a heightened degree of deference—the role of the courts is not to balance asserted burdens against intended benefits as it is in other fields. Compare Raymond Motor Transportation, Inc. v. Rice, 434 U.S. 429, 449 (1978) (Blackmun, J., concurring) (safety regulation) with Pike v. Bruce Church, Inc., 397 U.S. 137, 143 (1970) (regulation intended "to protect and enhance the reputation of growers within the State"). In the field of safety, once the court has established that the intended safety benefit is not illusory, insubstantial, or nonexistent, it must defer to the State's lawmakers on the appropriate balance to be struck against other interests. I therefore disagree with my Brother Powell when he asserts that the degree of interference with interstate commerce may in the first instance be "weighed" against the State's safety interests . . . .

[3] My Brother Rehnquist claims that the "argument" that a Court should defer to the actual purposes of the lawmakers rather than to the *post hoc* justifications of counsel "has been consistently rejected by the Court in other contexts." . . .

. . . .

If, as here, the only purpose ever articulated by the State's lawmakers for maintaining a regulation is illegitimate, I consider it contrary to precedent as well as to sound principles of constitutional adjudication for the courts to base their analysis on purposes never conceived by the lawmakers. This is especially true where, as the dissent's strained analysis of the relative safety of 65-foot doubles to shorter trucks amply demonstrates, the *post hoc* justifications are implausible as well as imaginary. I would emphasize that, although my Brother Powell's plurality opinion does not give as much weight to the illegitimacy of Iowa's actual purpose as I do, see Part III, infra, both that opinion and this concurrence have found the actual motivation of the Iowa lawmakers in maintaining the truck-length regulation highly relevant to, if not dispositive of, the case.

added). Following the proposals of the American Association of State Highway and Transportation Officials, the State has gradually increased the permissible length of trucks from 45 feet in 1947 to the present limit of 60 feet.

In 1974, the Iowa legislature again voted to increase the permissible length of trucks to conform to uniform standards then in effect in most other States. This legislation, House Bill 671, would have increased the maximum length of twin trailer trucks operable in Iowa from 60 to 65 feet. But Governor Ray broke from prior state policy, and vetoed the legislation. The legislature did not override the veto, and the present regulation was thus maintained. In his veto, Governor Ray did not rest his decision on the conclusion that 55-foot singles and 60-foot doubles are any safer than 65-foot doubles, or on any other safety consideration inherent in the type or size of the trucks. Rather, his principal concern was that to allow 65-foot doubles would "basically ope[n] our state to literally thousands and thousands more trucks per year." This increase in interstate truck traffic would, in the Governor's estimation, greatly increase highway maintenance costs, which are borne by the citizens of the State, and increase the number of accidents and fatalities within the State. The legislative response was not to override the veto, but to accede to the Governor's action, and in accord with his basic premise, to enact a "border cities exemption." This permitted cities within border areas to allow 65-foot doubles while otherwise maintaining the 60-foot limit throughout the State to discourage interstate truck traffic.

Although the Court has stated that "[i]n no field has . . . deference to state regulation been greater than that of highway safety," Raymond Motor Transportation, Inc. v. Rice, supra, 434 U.S., at 443, it has declined to go so far as to presume that size restrictions are inherently tied to public safety. The Court has emphasized that the "strong presumption of validity" of size restrictions "cannot justify a court in closing its eyes to uncontroverted evidence of record,"—here the obvious fact that the safety characteristics of 65-foot doubles did not provide the motivation for either legislators or Governor in maintaining the regulation.

III

Though my Brother Powell recognizes that the State's actual purpose in maintaining the truck-length regulation was "to limit the use of its highways by deflecting some through traffic," he fails to recognize that this purpose, being *protectionist* in nature, is *impermissible* under the Commerce Clause. The Governor admitted that he blocked legislative efforts to raise the length of trucks because the change "would benefit only a few Iowa-based companies while providing a great advantage for out-of-state trucking firms and competitors at the expense of our Iowa citizens." Appellant Raymond Kassel, Director of the Iowa Department of Transportation, while admitting that the greater 65-foot length standard would be *safer* overall, defended the more restrictive regulations because of their benefits *within Iowa* . . .

Iowa may not shunt off its fair share of the burden of maintaining interstate truck routes, nor may it create increased hazards on the highways of neighboring States in order to decrease the hazards on Iowa highways. Such an attempt has all the hallmarks of the "simple . . . protectionism" this Court has condemned in the economic area. Philadelphia v. New Jersey, 437 U.S. 617, 624 (1978). Just as a State's attempt to avoid interstate competition in economic goods may damage the prosperity of the Nation as a whole, so Iowa's attempt to deflect interstate truck traffic has been found to make the Nation's highways as a whole more hazardous. That attempt should therefore be subject to "a virtually *per se* rule of invalidity." Ibid.

This Court's heightened deference to the judgments of state lawmakers in the field of safety, is largely attributable to a judicial disinclination to weigh the interests of safety against other societal interests, such as the economic interest in the free flow of commerce.   Thus, "if safety justifications are not illusory, the Court will not second-guess legislative judgment about their importance *in comparison with related burdens on interstate commerce.*"   Raymond Motor Transportation, Inc. v. Rice, supra, at 449 (Blackmun, J., concurring) (emphasis added). Here, the decision of Iowa's lawmakers to promote *Iowa's* safety and other interests at the direct expense of the safety and other interests of neighboring States merits no such deference.   No special judicial acuity is demanded to perceive that this sort of parochial legislation violates the Commerce Clause.   As Justice Cardozo has written, the Commerce Clause "was framed upon the theory that the peoples of the several states must sink or swim together, and that in the long run prosperity and salvation are in union and not division."   Baldwin v. G.A.F. Seelig, Inc., 294 U.S. 511, 523 (1935).

I therefore concur in the judgment.

Justice Rehnquist, with whom The Chief Justice and Justice Stewart join, dissenting.

The result in this case suggests, to paraphrase Justice Jackson, that the only state truck-length limit "that is valid is one which this court has not been able to get its hands on."   Jungersen v. Ostby & Barton Co., 335 U.S. 560, 572 (1949) (dissenting opinion).   Although the plurality and concurring opinions strike down Iowa's law by different routes, I believe the analysis in both opinions oversteps our "limited authority to review state legislation under the commerce clause," Brotherhood of Locomotive Firemen v. Chicago, R.I. & P.R. Co., 393 U.S. 129, 136 (1968), and seriously intrudes upon the fundamental right of the States to pass laws to secure the safety of their citizens.   Accordingly, I dissent.

I

It is necessary to elaborate somewhat on the facts as presented in the plurality opinion to appreciate fully what the Court does today.   Iowa's action in limiting the length of trucks which may travel on its highways is in no sense unusual.   Every State in the Union regulates the length of vehicles permitted to use the public roads.   Nor is Iowa a renegade in having length limits which operate to exclude the 65-foot doubles favored by Consolidated.   These trucks are prohibited in other areas of the country as well, some 17 States and the District of Columbia, including all of New England and most of the Southeast. While pointing out that Consolidated carries commodities through Iowa on Interstate 80, "the principal east-west route linking New York, Chicago, and the west coast," the plurality neglects to note that both Pennsylvania and New Jersey, through which Interstate 80 runs before reaching New York, also ban 65-foot doubles.   In short, the persistent effort in the plurality opinion to paint Iowa as an oddity standing alone to block commerce carried in 65-foot doubles is simply not supported by the facts.

Nor does the plurality adequately convey the extent to which the lower courts permitted the 65-foot doubles to operate in Iowa.   Consolidated sought to have the 60-foot length limit declared an unconstitutional burden on commerce when applied to the seven Interstate Highways in Iowa and "access routes to and from Plaintiff's terminals, and reasonable access from said Interstate Highways to facilities for food, fuel, repairs, or rest."   The lower courts granted this relief, permitting the 65-foot doubles to travel *off the Interstates* as far as five miles for access to terminal and other facilities, or less if closer facilities were available.   475 F.Supp. 544, 553–554 (SD Iowa 1979).   To the extent the plurality relies on characteristics of the Interstate Highways in rejecting

Iowa's asserted safety justifications, it fails to recognize the scope of the District Court order it upholds.

With these additions to the relevant facts, we can now examine the appropriate analysis to be applied.

II

. . .

A determination that a state law is a rational safety measure does not end the Commerce Clause inquiry. A "sensitive consideration" of the safety purpose in relation to the burden on commerce is required. *Raymond,* supra, at 441. When engaging in such a consideration the Court does not directly compare safety benefits to commerce costs and strike down the legislation if the latter can be said in some vague sense to "outweigh" the former. Such an approach would make an empty gesture of the strong presumption of validity accorded state safety measures, particularly those governing highways. It would also arrogate to this Court functions of forming public policy, functions which, in the absence of congressional action, were left by the Framers of the Constitution to state legislatures. . . .

The purpose of the "sensitive consideration" referred to above is rather to determine if the asserted safety justification, although rational, is merely a pretext for discrimination against interstate commerce. We will conclude that it is if the safety benefits from the regulation are demonstrably trivial while the burden on commerce is great. Thus the Court in *Bibb* stated that the "strong presumption of validity" accorded highway safety measures could be overcome only when the safety benefits were "slight or problematical," 359 U.S., at 524.

. . . .

III

Iowa defends its statute as a highway safety regulation. There can be no doubt that the challenged statute is a valid highway safety regulation and thus entitled to the strongest presumption of validity against Commerce Clause challenges. As noted, all 50 States regulate the length of trucks which may use their highways. . . . There can also be no question that the particular limit chosen by Iowa—60 feet—is rationally related to Iowa's safety objective. Most truck limits are between 55 and 65 feet, and Iowa's choice is thus well within the widely accepted range.

Iowa adduced evidence supporting the relation between vehicle length and highway safety. . . .

. . . In sum, there was sufficient evidence presented at trial to support the legislative determination that length is related to safety, and nothing in Consolidated's evidence undermines this conclusion.

The District Court approached the case as if the question were whether Consolidated's 65-foot trucks were as safe as others permitted on Iowa highways, and the Court of Appeals as if its task were to determine if the District Court's factual findings in this regard were "clearly erroneous." 612 F.2d, at 1069. The question, however, is whether the Iowa Legislature has acted rationally in regulating vehicle lengths and whether the safety benefits from this regulation are more than slight or problematical. . . . "Since the adoption of one weight or width regulation, rather than another, is a legislative and not a judicial choice, its constitutionality is not to be determined by weighing in the judicial scales the merits of the legislative choice and rejecting it if the weight of evidence presented in court appears to favor a different standard." Barnwell Brothers, 303 U.S., at 191.

. . . .

It must be emphasized that there is nothing in the laws of nature which make 65-foot doubles an obvious norm. Consolidated operates 65-foot doubles on many of its routes simply because that is the largest size permitted in many States through which Consolidated travels. Doubles can and do come in smaller sizes; indeed, when Iowa adopted the present 60-foot limit in 1963, it was in accord with AASHTO recommendations. Striking down Iowa's law because Consolidated has made a voluntary business decision to employ 65-foot doubles, a decision based on the actions of other state legislatures, would essentially be compelling Iowa to yield to the policy choices of neighboring States. Under our constitutional scheme, however, there is only one legislative body which can pre-empt the rational policy determination of the Iowa Legislature and that is Congress. Forcing Iowa to yield to the policy choices of neighboring States perverts the primary purpose of the Commerce Clause, that of vesting power to regulate interstate commerce in Congress, where all the States are represented. . . .

   . . .

My Brother Brennan argues that the Court should consider only *the* purpose the Iowa legislators *actually* sought to achieve by the length limit, and not the purposes advanced by Iowa's lawyers in defense of the statute. . . . The argument has been consistently rejected by the Court in other contexts, compare, e.g., United States Railroad Retirement Board v. Fritz, 449 U.S. 166, 187–188 (1980) with id., at 187–188 (Brennan, J., dissenting) and Michael M. v. Superior Court of Sonoma County, [450 U.S.] at 469–470, (1981) (plurality opinion) with id., at 494–496 (Brennan, J., dissenting), and Justice Brennan can cite no authority for the proposition that possible legislative purposes suggested by a State's lawyers should not be considered in Commerce Clause cases. The problems with a view such as that advanced in the opinion concurring in the judgment are apparent. To name just a few, it assumes that individual legislators are motivated by one discernible "actual" purpose, and ignores the fact that different legislators may vote for a single piece of legislation for widely different reasons. . . . How, for example, would a court adhering to the views expressed in the opinion concurring in the judgment approach a statute, the legislative history of which indicated that 10 votes were based on safety considerations, 10 votes were based on protectionism, and the statute passed by a vote of 40–20? What would the *actual* purpose of the *legislature* have been in that case? This Court has wisely "never insisted that a legislative body articulate its reasons for enacting a statute." *Fritz,* supra, at 461.

Both the plurality and concurring opinions attach great significance to the Governor's veto of a bill passed by the Iowa Legislature permitting 65-foot doubles. Whatever views one may have about the significance of legislative motives, it must be emphasized that the law which the Court strikes down today was not passed to achieve the protectionist goals the plurality and the concurrence ascribe to the Governor. Iowa's 60-foot length limit was established in 1963, at a time when very few States permitted 65-foot doubles. Striking down legislation on the basis of asserted legislative motives is dubious enough, but the plurality and concurrence strike down the legislation involved in this case because of asserted impermissible motives for *not* enacting *other* legislation, motives which could not possibly have been present when the legislation under challenge here was considered and passed. Such action is, so far as I am aware, unprecedented in this Court's history.

Furthermore, the effort in both the plurality and concurring opinions to portray the legislation involved here as protectionist is in error. Whenever a State enacts more stringent safety measures than its neighbors, in an area which affects commerce, the safety law will have the incidental effect of deflecting interstate commerce to the neighboring States. Indeed, the safety and protectionist motives cannot be separated: The whole purpose of safety regulation of vehicles is to *protect* the State from unsafe vehicles. If a neighboring State chooses *not* to protect its citizens from the danger discerned by the enacting State, that is its business, but the enacting State should not be penalized when the vehicles it considers unsafe travel through the neighboring State.

The other States with truck-length limits that exclude Consolidated's 65-foot doubles would not at all be paranoid in assuming that they might be next on Consolidated's "hit list." The true problem with today's decision is that it gives no guidance whatsoever to these States as to whether their laws are valid or how to defend them. For that matter, the decision gives no guidance to Consolidated or other trucking firms either. Perhaps, after all is said and done, the Court today neither says nor does very much at all. We know only that Iowa's law is invalid and that the jurisprudence of the "negative side" of the Commerce Clause remains hopelessly confused.

FEDERAL REGULATION OF TRUCK SIZES

In 1983 Congress provided that states must allow twin trailer combinations with each trailer 28 feet long (approximate total length 65 feet) and 102 inches wide to use the interstate highway system and federal aided primary highways designated by the Secretary of Transportation. 49 U.S.C. §§ 2311, 2316. On April 6, 1983, the Federal Highway Administration designated about 140,000 miles of federally aided highways in addition to 42,000 miles of interstate highways upon which the larger trucks must be allowed to operate. 48 Fed. Reg. 14844 (1983).

SECTION 2.   IMPLIED RESTRICTIONS OF THE COMMERCE CLAUSE—PRODUCTION AND TRADE

A.   RESTRICTING IMPORTATION AND INSULATING IN-STATE BUSINESS FROM OUT-OF-STATE COMPETITION

STATE QUARANTINE AND INSPECTION LAWS

From the days of Chief Justice Marshall, the Court has repeatedly asserted that the Commerce Clause, in the absence of action by Congress, does not prevent the states from constitutionally enacting quarantine or inspection laws that affect interstate and foreign commerce, although the result has been rationalized in different ways at different times. In Hannibal & St. Joseph R.R. Co. v. Husen, 95 U.S. 465 (1877), the question was the validity of a Missouri statute providing that no Texas, Mexican, or Indian cattle should be driven or transported into or remain in, the state between March 1 and November 1 of each year. The Court said: "While we unhesitatingly admit that a State may pass sanitary laws, and laws for the protection of life, liberty, health, or property within its borders; while it may prevent persons and animals suffering under contagious or infectious diseases, or convicts, etc., from entering the State; while for the purpose of self-protection it may establish quarantine, and reasonable inspection laws, it may not interfere with transportation into or through the State, beyond what is absolutely necessary for its self-protection. It may not, under the cover of exerting its police powers, substantially prohibit or burden either foreign or interstate commerce." The Court did not believe that the statute was a legitimate quarantine or inspection law because of the unconditional character of the prohibition on bringing cattle into the state during the specified months of the year; consequently the act was held invalid.

However, in Kimmish v. Ball, 129 U.S. 217 (1889), the Court held valid an Iowa statute making liable in damages any person having possession of "Texas cattle" that had not wintered north of the southern boundary of Missouri or Kansas. In the opinion by Justice Field it is said: "the case is, therefore, reduced to this, whether the State may not provide that whoever permits diseased cattle in his possession to run at large within its limits shall be liable for any damages caused by the spread of the disease occasioned thereby; and upon that question we do not entertain the slightest doubt."

––––––––––

MINTZ v. BALDWIN, 289 U.S. 346 (1933). A New York regulation designed to guard against Bang's disease required cattle imported into New York for dairy and breeding purposes and the herds from which they came to be certified free from the disease by the chief sanitary official of the state of origin. A Wisconsin cattle breeder shipped 20 head of cattle from Wisconsin to a purchaser in New York. They were accompanied by a certificate that they were free of Bang's disease but there was nothing to show that the herd from which they came was free of the disease. The New York commissioner of agriculture refused to permit the cattle to be delivered. The shipper brought suit in a federal district court seeking an injunction against enforcement of the order. The court dismissed the suit. It made special findings to the effect that Bang's disease prevails throughout the United States, causing limitations on reproduction and milk yield and creating the risk of undulant fever in humans drinking raw milk. It also found that there was a body of expert opinion that cattle should be admitted to a state only when certified to have come from a clean herd because tests on individual cattle might not disclose the disease in its incubative stage.

The Supreme Court affirmed, stating: "The order is an inspection measure. Undoubtedly it was promulgated in good faith and is appropriate for the prevention of further spread of the disease among dairy cattle and to safeguard public health. It cannot be maintained therefore that the order so unnecessarily burdens interstate transportation as to contravene the commerce clause."

––––––––––

BALDWIN v. G.A.F. SEELIG, INC., 294 U.S. 511 (1935). The Great Depression of the 1930s had a particularly disastrous impact on dairy farmers. Prices paid to producers for milk in the New York area fell by some 61 percent and the milk supply was threatened as farmers slaughtered cattle rather than remain in a losing business. New York enacted the Milk Control Act of 1933 in an attempt to remedy the situation. A Milk Control Board was empowered to fix both the retail price of milk and the price paid to producers. The statute made it unlawful to sell milk which had been purchased from out-of-state producers at prices less than those required to be paid to farmers within the state.

Seelig was engaged in business as a milk dealer in New York City, buying milk in Vermont and transporting it to New York. Seelig purchased the milk in Vermont at prices lower than the minimum payable to New York producers under the New York law. The State Commissioner of Farms and Markets refused to grant Seelig a milk dealer's license to sell milk purchased from producers at prices below the minimum required by the law. Seelig brought suit to restrain the enforcement of the Milk Control Act. The Supreme Court held that an injunction should issue.

Justice Cardozo, speaking for a unanimous Court, said: "Such a power, if exerted, will set a barrier to traffic between one state and another as effective as if customs duties, equal to the price differential, had been laid upon the thing transported. . . . Nice distinctions have been made at times between direct and indirect burdens [on commerce]. They are irrelevant when the avowed purpose of the obstruction, as well as its necessary tendency, is to suppress or mitigate the consequences of competition between the states. . . . If New York in order to promote the economic welfare of her farmers, may guard them against competition with the cheaper prices of Vermont, the door has been opened to rivalries and reprisals that were meant to be averted by subjecting commerce between the states to the power of the nation."

On behalf of the state it was argued that a major objective of the Milk Control Act was the maintenance of a regular and adequate supply of pure and wholesome milk. The Court replied: "This would be to eat up the rule under the guise of an exception. Economic welfare is always related to health, for there can be no health if men are starving. Let such an exception be admitted, and all that a state will have to do in times of stress and strain is to say that its farmers and merchants and workmen must be protected against competition from without, lest they go upon the poor relief lists or perish altogether. To give entrance to that excuse would be to invite a speedy end of our national solidarity. The Constitution was framed under the dominion of a political philosophy less parochial in range. It was framed upon the theory that the peoples of the several states must sink or swim together, and that in the long run prosperity and salvation are in union and not division. . . . The line of division between direct and indirect restraints of commerce involves in its marking a reference to considerations of degree. Even so, the borderland is wide between the restrains upheld as incidental and those attempted here. . . . None of these statutes [upheld by the Court]—inspection laws, game laws, laws intended to curb fraud or exterminate disease—approaches in drastic quality the statute here in controversy which would neutralize the economic consequences of free trade among the states."

DEAN MILK CO. v. CITY OF MADISON

340 U.S. 349, 71 S.Ct. 295, 95 L.Ed. 329 (1951).

Mr. Justice Clark delivered the opinion of the Court.

This appeal challenges the constitutional validity of two sections of an ordinance of the City of Madison, Wisconsin, regulating the sale of milk and milk products within the municipality's jurisdiction. One section in issue makes it unlawful to sell any milk as pasteurized unless it has been processed and bottled at an approved pasteurization plant within a radius of five miles from the central square of Madison. Another section, which prohibits the sale of milk, or the importation, receipt or storage of milk for sale, in Madison unless from a source of supply possessing a permit issued after inspection by Madison officials, is attacked insofar as it expressly relieves municipal authorities from any duty to inspect farms located beyond twenty-five miles from the center of the city.

Appellant is an Illinois corporation engaged in distributing milk and milk products in Illinois and Wisconsin. It contended below, as it does here, that both the five-mile limit on pasteurization plants and the twenty-five-mile limit on sources of milk violate the Commerce Clause and the Fourteenth Amendment to the Federal Constitution. The Supreme Court of Wisconsin upheld the five-mile limit on pasteurization. As to the twenty-five-mile limitation the court ordered the complaint dismissed for want of a justiciable controversy. This appeal [contests] both rulings. . . .

The City of Madison is the county seat of Dane County. Within the county are some 5,600 dairy farms with the total raw milk production . . . more than ten times the requirements of Madison. Aside from the milk supplied to Madison, fluid milk produced in the county moves in large quantities to Chicago and more distant consuming areas, and the remainder is used in making cheese, butter and other products. At the time of trial the Madison milkshed was not of "Grade A" quality by the standards recommended by the United States Public Health Service, and no milk labeled "Grade A" was distributed in Madison.

The area defined by the ordinance with respect to milk sources encompasses practically all of Dane County and includes some 500 farms which supply milk for Madison. Within the five-mile area for pasteurization are plants of five processors, only three of which are engaged in the general wholesale and retail trade in Madison. Inspection of these farms and plants is scheduled once every thirty days and is performed by two municipal inspectors, one of whom is full-time. The courts below found that the ordinance in question promotes convenient, economical and efficient plant inspection.

Appellant purchases and gathers milk from approximately 950 farms in northern Illinois and southern Wisconsin, none being within twenty-five miles of Madison. Its pasteurization plants are located at Chemung and Huntley, Illinois, about 65 and 85 miles respectively from Madison. Appellant was denied a license to sell its products within Madison solely because its pasteurization plants were more than five miles away.

It is conceded that the milk which appellant seeks to sell in Madison is supplied from farms and processed in plants licensed and inspected by public health authorities of Chicago, and is labeled "Grade A" under the Chicago ordinance which adopts the rating standards recommended by the United States Public Health Service. Both the Chicago and Madison ordinances, though not the sections of the latter here in issue, are largely patterned after the Model Milk Ordinance of the Public Health Service. However, Madison contends and we assume that in some particulars its ordinance is more rigorous than that of Chicago.

Upon these facts we find it necessary to determine only the issue raised under the Commerce Clause, for we agree with appellant that the ordinance imposes an undue burden on interstate commerce.

This is not an instance in which an enactment falls because of federal legislation which, as a proper exercise of paramount national power over commerce, excludes measures which might otherwise be within the police power of the states. There is no pertinent national regulation by the Congress,
. . . .

Nor can there be objection to the avowed purpose of this enactment. We assume that difficulties in sanitary regulation of milk and milk products originating in remote areas may present a situation in which "upon a consideration of all the relevant facts and circumstances it appears that the matter is one which may appropriately be regulated in the interest of the safety, health and well-being of local communities . . . ." . . . We also assume that since Congress has not spoken to the contrary, the subject matter of the ordinance lies within the sphere of state regulation even though interstate commerce may be affected.
. . . .

But this regulation, . . . in practical effect excludes from distribution in Madison wholesome milk produced and pasteurized in Illinois. . . . In thus erecting an economic barrier protecting a major local industry against competition from without the State, Madison plainly discriminates against interstate commerce.[4] This it cannot do, even in the exercise of its unquestioned power to protect the health and safety of its people, if reasonable nondiscriminatory alternatives, adequate to conserve legitimate local interest, are available. . . . A different view, that the ordinance is valid simply because it professes to be a health measure, would mean that the Commerce Clause of itself imposes no limitations on state action other than those laid down by the Due Process Clause, save for the rare instance where a state artlessly discloses an avowed purpose to discriminate against interstate goods. Our issue then is whether the discrimination inherent in the Madison ordinance can be justified in view of the character of the local interests and the available methods of protecting them. . . . .

It appears that reasonable and adequate alternatives are available. If the City of Madison prefers to rely upon its own officials for inspection of distant milk sources, such inspection is readily open to it without hardship for it could charge the actual and reasonable cost of such inspection to the importing producers and processors. . . . Moreover, appellee Health Commissioner of Madison testified that as proponent of the local milk ordinance he had submitted the provisions here in controversy and an alternative proposal based on § 11 of the Model Milk Ordinance recommended by the United States Public Health Service. The model provision imposes no geographical limitation on location of milk sources and processing plants but excludes from the municipality milk not produced and pasteurized conformably to standards as high as those enforced by the receiving city. In implementing such an ordinance, the importing city obtains milk ratings based on uniform standards and established by health authorities in the jurisdiction where production and processing occur. The receiving city may determine the extent of enforcement of sanitary standards in the exporting area by verifying the accuracy of safety ratings of specific plants or of the milkshed in the distant jurisdiction through the United States Public Health Service, which routinely and on request spot checks the local ratings. The Commissioner testified that Madison consumers "would be safeguarded adequately" under either proposal and that he had expressed no preference. The milk sanitarium of the Wisconsin State Board of Health testified that the State Health Department recommends the adoption of a provision based on the Model Ordinance. Both officials agreed that a local health officer would be justified in relying upon the evaluation by the Public Health Service of enforcement conditions in remote producing areas.

To permit Madison to adopt a regulation not essential for the protection of local health interests and placing a discriminatory burden on interstate commerce would invite a multiplication of preferential trade areas destructive of the very purpose of the Commerce Clause. Under the circumstances here presented, the regulation must yield to the principle that "one state in its dealings with another may not place itself in a position of economic isolation."

For these reasons we conclude that the judgment below sustaining the five-mile provision as to pasteurization must be reversed.

The Supreme Court of Wisconsin thought it unnecessary to pass upon the validity of the twenty-five-mile limitation, apparently in part for the reason that this issue was made academic by its decision upholding the five-mile section. In view of our conclusion as to the latter provision, a determination of appellant's contention as to the other section is now necessary. As to this issue, therefore, we vacate the judgment below and remand for further proceedings not inconsistent with the principles announced in this opinion. It is so ordered.

Judgment vacated and cause remanded.

[4] It is immaterial that Wisconsin milk from outside the Madison area is subjected to the same proscription as that moving in interstate commerce. . . .

Mr. Justice Black, with whom Mr. Justice Douglas and Mr. Justice Minton concur, dissenting.

Today's holding invalidates § 7.21 of the Madison, Wisconsin, ordinance on the following reasoning: (1) the section excludes wholesome milk coming from Illinois; (2) this imposes a discriminatory burden on interstate commerce; (3) such a burden cannot be imposed where, as here, there are reasonable, nondiscriminatory and adequate alternatives available. I disagree with the Court's premises, reasoning, and judgment.

(1) This ordinance does not exclude wholesome milk coming from Illinois or anywhere else. It does require that all milk sold in Madison must be pasteurized within five miles of the center of the city. But there was no finding in the state courts, nor evidence to justify a finding there or here, that appellant, Dean Milk Company, is unable to have its milk pasteurized within the defined geographical area. As a practical matter, so far as the record shows, Dean can easily comply with the ordinance whenever it wants to. Therefore, Dean's personal preference to pasteurize in Illinois, not the ordinance, keeps Dean's milk out of Madison.

(2) Characterization of § 7.21 as a "discriminatory burden" on interstate commerce is merely a statement of the Court's result, which I think incorrect. The section does prohibit the sale of milk in Madison by interstate and intrastate producers who prefer to pasteurize over five miles distant from the city. But both state courts below found that § 7.21 represents a good-faith attempt to safeguard public health by making adequate sanitation inspection possible. While we are not bound by these findings, I do not understand the Court to overturn them. Therefore, the fact that § 7.21, like all health regulations, imposes some burden on trade, does not mean that it "discriminates" against commerce.

(3) This health regulation should not be invalidated merely because the Court believes that alternative milk-inspection methods might insure the cleanliness and healthfulness of Dean's Illinois milk. . . . Since the days of Chief Justice Marshall, federal courts have left states and municipalities free to pass bona fide health regulations subject only "to the paramount authority of Congress if it decides to assume control . . . ." . . . No case is cited, and I have found none, in which a bona fide health law was struck down on the ground that some other method of safeguarding health would be as good as, or better than, the one the Court was called on to review. In my view, to use this ground now elevates the right to traffic in commerce for profit above the power of the people to guard the purity of their daily diet of milk.

If, however, the principle announced today is to be followed, the Court should not strike down local health regulations unless satisfied beyond a reasonable doubt that the substitutes it proposes would not lower health standards. I do not think that the Court can so satisfy itself on the basis of its judicial knowledge. And the evidence in the record leads me to the conclusion that the substitute health measures suggested by the Court do not insure milk as safe as the Madison ordinance requires. . . .

From what this record shows, and from what it fails to show, I do not think that either of the alternatives suggested by the Court would assure the people of Madison as pure a supply of milk as they receive under their own ordinance. On this record I would uphold the Madison law. At the very least, however, I would not invalidate it without giving the parties a chance to present evidence and get findings on the ultimate issues the Court thinks crucial—namely, the relative merits of the Madison ordinance and the alternatives suggested by the Court today.

HUNT v. WASHINGTON STATE APPLE ADVERTISING COMMISSION

432 U.S. 333, 97 S.Ct. 2434, 53 L.Ed.2d 383 (1977).

Mr. Chief Justice Burger delivered the opinion of the Court.

In 1973, North Carolina enacted a statute which required, *inter alia,* all closed containers of apples sold, offered for sale or shipped into the State to bear "no grade other than the applicable U.S. grade or standard." N.C.Gen. Stat. § 106–189.1 (1973). In an action brought by the Washington State Apple Advertising Commission (Commission), a three-judge Federal District Court invalidated the statute insofar as it prohibited the display of Washington State apple grades on the ground that it unconstitutionally discriminated against interstate commerce.

. . .

Washington State is the Nation's largest producer of apples, its crops accounting for approximately 30% of all apples grown domestically and nearly half of all apples shipped in closed containers in interstate commerce. As might be expected, the production and sale of apples on this scale is a multimillion dollar enterprise which plays a significant role in Washington's economy. Because of the importance of the apple industry to the State, its legislature has undertaken to protect and enhance the reputation of Washington apples by establishing a stringent, mandatory inspection program, administered by the State's Department of Agriculture, which requires all apples shipped in interstate commerce to be tested under strict quality standards and graded accordingly. In all cases, the Washington State grades, which have gained substantial acceptance in the trade, are the equivalent of, or superior to, the comparable grades and standards adopted by the United States Department of Agriculture.

. . .

. . .

In 1972, the North Carolina Board of Agriculture adopted an administrative regulation, unique in the 50 states, which in effect required all closed containers of apples shipped into or sold in the State to display the applicable U.S.D.A. grade or a notice indicating no classification. State grades were expressly prohibited.

. . .

[The Court held that the Commission had standing to maintain the action on behalf of Washington growers and dealers.]

We turn finally to the appellants' claim that the District Court erred in holding that the North Carolina statute violated the Commerce Clause insofar as it prohibited the display of Washington State grades on closed containers of apples shipped into the State. Appellants do not really contest the District Court's determination that the challenged statute burdened the Washington apple industry by increasing its costs of doing business in the North Carolina market and causing it to lose accounts there. Rather, they maintain that any such burdens on the interstate sale of Washington apples were far outweighed by the local benefits flowing from what they contend was a valid exercise of North Carolina's inherent police powers designed to protect its citizenry from fraud and deception in the marketing of apples.

Prior to the statute's enactment, appellants point out, apples from 13 different states were shipped into North Carolina for sale. Seven of those states, including the State of Washington, had their own grading systems which, while differing in their standards, used similar descriptive labels (e.g., fancy, extra fancy, etc.). This multiplicity of inconsistent state grades, as the District

Court itself found, posed dangers of deception and confusion not only in the North Carolina market, but in the Nation as a whole. The North Carolina statute, appellants claim, was enacted to eliminate this source of deception and confusion by replacing the numerous state grades with a single uniform standard. Moreover, it is contended that North Carolina sought to accomplish this goal of uniformity in an evenhanded manner as evidenced by the fact that its statute applies to all apples sold in closed containers in the State without regard to their point of origin. . . .

As the District Court correctly found, the challenged statute has the practical effect of not only burdening interstate sales of Washington apples, but also discriminating against them. This discrimination takes various forms. The first, and most obvious, is the statute's consequence of raising the costs of doing business in the North Carolina market for Washington apple growers and dealers, while leaving those of their North Carolina counterparts unaffected. [T]his disparate effect results from the fact that North Carolina apple producers, unlike their Washington competitors, were not forced to alter their marketing practices in order to comply with the statute. They were still free to market their wares under the U.S.D.A. grade or none at all as they had done prior to the statute's enactment. Obviously, the increased costs imposed by the statute would tend to shield the local apple industry from the competition of Washington apple growers and dealers who are already at a competitive disadvantage because of their great distance from the North Carolina market.

Second, the statute has the effect of stripping away from the Washington apple industry the competitive and economic advantages it has earned for itself through its expensive inspection and grading system. The record demonstrates that the Washington apple grading system has gained nationwide acceptance in the apple trade. Indeed, it contains numerous affidavits from apple brokers and dealers located both inside and out of North Carolina who state their preference, and that of their customers, for apples graded under the Washington, as opposed to the U.S.D.A. system because of the former's greater consistency, its emphasis on color, and its supporting mandatory inspections. Once again, the statute had no similar impact on the North Carolina apple industry and thus operated to its benefit.

Third, by prohibiting Washington growers and dealers from marketing apples under their State's grades, the statute has a leveling effect which insidiously operates to the advantage of local apple producers. As noted earlier, the Washington State grades are equal or superior to the U.S.D.A. grades in all corresponding categories. Hence, with free market forces at work, Washington sellers would normally enjoy a distinct market advantage vis-a-vis local producers in those categories where the Washington grade is superior. However, because of the statute's operation, Washington apples which would otherwise qualify for, and be sold under the superior Washington grades will now have to be marketed under their inferior U.S.D.A. counterparts. Such "downgrading" offers the North Carolina apple industry the very sort of protection against competing out-of-state products that the Commerce Clause was designed to prohibit. At worst, it will have the effect of an embargo against those Washington apples in the superior grades as Washington dealers withhold them from the North Carolina market. At best, it will deprive Washington sellers of the market premium that such apples would otherwise command.

Despite the statute's facial neutrality, the Commission suggests that its discriminatory impact on interstate commerce was not an unintended byproduct and there are some indications in the record to that effect. The most glaring is the response of the North Carolina Agriculture Commissioner to the Commission's request for an exemption following the statute's passage in which he indicated that before he could support such an exemption, he would "want to have the sentiment from our apple producers *since they were mainly responsible for this legislation being passed . . . .*" Moreover, we find it somewhat suspect that North Carolina singled out only closed containers of apples, the very means by which apples are transported in commerce, to effectuate the statute's ostensible consumer protection purpose when apples are not generally sold at retail in their shipping containers. However, we need not ascribe an economic protection motive to the North Carolina Legislature to resolve this case; we conclude that the challenged statute cannot stand insofar as it prohibits the display of Washington State grades even if enacted for the declared purpose of protecting consumers from deception and fraud in the marketplace.

When discrimination against commerce of the type we have found is demonstrated, the burden falls on the State to justify it both in terms of the local benefits flowing from the statute and the unavailability of nondiscriminatory alternatives, adequate to preserve the local interests at stake. Dean Milk Co. v. Madison, 340 U.S. at 354. North Carolina has failed to sustain that burden on both scores.

The several States unquestionably possess a substantial interest in protecting their citizens from confusion and deception in the marketing of foodstuffs, but the challenged statute does remarkably little to further that laudable goal at least with respect to Washington apples and grades. The statute, as already noted, permits the marketing of closed containers of apples under *no* grades at all. Such a result can hardly be thought to eliminate the problems of deception and confusion created by the multiplicity of differing state grades; indeed, it magnifies them by depriving purchasers of all information concerning the quality of the contents of closed apple containers. Moreover, although the statute is ostensibly a consumer protection measure, it directs its primary efforts, not at the consuming public at large, but at apple wholesalers and brokers who are the principal purchasers of closed containers of apples. And those individuals are presumably the most knowledgeable individuals in this area. Since the statute does nothing at all to purify the flow of information at the retail level, it does little to protect consumers against the problems it was designed to eliminate. Finally, we note that any potential for confusion and deception created by the Washington grades was not of the type that led to the statute's enactment. Since Washington grades are in all cases equal or superior to their U.S.D.A. counterparts, they could only "deceive" or "confuse" a consumer to his benefit, hardly a harmful result.

In addition, it appears that nondiscriminatory alternatives to the outright ban of Washington State grades are readily available. For example, North Carolina could effectuate its goal by permitting out-of-state growers to utilize state grades only if they also marked their shipments with the applicable U.S.D.A. label. In that case, the U.S.D.A. grade would serve as a benchmark against which the consumer could evaluate the quality of the various state grades. If this alternative was for some reason inadequate to eradicate problems caused by state grades inferior to those adopted by the U.S.D.A., North Carolina might consider banning those state grades which, unlike Washington's, could not be demonstrated to be equal or superior to the corresponding U.S.D.A. categories. Concededly, even in this latter instance, some potential for "confusion" might persist. However, it is the type of "confusion" that the national interest in the free flow of goods between the states demands be tolerated.

The judgment of the District Court is affirmed.

Mr. Justice Rehnquist took no part in the consideration or decision of the case.

MINNESOTA v. CLOVER LEAF CREAMERY CO.

449 U.S. 456, 101 S.Ct. 715, 66 L.Ed.2d 659 (1981).

Justice Brennan delivered the opinion of the Court:

In 1977, the Minnesota Legislature enacted a statute banning the retail sale of milk in plastic nonreturnable, nonrefillable containers, but permitting such sale in other nonreturnable, nonrefillable containers, such as paperboard milk cartons. 1977, Minn.Laws, ch. 268, Minn.Stat., § 116F.21 (1978). Respondents [1] contend that the statute violates the Equal Protection and Commerce Clauses of the Constitution.

I

The purpose of the Minnesota statute is set out as § 1:

"The legislature finds that the use of nonreturnable, nonrefillable containers for the packaging of milk and other milk products presents a solid waste management problem for the state, promotes energy waste, and depletes natural resources. The legislature therefore, in furtherance of the policies stated in Minnesota Statutes, Section 116F.01, determines that the use of nonreturnable, nonrefillable containers for packaging milk and other milk products should be discouraged and that the use of returnable and reusable packaging for these products is preferred and should be encouraged." Minn.Laws 1977, ch. 268, § 1, codified as Minn.Stat., § 116F.21.

Section 2 of the Act forbids the retail sale of milk and fluid milk products, other than sour cream, cottage cheese, and yogurt, in nonreturnable, nonrefillable rigid or semirigid containers composed at least 50% of plastic.

The Act was introduced with the support of the state Pollution Control Agency, Department of Natural Resources, Department of Agriculture, Consumer Services Division, and Energy Agency, and debated vigorously in both houses of the state legislature. Proponents of the legislation argued that it would promote resource conservation, ease solid waste disposal problems, and conserve energy. Relying on the results of studies and other information, they stressed the need to stop introduction of the plastic nonreturnable container before it became entrenched in the market. Opponents of the Act, also presenting empirical evidence, argued that the Act would not promote the goals asserted by the proponents, but would merely increase costs of retail milk products and prolong the use of ecologically undesirable paperboard milk cartons.

After the Act was passed, respondents filed suit in Minnesota District Court, seeking to enjoin its enforcement. The Court conducted extensive evidentiary hearings into the Act's probable consequences, and found the evidence "in sharp conflict." Nevertheless, finding itself, "as factfinder . . . obliged to weigh and evaluate this evidence," the Court resolved the evidentiary conflicts in favor of respondents, and concluded that the Act "will not succeed in effecting the Legislature's published policy goals. . . ." The court further found that, contrary to the statement of purpose in § 1, the "actual basis" for the Act "was to promote the economic interests of certain segments of the local dairy and pulpwood industries at the expense of the economic interests of other

[1] Respondents, plaintiffs below, are a Minnesota dairy that owns equipment for producing plastic nonreturnable milk jugs, a Minnesota dairy that leases such equipment, a non-Minnesota company that manufactures such equipment, a Minnesota company that produces plastic nonreturnable milk jugs, a non-Minnesota dairy that sells milk products in Minnesota in plastic nonreturnable milk jugs, a Minnesota milk retailer, a non-Minnesota manufacturer of polyethylene resin that sells such resin in many States, including Minnesota, and a plastics industry trade association.

segments of the dairy industry and the plastics industry." The court therefore declared the Act "null, void, and unenforceable" and enjoined its enforcement, basing the judgment on substantive due process under the Fourteenth Amendment to the United States Constitution and Art. I, § 7, of the Minnesota Constitution; equal protection under the Fourteenth Amendment; and prohibition of unreasonable burdens on interstate commerce under Art. I, § 8, of the United States Constitution.

The State appealed to the Supreme Court of Minnesota, which affirmed the District Court on the federal equal protection and due process grounds, without reaching the Commerce Clause or state-law issues. 289 N.W.2d 79 (1979). Unlike the District Court, the State Supreme Court found that the purpose of the Act was "to promote the state interests of encouraging the reuse and recycling of materials and reducing the amount and type of material entering the solid waste stream," and acknowledged the legitimacy of this purpose. Id., at 82. Nevertheless, relying on the District Court's findings of fact, the full record, and an independent review of documentary sources, the State Supreme Court held that "the evidence conclusively demonstrates that the discrimination against plastic nonrefillables is not rationally related to the Act's objectives." Ibid. We granted certiorari, 445 U.S. 949, and now reverse.

II

The parties agree that the standard of review applicable to this case under the Equal Protection Clause is the familiar "rational basis" test. . . . Moreover, they agree that the purposes of the Act cited by the legislature— promoting resource conservation, easing solid waste disposal problems, and conserving energy—are legitimate state purposes. Thus, the controversy in this case centers on the narrow issue whether the legislative classification between plastic and nonplastic nonreturnable milk containers is rationally related to achievement of the statutory purposes.

. . .

We therefore conclude that the ban on plastic nonreturnable milk containers bears a rational relation to the State's objectives, and must be sustained under the Equal Protection Clause.

III

The District Court also held that the Minnesota statute is unconstitutional under the Commerce Clause because it imposes an unreasonable burden on interstate commerce.[14] We cannot agree.

When legislating in areas of legitimate local concern, such as environmental protection and resource conservation, States are nonetheless limited by the Commerce Clause. . . . If a state law purporting to promote environmental purposes is in reality "simple economic protectionism," we have applied a "virtually *per se* rule of invalidity." Philadelphia v. New Jersey, 437 U.S. 617, 624 (1978).[15] Even if a statute regulates "even handedly," and imposes only "incidental" burdens on interstate commerce, the courts must nevertheless strike

---

[14] The Minnesota Supreme Court did not reach the Commerce Clause issue. 289 N.W.2d, at 87, n. 20. The parties and *amici* have fully briefed and argued the question, and because of the obvious factual connection between the rationality analysis under the Equal Protection Clause and the balancing of interests under the Commerce Clause, we will reach and decide the question. See New York City Transit Authority v. Beazer, 440 U.S. 568, 583, n. 24 (1979).

[15] A court may find that a state law constitutes "economic protectionism" on proof either of discriminatory effect, see Philadelphia v. New Jersey, or of discriminatory purpose, see Hunt v. Washington State Apple Advertising Comm'n, 432 U.S., at 352–353 (1977). Respondents advance a "discriminatory purpose" argument, relying on a finding by the District Court that the Act's "actual basis was to promote the economic interests of certain segments of the local dairy and pulpwood industries at the expense of the economic interests of other segments of the dairy industry and the

it down if "the burden imposed on such commerce is clearly excessive in relation to the putative local benefits." Pike v. Bruce Church, Inc., 397 U.S. 137, 142 (1970). Moreover, "the extent of the burden that will be tolerated will of course depend on the nature of the local interest involved, and on whether it could be promoted as well with a lesser impact on interstate activities." Ibid.

Minnesota's statute does not effect "simple protectionism," but "regulates evenhandedly" by prohibiting all milk retailers from selling their products in plastic, nonreturnable milk containers, without regard to whether the milk, the containers, or the sellers are from outside the State. This statute is therefore unlike statutes discriminating against interstate commerce, which we have consistently struck down. . . .

Since the statute does not discriminate between interstate and intrastate commerce, the controlling question is whether the incidental burden imposed on interstate commerce by the Minnesota Act is "clearly excessive in relation to the putative local benefits." Pike v. Bruce Church, Inc., supra, at 142. We conclude that it is not.

The burden imposed on interstate commerce by the statute is relatively minor. Milk products may continue to move freely across the Minnesota border, and since most dairies package their products in more than one type of containers, the inconvenience of having to conform to different packaging requirements in Minnesota and the surrounding States should be slight. . . . Within Minnesota, business will presumably shift from manufacturers of plastic nonreturnable containers to producers of paperboard cartons, refillable bottles, and plastic pouches, but there is no reason to suspect that the gainers will be Minnesota firms, or the losers out-of-state firms. Indeed, two of the three dairies, the sole milk retailer, and the sole milk container producer challenging the statute in this litigation are Minnesota firms.[17]

Pulpwood producers are the only Minnesota industry likely to benefit significantly from the Act at the expense of out-of-state firms. Respondents point out that plastic resin, the raw material used for making plastic nonreturnable milk jugs, is produced entirely by non-Minnesota firms, while pulpwood, used for making paperboard, is a major Minnesota product. Nevertheless, it is clear that respondents exaggerate the degree of burden on out-of-state interests, both because plastics will continue to be used in the production of plastic pouches, plastic returnable bottles, and paperboard itself, and because out-of-state pulpwood producers will presumably absorb some of the business generated by the Act.

Even granting that the out-of-state plastics industry is burdened relatively more heavily than the Minnesota pulpwood industry, we find that this burden is not "clearly excessive" in light of the substantial state interest in promoting conservation of energy and other natural resources and easing solid waste disposal problems, which we have already reviewed in the context of equal protection analysis. We find these local benefits ample to support Minnesota's decision under the Commerce Clause. Moreover, we find that no approach

plastics industry." We have already considered and rejected this argument in the equal protection context, see n. 7, supra, and do so in this context as well.

[In note 7 the Court said, in part: "Here, a review of the legislative history supports the Minnesota Supreme Court's conclusion that the principal purposes of the Act were to promote conservation and ease solid waste disposal problems. The contrary evidence cited by respondents is easily understood, in context, as economic defense of an Act genuinely proposed for environmental reasons. We will not invalidate a state statute under the Equal Protection Clause merely because some legislators sought to obtain votes for the measure on the basis of its beneficial side effects on state industry."]

[17] See n. 1, supra. The existence of major in-state interests adversely affected by the Act is a powerful safeguard against legislative abuse. South Carolina State Highway Dept. v. Barnwell Bros., Inc., 303 U.S. 177, 187 (1938).

with "a lesser impact on interstate activities," Pike v. Bruce Church, Inc., supra, 397 U.S., at 142, is available. Respondents have suggested several alternative statutory schemes, but these alternatives are either more burdensome on commerce than the Act (as, for example, banning all nonreturnables) or less likely to be effective (as, for example, providing incentives for recycling).

In Exxon Corp. v. Governor of Maryland, 437 U.S. 117 (1978), we upheld a Maryland statute barring producers and refiners of petroleum products—all of which were out-of-state businesses—from retailing gasoline in the State. We stressed that the Commerce Clause "protects the interstate market, not particular interstate firms, from prohibitive or burdensome regulations." Id., at 127–128. A nondiscriminatory regulation serving substantial state purposes is not invalid simply because it causes some business to shift from a predominantly out-of-state industry to a predominantly in-state industry. Only if the burden on interstate commerce clearly outweighs the State's legitimate purposes does such a regulation violate the Commerce Clause.

The judgment of the Minnesota Supreme Court is
Reversed.

Justice Rehnquist took no part in the consideration or decision of this case.

Justice Powell, concurring in part and dissenting in part.

. . .

. . . I concur in the view that the statute survives equal protection challenge, and therefore join the judgment of reversal on this ground. . . .

I would not, however, reach the Commerce Clause issue, but would remand it for consideration by the Supreme Court of Minnesota. . . .

Justice Stevens, dissenting.

[Justice Stevens did not disagree with the Court's equal protection or commerce clause analysis. He claimed instead that the Court was not free to reject the factual conclusions reached by the Supreme Court of Minnesota and claimed that those conclusions justified a holding that the statute was in violation of the equal protection clause.]

B. REQUIRING BUSINESS OPERATIONS TO BE PERFORMED IN THE HOME STATE

MINNESOTA v. BARBER, 136 U.S. 313 (1890). A Minnesota statute prohibited the sale for human food of fresh meat not taken from animals inspected in Minnesota within 24 hours before being slaughtered. The case involved the sale in Minnesota of fresh beef slaughtered in Illinois but not inspected in Minnesota as required by the statute. In support of the legislation it was argued that inspection on the hoof, within a very short time before animals are slaughtered, was necessary to ascertain their condition with certainty.

The Court stated: "[I]f, as alleged, the inspection of fresh beef, veal, mutton, lamb or pork will not necessarily show whether the animal from which it was taken was diseased when slaughtered, it would not follow that a statute like the one before us is within the constitutional power of the State to enact. On the contrary, the enactment of a similar statute by each one of the States composing the Union would result in the destruction of commerce among the several States, so far as such commerce is involved in the transportation from one part of the country to another of animal meats designed for human food, and entirely free from disease. A careful examination of the Minnesota Act will place this construction of it beyond question. . . . As the inspection must take place within the twenty-four hours immediately before the slaughtering, the act, by its necessary operation, excludes from the Minnesota market practically all fresh beef, veal, mutton, lamb or pork—in whatever form, and although entirely sound, healthy and fit for human food—taken from animals slaughtered in other States; and directly tends to restrict the slaughtering of animals, whose meat is to be sold in Minnesota for human food, to those engaged in such business in that State. . . . It will not do to say—certainly no judicial tribunal can, with propriety, assume—that the people of Minnesota may not, with due regard to their health, rely upon inspections in other States of animals there slaughtered for purposes of human food. . . . [A] law providing for the inspection of animals whose meats are designed for human food cannot be regarded as a rightful exertion of the police powers of the State, if the inspection prescribed is of such a character, or is burdened with such conditions, as will prevent altogether the introduction into the State of sound meats, the product of animals slaughtered in other States."

The statute was held invalid as applied in the case.

FOSTER–FOUNTAIN PACKING CO. v. HAYDEL, 278 U.S. 1 (1928). A Louisiana statute declared all shrimp in Louisiana waters to be the property of the state but authorized the taking of shrimp on certain conditions. Among these conditions was the provision that no shipment out of state could be made of shrimp from which the heads and hulls had not been removed or of the raw heads and hulls "as they are required to be manufactured into fertilizer or used for an element in chicken feed." No restriction was placed on the shipment out of the state of fertilizer or chicken feed. The Court held the statute invalid, saying:

"As the representative of its people, the state might have retained the shrimp for consumption and use therein. But, in direct opposition to conservation for intrastate use, this enactment permits all parts of the shrimp to be shipped and sold outside the state. The purpose is not to retain the shrimp for the use of the people of Louisiana; it is to favor the canning of the meat and the manufacture of bran in Louisiana by withholding raw or unshelled shrimp from the Biloxi [Mississippi] plants. But by permitting its shrimp to be taken and all the products thereof to be shipped and sold in interstate commerce, the state necessarily releases its hold . . . . And those taking the shrimp . . . become entitled to the rights of private ownership and the protection of the commerce clause."

PIKE v. BRUCE CHURCH, INC., 397 U.S. 137 (1970). Appellee grows cantaloupes of superior quality in Parker, Arizona. Since the company lacked packing sheds in Parker, it transported the cantaloupes to nearby facilities in California where they were packed under regulations similar to those of Arizona, but shipped in containers bearing the name of the California packer. Pike, a State official acting under the Arizona Fruit and Vegetable Standardization Act, which was designed to prevent deceptive packaging, entered an order prohibiting the company from shipping its cantaloupes outside the State unless they were packed in containers approved by him. He contended that his order was necessary to ensure that the cantaloupes be identified as of Arizona origin. The company sought injunctive relief, claiming that the order would require it to build packing facilities in or near Parker at a cost of about $200,000 and this would constitute an unconstitutional burden on interstate commerce. A three-judge court granted relief. The Court unanimously affirmed, saying:

". . . Although the criteria for determining the validity of state statutes affecting interstate commerce have been variously stated, the general rule that emerges can be phrased as follows: Where the statute regulates even-handedly to effectuate a legitimate local public interest, and its effects on interstate commerce are only incidental, it will be upheld unless the burden imposed on such commerce is clearly excessive in relation to the putative local benefits. Huron Cement Co. v. Detroit, 362 U.S. 440, 443. If a legitimate local purpose is found, then the question becomes one of degree. And the extent of the burden that will be tolerated will of course depend on the nature of the local interest involved, and on whether it could be promoted as well with a lesser impact on interstate activities. Occasionally the Court has candidly undertaken a balancing approach in resolving these issues, Southern Pacific Co. v. Arizona, 325 U.S. 761, but more frequently it has spoken in terms of 'direct' and 'indirect' effects and burdens. . . ."

Referring to the stipulation of the State that the primary purpose of the Arizona law was to protect the reputation of Arizona growers by prohibiting deceptive packaging, the Court continued: "We are not, then, dealing here with 'state legislation in the field of safety where the propriety of local regulation has long been recognized,' or with an Act designed to protect consumers in Arizona from contaminated or unfit goods. Its purpose and design are simply to protect and enhance the reputation of growers within the State. These are surely legitimate state interests. Sligh v. Kirkwood, 237 U.S. 52, 61. We have upheld a State's power to require that produce packaged in the State be packaged in a particular kind of receptacle, Pacific States Box & Basket Co. v. White, 296 U.S. 176. And we have recognized the legitimate interest of a State in maximizing the financial return to an industry within it. Parker v. Brown, 317 U.S. 341.[a] . . .

"But application of the Act through the appellant's order to the appellee company has a far different impact, and quite a different purpose. . . . The appellant . . . is not complaining because the company is putting the good name of Arizona on an inferior or deceptively packaged product, but because it is not putting that name on a product that is superior and well packaged. . . . [T]he State's tenuous interest in having the company's cantaloupes identified as originating in Arizona cannot constitutionally justify the requirement that the company build and operate an unneeded $200,000 packing plant in the State. The nature of that burden is, constitutionally, more significant than its extent. For the Court has viewed with particular suspicion state statutes requiring business operations to be performed in the home State that could more efficiently be performed elsewhere. Even where the State is pursuing a clearly legitimate local interest, this particular burden on commerce has been declared to be virtually *per se* illegal. Foster-Fountain Packing Co. v. Haydel, 278 U.S. 1. . . ."

C. PRESERVING RESOURCES FOR IN–STATE CONSUMPTION

PENNSYLVANIA v. WEST VIRGINIA, 262 U.S. 553 (1923). In the early years of this century West Virginia was the major producing state for natural gas. Production exceeded local needs and the state permitted pipeline corporations to purchase natural gas and transport it to customers in Pennsylvania and Ohio. Large numbers of residential and industrial consumers in

---

[a] *Parker* (1943) sustained the California Agricultural Prorate Act as applied to a raisin producer most of whose product was marketed interstate. The Court (per Stone, C.J.) said: "[T]he adoption of legislative measures to prevent the demoralization of the industry by stabilizing the marketing of the raisin crop is a matter of state as well as national concern and, in the absence of inconsistent Congressional action, is a problem whose solution is peculiarly within the province of the state." Such legislation was not invalid because it "affected the commerce by increasing the interstate price of raisins and curtailing interstate shipments to some undetermined extent."

those states became dependent on the supply of gas from West Virginia. The time came when the demand for the gas exceeded the supply and that the only way more gas could be provided in one of the states was to reduce the amount supplied in the others.

West Virginia passed a statute requiring every pipeline company transporting gas produced in West Virginia to satisfy the needs, domestic or industrial, of all West Virginia customers, old or new, willing to pay for the gas and use it within the state. The states of Pennsylvania and Ohio brought suit to enjoin West Virginia from enforcing this statute. The Court held the statute invalid.

Justice Van Devanter, writing for the Court, said in part:

"Natural gas is a lawful article of commerce, and its transmission from one state to another for sale and consumption in the latter is interstate commerce. A state law, whether of the state where the gas is produced or that where it is to be sold, which by its necessary operation prevents, obstructs or burdens such transmission is a regulation of interstate commerce—a prohibited interference.

. . .

"But it is urged that there are special considerations which take the act out of the general rule and sustain its validity, even though there be an interference.

. . .

"[One such consideration] is that the gas is a natural product of the state and has become a necessity therein, that the supply is waning and no longer sufficient to satisfy local needs and be used abroad, and that the act is therefore a legitimate measure of conservation in the interest of the people of the state. If the situation be as stated, it affords no ground for the assumption by the state of power to regulate interstate commerce, which is what the act attempts to do. That power is lodged elsewhere."

In a dissenting opinion Justice Holmes said: "I see nothing in the commerce clause to prevent a State from giving a preference to its inhabitants in the enjoyment of its natural advantages."

H. P. HOOD & SONS v. DU MOND

336 U.S. 525, 69 S.Ct. 657, 93 L.Ed. 865 (1949).

[Hood & Sons has long distributed milk and milk products to the Boston area which obtains about 90% of its milk from states other than Massachusetts. For some time Hood has obtained milk in New York State for shipment to Boston and for this purpose has operated three receiving depots in the state. It now proposes to open a fourth at Greenwich, New York, in an area which has been developed by Hood and a competitor as part of the Boston Milkshed. Greenwich is ten miles from Salem and twelve miles from Eagle Bridge where two of Hood's existing depots are located. Hood applied for a license to open the new depot, as required by the New York law which provided that, before issuing the license, the Commission of Agriculture and Markets should be satisfied "that the issuance of a license will not tend to a destructive competition in a market already adequately served, and that the issuance of the license is in the public interest." Pursuant to this provision, the Commissioner refused to issue the license although Hood met all the other statutory requirements.]

Mr. Justice Jackson delivered the opinion of the Court. . . .

The Commissioner found that Hood, if licensed at Greenwich, would permit its present suppliers, at their option, to deliver at the new plant rather than the old ones and for a substantial number this would mean shorter hauls and savings in delivery costs. The new plant also would attract twenty to thirty producers, some of whose milk Hood anticipates will or may be diverted from other buyers. Other large milk distributors have plants within the general area and dealers serving Troy obtain milk in the locality. He found that Troy was inadequately supplied during the preceding short season.

. . .

Pennsylvania enacted a law including provisions to protect producers which were very similar to those of this New York Act. A concern which operated a receiving plant in Pennsylvania from which it shipped milk to the New York City market challenged the Act upon grounds thus defined by this Court: "The respondent contends that the act, if construed to require it to obtain a license, to file a bond for the protection of producers, and to pay the farmers the prices prescribed by the Board, unconstitutionally regulates and burdens interstate commerce." Milk Control Bd. v. Eisenberg Co., 306 U.S. 346, 350. This Court, specifically limiting its judgment to the Act's provisions with respect to license, bond and regulation of prices to be paid to producers, Id. at 306 U.S. at 352, considered their effect on interstate commerce "incidental and not forbidden by the Constitution, in the absence of regulation by Congress." Id. at 306 U.S. at 353.

The present controversy begins where the Eisenberg decision left off. New York's regulations, designed to assure producers a fair price and a responsible purchaser, and consumers a sanitary and modernly equipped handler, are not challenged here but have been complied with. It is only additional restrictions, imposed for the avowed purpose and with the practical effect of curtailing the volume of interstate commerce to aid local economic interests, that are in question here, and no such measures were attempted or such ends sought to be served in the Act before the Court in the Eisenberg case.

Our decision in a milk litigation most relevant to the present controversy deals with the converse of the present situation. Baldwin v. G. A. F. Seelig, Inc., 294 U.S. 511, . . . is an explicit, impressive, recent and unanimous condemnation by this Court of economic restraints on interstate commerce for local economic advantage, but it does not stand alone. This Court consistently has rebuffed attempts of states to advance their own commercial interests by curtailing the movement of articles of commerce, either into or out of the state, while generally supporting their right to impose even burdensome regulations in the interests of local health and safety. As most states serve their own interests best by sending their produce to market, the cases in which this Court has been obligated to deal with prohibitions or limitations by states upon exports of articles of commerce are not numerous. . . .

[The] principle that our economic unit is the Nation, which alone has the gamut of powers necessary to control of the economy, including the vital power of erecting customs barriers against foreign competition, has as its corollary that the states are not separable economic units. As the Court said in Baldwin v. G. A. F. Seelig, Inc., 294 U.S. 511, 527, "What is ultimate is the principle that one state in its dealings with another may not place itself in a position of economic isolation." In so speaking it but followed the principle that the state may not use its admitted powers to protect the health and safety of its people as a basis for suppressing competition. In Buck v. Kuykendall, 267 U.S. 307, the Court struck down a state act because, in the language of Mr. Justice Brandeis, "Its primary purpose is not regulation with a view to safety or to conservation of the highways, but the prohibition of competition." The same argument here advanced, that limitation of competition would itself contribute to safety and conservation, and therefore indirectly serve an end permissible to the state, was there declared "not sound." 267 U.S. 307, 315. It is no better here. . . .

The material success that has come to inhabitants of the states which make up this federal free trade unit has been the most impressive in the history of commerce, but the established interdependence of the states only emphasizes the necessity of protecting interstate movement of goods against local burdens and repressions. . . .

Our system, fostered by the Commerce Clause, is that every farmer and every craftsman shall be encouraged to produce by the certainty that he will have free access to every market in the Nation, that no home embargoes will withhold his export, and no foreign state will by customs duties or regulations exclude them. Likewise, every consumer may look to the free competition from every producing area in the Nation to protect him from exploitation by any. Such was the vision of the Founders; such has been the doctrine of this Court which has given it reality. . . .

Since the statute as applied violates the Commerce Clause and is not authorized by federal legislation pursuant to that Clause, it cannot stand. The judgment is reversed and the cause remanded for proceedings not inconsistent with this opinion. It is so ordered.

Reversed and remanded.

Mr. Justice Frankfurter, with whom Mr. Justice Rutledge joins, dissenting. . . .

. . .

Mr. Justice Black, dissenting.

In this case the Court sets up a new constitutional formula for invalidation of state laws regulating local phases of interstate commerce. I believe the New York law is invulnerable to constitutional attack under constitutional rules which the majority of this Court have long accepted. The new formula subjects state regulations of local business activities to greater constitutional hazards than they have ever had to meet before. The consequences of the new formula, as I understand it, will not merely leave a large area of local business activities free from state regulation. All local activities that fall within the scope of this new formula will be free from any regulatory control whatever. For it is inconceivable that Congress could pass uniform national legislation capable of adjustment and application to all the local phases of interstate activities that take place in the 48 states. It is equally inconceivable that Congress would attempt to control such diverse local activities through a "swarm of statutes only locally applicable, and utterly inconsistent." Kidd v. Pearson, 128 U.S. 1, 21. . . .

. . .

The language of this state Act is not discriminatory, the legislative history shows it was not so intended, and the commissioner has not administered it with a hostile eye. . . .

The basic question here is not the greatness of the commerce clause concept, but whether all local phases of interstate business are to be judicially immunized from state laws against destructive competitive business practices such as those prohibited by New York's law. Of course, there remains the bare possibility Congress might attempt to federalize all such local business activities in the forty-eight states. While I have doubt about the wisdom of this New York law, I do not conceive it to be the function of this Court to revise that state's economic judgments. Any doubt I may have concerning the wisdom of New York's law is far less, however, than is my skepticism concerning the ability of the Federal Government to reach out and effectively regulate all the local business activities in the forty-eight states.

I would leave New York's law alone.

Mr. Justice Murphy joins in this opinion.

PHILADELPHIA v. NEW JERSEY

437 U.S. 617, 98 S.Ct. 2531, 57 L.Ed.2d 475 (1978).

Mr. Justice Stewart delivered the opinion of the Court.

A New Jersey law prohibits the importation of most "solid or liquid waste which originated or was collected outside the territorial limits of the State. . . ." In this case we are required to decide whether this statutory prohibition violates the Commerce Clause of the United States Constitution.

. . .

[Operators of private landfills in New Jersey and several cities in other states that had agreements with these operators for waste disposal brought suit against New Jersey in state court challenging the validity of the statute and regulations issued under it. The New Jersey Supreme Court upheld the legislation. The plaintiffs appealed to the United States Supreme Court.]

III.

A.

. . .

The opinions of the Court through the years have reflected an alertness to the evils of "economic isolation" and protectionism, while at the same time recognizing that incidental burdens on interstate commerce may be unavoidable when a State legislates to safeguard the health and safety of its people. Thus, where simple economic protectionism is effected by state legislation, a virtually per se rule of invalidity has been erected. See, e.g., Hood & Sons v. Du Mond, supra; Toomer v. Witsell, 334 U.S. 385, 403–406; Baldwin v. G. A. F. Seelig, supra; Buck v. Kuykendall, 267 U.S. 307, 315–316. The clearest example of such legislation is a law that overtly blocks the flow of interstate commerce at a State's borders. Cf. Welton v. Missouri, 91 U.S. 275. But where other legislative objectives are credibly advanced and there is no patent discrimination against interstate trade, the Court has adopted a much more flexible approach, the general contours of which were outlined in Pike v. Bruce Church, Inc., 397 U.S. 137, 142:

. . . The crucial inquiry, therefore, must be directed to determining whether ch. 363 is basically a protectionist measure, or whether it can fairly be viewed as a law directed to legitimate local concerns, with effects upon interstate commerce that are only incidental.

B.

The purpose of ch. 363 is set out in the statute itself as follows:

"The Legislature finds and determines that . . . the volume of solid and liquid waste continues to rapidly increase, that the treatment and disposal of these wastes continues to pose an even greater threat to the quality of the environment of New Jersey, that the available and appropriate land fill sites within the State are being diminished, that the environment continues to be threatened by the treatment and disposal of waste which originated or was collected outside the State and that the public health, safety and welfare require that the treatment and disposal within this State of all wastes generated outside of the State be prohibited."

The New Jersey Supreme Court accepted this statement of the state legislature's purpose. The state court additionally found that New Jersey's existing landfill sites will be exhausted within a few years; that to go on using these sites or to develop new ones will take a heavy environmental toll, both from pollution and from loss of scarce open lands; that new techniques to divert

waste from landfills to other methods of disposal and resource recovery processes are under development, but that these changes will require time; and finally,
that "the extension of the lifespan of existing landfills, resulting from the
exclusion of out-of-state waste, may be of crucial importance in preventing
further virgin wetlands or other undeveloped lands from being devoted to
landfill purposes." 68 N.J., at 460–465, 348 A.2d, at 509–512. Based on
these findings, the court concluded that ch. 363 was designed to protect not the
State's economy, but its environment, and that its substantial benefits outweigh
its "slight" burden on interstate commerce. Id., at 471–478, 348 A.2d, at 515–
519.

The appellants strenuously contend that ch. 363, "while outwardly cloaked
'in the currently fashionable garb of environmental protection,' . . . is
actually no more than a legislative effort to suppress competition and stabilize
the cost of solid waste disposal for New Jersey residents. . . ."

. . .

The appellees, on the other hand, deny that ch. 363 was motivated by
financial concerns or economic protectionism. . . .

This dispute about ultimate legislative purpose need not be resolved, because its resolution would not be relevant to the constitutional issue to be
decided in this case. Contrary to the evident assumption of the state court and
the parties, the evil of protectionism can reside in legislative means as well as
legislative ends. Thus, it does not matter whether the ultimate aim of ch. 363 is
to reduce the waste disposal costs of New Jersey residents or to save remaining
open lands from pollution, for we assume New Jersey has every right to protect
its residents' pocketbooks as well as their environment. And it may be assumed
as well that New Jersey may pursue those ends by slowing the flow of all waste
into the State's remaining landfills, even though interstate commerce may
incidentally be affected. But whatever New Jersey's ultimate purpose, it may
not be accomplished by discriminating against articles of commerce coming from
outside the State unless there is some reason, apart from their origin, to treat
them differently. Both on its face and in its plain effect, ch. 363 violates this
principle of nondiscrimination.

The Court has consistently found parochial legislation of this kind to be
constitutionally invalid, whether the ultimate aim of the legislation was to assure
a steady supply of milk by erecting barriers to allegedly ruinous outside
competition, Baldwin v. G. A. F. Seelig, supra, at 522–524; or to create jobs by
keeping industry within the State, Foster Packing Co. v. Haydel, 278 U.S. 1, 10;
Johnson v. Haydel, 278 U.S. 16; Toomer v. Witsell, supra, at 403–404; or to
preserve the State's financial resources from depletion by fencing out indigent
immigrants, Edwards v. California, 314 U.S. 160, 173–174. In each of these
cases, a presumably legitimate goal was sought to be achieved by the illegitimate
means of isolating the State from the national economy.

Also relevant here are the Court's decisions holding that a State may not
accord its own inhabitants a preferred right of access over consumers in other
States to natural resources located within its borders. Oklahoma v. Kansas
Natural Gas Co., 221 U.S. 229; Pennsylvania v. West Virginia, 262 U.S. 553.
These cases stand for the basic principle that a "State is without power to
prevent privately owned articles of trade from being shipped and sold in
interstate commerce on the ground that they are required to satisfy local
demands or because they are needed by the people of the State." Foster
Packing Co. v. Haydel, supra, at 10.

The New Jersey law at issue in this case falls squarely within the area that the
Commerce Clause puts off-limits to state regulation. On its face, it imposes on
out-of-state commercial interests the full burden of conserving the State's

remaining landfill space. It is true that in our previous cases the scarce natural resource was itself the article of commerce, whereas here the scarce resource and the article of commerce are distinct. But that difference is without consequence. In both instances, the State has overtly moved to slow or freeze the flow of commerce for protectionist reasons. It does not matter that the State has shut the article of commerce inside the State in one case and outside the State in the other. What is crucial is the attempt by one State to isolate itself from a problem common to many by erecting a barrier against the movement of interstate trade.

The appellees argue that not all laws which facially discriminate against out-of-state commerce are forbidden protectionist regulations. In particular, they point to quarantine laws, which this Court has repeatedly upheld even though they appear to single out interstate commerce for special treatment. See Baldwin v. G. A. F. Seelig, supra, at 525; Bowman v. Chicago & Northwestern R. Co., supra, at 489. In the appellees' view, ch. 363 is analogous to such health-protective measures, since it reduces the exposure of New Jersey residents to the allegedly harmful effects of landfill sites.

It is true that certain quarantine laws have not been considered forbidden protectionist measures, even though they were directed against out-of-state commerce. . . . But those quarantine laws banned the importation of articles such as diseased livestock that required destruction as soon as possible because their very movement risked contagion and other evils. Those laws thus did not discriminate against interstate commerce as such, but simply prevented traffic in noxious articles, whatever their origin.

The New Jersey statute is not such a quarantine law. There has been no claim here that the very movement of waste into or through New Jersey endangers health, or that waste must be disposed of as soon and as close to its point of generation as possible. The harms caused by waste are said to arise after its disposal in landfill sites, and at that point, as New Jersey concedes, there is no basis to distinguish out-of-state waste from domestic waste. If one is inherently harmful, so is the other. Yet New Jersey has banned the former while leaving its landfill sites open to the latter. The New Jersey law blocks the importation of waste in an obvious effort to saddle those outside the State with the entire burden of slowing the flow of refuse into New Jersey's remaining landfill sites. That legislative effort is clearly impermissible under the Commerce Clause of the Constitution.

Today, cities in Pennsylvania and New York find it expedient or necessary to send their waste into New Jersey for disposal, and New Jersey claims the right to close its borders to such traffic. Tomorrow, cities in New Jersey may find it expedient or necessary to send their waste into Pennsylvania or New York for disposal, and those States might then claim the right to close their borders. The Commerce Clause will protect New Jersey in the future, just as it protects her neighbors now, from efforts by one State to isolate itself in the stream of interstate commerce from a problem shared by all.

The judgment is reversed.

Mr. Justice Rehnquist, with whom The Chief Justice joins, dissenting.

. . .

[T]he Court implies that the challenged laws must be invalidated because New Jersey has left its landfills open to domestic waste. But, as the Court notes . . . this Court has repeatedly upheld quarantine laws "even though they appear to single out interstate commerce for special treatment." The fact that New Jersey has left its landfill sites open for domestic waste does not, of course, mean that solid waste is not innately harmful. Nor does it mean that New Jersey prohibits importation of solid waste for reasons other than the health and safety of its population. New Jersey must out of sheer necessity treat and dispose of its solid waste in some fashion, just as it must treat New Jersey cattle suffering from hoof-and-mouth disease. It does not follow that New Jersey must, under the Commerce Clause, accept solid waste or diseased cattle from outside its borders and thereby exacerbate its problems.

The Supreme Court of New Jersey expressly found that ch. 363 was passed "to preserve the health of New Jersey residents by keeping their exposure to solid waste and landfill areas to a minimum." . . . The Court points to absolutely no evidence that would contradict this finding by the New Jersey Supreme Court. Because I find no basis for distinguishing the laws under challenge here from our past cases upholding state laws that prohibit the importation of items that could endanger the population of the State, I dissent.

HUGHES v. OKLAHOMA

441 U.S. 322, 99 S.Ct. 1727, 60 L.Ed.2d 250 (1979).

Mr. Justice Brennan delivered the opinion of the Court.

The question presented for decision is whether Okla.Stat., Tit. 29, § 4–115(B) (Supp.1978) violates the Commerce Clause, Art. I, § 8, cl. 3, of the United States Constitution, insofar as it provides that "No person may transport or ship minnows for sale outside the state which were seined or procured within the waters of this state . . . ."[1]

Appellant William Hughes holds a Texas license to operate a commercial minnow business near Wichita Falls, Tex. An Oklahoma Game Ranger arrested him on a charge of violating § 4–115(B) by transporting from Oklahoma to Wichita Falls a load of natural minnows purchased from a minnow dealer licensed to do business in Oklahoma. Hughes' defense that § 4–115(B) was unconstitutional because it was repugnant to the Commerce Clause was rejected, and he was convicted and fined. The Oklahoma Court of Criminal Appeals affirmed, . . . We noted probable jurisdiction, 439 U.S. 815 (1978). We reverse. Geer v. Connecticut [161 U.S. 519 (1896)] on which the Court of Criminal Appeals relied, is overruled. In that circumstance, § 4–115(B) cannot survive appellant's Commerce Clause attack.

I.

The few simple words of the Commerce Clause—"The Congress shall have Power . . . To regulate Commerce . . . among the several States . . . ."—reflected a central concern of the Framers that was an immediate reason for calling the Constitutional Convention: the conviction that in order to succeed, the new union would have to avoid the tendencies toward economic Balkanization that had plagued relations among the Colonies and later among the States under the Articles of Confederation. See H. P. Hood & Sons, Inc. v. Du Mond, 336 U.S. 525, 533–534 (1949). The Commerce Clause has accordingly been interpreted by this Court not only as an authorization for congressional action, but, even in the absence of a conflicting federal statute, as a restriction on permissible state regulation. The cases defining the scope of permissible state regulation in areas of congressional silence reflect an often controversial evolution of rules to accommodate federal and state interests. Geer v. Connecticut was decided relatively early in that evolutionary process.

---

[1] . . . The prohibition against transportation out of State for sale thus does not apply to hatchery-bred minnows, but only to "natural" minnows seined or procured from waters within the State.

We hold that time has revealed the error of the early resolution reached in that case, and accordingly *Geer* is today overruled.

A.

Geer sustained against a Commerce Clause challenge a statute forbidding the transportation beyond the State of game birds that had been lawfully killed within the State. The decision rested on the holding that no interstate commerce was involved. This conclusion followed in turn from the view that the State had the power, as representative for its citizens, who "owned" in common all wild animals within the State, to control not only the *taking* of game but the *ownership* of game that had been lawfully reduced to possession. By virtue of this power, Connecticut could qualify the ownership of wild game taken within the State by, for example, prohibiting its removal from the State: "The common ownership imports the right to keep the property, if the sovereign so chooses, always within its jurisdiction for every purpose." Accordingly, the State's power to qualify ownership raised serious doubts whether the sale or exchange of wild game constituted "commerce" at all; in any event the Court held that the qualification imposed by the challenged statute removed any transactions involving wild game killed in Connecticut from *interstate* commerce.

Mr. Justice Field and the first Mr. Justice Harlan dissented, rejecting as artificial and formalistic the Court's analysis of "ownership" and "commerce" in wild game. They would have affirmed the State's power to provide for the protection of wild game, but only "so far as such protection . . . does not contravene the power of Congress in the regulation of interstate commerce." Their view was that "[w]hen an animal . . . is lawfully killed for the purposes of food or other uses of man, it becomes an article of commerce, and its use cannot be limited to the citizens of one state to the exclusion of citizens of another state."

B.

The view of the *Geer* dissenters increasingly prevailed in subsequent cases. Indeed, not only has the *Geer* analysis been rejected when natural resources other than wild game were involved, but even state regulations of wild game have been held subject to the strictures of the Commerce Clause under the pretext of distinctions from *Geer*.

. . .

C.

The case before us is the first in modern times to present facts essentially on all fours with *Geer*. We now conclude that challenges under the Commerce Clause to state regulations of wild animals should be considered according to the same general rule applied to state regulations of other natural resources, and therefore expressly overrule *Geer*. We thus bring our analytical framework into conformity with practical realities. Overruling *Geer* also eliminates the anomaly, created by the decisions distinguishing *Geer*, that statutes imposing the most extreme burdens on interstate commerce (essentially total embargoes) were the most immune from challenge. At the same time, the general rule we adopt in this case makes ample allowance for preserving, in ways not inconsistent with the Commerce Clause, the legitimate state concerns for conservation and protection of wild animals underlying the 19th century legal fiction of state ownership.

II.

We turn then to the question whether the burden imposed on interstate commerce in wild game by § 4–115(B) is permissible under the general rule articulated in our precedents governing other types of commerce. See, e.g., Pike v. Bruce Church, supra, 397 U.S., at 142, . . .

Section 4–115(B) on its face discriminates against interstate commerce. It forbids the transportation of natural minnows out of the State for purposes of sale, and thus "overtly blocks the flow of interstate commerce at [the] State's border." Philadelphia v. New Jersey, supra, 437 U.S., at 624. Such facial discrimination by itself may be a fatal defect, regardless of the State's purpose, because "the evil of protectionism can reside in legislative means as well as legislative ends." Id., at 626. At a minimum such facial discrimination invokes the strictest scrutiny of any purported legitimate local purpose and of the absence of nondiscriminatory alternatives.

Oklahoma argues that § 4–115(B) serves a legitimate local purpose in that it is "readily apparent as a conservation measure." The State's interest in maintaining the ecological balance in state waters by avoiding the removal of inordinate numbers of minnows may well qualify as a legitimate local purpose. . . . But the scope of legitimate state interests in "conservation" is narrower under this analysis than it was under *Geer*. A State may no longer "keep the property, if the sovereign so chooses, always within its jurisdiction for every purpose." Geer v. Connecticut, supra, 161 U.S., at 530. The fiction of state ownership may no longer be used to force those outside the State to bear the full costs of "conserving" the wild animals within its borders when equally effective nondiscriminatory conservation measures are available.

Far from choosing the least discriminatory alternative, Oklahoma has chosen to "conserve" its minnows in the way that most overtly discriminates against interstate commerce. The State places no limits on the numbers of minnows that can be taken by licensed minnow dealers; nor does it limit in any way how these minnows may be disposed of within the State. Yet it forbids the transportation of any commercially significant number of natural minnows out of the State for sale. Section 4–115(B) is certainly not a "last ditch" attempt at conservation after nondiscriminatory alternatives have proven unfeasible. It is rather a choice of the most discriminatory means even though nondiscriminatory alternatives would seem likely to fulfill the State's purported legitimate local purpose more effectively.

We therefore hold that § 4–115(B) is repugnant to the Commerce Clause.

III.

The overruling of *Geer* does not leave the States powerless to protect and conserve wild animal life within their borders. Today's decision makes clear, however, that States may promote this legitimate purpose only in ways consistent with the basic principle that "our economic unit is the Nation," H. P. Hood & Sons, Inc. v. Du Mond, supra, 336 U.S., at 537, and that when a wild animal "becomes an article of commerce . . . its use cannot be limited to the citizens of one State to the exclusion of citizens of another State." Geer v. Connecticut, supra, 161 U.S., at 538 (Field, J., dissenting).

Reversed.[a]

---

[a] Apparently Oklahoma did not argue nor did the Court consider the relevance of 16 U.S.C. § 852 making it unlawful for any person knowingly "to transport . . . in interstate or foreign commerce, any black bass and other fish, if such . . . transportation is contrary to the law of the State . . . from which such black bass is transported." See Hellerstein, Hughes v. Oklahoma: The Court, The Commerce Clause, and State Control of Natural Resources, 1979 Sup.Ct.Rev. 51, 54.

Mr. Justice Rehnquist, with whom the Chief Justice joins, dissenting.
. . .

Contrary to the view of the Court, I do not think that Oklahoma's regulation of the commercial exploitation of natural minnows either discriminates against out-of-state enterprises in favor of local businesses or that it burdens the interstate commerce in minnows. At least, no such showing has been made on the record before us. . . . This is not a case where a State's regulation permits residents to export naturally seined minnows but prohibits nonresidents from so doing. No person is allowed to export natural minnows for sale outside of Oklahoma; the statute is evenhanded in its application. See Okla. Stat., Tit. 29, § 4–115(B). The State has not used its power to protect its own citizens from outside competition. . . . Nor is this a case where a State requires a nonresident business, as a condition to exporting minnows, to move a significant portion of its operations to the State or to use certain State resources in pursuit of its business for the benefit of the local economy. . . . And, notwithstanding the Court's protestations to the contrary, Oklahoma has not blocked the flow of interstate commerce in minnows at the State's borders. . . . Petitioner, or anyone else, may freely export as many minnows as he wishes, so long as the minnows so transported are hatchery minnows and not naturally seined minnows. On this record, I simply fail to see how interstate commerce in minnows, the commodity at issue here, is impeded in the least by Oklahoma's regulatory scheme.

Oklahoma does regulate the manner in which both residents and nonresidents procure minnows to be sold outside the State. But there is no showing in this record that requiring petitioner to purchase his minnows from hatcheries instead of from persons licensed to seine minnows from the State's waters in any way increases petitioner's costs of doing business. There also is nothing in the record to indicate that naturally seined minnows are any more desirable as items of commerce than hatchery minnows. So far as the record before us indicates, hatchery minnows and naturally seined minnows are fungible. Accordingly, any minimal burden that may result from requiring petitioner to purchase minnows destined for sale out of state from hatcheries instead of from those licensed to seine minnows is, in my view, more than outweighed by Oklahoma's substantial interest in conserving and regulating exploitation of its natural minnow population. I therefore would affirm the judgment of the Oklahoma Court of Criminal Appeals.

———

NEW ENGLAND POWER CO. v. NEW HAMPSHIRE, 455 U.S. 331 (1982). A power company generated large amounts of power in New Hampshire and sold most of it in other states. The state attempted to apply to this utility a statute that required corporations engaged in power production by water to obtain a commission order permitting them to do so and empowering the commission to deny a permit when it determines that the energy "is reasonably required for use within this state and that the public good requires that it be delivered for such use." The Supreme Court held the statute invalid. "Our cases consistently have held that the Commerce Clause . . . precludes a State from mandating that its residents be given a preferred right of access, over out-of-state consumers, to natural resources located within its borders or to the products derived therefrom. . . .

"The order of the New Hampshire Commission, prohibiting New England Power from selling its hydroelectric energy outside the State of New Hampshire is precisely the sort of protectionist regulation that the Commerce Clause

For an application of that Act to enforce a state ban on the export of fish, see United States v. Howard, 352 U.S. 212 (1957).

declares off-limits to the States. The Commission has made it clear that its order is designed to gain an economic advantage for New Hampshire citizens at the expense of New England Power's customers in neighboring States. Moreover, it cannot be disputed that the Commission's 'exportation ban' places direct and substantial burdens on transactions in interstate commerce . . . . Such state-imposed burdens cannot be squared with the Commerce Clause when they serve only to advance 'simple economic protectionism.' "

The Court then went on to hold that the Federal Power Act did not permit the state to impose such a ban.

SPORHASE v. NEBRASKA, 458 U.S. 941 (1982). Appellants jointly own contiguous tracts of land in Nebraska and Colorado. A well physically located on the Nebraska tract pumps ground water used for irrigation in both the Nebraska and Colorado tracts. Appellants did not seek a permit pursuant to a Nebraska statute which requires a permit to transport ground water taken in the state for use in another state and specifies that the permit should be granted only if the withdrawal of ground water "is reasonable, is not contrary to the conservation and use of ground water, and is not otherwise detrimental to the public welfare" and if the state in which the water is used grants reciprocal rights to withdraw water for use in Nebraska. Nebraska brought suit in the state court to enjoin appellants from transferring the water across the border without a permit. The Nebraska trial court granted the injunction and the Nebraska Supreme Court affirmed.

In an opinion written by Justice Stevens, the Supreme Court invalidated the portion of the statute requiring the other state to provide reciprocity. In the first part of the opinion, the Court addressed the question whether ground water is an article of commerce, concluded that it was and that "[g]round water overdraft is a national problem and Congress has the power to deal with it on that scale." In a third part of the opinion the Court held that Congress had not affirmatively authorized the state to impose otherwise impermissible burdens on interstate commerce in ground water.

In the middle section of the opinion the Court appeared to be saying that only the reciprocity requirement of the statute was invalid and that the remainder would survive if the state court found the invalid provision separable. Opening its discussion with the standard quotation from Pike v. Bruce Church, Inc., the Court then said:

"The only purpose that appellee advances . . . is to conserve and preserve diminishing sources of ground water. The purpose is unquestionably legitimate and highly important, and the other aspects of Nebraska's ground water regulation demonstrate that it is genuine. Appellants' land in Nebraska is located within the boundaries of the Upper Republican Ground Water Control Area, which was designated as such by the Director of the Nebraska Department of Water Resources based upon a determination 'that there is an inadequate ground water supply to meet present or reasonably foreseeable needs for beneficial use of such water supply.' Neb.Rev.Stat. § 46–658(1); . . . [T]he Upper Republican Natural Resources District has promulgated special rules and regulations governing ground water withdrawal and use. The rules and regulations define as 'critical' those townships in the control area in which the annual decline of the ground water table exceeds a fixed percentage; appellants' Nebraska tract is located within a critical township. The rules and regulations require the installation of flow meters on every well within the control area, specify the amount of water per acre that may be used for irrigation, and set the spacing that is required between wells. They also strictly limit the intrastate transfer of ground water: transfers are only permitted between lands controlled by the same ground water user, and all transfers must be approved by the district board of directors.

"The State's interest in conservation and preservation of ground water is advanced by the first three conditions . . . for the withdrawal of water for an interstate transfer. Those requirements are 'that the withdrawal of the ground water requested is reasonable, is not contrary to the conservation and use of ground water, and is not otherwise detrimental to the public welfare.' Although Commerce Clause concerns are implicated by the fact that [the statute] applies to interstate transfers but not to intrastate transfers, there are legitimate reasons for the special treatment accorded requests to transport ground water across state lines. Obviously, a State that imposes severe withdrawal and use restrictions on its own citizens is not discriminating against interstate commerce when it seeks to prevent the uncontrolled transfer of water out of the State. An exemption for interstate transfers would be inconsistent with the ideal of evenhandedness in regulation. At least in the area in which appellants' Nebraska tract is located, the first three standards . . . may well be no more strict in application than the limitations upon intrastate transfers imposed by the Upper Republican Natural Resources District.

"Moreover, in the absence of a contrary view expressed by Congress, we are reluctant to condemn as unreasonable measures taken by a State to conserve and preserve for its own citizens this vital resource in times of severe shortage. Our reluctance stems from the 'confluence of [several] realities.' Hicklin v. Orbeck, 437 U.S. 518, 534 (1978). First, a State's power to regulate the use of water in times and places of shortage for the purpose of protecting the health of its citizens—and not simply the health of its economy—is at the core of its police power. For Commerce Clause purposes, we have long recognized a difference between economic protectionism, on the one hand, and health and safety regulation, on the other. See H. P. Hood & Sons v. Du Mond, 336 U.S. 525, 533 (1949). Second, the legal expectation that under certain circumstances each State may restrict water within its borders has been fostered over the years not only by our equitable apportionment decrees, see, e.g., Wyoming v. Colorado, 353 U.S. 953 (1957), but also by the negotiation and enforcement of interstate compacts. Our law therefore has recognized the relevance of state boundaries in the allocation of scarce water resources. Third, although appellee's claim to public ownership of Nebraska ground water cannot justify a total denial of federal regulatory power, it may support a limited preference for its own citizens in the utilization of the resource. See Hicklin v. Orbeck, supra, at 533–534. In this regard, it is relevant that appellee's claim is logically more substantial than claims to public ownership of other natural resources. Finally, given appellee's conservation efforts, the continuing availability of ground water in Nebraska is not simply happenstance; the natural resource has some indicia of a good publicly produced and owned in which a State may favor its own citizens in times of shortage. See Reeves, Inc. v. Stake, 447 U.S. 429 (1980); . . . . A facial examination of the first three conditions set forth in § 46–613.01 does not, therefore, indicate that they impermissibly burden interstate commerce. Appellants, indeed, seem to concede their reasonableness.

"Appellants, however, do challenge the requirement that 'the state in which the water is to be used grants reciprocal rights to withdraw and transport ground water from that state for use in the State of Nebraska' . . . . Because Colorado forbids the exportation of its ground water, the reciprocity provision operates as an explicit barrier to commerce between the two States. The State therefore bears the initial burden of demonstrating a close fit between the reciprocity requirement and its asserted local purpose.

"The reciprocity requirement fails to clear this initial hurdle. For there is no evidence that this restriction is narrowly tailored to the conservation and preservation rationale. Even though the supply of water in a particular well may be abundant, or perhaps even excessive, and even though the most beneficial use of that water might be in another State, such water may not be shipped into a neighboring State that does not permit its water to be used in Nebraska. If it could be shown that the State as a whole suffers a water shortage, that the intrastate transportation of water from areas of abundance to areas of shortage is feasible regardless of distance, and that the importation of water from adjoining States would roughly compensate for any exportation to those States, then the conservation and preservation purpose might be credibly advanced for the reciprocity provision. A demonstrably arid state conceivably might be able to marshall evidence to establish a close means-end relationship between even a total ban on the exportation of water and a purpose to conserve and preserve water. Appellee, however, does not claim that such evidence exists. We therefore are not persuaded that the reciprocity requirement—when superimposed on the first three restrictions in the statute—significantly advances the State's legitimate conservation and preservation interest; it surely is not narrowly tailored to serve that purpose. The reciprocity requirement does not survive the 'strictest scrutiny' reserved for facially discriminatory legislation."

Justices Rehnquist and O'Connor dissented.

D. PRESERVING STATE–OWNED RESOURCES FOR IN–STATE USE

REEVES, INC. v. STAKE

447 U.S. 429, 100 S.Ct. 2271, 65 L.Ed.2d 244 (1980).

Mr. Justice Blackmun delivered the opinion of the Court.

The issue in this case is whether, consistent with the Commerce Clause, U.S. Const., Art. I, § 8, ch. 3, the State of South Dakota, in a time of shortage, may confine the sale of the cement it produces solely to its residents.

I.

In 1919, South Dakota undertook plans to build a cement plant. The project, a product of the State's then prevailing Progressive political movement, was initiated in response to recent regional cement shortages that "interfered with and delayed both public and private enterprises," and that were "threatening the people of this state." Eakin v. South Dakota State Cement Comm'n, 44 S.D. 268, 272, 183 N.W. 651, 652 (1921). In 1920, the South Dakota Cement Commission anticipated "[t]hat there would be a ready market for the entire output of the plant within the state." Report of State Cement Commission 9 (1920). The plant, however, located at Rapid City, soon produced more cement than South Dakotans could use. Over the years, buyers in no less than nine nearby States purchased cement from the State's plant. Between 1970 and 1977, some 40% of the plant's output went outside the State.

The plant's list of out-of-state cement buyers included petitioner Reeves, Inc. Reeves is a ready-mix concrete distributor organized under Wyoming law and with facilities in Buffalo, Gillette, and Sheridan, Wyo. From the beginning of its operations in 1958, and until 1978, Reeves purchased about 95% of its cement from the South Dakota plant. In 1977, its purchases were $1,172,000.

In turn, Reeves has supplied three northwestern Wyoming counties with more than half their ready-mix concrete needs. For 20 years the relationship between Reeves and the South Dakota cement plant was amicable, uninterrupted, and mutually profitable.

As the 1978 construction season approached, difficulties at the plant slowed production. Meanwhile, a booming construction industry spurred demand for cement both regionally and nationally. The plant found itself unable to meet all orders. Faced with the same type of "serious cement shortage" that inspired the plant's construction, the Commission "reaffirmed its policy of supplying all South Dakota customers first and to honor all contract commitments, with the remaining volume allocated on a first come, first served basis."

Reeves, which had no pre-existing long-term supply contract, was hit hard and quickly by this development. On June 30, 1978, the plant informed Reeves that it could not continue to fill Reeves' orders, and on July 5, it turned away a Reeves truck. Unable to find another supplier, Reeves was forced to cut production by 76% in mid-July.

On July 19, Reeves brought this suit against the Commission, challenging the plant's policy of preferring South Dakota buyers, and seeking injunctive relief. After conducting a hearing and receiving briefs and affidavits, the District Court found no substantial issue of material fact and permanently enjoined the Commission's practice. The court reasoned that South Dakota's "hoarding" was inimical to the national free market envisioned by the Commerce Clause.

The United States Court of Appeals for the Eighth Circuit reversed. . . . We granted Reeves' petition for certiorari to consider once again the impact of the Commerce Clause on state proprietary activity. 444 U.S. 1031 (1980).

II.

A.

Alexandria Scrap concerned a Maryland program designed to remove abandoned automobiles from the State's roadways and junkyards. To encourage recycling, a "bounty" was offered for every Maryland-titled junk car converted into scrap. Processors located both in and outside Maryland were eligible to collect these subsidies. The legislation, as initially enacted in 1969, required a processor seeking a bounty to present documentation evidencing ownership of the wrecked car. This requirement however, did not apply to "hulks," inoperable automobiles over eight years old. In 1974, the statute was amended to extend documentation requirements to hulks, which comprised a large majority of the junk cars being processed. Departing from prior practice, the new law imposed more exacting documentation requirements on out-of-state than in-state processors. By making it less remunerative for suppliers to transfer vehicles outside Maryland, the reform triggered a "precipitate decline in the number of bounty-eligible hulks supplied to appellee's [Virginia] plant from Maryland sources." 426 U.S., at 801. Indeed, "[t]he practical effect was substantially the same as if Maryland had withdrawn altogether the availability of bounties on hulks delivered by unlicensed suppliers to licensed non-Maryland processors." Id., at 803, n. 13; see id., at 819 (dissenting opinion).

Invoking the Commerce Clause, a three-judge District Court struck down the legislation. 391 F.Supp. 46 (Md.1975). It observed that the amendment imposed "substantial burdens upon the free flow of interstate commerce," id., at 62, and reasoned that the discriminatory program was not the least disruptive means of achieving the State's articulated objective. Id., at 63. See generally Pike v. Bruce Church, Inc., 397 U.S. 137, 142 (1970).

This Court reversed. It recognized the persuasiveness of the lower court's analysis if the inherent restrictions of the Commerce Clause were deemed applicable. In the Court's view, however, *Alexandria Scrap* did not involve "the kind of action with which the Commerce Clause is concerned." 426 U.S., at 805. Unlike prior cases voiding state laws inhibiting interstate trade, "Maryland has not sought to prohibit the flow of hulks, or to regulate the conditions under which it may occur. Instead, it has entered into the market itself to bid up their price," id., at 806, "as a purchaser, in effect, of a potential article of interstate commerce," and has restricted "its trade to its own citizens or businesses within the State." Id., at 808.

Having characterized Maryland as a market participant, rather than as a market regulator, the Court found no reason to "believe the Commerce Clause was intended to require independent justification for [the State's] action." Id., at 809. The Court couched its holding in unmistakably broad terms. "Nothing in the purposes animating the Commerce Clause prohibits a State, in the absence of congressional action, from participating in the market and exercising the right to favor its own citizens over others." Id., at 810 (footnote omitted).

B.

The basic distinction drawn in *Alexandria Scrap* between States as market participants and States as market regulators makes good sense and sound law. As that case explains, the Commerce Clause responds principally to state taxes and regulatory measures impeding free private trade in the national marketplace. 426 U.S., at 807–808, citing H. P. Hood & Sons v. Du Mond, 336 U.S. 525, 539 (1949) (referring to "home embargoes," "customs duties," and "regulations" excluding imports). There is no indication of a constitutional plan to limit the ability of the States themselves to operate freely in the free market. See L. Tribe, American Constitutional Law 336 (1978) ("the commerce clause was directed, as an historical matter, only at regulatory and taxing actions taken by states in their sovereign capacity"). The precedents comport with this distinction.

Restraint in this area is also counseled by considerations of state sovereignty,[10] the role of each State " 'as guardian and trustee for its people,' " Heim v. McCall, 239 U.S. 175, 191 (1915), quoting Atkin v. Kansas, 191 U.S. 207, 222–223 (1903), and "the long recognized right of trader or manufacturer, engaged in an entirely private business, freely to exercise his own independent discretion as to parties with whom he will deal." United States v. Colgate & Co., 250 U.S. 300, 307 (1919). Moreover, state proprietary activities may be, and often are, burdened with the same restrictions imposed on private market participants. Evenhandedness suggests that, when acting as proprietors, States should similarly share existing freedoms from federal constraints, including the inherent limits of the Commerce Clause. . . . Finally, as this case illustrates, the competing considerations in cases involving state proprietary action often will be subtle, complex, politically charged, and difficult to assess under traditional Commerce Clause analysis. Given these factors, *Alexandria Scrap* wisely recognizes that, as a rule, the adjustment of interests in this context is a task better suited for Congress than this Court.

[10] . . . Considerations of sovereignty independently dictate that marketplace actions involving "integral operations in areas of traditional governmental functions"—such as the employment of certain state workers—may not be subject even to congressional regulation pursuant to the commerce power. National League of Cities v. Usery, 426 U.S. 833, 852 (1976). It follows easily that the intrinsic limits of the Commerce Clause do not prohibit state marketplace conduct that falls within this sphere. Even where "integral operations" are not implicated, States may fairly claim some measure of a sovereign interest in retaining freedom to decide how, with whom, and for whose benefit to deal. The Supreme Court, 1975 Term, 90 Harv.L.Rev. 56, 63 (1976).

III.

South Dakota, as a seller of cement, unquestionably fits the "market participant" label more comfortably than a State acting to subsidize local scrap processors. Thus, the general rule of *Alexandria Scrap* plainly applies here. Petitioner argues, however, that the exemption for marketplace participation necessarily admits of exceptions. While conceding that possibility, we perceive in this case no sufficient reason to depart from the general rule.

A.

In finding a Commerce Clause violation, the District Court emphasized "that the Commission . . . made an election to become part of the interstate commerce system." The gist of this reasoning, repeated by petitioner here, is that one good turn deserves another. Having long exploited the interstate market, South Dakota should not be permitted to withdraw from it when a shortage arises. This argument is not persuasive. It is somewhat self-serving to say that South Dakota has "exploited" the interstate market. An equally fair characterization is that neighboring States long have benefited from South Dakota's foresight and industry. Viewed in this light, it is not surprising that *Alexandria Scrap* rejected an argument that the 1974 Maryland legislation challenged there was invalid because cars abandoned in Maryland had been processed in neighboring States for five years. As in *Alexandria Scrap,* we must conclude that "this chronology does not distinguish the case, for Commerce Clause purposes, from one in which a State offered [cement] only to domestic [buyers] from the start." 426 U.S., at 809.

Our rejection of petitioner's market-exploitation theory fundamentally refocuses analysis. It means that to reverse we would have to void a South Dakota "residents only" policy even if it had been enforced from the plant's very first days. Such a holding, however, would interfere significantly with a State's ability to structure relations exclusively with its own citizens. It would also threaten the future fashioning of effective and creative programs for solving local problems and distributing government largesse. See n. 1, supra. A healthy regard for federalism and good government renders us reluctant to risk these results. . . . .

B.

Undaunted by these considerations, petitioner advances four more arguments for reversal:

First, petitioner protests that South Dakota's preference for its residents responds solely to the "non-governmental objective[ ]" of protectionism. Therefore, petitioner argues, the policy is *per se* invalid. See Philadelphia v. New Jersey, 437 U.S. 617, 624 (1978).

We find the label "protectionism" of little help in this context. The State's refusal to sell to buyers other than South Dakotans is "protectionist" only in the sense that it limits benefits generated by a state program to those who fund the state treasury and whom the State was created to serve. Petitioner's argument apparently also would characterize as "protectionist" rules restricting to state residents the enjoyment of state educational institutions, energy generated by a state-run plant, police and fire protection, and agricultural improvement and business development programs. Such policies, while perhaps "protectionist" in a loose sense, reflect the essential and patently unobjectionable purpose of state government—to serve the citizens of the State.

Second, petitioner echoes the District Court's warning:

"If a state in this union, were allowed to hoard its commodities or resources for the use of their own residents only, a drastic situation might evolve. For example, Pennsylvania or Wyoming might keep their coal, the northwest its timber, and the mining states their minerals. The result being that embargo may be retaliated by embargo and commerce would be halted at state lines."

See, e.g., Baldwin v. Montana Fish & Game Comm'n, 436 U.S. 371, 385–386 (1978). This argument, although rooted in the core purpose of the Commerce Clause, does not fit the present facts. Cement is not a natural resource, like coal, timber, wild game, or minerals. Cf. Hughes v. Oklahoma, 441 U.S. 322 (1979) (minnows); Philadelphia v. New Jersey, supra (landfill sites); Pennsylvania v. West Virginia, 262 U.S. 553 (1923) (natural gas); West v. Kansas Natural Gas Co., 221 U.S. 229 (1911) (same); Note, 32 Rutgers L.Rev. 741 (1979). It is the end-product of a complex process whereby a costly physical plant and human labor act on raw materials. South Dakota has not sought to limit access to the State's limestone or other materials used to make cement. Nor has it restricted the ability of private firms or sister States to set up plants within its borders. Moreover, petitioner has not suggested that South Dakota possesses unique access to the materials needed to produce cement. Whatever limits might exist on a State's ability to invoke the *Alexandria Scrap* exemption to hoard resources which by happenstance are found there, those limits do not apply here.

Third, it is suggested that the South Dakota program is infirm because it places South Dakota suppliers of ready-mix concrete at a competitive advantage in the out-of-state market; Wyoming suppliers, such as petitioner, have little chance against South Dakota suppliers who can purchase cement from the State's plant and freely sell beyond South Dakota's borders.

The force of this argument is seriously diminished, if not eliminated, by several considerations. The argument necessarily implies that the South Dakota scheme would be unobjectionable if sales in other States were totally barred. It therefore proves too much, for it would tolerate even a greater measure of protectionism and stifling of interstate commerce than the challenged system allows. . . . Nor is it to be forgotten that *Alexandria Scrap* approved a state program that "not only . . . effectively protect[ed] scrap processors with existing plants in Maryland from the pressures of competitors with nearby out-of-state plants, but [that] implicitly offer[ed] to extend similar protection to any competitor . . . willing to erect a scrap processing facility within Maryland's boundaries." 391 F.Supp., at 63. Finally, the competitive plight of out-of-state ready-mix suppliers cannot be laid solely at the feet of South Dakota. It is attributable as well to their own States' not providing or attracting alternative sources of supply and to the suppliers' own failure to guard against shortages by executing long-term supply contracts with the South Dakota plant.

In its last argument, petitioner urges that, had South Dakota not acted, free market forces would have generated an appropriate level of supply at free market prices for all buyers in the region. Having replaced free market forces, South Dakota should be forced to replicate how the free market would have operated under prevailing conditions.

This argument appears to us to be simplistic and speculative. The very reason South Dakota built its plant was because the free market had failed adequately to supply the region with cement. There is no indication, and no way to know, that private industry would have moved into petitioner's market area, and would have ensured a supply of cement to petitioner either prior to or during the 1978 construction season. Indeed, it is quite possible that petitioner would never have existed—far less operated successfully for 20 years—had it not been for South Dakota cement.

C.

We conclude, then, that the arguments for invalidating South Dakota's resident-preference program are weak at best. Whatever residual force inheres in them is more than offset by countervailing considerations of policy and fairness. Reversal would discourage similar state projects, even though this project demonstrably has served the needs of state residents and has helped the entire region for more than a half century. Reversal also would rob South Dakota of the intended benefit of its foresight, risk, and industry. Under these circumstances, there is no reason to depart from the general rule of *Alexandria Scrap.*

The judgment of the United States Court of Appeals is affirmed.

It is so ordered.

Mr. Justice Powell, with whom Mr. Justice Brennan, Mr. Justice White, and Mr. Justice Stevens join, dissenting.

The South Dakota Cement Commission has ordered that in times of shortage the state cement plant must turn away out-of-state customers until all orders from South Dakotans are filled. This policy represents precisely the kind of economic protectionism that the Commerce Clause was intended to prevent. The Court, however, finds no violation of the Commerce Clause, solely because the State produces the cement. I agree with the Court that the State of South Dakota may provide cement for its public needs without violating the Commerce Clause. But I cannot agree that South Dakota may withhold its cement from interstate commerce in order to benefit private citizens and businesses within the State.

. . .

I share the Court's desire to preserve state sovereignty. But the Commerce Clause long has been recognized as a limitation on that sovereignty, consciously designed to maintain a national market and defeat economic provincialism. The Court today approves protectionist state policies. In the absence of contrary congressional action, those policies now can be implemented as long as the State itself directly participates in the market.

By enforcing the Commerce Clause in this case, the Court would work no unfairness on the people of South Dakota. They still could reserve cement for public projects and share in whatever return the plant generated. They could not, however, use the power of the State to furnish themselves with cement forbidden to the people of neighboring States.

The creation of a free national economy was a major goal of the States when they resolved to unite under the Federal Constitution. The decision today cannot be reconciled with that purpose.

WHITE v. MASSACHUSETTS COUNCIL OF CONSTRUCTION EMPLOYERS

460 U.S. 204, 103 S.Ct. 1042, 75 L.Ed.2d 1 (1983).

Justice Rehnquist delivered the opinion of the Court.

In 1979 the mayor of Boston, Massachusetts, issued an executive order which required that all construction projects funded in whole or in part by city funds, or funds which the city had the authority to administer, should be performed by a work force consisting of at least half *bona fide* residents of Boston. The Supreme Judicial Court of Massachusetts decided that the order was unconstitutional, observing that the Commerce Clause "presents a clear obstacle to the city's order." 384 Mass. 446, 425 N.E.2d 346 (1981). We granted certiorari to decide whether the Commerce Clause of the United States Constitution, Art. I, § 8, cl. 3, prevents the city from giving effect to the mayor's order. 455 U.S. 919 (1982). We now conclude that it does not and reverse.

I

. . .

Alexandria Scrap and *Reeves* . . . stand for the proposition that when a state or local government enters the market as a participant it is not subject to the restraints of the Commerce Clause. As we said in *Reeves,* in this kind of case there is "a single inquiry: whether the challenged 'program constituted direct state participation in the market.'" Id., at 436, n. 7. We reaffirm that principle now.

The Supreme Judicial Court of Massachusetts concluded that the City of Boston is not participating in the market in the sense described in *Alexandria Scrap Corp.* and *Reeves* because the order applies where the city is acting in a nonproprietary capacity, has a significant impact on interstate commerce, is more sweeping than necessary to achieve its objectives, and applies to funds the city receives from federal grants. 384 Mass., at ___, 425 N.E.2d, at 354–355. For the same reasons the court found that the city is not a market participant, it concluded that the executive order violated the substantive restraints of the Commerce Clause. Ibid.

II

. . . The only issues before us . . . are the propriety of applying the mayor's executive order to projects funded wholly with city funds and projects funded in part with federal funds. We address first the application of the order to city funded projects.

The Supreme Judicial Court of Massachusetts expressed reservations as to the application of the "market participation" principle to the city here, reasoning that "the implementation of the mayor's order will have a significant impact on those firms which engage in specialized areas of construction and employ permanent works crews composed of out-of-State residents." 384 Mass., at ___, 425 N.E.2d, at 354. Even if this conclusion is factually correct it is not relevant to the inquiry of whether the city is participating in the marketplace when it provides city funds for building construction. If the city is a market participant, then the Commerce Clause establishes no barrier to conditions such as these which the city demands for its participation. Impact on out-of-state residents figures in the equation only after it is decided that the city is regulating the market rather than participating in it, for only in the former case need it be determined whether any burden on interstate commerce is permitted by the Commerce Clause.

. . . .

The Supreme Judicial Court of Massachusetts also observed that "a significant percentage of the funds affected by the order are received from Federal sources." 384 Mass., at ___, 425 N.E.2d, at 354. The record does indicate that of approximately $54 million expended on projects affected by the mayor's executive order, some $34 million represented projects being funded in part through Urban Development Action Grants (UDAGs). While the record assigns specific dollar amounts only for UDAGs, the parties also have stipulated that the executive order applies to Community Development Block Grants (CDBGs) and Economic Development Administration Grants (EDAGs).

But all of this proves too much. The Commerce Clause is a grant of authority to Congress, and not a restriction on the authority of that body. See

American Power & Light Co. v. SEC, 329 U.S. 90 (1946); Gibbons v. Ogden, 9 Wheat. 1 (1824). Congress, unlike a state legislature authorizing similar expenditures, is not limited by any negative implications of the Commerce Clause in the exercise of its spending power. Where state or local government action is specifically authorized by Congress, it is not subject to the Commerce Clause even if it interferes with interstate commerce. Southern Pacific Co. v. Arizona, 325 U.S. 761, 769 (1945). Thus, if the restrictions imposed by the city on construction projects financed in part by federal funds are directed by Congress then no dormant Commerce Clause issue is presented.

An examination of the applicable statutes reveals that these federal programs were intended to encourage economic revitalization, including improved opportunities for the poor, minorities, and unemployed. Examination of the regulations set forth in the margin indicates that the mayor's executive order sounds a harmonious note; the federal regulations for each program affirmatively permit the type of parochial favoritism expressed in the order.

III

We hold that on the record before us the application of the mayor's executive order to the contracts in question did not violate the Commerce Clause of the United States Constitution.[12] Insofar as the city expended only its own funds in entering into construction contracts for public projects, it was a market participant and entitled to be treated as such under the rule of Hughes v. Alexandria Scrap Corp., supra. Insofar as the mayor's executive order was applied to projects funded in part with funds obtained from the federal programs described above, the order was affirmatively sanctioned by the pertinent regulations of those programs. The judgment of the Supreme Judicial Court of Massachusetts is therefore reversed, and the case is remanded to that court for proceedings not inconsistent with this opinion.

It is so ordered.

Justice Blackmun, with whom Justice White joins, concurring in part and dissenting in part.

. . . .

SOUTH–CENTRAL TIMBER DEVELOPMENT v. WUNNICKE

__ U.S. __, 104 S.Ct. 2237, 81 L.Ed.2d 71 (1984).

Justice White delivered the opinion of the Court with respect to Parts I and II, and delivered an opinion with respect to Parts III and IV, in which Justice Brennan, Justice Blackmun, and Justice Stevens joined.

We granted certiorari in this case to review a decision of the Court of Appeals for the Ninth Circuit that held that Alaska's requirement that timber taken from state lands be processed within the State prior to export was "implicitly authorized" by Congress and therefore does not violate the Commerce Clause. We hold that it was not authorized and reverse the judgment of the Court of Appeals.

---

[12] Respondents ask us to decide whether the executive order offends the Privileges and Immunities Clause of Art. IV, § 2, cl. 1, which provides: "The Citizens of each State shall be entitled to all Privileges and Immunities of Citizens in several States." . . .

This question has not been, to any great extent, briefed or argued in this Court. We did not grant certiorari on the issue and remand without passing on its merits. . . . [On the Privileges and Immunities issue, see United Building and Construction Trades Council v. City of Camden, infra p. 318.]

I

In September 1980, the Alaska Department of Natural Resources published a notice that it would sell approximately 49 million board-feet of timber in the area of Icy Cape, Alaska, on October 23, 1980. The notice of sale, the prospectus, and the proposed contract for the sale all provided, pursuant to 11 Alaska Admin.Code § 76.130, that "primary manufacture within the State of Alaska will be required as a special provision of the contract." Under the primary-manufacture requirement, the successful bidder must partially process the timber prior to shipping it outside of the State. The requirement is imposed by contract and does not limit the export of unprocessed timber not owned by the State. The stated purpose of the requirement is to "protect existing industries, provide for the establishment of new industries, derive revenue from all timber resources, and manage the State's forests on a sustained yield basis." Governor's Policy Statement. When it imposes the requirement, the State charges a significantly lower price for the timber than it otherwise would.

The major method of complying with the primary-manufacture requirement is to convert the logs into *cants,* which are logs slabbed on at least one side. In order to satisfy the Alaska requirement, cants must be either sawed to a maximum thickness of 12 inches or squared on four sides along their entire length.

Petitioner, South-Central Timber Development, Inc., is an Alaska corporation engaged in the business of purchasing standing timber, logging the timber, and shipping the logs into foreign commerce, almost exclusively to Japan.[4] It does not operate a mill in Alaska and customarily sells unprocessed logs. When it learned that the primary-manufacture requirement was to be imposed on the Icy Cape sale, it brought an action in Federal District Court seeking an injunction, arguing that the requirement violated the negative implications of the Commerce Clause.[5] The District Court agreed and issued an injunction. South-Central Timber Development, Inc. v. LeResche, 511 F.Supp. 139 (D.Alaska 1981). The Court of Appeals for the Ninth Circuit reversed, finding it unnecessary to reach the question whether, standing alone, the requirement would violate the Commerce Clause, because it found implicit congressional authorization in the federal policy of imposing a primary-manufacture requirement on timber taken from federal land in Alaska. South-Central Timber Development, Inc. v. LeResche, 693 F.2d 890 (C.A.9, 1982).

We must first decide whether the court was correct in concluding that Congress has authorized the challenged requirement. If Congress has not, we must respond to respondent's submission that we should affirm the judgment on two grounds not reached by the Court of Appeals: 1) whether in the absence of congressional approval Alaska's requirement is permissible because Alaska is acting as a market participant, rather than as a market regulator; and 2) if not, whether the local-processing requirement is forbidden by the Commerce Clause.

II

Although the Commerce Clause is by its text an affirmative grant of power to Congress to regulate interstate and foreign commerce, the Clause has long

---

[4] Apparently, there is virtually no interstate market in Alaska timber because of the high shipping costs associated with shipment between American ports. Consequently, over 90% of Alaska timber is exported to Japan.

[5] Although it would appear at first blush that it would be economically more efficient to have the primary processing take place within Alaska, that is apparently not the case. Material appearing in the record suggests that the slabs removed from the log in the process of making cants are often quite valuable, but apparently cannot be used and are burned. It appears that because of the wasted wood, cants are actually worth *less* than the unprocessed logs. . . .

been recognized as a self-executing limitation on the power of the States to enact laws imposing substantial burdens on such commerce. . . . It is equally clear that Congress "may redefine the distribution of power over interstate commerce" by "permit[ting] the states to regulate the commerce in a manner which would otherwise not be permissible." Southern Pacific Co. v. Arizona, 325 U.S. 761, 769 (1945). . . . The Court of Appeals held the Congress had done just that by consistently endorsing primary-manufacture requirements on timber taken from *federal* land. . . . [T]he Court of Appeals was incorrect in concluding either that there is a clearly delineated federal policy approving Alaska's local-processing requirement or that Alaska's policy with respect to its timber lands is authorized by the existence of a "parallel" federal policy with respect to federal lands.

. . . .

The fact that the state policy in this case appears to be consistent with federal policy—or even that state policy furthers the goals we might believe that Congress had in mind—is an insufficient indicium of congressional intent. Congress acted only with respect to federal lands; we cannot infer from that fact that it intended to authorize a similar policy with respect to state lands. Accordingly, we reverse the contrary judgment of the Court of Appeals.

III

We now turn to the issues left unresolved by the Court of Appeals. The first of these issues is whether Alaska's restrictions on export of unprocessed timber from state-owned lands are exempt from Commerce Clause scrutiny under the "market-participant doctrine."

Our cases make clear that if a State is acting as a market participant, rather than as a market regulator, the dormant Commerce Clause places no limitation on its activities. See White v. Massachusetts Council of Construction Employers, Inc.; Reeves, Inc. v. Stake, 447 U.S. 429, 436–437 (1980); Hughes v. Alexandria Scrap Corp., 426 U.S. 794, 810 (1976). The precise contours of the market-participant doctrine have yet to be established, however, the doctrine having been applied in only three cases of this Court to date.

. . . .

The State of Alaska contends that its primary-manufacture requirement fits squarely within the market-participant doctrine, arguing that "Alaska's entry into the market may be viewed as precisely the same type of subsidy to local interests that the Court found unobjectionable in *Alexandria Scrap.*" However, when Maryland became involved in the scrap market it was as a purchaser of scrap; Alaska, on the other hand, participates in the timber market, but imposes conditions downstream in the timber-processing market. Alaska is not merely subsidizing local timber processing in an amount "roughly equal to the difference between the price the timber would fetch in the absence of such a requirement and the amount the state actually receives." If the State directly subsidized the timber-processing industry by such an amount, the purchaser would retain the option of taking advantage of the subsidy by processing timber in the State or forgoing the benefits of the subsidy and exporting unprocessed timber. Under the Alaska requirement, however, the choice is made for him: if he buys timber from the State he is not free to take the timber out of state prior to processing.

The State also would have us find *Reeves* controlling. It states that "*Reeves* made it clear that the Commerce Clause imposes no limitation on Alaska's power to choose the terms on which it will sell its timber." Such an unrestrained reading of *Reeves* is unwarranted. Although the Court in *Reeves* did strongly endorse the right of a State to deal with whomever it chooses when it participates in the market, it did not—and did not purport to—sanction the imposition of any terms that the State might desire. For example, the Court expressly noted in *Reeves* that "Commerce Clause scrutiny may well be more rigorous when a restraint on foreign commerce is alleged,"; that a natural resource "like coal, timber, wild game, or minerals," was not involved, but instead the cement was "the end product of a complex process whereby a costly physical plant and human labor act on raw materials,"; and that South Dakota did not bar resale of South Dakota cement to out-of-state purchasers. In this case, all three of the elements that were not present in *Reeves*—foreign commerce, a natural resource, and restrictions on resale—are present.

Finally, Alaska argues that since the Court in *White* upheld a requirement that reached beyond "the boundary of formal privity of contract," then, *a fortiori,* the primary-manufacture requirement is permissible, because the State is not regulating contracts for resale of timber or regulating the buying and selling of timber, but is instead "a seller of timber, pure and simple." Yet it is clear that the State is more than merely a seller of timber. In the commercial context, the seller usually has no say over, and no interest in, how the product is to be used after sale; in this case, however, payment for the timber does not end the obligations of the purchaser, for, despite the fact that the purchaser has taken delivery of the timber and has paid for it, he cannot do with it as he pleases. Instead, he is obligated to deal with a stranger to the contract after completion of the sale.

That privity of contract is not always the outer boundary of permissible state activity does not necessarily mean that the Commerce Clause has no application within the boundary of formal privity. The market-participant doctrine permits a State to influence "a discrete, identifiable class of economic activity in which [it] is a major participant." White v. Massachusetts Council of Construction Workers, Inc. Contrary to the State's contention, the doctrine is not *carte blanche* to impose any conditions that the State has the economic power to dictate, and does not validate any requirement merely because the State imposes it upon someone with whom it is in contractual privity.

The limit of the market-participant doctrine must be that it allows a State to impose burdens on commerce within the market in which it is a participant, but allows it to go no further. The State may not impose conditions, whether by statute, regulation, or contract, that have a substantial regulatory effect outside of that particular market.[10] Unless the "market" is relatively narrowly defined, the doctrine has the potential of swallowing up the rule that States may not impose substantial burdens on interstate commerce even if they act with the permissible state purpose of fostering local industry.

At the heart of the dispute in this case is disagreement over the definition of the market. Alaska contends that it is participating in the processed timber market, although it acknowledges that it participates in no way in the actual processing. South-Central argues, on the other hand, that although the State may be a participant in the timber market, it is using its leverage in that market to exert a regulatory effect in the processing market, in which it is not a participant. We agree with the latter position.

There are sound reasons for distinguishing between a State's preferring its own residents in the initial disposition of goods when it is a market participant

[10] The view of the market-participant doctrine expressed by Justice Rehnquist would validate under the Commerce Clause any contractual condition that the State had the economic power to impose, without regard to the relationship of the subject matter of the contract and the condition imposed. If that were the law, it would have been irrelevant that the employees in White v. Massachusetts Council of Construction Workers, Inc., 460 U.S. 204 (1983), were in effect "working for the city." If the only question were whether the condition is imposed by contract, a residency requirement could have been imposed with respect to the work force on all projects of any employer doing business with the city.

and a State's attachment of restrictions on dispositions subsequent to the goods coming to rest in private hands.   First, simply as a matter of intuition a State market participant has a greater interest as a "private trader" in the immediate transaction than it has in what its purchaser does with the goods after the State no longer has an interest in them.   The common law recognized such a notion in the doctrine of restraints on alienation.   .   .   .   Similarly, the antitrust laws place limits on vertical restraints.   It is no defense in an action charging vertical trade restraints that the same end could be achieved through vertical integration;   if it were, there would be virtually no antitrust scrutiny of vertical arrangements.   We reject the contention that a State's action as a market regulator may be upheld against Commerce Clause challenge on the ground that the State could achieve the same end as a market participant.   We therefore find it unimportant for present purposes that the State could support its processing industry by selling only to Alaska processors, by vertical integration, or by direct subsidy.

Second, downstream restrictions have a greater regulatory effect than do limitations on the immediate transaction.   Instead of merely choosing its own trading partners, the State is attempting to govern the private, separate economic relationships of its trading partners;   that is, it restricts the post-purchase activity of the purchaser, rather than merely the purchasing activity.   In contrast to the situation in *White,* this restriction on private economic activity takes place after the completion of the parties' direct commercial obligations, rather than during the course of an ongoing commercial relationship in which the city retained a continuing proprietary interest in the subject of the contract.   In sum, the State may not avail itself of the market-participant doctrine to immunize its downstream regulation of the timber-processing market in which it is not a participant.

IV

Finally, the State argues that even if we find that Congress did not authorize the processing restriction, and even if we conclude that its actions do not qualify for the market-participant exception, the restriction does not substantially burden interstate or foreign commerce under ordinary Commerce Clause principles.   We need not labor long over that contention.

Viewed as a naked restraint on export of unprocessed logs, there is little question that the processing requirement cannot survive scrutiny under the precedents of the Court.   For example, in Pike v. Bruce Church, Inc., 397 U.S. 137 (1970), we invalidated a requirement of the State of Arizona that all Arizona cantaloupes be packed within the State.   The Court noted that the State's purpose was "to protect and enhance the reputation of growers within the State," a purpose we described as "surely legitimate."   We observed:

> "[T]he Court has viewed with particular suspicion state statutes requiring business operations to be performed in the home State that could more efficiently be performed elsewhere.   Even where the State is pursuing a clearly legitimate local interest, this particular burden on commerce has been declared to be virtually *per se* illegal.   Foster-Fountain Packing Co. v. Haydel, 278 U.S. 1; Johnson v. Haydel, 278 U.S. 16; Toomer v. Witsell, 334 U.S. 385."

We held that if the Commerce Clause forbids a State to require work to be done within the State for the purpose of promoting employment, then, *a fortiori,* it forbids a State from imposing such a requirement to enhance the reputation of its producers.   Because of the protectionist nature of Alaska's local-processing requirement and the burden on commerce resulting therefrom, we conclude that it falls within the rule of virtual *per se* invalidity of laws that "bloc[k] the flow of interstate commerce at a State's borders." City of Philadelphia v. New Jersey, 437 U.S. 617, 624 (1978).

We are buttressed in our conclusion that the restriction is invalid by the fact that foreign commerce is burdened by the restriction. It is a well-accepted rule that state restrictions burdening foreign commerce are subjected to a more rigorous and searching scrutiny. It is crucial to the efficient execution of the Nation's foreign policy that "the Federal Government . . . speak with one voice when regulating commercial relations with foreign governments." Michelin Tire Corp. v. Wages, 423 U.S. 276, 285 (1976); see also Japan Line, Ltd. v. County of Los Angeles, 441 U.S. 434 (1979). In light of the substantial attention given by Congress to the subject of export restrictions on unprocessed timber, it would be peculiarly inappropriate to permit state regulation of the subject. See Prohibit Export of Unprocessed Timber: Hearing on H.R. 639 Before the Subcomm. on Forests, Family Farms, and Energy of the House Comm. on Agriculture, 97th Cong., 1st Sess. (1981).

The judgment of the Court of Appeals is reversed and the case is remanded for proceedings consistent with the opinion of this Court.

It is so ordered.

Justice Marshall took no part in the decision of this case.

Justice Brennan, concurring.

I join Justice White's opinion in full because I believe Alaska's in-state processing requirement constitutes market regulation that is not authorized by Congress. In my view, Justice White's treatment of the market-participant doctrine and the response of Justice Rehnquist point up the inherent weakness of the doctrine. See Hughes v. Alexandria Scrap Corp., 426 U.S. 794, 817 (1976) (Brennan, J., dissenting).

Justice Powell, with whom Chief Justice Burger joins, concurring in part and concurring in the judgment.

I join Parts I and II of Justice White's opinion. I would remand the case to the Court of Appeals to allow that court to consider whether Alaska was acting as a "market participant" and whether Alaska's primary-manufacture requirement substantially burdened interstate commerce under the holding of Pike v. Bruce Church, Inc., 397 U.S. 137 (1970).

Justice Rehnquist, with whom Justice O'Connor joins, dissenting.

In my view, the line of distinction drawn in the plurality opinion between the State as market participant and the State as market regulator is both artificial and unconvincing. The plurality draws this line "simply as a matter of intuition," but then seeks to bolster its intuition through a series of remarks more appropriate to antitrust law than to the Commerce Clause.* For example, the plurality complains that the State is using its "leverage" in the timber market to distort consumer choice in the timber processing market, a classic example of a tying arrangement. See, e.g., United States Steel Corp. v. Fortner Enterprises, 429 U.S. 610, 619–621 (1977). And the plurality cites the common law doctrine of restraints on alienation and the antitrust limits on vertical restraints

---

* The plurality does offer one other reason for its demarcation of the boundary between these two concepts.

"[D]ownstream restrictions have a greater regulatory effect than do limitations on the immediate transaction. Instead of merely choosing its own trading partners, the State is attempting to govern the private, separate economic relationships of its trading partners; that is, it restricts the post-purchase activity of the purchaser, rather than merely the purchasing activity."

But, of course, this is not a "reason" at all, but merely a restatement of the conclusion. The line between participation and regulation is what we are trying to determine. To invoke that very distinction in support of the line drawn is merely to fall back again on intuition.

in dismissing the State's claim that it could accomplish exactly the same result in other ways.

Perhaps the State's actions do raise antitrust problems. But what the plurality overlooks is that the antitrust laws apply to a State only when it is acting as a market participant. See, e.g., Jefferson County Pharmaceutical Assoc., Inc. v. Abbott Labs, 460 U.S. 150, 154 (1983) (state action immunity "does not apply where a State has chosen to compete in the private retail market"). When the State acts as a market regulator, it is immune from antitrust scrutiny. See Parker v. Brown, 317 U.S. 341, 350–352 (1943). Of course, the line of distinction in cases under the Commerce Clause need not necessarily parallel the line drawn in antitrust law. But the plurality can hardly justify placing Alaska in the market-regulator category, in this Commerce Clause case, by relying on antitrust cases that are relevant only if the State is a market participant.

The contractual term at issue here no more transforms Alaska's sale of timber into "regulation" of the processing industry than the resident-hiring preference imposed by the city of Boston in White v. Massachusetts Council of Const. Employers, 460 U.S. 204 (1983), constituted regulation of the construction industry. Alaska is merely paying the buyer of the timber indirectly, by means of a reduced price, to hire Alaska residents to process the timber. Under existing precedent, the State could accomplish that same result in any number of ways. For example, the State could choose to sell its timber only to those companies that maintain active primary-processing plants in Alaska. Reeves, Inc. v. Stake, 447 U.S. 429 (1980). Or the State could directly subsidize the primary-processing industry within the State. Hughes v. Alexandria Scrap Corp., 426 U.S. 794 (1976). The State could even pay to have the logs processed and then enter the market only to sell processed logs. It seems to me unduly formalistic to conclude that the one path chosen by the State as best suited to promote its concerns is the path forbidden it by the Commerce Clause.

For these reasons, I would affirm the judgment of the Court of Appeals.

E. LIMITS ON BUSINESS ENTRY

LEWIS v. BT INVESTMENT MANAGERS, INC.

447 U.S. 27, 100 S.Ct. 2009, 64 L.Ed.2d 702 (1980).

Mr. Justice Blackmun delivered the opinion of the Court.

. . .

I.

Appellee Bankers Trust New York Corporation (Bankers Trust) is a corporation organized under the laws of the State of New York. It maintains its principal place of business in that State. It is a bank holding company within the meaning of § 2(a) of the Bank Holding Company Act of 1956, 70 Stat. 133, as amended, 12 U.S.C. § 1841(a) (1976 ed. and Supp. II) (the Act). Accordingly, it is subject to federal restrictions on the kinds of subsidiaries it may own or control. . . .

In 1972, the management of Bankers Trust decided to seek the Board [of Governors of the Federal Reserve System's] approval for an investment management subsidiary to operate in Florida. On October 3 of that year, Bankers Trust filed a formal proposal for such a subsidiary, which it planned to operate from offices in Palm Beach. Appellee BT Investment Managers, Inc. (BTIM), was Bankers Trust's intended vehicle for entry into the Florida market. It was incorporated under the laws of the State of Delaware as a wholly owned subsidiary on November 24, 1972. Three days later it qualified to do business in Florida. The application to the Board proposed that BTIM would provide "portfolio investment advice," as well as "general economic information and advice, general economic statistical forecasting services and industry studies" to persons other than banks. . . .

When Bankers Trust filed its application with the Board, certain Florida statutes restricted the ability of out-of-state bank holding companies to compete in the State's financial market. At that time Fla.Stat. § 659.141(1), added by 1972 Fla.Laws, ch. 72–96, § 1, and effective March 28, 1972, prohibited Bankers Trust from owning or controlling a bank or trust company located within the State; the same statute also prohibited it from owning businesses furnishing investment advisory services to local banks or trust companies. In addition, Fla.Stat. § 660.10 prohibited any corporation, other than a state-chartered bank and trust company or a national banking association located in Florida, from performing certain trust and fiduciary functions. Neither statute, however, directly prohibited an out-of-state bank holding company from owning or controlling a business furnishing investment advisory services to the general public. Thus, at the time Bankers Trust filed its application with the Board, it appeared that ownership of BTIM would not violate Florida law, although BTIM would be restricted in the types of financial services it could perform and the customers it could serve.

The reaction of the Florida financial community to Bankers Trust's proposed investment subsidiary was decidedly negative. The State Comptroller, the Florida Bankers Association, and the Palm Beach County Bankers Association, Inc., all filed comments with the Board objecting to the Bankers Trust proposal. More importantly for present purposes, the state legislature was persuaded to take action. On November 30, 1972, shortly after BTIM had qualified to do business in the State, a special session of the legislature amended Fla.Stat. § 659.141(1). That statute, which had been on the books only since March 28 of that year, was expanded to prohibit an out-of-state bank holding company from owning or controlling a business within the State that sells investment advisory services to any customer, rather than just to "trust companies or banks" in Florida, as the statute theretofore had read. This amendment took effect, without the Governor's approval, on December 21, 1972. There is evidence that the amendment was a direct response to Bankers Trust's pending application, and that it had the strong backing of the local financial community.

On April 26, 1973, the Board rejected Bankers Trust's proposal on the ground that it would conflict with state law. 59 Fed.Res.Bull. 364. The Board observed that the proposal contemplated *de novo* entry into the Florida investment management market rather than acquisition of an existing concern, and it noted that *de novo* entry ordinarily has a desirable procompetitive impact. Absent evidence of a contrary effect in this case, the Board intimated that it would have been favorably inclined toward the proposal. But it found that the December amendment to Fla.Stat. § 659.141(1) "was intended to, and does, prohibit the performance of investment advisory services in Florida by non-Florida bank holding companies." 59 Fed.Res.Bull. 365. In view of its obligation to respect the dictates of state law, the Board found itself constrained to reject the proposal. . . .

Within six months of the Board's decision, the two appellees filed this action seeking declaratory and injunctive relief. Count I of their complaint alleged that Fla.Stat. § 659.141(1) "is not designed to promote lawful regulatory objectives, but is intended to shelter those organizations presently conducting an investment advisory business in Florida from competition by [BTIM]." The complaint alleged violations of the due process and equal protection guarantees of the Fourteenth Amendment, as well as violation of the Commerce Clause. Count II alleged similar constitutional defects as the result of the joint operation of §§ 659.141(1), and 660.10. Appellees alleged that "[b]ut for the existence of the challenged statutes," Bankers Trust would seek authority from the Board to establish "a subsidiary trust company having a national bank charter or a Florida state charter" that would engage exclusively in one or more of the functions regulated by § 660.10. A three-judge court was convened pursuant to 28 U.S.C. § 2281, and the case was submitted for summary judgment on a stipulated set of facts.

[T]he District Court held that the challenged portions of the two statutes violate the Commerce Clause. 461 F.Supp. 1187 (1979). Without reaching appellees' due process and equal protection arguments, it found that the statutes under attack discriminate against interstate commerce. The court reasoned that § 659.141(1) "erects an insuperable barrier to the entry of foreign-based bank holding companies, through their subsidiaries, into the Florida investment advisory market," and that § 660.10 "similarly cordons off Florida trust companies from competition by out-of-state concerns." Id., at 1196. It ruled that the statutes are "parochial legislation" that "must be deemed per se unconstitutional." Ibid. Moreover, it held that the legislative purposes proffered by appellant, including a purported desire to curb anticompetitive abuses arising from agglomeration of financial power, failed to justify the discriminatory impact of the statutes.

Finally, the District Court held that the federal Bank Holding Company Act does not foster or permit the types of discrimination against out-of-state bank holding companies reflected in the Florida statutes. . . .

The court issued an order granting declaratory relief against both statutes . . . . .

II.

This appeal presents two distinct but related questions with respect to the validity of the challenged Florida statutes. The first is whether the statutes, viewed independently of federal legislation regulating the banking industry, burden interstate commerce in a manner contrary to the Commerce Clause. The second is whether Congress, by its own legislation in this area, has created an area in which the States may regulate free from Commerce Clause restraints. Since there is no contention that federal legislation preempts the state laws in question, federal law becomes important only if it appears that the Florida statutes cannot survive without federal authorization. Thus, the second question becomes pertinent only if we reach an affirmative answer to the first.

These questions arise against a backdrop of familiar principles. . . . .

Over the years, the Court has used a variety of formulations for the Commerce Clause limitation upon the States, but it consistently has distinguished between outright protectionism and more indirect burdens on the free flow of trade. The Court has observed that "where simple economic protectionism is effected by state legislation, a virtually *per se* rule of invalidity has been erected." Id., at 624. In contrast, legislation that visits its effects equally upon both interstate and local business may survive constitutional scrutiny if it is narrowly drawn. The Court stated in Pike v. Bruce Church, Inc., 397 U.S. 137 (1970):

"Where the statute regulates evenhandedly to effectuate a legitimate local public interest, and its effects on interstate commerce are only incidental, it will be upheld unless the burden imposed on such commerce is clearly excessive in relation to the putative local benefits. . . . If a legitimate local purpose is found, then the question becomes one of degree. And the extent of the burden that will be tolerated will of course depend on the nature of the local interest involved, and on whether it could be promoted as well with a lesser impact on interstate activities." Id., at 142.

. . . The principal focus of inquiry must be the practical operation of the statute, since the validity of state laws must be judged chiefly in terms of their probable effects. . . .

III.

With these principles in mind, we first turn to § 659.141(1). This statute has been the chief object of controversy, since it is the statute that prevents appellees from setting up their projected investment advisory business within Florida. The statute prohibits ownership of local investment or trust businesses by firms possessing two characteristics: a certain kind of business organization and purpose, whether it be as a bank, trust company, or a bank holding company; and location of principal operations outside Florida.

Appellant and the *amici* supporting his position argue that the District Court's analysis of § 659.141(1) is flawed in three respects: First, the statute assertedly affects only matters of local character that have insufficient interstate attributes to bring federal constitutional limitations into play. Second, the District Court erroneously labeled the statute protectionist legislation and thus incorrectly relied upon the *"per se* rule of invalidity" identified in Philadelphia v. New Jersey, 437 U.S., at 624. Appellant argues that the statute should be treated as neutral legislation subject to the less stringent standards of Pike v. Bruce Church, Inc., supra, and he argues that it meets this test. Third, the District Court failed to accord proper significance, in appellant's view, to the Bank Holding Company Act of 1956. Appellant argues that the Act grants authority to the States to prohibit out-of-state bank holding companies from owning local subsidiaries that provide bank-related services.

A.

The first of these arguments needs only brief mention. We readily accept the submission that, both as a matter of history and as a matter of present commercial reality, banking and related financial activities are of profound local concern. As appellees freely concede, sound financial institutions and honest financial practices are essential to the health of any State's economy and to the well-being of its people. Thus, it is not surprising that ever since the early days of our Republic, the States have chartered banks and have actively regulated their activities.

Nonetheless, it does not follow that these same activities lack important interstate attributes. . . .

B.

The contentions that the District Court erred by applying too stringent a standard in defining the limits of Florida's regulatory authority, and that § 659.141(1) is evenhanded local regulation, are more substantial. We nonetheless agree with the District Court's conclusion that this statute is "parochial" in the sense that it overtly prevents foreign enterprises from competing in local markets.

The statute makes the out-of-state location of a bank holding company's principal operations an explicit barrier to the presence of an investment subsidiary within the State. As Bankers Trust's application before the Board itself indicates, it thus prevents competition in local markets by out-of-state firms with the kinds of resources and business interests that make them likely to attempt *de novo* entry.   Appellant virtually concedes this effect, and the circumstances of enactment suggest that it was the legislature's principal objective.

Appellant argues, however, that the statute ought not to be declared *per se* invalid because it does not prevent all out-of-state investment enterprises from entering local markets.   Investment enterprises that are *not* bank holding companies, banks, or trust companies either may own investment subsidiaries in Florida or may enter the state investment market directly by obtaining a license to do business.   Furthermore, locally incorporated bank holding companies are subject to the same restrictions as their foreign counterparts if they maintain their principal operations elsewhere.   Appellant thus analogizes § 659.141(1) to the Maryland statute prohibiting local retail operations by vertically integrated petroleum companies that the Court upheld in Exxon Corp. v. Governor of Maryland, 437 U.S. 117 (1978).   The statute, it is said, discriminates against a particular kind of corporate organizational structure more than it does against the origin or citizenship of a particular business enterprise.

The statute involved in *Exxon* flatly prohibited producers and refiners of petroleum products from opening or operating retail services within Maryland under a variety of corporate or contractual arrangements.   It was enacted in response to perceived inequities in the allocation of petroleum products to retail outlets during the fuel shortage of 1973.   Various oil companies, all of which engaged in production and refining as well as in sale of petroleum products, challenged the statute on a number of grounds.   Among other arguments, they claimed that the statute violated the Commerce Clause because it discriminated against producers and refiners, all of which were interstate concerns, in favor of independent retailers, most of which were local businesses.

The Court rejected this contention.   After holding that the statute served the legitimate state purpose of "controlling the gasoline retail market," the Court separately analyzed its effect on interstate commerce in the producing-refining and retailing ends of the petroleum industry.   The Court concluded that the statute could not discriminate against interstate petroleum producers and refiners in favor of locally based competitors because, as a matter of fact, there were no such local producers or refiners to be favored.   For the same reason, it concluded that the flow of petroleum products in interstate commerce would not be reduced.   It also rejected a claim of discrimination at the retail level because the statute placed "no barriers whatsoever" on competition in local markets by "interstate independent dealers" that did not own production or refining facilities.   Despite the fact that the number of stations operated by independent dealers was small relative to the number operated by producer-refiners, the Court concluded that neither the placing of a disparate burden on some interstate competitors nor the shifting of business from one part of the interstate market to another was enough, under the circumstances, to establish a Commerce Clause violation.

There are some points of similarity between *Exxon* and the present case.   In the former, the statute in issue discriminated against vertical organization in the petroleum industry.   Section 659.141(1) similarly discriminates against a particular kind of conglomerate organization in the investment and financial industries.   And the Maryland statute permitted some kinds of interstate competitors free entry into the local market, as does the Florida statute at issue here.

We disagree, however, with the suggestion that *Exxon* should be treated as controlling precedent for this case.   Section 659.141(1) engages in an additional form of discrimination that is highly significant for purposes of Commerce Clause analysis.   Under the Florida statute, discrimination against affected business organizations is *not* evenhanded because only banks, bank holding companies, and trust companies with principal operations *outside* Florida are prohibited from operating investment subsidiaries or giving investment advice within the State.   It follows that § 659.141(1) discriminates *among* affected business entities according to the extent of their contacts with the local economy. The absence of a similar discrimination between interstate and local producer-refiners was a most critical factor in *Exxon*. Both on its face and in actual effect, § 659.141(1) thus displays a local favoritism or protectionism that significantly alters its Commerce Clause status. See Philadelphia v. New Jersey, 437 U.S., at 626–627; Baldwin v. G.A.F. Seelig, Inc., 294 U.S., at 527.

We need not decide whether this difference is sufficient to render the Florida legislation *per se* invalid, for we are convinced that the disparate treatment of out-of-state bank holding companies cannot be justified as an incidental burden necessitated by legitimate local concerns. In the District Court and to some extent on this appeal, appellant and supporting *amici* have argued that the Florida legislation advances several important state policies. Among those that have been specifically identified are an interest in discouraging undue economic concentration in the arena of high finance; an interest in regulating financial practices, presumably to protect local residents from fraud; and an interest in maximizing local control over locally based financial activities. We think that these alleged purposes fail to justify the extent of the burden placed upon out-of-state bank holding companies.

Discouraging economic concentration and protecting the citizenry against fraud are undoubtedly legitimate state interests. But we are not persuaded that these interests justify the heavily disproportionate burden this statute places on bank holding companies that operate principally outside the State. Appellant has demonstrated no basis for an inference that all out-of-state bank holding companies are likely to possess the evils of monopoly power, that they are more likely to do so than their home-grown counterparts, or that they are any more inclined to engage in sharp practices than bank holding companies that are locally based. Nor is there any reason to conclude that outright prohibition of entry, rather than some intermediate form of regulation, is the only effective method of protecting against the presumed evils, particularly when other out-of-state businesses that may be just as large or far-flung are permitted to compete in the local market. We conclude that these asserted state interests simply do not suffice to eliminate § 659.141(1)'s apparent constitutional defect. . . .

With regard to the asserted interest in promoting local control over financial institutions, we doubt that the interest itself is entirely clear of any tinge of local parochialism. In almost any Commerce Clause case it would be possible for a State to argue that it has an interest in bolstering local ownership, or wealth, or control of business enterprise. Yet these arguments are at odds with the general principle that the Commerce Clause prohibits a State from using its regulatory power to protect its own citizens from outside competition. See H. P. Hood & Sons, Inc. v. Du Mond, 336 U.S., at 538; Buck v. Kuykendall, 267 U.S. 307, 315–316 (1925); cf. Toomer v. Witsell, 334 U.S. 385, 403–404 (1948). In any event, the interest is not well-served by the present legislation. The statute, for example, does not restrict out-of-state ownership of local bank holding companies. Nor, as appellant concedes does it prevent entry by out-of-state entities other than those having the prohibited organizational forms. There is thus no reason to believe that the State's interest in local control, to the extent it legitimately exists, has been significantly or evenhandedly advanced by the statutory means that have been employed.

For these reasons, we conclude that the District Court did not err in holding that § 659.141(1) directly burdens interstate commerce in a manner that contravenes the Commerce Clause's implicit limitation on state power.

C.

Ordinarily, at this point we would have reached the end of our inquiry. But in this instance appellant has another string to his bow: the contention that by act of Congress the State has been given additional authority to regulate entry by bank holding companies into the local investment advisory market. Congress, of course, has power to regulate the flow of interstate commerce in ways that the States, acting independently, may not. And Congress, if it chooses, may exercise this power indirectly by conferring upon the States an ability to restrict the flow of interstate commerce that they would not otherwise enjoy. See H. P. Hood & Sons, Inc. v. Du Mond, 336 U.S., at 542–543; Prudential Insurance Co. v. Benjamin, 328 U.S. 408, 423–424 (1946); International Shoe Co. v. Washington, 326 U.S. 310, 315, (1945). It is appellant's view that the Bank Holding Company Act of 1956, as amended, is enabling legislation of this very kind, and that it authorizes the restrictions on bank holding companies embodied in § 659.141(1).

This argument rests on two provisions in the federal legislation. . . .

. . .

Since neither of these provisions authorizes state legislation of the variety contained in the challenged portions of § 659.141(1), we agree with the District Court that appellant's reliance on the Bank Holding Company Act is misplaced. The effects of the Florida statute on interstate commerce have not been permitted by Congress and its Commerce Clause defects have not been removed. Therefore, the District Court's injunction against enforcement of the statute must be sustained.

IV.

This brings us, finally, to § 660.10. That statute prohibits all corporations except state chartered banks and national banks having their operations in Florida from performing specified fiduciary functions. It does not purport to regulate the ownership of such institutions by bank holding companies. For the reasons stated below, we conclude that its constitutionality has been neither fully placed in issue nor fully determined by the District Court's decision. We therefore vacate the judgment with respect to § 660.10 and remand for such further proceedings as may be necessary in light of this opinion.

. . .

V.

In summary, we affirm the judgment of the District Court insofar as it declares unconstitutional the challenged portions of § 659.141(1) and enjoins their enforcement. We vacate that portion of the judgment that relates to the constitutionality of § 660.10, and we remand the case for such further proceedings as are appropriate and consistent with this opinion.

It is so ordered.

EDGAR v. MITE CORP., 457 U.S. 624 (1982). The Illinois Business Takeover Act requires takeover offers for acquisition of shares in Illinois-affiliated target companies [1] to be registered with the Illinois Secretary of State twenty days before the offer becomes effective. During the twenty-day period, the offeror may not communicate with shareholders, but the target company is free to disseminate information to its shareholders. The Secretary can refuse registration, after hearing, if the offer is not accompanied by full and fair disclosure, or the offer is inequitable or fraudulent. The Court held that the Illinois statute imposed an unconstitutional burden on interstate commerce.

[1] The Act applies where Illinois residents own 10% of the securities subject to the offer. It also applies where two of three conditions are met: (1) the target company's principal executive office is in Illinois; (2) the target company is organized under Illinois law; (3) 10% of the target company's stated capital and surplus is represented within Illinois.

Justice White's opinion offered two distinct rationales, only one of which commanded the votes of five Justices.[2] Part V.B. of the opinion, which had the votes of five Justices, was premised squarely on the "balancing approach" articulated in Pike v. Bruce Church (p. 281, supra). On this point, Justice White's opinion for the Court said in part:

"The effects of allowing the Illinois Secretary of State to block a nationwide tender offer are substantial. Shareholders are deprived of the opportunity to sell their shares at a premium. The reallocation of economic resources to their highest-valued use, a process which can improve efficiency and competition, is hindered. The incentive the tender offer mechanism provides incumbent management to perform well so that stock prices remain high is reduced.

"Appellant claims the Illinois Act . . . seeks to protect resident security holders . . .. We agree with the Court of Appeals that [this interest is] insufficient to outweigh the burdens Illinois imposes on interstate commerce.

"While protecting local investors is plainly a legitimate state objective, the state has no legitimate interest in protecting non-resident shareholders. Insofar as the Illinois law burdens out-of-state transactions, there is nothing to be weighed in the balance to sustain the law. We note, furthermore, that the Act completely exempts from coverage a corporation's acquisition of its own shares. . . . Thus Chicago Rivet was able to make a competing tender offer for its own stock without complying with the Illinois Act, leaving Chicago Rivet's shareholders to depend only on the protections afforded them by federal securities law, protections which Illinois views as inadequate to protect investors in other contexts. This distinction is at variance with Illinois' asserted legislative purpose, and tends to undermine appellant's justification for the burdens the statute imposes on interstate commerce.

"We are also unconvinced that the Illinois Act substantially enhances the shareholders' position. The Illinois Act seeks to protect shareholders of a company subject to a tender offer by requiring disclosures regarding the offer, assuring that shareholders have adequate time to decide whether to tender their shares, and according shareholders withdrawal, proration and equal considera- tion rights. . . . As the Court of Appeals noted, the disclosures required by the Illinois Act which go beyond those mandated by the Williams Act and the regulations pursuant to it may not substantially enhance the shareholders' ability to make informed decisions. It also was of the view that the possible benefits of the potential delays required by the Act may be outweighed by the increased risk that the tender offer will fail due to defensive tactics employed by incumbent management. We are unprepared to disagree with the Court of Appeals in these respects, and conclude that the protections the Illinois Act affords resident security holders are, for the most part, speculative.

F. INTERSTATE MOBILITY OF PERSONS

Shortly after the Civil War the Court was called upon to consider the constitutional freedom of persons to move from state to state. Nevada had enacted a statute levying a capitation tax of one dollar upon every person

---

[2] Part V.A. of Justice White's opinion concluded that the Illinois statute placed an impermissible burden on interstate commerce because of its extraterritorial effect, regulating transactions across state lines with out-of-state shareholders. Justice Powell, one of the five Justices to join part V.B. of the opinion, did not join part V.A., which thus received the votes of only four Justices. Justice Powell explained that he joined part V.B. (and not V.A.) because its rationale "leaves some room for state regulation of tender offers." Justice White's opinion also took the position that the Illinois Act was preempted by the Williams Act, a 1968 amendment to the Federal Securities and Exchange Act. Only Chief Justice Burger and Justice Blackmun concurred in this portion of the opinion. Justice Blackmun took no position on the commerce clause issue. Justices Brennan, Marshall and Rehnquist argued that the case was moot and did not express a position on the merits of either the commerce clause or preemption issues.

leaving the state by railroad, stage coach or other vehicle employed in the business of transporting persons for hire. The carrier was required to report the persons so transported and pay the tax. In Crandall v. Nevada, 6 Wall. 35 (1868), the Court held this act invalid. The majority of the Court did not place the decision on the commerce clause, but stated:

"The people of these United States constitute one nation. They have a government in which all of them are deeply interested. This government has necessarily a capital established by law, where its principal operations are conducted. Here sits its legislature, composed of senators and representatives, from the States and from the people of the States. Here resides the President directing through thousands of agents, the execution of the laws over all this vast country. Here is the seat of the supreme judicial power of the nation, to which all its citizens have a right to resort to claim justice at its hands. Here are the great executive departments, administering the offices of the mails, or the public lands, of the collection and distribution of the public revenues, and of our foreign relations. These are all established and conducted under the admitted powers of the Federal government. That government has a right to call to this point any or all of its citizens to aid in its service, as members of the Congress, of the courts, of the executive departments, and to fill all its other offices; and this right cannot be made to depend upon the pleasure of a State over whose territory they must pass to reach the point where these services must be rendered. The government, also, has its offices of secondary importance in all other parts of the country. On the sea-coasts and on the rivers it has its ports of entry. In the interior it has its land offices, its revenue offices, and its sub-treasuries. In all these it demands the services of its citizens, and is entitled to bring them to those points from all quarters of the nation, and no power can exist in a State to obstruct this right that would not enable it to defeat the purposes for which the government was established. . . .

"But if the government has these rights on her own account, the citizen also has correlative rights. He has the right to come to the seat of government to assert any claim he may have upon that government, or to transact any business he may have with it. To seek its protection, to share its offices, to engage in administering its functions. He has a right to free access to its sea-ports, through which all the operations of foreign trade and commerce are conducted, to the sub-treasuries, the land offices, the revenue offices, and the courts of justice in the several States, and this right is in its nature independent of the will of any State over whose soil he must pass in the exercise of it. . . ."

The question of interstate mobility arose again in Edwards v. California, 314 U.S. 160 (1941) where the Court struck down a law making it a misdemeanor to bring into California "any indigent person who is not a resident of the State, knowing him to be an indigent person." Resting the decision on the commerce clause the majority of the Court quoted the Baldwin v. Seelig statement that the Constitution "was framed upon the theory that the peoples of the several states must sink or swim together." Referring to the language in New York v. Miln regarding the "moral pestilence of paupers," the Court said: "Whatever may have been the notion then prevailing, we do not think that it will now be seriously contended that because a person is without employment and without funds he constitutes a 'moral pestilence'."

But four of the Justices (Douglas, Black, Murphy and Jackson) were not willing to place their concurrence on the commerce clause. They believed that the right of persons "to move freely from state to state is an incident of national citizenship protected by the privileges and immunities clause of the Fourteenth Amendment" and added Justice Jackson: "[T]he migrations of a human being do not fit easily into my notions as to what is commerce. To hold that the measure of his rights is the commerce clause is likely to result eventually in distorting the commercial law or in denaturing human rights."

The constitutional freedom of interstate migration will be met again later. See Chapter 11.

SECTION 3. EFFECT OF OTHER CONSTITUTIONAL PROVISIONS ON STATE REGULATORY POWER

A. THE PRIVILEGES AND IMMUNITIES CLAUSE OF ARTICLE IV, SECTION 2

Article IV, Section 2 provides: "The Citizens of each State shall be entitled to all Privileges and Immunities of Citizens in the several States." The progenitor of this provision was the Fourth of the Articles of Confederation which read as follows:

"The better to secure and perpetuate mutual friendship and intercourse among the people of the different States in this Union, the free inhabitants of each of these states, paupers, vagabonds and fugitives from justice excepted, shall be entitled to all privileges and immunities of free citizens in the several States; and the people of each State shall have free ingress and regress to and from any other State, and shall enjoy therein all the privileges of trade and commerce, subject to the same duties, impositions and restrictions as the inhabitants thereof respectively . . .".

These provisions were prompted by a fundamental problem of the federal system of government—how to reconcile the advantages of a common citizenship with a dispersed sovereignty in a number of independent, or largely independent, states. The basic character of the problem is illustrated by the fact that the Constitution of Australia contains a similar provision (Sec. 117) which reads: "A subject of the Queen, resident in any State, shall not be subject in any other State, to any disability or discrimination which would not be equally applicable to him if he were a subject of the Queen resident in such other State."

The first opinion on Article IV, Section 2, was given in Corfield v. Coryell, 4 Wash.C.C. 371, Fed.Cas. No. 3,230 (1825), by Justice Washington of the Supreme Court when on circuit. A New Jersey statute of 1820 made it unlawful for any person who was not "an actual inhabitant and resident" of the state to rake or gather clams, oysters, or shells in any of the rivers, bays, or waters of the state. The question was the validity of this statute as applied to a Pennsylvania citizen who was gathering oysters in New Jersey waters. Justice Washington declared that the phrase "privileges and immunities of citizens in the several states" should be confined to "those privileges and immunities which are, in their nature, *fundamental*" and "which belong, of right, to the citizens of all free governments." Among these, he said, were the "right of a citizen of one State to pass through, or to reside in any other State, for the purposes of trade, agriculture, professional pursuits, or otherwise;" the right "to take, hold and dispose of property, either real or personal; and an exemption from higher taxes or impositions than are paid by the other citizens of the State."

"But," he continued, "We cannot accede to the proposition which was insisted on by the counsel, that, under this provision of the Constitution, the citizens of the several States are permitted to participate in all *the rights* which belong exclusively to the citizens of any other particular State, merely upon the ground that they are enjoyed by those citizens; much less, that in regulating the use of the common property of the citizens of such State, the legislature is bound to extend to the citizens of all the other States the same advantages as are secured to their own citizens." The right to fish in the waters of the state for running fish or stationary shell fish, when not ceded by the state, he regarded as the common property of all the citizens of the state. "[I]t would, in our opinion, be going quite too far to construe the grant of privileges and immunities of citizens, as amounting to a grant of a co-tenancy in the common property of the State, to the citizens of all the other states."

The statute was sustained.

Justice Washington's reasoning was followed in McCready v. Virginia, 94 U.S. 391 (1877), which upheld the power of a state to limit to its own citizens the right to plant oysters in public waters.

The statute challenged in the Corfield case drew the line on the basis of "residence" rather than citizenship, but no point was made of this in the opinion. After the adoption of the Fourteenth Amendment it became even more difficult to distinguish between residence and state citizenship, for that Amendment provides that "All persons born or naturalized in the United States, and subject to the jurisdiction thereof, are citizens of the United States *and of the State wherein they reside.*" (Emphasis added.)

It was early held that the clause protected only individuals who are citizens and that a corporation could not claim the protection of the clause even though all of its incorporators were citizens of the state of incorporation. Bank of Augusta v. Earle, 38 U.S. (13 Pet.) 519 (1839).

UNITED BUILDING AND CONSTRUCTION TRADES COUNCIL OF CAMDEN COUNTY AND VICINITY v. MAYOR AND COUNCIL OF THE CITY OF CAMDEN

— U.S. —, 104 S.Ct. 1020, 79 L.Ed.2d 249 (1984).

Justice Rehnquist delivered the opinion of the Court.

A municipal ordinance of the city of Camden, New Jersey requires that at least 40% of the employees of contractors and subcontractors working on city construction projects be Camden residents. Appellant, the United Building and Construction Trades Council of Camden and Vicinity (the Council), challenges that ordinance as a violation of the Privileges and Immunities Clause, Article IV, § 2, of the United States Constitution. The Supreme Court of New Jersey rejected appellant's privileges and immunities attack on the ground that the ordinance discriminates on the basis of *municipal,* not state, residency. The court "decline[d] to apply the Privileges and Immunities Clause in the context of a municipal ordinance that has identical effects upon out-of-state citizens and New Jersey citizens not residing in the locality." 88 N.J. 317, 342, 443 A.2d 148, 160 (1982). We conclude that the challenged ordinance is properly subject to the strictures of the Clause. We therefore reverse the judgment of the Supreme Court of New Jersey and remand the case for a determination of the validity of the ordinance under the appropriate constitutional standard.

On August 28, 1980, the Camden City Council, acting pursuant to a state-wide affirmative action program, adopted an ordinance setting minority hiring "goals" on all public works contracts. The ordinance also created a hiring preference for Camden residents . . .. As subsequently amended, the ordinance requires that on all construction projects funded by the city:

> "The developer/contractor, in hiring for jobs, shall make every effort to employ persons residing within the City of Camden but, in no event, shall less than forty percent (40%) of the entire labor force be residents of the City of Camden."

The contractor is also obliged to ensure that any subcontractors working on such projects adhere to the same requirement.

. . .

. . . We first address the argument, accepted by the Supreme Court of New Jersey, that the Clause does not even apply to a *municipal* ordinance such as this. Two separate contentions are advanced in support of this position: first, that the Clause only applies to laws passed by a *State* and, second, that the Clause only applies to laws that discriminate on the basis of *state* citizenship.

The first argument can be quickly rejected. The fact that the ordinance in question is a municipal, rather than a state, law does not somehow place it outside the scope of the Privileges and Immunities Clause. First of all, one cannot easily distinguish municipal from state action in this case: the municipal ordinance would not have gone into effect without express approval by the State Treasurer. . . . The constitutional challenge to the resident hiring preference, therefore, must also "be interpreted as a challenge to the State Treasurer's general power" to adopt such a preference. . . .

More fundamentally, a municipality is merely a political subdivision of the State from which its authority derives. City of Trenton v. New Jersey, 262 U.S. 182, 187 (1923). It is as true of the Privileges and Immunities Clause as of the Equal Protection Clause that what would be unconstitutional if done directly by the State can no more readily be accomplished by a city deriving its authority from the State. . . . Thus, even if the ordinance had been adopted solely by Camden, and not pursuant to a state program or with state approval, the hiring preference would still have to comport with the Privileges and Immunities Clause.

The second argument merits more consideration. The New Jersey Supreme Court concluded that the Privileges and Immunities Clause does not apply to an ordinance that discriminates solely on the basis of *municipal* residency. The Clause is phrased in terms of *state* citizenship and was designed "to place the citizens of each State upon the same footing with citizens of other States, so far as the advantages resulting from citizenship in those States are concerned." Paul v. Virginia, 8 Wall. 168, 180 (1869). . . .

> "The primary purpose of this clause, like the clauses between which it is located—those relating to full faith and credit and to interstate extradition of fugitives from justice—was to help fuse into one Nation a collection of independent, sovereign States. It was designed to insure to a citizen of State A who ventures into State B the same privileges which the citizens of State B enjoy. For protection of such equality the citizen of State A was not to be restricted to the uncertain remedies afforded by diplomatic processes and official retaliation." Toomer v. Witsell, 334 U.S. 385, 395 (1948).

Municipal residency classifications, it is argued, simply do not give rise to the same concerns.

We cannot accept this argument. We have never read the Clause so literally as to apply it only to distinctions based on state citizenship. For example, in Mullaney v. Anderson, 342 U.S. 415, 419–420 (1952), the Court held that the Alaska Territory had no more freedom to discriminate against those not residing in the Territory than did any State to favor its own citizens. And despite some initial uncertainty, . . ., it is now established that the terms "citizen" and "resident" are "essentially interchangeable," Austin v. New Hampshire, 420 U.S. 656, 662, n. 8 (1975), for purposes of analysis of most cases under the Privileges and Immunities Clause. See Hicklin v. Orbeck, 437 U.S. 518, 524, n. 8 (1978); Toomer v. Witsell, 334 U.S. 385, 397 (1948). A person who is not residing in a given State is *ipso facto* not residing in a city within that State.

Thus, whether the exercise of a privilege is conditioned on state residency or on municipal residency he will just as surely be excluded.

Given the Camden ordinance, an out-of-state citizen who ventures into New Jersey will not enjoy the same privileges as the New Jersey citizen residing in Camden. It is true that New Jersey citizens not residing in Camden will be affected by the ordinance as well as out-of-state citizens. And it is true that the disadvantaged New Jersey residents have no claim under the Privileges and Immunities Clause. The Slaughter-House Cases, 16 Wall. 36, 77 (1872). But New Jersey residents at least have a chance to remedy at the polls any discrimination against them. Out-of-state citizens have no similar opportunity, Austin v. New Hampshire, 420 U.S. 656, 662 (1975), and they must "not be restricted to the uncertain remedies afforded by diplomatic processes and official retaliation." Toomer v. Witsell, 334 U.S. 385, 395 (1948).[9] We conclude that Camden's ordinance is not immune from constitutional review at the behest of out-of-state residents merely because some in-state residents are similarly disadvantaged.

Application of the Privileges and Immunities Clause to a particular instance of discrimination against out-of-state residents entails a two-step inquiry. As an initial matter, the court must decide whether the ordinance burdens one of those privileges and immunities protected by the Clause. Baldwin v. Montana Fish and Game Comm'n, 436 U.S. 371, 383 (1978). Not all forms of discrimination against citizens of other States are constitutionally suspect.

> "Some distinctions between residents and nonresidents merely reflect the fact that this is a Nation composed of individual States, and are permitted; other distinctions are prohibited because they hinder the formation, the purpose, or the development of a single Union of those States. Only with respect to those 'privileges' and 'immunities' bearing upon the vitality of the Nation as a single entity must the State treat all citizens, resident and nonresident, equally."

As a threshold matter, then, we must determine' whether an out-of-state resident's interest in employment on public works contracts in another State is sufficiently "fundamental" to the promotion of interstate harmony so as to "fall within the purview of the Privileges and Immunities Clause." Id., at 388.
. . .

Certainly, the pursuit of a common calling is one of the most fundamental of those privileges protected by the Clause. Baldwin v. Montana Fish and Game Comm'n, 436 U.S. 371, 387 (1978). Many, if not most, of our cases expounding the Privileges and Immunities Clause have dealt with this basic and essential activity. See, e.g., Hicklin v. Orbeck, 437 U.S. 518 (1978); Austin v. New Hampshire, 420 U.S. 656 (1975); Mullaney v. Anderson, 342 U.S. 415 (1952); Toomer v. Witsell, 334 U.S. 385 (1948); Ward v. Maryland, 79 U.S. 418 (1871). Public employment, however, is qualitatively different from employment in the private sector; it is a subspecies of the broader opportunity to pursue a common calling. We have held that there is no fundamental right to government employment for purposes of the Equal Protection Clause. Massachusetts v. Murgia, 427 U.S. 307, 313 (1976) (per curiam). Cf. McCarthy v. Philadelphia Civil Service Comm'n, 424 U.S. 645 (1976) (per curiam)

---

[9] The dissent suggests that New Jersey citizens not residing in Camden will adequately protect the interests of out-of-state residents and that the scope of the Privileges and Immunities Clause should be measured in light of this political reality. . . . What the dissent fails to appreciate is that the Camden ordinance at issue in this case was adopted pursuant to a comprehensive, state-wide program applicable in all New Jersey cities. The Camden resident-preference ordinance has already received state sanction and approval, and every New Jersey city is free to adopt a similar protectionist measure. Some have already done so. Thus, it is hard to see how New Jersey residents living outside Camden will protect the interests of out-of-state citizens.
. . .

(rejecting equal protection challenge to municipal residency requirement for municipal workers). And in *White,* 103 S.Ct., at 1046, n. 7, we held that for purposes of the Commerce Clause everyone employed on a city public works project is, "in a substantial if informal sense, 'working for the city.'"

It can certainly be argued that for purposes of the Privileges and Immunities Clause everyone affected by the Camden ordinance is also "working for the city" and, therefore, has no grounds for complaint when the city favors its own residents. But we decline to transfer mechanically into this context an analysis fashioned to fit the Commerce Clause. Our decision in *White* turned on a distinction between the city acting as a market participant and the city acting as a market regulator. The question whether employees of contractors and subcontractors on public works projects were or were not, in some sense, working for the city was crucial to that analysis. The question had to be answered in order to chart the boundaries of the distinction. But the distinction between market participant and market regulator relied upon in *White* to dispose of the Commerce Clause challenge is not dispositive in this context. The two Clauses have different aims and set different standards for state conduct.

The Commerce Clause acts as an implied restraint upon state regulatory powers. Such powers must give way before the superior authority of Congress to legislate on (or leave unregulated) matters involving interstate commerce. When the State acts solely as a market participant, no conflict between state *regulation* and federal regulatory authority can arise. *White,* 103 S.Ct., at 1044; Reeves, Inc. v. Stake, 447 U.S. 429, 436–437 (1980); Hughes v. Alexandria Scrap Corp., 426 U.S. 794, 810 (1976). The Privileges and Immunities Clause, on the other hand, imposes a direct restraint on state action in the interests of interstate harmony. Hicklin v. Orbeck, 437 U.S. 518, 523–524 (1978); Ward v. Maryland, 79 U.S. 418, 430 (1871); Paul v. Virginia, 8 Wall. 168, 180 (1869). This concern with comity cuts across the market regulator-market participant distinction that is crucial under the Commerce Clause. It is discrimination against out-of-state residents on matters of fundamental concern which triggers the Clause, not regulation affecting interstate commerce. Thus, the fact that Camden is merely setting conditions on its expenditures for goods and services in the marketplace does not preclude the possibility that those conditions violate the Privileges and Immunities Clause.

In Hicklin v. Orbeck, 437 U.S. 518 (1978), we struck down as a violation of the Privileges and Immunities Clause an "Alaska Hire" statute containing a resident hiring preference for all employment related to the development of the State's oil and gas resources. Alaska argued in that case "that because the oil and gas that are the subject of Alaska Hire are *owned* by the State, this ownership, of itself, is sufficient justification for the Act's discrimination against nonresidents, and takes the Act totally without the scope of the Privileges and Immunities Clause." We concluded, however, that the State's interest in controlling those things it claims to own is not absolute. "Rather than placing a statute completely beyond the Clause, a State's ownership of the property with which the statute is concerned is a factor—although often the crucial factor—to be considered in evaluating whether the statute's discrimination against noncitizens violates the Clause." . . . Much the same analysis, we think, is appropriate to a city's efforts to bias private employment decisions in favor of its residents on construction projects funded with public monies. The fact that Camden is expending its own funds or funds it administers in accordance with the terms of a grant is certainly a factor—perhaps the crucial factor—to be considered in evaluating whether the statute's discrimination violates the Privileges and Immunities Clause. But it does not remove the Camden ordinance completely from the purview of the Clause.

In sum, Camden may, without fear of violating the Commerce Clause, pressure private employers engaged in public works projects funded in whole or in part by the city to hire city residents. But that same exercise of power to bias the employment decisions of private contractors and subcontractors against out-of-state residents may be called to account under the Privileges and Immunities Clause. A determination of whether a privilege is "fundamental" for purposes of that Clause does not depend on whether the employees of private contractors and subcontractors engaged in public works projects can or cannot be said to be "working for the city." The opportunity to seek employment with such private employers is "sufficiently basic to the livelihood of the Nation," Baldwin v. Montana Fish and Game Comm'n, 436 U.S. 371, 388 (1978), as to fall within the purview of the Privileges and Immunities Clause even though the contractors and subcontractors are themselves engaged in projects funded in whole or part by the city.

The conclusion that Camden's ordinance discriminates against a protected privilege does not, of course, end the inquiry. We have stressed in prior cases that "[l]ike many other constitutional provisions, the privileges and immunities clause is not an absolute." Toomer v. Witsell, 334 U.S. 385, 396 (1948). It does not preclude discrimination against citizens of other States where there is a "substantial reason" for the difference in treatment. "[T]he inquiry in each case must be concerned with whether such reasons do exist and whether the degree of discrimination bears a close relation to them." As part of any justification offered for the discriminatory law, nonresidents must somehow be shown to "constitute a peculiar source of the evil at which the statute is aimed."

The city of Camden contends that its ordinance is necessary to counteract grave economic and social ills. Spiralling unemployment, a sharp decline in population, and a dramatic reduction in the number of businesses located in the city have eroded property values and depleted the city's tax base. The resident hiring preference is designed, the city contends, to increase the number of employed persons living in Camden and to arrest the "middle class flight" currently plaguing the city. The city also argues that all nonCamden residents employed on city public works projects, whether they reside in New Jersey or Pennsylvania, constitute a "source of the evil at which the statute is aimed." That is, they "live off" Camden without "living in" Camden. Camden contends that the scope of the discrimination practiced in the ordinance, with its municipal residency requirement, is carefully tailored to alleviate this evil without unreasonably harming nonresidents, who still have access to 60% of the available positions.

Every inquiry under the Privileges and Immunities Clause "must . . . be conducted with due regard for the principle that the states should have considerable leeway in analyzing local evils and in prescribing appropriate cures." Toomer v. Witsell, 334 U.S. 385, 396 (1948). This caution is particularly appropriate when a government body is merely setting conditions on the expenditure of funds it controls. The Alaska Hire statute at issue in Hicklin v. Orbeck, 437 U.S. 518 (1978), swept within its strictures not only contractors and subcontractors dealing directly with the State's oil and gas; it also covered suppliers who provided goods and services to those contractors and subcontractors. We invalidated the Act as "an attempt to force virtually all businesses that benefit in some way from the economic ripple effect of Alaska's decision to develop its oil and gas resources to bias their employment practices in favor of the State's residents." No similar "ripple effect" appears to infect the Camden ordinance. It is limited in scope to employees working directly on city public works projects.

Nonetheless, we find it impossible to evaluate Camden's justification on the record as it now stands. No trial has ever been held in the case. No findings of fact have been made. The Supreme Court of New Jersey certified the case for direct appeal after the brief administrative proceedings that led to approval of the ordinance by the State Treasurer. It would not be appropriate for this Court either to make factual determinations as an initial matter or to take judicial notice of Camden's decay. We, therefore, deem it wise to remand the case to the New Jersey Supreme Court. That court may decide, consistent with state procedures, on the best method for making the necessary findings.

The judgment of the Supreme Court of New Jersey is reversed, and the case is remanded for proceedings not inconsistent with this opinion.

Reversed and Remanded.

Justice Blackmun, dissenting.

For over a century the underlying meaning of the Privileges and Immunities Clause of the Constitution's Article IV has been regarded as settled: at least absent some substantial, noninvidious justification, a State may not discriminate between its own residents and residents of other States on the basis of state citizenship . . .

Today, however, the Court casually extends the scope of the Clause by holding that it applies to laws that discriminate *among* state residents on the basis of *municipal* residence, simply because discrimination on the basis of municipal residence disadvantages citizens of other States *"ipso facto."* This novel interpretation arrives accompanied by little practical justification and no historical or textual support whatsoever. Because I believe that the Privileges and Immunities Clause was not intended to apply to the kind of municipal discrimination presented by this case, I would affirm the judgment of the Supreme Court of New Jersey.

. . . .

Contrary to the Court's tacit assumption, discrimination on the basis of municipal residence is substantially different in this regard from discrimination on the basis of state citizenship. The distinction is simple but fundamental: discrimination on the basis of municipal residence penalizes persons within the State's political community as well as those without. The Court itself points out that while New Jersey citizens who reside outside Camden are not protected by the Privileges and Immunities Clause, they may resort to the State's political processes to protect themselves. What the Court fails to appreciate is that this avenue of relief for New Jersey residents works to protect residents of other States as well; disadvantaged state residents who turn to the state legislature to displace ordinances like Camden's further the interests of nonresidents as well as their own. Nor is this mechanism for relief merely a theoretical one; in the past decade several States, including California and Georgia, have repealed or forbidden protectionist ordinances like the one at issue here. In short, discrimination on the basis of municipal residence simply does not consign residents of other States, in the words of *Toomer,* supra, to "the uncertain remedies afforded by diplomatic processes and official retaliation." The Court thus has applied the Privileges and Immunities Clause without regard for the political ills that it was designed to cure.

. . . .

B.   THE TWENTY–FIRST AMENDMENT

Introduction. The relation of the Twenty-First Amendment to the commerce clause is quite different from that of Article IV, Section 2. Does the Amendment nullify the commerce clause as applied to the liquor trade?

BACCHUS IMPORTS, LTD. v. DIAS

___ U.S. ___, 104 S.Ct. 3049, 82 L.Ed.2d 200 (1984)

Justice White delivered the opinion of the Court.

Appellants challenge the constitutionality of the Hawaii Liquor Tax, which is a 20% excise tax imposed on sales of liquor at wholesale. Specifically at issue are exemptions from the tax for certain locally produced alcoholic beverages. The Supreme Court of Hawaii upheld the tax against challenges based upon the Equal Protection Clause, the Import-Export Clause, and the Commerce Clause. . . . We . . . reverse.

I

The Hawaii Liquor Tax was originally enacted in 1939 to defray the costs of police and other governmental services that the Hawaii legislature concluded had been increased due to the consumption of liquor. At its inception the statute contained no exemptions. However, because the legislature sought to encourage development of the Hawaiian liquor industry, it enacted an exemption for *okolehao* from May 17, 1971, until June 20, 1981, and an exemption for fruit wine from May 17, 1976, until June 30, 1981. . . .

Appellants—Bacchus Imports, Ltd., and Eagle Distributors, Inc.—are liquor wholesalers who sell to licensed retailers. They sell the liquor at their wholesale price plus the 20% excise tax imposed by § 244-4, plus a one-half percent tax imposed by Hawaii Rev.Stat. § 237-13. Pursuant to Hawaii Rev.Stat. § 40-35, which authorizes a taxpayer to pay taxes under protest and to commence an action in the Tax Appeal Court for the recovery of disputed sums, the wholesalers initiated protest proceedings and sought refunds of all taxes paid. Their complaint alleged that the Hawaii liquor tax was unconstitutional because it violates both the Import-Export Clause and the Commerce Clause of the United States Constitution. The wholesalers sought a refund of approximately $45 million, representing all of the liquor tax paid by them for the years in question.

The Tax Appeal Court rejected both constitutional claims. On appeal, the Supreme Court of Hawaii affirmed the decision of the Tax Appeal Court and rejected an equal protection challenge as well. . . .

. . .

III

A cardinal rule of Commerce Clause jurisprudence is that "[n]o State, consistent with the Commerce Clause, may 'impose a tax which discriminates against interstate commerce . . . by providing a direct commercial advantage to local business.'" Boston Stock Exchange v. State Tax Commission, 429 U.S. 318, 329 (1977) (quoting Northwestern States Portland Cement Co. v. Minnesota, 358 U.S. 450, 457 (1959). Despite the fact that the tax exemption here at issue seems clearly to discriminate on its face against interstate commerce by bestowing a commercial advantage on okolehao and pineapple wine, the State argues—and the Hawaii Supreme Court held—that there is no improper discrimination.

A

Much of the State's argument centers on its contention that okolehao and pineapple wine do not compete with the other products sold by the wholesalers. On the stipulated facts in this case, we are unwilling to conclude that no competition exists between the exempted and the nonexempted liquors. . . .

. . . . On the stipulated facts in this case, we are unwilling to conclude that no competition exists between the exempted and the nonexempted liquors.

B

. . . .

. . . . [W]e need not guess at the legislature's motivation, for it is undisputed that the purpose of the exemption was to aid Hawaiian industry. Likewise, the effect of the exemption is clearly discriminatory, in that it applies only to locally produced beverages, even though it does not apply to all such products. Consequently, as long as there is some competition between the locally produced exempt products and nonexempt products from outside the State, there is a discriminatory effect.

. . . .

We therefore conclude that the Hawaii Liquor Tax exemption for okolehao and pineapple wine violated the Commerce Clause because it had both the purpose and effect of discriminating in favor of local products.

IV

The State argues in this Court that even if the tax exemption violates ordinary Commerce Clause principles, it is saved by the Twenty-first Amendment to the Constitution. . . .

Despite broad language in some of the opinions of this Court written shortly after enactment of the Amendment,[13] more recently we have recognized the obscurity of the legislative history of § 2. See California Retail Liquor Dealers Assn. v. Midcal Aluminum, Inc., 445 U.S. 97, 107 n. 10 (1980). No clear consensus concerning the meaning of the provision is apparent. Indeed, Senator Blaine, the Senate sponsor of the Amendment resolution, appears to have espoused varying interpretations. In reporting the view of the Senate Judiciary Committee, he said that the purpose of § 2 was "to restore to the States . . . absolute control over interstate commerce affecting intoxicating liquors. . . ." 76 Cong.Rec. 4143 (1933). On the other hand, he also expressed a narrower view: "So to assure the so-called dry States against the importation of intoxicating liquor into those States, it is proposed to write permanently into the Constitution a prohibition along that line." Id., at 4141.

It is by now clear that the Amendment did not entirely remove state regulation of alcoholic beverages from the ambit of the Commerce Clause.

. . . .

Approaching the case in this light, we are convinced that Hawaii's discriminatory tax cannot stand. Doubts about the scope of the Amendment's authorization notwithstanding, one thing is certain: The central purpose of the provision was not to empower States to favor local liquor industries by erecting barriers to competition. It is also beyond doubt that the Commerce Clause itself furthers strong federal interests in preventing economic Balkanization.

---

[13] For example, in State Board of Equalization v. Young's Market Co., 299 U.S. 59, 62 (1936), the Court stated:

"The plaintiffs ask us to limit this broad command. They request us to construe the Amendment as saying, in effect: The State may prohibit the importation of intoxicating liquors provided it prohibits the manufacture and sale within its borders; but if it permits such manufacture and sale, it must let imported liquors compete with the domestic on equal terms. To say that, would involve not a construction of the Amendment, but a rewriting of it."

The Court went on to observe, however, that a high license fee for importation may "serve as an aid in policing the liquor traffic." Id., at 63.

See also Mahoney v. Joseph Triner Corp., 304 U.S. 401, 403 (1938) ("since the adoption of the Twenty-first Amendment, the equal protection clause is not applicable to imported intoxicating liquor"). Cf. Craig v. Boren, 429 U.S. 190 (1976).

. . . State laws that constitute mere economic protectionism are therefore not entitled to the same deference as laws enacted to combat the perceived evils of an unrestricted traffic in liquor. Here, the State does not seek to justify its tax on the ground that it was designed to promote temperance or to carry out any other purpose of the Twenty-first Amendment, but instead acknowledges that the purpose was "to promote a local industry." Consequently, because the tax violates a central tenet of the Commerce Clause but is not supported by any clear concern of the Twenty-first Amendment, we reject the State's belated claim based on the Amendment.

V

. . .

These refund issues, which are essentially issues of remedy for the imposition of a tax that unconstitutionally discriminated against interstate commerce, were not addressed by the state courts. Also, the Federal constitutional issues involved may well be intertwined with, or their consideration obviated by, issues of state law. Also, resolution of those issues, if required at all, may necessitate more of a record than so far has been made in this case. We are reluctant, therefore, to address them in the first instance. Accordingly, we reverse the judgment of the Supreme Court of Hawaii and remand for further proceedings not inconsistent with this opinion.

So ordered.

Justice Brennan took no part in the consideration or decision of this case.

Justice Stevens, with whom Justice Rehnquist and Justice O'Connor join, dissenting.

. . . I would affirm the judgment of the Supreme Court of Hawaii because the wholesalers' Commerce Clause claim is squarely foreclosed by the Twenty-first Amendment to the United States Constitution.

. . .

III

Today the Court, in essence, holds that the Hawaii tax is unconstitutional because it places a burden on intoxicating liquors that have been imported into Hawaii for use therein that is not imposed on liquors that are produced locally. As I read the text of the Amendment, it expressly authorizes this sort of burden. Moreover, as I read Justice Brandeis' opinion for the Court in the seminal case of State Board of Equalization v. Young's Market Co., 299 U.S. 59 (1936), the Court has squarely so decided.

In *Young's Market,* the Court upheld a California statute that imposed a license fee on the privilege of importing beer to any place in California. After noting that the statute would have been obviously unconstitutional prior to the Twenty-first Amendment, the Court explained that the Amendment enables a State to establish a local monopoly and to prevent or discourage competition from imported liquors. . . .

. . .

As a matter of pure constitutional power, Hawaii may surely prohibit the importation of all intoxicating liquors. It seems clear to me that it may do so without prohibiting the local sale of liquors that are produced within the State. In other words, even though it seems unlikely that the okolehao lobby could persuade it to do so, the Hawaii Legislature surely has the power to create a local monopoly by prohibiting the sale of any other alcoholic beverage. If the State has the constitutional power to create a total local monopoly—thereby imposing the most severe form of discrimination on competing products originating elsewhere—I believe it may also engage in a less extreme form of discrimination that merely provides a special benefit, perhaps in the form of a subsidy or a tax exemption, for locally produced alcoholic beverages.

The Court's contrary conclusion is based on the "obscurity of the legislative history" of § 2. What the Court ignores is that it was argued in *Young's Market* that a "limitation of the broad language" of § 2 was "sanctioned by its history," but the Court, observing that the language of the Amendment was "clear," determined that it was unnecessary to consider the history, 299 U.S., at 63–64—the history which the Court today considers unclear. But now, according to the Court, the force of the Twenty-first Amendment contention in this case is diminished because the "central purpose of the provision was not to empower States to favor local liquor industries by erecting barriers to competition." It follows, according to the Court, that "state laws that constitute mere economic protectionism are not entitled to the same deference as laws enacted to combat the perceived evils of an unrestricted traffic in liquor." This is a totally novel approach to the Twenty-first Amendment. The question is not one of "deference," nor one of "central purposes;" the question is whether the provision in this case is an exercise of a power expressly conferred upon the States by the Constitution. It plainly is.

Accordingly, I respectfully dissent.

CAPITAL CITIES CABLE, INC. v. CRISP

___ U.S. ___, 104 S.Ct. 2694, 81 L.Ed.2d 580 (1984).

Justice Brennan delivered the opinion of the Court.

The question presented in this case is whether Oklahoma may require cable television operators in that State to delete all advertisements for alcoholic beverages contained in the out-of-state signals that they retransmit by cable to their subscribers. Petitioners contend that Oklahoma's requirement abridges their rights under the First and Fourteenth Amendments and is pre-empted by federal law. Because we conclude that this state regulation is pre-empted, we reverse the judgment of the Court of Appeals for the Tenth Circuit and do not reach the First Amendment question.

. . . .

II

Petitioners and the FCC contend that the federal regulatory scheme for cable television systems administered by the Commission is intended to pre-empt any state regulation of the signals carried by cable system operators. Respondent apparently concedes that enforcement of the Oklahoma statute in this case conflicts with federal law, but argues that because the State's advertising ban was adopted pursuant to the broad powers to regulate the transportation and importation of intoxicating liquor reserved to the States by the Twenty-first Amendment, the statute should prevail notwithstanding the conflict with federal law. As in California Retail Liquor Dealers Assn. v. Midcal Aluminum, Inc., 445 U.S. 97 (1980), where we held that a California wine pricing program violated the Sherman Act notwithstanding the State's reliance upon the Twenty-first Amendment in establishing that system, we turn first before assessing the impact of the Twenty-first Amendment to consider whether the Oklahoma statute does in fact conflict with federal law.

. . . .

III

Respondent contends that even if the Oklahoma advertising ban is invalid under normal pre-emption analysis, the fact that the ban was adopted pursuant to the Twenty-first Amendment rescues the statute from pre-emption. A similar claim was advanced in California Retail Liquor Dealers Assn. v. Midcal Aluminum, Inc., 445 U.S. 97 (1980). In that case, after finding that a California wine pricing program violated the Sherman Act, we considered whether § 2 of the Twenty-first Amendment, which reserves to the States certain power to regulate traffic in liquor, "permits California to countermand the congressional policy—adopted under the commerce power—in favor of competition." 445 U.S., at 106. Here, we must likewise consider whether § 2 permits Oklahoma to override the federal policy, as expressed in FCC rulings and regulations, in favor of promoting the widespread development of cable communication.

The States enjoy broad power under § 2 of the Twenty-first Amendment to regulate the importation and use of intoxicating liquor within their borders. Ziffrin, Inc. v. Reeves, 308 U.S. 132 (1939). At the same time, our prior cases have made clear that the Amendment does not license the States to ignore their obligations under other provisions of the Constitution. See, e.g., Larkin v. Grendel's Den, 459 U.S. 116, 122 n. 5 (1982); California v. LaRue, 409 U.S. 109, 115 (1973); Wisconsin v. Constantineau, 400 U.S. 433, 436 (1971); Department of Revenue v. James B. Beam Distilling Co., 377 U.S. 341, 345–346 (1964). Indeed, "[t]his Court's decisions   .   .   .   have confirmed that the Amendment primarily created an exception to the normal operation of the Commerce Clause." Craig v. Boren, 429 U.S. 190, 206 (1976). Thus, as the Court explained in Hostetter v. Idlewild Bon Voyage Liquor Corp., 377 U.S. 324 (1964), § 2 reserves to the States power to impose burdens on interstate commerce in intoxicating liquor that, absent the Amendment, would clearly be invalid under the Commerce Clause. Id., at 330; State Board of Equalization v. Young's Market Co., 299 U.S. 59, 62–63 (1936). We have cautioned, however, that "[t]o draw a conclusion   .   .   .   that the Twenty-first Amendment has somehow operated to 'repeal' the Commerce Clause wherever regulation of intoxicating liquors is concerned would   .   .   .   be an absurd oversimplification." Hostetter, supra, at 331–332. Notwithstanding the Amendment's broad grant of power to the States, therefore, the Federal Government plainly retains authority under the Commerce Clause to regulate even interstate commerce in liquor.   .   .   .

In rejecting the claim that the Twenty-first Amendment ousted the Federal Government of all jurisdiction over interstate traffic in liquor, we have held that when a State has not attempted directly to regulate the sale or use of liquor within its borders—the core § 2 power—a conflicting exercise of federal authority may prevail. In Hostetter, for example, the Court found that in-state sales of intoxicating liquor intended to be used only in foreign countries could be made under the supervision of the federal Bureau of Customs, despite contrary state law, because the state regulation was not aimed at preventing unlawful use of alcoholic beverages within the state, but rather was designed "totally to prevent transactions carried on under the aegis of a law passed by Congress in the exercise of its explicit power under the Constitution to regulate commerce with foreign nations." Similarly, in Midcal Aluminum, supra, we found that "the Twenty-first Amendment provides no shelter for the violation of the Sherman Act caused by the State's wine pricing program," because the State's interest in promoting temperance through the program was not substantial and was therefore clearly outweighed by the important federal objectives of the Sherman Act.

Of course, our decisions in *Hostetter* and *Midcal Aluminum* were concerned only with conflicting state and federal efforts to regulate transactions involving liquor. In this case, by contrast, we must resolve a clash between an express federal decision to pre-empt all state regulation of cable signal carriage and a state effort to apply its ban on alcoholic beverage advertisements to wine commercials contained in out-of-state signals carried by cable systems. Nonetheless, the central question presented in those cases is essentially the same as the one before us here: whether the interests implicated by a state regulation are so closely related to the powers reserved by the Twenty-first Amendment that the regulation may prevail, notwithstanding that its requirements directly conflict with express federal policies. As in *Hostetter* and *Midcal Aluminum,* resolution of this question requires a "pragmatic effort to harmonize state and federal powers" within the context of the issues and interests at stake in each case. 445 U.S., at 109.

There can be little doubt that the comprehensive regulations developed over the past twenty years by the FCC to govern signal carriage by cable television systems reflect an important and substantial federal interest. . . .

On the other hand, application of Oklahoma's advertising ban to out-of-state signals carried by cable operators in that State is designed principally to further the State's interest in discouraging consumption of intoxicating liquor. Although the District Court found that "consumption of alcoholic beverages in Oklahoma has increased substantially in the last 20 years despite the ban on advertising of such beverages," we may nevertheless accept Oklahoma's judgment that restrictions on liquor advertising represent at least a reasonable, albeit limited, means of furthering the goal of promoting temperance in the State. The modest nature of Oklahoma's interests may be further illustrated by noting that Oklahoma has chosen not to press its campaign against alcoholic beverage advertising on all fronts. For example, the State permits both print and broadcast commercials for beer, as well as advertisements for all alcoholic beverages contained in newspapers, magazines and other publications printed outside of the State. The ban at issue in this case is directed only at wine commercials that occasionally appear on out-of-state signals carried by cable operators. By their own terms, therefore, the State's regulatory aims in this area are narrow. Although a state regulatory scheme obviously need not amount to a comprehensive attack on the problems of alcohol consumption in order to constitute a valid exercise of state power under the Twenty-first Amendment, the selective approach Oklahoma has taken toward liquor advertising suggests limits on the substantiality of the interests it asserts here. In contrast to state regulations governing the conditions under which liquor may be imported or sold within the state, therefore, the application of Oklahoma's advertising ban to the importation of distant signals by cable television operators engages only indirectly the central power reserved by § 2 of the Twenty-first Amendment—that of exercising "control over whether to permit importation or sale of liquor and how to structure the liquor distribution system." *Midcal Aluminum,* 445 U.S., at 110.

When this limited interest is measured against the significant interference with the federal objective of ensuring widespread availability of diverse cable services throughout the United States—an objective that will unquestionably be frustrated by strict enforcement of the Oklahoma statute—it is clear that the state's interest is not of the same stature as the goals identified in the FCC's rulings and regulations. As in *Midcal Aluminum,* therefore, we hold that when, as here, a state regulation squarely conflicts with the accomplishment and execution of the full purposes of federal law, and the state's central power under the Twenty-first Amendment of regulating the times, places, and manner under which liquor may be imported and sold is not directly implicated, the balance between state and federal power tips decisively in favor of the federal law, and enforcement of the state statute is barred by the Supremacy Clause.[16]

IV

We conclude that the application of Oklahoma's alcoholic beverage advertising ban to out-of-state signals carried by cable operators in that State is preempted by federal law and that the Twenty-first Amendment does not save the regulation from pre-emption. The judgment of the Court of Appeals is

Reversed.

SECTION 4. PREEMPTION OF STATE LEGISLATION BY FEDERAL LEGISLATION—THE IMPACT OF THE SUPREMACY CLAUSE

Introduction. We first met the preemption problem in Gibbons v. Ogden, supra p. 168, where the Court held the New York grant of a monopoly on a steamboat route to be inconsistent with the grant of a federal license to another steamboat to operate on the route. Marshall stated the ultimate principle— should there be a "collision" between an Act of Congress passed pursuant to the Constitution and a state statute, the state law "must yield to the law of Congress."

While simple to state, the principle is difficult to apply. The Supreme Court has applied a variety of verbal formulas over the years in seeking to determine when there is such a "collision" that the state law must fall. In many early cases it took a broad view of the subject, suggesting that merely by regulating in an area Congress should be taken as having "occupied the field" and determined that the states should not regulate in that field. See, e.g., Napier v. Atlantic Coast Line R.R. Co., 272 U.S. 605 (1926), in which the Court held that by granting power to the Interstate Commerce Commission to prescribe rules governing the safety of locomotives, Congress "intended to occupy the field" and state statutes requiring cab curtains and particular types of firebox doors were invalid even though the Commission had not issued any rules relating to cab curtains and firebox doors.

More recently the Court has been less likely to imply Congressional intent to supersede state laws in the absence of fairly direct conflict. In Rice v. Santa Fe Elevator Corp., 331 U.S. 218, 230 (1947), e.g., the Court said that when Congress has legislated "in a field which the States have traditionally occupied," we "start with the assumption that the historic police powers of the States were not to be superseded by the Federal Act unless that was the clear and manifest purpose of Congress . . . . Such a purpose may be evidenced in several ways. The scheme of federal regulation may be so pervasive as to make reasonable the inference that Congress left no room for the States to supplement it . . . . Or the Act of Congress may touch a field in which the federal interest is so dominant that the federal system will be assumed to preclude enforcement of state laws on the same subject. Likewise, the object sought to be obtained by the federal law and the character of obligations imposed by it may reveal the same purpose . . . . Or the state policy may produce a result inconsistent with the objective of the federal statute . . . . It is often a perplexing question whether Congress has precluded state action or by the choice of selective regulatory measures has left the police power of the States undisturbed except as the state and federal regulations collide."

[16] Because we have resolved the pre-emption and Twenty-first Amendment issues in petitioners' favor, we need not consider the additional question whether Oklahoma's advertising ban constitutes an invalid restriction on protected commercial speech, and we therefore express no view on that issue.

A useful law review note—*Pre-emption as a Preferential Ground: A New Canon of Construction,* 12 Stan.L.Rev. 308 (1959), Selected Essays on Constitutional Law, 1938–1962 (1963), 310—contains the following paragraph:

"[T]he Court has adopted the same weighing of interests approach in pre-emption cases that it uses to determine whether a state law unjustifiably burdens interstate commerce. In a number of situations the Court has invalidated statutes on the pre-emption ground when it appeared that the state laws sought to favor local economic interests at the expense of the interstate market. On the other hand, when the Court has been satisfied that valid local interests, such as those in safety or in the reputable operation of local business, outweigh the restrictive effect on interstate commerce, the Court has rejected the pre-emption argument and allowed state regulation to stand   .   .   .   ."

The case that follows is an illustration of the Court's approach to pre-emption cases. It is relevant to note that while the case presented here involves state regulation of interstate commerce, pre-emption problems may arise in any area where federal regulations are present. See, e.g., DeCanas v. Bica, 424 U.S. 351 (1976) involving an alleged conflict between a California statute regulating employment of illegal aliens and the federal immigration laws.

RAY v. ATLANTIC RICHFIELD CO.

435 U.S. 151, 98 S.Ct. 988, 55 L.Ed.2d 179 (1978).

Mr. Justice White delivered the opinion of the Court.

Pursuant to the Ports and Waterways Safety Act of 1972 (PWSA), 86 Stat. 424, 33 U.S.C. § 1221 et seq. (1970 ed., Supp. V), and 46 U.S.C. § 391a (1970 ed., Supp. V), navigation in Puget Sound, a body of inland water lying along the northwest coast of the State of Washington, is controlled in major respects by federal law. The PWSA also subjects to federal rule the design and operating characteristics of oil tankers.

This case arose when Chapter 125, Laws of Washington, 1975, First Extraordinary Session, Wash.Rev.Code § 88.16.170 et seq. (Tanker Law), was adopted with the aim of regulating in particular respects the design, size, and movement of oil tankers in Puget Sound. In response to the constitutional challenge to the law brought by the appellees herein, the District Court held that under the Supremacy Clause, Art. VI, cl. 2, of the Constitution, which declares that the federal law "shall be the supreme Law of the Land," the Tanker Law could not coexist with the PWSA and was totally invalid. Atlantic Richfield v. Evans, No. C–75–648–M (WD Wash. Sept. 24, 1976).

I.

Located adjacent to Puget Sound are six oil refineries having a total combined processing capacity of 359,500 barrels of oil per day. In 1971, appellee Atlantic Richfield Company (ARCO) began operating an oil refinery at Cherry Point, situated in the northern part of the Sound. Since then, the crude oil processed at that refinery has been delivered principally by pipeline from Canada and by tankers from the Persian Gulf; tankers will also be used to transport oil there from the terminus of the Trans-Alaska Pipeline at Valdez, Alaska. Of the 105 tanker deliveries of crude oil to the Cherry Point refinery from 1972 through 1975, 95 were by means of tankers in excess of 40,000 deadweight tons (DWT), and, prior to the effective date of the Tanker Law, 15 of them were by means of tankers in excess of 125,000 DWT.

Appellee Seatrain Lines, Inc. (Seatrain), owns or charters 12 tanker vessels in domestic and foreign commerce, of which four exceed 125,000 DWT. Seatrain also operates through a wholly owned subsidiary corporation a shipbuilding facility in New York City, where it has recently constructed or is constructing four tankers, each with a 225,000 DWT capacity.

On the day the Tanker Law became effective, ARCO brought suit in the United States District Court for the Western District of Washington, seeking a judgment declaring the statute unconstitutional and enjoining its enforcement. Seatrain was later permitted to intervene as a plaintiff. Named as defendants were the state and local officials responsible for the enforcement of the Tanker Law. The complaint alleged that the statute was pre-empted by federal law, in particular the PWSA, and that it was thus invalid under the Supremacy Clause. It was also alleged that the law imposed an undue burden on interstate commerce in violation of the Commerce Clause, Art. I, § 8, cl. 3, and that it interfered with the federal regulation of foreign affairs. Pursuant to 28 U.S.C. §§ 2281, 2284, a three-judge court was convened to determine the case.

. . . The three-judge court . . . rul[ed] that all of the operative provisions of the Tanker Law were pre-empted, and enjoining appellants and their successors from enforcing the chapter. We noted probable jurisdiction of the State's appeal, 430 U.S. 905 (1977), meanwhile having stayed the injunction. 429 U.S. 1035 (1977).

II.

The Court's prior cases indicate that when a State's exercise of its police power is challenged under the Supremacy Clause, "we start with the assumption that the historic police powers of the States were not to be superseded by the Federal Act unless that was the clear and manifest purpose of Congress." Rice v. Santa Fe Elevator Corp., 331 U.S. 218, 230 (1947) . . . . Under the relevant cases, one of the legitimate inquiries is whether Congress has either explicitly or implicitly declared that the States are prohibited from regulating the various aspects of oil-tanker operations and design with which the Tanker Law is concerned. As the Court noted in *Rice,* supra, 331 U.S. at 230:

"[The congressional] purpose may be evidenced in several ways. The scheme of federal regulation may be so pervasive as to make reasonable the inference that Congress left no room for the States to supplement it. Or the Act of Congress may touch a field in which the federal interest is so dominant that the federal system will be assumed to preclude enforcement of state laws of the same subject. Likewise, the object sought to be obtained by the federal law and the character of obligations imposed by it may reveal the same purpose."

Even if Congress has not completely foreclosed state legislation in a particular area, a state statute is void to the extent that it actually conflicts with a valid federal statute. A conflict will be found "where compliance with both federal and state regulations is a physical impossibility . . .," or where the state "law stands as an obstacle to the accomplishment and execution of the full purposes and objectives of Congress."

III.

With these principles in mind, we turn to an examination of each of the three operative provisions of the Tanker Law. We address first § 88.16.180, which requires both enrolled and registered[7] oil tankers of at least 50,000

---

[7] Enrolled vessels are those "engaged in domestic or coastwide trade or used for fishing," whereas registered vessels are those engaged in trade with foreign countries. Douglas v. Seacoast Products, Inc., 431 U.S. 265, 272–273 (1977).

DWT to take on a pilot licensed by the State of Washington while navigating Puget Sound. The District Court held that insofar as the law required a tanker "enrolled in the coastwise trade" to have a local pilot on board, it was in direct conflict with 46 U.S.C. §§ 215, 364. We agree.

Section 364 provides that "every coastwise seagoing steam vessel subject to the navigation laws of the United States, . . . not sailing under register, shall, when under way . . . be under the control and direction of pilots licensed by the Coast Guard." Section 215 adds that "[n]o State or municipal government shall impose upon pilots of steam vessels any obligation to procure a State or other license in addition to that issued by the United States . . . ." It goes on to explain that the statute shall not be construed to "affect any regulation established by the laws of any State, requiring vessels entering or leaving a port of any such State, *other than coastwise steam vessels,* to take a pilot duly licensed or authorized by the laws of such State . . . ." (Emphasis added.) The Court has long held that these two statutes read together give the Federal Government exclusive authority to regulate pilots on enrolled vessels and that they preclude a State from imposing its own pilotage requirements upon them. Thus, to the extent that the Tanker Law requires enrolled tankers to take on state-licensed pilots, the District Court correctly concluded, as the State now concedes, that it was in conflict with federal law and was therefore invalid.

. . . [J]ust as it is clear that States may not regulate the pilots of enrolled vessels, it is equally clear that they are free to impose pilotage requirements on registered vessels entering and leaving their ports. Not only does 46 U.S.C. § 215 so provide, as was noted above, but so also does § 101(5) of the PWSA, 33 U.S.C. § 1221(5) (1970 ed., Supp. V), which authorizes the Secretary of Transportation to "require pilots on self-propelled vessels engaged in the foreign trades in areas and under circumstances where a pilot is not otherwise required by State law to be on board until the State having jurisdiction of an area involved establishes a requirement for a pilot in that area or under the circumstances involved . . . ." Accordingly, as appellees now agree, the State was free to require registered tankers in excess of 50,000 DWT to take on a state-licensed pilot upon entering Puget Sound.

IV.

We next deal with § 88.16.190(2) of the Tanker Law, which requires enrolled and registered oil tankers of from 40,000 to 125,000 DWT to possess all of the following "standard safety features":

"(a) Shaft horsepower in the ratio of one horsepower to each two and one-half deadweight tons; and

"(b) Twin screws; and

"(c) Double bottoms, underneath all oil and liquid cargo compartments; and

"(d) Two radars in working order and operating, one of which must be collision avoidance radar; and

"(e) Such other navigational position location systems as may be prescribed from time to time by the board of pilotage commissioners . . . ."

This section contains a proviso, however, stating that if the "tanker is in ballast or is under escort of a tug or tugs with an aggregate shaft horsepower equivalent to five percent of the deadweight tons of that tanker . . . ," the design requirements are not applicable. The District Court held invalid this alternative design/tug requirement of the Tanker Law. We agree insofar as we hold that the foregoing design requirements, standing alone, are invalid in the light of the PWSA and its regulatory implementation.

The PWSA contains two titles representing somewhat overlapping provisions designed to insure vessel safety and the protection of the navigable waters, their resources, and shore areas from tanker cargo spillage. The focus of Title I, 33 U.S.C. §§ 1221–1227 (1970 ed., Supp. V), is traffic control at local ports; Title II's principal concern is tanker design and construction.

Title II begins by declaring that the protection of life, property, and the marine environment from harm requires the promulgation of "comprehensive minimum standards of design, construction, alteration, repair, maintenance, and operation" for vessels carrying certain cargoes in bulk, primarily oil and fuel tankers. § 391a(1). To implement the twin goals of providing for vessel safety and protecting the marine environment, it is provided that the Secretary of the Department in which the Coast Guard is located "shall establish" such rules and regulations as may be necessary with respect to the design, construction, and operation of the covered vessels and with respect to a variety of related matters. § 391a(3). In issuing regulations, the Secretary is to consider the kinds and grades of cargo permitted to be on board such vessels, to consult with other federal agencies, and to identify separately the regulations established for vessel safety and those to protect marine environment. Ibid.

Section 391a(5) provides for inspection of vessels for compliance with the Secretary's safety regulations. No vessel subject to Title II may have on board any of the specified cargoes until a certificate of inspection has been issued to the vessel and a permit endorsed thereon "indicating that such vessel is in compliance with the provisions of this section and the rules and regulations for vessel safety established hereunder, and showing the kinds and grades of such cargo that such vessel may have on board or transport." It is provided that in lieu of inspection under this section the Secretary is to accept from vessels of foreign nations valid certificates of inspection "recognized under law or treaty by the United States."

Title II also directs the Secretary to inspect tank vessels for compliance with the regulations which he is required to issue for the protection of the marine environment. § 391a(6). . . .

This statutory pattern shows that Congress, insofar as design characteristics are concerned, has entrusted to the Secretary the duty of determining which oil tankers are sufficiently safe to be allowed to proceed in the navigable waters of the United States. This indicates to us that Congress intended uniform national standards for design and construction of tankers that would foreclose the imposition of different or more stringent state requirements. In particular, as we see it, Congress did not anticipate that a vessel found to be in compliance with the Secretary's design and construction regulations and holding a Secretary's permit, or its equivalent, to carry the relevant cargo would nevertheless be barred by state law from operating in the navigable waters of the United States on the ground that its design characteristics constitute an undue hazard.

We do not question in the slightest the prior cases holding that enrolled and registered vessels must conform to "reasonable, nondiscriminatory conservation and environmental protection measures . . ." imposed by a State. Similarly, the mere fact that a vessel has been inspected and found to comply with the Secretary's vessel safety regulations does not prevent a State or city from enforcing local laws having other purposes, such as a local smoke abatement law. But in none of the relevant cases sustaining the application of state laws to federally licensed or inspected vessels did the federal licensing or inspection procedure implement a substantive rule of federal law addressed to the object also sought to be achieved by the challenged state regulation. Huron Portland Cement Co. v. Detroit [362 U.S. 440 (1960)] for example, made it plain that there was "no overlap between the scope of the federal ship inspection laws and that of the municipal ordinance . . ." there involved. The purpose of the "federal inspection statutes [was] to insure the seagoing safety of vessels . . . . to [afford] protection from the perils of marine navigation," while "[b]y contrast, the sole aim of the Detroit ordinance [was] the elimination of air pollution to protect the health and enhance the cleanliness of the local community."

Kelly v. Washington, 302 U.S. 1 (1937), involved a similar situation. There, the Court concluded that the Federal Motor Boat Act, although applicable to the vessels in question, was of limited scope and did not include provision for "the inspection of the hull and machinery of respondents' motor-driven tugs in order to insure safety or determine seaworthiness . . .," as long as the tugs did not carry passengers, freight, or inflammable liquid cargo. It followed that state inspection to insure safety was not in conflict with federal law, the Court also holding that the limited federal regulations did not imply an intent to exclude state regulation of those matters not touched by the federal statute.

Here, we have the very situation, that Huron Portland Cement Co. v. Detroit and Kelly v. Washington put aside. Title II aims at insuring vessel safety and protecting the marine environment; and the Secretary must issue all design and construction regulations that he deems necessary for these ends, after considering the specified statutory standards. The federal scheme thus aims precisely at the same ends as does § 88.16.190(2) of the Washington Law. Furthermore, under the PWSA, after considering the statutory standards and issuing all design requirements that in his judgment are necessary, the Secretary inspects and certifies each vessel as sufficiently safe to protect the marine environment and issues a permit or its equivalent to carry tank-vessel cargoes. Refusing to accept the federal judgment, however, the State now seeks to exclude from Puget Sound vessels certified by the Secretary as having acceptable design characteristics, unless they satisfy the different and higher design requirements imposed by state law. The Supremacy Clause dictates that the federal judgment that a vessel is safe to navigate United States waters prevail over the contrary state judgment.

Enforcement of the state requirements would at least frustrate what seems to us to be the evident congressional intention to establish a uniform federal regime controlling the design of oil tankers. The original Tank Vessel Act, amended by Title II, sought to effect a "reasonable and uniform set of rules and regulations concerning ship construction . . .," H.R.Rep. No. 2962, 74th Cong., 2d Sess., 2 (1936); and far from evincing a different purpose, the Title II amendments strongly indicate that insofar as tanker design is concerned, Congress anticipated the enforcement of federal standards that would pre-empt state efforts to mandate different or higher design requirements.

That the Nation was to speak with one voice with respect to tanker design standards is supported by the legislative history of Title II, particularly as it reveals a decided congressional preference for arriving at international standards for building tank vessels. . . .

Congress expressed a preference for international action and expressly anticipated that foreign vessels would or could be considered sufficiently safe for certification by the Secretary if they satisfied the requirements arrived at by treaty or convention; it is therefore clear that Title II leaves no room for the States to impose different or stricter design requirements than those which Congress has enacted with the hope of having them internationally adopted or has accepted as the result of international accord. A state law in this area, such as the first part of § 88.16.190(2), would frustrate the congressional desire of achieving uniform, international standards and is thus at odds with "the object sought to be obtained by [Title II] and the character of obligations imposed by it . . .." Rice v. Santa Fe Elevator Corp., 331 U.S., at 230. In this respect, the District Court was quite correct.

V.

Of course, that a tanker is certified under federal law as a safe vessel insofar as its design and construction characteristics are concerned does not mean that it is free to ignore otherwise valid state or federal rules or regulations that do not constitute design or construction specifications. Registered vessels, for example, as we have already indicated, must observe Washington's pilotage requirement. In our view, both enrolled and registered vessels must also comply with the provision of the Tanker Law that requires tug escorts for tankers over 40,000 DWT that do not satisfy the design provisions specified in § 88.16.190(2). This conclusion requires analysis of Title I of the PWSA, 33 U.S.C. §§ 1221–1227 (1970 ed., Supp. V).

. . .

VI.

We cannot arrive at the same conclusion with respect to the remaining provision of the Tanker Law at issue here. Section 88.16.190(1) excludes from Puget Sound under any circumstances any tanker in excess of 125,000 DWT. In our view, this provision is invalid in light of Title I and the Secretary's actions taken thereunder.

We begin with the premise that the Secretary has the authority to establish "vessel size and speed limitations," § 1221(3)(iii), and that local Coast Guard officers have been authorized to exercise this power on his behalf. Furthermore, § 1222(b), by permitting the State to impose higher equipment or safety standards "for structures only," impliedly forbids higher state standards for vessels. The implication is strongly supported by the legislative history of the PWSA. The House Report explains that the original wording of the bill did "not make it absolutely clear that the Coast Guard regulation of vessels pre-empts state action in this field" and says that § 1222(b) was amended to provide "a positive statement retaining State jurisdiction over structures and making clear that State regulation of vessels is not contemplated." House Report, at 15.

. . .

Our conclusion as to the State's ban on large tankers is consistent with the legislative history of Title I. In exercising his authority under the Title, the Secretary is directed to consult with other agencies in order "to assure consistency of regulations, . . ." § 1222(c), and also to "consider fully the wide variety of interests which may be affected . . ." § 1222(e). These twin themes—consistency of regulation and thoroughness of consideration—reflect the substance of the Committee Reports. . . .

. . .

We read these statements by Congress as indicating that it desired someone with an overview of all the possible ramifications of the regulation of oil tankers to promulgate limitations on tanker size and that he should act only after balancing all of the competing interests. While it was not anticipated that the final product of this deliberation would be the promulgation of traffic safety systems applicable across-the-board to all United States ports, it was anticipated that there would be a single decisionmaker, rather than a different one in each State.

Against this background, we think the pre-emptive impact of § 1222(b) is an understandable expression of congressional intent. Furthermore, even without § 1222(b), we would be reluctant to sustain the Tanker Law's absolute ban on tankers larger than 125,000 DWT. The Court has previously recognized that "where failure of . . . federal officials affirmatively to exercise their full authority takes on the character of a ruling that no such regulation is appropriate or approved pursuant to the policy of the statute," States are not permitted to use their police power to enact such a regulation. We think that in this case the Secretary's failure to promulgate a ban on the operations of oil tankers in excess of 125,000 DWT in Puget Sound takes on such a character. As noted above, a clear policy of the statute is that the Secretary shall carefully consider "the wide variety of interests which may be affected by the exercise of his authority," § 1222(e), and that he shall restrict the application of vessel size limitations to those areas where they are particularly necessary. In the case of Puget Sound, the Secretary has exercised his authority in accordance with the statutory directives and has promulgated a vessel traffic control system which contains only a narrow limitation on the operation of supertankers. This being the case, we conclude that Washington is precluded from enforcing the size limitation contained in the Tanker Law.

VII.

We also reject appellees' additional constitutional challenges to the State's tug escort requirement for vessels not satisfying its design standards. Appellees contend that this provision, even if not preempted by the PWSA, violates the Commerce Clause because it is an indirect attempt to regulate the design and equipment of tankers, an area of regulation that appellees contend necessitates a uniform national rule. We have previously rejected this claim, concluding that the provision may be viewed as simply a tug requirement since it does not have the effect of forcing compliance with the design specifications set forth in the provision. See supra, at n. 25. So viewed, it becomes apparent that the Commerce Clause does not prevent a State from enacting a regulation of this type. Similar in its nature to a local pilotage requirement, a requirement that a vessel take on a tug escort when entering a particular body of water is not the type of regulation that demands a uniform national rule. See Cooley v. Board of Wardens, 12 How. 299, 13 L.Ed. 996 (1851). Nor does it appear from the record that the requirement impedes the free and efficient flow of interstate and foreign commerce, for the cost of the tug escort for a 120,000 DWT tanker is less than one cent per barrel of oil and the amount of oil processed at Puget Sound refineries has not declined as a result of the provision's enforcement. App. 68. Accordingly, we hold that § 88.16.190(2) of the Tanker Law is not invalid under the Commerce Clause.

. . .

Accordingly, the judgment of the three-judge District Court is affirmed in part and reversed in part, and the case is remanded for further proceedings consistent with this opinion.

It is so ordered.

Mr. Justice Marshall, with whom Mr. Justice Brennan and Mr. Justice Rehnquist join, concurring in part and dissenting in part.

The Washington Tanker Law at issue here has three operative provisions: (1) a requirement that every oil tanker of 50,000 deadweight tons (DWT) or larger employ a pilot licensed by the State of Washington while navigating Puget Sound and adjacent waters, Wash.Rev.Code § 88.16.180 (Supp.1975); (2) a requirement that every oil tanker of from 40,000 to 125,000 DWT either possess certain safety features or utilize tug escorts while operating in Puget Sound, id., § 88.16.190(2); and (3) a size limitation, barring tankers in excess of 125,000 DWT from the Sound, id., § 88.16.190(1).

I agree with the Court that the pilotage requirement is pre-empted only with respect to enrolled vessels. I also agree that the tug escort requirement is fully valid, at least until such time as the Secretary of Transportation or his delegate promulgates a federal tug escort rule or decides, after full consideration, that no such rule is necessary. I therefore join Parts I, II, III, V, and VII of the Court's opinion.

In the current posture of this case, however, I see no need to speculate, as the Court does, on the validity of the safety features alternative to the tug requirement. . . . Accordingly, I cannot join Part IV of the Court's opinion.

I also cannot agree with the Court's conclusion in Part VI of its opinion that the size limitation contained in the Tanker Law is invalid under the Supremacy Clause. To reach this conclusion, the Court relies primarily on an analysis of Title I of the PWSA and the Secretary of Transportation's actions thereunder. I agree with the Court that the Secretary has authority to establish vessel size limitations based on the characteristics of particular waters, and that a State is not free to impose more stringent requirements once the Secretary has exercised that authority or has decided, after balancing all of the relevant factors, that a size limitation would not be appropriate. On the other hand, Title I does not by its own force pre-empt all state regulation of vessel size, since it "merely authorizes and does not require the Secretary to issue regulations to implement the provisions of the Title." Thus, as the Court notes, "[t]he pertinent inquiry at this point . . . [is] whether the Secretary, through his delegate, has addressed and acted upon the question of size limitations."

The Court concludes that the Secretary's delegate, the Coast Guard, has in fact considered the issue of size limitations for Puget Sound and reached a judgment contrary to the one embodied in the Tanker Law. Under well-established principles, however, state law should be displaced " 'only to the extent necessary to protect the achievement of the aims of' " federal law; whenever possible, we should "reconcile 'the operation of both statutory schemes with one another rather than holding [the State scheme] completely ousted.' " Viewed in light of these principles, the record simply does not support the Court's finding of conflict between state and federal law.

. . . .

For similar reasons, I would hold that Washington's size regulation does not violate the Commerce Clause. Since water depth and other navigational conditions vary from port to port, local regulation of tanker access—like pilotage and tug requirements, and other harbor and river regulation—is certainly appropriate, and perhaps even necessary, in the absence of determinative federal action. . . . Appellees have not demonstrated that the Tanker Law's size limit is an irrational or ineffective means of promoting safety and environmental protection, nor have they shown that the provision imposes any substantial burden on interstate or foreign commerce. Consequently, it is clear that appellees have not carried their burden of showing that the provision's impact on interstate or foreign commerce "is clearly excessive in relation to the putative local benefits." Pike v. Bruce Church, Inc., 397 U.S. 137, 142 (1970).

I do not find any of appellees' other arguments persuasive. I would therefore sustain the size limitation imposed by the Tanker Law.

Mr. Justice Stevens, with whom Mr. Justice Powell joins, concurring in part and dissenting in part.

The federal interest in uniform regulation of commerce on the high seas, reinforced by the Supremacy Clause, "dictates that the federal judgment that a vessel is safe to navigate United States waters prevail over the contrary state judgment." For that reason, as the Court explains in Part IV of its opinion, we must reject the judgment expressed by the Legislature of the State of Washington that an oil tanker of 40,000 to 125,000 tons cannot safely navigate in Puget

Sound unless it possesses the "standard safety features" prescribed by § 88.16.190(2) of the Washington Code. As the Court holds, the state statute imposing those design requirements is invalid. It follows, I believe, that the State may not impose any special restrictions on vessels which do not satisfy these invalid criteria.

The Court correctly holds that the State may not exclude vessels in that category from Puget Sound but it inconsistently allows the State to impose a costly tug escort requirement on these vessels and no others. . . .

If the federal interest in uniformity is to be vindicated, the magnitude of the special burden imposed by any one State's attempt to penalize noncompliance with its invalid rules is of no consequence. The tug escort penalty imposed by Washington will cost appellee approximately $277,500 per year. The significance of that cost cannot be determined simply by comparison with the capital investment which would be involved in complying with Washington's invalid design specifications. Rather, it should be recognized that this initial burden is subject to addition and multiplication by similar action in other States. Moreover, whether or not so multiplied, the imposition of any special restriction impairs the congressional determination to provide uniform standards for vessel design and construction.

Since I am persuaded that the tug escort requirement is an inseparable appendage to the invalid design requirements, the invalidity of one necessarily infects the other. I therefore respectfully dissent from Parts V and VII of the Court's opinion.

Chapter 6

THE SCOPE OF STATE POWER—TAXATION

SECTION 1. INTRODUCTION

Over the years the Supreme Court has decided several hundred cases involving state taxation of interstate commerce. Because these cases have developed doctrines substantially different from those involved in regulation cases it is necessary to look at them separately. But it is not possible to examine in any detail in a general book on constitutional law the elaborate and complex jurisprudence of the tax cases. Instead, the attempt will be made to give a general perspective, emphasizing the major themes in the cases. Fortunately a series of recent decisions have put to rest many of the doctrinal disputes of the past and they will serve as the core of the materials for this chapter.

SCOPE OF IMMUNITY OF INTERSTATE AND FOREIGN COMMERCE FROM STATE TAXATION

Ever since its first case dealing with state taxation of commerce—Brown v. Maryland, 25 U.S. (12 Wheat.) 419, decided in 1827—the Court has been struggling with the question whether the constitution intended that property moving in interstate and foreign commerce or businesses engaged in such commerce should be to some extent, at least, immune from state taxation. With respect to interstate commerce the question arises under the general grant of power to Congress to regulate commerce among the states. With respect to foreign commerce the question arises under the general power of Congress to regulate commerce with foreign nations and under the provision in Art. I, § 10: "No State shall, without the Consent of the Congress, lay any Imposts or Duties on Imports or Exports, except what may be absolutely necessary for executing its inspection Laws. . . ."

The cases have been clear from the earliest times that taxes which formally discriminate against interstate or foreign commerce are forbidden. The import-export clause obviously was intended at least to preclude states from erecting tariff barriers on goods from abroad. In Welton v. Missouri, 91 U.S. 275 (1876) the Court firmly stated the rule against discrimination in invalidating a statute which imposed a special license tax on peddlers who sold goods "which are not the growth, produce, or manufacture of the state." Most recently the Court has restated the rule in Armco, Inc. v. Hardesty, 104 S.Ct. 2620 (1984) (set out infra this chapter) and Bacchus Imports, Ltd. v. Dias, 104 S.Ct. 3049 (1984) (set out supra Chapter 5.)

But the question which has given enormous difficulty is whether there is an immunity beyond that against discrimination. Are the states precluded from imposing nondiscriminatory taxes on goods or instrumentalities of commerce physically present within their borders merely because they are moving in interstate commerce? Are the states precluded from imposing nondiscriminatory taxes on either the net or the gross proceeds from interstate commerce activity which takes place within their borders?

In the major cases of the last century the Court, reflecting the early suggestions in the state regulation cases that the power given to Congress by the commerce clause was exclusive, tended to find a wide scope of immunity against any state taxes which could be said to bear directly upon interstate or foreign commerce. For example, in Philadelphia & Reading Ry. Co. v. Pennsylvania (Case of the State Freight Tax), 82 U.S. 232, 279–80 (1873) the Court, in invalidating a tax which it found to be one directly on freight carried in interstate commerce, stated its general views as follows:

"If, then, this is a tax upon freight carried between states, and a tax because of its transportation, and if such a tax is in effect a regulation of interstate commerce, the conclusion seems to be inevitable that it is in conflict with the Constitution of the United States. It is not necessary to the present case to go at large into the much-debated question whether the power given to Congress by the Constitution to regulate commerce among the states is exclusive. In the early decisions of this court it was said to have been so entirely vested in Congress that no part of it can be exercised by a state. Gibbons v. Ogden, 9 Wheat. 1; Passenger Cases, 7 How. 283. It has, indeed, often been argued, and sometimes intimated, by the court, that so far as Congress has not legislated on the subject the states may legislate respecting interstate commerce. Yet, if they can, why may they not add regulations to commerce with foreign nations beyond those made by Congress, if not inconsistent with them, for the power over both foreign and interstate commerce is conferred upon the Federal legislature by the same words. And certainly it has never yet been decided by this court that the power to regulate interstate, as well as foreign commerce, is not exclusively in Congress. Cases that have sustained state laws, alleged to be regulations of commerce among the states, have been such as related to bridges or dams across streams wholly within a state, police or health laws, or subjects of a kindred nature, not strictly commercial regulations. . . . However this may be, the rule has been asserted with great clearness, that whenever the subjects over which a power to regulate commerce is asserted are in their nature national, or admit of one uniform system or plan of regulation, they may justly be said to be of such a nature as to require exclusive legislation by Congress. Cooley v. Port Wardens, 12 How. 299. Surely transportation of passengers or merchandise through a state, or from one state to another, is of this nature. It is of national importance that over that subject there should be but one regulating power, for if one state can directly tax persons or property passing through it, or tax them indirectly by levying a tax upon their transportation, every other may, and thus commercial intercourse between states remote from each other may be destroyed. The produce of western states may thus be effectually excluded from eastern markets, for though it might bear the imposition of a single tax, it would be crushed under the load of many. It was to guard against the possibility of such commercial embarrassments, no doubt, that the power of regulating commerce among other states was conferred upon the Federal government."

However, the Court did not go so far as to hold that states never could secure revenue from interstate business. A broad immunity would have placed the states in the position of being required to provide governmental services to property and business within their borders without being able to secure any contribution from such property and business to the cost of government. Hence, the states sought to devise means to secure such revenues and the Court began to draw lines between permissible and impermissible taxes on commerce. Originally, the lines drawn were largely formal. A state could impose a tax on the net proceeds from interstate activity within its borders but not on gross proceeds because the former bore only indirectly upon commerce while the latter bore directly. United States Glue Co. v. Town of Oak Creek, 247 U.S. 321 (1918). A state could impose a tax on the privilege of doing business and measure it by net income, including net income from interstate commerce attributable to the state, if the company did some local business but not if all of its activity within the state was interstate commerce. Spector Motor Serv. v. O'Connor, 340 U.S. 602 (1951).

In Western Livestock v. Bureau of Revenue, 303 U.S. 250, 254, 255 (1938), the Court began the search for a less formalistic basis upon which to decide the cases. It enunciated what has become known as the "multiple burdens" doctrine. First, the Court said "it was not the purpose of the commerce clause to relieve those engaged in interstate commerce from their just share of state tax burden even though it increases the cost of doing the business." Second, the Court indicated that the commerce clause should be construed to protect commerce against the multiple burdens which would result if more states than one could tax the same property or activity. In essence, the Court was simply restating the rule against discrimination when it attempted to rationalize prior cases: "The vice characteristic of those which have been held invalid is that they have placed on the commerce burdens of such a nature as to be capable in point of substance, of being imposed . . . with equal right by every state which the commerce touches, merely because interstate commerce is being done, so that without the protection of the commerce clause it would bear cumulative burdens not imposed on local commerce."

The decision in *Western Livestock* did not, however, mark an end to the older idea that interstate commerce itself could not be directly taxed. As recently as 1946 in Freeman v. Hewit, 329 U.S. 249, 256 (1946) the Court would say: "Nor is there any warrant in the constitutional principles heretofore applied by this Court to support the notion that a State may be allowed one single tax-worth of direct interference with the free flow of commerce. An exaction by a State from interstate commerce falls not because of a proven increase in the cost of the product. What makes the tax invalid is the fact that there is interference by a State with the freedom of interstate commerce . . . .. Trade being a sensitive plant, a direct tax upon it to some extent at least deters trade even if its effect is not precisely calculable." For nearly three decades after *Western Livestock* the cases continued to reflect first one and then the other of these conflicting approaches.

In reading the cases in this chapter it is useful to ask the question whether the Court now has put the old formal notions completely to rest. Is the relevant question now simply whether validating the challenged state tax would create the risk of placing commerce at a competitive disadvantage if other states imposed a similar tax? Do the answers differ when foreign commerce is involved?

LIMITS ON THE POWER OF STATES TO TAX PROPERTY AND ACTIVITIES OUTSIDE THEIR BORDERS

The second major theme which appears in the state taxation cases is one of jurisdiction. In State Tax on Foreign-held Bonds, 82 U.S. 300, 319 (1873) the Court said that "property lying beyond the jurisdiction of the state is not a subject upon which her taxing power can be legitimately exercised. Indeed, it would seem that no adjudication should be necessary to establish so obvious a proposition." By the turn of the century the Court placed this jurisdictional limitation under the due process clause. In Louisville & Jefferson Ferry Co. v. Kentucky, 188 U.S. 385, 396–397 (1903) the Court, in holding that Kentucky could not tax a franchise granted a ferry by Indiana to convey passengers from Indiana to Kentucky, first said that the taxing power of the states "is limited by a principle inhering in the very nature of constitutional government, namely, that the taxation imposed must have relation to a subject within the jurisdiction of the taxing government." It went on to assert that the taxation of the franchise by Kentucky is "a deprivation by that state of the property of the ferry company without due process of law in violation of the 14th Amendment of the Constitution of the United States; as much so as if that state taxed the real estate owned by that company in Indiana."

The earliest jurisdictional cases relating to commerce involved attempts by states to impose property taxes on the movable instrumentalities of interstate commerce—railroad rolling stock, ships and barges, and, at a later time, airplanes and trucks. In order to avoid problems of ascertaining the exact number of railroad cars, e.g., in the state on tax day, the practice arose of using formulas such as allocating to a state that portion of the value of all the cars owned by a company that the number of miles of track over which the cars were run in the state bore to the total miles of track over which they were run. The Court early rejected on due process grounds attempts by domiciliary states to tax the total value of railroad cars and upheld the apportionment method so long as it fairly allocated values to the taxing state. For an early case, see Union Refrigerator Transit Co. v. Kentucky, 199 U.S. 194 (1905). A more recent case discussing broadly the power of states to allocate values of property used in interstate commerce for purposes of imposing property taxes is Norfolk & Western Ry. Co. v. Missouri State Tax Comm'n, 390 U.S. 317 (1968). The Court's most recent exploration of this problem in the context of foreign commerce is in Japan Line v. County of Los Angeles, 441 U.S. 434 (1979), set out infra this chapter.

The jurisdictional problem also arises in cases involving state privilege taxes measured by net or gross income. The states characteristically have rejected the use of corporate accounting systems purporting to assign income to activities in particular states and have used instead a variety of apportionment formulas. Two kinds of jurisdictional problems have arisen. The first is the question whether the taxpayer conducts sufficient activities within a state to justify any tax at all. The second is whether the apportionment formula has the effect of reaching out and taxing values beyond the state. The Court has recently given exhaustive attention to the apportionment problem. Moorman Mfg. Co. v. Bair, 437 U.S. 267 (1978); Mobil Oil Corp. v. Commissioner of Taxes of Vermont, 445 U.S. 425 (1980); Exxon Corp. v. Wisconsin Dept. of Revenue, 447 U.S. 207 (1980); Container Corp. of America v. Franchise Tax Board, 104 S.Ct. 265 (1984). *Moorman* and *Container Corp.* are set out infra this chapter.

Sales and use tax cases have also given rise to jurisdictional issues. When the buyer and the seller are in the same state and delivery takes place there the sale is held to be local and taxable even though the goods come from outside the state. But when the seller is in one state and the buyer in another, the question has arisen whether the buyer's state can impose a tax on the sale. Where the seller does no more than solicit in the buyer's state by salespersons or by mail and delivery is via common carrier direct from seller to buyer, the Court has held that the state of the buyer can not impose a sales tax because to do so "would be to project its powers beyond its boundaries and to tax an interstate transaction." McLeod v. Dilworth Co., 322 U.S. 327, 330 (1944). But the Court has also held that the state of the buyer can impose a tax on the first use of goods purchased from out-of-state buyers—a tax which in substance is the same as the sales tax—because the use takes place within the taxing state. General Trading Co. v. State Tax Comm'n, 322 U.S. 335 (1944). But in order effectively to collect use taxes it is essential that the state of the buyer be able to compel the seller to collect and remit the tax. A number of cases have dealt with the due process problem of determining how much contact a seller must have with a state before the burden of collection can be imposed upon it. The most recent case, National Geographic Soc'y v. California Bd. of Equalization, 430 U.S. 551 (1977) is set out infra this chapter.

Often the due process and the commerce problems overlap. For example, if a state seeks to tax income of an interstate business which is fairly attributable to activities outside the state, the tax can be invalidated either as an assertion of jurisdiction over out-of-state activities or as creating the risk that interstate commerce will be disadvantaged because more than one state may be able to tax the same income. In other types of cases, however, there is no overlap. The question whether a state can impose its property tax on property moving in interstate commerce but physically within the state on tax day involves only the commerce clause. The physical presence provides adequate jurisdiction to tax. The question whether a state can tax property located outside its boundary when the property is not involved in interstate commerce presents only a due process problem. In reading the cases which follow, attention should be given to the question whether the commerce clause adds significant restrictions beyond those of the due process clause.

See generally, Hartman, *Federal Limitations on State and Local Taxation* (1981).

SECTION 2. THE GENERAL SCOPE OF THE LIMITATIONS IMPOSED ON STATE TAXATION OF INTERSTATE AND FOREIGN COMMERCE BY THE COMMERCE AND IMPORT–EXPORT CLAUSES

ARMCO, INC. v. HARDESTY

___ U.S. ___, 104 S.Ct. 2620, 81 L.Ed.2d 540 (1984).

Justice Powell delivered the opinion of the Court.

In this appeal an Ohio corporation claims that West Virginia's wholesale gross receipts tax, from which local manufacturers are exempt, unconstitutionally discriminates against interstate commerce. We agree and reverse the state court's judgment upholding the tax.

. . . .

II

It long has been established that the Commerce Clause of its own force protects free trade among the States. Boston Stock Exchange v. State Tax Comm'n, 429 U.S. 318, 328 (1977); Freeman v. Hewit, 329 U.S. 249, 252 (1946). One aspect of this protection is that a State "may not discriminate between transactions on the basis of some interstate element." *Boston Stock Exchange,* supra, 429 U.S., at 332, n. 12. That is, a State may not tax a transaction or incident more heavily when it crosses state lines than when it occurs entirely within the State.

On its face, the gross receipts tax at issue here appears to have just this effect. The tax provides that two companies selling tangible property at wholesale in West Virginia will be treated differently depending on whether the taxpayer conducts manufacturing in the State or out of it. Thus, if the property was manufactured in the State, no tax on the sale is imposed. If the property was manufactured out of the State and imported for sale, a tax of 0.27% is imposed on the sale price. . . .

The court below was of the view that no such discrimination in favor of local, intrastate commerce occurred because taxpayers manufacturing in the State were subject to a far higher tax of 0.88% of the sale price. This view is mistaken. The gross sales tax imposed on Armco cannot be deemed a "compensating tax" for the manufacturing tax imposed on its West Virginia competitors. In Maryland v. Louisiana, 451 U.S. 725, 758–759 (1981), the Court refused to consider a tax on the first use in Louisiana of gas brought in from out of State to be a complement of a severance tax in the same amount imposed on gas produced in the State. Severance and first use or processing were not "substantially equivalent event[s]" on which compensating taxes might be imposed. Here, too, manufacturing and wholesaling are not "substantially equivalent events" such that the heavy tax on in-state manufacturers can be said to compensate for the admittedly lighter burden placed on wholesalers from out of state. Manufacturing frequently entails selling in the State, but we cannot say which portion of the manufacturing tax is attributable to manufacturing, and which portion to sales. The fact that the manufacturing tax is not reduced when a West Virginia manufacturer sells its goods out of state, and that it is reduced when part of the manufacturing takes place out of state, makes clear that the manufacturing tax is just that, and not in part a proxy for the gross receipts tax imposed on Armco and other sellers from other States.

Moreover, when the two taxes are considered together, discrimination against interstate commerce persists. If Ohio or any of the other 48 States imposes a like tax on its manufacturers—which they have every right to do—then Armco and others from out of state will pay both a manufacturing tax and a wholesale tax while sellers resident in West Virginia will pay only the manufacturing tax. For example, if Ohio were to adopt the precise scheme here, then an interstate seller would pay the manufacturing tax of .88% *and* the gross receipts tax of 0.27%; a purely intrastate seller would pay only the manufacturing tax of 0.88% and would be exempt from the gross receipts tax.

Appellee suggests that we should require Armco to prove actual discriminatory impact on it by pointing to a State that imposes a manufacturing tax that results in a total burden higher than that imposed on Armco's competitors in West Virginia. This is not the test. In Container Corp. of America v. Franchise Tax Board, 463 U.S. 159, —— (1983), the Court noted that a tax must have "what might be called internal consistency—that is the [tax] must be such that, if applied by every jurisdiction," there would be no impermissible interference with free trade. In that case, the Court was discussing the requirement that a tax be fairly apportioned to reflect the business conducted in the State. A similar rule applies where the allegation is that a tax on its face discriminates against interstate commerce. A tax that unfairly apportions income from other States is a form of discrimination against interstate commerce. Any other rule would mean that the constitutionality of West Virginia's tax laws would depend on the shifting complexities of the tax codes of 49 other States, and that the validity of the taxes imposed on each taxpayer would depend on the particular other States in which it operated.

It is true, as the State of Washington appearing as *amicus curiae* points out, that Armco would be faced with the same situation that it complains of here if Ohio (or some other State) imposed a tax only upon manufacturing, while West Virginia imposed a tax only upon wholesaling. In that situation, Armco would bear two taxes, while West Virginia sellers would bear only one. But such a result would not arise from impermissible discrimination against interstate commerce but from fair encouragement of in-state business. What we said in *Boston Stock Exchange,* 429 U.S., at 336–337, is relevant here as well:

> "Our decision today does not prevent the States from structuring their tax systems to encourage the growth and development of intrastate commerce and industry. Nor do we hold that a State may not compete with other States for a share of interstate commerce; such competition lies at the heart of a free trade policy. We hold only that in the process of competition no State may discriminatorily tax the products manufactured or the business operations performed in any other State."

The judgment below is reversed.

It is so ordered.

Justice Rehnquist, dissenting.

The Court today strikes down West Virginia's wholesale gross receipts tax, finding that the wholesale tax unconstitutionally discriminates against interstate commerce, because local manufacturers are granted an exemption from the wholesale tax if they pay a manufacturing tax on their gross manufacturing receipts. Appellant's arguments, however, effectively rest on the hypothetical burden it might face if another State levied a corresponding tax on its manufactures. Because appellants have not shown that the taxes paid by out-of-state wholesalers on the same goods are higher than the taxes paid by in-state manufacturer-wholesalers, I would affirm the decision below.

. . .

THE TWENTY-FIRST AMENDMENT AND DISCRIMINATORY STATE TAXES

The Supreme Court early interpreted the twenty-first amendment as authorizing states to impose special license taxes on the importation of intoxicating beverages from other states. State Board of Equalization v. Young's Market Co., 299 U.S. 59 (1936). However, in Department of Revenue v. James Beam Distilling Co., 377 U.S. 341 (1964), the Court held that the twenty-first amendment did not repeal the explicit limitation of the export-import clause and so a state could not require an importer of liquor from abroad to secure a license and pay a fee. For speculation that the Court may be withdrawing from its original position that the power given to states to forbid the importation and sale of intoxicating beverages carries with it the power to impose taxes discriminating against interstate commerce in favor of local commerce, see Note, *The Effect of the Twenty-First Amendment on State Authority to Control Intoxicating Liquors*, 75 Colum.L.Rev. 1578 (1975).

BACCHUS IMPORTS, LIMITED v. DIAS

___ U.S. ___, 104 S.Ct. 3049, 82 L.Ed.2d 200 (1984).

[The report in this case appears, supra at p. 324]

OTHER CONSTITUTIONAL LIMITATIONS ON DISCRIMINATORY TAXATION—PRIVILEGES AND IMMUNITIES AND EQUAL PROTECTION

Discriminatory taxation may be challenged in situations where interstate commerce is not burdened. The principal constitutional limitations on such taxes are the privileges and immunities clause of Article IV and the equal protection clause. The cases which follow suggest the scope of the protection given by those clauses. In certain circumstances they serve to protect multistate businesses and hence perform functions related to the commerce limitation.

AUSTIN v. NEW HAMPSHIRE, 420 U.S. 656 (1975). The case involved a challenge to the New Hampshire Commuters Income Tax which had the effect of imposing an income tax only on the incomes of nonresidents working in New Hampshire. The Court held it invalid under Art. IV, § 2, cl. 1: "The Citizens of each State shall be entitled to all Privileges and Immunities of Citizens in the several States." The opinion included the following paragraphs:

"In resolving constitutional challenges to state tax measures this Court has made it clear that 'in taxation, even more than in other fields, legislatures possess the greatest freedom in classification.' Madden v. Kentucky, 309 U.S. 83, 88 (1940). See Lehnhausen v. Lake Shore Auto Parts Co., 410 U.S. 356 (1973). Our review of tax classifications has generally been concomitantly narrow, therefore, to fit the broad discretion vested in the state legislatures. When a tax measure is challenged as an undue burden on an activity granted special constitutional recognition, however, the appropriate degree of inquiry is that necessary to protect the competing constitutional value from erosion. See Lehnhausen v. Lake Shore Auto Parts Co., supra, 410 U.S., at 359.

"This consideration applies equally to the protection of individual liberties, see Grosjean v. American Press Co., 297 U.S. 233 (1936), and to the maintenance of our constitutional federalism. See Michigan-Wisconsin Pipe Line Co. v. Calvert, 347 U.S. 157, 164 (1954). The Privileges and Immunities Clause, by making noncitizenship or nonresidence an improper basis for locating a special burden, implicates not only the individual's right to nondiscriminatory treatment but also, perhaps more so, the structural balance essential to the concept of federalism. Since nonresidents are not represented in the taxing State's legislative halls, cf. Allied Stores of Ohio, Inc. v. Bowers, 358 U.S. 522, 532–533 (1959) (Brennan, J., concurring), judicial acquiescence in taxation schemes that burden them particularly would remit them to such redress as they could secure through their own State; but 'to prevent [retaliation] was one of the chief ends sought to be accomplished by the adoption of the Constitution.' Travis v. Yale & Towne Mfg. Co., 252 U.S. 60, 82 (1920). Our prior cases, therefore, reflect an appropriately heightened concern for the integrity of the Privileges and Immunities Clause by erecting a standard of review substantially more rigorous than that applied to state tax distinctions among, say, forms of business organizations or different trades and professions. . . ."

The privileges and immunities clause does not apply to corporations. Hence although states may not prevent corporations created in other states from entering to engage in interstate commerce, Allenberg Cotton Co., Inc. v. Pittman, 419 U.S. 20 (1974), they may prevent them from doing intrastate business or impose special entry fees for the doing of such business. Atlantic Refining Co. v. Virginia, 320 U.S. 22 (1937) (upholding special entry fee on foreign corporation.)

———

WESTERN AND SOUTHERN LIFE INSURANCE CO. v. STATE BOARD OF EQUALIZATION, 451 U.S. 648 (1981). California imposed two taxes on insurance companies doing business in the state: one applicable to both foreign and domestic insurance companies and a second "retaliatory" tax imposed on out-of-state insurers doing business in California whose state of incorporation imposed higher taxes on California insurers doing business in that state than California assessed for business done in California. The purpose of the retaliatory tax was to promote the interstate business of domestic insurers by deterring other states from enacting discriminatory or excessive taxes. The California courts upheld the validity of the retaliatory tax and the Supreme Court affirmed.

First, the Court rejected the argument that the tax was invalid under the commerce clause because it discriminated against the out-of-state insurance companies. It held that "Congress removed all Commerce Clause limitations on the authority of the States to regulate and tax the business of insurance when it passed the McCarran-Ferguson Act."

Second, it noted that the privileges and immunities clause did not apply because the insurance companies were corporations.

Third, it discussed at length the applicability of the equal protection clause to discriminatory taxes on foreign corporations. It concluded that while a state was free to exclude foreign corporations from doing intrastate business or to impose discriminatory entry fees, the state could not impose special taxes after entry without meeting the equal protection clause restricting the right of the state to impose special taxes after permission to do local business had been granted. "We consider it now established that, whatever the extent of a State's authority to exclude foreign corporations from doing business within its boundaries, that authority does not justify—imposition of more onerous taxes or other burdens on foreign corporations than those imposed on domestic corporations, unless the discrimination between foreign and domestic corporations bears a rational relation to a legitimate state purpose."

The Court went on to hold that the retaliatory tax was rationally related to achievement of a legitimate state purpose and so did not violate the equal protection clause. The Court noted that the tax was based on a model statute drafted by the insurance industry and was virtually identical to statutes adopted in many other states. Whether it actually worked to promote domestic insurance companies by deterring barriers to interstate business was questionable. But "[p]arties challenging legislation under the Equal Protection Clause cannot prevail so long as 'it is evident from all the considerations presented to [the legislature], and those of which we may take judicial notice, that the question is at least debatable' . . . On this standard, we cannot but conclude that the California retaliatory insurance tax withstands the strictures of the Fourteenth Amendment."

Justices Stevens and Blackmun dissented arguing that there was no legitimate purpose and so the tax violated equal protection.

NOTE

Occasionally, Congress intervenes to give greater protection to interstate businesses. In Nashville, Chattanooga & St. Louis Ry. v. Browning, 310 U.S. 362 (1940), the Court held that it was not a denial of equal protection of the laws for the state to collect a property tax from railroads with property assessed at full value while all other property was assessed at far less than full value. In the late 1970s Congress enacted statutes forbidding states from collecting property taxes on property belonging to railroads and to motor carriers higher than those imposed on other property. 49 U.S.C. §§ 11503, 11503a.

An argument can be made that tax classifications like those in *Nashville* should be subject to challenge under the commerce clause because they may be utilized to impose special burdens on predominantly interstate enterprises. Thomas Reed Powell once observed:

"When a statute picks a special subject for a special tax, the object of its desire is practically certain to be forced into a generosity in excess of that indulged in by property and business generally. If this special subject is interstate commerce or includes interstate commerce, enterprise which straddles a state line is paying more than some or all of the enterprise that is of interest only to the taxing state. The danger that the taxing state will heed the monition that charity beginneth at home is sufficient to justify the court in looking askance at any exaction on interstate commerce that is not certain to be matched by equivalent exactions on all local commerce." *State Income Taxes and the Commerce Clause*, 31 Yale L.J. 799, 801 (1922).

For an argument that the Court should regard with suspicion any special tax which lends itself to the imposition of special tax burdens on interstate commerce or upon predominantly interstate businesses, see Barrett, *"Substance" vs. "Form" in the Application of the Commerce Clause to State Taxation,* 101 U.Pa.L.Rev. 740, 749–754 (1953). For a suggestion that the Court today might be willing to listen to such an argument, see note 15 in Complete Auto Transit, Inc. v. Brady, 430 U.S. 274, 288 (1977), set out below.

COMPLETE AUTO TRANSIT, INC. v. BRADY

430 U.S. 274, 97 S.Ct. 1076, 51 L.Ed.2d 326 (1977).

Mr. Justice Blackmun delivered the opinion of the Court.

Once again we are presented with " 'the perennial problem of the validity of a state tax for the privilege of carrying on, within a state, certain activities' relating to a corporation's operation of an interstate business." The issue in this case is whether Mississippi runs afoul of the Commerce Clause, Const., Art. I, § 8, cl. 3, when it applies the tax it imposes on "the privilege of . . . doing business" within the State to appellant's activity in interstate commerce. The Supreme Court of Mississippi unanimously sustained the tax against appellant's constitutional challenge. 330 So.2d 268 (1976). We noted probable jurisdiction in order to consider anew the applicable principles in this troublesome area.

I.

The taxes in question are sales taxes assessed by the Mississippi State Tax Commission against the appellant, Complete Auto Transit, Inc., for the period from August 1, 1968, through July 31, 1972. The assessments were made pursuant to the following Mississippi statutes:

"There is hereby levied and assessed and shall be collected privilege taxes for the privilege of engaging or continuing in business or doing business within this state to be determined by the application of rates against gross proceeds of sales or gross income or values, as the case may be, as provided in the following sections." Miss.Code Ann. § 10105 (1942), as amended.

"Upon every person operating a pipeline, railroad, airplane, bus, truck, or any other transportation business for the transportation of persons or property for compensation or hire between points within this State, there is hereby levied, assessed, and shall be collected, a tax equal to five per cent (5%) of the gross income of such business. . . ." Id., § 10109(2), as amended.

Any person liable for the tax is required to add it to the gross sales price and, "insofar as practicable," to collect it at the time the sale price is collected. Section 10117, as amended.

Appellant is a Michigan corporation engaged in the business of transporting motor vehicles by motor carrier for General Motors Corporation. General Motors assembles outside Mississippi vehicles that are destined for dealers within the State. The vehicles are then shipped by rail to Jackson, Miss., where, usually within 48 hours, they are loaded onto appellant's trucks and transported by appellant to the Mississippi dealers. Appellant is paid on a contract basis for the transportation from the railhead to the dealers.

By letter dated October 5, 1971, the Mississippi Tax Commission informed appellant that it was being assessed taxes and interest totalling $122,160.59 for the sales of transportation services during the three-year period from August 1, 1968, through July 31, 1971. . . . By similar letter dated December 28,

1972, the Commission advised appellant of an assessment of $42,990.89 for the period from August 1, 1971, through July 31, 1972. Appellant paid the assessments under protest and, in April 1973, instituted the present refund action in the Chancery Court of the First Judicial District of Hinds County.

Appellant claimed that its transportation was but one part of an interstate movement, and that the taxes assessed and paid were unconstitutional as applied to operations in interstate commerce. The Chancery Court, in an unreported opinion, sustained the assessments.

The Mississippi Supreme Court affirmed. . . .

Appellant, in its complaint in Chancery Court, did *not* allege that its activity which Mississippi taxes does not have a sufficient nexus with the State; or that the tax discriminates against interstate commerce; or that the tax is unfairly apportioned; or that it is unrelated to services provided by the State. No such claims were made before the Mississippi Supreme Court, and although appellant argues here that a tax on "the privilege of doing interstate commerce" creates an unacceptable risk of discrimination and undue burdens, it does not claim that discrimination or undue burdens exist in fact.

Appellant's attack is based solely on decisions of this Court holding that a tax on the "privilege" of engaging in an activity in the State may not be applied to an activity that is part of interstate commerce. See, e.g., Spector Motor Service v. O'Connor, 340 U.S. 602 (1951); Freeman v. Hewit, 329 U.S. 249 (1946). This rule looks only to the fact that the incidence of the tax is the "privilege of doing business"; it deems irrelevant any consideration of the practical effect of the tax. The rule reflects an underlying philosophy that interstate commerce should enjoy a sort of "free trade" immunity from state taxation.[7]

Appellee, in its turn, relies on decisions of this Court stating that "[i]t was not the purpose of the commerce clause to relieve those engaged in interstate commerce from their just share of state tax burden even though it increases the cost of doing the business," Western Live Stock v. Bureau of Revenue, 303 U.S. 250, 254 (1938). These decisions have considered not the formal language of the tax statute, but rather its practical effect, and have sustained a tax against Commerce Clause challenge when the tax is applied to an activity with a substantial nexus with the taxing state, is fairly apportioned, does not discriminate against interstate commerce, and is fairly related to the services provided by the State.

Over the years, the Court has applied this practical analysis in approving many types of tax that avoided running afoul of the prohibition against taxing the "privilege of doing business," but in each instance it has refused to overrule the prohibition. Under the present state of the law, the *Spector* rule, as it has come to be known, has no relationship to economic realities. Rather it stands only as a trap for the unwary draftsman.

II.

The modern origin of the *Spector* rule may be found in Freeman v. Hewit, supra. At issue in *Freeman* was the application of an Indiana tax upon "the receipt of the entire gross income" of residents and domiciliaries. 329 U.S., at

---

[7] The Court summarized the "free trade" view in Freeman v. Hewit, 329 U.S., at 252:

"[T]he Commerce Clause was not merely an authorization to Congress to enact laws for the protection and encouragement of commerce among the States, but by its own force created an area of trade free from interference by the States. In short, the Commerce Clause even without implementing legislation by Congress is a limitation upon the power of the States . . . . This limitation on State power . . . does not merely forbid a State to single out interstate commerce for hostile action. A State is also precluded from taking any action which may fairly be deemed to have the effect of impeding the free flow of trade between States. It is immaterial that local commerce is subjected to a similar encumbrance."

250. Indiana sought to impose this tax on income generated when a trustee of an Indiana estate instructed his local stockbroker to sell certain securities. The broker arranged with correspondents in New York to sell the securities on the New York Stock Exchange. The securities were sold, and the New York brokers, after deducting expenses and commission, transmitted the proceeds to the Indiana broker who in turn delivered them, less his commission, to the trustee. The Indiana Supreme Court sustained the tax, but this Court reversed.

Mr. Justice Frankfurter, speaking for five Members of the Court, announced a blanket prohibition against any state taxation imposed directly on an interstate transaction. He explicitly deemed unnecessary to the decision of the case any showing of discrimination against interstate commerce or error in apportionment of the tax. He recognized that a State could constitutionally tax local manufacture, impose license taxes on corporations doing business in the State, tax property within the State, and tax the privilege of residence in the State and measure the privilege by net income, including that derived from interstate commerce. Nevertheless, a direct tax on interstate sales, even if fairly apportioned and nondiscriminatory, was held to be unconstitutional *per se.*

Mr. Justice Rutledge, in a lengthy concurring opinion, argued that the tax should be judged by its economic effects rather than by its formal phrasing. After reviewing the Court's prior decisions, he concluded: "The fact is that 'direct incidence' of a state tax or regulation . . . has long since been discarded as being in itself sufficient to outlaw state legislation." In his view, a state tax is unconstitutional only if the activity lacks the necessary connection with the taxing state to give "jurisdiction to tax," or if the tax discriminates against interstate commerce, or if the activity is subject to multiple taxation.

The rule announced in *Freeman* was viewed in the commentary as a triumph of formalism over substance, providing little guidance even as to formal requirements. See P. Hartman, State Taxation of Interstate Commerce 200–204 (1953); Dunham, "Gross Receipts Taxes on Interstate Transactions," 47 Col.L.Rev. 211 (1947). Although the rule might have been utilized as the keystone of a movement toward absolute immunity of interstate commerce from state taxation, the Court consistently has indicated that "interstate commerce may be made to pay its way," and has moved toward a standard of permissibility of state taxation based upon its actual effect rather than its legal terminology.

. . . .

The prohibition against state taxation of the "privilege" of engaging in commerce that is interstate was reaffirmed in Spector Motor Service v. O'Connor, 340 U.S. 602 (1951), a case similar on its facts to the instant case. The taxpayer there was a Missouri corporation engaged exclusively in interstate trucking. Some of its shipments originated or terminated in Connecticut. Connecticut imposed on a corporation a "tax or excise upon its franchise for the privilege of carrying on or doing business within the state," measured by apportioned net income. Spector brought suit in federal court to enjoin collection of the tax as applied to its activities. The District Court issued the injunction. The Second Circuit reversed. This Court, with three Justices in dissent, in turn reversed the Court of Appeals and held the tax unconstitutional as applied.

The Court recognized that "where a taxpayer is engaged both in intrastate and interstate commerce, a state may tax the privilege of carrying on intrastate business and, within reasonable limits, may compute the amount of the charge by applying the tax rate to a fair proportion of the taxpayer's business done within the state, including both interstate and intrastate." It held, nevertheless, that a tax on the "privilege" of doing business is unconstitutional if applied against what is exclusively interstate commerce. The dissenters argued, on the other hand, that there is no constitutional difference between an "exclusively interstate" business and a "mixed" business, and that a fairly apportioned and nondiscriminatory tax on either type is not prohibited by the Commerce Clause.

The *Spector* rule was applied in Railway Express Agency v. Virginia, 347 U.S. 359 (1954) (*Railway Express I*), to declare unconstitutional a State's "annual license tax" levied on gross receipts for the "privilege of doing business in this State." The Court, by a 5 to 4 vote, held that the tax on gross receipts was a tax on the privilege of doing business rather than a tax on property in the State, as Virginia contended.

Virginia thereupon revised the wording of its statute to impose a "franchise tax" on "intangible property" in the form of "going concern" value as measured by gross receipts. The tax was again asserted against the Agency which in Virginia was engaged exclusively in interstate commerce. This Court's opinion, buttressed by two concurring opinions and one concurrence in the result, upheld the reworded statute as not violative of the *Spector* rule. Railway Express Agency v. Virginia, 358 U.S. 434 (1959) (*Railway Express II*). In upholding the statute, the Court's opinion recognized that the rule against taxing the "privilege" of doing interstate business had created a situation where "the use of magic words or labels" could "disable an otherwise constitutional levy."

There was no real economic difference between the statutes in *Railway Express I* and *Railway Express II*. The Court long since had recognized that interstate commerce may be made to pay its way. Yet under the *Spector* rule, the economic realities in *Railway Express I* became irrelevant. The *Spector* rule had come to operate only as a rule of draftsmanship, and served only to distract the courts and parties from their inquiry into whether the challenged tax produced results forbidden by the Commerce Clause.

On the day it announced *Railway Express II,* the Court further confirmed that a State, with proper drafting, may tax exclusively interstate commerce so long as the tax does not create any effect forbidden by the Commerce Clause. In Northwestern Cement Co. v. Minnesota, 358 U.S. 450 (1959), the Court held that net income from the interstate operations of a foreign corporation may be subjected to state taxation, provided the levy is not discriminatory and is properly apportioned to local activities within the taxing State forming sufficient nexus to support the tax. Limited in that way, the tax could be levied even though the income was generated exclusively by interstate sales. *Spector* was distinguished, briefly and in passing, as a case in which "the incidence" of the tax "was the privilege of doing business."

Thus, applying the rule of *Northwestern Cement* to the facts of *Spector,* it is clear that Connecticut could have taxed the apportioned net income derived from the exclusively interstate commerce. It could not, however, tax the "privilege" of doing business as measured by the apportioned net income. The reason for attaching constitutional significance to a semantic difference is difficult to discern.

The unsatisfactory operation of the *Spector* rule is well demonstrated by our recent case of Colonial Pipeline Co. v. Traigle, 421 U.S. 100 (1975). Colonial was a Delaware corporation with an interstate pipeline running through Louisiana for approximately 258 miles. It maintained a work force and pumping stations in Louisiana to keep the pipeline flowing, but it did no intrastate business in that State. In 1962, Louisiana imposed on Colonial a franchise tax for "the privilege of carrying on or doing business" in the State. The Louisiana Court of Appeal invalidated the tax as violative of the rule of *Spector.* 228 So.2d 718 (1969). The Supreme Court of Louisiana refused review. 255 La. 474, 231 So.2d 393 (1970). The Louisiana Legislature, perhaps recognizing that it had run afoul of a rule of words rather than a rule of substance, then redrafted the statute to levy the tax, as an alternative incident, on the "qualification to carry on or do business in this state or the actual doing of business within this state in a corporate form." Again, the Court of Appeal held the tax unconstitutional as applied to the appellant. 275 So.2d 834 (1973). But this time the Louisiana Supreme Court upheld the new tax. 289 So.2d 93 (1974).

By a 7 to 1 vote, this Court affirmed. No question had been raised as to the propriety of the apportionment of the tax, and no claim was made that the tax was discriminatory. The Court noted that the tax was imposed on that aspect of interstate commerce to which the State bore a special relation, and that the State bestowed powers, privileges, and benefits sufficient to support a tax on doing business in the corporate form in Louisiana. Accordingly, on the authority of *Memphis Gas,* the tax was held to be constitutional. The Court distinguished *Spector* on the familiar ground that it involved a tax on the privilege of carrying on interstate commerce, while the Louisiana Legislature, in contrast, had worded the statute at issue "narrowly to confine the impost to one related to appellant's activities within the State in the corporate form."

. . . One commentator concluded: "After reading *Colonial,* only the most sanguine taxpayer would conclude that the Court maintains a serious belief in the doctrine that the privilege of doing interstate business is immune from state taxation." W. Hellerstein, "State Taxation of Interstate Business and the Supreme Court, 1974 Term: Standard Pressed Steel and Colonial Pipeline," 62 Va.L.Rev. 149, 188 (1976).

III.

In this case, of course, we are confronted with a situation like that presented in *Spector.* The tax is labeled a privilege tax "for the privilege of . . . doing business" in Mississippi, § 10105 of the State's 1942 Code, as amended, and the activity taxed is, or has been assumed to be, interstate commerce. We note again that no claim is made that the activity is not sufficiently connected to the State to justify a tax, or that the tax is not fairly related to benefits provided the taxpayer, or that the tax discriminates against interstate commerce, or that the tax is not fairly apportioned.

The view of the Commerce Clause that gave rise to the rule of *Spector* perhaps was not without some substance. Nonetheless, the possibility of defending it in the abstract does not alter the fact that the Court has rejected the proposition that interstate commerce is immune from state taxation:

"It is a truism that the mere act of carrying on business in interstate commerce does not exempt a corporation from state taxation. 'It was not the purpose of the commerce clause to relieve those engaged in interstate commerce from their just share of state tax burden even though it increases the cost of doing business.' Western Live Stock v. Bureau of Revenue, 303 U.S. 250, 254 (1938)." Colonial Pipeline Co. v. Traigle, 421 U.S., at 108.

Not only has the philosophy underlying the rule been rejected, but the rule itself has been stripped of any practical significance. If Mississippi had called its tax one on "net income" or on the "going concern value" of appellant's business, the *Spector* rule could not invalidate it. There is no economic consequence that follows necessarily from the use of the particular words, "privilege of doing business," and a focus on that formalism merely obscures the question whether the tax produces a forbidden effect. Simply put, the *Spector* rule does not address the problems with which the Commerce Clause is concerned.[15] Accordingly, we now reject the rule of Spector Motor Service,

---

[15] It might be argued that "privilege" taxes, by focusing on the doing of business, are easily tailored to single out interstate businesses and subject them to effects forbidden by the Commerce Clause, and that, therefore, "privilege" taxes should be subjected to a *per se* rule against their imposition on interstate business. Yet property taxes also may be tailored to differentiate between property used in transportation and other types of property, see *Railway Express II,* supra; an income tax could use

Inc. v. O'Connor, supra, that a state tax on the "privilege of doing business" is *per se* unconstitutional when it is applied to interstate commerce, and that case is overruled.

There being no objection to Mississippi's tax on appellant except that it was imposed on nothing other than the "privilege of doing business" that is interstate, the judgment of the Supreme Court of Mississippi is affirmed.

It is so ordered.

COMMONWEALTH EDISON CO. v. MONTANA

453 U.S. 609, 101 S.Ct. 2946, 69 L.Ed.2d 884 (1981).

Justice Marshall delivered the opinion of the Court.

Montana, like many other States, imposes a severance tax on mineral production in the State. In this appeal, we consider whether the tax Montana levies on each ton of coal mined in the State, Mont.Code § 15–35–101 et seq. (1979), violates the Commerce and Supremacy Clauses of the United States Constitution.

I

Buried beneath Montana are large deposits of low sulfur coal, most of it on federal land. Since 1921, Montana has imposed a severance tax on the output of Montana coal mines, including coal mined on federal land. . . . [I]n 1975, the Montana Legislature enacted the tax schedule at issue in this case. Mont.Code § 15–35–103 (1979). The tax is levied at varying rates depending on the value, energy content, and method of extraction of the coal, and may equal at a maximum, 30% of the "contract sales price." Under the terms of a 1976 amendment to the Montana Constitution, after Dec. 31, 1979, at least 50% of the revenues generated by the tax must be paid into a permanent trust fund, the principal of which may be appropriated only by a vote of three-fourths of the members of each house of the legislature. Montana Const. Art. IX, § 5.

Appellants, 4 Montana coal producers and 11 of their out-of-state utility company customers, filed these suits in Montana state court in 1978. They sought refunds of over $5.4 million in severance taxes paid under protest, a declaration that the tax is invalid under the Supremacy and Commerce Clauses, and an injunction against further collection of the tax. Without receiving any evidence, the court upheld the tax and dismissed the complaints.

On appeal, the Montana Supreme Court affirmed the judgment of the trial court. —— Mont. ——, 615 P.2d 847 (1980). . . .

We noted probable jurisdiction to consider the important issues raised. We now affirm.

---

different rates for different types of business; and a tax on the "privilege of doing business in corporate form" could be made to change with the nature of the corporate activity involved. Any tailored tax of this sort creates an increased danger of error in apportionment of discrimination against interstate commerce, and of a lack of relationship to the services provided by the State. See *Freeman v. Hewit*, 329 U.S., at 265–266, n. 13 (concurring opinion). A tailored tax, however accomplished, must receive the careful scrutiny of the courts to determine whether it produces a forbidden effect on interstate commerce. We perceive no reason, however, why a tax on the "privilege of doing business" should be viewed as creating a qualitatively different danger so as to require a *per se* rule of unconstitutionality.

It might also be argued that adoption of a rule of absolute immunity for interstate commerce (a rule that would, of course, go beyond *Spector*) would relieve this Court of difficult judgments that on occasion will have to be made. We believe, however, that administrative convenience, in this instance, is insufficient justification for abandoning the principle that "interstate commerce may be made to pay its way."

II

A

As an initial matter, appellants assert that the Montana Supreme Court erred in concluding that the Montana tax is not subject to the strictures of the Commerce Clause. In appellants' view, *Heisler*'s "mechanical" approach, which looks to whether a state tax is levied on goods prior to their entry into interstate commerce, no longer accurately reflects the law. Appellants contend that the correct analysis focuses on whether the challenged tax substantially affects interstate commerce, in which case it must be scrutinized under the *Complete Auto Transit* test.

We agree that *Heisler*'s reasoning has been undermined by more recent cases.

. . .

. . .

We therefore hold that a state severance tax is not immunized from Commerce Clause scrutiny by a claim that the tax is imposed on goods prior to their entry into the stream of interstate commerce. Any contrary statements in *Heisler* and its progeny are disapproved. We agree with appellants that the Montana tax must be evaluated under *Complete Auto Transit*'s four-part test. Under that test, a state tax does not offend the Commerce Clause if it "is applied to an activity with a substantial nexus with the taxing State, is fairly apportioned, does not discriminate against interstate commerce, and is fairly related to services provided by the State." 430 U.S., at 279.

B

Appellants do not dispute that the Montana tax satisfies the first two prongs of *Complete Auto Transit* test. As the Montana Supreme Court noted, "there can be no argument here that a substantial, in fact, the only nexus of the severance of coal is established in Montana." Nor is there any question here regarding apportionment or potential multiple taxation, for as the state court observed, "the severance can occur in no other state" and "no other state can tax the severance." Appellants do contend, however, that the Montana tax is invalid under the third and fourth prongs of the *Complete Auto Transit* test.

Appellants assert that the Montana tax "discriminate[s] against interstate commerce" because 90% of Montana coal is shipped to other States under contracts that shift the tax burden primarily to non-Montana utility companies and thus to citizens of other States. But the Montana tax is computed at the same rate regardless of the final destination of the coal, and there is no suggestion here that the tax is administered in a manner that departs from this even-handed formula. We are not, therefore, confronted here with the type of differential tax treatment of interstate and intrastate commerce that the Court has found in other "discrimination" cases. See, e.g., Maryland v. Louisiana, 451 U.S. 725 (1981); Boston Stock Exchange v. State Tax Comm'n, 429 U.S. 318 (1977); cf. Lewis v. BT Investment Managers, Inc., 447 U.S. 27 (1980); Philadelphia v. New Jersey, 437 U.S. 617 (1978).

Instead, the gravamen of appellants' claim is that a state tax must be considered discriminatory for purposes of the Commerce Clause if the tax burden is borne primarily by out-of-state consumers. Appellants do not suggest that this assertion is based on any of this Court's prior discriminatory tax cases. In fact, a similar claim was considered and rejected in *Heisler*. There, it was argued that Pennsylvania had a virtual monopoly of anthracite coal and that, because 80% of the coal was shipped out of State, the tax discriminated against and impermissibly burdened interstate commerce. 260 U.S. 251–253. The Court, however, dismissed these factors as "adventitious considerations." 260

U.S., at 259. We share the *Heisler* Court's misgivings about judging the validity of a state tax by assessing the State's "monopoly" position or its "exportation" of the tax burden out of State.

The premise of our discrimination cases is that "[t]he very purpose of the Commerce Clause was to create an area of free trade among the several States." McLeod v. J.E. Dilworth Co., 322 U.S. 327, 330 (1944). See Hunt v. Washington State Apple Advertising Comm'n, 432 U.S. 333, 350 (1977); Boston Stock Exchange v. State Tax Comm'n, supra, 429 U.S., at 328. Under such a regime, the boarders between the States are essentially irrelevant. . . . Consequently, to accept appellants' theory and invalidate the Montana tax solely because most of Montana's coal is shipped across the very state borders that ordinarily are to be considered irrelevant would require a significant and, in our view, unwarranted departure from the rationale of our prior discrimination cases.

Furthermore, appellants' assertion that Montana may not "exploit" its "monopoly" position by exporting tax burdens to other States, cannot rest on a claim that there is need to protect the out-of-state consumers of Montana coal from discriminatory tax treatment. As previously noted, there is no real discrimination in this case; the tax burden is borne according to the amount of coal consumed and not according to any distinction between in-state and out-of-state consumers. Rather, appellants assume that the Commerce Clause gives residents of one State a right of access at "reasonable" prices to resources located in another State that is richly endowed with such resources, without regard to whether and on what terms residents of the resource-rich State have access to the resources. We are not convinced that the Commerce Clause, of its own force, gives the residents of one State the right to control in this fashion the terms of resource development and depletion in a sister State. Cf. Philadelphia v. New Jersey, supra, 437 U.S., at 626.

In any event, appellants' discrimination theory ultimately collapses into their claim that the Montana tax is invalid under the fourth prong of the *Complete Auto Transit* test: that the tax is not "fairly related to the services provided by the State." 430 U.S., at 279. Because appellants concede that Montana may impose *some* severance tax on coal mined in the State, the only remaining foundation for their discrimination theory is a claim that the tax burden borne by the out-of-state consumers of Montana coal is excessive. This is, of course, merely a variant of appellants' assertion that the Montana tax does not satisfy the "fairly related" prong of the *Complete Auto Transit* test, and is to this contention that we now turn.

Appellants argue that they are entitled to an opportunity to prove that the amount collected under the Montana tax is not fairly related to the additional costs the State incurs because of coal mining. Thus, appellants' objection is to the *rate* of the Montana tax, and even then, their only complaint is that the *amount* the State receives in taxes far exceeds the *value* of the services provided to the coal mining industry. In objecting to the tax on this ground, appellants may be assuming that the Montana tax is, in fact, intended to reimburse the State for the cost of specific services furnished to the coal mining industry. Alternatively, appellants could be arguing that a State's power to tax an activity connected to interstate commerce cannot exceed the value of the services specifically provided to the activity. Either way, the premise of appellants' argument is invalid. Furthermore, appellants have completely misunderstood the nature of the inquiry under the fourth prong of the *Complete Auto Transit* test.

The Montana Supreme Court held that the coal severance tax is "imposed for the general support of the government" and we have no reason to question this characterization of the Montana tax as a general revenue tax. Consequently, in reviewing appellants' contentions, we put to one side those cases in which the Court reviewed challenges to "user" fees or "taxes" that were designed and defended as a specific charge imposed by the State for the use of state-owned or state-provided transportation or other facilities and services. See, e.g., Evansville-Vanderburgh Airport Authority Dist. v. Delta Airlines, Inc., 405 U.S. 707 (1972); Clark v. Paul Gray, Inc., 306 U.S. 583 (1939); Ingels v. Morf, 300 U.S. 290 (1937).

This Court has indicated that States have considerable latitude in imposing general revenue taxes. The Court has, for example, consistently rejected claims that the Due Process Clause of the Fourteenth Amendment stands as a barrier against taxes that are "unreasonable" or "unduly burdensome." . . . Moreover, there is no requirement under the Due Process Clause that the amount of general revenue taxes collected from a particular activity must be reasonably related to the value of the services provided to the activity. . . .

There is no reason to suppose that this latitude afforded the States under the Due Process Clause is somehow divested by the Commerce Clause merely because the taxed activity has some connection to interstate commerce; particularly when the tax is levied on an activity conducted within the State. . . . To accept appellants' apparent suggestion that the Commerce Clause prohibits the States from requiring an activity connected to interstate commerce to contribute to the general cost of providing governmental services, as distinct from those costs attributable to the taxed activity, would place such commerce in a privileged position. . . .

Furthermore, there can be no question that Montana may constitutionally raise general revenue by imposing a severance tax on coal mined in the State. The entire value of the coal, before transportation, originates in the State, and mining of the coal depletes the resource base and wealth of the State, thereby diminishing a future source of taxes and economic activity. Cf. Maryland v. Louisiana, 451 U.S., at 758–759. In many respects, a severance tax is like a real property tax, which has never been doubted as a legitimate means of raising revenue by the situs State (quite apart from the right of that or any other State to tax income derived from use of the property). . . . When, as here, a general revenue tax does not discriminate against interstate commerce and is apportioned to activities occurring within the State, the State "is free to pursue its own fiscal policies, unembarrassed by the Constitution, if by the practical operation of a tax the state has exerted its power in relation to opportunities which it has given, to protection which it has afforded, to benefits which it has conferred by the fact of being an orderly, civilized society." Wisconsin v. J.C. Penney Co., 311 U.S. 435, 444 (1940). . . .

The relevant inquiry under the fourth prong of the *Complete Auto Transit* test is not, as appellants suggest, the *amount* of the tax or the *value* of the benefits allegedly bestowed as measured by the costs the State incurs on account of the taxpayer's activities. Rather, the test is closely connected to the first prong of the *Complete Auto Transit* test. Under this threshold test, the interstate business must have a substantial nexus with the State before *any* tax may be levied on it. See National Bellas Hess, Inc. v. Illinois Revenue Dept., 386 U.S. 753 (1967). Beyond that threshold requirement, the fourth prong of the *Complete Auto Transit* test imposes the additional limitation that the *measure* of the tax must be reasonably related to the extent of the contact, since it is the activities or presence of the taxpayer in the State that may properly be made to bear a "just share of state tax burden," Western Live Stock Bureau v. Bureau of Revenue, 303 U.S., at 254. . . .

Against this background, we have little difficulty concluding that the Montana tax satisfies the fourth prong of the *Complete Auto Transit* test. The "operating incidence" of the tax is on the mining of coal within Montana.

Because it is measured as a percentage of the value of the coal taken, the Montana tax is in "proper proportion" to appellants' activities within the State and, therefore, to their "consequent enjoyment of the opportunities and protections which the State has afforded" in connection to those activities. Id., at 441. Compare Nippert v. City of Richmond, 327 U.S., at 427. When a tax is assessed in proportion to a taxpayer's activities or presence in a State, the taxpayer is shouldering its fair share of supporting the State's provision of "police and fire protection, the benefit of a trained work force, and 'the advantages of a civilized society.'" Exxon Corp. v. Wisconsin Dept. of Revenue, 447 U.S., at 228, quoting Japan Line, Ltd. v. County of Los Angeles, 441 U.S., at 445.

Appellants argue, however, that the fourth prong of the *Complete Auto Transit* test must be construed as requiring a factual inquiry into the relationship between the revenues generated by a tax and costs incurred on account of the taxed activity, in order to provide a mechanism for judicial disapproval under the Commerce Clause of state taxes that are excessive. This assertion reveals that appellants labor under a misconception about a court's role in cases such as this. The simple fact is that the appropriate level or rate of taxation is essentially a matter for legislative, and not judicial, resolution. . . . In essence, appellants ask this Court to prescribe a test for the validity of state taxes that would require state and federal courts, as a matter of federal constitutional law, to calculate acceptable rates or levels of taxation of activities that are conceded to be legitimate subjects of taxation. This we decline to do.

In the first place, it is doubtful whether any legal test could adequately reflect the numerous and competing economic, geographic, demographic, social, and political considerations that must inform a decision about an acceptable rate or level of state taxation, and yet be reasonably capable of application in a wide variety of individual cases. But even apart from the difficulty of the judicial undertaking, the nature of the factfinding and judgment that would be required of the courts merely reinforces the conclusion that questions about the appropriate level of state taxes must be resolved through the political process. Under our federal system, the determination is to be made by state legislatures in the first instance and, if necessary, by Congress, when particular state taxes are thought to be contrary to federal interests. Cf. Mobil Oil Corp. v. Commissioner of Taxes, 445 U.S., at 448–449; Moorman Manufacturing Co. v. Bair, 437 U.S., at 280.

Furthermore, the reference in the cases to police and fire protection and other advantages of civilized society is not, as appellants suggest, a disingenuous incantation designed to avoid a more searching inquiry into the relationship between the *value* of the benefits conferred on the taxpayer and the *amount* of taxes it pays. Rather, when the measure of a tax is reasonably related to the taxpayer's activities or presence in the State—from which it derives some benefit such as the substantial privilege of mining coal—the taxpayer will realize, in proper proportion to the taxes it pays, "[t]he only benefit to which it is constitutionally entitled . . .[:] that derived from his enjoyment of the privileges of living in an organized society, established and safeguarded by the devotion of taxes to public purposes." Carmichael v. Southern Coal & Coke Co., 301 U.S., at 522. Correspondingly, when the measure of a tax bears no relationship to the taxpayers presence or activities in a State, a court may properly conclude under the fourth prong of the *Complete Auto Transit* test that the State is imposing an undue burden on interstate commerce. See Nippert v. City of Richmond, 327 U.S., at 427; cf. Michigan-Wisconsin Pipe Line Co. v. Calvert, 347 U.S. 157 (1954). We are satisfied that the Montana tax, assessed under a formula that relates the tax liability to the value of appellant coal producers' activities within the State, comports with the requirements of the

Complete Auto Transit test. We therefore turn to appellants' contention that the tax is invalid under the Supremacy Clause.

. . .

[The Court rejected the supremacy clause argument.]

IV

In sum, we conclude that appellants have failed to demonstrate either that the Montana tax suffers from any of the constitutional defects alleged in their complaints, or that a trial is necessary to resolve the issue of the constitutionality of the tax. Consequently, the judgment of the Supreme Court of Montana is affirmed.

So ordered.

Justice White, concurring.

This is a very troublesome case for me, and I join the Court's opinion with considerable doubt and with the realization that Montana's levy on consumers in other States may in the long run prove to be an intolerable and unacceptable burden on commerce. Indeed, there is particular force in the argument that the tax is here and now unconstitutional. Montana collects most of its tax from coal lands owned by the Federal Government and hence by all of the people of this country, while at the same time sharing equally and directly with the Federal Government all of the royalties reserved under the leases the United States has negotiated on its land in the State of Montana. This share is intended to compensate the State for the burdens that coal mining may impose upon it. Also, as Justice Blackmun cogently points out, . . . another 40% of the federal revenue from mineral leases is indirectly returned to the States through a reclamation fund. In addition, there is statutory provision for federal grants to areas affected by increased coal production.

But this very fact gives me pause and counsels withholding our hand, at least for now. Congress has the power to protect interstate commerce from intolerable or even undesirable burdens. It is also very much aware of the Nation's energy needs, of the Montana tax and of the trend in the energy-rich States to aggrandize their position and perhaps lessen the tax burdens on their own citizens by imposing unusually high taxes on mineral extraction. Yet, Congress is so far content to let the matter rest, and we are counseled by the Executive Branch through the Solicitor General not to overturn the Montana tax as inconsistent with either the Commerce Clause or federal statutory policy in the field of energy or otherwise. The constitutional authority and the machinery to thwart efforts such as those of Montana, if thought unacceptable, are available to Congress, and surely Montana and other similarly situated States do not have the political power to impose their will on the rest of the country. As I presently see it, therefore, the better part of both wisdom and valor is to respect the judgment of the other branches of the Government. I join the opinion and the judgment of the Court.

Justice Blackmun, with whom Justice Powell and Justice Stevens join, dissenting.

In Complete Auto Transit, Inc. v. Brady, 430 U.S. 274 (1977), a unanimous Court observed: "A tailored tax, however accomplished, must receive the careful scrutiny of the courts to determine whether it produces a forbidden effect upon interstate commerce." In this case, appellants have alleged that Montana's severance tax on coal is tailored to single out interstate commerce, and that it produces a forbidden effect on that commerce because the tax bears no "relationship to the services provided by the State." Ibid. The Court today concludes that appellants are not entitled to a *trial* on this claim. Because I believe that the "careful scrutiny" due a tailored tax makes a trial here necessary, I respectfully dissent.

. . .

DEPARTMENT OF REVENUE OF WASHINGTON v. ASSOCIATION OF WASHINGTON STEVEDORING COMPANIES

435 U.S. 734, 98 S.Ct. 1388, 55 L.Ed.2d 682 (1978).

Mr. Justice Blackmun delivered the opinion of the Court.

. . .

[The state of Washington applied its general tax "for the act or privilege of engaging in business activities" measured by one percent of gross receipts to the total gross receipts of certain stevedoring companies. The companies derived all of their gross receipts from loading and unloading ships at ports located in Washington. The ships were engaged in interstate and foreign commerce. The Washington Supreme Court entered a declaratory judgment to the effect that the tax was invalid, relying on an earlier case so holding, Puget Sound Stevedoring Co. v. State Tax Commission, 302 U.S. 90 (1937).]

II. THE COMMERCE CLAUSE

A.

In *Puget Sound Stevedoring Co. v. State Tax Comm'n,* supra, the Court invalidated the Washington business and occupation tax on stevedoring only because it applied directly to interstate commerce. . . .

The petitioners (officers of the city of New York) in Joseph v. Carter & Weekes Stevedoring Co., [330 U.S. 422 (1947)] urged the Court to overrule *Puget Sound.* They argued that intervening cases had permitted local taxation of gross proceeds derived from interstate commerce. They concluded, therefore, that the Commerce Clause did not preclude the application to stevedoring of the New York City business tax on the gross receipts of a stevedoring corporation. The Court disagreed on the theory that the intervening cases permitted taxation only of local activity separate and distinct from interstate commerce. This separation theory was necessary, said the Court, because it served to diminish the threat of multiple taxation on commerce; if the tax actually fell on intrastate activity, there was less likelihood that other taxing jurisdictions could duplicate the levy. Stevedoring, however, was not separated from interstate commerce because, as previously enunciated in *Puget Sound,* it was interstate commerce:

"Stevedoring, we conclude, is essentially a part of the commerce itself and therefore a tax upon its gross receipts or upon the privilege of conducting the business of stevedoring for interstate and foreign commerce, measured by those gross receipts, is invalid. We reaffirm the rule of *Puget Sound Stevedoring Company.* 'What makes the tax invalid is the fact that there is interference by a State with the freedom of interstate commerce.' Freeman v. Hewit [329 U.S. 249,] 256." 330 U.S., at 433.

Because the tax in the present case is indistinguishable from the taxes at issue in *Puget Sound* and in *Carter & Weekes,* the *Stevedoring Cases* control today's decision on the Commerce Clause issue unless more recent precedent and a new analysis require rejection of their reasoning.

We conclude that Complete Auto Transit, Inc. v. Brady, [430 U.S. 274 (1977)], where the Court held that a State under appropriate conditions may tax directly the privilege of conducting interstate business, requires such rejection. . . .

The principles of *Complete Auto* also lead us now to question the underpinnings of *Puget Sound* and *Carter & Weekes*. First, *Puget Sound* invalidated the Washington tax on stevedoring activity only because it burdened the privilege of engaging in interstate commerce. Because *Complete Auto* permits a State properly to tax the privilege of engaging in interstate commerce, the basis for the holding in *Puget Sound* is removed completely.

Second, *Carter & Weekes* supported its reaffirmance of *Puget Sound* by arguing that a direct privilege tax would threaten multiple burdens on interstate commerce to a greater extent than would taxes on local activity connected to commerce. But *Complete Auto* recognized that errors of apportionment that may lead to multiple burdens may be corrected when they occur.

The argument of *Carter & Weekes* was an abstraction. No multiple burdens were demonstrated. When a general business tax levies only on the value of services performed within the State, the tax is properly apportioned and multiple burdens logically cannot occur. The reasoning of *Carter & Weekes*, therefore, no longer supports automatic tax immunity for stevedoring from a levy such as the Washington business and occupation tax.

Third, *Carter & Weekes* reaffirmed *Puget Sound* on a basis rejected by *Complete Auto* and previous cases. *Carter & Weekes* considered *any* direct tax on interstate commerce to be unconstitutional because it burdened or interfered with commerce. In support of that conclusion, the Court there cited only Southern Pacific Co. v. Arizona, 325 U.S. 761, 767 (1945), the case where Arizona's limitations on the length of trains were invalidated. In *Southern Pacific,* however, the Court had not struck down the legislation merely because it burdened interstate commerce. Instead, it weighed the burden against the State's interests in limiting the size of trains:

> "The decisive question is whether in the circumstances the total effect of the law as a safety measure in reducing accidents and casualties is so slight or problematical as not to outweigh the national interest in keeping interstate commerce free . . . ."

Only after concluding that railroad safety was not advanced by the regulations, did the Court invalidate them. They contravened the Commerce Clause because the burden on interstate commerce outweighed the State's interests.

Although the balancing of safety interests naturally differs from the balancing of state financial needs, *Complete Auto* recognized that a State has a significant interest in exacting from interstate commerce its fair share of the cost of state government. All tax burdens do not impermissibly impede interstate commerce. The Commerce Clause balance tips against the tax only when it unfairly burdens commerce by exacting more than a just share from the interstate activity. Again, then, the analysis of *Carter & Weekes* must be rejected.

B.

. . .

Consistent with *Complete Auto,* then, we hold that the Washington business and occupation tax does not violate the Commerce Clause by taxing the interstate commerce activity of stevedoring. To the extent that Puget Sound Stevedoring Co. v. State Tax Comm'n and Joseph v. Carter & Weekes Stevedoring Co. stand to the contrary, each is overruled.

C.

With the distinction between direct and indirect taxation of interstate commerce thus discarded, the constitutionality under the Commerce Clause of the application of the Washington business and occupation tax to stevedoring depends upon the practical effect of the exaction. As was recognized in

Western Live Stock v. Bureau of Revenue, supra, interstate commerce must bear its fair share of the state tax burden. The Court repeatedly has sustained taxes that are applied to activity with substantial nexus with the State, that are fairly apportioned, that do not discriminate against interstate commerce, and that are fairly related to the services provided by the State. . . .

Respondents proved no facts in the Superior Court that, under the above test, would justify invalidation of the Washington tax. The record contains nothing that minimizes the obvious nexus between Washington and respondents; indeed, respondents conduct their entire stevedoring operations within the State. Nor have respondents successfully attacked the apportionment of the Washington system. The tax under challenge was levied solely on the value of the loading and unloading that occurred in Washington. Although the rate of taxation varies with the type of business activity, respondents have not demonstrated how the 1% rate, which applies to them and generally to businesses rendering services, discriminates against interstate commerce. Finally, nothing in the record suggests that the tax is not fairly related to services and protection provided by the State. In short, because respondents relied below on the *per se* approach of *Puget Sound* and *Carter & Weekes,* they developed no factual basis on which to declare the Washington tax unconstitutional as applied to their members and their stevedoring activities.

III.   THE IMPORT–EXPORT CLAUSE

Having decided that the Commerce Clause does not *per se* invalidate the application of the Washington tax to stevedoring, we must face the question whether the tax contravenes the Import-Export Clause. Although the parties dispute the meaning of the prohibition of "Imposts or Duties on Imports or Exports," they agree that it differs from the ban the Commerce Clause erects against burdens and taxation on interstate commerce. The Court has noted before that the Import-Export Clause states an absolute ban, whereas the Commerce Clause merely grants power to Congress. Richfield Oil Corp. v. State Board, 329 U.S. 69, 75 (1946). On the other hand, the Commerce Clause touches all state taxation and regulation of interstate and foreign commerce, whereas the Import-Export Clause bans only "Imposts or Duties on Imports or Exports." Michelin Tire Corp. v. Wages, 423 U.S. 276, 279, 290–294 (1976). The resolution of the Commerce Clause issue, therefore, does not dispose of the Import-Export Clause question.

A.

In *Michelin* the Court upheld the application of a general ad valorem property tax to imported tires and tubes. The Court surveyed the history and purposes of the Import-Export Clause to determine, for the first time, which taxes fell within the absolute ban on "Imposts or Duties." Previous cases had assumed that all taxes on imports and exports and on the importing and exporting processes were banned by the Clause. Before *Michelin,* the primary consideration was whether the tax under review reached imports or exports. With respect to imports, the analysis applied the original package doctrine of Brown v. Maryland, 12 Wheat. 419, 6 L.Ed. 678 (1827). So long as the goods retained their status as imports by remaining in their import packages, they enjoyed immunity from state taxation. With respect to exports, the dispositive question was whether the goods had entered the "export stream," the final, continuous journey out of the country. As soon as the journey began, tax immunity attached.

Michelin initiated a different approach to Import-Export Clause cases. It ignored the simple question whether the tires and tubes were imports. Instead, it analyzed the nature of the tax to determine whether it was an "Impost or

Duty." Specifically, the analysis examined whether the exaction offended any of the three policy considerations leading to the presence of the Clause:

> "The Framers of the Constitution thus sought to alleviate three main concerns . . .: the Federal Government must speak with one voice when regulating commercial relations with foreign governments, and tariffs, which might affect foreign relations, could not be implemented by the States consistently with that exclusive power; import revenues were to be the major source of revenue of the Federal Government and should not be diverted to the States; and harmony among the States might be disturbed unless seaboard States, with their crucial ports of entry, were prohibited from levying taxes on citizens of other States by taxing goods merely flowing through their ports to the other States not situated as favorably geographically."

The ad valorem property tax there at issue offended none of these policies. It did not usurp the Federal Government's authority to regulate foreign relations since it did not "fall on imports as such because of their place of origin." As a general tax applicable to all property in the State, it could not have been used to create special protective tariffs and could not have been applied selectively to encourage or discourage importation in a manner inconsistent with federal policy. Further, the tax deprived the Federal Government of no revenues to which it was entitled. The exaction merely paid for services, such as fire and police protection, supplied by the local government. Although the tax would increase the cost of the imports to consumers, its effect on the demand for Michelin tubes and tires was insubstantial. The tax, therefore, would not significantly diminish the number of imports on which the Federal Government could levy import duties and would not deprive it of income indirectly. Finally, the tax would not disturb harmony among the States because the coastal jurisdictions would receive compensation only for services and protection extended to the imports. Although intending to prevent coastal States from abusing their geographical positions, the Framers also did not expect residents of the ports to subsidize commerce headed inland. The Court therefore concluded that the Georgia ad valorem property tax was not an "Impost or Duty," within the meaning of the Import-Export Clause, because it offended none of the policies behind that Clause.

A similar approach demonstrates that the application of the Washington business and occupation tax to stevedoring threatens no Import-Export Clause policy. First, the tax does not restrain the ability of the Federal Government to conduct foreign policy. As a general business tax that applies to virtually all businesses in the State, it has not created any special protective tariff. The assessments in this case are only upon business conducted entirely within Washington. No foreign business or vessel is taxed. Respondents, therefore, have demonstrated no impediment posed by the tax upon the regulation of foreign trade by the United States.

Second, the effect of the Washington tax on federal import revenues is identical to the effect in *Michelin*. The tax merely compensates the State for services and protection extended by Washington to the stevedoring business. Any indirect effect on the demand for imported goods because of the tax on the value of loading and unloading them from their ships is even less substantial than the effect of the direct ad valorem property tax on the imported goods themselves.

Third, the desire to prevent interstate rivalry and friction does not vary significantly from the primary purpose of the Commerce Clause. See P. Hartman, State Taxation of Interstate Commerce 2–3 (1953). The third Import-Export Clause policy, therefore, is vindicated if the tax falls upon a taxpayer with reasonable nexus to the State, is properly apportioned, does not discriminate, and relates reasonably to services provided by the State. As has been explained in Part II–B, supra, the record in this case, as presently developed, reveals the presence of all these factors.

Under the analysis of *Michelin*, then, the application of the Washington business and occupation tax to stevedoring violates no Import-Export Clause policy and therefore should not qualify as an "Impost or Duty" subject to the absolute ban of the Clause.

B.

The Court in *Michelin* qualified its holding with the observation that Georgia had applied the property tax to goods "no longer in transit." Because the goods were no longer in transit, however, the Court did not have to face the question whether a tax relating to goods in transit would be an "Impost or Duty" even if it offended none of the policies behind the Clause. Inasmuch as we now face this inquiry, we note two distinctions between this case and *Michelin*. First, the activity taxed here occurs while imports and exports are in transit. Second, however, the tax does not fall on the goods themselves. The levy reaches only the business of loading and unloading ships or, in other words, the business of transporting cargo within the State of Washington. Despite the existence of the first distinction, the presence of the second leads to the conclusion that the Washington tax is not a prohibited "Impost or Duty" when it violates none of the policies.

In Canton R. Co. v. Rogan, 340 U.S. 511, the Court upheld a gross receipts tax on a steam railroad operating exclusively within the Port of Baltimore. The railroad operated a marine terminal and owned rail lines connecting the docks to the trunk lines of major railroads. It switched and pulled cars, stored imports and exports pending transport, supplied wharfage, weighed imports and exports, and rented a stevedoring crane. Somewhat less than half of the company's 1946 gross receipts were derived from the transport of imports or exports. The company contended that this income was immune, under the Import-Export Clause, from the state tax. The Court rejected that argument primarily on the ground that immunity of services incidental to importing and exporting was not so broad as the immunity of the goods themselves:

> "The difference is that in the present case the tax is not on the *goods*, but on the *handling* of them at the port. An article may be an export and immune from a tax long before or long after it reaches the port. But when the tax is on activities connected with the export or import the range of immunity cannot be so wide.

> ". . . The broader definition which appellant tenders distorts the ordinary meaning of the terms. It would lead back to every forest, mine, and factory in the land and create a zone of tax immunity never before imagined."

In *Canton Railroad* the Court did not have to reach the question about taxation of stevedoring because the company did not load or unload ships. As implied in the opinion, however, the only distinction between stevedoring and the railroad services was that the loading and unloading of ships crossed the water line. This is a distinction without economic significance in the present context. The transportation services in both settings are necessary to the import-export process. Taxation in neither setting relates to the value of the goods, and therefore in neither can it be considered taxation upon the goods themselves. The force of *Canton Railroad* therefore prompts the conclusion that the *Michelin* policy analysis should not be discarded merely because the goods are in transit, at least where the taxation falls upon a service distinct from the goods and their value.[23]

C.

Another factual distinction between this case and *Michelin* is that here the stevedores load and unload imports and exports whereas in *Michelin* the Georgia tax touched only imports. As noted in Part III–A, supra, the analysis in the export cases has differed from that in the import cases. In the former, the question was when did the export enter the export stream; in the latter, the question was when did the goods escape their original package. The questions differed, for example, because an export could enter its export package and not secure tax immunity until later when it began its journey out of the country. Until *Michelin,* an import retained its immunity so long as it remained in its original package.

Despite these formal differences, the *Michelin* approach should apply to taxation involving exports as well as imports. The prohibition on the taxation of exports is contained in the same clause as that regarding imports. The export tax ban vindicates two of the three policies identified in *Michelin.* It precludes state disruption of the United States foreign policy. It does not serve to protect federal revenues, however, because the Constitution forbids federal taxation of exports. U.S. Const., Art. I, § 9, cl. 5; see United States v. Hvoslef, 237 U.S. 1 (1915). But it does avoid friction and trade barriers among the States. As a result, any tax relating to exports can be tested for its conformance with the first and third policies. If the constitutional interests are not disturbed, the tax should not be considered an "Impost or Duty" any more than should a tax related to imports. This approach is consistent with *Canton Railroad,* which permitted taxation of income from services connected to both imports and exports. The respondents' gross receipts from loading exports, therefore, are as subject to the Washington business and occupation tax as are the receipts from unloading imports.

D.

None of respondents' additional arguments convinces us that the *Michelin* approach should not be applied in this case to sustain the tax.

. . .

Third, respondents submit that the Washington tax imposes a transit fee upon inland consumers. Regardless of the validity of such a toll under the Commerce Clause, respondents conclude that it violates the Import-Export Clause. The problem with that analysis is that it does not explain how the policy of preserving harmonious commerce among the States and of preventing interstate tariffs, rivalries, and friction, differs as between the two Clauses. After years of development of Commerce Clause jurisprudence, the Court has concluded that interstate friction will not chafe when commerce pays for the governmental services it enjoys. See Part II, supra. Requiring coastal States to subsidize the commerce of inland consumers may well exacerbate, rather than diminish, rivalries and hostility. Fair taxation will be assured by the prohibition on discrimination and the requirements of apportionment, nexus, and reasonable relationship between tax and benefits. To the extent that the Import-Export

---

[23] We do not reach the question of the applicability of the *Michelin* approach when a State directly taxes imports or exports in transit.

Our Brother Powell, as his concurring opinion indicates, obviously would prefer to reach the issue today, even though the facts of the present case, as he agrees, do not present a case of a tax on goods in transit. As in *Michelin,* decided less than three years ago, we prefer to defer decision until a case with pertinent facts is presented. At that time, with full argument, the issue with all its ramifications may be decided.

Clause was intended to preserve interstate harmony, the four safeguards will vindicate the policy. To the extent that other policies are protected by the Import-Export Clause, the analysis of an Art. I, § 10, challenge must extend beyond that required by a Commerce Clause dispute. But distinctions not based on differences in constitutional policy are not required. Because respondents identify no such variation in policy, their transit fee argument must be rejected.

E.

The Washington Business and Occupation Tax, as applied to stevedoring, reaches services provided wholly within the State of Washington to imports, exports, and other goods. The application violates none of the constitutional policies identified in *Michelin*. It is, therefore, not among the "Imposts or Duties" within the prohibition of the Import-Export Clause.

IV.

The judgment of the Supreme Court of Washington is reversed, and the case is remanded for further proceedings not inconsistent with this opinion.

It is so ordered.

Mr. Justice Brennan took no part in the consideration or decision of this case.

Mr. Justice Powell, concurring in part and concurring in the result.

I join the opinion of the Court with the exception of Part III–B. As that section of the Court's opinion appears to resurrect the discarded "direct-indirect" test, I cannot join it.

. . . . .

NOTE

In Limbach v. Hooven & Allison Co., 104 S.Ct. 1837 (1984) the Court held unanimously that *Michelin* overruled Hooven & Allison Co. v. Evatt, 324 U.S. 652 (1945) and that Ohio could tax bales of fibres imported and held in their original packages for future use.

––––––––

JAPAN LINE, LIMITED v. COUNTY OF LOS ANGELES

441 U.S. 434, 99 S.Ct. 1813, 60 L.Ed.2d 336 (1979).

Mr. Justice Blackmun delivered the opinion of the Court.

This case presents the question whether a State, consistently with the Commerce Clause of the Constitution, may impose a nondiscriminatory ad valorem property tax on foreign-owned instrumentalities (cargo containers) of international commerce.

I.

. . . .

Appellants are six Japanese shipping companies; they are incorporated under the laws of Japan, and they have their principal places of business and commercial domiciles in that country. Appellants operate vessels used exclusively in foreign commerce; these vessels are registered in Japan and have their home ports there. The vessels are specifically designed and constructed to accommodate large cargo shipping containers. The containers, like the ships, are owned by appellants, have their home ports in Japan, and are used exclusively for hire in the transportation of cargo in foreign commerce. Each container is in constant transit save for time spent undergoing repair or awaiting loading and unloading of cargo. All appellants' containers are subject to property tax in Japan and, in fact, are taxed there.

Appellees are political subdivisions of the State of California. Appellants' containers, in the course of their international journeys, pass through appellees' jurisdictions intermittently. Although none of appellants' containers stays permanently in California, some are there at any given time; a container's average stay in the State is less than three weeks. The containers engage in no intrastate or interstate transportation of cargo except as continuations of international voyages. Any movements or periods of nonmovement of containers in appellees' jurisdictions are essential to, and inseparable from, the containers' efficient use as instrumentalities of foreign commerce.

Property present in California on March 1 (the "lien date" under California law) of any year is subject to ad valorem property tax. Cal.Rev. & Tax.Code Ann. §§ 117, 405, 2192 (West 1970 & Supp.1978). A number of appellants' containers were physically present in appellees' jurisdictions on the lien dates in 1970, 1971, and 1972; this number was fairly representative of the containers' "average presence" during each year. Appellees levied property taxes in excess of $550,000 on the assessed value of the containers present on March 1 of the three years in question. During the same period, similar containers owned or controlled by steamship companies domiciled in the United States, that appeared from time to time in Japan during the course of international commerce, were not subject to property taxation in Japan, and therefore were not, in fact, taxed in that country.

Appellants paid the taxes, so levied, under protest and sued for their refund in the Superior Court for the County of Los Angeles. That court awarded judgment in appellants' favor. The court found that appellants' containers were instrumentalities of foreign commerce that had their home ports in Japan where they were taxed. The federal courts, however, in the trial court's view, had "consistently held that vessels which are instrumentalities of foreign commerce and engaged in foreign commerce can be taxed in their home port only." This rule, said the court, was necessary to avoid multiple taxation; whereas apportionment of taxes can be used to prevent duplicative taxation in interstate commerce, apportionment is "not practical" when one of the taxing entities is a foreign sovereign. . . .

.   .   .

The California Supreme Court .   .   . reversed the judgment of the Superior Court, ... 20 Cal.3d 180, 141 Cal.Rptr. 905, 571 P.2d 254 (1977). It concluded that "the threat of double taxation from foreign taxing authorities has no role in commerce clause considerations of multiple burdens, since burdens in international commerce are not attributable to discrimination by the taxing state and are matters for international agreement." Deeming the containers' foreign ownership and use irrelevant for purposes of constitutional analysis, the court rejected appellants' Commerce Clause challenge and sustained the validity of the tax as applied.

Appellants appealed. .   .   .

.   .   .

III.

A.

The "home port doctrine" was first alluded to in Hays v. Pacific Mail S.S. Co., 17 How. 596, 58 U.S. 596 (1854). In *Hays,* California sought to impose property taxes on ocean-going vessels intermittently touching its ports. The vessels' home port was New York City, where they were owned, registered, and

based; they engaged in intercoastal commerce by way of the Isthmus of
Panama, and remained in California briefly to unload cargo and undergo
repairs. This Court held that the ships had established no tax situs in California:

> "We are satisfied that the State of California had no jurisdiction over
> these vessels for the purpose of taxation; they were not, properly, abiding
> within its limits, so as to become incorporated with the other personal
> property of the State; they were there but temporarily, engaged in lawful
> trade and commerce, with their *situs* at the home port, where the vessels
> belonged, and where the owners were liable to be taxed for the capital
> invested, and where the taxes had been paid."

Because the vessels were properly taxable in their home port, this Court
concluded, they could not be taxed in California at all.

The "home port doctrine" enunciated in *Hays* was a corollary of the
medieval maxim *mobilia sequuntur personam* ("movables follow the person," see
Black's Law Dictionary 1154 (rev. 4th ed. 1968)) and resulted in personal
property being taxable in full at the domicile of the owner. This theory of
taxation, of course, has fallen into desuetude, and the "home port doctrine," as
a rule for taxation of moving equipment, has yielded to a rule of fair apportionment among the States. This Court, accordingly, has held that various instrumentalities of commerce may be taxed, on a properly apportioned basis, by the
nondomiciliary States through which they travel. E.g., Pullman's Palace Car
Co. v. Pennsylvania, 141 U.S. 18 (1891); Ott v. Mississippi Valley Barge Line
Co., 336 U.S. 169 (1949); Braniff Airways, Inc. v. Nebraska State Bd. of
Equalization, 347 U.S. 590 (1954). In discarding the "home port" theory for
the theory of apportionment, however, the Court consistently has distinguished
the case of ocean-going vessels. . . . Relying on these cases, appellants
argue that the "home port doctrine," yet vital, continues to prescribe the proper
rule for state taxation of ocean-going ships. Since containers are "functionally a
part of the ship," appellants conclude, the containers, like the ships, may be
taxed only at their home ports in Japan, and thus are immune from tax in
California.

Although appellants' argument, as will be seen below, has an inner logic, we
decline to cast our analysis of the present case in this mold. The "home port
doctrine" can claim no unequivocal constitutional source; in assessing the
legitimacy of California's tax, the *Hays* Court did not rely on the Commerce
Clause, nor could it, in 1854, have relied on the Due Process Clause of the
Fourteenth Amendment. The basis of the "home port doctrine," rather, was
common-law jurisdiction to tax. Given its origins, the doctrine could be said to
be "anachronistic"; given its underpinnings, it may indeed be said to have been
"abandoned." Northwest Airlines, Inc. v. Minnesota, 322 U.S. 292, 320
(1944) (Stone, C.J., dissenting). As a theoretical matter, then, to rehabilitate
the "home port doctrine" as a tool of Commerce Clause analysis would be
somewhat odd. More importantly, to hold in this case that the "home port
doctrine" survives would be to prove too much. If an ocean-going vessel could
indeed be taxed only at its home port, taxation by a nondomiciliary State
logically would be barred, regardless of whether the vessel were domestically-
or foreign-owned, and regardless of whether it were engaged in domestic or
foreign commerce. In *Hays* itself, the vessel was owned in New York and was
engaged in interstate commerce through international waters. There is no need
in this case to decide currently the broad proposition whether mere use of
international routes is enough, under the "home port doctrine," to render an
instrumentality immune from tax in a nondomiciliary State. The question here
is a much more narrow one, that is, whether instrumentalities of commerce that
are owned, based, and registered abroad and that are used exclusively in

international commerce, may be subjected to apportioned ad valorem property taxation by a State.[7]

B.

The Constitution provides that "Congress shall have Power . . . To regulate Commerce with foreign Nations, and among the several States, and with the Indian Tribes." Art. I, § 8, cl. 3. In construing Congress' power to "regulate Commerce . . . among the several States," the Court recently has affirmed that the Constitution confers no immunity from state taxation, and that "interstate commerce must bear its fair share of the state tax burden." Washington Revenue Dept. v. Association of Wash. Stevedoring Cos., 435 U.S. 734, 750 (1978). Instrumentalities of interstate commerce are no exception to this rule, and the Court regularly has sustained property taxes as applied to various forms of transportation equipment. See *Pullman's Palace,* supra (railroad rolling stock); *Ott,* supra (barges on inland waterways); *Braniff,* supra (domestic aircraft). Cf. Central Greyhound Lines v. Mealey, 334 U.S. 653, 663 (1948) (motor vehicles). If the state tax "is applied to an activity with a substantial nexus with the taxing State, is fairly apportioned, does not discriminate against interstate commerce, and is fairly related to the services provided by the State," no impermissible burden on interstate commerce will be found. Complete Auto Transit, Inc. v. Brady, 430 U.S. 274, 279 (1977); *Washington Revenue Dept.,* 435 U.S., at 750.

Appellees contend that cargo shipping containers, like other vehicles of commercial transport, are subject to property taxation, and that the taxes imposed here meet *Complete Auto's* four-fold requirements. The containers, they argue, have a "substantial nexus" with California because some of them are present in that State at all times; jurisdiction to tax is based on "the habitual employment of the property within the State," *Braniff,* 347 U.S., at 601, and appellants' containers habitually are so employed. The tax, moreover, is "fairly apportioned," since it is levied only on the containers' "average presence" in California.[8] The tax "does not discriminate," thirdly, since it falls evenhandedly on all personal property in the State; indeed, as an ad valorem tax of general application, it is of necessity nondiscriminatory. The tax, finally, is "fairly related to the services provided by" California, services that include not only police and fire protection, but the benefits of a trained work force and the advantages of a civilized society.

These observations are not without force. We may assume that, if the containers at issue here were instrumentalities of purely interstate commerce, *Complete Auto* would apply and be satisfied, and our Commerce Clause inquiry would be at an end. Appellants' containers, however, are instrumentalities of foreign commerce, both as a matter of fact and as a matter of law. The premise of appellees' argument is that the Commerce Clause analysis is identical, regardless of whether interstate or foreign commerce is involved. This premise, we have concluded, must be rejected. When construing Congress' power to

---

[7] Accordingly, we do not reach questions as to the taxability of foreign-owned instrumentalities engaged in interstate commerce, or of domestically-owned instrumentalities engaged in foreign commerce. Cf. Sea-Land Service, Inc. v. County of Alameda, 12 Cal.3d 772, 117 Cal.Rptr. 448, 528 P.2d 56 (1974) (domestically-owned containers used in intercoastal and foreign commerce held subject to apportioned property tax); Flying Tiger Line, Inc. v. County of Los Angeles, 51 Cal.2d 314, 333 P. 323 (1958) (domestically-owned aircraft used in foreign commerce held subject to apportioned property tax).

[8] By taxing property present on the "lien date," California roughly apportions its property tax for mobile goods like containers. For example, if each of appellants' containers is in California for three weeks a year, the number present on any arbitrarily selected date would be roughly $\frac{3}{52}$ of the total entering the State that year. Taxing $\frac{3}{52}$ of the containers at full value, however, is the same as taxing all the containers at $\frac{3}{52}$ value. Thus, California effectively apportions its tax to reflect the containers' "average presence," i.e., the time each container spends in the State per year.

"regulate Commerce with foreign Nations," a more extensive constitutional inquiry is required.

When a State seeks to tax the instrumentalities of foreign commerce, two additional considerations, beyond those articulated in *Complete Auto,* come into play. The first is the enhanced risk of multiple taxation. It is a commonplace of constitutional jurisprudence that multiple taxation may well be offensive to the Commerce Clause. In order to prevent multiple taxation of interstate commerce, this Court has required that taxes be apportioned among taxing jurisdictions, so that no instrumentality of commerce is subjected to more than one tax on its full value. The corollary of the apportionment principle, of course, is that no jurisdiction may tax the instrumentality in full. "The rule which permits taxation by two or more states on an apportionment basis precludes taxation of all of the property by the state of the domicile. . . . Otherwise there would be multiple taxation of interstate operations." Standard Oil Co. v. Peck, 342 U.S., at 384–385; *Braniff,* 347 U.S., at 601.

The basis for this Court's approval of apportioned property taxation, in other words, has been its ability to enforce full apportionment by all potential taxing bodies.

Yet neither this Court nor this Nation can ensure full apportionment when one of the taxing entities is a foreign sovereign. If an instrumentality of commerce is domiciled abroad, the country of domicile may have the right, consistently with the custom of nations, to impose a tax on its full value.[11] If a State should seek to tax the same instrumentality on an apportioned basis, multiple taxation inevitably results. Hence, whereas the fact of apportionment in interstate commerce means that "multiple burdens logically cannot occur," *Washington Revenue Dept.,* 435 U.S., at 746–747 the same conclusion, as to foreign commerce, logically cannot be drawn. Due to the absence of an authoritative tribunal capable of ensuring that the aggregation of taxes is computed on no more than one full value, a state tax, even though "fairly apportioned" to reflect an instrumentality's presence within the State, may subject foreign commerce " 'to the risk of a double tax burden to which [domestic] commerce is not exposed, and which the commerce clause forbids.' "

Second, a state tax on the instrumentalities of foreign commerce may impair federal uniformity in an area where federal uniformity is essential. Foreign commerce is pre-eminently a matter of national concern. . . . Although the Constitution, Art. I, § 8, cl. 3, grants Congress power to regulate commerce "with foreign Nations" and "among the several States" in parallel phrases, there is evidence that the Founders intended the scope of the foreign commerce power to be the greater. . . . Finally, in discussing the Import-Export Clause, this Court, in Michelin Tire Corp. v. Wages, 423 U.S. 276, 285 (1976), spoke of the Framers' overriding concern that "the Federal Government must speak with one voice when regulating commercial relations with foreign governments." The need for federal uniformity is no less paramount in ascertaining the negative implications of Congress' power to "regulate Commerce with foreign Nations" under the Commerce Clause.

. . . .

For these reasons, we believe that an inquiry more elaborate than that mandated by *Complete Auto* is necessary when a State seeks to tax the instrumen-

---

[11] Ocean-going vessels, for example, are generally taxed only in their nation of registry; this fact in part explains the phenomenon of "flags of convenience" (a term deemed derogatory in some quarters), whereby vessels are registered under the flags of countries that permit the operation of ships "at a nominal level of taxation." See B. Boczek, Flags of Convenience, 5, 56–57 (1962). Aircraft engaged in international traffic, apparently, are likewise "subject to taxation on an unapportioned basis by their country of origin." Note, 11 Stan.L.Rev., at 519, and n. 11. See, e.g., *SAS,* 56 Cal.3d, at 17, and n. 3, 14 Cal.Rptr., at 28, 363 P.2d, at 28, and n. 3.

talities of foreign, rather than of interstate, commerce. In addition to answering the nexus, apportionment, and nondiscrimination questions posed in *Complete Auto,* a court must also inquire, first, whether the tax, notwithstanding apportionment, creates a substantial risk of international multiple taxation, and, second, whether the tax prevents the Federal Government from "speaking with one voice when regulating commercial relations with foreign governments." If a state tax contravenes either of these precepts, it is unconstitutional under the Commerce Clause.

C.

Analysis of California's tax under these principles dictates that the tax, as applied to appellants' containers, is impermissible. Assuming, *arguendo,* that the tax passes muster under *Complete Auto,* it cannot withstand scrutiny under either of the additional tests that a tax on foreign commerce must satisfy.

First, California's tax results in multiple taxation of the instrumentalities of foreign commerce. . . .

Second, California's tax prevents this Nation from "speaking with one voice" in regulating foreign trade. The desirability of uniform treatment of containers used exclusively in foreign commerce is evidenced by the Customs Convention on Containers, which the United States and Japan have signed. Under this Convention, containers temporarily imported are admitted free of "all duties and taxes whatsoever chargeable by reason of importation." 20 U.S.T., at 304. The Convention reflects a national policy to remove impediments to the use of containers as "instruments of international traffic." 19 U.S.C. § 1322(a). California's tax, however, will frustrate attainment of federal uniformity. It is stipulated that American-owned containers are not taxed in Japan. California's tax thus creates an asymmetry in international maritime taxation operating to Japan's disadvantage. The risk of retaliation by Japan, under these circumstances, is acute, and such retaliation of necessity would be felt by the Nation as a whole. If other States follow California's example (Oregon already has done so), foreign-owned containers will be subjected to various degrees of multiple taxation, depending on which American ports they enter. This result, obviously, would make "speaking with one voice" impossible. California, by its unilateral act, cannot be permitted to place these impediments before this Nation's conduct of its foreign relations and its foreign trade.

Because California's ad valorem tax, as applied to appellants' containers, results in multiple taxation of the instrumentalities of foreign commerce, and because it prevents the Federal Government from "speaking with one voice" in international trade, the tax is inconsistent with Congress' power to "regulate Commerce with foreign Nations." We hold the tax, as applied, unconstitutional under the Commerce Clause.

. . .

The judgment of the Supreme Court of California is reversed.

It is so ordered.

Substantially for the reasons set forth by Justice Manuel in his opinion for the unanimous Supreme Court of California, Mr. Justice Rehnquist is of the opinion that the judgment of that court should be affirmed.

SECTION 3. JURISDICTION TO TAX AND APPORTIONMENT

A. INCOME TAXES

THE FEDERAL STATUTORY LIMITATION

Prior to 1959 it was possible for an interstate enterprise to arrange its affairs to minimize the number of states to which it was obligated to report income and pay taxes. In particular under the doctrine of Spector Motor Serv. v. O'Connor, 340 U.S. 602 (1951), a company could not be subjected to an income tax by a state in which it did no more than solicit sales by solicitors or by mail—activities which were held to be exclusively interstate commerce. However, in Northwestern States Portland Cement Co. v. Minnesota, 358 U.S. 450 (1959) by holding that states validly could impose taxes on the receipt of income even though exclusively interstate commerce was done, the Court opened up the possibility that every state in which sales were made could impose an income tax. Justice Frankfurter, dissenting, indicated the problems he saw in such a holding:

"It will not, I believe, be gainsaid that there are thousands of relatively small or moderate size corporations doing exclusively interstate business spread over several States. To subject these corporations to a separate income tax in each of these States means that they will have to keep books, make returns, store records, and engage legal counsel, all to meet the divers and variegated tax laws of forty-nine States, with their different times for filing returns, different tax structures, different modes for determining 'net income' and different, often conflicting, formulas of apportionment. This will involve large increases in bookkeeping, accounting, and legal paraphernalia to meet these new demands. The cost of such far-flung scheme for complying with the taxing requirements of the different States may well exceed the burden of the taxes themselves, especially in the case of small companies doing a small volume of business in several States." 358 U.S. at 474.

Congress reacted to the *Northwestern* decision by enacting 15 U.S.C. § 381— one of the few occasions on which Congress has exercised authority to restrict state taxation. The effect of the statute is to preclude a state or local government from imposing a net income tax on a nonresident or nondomiciliary corporation if the only business done in the state is the "solicitation of orders by such person, or his representative, in such State for sales of tangible personal property, which orders are sent outside the State for approval or rejection, and, if approved, are filled by shipment or delivery from a point outside the State." Any added activity—such as the maintenance of an office or the delivery of goods by the seller within the state—serves to give jurisdiction to tax. For a discussion of problems of interpretation under the act, see Hartman, *"Solicitation" and "Delivery" Under Public Law 86–272: An Uncharted Course,* 29 Vand.L. Rev. 353 (1976).

THE MULTISTATE COMPACT

Over the past 15 years attempts have been made to secure action by Congress which not only would limit the states having jurisdiction to impose income taxes on multistate business but would also establish a uniform formula for allocating income. For an account of the early developments see Johnson & Visher, *State and Local Government Taxation of Multistate Corporations: A Survey of Legislative Developments,* 3 Urban Lawyer 1 (1971). To date, however, the states have been able to defeat such legislation, preferring to work out solutions through the medium of a multistate compact.

On January 20, 1967, the Council of State Governments proposed to the States a Multistate Tax Compact to go into effect on being enacted into law in seven states. As of July, 1984, twenty-five states were members of the Compact. The Compact deals primarily with the allocation of income for net income tax purposes. Its major provisions are:

(a) Taxpayers subject to income taxes may elect each year whether to apportion and allocate income in accordance with the laws of any particular state or subdivision or in accordance with the uniform formula provided in the Compact.

(b) Detailed allocation and apportionment provisions are set forth, with a three-factor formula for apportioning income based on property, payroll and sales. Sales for this purpose are allocated to the state in which the property is delivered to the purchaser unless the taxpayer is not subject to tax in that state in which case they are allocated to the state from which they are shipped.

(c) Full credit for sales and use taxes paid in one state is extended to use tax liability in another state. Also sellers are permitted good faith reliance on resale or other exemption certificates provided by purchasers.

(d) A taxpayer whose income in a state is derived solely from sales not in excess of $100,000 may elect to report any tax due on the basis of a percentage of such volume with rates to be set so as to reasonably approximate the tax otherwise due.

(e) A Multistate Tax Commission is established with certain duties of study and recommendation along with the maintenance of an arbitration panel for settlement of disputes concerning apportionment.

(f) Member states which specifically enact the interstate audit provisions of the Compact may individually or jointly request that the Commission perform an audit of any records or papers on their behalf. If it elects to perform the audit, the Commission may utilize the compulsory process of the courts of any state adopting the Compact's audit provisions to coerce the attendance of any person or the delivery for inspection of any relevant documents. The Commission may itself offer to audit the fiscal affairs of any taxpayer if it believes such an examination would be of interest to a number of states.

In United States Steel Corp. v. Multistate Tax Comm'n, 434 U.S. 452 (1978) the Supreme Court held the Compact to be valid even though it had not received the consent of Congress.

The Multistate Tax Compact is set out in 29 Vand.L.Rev. 470 (1976). For general discussions see Cappetta, *Joint Audit Program of the Multistate Tax Comm.,* 33 N.Y.U.Inst.Fed.Tax. 961 (1975); Corrigan, *Interstate Corporate Income Taxation—Recent Revolutions and a Modern Response,* 29 Vand.L.Rev. 423 (1976).

MOORMAN MFG. CO. v. BAIR

437 U.S. 267, 98 S.Ct. 2340, 57 L.Ed.2d 197 (1978).

Mr. Justice Stevens delivered the opinion of the Court.

The question in this case is whether the single-factor sales formula employed by Iowa to apportion the income of an interstate business for income tax purposes is prohibited by the Federal Constitution.

I.

Appellant, Moorman Manufacturing Company, is an Illinois corporation engaged in the manufacture and sale of animal feeds. Although the products it sells to Iowa customers are manufactured in Illinois, appellant has over 500 salesmen in Iowa and it owns six warehouses in the State from which deliveries are made to Iowa customers. Iowa sales account for about 20% of appellant's total sales.

Corporations, both foreign and domestic, doing business in Iowa are subject to the State's income tax. The taxable income for federal income tax purposes, with certain adjustments, is treated as the corporation's "net income" under the Iowa statute. If a corporation's business is not conducted entirely within Iowa, the statute imposes a tax only on the portion of its income "reasonably attributable" to the business within the State.

There are essentially two steps in computing the share of a corporation's income "reasonably attributable" to Iowa. First, certain income, "the geographical source of which is easily identifiable," is attributed entirely to a particular State. Second, if the remaining income is derived from the manufacture or sale of tangible personal property, "the part thereof attributable to business within the state shall be in that proportion which the gross sales made within the state bear to the total gross sales." This is the single-factor formula that appellant challenges in this case.

If the taxpayer believes that application of this formula subjects it to taxation on a greater portion of its net income than is "reasonably attributable" to business within the State, it may file a statement of objections and submit an alternative method of apportionment. If the evidence submitted by the taxpayer persuades the Director of Revenue that the statute is "inapplicable and inequitable" as applied to it, he may recalculate the corporation's taxable income.

During the fiscal years 1949 through 1960, the State Tax Commission allowed appellant to compute its Iowa income on the basis of a formula consisting of three, equally weighted factors—property, payroll and sales—rather than the formula prescribed by statute.[3] For the fiscal years 1961 through 1964, appellant complied with a directive of the State Tax Commission to compute its income in accordance with the statutory formula. Since 1965, however, appellant has resorted to the three-factor formula without the consent of the Commission.

In 1974, the Iowa Director of Revenue revised appellant's tax assessment for the fiscal years 1968 through 1972. This assessment was based on the statutory formula, which produced a higher percentage of taxable income than appellant, using the three-factor formula, had reported on its return in each of the disputed years.[4] The higher percentages, of course produced a correspondingly greater tax obligation for those years.

[3] The operation of the two formulas may be briefly described. The single-factor sales formula yields a percentage representing a ratio of gross sales in Iowa to total gross sales. The three-factor formula yields a percentage representing an average of three ratios: property within the State to total property, payroll within the State to total payroll, and sales within the State to total sales.

These percentages are multiplied by the adjusted total net income to arrive at Iowa taxable net income. This net income figure is then multiplied by the tax rate to compute the actual tax obligation of the taxpayer.

[4] For those years the two formulas resulted in the following percentages:

Fiscal Year Ended	Sales Factor Percentage	Three-Factor Percentage
3/31/68	21.8792%	14.1088%
3/31/69	21.2134%	14.3856%
3/31/70	19.9492%	14.0200%
3/31/71	18.9544%	13.2186%
3/31/72	18.6713%	12.2343%

For a description of how these percentages are computed, see n. 3, supra.

After the Tax Commission had rejected Moorman's appeal from the revised assessment, appellant challenged the constitutionality of the single-factor formula in the Iowa District Court for Polk County. That court held the formula invalid under the Due Process Clause and the Commerce Clause. The Supreme Court of Iowa reversed, holding that an apportionment formula that is necessarily only a rough approximation of the income properly attributable to the taxing State is not subject to constitutional attack unless the taxpayer proves that the formula has produced an income attribution "out of all proportion to the business transacted" within the State. The court concluded that appellant had not made such a showing.

We . . . affirm.

II.

Appellant contends that Iowa's single-factor formula results in extraterritorial taxation in violation of the Due Process Clause. This argument rests on two premises: first, that appellant's Illinois operations were responsible for some of the profits generated by sales in Iowa; and, second, that a formula that reaches any income not in fact earned within the borders of the taxing State violates due process. The first premise is speculative and the second is foreclosed by prior decisions of this Court.

.   .   .

The Due Process Clause places two restrictions on a State's power to tax income generated by the activities of an interstate business. First, no tax may be imposed, unless there is some minimal connection between those activities and the taxing State. National Bellas Hess, Inc. v. Department of Revenue, 386 U.S. 753, 756. This requirement was plainly satisfied here. Second, the income attributed to the State for tax purposes must be rationally related to "values connected with the taxing state." Norfolk & Western R. Co. v. Missouri, 390 U.S. 317, 325.

Since 1934 Iowa has used the formula method of computing taxable income. This method, unlike separate accounting, does not purport to identify the precise geographical source of a corporation's profits; rather, it is employed as a rough approximation of a corporation's income that is reasonably related to the activities conducted within the taxing State. The single-factor formula used by Iowa, therefore, generally will not produce a figure that represents the actual profits earned within the State. But the same is true of the Illinois three-factor formula. Both will occasionally over-reflect or under-reflect income attributable to the taxing State. Yet despite this imprecision, the Court has refused to impose strict constitutional restraints on a State's selection of a particular formula.

Thus, we have repeatedly held that a single-factor formula is presumptively valid. In Underwood Typewriter Co. v. Chamberlain, 254 U.S. 113, for example, the taxpayer challenged Connecticut's use of such a formula to apportion its net income. Underwood's manufacturing operations were conducted entirely within Connecticut. Its main office, however was in New York City and it had branch offices in many States where its typewriters were sold and repaired. Applying a single-factor property formula, Connecticut taxed 47% of the company's net income. Claiming that 97% of its profits were generated by transactions in tangible personal property outside Connecticut, Underwood contended that the formula taxed "income arising from business conducted beyond the boundaries of the State" in violation of the Due Process Clause.

Rejecting this claim the Court noted that Connecticut "adopted a method of apportionment which, for all that appears in this record, reached, and was meant to reach, only the profits earned within the State," and held that the taxpayer had failed to carry its burden of proving that "the method of apportionment adopted by the state was inherently arbitrary, or that its application to this corporation produced an unreasonable result."

In individual cases, it is true, the Court has found that the *application* of a single-factor formula to a particular taxpayer violated due process. See Hans Rees' Sons v. North Carolina, 283 U.S. 123; Norfolk & Western R. Co. v. State Tax Commission, 390 U.S. 317. In *Hans Rees'*, for example, the Court concluded that proof that the formula produced a tax on 83% of the taxpayer's income when only 17% of that income actually had its source in the State would suffice to invalidate the assessment under the Due Process Clause. But in neither *Hans Rees'* nor *Norfolk & Western* did the Court depart from the basic principles that the States have wide latitude in the selection of apportionment formulas and that a formula-produced assessment will only be disturbed when the taxpayer has proved by "clear and cogent evidence" that the income attributed to the State is in fact "out of all appropriate proportion to the business transacted . . . in that State," or has "led to a grossly distorted result."
. . .

The Iowa statute afforded appellant an opportunity to demonstrate that the single-factor formula produced an arbitrary result in its case. But this record contains no such showing and therefore the Director's assessment is not subject to challenge under the Due Process Clause.

III.

Appellant also contends that during the relevant years Iowa and Illinois imposed a tax on a portion of the income derived from the Iowa sales that was also taxed by the other State in violation of the Commerce Clause. Since most States use the three-factor formula that Illinois adopted in 1970, appellant argues that Iowa's longstanding single-factor formula must be held responsible for the alleged duplication and declared unconstitutional. We cannot agree.

In the first place, this record does not establish the essential factual predicate for a claim of duplicative taxation. Appellant's net income during the years in question was approximately $9 million. Since appellant did not prove the portion derived from sales to Iowa customers, rather than sales to customers in other States, we do not know whether Illinois and Iowa together imposed a tax on more than 100% of the relevant net income. The income figure that appellant contends was subject to duplicative taxation was computed by comparing gross sales in Iowa to total gross sales. As already noted, however, this figure does not represent *actual* profits earned from Iowa sales. Obviously, all sales are not equally profitable. Sales in Iowa, although only 20% of gross sales, may have yielded a much higher percentage of appellant's profits. Thus, profits from Iowa sales may well have exceeded the $2.5 million figure that appellant contends was taxed by the two States. If so, there was no duplicative taxation of the net income generated by Iowa sales. In any event, on this record its existence is speculative.

Even assuming some overlap, we could not accept appellant's argument that Iowa, rather than Illinois, was necessarily at fault in a constitutional sense. It is of course true that if Iowa had used Illinois' three-factor formula, a risk of duplication in the figures computed by the two States might have been avoided. But the same would be true had Illinois used the Iowa formula. Since the record does not reveal the sources of appellant's profits, its Commerce Clause claim cannot rest on the premise that profits earned in Illinois were included in its Iowa taxable income and therefore the Iowa formula was at fault for whatever overlap may have existed. Rather, the claim must be that even if the presumptively valid Iowa formula yielded no profits other than those properly attributable to appellant's activities within Iowa, the importance of avoiding any risk of duplication in the taxable income of an interstate concern justifies invalidation of the Iowa statute.

Appellant contends that to the extent this overlap is permitted the corporation that does business in more than one State shoulders a tax burden not shared by those operating entirely within a State. To alleviate the burden, appellant invites us to hold that the Commerce Clause itself, without implementing legislation by Congress, requires Iowa to compute corporate net income under the Illinois equally weighted, three-factor formula. For the reasons that follow, we hold that the Constitution does not require such a result.

The only conceivable constitutional basis for invalidating the Iowa statute would be that the Commerce Clause prohibits any overlap in the computation of taxable income by the States. If the Constitution were read to mandate such precision in interstate taxation, the consequences would extend far beyond this particular case. For some risk of duplicative taxation exists whenever the States in which a corporation does business do not follow identical rules for the division of income. Accepting appellant's view of the Constitution, therefore, would require extensive judicial lawmaking. Its logic is not limited to a prohibition on use of a single-factor apportionment formula. The asserted constitutional flaw in that formula is that it is different from that presently employed by a majority of States and that difference creates a risk of duplicative taxation. But a host of other division of income problems create precisely the same risk and would similarly rise to constitutional proportions.

Thus, it would be necessary for this Court to prescribe a uniform definition of each category in the three-factor formula. For if the States in which a corporation does business have different rules regarding where a "sale" takes place, and each includes the same sale in its three-factor computation of the corporation's income, there will be duplicative taxation despite the apparent identity of the formulas employed. A similar risk of multiple taxation is created by the diversity among the States in the attribution of "non-business" income, generally defined as that portion of a taxpayer's income that does not arise from activities in the regular course of its business. Some States do not distinguish between business and nonbusiness income for apportionment purposes. Other States, however, have adopted special rules that attribute nonbusiness income to specific locations. Moreover, even among the latter, there is diversity in the definition of nonbusiness income and in the designation of the locations to which it is deemed attributable. The potential for attribution of the same income to more than one State is plain.

The prevention of duplicative taxation, therefore, would require national uniform rules for the division of income. Although the adoption of a uniform code would undeniably advance the policies that underlie the Commerce Clause, it would require a policy decision based on political and economic considerations that vary from State to State. The Constitution, however, is neutral with respect to the content of any uniform rule. If division of income problems were to be constitutionalized, therefore, they would have to be resolved in the manner suggested by appellant for resolution of formula diversity—the prevalent practice would be endorsed as the constitutional rule. This rule would at best be an amalgam of independent State decisions, based on considerations unique to each State. Of most importance, it could not reflect the national interest, because the interests of those States whose policies are subordinated in the quest for uniformity would be excluded from the calculation.

While the freedom of the States to formulate independent policy in this area may have to yield to an overriding national interest in uniformity, the content of any uniform rules to which they must subscribe should be determined only after due consideration is given to the interests of all affected States. It is clear that the legislative power granted to Congress by the Commerce Clause of the Constitution would amply justify the enactment of legislation requiring all States to adhere to uniform rules for the division of income. It is to that body, and not this Court, that the Constitution has committed such policy decisions.

. . .

Accordingly, until Congress prescribes a different rule, Iowa is not constitutionally prohibited from requiring taxpayers to prove that application of the single-factor formula has produced arbitrary results in a particular case.

The judgment of the Iowa Supreme Court is affirmed.

Mr. Justice Brennan, dissenting.

. . .

Mr. Justice Blackmun, dissenting.

The unspoken, but obvious, premise of the majority opinion is the fear that a Commerce Clause invalidation of Iowa's single-factor sales formula will lead the Court into problems and difficulties in other cases yet to come. I reject that premise.

I agree generally with the content of Mr. Justice Powell's opinion in dissent. I join that opinion because I, too, feel that the Court has a duty to resolve, not to avoid, these problems of "delicate adjustment," Boston Stock Exchange v. State Tax Comm'n, 429 U.S. 318, 329 (1977), and because the opinion well demonstrates that Iowa's now anachronistic single-factor sales formula runs headlong into overriding Commerce Clause considerations and demands.

Today's decision is bound to be regressive. Single-factor formulas are relics of the early days of state income taxation. The three-factor formulas were inevitable improvements and, while not perfect, reflect more accurately the realities of the business and tax world. With their almost universal adoption by the States, the Iowa system's adverse and parochial impact on commerce comes vividly into focus. But with its single-factor formula now upheld by the Court, there is little reason why other States, perceiving or imagining a similar advantage to local interests, may not go back to the old ways. The end result, in any event, is to exacerbate what the Commerce Clause, absent governing congressional action, was devised to avoid.

Mr. Justice Powell, with whom Mr. Justice Blackmun joins, dissenting.

. . .

CONTAINER CORPORATION OF AMERICA v. FRANCHISE TAX BOARD

463 U.S. 159, 103 S.Ct. 2933, 77 L.Ed.2d 545 (1983).

Justice Brennan delivered the opinion of the Court.

This is another appeal claiming that the application of a State taxing scheme violates the Due Process and Commerce Clauses of the Federal Constitution. California imposes a corporate franchise tax geared to income. In common with a large number of other States, it employs the "unitary business" principle and formula apportionment in applying that tax to corporations doing business both inside and outside the State. Appellant is a Delaware corporation headquartered in Illinois and doing business in California and elsewhere. It also has a number of overseas subsidiaries incorporated in the countries in which they operate. Appellee is the California authority charged with administering the state's franchise tax. This appeal presents three questions for review: (1) Was it improper for appellee and the state courts to find that appellant and its overseas subsidiaries constituted a "unitary business" for purposes of the state tax? (2) Even if the unitary business finding was proper, do certain salient differences among national economies render the standard three-factor apportionment formula used by California so inaccurate as applied to the multinational enterprise consisting of appellant and its subsidiaries as to violate the constitutional requirement of "fair apportionment"? (3) In any event, did California have an obligation under the Foreign Commerce Clause, U.S. Const., Art. I, § 8, cl. 3, to employ the "arm's-length" analysis used by the federal government and most foreign nations in evaluating the tax consequences of inter-corporate relationships?

I

A

Various aspects of state tax systems based on the "unitary business" principle and formula apportionment have provoked repeated constitutional litigation in this Court. See, e.g., ASARCO, Inc. v. Idaho State Tax Comm'n, 458 U.S. 307 (1982); F.W. Woolworth Co. v. Taxation and Revenue Dept., 458 U.S. 354 (1982); Exxon Corp. v. Wisconsin Dept. of Revenue, 447 U.S. 207 (1980); Mobil Oil Corp. v. Commissioner of Taxes, 445 U.S. 425 (1980); Moorman Mfg. Co. v. Bair, 437 U.S. 267 (1978); General Motors Corp. v. Washington, 377 U.S. 436 (1964); Butler Bros. v. McColgan, 315 U.S. 501 (1942); Bass, Ratcliff & Gretton, Ltd. v. State Tax Comm'n, 266 U.S. 271 (1924); Underwood Typewriter Co. v. Chamberlain, 254 U.S. 113 (1920).

Under both the Due Process and the Commerce Clauses of the Constitution, a state may not, when imposing an income-based tax, "tax value earned outside its borders." ASARCO, supra, at ——. In the case of a more-or-less integrated business enterprise operating in more than one State, however, arriving at precise territorial allocations of "value" is often an elusive goal, both in theory and in practice. . . . For this reason and others, we have long held that the Constitution imposes no single formula on the States, Wisconsin v. J.C. Penney Co., 311 U.S. 435, 445 (1940), and that the taxpayer has the "distinct burden of showing by 'clear and cogent evidence' that [the state tax] results in extraterritorial values being taxed . . . ." Exxon Corp., supra, at 221, . . .

One way of deriving locally taxable income is on the basis of formal geographical or transactional accounting. The problem with this method is that formal accounting is subject to manipulation and imprecision, and often ignores or captures inadequately the many subtle and largely unquantifiable transfers of value that take place among the components of a single enterprise. See generally Mobil Oil Corp., 445 U.S., at 438–439, and sources cited. The unitary business/formula apportionment method is a very different approach to the problem of taxing businesses operating in more than one jurisdiction. It rejects geographical or transactional accounting, and instead calculates the local tax base by first defining the scope of the "unitary business" of which the taxed enterprise's activities in the taxing jurisdiction form one part, and then apportioning the total income of that "unitary business" between the taxing jurisdiction and the rest of the world on the basis of a formula taking into account objective measures of the corporation's activities within and without the jurisdiction. This Court long ago upheld the constitutionality of the unitary business/formula apportionment method, although subject to certain constraints. See, e.g., Hans Rees' Sons, Inc. v. North Carolina ex rel. Maxwell, 283 U.S. 123 (1931); Bass, Ratcliff & Gretton, Ltd. v. State Tax Comm'n, 266 U.S. 271 (1924); Underwood Typewriter Co. v. Chamberlain, 254 U.S. 113 (1920). The method has now gained wide acceptance, and is in one of its forms the basis for the Uniform Division of Income for Tax Purposes Act (Uniform Act), which has at last count been substantially adopted by 23 States, including California.

B

Two aspects of the unitary business/formula apportionment method have traditionally attracted judicial attention. These are, as one might easily guess, the notions of "unitary business" and "formula apportionment," respectively.

(1)

The Due Process and Commerce Clauses of the Constitution do not allow a State to tax income arising out of interstate activities—even on a proportional basis—unless there is a " 'minimal connection' or 'nexus' between the interstate activities and the taxing State, and 'a rational relationship between the income attributed to the State and the intrastate values of the enterprise.' " Exxon Corporation v. Wisconsin Dept. of Revenue, 447 U.S., at 219–220, quoting Mobil Oil Corp. v. Commissioner of Taxes, 445 U.S., at 436, 437. At the very least, this set of principles imposes the obvious and largely self-executing limitation that a State not tax a purported "unitary business" unless at least some part of it is conducted in the State. See *Exxon Corp.*, 447 U.S., at 220; Wisconsin v. J.C. Penney Co., 311 U.S. 435, 444 (1940). It also requires that there be some bond of ownership or control uniting the purported "unitary business." See *ASARCO*, 458 U.S., at ——.

In addition, the principles we have quoted require that the out-of-State activities of the purported "unitary business" be related in some concrete way to the in-State activities. The functional meaning of this requirement is that there be some sharing or exchange of value not capable of precise identification or measurement—beyond the mere flow of funds arising out of a passive investment or a distinct business operation—which renders formula apportionment a reasonable method of taxation. . . .

The California statute at issue in this case, and the Uniform Act from which most of its relevant provisions are derived, tracks in large part the principles we have just discussed. In particular, the statute distinguishes between the "business income" of a multi-jurisdictional enterprise, which is apportioned by formula, Cal.Rev. & Tax.Code Ann. §§ 25128–25136, and its "non-business" income, which is not.[1] Although the statute does not explicitly require that income from distinct business enterprises be apportioned separately, this requirement antedated adoption of the Uniform Act, and has not been abandoned.

(2)

Having determined that a certain set of activities constitute a "unitary business," a State must then apply a formula apportioning the income of that business within and without the State. Such an apportionment formula must, under both the Due Process and Commerce Clauses, be fair. See *Exxon Corp.*, 447 U.S., at 219, 227–228; *Moorman Mfg. Co.*, 437 U.S., at 272–273; *Hans Rees' Sons, Inc.*, 283 U.S. at 134. The first, and again obvious, component of fairness in an apportionment formula is what might be called internal consistency—that is the formula must be such that, if applied by every jurisdiction, it would result in no more than all of the unitary business's income being taxed. The second and more difficult requirement is what might be called external consistency—the factor or factors used in the apportionment formula must

---

[1] Certain forms of non-business income, such as dividends, are allocated on the basis of the taxpayer's commercial domicile. Other forms of non-business income, such as capital gains on sales of real property, are allocated on the basis of situs. See Cal.Rev. & Tax.Code Ann. §§ 25123–25127 (West 1979).

actually reflect a reasonable sense of how income is generated. The Constitution does not "invalidat[e] an apportionment formula whenever it *may* result in taxation of some income that did not have its source in the taxing State . . . ." *Moorman Mfg. Co.,* supra, at 272 (emphasis added). See *Underwood Typewriter Co.,* 254 U.S., at 120–121. Nevertheless, we will strike down the application of an apportionment formula if the taxpayer can prove "by 'clear and cogent evidence' that the income attributed to the State is in fact 'out of all appropriate proportions to the business transacted in that State,' [*Hans Rees' Sons, Inc.,*] 283 U.S., at 135 or has 'led to a grossly distorted result,' [Norfolk & Western R. Co. v. State Tax Comm'n, 390 U.S. 317, 326 (1968)]." *Moorman Mfg. Co.,* supra, at 274.

California and the other States that have adopted the Uniform Act use a formula—commonly called the "three-factor" formula—which is based, in equal parts, on the proportion of a unitary business's total payroll, property, and sales which are located in the taxing State. See Cal.Code Ann. §§ 25128–25136 (West 1979). We approved the three-factor formula in Butler Bros. v. McCoglan, supra. Indeed, not only has the three-factor formula met our approval, but it has become, for reasons we discuss in more detail infra, something of a benchmark against which other apportionment formulas are judged. . . .

Besides being fair, an apportionment formula must, under the Commerce Clause, also not result in discrimination against interstate or foreign commerce. See *Mobil Oil Corp.,* 445 U.S., at 444; cf. Japan Line, Ltd. v. County of Los Angeles, 441 U.S. 434, 444–448 (1979) (property tax). Aside from forbidding the obvious types of discrimination against interstate or foreign commerce, this principle might have been construed to require that a state apportionment formula not differ so substantially from methods of allocation used by other jurisdictions in which the taxpayer is subject to taxation so as to produce double taxation of the same income, and a resultant tax burden higher than the taxpayer would incur if its business were limited to any one jurisdiction. At least in the interstate commerce context, however, the antidiscrimination principle has not in practice required much in addition to the requirement of fair apportionment. In Moorman Mfg. Co. v. Bair, supra, in particular, we explained that eliminating all overlapping taxation would require this Court to establish not only a single constitutionally mandated method of taxation, but also rules regarding the application of that method in particular cases. 437 U.S., at 278–280. Because that task was thought to be essentially legislative, we declined to undertake it, and held that a fairly apportioned tax would not be found invalid simply because it differed from the prevailing approach adopted by the States. As we discuss infra, however, a more searching inquiry is necessary when we are confronted with the possibility of international double taxation.

II

A

Appellant is in the business of manufacturing custom-ordered paperboard packaging. Its operation is vertically integrated, and includes the production of paperboard from raw timber and wastepaper as well as its composition into the finished products ordered by customers. The operation is also largely domestic. During the years at issue in this case—1963, 1964, and 1965—appellant controlled 20 foreign subsidiaries located in four Latin American and four European countries. Its percentage ownership of the subsidiaries (either directly or through other subsidiaries) ranged between 66.7% and 100%. In those instances (about half) in which appellant did not own a 100% interest in the subsidiary, the remainder was owned by local nationals. One of the subsidiaries was a holding company that had no payroll, sales, or property, but did have book income. Another was inactive. The rest were all engaged—in their respective local markets—in essentially the same business as appellant.

Most of appellant's subsidiaries were, like appellant itself, fully integrated, although a few bought paperboard and other intermediate products elsewhere. Sales of materials from appellant to its subsidiaries accounted for only about 1% of the subsidiaries' total purchases. The subsidiaries were also relatively autonomous with respect to matters of personnel and day-to-day management. For example, transfers of personnel from appellant to its subsidiaries were rare, and occurred only when a subsidiary could not fill a position locally. There was no formal United States training program for the subsidiaries' employees, although groups of foreign employees occasionally visited the United States for 2–6 week periods to familiarize themselves with appellant's methods of operation. Appellant charged one senior vice-president and four other officers with the task of overseeing the operations of the subsidiaries. These officers established general standards of professionalism, profitability, and ethical practices and dealt with major problems and long-term decisions; day-to-day management of the subsidiaries, however, was left in the hands of local executives who were always citizens of the host country. Although local decisions regarding capital expenditures were subject to review by appellant, problems were generally worked out by consensus rather than outright domination. Appellant also had a number of its directors and officers on the boards of directors of the subsidiaries, but they did not generally play an active role in management decisions.

Nevertheless, in certain respects, the relationship between appellant and its subsidiaries was decidedly close. For example, approximately half of the subsidiaries' long-term debt was either held directly, or guaranteed, by appellant. Appellant also provided advice and consultation regarding manufacturing techniques, engineering, design, architecture, insurance, and cost accounting to a number of its subsidiaries, either by entering into technical service agreements with them or by informal arrangement. Finally, appellant occasionally assisted its subsidiaries in their procurement of equipment, either by selling them used equipment of its own or by employing its own purchasing department to act as an agent for the subsidiaries.

B

During the tax years at issue in this case, appellant filed California franchise tax returns. In 1969, after conducting an audit of appellant's returns for the years in question, appellee issued notices of additional assessments for each of those years. The respective approaches and results reflected in appellant's initial returns and in appellee's notices of additional assessments capture the legal differences at issue in this case.

In calculating the total unapportioned taxable income of its unitary business, appellant included its own corporate net earnings as derived from its federal tax form (subject to certain adjustments not relevant here), but did not include any income of its subsidiaries. It also deducted—as it was authorized to do under state law—all dividend income, non-business interest income, and gains on sales of assets not related to the unitary business. In calculating the share of its net income which was apportionable to California under the three-factor formula, appellant omitted all of its subsidiaries' payroll, property, and sales. The results of these calculations are summarized in the margin.[11]

The gravamen of the notices issued by appellee in 1969 was that appellant should have treated its overseas subsidiaries as part of its unitary business rather than as passive investments. Including the overseas subsidiaries in appellant's

11. See note 11 on page 383.

unitary business had two primary effects: it increased the income subject to apportionment by an amount equal to the total income of those subsidiaries (less inter-subsidiary dividends), and it decreased the percentage of that income which was apportionable to California. The net effect, however, was to increase appellant's tax liability in each of the three years.[12]

Appellant paid the additional amounts under protest, and then sued in California Superior Court for a refund, raising the issues now before this Court. The case was tried on stipulated facts, and the Superior Court upheld appellee's assessments. On appeal, the California Court of Appeal affirmed, 117 Cal.App. 3d 988, 173 Cal.Rptr. 121 (1981), and the California Supreme Court refused to exercise discretionary review. We noted probable jurisdiction. 456 U.S. 960 (1982).

III

A

We address the unitary business issue first. As previously noted, the taxpayer always has the "distinct burden of showing by 'clear and cogent evidence' that [the state tax] results in extraterritorial values being taxed." One necessary corollary of that principle is that this Court will, if reasonably possible, defer to the judgment of state courts in deciding whether a particular set of activities constitutes a "unitary business." . . .

.   .   .

C

The state Court of Appeal relied on a large number of factors in reaching its judgment that appellant and its foreign subsidiaries constituted a unitary business. These included appellant's assistance to its subsidiaries in obtaining used and new equipment and in filling personnel needs that could not be met locally, the substantial role played by appellant in loaning funds to the subsidiaries and guaranteeing loans provided by others, the "considerable interplay between appellant and its foreign subsidiaries in the area of corporate expansion," 117 Cal.App.3d, at 997, 173 Cal.Rptr., at 127, the "substantial" technical assistance provided by appellant to the subsidiaries, id., at 998–999, and the supervisory role played by appellant's officers in providing general guidance to the subsidiaries. In each of these respects, this case differs from *ASARCO* and *F.W. Woolworth,* and clearly comes closer than those cases did to presenting a

11

	1963	1964	1965
Total income of unitary business	$26,870,427.00	$28,774,320.48	$32,280,842.90
Percentage attributed to Calif.	11.041%	10.6422%	9.8336%
Amount attributed to Calif.	2,966,763.85	3,062,220.73	3,174,368.97
Tax (5.5%)	163,172.01	168,422.14	174,590.29

[12] According to the notices, appellant's actual tax obligations were as follows:

	1963	1964	1965
Total income of unitary business	$37,348,183.00	$44,245,879.00	$46,884,966.00
Percentage attributed to Calif.	8.6886%	8.3135%	7.6528%
Amount attributed to Calif.	3,245,034.23	3,673,381.15	3,588,012.68
Tax (5.5%)	178,476.88	202,310.95	197,340.70

"functionally integrated enterprise," *Mobil,* 445 U.S., at 440, which the State is entitled to tax as a single entity. We need not decide whether any one of these factors would be sufficient as a constitutional matter to prove the existence of a unitary business. Taken in combination, at least, they clearly demonstrate that the state court reached a conclusion "within the realm of permissible judgment."

IV

We turn now to the question of fair apportionment. Once again, appellant has the burden of proof; it must demonstrate that "there is no rational relationship between the income attributed to the State and the intrastate values of the enterprise," *Exxon Corp.,* 447 U.S., at 220, quoting *Mobil,* 445 U.S., at 436, by proving that the income apportioned to California under the statute is "out of all appropriate proportions to the business transacted in that State," *Hans Rees' Sons, Inc.,* 283 U.S., at 135.

Appellant challenges the application of California's three-factor formula to its business on two related grounds, both arising as a practical (although not a theoretical) matter out of the international character of the enterprise. First, appellant argues that its foreign subsidiaries are significantly more profitable than it is, and that the three-factor formula, by ignoring that fact and relying instead on indirect measures of income such as payroll, property, and sales, systematically distorts the true allocation of income between appellant and the subsidiaries. The problem with this argument is obvious: the profit figures relied on by appellant are based on precisely the sort of formal geographical accounting whose basic theoretical weaknesses justify resort to formula apportionment in the first place. . . .

Appellant's second argument is related, and can be answered in the same way. Appellant contends that:

> "The costs of production in foreign countries are generally significantly
> lower than in the United States, primarily as a result of the lower wage rates
> of workers in countries other than the United States. Because wages are
> one of the three factors used in formulary apportionment, the use of the
> formula unfairly inflates the amount of income apportioned to United States
> operations, where wages are higher."

Appellant supports this argument with various statistics that appear to demonstrate, not only that wage rates are generally lower in the foreign countries in which its subsidiaries operate, but also that those lower wages are not offset by lower levels of productivity. Indeed, it is able to show that at least one foreign plant had labor costs per thousand square feet of corrugated container that were approximately 40% of the same costs in appellant's California plants.

The problem with all this evidence, however, is that it does not by itself come close to impeaching the basic rationale behind the three-factor formula. Appellant and its foreign subsidiaries have been determined to be a unitary business. It therefore may well be that in addition to the foreign payroll going into the production of any given corrugated container by a foreign subsidiary, there is also California payroll, as well as other California factors, contributing— albeit more indirectly—to the same production. The mere fact that this possibility is not reflected in appellant's accounting does not disturb the underlying premises of the formula apportionment method.

Both geographical accounting and formula apportionment are imperfect proxies for an ideal which is not only difficult to achieve in practice, but also difficult to describe in theory. . . .

The three-factor formula used by California has gained wide approval precisely because payroll, property, and sales appear in combination to reflect a very large share of the activities by which value is generated. . . .

Of course, even the three-factor formula is necessarily imperfect. But we have seen no evidence demonstrating that the margin of error (systematic or not) inherent in the three-factor formula is greater than the margin of error (systematic or not) inherent in the sort of separate accounting urged upon us by appellant. Indeed, it would be difficult to come to such a conclusion on the basis of the figures in this case: for all of appellant's statistics showing allegedly enormous distortions caused by the three-factor formula, the tables we set out at nn. 11–12, supra, reveal that the percentage increase in taxable income attributable to California between the methodology employed by appellant and the methodology employed by appellee comes to approximately 14%, a far cry from the more than 250% difference which led us to strike down the state tax in *Hans Rees' Sons, Inc.,* and a figure certainly within the substantial margin of error inherent in any method of attributing income among the components of a unitary business.

V

For the reasons we have just outlined, we conclude that California's application of the unitary business principle to appellant and its foreign subsidiaries was proper, and that its use of the standard three-factor formula to apportion the income of that unitary business was fair. This proper and fair method of taxation happens, however, to be quite different from the method employed both by the Federal Government in taxing appellant's business, and by each of the relevant foreign jurisdictions in taxing the business of appellant's subsidiaries. Each of these other taxing jurisdictions has adopted a qualified separate accounting approach—often referred to as the "arm's-length" approach—to the taxation of related corporations. Under the arm's-length approach, every corporation, even if closely tied to other corporations, is treated for most—but decidedly not all—purposes as if it were an independent entity dealing at arm's length with its affiliated corporations, and subject to taxation only by the jurisdictions in which it operates and only for the income it realizes on its own books.

If the unitary business consisting of appellant and its subsidiaries were entirely domestic, the fact that different jurisdictions applied different methods of taxation to it would probably make little constitutional difference, for the reasons we discuss supra. Given that it is international, however, we must subject this case to the additional scrutiny required by the Foreign Commerce Clause. See *Mobil Oil Corp.,* 445 U.S., at 446; *Japan Line, Ltd.,* 441 U.S., 446; Bowman v. Chicago & N.W.R. Co., 125 U.S. 465, 482 (1888). The case most relevant to our inquiry is *Japan Line.*

. . . .

This case is similar to *Japan Line* in a number of important respects. First, the tax imposed here, like the tax imposed in *Japan Line,* has resulted in actual double taxation, in the sense that some of the income taxed without apportionment by foreign nations as attributable to appellant's foreign subsidiaries was also taxed by California as attributable to the State's share of the total income of the unitary business of which those subsidiaries are a part. Second, that double taxation stems from a serious divergence in the taxing schemes adopted by California and the foreign taxing authorities. Third, the taxing method adopted by those foreign taxing authorities is consistent with accepted international practice. Finally, our own Federal Government, to the degree it has spoken, seems to prefer the taxing method adopted by the international community to the taxing method adopted by California.

Nevertheless, there are also a number of ways in which this case is clearly distinguishable from *Japan Line*. First, it involves a tax on income rather than a tax on property. We distinguished property from income taxation in *Mobil Oil Corp.*, 445 U.S., at 444–446, and *Exxon Corp.*, 447 U.S., at 228–229, suggesting that "[t]he reasons for allocation to a single situs that often apply in the case of property taxation carry little force" in the case of income taxation. 445 U.S., at 445. Second, the double taxation in this case, although real, is not the "inevitabl[e]" result of the California taxing scheme. Cf. *Japan Line*, 441 U.S., at 447. In *Japan Line*, we relied strongly on the fact that one taxing jurisdiction claimed the right to tax a given value in full, and another taxing jurisdiction claimed the right to tax the same entity in part—a combination resulting necessarily in double taxation. 441 U.S., at 447, 452, 455. Here, by contrast, we are faced with two distinct methods of allocating the income of a multi-national enterprise. The "arm's-length" approach divides the pie on the basis of formal accounting principles. The formula apportionment method divides the same pie on the basis of a mathematical generalization. Whether the combination of the two methods results in the same income being taxed twice or in some portion of income not being taxed at all is dependent solely on the facts of the individual case. The third difference between this case and *Japan Line* is that the tax here falls, not on the foreign owners of an instrumentality of foreign commerce, but on a corporation domiciled and headquartered in the United States. We specifically left open in *Japan Line* the application of that case to "domestically owned instrumentalities engaged in foreign commerce," 441 U.S., at 444, n. 7, and—to the extent that corporations can be analogized to cargo containers in the first place—this case falls clearly within that reservation.

In light of these considerations, our task in this case must be to determine whether the distinctions between the present tax and the tax at issue in *Japan Line* add up to a constitutionally significant difference. For the reasons we are about to explain, we conclude that they do.

. . . .

VI

The judgment of the California Court of Appeal is
Affirmed.

Justice Stevens took no part in the consideration or decision of this case.

———

Justice Powell, with whom The Chief Justice and Justice O'Connor join, dissenting.

The Court's opinion addresses the several questions presented in this case with commendable thoroughness. In my view, however, the California tax clearly violates the Foreign Commerce Clause—just as did the tax in Japan Line, Ltd. v. County of Los Angeles, 441 U.S. 434 (1979). I therefore do not consider whether appellant and its foreign subsidiaries constitute a "unitary business" or whether the State's apportionment formula is fair.

With respect to the Foreign Commerce Clause issue, the Court candidly concedes: (i) "double taxation is a constitutionally disfavored state of affairs, particularly in the international context"; (ii) "like the tax imposed in *Japan Line*, [California's tax] has resulted in actual double taxation,"; and therefore (iii) this tax "deserves to receive close scrutiny". The Court also concedes that "[t]his case is similar to *Japan Line* in a number of important respects,", and that the Federal Government "seems to prefer the [arm's-length] taxing method adopted by the international community". The Court identifies several distinctions between this case and *Japan Line*, however, and sustains the validity of the

California tax despite the inevitable double taxation and the incompatability with the method of taxation accepted by the international community.

In reaching its result, the Court fails to apply "close scrutiny" in a manner that meets the requirements of that exacting standard of review. Although the facts of *Japan Line* differ in some respects, they are identical on the critical questions of double taxation and federal uniformity. The principles enunciated in that case should be controlling here: a state tax is unconstitutional if it either "creates a substantial risk of international multiple taxation" or "prevents the Federal Government from 'speaking with one voice when regulating commercial relations with foreign governments.'" 441 U.S., at 451.

. . .

NOTE

Container Corp. has sparked a major controversy. Foreign governments—such as England, West Germany, and Japan—are vigorously protesting the unitary tax. Legislation is pending in Congress and President Reagan has established a working group to look into the problem. For a brief discussion of developments, see Kiesel, *Tax Wars—Unitary Tax Bite Felt Abroad,* 70 A.B.A.J. 38 (1984). See generally, Hartman, *Constitutional Limitations on State Taxation of Corporate Income From Multinational Corporations,* 37 Vand.L.Rev. 218 (1984).

B. SALES AND USE TAXES

NATIONAL GEOGRAPHIC SOCIETY v. CALIFORNIA BOARD OF EQUALIZATION

430 U.S. 551, 97 S.Ct. 1386, 51 L.Ed.2d 631 (1977).

Mr. Justice Brennan delivered the opinion of the Court.

Appellant National Geographic Society, a nonprofit scientific and educational corporation of the District of Columbia, maintains two offices in California that solicit advertising copy for the Society's monthly magazine, the National Geographic Magazine. However, the offices perform no activities related to the Society's operation of a mail-order business for the sale from the District of Columbia of maps, atlases, globes, and books. Orders for these items are mailed from California directly to appellant's Washington, D.C., headquarters on coupons or forms enclosed with announcements mailed to Society members and magazine subscribers or on order forms contained in the magazine. Deliveries are made by mail from the Society's Washington, D.C., or Maryland offices. Payment is either by cash mailed with the order or after a mailed billing following receipt of the merchandise. Such mail-order sales to California residents during the period involved in this suit aggregated $83,596.48.

California Rev. & Tax.Code § 6203 (West Supp.1976) requires every "retailer engaged in business in this state and making sales of tangible personal property for storage, use, or other consumption in this state" to collect from the purchaser a use tax in lieu of the sales tax imposed upon local retailers. The California Supreme Court held that appellant is subject to the statute as a "'retailer engaged in business in this state'", because its maintenance of the two offices brings appellant within the definition under § 6203(a) that includes "'[a]ny retailer maintaining . . . an office . . . .'" 16 Cal.3d 637, 642, 128 Cal.Rptr. 682, 685, 547 P.2d 458, 460–461 (1976). Section 6204 makes the retailer liable to the State for any taxes required to be collected regardless of whether he collects the tax. See Bank of America v. State Bd. of Equalization, 209 Cal.App.2d 780, 793, 26 Cal.Rptr. 348, 355 (1962).

The question presented by this case is whether the Society's activities at the offices in California provided sufficient nexus between the out-of-state seller appellant and the State—as required by the Due Process Clause of the Fourteenth Amendment and the Commerce Clause—to support the imposition upon the Society of a use-tax-collection liability pursuant to §§ 6203 and 6204, measured by the $83,596.48 of mail-order sales of merchandise from the District of Columbia and Maryland. The California Supreme Court held that the imposition of use-tax-collection liability on the Society violated neither Clause, 16 Cal.3d 637, 128 Cal.Rptr. 682, 547 P.2d 458 (1976). We noted probable jurisdiction. 429 U.S. 883 (1976). We affirm.

I.

All States that impose sales taxes also impose a corollary use tax on tangible property bought out of State to protect sales tax revenues and put local retailers subject to the sales tax on a competitive parity with out-of-state retailers exempt from the sales tax. H.R.Rep. No. 565, 89th Cong., 1st Sess., 614 (1965). The constitutionality of such state schemes is settled. Henneford v. Silas Mason Co., 300 U.S. 577, 581 (1937); Monamotor Oil Co. v. Johnson, 292 U.S. 86 (1934).

But the limitation of use taxes to consumption within the State so as to avoid problems of due process that might arise from the extension of the sales tax to interstate commerce, see, e.g., Nelson v. Sears, Roebuck & Co., 312 U.S. 359, 363 (1941); Monamotor Oil Co. v. Johnson, supra, at 95, does not avoid all constitutional difficulties. States necessarily impose the burden of collecting the tax on the out-of-state seller; the impracticability of its collection from the multitude of individual purchasers is obvious. Miller Bros. Co. v. Maryland, 347 U.S. 340, 343 (1954). However, not every out-of-state seller may constitutionally be made liable for payment of the use tax on merchandise sold to purchasers in the State. The California Supreme Court concluded, based on its survey of the relevant decisions of this Court, that the "slightest presence" of the seller in California established sufficient nexus between the State and the seller constitutionally to support the imposition of the duty to collect and pay the tax. . . .

Our affirmance of the California Supreme Court is not to be understood as implying agreement with that court's "slightest presence" standard of constitutional nexus. Appellant's maintenance of two offices in the State and solicitation by employees assigned to those offices of advertising copy in the range of $1 million annually, establish a much more substantial presence than the expression "slightest presence" connotes. Our affirmance thus rests upon our conclusion that appellant's maintenance of the two offices in California and activities there adequately establish a relationship or "nexus" between the Society and the State that renders constitutional the obligations imposed upon appellant pursuant to §§ 6203 and 6204. This conclusion is supported by several of our decisions.

The requisite nexus was held to be shown when the out-of-state sales were arranged by the seller's local agents working in the taxing State, Felt & Tarrant Co. v. Gallagher, 306 U.S. 62 (1939); General Trading Co. v. Tax Comm'n, 322 U.S. 335 (1944), and in cases of maintenance in the State of local retail store outlets by out-of-state mail-order sellers. Nelson v. Sears, Roebuck & Co., supra; Nelson v. Montgomery Ward, 312 U.S. 373 (1941). In Scripto, Inc. v. Carson, 362 U.S. 207 (1960), the necessary basis was found in the case of a Georgia-based company that had "10 wholesalers, jobbers, or 'salesmen' conducting continuous local solicitation in Florida and forwarding the resulting orders from that State to Atlanta for shipment of the ordered goods," id., at

211, although maintaining no office or place of business in Florida, and having no property or regular full-time employees there.

Standard Pressed Steel Co. v. Washington Rev. Dept., 419 U.S. 560 (1975), is also instructive. That case involved a direct tax upon the gross receipts of a foreign corporation resulting from sales to a State of Washington customer, and not imposition of use-tax-collection duties. Although "a vice in a tax on gross receipts of a corporation doing an interstate business is the risk of multiple taxation . . .," a concern not present when only imposition of use-tax-collection duty is involved, *Standard Pressed Steel* held that maintenance in the taxing State of a single employee, an engineer whose office was in his Washington home and whose primary responsibility was to consult with the Washington-based customer regarding its anticipated needs for the out-of-state supplier's product, established a sufficient relation to activities within the State producing the gross receipts as to support imposition of the tax. It is particularly significant for our purposes in this case that the Court characterized as "frivolous" the argument that the seller's in-state activities were so thin and inconsequential that the tax had no reasonable relation to the protection and benefits conferred by the taxing State, for the employee "made possible the realization and continuance of valuable contractual relations between [the seller and its Washington customer]." 419 U.S., at 562. Other fairly apportioned, nondiscriminatory direct taxes have also been sustained when the taxes have been shown to be fairly related to the services provided the out-of-state seller by the taxing State. Complete Auto Transit, Inc. v. Brady, 430 U.S. 274 (1977).

The case for the validity of the imposition upon the out-of-state seller enjoying such services of a duty to collect a use tax is even stronger. The out-of-state seller runs no risk of double taxation. The consumer's identification as a resident of the taxing State is self-evident. The out-of-state seller becomes liable for the tax only by failing or refusing to collect the tax from that resident consumer. Thus, the sole burden imposed upon the out-of-state seller by statutes like §§ 6203 and 6204 is the administrative one of collecting it.

Two decisions that have held fact patterns deficient to establish the necessary nexus to impose the duty to collect the use tax highlight the significance of the inquiry whether the out-of-state seller enjoys services of the taxing State. Miller Bros. Co. v. Maryland, 347 U.S. 340 (1954), struck down a Maryland assessment against a Delaware store near the border between the two States. The store had made over-the-counter sales to Maryland residents and occasionally shipped or delivered goods by truck into that State. The store advertised in Delaware by newspaper and radio, and some of these advertisements reached Maryland residents. These advertisements were sometimes supplemented with "flyers" mailed to customers, some of whom lived in Maryland. The Court concluded that Maryland could not satisfy the due process requirement. In addition to the almost total lack of contacts between Maryland and the Delaware store—Marylanders went to Delaware to make purchases, the seller did not go to Maryland to make sales—the seller obviously could not know whether the goods sold over the counter in Delaware were transported to Maryland prior to their use.

National Bellas Hess, Inc. v. Illinois Rev. Dept., 386 U.S. 753 (1967), presented the question in the case of an out-of-state seller whose only connection with customers in the taxing State was by common carrier or mail. Illinois subjected appellant Bellas Hess, a national mail-order house centered in Missouri, to use tax liability based upon mail-order sales to customers in that State. Bellas Hess owned no tangible property in Illinois, had no sales outlets, representatives, telephone listings, or solicitors in that State, and did not advertise there by radio, television, billboards, or newspapers. It communicated with potential customers by mailing catalogues throughout the United States, including Illinois, twice a year and occasionally supplemented this effort by mailing out "flyers." All orders for merchandise were mailed to Bellas Hess' Missouri plant, and the goods were sent to customers by mail or common carrier. *Bellas Hess* held that, constitutionally, the basis for the requisite nexus was not to be found solely in Bellas Hess' mail-order activities in the State. The Court's opinion carefully underscored, however, the "sharp distinction . . . between mail order sellers with retail outlets, solicitors, or property within [the taxing] State, and those [like Bellas Hess] who do no more than communicate with customers in the State by mail or common carrier as part of a general interstate business." Id., at 758. Appellant Society clearly falls into the former category.

II.

The Society argues, however, that its contacts with customers in California were related solely to its mail-order sales by means of common carrier or the mail, that the two offices played no part in that activity, and that therefore this case is controlled by *Bellas Hess.* The Society argues in other words that there must exist a nexus or relationship not only between the seller and the taxing State, but also between the activity of the seller sought to be taxed and the seller's activity within the State. We disagree. However fatal to a direct tax a "showing that particular transactions are dissociated from the local business . . . .," such dissociation does not bar the imposition of the use-tax-collection duty. . . . [T]he relevant constitutional test to establish the requisite nexus for requiring an out-of-state seller to collect and pay the use tax is not whether the duty to collect the use tax relates to the seller's activities carried on within the State, but simply whether the facts demonstrate "some definite link, some minimum connection, between [the State and] the *person* . . . it seeks to tax." Miller Bros. v. Maryland, 347 U.S., at 344–345. (Emphasis added.) Here the Society's two offices, without regard to the nature of their activities, had the advantage of the same municipal services—fire and police protection, and the like—as they would have had if their activities, as in *Sears* and *Montgomery Ward,* included assistance to the mail-order operations that generated the use taxes.

. . . We conclude that the Society's continuous presence in California in offices that solicit advertising for its magazine provides a sufficient nexus to justify that State's imposition upon the Society of the duty to act as collector of the use tax.

Affirmed.

The Chief Justice and Mr. Justice Rehnquist took no part in the consideration or decision of this case.

Mr. Justice Blackmun, concurring in the result.

Chapter 7

INTERGOVERNMENTAL RELATIONSHIPS WITHIN THE FEDERAL SYSTEM

SECTION 1. INTERGOVERNMENTAL TAX IMMUNITY

A. FEDERAL IMMUNITY

McCULLOCH v. MARYLAND

17 U.S. (4 Wheat.) 316, 4 L.Ed. 579 (1819).

[The report in this case appears supra at p. 185.]

UNITED STATES v. NEW MEXICO

455 U.S. 720, 102 S.Ct. 1373, 71 L.Ed.2d 580 (1982).

Justice Blackmun delivered the opinion of the Court.

We are presented here with a recurring problem: to what extent may a State impose taxes on contractors that conduct business with the Federal Government?

I

A

This case concerns the contractual relationships between three private entities and the United States. The three agreements involved are typical in most respects of management contracts devised by the Atomic Energy Commission (AEC), now the Department of Energy (DOE). Like many of the Government's contractual undertakings, DOE management contracts generally provide the private contractor with its costs plus a fixed fee. . . . While subject to the general direction of the Government, the contractors are vested with substantial autonomy in their operations and procurement practices.

The first of the contractors, Sandia Corporation, . . . a subsidiary of Western Electric Company, . . . manages the government-owned Sandia Laboratories in Albuquerque, N.M., . . . It receives no fee under its contract, and owns no property except for $1000 in United States bonds that constitute its paid-in capital. But Sandia and Western Electric are guaranteed royalty-free, irrevocable licenses for any communications-related discoveries or inventions developed by most Sandia employees during the course of the contract, and the company receives complete reimbursements for salary outlays and other expenditures.

The Zia Company, another of the contractors, . . . has performed a variety of management, maintenance, and related functions at the Government's Los Alamos Scientific Laboratory, for which it receives its costs as well as a fixed annual fee. . . .

The third contractor is Los Alamos Constructors, Inc. (LACI), since 1953 a subsidiary of Zia. LACI's operations are limited to construction and repair work at the Los Alamos facility. The company owns no tangible personal property and makes no purchases; it procures needed property and equipment through its parent, Zia. And like Zia, LACI receives its costs plus a fixed annual fee from the Government.

The management contracts between the Government and the three contractors have a number of significant features in common. As in most DOE atomic facility management agreements, the contracts provide that title to all tangible personal property purchased by the contractors passes directly from the vendor to the Government. Similarly, the Government bears the risk of loss for property procured by the contractors. Zia and LACI must submit an annual voucher of expenditures for Government approval. And the agreements give the Government control over the disposition of all property purchased under the contracts, as well as over each contractor's property management procedures. Disputes under the contracts are to be resolved by a DOE contracting official.

On the other hand, the contractors place orders with third-party suppliers in their own names, and identify themselves as the buyers. Indeed, the Government acknowledged during discovery that Sandia, Zia, and LACI "may be . . . 'independent contractor[s],' rather than . . . 'servant[s]' for . . . given 'function[s] under' the contract[s] . . ." and the Government does not claim that the contractors are federal instrumentalities. . . . Finally, and most importantly, the contracts use a so-called "advanced funding" procedure to meet contractor costs. . . . The procedure allows contractors to pay creditors and employees with drafts drawn on a special bank account in which United States Treasury funds are deposited.

. . . [O]nly federal funds are expended when the contractor makes purchases. If the Government fails to provide funding, the contractor is excused from performance of the contract, and the Government is liable for all properly incurred claims.

Prior to July 1, 1977, the Government's contracts with Sandia, Zia, and LACI did not refer to the contractors as federal "agents." On that date—some two years *after* the commencement of this litigation—the agreements were modified to state that each contractor "acts as an agent [of the Government] . . . for certain purposes," including the disbursement of Government funds and the "purchase, lease, or other acquisition" of property. This was designed to recognize what was described as the "long-standing agency status and authority" of the contractors. . . . At the same time, however, the United States denied any intent "formally and directly [to] designat[e] the contractors as agents," and each modification stated that it did not "create rights or obligations not otherwise provided for in the contract."

B

New Mexico imposes a gross receipts tax and a compensating use tax on those doing business within the State. With limited exceptions, "[f]or the privilege of engaging in business, an excise tax equal to four per cent [4%] of gross receipts is imposed on any person engaging in business in New Mexico." N.M.Stat.Ann. § 72–16A–4 (Supp.1975). In effect, the gross receipts tax operates as a tax on the sale of goods and services. The State also levies a compensating use tax, equivalent in amount to the gross receipts tax, "[f]or the privilege of using property in New Mexico." § 72–16A–7. This is imposed on property acquired out-of-state in a "transaction that would have been subject to the gross receipts tax had it occurred within [New Mexico]." § 72–16A–7(A)(2). Thus the compensating use tax functions as an enforcement mechanism for the gross receipts tax by imposing a levy on the use of all property that has not already been taxed; the State collects the same percentage regardless of where the property is purchased. Neither tax, however, is imposed on the "receipts of the United States or any agency or instrumentality thereof," or on the "use of property by the United States or any agency or instrumentality thereof." §§ 72–16A–12.1, 72–16A–12.2.

Without objection, Zia and LACI each year paid the New Mexico gross receipts tax on the fixed fees they received from the Federal Government. But the Government argued that the contractors' other expenditures and operations are constitutionally immune from state taxation. . . . [T]he United States [sought] a declaratory judgment that advanced funds are not taxable gross receipts to the contractors; that the receipts of vendors selling tangible property to the United States through the contractors cannot be taxed by the State; and that the use of Government-owned property by the contractors is not subject to the State's compensating use tax.

The District Court granted the United States summary judgment. . . .

The United States Court of Appeals for the Tenth Circuit reversed. 624 F.2d 111 (1980). . . .

The United States sought certiorari, and we granted the writ to consider the seemingly intractable problems posed by State taxation of federal contractors. 450 U.S. 909 (1981).

II

A

With the famous declaration that "the power to tax involves the power to destroy," McCulloch v. Maryland, 4 Wheat. 316, 431 (1819), Chief Justice Marshall announced for the Court the doctrine of federal immunity from state taxation. In so doing he introduced the Court to what has become a "much litigated and often confused field," United States v. City of Detroit, 355 U.S. 466, 473 (1958), one that has been marked from the beginning by inconsistent decisions and excessively delicate distinctions.

McCulloch itself relied on generalized notions of federal supremacy to invalidate a state tax on the Second Bank of the United States. The Court gave broad scope to state power: the opinion declined to "deprive the States of any resources which they originally possessed. It does not extend to . . . a tax imposed on the interest which citizens of Maryland may hold in [the Bank], in common with other property of the same description throughout the State." 4 Wheat., at 436. Not long afterwards, however, Chief Justice Marshall, speaking for the Court, seemingly disregarded the *McCulloch* dictum in striking down a state tax on interest income from federal bonds, explaining that such levies cannot constitutionally fall on an "operation essential to the important objects for which the government was created." Weston v. Charleston, 2 Pet. 449, 467 (1829). During the following century the Court took to heart *Weston's* expansive analysis of federal tax immunity, invalidating, among many others, state taxes on the income of federal employees, Dobbins v. Commissioners, 16 Pet. 435 (1842); on income derived from property leased from the Federal Government, Gillespie v. Oklahoma, 257 U.S. 501 (1922); and on sales to the United States, Panhandle Oil Co. v. Mississippi ex rel. Knox, 277 U.S. 218 (1928).[10]

_____

[10] It is in the case last cited that Justice Holmes in dissent, joined by Justice Brandeis and Justice Stone, countered the great Chief Justice's observation with other well known words: "The power to tax is not the power to destroy while this Court sits." 277 U.S., at 223. Justice Frankfurter, concurring, in Graves v. New York ex rel. O'Keefe, 306 U.S. 466, 490 (1939), observed: "The web of

These decisions, it has been said, were increasingly divorced both from the constitutional foundations of the immunity doctrine and from "the actual workings of our federalism," Graves v. New York ex rel. O'Keefe, 306 U.S. 466, 490 (1939) (Frankfurter, J., concurring), and in James v. Dravo Contracting Co., 302 U.S. 134 (1937), by a 5–4 vote, the Court marked a major change in course. Over the dissent's justifiable objections that it was "overrul[ing], *sub silentio,* a century of precedents," id., at 161, the Court upheld a state tax on the gross receipts of a contractor providing services to the Federal Government:

> "[I]t is not necessary to cripple [the State's power to tax] by extending the constitutional exemption from taxation to those subjects which fall within the general application of non-discriminatory laws, and where no direct burden is laid upon the governmental instrumentality, and there is only a remote, if any, influence upon the exercise of the functions of government."

The Court's more recent cases involving federal contractors generally have hewed to the *James* analysis. Alabama v. King & Boozer, 314 U.S. 1 (1941), upheld a state tax on sales to a federal contractor, overruling Panhandle Oil Co. v. Mississippi ex rel. Knox, supra. Decisions such as United States v. City of Detroit, supra, have validated state use taxes on private entities holding federal property.

Even the Court's post-*James* decisions, however, cannot be set in an entirely unwavering line. United States v. Allegheny County, 322 U.S. 174 (1944), invalidated a state property tax that included in the assessment the value of federal machinery held by a private party; fourteen years later that decision in large part was overruled by United States v. City of Detroit, supra. See United States v. County of Fresno, 429 U.S. 452, 462–463, n. 10 (1977). In Livingston v. United States, 364 U.S. 281 (1960), summarily aff'g 179 F.Supp. 9 (EDSC 1959), the Court, without opinion or citation, approved the invalidation of a state use tax as applied to a federal contractor. Yet United States v. Boyd, supra, upheld a virtually identical state tax, seemingly confining *Livingston* to its "extraordinary" facts. 378 U.S., at 45, n. 6.

Similarly, the decisions fail to speak with one voice on the relevance of traditional agency rules in determining the tax-immunity status of federal contractors. . . .

B

We have concluded that the confusing nature of our precedents counsels a return to the underlying constitutional principle. The one constant here, of course, is simple enough to express: a State may not, consistent with the Supremacy Clause, U.S. Const., Art. VI, cl. 2, lay a tax "directly upon the United States." Mayo v. United States, 319 U.S. 441, 447 (1943). While "[o]ne could, and perhaps should, read *McCulloch* . . . simply for the principle that the Constitution prohibits a State from taxing discriminatorily a federally established instrumentality," First Agricultural Bank v. State Tax Comm'n, 392 U.S. 339, 350 (1968) (dissenting opinion), the Court has never questioned the propriety of absolute federal immunity from state taxation. And after 160 years, the doctrine has gathered "a momentum of authority that reflects, if not a detailed exposition of considerations of policy demanded by our federal system, certainly a deep instinct that there are such considerations. . . ." City of Detroit v. Murray Corp., 355 U.S. 489, 503–504 (1958) (opinion of Frankfurter, J.).

But the limits on the immunity doctrine are, for present purposes, as significant as the rule itself. Thus, immunity may not be conferred simply

unreality spun from Marshall's famous dictum was brushed away by one stroke of Mr. Justice Holmes' pen."

because the tax has an effect on the United States, or even because the Federal Government shoulders the entire economic burden of the levy. That is the import of Alabama v. King & Boozer, where a sales tax was imposed on the gross receipts of a vendor selling to a cost-plus Government contractor. . . . That the contractor is purchasing property for the Government is similarly irrelevant; in *King & Boozer,* title to goods purchased by the contractor vested in the United States immediately upon shipment by the seller. Id., at 13.

Similarly, immunity cannot be conferred simply because the state tax falls on the earnings of a contractor providing services to the Government. James v. Dravo Contracting Co., supra. And where a use tax is involved, immunity cannot be conferred simply because the State is levying the tax on the use of federal property in private hands, United States v. City of Detroit, supra, even if the private entity is using the Government property to provide the United States with goods, United States v. Township of Muskegon, supra; City of Detroit v. Murray Corp., supra, or services, Curry v. United States, 314 U.S. 14 (1941); United States v. Boyd, supra. . . . Indeed, immunity cannot be conferred simply because the tax is paid with Government funds; that was apparently the case in *Boyd,* where the contractor made expenditures under an advanced funding arrangement similar to the one involved here.

What the Court's cases leave room for, then, is the conclusion that tax immunity is appropriate in only one circumstance: when the levy falls on the United States itself, or on an agency or instrumentality so closely connected to the Government that the two cannot realistically be viewed as separate entities, at least insofar as the activity being taxed is concerned. This view, we believe, comports with the principal purpose of the immunity doctrine, that of forestalling "clashing sovereignty," McCulloch v. Maryland, 4 Wheat., at 430, by preventing the States from laying demands directly on the Federal Government. See City of Detroit v. Murray Corp., 355 U.S., at 504–505 (opinion of Frankfurter, J.). As the federal structure—along with the workings of the tax immunity doctrine [11]—has evolved, this command has taken on essentially symbolic importance, as the visible "consequence of that [federal] supremacy which the constitution has declared." M'Culloch v. Maryland, 4 Wheat., at 436. At the same time, a narrow approach to governmental tax immunity accords with competing constitutional imperatives, by giving full range to each sovereign's taxing authority. See Graves v. New York ex rel. O'Keefe, 306 U.S., at 483.

Thus, a finding of constitutional tax immunity requires something more than the invocation of traditional agency notions: to resist the State's taxing power, a private taxpayer must actually "stand in the Government's shoes." . . . [T]he point is settled by *Boyd,* the Court's most recent decision in the field. There, the Government argued that its contractors were tax-exempt because they were federal agents. Without any discussion of traditional agency rules the Court rejected that suggestion out-of-hand, declaring that "we cannot believe that [the contractors are] 'so assimilated by the Government as to become one of its constituent parts.'" 378 U.S., at 47, quoting United States v. Township of Muskegon, 355 U.S., at 486. And the Court continued:

> "Should the [Atomic Energy] Commission intend to build or operate the plant with its own servants and employees, it is well aware that it may do so and familiar with the ways of doing it. It chose not to do so here. We

---

[11] With the abandonment of the notion that the economic—as opposed to the legal—incidence of the tax is relevant, it becomes difficult to maintain that federal tax immunity is designed to insulate federal operations from the effects of state taxation. It remains true, of course, that state taxes on contractors are constitutionally invalid if they discriminate against the Federal Government, or substantially interfere with its activities. See United States v. County of Fresno, 429 U.S. 452, 463 n. 11, 464 (1977); Moses Lake Homes, Inc. v. Grant County, 365 U.S. 744 (1961); City of Detroit v. Murray Corp., 355 U.S. 489, 495 (1958). New Mexico, however, is not discriminating here.

cannot conclude that [the contractors], both cost-plus contractors for profit, have been so incorporated into the government structure as to become instrumentalities of the United States and thus enjoy governmental immunity." 378 U.S., at 48.

. . .

Granting tax immunity only to entities that have been "incorporated into the government structure" can forestall, at least to a degree, some of the manipulation and wooden formalism that occasionally have marked tax litigation—and that have no proper place in determining the allocation of power between co-existing sovereignties. In this case, for example, the Government and its contractors modified their agreements two years into the litigation in an obvious attempt to strengthen the case for nonliability. Yet the Government resists using its own employees for the tasks at hand—or, indeed, even formally designating Sandia, Zia, and LACI as agents—because it seeks to tap the expertise of industry, without subjecting its contractors to burdensome federal procurement regulations. . . .

If the immunity of federal contractors is to be expanded beyond its narrow constitutional limits, it is Congress that must take responsibility for the decision. . . . And this allocation of responsibility is wholly appropriate, for the political process is "uniquely adapted to accommodating the competing demands" in this area. . . .

III

It remains to apply these principles to the Sandia, Zia, and LACI contracts. The Government concedes that the legal incidence of the gross receipts and use taxes falls on the contractors, and we do not disagree. . . . The issue, then, is whether the contractors can realistically be considered entities independent of the United States. If so, a tax on them cannot be viewed as a tax on the United States itself.

So far as the use tax is concerned, United States v. Boyd, supra, controls this case. The contracts at issue in *Boyd* were standard AEC management contracts, in all relevant respects identical to the ones here. . . .

. . .

. . . The tax, the taxed activity, and the contractual relationships do not differ from those involved in *Boyd*. The contractors here are privately owned corporations; . . . In contrast to federal employees, then, Sandia and its fellow contractors cannot be termed "constituent parts" of the Federal Government. . . .

For similar reasons, the New Mexico gross receipts tax must be upheld as applied to funds received by the contractors to meet salaries and internal costs. Once it is conceded that the contractors are independent taxable entities, it cannot be disputed that their gross income is taxable. . . . And despite the Government's arguments, the use of advanced funding does not change the analysis. That device is, at heart, an efficient method of reimbursing contractors—something the Government has apparently recognized in contexts other than tax litigation. If receipt of advanced funding is coextensive with status as a federal instrumentality, virtually every federal contractor is, or could easily become, immune from state taxation.

New Mexico's tax on sales to the contractors presents a more complex problem. So far as the use tax discussed above is concerned, the subject of the levy is the taxed entity's beneficial use of the property involved. See United States v. Boyd, 378 U.S., at 44. Unless the entity as a whole is one of the Government's "constituent parts," then, a tax on its use of property should not be seen as falling on the United States; in that situation the property is being used in furtherance of the contractor's essentially independent commercial enterprise. In the case of a sales tax, however, it is arguable that an entity serving as a federal procurement agent can be so closely associated with the Government, and so lack an independent role in the purchase, as to make the sale—in both a real and a symbolic sense—a sale to the United States, even though the purchasing agent has not otherwise been incorporated into the Government structure.

Such was the Court's conclusion in Kern-Limerick, Inc. v. Scurlock, supra, a decision on which the Government heavily relies. The contractor in that case identified itself as a federal procurement agent, and when it made purchases title passed directly to the Government; the purchase orders themselves declared that the purchase was made by the Government and that the United States was liable on the sale. Equally as important, the contractor itself was *not* liable for the purchase price, and it required specific Government approval for each transaction. See 347 U.S., at 120–121. And, as the Court emphasized, the statutory procurement scheme envisioned the use of federal purchasing agents. Id., at 114. The Court concluded that a sale to the contractor was in effect a sale to the United States, and therefore not a proper subject for the Arkansas sales tax. As we have noted elsewhere, *Kern-Limerick* "stands only for the proposition that the State may not impose a tax the legal incidence of which falls on the Federal Government." United States v. County of Fresno, 429 U.S., at 459–460, n. 7.

We think it evident that the *Kern-Limerick* principle does not invalidate New Mexico's sales tax as applied to purchases made by the contractors here. Even accepting the Government's representation that it is directly liable to vendors for the purchase price, Sandia and Zia nevertheless make purchases in their own names—Sandia, in fact, is contractually obligated to do so, and presumably they are themselves liable to the vendors. Vendors are not informed that the Government is the only party with an independent interest in the purchase, as was true in *Kern-Limerick*, and the Government disclaims any formal intention to denominate the contractors as purchasing agents. Similarly, Sandia and Zia need not obtain advance Government approval for each purchase. These factors demonstrate that the contractors have a substantial independent role in making purchases, and that the identity of interests between the Government and the contractors is far from complete. As a result, sales to Zia and Sandia are in neither a real nor a symbolic sense sales to the "United States itself." It is true that title passes directly from the vendor to the Federal Government, but that factor alone cannot make the transaction a purchase by the United States, so long as the purchasing entity, in its role as a purchaser, is sufficiently distinct from the Government. Alabama v. King & Boozer, 314 U.S., at 13.

There is a final irony in this case. In Carson v. Roane-Anderson Co., 342 U.S. 232 (1952), the Court considered a state sales and use tax imposed on AEC management contractors. The terms of the contracts were in most relevant respects identical to the ones here, and insofar as they differed they established an even closer relationship between the Government and the contractors. The Court held that in the last sentence of § 9(b) of the Atomic Energy Act of 1946, 60 Stat. 765—which barred state or local taxation of AEC "activities"—Congress had statutorily exempted the contractors from state taxation, because the operations of management contractors were Commission activities. 342 U.S., at 234. Congress responded by repealing the last sentence of § 9(b), Pub.L. 262, 67 Stat. 575, in an attempt to "place the Commission and its activities on the same basis, with respect to immunity from State and local taxation, as other Federal agencies." S.Rep. No. 694, 83d Cong., 1st Sess., 3 (1953). In doing so, Congress endorsed the principle that "constitutional immunity does not extend to cost-plus-fixed-fee contractors of the Federal

Government, but is limited to taxes imposed directly upon the United States."
Id., at 2.

We do not suggest that the repeal of § 9(b) waives the Government's constitutional tax immunity; Congress intended AEC contractors to be shielded by constitutional immunity principles "as interpreted by the courts." S.Rep. No. 694, at 3. But it is worth remarking that DOE is asking us to establish as a constitutional rule something that it was unable to obtain statutorily from Congress. For the reasons set out above, we conclude that the contractors here are not protected by the Constitution's guarantee of federal supremacy. If political or economic considerations suggest that a broader immunity rule is appropriate, "[s]uch complex problems are ones which Congress is best qualified to resolve." United States v. City of Detroit, 355 U.S., at 474.

Accordingly, the judgment of the Court of Appeals is

Affirmed.

CONGRESSIONAL POWER TO BROADEN OR CONSTRICT FEDERAL IMMUNITY FROM STATE TAXATION

It has long been settled that federal statutes can waive immunity from state taxation by consenting to state taxes that would otherwise be unconstitutional. As the last sentence in the Court's opinion in United States v. New Mexico suggests, Congress also has power to broaden the scope of federal immunity. In Pittman v. Home Owner's Loan Corp., 308 U.S. 21 (1939), for example, the Court sustained a federal statute immunizing the franchise, capital, reserves, surplus, loans, and income of the Federal Home Owner's Loan Corporation from state taxation. The Court rejected an argument that Congress could not create immunity from taxation greater than the constitutional immunity. Congress' power to create the corporation included "the power to protect the operations thus validly authorized."

B.　STATE IMMUNITY

MASSACHUSETTS v. UNITED STATES

435 U.S. 444, 98 S.Ct. 1153, 55 L.Ed.2d 403 (1978).

Mr. Justice Brennan delivered the opinion of the Court.*

As part of a comprehensive program to recoup the costs of federal aviation programs from those who use the national airsystem, Congress in 1970 imposed an annual registration tax on all civil aircraft that fly in the navigable airspace of the United States. 26 U.S.C. § 4491. The constitutional question presented in this case is whether this tax, as applied to an aircraft owned by a State and used by it exclusively for police functions, violates the implied immunity of a state government from federal taxation. We hold that it does not.

. . . .

II.

A review of the development of the constitutional doctrine of state immunity from federal taxation is a necessary preface to decision of this case. For while the Commonwealth concedes that certain types of user fees may constitutionally be applied to its essential activities, it urges that the decisions of this Court teach

---

* Mr. Justice Stewart and Mr. Justice Powell join only Parts I, II–C, and III of this opinion. Mr. Justice White, Mr. Justice Marshall, and Mr. Justice Stevens join the entire opinion.

that the validity of any impost levied against a State must be judged by a "bright-line" test: if the measure is labelled a tax and/or imposed or collected pursuant to the Internal Revenue Code, it is unconstitutional as applied to an essential state function even if the revenue measure operates as a user fee. . . . And the Commonwealth maintains that § 4491 is invalid for the additional reason that the values furthered by this constitutional doctrine necessarily require the invalidation of a levy such as that under § 4491 which, as an annual fee, is not directly related to use. . . . Neither contention has merit. The principles that have animated the development of the doctrine of state tax immunity and the decisions of this Court in analogous contexts persuade us that a State enjoys no constitutional immunity from a nondiscriminatory revenue measure, like § 4491, which operates only to ensure that each member of a class of special beneficiaries of a federal program pays a reasonable approximation of its fair share of the cost of the program to the National Government. Like the Court of Appeals, we have no occasion to decide either the present vitality of the doctrine of state tax immunity or the conditions under which it might be invoked.

A.

That the existence of the States implies some restriction on the national taxing power was first decided in Collector v. Day, 11 Wall. 113. There this Court held that the immunity that federal instrumentalities and employees then enjoyed from state taxation, . . . was to some extent reciprocal and that the salaries paid state judges were immune from a nondiscriminatory federal tax. This immunity of State and Federal governments from taxation by each other was expanded in decisions over the last third of the 19th Century and the first third of this century, . . . but more recent decisions of this Court have confined the scope of the doctrine.

The immunity of the Federal Government from state taxation is bottomed on the Supremacy Clause, but the States' immunity from federal taxes was judicially implied from the States' role in the constitutional scheme. Collector v. Day, supra, emphasized that the States had been in existence as independent sovereigns when the Constitution was adopted, and that the Constitution presupposes and guarantees the continued existence of the States as governmental bodies performing traditional sovereign functions. 11 Wall., at 125–126. To implement this aspect of the constitutional plan, Collector v. Day concluded that it was imperative absolutely to prohibit any federal taxation that directly affected a traditional state function, quoting Chief Justice Marshall's aphorisms that "the power of taxing . . . may be exercised so far as to destroy," id., at 123, quoting McCulloch v. Maryland, supra, at 427, and "a right [to tax], in its nature, acknowledges no limits." Ibid., quoting Weston v. Charleston, 2 Pet. 449, 466 (1829). The Court has more recently remarked that these maxims refer primarily to two attributes of the taxing power. *First,* in imposing a tax to support the services a government provides to the public at large, a legislature need not consider the value of particular benefits to a taxpayer, but may assess the tax solely on the basis of taxpayers' ability to pay. *Second* (of perhaps greater concern in the present context), a tax is a powerful regulatory device; a legislature can discourage or eliminate a particular activity that is within its regulatory jurisdiction simply by imposing a heavy tax on its exercise. . . . Collector v. Day, like the earlier *McCulloch v. Maryland,* reflected the view that the awesomeness of the taxing power required a flat and absolute prohibition against a tax implicating an essential state function because the ability of the federal courts to determine whether particular revenue measures would or would not destroy such an essential function was to be doubted.

As the contours of the principle evolved in later decisions, "cogent reasons" were recognized for narrowly limiting the immunity of the States from federal imposts. See Helvering v. Gerhardt, 304 U.S. 405, 416 (1938). The first is that any immunity for the protection of state sovereignty is at the expense of the sovereign power of the National Government to tax. Therefore, when the scope of the States' constitutional immunity is enlarged beyond that necessary to protect the continued ability of the States to deliver traditional governmental services, the burden of the immunity is thrown upon the National Government without any corresponding promotion of the constitutionally protected values. . . . The second, also recognized by Chief Justice Marshall in McCulloch v. Maryland, supra, at 435–436, is that the political process is uniquely adapted to accommodating the competing demands "for national revenue, on the one hand, and for reasonable scope for the independence of state action, on the other," Helvering v. Gerhardt, supra, 304 U.S., at 416: The Congress, composed as it is of members chosen by state constituencies, constitutes an inherent check against the possibility of abusive taxing of the States by the National Government.[13] Rather, the majority reasoned that a nondiscriminatory tax may be applied to a State business activity where . . . the recognition of immunity would "accomplish a withdrawal from the taxing power of the nation a subject of taxation of a nature which has traditionally been within that power from the beginning. . . .

In tacit, and at times explicit, recognition of these considerations, decisions of the Court either have declined to enlarge the scope of state immunity or have in fact restricted its reach. Typical of this trend are decisions holding that the National Government may tax revenue generating activities of the States that are of the same nature as those traditionally engaged in by private persons. See, e.g., New York v. United States, 326 U.S. 572 (1946) (tax on water bottled and sold by State upheld); . . . . It is true that some of the opinions speak of the state activity taxed as "proprietary" and thus not an immune essential *governmental* activity, but the opinions of the Members of the Court in New York v. United States supra, the most recent decision, rejected the governmental-proprietary distinction as untenable.

Illustrative of decisions actually restricting the scope of the immunity is the line of cases that culminated in the overruling of Collector v. Day in Graves v. New York ex rel. O'Keefe, 306 U.S. 466 (1939). . . . Collector v. Day, of course, involved a nondiscriminatory tax that was imposed not directly on the State but rather on the salary earned by a judicial officer. Neither Collector v. Day itself nor its progeny or precursors made clear how such a taxing measure could be employed to preclude the States from performing essential functions. In any case, in the line of decisions that culminated in Graves v. New York ex rel. O'Keefe, supra, the Court demonstrated that an immunity for the salaries paid key state officials is not justifiable. Although key state officials are agents of the State, they are also citizens of the United States, so their income is a natural subject for income taxation. . . .

More significantly, because the taxes imposed were nondiscriminatory and thus also applicable to income earned by persons in private employment, the risk was virtually nonexistent that such revenue provisions could significantly impede a State's ability to hire able persons to perform its essential functions. . . . The only advantage conceivably to be lost by denying the States such an

---

[13] Although the opinion for the Court in National League of Cities v. Usery, 426 U.S. 833, (1976), rejects the argument that the operation of the political process eliminates any reason for reviewing federalism based challenges to federal regulation of the States qua States, we do not believe it follows that the existence of "political checks" has no relevance to a determination of the proper scope of a State's immunity from federal taxation. We have regularly relied upon the existence of such political checks in considering the scope of the National Government's immunity from state taxation. See, e.g., United States v. County of Fresno, 429 U.S. 452 (1977).

immunity is that essential state functions might be obtained at a lesser cost because employees exempt from taxation might be willing to work for lesser salaries. See ibid. But that was regarded as an inadequate ground for sustaining the immunity and preventing the National Government from requiring these citizens to support its activities. The purpose of the implied constitutional restriction on the national taxing power is not to give an advantage to the States by enabling them to engage employees at a lower charge than those paid by private entities, but rather is solely to protect the States from undue interference with their traditional governmental functions. While a tax on the salary paid key state officers may increase the cost of government, it will no more preclude the States from performing traditional functions than it will prevent private entities from performing their missions. . . .

These two lines of decisions illustrate the "practical construction" that the Court now gives the limitation the existence of the States constitutionally imposes on the national taxing power; "that limitation cannot be so varied or extended as seriously to impair either the taxing power of the government imposing the tax . . . or the appropriate exercise of the functions of the government affected by it." New York v. United States, supra, 326 U.S., at 589–590 (Stone, C.J., concurring) quoting Metcalf & Eddy v. Mitchell, supra, 269 U.S., at 523–524. Where the subject of tax is a natural and traditional source of federal revenue and where it is inconceivable that such a revenue measure could ever operate to preclude traditional state activities, the tax is valid. While the Court has by no means abandoned its doubts concerning its ability to make particularized assessments of the impact of revenue measures on essential state operations, . . . it has recognized that some generic types of revenue measures could never seriously threaten the continued functioning of the States and hence are outside the scope of the implied tax immunity.

B.

A nondiscriminatory taxing measure that operates to defray the cost of a federal program by recovering a fair approximation of each beneficiary's share of the cost is surely no more offensive to the constitutional scheme than is either a tax on the income earned by state employees or a tax on a State's sale of bottled water. The National Government's interest in being compensated for its expenditures is only too apparent. More significantly perhaps, such revenue measures by their very nature cannot possess the attributes that led Chief Justice Marshall to proclaim that the power to tax is the power to destroy. There is no danger that such measures will not be based on benefits conferred or that they will function as regulatory devices unduly burdening essential state activities. It is of course, the case that a revenue provision that forces a State to pay its own way when performing an essential function will increase the cost of the state activity. But Graves v. New York ex rel. O'Keefe, supra, and its precursors, . . . teach that an economic burden on traditional state functions without more is not a sufficient basis for sustaining a claim of immunity. . . .

Our decisions in analogous contexts support this conclusion. We have repeatedly held that the Federal Government may impose appropriate conditions on the use of federal property or privileges and may require that state instrumentalities comply with conditions that are reasonably related to the federal interest in particular national projects or programs. . . . A requirement that States, like all other users, pay a portion of the costs of the benefits they enjoy from federal programs is surely permissible since it is closely related to the federal interest in recovering costs from those who benefit and since it effects no greater interference with state sovereignty than do the restrictions which this Court has approved.

A clearly analogous line of decisions is that interpreting provisions in the Constitution that also place limitations on the taxing power of government. See, e.g., U.S. Const., Art. I, § 8, cl. 3 (restricting power of States to tax interstate commerce); § 10, cl. 3 (prohibiting any state tax that operates "to impose a charge for the privilege of entering in, trading in, or lying in port." . . . These restrictions, like the implied state tax immunity, exist to protect constitutionally valued activity from the undue and perhaps destructive interference that could result from certain taxing measures. . . .

Our decisions implementing these constitutional provisions have consistently recognized that the interests protected by these Clauses are not offended by revenue measures that operate only to compensate a government for benefits supplied. . . . Evansville-Vanderburgh Airport Authority v. Delta Airlines, Inc., 405 U.S. 707 (1972) ($1 head tax on enplaning commercial air passengers upheld under the Commerce Clause because designed to recoup cost of airport facilities). . . .

C.

Having established that taxes that operate as user fees may constitutionally be applied to the States, we turn to consider the Commonwealth's argument that § 4491 should not be treated as a user fee because the amount of the tax is a flat annual fee and hence is not directly related to the degree of use of the airways. . . .

. . . .

We note first that it is doubtful that the National Government could recover the costs of its aviation activities from those direct beneficiaries without making at least some use of annual flat fees. . . .

But even if it were feasible to recover all costs through charges for measurable amounts of use of Government facilities, we fail to see how such a requirement would appreciably advance the policies embodied in the doctrine of state tax immunity. Since a State has no constitutional complaint when it is required to pay the cost of benefits received, the Commonwealth's only legitimate fear is that the flat fee requirement may result in the collection from it of more than its actual "fair share." We observe first that where the charges imposed by the Federal Government apply to large numbers of private parties as well as to state activities, it is as likely as not that the user fee will result in exacting less money from the State than it would have to pay under a perfect user fee system. . . . But the complete answer to the Commonwealth's concern is that even if the flat fee does cost it somewhat more than it would have to pay under a perfect user fee system, there is still no interference with the values protected by the implied constitutional tax immunity of the States. The possibility of a slight overcharge is no more offensive to the constitutional structure than is the increase in the cost of essential operations that results either from the fact that those who deal with the State may be required to pay nondiscriminatory taxes on the money they receive or from the fact a jury may award an eminent domain claimant an amount in excess of what would be "just compensation" in an ideal system of justice.

Whatever the present scope of the principle of state tax immunity, a State can have no constitutional objection to a revenue measure that satisfies the three-prong test of Evansville-Vanderburgh Airport Authority v. Delta Airlines, Inc., supra—substituting "state function" for "interstate commerce" in that test. So long as the charges do not discriminate against state functions, are based on a fair approximation of use of the system, and are structured to produce revenues that will not exceed the total cost to the Federal Government of the benefits to be supplied, there can be no substantial basis for a claim that the National Government will be using its taxing powers to control, unduly interfere with, or destroy a State's ability to perform essential services. The requirement that total revenues not exceed expenditures places a natural ceiling on the total amount that such charges may generate and the further requirement that the measure be reasonable and nondiscriminatory precludes the adoption of a charge that will unduly burden state activities.

III.

Applying these principles to this case demonstrates that the Commonwealth's claim of constitutional immunity is particularly insubstantial. First, there is no question but that the tax imposed by § 4491 is nondiscriminatory. . . .

Second, the tax satisfies the requirement that it be a fair approximation of the cost of the benefits civil aircraft receive from the federal activities. . . . A more precisely calibrated formula—which would include landing fees, charges for specific services received, and less reliance on annual flat fees . . . would, of course be administratively more costly.

It follows that a State may not complain of the application of § 4491 on the ground it is not a fair approximation of use. . . .

Finally, the tax is not excessive in relation to the cost of the government benefits supplied. . . .

Affirmed.

Mr. Justice Blackmun took no part in the consideration or decision of this case.

Mr. Justice Stewart and Mr. Justice Powell, concurring in part and concurring in the judgment.

The petitioner has conceded that a nondiscriminatory user fee may constitutionally be imposed upon a State, and, for substantially the reasons stated in Part II–B of the Court's opinion, we agree. Moreover, we agree with the Court that the aircraft registration tax imposed by 26 U.S.C. § 4491 is such a user fee. We therefore see no need to discuss the general contours of state immunity from federal taxation, as the Court does in Part II–A of its opinion.

On this basis we join Parts I, II–C, and III of the Court's opinion and concur in its judgment.

Mr. Justice Rehnquist, with whom The Chief Justice joins, dissenting.

. . .

The United States has defended its judgment in this Court solely on the basis that the Court of Appeals was correct in concluding that the exaction in question was a user charge. . . . It is therefore somewhat surprising to find Part II–A of today's opinion (which is joined by only four Justices) discussing at length the scope of intergovernmental tax immunity. Petitioner insists that it may be able to prove at a trial of the action that the charge is not in fact a user fee; respondent insists that it is a user fee, apparently as a matter of law. This is the issue before the Court, and the only issue before it.

I agree with the Court that respondent would have a valid defense to this action if it had established, or could establish, that the charge imposed was reasonably related to services rendered to the petitioner by agencies of the Federal Government. I further conclude that the United States would have a valid defense to this action if it could establish that the charge was based on use by the petitioner of some property which respondent owned or in which it had some other type of proprietary interest. . . . I am at a loss to know why the Court feels obligated to draw on cases decided under the Commerce Clause, U.S.Const., Art. I, § 8, cl. 3, to establish its vague and convoluted three-part test to determine whether the user fee is valid, since cases regarding intergovernmental relations raise significantly different considerations. Commerce

Clause cases, while no doubt useful analogies, are not required to deal with the fact that the payer of the user fee is a State in our constitutional structure, and that its essential sovereign interests are entitled to greater deference than is due to ordinary business enterprises which may be regulated by both State and Federal governments. Since the United States concedes that the absence of intergovernmental immunity to user fees is a reciprocal one, . . . it stands to lose as much from the vagueness of the Court's test as do petitioner and her sister States.

Regardless of the phrasing of the test, I cannot accept the Court's conclusion that the Commonwealth need not be given the opportunity to prove that the test has not been satisfied. . . .

. . .

SECTION 2. INTERGOVERNMENTAL REGULATORY IMMUNITY

A. FEDERAL IMMUNITY

MILLER v. ARKANSAS

352 U.S. 187, 77 S.Ct. 257, 1 L.Ed.2d 231 (1956).

Per Curiam.

Appellant submitted a bid in May 1954 for construction of facilities at an Air Force Base in Arkansas over which the United States had not acquired jurisdiction pursuant to 54 Stat. 19, 40 U.S.C. § 255. The United States accepted appellant's bid, and in June appellant began work on the project. In September, the State of Arkansas filed an information accusing appellant of violation of Ark.Stat., 1947, §§ 71–701 through 71–721, for submitting a bid, executing a contract, and commencing work as a contractor in the State of Arkansas without having obtained a license under Arkansas law for such activity from its Contractors Licensing Board. The case was tried on stipulated facts. Appellant was found guilty and fined. The trial court's judgment was affirmed by the Arkansas Supreme Court, 225 Ark. 285, 281 S.W.2d 946, and the case came here on appeal. 351 U.S. 948. Appellant and the United States as *amicus curiae* contend that the application of the Arkansas statute to this contractor interferes with the Federal Government's power to select contractors and schedule construction and is in conflict with the federal law regulating procurement.

Congress provided in § 3 of the Armed Services Procurement Act of 1947, 62 Stat. 21, 23, 41 U.S.C. § 152, that awards on advertised bids "shall be made . . . to that responsible bidder whose bid, conforming to the invitation for bids, will be most advantageous to the Government, price and other factors considered . . . . ." The report from the Committee on Armed Services of the House of Representatives indicated some of the factors to be considered: "The question whether a particular bidder is a 'responsible bidder' requires some business judgment, and involves an evaluation of the bidder's experience, facilities, technical organization, reputation, financial resources, and other factors." H.R.Rep. No. 109, 80th Cong., 1st Sess. 18; see S.Rep. No. 571, 80th Cong., 1st Sess. 16. The Armed Services Procurement Regulations, promulgated under the Act, set forth a list of guiding considerations, defining a responsible contractor as one who

"(a) Is a manufacturer, construction contractor, or regular dealer.

. . . .

"(b) Has adequate financial resources, or ability to secure such resources;

"(c) Has the necessary experience, organization, and technical qualifications, and has or can acquire the necessary facilities (including probable subcontractor arrangements) to perform the proposed contract;

"(d) Is able to comply with the required delivery or performance schedule (taking into consideration all existing business commitments);

"(e) Has a satisfactory record of performance, integrity, judgment, and skills; and

"(f) Is otherwise qualified and eligible to receive an award under applicable laws and regulations." 32 CFR § 1.307; see also 32 CFR § 2.406–3. Under the Arkansas licensing law similar factors are set forth to guide the Contractors Licensing Board:

> "The Board, in determining the qualifications of any applicant for original license . . . shall, among other things, consider the following: (a) experience, (b) ability, (c) character, (d) the manner of performance of previous contracts, (e) financial condition, (f) equipment, (g) any other fact tending to show ability and willingness to conserve the public health and safety, and (h) default in complying with the provisions of this act . . . or any other law of the State. . . ." Ark.Stat., 1947, § 71–709.

Mere enumeration of the similar grounds for licensing under the state statute and for finding "responsibility" under the federal statute and regulations is sufficient to indicate conflict between this license requirement which Arkansas places on a federal contractor and the action which Congress and the Department of Defense have taken to insure the reliability of persons and companies contracting with the Federal Government. Subjecting a federal contractor to the Arkansas contractor license requirements would give the State's licensing board a virtual power of review over the federal determination of "responsibility" and would thus frustrate the expressed federal policy of selecting the lowest responsible bidder. In view of the federal statute and regulations, the rationale of Johnson v. Maryland, 254 U.S. 51, 57, is applicable:

"It seems to us that the immunity of the instruments of the United States from state control in the performance of their duties extends to a requirement that they desist from performance until they satisfy a state officer upon examination that they are competent for a necessary part of them and pay a fee for permission to go on. Such a requirement does not merely touch the Government servants remotely by a general rule of conduct; it lays hold of them in their specific attempt to obey orders and requires qualifications in addition to those that the Government has pronounced sufficient. It is the duty of the Department to employ persons competent for their work and that duty it must be presumed has been performed. . . ."

The judgment of the Supreme Court of Arkansas is reversed and the cause is remanded for further proceedings not inconsistent with this opinion.

Reversed and remanded.

PUBLIC UTILITIES COMMISSION OF CALIFORNIA v. UNITED STATES, 355 U.S. 534 (1958). The federal government had followed the practice of negotiating special rates with common carriers for the shipment of government property. A California statute required the United States to apply to the California Public Utilities Commission for approval of the freight rates to be applied to shipments within California. The Court held this statute unconstitutional. The opinion, by Justice Douglas, emphasized the fact that published rate schedules did not well accommodate the types of freight—ofttimes unique or secret military equipment—which the government often ships, and that delay and burden would be involved in securing approvals from 48 state commissions. Justice Harlan (joined by Chief Justice Warren and Justice Burton) dissented, stressing that it was premature to predict the burden involved until after application to the California commission for an efficient system for arriving at rates for government shipments. Cf. Paul v. United States, 371 U.S. 245 (1963) (state minimum price regulations for milk could not be enforced against bidder on sales to United States when Act of Congress required that purchases be made by competitive bidding).

———

HANCOCK v. TRAIN, 426 U.S. 167 (1976). The question before the Court was whether a state whose federally approved implementation plan forbids an air contaminant source to operate without a state permit may require existing federally owned or operated installations to secure such a permit. The specific question was whether obtaining a permit to operate is among those "requirements respecting control and abatement of air pollution" with which existing federal facilities must comply under § 118 of the federal Clean Air Act. The Court held that federal installations did not have to acquire state permits, prefacing its statutory construction discussion as follows:

"It is a seminal principle of our law 'that the constitution and the laws made in pursuance thereof are supreme; that they control the constitution and laws of the respective states and cannot be controlled by them.' McCulloch v. Maryland, 4 Wheat. 316, 426 (1819). From this principle is deduced the corollary that

' [i]t is the very essence of supremacy to remove all obstacles to its action within its own sphere, and so to modify every power vested in subordinate governments, as to exempt its own operation from their own influence.' Id., at 427.

"The effect of this corollary, which derives from the Supremacy Clause and is exemplified in the Plenary Powers Clause giving Congress exclusive legislative authority over federal enclaves purchased with the consent of a State, is 'that the activities of the Federal Government are free from regulation by any State.' As Mr. Justice Holmes put it in Johnson v. Maryland, 254 U.S. 51, 57 (1920),

'the immunity of the instruments of the United States from state control in the performance of their duties extends to a requirement that they desist from performance until they satisfy a state officer upon examination that they are competent for a necessary part of them . . . . .'

"Taken with the 'old and well-known rule that statutes which in general terms divest pre-existing rights or privileges will not be applied to the sovereign' 'without a clear expression or implication to that effect,' this immunity means that where 'Congress does not affirmatively declare its instrumentalities or property subject to regulation,' 'the federal function must be left free' of regulation. Particular deference should be accorded that 'old and well-known rule' where, as here, the rights and privileges of the Federal Government at stake not only find their origin in the Constitution, but are to be divested in favor of and subjected to regulation by a subordinate sovereign. Because of the fundamental importance of the principles shielding federal installations and activities from regulation by the States, an authorization of state regulation is found only when and to the extent there is 'a clear congressional mandate,' 'specific congressional action' that makes this authorization of state regulation 'clear and unambiguous.'

". . . [I]t is clear from the record that prohibiting operation of the air contaminant sources for which the State seeks to require permits, is tantamount to prohibiting operation of the federal installations on which they are located.

". . . We are unable to find in § 118, on its face or in relation to the Clean Air Act as a whole, or to derive from the legislative history of the Amendments any clear and unambiguous declaration by the Congress that federal installations may not perform their activities unless a state official issues a permit. Nor can congressional intention to submit federal activity to state control be implied from the claim that under Kentucky's EPA-approved implementation plan it is only through the permit system that compliance schedules and other requirements may be administratively enforced against federal installations."

B.   STATE IMMUNITY

STATE IMMUNITY FROM FEDERAL REGULATION—

1936–1976

United States v. California, 297 U.S. 175 (1936), sustained a penalty imposed on a state-owned railroad for violation of the Federal Safety Appliance Act. It was not necessary to address California's argument that the non-profit operation of the railroad was performance of "a public function in its sovereign capacity." It was irrelevant whether operation of the railroad was in a sovereign or private capacity. "The sovereign power of the states is necessarily diminished to the extent of the grants of power to the federal government in the Constitution." Id. at 184. Chief Justice Stone's opinion for the Court also rejected any analogy to a state's constitutional immunity from federal taxation. "[W]e look to the activities in which the states have traditionally engaged as marking the boundary of the restriction upon the federal taxing power. But there is no such limitation upon the plenary power to regulate commerce. The state can no more deny the power if its exercise has been authorized by Congress than can an individual." Id. at 185.

Until 1976, constitutional attacks on application of federal regulatory statutes to state activities were uniformly rejected. Case v. Bowles, 327 U.S. 92 (1946), upheld application of a maximum price under the Emergency Price Control Act as applied to a timber sale by the State of Washington. California v. Taylor, 353 U.S. 553 (1957), rejected a challenge to application of the Railway Labor Act to a state owned railroad. (The Act made wages and working conditions subject to a collective bargaining agreement rather than state civil service laws.) Parden v. Terminal Ry. Co., 377 U.S. 184 (1964), held that a state owned railroad was subject to liability to an injured employee under the Federal Employers' Liability Act. Maryland v. Wirtz, 392 U.S. 183 (1968), sustained application of the wage and hour provisions of the Fair Labor Standards Act to employees of public schools and hospitals. Fry v. United States, 421 U.S. 542 (1975) sustained application of the Economic Stabilization Act to limit wage increases of public employees.

Significantly, however, Justices Douglas and Stewart dissented in Maryland v. Wirtz, arguing that the commerce power could not be exercised in a way that unreasonably interfered with a state's sovereign power. Justice Rehnquist's dissent in Fry v. United States argued that Maryland v. Wirtz should be overruled. Finally, a footnote to Justice Marshall's opinion for the Court in *Fry* contained this statement: "While the Tenth Amendment has been characterized as 'a truism,' . . . United States v. Darby, 312 U.S. 100, 124 (1941), it is not without significance. The Amendment expressly declares the constitutional policy that Congress may not exercise power in a fashion that impairs the States' integrity or their ability to function effectively in a federal system. . . ." 427 U.S. at 547, n. 7.

———

NATIONAL LEAGUE OF CITIES v. USERY

426 U.S. 833, 96 S.Ct. 2465, 49 L.Ed.2d 245 (1976).

Mr. Justice Rehnquist delivered the opinion for the Court.

. . .

The original Fair Labor Standards Act passed in 1938 specifically excluded the States and their political subdivisions from its coverage. In 1974, however, Congress enacted the most recent of a series of broadening amendments to the Act. By these amendments Congress has extended the minimum wage and maximum hour provisions to almost all public employees employed by the States and by their various political subdivisions. Appellants in these cases include individual cities and States, the National League of Cities, and the National Governors' Conference; they brought an action in the District Court for the District of Columbia which challenged the validity of the 1974 amendments. They asserted in effect that when Congress sought to apply the Fair Labor Standards Act provisions virtually across the board to employees of state and municipal governments it "infringed a constitutional prohibition" running in favor of the States *as States.* The gist of their complaint was not that the conditions of employment of such public employees were beyond the scope of the commerce power had those employees been employed in the private sector, but that the established constitutional doctrine of intergovernmental immunity consistently recognized in a long series of our cases affirmatively prevented the exercise of this authority in the manner which Congress chose in the 1974 Amendments.

I.

. . .

. . . By its 1974 amendments, then, Congress has now entirely removed the exemption previously afforded States and their political subdivisions, substituting only the Act's general exemption for executive, administrative, or professional personnel, 29 U.S.C. § 213(a)(1), which is supplemented by provisions excluding from the Act's coverage those individuals holding public elective office or serving such an officeholder in one of several specific capacities. 29 U.S.C. § 203(e)(2)(C). The Act thus imposes upon almost all public employment the minimum wage and maximum hour requirements previously restricted to employees engaged in interstate commerce. These requirements are essentially identical to those imposed upon private employers, although the Act does attempt to make some provision for public employment relationships which are without counterpart in the private sector, such as those presented by fire protection and law enforcement personnel. See 29 U.S.C. § 207(k).

Challenging these 1974 amendments in the District Court, appellants sought both declaratory and injunctive relief against the amendments' application to them, and a three-judge court was accordingly convened pursuant to 28 U.S.C. § 2282. That court, after hearing argument on the law from the parties, granted appellee Secretary of Labor's motion to dismiss the complaint for failure to state a claim upon which relief might be granted. . . .

. . . We agree with the District Court that the appellants' contentions are substantial. Indeed upon full consideration of the question we have decided that the "far-reaching implications" of *Wirtz,* should be overruled, and that the judgment of the District Court must be reversed.

II.

.   .   .

Appellants in no way challenge   .   .   .   decisions establishing the breadth of authority granted Congress under the commerce power.   Their contention, on the contrary, is that when Congress seeks to regulate directly the activities of States as public employers, it transgresses an affirmative limitation on the exercise of its power akin to other commerce power affirmative limitations contained in the Constitution.   Congressional enactments which may be fully within the grant of legislative authority contained in the Commerce Clause may nonetheless be invalid because found to offend against the right to trial by jury contained in the Sixth Amendment, United States v. Jackson, 390 U.S. 570 (1968), or the Due Process Clause of the Fifth Amendment, Leary v. United States, 395 U.S. 6 (1969).   Appellants' essential contention is that the 1974 amendments to the Act, while undoubtedly within the scope of the Commerce Clause, encounter a similar constitutional barrier because they are to be applied directly to the States and subdivisions of States as employers.[12]

This Court has never doubted that there are limits upon the power of Congress to override state sovereignty, even when exercising its otherwise plenary powers to tax or to regulate commerce which are conferred by Art. I of the Constitution.   In *Wirtz,* for example, the Court took care to assure the appellants that it had "ample power to prevent   .   .   .   'the utter destruction of the State as a sovereign political entity.' " which they feared.   392 U.S., at 196. Appellee Secretary in this case, both in his brief and upon oral argument, has agreed that our federal system of government imposes definite limits upon the authority of Congress to regulate the activities of the States as States by means of the commerce power.   In *Fry,* supra, the Court recognized that an express declaration of this limitation is found in the Tenth Amendment:

"While the Tenth Amendment has been characterized as a 'truism,' stating merely that 'all is retained which has not been surrendered,' United States v. Darby, 312 U.S. 100, 124 (1941), it is not without significance.   The Amendment expressly declares the constitutional policy that Congress may not exercise power in a fashion that impairs the States' integrity or their

---

[12] The dissent intimates, that guarantees of individual liberties are the only sort of constitutional restrictions which this Court will enforce as against congressional action.   It reasons that "Congress is constituted of representatives in both the Senate and House *elected from the States.*   .   .   .   Decisions upon the extent of federal intervention under the Commerce Clause into the affairs of the States are in that sense decisions of the States themselves."   Precisely what is meant by the phrase "are in that sense decisions of the States themselves" is not entirely clear from this language; it is indisputable that a common constituency of voters elects both a State's governor and its two United States Senators.   It is equally indisputable that since the enactment of the Seventeenth Amendment those Senators are not dependent upon state legislators for their election.   But in any event the intimation which this reasoning is used to support is incorrect.

In Myers v. United States, 272 U.S. 52 (1926), the Court held that Congress could not by law limit the authority of the President to remove at will an officer of the Executive Branch appointed by him. In Buckley v. Valeo, 424 U.S. 1 (1976), the Court held that Congress could not constitutionally require that members of the Federal Elections Commission be appointed by officers of the House and of the Senate, and that all such appointments must be made by the President.   In each of these cases, an even stronger argument than that made in the dissent could be made to the effect that since each of these bills had been signed by the President, the very officer who challenged them had consented to their becoming law and it was therefore no concern of this Court that the law violated the Constitution.   Just as the dissent contends that "the States are fully able to protect their own interests .   .   .," it could have been contended that the President, armed with the mandate of a national constituency and with the veto power, was able to protect *his* own interests.   Nonetheless, in both cases the laws were held unconstitutional, because they trenched on the authority of the Executive Branch.

ability to function effectively in a federal system. . . ." 421 U.S., at 547, n. 7.

In New York v. United States, 326 U.S. 572 (1946), Chief Justice Stone, speaking for four Members of an eight-Member Court in rejecting the proposition that Congress could impose taxes on the States so long as it did so in a nondiscriminatory manner, observed:

"A State may, like a private individual, own real property and receive income. But in view of our former decisions we could hardly say that a general nondiscriminatory real estate tax (apportioned), or an income tax laid upon citizens and States alike could be constitutionally applied to the State's capitol, its State-house, its public school houses, public parks, or its revenues from taxes or school lands, even though all real property and all income of the citizen is taxed." Id. at 587–588.[14]

The expressions in these more recent cases trace back to earlier decisions of this Court recognizing the essential role of the States in our federal system of government. . . .

Appellee Secretary argues that the cases in which this Court has upheld sweeping exercises of authority by Congress, even though those exercises preempted state regulation of the private sector, have already curtailed the sovereignty of the States quite as much as the 1974 amendments to the Fair Labor Standards Act. We do not agree. It is one thing to recognize the authority of Congress to enact laws regulating individual businesses necessarily subject to the dual sovereignty of the government of the Nation and of the State in which they reside. It is quite another to uphold a similar exercise of congressional authority directed not to private citizens, but to the States as States. We have repeatedly recognized that there are attributes of sovereignty attaching to every state government which may not be impaired by Congress, not because Congress may lack an affirmative grant of legislative authority to reach the matter, but because the Constitution prohibits it from exercising the authority in that manner. In Coyle v. Smith, 221 U.S. 559 (1911), the Court gave this example of such an attribute

"The power to locate its own seat of government and to determine when and how it shall be changed from one place to another, and to appropriate its own public funds for that purpose, are essentially and peculiarly state powers. That one of the original thirteen States could now be shorn of such powers by an Act of Congress would not be for a moment entertained." Id. at 565.

One undoubted attribute of state sovereignty is the States' power to determine the wages which shall be paid to those whom they employ in order to carry out their governmental functions, what hours those persons will work, and what compensation will be provided where these employees may be called upon to work overtime. The question we must resolve in this case, then, is whether these determinations are "functions essential to separate and independent existence," Coyle v. Smith, supra, at 580, . . . so that Congress may not abrogate the State's otherwise plenary authority to make them.

In their complaint appellants advanced estimates of substantial costs which will be imposed upon them by the 1974 amendments. Since the District Court

---

[14] Mr. Justice Brennan suggests that "the Chief Justice was addressing not the question of a state sovereignty restraint upon the exercise of the commerce power, but rather the principle of implied immunity of the States and federal government from taxation by the other. . . ." The asserted distinction, however, escapes us. Surely the federal power to tax is no less a delegated power than is the commerce power: both find their genesis in Art. I, § 8. Nor can characterizing the limitation recognized upon the federal taxing power as an "implied immunity" obscure the fact that this "immunity" is derived from the sovereignty of the States and the concomitant barriers which such sovereignty presents to otherwise plenary federal authority.

dismissed their complaint, we take its well-pleaded allegations as true, although it appears from appellee's submissions in the District Court and in this Court that resolution of the factual disputes as to the effect of the amendments is not critical to our disposition of the case.

Judged solely in terms of increased costs in dollars, these allegations show a significant impact on the functioning of the governmental bodies involved. . . . The State of California, which must devote significant portions of its budget to fire suppression endeavors, estimated that application of the Act to its employment practices will necessitate an increase in its budget of between $8 million and $16 million.

Increased costs are not, of course, the only adverse effects which compliance with the Act will visit upon state and local governments, and in turn upon the citizens who depend upon those governments. In its complaint in intervention, for example, California asserted that it could not comply with the overtime costs (approximately $750,000 per year) which the Act required to be paid to California Highway Patrol cadets during their academy training program. California reported that it had thus been forced to reduce its academy training program from 2,080 hours to only 960 hours, a compromise undoubtedly of substantial importance to those whose safety and welfare may depend upon the preparedness of the California Highway Patrol.

This type of forced relinquishment of important governmental activities is further reflected in the complaint's allegation that the City of Inglewood, California, has been forced to curtail its affirmative action program for providing employment opportunities for men and women interested in a career in law enforcement. . . .

Quite apart from the substantial costs imposed upon the States and their political subdivisions, the Act displaces state policies regarding the manner in which they will structure delivery of those governmental services which their citizens require. The Act, speaking directly to the States *qua* States, requires that they shall pay all but an extremely limited minority of their employees the minimum wage rates currently chosen by Congress. It may well be that as a matter of economic policy it would be desirable that States, just as private employers, comply with these minimum wage requirements. But it cannot be gainsaid that the federal requirement directly supplants the considered policy choices of the States' elected officials and administrators as to how they wish to structure pay scales in state employment. The State might wish to employ persons with little or no training, or those who wish to work on a casual basis, or those who for some other reason do not possess minimum employment requirements, and pay them less than the federally prescribed minimum wage. It may wish to offer part time or summer employment to teenagers at a figure less than the minimum wage, and if unable to do so may decline to offer such employment at all. But the Act would forbid such choices by the States. The only "discretion" left to them under the Act is either to attempt to increase their revenue to meet the additional financial burden imposed upon them by paying congressionally prescribed wages to their existing complement of employees, or to reduce that complement to a number which can be paid the federal minimum wage without increasing revenue.

This dilemma presented by the minimum wage restrictions may seem not immediately different from that faced by private employers, who have long been covered by the Act and who must find ways to increase their gross income if they are to pay higher wages while maintaining current earnings. The difference, however is that a State is not merely a factor in the "shifting economic arrangements" of the private sector of the economy, Kovacs v. Cooper, 336 U.S. 77, 95 (1949) (Frankfurter, J., concurring), but is itself a coordinate element in the system established by the framers for governing our Federal Union.

The degree to which the FLSA amendments would interfere with traditional aspects of state sovereignty can be seen even more clearly upon examining the overtime requirements of the Act. The general effect of these provisions is to require the States to pay their employees at premium rates whenever their work exceeds a specified number of hours in a given period. The asserted reason for these provisions is to provide a financial disincentive upon using employees beyond the work period deemed appropriate by Congress. . . . We do not doubt that this may be a salutary result, and that it has a sufficiently rational relationship to commerce to validate the application of the overtime provisions to private employers. But, like the minimum wage provisions, the vice of the Act as sought to be applied here is that it directly penalizes the States for choosing to hire governmental employees on terms different from those which Congress has sought to impose.

This congressionally imposed displacement of state decisions may substantially restructure traditional ways in which the local governments have arranged their affairs. . . .

Our examination of the effect of the 1974 amendments, as sought to be extended to the States and their political subdivisions, satisfies us that both the minimum wage and the maximum hour provisions will impermissibly interfere with the integral governmental functions of these bodies. We earlier noted some disagreement between the parties regarding the precise effect the amendments will have in application. We do not believe particularized assessments of actual impact are crucial to resolution of the issue presented, however. For even if we accept appellee's assessments concerning the impact of the amendments, their application will nonetheless significantly alter or displace the States' abilities to structure employer-employee relationships in such areas as fire prevention, police protection, sanitation, public health, and parks and recreation. These activities are typical of those performed by state and local governments in discharging their dual functions of administering the public law and furnishing public services.[16] Indeed, it is functions such as these which governments are created to provide, services such as these which the States have traditionally afforded their citizens. If Congress may withdraw from the States the authority to make those fundamental employment decisions upon which their systems for performance of these functions must rest, we think there would be little left of the States' "separate and independent existence." *Coyle,* 221 U.S., at 580. Thus, even if appellants may have overestimated the effect which the Act will have upon their current levels and patterns of governmental activity, the dispositive factor is that Congress has attempted to exercise its Commerce Clause authority to prescribe minimum wages and maximum hours to be paid by the States in their capacities as sovereign governments. In so doing, Congress has sought to wield its power in a fashion that would impair the States' "ability to function effectively within a federal system," *Fry,* 421 U.S., at 547 n.7. This exercise of congressional authority does not comport with the federal system of government embodied in the Constitution. We hold that insofar as the challenged amendments operate to directly displace the States' freedom to structure integral operations in areas of traditional governmental functions, they are not within the authority granted Congress by Art. I, § 8, cl. 3.[17]

---

[16] These examples are obviously not an exhaustive catalogue of the numerous line and support activities which are well within the area of traditional operations of state and local governments.

[17] We express no view as to whether different results might obtain if Congress seeks to affect integral operations of state governments by exercising authority granted it under other sections of the Constitution such as the spending power. Art. I, § 8, cl. 1, or § 5 of the Fourteenth Amendment.

III.

One final matter requires our attention. Appellee has vigorously urged that we cannot, consistently with the Court's decisions in Maryland v. Wirtz, 392 U.S. 183 (1968), and *Fry,* supra, rule against him here. It is important to examine this contention so that it will be clear what we hold today, and what we do not.

With regard to *Fry,* we disagree with appellee. There the Court held that the Economic Stabilization Act of 1970 was constitutional as applied to temporarily freeze the wages of state and local government employees. The Court expressly noted that the degree of intrusion upon the protected area of state sovereignty was in that case even less than that worked by the amendments to the FLSA which were before the Court in *Wirtz.* The Court recognized that the Economic Stabilization Act was "an emergency measure to counter severe inflation that threatened the national economy." 421 U.S., at 548.

We think our holding today quite consistent with *Fry.* The enactment at issue there was occasioned by an extremely serious problem which endangered the well-being of all the component parts of our federal system and which only collective action by the National Government might forestall. The means selected were carefully drafted so as not to interfere with the States' freedom beyond a very limited, specific period of time. The effect of the across-the-board freeze authorized by that Act, moreover, displaced no state choices as to how governmental operations should be structured nor did it force the States to remake such choices themselves. Instead, it merely required that the wage scales and employment relationships which the States themselves had chosen be maintained during the period of the emergency. Finally, the Economic Stabilization Act operated to reduce the pressures upon state budgets rather than increase them. These factors distinguish the statute in *Fry* from the provisions at issue here. The limits imposed upon the commerce power when Congress seeks to apply it to the States are not so inflexible as to preclude temporary enactments tailored to combat a national emergency. "[A]lthough an emergency may not call into life a power which has never lived, nevertheless emergency may afford a reason for the exertion of a living power already enjoyed." Wilson v. New, 243 U.S. 332, 348 (1917).

With respect to the Court's decision in *Wirtz,* we reach a different conclusion. Both appellee and the District Court thought that decision required rejection of appellants' claims. Appellants, in turn, advance several arguments by which they seek to distinguish the facts before the Court in *Wirtz* from those presented by the 1974 amendments to the Act. There are undoubtedly factual distinctions between the two situations, but in view of the conclusions expressed earlier in this opinion we do not believe the reasoning in *Wirtz* may any longer be regarded as authoritative.

Wirtz relied heavily on the Court's decision in United States v. California, 297 U.S. 175 (1936). The opinion quotes the following language from that case:

> "'[We] look to the activities to which the states have traditionally engaged as marking the boundary of the restriction upon the federal taxing power. But there is no such limitation upon the plenary power to regulate commerce. The State can no more deny the power if its exercise has been authorized by Congress than can an individual.' 297 U.S., at 185." 392 U.S., at 198.

But we have reaffirmed today that the States as States stand on a quite different footing than an individual or a corporation when challenging the exercise of Congress' power to regulate commerce. We think the dicta [18] from United States v. California, simply wrong. Congress may not exercise that power so as to force directly upon the States its choices as to how essential decisions regarding the conduct of integral governmental functions are to be made. We agree that such assertions of power, if unchecked, would indeed, as Mr. Justice Douglas cautioned in his dissent in *Wirtz*, allow "the National Government [to] devour the essentials of state sovereignty." 392 U.S., at 205, and would therefore transgress the bounds of the authority granted Congress under the Commerce Clause. While there are obvious differences between the schools and hospitals involved in *Wirtz*, and the fire and police departments affected here, each provides an integral portion of those governmental services which the States and their political subdivisions have traditionally afforded their citizens.[20] We are therefore persuaded that *Wirtz* must be overruled.

The judgment of the District Court is accordingly reversed and the cases are remanded for further proceedings consistent with this opinion.

So ordered.

Mr. Justice Blackmun, concurring.

The Court's opinion and the dissents indicate the importance and significance of this case as it bears upon the relationship between the Federal Government and our States. Although I am not untroubled by certain possible implications of the Court's opinion—some of them suggested by the dissents—I do not read the opinion so despairingly as does my Brother Brennan. In my view, the result with respect to the statute under challenge here is necessarily correct. I may misinterpret the Court's opinion, but it seems to me that it adopts a balancing approach, and does not outlaw federal power in areas such as environmental protection, where the federal interest is demonstrably greater and where state facility compliance with imposed federal standards would be essential. . . . With this understanding on my part of the Court's opinion, I join it.

Mr. Justice Brennan, with whom Mr. Justice White and Mr. Justice Marshall join, dissenting.

The Court concedes, as of course it must, that Congress enacted the 1974 amendments pursuant to its exclusive power under Art. I, § 8, cl. 3, of the Constitution "To regulate Commerce . . . among the several States." It must therefore be surprising that my Brethren should choose this Bicentennial year of our independence to repudiate principles governing judicial interpreta-

---

[18] The holding of United States v. California, as opposed to the language quoted in the text, is quite consistent with our holding today. There California's activity to which the congressional command was directed was not in an area that the States have regarded as integral parts of their governmental activities. It was, on the contrary, the operation of a railroad engaged in "common carriage by rail in interstate commerce . . . ." 297 U.S., at 182.

For the same reasons, despite Mr. Justice Brennan's claims to the contrary, the holdings in Parden v. Terminal R. Co., 377 U.S. 184 (1964), and California v. Taylor, 353 U.S. 553 (1957), are likewise unimpaired by our decision today. It also seems appropriate to note that Case v. Bowles, 327 U.S. 92 (1946), has not been overruled as the dissent asserts. Indeed that decision, upon which our Brother heavily relies, has no direct application to the questions we consider today at all. For there the Court sustained an application of the Emergency Price Control Act to a sale of timber by the State of Washington, expressly noting that the "only question is whether the State's power to make the sales must be in subordination to the power of Congress to fix maximum prices in order to carry on war." Id. at 102. The Court rejected the State's claim of immunity on the ground that sustaining it would impermissibly "impair a prime purpose of the Federal Government's establishment." Ibid. Nothing we say in this opinion addresses the scope of Congress' authority under its war power. Cf. n. 17, supra.

[20] As the denomination "political subdivision" implies, the local governmental units which Congress sought to bring within the Act derive their authority and power from their respective States. Interference with integral governmental services provided by such subordinate arms of a state government is therefore beyond the reach of congressional power under the Commerce Clause just as if such services were provided by the State itself.

tion of our Constitution settled since the time of Mr. Chief Justice John Marshall, discarding his postulate that the Constitution contemplates that restraints upon exercise by Congress of its plenary commerce power lie in the political process and not in the judicial process.   . . .

. . .

. . . This Court is simply not at liberty to erect a mirror of its own conception of a desirable governmental structure.   If the 1974 amendments have any "vice," my Brother Stevens is surely right that it represents "merely . . . a policy issue which has been firmly resolved by the branches of government having power to decide such questions."   It bears repeating "that effective restraints on . . . exercise [of the commerce power] must proceed from political rather than from judicial processes."   Wickard v. Filburn, 317 U.S., at 120.

It is unacceptable that the judicial process should be thought superior to the political process in this area.   Under the Constitution the judiciary has no role to play beyond finding that Congress has not made an unreasonable legislative judgment respecting what is "commerce."   My Brother Blackmun suggests that controlling judicial supervision of the relationship between the States and our National Government by use of a balancing approach diminishes the ominous implications of today's decision.   Such an approach, however, is a thinly veiled rationalization for judicial supervision of a policy judgment that our system of government reserves to Congress.

Judicial restraint in this area merely recognizes that the political branches of our Government are structured to protect the interests of the States, as well as the Nation as a whole, and that the States are fully able to protect their own interests in the premises.   . . .

We are left then with a catastrophic judicial body blow at Congress' power under the Commerce Clause.   Even if Congress may nevertheless accomplish its objectives—for example by conditioning grants of federal funds upon compliance with federal minimum wage and overtime standards, cf. Oklahoma v. CSC, 330 U.S. 127, 144 (1947)—there is an ominous portent of disruption of our constitutional structure implicit in today's mischievous decision.   I dissent.

Mr. Justice Stevens, dissenting.

The Court holds that the Federal Government may not interfere with a sovereign state's inherent right to pay a substandard wage to the janitor at the state capitol.   The principle on which the holding rests is difficult to perceive.

The Federal Government may, I believe, require the State to act impartially when it hires or fires the janitor, to withhold taxes from his pay check, to observe safety regulations when he is performing his job, to forbid him from burning too much soft coal in the capitol furnace, from dumping untreated refuse in an adjacent waterway, from overloading a state-owned garbage truck or from driving either the truck or the governor's limousine over 55 miles an hour.   Even though these and many other activities of the capitol janitor are activities of the State *qua* State, I have no doubt that they are subject to federal regulation.

I agree that it is unwise for the Federal Government to exercise its power in the ways described in the Court's opinion.   For the proposition that regulation of the minimum price of a commodity—even labor—will increase the quantity consumed is not one that I can readily understand.   That concern, however, applies with even greater force to the private sector of the economy where the exclusion of the marginally employable does the greatest harm and, in all events, merely reflects my views on a policy issue which has been firmly resolved by the branches of government having power to decide such questions. As far as the complexities of adjusting police and fire departments to this sort of federal control are concerned, I presume that appropriate tailor-made regulations would soon solve their most pressing problems. After all, the interests adversely affected by this legislation are not without political power.

My disagreement with the wisdom of this legislation may not, of course, affect my judgment with respect to its validity. On this issue there is no dissent from the proposition that the Federal Government's power over the labor market is adequate to embrace these employees. Since I am unable to identify a limitation on that federal power that would not also invalidate federal regulation of state activities that I consider unquestionably permissible, I am persuaded that this statute is valid. Accordingly, with respect and a great deal of sympathy for the views expressed by the Court, I dissent from its constitutional holding.

UNITED TRANSPORTATION UNION v. LONG ISLAND RAILROAD CO., 455 U.S. 678 (1982). The Court held that a state-owned railroad was not immune from application of the federal Railway Labor Act, reaffirming United States v. California, 297 U.S. 175 (1936), California v. Taylor, 353 U.S. 553 (1957), and Parden v. Terminal Railway Co., 377 U.S. 184 (1964). Chief Justice Burger, writing for a unanimous Court, emphasized that the key question in applying National League of Cities v. Usery was whether state compliance with federal law impaired a state's ability "to structure integral operations in areas of traditional functions." He explained that the emphasis on *traditional* state functions was not meant to impose a static historical view of state functions immune from federal regulation, but was meant to focus inquiry on whether federal regulation "would be likely to hamper the state government's ability to fulfill its role in the Union." Nevertheless, the opinion relied on the lengthy history of federal railroad regulation, and the historical absence of state regulation of collective bargaining in the railroad industry. "To allow individual States, by acquiring railroads, to circumvent the federal system of railroad bargaining, or any of the other elements of federal regulation of railroads, would destroy the uniformity thought essential by Congress and would endanger the efficient operation of the interstate rail system."

EQUAL EMPLOYMENT OPPORTUNITY COMMISSION
v. WYOMING

460 U.S. 226, 103 S.Ct. 1054, 75 L.Ed.2d 18 (1983).

Justice Brennan delivered the opinion of the Court.

Under the Age Discrimination in Employment Act of 1967, 81 Stat. 602, as amended, 29 U.S.C. § 621 et seq. (1976 ed. and Supp. IV) (ADEA or Act), it is unlawful for an employer to discriminate against any employee or potential employee on the basis of age, except "where age is a bona fide occupational qualification reasonably necessary to the normal operation of the particular business, or where the differentiation is based on reasonable factors other than age." The question presented in this case is whether Congress acted constitutionally when, in 1974, it extended the definition of "employer" under § 11(b) of the Act to include state and local governments. The United States District Court for the District of Wyoming, in an enforcement action brought by the Equal Employment Opportunity Commission (EEOC or Commission), held that, at least as applied to certain classes of state workers, the extension was unconstitutional. 514 F.Supp. 595 (1981). The Commission filed a direct appeal under 28 U.S.C. § 1252, and we noted probable jurisdiction.

We now reverse.

I

.   .   .

.   .   .   The provisions of the Act as relevant here prohibited various forms of age discrimination in employment, including the discharge of workers on the basis of their age. Section 4(a), 29 U.S.C. § 623(a). The protection of the Act was limited, however, to workers between the ages of 40 and 65, § 12(a), 29 U.S.C. § 631, raised to age in 70 in 1978, Age Discrimination in Employment Act Amendments of 1978, § 3, 92 Stat. 189. Moreover, in order to insure that employers were permitted to use neutral criteria not directly dependent on age, and in recognition of the fact that even criteria that are based on age are occasionally justified, the Act provided that certain otherwise prohibited employment practices would not be unlawful "where age is a bona fide occupational qualification reasonably necessary to the normal operation of the particular business, or where the differentiation is based on reasonable factors other than age." Section 4(f)(1), 29 U.S.C. § 623(f)(1).

The ADEA, as originally passed in 1967, did not apply to the Federal Government, to the States or their political subdivisions, or to employers with fewer than 25 employees. .   .   .   In 1974, Congress extended the substantive prohibitions of the Act to employers having at least 20 workers, and to the Federal and State Governments.

II

Prior to the district court decision in this case, every federal court that considered the question upheld the constitutionality of the 1974 extension of the Age Discrimination in Employment Act to state and local workers as an exercise of Congress's power under either the Commerce Clause or § 5 of the Fourteenth Amendment.

This case arose out of the involuntary retirement at age 55 of Bill Crump, a District Game Division supervisor for the Wyoming Game and Fish Department. Crump's dismissal was based on a Wyoming statute that conditions further employment for Game and Fish Wardens who reach the age of 55 on "the approval of [their] employer." Crump filed a complaint with the EEOC, alleging that the Game and Fish Department had violated the Age Discrimination in Employment Act. .   .   .

.   .   .

III

The appellees have not claimed either in the District Court or in this Court that Congress exceeded the scope of its affirmative grant of power under the Commerce Clause in enacting the ADEA. .   .   .   Rather, the District Court held and appellees argue that, at least with respect to state game wardens, application of the ADEA to the States is precluded by virtue of external constraints imposed on Congress's commerce powers by the Tenth Amendment.

A

.   .   .

Hodel v. Virginia Surface Mining & Reclamation Assn., Inc., [452 U.S. 264 (1981)], summarized the hurdles that confront any claim that a state or local governmental unit should be immune from an otherwise legitimate exercise of the federal power to regulate commerce: .   .   .   The first requirement—that the challenged federal statute regulate the "States as States"—is plainly met in this case. The second requirement—that the federal statute address an "undoubted attribute of state sovereignty"—poses significantly more difficulties.

We need not definitively resolve this issue, however, nor do we have any occasion to reach the final balancing step of the inquiry described in *Hodel,* for we are convinced that, even if Wyoming's decision to impose forced retirement on its game wardens does involve the exercise of an attribute of state sovereignty, the Age Discrimination in Employment Act does not "directly impair" the State's ability to "structure integral operations in areas of traditional governmental functions."

B

The management of state parks is clearly a traditional state function. *National League of Cities,* supra, at 851. As we have already emphasized, however, the purpose of the doctrine of immunity articulated in *National League of Cities* was to protect States from federal intrusions that might threaten their "separate and independent existence." Ibid. Our decision as to whether the federal law at issue here directly impairs the States' ability to structure their integral operations must therefore depend, as it did in *National League of Cities* itself, on considerations of degree. . . . We conclude that the degree of federal intrusion in this case is sufficiently less serious than it was in *National League of Cities* so as to make it unnecessary for us to override Congress's express choice to extend its regulatory authority to the States.

In this case, appellees claim no substantial stake in their retirement policy other than "assur[ing] the physical preparedness of Wyoming game wardens to perform their duties." Under the ADEA, however, the State may still, at the very least, assess the fitness of its game wardens and dismiss those wardens whom it reasonably finds to be unfit. Put another way, the Act requires the State to achieve its goals in a more individualized and careful manner than would otherwise be the case, but it does not require the State to abandon those goals, or to abandon the public policy decisions underlying them. . . .

Perhaps more important, appellees remain free under the ADEA to continue to do *precisely what they are doing now,* if they can demonstrate that age is a "bona fide occupational qualification" for the job of game warden. Thus, in distinct contrast to the situation in *National League of Cities,* . . . even the State's discretion to achieve its goals *in the way it thinks best* is not being overridden entirely, but is merely being tested against a reasonable federal standard.

Finally, the Court's concern in *National League of Cities* was not only with the effect of the federal regulatory scheme on the particular decisions it was purporting to regulate, but also with the potential impact of that scheme on the States' ability to structure operations and set priorities over a wide range of decisions. . . . Indeed, *National League of Cities* spelled out in some detail how application of the federal wage and hour statute to the States threatened a virtual chain reaction of substantial and almost certainly unintended consequential effects on state decisionmaking. . . . Nothing in this case, however, portends anything like the same wide-ranging and profound threat to the structure of State governance.

The most tangible consequential effect identified in *National League of Cities* was financial: forcing the States to pay their workers a minimum wage and an overtime rate would leave them with less money for other vital state programs. The test of such financial effect as drawn in *National League of Cities* does not depend, however, on "particularized assessments of actual impact," which may vary from State to State and time to time, but on a more generalized inquiry, essentially legal rather than factual, into the direct and obvious effect of the federal legislation on the ability of the States to allocate their resources. . . . In this case, we cannot conclude from the nature of the ADEA that it will have either a direct or an obvious negative effect on state finances. Older workers with seniority may tend to get paid more than the younger workers without seniority, and may by their continued employment accrue increased benefits when they do retire.   But these increased costs, even if they were not largely speculative in their own right, might very well be outweighed by a number of other factors: Those same older workers, as long as they remain employed, will not have to be paid any pension benefits at all, and will continue to contribute to the pension fund.   And, when they do retire, they will likely, as an actuarial matter, receive benefits for fewer years than workers who retire early.   Admittedly, as some of the *amici* point out, the costs of certain state health and other benefit plans would increase if they were automatically extended to older workers now forced to retire at an early age.   But Congress, in passing the ADEA, included a provision specifically disclaiming a construction of the Act which would require that the health and similar benefits received by older workers be in all respects identical to those received by younger workers. ADEA § 4(f)(2), 29 U.S.C. § 623(f)(2) (1976 ed. and Supp. IV).

The second consequential effect identified in *National League of Cities* was on the States' ability to use their employment relationship with their citizens as a tool for pursuing social and economic policies beyond their immediate managerial goals.   See, e.g., 426 U.S., at 848 (offering jobs at below the minimum wage to persons who do not possess "minimum employment requirements"). Appellees, however, have claimed no such purposes for Wyoming's involuntary retirement statute.   Moreover, whatever broader social or economic purposes could be imagined for this particular Wyoming statute would not, we are convinced, bring with them either the breadth or the importance of the state policies identified in *National League of Cities.*

IV

The extension of the ADEA to cover state and local governments, both on its face and as applied in this case, was a valid exercise of Congress's powers under the Commerce Clause.   We need not decide whether it could also be upheld as an exercise of Congress's powers under § 5 of the Fourteenth Amendment.[18]   The judgment of the District Court is reversed, and the case is remanded for further proceedings consistent with this opinion.[a]

So ordered.

Justice Stevens, concurring.

While I join the Court's opinion, a complete explanation of my appraisal of the case requires these additional comments about the larger perspective in which I view the underlying issues.

[18] We do reaffirm that when properly exercising its power under § 5, Congress is not limited by the same Tenth Amendment constraints that circumscribe the exercise of its Commerce Clause powers. City of Rome v. United States, 446 U.S. 156, 179 (1980).   We also note that, whatever else may be said about the § 5 question in this case, the District Court erred in reading Pennhurst State School v. Halderman, 451 U.S. 1 (1981), as holding that Congressional action could not be upheld on the basis of § 5 unless Congress "expressly articulated its intent to legislate under § 5," and in disposing of the § 5 argument on the sole basis that "nothing in the 1974   .   .   .   Amendments [to the ADEA] or their legislative history   .   .   .   suggest[s] that Congress acted pursuant to any other power than the Commerce Clause," 514 F.Supp., at 600.

It is in the nature of our review of congressional legislation defended on the basis of Congress's powers under § 5 of the Fourteenth Amendment that we be able to discern some legislative purpose or factual predicate that supports the exercise of that power.   That does not mean, however, that Congress need anywhere recite the words "section 5" or "Fourteenth Amendment" or "equal protection," see e.g., Fullilove v. Klutznick, 448 U.S. 448, 476–478 (1980) (Burger, C.J.), for "[t]he constitutionality of action taken by Congress does not depend on recitals of the power which it undertakes to exercise."   Woods v. Miller, 333 U.S. 138, 144 (1948).

[a] The scope of Congress' power to constrain states under § 5 of the Fourteenth Amendment is discussed, infra beginning at p. 1040.

I

There have been occasions when the Court has given a miserly construction to the Commerce Clause. But as the needs of a dynamic and constantly expanding national economy have changed, this Court has construed the Commerce Clause to reflect the intent of the Framers of the Constitution—to confer a power on the national government adequate to discharge its central mission. In this process the Court has repeatedly repudiated cases that had narrowly construed the clause. The development of judicial doctrine has accommodated the transition from a purely local, to a regional, and ultimately to a national economy. Today, of course, our economy is merely a part of an international mechanism no single nation could possibly regulate.

. . .

Congress may not, of course, transcend specific limitations on its exercise of the commerce power that are imposed by other provisions of the Constitution. But there is no limitation in the text of the Constitution that is even arguably applicable to this case. . . . I believe that the law would be well served by a prompt rejection of *National League of Cities'* modern embodiment of the spirit of the Articles of Confederation.

II

My conviction that Congress had ample power to enact this statute, as well as the statute at issue in *National League of Cities,* is unrelated to my views about the merits of either piece of legislation. As I intimated in my dissent in that case, I believe that federal regulation that enhances the minimum price of labor inevitably reduces the number of jobs available to people who are ready, willing, and able to engage in productive work—and thereby aggravates rather than ameliorates our unemployment problems. I also believe, contrary to the popular view, that the burdens imposed on the national economy by legislative prohibitions against mandatory retirement on account of age exceed the potential benefits. My personal views on such matters are, however, totally irrelevant to the judicial task I am obligated to perform. . . .

The question in this case is purely one of constitutional power. In exercising its power to regulate the national market for the services of individuals—either by prescribing the minimum price for such services or by prohibiting employment discrimination on account of age—may Congress regulate both the public sector and the private sector of that market, or must it confine its regulation to the private sector? If the power is to be adequate to enable the national government to perform its central mission, that question can have only one answer.

Chief Justice Burger, with whom Justice Powell, Justice Rehnquist, and Justice O'Connor join, dissenting.

The Court decides today that Congress may dictate to the states, and their political subdivisions, detailed standards governing the selection of state employees, including those charged with protecting people and homes from crimes and fires. Although the opinion reads the Constitution to allow Congress to usurp this fundamental state function, I have reexamined that document and I fail to see where it grants to the national government the power to impose such strictures on the states either expressly or by implication. Those strictures are not required by any holding of this Court, and it is not wholly without significance that Congress has not placed similar limits on itself in the exercise of its own sovereign powers. Accordingly, I would hold the Age Discrimination in Employment Act (Age Act) unconstitutional as applied to the states, and affirm the judgment of the District Court.

I

I begin by analyzing the Commerce Clause rationale, for it was upon this power that Congress expressly relied when it originally enacted the Age Act in 1967, see 29 U.S.C. § 621, and when it extended its protections to state and local government employers, see H.R.Rep. No. 93–913, 93d Cong., 2d Sess. 1–2 (1974).

.   .   .

The third prong of the *National League of Cities* test is that the federal intrusion must impair the ability of the state to structure integral operations. Wyoming cites several ways in which the Age Act interferes with its ability to structure state services, and several *amici* inform us of additional difficulties, some economic, some not, that are engendered by the Act.

It is beyond dispute that the statute can give rise to increased employment costs caused by forced employment of older individuals. Since these employees tend to be at the upper end of the pay scale, the cost of their wages while they are still in the work force is greater. And since most pension plans calculate retirement benefits on the basis of maximum salary or number of years of service, pension costs are greater when an older employee retires. The employer is also forced to pay more for insuring the health of older employees because, as a group, they inevitably carry a higher-than-average risk of illness. .   .   . Since they are—especially in law enforcement—also more prone to on-the-job injuries, it is reasonable to conclude that the employer's disability costs are increased. .   .   .

Non-economic hardships are equally severe. Employers are prevented from hiring those physically best able to do the job. Since older workers occupy a disproportionate share of the upper-level and supervisory positions, a bar on mandatory retirement also impedes promotion opportunities. Lack of such opportunities tends to undermine younger employees' incentive to strive for excellence, and impedes the state from fulfilling affirmative action objectives.

.   .   . I find it impossible to say that § 623(f)(1) provides an adequate method for avoiding significant impairment to the state's ability to structure its integral governmental operations.

Since I am satisfied that the Age Act runs afoul of the three prongs of the *National League of Cities* test, I turn to the balancing test alluded to in Justice Blackmun's concurring opinion in *National League of Cities,* and in *Hodel.* The Commission argues that the federal interest in preventing unnecessary demands on the social security system and other maintenance programs, in protecting employees from arbitrary discrimination, and in eliminating unnecessary burdens on the free flow of commerce "is more than sufficient in the face of Wyoming's bald assertion of a prerogative to be arbitrary."

It is simply not accurate to state that Wyoming is resting its challenge to the Age Act on a "sovereign" right to discriminate; as I read it, Wyoming is asserting a right to set standards to meet local needs. Nor do I believe that these largely theoretical benefits to the Federal Government outweigh the very real danger that a fire may burn out of control because the firefighters are not physically able to cope; or that a criminal may escape because a law-enforcement officer's reflexes are too slow to react swiftly enough to apprehend an offender; or that an officer may be injured or killed for want of capacity to defend himself. These factors may not be real to Congress but it is not Congress' responsibility to prevent them; they are nonetheless real to the states. I would hold that Commerce Clause powers are wholly insufficient to bar the states from dealing with or preventing these dangers in a rational manner. Wyoming's solution is plainly a rational means.

II

Since it was ratified after the Tenth Amendment, the Fourteenth Amendment is not subject to the constraints discussed earlier in connection with the Commerce Clause. Indeed, it is well established that Congress may, under the powers bestowed by § 5, enact legislation affecting the states, Ex Parte Virginia, 100 U.S. 339, 345 (1880); Fitzpatrick v. Bitzer, 427 U.S. 445 (1976). But this does not mean that Congress has been given a "blank check" to intrude into details of states' governments at will. The Tenth Amendment was not, after all repealed when the Fourteenth Amendment was ratified: it was merely limited. The question then becomes whether the Fourteenth Amendment operates to transfer from the states to the Federal Government the essentially local governmental function of deciding who will protect citizens from lawbreakers.

The outer reaches of congressional power under the civil war amendments have always been uncertain. One factor is, however, clear: Congress may act only where a violation lurks. The flaw in the Commission's analysis is that in this instance, no one—not the Court, not the Congress—has determined that mandatory retirement plans violate any rights protected by these amendments. We cannot say that the Judiciary made this determination, for we have considered the constitutionality of mandatory retirement schemes twice, in Massachusetts Board of Retirement v. Murgia, 427 U.S. 307 (1976), for state police, and Vance v. Bradley, 440 U.S. 93 (1979), for Foreign Service officers; we rejected both equal protection challenges. In both instances, we arrived at our conclusion by examining, *arguendo,* the retirement schemes under the rational-basis standard. It was not necessary that we be convinced that equal protection guarantees extend to classes defined by age because governmental employment is not a fundamental right and those who are mandatorily retired are not a suspect class.

. . .

Nor can appellant claim that Congress has used the powers we recognized in City of Rome v. United States, 446 U.S. 156, 176–177 (1980); Oregon v. Mitchell, supra; Jones v. Alfred H. Mayer Co., 392 U.S. 409, 437–444 (1968); South Carolina v. Katzenbach, 383 U.S. 301 (1966); Katzenbach v. Morgan, 384 U.S. 641 (1966), to enact legislation that prohibits conduct not in itself unconstitutional because it considered the prohibition necessary to guard against encroachment of guaranteed rights or to rectify past discrimination. There has been no finding, as there was in South Carolina v. Katzenbach, supra, at 309, that the abrogated state law infringed on rights identified by this Court.[7] Nor did Congress use, as it did in Katzenbach v. Morgan, supra, 384 U.S., at 656, its "specially informed legislative competence" to decide that the state law it invalidated was too intrusive on federal rights to be an appropriate means to achieve the ends sought by the state. Instead, the Age Act can be sustained only if we assume first, that Congress can define rights wholly independently of

---

[7] At oral argument, the Solicitor General argued that in applying the rational-basis test in *Murgia* and *Bradley,* the Court *sub silentio* agreed that age discrimination is protected by the Equal Protection Clause, and that Congress has merely altered the burden needed to prove compliance with its guarantees. I do not read these decisions to support this notion. *Murgia* and *Bradley* presented us with no occasion to determine the scope of the equal protection guarantee because we found the legislation challenged there sustainable even if we assumed the class was protected.

This is not to say definitively that age discrimination is not protected by the Fourteenth Amendment because this case does not squarely raise that issue. Rather, I am pointing out that since this Court has not decided the question, the Government cannot support this enactment on the ground that Congress was attempting to establish further safeguards for a class we have found to be constitutionally protected.

our case law, and second, that Congress has done so here. I agree with neither proposition.

Allowing Congress to protect constitutional rights statutorily that it has independently defined fundamentally alters our scheme of government. Although the South Carolina v. Katzenbach line of cases may be read to allow Congress a degree of flexibility in deciding what the Fourteenth Amendment safeguards, I have always read Oregon v. Mitchell as finally imposing a limitation on the extent to which Congress may substitute its own judgment for that of the states and assume this Court's "role of final arbiter," *Mitchell,* at 205 (Harlan, J., dissenting). *Mitchell,* after all, involved legislation in the area of suffrage, where Congress had special competence and special reasons to limit the powers of the states. It is significant, however, that while we there sustained the portions of the Voting Rights Act of 1970 lowering the minimum age of voters from 21 to 18 in federal elections, barring literacy tests in state and federal elections, and forbidding states from disqualifying voters in presidential elections for failure to meet state residency requirements, a majority of the *Mitchell* Court did not agree to allow Congress to alter voting requirements in *state* elections. We struck that portion of the Voting Rights Act because we thought it a "plain fact of history" that Congress lacked this power, see id., at 125 and 294 (Black and Stewart, JJ.); id., 400 U.S., at 154–215 (Harlan, J.); and because we thought that the Fourteenth Amendment was not a license to "overstep the letter or spirit of any constitutional restriction," id., 400 U.S., at 287 (Stewart, J.).

For me, this same reasoning leads inevitably to the conclusion that Congress lacked power to apply the Age Act to the states. There is no hint in the body of the Constitution ratified in 1789 or in the relevant amendments that every classification based on age is outlawed. Yet there is much in the Constitution and the relevant amendments to indicate that states retain sovereign powers not expressly surrendered, and these surely include the power to choose the employees they feel are best able to serve and protect their citizens.[8]

And even were we to assume, *arguendo,* that Congress could redefine the Fourteenth Amendment, I would still reject the power of Congress to impose the Age Act on the states when Congress, in the same year that the Age Act was extended to the states, passed mandatory retirement legislation of its own, Pub. L. 93–350, 88 Stat. 356, codified at 5 U.S.C. § 8335, for law enforcement officers and firefighters. Over eight years have elapsed since the Age Act was extended to the states, yet early retirement is still required of federal air traffic controllers, 5 U.S.C. § 8335(a), federal law enforcement officers, § 8335(b), federal firefighters, id., employees of the Panama Canal Commission and the Alaska Railroad, § 8335(c), members of the Foreign Service, 22 U.S.C. § 4052, and members of the Armed Services, 10 U.S.C. § 1251.

III

. . .

The reserved powers of the states and Justice Brandeis' classic conception of the states as laboratories, New State Ice Co. v. Liebmann, 285 U.S. 262, 311 (1932) (Brandeis, J., dissenting), are turned on their heads when national rather than state governments assert the authority to make decisions on the age

---

[8] It has been suggested that where a congressional resolution of a policy question hinges on legislative facts, the Court should defer to Congress's judgment because Congress is in a better position than the Court to find the relevant facts. Cox, The Role of Congress in Constitutional Determinations, 40 U.Cinn.L.Rev. 187, 229–230 (1971). While this theory may have some importance in matters of strictly federal concern, it has no place in deciding between the legislative judgments of Congress and that of the Wyoming Legislature. Congress is simply not as well equipped as state legislators to make decisions involving purely local needs.

standard of state law enforcement officers. Flexibility for experimentation not only permits each state to find the best solutions to its own problems, it is the means by which each state may profit from the experiences and activities of all the rest. Nothing in the Constitution permits Congress to force the states into a Procrustean national mold that takes no account of local needs and conditions. That is the antithesis of what the authors of the Constitution contemplated for our federal system.

Justice Powell, with whom Justice O'Connor joins, dissenting.

I join The Chief Justice's dissenting opinion, but write separately to record a personal dissent from Justice Stevens' novel view of our Nation's history.

. . .

III

One would never know from the concurring opinion that the Constitution formed a federal system, comprising a national government with delegated powers and state governments that retained a significant measure of sovereign authority. This is clear from the Constitution itself, from the debates surrounding its adoption and ratification, from the early history of our constitutional development, and from the decisions of this Court. It is impossible to believe that the Constitution would have been recommended by the Convention, much less ratified, if it had been understood that the Commerce Clause embodied the national government's "central mission," a mission to be accomplished even at the expense of regulating the personnel practices of state and local governments.

. . . .

IV

Justice Stevens' concurring opinion recognizes no limitation on the ability of Congress to override state sovereignty in exercising its powers under the Commerce Clause. His opinion does not mention explicitly either federalism or state sovereignty. Instead it declares that "[t]he *only* basis for questioning the federal statute at issue here is the pure judicial fiat found in this Court's opinion in National League of Cities v. Usery." Under this view it is not easy to think of any state function—however sovereign—that could not be preempted.

HODEL v. VIRGINIA SURFACE MINING & RECLAMATION AS-SOCIATION, INC., 452 U.S. 264 (1981). The Surface Mining Control and Reclamation Act of 1977 required the Secretary of the Interior to adopt a regulatory program for surface mining of coal in each state, either by a state program meeting minimum federal standards or by adoption of a federal program for states not submitting a qualifying program. The lower federal court, relying on National League of Cities v. Usery, held portions of the Act invalid as interfering with state autonomy. The Supreme Court reversed, concluding that *Usery* was inapplicable since the statute regulated private activity and not the "States as States." On this issue, Justice Marshall's opinion for the Court said in part:

"As the District Court itself acknowledged, the steep-slope provisions of the Surface Mining Act govern only the activities of coal mine operators who are private individuals and businesses. Moreover, the States are not compelled to enforce the steep-slope standards, to expend any state funds, or to participate in the federal regulatory program in any manner whatsoever. If a State does not wish to submit a proposed permanent program that complies with the Act and implementing regulations, the full regulatory burden will be borne by the Federal Government. Thus, there can be no suggestion that the Act commandeers the legislative processes of the States by directly compelling them to enact and enforce a federal regulatory program. Cf. Maryland v. EPA, 530 F.2d 215, 224–228 (CA4 1975), vacated and remanded sub nom. EPA v. Brown, 431 U.S. 99 (1977); . . . The most that can be said is that the Surface Mining Act establishes a program of cooperative federalism that allows the States, within limits established by federal minimum standards, to enact and administer their own regulatory programs, structured to meet their own particular needs. . . . In this respect, the Act resembles a number of other federal statutes that have survived Tenth Amendment challenges in the lower federal courts.

"Appellees argue, however, that the threat of federal usurpation of their regulatory roles coerces the States into enforcing the Surface Mining Act. Appellees also contend that the Act directly regulates the States as States because it establishes mandatory minimum federal standards. In essence, appellees urge us to join the District Court in looking beyond the activities actually regulated by the Act to its conceivable effects on the States' freedom to make decisions in areas of 'integral governmental functions.' And appellees emphasize, as did the court below, that the Act interferes with the States ability to exercise their police powers by regulating land use.

. . . .

". . . Congress could constitutionally have enacted a statute prohibiting any state regulation of surface coal mining. We fail to see why the Surface Mining Act should become constitutionally suspect simply because Congress chose to allow the States a regulatory role. Contrary to the assumption by both the District Court and appellees, nothing in *National League of Cities* suggests that the Tenth Amendment shields the States from pre-emptive federal regulation of *private* activities affecting interstate commerce. To the contrary, *National League of Cities* explicitly reaffirmed the teaching of earlier cases that Congress may, in regulating private activities pursuant to the commerce power, 'pre-empt express state-law determinations contrary to the result which has commended itself to the collective wisdom of Congress. . . .' Id., 426 U.S., at 840. The only limitation on congressional authority in this regard is the requirement that the means selected be reasonably related to the goal of regulating interstate commerce. Ibid. We have already indicated that the Act satisfies this test."

FEDERAL ENERGY REGULATORY COMMISSION v. MISSISSIPPI

456 U.S. 742, 102 S.Ct. 2126, 72 L.Ed.2d 532 (1982).

Justice Blackmun delivered the opinion of the Court.

In this case, appellees successfully challenged the constitutionality of Titles I and III, and of § 210 of Title II, of the Public Utility Regulatory Policies Act of 1978, Pub.L. No. 95–617, 92 Stat. 3117 (PURPA or Act). We conclude that appellees' challenge lacks merit and we reverse the judgment below.

I

On November 9, 1978, President Carter signed PURPA into law. The Act was part of a package of legislation, approved the same day, designed to combat the nationwide energy crisis. . . . Congress . . . determined that conservation by electricity utilities of oil and natural gas was essential to the success of any effort to lessen the country's dependence on foreign oil, to avoid a repetition of the shortage of natural gas that had been experienced in 1977, and to control consumer costs.

[Section 210 of Title II was designed to encourage development of co-generation and small power production facilities. It authorized the FERC to exempt those facilities from certain state regulations that imposed financial burdens discouraging their development. In order to encourage traditional electric companies to purchase and sell power to these non-traditional facilities, FERC was also directed to promulgate rules requiring those purchases and sales. In adopting those regulations, FERC provided that state regulatory commissions must enforce them either by issuing regulations, resolving disputes on a case-by-case basis, or taking any other action reasonably designed to enforce the FERC rules.

Titles I and III require state regulatory agencies to consider specified policies to encourage conservation and optimal use of facilities. These include such approaches as adopting time-of-day, seasonal, and interruptible rates, requiring individual meters in new buildings, and prohibiting utilities from recovering advertising costs from consumers. No state agency is required to adopt these policies but certain procedures are required in the mandated state regulatory proceedings to consider their adoption. For example, there must be public hearings, adequate notice, and a written statement of reasons for action taken. After specifying who may intervene in the administrative proceedings, PURPA further provides that participants may obtain judicial review in state court.]

II

In April 1979, the State of Mississippi and the Mississippi Public Service Commission, appellees here, filed this action in the United States District Court for the Southern District of Mississippi against FERC and the Secretary of Energy, seeking a declaratory judgment that PURPA's Titles I and III and § 210 are unconstitutional. Appellees maintained that PURPA was beyond the scope of congressional power under the Commerce Clause and that it constituted an invasion of state sovereignty in violation of the Tenth Amendment.

Following cross-motions for summary judgment, the District Court, in an unreported opinion, held that in enacting PURPA Congress had exceeded its powers under the Commerce Clause. . . .

Relying on National League of Cities v. Usery, 426 U.S. 833 (1976), the court also concluded that PURPA trenches on state sovereignty. . . .

FERC and the Secretary of Energy appealed directly to this Court pursuant to 28 U.S.C. § 1252. . . .

III

The Commerce Clause

We readily conclude that the District Court's analysis and the appellees' arguments are without merit so far as they concern the Commerce Clause. . . .

IV

The Tenth Amendment

Unlike the Commerce Clause question, the Tenth Amendment issue presented here is somewhat novel. This case obviously is related to National League of Cities v. Usery, 426 U.S. 833 (1976), insofar as both concern principles of state sovereignty. But there is a significant difference as well. *National League of Cities,* like Fry v. United States, 421 U.S. 542 (1975), presented a problem the Court often confronts: the extent to which state sovereignty shields the States from generally applicable federal regulations. In PURPA, in contrast, the Federal Government attempts to use state regulatory machinery to advance federal goals. To an extent, this presents an issue of first impression.

PURPA, for all its complexity, contains essentially three requirements: (1) § 210 has the States enforce standards promulgated by FERC; (2) Titles I and III direct the States to consider specified rate-making standards; and (3) those Titles impose certain procedures on state commissions. We consider these three requirements in turn:

A. Section 210. On its face, this appears to be the most intrusive of PURPA's provisions. The question of its constitutionality, however, is the easiest to resolve. Insofar as § 210 authorizes FERC to exempt qualified power facilities from "State laws and regulations," it does nothing more than pre-empt conflicting state enactments in the traditional way. Clearly, Congress can pre-empt the States completely in the regulation of retail sales by electricity and gas utilities and in the regulation of transactions between such utilities and cogenerators. . . . The propriety of this type of regulation—so long as it is a valid exercise of the commerce power—was made clear in *National League of Cities,* and was reaffirmed in Hodel v. Virginia Surface Min. & Recl. Assn.: the Federal Government may displace state regulation even though this serves to "curtail or prohibit the States' prerogatives to make legislative choices respecting subjects the States may consider important. 452 U.S., at 290.

Section 210's requirement that "each State regulatory authority shall, after notice and opportunity for public hearing, *implement* such rule (or revised rule) for each electric utility for which it has ratemaking authority," 16 U.S.C. § 824a-3(f)(1) (emphasis added), is more troublesome. The statute's substantive provisions require electricity utilities to purchase electricity from, and to sell it to, qualifying cogenerator and small power production facilities. § 824a-3(a). Yet FERC has declared that state commissions may implement this by, among other things, "an undertaking to resolve disputes between qualifying facilities and electric utilities arising under [PURPA]." 18 CFR § 292.401(a) (1980). In essence, then, the statute and the implementing regulations simply require the Mississippi authorities to adjudicate disputes arising under the statute. Dispute resolution of this kind is the very type of activity customarily engaged in by the Mississippi Public Service Commission. . . .

Testa v. Katt, 330 U.S. 386 (1947), is instructive and controlling on this point. There, the Emergency Price Control Act, 56 Stat. 34, as amended, created a treble damages remedy, and gave jurisdiction over claims under the Act to state as well as federal courts. The courts of Rhode Island refused to entertain such claims, although they heard analogous state causes of action. This Court upheld the federal program. It observed that state courts have a unique role in enforcing the body of federal law, and that the Rhode Island courts had "jurisdiction adequate and appropriate under established local law to adjudicate this action." 330 U.S., at 394. Thus the state courts were directed to heed the constitutional command that "the policy of the federal Act is the prevailing policy in every state," id., at 393, " 'and should be respected accordingly in the courts of the State.' " Id., at 392, quoting Mondou v. New York, N.H. & H.R. Co., 223 U.S. 1, 57, (1912).

So it is here. The Mississippi Commission has jurisdiction to entertain claims analogous to those granted by PURPA, and it can satisfy § 210's requirements simply by opening its doors to claimants. That the Commission has administrative as well as judicial duties is of no significance. Any other conclusion would allow the States to disregard both the preeminent position held by federal law throughout the Nation, cf. Martin v. Hunter's Lessee, 1 Wheat. 304, 340–341 (1816), and the congressional determination that the federal rights granted by PURPA can appropriately be enforced through state adjudicatory machinery. Such an approach, *Testa* emphasized, "flies in the face of the fact that the States of the Union constitute a nation," and "disregards the purpose and effect of Article VI of the Constitution." 330 U.S., at 389.

B. Mandatory Consideration of Standards. We acknowledge that "the authority to make . . . fundamental . . . decisions" is perhaps the quintessential attribute of sovereignty. See National League of Cities v. Usery, 426 U.S., at 851. Indeed, having the power to make decisions and to set policy is what gives the State its sovereign nature. . . . It would follow that the ability of a state legislature (or, as here, administrative) body—which makes decisions and sets policy for the State as a whole—to consider and promulgate regulations of its choosing must be central to a State's role in the federal system. Indeed, the nineteenth century view, expressed in a well known slavery case, was that Congress "has no power to impose upon a State officer, as such, any duty whatever, and compel him to perform it." Kentucky v. Dennison, 24 How. 66, 107 (1861).

Recent cases, however, demonstrate that this rigid and isolated statement from Kentucky v. Dennison—which suggests that the States and the Federal Government in all circumstances must be viewed as co-equal sovereigns—is not representative of the law today. While this Court never has sanctioned explicitly a federal command to the States to promulgate and enforce laws and regulations, . . . there are instances where the Court has upheld federal statutory structures that in effect directed state decision-makers to take or to refrain from taking certain actions. In Fry v. United States, 421 U.S. 542 (1975), for example, state executives were held restricted, with respect to state employees, to the wage and salary limitations established by the Economic Stabilization Act of 1970. Washington v. Fishing Vessel Assn., 443 U.S. 658 (1979), acknowledged a federal court's power to enforce a treaty by compelling a state agency to "prepare" certain rules "even if state law withholds from [it] the power to do so." Id., at 695. And certainly Testa v. Katt, supra, by declaring that "the policy of the federal Act is the prevailing policy in every state," 330 U.S., at 393 reveals that the Federal Government has some power to enlist a branch of state government—there the judiciary—to further federal ends. In doing so, Testa clearly cut back on both the quoted language and the analysis of the Dennison case of the preceding century.

Whatever all this may forebode for the future, or for the scope of federal authority in the event of a crisis of national proportions, it plainly is not necessary for the Court in this case to make a definitive choice between competing views of federal power to compel state regulatory activity. Titles I and III of PURPA require only *consideration* of federal standards. And if a State has no utilities commission, or simply stops regulating in the field, it need not even entertain the federal proposals. As we have noted, the commerce power permits Congress to pre-empt the States entirely in the regulation of private utilities. In a sense, then, this case is only one step beyond Hodel v. Virginia Surface Min. & Recl. Assn., supra. There, the Federal Government could have pre-empted all surface mining regulations; instead, it allowed the States to enter the field if they promulgated regulations consistent with federal standards. In the Court's view, this raised no Tenth Amendment problem. . . .

Similarly here, Congress could have pre-empted the field, at least insofar as private rather than state activity is concerned; PURPA should not be invalid simply because, out of deference to state authority, Congress adopted a less intrusive scheme and allowed the States to continue regulating in the area on the condition that they *consider* the suggested federal standards. While the condition here is affirmative in nature—that is, it directs the States to entertain proposals—nothing in this Court's cases suggests that the nature of the condition makes it a constitutionally improper one. There is nothing in PURPA "directly compelling" the States to enact a legislative program. In short, because the two challenged Titles simply condition continued state involvement in a pre-emptible area on the consideration of federal proposals, they do not threaten the States' "separate and independent existence," . . . and do not impair the ability of the States "to function effectively in a federal system." . . . To the contrary, they offer the States a vehicle for remaining active in an area of overriding concern.

We recognize, of course, that the choice put to the States—that of either abandoning regulation of the field altogether or considering the federal standards—may be a difficult one. And that is particularly true when Congress, as is the case here, has failed to provide an alternative regulatory mechanism to police the area in the event of state default. Yet in other contexts the Court has recognized that valid federal enactments may have an effect on state policy—and may, indeed, be designed to induce state action in areas that otherwise would be beyond Congress' regulatory authority. Thus in Oklahoma v. Civil Service Comm'n, 330 U.S. 127 (1947), the Court upheld Congress' power to attach conditions to grants-in-aid received by the States, although the condition under attack involved an activity that "the United States is not concerned with, and has no power to regulate." Id., at 143. The Tenth Amendment, the Court declared, "has been consistently construed 'as not depriving the national government of authority to resort to all means for the exercise of a granted power which are appropriate and plainly adapted to the permitted end,' " ibid, quoting United States v. Darby, 312 U.S. 100 (1941)—the end there being the disbursement of federal funds. Thus it cannot be constitutionally determinative that the federal regulation is likely to move the States to act in a given way, or even to "coerc[e] the States" into assuming a regulatory role by affecting their "freedom to make decisions in areas of 'integral governmental functions.' " Hodel v. Virginia Surface Min. & Recl. Assn., 452 U.S., at 289.

. . . [I]t may be unlikely that the States will or easily can abandon regulation of public utilities to avoid PURPA's requirements. But this does not change the constitutional analysis: as in Hodel v. Virginia Surface Min. & Recl. Assn., "[t]he most that can be said is that the . . . Act establishes a program of cooperative federalism that allows the States, within limits established by federal minimum standards, to enact and administer their own regulatory programs, structured to meet their own particular needs." Id., at 289.

. . . .

. . . As we read them, Titles I and III simply establish requirements for continued state activity in an otherwise preemptible field. Whatever the constitutional problems associated with more intrusive federal programs, the "mandatory consideration" provisions of Titles I and III must be validated under the principle of Hodel v. Virginia Surface Min. & Recl. Assn.

C. The Procedural Requirements. Titles I and III also require state commissions to follow certain notice and comment procedures when acting on the proposed federal standards. In a way, these appear more intrusive than the "consideration" provisions; while the latter are essentially hortatory, the procedural provisions obviously are prescriptive. Appellants and *amici* Maryland, et al., argue that the procedural requirements simply establish minimum due process standards, something Mississippi appears already to provide, and therefore may be upheld as an exercise of Congress' Fourteenth Amendment powers. We need not go that far, however, for we uphold the procedural requirements under the same analysis employed above in connection with the "consideration" provisions. If Congress can require a state administrative body to consider proposed regulations as a condition to its continued involvement in a pre-emptible field—and we hold today that it can—there is nothing unconstitutional about Congress' requiring certain procedural minima as that body goes about undertaking its tasks. The procedural requirements obviously do not compel the exercise of the State's sovereign powers, and do not purport to set standards to be followed in all areas of the state commission's endeavors.

The judgment of the District Court is reversed.

It is so ordered.

Justice Powell, concurring and dissenting.

. . .

II

. . . I know of no other attempt by the Federal Government to supplant state prescribed procedures that in part define the nature of their administrative agencies. If Congress may do this, presumably it has the power to preempt state court rules of civil procedure and judicial review in classes of cases found to affect commerce. This would be the type of gradual encroachment hypothesized by Professor Tribe: "Of course, no one expects Congress to obliterate the states, at least in one fell swoop. If there is any danger, it lies in the tyranny of small decisions—in the prospect that Congress will nibble away at state sovereignty, bit by bit, until someday essentially nothing is left but a gutted shell."

I limit this dissent to the provisions of the PURPA identified above. Despite the appeal—and indeed wisdom—of Justice O'Connor's evocation of the principles of federalism, I believe precedents of this Court support the constitutionality of the substantive provisions of this Act on this facial attack.

. . .

Justice O'Connor, with whom the Chief Justice and Justice Rehnquist join, concurring in part in the judgment and dissenting in part.

I agree with the Court that the Commerce Clause supported Congress' enactment of the Public Utility Regulatory Policies Act of 1978, Pub.L. No. 95–617, 92 Stat. 3117 (PURPA). I disagree, however, with much of the Court's Tenth Amendment Analysis. Titles I and III of PURPA conscript state utility commissions into the national bureaucratic army. This result is contrary to the principles of National League of Cities v. Usery, 426 U.S. 833 (1976), antithetical to the values of federalism, and inconsistent with our constitutional history. Accordingly, I dissent from subsections IVB and C of the Court's opinion.

I

. . .

If Congress routinely required the state legislatures to debate bills drafted by congressional committees, it could hardly be questioned that the practice would affect an attribute of state sovereignty. PURPA, which sets the agendas of agencies exercising delegated legislative power in a specific field, has a similarly intrusive effect.

. . .

The Court sidesteps this analysis, suggesting that the States may escape PURPA simply by ceasing regulation of public utilities. Even the Court recognizes that this choice "may be a difficult one," and that "it may be unlikely that the States will or easily can abandon regulation of public utilities to avoid PURPA's requirements." In fact, the Court's "choice" is an absurdity, for if its analysis is sound, the Constitution no longer limits federal regulation of state governments. Under the Court's analysis, for example, National League of Cities v. Usery, 426 U.S. 833 (1976), would have been wrongly decided, because the States could have avoided the Fair Labor Standards Act by "choosing" to fire all employees subject to that Act and to close those branches of state government. Similarly, Congress could dictate the agendas and meeting places of state legislatures, because unwilling States would remain free to abolish their legislative bodies. I do not agree that this dismemberment of state government is the correct solution to a Tenth Amendment challenge.

The choice put to the States by the Surface Mining Control and Reclamation Act of 1977, 30 U.S.C. § 1201 et seq. (1976 ed., Supp. III), the federal statute upheld in Hodel v. Virginia Surface Mining & Reclamation Association, 452 U.S. 264 (1981), is quite different from the decision PURPA mandates. . . . The Surface Mining Act does not force States to choose between performing tasks set by Congress and abandoning all mining or land use regulation. That statute is "a program of cooperative federalism," *Hodel,* supra, at 289, because it allows the States to choose either to work with Congress in pursuit of federal surface mining goals or to devote their legislative resources to other mining and land use problems. By contrast, there is nothing "cooperative" about a federal program that compels state agencies either to function as bureaucratic puppets of the Federal Government or to abandon regulation of an entire field traditionally reserved to state authority. Yet this is the "choice" the Court today forces upon the States.

The Court defends its novel decision to permit federal conscription of state legislative power by citing three cases upholding statutes that "in effect directed state decision-makers to take or to refrain from taking certain actions." Testa v. Katt, 330 U.S. 386 (1947), is the most suggestive of these decisions. In *Testa,* the Court held that state trial courts may not refuse to hear a federal claim if "th[e] same type of claim arising under [state] law would be enforced by that State's courts." Id., at 394. A facile reading of *Testa* might suggest that state legislatures must also entertain congressionally sponsored business, as long as the federal duties are similar to existing state obligations. Application of *Testa* to legislative power, however, vastly expands the scope of that decision. Because trial courts of general jurisdiction do not choose the cases that they hear, the requirement that they evenhandedly adjudicate state and federal claims falling within their jurisdiction does not infringe any sovereign authority to set an agenda. As explained above, however, the power to choose subjects for legislation is a fundamental attribute of legislative power, and interference with this power unavoidably undermines state sovereignty. Accordingly, the existence of a congressional authority to "enlist . . . the [state] judiciary . . . to further federal ends," does not imply an equivalent power to impress state legislative bodies into federal service.

The Court, finally, reasons that because Congress could have preempted the entire field of intrastate utility regulation, the Constitution should not forbid PURPA's "less intrusive scheme." The Court's evaluation of intrusiveness, however, is simply irrelevant to the constitutional inquiry. The Constitution permits Congress to govern only through certain channels. If the Tenth Amendment principles articulated in National League of Cities v. Usery, 426 U.S. 833 (1976), and Hodel v. Virginia Surface Mining & Reclamation Association, 452 U.S. 264 (1981), foreclose PURPA's approach, it is no answer to argue that Congress could have reached the same destination by a different route. This Court's task is to enforce constitutional limits on congressional power, not to decide whether alternative courses would better serve state and federal interests.

I do not believe, moreover, that Titles I and III of PURPA are less intrusive than preemption. When Congress preempts a field, it precludes only state legislation that conflicts with the national approach. The States usually retain the power to complement congressional legislation, either by regulating details unsupervised by Congress or by imposing requirements that go beyond the national threshold. Most importantly, after Congress preempts a field, the

States may simply devote their resources elsewhere. This country does not lack for problems demanding legislative attention. PURPA, however, drains the inventive energy of state governmental bodies by requiring them to weigh its detailed standards, enter written findings, and defend their determinations in state court. While engaged in these congressionally mandated tasks, state utility commissions are less able to pursue local proposals for conserving gas and electric power. The States might well prefer that Congress simply impose the standards described in PURPA; this, at least, would leave them free to exercise their power in other areas.

.   .   .

II

As explained above, the Court's decision to uphold Titles I and III violates the principles of National League of Cities v. Usery, 426 U.S. 833 (1976), and threatens the values promoted by our federal system. The Court's result, moreover, is at odds with our constitutional history, which demonstrates that the Framers consciously rejected a system in which the national legislature would employ state legislative power to achieve national ends.

The principal defect of the Articles of Confederation, eighteenth century writers agreed, was that the new National Government lacked the power to compel individual action. Instead, the central government had to rely upon the cooperation of state legislatures to achieve national goals. .   .   .

The Constitution cured this defect by permitting direct contact between the National Government and the individual citizen, .   .   .

.   .   .

Thus, the Framers concluded that government by one sovereign through the agency of a second cannot be satisfactory. At one extreme, as under the Articles of Confederation, such a system is simply ineffective. At the other, it requires a degree of military force incompatible with stable government and civil liberty. For this reason, the Framers concluded that "the execution of the laws of the national government .   .   . should not require the intervention of the State Legislatures," The Federalist No. 16, p. 103, and abandoned the Articles of Confederation in favor of direct national legislation.

.   .   .

While this history demonstrates the Framers' commitment to a strong central government, the means that they adopted to achieve that end are as instructive as the end itself. Under the Articles of Confederation, the national legislature operated through the States. The Framers could have fortified the central government, while still maintaining the same system, if they had increased Congress' power to demand obedience from state legislatures. In time, this scheme might have relegated the States to mere departments of the National Government, a status the Court appears to endorse today. The Framers, however, eschewed this course, choosing instead to allow Congress to pass laws directly affecting individuals, and rejecting proposals that would have given Congress military or legislative power over state governments. In this way, the Framers established independent state and national sovereigns. The National Government received the power to enact its own laws and to enforce those laws over conflicting state legislation. The States retained the power to govern as sovereigns in fields that Congress cannot or will not preempt. This product of the Constitutional Convention, I believe, is fundamentally inconsistent with a system in which either Congress or a state legislature harnesses the legislative powers of the other sovereign.[a]

.   .   .

---

[a] For an exhaustive review of the lower court decisions, and an argument that political restraints are ineffective when Congress requires states to enforce Federal policies, see La Pierre, *The Political*

SECTION 3.   GOVERNMENTAL RELATIONSHIPS
AMONG THE STATES

INTERSTATE COMPACTS

The creation of governmental units by agreement among states is recognized, in a back-handed manner, by Article I, Section 10, of the Constitution, which provides: "No State shall . . . without the consent of Congress, . . . enter into any Agreement or Compact with another State, or with a foreign Power. . . ." Despite the difficulties of reaching agreement between states and Congress, and of running governmental units resting on agreement, the compact has been used at an accelerating pace.[1]

Compacts can serve two purposes. One purpose is limited regional government. The federal system created by the Constitution recognizes only states and the national government, but there are problems that affect geographic regions or multi-state metropolitan centers better served by decisions that reach across state lines, but are not national in scope. An early use of the compact was in the creation of multi-state transportation facilities, such as bridges—and later tunnels—traversing rivers marking state boundaries. Another example is provided by marine fisheries compacts that have been created for the Atlantic Coast States, the Gulf States, and the Pacific States, respectively.[2] A second purpose of compacts has been in national cooperation among the states.[3] For example, in 1934 Congress gave consent in advance for "any two or more states to enter into agreements or compacts for cooperative effort and mutual assistance in the prevention of crime and in the enforcement of their respective criminal laws and policies, and to establish such agencies, joint or otherwise, as they may deem desirable for making effective such agreements and compacts." Under this authority, the Interstate Compact for the Supervision of Parolees and Probationers has been widely ratified by the states.[4]

There are a number of important and unsolved problems concerning the extent to which effective governmental powers can be conferred by compact on interstate commissions. Significant fiscal powers have been created by transferring revenue-producing property, such as toll bridges and tunnels, to interstate agencies. But can an interstate commission be given the power to tax or promulgate binding regulations? Can Congress make violations of such regulations subject to enforcement in the federal courts?

One question that has arisen concerns the extent to which the power to enter into binding interstate compacts can be restricted by state law. In West Virginia v. Sims, 341 U.S. 22 (1951), the West Virginia Supreme Court of Appeals had refused to order the state auditor to issue a warrant to pay the State's annual appropriation to the Ohio River Valley Water Sanitation Compact. The court concluded that the West Virginia statute approving the State's adherence to the compact violated the State constitution. The Supreme Court reversed. The Court did not reach the question whether the compact clause precludes states from limiting their power to enter into a compact to which Congress had

---

Safeguards of Federalism Redux: Intergovernmental Immunity and the States as Agent of the Nation, 60 Wash.U.L.Q. 779 (1982).

[1] A useful study of several major compacts is Ridgeway, *Interstate Compacts: A question of Federalism* (1971). For a list of interstate compacts, see Council of State Governments, *Interstate Compacts* (1983).

[2] Thursby, *Interstate Cooperation* 103 (1953).

[3] Interstate cooperation can also be facilitated through uniform laws with reciprocal obligations. One of these, the Uniform Law to Secure the Attendance of Witnesses from Within or Without a State in Criminal Proceedings, was sustained in New York v. O'Neill, 359 U.S. 1 (1959).

[4] 48 Stat. 908. Thursby, *supra* at 99.

consented. Because, however, compacts are a means of safeguarding national interests, and state court decisions in this field necessarily involve the rights of other states, the interpretation of any purported state law limitation on entry into a compact was for the United States Supreme Court. The Court concluded that the West Virginia constitution was not violated by the State's entry into the compact.

Another issue concerns the necessity for Congressional consent to interstate agreements. Despite the breadth of the phrase "any agreement or Compact" in Article I, Section 10, many agreements among states do not require Congressional approval. In New Hampshire v. Maine, 426 U.S. 363 (1976), the Court followed earlier cases in concluding that an agreement between two states to settle the disputed boundary between them did not require Congressional consent. The Court noted that Congressional consent was needed only when the agreeing states enhance their "power in any sense that threatens the supremacy of the Federal Government." The most ambitious multi-state agreement without Congressional consent, The Multistate Tax Compact, was held not to require Congressional consent in United States Steel Corp. v. Multistate Tax Comm'n, 434 U.S. 452 (1978). (As of 1983, 30 states were members of the compact, designed to facilitate the collection of taxes from and the avoidance of duplicative taxation of, multi-state corporations.) The Court conceded that there was "some incremental increase in the bargaining power of member states" in their dealings with corporations subject to their taxing jurisdiction. Still, the compact did not enhance the power of those states with reference to the national government, since it "did not purport to authorize the member States to exercise any powers they could not exercise in its absence." The dissenters argued that the compact did encroach on national authority, because it involved "encroachments on the authority and power of non-Compact states."

OTHER INTERGOVERNMENTAL RELATIONSHIPS AMONG STATES

The Constitution contains a number of specific provisions dealing with states' obligations to each other. For example, Article IV, Section 1, requires each state to give "full faith and credit" to the "public acts, records, and judicial proceedings" of other states and Article IV, Section 2, requires states to "deliver up" persons charged with crime in other states.[1]

An issue not provided for in the Constitution is whether one state might be subject to suit in courts of another state. In Nevada v. Hall, 440 U.S. 410 (1979), California courts permitted a personal injury suit to proceed against the State of Nevada, when a Nevada-owned vehicle was involved in an automobile accident in California. The Supreme Court concluded that the Eleventh Amendment, applicable only to suits in federal court, did not immunize Nevada from suits in a state court, and that the full faith and credit clause did not require California to honor Nevada's immunity from suit under Nevada law. Nevada argued further that the Constitution implicitly required each state to respect the sovereignty of other states. The Court stated that the existence of express limitations on state sovereignty in the Constitution "may equally imply that caution should be exercised before concluding that unstated limitations on state power were intended by the Framers." Dissenting, Justice Rehnquist argued that "when the Constitution is ambiguous or silent on a particular issue,

---

[1] Chief Justice Taney's opinion for the Court in Kentucky v. Dennison, 65 U.S. (24 How.) 66 (1861), concluded, however, that a state's constitutional obligation to honor an extradition request rested on "a sense of justice and mutual interest" and could not be enforced by the federal government "either through the judicial department or any other department."

this Court has often relied on notions of a constitutional plan—the implicit ordering of relationships within the federal system necessary to make the Constitution a workable governing charter . . ." (He cited McCulloch v. Maryland and National League of Cities v. Usery at this point in his opinion.)

Chapter 8

SEPARATION OF POWERS

Introduction. James Madison, writing in the Federalist No. 47, asserted that the Constitution was true to Montesquieu's well-known maxim that the legislative, executive, and judicial departments ought to be separate and distinct:

"The reasons on which Montesquieu grounds his maxim are a further demonstration of his meaning. 'When the legislative and executive powers are united in the same person or body,' says he, 'there can be no liberty, because apprehensions may arise lest *the same* monarch or senate should *enact* tyrannical laws to execute them in a tyrannical manner.' Again: 'Were the power of judging joined with the legislative, the life and liberty of the subject would be exposed to arbitrary control, for *the judge* would then be *the legislator*. Were it joined to the executive power, *the judge* might behave with all the violence of *an oppressor*.' Some of these reasons are more fully explained in other passages; but briefly stated as they are here, they sufficiently establish the meaning which we have put on this celebrated maxim of this celebrated author."

Chief Justice Taft, writing for the Court in Hampton & Co. v. United States, 276 U.S. 394, 406 (1928), said:

"The Federal Constitution and state Constitutions of this country divide the governmental power into three branches. . . . This is not to say that the three branches are not co-ordinate parts of one government and that each in the field of its duties may not invoke the action of the two other branches in so far as the action invoked shall not be an assumption of the constitutional field of action of another branch. In determining what it may do in seeking assistance from another branch, the extent and character of that assistance must be fixed according to common sense and the inherent necessities of the governmental co-ordination."

This chapter focuses on issues of division of power between the President and Congress. The coverage is, of necessity, both introductory and very selective, since the topic could easily be the sole concern of many volumes.[1] Section 1 raises the question of the extent to which the President has the power to determine national policies, with particular attention to the President's power over international relations, and the President's power to commit the nation to a war. Section 2 deals with the other side of the coin, examining some instances where it is claimed that Congress has interfered with recognized Presidential powers. The specific topics included are Congressional avoidance of the Presidential veto and usurpation of the President's power to appoint "officers of the United States." Section 3 is concerned primarily with Presidential immunity from Congressional and judicial process.

SECTION 1. THE PRESIDENT'S POWER TO DETERMINE NATIONAL POLICY

A. IN GENERAL

Introduction. As shown in the quote from the Federalist with which this chapter begins, a simplistic description of the division of powers between the

[1] For an overview of many of the issues discussed in this chapter, see Strauss, *The Place of Agencies in Government: Separation of Powers and the Fourth Branch*, 84 Colum.L.Rev. 573 (1984).

legislature and the executive is that a nation's policies are set by the legislature in the laws, and carried into force by the executive. Even the casual student of American history knows that the reality of the division of authority between the President and Congress has been much more complex.

YOUNGSTOWN SHEET & TUBE CO. v. SAWYER
[The Steel Seizure Case]
343 U.S. 579, 72 S.Ct. 863, 96 L.Ed. 1153 (1952).

[This important decision emerged from a tangled background of labor legislation, price and wage negotiation in the steel industry, unhappiness between Congress and President Truman and the frustrating inability of the government to find an end for the war in Korea, then in its third year. The opinions of the justices run to 130 pages; nevertheless, additional facts are needed to help us see the controversy in the round.[a]

[Part of the setting was disagreement between Congress and President Truman over the means of resolving major labor disputes. In 1947 Congress, over President Truman's veto, had passed the Taft-Hartley Act subjecting union practices to national control; one part of the Act provided that if a strike would endanger national health and safety the President was authorized to seek an injunction against the strike during a cooling-off period of eighty days during which a secret ballot of the workers could be held. These various provisions were bitterly resisted by labor. While this law was under consideration in Congress an amendment was offered for government seizure of industries to avoid serious shut-downs; Congress rejected the proposal. In his hard-hitting and astonishingly successful 1948 campaign for reelection, Truman slashed at the "do-nothing" record of this session of Congress, and called for repeal of the "oppressive" Taft-Hartley Act.

[Another dimension to the problem was the Administration's controversy with the steel industry. Wage negotiations between the United Steel Workers and the industry had been opened in November 1951, five months before the final crisis. The negotiations were deadlocked, and in December the President referred this controversy to the Wage Stabilization Board—which was part of the program of controls over wages and prices that had been established during the Korean War. The Board did not have authority to dictate a settlement; its chief sanction was to decide the extent to which labor cost increases could be taken into account by the Office of Price Stabilization in acting on requests for increases in ceiling prices. The Wage Stabilization Board recommended certain wage increases; the steel industry rejected this recommendation unless it received a $12 per ton increase in the ceiling price. The stabilization officials refused to approve this increase on the ground that high earnings of the steel industry permitted the absorption of at least a part of the increase in labor costs.

[On April 3, Philip Murray, President of the United Steelworkers, called a general steel strike for 12:01 a.m., April 9. On the night of April 8, following a radio address to the nation, President Truman issued Executive Order 10340 directing the Secretary of Commerce "to take possession" and "to operate or arrange for the operation" of the production facilities of the steel industry. The Order outlined the vital part of steel in the war effort, and concluded that "a work stoppage would immediately jeopardize and imperil our national defense."

-----

[a] The setting was known to the Court—and to all concerned Americans. The fullest account of the case in context is Westin, The Anatomy of a Constitutional Law Case (1958). Other accounts on which this discussion draws are Kauper, The Steel Seizure Case, 51 Mich.L.Rev. 141 (1952), Selected Essays, 129 (1963), cited as Kauper. See also: Freund, Foreword: The Year of the Steel Case, 66 Harv.L.Rev. 89 (1952); McConnell, The Steel Seizure of 1952 (1958); The Steel Seizure Case, 82d Cong., 2d Sess., H.Doc.No. 534.

The Secretary of Commerce was instructed to leave control, insofar as possible, in the hands of the present management, but the Order included a pointed authorization to "determine and prescribe terms and conditions of employment." [b] The next morning, President Truman sent Congress a message reporting on this action and stating that if Congress preferred a different course of action, "That is a matter for the Congress to determine."

[Just before midnight on April 8, within an hour after the President's Order, attorneys for the steel companies arrived at the home of a United States District Judge with a motion for immediate relief; a hearing was set for 11:30 the next morning. The relief initially requested by the companies was the prevention of a change in wage rates during government management—a move designed to block the government's plan to force a settlement by establishing a new wage level that, as a practical matter, would be irreversible; but the case quickly reached larger dimensions and on April 29 District Judge David Pine held the seizure illegal and enjoined government officials from remaining in control of the industry. The case was rapidly carried to the Supreme Court.]

Mr. Justice Black delivered the opinion of the Court.

We are asked to decide whether the President was acting within his constitutional power when he issued an order directing the Secretary of Commerce to take possession of and operate most of the Nation's steel mills. The mill owners argue that the President's order amounts to lawmaking, a legislative function which the Constitution has expressly confided to the Congress and not to the President. The Government's position is that the order was made on findings of the President that his action was necessary to avert a national catastrophe which would inevitably result from a stoppage of steel production, and that in meeting this grave emergency the President was acting within the aggregate of his constitutional powers as the Nation's Chief Executive and the Commander-in-Chief of the Armed Forces of the United States. The issue emerges here from the following series of events:

In the latter part of 1951, a dispute arose between the steel companies and their employees over terms and conditions that should be included in new collective bargaining agreements. Long-continued conferences failed to resolve the dispute. On December 18, 1951, the employees' representative, United Steelworkers of America, C.I.O., gave notice of an intention to strike when the existing bargaining agreements expired on December 31. The Federal Mediation and Conciliation Service then intervened in an effort to get labor and management to agree. This failing, the President on December 22, 1951, referred the dispute to the Federal Wage Stabilization Board to investigate and make recommendations for fair and equitable terms of settlement. This Board's report resulted in no settlement. On April 4, 1952, the Union gave notice of a nation-wide strike called to begin at 12:01 a.m. April 9. The indispensability of steel as a component of substantially all weapons and other war materials led the President to believe that the proposed work stoppage would immediately jeopardize our national defense and that governmental seizure of the steel mills was necessary in order to assure the continued availability of steel. Reciting these considerations for his action, the President, a few hours before the strike was to begin, issued Executive Order 10340, ... The order directed the

---

[b] 17 Fed.Reg. 3139 (April 8, 1952); 343 U.S. 589–592. President Truman, in his radio address to the nation the evening of the seizure, emphasized the vital part played by steel in supplying the fighting forces. After discussing the above-mentioned wage recommendation of the Wage Stabilization Board, which the industry had rejected, the President added: "I think [the companies] realize that the board's recommendations on wages are reasonable, and that they are raising all this hullabaloo in an attempt to force the Government to give them a big boost in prices." The profits being made by the industry were described; after noting that the companies insisted on a price increase of $12 per ton, the President exclaimed: "That's about the most outrageous thing I ever heard of . . . they want to double their money on the deal".

Secretary of Commerce to take possession of most of the steel mills and keep them running. The Secretary immediately issued his own possessory orders, calling upon the presidents of the various seized companies to serve as operating managers for the United States. They were directed to carry on their activities in accordance with regulations and directions of the Secretary. The next morning the President sent a message to Congress reporting his action. . . . Twelve days later he sent a second message. . . . Congress has taken no action.

Obeying the Secretary's orders under protest, the companies brought proceedings against him in the District Court. Their complaints charged that the seizure was not authorized by an act of Congress or by any constitutional provisions. The District Court was asked to declare the orders of the President and the Secretary invalid and to issue preliminary and permanent injunctions restraining their enforcement. . . . [T]he United States asserted that a strike disrupting steel production for even a brief period would so endanger the well-being and safety of the Nation that the President had "inherent power" to do what he had done—power "supported by the Constitution, by historical precedent, and by court decisions." . . . [T]he District Court on April 30 issued a preliminary injunction restraining the Secretary from "continuing the seizure and possession of the plants . . . and from acting under the purported authority of Executive Order No. 10340." On the same day the Court of Appeals stayed the District Court's injunction. Deeming it best that the issues raised be promptly decided by this Court, we granted certiorari on May 3 and set the cause for argument on May 12.[a] . . .

The President's power, if any, to issue the order must stem either from an act of Congress or from the Constitution itself. There is no statute that expressly authorizes the President to take possession of property as he did here. Nor is there any act of Congress to which our attention has been directed from which such a power can fairly be implied. . . .

Moreover, the use of the seizure technique to solve labor disputes in order to prevent work stoppages was not only unauthorized by any congressional enactment; prior to this controversy, Congress had refused to adopt that method of settling labor disputes. When the Taft-Hartley Act was under consideration in 1947, Congress rejected an amendment which would have authorized such governmental seizures in cases of emergency. . . . Instead, the plan sought to bring about settlements by use of the customary devices of mediation, conciliation, investigation by boards of inquiry, and public reports. In some instances temporary injunctions were authorized to provide cooling-off periods. All this failing, unions were left free to strike after a secret vote by employees as to whether they wished to accept their employers' final settlement offer.

It is clear that if the President had authority to issue the order he did, it must be found in some provision of the Constitution. And it is not claimed that express constitutional language grants this power to the President. The contention is that presidential power should be implied from the aggregate of his powers under the Constitution. Particular reliance is placed on provisions in Article II which say that "the executive Power shall be vested in a President . . . ."; that "he shall take Care that the Laws be faithfully executed"; and that he "shall be Commander in Chief of the Army and Navy of the United States."

The order cannot properly be sustained as an exercise of the President's military power as Commander in Chief of the Armed Forces. The Government attempts to do so by citing a number of cases upholding broad powers in

[a] The decision of the Supreme Court came on June 2, only 34 days after the trial court issued its injunction!

military commanders engaged in day-to-day fighting in a theater of war. Such cases need not concern us here. Even though "theater of war" be an expanding concept, we cannot with faithfulness to our constitutional system hold that the Commander in Chief of the Armed Forces has the ultimate power as such to take possession of private property in order to keep labor disputes from stopping production. This is a job for the Nation's lawmakers, not for its military authorities.

Nor can the seizure order be sustained because of the several constitutional provisions that grant executive power to the President. In the framework of our Constitution, the President's power to see that the laws are faithfully executed refutes the idea that he is to be a lawmaker. The Constitution limits his functions in the lawmaking process to the recommending of laws he thinks wise and the vetoing of laws he thinks bad. And the Constitution is neither silent nor equivocal about who shall make laws which the President is to execute. The first section of the first article says that "All legislative Powers herein granted shall be vested in a Congress of the United States . . . ." After granting many powers to the Congress, Article I goes on to provide that Congress may "make all Laws which shall be necessary and proper for carrying into Execution the foregoing Powers and all other Powers vested by this Constitution in the Government of the United States, or in any Department or Officer thereof."

The President's order does not direct that a congressional policy be executed in a manner prescribed by Congress—it directs that a presidential policy be executed in a manner prescribed by the President. The preamble of the order itself, like that of many statutes, sets out reasons why the President believes certain policies should be adopted, proclaims these policies as rules of conduct to be followed, and again, like a statute, authorizes a government official to promulgate additional rules and regulations consistent with the policy proclaimed and needed to carry that policy into execution. The power of Congress to adopt such public policies as those proclaimed by the order is beyond question. It can authorize the taking of private property for public use. It can make laws regulating the relationships between employers and employees, prescribing rules designed to settle labor disputes, and fixing wages and working conditions in certain fields of our economy. The Constitution does not subject this lawmaking power of Congress to presidential or military supervision or control.

It is said that other Presidents without congressional authority have taken possession of private business enterprises in order to settle labor disputes. But even if this be true, Congress has not thereby lost its exclusive constitutional authority to make laws necessary and proper to carry out the powers vested by the Constitution "in the Government of the United States, or in any Department or Officer thereof."

The Founders of this Nation entrusted the lawmaking power to the Congress alone in both good and bad times. It would do no good to recall the historical events, the fears of power and the hopes for freedom that lay behind their choice. Such a review would but confirm our holding that this seizure order cannot stand.

The judgment of the District Court is affirmed.

Affirmed.

[All of the Justices who joined Justice Black's opinion for the Court also wrote individual concurring opinions. Justice Frankfurter stated that questions concerning the extent of Presidential power in the absence of legislation were not before the Court. The Labor Management Relations Act of 1947 was equivalent to an explicit Congressional negation of the authority asserted by the seizure. Justice Burton stated that the "controlling fact" was that Congress had prescribed specific procedures, which did not include seizure, for the present type of emergency. Justice Douglas emphasized the fifth amendment's requirement of compensation for takings of property, arguing that Congress, as the only branch with power to appropriate money to compensate for seizures, was the only branch with power to authorize or ratify them. A few often-quoted passages from Justice Jackson's lengthy concurring opinion follow.]

Mr. Justice Jackson, concurring in the judgment and opinion of the Court.

. . .

The actual art of governing under our Constitution does not and cannot conform to judicial definitions of the power of any of its branches based on isolated clauses or even single Articles torn from context. While the Constitution diffuses power the better to secure liberty, it also contemplates that practice will integrate the dispersed powers into a workable government. It enjoins upon its branches separateness but interdependence, autonomy but reciprocity. Presidential powers are not fixed but fluctuate, depending upon their disjunction or conjunction with those of Congress. We may well begin by a somewhat over-simplified grouping of practical situations in which a President may doubt, or others may challenge, his powers, and by distinguishing roughly the legal consequences of this factor of relativity.

1. When the President acts pursuant to an express or implied authorization of Congress, his authority is at its maximum, for it includes all that he possesses in his own right plus all that Congress can delegate. In these circumstances, and in these only, may he be said (for what it may be worth), to personify the federal sovereignty. If his act is held unconstitutional under these circumstances, it usually means that the Federal Government as an undivided whole lacks power. A seizure executed by the President pursuant to an Act of Congress would be supported by the strongest of presumptions and the widest latitude of judicial interpretation, and the burden of persuasion would rest heavily upon any who might attack it.

2. When the President acts in absence of either a congressional grant or denial of authority, he can only rely upon his own independent powers, but there is a zone of twilight in which he and Congress may have concurrent authority, or in which its distribution is uncertain. Therefore, congressional inertia, indifference or quiescence may sometimes, at least as a practical matter, enable, if not invite, measures on independent presidential responsibility. In this area, any actual test of power is likely to depend on the imperatives of events and contemporary imponderables rather than on abstract theories of law.

3. When the President takes measures incompatible with the expressed or implied will of Congress, his power is at its lowest ebb, for then he can rely only upon his own constitutional powers minus any constitutional powers of Congress over the matter. Courts can sustain exclusive Presidential control in such a case only by disabling the Congress from acting upon the subject. Presidential claim to a power at once so conclusive and preclusive must be scrutinized with caution, for what is at stake is the equilibrium established by our constitutional system.

Into which of these classifications does this executive seizure of the steel industry fit? It is eliminated from the first by admission, for it is conceded that no congressional authorization exists for this seizure. That takes away also the support of the many precedents and declarations which were made in relation, and must be confined, to this category.

Can it then be defended under flexible tests available to the second category? It seems clearly eliminated from that class because Congress has not left seizure of private property an open field but has covered it by three statutory policies inconsistent with this seizure. . . .

This leaves the current seizure to be justified only by the severe tests under the third grouping, where it can be supported only by any remainder of executive power after subtraction of such powers as Congress may have over the subject. In short, we can sustain the President only by holding that seizure of such strike-bound industries is within his domain and beyond control by Congress. Thus, this Court's first review of such seizures occurs under circumstances which leave Presidential power most vulnerable to attack and in the least favorable of possible constitutional postures.

. . .

But I have no illusion that any decision by this Court can keep power in the hands of Congress if it is not wise and timely in meeting its problems. A crisis that challenges the President equally, or perhaps primarily, challenges Congress. If not good law, there was worldly wisdom in the maxim attributed to Napoleon that "The tools belong to the man who can use them." We may say that power to legislate for emergencies belongs in the hands of Congress, but only Congress itself can prevent power from slipping through its fingers.

. . .

Mr. Justice Clark, concurring in the judgment of the Court . . .

I conclude that where Congress has laid down specific procedures to deal with the type of crisis confronting the President, he must follow those procedures in meeting the crisis; but that in the absence of such action by Congress, the President's independent power to act depends upon the gravity of the situation confronting the nation. I cannot sustain the seizure in question because here, as in Little v. Barreme, 2 Cranch 170, Congress had prescribed methods to be followed by the President in meeting the emergency at hand.

. . . .

Mr. Chief Justice Vinson, with whom Mr. Justice Reed and Mr. Justice Minton join, dissenting. . . .

[The dissenting opinion described legislation authorizing the supplying of the forces then engaged in the Korean War and other procurement and foreign aid legislation.]

The President has the duty to execute the foregoing legislative programs. Their successful execution depends upon continued production of steel and stabilized prices for steel. . . .

Secretary of Defense Lovett swore that "a work stoppage in the steel industry will result immediately in serious curtailment of production of essential weapons and munitions of all kinds." He illustrated by showing that 84% of the national production of certain alloy steel is currently used for production of military-end items and that 35% of total production of another form of steel goes into ammunition, 80% of such ammunition now going to Korea. The Secretary of Defense stated that: "We are holding the line [in Korea] with ammunition and not with the lives of our troops." . . .

One is not here called upon even to consider the possibility of executive seizure of a farm, a corner grocery store or even a single industrial plant. Such considerations arise only when one ignores the central fact of this case—that the Nation's entire basic steel production would have shut down completely if there had been no Government seizure. . . .

[W]e are not called upon today to expand the Constitution to meet a new situation. For, in this case, we need only look to history and time-honored principles of constitutional law—principles that have been applied consistently by all branches of the Government throughout our history. . . .

A review of executive action demonstrates that our Presidents have on many occasions exhibited the leadership contemplated by the Framers when they made the President Commander in Chief, and imposed upon him the trust to "take Care that the Laws be faithfully executed." With or without explicit statutory authorization, Presidents have at such times dealt with national emergencies by acting promptly and resolutely to enforce legislative programs, at least to save those programs until Congress could act. Congress and the courts have responded to such executive initiative with consistent approval. . . .

[A summary of episodes from Presidents Washington to Roosevelt is omitted.]

. . .

This is but a cursory summary of executive leadership. But it amply demonstrates that Presidents have taken prompt action to enforce the laws and protect the country whether or not Congress happened to provide in advance for the particular method of execution. . . .

Focusing now on the situation confronting the President on the night of April 8, 1952, we cannot but conclude that the President was performing his duty under the Constitution to "take Care that the Laws be faithfully executed"—a duty described by President Benjamin Harrison as "the central idea of the office." . . .

. . . Faced with the duty of executing the defense programs which Congress had enacted and the disastrous effects that any stoppage in steel production would have on those programs, the President acted to preserve those programs by seizing the steel mills. There is no question that the possession was other than temporary in character and subject to congressional direction— either approving, disapproving or regulating the manner in which the mills were to be administered and returned to the owners. The President immediately informed Congress of his action and clearly stated his intention to abide by the legislative will. No basis for claims of arbitrary action, unlimited powers or dictatorial usurpation of congressional power appears from the facts of this case. On the contrary, judicial, legislative and executive precedents throughout our history demonstrate that in this case the President acted in full conformity with his duties under the Constitution. Accordingly, we would reverse the order of the District Court.

B. INTERNATIONAL RELATIONS

Introduction. Most of the constitutional grants of power to the federal government relating to foreign affairs appear in the enumeration of executive powers: the President is made "Commander-in-Chief" of the armed forces; he is given the power, with the approval of two-thirds of the Senate, "to make Treaties"; and, with the "advice and consent" of the Senate, he "shall appoint Ambassadors, other public Ministers and Consuls," i.e., our representatives abroad (Art. II, § 2). Also, "he shall receive Ambassadors and other public Ministers" (Art. II, § 3). Those spare provisions, however, hardly begin to capture the scope of "the executive power" to conduct the nation's foreign affairs.

United States v. Curtiss-Wright Export Corp., 299 U.S. 304, 320 (1936), concerned the validity of a delegation of power from Congress to the President. In the course of upholding the delegation the Court noted that the legislative power was combined with "the very delicate, plenary and exclusive power of the President as the sole organ of the Federal government in the field of international relations—a power which does not require as a basis for its exercise an act of Congress, but which, of course, like every other governmental power, must be exercised in subordination to the applicable provisions of the Constitution. It is quite apparent that if, in the maintenance of our international relations, embarrassment—perhaps serious embarrassment—is to be avoided and success for our aims achieved, congressional legislation which is to be made effective through negotiation and inquiry within the international field must often accord to the President a degree of discretion and freedom from statutory restriction which would not be admissible were domestic affairs alone involved. Moreover, he, not Congress, has the better opportunity of knowing the conditions which prevail in foreign countries, and especially is this true in time of war. He has his confidential sources of information. He has his agents in the form of diplomatic, consular and other officials. Secrecy in respect of information gathered by them may be highly necessary, and the premature disclosure of it productive of harmful results. Indeed, so clearly is this true that the first President refused to accede to a request to lay before the House of Representatives the instructions, correspondence and documents relating to the negotiation of the Jay Treaty—a refusal the wisdom of which was recognized by the House itself and has never since been doubted."

For an excellent and full discussion of the powers of the President in the conduct of foreign affairs, see Henkin, *Foreign Affairs and the Constitution* 37–65 (1972).

INTERNATIONAL AGREEMENTS

The scope of national power to override state law and policy through the use of international agreements was discussed in Chapter 4. In that connection we looked at United States v. Belmont, supra p. 237, and United States v. Pink, supra p. 238, relating to the power of the President to consummate international agreements without going through the process of having formal treaties ratified by the Senate and the effect of such agreements on state law.

Belmont and *Pink* raised a separate issue which has proved highly controversial—the extent to which executive agreements can be employed to circumvent the role of the Senate embodied in Article 2 of the Constitution. Some commentators were critical. Borchard, *Shall the Executive Agreement Replace the Treaty?*, 53 Yale L.J. 664 (1944), 54 Yale L.J. 616 (1945). Others supported the use of executive agreements (buttressed in some cases by joint action by the two houses of Congress) as a well-established means to provide flexibility in dealing with international relations. McDougal & Lans, *Treaties and Congressional-Executive or Presidential Agreements: Interchangeable Instruments of National Policy*, 54 Yale L.J. 181, 534 (1945). This dispute does not concern the propriety of the bulk of agreements made between the heads of governments in their day-to-day handling of routine arrangements (like an agreement for the exchange of visits by naval vessels) or military arrangements like the line in conquered territory where allied armies will meet. Some such arrangements may fall within the independent power of the President as "commander-in-chief", others within "the executive power" of the President to conduct the day-to-day business of foreign relations. But one of the questions stirred by the *Belmont* and *Pink* cases is whether the President might use executive agreements for basic long-range commitments of the nation—possibly because of the fear that it might be impossible to obtain the two-thirds vote of the Senate which the Constitution requires for treaty ratification.

DAMES & MOORE v. REGAN, 453 U.S. 654 (1981). On January 20, 1981, Iran released hostages captured in the seizure of the American Embassy, in Teheran, pursuant to an agreement with the United States. One provision of the agreement provided for termination of litigation in American courts against Iran, with the arbitration of those claims before an international claims tribunal. On January 19, 1981, President Carter issued Executive Orders providing for transfer of blocked Iranian funds in the United States, and nullifying attachments issued against those funds. On February 24, 1981, President Reagan ratified the January 19th Executive Orders, and suspended all claims filed in United States courts that could be presented to the claims tribunal.

Petitioner was a company that had procured a judgment against Iran in a federal trial court for breach of its contract to conduct studies for a proposed nuclear plant in Iran. This case was an action against the Secretary of the Treasury, seeking to prevent enforcement of the Executive Orders. Reserving questions whether the Executive Orders' suspension of claims constituted an uncompensated taking of property, the Court held that the Executive Orders did not exceed Presidential powers.

The provisions of the Executive Orders suspending attachments against persons holding blocked Iranian funds, and directing the transfer of those funds to Iran, were held to be authorized by provisions of the International Emergency Economic Powers Act (IEEPA). The Court concluded, however, that neither IEEPA, nor the Hostage Act of 1868,[1] specifically authorized the President to suspend claims pending in United States Courts. In upholding the validity of this aspect of the Executive Orders, Justice Rehnquist's opinion for the Court said, in part:

"Concluding that neither the IEEPA nor the Hostage Act constitutes specific authorization of the President's action suspending claims, however, is not to say that these statutory provisions are entirely irrelevant to the question of the validity of the President's action. We think both statutes highly relevant in the looser sense of indicating congressional acceptance of a broad scope for executive action in circumstances such as those presented in this case. . . . [T]he IEEPA delegates broad authority to the President to act in times of national emergency with respect to property of a foreign country. The Hostage Act similarly indicates congressional willingness that the President have broad discretion when responding to the hostile acts of foreign sovereigns. . . .

"Although we have declined to conclude that the IEEPA or the Hostage Act directly authorizes the President's suspension of claims for the reasons noted, we cannot ignore the general tenor of Congress' legislation in this area in trying to determine whether the President is acting alone or at least with the acceptance of Congress. As we have noted, Congress cannot anticipate and legislate with regard to every possible action the President may find it necessary to take or every possible situation in which he might act. Such failure of Congress specifically to delegate authority does not, 'especially . . . in the areas of foreign policy and national security,' imply 'congressional disapproval' of action taken by the Executive. Haig v. Agee, 453 U.S. 280, 288 (1981). On the contrary, the enactment of legislation closely related to the question of the President's authority in a particular case which evinces legislative intent to accord the President broad discretion may be considered to 'invite' 'measures on independent presidential responsibility.' *Youngstown,* 343 U.S., at 637 (Jackson, J., conferring). At least this is so where there is no contrary indication of legislative intent and when, as here, there is a history of congressional acquiescence in conduct of the sort engaged in by the President. It is to that history which we now turn.

"Not infrequently in affairs between nations, outstanding claims by nationals of one country against the government of another country are 'sources of friction' between the two sovereigns. United States v. Pink, 315 U.S. 203, 225 (1942). To resolve these difficulties, nations have often entered into agreements settling the claims of their respective nationals. As one treatise writer puts it, international agreements settling claims by nationals of one state against the government of another 'are established international practice reflecting

---

[1] The Act provides that, in securing release of American citizens unjustly held by foreign governments, "the President shall use such means, not amounting to acts of war, as he may think necessary and proper to obtain or effectuate the release."

traditional international theory.' L. Henkin, Foreign Affairs and the Constitution 262 (1972). Consistent with that principle, the United States has repeatedly exercised its sovereign authority to settle the claims of its nationals against foreign countries. Though those settlements have sometimes been made by treaty, there has also been a longstanding practice of settling such claims by executive agreement without the advice and consent of the Senate. . . .

"Crucial to our decision today is the conclusion that Congress has implicitly approved the practice of claim settlement by executive agreement. This is best demonstrated by Congress' enactment of the International Claims Settlement Act of 1949, 22 U.S.C. § 1621 et seq., as amended (1980). . . . Congress created the International Claims Commission, now the Foreign Claims Settlement Commission, and gave it jurisdiction to make final and binding decisions with respect to claims by United States nationals against settlement funds. 22 U.S.C. § 1623(a). By creating a procedure to implement future settlement agreements, Congress placed its stamp of approval on such agreements. . . .

"Over the years Congress has frequently amended the International Claims Settlement Act to provide for particular problems arising out of settlement agreements, thus demonstrating Congress' continuing acceptance of the President's claim settlement authority. . . . Finally, the legislative history of the IEEPA further reveals that Congress has accepted the authority of the Executive to enter into settlement agreements. . . .

"In addition to congressional acquiescence in the President's power to settle claims, prior cases of this Court have also recognized that the President does have some measure of power to enter into executive agreements without obtaining the advice and consent of the Senate. In United States v. Pink, 315 U.S. 203 (1942), for example, the Court upheld the validity of the Litvinov Assignment, which was part of an Executive Agreement whereby the Soviet Union assigned to the United States amounts owed to it by American nationals so that outstanding claims of other American nationals could be paid. The Court explained that the resolution of such claims was integrally connected with normalizing United States' relations with a foreign state. . . .

"In light of all of the foregoing—the inferences to be drawn from the character of the legislation Congress has enacted in the area, such as the IEEPA and the Hostage Act, and from the history of acquiescence in executive claims settlement—we conclude that the President was authorized to suspend pending claims pursuant to Executive Order No. 12294. As Justice Frankfurter pointed out in *Youngstown*, 343 U.S. at 610–611, 'a systematic unbroken executive practice, long pursued to the knowledge of Congress and never before questioned . . . may be treated as a gloss on "Executive Power" vested in the President by § 1 of Art. II.' Past practice does not, by itself, create power, but 'long-continued practice, known to and acquiesced in by Congress, would raise a presumption that the [action] has been [taken] in pursuance of its consent. . . .' United States v. Midwest Oil Co., 236 U.S. 459, 469 (1915). See Haig v. Agee, 453 U.S., at 297, 298. Such practice is present here and such a presumption is also appropriate. In light of the fact that Congress may be considered to have consented to the President's action in suspending claims, we cannot say that action exceeded the President's powers.

. . .

"Just as importantly, Congress has not disapproved of the action taken here. Though Congress has held hearings on the Iranian Agreement itself, Congress has not enacted legislation, or even passed a resolution, indicating its displeasure with the Agreement. Quite the contrary, the relevant Senate Committee has stated that the establishment of the Tribunal is 'of vital importance to the United States.' S.Rep.No. 97–71, 97th Cong., 1st Sess., 5 (1981). We are thus clearly not confronted with a situation in which Congress has in some way resisted the exercise of presidential authority.

"Finally, we re-emphasize the narrowness of our decision. We do not decide that the President possesses plenary power to settle claims, even as against foreign governmental entities. As the Court of Appeals for the First Circuit stressed, 'the sheer magnitude of such a power, considered against the background of the diversity and complexity of modern international trade, cautions against any broader construction of authority than is necessary.' Chas. T. Main Int'l, Inc. v. Khuzestan Water & Power Authority, 651 F.2d, at 814. But where, as here, the settlement of claims has been determined to be a necessary incident to the resolution of a major foreign policy dispute between our country and another, and where, as here, we can conclude that Congress acquiesced in the President's action, we are not prepared to say that the President lacks the power to settle such claims."

C. WAR AND NATIONAL DEFENSE

Introduction. The Constitution is not silent about Congressional participation in one aspect of foreign affairs. Article I, Section 8, Clause 11, of the Constitution specifies that it is a Congressional prerogative "to declare war."

THE PRIZE CASES

67 U.S. (2 Black) 635, 17 L.Ed. 459 (1863).

[In April, 1861, President Lincoln declared a blockade of southern ports. Pursuant to this blockade, in May and July, 1861, Union ships seized merchant vessels and cargoes of foreign neutrals and residents of the southern states. The ships were condemned by federal court order. The owners of the ships and cargo appealed. The Supreme Court regarded the first question to be: Had the President authority to institute a blockade of southern ports which neutrals were bound to respect? The following excerpts are addressed to that question.]

Mr. Justice Grier

. . .

By the Constitution, Congress alone has the power to declare a national or foreign war. It cannot declare war against a State or any number of States, by virtue of any clause in the Constitution. The Constitution confers on the President the whole executive power. He is bound to take care that the laws be faithfully executed. He is Commander-in-Chief of the Army and Navy of the United States, and of the militia of the several States when called into the actual service of the United States. He has no power to initiate or declare a war either against a foreign nation or a domestic State. But by the Acts of Congress of Feb. 28th, 1795 and 3d of March, 1807, he is authorized to call out the militia and use the military and naval forces of the United States in case of invasion by foreign nations, and to suppress insurrection against the government of a State or of the United States.

If a war be made by invasion of a foreign nation, the President is not only authorized but bound to resist force, by force. He does not initiate the war, but is bound to accept the challenge without waiting for any special legislative authority. And whether the hostile party be a foreign invader, or States organized in rebellion, it is none the less a war, although the declaration of it be *"unilateral."* Lord Stowell (*The Eliza Ann,* 1 Dod., 247) observes, "It is not the less a war on that account, for war may exist without declaration on either side. It is so laid down by the best writers on the law of nations. A declaration of war by one country only, is not a mere challenge to be accepted or refused at pleasure by the other."

The battles of Palo Alto and Resaca de la Palma had been fought before the passage of the Act of Congress of May 13th, 1846, ch. 16 (9 Stat. at L., 9), which recognized "a state of war as existing by the Act of the Republic of Mexico." This Act not only provided for the future prosecution of the war, but was itself a vindication and ratification of the Act of the President in accepting the challenge without a previous formal declaration of war by Congress.

This greatest of civil wars was not gradually developed by popular commotion, tumultuous assemblies, or local unorganized insurrections. However long may have been its previous conception, it nevertheless sprung forth suddenly from the parent brain, a Minerva in the full panoply of war. The President was bound to meet it in the shape it presented itself, without waiting for Congress to baptize it with a name; and no name given to it by him or them could change the fact. . . .

Whether the President in fulfilling his duties, as Commander-in-Chief, in suppressing an insurrection, has met with such armed hostile resistance, and a civil war of such alarming proportions as will compel him to accord to them the character of belligerents, is a question to be decided by him, and this court must be governed by the decisions and acts of the Political Department of the government to which this power was intrusted. "He must determine what degree of force the crisis demands." The proclamation of blockade is, itself, official and conclusive evidence to the court that a state of war existed which demanded and authorized a recourse to such a measure, under the circumstances peculiar to the case.

. . .

If it were necessary to the technical existence of a war, that it should have a legislative sanction, we find it in almost every Act passed at the extraordinary session of the Legislature of 1861, which was wholly employed in enacting laws to enable the government to prosecute the war with vigor and efficiency. And finally, in 1861, we find Congress *"ex majore cautela"* and in anticipation of such astute objections, passing an Act "approving, legalizing and making valid all the acts, proclamations, and orders of the President, &c., as if they had been issued and done under the previous express authority and direction of the Congress of the United States."

Without admitting that such an Act was necessary under the circumstances, it is plain that if the President had in any manner assumed powers which it was necessary should have the authority or sanction of Congress, that on the well known principal of law, *"omnis ratihabitio retrotrahitur et mandato equiparatur,"* this ratification has operated to perfectly cure the defect. . . .

[The decrees of condemnation were affirmed except for certain cargoes which were bought and paid for in the South before the war broke out and which were being removed shortly thereafter.]

Mr. Justice Nelson [joined by Chief Justice Taney and Justices Catron and Clifford, dissenting]. . . .

The Acts of 1795 and 1807 did not, and could not, under the Constitution, confer on the President the power of declaring war against a State of this Union, or of deciding that war existed, and upon that ground authorize the capture and confiscation of the property of every citizen of the State whenever it was found on the waters. The laws of war, whether the war be civil or *inter gentes,* as we have seen, convert every citizen of the hostile State into a public enemy, and treat him accordingly, whatever may have been his previous conduct. This great power over the business and property of the citizen is reserved to the Legislative Department by the express words of the Constitution. It cannot be delegated or surrendered to the Executive. Congress alone can determine whether war exists or should be declared, and until they have acted, no citizen of the State can be punished in his person or property, unless he has committed some offense against a law of Congress passed before the act was committed, which made it a crime, and defined the punishment. The penalty of confiscation for the acts of others with which he had no concern cannot lawfully be inflicted. . . .

[This dissenting opinion also came to the conclusion that congressional ratification of the seizures was an *ex post facto* law and hence invalid.]

MORA v. McNAMARA

389 U.S. 934, 88 S.Ct. 282, 19 L.Ed.2d 287 (1967).

Petition for writ of certiorari to the United States Court of Appeals for the District of Columbia Circuit.

Nov. 6, 1967. Denied.

Mr. Justice Marshall took no part in the consideration or decision of this petition.

Mr. Justice Stewart, with whom Mr. Justice Douglas joins, dissenting.

The petitioners were drafted into the United States Army in late 1965, and six months later were ordered to a West Coast replacement station for shipment to Vietnam. They brought this suit to prevent the Secretary of Defense and the Secretary of the Army from carrying out those orders, and requested a declaratory judgment that the present United States military activity in Vietnam is "illegal." The District Court dismissed the suit, and the Court of Appeals affirmed.

There exist in this case questions of great magnitude. Some are akin to those referred to by Mr. Justice Douglas in Mitchell v. United States, 386 U.S. 972. But there are others:

I. Is the present United States military activity in Vietnam a "war" within the meaning of Article I, Section 8, Clause 11 of the Constitution?

II. If so, may the Executive constitutionally order the petitioners to participate in that military activity, when no war has been declared by the Congress?

III. Of what relevance to Question II are the present treaty obligations of the United States?

IV. Of what relevance to Question II is the Joint Congressional ("Tonkin Gulf") Resolution of August 10, 1964? [a]

(a) Do present United States military operations fall within the terms of the Joint Resolution?

(b) If the Joint Resolution purports to give the Chief Executive authority to commit United States forces to armed conflict limited in scope only by his own absolute discretion, is the Resolution a constitutionally impermissible delegation of all or part of Congress' power to declare war?

These are large and deeply troubling questions. Whether the Court would ultimately reach them depends, of course, upon the resolution of serious

------

[a] The Tonkin Gulf Resolution was enacted at the request of President Johnson as a result of specific naval incidents in the Gulf of Tonkin. It stated that "Congress approves and supports the determination of the President, as Commander-in-Chief, to take all necessary measures to repel any armed attack against the forces of the United States and to prevent further aggression." H.R.J.Res. 1145, 88th Cong., 2d Sess., 78 Stat. 384 (1964). It was repealed December 31, 1970. Did the repeal have any effect on the President's powers to continue operations in Vietnam?

preliminary issues of justiciability. We cannot make these problems go away simply by refusing to hear the case of three obscure Army privates. I intimate not even tentative views upon any of these matters, but I think the Court should squarely face them by granting certiorari and setting this case for oral argument.

Mr. Justice Douglas, with whom Mr. Justice Stewart concurs, dissenting.

The questions posed by Mr. Justice Stewart cover the wide range of problems which the Senate Committee on Foreign Relations recently explored, in connection with the SEATO treaty of February 19, 1955, and the Tonkin Gulf Resolution.

Mr. Katzenbach, representing the Administration, testified that he did not regard the Tonkin Gulf Resolution to be "a declaration of war" and that while the Resolution was not "constitutionally necessary" it was "politically, from an international viewpoint and from a domestic viewpoint, extremely important." He added:

"The use of the phrase 'to declare war' as it was used in the Constitution of the United States had a particular meaning in terms of the events and the practices which existed at the time it was adopted. . . .

"[I]t was recognized by the Founding Fathers that the President might have to take emergency action to protect the security of the United States, but that if there was going to be another use of the armed forces of the United States, that was a decision which Congress should check the Executive on, which Congress should support. It was for that reason that the phrase was inserted in the Constitution.

"Now, over a long period of time, . . . there have been many uses of the military forces of the United States for a variety of purposes without a congressional declaration of war. But it would be fair to say that most of these were relatively minor uses of force. . . .

"A declaration of war would not, I think, correctly reflect the very limited objectives of the United States with respect to Vietnam. It would not correctly reflect our efforts there, what we are trying to do, the reasons why we are there, to use an outmoded phraseology, to declare war."

The view that Congress was intended to play a more active role in the initiation and conduct of war than the above statements might suggest has been espoused by Senator Fulbright (Cong.Rec. Oct. 11, 1967, 14683–14690), quoting Thomas Jefferson who said:

"We have already given in example one effectual check to the Dog of war by transferring the power of letting him loose from the Executive to the Legislative body, from those who are to spend to those who are to pay."

These opposed views are reflected in the Prize Cases, 2 Black 635, a five-to-four decision rendered in 1863. Mr. Justice Grier, writing for the majority, emphasized the arguments for strong presidential powers. Justice Nelson, writing for the minority of four, read the Constitution more strictly, emphasizing that what is war in actuality may not constitute war in the constitutional sense. During all subsequent periods in our history—through the Spanish-American War, the Boxer Rebellion, two World Wars, Korea, and now Vietnam—the two points of view urged in the *Prize Cases* have continued to be voiced. . . .

THE COURT AND THE VIETNAM CONTROVERSY

After the *Mora* decision, efforts to obtain a Supreme Court ruling on whether or not American military operations in Vietnam amounted to an "unconstitutional" war continued, but without success. The lower courts generally ruled that the issue was not justiciable.

Orlando v. Laird, 443 F.2d 1039 (2d Cir.1971) cert. denied 404 U.S. 869 (1971), is a notable instance in which a challenge to United States military activity in Vietnam was held to present a justicable question. Reaching the merits of the case, the court concluded that some mutual participation of Congress in a war of this kind was required but that Congress had sufficiently authorized our South-East Asian commitments.

Dissenting again from denial of certiorari in Da Costa v. Laird, 405 U.S. 979 (1972) Justice Douglas said: "[I]t is argued that the Constitution gives to Congress the *exclusive* power to determine when it has declared war. But if there is such a 'textually demonstrable constitutional commitment,' . . . it is for this Court to determine its scope."

Professor Henkin argues that the "courts, despite sometimes-misguided efforts to compel them to do so (as on Vietnam), are not likely to step into intense confrontations between President and Congress, or inhibit either when the other does not object. Whether from the sense that the boundary between Congress and President . . ., cannot be defined by law, whether from realization of the inherent limitations of judicial power or from prudence, whether under a doctrine of 'political questions' or by other judicial devices and formulae for abstention, courts will not make certain what was left uncertain, will not curtail the power of the political branches, will not arbitrate their differences. Then, in time, the issues will recede, stirring neither controversy nor case." *Foreign Affairs and the Constitution,* 274–275 (1972).

SECTION 2. CONGRESSIONAL INTERFERENCE WITH PRESIDENTIAL PREROGATIVES

A. THE LEGISLATIVE VETO

IMMIGRATION AND NATURALIZATION SERVICE v. CHADHA

462 U.S. 919, 103 S.Ct. 2764, 77 L.Ed.2d 317 (1983).

Chief Justice Burger delivered the opinion of the Court.

. . . [These cases present] a challenge to the constitutionality of the provision in § 244(c)(2) of the Immigration and Nationality Act, 8 U.S.C. § 1254(c)(2), authorizing one House of Congress, by resolution, to invalidate the decision of the Executive Branch, pursuant to authority delegated by Congress to the Attorney General of the United States, to allow a particular deportable alien to remain in the United States.

I

Chadha is an East Indian who was born in Kenya and holds a British passport. He was lawfully admitted to the United States in 1966 on a non-immigrant student visa. His visa expired on June 30, 1972. On October 11, 1973, the District Director of the Immigration and Naturalization Service ordered Chadha to show cause why he should not be deported for having "remained in the United States for a longer time than permitted." App. 6. Pursuant to § 242(b) of the Immigration and Nationality Act (Act), 8 U.S.C. § 1254(b), a deportation hearing was held before an immigration judge on January 11, 1974. Chadha conceded that he was deportable for overstaying his visa and the hearing was adjourned to enable him to file an application for suspension of deportation under § 244(a)(1) of the Act, 8 U.S.C. § 1254(a) (1). Section 244(a)(1) provides:

"(a) As hereinafter prescribed in this section, the Attorney General may, in his discretion, suspend deportation and adjust the status to that of an alien lawfully admitted for permanent residence, in the case of an alien who applies to the Attorney General for suspension of deportation and—

(1) is deportable under any law of the United States except the provisions specified in paragraph (2) of this subsection; has been physically present in the United States for a continuous period of not less than seven years immediately preceding the date of such application, and proves that during all of such period he was and is a person of good moral character; and is a person whose deportation would, in the opinion of the Attorney General, result in extreme hardship to the alien or to his spouse, parent, or child, who is a citizen of the United States or an alien lawfully admitted for permanent residence."

After Chadha submitted his application for suspension of deportation, the deportation hearing was resumed on February 7, 1974. On the basis of evidence adduced at the hearing, affidavits submitted with the application, and the results of a character investigation conducted by the INS, the immigration judge, on June 25, 1974, ordered that Chadha's deportation be suspended. The immigration judge found that Chadha met the requirements of § 244(a) (1): he had resided continuously in the United States for over seven years, was of good moral character, and would suffer "extreme hardship" if deported.

Pursuant to § 244(c)(1) of the Act, 8 U.S.C. § 1254(c)(1), the immigration judge suspended Chadha's deportation and a report of the suspension was transmitted to Congress. Section 244(c)(1) provides:

"Upon application by any alien who is found by the Attorney General to meet the requirements of subsection (a) of this section the Attorney General may in his discretion suspend deportation of such alien. If the deportation of any alien is suspended under the provisions of this subsection, a complete and detailed statement of the facts and pertinent provisions of law in the case shall be reported to the Congress with the reasons for such suspension. Such reports shall be submitted on the first day of each calendar month in which Congress is in session."

Once the Attorney General's recommendation for suspension of Chadha's deportation was conveyed to Congress, Congress had the power under § 244(c) (2) of the Act, 8 U.S.C. § 1254(c)(2), to veto the Attorney General's determination that Chadha should not be deported. Section 244(c)(2) provides:

"(2) In the case of an alien specified in paragraph (1) of subsection (a) of this subsection—

if during the session of the Congress at which a case is reported, or prior to the close of the session of the Congress next following the session at which a case is reported, either the Senate or the House of Representatives passes a resolution stating in substance that it does not favor the suspension of such deportation, the Attorney General shall thereupon deport such alien or authorize the alien's voluntary departure at his own expense under the order of deportation in the manner provided by law. If, within the time above specified, neither the Senate nor the House of Representatives shall pass such a resolution, the Attorney General shall cancel deportation proceedings."

The June 25, 1974 order of the immigration judge suspending Chadha's deportation remained outstanding as a valid order for a year and a half. For reasons not disclosed by the record, Congress did not exercise the veto authority reserved to it under § 244(c)(2) until the first session of the 94th Congress. This was the final session in which Congress, pursuant to § 244(c)(2), could act to veto the Attorney General's determination that Chadha should not be deported. . . .

On December 12, 1975, Representative Eilberg, Chairman of the Judiciary Subcommittee on Immigration, Citizenship, and International Law, introduced a resolution opposing "the granting of permanent residence in the United States to [six] aliens", including Chadha.   H.R.Res. 926, 94th Cong., 1st Sess.; 121 Cong.Rec. 40247 (1975).   The resolution was referred to the House Committee on the Judiciary.   On December 16, 1975, the resolution was discharged from further consideration by the House Committee on the Judiciary and submitted to the House of Representatives for a vote.   121 Cong.Rec. 40800. The resolution had not been printed and was not made available to other Members of the House prior to or at the time it was voted on.   Ibid.   So far as the record before us shows, the House consideration of the resolution was based on Representative Eilberg's statement from the floor that

"[i]t was the feeling of the committee, after reviewing 340 cases, that the aliens contained in the resolution [Chadha and five others] did not meet these statutory requirements, particularly as it relates to hardship; and it is the opinion of the committee that their deportation should not be suspended."   Ibid.

The resolution was passed without debate or recorded vote.   Since the House action was pursuant to § 244(c)(2), the resolution was not treated as an Article I legislative act; it was not submitted to the Senate or presented to the President for his action.

After the House veto of the Attorney General's decision to allow Chadha to remain in the United States, the immigration judge reopened the deportation proceedings to implement the House order deporting Chadha.   Chadha moved to terminate the proceedings on the ground that § 244(c)(2) is unconstitutional. The immigration judge held that he had no authority to rule on the constitutional validity of § 244(c)(2).   On November 8, 1976, Chadha was ordered deported pursuant to the House action.

Chadha appealed the deportation order to the Board of Immigration Appeals again contending that § 244(c)(2) is unconstitutional.   The Board held that it had "no power to declare unconstitutional an act of Congress" and Chadha's appeal was dismissed.

Pursuant to § 106(a) of the Act, 8 U.S.C. § 1105a(a), Chadha filed a petition for review of the deportation order in the United States Court of Appeals for the Ninth Circuit.   The Immigration and Naturalization Service agreed with Chadha's position before the Court of Appeals and joined him in arguing that § 244(c)(2) is unconstitutional.   In light of the importance of the question, the Court of Appeals invited both the Senate and the House of Representatives to file briefs *amici curiae.*

After full briefing and oral argument, the Court of Appeals held that the House was without constitutional authority to order Chadha's deportation; accordingly it directed the Attorney General "to cease and desist from taking any steps to deport this alien based upon the resolution enacted by the House of Representatives."   Chadha v. INS, 634 F.2d 408, 436 (CA9 1980).   The essence of its holding was that § 244(c)(2) violates the constitutional doctrine of separation of powers.

. . . [W]e now affirm.

II

Before we address the important question of the constitutionality of the one-House veto provision of § 244(c)(2), we first consider several challenges to the authority of this Court to resolve the issue raised.

. . .

B

Severability

Congress . . . contends that the provision for the one-House veto in § 244(c)(2) cannot be severed from § 244. Congress argues that if the provision for the one-House veto is held unconstitutional, all of § 244 must fall. If § 244 in its entirety is violative of the Constitution, it follows that the Attorney General has no authority to suspend Chadha's deportation under § 244(a)(1) and Chadha would be deported. From this, Congress argues that Chadha lacks standing to challenge the constitutionality of the one-House veto provision because he could receive no relief even if his constitutional challenge proves successful.

. . . Congress itself has provided the answer to the question of severability in § 406 of the Immigration and Nationality Act, 8 U.S.C. § 1101, which provides:

"If *any* particular provision of this Act, or the application thereof to *any* person or circumstance, is held invalid, *the remainder of the Act and the application of such proposition to other persons or circumstances shall not be affected thereby.*" (Emphasis added.)

. . .

. . . Plainly, Congress' desire to retain a veto in this area cannot be considered in isolation but must be viewed in the context of Congress' irritation with the burden of private immigration bills. This legislative history is not sufficient to rebut the presumption of severability raised by § 406 because there is insufficient evidence that Congress would have continued to subject itself to the onerous burdens of private bills had it known that § 244(c)(2) would be held unconstitutional.

. . . Absent the passage of a bill to the contrary, deportation proceedings will be cancelled when the period specified in § 244(c)(2) has expired. Clearly, § 244 survives as a workable administrative mechanism without the one-House veto.

. . .

F

Case or Controversy

It is also contended that this is not a genuine controversy but "a friendly, non-adversary, proceeding," Ashwander v. Tennessee Valley Authority, supra, 297 U.S., at 346 (Brandeis, J., concurring), upon which the Court should not pass. This argument rests on the fact that Chadha and the INS take the same position on the constitutionality of the one-House veto. But it would be a curious result if, in the administration of justice, a person could be denied access to the courts because the Attorney General of the United States agreed with the legal arguments asserted by the individual.

. . . [T]he INS's agreement with Chadha's position does not alter the fact that the INS would have deported Chadha absent the Court of Appeals' judgment. We agree with the Court of Appeals that "Chadha has asserted a concrete controversy, and our decision will have real meaning: if we rule for

Chadha, he will not be deported; if we uphold § 244(c)(2), the INS will execute its order and deport him." 634 F.2d, at 419.

Of course, there may be prudential, as opposed to Art. III, concerns about sanctioning the adjudication of this case in the absence of any participant supporting the validity of § 244(c)(2). The Court of Appeals properly dispelled any such concerns by inviting and accepting briefs from both Houses of Congress. We have long held that Congress is the proper party to defend the validity of a statute when an agency of government, as a defendant charged with enforcing the statute, agrees with plaintiffs that the statute is inapplicable or unconstitutional. See Cheng Fan Kwok v. INS, supra, 392 U.S., at 210 n. 9; United States v. Lovett, 328 U.S. 303 (1946).

G

Political Question

It is also argued that this case presents a nonjusticiable political question because Chadha is merely challenging Congress' authority under the Naturalization Clause, U.S. Const. art. I, § 8, cl. 4, and the Necessary and Proper Clause, U.S. Const. art. I, § 8, cl. 18. It is argued that Congress' Article I power "To establish a uniform Rule of Naturalization", combined with the Necessary and Proper Clause, grants it unreviewable authority over the regulation of aliens. The plenary authority of Congress over aliens under Art. I, § 8, cl. 4 is not open to question, but what is challenged here is whether Congress has chosen a constitutionally permissible means of implementing that power. As we made clear in Buckley v. Valeo, 424 U.S. 1 (1976); "Congress has plenary authority in all cases in which it has substantive legislative jurisdiction, McCulloch v. Maryland, 4 Wheat. 316 (1819), so long as the exercise of that authority does not offend some other constitutional restriction." Id., at 132.

.   .   .

It is correct that this controversy may, in a sense, be termed "political." But the presence of constitutional issues with significant political overtones does not automatically invoke the political question doctrine. Resolution of litigation challenging the constitutional authority of one of the three branches cannot be evaded by courts because the issues have political implications in the sense urged by Congress. Marbury v. Madison, 1 Cranch 137 (1803), was also a "political" case, involving as it did claims under a judicial commission alleged to have been duly signed by the President but not delivered. But "courts cannot reject as 'no law suit' a bona fide controversy as to whether some action denominated 'political' exceeds constitutional authority." Baker v. Carr, supra, 369 U.S. at 217.

.   .   .

III

A

We turn now to the question whether action of one House of Congress under § 244(c)(2) violates strictures of the Constitution. We begin, of course, with the presumption that the challenged statute is valid. . . .

By the same token, the fact that a given law or procedure is efficient, convenient, and useful in facilitating functions of government, standing alone, will not save it if it is contrary to the Constitution. Convenience and efficiency are not the primary objectives—or the hallmarks—of democratic government and our inquiry is sharpened rather than blunted by the fact that Congressional veto provisions are appearing with increasing frequency in statutes which delegate authority to executive and independent agencies:

"Since 1932, when the first veto provision was enacted into law, 295 congressional veto-type procedures have been inserted in 196 different statutes as follows: from 1932 to 1939, five statutes were affected; from 1940–49, nineteen statutes; between 1950–59, thirty-four statutes; and from 1960–69, forty-nine. From the year 1970 through 1975, at least one hundred sixty-three such provisions were included in eighty-nine laws." Abourezk, The Congressional Veto: A Contemporary Response to Executive Encroachment on Legislative Prerogatives, 52 Ind.L.Rev. 323, 324 (1977).

Justice White undertakes to make a case for the proposition that the one-House veto is a useful "political invention," and we need not challenge that assertion. We can even concede this utilitarian argument although the long range political wisdom of this "invention" is arguable. It has been vigorously debated and it is instructive to compare the views of the protagonists. See, e.g., Javits & Klein, Congressional Oversight and the Legislative Veto: A Constitutional Analysis, 52 N.Y.U.L.Rev. 455 (1977), and Martin, The Legislative Veto and the Responsible Exercise of Congressional Power, 68 Va.L.Rev. 253 (1982). But policy arguments supporting even useful "political inventions" are subject to the demands of the Constitution which defines powers and, with respect to this subject, sets out just how those powers are to be exercised.

Explicit and unambiguous provisions of the Constitution prescribe and define the respective functions of the Congress and of the Executive in the legislative process. Since the precise terms of those familiar provisions are critical to the resolution of this case, we set them out verbatim. Art. I provides:

"All legislative Powers herein granted shall be vested in a Congress of the United States, which shall consist of a Senate *and* a House of Representatives." Art. I, § 1. (Emphasis added).

"Every Bill which shall have passed the House of Representatives *and* the Senate, *shall,* before it become a Law, be presented to the President of the United States; . . ." Art. I, § 7, cl. 2. (Emphasis added).

"*Every* Order, Resolution, or Vote to which the Concurrence of the Senate and House of Representatives may be necessary (except on a question of Adjournment) *shall be* presented to the President of the United States; and before the Same shall take Effect, *shall be* approved by him, or being disapproved by him, *shall be* repassed by two thirds of the Senate and House of Representatives, according to the Rules and Limitations prescribed in the Case of a Bill." Art. I, § 7, cl. 3. (Emphasis added).

. . . [T]he purposes underlying the Presentment Clauses, Art. I, § 7, cls. 2, 3, and the bicameral requirement of Art. I, § 1 and § 7, cl. 2, guide our resolution of the important question presented in this case. The very structure of the articles delegating and separating powers under Arts. I, II, and III exemplify the concept of separation of powers and we now turn to Art. I.

B

The Presentment Clauses

The records of the Constitutional Convention reveal that the requirement that all legislation be presented to the President before becoming law was uniformly accepted by the Framers. Presentment to the President and the Presidential veto were considered so imperative that the draftsmen took special pains to assure that these requirements could not be circumvented. During the final debate on Art. I, § 7, cl. 2, James Madison expressed concern that it might easily be evaded by the simple expedient of calling a proposed law a "resolution" or "vote" rather than a "bill." 2 M. Farrand, The Records of the Federal Convention of 1787 301–302. As a consequence, Art. I, § 7, cl. 3, was added. Id., at 304–305.

The decision to provide the President with a limited and qualified power to nullify proposed legislation by veto was based on the profound conviction of the Framers that the powers conferred on Congress were the powers to be most carefully circumscribed. It is beyond doubt that lawmaking was a power to be shared by both Houses and the President. . . .

The President's role in the lawmaking process also reflects the Framers' careful efforts to check whatever propensity a particular Congress might have to enact oppressive, improvident, or ill-considered measures. . . . Presentment Clauses serve the important purpose of assuring that a "national" perspective is grafted on the legislative process. . . .

C

Bicameralism

The bicameral requirement of Art. I, §§ 1, 7 was of scarcely less concern to the Framers than was the Presidential veto and indeed the two concepts are interdependent. By providing that no law could take effect without the concurrence of the prescribed majority of the Members of both Houses, the Framers reemphasized their belief, already remarked upon in connection with the Presentment Clauses, that legislation should not be enacted unless it has been carefully and fully considered by the Nation's elected officials. . . .

. . .

However familiar, it is useful to recall that apart from their fear that special interests could be favored at the expense of public needs, the Framers were also concerned, although not of one mind, over the apprehensions of the smaller states. Those states feared a commonality of interest among the larger states would work to their disadvantage; representatives of the larger states, on the other hand, were skeptical of a legislature that could pass laws favoring a minority of the people. See 1 M. Farrand, supra, 176–177, 484–491. It need hardly be repeated here that the Great Compromise, under which one House was viewed as representing the people and the other the states, allayed the fears of both the large and small states.

We see therefore that the Framers were acutely conscious that the bicameral requirement and the Presentment Clauses would serve essential constitutional functions. The President's participation in the legislative process was to protect the Executive Branch from Congress and to protect the whole people from improvident laws. The division of the Congress into two distinctive bodies assures that the legislative power would be exercised only after opportunity for full study and debate in separate settings. The President's unilateral veto power, in turn, was limited by the power of two thirds of both Houses of Congress to overrule a veto thereby precluding final arbitrary action of one person. See 1 M. Farrand, supra, at 99–104. It emerges clearly that the prescription for legislative action in Art. I, §§ 1, 7 represents the Framers' decision that the legislative power of the Federal government be exercised in accord with a single, finely wrought and exhaustively considered, procedure.

IV

. . . [W]e must . . . establish that the challenged action under § 244(c)(2) is of the kind to which the procedural requirements of Art. I, § 7 apply. Not every action taken by either House is subject to the bicameralism and presentment requirements of Art. I. Whether actions taken by either

House are, in law and fact, an exercise of legislative power depends not on their form but upon "whether they contain matter which is properly to be regarded as legislative in its character and effect." S.Rep. No. 1335, 54th Cong., 2d Sess., 8 (1897).

Examination of the action taken here by one House pursuant to § 244(c)(2) reveals that it was essentially legislative in purpose and effect. In purporting to exercise power defined in Art. I, § 8, cl. 4 to "establish an uniform Rule of Naturalization," the House took action that had the purpose and effect of altering the legal rights, duties and relations of persons, including the Attorney General, Executive Branch officials and Chadha, all outside the legislative branch. . . .

The legislative character of the one-House veto in this case is confirmed by the character of the Congressional action it supplants. Neither the House of Representatives nor the Senate contends that, absent the veto provision in § 244(c)(2), either of them, or both of them acting together, could effectively require the Attorney General to deport an alien once the Attorney General, in the exercise of legislatively delegated authority,[16] had determined the alien should remain in the United States. Without the challenged provision in § 244(c)(2), this could have been achieved, if at all, only by legislation requiring deportation. Similarly, a veto by one House of Congress under § 244(c)(2) cannot be justified as an attempt at amending the standards set out in § 244(a)(1), or as a repeal of § 244 as applied to Chadha. Amendment and repeal of statutes, no less than enactment, must conform with Art. I.

The nature of the decision implemented by the one-House veto in this case further manifests its legislative character. After long experience with the clumsy, time consuming private bill procedure, Congress made a deliberate choice to delegate to the Executive Branch, and specifically to the Attorney General, the authority to allow deportable aliens to remain in this country in certain specified circumstances. It is not disputed that this choice to delegate authority is precisely the kind of decision that can be implemented only in accordance with the procedures set out in Art. I. Disagreement with the Attorney General's decision on Chadha's deportation—that is, Congress' decision to deport Chadha—no less than Congress' original choice to delegate to the Attorney General the authority to make that decision, involves determinations of policy that Congress can implement in only one way; bicameral passage followed by presentment to the President. Congress must abide by its delegation of authority until that delegation is legislatively altered or revoked.[19]

[16] Congress protests that affirming the Court of Appeals in this case will sanction "lawmaking by the Attorney General. . . . Why is the Attorney General exempt from submitting his proposed changes in the law to the full bicameral process?" To be sure, some administrative agency action—rule making for example—may resemble "lawmaking." See 5 U.S.C. § 551(4), which defines an agency's "rule" as "the whole or part of an agency statement of general or particular applicability and future effect designed to implement, interpret, or prescribe *law* or policy. . . ." Executive action under legislatively delegated authority that might resemble "legislative" action in some respects is not subject to the approval of both Houses of Congress and the President for the reason that the Constitution does not so require. That kind of Executive action is always subject to check by the terms of the legislation that authorized it; and if that authority is exceeded it is open to judicial review as well as the power of Congress to modify or revoke the authority entirely. A one-House veto is clearly legislative in both character and effect and is not so checked; the need for the check provided by Art. I, §§ 1, 7 is therefore clear. Congress' authority to delegate portions of its power to administrative agencies provides no support for the argument that Congress can constitutionally control administration of the laws by way of a Congressional veto.

[19] This does not mean that Congress is required to capitulate to "the accretion of policy control by forces outside its chambers." Javits and Klein, Congressional Oversight and the Legislative Veto: A Constitutional Analysis, 52 N.Y.U.L.Rev. 455, 462 (1977). The Constitution provides Congress with abundant means to oversee and control its administrative creatures. Beyond the obvious fact that Congress ultimately controls administrative agencies in the legislation that creates them, other means of control, such as durational limits on authorizations and formal reporting requirements, lie well

. . .

Since it is clear that the action by the House under § 244(c)(2) was not within any of the express constitutional exceptions authorizing one House to act alone, and equally clear that it was an exercise of legislative power, that action was subject to the standards prescribed in Article I.[21] . . .

The veto authorized by § 244(c)(2) doubtless has been in many respects a convenient shortcut; the "sharing" with the Executive by Congress of its authority over aliens in this manner is, on its face, an appealing compromise. In purely practical terms, it is obviously easier for action to be taken by one House without submission to the President; but it is crystal clear from the records of the Convention, contemporaneous writings and debates, that the Framers ranked other values higher than efficiency. The records of the Convention and debates in the States preceding ratification underscore the common desire to define and limit the exercise of the newly created federal powers affecting the states and the people. There is unmistakable expression of a determination that legislation by the national Congress be a step-by-step, deliberate and deliberative process.

. . .

V

We hold that the Congressional veto provision in § 244(c)(2) is severable from the Act and that it is unconstitutional. Accordingly, the judgment of the Court of Appeals is

Affirmed.

Justice Powell, concurring in the judgment.

The Court's decision, based on the Presentment Clauses, Art. I, § 7, cl. 2 and 3, apparently will invalidate every use of the legislative veto. The breadth of this holding gives one pause. Congress has included the veto in literally hundreds of statutes, dating back to the 1930s. Congress clearly views this procedure as essential to controlling the delegation of power to administrative agencies. One reasonably may disagree with Congress' assessment of the veto's utility, but the respect due its judgment as a coordinate branch of Government cautions that our holding should be no more extensive than necessary to decide this case. In my view, the case may be decided on a narrower ground. When Congress finds that a particular person does not satisfy the statutory criteria for permanent residence in this country it has assumed a judicial function in violation of the principle of separation of powers. Accordingly, I concur in the judgment.

. . .

II

. . .

On its face, the House's action appears clearly adjudicatory. The House did not enact a general rule; rather it made its own determination that six specific

within Congress' constitutional power. See id., at 460–461; Kaiser, Congressional Action to Overturn Agency Rules: Alternatives to the "Legislative Veto", 32 Ad.L.Rev. 667 (1980).

[21] Justice Powell's position is that the one-House veto in this case is a *judicial* act and therefore unconstitutional as beyond the authority vested in Congress by the Constitution. We agree that there is a sense in which one-House action pursuant to § 244(c)(2) has a judicial cast, since it purports to "review" Executive action. . . . But the attempted analogy between judicial action and the one-House veto is less than perfect. Federal courts do not enjoy a roving mandate to correct alleged excesses of administrative agencies; we are limited by Art. III to hearing cases and controversies and no justiciable case or controversy was presented by the Attorney General's decision to allow Chadha to remain in this country. We are aware of no decision, and Justice Powell has cited none, where a federal court has reviewed a decision of the Attorney General suspending deportation of an alien pursuant to the standards set out in § 244(a)(1). This is not surprising, given that no party to such action has either the motivation or the right to appeal from it. . . .

persons did not comply with certain statutory criteria. It thus undertook the type of decision that traditionally has been left to other branches. Even if the House did not make a *de novo* determination, but simply reviewed the Immigration and Naturalization Service's findings, it still assumed a function ordinarily entrusted to the federal courts. . . .

The impropriety of the House's assumption of this function is confirmed by the fact that its action raises the very danger the Framers sought to avoid—the exercise of unchecked power. In deciding whether Chadha deserves to be deported, Congress is not subject to any internal constraints that prevent it from arbitrarily depriving him of the right to remain in this country.[9] Unlike the judiciary or an administrative agency, Congress is not bound by established substantive rules. Nor is it subject to the procedural safeguards, such as the right to counsel and a hearing before an impartial tribunal, that are present when a court or an agency adjudicates individual rights. The only effective constraint on Congress' power is political, but Congress is most accountable politically when it prescribes rules of general applicability. When it decides rights of specific persons, those rights are subject to "the tyranny of a shifting majority."

Chief Justice Marshall observed: "It is the peculiar province of the legislature to prescribe general rules for the government of society; the application of those rules would seem to be the duty of other departments." Fletcher v. Peck, 6 Cranch 87, 136 (1810). In my view, when Congress undertook to apply its rules to Chadha, it exceeded the scope of its constitutionally prescribed authority. I would not reach the broader question whether legislative vetoes are invalid under the Presentment Clauses.

Justice White, dissenting.

Today the Court not only invalidates § 244(c)(2) of the Immigration and Nationality Act, but also sounds the death knell for nearly 200 other statutory provisions in which Congress has reserved a "legislative veto." For this reason, the Court's decision is of surpassing importance. And it is for this reason that the Court would have been well-advised to decide the case, if possible, on the narrower grounds of separation of powers, leaving for full consideration the constitutionality of other congressional review statutes operating on such varied matters as war powers and agency rulemaking, some of which concern the independent regulatory agencies.

The prominence of the legislative veto mechanism in our contemporary political system and its importance to Congress can hardly be overstated. It has become a central means by which Congress secures the accountability of executive and independent agencies. Without the legislative veto, Congress is faced with a Hobson's choice: either to refrain from delegating the necessary authority, leaving itself with a hopeless task of writing laws with the requisite specificity to cover endless special circumstances across the entire policy landscape, or in the alternative, to abdicate its lawmaking function to the executive branch and independent agencies. To choose the former leaves major national problems unresolved; to opt for the latter risks unaccountable policymaking by those not elected to fill that role. Accordingly, over the past five decades, the legislative veto has been placed in nearly 200 statutes. The device is known in every field of governmental concern: reorganization, budgets, foreign affairs,

---

[9] When Congress grants particular individuals relief or benefits under its spending power, the danger of oppressive action that the separation of powers was designed to avoid is not implicated. Similarly, Congress may authorize the admission of individual aliens by special acts, but it does not follow that Congress unilaterally may make a judgment that a particular alien has no legal right to remain in this country. See Memorandum Concerning H.R. 9766 Entitled "An Act to Direct the Deportation of Harry Renton Bridges," reprinted in S.Rep. No. 2031, pt. 1, 76th Cong., 3d Sess., 8 (1940). As Attorney General Robert Jackson remarked, such a practice "would be an historical departure from an unbroken American practice and tradition." S.Rep. No. 2031, supra, at 9.

war powers, and regulation of trade, safety, energy, the environment and the economy.

I

. . .

During the 1970's the legislative veto was important in resolving a series of major constitutional disputes between the President and Congress over claims of the President to broad impoundment, war, and national emergency powers. The key provision of the War Powers Resolution, 50 U.S.C. § 1544(c), authorizes the termination by concurrent resolution of the use of armed forces in hostilities. A similar measure resolved the problem posed by Presidential claims of inherent power to impound appropriations. Congressional Budget and Impoundment Control Act of 1974, 31 U.S.C. § 1403. In conference, a compromise was achieved under which permanent impoundments, termed "rescissions," would require approval through enactment of legislation. In contrast, temporary impoundments, or "deferrals," would become effective unless disapproved by one House. This compromise provided the President with flexibility, while preserving ultimate Congressional control over the budget. Although the War Powers Resolution was enacted over President Nixon's veto, the Impoundment Control Act was enacted with the President's approval. These statutes were followed by others resolving similar problems: the National Emergencies Act, § 202, 90 Stat. 1255, 50 U.S.C. § 1622 (1976), resolving the longstanding problems with unchecked Executive emergency power; the Arms Export Control Act, § 211, 90 Stat. 729, 22 U.S.C. § 2776(b) (1976), resolving the problem of foreign arms sales; and the Nuclear Non-Proliferation Act of 1978, §§ 303, 304(a), 306, 307, 401, 92 Stat. 120, 130, 134, 137, 139, 144–145, 42 U.S.C. §§ 2160(f), 2155(b), 2157(b), 2158, 2153(d) (Supp. IV, 1980), resolving the problem of exports of nuclear technology.

. . .

. . . [T]he legislative veto is more than "efficient, convenient, and useful." It is an important if not indispensable political invention that allows the President and Congress to resolve major constitutional and policy differences, assures the accountability of independent regulatory agencies, and preserves Congress' control over lawmaking. Perhaps there are other means of accommodation and accountability, but the increasing reliance of Congress upon the legislative veto suggests that the alternatives to which Congress must now turn are not entirely satisfactory.

The history of the legislative veto also makes clear that it has not been a sword with which Congress has struck out to aggrandize itself at the expense of the other branches—the concerns of Madison and Hamilton. Rather, the veto has been a means of defense, a reservation of ultimate authority necessary if Congress is to fulfill its designated role under Article I as the nation's lawmaker. While the President has often objected to particular legislative vetoes, generally those left in the hands of congressional committees, the Executive has more often agreed to legislative review as the price for a broad delegation of authority. To be sure, the President may have preferred unrestricted power, but that could be precisely why Congress thought it essential to retain a check on the exercise of delegated authority.

II

For all these reasons, the apparent sweep of the Court's decision today is regretable. The Court's Article I analysis appears to invalidate all legislative vetoes irrespective of form or subject. Because the legislative veto is commonly found as a check upon rulemaking by administrative agencies and upon broad-based policy decisions of the Executive Branch, it is particularly unfortunate that the Court reaches its decision in a case involving the exercise of a veto over deportation decisions regarding particular individuals. . . . Unfortunately, today's holding is not so limited.

If the legislative veto were as plainly unconstitutional as the Court strives to suggest, its broad ruling today would be more comprehensible. But, the constitutionality of the legislative veto is anything but clearcut. The issue divides scholars, courts, attorneys general, and the two other branches of the National Government. If the veto devices so flagrantly disregarded the requirements of Article I as the Court today suggests, I find it incomprehensible that Congress, whose members are bound by oath to uphold the Constitution, would have placed these mechanisms in nearly 200 separate laws over a period of 50 years.

The reality of the situation is that the constitutional question posed today is one of immense difficulty over which the executive and legislative branches—as well as scholars and judges—have understandably disagreed. That disagreement stems from the silence of the Constitution on the precise question: The Constitution does not directly authorize or prohibit the legislative veto. Thus, our task should be to determine whether the legislative veto is consistent with the purposes of Art. I and the principles of Separation of Powers which are reflected in that Article and throughout the Constitution. . . .

. . . .

III

The Court holds that the disapproval of a suspension of deportation by the resolution of one House of Congress is an exercise of legislative power without compliance with the prerequisites for lawmaking set forth in Art. I of the Constitution. Specifically, the Court maintains that the provisions of § 244(c) (2) are inconsistent with the requirement of bicameral approval, implicit in Art. I, § 1, and the requirement that all bills and resolutions that require the concurrence of both Houses be presented to the President, Art. I, § 7, cl. 2 and 3.

I do not dispute the Court's truismatic exposition of these clauses. . . .

It does not, however, answer the constitutional question before us. The power to exercise a legislative veto is not the power to write new law without bicameral approval or presidential consideration. The veto must be authorized by statute and may only negative what an Executive department or independent agency has proposed. On its face, the legislative veto no more allows one House of Congress to make law than does the presidential veto confer such power upon the President. Accordingly, the Court properly recognizes that it "must establish that the challenged action under § 244(c)(2) is of the kind to which the procedural requirements of Art. I, § 7 apply" and admits that "not every action taken by either House is subject to the bicameralism and presentation requirements of Art. I."

A

The terms of the Presentment Clauses suggest only that bills and their equivalent are subject to the requirements of bicameral passage and presentment to the President. . . .

B

. . . . The Court's holding today that all legislative-type action must be enacted through the lawmaking process ignores that legislative authority is routinely delegated to the Executive branch, to the independent regulatory agencies, and to private individuals and groups. . . .

This Court's decisions sanctioning such delegations make clear that Article I does not require all action with the effect of legislation to be passed as a law.

Theoretically, agencies and officials were asked only to "fill up the details," and the rule was that "Congress cannot delegate any part of its legislative power except under a limitation of a prescribed standard." United States v. Chicago, Milwaukee R. Co., 282 U.S. 311, 324 (1931). Chief Justice Taft elaborated the standard in J.W. Hampton & Co. v. United States, 276 U.S. 394, 409 (1928): "If Congress shall lay down by legislative act an intelligible principle to which the person or body authorized to fix such rates is directed to conform, such legislative action is not a forbidden delegation of legislative power." In practice, however, restrictions on the scope of the power that could be delegated diminished and all but disappeared. In only two instances did the Court find an unconstitutional delegation. Panama Refining Co. v. Ryan, 293 U.S. 388 (1935); Schechter Poultry Corp. v. United States, 295 U.S. 495 (1935). In other cases, the "intelligible principle" through which agencies have attained enormous control over the economic affairs of the country was held to include such formulations as "just and reasonable," Tagg Bros. & Moorhead v. United States, 280 U.S. 420 (1930), "public interest," New York Central Securities Corp. v. United States, 287 U.S. 12 (1932), "public convenience, interest, or necessity," Federal Radio Comm. v. Nelson Bros. Bond & Mortgage Co., 289 U.S. 266, 285 (1933), and "unfair methods of competition." FTC v. Gratz, 253 U.S. 421 (1920).

The wisdom and the constitutionality of these broad delegations are matters that still have not been put to rest. . . . . There is no question but that agency rulemaking is lawmaking in any functional or realistic sense of the term.

. . .

If Congress may delegate lawmaking power to independent and executive agencies, it is most difficult to understand Article I as forbidding Congress from also reserving a check on legislative power for itself. Absent the veto, the agencies receiving delegations of legislative or quasi-legislative power may issue regulations having the force of law without bicameral approval and without the President's signature. It is thus not apparent why the reservation of a veto over the exercise of that legislative power must be subject to a more exacting test. In both cases, it is enough that the initial statutory authorizations comply with the Article I requirements.

. . .

. . . If the effective functioning of a complex modern government requires the delegation of vast authority which, by virtue of its breadth, is legislative or "quasi-legislative" in character, I cannot accept that Article I— which is, after all, the source of the non-delegation doctrine—should forbid Congress from qualifying that grant with a legislative veto.

. . .

IV

. . . [T]he history of the separation of powers doctrine is . . . a history of accommodation and practicality. Apprehensions of an overly powerful branch have not led to undue prophylactic measures that handicap the effective working of the national government as a whole. The Constitution does not contemplate total separation of the three branches of Government.

. . .

. . .

I do not suggest that all legislative vetoes are necessarily consistent with separation of powers principles. A legislative check on an inherently executive function, for example that of initiating prosecutions, poses an entirely different question. But the legislative veto device here—and in many other settings—is far from an instance of legislative tyranny over the Executive. It is a necessary check on the unavoidably expanding power of the agencies, both executive and independent, as they engage in exercising authority delegated by Congress.

V

I regret that I am in disagreement with my colleagues on the fundamental questions that this case presents. But even more I regret the destructive scope of the Court's holding. It reflects a profoundly different conception of the Constitution than that held by the Courts which sanctioned the modern administrative state. Today's decision strikes down in one fell swoop provisions in more laws enacted by Congress than the Court has cumulatively invalidated in its history. I fear it will now be more difficult "to insure that the fundamental policy decisions in our society will be made not by an appointed official but by the body immediately responsible to the people," Arizona v. California, 373 U.S. 546, 626 (1963) (Harlan, J., dissenting). I must dissent.

Justice Rehnquist, with whom Justice White joins, dissenting.

. . .

By severing § 244(c)(2), the Court permits suspension of deportation in a class of cases where Congress never stated that suspension was appropriate. I do not believe we should expand the statute in this way without some clear indication that Congress intended such an expansion. . . .

The Court finds that the legislative history of § 244 shows that Congress intended § 244(c)(2) to be severable because Congress wanted to relieve itself of the burden of private bills. But the history elucidated by the Court shows that Congress was unwilling to give the Executive Branch permission to suspend deportation on its own. Over the years, Congress consistently rejected requests from the Executive for complete discretion in this area. Congress always insisted on retaining ultimate control, whether by concurrent resolution, as in the 1948 Act, or by one-House veto, as in the present Act. Congress has never indicated that it would be willing to permit suspensions of deportation unless it could retain some sort of veto.

It is doubtless true that Congress has the power to provide for suspensions of deportation without a one-House veto. But the Court has failed to identify any evidence that Congress intended to exercise that power. On the contrary, Congress' continued insistence on retaining control of the suspension process indicates that it has never been disposed to give the Executive Branch a free hand. By severing § 244(c)(2) the Court has "confounded" Congress' "intention" to permit suspensions of deportation "with their power to carry that intention into effect." . . .

Because I do not believe that § 244(c)(2) is severable. I would reverse the judgment of the Court of Appeals.

B. APPOINTMENT OF "OFFICERS OF THE UNITED STATES"

BUCKLEY v. VALEO
424 U.S. 1, 96 S.Ct. 612, 46 L.Ed.2d 659 (1976).

[A suit was brought in the United States District Court for the District of Columbia pursuant to a special statutory provision for judicial review challenging on many grounds the constitutionality of the Federal Election Campaign Act

of 1971, as amended in 1974.   The portion of the opinion relating to separation
of powers is set out below.]
Per Curiam.

.   .   .

IV.   THE FEDERAL ELECTION COMMISSION

The 1974 Amendments to the Act created an eight-member Federal Election
Commission, and vest in it primary and substantial responsibility for administering and enforcing the Act.   The question that we address in this portion of the
opinion is whether, in view of the manner in which a majority of its members
are appointed, the Commission may under the Constitution exercise the powers
conferred upon it.   .   .   .

Beyond   .   .   .   recordkeeping, disclosure, and investigative functions,
however, the Commission is given extensive rulemaking and adjudicative powers.   .   .   .

The Commission's enforcement power is both direct and wide-ranging.

.   .   .

The body in which this authority is reposed consists of eight members.   The
Secretary of the Senate and the Clerk of the House of Representatives are *ex
officio* members of the Commission without the right to vote.   Two members are
appointed by the President *pro tempore* of the Senate "upon the recommendations of the majority leader of the Senate and the minority leader of the
Senate."   Two more are to be appointed by the Speaker of the House of
Representatives, likewise upon the recommendations of its respective majority
and minority leaders.   The remaining two members are appointed by the
President.   Each of the six voting members of the Commission must be
confirmed by the majority of both Houses of Congress, and each of the three
appointing authorities is forbidden to choose both of their appointees from the
same political party.   .   .   .

B.   The Merits

Appellants urge that since Congress has given the Commission wide-ranging
rule-making and enforcement powers with respect to the substantive provisions
of the Act, Congress is precluded under the principle of separation of powers
from vesting in itself the authority to appoint those who will exercise such
authority.   Their argument is based on the language of Art. II, § 2, cl. 2, of the
Constitution, which provides in pertinent part as follows:

"[The President] shall nominate, and by and with the Advice and Consent of
the Senate, shall appoint   .   .   .   all other Officers of the United States,
whose Appointments are not herein otherwise provided for, and which shall
be established by Law: but the Congress may by Law vest the Appointment
of such inferior Officers, as they think proper, in the President alone, in the
Courts of Law, or in the Heads of Departments."

.   .   .

1.   Separation of Powers

.   .   .

The Framers regarded the checks and balances that they had built into the
tripartite Federal Government as a self-executing safeguard against the encroachment or aggrandizement of one branch at the expense of the other.   .   .   .

This Court has not hesitated to enforce the principle of separation of powers
embodied in the Constitution when its application has proved necessary for the
decisions of cases and controversies properly before it.   The Court has held that
executive or administrative duties of a nonjudicial nature may not be imposed
on judges holding office under Art. III of the Constitution.   United States v.

Ferreira, 13 How. 40 (1852); Hayburn's Case, 2 Dall. 409 (1792). The Court has held that the President may not execute and exercise legislative authority belonging only to Congress. Youngstown Co. v. Sawyer, supra [343 U.S. 579].
. . .

More closely in point to the facts of the present case is this Court's decision in Springer v. Philippine Islands, [277 U.S. 189 (1928)], where the Court held that the legislature of the Philippine Islands could not provide for legislative appointment to executive agencies.

2. The Appointments Clause
. . .

We think that the term "Officers of the United States" as used in Art. II, . . . is a term intended to have substantive meaning. We think its fair import is that any appointee exercising significant authority pursuant to the laws of the United States is an Officer of the United States, and must, therefore, be appointed in the manner prescribed by § 2, cl. 2 of that Article.

If "all persons who can be said to hold an office under the government about to be established under the Constitution were intended to be included within one or the other of these modes of appointment," United States v. Germaine, supra, it is difficult to see how the members of the Commission may escape inclusion. If a Postmaster first class, Myers v. United States, 272 U.S. 52 (1926), and the Clerk of a District Court, Matter of Hennen, 13 Pet. 230 (1839), are inferior officers of the United States within the meaning of the Appointments Clause, as they are, surely the Commissioners before us are at the very least such "inferior Officers" within the meaning of that Clause.[162] . . .

Appellee Commission and amici finally contend, and the majority of the Court of Appeals agreed with them, that whatever shortcomings the provisions for the appointment of members of the Commission might have under Art. II, Congress had ample authority under the Necessary and Proper Clause of Art. I to effectuate this result. We do not agree. . . .

. . . Congress could not, merely because it concluded that such a measure was "necessary and proper" to the discharge of its substantive legislative authority, pass a bill of attainder or ex post facto law contrary to the prohibitions contained in § 9 of Art. I. No more may it vest in itself, or in its officers, the authority to appoint officers of the United States when the Appointments Clause by clear implication prohibits it from doing so.

The trilogy of cases from this Court dealing with the constitutional authority of Congress to circumscribe the President's power to *remove* officers of the United States is entirely consistent with this conclusion. In Myers v. United States, 272 U.S. 52 (1926), the Court held that Congress could not by statute divest the President of the power to remove an officer in the Executive Branch whom he was initially authorized to appoint. . . .

. . .

In the later case of *Humphrey's Executor,* where it was held that Congress could circumscribe the President's power to remove members of independent regulatory agencies, the Court was careful to note that it was dealing with an agency intended to be independent of executive authority *"except in its selection."* 295 U.S., at 625 (emphasis in original). Weiner v. United States, 357 U.S. 349 (1958), which applied the holding in *Humphrey's Executor* to a member of the

---

[162] "Officers of the United States" do not include all employees of the United States, but there is no claim made that the Commissioners are employees of the United States rather than officers. Employees are lesser functionaries subordinate to officers of the United States see Auffmordt v. Hedden, 137 U.S. 310, 327 (1890); United States v. Germaine, supra, whereas the Commissioners, appointed for a statutory term, are not subject to the control or direction of any other executive, judicial, or legislative authority.

War Crimes Commission, did not question in any respect that members of independent agencies are not independent of the executive with respect to their appointments. . . .

3. The Commission's Powers

.   . .

Insofar as the powers confided in the Commission are essentially of an investigative and informative nature, falling in the same general category as those powers which Congress might delegate to one of its own committees, there can be no question that the Commission as presently constituted may exercise them. . . .

But when we go beyond this type of authority to the more substantial powers exercised by the Commission, we reach a different result. The Commission's enforcement power, exemplified by its discretionary power to seek judicial relief, is authority that cannot possibly be regarded as merely in aid of the legislative function of Congress. A lawsuit is the ultimate remedy for a breach of the law, and it is to the President, and not to the Congress, that the Constitution entrusts the responsibility to "take Care that the Laws be faithfully executed." Art. II, § 3. . . .

All aspects of the Act are brought within the Commission's broad administrative powers: rule-making, advisory opinions, and determinations of eligibility for funds and even for federal elective office itself. These functions, exercised free from day-to-day supervision of either Congress or the Executive Branch, are more legislative and judicial in nature than are the Commission's enforcement powers, and are of kinds usually performed by independent regulatory agencies or by some department in the Executive Branch under the direction of an Act of Congress. Congress viewed these broad powers as essential to effective and impartial administration of the entire substantive framework of the Act. Yet each of these functions also represents the performance of a significant governmental duty exercised pursuant to a public law. While the President may not insist that such functions be delegated to an appointee of his removable at will, Humphrey's Executor v. United States, supra, none of them operates merely in aid of congressional authority to legislate or is sufficiently removed from the administration and enforcement of public law to allow it to be performed by the present Commission. These administrative functions may therefore be exercised only by persons who are "Officers of the United States." . . .

———

C. IMPEACHMENT

Article II, Section 4, of the Constitution provides that the President, the Vice President "and all civil officers of the United States" may be removed from office on impeachment for, and conviction of "treason, bribery or other high crimes and misdemeanors." Article I, Section 2, provides that the House of Representatives "shall have the sole power of impeachment" and Article I, Section 3, vests "the sole power to try all impeachments" in the Senate.[1] The aborted proceedings looking toward the impeachment of President Nixon in 1974 raised two major unresolved legal issues. Are only violations of the criminal law "high crimes and misdemeanors"? May a person impeached and convicted obtain judicial review? The Report of the Committee on Federal Legislation of the Association of the Bar of the City of New York, *The Law of Presidential Impeachment*, 29 The Record 154 (1974), concludes that: grounds

———

[1] There have been only twelve impeachments in United States history. Nine of the impeachments have been of federal judges, with four convictions. The two executive officers impeached—neither convicted—were President Andrew Johnson (1868) and Secretary of War William Belknap (1876). Senator William Blount was impeached in 1797, but not convicted.

for impeachment are not limited to or synonymous with criminal offenses, but are acts that "undermine the integrity of government"; judicial review is inappropriate both because the Constitution textually commits the issues to the House and Senate, and because those issues are not judicially manageable.[2]

SECTION 3. PRESIDENTIAL AND CONGRESSIONAL IMMUNITIES

UNITED STATES v. NIXON

418 U.S. 683, 94 S.Ct. 3090, 41 L.Ed.2d 1039 (1974).

Mr. Chief Justice Burger delivered the opinion of the Court.

This litigation presents for review the denial of a motion, filed on behalf of the President of the United States, in the case of United States v. Mitchell et al. (D.C.Crim. No. 74–110), to quash a third-party subpoena *duces tecum* issued by the United States District Court for the District of Columbia, pursuant to Fed. Rule Crim.Proc. 17(c). The subpoena directed the President to produce certain tape recordings and documents relating to his conversations with aides and advisers. The court rejected the President's claims of absolute executive privilege, of lack of jurisdiction, and of failure to satisfy the requirements of Rule 17(c). The President appealed to the Court of Appeals. We granted the United States' petition for certiorari before judgment, . . . because of the public importance of the issues presented and the need for their prompt resolution, 417 U.S. 927 and 960 (1974).

On March 1, 1974, a grand jury of the United States District Court for the District of Columbia returned an indictment charging seven named individuals[3] with various offenses, including conspiracy to defraud the United States and to obstruct justice. Although he was not designated as such in the indictment, the grand jury named the President, among others, as an unindicted coconspirator. On April 18, 1974, upon motion of the Special Prosecutor, a subpoena *duces tecum* was issued pursuant to Rule 17(c) to the President by the United States District Court and made returnable on May 2, 1974. This subpoena required the production, in advance of the September 9 trial date, of certain tapes, memoranda, papers, transcripts, or other writings relating to certain precisely identified meetings between the President and others. The Special Prosecutor was able to fix the time, place and persons present at these discussions because the White House daily logs and appointment records had been delivered to him. On April 30, the President publicly released edited transcripts of 43 conversations; portions of 20 conversations subject to subpoena in the present case were included. On May 1, 1974, the President's counsel, filed a "special appearance" and a motion to quash the subpoena, under Rule 17(c). This motion was accompanied by a formal claim of privilege. At a subsequent hearing, further motions to expunge the grand jury's action naming the President as an unindicted coconspirator and for protective orders against the disclosure of that information were filed or raised orally by counsel for the President.

On May 20, 1974, the District Court denied the motion to quash and the motions to expunge and for protective orders, 377 F.Supp. 1326 (1974). It

---

[2] The possible Nixon impeachment also renewed interest in the many procedural problems involved in House impeachment and Senate trial. See Firmage & Mangrum, *Removal of the President: Resignation and the Procedural Law of Impeachment,* 1974 Duke L.J. 1023.

[3] The seven defendants were John N. Mitchell, H.R. Haldeman, John D. Ehrlichman, Charles W. Colson, Robert C. Mardian, Kenneth W. Parkinson, and Gordon Strachan. Each had occupied either a position of responsibility on the White House staff or the Committee for the Re-election of the President. Colson entered a guilty plea on another charge and is no longer a defendant.

further ordered "the President or any subordinate officer, official or employee with custody or control of the documents or objects subpoenaed," to deliver to the District Court, on or before May 31, 1974, the originals of all subpoenaed items, as well as an index and analysis of those items, together with tape copies of those portions of the subpoenaed recordings for which transcripts had been released to the public by the President on April 30. . . .

The District Court held that the judiciary, not the President, was the final arbiter of a claim of executive privilege. The court concluded that, under the circumstances of this case, the presumptive privilege was overcome by the Special Prosecutor's prima facie "demonstration of need sufficiently compelling to warrant judicial examination in chambers . . . ." 377 F.Supp., at 1330. . . .

On May 24, 1974, the President filed a timely notice of appeal from the District Court order, and the certified record from the District Court was docketed in the United States Court of Appeals for the District of Columbia Circuit. . . .

Later on May 24, the Special Prosecutor also filed, in this Court, a petition for a writ of certiorari before judgment. On May 31, the petition was granted with an expedited briefing schedule. 417 U.S. 927 (1974). On June 6, the President filed, under seal, a cross-petition for writ of certiorari before judgment. This cross-petition was granted June 15, 1974, 417 U.S. 960 (1974), and the case was set for argument on July 8, 1974.

. . .

II. JUSTICIABILITY

In the District Court, the President's counsel argued that the court lacked jurisdiction to issue the subpoena because the matter was an intrabranch dispute between a subordinate and superior officer of the Executive Branch and hence not subject to judicial resolution. That argument has been renewed in this Court with emphasis on the contention that the dispute does not present a "case" or "controversy" which can be adjudicated in the federal courts. The President's counsel argues that the federal courts should not intrude into areas committed to the other branches of Government. He views the present dispute as essentially a "jurisdictional" dispute within the Executive Branch which he analogizes to a dispute between two congressional committees. . . .

. . .

Our starting point is the nature of the proceeding for which the evidence is sought—here a pending criminal prosecution. It is a judicial proceeding in a federal court alleging violation of federal laws and is brought in the name of the United States as sovereign. . . . Under the authority of Art. II, § 2, Congress has vested in the Attorney General the power to conduct the criminal litigation of the United States Government. 28 U.S.C. § 516. It has also vested in him the power to appoint subordinate officers to assist him in the discharge of his duties. 28 U.S.C. §§ 509, 510, 515, 533. Acting pursuant to those statutes, the Attorney General has delegated the authority to represent the United States in these particular matters to a Special Prosecutor with unique authority and tenure. The regulation gives the Special Prosecutor explicit power to contest the invocation of executive privilege in the process of seeking evidence deemed relevant to the performance of these specially delegated duties. 38 Fed.Reg. 30739, as amended by 38 Fed.Reg. 32805.

So long as this regulation is extant it has the force of law. . . .

. . . . [I]t is theoretically possible for the Attorney General to amend or revoke the regulation defining the Special Prosecutor's authority. But he has not done so. So long as this regulation remains in force the Executive Branch is bound by it, and indeed the United States as the sovereign composed of the three branches is bound to respect and to enforce it. Moreover, the delegation of authority to the Special Prosecutor in this case is not an ordinary delegation by the Attorney General to a subordinate officer: with the authorization of the President, the Acting Attorney General provided in the regulation that the Special Prosecutor was not to be removed without the "consensus" of eight designated leaders of Congress.

.   .   .

IV. THE CLAIM OF PRIVILEGE

A.

.   .   . [W]e turn to the claim that the subpoena should be quashed because it demands "confidential conversations between a President and his close advisors that it would be inconsistent with the public interest to produce." The first contention is a broad claim that the separation of powers doctrine precludes judicial review of a President's claim of privilege. The second contention is that if he does not prevail on the claim of absolute privilege, the court should hold as a matter of constitutional law that the privilege prevails over the subpoena *duces tecum*.

In the performance of assigned constitutional duties each branch of the Government must initially interpret the Constitution, and the interpretation of its powers by any branch is due great respect from the others. The President's counsel, as we have noted, reads the Constitution as providing an absolute privilege of confidentiality for all presidential communications. Many decisions of this Court, however, have unequivocally reaffirmed the holding of Marbury v. Madison, 1 Cranch 137 (1803), that "it is emphatically the province and duty of the judicial department to say what the law is." Id., at 177.

.   .   .

Notwithstanding the deference each branch must accord the others, the "judicial Power of the United States" vested in the federal courts by Art. III, § 1 of the Constitution can no more be shared with the Executive Branch than the Chief Executive, for example, can share with the Judiciary the veto power, or the Congress share with the Judiciary the power to override a presidential veto. Any other conclusion would be contrary to the basic concept of separation of powers and the checks and balances that flow from the scheme of a tripartite government. The Federalist, No. 47, p. 313 (C.F. Mittel ed. 1938). We therefore reaffirm that it is "emphatically the province and the duty" of this Court "to say what the law is" with respect to the claim of privilege presented in this case. Marbury v. Madison, supra, at 177.

B.

In support of his claim of absolute privilege the President's counsel urges two grounds one of which is common to all governments and one of which is peculiar to our system of separation of powers. The first ground is the valid need for protection of communications between high Government officials and those who advise and assist them in the performance of their manifold duties; the importance of this confidentiality is too plain to require further discussion. Human experience teaches that those who expect public dissemination of their remarks may well temper candor with a concern for appearances and for their own interests to the detriment of the decisionmaking process. Whatever the nature of the privilege of confidentiality of presidential communications in the exercise of Art. II powers, the privilege can be said to derive from the supremacy of each branch within its own assigned area of constitutional duties. Certain powers and privileges flow from the nature of enumerated powers; the protection of the confidentiality of Presidential communications has similar constitutional underpinnings.

The second ground asserted by the President's counsel in support of the claim of absolute privilege rests on the doctrine of separation of powers. Here it is argued that the independence of the Executive Branch within its own sphere insulates a president from a judicial subpoena in an ongoing criminal prosecution, and thereby protects confidential Presidential communications.

However, neither the doctrine of separation of powers, nor the need for confidentiality of high level communications without more, can sustain an absolute, unqualified Presidential privilege of immunity from judicial process under all circumstances. The President's need for complete candor and objectivity from advisers calls for great deference from the courts. However, when the privilege depends solely on the broad, undifferentiated claim of public interest in the confidentiality of such conversations, a confrontation with other values arises. Absent a claim of need to protect military, diplomatic or sensitive national security secrets, we find it difficult to accept the argument that even the very important interest in confidentiality of Presidential communications is significantly diminished by production of such material for *in camera* inspection with all the protection that a district court will be obliged to provide.

The impediment that an absolute, unqualified privilege would place in the way of the primary constitutional duty of the Judicial Branch to do justice in criminal prosecutions would plainly conflict with the function of the courts under Art. III. In designing the structure of our Government and dividing and allocating the sovereign power among three coequal branches, the Framers of the Constitution sought to provide a comprehensive system, but the separate powers were not intended to operate with absolute independence. . . . To read the Art. II powers of the President as providing an absolute privilege as against a subpoena essential to enforcement of criminal statutes on no more than a generalized claim of the public interest in confidentiality of nonmilitary and nondiplomatic discussions would upset the constitutional balance of "a workable government" and gravely impair the role of the courts under Art. III.

C.

Since we conclude that the legitimate needs of the judicial process may outweigh Presidential privilege, it is necessary to resolve those competing interests in a manner that preserves the essential functions of each branch. The right and indeed the duty to resolve that question does not free the Judiciary from according high respect to the representations made on behalf of the President. . . .

. . . The privilege is fundamental to the operation of Government and inextricably rooted in the separation of powers under the Constitution. In Nixon v. Sirica, 159 U.S.App.D.C. 58, 487 F.2d 700 (1973), the Court of Appeals held that such Presidential communications are "presumptively privileged," and this position is accepted by both parties in the present litigation. We agree with Mr. Chief Justice Marshall's observation, therefore, that "in no case of this kind would a court be required to proceed against the president as against an ordinary individual." United States v. Burr, 25 F.Cas. at 192 (No. 14,694) (C.C.D.Va.1807).

But this presumptive privilege must be considered in light of our historic commitment to the rule of law. . . . The very integrity of the judicial system and public confidence in the system depend on full disclosure of all the facts, within the framework of the rules of evidence. To ensure that justice is done, it is imperative to the function of courts that compulsory process be available for the production of evidence needed either by the prosecution or by the defense.

. . . .

In this case the President . . . does not place his claim of privilege on the ground they are military or diplomatic secrets. As to these areas of Art. II duties the courts have traditionally shown the utmost deference to Presidential responsibilities. . . .

No case of the Court, however, has extended this high degree of deference to a President's generalized interest in confidentiality. Nowhere in the Constitution, as we have noted earlier, is there any explicit reference to a privilege of confidentiality, yet to the extent this interest relates to the effective discharge of a President's powers, it is constitutionally based.

. . . .

In this case we must weigh the importance of the general privilege of confidentiality of Presidential communications in performance of the President's responsibilities against the inroads of such a privilege on the fair administration of criminal justice. The interest in preserving confidentiality is weighty indeed and entitled to great respect. However we cannot conclude that advisers will be moved to temper the candor of their remarks by the infrequent occasions of disclosure because of the possibility that such conversations will be called for in the context of a criminal prosecution.

. . . .

We conclude that when the ground for asserting privilege as to subpoenaed materials sought for use in a criminal trial is based only on the generalized interest in confidentiality, it cannot prevail over the fundamental demands of due process of law in the fair administration of criminal justice. The generalized assertion of privilege must yield to the demonstrated, specific need for evidence in a pending criminal trial.

. . . .

Since this matter came before the Court during the pendency of a criminal prosecution, and on representations that time is of the essence, the mandate shall issue forthwith.

Affirmed [a]

Mr. Justice Rehnquist took no part in the consideration or decision of these cases.

———

NIXON v. ADMINISTRATOR OF GENERAL SERVICES, 433 U.S. 425 (1977). The Presidential Recordings and Materials Preservation Act of 1974 directed the Administrator to take custody of former President Nixon's papers and tapes, to provide for their screening by archivists for the purpose of returning personal and private materials, and to determine conditions for public access. The public access regulations were to take into account seven factors, including "the need to protect any party's opportunity to assert any legally or constitutionally based right or privilege. . . . " The day after the Act was signed into law by President Ford, this suit was brought in the District Court for the District of Columbia, challenging the constitutionality of the law on numerous grounds, including separation of powers and Presidential privilege. The Court affirmed the lower court's dismissal of the complaint. On the issue of separation of powers, the Court noted that the Act entrusted the documents to the Executive Branch, and, as with other statutory requirements for disclosure of documents in possession of the Executive Branch (such as the Freedom of Information Act), regulation of material generated in the Executive Branch had

[a] For discussions of United States v. Nixon, see *Symposium: United States v. Nixon*, 22 UCLA L.Rev. 4–140 (1974); Freund, *On Presidential Privilege*, 88 Harv.L.Rev. 13 (1974); Cox, *Executive Privilege*, 122 U.Pa.L.Rev. 1383 (1974).

never been considered an invasion of its autonomy. With respect to the claim of Presidential privilege, the Court rejected an argument that the privilege could be claimed only by the incumbent President. On the other hand, the fact that neither President Ford nor President Carter supported President Nixon's claim of Presidential privilege "detracts from the weight of his contention that the Act impermissibly intrudes into the executive function." Justice Brennan's opinion for the Court continued:

"The appellant bases his claim of Presidential privilege in this case on the assertion that the potential disclosure of communications given to the appellant in confidence would adversely affect the ability of future Presidents to obtain the candid advice necessary for effective decisionmaking. We are called upon to adjudicate that claim, however, only with respect to the process by which the materials will be screened and catalogued by professional archivists. For any eventual public access will be governed by the guidelines of § 104, ...

"[T]here is no reason to believe that the restriction on public access ultimately established by regulation will not be adequate to preserve executive confidentiality. An absolute barrier to all outside disclosure is not practically or constitutionally necessary. As the careful research by the District Court clearly demonstrates, there has never been an expectation that the confidences of the Executive Office are absolute and unyielding. All former Presidents from President Hoover to President Johnson have deposited their papers in Presidential libraries (an example appellant has said he intended to follow) for governmental preservation and eventual disclosure. The screening processes for sorting materials for lodgment in these libraries also involved comprehensive review by archivists, often involving materials upon which access restrictions ultimately have been imposed. The expectation of the confidentiality of executive communications thus has always been limited and subject to erosion over time after an administration leaves office.

"We are thus left with the bare claim that the mere screening of the materials by the archivists will impermissibly interfere with candid communication of views by Presidential advisers. We agree with the District Court that, thus framed, the question is readily resolved. The screening constitutes a very limited intrusion by personnel in the Executive Branch sensitive to executive concerns. These very personnel have performed the identical task in each of the Presidential libraries without any suggestion that such activity has in any way interfered with executive confidentiality. . . .

.   .   .

"In short, we conclude that the screening process contemplated by the Act will not constitute a more severe intrusion into Presidential confidentiality than the *in camera* inspection by the District Court approved in United States v. Nixon, 418 U.S., at 706. We must of course presume that the Administrator and the career archivists concerned will carry out the duties assigned to them by the Act. Thus, there is no basis for appellant's claim that the Act 'reverses' the presumption in favor of confidentiality of Presidential papers recognized in United States v. Nixon. Appellant's right to assert the privilege is specifically preserved by the Act. The guideline provisions on their face are as broad as the privilege itself. If the broadly written protections of the Act should nevertheless prove inadequate to safeguard appellant's rights or to prevent usurpation of executive powers, there will be time enough to consider that problem in a specific factual context. For the present, we hold, in agreement with the District Court, that the Act on its face does not violate the Presidential privilege."

Justices Powell and Blackmun concurred in the judgment. Justice Powell noted that "the difficult constitutional questions lie ahead" when regulations governing access are promulgated, since the Court's decision was limited to the facial validity of the Act. The Chief Justice and Justice Rehnquist dissented. As to the issue of confidential Presidential communications, Justice Rehnquist said, in part:

"The critical factor in all of this is not that confidential material might be disclosed, since the President himself might choose to 'go public' with it. The critical factor is that the determination as to whether to disclose is wrested by the Act from the President. When one speaks in confidence to a President, he necessarily relies upon the President's discretion not to disclose the sensitive. The President similarly relies on the discretion of a subordinate when instructing him. Thus it is no answer to suggest, as does the Court, that the expectation of confidentiality has always been limited because Presidential papers have in the past been turned over to Presidential libraries or otherwise subsequently disclosed. In those cases, ultimate reliance was upon the discretion of the President to cull the sensitive before disclosure. But when, as is the case under this Act, the decision whether to disclose no longer resides in the President, communication will inevitably be restrained.

.   .   .   .

NIXON v. FITZGERALD, 457 U.S. 731 (1982). The Court held that the President is absolutely immune from damage claims for any acts within the "outer perimeter" of his official responsibility. The Court concluded that lesser immunity would "subject the President to trial on virtually every allegation that an action was unlawful, or was taken for a forbidden purpose." Justice Powell's opinion for the Court concluded:

"A rule of absolute immunity for the President will not leave the Nation without sufficient protection against misconduct on the part of the chief executive. There remains the constitutional remedy of impeachment. In addition, there are formal and informal checks on Presidential action that do not apply with equal force to other executive officials. The President is subjected to constant scrutiny by the press. Vigilant oversight by Congress also may serve to deter Presidential abuses of office, as well as to make credible the threat of impeachment. Other incentives to avoid misconduct may include a desire to earn re-election, the need to maintain prestige as an element of Presidential influence, and a President's traditional concern for his historical stature.

"The existence of alternative remedies and deterrents establishes that absolute immunity will not place the President 'above the law.' For the President, as for judges and prosecutors, absolute immunity merely precludes a particular private remedy for alleged misconduct in order to advance compelling public ends."

The four dissenting Justices (White, Brennan, Marshall and Blackmun) argued that the President should enjoy only qualified immunity, in the absence of a showing "that the absence of absolute immunity will substantially impair his ability to carry out particular functions that are his Constitutional responsibility." [1]

In a footnote, the Court reserved the question whether Congress could expressly create a damage action against the President on behalf of wronged individuals. The dissent argued, however, that the Court's rationale would also invalidate Congressional efforts to create a statutory action against the President. In a separate concurrence, Chief Justice Burger argued that absolute Presidential

---

[1] In a companion case, Harlow v. Fitzgerald, 457 U.S. 800 (1982), the Court held that Presidential aides were entitled to only qualified immunity absent a showing that: (1) the aide's responsibilities embraced a function so sensitive as to require absolute immunity from civil actions; and (2) the act for which liability is claimed was in discharge of that sensitive function.

immunity from civil claims is mandated by the "constitutional doctrine of separation of powers."

THE SPEECH OR DEBATE CLAUSE

Article I, Section 6, of the Constitution provides that "for any speech or debate in either House, [Senators and Representatives] shall not be questioned in any other place." The Court has read this provision broadly to provide immunity against civil and criminal actions, and against actions brought by individuals as well as the executive. In Eastland v. United States Servicemen's Fund, 421 U.S. 491 (1975), for example, the clause was held to bar an injunction action seeking to block enforcement of a subpoena *duces tecum* issued by a Senate subcommittee. On the other hand, the clause only immunizes Senators and members of Congress, and their aides, from judicial inquiry into and sanctions imposed on "legislative acts." Thus the clause provided no immunity for a Senator's aide from grand jury questioning concerning arrangements for private publication of the Pentagon Papers [1], for a Senator from suit for defamation arising from statements in press releases and newsletters,[2] or for a member of Congress from prosecution for accepting a bribe in exchange for a promise to perform a legislative act in the future.[3]

In Davis v. Passman, 442 U.S. 228 (1979), the Court raised, but did not decide, the question whether the clause provided a member of Congress immunity from suit for discharge of an employee, who claimed that her discharge constituted unconstitutional gender discrimination. Justice Powell (joined by Chief Justice Burger and Justice Rehnquist) argued in dissent, however, that, whether or not the defendant's conduct was immunized by the speech or debate clause, "[a] Congressman simply cannot perform his constitutional duties effectively, or serve his constituents properly, unless he is supported by a staff in which he has total confidence."

[1] Gravel v. United States, 408 U.S. 606 (1972).

[2] Hutchinson v. Proxmire, 443 U.S. 111 (1979).

[3] United States v. Brewster, 408 U.S. 501 (1972). The clause, however, precludes the United States from proving in the bribery prosecution that the promised legislative act was performed, because this would inquire into a past legislative act, and the motives for performing it. United States v. Helstoski, 442 U.S. 477 (1979).

Part III

GOVERNMENT AND THE INDIVIDUAL: THE PROTECTION OF LIBERTY AND PROPERTY UNDER THE DUE PROCESS AND EQUAL PROTECTION CLAUSES

In this Part, the emphasis shifts from exploring the constitutional relationship between different parts of the governmental structure, to the protection of individual rights from interference by all levels and branches of government. The central question is definition of the proper judicial role in giving content to the vague language of the due process clauses of the fifth and fourteenth amendments, and of the equal protection clause of the fourteenth amendment.

Chapter 9 concerns the interrelationship between the bill rights and the Civil War amendments to the Constitution. Chapter 10 deals with the application of the due process clause. Chapter 11 discusses the equal protection clause. Chapter 12 completes the analysis with an examination of constitutional norms of fair procedure. (The discrete problems of constitutional protection of speech and conscience under the first amendment are reserved for Part IV.)

Chapter 13 returns to an issue of division of national and state power. After examining the application of the Civil War amendments to private conduct, the bulk of this chapter concerns the extent of Congressional power to enforce the amendments.

Chapter 9

THE BILL OF RIGHTS, THE CIVIL WAR AMENDMENTS AND THEIR INTER–RELATIONSHIP

Introduction. In Chapter 1 it was noted that the original constitution included only a few limitations upon power of government to regulate life, liberty and property. The principal restraints on state regulation were those forbidding the impairment of the obligation of contracts (Art. I, § 10), banning bills of attainder and ex post facto laws (Art. I, § 10), and guaranteeing citizens of one state the right to enjoy in another state "all the Privileges and Immunities" of its own citizens (Art. IV, § 2).

The Bill of Rights (Amendments 1–10) adopted in 1791 imposed a substantial series of protections for the individual against government. Almost 80 years later the Civil War Amendments (13, 14, and 15) specifically imposed restraints on the power of states to regulate the personal and property interests of their citizens.

The purpose of this Chapter is to give a brief historical introduction to the Court's application of these three sets of restraints on the power of government to regulate liberty and property. A major focus will be on the dispute over the interrelationship between the Bill of Rights and the Civil War Amendments.

SECTION 1. THE PRE–CIVIL WAR BACKGROUND

A. THE CONTRACT CLAUSE AND THE PRIVILEGES AND IMMUNITIES CLAUSE OF ARTICLE IV— EARLY INTERPRETATIONS

THE CONTRACT CLAUSE

The first case in which the Supreme Court held a state statute to be in conflict with the constitution involved the contract clause. In Fletcher v. Peck, 10 U.S. (6 Cranch.) 87 (1810) the Court held invalid an act of the Georgia legislature rescinding a sale of land which it had previously approved. Marshall writing for the Court held that the contract clause applied to public contracts and that a grant of land constituted a contract not to reassert rights over the land granted. In invalidating the law he relied both on the contract clause and on the more general notion that "the nature of society and of government [ ] prescribe some limits to the legislative power."

The Court went on to decide a large number of cases under the contract clause.

"During the nineteenth century no constitutional clause was so frequently the basis of decision by the Supreme Court of the United States as that forbidding the states to pass laws impairing the obligation of contracts. If we exclude the commerce clause as being primarily a grant of power to the national government, although it is significant because of its treatment as a restriction on state powers, the contract clause was the constitutional justification for more cases involving the validity of state laws than all of the other clauses of the Constitution together."

Wright, *The Contract Clause of the Constitution* xi (1938).

No attempt is made here to review the early cases. Much of the historical material is discussed in two modern cases, Allied Structural Steel Co. v. Spannas, 438 U.S. 234 (1978), and United States Trust Co. of New York v. New Jersey, 431 U.S. 1 (1977), both set out, infra, Chapter 10.

THE PRIVILEGES AND IMMUNITIES CLAUSE OF ARTICLE IV

CORFIELD v. CORYELL, 4 Wash.C.C. 371, Fed.Cas.No.3,230 (1825). A New Jersey statute of 1820 made it unlawful for any person who was not "an actual inhabitant and resident" of the state to rake or gather clams, oysters, or shells in any of the rivers, bays, or waters of the state. The statute was challenged by a Pennsylvania citizen who was gathering oysters in New Jersey waters. In disposing of the claim made under Article IV, Section 2, Justice Washington of the Supreme Court, sitting on circuit, said:

"The next question is, whether this act infringes that section of the constitution which declares that 'the citizens of each state shall be entitled to all the privileges and immunities of citizens in the several states?' The inquiry is, what are the privileges and immunities of citizens in the several states? We feel no hesitation in confining these expressions to those privileges and immunities which are, in their nature, fundamental; which belong, of right, to the citizens of all free governments; and which have, at all times, been enjoyed by the citizens of the several states which compose this Union, from the time of their becoming free, independent, and sovereign. What these fundamental principles are, it would perhaps be more tedious than difficult to enumerate. They may, however, be all comprehended under the following general heads: Protection by the government; the enjoyment of life and liberty, with the right to acquire and possess property of every kind, and to pursue and obtain happiness and safety; subject nevertheless to such restraints as the government may justly prescribe for the general good of the whole. The right of a citizen of one state to pass through, or to reside in any other state, for purposes of trade, agriculture, professional pursuits, or otherwise; to claim the benefit of the writ of habeas corpus; to institute and maintain actions of any kind in the courts of the state; to take hold and dispose of property, either real or personal; and an exemption from higher taxes or impositions than are paid by the other citizens of the state; may be mentioned as some of the particular privileges and immunities of citizens, which are clearly embraced by the general description of privileges deemed to be fundamental: to which may be added, the elective franchise, as regulated and established by the laws or constitution of the state in which it is to be exercised. These, and many others which might be mentioned, are, strictly speaking, privileges and immunities, and the enjoyment of them by the citizens of each state, in every other state, was manifestly calculated (to use the expressions of the preamble of the corresponding provision in the old articles of confederation) 'the better to secure and perpetuate mutual friendship and intercourse among the people of the different states of the Union.' But we cannot accede to the proposition which was insisted on by the counsel, that, under this provision of the constitution, the citizens of the several states are permitted to participate in all the rights which belong exclusively to the citizens of any other particular state, merely upon the ground that they are enjoyed by those citizens; much less, that in regulating the use of the common property of the citizens of such state, the legislature is bound to extend to the citizens of all the other states the same advantages as are secured to their own citizens. A several fishery, either as the right to it respects running fish, or such as are stationary, such as oysters, clams, and the like, is as much the property of the individual to whom it belongs, as dry land, or land covered by water; and is equally protected by the laws of the state against the aggressions of others, whether citizens or strangers. Where those private rights do not exist to the exclusion of the common right, that of fishing belongs to all the citizens or subjects of the state. It is the property of all; to be enjoyed by them in subordination to the laws which regulate its use. They may be considered as tenants in common of this property; and they are so exclusively entitled to the use of it, that it cannot be enjoyed by others without the tacit consent, or the express permission of the sovereign who has the power to regulate its use."

PAUL v. VIRGINIA, 75 U.S. (8 Wall.) 168, 180 (1869). The Court upheld a state law imposing special burdens on insurance companies incorporated in other states as a condition of doing business on the ground that a corporation is not a citizen protected by the privileges and immunities clause of Article IV. In construing the clause the Court said:

"It was undoubtedly the object of the clause in question to place the citizens of each State upon the same footing with citizens of other States, so far as the advantages resulting from citizenship in those States are concerned. It relieves them from the disabilities of alienage in other States; it inhibits discriminating legislation against them by other States; it gives them the right of free ingress into other States, and egress from them; it insures to them in other States the same freedom possessed by the citizens of those States in the acquisition and enjoyment of property and in the pursuit of happiness; and it secures to them in other States the equal protection of their laws. It has been justly said that no provision in the Constitution has tended so strongly to constitute the citizens of the United States one people as this. Lemmon v. People, 20 N.Y. 607.

"Indeed, without some provision of the kind removing from the citizens of each State the disabilities of alienage in the other States, and giving them equality of privilege with citizens of those States, the Republic would have constituted little more than a league of States; it would not have constituted the Union which now exists.

"But the privileges and immunities secured to citizens of each State in the several States, by the provision in question, are those privileges and immunities which are common to the citizens in the latter States under their Constitution and laws by virtue of their being citizens. Special privileges enjoyed by citizens in their own States are not secured in other States by this provision. It was not intended by the provision to give to the laws of one State any operation in other States. They can have no such operation, except by the permission, express or implied, of those States. The special privileges which they confer must, therefore, be enjoyed at home, unless the assent of other States to their enjoyment therein be given."

B. THE BILL OF RIGHTS

BARRON v. MAYOR AND CITY COUNCIL OF BALTIMORE

7 Pet. 243, 8 L.Ed. 672 (1833).

[Barron brought an action on the case against the City of Baltimore. Barron presented evidence that municipal street construction diverted the flow of streams so that they deposited silt in front of his wharf; this made the water so shallow that vessels could no longer reach the wharf. In the County Court Barron obtained a verdict for $45,000 which was reversed on appeal by the Maryland Circuit Court. By writ of error in the United States Supreme Court Barron presented the contention that the state court had failed to grant his property the protection guaranteed it by the Fifth Amendment to the United States Constitution.]

Marshall, Ch. J., delivered the opinion of the court.

The judgment brought up by this writ of error having been rendered by the court of a state, this tribunal can exercise no jurisdiction over it, unless it be shown to come within the provisions of the 25th section of the judicial act. The plaintiff in error contends that it comes within that clause in the fifth amendment to the constitution, which inhibits the taking of private property for public use, without just compensation. He insists that this amendment, being in favor of the liberty of the citizen, ought to be so construed as to restrain the legislative power of a state, as well as that of the United States. If this proposition be untrue, the court can take no jurisdiction of the cause.

The question thus presented is, we think, of great importance, but not of much difficulty. The constitution was ordained and established by the people of the United States for themselves, for their own government, and not for the government of the individual states. Each state established a constitution for itself, and in that constitution, provided such limitations and restrictions on the powers of its particular government, as its judgment dictated. The people of the United States framed such a government for the United States as they supposed best adapted to their situation and best calculated to promote their interests. The powers they conferred on this government were to be exercised by itself; and the limitations on power, if expressed in general terms, are naturally, and, we think, necessarily, applicable to the government created by the instrument. They are limitations of power granted in the instrument itself; not of distinct governments, framed by different persons and for different purposes.

If these propositions be correct, the fifth amendment must be understood as restraining the power of the general government, not as applicable to the states. In their several constitutions, they have imposed such restrictions on their respective governments, as their own wisdom suggested; such as they deemed most proper for themselves. It is a subject on which they judge exclusively, and with which others interfere no further than they are supposed to have a common interest.

. . .

Had the people of the several states, or any of them, required changes in their constitutions; had they required additional safe-guards to liberty from the apprehended encroachments of their particular governments; the remedy was in their own hands, and could have been applied by themselves. A convention could have been assembled by the discontented state, and the required improvements could have been made by itself. The unwieldy and cumbrous machinery of procuring a recommendation from two-thirds of congress, and the assent of three-fourths of their sister states, could never have occurred to any human being, as a mode of doing that which might be effected by the state itself. Had the framers of these amendments intended them to be limitations on the powers of the state governments, they would have imitated the framers of the original constitution, and have expressed that intention. Had congress engaged in the extraordinary occupation of improving the constitutions of the several states, by affording the people additional protection from the exercise of power by their own governments, in matters which concerned themselves alone, they would have declared this purpose in plain and intelligible language.

But it is universally understood, it is a part of the history of the day, that the great revolution which established the constitution of the United States, was not effected without immense opposition.   Serious fears were extensively entertained, that those powers which the patriot statesmen, who then watched over the interests of our country, deemed essential to union, and to the attainment of those invaluable objects for which union was sought, might be exercised in a manner dangerous to liberty.   In almost every convention by which the constitution was adopted, amendments to guard against the abuse of power were recommended.   These amendments demanded security against the apprehended encroachments of the general government—not against those of the local governments.   In compliance with a sentiment thus generally expressed, to quiet fears thus extensively entertained, amendments were proposed by the required majority in congress, and adopted by the states.   These amendments contain no expression indicating an intention to apply them to the state governments.   This court cannot so apply them.

We are of opinion, that the provision in the fifth amendment to the constitution, declaring that private property shall not be taken for public use, without just compensation, is intended solely as a limitation on the exercise of power by the government of the United States, and is not applicable to the legislation of the states.   We are, therefore, of opinion, that there is no repugnancy between the several acts of the general assembly of Maryland, given in evidence by the defendants at the trial of this cause, in the court of that state, and the constitution of the United States.   This court, therefore, has no jurisdiction of the cause, and it is dismissed.

PRE-CIVIL WAR INTERPRETATIONS OF THE BILL OF RIGHTS

The decision in Barron v. Baltimore that the Bill of Rights was not designed to restrict actions of the states has been repeatedly affirmed by the Supreme Court.   What is more striking is the fact that in the three-quarters of a century prior to the Civil War there were only a small handful of cases in which the Bill of Rights was invoked to challenge actions of the national government.   See Wright, *The Growth of American Constitutional Law*, 77–78 (1942).

On two occasions, however, the Court did attempt to define the scope of the words "due process of law" in the fifth amendment.   In Murray's Lessee v. Hoboken Land & Improvement Co., 56 U.S. (18 How.) 272 (1856), a fifth amendment challenge was made to a summary procedure used by the United States treasury to fix a lien on the property of a customs collector whose accounts were found to be short by over a million dollars.   In upholding the procedure the Court said:

"The words, 'due process of law,' were undoubtedly intended to convey the same meaning as the words, 'by the law of the land,' in *Magna Charta*.   Lord Coke, in his commentary on those words, (2 Inst. 50,) says they mean due process of law.   The constitutions which had been adopted by the several States before the formation of the federal constitution, following the language of the great charter more closely, generally contained the words, 'but by the judgment of his peers, or the law of the land.'   The ordinance of congress of July 13, 1787, for the government of the territory of the United States northwest of the River Ohio, used the same words.

"The constitution of the United States, as adopted, contained the provision, that 'the trial of all crimes, except in cases of impeachment, shall be by jury.'   When the fifth article of amendment containing the words now in question was made, the trial by jury in criminal cases had thus already been provided for.   By the sixth and seventh articles of amendment, further special provisions were separately made for that mode of trial in civil and criminal cases. To have followed, as in the state constitutions, and in the ordinance of 1787, the words of *Magna Charta*, and declared that no person shall be deprived of his life, liberty, or property but by the judgment of his peers or the law of the land, would have been in part superfluous and inappropriate. To have taken the clause, 'law of the land' without its immediate context, might possibly have given rise to doubts, which would be effectually dispelled by using those words which the great commentator on *Magna Charta* had declared to be the true meaning of the phrase, 'law of the land,' in that instrument, and which were undoubtedly then received as their true meaning.

"That the warrant now in question is legal process, is not denied. It was issued in conformity with an act of Congress. But is it 'due process of law?' The constitution contains no description of those processes which it was intended to allow or forbid. It does not even declare what principles are to be applied to ascertain whether it be due process. It is manifest that it was not left to the legislative power to enact any process which might be devised. The article is a restraint on the legislative as well as on the executive and judicial powers of the government, and cannot be so construed as to leave congress free to make any process 'due process of law,' by its mere will. To what principles, then, are we to resort to ascertain whether this process, enacted by congress, is due process? To this the answer must be twofold. We must examine the constitution itself, to see whether this process be in conflict with any of its provisions. If not found to be so, we must look to those settled usages and modes of proceeding existing in the common and statute law of England, before the emigration of our ancestors, and which are shown not to have been unsuited to their civil and political condition by having been acted on by them after the settlement of this country. . . . .

"Tested by the common and statute law of England prior to the emigration of our ancestors, and by the laws of many of the States at the time of the adoption of this amendment, the proceedings authorized by the act of 1820 cannot be denied to be due process of law, when applied to the ascertainment and recovery of balances due to the government from a collector of customs, unless there exists in the constitution some other provision which restrains congress from authorizing such proceedings. For, though 'due process of law' generally implies and includes *actor, reus, judex,* regular allegations, opportunity to answer, and a trial according to some settled course of judicial proceedings, (2 Inst. 47, 50; Hoke v. Henderson, 4 Dev.N.C.Rep. 15; Taylor v. Porter, 4 Hill, 146; Van Zandt v. Waddel, 2 Yerger, 260; State Bank v. Cooper, Ibid. 599; Jones's Heirs v. Perry, 10 Ibid. 59; Greene v. Briggs, 1 Curtis, 311,) yet, this is not universally true. There may be, and we have seen that there are cases, under the law of England after *Magna Charta*, and as it was brought to this country and acted on here, in which process, in its nature final, issues against the body, lands, and goods of certain public debtors without any such trial; and this brings us to the question, whether those provisions of the constitution which relate to the judicial power are incompatible with these proceedings?"[a]

---

[a] During this period there were a few state court opinions applying state constitutional phrases such as "due process of law" and "the law of the land" not only to require fair procedure but also to invalidate special or "class" legislation and retroactive impairment of "vested rights". See, e.g., Wynehamer v. The People, 13 N.Y. 378, 393–395 (1856), quoting comparable approaches by the courts of Pennsylvania and North Carolina. For general discussion see: Corwin, *Liberty against Government* 75–82, 91–110 (1948); Mott, *Due Process of Law* 241–274 (1926); Howe, *The Meaning of "Due Process of Law" Prior to the Adoption of the Fourteenth Amendment,* 18 Calif.L.Rev. 583, 596–610 (1930).

In Dred Scott v. Sanford, 60 U.S. (19 How.) 393 (1857) the Court had before it a challenge to the validity of the Act of Congress known as the Missouri Compromise which excluded slavery from specified northern portions of the United States territory. The opinion of the court, by Chief Justice Taney, after referring to the free speech and other guaranties of the Bill of Rights, continued:

"These powers, and others in relation to rights of person, which it is not necessary here to enumerate, are, in express and positive terms, denied to the general government; and the rights of private property have been guarded with equal care. Thus the rights of property are united with the rights of person, and placed on the same ground by the fifth amendment to the Constitution, which provides that no person shall be deprived of life, liberty and property, without due process of law. And an Act of Congress which deprives a citizen of the United States of his liberty or property, merely because he came himself or brought his property into a particular Territory of the United States, and who had committed no offense against the laws, could hardly be dignified with the name of due process of law."

SECTION 2. THE INITIAL INTERPRETATION OF THE CIVIL WAR AMENDMENTS

SLAUGHTER–HOUSE CASES

16 Wall. 36, 21 L.Ed. 394 (1872).

[The Louisiana legislature chartered a corporation and granted to it, for twenty-five years, an exclusive right to operate facilities in New Orleans for the landing, keeping, and slaughter of livestock. All competing plants were required to cease operation, and independent butchers were given a right to slaughter at the corporation's plant on paying maximum charges which were fixed by statute.

New Orleans butchers sued in the state courts to have the act declared invalid as a violation of both the Thirteenth and Fourteenth Amendments. The statute was upheld by the Louisiana Supreme Court.]

Mr. Justice Miller delivered the opinion of the court. . . .

This statute is denounced not only as creating a monopoly and conferring odious and exclusive privileges upon a small number of persons at the expense of the great body of the community of New Orleans, but it is asserted that it deprives a large and meritorious class of citizens—the whole of the butchers of the city—of the right to exercise their trade, the business to which they have been trained and on which they depend for the support of themselves and their families; and that the unrestricted exercise of the business of butchering is necessary to the daily subsistence of the population of the city.

But a critical examination of the act hardly justifies these assertions. . . .

The power here exercised by the legislature of Louisiana is, in its essential nature, one which has been, up to the present period in the constitutional history of this country, always conceded to belong to the States, however it may *now* be questioned in some of its details. . . . This is called the police power; and it is declared by Chief Justice Shaw that it is much easier to perceive and realize the existence and sources of it than to mark its boundaries, or prescribe limits to its exercise.

This power is, and must be from its very nature, incapable of any very exact definition or limitation. Upon it depends the security of social order, the life and health of the citizen, the comfort of an existence in a thickly populated community, the enjoyment of private and social life, and the beneficial use of property. . . .

It may, therefore, be considered as established, that the authority of the legislature of Louisiana to pass the present statute is ample, unless some restraint in the exercise of that power be found in the constitution of that State or in the amendments to the Constitution of the United States, adopted since the date of the decisions we have already cited. . . .

The plaintiffs in error accepting this issue, allege that the statute is a violation of the Constitution of the United States in these several particulars:

That it creates an involuntary servitude forbidden by the thirteenth article of amendment;

That it abridges the privileges and immunities of citizens of the United States;

That it denies to the plaintiffs the equal protection of the laws; and,

That it deprives them of their property without due process of law; contrary to the provisions of the first section of the fourteenth article of amendment.

This court is thus called upon for the first time to give construction to these articles.

We do not conceal from ourselves the great responsibility which this duty devolves upon us. No questions so far-reaching and pervading in their consequences, so profoundly interesting to the people of this country, and so important in their bearing upon the relations of the United States, and of the several States to each other and to the citizens of the States and of the United States, have been before this court during the official life of any of its present members. . . .

Twelve articles of amendment were added to the Federal Constitution soon after the original organization of the government under it in 1789. Of these all but the last were adopted so soon afterwards as to justify the statement that they were practically contemporaneous with the adoption of the original; and the twelfth, adopted in eighteen hundred and three, was so nearly so as to have become, like all the others, historical and of another age. But within the last eight years three other articles of amendment of vast importance have been added by the voice of the people to that now venerable instrument.

The most cursory glance at these articles discloses a unity of purpose, when taken in connection with the history of the times, which cannot fail to have an important bearing on any question of doubt concerning their true meaning. Nor can such doubts, when any reasonably exist, be safely and rationally solved without a reference to that history; for in it is found the occasion and the necessity for recurring again to the great source of power in this country, the people of the States, for additional guarantees of human rights; additional powers to the Federal government; additional restraints upon those of the States. Fortunately that history is fresh within the memory of us all, and its leading features, as they bear upon the matter before us, free from doubt.

The institution of African slavery, as it existed in about half the States of the Union, and the contests pervading the public mind for many years, between those who desired its curtailment and ultimate extinction and those who desired additional safeguards for its security and perpetuation, culminated in the effort, on the part of most of the States in which slavery existed, to separate from the Federal government, and to resist its authority. This constituted the war of the rebellion, and whatever auxiliary causes may have contributed to bring about this war, undoubtedly the overshadowing and efficient cause was African slavery.

In that struggle slavery, as a legalized social relation, perished. It perished as a necessity of the bitterness and force of the conflict. When the armies of freedom found themselves upon the soil of slavery they could do nothing less than free the poor victims whose enforced servitude was the foundation of the quarrel. And when hard pressed in the contest these men (for they proved themselves men in that terrible crisis) offered their services and were accepted by thousands to aid in suppressing the unlawful rebellion, slavery was at an end wherever the Federal government succeeded in that purpose. The proclamation of President Lincoln expressed an accomplished fact as to a large portion of the insurrectionary districts, when he declared slavery abolished in them all. But the war being over, those who had succeeded in re-establishing the authority of the Federal government were not content to permit this great act of emancipation to rest on the actual results of the contest or the proclamation of the Executive, both of which might have been questioned in after times, and they determined to place this main and most valuable result in the Constitution of the restored Union as one of its fundamental articles. Hence the thirteenth article of amendment of that instrument. Its two short sections seem hardly to admit of construction, so vigorous is their expression and so appropriate to the purpose we have indicated.

. . .

To withdraw the mind from the contemplation of this grand yet simple declaration of the personal freedom of all the human race within the jurisdiction of this government—a declaration designed to establish the freedom of four millions of slaves—and with a microscopic search endeavor to find in it a reference to servitudes, which may have been attached to property in certain localities, requires an effort, to say the least of it.

That a personal servitude was meant is proved by the use of the word "involuntary," which can only apply to human beings. The exception of servitude as a punishment for crime gives an idea of the class of servitude that is meant. The word servitude is of larger meaning than slavery, as the latter is popularly understood in this country, and the obvious purpose was to forbid all shades and conditions of African slavery. It was very well understood that in the form of apprenticeship for long terms, as it had been practiced in the West India Islands, on the abolition of slavery by the English government, or by reducing the slaves to the condition of serfs attached to the plantation, the purpose of the article might have been evaded, if only the word slavery had been used. The case of the apprentice slave, held under a law of Maryland, liberated by Chief Justice Chase, on a writ of habeas corpus under this article, illustrates this course of observation. And it is all that we deem necessary to say on the application of that article to the statute of Louisiana, now under consideration.

The process of restoring to their proper relations with the Federal government and with the other States those which had sided with the rebellion, undertaken under the proclamation of President Johnson in 1865, and before the assembling of Congress, developed the fact that, notwithstanding the formal recognition by those States of the abolition of slavery, the condition of the slave race would, without further protection of the Federal government, be almost as bad as it was before. Among the first acts of legislation adopted by several of the States in the legislative bodies which claimed to be in their normal relations with the Federal government, were laws which imposed upon the colored race onerous disabilities and burdens, and curtailed their rights in the pursuit of life, liberty, and property to such an extent that their freedom was of little value, while they had lost the protection which they had received from their former owners from motives both of interest and humanity.

They were in some States forbidden to appear in the towns in any other character than menial servants. They were required to reside on and cultivate the soil without the right to purchase or own it. They were excluded from many occupations of gain, and were not permitted to give testimony in the courts in any case where a white man was a party. It was said that their lives were at the mercy of bad men, either because the laws for their protection were insufficient or were not enforced.

These circumstances, whatever of falsehood or misconception may have been mingled with their presentation, forced upon the statesmen who had conducted the Federal government in safety through the crisis of the rebellion, and who supposed that by the thirteenth article of amendment they had secured the result of their labors, the conviction that something more was necessary in the way of constitutional protection to the unfortunate race who had suffered so much. They accordingly passed through Congress the proposition for the fourteenth amendment, and they declined to treat as restored to their full participation in the government of the Union the States which had been in insurrection, until they ratified that article by a formal vote of their legislative bodies.

Before we proceed to examine more critically the provisions of this amendment, on which the plaintiffs in error rely, let us complete and dismiss the history of the recent amendments, as that history relates to the general purpose which pervades them all. A few years' experience satisfied the thoughtful men who had been the authors of the other two amendments that, notwithstanding the restraints of those articles on the States, and the laws passed under the additional powers granted to Congress, these were inadequate for the protection of life, liberty, and property, without which freedom to the slave was no boon. They were in all those States denied the right of suffrage. The laws were administered by the white man alone. It was urged that a race of men distinctively marked as was the negro, living in the midst of another and dominant race, could never be fully secured in their person and their property without the right of suffrage.

Hence the fifteenth amendment, which declares that "the right of a citizen of the United States to vote shall not be denied or abridged by any State on account of race, color, or previous condition of servitude." The negro having, by the fourteenth amendment, been declared to be a citizen of the United States, is thus made a voter in every State of the Union.

We repeat, then, in the light of this recapitulation of events, almost too recent to be called history, but which are familiar to us all; and on the most casual examination of the language of these amendments, no one can fail to be impressed with the one pervading purpose found in them all, lying at the foundation of each, and without which none of them would have been even suggested; we mean the freedom of the slave race, the security and firm establishment of that freedom, and the protection of the newly-made freeman and citizen from the oppressions of those who had formerly exercised unlimited dominion over him. It is true that only the fifteenth amendment, in terms, mentions the negro by speaking of his color and his slavery. But it is just as true that each of the other articles was addressed to the grievances of that race, and designed to remedy them as the fifteenth.

We do not say that no one else but the negro can share in this protection. Both the language and spirit of these articles are to have their fair and just weight in any question of construction. Undoubtedly while negro slavery alone was in the mind of the Congress which proposed the thirteenth article, it forbids any other kind of slavery, now or hereafter. If Mexican peonage or the Chinese coolie labor system shall develop slavery of the Mexican or Chinese race within our territory, this amendment may safely be trusted to make it void. And so if other rights are assailed by the States which properly and necessarily fall within the protection of these articles, that protection will apply, though the party interested may not be of African descent. But what we do say, and what we wish to be understood is, that in any fair and just construction of any section or phrase of these amendments, it is necessary to look to the purpose which we have said was the pervading spirit of them all, the evil which they were designed to remedy, and the process of continued addition to the Constitution, until that purpose was supposed to be accomplished, as far as constitutional law can accomplish it.

The first section of the fourteenth article, to which our attention is more specially invited, opens with a definition of citizenship—not only citizenship of the United States, but citizenship of the States. No such definition was previously found in the Constitution, nor had any attempt been made to define it by act of Congress. It had been the occasion of much discussion in the courts, by the executive departments, and in the public journals. It had been said by eminent judges that no man was a citizen of the United States, except as he was a citizen of one of the States composing the Union. Those, therefore, who had been born and resided always in the District of Columbia or in the Territories, though within the United States, were not citizens. Whether this proposition was sound or not had never been judicially decided. But it had been held by this court, in the celebrated Dred Scott case, only a few years before the outbreak of the civil war, that a man of African descent, whether a slave or not, was not and could not be a citizen of a State or of the United States. This decision, while it met the condemnation of some of the ablest statesmen and constitutional lawyers of the country, had never been overruled; and if it was to be accepted as a constitutional limitation of the right of citizenship, then all the negro race who had recently been made freemen, were still, not only not citizens, but were incapable of becoming so by anything short of an amendment to the Constitution.

To remove this difficulty primarily, and to establish a clear and comprehensive definition of citizenship which should declare what should constitute citizenship of the United States, and also citizenship of a State, the first clause of the first section was framed.

"All persons born or naturalized in the United States, and subject to the jurisdiction thereof, are citizens of the United States and of the State wherein they reside."

The first observation we have to make on this clause is, that it puts at rest both the questions which we stated to have been the subject of differences of opinion. It declares that persons may be citizens of the United States without regard to their citizenship, of a particular State, and it overturns the Dred Scott decision by making *all persons* born within the United States and subject to its jurisdiction citizens of the United States. That its main purpose was to establish the citizenship of the negro can admit of no doubt. The phrase, "subject to its jurisdiction" was intended to exclude from its operation children of ministers, consuls, and citizens or subjects of foreign States born within the United States.

The next observation is more important in view of the arguments of counsel in the present case. It is, that the distinction between citizenship of the United States and citizenship of a State is clearly recognized and established. Not only may a man be a citizen of the United States without being a citizen of a State, but an important element is necessary to convert the former into the latter. He must reside within the State to make him a citizen of it, but it is only necessary that he should be born or naturalized in the United States to be a citizen of the Union.

It is quite clear, then, that there is a citizenship of the United States, and a citizenship of a State, which are distinct from each other, and which depend upon different characteristics or circumstances in the individual.

We think this distinction and its explicit recognition in this amendment of great weight in this argument, because the next paragraph of this same section, which is the one mainly relied on by the plaintiffs in error, speaks only of privileges and immunities of citizens of the United States, and does not speak of those of citizens of the several States. The argument, however, in favor of the plaintiffs rests wholly on the assumption that the citizenship is the same, and the privileges and immunities guaranteed by the clause are the same.

The language is, "No State shall make or enforce any law which shall abridge the privileges or immunities of citizens of *the United States.*" It is a little remarkable, if this clause was intended as a protection to the citizen of a State against the legislative power of his own State, that the word citizen of the State should be left out when it is so carefully used, and used in contradistinction to citizens of the United States, in the very sentence which precedes it. It is too clear for argument that the change in phraseology was adopted understandingly and with a purpose.

Of the privileges and immunities of the citizen of the United States, and of the privileges and immunities of the citizen of the State, and what they respectively are, we will presently consider; but we wish to state here that it is only the former which are placed by this clause under the protection of the Federal Constitution, and that the latter, whatever they may be, are not intended to have any additional protection by this paragraph of the amendment.

If, then, there is a difference between the privileges and immunities belonging to a citizen of the United States as such, and those belonging to the citizen of the State as such, the latter must rest for their security and protection where they have heretofore rested; for they are not embraced by this paragraph of the amendment.

The first occurrence of the words "privileges and immunities" in our constitutional history, is to be found in the fourth of the articles of the old Confederation.

It declares "that the better to secure and perpetuate mutual friendship and intercourse among the people of the different States in this Union, the free inhabitants of each of these States, paupers, vagabonds, and fugitives from justice excepted, shall be entitled to all the privileges and immunities of free citizens in the several States; and the people of each State shall have free ingress and regress to and from any other State, and shall enjoy therein all the privileges of trade and commerce, subject to the same duties, impositions, and restrictions as the inhabitants thereof respectively."

In the Constitution of the United States, which superseded the Articles of Confederation, the corresponding provision is found in section two of the fourth article, in the following words: "The citizens of each State shall be entitled to all the privileges and immunities of citizens of the several States."

There can be but little question that the purpose of both these provisions is the same, and that the privileges and immunities intended are the same in each. In the article of the Confederation we have some of these specifically mentioned, and enough perhaps to give some general idea of the class of civil rights meant by the phrase.

Fortunately we are not without judicial construction of this clause of the Constitution. The first and the leading case on the subject is that of Corfield v. Coryell, decided by Mr. Justice Washington in the Circuit Court for the District of Pennsylvania in 1823.

"The inquiry," he says, "is, what are the privileges and immunities of citizens of the several States? We feel no hesitation in confining these expressions to those privileges and immunities which are *fundamental;* which belong of right to the citizens of all free governments, and which have at all times been enjoyed by citizens of the several States which compose this Union, from the time of their becoming free, independent, and sovereign. What these fundamental principles are, it would be more tedious than difficult to enumerate. They may all, however, be comprehended under the following general heads:

protection by the government, with the right to acquire and possess property of every kind, and to pursue and obtain happiness and safety, subject, nevertheless, to such restraints as the government may prescribe for the general good of the whole."

. . . The description, when taken to include others not named, but which are of the same general character, embraces nearly every civil right for the establishment and protection of which organized government is instituted. They are, in the language of Judge Washington, those rights which are fundamental. Throughout his opinion, they are spoken of as rights belonging to the individual as a citizen of a State. They are so spoken of in the constitutional provision which he was construing. And they have always been held to be the class of rights which the State governments were created to establish and secure.

. . . [Article IV] did not create those rights, which it called privileges and immunities of citizens of the States. It threw around them in that clause no security for the citizen of the State in which they were claimed or exercised. Nor did it profess to control the power of the State governments over the rights of its own citizens.

Its sole purpose was to declare to the several States, that whatever those rights, as you grant or establish them to your own citizens, or as you limit or qualify, or impose restrictions on their exercise, the same, neither more nor less, shall be the measure of the rights of citizens of other States within your jurisdiction.

It would be the vainest show of learning to attempt to prove by citations of authority, that up to the adoption of the recent amendments, no claim or pretence was set up that those rights depended on the Federal government for their existence or protection, beyond the very few express limitations which the Federal Constitution imposed upon the States—such, for instance, as the prohibition against ex post facto laws, bills of attainder, and laws impairing the obligation of contracts. But with the exception of these and a few other restrictions, the entire domain of the privileges and immunities of citizens of the States, as above defined, lay within the constitutional and legislative power of the States, and without that of the Federal government. Was it the purpose of the fourteenth amendment, by the simple declaration that no State should make or enforce any law which shall abridge the privileges and immunities of *citizens of the United States,* to transfer the security and protection of all the civil rights which we have mentioned, from the States to the Federal government? And where it is declared that Congress shall have the power to enforce that article, was it intended to bring within the power of Congress the entire domain of civil rights heretofore belonging exclusively to the States?

All this and more must follow, if the proposition of the plaintiffs in error be sound. For not only are these rights subject to the control of Congress whenever in its discretion any of them are supposed to be abridged by State legislation, but that body may also pass laws in advance, limiting and restricting the exercise of legislative power by the States, in their most ordinary and usual functions, as in its judgment it may think proper on all such subjects. And still further, such a construction followed by the reversal of the judgments of the Supreme Court of Louisiana in these cases, would constitute this court a perpetual censor upon all legislation of the States, on the civil rights of their own citizens, with authority to nullify such as it did not approve as consistent with those rights, as they existed at the time of the adoption of this amendment. The argument we admit is not always the most conclusive which is drawn from the consequences urged against the adoption of a particular construction of an instrument. But when, as in the case before us, these consequences are so serious, so far-reaching and pervading, so great a departure from the structure and spirit of our institutions; when the effect is to fetter and degrade the State governments by subjecting them to the control of Congress, in the exercise of powers heretofore universally conceded to them of the most ordinary and fundamental character; when in fact it radically changes the whole theory of the relations of the State and Federal governments to each other and of both these governments to the people; the argument has a force that is irresistible, in the absence of language which expresses such a purpose too clearly to admit of doubt.

We are convinced that no such results were intended by the Congress which proposed these amendments, nor by the legislatures of the States which ratified them.

Having shown that the privileges and immunities relied on in the argument are those which belong to citizens of the States as such, and that they are left to the State governments for security and protection, and not by this article placed under the special care of the Federal government, we may hold ourselves excused from defining the privileges and immunities of citizens of the United States which no State can abridge, until some case involving those privileges may make it necessary to do so.

But lest it should be said that no such privileges and immunities are to be found if those we have been considering are excluded, we venture to suggest some which owe their existence to the Federal government, its National character, its Constitution, or its laws.

One of these is well described in the case of Crandall v. Nevada. It is said to be the right of the citizen of this great country, protected by implied guarantees of its Constitution, "to come to the seat of government to assert any claim he may have upon that government, to transact any business he may have with it, to seek its protection, to share its offices, to engage in administering its functions. He has the right of free access to its seaports, through which all operations of foreign commerce are conducted, to the sub-treasuries, land offices, and courts of justice in the several States." And quoting from the language of Chief Justice Taney in another case, it is said "that *for all the great purposes for which the Federal government* was established, we are one people, with one common country, *we are all citizens of the United States;*" and it is, as such citizens, that their rights are supported in this court in Crandall v. Nevada.

Another privilege of a citizen of the United States, is to demand the care and protection of the Federal government over his life, liberty, and property when on the high seas or within the jurisdiction of a foreign government. Of this there can be no doubt, nor that the right depends upon his character as a citizen of the United States. The right to peaceably assemble and petition for redress of grievances, the privilege of the writ of *habeas corpus,* are rights of the citizen guaranteed by the Federal Constitution. The right to use the navigable waters of the United States, however they may penetrate the territory of the several States, all rights secured to our citizens by treaties with foreign nations, are dependent upon citizenship of the United States, and not citizenship of a State. One of these privileges is conferred by the very article under consideration. It is that a citizen of the United States can, of his own volition, become a citizen of any State of the Union by a *bona fide* residence therein, with the same rights as other citizens of that State. To these may be added the rights secured by the thirteenth and fifteenth articles of amendment, and by the other clause of the fourteenth, next to be considered.

But it is useless to pursue this branch of the inquiry, since we are of opinion that the rights claimed by these plaintiffs in error, if they have any existence, are not privileges and immunities of citizens of the United States within the meaning of the clause of the fourteenth amendment under consideration.
. . . .

The argument has not been much pressed in these cases that the defendant's charter deprives the plaintiffs of their property without due process of law, or that it denies to them the equal protection of the law. The first of these paragraphs has been in the Constitution since the adoption of the fifth amendment, as a restraint upon the Federal power. It is also to be found in some form of expression in the constitutions of nearly all the States, as a restraint upon the power of the States. This law then, has practically been the same as it now is during the existence of the government, except so far as the present amendment may place the restraining power over the States in this matter in the hands of the Federal government.

We are not without judicial interpretation, therefore, both State and National, of the meaning of this clause. And it is sufficient to say that under no construction of that provision that we have ever seen, or any that we deem admissible, can the restraint imposed by the State of Louisiana upon the exercise of their trade by the butchers of New Orleans be held to be a deprivation of property within the meaning of that provision.

"Nor shall any State deny to any person within its jurisdiction the equal protection of the laws."

In the light of the history of these amendments, and the pervading purpose of them, which we have already discussed, it is not difficult to give a meaning to this clause. The existence of laws in the States where the newly emancipated negroes resided, which discriminated with gross injustice and hardship against them as a class, was the evil to be remedied by this clause, and by it such laws are forbidden.

If, however, the States did not conform their laws to its requirements, then by the fifth section of the article of amendment Congress was authorized to enforce it by suitable legislation. We doubt very much whether any action of a State not directed by way of discrimination against the negroes as a class, or on account of their race, will ever be held to come within the purview of this provision. It is so clearly a provision for that race and that emergency, that a strong case would be necessary for its application to any other. But as it is a State that is to be dealt with, and not alone the validity of its laws, we may safely leave that matter until Congress shall have exercised its power, or some case of State oppression, by denial of equal justice in its courts, shall have claimed a decision at our hands. We find no such case in the one before us, and do not deem it necessary to go over the argument again, as it may have relation to this particular clause of the amendment.

In the early history of the organization of the government, its statesmen seem to have divided on the line which should separate the powers of the National government from those of the State governments, and though this line has never been very well defined in public opinion, such a division has continued from that day to this.

The adoption of the first eleven amendments to the Constitution so soon after the original instrument was accepted, shows a prevailing sense of danger at that time from the Federal power. And it cannot be denied that such a jealousy continued to exist with many patriotic men until the breaking out of the late civil war. It was then discovered that the true danger to the perpetuity of the Union was in the capacity of the State organizations to combine and concentrate all the powers of the State, and of contiguous States, for a determined resistance to the General Government.

Unquestionably this has given great force to the argument, and added largely to the number of those who believe in the necessity of a strong National government.

But, however pervading this sentiment, and however it may have contributed to the adoption of the amendments we have been considering, we do not see in those amendments any purpose to destroy the main features of the general system. Under the pressure of all the excited feeling growing out of the war, our statesmen have still believed that the existence of the States with powers for domestic and local government, including the regulation of civil rights—the rights of person and of property—was essential to the perfect working of our complex form of government, though they have thought proper to impose additional limitations on the States, and to confer additional power on that of the Nation.

But whatever fluctuations may be seen in the history of public opinion on this subject during the period of our national existence, we think it will be found that this court, so far as its functions required, has always held with a steady and an even hand the balance between State and Federal power, and we trust that such may continue to be the history of its relation to that subject so long as it shall have duties to perform which demand of it as construction of the Constitution, or of any of its parts.

The judgments of the Supreme Court of Louisiana in these cases are

Affirmed.

Mr. Justice Field, dissenting:

. . .

The act of Louisiana presents the naked case, unaccompanied by any public considerations, where a right to pursue a lawful and necessary calling, previously enjoyed by every citizen, and in connection with which a thousand persons were daily employed, is taken away and vested exclusively for twenty-five years, for an extensive district and a large population, in a single corporation, or its exercise is for that period restricted to the establishments of the corporation, and there allowed only upon onerous conditions. . . .

The question presented is, therefore, one of the gravest importance, not merely to the parties here, but to the whole country. It is nothing less than the question whether the recent amendments to the Federal Constitution protect the citizens of the United States against the deprivation of their common rights by State legislation. In my judgment the fourteenth amendment does afford such protection, and was so intended by the Congress which framed and the States which adopted it. . . .

The amendment does not attempt to confer any new privileges or immunities upon citizens, or to enumerate or define those already existing. It assumes that there are such privileges and immunities which belong of right to citizens as such, and ordains that they shall not be abridged by State legislation. If this inhibition has no reference to privileges and immunities of this character, but only refers, as held by the majority of the court in their opinion, to such privileges and immunities as were before its adoption specially designated in the Constitution or necessarily implied as belonging to citizens of the United States, it was a vain and idle enactment, which accomplished nothing, and most unnecessarily excited Congress and the people on its passage. With privileges and immunities thus designated or implied no State could ever have interfered by its laws, and no new constitutional provision was required to inhibit such interference. The supremacy of the Constitution and the laws of the United States always controlled any State legislation of that character. But if the amendment refers to the natural and inalienable rights which belong to all citizens, the inhibition has a profound significance and consequence.

What, then, are the privileges and immunities which are secured against abridgment by State legislation?

In the first section of the Civil Rights Act Congress has given its interpretation to these terms, or at least has stated some of the rights which, in its judgment, these terms include; it has there declared that they include the right "to make and enforce contracts, to sue, be parties and give evidence, to inherit, purchase, lease, sell, hold, and convey real and personal property, and to full and equal benefit of all laws and proceedings for the security of person and property." . . .

The common law of England . . . condemned all monopolies in any known trade or manufacture, and declared void all grants of special privileges whereby others could be deprived of any liberty which they previously had, or be hindered in their lawful trade. The statute of James I, to which I have referred, only embodied the law as it had been previously declared by the courts of England, although frequently disregarded by the sovereigns of that country.

The common law of England is the basis of the jurisprudence of the United States. . . . And when the Colonies separated from the mother country no privilege was more fully recognized or more completely incorporated into the fundamental law of the country than that every free subject in the British empire was entitled to pursue his happiness by following any of the known established trades and occupations of the country, subject only to such restraints as equally affected all others. . . .

[The dissenting opinion discussed state court decisions in Illinois, Connecticut and New York striking down monopolies and exclusive privileges.]

. . .

This equality of right, with exemption from all disparaging and partial enactments, in the lawful pursuits of life, throughout the whole country, is the distinguishing privilege of citizens of the United States. To them, everywhere, all pursuits, all professions, all avocations are open without other restrictions than such as are imposed equally upon all others of the same age, sex, and condition. The State may prescribe such regulations for every pursuit and calling of life as will promote the public health, secure the good order and advance the general prosperity of society, but when once prescribed the pursuit or calling must be free to be followed by every citizen who is within the conditions designated, and will conform to the regulations. This is the fundamental idea upon which our institutions rest, and unless adhered to in the legislation of the country our government will be a republic only in name. The fourteenth amendment, in my judgment, makes it essential to the validity of the legislation of every State that this equality of right should be respected. How widely this equality has been departed from, how entirely rejected and trampled upon by the act of Louisiana, I have already shown. And it is to me a matter of profound regret that its validity is recognized by a majority of this court, for by it the right of free labor, one of the most sacred and imprescriptible rights of man, is violated. As stated by the Supreme Court of Connecticut, in the case cited, grants of exclusive privileges, such as is made by the act in question, are opposed to the whole theory of free government, and it requires no aid from any bill of rights to render them void. That only is a free government, in the American sense of the term, under which the inalienable right of every citizen to pursue his happiness is unrestrained, except by just, equal, and impartial laws.

I am authorized by the Chief Justice [Chase], Mr. Justice Swayne, and Mr. Justice Bradley, to state that they concur with me in this dissenting opinion.

[Justices Bradley and Swayne also filed dissenting opinions.]

———

THE PRIVILEGES AND IMMUNITIES CLAUSE OF THE FOURTEENTH AMENDMENT

Does the 14th amendment privileges and immunities clause have any independent significance as interpreted by the Court in the Slaughterhouse Cases? Would any case be decided differently because of the presence of that clause? How does it differ from the privileges and immunities clause in Art. IV?

The conventional interpretations of the Art. IV clause would render unconstitutional an attempt by a state to impose higher taxes on nonresidents doing business in the state than upon residents. See, e.g., Austin v. New Hampshire, 420 U.S. 656 (1975). In Madden v. Kentucky, 309 U.S. 83 (1940) the Court had before it a challenge to a state tax which required residents of that state to pay a higher tax on deposits in banks outside the state than in local banks. The argument was made that the privileges and immunities clause of the 14th amendment protected a resident of a state against this discrimination against property and activities outside the state. The Court rejected this argument: "[T]he privileges and immunities clause protects all citizens against abridgment by states of rights of national citizenship as distinct from the fundamental or natural rights inherent in state citizenship. . . . We think it quite clear that the right to carry out an incident to a trade, business or calling such as the deposit of money in banks is not a privilege of national citizenship."

DUE PROCESS AND JURISDICTION

Even prior to the adoption of the fourteenth amendment the Court applied restrictions on the jurisdiction of state legislatures and state courts without any clear constitutional basis for the restrictions. The Court held, e.g., in Baldwin v. Hale, 68 U.S. (1 Wall.) 223, 234 (1864), that "[i]nsolvent laws of one State cannot discharge the contracts of citizens of other States, because they have no extraterritorial operation, and consequently the tribunal sitting under them, unless in cases where a citizen of such other State voluntarily becomes a party to the proceedings, has no jurisdiction in the case. Legal notice cannot be given and, consequently, there can be no obligation to appear, and of course, there can be no legal default." And in State Tax on Foreign-held Bonds, 82 U.S. (15 Wall.) 300, 319 (1873), the Court referred to an earlier case as establishing the proposition that "property lying beyond the jurisdiction of the state is not a subject upon which her taxing power can be legitimately exercised. Indeed, it would seem that no adjudication should be necessary to establish so obvious a proposition."

The requirement of personal service of process within the jurisdiction or voluntary appearance as a basis for securing a valid judgment in personam was early brought under the due process rubric in Pennoyer v. Neff, 95 U.S. 714, 732 (1878). The Court said that "[s]ince the adoption of the Fourteenth Amendment" the validity of judgments of state courts may be questioned "on the ground that proceedings in a court of justice to determine the personal rights and obligations of parties over whom that court has no jurisdiction, do not constitute due process of law."

It was not until the turn of the century, however, that the Court placed under the due process clause limitations on the jurisdiction of the states to tax tangible property located outside the state. In Louisville & Jefferson Ferry Co. v. Kentucky, 188 U.S. 385, 396, 397 (1903), the Court, in holding that Kentucky could not tax a franchise granted a ferry by Indiana to convey passengers from Indiana to Kentucky, first said that the taxing power of the states "is limited by a principle inhering in the very nature of constitutional government, namely, that the taxation imposed must have relation to a subject within the jurisdiction of the taxing government." It went on, however, to assert that the taxation of the franchise by Kentucky is "a deprivation by that state of the property of the ferry company without due process of law in violation of the 14th Amendment of the Constitution of the United States; as much so as if that state taxed the real estate owned by that company in Indiana." See also Union Refrigerator Transit Co. v. Kentucky, 199 U.S. 194 (1905) where the Court clearly made jurisdiction to tax a due process issue even though Justice Holmes noted that he and Chief Justice Fuller could not "understand" how the result "can be deduced from the 14th Amendment."

DUE PROCESS AND FAIR PROCEDURE

In 1856 in *Murray's Lessee,* supra p. 481, the Court started to mark out the limits imposed by the due process clause of the fifth amendment on procedures devised by Congress. But in 1864 the Court was still finding limits on the powers of the states to establish procedures for civil cases without any definite constitutional basis. Thus in Baldwin v. Hale, 68 U.S. (1 Wall.) 223, 233 (1864), the Court said: "Parties whose rights are to be affected are entitled to be heard; and in order that they may enjoy that right they must first be notified. Common justice requires that no man shall be condemned in his person or property without notice and an opportunity to make his defense."

After the adoption of the fourteenth amendment, however, the Court quickly placed the guarantee of fair procedures in the states firmly on the due process clause of that amendment. In Hagar v. Reclamation District, 111 U.S. 701, 708 (1884), the Court said: "Undoubtedly, where life and liberty are involved, due process requires that there be a regular course of judicial proceedings, which imply that the party to be affected shall have notice and an opportunity to be heard; so, also, where title or possession of property is involved." And in Hurtado v. California, 110 U.S. 516, 534 (1884), the Court, in holding that a state could substitute a preliminary hearing for indictment by grand jury in criminal cases, said that the due process clause in the fourteenth amendment meant the same as it did in the fifth amendment and that any state proceeding constituted due process of law if it was "exerted within the limits of those fundamental principles of liberty and justice which lie at the base of all our civil and political institutions . . . ."

SECTION 3. THE FOURTEENTH AMENDMENT
AND CITIZENSHIP

The distinction between alienage and citizenship is fundamental and vitally important issues turn on it. A citizen may not be deported nor excluded from the United States. United States v. Wong Kim Ark, 169 U.S. 649 (1898) held, for example, that a person born in the United States and therefore a citizen could not be excluded from the country when he attempted to enter even though his foreign-born parents were not eligible for naturalization. An alien, on the other hand, may be deported for any of a substantial list of reasons. 8 U.S.C. § 1251. In Harisiades v. Shaughnessy, 342 U.S. 580 (1952), it was held that an alien (resident of the United States for thirty years) could be deported because of Communist Party membership even though this membership had terminated before enactment of the deportation statute. See also Galvan v. Press, 347 U.S. 522 (1954); Rowoldt v. Perfetto, 355 U.S. 115 (1957). Aliens may also be excluded from the United States for an even longer list of reasons. 8 U.S.C. § 1182. An alien seeking entry into the United States has no constitutional right to a hearing and the exercise of power by the Attorney General to deny admission without a hearing has been upheld. United States ex rel. Knauff v. Shaughnessy, 338 U.S. 537 (1950). However, an administrative hearing is provided by statute for most exclusion cases. 8 U.S.C. § 1226.

In Landon v. Plasencia, 459 U.S. 21 (1982) the Court addressed the question of what hearing might be required under due process for a permanent resident alien returning from a brief trip abroad. The Court held that such an alien was not entitled to a deportation hearing. However, the Court went on to hold that such an alien did have a due process right to a fair exclusion hearing. The Court said:

"This Court has long held that an alien seeking initial admission to the United States requests a privilege and has no constitutional rights regarding his application, for the power to admit or exclude aliens is a sovereign prerogative. See, e.g., United States ex rel. Knauff v. Shaughnessy, 338 U.S. 537, 542 (1950); Nishimura Ekiu v. United States, 142 U.S. 651, 659–660 (1892). Our recent decisions confirm that view. See, e.g., Fiallo v. Bell, 430 U.S. 787, 792 (1977); Kleindienst v. Mandel, 408 U.S. 753 (1972). As we explained in Johnson v. Eisentrager, 339 U.S. 763, 770 (1950), however, once an alien gains admission to our country and begins to develop the ties that go with permanent residence his constitutional status changes accordingly. Our cases have frequently suggested that a continuously present resident alien is entitled to a fair hearing when threatened with deportation . . . and, although we have only rarely held that the procedures provided by the executive were inadequate, we developed the rule that a continuously present permanent resident alien has a right to due process in such a situation. . . .

"The question of the procedures due a returning resident alien arose in Kwong Hai Chew v. Colding, supra. There, the regulations permitted the exclusion of an arriving alien without a hearing. We interpreted those regulations not to apply to Chew, a permanent resident alien who was returning from a five-month voyage abroad as a crewman on an American merchant ship. We reasoned that, 'For purposes of his constitutional right to due process, we assimilate petitioner's status to that of an alien continuously residing and physically present in the United States.' 344 U.S., at 596. Then, to avoid constitutional problems, we construed the regulation as inapplicable. Although the holding was one of regulatory interpretation, the rationale was one of constitutional law. Any doubts that Chew recognized constitutional rights in the resident alien returning from a brief trip abroad were dispelled by Rosenberg v. Fleuti, supra, where we described Chew as holding 'that the returning resident alien is entitled as a matter of due process to a hearing on the charges underlying any attempt to exclude him.' 374 U.S., at 460.

"If the permanent resident alien's absence is extended, of course, he may lose his entitlement to 'assimilat[ion of his] status,' Kwong Hai Chew v. Colding, supra, 344 U.S., at 596, to that of an alien continuously residing and physically present in the United States. In Shaughnessy v. United States ex rel. Mezei, 345 U.S. 206 (1953), this Court rejected the argument of an alien who had left the country for some twenty months that he was entitled to due process in assessing his right to admission on his return. We did not suggest that no returning resident alien has a right to due process, for we explicitly reaffirmed Chew. We need not now decide the scope of Mezei; it does not govern this case, for Plasencia was absent from the country only a few days, and the United States has conceded that she has a right to due process, ..."

In view of the importance of citizenship it is surprising that the constitution originally did not define it. However, the desire to assure citizenship to former slaves (who had been held not to be citizens in Dred Scott v. Sandford, 60 U.S.

(19 How.) 393 (1857)) led to the definition contained in the opening sentence of the fourteenth amendment: "All persons born or naturalized in the United States, and subject to the jurisdiction thereof, are citizens of the United States and of the State wherein they reside." In United States v. Wong Kim Ark, 169 U.S. 649 (1898), it was stated that the phrase, "and subject to the jurisdiction thereof" excluded "by the fewest and fittest words (besides children of members of the Indian tribes, standing in a peculiar relation to the National Government, unknown to the common law) the two classes of cases—children born of alien enemies in hostile occupation, and children of diplomatic representatives of a foreign state. . . . ."

Congress has added by statute to the constitutional definition of citizenship. Three principal categories have been added: (1) persons born in the United States to members of Indian, Eskimo, Aleutian, or other aboriginal tribes; (2) persons born outside the United States of parents both of whom are citizens and one of whom has had a residence in the United States prior to birth of such person; and (3) persons born outside the United States where only one parent is a citizen and that parent has resided in the United States for a prescribed period. See generally 8 U.S.C. § 1401.

Congress has long recognized the right of citizens to renounce their United States citizenship. 8 U.S.C. § 1481(a)(6), (7). Major problems have arisen, however, as a result of statutory provisions providing for loss of nationality upon the doing of certain acts—e.g. obtaining naturalization in a foreign state, taking an oath of allegiance to a foreign state, entering and serving in the armed forces of a foreign state without official consent. 8 U.S.C. § 1481. The Court holds that a person who acquires citizenship by virtue of the fourteenth amendment (one who is born in the United States or one who is naturalized) may not be stripped of citizenship for any reason. A more subtle question is whether Congress may presume an intent to renounce citizenship from performance of certain acts, e.g., taking an oath of allegiance to a foreign state. The case which follows is the most recent to explore the issue.

VANCE v. TERRAZAS, 444 U.S. 252 (1980). Terrazas, who was born in the United States as the son of a Mexican citizen, acquired at birth both United States and Mexican citizenship. At the age of 22 while in Mexico he applied for a certificate of Mexican nationality, swearing adherence to the laws of Mexico and "expressly renounc[ing] United States citizenship . . . .." The State Department determined that he had lost his United States citizenship by so doing and issued a certificate of loss of nationality. Terrazas brought suit against the Secretary of State for a declaration of his United States nationality. The trial court applied the statutory standard that the burden on the government to establish an intent to renounce citizenship was that of a preponderance of the evidence and found for the government. The court of appeals reversed holding that clear and convincing evidence was required. The Supreme Court, in an opinion by Justice White, reversed the court of appeals.

In its opinion the Court first rejected a claim by the government that it was sufficient to prove that the plaintiff had voluntarily executed the oath of allegiance to Mexico. It referred to the earlier case of Afroyim v. Rusk, 387 U.S. 253 (1967) in which it had rejected the idea that "Congress has any general power, express or implied, to take away an American citizen's citizenship without his assent" and stated that § 1 of the fourteenth amendment is "most reasonably . . . read as defining a citizenship which a citizen keeps unless he voluntarily relinquishes it." Hence, the Court held that in addition to proving that the plaintiff had taken the oath of allegiance voluntarily the government also had to prove that he did so intending to relinquish his citizenship.

However, the Court went on to hold that it was constitutional for Congress to provide that the burden on the government in establishing intent to renounce was that of a preponderance of the evidence. It also considered the effect of a statutory presumption that plaintiff by taking the Mexican oath had done so voluntarily, holding that it was constitutional to have such a rebuttable presumption that the act was voluntary so long as there was no presumption of intention to renounce United States Citizenship. The opinion concluded:

"In sum, we hold that in proving expatriation, an expatriating act and an intent to relinquish citizenship must be proved by a preponderance of the evidence. We also hold that when one of the statutory expatriating acts is proved, it is constitutional to presume it to have been a voluntary act until and unless proved otherwise by the actor. If he succeeds, there can be no expatriation. If he fails, the question remains whether on all the evidence the Government has satisfied its burden of proof that the expatriating act was performed with the necessary intent to relinquish citizenship."

Justices Marshall and Stevens dissented from the Court's holding that intent to renounce could be established by only a preponderance of the evidence. Justice Brennan dissented on two grounds. First, he contended that expatriating acts were irrelevant and only formal renunciation of citizenship before a United States official could result in expatriation. Second, he contended that where a dual citizen takes an oath of allegiance to the other country of which he is a citizen the act adds nothing to his foreign citizenship and cannot be expatriating. Justice Stewart dissented for the second reason given by Justice Brennan.

SECTION 4. APPLICATION OF THE BILL OF RIGHTS TO THE STATES

Introduction. Early in the process of giving content to the due process clause of the fourteenth amendment the question arose as to the relationship between the Bill of Rights and the fourteenth amendment. An early example of the Court's approach was Twining v. New Jersey, 211 U.S. 78 (1908). The question posed was whether the provision in the fifth amendment that no person "shall be compelled in any criminal case to be a witness against himself" applied to restrain the states. Twining argued first that the "privileges and immunities of citizens of the United States" protected against state action by the fourteenth amendment included those fundamental personal rights which were protected against national action by the first eight Amendments; that this was the intention of the framers of the fourteenth amendment. The Court rejected this argument, relying on the interpretation of the privileges and immunities clause in the Slaughterhouse Cases. Second, Twining argued that a denial of the privilege against self-incrimination constituted a denial of due process of law. The Court rejected this argument, holding that the privilege against self-incrimination was not "an immutable principle of justice which is the inalienable possession of every citizen of a free government" and hence to deny it was not to deny due process.

The question whether the first eight amendments could be utilized to make more specific the meaning of "due process of law" was not settled by *Twining*. The subsequent cases involved primarily criminal procedure, and detailed consideration of those cases is left to the courses in criminal procedure. All that will be presented here is a few of the principal cases illustrating the dispute over the incorporation problem, and over the nature of judicial review itself.

One aspect of the incorporation doctrine has become the foundation for most of the modern developments concerning freedom of speech, press, and religion. Almost casually, the Court in 1925 asserted in Gitlow v. New York,

268 U.S. 652, 666: "For present purposes we may and do assume that freedom of speech and of the press—which are protected by the 1st Amendment from abridgment by Congress—are among the fundamental personal rights and 'liberties' protected by the due process clause of the 14th Amendment from impairment by the states."

THE INCORPORATION DOCTRINE

In Chapter 10 we will see how the Court gave an early expansive meaning to such fourteenth amendment terms as "liberty", "property", and "due process of law" in the context of judicial review of the substance of economic regulations. We will also see the Court's withdrawal from that expansive interpretation in recent decades.

In the field of procedure (primarily procedure in criminal cases) there was a similar development, but with a different twist. In the early years the Court found in the fourteenth amendment restrictions upon state procedures which denied "immutable principles of justice" which are "the inalienable possession of every citizen of a free government" or which deprived the accused of "sufficient notice of the accusation" and "an adequate opportunity to defend himself". These expansive terms, and others, tended to limit rather than to expand (as was the case with respect to the substance of economic regulations) the scope of Court review of state procedures. More recently, through the idea that the fourteenth amendment applies to the states the more specific procedural guaranties in the Bill of Rights, the Court has expanded the scope of review of state court procedures while making somewhat more specific the applicable standards.

This section is designed to show the development of the incorporation doctrine and to underline the dispute within the Court as to the wisdom of seeking to restrain judicial review by confining it to the areas covered by the Bill of Rights. In reading the cases the student should consider how successful the Court has been in achieving more specific standards.

PALKO v. CONNECTICUT

302 U.S. 319, 58 S.Ct. 149, 82 L.Ed. 288 (1937).

Mr. Justice Cardozo delivered the opinion of the Court.

A statute of Connecticut permitting appeals in criminal cases to be taken by the state is challenged by appellant as an infringement of the Fourteenth Amendment of the Constitution of the United States. Whether the challenge should be upheld is now to be determined.

Appellant was indicted in Fairfield County, Conn., for the crime of murder in the first degree. A jury found him guilty of murder in the second degree, and he was sentenced to confinement in the state prison for life. Thereafter the State of Connecticut, with the permission of the judge presiding at the trial, gave notice of appeal to the Supreme Court of Errors. This it did pursuant to an act adopted in 1886. . . . Upon such appeal, the Supreme Court of Errors reversed the judgment and ordered a new trial. . . .

Pursuant to the mandate of the Supreme Court of Errors, defendant was brought to trial again. Before a jury was impaneled, and also at later stages of the case, he made the objection that the effect of the new trial was to place him twice in jeopardy for the same offense, and in so doing to violate the Fourteenth Amendment of the Constitution of the United States. Upon the overruling of the objection the trial proceeded. The jury returned a verdict of murder in the first degree, and the court sentenced the defendant to the punishment of death.

The Supreme Court of Errors affirmed the judgment of conviction (122 Conn. 529, 191 A. 320). . . .

1. The execution of the sentence will not deprive appellant of his life without the process of law assured to him by the Fourteenth Amendment of the Federal Constitution.

The argument for appellant is that whatever is forbidden by the Fifth Amendment is forbidden by the Fourteenth also. The Fifth Amendment, which is not directed to the States, but solely to the federal government, creates immunity from double jeopardy. No person shall be "subject for the same offense to be twice put in jeopardy of life or limb." The Fourteenth Amendment ordains, "nor shall any State deprive any person of life, liberty, or property, without due process of law." To retry a defendant, though under one indictment and only one, subjects him, it is said, to double jeopardy in violation of the Fifth Amendment, if the prosecution is one on behalf of the United States. From this the consequence is said to follow that there is a denial of life or liberty without due process of law, if the prosecution is one on behalf of the people of a state. . . .

We do not find it profitable to mark the precise limits of the prohibition of double jeopardy in federal prosecutions. The subject was much considered in Kepner v. United States, 195 U.S. 100, decided in 1904 by a closely divided court. The view was there expressed for a majority of the court that the prohibition was not confined to jeopardy in a new and independent case. It forbade jeopardy in the same case if the new trial was at the instance of the government and not upon defendant's motion. . . .

We have said that in appellant's view the Fourteenth Amendment is to be taken as embodying the prohibitions of the Fifth. His thesis is even broader. Whatever would be a violation of the original bill of rights (Amendments 1 to 8) if done by the federal government is now equally unlawful by force of the Fourteenth Amendment if done by a state. There is no such general rule.

The Fifth Amendment provides, among other things, that no person shall be held to answer for a capital or otherwise infamous crime unless on presentment or indictment of a grand jury. This court has held that, in prosecutions by a state, presentment or indictment by a grand jury may give way to informations at the instance of a public officer. Hurtado v. California, 110 U.S. 516. . . . The Fifth Amendment provides also that no person shall be compelled in any criminal case to be a witness against himself. This court has said that, in prosecutions by a state, the exemption will fail if the state elects to end it. Twining v. New Jersey, 211 U.S. 78, 106, 111, 112. . . . The Sixth Amendment calls for a jury trial in criminal cases and the Seventh for a jury trial in civil cases at common law where the value in controversy shall exceed $20. This court has ruled that consistently with those amendments trial by jury may be modified by a state or abolished altogether. Walker v. Sauvinet, 92 U.S. 90; Maxwell v. Dow, 176 U.S. 581. . . .

On the other hand, the due process clause of the Fourteenth Amendment may make it unlawful for a state to abridge by its statutes the freedom of speech which the First Amendment safeguards against encroachment by the Congress . . . or the like freedom of the press, . . . or the free exercise of religion, . . . or the right of peaceable assembly, without which speech would be unduly trammeled, . . . or the right of one accused of crime to the benefit of counsel (Powell v. Alabama, 287 U.S. 45). In these and other situations immunities that are valid as against the federal government by force of the specific pledges of particular amendments have been found to be implicit in the concept of ordered liberty, and thus, through the Fourteenth Amendment, become valid as against the states.

The line of division may seem to be wavering and broken if there is a hasty catalogue of the cases on the one side and the other. Reflection and analysis will induce a different view. There emerges the perception of a rationalizing principle which gives to discrete instances a proper order and coherence. The right to trial by jury and the immunity from prosecution except as the result of an indictment may have value and importance. Even so, they are not of the very essence of a scheme of ordered liberty. To abolish them is not to violate a "principle of justice so rooted in the traditions and conscience of our people as to be ranked as fundamental." Snyder v. Massachusetts, supra, 291 U.S. 97, at page 105; Brown v. Mississippi, 297 U.S. 278, at page 285; Hebert v. Louisiana, 272 U.S. 312, 316. Few would be so narrow or provincial as to maintain that a fair and enlightened system of justice would be impossible without them. What is true of jury trials and indictments is true also, as the cases show, of the immunity from compulsory self-incrimination. Twining v. New Jersey, supra. This too might be lost, and justice still be done. Indeed, today as in the past there are students of our penal system who look upon the immunity as a mischief rather than a benefit, and who would limit its scope, or destroy it altogether.[3] No doubt there would remain the need to give protection against torture, physical or mental. Brown v. Mississippi, supra. Justice, however, would not perish if the accused were subject to a duty to respond to orderly inquiry. The exclusion of these immunities and privileges from the privileges and immunities protected against the action of the States has not been arbitrary or casual. It has been dictated by a study and appreciation of the meaning, the essential implications, of liberty itself.

We reach a different plane of social and moral values when we pass to the privileges and immunities that have been taken over from the earlier articles of the Federal Bill of Rights and brought within the Fourteenth Amendment by a process of absorption. These in their origin were effective against the federal government alone. If the Fourteenth Amendment has absorbed them, the process of absorption has had its source in the belief that neither liberty nor justice would exist if they were sacrificed. . . . This is true, for illustration, of freedom of thought and speech. Of that freedom one may say that it is the matrix, the indispensable condition, of nearly every other form of freedom. With rare aberrations a pervasive recognition of that truth can be traced in our history, political and legal. So it has come about that the domain of liberty, withdrawn by the Fourteenth Amendment from encroachment by the states, has been enlarged by latter-day judgments to include liberty of the mind as well as liberty of action. The extension became, indeed, a logical imperative when once it was recognized, as long ago it was, that liberty is something more than exemption from physical restraint, and that even in the field of substantive rights and duties the legislative judgment, if oppressive and arbitrary, may be overridden by the courts. . . . Fundamental too in the concept of due process and so in that of liberty, is the thought that condemnation shall be rendered only after trial. . . . The hearing, moreover, must be a real one, not a sham, or a pretense. Moore v. Dempsey, 261 U.S. 86; Mooney v. Holohan, 294 U.S. 103. For that reason, ignorant defendants in a capital case were held to have been condemned unlawfully when in truth, though not in form, they were refused the aid of counsel. Powell v. Alabama, supra, 287 U.S. 45, at pages 67, 68. The decision did not turn upon the fact that the benefit of counsel would

---

[3] See, e.g., Bentham, Rationale of Judicial Evidence, Book IX, Pt. 4, c. III; Glueck, Crime and Justice, p. 94. Cf. Wigmore, Evidence, vol. 4, § 2251.

Compulsory self-incrimination is part of the established procedure in the law of Continental Europe. Wigmore, supra, p. 824; Garner, Criminal Procedure in France, 25 Yale L.J. 255, 260; Sherman, Roman Law in the Modern World, vol. 2, pp. 493, 494; Stumberg, Guide to the Law and Legal Literature of France, p. 184. Double jeopardy too is not everywhere forbidden. Radin, Anglo American Legal History, p. 228.

have been guaranteed to the defendants by the provisions of the Sixth Amendment if they had been prosecuted in a federal court. The decision turned upon the fact that in the particular situation laid before us in the evidence the benefit of counsel was essential to the substance of a hearing.

Our survey of the cases serves, we think, to justify the statement that the dividing line between them, if not unfaltering throughout its course, has been true for the most part to a unifying principle. On which side of the line the case made out by the appellant has appropriate location must be the next inquiry and the final one. Is that kind of double jeopardy to which the statute has subjected him a hardship so acute and shocking that our polity will not endure it? Does it violate those "fundamental principles of liberty and justice which lie at the base of all our civil and political institutions"? Hebert v. Louisiana, supra. The answer surely must be "no." What the answer would have to be if the state were permitted after a trial free from error to try the accused over again or to bring another case against him, we have no occasion to consider. We deal with the statute before us and no other. The state is not attempting to wear the accused out by a multitude of cases with accumulated trials. It asks no more than this, that the case against him shall go on until there shall be a trial free from the corrosion of substantial legal error. . . . This is not cruelty at all, nor even vexation in any immoderate degree. If the trial had been infected with error adverse to the accused, there might have been review at his instance, and as often as necessary to purge the vicious taint. A reciprocal privilege, subject at all times to the discretion of the presiding judge . . . has now been granted to the state. There is here no seismic innovation. The edifice of justice stands, its symmetry, to many, greater than before.

2. The conviction of appellant is not in derogation of any privileges or immunities that belong to him as a citizen of the United States.

There is argument in his behalf that the privileges and immunities clause of the Fourteenth Amendment as well as the due process clause has been flouted by the judgment.

Maxwell v. Dow, supra, 176 U.S. 581, at page 584, gives all the answer that is necessary.

The judgment is affirmed.

Mr. Justice Butler dissents.

ADAMSON v. CALIFORNIA, 332 U.S. 46 (1947). Defendant was convicted of murder in the first degree. As permitted by California law the judge and the prosecutor commented on the failure of the defendant to explain or deny evidence against him. Under California law the jury could have been made aware on cross-examination of prior convictions of the defendant if he had taken the stand. In the Supreme Court the defendant argued both that his conviction under this procedure was a denial of the Fifth Amendment privilege against self-incrimination and that it denied him a fair trial in contravention of the due process clause of the Fourteenth Amendment. The Court affirmed the conviction. Speaking for the Court, Justice Reed stated the holding as follows:

(1) The privilege against self-incrimination is not a privilege of national citizenship protected by the Fourteenth Amendment. "The Slaughter-House Cases decided . . . that these rights, as privileges and immunities of state citizenship, remained under the sole protection of the state governments. . . . This construction has become embedded in our federal system as a functioning element in preserving the balance between national and state power."

(2) The privilege against self-incrimination does not to its full scope inhere in the right to a fair trial protected by the due process clause of the Fourteenth Amendment. "Nothing has been called to our attention that either the framers of the Fourteenth Amendment or the states that adopted intended its due process clause to draw within its scope the earlier amendments to the Constitution."

(3) The particular state procedure involved here did not violate "the protection against state action that the due process clause does grant to an accused. The due process clause forbids compulsion to testify by fear of hurt, torture or exhaustion. It forbids any other type of coercion that falls within the scope of due process."

Justice Frankfurter, concurring, said, in part:

"The short answer to the suggestion that the provision of the Fourteenth Amendment, which ordains 'nor shall any State deprive any person of life, liberty, or property, without due process of law,' was a way of saying that every State must thereafter initiate prosecutions through indictment by a grand jury, must have a trial by a jury of 12 in criminal cases, and must have trial by such a jury in common law suits where the amount in controversy exceeds $20, is that it is a strange way of saying it. It would be extraordinarily strange for a Constitution to convey such specific commands in such a roundabout and inexplicit way. After all, an amendment to the Constitution should be read in a '"sense most obvious to the common understanding at the time of its adoption." . . . For it was for public adoption that it was proposed.' . . . Those reading the English language with the meaning which it ordinarily conveys, those conversant with the political and legal history of the concept of due process, those sensitive to the relations of the States to the central government as well as the relation of some of the provisions of the Bill of Rights to the process of justice, would hardly recognize the Fourteenth Amendment as a cover for the various explicit provisions of the first eight Amendments. Some of these are enduring reflections of experience with human nature, while some express the restricted views of Eighteenth-Century England regarding the best methods for the ascertainment of facts. The notion that the Fourteenth Amendment was a covert way of imposing upon the States all the rules which it seemed important to Eighteenth Century statesmen to write into the Federal Amendments, was rejected by judges who were themselves witnesses of the process by which the Fourteenth Amendment became part of the Constitution. Arguments that may now be adduced to prove that the first eight Amendments were concealed within the historic phrasing of the Fourteenth Amendment were not unknown at the time of its adoption. A surer estimate of their bearing was possible for judges at the time than distorting distance is likely to vouchsafe. Any evidence of design or purpose not contemporaneously known could hardly have influenced those who ratified the Amendment. Remarks of a particular proponent of the Amendment, no matter how influential, are not to be deemed part of the Amendment. What was submitted for ratification was his proposal, not his speech. Thus, at the time of the ratification of the Fourteenth Amendment the constitutions of nearly half of the ratifying States did not have the rigorous requirements of the Fifth Amendment for instituting criminal proceedings through a grand jury. It could hardly have occurred to these States that by ratifying the Amendment they uprooted their established methods for prosecuting crime and fastened upon themselves a new prosecutorial system.

"Indeed, the suggestion that the Fourteenth Amendment incorporates the first eight Amendments as such is not unambiguously urged. Even the boldest innovator would shrink from suggesting to more than half the States that they may no longer initiate prosecutions without indictment by grand jury, or that thereafter all the States of the Union must furnish a jury of 12 for every case involving a claim above $20. There is suggested merely a selective incorporation of the first eight Amendments into the Fourteenth Amendment. Some are in and some are out, but we are left in the dark as to which are in and which are out. Nor are we given the calculus for determining which go in and which stay out. If the basis of selection is merely that those provisions of the first eight Amendments are incorporated which commend themselves to individual justices as indispensable to the dignity and happiness of a free man, we are thrown back to a merely subjective test. The protection against unreasonable search and seizure might have primacy for one judge, while trial by a jury of 12 for every claim above $20 might appear to another as an ultimate need in a free society. In the history of thought 'natural law' has a much longer and much better founded meaning and justification than such subjective selection of the first eight Amendments for incorporation into the Fourteenth. If all that is meant is that due process contains within itself certain minimal standards which are 'of the very essence of a scheme of ordered liberty,' Palko v. Connecticut, 302 U.S. 319, 325, putting upon this Court the duty of applying these standards from time to time, then we have merely arrived at the insight which our predecessors long ago expressed. We are called upon to apply to the difficult issues of our own day the wisdom afforded by the great opinions in this field. . . . This guidance bids us to be duly mindful of the heritage of the past, with its great lessons of how liberties are won and how they are lost. As judges charged with the delicate task of subjecting the government of a continent to the Rule of Law, we must be particularly mindful that it is 'a *constitution* we are expounding,' so that it should not be imprisoned in what are merely legal forms even though they have the sanction of the Eighteenth Century. . . .

"And so, when, as in a case like the present, a conviction in a State court is here for review under a claim that a right protected by the Due Process Clause of the Fourteenth Amendment has been denied, the issue is not whether an infraction of one of the specific provisions of the first eight Amendments is disclosed by the record. The relevant question is whether the criminal proceedings which resulted in conviction deprived the accused of the due process of law to which the United States Constitution entitled him. Judicial review of that guaranty of the Fourteenth Amendment inescapably imposes upon this Court an exercise of judgment upon the whole course of the proceedings in order to ascertain whether they offend those canons of decency and fairness which express the notions of justice of English-speaking peoples even toward those charged with the most heinous offenses. These standards of justice are not authoritatively formulated anywhere as though they were prescriptions in a pharmacopoeia. But neither does the application of the Due Process Clause imply that judges are wholly at large. The judicial judgment in applying the Due Process Clause must move within the limits of accepted notions of justice and is not to be based upon the idiosyncrasies of a merely personal judgment. The fact that judges among themselves may differ whether in a particular case a trial offends accepted notions of justice is not disproof that general rather than idiosyncratic standards are applied. An important safeguard against such merely individual judgment is an alert deference to the judgment of the State court under review."

Justices Murphy and Rutledge, dissenting, noted:

"While in substantial agreement with the views of Mr. Justice Black, I have one reservation and one addition to make.

"I agree that the specific guarantees of the Bill of Rights should be carried over intact into the first section of the Fourteenth Amendment. But I am not prepared to say that the latter is entirely and necessarily limited by the Bill of Rights. Occasions may arise where a proceeding falls so far short of conforming to fundamental standards of procedure as to warrant constitutional condemnation in terms of a lack of due process despite the absence of a specific provision in the Bill of Rights." . . .

Justice Black joined by Justice Douglas delivered a long dissenting opinion. The following paragraphs illustrate his thesis:

"This decision reasserts a constitutional theory spelled out in Twining v. New Jersey, 211 U.S. 78, that this Court is endowed by the Constitution with boundless power under 'natural law' periodically to expand and contract constitutional standards to conform to the Court's conception of what at a particular time constitutes 'civilized decency' and 'fundamental principles of liberty and justice.' Invoking this Twining rule, the Court concludes that although comment upon testimony in a federal court would violate the Fifth Amendment, identical comment in a state court does not violate today's fashion in civilized decency and fundamentals and is therefore not prohibited by the Federal Constitution as amended.

"The Twining case was the first, as it is the only decision of this Court, which has squarely held that states were free, notwithstanding the Fifth and Fourteenth Amendments, to extort evidence from one accused of crime. I agree that if Twining be reaffirmed, the result reached might appropriately follow. But I would not reaffirm the Twining decision. I think that decision and the 'natural law' theory of the Constitution upon which it relies, degrade the constitutional safeguards of the Bill of Rights and simultaneously appropriate for this Court a broad power which we are not authorized by the Constitution to exercise. . . . My reasons for believing that the Twining decision should not be revitalized can best be understood by reference to the constitutional, judicial, and general history that preceded and followed the case. That reference must be abbreviated far more than is justified but for the necessary limitations of opinion-writing. . . .

"My study of the historical events that culminated in the Fourteenth Amendment, and the expressions of those who sponsored and favored, as well as those who opposed its submission and passage, persuades me that one of the chief objects that the provisions of the Amendment's first section, separately, and as a whole, were intended to accomplish was to make the Bill of Rights applicable to the states. With full knowledge of the import of the Barron decision, the framers and backers of the Fourteenth Amendment proclaimed its purpose to be to overturn the constitutional rule that case had announced. This historical purpose has never received full consideration or exposition in any opinion of this Court interpreting the Amendment. . . .

"For this reason, I am attaching to this dissent, an appendix which contains a résumé, by no means complete, of the Amendment's history. In my judgment that history conclusively demonstrates that the language of the first section of the Fourteenth Amendment, taken as a whole, was thought by those responsible for its submission to the people, and by those who opposed its submission, sufficiently explicit to guarantee that thereafter no state could deprive its citizens of the privileges and protections of the Bill of Rights. Whether this Court ever will, or whether it now should, in the light of past decisions, give full effect to what the Amendment was intended to accomplish is not necessarily essential to a decision here. However that may be, our prior decisions, including Twining, do not prevent our carrying out that purpose, at least to the extent of making applicable to the states, not a mere part, as the Court has, but the full protection of the Fifth Amendment's provision against compelling evidence from an accused to convict him of crime. And I further contend that the 'natural law' formula which the Court uses to reach its conclusion in this case should be abandoned as an incongruous excrescence on our Constitution. I believe that formula to be itself a violation of our Constitution, in that it subtly conveys to courts, at the expense of legislatures, ultimate power over public policies in fields where no specific provision of the Constitution limits legislative power. . . .

"I cannot consider the Bill of Rights to be an outworn 18th Century 'strait jacket' as the Twining opinion did. Its provisions may be thought outdated abstractions by some. And it is true that they were designed to meet ancient evils. But they are the same kind of human evils that have emerged from century to century wherever excessive power is sought by the few at the expense of the many. In my judgment the people of no nation can lose their liberty so long as a Bill of Rights like ours survives and its basic purposes are conscientiously interpreted, enforced and respected so as to afford continuous protection against old, as well as new, devices and practices which might thwart those purposes. I fear to see the consequences of the Court's practice of substituting its own concepts of decency and fundamental justice for the language of the Bill of Rights at its point of departure in interpreting and enforcing that Bill of Rights. If the choice must be between the selective process of the Palko decision applying some of the Bill of Rights to the States, or the Twining rule applying none of them, I would choose the Palko selective process. But rather than accept either of these choices, I would follow what I believe was the original purpose of the Fourteenth Amendment—to extend to all the people of the nation the complete protection of the Bill of Rights. To hold that this Court can determine what, if any, provisions of the Bill of Rights will be enforced, and if so to what degree, is to frustrate the great design of a written Constitution. . . .

"It is an illusory apprehension that literal application of some or all of the provisions of the Bill of Rights to the States would unwisely increase the sum total of the powers of this Court to invalidate state legislation. The Federal Government has not been harmfully burdened by the requirement that enforcement of federal laws affecting civil liberty conform literally to the Bill of Rights. Who would advocate its repeal? It must be conceded, of course, that the natural-law-due-process formula, which the Court today reaffirms, has been interpreted to limit substantially this Court's power to prevent state violations of the individual civil liberties guaranteed by the Bill of Rights. But this formula also has been used in the past and can be used in the future, to license this Court, in considering regulatory legislation, to roam at large in the broad expanses of policy and morals and to trespass, all too freely, on the legislative domain of the States as well as the Federal Government.

"Since Marbury v. Madison, 1 Cranch 137, was decided, the practice has been firmly established for better or worse, that courts can strike down legislative enactments which violate the Constitution. This process, of course, involves interpretation, and since words can have many meanings, interpretation obviously may result in contraction or extension of the original purpose of a constitutional provision thereby affecting policy. But to pass upon the constitutionality of statutes by looking to the particular standards enumerated in the Bill of Rights and other parts of the Constitution is one thing; to invalidate statutes because of application of 'natural law' deemed to be above and undefined by the Constitution is another. 'In the one instance, courts proceeding within clearly marked constitutional boundaries seek to execute policies written into the Constitution; in the other they roam at will in the limitless area of their own beliefs as to reasonableness and actually select policies, a responsibility which the Constitution entrusts to the legislative representatives of the people.' Federal Power Commission v. Natural Gas Pipeline Co., 315 U.S. 575, 599, 601, n. 4."

THE HISTORICAL DEBATE

Justice Black's historical thesis is more fully set out in an Appendix in *Adamson* found at 332 U.S. 92. See also the discussion in the opinions of Justices Black and Harlan in Duncan v. Louisiana, set out infra. Scholars attempting to discover the true intent of the framers of the fourteenth amendment have consulted many sources, including: The pre-Civil War literature and party platforms of abolitionist groups. Judicial and legislative pronouncements in the foreground when the amendment was drafted: Barron v. Baltimore, 7 Pet. 243 (1833), Murray's Lessee v. Hoboken, 18 How. 272 (1856), and Dred Scott v. Sanford, 19 How. 393 (1857), and the provisions of the Freedman's Bureau bill and the Civil Rights Act. Debates in the Congress and the state ratification bodies. Newspaper and magazine comment of the time. Post-ratification statements purporting to explain the meaning of the amendment by two of the draftsmen, John A. Bingham and Roscoe Conkling.

Out of this vast body of material, diverse conclusions have been drawn as to the import of almost every clause of the amendment. On the specific issue of the amendment's incorporation of the first eight amendments to the federal constitution, historical support can be mustered both for the majority and the dissenting opinions in *Adamson*. The argument for incorporation rests on the known aversion of some of the framers to Barron v. Baltimore, and focuses on the 1871 speech of Bingham stating this as the meaning of the privileges and immunities clause. This position is documented in the works of Guthrie, *The Fourteenth Article of Amendment to the Constitution of the United States* (1898); Flack, *The Adoption of the Fourteenth Amendment* (1908); 2 Crosskey, *Politics and the Constitution* chs. XXXI, XXXII (1953); Boudin, *Truth and Fiction about the Fourteenth Amendment*, 16 N.Y.U.L.Q.Rev. 19 (1938) (with additional support from the due process clause). Equally assiduous work by other researchers has led them to conclude that no such specific content was contemplated for the fourteenth amendment. The writers who argue from abolitionist history point to a greater concern for substantive protection of rights vaguely categorized as principles of natural law than to any particular set of rules for the conduct of trials. Ten Broek, *The Antislavery Origins of the Fourteenth Amendment* (1951); Graham, *The "Conspiracy Theory" of the Fourteenth Amendment*, 47 Yale L.J. 371 (1938) and Graham, *The Early Antislavery Background of the Fourteenth Amendment*, 1950 Wis.L.Rev. 479, 610. Other authors have pointed to the lack of specific debate on this point as indicative of absence of intent to achieve incorporation. They maintain that such a revolutionary change of state procedures, already then divergent from the federal model, would certainly not have been accepted *sub silentio* by the state conventions, if they had so understood the amendment. Fairman and Morrison, *Does the Fourteenth Amendment Incorporate the Bill of Rights*, 2 Stan.L.Rev. 5, 140 (1949); and see Meyer, *The Blaine Amendment and the Bill of Rights*, 64 Harv.L.Rev. 939 (1951).

For a recent debate of the historical materials, see Curtis, *The Bill of Rights as a Limitation on State Authority: A Reply to Professor Berger*, 16 Wake Forest L.Rev. 45 (1980); Berger, *Incorporation of the Bill of Rights in the Fourteenth Amendment: A Nine-Lived Cat*, 42 Ohio St.L.J. 435 (1981); Curtis, *Further Adventures of the Nine Lived Cat: A Response to Mr. Berger on Incorporation of the Bill of Rights*, 43 Ohio St.L.J. 89 (1982); Berger, *Incorporation of the Bill of Rights: A Reply to Michael Curtis' Response*, 44 Ohio St.L.J. 1 (1983).

In appraising these historical analyses of the fourteenth amendment, you should ask yourself what the utility and relevance of conclusions derived from ambiguous historical records are for present day constitutional law. How can we validly infer the intent of Congress and the ratifying states from the speeches of individual supporters and opponents of the amendment? How can the enactment of the first section of the amendment be separated from the furor and passion accompanying the other sections, then perhaps deemed more important, and now dead letters?

DUNCAN v. LOUISIANA

391 U.S. 145, 88 S.Ct. 1444, 20 L.Ed.2d 491 (1968).

Mr. Justice White delivered the opinion of the Court.

Appellant, Gary Duncan, was convicted of simple battery in the Twenty-fifth Judicial District Court of Louisiana. Under Louisiana law simple battery is a misdemeanor, punishable by two years' imprisonment and a $300 fine. Appellant sought trial by jury, but because the Louisiana Constitution grants jury trials only in cases in which capital punishment or imprisonment at hard labor may be imposed, the trial judge denied the request. Appellant was convicted and sentenced to serve 60 days in the parish prison and pay a fine of $150. Appellant sought review in the Supreme Court of Louisiana, asserting that the denial of jury trial violated rights guaranteed to him by the United States Constitution. The Supreme Court, finding "no error of law in the ruling complained of," denied appellant a writ of certiorari. Pursuant to 28 U.S.C. § 1257(2) appellant sought review in this Court, alleging that the Sixth and Fourteenth Amendments to the United States Constitution secure the right to jury trial in state criminal prosecutions where a sentence as long as two years may be imposed. We noted probable jurisdiction . . .

I.

The Fourteenth Amendment denies the States the power to "deprive any person of life, liberty, or property, without due process of law." In resolving conflicting claims concerning the meaning of this spacious language, the Court has looked increasingly to the Bill of Rights for guidance; many of the rights guaranteed by the first eight Amendments to the Constitution have been held to be protected against state action by the Due Process Clause of the Fourteenth Amendment. That clause now protects the right to compensation for property taken by the State; the rights of speech, press, and religion covered by the First Amendment; the Fourth Amendment rights to be free from unreasonable searches and seizures and to have excluded from criminal trials any evidence illegally seized; the right guaranteed by the Fifth Amendment to be free of compelled self-incrimination; and the Sixth Amendment rights to counsel to a speedy and public trial, to confrontation of opposing witnesses, and to compulsory process for obtaining witnesses.

The test for determining whether a right extended by the Fifth and Sixth Amendments with respect to federal criminal proceedings is also protected against state action by the Fourteenth Amendment has been phrased in a variety of ways in the opinions of this Court. The question has been asked whether a right is among those " 'fundamental principles of liberty and justice which lie at the base of all our civil and political institutions,' " Powell v. Alabama, 287 U.S. 45, 67 (1932); whether it is "basic in our system of jurisprudence," In re Oliver, 333 U.S. 257, 273 (1948); and whether it is "a fundamental right, essential to a fair trial," Gideon v. Wainwright, 372 U.S. 335, 343–344 (1963); Malloy v. Hogan, 378 U.S. 1, 6 (1964); Pointer v. Texas, 380 U.S. 400, 403 (1965). The claim before us is that the right to trial by jury guaranteed by the Sixth Amendment meets these tests. The position of Louisiana, on the other hand, is that the Constitution imposes upon the States no duty to give a jury trial in any criminal case, regardless of the seriousness of the crime or the size of the punishment which may be imposed. Because we believe that trial by jury in criminal cases is fundamental to the American scheme of justice, we hold that the Fourteenth Amendment guarantees a right of jury trial in all criminal cases which—were they to be tried in a federal court—would come within the Sixth Amendment's guarantee.[14] Since we consider the appeal before us to be such a case, we hold that the Constitution was violated when appellant's demand for jury trial was refused.

The history of trial by jury in criminal cases has been frequently told. . . .

. . .

Even such skeletal history is impressive support for considering the right to jury trial in criminal cases to be fundamental to our system of justice, an importance frequently recognized in the opinions of this Court. . . .

Jury trial continues to receive strong support. The laws of every State guarantee a right to jury trial in serious criminal cases; no State has dispensed with it; nor are there significant movements underway to do so. . . .

We are aware of prior cases in this Court in which the prevailing opinion contains statements contrary to our holding today that the right to jury trial in serious criminal cases is a fundamental right and hence must be recognized by the States as part of their obligation to extend due process of law to all persons within their jurisdiction. . . . None of these cases, however, dealt with a State which had purported to dispense entirely with a jury trial in serious criminal cases. . . . Respectfully, we reject the prior dicta regarding jury trial in criminal cases.

[14] In one sense recent cases applying provisions of the first eight amendments to the States represent a new approach to the "incorporation" debate. Earlier the Court can be seen as having asked, when inquiring into whether some particular procedural safeguard was required of a State, if a civilized system could be imagined that would not accord the particular protection. For example, Palko v. Connecticut, 302 U.S. 319, 325 (1937), stated: "The right to trial by jury and the immunity from prosecution except as the result of an indictment may have value and importance. Even so, they are not of the very essence of a scheme of ordered liberty . . . . . Few would be so narrow or provincial as to maintain that a fair and enlightened system of justice would be impossible without them." The recent cases, on the other hand, have proceeded upon the valid assumption that state criminal processes are not imaginary and theoretical schemes but actual systems bearing virtually every characteristic of the common-law system that has been developing contemporaneously in England and in this country. The question thus is whether given this kind of system a particular procedure is fundamental—whether, that is, a procedure is necessary to an Anglo-American regime of ordered liberty. It is this sort of inquiry that can justify the conclusions that state courts must exclude evidence seized in violation of the Fourth Amendment, Mapp v. Ohio, 367 U.S. 643 (1961); that state prosecutors may not comment on a defendant's failure to testify, Griffin v. California, 380 U.S. 609 (1965); and that criminal punishment may not be imposed for the status of narcotics addiction, Robinson v. California, 370 U.S. 660 (1962). Of immediate relevance for this case are the Court's holdings that the States must comply with certain provisions of the Sixth Amendment, specifically that the States may not refuse a speedy trial, confrontation of witnesses, and the assistance, at state expense if necessary, of counsel. See cases cited in nn. 8–12, supra. Of each of these determinations that a constitutional provision originally written to bind the Federal Government should bind the States as well it might be said that the limitation in question is not necessarily fundamental to fairness in every criminal system that might be imagined but is fundamental in the context of the criminal processes maintained by the American States.

When the inquiry is approached in this way the question whether the States can impose criminal punishment without granting a jury trial appears quite different from the way it appeared in the older cases opining that States might abolish jury trial. See, e.g., Maxwell v. Dow, 176 U.S. 581 (1900). A criminal process which was fair and equitable but used no juries is easy to imagine. It would make use of alternative guarantees and protections which would serve the purposes that the jury serves in the English and American systems. Yet no American State has undertaken to construct such a system. Instead, every American State, including Louisiana, uses the jury extensively, and imposes very serious punishments only after a trial at which the defendant has a right to a jury's verdict. In every State, including Louisiana, the structure and style of the criminal process—the supporting framework and the subsidiary procedures—are of the sort that naturally complement jury trial, and have developed in connection with and in reliance upon jury trial.

The guarantees of jury trial in the Federal and State Constitutions reflect a profound judgment about the way in which law should be enforced and justice administered. A right to jury trial is granted to criminal defendants in order to prevent oppression by the Government. . . . The deep commitment of the Nation to the right of jury trial in serious criminal cases as a defense against arbitrary law enforcement qualifies for protection under the Due Process Clause of the Fourteenth Amendment, and must therefore be respected by the States.

Of course jury trial has "its weaknesses and the potential for misuse," Singer v. United States, 380 U.S. 24, 35 (1965). We are aware of the long debate, especially in this century, among those who write about the administration of justice, as to the wisdom of permitting untrained laymen to determine the facts in civil and criminal proceedings.[24] Although the debate has been intense, with powerful voices on either side, most of the controversy has centered on the jury in civil cases. Indeed, some of the severest critics of civil juries acknowledge that the arguments for criminal juries are much stronger. . . .

The State of Louisiana urges that holding that the Fourteenth Amendment assures a right to jury trial will cast doubt on the integrity of every trial conducted without a jury. Plainly, this is not the import of our holding. Our conclusion is that in the American States, as in the federal judicial system, a general grant of jury trial for serious offenses is a fundamental right, essential for preventing miscarriages of justice and for assuring that fair trials are provided for all defendants. We would not assert, however, that every criminal trial—or any particular trial—held before a judge alone is unfair or that a defendant may never be as fairly treated by a judge as he would be by a jury. Thus we hold no constitutional doubts about the practices, common in both federal and state courts, of accepting waivers of jury trial and prosecuting petty crimes without extending a right to jury trial. However, the fact is that in most places more trials for serious crimes are to juries than to a court alone; a great many defendants prefer the judgment of a jury to that of a court. Even where defendants are satisfied with bench trials, the right to a jury trial very likely serves its intended purpose of making judicial or prosecutorial unfairness less likely.[30]

---

[24] A thorough summary of the arguments that have been made for and against jury trial and an extensive bibliography of the relevant literature is available at Hearings on Recording of Jury Deliberations before the Subcommittee to Investigate the Administration of the Internal Security Act of the Senate Committee on the Judiciary, 84th Cong., 1st Sess., pp. 63–81 (1955). A more selective bibliography appears at H. Kalven, Jr. & H. Zeisel, The American Jury 4, n. 2 (1966).

[30] Louisiana also asserts that if due process is deemed to include the right to jury trial, States will be obligated to comply with all past interpretations of the Sixth Amendment, an amendment which in its inception was designed to control only the federal courts and which throughout its history has operated in this limited environment where uniformity is a more obvious and immediate consideration. In particular, Louisiana objects to application of the decisions of this Court interpreting the Sixth Amendment as guaranteeing a 12-man jury in serious criminal cases, Thompson v. Utah, 170 U.S. 343 (1898); as requiring a unanimous verdict before guilt can be found, Maxwell v. Dow, 176 U.S. 581, 586 (1900); and as barring procedures by which crimes subject to the Sixth Amendment jury trial provision are tried in the first instance without a jury but at the first appellate stage by *de novo* trial with a jury, Callan v. Wilson, 127 U.S. 540, 557 (1888). It seems very unlikely to us that our decision today will require widespread changes in state criminal processes. First, our decisions interpreting the Sixth Amendment are always subject to reconsideration, a fact amply demonstrated by the instant decision. In addition, most of the States have provisions for jury trials equal in breadth to the Sixth Amendment, if that amendment is construed, as it has been, to permit the trial of petty crimes and offenses without a jury. Indeed, there appear to be only four States in which juries of fewer than 12 can be used without the defendant's consent for offenses carrying a maximum penalty of greater than one year. Only in Oregon and Louisiana can a less-than-unanimous jury convict for an offense with a maximum penalty greater than one year. However 10 States authorize first-stage trials without juries for crimes carrying lengthy penalties; these States give a convicted defendant the right to a *de novo* trial before a jury in a different court. The statutory provisions are listed in the briefs filed in this case.

II.

Louisiana's final contention is that even if it must grant jury trials in serious criminal cases, the conviction before us is valid and constitutional because here the petitioner was tried for simple battery and was sentenced to only 60 days in the parish prison. We are not persuaded. It is doubtless true that there is a category of petty crimes or offenses which is not subject to the Sixth Amendment jury trial provision and should not be subject to the Fourteenth Amendment jury trial requirement here applied to the States. Crimes carrying possible penalties up to six months do not require a jury trial if they otherwise qualify as petty offenses, Cheff v. Schnackenberg, 384 U.S. 373 (1966). But the penalty authorized for a particular crime is of major relevance in determining whether it is serious or not and may in itself, if severe enough, subject the trial to the mandates of the Sixth Amendment. District of Columbia v. Clawans, 300 U.S. 617 (1937). The penalty authorized by the law of the locality may be taken "as a gauge of its social and ethical judgments," 300 U.S., at 628 of the crime in question. In *Clawans* the defendant was jailed for 60 days, but it was the 90-day authorized punishment on which the Court focused in determining that the offense was not one for which the Constitution assured trial by jury. In the case before us the Legislature of Louisiana has made simple battery a criminal offense punishable by imprisonment for two years and a fine. The question, then is whether a crime carrying such a penalty is an offense which Louisiana may insist on trying without a jury.

We think not. . . .

. . . .

The judgment below is reversed and the case is remanded for proceedings not inconsistent with this opinion.

Mr. Justice Black, with whom Mr. Justice Douglas joins, concurring.

The Court today holds that the right to trial by jury guaranteed defendants in criminal cases in federal courts by Art. III of the United States Constitution and by the Sixth Amendment is also guaranteed by the Fourteenth Amendment to defendants tried in state courts. With this holding I agree for reasons given by the Court. I also agree because of reasons given in my dissent in Adamson v. California, 332 U.S. 46, 68. . . . In this situation I said in Adamson v. California, 332 U.S., at 89, 67 S.Ct., at 1695, that while "I would extend to all the people of the nation the complete protection of the Bill of Rights," that "[i]f the choice must be between the selective process of the *Palko* decision applying some of the Bill of Rights to the States, or the *Twining* rule applying none of them, I would choose the *Palko* selective process." See Gideon v. Wainwright, 372 U.S. 335, 83 S.Ct. 792, 9 L.Ed.2d 799. And I am very happy to support this selective process through which our Court has since the *Adamson* case held most of the specific Bill of Rights' protections applicable to the States to the same extent they are applicable to the Federal Government. Among these are the right to trial by jury decided today, the right against compelled self-incrimination, the right to counsel, the right to compulsory process for witnesses, the right to confront witnesses, the right to a speedy and public trial, and the right to be free from unreasonable searches and seizures.

All of these holdings making Bill of Rights' provisions applicable as such to the States mark, of course, a departure from the *Twining* doctrine holding that none of those provisions were enforceable as such against the States. The dissent in this case, however, makes a spirited and forceful defense of that now discredited doctrine. I do not believe that it is necessary for me to repeat the historical and logical reasons for my challenge to the *Twining* holding contained in my *Adamson* dissent and Appendix to it. What I wrote there in 1947 was the product of years of study and research. My appraisal of the legislative history followed 10 years of legislative experience as a Senator of the United States, not a bad way, I suspect, to learn the value of what is said in legislative debates, committee discussions, committee reports, and various other steps taken in the course of passage of bills, resolutions, and proposed constitutional amendments. My Brother Harlan's objections to my *Adamson* dissent history, like that of most of the objectors, relies most heavily on a criticism written by Professor Charles Fairman and published in the Stanford Law Review. 2 Stan.L.Rev. 5 (1949). I have read and studied this article extensively, including the historical references, but am compelled to add that in my view it has completely failed to refute the inferences and arguments that I suggested in my *Adamson* dissent. Professor Fairman's "history" relies very heavily on what was *not* said in the state legislatures that passed on the Fourteenth Amendment. Instead of relying on this kind of negative pregnant, my legislative experience has convinced me that it is far wiser to rely on what *was* said, and most importantly, said by the men who actually sponsored the Amendment in the Congress. I know from my years in the United States Senate that it is to men like Congressman Bingham, who steered the Amendment through the House, and Senator Howard, who introduced it in the Senate, that members of Congress look when they seek the real meaning of what is being offered. And they vote for or against a bill based on what the sponsors of that bill and those who oppose it tell them it means. The historical appendix to my *Adamson* dissent leaves no doubt in my mind that both its sponsors and those who opposed it believed the Fourteenth Amendment made the first eight Amendments of the Constitution (The Bill of Rights) applicable to the States.

In addition to the adoption of Professor Fairman's "history," the dissent states that "the great words of the four clauses of the first section of the Fourteenth Amendment would have been an exceedingly peculiar way to say that 'The rights heretofore guaranteed against federal intrusion by the first eight amendments are henceforth guaranteed against State intrusion as well.'" Dissenting opinion, n. 9. In response to this I can say only that the words "No State shall make or enforce any law which shall abridge the privileges or immunities of citizens of the United States" seems to me an eminently reasonable way of expressing the idea that henceforth the Bill of Rights shall apply to the States.[1] What more precious "privilege" of American citizenship could there be than that privilege to claim the protections of our great Bill of Rights? I suggest that any reading of "privileges or immunities of citizens of the United States" which excludes the Bill of Rights' safeguards renders the words of this section of the Fourteenth Amendment meaningless. . . .

While I do not wish at this time to discuss at length my disagreement with Brother Harlan's forthright and frank restatement of the now discredited *Twining* doctrine, I do want to point out what appears to me to be the basic difference between us. His view, as was indeed the view of *Twining*, is that "due process is an evolving concept" and therefore that it entails a "gradual process of judicial inclusion and exclusion" to ascertain those "immutable principles of free government which no member of the Union may disregard." Thus the Due Process Clause is treated as prescribing no specific and clearly ascertainable constitutional command that judges must obey in interpreting the Constitution, but rather as leaving judges free to decide at any particular time whether a particular rule or judicial formulation embodies an "immutable principle[s] of free government" or "is implicit in the concept of ordered liberty," or whether certain conduct "shocks the judge's conscience" or runs counter to some other similar, undefined and undefinable standard. Thus due

---

[1] My view has been and is that the Fourteenth Amendment, *as a whole*, makes the Bill of Rights applicable to the States. This would certainly include the language of the Privileges and Immunities Clause, as well as the Due Process Clause.

process, according to my Brother Harlan, is to be a word with no permanent meaning, but one which is found to shift from time to time in accordance with judges' predilections and understandings of what is best for the country. If due process means this, the Fourteenth Amendment, in my opinion, might as well have been written that "no person shall be deprived of life, liberty or property except by laws that the judges of the United States Supreme Court shall find to be consistent with the immutable principles of free government." It is impossible for me to believe that such unconfined power is given to judges in our Constitution that it is a written one in order to limit governmental power.

Another tenet of the *Twining* doctrine as restated by my Brother Harlan is that "due process of law requires only fundamental fairness." But the "fundamental fairness" test is one on a par with that of shocking the conscience of the Court. Each of such tests depends entirely on the particular judge's idea of ethics and morals instead of requiring him to depend on the boundaries fixed by the written words of the Constitution. Nothing in the history of the phrase "due process of law" suggests that constitutional controls are to depend on any particular judge's sense of values. . . .

Finally I want to add that I am not bothered by the argument that applying the Bill of Rights to the States, "according to the same standards that protect those rights against federal encroachment," interferes with our concept of federalism in that it may prevent States from trying novel social and economic experiments. I have never believed that under the guise of federalism the States should be able to experiment with the protections afforded our citizens through the Bill of Rights. . . . It seems to me totally inconsistent to advocate on the one hand, the power of this Court to strike down any state law or practice which it finds "unreasonable" or "unfair," and on the other hand urge that the States be given maximum power to develop their own laws and procedures. Yet the due process approach of my Brothers Harlan and Fortas (see other concurring opinion) does just that since in effect it restricts the States to practices which a majority of this Court is willing to approve on a case-by-case basis. No one is more concerned than I that the States be allowed to use the full scope of their powers as their citizens see fit. And that is why I have continually fought against the expansion of this Court's authority over the States through the use of a broad, general interpretation of due process that permits judges to strike down state laws they do not like.

In closing I want to emphasize that I believe as strongly as ever that the Fourteenth Amendment was intended to make the Bill of Rights applicable to the States. I have been willing to support the selective incorporation doctrine, however, as an alternative, although perhaps less historically supportable than complete incorporation. The selective incorporation process, if used properly, does limit the Supreme Court in the Fourteenth Amendment field to specific Bill of Rights' protections only and keeps judges from roaming at will in their own notions of what policies outside the Bill of Rights are desirable and what are not. And, most importantly for me, the selective incorporation process has the virtue of having already worked to make most of the Bill of Rights' protections applicable to the States.

Mr. Justice Fortas, concurring.

I join the judgments and opinions of the Court in these cases because I agree that the Due Process Clause of the Fourteenth Amendment requires that the States accord the right to jury trial in prosecutions for offenses that are not petty. . . .

. . . .

Mr. Justice Harlan, whom Mr. Justice Stewart joins, dissenting.

Every American jurisdiction provides for trial by jury in criminal cases. The question before us is not whether jury trial is an ancient institution, which it is; nor whether it plays a significant role in the administration of criminal justice, which it does; nor whether it will endure, which it shall. The question in this case is whether the State of Louisiana, which provides trial by jury for all felonies, is prohibited by the Constitution from trying charges of simple battery to the court alone. In my view, the answer to that question, mandated alike by our constitutional history and by the longer history of trial by jury, is clearly "no."

. . . .

I.

I believe I am correct in saying that every member of the Court for at least the last 135 years has agreed that our Founders did not consider the requirements of the Bill of Rights so fundamental that they should operate directly against the States. They were wont to believe rather that the security of liberty in America rested primarily upon the dispersion of governmental power across a federal system. The Bill of Rights was considered unnecessary by some but insisted upon by others in order to curb the possibility of abuse of power by the strong central government they were creating.

The Civil War Amendments dramatically altered the relation of the Federal Government to the States. The first section of the Fourteenth Amendment imposes highly significant restrictions on state action. But the restrictions are couched in very broad and general terms: citizenship, privileges and immunities; due process of law; equal protection of the laws. Consequently, for 100 years this Court has been engaged in the difficult process Professor Jaffe has well called "the search for intermediate premises." The question has been, "Where does the Court properly look to find the specific rules that define and give content to such terms as 'life, liberty, or property' and 'due process of law'?"

A few members of the Court have taken the position that the intention of those who drafted the first section of the Fourteenth Amendment was simply, and exclusively, to make the provisions of the first eight amendments applicable to state action. This view has never been accepted by this Court. In my view, often expressed elsewhere, the first section of the Fourteenth Amendment was meant neither to incorporate, nor to be limited to, the specific guarantees of the first eight amendments. The overwhelming historical evidence marshalled by Professor Fairman demonstrates, to me conclusively, that the Congressmen and state legislators who wrote, debated, and ratified the Fourteenth Amendment did not think they were "incorporating" the Bill of Rights [9] and the very breadth and generality of the Amendment's provisions suggests that its authors

---

[9] Fairman, Does the Fourteenth Amendment Incorporate the Bill of Rights? The Original Understanding, 2 Stan.L.Rev. 5 (1949). Professor Fairman was not content to rest upon the overwhelming fact that the great words of the four clauses of the first section of the Fourteenth Amendment would have been an exceedingly peculiar way to say that "The rights heretofore guaranteed against federal intrusion by the first eight Amendments are henceforth guaranteed against state intrusion as well." He therefore sifted the mountain of material comprising the debates and committee reports relating to the Amendment in both Houses of Congress and in the state legislatures that passed upon it. He found that in the immense corpus of comments on the purpose and effects of the proposed amendment, and on its virtues and defects, there is almost no evidence whatever for "incorporation." The first eight amendments are so much as mentioned by only two members of Congress, one of whom effectively demonstrated (a) that he did not understand Barron v. Baltimore, 7 Pet. 243, and therefore did not understand the question of incorporation, and (b) that he was not himself understood by his colleagues. One state legislative committee report, rejected by the legislature as a whole, found § I of the Fourteenth Amendment superfluous because it duplicated the Bill of Rights: the committee obviously did not understand Barron v. Baltimore either. That is all

did not suppose that the Nation would always be limited to mid-19th century conceptions of "liberty" and "due process of law" but that the increasing experience and evolving conscience of the American people would add new "intermediate premises." In short, neither history, nor sense, supports using the Fourteenth Amendment to put the States in a constitutional straitjacket with respect to their own development in the administration of criminal or civil law.

Although I therefore fundamentally disagree with the total incorporation view of the Fourteenth Amendment, it seems to me that such a position does at least have the virtue, lacking in the Court's selective incorporation approach, of internal consistency: we look to the Bill of Rights, word for word, clause for clause, precedent for precedent because, it is said, the men who wrote the Amendment wanted it that way. For those who do not accept this "history," a different source of "intermediate premises" must be found. The Bill of Rights is not necessarily irrelevant to the search for guidance in interpreting the Fourteenth Amendment, but the reason for and the nature of its relevance must be articulated.

Apart from the approach taken by the absolute incorporationists, I can see only one method of analysis that has any internal logic. That is to start with the words "liberty" and "due process of law" and attempt to define them in a way that accords with American traditions and our system of government. This approach, involving a much more discriminating process of adjudication than does "incorporation," is, albeit difficult, the one that was followed throughout the Nineteenth and most of the present century. It entails a "gradual process of judicial inclusion and exclusion," seeking, with due recognition of constitutional tolerance for state experimentation and disparity, to ascertain those "immutable principles of free government which no member of the Union may disregard."

. . .

. . .

Today's Court still remains unwilling to accept the total incorporationists' view of the history of the Fourteenth Amendment. This, if accepted, would afford a cogent reason for applying the Sixth Amendment to the States. The Court is also, apparently, unwilling to face the task of determining whether denial of trial by jury in the situation before us, or in other situations, is fundamentally unfair. Consequently, the Court has compromised on the ease of the incorporationist position, without its internal logic. It has simply assumed that the question before us is whether the Jury Trial Clause of the Sixth Amendment should be incorporated into the Fourteenth, jot-for-jot and case-for-case, or ignored. Then the Court merely declares that the clause in question is "in" rather than "out."

. . .

The Court has justified neither its starting place nor its conclusion. . . .

II.

Since, as I see it, the Court has not even come to grips with the issues in this case, it is necessary to start from the beginning. When a criminal defendant contends that his state conviction lacked "due process of law," the question before this Court, in my view, is whether he was denied any element of

Professor Fairman could find, in hundreds of pages of legislative discussion prior to passage of the Amendment, that even suggests incorporation.

To this negative evidence the judicial history of the Amendment could be added. For example, it proved possible for a court whose members had lived through Reconstruction to reiterate the doctrine of Barron v. Baltimore, that the Bill of Rights did not apply to the States, without so much as questioning whether the Fourteenth Amendment had any effect on the continued validity of that principle. E.g., Walker v. Sauvinet, 92 U.S. 90; see generally Morrison. Does the Fourteenth Amendment Incorporate the Bill of Rights? The Judicial Interpretation, 2 Stan.L.Rev. 140 (1949).

fundamental procedural fairness. Believing, as I do, that due process is an evolving concept and that old principles are subject to re-evaluation in light of later experience, I think it appropriate to deal on its merits with the question whether Louisiana denied appellant due process of law when it tried him for simple assault without a jury. . . .

In sum, there is a wide range of views on the desirability of trial by jury, and on the ways to make it most effective when it is used; there is also considerable variation from State to State in local conditions such as the size of the criminal caseload, the ease or difficulty of summoning jurors, and other trial conditions bearing on fairness. We have before us, therefore, an almost perfect example of a situation in which the celebrated dictum of Mr. Justice Brandeis should be invoked. It is, he said,

> "one of the happy incidents of the federal system that a single courageous State may, if its citizens choose, serve as a laboratory . . . ." New State Ice Co. v. Liebmann, 285 U.S. 262, 280, 311 (dissenting opinion).

This Court, other courts, and the political process are available to correct any experiments in criminal procedure that prove fundamentally unfair to defendants. That is not what is being done today: instead, and quite without reason, the Court has chosen to impose upon every State one means of trying criminal cases; it is a good means, but it is not the only fair means, and it is not demonstrably better than the alternatives States might devise.

I would affirm the judgment of the Supreme Court of Louisiana.

INCORPORATION AND THE JURY TRIAL CASES

Prior to *Duncan* it had been assumed that the jury trial guaranteed in the sixth and seventh amendments was the traditional unanimous jury of twelve. Footnote 30 in *Duncan* opened the door to reconsideration of that assumption. The results are worth reporting.

In Williams v. Florida, 399 U.S. 78 (1969) the Court upheld as consistent with the sixth amendment, as made applicable to the states through the fourteenth, a state law permitting conviction by a unanimous jury of six in all non-capital criminal cases. Justice Harlan, concurring, accused the Court of diluting "a federal guarantee in order to reconcile the logic of 'incorporation,' the 'jot-for-jot and case-for-case' application of the federal right to the States, with the reality of federalism. Can one doubt that had Congress tried to undermine the common law right to trial by jury before *Duncan* came on the books the history today recited would have barred such action? Can we expect repeat performances when this Court is called upon to give definition and meaning to other federal guarantees that have been 'incorporated'?" Justice Black, concurring, responded: "Today's decision is in no way attributable to any desire to dilute the Sixth Amendment in order more easily to apply it to the States, but follows solely as a necessary consequence of our duty to re-examine prior decisions to reach the correct constitutional meaning in each case." In Colgrove v. Battin, 413 U.S. 149 (1973) the Court applied the logic of *Williams* in holding that a jury of six persons in a civil case in the federal courts was not in violation of the seventh amendment. However, in Ballew v. Georgia, 435 U.S. 223 (1978) the Court held that the constitutional minimum size for a jury in non-petty criminal offenses was six, invalidating a state statute providing for conviction by unanimous vote of a jury of five.

In Apodaca v. Oregon, 406 U.S. 404 (1972) the Court upheld an Oregon statute providing for conviction in criminal cases by a vote of 10 persons out of a jury of twelve. Justice Powell repeated Justice Harlan's objection in *Williams* that the Court was diluting the scope of sixth amendment rights in the federal courts in order to avoid imposing "unnecessarily rigid" requirements on the states. Most recently in Burch v. Louisiana, 441 U.S. 130 (1979) the Court held invalid a statute providing for trial "before a jury of six persons, five of whom must concur to render a verdict." The Court recognized that "having already departed from the strictly historical requirements of jury trial, it is inevitable that lines must be drawn somewhere if the substance of jury trial right is to be preserved." The Court left open the question whether it would be consistent with the sixth amendment to provide for a nonunanimous vote by any jury of less than twelve but more than six.

(10?)

DUE PROCESS AS A LIMITATION ON PROCEDURES NOT FORBIDDEN BY THE BILL OF RIGHTS

Justice Black substantially won his argument that the fourteenth amendment should be construed to make the Bill of Rights applicable to the states. As the following case indicates, however, he lost his battle to confine Court review of state procedures to the "specific" provisions of the Bill of Rights.

IN RE WINSHIP, 397 U.S. 358 (1970). In a case involving the question of what process must be accorded in juvenile proceedings, the Court examined the requirement that proof of criminal charges be beyond a reasonable doubt, concluding that it "plays a vital role in the American scheme of criminal procedure" and that its use "is indispensable to command the respect and confidence of the community in applications of the criminal law." Based on such judgments as to the importance of the standard, the Court said:

"Lest there remain any doubt about the constitutional stature of the reasonable-doubt standard, we explicitly hold that the Due Process Clause protects the accused against conviction except upon proof beyond a reasonable doubt of every fact necessary to constitute the crime with which he is charged."

Justice Harlan concurred in the opinion and judgment. Justice Black dissented at length, opening his opinion with the following:

". . . The Court has never clearly held . . . that proof beyond a reasonable doubt is either expressly or impliedly commanded by any provision of the Constitution. The Bill of Rights, which in my view is made fully applicable to the States by the Fourteenth Amendment, see Adamson v. California, 332 U.S. 46, 71–75 (1947) (dissenting opinion), does by express language provide for, among other things, a right to counsel in criminal trials, a right to indictment, and the right of a defendant to be informed of the nature of the charges against him. And in two places the Constitution provides for trial by jury, but nowhere in that document is there any statement that conviction of crime requires proof of guilt beyond a reasonable doubt. The Constitution thus goes into some detail to spell out what kind of trial a defendant charged with crime should have, and I believe the Court has no power to add to or subtract from the procedures set forth by the Founders. I realize that it is far easier to substitute individual judges' ideas of 'fairness' for the fairness prescribed by the Constitution, but I shall not at any time surrender my belief that that document itself should be our guide, not our own concept of what is fair, decent, and right. That this old 'shock-the-conscience' test is what the Court is relying on, rather than the words of the Constitution, is clearly enough revealed by the reference of the majority to 'fair treatment' and to the statement by the dissenting judges in the New York Court of Appeals that failure to require proof beyond a reasonable doubt amounts to a 'lack of fundamental fairness.' As I have said time and time again, I prefer to put my faith in the words of the written Constitution itself rather than to rely on the shifting, day-to-day standards of fairness of individual judges."

"INCORPORATION"—ITS CURRENT SCOPE

Which portions of the Bill of Rights have been "incorporated" by the fourteenth amendment so as to be applicable against the states? The current situation is outlined below.

(1) **The First Amendment.** The Court has long applied to the states under the fourteenth amendment the same restrictions upon regulations relating to speech, religion, and association as it applies to the federal government under the first amendment. See, e.g., West Virginia State Board of Education v. Barnette, 319 U.S. 624 (1943); Everson v. Board of Education, 330 U.S. 1 (1947); Edwards v. California, 372 U.S. 229 (1963). For a case in which there was a dissent from the application of identical standards to the states as to the federal government, see Roth v. United States, 354 U.S. 476 (1957).

(2) **The Fourth Amendment.** *Arrest and Search.* That the fourth amendment applies to the states with the same coverage as it has with respect to the federal government was decided in Mapp v. Ohio, 367 U.S. 643 (1961), and Kerr v. California, 374 U.S. 23 (1963).

(3) **The Fifth Amendment**

Indictment. The Court held in Hurtado v. California, 110 U.S. 516 (1884) that states could permit prosecutions on the basis of information filed by district attorneys rather than indictments by grand juries. In Alexander v. Louisiana, 405 U.S. 625 (1972) the Court in refusing to permit a male defendant to challenge an exemption of women from the grand jury, said: "Although the Due Process Clause guarantees petitioner a fair trial, it does not require the States to observe the Fifth Amendment's provision for presentment or indictment by a grand jury. . . . the Court has never held that federal concepts of a 'grand jury', binding on the federal courts under the Fifth Amendment, are obligatory for the States. Hurtado v. California . . . ."

Double Jeopardy. In Benton v. Maryland, 395 U.S. 784 (1969) the Court held that charges of double jeopardy in state proceedings "must be judged not by the watered-down standard enunciated in Palko, but under this Court's interpretations of the Fifth Amendment double jeopardy provision." In Ashe v. Swenson, 397 U.S. 436 (1970) the Court held that the doctrine of collateral estoppel is included in the fifth amendment guaranty and made applicable to the states.

Privilege Against Self-incrimination. "The Fifth Amendment's exception from compulsory self-incrimination is also protected by the Fourteenth Amendment against abridgment by the States." Malloy v. Hogan, 378 U.S. 1 (1964). See also Griffin v. California, 380 U.S. 609 (1965); Williams v. Florida, 399 U.S. 78 (1970); California v. Byers, 402 U.S. 424 (1971).

Taking of Property Without Just Compensation. The "taking" clause has long been held applicable to the states. In Penn Central Transportation Co. v. New York City, 438 U.S. 104 (1978) the Court said that "of course" the taking clause "is made applicable to the States through the Fourteenth Amendment," citing Chicago, B. & Q.R. Co. v. Chicago, 166 U.S. 226 (1897).

(4) **The Sixth Amendment**

Speedy Trial. Klopfer v. North Carolina, 386 U.S. 213, 223 (1967): "We hold here that the right to a speedy trial is as fundamental as any of the rights secured by the Sixth Amendment." The Court reversed an order under a state procedure which permitted the prosecutor to bring a case to trial at any time on his own motion.

Public Trial. The Court first held that the fourteenth amendment guaranteed to defendants a public trial in In re Oliver, 333 U.S. 257 (1948). In Estes v. Texas, 381 U.S. 532, 538 (1965) dealing with a state prosecution the Court said: "We start with the proposition that it is a 'public trial' that the Sixth Amendment guarantees to the 'accused.'"

Jury Trial. See Duncan v. Louisiana, 391 U.S. 145 (1968), supra.

Notice of Charge. "No principle of procedural due process is more clearly established than that notice of the specific charge, and a chance to be heard in a trial of the issues raised by that charge, if desired, are among the constitutional rights of every accused in a criminal proceeding in all courts, state or federal." Cole v. Arkansas, 333 U.S. 196, 201 (1948). See also In re Oliver, 333 U.S. 257 (1948); In re Gault, 387 U.S. 1, 31 (1967).

Confrontation of Witnesses. In Pointer v. Texas, 380 U.S. 400 (1965) the Court reversed a conviction where the transcript of the testimony of a witness whom the defendant had not had a fair opportunity to cross-examine was used at the trial. "We hold today that the Sixth Amendment's right of an accused to confront the witnesses against him is likewise a fundamental right and is made obligatory on the States by the Fourteenth Amendment." See also Parker v. Gladden, 385 U.S. 363 (1966).

Compulsory Process for Obtaining Witnesses. In Washington v. Texas, 388 U.S. 14 (1967) the Court reversed a conviction where the application of a state statute forbidding persons charged as principals, accomplices, or accessories in the same crime to be witnesses for each other deprived defendant of the testimony of the only other witness to the crime. "The right of an accused to have compulsory process for obtaining witnesses in his favor stands on no lesser footing than the other Sixth Amendment rights that we have previously held applicable to the States."

Right to Counsel. The Court first held that the sixth amendment guaranty of the right to counsel applied as such to the states through the Fourteenth Amendment in Gideon v. Wainwright, 372 U.S. 335 (1963).

(5) **The Seventh Amendment.** The Court held in Walker v. Sauvinet, 92 U.S. 90 (1876), that the fourteenth amendment did not require the states to provide a jury in civil cases. In Palko v. Connecticut, 302 U.S. 319, 324 (1937), the Court said that trial by jury in civil cases can be abolished altogether. This interpretation has not been modified and the states have been left free to construct their own systems for providing jury trial in civil cases.

(6) **The Eighth Amendment**

Bail. The question whether the states are under federal constitutional constraints with reference to bail was raised but not decided in New York v. O'Neill, 359 U.S. 1 (1959).

Cruel and Unusual Punishment. In Robinson v. California, 370 U.S. 660, 667 (1962) the Court held that "a state law which imprisons a person (afflicted with the illness of narcotic addiction) as a criminal, even though he has never touched any narcotic drug within the State or been guilty of any irregular behavior there, inflicts a cruel and unusual punishment in violation of the Fourteenth Amendment." In Furman v. Georgia, 408 U.S. 238 (1972) the court held "that the imposition and carrying out of the death penalty in these cases constitutes cruel and unusual punishment in violation of the Eighth and Fourteenth Amendments."

Chapter 10

THE DUE PROCESS, CONTRACT, AND JUST COMPENSATION CLAUSES AND THE REVIEW OF THE REASONABLENESS OF LEGISLATION

SECTION 1. ECONOMIC REGULATORY LEGISLATION

A. THE RISE AND FALL OF DUE PROCESS

DUE PROCESS AS A RESTRAINT ON THE SUBSTANCE OF LEGISLATION

The due process clauses of the Fifth and Fourteenth Amendments presented two major initial problems of interpretation: (1) Were the clauses, like Magna Charta, intended only as a restraint upon the executive? Did they operate only to provide that the executive branch of the government shall operate in accordance with the common or statutory law in force? Or were they intended in the context of the United States to function as limitations upon the powers of Congress and of the state legislatures? (2) If they were intended to limit the legislatures, did they serve to restrain only the enactment of procedures which are not "due" or "fair"? Or did they serve to impose restraints on the substance of legislation?

In two cases arising under the fifth amendment prior to the Civil War the Court almost casually gave answers to these questions. In 1856 in Murray's Lessee v. Hoboken Land & Improvement Co., 18 How. 272, 276 (1856), the Court answered the first question: "It is manifest that it was not left to the legislative power to enact any process which might be devised. The article is a restraint on the legislative as well as on the executive and judicial powers of government, and cannot be so constructed as to leave congress free to make any process 'due process of law' by its mere will." In 1857 in Dred Scott v. Sanford, 19 How. 393, 450 (1857), the Court with equal casualness gave a substantive content to the clause: "And an Act of Congress which deprives a citizen of the United States of his liberty or property, merely because he came himself or brought his property into a particular Territory of the United States, and who had committed no offense against the laws, could hardly be dignified with the name of due process of law."

In the Slaughter-House Cases in 1872, set out supra p. 483, the Court summarily rejected a challenge to a law granting a monopoly based on due process, in the face of a dissent by Justice Bradley arguing that "a law which prohibits a large class of citizens from adopting a lawful employment, or from following a lawful employment previously adopted, does deprive them of liberty as well as property, without due process of law. Their right of choice is a portion of their liberty; their occupation is their property."

The Court addressed the issues again in 1878 in Davidson v. New Orleans, 96 U.S. 97 (1878). The Court upheld an application of a Louisiana statute providing for a special assessment against property for drainage purposes. In discussing the meaning of the due process clause the Court said: "It is easy to see that when the great Barons of England wrung from King John, at the point of the sword, the concession that neither their lives nor their property should be disposed of by the Crown, except as provided by the law of the land, they meant by 'law of the land' the ancient and customary laws of the English people, or laws enacted by the Parliament of which those Barons were a controlling element. It was not in their minds, therefore, to protect themselves against the enactment of laws by the Parliament of England. But when, in the year of grace 1866, there is placed in the Constitution of the United States a declaration that 'No State shall deprive any person of life, liberty, or property without due process of law,' can a State make anything due process of law which, by its own legislation, it chooses to declare such? To affirm this is to hold that the prohibition to the States is of no avail, or has no application where the invasion of private rights is affected under the forms of state legislation. It seems to us that a statute which declared in terms, and without more, that the full and exclusive title of a described piece of land, which is now in A, shall be and is hereby vested in B, would, if effectual, deprive A of his property without due process of law, within the meaning of the constitutional provision. . . ."

THE FLOWERING OF ECONOMIC DUE PROCESS

In the first few economic regulation cases to come before it under the fourteenth amendment the Court indicated a very limited scope for due process review. A challenge to a statutory monopoly was rejected in the Slaughter-House Cases, supra. In Munn v. Illinois, 94 U.S. 113 (1877), the Court upheld an Illinois statute fixing maximum charges for the storage of grain in warehouses. The Court concluded that such warehouses were sufficiently related to the public interest that they would be governed by the common law rule requiring charges to be reasonable. Hence, whatever might be the case with respect to merely private contracts this type could be regulated and the determination as to reasonableness of the price could be made legislatively rather than judicially. "Rights of property which have been created by the common law cannot be taken away without due process; but the law itself, as a rule of conduct, may be changed at the will, or even at the whim, of the legislature, unless prevented by constitutional limitations. Indeed, the great office of statutes is to remedy defects in the common law as they are developed, and to adapt it to the changes of time and circumstances. . . . We know that this is a power which may be abused; but that is no argument against its existence. For protection against abuses by Legislatures the people must resort to the polls, not the courts." Justices Field and Strong dissented.

Between 1877 and 1900, the Court gradually broadened its interpretation of the meaning of the due process clause with reference to economic regulations. During this period the membership of the Court changed completely—by 1898 not a single judge remained who had sat at the time of Munn v. Illinois. The expressed opinions of the leaders of the bar helped create a favorable climate for this broadened interpretation. See Twiss, *Lawyers and the Constitution* (1942).

A major step was the decision that corporations were "persons" within the meaning of the fourteenth amendment and hence able to claim under the due process and equal protection clauses. The point was first argued to the Court, but not decided, in San Mateo County v. Southern Pacific R.R. Co., 116 U.S. 138 (1885). It was decided without argument or opinion in Santa Clara County v. Southern Pacific R.R. Co., 118 U.S. 394 (1886) when Chief Justice

Waite announced: "The Court does not wish to hear argument on the question whether the provision in the Fourteenth Amendment to the Constitution, which forbids a State to deny to any person within its jurisdiction the equal protection of the laws, applies to these Corporations. We are all of the opinion that it does." For the story behind this decision, see Graham, *The "Conspiracy Theory" of the Fourteenth Amendment,* 47 Yale L.J. 371 (1938), 48 id. 171 (1938).

The Court's more expansive view was signaled in Mugler v. Kansas, 123 U.S. 623 (1887). While it upheld a state law prohibiting the manufacture and sale of alcoholic beverages, it stated that not every regulatory statute "is to be accepted as a legitimate exertion of the police powers of the State. There are, of necessity, limits beyond which legislation cannot rightfully go. . . . The courts are not bound by mere forms, nor are they to be misled by mere pretenses. They are at liberty—indeed, are under a solemn duty—to look at the substance of things, whenever they enter upon the inquiry whether the Legislature has transcended the limits of its authority. If therefore, a statute purporting to have been enacted to protect the public health, the public morals, or the public safety, has no real or substantial relations to those objects, or is a palpable invasion of rights secured by the fundamental law, it is the duty of the courts to so adjudge, and thereby give effect to the Constitution."

The first major use of the due process clause to invalidate state economic regulations arose in the context of state regulation of railroad rates. In Chicago, M. & St. P.R. Co. v. Minnesota, 134 U.S. 418 (1890), the Court held unconstitutional a Minnesota statute which authorized a state commission to fix rates to be charged by railroads and forbade any judicial review of the rates set. The Court said that under the due process clause the railroad companies were entitled to a judicial hearing on the question whether the rates set were reasonable. "The question of the reasonableness of a rate of charge for transportation by a railroad company, involving as it does the element of reasonableness both as regards the company and as regards the public, is eminently a question for judicial investigation, requiring due process of law for its determination. If the company is deprived of the power of charging reasonable rates for the use of its property, and such deprivation takes place in the absence of an investigation by judicial machinery, it is deprived of the lawful use of its property, and thus, in substance and effect, of the property itself, without due process of law and in violation of the Constitution of the United States. . . ."

In Smyth v. Ames, 169 U.S. 466, 546 (1898) the Court established a constitutional standard to be applied in reviewing rate regulations: "We hold . . . that the basis of all calculations as to the reasonableness of rates to be charged by a corporation maintaining a highway under legislative sanction must be the fair value of the property being used by it for the convenience of the public." [1]

ALLGEYER v. LOUISIANA, 165 U.S. 578 (1897). The Court held that under the due process clause the state of Louisiana could not make it a misdemeanor for a resident of Louisiana to use the mails to enter into a contract in New York with an insurance company not licensed to do business in Louisiana to insure goods shipped from Louisiana to Europe. The Court said: "The Supreme Court of Louisiana says that the act of writing within that State the letter of notification, was an act therein done to effect an insurance on

---

[1] The long and complicated history of the attempt by the courts to apply this doctrine is summarized in Cook, *History of Rate-Determination Under Due Process Clauses,* 11 U.Chi.L.Rev. 297 (1944); Jourolmon, *The Life and Death of Smyth v. Ames,* 18 Tenn.L.Rev. 347, 663, 756 (1944–45); Dakin, *The Changing Nature of Public Utility Rate Regulation: Just Compensation, Due Process, and Equal Protection,* 36 Tulane L.Rev. 401, 711 (1962).

property then in the State, in a marine insurance company which had not complied with its laws, and such act was, therefore, prohibited by the statute. As so construed we think the statute is a violation of the Fourteenth Amendment of the Federal Constitution, in that it deprives the defendants of their liberty without due process of law. The statute which forbids such act does not become due process of law, because it is inconsistent with the provisions of the Constitution of the Union. The liberty mentioned in that amendment means not only the right of the citizen to be free from the mere physical restraint of his person, as by incarceration, but the term is deemed to embrace the right of the citizen to be free in the enjoyment of all his faculties; to be free to use them in all lawful ways; to live and work where he will; to earn his livelihood by any lawful calling; to pursue any livelihood or avocation, and for that purpose to enter into all contracts which may be proper, necessary and essential to his carrying out to a successful conclusion the purposes above mentioned."

LOCHNER v. NEW YORK

198 U.S. 45, 25 S.Ct. 539, 49 L.Ed. 937 (1905).

Mr. Justice Peckham delivered the opinion of the Court. . . .

The indictment, it will be seen, charges that the plaintiff in error violated the 110th section of article 8, chapter 415, of the Laws of 1897, known as the labor law of the state of New York, in that he wrongfully and unlawfully required and permitted an employee working for him to work more than sixty hours in one week. . . .

It is not an act merely fixing the number of hours which shall constitute a legal day's work, but an absolute prohibition upon the employer permitting, under any circumstances, more than ten hours' work to be done in his establishment. The employee may desire to earn the extra money which would arise from his working more than the prescribed time, but this statute forbids the employer from permitting the employee to earn it.

The statute necessarily interferes with the right of contract between the employer and employees, concerning the number of hours in which the latter may labor in the bakery of the employer. The general right to make a contract in relation to his business is part of the liberty of the individual protected by the 14th Amendment of the Federal Constitution. Allgeyer v. Louisiana, 165 U.S. 578. Under that provision no state can deprive any person of life, liberty, or property without due process of law. The right to purchase or to sell labor is part of the liberty protected by this amendment, unless there are circumstances which exclude the right. There are, however, certain powers, existing in the sovereignty of each state in the Union, somewhat vaguely termed police powers, the exact description and limitation of which have not been attempted by the courts. Those powers, broadly stated, and without, at present, any attempt at a more specific limitation, relate to the safety, health, morals, and general welfare of the public. Both property and liberty are held on such reasonable conditions as may be imposed by the governing power of the state in the exercise of those powers, and with such conditions the 14th Amendment was not designed to interfere. Mugler v. Kansas, 123 U.S. 623. . . .

Therefore, when the state, by its legislature, in the assumed exercise of its police powers, has passed an act which seriously limits the right to labor or the right of contract in regard to their means of livelihood between persons who are *sui juris* (both employer and employee), it becomes of great importance to determine which shall prevail,—the right of the individual to labor for such time as he may choose, or the right of the state to prevent the individual from laboring, or from entering into any contract to labor, beyond a certain time prescribed by the state.

This court has recognized the existence and upheld the exercise of the police powers of the states in many cases which might fairly be considered as border ones, and it has, in the course of its determination of questions regarding the asserted invalidity of such statutes, on the ground of their violation of the rights secured by the Federal Constitution, been guided by rules of a very liberal nature, the application of which has resulted, in numerous instances, in upholding the validity of state statutes thus assailed. Among the later cases where the state law has been upheld by this court is that of Holden v. Hardy, 169 U.S. 366. A provision in the act of the legislature of Utah was there under consideration, the act limiting the employment of workmen in all underground mines or workings, to eight hours per day, "except in cases of emergency, where life or property is in imminent danger." It also limited the hours of labor in smelting and other institutions for the reduction or refining of ores or metals to eight hours per day, except in like cases of emergency. The act was held to be a valid exercise of the police powers of the state. . . .

It must, of course, be conceded that there is a limit to the valid exercise of the police power by the state. . . . In every case that comes before this court, therefore, where legislation of this character is concerned, and where the protection of the Federal Constitution is sought, the question necessarily arises: Is this a fair, reasonable, and appropriate exercise of the police power of the state, or is it an unreasonable, unnecessary, and arbitrary interference with the right of the individual to his personal liberty, or to enter into those contracts in relation to labor which may seem to him appropriate or necessary for the support of himself and his family? Of course the liberty of contract relating to labor includes both parties to it. The one has as much right to purchase as the other to sell labor.

This is not a question of substituting the judgment of the court for that of the legislature. If the act be within the power of the state it is valid, although the judgment of the court might be totally opposed to the enactment of such a law. But the question would still remain: Is it within the police power of the state? and that question must be answered by the court.

The question whether this act is valid as a labor law, pure and simple, may be dismissed in a few words. There is no reasonable ground for interfering with the liberty of persons or the right of free contract, by determining the hours of labor, in the occupation of a baker. . . . Viewed in the light of a purely labor law with no reference whatever to the question of health, we think that a law like the one before us involves neither the safety, the morals, nor the welfare of the public, and that the interest of the public is not in the slightest degree affected by such an act. The law must be upheld, if at all, as a law pertaining to the health of the individual engaged in the occupation of a baker. . . . .

We think the limit of the police power has been reached and passed in this case. There is, in our judgment, no reasonable foundation for holding this to be necessary or appropriate as a health law to safeguard the public health, or the health of the individuals who are following the trade of a baker. . . .

It is also urged, pursuing the same line of argument, that it is to the interest of the state that its population should be strong and robust, and therefore any legislation which may be said to tend to make people healthy must be valid as health laws, enacted under the police power. If this be a valid argument and a justification for this kind of legislation, it follows that the protection of the Federal Constitution from undue interference with liberty of person and freedom of contract is visionary, wherever the law is sought to be justified as a valid exercise of the police power. Scarcely any law but might find shelter under such assumptions, and conduct, properly so called, as well as contract, would come under the restrictive sway of the legislature. Not only the hours of employees, but the hours of employers, could be regulated, and doctors, lawyers, scientists, all professional men, as well as athletes and artisans, could be forbidden to fatigue their brains and bodies by prolonged hours of exercise, lest the fighting strength of the state be impaired. We mention these extreme cases because the contention is extreme. We do not believe in the soundness of the views which uphold this law. . . . Statutes of the nature of that under review, limiting the hours in which grown and intelligent men may labor to earn their living, are mere meddlesome interferences with the rights of the individual, and they are not saved from condemnation by the claim that they are passed in the exercise of the police power and upon the subject of the health of the individual whose rights are interfered with, unless there be some fair ground, reasonable in and of itself, to say that there is material danger to the public health, or to the health of the employees, if the hours of labor are not curtailed. . . .

It is impossible for us to shut our eyes to the fact that many of the laws of this character, while passed under what is claimed to be the police power for the purpose of protecting the public health or welfare, are, in reality, passed from other motives. We are justified in saying so when, from the character of the law and the subject upon which it legislates, it is apparent that the public health or welfare bears but the most remote relation to the law. The purpose of a statute must be determined from the natural and legal effect of the language employed; and whether it is or is not repugnant to the Constitution of the United States must be determined from the natural effect of such statutes when put into operation, and not from their proclaimed purpose. . . .

It is manifest to us that the limitation of the hours of labor as provided for in this section of the statute under which the indictment was found, and the plaintiff in error convicted, has no such direct relation to, and no such substantial effect upon, the health of the employee, as to justify us in regarding the section as really a health law. It seems to us that the real object and purpose were simply to regulate the hours of labor between the master and his employees (all being men, *sui juris*), in a private business, not dangerous in any degree to morals, or in any real and substantial degree to the health of the employees. Under such circumstances the freedom of master and employee to contract with each other in relation to their employment, and in defining the same, cannot be prohibited or interfered with, without violating the Federal Constitution.

The judgment of the Court of Appeals of New York, as well as that of the Supreme Court and of the County Court of Oneida County, must be reversed and the case remanded to the County Court for further proceedings not inconsistent with this opinion.

Reversed.

Mr. Justice Harlan (with whom Mr. Justice White and Mr. Justice Day concurred) dissenting:

. . . .

I take it to be firmly established that what is called the liberty of contract may, within certain limits, be subjected to regulations designed and calculated to promote the general welfare, or to guard the public health, the public morals, or the public safety. "The liberty secured by the Constitution of the United States to every person within its jurisdiction does not import," this court has recently said, "an absolute right in each person to be at all times and in all circumstances wholly freed from restraint. There are manifold restraints to which every person is necessarily subject for the common good." . . .

Granting, then, that there is a liberty of contract which cannot be violated even under the sanction of direct legislative enactment, but assuming, as according to settled law we may assume, that such liberty of contract is subject to such regulations as the state may reasonably prescribe for the common good and the well-being of society, what are the conditions under which the judiciary may declare such regulations to be in excess of legislative authority and void? Upon this point there is no room for dispute; for the rule is universal that a legislative enactment, Federal or state, is never to be disregarded or held invalid unless it be, beyond question, plainly and palpably in excess of legislative power. . . . If there be doubt as to the validity of the statute, that doubt must therefore be resolved in favor of its validity and the courts must keep their hands off leaving the legislature to meet the responsibility for unwise legislation. If the end which the legislature seeks to accomplish be one to which its power extends, and if the means employed to that end, although not the wisest or best, are yet not plainly and palpably unauthorized by law, then the court cannot interfere. In other words, when the validity of a statute is questioned, the burden of proof, so to speak, is upon those who assert it to be unconstitutional. McCulloch v. Maryland, 4 Wheat. 316, 421.

Let these principles be applied to the present case. By the statute in question it is provided that "no employee shall be required, or permitted, to work in a biscuit, bread, or cake bakery, or confectionery establishment, more than sixty hours in any one week, or more than ten hours in any one day, unless for the purpose of making a shorter work day on the last day of the week; nor more hours in any one week than will make an average of ten hours per day for the number of days during such week in which such employee shall work."

It is plain that this statute was enacted in order to protect the physical well-being of those who work in bakery and confectionery establishments. It may be that the statute had its origin, in part, in the belief that employers and employees in such establishments were not upon an equal footing, and that the necessities of the latter often compelled them to submit to such exactions as unduly taxed their strength. Be this as it may, the statute must be taken as expressing the belief of the people of New York that, as a general rule, and in the case of the average man, labor in excess of sixty hours during a week in such establishments may endanger the health of those who thus labor. Whether or not this be wise legislation it is not the province of the court to inquire. Under our systems of government the courts are not concerned with the wisdom or policy of legislation. So that, in determining the question of power to interfere with liberty of contract, the court may inquire whether the means devised by the state are germane to an end which may be lawfully accomplished and have a real or substantial relation to the protection of health, as involved in the daily work of the persons, male and female, engaged in bakery and confectionery establishments. But when this inquiry is entered upon I find it impossible, in view of common experience, to say that there is here no real or substantial relation between the means employed by the state and the end sought to be accomplished by its legislation. Mugler v. Kansas, 123 U.S. 623, 661. Nor can I say that the statute has no appropriate or direct connection with that protection to health which each state owes to her citizens . . . or that it is not promotive of the health of the employees in question . . . or that the regulation prescribed by the state is utterly unreasonable and extravagant or wholly arbitrary. . . . Still less can I say that the statute, is, beyond question, a plain, palpable invasion of rights, secured by the fundamental law. . . .
Therefore I submit that this court will transcend its functions if it assumes to annul the statute of New York. It must be remembered that this statute does not apply to all kinds of business. It applies only to work in bakery and confectionery establishments, in which, as all know, the air constantly breathed

by workmen is not as pure and healthful as that to be found in some other establishments or out of doors.

.   .   .

Mr. Justice Holmes dissenting:

I regret sincerely that I am unable to agree with the judgment in this case, and that I think it my duty to express my dissent.

This case is decided upon an economic theory which a large part of the country does not entertain. If it were a question whether I agreed with that theory, I should desire to study it further and long before making up my mind. But I do not conceive that to be my duty, because I strongly believe that my agreement or disagreement has nothing to do with the right of a majority to embody their opinions in law. It is settled by various decisions of this court that state constitutions and state laws may regulate life in many ways which we as legislators might think as injudicious, or if you like as tyrannical, as this, and which, equally with this, interfere with the liberty to contract. Sunday laws and usury laws are ancient examples. A more modern one is the prohibition of lotteries. The liberty of the citizen to do as he likes so long as he does not interfere with the liberty of others to do the same, which has been a shibboleth for some well-known writers, is interfered with by school laws, by the Postoffice, by every state or municipal institution which takes his money for purposes thought desirable, whether he likes it or not. The 14th Amendment does not enact Mr. Herbert Spencer's Social Statics. The other day we sustained the Massachusetts vaccination law. Jacobson v. Massachusetts, 197 U.S. 11. United States and state statutes and decisions cutting down the liberty to contract by way of combination are familiar to this court. Northern Securities Co. v. United States, 193 U.S. 197. Two years ago we upheld the prohibition of sales of stock on margins, or for future delivery, in the Constitution of California. Otis v. Parker, 187 U.S. 606. The decision sustaining an eight-hour law for miners is still recent. Holden v. Hardy, 169 U.S. 366. Some of these laws embody convictions or prejudices which judges are likely to share. Some may not. But a Constitution is not intended to embody a particular economic theory, whether of paternalism and the organic relation of the citizen to the state or of *laissez faire*. It is made for people of fundamentally differing views, and the accident of our finding certain opinions natural and familiar, or novel, and even shocking, ought not to conclude our judgment upon the question whether statutes embodying them conflict with the Constitution of the United States.

General propositions do not decide concrete cases. The decision will depend on a judgment or intuition more subtle than any articulate major premise. But I think that the proposition just stated, if it is accepted, will carry us far toward the end. Every opinion tends to become a law. I think that the word "liberty," in the 14th Amendment, is perverted when it is held to prevent the natural outcome of a dominant opinion, unless it can be said that a rational and fair man necessarily would admit that the statute proposed would infringe fundamental principles as they have been understood by the traditions of our people and our law. It does not need research to show that no such sweeping condemnation can be passed upon the statute before us. A reasonable man might think it a proper measure on the score of health. Men whom I certainly could not pronounce unreasonable would uphold it as a first instalment of a general regulation of the hours of work. Whether in the latter aspect it would be open to the charge of inequality I think it unnecessary to discuss.

———

THE POST–LOCHNER DEVELOPMENTS

(1) Liberty of Contract and Labor Legislation.

Maximum hours.   In Muller v. Oregon, 208 U.S. 412 (1908), the Court upheld the validity of a statute forbidding the employment of women in factories or laundries more than 10 hours per day as applied to a laundry.   The Court distinguished *Lochner* on the ground that the state had a stronger interest in regulating the hours of work of women than of men.   The physical differences between women and men were emphasized and the Court said that "history discloses the fact that woman has always been dependent upon man." The Court, in taking judicial notice of the general belief that "woman's physical structure, and the functions she performs in consequence thereof, justify special legislation restricting or qualifying the conditions under which she should be permitted to toil," relied on a brief filed in the Court by Mr. Louis D. (later Justice) Brandeis which included a large collection of opinions from non-judicial sources.[1]   It then said: "Constitutional questions . . . are not settled by even a consensus of present public opinion, for it is the peculiar value of a written constitution that it places in unchanging form limitations upon legislative action, and thus gives a permanence and stability to popular government which otherwise would be lacking.   At the same time, when a question of fact is debated and debatable, and the extent to which a special constitutional limitation goes is affected by the truth in respect to that fact, a widespread and long continued belief concerning it is worthy of consideration."   Several years later, without mentioning *Lochner,* the Court upheld a law providing a maximum 10-hour day for factory workers of both sexes which also permitted up to three hours a day overtime at time-and-a-half rate.   Bunting v. Oregon, 243 U.S. 426 (1917).

"Yellow-Dog" Contracts.   In Adair v. United States, 208 U.S. 161 (1908) and Coppage v. Kansas, 236 U.S. 1 (1915), the Court held invalid federal and state legislation forbidding employers to require employees to agree not to become or remain members of any labor organizations during the period of their employment.   In *Coppage* the Court said: "An interference with this liberty [to make contracts] so serious as that now under consideration, and so disturbing of equality of right, must be deemed to be arbitrary, unless it be supportable as a reasonable exercise of the police power of the State."   The Court went on to reject the argument of the state that such legislation was necessary to protect the interests of employees who were not financially as able to be independent in making contracts as employers, saying: "[S]ince it is self-evident that, unless all things are held in common, some persons must have more property than others, it is from the nature of things impossible to uphold freedom of contract and the right of private property without at the same time recognizing as legitimate those inequalities of fortune that are the necessary result of the exercise of those rights."

Minimum Wages.   Adkins v. Children's Hosp., 261 U.S. 525 (1923), involved an Act of Congress prescribing minimum wages for women and children in the District of Columbia.   The Court held the statute invalid when challenged by a hospital which employed women at lower than the minimum rate and by a woman elevator operator who was discharged by her employer to avoid the penalties of the act.   The Court prefaced its discussion by saying:

[1] The famous "Brandeis Brief" has been lauded as introducing the Court "to a new technique in the weighing of constitutional issues.   This occurred when Mr. Louis D. Brandeis handed the Court . . . his famous brief, three pages of which were devoted to a statement of the constitutional principles involved and 113 pages of which were devoted to the presentation of facts and statistics, backed by scientific authorities, to show the evil effects of too long hours on women, 'the mothers of the race'."   Johnson, *Social Planning Under the Constitution,* 2 Selected Essays (1938) 131, 145.

"There is, of course, no such thing as absolute freedom of contract. It is subject to a great variety of restraints. But freedom of contract is, nevertheless, the general rule and restraint the exception; and the exercise of legislative authority to abridge it can be justified only by the existence of exceptional circumstances." In distinguishing Muller v. Oregon, the Court said:

"But the ancient inequality of the sexes, otherwise than physical, as suggested in the *Muller* case, has continued 'with diminishing intensity.' In view of the great—not to say revolutionary—changes which have taken place since that utterance, in the contractual, political and civil status of women, culminating in the Nineteenth Amendment, it is not unreasonable to say that these differences have now come almost, if not quite, to the vanishing point. In this aspect of the matter, while the physical differences must be recognized in appropriate cases, and legislation fixing hours or conditions of work may properly take them into account, we cannot accept the doctrine that women of mature age, sui juris, require or may be subjected to restrictions upon their liberty of contract which could not lawfully be imposed in the case of men under similar circumstances."

It then went on to say that the statute could not be justified as safeguarding the morals of women because it "cannot be shown that well paid women safeguard their morals more carefully than those who are poorly paid." It concluded that the real flaw in the statute was that "it exacts from the employer an arbitrary payment for a purpose and upon a basis having no causal connection with his business or the contract or the work the employee engages to do." This, the Court said, "is so clearly the product of a naked, arbitrary exercise of power that it cannot be allowed to stand under the Constitution of the United States."

Justice Holmes in dissent said: "It will need more than the Nineteenth Amendment to convince me that there are no differences between men and women, or that legislation cannot take those differences into account. I should not hesitate to take them into account if I thought it necessary to sustain this act. . . . But after Bunting v. Oregon, 243 U.S. 426, I had supposed that it was not necessary, and that Lochner v. New York, 198 U.S. 45, would be allowed a deserved repose."

(2) Liberty of Contract and Business Regulations Relating to Prices and Other Economic Issues.

Price Fixing. In Tyson & Brother v. Banton, 273 U.S. 418 (1927), the court held invalid a statute regulating the prices of theater tickets. The Court said "that the right of the owner to fix a price at which his property shall be sold or used is an inherent attribute of the property itself." Hence, the power to fix prices "does not exist in respect of merely private property or business . . . but exists only where the business or the property involved has become 'affected with a public interest.'" A long line of cases developed marking out the distinction between ordinary businesses and those "affected with a public interest" and so subject to price regulations. See, e.g., Williams v. Standard Oil Co., 278 U.S. 235 (1929), holding invalid a state statute regulating the price of gasoline. For later modifications of this doctrine, see Nebbia v. New York, 291 U.S. 502 (1934), set out infra p. 536.

Restrictions on Business Entry. The Court applied an approach similar to that in the price fixing cases with regard to legislation restricting entry into particular businesses. In New State Ice Co. v. Liebmann, 285 U.S. 262 (1932), it held invalid a statute requiring any person desiring to engage in the ice business to obtain a certificate of public convenience and necessity. It said that the question was "whether the business is so charged with a public use as to justify" the restriction. It also said: "Plainly, a regulation which has the effect of denying or unreasonably curtailing the common right to engage in a lawful private business, such as that under review, cannot be upheld consistent with the 14th Amendment."

(3) **Regulations of Business Designed to Protect Public Health and Safety.** Most business regulations which came before the court were upheld where the legislative objective was to protect public health and safety rather than to interfere with the free market. However, in some cases the Court held regulations invalid because they were not sufficiently related to the legislative objectives. In Weaver v. Palmer Bros. Co., 270 U.S. 402 (1926), e.g., the Court held invalid a statute which forbade completely the use of shoddy (cut up fabrics) in the manufacture of bedding and provided for the use of other second-hand materials and feathers only if sterilized. It was conceded by the parties that shoddy could be made harmless by disinfection or sterilization and there was no evidence to show that sickness or disease had been caused by the use of shoddy. The Court recognized that state regulations designed to protect public health and to protect the public from deception were generally valid but held that this statute did not sufficiently serve those ends. The measure could not be sustained as a measure to protect health because sterilization would eliminate the danger. Nor could it be sustained as a measure to protect deception because the regulation provided for adequate notice to the public of the contents of the bedding. It then concluded: "The constitutional guarantees may not be made to yield to mere convenience . . . The business here involved is legitimate and useful; and, while it is subject to all reasonable regulation, the absolute prohibition of the use of shoddy in the manufacture of comfortables is purely arbitrary and violates the due process clause of the Fourteenth Amendment.

NEBBIA v. NEW YORK

291 U.S. 502, 54 S.Ct. 505, 78 L.Ed. 940 (1934).

Mr. Justice Roberts delivered the opinion of the Court.

. . .

[A New York statute provided for the fixing of maximum and minimum prices for the sale of milk. Nebbia, owner of a grocery store, was convicted for selling milk at a price below the minimum fixed. He contended, inter alia, that the statute deprived him of due process of law. The Court upheld the law by a vote of 5 to 4. Excerpts from Justice Roberts' long opinion follow.]

The reports of our decisions abound with cases in which the citizen, individual or corporate, has vainly invoked the Fourteenth Amendment in resistance to necessary and appropriate exertion of the police power.

. . .

But we are told that because the law essays to control prices it denies due process. . . . The argument runs that the public control of rates or prices is per se unreasonable and unconstitutional save as applied to businesses affected with a public interest; that a business so affected is one in which property is devoted to an enterprise of a sort which the public itself might appropriately undertake, or one whose owner relies on a public grant or franchise for the right to conduct the business, or in which he is bound to serve all who apply; in short, such as is commonly called a public utility; or a business in its nature a monopoly. The milk industry, it is said, possesses none of these characteristics, and therefore, not being affected with a public interest, its charges may not be controlled by the state. Upon the soundness of this contention the appellant's case against the statute depends.

We may as well say at once that the dairy industry is not, in the accepted sense of the phrase, a public utility. We think the appellant is also right in asserting that there is in this case no suggestion of any monopoly or monopolistic practice. It goes without saying that those engaged in the business are in no way dependent upon public grants or franchises for the privilege of conducting their activities. But if, as must be conceded, the industry is subject to regulation in the public interest, what constitutional principle bars the state from correcting existing maladjustments by legislation touching prices? We think there is no such principle. The due process clause makes no mention of sales or of prices any more than it speaks of business or contracts or buildings or other incidents of property. The thought seems nevertheless to have persisted that there is something peculiarly sacrosanct about the price one may charge for what he makes or sells, and that, however able to regulate other elements of manufacture or trade, with incidental effect upon price, the state is incapable of directly controlling the price itself. This view was negatived many years also. Munn v. Illinois, 94 U.S. 113. . . .

It is clear that there is no closed class or category of businesses affected with a public interest, and the function of courts in the application of the Fifth and Fourteenth Amendments is to determine in each case whether circumstances vindicate the challenged regulation as a reasonable exertion of governmental authority or condemn it as arbitrary or discriminatory. Wolff Packing Co. v. Court of Industrial Relations, 262 U.S. 522, 535. The phrase "affected with a public interest" can, in the nature of things, mean no more than that an industry, for adequate reason, is subject to control for the public good. In several of the decisions of this court wherein the expressions "affected with a public interest," and "clothed with a public use," have been brought forward as the criteria of the validity of price control, it has been admitted that they are not susceptible of definition and form an unsatisfactory test of the constitutionality of legislation directed at business practices or prices. These decisions must rest, finally, upon the basis that the requirements of due process were not met because the laws were found arbitrary, in their operation and effect. But there can be no doubt that upon proper occasion and by appropriate measures the state may regulate a business in any of its aspects, including the prices to be charged for the products or commodities it sells.

So far as the requirement of due process is concerned, and in the absence of other constitutional restriction, a state is free to adopt whatever economic policy may reasonably be deemed to promote public welfare, and to enforce that policy by legislation adapted to its purpose. The courts are without authority either to declare such policy, or, when it is declared by the legislature, to override it. If the laws passed are seen to have a reasonable relation to a proper legislative purpose, and are neither arbitrary nor discriminatory, the requirements of due process are satisfied, and judicial determination to that effect renders a court functus officio. . . . With the wisdom of the policy adopted, with the adequacy or practicability of the law enacted to forward it, the courts are both incompetent and unauthorized to deal. The course of decision in this court exhibits a firm adherence to these principles. Times without number we have said that the Legislature is primarily the judge of the necessity of such an enactment, that every possible presumption is in favor of its validity, and that though the court may hold views inconsistent with the wisdom of the law, it may not be annulled unless palpably in excess of legislative power. . . . Price control, like any other form of regulation, is unconstitutional only if arbitrary, discriminatory, or demonstrably irrelevant to the policy the Legislature is free to adopt, and hence an unnecessary and unwarranted interference with individual liberty.

THE OVERTURNING OF ADKINS v.
CHILDREN'S HOSPITAL

In Morehead v. New York ex rel. Tipaldo, 298 U.S. 587 (1936), Justice Roberts, author of the opinion in *Nebbia,* joined with the *Nebbia* dissenters in applying *Adkins* to hold invalid a New York law providing for minimum wages for women workers. The Court noted that the petitioner had not asked the Court to reconsider the constitutional question decided in *Adkins.* Finding no sufficient basis for distinction, the Court held the statute invalid.

The next year, however, the Court, by a vote of 5 to 4 with Justice Roberts joining the majority, specifically overruled Adkins v. Children's Hospital. West Coast Hotel Co. v. Parrish, 300 U.S. 379 (1937). The Court responded to the argument based on freedom of contract by saying: "What is freedom? The Constitution does not speak of freedom of contract. It speaks of liberty and prohibits the deprivation of liberty without due process of law. . . . But the liberty safeguarded is liberty in a social organization which requires the protection of law against the evils which menace the health, safety, morals and welfare of the people. Liberty under the constitution is thus necessarily subject to the restraints of due process, and regulation which is reasonable in relation to its subject and is adopted in the interests of the community is due process. This essential limitation of liberty in general governs freedom of contract in particular."

It should be noted that the decision in *West Coast Hotel* was announced while President Roosevelt's "Court packing" proposal was pending in Congress. For a reference to the question whether this decision was intended to have an impact on that proposal, see n. 1, supra p. 200.

UNITED STATES v. CAROLENE PRODUCTS CO.

304 U.S. 144, 58 S.Ct. 778, 82 L.Ed. 1234 (1938).

Mr. Justice Stone delivered the opinion of the Court.

The question for decision is whether the "Filled Milk Act" of Congress of March 4, 1923 . . . , which prohibits the shipment in interstate commerce of skimmed milk compounded with any fat or oil other than milk fat, so as to resemble milk or cream, transcends the power of Congress to regulate interstate commerce or infringes the Fifth Amendment. . . .

[The defendant was indicted for shipping in interstate commerce packages of "Milnut," a compound of condensed skimmed milk and coconut oil made in imitation or semblance of condensed milk or cream. The indictment stated in the words of the statute that Milnut "is an adulterated article of food, injurious to the public health." The trial court sustained a demurrer to the indictment and the government appealed to the Supreme Court. After upholding the statute as being within the power of Congress to regulate commerce, the Court addressed the due process issue.]

The prohibition of shipment of appellee's product in interstate commerce does not infringe the Fifth Amendment. Twenty years ago this Court in Hebe Co. v. Shaw, 248 U.S. 297, held that a state law which forbids the manufacture and sale of a product assumed to be wholesome and nutritive, made of condensed skimmed milk, compounded with coconut oil, is not forbidden by the Fourteenth Amendment. The power of the Legislature to secure a minimum of particular nutritive elements in a widely used article of food and to protect the public from fraudulent substitutions, was not doubted; and the Court thought that there was ample scope for the legislative judgment that prohibition of the offending article was an appropriate means of preventing injury to the public.

We see no persuasive reason for departing from that ruling here, where the Fifth Amendment is concerned; and since none is suggested, we might rest decision wholly on the presumption of constitutionality. But affirmative evidence also sustains the statute. In twenty years evidence has steadily accumulated of the danger to the public health from the general consumption of foods which have been stripped of elements essential to the maintenance of health. The Filled Milk Act was adopted by Congress after committee hearings, in the course of which eminent scientists and health experts testified. An extensive investigation was made of the commerce in milk compounds in which vegetable oils have been substituted for natural milk fat, and of the effect upon the public health of the use of such compounds as a food substitute for milk. The conclusions drawn from evidence presented at the hearings were embodied in reports of the House Committee on Agriculture, H.R. No. 365, 67th Cong., 1st Sess., and the Senate Committee on Agriculture and Forestry, Sen.Rep. No. 987, 67th Cong., 4th Sess. Both committees concluded, as the statute itself declares, that the use of filled milk as a substitute for pure milk is generally injurious to health and facilitates fraud on the public.

There is nothing in the Constitution which compels a Legislature, either national or state, to ignore such evidence, nor need it disregard the other evidence which amply supports the conclusions of the Congressional committees that the danger is greatly enhanced where an inferior product, like appellee's, is indistinguishable from a valuable food of almost universal use, thus making fraudulent distribution easy and protection of the consumer difficult.

Here the prohibition of the statute is inoperative unless the product is "in imitation or semblance of milk, cream, or skimmed milk, whether or not condensed." Section 1(c), 21 U.S.C. § 61(c). Whether in such circumstances the public would be adequately protected by the prohibition of false labels and false branding imposed by the Pure Food and Drugs Act, 21 U.S.C. § 1 et seq., or whether it was necessary to go farther and prohibit a substitute food product thought to be injurious to health if used as a substitute when the two are not distinguishable, was a matter for the legislative judgment and not that of courts. . . . It was upon this ground that the prohibition of the sale of oleomargarine made in imitation of butter was held not to infringe the Fourteenth Amendment in Powell v. Pennsylvania, 127 U.S. 678; Capital City Dairy Co. v. Ohio, 183 U.S. 238. Compare McCray v. United States, 195 U.S. 27, 63; Purity Extract & Tonic Co. v. Lynch, 226 U.S. 192.

. . .

Third. We may assume for present purposes that no pronouncement of a Legislature can forestall attack upon the constitutionality of the prohibition which it enacts by applying opprobrious epithets to the prohibited act, and that a statute would deny due process which precluded the disproof in judicial proceedings of all facts which would show or tend to show that a statute depriving the suitor of life, liberty, or property had a rational basis.

But such we think is not the purpose or construction of the statutory characterization of filled milk as injurious to health and as a fraud upon the public. There is no need to consider it here as more than a declaration of the legislative findings deemed to support and justify the action taken as a constitutional exertion of the legislative power, aiding informed judicial review, as do the reports of legislative committees, by revealing the rationale of the legislation. Even in the absence of such aids, the existence of facts supporting the legislative judgment is to be presumed, for regulatory legislation affecting ordinary commercial transactions is not to be pronounced unconstitutional unless in the light of the facts made known or generally assumed it is of such a character as to preclude the assumption that it rests upon some rational basis within the knowledge and experience of the legislators.[4] . . . .

Where the existence of a rational basis for legislation whose constitutionality is attacked depends upon facts beyond the sphere of judicial notice, such facts may properly be made the subject of judicial inquiry, . . . and the constitutionality of a statute predicated upon the existence of a particular state of facts may be challenged by showing to the court that those facts have ceased to exist. . . . Similarly we recognize that the constitutionality of a statute, valid on its face, may be assailed by proof of facts tending to show that the statute as applied to a particular article is without support in reason because the article, although within the prohibited class, is so different from others of the class as to be without the reason for the prohibition . . . . But by their very nature such inquiries, where the legislative judgment is drawn in question, must be restricted to the issue whether any state of facts either known or which could reasonably be assumed affords support for it. Here the demurrer challenges the validity of the statute on its face and it is evident from all the considerations presented to Congress, and those of which we may take judicial notice, that the question is at least debatable whether commerce in filled milk should be left unregulated, or in some measure restricted, or wholly prohibited. As that decision was for Congress, neither the finding of a court arrived at by weighing the evidence, nor the verdict of a jury can be substituted for it.

. . . .

Reversed.

Mr. Justice Black concurs in the result and in all of the opinion except the part marked "Third."

Mr. Justice McReynolds thinks that the judgment should be affirmed.

Mr. Justice Cardozo and Mr. Justice Reed took no part in the consideration or decision of this case.

Mr. Justice Butler.

I concur in the result. . . .[a]

_____

[4] There may be narrower scope for operation of the presumption of constitutionality when legislation appears on its face to be within a specific prohibition of the Constitution, such as those of the first ten Amendments, which are deemed equally specific when held to be embraced within the Fourteenth. See Stromberg v. California, 283 U.S. 359, 369, 370; Lovell v. Griffin, 303 U.S. 444.

It is unnecessary to consider now whether legislation which restricts those political processes which can ordinarily be expected to bring about repeal of undesirable legislation, is to be subjected to more exacting judicial scrutiny under the general prohibitions of the Fourteenth Amendment than are most other types of legislation. On restrictions upon the right to vote, see Nixon v. Herndon, 273 U.S. 536; Nixon v. Condon, 286 U.S. 73; on restraints upon the dissemination of information, see Near v. Minnesota, 283 U.S. 697, 713–714, 718–720, 722; Grosjean v. American Press Co., 297 U.S. 233; Lovell v. Griffin, supra; on interferences with political organizations, see Stromberg v. California, supra, 283 U.S. 359, 369; Fiske v. Kansas, 274 U.S. 380; Whitney v. California, 274 U.S. 357, 373–378; Herndon v. Lowry, 301 U.S. 242, and see Holmes, J., in Gitlow v. New York, 268 U.S. 652, 673; as to prohibition of peaceable assembly, see De Jonge v. Oregon, 299 U.S. 353, 365.

Nor need we enquire whether similar considerations enter into the review of statutes directed at particular religious, Pierce v. Society of Sisters, 268 U.S. 510, or national, Meyer v. Nebraska, 262 U.S. 390; Bartels v. Iowa, 262 U.S. 404; Farrington v. Tokushige, 273 U.S. 284, or racial minorities. Nixon v. Herndon, supra; Nixon v. Condon, supra: whether prejudice against discrete and insular minorities may be a special condition, which tends seriously to curtail the operation of those political processes ordinarily to be relied upon to protect minorities, and which may call for a correspondingly more searching judicial inquiry. Compare McCulloch v. Maryland, 4 Wheat. 316, 428; South Carolina State Highway Department v. Barnwell Bros., 303 U.S. 177, and cases cited.

[a] For recent discussions of the famous footnote 4, see Lusky, *Footnote Redux: A* Carolene Products *Reminiscence,* 82 Colum.L.Rev. 1093 (1982); Powell, Carolene Products *Revisited,* 82 Colum.L.Rev. 1087 (1982).

THE DEMISE OF LIBERTY OF CONTRACT

During the 1940s the Supreme Court (which received seven new members between 1937 and 1941) overturned the old precedents and rejected all challenges to legislation based on assertions of a constitutional preference for a free economic market place.

In United States v. Darby, 312 U.S. 100 (1941), the Court upheld the provisions of the Fair Labor Standards Act fixing maximum hours and minimum wages for all covered employees. The Court said that "it is no longer open to question" that it is within the legislative power to fix wages and hours for men as well as women.

In Phelps Dodge Corp. v. Nat'l Labor Relations Bd., 313 U.S. 177 (1941), the Court upheld the provision of the N.L.R.A. making it an unfair labor practice for an employer to encourage or discourage membership in any labor union, saying that "[t]he course of decisions in this Court since Adair v. United States . . . and Coppage v. Kansas . . . have completely sapped those cases of their authority.

In Olsen v. Nebraska, 313 U.S. 236 (1941), the Court upheld a state statute fixing the fees chargeable by a private employment agency and in Lincoln Fed. Labor Union v. Northwestern Iron & Metal Co., 335 U.S. 525 (1949), upheld a state law providing that no person should be denied an opportunity to obtain employment because he was or was not a member of a labor union. In the latter case it rejected a claim by a labor union that the "open shop" law was invalid by saying: "Just as we have held that the due process clause erects no obstacle to block legislative protection of union members, we now hold that legislative protection can be afforded non-union members."

In Daniel v. Family Sec. Life Ins. Co., 336 U.S. 220 (1949), the Court upheld a statute which prohibited life insurance companies and their agents from engaging in the undertaking business and undertakers from acting as life insurance agents. The statute was challenged by an undertaker selling "funeral insurance." His claim that the statute resulted from the activities of the "insurance lobby" was rejected by the Court: "[A] judiciary must judge by results, not by the varied factors which may have determined legislators' votes. We cannot undertake a search for motive in testing constitutionality." In rejecting the claim that the statute was arbitrary and unreasonable, the Court said: "Looking through the form of this plea to its essential basis, we cannot fail to recognize it as an argument for invalidity because this Court disagrees with the desirability of the legislation. We rehearse the obvious when we say that our function is thus misconceived. We are not equipped to decide desirability; and a court cannot eliminate measures which do not happen to suit its tastes if it seeks to maintain a democratic system. The forum for the correction of ill-considered legislation is a responsive legislature.

"We cannot say that South Carolina is not entitled to call the funeral insurance business an evil. Nor can we say that the statute has no relation to the elimination of those evils. There our inquiry must stop."

WILLIAMSON v. LEE OPTICAL OF OKLAHOMA

348 U.S. 483, 75 S.Ct. 461, 99 L.Ed. 563 (1955).

Mr. Justice Douglas delivered the opinion of the Court.

This suit was instituted in the District Court to have an Oklahoma law, . . . declared unconstitutional and to enjoin state officials from enforcing it, . . . for the reason that it allegedly violated various provisions of the Federal

Constitution. The matter was heard by a district Court of three judges,
. . .. That court held certain provisions of the law unconstitutional. 120
F.Supp. 128. The case is here by appeal. . . .

The District Court held unconstitutional portions of three sections of the
Act. First, it held invalid under the Due Process Clause of the Fourteenth
Amendment the portions of § 2 which make it unlawful for any person not a
licensed optometrist or ophthalmologist to fit lenses to a face or to duplicate or
replace into frames lenses or other optical appliances, except upon written
prescriptive authority of an Oklahoma licensed ophthalmologist or optometrist.

An ophthalmologist is a duly licensed physician who specializes in the care of
the eyes. An optometrist examines eyes for refractive error, recognizes (but
does not treat) diseases of the eye, and fills prescriptions for eyeglasses. The
optician is an artisan qualified to grind lenses, fill prescriptions, and fit frames.

The effect of § 2 is to forbid the optician from fitting or duplicating lenses
without a prescription from an ophthalmologist or optometrist. In practical
effect, it means that no optician can fit old glasses into new frames or supply a
lens, whether it be a new lens or one to duplicate a lost or broken lens, without
a prescription. The District Court conceded that it was in the competence of
the police power of a State to regulate the examination of the eyes. But it
rebelled at the notion that a State could require a prescription from an
optometrist or ophthalmologist "to take old lenses and place them in new
frames and then fit the completed spectacles to the *face* of the eyeglass wearer."
. . . It held that such a requirement was not "reasonably and rationally
related to the health and welfare of the people." . . . The court found that
through mechanical devices and ordinary skills the optician could take a broken
lens or a fragment thereof, measure its power, and reduce it to prescriptive
terms. The court held that "Although on this precise issue of duplication, the
legislature in the instant regulation was dealing with a matter of public interest,
the particular means chosen are neither reasonably necessary nor reasonably
related to the end sought to be achieved." . . . It was, accordingly, the
opinion of the court that this provision of the law violated the Due Process
Clause by arbitrarily interfering with the optician's right to do business.

. . . .

The Oklahoma law may exact a needless, wasteful requirement in many
cases. But it is for the legislature, not the courts, to balance the advantages and
disadvantages of the new requirement. It appears that in many cases the
optician can easily supply the new frames or new lenses without reference to the
old written prescription. It also appears that many written prescriptions contain
no directive data in regard to fitting spectacles to the face. But in some cases
the directions contained in the prescription are essential, if the glasses are to be
fitted so as to correct the particular defects of vision or alleviate the eye
condition. The legislature might have concluded that the frequency of occasions when a prescription is necessary was sufficient to justify this regulation of
the fitting of eyeglasses. Likewise, when it is necessary to duplicate a lens, a
written prescription may or may not be necessary. But the legislature might
have concluded that one was needed often enough to require one in every case.
Or the legislature may have concluded that eye examinations were so critical,
not only for correction of vision but also for detection of latent ailments or
diseases, that every change in frames and every duplication of a lens should be
accompanied by a prescription from a medical expert. To be sure, the present
law does not require a new examination of the eyes every time the frames are
changed or the lenses duplicated. For if the old prescription is on file with the
optician, he can go ahead and make the new fitting or duplicate the lenses. But
the law need not be in every respect logically consistent with its aims to be
constitutional. It is enough that there is an evil at hand for correction, and that

it might be thought that the particular legislative measure was a rational way to correct it.

The day is gone when this Court uses the Due Process Clause of the Fourteenth Amendment to strike down state laws, regulatory of business and industrial conditions, because they may be unwise, improvident, or out of harmony with a particular school of thought. . . .

We emphasize again what Chief Justice Waite said in Munn v. State of Illinois, 94 U.S. 113, 134, "For protection against abuses by legislatures the people must resort to the polls, not to the courts."

. . .

Third, the District Court held unconstitutional, as violative of the Due Process Clause of the Fourteenth Amendment, that portion of § 3 which makes it unlawful "to solicit the sale of . . . frames, mountings . . . or any other optical appliances." The court conceded that state regulation of advertising relating to eye examinations was a matter "rationally related to the public health and welfare", 120 F.Supp. at 140, and therefore subject to regulation . . . .. But regulation of the advertising of eyeglass frames was said to intrude "into a mercantile field only casually related to the visual care of the public" and restrict "an activity which in no way can detrimentally affect the people."

An eyeglass frame, considered in isolation, is only a piece of merchandise. But an eyeglass frame is not used in isolation, as Judge Murrah said in dissent below; it is used with lenses; and lenses, pertaining as they do to the human eye, enter the field of health. Therefore, the legislature might conclude that to regulate one effectively it would have to regulate the other. Or it might conclude that both the sellers of frames and the sellers of lenses were in a business where advertising should be limited or even abolished in the public interest. . . . The advertiser of frames may be using his ads to bring in customers who will buy lenses. If the advertisement of lenses is to be abolished or controlled, the advertising of frames must come under the same restraints; or so the legislature might think. We see no constitutional reason why a State may not treat all who deal with the human eye as members of a profession who should use no merchandising methods for obtaining customers.

Fourth, the District Court held unconstitutional, as violative of the Due Process Clause of the Fourteenth Amendment, the provision of § 4 of the Oklahoma Act which reads as follows:

> "No person, firm, or corporation engaged in the business of retailing merchandise to the general public shall rent space, sublease departments, or otherwise permit any person purporting to do eye examination or visual care to occupy space in such retail store."

It seems to us that this regulation is on the same constitutional footing as the denial to corporations of the right to practice dentistry. Semler v. Oregon State Board of Dental Examiners, supra, 294 U.S. at 611. It is an attempt to free the profession, to as great an extent as possible, from all taints of commercialism. It certainly might be easy for an optometrist with space in a retail store to be merely a front for the retail establishment. In any case, the opportunity for that nexus may be too great for safety, if the eye doctor is allowed inside the retail store. Moreover, it may be deemed important to effective regulation that the eye doctor be restricted to geographical locations that reduce the temptations of commercialism. Geographical location may be an important consideration in a legislative program which aims to raise the treatment of the human eye to a strictly professional level. We cannot say that the regulation has no rational relation to that objective and therefore is beyond constitutional bounds.

What we have said is sufficient to dispose of the appeal in No. 185 from the conclusion of the District Court that that portion of § 3 which makes it unlawful to solicit the sale of spectacles, eyeglasses, lenses, and prisms by the use of advertising media is constitutional.

The other contentions urged by appellants in No. 185 are without merit.

Affirmed in part and reversed in part.

Mr. Justice Harlan took no part in the consideration or decision of this case.

FERGUSON v. SKRUPA

372 U.S. 726, 83 S.Ct. 1028, 10 L.Ed.2d 93 (1963).

Mr. Justice Black delivered the opinion of the Court.

In this case, . . . we are asked to review the judgment of a three-judge District Court enjoining, as being in violation of the Due Process Clause of the Fourteenth Amendment, a Kansas statute making it a misdemeanor for any person to engage "in the business of debt adjusting" except as an incident to "the lawful practice of law in this state." The statute defines "debt adjusting" as "the making of a contract, express, or implied with a particular debtor whereby the debtor agrees to pay a certain amount of money periodically to the person engaged in the debt adjusting business who shall for a consideration distribute the same among certain specified creditors in accordance with a plan agreed upon."

The complaint, filed by appellee Skrupa doing business as "Credit Advisors," alleged that Skrupa was engaged in the business of "debt adjusting" as defined by the statute, that his business was a "useful and desirable" one, that his business activities were not "inherently immoral or dangerous" or in any way contrary to the public welfare, and that therefore the business could not be "absolutely prohibited" by Kansas. The three-judge court heard evidence by Skrupa tending to show the usefulness and desirability of his business and evidence by the state officials tending to show that "debt adjusting" lends itself to grave abuses against distressed debtors, particularly in the lower income brackets, and that these abuses are of such gravity that a number of States have strictly regulated "debt adjusting" or prohibited it altogether. The court found that Skrupa's business did fall within the Act's proscription and concluded, one judge dissenting, that the Act was prohibitory, not regulatory, but that even if construed in part as regulatory it was an unreasonable regulation of a "lawful business," which the court held amounted to a violation of the Due Process Clause of the Fourteenth Amendment. The court accordingly enjoined enforcement of the statute.

The only case discussed by the court below as support for its invalidation of the statute was Commonwealth v. Stone, 191 Pa.Super. 117, 155 A.2d 453 (1959), in which the Superior Court of Pennsylvania struck down a statute almost identical to the Kansas act involved here. . . . In doing so, the Pennsylvania court relied heavily on Adams v. Tanner, 244 U.S. 590 (1917), which held that the Due Process Clause forbids a State to prohibit a business which is "useful" and not "inherently immoral or dangerous to public welfare."

Both the District Court in the present case and the Pennsylvania court in Stone adopted the philosophy of Adams v. Tanner, and cases like it, that it is the province of courts to draw on their own views as to the morality, legitimacy, and usefulness of a particular business in order to decide whether a statute bears too heavily upon that business and by so doing violates due process. Under the system of government created by our Constitution, it is up to legislatures, not courts, to decide on the wisdom and utility of legislation. There was a time when the Due Process Clause was used by this Court to strike down laws which were thought unreasonable, that is, unwise or incompatible with some particular economic or social philosophy.   In this manner the Due Process Clause was used, for example, to nullify laws prescribing maximum hours for work in bakeries, Lochner v. New York, 198 U.S. 45 (1905), outlawing "yellow dog" contracts, Coppage v. Kansas, 236 U.S. 1 (1915), setting minimum wages for women, Adkins v. Children's Hospital, 261 U.S. 525 (1923), and fixing the weight of loaves of bread, Jay Burns Baking Co. v. Bryan, 264 U.S. 504 (1924).   This intrusion by the judiciary into the realm of legislative value judgments was strongly objected to at the time, particularly by Mr. Justice Holmes and Mr. Justice Brandeis.   . . .

The doctrine that prevailed in *Lochner, Coppage, Adkins, Burns,* and like cases—that due process authorizes courts to hold laws unconstitutional when they believe the legislature has acted unwisely—has long since been discarded. We have returned to the original constitutional proposition that courts do not substitute their social and economic beliefs for the judgment of legislative bodies, who are elected to pass laws.   . . .

In the face of our abandonment of the use of the "vague contours" of the Due Process Clause to nullify laws which a majority of the Court believed to be economically unwise, reliance on Adams v. Tanner is as mistaken as would be adherence to Adkins v. Children's Hospital, overruled by West Coast Hotel Co. v. Parrish, 300 U.S. 379 (1937) . . ..   We conclude that the Kansas Legislature was free to decide for itself that legislation was needed to deal with the business of debt adjusting.   Unquestionably, there are arguments showing that the business of debt adjusting has social utility, but such arguments are properly addressed to the legislature, not to us.   We refuse to sit as a "superlegislature to weigh the wisdom of legislation," and we emphatically refuse to go back to the time when courts used the Due Process Clause "to strike down state laws, regulatory of business and industrial conditions, because they may be unwise, inprovident, or out of harmony with a particular school of thought."   Nor are we able or willing to draw lines by calling a law "prohibitory" or "regulatory."   Whether the legislature takes for its textbook Adam Smith, Herbert Spencer, Lord Keynes, or some other is no concern of ours. The Kansas debt adjusting statute may be wise or unwise.   But relief, if any be needed, lies not with us but with the body constituted to pass laws for the State of Kansas.

. . .

Reversed.

Mr. Justice Harlan concurs in the judgment on the ground that this state measure bears a rational relation to a constitutionally permissible objective.   See Williamson v. Lee Optical Co., 348 U.S. 483, 491.

DOES THE DUE PROCESS CLAUSE TODAY IMPOSE ANY LIMITATIONS ON THE SUBSTANCE OF ECONOMIC REGULATORY LEGISLATION?

Does the decision in Ferguson v. Skrupa constitute a complete abandonment by the Court of the use of due process to impose a minimum standard of rationality on legislation?   Does Justice Harlan's concurring opinion indicate that he thought the Court was no longer going to insist that legislation "bear a rational relationship to a constitutionally permissible objective"?

If one looks only at the outcome of cases challenging economic regulatory legislation under due process, the answer would appear to be that no effective review is undertaken by the Court.   No economic regulatory statute has been held invalid under due process since 1937.   Only in cases where the Court has been able to find a "taking" of property without just compensation in violation of the taking clause of the fifth amendment or an impairment of contract within the meaning of the contract clause has it invalidated legislation in the economic area.

However, the Court continues to write opinions in which it states that it is applying a due process standard which requires legislation to bear a rational relationship to a legitimate state objective. In Exxon Corp. v. Governor of Maryland, 437 U.S. 117, 125 (1978), the Court, in upholding a statute prohibiting producers or refiners of petroleum products from operating retail service stations in the state, rejected a due process objection stating: "[W]e have no hesitancy in concluding that it bears a reasonable relation to the State's legitimate purpose in controlling the gasoline retail market." And in Pruneyard Shopping Center v. Robins, 447 U.S. 74 (1980), the Court rejected a due process challenge to state court judgment ordering a private property owner to permit use of a portion of that property by persons soliciting signatures on petitions. It quoted from Nebbia v. New York, set out supra p. 530: "The guaranty of due process . . . demands only that the law shall not be unreasonable, arbitrary or capricious, and that the means selected shall have a real and substantial relation to the objective sought to be [obtained]." The Court then added: "Appellants have failed to provide sufficient justification for concluding that this test is not satisfied by the State's asserted interest in promoting more expansive rights of free speech and petition than conferred by the Federal Constitution."

What does the following case add?

PENSION BENEFIT GUARANTY CORP. v. R.A. GRAY & CO., 104 S.Ct. 2709 (1984). In 1980 Congress enacted the Multiemployer Pension Plan Amendments Act (MPPAA) requiring that an employer withdrawing from a multiemployer pension plan pay a fixed and certain debt to the pension plan. The statute provided that the withdrawal liability provisions took effect five months before the statute was enacted into law. R.A. Gray & Co. withdrew from a multiemployer pension plan about four months prior to the enactment of the MPPAA and was assessed a withdrawal liability under the statute. Gray filed suit seeking declaratory and injunctive relief against the application of the statute to it. The Supreme Court rejected his claim in a unanimous opinion.

The Court said, in part:

II

"The starting point for analysis is our decision in Usery v. Turner Elkhorn Mining Co., 428 U.S. 1 (1976). In *Turner Elkhorn*, we considered a constitutional challenge to the retroactive effects of the Federal Coal Mine Health and Safety Act of 1969 as amended by the Black Lung Benefits Act of 1972. Under Title IV of that Act, coal mine operators were required to compensate former employees disabled by pneumoconiosis even though those employees had terminated their work in the industry before the statute was enacted. We nonetheless had little difficulty in upholding the statute against constitutional attack under the Due Process Clause. . . .

"We . . . explained that the strong deference accorded legislation in the field of national economic policy is no less applicable when that legislation is applied retroactively. Provided that the retroactive application of a statute is supported by a legitimate legislative purpose furthered by rational means, judgments about the wisdom of such legislation remain within the exclusive province of the legislative and executive branches:

'[I]nsofar as the Act requires compensation for disabilities bred during employment terminated before the date of enactment, the Act has some retrospective effect—although, as we have noted, the Act imposed no liability on operators until [after its enactment]. And it may be that the liability imposed by the Act for disabilities suffered by former employees was not anticipated at the time of actual employment. But our cases are clear that legislation readjusting rights and burdens is not unlawful solely because it upsets otherwise settled expectations. See Fleming v. Rhodes, 331 U.S. 100 (1947); Carpenter v. Wabash R. Co., 309 U.S. 23 (1940); Norman v. Baltimore & Ohio R. Co., 294 U.S. 240 (1935); Home Bldg. & Loan Assn. v. Blaisdell, 290 U.S. 398 (1934); Louisville & Nashville R. Co. v. Mottley, 219 U.S. 467 (1911). This is true even though the effect of the legislation is to impose a new duty or liability based on past acts. See Lichter v. United States, 334 U.S. 742 (1948); Welch v. Henry, 305 U.S. 134 (1938); Funkhouser v. Preston Co., 290 U.S. 163 (1933).'

"To be sure, we went on to recognize that retroactive legislation does have to meet a burden not faced by legislation that has only future effects. 'It does not follow . . . that what Congress can legislate prospectively it can legislate retrospectively. The retroactive aspects of legislation, as well as the prospective aspects, must meet the test of due process, and the justifications for the latter may not suffice for the former.' But that burden is met simply by showing that the retroactive application of the legislation is itself justified by a rational legislative purpose.

"For example, in *Turner Elkhorn* we found that 'the imposition of liability for the effects of disabilities bred in the past is justified as a rational measure to spread the costs of the employees' disabilities to those who have profited from the fruits of their labor—the operators and the coal consumers.' Similarly, in these cases, a rational legislative purpose supporting the retroactive application of the MPPAA's withdrawal liability provisions is easily identified. Indeed, Congress was quite explicit when explaining the reason for the statute's retroactivity.

"In particular, we believe it was eminently rational for Congress to conclude that the purposes of the MPPAA could be more fully effectuated if its withdrawal liability provisions were applied retroactively. One of the primary problems Congress identified under ERISA was that the statute encouraged employer withdrawals from multiemployer plans. And Congress was properly concerned that employers would have an even greater incentive to withdraw if they knew that legislation to impose more burdensome liability on withdrawing employers was being considered. . . . Withdrawals occurring during the legislative process not only would have required that remaining employers increase their contributions to existing pension plans, but also could have ultimately affected the stability of the plans themselves. Congress therefore utilized retroactive application of the statute to prevent employers from taking advantage of a lengthy legislative process and withdrawing while Congress debated necessary revisions in the statute. . . . As we recently noted when upholding the retroactive application of an income tax statute in United States v. Darusmont, 449 U.S. 292, 296–297 (1981) (per curiam), the enactment of retroactive statutes 'confined to short and limited periods required by the practicalities of producing national legislation . . . is a customary congressional practice.' We are loathe to reject such a common practice when conducting the limited judicial review accorded economic legislation under the Fifth Amendment's Due Process Clause.

III

"Gray and its supporting *amici* offer several reasons for subjecting the retroactive application of the MPPAA to some form of heightened judicial scrutiny. We are not persuaded, however, by any of their arguments.

.   .   .

"Second, it is suggested that we apply constitutional principles that have been developed under the Contract Clause .   .   ., when reviewing this federal legislation. See, e.g., Energy Resources Group, Inc. v. Kansas Power & Light Co., 459 U.S. 400 (1983); Allied Structural Steel Co. v. Spannaus, 438 U.S. 234 (1978). We have never held, however, that the principles embodied in the Fifth Amendment's Due Process Clause are coextensive with prohibitions existing against state impairments of pre-existing contracts. See, e.g., Philadelphia, Baltimore & Washington Railroad v. Schubert, 224 U.S. 603 (1912). Indeed, to the extent that recent decisions of the Court have addressed the issue, we have contrasted the limitations imposed on States by the Contract Clause with the less searching standards imposed on economic legislation by the Due Process Clauses. See United States Trust Co. v. New Jersey, 431 U.S. 1, 17, n. 13 (1977). And, although we have noted that retrospective civil legislation may offend due process if it is 'particularly "harsh and oppressive,"' *ibid.* (quoting Welch v. Henry, 305 U.S. 134, 147 (1938), and citing *Turner Elkhorn,* supra, at 14–20), that standard does not differ from the prohibition against arbitrary and irrational legislation that we clearly enunciated in *Turner Elkhorn.*

.   .   .

IV

"We conclude that Congress' decision to apply the withdrawal liability provisions of the Multiemployer Pension Plan Amendments Act to employers withdrawing from pension plans during the five-month period preceding enactment of the Act is supported by a rational legislative purpose, and therefore withstands attack under the Due Process Clause of the Fifth Amendment."

———

STATE COURTS AND BUSINESS REGULATIONS

Many state courts have refused to go as far as the United States Supreme Court in abandoning judicial control of economic legislation. For example, the Supreme Court in Day-Brite Lighting v. Missouri, 342 U.S. 421 (1952), held valid a Missouri statute providing that an employee could absent himself from his employment without loss of pay for up to four hours on election day for the purpose of voting. In Heimgaertner v. Benjamin Elec. Mfg. Co., 6 Ill.2d 152, 128 N.E.2d 691 (1955), however, the Supreme Court of Illinois refused to follow the Day-Brite decision and held a similar law invalid under the due process clause of the state constitution. The court rejected the Day-Brite decision with the following statement:

"Although the decision eliminates the Federal aspects of the problems surrounding such regulations, it serves to reaffirm that it is for each State to determine if its legislature is empowered to enact such a statute and to determine if the means selected to further the public welfare bear a real and substantial relation to the objects sought to be obtained. It is the duty of each State to pass upon the validity of its own legislation and, if no Federal question is involved, the United States Supreme Court will adopt and follow the decision of the State court."

For a comprehensive review of the cases, see Hetherington, *State Economic Regulation and Substantive Due Process of Law,* 53 Northwest U.L.Rev. 13, 226

(1958); *Developments in the Law—The Interpretation of State Constitutional Rights,* 95 Harv.L.Rev. 1324, 1463–1493 (1982). See also Carpenter, *Our Constitutional Heritage: Economic Due Process and the State Courts,* 45 A.B.A.J. 1027 (1959); Linde, *Constitutional Law—1959 Oregon Survey,* 39 Ore.L.Rev. 138, 143–160 (1960); Paulsen, *The Persistence of Substantive Due Process in the States,* 34 Minn.L. Rev. 91 (1950); Note, 53 Col.L.Rev. 827 (1953); Note, 18 Ohio St.L.J. 384 (1957). For a discussion of state cases which advocates greater review of economic regulations by the United States Supreme Court see Struve, *The Less-Restrictive-Alternative Principle and Economic Due Process,* 80 Harv.L.Rev. 1463 (1967).

B. THE CONTRACT CLAUSE—WHAT DOES IT ADD TO THE DUE PROCESS LIMITATION?

UNITED STATES TRUST CO. OF NEW YORK v. NEW JERSEY

431 U.S. 1, 97 S.Ct. 1505, 52 L.Ed.2d 92 (1977).

[The New York and New Jersey Port Authority was formed by compact of the two States in 1921, as a financially independent agency. The Authority's income from bridge and tunnel tolls was pledged to the retirement of bonds issued by the Authority. In 1960, the Authority took over the Hudson & Manhattan Railroad, a financially troubled, privately owned commuter train that operated through the Hudson tunnel. Concern that use of tolls to finance the railroad's deficits would conflict with rights of holders of the Authority's bonds led to the 1962 "Statutory Covenant," enacted into law in both States. The statutes provided that "the 2 States covenant and agree with each other and with the holders of any affected bonds" not to finance railroad deficits with revenue pledged to pay bonds, except as permitted by exceptions in the 1962 statutes. In 1974, New York and New Jersey retroactively repealed the 1962 covenant, in order to permit greater use of bridge and tunnel tolls to subsidize mass transit. Appellant, trustee and holder of Authority bonds, brought suit in a New Jersey State court for a declaratory judgment that New Jersey's repeal of the 1962 covenant was prohibited by the Contract Clause. The trial court's decision, that the repeal was a reasonable exercise of New Jersey's police power and not in violation of the Contract Clause, was affirmed by the Supreme Court of New Jersey.]

Mr. Justice Blackmun delivered the opinion of the court.

. . .

II.

At the time the Constitution was adopted, and for nearly a century thereafter, the Contract Clause was one of the few express limitations on state power. The many decisions of this Court involving the Contract Clause are evidence of its important place in our constitutional jurisprudence. Over the last century, however, the Fourteenth Amendment has assumed a far larger place in constitutional adjudication concerning the States. We feel that the present role of the Contract Clause is largely illuminated by two of this Court's decisions. In each, legislation was sustained despite a claim that it had impaired the obligations of contracts.

Home Building & Loan Assn. v. Blaisdell, 290 U.S. 398 (1934), is regarded as the leading case in the modern era cf Contract Clause interpretation. At issue was the Minnesota Mortgage Moratorium Law, enacted in 1933, during the depth of the Depression and when that state was under severe economic stress, and appeared to have no effective alternative. The statute was a temporary measure that allowed judicial extension of the time for redemption; a mortgagor who remained in possession during the extension period was required to pay a reasonable income or rental value to the mortgagee. A closely divided Court, in an opinion by Mr. Chief Justice Hughes, observed that "emergency may furnish the occasion for the exercise of power" and that the "constitutional question presented in the light of an emergency is whether the power possessed embraces the particular exercise of it in response to particular conditions." It noted that the debates in the Constitutional Convention were of little aid in the construction of the Contract Clause, but that the general purpose of the Clause was clear: to encourage trade and credit by promoting confidence in the stability of contractual obligations. Nevertheless, a State "continues to possess authority to safeguard the vital interests of its people. . . . This principle of harmonizing the constitutional prohibition with the necessary residuum of state power has had progressive recognition in the decisions of this Court." The great clauses of the Constitution are to be considered in the light of our whole experience, and not merely as they would be interpreted by its Framers in the conditions and with the outlook of their time.

This Court's most recent Contract Clause decision is El Paso v. Simmons, 379 U.S. 497 (1965). That case concerned a 1941 Texas statute that limited to a 5-year period the reinstatement rights of an interest-defaulting purchaser of land from the State. For many years prior to the enactment of that statute, such a defaulting purchaser, under Texas law, could have reinstated his claim to the land upon written request and payment of delinquent interest, unless rights of third parties had intervened. This Court held that "it is not every modification of a contractual promise that impairs the obligation of contract under federal law." It observed that the State "has the 'sovereign right . . . to protect the . . . general welfare of the people'" and "'we must respect the "wide discretion on the part of the legislature in determining what is and what is not necessary,"'" quoting East New York Savings Bank v. Hahn, 326 U.S. 230, 232–233 (1945). The Court recognized that "the power of a State to modify or affect the obligation of contract is not without limit," but held that "the objects of the Texas statute make abundantly clear that it impairs no protected right under the Contract Clause."

Both of these cases eschewed a rigid application of the Contract Clause to invalidate state legislation. Yet neither indicated that the Contract Clause was without meaning in modern constitutional jurisprudence, or that its limitation on state power was illusory. Whether or not the protection of contract rights comports with current views of wise public policy, the Contract Clause remains a part of our written Constitution. We therefore must attempt to apply that constitutional provision to the instant case with due respect for its purpose and the prior decisions of this Court.

III.

We first examine appellant's general claim that repeal of the 1962 covenant impaired the obligation of the States' contract with the bondholders. It long has been established that the Contract Clause limits the power of the States to modify their own contracts as well as to regulate those between private parties. Fletcher v. Peck, 6 Cranch 87, 137–139 (1810); Dartmouth College v. Woodward, 4 Wheat. 518 (1819). Yet the Contract Clause does not prohibit the States from repealing or amending statutes generally, or from enacting legislation with retroactive effects.[13] Thus, as a preliminary matter, appellant's

[13] The Contract Clause is in the phrase of the Constitution which contains the prohibition against any State's enacting a bill of attainder or *ex post facto* law. Notwithstanding Mr. Chief Justice Marshall's reference to these two other forbidden categories in Fletcher v. Peck, 6 Cranch, at 138–139,

claim requires a determination that the repeal has the effect of impairing a contractual obligation.

In this case the obligation was itself created by a statute, the 1962 legislative covenant. It is unnecessary, however, to dwell on the criteria for determining whether state legislation gives rise to a contractual obligation. The trial court found, . . . and appellees do not deny, that the 1962 covenant constituted a contract between the two States and the holders of the Consolidated Bonds issued between 1962 and the 1973 prospective repeal. . . .

The trial court recognized that there was an impairment in this case: "To the extent that the repeal of the covenant authorizes the Authority to assume greater deficits for such purposes, it permits a diminution of the pledged revenues and reserves and may be said to constitute an impairment of the states' contract with the bondholders." . . .

Having thus established that the repeal impaired a contractual obligation of the States, we turn to the question whether that impairment violated the Contract Clause.

IV.

Although the Contract Clause appears literally to proscribe "any" impairment, this Court observed in *Blaisdell* that "the prohibition is not an absolute one and is not to be read with literal exactness like a mathematical formula." Thus, a finding that there has been a technical impairment is merely a preliminary step in resolving the more difficult question whether that impairment is permitted under the Constitution. In the instant case, as in *Blaisdell*, we must attempt to reconcile the strictures of the Contract Clause with the "essential attributes of sovereign power," necessarily reserved by the States to safeguard the welfare of their citizens.

The trial court concluded that repeal of the 1962 covenant was a valid exercise of New Jersey's police power because repeal served important public interests in mass transportation, energy conservation, and environmental protection. Yet the Contract Clause limits otherwise legitimate exercises of state legislative authority, and the existence of an important public interest is not always sufficient to overcome that limitation. "Undoubtedly, whatever is reserved of state power must be consistent with the fair intent of the constitutional limitation of that power." *Blaisdell*, 290 U.S., at 439. Moreover, the scope of the State's reserved power depends on the nature of the contractual relationship with which the challenged law conflicts.

The States must possess broad power to adopt general regulatory measures without being concerned that private contracts will be impaired, or even destroyed, as a result. Otherwise, one would be able to obtain immunity from the state regulation by making private contractual arrangements. This principle is summarized in Mr. Justice Holmes' well-known dictum: "One whose rights, such as they are, are subject to state restriction, cannot remove them from the power of the State by making a contract about them." Hudson Water Co. v. McCarter, 209 U.S. 349, 357.

Yet private contracts are not subject to unlimited modification under the police power. The Court in *Blaisdell* recognized that laws intended to regulate existing contractual relationships must serve a legitimate public purpose. A State could not "adopt as its policy the repudiation of debts or the destruction of

it is clear that they limit the powers of the States only with regard to the imposition of punishment. Cummings v. Missouri, 4 Wall. 277, 322–326, 18 L.Ed. 356 (1867); Calder v. Bull, 3 Dall. 386, 390–391, 1 L.Ed. 648 (1798). The Due Process Clause of the Fourteenth Amendment generally does not prohibit retrospective civil legislation, unless the consequences are particularly "harsh and oppressive." Welch v. Henry, 305 U.S. 134, 147 (1938). See Usery v. Turner Elkhorn Mining Co., 428 U.S. 1, 14–20 (1976).

contracts or the denial of means to enforce them." Legislation adjusting the rights and responsibilities of contracting parties must be upon reasonable conditions and of a character appropriate to the public purpose justifying its adoption. As is customary in reviewing economic and social regulation, however, courts properly defer to legislative judgment as to the necessity and reasonableness of a particular measure.

. . . .

When a State impairs the obligation of its own contract, the reserved-powers doctrine has a different basis. The initial inquiry concerns the ability of the State to enter into an agreement that limits its power to act in the future. As early as Fletcher v. Peck, the Court considered the argument that "one legislature cannot abridge the powers of a succeeding legislature." 6 Cranch, at 135. It is often stated that "the legislature cannot bargain away the police power of a State." Stone v. Mississippi, 101 U.S. 814, 817 (1880).[20] This doctrine requires a determination of the State's power to create irrevocable contract rights in the first place, rather than an inquiry into the purpose or reasonableness of the subsequent impairment. In short, the Contract Clause does not require a State to adhere to a contract that surrenders an essential attribute of its sovereignty.

In deciding whether a State's contract was invalid *ab initio* under the reserved powers doctrine, earlier decisions relied on distinctions among the various powers of the State. Thus, the police power and the power of eminent domain were among those that could not be "contracted away," but the State could bind itself in the future exercise of the taxing and spending powers.[21] Such formalistic distinctions perhaps cannot be dispositive, but they contain an important element of truth. Whatever the propriety of a State's binding itself to a future course of conduct in other contexts, the power to enter into effective financial contracts cannot be questioned. Any financial obligation could be regarded in theory as a relinquishment of the State's spending power, since money spent to repay debts is not available for other purposes. Similarly, the taxing power may have to be exercised if debts are to be repaid. Notwithstanding these effects, the Court has regularly held that the States are bound by their debt contracts.

The instant case involves a financial obligation and thus as a threshold matter may not be said automatically to fall within the reserved powers that cannot be contracted away. Not every security provision, however, is necessarily financial. For example, a revenue bond might be secured by the State's promise to continue operating the facility in question; yet such a promise surely could not validly be construed to bind the State never to close the facility for health or safety reasons. The security provision at issue here, however, is different: the States promised that revenues and reserves securing the bonds would not be depleted by the Port Authority's operation of deficit-producing passenger railroads beyond the level of "permitted deficits." Such a promise is purely financial and thus not necessarily a compromise of the State's reserved powers.

---

[20] Stone v. Mississippi sustained the State's revocation of a 25-year charter to operate a lottery. Other cases similarly have held that a State is without power to enter into binding contracts not to exercise its police power in the future. . . . .

[21] In New Jersey v. Wilson, 7 Cranch 164 (1812), the Court held that a State could properly grant a permanent tax exemption and that the Contract Clause prohibited any impairment of such an agreement. This holding has never been repudiated, although tax exemption contracts generally have not received a sympathetic construction. See B. Wright, The Contract Clause of the Constitution 179–194 (1938).

By contrast, the doctrine that a State cannot contract away the power of eminent domain has been established since West River Bridge Co. v. Dix, 6 How. 507 (1848). See Contributors to Pennsylvania Hospital v. Philadelphia, 245 U.S., at 23–24. The doctrine that a State cannot be bound to a contract forbidding the exercise of its police power is almost as old. See n. 20, supra.

Of course, to say that the financial restrictions of the 1962 covenant were valid when adopted does not finally resolve this case. The Contract Clause is not an absolute bar to subsequent modification of a State's own financial obligations. As with laws impairing the obligations of private contracts, an impairment may be constitutional if it is reasonable and necessary to serve an important public purpose. In applying this standard, however, complete deference to a legislative assessment of reasonableness and necessity is not appropriate because the State's self-interest is at stake. A governmental entity can always find a use for extra money, especially when taxes do not have to be raised. If a State could reduce its financial obligations whenever it wanted to spend the money for what it regarded as an important public purpose, the Contract Clause would provide no protection at all.

The trial court recognized to an extent the special status of a State's financial obligations when it held that *total* repudiation, presumably for even a worthwhile public purpose, would be unconstitutional. But the trial court regarded the protection of the Contract Clause as available only in such an extreme case: "The states' inherent power to protect the public welfare may be validly exercised under the Contract Clause even if it impairs a contractual obligation so long as it does not destroy it."

The trial court's "total destruction" test is based on what we think is a misreading of W.B. Worthen Co. v. Kavanaugh, 295 U.S. 56 (1935). In the first place, the impairment held unconstitutional in *Kavanaugh* was one that affected the value of a security provision, and certainly not every bond would have been worthless. More importantly, Mr. Justice Cardozo needed only to state an "outermost limits" test in the Court's opinion, because the impairment was so egregious. He expressly recognized that the actual line between permissible and impermissible impairments could well be drawn more narrowly. Thus the trial court was not correct when it drew the negative inference that any impairment less oppressive than the one in *Kavanaugh* was necessarily constitutional. The extent of impairment is certainly a relevant factor in determining its reasonableness. But we cannot sustain the repeal of the 1962 covenant simply because the bondholders' rights were not totally destroyed.

. . .

V.

Mass transportation, energy conservation, and environmental protection are goals that are important and of legitimate public concern. Appellees contend that these goals are so important that any harm to bondholders from repeal of the 1962 covenant is greatly outweighed by the public benefit. We do not accept this invitation to engage in a utilitarian comparison of public benefit and private loss. Contrary to Mr. Justice Black's fear expressed on sole dissent in El Paso v. Simmons, 379 U.S., at 517, the Court has not "balanced away" the limitation on state action imposed by the Contract Clause. Thus a State cannot refuse to meet its legitimate financial obligations simply because it would prefer to spend the money to promote the public good rather than the private welfare of its creditors. We can only sustain the repeal of the 1962 covenant if that impairment was both reasonable and necessary to serve the admittedly important purposes claimed by the State.[27]

The more specific justification offered for the repeal of the 1962 covenant was the States' plan for encouraging users of private automobiles to shift to

---

[27] The dissent suggests that such careful scrutiny is unwarranted in this case because the harm to bondholders is relatively small. For the same reason, however, contractual obligations of this magnitude need not impose barriers to changes in public policy. The States remain free to exercise their powers of eminent domain to abrogate such contractual rights, upon payment of just compensation.

public transportation. The States intended to discourage private automobile use by raising bridge and tunnel tolls and to use the extra revenue from those tolls to subsidize improved commuter railroad service. Appellees contend that repeal of the 1962 covenant was necessary to implement this plan because the new mass transit facilities could not possibly be self-supporting and the covenant's "permitted deficits" level had already been exceeded. We reject this justification because the repeal was neither necessary to achievement of the plan nor reasonable in light of the circumstances.

The determination of necessity can be considered on two levels. First, it cannot be said that total repeal of the covenant was essential; a less drastic modification would have permitted the contemplated plan without entirely removing the covenant's limitations on the use of Port Authority revenues and reserves to subsidize commuter railroads.[28] Second, without modifying the covenant at all, the States could have adopted alternative means of achieving their twin goals of discouraging automobile use and improving mass transit. Appellees contend, however, that choosing among these alternatives is a matter for legislative discretion. But a State is not completely free to consider impairing the obligations of its own contracts on a par with other policy alternatives. Similarly, a State is not free to impose a drastic impairment when an evident and more moderate course would serve its purposes equally well. In El Paso v. Simmons, supra, the . . . Court held that adoption of a statute of limitation was a reasonable means to "restrict a party to those gains reasonably to be expected from the contract" when it was adopted.

By contrast, in the instant case the need for mass transportation in the New York metropolitan area was not a new development, and the likelihood that publicly owned commuter railroads would produce substantial deficits was well known. As early as 1922, over a half century ago, there were pressures to involve the Port Authority in mass transit. It was with full knowledge of these concerns that the 1962 covenant was adopted. Indeed, the covenant was specifically intended to protect the pledged revenues and reserves against the possibility that such concerns would lead the Port Authority into greater involvement in deficit mass transit.

During the 12-year period between adoption of the covenant and its repeal, public perception of the importance of mass transit undoubtedly grew because of increased general concern with environmental protection and energy conservation. But these concerns were not unknown in 1962, and the subsequent changes were of degree and not of kind. We cannot say that these changes caused the covenant to have a substantially different impact in 1974 than when it was adopted in 1962. And we cannot conclude that the repeal was reasonable in the light of changed circumstances.

We therefore hold that the Contract Clause of the United States Constitution prohibits the retroactive repeal of the 1962 covenant. The judgment of the Supreme Court of New Jersey is reversed.

It is so ordered.

Mr. Justice Stewart took no part in the decision of this case.

Mr. Justice Powell took no part in the consideration or decision of this case.

Mr. Chief Justice Burger, concurring.

. . .

For emphasis, I note that the Court pointedly does not hold that, on the facts of this case, any particular "less drastic modification" would pass constitutional muster, n. 28.

---

[28] Of course, we express no opinion as to whether any of these lesser impairments would be constitutional.

Mr. Justice Brennan, with whom Mr. Justice White and Mr. Justice Marshall join, dissenting.

Decisions of this Court for at least a century have construed the Contract Clause largely to be powerless in binding a State to contracts limiting the authority of successor legislatures to enact laws in furtherance of the health, safety, and similar collective interests of the polity. In short, those decisions established the principle that lawful exercises of a State's police powers stand paramount to private rights held under contract. Today's decision, in invalidating the New Jersey Legislature's 1974 repeal of its predecessor's 1962 covenant, rejects this previous understanding and remolds the Contract Clause into a potent instrument for overseeing important policy determinations of the state legislature. At the same time, by creating a constitutional safe haven for property rights embodied in a contract, the decision substantially distorts modern constitutional jurisprudence governing regulation of private economic interests. I might understand, though I could not accept, this revival of the Contract Clause were it in accordance with some coherent and constructive view of public policy. But elevation of the clause to the status of regulator of the municipal bond market at the heavy price of frustration of sound legislative policymaking is as demonstrably unwise as it is unnecessary. The justification for today's decision, therefore, remains a mystery to me, and I respectfully dissent.

. . . .

Thus, as I had occasion to remark only last Term, the Court again offers a constitutional analysis that rests upon "abstraction[s] without substance," National League of Cities v. Usery, 426 U.S. 833, 860 (1976) (Brennan, J., dissenting). Given that this is the first case in some 40 years in which this Court has seen fit to invalidate purely economic and social legislation on the strength of the Contract Clause, one may only hope that it will prove a rare phenomenon, turning on the Court's particularized appraisal of the facts before it. But there also is reason for broader concern. It is worth remembering that there is nothing sacrosanct about a contract. All property rights, no less than a contract, are rooted in certain "expectations" about the sanctity of one's right of ownership. . . . And other constitutional doctrines are akin to the Contract Clause in directing their protections to the property interests of private parties. Hence the command of the Fifth Amendment that "private property [shall not] be taken for public use, without just compensation" also "remains a part of our written Constitution." Ante, at 1515. And during the heyday of economic due process associated with Lochner v. New York, 198 U.S. 45 (1905), and similar cases long since discarded, see Whalen v. Roe, supra, 429 U.S. 589, 597 (1977), this Court treated "the liberty of contract" under the Due Process Clause as virtually indistinguishable from the Contract Clause. G. Gunther, Constitutional Law, at 603–604 (1975); Hale, The Supreme Court and the Contract Clause: III, 57 Harv.L.Rev. 852, 890–891 (1944). In more recent times, however, the Court wisely has come to embrace a coherent, unified interpretation of all such constitutional provisions, and has granted wide latitude to "a valid exercise of [the States'] police powers," Goldblatt v. Hempstead, 369 U.S. 590, 592 (1962), even if it results in severe violations of property rights. . . . If today's case signals a return to substantive constitutional review of States' policies, and a new resolve to protect property owners whose interest or circumstances may happen to appeal to Members of this Court, then more than the citizens of New Jersey and New York will be the losers.

I would not want to be read as suggesting that the States should blithely proceed down the path of repudiating their obligations, financial or otherwise. Their credibility in the credit market obviously is highly dependent on exercising their vast lawmaking powers with self-restraint and discipline, and I, for one, have little doubt that few, if any, jurisdictions would choose to use their authority "so foolish[ly] as to kill a goose that lays golden eggs for them." But in the final analysis, there is no reason to doubt that appellant's financial welfare is being adequately policed by the political processes and the bond marketplace itself. The role to be played by the Constitution is at most a limited one. For this Court should have learned long ago that the Constitution—be it through the Contract or Due Process Clause—can actively intrude into such economic and policy matters only if my Brethren are prepared to bear enormous institutional and social costs. Because I consider the potential dangers of such judicial interference to be intolerable, I dissent.

ALLIED STRUCTURAL STEEL CO. v. SPANNAUS

438 U.S. 234, 98 S.Ct. 2716, 57 L.Ed.2d 727 (1978).

Mr. Justice Stewart delivered the opinion of the Court.

The issue in this case is whether the application of Minnesota's Private Pension Benefits Protection Act to the appellant violates the Contract Clause of the United States Constitution.

I.

In 1974 appellant Allied Structural Steel Company (the company), a corporation with its principal place of business in Illinois, maintained an office in Minnesota with 30 employees. Under the company's general pension plan, adopted in 1963 and qualified as a single-employer plan under § 401 of the Internal Revenue Code, salaried employees were covered as follows: At age 65 an employee was entitled to retire and receive a monthly pension generally computed by multiplying 1% of his average monthly earnings by the total number of his years of employment with the company. Thus an employee aged 65 or more could retire without satisfying any particular length of service requirement, but the size of his pension would reflect the length of his service with the company. An employee could also become entitled to receive a pension, payable in full at age 65, if he met any one of the following requirements: (1) he had worked 15 years for the company and reached the age of 60; or (2) he was at least 55 years old and the sum of his age and his years of service with the company was at least 75; or (3) he was less than 55 years old but the sum of his age and his years of service with the company was at least 80. Once an employee satisfied any one of these conditions, his pension right became vested in the sense that any subsequent termination of employment would not affect his right to receive a monthly pension when he reached 65. Those employees who quit or were discharged before age 65 without fulfilling one of the other three conditions did not acquire any pension rights.

. . .

The company not only retained a virtually unrestricted right to amend the plan in whole or in part, but was also free to terminate the plan and distribute the trust assets at any time and for any reason. . . . The plan also specifically advised employees that neither its existence nor any of its terms were to be understood as implying any assurance that employees could not be dismissed from their employment with the company at any time.

In sum, an employee who did not die, did not quit, and was not discharged before meeting one of the requirements of the plan would receive a fixed pension at age 65 if the company remained in business and elected to continue the pension plan in essentially its existing form.

On April 9, 1974, Minnesota enacted the law here in question, the Private Pension Benefits Protection Act, Minn.Stat. §§ 181B.01–181B.17. Under the Act, a private employer of 100 employees or more—at least one of whom was a Minnesota resident—who provided pension benefits under a plan meeting the qualifications of § 401 of the Internal Revenue Code, was subject to a "pension funding charge" if he either terminated the plan or closed a Minnesota office. The charge was assessed if the pension funds were not sufficient to cover full pensions for all employees who had worked at least 10 years. The Act required the employer to satisfy the deficiency by purchasing deferred annuities, payable to the employees at their normal retirement age. A separate provision specified that periods of employment prior to the effective date of the Act were to be included in the 10-year employment criterion.

During the summer of 1974 the company began closing its Minnesota office. On July 31, it discharged 11 of its 30 Minnesota employees, and the following month it notified the Minnesota Commissioner of Labor and Industry, as required by the Act, that it was terminating an office in the State. At least nine of the discharged employees did not have any vested pension rights under the company's plan, but had worked for the company for 10 years or more and thus qualified as pension obligees of the company under the law that Minnesota had enacted a few months earlier. On August 18, the State notified the company that it owed a pension funding charge of approximately $185,000 under the provisions of the Private Pension Benefits Protection Act.

The company brought suit in a federal district court asking for injunctive and declaratory relief. It claimed that the Act unconstitutionally impaired its contractual obligations to its employees under its pension agreement. The three-judge court upheld the constitutional validity of the Act as applied to the company, . . . and an appeal was brought to this Court, under 28 U.S.C. § 1253. We noted probable jurisdiction. . . .

II.

A.

There can be no question of the impact of the Minnesota Private Pension Benefits Protection Act upon the company's contractual relationships with its employees. The Act substantially altered those relationships by superimposing pension obligations upon the company conspicuously beyond those that it had voluntarily agreed to undertake. But it does not inexorably follow that the Act, as applied to the company, violates the Contract Clause of the Constitution.

The language of the Contract Clause appears unambiguously absolute: "No State shall . . . pass any . . . Law impairing the Obligation of Contracts." U.S. Const. Art. 1, § 10. The Clause is not, however, the draconian provision that its words might seem to imply. As the Court has recognized, "literalism in the construction of the contract clause . . . would make it destructive of the public interest by depriving the State of its prerogative of self-protection." W.B. Worthen Co. v. Thomas, 292 U.S. 426, 433.

Although it was perhaps the strongest single constitutional check on state legislation during our early years as a Nation, the Contract Clause receded into comparative desuetude with the adoption of the Fourteenth Amendment, and particularly with the development of the large body of jurisprudence under the Due Process Clause of that Amendment in modern constitutional history. Nonetheless, the Contract Clause remains part of the Constitution. It is not a dead letter. And its basic contours are brought into focus by several of this Court's 20th century decisions.

First of all, it is to be accepted as a commonplace that the Contract Clause does not operate to obliterate the police power of the States. "It is the settled law of this court that the interdiction of statutes impairing the obligation of contracts does not prevent the State from exercising such powers as are vested in it for the promotion of the common weal, or are necessary for the general good of the public, though contracts previously entered into between individuals may thereby be affected. This power, which in its various ramifications is known as the police power, is an exercise of the sovereign right of the Government to protect the lives, health, morals, comfort and general welfare of the people, and is paramount to any rights under contracts between individuals." Manigault v. Springs, 199 U.S. 473, 480. As Mr. Justice Holmes succinctly put the matter in his opinion for the Court in Hudson Water Co. v. McCarter, 209 U.S. 349, 357: "One whose rights, such as they are, are subject to state restriction, cannot remove them from the power of the State by making a contract about them. The contract will carry with it the infirmity of the subject matter."

B.

If the Contract Clause is to retain any meaning at all, however, it must be understood to impose some limits upon the power of a State to abridge existing contractual relationships, even in the exercise of its otherwise legitimate police power. The existence and nature of those limits were clearly indicated in a series of cases in this Court arising from the efforts of the States to deal with the unprecedented emergencies brought on by the severe economic depression of the early 1930's.

In Home Building & Loan Assn. v. Blaisdell, 290 U.S. 398, the Court upheld against a Contract Clause attack a mortgage moratorium law that Minnesota had enacted to provide relief for homeowners threatened with foreclosure. Although the legislation conflicted directly with lenders' contractual foreclosure rights, the Court there acknowledged that, despite the Contract Clause, the States retain residual authority to enact laws "to safeguard the vital interests of [their] people." . . . In upholding the state mortgage moratorium law, the Court found five factors significant. First, the state legislature had declared in the Act itself that an emergency need for the protection of homeowners existed. . . . Second, the state law was enacted to protect a basic societal interest, not a favored group. . . . Third, the relief was appropriately tailored to the emergency that it was designed to meet. . . . Fourth, the imposed conditions were reasonable. . . . And, finally, the legislation was limited to the duration of the emergency. . . .

The *Blaisdell* opinion thus clearly implied that if the Minnesota moratorium legislation had not possessed the characteristics attributed to it by the Court, it would have been invalid under the Contract Clause of the Constitution. These implications were given concrete force in three cases that followed closely in *Blaisdell's* wake.

In W.B. Worthen Co. v. Thomas, 292 U.S. 426, the Court dealt with an Arkansas law that exempted the proceeds of a life insurance policy from collection by the beneficiary's judgment creditors. Stressing the retroactive effect of the state law, the Court held that it was invalid under the Contract Clause, since it was not precisely and reasonably designed to meet a grave temporary emergency in the interest of the general welfare. In W.B. Worthen Co. v. Kavanaugh, 295 U.S. 56, the Court was confronted with another Arkansas law that diluted the rights and remedies of mortgage bondholders. The Court held the law invalid under the Contract Clause. "Even when the public welfare is invoked as an excuse," Mr. Justice Cardozo wrote for the Court, the security of a mortgage cannot be cut down "without moderation or reason or in a spirit of oppression." . . . And finally, in Treigle v. Acme Homestead Assn., 297 U.S. 189, the Court held invalid under the Contract Clause a Louisiana law that modified the existing withdrawal rights of the members of a building and loan association. "Such an interference with the right of contract," said the Court, "cannot be justified by saying that in the public interest the operations of building associations may be controlled and regulated, or that in the same interest their charters may be amended."

. . .

III.

In applying these principles to the present case, the first inquiry must be whether the state law has, in fact, operated as a substantial impairment of a contractual relationship.[16] The severity of the impairment measures the height of the hurdle the state legislation must clear. Minimal alteration of contractual obligations may end the inquiry at its first stage. Severe impairment on the other hand, will push the inquiry to a careful examination of the nature and purpose of the state legislation.

The severity of an impairment of contractual obligations can be measured by the factors that reflect the high value the Framers placed on the protection of private contracts. Contracts enable individuals to order their personal and business affairs according to their particular needs and interests. Once arranged, those rights and obligations are binding under the law, and the parties are entitled to rely on them.

Here, the company's contracts of employment with its employees included as a fringe benefit or additional form of compensation, the pension plan. The company's maximum obligation was to set aside each year an amount based on the plan's requirements for vesting. The plan satisfied the current federal income tax code and was subject to no other legislative requirements. And, of course, the company was free to amend or terminate the pension plan at any time. The company thus had no reason to anticipate that its employees' pension rights could become vested except in accordance with the terms of the plan. It relied heavily, and reasonably, on this legitimate contractual expectation in calculating its annual contributions to the pension fund.

The effect of Minnesota's Private Pension Benefits Protection Act on this contractual obligation was severe. The company was required in 1974 to have made its contributions throughout the pre-1974 life of its plan as if employees' pension rights had vested after 10 years, instead of vesting in accord with the terms of the plan. Thus a basic term of the pension contract—one on which the company had relied for 10 years—was substantially modified. The result was that although the company's past contributions were adequate when made, they were not adequate when computed under the 10-year statutory vesting requirement. The Act thus forced a current recalculation of the past 10 years' contributions based on the new, unanticipated 10-year vesting requirement.

Not only did the state law thus retroactively modify the compensation that the company had agreed to pay its employees from 1963 to 1974, but it did so by changing the company's obligations in an area where the element of reliance was vital—the funding of a pension plan. . . .

Moreover, the retroactive state-imposed vesting requirement was applied only to those employers who terminated their pension plans or who, like the company, closed their Minnesota offices. The company was thus forced to

---

[16] The novel construction of the Contract Clause expressed in the dissenting opinion is wholly contrary to the decisions of this Court. The narrow view that the Clause forbids only state laws that diminish the duties of a contractual obligor and not laws that increase them, a view arguably suggested by *Satterlee v. Matthewson,* 2 Pet. 380, has since been expressly repudiated. . . . Moreover, in any bilateral contract the diminution of duties on one side effectively increases the duties on the other.

The even narrower view that the Clause is limited in its application to state laws relieving debtors of obligations to their creditors is, as the dissent recognizes, . . . completely at odds with this Court's decisions. See *Dartmouth College v. Woodward,* 4 Wheat. 518. . . .

make all the retroactive changes in its contractual obligations at one time. By simply proceeding to close its office in Minnesota, a move that had been planned before the passage of the Act, the company was assessed an immediate pension funding charge of approximately $185,000.

Thus, the statute in question here nullifies express terms of the company's contractual obligations and imposes a completely unexpected liability in potentially disabling amounts. There is not even any provision for gradual applicability or grace periods. Compare the Employee Retirement Income Security Act, 29 U.S.C. §§ 1061(b)(2), 1086(b), and 1144. See n. 23, infra. Yet there is no showing in the record before us that this severe disruption of contractual expectations was necessary to meet an important general social problem. The presumption favoring "legislative judgment as to the necessity and reasonableness of a particular measure," . . . simply cannot stand in this case.

. . .

Entering a field it had never before sought to regulate, the Minnesota Legislature grossly distorted the company's existing contractual relationships with its employees by superimposing retroactive obligations upon the company substantially beyond the terms of its employment contracts. And that burden was imposed upon the company only because it closed its office in the State.

This Minnesota law simply does not possess the attributes of those state laws that in the past have survived challenge under the Contract Clause of the Constitution. The law was not even purportedly enacted to deal with a broad, generalized economic or social problem. Cf. Home Building & Loan Assn. v. Blaisdell, 290 U.S., at 445. It did not operate in an area already subject to state regulation at the time the company's contractual obligations were originally undertaken, but invaded an area never before subject to regulation by the State. Cf. Veix v. Sixth Ward Assn., 310 U.S., at 38. It did not effect simply a temporary alteration of the contractual relationships of those within its coverage, but worked a severe, permanent, and immediate change in those relationships—irrevocably and retroactively. . . . And its narrow aim was levelled not at every Minnesota employer, not even at every Minnesota employer who left the State, . . . but only at those who had in the past been sufficiently enlightened as voluntarily to agree to establish pension plans for their employees.

"Not Blaisdell's case, but Worthen's (W.B. Worthen Co. v. Thomas, [292 U.S. 426]) supplies the applicable rule" here. W.B. Worthen Co. v. Kavanaugh, 295 U.S. 56, 63. It is not necessary to hold that the Minnesota law impaired the obligation of the company's employment contracts "without moderation or reason or in a spirit of oppression." . . . But we do hold that if the Contract Clause means anything at all, it means that Minnesota could not constitutionally do what it tried to do to the company in this case.

The judgment of the District Court is reversed.

It is so ordered.

Mr. Justice Blackmun took no part in the consideration or decision of this case.

Mr. Justice Brennan, with whom Mr. Justice White and Mr. Justice Marshall join, dissenting.

. . .

Today's decision greatly expands the reach of the [Contract] Clause. The Minnesota Private Pension Benefits Protection Act (Act) does not abrogate or dilute any obligation due a party to a private contract; rather, like all positive social legislation, the Act imposes new, additional obligations on a particular class of persons. In my view, any constitutional infirmity in the law must therefore derive, not from the Contract Clause, but from the Due Process

Clause of the Fourteenth Amendment. I perceive nothing in the Act that works a denial of Due Process and therefore I dissent.

.   .   .

II.

The primary question in this case is whether the Contract Clause is violated by state legislation enacted to protect employees covered by a pension plan by requiring an employer to make outlays—which, although not in this case, will largely be offset against future savings—to provide terminated employees with the equivalent of benefits reasonably to be expected under the plan. The Act does not relieve either the employer or his employees of any existing contract obligation. Rather, the Act simply creates an additional, supplemental duty of the employer, no different in kind from myriad duties created by a wide variety of legislative measures which defeat settled expectations but which have nonetheless been sustained by this Court. See, e.g., Usery v. Turner Elkhorn Mining Co., 428 U.S. 1 (1976); Hadacheck v. Sebastian, 239 U.S. 394 (1915). For this reason, the Minnesota Act, in my view, does not implicate the Contract Clause in any way. The basic fallacy of today's decision is its mistaken view that the Contract Clause protects all contract based expectations, including that of an employer that his obligations to his employees will not be legislatively enlarged beyond those explicitly provided in his pension plan.

.   .   .

C.

The Court seems to attempt to justify its distortion of the meaning of the Contract Clause on the ground that imposing new duties on one party to a contract can upset his contract based expectations as much as can laws that effectively relieve the other party of any duty to perform. But it is no more anomalous to give effect to the term "impairment" and deny a claimant protection under the Contract Clause when new duties are created than it is to give effect to the Clause's inapplicability to acts of the National Government and deny a Contract Clause remedy when an act of Congress denies a creditor the ability to enforce a contract right to payment. Both results are simply consequences of the fact that the Clause does not protect all contract based expectations.

More fundamentally, the Court's distortion of the meaning of the Contract Clause creates anomalies of its own and threatens to undermine the jurisprudence of property rights developed over the last 40 years. The Contract Clause, of course, is but one of several clauses in the Constitution that protect existing economic values from governmental interference. The Fifth Amendment's command that "private property [shall not] be taken for public use, without just compensation" is such a clause. A second is the Due Process Clause, which during the heyday of substantive due process, see Lochner v. New York, 198 U.S. 45 (1905), largely supplanted the Contract Clause in importance and operated as a potent limitation on Government's ability to interfere with economic expectations. . . . Decisions over the past 50 years have developed a coherent, unified interpretation of all the constitutional provisions that may protect economic expectations and these decisions have recognized a broad latitude in States to effect even severe interference with existing economic values when reasonably necessary to promote the general welfare. See Penn Central Transp. Co. v. New York City, 438 U.S. 104 . . . .. At the same time the prohibition of the Contract Clause, consistently with its wording and historic purposes, has been limited in application to state laws that diluted, with utter indifference to the legitimate interests of the beneficiary of a contract duty, the existing contract obligation. . . .

Today's conversion of the Contract Clause into a limitation on the power of States to enact laws that impose duties additional to obligations assumed under private contracts must inevitably produce results difficult to square with any rational conception of a constitutional order. Under the Court's opinion, any law that may be characterized as "superimposing" new obligations on those provided for by contract is to be regarded as creating "sudden, substantial, and unanticipated burdens" and then to be subjected to the most exacting scrutiny. The validity of such a law will turn upon whether judges see it as a law that deals with a generalized social problem, whether it is temporary (as few will be) or permanent, whether it operates in an area previously subject to regulation, and, finally, whether its duties apply to a broad class of persons. . . . The necessary consequence of the extreme malleability of these rather vague criteria is to vest judges with broad subjective discretion to protect property interests that happen to appeal to them.

To permit this level of scrutiny of laws that interfere with contract based expectations is an anomaly. There is nothing sancrosanct about expectations rooted in contract that justify according them a constitutional immunity denied other property rights. Laws that interfere with settled expectations created by state property law (and which impose severe economic burdens) are uniformly held constitutional where reasonably related to the promotion of the general welfare. Hadacheck v. Sebastian, 239 U.S. 394 (1915) is illustrative. There a property owner had established on a particular parcel of land a perfectly lawful business of a brickyard, and, in reliance on the existing law, continued to operate that business for a number of years. However, a local ordinance was passed prohibiting the operation of brickyards in the particular locale and diminishing the value of the claimant's parcel and thus of his investment by nearly 90%. Notwithstanding the effect of the ordinance on the value of the investment, the ordinance was sustained against a taking claim. See also Miller v. Schoene, 276 U.S. 272 (1928) (statute required cutting down ornamental red cedar trees because they had cedar rust which would be harmful to apple trees in the vicinity).

There is no logical or rational basis for sustaining the duties created by the laws in *Miller* and *Hadacheck,* but invalidating the duty created by the Minnesota Act. Surely, the Act effects no greater interference with reasonable reliance interests than did these other laws. Moreover, the laws operate identically: they all create duties that burden one class of persons and benefit another. The only difference between the present case and *Hadacheck* or *Miller* is that here there was a prior contractual relationship between the members of the benefited and burdened classes. I simply cannot accept that this difference should possess constitutional significance. The only means of avoiding this anomaly is to construe the Contract Clause consistently with its terms and the original understanding and hold it is inapplicable to laws which create new duties.

. . .

ENERGY RESERVES GROUP, INC. v. KANSAS POWER & LIGHT CO., 459 U.S. 400 (1983). In 1975 Kansas Power & Light Co. (KPL) entered into two contracts with the predecessor-in-interest of Energy Reserves Group, Inc. (ERG) to purchase natural gas from wells in Kansas. The initial price was $1.50 per thousand cubic feet (Mcf) of gas but the contracts contained a government price escalation clause under which the price would rise to any price fixed by a governmental authority.

Congress passed the Natural Gas Policy Act of 1978. Section 102 of the Act fixed a gradually increasing price for newly discovered natural gas which in December, 1978, was $2.078 per million British thermal units. Section 109 of the Act set a price for gas not otherwise covered at $1.63 per million Btus. The Act also for the first time regulated intrastate gas sales, fixing as a maximum price that under § 102 and permitting state regulation so long as prices fixed did not exceed the § 102 price. It is agreed that the gas contracts under dispute here were intrastate and governed by this latter provision.

Kansas promptly passed a statute applicable to natural gas contracts entered before 1977 and controlling gas prices only until 1984. It specifically prohibited gas price contracts to operate so as to increase the prices of old intrastate gas beyond those set in § 109 of the federal act.

ERG took the position that under the contracts the price escalated to that of § 102 under the federal act and that the state could not change the contracts. KPL contended that the state act applied and the price should be that under § 109 of the federal act. ERG brought a suit in Kansas courts which held that the Kansas act applied and that the contract clause did not require otherwise. The Supreme Court, in an opinion written by Justice Blackmun, unanimously agreed with the Kansas courts.

A

"Although the language of the Contract Clause is facially absolute, its prohibition must be accommodated to the inherent police power of the State 'to safeguard the vital interests of its people.' Home Bldg. & Loan Ass'n v. Blaisdell, 290 U.S. 398, 434 (1934). . . .

. . . .

"The threshold inquiry is 'whether the state law has, in fact, operated as a substantial impairment of a contractual relationship.' *Allied Structural Steel Co.,* 438 U.S., at 244. See *United States Trust Co.,* 431 U.S., at 17. The severity of the impairment is said to increase the level of scrutiny to which the legislation will be subjected. *Allied Structural Steel Co.,* 438 U.S., at 245. Total destruction of contractual expectations is not necessary for a finding of substantial impairment. *United States Trust Co.,* 431 U.S., at 26–27. On the other hand, state regulation that restricts a party to gains it reasonably expected from the contract does not necessarily constitute a substantial impairment. Id., at 31, citing El Paso v. Simmons, 379 U.S. 497, 515 (1965). In determining the extent of the impairment, we are to consider whether the industry the complaining party has entered has been regulated in the past. *Allied Structural Steel Co.,* 438 U.S., at 242, n. 13, citing Veix v. Sixth Ward Bldg. & Loan Ass'n, 310 U.S. 32, 38 (1940) ('When he purchased into an enterprise already regulated in the particular to which he now objects, he purchased subject to further legislation upon the same topic'). The Court long ago observed: 'One whose rights, such as they are, are subject to state restriction, cannot remove them from the power of the State by making a contract about them.' Hudson Water Co. v. McCarter, 209 U.S. 349, 357 (1908).

"If the state regulation constitutes a substantial impairment, the State, in justification, must have a significant and legitimate public purpose behind the regulation, *United States Trust Co.,* 431 U.S., at 22, such as the remedying of a broad and general social or economic problem. *Allied Structural Steel Co.,* 438 U.S., at 247, 249. Furthermore, since *Blaisdell,* the Court has indicated that the public purpose need not be addressed to an emergency or temporary situation. *United States Trust Co.,* 431 U.S., at 22, n. 19; Veix v. Sixth Ward Bldg. & Loan Ass'n, 310 U.S., at 39–40. One legitimate state interest is the elimination of unforeseen windfall profits. *United States Trust Co.,* 431 U.S., at 31, n. 30. The requirement of a legitimate public purpose guarantees that the State is exercising its police power, rather than providing a benefit to special interests.

"Once a legitimate public purpose has been identified, the next inquiry is whether the adjustment of 'the rights and responsibilities of contracting parties [is based] upon reasonable conditions and [is] of a character appropriate to the public purpose justifying [the legislation's] adoption.' *United States Trust Co.,* 431 U.S., at 22. Unless the State itself is a contracting party, see id., at 23 [14] '[a]s is customary in reviewing economic and social regulation, ... courts properly defer to legislative judgment as to the necessity and reasonableness of a particular measure.' Id., at 22–23.

B

"The threshold determination is whether the Kansas Act has impaired substantially ERG's contractual rights. Significant here is the fact that the parties are operating in a heavily regulated industry. . . .

. . . .

"Moreover, the contracts expressly recognize the existence of extensive regulation by providing that any contractual terms are subject to relevant present and future state and federal law. This latter provision could be interpreted to incorporate all future state price regulation, and thus dispose of the Contract Clause claim. Regardless of whether this interpretation is correct, the provision does suggest that ERG knew its contractual rights were subject to alteration by state price regulation. Price regulation existed and was foreseeable as the type of law that would alter contract obligations. Reading the Contract Clause as ERG does would mean that indefinite price escalator clauses could exempt ERG from any regulatory limitation of prices whatsoever. Such a result cannot be permitted. Hudson Water Co. v. McCarter, 209 U.S., at 357. In short, ERG's reasonable expectations have not been impaired by the Kansas Act. See El Paso v. Simmons, 379 U.S., at 515.

C

"To the extent, if any, the Kansas Act impairs ERG's contractual interests, the Kansas Act rests on, and is prompted by, significant and legitimate state interests. . . .

". . . There can be little doubt about the legitimate public purpose behind the Act.

"Nor are the means chosen to implement these purposes deficient, particularly in light of the deference to which the Kansas Legislature's judgment is entitled.

"We thus resolve the constitutional issue against ERG."

. . . .

"**Justice Powell, with whom The Chief Justice and Justice Rehnquist join, concurring.**

"I concur in the judgment and all of the Court's opinion except Part II–C. The Court concludes in Part II–B that there has been no substantial impairment of ERG's contractual rights. The closing sentence states that 'ERG's reasonable expectations have not been impaired by the Kansas Act.' This conclusion is

---

[14] See, generally, Note, A Process-Oriented Approach to the Contract Clause, 89 Yale L.J. 1623, 1647–1648 (1980) (distinguishing public from private contracts). In *United States Trust Co.,* but not in *Allied Structural Steel Co.,* the State was one of the contracting parties. When a State itself enters into a contract, it cannot simply walk away from its financial obligations. In almost every case, the Court has held a governmental unit to its contractual obligations when it enters financial or other markets. See *United States Trust Co.,* 431 U.S., at 25–28. . . . When the State is a party to the contract, "complete deference to a legislative assessment of reasonableness and necessity is not appropriate because the State's self-interest is at stake." *United States Trust Co.,* 431 U.S., at 26. In the present case, of course, the stricter standard of *United States Trust Co.* does not apply because Kansas has not altered its own contractual obligations.

dispositive, and it is unnecessary for the Court to address the question of whether, if there were an impairment of contractual rights, it would constitute a violation of the Contract Clause. See Allied Structural Steel Co. v. Spannaus, 438 U.S. 234, 245 (1978)."

———

EXXON CORP. v. EAGERTON, 462 U.S. 176 (1983). Alabama increased its severance tax on oil and gas and prohibited passing on the increase to purchasers. Some producers of oil and gas were parties to contracts made before the tax increase under which they were permitted to include in their price to customers any increase in severance taxes. The Court held unanimously that application of the pass-through prohibition to those contracts did not violate the contract clause. The Court said: "The prohibition applied to all oil and gas producers, regardless of whether they happened to be parties to sale contracts that contained a provision permitting them to pass tax increases through to their purchasers. The effect of the pass-through prohibition on existing contracts that did contain such a provision was incidental to its main effect of shielding consumers from the burden of the tax increase."

C. THE JUST COMPENSATION CLAUSE OF THE FIFTH AMENDMENT—WHAT DOES IT ADD TO DUE PROCESS?

———

PENN CENTRAL TRANSPORTATION CO. v. CITY OF NEW YORK

438 U.S. 104, 98 S.Ct. 2646, 57 L.Ed.2d 631 (1978).

Mr. Justice Brennan delivered the opinion of the Court.

The question presented is whether a city may, as part of a comprehensive program to preserve historic landmarks and historic districts, place restrictions on the development of individual historic landmarks—in addition to those imposed by applicable zoning ordinances—without effecting a "taking" requiring the payment of "just compensation." Specifically, we must decide whether the application of New York City's Landmarks Preservation Law to the parcel of land occupied by Grand Central Terminal has "taken" its owners' property in violation of the Fifth and Fourteenth Amendments.

I.

A.

Over the past 50 years, all 50 States and over 500 municipalities have enacted laws to encourage or require the preservation of buildings and areas with historic or aesthetic importance. These nationwide legislative efforts have been precipitated by two concerns. The first is recognition that, in recent years, large numbers of historic structures, landmarks, and areas have been destroyed without adequate consideration of either the values represented therein or the possibility of preserving the destroyed properties for use in economically productive ways. The second is a widely shared belief that structures with special historic, cultural, or architectural significance enhance the quality of life for all. Not only do these buildings and their workmanship represent the lessons of the past and embody precious features of our heritage, they serve as examples of quality for today. "[H]istoric conservation is but one aspect of the much larger problem, basically an environmental one, of enhancing—or perhaps developing for the first time—the quality of life for people."

New York City, responding to similar concerns and acting pursuant to a New York state enabling act, adopted its Landmarks Preservation Law in 1965.
.   .   .   .

The New York City law is typical of many urban landmark laws in that its primary method of achieving its goals is not by acquisitions of historic properties, but rather by involving public entities in land use decisions affecting these properties and providing services, standards, controls, and incentives that will encourage preservation by private owners and users. While the law does place special restrictions on landmark properties as a necessary feature to the attainment of its larger objectives, the major theme of the Act is to ensure the owners of any such properties both a "reasonable return" on their investments and maximum latitude to use their parcels for purposes not inconsistent with the preservation goals.

.   .   .

Although the designation of a landmark and landmark site restricts the owner's control over the parcel, designation also enhances the economic position of the landmark owner in one significant respect. Under New York City's zoning laws, owners of real property who have not developed their property to the full extent permitted by the applicable zoning laws are allowed to transfer development rights to contiguous parcels on the same city block.   .   .   .

B.

This case involves the application of New York City's Landmark Preservation Law to Grand Central Terminal (Terminal). The Terminal, which is owned by the Penn Central Transportation Company and its affiliates (Penn Central), is one of New York City's most famous buildings. Opened in 1913, it is regarded not only as providing an ingenious engineering solution to the problems presented by urban railroad stations, but also as a magnificent example of the French Beaux Arts style.

The Terminal is located in midtown Manhattan. Its south facade faces 42nd Street and that street's intersection with Park Avenue. At street level, the Terminal is bounded on the west by Vanderbilt Avenue, on the east by the Commodore Hotel, and on the north by the Pan-American Building. Although a 20-story office tower, to have been located above the Terminal, was part of the original design, the planned tower was never constructed. The Terminal itself is an eight-story structure which Penn Central uses as a railroad station and in which it rents space not needed for railroad purposes to a variety of commercial interests. The Terminal is one of a number of properties owned by appellant Penn Central in this area of midtown Manhattan. The other include the Barclay, Biltmore, Commodore, Roosevelt, and Waldorf-Astoria Hotels, the Pan-American Building and other office buildings along Park Avenue, and the Yale Club. At least eight of these are eligible to be recipients of development rights afforded the Terminal by virtue of landmark designation.

On August 2, 1967, following a public hearing, the Commission designated the Terminal a "landmark" and designated the "city tax block" it occupies a "landmark site." The Board of Estimate confirmed this action on September 21, 1967. Although appellant Penn Central had opposed the designation before the Commission, it did not seek judicial review of the final designation decision.

On January 22, 1968, appellant Penn Central, to increase its income, entered into a renewable 50-year lease and sublease agreement with appellant UGP Properties, Inc. (UGP), a wholly owned subsidiary of Union General Properties, Ltd., a United Kingdom corporation. Under the terms of the agreement, UGP was to construct a multistory office building above the Terminal. UGP promised to pay Penn Central $1 million annually during construction and at least $3 million annually thereafter. The rentals would be offset in part by a loss of some $700,000 to $1 million in net rentals presently received from concessionaires displaced by the new building.

Appellants UGP and Penn Central then applied to the Commission for permission to construct an office building atop the Terminal. Two separate plans, both designed by architect Marcel Breuer and both apparently satisfying the terms of the applicable zoning ordinance, were submitted to the Commission for approval. The first, Breuer I, provided for the construction of a 55-story office building, to be cantilevered above the existing facade and to rest on the roof of the Terminal. The second, Breuer II Revised, called for tearing down a portion of the Terminal that included the 42nd Street facade, stripping off some of the remaining features of the Terminal's facade, and constructing a 53-story office building. The Commission denied a certificate of no exterior effect on September 20, 1968. Appellants then applied for a certificate of "appropriateness" as to both proposals. After four days of hearings at which over 80 witnesses testified, the Commission denied this application as to both proposals.

. . . .

Appellants did not seek judicial review of the denial of either certificate. . . . Instead, appellants filed suit in New York Supreme Court, Trial Term, claiming, *inter alia,* that the application of the Landmarks Preservation Law had "taken" their property without just compensation in violation of the Fifth and Fourteenth Amendments and arbitrarily deprived them of their property without Due Process of law in violation of the Fourteenth Amendment. Appellants sought a declaratory judgment, injunctive relief barring the city from using the Landmarks Law to impede the construction of any structure that may otherwise lawfully be constructed on the Terminal site, and damages for the "temporary taking" that occurred between August 2, 1967, the designation date, and the date when the restrictions arising from the Landmarks Law are lifted. The trial court granted the injunctive and declaratory relief, but severed the question of damages for a "temporary taking."

Appellee, the city, appealed, and the New York Supreme Court, Appellate Division, reversed. . . .

The New York Court of Appeals affirmed. . . .

. . . We noted probable jurisdiction. 434 U.S. 983 (1977). We affirm.

II.

The issues presented by appellants are (1) whether the restrictions imposed by New York City's law upon appellants' exploitation of the Terminal site effect a "taking" of appellants' property for a public use within the meaning of the Fifth Amendment, which of course is made applicable to the States through the Fourteenth Amendment, see Chicago B. & Q.R. Co. v. Chicago, 166 U.S. 226, 239 (1897) and, (2) if so, whether the transferable development rights afforded appellants constitute "just compensation" within the meaning of the Fifth Amendment. We need only address the question whether a "taking" has occurred.[25]

A.

Before considering appellants' specific contentions, it will be useful to review the factors that have shaped the jurisprudence of the Fifth Amendment injunction "nor shall private property be taken for public use, without just compensation." The question of what constitutes a "taking" for purposes of the

---

[25] As is implicit in our opinion, we do not embrace the proposition that a "taking" can never occur unless Government has transferred physical control over a portion of a parcel.

Fifth Amendment has proved to be a problem of considerable difficulty. While this Court has recognized that the "Fifth Amendment's guarantee [is] designed to bar Government from forcing some people alone to bear public burdens which, in all fairness and justice, should be borne by the public as a whole," Armstrong v. United States, 364 U.S. 40, 49 (1960), this Court, quite simply, has been unable to develop any "set formula" for determining when "justice and fairness" require that economic injuries caused by public action be compensated by the Government, rather than remain disproportionately concentrated on a few persons. See Goldblatt v. Hempstead, 369 U.S. 590, 594 (1962). Indeed, we have frequently observed that whether a particular restriction will be rendered invalid by the Government's failure to pay for any losses proximately caused by it depends largely "upon the particular circumstances [in that] case." United States v. Central Eureka Mining Co., 357 U.S. 155, 168 (1958)
. . . .

In engaging in these essentially ad hoc, factual inquiries, the Court's decisions have identified several factors that have particular significance. The economic impact of the regulation on the claimant and, particularly, the extent to which the regulation has interfered with distinct investment backed expectations are of course relevant considerations. . . . So too is the character of the governmental action. A "taking" may more readily be found when the interference with property can be characterized as a physical invasion by Government, see, e.g., Causby v. United States, 328 U.S. 256 (1946), than when interference arises from some public program adjusting the benefits and burdens of economic life to promote the common good.

"Government could hardly go on if to some extent values incident to property could not be diminished without paying for every such change in the general law," Pennsylvania Coal Co. v. Mahon, 260 U.S. 393, 413 (1922), and this Court has accordingly recognized, in a wide variety of contexts, that Government may execute laws or programs that adversely affect recognized economic values. Exercises of the taxing power are one obvious example. A second are the decisions in which this Court has dismissed "taking" challenges on the ground that, while the challenged Government action caused economic harm, it did not interfere with interests that were sufficiently bound up with the reasonable expectations of the claimant to constitute "property" for Fifth Amendment purposes. See, e.g., United States v. Willow River Power Co., 324 U.S. 499 (1945) (interest in high water level of river for run off for tail waters to maintain power head is not property); United States v. Chandler-Dunbar Water Power Co., 229 U.S. 53 (1913) (no property interest can exist in navigable waters); see also . . . .; Sax, Takings and the Police Power, 74 Yale L.J. 36, 61–62 (1963).

More importantly for the present case, in instances in which a state tribunal reasonably concluded that "the health, safety, morals or general welfare" would be promoted by prohibiting particular contemplated uses of land, this Court has upheld land use regulations that destroyed or adversely affected recognized real property interests. See Nectow v. City of Cambridge, 277 U.S. 183, 188 (1928). Zoning laws are of course the classic example, see Euclid v. Ambler Realty Co., 272 U.S. 365 (1926) (prohibition of industrial use); Gorieb v. Fox, 274 U.S. 603, 608 (1927) (requirement that portions of parcels be left unbuilt); Welch v. Swasey, 214 U.S. 91 (1909) (height restriction), which have been viewed as permissible governmental action even when prohibiting the most beneficial use of the property. . . .

Zoning laws generally do not affect existing uses of real property, but taking challenges have also been held to be without merit in a wide variety of situations when the challenged governmental actions prohibited a beneficial use to which individual parcels had previously been devoted and thus caused

substantial individualized harm.   Miller v. Schoene, 276 U.S. 272 (1928), is
illustrative.   In that case, a state entomologist, acting pursuant to a state statute,
ordered the claimants to cut down a large number of ornamental red cedar trees
because they produced cedar rust fatal to apple trees cultivated nearby.   Although the statute provided for recovery of any expense incurred in removing
the cedars, and permitted claimants to use the felled trees, it did not provide
compensation for the value of the standing trees or for the resulting decrease in
market value of the properties as a whole.   A unanimous Court held that this
latter omission did not render the statute invalid.   The Court held that the State
might properly make "a choice between the preservation of one class of
property and that of the other" and since the apple industry was important in
the State involved, concluded that the State had not exceeded "its constitutional
powers by deciding upon the destruction of one class of property [without
compensation] in order to save another, which, in the judgment of the legislature, is of greater value to the public."

Again, Hadacheck v. Sebastian, 239 U.S. 394 (1915), upheld a law prohibiting the claimant from continuing his otherwise lawful business of operating a
brickyard in a particular physical community on the ground that the legislature
had reasonably concluded that the presence of the brickyard was inconsistent
with neighboring uses.   See also United States v. Central Eureka Mining Co.,
supra (government order closing gold mines so that skilled miners would be
available for other mining work held not a taking); Atchison, T. & S.F.R. Co. v.
Public Utilities Comm., 346 U.S. 346 (1953) (railroad may be required to pay
cost of constructing railroad grade crossing); Walls v. Midland Carbon Co., 254
U.S. 300 (1920) (law prohibiting manufacture of carbon black upheld); Rein-
man v. Little Rock, 237 U.S. 171 (1915) (law prohibiting livery stable upheld);
Mugler v. Kansas, 123 U.S. 623 (1887) (law prohibiting liquor business
upheld).

Goldblatt v. Hempstead, supra, is a recent example.   There, a 1958 city
safety ordinance banned any excavations below the water table and effectively
prohibited the claimant from continuing a sand and gravel mining business that
had been operated on the particular parcel since 1927.   The Court upheld the
ordinance against a "taking" challenge, although the ordinance prohibited the
present and presumably most beneficial use of the property and had, like the
regulations in *Miller* and *Hadacheck,* impacted severely on a particular owner.
The Court assumed that the ordinance did not prevent the owner's reasonable
use of the property since the owner made no showing for an adverse effect on
the value of the land.   Because the restriction served a substantial public
purpose, the Court thus held no taking had occurred.   It is of course implicit in
Goldblatt that a use restriction on real property may constitute a "taking" if not
reasonably necessary to the effectuation of a substantial public purpose . . .
or perhaps if it has an unduly harsh impact upon the owner's use of the
property.

Pennsylvania Coal Co. v. Mahon, 260 U.S. 393 (1922), is the leading case
for the proposition that a state statute that substantially furthers important public
policies may so frustrate distinct investment-backed expectations as to amount to
a "taking."   There the claimant had sold the surface rights to particular parcels
of property, but expressly reserved the right to remove the coal thereunder.   A
Pennsylvania statute, enacted after the transactions, forbade any mining of coal
that caused the subsidence of any house, unless the house was the property of
the owner of the underlying coal and was more than 150 feet from the
improved property of another.   Because the statute made it commercially
impracticable to mine the coal, and thus had nearly the same effect as the
complete destruction of rights claimant had purchased from the owners of the
surface land, the Court held that the statute was invalid as effecting a "taking"

without just compensation. See also Armstrong v. United States, supra. (Government's complete destruction of a materialman's lien in certain property held a "taking"); Hudson Water Co. v. McCarter, 209 U.S. 349, 355 (1908) (if height restriction makes property wholly useless "the right of property prevails over the public interest" and compensation is required). See generally Michelman, Property, Utility, and Fairness: Comments on the Ethical Foundations of "Just Compensation" Law, 80 Harv.L.Rev. 1165, 1229–1234 (1967).

Finally, Government actions that may be characterized as acquisitions of resources to permit or facilitate uniquely public functions have often been held to constitute "takings." Causby v. United States, supra, is illustrative. In holding that direct overflights above the claimant's land, that destroyed the present use of the land as a chicken farm, constituted a "taking." *Causby* emphasized that Government had not "merely destroyed property [but was] using a part of it for the flight of its planes." See also Griggs v. Allegheny County, 369 U.S. 84 (1962) (overflights held a taking); Portsmouth Co. v. United States, 260 U.S. 327 (1922) (United States' military installations repeated firing of guns over claimant's land is a taking); United States v. Cress, 243 U.S. 316 (1917) (repeated floodings of land caused by water project is taking); but see YMCA v. United States, 395 U.S. 85 (1969) (damage caused to building when federal officers who were seeking to protect building were attacked by rioters held not a taking). See generally Michelman, 80 Harv.L. Rev. 1165, 1226–1229 (1967); Sax, 74 Yale L.J. 36 (1963).

B.

In contending that the New York City law has "taken" their property in violation of the Fifth and Fourteenth Amendments, appellants make a series of arguments, which, while tailored to the facts of this case, essentially urge that any substantial restriction imposed pursuant to a landmark law must be accompanied by just compensation if it is to be constitutional. Before considering these, we emphasize what is not in dispute. Because this Court has recognized, in a number of settings, that States and cities may enact land use restrictions or controls to enhance the quality of life by preserving the character and desirable aesthetic features of a city, . . . appellants do not contest that New York City's objective of preserving structures and areas with special historic, architectural, or cultural significance is an entirely permissible governmental goal. They also do not dispute that the restrictions imposed on its parcel are appropriate means of securing the purposes of the New York City law. Finally, appellants do not challenge any of the specific factual premises of the decision below. They accept for present purposes both that the parcel of land occupied by Grand Central Terminal must, in its present state, be regarded as capable of earning a reasonable return, and that the transferable development rights afforded appellants by virtue of the Terminal's designation as a landmark are valuable, even if not as valuable as the rights to construct above the Terminal. In appellants' view none of these factors derogate from their claim that New York City's law has effected a "taking."

They first observe that the airspace above the Terminal is a valuable property interest, citing United States v. Causby, supra. They urge that the Landmark Law has deprived them of any gainful use of their "air rights" above the Terminal and that, irrespective of the value of the remainder of their parcel the city has "taken" their right to this superadjacent air space, thus entitling them to "just compensation" measured by the fair market value of these air rights.

Apart from our own disagreement with appellants' characterization of the effect of the New York law, see infra, the submission that appellants may establish a "taking" simply by showing that they have been denied the ability to exploit a property interest that they heretofore had believed was available for development is quite simply untenable. Were this the rule, this Court would have erred not only in upholding laws restricting the development of air rights, see Welch v. Swasey, supra, but also in approving those prohibiting both the subjacent, see Goldblatt v. Hempstead, supra, and the lateral development, see Gorieb v. Fox, supra, of particular parcels.[27] "Taking" jurisprudence does not divide a single parcel into discrete segments and attempt to determine whether rights in a particular segment have been entirely abrogated. In deciding whether a particular governmental action has effected a taking, this Court focuses rather both on the character of the action and on the nature and extent of the interference with rights in the parcel as a whole, here, the city tax block designated as the "landmark site."

Secondly, appellants, focusing on the character and impact of the New York City law, argue that it effects a "taking" because its operation has significantly diminished the value of the Terminal site. Appellants concede that the decisions sustaining other land use regulations, which, like the New York law, are reasonably related to the promotion of the general welfare, uniformly reject the proposition that diminution in property value, standing alone, can establish a taking, see Euclid v. Ambler Realty Co., supra (75% diminution in value caused by zoning law); Hadacheck v. Sebastian, supra (87½% diminution in value); cf. Eastlake v. Forest City Enterprises, Inc., 426 U.S., at 476 n. 8, and that the taking issue in these contexts is resolved by focusing on the uses the regulations permit. See also Goldblatt v. Hempstead, supra. Appellants, moreover, also do not dispute that a showing of diminution in property value would not establish a taking if the restriction had been imposed as a result of historic district legislation, see generally Maher v. City of New Orleans, 516 F.2d 1051 (5th Cir.1975), but appellants argue that New York City's regulation of individual landmarks is fundamentally different from zoning or from historic district legislation because the controls imposed by New York City's law apply only to individuals who own selected properties.

Stated baldly, appellants' position appears to be that the only means of ensuring that selected owners are not singled out to endure financial hardship for no reason is to hold that any restriction imposed on individual landmarks pursuant to the New York scheme is a "taking" requiring the payment of "just compensation." Agreement with this argument would of course invalidate not just New York City's law, but all comparable landmark legislation in the Nation. We find no merit in it.

It is true, as appellants emphasize, that both historic district legislation and zoning laws regulate all properties within given physical communities whereas landmark laws apply only to selected parcels. But, contrary to appellants' suggestions, landmark laws are not like discriminatory, or "reverse spot," zoning: that is, a land use decision which arbitrarily singles out a particular parcel for different, less favorable treatment than the neighboring ones. See 2 Rathkopf, The Law of Zoning and Planning 26–4 and 26–4—26–5, n. 6 (2d Ed. 1977). In contrast to discriminatory zoning, which is the antithesis of land use control as part of some comprehensive plan, the New York City law embodies a comprehensive plan to preserve structures of historic or aesthetic interest wherever they might be found in the city, and as noted, over 400 landmarks and 31 historic districts have been designated pursuant to this plan.

---

[27] These cases dispose of any contention that might be based on Pennsylvania Coal Co. v. Mahon, supra, that full use of air rights is so bound up with the investment backed expectations of appellants that Governmental deprivation of these rights invariably—i.e., irrespective of the impact of the restriction on the value of the parcel as a whole—constitutes a "taking." Similarly, *Welch, Goldblatt,* and *Gorieb* illustrate the fallacy of appellants' related contention that a "taking" must be found to have occurred whenever the land use restriction may be characterized as imposing a "servitude" on the claimant's parcel.

Equally without merit is the related argument that the decision to designate a structure as a landmark "is inevitably arbitrary or at least subjective because it basically is a matter of taste," . . . thus unavoidably singling out individual landowners for disparate and unfair treatment. The argument has a particularly hollow ring in this case. For appellants not only did not seek judicial review of either the designation or of the denials of the certificates of appropriateness and of no exterior effect, but do not even now suggest that the Commission's decisions concerning the Terminal were in any sense arbitrary or unprincipled. But, in any event, a landmark owner has a right to judicial review of any Commission decision, and, quite simply, there is no basis whatsoever for a conclusion that courts will have any greater difficulty identifying arbitrary or discriminatory action in the context of landmark regulation than in the context of classic zoning or indeed in any other context.

Next, appellants observe that New York City's law differs from zoning laws and historic district ordinances in that the Landmark Law does not impose identical or similar restrictions on all structures located in particular physical communities. It follows, they argue, that New York City's law is inherently incapable of producing the fair and equitable distribution of benefits and burdens of governmental action which is characteristic of zoning laws and historic district legislation and which they maintain is a constitutional requirement if "just compensation" is not to be afforded. It is of course true that the Landmark Law has a more severe impact on some landowners than on others, but that in itself does not mean that the law effects a "taking." Legislation designed to promote the general welfare commonly burdens some more than others. The owners of the brickyard in *Hadacheck*, of the cedar trees in Miller v. Schoene, and of the gravel and sand mine in Goldblatt v. Hempstead, were uniquely burdened by the legislation sustained in those cases.[30] Similarly, zoning laws often impact more severely on some property owners than others but have not been held to be invalid on that account. For example, the property owner in *Euclid* who wished to use his property for industrial purposes was affected far more severely by the ordinance than his neighbors who wished to use their land for residences.

In any event, appellants' repeated suggestions that they are solely burdened and unbenefited is factually inaccurate. This contention overlooks the fact that the New York City law applies to vast numbers of structures in the city in addition to the Terminal—all the structures contained in the 31 historic districts and over 400 individual landmarks, many of which are close to the Terminal. Unless we are to reject the judgment of the New York City Council that the preservation of landmarks benefit all New York citizens and all structures, both economically and by improving the quality of life in the city as a whole—which we are unwilling to do—we cannot conclude that the owners of the Terminal have in no sense been benefited by the Landmark Law. Doubtless appellants

---

[30] Appellants attempt to distinguish these cases on the ground that, in each, Government was prohibiting a "noxious" use of land and that in the present case, in contrast, appellants' proposed construction above the Terminal would be beneficial. We observe that the uses in issue in *Hadacheck, Miller,* and *Goldblatt* were perfectly lawful in themselves. They involved no "blameworthiness, ... moral wrongdoing, or conscious act of dangerous risk-taking which induce[d society] to shift the cost to a particular individual." Sax, 74 Yale L.J. 36, 50 (1964). These cases are better understood as resting not on any supposed "noxious" quality of the prohibited uses but rather on the ground that the restrictions were reasonably related to the implementation of a policy—not unlike historic preservation—expected to produce a widespread public benefit and applicable to all similarly situated property.

Nor, correlatively, can it be asserted that the destruction or fundamental alteration of a historic landmark is not harmful. The suggestion that the beneficial quality of appellants' proposed construction is established by the fact the construction would have been consistent with applicable zoning laws ignores the development in sensibilities and ideals reflected in landmark legislation like New York City's. . . .

believe they are more burdened than benefited by the law, but that must have been true too of the property owners in *Miller, Hadacheck, Euclid,* and *Goldblatt.*[32]

Appellants' final broad-based attack would have us treat the law as an instance, like that in United States v. Causby, supra, in which Government, acting in an enterprise capacity, has appropriated part of their property for some strictly governmental purpose. Apart from the fact that *Causby* was a case of invasion of airspace that destroyed the use of the farm beneath and this New York City law has in no wise impaired the present use of the Terminal, the Landmark Law neither exploits appellants' parcel for city purposes nor facilitates nor arises from any entrepreneurial operations of the city. The situation is not remotely like that in *Causby* when the airspace above the Terminal was in the flight pattern for military aircraft. The Landmark Law's effect is simply to prohibit appellants or anyone else from occupying portions of the airspace above the Terminal, while permitting appellants to use the remainder of the parcel in a gainful fashion. This is no more an appropriation of property by Government for its own uses than is a zoning law prohibiting, for "aesthetic" reasons, two or more adult theatres within a specified area, see Young v. American Mini Theatres, Inc., supra, or a safety regulation prohibiting excavations below a certain level. See Goldblatt v. City of Hempstead, supra.

C.

Rejection of appellants' broad arguments is not however the end of our inquiry, for all we thus far have established is that the New York law is not rendered invalid by its failure to provide "just compensation" whenever a landmark owner is restricted in the exploitation of property interests, such as air rights, to a greater extent than provided for under applicable zoning laws. We now must consider whether the interference with appellants' property is of such a magnitude that "there must be an exercise of eminent domain and compensation to sustain [it]." Pennsylvania Coal Co. v. Mahon, 260 U.S., at 413. That inquiry may be narrowed to the question of the severity of the impact of the law on appellants' parcel, and its resolution in turn requires a careful assessment of the impact of the regulation on the Terminal site.

Unlike the governmental acts in *Goldblatt, Miller, Causby, Griggs,* and *Hadacheck,* the New York City law does not interfere in any way with the present uses of the Terminal. Its designation as a landmark not only permits but contemplates that appellants may continue to use the property precisely as it has for the past 65 years: as a railroad terminal containing office space and concessions. So the law does not interfere with what must be regarded as Penn Central's primary expectation concerning the use of the parcel. More importantly, on this record, we must regard the New York City law as permitting Penn Central not only to profit from the Terminal but to obtain a "reasonable return" on its investment.

Appellants, moreover, exaggerate the effect of the Act on its ability to make use of the air rights above the Terminal in two respects. First, it simply cannot be maintained, on this record, that appellants have been prohibited from occupying *any* portion of the airspace above the Terminal. . . . Since appellants have not sought approval for the construction of a smaller structure, we do not know that appellants will be denied any use of any portion of the airspace above the Terminal.

Second, to the extent appellants have been denied the right to build above the Terminal, it is not literally accurate to say that they have been denied *all* use

---

[32] It is of course true that the fact the duties imposed by zoning and historic district legislation apply throughout particular physical communities provides assurances against arbitrariness, but the applicability of the landmarks law to large number of parcels in the city, in our view, provides comparable, if not identical, assurances.

of even those pre-existing air rights. Their ability to use these rights has not been abrogated; they are made transferable to at least eight parcels in the vicinity of the Terminal, one or two of which have been found suitable for the construction of new office buildings. Although appellants and others have argued that New York City's transferable development rights program is far from ideal, the New York courts here supportably found that, at least in the case of the Terminal, the rights afforded are valuable. While these rights may well not have constituted "just compensation" if a "taking" had occurred, the rights nevertheless undoubtedly mitigate whatever financial burdens the law has imposed on appellants and, for that reason, are to be taken into account in considering the impact of regulation. . . .

On this record we conclude that the application of New York City's Landmark Preservation Law has not effected a "taking" of appellants' property. The restrictions imposed are substantially related to the promotion of the general welfare and not only permit reasonable beneficial use of the landmark site but afford appellants opportunities further to enhance not only the Terminal site proper but also other properties.[36]

Affirmed.

Mr. Justice Rehnquist, with whom The Chief Justice and Mr. Justice Stevens join, dissenting.

. . .

I.

The Fifth Amendment provides in part: "nor shall private property be taken for public use, without just compensation." In a very literal sense, the actions of appellees violated this constitutional prohibition. Before the city of New York declared Grand Central Terminal to be a Landmark, Penn Central could have used its "air rights" over the Terminal to building a multistory office building, at an apparent value of several million dollars per year. Today, the Terminal cannot be modified in *any* form, including the erection of additional stories, without the permission of the Landmark Preservation Commission, a permission which appellants, despite good-faith attempts, have so far been unable to obtain. . . .

. . .

II.

Over 50 years ago, Justice Holmes, speaking for the Court, warned that the courts were "in danger of forgetting that a strong public desire to improve the public condition is not enough to warrant achieving the desire by a shorter cut than the constitutional way of paying for the change." Pennsylvania Coal Co. v. Mahon, 260 U.S., at 416. The Court's opinion in this case demonstrates that the danger thus foreseen has not abated. The city of New York is in a precarious financial state, and some may believe that the costs of landmark preservation will be more easily borne by corporations such as Penn Central than the overburdened individual taxpayers of New York. But these concerns do not allow us to ignore past precedents construing the Eminent Domain Clause to the end that the desire to improve the public condition is, indeed, achieved by a shorter cut than the constitutional way of paying for the damage.

---

[36] We emphasize that our holding today is on the present record which in turn is based on Penn Central's present ability to use the Terminal for its intended purposes and in a gainful fashion. The city conceded at oral argument that if appellants can demonstrate at some point in the future that circumstances have changed such that the Terminal ceases to be, in the city's counsel's words, "economically viable," appellants may obtain relief.

PRUNEYARD SHOPPING CENTER v. ROBINS, 447 U.S. 74 (1980). The California Supreme Court held that the free speech provision of the California constitution compelled the owner of a large shopping center to permit a group of students to set up a card table in a corner of the central courtyard to solicit support for their opposition to a United Nations resolution against "Zionism." One argument made against the result below was that it constituted a taking of private property without just compensation. On this issue the Court said:

"Appellants next contend that a right to exclude others underlies the Fifth Amendment guarantee against the taking of property without just compensation and the Fourteenth Amendment guarantee against the deprivation of property without due process of law.

"It is true that one of the essential sticks in the bundle of property rights is the right to exclude others. Kaiser Aetna v. United States, 444 U.S. 164, 176, 177 (1979). And here there has literally been a 'taking' of that right to the extent that the California Supreme Court has interpreted the state constitution to entitle its citizens to exercise free expression and petition rights on shopping center property. But it is well-established that 'not every destruction or injury to property by governmental action has been held to be a "taking" in the constitutional sense.' Armstrong v. United States, 364 U.S. 40, 48 (1960). Rather, the determination whether a state law unlawfully infringes a landowner's property in violation of the Taking Clause requires an examination of whether the restriction on private property 'forc[es] some people alone to bear public burdens which, in all fairness and justice, should be borne by the public as a whole.' Id., at 49. This examination entails inquiry into such factors as the character of the governmental action, its economic impact, and its interference with reasonable investment backed expectations. Kaiser Aetna v. United States, 444 U.S., at 164. When 'regulation goes too far it will be recognized as a taking.' Pennsylvania Coal Co. v. Mahon, 260 U.S., at 415.

"Here the requirement that appellants permit appellees to exercise state-protected rights of free expression and petition on shopping center property clearly does not amount to an unconstitutional infringement of appellants' property rights under the Taking Clause. There is nothing to suggest that preventing appellants from prohibiting this sort of activity will unreasonably impair the value or use of their property as a shopping center. The PruneYard is a large commercial complex that covers several city blocks, contains numerous separate business establishments, and is open to the public at large. The decision of the California Supreme Court makes it clear that the PruneYard may restrict expressive activity by adopting time, place and manner regulations that will minimize any interference with its commercial functions. Appellees were orderly, and they limited their activity to the common areas of the shopping center. In these circumstances, the fact that they may have 'physically invaded' appellants' property cannot be viewed as determinative.

"This case is quite different from Kaiser Aetna v. United States, supra. Kaiser Aetna was a case in which the owners of a private pond had invested substantial amounts of money in dredging the pond, developing it into an exclusive marina, and building a surrounding marina community. The marina was open only to fee-paying members, and the fees were paid in part 'to maintain the privacy and security of the pond.' Id., 444 U.S., at 166–168. The Federal Government sought to compel free public use of the private marina on the ground that the marina became subject to the federal navigational servitude because the owners had dredged a channel connecting it to 'navigable water.'

"The Government's attempt to create a public right of access to the improved pond interfered with Kaiser Aetna's 'reasonable investment backed expectations.' We held that it went 'so far beyond ordinary regulation or improvement for navigation as to amount to a taking. . . .' Id., 444 U.S., at 177–179. Nor as a general proposition is the United States, as opposed to the several States, possessed of residual authority that enables it to define 'property' in the first instance. A State is, of course, bound by the Just Compensation Clause of the Fifth Amendment, Chicago, Burlington & Quincy Railroad Co. v. Chicago, 166 U.S. 226, 233, 236–237 (1897), but here appellants have failed to demonstrate that the 'right to exclude others' is so essential to the use or economic value of their property that the State-authorized limitation of it amounted to a 'taking.' "

WEBB'S FABULOUS PHARMACIES, INC. v. BECKWITH, 449 U.S. 155 (1980). An interpleader fund was deposited in the registry of the county court to be subjected to the claims of creditors. Under the applicable state statute the clerk of the court received a fee calculated with reference to the size of the fund plus all interest accruing on the fund while on deposit. A receiver was appointed who claimed that the interest on the fund (over $100,000) belonged to the creditors not the clerk. The Supreme Court unanimously held the statute invalid insofar as it provided that the clerk should retain the interest in addition to the fee provided for the clerk's services. The Court said:

". . . The earnings of a fund are incidents of ownership of the fund itself and are property just as the fund itself is property. The state statute has the practical effect of appropriating for the county the value of the use of the fund for the period in which it is held in the registry.

"To put it another way: A State, by *ipse dixit,* may not transform private property into public property without compensation, even for the limited duration of the deposit in court. This is the very kind of thing that the Taking Clause of the Fifth Amendment was meant to prevent. That Clause stands as a shield against the arbitrary use of government property."

LORETTO v. TELEPROMPTER MANHATTAN CATV CORP., 458 U.S. 419 (1982). A New York law, passed in 1973 to facilitate tenant access to cable TV, requires property owners to permit the installation of cable facilities on their properties at a one-time payment of $1. This suit was brought in the state court alleging that such cable installations were trespasses and takings of property without just compensation. The New York courts upheld the law, the Court of Appeals stating that it served the legitimate public purpose of "rapid development of and maximum penetration by a means of communication which has important educational and community aspects."

The Supreme Court, in an opinion by Justice Marshall, reversed, concluding "that a permanent physical occupation authorized by government is a taking without regard to the public interests that it may serve." First, the opinion examined prior cases and concluded: "In short, when the 'character of the governmental action,' . . . is a permanent physical occupation of property, our cases uniformly have found a taking to the extent of the occupation, without regard to whether the action achieves an important public benefit or has only minimal economic impact on the owner." Second, the opinion asserted that the "historical rule that a permanent physical occupation of another's property is a taking has more than tradition to commend it. Such an appropriation is perhaps the most serious form of an invasion of an owner's property interest . . . . [T]he government does not simply take a single 'strand' from the 'bundle' of property rights: it chops through the bundle, taking a slice of every strand." Third, the Court concluded that this kind of permanent cable installation constitutes a taking under the traditional test.

The Court concluded:

"Our holding today is very narrow. We affirm the traditional rule that a permanent physical occupation of property is a taking. In such a case, the property owner entertains an historically-rooted expectation of compensation, and the character of the invasion is qualitatively more intrusive than perhaps any other category of property regulation. We do not, however, question the equally substantial authority upholding a State's broad power to impose appropriate restrictions upon an owner's *use* of his property."

Justice Blackmun, joined by Justices Brennan and White, dissented. His position is suggested by the opening paragraphs of the opinion:

"If the Court's decisions construing the Takings Clause state anything clearly, it is that '[t]here is no set formula to determine where regulation ends and taking begins.' Goldblatt v. Town of Hempstead, 369 U.S. 590, 594 (1962).

"In a curiously anachronistic decision, the Court today acknowledges its historical disavowal of set formulae in almost the same breath as it constructs a rigid *per se* takings rule: 'a permanent physical occupation authorized by government is a taking without regard to the public interests that it may serve.' To sustain its rule against our recent precedents, the Court erects a strained and untenable distinction between 'temporary physical invasions,' whose constitutionality concededly 'is subject to a balancing process,' and 'permanent physical occupations,' which are 'taking[s] without regard to other factors that a court might ordinarily examine.'

"In my view, the Court's approach 'reduces the constitutional issue to a formalistic quibble' over whether property has been 'permanently occupied' or 'temporarily invaded.' Sax, Takings and the Police Power, 74 Yale L.J. 36, 37 (1964). The Court's application of its formula to the facts of this case vividly illustrates that its approach is potentially dangerous as well as misguided. Despite its concession that 'States have broad power to regulate . . . the landlord-tenant relationship . . . without paying compensation for all economic injuries that such regulation entails,' the Court uses its rule to undercut a carefully-considered legislative judgment concerning landlord-tenant relationships. I therefore respectfully dissent."

RUCKELSHAUS v. MONSANTO COMPANY

___ U.S. ___, 104 S.Ct. 2862, 81 L.Ed.2d 815 (1984).

Justice Blackmun delivered the opinion of the Court.

[Monsanto Co. brought a suit seeking injunctive and declaratory relief against various provisions of the Federal Insecticide, Fungicide, and Rodenticide Act. The statute prior to 1972 required that pesticides be registered and that test data be submitted to support claims on the label. Nothing was said in the statute about the disclosure of any of the health and safety data submitted. In 1972 the statute was amended and provided that the EPA could not publicly disclose information containing or relating to trade secrets or commercial or financial information. It allowed EPA to consider data submitted by one applicant for registration to support another application pertaining to a similar chemical if the subsequent applicant offered to compensate the applicant who originally submitted the data. In 1978 the bill was amended again to provide that applicants for registration be granted a 10-year period of exclusive use for data on new active ingredients contained in pesticides. It also provided that other data submitted could be used to support another application for 15 years after the original submission if the applicant offered to compensate the original submitter. If the parties could not agree on the amount of the compensation a binding arbitration proceeding was provided. Also in 1978 it was provided that the EPA could disclose all health, safety, and environmental data to qualified requesters, notwithstanding the prohibition against disclosure of trade secrets.]

. . .

III

In deciding this case, we are faced with four questions: (1) Does Monsanto have a property interest protected by the Fifth Amendment's Taking Clause in the health, safety, and environmental data it has submitted to EPA? (2) If so, does EPA's use of the data to evaluate the applications of others or EPA's disclosure of the data to qualified members of the public effect a taking of that property interest? (3) If there is a taking, is it a taking for a public use? (4) If there is a taking for a public use, does the statute adequately provide for just compensation?

. . . [W]e address the question whether the data at issue here can be considered property for the purposes of the Taking Clause of the Fifth Amendment.

This Court never has squarely addressed the applicability of the protections of the Taking Clause of the Fifth Amendment to commercial data of the kind involved in this case. In answering the question now, we are mindful of the basic axiom that " '[p]roperty interests . . . are not created by the Constitution. Rather, they are created and their dimensions are defined by existing rules or understandings that stem from an independent source such as state law.' " Webb's Fabulous Pharmacies, Inc. v. Beckwith, 449 U.S. 155, 161 (1980), quoting Board of Regents v. Roth, 408 U.S. 564, 577 (1972). Monsanto asserts that the health, safety, and environmental data it has submitted to EPA are property under Missouri law, which recognizes trade secrets, as defined in § 757, Comment *b*, of the Restatement of Torts, as property. . . .

Because of the intangible nature of a trade secret, the extent of the property right therein is defined by the extent to which the owner of the secret protects his interest from disclosure to others. . . . Information that is public knowledge or that is generally known in an industry cannot be a trade secret. . . .

Trade secrets have many of the characteristics of more tangible forms of property. A trade secret is assignable. . . . A trade secret can form the *res* of a trust . . . and it passes to a trustee in bankruptcy. . . .

. . .

Although this Court never has squarely addressed the question whether a person can have a property interest in a trade secret, which is admittedly intangible, the Court has found other kinds of intangible interests to be property for purposes of the Fifth Amendment's Taking Clause. . . . That intangible property rights protected by state law are deserving of the protection of the Taking Clause has long been implicit in the thinking of this Court. . . .

We therefore hold that to the extent that Monsanto has an interest in its health, safety, and environmental data cognizable as a trade-secret property right under Missouri law, that property right is protected by the Taking Clause of the Fifth Amendment.

IV

Having determined that Monsanto has a property interest in the data it has submitted to EPA, we confront the difficult question whether a "taking" will occur when EPA discloses that data or considers the data in evaluating another application for registration. The question of what constitutes a "taking" is one with which this Court has wrestled on many occasions. It has never been the rule that only governmental acquisition or destruction of the property of an individual constitutes a taking. . . .

As has been admitted on numerous occasions, "this Court has generally 'been unable to develop any "set formula" for determining when "justice and fairness" require that economic injuries caused by public action' " must be deemed a compensable taking. Kaiser Aetna v. United States, 444 U.S. 164, 175 (1979), quoting Penn Central Transportation Co. v. New York City, 438 U.S. 104, 124 (1978); accord, Hodel v. Virginia Surface Mining and Recl. Assn., 452 U.S. 264, 295 (1981). The inquiry into whether a taking has occurred is essentially an "ad hoc, factual" inquiry. *Kaiser Aetna,* 444 U.S., at 175. The Court, however, has identified several factors that should be taken into account when determining whether a governmental action has gone beyond "regulation" and effects a "taking." Among those factors are: "the character of the governmental action, its economic impact, and its interference with reasonable investment-backed expectations." PruneYard Shopping Center v. Robins, 447 U.S., at 83; see *Kaiser Aetna,* 444 U.S., at 175; Penn Central, 438 U.S., at 124. It is to the last of these three factors that we now direct our attention, for we find that the force of this factor is so overwhelming, at least with respect to certain of the data submitted by Monsanto to EPA, that it disposes of the taking question regarding that data.

A

A "reasonable investment-backed expectation" must be more than a "unilateral expectation or an abstract need." *Webb's Fabulous Pharmacies,* 449 U.S., at 161. We find that with respect to any health, safety, and environmental data that Monsanto submitted to EPA after the effective date of the 1978 FIFRA amendments—that is, on or after October 1, 1978—Monsanto could not have had a reasonable, investment-backed expectation that EPA would keep the data confidential beyond the limits prescribed in the amended statute itself. Monsanto was on notice of the manner in which EPA was authorized to use and disclose any data turned over to it by an applicant for registration.

. . . If, despite the data-consideration and data-disclosure provisions in the statute, Monsanto chose to submit the requisite data in order to receive a registration, it can hardly argue that its reasonable investment-backed expectations are disturbed when EPA acts to use or disclose the data in a manner that was authorized by law at the time of the submission.

. . .

Thus, as long as Monsanto is aware of the conditions under which the data are submitted, and the conditions are rationally related to a legitimate government interest, a voluntary submission of data by an applicant in exchange for the economic advantages of a registration can hardly be called a taking. . . .

B

Prior to the 1972 amendments, FIFRA was silent with respect to EPA's authorized use and disclosure of data submitted to it in connection with an application for registration. . . .

. . . [T]he Trade Secrets Act cannot be construed as any sort of assurance against internal agency use of submitted data during consideration of the application of a subsequent applicant for registration. Indeed, there is some evidence that the practice of using data submitted by one company during consideration of the application of a subsequent applicant was widespread and well known. Thus, with respect to any data that Monsanto submitted to EPA prior to the effective date of the 1972 amendments to FIFRA, we hold that

Monsanto could not have had a "reasonable investment-backed expectation" that EPA would maintain that data in strictest confidence and would use it exclusively for the purpose of considering the Monsanto application in connection with which the data were submitted.

C

The situation may be different, however, with respect to data submitted by Monsanto to EPA during the period from October 22, 1972, through September 30, 1978. Under the statutory scheme then in effect, a submitter was given an opportunity to protect its trade secrets from disclosure by designating them as trade secrets at the time of submission. When Monsanto provided data to EPA during this period, it was with the understanding, embodied in FIFRA, that EPA was free to use any of the submitted data that were not trade secrets in considering the application of another, provided that EPA required the subsequent applicant to pay "reasonable compensation" to the original submitter. § 3(c)(1)(D), 86 Stat. 979. But the statute also gave Monsanto explicit assurance that EPA was prohibited from disclosing publicly, or considering in connection with the application of another, any data submitted by an applicant if both the applicant and EPA determined the data to constitute trade secrets. § 10, 86 Stat. 989. Thus, with respect to trade secrets submitted under the statutory regime in force between the time of the adoption of the 1972 amendments and the adoption of the 1978 amendments, the Federal Government had explicitly guaranteed to Monsanto and other registration applicants an extensive measure of confidentiality and exclusive use. This explicit governmental guarantee formed the basis of a reasonable investment-backed expectation. . . .

The right to exclude others is generally "one of the most essential sticks in the bundle of rights that are commonly characterized as property." *Kaiser Aetna,* 444 U.S., at 176. With respect to a trade secret, the right to exclude others is central to the very definition of the property interest. Once the data that constitutes a trade secret is disclosed to others, or others are allowed to use that data, the holder of the trade secret has lost his property interest in the data. . . . The economic value of that property right lies in the competitive advantage over others that Monsanto enjoys by virtue of its exclusive access to the data, and disclosure or use by others of the data would destroy that competitive edge.

. . .

If a negotiation or arbitration pursuant to § 3(c)(1)(D)(ii) were to yield just compensation to Monsanto for the loss in the market value of its trade-secret data suffered because of EPA's consideration of the data in connection with another application, then Monsanto would have no claim against the Government for a taking. Since no arbitration has yet occurred with respect to any use of Monsanto's data, any finding that there has been an actual taking would be premature.

In summary, we hold that EPA's consideration or disclosure of data submitted by Monsanto to the agency prior to October 22, 1972, or after September 30, 1978, does not effect a taking. We further hold that EPA consideration or disclosure of health, safety, and environmental data will constitute a taking if Monsanto submitted the data to EPA between October 22, 1972, and September 30, 1978; the data constituted trade secrets under Missouri law; Monsanto had designated the data as trade secrets at the time of its submission; the use of disclosure conflicts with the explicit assurance of confidentiality or exclusive use contained in the statute during that period; and the operation of the arbitration provision does not adequately compensate for the loss in market value of the data that Monsanto suffers because of EPA's use or disclosure of the trade secrets.

V

We must next consider whether any taking of private property that may occur by operation of the data-disclosure and data-consideration provisions of FIFRA is a taking for a "public use." We have recently stated that the scope of the "public use" requirement of the Taking Clause is "coterminus with the scope of a sovereign's police powers." Hawaii Housing Authority v. Midkiff, ___ U.S. ___, ___ (1984); see Berman v. Parker, 348 U.S. 26, 33 (1954). The role of the courts in second-guessing the legislature's judgment of what constitutes a public use is extremely narrow. *Midkiff,* supra; *Berman,* supra, at 32.

The District Court found that EPA's action pursuant to the data-consideration provisions of FIFRA would effect a taking for a private use, rather than a public use, because such action benefits subsequent applicants by forcing original submitters to share their data with later applicants. 564 F.Supp., at 566. It is true that the most direct beneficiaries of EPA actions under the data-consideration provisions of FIFRA will be the later applicants who will support their applications by citation to data submitted by Monsanto or some other original submitter. Because of the data-consideration provisions, later applicants will not have to replicate the sometimes intensive and complex research necessary to produce the requisite data. This Court, however, has rejected the notion that a use is a public use only if the property taken is put to use for the general public. *Midkiff,* ___ U.S., at ___; Rindge Co. v. Los Angeles, 262 U.S. 700, 707 (1923); Block v. Hirsh, 256 U.S. 135, 155 (1921).

So long as the taking has a conceivable public character, "the means by which it will be attained is . . . for Congress to determine." *Berman,* 348 U.S., at 33. Here, the public purpose behind the data-consideration provision is clear from the legislative history. Congress believed that the provisions would eliminate costly duplication of research and streamline the registration process, making new end-use products available to consumers more quickly. Allowing applicants for registration, upon payment of compensation, to use data already accumulated by others, rather than forcing them to go through the time-consuming process of repeating the research, would eliminate a significant barrier to entry into the pesticide market, thereby allowing greater competition among producers of end-use products. . . . Such a procompetitive purpose is well within the police power of Congress. See *Midkiff,* ___ U.S., at ___.

.   .   .

We therefore hold that any taking of private property that may occur in connection with EPA's use or disclosure of data submitted to it by Monsanto between October 22, 1972, and September 30, 1978, is a taking for a public use.

.   .   .

VIII

We find no constitutional infirmity in the challenged provisions of FIFRA. Operation of the provisions may effect a taking with respect to certain health, safety, and environmental data constituting trade secrets under state law and designated by Monsanto as trade secrets upon submission to EPA between October 22, 1972, and September 30, 1978. But whatever taking may occur is one for a public use, and a Tucker Act remedy is available to provide Monsanto with just compensation. Once a taking has occurred, the proper forum for Monsanto's claim is the Claims Court. Monsanto's challenges to the constitutionality of the arbitration procedure are not yet ripe for review. The judgment of the District Court is therefore vacated and the case is remanded for further proceedings consistent with this opinion.

It is so ordered.

Justice White took no part in the consideration or decision of this case.

Justice O'Connor, concurring in part and dissenting in part.

I join all of the Court's opinion except for Part IV–B and the Court's conclusion, that "EPA's consideration or disclosure of data submitted by Monsanto to the agency prior to October 22, 1972 . . . does not effect a taking." In my view public disclosure of pre-1972 data would effect a taking. . . .

SAN DIEGO GAS & ELECTRIC CO. v. CITY OF SAN DIEGO, 450 U.S. 621 (1981). Plaintiff challenged an ordinance rezoning much of plaintiff's property from industrial use to open-space land as constituting a taking and asserted a right to compensation for damages suffered. It specifically raised the issue . . . whether the state could limit the remedies for a regulatory taking to mandamus and declaratory judgment. Five members of the Court concluded that the appeals must be dismissed because of the lack of a final judgment below. Justices Brennan, Stewart, Marshall, and Powell concluded that there was a final judgment and reached the merits. Since Justice Rehnquist who concluded that there was not a final judgment also indicated in a concurring opinion that he "would have little difficulty in agreeing with much of what is said in the dissenting opinion of Justice Brennan," the dissent may indicate the ultimate views of the Court on the merits.

The dissent concluded that mere invalidation of a regulatory statute which constituted a taking "would fall far short of fulfilling the fundamental purpose of the Just Compensation Clause. That guarantee was designed to bar the government from forcing some individuals to bear burdens which, in all fairness, should be borne by the public as a whole. . . . If the regulation denies the private property owner the use and enjoyment of his land and is found to effect a 'taking,' it is only fair that the public bear the cost of benefits received during the interim period between application of the regulation and the government entity's rescission of it. The payment of just compensation serves to place the landowner in the same position monetarily as he would have occupied if his property had not been taken."

The dissent rejected, however, the plaintiff's claim that the city must formally condemn its property and pay full market value. "[N]othing in the Just Compensation Clause empowers a court to order a government entity to condemn the property and pay its full fair market value, where the 'taking' already effected is temporary and reversible and the government wants to halt the 'taking.' Just as the government may cancel condemnation proceedings before passage of title, . . . or abandon property it has temporarily occupied or invaded, . . . it must have the same power to rescind a regulatory 'taking.' . . .

"The constitutional rule I propose requires that, once a court finds that a police power regulation has effected a 'taking,' the government entity must pay just compensation for the period commencing on the date the regulation first effected the 'taking,' and ending on the date the government entity chooses to rescind or otherwise amend the regulation. Ordinary principles determining the proper measure of just compensation, regularly applied in cases of permanent and temporary 'takings' involving formal condemnation proceedings, occupations, and physical invasions, should provide guidance to the courts in the award of compensation for a regulatory 'taking.' "

JUST COMPENSATION

The problem of according the just compensation directed to be paid upon a taking for a public use presents great difficulties. The ground rules—that the owner's loss and not the taker's gain is the measure of compensation, United States v. Miller, 317 U.S. 369, 375 (1943); that where fair market value can be determined it is the normal measure of recovery, United States ex rel. T.V.A. v. Powelson, 319 U.S. 266, 275 (1943); and that fair market value is "what a willing buyer would pay in cash to a willing seller," United States v. Miller, supra—are suggestive of the varying considerations present in determining just compensation. Problems of peculiar value to the owner, of consequential damages, of enhanced value brought about by the project for which the land is condemned, of compensation for interests less than a fee, and myriads of others complicate the determination of what is just compensation. For a comprehensive study see 4 Nichols, *The Law of Eminent Domain* (rev. 3rd ed. 1962).

SECTION 2. PROTECTION OF PERSONAL LIBERTIES

———

A. INTRODUCTION

In Section 1 of this chapter we saw how the Court determined that the word "liberty" in the due process clause gave special protection to the liberty to contract so that restrictions on that liberty, especially as reflected in labor legislation, were invalid unless specially justified by the state.

The liberty of contract cases have long since been overruled. But currently the Court is in the process of deriving from the word liberty a special constitutional protection for privacy, personal autonomy, and some family relationships which requires special justification for state infringements on those interests. The process by which an interest is singled out by the Court for special constitutional protection is worthy of examination as a means of understanding how general constitutional phrases become limitations on the power of legislatures.

Some issues that relate to privacy are governed by special constitutional language. The fourth amendment (incorporated by the fourteenth amendment against the states) protects persons, places, and possessions against indiscriminate searches and seizures. The fifth amendment protects against self-incrimination. But no language in the Constitution talks about privacy, family life, or personal autonomy.

In reading these cases ask yourself whether the Court adduces a principled basis for singling out these particular interests from all the other aspects of liberty which might be similarly protected.

Try also to determine what is the scope of this special protection. What kinds of regulations can be brought within the privacy rubric so as to require special state justification?

For useful general discussion, see Dixon, *The "New" Substantive Due Process and the Democratic Ethic: A Prolegomenon*, 1976 B.Y.U.L.Rev. 43; Henkin, *Privacy and Autonomy*, 74 Colum.L.Rev. 1410 (1974).

Two early cases from the *Lochner* era are frequently cited in current opinions. In Meyer v. Nebraska, 262 U.S. 390 (1923), a parochial school language teacher had been convicted of violating a law prohibiting the teaching of any subject in a language other than English in the first eight grades of public and private schools. In reversing his conviction, the Court said that the liberty protected by due process "denotes not merely freedom from bodily restraint, but also the right of the individual to contract, to engage in any of the common occupations of life, to acquire useful knowledge, to marry, establish a home and bring up children, to worship God according to the dictates of his own conscience, and, generally, to enjoy those privileges long recognized at common law as essential to the orderly pursuit of happiness by free men." The right of Meyer to teach German and the right of parents to engage him were within that zone of constitutionally-protected liberty. The Court concluded that, because no justifications for the complete abolition of the right to teach foreign languages had been shown, "the statute as applied is arbitrary, and without reasonable relation to any end within the competency of the state."

In Pierce v. Soc'y of Sisters, 268 U.S. 510 (1925), the Court upheld a trial court injunction against the enforcement of an Oregon statute requiring parents to send children between the ages of 8 and 16 to a public school. The suit was brought by a Catholic society operating a school and a private corporation operating a military academy. The Court noted that the effect of the act would be to force private schools out of business. It then said that under the doctrine of *Meyer* "we think it entirely plain that the [statute] unreasonably interferes with the liberty of parents and guardians to direct the upbringing and education of children under their control. . . . The fundamental theory of liberty upon which all governments in this Union repose excludes any general power of the state to standardize its children by forcing them to accept instruction from public teachers only. The child is not the mere creature of the state; those who nurture him and direct his destiny have the right, coupled with the high duty, to recognize and prepare him for additional obligations."

Another case prior to Griswold v. Connecticut that referred to special constitutional protection for interests relating to personal autonomy and family relationships was Skinner v. Oklahoma, 316 U.S. 535 (1942). The Court held invalid under equal protection a statute providing for compulsory sterilization of criminals convicted two or more times of crimes of moral turpitude. Since the statute made grand larceny a felony of moral turpitude, while embezzlement was not, it violated the equal protection clause. The Court, in an opinion by Justice Douglas, began its discussion of the equal protection issue by saying: "We are dealing here with legislation which involves one of the basic civil rights of man. Marriage and procreation are fundamental to the very existence and survival of the race. The power to sterilize, if exercised, may have subtle, far-reaching and devastating effects. . . . There is no redemption for the individual whom the law touches. Any experiment which the State conducts is to his irreparable injury. He is forever deprived of a basic liberty. We mention these matters not to reexamine the scope of the police power of the States. We advert to them merely in emphasis of our view that strict scrutiny of the classification which a State makes in a sterilization law is essential. . . ."

GRISWOLD v. CONNECTICUT

381 U.S. 479, 85 S.Ct. 1678, 14 L.Ed.2d 510 (1965).

Mr. Justice Douglas delivered the opinion of the Court.

Appellant Griswold is Executive Director of the Planned Parenthood League of Connecticut. Appellant Buxton is a licensed physician and a professor at the Yale Medical School who served as Medical Director for the League at its Center in New Haven—a center open and operating from November 1 to November 10, 1961, when appellants were arrested.

They gave information, instruction, and medical advice to *married persons* as to the means of preventing conception. They examined the wife and prescribed the best contraceptive device or material for her use. Fees were usually charged, although some couples were serviced free.

The statutes whose constitutionality is involved in this appeal are §§ 53–32 and 54–196 of the General Statutes of Connecticut (1938). The former provides:

> "Any person who uses any drug, medicinal article or instrument for the purpose of preventing conception shall be fined not less than fifty dollars or imprisoned not less than sixty days nor more than one year or be both fined and imprisoned."

Section 54–196 provides:

> "Any person who assists, abets, counsels, causes, hires or commands another to commit any offense may be prosecuted and punished as if he were the principal offender."

The appellants were found guilty as accessories and fined $100 each, against the claim that the accessory statute as so applied violated the Fourteenth Amendment. The Appellate Division of the Circuit Court affirmed. The Court of Errors affirmed that judgment. 151 Conn. 544, 200 A.2d 479. We noted probable jurisdiction. 379 U.S. 926.

   . . .

Coming to the merits, we are met with a wide range of questions that implicate the Due Process Clause of the Fourteenth Amendment. Overtones of some arguments suggest that Lochner v. State of New York, 198 U.S. 45, should be our guide. But we decline that invitation as we did in West Coast Hotel Co. v. Parrish, 300 U.S. 379; Olsen v. State of Nebraska, 313 U.S. 236; Lincoln Federal Labor Union v. Northwestern Co., 335 U.S. 525; Williamson v. Lee Optical Co., 348 U.S. 483; Giboney v. Empire Storage Co., 336 U.S. 490. We do not sit as a super-legislature to determine the wisdom, need, and propriety of laws that touch economic problems, business affairs, or social conditions. This law, however, operates directly on an intimate relation of husband and wife and their physician's role in one aspect of that relation.

The association of people is not mentioned in the Constitution nor in the Bill of Rights. The right to educate a child in a school of the parents' choice—whether public or private or parochial—is also not mentioned. Nor is the right to study any particular subject or any foreign language. Yet the First Amendment has been construed to include certain of those rights.

By Pierce v. Society of Sisters, supra, the right to educate one's children as one chooses is made applicable to the States by the force of the First and Fourteenth Amendments. By Meyer v. State of Nebraska, supra, the same dignity is given the right to study the German language in a private school. In other words, the State may not, consistently with the spirit of the First Amendment, contract the spectrum of available knowledge. The right of freedom of speech and press includes not only the right to utter or to print, but the right to distribute, the right to receive, the right to read (Martin v. City of Struthers, 319 U.S. 141, 143) and freedom of inquiry, freedom of thought, and freedom to teach (see Wieman v. Updegraff, 344 U.S. 183, 195)—indeed the freedom of the entire university community. Sweezy v. State of New Hampshire, 354 U.S. 234, 249–250, 261–263; Barenblatt v. United States, 360 U.S. 109, 112; Baggett v. Bullitt, 377 U.S. 360, 369. Without those peripheral rights the specific rights would be less secure. And so we reaffirm the principle of the *Pierce* and the *Meyer* cases.

   . . .

The foregoing cases suggest that specific guarantees in the Bill of Rights have penumbras, formed by emanations from those guarantees that help give them life and substance. See Poe v. Ullman, 367 U.S. 497, 516–522 (dissenting opinion). Various guarantees create zones of privacy. The right of association contained in the penumbra of the First Amendment is one, as we have seen. The Third Amendment in its prohibition against the quartering of soldiers "in any house" in time of peace without the consent of the owner is another facet of that privacy. The Fourth Amendment explicitly affirms the "right of the people to be secure in their persons, houses, papers, and effects, against unreasonable searches and seizures." The Fifth Amendment in its Self-Incrimination Clause enables the citizen to create a zone of privacy which government may not force him to surrender to his detriment. The Ninth Amendment provides: "The enumeration in the Constitution, of certain rights, shall not be construed to deny or disparage others retained by the people."

The Fourth and Fifth Amendments were described in Boyd v. United States, 116 U.S. 616, 630, as protection against all governmental invasions "of the sanctity of a man's home and the privacies of life." We recently referred in Mapp v. Ohio, 367 U.S. 643, 656, to the Fourth Amendment as creating a "right to privacy, no less important than any other right carefully and particularly reserved to the people." See Beaney, The Constitutional Right to Privacy, 1962 Sup.Ct.Rev. 212; Griswold, The Right to be Let Alone, 55 N.W.U.L. Rev. 216 (1960).

We have had many controversies over these penumbral rights of "privacy and repose." . . . These cases bear witness that the right of privacy which presses for recognition here is a legitimate one.

The present case, then, concerns a relationship lying within the zone of privacy created by several fundamental constitutional guarantees. And it concerns a law which, in forbidding the *use* of contraceptives rather than regulating their manufacture or sale, seeks to achieve its goals by means having a maximum destructive impact upon that relationship. Such a law cannot stand in light of the familiar principle, so often applied by this Court, that a "governmental purpose to control or prevent activities constitutionally subject to state regulation may not be achieved by means which sweep unnecessarily broadly and thereby invade the area of protected freedoms." NAACP v. Alabama, 377 U.S. 288, 307. Would we allow the police to search the sacred precincts of marital bedrooms for telltale signs of the use of contraceptives? The very idea is repulsive to the notions of privacy surrounding the marriage relationship.

We deal with a right of privacy older than the Bill of Rights—older than our political parties, older than our school system. Marriage is a coming together for better or for worse, hopefully enduring, and intimate to the degree of being sacred. It is an association that promotes a way of life, not causes; a harmony in living, not political faiths; a bilateral loyalty, not commercial or social projects. Yet it is an association for as noble a purpose as any involved in our prior decisions.

Reversed.

Mr. Justice Goldberg, whom The Chief Justice and Mr. Justice Brennan join, concurring.

I agree with the Court that Connecticut's birth control law unconstitutionally intrudes upon the right of marital privacy, and I join in its opinion and judgment. Although I have not accepted the view that " 'due process' as used in the Fourteenth Amendment includes all of the first eight Amendments," id., 367 U.S. at 516 (see my concurring opinion in Pointer v. Texas, 380 U.S. 400, 410, and the dissenting opinion of Mr. Justice Brennan in Cohen v. Hurley, 366 U.S. 117), I do agree that the concept of liberty protects those personal rights that are fundamental, and is not confined to the specific terms of the Bill of Rights. My conclusion that the concept of liberty is not so restricted and that it embraces the right of marital privacy though that right is not mentioned explicitly in the Constitution is supported both by numerous decisions of this Court, referred to in the Court's opinion, and by the language and history of the Ninth Amendment. In reaching the conclusion that the right of marital privacy is protected, as being within the protected penumbra of specific guarantees of the Bill of Rights, the Court refers to the Ninth Amendment. I add these words to emphasize the relevance of that Amendment to the Court's holding.

.   .   .

The Ninth Amendment reads, "The enumeration in the Constitution, of certain rights, shall not be construed to deny or disparage others retained by the people."   .   .   .

While this Court has had little occasion to interpret the Ninth Amendment,[6] "[i]t cannot be presumed that any clause in the constitution is intended to be without effect." Marbury v. Madison, 1 Cranch 137, 174. In interpreting the Constitution, "real effect should be given to all the words it uses." Myers v. United States, 272 U.S. 52, 151. The Ninth Amendment to the Constitution may be regarded by some as a recent discovery but since 1791 it has been a basic part of the Constitution which we are sworn to uphold. To hold that a right so basic and fundamental and so deep-rooted in our society as the right of privacy in marriage may be infringed because that right is not guaranteed in so many words by the first eight amendments to the Constitution is to ignore the Ninth Amendment and to give it no effect whatsoever. Moreover, a judicial construction that this fundamental right is not protected by the Constitution because it is not mentioned in explicit terms by one of the first eight amendments or elsewhere in the Constitution would violate the Ninth Amendment, which specifically states that "[t]he enumeration in the Constitution, of certain rights shall not be *construed* to deny or disparage others retained by the people." (Emphasis added.)

.   .   .

The entire fabric of the Constitution and the purposes that clearly underlie its specific guarantees demonstrate that the rights to marital privacy and to marry and raise a family are of similar order and magnitude as the fundamental rights specifically protected.

Although the Constitution does not speak in so many words of the right of privacy in marriage, I cannot believe that it offers these fundamental rights no protection. The fact that no particular provision of the Constitution explicitly forbids the State from disrupting the traditional relation of the family—a relation as old and as fundamental as our entire civilization—surely does not show that the Government was meant to have the power to do so. Rather, as the Ninth Amendment expressly recognizes, there are fundamental personal rights such as this one, which are protected from abridgment by the Government though not specifically mentioned in the Constitution.

.   .   .

The logic of the dissents would sanction federal or state legislation that seems to me even more plainly unconstitutional than the statute before us. .   .   . [I]f upon a showing of a slender basis of rationality, a law outlawing voluntary birth control by married persons is valid, then, by the same reasoning, a law requiring compulsory birth control also would seem to be valid. In my

---

[6] This Amendment has been referred to as "The Forgotten Ninth Amendment," in a book with that title by Bennet B. Patterson (1955). Other commentary on the Ninth Amendment includes Redlich, Are There "Certain Rights . . . Retained by the People"? 37 N.Y.U.L.Rev. 787 (1962), and Kelsey, The Ninth Amendment of the Federal Constitution, 11 Ind.L.J. 309 (1936). As far as I am aware, until today this Court has referred to the Ninth Amendment only in United Public Workers v. Mitchell, 330 U.S. 75, 94–95; Tennessee Electric Power Co. v. TVA, 306 U.S. 118, 143–144; and Ashwander v. TVA, 297 U.S. 288, 330–331. See also Calder v. Bull, 3 Dall. 386, 388; Loan Ass'n v. City of Topeka, 20 Wall. 655, 662–663. . . .

view, however, both types of law would unjustifiably intrude upon rights of marital privacy which are constitutionally protected.

. . .

In sum, I believe that the right of privacy in the marital relation is fundamental and basic—a personal right "retained by the people" within the meaning of the Ninth Amendment.   Connecticut cannot constitutionally abridge this fundamental right, which is protected by the Fourteenth Amendment from infringement by the States.   I agree with the Court that petitioners' convictions must therefore be reversed.

Mr. Justice Harlan, concurring in the judgment.

I fully agree with the judgment of reversal, but find myself unable to join the Court's opinion.   The reason is that it seems to me to evince an approach to this case very much like that taken by my Brothers Black and Stewart in dissent, namely: the Due Process Clause of the Fourteenth Amendment does not touch this Connecticut statute unless the enactment is found to violate some right assured by the letter or penumbra of the Bill of Rights.

In other words, what I find implicit in the Court's opinion is that the "incorporation" doctrine may be used to *restrict* the reach of Fourteenth Amendment Due Process.   For me this is just as unacceptable constitutional doctrine as is the use of the "incorporation" approach to *impose* upon the States all the requirements of the Bill of Rights as found in the provisions of the first eight amendments and in the decisions of this Court interpreting them.   . . .

Mr. Justice White, concurring in the judgment.

In my view this Connecticut law as applied to married couples deprives them of "liberty" without due process of law, as that concept is used in the Fourteenth Amendment.   I therefore concur in the judgment of the Court reversing these convictions under Connecticut's aiding and abetting statute.

. . .

Mr. Justice Black, with whom Mr. Justice Stewart joins, dissenting.

I agree with my Brother Stewart's dissenting opinion.   And like him I do not to any extent whatever base my view that this Connecticut law is constitutional on a belief that the law is wise or that its policy is a good one.   In order that there may be no room at all to doubt why I vote as I do, I feel constrained to add that the law is every bit as offensive to me as it is to my Brethren of the majority and my Brothers Harlan, White and Goldberg who, reciting reasons why it is offensive to them, hold it unconstitutional.   There is no single one of the graphic and eloquent strictures and criticisms fired at the policy of this Connecticut law either by the Court's opinion or by those of my concurring Brethren to which I cannot subscribe—except their conclusion that the evil qualities they see in the law make it unconstitutional.

. . .

The Court talks about a constitutional "right of privacy" as though there is some constitutional provision or provisions forbidding any law ever to be passed which might abridge the "privacy" of individuals.   But there is not.   . . .

. . .

I realize that many good and able men have eloquently spoken and written, sometimes in rhapsodical strains, about the duty of this Court to keep the Constitution in tune with the times.   The idea is that the Constitution must be changed from time to time and that this Court is charged with a duty to make those changes.   For myself, I must with all deference reject that philosophy.   The Constitution makers knew the need for change and provided for it.   Amendments suggested by the people's elected representatives can be submitted to the people or their selected agents for ratification.   That method of change was good for our Fathers, and being somewhat old-fashioned I must add it is good enough for me. And so, I cannot rely on the Due Process Clause or the Ninth Amendment or any mysterious and uncertain natural law concept as a reason for striking down this state law. The Due Process Clause with an "arbitrary and capricious" or "shocking to the conscience" formula was liberally used by this Court to strike down economic legislation in the early decades of this century, threatening, many people thought, the tranquility and stability of the nation. See, e.g., Lochner v. State of New York, 198 U.S. 45. That formula, based on subjective considerations of "natural justice," is no less dangerous when used to enforce this Court's views about personal rights than those about economic rights. I had thought that we had laid that formula, as a means for striking down state legislation, to rest once and for all in cases like West Coast Hotel Co. v. Parrish, 300 U.S. 379; Olsen v. State of Nebraska ex rel. Western Reference & Bond Assn., 313 U.S. 236, and many other opinions.

. . .

. . . . The late Judge Learned Hand, after emphasizing his view that judges should not use the due process formula suggested in the concurring opinions today or any other formula like it to invalidate legislation offensive to their "personal preferences," [22] made the statement, with which I fully agree, that:

"For myself it would be most irksome to be ruled by a bevy of Platonic Guardians, even if I knew how to choose them, which I assuredly do not."

So far as I am concerned, Connecticut's law as applied here is not forbidden by any provision of the Federal Constitution as that Constitution was written, and I would therefore affirm.

Mr. Justice Stewart, whom Mr. Justice Black joins, dissenting.

Since 1879 Connecticut has had on its books a law which forbids the use of contraceptives by anyone. I think this is an uncommonly silly law. As a practical matter, the law is obviously unenforceable, except in the oblique context of the present case. As a philosophical matter, I believe the use of contraceptives in the relationship of marriage should be left to personal and private choice, based upon each individual's moral, ethical, and religious beliefs. As a matter of social policy, I think professional counsel about methods of birth control should be available to all, so that each individual's choice can be meaningfully made. But we are not asked in this case to say whether we think this law is unwise, or even asinine. We are asked to hold that it violates the United States Constitution. And that I cannot do.

. . .

What provision of the Constitution, then, does make this state law invalid? The Court says it is the right of privacy "created by several fundamental constitutional guarantees." With all deference, I can find no such general right of privacy in the Bill of Rights, in any other part of the Constitution, or in any case ever before decided by this Court.[a]

. . .

----

[22] Hand, The Bill of Rights (1958) 70. . . .

[a] Helpful discussion of the Court's approach to the Griswold case may be found in: *Symposium on the Griswold Case and the Right of Privacy,* 64 Mich.L.Rev. 197 (1965); Beaney, *The Griswold Case and the Expanding Right to Privacy,* 1966 Wis.L.Rev. 979; Katin, *Griswold v. Connecticut: The Justices and Connecticut's "Uncommonly Silly Law,"* 42 Notre Dame L. 680 (1967); Franklin, *The Ninth Amendment as Civil Law Method and Its Implications for a Republican Form of Government,* 40 Tul.L.Rev. 487 (1966).

PRIVACY AS AUTONOMY VERSUS PRIVACY AS FREEDOM FROM INTRUSION AND DISCLOSURE

In *Griswold* the Court appeared to use the term "privacy" in the sense of protecting private matters from disclosure. It emphasized intrusion into "the sacred precincts of marital bedrooms." But in Roe v. Wade, infra p. 585, the Court gave the term a broader meaning protecting personal autonomy. In fact, in Carey v. Population Services Int'l., 431 U.S. 678, 687 (1977), the Court said that later decisions had "put *Griswold* in proper perspective. *Griswold* may no longer be read as holding only that a State may not prohibit a married couple's use of contraceptives. Read in the light of its progeny, the teaching of *Griswold* is that the Constitution protects individual decisions in matters of childbearing from unjustified intrusion by the State."

The Court has decided only one case since *Griswold* involving claims that the state had unconstitutionally invaded privacy in the sense of requiring disclosure of personal matters. Whalen v. Roe, 429 U.S. 589 (1977), presented the question whether a state could record, in a centralized computer file, the names and addresses of all persons who had obtained, pursuant to a doctor's prescription, certain drugs for which there was both a lawful and an unlawful market. In response to an argument that the state requirement invaded a constitutionally protected zone of privacy, the Court noted: "The cases sometimes characterized as protecting 'privacy' have in fact involved at least two different kinds of interests. One is the individual interest in avoiding disclosure of personal matters, and another is the interest in independence in making certain kinds of important decisions." The Court upheld the statute on the ground that the state protections against public disclosure of the data were sufficient to avoid a serious threat to either interest. It concluded its opinion with the following paragraph:

> "A final word about issues we have not decided. We are not unaware of the threat to privacy implicit in the accumulation of vast amounts of personal information in computerized data banks or other massive government files. The collection of taxes, the distribution of welfare and social security benefits, the supervision of public health, the direction of our armed forces and the enforcement of the criminal laws, all require the orderly preservation of great quantities of information, much of which is personal in character and potentially embarrassing or harmful if disclosed. The right to collect and use such data for public purposes is typically accompanied by a concomitant statutory or regulatory duty to avoid unwarranted disclosures. Recognizing that in some circumstances that duty arguably has its roots in the Constitution, nevertheless New York's statutory scheme, and its implementing administrative procedures, evidence a proper concern with, and protection of, the individual's interest in privacy. We therefore need not, and do not, decide any question which might be presented by the unwarranted disclosure of accumulated private data—whether intentional or unintentional—or by a system that did not contain comparable security provisions. We simply hold that this record does not establish an invasion of any right or liberty protected by the Fourteenth Amendment."

B. PERSONAL AUTONOMY

EISENSTADT v. BAIRD, 405 U.S. 438 (1972). In a prosecution of a defendant for giving a contraceptive to an unmarried person the Court had before it, among others, the question whether it was a denial of equal protection of the laws to permit the distribution of contraceptives to married persons but not to unmarried. One argument made to sustain the classification was that contraceptives were considered immoral. The counter argument was that under Griswold v. Connecticut it would be a denial of due process to prohibit the distribution of contraceptives. The Court said it did not need to decide the issue, but did make the following observation: "If the right of privacy means anything, it is the right of the *individual,* married or single, to be free from unwarranted governmental intrusion into matters so fundamentally affecting a person as the decision whether to bear or beget a child."

ROE v. WADE

410 U.S. 113, 93 S.Ct. 705, 35 L.Ed.2d 147 (1973).

Mr. Justice Blackmun delivered the opinion of the Court.

This Texas federal appeal and its Georgia companion, Doe v. Bolton, post, 410 U.S. 179, present constitutional challenges to state criminal abortion legislation. The Texas statutes under attack here are typical of those that have been in effect in many States for approximately a century. The Georgia statutes, in contrast, have a modern cast and are a legislative product that, to an extent at least, obviously reflects the influences of recent attitudinal change, of advancing medical knowledge and techniques, and of new thinking about an old issue.

We forthwith acknowledge our awareness of the sensitive and emotional nature of the abortion controversy, of the vigorous opposing views, even among physicians, and of the deep and seemingly absolute convictions that the subject inspires. One's philosophy, one's experiences, one's exposure to the raw edges of human existence, one's religious training, one's attitudes toward life and family and their values, and the moral standards one establishes and seeks to observe, are all likely to influence and to color one's thinking and conclusions about abortion.

In addition, population growth, pollution, poverty, and racial overtones tend to complicate and not to simplify the problem.

Our task, of course, is to resolve the issue by constitutional measurement free of emotion and of predilection. We seek earnestly to do this, and, because we do, we have inquired into, and in this opinion place some emphasis upon, medical and medical-legal history and what that history reveals about man's attitudes toward the abortive procedure over the centuries. We bear in mind, too, Mr. Justice Holmes' admonition in his now vindicated dissent in Lochner v. New York, 198 U.S. 45, 76 (1905):

"It [the Constitution] is made for people of fundamentally differing views, and the accident of our finding certain opinions natural and familiar, or novel, and even shocking, ought not to conclude our judgment upon the question whether statutes embodying them conflict with the Constitution of the United States."

I.

The Texas statutes that concern us here are Arts. 1191–1194 and 1196 of the State's Penal Code, Vernon's Ann.P.C. These make it a crime to "procure an abortion," as therein defined, or to attempt one, except with respect to "an abortion procured or attempted by medical advice for the purpose of saving the life of the mother." Similar statutes are in existence in a majority of the States.

.   .   .   .

V.

The principal thrust of appellant's attack on the Texas statutes is that they improperly invade a right, said to be possessed by the pregnant woman, to choose to terminate her pregnancy. Appellant would discover this right in the concept of personal "liberty" embodied in the Fourteenth Amendment's Due Process Clause; or in personal, marital, familial, and sexual privacy said to be protected by the Bill of Rights or its penumbras, see Griswold v. Connecticut, 381 U.S. 479 (1965); Eisenstadt v. Baird, 405 U.S. 438 (1972); id., at 460 (White, J., concurring); or among those rights reserved to the people by the Ninth Amendment, Griswold v. Connecticut, 381 U.S., at 486 (Goldberg, J., concurring). Before addressing this claim, we feel it desirable briefly to survey, in several aspects, the history of abortion, for such insight as that history may afford us, and then to examine the state purposes and interests behind the criminal abortion laws.

. . .

[The Court's long historical discussion is omitted.]

VII.

Three reasons have been advanced to explain historically the enactment of criminal abortion laws in the 19th century and to justify their continued existence.

It has been argued occasionally that these laws were the product of a Victorian social concern to discourage illicit sexual conduct. Texas, however, does not advance this justification in the present case, and it appears that no court or commentator has taken the argument seriously. . . .

A second reason is concerned with abortion as a medical procedure. When most criminal abortion laws were first enacted, the procedure was a hazardous one for the woman. . . .

Modern medical techniques have altered this situation. Appellants and various *amici* refer to medical data indicating that abortion in early pregnancy, that is, prior to the end of first trimester, although not without its risk, is now relatively safe. Mortality rates for women undergoing early abortions, where the procedure is legal, appear to be as low as or lower than the rates for normal childbirth. Consequently, any interest of the State in protecting the woman from an inherently hazardous procedure, except when it would be equally dangerous for her to forgo it, has largely disappeared. Of course, important state interests in the area of health and medical standards do remain. The State has a legitimate interest in seeing to it that abortion, like any other medical procedure, is performed under circumstances that insure maximum safety for the patient. This interest obviously extends at least to the performing physician and his staff, to the facilities involved, to the availability of after-care, and to adequate provision for any complication or emergency that might arise. The prevalence of high mortality rates at illegal "abortion mills" strengthens, rather than weakens, the State's interest in regulating the conditions under which abortions are performed. Moreover, the risk to the woman increases as her pregnancy continues. Thus the State retains a definite interest in protecting the woman's own health and safety when an abortion is proposed at a late stage of pregnancy.

The third reason is the State's interest—some phrase it in terms of duty—in protecting prenatal life. Some of the argument for this justification rests on the theory that a new human life is present from the moment of conception. The State's interest and general obligation to protect life then extends, it is argued, to prenatal life. Only when the life of the pregnant mother herself is at stake, balanced against the life she carries within her, should the interest of the embryo or fetus not prevail. Logically, of course, a legitimate state interest in this area need not stand or fall on acceptance of the belief that life begins at conception or at some other point prior to live birth. In assessing the State's interest, recognition may be given to the less rigid claim that as long as at least *potential* life is involved, the State may assert interests beyond the protection of the pregnant woman alone.

Parties challenging state abortion laws have sharply disputed in some courts the contention that a purpose of these laws, when enacted, was to protect prenatal life. Pointing to the absence of legislative history to support the contention, they claim that most state laws were designed solely to protect the woman. Because medical advances have lessened this concern, at least with respect to abortion in early pregnancy, they argue that with respect to such abortions the laws can no longer be justified by any state interest. There is some scholarly support for this view of original purpose. The few state courts called upon to interpret their laws in the late 19th and early 20th centuries did focus on the State's interest in protecting the woman's health rather than in preserving the embryo and fetus. Proponents of this view point out that in many States, including Texas, by statute or judicial interpretation, the pregnant woman herself could not be prosecuted for self-abortion or for cooperating in an abortion performed upon her by another. They claim that adoption of the "quickening" distinction through received common law and state statutes tacitly recognizes the greater health hazards inherent in late abortion and impliedly repudiates the theory that life begins at conception.

It is with these interests, and the weight to be attached to them, that this case is concerned.

VIII.

The Constitution does not explicitly mention any right of privacy. In a line of decisions, however, going back perhaps as far as Union Pacific R. Co. v. Botsford, 141 U.S. 250, 251 (1891), the Court has recognized that a right of personal privacy, or a guarantee of certain areas or zones of privacy, does exist under the Constitution. In varying contexts the Court or individual Justices have indeed found at least the roots of that right in the First Amendment, Stanley v. Georgia, 394 U.S. 557, 564 (1969); in the Fourth and Fifth Amendments, Terry v. Ohio, 392 U.S. 1, 8–9 (1968), Katz v. United States, 389 U.S. 347, 350 (1967); Boyd v. United States, 116 U.S. 616 (1886), see Olmstead v. United States, 277 U.S. 438, 478 (1928) (Brandeis, J., dissenting); in the penumbras of the Bill of Rights, Griswold v. Connecticut, 381 U.S. 479, 484–485 (1965); in the Ninth Amendment, id., at 486 (Goldberg, J., concurring); or in the concept of liberty guaranteed by the first section of the Fourteenth Amendment, see Meyer v. Nebraska, 262 U.S. 390, 399 (1923). These decisions make it clear that only personal rights that can be deemed "fundamental" or "implicit in the concept of ordered liberty," Palko v. Connecticut, 302 U.S. 319, 325 (1937), are included in this guarantee of personal privacy. They also make it clear that the right has some extension to activities relating to marriage, Loving v. Virginia, 388 U.S. 1, 12 (1967), procreation, Skinner v. Oklahoma, 316 U.S. 535 (1942), contraception, Eisenstadt v. Baird, 405 U.S. 438, 453–454 (1972); id., at 460, 463–465 (White, J., concurring), family relationships, Prince v. Massachusetts, 321 U.S. 158, 166 (1944), and child rearing and education, Pierce v. Society of Sisters, 268 U.S. 510, 535 (1925), Meyer v. Nebraska, supra.

This right of privacy, whether it be founded in the Fourteenth Amendment's concept of personal liberty and restrictions upon state action, as we feel it is, or, as the District Court determined, in the Ninth Amendment's reservation of rights to the people, is broad enough to encompass a woman's decision whether or not to terminate her pregnancy. The detriment that the State would impose upon the pregnant woman by denying this choice altogether is apparent. Specific and direct harm medically diagnosable even in early pregnancy may be involved. Maternity, or additional offspring, may force upon the woman a distressful life and future. Psychological harm may be imminent. Mental and physical health may be taxed by child care. There is also the distress, for all concerned, associated with the unwanted child, and there is the problem of bringing a child into a family already unable, psychologically and otherwise, to care for it. In other cases, as in this one, the additional difficulties and continuing stigma of unwed motherhood may be involved. All these are factors the woman and her responsible physician necessarily will consider in consultation.

On the basis of elements such as these, appellants and some *amici* argue that the woman's right is absolute and that she is entitled to terminate her pregnancy at whatever time, in whatever way, and for whatever reason she alone chooses. With this we do not agree. Appellants' arguments that Texas either has no valid interest at all in regulating the abortion decision, or no interest strong enough to support any limitation upon the woman's sole determination, is unpersuasive. The Court's decisions recognizing a right of privacy also acknowledge that some state regulation in areas protected by that right is appropriate. As noted above, a state may properly assert important interests in safeguarding health, in maintaining medical standards, and in protecting potential life. At some point in pregnancy, these respective interests become sufficiently compelling to sustain regulation of the factors that govern the abortion decision. The privacy right involved, therefore, cannot be said to be absolute. In fact, it is not clear to us that the claim asserted by some *amici* that one has an unlimited right to do with one's body as one pleases bears a close relationship to the right of privacy previously articulated in the Court's decisions. The Court has refused to recognize an unlimited right of this kind in the past. Jacobson v. Massachusetts, 197 U.S. 11 (1905) (vaccination); Buck v. Bell, 274 U.S. 200 (1927) (sterilization).

We therefore conclude that the right of personal privacy includes the abortion decision, but that this right is not unqualified and must be considered against important state interests in regulation.

We note that those federal and state courts that have recently considered abortion law challenges have reached the same conclusion. A majority, in addition to the District Court in the present case, have held state laws unconstitutional, at least in part, because of vagueness or because of overbreadth and abridgement of rights. . . .

Although the results are divided, most of these courts have agreed that the right of privacy, however based, is broad enough to cover the abortion decision; that the right, nonetheless, is not absolute and is subject to some limitations; and that at some point the state interests as to protection of health, medical standards, and prenatal life, become dominant. We agree with this approach.

Where certain "fundamental rights" are involved, the Court has held that regulation limiting these rights may be justified only by a "compelling state interest," Kramer v. Union Free School District, 395 U.S. 621, 627 (1969); Shapiro v. Thompson, 394 U.S. 618, 634 (1969); Sherbert v. Verner, 374 U.S. 398, 406 (1963), and that legislative enactments must be narrowly drawn to express only the legitimate state interests at stake. Griswold v. Connecticut, 381 U.S. 479, 485 (1965); Aptheker v. Secretary of State, 378 U.S. 500, 508 (1964); Cantwell v. Connecticut, 310 U.S. 296, 307–308 (1940); see Eisenstadt v. Baird, 405 U.S. 438, 460, 463–464 (1972) (White, J., concurring).

In the recent abortion cases, cited above, courts have recognized these principles. Those striking down state laws have generally scrutinized the State's interest in protecting health and potential life and have concluded that neither interest justified broad limitations on the reasons for which a physician and his pregnant patient might decide that she should have an abortion in the early stages of pregnancy. Courts sustaining state laws have held that the State's determinations to protect health or prenatal life are dominant and constitutionally justifiable.

IX.

The District Court held that the appellee failed to meet his burden of demonstrating that the Texas statute's infringement upon Roe's rights was necessary to support a compelling state interest, and that, although the defendant presented "several compelling justifications for state presence in the area of abortions," the statutes outstripped these justifications and swept "far beyond any areas of compelling state interest." 314 F.Supp., at 1222–1223. Appellant and appellee both contest that holding. Appellant, as has been indicated, claims an absolute right that bars any state imposition of criminal penalties in the area. Appellee argues that the State's determination to recognize and protect prenatal life from and after conception constitutes a compelling state interest. As noted above, we do not agree fully with either formulation.

A. The appellee and certain *amici* argue that the fetus is a "person" within the language and meaning of the Fourteenth Amendment. In support of this they outline at length and in detail the well-known facts of fetal development. If this suggestion of personhood is established, the appellant's case, of course, collapses, for the fetus' right to life is then guaranteed specifically by the Amendment. The appellant conceded as much on reargument. On the other hand, the appellee conceded on reargument that no case could be cited that holds that a fetus is a person within the meaning of the Fourteenth Amendment.

The Constitution does not define "person" in so many words. Section 1 of the Fourteenth Amendment contains three references to "person." The first, in defining "citizens," speaks of "persons born or naturalized in the United States." The word also appears both in the Due Process Clause and in the Equal Protection Clause. "Person" is used in other places in the Constitution: in the listing of qualifications for representatives and senators, Art. I, § 2, cl. 2, and § 3, cl. 3; in the Apportionment Clause, Art. I, § 2, cl. 3; in the Migration and Importation provision, Art. I, § 9, cl. 1; in the Emolument Clause, Art. I, § 9, cl. 8; in the Electors provisions, Art. II, § 1, cl. 2, and the superseded cl. 3; in the provision outlining qualifications for the office of President, Art. II, § 1, cl. 5; in the Extradition provisions, Art. IV, § 2, cl. 2, and the superseded Fugitive Slave cl. 3; and in the Fifth, Twelfth, and Twenty-second Amendments as well as in §§ 2 and 3 of the Fourteenth Amendment. But in nearly all these instances, the use of the word is such that it has application only postnatally. None indicates, with any assurance, that it has any possible prenatal application.[54]

---

[54] When Texas urges that a fetus is entitled to Fourteenth Amendment protection as a person, it faces a dilemma. Neither in Texas nor in any other State are all abortions prohibited. Despite broad proscription, an exception always exists. The exception contained in Art. 1196, for an abortion procured or attempted by medical advice for the purpose of saving the life of the mother, is typical. But if the fetus is a person who is not to be deprived of life without due process of law, and if the mother's condition is the sole determinant, does not the Texas exception appear to be out of line with the Amendment's command?

There are other inconsistencies between Fourteenth Amendment status and the typical abortion statute. It has already been pointed out, that in Texas the woman is not a principal or an accomplice with respect to an abortion upon her. If the fetus is a person, why is the woman not a principal or an accomplice? Further, the penalty for criminal abortion specified by Art. 1195 is significantly less than

All this, together with our observation, supra, that throughout the major portion of the 19th century prevailing legal abortion practices were far freer than they are today, persuades us that the word "person," as used in the Fourteenth Amendment, does not include the unborn. . . .

This conclusion, however, does not of itself fully answer the contentions raised by Texas, and we pass on to other considerations.

B.   The pregnant woman cannot be isolated in her privacy.   She carries an embryo and, later, a fetus, if one accepts the medical definitions of the developing young in the human uterus.   See Dorland's Illustrated Medical Dictionary, 478–479, 547 (24th ed. 1965).   The situation therefore is inherently different from marital intimacy, or bedroom possession of obscene material, or marriage, or procreation, or education, with which *Eisenstadt, Griswold, Stanley, Loving, Skinner, Pierce,* and *Meyer* were respectively concerned.   As we have intimated above, it is reasonable and appropriate for a State to decide that at some point in time another interest, that of health of the mother or that of potential human life, becomes significantly involved.   The woman's privacy is no longer sole and any right of privacy she possesses must be measured accordingly.

Texas urges that, apart from the Fourteenth Amendment, life begins at conception and is present throughout pregnancy, and that, therefore, the State has a compelling interest in protecting that life from and after conception.   We need not resolve the difficult question of when life begins.   When those trained in the respective disciplines of medicine, philosophy, and theology are unable to arrive at any consensus, the judiciary, at this point in the development of man's knowledge, is not in a position to speculate as to the answer.

It should be sufficient to note briefly the wide divergence of thinking on this most sensitive and difficult question.   There has always been strong support for the view that life does not begin until live birth.   This was the belief of the Stoics.   It appears to be the predominant, though not the unanimous, attitude of the Jewish faith.   It may be taken to represent also the position of a large segment of the Protestant community, insofar as that can be ascertained; organized groups that have taken a formal position on the abortion issue have generally regarded abortion as a matter for the conscience of the individual and her family.   As we have noted, the common law found greater significance in quickening.   Physicians and their scientific colleagues have regarded that event with less interest and have tended to focus either upon conception or upon live birth or upon the interim point at which the fetus becomes "viable," that is, potentially able to live outside the mother's womb, albeit with artificial aid.[59]   Viability is usually placed at about seven months (28 weeks) but may occur earlier, even at 24 weeks.[60]   The Aristotelian theory of "mediate animation," that held sway throughout the Middle Ages and the Renaissance in Europe, continued to be official Roman Catholic dogma until the 19th century, despite opposition to this "ensoulment" theory from those in the Church who would recognize the existence of life from the moment of conception.   The latter is now, of course, the official belief of the Catholic Church.   As one of the briefs *amicus* discloses, this is a view strongly held by many non-Catholics as well, and by many physicians.   Substantial problems for precise definition of this view are posed, however, by new embryological data that purport to indicate that conception is a "process" over time, rather than an event, and by new medical

the maximum penalty for murder prescribed by Art. 1257 of the Texas Penal Code.   If the fetus is a person, may the penalties be different?

[59] L. Hellman & J. Pritchard, Williams Obstetrics 493 (14th ed. 1971); Dorland's Illustrated Medical Dictionary 1689 (24th ed. 1965).

[60] Hellman & Pritchard, supra, n. 59, at 493.

techniques such as menstrual extraction, the "morning-after" pill, implantation of embryos, artificial insemination, and even artificial wombs.

In areas other than criminal abortion the law has been reluctant to endorse any theory that life, as we recognize it, begins before live birth or to accord legal rights to the unborn except in narrowly defined situations and except when the rights are contingent upon live birth. For example, the traditional rule of tort law had denied recovery for prenatal injuries even though the child was born alive. That rule has been changed in almost every jurisdiction. In most States recovery is said to be permitted only if the fetus was viable, or at least quick, when the injuries were sustained, though few courts have squarely so held. In a recent development, generally opposed by the commentators, some States permit the parents of a stillborn child to maintain an action for wrongful death because of prenatal injuries. Such an action, however, would appear to be one to vindicate the parents' interest and is thus consistent with the view that the fetus, at most, represents only the potentiality of life. Similarly, unborn children have been recognized as acquiring rights or interests by way of inheritance or other devolution of property, and have been represented by guardians *ad litem*. Perfection of the interests involved, again, has generally been contingent upon live birth. In short, the unborn have never been recognized in the law as persons in the whole sense.

X.

In view of all this, we do not agree that, by adopting one theory of life, Texas may override the rights of the pregnant woman that are at stake. We repeat, however, that the State does have an important and legitimate interest in preserving and protecting the health of the pregnant woman, whether she be a resident of the State or a non-resident who seeks medical consultation and treatment there, and that it has still *another* important and legitimate interest in protecting the potentiality of human life. These interests are separate and distinct. Each grows in substantiality as the woman approaches term and, at a point during pregnancy, each becomes "compelling."

With respect to the State's important and legitimate interest in the health of the mother, the "compelling" point, in the light of present medical knowledge, is at approximately the end of the first trimester. This is so because of the now established medical fact, referred to above . . . that until the end of the first trimester mortality in abortion is less than mortality in normal childbirth. It follows that, from and after this point, a State may regulate the abortion procedure to the extent that the regulation reasonably relates to the preservation and protection of maternal health. Examples of permissible state regulation in this area are requirements as to the qualifications of the person who is to perform the abortion; as to the licensure of that person; as to the facility in which the procedure is to be performed, that is, whether it must be a hospital or may be a clinic or some other place of less-than-hospital status; as to the licensing of the facility; and the like.

This means, on the other hand, that, for the period of pregnancy prior to this "compelling" point, the attending physician, in consultation with his patient, is free to determine, without regulation by the State, that in his medical judgment the patient's pregnancy should be terminated. If that decision is reached, the judgment may be effectuated by an abortion free of interference by the State.

With respect to the State's important and legitimate interest in potential life, the "compelling" point is at viability. This is so because the fetus then presumably has the capability of meaningful life outside the mother's womb. State regulation protective of fetal life after viability thus has both logical and biological justifications. If the State is interested in protecting fetal life after viability, it may go so far as to proscribe abortion during that period except when it is necessary to preserve the life or health of the mother.

Measured against these standards, Art. 1196 of the Texas Penal Code, in restricting legal abortions to those "procured or attempted by medical advice for the purpose of saving the life of the mother," sweeps too broadly. The statute makes no distinction between abortions performed early in pregnancy and those performed later, and it limits to a single reason, "saving" the mother's life, the legal justification for the procedure. The statute, therefore, cannot survive the constitutional attack made upon it here.

This conclusion makes it unnecessary for us to consider the additional challenge to the Texas statute asserted on grounds of vagueness. See United States v. Vuitch, 402 U.S. 62, 67–72 (1971).

XI.

To summarize and to repeat:

1. A state criminal abortion statute of the current Texas type, that excepts from criminality only a *life saving* procedure on behalf of the mother, without regard to pregnancy stage and without recognition of the other interests involved, is violative of the Due Process Clause of the Fourteenth Amendment.

(a) For the stage prior to approximately the end of the first trimester, the abortion decision and its effectuation must be left to the medical judgment of the pregnant woman's attending physician.

(b) For the stage subsequent to approximately the end of the first trimester, the State, in promoting its interest in the health of the mother, may, if it chooses, regulate the abortion procedure in ways that are reasonably related to maternal health.

(c) For the stage subsequent to viability the State, in promoting its interest in the potentiality of human life, may, if it chooses, regulate, and even proscribe, abortion except where it is necessary, in appropriate medical judgment, for the preservation of the life or health of the mother.

2. The State may define the term "physician," as it has been employed in the preceding numbered paragraphs of this Part XI of this opinion, to mean only a physician currently licensed by the State, and may proscribe any abortion by a person who is not a physician as so defined.

In Doe v. Bolton, 410 U.S. 179, procedural requirements contained in one of the modern abortion statutes are considered. That opinion and this one, of course, are to be read together.

This holding, we feel, is consistent with the relative weights of the respective interests involved, with the lessons and example of medical and legal history, with the lenity of the common law, and with the demands of the profound problems of the present day. The decision leaves the State free to place increasing restrictions on abortion as the period of pregnancy lengthens, so long as those restrictions are tailored to the recognized state interests. The decision vindicates the right of the physician to administer medical treatment according to his professional judgment up to the points where important state interests provide compelling justifications for intervention. Up to those points the abortion decision in all its aspects is inherently, and primarily, a medical decision, and basic responsibility for it must rest with the physician. If an individual practitioner abuses the privilege of exercising proper medical judgment, the usual remedies, judicial and intra-professional, are available.

. . . .

The judgment of the District Court as to intervenor Hallford is reversed, and Dr. Hallford's complaint in intervention is dismissed. In all other respects the judgment of the District Court is affirmed. Costs are allowed to the appellee.

Mr. Justice Stewart, concurring.

. . .

Mr. Justice Rehnquist, dissenting.

The Court's opinion brings to the decision of this troubling question both extensive historical fact and a wealth of legal scholarship. While its opinion thus commands my respect, I find myself nonetheless in fundamental disagreement with those parts of it which invalidate the Texas statute in question, and therefore dissent.

. . .

I have difficulty in concluding, as the Court does, that the right of "privacy" is involved in this case. Texas by the statute here challenged bars the performance of a medical abortion by a licensed physician on a plaintiff such as Roe. A transaction resulting in an operation such as this is not "private" in the ordinary usage of that word. Nor is the "privacy" which the Court finds here even a distant relative of the freedom from searches and seizures protected by the Fourth Amendment to the Constitution which the Court has referred to as embodying a right to privacy. Katz v. United States, 389 U.S. 347 (1967).

. . .

The Court eschews the history of the Fourteenth Amendment in its reliance on the "compelling state interest" test. See Weber v. Aetna Cas. & Sur. Co., 406 U.S. 164, 179 (1972) (dissenting opinion). But the Court adds a new wrinkle to this test by transposing it from the legal considerations associated with the Equal Protection Clause of the Fourteenth Amendment to this case arising under the Due Process Clause of the Fourteenth Amendment. Unless I misapprehend the consequences of this transplanting of the "compelling state interest test," the Court's opinion will accomplish the seemingly impossible feat of leaving this area of the law more confused than it found it.

While the Court's opinion quotes from the dissent of Mr. Justice Holmes in Lochner v. New York, 198 U.S. 45 (1905), the result it reaches is more closely attuned to the majority opinion of Mr. Justice Peckham in that case. As in *Lochner* and similar cases, applying substantive due process standards to economic and social welfare legislation, the adoption of the compelling state interest standard will inevitably require this Court to examine the legislative policies and pass on the wisdom of these policies in the very process of deciding whether a particular state interest put forward may or may not be "compelling." The decision here to break the term of pregnancy into three distinct terms and to outline the permissible restrictions the State may impose in each one, for example, partakes more of judicial legislation than it does of a determination of the intent of the drafters of the Fourteenth Amendment.

The fact that a majority of the States, reflecting after all the majority sentiment in those States, have had restrictions on abortions for at least a century is a strong indication, it seems to me, that the asserted right to an abortion is not "so rooted in the traditions and conscience of our people as to be ranked as fundamental," Snyder v. Massachusetts, 291 U.S. 97, 105 (1934). Even today, when society's views on abortion are changing, the very existence of the debate is evidence that the "right" to an abortion is not so universally accepted as the appellants would have us believe.[a]

---

[a] For an early view criticizing the method by which the Court reached its result in the original abortion decisions, see Ely, *The Wages of Crying Wolf: A Comment on Roe v. Wade,* 82 Yale L.J. 920 (1973). For other useful commentary at the time see Epstein, *Substantive Due Process by Any Other*

[In the companion case of Doe v. Bolton, 410 U.S. 179 (1973), the Court held invalid a number of provisions of the Georgia statute regulating medical practice in abortion cases. The concurring and dissenting opinions which follow were addressed to both cases.]

Mr. Chief Justice Burger, concurring [in *Wade* and *Bolton*].

I agree that, under the Fourteenth Amendment to the Constitution, the abortion statutes of Georgia and Texas impermissibly limit the performance of abortions necessary to protect the health of pregnant women, using the term health in its broadest medical context. See United States v. Vuitch, 402 U.S. 62, 71–72 (1971). I am somewhat troubled that the Court has taken notice of various scientific and medical data in reaching its conclusion; however, I do not believe that the Court has exceeded the scope of judicial notice accepted in other contexts.

. . .

I do not read the Court's holding today as having the sweeping consequences attributed to it by the dissenting Justices; the dissenting views discount the reality that the vast majority of physicians observe the standards of their profession, and act only on the basis of carefully deliberated medical judgments relating to life and health. Plainly, the Court today rejects any claim that the Constitution requires abortion on demand.

Mr. Justice Douglas, concurring [in *Wade* and *Bolton*].

While I join the opinion of the Court, I add a few words.

The questions presented in the present cases go far beyond the issues of vagueness, which we considered in United States v. Vuitch, 402 U.S. 62. They involve the right of privacy, one aspect of which we considered in Griswold v. Connecticut, 381 U.S. 479, 484, when we held that various guarantees in the Bill of Rights create zones of privacy. . . .

The Ninth Amendment obviously does not create federally enforceable rights. It merely says, "The enumeration in the Constitution of certain rights, shall not be construed to deny or disparage others retained by the people." But a catalogue of these rights includes customary, traditional, and time-honored rights, amenities, privileges, and immunities that come within the sweep of "the Blessings of Liberty" mentioned in the preamble to the Constitution. Many of them in my view come within the meaning of the term "liberty" as used in the Fourteenth Amendment.

First is the autonomous control over the development and expression of one's intellect, interests, tastes, and personality.

These are rights protected by the First Amendment and in my view they are absolute, permitting of no exceptions. . . .

Second is freedom of choice in the basic decisions of one's life respecting marriage, divorce, procreation, contraception, and the education and upbringing of children.

These rights, unlike those protected by the First Amendment, are subject to some control by the police power. Thus the Fourth Amendment speaks only of "unreasonable searches and seizures" and of "probable cause." These rights are "fundamental" and we have held that in order to support legislative action the statute must be narrowly and precisely drawn and that a "compelling state interest" must be shown in support of the limitation. . . .

The liberty to marry a person of one's own choosing, Loving v. Virginia, 388 U.S. 1; the right of procreation, Skinner v. Oklahoma, 316 U.S. 535; the liberty to direct the education of one's children, Pierce v. Soc'y of Sisters, 268

Name: The Abortion Cases, 1973 Sup.Ct.Rev. 159; Tribe, *Forward: Toward a Model of Roles in the Due Process of Life and Law,* 87 Harv.L.Rev. 1 (1973).

U.S. 510, and the privacy of the marital relation, Griswold v. Connecticut, supra, are in this category. . . .

This right of privacy was called by Mr. Justice Brandeis the right "to be let alone." Olmstead v. United States, 277 U.S. 438, 478. That right includes the privilege of an individual to plan his own affairs, for, "outside areas of plainly harmful conduct, every American is left to shape his own life as he thinks best, do what he pleases, go where he pleases." Kent v. Dulles, 357 U.S. 116, 126.

Third is the freedom to care for one's health and person, freedom from bodily restraint or compulsion, freedom to walk, stroll, or loaf.

These rights, though fundamental, are likewise subject to regulation on a showing of "compelling state interest." . . .

The present statute has struck the balance between the woman and the State's interests wholly in favor of the latter. I am not prepared to hold that a State may equate, as Georgia has done, all phases of maturation preceding birth. . . .

In summary, the enactment is overbroad. It is not closely correlated to the aim of preserving pre-natal life. In fact, it permits its destruction in several cases, including pregnancies resulting from sex acts in which unmarried females are below the statutory age of consent. At the same time, however, the measure broadly proscribes aborting other pregnancies which may cause severe mental disorders. Additionally, the statute is overbroad because it equates the value of embryonic life immediately after conception with the worth of life immediately before birth. . . .

I also agree that the superstructure of medical supervision which Georgia has erected violates the patient's right of privacy inherent in her choice of her own physician.

Mr. Justice White, with whom Mr. Justice Rehnquist joins, dissenting [in *Wade* and *Bolton*]. . . .

With all due respect, I dissent. I find nothing in the language or history of the Constitution to support the Court's judgment. The Court simply fashions and announces a new constitutional right for pregnant mothers and, with scarcely any reason or authority for its action, invests that right with sufficient substance to override most existing state abortion statutes. The upshot is that the people and the legislatures of the 50 States are constitutionally disentitled to weigh the relative importance of the continued existence and development of the fetus on the one hand against a spectrum of possible impacts on the mother on the other hand. As an exercise of raw judicial power, the Court perhaps has authority to do what it does today; but in my view its judgment is an improvident and extravagant exercise of the power of judicial review which the Constitution extends to this Court.

The Court apparently values the convenience of the pregnant mother more than the continued existence and development of the life or potential life which she carries. Whether or not I might agree with that marshalling of values, I can in no event join the Court's judgment because I find no constitutional warrant for imposing such an order of priorities on the people and legislatures of the States. In a sensitive area such as this, involving as it does issues over which reasonable men may easily and heatedly differ, I cannot accept the Court's exercise of its clear power of choice by interposing a constitutional barrier to state efforts to protect human life and by investing mothers and doctors with the constitutionally protected right to exterminate it. This issue, for the most part, should be left with the people and to the political processes the people have devised to govern their affairs.

It is my view, therefore, that the Texas statute is not constitutionally infirm because it denies abortions to those who seek to serve only their convenience rather than to protect their life or health. . . .

———

REQUIREMENT OF CONSENT OF SPOUSE TO ABORTION

In Planned Parenthood v. Danforth, supra, the Court by a vote of 6 to 3 held invalid a requirement of the written consent of the spouse of a woman seeking an abortion during the first twelve weeks of pregnancy. Justice Blackmun, writing for the Court, said:

"Clearly, since the State cannot regulate or proscribe abortion during the first stage, when the physician and his patient make that decision, the State cannot delegate authority to any particular person, even the spouse, to prevent abortion during that same period.

. . .

"It seems manifest that, ideally, the decision to terminate a pregnancy should be one concurred in by both the wife and her husband. No marriage may be viewed as harmonious or successful if the marriage partners are fundamentally divided on so important and vital an issue. But it is difficult to believe that the goal of fostering mutuality and trust in a marriage, and of strengthening the marital relationship and the marriage institution, will be achieved by giving the husband a veto power exercisable for any reason whatsoever or for no reason at all. . . .

"We recognize, of course, that when a woman, with the approval of her physician but without the approval of her husband, decides to terminate her pregnancy, it could be said that she is acting unilaterally. The obvious fact is that when the wife and the husband disagree on this decision, the view of only one of the two marriage partners can prevail. Since it is the woman who physically bears the child and who is the more directly and immediately affected by the pregnancy, as between the two, the balance weighs in her favor. Cf. Roe v. Wade, 410 U.S., at 153."

Justice White, joined by Chief Justice Burger and Justice Rehnquist, dissented, saying:

. . . "It is truly surprising that the majority finds in the United States Constitution, as it must in order to justify the result it reaches, a rule that the State must assign a greater value to a mother's decision to cut off a potential human life by abortion than to a father's decision to let it mature into a live child. Such a rule cannot be found there, nor can it be found in Roe v. Wade, supra. These are matters which a State should be able to decide free from the suffocating power of the federal judge, purporting to act in the name of the Constitution.

"In describing the nature of a mother's interest in terminating a pregnancy, the Court in Roe v. Wade mentioned only the post-birth burdens of rearing a child, id., at p. 153, and rejected a rule based on her interest in controlling her own body during pregnancy. Id., at 154. Missouri has a law which prevents a woman from putting a child up for adoption over her husband's objection, § 453.030 R.S.Mo.1969. This law represents a judgment by the State that the mother's interest in avoiding the burdens of child rearing do not outweigh or snuff out the father's interest in participating in bringing up his own child. That law is plainly valid, but no more so than § 3(3) of the Act now before us, resting as it does on precisely the same judgment."

LIMITATIONS ON THE ACCESS OF MINORS TO ABORTIONS AND CONTRACEPTIVES

In Planned Parenthood v. Danforth, supra, the Court, by a vote of 5 to 4, held invalid a requirement that a parent or person *in loco parentis* consent to abortions by minors unless the abortion was necessary to preserve the life of the mother. Justice Blackmun, speaking for the Court, said:

"Just as with the requirement of consent from the spouse, so here, the State does not have the constitutional authority to give a third party an absolute, and possibly arbitrary, veto over the decision of the physician and his patient to terminate the patient's pregnancy, regardless of the reason for withholding the consent.

"Constitutional rights do not mature and come into being magically only when one attains the state-defined age of majority. Minors, as well as adults, are protected by the Constitution and possess constitutional rights. See, e.g., Breed v. Jones, 421 U.S. 519 (1975); Goss v. Lopez, 419 U.S. 565 (1975); Tinker v. Des Moines School District, 393 U.S. 503 (1969); In re Gault, 387 U.S. 1 (1967). The Court indeed, however, long has recognized that the State has somewhat broader authority to regulate the activities of children than of adults. Prince v. Massachusetts, 321 U.S., at 170; Ginsberg v. New York, 390 U.S. 629 (1968). It remains, then, to examine whether there is any significant state interest in conditioning an abortion on the consent of a parent or person *in loco parentis* that is not present in the case of an adult.

"One suggested interest is the safeguarding of the family unit and of parental authority. 392 F.Supp., at 1370. It is difficult, however, to conclude that providing a parent with absolute power to overrule a determination, made by the physician and his minor patient, to terminate the patient's pregnancy will serve to strengthen the family unit. Neither is it likely that such veto power will enhance parental authority or control where the minor and the nonconsenting parent are so fundamentally in conflict and the very existence of the pregnancy already has fractured the family structure. Any independent interest the parent may have in the termination of the minor daughter's pregnancy is no more weighty than the right of privacy of the competent minor mature enough to have become pregnant.

"We emphasize that our holding that § 3(4) is invalid does not suggest that every minor, regardless of age or maturity, may give effective consent for termination of her pregnancy. See Bellotti v. Baird, post. The fault with § 3(4) is that it imposes a special consent provision, exercisable by a person other than the woman and her physician, as a prerequisite to a minor's termination of her pregnancy and does so without a sufficient justification for restriction. It violates the strictures of *Roe* and *Doe*."

Justice White, joined by Chief Justice Burger, and Justice Rehnquist, dissenting, said:

"[T]he purpose of the parental consent requirement is not merely to vindicate any interest of the parent or of the State. The purpose of the requirement is to vindicate the very right created in Roe v. Wade, supra— the right of the pregnant woman to decide 'whether *or not* to terminate her pregnancy'. Id., at 153 (emphasis added). The abortion decision is unquestionably important and has irrevocable consequences whichever way it is made. Missouri is entitled to protect the minor unmarried woman from making the decision in a way which is not in her own best interests, and it seeks to achieve this goal by requiring parental consultation and consent. This is the traditional way by which States have sought to protect children from their own immature and improvident decisions; and there is absolutely no reason expressed by the majority why the State may not utilize that method here."

Justice Stevens also dissented on this point, saying in part:

". . . [T]he holding in Roe v. Wade that the abortion decision is entitled to constitutional protection merely emphasizes the importance of the decision; it does not lead to the conclusion that the state legislature has no power to enact legislation for the purpose of protecting a young pregnant woman from the consequences of an incorrect decision.

"The abortion decision is, of course, more important than the decision to attend or to avoid an adult motion picture, or the decision to work long hours in a factory. It is not necessarily any more important than the decision to run away from home or the decision to marry. But even if it is the most important kind of a decision a young person may ever make, that assumption merely enhances the quality of the State's interest in maximizing the probability that the decision be made correctly and with full understanding of the consequences of either alternative.

"The Court recognizes that the State may insist that the decision not be made without the benefit of medical advice. But since the most significant consequences of the decision are not medical in character, it would seem to me that the State may, with equal legitimacy, insist that the decision be made only after other appropriate counsel has been had as well. Whatever choice a pregnant young woman makes—to marry, to abort, to bear her child out of wedlock—the consequences of her decision may have a profound impact on her entire future life. A legislative determination that such a choice will be made more wisely in most cases if the advice and moral support of a parent play a part in the decisionmaking process is surely not irrational. Moreover, it is perfectly clear that the parental consent requirement will necessarily involve a parent in the decisional process."

In Carey v. Population Services International, 431 U.S. 678 (1977), the Court held invalid a law forbidding the distribution of contraceptives to persons under age 16. There was no opinion for the Court. Justice Brennan's opinion joined by Justices Stewart, Marshall and Blackmun, said:

"Since the State may not impose a blanket prohibition, or even a blanket requirement of parental consent, on the choice of a minor to terminate her pregnancy, the constitutionality of a blanket prohibition of the distribution of contraceptives to minors is *a fortiori* foreclosed. The State's interests in protection of the mental and physical health of the pregnant minor, and in protection of potential life are clearly more implicated by the abortion decision than by the decision to use a nonhazardous contraceptive."

The concurring Justices were concerned with implications of the plurality opinion as to the level of scrutiny applicable to state laws forbidding premarital sexual activity by minors. Justices White and Stevens described the argument that minors have a constitutional right to engage in premarital intercourse as frivolous. Justice White concurred in the result on the ground that there was insufficient demonstration that prohibition on distribution of contraceptives deters sexual activity. Justice Stevens argued further that New York had denied minors the means of reducing exposure to venereal disease and pregnancy. "It is as though a State decided to dramatize its disapproval of motorcycles by forbidding the use of safety helmets." Justice Powell concluded that the vice of the New York law was in its prohibitions on parental distribution of contraceptives, and on distribution to married females between the ages of 14 and 16.

Chief Justice Burger and Justice Rehnquist dissented.

In Bellotti v. Baird, 443 U.S. 622 (1979), the Court held invalid a Massachusetts statute regulating abortions for unmarried minors. The law provided that if one or both of the minor's parents refused consent, the abortion may be obtained by order of a judge "for good cause shown." The Court concluded that the law was invalid because, if the parents refused consent, judicial authorization could still be withheld even if the minor was mature and capable of informed decisionmaking. Justice Powell's opinion, joined by Chief Justice Burger, and Justices Stewart and Rehnquist, concluded that the statute was also invalid in requiring parental consultation or notification in every instance, whether or not in the minor's best interest. The opinion concluded that a valid law requiring parental consent must provide an alternative authorization procedure allowing the minor to show she was mature enough to make the decision, in consultation with her physician, independent of her parents' wishes, or that the desired abortion was in her best interest. Moreover, the alternative procedure must assure anonymity and sufficient expedition so that the parental consent requirement did not amount, in fact, to an absolute veto. Justice Stevens, joined by Justices Brennan, Marshall and Blackmun, concurred in the conclusion that the judge's authority to deny an abortion contrary to the minor's informed and reasonable decision was unconstitutional because it amounted to an absolute third party veto. "Because [Justice Powell's] opinion goes further, however, and addresses the constitutionality of an abortion statute that Massachusetts has not enacted, I decline to join his opinion." Justice White dissented.

H.L. v. Matheson, 450 U.S. 398 (1981), concerned the validity of a Utah statute requiring a physician to "notify, if possible" the parents of a minor upon whom an abortion was to be performed. The Court held that plaintiff lacked standing to challenge the statute as applied to minors who were mature or emancipated. In a narrow holding, the Court upheld the statute as applied to a minor living with and dependent upon her parents, where there was no showing of maturity or of the details of her relationship to her parents. The Court's opinion distinguished between parental veto, and a "mere requirement of parental notice." Justices Powell and Stewart, who joined the Court's opinion, also wrote separately, concluding that "a State may not validly require notice to parents in all cases, without providing an independent decisionmaker to whom a pregnant minor can have recourse if she believes that she is mature enough to make the abortion decision independently or that notification otherwise would not be in her best interests." In a footnote, he explained that the rationale of his plurality opinion in the 1979 *Bellotti* decision was as applicable to requirements of parental notice as to requirements of parental consent. Justice Marshall, joined by Justices Brennan and Blackmun, dissented. The dissent argued that the statute, which required parental notification in all cases, should be tested for constitutionality "on its face." The statute was "plainly overbroad" in requiring parental notification in all cases.

Parham v. J.R., 442 U.S. 584 (1979), should be compared with the abortion and contraception cases. The Court upheld a Georgia statute permitting a parent or guardian to commit a minor to a mental institution for detention and treatment if the superintendent of the facility determined that the minor had a treatable mental illness. No hearing was provided in which the child's interests would be directly represented. The majority opinion (representing the views of Chief Justice Burger, and Justices White, Blackmun, Powell, and Rehnquist) contained the following discussion of the rights of parents to make decisions for their children:

"We next deal with the interests of the parents who have decided, on the basis of their observations and independent professional recommendations, that their child needs institutional care. Appellees argue that the constitutional rights of the child are of such magnitude and the likelihood of parental abuse is so great that the parents' traditional interests in and responsibility for the upbringing of their child must be subordinated at least to the extent of providing a formal adversary hearing prior to a voluntary commitment.

"Our jurisprudence historically has reflected Western Civilization concepts of the family as a unit with broad parental authority over minor children. Our cases have consistently followed that course; our constitutional system long ago rejected any notion that a child is 'the mere creature of the State' and, on the contrary, asserted that parents generally 'have the right, coupled with the high duty, to recognize and prepare [their children] for additional obligations.' Pierce v. Soc'y of Sisters, 268 U.S. 510, 535 (1924). See also Wisconsin v. Yoder, 406 U.S. 205, 213 (1972); Prince v. Massachusetts, 321 U.S. 158, 166 (1944); Meyer v. Nebraska, 262 U.S. 390, 400 (1923). Surely, this includes a 'high duty' to recognize symptoms of illness and to seek and follow medical advice. The law's concept of the family rests on a presumption that parents possess what a child lacks in maturity, experience, and capacity for judgment required for making life's difficult decisions. More important, historically it has recognized that natural bonds of affection lead parents to act in the best interests of their children. 1 W. Blackstone, *Commentaries* * 447; 2 Kent, *Commentaries on American Law* * 190.

"As with so many other legal presumptions, experience and reality may rebut what the law accepts as a starting point; the incidence of child neglect and abuse cases attests to this. That some parents 'may at times be acting against the interests of their child' . . . creates a basis for caution, but is hardly a reason to discard wholesale those pages of human experience that teach that parents generally do act in the child's best interests. . . . The statist notion that governmental power should supersede parental authority in *all* cases because *some* parents abuse and neglect children is repugnant to American tradition.

"Nonetheless, we have recognized that a state is not without constitutional control over parental discretion in dealing with children when their physical or mental health is jeopardized. . . . Moreover, the Court recently declared unconstitutional a state statute that granted parents an absolute veto over a minor child's decision to have an abortion. Planned Parenthood of Missouri v. Danforth, 428 U.S. 52 (1976). Appellees urge that these precedents limiting the traditional rights of parents, if viewed in the context of the liberty interest of the child and the likelihood of parental abuse, require us to hold that the parents' decision to have a child admitted to a mental hospital must be subjected to an exacting constitutional scrutiny, including a formal, adversary, preadmission hearing.

"Appellees' argument, however, sweeps too broadly. Simply because the decision of a parent is not agreeable to a child or because it involves risks does not automatically transfer the power to make that decision from the parents to some agency or officer of the state. The same characterizations can be made for a tonsillectomy, appendectomy or other medical procedure. Most children, even in adolescence, simply are not able to make sound judgments concerning many decisions, including their need for medical care or treatment. Parents can and must make those judgments. Here there is no finding by the District Court of even a single instance of bad faith by any parent of any member of appellees' class. We cannot assume that the result in Meyer v. Nebraska, supra, and Pierce v. Soc'y of Sisters, supra, would have been different if the children there had announced a preference to learn only English or a preference to go to a public, rather than a church, school. The fact that a child may balk at hospitalization or complain about a parental refusal to provide cosmetic surgery does not diminish the parents' authority to decide what is best for the child. See generally Goldstein,

Medical Case for the Child at Risk: On State Supervention of Parental Autonomy, 86 Yale L.J. 645, 664–668 (1977). Bennett, *Allocation of Child Medical Care Decision-making Authority: A Suggested Interest Analysis,* 62 Va.L.Rev. 285, 308 (1976). Neither state officials nor federal courts are equipped to review such parental decisions.

"Appellees place particular reliance on *Planned Parenthood,* arguing that its holding indicates how little deference to parents is appropriate when the child is exercising a constitutional right. The basic situation in that case, however, was very different; *Planned Parenthood* involved an absolute parental veto over the child's ability to obtain an abortion. Parents in Georgia in no sense have an absolute right to commit their children to state mental hospitals; the statute requires the superintendent of each regional hospital to exercise independent judgment as to the child's need for confinement.

"In defining the respective rights and prerogatives of the child and parent in the voluntary commitment setting, we conclude that our precedents permit the parents to retain a substantial, if not the dominant, role in the decision, absent a finding of neglect or abuse, and that the traditional presumption that the parents act in the best interests of their child should apply. We also conclude, however, that the child's rights and the nature of the commitment decision are such that parents cannot always have absolute and unreviewable discretion to decide whether to have a child institutionalized. They, of course, retain plenary authority to seek such care for their children, subject to a physician's independent examination and medical judgment."

RESTRICTIONS ON PRIVATE CONSENSUAL SEXUAL BEHAVIOR

Can the protection of privacy and personal autonomy articulated in Roe v. Wade be extended to protect private consensual sexual behavior outside the norms of the marriage relationship? In Carey v. Population Serv. Int'l, 431 U.S. 678 (1977) the Court said in a footnote: "Appellees argue that . . . the right to privacy comprehends a right of minors as well as adults to engage in private consensual sexual behavior. We observe that the Court has not definitively answered the difficult question whether and to what extent the Constitution prohibits state statutes regulating such behavior among adults. See generally Note, On Privacy: Constitutional Protection for Personal Liberty, 48 N.Y. U.L.Rev. 670, 719–738 (1973)." Justice Powell expressed his concern that the Court "would subject all state regulation affecting adult sexual relations to the strictest standard of judicial review." Justice Rehnquist asserted that while the Court had not "ruled on every conceivable regulation affecting such conduct the facial constitutional validity of criminal statutes prohibiting certain consensual acts has been 'definitively' established." For that statement he relied on Doe v. Commonwealth's Attorney, 425 U.S. 901 (1976), in which the Court summarily affirmed a district court dismissal of a challenge by male homosexuals to Virginia's sodomy law.

In New York v. Uplinger, 104 S.Ct. 2332 (1984) the Court granted certiorari to review a decision of the New York Court of Appeals holding unconstitutional a state statute forbidding loitering in a public place for the purpose of engaging in deviate sexual intercourse. After the case was briefed and argued on the merits, the Court, by a vote of 5 to 4, dismissed the writ of certiorari as improvidently granted.

AKRON v. AKRON CENTER FOR REPRODUCTIVE HEALTH, INC.

462 U.S. 416, 103 S.Ct. 2481, 76 L.Ed.2d 687 (1983).

Justice Powell delivered the opinion of the Court.

In this litigation we must decide the constitutionality of several provisions of an ordinance enacted by the city of Akron, Ohio, to regulate the performance of abortions. Today we also review abortion regulations enacted by the State of Missouri, see Planned Parenthood Ass'n of Kansas City, Mo., Inc. v. Ashcroft, 462 U.S. 476, and by the State of Virginia, see Simopoulos v. Virginia, 462 U.S. 506.

These cases come to us a decade after we held in Roe v. Wade, 410 U.S. 113 (1973), that the right of privacy, grounded in the concept of personal liberty guaranteed by the Constitution, encompasses a woman's right to decide whether to terminate her pregnancy. Legislative responses to the Court's decision have required us on several occasions, and again today, to define the limits of a State's authority to regulate the performance of abortions. And arguments continue to be made, in these cases as well, that we erred in interpreting the Constitution. Nonetheless, the doctrine of *stare decisis,* while perhaps never entirely persuasive on a constitutional question, is a doctrine that demands respect to a society governed by the rule of law.[1] We respect it today, and reaffirm Roe v. Wade.

I

In February 1978 the city council of Akron enacted Ordinance No. 160–1978, entitled "Regulation of Abortions." The ordinance sets forth 17 provisions that regulate the performance of abortions, see Akron Codified Ordinances ch. 1870, five of which are at issue in this case:

---

[1] There are especially compelling reasons for adhering to *stare decisis* in applying the principles of Roe v. Wade. That case was considered with special care. It was first argued during the 1971 Term, and reargued—with extensive briefing—the following Term. The decision was joined by the Chief Justice and six other Justices. Since *Roe* was decided in February 1973, the Court repeatedly and consistently has accepted and applied the basic principle that a woman has a fundamental right to make the highly personal choice whether or not to terminate her pregnancy. See Connecticut v. Menillo, 423 U.S. 9 (1975); Planned Parenthood of Central Mo. v. Danforth, 428 U.S. 52 (1976); Bellotti v. Baird, 428 U.S. 132 (1976); Beal v. Doe, 432 U.S. 438 (1977); Maher v. Roe, 432 U.S. 464 (1977); Colautti v. Franklin, 439 U.S. 379 (1979); Bellotti v. Baird, 443 U.S. 622 (1979); Harris v. McRae, 448 U.S. 297 (1980); H.L. v. Matheson, 450 U.S. 398 (1981).

Today, however, the dissenting opinion rejects the basic premise of *Roe* and its progeny. The dissent stops short of arguing flatly that *Roe* should be overruled. Rather, it adopts reasoning that, for all practical purposes, would accomplish precisely that result. The dissent states that "[e]ven assuming that there is a fundamental right to terminate pregnancy in some situations," the State's compelling interests in maternal health and potential human life "are present *throughout* pregnancy." (emphasis in original). The existence of these compelling interests turns out to be largely unnecessary, however, for the dissent does not think that even one of the numerous abortion regulations at issue imposes a sufficient burden on the "limited" fundamental right to require heightened scrutiny. Indeed, the dissent asserts that, regardless of cost, "[a] health regulation, such as the hospitalization requirement, simply does not rise to the level of 'official interference' with the abortion decision." The dissent therefore would hold that a requirement that all abortions be performed in an acute-care, general hospital does not impose an unacceptable burden on the abortion decision. It requires no great familiarity with the cost and limited availability of such hospitals to appreciate that the effect of the dissent's views would be to drive the performance of many abortions back underground free of effective regulation and often without the attendance of a physician.

In sum, it appears that the dissent would uphold virtually any abortion regulation under a rational-basis test. It also appears that even where heightened scrutiny is deemed appropriate, the dissent would uphold virtually any abortion-inhibiting regulation because of the State's interest in preserving potential human life. See post, (arguing that a 24-hour waiting period is justified in part because the abortion decision "has grave consequences for the fetus"). This analysis is wholly incompatible with the existence of the fundamental right recognized in Roe v. Wade.

(i) Section 1870.03 requires that all abortions performed after the first trimester of pregnancy be performed in a hospital.

(ii) Section 1870.05 sets forth requirements for notification of and consent by parents before abortions may be performed on unmarried minors.

(iii) Section 1870.06 requires that the attending physician make certain specified statements to the patient "to insure that the consent for an abortion is truly informed consent."

(iv) Section 1870.07 requires a 24-hour waiting period between the time the woman signs a consent form and the time the abortion is performed.

(v) Section 1870.16 requires that fetal remains be "disposed of in a humane and sanitary manner."

A violation of any section of the ordinance is punishable as a criminal misdemeanor. § 1870.18. If any provision is invalidated, it is to be severed from the remainder of the ordinance. The ordinance became effective on May 1, 1978.

. . .

[A lawsuit was brought in the federal district court by abortion clinics and a doctor against the City of Akron and three city officials challenging the validity of the ordinance. On appeal challenges to the five regulations set out above were at issue. The Court held all five to be unconstitutional.]

II

In Roe v. Wade, the Court held that the "right of privacy, . . . founded in the Fourteenth Amendment's concept of personal liberty and restrictions upon state action, . . . is broad enough to encompass a woman's decision whether or not to terminate her pregnancy." 410 U.S., at 153. . . .

At the same time, the Court in *Roe* acknowledged that the woman's fundamental right "is not unqualified and must be considered against important state interests in abortion." *Roe,* 410 U.S., at 154. But restrictive state regulation of the right to choose abortion, as with other fundamental rights subject to searching judicial examination, must be supported by a compelling state interest. We have recognized two such interests that may justify state regulation of abortions.

First, a State has an "important and legitimate interest in protecting the potentiality of human life." Although this interest exists "throughout the course of the woman's pregnancy," Beal v. Doe, 432 U.S. 438, 446 (1977), it becomes compelling only at viability, the point at which the fetus "has the capability of meaningful life outside the mother's womb," *Roe,* 410 U.S., at 163. See Planned Parenthood of Central Mo. v. Danforth, 428 U.S. 52, 63–65 (1976). At viability this interest in protecting the potential life of the unborn child is so important that the State may proscribe abortions altogether, "except when it is necessary to preserve the life or health of the mother." *Roe,* 410 U.S. at 164.

Second, because a State has a legitimate concern with the health of women who undergo abortions, "a State may properly assert important interests in safeguarding health [and] in maintaining medical standards." We held in *Roe,* however, that this health interest does not become compelling until "approximately the end of the first trimester" of pregnancy.[11] Until that time, a pregnant woman must be permitted, in consultation with her physician, to

---

[11] *Roe* identified the end of the first trimester as the compelling point because until that time—according to the medical literature available in 1973—"mortality in abortion may be less than mortality in normal childbirth." 410 U.S., at 163. There is substantial evidence that developments in the past decade, particularly the development of a much safer method for performing second-trimester abortions, have extended the period in which abortions are safer than childbirth. See, e.g., LeBolt, et

decide to have an abortion and to effectuate that decision "free of interference by the State."

This does not mean that a State never may enact a regulation touching on the woman's abortion right during the first weeks of pregnancy. Certain regulations that have no significant impact on the woman's exercise of her right may be permissible where justified by important state health objectives. In *Danforth,* supra, we unanimously upheld two Missouri statutory provisions, applicable to the first trimester, requiring the woman to provide her informed written consent to the abortion and the physician to keep certain records, even though comparable requirements were not imposed on most other medical procedures. The decisive factor was that the State met its burden of demonstrating that these regulations furthered important health-related State concerns. But even these minor regulations on the abortion procedure during the first trimester may not interfere with physician-patient consultation or with the woman's choice between abortion and childbirth.

From approximately the end of the first trimester of pregnancy, the State "may regulate the abortion procedure to the extent that the regulation reasonably relates to the preservation and protection of maternal health." *Roe,* 410 U.S., at 163. The State's discretion to regulate on this basis does not, however, permit it to adopt abortion regulations that depart from accepted medical practice. We have rejected a State's attempt to ban a particular second-trimester abortion procedure, where the ban would have increased the costs and limited the availability of abortions without promoting important health benefits. See *Danforth,* 428 U.S., at 77–78. If a State requires licensing or undertakes to regulate the performance of abortions during this period, the health standards adopted must be "legitimately related to the objective the State seeks to accomplish." *Doe,* 410 U.S., at 195.

III

Section 1870.03 of the Akron ordinance requires that any abortion performed "upon a pregnant woman subsequent to the end of the first trimester of her pregnancy" [15] must be "performed in a hospital." A "hospital" is "a

al., Mortality from Abortion and Childbirth: Are the Populations Comparable?, 248 J.A.M.A. 188, 191 (1982) (abortion may be safer than childbirth up to gestational ages of 16 weeks).

We think it prudent, however, to retain *Roe's* identification of the beginning of the second trimester as the approximate time at which the State's interest in maternal health becomes sufficiently compelling to justify significant regulation of abortion. We note that the medical evidence suggests that until approximately the end of the first trimester, the State's interest in maternal health would not be served by regulations that restrict the manner in which abortions are performed by a licensed physician. See, e.g., American College of Obstetricians and Gynecologists (ACOG), Standards for Obstetric-Gynecologic Services 54 (5th ed. 1982) (hereinafter ACOG Standards) (uncomplicated abortions generally may be performed in a physician's office or an outpatient clinic up to 14 weeks from the first day of the last menstrual period); ACOG Technical Bulletin No. 56, Methods of Mid-Trimester Abortion (Dec. 1979) ("Regardless of advances in abortion technology, midtrimester terminations will likely remain more hazardous, expensive, and emotionally disturbing for women than earlier abortions.").

The *Roe* trimester standard thus continues to provide a reasonable legal framework for limiting a State's authority to regulate abortions. Where the State adopts a health regulation governing the performance of abortions during the second trimester, the determinative question should be whether there is a reasonable medical basis for the regulation. See *Roe,* supra, at 163. The comparison between abortion and childbirth mortality rates may be relevant only where the State employs a health rationale as a justification for a complete prohibition on abortions in certain circumstances. See *Danforth,* 428 U.S., at 78–79 (invalidating state ban on saline abortions, a method that was "safer, with respect to maternal mortality, than even continuation of the pregnancy until normal childbirth").

[15] The Akron ordinance does not define "first trimester," but elsewhere suggests that the age of the fetus should be measured from the date of conception. See § 1870.06(B)(2) (physician must inform woman of the number of weeks elapsed since conception); § 1870.06(B)(4) (physician must inform woman that a fetus may be viable after 22 weeks from conception). An average pregnancy lasts approximately 38 weeks from the time of conception or, as more commonly measured, 40 weeks from

general hospital or special hospital devoted to gynecology or obstetrics which is accredited by the Joint Commission on Accreditation of Hospitals or by the American Osteopathic Association." § 1870.1(B). Accreditation by these organizations requires compliance with comprehensive standards governing a wide variety of health and surgical services. The ordinance thus prevents the performance of abortions in outpatient facilities that are not part of an acute-care, full-service hospital.

. . . We . . . now hold that § 1870.03 is unconstitutional.

A

In Roe v. Wade the Court held that after the end of the first trimester of pregnancy the State's interest becomes compelling . . . .

We reaffirm today that a State's interest in health regulation becomes compelling at approximately the end of the first trimester. The existence of a compelling state interest in health, however, is only the beginning of the inquiry. The State's regulation may be upheld only if it is reasonably designed to further that state interest. See *Doe,* 410 U.S., at 195. And the Court in *Roe* did not hold that it always is reasonable for a State to adopt an abortion regulation that applies to the entire second trimester. A State necessarily must have latitude in adopting regulations of general applicability in this sensitive area. But if it appears that during a substantial portion of the second trimester the State's regulation "depart[s] from accepted medical practice," the regulation may not be upheld simply because it may be reasonable for the remaining portion of the trimester. Rather, the State is obligated to make a reasonable effort to limit the effect of its regulations to the period in the trimester during which its health interest will be furthered.

B

There can be no doubt that § 1870.03's second-trimester hospitalization requirement places a significant obstacle in the path of women seeking an abortion. A primary burden created by the requirement is additional cost to the woman. The Court of Appeals noted that there was testimony that a second-trimester abortion costs more than twice as much in a hospital as in a clinic. . . . Moreover, the court indicated that second-trimester abortions were rarely performed in Akron hospitals. . . . Thus, a second-trimester hospitalization requirement may force women to travel to find available facilities, resulting in both financial expense and additional health risk. It therefore is apparent that a second-trimester hospitalization requirement may significantly limit a woman's ability to obtain an abortion.

Akron does not contend that § 1870.03 imposes only an insignificant burden on women's access to abortion, but rather defends it as a reasonable health regulation. This position had strong support at the time of Roe v. Wade, as hospitalization for second-trimester abortions was recommended by the American Public Health Association (APHA), see *Roe,* 410 U.S., at 143–146, and the American College of Obstetricians and Gynecologists (ACOG), see Standards for Obstetric-Gynecologic Services 65 (4th ed. 1974). Since then,

the beginning of the woman's last menstrual period. Under both methods there may be more than a two-week deviation either way.

Because of the approximate nature of these measurements, there is no certain method of delineating "trimesters." Frequently, the first trimester is estimated as 12 weeks following conception, or 14 weeks following the last menstrual period. We need not attempt to draw a precise line, as this Court—for purposes of analysis—has identified the "compelling point" for the State's interest in health as "approximately the end of the first trimester." *Roe,* 410 U.S., at 163. Unless otherwise indicated, all references in this opinion to gestational age are based on the time from the beginning of the last menstrual period.

however, the safety of second-trimester abortions has increased dramatically. The principal reason is that the D & E procedure is now widely and successfully used for second-trimester abortions.[23] The Court of Appeals found that there was "an abundance of evidence that D & E is the safest method of performing post-first trimester abortions today." 651 F.2d, at 1209. The availability of the D & E procedure during the interval between approximately 12 and 16 weeks of pregnancy, a period during which other second-trimester abortion techniques generally cannot be used,[24] has meant that women desiring an early second-trimester abortion no longer are forced to incur the health risks of waiting until at least the sixteenth week of pregnancy.

For our purposes, an even more significant factor is that experience indicates that D & E may be performed safely on an outpatient basis in appropriate nonhospital facilities. The evidence is strong enough to have convinced the APHA to abandon its prior recommendation of hospitalization for all second-trimester abortions:

> "Current data show that abortions occurring in the second trimester can be safely performed by the Dilatation and Evacuation (D and E) procedure. . . . Requirements that all abortions after 12 weeks of gestation be performed in hospitals increase the expense and inconvenience to the woman without contributing to the safety of the procedure." APHA Recommended Program Guide for Abortion Services (Revised 1979), 70 Am.J.Public Health 652, 654 (1980) (hereinafter APHA Recommended Guide).

Similarly, the ACOG no longer suggests that all second-trimester abortions be performed in a hospital. It recommends that abortions performed in a physician's office or outpatient clinic be limited to 14 weeks of pregnancy, but it indicates that abortions may be performed safely in "a hospital-based or in a free-standing ambulatory surgical facility, or in an outpatient clinic meeting the criteria required for a free-standing surgical facility," until 18 weeks of pregnancy. ACOG, Standards for Obstetric-Gynecologic Services 54 (5th ed. 1982).

These developments, and the professional commentary supporting them, constitute impressive evidence that—at least during the early weeks of the second trimester—D & E abortions may be performed as safely in an outpatient clinic as in a full-service hospital. We conclude, therefore, that "present medical knowledge," *Roe,* 410 U.S., at 163, convincingly undercuts Akron's justification for requiring that *all* second-trimester abortions be performed in a hospital.

Akron nonetheless urges that "[t]he fact that some mid-trimester abortions may be done in a minimally equipped clinic does not invalidate the regulation." [27] It is true that a state abortion regulation is not unconstitutional simply because it does not correspond perfectly in all cases to the asserted state interest. But the lines drawn in a state regulation must be reasonable, and this cannot be said of § 1870.03. By preventing the performance of D & E abortions in an

---

[23] At the time *Roe* was decided, the D & E procedure was used only to perform first-trimester abortions.

[24] Instillation procedures, the primary means of performing a second-trimester abortion before the development of D & E, generally cannot be performed until approximately the 16th week of pregnancy because until that time the amniotic sac is too small. See Grimes & Cates, Dilatation and Evacuation, published in Second Trimester Abortion 121.

[27] The city thus implies that its hospital requirement may be sustained because it is reasonable as applied to later D & E abortions or to all second-trimester instillation abortions. We do not hold today that a State in no circumstances may require that some abortions be performed in a full-service hospital. Abortions performed by D & E are much safer, up to a point in the development of the fetus, than those performed by instillation methods. See Cates & Grimes, Morbidity and Mortality, published in Second Trimester Abortion 166–169. The evidence before us as to the need for hospitalization concerns only the D & E method performed in the early weeks of the second trimester. See 651 F.2d, at 1208–1210.

appropriate nonhospital setting, Akron has imposed a heavy, and unnecessary, burden on women's access to a relatively inexpensive, otherwise accessible, and safe abortion procedure. Section 1870.03 has "the effect of inhibiting . . . the vast majority of abortions after the first 12 weeks," *Danforth,* 428 U.S., at 79, and therefore unreasonably infringes upon a woman's constitutional right to obtain an abortion.

IV

We turn next to § 1870.05(B), the provision prohibiting a physician from performing an abortion on a minor pregnant woman under the age of 15 unless he obtains "the informed written consent of one of her parents or her legal guardian" or unless the minor obtains "an order from a court having jurisdiction over her that the abortion be performed or induced."

The relevant legal standards are not in dispute. The Court has held that "the State may not impose a blanket provision . . . requiring the consent of a parent or person *in loco parentis* as a condition for abortion of an unmarried minor." *Danforth,* 428 U.S., at 74. In Bellotti v. Baird, 443 U.S. 622 (1979) (*Bellotti II*), a majority of the Court indicated that a State's interest in protecting immature minors will sustain a requirement of a consent substitute, either parental or judicial. . . . The *Bellotti II* plurality cautioned, however, that the State must provide an alternative procedure whereby a pregnant minor may demonstrate that she is sufficiently mature to make the abortion decision herself or that, despite her immaturity, an abortion would be in her best interests. Under these decisions, it is clear that Akron may not make a blanket determination that *all* minors under the age of 15 are too immature to make this decision or that an abortion never may be in the minor's best interests without parental approval.

Akron's ordinance does not create expressly the alternative procedure required by *Bellotti II.*   .   .   .

.   .   . [W]e do not think that the Akron ordinance, as applied in Ohio juvenile proceedings, is reasonably susceptible of being construed to create an "opportunity for case-by-case evaluations of the maturity of pregnant minors." *Bellotti II,* 443 U.S., at 643, n. 23 (plurality opinion). We therefore affirm the Court of Appeals' judgment that § 1870.05(B) is unconstitutional.

V

The Akron ordinance provides that no abortion shall be performed except "with the informed written consent of the pregnant woman, .   .   . given freely and without coercion." § 1870.06(A). Furthermore, "in order to insure that the consent for an abortion is truly informed consent," the woman must be "orally informed by her attending physician" of the status of her pregnancy, the development of her fetus, the date of possible viability, the physical and emotional complications that may result from an abortion, and the availability of agencies to provide her with assistance and information with respect to birth control, adoption, and childbirth. § 1870.06(B). In addition, the attending physician must inform her "of the particular risks associated with her own pregnancy and the abortion technique to be employed .   .   . [and] other information which in his own medical judgment is relevant to her decision as to whether to have an abortion or carry her pregnancy to term." § 1870.06(C).

The District Court found that § 1870.06(B) was unconstitutional, but that § 1870.06(C) was related to a valid state interest in maternal health. See 479 F.Supp., at 1203–1204. The Court of Appeals concluded that both provisions were unconstitutional. See 651 F.2d, at 1207. We affirm.

A

In *Danforth,* supra, we upheld a Missouri law requiring a pregnant woman to "certif[y] in writing her consent to the abortion and that her consent is informed and freely given and is not the result of coercion." 428 U.S., at 85. We explained:

"The decision to abort . . . is an important, and often a stressful one, and it is desirable and imperative that it be made with full knowledge of its nature and consequences. The woman is the one primarily concerned, and her awareness of the decision and its significance may be assured, constitutionally, by the State to the extent of requiring her prior written consent."

We rejected the view that "informed consent" was too vague a term, construing it to mean "the giving of information to the patient as to just what would be done and as to its consequences. To abscribe more meaning than this might well confine the attending physician in an undesired and uncomfortable straitjacket in the practice of his profession."

The validity of an informed consent requirement thus rests on the State's interest in protecting the health of the pregnant woman. The decision to have an abortion has "implications far broader than those associated with most other kinds of medical treatment," *Bellotti II,* 443 U.S., at 649 (plurality opinion), and thus the State legitimately may seek to ensure that it has been made "in the light of all attendant circumstances—psychological and emotional as well as physical— that might be relevant to the well-being of the patient." Colautti v. Franklin, 439 U.S. 379, 394 (1979).[32] This does not mean, however, that a State has unreviewable authority to decide what information a woman must be given before she chooses to have an abortion. It remains primarily the responsibility of the physician to ensure that appropriate information is conveyed to his patient, depending on her particular circumstances. *Danforth's* recognition of the State's interest in ensuring that this information be given will not justify abortion regulations designed to influence the woman's informed choice between abortion or childbirth.[33]

B

Viewing the city's regulations in this light, we believe that § 1870.06(B) attempts to extend the State's interest in ensuring "informed consent" beyond permissible limits. First, it is fair to say that much of the information required is designed not to inform the woman's consent but rather to persuade her to withhold it altogether. Subsection (3) requires the physician to inform his patient that "the unborn child is a human life from the moment of conception," a requirement inconsistent with the Court's holding in Roe v. Wade that a State may not adopt one theory of when life begins to justify its regulation of abortions. . . .

An additional, and equally decisive, objection to § 1870.06(B) is its intrusion upon the discretion of the pregnant woman's physician. . . . Akron has gone far beyond merely describing the general subject matter relevant to informed consent. By insisting upon recitation of a lengthy and inflexible list of

[32] In particular, we have emphasized that a State's interest in protecting immature minors and in promoting family integrity gives it a special interest in ensuring that the abortion decision is made with understanding and after careful deliberation. See, e.g., H.L. v. Matheson, 450 U.S. 398, 411 (1981); id. at 419–420 (Powell, J., concurring); id., at 421–424 (Stevens, J., concurring in judgment).

[33] A State is not always foreclosed from asserting an interest in whether pregnancies end in abortion or childbirth. In Maher v. Roe, 432 U.S. 464 (1977), and Harris v. McRae, 448 U.S. 297 (1980), we upheld governmental spending statutes that reimbursed indigent women for childbirth but not abortion. This legislation to further an interest in preferring childbirth over abortion was permissible, however, only because it did not add any "restriction on access to abortion that was not already there." *Maher,* 432 U.S., at 474.

information, Akron unreasonably has placed "obstacles in the path of the doctor upon whom [the woman is] entitled to rely for advice in connection with her decision." Whalen v. Roe, 429 U.S. 589, 604, n. 33 (1977).

C

Section 1870.06(C) presents a different question. Under this provision, the "attending physician" must inform the woman

"of the particular risks associated with her own pregnancy and the abortion technique to be employed including providing her with at least a general description of the medical instructions to be followed subsequent to the abortion in order to insure her safe recovery, and shall in addition provide her with such other information which in his own medical judgment is relevant to her decision as to whether to have an abortion or carry her pregnancy to term."

The information required clearly is related to maternal health and to the State's legitimate purpose in requiring informed consent. . . .

The Court of Appeals also held, however, that § 1870.06(C) was invalid because it required that the disclosure be made by the "attending physician." . . .

Requiring physicians personally to discuss the abortion decision, its health risks, and consequences with each patient may in some cases add to the cost of providing abortions, though the record here does not suggest that ethical physicians will charge more for adhering to this typical element of the physician-patient relationship. Yet in *Roe* and subsequent cases we have "stressed repeatedly the central role of the physician, both in consulting with the woman about whether or not to have an abortion, and in determining how any abortion was to be carried out." Colautti v. Franklin, 439 U.S. 379, 387 (1979). Moreover, we have left no doubt that, to ensure the safety of the abortion procedure, the States may mandate that only physicians perform abortions. See Connecticut v. Menillo, 423 U.S. 9, 11 (1975); *Roe,* 410 U.S., at 165.

We are not convinced, however, that there is as vital a state need for insisting that the physician performing the abortion, or for that matter any physician, personally counsel the patient in the absence of a request. The State's interest is in ensuring that the woman's consent is informed and unpressured; the critical factor is whether she obtains the necessary information and counseling from a qualified person, not the identity of the person from whom she obtains it. . . .

In so holding, we do not suggest that the State is powerless to vindicate its interest in making certain the "important" and "stressful" decision to abort "is made with full knowledge of its nature and consequences." *Danforth,* 428 U.S., at 67. Nor do we imply that a physician may abdicate his essential role as the person ultimately responsible for the medical aspects of the decision to perform the abortion.[39] A State may define the physician's responsibility to include verification that adequate counseling has been provided and that the woman's consent is informed. In addition, the State may establish reasonable minimum qualifications for those people who perform the primary counseling function. See, e.g., *Doe,* 410 U.S., at 195 (State may require a medical facility "to possess all the staffing and services necessary to perform an abortion safely"). In light of these alternatives, we believe that it is unreasonable for a State to insist that only a physician is competent to provide the information and counseling

---

[39] This Court's consistent recognition of the critical role of the physician in the abortion procedure has been based on the model of the competent, conscientious, and ethical physician. See *Doe,* 410 U.S., at 196–197. We have no occasion in this case to consider conduct by physicians that may depart from this model. Cf. *Danforth,* 428 U.S., at 91–92, n. 2 (Stewart, J., concurring).

relevant to informed consent. We affirm the judgment of the Court of Appeals that § 1870.06(C) is invalid.

VI

The Akron ordinance prohibits a physician from performing an abortion until 24 hours after the pregnant woman signs a consent form. § 1870.07. . . .

We find that Akron has failed to demonstrate that any legitimate state interest is furthered by an arbitrary and inflexible waiting period. There is no evidence suggesting that the abortion procedure will be performed more safely. Nor are we convinced that the State's legitimate concern that the woman's decision be informed is reasonably served by requiring a 24-hour delay as a matter of course. The decision whether to proceed with an abortion is one as to which it is important to "affor[d] the physician adequate discretion in the exercise of his medical judgment." Colautti v. Franklin, 439 U.S. 379, 387 (1979). In accordance with the ethical standards of the profession, a physician will advise the patient to defer the abortion when he thinks this will be beneficial to her. But if a woman, after appropriate counseling, is prepared to give her written informed consent and proceed with the abortion, a State may not demand that she delay the effectuation of that decision.

VII

Section 1870.16 of the Akron ordinance requires physicians performing abortions to "insure that the remains of the unborn child are disposed of in a humane and sanitary manner." The Court of Appeals found that the word "humane" was impermissibly vague as a definition of conduct subject to criminal prosecution. The court invalidated the entire provision, declining to sever the word "humane" in order to uphold the requirement that disposal be "sanitary." See 651 F.2d at 1211. We affirm this judgment.

. . .

Justice O'Connor, with whom Justice White and Justice Rehnquist join, dissenting.

In Roe v. Wade, 410 U.S. 113 (1973), the Court held that the "right of privacy . . . founded in the Fourteenth Amendment's concept of personal liberty and restrictions upon state action . . . is broad enough to encompass a woman's decision whether or not to terminate her pregnancy." Id., at 153. The parties in these cases have not asked the Court to re-examine the validity of that holding and the court below did not address it. Accordingly, the Court does not re-examine its previous holding. Nonetheless, it is apparent from the Court's opinion that neither sound constitutional theory nor our need to decide cases based on the application of neutral principles can accommodate an analytical framework that varies according to the "stages" of pregnancy, where those stages, and their concomitant standards of review, differ according to the level of medical technology available when a particular challenge to state regulation occurs. The Court's analysis of the Akron regulations is inconsistent both with the methods of analysis employed in previous cases dealing with abortion, and with the Court's approach to fundamental rights in other areas.

Our recent cases indicate that a regulation imposed on "a lawful abortion 'is not unconstitutional unless it unduly burdens the right to seek an abortion.'" Maher v. Roe, 432 U.S. 464, 473 (1977) (quoting Bellotti v. Baird, 428 U.S. 132, 147 (1977) (*Bellotti I*)). See also Harris v. McRae, 448 U.S. 297, 314 (1980). In my view, this "unduly burdensome" standard should be applied to the challenged regulations throughout the entire pregnancy without reference to the particular "stage" of pregnancy involved. If the particular regulation does not "unduly burden[ ]" the fundamental right, *Maher,* supra, at 473, then our evaluation of that regulation is limited to our determination that the regulation rationally relates to a legitimate state purpose.   Irrespective of what we may believe is wise or prudent policy in this difficult area, "the Constitution does not constitute us as 'Platonic Guardians' nor does it vest in this Court the authority to strike down laws because they do not meet our standards of desirable social policy, 'wisdom,' or 'common sense.'"   Plyler v. Doe, 457 U.S. 202, 242 (1982) (Burger, C.J., dissenting).

I

The trimester or "three-stage" approach adopted by the Court in *Roe,* and, in a modified form, employed by the Court to analyze the state regulations in these cases, cannot be supported as a legitimate or useful framework for accommodating the woman's right and the State's interests.   The decision of the Court today graphically illustrates why the trimester approach is a completely unworkable method of accommodating the conflicting personal rights and compelling state interests that are involved in the abortion context.

As the Court indicates today, the State's compelling interest in maternal health changes as medical technology changes, and any health regulation must not "depart from accepted medical practice."   In applying this standard, the Court holds that "the safety of second-trimester abortions has increased dramatically" since 1973, when *Roe* was decided.   Although a regulation such as one requiring that all second-trimester abortions be performed in hospitals "had strong support" in 1973 "as a reasonable health regulation," this regulation can no longer stand because, according to the Court's diligent research into medical and scientific literature, the dilation and evacuation procedure (D & E), used in 1973 only for first-trimester abortions, "is now widely and successfully used for second trimester abortions."   Further, the medical literature relied on by the Court indicates that the D & E procedure may be performed in an appropriate non-hospital setting for "at least .   .   . the early weeks of the second trimester .   .   .."   The Court then chooses the period of 16 weeks of gestation as that point at which D & E procedures may be performed safely in a non-hospital setting, and thereby invalidates the Akron hospitalization regulation.

It is not difficult to see that despite the Court's purported adherence to the trimester approach adopted in *Roe,* the lines drawn in that decision have now been "blurred" because of what the Court accepts as technological advancement in the safety of abortion procedure.   The State may no longer rely on a "bright line" that separates permissible from impermissible regulation, and it is no longer free to consider the second trimester as a unit and weigh the risks posed by all abortion procedures throughout that trimester.   Rather, the State must continuously and conscientiously study contemporary medical and scientific literature in order to determine whether the effect of a particular regulation is to "depart from accepted medical practice" insofar as particular procedures and particular periods within the trimester are concerned.   Assuming that legislative bodies are able to engage in this exacting task, it is difficult to believe that our Constitution *requires* that they do it as a prelude to protecting the health of their citizens.   It is even more difficult to believe that this Court, without the resources available to those bodies entrusted with making legislative choices, believes itself competent to make these inquiries and to revise these standards every time the American College of Obstetricians and Gynecologists (ACOG) or similar group revises its views about what is and what is not appropriate medical procedure in this area.   Indeed, the ACOG standards on which the Court relies were changed in 1982 after trial in the present cases.   Before ACOG changed its standards in 1982, it recommended that all mid-trimester abortions be performed in a hospital.   .   .   .   As today's decision indicates, medical technology is changing, and this change will necessitate our continued functioning as the nation's *"ex officio* medical board with powers to approve or disapprove medical and operative practices and standards throughout the United States." Planned Parenthood v. Danforth, 428 U.S. 52, 99 (1976) (White, J., concurring in part and dissenting in part).

Just as improvements in medical technology inevitably will move *forward* the point at which the State may regulate for reasons of maternal health, different technological improvements will move *backward* the point of viability at which the State may proscribe abortions except when necessary to preserve the life and health of the mother.

In 1973, viability before 28 weeks was considered unusual. The fourteenth edition of L. Hellman & J. Pritchard, Williams Obstetrics, on which the Court relied in *Roe* for its understanding of viability, stated that "[a]ttainment of a [fetal] weight of 1,000 g [or a fetal age of approximately 28 weeks gestation] is . . . . widely used as the criterion of viability." Id., at 493. However, recent studies have demonstrated increasingly earlier fetal viability. It is certainly reasonable to believe that fetal viability in the first trimester of pregnancy may be possible in the not too distant future. Indeed, the Court has explicitly acknowledged that *Roe* left the point of viability "flexible for anticipated advancements in medical skill." Colautti v. Franklin, 439 U.S. 379, 387 (1979). "[W]e recognized in *Roe* that viability was a matter of medical judgment, skill, and technical ability, and we preserved the flexibility of the term." *Danforth,* supra, 428 U.S., at 64.

The *Roe* framework, then, is clearly on a collision course with itself. As the medical risks of various abortion procedures decrease, the point at which the State may regulate for reasons of maternal health is moved further forward to actual childbirth. As medical science becomes better able to provide for the separate existence of the fetus, the point of viability is moved further back toward conception. Moreover, it is clear that the trimester approach violates the fundamental aspiration of judicial decision making through the application of neutral principles "sufficiently absolute to give them roots throughout the community and continuity over significant periods of time . . . ." A. Cox, The Role of the Supreme Court in American Government 114 (1976). The *Roe* framework is inherently tied to the state of medical technology that exists whenever particular litigation ensues. Although legislatures are better suited to make the necessary factual judgments in this area, the Court's framework forces legislatures, as a matter of constitutional law, to speculate about what constitutes "accepted medical practice" at any given time. Without the necessary expertise or ability, courts must then pretend to act as science review boards and examine those legislative judgments.

The Court adheres to the *Roe* framework because the doctrine of *stare decisis* "demands respect in a society governed by the rule of law." Although respect for *stare decisis* cannot be challenged, "this Court's considered practice [is] not to apply *stare decisis* as rigidly in constitutional as in nonconstitutional cases." Glidden Company v. Zdanok, 370 U.S. 530, 543 (1962). Although we must be mindful of the "desirability of continuity of decision in constitutional questions. . . . when convinced of former error, this Court has never felt constrained to follow precedent. In constitutional questions, when correction depends on amendment and not upon legislative action this Court throughout its history has freely exercised its power to reexamine the basis of its constitutional decisions." Smith v. Allwright, 321 U.S. 649, 665 (1944) (footnote omitted).

Even assuming that there is a fundamental right to terminate pregnancy in some situations, there is no justification in law or logic for the trimester framework adopted in *Roe* and employed by the Court today on the basis of *stare decisis.* For the reasons stated above, that framework is clearly an unworkable means of balancing the fundamental right and the compelling state interests that are indisputably implicated.

II

The Court in *Roe* correctly realized that the State has important interests "in the areas of health and medical standards" and that "[t]he State has a legitimate interest in seeing to it that abortion, like any other medical procedure, is performed under circumstances that insure maximum safety for the patient." 410 U.S., at 149, 150. The Court also recognized that the State has *"another* important and legitimate interest in protecting the potentiality of human life." I agree completely that the State has these interests, but in my view, the point at which these interests become compelling does not depend on the trimester of pregnancy. Rather, these interests are present *throughout* pregnancy.

This Court has never failed to recognize that "a State may properly assert important interests in safeguarding health [and] in maintaining medical standards." 410 U.S., at 154. It cannot be doubted that as long as a state statute is within "the bounds of reason and [does not] assume[ ] the character of a merely arbitrary fiat. . . . [then] [t]he State . . . must decide upon measures that are needful for the protection of its people . . . ." Purity Extract and Tonic Co. v. Lynch, 226 U.S. 192, 204–205 (1912). "There is nothing in the United States Constitution which limits the State's power to require that medical procedures be done safely . . . ." Sendak v. Arnold, 429 U.S. 968, 969 (White, J., dissenting). "The mode and procedure of medical diagnostic procedures is not the business of judges." Parham v. J.R., 442 U.S. 584, 607–608 (1979). Under the *Roe* framework, however, the state interest in maternal health cannot become compelling until the onset of the second trimester of pregnancy because "until the end of the first trimester mortality in abortion may be less than mortality in normal childbirth." Before the second trimester, the decision to perform an abortion "must be left to the medical judgment of the pregnant woman's attending physician." Id., at 164.[6]

The fallacy inherent in the *Roe* framework is apparent: just because the State has a compelling interest in ensuring maternal safety once an abortion may be more dangerous than childbirth, it simply does not follow that the State has *no* interest before that point that justifies state regulation to ensure that first-trimester abortions are performed as safely as possible.

The state interest in potential human life is likewise extant throughout pregnancy. In *Roe,* the Court held that although the State had an important and legitimate interest in protecting potential life, that interest could not become compelling until the point at which the fetus was viable. The difficulty with this analysis is clear: *potential* life is no less potential in the first weeks of pregnancy than it is at viability or afterward. At any stage in pregnancy, there is the *potential* for human life. Although the Court refused to "resolve the difficult question of when life begins," id., at 159, the Court chose the point of viability—when the fetus is *capable* of life independent of its mother—to permit the complete proscription of abortion. The choice of viability as the point at which the state interest in *potential* life becomes compelling is no less arbitrary than choosing any point before viability or any point afterward. Accordingly, I believe that the State's interest in protecting potential human life exists throughout the pregnancy.

---

[6] Interestingly, the Court in *Danforth* upheld a recordkeeping requirement as well as the consent provision even though these requirements were imposed on first-trimester abortions and although the State did not impose comparable requirements on most other medical procedures. See *Danforth,* supra, 428 U.S., at 65–67, 79–81 (1976). *Danforth,* then, must be understood as a retreat from the position ostensibly adopted in *Roe* that the State had *no* compelling interest in regulation during the first trimester of pregnancy that would justify restrictions imposed on the abortion decision.

III

Although the State possesses compelling interests in the protection of potential human life and in maternal health throughout pregnancy, not every regulation that the State imposes must be measured against the State's compelling interests and examined with strict scrutiny. This Court has acknowledged that "the right in Roe v. Wade can be understood only by considering both the woman's interest and the nature of the State's interference with it. *Roe* did not declare an unqualified 'constitutional right to an abortion,' . . . . Rather, the right protects the woman from unduly burdensome interference with her freedom to decide whether to terminate her pregnancy." *Maher,* supra, 432 U.S., at 473–474. The Court and its individual Justices have repeatedly utilized the "unduly burdensome" standard in abortion cases.

The requirement that state interference "infringe substantially" or "heavily burden" a right before heightened scrutiny is applied is not novel in our fundamental-rights jurisprudence, or restricted to the abortion context. In San Antonio Independent School District v. Rodriguez, 411 U.S. 1, 37, 38 (1973), we observed that we apply "strict judicial scrutiny" only when legislation may be said to have " 'deprived,' 'infringed,' or 'interfered' with the free exercise of some such fundamental personal right or liberty." If the impact of the regulation does not rise to the level appropriate for our strict scrutiny, then our inquiry is limited to whether the state law bears "some rational relationship to legitimate state purposes." Id., at 40. Even in the First Amendment context, we have required in some circumstances that state laws "infringe substantially" on protected conduct, Gibson v. Florida Legislative Investigation Committee, 372 U.S. 539, 545 (1963), or that there be "a significant encroachment upon personal liberty," Bates v. City of Little Rock, 361 U.S. 516, 524 (1960).

In Carey v. Population Services International, 431 U.S. 678 (1977), we eschewed the notion that state law had to meet the exacting "compelling state interest" test " 'whenever it implicates sexual freedom.' " Id., at 688, n. 5. Rather, we required that before the "strict scrutiny" standard was employed, it was necessary that the state law "impose[ ] a significant burden" on a protected right, id., at 689, or that it "burden an individual's right to prevent conception or terminate pregnancy by *substantially* limiting access to the means of effectuating that decision . . . ." Id., at 688 (emphasis added). The Court stressed that "even a burdensome regulation may be validated by a sufficiently compelling state interest." Id., at 686. Finally, Griswold v. Connecticut, 381 U.S. 479, 485 (1965) recognized that a law banning the use of contraceptives by married persons had "a maximum destructive impact" on the marital relationship.

Indeed, the Court today follows this approach. Although the Court does not use the expression "undue burden," the Court recognizes that even a "significant obstacle" can be justified by a "reasonable" regulation.

The "undue burden" required in the abortion cases represents the required threshold inquiry that must be conducted before this Court can require a State to justify its legislative actions under the exacting "compelling state interest" standard. "[A] test so severe that legislation can rarely meet it should be imposed by courts with deliberate restraint in view of the respect that properly should be accorded legislative judgments." *Carey,* supra, 431 U.S., at 705 (Powell, J., concurring in part and concurring in the judgment).

The "unduly burdensome" standard is particularly appropriate in the abortion context because of the *nature* and *scope* of the right that is involved. The privacy right involved in the abortion context "cannot be said to be absolute." *Roe,* supra, 410 U.S., at 154. "*Roe* did not declare an unqualified 'constitutional right to an abortion.' " *Maher,* supra, 432 U.S., at 473. Rather, the *Roe* right is intended to protect against state action "drastically limiting the availability and safety of the desired service," id., at 472, against the imposition of an "absolute obstacle" on the abortion decision, *Danforth,* supra, 428 U.S., at 70–71, n. 11, or against "official interference" and "coercive restraint" imposed on the abortion decision, *Harris,* supra, 448 U.S. at 328 (White, J., concurring). That a state regulation may "inhibit" abortions to some degree does not require that we find that the regulation is invalid. See H.L. v. Matheson, 450 U.S. 398, 413 (1981).

The abortion cases demonstrate that an "undue burden" has been found for the most part in situations involving absolute obstacles or severe limitations on the abortion decision. In *Roe,* the Court invalidated a Texas statute that criminalized *all* abortions except those necessary to save the life of the mother. In *Danforth,* supra, the Court invalidated a state prohibition of abortion by saline amniocentesis because the ban had "the effect of inhibiting . . . the vast majority of abortions after the first 12 weeks." 428 U.S., at 79. The Court today acknowledges that the regulation in *Danforth* effectively represented "a *complete* prohibition of abortions in certain circumstances." In *Danforth,* supra, the Court also invalidated state regulations requiring parental or spousal consent as a prerequisite to a first-trimester abortion because the consent requirements effectively and impermissibly delegated a "veto power" to parents and spouses during the first trimester of pregnancy. In both *Bellotti I,* supra, and Bellotti v. Baird, 443 U.S. 622 (1979) (*Bellotti II*), the Court was concerned with effective parental veto over the abortion decision.

In determining whether the State imposes an "undue burden," we must keep in mind that when we are concerned with extremely sensitive issues, such as the one involved here, "the appropriate forum for their resolution in a democracy is the legislature. We should not forget that 'legislatures are ultimate guardians of the liberties and welfare of the people in quite as great a degree as the courts.' Missouri, K. & T.R. Co. v. May, 194 U.S. 267, 270 (1904) (Holmes, J.)." *Maher,* supra, 432 U.S., at 479–480 (footnote omitted). This does not mean that in determining whether a regulation imposes an "undue burden" on the *Roe* right that we defer to the judgments made by state legislatures. "The point is, rather, that when we face a complex problem with many hard questions and few easy answers we do well to pay careful attention to how the other branches of Government have addressed the same problem." Columbia Broadcasting System, Inc. v. Democratic National Committee, 412 U.S. 94, 103 (1973).

We must always be mindful that "[t]he Constitution does not compel a state to fine-tune its statutes so as to encourage or facilitate abortions. To the contrary, state action 'encouraging childbirth except in the most urgent circumstances' is 'rationally related to the legitimate government objective of protecting potential life.' Harris v. McRae, 448 U.S., at 325. . . ."

IV

A

Section 1870.03 of the Akron ordinance requires that second-trimester abortions be performed in hospitals. The Court holds that this requirement imposes a "significant obstacle" in the form of increased cost and decreased availability of abortions, and the Court rejects the argument offered by the State that the requirement is a reasonable health regulation under *Roe,* supra, 410 U.S., at 163.

For the reasons stated above, I find no justification for the trimester approach used by the Court to analyze this restriction. I would apply the "unduly burdensome" test and find that the hospitalization requirement does not impose an undue burden on that decision.

. . .

The hospitalization requirement does not impose an undue burden, and it is not necessary to apply an exacting standard of review. Further, the regulation has a "rational relation" to a valid state objective of ensuring the health and welfare of its citizens. See Williamson v. Lee Optical Co., 348 U.S. 483, 491 (1955).[11]

. . .

V

For the reasons set forth above, I dissent from the judgment of the Court in these cases.

PLANNED PARENTHOOD ASSOCIATION OF KANSAS CITY v. ASHCROFT, 462 U.S. 476 (1983). A challenge was made to several sections of Missouri statutes regulating abortions. The Court disposed of the challenges as follows:

(1) A requirement that all abortions after 12 weeks of pregnancy be performed in a hospital was held invalid by a vote of 6 to 3, relying on the *Akron* opinion.

(2) Missouri permits post-viability abortions only when necessary to preserve the life or health of the woman. It requires that a second physician be present in all such abortions with the duty of taking steps necessary to preserve the life and health of the viable unborn child. The Court upheld the second-physician requirement by a vote of 5 to 4. Justice Powell, joined by the Chief Justice, held that the state's interest in preserving life justified the requirement. Justices O'Connor, White and Rehnquist concurred in the judgment, saying: "I agree that second-physician requirement . . . is constitutional because the State possesses a compelling interest in protecting and preserving fetal life, but I believe that this state interest is extant throughout pregnancy." Justices Blackmun, Brennan, Marshall, and Stevens dissented.

(3) A Missouri statute required that all tissue surgically removed (with minor exceptions) in hospitals shall be examined by a pathologist. With respect to abortions, it required submission to a pathologist whether performed in a hospital or outside a hospital. This procedure was upheld by a vote of 5 to 4. Justices Powell and the Chief Justice said that the comparatively small cost of this procedure was not sufficient to require that the state subordinate its health

[11] . . . The Court has never required that state regulation that burdens the abortion decision be "narrowly drawn" to express only the relevant state interest. In *Roe*, the Court mentioned "narrowly drawn" legislative enactments, 410 U.S., at 155, but the Court never actually adopted this standard in the *Roe* analysis. In its decision today, the Court fully endorses the *Roe* requirement that a burdensome health regulation, or as the Court appears to call it, a "significant obstacle," be "reasonably related" to the state compelling interest. The Court recognizes that "[a] State necessarily must have latitude in adopting regulations of general applicability in this sensitive area." See also Simopoulos v. Virginia, post. Nevertheless, the Court fails to apply the "reasonably related" standard. The hospitalization requirement "reasonably relates" to its compelling interest in protection and preservation of maternal health under any normal understanding of what "reasonably relates" signifies.

The Court concludes that the regulation must fall because "it appears that during a substantial portion of the second trimester the State's regulation 'depart[s] from accepted medical practice'." It is difficult to see how the Court concludes that the regulation "depart[s] from accepted medical practice" during "a substantial portion of the second trimester," in light of the fact that the Court concludes that D & E abortions may be performed safely in an outpatient clinic through 16 weeks, or 4 weeks into the second trimester. Four weeks is hardly a "substantial portion" of the second trimester.

interest. Justices O'Connor, White, and Rehnquist concurred in the judgment.
Justices Blackmun, Brennan, Marshall, and Stevens dissented.

(4) The Court upheld a provision requiring minors to obtain either parental
or judicial consent. Justice Powell and the Chief Justice said that a statute
would be valid if it provided a sufficient alternative procedure by which the
pregnant minor may demonstrate that she is sufficiently mature to make the
abortion decision herself or that despite her immaturity, an abortion would be in
her best interests. He found that the judicial procedure set out here met that
standard. Justices O'Connor, White, and Rehnquist concurred in the judgment.
Justices Blackmun, Brennan, Marshall, and Stevens dissented.

———

SIMOPOULOS v. VIRGINIA, 462 U.S. 506 (1983). Dr. Simopoulos
aborted a 17-year old woman by a saline injection given in his unlicensed clinic.
He was convicted of violating a Virginia statute requiring that second-trimester
abortions be performed only in licensed hospitals. The Court affirmed his
conviction.

Justice Powell, writing for the Court, noted that the Virginia statutes defined
a "hospital" to include outpatient surgical clinics which met defined standards
and were licensed. He said there appeared no doubt that an adequately
equipped clinic could obtain an outpatient hospital license permitting the
performance of second-trimester abortions. "We conclude that Virginia's requirement that second-trimester abortions be performed in licensed clinics is not
an unreasonable means of furthering the State's compelling interest in 'protecting the woman's own health and safety.' *Roe,* 410 U.S., at 150. . . .
Unlike the provisions at issue in *City of Akron* and *Ashcroft,* Virginia's statute and
regulations do not require that the patient be hospitalized as an inpatient or that
the abortion be performed in full-service, acute-care hospital. Rather, the
State's requirement that second-trimester abortions be performed in licensed
clinics appears to comport with accepted medical practice, and leaves the
method and time of the abortion precisely where they belong—with the
physician and the patient."

Justices O'Connor, White, and Rehnquist concurred in the judgment saying:
"[I] do not agree that the constitutional validity of the Virginia mandatory
hospitalization requirement is contingent in any way on the trimester in which it
is imposed. Rather, I believe that the requirement in this case is not an undue
burden on the decision to undergo an abortion."

Justice Stevens dissented, arguing that the case be sent back to Virginia for
construction of the state statute.

C. FAMILY RELATIONSHIPS

———

MOORE v. CITY OF EAST CLEVELAND

431 U.S. 494, 97 S.Ct. 1932, 52 L.Ed.2d 531 (1977).

**Mr. Justice Powell announced the judgment of the Court, and deliv-
ered an opinion in which Mr. Justice Brennan, Mr. Justice Marshall, and
Mr. Justice Blackmun joined.**

East Cleveland's housing ordinance, like many throughout the country, limits
occupancy of a dwelling unit to members of a single family. § 1351.02. But
the ordinance contains an unusual and complicated definitional section that
recognizes as a "family" only a few categories of related individuals,

§ 1341.08.[2] Because her family, living together in her home, fits none of those categories, appellant stands convicted of a criminal offense. The question in this case is whether the ordinance violates the Due Process Clause of the Fourteenth Amendment.

I.

Appellant, Mrs. Inez Moore, lives in her East Cleveland home together with her son, Dale Moore Sr., and her two grandsons, Dale, Jr., and John Moore, Jr. The two boys are first cousins rather than brothers; we are told that John came to live with his grandmother and with the elder and younger Dale Moores after his mother's death.

In early 1973, Mrs. Moore received a notice of violation from the city, stating that John was an "illegal occupant" and directing her to comply with the ordinance. When she failed to remove him from her home, the city filed a criminal charge. Mrs. Moore moved to dismiss, claiming that the ordinance was constitutionally invalid on its face. Her motion was overruled, and upon conviction she was sentenced to five days in jail and a $25 fine. The Ohio Court of Appeals affirmed after giving full consideration to her constitutional claims, and the Ohio Supreme Court denied review. We noted probable jurisdiction of her appeal, 425 U.S. 949 (1976).

II.

The city argues that our decision in Village of Belle Terre v. Boraas, 416 U.S. 1 (1974), requires us to sustain the ordinance attacked here. Belle Terre, like East Cleveland, imposed limits on the types of groups that could occupy a single dwelling unit. Applying the constitutional standard announced in this Court's leading land-use case, Euclid v. Ambler Realty Co., 272 U.S. 365 (1926), we sustained the Belle Terre ordinance on the ground that it bore a rational relationship to permissible state objectives.

But one overriding factor sets this case apart from *Belle Terre.* The ordinance there affected only *unrelated* individuals. It expressly allowed all who were related by "blood, adoption, or marriage" to live together, and in sustaining the ordinance we were careful to note that it promoted "family needs" and "family values." East Cleveland, in contrast, has chosen to regulate the occupancy of its housing by slicing deeply into the family itself. This is no mere incidental result of the ordinance. On its face it selects certain categories of relatives who may live together and declares that others may not. In particular, it makes a crime of a grandmother's choice to live with her grandson in circumstances like those presented here.

---

[2] Section 1341.08 (1966) provides:

" 'Family' means a number of individuals related to the nominal head of the household or to the spouse of the nominal head of the household living as a single housekeeping unit in a single dwelling unit, but limited to the following:

"(a) Husband or wife of the nominal head of the household.

"(b) Unmarried children of the nominal head of the household or of the spouse of the nominal head of the household, provided, however, that such unmarried children have no children residing with them.

"(c) Father or mother of the nominal head of the household or of the spouse of the nominal head of the household.

"(d) Notwithstanding the provisions of subsection (b) hereof, a family may include not more than one dependent married or unmarried child of the nominal head of the household or of the spouse of the nominal head of the household and the spouse and dependent children of such dependent child. For the purpose of this subsection, a dependent person is one who has more than fifty percent of his total support furnished for him by the nominal head of the household and the spouse of the nominal head of the household.

"(e) A family may consist of one individual."

When a city undertakes such intrusive regulation of the family, neither *Belle Terre* nor *Euclid* governs; the usual judicial deference to the legislature is inappropriate. "This Court has long recognized that freedom of personal choice in matters of marriage and family life is one of the liberties protected by the Due Process Clause of the Fourteenth Amendment." . . . A host of cases, tracing their lineage to Meyer v. Nebraska, 262 U.S. 390, 399–401 (1923), and Pierce v. Society of Sisters, 268 U.S. 510, 534–535 (1925), have consistently acknowledged a "private realm of family life which the state cannot enter." Prince v. Massachusetts, 321 U.S. 158, 166 (1944). . . . Of course, the family is not beyond regulation. See Prince v. Massachusetts. But when the government intrudes on choices concerning family living arrangements, this Court must examine carefully the importance of the governmental interests advanced and the extent to which they are served by the challenged regulation. See Poe v. Ullman (Harlan, J., dissenting).

When thus examined, this ordinance cannot survive. The city seeks to justify it as a means of preventing overcrowding, minimizing traffic and parking congestion, and avoiding an undue financial burden on East Cleveland's school system. Although these are legitimate goals, the ordinance before us serves them marginally, at best. For example, the ordinance permits any family consisting only of husband, wife, and unmarried children to live together, even if the family contains a half-dozen licensed drivers, each with his or her own car. At the same time it forbids an adult brother and sister to share a household, even if both faithfully use public transportation. The ordinance would permit a grandmother to live with a single dependent son and children, even if his school-age children number a dozen, yet it forces Mrs. Moore to find another dwelling for her grandson John, simply because of the presence of his uncle and cousin in the same household. We need not labor the point. Section 1341.08 has but a tenuous relation to alleviation of the conditions mentioned by the city.

III.

The city would distinguish the cases based on *Meyer* and *Pierce*. It points out that none of them "gives grandmothers any fundamental rights with respect to grandsons," and suggests that any constitutional right to live together as a family extends only to the nuclear family—essentially a couple and its dependent children.

To be sure, these cases did not expressly consider the family relationship presented here. They were immediately concerned with freedom of choice with respect to childbearing, e.g., *LaFleur,* Roe v. Wade, *Griswold,* supra, or with the rights of parents to the custody and companionship of their own children, Stanley v. Illinois, supra, or with traditional parental authority in matters of child rearing and education. *Yoder, Ginsberg, Pierce, Meyer,* supra. But unless we close our eyes to the basic reasons why certain rights associated with the family have been accorded shelter under the Fourteenth Amendment's Due Process Clause, we cannot avoid applying the force and rationale of these precedents to the family choice involved in this case.

. . . .

Substantive due process has at times been a treacherous field for this Court. There *are* risks when the judicial branch gives enhanced protection to certain substantive liberties without the guidance of the more specific provisions of the Bill of Rights. As the history of the *Lochner* era demonstrates, there is reason for concern lest the only limits to such judicial intervention become the predilections of those who happen at the time to be Members of this Court. That history counsels caution and restraint. But it does not counsel abandonment, nor does it require what the city urges here: cutting off any protection of family rights at the first convenient, if arbitrary boundary—the boundary of the nuclear family.

Appropriate limits on substantive due process come not from drawing arbitrary lines but rather from careful "respect for the teachings of history [and] solid recognition of the basic values that underlie our society." Griswold v. Connecticut, 381 U.S., at 501 (Harlan, J., concurring). . . . Our decisions establish that the Constitution protects the sanctity of the family precisely because the institution of the family is deeply rooted in this Nation's history and tradition. It is through the family that we inculcate and pass down many of our most cherished values, moral and cultural.

Ours is by no means a tradition limited to respect for the bonds uniting the members of the nuclear family. The tradition of uncles, aunts, cousins, and especially grandparents sharing a household along with parents and children has roots equally venerable and equally deserving of constitutional recognition. Over the years millions of our citizens have grown up in just such an environment, and most, surely, have profited from it. Even if conditions of modern society have brought about a decline in extended family households, they have not erased the accumulated wisdom of civilization, gained over the centuries and honored throughout our history, that supports a larger conception of the family. Out of choice, necessity, or a sense of family responsibility, it has been common for close relatives to draw together and participate in the duties and the satisfactions of a common home. Decisions concerning child rearing, which *Yoder, Meyer, Pierce* and other cases have recognized as entitled to constitutional protection, long have been shared with grandparents or other relatives who occupy the same household—indeed who may take on major responsibility for the rearing of the children. Especially in times of adversity, such as the death of a spouse or economic need, the broader family has tended to come together for mutual sustenance and to maintain or rebuild a secure home life. This is apparently what happened here.

Whether or not such a household is established because of personal tragedy, the choice of relatives in this degree of kinship to live together may not lightly be denied by the State. *Pierce* struck down an Oregon law requiring all children to attend the State's public schools, holding that the Constitution "excludes any general power of the State to standardize its children by forcing them to accept instruction from public teachers only." 268 U.S., at 535. By the same token the Constitution prevents East Cleveland from standardizing its children—and its adults—by forcing all to live in certain narrowly defined family patterns.

Reversed.

Mr. Justice Brennan, with whom Mr. Justice Marshall joins, concurring.

I join the plurality's opinion. . . .

In today's America, the "nuclear family" is the pattern so often found in much of white suburbia. Sanden, Sociology: A Systematic Approach, p. 320 (1965). The Constitution cannot be interpreted, however, to tolerate the imposition by government upon the rest of us of white suburbia's preference in patterns of family living. The "extended family" that provided generations of early Americans with social services and economic and emotional support in times of hardship, and was the beachhead for successive waves of immigrants who populated our cities, remains not merely still a pervasive living pattern, but under the goad of brutal economic necessity, a prominent pattern—virtually a means of survival—for large numbers of the poor and deprived minorities of our society. For them compelled pooling of scant resources requires compelled sharing of a household.

The "extended" form is especially familiar among black families. . . .

I do not wish to be understood as implying that East Cleveland's enforcement of its ordinance is motivated by a racially discriminatory purpose: the record of this case would not support that implication. But the prominence of other than nuclear families among ethnic and racial minority groups, including our black citizens, surely demonstrates that the "extended family" pattern remains a vital tenet of our society. It suffices that in prohibiting this pattern of family living as a means of achieving its objectives, appellee city has chosen a device that deeply intrudes into family associational rights that historically have been central, and today remain central, to a large proportion of our population.

. . .

Mr. Justice Stevens, concurring in the judgment.

In my judgment the critical question presented by this case is whether East Cleveland's housing ordinance is a permissible restriction on appellant's right to use her own property as she sees fit.

. . .

Mr. Justice Stewart, with whom Mr. Justice Rehnquist joins, dissenting.

. . .

. . . The question presented, as I view it, is whether the decision in *Belle Terre* is controlling, or whether the Constitution compels a different result because East Cleveland's definition of "family" is more restrictive than that before us in the *Belle Terre* case.

. . . The *Belle Terre* decision disposes of the appellant's contentions to the extent they focus not on her blood relationships with her sons and grandsons but on more general notions about the "privacy of the home." Her suggestion that every person has a constitutional right permanently to share his residence with whomever he pleases, and that such choices are "beyond the province of legitimate governmental intrusion," amounts to the same argument that was made and found unpersuasive in *Belle Terre.*

To be sure, the ordinance involved in *Belle Terre* did not prevent blood relatives from occupying the same dwelling, and the Court's decision in that case does not, therefore, foreclose the appellant's arguments based specifically on the ties of kinship present in this case. Nonetheless, I would hold, for the reasons that follow, that the existence of those ties does not elevate either the appellant's claim of associational freedom or her claim of privacy to a level invoking constitutional protection.

. . .

The "association" in this case is not for any purpose relating to the promotion of speech, assembly, the press, or religion. And wherever the outer boundaries of constitutional protection of freedom of association may eventually turn out to be, they surely do not extend to those who assert no interest other than the gratification, convenience, and economy of sharing the same residence.

The appellant is considerably closer to the constitutional mark in asserting that the East Cleveland ordinance intrudes upon "the private realm of family life which the state cannot enter." . . .

Although the appellant's desire to share a single-dwelling unit also involves "private family life" in a sense, that desire can hardly be equated with any of the interests protected in [previous cases.] The ordinance about which the appellant complains did not impede her choice to have or not to have children, and it did not dictate to her how her own children were to be nurtured and reared. The ordinance clearly does not prevent parents from living together or living with their unemancipated offspring.

. . . When the Court has found that the Fourteenth Amendment placed a substantive limitation on a State's power to regulate, it has been in those rare cases in which the personal interests at issue have been deemed "implicit in the concept of ordered liberty." See Roe v. Wade, supra, at 152, quoting Palko v. Connecticut, 302 U.S. 319, 325. The interest that the appellant may have in permanently sharing a single kitchen and a suite of contiguous rooms with some of her relatives simply does not rise to that level. To equate this interest with the fundamental decisions to marry and to bear and raise children is to extend the limited substantive contours of the Due Process Clause beyond recognition.

The appellant also challenges the single-family occupancy ordinance on equal protection grounds. Her claim is that the city has drawn an arbitrary and irrational distinction between groups of people who may live together as a "family" and those who may not. . . .

Obviously, East Cleveland might have as easily and perhaps as effectively hit upon a different definition of "family." But a line could hardly be drawn that would not sooner or later become the target of a challenge like the appellant's. If "family" included all of the householder's grandchildren there would doubtless be the hard case of an orphaned niece or nephew. If, as the appellant suggests, a "family" must include all blood relatives, what of longtime friends? The point is that any definition would produce hardships in some cases without materially advancing the legislative purpose. . . .

. . .

For these reasons, I think the Ohio courts did not err in rejecting the appellant's constitutional claims. Accordingly, I respectfully dissent.

Mr. Justice White, dissenting.

. . .

. . . Realizing that the present construction of the Due Process Clause represents a major judicial gloss on its terms, as well as on the anticipation of the Framers, and that much of the underpinning for the broad, substantive application of the Clause disappeared in the conflict between the executive and the judiciary in the 1930's and 1940's, the Court should be extremely reluctant to breathe still further substantive content into the Due Process Clause so as to strike down legislation adopted by a State or city to promote its welfare. Whenever the judiciary does so, it unavoidably pre-empts for itself another part of the governance of the country without express constitutional authority.

Accepting the cases as they are and the Due Process Clause as construed by them, however, I think it evident that the threshold question in any due process attack on legislation, whether the challenge is procedural or substantive, is whether there is a deprivation of life, liberty or property. . . .

It seems to me that Mr. Justice Douglas was closest to the mark in Poe v. Ullman, supra, at 517, when he said that the trouble with the holdings of the "old Court" was not in its definition of liberty but in its definition of the protections guaranteed to that liberty—"not in entertaining inquiries concerning the constitutionality of social legislation but in applying the standards that it did."

The term "liberty" is not, therefore, to be given a crabbed construction. I have no more difficulty than Mr. Justice Powell apparently does in concluding that petitioner in this case properly asserts a liberty interest within the meaning of the Due Process Clause. The question is not one of liberty, *vel non*. Rather, there being no procedural issue at stake, the issue is whether the precise interest involved—the interest in having more than one set of grandchildren live in her home—is entitled to such substantive protection under the Due Process Clause that this ordinance must be held invalid.

. . .

[T]he general principle [is] that "liberty may not be interfered with, under the guise of protecting the public interest, by legislative action which is arbitrary or without reasonable relation to some purpose within the competency of the state to effect." Meyer v. Nebraska, supra, at 399–400. This means-end test appears to require that any statute restrictive of liberty have an ascertainable purpose and represent a rational means to achieve that purpose, whatever the nature of the liberty interest involved. . . .

There are various "liberties," however, which require that infringing legislation be given closer judicial scrutiny, not only with respect to existence of a purpose and the means employed, but also with respect to the importance of the purpose itself relative to the invaded interest. Some interests would appear almost impregnable to invasion, such as the freedoms of speech, press, and religion, and the freedom from cruel and unusual punishments. Other interests, for example, the right of association, the right to vote, and various claims sometimes referred to under the general rubric of the right to privacy, also weigh very heavily against state claims of authority to regulate. It is this category of interests which, as I understand it, Mr. Justice Stewart refers to as "implicit in the concept of ordered liberty." Because he would confine the reach of substantive due process protection to interests such as these and because he would not classify in this category the asserted right to share a house with the relatives involved here, he rejects the due process claim.

Given his premise, he is surely correct. Under our cases, the Due Process Clause extends substantial protection to various phases of family life, but none requires that the claim made here be sustained. I cannot believe that the interest in residing with more than one set of grandchildren is one that calls for any kind of heightened protection under the Due Process Clause. . . .

Mr. Justice Powell would apparently construe the Due Process Clause to protect from all but quite important state regulatory interests any right or privilege that in his estimate is deeply rooted in the country's traditions. For me, this suggests a far too expansive charter for this Court and a far less meaningful and less confining guiding principle than Mr. Justice Stewart would use for serious substantive due process review. . . .

. . . Had it been our task to legislate, we might have approached the problem in a different manner than did the drafters of this ordinance; but I have no trouble in concluding that the normal goals of zoning regulation are present here and that the ordinance serves these goals by limiting, in identifiable circumstances, the number of people who can occupy a single household. The ordinance does not violate the Due Process Clause.

For very similar reasons, the equal protection claim must fail, since it is not to be judged by the strict scrutiny standard employed when a fundamental interest or suspect classification is involved. . . .

[A dissenting opinion by Chief Justice Burger is omitted.] [a]

D. RIGHTS OF PERSONS CONFINED IN STATE INSTITUTIONS

YOUNGBERG v. ROMEO, 457 U.S. 307 (1982). The case presented the question of what rights a person involuntarily committed to a state institution for the mentally retarded has under the due process clause. The state conceded that such a person has a right to adequate food, shelter, clothing, and

---

[a] For a full discussion see *Developments in the Law—The Constitution and the Family,* 93 Harv.L. Rev. 1156 (1980).

medical care. The argument was about whether liberty interests also exist in safety, freedom of movement, and training. As to the first two liberty interests, the Court said:

"Respondent's first two claims involve liberty interests recognized by prior decisions of this Court, interests that involuntary commitment proceedings do not extinguish. The first is a claim to safe conditions. In the past, this Court has noted that the right to personal security constitutes an 'historic liberty interest' protected substantively by the Due Process Clause. Ingraham v. Wright, 430 U.S. 651, 673 (1977). And that right is not extinguished by lawful confinement, even for penal purposes. See Hutto v. Finney, 437 U.S. 678 (1978). If it is cruel and unusual punishment to hold convicted criminals in unsafe conditions, it must be unconstitutional to confine the involuntarily committed—who may not be punished at all—in unsafe conditions.

"Next, respondent claims a right to freedom from bodily restraint. In other contexts, the existence of such an interest is clear in the prior decisions of this Court. Indeed, '[l]iberty from bodily restraint always has been recognized as the core of the liberty protected by the Due Process Clause from arbitrary governmental action.' Greenholtz v. Nebraska Penal Inmates, 442 U.S. 1, 18 (1979) (Powell, J., concurring). This interest survives criminal conviction and incarceration. Similarly, it must also survive involuntary commitment."

As to the alleged right to training the Court had more difficulty. Some training may be necessary to make possible other needs to bodily safety and a minimum of physical restraint. Such training the Court held required. But as to the question whether training beyond what is necessary to ensure safety and freedom from undue restraint is required, the Court decided that the issue was not before it and so left it unresolved.

The Court went on to say:

"We have established that Romeo retains liberty interests in safety and freedom from bodily restraint. Yet these interests are not absolute; indeed to some extent they are in conflict. In operating an institution such as Pennhurst, there are occasions in which it is necessary for the State to restrain the movement of residents—for example, to protect them as well as others from violence. Similar restraints may also be appropriate in a training program. And an institution cannot protect its residents from all danger of violence if it is to permit them to have any freedom of movement. The question then is not simply whether a liberty interest has been infringed but whether the extent or nature of the restraint or lack of absolute safety is such as to violate due process."

The Court then discussed the kind of a hearing necessary to determine what is reasonable, concluding: "[T]he decision, if made by a professional, is presumptively valid. Liability may be imposed only when the decision by the professional is such a substantial departure from accepted professional judgment, practice or standards as to demonstrate that the person responsible actually did not base the decision on such judgment."

E. PROVISION OF ESSENTIAL GOVERNMENTAL BENEFITS AND SERVICES TO THE POOR

The general question raised here is whether the constitution provides a basis for a higher level of judicial scrutiny of legislation which relates to the provision by government to the poor of basic human necessities—food, medical care, education, housing—than it does to economic regulations. Three separate constitutional arguments may be made to support an affirmative answer to that question.

(1) Does the constitution (through the due process clause or otherwise) guarantee some minimum entitlement by the poor to the basic necessities of life? Is the due process clause not only a shield against governmental deprivations of liberty and property but also a sword which imposes affirmative obligations on government? Professor Michelman, *On Protecting the Poor Through the Fourteenth Amendment,* 83 Harv.L.Rev. 7, 9 (1969) argues that the purposes of the Supreme Court decisions dealing with equal protection and wealth classifications "could be more soundly and satisfyingly understood as vindication of a state's duty to protect against certain hazards which are endemic in an unequal society, rather than vindication of a duty to avoid complicity in unequal treatment." He goes on to elaborate the proposition that the Court should be talking of "minimum protection against economic hazard" rather than "equal protection." Professor Tribe refers to "[e]merging notions that government has an affirmative obligation somehow to provide at least a minimally decent subsistence with respect to the most basic human needs, subject to all of the familiar difficulties with judicial enforcement of affirmative duties." *American Constitutional Law* 919 (1978). Professor Michelman restated his thesis in *Welfare Rights in a Constitutional Democracy,* 1979 Wash.U.L.Q. 659. In commentary on that restatement Professor Bork asserts "that the argument for welfare rights is unconnected with either the Constitution or its history" and therefore "offers inadequate guidelines and so requires political decision making by the judiciary." *The Impossibility of Finding Welfare Rights in the Constitution,* 1979 Wash.U.L.Q. 695. See also Appleton, *Professor Michelman's Quest for a Constitutional Welfare Right,* 1979 Wash.U.L.Q. 715.

(2) Should classifications in statutes providing governmental services to the poor be subject to a heightened standard of review under the equal protection clause because they involve the basic economic needs of impoverished human beings? This argument is discussed infra in the equal protection chapter, pp. 895 to 911.

(3) Should classifications based on wealth be held to be constitutionally "suspect" and hence to require special justification in order to be valid? This argument is discussed infra in the equal protection chapter, pp. 750 to 751.

The materials that follow show a few situations in which the Court has looked at the problem in due process terms though even then with equal protection arguments also made.

THE RIGHTS OF THE POOR DEFENDANT IN THE CRIMINAL JUSTICE SYSTEM

During the past 20 years the Court has had before it a number of cases involving the criminal appellate process. It invalidated a series of state statutes which by requiring filing fees and transcripts barred access to appeal by a defendant who was indigent. See, e.g., Griffin v. Illinois, 351 U.S. 12 (1956); Draper v. Washington, 372 U.S. 487 (1963). In Douglas v. California, 372 U.S. 353 (1963) the Court also held that a state had a duty to furnish counsel to an indigent taking his first appeal as of right. In Ross v. Moffitt, 417 U.S. 600 (1974), however, the Court held that an indigent defendant was not entitled to have counsel provided in taking a discretionary appeal to the highest state court or in petitioning for certiorari in the United States Supreme Court.

The Court said:

"The precise rationale for the *Griffin* and *Douglas* line of case has never been explicitly stated, some support being derived from the Equal Protection Clause of the Fourteenth Amendment, and some from the Due Process Clause of that Amendment. Neither clause by itself provides an entirely satisfactory basis for the result reached, each depending on a different inquiry which emphasizes different factors. 'Due process' emphasizes fairness between the State and the individual dealing with the State, regardless of how other individuals in the same situation may be treated. 'Equal protection,' on the other hand, emphasizes disparity in treatment by a State between classes of individuals whose situations are arguably indistinguishable."

The Court went on to hold that the denial of counsel in this case was constitutional under either constitutional clause. The Court concluded:

"[T]he fact that a particular service might be of benefit to an indigent defendant does not mean that the service is constitutionally required. The duty of the State under our cases is not to duplicate the legal arsenal that may be privately retained by a criminal defendant in a continuing effort to reverse his conviction, but only to assure the indigent defendant an adequate opportunity to present his claims fairly in the context of the State's appellate process."

Justices Douglas, Brennan and Marshall, dissented.

ACCESS OF THE POOR TO THE COURTS IN
CIVIL CASES

BODDIE v. CONNECTICUT, 401 U.S. 371 (1971). A welfare recipient brought an action challenging the state procedures under which a plaintiff in a divorce action was required to pay fees of about $60 in order to file the action. The Court discussed the case as one involving procedural due process, concluding "that the State's refusal to admit these appellants to its courts, the sole means in Connecticut for obtaining a divorce, must be regarded as the equivalent of denying them an opportunity to be heard upon their claimed right to a dissolution of their marriages, and, in the absence of a sufficient countervailing justification for the State's action, a denial of due process." Justices Douglas and Brennan in concurring opinions argued that the decision should have been rested on the equal protection clause because of discrimination against the poor. Justice Black dissented. For a discussion which preceded *Boddie,* see Goodpaster, *The Integration of Equal Protection, Due Process Standards, and the Indigent's Right of Free Access to the Courts,* 56 Iowa L.Rev. 223 (1970).

UNITED STATES v. KRAS, 409 U.S. 434 (1973). An indigent petitioner seeking voluntary bankruptcy sought to proceed without paying the fees (not more than $50 in this case) which were a condition of discharge. The district court found for the petitioner, relying on *Boddie.* The Supreme Court reversed, Justice Blackmun, speaking for the Court, said, in part:

"We agree with the Government that our decision in *Boddie* does not control the disposition of this case and that the District Court's reliance upon *Boddie* is misplaced.

"A. *Boddie* was based on the notion that a State cannot deny access, simply because of one's poverty, to a 'judicial proceeding [that is] the only effective means of resolving the dispute at hand.' 401 U.S., at 376. Throughout the opinion there is constant and recurring reference to Connecticut's exclusive control over the establishment, enforcement, and dissolution of the marital relationship. The Court emphasized that 'marriage involves interests of basic importance in our society' ibid., and spoke of 'state monopolization of the means for legally dissolving this relationship.' '[R]esort to the state courts [was] the only avenue to dissolution of . . . marriages,' which was 'not only the paramount dispute-settlement technique, but, in fact the only available one.' . . .. In the light of all this, we concluded that resort to the judicial process was 'no more voluntary in a realistic sense than that of the defendant called upon to defend his interests in court' and we resolved the case 'in light of the principles enunciated in our due process decisions that delimit rights of defendants compelled to litigate their differences in the judicial forum.'

"B. The appellants in *Boddie,* on the one hand, and Robert Kras, on the other stand in materially different postures. The denial of access to the judicial forum in *Boddie* touched directly, as has been noted, on the marital relationship and on the associational interests that surround the establishment and dissolution of that relationship. On many occasions we have recognized the fundamental importance of these interests under our Constitution. See, for example, Loving v. Virginia, 388 U.S. 1 (1967) . . .. The *Boddie* appellants' inability to dissolve their marriages seriously impaired their freedom to pursue other protected associational activities. Kras' alleged interest in the elimination of his debt burden, and in obtaining his desired new start in life, although important and so recognized by the enactment of the Bankruptcy Act, does not rise to the same constitutional level. See Dandridge v. Williams, 397 U.S. 471 (1970); Richardson v. Belcher, 404 U.S. 78 (1971). If Kras is not discharged in bankruptcy, his position will not be materially altered in any constitutional sense. Gaining or not gaining a discharge will effect no change with respect to basic necessities. We see no fundamental interest that is gained or lost depending on the availability of a discharge in bankruptcy.

"C. Nor is the government's control over the establishment, enforcement, or dissolution of debts nearly so exclusive as Connecticut's control over the marriage relationship in *Boddie.* In contrast with divorce, bankruptcy is not the only method available to a debtor for the adjustment of his legal relationship with his creditors. The utter exclusiveness of court access and court remedy, as has been noted, was a potent factor in *Boddie.* But '[w]ithout a prior judicial imprimatur, individuals may freely enter into and rescind commercial contracts. . . .' 401 U.S., at 376.

"However unrealistic the remedy may be in a particular situation, a debtor, in theory, and often in actuality, may adjust his debts by negotiated agreement with his creditors. At times the happy passage of the applicable limitation period, or other acceptable creditor arrangement, will provide the answer. Government's role with respect to the private commercial relationship is qualitatively and quantitatively different than its role in the establishment, enforcement, and dissolution of marriage.

"Resort to the Court, therefore, is not Kras' sole path to relief. *Boddie's* emphasis on exclusivity finds no counterpart in the bankrupt's situation. . . .

"D. We are also of the opinion that the filing fee requirement does not deny Kras the equal protection of the laws. Bankruptcy is hardly akin to free speech or marriage or to those other rights, so many of which are imbedded in the First Amendment, that the Court has come to regard as fundamental and that demand the lofty requirement of a compelling governmental interest before they may be significantly regulated. See Shapiro v. Thompson, 394 U.S. 618, 638 (1969). Neither does it touch upon what has been said to be the suspect criteria of race, nationality or alienage. Graham v. Richardson, 403 U.S. 365, 375 (1971). Instead, bankruptcy legislation is in the area of economics and social welfare. See Dandridge v. Williams, 397 U.S., at 484–485; Richardson v. Belcher, 404 U.S., at 81; Lindsey v. Normet, 405 U.S. 56, 74 (1972); Jefferson v. Hackney, 406 U.S. 535, 546 (1972). This being so, the applicable standard, in measuring the propriety of Congress' classification, is that of rational justification."

Justices Stewart, Douglas, and Marshall, dissented.

ORTWEIN v. SCHWAB, 410 U.S. 656 (1973). Ortwein, a recipient of old-age assistance had his award reduced by the county welfare agency. As provided by state law he appealed to the state public welfare agency which held a hearing and upheld the county agency's decision. Judicial review of the state agency decision was provided by law in the state appellate court. Ortwein sought to appeal to that court without paying the $25 filing fee required in all civil cases filed in that court, alleging that he was indigent and unable to pay the fee. The state court denied this contention and refused to hear the appeal without the fee. The Supreme Court, in a *per curiam* opinion, affirmed, indicating that *Kras* rather than *Boddie* was the controlling precedent. The Court gave three principal reasons for its decision:

(1) The interest in increased welfare benefits "has far less constitutional significance" than the inability to dissolve one's marriage except through the courts.

(2) Ortwein did receive a pre-termination evidentiary hearing (the required due process minimum) not conditioned on the payment of a fee. "This Court has long recognized that, even in criminal cases, due process does not require a State to provide an appellate system."

(3) The filing fee does not violate the Equal Protection Clause by discriminating against the poor. The litigation, which deals with welfare payments, is in the area of economics and social welfare. "No suspect classification, such as race, nationality, or alienage, is present . . . .. The applicable standard is that of rational justification." The filing fee makes a contribution toward the cost of operating the court system, hence the "requirement of rationality is met."

Justices Stewart, Douglas, Brennan and Marshall dissented.

LITTLE v. STREATER, 452 U.S. 1 (1981). A unanimous Court concluded that refusal to furnish blood grouping tests to an indigent defendant in a civil paternity case denied that defendant "a meaningful opportunity to be heard" within the rationale of Boddie v. Connecticut. The Court relied on these factors: this action was not simply a civil proceeding between private parties since the child's mother was compelled to bring the action by State welfare officials and the State Attorney General was a party to the action; under State law, the defendant's testimony in a paternity action, standing alone, was insufficient to overcome the mother's testimony.

LASSITER v. DEPARTMENT OF SOCIAL SERVICES, 452 U.S. 18 (1981). A majority of the Court concluded that due process required the appointment of counsel, for an indigent parent in a proceeding brought by the state to terminate parental status, only in appropriate circumstances. The majority held that in this case, those special factors requiring the appointment of counsel were not present in that: no allegations of neglect or abuse had been made; no expert witness testified; and the presence of counsel could not have made a determinative difference in the result. The four dissenting Justices (Blackmun, Brennan, Marshall and Stevens) argued that due process should require the appointment of counsel for indigents in all proceedings brought by the state to terminate parental rights.

Chapter 11

THE EQUAL PROTECTION CLAUSE AND THE REVIEW OF THE REASONABLENESS OF LEGISLATION

SECTION 1. INTRODUCTION—THE SCOPE OF EQUAL PROTECTION

The fourteenth amendment provision that no state shall "deny to any person within its jurisdiction the equal protection of the laws," raises a host of difficult analytical problems. It can hardly be taken to be a guarantee that every law shall apply equally to every person, for almost all legislation involves classifications placing special burdens on or granting special benefits to individuals or groups. But if laws may classify, what content can be given to a guarantee of "equal protection of the laws"?

THE ORIGINAL UNDERSTANDING

The Supreme Court originally took a narrow view of the scope of the equal protection clause. In the Slaughter-House Cases, 83 U.S. (16 Wall.) 36, 81 (1872) the Court said: "We doubt very much whether any action of a State not directed by way of discrimination against the negroes as a class, or on account of their race, will ever be held to come within the purview of this provision. It is so clearly a provision for that race and that emergency, that a strong case would be necessary for its application to any other." In Strauder v. West Virginia, 100 U.S. 303, 306, 307 (1880), in invalidating a statute limiting jury service to whites, the Court said: "[The fourteenth amendment] was designed to assure to the colored race the enjoyment of all the civil rights that under the law are enjoyed by white persons, and to give to that race the protection of the General Government, in that enjoyment, whenever it should be denied by the States." In referring to the equal protection clause the Court said: "What is this but declaring that the law in the States shall be the same for the black as for the white; that all persons whether colored or white, shall stand equal before the laws of the States and, in regard to the colored race, for whose protection the Amendment was primarily designed, that no discrimination shall be made against them by law because of their color."

However, the Court shortly expanded its view in a way which brought the full range of legislative classification within the restrictions of the clause. In Barbier v. Connolly, 113 U.S. 27 (1885), the Court upheld a statute prohibiting the operation of laundries from 10 p.m. to 6 a.m., but assumed that the equal protection clause applied. The Court said that the equal protection clause guaranteed, inter alia, that "all persons should be equally entitled to pursue their happiness and acquire and enjoy property;" that "no impediment should be interposed to the pursuits of any one except as applied to the same pursuits by others under like circumstances;" and that "no greater burdens should be laid upon one than are laid upon others in the same calling or condition." The promise of *Barbier* that the equal protection clause would be applied to economic regulations was fulfilled in the following case.

GULF, COLORADO & SANTA FE RAILROAD CO. v. ELLIS, 165 U.S. 150 (1897). A statute provided that successful plaintiffs in certain kinds of suits against railroad companies should receive in addition to costs reasonable attorney's fees "not to exceed $10." The Court held the statute unconstitutional. The following passages suggest its reasoning:

". . . The act singles out a certain class of debtors and punishes them when for like delinquencies it punishes no others. They are not treated as other debtors, or equally with other debtors. They cannot appeal to the courts as other litigants under like conditions and with like protection. If litigation terminates adversely to them, they are mulcted in the attorney's fees of the successful plaintiff; if it terminates in their favor, they recover no attorney's fees. It is no sufficient answer to say that they are punished only when adjudged to be in the wrong. They do not enter the courts upon equal terms. They must pay attorney's fees if wrong; they do not recover any if right; while their adversaries recover if right and pay nothing if wrong. In the suits, therefore, to which they are parties they are discriminated against, and are not treated as others. They do not stand equal before the law. They do not receive its equal protection. All this is obvious from a mere inspection of the statute.

. . .

"While good faith and a knowledge of existing conditions on the part of a legislature is to be presumed, yet to carry that presumption to the extent of always holding that there must be some undisclosed and unknown reason for subjecting certain individuals or corporations to hostile and discriminating legislation is to make the protecting clauses of the Fourteenth Amendment a mere rope of sand, in no manner restraining state action.

. . .

"But it is said that it is not within the scope of the Fourteenth Amendment to withhold from States the power of classification, and that if the law deals alike with all of a certain class it is not obnoxious to the charge of a denial of equal protection. While, as a general proposition, this is undeniably true, . . . yet it is equally true that such classification cannot be made arbitrarily. The State may not say that all white men shall be subjected to the payment of the attorney's fees of parties successfully suing them and all black men not. It may not say that all men beyond a certain age shall be alone thus subjected, or all men possessed of a certain wealth. These are distinctions which do not furnish any proper basis for the attempted classification. That must always rest upon some difference which bears a reasonable and just relation to the act in respect to which the classification is proposed, and can never be made arbitrarily and without any such basis."

. . .

THE DOCTRINE OF REASONABLE CLASSIFICATION

In *Ellis* the Court articulated a doctrine of reasonable classification. To be valid a classification must be reasonably related to the object of the legislation and cannot be arbitrary. But how do you determine whether a classification is reasonable?

The following classic discussion of equal protection theory provides a framework of analysis. Tussman and ten-Broek, *The Equal Protection of the Laws* 37 Calif.L.Rev. 341 (1949):

"Here, then, is a paradox: The equal protection of the laws is a 'pledge of the protection of equal laws.' But laws may classify. And 'the very idea of classification is that of inequality.' In tackling this paradox the Court has neither abandoned the demand for equality nor denied the legislative right to classify. It has taken a middle course. It has resolved the contradictory demands of legislative specialization and constitutional generality by a doctrine of reasonable classification.

"The essence of that doctrine can be stated with deceptive simplicity. The Constitution does not require that things different in fact be treated in law as though they were the same. But it does require, in its concern for equality, that those who are similarly situated be similarly treated. The measure of the reasonableness of a classification is the degree of its success in treating similarly those similarly situated. . . .

. . .

". . . [W]here are we to look for the test of similarity of situation which determines the reasonableness of a classification? The inescapable answer is that we must look beyond the classification to the purpose of the law. A reasonable classification is one which includes all persons who are similarly situated with respect to the purpose of the law.

"The purpose of a law may be either the elimination of a public 'mischief' or the achievement of some positive public good. To simplify the discussion we shall refer to the purpose of a law in terms of the elimination of mischief, since the same argument holds in either case. We shall speak of the defining character or characteristics of the legislative classification as the trait. We can thus speak of the relation of the classification to the purpose of the law as the relation of the Trait to the Mischief.

. . .

"In other words, we are really dealing with the relation of two classes to each other. The first class consists of all individuals possessing the defining Trait; the second class consists of all individuals possessing, or rather, tainted by, the Mischief at which the law aims. The former is the legislative classification; the latter is the class of those similarly situated with respect to the purpose of the law. We shall refer to these two classes as T and M respectively.

"Now, since the reasonableness of any class T depends entirely upon its relation to a class M, it is obvious that it is impossible to pass judgment on the reasonableness of a classification without taking into consideration, or identifying, the purpose of the law. . . .

"There are five possible relationships between the class defined by the Trait and the class defined by the Mischief. These relationships can be indicated by the following diagrams:

(1)   : All *T*'s are *M*'s and all *M*'s are *T*'s

(2)   : No *T*'s are *M*'s

(3)   : All *T*'s are *M*'s but some *M*'s are not *T*'s

(4)   : All *M*'s are *T*'s but some *T*'s are not *M*'s

(5)   : Some *T*'s are *M*'s; some *T*'s are not *M*'s; and some *M*'s are not *T*'s

[C2555]

One of these five relationships holds in fact in any case of legislative classification, and we will consider each from the point of view of its 'reasonableness.'

"The first two situations represent respectively the ideal limits of reasonableness and unreasonableness. . . .

"Classification of the third type may be called 'under-inclusive.' All who are included in the class are tainted with the mischief, but there are others also tainted whom the classification does not include. Since the classification does not include all who are similarly situated with respect to the purpose of the law, there is a prima facie violation of the equal protection requirement of reasonable classification.

"But the Court has recognized the very real difficulties under which legislatures operate—difficulties arising out of both the nature of the legislative process and of the society which legislation attempts perennially to reshape—and it has refused to strike down indiscriminately all legislation embodying the classificatory inequality here under consideration.

"In justifying this refusal, the Court has defended under-inclusive classifications on such grounds as: the legislature may attack a general problem in a piecemeal fashion; 'some play must be allowed for the joints of the machine'; 'a statute aimed at what is deemed an evil, and hitting it presumably where experience shows it to be most felt, is not to be upset . . . .'; 'the law does all that is needed when it does all that it can . . . .'; and—perhaps with some impatience—the equal protection clause is not 'a pedagogic requirement of the impracticable.'

"These generalities, while expressive of judicial tolerance, are not, however, very helpful. They do not constitute a clear statement of the circumstances and conditions which justify such tolerance—which justify a departure from the strict requirements of the principle of equality. . . .

"The fourth type of classification imposes a burden upon a wider range of individuals than are included in the class of those tainted with the mischief at which the law aims. It can thus be called 'over-inclusive.' Herod, ordering the death of all male children born on a particular day because one of them would some day bring about his downfall, employed such a classification. It is exemplified by the quarantine and the dragnet. The wartime treatment of American citizens of Japanese ancestry is a striking recent instance of the imposition of burdens upon a large class of individuals because some of them were believed to be disloyal.

"The prima facie case against such departures from the ideal standards of reasonable classification is stronger than the case against under-inclusiveness. For in the latter case, all who are included in the class are at least tainted by the mischief at which the law aims; while over-inclusive classifications reach out to the innocent bystander, the hapless victim of circumstance or association." [a]

APPLICATION OF THE EQUAL PROTECTION LIMITATION TO THE FEDERAL GOVERNMENT THROUGH THE DUE PROCESS CLAUSE OF THE FIFTH AMENDMENT

Originally the Supreme Court took the position that "[u]nlike the Fourteenth Amendment, the Fifth contains no equal protection clause and it provides no guaranty against discriminatory legislation by Congress." Detroit Bank v. United States, 317 U.S. 329, 337 (1943). At the same time the Court indicated that discriminatory legislation "may be so arbitrary and injurious in character as to violate the due process clause of the Fifth Amendment." Id. at 338.

However, in Bolling v. Sharpe, 347 U.S. 497, 499 (1954) (a companion case to Brown v. Board of Educ., 347 U.S. 483 (1954)) the Court, in invalidating racial segregation in the District of Columbia schools, said:

[a] Copyright ©, 1949, California Law Review, Inc. Reprinted by Permission.

Also see generally Note, *Developments in the Law—Equal Protection,* 82 Harv.L.Rev. 1065 (1969).

"The Fifth Amendment which is applicable in the District of Columbia does not contain an equal protection clause as does the Fourteenth Amendment which applies only to the states. But the concepts of equal protection and due process, both stemming from our American ideal of fairness, are not mutually exclusive. The 'equal protection of the laws' is a more explicit safeguard of prohibited unfairness than 'due process of law,' and, therefore, we do not imply that the two are always interchangeable phrases. But, as this Court has recognized, discrimination may be so unjustifiable as to be violative of due process."

By 1975 the Court went so far as to say, in invalidating a gender classification in the Social Security Act: "This Court's approach to Fifth Amendment equal protection claims has always been precisely the same as to equal protection claims under the Fourteenth Amendment." Weinberger v. Wiesenfeld, 420 U.S. 636, 639, n. 2 (1975). However, the next year the Court, in holding invalid a federal regulation barring resident aliens from employment in the federal competitive civil service, distinguished decisions holding similar state laws to be a violation of equal protection by saying: "The concept of equal justice under law is served by the Fifth Amendment's guarantee of due process, as well as by the Equal Protection Clause of the Fourteenth Amendment. Although both Amendments require the same type of analysis, . . . the Court of Appeals correctly stated that the two protections are not always coextensive. Not only does the language of the two Amendments differ, but more importantly, there may be overriding national interests which justify selective federal legislation that would be unacceptable for an individual State." Hampton v. Mow Sun Wong, 426 U.S. 88, 100 (1976).

More recently the Court began its consideration of the validity of a federal statute by saying that the "issue presented is whether Congress violates the equal protection component of the Fifth Amendment's Due Process Clause." Vance v. Bradley, 440 U.S. 93, 94 (1979). In a footnote to that statement the Court said: "Concern with assuring equal protection was part of the fabric of our Constitution even before the Fourteenth Amendment expressed it most directly in applying it to the States . . . .. Accordingly, the Court has held that the Due Process Clause of the Fifth Amendment forbids the Federal Government from denying equal protection of the laws."

THE STANDARD OF REVIEW

The Tussman and tenBroek excerpt does not address directly the question of the standard of review to be applied in equal protection cases. How closely must a classification be related to the purpose? How important must the purpose be? Who has the burden of proof on the issue of reasonableness of the classification?

In Lindsley v. Natural Carbonic Gas Co., 220 U.S. 61, 78 (1911), the Court stated a standard which gave substantial deference to the legislative judgment in making classifications:

"The rules by which [the contention that a statutory classification violates the equal protection clause] must be tested, as is shown by repeated decisions of this court, are these: 1. The equal protection clause of the 14th Amendment does not take from the state the power to classify in the adoption of police laws, but admits of the exercise of a wide scope of discretion in that regard, and avoids what is done only when it is without any reasonable basis, and therefore is purely arbitrary. 2. A classification having some reasonable basis does not offend against that clause merely because it is not made with mathematical nicety, or because in practice it results in some inequality. 3. When the classification in such a law is called in question, if any state of facts reasonably can be conceived that would sustain it, the existence of that state of facts at the time the law was enacted must be assumed. 4. One who assails the classification in such a law must carry the burden of showing that it does not rest upon any reasonable basis, but is essentially arbitrary."

However, in the 1920s and early 1930s the Court invalidated a substantial number of statutes under equal protection—particularly statutes discriminating against corporations and statutes making unusual tax classifications. In many of these cases the Court, as in the due process cases of the period set out in Chapter 10, supra, appeared to be placing the burden of justifying the classifications on the state, without specifying how great that burden was. In Quaker City Cab Co. v. Pennsylvania, 277 U.S. 389, 402 (1928), e.g., the Court invalidated a law imposing a tax on corporations engaged in the transportation business but not on individuals engaged in the same businesses. The Court said: "The tax is imposed merely because the owner is a corporation. The discrimination is not justified by any difference in the source of the receipts or in the situation or character of the property employed. It follows that the section fails to meet the requirement that a classification to be consistent with the equal protection clause must be based on a real and substantial difference having reasonable relation to the subject of the legislation . . . No decision of this court gives support to such a classification. In no view can it be held to have more than an arbitrary basis . . .. The tax cannot be sustained."

Two cases decided on the same day in 1936 further illustrate the failure of the Court to articulate a consistent standard of review in equal protection cases. In Borden's Farm Products Co. v. Ten Eyck, 297 U.S. 251, 263 (1936), the Court, in upholding a provision of the New York Milk Control Law which fixed a differential of one cent per quart on sales to stores in favor of milk dealers not having a well-advertised trade name, said: "In the light of the facts found the legislature might reasonably have thought trade conditions existed justifying the fixing of a differential. Judicial inquiry does not concern itself with the accuracy of the legislative finding, but only with the question whether it so lacks any reasonable basis as to be arbitrary." In Mayflower Farms, Inc. v. Ten Eyck, 297 U.S. 266, 274 (1936), however, the Court invalidated another provision of the New York law which limited the one cent per quart differential to milk dealers who had been continuously in business since April 10, 1933, saying:

"The challenged provision . . . is not a regulation of a business or activity in the interest of, or for the protection of, the public, but an attempt to give an economic advantage to those engaged in a given business at an arbitrary date as against all those who enter the industry after that date. The appellees do not intimate that the classification bears any relation to the public health or welfare generally; that the provision will discourage monopoly; or that it was aimed at any abuse, cognizable by law, in the milk business. In the absence of any such showing, we have no right to conjure up possible situations which might justify the discrimination. The classification is arbitrary and unreasonable and denies the appellant the equal protection of the law."

In 1937 the Court's approach to the application of equal protection changed as did its approach to the application of due process. With respect to ordinary social and economic legislation, the standard of review is low and the cases will be reviewed in Section 2. Higher standards of review are applied to cases in which the bases of classification—race, nationality, alienage, gender, legitimacy—are held to be "suspect" and to require special justification. These cases will be reviewed in Section 3. And finally in Section 4 we will examine cases in which the Court holds that legislative classifications which burden constitutionally protected interests are invalid if not closely related to important or substantial governmental interests.

As we pursue the three strands of equal protection through this chapter, it may be helpful to have a brief overview of the analytical differences among them. Consider the implications of the following three cases.

In the first, a statute excluding resident aliens from the receipt of welfare benefits was held invalid because "classifications based on alienage, like those based on nationality or race, are inherently suspect and subject to close judicial scrutiny." Graham v. Richardson, 403 U.S. 365, 372 (1971). In the second, a statute denying welfare assistance to residents who had not resided within the state for a year was held invalid because it served "to penalize the exercise" of the constitutionally protected "right" to travel and the state had not shown that the statutory scheme was "necessary to promote a *compelling* governmental interest." Shapiro v. Thompson, 394 U.S. 618, 634 (1969). In the third, a statute providing lower welfare payments for dependent children than for the aged was upheld because it did not use a suspect classification, burden a constitutionally protected interest, or fail the general test of rationality—there was some relationship between the classification and the state objective. Jefferson v. Hackney, 406 U.S. 535, 546, 549 (1972).

SECTION 2.   SOCIAL AND ECONOMIC REGULATORY LEGISLATION

RAILWAY EXPRESS AGENCY v. NEW YORK

336 U.S. 106, 69 S.Ct. 463, 93 L.Ed. 533 (1949).

Mr. Justice Douglas delivered the opinion of the Court.

Section 124 of the Traffic Regulations of the City of New York promulgated by the Police Commissioner provides:

"No person shall operate, or cause to be operated, in or upon any street an advertising vehicle; provided that nothing herein contained shall prevent the putting of business notices upon business delivery vehicles, so long as such vehicles are engaged in the usual business or regular work of the owner and not used merely or mainly for advertising."

Appellant is engaged in a nation-wide express business. It operates about 1,900 trucks in New York City and sells the space on the exterior sides of these trucks for advertising. That advertising is for the most part unconnected with its own business. It was convicted in the magistrates court and fined. The judgment of conviction was sustained in the Court of Special Sessions. . . . The Court of Appeals affirmed without opinion by a divided vote. . . . The case is here on appeal . . .

The Court of Special Sessions concluded that advertising on vehicles using the streets of New York City constitutes a distraction to vehicle drivers and to pedestrians alike and therefore affects the safety of the public in the use of the streets. We do not sit to weigh evidence on the due process issue in order to determine whether the regulation is sound or appropriate; nor is it our function to pass judgment on its wisdom. See Olsen v. State of Nebraska, 313 U.S. 236. We would be trespassing on one of the most intensely local and specialized of all municipal problems if we held that this regulation had no relation to the traffic problem of New York City. It is the judgment of the local authorities that it does have such a relation. And nothing has been advanced which shows that to be palpably false.

The question of equal protection of the laws is pressed more strenuously on us. It is pointed out that the regulation draws the line between advertisements of products sold by the owner of the truck and general advertisements. It is argued that unequal treatment on the basis of such a distinction is not justified by the aim and purpose of the regulation. It is said, for example, that one of appellant's trucks carrying the advertisement of a commercial house would not cause any greater distraction of pedestrians and vehicle drivers than if the commercial house carried the same advertisement on its own truck. Yet the regulation allows the latter to do what the former is forbidden from doing. It is therefore contended that the classification which the regulation makes has no relation to the traffic problem since a violation turns not on what kind of advertisements are carried on trucks but on whose trucks they are carried.

That, however, is a superficial way of analyzing the problem, even if we assume that it is premised on the correct construction of the regulation. The local authorities may well have concluded that those who advertised their own wares on their trucks do not present the same traffic problem in view of the nature or extent of the advertising which they use. It would take a degree of omniscience which we lack to say that such is not the case. If that judgment is correct, the advertising displays that are exempt have less incidence on traffic than those of appellants.

We cannot say that that judgment is not an allowable one. Yet if it is, the classification has relation to the purpose for which it is made and does not contain the kind of discrimination against which the Equal Protection Clause affords protection. It is by such practical considerations based on experience rather than by theoretical inconsistencies that the question of equal protection is to be answered. Patsone v. Commonwealth of Pennsylvania, 232 U.S. 138, 144. . . . And the fact that New York City sees fit to eliminate from traffic this kind of distraction but does not touch what may be even greater ones in a different category, such as the vivid displays on Times Square, is immaterial. It is no requirement of equal protection that all evils of the same genus be eradicated or none at all. . . .

Affirmed.

Mr. Justice Rutledge acquiesces in the Court's opinion and judgment, dubitante on the question of equal protection of the laws.

Mr. Justice Jackson, concurring.

There are two clauses of the Fourteenth Amendment which this Court may invoke to invalidate ordinances by which municipal governments seek to solve their local problems. One says that no state shall "deprive any person of life, liberty, or property, without due process of law". The other declares that no state shall "deny to any person within its jurisdiction the equal protection of the laws."

My philosophy as to the relative readiness with which we should resort to these two clauses is almost diametrically opposed to the philosophy which prevails on this Court. While claims of denial of equal protection are frequently asserted, they are rarely sustained. But the Court frequently uses the due process clause to strike down measures taken by municipalities to deal with activities in their streets and public places which the local authorities consider to create hazards, annoyances or discomforts to their inhabitants. . . .

The burden should rest heavily upon one who would persuade us to use the due process clause to strike down a substantive law or ordinance. Even its provident use against municipal regulations frequently disables all government—state, municipal and federal—from dealing with the conduct in question because the requirement of due process is also applicable to State and Federal Governments. Invalidation of a statute or an ordinance on due process grounds leaves ungoverned and ungovernable conduct which many people find objectionable.

Invocation of the equal protection clause, on the other hand, does not disable any governmental body from dealing with the subject at hand. It merely means that the prohibition or regulation must have a broader impact. I regard it as a salutary doctrine that cities, states and the Federal Government must exercise their powers so as not to discriminate between their inhabitants except upon some reasonable differentiation fairly related to the object of regulation. This equality is not merely abstract justice. The framers of the Constitution knew, and we should not forget today, that there is no more effective practical guaranty against arbitrary and unreasonable government than to require that the principles of law which officials would impose upon a minority must be imposed generally. Conversely, nothing opens the door to arbitrary action so effectively as to allow those officials to pick and choose only a few to whom they will apply legislation and thus to escape the political retribution that might be visited upon them if larger numbers were affected. Courts can take no better measure to assure that laws will be just than to require that laws be equal in operation. . . .

In this case, if the City of New York should assume that display of any advertising on vehicles tends and intends to distract the attention of persons using the highways and to increase the dangers of its traffic, I should think it fully within its constitutional powers to forbid it all. The same would be true if the City should undertake to eliminate or minimize the hazard by any generally applicable restraint, such as limiting the size, color, shape or perhaps to some extent the contents of vehicular advertising. Instead of such general regulation of advertising, however, the City seeks to reduce the hazard only by saying that while some may, others may not exhibit such appeals. The same display, for example, advertising cigarettes, which this appellant is forbidden to carry on its trucks, may be carried on the trucks of a cigarette dealer and might on the trucks of this appellant if it dealt in cigarettes. And almost an identical advertisement, certainly one of equal size, shape, color and appearance, may be carried by this appellant if it proclaims its own offer to transport cigarettes. But it may not be carried so long as the message is not its own but a cigarette dealer's offer to sell the same cigarettes.

. . .

The question in my mind comes to this. Where individuals contribute to an evil or danger in the same way and to the same degree, may those who do so for hire be prohibited, while those who do so for their own commercial ends but not for hire be allowed to continue? I think the answer has to be that the hireling may be put in a class by himself and may be dealt with differently than those who act on their own. But this is not merely because such a discrimination will enable the lawmaker to diminish the evil. That might be done by many classifications, which I should think wholly unsustainable. It is rather because there is a real difference between doing in self-interest and doing for hire, so that it is one thing to tolerate action from those who act on their own and it is another thing to permit the same action to be promoted for a price.

. . .

WILLIAMSON v. LEE OPTICAL CO. OF OKLAHOMA, 348 U.S. 483 (1955). The due process portions of this case are set out supra, p. 535. The Court disposed of an equal protection objection to the portion of the law which exempted sellers of ready-to-wear glasses from regulations imposed on opticians as follows:

"The problem of legislative classification is a perennial one, admitting of no doctrinaire definition. Evils in the same field may be of different dimensions and propositions, requiring different remedies. Or so the legislature may think. . . . Or the reform may take one step at a time, addressing itself to the phase of the problem which seems most acute to the legislative mind. . . . The legislature may select one phase of one field, and apply a remedy there, neglecting the others. . . . The prohibition of the Equal Protection Clause goes no further than the individious discrimination. We cannot say that that point has been reached here. For all this record shows, the ready-to-wear branch of this business may not loom large in Oklahoma or may present problems of regulation distinct from the other branch."

MOREY v. DOUD, 354 U.S. 457 (1957). An Illinois statute imposed a requirement of licensing and submission to certain regulations of private firms engaged in the business of selling or issuing money orders "other than . . . American Express Company money order[s]." The Court held that because of the exception provided for the American Express Company the statute could not validly be applied to other firms issuing money orders. In arriving at its result the Court cited *Lee Optical* for the proposition that only individious discriminations are prohibited by equal protection but proceeded to rely on cases from the 1930s, such as Smith v. Cahoon, 283 U.S. 553 (1931), and Hartford Steam Boiler Inspection & Ins. Co. v. Harrison, 301 U.S. 459 (1937), for the proposition that statutory discriminations must be "based on differences that are reasonably related to the purposes" of the statute under review. After examining the asserted purposes of the act and the relationship of the classification to those purposes, the Court concluded:

"Taking all of these factors in conjunction—the remote relationship of the statutory classification to the Act's purpose or to business characteristics, and the creation of a closed class by the singling out of the money orders of a named company, with accompanying economic advantages—we hold that the application of the Act to appellees deprives them of equal protection of the laws."

Justice Black, dissenting, said the classification here could hardly be called "invidious" and expressed his objection "to the use of general provisions of the Constitution to restrict narrowly state power over state domestic economic affairs." Justice Frankfurter, joined by Justice Harlan, also dissented. He noted that "[c]lassification is inherent in legislation; the Equal Protection Clause has not forbidden it. To recognize marked differences that exist in fact is living law; to disregard practical differences and concentrate on some abstract identities is lifeless logic." He stated that the *Coleman* and *Harrison* cases relied on by the Court are "false leads"—"both manifest the requirement of nondiscriminatory classifications as an exercise in logical abstractions." He concluded that the decisive fact which should lead to upholding the legislation was that "the American Express Co. is decisively different from those money order issuers that are within the regulatory scheme."

NEW ORLEANS v. DUKES

427 U.S. 297, 96 S.Ct. 2513, 49 L.Ed.2d 511 (1976).

Per Curiam.

The question presented by this case is whether the provision of a New Orleans ordinance, as amended in 1972, that excepts from the ordinance's prohibition against vendors' selling of foodstuffs from pushcarts in the Vieux Carre, or French Quarter, "vendors who have continually operated the same business within the Vieux Carre . . . for eight years prior to January 1, 1972 . . ." denied appellee vendor equal protection of the laws in violation of the Fourteenth Amendment.

Appellee operates a vending business from pushcarts throughout New Orleans but had carried on that business in the Vieux Carre for only two years when the ordinance was amended in 1972 and barred her from continuing operations there.   She had previously filed an action in the District Court for the Eastern District of Louisiana attacking the validity of the former version of the ordinance, and amended her complaint to challenge the application of the ordinance's "grandfather clause"—the eight years or more provision—as a denial of equal protection.   She prayed for an injunction and declaratory judgment.   On cross-motions for summary judgment, the District Court, without opinion, granted appellant city's motion.   The Court of Appeals for the Fifth Circuit reversed.   501 F.2d 706 (1974). . . .   We hold that we have jurisdiction of appellant's appeal, and on the merits reverse the judgment of the Court of Appeals.

. . .

Chapter 46 of the Code of the City of New Orleans sets up a comprehensive scheme of permits for the conduct of various businesses in the city.   In 1972, the Code was amended to restrict the validity of many of these permits to points outside the Vieux Carre.   However, even as to those occupations—including all pushcart food vendors—which were to be banned from the Vieux Carre during seasons other than Mardi Gras, the city council made the "grandfather provision" exception.   Two pushcart food vendors—one engaged in the sale of hot dogs and the other an ice cream vendor—had operated in the Vieux Carre for 20 or more years and therefore qualified under the "grandfather clause" and continued to operate there. . . .

II.

The record makes abundantly clear that the amended ordinance, including the "grandfather provision," is solely an economic regulation aimed at enhancing the vital role of the French Quarter's tourist-oriented charm in the economy of New Orleans.

When local economic regulation is challenged solely as violating the Equal Protection Clause, this Court consistently defers to legislative determinations as to the desirability of particular statutory discriminations.   See, e.g., Lehnhausen v. Lake Shore Auto Parts Co., 410 U.S. 356 (1973). . . .   In short, the judiciary may not sit as a superlegislature to judge the wisdom or desirability of legislative policy determinations made in areas that neither affect fundamental rights nor proceed along suspect lines, see, e.g., Day-Brite Lighting, Inc. v. Missouri, 342 U.S. 421, 423 (1952); in the local economic sphere, it is only the invidious discrimination, the wholly arbitrary act, which cannot stand consistently with the Fourteenth Amendment.   See, e.g., Ferguson v. Skrupa, 372 U.S. 726, 732 (1963).

The Court of Appeals held in this case, however, that the "grandfather provision" failed even the rationality test.   We disagree.   The city's classification rationally furthers the purpose which the Court of Appeals recognized the city had identified as its objective in enacting the provision, that is, as a means "to preserve the appearance and custom valued by the Quarter's residents and attractive to tourists."   501 F.2d, at 709.   The legitimacy of that objective is obvious. . . .

It is suggested that the "grandfather provision," allowing the continued operation of some vendors was a totally arbitrary and irrational method of achieving the city's purpose.   But rather than proceeding by the immediate and absolute abolition of all pushcart food vendors, the city could rationally choose initially to eliminate vendors of more recent vintage. This gradual approach to the problem is not constitutionally impermissible. . . . The city could reasonably decide that newer businesses were less likely to have built up substantial reliance interests in continued operation in the Vieux Carre and that the two vendors which qualified under the "grandfather clause"—both of which had operated in the area for over 20 years rather than only eight—had themselves become part of the distinctive character and charm that distinguishes the Vieux Carre. We cannot say that these judgments so lack rationality that they constitute a constitutionally impermissible denial of equal protection.

Nevertheless, relying on Morey v. Doud, supra, as its "chief guide," the Court of Appeals held that even though the exemption of the two vendors was rationally related to legitimate city interests on the basis of facts extant when the ordinance was amended, the "grandfather clause" still could not stand because "the hypothesis that a present eight-year veteran of the pushcart hot dog market in the Vieux Carre will continue to operate in a manner more consistent with the traditions of the Quarter than would any other operator is without foundation." 501 F.2d, at 711. Actually, the reliance on the statute's potential irrationality in Morey v. Doud, as the dissenters in that case correctly pointed out, see 354 U.S., at 474–475 (Frankfurter, J., dissenting), was a needlessly intrusive judicial infringement on the State's legislative powers, and we have concluded that the equal protection analysis employed in that opinion should no longer be followed. *Morey* was the only case in the last half century to invalidate a wholly economic regulation solely on equal protection grounds, and we are now satisfied that the decision was erroneous. *Morey* is, as appellee and the Court of Appeals properly recognized, essentially indistinguishable from this case, but the decision so far departs from proper equal protection analysis in cases of exclusively economic regulation that it should be, and it is, overruled.

The judgment of the Court of Appeals is reversed and the case is remanded for further proceedings consistent with this opinion.

It is so ordered.

Mr. Justice Marshall joins in the judgment.

Mr. Justice Stevens took no part in the consideration or decision of this case.

UNITED STATES RAILROAD RETIREMENT BOARD v. FRITZ

449 U.S. 166, 101 S.Ct. 453, 66 L.Ed.2d 368 (1980).

Justice Rehnquist delivered the opinion of the Court.

The United States District Court for the Southern District of Indiana held unconstitutional a section of the Railroad Retirement Act of 1974, 45 U.S.C. § 231 et seq., and the United States Railroad Retirement Board has appealed to this Court pursuant to 28 U.S.C. § 1252.

The 1974 Act fundamentally restructured the railroad retirement system. The Act's predecessor statute, adopted in 1937, provided a system of retirement and disability benefits for persons who pursued careers in the railroad industry. Under that statute, a person who worked for both railroad and nonrailroad employers and who qualified for railroad retirement benefits and social security benefits, 42 U.S.C. § 401 et seq., received retirement benefits under both systems and an accompanying "windfall" benefit. The legislative history of the 1974 Act shows that the payment of windfall benefits threatened the railroad retirement system with bankruptcy by the year 1981. Congress therefore determined to place the system on a "sound financial basis" by eliminating future accruals of those benefits. Congress also enacted various transitional provisions, including a grandfather provision, § 231b(h) which expressly preserved windfall benefits for some classes of employees.

In restructuring the Railroad Retirement Act in 1974, Congress divided employees into various groups. *First*, those employees who lacked the requisite 10 years of railroad employment to qualify for railroad retirement benefits as of January 1, 1975, the changeover date, would have their retirement benefits computed under the new system and would not receive any windfall benefit. *Second*, those individuals already retired and already receiving dual benefits as of the changeover date would have their benefits computed under the old system and would continue to receive a windfall benefit. *Third*, those employees who had qualified for both railroad and social security benefits as of the changeover date, but who had not yet retired as of that date (and thus were not yet receiving dual benefits), were entitled to windfall benefits if they had (1) performed some railroad service in 1974 or (2) had a "current connection" with the railroad industry as of December 31, 1974, or (3) completed 25 years of railroad service as of December 31, 1974. 45 U.S.C. § 231b(h)(1). *Fourth*, those employees who had qualified for railroad benefits as of the changeover date, but lacked a current connection with the railroad industry in 1974 and lacked 25 years of railroad employment, could obtain a lesser amount of windfall benefit if they had qualified for social security benefits as of the year (prior to 1975) they left railroad employment. 45 U.S.C. § 231b(h)(2).

Thus, an individual who, as of the changeover date, was unretired and had 11 years of railroad employment and sufficient nonrailroad employment to qualify for social security benefits is eligible for the full windfall amount if he worked for the railroad in 1974 or had a current connection with the railroad as of December 31, 1974, or his later retirement date. But an unretired individual with 24 years of railroad service and sufficient nonrailroad service to qualify for social security benefits is not eligible for a full windfall amount unless he worked for the railroad in 1974, or had a current connection with the railroad as of December 31, 1974 or his later retirement date. And an employee with 10 years of railroad employment who qualified for social security benefits only after leaving the railroad industry will not receive a reduced windfall benefit while an employee who qualified for social security benefits prior to leaving the railroad industry would receive a reduced benefit. It was with these complicated comparisons that Congress wrestled in 1974.

Appellees filed this class action in the United States District Court for the Southern District of Indiana, seeking a declaratory judgment that 45 U.S.C. § 231b(h) is unconstitutional under the Due Process Clause of the Fifth Amendment because it irrationally distinguishes between classes of annuitants. The District Court eventually certified a class of all persons eligible to retire between January 1, 1975 and January 31, 1977, who were permanently insured under the Social Security Act as of December 31, 1974, but who were not eligible to receive any "windfall component" because they had left the railroad industry before 1974, had no "current connection" with it at the end of 1974, and had less than 25 years of railroad service. Appellees contended below that it was irrational for Congress to have drawn a distinction between employees who had more than 10 years but less than 25 years of railroad employment simply on the basis of whether they had a "current connection" with the railroad industry as of the changeover date or as of the date of retirement.

The District Court agreed with appellees that a differentiation based solely on whether an employee was "active" in the railroad business as of 1974 was not "rationally related" to the congressional purposes of insuring the solvency of the railroad retirement system and protecting vested benefits. We disagree and reverse.

The initial issue presented by this case is the appropriate standard of judicial review to be applied when social and economic legislation enacted by Congress is challenged as being violative of the Fifth Amendment to the United States Constitution. . . .

. . .

In more recent years, however, the Court in cases involving social and economic benefits has consistently refused to invalidate on equal protection grounds legislation which it simply deemed unwise or unartfully drawn.

Thus in Dandridge v. Williams, 397 U.S. 471, 485–486 (1970), the Court rejected a claim that Maryland welfare legislation violated the Equal Protection Clause of the Fourteenth Amendment. It said:

"In the area of economic and social welfare, a State does not violate the Equal Protection Clause merely because the classifications made by its law are imperfect. If the classification has some 'reasonable basis', it does not offend the Constitution simply because the classification 'is not made with mathematical nicety or because in practice it results in some inequality.' Lindsley v. National Carbonic Gas Co., 220 U.S. 61, 78. 'The problems of government are practical ones and may justify, if they do not require, rough accommodations—illogical, it may be, and unscientific.' Metropolis Theatre Co. v. City of Chicago, 228 U.S. 61, 68–70 . . ..

"[The rational basis standard] is true to the principle that the Fourteenth Amendment gives the federal courts no power to impose upon the States their views of what constitutes wise economic or social policy."

Of like tenor are Vance v. Bradley, 440 U.S. 93, 97 (1979) [a] and New Orleans v. Dukes, 427 U.S. 297, 303 (1975). . . .

Applying those principles to this case, the plain language of § 231b(h) marks the beginning and end of our inquiry.[10] There Congress determined that some of those who in the past received full windfall benefits would not continue to do so. Because Congress could have eliminated windfall benefits for all classes of employees, it is not constitutionally impermissible for Congress to have drawn lines between groups of employees for the purpose of phasing out those benefits. New Orleans v. Dukes, 427 U.S., at 305.

The only remaining question is whether Congress achieved its purpose in a patently arbitrary or irrational way. The classification here is not arbitrary, says

---

[a] In the *Bradley* case the Court upheld a federal statute requiring retirement at age 60 of federal employees covered by the Foreign Service retirement and disability system but not those covered by the Civil Service retirement and disability system.

[10] This opinion and Justice Brennan's dissent cite a number of equal protection cases including Lindsley v. Natural Carbonic Gas Co., 220 U.S. 16 (1911), Royster Guano Co. v. Virginia, 253 U.S. 412 (1920), Morey v. Doud, 354 U.S. 457 (1957), Flemming v. Nestor, 363 U.S. 603 (1960), Massachusetts Board of Retirement v. Murgia, 427 U.S. 307 (1976), New Orleans v. Dukes, 427 U.S. 297 (1976), Johnson v. Robison, 415 U.S. 361 (1974), U.S. Dept. of Agriculture v. Moreno, 413 U.S. 528 (1973), United States Dept. of Agriculture v. Murry, 413 U.S. 508 (1973). Weinberger v. Wiesenfeld, 420 U.S. 636 (1975), and James v. Strange, 407 U.S. 128 (1972). The most arrogant legal scholar would not claim that all of these cases applied a uniform or consistent test under the Equal Protection Clause. And realistically speaking, we can be no more certain that this opinion will remain undisturbed than were those who joined the opinion in Lindsley, supra, Royster Guano Co., supra, or any of the other cases referred to in this opinion and in the dissenting opinion. But like our predecessors and our successors, we are obliged to apply the equal protection component of the Fifth Amendment as we believe the Constitution requires and in so doing we have no hesitation in asserting, contrary to the dissent, that where social or economic regulations are involved Dandridge v. Williams, 397 U.S. 41 (1970), and Jefferson v. Hackney, 406 U.S. 435 (1972), together with this case, state the proper application of the test. The comments in the dissenting opinion about the proper cases for which to look for the correct statement of the equal protection rational basis standard, and about which cases limit earlier cases, are just that: comments in a dissenting opinion.

appellant, because it is an attempt to protect the relative equities of employees and to provide benefits to career railroad employees. Congress fully protected, for example, the expectations of those employees who had already retired and those unretired employees who had 25 years of railroad employment. Conversely, Congress denied all windfall benefits to those employees who lacked 10 years of railroad employment. Congress additionally provided windfall benefits, in lesser amount, to those employees with 10 years railroad employment who had qualified for social security benefits at the time they had left railroad employment, regardless of a current connection with the industry in 1974 or on their retirement date.

Thus, the only eligible former railroad employees denied full windfall benefits are those, like appellees, who had no statutory entitlement to dual benefits at the time they left the railroad industry, but thereafter became eligible for dual benefits when they subsequently qualified for social security benefits. Congress could properly conclude that persons who had actually acquired statutory entitlement to windfall benefits while still employed in the railroad industry had a greater equitable claim to those benefits than the members of appellees' class who were no longer in railroad employment when they became eligible for dual benefits. Furthermore, the "current connection" test is not a patently arbitrary means for determining which employees are "career railroaders," particularly since the test has been used by Congress elsewhere as an eligibility requirement for retirement benefits. Congress could assume that those who had a current connection with the railroad industry when the Act was passed in 1974, or who returned to the industry before their retirement, were more likely than those who had left the industry prior to 1974, and who never returned to be among the class of persons who pursue careers in the railroad industry, the class for whom the Railroad Retirement Act was designed. Hisquierdo v. Hisquierdo, 439 U.S. 572, 573 (1979).

Where, as here, there are plausible reasons for Congress' action, our inquiry is at an end. It is, of course, "constitutionally irrelevant whether this reasoning in fact underlay the legislative decision," Flemming v. Nestor, 363 U.S., at 612, because this Court has never insisted that a legislative body articulate its reasons for enacting a statute. This is particularly true where the legislature must necessarily engage in a process of line drawing. The "task of classifying persons for . . . benefits . . . inevitably requires that some persons who have an almost equally strong claim to favorite treatment be placed on different sides of the line," Mathews v. Diaz, 426 U.S. 67, 83–84 (1970), and the fact the line might have been drawn differently at some points is a matter for legislative, rather than judicial, consideration.

Finally, we disagree with the District Court's conclusion that Congress was unaware of what it accomplished or that it was misled by the groups that appeared before it. If this test were applied literally to every member of any legislature that ever voted on a law, there would be very few laws which would survive it. The language of the statute is clear, and we have historically assumed that Congress intended what it enacted. To be sure, appellees lost a political battle in which they had a strong interest, but this is neither the first nor the last time that such a result will occur in the legislative forum. What we have said is enough to dispose of the claims that Congress not only failed to accept appellees argument as to restructuring *in toto,* but that such failure denied them equal protection of the laws guaranteed by the Fifth Amendment.[12]

---

[12] As we have recently stated, "The Constitution presumes that, absent some reason to infer antipathy, even improvident decision will eventually be rectified by the democratic processes and that judicial intervention is generally unwarranted no matter how unwisely we may think a political branch has acted." Vance v. Bradley, 440 U.S. 93, 97 (1979).

For the foregoing reasons, the judgment of the District Court is Reversed.

Justice Stevens, concurring in the judgment.

In my opinion Justice Brennan's criticism of the Court's approach to this case merits a more thoughtful response than that contained in footnote 10, ante. Justice Brennan correctly points out that if the analysis of legislative purpose requires only a reading of the statutory language in a disputed provision, and if any "conceivable basis" for a discriminatory classification will repel a constitutional attack on the statute, judicial review will constitute a mere tautological recognition of the fact that Congress did what it intended to do. Justice Brennan is also correct in reminding us that even though the statute is an example of "social and economic legislation," the challenge here is mounted by individuals whose legitimate expectations of receiving a fixed retirement income are being frustrated by, in effect, a breach of a solemn commitment by their government. When Congress deprives a small class of persons of vested rights that are protected—and, indeed, even enhanced [1]—for others who are in a similar though not identical position, I believe the Constitution requires something more than merely a "conceivable" or a "plausible" explanation for the unequal treatment.

I do not, however, share Justice Brennan's conclusion that every statutory classification must further an objective that can be confidently identified as the "actual purpose" of the legislature. Actual purpose is sometimes unknown. Moreover, undue emphasis on actual motivation may result in identically worded statutes being held valid in one State and invalid in a neighboring State. I therefore believe that we must discover a correlation between the classification and either the actual purpose of the statute or a legitimate purpose that we may reasonably presume to have motivated an impartial legislature. If the adverse impact on the disfavored class is an apparent aim of the legislature, its impartiality would be suspect. If, however, the adverse impact may reasonably be viewed as an acceptable cost of achieving a larger goal, an impartial lawmaker could rationally decide that that cost should be incurred.

In this case, however, we need not look beyond the actual purpose of the legislature. As is often true, this legislation is the product of multiple and somewhat inconsistent purposes that led to certain compromises. One purpose was to eliminate in the future the benefit that is described by the Court as a "windfall benefit" and by Justice Brennan as an "earned dual benefit." That aim was incident to the broader objective of protecting the solvency of the entire railroad retirement program. Two purposes that conflicted somewhat with this broad objective were the purposes of preserving those benefits that had already vested and of increasing the level of payments to beneficiaries whose rights were not otherwise to be changed. As Justice Brennan emphasizes, Congress originally intended to protect *all* vested benefits, but it ultimately sacrificed some benefits in the interest of achieving other objectives.

Given these conflicting purposes, I believe the decisive questions are (1) whether Congress can rationally reduce the vested benefits of some employees to improve the solvency of the entire program while simultaneously increasing the benefits of others; and (2) whether, in deciding which vested benefits to reduce, Congress may favor annuitants whose railroad service was more recent than that of disfavored annuitants who had an equal or greater quantum of employment.

My answer to both questions is in the affirmative. The congressional purpose to eliminate dual benefits is unquestionably legitimate; that legitimacy

---

[1] The 1974 Act provided increased benefits for spouses, widows, survivors and early retirees. See 45 U.S.C. § 231c(g).

is not undermined by the adjustment in the level of remaining benefits in response to inflation in the economy.   As for the second question, some hardship—in the form of frustrated long-term expectations—must inevitably result from any reduction in vested benefits.   Arguably, therefore, Congress had a duty—and surely it had the right to decide—to eliminate no more vested benefits than necessary to achieve its fiscal purpose.   Having made that decision, any distinction it chose within the class of vested beneficiaries would involve a difference of degree rather that a difference in entitlement.   I am satisfied that a distinction based upon currency of railroad employment represents an impartial method of identifying that sort of difference.   Because retirement plans frequently provide greater benefits for recent retirees than for those who retired years ago—and thus give a greater reward for recent service than for past service of equal duration—the basis for the statutory discrimination is supported by relevant precedent.   It follows, in my judgment, that the timing of the employees' railroad service is a "reasonable basis" for the classification as that term is used in *Linsley,* and *Dandridge,* as well as a "ground of difference having a fair and substantial relation to the object of the legislation," as those words are used in *Royster Guano.*

Accordingly, I concur in the judgment.

Justice Brennan, with whom Justice Marshall joins, dissenting.

.   .   .

The only question in this case is whether the equal protection component of the Fifth Amendment bars Congress from allocating pension benefits in this manner.   The answer to this question turns in large part on the way in which the strictures of equal protection are conceived by this Court.   .   .   .   The parties agree that the legal standard applicable to this case is the "rational basis" test.   .   .   .   The Court today purports to apply this standard, but in actuality fails to scrutinize the challenged classification in the manner established by our governing precedents.   I suggest that the mode of analysis employed by the Court in this case virtually immunizes social and economic legislative classifications from judicial review.

I.

A legislative classification may be upheld only if it bears a rational relationship to a legitimate state purpose.   .   .   .

Nonetheless, the rational basis standard "is not a toothless one," ibid., and will not be satisfied by flimsy or implausible justifications for the legislative classification, proffered after the fact by Government attorneys.   See, e.g., Jimenez v. Weinberger, 417 U.S. 628 (1974); U.S. Dept. of Agriculture v. Moreno, 413 U.S. 528 (1973); U.S. Dept. of Agriculture v. Murry, 413 U.S. 508 (1973); James v. Strange, 407 U.S. 128 (1972).   When faced with a challenge to a legislative classification under the rational basis test, the court should ask, first, what the purposes of the statute are, and second, whether the classification is rationally related to achievement of those purposes.

II.

The purposes of the Railroad Retirement Act of 1974 are clear, because Congress has commendably stated them in the House and Senate reports accompanying the Act.   .   .   .

Thus, a "principal purpose" of the Railroad Retirement Act of 1974, as explicitly stated by Congress, was to preserve the vested earned benefits of retirees who had already qualified for them.   The classification at issue here, which deprives some retirees of vested dual benefits, that they had earned prior to 1974, directly conflicts with Congress' stated purpose.   As such, the classification is not only rationally unrelated to the congressional purpose; it is inimical to it.

III.

The Court today avoids the conclusion that § 231b(h) must be invalidated by deviating in three ways from traditional rational basis analysis. First, the Court adopts a tautological approach to statutory purpose, thereby avoiding the necessity for evaluating the relationship between the challenged classification and the legislative purpose. Second, it disregards the actual stated purpose of Congress in favor of a justification which was never suggested by any Representative or Senator, and which in fact conflicts with the stated congressional purpose. Third, it upholds the classification without any analysis of its rational relationship to the identified purpose.

A.

The Court states that "the plain language of § 231b(h) marks the beginning and end of our inquiry." This statement is strange indeed, for the "plain language" of the statute can tell us only what the classification is; it can tell us nothing about the purpose of the classification, let alone the relationship between the classification and that purpose. Since § 231b(h) of the Act deprives appellees of their vested earned dual benefits, the Court apparently assumes that Congress must have *intended* that result. But by presuming purpose from result, the Court reduces analysis to tautology. It may always be said that Congress intended to do what it in fact did. If that were the extent of our analysis, we would find every statute, no matter how arbitrary or irrational, perfectly tailored to achieve its purpose. But equal protection scrutiny under the rational basis test requires the courts first to deduce the independent objectives of the statute, usually from statements of purpose and other evidence in the statute and legislative history, and second to analyze whether the challenged classification rationally furthers achievement of those objectives. The Court's tautological approach will not suffice.

B.

The Court analyzes the rationality of § 231b(h) in terms of a justification suggested by Government attorneys, but never adopted by Congress. The Court states that it is "constitutionally irrelevant whether this reasoning in fact underlay the legislative decision." (Quoting Flemming v. Nestor, 363 U.S. 603, 612 (1960)). . . .

. . . .

From these cases and others it is clear that this Court will no longer sustain a challenged classification under the rational basis test merely because Government attorneys can suggest a "conceivable basis" upon which it might be thought rational. The standard we have applied is properly deferential to the Legislative Branch: where Congress has articulated a legitimate governmental objective, and the challenged classification rationally furthers that objective, we must sustain the provision. In other cases, however, the courts must probe more deeply. Where Congress has expressly stated the purpose of a piece of legislation, but where the challenged classification is either irrelevant to or counter to that purpose, we must view any *post hoc* justifications proffered by Government attorneys with skepticism. A challenged classification may be sustained only if it is rationally related to achievement of an *actual* legitimate governmental purpose.

. . . .

. . . . Congress asked railroad management and labor representatives to negotiate and submit a bill to restructure the Railroad Retirement system, which should "take into account the specific recommendations of the Commission on Railroad Retirement." Pub.L. 69, § 107, 93d Cong., 1st Sess. (1973); 87 Stat. 165. The members of this Joint Labor-Management Negotiating Committee were not appointed by public officials, nor did they represent the interests of the appellee class, who were no longer active railroaders or union members.

In an initial proposed restructuring of the system, the Joint Committee devised a means whereby the system's deficit could be completely eliminated without depriving retirees of vested earned benefits. However, labor representatives demanded that benefits be increased for their current members, the cost to be offset by divesting the appellee class of a portion of the benefits they had earned under prior law.

.   .   .

Congress conducted hearings to consider the Joint Committee's recommendations, but never directed its attention to their effect on persons in appellees' situation. In fact, the Joint Committee negotiators and Railroad Retirement Board members who testified at congressional hearings perpetuated the inaccurate impression that all retirees with earned vested dual benefits under prior law would retain their benefits unchanged.   .   .   .

Most striking is the following colloquy between Representative Dingell and Mr. Dempsey:

"Mr. DINGELL: Who is going to be adversely affected? Somebody has to get it in the neck on this. Who is going to be that lucky fellow?

"Mr. DEMPSEY: Well, I don't think so really. I think this is the situation in which every one wins. Let me explain.

.   .   .

"Mr. DINGELL: Mr. Dempsey, I see some sleight of hand here but I don't see how it is happening. I applaud it but I would like to understand it. My problem is that you are going to go to a realistic system that is going to cost less but pay more in benefits. Now if you have accomplished this, I suggest we should put you in charge of the social security system."

The Act was passed in the form drafted by the Joint Committee without any amendment relevant to this case.

Of course, a misstatement or several misstatements by witnesses before Congress would not ordinarily lead us to conclude that Congress misapprehended what it was doing. In this instance, however, where complex legislation was drafted by outside parties and Congress relied on them to explain it, where the misstatements are frequent and unrebutted, and where no Member of Congress can be found to have stated the effect of the classification correctly, we are entitled to suspect that Congress may have been misled. As the District Court found: "At no time during the hearings did Congress even give a hint that it understood that the bill by its language eliminated an earned benefit of plaintiff's class."

Therefore, I do not think that this classification was rationally related to an *actual* governmental purpose.

C.

The third way in which the Court has deviated from the principles of rational basis scrutiny is its failure to analyze whether the challenged classification is genuinely related to the purpose identified by the Court. Having suggested that "equitable considerations" underlay the challenged classification—in direct contradiction to Congress' evaluation of those considerations, and in the face of evidence that the classification was the product of private negotiation by interested parties, inadequately examined and understood by Congress—the Court proceeds to accept that suggestion without further analysis.

I therefore conclude that the Government's proffered justification of "equitable considerations," accepted without question by the Court, cannot be defended. Rather, as the legislative history repeatedly states, equity and fairness demand that appellees, like their coworkers, retain the vested dual benefits they earned prior to 1974. A conscientious application of rational basis scrutiny demands, therefore, that § 231b(h) be invalidated.

IV

Equal protection rationality analysis does not empower the courts to second-guess the wisdom of legislative classifications. On this we are agreed, and have been for over 40 years. On the other hand, we are not powerless to probe beneath claims by Government attorneys concerning the means and ends of Congress. Otherwise, we would defer not to the considered judgment of Congress, but to the arguments of litigators. The instant case serves as an example of the unfortunate consequence of such misplaced deference. Because the Court is willing to accept a tautological analysis of congressional purpose, an assertion of "equitable" considerations contrary to the expressed judgment of Congress, and a classification patently unrelated to achievement of the identified purpose, it succeeds in effectuating neither equity nor congressional intent.

I respectfully dissent.

SCHWEIKER v. WILSON, 450 U.S. 221 (1981). Congress created the Supplemental Security Income program to aid those who cannot work because of age, blindness, or disability. From the beginning, however, the program did not make payments to persons who are inmates of public institutions, but with the partial exception to this exclusion providing a small amount of money (not over $300 per year) to any qualified person in an institution receiving payments with respect to the individual under a state plan approved under the Medicaid program. The major group of people not receiving these small benefits while institutionalized were persons aged 21 to 64 residing in public mental institutions since such treatment was not funded under Medicaid. There were, however, other groups excluded because they were in prisons or in other institutions not funded under Medicaid.

A suit was brought by mentally ill people in mental hospitals challenging the failure to pay them the small comfort allowance. The Court rejected their claims. Justice Blackmun, writing for the Court, first held that this statute did not classify in terms of mental health and it was not necessary to decide whether such a classification might require a higher standard of review. Second, he held that the statute was valid under the equal protection standard as applied to ordinary economic and social legislation. The opinion said, in part:

"Thus, the pertinent inquiry is whether the classification employed in § 1611(e)(1)(B) advances legitimate legislative goals in a rational fashion. The Court has said that, although this rational-basis standard is 'not a toothless one,' Mathews v. Lucas, 427 U.S. 495, 510 (1976), it does not allow us to substitute our personal notions of good public policy for those of Congress. . . .

. . . .

"We believe that the decision to incorporate the Medicaid eligibility standards into the SSI scheme must be considered Congress' deliberate, considered choice. The legislative record, although sparse, appears to be unequivocal. Both House and Senate Reports on the initial SSI bill noted the exclusion in no uncertain terms. . . . .

. . .

"Having found the adoption of the Medicaid standards intentional, we deem it logical to infer from Congress' deliberate action an intent to further the same subsidiary purpose that lies behind the Medicaid exclusion, which, as no party denies, was adopted because Congress believed the States to have a 'traditional' responsibility to care for those institutionalized in public mental institutions.

. . .

"Although we understand and are inclined to be sympathetic with appellees' and their supporting *amici's* assertions as to the beneficial effects of a patient's receiving the reduced stipend, we find this a legislative, and not a legal, argument. Congress rationally may elect to shoulder only part of the burden of supplying this allowance, and may rationally limit the grant to Medicaid recipients, for whose care the Federal Government already has assumed the major portion of the expense. The limited gratuity represents a partial solution to a far more general problem, and Congress legitimately may assume that the States would, or should, provide an equivalent, either in funds or in basic care. See Baur v. Mathews, 578 F.2d 228, 233 (CA9 1978). This Court has granted a 'strong presumption of constitutionality' to legislation conferring monetary benefits. Mathews v. De Castro, 429 U.S., at 185, because it believes that Congress should have discretion in deciding how to expend necessarily limited resources. Awarding this type of benefits inevitably involves the kind of line-drawing that will leave some comparably needy person outside the favored circle. We cannot say that it was irrational of Congress, in view of budgetary constraints, to decide that it is the Medicaid recipients in public institutions that are the most needy and the most deserving of the small monthly supplement."

Justice Powell, joined by Justices Brennan, Marshall, and Stevens, dissented. A few paragraphs from the dissent follow:

"The deference to which legislative accommodation of conflicting interests is entitled rests in part upon the principle that the political process of our majoritarian democracy responds to the wishes of the people. Accordingly, an important touchstone for equal protection review of statutes is how readily a policy can be discerned which the legislature intended to serve. . . . When a legitimate purpose for a statute appears in the legislative history or is implicit in the statutory scheme itself, a court has some assurance that the legislature has made a conscious policy choice. Our democratic system requires that legislation intended to serve a discernable purpose receive the most respectful deference. See Harris v. McRae, 448 U.S. 297 (1980); Maher v. Roe, 432 U.S. 464, 479 (1977); Weinberger v. Salfi, 422 U.S. 749 (1975). Yet, the question of whether a statutory classification discriminates arbitrarily cannot be divorced from whether it was enacted to serve an identifiable purpose. When a legislative purpose can be suggested only by the ingenuity of a government lawyer litigating the constitutionality of a statute, a reviewing court may be presented not so much with a legislative policy choice as its absence.

"In my view, the Court should receive with some skepticism *post hoc* hypotheses about legislative purpose, unsupported by the legislative history.[6] When no indication of legislative purpose appears other than the current

---

[6] Some of our cases suggest that the actual purpose of a statute is irrelevant, Flemming v. Nestor, 363 U.S. 603, 612 (1960), and that the statute must be upheld "if any state of facts reasonably may be conceived to justify" its discrimination, McGowan v. Maryland, 366 U.S. 420, 426 (1961). Although these cases preserve an important caution, they do not describe the importance of actual legislative purpose in our analysis. We recognize that a legislative body rarely acts with a single mind and that compromises blur purpose. Therefore, it is appropriate to accord some deference to the executive's view of legislative intent, as similarly we accord deference to the consistent construction of a statute by the administrative agency charged with its enforcement. E.g., Udall v. Tallman, 380 U.S. 1, 16 (1965). Ascertainment of actual purpose to the extent feasible, however, remains an essential step in equal protection.

position of the Secretary, the Court should require that the classification bear a 'fair and substantial relation' to the asserted purpose. See F.S. Royster Guano Co. v. Virginia, 253 U.S. 412, 415 (1920). This marginally more demanding scrutiny indirectly would test the plausibility of the tendered purpose, and preserve equal protection review as something more than 'a mere tautological recognition of the fact that Congress did what it intended to do.' *Fritz,* supra, at 180 (Stevens J., concurring).

. . . .

"I conclude that Congress had no rational reason for refusing to pay a comfort allowance to appellees, while paying it to numerous otherwise identically situated disabled indigents. This unexplained difference in treatment must have been a legislative oversight. I therefore dissent."

────────

LOGAN v. ZIMMERMAN BRUSH CO., 455 U.S. 422 (1982): An Illinois statute barred employment discrimination on the basis of physical handicap unrelated to ability. A person claiming discrimination was to file a charge before the Illinois Fair Employment Practices Commission within 180 days of the alleged discriminatory act. The Commission was given 120 days to convene a fact-finding conference. Thereafter the case went through a variety of procedures ending up with a final order of the Commission which then could be taken to court for review. In this case the Commission scheduled its fact-finding conference 5 days after expiration of the statutory 120 days. At the hearing the employer of the complainant moved to dismiss on the ground that the conference was not held within the statutory period. The Commission rejected the motion and the company took the case to the Supreme Court of Illinois which held that the 120 day period was jurisdictional—even though neither the complainant nor the employer could see that the claim was heard in time—and constitutional.

The Supreme Court, in an opinion by Justice Blackmun, held the statute invalid as depriving the complainant of property without due process of law. See discussion of that opinion in Chapter 12 infra. Justice Blackmun then filed a separate opinion, joined by Justices Brennan, Marshall, and O'Connor, asserting that the statute also violated the equal protection clause, saying in part:

"The Court's opinion considers appellant Logan's due process claim and decides that issue in his favor. As has been noted, Logan also raised an equal protection claim and that issue has been argued and briefed here. Although the Court considered that it was unnecessary to discuss and dispose of the equal protection claim when the due process issue was being decided in Logan's favor, I regard the equal protection issue as sufficiently important to require comment on my part, particularly inasmuch as a majority of the Members of the Court are favorably inclined toward the claim, although, to be sure, that majority is not the one that constitutes the Court for the controlling opinion.

"On its face, Logan's equal protection claim is an unconventional one. The Act's ¶ 858(b) establishes no explicit classifications and does not expressly distinguish between claimants, and the company therefore argues that Logan has no more been deprived of equal protection than anyone would be who is injured by a random act of governmental misconduct. As the Illinois Supreme Court interpreted the statute, however, ¶ 858(b) unambiguously divides claims—and thus, necessarily, claimants—into two discrete groups that are accorded radically disparate treatment. Claims processed within 120 days are given full consideration on the merits, and complainants bringing such charges are awarded the opportunity for full administrative and judicial review. In contrast, otherwise identical claims that do not receive a hearing within the statutory period are unceremoniously, and finally, terminated. Because the

Illinois court recognized, in so many words, that the FEPA establishes two categories of claims, one may proceed to determine whether the classification drawn by the statute is consistent with the Fourteenth Amendment.

"For over a century, the Court has engaged in a continuing and occasionally almost metaphysical effort to identify the precise nature of the Equal Protection Clause's guarantees. At the minimum level, however, the Court 'consistently has required that legislation classify the persons it affects in a manner rationally related to legitimate governmental objectives.' Schweiker v. Wilson, 450 U.S. 221, 230 (1981). This is not a difficult standard for a State to meet, when it is attempting to act sensibly and in good faith. But the 'rational-basis standard is "not a toothless one," ' id., at 234, quoting Mathews v. Lucas, 427 U.S. 495, 510 (1976); the classificatory scheme must 'rationally advanc[e] a reasonable and identifiable governmental objective.' Schweiker v. Wilson, 450 U.S., at 235. I see no need to explore the outer bounds of this test, for I find that the Illinois statute runs afoul of the lowest level of permissible equal protection scrutiny.

.   .   .

"In its opinion, . . . the Illinois Supreme Court recognized a third rationale for ¶ 858(b): that provision, according to the court, was designed to further the 'just and expeditious resolutio[n]' of employment disputes. 82 Ill. 2d, at 107, 44 Ill.Dec., at 313, 411 N.E.2d, at 282. Insofar as the court meant to suggest that a factfinding conference may help settle controversies and frame issues for a more efficient future resolution, it was undoubtedly correct. But I cannot agree that terminating a claim that the State itself has misscheduled is a rational way of expediting the resolution of disputes.

.   .   .

"It is true, of course, that ¶ 858(b) serves to expedite the resolution of certain claims—those not processed within 120 days—in a most obvious way, and in that sense it furthers the purpose of terminating disputes expeditiously. But it is not enough, under the Equal Protection Clause, to say that the legislature sought to terminate certain claims and succeeded in doing so, for that is 'a mere tautological recognition of the fact that [the legislature] did what it intended to do.' U.S. Railroad Retirement Bd. v. Fritz, 449 U.S., at 180 (Stevens, J., concurring in the judgment). This Court still has an obligation to view the classificatory *system,* in an effort to determine whether the disparate treatment accorded the affected classes is arbitrary. Rinaldi v. Yeager, 384 U.S., at 308 ('The Equal Protection Clause requires more of a state law than nondiscriminatory application within the class it establishes.') Cf. U.S. Retirement Bd. v. Fritz, 449 U.S., at 178.

"Here, that inquiry yields an affirmative result. So far as the State's purpose is concerned, every FEPA claimant's charge, when filed with the Commission, stands on the same footing. Yet certain randomly selected claims, because processed too slowly by the State, are irrevocably terminated without review. In other words, the State converts similarly situated claims into dissimilarly situated ones, and then uses this distinction as the basis for its classification. This, I believe, is the very essence of arbitrary state action. '[T]he Equal Protection Clause "imposes a requirement of some rationality in the nature of the class singled out" ' James v. Strange, 407 U.S. 128, 140 (1972), quoting Rinaldi, 384 U.S., at 308–309, and that rationality is absent here. The Court faced an analogous situation in a case involving sex-based classifications, and its conclusion there is applicable to the case before us now: giving preference to a discrete class 'merely to accomplish the elimination of hearings on the merits, is to make the very kind of arbitrary legislative choice forbidden by the Equal Protection Clause. . . .' Reed v. Reed, 404 U.S. 71, 76 (1971).

"Finally, it is possible that the Illinois Supreme Court meant to suggest that the deadline contained in ¶ 858(b) can be justified as a means of thinning out the Commission's caseload, with the aim of encouraging the Commission to convene timely hearings. This rationale, however, suffers from the defect outlined above: it draws an arbitrary line between otherwise identical claims. In any event, the State's method of furthering this purpose—if this was in fact the legislative end—has so speculative and attenuated a connection to its goal as to amount to arbitrary action. The State's rationale must be something more than the exercise of a strained imagination; while the connection between means and ends need not be precise, it, at the least, must have some objective basis. That is not so here.

"I thus agree with appellant Logan that the Illinois scheme also deprives him of his Fourteenth Amendment right to the equal protection of the laws."

Justice Powell, joined by Justice Rehnquist, concurred in the judgment. He discussed the equal protection claim briefly, concluding: "This Court has held repeatedly that state created classifications must bear a rational relationship to legitimate governmental objectives. . . . Although I do not join Justice Blackmun's separate opinion, I agree that the challenged statute, as construed and applied in this case, fails to comport with this minimal standard."

SCOPE AND LEGITIMACY OF JUDICIAL REVIEW OF THE RATIONALITY OF LEGISLATION UNDER EQUAL PROTECTION

Constitutional law scholars are sharply divided on the question whether the courts should examine ordinary economic legislation under the equal protection clause to insure that such legislation is at least minimally related to some general good. Three general views are identifiable.

Some scholars assert the view that courts should examine both the means and the ends of legislation. They state that courts cannot escape the burden of examining the outcomes of the legislative process to determine whether the regulations are reasonably related to legitimate public purposes. See, e.g. Tribe, *American Constitutional Law* 451, 452, 995, 999 (1978); Tussman and ten Broek, *Equal Protection of the Laws,* 37 Calif.L.Rev. 341, 350 (1949).

Others assert that courts should not reexamine legislative choices as to the ends to be served by legislation but should engage in a real inquiry to determine whether the means selected have a real and substantial relation to the object sought to be attained. See, e.g., Gunther, *Forward: In Search of Evolving Doctrine on a Changing Court: A Model for a Newer Equal Protection,* 86 Harv.L. Rev. 1 (1972).

A third view is that the proper role of the courts is to police the structural and procedural limitations which the Constitution puts on the legislative process but not to scrutinize the outcomes for reasonableness. The proponents of this view state that, except for those constitutional provisions which place substantive limits on legislative outcomes by extending special protection to interests against the legislative process, the reach and limits of otherwise valid laws are assumed to be adequately explained by the conflicting forces within the legislative process which shaped them. See, e.g., Linde, *Due Process of Lawmaking,* 55 Neb. L.Rev. 197 (1975); Barrett, *The Rational Basis Standard for Equal Protection Review of Ordinary Legislative Classifications,* 68 Ky.L.Rev. 845 (1980).

SECTION 3.　SUSPECT CLASSIFICATIONS

Introduction.　This section presents the cases where the classifying factor rather than the burden on a fundamental interest gives rise to a heightened standard of review.　Subsection A deals with the most clearly suspect classification—those disadvantaging racial minorities.　Subsection B involves a special application of the racial classification doctrine to official racial segregation of schools and other public facilities.

Subsections C, D, and E, dealing with classifications involving aliens, non-marital children, and gender, present cases where the Court uses the classifying factor to justify a heightened standard of review but one which is not as rigorous as that applied to racial classifications.　Subsection F discusses the possibility that other classifying factors may trigger heightened scrutiny.

The cases in Subsection G typically involve legislation which does not facially involve suspect classifications but which has a differential impact on particular groups.　The question addressed is whether "suspectness" turns on the "impact" of laws or the "intent" with which they are enacted.

Subsection H discusses the most controversial and divisive issue before the Court under the equal protection clause—the validity of the use of gender and racial classifications for the purpose of aiding women or minority groups.

A.　CLASSIFICATIONS DISADVANTAGING RACIAL MINORITIES

LOVING v. VIRGINIA

388 U.S. 1, 87 S.Ct. 1817, 18 L.Ed.2d 1010 (1967).

Mr. Chief Justice Warren delivered the opinion of the Court.

This case presents a constitutional question never addressed by this Court: whether a statutory scheme adopted by the State of Virginia to prevent marriages between persons solely on the basis of racial classifications violates the Equal Protection and Due Process Clauses of the Fourteenth Amendment.　For reasons which seem to us to reflect the central meaning of those constitutional commands, we conclude that these statutes cannot stand consistently with the Fourteenth Amendment.

In June 1958, two residents of Virginia, Mildred Jeter, a Negro woman, and Richard Loving, a white man, were married in the District of Columbia pursuant to its laws.　Shortly after their marriage, the Lovings returned to Virginia and established their marital abode in Caroline County.　At the October Term, 1958, of the Circuit Court of Caroline County, a grand jury issued an indictment charging the Lovings with violating Virginia's ban on interracial marriages.　On January 6, 1959, the Lovings pleaded guilty to the charge and were sentenced to one year in jail; however, the trial judge suspended the sentence for a period of 25 years on the condition that the Lovings leave the State and not return to Virginia together for 25 years, stating that:

> "Almighty God created the races white, black, yellow, malay, and red, and he placed them on separate continents.　And but for the interference with his arrangement there would be no cause for such marriages.　The fact that he separated the races shows that he did not intend for the races to mix."

After their convictions the Lovings took up residence in the District of Columbia.　On November 6, 1963, they filed a motion in the state trial court to vacate the judgment and set aside the sentence on the ground that the statutes which they had violated were repugnant to the Fourteenth Amendment.　The motion not having been decided by October 28, 1964, the Lovings instituted a class action in the United States District Court for the Eastern District of Virginia requesting that a three-judge court be convened to declare the Virginia antimiscegenation statutes unconstitutional and to enjoin state officials from enforcing their convictions.   On January 22, 1965, the state trial judge denied the motion to vacate the sentences, and the Lovings perfected an appeal to the Supreme Court of Appeals of Virginia.   On February 11, 1965, the three-judge District Court continued the case to allow the Lovings to present their constitutional claims to the highest state court.

The Supreme Court of Appeals upheld the constitutionality of the antimiscegenation statutes and, after modifying the sentence, affirmed the convictions. The Lovings appealed this decision, and we noted probable jurisdiction on December 12, 1966.

The two statutes under which appellants were convicted and sentenced are part of a comprehensive statutory scheme aimed at prohibiting and punishing interracial marriages.   The Lovings were convicted of violating § 20–58 of the Virginia Code:

> "*Leaving State to Evade Law.*   If any white person and colored person shall go out of this State, for the purpose of being married, and with the intention of returning, and be married out of it, and afterwards return to and reside in it, cohabiting as man and wife, they shall be punished as provided in § 20–59, and the marriage shall be governed by the same law as if it had been solemnized in this State.   The fact of their cohabitation here as man and wife shall be evidence of their marriage."

Section 20–59, which defines the penalty for miscegenation, provides:

> "*Punishment for Marriage.*   If any white person intermarry with a colored person, or any colored person intermarry with a white person, he shall be guilty of a felony and shall be punished by confinement in the penitentiary for not less than one nor more than five years."

Other central provisions in the Virginia statutory scheme are § 20–57, which automatically voids all marriages between "a white person and a colored person" without any judicial proceeding, and §§ 20–54 and 1–14 which, respectively, define "white persons" and "colored persons and Indians" for purposes of the statutory prohibitions.   The Lovings have never disputed in the course of this litigation that Mrs. Loving is a "colored person" or that Mr. Loving is a "white person" within the meanings given those terms by the Virginia statutes.

Virginia is now one of 16 States which prohibit and punish marriages on the basis of racial classifications.   Penalties for miscegenation arose as an incident to slavery and have been common in Virginia since the colonial period.   The present statutory scheme dates from the adoption of the Racial Integrity Act of 1924, passed during the period of extreme nativism which followed the end of the First World War.   The central features of this Act, and current Virginia law, are the absolute prohibition of a "white person" marrying other than another "white person," a prohibition against issuing marriage licenses until the issuing official is satisfied that the applicants' statements as to their race are correct, certificates of "racial composition" to be kept by both local and state registrars, and the carrying forward of earlier prohibitions against racial intermarriage.

I.

In upholding the constitutionality of these provisions in the decision below, the Supreme Court of Appeals of Virginia referred to its 1955 decision in Naim v. Naim, 197 Va. 80, 87 S.E.2d 749, as stating the reasons supporting the validity of these laws.   In *Naim,* the state court concluded that the State's legitimate purposes were "to preserve the racial integrity of its citizens," and to prevent "the corruption of blood," "a mongrel breed of citizens," and "the obliteration of racial pride," obviously an endorsement of the doctrine of White Supremacy. 87 S.E.2d, at 756. The court also reasoned that marriage has traditionally been subject to state regulation without federal intervention, and, consequently, the regulation of marriage should be left to exclusive state control by the Tenth Amendment.

While the state court is no doubt correct in asserting that marriage is a social relation subject to the State's police power, Maynard v. Hill, 125 U.S. 190 (1888), the State does not contend in its argument before this Court that its powers to regulate marriage are unlimited notwithstanding the commands of the Fourteenth Amendment. Nor could it do so in light of Meyer v. State of Nebraska, 262 U.S. 390 (1923), and Skinner v. State of Oklahoma, 316 U.S. 535 (1942). Instead, the State argues that the meaning of the Equal Protection Clause, as illuminated by the statements of the Framers, is only that state penal laws containing an interracial element as part of the definition of the offense must apply equally to whites and Negroes in the sense that members of each race are punished to the same degree. Thus, the State contends that, because its miscegenation statutes punish equally both the white and the Negro participants in an interracial marriage, these statutes, despite their reliance on racial classifications do not constitute an invidious discrimination based upon race. The second argument advanced by the State assumes the validity of its equal application theory. The argument is that, if the Equal Protection Clause does not outlaw miscegenation statutes because of their reliance on racial classifications, the question of constitutionality would thus become whether there was any rational basis for a State to treat interracial marriages differently from other marriages. On this question, the State argues, the scientific evidence is substantially in doubt and, consequently, this Court should defer to the wisdom of the state legislature in adopting its policy of discouraging interracial marriages.

Because we reject the notion that the mere "equal application" of a statute containing racial classifications is enough to remove the classifications from the Fourteenth Amendment's proscription of all invidious racial discriminations, we do not accept the State's contention that these statutes should be upheld if there is any possible basis for concluding that they serve a rational purpose. The mere fact of equal application does not mean that our analysis of this statute should follow the approach we have taken in cases involving no racial discrimination where the Equal Protection Clause has been arrayed against a statute discriminating between the kinds of advertising which may be displayed on trucks in New York City, Railway Express Agency, Inc. v. People of State of New York, 336 U.S. 106 (1949), or an exemption in Ohio's ad valorem tax for merchandise owned by a non-resident in a storage warehouse, Allied Stores of Ohio, Inc. v. Bowers, 358 U.S. 522 (1959). In these cases, involving distinctions not drawn according to race, the Court has merely asked whether there is any rational foundation for the discriminations, and has deferred to the wisdom of the state legislatures. In the case at bar, however, we deal with statutes containing racial classifications, and the fact of equal application does not immunize the statute from the very heavy burden of justification which the Fourteenth Amendment has traditionally required of state statutes drawn according to race.

The State argues that statements in the Thirty-ninth Congress about the time of the passage of the Fourteenth Amendment indicate that the Framers did not intend the Amendment to make unconstitutional state miscegenation laws. Many of the statements alluded to by the State concern the debates over the Freemen's Bureau Bill, which President Johnson vetoed, and the Civil Rights Act of 1966, enacted over his veto. While these statements have some relevance to the intention of Congress in submitting the Fourteenth Amendment, it must be understood that they pertained to the passage of specific statutes and not to the broader, organic purpose of a constitutional amendment. As for the various statements directly concerning the Fourteenth Amendment, we have said in connection with a related problem, that although these historical sources "cast some light" they are not sufficient to resolve the problem; "[a]t best, they are inconclusive. The most avid proponents of the post-War Amendments undoubtedly intended them to remove all legal distinctions among 'all persons born or naturalized in the United States.' Their opponents, just as certainly, were antagonistic to both the letter and the spirit of the Amendments and wished them to have the most limited effect." Brown et al. v. Board of Education of Topeka, et al., 347 U.S. 483 (1954). See also Strauder v. West Virginia, 100 U.S. 303, 310 (1880). We have rejected the proposition that the debates in the Thirty-ninth Congress or in the state legislatures which ratified the Fourteenth Amendment supported the theory advanced by the State, that the requirement of equal protection of the laws is satisfied by penal laws defining offenses based on racial classifications so long as white and Negro participants in the offense were similarly punished. McLaughlin et al. v. State of Florida, 379 U.S. 184 (1964).

The State finds support for its "equal application" theory in the decision of the Court in Pace v. Alabama, 106 U.S. 583 (1882). In that case, the Court upheld a conviction under an Alabama statute forbidding adultery or fornication between a white person and a Negro which imposed a greater penalty than that of a statute proscribing similar conduct by members of the same race. The Court reasoned that the statute could not be said to discriminate against Negroes because the punishment for each participant in the offense was the same. However, as recently as the 1964 Term, in rejecting the reasoning of that case, we stated "*Pace* represents a limited view of the Equal Protection Clause which has not withstood analysis in the subsequent decisions of this Court." McLaughlin et al. v. Florida, supra, 379 U.S. at 188. As we there demonstrated, the Equal Protection Clause requires the consideration of whether the classifications drawn by any statute constitute an arbitrary and invidious discrimination. The clear and central purpose of the Fourteenth Amendment was to eliminate all official state sources of invidious racial discrimination in the States. Slaughter-House Cases, 16 Wall. 36, 71 (1873); Strauder v. State of West Virginia, 100 U.S. 303, 307–308 (1880); Ex parte Virginia, 100 U.S. 339, 344–345 (1880); Shelley v. Kraemer, 334 U.S. 1 (1948); Burton v. Wilmington Parking Authority, 365 U.S. 715 (1961).

There can be no question but that Virginia's miscegenation statutes rest solely upon distinctions drawn according to race. The statutes proscribe generally accepted conduct if engaged in by members of different races. Over the years, this Court has consistently repudiated "[d]istinctions between citizens solely because of their ancestry" as being "odious to a free people whose institutions are founded upon the doctrine of equality." Hirabayashi v. United States, 320 U.S. 81, 100 (1943). At the very least, the Equal Protection Clause demands that racial classifications, especially suspect in criminal statutes, be subjected to the "most rigid scrutiny," Korematsu v. United States, 323 U.S. 214, 216 (1944), and, if they are ever to be upheld, they must be shown to be necessary to the accomplishment of some permissible state objective, independent of the racial discrimination which it was the object of the Fourteenth Amendment to eliminate. Indeed, two members of this Court have already stated that they "cannot conceive of a valid legislative purpose . . . which makes the color of a person's skin the test of whether his conduct is a criminal offense." McLaughlin v. Florida, supra, 379 U.S. at 198 (Stewart, J., joined by Douglas, J., concurring).

There is patently no legitimate overriding purpose independent of invidious racial discrimination which justifies this classification. The fact that Virginia only prohibits interracial marriages involving white persons demonstrates that the racial classifications must stand on their own justification, as measures designed to maintain White Supremacy.[11] We have consistently denied the constitutionality of measures which restrict the rights of citizens on account of race. There can be no doubt that restricting the freedom to marry solely because of racial classifications violates the central meaning of the Equal Protection Clause.

. . .

These convictions must be reversed. It is so ordered.

Mr. Justice Stewart, concurring.

I have previously expressed the belief that "it is simply not possible for a state law to be valid under our Constitution which makes the criminality of an act depend upon the race of the actor." McLaughlin v. State of Florida, 379 U.S. 184, 198 (concurring opinion). Because I adhere to that belief, I concur in the judgment of the Court.

PALMOR v. SIDOTI

___ U.S. ___, 104 S.Ct. 1879, 80 L.Ed.2d 421 (1984).

Chief Justice Burger delivered the opinion of the Court.

We granted certiorari to review a judgment of a state court divesting a natural mother of the custody of her infant child because of her remarriage to a person of a different race.

I

When petitioner Linda Sidoti Palmore and respondent Anthony J. Sidoti, both Caucasians, were divorced in May 1980 in Florida, the mother was awarded custody of their three-year-old daughter.

In September 1981 the father sought custody of the child by filing a petition to modify the prior judgment because of changed conditions. The change was that the child's mother was then cohabiting with a Negro, Clarence Palmore, Jr., whom she married two months later. Additionally, the father made several allegations of instances in which the mother had not properly cared for the child.

After hearing testimony from both parties and considering a court counselor's investigative report, the court noted that the father had made allegations about the child's care, but the court made no findings with respect to these allegations. On the contrary, the court made a finding that "there is no issue as to either party's devotion to the child, adequacy of housing facilities, or respect[a]bility of the new spouse of either parent."

The court then addressed the recommendations of the court counselor, who had made an earlier report "in [another] case coming out of this circuit also

---

[11] Appellants point out that the State's concern in these statutes, as expressed in the words of the 1924 Act's title, "An Act to Preserve Racial Integrity," extends only to the integrity of the white race. While Virginia prohibits whites from marrying any nonwhite (subject to the exception for the descendants of Pocahontas), Negroes, Orientals, and any other racial class may intermarry without statutory interference. Appellants contend that this distinction renders Virginia's miscegenation statutes arbitrary and unreasonable even assuming the constitutional validity of an official purpose to preserve "racial integrity." We need not reach this contention because we find the racial classifications in these statutes repugnant to the Fourteenth Amendment, even assuming an even-handed state purpose to protect the "integrity" of all races.

involving the social consequences of an interracial marriage. Niles v. Niles, 299 So.2d 162." From this vague reference to that earlier case, the court turned to the present case and noted the counselor's recommendation for a change in custody because "[t]he wife [petitioner] has chosen for herself and for her child, a life-style unacceptable to her father *and to society.* . . . The child . . . . is, or at school age will be, subject to environmental pressures not of choice."

The court then concluded that the best interests of the child would be served by awarding custody to the father. The court's rationale is contained in the following:

"The father's evident resentment of the mother's choice of a black partner is not sufficient to wrest custody from the mother. It is of some significance, however, that the mother did see fit to bring a man into her home and carry on a sexual relationship with him without being married to him. Such action tended to place gratification of her own desires ahead of her concern for the child's future welfare. *This Court feels that despite the strides that have been made in bettering relations between the races in this country, it is inevitable that Melanie will, if allowed to remain in her present situation and attains school age and thus more vulnerable to peer pressures, suffer from the social stigmatization that is sure to come.*"

The Second District Court of Appeal affirmed without opinion, thus denying the Florida Supreme Court jurisdiction to review the case. . . . We granted certiorari, ___ U.S. ___ (1983), and we reverse.

II

The judgment of a state court determining or reviewing a child custody decision is not ordinarily a likely candidate for review by this Court. However, the court's opinion, after stating that the "father's evident resentment of the mother's choice of a black partner is not sufficient" to deprive her of custody, then turns to what it regarded as the damaging impact on the child from remaining in a racially-mixed household. This raises important federal concerns arising from the Constitution's commitment to eradicating discrimination based on race.

The Florida court did not focus directly on the parental qualifications of the natural mother or her present husband, or indeed on the father's qualifications to have custody of the child. The court found that "there is no issue as to either party's devotion to the child, adequacy of housing facilities, or respect[a]bility of the new spouse of either parent." This, taken with the absence of any negative finding as to the quality of the care provided by the mother, constitutes a rejection of any claim of petitioner's unfitness to continue the custody of her child.

The court correctly stated that the child's welfare was the controlling factor. But that court was entirely candid and made no effort to place its holding on any ground other than race. Taking the court's findings and rationale at face value, it is clear that the outcome would have been different had petitioner married a Caucasian male of similar respectability.

A core purpose of the Fourteenth Amendment was to do away with all governmentally-imposed discrimination based on race. See Strauder v. West Virginia, 100 U.S. 303, 307–308, 310 (1880). Classifying persons according to their race is more likely to reflect racial prejudice than legitimate public concerns; the race, not the person, dictates the category. See Personnel Administrator v. Feeney, 442 U.S. 256, 272 (1979). Such classifications are subject to the most exacting scrutiny; to pass constitutional muster, they must be justified by a compelling governmental interest and must be "necessary . . .

to the accomplishment" of its legitimate purpose, McLaughlin v. Florida, 379 U.S. 184, 196 (1964). See Loving v. Virginia, 388 U.S. 1, 11 (1967).

The State, of course, has a duty of the highest order to protect the interests of minor children, particularly those of tender years. In common with most states, Florida law mandates that custody determinations be made in the best interests of the children involved. Fla.Stat. § 61.13(2)(b)(1) (1983). The goal of granting custody based on the best interests of the child is indisputably a substantial governmental interest for purposes of the Equal Protection Clause.

It would ignore reality to suggest that racial and ethnic prejudices do not exist or that all manifestations of those prejudices have been eliminated. There is a risk that a child living with a step-parent of a different race may be subject to a variety of pressures and stresses not present if the child were living with parents of the same racial or ethnic origin.

The question, however, is whether the reality of private biases and the possible injury they might inflict are permissible considerations for removal of an infant child from the custody of its natural mother. We have little difficulty concluding that they are not. The Constitution cannot control such prejudices but neither can it tolerate them. Private biases may be outside the reach of the law, but the law cannot, directly or indirectly, give them effect. "Public officials sworn to uphold the Constitution may not avoid a constitutional duty by bowing to the hypothetical effects of private racial prejudice that they assume to be both widely and deeply held." Palmer v. Thompson, 403 U.S. 217, 260–261 (1971) (White, J., dissenting).

This is by no means the first time that acknowledged racial prejudice has been invoked to justify racial classifications. In Buchanan v. Warley, 245 U.S. 60 (1917), for example, this Court invalidated a Kentucky law forbidding Negroes from buying homes in white neighborhoods.

> "It is urged that this proposed segregation will promote the public peace by preventing race conflicts. Desirable as this is, and important as is the preservation of the public peace, this aim cannot be accomplished by laws or ordinances which deny rights created or protected by the Federal Constitution."

Whatever problems racially-mixed households may pose for children in 1984 can no more support a denial of constitutional rights than could the stresses that residential integration was thought to entail in 1917. The effects of racial prejudice, however real, cannot justify a racial classification removing an infant child from the custody of its natural mother found to be an appropriate person to have such custody.

The judgment of the District Court of Appeal is reversed.

It is so ordered.

THE JAPANESE CURFEW AND EVACUATION CASES

At the outset of World War II, it was believed by military authorities that citizens as well as aliens of Japanese ancestry on the West Coast posed a security threat; that there was among them an actual or incipient fifth column. On February 19, 1942, President Roosevelt, acting as President and Commander-in-Chief, issued Executive Order No. 9066 authorizing such military commanders as he might designate to prescribe military areas from which any or all persons might be excluded as a security measure. Pursuant to this order he designated General DeWitt as Military Commander of the Western Defense Command. Acting under the Executive Order, the General, on March 2, 1942, established Military Area No. 1 which included the Pacific Coast states. Not willing to have these security measures entirely a matter of executive and military power, Congress, by the Act of March 21, 1942, made criminal the violation of enforcement orders issued under Executive Order 9066. Beginning on March 24, 1942, General DeWitt issued a series of orders applying to persons of Japanese ancestry residing in Military Area No. 1. One of these established a curfew for such persons between the hours of 8:00 p.m. and 6:00 a.m.; others were "exclusion orders" requiring persons of Japanese ancestry to remove from designated districts in the Military Area to "relocation centers" established further inland.

HIRABAYASHI v. UNITED STATES, 320 U.S. 81 (1943). Appellant, an American citizen of Japanese ancestry, was convicted in a federal district court of violating the curfew order and therefore the Act of March 21, 1942, by failing to remain in his residence between the hours of 8:00 p.m. and 6:00 a.m. The Court affirmed in an opinion by Chief Justice Stone, saying: "Distinctions between citizens solely because of their ancestry are by their very nature odious to a free people whose institutions are founded upon the doctrine of equality." However, the Court held that while racial discriminations are in most cases irrelevant, there was an adequate showing in this case that persons of Japanese descent presented a special danger to the community in the context of the war with Japan and that it was not feasible to determine loyalty on an individual basis.

KOREMATSU v. UNITED STATES, 323 U.S. 214 (1944). Petitioner, an American citizen of Japanese descent, was convicted in a federal district court for remaining in San Leandro, California, contrary to General DeWitt's Civilian Exclusion Order No. 34. No question was raised as to petitioner's loyalty to the United States. The Court upheld the conviction. It refused to rule on the validity of other orders which required the detention of excluded persons in relocation centers. Justice Black, speaking for the Court, said: "[A]ll legal restrictions which curtail the civil rights of a single racial group are immediately suspect. That is not to say that all such restrictions are unconstitutional. It is to say that courts must subject them to the most rigid scrutiny. Pressing public necessity may sometimes justify the existence of such restrictions; racial antagonism never can." He concluded his opinion by saying:

"To cast this case into outlines of racial prejudice, without reference to the real military dangers which were presented, merely confuses the issue. Korematsu was not excluded from the Military Area because of hostility to him or his race. He *was* excluded because we are at war with the Japanese Empire, because the properly constituted military authorities feared an invasion of our West Coast and felt constrained to take proper security measures, because they decided that the military urgency of the situation demanded that all citizens of Japanese ancestry be segregated from the West Coast temporarily, and finally, because Congress, reposing its confidence in this time of war in our military leaders—as inevitably it must—determined they should have the power to do just this. There was evidence of disloyalty on the part of some, the military authorities considered that the need for action was great, and time was short. We cannot—by availing ourselves of the calm perspective of hindsight—now say that at that time these actions were unjustified."

Justices Roberts, Murphy, and Jackson all dissented on the ground that the order constituted unjustified discrimination against loyal Japanese citizens on the basis of race. Justice Jackson noted the practical inability of the courts to interfere with military actions of this kind taken during times of war but said:

"[O]nce a judicial opinion . . . rationalizes the Constitution to show that the Constitution sanctions such an order, the Court for all time has validated the principle of racial discrimination in criminal procedure and of transplanting American citizens. The principle then lies about like a loaded weapon ready for the hand of any authority that can bring forward a plausible claim of an urgent need."

EX PARTE ENDO, 323 U.S. 283 (1944). This case was decided the same day as *Korematsu* and involved a later phase of the Japanese relocation program, i.e. the continued detention of concededly loyal persons of Japanese ancestry in the relocation centers. This raised a question which had been expressly left open in *Korematsu*. Appellant, an American citizen of Japanese ancestry and unquestioned loyalty, was evacuated from Sacramento, California in 1942 and placed in an evacuation center, first in Modoc County, California, and then in Utah. In July, 1942, she filed a petition for writ of habeas corpus in the district court which denied it in July, 1943. An appeal was taken to the circuit court of appeals which certified certain questions to the Supreme Court. Justice Douglas, for the Court, said that whatever power the War Relocation Authority had to detain persons of Japanese ancestry initially, or to detain those whose loyalty was questioned, it had no authority to subject concededly loyal citizens to its "leave" procedure. The detainee seeking "indefinite leave" had to meet a number of conditions, including a showing that "public sentiment" at the detainee's "proposed destination" had been investigated and approved. The Court's decision was rested on the conclusion that the detention of a loyal citizen under these circumstances exceeded what was authorized by the Act of March 21, 1942, and the President's executive orders, but there were constitutional overtones in the opinion: ". . . We must assume that the Chief Executive and members of Congress, as well as the courts, are sensitive to and respectful of the liberties of the citizen. In interpreting a wartime measure we must assume that their purpose was to allow for the greatest possible accommodation between those liberties and the exigencies of war. . . . The purpose and objective of the Act and of these orders are plain. Their single aim was the protection of the war effort against espionage and sabotage. It is in light of that one objective that the powers conferred by the orders must be construed. . . . A citizen who is concededly loyal presents no problem of espionage or sabotage. . . . When the power to detain is derived from the power to protect the war effort against espionage and sabotage, detention which has no relationship to that objective is unauthorized. . . . If we assume (as we do) that the original evacuation was justified, its lawful character was derived from the fact that it was an espionage and sabotage measure, not that there was community hostility to this group of American citizens. The evacuation program rested explicitly on the former ground not on the latter as the underlying legislation shows. The authority to detain a citizen or to grant him a conditional release as protection against espionage or sabotage is exhausted at least when his loyalty is conceded. . . ."

The district court was reversed; Roberts and Murphy, JJ., concurred but stressed their view that the entire evacuation program was unconstitutional.[a]

---

[a] The Japanese evacuation cases have been subject to great criticism: Girdner & Loftis, *The Great Betrayal* (1969); Rostow, *The Japanese-American Cases—A Disaster, in the Sovereign Prerogative* 193 (1962); Dembitz, *Racial Discrimination and the Military Judgment,* 45 Colum.L.Rev. 175 (1945).

Cf. Chief Justice Warren, *The Bill of Rights and the Military,* in *Great Rights* 89 (Cahn ed. 1963).

For a comprehensive study of Japanese-American evacuation, see ten Broek, Barnhart & Matson, *Prejudice, War and the Constitution* (1954).

WHAT GROUPS ARE SPECIALLY PROTECTED AGAINST DISCRIMINATION?

In the Slaughter-House Cases, 83 U.S. (16 Wall.) 36 (1872), set out supra, p. 486, the Court said: "We doubt very much whether any action of a State not directed by way of discrimination against the negroes as a class, or on account of their race, will ever be held to come within the purview of this provision. It is so clearly a provision for that race and that emergency, that a strong case would be necessary for its application to any other." A decade and a half later, however, the Court in Yick Wo v. Hopkins, 118 U.S. 356 (1886), invalidated a classification found to discriminate against aliens of Chinese ancestry, saying: "[The provisions of the fourteenth amendment] are universal in their application, to all persons within the territorial jurisdiction, without regard to any differences of race, or color, or of nationality." In Hernandez v. Texas, 347 U.S. 475 (1954) it was held a violation of the equal protection clause to subject a person of Mexican descent to trial before a jury from which persons of similar ancestry had been systematically excluded. In response to an argument by the state that the equal protection clause contemplated only two classes—white and Negro—the Court said:

"Throughout our history differences in race and color have defined easily identifiable groups which have at times required the aid of the courts in securing equal treatment under the laws. But community prejudices are not static, and from time to time other differences from the community norm may define other groups which need the same protection. Whether such a group exists within a community is a question of fact. When the existence of a distinct class is demonstrated, and it is further shown that the laws, as written or as applied, single out that class for different treatment not based on some reasonable classification, the guarantees of the Constitution have been violated. The Fourteenth Amendment is not directed solely against discrimination due to a 'two-class theory'—that is, based upon differences between 'white' and Negro."

ASCERTAINING THE EXISTENCE OF A RACIAL CLASSIFICATION

When the statute makes the racial classification on its face, as was true in *Loving,* no problem arises. But under what circumstances may racial discrimination be found even though the statute on its face makes no racial classification. Two distinct situations are involved.

First, a statute fair on its face may be administered in a way which results in racial discrimination. In Yick Wo v. Hopkins, supra, for example, the Court had before it an ordinance which made it unlawful to operate a laundry in a wooden building without a permit from the board of supervisors. A laundryman of Chinese descent who had been denied a permit to operate his laundry in a wooden building showed that the board had denied permits to the 200 Chinese who had petitioned but granted them to 80 non-Chinese. In holding that this constituted a violation of equal protection the Court said: "Though the

For a full recent review of the Japanese relocation see Report of the Commission on Wartime Relocation and Internment of Civilians, *Personal Justice Denied* (1982).

In 1983 Gordon Hirabayashi, Fred Korematsu, and Minoru Yasui, all defendants in the original cases decided in the 1940's, filed petitions for writs of error coram nobis in federal courts in San Francisco, Portland, and Seattle, charging that their original convictions were tainted with fundamental error and manifest injustice. In April, 1984, a federal district judge in San Francisco issued an order in Korematsu's case vacating his conviction. For a full account of the original trials and how they were prosecuted and defended, see Irons, *Justice at War* (1983).

law itself be fair on its face, and impartial in appearance, yet, if it is applied and administered by public authority with an evil eye and an unequal hand, so as practically to make unjust and illegal discriminations between persons in similar circumstances, material to their rights, the denial of equal justice is still within the prohibition of the constitution."

Second, the contention may be that a statute which does not on its face make a racial classification was in fact designed to discriminate against a racial group. At one extreme are cases where it is apparent from the face of the statute that an ostensibly nondiscriminatory classification in fact is based on race. See, e.g., Guinn v. United States, 238 U.S. 347 (1915). The Oklahoma Constitution was amended in 1910 to provide that no person shall be registered to vote unless able to read and write a section of that Constitution, but that no person who on Jan. 1, 1866, or any time prior thereto was entitled to vote under any form of government, and no lineal descendant of such person, shall be denied the right to vote because of inability to read and write a section of the Constitution. In holding the provision invalid as a forbidden racial discrimination in voting, the Court said that the discrimination appears from the mere statement of the text. "It is true it contains no express words of an exclusion from the standard which is established of any person on account of race, color, or previous condition of servitude, prohibited by the 15th Amendment, but the standard itself inherently brings that result into existence since it is based purely upon a period of time before the enactment of the 15th Amendment, and makes that period the controlling and dominant test of the right of suffrage." At the other extreme are cases where a statute which does not make a racial classification is shown to have a disproportionate impact on a particular racial group. See, e.g., Jefferson v. Hackney, 406 U.S. 535 (1972), in which the Court upheld a state welfare statute which funded old age assistance at 100% of recognized need but aid to dependent children at 75% of such need. The Court held that a showing that 40% of the recipients of old age assistance were Negroes and Mexican-Americans while 87% of the recipients of aid to dependent children were from such groups was not sufficient to establish that the classification was based on race.

Because the problems of establishing the existence of the discrimination also arises in cases involving classifications based on gender, the cases dealing with proof of discriminatory purpose are postponed for consideration to page 751, infra.

B. RACIAL SEGREGATION IN SCHOOLS AND OTHER PUBLIC FACILITIES

PLESSY v. FERGUSON

163 U.S. 537, 16 S.Ct. 1138, 41 L.Ed. 256 (1896).

Mr. Justice Brown delivered the opinion of the court.

This case turns upon the constitutionality of an act of the general assembly of the state of Louisiana, passed in 1890, providing for separate railway carriages for the white and colored races. Acts 1890, No. 111, p. 152. . . .

. . . .

The petition for the writ of prohibition averred that petitioner was seven-eighths Caucasian and one-eighth African blood; that the mixture of colored blood was not discernible in him; and that he was entitled to every right, privilege, and immunity secured to citizens of the United States of the white race; and that, upon such theory, he took possession of a vacant seat in a coach where passengers of the white race were accommodated, and was ordered by the conductor to vacate said coach, and take a seat in another, assigned to persons of the colored race, and, having refused to comply with such demand, he was forcibly ejected, with the aid of a police officer, and imprisoned in the parish jail to answer a charge of having violated the above act.

The constitutionality of this act is attacked upon the ground that it conflicts . . . with . . . the fourteenth amendment. . . .

. . .

The object of the amendment was undoubtedly to enforce the absolute equality of the two races before the law, but, in the nature of things, it could not have been intended to abolish distinctions based upon color, or to enforce social, as distinguished from political, equality, or a commingling of the two races upon terms unsatisfactory to either. Laws permitting, and even requiring, their separation, in places where they are liable to be brought into contact, do not necessarily imply the inferiority of either race to the other, and have been generally, if not universally, recognized as within the competency of the state legislatures in the exercise of their police power. The most common instance of this is connected with the establishment of separate schools for white and colored children, which have been held to be a valid exercise of the legislative power even by courts of states where the political rights of the colored race have been longest and most earnestly enforced.

. . .

Laws forbidding the intermarriage of the two races may be said in a technical sense to interfere with the freedom of contract, and yet have been universally recognized as within the police power of the state. State v. Gibson, 36 Ind. 389. . . .

. . .

In this connection, it is also suggested by the learned counsel for the plaintiff in error that the same argument that will justify the state legislature in requiring railways to provide separate accommodations for the two races will also authorize them to require separate cars to be provided for people whose hair is of a certain color, or who are aliens, or who belong to certain nationalities, or to enact laws requiring colored people to walk upon one side of the street, and white people upon the other, or requiring white men's houses to be painted white, and colored men's black, or their vehicles or business signs to be of different colors, upon the theory that one side of the street is as good as the other, or that a house or vehicle of one color is as good as one of another color. The reply to all this is that every exercise of the police power must be reasonable, and extend only to such laws as are enacted in good faith for the promotion of the public good, and not for the annoyance or oppression of a particular class. . . .

So far, then, as a conflict with the fourteenth amendment is concerned, the case reduces itself to the question whether the statute of Louisiana is a reasonable regulation, and with respect to this there must necessarily be a large discretion on the part of the legislature. In determining the question of reasonableness, it is at liberty to act with reference to the established usages, customs, and traditions of the people, and with a view to the promotion of their comfort, and the preservation of the public peace and good order. Gauged by this standard, we cannot say that a law which authorizes or even requires the separation of the two races in public conveyances is unreasonable, or more obnoxious to the fourteenth amendment than the acts of congress requiring separate schools for colored children in the District of Columbia, the constitutionality of which does not seem to have been questioned or the corresponding acts of state legislatures.

We consider the underlying fallacy of the plaintiff's argument to consist in the assumption that the enforced separation of the two races stamps the colored race with a badge of inferiority. If this be so, it is not by reason of anything found in the act, but solely because the colored race chooses to put that construction upon it. The argument necessarily assumes that if, as has been more than once the case, and is not unlikely to be so again, the colored race should become the dominant power in the state legislature, and should enact a law in precisely similar terms, it would thereby relegate the white race to an inferior position. We imagine that the white race, at least, would not acquiesce in this assumption. The argument also assumes that social prejudices may be overcome by legislation, and that equal rights cannot be secured to the negro except by an enforced commingling of the two races. We cannot accept this proposition. If the two races are to meet upon terms of social equality, it must be the result of natural affinities, a mutual appreciation of each other's merits, and a voluntary consent of individuals. . . . Legislation is powerless to eradicate racial instincts, or to abolish distinctions based upon physical differences, and the attempt to do so can only result in accentuating the difficulties of the present situation. If the civil and political rights of both races be equal, one cannot be inferior to the other civilly or politically. If one race be inferior to the other socially, the constitution of the United States cannot put them upon the same plane. . . .

The judgment of the court below is therefore affirmed.

Mr. Justice Brewer did not hear the argument or participate in the decision of this case.

Mr. Justice Harlan dissenting. . . .

In respect of civil rights, common to all citizens, the constitution of the United States does not, I think, permit any public authority to know the race of those entitled to be protected in the enjoyment of such rights. Every true man has pride of race, and under appropriate circumstances, when the rights of others, his equals before the law, are not to be affected, it is his privilege to express such pride and to take such action based upon it as to him seems proper. But I deny that any legislative body or judicial tribunal may have regard to the race of citizens when the civil rights of those citizens are involved. Indeed, such legislation as that here in question is inconsistent not only with that equality of rights which pertains to citizenship, national and state, but with the personal liberty enjoyed by every one within the United States. . . .

[The thirteenth, fourteenth, and fifteenth amendments] were welcomed by the friends of liberty throughout the world. They removed the race line from our governmental systems. . . .

It was said in argument that the statute of Louisiana does not discriminate against either race, but prescribes a rule applicable alike to white and colored citizens. But this argument does not meet the difficulty. Everyone knows that the statute in question had its origin in the purpose, not so much to exclude white persons from railroad cars occupied by blacks; as to exclude colored people from coaches occupied by or assigned to white persons. Railroad corporations of Louisiana did not make discrimination among whites in the matter of accommodation for travelers. The thing to accomplish was, under the guise of giving equal accommodation for whites and blacks, to compel the latter to keep to themselves while traveling in railroad passenger coaches. No one would be so wanting in candor as to assert the contrary. The fundamental objection, therefore, to the statute, is that it interferes with the personal freedom of citizens. . . . If a white man and a black man choose to occupy the same public conveyance on a public highway, it is their right to do so; and no government, proceeding alone on grounds of race, can prevent it without infringing the personal liberty of each. . . .

The white race deems itself to be the dominant race in this country. And so it is, in prestige, in achievements, in education, in wealth, and in power. So, I doubt not, it will continue to be for all time, if it remains true to its great heritage, and holds fast to the principles of constitutional liberty. But in view of the constitution, in the eye of the law, there is in this country no superior, dominant, ruling class of citizens. There is no caste here. Our constitution is color-blind, and neither knows nor tolerates classes among citizens. In respect of civil rights, all citizens are equal before the law. The humblest is the peer of the most powerful. The law regards man as man, and takes no account of his surroundings or of his color when his civil rights as guaranteed by the supreme law of the land are involved. It is therefore to be regretted that this high tribunal, the final expositor of the fundamental law of the land, has reached the conclusion that it is competent for a state to regulate the enjoyment by citizens of their civil rights solely upon the basis of race.

. . . .

If evils will result from the commingling of the two races upon public highways established for the benefit of all, they will be infinitely less than those that will surely come from state legislation regulating the enjoyment of civil rights upon the basis of race. We boast of the freedom enjoyed by our people above all other peoples. But it is difficult to reconcile that boast with a state of the law which, practically, puts the brand of servitude and degradation upon a large class of our fellow citizens,—our equals before the law. The thin disguise of "equal" accommodations for passengers in railroad coaches will not mislead any one, nor atone for the wrong this day done. . . .

————

BROWN v. BOARD OF EDUCATION OF TOPEKA

347 U.S. 483, 74 S.Ct. 686, 98 L.Ed. 873 (1954).

Mr. Chief Justice Warren delivered the opinion of the Court.

These cases come to us from the States of Kansas, South Carolina, Virginia, and Delaware. They are premised on different facts and different local conditions, but a common legal question justifies their consideration together in this consolidated opinion.

In each of the cases, minors of the Negro race, through their legal representatives, seek the aid of the courts in obtaining admission to the public schools of their community on a nonsegregated basis. In each instance, they have been denied admission to schools attended by white children under laws requiring or permitting segregation according to race. This segregation was alleged to deprive the plaintiffs of the equal protection of the laws under the Fourteenth Amendment. In each of the cases other than the Delaware case, a three-judge federal district court denied relief to the plaintiffs on the so-called "separate but equal" doctrine announced by this Court in Plessy v. Ferguson, 163 U.S. 537. Under that doctrine, equality of treatment is accorded when the races are provided substantially equal facilities, even though these facilities be separate. In the Delaware case, the Supreme Court of Delaware adhered to that doctrine, but ordered that the plaintiffs be admitted to the white schools because of their superiority to the Negro schools.

The plaintiffs contend that segregated public schools are not "equal" and cannot be made "equal," and that hence they are deprived of the equal protection of the laws. Because of the obvious importance of the question presented, the Court took jurisdiction. Argument was heard in the 1952 Term, and reargument was heard this Term on certain questions propounded by the Court.

Reargument was largely devoted to the circumstances surrounding the adoption of the Fourteenth Amendment in 1868. It covered exhaustively consideration of the Amendment in Congress, ratification by the states, then existing practices in racial segregation, and the views of proponents and opponents of the Amendment. This discussion and our own investigation convince us that, although these sources cast some light, it is not enough to resolve the problem with which we are faced. At best, they are inconclusive. The most avid proponents of the post-War Amendments undoubtedly intended them to remove all legal distinctions among "all persons born or naturalized in the United States." Their opponents, just as certainly were antagonistic to both the letter and the spirit of the Amendments and wished them to have the most limited effect. What others in Congress and the state legislatures had in mind cannot be determined with any degree of certainty.

An additional reason for the inconclusive nature of the Amendment's history, with respect to segregated schools, is the status of public education at that time. In the South, the movement toward free common schools, supported by general taxation, had not yet taken hold. Education of white children was largely in the hands of private groups. Education of Negroes was almost nonexistent, and practically all of the race were illiterate. In fact, any education of Negroes was forbidden by law in some states. Today, in contrast, many Negroes have achieved outstanding success in the arts and sciences as well as in the business and professional world. It is true that public school education at the time of the Amendment had advanced further in the North, but the effect of the Amendment on Northern States was generally ignored in the congressional debates. Even in the North, the conditions of public education did not approximate those existing today. The curriculum was usually rudimentary; ungraded schools were common in rural areas; the school term was but three months a year in many states; and compulsory school attendance was virtually unknown. As a consequence, it is not surprising that there should be so little in the history of the Fourteenth Amendment relating to its intended effect on public education.

In the first cases in this Court construing the Fourteenth Amendment, decided shortly after its adoption, the Court interpreted it as proscribing all state-imposed discriminations against the Negro race. The doctrine of "separate but equal" did not make its appearance in this Court until 1896 in the case of Plessy v. Ferguson, supra, involving not education but transportation. American courts have since labored with the doctrine for over half a century. In this Court, there have been six cases involving the "separate but equal" doctrine in the field of public education. In Cumming v. Board of Education of Richmond County, 175 U.S. 528, and Gong Lum v. Rice, 275 U.S. 78, the validity of the doctrine itself was not challenged. In more recent cases, all on the graduate school level, inequality was found in that specific benefits enjoyed by white students were denied to Negro students of the same educational qualifications. State of Missouri ex rel. Gaines v. Canada, 305 U.S. 337; Sipuel v. Board of Regents of University of Oklahoma, 332 U.S. 631; Sweatt v. Painter, 339 U.S. 629; McLaurin v. Oklahoma State Regents, 339 U.S. 637. In none of these cases was it necessary to reexamine the doctrine to grant relief to the Negro plaintiff. And in Sweatt v. Painter, supra, the Court expressly reserved decision on the question whether Plessy v. Ferguson should be held inapplicable to public education.

In the instant cases, that question is directly presented. Here, unlike Sweatt v. Painter, there are findings below that the Negro and white schools involved have been equalized, or are being equalized, with respect to buildings, curricula, qualifications and salaries of teachers, and other "tangible" factors. Our decision, therefore, cannot turn on merely a comparison of these tangible factors in the Negro and white schools involved in each of the cases. We must look instead to the effect of segregation itself on public education.

In approaching this problem, we cannot turn the clock back to 1868 when the Amendment was adopted, or even to 1896 when Plessy v. Ferguson was written. We must consider public education in the light of its full development and its present place in American life throughout the Nation. Only in this way can it be determined if segregation in public schools deprives these plaintiffs of the equal protection of the laws.

Today, education is perhaps the most important function of state and local governments. Compulsory school attendance laws and the great expenditures for education both demonstrate our recognition of the importance of education to our democratic society. It is required in the performance of our most basic public responsibilities, even service in the armed forces. It is the very foundation of good citizenship. Today it is a principal instrument in awakening the child to cultural values, in preparing him for later professional training, and in helping him to adjust normally to his environment. In these days, it is doubtful that any child may reasonably be expected to succeed in life if he is denied the opportunity of an education. Such an opportunity, where the state has undertaken to provide it, is a right which must be made available to all on equal terms.

We come then to the question presented: Does segregation of children in public schools solely on the basis of race, even though the physical facilities and other "tangible" factors may be equal, deprive the children of the minority group of equal educational opportunities? We believe that it does.

In Sweatt v. Painter, supra, in finding that a segregated law school for Negroes could not provide them equal educational opportunities, this Court relied in large part on "those qualities which are incapable of objective measurement but which make for greatness in a law school." In McLaurin v. Oklahoma State Regents, supra, the Court, in requiring that a Negro admitted to a white graduate school be treated like all other students, again resorted to intangible considerations: ". . . his ability to study, to engage in discussions and exchange views with other students, and, in general, to learn his profession." Such considerations apply with added force to children in grade and high schools. To separate them from others of similar age and qualifications solely because of their race generates a feeling of inferiority as to their status in the community that may affect their hearts and minds in a way unlikely ever to be undone. The effect of this separation on their educational opportunities was well stated by a finding in the Kansas case by a court which nevertheless felt compelled to rule against the Negro plaintiffs:

"Segregation of white and colored children in public schools has a detrimental effect upon the colored children. The impact is greater when it has the sanction of the law; for the policy of separating the races is usually interpreted as denoting the inferiority of the negro group. A sense of inferiority affects the motivation of a child to learn. Segregation with the sanction of law, therefore, has a tendency to [retard] the educational and mental development of negro children and to deprive them of some of the benefits they would receive in a racial[ly] integrated school system."

Whatever may have been the extent of psychological knowledge at the time of Plessy v. Ferguson, this finding is amply supported by modern authority.[11] Any language in Plessy v. Ferguson contrary to this finding is rejected.

---

[11] K.B. Clark, Effect of Prejudice and Discrimination on Personality Development (Midcentury White House Conference on Children and Youth, 1950); Witmer and Kotinsky, Personality in the Making (1952), c. VI; Deutscher and Chein, The Psychological Effects of Enforced Segregation: A Survey of Social Science Opinion, 26 J.Psychol. 259 (1948); Chein, What are the Psychological Effects of Segregation Under Conditions of Equal Facilities?, 3 Int.J.Opinion and Attitude Res. 229 (1949);

We conclude that in the field of public education the doctrine of "separate but equal" has no place. Separate educational facilities are inherently unequal. Therefore, we hold that the plaintiffs and others similarly situated for whom the actions have been brought are, by reason of the segregation complained of, deprived of the equal protection of the laws guaranteed by the Fourteenth Amendment. This disposition makes unnecessary any discussion whether such segregation also violates the Due Process Clause of the Fourteenth Amendment.

Because these are class actions, because of the wide applicability of this decision, and because of the great variety of local conditions, the formulation of decrees in these cases presents problems of considerable complexity. On reargument, the consideration of appropriate relief was necessarily subordinated to the primary question—the constitutionality of segregation in public education. We have now announced that such segregation is a denial of the equal protection of the laws. In order that we may have the full assistance of the parties in formulating decrees, the cases will be restored to the docket, and the parties are requested to present further argument on Questions 4 and 5 previously propounded by the Court for the reargument this Term. The Attorney General of the United States is again invited to participate. The Attorneys General of the states requiring or permitting segregation in public education will also be permitted to appear as *amici curiae* upon request to do so by September 15, 1954, and submission of briefs by October 1, 1954.

It is so ordered.

BOLLING v. SHARPE

347 U.S. 497, 74 S.Ct. 693, 98 L.Ed. 884 (1954).

Mr. Chief Justice Warren delivered the opinion of the Court.

This case challenges the validity of segregation in the public schools of the District of Columbia. The petitioners, minors of the Negro race, allege that such segregation deprives them of due process of law under the Fifth Amendment. They were refused admission to a public school attended by white children solely because of their race. They sought the aid of the District Court for the District of Columbia in obtaining admission. That court dismissed their complaint. The Court granted a writ of certiorari before judgment in the Court of Appeals because of the importance of the constitutional question presented. 344 U.S. 873.

We have this day held that the Equal Protection Clause of the Fourteenth Amendment prohibits the states from maintaining racially segregated public schools. The legal problem in the District of Columbia is somewhat different, however. The Fifth Amendment, which is applicable in the District of Columbia, does not contain an equal protection clause as does the Fourteenth Amendment which applies only to the states. But the concepts of equal protection and due process, both stemming from our American ideal of fairness, are not mutually exclusive. The "equal protection of the laws" is a more explicit safeguard of prohibited unfairness than "due process of law," and, therefore, we do not imply that the two are always interchangeable phrases. But, as this Court has recognized, discrimination may be so unjustifiable as to be violative of due process.

Classifications based solely upon race must be scrutinized with particular care, since they are contrary to our traditions and hence constitutionally suspect.

Brameld, Educational Costs, in Discrimination and National Welfare (MacIver, ed., 1949), 44–48; Frazier, The Negro in the United States (1949), 674–681. And see generally Myrdal, An American Dilemma (1944).

As long ago as 1896, this Court declared the principle "that the constitution of the United States, in its present form, forbids, so far as civil and political rights are concerned, discrimination by the general government, or by the states, against any citizen because of his race." And in Buchanan v. Warley, 245 U.S. 60, the Court held that a statute which limited the right of a property owner to convey his property to a person of another race was, as an unreasonable discrimination, a denial of due process of law.

Although the Court has not assumed to define "liberty" with any great precision, that term is not confined to mere freedom from bodily restraint. Liberty under law extends to the full range of conduct which the individual is free to pursue, and it cannot be restricted except for a proper governmental objective. Segregation in public education is not reasonably related to any proper governmental objective, and thus it imposes on Negro children of the District of Columbia a burden that constitutes an arbitrary deprivation of their liberty in violation of the Due Process Clause.

In view of our decision that the Constitution prohibits the states from maintaining racially segregated public schools, it would be unthinkable that the same Constitution would impose a lesser duty on the Federal Government. We hold that racial segregation in the public schools of the District of Columbia is a denial of the due process of law guaranteed by the Fifth Amendment to the Constitution.

For the reasons set out in Brown v. Board of Education, this case will be restored to the docket for reargument on Questions 4 and 5 previously propounded by the Court. 345 U.S. 972.

It is so ordered.

BROWN AND THE RELEVANCE OF SOCIAL SCIENCE AND HISTORICAL MATERIALS

The Court in *Brown* relied to some extent on studies by psychologists and social scientists to support the conclusion that placing Negro children in separate schools generates feelings of inferiority unlikely to be undone. The Court's reference to this data generated immediate controversy among lawyers as to its propriety and relevance. Compare Cahn, *Science or Common Sense? A Dangerous Myth, in 1954 Annual Survey of American Law: Jurisprudence,* 30 N.Y.U.L.Rev. 150 (1955) with Honnold, *Book Review,* 33 Ind.L.J. 612, 614 (1958). More recent and elaborate consideration will be found in two symposia: *The Courts, Social Science, and School Desegregation,* 39 Law & Contemp.Prob. (No. 1, Winter, 1975, and No. 2, Spring, 1975); *School Desegregation: Lessons of the First Twenty-Five Years,* 42 Law & Contemp.Prob. (Summer 1978 and Autumn 1978).

The Court in *Brown* also directed attention to the historical background of the fourteenth amendment. For a discussion of the historical record, see Bickel, *The Original Understanding and the Segregation Decisions,* 69 Harv.L.Rev. 1 (1955), *Selected Essays on Constitutional Law,* 1938–1962 (1963) 853.

For some of the voluminous literature which followed the desegregation cases and probed their implications, see Wechsler, *Toward Neutral Principles of Constitutional Law,* 73 Harv.L.Rev. 1 (1959); Black, *The Lawfulness of the Segregation Decisions,* 69 Yale L.J. 421 (1960); Pollak, *Racial Discrimination and Judicial Integrity,* 108 U.Pa.L.Rev. 1 (1959). These articles are reprinted in *Selected Essays on Constitutional Law,* 1938–1962 (1963) at 463, 844, and 819.

SEGREGATION IN PUBLIC FACILITIES OTHER
THAN SCHOOLS

In *Brown* the Court emphasized the importance of education and gave reasons why segregation in schools was inherently unequal. When presented with the question whether the same reasoning would serve to invalidate segregation in other public facilities, the Court held such segregation invalid in a series of per curiam orders without explanatory opinions. In Mayor and City Council of Baltimore City v. Dawson, 350 U.S. 877 (1955) it summarily affirmed an order enjoining racial segregation in public beaches and bathhouses. In Holmes v. Atlanta, 350 U.S. 879 (1955) the Court summarily reversed a lower court order which appeared to permit the city to allocate a municipal golf course to different races on alternate days. In Gayle v. Browder, 352 U.S. 903 (1956) it summarily affirmed a judgment enjoining enforcement of racial segregation on city buses. Similar dispositions were made in cases involving other public facilities in New Orleans City Parks Improvement Ass'n v. Detiege, 358 U.S. 54 (1958) (golf course and parks); State Athletic Comm'n v. Dorsey, 359 U.S. 533 (1959); (participation in athletic contests); Schiro v. Bynum, 375 U.S. 395 (1964) (municipal auditorium).

In Johnson v. Virginia, 373 U.S. 61 (1963) the Court wrote a brief per curiam opinion reversing a conviction of a defendant for sitting in a section of a segregated courtroom reserved for whites. The Court said, without further elaboration: "Such a conviction cannot stand for it is no longer open to question that a State may not constitutionally require segregation of public facilities." [1]

BROWN v. BOARD OF EDUCATION OF TOPEKA

349 U.S. 294, 75 S.Ct. 753, 99 L.Ed. 1083 (1955).

Mr. Chief Justice Warren delivered the opinion of the Court.

These cases were decided on May 17, 1954. The opinions of that date, declaring the fundamental principle that racial discrimination in public education is unconstitutional, are incorporated herein by reference. All provisions of federal, state, or local law requiring or permitting such discrimination must yield to this principle. There remains for consideration the manner in which relief is to be accorded.

Because these cases arose under different local conditions and their disposition will involve a variety of local problems, we requested further argument on the question of relief. In view of the nationwide importance of the decision, we invited the Attorney General of the United States and the Attorneys General of all states requiring or permitting racial discrimination in public education to present their views on that question. The parties, the United States, and the States of Florida, North Carolina, Arkansas, Oklahoma, Maryland, and Texas filed briefs and participated in the oral argument.

These presentations were informative and helpful to the Court in its consideration of the complexities arising from the transition to a system of public education freed of racial discrimination. . . .

Full implementation of these constitutional principles may require solution of varied local school problems. School authorities have the primary responsibility for elucidating, assessing, and solving these problems; courts will have to consider whether the action of school authorities constitutes good faith imple-

[1] For observations on the extent to which the Court uses per curiam decisions, see Brown, Process of Law, 72 Harv.L.Rev. 77 (1958).

mentation of the governing constitutional principles. Because of their proximity to local conditions and the possible need for further hearings, the courts which originally heard these cases can best perform this judicial appraisal. Accordingly, we believe it appropriate to remand the cases to those courts.

In fashioning and effectuating the decrees, the courts will be guided by equitable principles. Traditionally, equity has been characterized by a practical flexibility in shaping its remedies and by a facility for adjusting and reconciling public and private needs. These cases call for the exercise of these traditional attributes of equity power. At stake is the personal interest of the plaintiffs in admission to public schools as soon as practicable on a nondiscriminatory basis. To effectuate this interest may call for elimination of a variety of obstacles in making the transition to school systems operated in accordance with the constitutional principles set forth in our May 17, 1954, decision. Courts of equity may properly take into account the public interest in the elimination of such obstacles in a systematic and effective manner. But it should go without saying that the vitality of these constitutional principles cannot be allowed to yield simply because of disagreement with them.

While giving weight to these public and private considerations, the courts will require that the defendants make a prompt and reasonable start toward full compliance with our May 17, 1954, ruling. Once such a start has been made, the courts may find that additional time is necessary to carry out the ruling in an effective manner. The burden rests upon the defendants to establish that such time is necessary in the public interest and is consistent with good faith compliance at the earliest practicable date. To that end, the courts may consider problems related to administration, arising from the physical condition of the school plant, the school transportation system, personnel, revision of school districts and attendance areas into compact units to achieve a system of determining admission to the public schools on a nonracial basis, and revision of local laws and regulations which may be necessary in solving the foregoing problems. They will also consider the adequacy of any plans the defendants may propose to meet these problems and to effectuate a transition to a racially nondiscriminatory school system. During this period of transition, the courts will retain jurisdiction of these cases.

The judgments below, except that in the Delaware case, are accordingly reversed and remanded to the District Courts to take such proceedings and enter such orders and decrees consistent with this opinion as are necessary and proper to admit to public schools on a racially nondiscriminatory basis with all deliberate speed the parties to these cases. The judgment in the Delaware case—ordering the immediate admission of the plaintiffs to schools previously attended only by white children—is affirmed on the basis of the principles stated in our May 17, 1954, opinion, but the case is remanded to the Supreme Court of Delaware for such further proceedings as that court may deem necessary in light of this opinion.

It is so ordered.

SCHOOL DESEGREGATION FROM BROWN TO SWANN

It is not possible within the limited space available in a casebook to describe the events of this period. An excellent brief account which should be consulted is Read, *Judicial Evolution of the Law of School Integration Since Brown v. Board of Education,* 39 Law & Contemp.Prob. 7 (No. 1, Winter, 1975). Some of the events are summarized in *Swann.*

SWANN v. CHARLOTTE–MECKLENBURG
BOARD OF EDUCATION

402 U.S. 1, 91 S.Ct. 1267, 28 L.Ed.2d 554 (1971).

Mr. Chief Justice Burger delivered the opinion of the Court.

We granted certiorari in this case to review important issues as to the duties of school authorities and the scope of powers of federal courts under this Court's mandates to eliminate racially separate public schools established and maintained by state action. Brown v. Board of Education, 347 U.S. 483 (1954).

This case and those argued with it arose in states having a long history of maintaining two sets of schools in a single school system deliberately operated to carry out a governmental policy to separate pupils in schools solely on the basis of race. That was what Brown v. Board of Education was all about. These cases present us with the problem of defining in more precise terms than heretofore the scope of the duty of school authorities and district courts in implementing *Brown I* and the mandate to eliminate dual systems and establish unitary systems at once. Meanwhile district courts and courts of appeals have struggled in hundreds of cases with a multitude and variety of problems under this Court's general directive. Understandably, in an area of evolving remedies, those courts had to improvise and experiment without detailed or specific guidelines. This Court, in *Brown I,* appropriately dealt with the large constitutional principles; other federal courts had to grapple with the flinty, intractable realities of day-to-day implementation of those constitutional commands. Their efforts, of necessity, embraced a process of "trial and error," and our effort to formulate guidelines must take into account their experience.

I.

The Charlotte-Mecklenburg school system, the 43d largest in the Nation, encompasses the city of Charlotte and surrounding Mecklenburg County, North Carolina. The area is large—550 square miles—spanning roughly 22 miles east-west and 36 miles north-south. During the 1968–1969 school year the system served more than 84,000 pupils in 107 schools. Approximately 71% of the pupils were found to be white and 29% Negro. As of June 1969 there were approximately 24,000 Negro students in the system, of whom 21,000 attended schools within the city of Charlotte. Two-thirds of those 21,000—approximately 14,000 Negro students—attended 21 schools which were either totally Negro or more than 99% Negro.

[Pursuant to an order of a federal district court the school board adopted a desegregation plan which went so far in dealing with elementary schools as to group two or three outlying schools with one black inner city school, transporting black students from grades one through four to the outlying white schools, and transporting white students from the fifth and sixth grades to the inner city black school. Other aspects of the plan are discussed in the opinion.]

. . .

II.

Nearly 17 years ago this Court held, in explicit terms, that state-imposed segregation by race in public schools denies equal protection of the laws. At no time has the Court deviated in the slightest degree from that holding or its constitutional underpinnings. . . .

Over the 16 years since *Brown II,* many difficulties were encountered in implementation of the basic constitutional requirement that the State not discriminate between public school children on the basis of their race. Nothing in our national experience prior to 1955 prepared anyone for dealing with changes and adjustments of the magnitude and complexity encountered since then.   Deliberate resistance of some to the Court's mandates has impeded the good-faith efforts of others to bring school systems into compliance.   The detail and nature of these dilatory tactics have been noted frequently by this Court and other courts.

By the time the Court considered Green v. County School Board, 391 U.S. 430, in 1968, very little progress had been made in many areas where dual school systems had historically been maintained by operation of state laws.   In Green, the Court was confronted with a record of a freedom-of-choice program that the District Court had found to operate in fact to preserve a dual system more than a decade after Brown II.   While acknowledging that a freedom-of-choice concept could be a valid remedial measure in some circumstances, its failure to be effective in Green required that:

> "The burden on a school board today is to come forward with a plan that promises realistically to work   . . .   *now*   . . .   until it is clear that state-imposed segregation has been completely removed."

. . .

The problems encountered by the district courts and courts of appeals make plain that we should now try to amplify guidelines, however, incomplete and imperfect, for the assistance of school authorities and courts.[5]   The failure of local authorities to meet their constitutional obligations aggravated the massive problem of converting from the state-enforced discrimination of racially separate school systems.   This process has been rendered more difficult by changes since 1954 in the structure and patterns of communities, the growth of student population, movement of families, and other changes, some of which had marked impact on school planning, sometimes neutralizing or negating remedial action before it was fully implemented.   Rural areas accustomed for half a century to the consolidated school systems implemented by bus transportation could make adjustments more readily than metropolitan areas with dense and shifting population, numerous schools, congested and complex traffic patterns.

III.

The objective today remains to eliminate from the public schools all vestiges of state-imposed segregation.   Segregation was the evil struck down by *Brown I* as contrary to the equal protection guarantees of the Constitution.   That was the violation sought to be corrected by the remedial measures of *Brown II*.   That was the basis for the holding in *Green* that school authorities are "clearly charged with the affirmative duty to take whatever steps might be necessary to convert to a unitary system in which racial discrimination would be eliminated root and branch."   391 U.S., at 437–438.

If school authorities fail in their affirmative obligations under these holdings, judicial authority may be invoked.   Once a right and a violation have been shown, the scope of a district court's equitable powers to remedy past wrongs is broad, for breadth and flexibility are inherent in equitable remedies.   . . .

. . .

In seeking to define even in broad and general terms how far this remedial power extends it is important to remember that judicial powers may be exercised only on the basis of a constitutional violation.   Remedial judicial authority does not put judges automatically in the shoes of school authorities whose powers are plenary.   Judicial authority enters only when local authority defaults.

---

[5] The necessity for this is suggested by the situation in the Fifth Circuit where 166 appeals in school desegregation cases were heard between December 2, 1969, and September 24, 1970.

School authorities are traditionally charged with broad power to formulate and implement educational policy and might well conclude, for example, that in order to prepare students to live in a pluralistic society each school should have a prescribed ratio of Negro to white students reflecting the proportion for the district as a whole.   To do this as an educational policy is within the broad discretionary powers of school authorities; absent a finding of a constitutional violation, however, that would not be within the authority of a federal court. As with any equity case, the nature of the violation determines the scope of the remedy.   In default by the school authorities of their obligation to proffer acceptable remedies, a district court has broad power to fashion a remedy that will assure a unitary school system.

.   .   .

IV.

We turn now to the problem of defining with more particularity the responsibilities of school authorities in desegregating a state-enforced dual school system in light of the Equal Protection Clause.   Although the several related cases before us are primarily concerned with problems of student assignment, it may be helpful to begin with a brief discussion of other aspects of the process.

In *Green,* we pointed out that existing policy and practice with regard to faculty, staff, transportation, extracurricular activities, and facilities were among the most important indicia of a segregated system.   391 U.S., at 435.   Independent of student assignment, where it is possible to identify a "white school" or a "Negro school" simply by reference to the racial composition of teachers and staff, the quality of school buildings and equipment, or the organization of sports activities, a *prima facie* case of violation of substantive constitutional rights under the Equal Protection Clause is shown.

When a system has been dual in these respects, the first remedial responsibility of school authorities is to eliminate invidious racial distinctions.   With respect to such matters as transportation, supporting personnel, and extracurricular activities, no more than this may be necessary.   Similar corrective action must be taken with regard to the maintenance of buildings and the distribution of equipment.   In these areas, normal administrative practice should produce schools of like quality, facilities, and staffs.   Something more must be said, however, as to faculty assignment and new school construction.

In the companion *Davis* case, the Mobile school board has argued that the Constitution requires that teachers be assigned on a "color blind" basis.   It also argues that the Constitution prohibits district courts from using their equity power to order assignment of teachers to achieve a particular degree of faculty desegregation.   We reject that contention.

In United States v. Montgomery County Board of Education, 395 U.S. 225 (1969), the District Court set as a goal a plan of faculty assignment in each school with a ratio of white to Negro faculty members substantially the same throughout the system.   .   .   .

The District Court in *Montgomery* then proceeded to set an initial ratio for the whole system of at least two Negro teachers out of each 12 in any given school. The Court of Appeals modified the order by eliminating what it regarded as "fixed mathematical ratio" of faculty and substituted an initial requirement of "substantially or approximately" a five-to-one ratio.   .   .   ·.

We reversed the Court of Appeals and restored the District Court's order in its entirety, holding that the order of the District Judge

"was adopted in the spirit of this Court's opinion in *Green* . . . in that his plan 'promises realistically to work, and promises realistically to work *now.*' . . ."

The principles of *Montgomery* have been properly followed by the District Court and the Court of Appeals in this case.

The construction of new schools and the closing of old ones is one of the most important functions of local school authorities and also one of the most complex. They must decide questions of location and capacity in light of population growth, finances, land values, site availability, through an almost endless list of factors to be considered. The result of this will be a decision which, when combined with one technique or another of student assignment, will determine the racial composition of the student body in each school in the system. Over the long run, the consequences of the choices will be far reaching. People gravitate toward school facilities, just as schools are located in response to the needs of people. The location of schools may thus influence the patterns of residential development of a metropolitan area and have important impact on composition of inner city neighborhoods.

In the past, choices in this respect have been used as a potent weapon for creating or maintaining a state-segregated school system. . . .

In ascertaining the existence of legally imposed school segregation, the existence of a pattern of school construction and abandonment is thus a factor of great weight. In devising remedies where legally imposed segregation has been established, it is the responsibility of local authorities and district courts to see to it that future school construction and abandonment is not used and does not serve to perpetuate or re-establish the dual system. When necessary, district courts should retain jurisdiction to assure that these responsibilities are carried out. Cf. United States v. Board of Public Instruction, 395 F.2d 66 (C.A.5 1968); Brewer v. School Board, 397 F.2d 37 (C.A.4 1968).

V.

The central issue in this case is that of student assignment, and there are essentially four problem areas:

(1) to what extent racial balance or racial quotas may be used as an implement in a remedial order to correct a previously segregated system;

(2) whether every all-Negro and all-white school must be eliminated as an indispensable part of a remedial process of desegregation;

(3) what are the limits, if any, on the rearrangement of school districts and attendance zones, as a remedial measure; and

(4) what are the limits, if any, on the use of transportation facilities to correct state-enforced racial school segregation.

(1) *Racial Balances or Racial Quotas.* The constant theme and thrust of every holding from *Brown I* to date is that state-enforced separation of races in public schools is discrimination that violates the Equal Protection Clause. The remedy commanded was to dismantle dual school systems.

We are concerned in these cases with the elimination of the discrimination inherent in the dual school systems, not with myriad factors of human existence which can cause discrimination in a multitude of ways on racial, religious, or ethnic grounds. The target of the cases from *Brown I* to the present was the dual school system. The elimination of racial discrimination in public schools is a large task and one that should not be retarded by efforts to achieve broader purposes lying beyond the jurisdiction of school authorities. One vehicle can carry only a limited amount of baggage. It would not serve the important objective of *Brown I* to seek to use school desegregation cases for purposes beyond their scope, although desegregation of schools ultimately will have impact on other forms of discrimination. We do not reach in this case the question whether a showing that school segregation is a consequence of other types of state action, without any discriminatory action by the school authorities, is a constitutional violation requiring remedial action by a school desegregation decree. This case does not present that question and we therefore do not decide it.

Our objective in dealing with the issues presented by these cases is to see that school authorities exclude no pupil of a racial minority from any school, directly or indirectly, on account of race; it does not and cannot embrace all the problems of racial prejudice, even when those problems contribute to disproportionate racial concentrations in some schools.

In this case it is urged that the District Court has imposed a racial balance requirement of 71%–29% on individual schools. The fact that no such objective was actually achieved—and would appear to be impossible—tends to blunt that claim, yet in the opinion and order of the District Court of December 1, 1969, we find that court directing:

"that efforts should be made to reach a 71–29 ratio in the various schools so that there will be no basis for contending that one school is racially different from the others   .   .   ., that no school [should] be operated with an all-black or predominantly black student body, [and] that pupils of all grades [should] be assigned in such a way that as nearly as practicable the various schools at various grade levels have about the same proportion of black and white students."

The District Judge went on to acknowledge that variation "from that norm may be unavoidable." This contains intimations that the "norm" is a fixed mathematical racial balance reflecting the pupil constituency of the system. If we were to read the holding of the District Court to require, as a matter of substantive constitutional right, any particular degree of racial balance or mixing, that approach would be disapproved and we would be obliged to reverse. The constitutional command to desegregate schools does not mean that every school in every community must always reflect the racial composition of the school system as a whole.

.   .   .   .

We see therefore that the use made of mathematical ratios was no more than a starting point in the process of shaping a remedy, rather than an inflexible requirement. From that starting point the District Court proceeded to frame a decree that was within its discretionary powers, an equitable remedy for the particular circumstances. As we said in *Green,* a school authority's remedial plan or a district court's remedial decree is to be judged by its effectiveness. Awareness of the racial composition of the whole school system is likely to be a useful starting point in shaping a remedy to correct past constitutional violations. In sum, the very limited use made of mathematical ratios was within the equitable remedial discretion of the District Court.

(2) *One-Race Schools.* The record in this case reveals the familiar phenomenon that in metropolitan areas minority groups are often found concentrated in one part of the city. In some circumstances certain schools may remain all or largely of one race until new schools can be provided or neighborhood patterns change. Schools all or predominantly of one race in a district of mixed population will require close scrutiny to determine that school assignments are not part of state-enforced segregation.

In light of the above, it should be clear that the existence of some small number of one-race, or virtually one-race, schools within a district is not in and of itself the mark of a system which still practices segregation by law. The district judge or school authorities should make every effort to achieve the greatest possible degree of actual desegregation and will thus necessarily be concerned with the elimination of one-race schools. No *per se* rule can adequately embrace all the difficulties of reconciling the competing interests involved; but in a system with a history of segregation the need for remedial criteria of sufficient specificity to assure a school authority's compliance with its constitutional duty warrants a presumption against schools that are substantially disproportionate in their racial composition. Where the school authority's proposed plan for conversion from a dual to a unitary system contemplates the continued existence of some schools that are all or predominately of one race, they have the burden of showing that such school assignments are genuinely nondiscriminatory. The court should scrutinize such schools, and the burden upon the school authorities will be to satisfy the court that their racial composition is not the result of present or past discriminatory action on their part.

An optional majority-to-minority transfer provision has long been recognized as a useful part of every desegregation plan. Provision for optional transfer of those in the majority racial group of a particular school to other schools where they will be in the minority is an indispensable remedy for those students willing to transfer to other schools in order to lessen the impact on them of the state-imposed stigma of segregation. In order to be effective, such a transfer arrangement must grant the transferring student free transportation and space must be made available in the school to which he desires to move. Cf. Ellis v. Board of Public Instruction, 423 F.2d 203, 206 (C.A.5 1970). The court orders in this and the companion *Davis* case now provide such an option.

(3) *Remedial Altering of Attendance Zones.* The maps submitted in these cases graphically demonstrate that one of the principal tools employed by school planners and by courts to break up the dual school system has been a frank—and sometimes drastic—gerrymandering of school districts and attendance zones. An additional step was pairing, "clustering," or "grouping" of schools with attendance assignments made deliberately to accomplish the transfer of Negro students out of formerly segregated Negro schools and transfer of white students to formerly all-Negro schools. More often than not, these zones are neither compact nor contiguous; indeed they may be on opposite ends of the city. As an interim corrective measure, this cannot be said to be beyond the broad remedial powers of a court.

Absent a constitutional violation there would be no basis for judicially ordering assignment of students on a racial basis. All things being equal, with no history of discrimination, it might well be desirable to assign pupils to schools nearest their homes. But all things are not equal in a system that has been deliberately constructed and maintained to enforce racial segregation. The remedy for such segregation may be administratively awkward, inconvenient and even bizarre in some situations and may impose burdens on some; but all awkwardness and inconvenience cannot be avoided in the interim period when remedial adjustments are being made to eliminate the dual school systems.

No fixed or even substantially fixed guidelines can be established as to how far a court can go, but it must be recognized that there are limits. The objective is to dismantle the dual school system. "Racially neutral" assignment plans proposed by school authorities to a district court may be inadequate; such plans may fail to counteract the continuing effects of past school segregation resulting from discriminatory location of school sites or distortion of school size in order to achieve or maintain an artificial racial separation. When school authorities present a district court with a "loaded game board," affirmative action in the form of remedial altering of attendance zones is proper to achieve truly nondiscriminatory assignments. In short, an assignment plan is not acceptable simply because it appears to be neutral.

In this area, we must of necessity rely to a large extent, as this Court has for more than 16 years, on the informed judgment of the district courts in the first instance and on courts of appeals.

We hold that the pairing and grouping of non-contiguous school zones is a permissible tool and such action is to be considered in light of the objectives sought. . . .

(4) *Transportation of Students.* The scope of permissible transportation of students as an implement of a remedial decree has never been defined by this Court and by the very nature of the problem it cannot be defined with precision. No rigid guidelines as to student transportation can be given for application to the infinite variety of problems presented in thousands of situations. Bus transportation has been an integral part of the public education system for years, and was perhaps the single most important factor in the transition from the one-room schoolhouse to the consolidated school. Eighteen million of the nation's public school children, approximately 39% were transported to their schools by bus in 1969–1970 in all parts of the country.

The importance of bus transportation as a normal and accepted tool of educational policy is readily discernible in this and the companion case. The Charlotte school authorities did not purport to assign students on the basis of geographically drawn zones until 1965 and then they allowed almost unlimited transfer privileges. The District Court's conclusion that assignment of children to the school nearest their home serving their grade would not produce an effective dismantling of the dual system is supported by the record.

Thus the remedial techniques used in the District Court's order were within the court's power to provide equitable relief; implementation of the decree is well within the capacity of the school authority.

The decree provided that the buses used to implement the plan would operate on direct routes. Students would be picked up at schools near their homes and transported to the schools they were to attend. The trips for elementary school pupils average about seven miles and the District Court found that they would take "not over 35 minutes at the most." This system compares favorably with the transportation plan previously operated in Charlotte under which each day 23,600 students on all grade levels were transported an average of 15 miles one way for an average trip requiring over an hour. In these circumstances, we find no basis for holding that the local school authorities may not be required to employ bus transportation as one tool of school desegregation. Desegregation plans cannot be limited to the walk-in school.

An objection to transportation of students may have validity when the time or distance of travel is so great as to risk either the health of the children or significantly impinge on the educational process. District courts must weigh the soundness of any transportation plan in light of what is said in subdivisions (1), (2), and (3) above. It hardly needs stating that the limits on time of travel will vary with many factors, but probably with none more than the age of the students. The reconciliation of competing values in a desegregation case is, of course, a difficult task with many sensitive facets but fundamentally no more so than remedial measures courts of equity have traditionally employed.

VI.

The Court of Appeals, searching for a term to define the equitable remedial power of the district courts, used the term "reasonableness." In *Green, supra,* this Court used the term "feasible" and by implication, "workable," "effective," and "realistic" in the mandate to develop "a plan that promises realistically to work, and . . . to work *now.*" On the facts of this case, we are unable to conclude that the order of the District Court is not reasonable, feasible and workable. However, in seeking to define the scope of remedial power or the limits on remedial power of courts in an area as sensitive as we deal with here, words are poor instruments to convey the sense of basic fairness inherent in equity. Substance, not semantics, must govern, and we have sought to suggest the nature of limitations without frustrating the appropriate scope of equity.

At some point, these school authorities and others like them should have achieved full compliance with this Court's decision in *Brown I.* The systems will then be "unitary" in the sense required by our decisions in *Green* and *Alexander.*

It does not follow that the communities served by such systems will remain demographically stable, for in a growing, mobile society, few will do so. Neither school authorities nor district courts are constitutionally required to make year-by-year adjustments of the racial composition of student bodies once the affirmative duty to desegregate has been accomplished and racial discrimination through official action is eliminated from the system. This does not mean that federal courts are without power to deal with future problems; but in the absence of a showing that either the school authorities or some other agency of the State has deliberately attempted to fix or alter demographic patterns to affect the racial composition of the schools, further intervention by a district court should not be necessary.

For the reasons herein set forth, the judgment of the Court of Appeals is affirmed as to those parts in which it affirmed the judgment of the District Court. The order of the District Court dated August 7, 1970, is also affirmed. It is so ordered.

Judgment of Court of Appeals affirmed in part; order of District Court affirmed.[a]

KEYES v. SCHOOL DISTRICT NO. 1, DENVER, 413 U.S. 189 (1973). This case was the first occasion for the Court to explore problems of desegregation in the north. No legally based segregation had existed in Denver—in fact, the Colorado Constitution prohibited "any classification of pupils . . . on account of race or color." The complaint was, instead, that the school board had intentionally taken certain actions for the purpose of creating or maintaining segregated schools in the district. Much of the opinion of the Court, written by Justice Brennan, dealt with the questions which arise when the plaintiff proves intentional acts of segregation in one part of a school district and seeks to use them as a basis for obtaining an order desegregating the schools in another part of the district. On this issue the basic holding of the Court was that "a finding of intentionally segregative school board actions in a meaningful portion of a school system, as in this case, creates a presumption that other segregated schooling within the system is not adventitious. It establishes,

[a] In North Carolina State Bd. of Ed. v. Swann, 402 U.S. 43 (1971) the Court held unconstitutional a state statute providing that "No student shall be assigned or compelled to attend any school on account of race, creed, color or national origin, or for the purpose of creating a balance or ratio of race, religion or national origins." The Court said that the statute would obstruct the remedies utilized in the *Swann* case and added: "Just as the race of students must be considered in determining whether a constitutional violation has occurred, so also must race be considered in formulating a remedy. To forbid, at this stage, all assignments made on the basis of race would deprive school authorities of the one tool absolutely essential to fulfillment of their constitutional obligation to eliminate existing dual school systems." See also Davis v. Board of Sch. Comm'rs, 402 U.S. 33 (1971); McDaniel v. Barresi, 402 U.S. 39 (1971).

See generally Carter, *An Evaluation of Past and Current Legal Approaches to Vindication of the Fourteenth Amendment's Guarantee of Equal Educational Opportunity,* 1972 Wash.U.L.Q. 479; Karsh, *Not One Law at Rome and Another at Athens: The Fourteenth Amendment in Nationwide Application,* 1972 Wash.U.L.Q. 383.

in other words, a prima facie case of unlawful segregative design on the part of school authorities, and shifts to those authorities the burden of proving that other segregated schools within the system are not also the results of intentionally segregative actions."

The opinion was constructed on the assumption (not challenged by the parties) that in a school district without a history of legally imposed segregation the initial burden of a plaintiff seeking a desegregation order is to establish (1) intentional acts by the school board designed to create or maintain racially segregated schools and (2) the existence of currently segregated schools resulting from those acts. In the opinion the Court gave some indication of the kinds of proof which a plaintiff might adduce to establish intentional segregation by approving as a basis for a desegregation order findings of the district court that by the construction of a new, relatively small elementary school in the middle of the Negro community, by the gerrymandering of student attendance zones, by the use of so-called "optional zones," and by the excessive use of mobile classroom units, the school board had engaged in deliberate racial segregation.

The Court also discussed the question of how you establish the existence of segregated schools. Does the Courts' discussion—all of which follows—give adequate guidance to the district courts in determining when a plaintiff has established that schools are "segregated" in the sense that desegregation must be ordered?

"Before turning to the primary question we decide today, a word must be said about the District Court's method of defining a 'segregated' school. Denver is a tri-ethnic, as distinguished from a bi-racial, community. The overall racial and ethnic composition of the Denver public schools is 66% Anglo, 14% Negro and 20% Hispano. The District Court in assessing the question of *de jure* segregation in the core city schools, preliminarily resolved that Negroes and Hispanos should not be placed in the same category to establish the segregated character of a school. 313 F.Supp., at 69. Later, in determining the schools that were likely to produce an inferior educational opportunity, the court concluded that a school would be considered inferior only if it had 'a concentration of either Negro or Hispano students in the general area of 70 to 75 percent.' Id., at 77. We intimate no opinion whether the District Court's 70 to 75% requirement was correct. The District Court used those figures to signify educationally inferior schools, and there is no suggestion in the record that those same figures were or would be used to define a 'segregated' school in the *de jure* context. What is or is not a segregated school will necessarily depend on the facts of each particular case. In addition to the racial and ethnic composition of a school's student body, other factors such as the racial and ethnic composition of faculty and staff and the community and administration attitudes toward the school must be taken into consideration. The District Court has recognized these specific factors as elements of the definition of a 'segregated' school, id., at 74, and we may therefore infer that the court will consider them again on remand.

"We conclude, however, that the District Court erred in separating Negroes and Hispanos for purposes of defining a 'segregated' school. We have held that Hispanos constitute an identifiable class for purposes of the Fourteenth Amendment. Hernandez v. Texas, 347 U.S. 475 (1954). . . . Indeed the District Court recognized this in classifying predominantly Hispano schools as 'segregated' schools in their own right. But there is also much evidence that in the Southwest Hispanos and Negroes have a great many things in common. The United States Commission on Civil Rights has recently published two Reports on Hispano education in the Southwest. Focusing on students in the States of Arizona, California, Colorado, New Mexico, and Texas, the Commission concluded that Hispanos suffer from the same educational inequities as Negroes and American Indians. In fact, the District Court itself recognized that '[o]ne of the things which the Hispano has in common with the Negro is economic and cultural deprivation and discrimination.' 313 F.Supp., at 69. This is agreement that, though of different origins Negroes and Hispanos in Denver suffer identical discrimination in treatment when compared with the treatment afforded Anglo students. In that circumstance, we think petitioners are entitled to have schools with a combined predominance of Negroes and Hispanos included in the category of 'segregated' schools."

The Court also discussed the kind of proof by a school district which might rebut the prima facie case made when the plaintiff establishes intentional acts of segregation plus the existence of segregated schools:

. . . "Thus, be it a statutory dual system or an allegedly unitary system where a meaningful portion of the system is found to be intentionally segregated, the existence of subsequent or other segregated schooling within the same system justifies a rule imposing on the school authorities the burden of proving that this segregated schooling is not also the result of intentionally segregative acts.

"In discharging that burden, it is not enough, of course, that the school authorities rely upon some allegedly logical, racially neutral explanation for their actions. Their burden is to adduce proof sufficient to support a finding that segregative intent was not among the factors that motivated their actions. The courts below attributed much significance to the fact that many of the Board's actions in the core city area antedated our decision in *Brown.* We reject any suggestion that remoteness in time has any relevance to the issue of intent. If the actions of school authorities were to any degree motivated by segregative intent and the segregation resulting from those actions continues to exist, the fact of remoteness in time certainly does not make those actions any less 'intentional.'

"This is not to say, however, that the prima facie case may not be met by evidence supporting a finding that a lesser degree of segregated schooling in the core city area would not have resulted even if the Board had not acted as it did. In *Swann,* we suggested that at some point in time the relationship between past segregative acts and present segregation may become so attenuated as to be incapable of supporting a finding of *de jure* segregation warranting judicial intervention. 402 U.S. at 31–32. . . . We made it clear, however, that a connection between past segregative acts and present segregation may be present even when not apparent and that close examination is required before concluding that the connection does not exist. Intentional school segregation in the past may have been a factor in creating a natural environment for the growth of further segregation. Thus, if respondent School Board cannot disprove segregative intent, it can rebut the prima facie case only by showing that its past segregative acts did not create or contribute to the current segregated condition of the core city schools.

"The respondent School Board invoked at trial its 'neighborhood school policy' as explaining racial and ethnic concentrations within the core city schools, arguing that since the core city area population had long been Negro and Hispano, the concentrations were necessarily the result of residential patterns and not of purposefully segregative policies. We have no occasion to consider in this case whether a 'neighborhood school policy' of itself will justify racial or ethnic concentrations in the absence of a finding that school authorities have committed acts constituting *de jure* segregation. It is enough that we hold that the mere assertion of such a policy is not dispositive where, as in this case, the school authorities have been found to have practiced *de jure* segregation in a meaningful portion of the school system by techniques that indicate that the 'neighborhood school' concept has not been maintained free of manipulation."

Chief Justice Burger concurred in the result without opinion. Justice White took no part in the decision.

Justice Powell, concurring in part and dissenting in part, disagreed with the Court's assumption that northern schools should be free of any obligation to desegregate in the absence of a showing of intentional segregative acts. He said that "if our national concern is for those who attend [segregated] schools, rather than for perpetuating a legalism rooted in history rather than present reality, we must recognize that the evil of operating separate schools is no less in Denver than in Atlanta." He concluded on this point:

. . . "I would not, . . . perpetuate the *de jure/de facto* distinction nor would I leave to petitioners the initial tortuous effort of identifying 'segregative acts' and deducing 'segregatory intent.' I would hold, quite simply, that where segregated public schools exist within a school district to a substantial degree, there is a prima facie case that the duly constituted public authorities (I will usually refer to them collectively as the 'school board') are sufficiently responsible to impose upon them a nationally applicable burden to demonstrate they nevertheless are operating a genuinely integrated school system."

Justice Powell then discussed the limits he would impose upon remedial orders by the courts, North or South. Brief excerpts from his long opinion follow:

"Where school authorities have defaulted in their duty to operate an integrated school system, district courts must insure that affirmative desegregative steps ensue. Many of these can be taken effectively without damaging state and parental interests in having children attend schools within a reasonable vicinity of home. Where desegregative steps are possible within the framework of a system of 'neighborhood education' school authorities must pursue them.

. . .

. . . "School boards would, of course, be free to develop and initiate further plans to promote school desegregation. In a pluralistic society such as ours, it is essential that no racial minority feel demeaned or discriminated against and that students of all races learn to play, work, and cooperate with one another in their common pursuits and endeavors. Nothing in this opinion is meant to discourage school boards from exceeding minimal constitutional standards in promoting the values of an integrated school experience.

"A *constitutional requirement* of extensive student transportation solely to achieve integration presents a vastly more complex problem. It promises on the one hand a greater degree of actual desegregation, while it infringes on what may fairly be regarded as other important community aspirations and personal rights. Such a requirement is further likely to divert attention and resources from the foremost goal of any school system: the best quality education for all pupils. The Equal Protection Clause does indeed command that racial discrimination not be tolerated in the decisions of public school authorities. But it does not require that school authorities undertake widespread student transportation solely for the sake of maximizing integration.

. . .

"It is well to remember that the course we are running is a long one and the goal sought in the end—so often overlooked—is the best possible educational opportunity for all children. Communities deserve the freedom and the incentive to turn their attention and energies to this goal of quality education, free from protracted and debilitating battles over court-ordered student transportation. The single most disruptive element in education today is the widespread use of compulsory transportation, especially at elementary grade levels. This has risked distracting and diverting attention from basic educational ends, dividing and embittering communities, and exacerbating rather than ameliorating inter-racial friction and misunderstanding. It is time to return to a more balanced evaluation of the recognized interests of our society in achieving desegregation with other educational and societal interests a community may legitimately assert. This will help assure that integrated school systems will be established and maintained by rational action, will be better understood and supported by parents and children of both races, and will promote the enduring qualities of an integrated society so essential to its genuine success."

Justice Douglas, concurring in the opinion of the Court, also agreed with Justice Powell that cases from the North and the South should be treated the same. Justice Rehnquist dissented.

MAY COURTS COMPEL MAINTENANCE OF RACIAL BALANCE ONCE DESEGREGATION HAS BEEN ACHIEVED?

In Pasadena City Bd. of Educ. v. Spangler, 427 U.S. 424 (1976) the district court had entered a desegregation order which included a provision that by 1970 there should be no school in the district "with a majority of any minority students." The school board implemented the plan in 1970, fully carrying out the terms of the plan. Over the next several years as a result of demographic changes 5 out of 32 schools in the district came to have more than 50% black students. The school board returned to the district court and sought to have the decree modified to eliminate the requirement that there be no school with a majority of minority students. The district court refused and the court of appeals affirmed. The Supreme Court reversed. It noted that there was no contention that the post-1971 changes in the racial mix of the schools resulted from any segregative acts chargeable to the school district. Instead, the changes appeared to be the result of people randomly moving into, out of, and around the district. It concluded:

"In this case the District Court approved a plan designed to obtain racial neutrality in the attendance of students at Pasadena's public schools. No one disputes that the initial implementation of this plan accomplished *that* objective. That being the case, the District Court was not entitled to require the School District to rearrange its attendance zones each year so as to ensure that the racial mix desired by the court was maintained in perpetuity. For having once implemented a racially neutral attendance pattern in order to remedy the perceived constitutional violations on the part of the defendants, the District Court had fully performed its function of providing the appropriate remedy for previous racially discriminatory attendance patterns."

FINDING DE JURE SEGREGATION IN NORTHERN SCHOOLS

In the South schools had been desegregated by law. In the North the law did not require segregation and so in each case it was necessary to show that the school district had intentionally taken acts designed to separate students on racial grounds. In its two most recent segregation cases the Court appeared to be substantially reducing this difference between cases from the North and those from the South.

In Columbus Bd. of Educ. v. Penick, 443 U.S. 499 (1979); and Dayton Bd. of Educ. v. Brinkman, 443 U.S. 526 (1979) the Court had before it two cities in which despite the fact that the law did not compel segregation it was reasonably clear that prior to the decision in Brown v. Board of Education the school boards had intentionally taken a number of acts which created virtually a segregated school system. The Court in these cases upheld the conclusion of the court of appeals that the cities since the *Brown* case had been under a duty to disestablish the dual system and had not done so. A little of the flavor of the five-Justice majority opinion is presented in the following excerpt from the *Dayton* case.

"Petitioners next contend that, even if a dual system did exist a quarter of a century ago, the Court of Appeals erred in finding any wide-spread violations of constitutional duty since that time.

"Given intentionally segregated schools in 1954, however, the Court of Appeals was quite right in holding that the Board was thereafter under a continuing duty to eradicate the effects of that system and that the systemwide nature of the violation furnished prima facie proof that current segregation in the Dayton schools was caused at least in part by prior intentionally segregative official acts. Thus, judgment for the plaintiffs was authorized and required absent sufficient countervailing evidence by the defendant school officials. Keyes, supra, 413 U.S., at 211; Swann, supra, 402 U.S., at 26. At the time of trial, Dunbar High School and the three black elementary schools, or the schools that succeeded them, remained black schools; and most of the schools in Dayton were virtually one-race schools, as were 80% of the classrooms. 'Every school which was 90 percent or more black in 1951–52 *or* 1963–64 *or* 1971–72 and which is still in use today remains 90 percent or more black. Of the 25 white schools in 1972–73, *all* opened 90 percent or more white and, if open, were 90 percent or more white in 1971–72, 1963–64 and 1951–52.' 583 F.2d, at 254 (emphasis in original), quoting Brinkman v. Gilligan, 503 F.2d 684, 694–695 (CA6 1974). Against this background, the Court of Appeals held that '[t]he evidence of record demonstrates convincingly that defendants have failed to eliminate the continuing systemwide effects of their prior discrimination and have intentionally maintained a segregated school system down to the time the complaint was filed in the present case.' At the very least, defendants had failed to come forward with evidence to deny 'that the current racial composition of the school population reflects the systemwide impact' of the Board's prior discriminatory conduct.

"Part of the affirmative duty imposed by our cases . . . , is the obligation not to take any action that would impede the process of disestablishing the dual system and its effects. . . . The Dayton Board, however, had engaged in many post-Brown I actions that had the effect of increasing or perpetuating segregation. . . . But the measure of the post-Brown I conduct of a school board under an unsatisfied duty to liquidate a dual system is the effectiveness, not the purpose, of the actions in decreasing or increasing the segregation caused by the dual system. . . . As was clearly established in Keyes and Swann, the Board had to do more than abandon its prior discriminatory purpose. . . . The Board has had an affirmative responsibility to see that pupil assignment policies and school construction and abandonment practices 'are not used and do not serve to perpetuate or re-establish the dual school system,' . . . and the Board has a 'heavy burden' of showing that actions that increased or continued the effects of the dual system serve important and legitimate ends."

MAY SCHOOL DESEGREGATION ORDERS EXTEND BEYOND SCHOOL DISTRICT LINES?

MILLIKEN v. BRADLEY, 418 U.S. 717 (1974). Litigation was commenced in 1970 seeking desegregation of the Detroit school district. At that time there were 86 school districts in the Detroit metropolitan area enrolling a million children, with about 275,000 in the Detroit district alone. The racial composition of the area school population was 81% white, 19% black. The racial composition of the Detroit district was 64% black and 34% white. Within the Detroit district most of the schools were either predominantly black or predominantly white. The trial judge found numerous actions by the Detroit School Board taken for the purpose of maintaining segregation of the schools within the district. He also found a number of actions by the state which contributed to the segregation, including a failure to provide funds for busing within Detroit while providing them in the suburbs. Eventually the judge found that it would not be possible to desegregate the schools by any remedy confined to Detroit alone, and that any remedy possible would simply create a system composed all of predominantly black schools and cause further movement of white pupils out of the public school system. The judge then determined that only an interdistrict remedy would solve the problem. Relying on the involvement of the state and requiring no showing of any segregative acts by the suburban school districts (and providing only minimal opportunity for those districts to appear and contest the ruling) the court ordered an interdistrict remedy. He designated 53 of the 85 suburban school districts plus Detroit as the "desegregation area" and appointed a panel to prepare a plan. The plan was to be based on 15 clusters containing part of the Detroit system and two or more suburban districts to "achieve the greatest degree of actual desegregation to the end that, upon implementation, no school, grade or classroom [would be] substantially disproportionate to the overall pupil racial composition." He also ordered the state to purchase or lease at least 295 buses to provide transportation under an interim plan. The court of appeals affirmed. It said that the harm to black pupils from being confined to predominantly black schools surrounded by white schools was the same whether within a single district or within a multi-district metropolitan area. It also said that the state's general responsibility for education and the acts of segregation it had committed justified the interdistrict order without showing violations by the suburban districts.

The Supreme Court reversed. Chief Justice Burger, writing for the Court, began by noting that the "target of the *Brown* holding was clear and forthright: the elimination of state mandated or deliberately maintained dual school systems with certain schools for Negro pupils and others for White pupils." He relied on language in *Swann* as showing that desegregation "in the sense of dismantling a dual school system" does not require any particular racial balance. In a footnote he added: "Disparity in the racial composition of pupils within a single district may well constitute a 'signal' to a district court at the outset, leading to inquiry into the causes accounting for a pronounced racial identifiability of schools within one school system. . . . However, the use of significant racial imbalance in schools within an autonomous school district as a signal which operates simply to shift the burden of proof, is a very different matter from equating racial imbalance with a constitutional violation calling for a remedy."

On the basic issue of the propriety of the interdistrict remedy, he said:

"Here the District Court's approach to what constituted 'actual desegregation' raises the fundamental question, not presented in *Swann,* as to the circumstances in which a federal court may order desegregation relief that embraces more than a single school district. The court's analytical starting point was its conclusion that school district lines are no more than arbitrary lines on a map 'drawn for political convenience.' Boundary lines may be bridged where there has been a constitutional violation calling for inter-district relief, but, the notion that school district lines may be casually ignored or treated as a mere administrative convenience is contrary to the history of public education in our country. No single tradition in public education is more deeply rooted than local control over the operation of schools; local autonomy has long been thought essential both to the maintenance of community concern and support for public schools and to quality of the educational process. . . .

"The Michigan educational structure involved in this case, in common with most States, provides for a large measure of local control and a review of the scope and character of these local powers indicates the extent to which the inter-district remedy approved by the two courts could disrupt and alter the structure of public education in Michigan. The metropolitan remedy would require, in effect, consolidation of 54 independent school districts historically administered as separate units into a vast new super school district. . . . Entirely apart from the logistical and other serious problems attending large-scale transportation of students, the consolidation would give rise to an array of other problems in financing and operating this new school system. Some of the more obvious questions would be: What would be the status and authority of the present popularly elected school boards? Would the children of Detroit be within the jurisdiction and operating control of a school board elected by the parents and residents of other districts? What board or boards would levy taxes for school operations in these 54 districts constituting the consolidated metropolitan area? What provisions could be made for assuring substantial equality in tax levies among the 54 districts, if this were deemed requisite? What provisions would be made for financing? Would the validity of long-term bonds be jeopardized unless approved by all of the component districts as well as the State? What body would determine that portion of the curricula now left to the discretion of local school boards? Who would establish attendance zones, purchase school equipment, locate and construct new schools, and indeed attend to all the myriad day-to-day decisions that are necessary to school operations affecting potentially more than three quarters of a million pupils? . . .

. . . .

"Of course, no state law is above the Constitution. School district lines and the present laws with respect to local control, are not sacrosanct and if they conflict with the Fourteenth Amendment federal courts have a duty to prescribe appropriate remedies. See, e.g., Wright v. Council of City of Emporia, 407 U.S. 451; United States v. Scotland Neck Board of Education, 407 U.S. 484 (state or local officials prevented from carving out a new school district from an existing district that was in process of dismantling a dual school system); . . . But our prior holdings have been confined to violations and remedies within a single school district. We therefore turn to address, for the first time, the validity of a remedy mandating cross-district or inter-district consolidation to remedy a condition of segregation found to exist in only one district.

"The controlling principle consistently expounded in our holdings is that the scope of the remedy is determined by the nature and extent of the constitutional violation. *Swann,* supra, at 16. Before the boundaries of separate and autonomous school districts may be set aside by consolidating the separate units for remedial purposes or by imposing a cross-district remedy, it must first be shown that there has been a constitutional violation within one district that produces a significant segregative effect in another district. Specifically it must be shown that racially discriminatory acts of the state or local school districts, or of a single school district have been a substantial cause of inter-district segregation. Thus an inter-district remedy might be in order where the racially discriminatory acts of one or more school districts caused racial segregation in an adjacent district, or where district lines have been deliberately drawn on the basis of race. In such circumstances an inter-district remedy would be appropriate to eliminate the inter-district segregation directly caused by the constitutional violation.

Conversely, without an inter-district violation and inter-district effect, there is no constitutional wrong calling for an inter-district remedy.

   .   .   .

"In dissent Mr. Justice White and Mr. Justice Marshall undertake to demonstrate that agencies having statewide authority participated in maintaining the dual school system found to exist in Detroit. They are apparently of the view that once such participation is shown, the District Court should have a relatively free hand to reconstruct school districts outside of Detroit in fashioning relief. Our assumption, *arguendo* . . . that state agencies did participate in the maintenance of the Detroit system, should make it clear that it is not on this point that we part company. The difference between us arises instead from established doctrine laid down by our cases. *Brown,* supra, *Green,* supra, *Swann,* supra, *Scotland Neck,* supra, and *Emporia,* supra, each addressed the issue of constitutional wrong in terms of an established geographic and administrative school system populated by both Negro and White children. In such a context, terms such as 'unitary' and 'dual' systems, and 'racially identifiable schools,' have meaning, and the necessary federal authority to remedy the constitutional wrong is firmly established. But the remedy is necessarily designed, as all remedies are, to restore the victims of discriminatory conduct to the position they would have occupied in the absence of such conduct. Disparate treatment of White and Negro students occurred within the Detroit school system, and not elsewhere, and on this record the remedy must be limited to that system. *Swann,* supra, at 16.

"The constitutional right of the Negro respondents residing in Detroit is to attend a unitary school system in that district. Unless petitioners drew the district lines in a discriminatory fashion, or arranged for White students residing in the Detroit district to attend schools in Oakland and Macomb Counties, they were under no constitutional duty to make provisions for Negro students to do so. The view of the dissenters, that the existence of a dual system *in Detroit* can be made the basis for a decree requiring cross-district transportation of pupils cannot be supported on the grounds that it represents merely the devising of a suitably flexible remedy for the violation of rights already established by our prior decisions. It can be supported only by drastic expansion of the constitutional right itself, an expansion without any support in either constitutional principle or precedent."

Justice Stewart concurred in the opinion of the Court and wrote a separate opinion which included in a footnote the observation that it is the "essential fact of a predominantly Negro school population in Detroit—caused by unknown and perhaps unknowable factors such as in-migration, birth rates, economic changes, or cumulative acts of private racial fears—that accounts for the 'growing core of Negro schools,' a 'core' that had grown to include virtually the entire city." He then said that the courts have no authority to attempt to change this situation in the absence of proof that it was in any significant measure caused by governmental activity.

Justices White, Douglas, Brennan, and Marshall dissented. Justice White writing for all the dissenters indicated he thought the Court was in the name of administrative convenience permitting the state to insulate itself "from its duty to provide effective desegregation remedies by vesting sufficient power over its public schools in its local school districts." Justice Marshall, also writing for all the dissenters, observed:

"After 20 years of small, often difficult steps toward that great end, the Court today takes a giant step backwards. Notwithstanding a record showing widespread and pervasive racial segregation in the educational system provided by the State of Michigan for children in Detroit, this Court holds that the District Court was powerless to require the State to remedy its constitutional violation in any meaningful fashion. Ironically purporting to base its result on the principle that the scope of the remedy in a desegregation case should be determined by the nature and the extent of the constitutional violation, the Court's answer is to provide no remedy at all for the violation proved in this case, thereby guaranteeing that Negro children in Detroit will receive the same separate and inherently unequal education in the future as they have been unconstitutionally afforded in the past.

"I cannot subscribe to this emasculation of our constitutional guarantee of equal protection of the laws and must respectfully dissent. . . .

"The rights at issue in this case are too fundamental to be abridged on grounds as superficial as those relied on by the majority today. We deal here with the right of all of our children, whatever their race, to an equal start in life and to an equal opportunity to reach their full potential as citizens. Those children who have been denied that right in the past deserve better than to see fences thrown up to deny them that right in the future. Our Nation, I fear, will be ill-served by the Court's refusal to remedy separate and unequal education for unless our children begin to learn together, there is little hope that our people will ever learn to live together. . . .

"Because of the already high and rapidly increasing percentage of Negro students in the Detroit system, as well as the prospect of white flight, a Detroit-only plan simply has no hope of achieving actual desegregation. Under such a plan white and Negro students will not go to school together. Instead, Negro children will continue to attend all-Negro schools. The very evil that *Brown I* was aimed at will not be cured, but will be perpetuated for the future. . . .

"Desegregation is not and was never expected to be an easy task. Racial attitudes ingrained in our Nation's childhood and adolescence are not quickly thrown aside in its middle years. But just as the inconvenience of some cannot be allowed to stand in the way of the rights of others, so public opposition, enforcement of the constitutional principles at issue in this case. Today's holding, I fear, is more a reflection of a perceived public mood that we have gone far enough in enforcing the Constitution's guarantee of equal justice than it is the product of neutral principles of law. In the short run, it may seem to be the easier course to allow our great metropolitan areas to be divided up each into two cities—one white, the other black—but it is a course, I predict, our people will ultimately regret. I dissent." [a]

————

MILLIKEN v. BRADLEY (MILLIKEN II), 433 U.S. 267 (1977). On remand, the district court included in its decree remedial or compensatory education programs, including in-service training for teachers and administrators, guidance and counseling programs, and revised testing procedures. The cost of these programs was to be borne equally by the Detroit Board of Education and the State of Michigan. That portion of the district court's order was affirmed by the Court of Appeals, and those defendants representing the State appealed. The appellants argued that, since the constitutional violation was unlawful segregation, under the principles of *Milliken I* the court's decree must be limited to redressing that violation by pupil assignments. The Supreme Court rejected that argument and affirmed. Chief Justice Burger said, for the Court:

———

[a] For a careful argument to the effect that the Court should extend federal remedies across school district boundaries so as to achieve maximum racial mixing in metropolitan areas, see Strickman, *School Desegregation at the Crossroads,* 70 Nw.U.L.Rev. 725 (1975). See also Sedler, *Metropolitan Desegregation in the Wake of Milliken—On Losing Big Battles and Winning Small Wars: The View Largely from Within,* 1975 Wash.U.L.Rev. 535.

"In a word, discriminatory student assignment policies can themselves manifest and breed other inequalities built into a dual system founded on racial discrimination. Federal courts need not, and cannot, close their eyes to inequalities, shown by the record, which flow from a longstanding segregated system."

C. CLASSIFICATIONS DISADVANTAGING ALIENS

GRAHAM v. RICHARDSON

403 U.S. 365, 91 S.Ct. 1848, 29 L.Ed.2d 534 (1971).

Mr. Justice Blackmun delivered the opinion of the Court.

These are welfare cases. They provide yet another aspect of the widening litigation in this area. The issue here is whether the Equal Protection Clause of the Fourteenth Amendment prevents a State from conditioning welfare benefits either (a) upon the beneficiary's possession of United States citizenship, or (b) if the beneficiary is an alien, upon his having resided in this country for a specified number of years. The facts are not in dispute.

I.

.   .   .

[Aliens denied welfare benefits challenged an Arizona law which provided welfare to citizens but not to aliens unless they had resided in the United States for 15 years and a Pennsylvania law which excluded aliens from certain state funded welfare benefits. In each case a three-judge district court ruled that the statute violated the equal protection clause.]

II.

The appellants argue initially that the States, consistent with the Equal Protection Clause, may favor United States citizens over aliens in the distribution of welfare benefits. It is said that this distinction involves no "invidious discrimination" such as was condemned in King v. Smith, 392 U.S. 309 (1968), for the State is not discriminating with respect to race or nationality.

The Fourteenth Amendment provides, "[N]or shall any State deprive any person of life, liberty, or property, without due process of law; nor deny to any person within its jurisdiction the equal protection of the laws." It has long been settled, and it is not disputed here, that the term "person" in this context encompasses lawfully admitted resident aliens as well as citizens of the United States and entitles both citizens and aliens to the equal protection of the laws of the State in which they reside. Yick Wo v. Hopkins, 118 U.S. 356, 369 (1886); Truax v. Raich, 239 U.S. 33, 39 (1915); Takahashi v. Fish & Game Commission, 334 U.S., at 420. Nor is it disputed that the Arizona and Pennsylvania statutes in question create two classes of needy persons, indistinguishable except with respect to whether they are or are not citizens of this country. Otherwise qualified United States citizens living in Arizona are entitled to federally funded categorical assistance benefits without regard to length of national residency, but aliens must have lived in this country for 15 years in order to qualify for aid. United States citizens living in Pennsylvania, unable to meet the requirements for federally funded benefits, may be eligible for state supported general assistance, but resident aliens as a class are precluded from that assistance.

Under traditional equal protection principles, a State retains broad discretion to classify as long as its classification has a reasonable basis. . . . This is so in "the area of economics and social welfare." Dandridge v. Williams, 397 U.S. 471, 485 (1970). But the Court's decisions have established that classifications based on alienage, like those based on nationality or race, are inherently suspect and subject to close judicial scrutiny. Aliens as a class are a prime example of a "discrete and insular" minority (see United States v. Carolene Products Co., 304 U.S. 144, 152–153 n. 4 (1938)) for whom such heightened judicial solicitude is appropriate. Accordingly, it was said in Takahashi, 334 U.S., at 420, that ". . . the power of a state to apply its laws exclusively to its alien inhabitants as a class is confined within narrow limits."

Arizona and Pennsylvania seek to justify their restrictions on the eligibility of aliens for public assistance solely on the basis of a State's "special public interest" in favoring its own citizens over aliens in the distribution of limited resources such as welfare benefits. . . .

. . . [W]e conclude that a State's desire to preserve limited welfare benefits for its own citizens is inadequate to justify Pennsylvania's making noncitizens ineligible for public assistance, and Arizona's restricting benefits to citizens and longtime resident aliens. . . .

. . .

We agree with the three-judge court in the Pennsylvania case that the "justification of limiting expenses is particularly inappropriate and unreasonable when the discriminated class consists of aliens. . . ." There can be no "special public interest" in tax revenues to which aliens have contributed on an equal basis with the residents of the State.

Accordingly, we hold that a state statute that denies welfare benefits to resident aliens and one that denies them to aliens who have not resided in the United States for a specified number of years violates the Equal Protection Clause.

III.

An additional reason why the state statutes at issue in these cases do not withstand constitutional scrutiny emerges from the area of federal-state relations. The National Government has "broad constitutional powers in determining what aliens shall be admitted to the United States, the period they may remain, regulation of their conduct before naturalization, and the terms and conditions of their naturalization." Takahashi v. Fish & Game Commission, 334 U.S., at 419; Hines v. Davidowitz, 312 U.S. 52, 66 (1941); see also Chinese Exclusion Case, 130 U.S. 581 (1889); United States ex rel. Turner v. Williams, 194 U.S. 279 (1904); Fong Yue Ting v. United States, 149 U.S. 698 (1893); Harisiades v. Shaughnessy, 342 U.S. 580 (1952). Pursuant to that power, Congress has provided, as part of a comprehensive plan for the regulation of immigration and naturalization, that "[a]liens who are paupers, professional beggars, or vagrants" or aliens who "are likely at any time to become public charges" shall be excluded from admission into the United States, 8 U.S.C. §§ 1182(a)(8) and 1182(a)(15), and that any alien lawfully admitted shall be deported who "has within five years after entry become a public charge from causes not affirmatively shown to have arisen after entry . . . ." 8 U.S.C. § 1251(a)(8). Admission of aliens likely to become public charges may be conditioned upon the posting of a bond or cash deposit. 8 U.S.C. § 1138. But Congress has not seen fit to impose any burden or restriction on aliens who become indigent after their entry into the United States. Rather, it has broadly declared that "All persons within the jurisdiction of the United States shall have the same right in every State and Territory . . . to the full and equal benefit of all laws and proceedings for the security of persons and property as is enjoyed by white citizens . . . ." 42 U.S.C. § 1981. The protection of this statute has been held to extend to aliens as well as to citizens. *Takahashi*, 334 U.S., at 419 n. 7.

Moreover, this Court has made it clear that, whatever may be the scope of the constitutional right of interstate travel, aliens lawfully within this country have a right to enter and abide in any State in the Union "on an equality of legal privileges with all citizens under nondiscriminatory laws." *Takahashi,* 334 U.S., at 420.

State laws that restrict the eligibility of aliens for welfare benefits merely because of their alienage conflict with these overriding national policies in an area constitutionally entrusted to the Federal Government. . . . State alien residency requirements, that either deny welfare benefits to noncitizens or condition them on longtime residency, equate with the assertion of a right, inconsistent with federal policy, to deny entrance and abode. Since such laws encroach upon exclusive federal power, they are constitutionally impermissible.

. . .

The judgments appealed from are affirmed.

It is so ordered.

Mr. Justice Harlan joins in Parts III and IV of the Court's opinion, and in the judgment of the Court.

BERNAL v. FAINTER

___ U.S. ___, 104 S.Ct. 2312, 81 L.Ed.2d 175 (1984).

Justice Marshall delivered the opinion of the Court.

The question posed by this case is whether a statute of the State of Texas violates the Equal Protection Clause of the Fourteenth Amendment of the United States Constitution by denying aliens the opportunity to become notaries public. The Court of Appeals for the Fifth Circuit held that the statute does not offend the Equal Protection Clause. We . . . reverse.

I

Petitioner, a native of Mexico, is a resident alien who has lived in the United States since 1961. He works as a paralegal for Texas Rural Legal Aid, Inc., helping migrant farm workers on employment and civil rights matters. In order to administer oaths to these workers and to notarize their statements for use in civil litigation, petitioner applied in 1978 to become a notary public. Under Texas law, notaries public authenticate written instruments, administer oaths, and take out-of-court depositions. The Texas Secretary of State denied petitioner's application because he failed to satisfy the statutory requirement that a notary public be a citizen of the United States. Tex.Civ.Stat.Ann., Art. 5949(2) (Vernon) (hereafter Article 5949(2)). After an unsuccessful administrative appeal, petitioner brought suit in the federal district court, claiming that the citizenship requirement mandated by Article 5942(2) violated the federal Constitution.

The District Court ruled in favor of petitioner. . . . A divided panel of the Court of Appeals for the Fifth Circuit reversed, concluding that the proper standard for review was the rational relationship test and that Article 5949(2) satisfied that test because it "bears a rational relationship to the state's interest in the proper and orderly handling of a countless variety of legal documents of importance to the state." *Vargas v. Strake,* 710 F.2d 190, 195 (CA5 1983).

II

As a general matter, a State law that discriminates on the basis of alienage can be sustained only if it can withstand strict judicial scrutiny. In order to withstand strict scrutiny, the law must advance a compelling State interest by the least restrictive means available. Applying this principle, we have invalidated an array of State statutes that denied aliens the right to pursue various occupations. In Sugarman v. Dougall, 413 U.S. 634 (1973), we struck down a State statute barring aliens from employment in permanent positions in the competitive class of the State civil service. In In re Griffiths, 413 U.S. 717 (1973), we nullified a State law excluding aliens from eligibility for membership in the State bar. And in Examining Board v. Flores de Otero, 426 U.S. 572 (1976), we voided a State law that excluded aliens from the practice of civil engineering.

We have, however, developed a narrow exception to the rule that discrimination based on alienage triggers strict scrutiny. This exception has been labelled the "political function" exception and applies to laws that exclude aliens from positions intimately related to the process of democratic self-government. The contours of the "political function" exception are outlined by our prior decisions. In Foley v. Connelie, 435 U.S. 291 (1978), we held that a State may require police to be citizens because, in performing a fundamental obligation of government, police "are clothed with authority to exercise an almost infinite variety of discretionary powers" often involving the most sensitive areas of daily life. In Ambach v. Norwick, 441 U.S. 68 (1979), we held that a State may bar aliens who have not declared their intent to become citizens from teaching in the public schools because teachers, like police, possess a high degree of responsibility and discretion in the fulfillment of a basic governmental obligation. They have direct, day-to-day contact with students, exercise unsupervised discretion over them, act as role models and influence their students about the government and the political process. Finally, in Cabell v. Chavez-Salido, 454 U.S. 432 (1982), we held that a State may bar aliens from positions as probation officers because they, like police and teachers, routinely exercise discretionary power, involving a basic governmental function, that places them in a position of direct authority over other individuals.

The rationale behind the political function exception is that within broad boundaries a State may establish its own form of government and limit the right to govern to those who are full-fledged members of the political community. Some public positions are so closely bound up with the formulation and implementation of self-government that the State is permitted to exclude from those positions persons outside the political community, hence persons who have not become part of the process of democratic self-determination.

> "The exclusion of aliens from basic governmental processes is not a deficiency in the democratic system but a necessary consequence of the community's process of political self-definition. Self-government, whether direct or through representatives, begins by defining the scope of the community of the governed and thus of the governors as well: Aliens are by definition those outside of this community."

We have therefore lowered our standard of review when evaluating the validity of exclusions that entrust only to citizens important elective and nonelective positions whose operations "go to the heart of representative government." Sugarman v. Dougall, supra, 413 U.S., at 647. "While not retreating from the position that restrictions on lawfully resident aliens that primarily affect economic interests are subject to heightened judicial scrutiny . . . we have concluded that strict scrutiny is out of place when the restriction primarily serves a political function. . . ." Cabell v. Chavez-Salido, supra, 454 U.S., at 439.

To determine whether a restriction based on alienage fits within the narrow political function exception, we devised in *Cabell* a two-part test.

> "First, the specificity of the classification will be examined: a classification that is substantially overinclusive or underinclusive tends to undercut the

governmental claim that the classification serves legitimate political ends. . . . Second, even if the classification is sufficiently tailored, it may be applied in the particular case only to 'persons holding state elective or important nonelective executive, legislative, and judicial positions,' those officers who 'participate directly in the formulation, execution, or review of broad public policy' and hence 'perform functions that go right to the heart of representative government.' " [7]

III

We now turn to Article 5949(2) to determine whether it satisfies the *Cabell* test. The statute provides that "[t]o be eligible for appointment as a Notary Public, a person shall be a resident citizen of the United States and of this state . . . ." Unlike the statute invalidated in *Sugarman,* Article 5949(2) does not indiscriminately sweep within its ambit a wide range of offices and occupations but specifies only one particular post with respect to which the State asserts a right to exclude aliens. Clearly, then, the statute is not overinclusive; it applies narrowly to only one category of persons: those wishing to obtain appointments as notaries. Less clear is whether Article 5942(2) is fatally underinclusive. Texas does not require court reporters to be United States citizens even though they perform some of the same services as notaries. Nor does Texas require that its Secretary of State be a citizen, even though he holds the highest appointive position in the State and performs many important functions, including supervision of the licensing of all notaries public. We need not decide this issue, however, because of our decision with respect to the second prong of the *Cabell* test.

In support of the proposition that notaries public fall within that category of officials who perform functions that "go to the heart of representative government," the State emphasizes that notaries are designated as public officers by the Texas Constitution. Texas maintains that this designation indicates that the State views notaries as important officials occupying posts central to the State's definition of itself as a political community. This Court, however, has never deemed the *source* of a position—whether it derives from a State's statute or its Constitution—as the dispositive factor in determining whether a State may entrust the position only to citizens. Rather, this Court has always looked to the actual *function* of the position as the dispositive factor. The focus of our inquiry has been whether a position was such that the officeholder would necessarily exercise broad discretionary power over the formulation or execution of public policies importantly affecting the citizen population—power of the sort that a self-governing community could properly entrust only to full-fledged members of that community. As the Court noted in *Cabell,* in determining whether the function of a particular position brings the position within the narrow ambit of the exception, "the Court will look to the importance of the function as a factor giving substance to the concept of democratic self-government."

The State maintains that even if the actual function of a post is the touchstone of a proper analysis, Texas notaries public should still be classified among those positions from which aliens can properly be excluded because the duties of Texas notaries entail the performance of functions sufficiently consequential to be deemed "political." . . .

We recognize the critical need for a notary's duties to be carried out correctly and with integrity. But a notary's duties, important as they are, hardly implicate responsibilities that go to the heart of representative government.

---

[7] We emphasize, as we have in the past, that the political-function exception must be narrowly construed; otherwise the exception will swallow the rule and depreciate the significance that should attach to the designation of a group as a "discrete and insular" minority for whom heightened judicial solicitude is appropriate. See Nyquist v. Mauclet, 432 U.S. 1, 11 (1976).

Rather, these duties are essentially clerical and ministerial. In contrast to state troopers, Foley v. Connelie, notaries do not routinely exercise the State's monopoly of legitimate coercive force. Nor do notaries routinely exercise the wide discretion typically enjoyed by public school teachers when they present materials that educate youth respecting the information and values necessary for the maintenance of a democratic political system. See Ambach v. Norwick, 441 U.S., at 77. To be sure, considerable damage could result from the negligent or dishonest performance of a notary's duties. But the same could be said for the duties performed by cashiers, building inspectors, the janitors who clean up the offices of public officials, and numerous other categories of personnel upon whom we depend for careful, honest service. What distinguishes such personnel from those to which the political function exception is properly applied is that the latter are either invested with policy-making responsibility or broad discretion in the execution of public policy that requires the routine exercise of authority over individuals. Neither of these characteristics pertain to the functions performed by Texas notaries.

The inappropriateness of applying the political function exception to Texas notaries is further underlined by our decision in In re Griffiths, supra, in which we subjected to strict scrutiny a Connecticut statute that prohibited non-citizens from becoming members of the State bar. Along with the usual powers and privileges accorded to members of the bar, Connecticut gave to members of its bar additional authority that encompasses the very duties performed by Texas notaries—authority to "sign writs and subpoenas, take recognizances, administer oaths and take depositions and acknowledgement of deeds." In striking down Connecticut's citizenship requirement, we concluded that "[i]t in no way denigrates a lawyer's high responsibility to observe that [these duties] hardly involve matters of state policy or acts of such unique responsibility as to entrust them only to citizens." If it is improper to apply the political function exception to a citizenship requirement governing eligibility for membership in a State bar, it would be anomalous to apply the exception to the citizenship requirement that governs eligibility to become a Texas notary. We conclude, then, that the "political function" exception is inapplicable to Article 5949(2) and that the statute is therefore subject to strict judicial scrutiny.

IV

To satisfy strict scrutiny, the State must show that Article 5949(2) furthers a compelling State interest by the least restrictive means practically available. Respondent maintains that Article 5949(2) serves its "legitimate concern that notaries be reasonably familiar with state law and institutions" and "that notaries may be called upon years later to testify to acts they have performed." However both of these asserted justifications utterly fail to meet the stringent requirements of strict scrutiny. There is nothing in the record that indicates that resident aliens, as a class, are so incapable of familiarizing themselves with Texas law as to justify the State's absolute and class-wide exclusion. The possibility that some resident aliens are unsuitable for the position cannot justify a wholesale ban against all resident aliens. Furthermore, if the State's concern with ensuring a notary's familiarity with state law were truly "compelling," one would expect the State to give some sort of test actually measuring a person's familiarity with the law. The State, however, administers no such test. To become a notary public in Texas, one is merely required to fill out an application that lists one's name and address and that answers four questions pertaining to one's age, citizenship, residency and criminal record—nothing that reflects the State's asserted interest in insuring that notaries are familiar with Texas law. Similarly inadequate is the State's purported interest in insuring the later availability of notaries' testimony. This justification fails because the State fails to advance a factual showing that the unavailability of notaries' testimony presents a real, as opposed to a merely speculative, problem to the State. Without a factual underpinning, the State's asserted interest lacks the weight we have required of interests properly denominated as compelling.

V

We conclude that Article 5949(2) violates the Fourteenth Amendment of the United States Constitution. Accordingly the judgment of the Court of Appeals is reversed, and the case is remanded for further proceedings consistent with this opinion.

Justice Rehnquist, dissenting.

I dissent for the reasons stated in my dissenting opinion in Sugarman v. Dougall, 413 U.S. 634, 649 (1973).

MATHEWS v. DIAZ

426 U.S. 67, 96 S.Ct. 1883, 48 L.Ed.2d 478 (1976).

Mr. Justice Stevens delivered the opinion of the Court.

The question presented by the Secretary's appeal is whether Congress may condition an alien's eligibility for participation in a federal medical insurance program on continuous residence in the United States for a five-year period and admission for permanent residence. The District Court held that the first condition was unconstitutional and that it could not be severed from the second. Since we conclude that both conditions are constitutional, we reverse.

Each of the appellees is a resident alien who was lawfully admitted to the United States less than five years ago. Appellees Diaz and Clara are Cuban refugees who remain in this country at the discretion of the Attorney General; appellee Espinosa has been admitted for permanent residence. All three are over 65 years old and have been denied enrollment in the Medicare Part B supplemental medical insurance program established by § 1831 et seq. of the Social Security Act of 1935, 49 Stat. 620, as added, 79 Stat. 301, and as amended, 42 U.S.C. § 1395j et seq. (1970 ed. and Supp. IV). They brought this action to challenge the statutory basis for that denial. Specifically, they attack 42 U.S.C. § 1395*o*(2), which grants eligibility to resident citizens who are 65 or older but denies eligibility to such aliens unless they have been admitted for permanent residence and also have resided in the United States for at least five years. Appellees Diaz and Clara meet neither requirement; appellee Espinosa meets only the first. . . .

. . . . .

II.

There are literally millions of aliens within the jurisdiction of the United States. The Fifth Amendment, as well as the Fourteenth Amendment, protects every one of these persons from deprivation of life, liberty or property without due process of law. Wong Yang Sung v. McGrath, 339 U.S. 33, 48–51; Wong Wing v. United States, 163 U.S. 228, 238; see Russian Volunteer Fleet v. United States, 282 U.S. 481, 489. Even one whose presence in this country is unlawful, involuntary, or transitory, is entitled to that constitutional protection. Wong Yang Sung, supra; Wong Wing, supra.

The fact that all persons, aliens and citizens alike, are protected by the Due Process Clause does not lead to the further conclusion that all aliens are entitled to enjoy all the advantages of citizenship or, indeed, to the conclusion that all aliens must be placed in a single homogenous legal classification. For a host of constitutional and statutory provisions rest on the premise that a legitimate distinction between citizens and aliens may justify attributes and benefits for one class not accorded to the other; [12] and the class of aliens is itself a heterogenous multitude of persons with a wide-ranging variety of ties to this country.

In the exercise of its broad power over naturalization and immigration, Congress regularly makes rules that would be unacceptable if applied to citizens. The exclusion of aliens and the reservation of the power to deport have no permissible counterpart in the Federal Government's power to regulate the conduct of its own citizenry. The fact that an act of Congress treats aliens differently from citizens does not in itself imply that such disparate treatment is "invidious."

In particular, the fact that Congress has provided some welfare benefits for citizens does not require it to provide like benefits for *all aliens.* Neither the overnight visitor, the unfriendly agent of a hostile foreign power, the resident diplomat, nor the illegal entrant, can advance even a colorable constitutional claim to a share in the bounty that a conscientious sovereign makes available to its own citizens and *some* of its guests. The decision to share that bounty with our guests may take into account the character of the relationship between the alien and this country: Congress may decide that as the alien's tie grows stronger, so does the strength of his claim to an equal share of that munificence.

The real question presented by this case is not whether discrimination between citizens and aliens is permissible; rather, it is whether the statutory discrimination *within* the class of aliens—allowing benefits to some aliens but not to others—is permissible. We turn to that question.

III.

For reasons long recognized as valid, the responsibility for regulating the relationship between the United States and our alien visitors has been committed to the political branches of the Federal Government. Since decisions in these matters may implicate our relations with foreign powers, and since a wide variety of classifications must be defined in the light of changing political and economic circumstances, such decisions are frequently of a character more appropriate to either the legislature or the executive than to the judiciary. This very case illustrates the need for flexibility in policy choices rather than the rigidity often characteristic of constitutional adjudication. Appellees Diaz and Clara are but two of over 440,000 Cuban refugees who arrived in the United States between 1961 and 1972. And the Cuban parolees are but one of several categories of aliens who have been admitted in order to make a humane response to a natural catastrophe or an international political situation. Any rule of constitutional law that would inhibit the flexibility of the political branches of government to respond to changing world conditions should be adopted only with the greatest caution. The reasons that preclude judicial review of political questions also dictate a narrow standard of review of decisions made by the Congress or the President in the area of immigration and naturalization.

Since it is obvious that Congress has no constitutional duty to provide *all aliens* with the welfare benefits provided to citizens, the party challenging the

---

[12] The Constitution protects the privileges and immunities only of citizens, Amend. XIV, § 1; see Art. IV, § 2, cl. 1, and the right to vote only of citizens. Amends. XV, XIX, XXIV, XXVI. It requires that Representatives have been citizens for seven years, Art. I, § 2, cl. 2, and Senators citizens for nine, Art. I, § 3, cl. 3, and that the President be a "natural born Citizen." Art. II, § 1, cl. 5.

A multitude of federal statutes distinguish between citizens and aliens. The whole of Title 8 of the United States Code, regulating aliens and nationality, is founded on the legitimacy of distinguishing citizens and aliens. A variety of other federal statutes provide for disparate treatment of aliens and citizens. . . .

constitutionality of the particular line Congress has drawn has the burden of advancing principled reasoning that will at once invalidate that line and yet tolerate a different line separating some aliens from others. In this case the appellees have challenged two requirements, first that the alien be admitted as a permanent resident, and second that his residence be of a duration of at least five years. But if these requirements were eliminated, surely Congress would at least require that the alien's entry be lawful; even then, unless mere transients are to be held constitutionally entitled to benefits, *some* durational requirement would certainly be appropriate. In short, it is unquestionably reasonable for Congress to make an alien's eligibility depend on both the character and the duration of his residence. Since neither requirement is wholly irrational, this case essentially involves nothing more than a claim that it would have been more reasonable for Congress to select somewhat different requirements of the same kind.

We may assume that the five-year line drawn by Congress is longer than necessary to protect the fiscal integrity of the program. We may also assume that unnecessary hardship is incurred by persons just short of qualifying. But it remains true that some line is essential, that any line must produce some harsh and apparently arbitrary consequences, and, of greatest importance, that those who qualify under the test Congress has chosen may reasonably be presumed to have a greater affinity to the United States than those who do not. In short, citizens and those who are most like citizens qualify. Those who are less like citizens do not.

The task of classifying persons for medical benefits, like the task of drawing lines for federal tax purposes, inevitably requires that some persons who have an almost equally strong claim to favored treatment be placed on different sides of the line; the differences between the eligible and the ineligible are differences in degree rather than differences in the character of their respective claims. When this kind of policy choice must be made, we are especially reluctant to question the exercise of congressional judgment. In this case, since appellees have not identified a principled basis for prescribing a different standard than the one selected by Congress, they have, in effect, merely invited us to substitute our judgment for that of Congress in deciding which aliens shall be eligible to participate in the supplementary insurance program on the same conditions as citizens. We decline the invitation.

IV.

The cases on which appellees rely are consistent with our conclusion that this statutory classification does not deprive them of liberty or property without due process of law.

Graham v. Richardson, 403 U.S. 365, provides the strongest support for appellees' position. That case holds that state statutes that deny welfare benefits to resident aliens, or to aliens not meeting a requirement of durational residence within the United States, violate the Equal Protection Clause of the Fourteenth Amendment and encroach upon the exclusive federal power over the entrance and residence of aliens. Of course, the latter ground of decision actually supports our holding today that it is the business of the political branches of the Federal Government, rather than that of either the States or the federal judiciary, to regulate the conditions of entry and residence of aliens. The equal protection analysis also involves significantly different considerations because it concerns the relationship between aliens and the States rather than between aliens and the Federal Government.

Insofar as state welfare policy is concerned, there is little, if any, basis for treating persons who are citizens of another State differently from persons who are citizens of another country. Both groups are noncitizens as far as the State's interests in administering its welfare programs are concerned. Thus, a division by a State of the category of persons who are not citizens of that State into subcategories of United States citizens and aliens has no apparent justification, whereas, a comparable classification by the Federal Government is a routine and normally legitimate part of its business. Furthermore, whereas the Constitution inhibits every State's power to restrict travel across its own borders, Congress is explicitly empowered to exercise that type of control over travel across the borders of the United States.

.   .   .

We hold that § 1395*o*(2)(B) has not deprived appellees of liberty or property without due process of law.

The judgment of the District Court is reversed.

D. CLASSIFICATIONS DISADVANTAGING NON–MARITAL CHILDREN

THE STANDARD OF REVIEW FOR LEGITIMACY CLASSIFICATIONS

In Levy v. Louisiana, 391 U.S. 68 (1968) the Court held invalid a state statute which permitted legitimate but not illegitimate children to sue for wrongful death of their mother. The Court indicated that the classification did not meet the lowest standard of review. "Legitimacy or illegitimacy of birth has no relation to the nature of the wrong allegedly inflicted on the mother." In Labine v. Vincent, 401 U.S. 532 (1971) the Court upheld a statute under which illegitimate children acknowledged but not legitimated by the father could not take by intestate succession from the father. The next year, in Weber v. Aetna Cas. and Sur. Co., 406 U.S. 164 (1972), the Court held invalid a statute which did not permit dependent, unacknowledged children of a father to recover workers' compensation benefits for death of the father, saying that the classification "is justified by no legitimate state interest, compelling or otherwise." In the next three cases to come before it the Court invalidated legitimacy classifications: Gomez v. Perez, 409 U.S. 535 (1973) (father obligated to support legitimate but not illegitimate children); New Jersey Welfare Rights Organization v. Cahill, 411 U.S. 619 (1973) (state welfare statute); Jimenez v. Weinberger, 417 U.S. 628 (1974) (federal classification which did not permit some illegitimate children to obtain benefits under parent's disability insurance).

In Mathews v. Lucas, 427 U.S. 495 (1976), the Court upheld a provision of the Social Security Act which gave a survivor's benefit to a minor dependent child of a deceased parent, but extended a presumption of dependency to all children except certain classes of illegitimate children. Justice Blackmun, speaking for the Court, said that the trial judge was wrong in treating the classification as suspect requiring strict scrutiny:

"It is true, of course, that the legal status of illegitimacy, however defined, is like race or national origin, a characteristic determined by causes not within the control of the illegitimate individual, and it bears no relation to the individual's ability to participate in and contribute to society. The Court recognized in *Weber* that visiting condemnation upon the child in order to express society's disapproval of the parents' liaisons

'is illogical and unjust. Moreover, imposing disabilities on the illegitimate child is contrary to the basic concept of our system that legal burdens should bear some relationship to individual responsibility or wrongdoing. Obviously, no child is responsible for his birth and penalizing the illegitimate child is an ineffectual—as well as an unjust—way of deterring the parent.' (Footnote omitted.) 406 U.S., at 175.

But where the law is arbitrary in such a way, we have had no difficulty in finding the discrimination impermissible on less demanding standards than those advocated here. New Jersey Welfare Rights Organization v. Cahill, 411 U.S. 619 (1973); Richardson v. Davis, 409 U.S. 1069 (1972); Richardson v. Griffin, 409 U.S. 1069 (1972); *Weber,* supra; Levy v. Louisiana, 391 U.S. 68 (1968). And such irrationality in some classifications does not in itself demonstrate that other, possibly rational, distinctions made in part on the basis of legitimacy are inherently untenable. Moreover, while the law has long placed the illegitimate child in an inferior position relative to the legitimate in certain circumstances, particularly in regard to obligations of support or other aspects of family law, see generally, e.g., H. Krause, *Illegitimacy: Law and Social Policy* 21–42 (1971); Gray & Rudovsky, *The Court Acknowledges the Illegitimate: Levy v. Louisiana and Glona v. American Guarantee & Liability Insurance Co.,* 118 U.Pa.L.Rev. 1, 19–38 (1969), perhaps in part because the roots of the discrimination rest in the conduct of the parents rather than the child, and perhaps in part because illegitimacy does not carry an obvious badge, as race or sex do, this discrimination against illegitimates has never approached the severity or pervasiveness of the historic legal and political discrimination against women and Negroes. See Frontiero v. Richardson, 411 U.S. 677, 684–686 (1973) (plurality opinion).

"We therefore adhere to our earlier view, see Labine v. Vincent, 401 U.S. 532 (1971), that the Act's discrimination between individuals on the basis of their legitimacy does not 'command extraordinary protection from the majoritarian political process,' San Antonio Independent School District v. Rodriguez, 411 U.S. 1, 28 (1973), which our most exacting scrutiny would entail."

Later in the opinion he referred to the showing necessary to demonstrate that the relationship between the statutory classifications and the likelihood of dependency was not sufficiently material: "[T]he scrutiny by which their showing is to be judged is not a toothless one" but "the burden remains upon the appellees to demonstrate the insubstantiality of that relation."

LALLI v. LALLI

439 U.S. 259, 99 S.Ct. 518, 58 L.Ed.2d 503 (1978).

Mr. Justice Powell announced the judgment of the Court in an opinion, in which The Chief Justice and Mr. Justice Stewart join.

This case presents a challenge to the constitutionality of § 4–1.2 of New York's Estates, Powers, and Trusts Law, which requires illegitimate children who would inherit from their fathers by intestate succession to provide a particular form of proof of paternity. Legitimate children are not subject to the same requirement.

I.

Appellant Robert Lalli claims to be the illegitimate son of Mario Lalli who died intestate on January 7, 1973, in the State of New York. Appellant's mother, who died in 1968, never was married to Mario. After Mario's widow, Rosamond Lalli, was appointed administratrix of her husband's estate, appellant petitioned the Surrogate's Court for Westchester County for a compulsory accounting, claiming that he and his sister Maureen Lalli were entitled to inherit from Mario as his children. Rosamond Lalli opposed the petition. She argued that even if Robert and Maureen were Mario's children, they were not lawful distributees of the state because they had failed to comply with § 4–1.2, which provides in part:

> "An illegitimate child is the legitimate child of his father so that he and his issue inherit from his father if a court of competent jurisdiction has, during the lifetime of the father, made an order of filiation declaring paternity in a proceeding instituted during the pregnancy of the mother or within two years from the birth of the child."

Appellant conceded that he had not obtained an order of filiation during his putative father's lifetime. He contended, however, that § 4–1.2, by imposing this requirement, discriminated against him on the basis of his illegitimate birth . in violation of the Equal Protection Clause of the Fourteenth Amendment. Appellant tendered certain evidence of his relationship with Mario Lalli, including a notarized document in which Lalli, in consenting to appellant's marriage, referred to him as "my son," and several affidavits by persons who stated that Lalli had acknowledged openly and often that Robert and Maureen were his children.

The Surrogate's Court . . . ruled that appellant was properly excluded as a distributee of Lalli's estate and therefore lacked status to petition for a compulsory accounting.

On direct appeal the New York Court of Appeals affirmed. . . .

Appellant appealed the Court of Appeals' decision to this Court. While that case was pending here, we decided Trimble v. Gordon, 430 U.S. 762 (1977). Because the issues in these two cases were similar in some respects, we vacated and remanded to permit further consideration in light of *Trimble.*

On remand, the New York Court of Appeals, with one judge dissenting, adhered to its former disposition. . . .

Appellant again sought review here, and we noted probable jurisdiction. We now affirm.

II.

We begin our analysis with *Trimble.* At issue in that case was the constitutionality of an Illinois statute providing that a child born out of wedlock could inherit from his intestate father only if the father had "acknowledged" the child and the child had been legitimated by the intermarriage of the parents. The appellant in *Trimble* was a child born out of wedlock whose father had neither acknowledged her nor married her mother. He had, however, been found to be her father in a judicial decree ordering him to contribute to her support. When the father died intestate, the child was excluded as a distributee because the statutory requirements for inheritance had not been met.

We concluded that the Illinois statute discriminated against illegitimate children in a manner prohibited by the Equal Protection Clause. Although, as decided in Mathews v. Lucas, 427 U.S. 495 (1976), and reaffirmed in *Trimble,* classifications based on illegitimacy are not subject to "strict scrutiny," they nevertheless are invalid under the Fourteenth Amendment if they are not substantially related to permissible state interests. Upon examination, we found that the Illinois law failed that test.

Two state interests were proposed which the statute was said to foster: the encouragement of legitimate family relationships and the maintenance of an accurate and efficient method of disposing of an intestate decedent's property. Granting that the State was appropriately concerned with the integrity of the family unit, we viewed the statute as bearing "only the most attenuated relationship to the asserted goal." We again rejected the argument that "persons will shun illicit relationships because the offspring may not one day reap the benefits" that would accrue to them were they legitimate. Weber v. Aetna Casualty & Surety Co., 406 U.S. 164 (1972). The statute therefore was not defensible as an incentive to enter legitimate family relationships.

Illinois' interest in safeguarding the orderly disposition of property at death was more relevant to the statutory classification. We recognized that devising "an appropriate legal framework" in the furtherance of that interest "is a matter particularly within the competence of the individual States." An important aspect of that framework is a response to the often difficult problem of proving the paternity of illegitimate children and the related danger of spurious claims against intestate estates. These difficulties, we said, "might justify a more demanding standard for illegitimate children claiming under their fathers' estates than that required either for illegitimate children claiming under their mothers' estates or for legitimate children generally."

The Illinois statute, however, was constitutionally flawed, because, by insisting upon not only an acknowledgment by the father, but also the marriage of the parents, it excluded "at least some significant categories of illegitimate children of intestate men [whose] inheritance rights can be recognized without jeopardizing the orderly settlement of estates or the dependability of titles to property passing under intestacy laws." We concluded that the Equal Protection Clause required that a statute placing exceptional burdens on illegitimate children in the furtherance of proper State objectives must be more "carefully tuned to alternative considerations," than was true of the broad disqualification in the Illinois law.

III.

The New York statute, enacted in 1965, was intended to soften the rigors of previous law which permitted illegitimate children to inherit only from their mothers. By lifting the absolute bar to paternal inheritance, § 4–1.2 tended to achieve its desired effect. As in *Trimble,* however, the question before us is whether the remaining statutory obstacles to inheritance by illegitimate children can be squared with the Equal Protection Clause.

A.

At the outset we observe that § 4–1.2 is different in important respects from the statutory provision overturned in *Trimble.* The Illinois statute required, in addition to the father's acknowledgment of paternity, the legitimation of the child through the intermarriage of the parents as an absolute precondition to inheritance. This combination of requirements eliminated "the possibility of a middle ground between the extremes of complete exclusion and case-by-case determination of paternity." *Trimble,* supra. As illustrated by the facts in *Trimble,* even a judicial declaration of paternity was insufficient to permit inheritance.

Under § 4–1.2, by contrast, the marital status of the parents is irrelevant. The single requirement at issue here is an evidentiary one—that the paternity of the father be declared in a judicial proceeding sometime before his death. The child need not have been legitimated in order to inherit from his father. Had the appellant in *Trimble* been governed by § 4–1.2, she would have been a distributee of her father's estate.

A related difference between the two provisions pertains to the state interests said to be served by them. The Illinois law was defended, in part, as a means of encouraging legitimate family relationships. No such justification has been offered in support of § 4–1.2. The Court of Appeals disclaimed that the purpose of the statute, "even in small part, was to discourage illegitimacy, to mold human conduct or to set societal norms." The absence in § 4–1.2 of any requirement that the parents intermarry or otherwise legitimate a child born out of wedlock and our review of the legislative history of the statute confirm this view.

Our inquiry, therefore, is focused narrowly. We are asked to decide whether the discrete procedural demands that § 4–1.2 places on illegitimate children bear an evident and substantial relation to the particular state interests this statute is designed to serve.

B.

The primary state goal underlying the challenged aspects of § 4–1.2 is to provide for the just and orderly disposition of property at death. We long have recognized that this is an area with which the States have an interest of considerable magnitude.

This interest is directly implicated in paternal inheritance by illegitimate children because of the peculiar problems of proof that are involved. Establishing maternity is seldom difficult. . . . Proof of paternity, by contrast, frequently is difficult when the father is not part of a formal family unit. . . .

Thus, a number of problems arise that counsel against treating illegitimate children identically to all other heirs of an intestate father. These were the subject of a comprehensive study by the Temporary State Commission on the Modernization, Revision and Simplification of the Law of Estates. This group, known as the Bennett Commission, consisted of individuals experienced in the practical problems of estate administration. The Commission issued its report and recommendations to the Legislature in 1965. The statute now codified as § 4–1.2 was included.

Although the overarching purpose of the proposed statute was "to alleviate the plight of the illegitimate child," the Bennett Commission considered it necessary to impose the strictures of § 4–1.2 in order to mitigate serious difficulties in the administration of the estates of both testate and intestate decedents. The Commission's perception of some of these difficulties was described by Surrogate Sobel, a member of "the busiest [surrogate's] court in the State measured by the number of intestate estates which traffic daily through this court," and a participant in some of the Commission's deliberations:

> "An illegitimate, if made an unconditional distributee in intestacy, must be served with process in the estate of his parent or if he is a distributee in the estate of the kindred of a parent. . . . And, in probating the will of his parent (though not named a beneficiary) or in probating the will of any person who makes a class disposition to 'issue' of such parent, the illegitimate must be served with process. . . . How does one cite and serve an illegitimate of whose existence neither family nor personal representative may be aware? And of greatest concern, how achieve finality of decree in *any* estate when there always exists the possibility however remote of a secret illegitimate lurking in the buried past of a parent or an ancestor of a class of beneficiaries? . . . ."

Even where an individual claiming to be the illegitimate child of a deceased man makes himself known, the difficulties facing an estate are likely to persist. Because of the particular problems of proof, spurious claims may be difficult to expose. The Bennett Commission therefore sought to protect "innocent adults and those rightfully interested in their estates from fraudulent claims of heirship and harassing litigation instituted by those seeking to establish themselves as illegitimate heirs."

C.

As the State's interests are substantial, we now consider the means adopted by New York to further these interests. In order to avoid the problems described above, the Commission recommended a requirement designed to ensure the accurate resolution of claims of paternity and to minimize the potential for disruption of estate administration. Accuracy is enhanced by placing paternity disputes in a judicial forum during the lifetime of the father.

. . .

The administration of an estate will be facilitated, and the possibility of delay and uncertainty minimized, where the entitlement of an illegitimate child to notice and participation is a matter of judicial record before the administration commences. Fraudulent assertions of paternity will be much less likely to succeed, or even to arise, where the proof is put before a court of law at a time when the putative father is available to respond, rather than first brought to light when the distribution of the assets of an estate is in the offing.[8]

Appellant contends that § 4–1.2, like the statute at issue in *Trimble,* excludes "significant categories of illegitimate children" who could be allowed to inherit "without jeopardizing the orderly settlement" of their intestate fathers' estates. He urges that those in his position—"known" illegitimate children who, despite the absence of an order of filiation obtained during their fathers' lifetimes, can present convincing proof of paternity—cannot rationally be denied inheritance as they pose none of the risks § 4–1.2 was intended to minimize.

We do not question that there will be some illegitimate children who would be able to establish their relationship to their deceased fathers without serious disruption of the administration of estates and that, as applied to such individuals, § 4–1.2 appears to operate unfairly. But few statutory classifications are entirely free from the criticism that they sometimes produce inequitable results. Our inquiry under the Equal Protection Clause does not focus on the abstract "fairness" of a state law, but on whether the statute's relation to the state interests it is intended to promote is so tenuous that it lacks the rationality contemplated by the Fourteenth Amendment.

. . .

We conclude that the requirement imposed by § 4–1.2 on illegitimate children who would inherit from their fathers is substantially related to the important state interests the statute is intended to promote. We therefore find no violation of the Equal Protection Clause.

The judgment of the New York Court of Appeals is affirmed.

For the reasons stated in his dissent in Trimble v. Gordon, **Mr. Justice Rehnquist** concurs in the judgment of affirmance.

Mr. Justice Stewart, concurring.

It seems to me that Mr. Justice Powell's opinion convincingly demonstrates the significant differences between the New York law at issue here and the Illinois law at issue in Trimble v. Gordon. Therefore, I cannot agree with the view expressed in the concurring opinion that Trimble v. Gordon is now "a derelict," or with the implication that in deciding the two cases the way it has this Court has failed to give authoritative guidance to the courts and legislatures of the several States.

---

[8] In affirming the judgment below, we do not, of course, restrict a State's freedom to require proof of paternity by means other than a judicial decree. Thus a State may prescribe any *formal* method of proof, whether it be similar to that provided by § 4–1.2 or some other regularized procedure that would assure the authenticity of the acknowledgment.

Mr. Justice Blackmun, concurring in the judgment.

I agree with the result the Court has reached and concur in its judgment. I also agree with much that has been said in the plurality opinion. My point of departure, of course, is at the plurality's valiant struggle to distinguish, rather than overrule, Trimble v. Gordon, decided just last Term, and involving a small probate estate (an automobile worth approximately $2,500) and a sad and appealing fact situation. Four Members of the Court . . . were in dissent.

I would overrule *Trimble,* but the Court refrains from doing so on the theory that the result in *Trimble* is justified because of the peculiarities of the Illinois Probate Act there under consideration. This, of course, is an explanation, but, for me, it is an unconvincing one. I therefore must regard *Trimble* as a derelict, explainable only because of the overtones of its appealing facts and offering little precedent for constitutional analysis of State intestate succession laws. If *Trimble* is not a derelict, the corresponding statutes of other States will be of questionable validity until this Court passes them, one by one, as being on the *Trimble* side of the line, or the *Vincent-Lalli* side.

Mr. Justice Brennan, with whom Mr. Justice White, Mr. Justice Marshall, and Mr. Justice Stevens join, dissenting.

Trimble v. Gordon, declares that the state interest in the accurate and efficient determination of paternity can be adequately served by requiring the illegitimate child to offer into evidence a "formal acknowledgment of paternity." The New York statute is inconsistent with this command. Under the New York scheme, an illegitimate child may inherit intestate only if there has been a judicial finding of paternity during the lifetime of the father.

. . .

I see no reason to retreat from our decision in Trimble v. Gordon. The New York statute on review here, like the Illinois statute in *Trimble,* excludes "forms of proof which do not compromise the State['s] interests." The statute thus discriminates against illegitimates through means not substantially related to the legitimate interests that the statute purports to promote. I would invalidate the statute.

PICKETT v. BROWN, 462 U.S. 1 (1983). Tennessee makes the father of a child born out of wedlock liable for support of that child. Enforcement of this obligation depends on the establishment of paternity. A procedure is provided for determining paternity, but with a requirement that the action must be filed within two years after the birth of the child. In this case a suit to determine paternity was brought by the mother of the child ten years after the birth. The state courts upheld the statute of limitation and the Supreme Court reversed in a unanimous opinion by Justice Brennan.

The Court noted that it had held invalid a one year limitation period in Mills v. Habluetzel, 456 U.S. 91 (1982). Based on that case, the Court held the two-year statute also invalid. The Court determined that such a short period of limitation did not provide a reasonable opportunity for suits to be brought on behalf of the child. It also said that the time limitation was not substantially related to the state's interest in avoiding the litigation of stale or fraudulent claims. The Court did not need to decide how long a time the state must allow for the filing of paternity claims, but the tone of the opinion suggests that a long period, perhaps any time during the child's minority, would be required.

The Court also agreed upon the following statement as to the standard of review to be used in reviewing classifications disadvantaging non-marital children:

"In view of the history of treating illegitimate children less favorably than legitimate ones, we have subjected statutory classifications based on illegitimacy to a heightened level of scrutiny. Although we have held that classifications based on illegitimacy are not 'suspect,' or subject to 'our most exacting scrutiny,' Trimble v. Gordon, 430 U.S., at 767; Mathews v. Lucas, 427 U.S., at 506, the scrutiny applied to them 'is not a toothless one. . . .' In United States v. Clark, supra, we stated that a classification based on illegitimacy is unconstitutional unless it bears 'an evident and substantial relation to the particular . . . interests [the] statute is designed to serve.' 445 U.S., at 27. See also Lalli v. Lalli, 439 U.S., at 265 (plurality opinion) ('classifications based on illegitimacy . . . are invalid under the Fourteenth Amendment if they are not substantially related to permissible state interests'). We applied a similar standard of review to a classification based on illegitimacy last Term in Mills v. Habluetzel, 456 U.S. 91. We stated that restrictions on support suits by illegitimate children 'will survive equal protection scrutiny to the extent they are substantially related to a legitimate state interest.' "

PARENTAL RIGHTS OF FATHERS OF ILLEGITIMATE CHILDREN

It is a common statutory pattern for the father of an illegitimate child to be given fewer parental rights than the child's mother, or than the father of a child born in wedlock or legitimated. That statutory pattern has raised substantive due process questions concerning state regulation of the relationship between parent and child, as well as questions of procedural due process and equal protection.

In Stanley v. Illinois, 405 U.S. 645 (1972), the unmarried parents of three children lived together for 18 years prior to the mother's death. Upon the mother's death, the children were declared wards of the state under Illinois law, which provided that illegitimate children become wards of the State upon the mother's death. The Court held that denial of a hearing to Stanley on his fitness as a parent was a violation of procedural due process, as well as a denial of equal protection. As to the equal protection claim, "all Illinois parents are constitutionally entitled to a hearing on their fitness before their children are removed from their custody"; hence the distinction between unmarried fathers on the one hand, and unmarried mothers, married parents and divorced parents on the other, was contrary to the equal protection clause.

In Quilloin v. Walcott, 434 U.S. 246 (1978), the natural father had neither lived with the child's mother, nor had custody of the child. The child's mother consented to the child's adoption by her husband. State courts dismissed the father's objection to the adoption under a law requiring only the mother's consent for adoption of an illegitimate child. The Court's conclusion that the father had not been denied substantive due process was limited to the facts of the case—the father had not sought custody of the child, and the adoption recognized "a family unit already in existence." The Court also rejected an equal protection challenge based on the argument that a married father who was separated or divorced would have been permitted to veto the adoption. An argument that an unmarried father should, as matter of equal protection, be given the same rights as an unmarried mother, was not considered because it had not been properly presented.

That argument, however, proved crucial in Caban v. Mohammed, 441 U.S. 380 (1979). The father had lived with the children as their father in their early years. At the time of the petition for adoption by the children's mother and her husband, the father and mother were engaged in a legal battle for the children's custody. The Court held that New York's law, which permitted an unwed mother to block her child's adoption but gave no similar right to the father, was an unconstitutional distinction on the basis of gender. While Justice Powell's opinion for the Court rejected the argument that the gender distinction could be justified by the difference in maternal and paternal roles, it conceded that the distinction could be applied constitutionally in cases of adoption at birth or in cases where the father had not participated in the rearing of the child. Chief Justice Burger, and Justices Stewart, Rehnquist and Stevens dissented.

On the same day the *Caban* case was decided, Justice Powell concurred with the dissenters in that case to sustain a distinction between unwed mothers and fathers. Parham v. Hughes, 441 U.S. 347 (1979) involved a Georgia law which permitted the mother of an illegitimate child to sue for the wrongful death of a child, while denying that right to the child's father. The four *Caban* dissenters, in an opinion by Justice Stewart, argued that the gender based distinction was not invidious—the father's right to sue was not denied solely because of his male sex, but because he had taken no steps to legitimate the child. Justice Powell concurred in the result on the narrower ground that the gender-based distinction was justified by problems of proving paternity after an illegitimate child's death. Justice White's dissent, joined by Justices Brennan, Marshall and Blackmun, argued that Georgia's interest in rejecting spurious claims could not justify categorically eliminating all claims of fathers of illegitimate children "on the basis of sex."

The Court returned to the problem again in 1983 in Lehr v. Robertson, 463 U.S. 248 (1983). Lehr, an unmarried father, had lived with the mother prior to birth of the child, visited the mother and child in the hospital, but thereafter had little contact neither providing support nor offering to marry the mother. The mother married another man eight months after the child's birth and when the child was two years old the mother and her husband sought to adopt the child. No notice was given Lehr of the adoption proceeding and the court granted the adoption after it had become aware that Lehr had filed a paternity and visitation proceeding in another county. Lehr brought this action to set aside the adoption proceeding as violating the due process and equal protection clauses. The New York courts denied his claim and the Supreme Court affirmed.

Justice Stevens, writing for the majority, noted that New York maintains a "putative father registry" in which a person claiming to be the father may enter his name and have the right to receive notice of any proceeding to adopt the child. The law also provides notice to men who have been adjudicated to be fathers, who have been identified as fathers on the child's birth certificate, who live openly with the child and the child's mother and hold themselves out as fathers, who have been identified as father by the mother in a sworn written statement, and who were married to the child's mother before the child was six months old. This law, the Court said, adequately protected the opportunity of the putative father to establish a relationship with the illegitimate child. Lehr had not complied with that statute and had not established any relationship with the child. Under these circumstances it was not a denial of due process to enter the order of adoption without notice to Lehr, even though the judge in the adoption proceeding had knowledge of the paternity petition filed by Lehr. "Since the New York statutes adequately protected appellant's inchoate interest in establishing a relationship with . . . [the child], we find no merit in the claim that his constitutional rights were offended because the family court strictly complied with the notice provisions of the statute."

The Court went on to hold that there was no denial of equal protection. It said that the parents here were in a different position than those in Caban v. Mohammed, 441 U.S. 380 (1979). Lehr never established any custodial, personal, or financial relations with the child. "If one parent has an established custodial relationship with the child and the other parent has either abandoned or never established a relationship, the Equal Protection Clause does not prevent a state from according the two parents different legal rights."

Justices White, Marshall and Blackmun dissented, arguing that it was a denial of due process to deny notice and an opportunity to be heard in an adoption proceeding to a putative father when the state has actual notice of his existence, whereabouts, and interest in the child.

E. CLASSIFICATIONS BASED ON GENDER

REED v. REED

404 U.S. 71, 92 S.Ct. 251, 30 L.Ed.2d 225 (1971).

[Section 15–314 of Idaho code provided that in the choice of persons to administer an intestate estate "[o]f several persons claiming and equally entitled to administer, males must be preferred to females." Solely because of this statute an Idaho court appointed the father rather than the mother of a deceased child as administrator. The mother appealed the decision.]

Mr. Chief Justice Burger delivered the opinion of the Court.

. . .

Section 15–314 is restricted in its operation to those situations where competing applications for letters of administration have been filed by both male and female members of the same entitlement class established by § 15–312. In such situations, § 15–314 provides that different treatment be accorded to the applicants on the basis of their sex; it thus establishes a classification subject to scrutiny under the Equal Protection Clause.

In applying that clause, this Court has consistently recognized that the Fourteenth Amendment does not deny to States the power to treat different classes of persons in different ways. Barbier v. Connolly, 113 U.S. 27; Lindsley v. Natural Carbonic Gas Co., 220 U.S. 61 (1911); Railway Express Agency, Inc. v. New York, 336 U.S. 106 (1949); McDonald v. Board of Election Commissioners, 394 U.S. 802 (1968). The Equal Protection Clause of that Amendment does, however, deny to States the power to legislate that different treatment be accorded to persons placed by a statute into different classes on the basis of criteria wholly unrelated to the objective of that statute. A classification "must be reasonable, not arbitrary, and must rest upon some ground of difference having a fair and substantial relation to the object of the legislation, so that all persons similarly circumstanced shall be treated alike." Royster Guano Co. v. Virginia, 253 U.S. 412, 415 (1920). The question presented by this case, then, is whether a difference in the sex of competing applicants for letters of administration bears a rational relationship to a state objective that is sought to be advanced by the operation of §§ 15–312 and 15–314.

In upholding the latter section, the Idaho Supreme Court concluded that its objective was to eliminate one area of controversy when two or more persons, equally entitled under § 15–312, seek letters of administration and thereby present the probate court "with the issue of which one should be named." The court also concluded that where such persons are not of the same sex, the elimination of females from consideration "is neither an illogical nor arbitrary method devised by the legislature to resolve an issue that would otherwise require a hearing as to the relative merits . . . of the two or more petitioning relatives . . . ." 93 Idaho, at 514, 465 P.2d, at 638.

Clearly the objective of reducing the workload on probate courts by eliminating one class of contests is not without some legitimacy. The crucial question, however, is whether § 15–314 advances that objective in a manner consistent with the command of the Equal Protection Clause. We hold that it does not. To give a mandatory preference to members of either sex over members of the other, merely to accomplish the elimination of hearings on the merits, is to make the very kind of arbitrary legislative choice forbidden by the Equal Protection Clause of the Fourteenth Amendment; and whatever may be said as to the positive values of avoiding intrafamily controversy, the choice in this context may not lawfully be mandated solely on the basis of sex.

We note finally that if § 15–314 is viewed merely as a modifying appendage to § 15–312 and as aimed at the same objective, its constitutionality is not thereby saved. The objective of § 15–312 clearly is to establish degrees of entitlement of various classes of persons in accordance with their varying degrees and kinds of relationship to the intestate. Regardless of their sex, persons within any one of the enumerated classes of that section are similarly situated with respect to that objective. By providing dissimilar treatment for men and women who are thus similarly situated, the challenged section violates the Equal Protection Clause. Royster Guano Co. v. Virginia, supra.

The judgment of the Idaho Supreme Court is reversed and the case remanded for further proceedings not inconsistent with this opinion.

FRONTIERO v. RICHARDSON

411 U.S. 677, 93 S.Ct. 1764, 36 L.Ed.2d 583 (1973).

Mr. Justice Brennan announced the judgment of the Court in an opinion in which Mr. Justice Douglas, Mr. Justice White, and Mr. Justice Marshall join.

The question before us concerns the right of a female member of the uniformed services to claim her spouse as a "dependent" for the purposes of obtaining increased quarters allowances and medical and dental benefits under 37 U.S.C. §§ 401, 403, and 10 U.S.C. §§ 1072, 1076, on an equal footing with male members. Under these statutes, a serviceman may claim his wife as a "dependent" without regard to whether she is in fact dependent upon him for any part of her support. 37 U.S.C. § 401(1); 10 U.S.C. § 1072(2)(A). A servicewoman, on the other hand, may not claim her husband as a "dependent" under these programs unless he is in fact dependent upon her for over one-half of his support. 37 U.S.C. § 401; 10 U.S.C. § 1072(2)(C). Thus, the question for decision is whether this difference in treatment constitutes an unconstitutional discrimination against servicewomen in violation of the Due Process Clause of the Fifth Amendment. A three-judge District Court for the Middle District of Alabama, one judge dissenting, rejected this contention and sustained the constitutionality of the provisions of the statutes making this distinction. 341 F.Supp. 201 (1972). We noted probable jurisdiction. 409 U.S. 840 (1972). We reverse.

I.

In an effort to attract career personnel through reenlistment, Congress established, in 37 U.S.C. § 401 et seq., and 10 U.S.C. § 1071 et seq., a scheme for the provision of fringe benefits to members of the uniformed services on a competitive basis with business and industry. Thus, under 37 U.S.C. § 403, a member of the uniformed services with dependents is entitled to an increased "basic allowance for quarters" and, under 10 U.S.C. § 1076, a member's dependents are provided comprehensive medical and dental care.

Appellant Sharron Frontiero, a lieutenant in the United States Air Force, sought increased quarters allowances, and housing and medical benefits for her husband, appellant Joseph Frontiero, on the ground that he was her "dependent." Although such benefits would automatically have been granted with respect to the wife of a male member of the uniformed services, appellant's application was denied because she failed to demonstrate that her husband was dependent on her for more than one-half of his support. Appellants then commenced this suit, contending that, by making this distinction, the statutes unreasonably discriminate on the basis of sex in violation of the Due Process Clause of the Fifth Amendment. In essence, appellants asserted that the discriminatory impact of the statutes is two-fold: first, as a procedural matter, a female member is required to demonstrate her spouse's dependency, while no such burden is imposed upon male members; and second, as a substantive matter, a male member who does not provide more than one-half of his wife's support receives benefits, while a similarly situated female member is denied such benefits. Appellants therefore sought a permanent injunction against the continued enforcement of these statutes and an order directing the appellees to provide Lieutenant Frontiero with the same housing and medical benefits that a similarly situated male member would receive.

Although the legislative history of these statutes sheds virtually no light on the purposes underlying the differential treatment accorded male and female members, a majority of the three-judge District Court surmised that Congress might reasonably have concluded that, since the husband in our society is generally the "breadwinner" in the family—and the wife typically the "dependent" partner—"it would be more economical to require married female members claiming husbands to prove actual dependency than to extend the presumption of dependency to such members." 341 F.Supp., at 207. Indeed, given the fact that approximately 99% of all members of the uniformed services are male, the District Court speculated that such differential treatment might conceivably lead to a "considerable saving of administrative expense and manpower." Ibid.

II.

At the outset, appellants contend that classifications based upon sex, like classifications based upon race, alienage, and national origin, are inherently suspect and must therefore be subjected to close judicial scrutiny. We agree and, indeed, find at least implicit support for such an approach in our unanimous decision only last Term in Reed v. Reed, 404 U.S. 71 (1971). . . .

There can be no doubt that our Nation has had a long and unfortunate history of sex discrimination. Traditionally, such discrimination was rationalized by an attitude of "romantic paternalism" which, in practical effect, put women not on a pedestal, but in a cage. Indeed, this paternalistic attitude became so firmly rooted in our national consciousness that, exactly 100 years ago, a distinguished member of this Court was able to proclaim:

> "Man is, or should be, woman's protector and defender. The natural and proper timidity and delicacy which belongs to the female sex evidently unfits it for many of the occupations of civil life. The constitution of the family organization, which is founded in the divine ordinance, as well as in the nature of things, indicates the domestic sphere as that which properly belongs to the domain and functions of womanhood. The harmony, not to say identity, of interests and views which belong, or should belong, to the family institution is repugnant to the ideas of a woman adopting a distinct and independent career from that of her husband. . . .

". . . . The paramount destiny and mission of women are to fulfil the noble and benign offices of wife and mother. This is the law of the Creator." Bradwell v. Illinois, 83 U.S. [16 Wall.] 130, 141 (1873) (Bradley, J., concurring).

As a result of notions such as these, our statute books gradually became laden with gross, stereotypical distinctions between the sexes and, indeed, throughout much of the 19th century the position of women in our society was, in many respects, comparable to that of blacks under the pre-Civil War slave codes. Neither slaves nor women could hold office, serve on juries, or bring suit in their own names, and married women traditionally were denied the legal capacity to hold or convey property or to serve as legal guardians of their own children. See generally, L. Kantowitz, Women and the Law: The Unfinished Revolution 5–6 (1969); G. Mydral, An American Dilemma 1073 (2d ed. 1962). And although blacks were guaranteed the right to vote in 1870, women were denied even that right—which is itself "preservative of other basic civil and political rights"—until adoption of the Nineteenth Amendment half a century later.

It is true, of course, that the position of women in America has improved markedly in recent decades. Nevertheless, it can hardly be doubted that, in part because of the high visibility of the sex characteristic, women still face pervasive, although at times more subtle, discrimination in our educational institutions, on the job market and, perhaps most conspicuously, in the political arena.[17] See generally, K. Amundsen, The Silenced Majority: Women and American Democracy (1971); The President's Task Force on Women's Rights and Responsibilities, A Matter of Simple Justice (1970).

Moreover, since sex, like race and national origin, is an immutable characteristic determined solely by the accident of birth, the imposition of special disabilities upon the members of a particular sex because of their sex would seem to violate "the basic concept of our system that legal burdens should bear some relationship to individual responsibility . . . ." Weber v. Aetna Casualty & Surety Co., 406 U.S. 164, 175 (1972). And what differentiates sex from such nonsuspect statuses as intelligence or physical disability, and aligns it with the recognized suspect criteria, is that the sex characteristic frequently bears no relation to ability to perform or contribute to society. As a result, statutory distinctions between the sexes often have the effect of invidiously relegating the entire class of females to inferior legal status without regard to the actual capabilities of its individual members.

We might also note that, over the past decade, Congress has itself manifested an increasing sensitivity to sex-based classifications. In Tit. VII of the Civil Rights Act of 1964, for example, Congress expressly declared that no employer, labor union, or other organization subject to the provisions of the Act shall discriminate against any individual on the basis of "race, color, religion, *sex*, or national origin." Similarly, the Equal Pay Act of 1963 provides that no employer covered by the Act "shall discriminate . . . between employees on the basis of sex." And § 1 of the Equal Rights Amendment, passed by Congress on March 22, 1972, and submitted to the legislatures of the States for ratification, declares that "[e]quality of rights under the law shall not be denied or abridged by the United States or by any State on account of sex." Thus, Congress has itself concluded that classifications based upon sex are inherently

---

[17] It is true, of course, that when viewed in the abstract, women do not constitute a small and powerless minority. Nevertheless, in part because of past discrimination, women are vastly underrepresented in this Nation's decisionmaking councils. There has never been a female President, nor a female member of this Court. Not a single woman presently sits in the United States Senate, and only 14 women hold seats in the House of Representatives. And, as appellants point out, this underrepresentation is present throughout all levels of our State and Federal Government.

invidious, and this conclusion of a coequal branch of Government is not without significance to the question presently under consideration. . . .

With these considerations in mind, we can only conclude that classifications based upon sex, like classifications based upon race, alienage, or national origin, are inherently suspect, and must therefore be subjected to strict judicial scrutiny. Applying the analysis mandated by that stricter standard of review, it is clear that the statutory scheme now before us is constitutionally invalid.

III.

The sole basis of the classification established in the challenged statutes is the sex of the individuals involved. . . .

Moreover, the Government concedes that the differential treatment accorded men and women under these statutes serves no purpose other than mere "administrative convenience." In essence, the Government maintains that, as an empirical matter, wives in our society frequently are dependent upon their husbands, while husbands rarely are dependent upon their wives. Thus, the Government argues that Congress might reasonably have concluded that it would be both cheaper and easier simply conclusively to presume that wives of male members are financially dependent upon their husbands, while burdening female members with the task of establishing dependency in fact.[22]

The Government offers no concrete evidence, however, tending to support its view that such differential treatment in fact saves the Government any money. In order to satisfy the demands of strict judicial scrutiny, the Government must demonstrate, for example, that it is actually cheaper to grant increased benefits with respect to *all* male members, than it is to determine which male members are in fact entitled to such benefits and to grant increased benefits only to those members whose wives actually meet the dependency requirement. Here, however, there is substantial evidence that, if put to the test, many of the wives of male members would fail to qualify for benefits. And in light of the fact that the dependency determination with respect to the husbands of female members is presently made solely on the basis of affidavits rather than through the more costly hearing process, the Government's explanation of the statutory scheme is, to say the least, questionable.

In any case, our prior decisions make clear that, although efficacious administration of governmental programs is not without some importance, "the Constitution recognizes higher values than speed and efficiency." Stanley v. Illinois, 405 U.S. 645, 656 (1972). And when we enter the realm of "strict judicial scrutiny," there can be no doubt that "administrative convenience" is not a shibboleth, the mere recitation of which dictates constitutionality. See Shapiro v. Thompson, 394 U.S. 618 (1969); Carrington v. Rash, 380 U.S. 89 (1965). On the contrary, any statutory scheme which draws a sharp line between the sexes, *solely* for the purpose of achieving administrative convenience, necessarily commands "dissimilar treatment for men and women who are . . . similarly situated," and therefore involves the "very kind of arbitrary legislative choice forbidden by the [Constitution] . . . ." Reed v. Reed, 404 U.S., supra, at 77, 76. We therefore conclude that, by according differential treatment to male and female members of the uniformed services for the sole purpose of achieving administrative convenience, the challenged statutes violate the Due Process Clause of the Fifth Amendment insofar as they require a female member to prove the dependency of her husband.

Reversed.

---

[22] It should be noted that these statutes are not in any sense designed to rectify the effects of past discrimination against women. . . . On the contrary, these statutes seize upon a group—women— who have historically suffered discrimination in employment, and rely on the effects of this past discrimination as a justification for heaping on additional economic disadvantages . . . .

Mr. Justice Stewart concurs in the judgment, agreeing that the statutes before us work an invidious discrimination in violation of the Constitution. Reed v. Reed, 404 U.S. 71.

Mr. Justice Rehnquist dissents for the reasons stated by Judge Rives in his opinion for the District Court, Frontiero v. Laird, 341 F.Supp. 201 (1972).

Mr. Justice Powell, with whom The Chief Justice and Mr. Justice Blackmun join, concurring in the judgment.

I agree that the challenged statutes constitute an unconstitutional discrimination against service women in violation of the Due Process Clause of the Fifth Amendment, but I cannot join the opinion of Mr. Justice Brennan, which would hold that all classifications based upon sex, "like classifications based upon race, alienage, and national origin," are "inherently suspect and must therefore be subjected to close judicial scrutiny." Supra, at 1768. It is unnecessary for the Court in this case to characterize sex as a suspect classification, with all of the far-reaching implications of such a holding. Reed v. Reed, 404 U.S. 71 (1971), which abundantly supports our decision today, did not add sex to the narrowly limited group of classifications which are inherently suspect. In my view, we can and should decide this case on the authority of *Reed* and reserve for the future any expansion of its rationale.

There is another, and I find compelling, reason for deferring a general categorizing of sex classifications as invoking the strictest test of judicial scrutiny. The Equal Rights Amendment, which if adopted will resolve the substance of this precise question, has been approved by the Congress and submitted for ratification by the States. If this Amendment is duly adopted, it will represent the will of the people accomplished in the manner prescribed by the Constitution. By acting prematurely and unnecessarily, as I view it, the Court has assumed a decisional responsibility at the very time when state legislatures, functioning within the traditional democratic process, are debating the proposed Amendment. It seems to me that this reaching out to preempt by judicial action a major political decision which is currently in process of resolution does not reflect appropriate respect for duly prescribed legislative processes.

There are times when this Court, under our system, cannot avoid a constitutional decision on issues which normally should be resolved by the elected representatives of the people. But democratic institutions are weakened, and confidence in the restraint of the Court is impaired, when we appear unnecessarily to decide sensitive issues of broad social and political importance at the very time they are under consideration within the prescribed constitutional processes.

CRAIG v. BOREN

429 U.S. 190, 97 S.Ct. 451, 50 L.Ed.2d 397 (1976).

Mr. Justice Brennan delivered the opinion of the Court.

The interaction of two sections of an Oklahoma statute, 37 Okla.Stat. §§ 241 and 245, prohibits the sale of "nonintoxicating" 3.2% beer to males under the age of 21 and to females under the age of 18. The question to be decided is whether such a gender-based differential constitutes a denial to males 18–20 years of age of the Equal Protection of the Laws in violation of the Fourteenth Amendment.

This action was brought in the District Court for the Western District of Oklahoma on December 20, 1972, by appellant Craig, a male then between 18 and 21 years of age, and by appellant Whitener, a licensed vendor of 3.2% beer. The complaint sought declaratory and injunctive relief against enforcement of the gender-based differential on the ground that it constituted invidious discrimination against males 18–20 years of age. A three-judge court convened under 28 U.S.C. § 2281 sustained the constitutionality of the statutory differential and dismissed the action. 399 F.Supp. 1304 (1975). We noted probable jurisdiction of appellants' appeal, 423 U.S. 1947 (1976). We reverse.

. . .

II.

A.

Analysis may appropriately begin with the reminder that Reed v. Reed, supra, emphasized that statutory classifications that distinguish between males and females are "subject to scrutiny under the Equal Protection Clause." 404 U.S., at 75. To withstand constitutional challenge, previous cases establish that classifications by gender must serve important governmental objectives and must be substantially related to achievement of those objectives. Thus, in Reed, the objectives of "reducing the workload on probate courts," id., at 76, and "avoiding intra-family controversy," id., at 77, were deemed of insufficient importance to sustain use of an overt gender criterion in the appointment of intestate administrators. Decisions following Reed similarly have rejected administrative ease and convenience as sufficiently important objectives to justify gender-based classifications. See, e.g., Stanley v. Illinois, 405 U.S. 645, 656 (1972); Frontiero v. Richardson, 411 U.S. 677, 690 (1973); cf. Schlesinger v. Ballard, 419 U.S. 498, 506–507 (1975). And only two Terms ago Stanton v. Stanton, 421 U.S. 7 (1975), expressly stating that Reed v. Reed was "controlling," id., at 13, held that Reed required invalidation of a Utah differential age-of-majority statute, notwithstanding the statute's coincidence with and furtherance of the State's purpose of fostering "old notions" of role-typing and preparing boys for their expected performance in the economic and political worlds. Id., at 14–15.[6]

Reed v. Reed has also provided the underpinning for decisions that have invalidated statutes employing gender as an inaccurate proxy for other, more germane bases of classification. Hence, "archaic and overbroad" generalizations, Schlesinger v. Ballard, supra, 419 U.S., at 508, concerning the financial position of servicewomen, Frontiero v. Richardson, supra, 411 U.S., at 689 n. 3, and working women, Weinberger v. Wiesenfeld, 420 U.S. 636, 643 (1975), could not justify use of a gender line in determining eligibility for certain governmental entitlements. Similarly, increasingly outdated misconceptions concerning the role of females in the home rather than in the "marketplace and world of ideas" were rejected as loose-fitting characterizations incapable of supporting state statutory schemes that were premised upon their accuracy. Stanton v. Stanton, supra; Taylor v. Louisiana, 419 U.S. 522, 535 n. 17 (1975). In light of the weak congruence between gender and the characteristic or trait that gender purported to represent, it was necessary that the legislatures choose either to realign their substantive laws in a gender-neutral fashion, or to adopt procedures for identifying those instances where the sex-centered generalization actually comported to fact. See, e.g., Stanley v. Illinois, supra, 405 U.S., at 658; cf. Cleveland Board of Educ. v. LaFleur, 414 U.S. 632, 650 (1974).

In this case, too, "Reed we feel, is controlling . . . ," Stanton v. Stanton, supra, 421 U.S., at 13. We turn then to the question whether, under Reed, the difference between males and females with respect to the purchase of 3.2% beer

[6] Kahn v. Shevin, 416 U.S. 351 (1974) and Schlesinger v. Ballard, 419 U.S. 498 (1975), upholding the use of gender-based classifications, rested upon the Court's perception of the laudatory purposes of those laws as remedying disadvantageous conditions suffered by women in economic and military life. See 416 U.S., at 353–354; 419 U.S., at 508. Needless to say, in this case Oklahoma does not suggest that the age-sex differential was enacted to ensure the availability of 3.2% beer for women as compensation for previous deprivations.

warrants the differential in age drawn by the Oklahoma statute. We conclude that it does not.

B.

The District Court recognized that Reed v. Reed was controlling. In applying the teachings of that case, the Court found the requisite important governmental objective in the traffic-safety goal preferred by the Oklahoma Attorney General. It then concluded that the statistics introduced by the appellees established that the gender-based distinction was substantially related to achievement of that goal.

C.

We accept for purposes of discussion the District Court's identification of the objective underlying §§ 241 and 245 as the enhancement of traffic safety.[7] Clearly, the protection of public health and safety represents an important function of state and local governments. However, appellees' statistics in our view cannot support the conclusion that the gender-based distinction closely serves to achieve that objective and therefore the distinction cannot under *Reed* withstand equal protection challenge.

The appellees introduced a variety of statistical surveys. First, an analysis of arrest statistics for 1973 demonstrated that 18–20-year-old male arrests for "driving under the influence" and "drunkenness" substantially exceeded female arrests for that same age period.[8] Similarly, youths aged 17–21 were found to be overrepresented among those killed or injured in traffic accidents, with males again numerically exceeding females in this regard.[9] Third, a random roadside survey in Oklahoma City revealed that young males were more inclined to drive and drink beer than were their female counterparts.[10] Fourth, Federal Bureau of Investigation nationwide statistics exhibited a notable increase in arrests for "driving under the influence."[11] Finally, statistical evidence gathered in other jurisdictions, particularly Minnesota and Michigan, was offered to corroborate Oklahoma's experience by indicating the pervasiveness of youthful participation in motor vehicle accidents following the imbibing of alcohol. Conceding that "the case is not free from doubt," 399 F.Supp., at 1314, the District Court nonetheless concluded that this statistical showing substantiated "a rational basis

---

[7] That this was the true purpose is not at all self-evident. The purpose is not apparent from the face of the statute and the Oklahoma Legislature does not preserve statutory history materials capable of clarifying the objectives served by its legislative enactments. The District Court acknowledged the nonexistence of materials necessary "to reveal what the actual purpose of the legislature was," but concluded that "we feel it apparent that a major purpose of the legislature was to promote the safety of the young persons affected and the public generally." 399 F.Supp., at 1311 n. 6. Similarly, the attorney for Oklahoma, while proposing traffic safety as a legitimate rationale for the 3.2% beer law, candidly acknowledged at oral argument that he is unable to assert that traffic safety is "indeed the reason" for the gender line contained in § 245. For this appeal we find adequate the appellee's representation of legislative purpose, leaving for another day consideration of whether the statement of the State's Assistant Attorney General should suffice to inform this Court of the legislature's objectives, or whether the Court must determine if the litigant simply is selecting a convenient, but false, *post-hoc* rationalization.

[8] The disparities in 18–20-year-old male-female arrests were substantial for both categories of offenses: 427 versus 24 for driving under the influence of alcohol and 966 versus 102 for drunkenness. Even if we assume that a legislature may rely on such arrest data in some situations, these figures do not offer support for a differential age line, for the disproportionate arrests of males persisted at older ages; indeed, in the case of arrests for drunkenness, the figures for all ages indicated "even more male involvement in such arrests at later ages." 399 F.Supp., at 1309. See also n. 14, infra.

[9] This survey drew no correlation between the accident figures for any age group and levels of intoxication found in those killed or injured.

[10] For an analysis of the results of this exhibit, see n. 16, infra.

[11] The FBI made no attempt to relate these arrest figures either to beer drinking or to an 18–21 age differential, but rather found that male arrests for all ages exceeded 90% of the total.

for the legislative judgment underlying the challenged classification." Id., at 1307.

Even were this statistical evidence accepted as accurate, it nevertheless offers only a weak answer to the equal protection question presented here. The most focused and relevant of the statistical surveys, arrests of 18–20-year-olds for alcohol-related driving offenses, exemplifies the ultimate unpersuasiveness of this evidentiary record. Viewed in terms of the correlation between sex and the actual activity that Oklahoma seeks to regulate—driving while under the influence of alcohol—the statistics broadly establish that .18% of females and 2% of males in that age group were arrested for that offense. While such a disparity is not trivial in a statistical sense, it hardly can form the basis for employment of a gender line as a classifying device. Certainly if maleness is to serve as a proxy for drinking and driving a correlation of 2% must be considered an unduly tenuous "fit." Indeed, prior cases have consistently rejected the use of sex as a decisionmaking factor even though the statutes in question certainly rested on far more predictive empirical relationships than this.[13]

Moreover, the statistics exhibit a variety of other shortcomings that seriously impugn their value to equal protection analysis. Setting aside the obvious methodological problems,[14] the surveys do not adequately justify the salient features of Oklahoma's gender-based traffic-safety law. None purports to measure the use and dangerousness of 3.2% beer as opposed to alcohol generally, a detail that is of particular importance since, in light of its low alcohol level, Oklahoma apparently considers the 3.2% beverage to be "non-intoxicating." 37 Okla.Stat. § 163.1 (1971); see State ex rel. Springer v. Bliss, 199 Okla. 198, 185 P.2d 220 (1947). Moreover, many of the studies, while graphically documenting the unfortunate increase in driving while under the influence of alcohol, make no effort to relate their findings to age-sex differentials as involved here. Indeed, the only survey that explicitly centered its attention upon young drivers and their use of beer—albeit apparently not of the diluted 3.2% variety—reached results that hardly can be viewed as impressive in justifying either a gender or age classification.[16]

[13] For example, we can conjecture that in *Reed,* Idaho's apparent premise that women lacked experience in formal business matters (particularly compared to men) would have proved to be accurate in substantially more than 2% of all cases. And in both *Frontiero* and *Wiesenfeld,* we expressly found the government's empirical defense of mandatory dependency tests for men but not women to be unsatisfactory, even though we recognized that husbands still are far less likely to be dependent on their wives than vice versa. See, e.g., 411 U.S., at 688–690.

[14] The very social stereotypes that find reflection in age differential laws, see Stanton v. Stanton, supra, 421 U.S., at 114–15, are likely substantially to distort the accuracy of these comparative statistics. Hence "reckless" young men who drink and drive are transformed into arrest statistics, whereas their female counterparts are chivalrously escorted home. See, e.g., W. Reckless & B. Kay, The Female Offender 4, 7, 13, 16–17 (Report to Pres. Comm'n on Law Enforcement & Admin. of Justice, 1967). Moreover, the Oklahoma surveys, gathered under a regime where the age-differential law in question has been in effect, are lacking in controls necessary for appraisal of the actual effectiveness of the male 3.2% beer prohibition. In this regard, the disproportionately high arrest statistics for young males—and, indeed, the growing alcohol-related arrest figures for all ages and sexes—simply may be taken to document the relative futility of controlling driving behavior by the 3.2 beer statute and like legislation, although we obviously have no means of estimating how many individuals, if any, actually were prevented from drinking by these laws.

[16] The random roadside survey of drivers conducted in Oklahoma City during August of 1972 found that 78% of drivers under 20 were male. Turning to an evaluation of their drinking habits and factoring out nondrinkers, 84% of the males versus 77% of the females expressed a preference for beer. Further 16.5% of the men and 11.4% of the women had consumed some alcoholic beverage within two hours of the interview. Finally, a blood alcohol concentration greater than .1% was discovered in 14.6% of the males compared to 11.5% of the females. "The 1973 figures, although they contain some variations, reflect essentially the same pattern." 399 F.Supp., at 1309. Plainly these statistical disparities between the sexes are not substantial. Moreover, when the 18–20 age boundaries are lifted and all drivers analyzed, the 1972 roadside survey indicates that male drinking

There is no reason to belabor this line of analysis. It is unrealistic to expect either members of the judiciary or state officials to be well versed in the rigors of experimental or statistical technique. But this merely illustrates that proving broad sociological propositions by statistics is a dubious business, and one that inevitably is in tension with the normative philosophy that underlies the Equal Protection Clause. Suffice to say that the showing offered by the appellees does not satisfy us that sex represents a legitimate, accurate proxy for the regulation of drinking and driving. In fact, when it is further recognized that Oklahoma's statute prohibits only the selling of 3.2% beer to young males and not their drinking the beverage once acquired (even after purchase by their 18–20-year-old female companions), the relationship between gender and traffic safety becomes far too tenuous to satisfy *Reed's* requirement that the gender-based difference be substantially related to achievement of the statutory objective.

We hold, therefore, that under *Reed,* Oklahoma's 3.2% beer statute invidiously discriminates against males 18–20 years of age.

D.

Appellees argue, however, that §§ 241 and 245 enforce state policies concerning the sale and distribution of alcohol and by force of the Twenty-first Amendment should therefore be held to withstand the equal protection challenge. The District Court's response to this contention is unclear. . . . The Twenty-first Amendment repealed the Eighteenth Amendment in 1933. . . . This Court's decisions since have confirmed that the Amendment primarily created an exception to the normal operation of the Commerce Clause. See, e.g., Hostetter v. Idlewild Bon Voyage Liquor Corp., 377 U.S. 324, 330 (1964); . . . .

Once passing beyond consideration of the Commerce Clause, the relevance of the Twenty-first Amendment to other constitutional provisions becomes increasingly doubtful. . . . Cases involving individual rights protected by the Due Process Clause have been treated in sharp contrast. . . .

Following this approach, both federal and state courts uniformly have declared the unconstitutionality of gender lines that restrain the activities of customers of state-regulated liquor establishments irrespective of the operation of the Twenty-first Amendment. . . . Even when state officials have posited sociological or empirical justifications for these gender-based differentiations, the courts have struck down discriminations aimed at an entire class under the guise of alcohol regulation. In fact, social science studies that have uncovered quantifiable differences in drinking tendencies dividing along both racial and ethnic lines strongly suggest the need for application of the Equal Protection Clause in preventing discriminatory treatment that almost certainly would be perceived as invidious.[22] In sum, the principles embodied in the Equal Protec-

rose slightly whereas female exposure to alcohol remained relatively constant. Again, in 1973, the survey established that "compared to all drivers interviewed, . . . the under-20 age group generally showed a lower involvement with alcohol in terms of having drunk within the past two hours or having a significant BAC (blood alcohol content)." Id., at 1309. In sum, this survey provides little support for a gender line among teenagers and actually runs counter to the imposition of drinking restrictions based upon age.

[22] Thus, if statistics were to govern the permissibility of state alcohol regulation without regard to the Equal Protection Clause as a limiting principle, it might follow that States could freely favor Jews and Italian Catholics at the expense of all other Americans, since available studies regularly demonstrate that the former two groups exhibit the lowest rates of problem drinking. . . .

In the past, some States have acted upon their notions of the drinking propensities of entire groups in fashioning their alcohol policies. The most typical recipient of this treatment has been the American Indian; indeed, several States established criminal sanctions for the sale of alcohol to an Indian or "half or quarter breed Indian." See, e.g., Fla.Stat.Ann. § 569.07 (1962) (repealed in 1972); Iowa Code Ann. § 732.5 (1950) (repealed in 1967); Minn.Stat. § 340.82 (1947) (repealed in 1969); Neb.Rev.Stat. 53–181 (1944) (repealed in 1955); Utah Code Ann. § 76–34–1 (1953) (repealed in tion Clause are not to be rendered inapplicable by statistically measured but loose-fitting generalities concerning the drinking tendencies of aggregate groups. We thus hold that the operation of the Twenty-first Amendment does not alter the application of equal protection standards that otherwise govern this case.

We conclude that the gender-based differential contained in 37 Okla.Stat. § 245 constitutes a denial of the Equal Protection of the Laws to males aged 18–20 [23] and reverse the judgment of the District Court.[24]

Mr. Justice Stewart, concurring.

.   .   .

Mr. Justice Blackmun, concurring.

I join the Court's opinion except Part II–D thereof. I agree, however, that the Twenty-first Amendment does not save the challenged Oklahoma statute.

Mr. Justice Powell, concurring.

I join the opinion of the Court as I am in general agreement with it. I do have reservations as to some of the discussion concerning the appropriate standard for equal protection analysis and the relevance of the statistical evidence. Accordingly, I add this concurring statement.

With respect to the equal protection standard, I agree that Reed v. Reed, 404 U.S. 71 (1971), is the most relevant precedent. But I find it unnecessary, in deciding this case, to read that decision as broadly as some of the Court's language may imply. *Reed* and subsequent cases involving gender-based classifications make clear that the Court subjects such classifications to a more critical examination than is normally applied when "fundamental" constitutional rights and "suspect classes" are not present.*

.   .   .

Mr. Justice Stevens, concurring.

There is only one Equal Protection Clause. It requires every State to govern impartially. It does not direct the courts to apply one standard of review in some cases and a different standard in other cases. Whatever criticism

---

1955). Other statutes and constitutional provisions proscribed the introduction of alcoholic beverages onto Indian reservations. See, e.g., C. 310, § 2, 36 Stat. 558 (1910); Ariz.Ann.Const. Art. XX(3); N.M.Stat.Ann.Const. Art. XXI, § 8; Okla.Stat.Ann.Const. Art. I, § 7. While Indian-oriented provisions were the most common, state alcohol beverage prohibitions also have been directed at other groups, notably German, Italian, and Catholic immigrants. See, e.g., J. Higham, Strangers In the Land 25, 267–268, 295 (1975). The repeal of most of these laws signals society's perception of the unfairness and questionable constitutionality of singling out groups to bear the brunt of alcohol regulation.

[23] Insofar as Goesaert v. Cleary, 335 U.S. 464 (1948), may be inconsistent, that decision is disapproved.   .   .   .

[24] As noted in Stanton v. Stanton, supra, 421 U.S., at 17–18, the Oklahoma Legislature is free to redefine any cutoff age for the purchase and sale of 3.2 beer that it may choose, provided that the redefinition operates in a gender-neutral fashion.

* As is evident from our opinions, the Court has had difficulty in agreeing upon a standard of equal protection analysis that can be applied consistently to the wide variety of legislative classifications. There are valid reasons for dissatisfaction with the "two-tier" approach that has been prominent in the Court's decisions in the past decade. Although viewed by many as a result-oriented substitute for more critical analysis, that approach—with its narrowly limited "upper-tier"—now has substantial precedential support. As has been true of *Reed* and its progeny, our decision today will be viewed by some as a "middle-tier" approach. While I would not endorse that characterization and would not welcome a further subdividing of equal protection analysis, candor compels the recognition that the relatively deferential "rational basis" standard of review normally applied takes on a sharper focus when we address a gender-based classification. So much is clear from our recent cases. For thoughtful discussions of equal protection analysis, see, e.g., Gunther, The Supreme Court, 1971 Term—Foreword: In Search of Evolving Doctrine on a Changing Court: A Model for Newer Equal Protection, 86 Harv.L.Rev. 1 (1972); Wilkinson, The Supreme Court, the Equal Protection Clause, and the Three Faces of Constitutional Equality, 61 Va.L.Rev. 945 (1975).

may be levelled at a judicial opinion implying that there are at least three such standards applies with the same force to a double standard.

I am inclined to believe that what has become known as the two-tiered analysis of equal protection claims does not describe a completely logical method of deciding cases, but rather is a method the Court has employed to explain decisions that actually apply a single standard in a reasonably consistent fashion.   I also suspect that a careful explanation of the reasons motivating particular decisions may contribute more to an identification of that standard than an attempt to articulate it in all-encompassing terms.   It may therefore be appropriate for me to state the principal reasons which persuaded me to join the Court's opinion.

In this case, the classification is not as obnoxious as some the Court has condemned, nor as inoffensive as some the Court has accepted.   It is objectionable because it is based on an accident of birth, because it is a mere remnant of the now almost universally rejected tradition of discriminating against males in this age bracket, and because, to the extent it reflects any physical difference between males and females, it is actually perverse.   The question then is whether the traffic safety justification put forward by the State is sufficient to make an otherwise offensive classification acceptable.

The classification is not totally irrational.   For the evidence does indicate that there are more males than females in this age bracket who drive and also more who drink.   Nevertheless, there are several reasons why I regard the justification as unacceptable.   It is difficult to believe that the statute was actually intended to cope with the problem of traffic safety, since it has only a minimal effect on access to a not-very-intoxicating beverage and does not prohibit its consumption.   Moreover, the empirical data submitted by the State accentuates the unfairness of treating all 18–21-year-old males as inferior to their female counterparts.   The legislation imposes a restraint on one hundred percent of the males in the class allegedly because about 2% of them have probably violated one or more laws relating to the consumption of alcoholic beverages.   It is unlikely that this law will have a significant deterrent effect either on that 2% or on the law-abiding 98%.   But even assuming some such slight benefit, it does not seem to me that an insult to all of the young men of the State can be justified by visiting the sins of the 2% on the 98%.

Mr. Chief Justice Burger, dissenting.

I am in general agreement with Mr. Justice Rehnquist's dissent, but even at the risk of compounding the obvious confusion created by those voting to reverse the District Court, I will add a few words.

.   .   .

Though today's decision does not go so far as to make gender-based classifications "suspect," it makes gender a disfavored classification.   Without an independent constitutional basis supporting the right asserted or disfavoring the classification adopted, I can justify no substantive constitutional protection other than the normal McGowan v. Maryland, 366 U.S., at 425–426, protection afforded by the Equal Protection Clause.

.   .   .

Mr. Justice Rehnquist, dissenting.

The Court's disposition of this case is objectionable on two grounds.   First is its conclusion that *men* challenging a gender-based statute which treats them less favorably than women may invoke a more stringent standard of judicial review than pertains to most other types of classifications.   Second is the Court's enunciation of this standard, without citation to any source, as being that "classifications by gender must serve *important* governmental objectives and must be *substantially* related to achievement of those objectives."   Ante at 197 (emphasis added). The only redeeming feature of the Court's opinion, to my mind, is that it apparently signals a retreat by those who joined the plurality opinion in Frontiero v. Richardson, 411 U.S. 677 (1973), from their view that sex is a "suspect" classification for purposes of equal protection analysis. I think the Oklahoma statute challenged here need pass only the "rational basis" equal protection analysis expounded in cases such as McGowan v. Maryland, 366 U.S. 420 (1961), and Williamson v. Lee Optical Co., 348 U.S. 483 (1955), and I believe that it is constitutional under that analysis.

. . . .

CLASSIFICATIONS ADVANTAGING FEMALES

The Court in Craig v. Boren (in footnote 6) refers to cases such as Kahn v. Shevin, 416 U.S. 351 (1974) upholding classifications designed to remedy past discrimination against women. That case and others will be discussed in Subsection H, infra, dealing with "benign" discrimination in cases involving gender and in cases involving race.

WHAT CONSTITUTES DISCRIMINATION BASED ON GENDER?

In Geduldig v. Aiello, 417 U.S. 484 (1974) the Court rejected a challenge to the California disability insurance program which excluded from its coverage disabilities resulting from normal pregnancy. Justice Stewart, speaking for the Court, said, in part:

"The State has a legitimate interest in maintaining the self-supporting nature of its insurance program. Similarly, it has an interest in distributing the available resources in such a way as to keep benefit payments at an adequate level for disabilities that are covered, rather than to cover all disabilities inadequately. Finally, California has a legitimate concern in maintaining the contribution rate at a level that will not unduly burden participating employees, particularly low-income employees who may be most in need of the disability insurance.

"These policies provide an objective and wholly non-invidious basis for the State's decision not to create a more comprehensive insurance program than it has. There is no evidence in the record that the selection of the risks insured by the program worked to discriminate against any definable group or class in terms of the aggregate risk protection derived by that group or class from the program.[20] There is no risk from which men are protected

---

[20] The dissenting opinion to the contrary, this case is thus a far cry from cases like Reed v. Reed, 404 U.S. 71, and Frontiero v. Richardson, 411 U.S. 677, involving discrimination based upon gender as such. The California insurance program does not exclude anyone from benefit eligibility because of gender but merely removes one physical condition—pregnancy—from the list of compensable disabilities. While it is true that only women can become pregnant, it does not follow that every legislative classification concerning pregnancy is a sex-based classification like those considered in *Reed,* supra, and *Frontiero,* supra. Normal pregnancy is an objectively identifiable physical condition with unique characteristics. Absent a showing that distinctions involving pregnancy are mere pretexts designed to effect an invidious discrimination against the members of one sex or the other, lawmakers are constitutionally free to include or exclude pregnancy from the coverage of legislation such as this on any reasonable basis, just as with respect to any other physical condition.

The lack of identity between the excluded disability and gender as such under this insurance program becomes clear upon the most cursory analysis. The program divides potential recipients into two groups—pregnant women and nonpregnant persons. While the first group is exclusively female, the second includes members of both sexes. The fiscal and actuarial benefits of the program thus accrue to members of both sexes.

and women are not. Likewise, there is no risk from which women are protected and men are not.[21]

"The appellee simply contends that, although she has received insurance protection equivalent to that provided all other participating employees, she has suffered discrimination because she encountered a risk that was outside the program's protection. For the reasons we have stated, we hold that this contention is not a valid one under the Equal Protection Clause of the Fourteenth Amendment."

Justices Brennan, Douglas, and Marshall dissented on the ground that the *Reed* and *Frontiero* cases "mandate a stricter standard of scrutiny which the State's classification fails to satisfy."

In General Elec. Co. v. Gilbert, 429 U.S. 125 (1976) the Court had before it a challenge under Title VII of the Civil Rights Act of 1964 to the disability plan of a private company which excluded disabilities arising from pregnancy. The Court reaffirmed its holding in Geduldig v. Aiello that such a classification does not involve discrimination based on sex and held unwarranted by the statute an EEOC guideline stating that disabilities due to pregnancy should be included in such plans. The Court noted that the exclusion would be invalid if "it were in fact a subterfuge to accomplish a forbidden discrimination" but held that no such showing had been made.

In Nashville Gas Co. v. Satty, 434 U.S. 136 (1977) the Court had before it a challenge under Title VII of the Civil Rights Act of 1964 to the sick pay and seniority policies of a private company. The company required pregnant employees to take a leave of absence without pay, although sick leave pay was given to those disabled by nonoccupational disease or injury. Accumulated seniority was denied to female employees returning to work after a pregnancy leave though it was granted following sick leave for other causes.

The Court upheld the policy of not granting sick leave pay to pregnant employees as "legally indistinguishable from the disability insurance plan upheld in [General Electric Co. v.] Gilbert." However, the Court held invalid the provision denying seniority to female employees returning after pregnancy leave—a policy which in the instant case meant that the plaintiff was able to get only temporary employment on her return from leave. The Court distinguished *Gilbert* by saying that in that case no evidence was presented to show that men as a group received more benefits from the disability program than did women as a group. "Here, by comparison, petitioner has not merely refused to extend to women a benefit that men cannot and do not receive, but has imposed on women a substantial burden that men need not suffer. The distinction between benefits and burdens is more than one of semantics. We held in Gilbert that [the statute] did not require that greater economic benefits be paid to one sex or the other 'because of their differing roles in "the scheme of human existence,"' but that holding does not allow us to read [the statute] to permit an employer to burden female employees in such a way as to deprive them of employment opportunities because of their different roles."[1]

---

[21] Indeed, the appellant submitted to the District Court data that indicated that both the annual claim rate and the annual claim cost are greater for women than for men. As the District Court acknowledged, "women contribute 28 per cent of the total disability insurance fund and receive back about 38 per cent of the fund in benefits." 359 F.Supp., at 800. Several *amici curiae* have represented to the Court that they have had a similar experience under private disability insurance programs.

[1] In 1978 Congress amended Title VII of the Civil Rights Act of 1964 to provide: "The terms 'because of sex' or 'on the basis of sex' include, but are not limited to, because of or on the basis of pregnancy, childbirth, or related medical conditions; and women affected by pregnancy, childbirth, or related medical conditions shall be treated the same for all employment-related purposes, including receipt of benefits under fringe benefit programs, as other persons not so affected but similar in their ability or inability to work, ..." 42 U.S.C. § 2000e(k). The amendment goes on to provide that

With these cases involving the question whether classifications based on pregnancy shall be treated as gender classifications for the purpose of determining the appropriate standard of review, compare Mathews v. Lucas, 427 U.S. 495 (1976). In that case the Social Security Act provided a presumption of dependency on a deceased father for all legitimate children and for some (but not all) illegitimate children. The Court said: "That the statutory classifications challenged here discriminate among illegitimate children does not mean, of course, that they are not also properly described as discriminating between legitimate and illegitimate children."

A separate problem arises when a statute which on its face does not make a gender classification is challenged on the ground that it has a disparate impact on one sex. See, e.g., Personnel Adm'r of Massachusetts v. Feeney, 442 U.S. 256 (1979) in which a law providing job preferences to veterans was challenged by a showing that 98% of veterans were male. *Feeney* will be considered along with similar cases involving race in Section 7 of this chapter dealing with the requirement of showing a discriminatory purpose.

CITY OF LOS ANGELES, DEPARTMENT OF WATER AND POWER v. MANHART

435 U.S. 702, 98 S.Ct. 1370, 55 L.Ed.2d 657 (1978).

Mr. Justice Stevens delivered the opinion of the Court.

As a class, women live longer than men. For this reason, the Los Angeles Department of Water and Power required its female employees to make larger contributions to its pension fund than its male employees. We granted certiorari to decide whether this practice discriminated against individual female employees because of their sex in violation of § 703(a)(1) of the Civil Rights Act of 1964, as amended.

For many years the Department has administered retirement, disability, and death-benefit programs for its employees. Upon retirement each employee is eligible for a monthly retirement benefit computed as a fraction of his or her salary multiplied by years of service. The monthly benefits for men and women of the same age, seniority, and salary are equal. Benefits are funded entirely by contributions from the employees and the Department, augmented by the income earned on those contributions. No private insurance company is involved in the administration or payment of benefits.

Based on a study of mortality tables and its own experience, the Department determined that its 2,000 female employees, on the average, will live a few years longer than its 10,000 male employees. The cost of a pension for the average retired female is greater than for the average male retiree because more monthly payments must be made to the average woman. The Department therefore required female employees to make monthly contributions to the fund which were 14.84% higher than the contributions required of comparable male employees. Because employee contributions were withheld from paychecks, a female employee took home less pay than a male employee earning the same salary.

Since the effective date of the Equal Employment Opportunity Act of 1972, the Department has been an employer within the meaning of Title VII of the Civil Rights Act of 1964. See 42 U.S.C. § 2000e (1970 ed. Supp. V). In

an employer need not pay health insurance benefits for an abortion, except where the life of the mother would be endangered or where medical complications have arisen from an abortion.

For an application of this statutory change see Newport News Shipbuilding and Dry Dock Co. v. EEOC, 103 S.Ct. 2622 (1983). The Court held invalid a health plan which gave lesser benefits for pregnancy-related conditions to spouses of male employees than it gave to female employees.

1973, respondents brought this suit in the United States District Court for the Central District of California on behalf of a class of women employed or formerly employed by the Department. They prayed for an injunction and restitution of excess contributions.

. . .

There are both real and fictional differences between women and men. It is true that the average man is taller than the average woman; it is not true that the average woman driver is more accident prone than the average man. Before the Civil Rights Act of 1964 was enacted, an employer could fashion his personnel policies on the basis of assumptions about the differences between men and women, whether or not the assumptions were valid.

It is now well recognized that employment decisions cannot be predicated on mere "stereotyped" impressions about the characteristics of males or females. Myths and purely habitual assumptions about a woman's inability to perform certain kinds of work are no longer acceptable reasons for refusing to employ qualified individuals, or for paying them less. This case does not, however, involve a fictional difference between men and women. It involves a generalization that the parties accept as unquestionably true: Women, as a class, do live longer than men. The Department treated its women employees differently from its men employees because the two classes are in fact different. It is equally true, however, that all individuals in the respective classes do not share the characteristic that differentiates the average class representatives. Many women do not live as long as the average man and many men outlive the average woman. The question, therefore, is whether the existence or nonexistence of "discrimination" is to be determined by comparison of class characteristics or individual characteristics. A "stereotyped" answer to that question may not be the same as the answer that the language and purpose of the statute command.

The statute makes it unlawful "to discriminate against any *individual* with respect to his compensation, terms, conditions, or privileges of employment, because of such *individual's* race, color, religion, sex, or national origin." 42 U.S.C. § 2000e–2(a)(1) [42 USCS § 2000e–2(a)(1)] (emphasis added). The statute's focus on the individual is unambiguous. It precludes treatment of individuals as simply components of a racial, religious, sexual, or national class. If height is required for a job, a tall woman may not be refused employment merely because, on the average, women are too short. Even a true generalization about the class is an insufficient reason for disqualifying an individual to whom the generalization does not apply.

That proposition is of critical importance in this case because there is no assurance that any individual woman working for the Department will actually fit the generalization on which the Department's policy is based. Many of those individuals will not live as long as the average man. While they were working, those individuals received smaller paychecks because of their sex, but they will receive no compensating advantage when they retire.

It is true, of course, that while contributions are being collected from the employees, the Department cannot know which individuals will predecease the average woman. Therefore, unless women as a class are assessed an extra charge, they will be subsidized, to some extent, by the class of male employees. It follows, according to the Department, that fairness to its class of male employees justifies the extra assessment against all of its female employees.

But the question of fairness to various classes affected by the statute is essentially a matter of policy for the legislature to address. Congress has decided that classifications based on sex, like those based on national origin or race, are unlawful. Actuarial studies could unquestionably identify differences in life expectancy based on race or national origin, as well as sex. But a statute which was designed to make race irrelevant in the employment market, see Griggs v. Duke Power Co., 401 U.S. 424, 436, could not reasonably be construed to permit a take-home pay differential based on a racial classification.

Even if the statutory language were less clear, the basic policy of the statute requires that we focus on fairness to individuals rather than fairness to classes. Practices which classify employees in terms of religion, race, or sex tend to preserve traditional assumptions about groups rather than thoughtful scrutiny of individuals. The generalization involved in this case illustrates the point. Separate mortality tables are easily interpreted as reflecting innate differences between the sexes; but a significant part of the longevity differential may be explained by the social fact that men are heavier smokers than women.

. . . .

In *Gilbert* the Court held that the exclusion of pregnancy from an employer's disability benefit plan did not constitute sex discrimination within the meaning of Title VII. Relying on the reasoning in Geduldig v. Aiello, 417 U.S. 484, the Court first held that the General Electric plan did not involve "discrimination based upon gender as such." The two groups of potential recipients which that case concerned were pregnant women and nonpregnant persons. "While the first group is exclusively female, the second includes members of both sexes." 429 U.S., at 135. In contrast each of the two groups of employees involved in this case is composed entirely and exclusively of members of the same sex. On its face, this plan discriminates on the basis of sex whereas the General Electric plan discriminated on the basis of a special physical disability.

In *Gilbert* the Court did note that the plan as actually administered had provided more favorable benefits to women as a class than to men as a class. This evidence supported the conclusion that not only had plaintiffs failed to establish a prima facie case by proving that the plan was discriminatory on its face, but they had also failed to prove any discriminatory effect.

In this case, however, the Department argues that the absence of a discriminatory effect on women as a class justifies an employment practice which, on its face, discriminated against individual employees because of their sex. But even if the Department's actuarial evidence is sufficient to prevent plaintiffs from establishing a prima facie case on the theory that the effect of the practice on women as a class was discriminatory, that evidence does not defeat the claim that the practice, on its face, discriminated against every individual woman employed by the Department.

. . .

[On the question whether the retirement system violated the statute, Chief Justice Burger and Justice Rehnquist dissented. Justice Brennan took no part in the decision. Justice Blackmun concurred only in the judgment on that issue, saying, in part:]

Given the decisions in *Geduldig* and *General Electric*—the one constitutional, the other statutory—the present case just cannot be an easy one for the Court. I might have thought that those decisions would have required the Court to conclude that the critical difference in the Department's pension payments was based on life expectancy, a nonstigmatizing factor that demonstrably differentiates females from males and that is not measurable on an individual basis. I might have thought, too, that there is nothing arbitrary, irrational, or "discriminatory" about recognizing the objective and accepted . . . disparity in female-male life expectancies in computing rates for retirement plans. Moreover, it is unrealistic to attempt to force, as the Court does, an individualized analysis upon what is basically an insurance context. Unlike the possibility, for example, of properly testing job applicants for qualifications before employment, there is simply no way to determine in advance when a particular employee will die.

. . .

The Court's distinction between the present case and *General Electric*—that the permitted classes there were "pregnant women and nonpregnant persons," both female and male, . . . seems to me to be just too easy. It is probably the only distinction that can be drawn. For me, it does not serve to distinguish the case on any principled basis. I therefore must conclude that today's decision cuts back on *General Electric,* and inferentially on *Geduldig,* the reasoning of which was adopted there, . . . and, indeed, makes the recognition of those cases as continuing precedent somewhat questionable. I do not say that this is necessarily bad. If that is what Congress has chosen to do by Title VII—as the Court today with such assurance asserts—so be it. I feel, however, that we should meet the posture of the earlier cases head-on and not by thin rationalization that seeks to distinguish but fails in its quest.

――――――

ARIZONA GOVERNING COMMITTEE v. NORRIS, 103 S.Ct. 3492 (1983). Arizona's pension system for state employees made equal contributions to pensions of male and female employees. Employees were given the option of receiving benefits from one of several companies, selected by the employer— all of which paid lower pensions to females, using gender-based mortality tables. The Court held that Arizona had violated the gender discrimination provisions of Title VII. "We have no hesitation in holding . . . that the classification of employees on the basis of sex is no more permissible at the pay-out stage of a retirement plan than at the pay-in stage." In *Manhart,* the Court had stated that its opinion did not forbid equal employer contributions to all employees, with each retiree allowed to "purchase the largest benefits which his or her accumulated contribution could command in the open market." In this case, however, the employer selected the companies participating in the plan, entered into contracts with them, and did not permit employees to obtain benefits from other companies. Thus, the employer was "legally responsible for the discriminatory terms on which annuities are offered by the companies chosen to participate in the plan." Justice Powell dissented, joined by Chief Justice Burger and Justices Blackmun and Rehnquist.

A different majority of five Justices concluded that the decision would be applied only prospectively, to retirement benefits derived from contributions made after the decision. As explained by Justice O'Connor, the only Justice in both majorities, the "real danger of bankrupting pension funds requires that our decision be made prospective."

――――――

MICHAEL M. v. SUPERIOR COURT

450 U.S. 464, 101 S.Ct. 1200, 67 L.Ed.2d 437 (1981).

Justice Rehnquist announced the judgment of the Court and delivered an opinion in which The Chief Justice, Justice Stewart, and Justice Powell joined.

The question presented in this case is whether California's "statutory rape" law, § 261.5 of the Cal.Penal Code Ann. (West Supp.1981), violates the Equal Protection Clause of the Fourteenth Amendment. Section 261.5 defines unlawful sexual intercourse as "an act of sexual intercourse accomplished with a female not the wife of the perpetrator, where the female is under the age of 18 years." The statute thus makes men alone criminally liable for the act of sexual intercourse.

In July 1978, a complaint was filed in the Municipal Court of Sonoma County, Cal., alleging that petitioner, then a 17½-year-old male, had had

unlawful sexual intercourse with a female under the age of 18, in violation of
§ 261.5. . . . Prior to trial, petitioner sought to set aside the information
on both state and federal constitutional grounds, asserting that § 261.5 unlawfully discriminated on the basis of gender. The trial court and the California
Court of Appeal denied petitioner's request for relief and petitioner sought
review in the Supreme Court of California.

The Supreme Court held that "section 261.5 discriminates on the basis of
sex because only females may be victims, and only males may violate the
section." The court then subjected the classification to "strict scrutiny," stating
that it must be justified by a compelling state interest. It found that the
classification was "supported not by mere social convention but by the immutable physiological fact that it is the female exclusively who can become pregnant." Canvassing "the tragic human cost of illegitimate teenage pregnancies,"
including the large number of teenage abortions, the increased medical risk
associated with teenage pregnancies, and the social consequences of teenage
childbearing, the court concluded that the State has a compelling interest in
preventing such pregnancies. Because males alone can "physiologically cause
the result which the law properly seeks to avoid," the court further held that the
gender classification was readily justified as a means of identifying offender and
victim. For the reasons stated below, we affirm the judgment of the California
Supreme Court.

As is evident from our opinions, the Court has had some difficulty in
agreeing upon the proper approach and analysis in cases involving challenges to
gender-based classifications. The issues posed by such challenges range from
issues of standing, see Orr v. Orr, 440 U.S. 268 (1979), to the appropriate
standard of judicial review for the substantive classification. Unlike the California Supreme Court, we have not held that gender-based classifications are
"inherently suspect" and thus we do not apply so-called "strict scrutiny" to
those classifications. See Stanton v. Stanton, 421 U.S. 7 (1975). Our cases
have held, however, that the traditional minimum rationality test takes on a
somewhat "sharper focus" when gender-based classifications are challenged.
See Craig v. Boren, 429 U.S. 190, 210 n* (1976) (Powell, J., concurring). In
Reed v. Reed, 404 U.S. 71 (1971), for example, the Court stated that a gender-
based classification will be upheld if it bears a "fair and substantial relationship"
to legitimate state ends, while in Craig v. Boren, supra, at 197, the Court
restated the test to require the classification to bear a "substantial relationship"
to "important governmental objectives."

Underlying these decisions is the principle that a legislature may not "make
overbroad generalizations based on sex which are entirely unrelated to any
differences between men and women or which demean the ability or social
status of the affected class." Parham v. Hughes, 441 U.S. 347, 354 (1979)
(plurality opinion of Stewart, J.). But because the Equal Protection Clause does
not "demand that a statute necessarily apply equally to all persons" or require
" 'things which are different in fact . . . to be treated in law as though they
were the same,' " Rinaldi v. Yeager, 384 U.S. 305, 309 (1966), quoting Tigner
v. Texas, 310 U.S. 141, 147 (1940), this Court has consistently upheld statutes
where the gender classification is not invidious, but rather realistically reflects
the fact that the sexes are not similarly situated in certain circumstances.
Parham v. Hughes, supra; Califano v. Webster, 430 U.S. 313 (1977); Schlesinger v. Ballard, 419 U.S. 498 (1975); Kahn v. Shevin, 416 U.S. 351 (1974).
As the Court has stated, a legislature may "provide for the special problems of
women." Weinberger v. Wiesenfeld, 420 U.S. 636, 653 (1975).

Applying those principles to this case, the fact that the California Legislature
criminalized the act of illicit sexual intercourse with a minor female is a sure
indication of its intent or purpose to discourage that conduct. Precisely why the

legislature desired that result is of course somewhat less clear. This Court has long recognized that "[i]nquiries into congressional motives or purposes are a hazardous matter," United States v. O'Brien, 391 U.S. 367, 383–384 (1968); Palmer v. Thompson, 403 U.S. 217, 224 (1970), and the search for the "actual" or "primary" purpose of a statute is likely to be elusive. Arlington Heights v. Metropolitan Housing Dev. Corp., 429 U.S. 252, 265 (1977); McGinnis v. Royster, 410 U.S. 263, 276–277 (1973). Here, for example, the individual legislators may have voted for the statute for a variety of reasons. Some legislators may have been concerned about preventing teenage pregnancies, others about protecting young females from physical injury or from the loss of "chastity," and still others about promoting various religious and moral attitudes towards premarital sex.

The justification for the statute offered by the State, and accepted by the Supreme Court of California, is that the legislature sought to prevent illegitimate teenage pregnancies. That finding, of course, is entitled to great deference. Reitman v. Mulkey, 387 U.S. 369, 373–374 (1967). And although our cases establish that the State's asserted reason for the enactment of a statute may be rejected, if it "could not have been a goal of the legislation," Weinberger v. Wiesenfeld, supra, at 648, n. 16, this is not such a case.

We are satisfied not only that the prevention of illegitimate pregnancy is at least one of the "purposes" of the statute, but that the State has a strong interest in preventing such pregnancy. At the risk of stating the obvious, teenage pregnancies, which have increased dramatically over the last two decades, have significant social, medical and economic consequences for both the mother and her child, and the State. Of particular concern to the State is that approximately half of all teenage pregnancies end in abortion. And of those children who are born, their illegitimacy makes them likely candidates to become wards of the State.

We need not be medical doctors to discern that young men and young women are not similarly situated with respect to the problems and the risks of sexual intercourse. Only women may become pregnant, and they suffer disproportionately the profound physical, emotional, and psychological consequences of sexual activity. The statute at issue here protects women from sexual intercourse at an age when those consequences are particularly severe.[7]

The question thus boils down to whether a State may attack the problem of sexual intercourse and teenage pregnancy directly by prohibiting a male from having sexual intercourse with a minor female. We hold that such a statute is sufficiently related to the State's objectives to pass constitutional muster.

Because virtually all of the significant harmful and inescapably identifiable consequences of teenage pregnancy fall on the young female, a legislature acts

[7] Although petitioner concedes that the State has a "compelling" interest in preventing teenage pregnancy, he contends that the "true" purpose of § 261.5 is to protect the virtue and chastity of young women. As such, the statute is unjustifiable because it rests on archaic stereotypes. What we have said above is enough to dispose of that contention. The question for us—and the only question under the Federal Constitution—is whether the legislation violates the Equal Protection Clause of the Fourteenth Amendment, not whether its supporters may have endorsed it for reasons no longer generally accepted. Even if the preservation of female chastity were one of the motives of the statute, and even if that motive be impermissible, petitioner's argument must fail because "[i]t is a familiar practice of constitutional law that this court will not strike down an otherwise constitutional statute on the basis of an alleged illicit legislative motive." United States v. O'Brien, 391 U.S. 367, 383 (1968). In Orr v. Orr, 440 U.S. 268 (1979), for example, the Court rejected one asserted purpose as impermissible, but then considered other purposes to determine if they could justify the statute. Similarly, in Washington v. Davis, 426 U.S. 229, 243 (1976) the Court distinguished Palmer v. Thompson, 403 U.S. 217 (1971), on the grounds that the purposes of the ordinance there were not open to impeachment by evidence that the legislature was actually motivated by an impermissible purpose. See also Arlington Heights v. Metropolitan Housing Dev. Corp., 429 U.S. 252, 270, n. 21 (1977); Mobile v. Bolden, 446 U.S. 55, 91 (1980) (Stevens, J., concurring in judgment).

well within its authority when it elects to punish only the participant who, by nature, suffers few of the consequences of his conduct. It is hardly unreasonable for a legislature acting to protect minor females to exclude them from punishment. Moreover, the risk of pregnancy itself constitutes a substantial deterrence to young females. No similar natural sanctions deter males. A criminal sanction imposed solely on males thus serves to roughly "equalize" the deterrents on the sexes.

We are unable to accept petitioner's contention that the statute is impermissibly underinclusive and must, in order to pass judicial scrutiny, be *broadened* so as to hold the female as criminally liable as the male. It is argued that this statute is not *necessary* to deter teenage pregnancy because a gender-neutral statute, where both male and female would be subject to prosecution, would serve that goal equally well. The relevant inquiry, however, is not whether the statute is drawn as precisely as it might have been, but whether the line chosen by the California Legislature is within constitutional limitations. Kahn v. Shevin, 416 U.S., at 356, n. 10.

In any event, we cannot say that a gender-neutral statute would be as effective as the statute California has chosen to enact. The State persuasively contends that a gender-neutral statute would frustrate its interest in effective enforcement. Its view is that a female is surely less likely to report violations of the statute if she herself would be subject to criminal prosecution. In an area already fraught with prosecutorial difficulties, we decline to hold that the Equal Protection Clause requires a legislature to enact a statute so broad that it may well be incapable of enforcement.[10]

We similarly reject petitioner's argument that § 261.5 is impermissibly overbroad because it makes unlawful sexual intercourse with prepubescent females, who are, by definition, incapable of becoming pregnant. Quite apart from the fact that the statute could well be justified on the grounds that very young females are particularly susceptible to physical injury from sexual intercourse, see Rundlett v. Oliver, 607 F.2d 495 (CA1 1979), it is ludicrous to suggest that the Constitution requires the California Legislature to limit the scope of its rape statute to older teenagers and exclude young girls.

There remains only petitioner's contention that the statute is unconstitutional as it is applied to him because he, like Sharon, was under 18 at the time of sexual intercourse. Petitioner argues that the statute is flawed because it presumes that as between two persons under 18, the male is the culpable aggressor. We find petitioner's contentions unpersuasive. Contrary to his assertions, the statute does not rest on the assumption that males are generally the aggressors. It is instead an attempt by a legislature to prevent illegitimate teenage pregnancy by providing an additional deterrent for men. The age of the man is irrelevant since young men are as capable as older men of inflicting the harm sought to be prevented.

[10] The question whether a statute is *substantially* related to its asserted goals is at best an opaque one. It can be plausibly argued that a gender-neutral statute would produce fewer prosecutions than the statute at issue here. The dissent argues, on the other hand, that "even assuming that a gender-neutral statute would be more difficult to enforce. . . . [c]ommon sense . . . suggests that a gender-neutral statutory rape law is potentially a greater deterrent of sexual activity than a gender-based law, for the simple reason that a gender-neutral law subjects both men and women to criminal sanctions and thus arguably has a deterrent effect on twice as many potential violators."

Where such differing speculations as to the effect of a statute are plausible, we think it appropriate to defer to the decision of the California Supreme Court, "armed as it was with the knowledge of the facts and circumstances concerning the passage and potential impact of [the statute], and familiar with the milieu in which that provision would operate." Reitman v. Mulkey, 387 U.S. 369, 378–379 (1967).

.   .   .

In upholding the California statute we also recognize that this is not a case where a statute is being challenged on the grounds that it "invidiously discriminates" against females. To the contrary, the statute places a burden on males which is not shared by females. But we find nothing to suggest that men, because of past discrimination or peculiar disadvantages, are in need of the special solicitude of the courts. Nor is this a case where the gender classification is made "solely for . . . administrative convenience," as in Frontiero v. Richardson, 411 U.S. 677, 690 (1973) (emphasis omitted), or rests on "the baggage of sexual stereotypes" as in Orr v. Orr, 440 U.S., at 283. As we have held, the statute instead reasonably reflects the fact that the consequences of sexual intercourse and pregnancy fall more heavily on the female than on the male.

Accordingly the judgment of the California Supreme Court is

Affirmed.

Justice Stewart, concurring.

Section 261.5, on its face, classifies on the basis of sex. A male who engages in sexual intercourse with an underage female who is not his wife violates the statute; a female who engages in sexual intercourse with an underage male who is not her husband does not. The petitioner contends that this state law, which punishes only males for the conduct in question, violates his Fourteenth Amendment right to the equal protection of the law. The Court today correctly rejects that contention.

. . .

The Constitution is violated when government, state or federal, invidiously classifies similarly situated people on the basis of the immutable characteristics with which they were born. Thus, detrimental racial classifications by government always violate the Constitution, for the simple reason that, so far as the Constitution is concerned, people of different races are always similarly situated. See Fullilove v. Klutznick, 448 U.S. 448, 522 (dissenting opinion); McLaughlin v. Florida, 379 U.S. 184, 198 (concurring opinion); Brown v. Board of Ed., 347 U.S. 483; Plessy v. Ferguson, 163 U.S. 537, 552 (dissenting opinion). By contrast, while detrimental gender classifications by government often violate the Constitution, they do not always do so, for the reason that there are differences between males and females that the Constitution necessarily recognizes. In this case we deal with the most basic of these differences: females can become pregnant as the result of sexual intercourse; males cannot.

. . .

. . . Experienced observation confirms the common sense notion that adolescent males disregard the possibility of pregnancy far more than do adolescent females. And to the extent that § 261.5 may punish males for intercourse with prepubescent females, that punishment is justifiable because of the substantial physical risks for prepubescent females that are not shared by their male counterparts.

The petitioner argues that the California Legislature could have drafted the statute differently, so that its purpose would be accomplished more precisely. "But the issue, of course, is not whether the statute could have been drafted more wisely, but whether the lines chosen by the . . . [l]egislature are within constitutional limitations." Kahn v. Shevin, 416 U.S. 351, 356, n. 10. That other States may have decided to attack the same problems more broadly, with gender-neutral statutes, does not mean that every State is constitutionally compelled to do so.

. . .

In short, the Equal Protection Clause does not mean that the physiological differences between men and women must be disregarded. While those differences must never be permitted to become a pretext for invidious discrimination, no such discrimination is presented by this case. The Constitution surely does not require a State to pretend that demonstrable differences between men and women do not really exist.

Justice Blackmun, concurring in the judgment.

It is gratifying that the plurality recognizes that "[a]t the risk of stating the obvious, teenage pregnancies . . . have increased dramatically over the last two decades" and "have significant social, medical, and economic consequences for both the mother and her child, and the State." There have been times when I have wondered whether the Court was capable of this perception, particularly when it has struggled with the different but not unrelated problems that attend abortion issues. See, for example, the opinions (and the dissenting opinions) in Beal v. Doe, 432 U.S. 438 (1977); Maher v. Roe, 432 U.S. 464 (1977); Poelker v. Doe, 432 U.S. 519 (1977); Harris v. McRae, 448 U.S. 297 (1980); Williams v. Zbaraz, 448 U.S. 358 (1980); and today's opinion in H.L. v. Matheson, ante.

Some might conclude that the two uses of the criminal sanction—here flatly to forbid intercourse in order to forestall teenage pregnancies, and in *Matheson* to prohibit a physician's abortion procedure except upon notice to the parents of the pregnant minor—are vastly different proscriptions. But the basic social and privacy problems are much the same. Both Utah's statute in *Matheson* and California's statute in this case are legislatively created tools intended to achieve similar ends and addressed to the same societal concerns: the control and direction of young people's sexual activities. The plurality opinion impliedly concedes as much when it notes that "approximately half of all teenage pregnancies end in abortion," and that "those children who are born" are "likely candidates to become wards of the State."

I, however, cannot vote to strike down the California statutory rape law, for I think it is a sufficiently reasoned and constitutional effort to control the problem at its inception. . . . I am persuaded that, although a minor has substantial privacy rights in intimate affairs connected with procreation, California's efforts to prevent teenage pregnancy are to be viewed differently from Utah's efforts to inhibit a woman from dealing with pregnancy once it has become an inevitability.

Craig v. Boren, 429 U.S. 190 (1976), was an opinion which, in large part, I joined. The plurality opinion in the present case points out, the Court's respective phrasings of the applicable test in Reed v. Reed, 404 U.S. 71, 76 (1971), and in Craig v. Boren, 429 U.S., at 197. I vote to affirm the judgment of the Supreme Court of California and to uphold the State's gender-based classification on that test and as exemplified by those two cases and by Schlesinger v. Ballard, 419 U.S. 498 (1975); Weinberger v. Wiesenfeld, 420 U.S. 636 (1975); and Kahn v. Shevin, 416 U.S. 351 (1974).

. . . .

Justice Brennan, with whom Justices White and Marshall join, dissenting.

I

It is disturbing to find the Court so splintered on a case that presents such a straightforward issue: whether the admittedly gender-based classification in Cal. Penal Code Ann. § 261.5 (West Supp.1981) bears a sufficient relationship to the State's asserted goal of preventing teenage pregnancies to survive the "mid-level" constitutional scrutiny mandated by Craig v. Boren, 429 U.S. 190 (1976). Applying the analytical frame work provided by our precedents, I am convinced that there is only one proper resolution of this issue: the classification must be declared unconstitutional. I fear that the plurality and Justices Stewart and Blackmun reach the opposite result by placing too much emphasis on the desirability of achieving the State's asserted statutory goal—prevention of teenage pregnancy—and not enough emphasis on the fundamental question of whether the sex-based discrimination in the California statute is *substantially* related to the achievement of that goal.

.　.　.

The State of California vigorously asserts that the "important governmental objective" to be served by § 261.5 is the prevention of teenage pregnancy. It claims that its statute furthers this goal by deterring sexual activity by males—the class of persons it considers more responsible for causing those pregnancies. But even assuming that prevention of teenage pregnancy is an important governmental objective and that it is in fact an objective of § 261.5, California still has the burden of proving that there are fewer teenage pregnancies under its gender-based statutory rape law than there would be if the law were gender neutral. To meet this burden, the State must show that because its statutory rape law punishes only males, and not females, it more effectively deters minor females from having sexual intercourse.

The plurality assumes that a gender-neutral statute would be less effective than § 261.5 in deterring sexual activity because a gender-neutral statute would create significant enforcement problems. .　.　.

.　.　. [T]here are at least two serious flaws in the State's assertion that law enforcement problems created by a gender-neutral statutory rape law would make such a statute less effective than a gender-based statute in deterring sexual activity.

First, the experience of other jurisdictions, and California itself, belies the plurality's conclusion that a gender-neutral statutory rape law "may well be incapable of enforcement." .　.　.

.　.　.

The second flaw in the State's assertion is that even assuming that a gender-neutral statute would be more difficult to enforce, the State has still not shown that those enforcement problems would make such a statute less effective than a gender-based statute in deterring minor females from engaging in sexual intercourse. Common sense, however, suggests that a gender-neutral statutory rape law is potentially a *greater* deterrent of sexual activity than a gender-based law, for the simple reason that a gender-neutral law subjects both men and women to criminal sanctions and thus arguably has a deterrent effect on twice as many potential violators. .　.　.

III

Until very recently, no California court or commentator had suggested that the purpose of California's statutory rape law was to protect young women from the risk of pregnancy. Indeed, the historical development of § 261.5 demonstrates that the law was initially enacted on the premise that young women, in contrast to young men, were to be deemed legally incapable of consenting to an act of sexual intercourse. Because their chastity was considered particularly precious, those young women were felt to be uniquely in need of the State's protection. In contrast, young men were assumed to be capable of making such decisions for themselves; the law therefore did not offer them any special protection.

It is perhaps because the gender classification in California's statutory rape law was initially designed to further these outmoded sexual stereotypes, rather than to reduce the incidence of teenage pregnancies, that the State has been unable to demonstrate a substantial relationship between the classification and its newly asserted goal. Cf. Califano v. Goldfarb, supra, 430 U.S., at 223 (Stevens, J., concurring in judgment). But whatever the reason, the State has not shown that Cal.Penal Code § 261.5 is any more effective than a gender-neutral law would be in deterring minor females from engaging in sexual intercourse. It has therefore not met its burden of proving that the statutory classification is substantially related to the achievement of its asserted goal.

I would hold that § 261.5 violates the Equal Protection Clause of the Fourteenth Amendment and I would reverse the judgment of the California Supreme Court.

Justice Stevens, dissenting.

Local custom and belief—rather than statutory laws of venerable but doubtful ancestry—will determine the volume of sexual activity among unmarried teenagers. The empirical evidence cited by the plurality demonstrates the futility of the notion that a statutory prohibition will significantly affect the volume of that activity or provide a meaningful solution to the problems created by it. Nevertheless, as a matter of constitutional power, unlike my Brother Brennan, I would have no doubt about the validity of a state law prohibiting all unmarried teenagers from engaging in sexual intercourse. The societal interests in reducing the incidence of venereal disease and teenage pregnancy are sufficient, in my judgment, to justify a prohibition of conduct that increases the risk of those harms.

My conclusion that a nondiscriminatory prohibition would be constitutional does not help me answer the question whether a prohibition applicable to only half of the joint participants in the risk-creating conduct is also valid. It cannot be true that the validity of a total ban is an adequate justification for a selective prohibition; otherwise, the constitutional objection to discriminatory rules would be meaningless. The question in this case is whether the difference between males and females justifies this statutory discrimination based entirely on sex.

The fact that the Court did not immediately acknowledge that the capacity to become pregnant is what primarily differentiates the female from the male does not impeach the validity of the plurality's newly found wisdom. I think the plurality is quite correct in making the assumption that the joint act that this law seeks to prohibit creates a greater risk of harm for the female than for the male.

. . .

In my judgment, the fact that a class of persons is especially vulnerable to a risk that a statute is designed to avoid is a reason for making the statute applicable to that class. The argument that a special need for protection provides a rational explanation for an exemption is one I simply do not comprehend.

In this case, the fact that a female confronts a greater risk of harm than a male is a reason for applying the prohibition to her—not a reason for granting her a license to use her own judgment on whether or not to assume the risk.

. . .

. . .

Finally, even if my logic is faulty and there actually is some speculative basis for treating equally guilty males and females differently, I still believe that any such speculative justification would be outweighed by the paramount interest in evenhanded enforcement of the law. A rule that authorizes punishment of only one of two equally guilty wrongdoers violates the essence of the constitutional requirement that the sovereign must govern impartially.

I respectfully dissent.

———

ROSTKER v. GOLDBERG

453 U.S. 57, 101 S.Ct. 2646, 69 L.Ed.2d 478 (1981).

Justice Rehnquist delivered the opinion of the Court.

The question presented is whether the Military Selective Service Act, 50 U.S.C.App. § 451 et seq. (1976 ed. and Supp. III), violates the Fifth Amendment to the United States Constitution in authorizing the President to require the registration of males and not females.

I

.   .   .

[In 1980 President Carter determined that it was necessary to reactivate the draft registration process. He recommended to Congress that funds be provided for this purpose and that the Military Selective Service Act be amended to permit the registration and conscription of women as well as men. Congress refused to amend the Act and provided funds only for the registration of males. A law suit challenging the draft as involving forbidden gender-based discrimination, which had been pending for nearly a decade, was reactivated. The District Court held that the limitation of the draft to males was unconstitutional and enjoined the government from requiring registration under the Act. The case was appealed to the Supreme Court. A stay was granted pending disposition of the appeal.]

II

Whenever called upon to judge the constitutionality of an Act of Congress— "the gravest and most delicate duty that this Court is called upon to perform," Blodgett v. Holden, 275 U.S. 142, 148 (1927) (Holmes, J.)—the Court accords "great weight to the decisions of Congress." Columbia Broadcasting System, Inc. v. Democratic National Committee, 412 U.S. 94, 102 (1973). The Congress is a coequal branch of government whose Members take the same oath we do to uphold the Constitution of the United States. As Justice Frankfurter noted in Joint Anti-Fascist Refugee Committee v. McGrath, 341 U.S. 123, 164 (1951) (concurring opinion), we must have "due regard to the fact that this Court is not exercising a primary judgment but is sitting in judgment upon those who also have taken the oath to observe the Constitution and who have the responsibility for carrying on government." The customary deference accorded the judgments of Congress is certainly appropriate when, as here, Congress specifically considered the question of the Act's constitutionality.   .   .   .

This is not, however, merely a case involving the customary deference accorded congressional decisions. The case arises in the context of Congress' authority over national defense and military affairs, and perhaps in no other area has the Court accorded Congress greater deference. In rejecting the registration of women, Congress explicitly relied upon its constitutional powers under Art. I, § 8, cls. 12–14.   .   .   .   This Court has consistently recognized Congress' "broad constitutional power" to raise and regulate armies and navies, Schlesinger v. Ballard, 419 U.S. 498, 510 (1975).   .   .   .

Not only is the scope of Congress' constitutional power in this area broad, but the lack of competence on the part of the courts is marked.   .   .   .

The operation of a healthy deference to legislative and executive judgments in the area of military affairs is evident in several recent decisions of this Court.

.   .   .   .

.   .   .   .

None of this is to say that Congress is free to disregard the Constitution when it acts in the area of military affairs. In that area as any other Congress remains subject to the limitations of the Due Process Clause, see Ex parte Milligan, 4 Wall. 2 (1866); Hamilton v. Kentucky Distilleries & Warehouse Co., 251 U.S. 146, 156 (1919), but the tests and limitations to be applied may differ because of the military context. We of course do not abdicate our ultimate responsibility to decide the constitutional question, but simply recognize that the Constitution itself requires such deference to congressional choice. See Columbia Broadcasting System, Inc. v. Democratic National Committee, 412 U.S., at 103. In deciding the question before us we must be particularly careful not to substitute our judgment of what is desirable for that of Congress, or our own evaluation of evidence for a reasonable evaluation by the Legislative Branch.

The District Court purported to recognize the appropriateness of deference to Congress when that body was exercising its constitutionally delegated authority over military affairs, 509 F.Supp., at 596, but it stressed that "[w]e are not here concerned with military operations or day-to-day conduct of the military into which we have no desire to intrude." . . . We find these efforts to divorce registration from the military and national defense context, with all the deference called for in that context, singularly unpersuasive. . . . Congressional judgments concerning registration and the draft are based on judgments concerning military operations and needs . . . and the deference unquestionably due the latter judgments is necessarily required in assessing the former as well. . . . It would be blinking reality to say that our precedents requiring deference to Congress in military affairs are not implicated by the present case.

The Solicitor General argues, largely on the basis of the foregoing cases emphasizing the deference due Congress in the area of military affairs and national security, that this Court should scrutinize the MSSA only to determine if the distinction drawn between men and women bears a rational relation to some legitimate Government purpose, see U.S. Railroad Retirement Board v. Fritz, 449 U.S. 166 (1980), and should not examine the Act under the heightened scrutiny with which we have approached gender-based discrimination, see Michael M. v. Superior Court of Sonoma County, 450 U.S. 464 (1981); Craig v. Boren, 429 U.S. 190; Reed v. Reed, supra. We do not think that the substantive guarantee of due process or certainty in the law will be advanced by any further "refinement" in the applicable tests as suggested by the Government. Announced degrees of "deference" to legislative judgments, just as levels of "scrutiny" which this Court announces that it applies to particular classifications made by a legislative body, may all too readily become facile abstractions used to justify a result. In this case the courts are called upon to decide whether Congress, acting under an explicit constitutional grant of authority, has by that action transgressed an explicit guarantee of individual rights which limits the authority so conferred. Simply labelling the legislative decision "military" on the one hand or "gender-based" on the other does not automatically guide a court to the correct constitutional result.

No one could deny that under the test of Craig v. Boren, supra, the Government's interest in raising and supporting armies is an "important governmental interest." Congress and its committees carefully considered and debated two alternative means of furthering that interest: the first was to register only males for potential conscription, and the other was to register both sexes. Congress chose the former alternative. When that decision is challenged on equal protection grounds, the question a court must decide is not which alternative it would have chosen, had it been the primary decisionmaker, but whether that chosen by Congress denies equal protection of the laws.

Nor can it be denied that the imposing number of cases from this Court previously cited suggest that judicial deference to such congressional exercise of authority is at its apogee when legislative action under the congressional authority to raise and support armies and make rules and regulations for their governance is challenged. . . .

. . . In light of the floor debate and the Report of the Senate Armed Services Committee hereinafter discussed, it is apparent that Congress was fully aware not merely of the many facts and figures presented to it by witnesses who testified before its Committees, but of the current thinking as to the place of women in the Armed Services. In such a case, we cannot ignore Congress' broad authority conferred by the Constitution to raise and support armies when we are urged to declare unconstitutional its studied choice of one alternative in preference to another for furthering that goal.

III

This case is quite different from several of the gender-based discrimination cases we have considered in that, despite appellees' assertions, Congress did not act "unthinkingly" or "reflexively and not for any considered reason." The question of registering women for the draft not only received considerable national attention and was the subject of wide-ranging public debate, but also was extensively considered by Congress in hearings, floor debate, and in committee. Hearings held by both Houses of Congress in response to the President's request for authorization to register women adduced extensive testimony and evidence concerning the issue. . . . These hearings built on other hearings held the previous year addressed to the same question.

The House declined to provide for the registration of women when it passed the Joint Resolution allocating funds for the Selective Service System. See 126 Cong.Rec. 8601–8602, 8620 (1980). When the Senate considered the Joint Resolution, it defeated, after extensive debate, an amendment which in effect would have authorized the registration of women. Id. at 13876–13896. . . .

While proposals to register women were being rejected in the course of transferring funds to register males, committees in both Houses which had conducted hearings on the issue were also rejecting the registration of women. . . .

The foregoing clearly establishes that the decision to exempt women from registration was not the " 'accidental by-product of a traditional way of thinking about women.' " Califano v. Webster, 430 U.S. 313, 320 (1977) (quoting Califano v. Goldfarb, 430 U.S. 199, 233 (1977) (Stevens, J., concurring)). In Michael M., 450 U.S., at 471, n. 6 (plurality), we rejected a similar argument because of action by the California Legislature considering and rejecting proposals to make a statute challenged on discrimination grounds gender-neutral. The cause for rejecting the argument is considerably stronger here. The issue was considered at great length, and Congress clearly expressed its purpose and intent. Contrast Califano v. Westcott, 443 U.S. 76, 87 (1979) ("The gender qualification . . . escaped virtually unnoticed in the hearings and floor debates"). . . .

. . . Any assessment of the congressional purpose and its chosen means must . . . consider the registration scheme as a prelude to a draft in a time of national emergency. Any other approach would not be testing the Act in light of the purposes Congress sought to achieve.

Congress determined that any future draft, which would be facilitated by the registration scheme, would be characterized by a need for combat troops.

. . . . The purpose of registration, therefore, was to prepare for a draft *of combat troops*.

Women as a group, however, unlike men as a group, are not eligible for combat. The restrictions on the participation of women in combat in the Navy and Air Force are statutory. Under 10 U.S.C. § 6015 (1976 ed., Supp. III) "women may not be assigned to duty on vessels or in aircraft that are engaged in combat missions," and under 10 U.S.C. § 8549 female members of the Air Force "may not be assigned to duty in aircraft engaged in combat missions." The Army and Marine Corps preclude the use of women in combat as a matter of established policy. Congress specifically recognized and endorsed the exclusion of women from combat in exempting women from registration. In the words of the Senate Report:

> "The principle that women should not intentionally and routinely engage in combat is fundamental, and enjoys wide support among our people. It is universally supported by military leaders who have testified before the Committee. . . . Current law and policy exclude women from being assigned to combat in our military forces, and the Committee reaffirms this policy. S.Rep. No. 96–826, supra, at 157.

The Senate Report specifically found that "[w]omen should not be intentionally or routinely placed in combat positions in our military services." Id., at 160. See S.Rep. No. 96–226, supra, at 9. The President expressed his intent to continue the current military policy precluding women from combat . . .

The existence of the combat restrictions clearly indicates the basis for Congress' decision to exempt women from registration. The purpose of registration was to prepare for a draft of combat troops. Since women are excluded from combat, Congress concluded that they would not be needed in the event of a draft, and therefore decided not to register them. . . .

The District Court stressed that the military need for women was irrelevant to the issue of their registration. As that court put it: "Congress could not constitutionally require registration under the MSSA of only black citizens or only white citizens, or single out any political or religious group simply because those groups contained sufficient persons to fill the needs of the Selective Service System." 509 F.Supp., at 596. This reasoning is beside the point. The reason women are exempt from registration is not because military needs can be met by drafting men. This is not a case of Congress arbitrarily choosing to burden one of two similarly situated groups, such as would be the case with an all-black or all-white, or an all-Catholic or all-Lutheran, or an all-Republican or all-Democratic registration. Men and women, because of the combat restrictions on women, are simply not similarly situated for purposes of a draft or registration for a draft.

Congress' decision to authorize the registration of only men, therefore, does not violate the Due Process Clause. The exemption of women from registration is not only sufficiently but also closely related to Congress' purpose in authorizing registration. See Michael M., 450 U.S., at 472–473 (plurality opinion); Craig v. Boren, 429 U.S. 190 (1976); Reed v. Reed, 404 U.S. 71 (1971). The fact that Congress and the Executive have decided that women should not serve in combat fully justifies Congress in not authorizing their registration, since the purpose of registration is to develop a pool of potential combat troops. As was the case in Schlesinger v. Ballard, supra, "the gender classification is not invidious, but rather realistically reflects the fact that the sexes are not similarly situated" in this case. Michael M., supra, at 469 (plurality opinion). The Constitution requires that Congress treat similarly situated persons similarly, not that it engage in gestures of superficial equality.

In holding the MSSA constitutionally invalid the District Court relied heavily on the President's decision to seek authority to register women and the testimony of members of the Executive Branch and the military in support of that decision. . . .

Although the military experts who testified in favor of registering women uniformly opposed the actual drafting of women, see, e.g., Hearing on S. 109 and S. 226, supra, at 11 (Gen. Rogers), there was testimony that in the event of a draft of 650,000 the military could absorb some 80,000 female inductees. Hearings on S. 2294, at 1661, 1828. The 80,000 would be used to fill noncombat positions, freeing men to go to the front. In relying on this testimony in striking down the MSSA, the District Court palpably exceeded its authority when it ignored Congress' considered response to this line of reasoning.

In the first place, assuming that a small number of women could be drafted for noncombat roles, Congress simply did not consider it worth the added burdens of including women in draft and registration plans. . . .

Congress also concluded that whatever the need for women for noncombat roles during mobilization, whether 80,000 or less, it could be met by volunteers. . . .

Most significantly, Congress determined that staffing noncombat positions with women during a mobilization would be positively detrimental to the important goal of military flexibility. . . . The District Court was quite wrong in undertaking an independent evaluation of this evidence, rather than adopting an appropriately deferential examination of *Congress'* evaluation of that evidence.

In light of the foregoing, we conclude that Congress acted well within its constitutional authority when it authorized the registration of men, and not women, under the Military Selective Service Act. The decision of the District Court holding otherwise is accordingly

Reversed.

Justice White, with whom Justice Brennan joins, dissenting.

I assume what has not been challenged in this case—that excluding women from combat positions does not offend the Constitution. . . .

. . . .

As I understand the record, then, in order to secure the personnel it needs during mobilization, the Government cannot rely on volunteers and must register and draft not only to fill combat positions and those noncombat positions that must be filled by combat-trained men, but also to secure the personnel needed for jobs that can be performed by persons ineligible for combat without diminishing military effectiveness. The claim is that in providing for the latter category of positions, Congress is free to register and draft only men. I discern no adequate justification for this kind of discrimination between men and women. Accordingly, with all due respect, I dissent.

Justice Marshall, with whom Justice Brennan joins, dissenting.

The Court today places its imprimatur on one of the most potent remaining public expressions of "ancient canards about the proper role of women," Phillips v. Martin Marietta Corp., 400 U.S. 542, 545 (1971) (Marshall, J., concurring). It upholds a statute that requires males but not females to register for the draft, and which thereby categorically excludes women from a fundamental civic obligation. Because I believe the Court's decision is inconsistent with the Constitution's guarantee of equal protection of the laws, I dissent.

I

A

The background to this litigation is set out in the opinion of the Court, and I will not repeat that discussion here. It bears emphasis, however, that the only question presented by this case is whether the exclusion of women from registration under the Military Selective Service Act, 50 U.S.C.App. § 451 et seq. . . . (MSSA), contravenes the equal protection component of the Due Process Clause of the Fifth Amendment. Although the purpose of registration is to assist preparations for drafting civilians into the military, *we are not asked to rule on the constitutionality of a statute governing conscription.* With the advent of the All-Volunteer Armed Forces, the MSSA was specifically amended to preclude conscription as of July 1, 1973, . . . and reactivation of the draft would therefore require a legislative amendment. . . . Consequently, we are not called upon to decide whether either men or women can be drafted at all, whether they must be drafted in equal numbers, in what order they should be drafted, or, once inducted, how they are to be trained for their respective functions. In addition, this case does not involve a challenge to the statutes or policies that prohibit female members of the Armed Forces from serving in combat. It is with this understanding that I turn to the task at hand.

. . .

VI

After reviewing the discussion and findings contained in the Senate Report, the most I am able to say of the Report is that it demonstrates that drafting *very large numbers* of women would frustrate the achievement of a number of important governmental objectives that relate to the ultimate goal of maintaining "an adequate armed strength . . . to insure the security of this Nation," 50 U.S.C.App. § 451(b). Or to put it another way, the Senate Report establishes that induction of a large number of men but only a limited number of women, as determined by the military's personnel requirements, would be substantially related to important governmental interests. But the discussion and findings in the Senate Report do not enable the Government to carry its burden of demonstrating that *completely* excluding women from the draft by excluding them from registration substantially furthers important governmental objectives.

In concluding that the Government has carried its burden in this case, the Court adopts "an appropriately deferential examination of *Congress'* evaluation of [the] evidence," (emphasis in the original). The majority then proceeds to supplement Congress' actual findings with those the Court apparently believes Congress could (and should) have made. Beyond that, the Court substitutes hollow shibboleths about "deference to legislative decisions" for constitutional analysis. It is as if the majority has lost sight of the fact that "it is the responsibility of this Court to act as the ultimate interpreter of the Constitution." Powell v. McCormack, 395 U.S., at 549. See Baker v. Carr, 369 U.S., at 211. Congressional enactments in the area of military affairs must, like all other laws, be *judged* by the standards of the Constitution. For the Constitution is the supreme law of the land, and *all* legislation must conform to the principles it lays down. As the Court has pointed out, "the phrase 'war power' cannot be invoked as a talismanic incantation to support any exercise of congressional power which can be brought within its ambit." United States v. Robel, 389 U.S., at 263–264.

Furthermore, "[w]hen it appears that an Act of Congress conflicts with [a constitutional] provisio[n], we have no choice but to enforce the paramount commands of the Constitution. We are sworn to do no less. We cannot push back the limits of the Constitution merely to accommodate challenged legislation." Trop v. Dulles, 356 U.S. 86, 104 (1958) (plurality opinion). In some 106 instances since this Court was established it has determined that congressional action exceeded the bounds of the Constitution. I believe the same is true of this statute. In an attempt to avoid its constitutional obligation, the Court today "pushes back the limits of the Constitution" to accommodate an Act of Congress.

I would affirm the judgment of the District Court.

———

MISSISSIPPI UNIVERSITY FOR WOMEN v. HOGAN, 458 U.S. 718 (1982). The Court held invalid a state statute which excluded males from enrolling in a state-supported professional nursing school. Justice O'Connor, writing for the Court, said that the "test for determining the validity of a gender-based classification is straightforward." Without citing either *Michael M.* or *Rossiter* she said: "Our decisions . . . establish that the party seeking to uphold a statute that classifies individuals on the basis of their gender must carry the burden of showing an 'exceeding persuasive justification' for the classification. . . . The burden is met only by showing at least that the classification serves 'important governmental objectives and that the discriminatory means employed' are 'substantially related to the achievement of those objectives.'" She also noted that the "policy of excluding males from admission to the School of Nursing tends to perpetuate the stereotyped view of nursing as an exclusively women's job."

For a fuller treatment of this case, see infra p. 781.

———

WHO ARE DISCRIMINATED AGAINST— MALES OR FEMALES?

In Frontiero v. Richardson, supra, it was clear that the discrimination was against females. A serviceman who was married received increased quarters allowances and medical and dental benefits whether or not his wife was dependent on him while a married servicewoman received the benefits only if her husband was dependent on her.

But what of statutes like the one in Weinberger v. Wiesenfeld, 420 U.S. 636 (1975)? Social Security Act benefits of a deceased husband and father covered by the Act were payable both to the widow and the minor children in her care. Such benefits on the basis of the earnings of a deceased wife and mother covered by the Act however were paid only to the children and not to the father. Is this a discrimination against males because they receive no payments when the covered wife dies while the wife receives payments when the covered husband dies? Or is this a discrimination against women because women workers covered by the Act received less protection for their families than men workers? In *Wiesenfeld* the Court held that the discrimination was against women and held it unconstitutional.

The issue next arose in Califano v. Goldfarb, 430 U.S. 199 (1977). Under the Federal Old-Age, Survivors, and Disability Insurance Benefits program survivors benefits were paid to the widow of a deceased husband covered by the Act but were payable to a widower whose wife was covered only if he received one-half or more of his support from his deceased wife. The Court held the classification invalid—four Justices regarded it as discriminating against female workers and invalid, while the fifth, concurring Justice, regarded it as discriminating against male survivors but still invalid. The four dissenters analyzed the law as benefitting female survivors.

The case that follows is the last in this series. Who is discriminated against? Men? Women? Both?

WENGLER v. DRUGGISTS MUTUAL INSURANCE CO.

446 U.S. 142, 100 S.Ct. 1540, 64 L.Ed.2d 107 (1980).

Mr. Justice White delivered the opinion of the Court.

This case challenges under the Equal Protection Clause of the Fourteenth Amendment a provision of the Missouri workers' compensation laws, Mo.Ann. Stat. § 287.240 (Vernon 1979 Cum.Supp.), which is claimed to involve an invalid gender-based discrimination.

I.

The facts are not in dispute. On February 11, 1977, Ruth Wengler, wife of appellant Paul J. Wengler, died in a work-related accident in the parking lot of her employer, appellee Dicus Prescription Drugs, Inc. Appellant filed a claim for death benefits under Mo.Ann.Stat. § 287.240 (Vernon 1979 Cum.Supp.), under which a widower is not entitled to death benefits unless he either is mentally or physically incapacitated from wage earning or proves actual dependence on his wife's earnings. In contrast, a widow qualifies for death benefits without having to prove actual dependence on her husband's earnings.[2]

Appellant stipulated that he was neither incapacitated nor dependent on his wife's earnings, but argued that, owing to its disparate treatment of similarly situated widows and widowers, § 287.240 violated the Equal Protection Clause of the United States Constitution. The claim was administratively denied, but the Circuit Court of Madison County reversed, holding that § 287.240 violated the Equal Protection Clause because the statutory restriction on a widower's recovery of death benefits did not also apply to a surviving wife. Dicus and its insurer, appellee Druggists Mutual Insurance Company, were ordered to pay death benefits to appellant in the appropriate amount.

The Missouri Supreme Court, distinguishing certain cases in this Court, reversed the Circuit Court's decision. The equal protection challenge to § 287.240 failed because "the substantive difference in the economic standing of working men and women justifies the advantage that [§ 287.240] administratively gives to a widow." Wengler v. Druggists Mutual Ins. Co., 583 S.W.2d 162, 168 (Mo.1979).

Because the decision of the Supreme Court of Missouri arguably conflicted with our precedents, we noted probable jurisdiction. . . . We now reverse.[3]

II.

The Missouri law indisputably mandates gender-based discrimination. Although the Missouri Supreme Court was of the view that the law favored, rather than disfavored, women, it is apparent that the statute discriminates against both

---

[2] At the time of her death Mrs. Wengler's wages were $69 per week. Had appellant prevailed in his attempt to receive full death benefits under the statute, his compensation would have been $46 per week. App. to Juris. Statement A23; see Mo.Ann.Stat. § 287.240(2) (Vernon 1979 Cum.Supp.). These benefits would have continued until appellant's death or remarriage. Id., § 287.240(4)(a).

[3] Recent decisions in three States have held unconstitutional workers' compensation statutes with presumptions of dependency identical to that at issue in this case. Arp v. Workers' Compensation Appeals Board, 19 Cal.3d 395, 563 P.2d 849, 138 Cal.Rptr. 293 (1977); Passante v. Walden Printing Co., 53 A.D.2d 8, 385 N.Y.S.2d 178 (1976); Tomarchio v. Township of Greenwich, 75 N.J. 62, 379 A.2d 848 (1977). The workers' compensation laws of the vast majority of States now make no distinction between the eligibility of widows and widowers for death benefits.

men and women. The provision discriminates against a woman covered by the Missouri workers' compensation system since, in the case of her death, benefits are payable to her spouse only if he is mentally or physically incapacitated or was to some extent dependent upon her. Under these tests, Mrs. Wengler's spouse was entitled to no benefits. If Mr. Wengler had died, however, Mrs. Wengler would have been conclusively presumed to be dependent and would have been paid the statutory amount for life or until she remarried even though she may not in fact have been dependent on Mr. Wengler. The benefits, therefore, that the working woman can expect to be paid to her spouse in the case of her work-related death are less than those payable to the spouse of the deceased male wage earner.

It is this kind of discrimination against working women that our cases have identified and in the circumstances found unjustified. At issue in Weinberger v. Wiesenfeld, 420 U.S. 636 (1975), was a provision in the Social Security Act, 42 U.S.C. § 402(g), that granted survivors' benefits based on the earnings of a deceased husband and father covered by the Act both to his widow and to the couple's minor children in her care, but that granted benefits based on the earnings of a covered deceased wife and mother only to the minor children and not to the widower. In concluding that the provision violated the equal protection component of the Fifth Amendment, we noted that, "[o]bviously, the notion that men are more likely than women to be the primary supporters of their spouses and children is not entirely without empirical support." Weinberger v. Wiesenfeld, supra, at 645, citing Kahn v. Shevin, 416 U.S. 351, 354, n. 7 (1974).[4] But such a generalization could not itself justify the gender-based distinction found in the Act, for § 402(g) "clearly operate[d] . . . to deprive women of protection for their families which men receive as a result of their employment." The offensive assumption was "that male workers' earnings are vital to the support of their families, while the earnings of female wage earners do not significantly contribute to their families' support."

Similarly, in Califano v. Goldfarb, 430 U.S. 199 (1977), we dealt with a Social Security Act provision providing survivors' benefits to a widow regardless of dependency, but providing the same benefits to a widower only if he had been receiving at least half of his support from his deceased wife. 42 U.S.C. § 402(f)(1)(D). Mr. Justice Brennan's plurality opinion pointed out that, under the challenged section, "female insureds received less protection for their spouses solely because of their sex" and that, as in *Wiesenfeld,* the provision disadvantaged women as compared to similarly situated men by providing the female wage earner with less protection for her family than it provided the family of the male wage earner even though the family needs might be identical. Califano v. Goldfarb, supra, at 208. The plurality opinion, in the circumstances there, found the discrimination violative of the Fifth Amendment's equal protection guarantee.

Frontiero v. Richardson, 411 U.S. 677 (1973), involved a similar discrimination. There, a serviceman could claim his wife as a dependent without regard to whether she was in fact dependent upon him and so obtain increased quarters allowances and medical and dental benefits. A servicewoman, on the other hand, could not claim her husband as a dependent for these purposes unless he was in fact dependent upon her for over one-half of his support. This

---

[4] In Kahn v. Shevin, 416 U.S. 351 (1974), the Court upheld a Florida annual $500 real estate tax exemption for all widows in the face of an equal protection challenge. The Court believed that statistics established a lower median income for women than men, a discrepancy that justified "a state tax law reasonably designed to further the state policy of cushioning the financial impact of spousal loss upon the sex for which that loss imposes a disproportionately heavy burden." As in *Kahn* we accept the importance of the state goal of helping needy spouses but as described in text the Missouri law in our view is not "reasonably designed" to achieve this goal. Thus the holding in *Kahn* is in no way dispositive of the case at bar.

discrimination, devaluing the service of the woman as compared with that of the man, was invalidated.

The Missouri law, as the Missouri courts recognized, also discriminates against men who survive their employed wives dying in work-related accidents. To receive benefits, the surviving male spouse must prove his incapacity or dependency. The widow of a deceased wage earner, in contrast, is presumed dependent and is guaranteed a weekly benefit for life or until remarriage. It was this discrimination against the male survivor as compared with a similarly situated female that Mr. Justice Stevens identified in Califano v. Goldfarb, supra, as resulting in a denial of equal protection. 430 U.S., at 217–224 (opinion of Stevens, J.).

III.

However the discrimination is described in this case, our precedents require that gender-based discriminations must serve important governmental objectives and that the discriminatory means employed must be substantially related to the achievement of those objectives. Califano v. Westcott, 443 U.S. 76, 89 (1979); Orr v. Orr, 440 U.S. 268, 279 (1979); Califano v. Webster, 430 U.S. 313, 316–317 (1977); Craig v. Boren, 429 U.S. 190, 197 (1976).

Acknowledging that the discrimination involved here must satisfy the Craig v. Boren standard, Wengler v. Druggists Mutual Ins. Co., 583 S.W.2d 162, 164–165 (1979), the Missouri Supreme Court stated that "the purpose of the [law] was to favor widows, not to disfavor them" and that when the law was passed in 1925 the legislature no doubt believed that "a widow was more in need of prompt payment of death benefits upon her husband's death without drawn-out proceedings to determine the amount of dependency than was a widower." Hence, the conclusive presumption of dependency satisfied "a perceived need widows generally had, which need was not common to men whose wives might be killed while working." Ibid. The survivor's "hardship was seen by the legislature [ ] as more immediate and pronounced on women than on men," and "the substantive difference in the economic standing of working men and women justifies the advantage that [the law] administratively gives to the widow."

Providing for needy spouses is surely an important governmental objective, Orr v. Orr, 440 U.S. 268, 280 (1979), and the Missouri statute effects that goal by paying benefits to all surviving female spouses and to all surviving male spouses who prove their dependency. But the question remains whether the discriminatory means employed—discrimination against women wage earners and surviving male spouses—itself substantially serves the statutory end. Surely the needs of surviving widows and widowers would be completely served either by paying benefits to all members of both classes or by paying benefits only to those members of either class who can demonstrate their need. Why, then, employ the discriminatory means of paying all surviving widows without requiring proof of dependency, but paying only those widowers who make the required demonstration? The only justification offered by the state court or appellees for not treating males and females alike, whether viewed as wage earners or survivors of wage earners, is the assertion that most women are dependent on male wage earners and that it is more efficient to presume dependency in the case of women than to engage in case-to-case determination, whereas individualized inquiries in the postulated few cases in which men might be dependent are not prohibitively costly.

The burden, however, is on those defending the discrimination to make out the claimed justification, and this burden is not carried simply by noting that in 1925 the state legislature thought widows to be more in need of prompt help than men or that today "the substantive difference in the economic standing of working men and women justifies the advantage given to widows." Wengler v. Druggists Mutual Ins. Co., supra, at 168. It may be that there is empirical support for the proposition that men are more likely to be the principal supporters of their spouses and families, Weinberger v. Wiesenfeld, supra, at 645, but the bare assertion of this argument falls far short of justifying gender-based discrimination on the grounds of administrative convenience. Yet neither the court below nor appellees in this Court essay any persuasive demonstration as to what the economic consequences to the State or to the beneficiaries might be if, in one way or another, men and women, whether as wage earners or survivors, were treated equally under the workers' compensation law, thus eliminating the double-edged discrimination described in Part II of this opinion.

We think, then, that the claimed justification of administrative convenience fails, just as it has in our prior cases. In Frontiero v. Richardson, 411 U.S. 677, 689–690 (1973), the government claimed that, as an empirical matter, wives are so frequently dependent upon their husbands and husbands so rarely dependent upon their wives that it was cheaper to presume wives to be dependent upon their husbands while requiring proof of dependency in the case of the male. The Court found the claimed justification insufficient to save the discrimination. And in Reed v. Reed, 404 U.S. 71, 76 (1971), the Court said "[t]o give a mandatory preference to members of either sex over members of the other, merely to accomplish the elimination of hearings on the merits, is to make the very kind of arbitrary legislative choice forbidden by the Equal Protection Clause. . . ." See also Califano v. Goldfarb, supra, at 219–220 (opinion of Stevens, J.). It may be that there are levels of administrative convenience that will justify discriminations that are subject to heightened scrutiny under the Equal Protection Clause, but the requisite showing has not been made here by the mere claim that it would be inconvenient to individualize determinations about widows as well as widowers.

IV.

Thus we conclude that the Supreme Court of Missouri erred in upholding the constitutional validity of § 287.240. We are left with the question whether the defect should be cured by extending the presumption of dependence to widowers or by eliminating it for widows. Because state legislation is at issue, and because a remedial outcome consonant with the state legislature's overall purpose is preferable, we believe that state judges are better positioned to choose an appropriate method of remedying the constitutional violation. Accordingly, we reverse the decision of the Supreme Court of Missouri and remand the case to that court for further proceedings not inconsistent with this opinion.

So ordered.

Mr. Justice Rehnquist, continuing to believe that Califano v. Goldfarb, 430 U.S. 199 (1977), was wrongly decided, and that constitutional issues should be more readily reexamined under the doctrine of *stare decisis* than other issues, dissents and would affirm the judgment of the Supreme Court of Missouri.

Mr. Justice Stevens, concurring.

Nothing has happened since the decision in Califano v. Goldfarb, 430 U.S. 199, to persuade me that this kind of gender-based classification can simultaneously disfavor the male class and the female class.

To illustrate my difficulty with the analysis in Part II of the Court's opinion, it should be noted that there are three relevant kinds of marriages: (1) those in which the husband is dependent on the wife; (2) those in which the wife is dependent on the husband; and (3) those in which neither spouse is dependent on the other.

Under the Missouri statute, in either of the first two situations, if the dependent spouse survives, a death benefit will be paid regardless of whether the survivor is male or female; conversely, if the working spouse survives, no death benefit will be paid. The only difference in the two situations is that the surviving male, unlike the surviving female, must undergo the inconvenience of proving dependency. That surely is not a discrimination against females.

In the third situation, if one spouse dies, benefits are payable to a surviving female but not to a surviving male. In my view, that is a rather blatant discrimination against males. While both spouses remain alive, the prospect of receiving a potential death benefit upon the husband's demise reduces the wife's need for insurance on his life, whereas the prospect of *not* receiving a death benefit upon the wife's demise increases the husband's need for insurance on her life. That difference again places the husband at a disadvantage.

No matter how the statute is viewed, the class against which it discriminates is the male class. I therefore cannot joint Part II of the Court's opinion. I do, however, agree that Missouri has failed to justify the disparate treatment of persons who have as strong a claim to equal treatment as do similarly situated surviving spouses, see Califano v. Goldfarb, 430 U.S. 199, 223 (Stevens, J., concurring), and that its statute violates the Equal Protection Clause of the Fourteenth Amendment. For that reason I concur in the Court's judgment.

EQUAL RIGHTS AMENDMENT PROPOSED

On March 22, 1972, Congress passed and submitted to the legislatures of the states for ratification an amendment to the Constitution reading as follows:

"Section 1. Equality of rights under the law shall not be denied or abridged by the United States or by any State on account of sex.

"Section 2. The Congress shall have the power to enforce, by appropriate legislation, the provisions of this article.

"Section 3. This amendment shall take effect two years after the date of ratification."

The statute proposing the amendment provided that the ratifications must occur within seven years. By 1978, 35 states (3 less than the required three-fourths) had ratified, but three of them had rescinded their previous ratification. Congress then passed a statute extending the time for ratification to June 30, 1982. The necessary number of states did not ratify by that deadline.

F. ARE THERE OTHER SUSPECT CLASSIFICATIONS?

MASSACHUSETTS BOARD OF RETIREMENT v. MURGIA

427 U.S. 307, 96 S.Ct. 2562, 49 L.Ed.2d 520 (1976).

Per Curiam.

This case presents the question whether the provision of Mass.Gen.Laws Ann. c. 32, § 26(3)(a), that a uniformed State Police Officer "shall be retired . . . upon his attaining age fifty," denies appellee police officer equal protection of the laws in violation of the Fourteenth Amendment.

Appellee Robert Murgia was an officer in the Uniformed Branch of the Massachusetts State Police. The Massachusetts Board of Retirement retired him upon his 50th birthday. Appellee brought this civil action in the United States District Court for the District of Massachusetts, alleging that the operation of

§ 26(3)(a) denied him equal protection of the laws and requesting the convening of a three-judge court under 28 U.S.C. §§ 2281, 2284. . . .

The primary function of the Uniformed Branch of the Massachusetts State Police is to protect persons and property and maintain law and order. Specifically, uniformed officers participate in controlling prison and civil disorders, respond to emergencies and natural disasters, patrol highways in marked cruisers, investigate crime, apprehend criminal suspects, and provide back-up support for local law enforcement personnel. As the District Court observed, "service in this branch is, or can be arduous." 376 F.Supp., at 754. "[H]igh versatility is required, with few, if any, backwaters available for the partially superannuated." Ibid. Thus, "even [appellee's] experts concede that there is a general relationship between advancing age and decreasing physical ability to respond to the demands of the job." Id., at 755.

These considerations prompt the requirement that uniformed state officers pass a comprehensive physical examination biennially until age 40. After that, until mandatory retirement at age 50, uniformed officers must pass annually a more rigorous examination, including an electrocardiogram and tests for gastrointestinal bleeding. Appellee Murgia had passed such an examination four months before he was retired, and there is no dispute that, when he retired, his excellent physical and mental health still rendered him capable of performing the duties of a uniformed officer.

. . .

In assessing appellee's equal protection claim, the District Court found it unnecessary to apply a strict scrutiny test, see Shapiro v. Thompson, 394 U.S. 618 (1969), for it determined that the age classification established by the Massachusetts statutory scheme could not in any event withstand a test of rationality, see Dandridge v. Williams, 397 U.S. 471 (1970). Since there had been no showing that reaching age 50 forecast even "imminent change" in an officer's physical condition, the District Court held that compulsory retirement at age 50 was irrational under a scheme that assessed the capabilities of officers individually by means of comprehensive annual physical examinations. We agree that rationality is the proper standard by which to test whether compulsory retirement at age 50 violates equal protection. We disagree, however, with the District Court's determination that the age 50 classification is not rationally related to furthering a legitimate state interest.

I.

We need state only briefly our reasons for agreeing that strict scrutiny is not the proper test for determining whether the mandatory retirement provision denies appellee equal protection. San Antonio Independent School District v. Rodriguez, 411 U.S. 1, 16 (1973), reaffirmed that equal protection analysis requires strict scrutiny of a legislative classification only when the classification impermissibly interferes with the exercise of a fundamental right or operates to the peculiar disadvantage of a suspect class. Mandatory retirement at age 50 under the Massachusetts statute involves neither situation.

This Court's decisions give no support to the proposition that a right of governmental employment per se is fundamental. See San Antonio Independent School District v. Rodriguez, supra; Lindsey v. Normet, 405 U.S. 56, 73 (1972); Dandridge v. Williams, supra, at 485. Accordingly, we have expressly stated that a standard less than strict scrutiny "has consistently been applied to state legislation restricting the availability of employment opportunities." Ibid.

Nor does the class of uniformed state police officers over 50 constitute a suspect class for purposes of equal protection analysis. Rodriguez, supra, at 28, observed that a suspect class is one "saddled with such disabilities, or subjected to such a history of purposeful unequal treatment, or relegated to such a position of political powerlessness as to command extraordinary protection from the majoritarian political process." While the treatment of the aged in this Nation has not been wholly free of discrimination, such persons, unlike say, those who have been discriminated against on the basis of race or national origin, have not experienced a "history of purposeful unequal treatment" or been subjected to unique disabilities on the basis of stereotyped characteristics not truly indicative of their abilities. The class subject to the compulsory retirement feature of the Massachusetts statute consists of uniformed state police officers over the age of 50. It cannot be said to discriminate only against the elderly. Rather, it draws the line at a certain age in middle life. But even old age does not define a "discrete and insular" group, United States v. Carolene Products Co., 304 U.S. 144, 152–153, n. 4 (1938), in need of "extraordinary protection from the majoritarian political process." Instead, it marks a stage that each of us will reach if we live out our normal span. Even if the statute could be said to impose a penalty upon a class defined as the aged, it would not impose a distinction sufficiently akin to those classifications that we have found suspect to call for strict judicial scrutiny.

Under the circumstances, it is unnecessary to subject the State's resolution of competing interests in this case to the degree of critical examination that our cases under the Equal Protection Clause recently have characterized as "strict judicial scrutiny."

II.

We turn then to examine this state classification under the rational basis standard. This inquiry employs a relatively relaxed standard reflecting the Court's awareness that the drawing of lines that create distinctions is peculiarly a legislative task and an unavoidable one. Perfection in making the necessary classifications is neither possible nor necessary. Dandridge v. Williams, supra, at 485. Such action by a legislature is presumed to be valid.

In this case, the Massachusetts statute clearly meets the requirements of the Equal Protection Clause, for the State's classification rationally furthers the purpose identified by the State: Through mandatory retirement at age 50, the legislature seeks to protect the public by assuring physical preparedness of its uniformed police. Since physical ability generally declines with age, mandatory retirement at 50 serves to remove from police service those whose fitness for uniformed work presumptively has diminished with age. This clearly is rationally related to the State's objective. There is no indication that § 26(3)(a) has the effect of excluding from service so few officers who are in fact unqualified as to render age 50 a criterion wholly unrelated to the objective of the statute.

That the State chooses not to determine fitness more precisely through individualized testing after age 50 is not to say that the objective of assuring physical fitness is not rationally furthered by a maximum age limitation. It is only to say that with regard to the interest of all concerned, the State perhaps has not chosen the best means to accomplish this purpose. But where rationality is the test, a State "does not violate the Equal Protection Clause merely because the classifications made by its laws are imperfect." Dandridge v. Williams, 397 U.S., at 485.

We do not make light of the substantial economic and psychological effects premature and compulsory retirement can have on an individual; nor do we denigrate the ability of elderly citizens to continue to contribute to society. The problems of retirement have been well documented and are beyond serious dispute. But "[w]e do not decide today that the [Massachusetts statute] is wise, that it best fulfills the relevant social and economic objectives that [Massachusetts] might ideally espouse, or that a more just and humane system could not be devised." Id., at 487. We decide only that the system enacted by the Massachusetts Legislature does not deny appellee equal protection of the law.

The judgment is reversed.

Mr. Justice Stevens took no part in the consideration or decision of this case.

Mr. Justice Marshall, dissenting.

. . .

I.

Although there are signs that its grasp on the law is weakening, the rigid two-tier model still holds sway as the Court's articulated description of the equal protection test. Again, I must object to its perpetuation. The model's two fixed modes of analysis, strict scrutiny and mere rationality, simply do not describe the inquiry the Court has undertaken—or should undertake—in equal protection cases. Rather, the inquiry has been much more sophisticated and the Court should admit as much. It has focused upon the character of the classification in question, the relative importance to individuals in the class discriminated against of the governmental benefits that they do not receive, and the state interests asserted in support of the classification. . . .

Although the Court outwardly adheres to the two-tier model, it has apparently lost interest in recognizing further "fundamental" rights and "suspect" classes. See San Antonio School District v. Rodriguez, supra (rejecting education as a fundamental right); Frontiero v. Richardson, 411 U.S. 677 (1973) (declining to treat women as a suspect class). In my view, this result is the natural consequence of the limitations of the Court's traditional equal protection analysis. If a statute invades a "fundamental" right or discriminates against a "suspect" class, it is subject to strict scrutiny. If a statute is subject to strict scrutiny, the statute always, or nearly always, see Korematsu v. United States, 323 U.S. 214 (1944), is struck down. Quite obviously, the only critical decision is whether strict scrutiny should be invoked at all. It should be no surprise, then, that the Court is hesitant to expand the number of categories of rights and classes subject to strict scrutiny, when each expansion involves the invalidation of virtually every classification bearing upon a newly covered category.[1]

But however understandable the Court's hesitancy to invoke strict scrutiny, all remaining legislation should not drop into the bottom tier, and be measured by the mere rationality test. For that test, too, when applied as articulated, leaves little doubt about the outcome; the challenged legislation is always upheld. See New Orleans v. Dukes, 427 U.S. 297 (1976) (overruling Morey v. Doud, 354 U.S. 457 (1957), the only modern case in which this Court has struck down an economic classification as irrational). It cannot be gainsaid that there remain rights, not now classified as "fundamental," that remain vital to the flourishing of a free society, and classes, not now classified as "suspect," that are unfairly burdened by invidious discrimination unrelated to the individual worth of their members. Whatever we call these rights and classes, we simply cannot forgo all judicial protection against discriminatory legislation bearing upon

---

[1] Some classifications are so invidious that they should be struck down automatically absent the most compelling state interest, and by suggesting the limitations of strict scrutiny analysis I do not mean to imply otherwise. The analysis should be accomplished, however, not by stratified notions of "suspect" classes and "fundamental" rights, but by individualized assessments of the particular classes and rights involved in each case. Of course, the traditional suspect classes and fundamental rights would still rank at the top of the list of protected categories, so that in cases involving those categories analysis would be functionally equivalent to strict scrutiny. Thus, the advantages of the approach I favor do not appear in such cases, but rather emerge in those dealing with traditionally less protected classes and rights.

them, but for the rare instances when the legislative choice can be termed "wholly irrelevant" to the legislative goal. McGowan v. Maryland, 366 U.S. 420, 425 (1961).

While the Court's traditional articulation of the rational basis test does suggest just such an abdication, happily the Court's deeds have not matched its words. Time and again, met with cases touching upon the prized rights and burdened classes of our society, the Court has acted only after a reasonably probing look at the legislative goals and means, and at the significance of the personal rights and interests invaded. . . . These cases make clear that the court has rejected, albeit *sub silentio,* its most deferential statements of the rationality standard in assessing the validity under the Equal Protection Clause of much noneconomic legislation.

But there are problems with deciding cases based on factors not encompassed by the applicable standards. First, the approach is rudderless, affording no notice to interested parties of the standards governing particular cases and giving no firm guidance to judges who, as a consequence, must assess the constitutionality of legislation before them on an *ad hoc* basis. Second, and not unrelatedly, the approach is unpredictable and requires holding this Court to standards it has never publicly adopted. Thus, the approach presents the danger that, as I suggest has happened here, relevant factors will be misapplied or ignored. All interests not "fundamental" and all cases not "suspect" are not the same; and it is time for the Court to drop the pretense that, for purposes of the Equal Protection Clause, they are.

II.

The danger of the Court's verbal adherence to the rigid two-tier test, despite its effective repudiation of that test in the cases, is demonstrated by its efforts here. There is simply no reason why a statute that tells able-bodied police officers, ready and willing to work, that they no longer have the right to earn a living in their chosen profession merely because they are 50 years old should be judged by the same minimal standards of rationality that we use to test economic legislation that discriminates against business interests. See New Orleans v. Dukes, supra; Williamson v. Lee Optical Co., 348 U.S. 483 (1955). Yet, the Court today not only invokes the minimal level of scrutiny, it wrongly adheres to it. Analysis of the three factors I have identified above—the importance of the governmental benefits denied, the character of the class, and the asserted state interests—demonstrates the Court's error.

Whether "fundamental" or not, "the right of the individual . . . to engage in any of the common occupations of life" has been repeatedly recognized by this Court as falling within the concept of liberty guaranteed by the Fourteenth Amendment. Board of Regents v. Roth, 408 U.S. 564, 572 (1972), quoting Meyer v. Nebraska, 262 U.S. 390, 399 (1923). . . . Even if the right to earn a living does not include the right to work for the government, it is settled that because of the importance of the interest involved, we have always carefully looked at the reasons asserted for depriving a government employee of his job.

While depriving any government employee of his job is a significant deprivation, it is particularly burdensome when the person deprived is an older citizen. Once terminated, the elderly cannot readily find alternative employment. The lack of work is not only economically damaging, but emotionally and physically draining. Deprived of his status in the community and of the opportunity for meaningful activity, fearful of becoming dependent on others for his support, and lonely in his new-found isolation, the involuntarily retired person is susceptible to physical and emotional ailments as a direct consequence of his enforced idleness. Ample clinical evidence supports the conclusion that mandatory retirement poses a direct threat to the health and life expectancy of the retired person, and these consequences of termination for age are not disputed by appellant. Thus, an older person deprived of his job by the government loses not only his right to earn a living, but, too often, his health as well, in sad contradiction of Browning's promise, "The best is yet to be/The last of life, for which the first was made."

Not only are the elderly denied important benefits when they are terminated on the basis of age, but the classification of older workers is itself one that merits judicial attention. Whether older workers constitute a "suspect" class or not, it cannot be disputed that they constitute a class subject to repeated and arbitrary discrimination in employment. . . .

Of course, the Court is quite right in suggesting that distinctions exist between the elderly and traditional suspect classes such as Negroes, and between the elderly and "quasi-suspect" classes such as women or illegitimates. The elderly are protected not only by certain anti-discrimination legislation, but by legislation that provides them with positive benefits not enjoyed by the public at large. Moreover, the elderly are not isolated in society, and discrimination against them is not pervasive but is centered primarily in employment. The advantage of a flexible equal protection standard, however, is that it can readily accommodate such variables. The elderly are undoubtedly discriminated against, and when legislation denies them an important benefit—employment—I conclude that to sustain the legislation the Commonwealth must show a reasonably substantial interest and a scheme reasonably closely tailored to achieving that interest. . . . This inquiry, ultimately, is not markedly different from that undertaken by the Court in Reed v. Reed, supra.

Turning then, to the Commonwealth's arguments, I agree that the purpose of the mandatory retirement law is legitimate, and indeed compelling. The Commonwealth has every reason to assure that its state police officers are of sufficient physical strength and health to perform their jobs. In my view, however, the means chosen, the forced retirement of officers at age 50, is so overinclusive that it must fall.

All potential officers must pass a rigorous physical examination. Until age 40, this same examination must be passed every two years—when the officer re-enlists—and, after age 40, every year. The Commonwealth has conceded that "[w]hen a member passes his re-enlistment or annual physical, he is found to be qualified to perform all of the duties of the Uniformed Branch of the Massachusetts State Police." If a member fails the examination, he is immediately terminated or refused re-enlistment. Thus, the only members of the state police still on the force at age 50 are those who have been determined—repeatedly—by the Commonwealth to be physically fit for the job. Yet, all of these physically fit officers are automatically terminated at age 50. The Commonwealth does not seriously assert that its testing is no longer effective at age 50, nor does it claim that continued testing would serve no purpose because officers over 50 are no longer physically able to perform their jobs. Thus the Commonwealth is in the position of already individually testing its police officers for physical fitness, conceding that such testing be adequate to determine the physical ability of an officer to continue on the job, and conceding that that ability may continue after age 50. In these circumstances, I see no reason at all for automatically terminating those officers who reach the age of 50; indeed, that action seems the height of irrationality.

Accordingly, I conclude that the Commonwealth's mandatory retirement law cannot stand when measured against the significant deprivation the Commonwealth's action works upon the terminated employees. I would affirm the judgment of the District Court.[a]

WEALTH CLASSIFICATIONS

The Court has often stated that wealth classifications are not suspect. Two cases illustrate its approach.

In Ortwein v. Schwab, 410 U.S. 656 (1973) the Court held valid a state requirement of a $25 appellate court filing fee in cases challenging welfare agency determinations. The Court said:

"Appellants urge that the filing fee violates the Equal Protection Clause by unconstitutionally discriminating against the poor. . . . [T]his litigation, which deals with welfare payments, 'is in the area of economics and social welfare.' 409 U.S., at 446; See Dandridge v. Williams, 397 U.S., at 485–486. No suspect classification, such as race, nationality, or alienage, is present. See Graham v. Richardson, 403 U.S. 365, 372 (1971). The applicable standard is that of rational justification."

In Harris v. McRae, 448 U.S. 297 (1980) (set out fully infra p. 899) the Court upheld a federal statute prohibiting the expenditure of federal funds for abortions. On the suspect classification argument the Court said:

"[We now conclude that the Hyde Amendment] is not predicated on a constitutionally suspect classification. In reaching this conclusion, we again draw guidance from the Court's decision in Maher v. Roe. As to whether the Connecticut welfare regulation providing funds for childbirth but not for nontherapeutic abortions discriminated against a suspect class, the Court in Maher observed:

'An indigent woman desiring an abortion does not come within the limited category of disadvantaged classes so recognized by our cases. Nor does the fact that the impact of the regulation falls upon those who cannot pay lead to a different conclusion. In a sense, every denial of welfare to an indigent creates a wealth classification as compared to nonindigents who are able to pay for the desired goods or services. But this Court has never held that financial need alone identifies a suspect class for purposes of equal protection analysis.' 432 U.S., at 470–471, citing San Antonio School Dist. v. Rodriguez, 411 U.S. 1, 29; Dandridge v. Williams, 397 U.S. 471.

'Thus, the Court in Maher found no basis for concluding that the Connecticut regulation was predicated on a suspect classification.'

"It is our view that the present case is indistinguishable from Maher in this respect. Here, as in Maher, the principal impact of the Hyde Amendment falls on the indigent. But that fact does not itself render the funding restriction constitutionally invalid, for this Court has held repeatedly that poverty, standing alone, is not a suspect classification. See, e.g., James v. Valtierra, 402 U.S. 137."

Justice Marshall, dissenting, said:

"With all deference, I am unable to understand how the Court can afford the same level of scrutiny to the legislation involved here—whose cruel impact falls exclusively on indigent pregnant women—that it has given to legislation distinguishing opticians from ophthalmologists, or to other legislation that makes distinctions between economic interests more than able to protect themselves in the political process. . . . Heightened scrutiny of legislative classifications has always been designed to protect groups saddled with such disabilities or subjected to such a history of purposeful unequal treatment, or relegated to such

---

[a] On the question of age discrimination see also Vance v. Bradley, 440 U.S. 93 (1979).

a position of political powerlessness as to command extraordinary protection from the majoritarian political process. San Antonio School District v. Rodriguez, supra, at 28 (1973). And while it is now clear that traditional 'strict scrutiny' is unavailable to protect the poor against classifications that disfavor them, Dandridge v. Williams, 397 U.S. 471 (1970), I do not believe that legislation that imposes a crushing burden on indigent women can be treated with the same deference given to legislation distinguishing among business interests.

B.

. . . .

"The class burdened by the Hyde Amendment consists of indigent women, a substantial proportion of whom are members of minority races. As I observed in *Maher,* nonwhite women obtain abortions at nearly double the rate of whites. . . . In my view, the fact that the burden of the Hyde Amendment falls exclusively on financially destitute women suggests 'a special condition, which tends seriously to curtail the operation of those political processes ordinarily to be relied upon to protect minorities, and which may call for a correspondingly more searching judicial inquiry' United States v. Carolene Products, 304 U.S. 144, 152–153, n. 4 (1938). For this reason, I continue to believe that 'a showing that state action has a devastating impact on the lives of minority racial groups must be relevant' for purposes of equal protection analysis. Jefferson v. Hackney, 406 U.S. 535, 575–576 (1972) (Marshall, J., dissenting)."

G.　THE REQUIREMENT OF A DISCRIMINATORY PURPOSE—THE RELEVANCE OF DISCRIMINATORY IMPACT

WASHINGTON v. DAVIS

426 U.S. 229, 96 S.Ct. 2040, 48 L.Ed.2d 597 (1976).

Mr. Justice White delivered the opinion of the Court.

This case involves the validity of a qualifying test administered to applicants for positions as police officers in the District of Columbia Metropolitan Police Department. The test was sustained by the District Court but invalidated by the Court of Appeals. We are in agreement with the District Court and hence reverse the judgment of the Court of Appeals.

I.

This action began on April 10, 1970, when two Negro police officers filed suit against the then Commissioner of the District of Columbia, the Chief of the District's Metropolitan Police Department and the Commissioners of the United States Civil Service Commission. An amended complaint, filed December 10, alleged that the promotion policies of the Department were racially discriminatory and sought a declaratory judgment and an injunction. The respondents Harley and Sellers were permitted to intervene, their amended complaint asserting that their applications to become officers in the Department had been rejected, and that the Department's recruiting procedures discriminated on the basis of race against black applicants by a series of practices including, but not limited to, a written personnel test which excluded a disproportionately high number of Negro applicants. These practices were asserted to violate respondents' rights "under the due process clause of the Fifth Amendment to the United States Constitution, under 42 U.S.C. § 1981 and under D.C.Code § 1–320." Defendants answered, and discovery and various other proceedings followed. Respondents then filed a motion for partial summary judgment with respect to the recruiting phase of the case, seeking a declaration that the test administered to those applying to become police officers is "unlawfully discriminatory and therefore in violation of the Due Process Clause of the Fifth Amendment. . . . ." No issue under any statute or regulation was raised by the motion. The District of Columbia defendants, petitioners here, and the federal parties also filed motions for summary judgment with respect to the recruiting aspects of the case asserting that respondents were entitled to relief on neither constitutional nor statutory grounds. The District Court granted petitioners' and denied respondents' motions. Davis v. Washington, 348 F.Supp. 15 (D.C.1972).

According to the findings and conclusions of the District Court, to be accepted by the Department and to enter an intensive 17-week training program, the police recruit was required to satisfy certain physical and character standards, to be a high school graduate or its equivalent and to receive a grade of at least 40 on "Test 21," which is "an examination that is used generally throughout the federal service," which "was developed by the Civil Service Commission not the Police Department" and which was "designed to test verbal ability, vocabulary, reading and comprehension."

The validity of Test 21 was the sole issue before the court on the motions for summary judgment. The District Court noted that there was no claim of "an intentional discrimination or purposeful discriminatory actions" but only a claim that Test 21 bore no relationship to job performance and "has a highly discriminatory impact in screening out black candidates." Petitioners' evidence, the District Court said, warranted three conclusions: "(a) The number of black police officers, while substantial, is not proportionate to the population mix of the city. (b) A higher percentage of blacks fail the Test than whites. (c) The Test has not been validated to establish its reliability for measuring subsequent job performance." Ibid. This showing was deemed sufficient to shift the burden of proof to the defendants in the action, petitioners here; but the court nevertheless concluded that on the undisputed facts respondents were not entitled to relief. The District Court relied on several factors. Since August 1969, 44% of new police force recruits had been black; that figure also represented the proportion of blacks on the total force and was roughly equivalent to 20–29-year-old blacks in the 50-mile radius in which the recruiting efforts of the Police Department had been concentrated. It was undisputed that the Department had systematically and affirmatively sought to enroll black officers many of whom passed the test but failed to report for duty. The District Court rejected the assertion that Test 21 was culturally slanted to favor whites and was "satisfied that the undisputable facts prove the test to be reasonably and directly related to the requirements of the police recruit training program and that it is neither so designed nor operated to discriminate against otherwise qualified blacks." It was thus not necessary to show that Test 21 was not only a useful indicator of training school performance but had also been validated in terms of job performance—"the lack of job performance validation does not defeat the test, given its direct relationship to recruiting and the valid part it plays in this process." The District Court ultimately concluded that "the proof is wholly lacking that a police officer qualifies on the color of his skin rather than ability" and that the Department "should not be required on this showing to lower standards or to abandon efforts to achieve excellence."

Having lost on both constitutional and statutory issues in the District Court, respondents brought the case to the Court of Appeals claiming that their summary judgment motion, which rested on purely constitutional grounds, should have been granted. The tendered constitutional issue was whether the use of Test 21 invidiously discriminated against Negroes and hence denied them due process of law contrary to the commands of the Fifth Amendment. The Court of Appeals, addressing that issue, announced that it would be guided by Griggs v. Duke Power Co., 401 U.S. 424 (1971), a case involving the interpretation and application of Title VII of the Civil Rights Act of 1964, and held that the statutory standards elucidated in that case were to govern the due process question tendered in this one. 168 U.S.App.D.C. 42, 512 F.2d 956 (1975). The court went on to declare that lack of discriminatory intent in designing and administering Test 21 was irrelevant; the critical fact was rather that a far greater proportion of blacks—four times as many—failed the test than did whites. This disproportionate impact, standing alone and without regard to whether it indicated a discriminatory purpose, was held sufficient to establish a constitutional violation, absent proof by petitioners that the test was an adequate measure of job performance in addition to being an indicator of probable success in the training program, a burden which the court ruled petitioners had failed to discharge.

. . . .

II.

Because the Court of Appeals erroneously applied the legal standards applicable to Title VII cases in resolving the constitutional issue before it, we reverse its judgment in respondents' favor. Although the petition for certiorari did not present this ground for reversal, our Rule 40(1)(d)(2) provides that we "may notice a plain error not presented"; and this is an appropriate occasion to invoke the rule.

As the Court of Appeals understood Title VII, employees or applicants proceeding under it need not concern themselves with the employer's possibly discriminatory purpose but instead may focus solely on the racially differential impact of the challenged hiring or promotion practices. This is not the constitutional rule. We have never held that the constitutional standard for adjudicating claims of invidious racial discrimination is identical to the standards applicable under Title VII, and we decline to do so today.

The central purpose of the Equal Protection Clause of the Fourteenth Amendment is the prevention of official conduct discriminating on the basis of race. It is also true that the Due Process Clause of the Fifth Amendment contains an equal protection component prohibiting the United States from invidiously discriminating between individuals or groups. Bolling v. Sharpe, 347 U.S. 497 (1954). But our cases have not embraced the proposition that a law or other official act, without regard to whether it reflects a racially discriminatory purpose, is unconstitutional *solely* because it has a racially disproportionate impact.

Almost 100 years ago, Strauder v. West Virginia, 100 U.S. 303 (1879), established that the exclusion of Negroes from grand and petit juries in criminal proceedings violated the Equal Protection Clause, but the fact that a particular jury or a series of juries does not statistically reflect the racial composition of the community does not in itself make out an invidious discrimination forbidden by the Clause. "A purpose to discriminate must be present which may be proven by systematic exclusion of eligible jurymen of the prescribed race or by an unequal application of the law to such an extent as to show intentional discrimination." Akins v. Texas, 325 U.S. 398, 403–404 (1945). A defendant in a criminal case is entitled "to require that the State not deliberately and systematically deny to the members of his race the right to participate as jurors in the administration of justice." See also Carter v. Jury Commission, 396 U.S. 320, 335–337, 339 (1970); Cassell v. Texas, 339 U.S. 282, 287–290 (1950); Patton v. Mississippi, 332 U.S. 463, 468–469 (1947).

The rule is the same in other contexts. Wright v. Rockefeller, 376 U.S. 52 (1964), upheld a New York congressional apportionment statute against claims that district lines had been racially gerrymandered. The challenged districts were made up predominantly of whites or of minority races, and their boundaries were irregularly drawn. The challengers did not prevail because they failed to prove that the New York legislature "was either motivated by racial considerations or in fact drew the districts on racial lines"; the plaintiffs had not shown that the statute "was the product of a state contrivance to segregate on the basis of race or place of origin." 376 U.S., at 56, 58. The dissenters were in agreement that the issue was whether the "boundaries . . . were purposefully drawn on racial lines." 376 U.S., at 67.

The school desegregation cases have also adhered to the basic equal protection principle that the invidious quality of a law claimed to be racially discriminatory must ultimately be traced to a racially discriminatory purpose. That there are both predominantly black and predominantly white schools in a community is not alone violative of the Equal Protection Clause. The essential element of *de jure* segregation is "a current condition of segregation resulting from intentional state action . . . the differentiating factor between *de jure* segregation and so-called *de facto* segregation . . . is *purpose* or *intent* to segregate." Keyes v. School District No. 1, 413 U.S. 189, 205, 208 (1973). The Court has also recently rejected allegations of racial discrimination based solely on the statistically disproportionate racial impact of various provisions of the Social Security Act because "the acceptance of appellant's constitutional theory would render suspect each difference in treatment among the grant classes, however lacking the racial motivation and however rational the treatment might be." Jefferson v. Hackney, 406 U.S. 535, 548 (1972). And compare Hunter v. Erickson, 393 U.S. 385 (1969), with James v. Valtierra, 402 U.S. 137 (1971).

This is not to say that the necessary discriminatory racial purpose must be express or appear on the face of the statute, or that a law's disproportionate impact is irrelevant in cases involving Constitution-based claims of racial discrimination. A statute, otherwise neutral on its face, must not be applied so as invidiously to discriminate on the basis of race. Yick Wo v. Hopkins, 118 U.S. 356 (1886). It is also clear from the cases dealing with racial discrimination in the selection of juries that the systematic exclusion of Negroes is itself such an "unequal application of the law . . . as to show intentional discrimination." Akins v. Texas, supra, at 404. Smith v. Texas, 311 U.S. 128 (1940); Pierre v. Louisiana, 306 U.S. 354 (1939); Neal v. Delaware, 103 U.S. 370 (1881). A prima facie case of discriminatory purpose may be proved as well by the absence of Negroes on a particular jury combined with the failure of the jury commissioners to be informed of eligible Negro jurors in a community, Hill v. Texas, 316 U.S. 400, 404 (1942), or with racially nonneutral selection procedures, Alexander v. Louisiana, 405 U.S. 625 (1972); Avery v. Georgia, 345 U.S. 559 (1953); Whitus v. Georgia, 385 U.S. 545 (1967). With a prima facie case made out, "the burden of proof shifts to the State to rebut the presumption of unconstitutional action by showing that permissible racially neutral selection criteria and procedures have produced the monochromatic result." Alexander, supra, at 632. See also Turner v. Fouche, 396 U.S. 346, 361 (1970); Eubanks v. Louisiana, 356 U.S. 584, 587 (1958).

Necessarily, an invidious discriminatory purpose may often be inferred from the totality of the relevant facts, including the fact, if it is true, that the law bears more heavily on one race than another. It is also not infrequently true that the discriminatory impact—in the jury cases for example, the total or seriously disproportionate exclusion of Negroes from jury venires—may for all practical purposes demonstrate unconstitutionality because in various circumstances the discrimination is very difficult to explain on nonracial grounds. Nevertheless, we have not held that a law, neutral on its face and serving ends otherwise within the power of government to pursue, is invalid under the Equal Protection Clause simply because it may affect a greater proportion of one race than of another. Disproportionate impact is not irrelevant, but it is not the sole touchstone of an invidious racial discrimination forbidden by the Constitution. Standing alone, it does not trigger the rule, McLaughlin v. Florida, 379 U.S. 184 (1964), that racial classifications are to be subjected to the strictest scrutiny and are justifiable only by the weightiest of considerations.

There are some indications to the contrary in our cases. In Palmer v. Thompson, 403 U.S. 217 (1971), the city of Jackson, Miss., following a court decree to this effect, desegregated all of its public facilities save five swimming pools which had been operated by the city and which, following the decree, were closed by ordinance pursuant to a determination by the city council that closure was necessary to preserve peace and order and that integrated pools could not be economically operated. Accepting the finding that the pools were closed to avoid violence and economic loss, this Court rejected the argument that the abandonment of this service was inconsistent with the outstanding desegregation decree and that the otherwise seemingly permissible ends served by the ordinance could be impeached by demonstrating that racially invidious motivations had prompted the city council's action. The holding was that the city was not overtly or covertly operating segregated pools and was extending identical treatment to both whites and Negroes. The opinion warned against grounding decision on legislative purpose or motivation, thereby lending support for the proposition that the operative effect of the law rather than its purpose is the paramount factor. But the holding of the case was that the legitimate purposes of the ordinance—to preserve peace and avoid deficits— were not open to impeachment by evidence that the councilmen were actually motivated by racial considerations. Whatever dicta the opinion may contain, the decision did not involve, much less invalidate, a statute or ordinance having neutral purposes but disproportionate racial consequences.

Wright v. Council of the City of Emporia, 407 U.S. 451 (1972), also indicates that in proper circumstances, the racial impact of a law, rather than its discriminatory purpose, is the critical factor. That case involved the division of a school district. The issue was whether the division was consistent with an outstanding order of a federal court to desegregate the dual school system found to have existed in the area. The constitutional predicate for the District Court's invalidation of the divided district was "the enforcement until 1969 of racial segregation in the public school system of which Emporia had always been a part." Id., at 459. There was thus no need to find "an independent constitutional violation." Ibid. Citing Palmer v. Thompson, we agreed with the District Court that the division of the district had the effect of interfering with the federal decree and should be set aside.

That neither *Palmer* nor *Wright* was understood to have changed the prevailing rule is apparent from Keyes v. School District No. 1, supra, where the principal issue in litigation was whether and to what extent there had been purposeful discrimination resulting in a partially or wholly segregated school system. Nor did other later cases, Alexander v. Louisiana, supra, and Jefferson v. Hackney, supra, indicate that either *Palmer* or *Wright* had worked a fundamental change in equal protection law.[11]

---

[11] To the extent that *Palmer* suggests a generally applicable proposition that legislative purpose is irrelevant in constitutional adjudication, our prior cases—as indicated in the text—are to the contrary; and very shortly after *Palmer*, all Members of the Court majority in that case joined the Court's opinion in Lemon v. Kurtzman, 403 U.S. 602 (1971), which dealt with the issue of public financing for private schools and which announced, as the Court had several times before, that the validity of public aid to church-related schools includes close inquiry into the purpose of the challenged statute.

Both before and after Palmer v. Thompson, however, various Courts of Appeals have held in several contexts, including public employment, that the substantially disproportionate racial impact of a statute or official practice standing alone and without regard to discriminatory purpose, suffices to prove racial discrimination violating the Equal Protection Clause absent some justification going substantially beyond what would be necessary to validate most other legislative classifications. The cases impressively demonstrate that there is another side to the issue; but, with all due respect, to the extent that those cases rested on or expressed the view that proof of discriminatory racial purpose is unnecessary in making out an equal protection violation, we are in disagreement.

As an initial matter, we have difficulty understanding how a law establishing a racially neutral qualification for employment is nevertheless racially discriminatory and denies "any person equal protection of the laws" simply because a greater proportion of Negroes fail to qualify than members of other racial or ethnic groups. Had respondents, along with all others who had failed Test 21, whether white or black, brought an action claiming that the test denied each of them equal protection of the laws as compared with those who had passed with high enough scores to qualify them as police recruits, it is most unlikely that their challenge would have been sustained. Test 21, which is administered generally to prospective government employees, concededly seeks to ascertain whether those who take it have acquired a particular level of verbal skill; and it is untenable that the Constitution prevents the government from seeking modestly to upgrade the communicative abilities of its employees rather than to be satisfied with some lower level of competence, particularly where the job requires special ability to communicate orally and in writing. Respondents, as Negroes, could no more successfully claim that the test denied them equal protection than could white applicants who also failed. The conclusion would not be different in the face of proof that more Negroes than whites had been disqualified by Test 21. That other Negroes also failed to score well would, alone, not demonstrate that respondents individually were being denied equal protection of the laws by the application of an otherwise valid qualifying test being administered to prospective police recruits.

Nor on the facts of the case before us would the disproportionate impact of Test 21 warrant the conclusion that it is a purposeful device to discriminate against Negroes and hence an infringement of the constitutional rights of respondents as well as other black applicants. As we have said, the test is neutral on its face and rationally may be said to serve a purpose the government is constitutionally empowered to pursue. Even agreeing with the District Court that the differential racial effect of Test 21 called for further inquiry, we think the District Court correctly held that the affirmative efforts of the Metropolitan Police Department to recruit black officers, the changing racial composition of the recruit classes and of the force in general, and the relationship of the test to the training program negated any inference that the Department discriminated on the basis of race or that "a police officer qualifies on the color of his skin rather than ability." 348 F.Supp., at 18.

Under Title VII, Congress provided that when hiring and promotion practices disqualifying substantially disproportionate numbers of blacks are challenged, discriminatory purpose need not be proved, and that it is an insufficient response to demonstrate some rational basis for the challenged practices. It is necessary, in addition, that they be "validated" in terms of job performance in any one of several ways, perhaps by ascertaining the minimum skill, ability or potential necessary for the position at issue and determining whether the qualifying tests are appropriate for the selection of qualified applicants for the job in question. However this process proceeds, it involves a more probing judicial review of, and less deference to, the seemingly reasonable acts of administrators and executives than is appropriate under the Constitution where special racial impact, without discriminatory purpose, is claimed. We are not disposed to adopt this more rigorous standard for the purposes of applying the Fifth and the Fourteenth Amendments in cases such as this.

A rule that a statute designed to serve neutral ends is nevertheless invalid, absent compelling justification, if in practice it benefits or burdens one race more than another would be far reaching and would raise serious questions about, and perhaps invalidate, a whole range of tax, welfare, public service, regulatory, and licensing statutes that may be more burdensome to the poor and to the average black than to the more affluent white.[14]

Given that rule, such consequences would perhaps be likely to follow. However, in our view, extension of the rule beyond those areas where it is already applicable by reason of statute, such as in the field of public employment, should await legislative prescription.

As we have indicated, it was error to direct summary judgment for respondents based on the Fifth Amendment.

III.

We also hold that the Court of Appeals should have affirmed the judgment of the District Court granting the motions for summary judgment filed by petitioners and the federal parties. Respondents were entitled to relief on neither constitutional nor statutory grounds.

The submission of the defendants in the District Court was that Test 21 complied with all applicable statutory as well as constitutional requirements; and they appear not to have disputed that under the statutes and regulations governing their conduct standards similar to those obtaining under Title VII had to be satisfied. The District Court also assumed that Title VII standards were to control the case, identified the determinative issue as whether Test 21 was sufficiently job related and proceeded to uphold use of the test because it was "directly related to a determination of whether the applicant possesses sufficient skills requisite to the demands of the curriculum a recruit must master at the police academy." 348 F.Supp., at 17. The Court of Appeals reversed because the relationship between Test 21 and training school success, if demonstrated at all, did not satisfy what it deemed to be the crucial requirement of a direct relationship between performance on Test 21 and performance on the policeman's job.

We agree with petitioners and the federal respondents that this was error. The advisability of the police recruit training course informing the recruit about his upcoming job, acquainting him with its demands and attempting to impart a modicum of required skills seems conceded. It is also apparent to us, as it was to the District Judge, that some minimum verbal and communicative skill would be very useful, if not essential, to satisfactory progress in the training regimen. Based on the evidence before him, the District Judge concluded that Test 21 was directly related to the requirements of the police training program and that a positive relationship between the test and training course performance was sufficient to validate the former, wholly aside from its possible relationship to

---

[14] Goodman, De Facto School Segregation: Constitutional and Empirical Analysis, 60 Cal.L.Rev. 275, 300 (1972), suggests that disproportionate impact analysis might invalidate "tests and qualifications for voting, draft deferment, public employment, jury service and other government-conferred benefits and opportunities . . . .; [s]ales taxes, bail schedules, utility rates, bridge tolls, license fees, and other state-imposed charges." It has also been argued that minimum wage and usury laws as well as professional licensing requirements would require major modifications in light of the unequal impact rule. Silverman, Equal Protection, Economic Legislation and Racial Discrimination, 25 Vand. L.Rev. 1183 (1972). See also Demsetz, Minorities in the Market Place, 43 N.C.L.Rev. 271.

actual performance as a police officer. This conclusion of the District Judge that training-program validation may itself be sufficient is supported by regulations of the Civil Service Commission, by the opinion evidence placed before the District Judge and by the current views of the Civil Service Commissioners who were parties to the case. Nor is the conclusion foreclosed by either *Griggs* or Albemarle Paper Co. v. Moody, 422 U.S. 405 (1975); and it seems to us the much more sensible construction of the job relatedness requirement.

The District Court's accompanying conclusion that Test 21 was in fact directly related to the requirements of the police training program was supported by a validation study, as well as by other evidence of record; and we are not convinced that this conclusion was erroneous. . . .

The judgment of the Court of Appeals accordingly is reversed.

So ordered.

Mr. Justice Stewart joins Parts I and II of the Court's opinion.

Mr. Justice Stevens, concurring.

While I agree with the Court's disposition of this case, I add these comments on the constitutional issue discussed in Part II. . . .

. . .

Frequently the most probative evidence of intent will be objective evidence of what actually happened rather than evidence describing the subjective state of mind of the actor. . . .

My point in making this observation is to suggest that the line between discriminatory purpose and discriminatory impact is not nearly as bright, and perhaps not quite as critical, as the reader of the Court's opinion might assume. I agree, of course, that a constitutional issue does not arise every time some disproportionate impact is shown. On the other hand, when the disproportion is as dramatic as in *Gomillion* or *Yick Wo,* it really does not matter whether the standard is phrased in terms of purpose or effect. Therefore, although I accept the statement of the general rule in the Court's opinion, I am not yet prepared to indicate how that standard should be applied in the many cases which have formulated the governing standard in different language.

. . .

Mr. Justice Brennan, with whom Mr. Justice Marshall joins, dissenting.

. . .

[This opinion addressed only the statutory issues explored in Part III of the Court's opinion.]

VILLAGE OF ARLINGTON HEIGHTS v. METROPOLITAN HOUSING DEVELOPMENT CORP., 429 U.S. 252 (1977). Metropolitan Housing submitted a request for the rezoning of a 15-acre parcel from single-family to multiple-family classification for the purpose of building apartments for low and moderate income families. The apartments were to be constructed under a federal program which required an affirmative marketing plan to assure that the development would be racially integrated. Public hearings were held. Some persons objected to the introduction of low income racially integrated housing in the area. Many focussed on the fact the land had always been zoned for single-family housing and neighboring citizens built or purchased their homes relying on the classification. They also noted that the city's consistent policy had been to zone for multiple-family housing only in areas which would serve as a buffer between single-family and commercial developments whereas the parcel involved here did not adjoin any commercial district. The zoning request was denied and a suit was brought in the federal district court seeking declaratory and injunctive relief. The trial judge ruled for the city but the court of appeals reversed, finding that the "ultimate effect" of the denial was racially discriminatory. The Supreme Court reversed the court of appeals.

Mr. Justice Powell, speaking for the Court, said, in part:

III.

"Our decision last Term in Washington v. Davis, 426 U.S. 229 (1976), made it clear that official action will not be held unconstitutional solely because it results in a racially disproportionate impact. . . .

"*Davis* does not require a plaintiff to prove that the challenged action rested solely on racially discriminatory purposes. Rarely can it be said that a legislature or administrative body operating under a broad mandate made a decision motivated solely by a single concern, or even that a particular purpose was the 'dominant' or 'primary' one. In fact, it is because legislators and administrators are properly concerned with balancing numerous competing considerations that courts refrain from reviewing the merits of their decisions, absent a showing of arbitrariness or irrationality. But racial discrimination is not just another competing consideration. When there is a proof that a discriminatory purpose has been a motivating factor in the decision, this judicial deference is no longer justified.[12]

"Determining whether invidious discriminatory purpose was a motivating factor demands a sensitive inquiry into such circumstantial and direct evidence of intent as may be available. The impact of the official action—whether it 'bears more heavily on one race than another,' Washington v. Davis, 426 U.S., at 242—may provide an important starting point. Sometimes a clear pattern, unexplainable on grounds other than race, emerges from the effect of the state action even when the governing legislation appears neutral on its face. Yick Wo v. Hopkins, 118 U.S. 356 (1886); Guinn v. United States, 238 U.S. 347 (1915); Lane v. Wilson, 307 U.S. 268 (1939); Gomillion v. Lightfoot, 364 U.S. 339 (1960). The evidentiary inquiry is then relatively easy.[13] But such cases are rare. Absent a pattern as stark as that in *Gomillion* or *Yick Wo,* impact alone is not determinative,[14] and the Court must look to other evidence.[15]

"The historical background of the decision is one evidentiary source, particularly if it reveals a series of official actions taken for invidious purposes. . . . The specific sequence of events leading up to the challenged decision also may shed some light on the decisionmaker's purposes. . . . For example, if the property involved here always had been zoned R–5 but suddenly was changed to R–3 when the town learned of MHDC's plans to erect integrated housing, we would have a far different case. Departures from the normal procedural sequence also might afford evidence that improper purposes are playing a role. Substantive departures too may be relevant, particularly if the factors usually considered important by the decisionmaker strongly favor a decision contrary to the one reached.

[12] For a scholarly discussion of legislative motivation, see Brest, Palmer v. Thompson: An Approach to the Problem of Unconstitutional Legislative Motive, 1971 Sup.Ct.Rev. 95, 116–118.

[13] Several of our jury selection cases fall into this category. Because of the nature of the jury selection task, however, we have permitted a finding of constitutional violation even when the statistical pattern does not approach the extremes of Yick Wo or Gomillion. See, e.g., Turner v. Fouche, 396 U.S. 346, 359 (1970); Sims v. Georgia, 389 U.S. 404, 407 (1967).

[14] This is not to say that a consistent pattern of official racial discrimination is a necessary predicate to a violation of the equal protection clause. A single invidiously discriminatory governmental act— in the exercise of the zoning power as elsewhere—would not necessarily be immunized by the absence of such discrimination in the making of other comparable decisions. See City of Richmond v. United States, 422 U.S. 358, 378 (1975).

[15] In many instances, to recognize the limited probative value of disproportionate impact is merely to acknowledge the "heterogeneity" of the nation's population. Jefferson v. Hackney, 406 U.S. 535, 548 (1972); see also Washington v. Davis, 426 U.S., at 248.

"The legislative or administrative history may be highly relevant, especially where there are contemporary statements by members of the decision-making body, minutes of its meetings, or reports. In some extraordinary instances the members might be called to the stand at trial to testify concerning the purpose of the official action, although even then such testimony frequently will be barred by privilege. . . .[18]

"The foregoing summary identifies, without purporting to be exhaustive, subjects of proper inquiry in determining whether racially discriminatory intent existed. With these in mind, we now address the case before us.

IV.

.   .   .

"We also have reviewed the evidence. The impact of the Village's decision does arguably bear more heavily on racial minorities. Minorities comprise 18% of the Chicago area population, and 40% of the income groups said to be eligible for Lincoln Green. But there is little about the sequence of events leading up to the decision that would spark suspicion. The area around the Victorian property has been zoned R–3 since 1959, the year when Arlington Heights first adopted a zoning map. Single-family homes surround the 80-acre site, and the Village is undeniably committed to single-family homes as its dominant residential land use. The rezoning request progressed according to the usual procedures. The Plan Commission even scheduled two additional hearings, at least in part to accommodate MHDC and permit it to supplement its presentation with answers to questions generated at the first hearing.

"The statements by the Plan Commission and Village Board members, as reflected in the official minutes, focused almost exclusively on the zoning aspects of the MHDC petition, and the zoning factors on which they relied are not novel criteria in the Village's rezoning decisions. There is no reason to doubt that there has been reliance by some neighboring property owners on the maintenance of single-family zoning in the vicinity. The Village originally adopted its buffer policy long before MHDC entered the picture and has applied the policy too consistently for us to infer discriminatory purpose from its application in this case. Finally, MHDC called one member of the Village Board to the stand at trial. Nothing in her testimony supports an inference of invidious purpose.

"In sum, the evidence does not warrant overturning the concurrent findings of both courts below. Respondents simply failed to carry their burden of proving that discriminatory purpose was a motivating factor in the Village's decision.[21] This conclusion ends the constitutional inquiry. The Court of

---

[18] This Court has recognized, ever since Fletcher v. Peck, 6 Cranch 87, 130–131 (1810), that judicial inquiries into legislative or executive motivation represent a substantial intrusion into the workings of other branches of government. Placing a decisionmaker on the stand is therefore "usually to be avoided." Citizens to Preserve Overton Park v. Volpe, 401 U.S. 402, 420 (1971). The problems involved have prompted a good deal of scholarly commentary. See Tussman & tenBroek, The Equal Protection of the Laws, 37 Calif.L.Rev. 341, 356–361 (1949); A. Bickel, The Least Dangerous Branch, 208–221 (1962); Ely, Legislative and Administrative Motivation in Constitutional Law, 79 Yale L.J. 1205 (1970); Brest supra, n. 8.

[21] Proof that the decision by the Village was motivated in part by a racially discriminatory purpose would not necessarily have required invalidation of the challenged decision. Such proof would, however, have shifted to the Village the burden of establishing that the same decision would have resulted even had the impermissible purpose not been considered. If this were established, the complaining party in a case of this kind no longer fairly could attribute the injury complained of to improper consideration of a discriminatory purpose. In such circumstances, there would be no justification for judicial interference with the challenged decision. But in this case respondents failed to make the required threshold showing. See Mt. Healthy City School Dist. Bd. of Education v. Doyle, 429 U.S. 274.

Appeals' further finding that the Village's decision carried a discriminatory 'ultimate effect' is without independent constitutional significance."

Justices Marshall and Brennan concurred in Part III of the opinion set out above but indicated that in their view the case should be remanded to the court of appeals for it to reassess the evidence on discriminatory purpose. Justice White also dissented, calling for a remand to the court of appeals. Justice Stevens took no part in the decision.

PERSONNEL ADMINISTRATOR OF MASSACHUSETTS v. FEENEY, 442 U.S. 256 (1979). Massachusetts' veterans' preference for state civil service positions was challenged as unconstitutional gender discrimination. Under the law, all veterans had an "absolute lifetime preference"; veterans with passing scores for classified civil service jobs were ranked above *all* other candidates. Since 98% of veterans were male, and the preference for veterans with passing scores was absolute, the impact of the law was, obviously, to disqualify female eligibles from consideration in much greater proportion than male eligibles. The Court rejected the argument that Massachusetts had discriminated against women in violation of the Equal Protection Clause. Justice Stewart's opinion for the Court said, in part:

"The cases of Washington v. Davis, and Village of Arlington Heights v. Metropolitan Housing Development Corp., recognize that when a neutral law has a disparate impact upon a group that has historically been the victim of discrimination, an unconstitutional purpose may still be at work. But those cases signalled no departure from the settled rule that the Fourteenth Amendment guarantees equal laws, not equal results. . . .

"When a statute gender-neutral on its face is challenged on the ground that its effects upon women are disproportionately adverse, a two-fold inquiry is thus appropriate. The first question is whether the statutory classification is indeed neutral in the sense that it is not gender-based. If the classification itself, covert or overt, is not based upon gender, the second question is whether the adverse effect reflects invidious gender-based discrimination. . . . In this second inquiry, impact provides an 'important starting point,' but purposeful discrimination is 'the condition that offends the Constitution.' . . .

. . .

"The question whether ch. 31, § 23 establishes a classification that is overtly or covertly based upon gender must first be considered. The appellee has conceded that ch. 31, § 23 is neutral on its face. . . .

. . . Apart from the fact that the definition of "veterans" in the statute has always been neutral as to gender and that Massachusetts has consistently defined veteran status in a way that has been inclusive of women who have served in the military, this is not a law that can plausibly be explained only as a gender-based classification. Indeed, it is not a law that can rationally be explained on that ground. Veteran status is not uniquely male. Although few women benefit from the preference, the nonveteran class is not substantially all-female. To the contrary, significant numbers of nonveterans are men, and all nonveterans—male as well as female—are placed at a disadvantage. Too many men are affected to permit the inference that the statute is but a pretext for preferring men over women.

"Moreover, as the District Court implicitly found, the purposes of the statute provide the surest explanation for its impact. Just as there are cases in which impact alone can unmask an invidious classification, cf. Yick Wo v. Hopkins, there are others, in which—notwithstanding impact—the legitimate noninvidious purposes of a law cannot be missed. This is one. The distinction . . .

is, as it seems to be, quite simply between veterans and nonveterans, not between men and women.

"The dispositive question, then, is whether the appellee has shown that a gender-based discriminatory purpose has, at least in some measure, shaped the Massachusetts veterans' preference legislation.   . . .

"The contention that this veterans' preference is 'inherently non-neutral' or 'gender-based' presumes that the State, by favoring veterans, intentionally incorporated into its public employment policies the panoply of sex-based and assertedly discriminatory federal laws that have prevented all but a handful of women from becoming veterans.   There are two serious difficulties with this argument.   First, it is wholly at odds with the District Court's central finding that Massachusetts has not offered a preference to veterans for the purpose of discriminating against women.   Second, it cannot be reconciled with the assumption made by both the appellee and the District Court that a more limited hiring preference for veterans could be sustained.   Taken together, these difficulties are fatal.

. . . .

"To be sure, this case is unusual in that it involves a law that by design is not neutral.   The law overtly prefers veterans as such.   As opposed to the written test at issue in *Davis,* it does not purport to define a job related characteristic. To the contrary, it confers upon a specifically described group—perceived to be particularly deserving—a competitive head start.   But the District Court found, and the appellee has not disputed, that this legislative choice was legitimate. The basic distinction between veterans and nonveterans, having been found not gender-based, and the goals of the preference having been found worthy, ch. 31 must be analyzed as is any other neutral law that casts a greater burden upon women as a group than upon men as a group.   The enlistment policies of the armed services may well have discriminated on the basis of sex.   See Frontiero v. Richardson, 411 U.S. 677; cf. Schlesinger v. Ballard, 419 U.S. 498.   But the history of discrimination against women in the military is not on trial in this case.

"The appellee's ultimate argument rests upon the presumption, common to the criminal and civil law, that a person intends the natural and foreseeable consequences of his voluntary actions.   . . .

". . . [I]t cannot seriously be argued that the legislature of Massachusetts could have been unaware that most veterans are men.   It would thus be disingenuous to say that the adverse consequences of this legislation for women were unintended, in the sense that they were not volitional or in the sense that they were not foreseeable.

" 'Discriminatory purpose,' however, implies more than intent as volition or intent as awareness of consequences.   . . .   It implies that the decisionmaker, in this case a state legislature, selected or reaffirmed a particular course of action at least in part 'because of,' not merely 'in spite of,' its adverse effects upon an identifiable group.   Yet nothing in the record demonstrates that this preference for veterans was originally devised or subsequently re-enacted because it would accomplish the collateral goal of keeping women in a stereotypic and predefined place in the Massachusetts Civil Service."

Justice Stevens' concurring opinion, joined by Justice White, said:

"While I concur in the Court's opinion, I confess that I am not at all sure that there is any difference between the two questions posed   . . . ..   If a classification is not overtly based on gender, I am inclined to believe the question whether it is covertly gender-based is the same as the question whether its adverse effects reflect invidious gender-based discrimination.   However the question is phrased, for me the answer is largely provided by the fact that the number of males disadvantaged by Massachusetts' Veterans Preference (1,867,000) is sufficiently large—and sufficiently close to the number of disadvantaged females (2,954,000)—to refute the claim that the rule was intended to benefit males as a class over females as a class."

Justice Marshall's dissent, joined by Justice Brennan, concluded that Massachusetts' veterans' preference system constituted "intentional" gender-based discrimination. The foreseeable impact of the law had such a disproportionate impact that the State should have the burden to establish that "sex-based considerations played no part in the choice of the particular legislative scheme."

"Clearly, that burden was not sustained here. The legislative history of the statute reflects the Commonwealth's patent appreciation of the impact the preference system would have on women, and an equally evident desire to mitigate that impact only with respect to certain traditionally female occupations. Until 1971, the statute and implementing civil service regulations exempted from operation of the preference any job requisitions 'especially calling for women.' . . . In practice, this exemption, coupled with the absolute preference for veterans, has created a gender-based civil service hierarchy, with women occupying low grade clerical and secretarial jobs and men holding more responsible and remunerative positions.

"Thus, for over 70 years, the Commonwealth has maintained, as an integral part of its veteran's preference system, an exemption relegating female civil service applicants to occupations traditionally filled by women. Such a statutory scheme both reflects and perpetuates precisely the kind of archaic assumptions about women's roles which we have previously held invalid. . . ."

COLUMBUS BOARD OF EDUCATION v. PENICK, 443 U.S. 449 (1979). In this case the Court upheld a finding that schools were intentionally segregated based in large measure on a finding that the schools had been intentionally segregated in 1954 when *Brown* was decided and that they had failed in the intervening years to disestablish the dual system. One objection raised was that the lower courts had not found an intention to discriminate. As to this, the Court said:

"It is urged that the courts below failed to heed the requirements of Keyes, Washington v. Davis, 426 U.S. 229 (1976), and Village of Arlington Heights v. Metropolitan Housing Dev. Corp., 429 U.S. 252 (1977), that a plaintiff seeking to make out an equal protection violation on the basis of racial discrimination must show purpose. Both courts, it is argued, considered the requirement satisfied if it were shown that disparate impact would be the natural and foreseeable consequence of the practices and policies of the Board, which, it is said, is nothing more than equating impact with intent, contrary to the controlling precedent.

"The District Court, however, was amply cognizant of the controlling cases. It is understood that to prevail the plaintiffs were required to 'prove not only that segregated schooling exists but also that it was brought about or maintained by intentional state action,' that is, that the school officials had 'intended to segregate.' The District Court also recognized that under those cases disparate impact and foreseeable consequences, without more, do not establish a constitutional violation. Nevertheless, the District Court correctly noted that actions having foreseeable and anticipated disparate impact are relevant evidence to prove the ultimate fact, forbidden purpose. Those cases do not forbid 'the foreseeable effects standard from being utilized as one of the several kinds of proofs from which an inference of segregative intent may be properly drawn.' Adherence to a particular policy or practice, 'with full knowledge of the predictable effects of such adherence upon racial imbalance in a school system is one factor among many others which may be considered by a court in determining whether an inference of segregative intent should be drawn.' The District Court thus stayed well within the requirements of Washington v. Davis and *Arlington Heights.*"

ROGERS v. LODGE

458 U.S. 613, 102 S.Ct. 3272, 73 L.Ed.2d 1012 (1982).

Justice White delivered the opinion of the Court.

The issue in this case is whether the at-large system of elections in Burke County, Georgia violates the Fourteenth Amendment rights of Burke County's black citizens.

I

Burke County is a large, predominately rural county located in eastern Georgia. Eight hundred and thirty-one square miles in area, it is approximately two-thirds the size of the State of Rhode Island. According to the 1980 Census, Burke County had a total population of 19,349, of whom 10,385, or 53.6%, were black. The average age of blacks living there is lower than the average age of whites and therefore whites constitute a slight majority of the voting age population. As of 1978, 6,373 persons were registered to vote in Burke County, of whom 38% were black.

The Burke County Board of Commissioners governs the county. It was created in 1911, see 1911 Georgia Laws at 310–311, and consists of five members elected at large to concurrent four-year terms by all qualified voters in the county. The county has never been divided into districts, either for the purpose of imposing a residency requirement on candidates or for the purpose of requiring candidates to be elected by voters residing in a district. In order to be nominated or elected, a candidate must receive a majority of the votes cast in the primary or general election, and a runoff must be held if no candidate receives a majority in the first primary or general election. Ga.Code § 34–1513 (1980). Each candidate must run for a specific seat on the Board, Ga. Code § 34–1015 (1980), and a voter may vote only once for any candidate. No Negro has ever been elected to the Burke County Board of Commissioners.

Eight black citizens of Burke County filed this suit in 1976 in the United States District Court for the Southern District of Georgia. The suit was brought on behalf of all black citizens in Burke County. The class was certified in 1977. The complaint alleged that the County's system of at-large elections violates appellees' First, Thirteenth, Fourteenth and Fifteenth Amendment rights, as well as their rights under 42 U.S.C. §§ 1971, 1973, and 1983 by diluting the voting power of black citizens. Following a bench trial at which both sides introduced extensive evidence, the court issued an order on September 29, 1978 stating that appellees were entitled to prevail and ordering that Burke County be divided into five districts for purposes of electing County Commissioners. The court later issued detailed findings of fact and conclusions of law in which it stated that while the present method of electing County Commissioners was "racially neutral when adopted, [it] is being *maintained* for invidious purposes" in violation of appellees' Fourteenth and Fifteenth Amendment rights.

The Court of Appeals affirmed *sub nom.* Lodge v. Buxton, 639 F.2d 1358 (CA5 1981). It stated that while the proceedings in the District Court took place prior to the decision in Mobile v. Bolden, 446 U.S. 55 (1980), the District Court correctly anticipated *Mobile* and required appellees to prove that the at-large voting system was maintained for a discriminatory purpose. The

Court of Appeals also held that the District Court's findings not only were not clearly erroneous, but its conclusion that the at-large system was maintained for invidious purposes was "virtually mandated by the overwhelming proof." We noted probable jurisdiction and now affirm.

II

At-large voting schemes and multimember districts tend to minimize the voting strength of minority groups by permitting the political majority to elect *all* representatives of the district. A distinct minority, whether it be a racial, ethnic, economic, or political group, may be unable to elect any representatives in an at-large election, yet may be able to elect several representatives if the political unit is divided into single-member districts. The minority's voting power in a multimember district is particularly diluted when bloc voting occurs and ballots are cast along strict majority-minority lines. While multimember districts have been challenged for "their winner-take-all aspects, their tendency to submerge minorities and to overrepresent the winning party," Whitcomb v. Chavis, 403 U.S. 124, 158–159 (1971), this Court has repeatedly held that they are not unconstitutional *per se.* Mobile v. Bolden, supra, 446 U.S. at 66; White v. Regester, 412 U.S. 755, 765 (1973); Whitcomb v. Chavis, supra, 403 U.S. at 142. The Court has recognized, however, that multimember districts violate the Fourteenth Amendment if "conceived or operated as purposeful devises to further racial . . . discrimination" by minimizing, cancelling out or diluting the voting strength of racial elements in the voting population. Whitcomb v. Chavis, supra, 403 U.S. at 149. . . . Cases charging that multimember districts unconstitutionally dilute the voting strength of racial minorities are thus subject to the standard of proof generally applicable to Equal Protection Clause cases. Washington v. Davis, 426 U.S. 229 (1976), and Village of Arlington Heights v. Metropolitan Housing Development Corp., 429 U.S. 252 (1977), made it clear that in order for the Equal Protection Clause to be violated, "the invidious quality of a law claimed to be racially discriminatory must ultimately be traced to a racially discriminatory purpose." Washington v. Davis, supra, 426 U.S. at 240. Neither case involved voting dilution, but in both cases the Court observed that the requirement that racially discriminatory purpose or intent be proven applies to voting cases by relying upon, among others, Wright v. Rockefeller, 376 U.S. 52 (1964), a districting case, to illustrate that a showing of discriminatory intent has long been required in *all* types of equal protection cases charging racial discrimination. *Arlington Heights,* supra, 429 U.S. at 265; Washington v. Davis, supra, 426 U.S. at 240.[5]

Arlington Heights and Washington v. Davis both rejected the notion that a law is invalid under the Equal Protection Clause simply because it may affect a greater proportion of one race than another. *Arlington Heights,* supra, 429 U.S. at 265; Washington v. Davis, supra, 426 U.S. at 242. However, both cases recognized that discriminatory intent need not be proven by direct evidence. "Necessarily, an invidious discriminatory purpose may often be inferred from the totality of the relevant facts, including the fact, if it is true, that the law bears more heavily on one race than another." Ibid. Thus determining the existence of a discriminatory purpose "demands a sensitive inquiry into such circumstantial and direct evidence of intent as may be available." *Arlington Heights,* supra, 429 U.S. at 266.

In Mobile v. Bolden, supra, the Court was called upon to apply these principles to the at-large election system in Mobile, Alabama. Mobile is governed by three commissioners who exercise all legislative, executive, and

---

[5] Purposeful racial discrimination invokes the strictest scrutiny of adverse differential treatment. Absent such purpose, differential impact is subject only to the test of rationality. Washington v. Davis, supra, at 247–248.

administrative power in the municipality. Each candidate for the City Commission runs for one of three numbered posts in an at-large election and can only be elected by a majority vote. Plaintiffs brought a class action on behalf of all Negro citizens of Mobile alleging that the at-large scheme diluted their voting strength in violation of several statutory and constitutional provisions. The District Court concluded that the at-large system "violates the constitutional rights of the plaintiffs by improperly restricting their access to the political process," and ordered that the commission form of government be replaced by a mayor and a nine-member City Council elected from single-member districts. The Court of Appeals affirmed. This Court reversed.

Justice Stewart, writing for himself and three other Justices, noted that to prevail in their contention that the at-large voting system violates the Equal Protection Clause of the Fourteenth Amendment, plaintiffs had to prove the system was "conceived or operated as [a] purposeful devic[e] to further racial . . . discrimination." 446 U.S., at 66, quoting Whitcomb v. Chavis, 403 U.S., at 149.[6] Such a requirement "is simply one aspect of the basic principle that only if there is purposeful discrimination can there be a violation of the Equal Protection Clause of the Fourteenth Amendment," 446 U.S., at 66, and White v. Regester is consistent with that principle. Another Justice agreed with the standard of proof recognized by the plurality. Id., at 101 (White, J., dissenting).

The plurality went on to conclude that the District Court had failed to comply with this standard. The District Court had analyzed plaintiffs' claims in light of the standard which had been set forth in Zimmer v. McKeithen, 485 F.2d 1297 (CA5 1973), aff'd on other grounds *sub nom.* East Carroll Parish School Bd. v. Marshall, 424 U.S. 636 (1975) (*per curiam*). *Zimmer* set out a list of factors[8] gleaned from Whitcomb v. Chavis, supra, and White v. Regester, supra, that a court should consider in assessing the constitutionality of at-large and multimember district voting schemes. Under *Zimmer,* voting dilution is established "upon proof of the existence of an aggregate of these factors."

The plurality in *Mobile* was of the view that *Zimmer* was "decided upon the misunderstanding that it is not necessary to show a discriminatory purpose in order to prove a violation of the Equal Protection Clause—that proof of a discriminatory effect is sufficient." The plurality observed that while "the presence of the indicia relied on in *Zimmer* may afford some evidence of a discriminatory purpose," the mere existence of those criteria is not a substitute for a finding of discriminatory purpose. The District Court's standard in *Mobile* was likewise flawed. Finally, the plurality concluded that the evidence upon which the lower courts had relied was "insufficient to prove an unconstitutional-

---

[6] With respect to the Fifteenth Amendment, the plurality held that the Amendment prohibits only direct, purposefully discriminatory interference with the freedom of Negroes to vote. "Having found that Negroes in Mobile 'register and vote without hindrance,' the District Court and Court of Appeals were in error in believing that the appellants invaded the protection of [the Fifteenth] Amendment in the present case." Mobile v. Bolden, 446 U.S. 55, 65 (1980). Three Justices disagreed with the plurality's basis for putting aside the Fifteenth Amendment. Id., at 84, n. 3, (Stevens, J., concurring); Id., at 102 (White, J., dissenting); Id., at 125–135 (Marshall, J., dissenting). We express no view on the application of the Fifteenth Amendment to this case.

The plurality noted that plaintiffs' claim under § 2 of the Voting Rights Act, 79 Stat. 437, as amended, 42 U.S.C. § 1973, added nothing to their Fifteenth Amendment claim because the "legislative history of § 2 makes clear that it was intended to have an effect no different from that of the Fifteenth Amendment itself." Id., at 60–61.

[8] The primary factors listed in *Zimmer* include a lack of minority access to the candidate selection process, unresponsiveness of elected officials to minority interests, a tenuous state policy underlying the preference for multi-member or at-large districting, and the existence of past discrimination which precludes effective participation in the elector process. Factors which enhance the proof of voting dilution are the existence of large districts, anti-single shot voting provisions, and the absence of any provision for at-large candidates to run from geographic subdivisions.

ly discriminatory purpose in the present case." Justice Stevens rejected the intentional discrimination standard but concluded that the proof failed to satisfy the legal standard that in his view was the applicable rule. He therefore concurred in the judgment of reversal. Four other Justices, however, thought the evidence sufficient to satisfy the purposeful discrimination standard. One of them, Justice Blackmun, nevertheless concurred in the Court's judgment because he believed an erroneous remedy had been imposed.

Because the District Court in the present case employed the evidentiary factors outlined in *Zimmer,* it is urged that its judgment is infirm for the same reasons that led to the reversal in *Mobile.* We do not agree. First, and fundamentally, we are unconvinced that the District Court in this case applied the wrong legal standard. Not only was the District Court's decision rendered a considerable time after Washington v. Davis and *Arlington Heights,* but the trial judge also had the benefit of Nevett v. Sides, 571 F.2d 209 (CA5 1978), where the Court of Appeals for the Fifth Circuit assessed the impact of Washington v. Davis and *Arlington Heights* and held that "a showing of racially motivated discrimination is a necessary element in an equal protection voting dilution claim . . ." The court stated that "[t]he ultimate issue in a case alleging unconstitutional dilution of the votes of a racial group is whether the districting plan under attack exists because it was intended to diminish or dilute the political efficacy of that group." Id., at 226. The Court of Appeals also explained that although the evidentiary factors outlined in *Zimmer* were important considerations in arriving at the ultimate conclusion of discriminatory intent, the plaintiff is not limited to those factors. "The task before the fact finder is to determine, under all the relevant facts, in whose favor the 'aggregate' of the evidence preponderates. This determination is peculiarly dependent upon the facts of each case."

The District Court referred to Nevett v. Sides and demonstrated its understanding of the controlling standard by observing that a determination of discriminatory intent is "a requisite to a finding of unconstitutional vote dilution" under the Fourteenth and Fifteenth Amendments. Furthermore, while recognizing that the evidentiary factors identified in *Zimmer* were to be considered, the District Court was aware that it was "not limited in its determination only to the *Zimmer* factors" but could consider other relevant factors as well. The District Court then proceeded to deal with what it considered to be the relevant proof and concluded that the at-large scheme of electing commissioners, "although racially neutral when adopted, is being *maintained* for invidious purposes." That system "while neutral in origin . . . has been subverted to invidious purposes." For the most part, the District Court dealt with the evidence in terms of the factors set out in *Zimmer* and its progeny, but as the Court of Appeals stated:

> "Judge Alaimo employed the constitutionally required standard . . . [and] did not treat the *Zimmer* criteria as absolute, but rather considered them only to the extent they were relevant to the question of discriminatory intent."

Although a tenable argument can be made to the contrary, we are not inclined to disagree with the Court of Appeals' conclusion that the District Court applied the proper legal standard.

III

A

We are also unconvinced that we should disturb the District Court's finding that the at-large system in Burke County was being maintained for the invidious purpose of diluting the voting strength of the black population. In White v.

Regester, 412 U.S., at 769–770, we stated that we were not inclined to overturn the District Court's factual findings, "representing as they do a blend of history and an intensely local appraisal of the design and impact of the Bexar County multimember district in the light of past and present reality, political and otherwise." . . . We are of the view that the same clearly-erroneous standard applies to the trial court's finding in this case that the at-large system in Burke County is being maintained for discriminatory purposes, as well as to the court's subsidiary findings of fact. The Court of Appeals did not hold any of the District Court's findings of fact to be clearly erroneous, and this Court has frequently noted its reluctance to disturb findings of fact concurred in by two lower courts. . . . We agree with the Court of Appeals that on the record before us, none of the factual findings are clearly erroneous.

B

The District Court found that blacks have always made up a substantial majority of the population in Burke County, but that they are a distinct minority of the registered voters. There was also overwhelming evidence of bloc voting along racial lines. Hence, although there had been black candidates, no black had ever been elected to the Burke County commission. These facts bear heavily on the issue of purposeful discrimination. Voting along racial lines allows those elected to ignore black interests without fear of political consequences, and without bloc voting the minority candidates would not lose elections solely because of their race. Because it is sensible to expect that at least some blacks would have been elected in Burke County, the fact that none have ever been elected is important evidence of purposeful exclusion. See White v. Regester, supra, at 766.

Under our cases, however, such facts are insufficient in themselves to prove purposeful discrimination absent other evidence such as proof that blacks have less opportunity to participate in the political processes and to elect candidates of their choice. . . . Both the District Court and the Court of Appeals thought the supporting proof in this case was sufficient to support an inference of intentional discrimination. The supporting evidence was organized primarily around the factors which Nevett v. Sides, supra, had deemed relevant to the issue of intentional discrimination. These factors were primarily those suggested in Zimmer v. McKeithen, supra.

The District Court began by determining the impact of past discrimination on the ability of blacks to participate effectively in the political process. Past discrimination was found to contribute to low black voter registration because prior to the Voting Rights Act of 1965, blacks had been denied access to the political process by means such as literacy tests, poll taxes, and white primaries. The result was that "black suffrage in Burke County was virtually nonexistent." Black voter registration in Burke County has increased following the Voting Rights Act to the point that some 38 per cent of blacks eligible to vote are registered to do so. On that basis the District Court inferred that "past discrimination has had an adverse effect on black voter registration which lingers to this date." Past discrimination against blacks in education also had the same effect. Not only did Burke County schools discriminate against blacks as recently as 1969, but some schools still remain essentially segregated and blacks as a group have completed less formal education than whites.

The District Court found further evidence of exclusion from the political process. Past discrimination had prevented blacks from effectively participating in Democratic Party affairs and in primary elections. Until this law suit was filed, there had never been a black member of the County Executive Committee of the Democratic Party. There were also property ownership requirements that made it difficult for blacks to serve as chief registrar in the county. There had been discrimination in the selection of grand jurors, the hiring of county employees, and in the appointments to boards and committees which oversee the county government. The District Court thus concluded that historical discrimination had restricted the present opportunity of blacks effectively to participate in the political process. Evidence of historical discrimination is relevant to drawing an inference of purposeful discrimination, particularly in cases such as this one where the evidence shows that discriminatory practices were commonly utilized, that they were abandoned when enjoined by courts or made illegal by civil rights legislation, and that they were replaced by laws and practices which, though neutral on their face, serve to maintain the status quo.

Extensive evidence was cited by the District Court to support its finding that elected officials of Burke County have been unresponsive and insensitive to the needs of the black community, which increases the likelihood that the political process was not equally open to blacks. . . .

The District Court also considered the depressed socio-economic status of Burke County blacks. It found that proportionately more blacks than whites have incomes below the poverty level. . . .

Although finding that the state policy behind the at-large electoral system in Burke County was "neutral in origin," the District Court concluded that the policy "has been subverted to invidious purposes." As a practical matter, maintenance of the state statute providing for at-large elections in Burke County is determined by Burke County's state representatives, for the legislature defers to their wishes on matters of purely local application. The court found that Burke County's state representatives "have retained a system which has minimized the ability of Burke County Blacks to participate in the political system."

The trial court considered, in addition, several factors which this Court has indicated enhance the tendency of multimember districts to minimize the voting strength of racial minorities. See Whitcomb v. Chavis, supra, 403 U.S., at 143–144. It found that the sheer geographic size of the county, which is nearly two-thirds the size of Rhode Island, "has made it more difficult for Blacks to get to polling places or to campaign for office." The court concluded, as a matter of law, that the size of the county tends to impair the access of blacks to the political process. The majority vote requirement, Ga.Code § 34–1513 (1980), was found "to submerge the will of the minority" and thus "deny the minority's access to the system." The court also found the requirement that candidates run for specific seats, Ga.Code § 34–1015 (1980), enhances respondent's lack of access because it prevents a cohesive political group from concentrating on a single candidate. Because Burke County has no residency requirement, "[a]ll candidates could reside in Waynesboro, or in 'lilly-white' neighborhoods. To that extent, the denial of access becomes enhanced."

None of the District Court's findings underlying its ultimate finding of intentional discrimination appears to us to be clearly erroneous; and as we have said, we decline to overturn the essential finding of the District Court, agreed to by the Court of Appeals, that the at-large system in Burke County has been maintained for the purpose of denying blacks equal access to the political processes in the county. As in White v. Regester, 412 U.S., at 767, the District Court's findings were "sufficient to sustain [its] judgment . . . and, on this record, we have no reason to disturb them."

IV

We also find no reason to overturn the relief ordered by the District Court. Neither the District Court nor the Court of Appeals discerned any special

circumstances that would militate against utilizing single-member districts.
. . . .

The judgment of the Court of Appeals is
Affirmed.

Justice Powell, with whom Justice Rehnquist joins, dissenting.

I

Mobile v. Bolden, 446 U.S. 55 (1980), establishes that an at-large voting system must be upheld against constitutional attack unless maintained for a discriminatory purpose. In *Mobile* we reversed a finding of unconstitutional vote dilution because the lower courts had relied on factors insufficient as a matter of law to establish discriminatory intent. See 446 U.S., at 73 (plurality opinion of Stewart, J.). The District Court and Court of Appeals in this case based their findings of unconstitutional discrimination on the same factors held insufficient in *Mobile*. Yet the Court now finds their conclusion unexceptionable. The *Mobile* plurality also affirmed that the concept of "intent" was no mere fiction, and held that the District Court had erred in "its failure to identify the state officials whose intent it considered relevant." Id., at 74 n. 20. Although the courts below did not answer that question in this case, the Court today affirms their decision.

Whatever the wisdom of *Mobile,* the Court's opinion cannot be reconciled persuasively with that case. There are some variances in the largely sociological evidence presented in the two cases. But *Mobile* held that this *kind* of evidence was not enough. Such evidence, we found in *Mobile,* did not merely fall short, but "fell *far* short[,] of showing that [an at-large electoral scheme was] 'conceived or operated [as a] purposeful devic[e] to further racial . . . discrimination.' " Id. at 70 (emphasis added), quoting Whitcomb v. Chavis, 403 U.S. 124, 149 (1971). Because I believe that *Mobile* controls this case, I dissent.

II

The Court's decision today relies heavily on the capacity of the federal district courts—essentially free from any standards propounded by this Court—to determine whether at-large voting systems are "being maintained for the invidious purpose of diluting the voting strength of the black population." Federal courts thus are invited to engage in deeply subjective inquiries into the motivations of local officials in structuring local governments. Inquiries of this kind not only can be "unseemly," see Karst, The Costs of Motive-Centered Inquiry, 15 San Diego Law Rev. 1163, 1164 (1978); they intrude the federal courts—with only the vaguest constitutional direction—into an area of intensely local and political concern.

Emphasizing these considerations, Justice Stevens, argues forcefully that the Court's focus of inquiry is seriously mistaken. I agree with much of what he says. As I do not share his views entirely, however, I write separately.

A

As I understand it, Justice Stevens' critique of the Court's approach rests on three principles with which I am in fundamental agreement.

First, it is appropriate to distinguish between "state action that inhibits an individual's right to vote and state action that affects the political strength of various groups." Mobile v. Bolden, 446 U.S. 55, 83 (Stevens, J., concurring). Under this distinction, this case is fundamentally different from cases involving direct barriers to voting. There is no claim here that blacks may not register freely and vote for whom they choose. This case also differs from one-man, one-vote cases, in which districting practices make a person's vote less weighty in some districts than in others.

Second, I agree with Justice Stevens that vote dilution cases of this kind are difficult if not impossible to distinguish—especially in their remedial aspect— from other actions to redress gerrymanders.

Finally, Justice Stevens clearly is correct in arguing that the standard used to identify unlawful racial discrimination in this area should be defined in terms that are judicially manageable and reviewable. In the absence of compelling reasons of both law and fact, the federal judiciary is unwarranted in undertaking to restructure state political systems. This is inherently a political area, where the identification of a seeming violation does not necessarily suggest an enforceable judicial remedy—or at least none short of a system of quotas or group representation. Any such system, of course, would be antithetical to the principles of our democracy.

B

Justice Stevens would accommodate these principles by holding that subjective intent is irrelevant to the establishment of a case of racial vote dilution under the Fourteenth Amendment. Despite sharing the concerns from which his position is developed, I would not accept this view. "The central purpose of the Equal Protection Clause of the Fourteenth Amendment is the prevention of official conduct discriminating on the basis of race." Washington v. Davis, 426 U.S. 229, 239 (1976). Because I am unwilling to abandon this central principle in cases of this kind, I cannot join Justice Steven's opinion.

Nonetheless, I do agree with him that what he calls "objective" factors should be the focus of inquiry in vote-dilution cases. Unlike the considerations on which the lower courts relied in this case and in *Mobile,* the factors identified by Justice Stevens as "objective" in fact are direct, reliable, and unambiguous indices of discriminatory *intent.* If we held, as I think we should, that the district courts must place primary reliance on these factors to establish discriminatory intent, we would prevent federal court inquiries into the *subjective* thought processes of local officials—at least until enough objective evidence had been presented to warrant discovery into subjective motivations in this complex, politically charged area. By prescribing such a rule we would hold federal courts to a standard that was judicially manageable. And we would remain faithful to the central protective purpose of the Equal Protection Clause.

In the absence of proof of discrimination by reliance on the kind of objective factors identified by Justice Stevens, I would hold that the factors cited by the Court of Appeals are too attenuated as a matter of law to support an inference of discriminatory intent. I would reverse its judgment on that basis.

Justice Stevens, dissenting.

. . .

[Justice Stevens' long and interesting opinion is omitted.]

NOTE

On June 29, the day before the opinion was announced in *Rogers,* Congress passed the following amended version of Section 2 of the Voting Rights Act of 1965:

> "Sec. 2(a) No voting qualification or prerequisite to voting or standard, practice, or procedure shall be imposed or applied by any State or political subdivision in a manner which results in a denial or abridgement of the right of any citizen of the United States to vote on account of race or color, or in

contravention of the guarantees set forth in section 4(f)(2), as provided in subsection (b).

"(b) A violation of subsection (a) is established if, based on the totality of circumstances, it is shown that the political processes leading to nomination or election in the State or political subdivision are not equally open to participation by members of a class of citizens protected by subsection (a) in that its members have less opportunity than other members of the electorate to participate in the political process and to elect representatives of their choice. The extent to which members of a protected class have been elected to office in the State or political subdivision is one circumstance which may be considered: Provided, That nothing in this section establishes a right to have members of a protected class elected in numbers equal to their proportion in the population."

In the report of the Senate Committee on the Judiciary which accompanied the bill it was made clear that it was intended to restore the legal standard that governed voting discrimination cases prior to the Supreme Court's decision in Mobile v. Bolden, 446 U.S. 55 (1980).

CITY OF MEMPHIS v. GREENE, 451 U.S. 100 (1980). The city closed a street through a white residential community. Black residents of a nearby predominantly black neighborhood, who would be required by the closing to go around the community instead of taking a direct route through it, brought suit in federal court challenging the street closure. The district court entered judgment for the city, concluding that no racially discriminatory purpose had been proved. The Court of Appeals reversed, holding that the street closure was a "badge of slavery" under the thirteenth amendment and 42 U.S.C. § 1982, whether or not it was motivated by racial discrimination. The Supreme Court reversed the decision of the Court of Appeals.

The argument in the Supreme Court centered on the question whether proof of discriminatory intent was necessary in cases challenging official action under the thirteenth amendment and § 1982. (42 U.S.C. §§ 1981 and 1982 are fragments of the Civil Rights Act of 1866, which had been enacted pursuant to Congress' power to enforce the thirteenth amendment. See pages 22–23 of the casebook. Section 1982 provides that all citizens have "the same right . . . as is enjoyed by white citizens . . . to inherit, purchase, lease, sell, hold, and convey real and personal property.") Justice Stevens' opinion for the Court, however, did not decide whether thirteenth amendment or § 1982 claims required proof of an unlawful purpose. Section 1982 was inapplicable because plaintiffs' injury was not an impairment of "property interests." The thirteenth amendment was inapplicable because there was no badge of slavery. The "adverse impact on motorists" could not be compared "to the odious practice the Thirteenth Amendment was designed to eradicate."

Justice White's concurrence stated that "a violation of § 1982 requires some showing of racial animus or an intent to discriminate on the basis of race." (Justice White's position was adopted in the Court's later opinion in General Bldg. Contractors Ass'n v. Pennsylvania, 458 U.S. 375 (1982). That case held that liability could not be imposed on a private party for employment discrimination, under 42 U.S.C. § 1981, without proof of intentional discrimination. The Court's conclusion was based on the legislative history of the Civil Rights Act of 1866, particularly the fact that the 1866 Act was the product of the same Congress that proposed the fourteenth amendment.)[1]

---

[1] The question of the necessity for proving discriminatory intent under modern federal anti-discrimination laws has continued to be controversial. Title VI of the Civil Rights Act of 1964 forbids racial discrimination in activities receiving federal financial assistance. In Regents of the

Justices Marshall, Brennan and Blackmun dissented. The dissenters also did not reach the question whether proof of purposeful racially discrimination was necessary in § 1982 cases, concluding that the evidence "supports a strong inference that the operation of such prejudice is precisely what led to the closing." (Justices Marshall and Brennan dissented in the later *General Building Contractors* case, supra, arguing that claims under 42 U.S.C. § 1981 did not require proof of intent in employment discrimination cases "where proof of actual intent is nearly impossible to obtain.")

CASTANEDA v. PARTIDA, 430 U.S. 482 (1977). Partida filed suit in a federal district court challenging his conviction of crime in the state courts on the ground that the grand jury which indicted him resulted from a state grand jury selection process which discriminated against Mexican-Americans. The district judge found on the basis of statistical evidence that Partida had made out a bare prima facie case of invidious discrimination. However, he held that this was overcome by the state's showing that Mexican-Americans constituted the governing majority in the county, and dismissed the petition. The court of appeals reversed and the Supreme Court affirmed the court of appeals.

Justice Blackmun, speaking for the Court, reviewed the statistical evidence of racial disparities in jury panels and concluded that Partida established a prima facie case of discrimination against Mexican-Americans. He then went on to hold that the state did not dispel the presumption of purposeful discrimination by its governing majority showing, saying:

"Because of the many facets of human motivation, it would be unwise to presume as a matter of law that human beings of one definable group will not discriminate against other members of their group. Indeed, even the dissent of Mr. Justice Powell does not suggest that such a presumption would be appropriate. . . . The problem is a complex one, about which widely differing views can be held, and, as such, it would be somewhat precipitous to take judicial notice of one view over another on the basis of a record as barren as this.[20]

"Furthermore, the relevance of a governing majority of elected officials to the grand jury selection process is questionable. The fact that certain elected officials are Mexican-American demonstrates nothing about the motivations and methods of the grand jury commissioners who select persons for grand jury lists. The only arguably relevant fact in this record on the issue is that three of the five jury commissioners in respondent's case were Mexican-American. Knowing only this, we would be forced to rely on the reasoning that we have rejected—that human beings would not discriminate against their own kind—in order to find that the presumption of purposeful discrimination was rebutted. Without the benefit of this simple behavioral presumption, discriminatory intent can be rebutted only with evidence in the record about the way in which the commissioners operated and their reasons for doing so. It was the State's burden to supply such evidence, once respondent established his prima facie case. The State's failure in this regard leaves unchallenged respondent's proof of purposeful discrimination.

University of California v. Bakke, 438 U.S. 265 (1978), five Justices had stated in dicta that proof of intentional discrimination was required under Title VI. In Guardians Ass'n v. Civil Serv. Comm'n of the City of New York, 103 S.Ct. 3221 (1983), however, five Justices voted to uphold interpretive regulations of several federal agencies incorporating a disparate-impact standard for Title VI cases. (A different five vote majority in the same case held that plaintiffs in Title VI cases were limited to injunctive relief, and could not collect damages, in the absence of proof of discriminatory intent.)

[20] This is not a case where a majority is practicing benevolent discrimination in favor of a traditionally disfavored minority, although that situation illustrates that motivations not immediately obvious might enter into discrimination against "one's own kind."

"Finally, even if a 'governing majority' theory has general applicability in cases of this kind, the inadequacy of the record in this case does not permit such an approach. Among the evidentiary deficiencies are the lack of any indication of how long the Mexican-Americans have enjoyed 'governing majority' status, the absence of information about the relative power inherent in the elective offices held by Mexican-Americans, and the uncertain relevance of the general political power to the specific issue in this case. Even for the most recent time period, when presumably the political power of Mexican-Americans was at its greatest, the discrepancy between the number of Mexican-Americans in the total population and the number on the grand jury lists was substantial. Thus, under the facts presented in this case, the 'governing majority' theory is not developed fully enough to satisfy the State's burden of rebuttal."

Justice Marshall concurred, stating:

"I join fully Mr. Justice Blackmun's sensitive opinion for the Court. I feel compelled to write separately, however, to express my profound disagreement with the views expressed by Mr. Justice Powell in his dissent. . . .

"The sole basis for Mr. Justice Powell's conclusion lies in the third category of evidence presented: proof of the political dominance and control by the Mexican-American majority in Hidalgo County, ... Like the District Court, he appears to assume—without any basis in the record—that *all* Mexican-Americans, indeed *all* members of *all* minority groups, have an 'inclination to assure fairness' to other members of their group. . . . Although he concedes the possibility that minority group members will violate this 'inclination,' . . ., he apparently regards this possibility as more theoretical than real. Thus he would reject the inference of purposeful discrimination here absent any alternative explanation for the disparate results. I emphatically disagree.

"In the first place, Mr. Justice Powell's assumptions about human nature, plausible as they may sound, fly in the face of a great deal of social science theory and research. Social scientists agree that members of minority groups frequently respond to discrimination and prejudice by attempting to disassociate themselves from the group, even to the point of adopting the majority's negative attitudes towards the minority. Such behavior occurs with particular frequency among members of minority groups who have achieved some measure of economic or political success and thereby have gained some acceptability among the dominant group.

"But even if my Brother Powell's behavioral assumptions were more valid, I still could not agree to making them the foundation for a constitutional ruling. It seems to me that especially in reviewing claims of intentional discrimination, this Court has a solemn responsibility to avoid basing its decisions on broad generalizations concerning minority groups. If history has taught us anything, it is the danger of relying on such stereotypes. The question for decision here is not how Mexican-Americans treat other Mexican-Americans, but how the particular grand jury commissioners in Hidalgo County acted. The only reliable way to answer that question, as we have said so many times, is for the State to produce testimony concerning the manner in which the selection process operated. Because the State failed to do so after respondent established a prima facie case of discrimination, I join the Court's opinion affirming the Court of Appeals."

Mr. Justice Powell, joined by The Chief Justice and Mr. Justice Rehnquist, dissented. With respect to the governing majority issue, he said:

"In this case, the following critical facts are beyond dispute: the judge who appointed the jury commissioners and later presided over respondent's trial was Mexican-American; three of the five jury commissioners were Mexican-American; 10 of the 20 members of the grand jury array were Mexican-American; five of the 12 grand jurors who returned the indictment, including the foreman, were Mexican-American, and seven of the 12 petit jurors who returned the verdict of guilt were Mexican-American. In the year in which respondent was indicted, 52.5% of the persons on the grand jury list were Mexican-American. In addition, a majority of the elected officials in Hidalgo County were Mexican-American, as were a majority of the judges. That these positions of power and influence were so held is not surprising in a community where 80% of the population is Mexican-American. As was emphasized by District Judge Garza, the able Mexican-American jurist who presided over the habeas proceedings in the District Court, this case *is* unique. Every other jury discrimination case reaching this Court has involved a situation where the governing majority, and the resulting power over the jury selection process, was held by a white electorate and white officials.[6]

"The most significant fact in this case, all but ignored in the Court's opinion, is that a majority of the jury commissioners were Mexican-American. The jury commission is the body vested by Texas law with the authority to select grand jurors. Under the Texas selection system, as noted by the Court, the jury commission has the opportunity to identify in advance those potential jurors who have Spanish surnames. In these circumstances, where Mexican-Americans control both the selection of jurors and the political process, rational inferences from the most basic facts in a democratic society render improbable respondent's claim of an intent to discriminate against him and other Mexican-Americans. As Judge Garza observed, 'If people in charge can choose whom they want, it is unlikely they will discriminate against themselves.' 384 F.Supp. 79, 90.

"That individuals are more likely to discriminate in favor of, than against, those who share their own identifiable attributes is the premise that underlies the cases recognizing that the criminal defendant has a personal right under the Fourteenth Amendment not to have members of his own class excluded from jury service. Discriminatory exclusion of members of the defendant's class has been viewed as unfairly excluding persons who may be inclined to favor the defendant. See Strauder v. West Virginia, 100 U.S., at 309. Were it not for the perceived likelihood that jurors will favor defendants of their own class, there would be no reason to suppose that a jury selection process that systematically excluded persons of a certain race would be the basis of any legitimate complaint by criminal defendants of that race. Only the individuals excluded from jury service would have a personal right to complain.

". . . With all respect, I am compelled to say that the Court today *has* 'lightly' concluded that the grand jury commissioners of this county have disregarded not only their sworn duty but also their likely inclination to assure fairness to Mexican-Americans.[7]"

[6] I do not suggest, of course, that the mere fact that Mexican-Americans constitute a majority in Hidalgo County is dispositive. There are many communities in which, by virtue of historical or other reasons, a majority of the population may not be able at a particular time to control or significantly influence political decisions or the way the system operates. See Turner v. Fouche, supra. But no one can contend seriously that Hidalgo County is such a community. The classic situation in which a "minority group" may suffer discrimination in a community is where it is "relegated to . . . a position of political powerlessness." San Antonio School District v. Rodriguez, 411 U.S. 1, 28 (1973). Here the Mexican-Americans are not politically "powerless"; they *are* the majoritarian political element of the community, with demonstrated capability to elect and protect their own.

Nor do I suggest that persons in positions of power can never be shown to have discriminated against other members of the same ethnic or racial group. I would hold only that respondent's statistical evidence, without more, is insufficient to prove a claim of discrimination in this case.

[7] I agree with Mr. Justice Marshall that stereotypes concerning identifiable classes in our society have no place in the decisions of this Court. For that reason, I consider it inappropriate to characterize the Mexican-American majority in Hidalgo County as a "minority group" and on that

Mr. Chief Justice Burger, joined by Mr. Justice Powell and Mr. Justice Rehnquist, wrote a dissenting opinion challenging the adequacy of the statistical showing to make out a prima facie case of discrimination. Mr. Justice Stewart also dissented indicating that he was "in substantial agreement" with the other two dissenting opinions.

H. "BENIGN" DISCRIMINATION: AFFIRMATIVE ACTION, QUOTAS, PREFERENCES BASED ON GENDER OR RACE

1. CLASSIFICATIONS ADVANTAGING FEMALES

KAHN v. SHEVIN

416 U.S. 351, 94 S.Ct. 1734, 40 L.Ed.2d 189 (1974).

Mr. Justice Douglas delivered the opinion of the Court.

Since at least 1885, Florida has provided for some form of property tax exemption for widows. The current law granting all widows an annual $500 exemption, Fla.Stat. § 196.191(7), F.S.A., has been essentially unchanged since 1941. Appellant Kahn is a widower who lives in Florida and applied for the exemption to the Dade County Tax Assessor's Office. It was denied because the statute offers no analogous benefit for widowers. Kahn then sought a declaratory judgment in the Circuit Court for Dade County, Florida, and that court held the statute violative of the Equal Protection Clause of the Fourteenth Amendment because the classification "widow" was based upon gender. The Florida Supreme Court reversed, finding the classification valid because it has a "fair and substantial relation to the object of the legislation," that object being the reduction of "the disparity between the economic capabilities of a man and a woman." Kahn appealed here, . . . We affirm.

There can be no dispute that the financial difficulties confronting the lone woman in Florida or in any other State exceed those facing the man. Whether from overt discrimination or from the socialization process of a male dominated culture, the job market is inhospitable to the woman seeking any but the lowest paid jobs. There are of course efforts underway to remedy this situation. On the federal level Title VII of the Civil Rights Act of 1964 prohibits covered employers and labor unions from discrimination on the basis of sex, 42 U.S.C. § 2000e–2(a), (b), (c), as does the Equal Pay Act of 1963, 29 U.S.C. § 206(d). But firmly entrenched practices are resistant to such pressures, and indeed, data compiled by the Women's Bureau of the United States Department of Labor shows that in 1972 women working full time had a median income which was only 57.9% of the male median—a figure actually six points lower than had been achieved in 1955. Other data points in the same direction. The disparity is likely to be exacerbated for the widow. While the widower can usually continue in the occupation which preceded his spouse's death in many cases the widow will find herself suddenly forced into a job market with which she is unfamiliar, and in which, because of her former economic dependency, she will have fewer skills to offer.

There can be no doubt therefore that Florida's differing treatment of widows and widowers "rest[s] upon some ground of difference having a fair and

basis to suggest that these Mexican-Americans may have "adopt[ed] the majority's negative attitudes towards the minority." This type of speculation illustrates the lengths to which one must go to buttress a holding of purposeful discrimination that otherwise is based solely on a lack of proportional representation.

substantial relation to the object of the legislation." Reed v. Reed, 404 U.S. 71, 76 . . . .

This is not a case like Frontiero v. Richardson, 411 U.S. 677, where the Government denied its female employees both substantive and procedural benefits granted males *"solely* for administrative convenience." Id., at 690 (emphasis in original).[8] We deal here with a state tax law reasonably designed to further the state policy of cushioning the financial impact of spousal loss upon the sex for whom that loss imposes a disproportionately heavy burden. We have long held that "[w]here taxation is concerned and no specific federal right, apart from equal protection, is imperiled, the States have large leeway in making classifications and drawing lines which in their judgment produce reasonable systems of taxation." Lehnhausen v. Lake Shore Auto Parts Co., 410 U.S. 356, 359. A state tax law is not arbitrary although it "discriminate[s] in favor of a certain class . . . if the discrimination is founded upon a reasonable distinction, or difference in state policy," not in conflict with the Federal Constitution. Allied Stores v. Bowers, 358 U.S. 522, 528. This principle has weathered nearly a century of Supreme Court adjudication, and it applies here as well. The statute before us is well within those limits.[10]

Affirmed.

Mr. Justice Brennan, with whom Mr. Justice Marshall joins, dissenting.

. . . In my view, however, a legislative classification that distinguishes potential beneficiaries solely by reference to their gender-based status as widows or widowers, like classifications based upon race, alienage, and national origin, must be subjected to close judicial scrutiny, because it focuses upon generally immutable characteristics over which individuals have little or no control, and also because gender-based classifications too often have been inexcusably utilized to stereotype and stigmatize politically powerless segments of society. See Frontiero v. Richardson, 411 U.S. 677 (1973). The Court is not therefore free to sustain the statute on the ground that it rationally promotes legitimate governmental interests; rather, such suspect classifications can be sustained only when the State bears the burden of demonstrating that the challenged legislation serves overriding or compelling interests that cannot be achieved either by a more carefully tailored legislative classification or by the use of feasible less drastic means. While, in my view, the statute serves a compelling governmental interest by "cushioning the financial impact of spousal loss upon the sex for whom that loss imposes a disproportionately heavy burden," I think that the statute is invalid because the State's interest can be served equally well by a more narrowly drafted statute.

Gender-based classifications cannot be sustained merely because they promote legitimate governmental interests, such as efficacious administration of government. Frontiero v. Richardson, supra; Reed v. Reed, 404 U.S. 71

---

[8] And in *Frontiero* the plurality opinion also noted that the statutes there were "not in any sense designed to rectify the effects of past discrimination against women. On the contrary, these statutes seize upon a group—women—who have historically suffered discrimination in employment, and rely on the effects of this past discrimination as a justification for heaping on additional economic disadvantages." Frontiero v. Richardson, 411 U.S. 677, 689 n. 22 (citations omitted).

[10] The dissents argue that the Florida Legislature could have drafted the statute differently, so that its purpose would have been accomplished more precisely. But the issue of course is not whether the statute could have been drafted more wisely, but whether the lines chosen by the Florida Legislature are within constitutional limitations. The dissent would use the Equal Protection Clause as a vehicle for reinstating notions of substantive due process that have been repudiated. . . .

Gender has never been rejected as an impermissible classification in all instances. Congress has not so far drafted women into the Armed Services. 50 App.U.S.C. § 454. The famous Brandeis Brief in Muller v. Oregon, 208 U.S. 412, on which the court specifically relied, id., at 419–420, emphasized that the special physical organization of women has a bearing on the "conditions under which she should be permitted to toil." Id., at 420. These instances are pertinent to the problem in the tax field

. . . . .

(1971). For "when we enter the realm of 'strict judicial scrutiny,' there can be no doubt that 'administrative convenience' is not a shibboleth, the mere recitation of which dictates constitutionality. See Shapiro v. Thompson, 394 U.S. 618 (1969); Carrington v. Rash, 380 U.S. 89 (1965). On the contrary, any statutory scheme which draws a sharp line between the sexes, *solely* for the purpose of achieving administrative convenience, necessarily commands 'dissimilar treatment for men and women who are . . . similarly situated,' and therefore involves the 'very kind of arbitrary legislative choice forbidden by the [Constitution] . . ..' Reed v. Reed, 404 U.S., at 77, 76." Frontiero v. Richardson, supra, 411 U.S., at 690. But Florida's justification of § 196.191(7) is not that it serves administrative convenience or helps to preserve the public fisc. Rather, the asserted justification is that § 196.191(7) is an affirmative step toward alleviating the effects of past economic discrimination against women.

I agree that, in providing special benefits for a needy segment of society long the victim of purposeful discrimination and neglect, the statute serves the compelling state interest of achieving equality for such groups. No one familiar with this country's history of pervasive sex discrimination against women can doubt the need for remedial measures to correct the resulting economic imbalances. Indeed, the extent of the economic disparity between men and women is dramatized by the data cited by the Court. By providing a property tax exemption for widows, § 196.01(7) assists in reducing that economic disparity for a class of women particularly disadvantaged by the legacy of economic discrimination. In that circumstance, the purpose and effect of the suspect classification is ameliorative; the statute neither stigmatizes nor denigrates widowers not also benefited by the legislation. Moreover, inclusion of needy widowers within the class of beneficiaries would not further the State's overriding interest in remedying the economic effects of past sex discrimination for needy victims of that discrimination. While doubtless some widowers are in financial need, no one suggests that such need results from sex discrimination as in the case of widows.

The statute nevertheless fails to satisfy the requirements of equal protection, since the State has not borne its burden of proving that its compelling interest could not be achieved by a more precisely tailored statute or by use of feasible less drastic means. Section 196.191(7) is plainly overinclusive, for the $500 property tax exemption may be obtained by a financially independent heiress as well as by an unemployed widow with dependent children. The State has offered nothing to explain why inclusion of widows of substantial economic means was necessary to advance the State's interest in ameliorating the effects of past economic discrimination against women.

Moreover, alternative means of classification, narrowing the class of widow beneficiaries, appear readily available. The exemption is granted only to widows who complete and file with the tax assessor a form application establishing their status as widows. By merely redrafting that form to exclude widows who earn annual incomes, or possess assets, in excess of specified amounts, the State could readily narrow the class of beneficiaries to those widows for whom the effects of past economic discrimination against women have been a practical reality.

Mr. Justice White, dissenting.

The Florida tax exemption at issue here is available to all widows but not to widowers. The presumption is that all widows are financially more needy and less trained or less ready for the job market than men. It may be that most widows have been occupied as housewife, mother and homemaker and are not immediately prepared for employment. But there are many rich widows who need no largess from the State; many others are highly trained and have held lucrative positions long before the death of their husbands. At the same time, there are many widowers who are needy and who are in more desperate financial straits and have less access to the job market than many widows. Yet none of them qualifies for the exemption.

I find the discrimination invidious and violative of the Equal Protection Clause. There is merit in giving poor widows a tax break, but gender-based classifications are suspect and require more justification than the State has offered.

I perceive no purpose served by the exemption other than to alleviate current economic necessity, but the State extends the exemption to widows who do not need the help and denies it to widowers who do. It may be administratively inconvenient to make individual determinations of entitlement and to extend the exemption to needy men as well as needy women, but administrative efficiency is not an adequate justification for discriminations based purely on sex. Frontiero v. Richardson, 411 U.S. 677 (1973); Reed v. Reed, 404 U.S. 71 (1971).

It may be suggested that the State is entitled to prefer widows over widowers because their assumed need is rooted in past and present economic discrimination against women. But this is not a credible explanation of Florida's tax exemption; for if the State's purpose was to compensate for past discrimination against females, surely it would not have limited the exemption to women who are widows. Moreover, even if past discrimination is considered to be the criterion for current tax exemption, the State nevertheless ignores all those widowers who have felt the effects of economic discrimination, whether as a member of a racial group or as one of the many who cannot escape the cycle of poverty. It seems to me that the State in this case is merely conferring an economic benefit in the form of a tax exemption and has not adequately explained why women should be treated differently than men.

I dissent.

CALIFANO v. WEBSTER, 430 U.S. 313 (1977). A complex formula for computing retirement benefits under social security permitted a female wage earner to exclude from the computation of her "average monthly wage" three more lower earning years than a similarly situated male wage earner could exclude. This resulted in a higher level of monthly old-age benefits for the retired female wage earner. In a Per Curiam opinion the Court held the classification valid, saying, in part:

"To withstand scrutiny under the equal protection component of the Fifth Amendment's Due Process Clause, 'classifications by gender must serve important governmental objectives and must be substantially related to achievement of those objectives.' Craig v. Boren, 429 U.S. 190, 197 (1976). Reduction of the disparity in economic condition between men and women caused by the long history of discrimination against women has been recognized as such an important governmental objective. Schlesinger v. Ballard, 419 U.S. 498 (1975); Kahn v. Shevin, 416 U.S. 351 (1974). But 'the mere recitation of a benign, compensatory purpose is not an automatic shield which protects against any inquiry into the actual purposes underlying a statutory scheme.' Weinberger v. Wiesenfeld, 420 U.S. 636, 648 (1975). Accordingly, we have rejected attempts to justify gender classifications as compensation for past discrimination against women when the classifications in fact penalized women wage earners, Califano v. Goldfarb, 430 U.S. 199, Weinberger v. Wiesenfeld, supra, at 645, or when the statutory structure and its legislative history revealed that the classification was not enacted as compensation for past discrimination. . . .

"The statutory scheme involved here is more analogous to those upheld in *Kahn* and *Ballard* than to those struck down in *Wiesenfeld* and *Goldfarb*. The more favorable treatment of the female wage earner enacted here was not a result of 'archaic and overbroad generalizations' about women. Schlesinger v. Ballard, supra, at 508, or of 'the role-typing society has long imposed' upon women. Stanton v. Stanton, 421 U.S. 7, 15 (1975), such as casual assumptions that women are 'the weaker sex' or are more likely to be child-rearers or dependents. Cf. Califano v. Goldfarb, supra; Weinberger v. Wiesenfeld, supra. Rather, 'the only discernible purpose of [§ 215's more favorable treatment is] the permissible one of redressing our society's longstanding disparate treatment of women.' Califano v. Goldfarb, ante, at 209 n. 8.

"The challenged statute operated directly to compensate women for past economic discrimination. Retirement benefits under the Act are based on past earnings. But as we have recognized: 'Whether from overt discrimination or from the socialization process of a male-dominated culture, the job market is inhospitable to the woman seeking any but the lowest paid jobs.' Kahn v. Shevin, 416 U.S. at 353 . . . . Thus, allowing women, who as such have been unfairly hindered from earning as much as men, to eliminate additional low-earning years from the calculation of their retirement benefits works directly to remedy some part of the effect of past discrimination. Cf. Schlesinger v. Ballard, supra, at 508.

"The legislative history of § 215(b)(3) also reveals that Congress directly addressed the justification for differing treatment of men and women in the former version of that section and purposely enacted the more favorable treatment for female wage earners to compensate for past employment discrimination against women. . . . "

Chief Justice Burger, joined by Justices Stewart, Blackmun, and Rehnquist concurred in the judgment.

ORR v. ORR, 440 U.S. 268 (1979). The Court held unconstitutional Alabama's statutory scheme imposing alimony obligations on husbands but not wives. It rejected the argument that the gender distinction was justified, because of the disparity between the economic condition of men and women, to provide support for needy wives of broken marriages. Justice Brennan's opinion for the Court said in part:

"Ordinarily, we would begin the analysis of the 'needy spouse' objective by considering whether sex is a sufficiently 'accurate proxy' for dependency to establish that the gender classification rests ' "upon some ground of difference having a fair and substantial relation to the object of the legislation." ' Similarly, we would initially approach the 'compensation' rationale by asking whether women had in fact been significantly discriminated against in the sphere to which the statute applied a sex-based classification, leaving the sexes '*not* similarly situated with respect to opportunities' in that sphere.[11]

"But in this case, even if sex were a reliable proxy for need, and even if the institution of marriage did discriminate against women, these factors still would 'not adequately justify the salient features of' Alabama's statutory scheme. Under the statute, individualized hearings at which the parties' relative financial circumstances are considered *already* occur. There is no reason, therefore, to use sex as a proxy for need. Needy males could be helped along with needy females with little if any additional burden on the State. In such circumstances, not even an administrative convenience rationale exists to justify operating by

[11] We would also consider whether the purportedly compensatory "classifications in fact penalized women," and whether "the statutory structure and its legislative history revealed that the classification was not enacted as compensation for past discrimination."

generalization or proxy. Similarly, since individualized hearings can determine which women were in fact discriminated against vis à vis their husbands, as well as which family units defied the stereotype and left the husband dependent on the wife, Alabama's alleged compensatory purpose may be effectuated without placing burdens solely on husbands. Progress toward fulfilling such a purpose would not be hampered, and it would cost the State nothing more, if it were to treat men and women equally by making alimony burdens independent of sex. 'Thus, the gender-based distinction is gratuitous; without it the statutory scheme would only provide benefits to those men who are in fact similarly situated to the women the statute aids,' and the effort to help those women would not in any way be compromised.

"Moreover, use of a gender classification actually produces perverse results in this case. As compared to a gender-neutral law placing alimony obligations on the spouse able to pay, the present Alabama statutes give an advantage only to the financially secure wife whose husband is in need. Although such a wife might have to pay alimony under a gender-neutral statute, the present statutes exempt her from that obligation. Thus, '[t]he [wives] who benefit from the disparate treatment are those who were . . . nondependent on their husbands.' They are precisely those who are not 'needy spouses' and who are 'least likely to have been victims of . . . discrimination,' by the institution of marriage. A gender-based classification which, as compared to a gender-neutral one, generates additional benefits only for those it has no reason to prefer cannot survive equal protection scrutiny.

"Legislative classifications which distribute benefits and burdens on the basis of gender carry the inherent risk of reinforcing the stereotypes about the 'proper place' of women and their need for special protection. Thus, even statutes purportedly designed to compensate for and ameliorate the effects of past discrimination must be carefully tailored. Where, as here, the State's compensatory and ameliorative purposes are as well served by a gender-neutral classification as one that gender-classifies and therefore carries with it the baggage of sexual stereotypes, the State cannot be permitted to classify on the basis of sex. And this is doubly so where the choice made by the State appears to redound—if only indirectly—to the benefit of those without need for special solicitude.

"Having found Alabama's alimony statutes unconstitutional, we reverse the judgment below and remand the cause for further proceedings not inconsistent with this opinion. That disposition, of course, leaves the state courts free . . . on remand to consider whether Mr. Orr's stipulated agreement to pay alimony, or other grounds of gender-neutral state law, bind him to continue his alimony payments."

Chief Justice Burger, Justice Powell, and Justice Rehnquist, dissenting on other issues, did not reach the equal protection question.

———

MISSISSIPPI UNIVERSITY FOR WOMEN v. HOGAN

458 U.S. 718, 102 S.Ct. 3331, 73 L.Ed.2d 1090 (1982).

Justice O'Connor delivered the opinion of the Court.

This case presents the narrow issue of whether a state statute that excludes males from enrolling in a state-supported professional nursing school violates the Equal Protection Clause of the Fourteenth Amendment.

I

The facts are not in dispute. In 1884, the Mississippi legislature created the Mississippi Industrial Institute and College for the Education of White Girls of the State of Mississippi, now the oldest state-supported all-female college in the United States. 1884 Miss.Gen.Laws, Ch. XXX, § 6. The school, known today as Mississippi University for Women (MUW), has from its inception limited its enrollment to women.

In 1971, MUW established a School of Nursing, initially offering a two-year associate degree. Three years later, the school instituted a four-year baccalaureate program in nursing and today also offers a graduate program. The School of Nursing has its own faculty and administrative officers and establishes its own criteria for admission.

Respondent, Joe Hogan, is a registered nurse but does not hold a baccalaureate degree in nursing. Since 1974, he has worked as a nursing supervisor in a medical center in Columbus, the city in which MUW is located. In 1979, Hogan applied for admission to the MUW School of Nursing's baccalaureate program. Although he was otherwise qualified, he was denied admission to the School of Nursing solely because of his sex. School officials informed him that he could audit the courses in which he was interested, but could not enroll for credit.

Hogan filed an action in the United States District Court for the Northern District of Mississippi, claiming the single-sex admissions policy of MUW's School of Nursing violated the Equal Protection Clause of the Fourteenth Amendment. Hogan sought injunctive and declaratory relief, as well as compensatory damages.

Following a hearing, the District Court denied preliminary injunctive relief. . . .

The Court of Appeals for the Fifth Circuit reversed, holding that, because the admissions policy discriminates on the basis of gender, the District Court improperly used a "rational relationship" test to judge the constitutionality of the policy. Instead, the Court of Appeals stated, the proper test is whether the State has carried the heavier burden of showing that the gender-based classification is substantially related to an important governmental objective. . . .

On rehearing, the State contended that Congress, in enacting § 901(a)(5) of Title IX of the Education Amendments of 1972, Pub.L. 92–318, 86 Stat. 373, 20 U.S.C. § 1681 et seq., expressly had authorized MUW to continue its single-sex admissions policy by exempting public undergraduate institutions that traditionally have used single-sex admissions policies from the gender discrimination prohibition of Title IX. Through that provision, the State argued, Congress limited the reach of the Fourteenth Amendment by exercising its power under § 5 of the Amendment. The Court of Appeals rejected the argument, holding that § 5 of the Fourteenth Amendment does not grant Congress power to authorize States to maintain practices otherwise violative of the Amendment. 653 F.2d 223.

We granted certiorari and now affirm the judgment of the Court of Appeals.[7]

II

We begin our analysis aided by several firmly-established principles. Because the challenged policy expressly discriminates among applicants on the

---

[7] Although some statements in the Court of Appeals' decision refer to all schools within MUW, see 646 F.2d, at 1119, the factual underpinning of Hogan's claim for relief involved only his exclusion from the nursing program, and the Court of Appeals' holding applies only to Hogan's individual claim for relief. 646 F.2d, at 1119–1120. Additionally, during oral argument, counsel verified that Hogan sought only admission to the School of Nursing. Because Hogan's claim is thus limited, and because we review judgments, not statements in opinions, Black v. Cutter Laboratories, 351 U.S. 292 (1956), we decline to address the question of whether MUW's admissions policy, as applied to males seeking admission to schools other than the School of Nursing, violates the Fourteenth Amendment.

basis of gender, it is subject to scrutiny under the Equal Protection Clause of the Fourteenth Amendment. Reed v. Reed, 404 U.S. 71, 75 (1971). That this statute discriminates against males rather than against females does not exempt it from scrutiny or reduce the standard of review.[8] Caban v. Mohammed, 441 U.S. 380, 394 (1979); Orr v. Orr, 440 U.S. 268, 279 (1979). Our decisions also establish that the party seeking to uphold a statute that classifies individuals on the basis of their gender must carry the burden of showing an "exceedingly persuasive justification" for the classification. Kirchberg v. Feenstra, 450 U.S. 455, 461 (1981); Personnel Administrator of Massachusetts v. Feeney, 442 U.S. 256, 273 (1979). The burden is met only by showing at least that the classification serves "important governmental objectives and that the discriminatory means employed" are "substantially related to the achievement of those objectives." Wengler v. Druggists Mutual Insurance Co., 446 U.S. 142, 150 (1980).

Although the test for determining the validity of a gender-based classification is straightforward, it must be applied free of fixed notions concerning the roles and abilities of males and females. Care must be taken in ascertaining whether the statutory objective itself reflects archaic and stereotypic notions. Thus, if the statutory objective is to exclude or "protect" members of one gender because they are presumed to suffer from an inherent handicap or to be innately inferior, the objective itself is illegitimate. See Frontiero v. Richardson, 411 U.S. 677, 684–685 (1973) (plurality opinion).

If the State's objective is legitimate and important, we next determine whether the requisite direct, substantial relationship between objective and means is present. The purpose of requiring that close relationship is to assure that the validity of a classification is determined through reasoned analysis rather than through the mechanical application of traditional, often inaccurate, assumptions about the proper roles of men and women. The need for the requirement is amply revealed by reference to the broad range of statutes already invalidated by this Court, statutes that relied upon the simplistic, outdated assumption that gender could be used as a "proxy for other, more germane bases of classification," Craig v. Boren, 429 U.S. 190, 198 (1976), to establish a link between objective and classification.

Applying this framework, we now analyze the arguments advanced by the State to justify its refusal to allow males to enroll for credit in MUW's School of Nursing.

III

A

The State's primary justification for maintaining the single-sex admissions policy of MUW's School of Nursing is that it compensates for discrimination against women and, therefore, constitutes educational affirmative action. As applied to the School of Nursing, we find the State's argument unpersuasive.

In limited circumstances, a gender-based classification favoring one sex can be justified if it intentionally and directly assists members of the sex that is disproportionately burdened. See Schlesinger v. Ballard, 419 U.S. 498 (1975).

---

[8] Without question, MUW's admissions policy worked to Hogan's disadvantage. Although Hogan could have attended classes and received credit in one of Mississippi's state-supported coeducational nursing programs, none of which was located in Columbus, he could attend only by driving a considerable distance from his home. A similarly situated female would not have been required to choose between foregoing credit and bearing that inconvenience. Moreover, since many students enrolled in the School of Nursing hold full-time jobs, Hogan's female colleagues had available an opportunity, not open to Hogan, to obtain credit for additional training. The policy of denying males the right to obtain credit toward a baccalaureate degree thus imposed upon Hogan "a burden he would not bear were he female." Orr v. Orr, 440 U.S. 268, 273 (1979).

However, we consistently have emphasized that "the mere recitation of a benign, compensatory purpose is not an automatic shield which protects against any inquiry into the actual purposes underlying a statutory scheme." Weinberger v. Wiesenfeld, 420 U.S. 636, 648 (1975). The same searching analysis must be made, regardless of whether the State's objective is to eliminate family controversy, Reed v. Reed, supra, to achieve administrative efficiency, Frontiero v. Richardson, supra, or to balance the burdens borne by males and females.

It is readily apparent that a State can evoke a compensatory purpose to justify an otherwise discriminatory classification only if members of the gender benefited by the classification actually suffer a disadvantage related to the classification. We considered such a situation in Califano v. Webster, 430 U.S. 313 (1977), which involved a challenge to a statutory classification that allowed women to eliminate more low-earning years than men for purposes of computing Social Security retirement benefits. Although the effect of the classification was to allow women higher monthly benefits than were available to men with the same earning history, we upheld the statutory scheme, noting that it took into account that women "as such have been unfairly hindered from earning as much as men" and "work[ed] directly to remedy" the resulting economic disparity.

A similar pattern of discrimination against women influenced our decision in Schlesinger v. Ballard, 419 U.S. 498 (1975). There, we considered a federal statute that granted female Naval officers a 13-year tenure of commissioned service before mandatory discharge, but accorded male officers only a nine-year tenure. We recognized that, because women were barred from combat duty, they had had fewer opportunities for promotion than had their male counterparts. By allowing women an additional four years to reach a particular rank before subjecting them to mandatory discharge, the statute directly compensated for other statutory barriers to advancement.

In sharp contrast, Mississippi has made no showing that women lacked opportunities to obtain training in the field of nursing or to attain positions of leadership in that field when the MUW School of Nursing opened its door or that women currently are deprived of such opportunities. In fact, in 1970, the year before the School of Nursing's first class enrolled, women earned 94 percent of the nursing baccalaureate degrees conferred in Mississippi and 98.6 percent of the degrees earned nationwide. United States Department of Health, Education, and Welfare, Earned Degrees Conferred: 1969–1970, 388 (1972). . . . As one would expect, the labor force reflects the same predominance of women in nursing. When MUW's School of Nursing began operation, nearly 98 percent of all employed registered nurses were female. United States Bureau of the Census, 1981 Statistical Abstract of the United States 402 (1981).

Rather than compensate for discriminatory barriers faced by women, MUW's policy of excluding males from admission to the School of Nursing tends to perpetuate the sterotyped view of nursing as an exclusively women's job. By assuring that Mississippi allots more openings in its state-supported nursing schools to women than it does to men, MUW's admissions policy lends credibility to the old view that women, not men, should become nurses, and makes the assumption that nursing is a field for women a self-fulfilling prophecy. See Stanton v. Stanton, 421 U.S. 7 (1975). Thus, we conclude that, although the State recited a "benign, compensatory purpose," it failed to establish that the alleged objective is the actual purpose underlying the discriminatory classification.

The policy is invalid also because it fails the second part of the equal protection test, for the State has made no showing that the gender-based classification is substantially and directly related to its proposed compensatory objective. To the contrary, MUW's policy of permitting men to attend classes as auditors fatally undermines its claim that women, at least those in the School of Nursing, are adversely affected by the presence of men.

MUW permits men who audit to participate fully in classes. Additionally, both men and women take part in continuing education courses offered by the School of Nursing, in which regular nursing students also can enroll. The uncontroverted record reveals that admitting men to nursing classes does not affect teaching style, that the presence of men in the classroom would not affect the performance of the female nursing students, and that men in coeducational nursing schools do not dominate the classroom. In sum, the record in this case is flatly inconsistent with the claim that excluding men from the School of Nursing is necessary to reach any of MUW's educational goals.

Thus, considering both the asserted interest and the relationship between the interest and the methods used by the State, we conclude that the State has fallen far short of establishing the "exceedingly persuasive justification" needed to sustain the gender-based classification. Accordingly, we hold that MUW's policy denying males the right to enroll for credit in its School of Nursing violates the Equal Protection Clause of the Fourteenth Amendment.

. . .

IV

Because we conclude that the State's policy of excluding males from MUW's School of Nursing violates the Equal Protection Clause of the Fourteenth Amendment, we affirm the judgment of the Court of Appeals.

It is so ordered.

Chief Justice Burger, dissenting.

I agree generally with Justice Powell's dissenting opinion. I write separately, however, to emphasize that the Court's holding today is limited to the context of a professional nursing school. Since the Court's opinion relies heavily on its finding that women have traditionally dominated the nursing profession, it suggests that a State might well be justified in maintaining, for example, the option of an all-women's business school or liberal arts program.

Justice Blackmun, dissenting.

. . .

I have come to suspect that it is easy to go too far with rigid rules in this area of claimed sex discrimination, and to lose—indeed destroy—values that mean much to some people by forbidding the State from offering them a choice while not depriving others of an alternate choice. . . .

. . .

I hope that we do not lose all values that some think are worthwhile (and are not based on differences of race or religion) and relegate ourselves to needless conformity. The ringing words of the Equal Protection Clause of the Fourteenth Amendment—what Justice Powell aptly describes as its "liberating spirit,"—do not demand that price.

Justice Powell, with whom Justice Rehnquist joins, dissenting.

The Court's opinion bows deeply to conformity. Left without honor—indeed, held unconstitutional—is an element of diversity that has characterized much of American education and enriched much of American life. The Court in effect holds today that no State now may provide even a single institution of higher learning open only to women students. . . .

. . .

II

The issue in this case is whether a State transgresses the Constitution when—within the context of a public system that offers a diverse range of campuses, curricula, and educational alternatives—it seeks to acommodate the legitimate personal preferences of those desiring the advantages of an all-women's college. In my view, the Court errs seriously by assuming—without argument or discussion—that the equal protection standard generally applicable to sex discrimination is appropriate here. That standard was designed to free women from "archaic and overbroad generalizations . . . ." Schlesinger v. Ballard, 419 U.S. 498, 508 (1975). In no previous case have we applied it to invalidate state efforts to *expand* women's choices. Nor are there prior sex discrimination decisions by this Court in which a male plaintiff, as in this case, had the choice of an equal benefit. . . .

By applying heightened equal protection analysis to this case, the Court frustrates the liberating spirit of the Equal Protection Clause. It forbids the States from providing women with an opportunity to choose the type of university they prefer. And yet it is these women whom the Court regards as the *victims* of an illegal, stereotyped perception of the role of women in our society. The Court reasons this way in a case in which no woman has complained, and the only complainant is a man who advances no claims on behalf of anyone else. His claim, it should be recalled, is not that he is being denied a substantive educational opportunity, or even the right to attend an all-male or a coeducational college. It is *only* that the colleges open to him are located at inconvenient distances.

. . . .

IV

A distinctive feature of America's tradition has been respect for diversity. This has been characteristic of the peoples from numerous lands who have built our country. It is the essence of our democratic system. At stake in this case as I see it is the preservation of a small aspect of this diversity. But that aspect is by no means insignificant, given our heritage of available choice between single-sex and coeducational institutions of higher learning. The Court answers that there is discrimination—not just that which may be tolerable, as for example between those candidates for admission able to contribute most to an educational institution and those able to contribute less—but discrimination of constitutional dimension. But, having found "discrimination," the Court finds it difficult to identify the victims. It hardly can claim that women are discriminated against. A constitutional case is held to exist solely because one man found it inconvenient to travel to any of the other institutions made available to him by the State of Mississippi. In essence he insists that he has a right to attend a college in his home community. This simply is not a sex discrimination case. The Equal Protection Clause was never intended to be applied to this kind of case.

2. Classifications Advantaging Racial Minorities

REGENTS OF THE UNIVERSITY OF CALIFORNIA v. BAKKE

438 U.S. 265, 98 S.Ct. 2733, 57 L.Ed.2d 750 (1978).

Mr. Justice Powell announced the judgment of the Court.

This case presents a challenge to the special admissions program of the petitioner, the Medical School of the University of California at Davis, which is designed to assure the admission of a specified number of students from certain minority groups. The Superior Court of California sustained respondent's challenge, holding that petitioner's program violated the California Constitution, Title VI of the Civil Rights Act of 1964, 42 U.S.C. § 2000d, and the Equal Protection Clause of the Fourteenth Amendment. The court enjoined petitioner from considering respondent's race or the race of any other applicant in making admissions decisions. It refused, however, to order respondent's admission to the Medical School, holding that he had not carried his burden of proving that he would have been admitted but for the constitutional and statutory violations. The Supreme Court of California affirmed those portions of the trial court's judgment declaring the special admissions program unlawful and enjoining petitioner from considering the race of any applicant. It modified that portion of the judgment denying respondent's requested injunction and directed the trial court to order his admission.

For the reasons stated in the following opinion, I believe that so much of the judgment of the California court as holds petitioner's special admissions program unlawful and directs that respondent be admitted to the Medical School must be affirmed. For the reasons expressed in a separate opinion, my Brothers The Chief Justice, Mr. Justice Stewart, Mr. Justice Rehnquist, and Mr. Justice Stevens concur in this judgment.

I also conclude for the reasons stated in the following opinion that the portion of the court's judgment enjoining petitioner from according any consideration to race in its admissions process must be reversed. For reasons expressed in separate opinions, my Brothers Mr. Justice Brennan, Mr. Justice White, Mr. Justice Marshall, and Mr. Justice Blackmun concur in this judgment.

Affirmed in part and reversed in part.

I.†

The Medical School of the University of California at Davis opened in 1968 with an entering class of 50 students. In 1971, the size of the entering class was increased to 100 students, a level at which it remains. No admissions program for disadvantaged or minority students existed when the school opened, and the first class contained three Asians but no blacks, no Mexican-Americans, and no American Indians. Over the next two years, the faculty devised a special admissions program to increase the representation of "disadvantaged" students in each medical school class. The special program consisted of a separate admissions system operating in coordination with the regular admissions process.

Under the regular admissions procedure, a candidate could submit his application to the medical school beginning in July of the year preceding the academic year for which admission was sought. . . . Because of the large number of applications,[2] the admissions committee screened each one to select candidates for further consideration. Candidates whose overall undergraduate grade point averages fell below 2.5 on a scale of 4.0 were summarily rejected. . . . About one out of six applicants was invited for a personal interview. . . . Following the interviews, each candidate was rated on a scale of 1 to 100 by his interviewers and four other members of the admissions committee. The rating embraced the interviewers' summaries, the candidate's overall grade point average, grade point average in science courses, and scores on the Medical College Admissions Test (MCAT), letters of recommendation, extracurricular activities, and other biographical data. . . . The ratings were added together to arrive at each candidate's "benchmark" score. Since five committee

---

† Mr. Justice Brennan, Mr. Justice White, Mr. Justice Marshall, and Mr. Justice Blackmun join Parts I and V–C of this opinion. Mr. Justice White also joins Part III–A of this opinion.

[2] For the 1973 entering class of 100 seats, the Davis medical school received 2,464 applications. . . . For the 1974 entering class, 3,737 applications were submitted. . . .

members rated each candidate in 1973, a perfect score was 500; in 1974, six members rated each candidate, so that a perfect score was 600. The full committee then reviewed the file and scores of each applicant and made offers of admission on a "rolling" basis.[3] The chairman was responsible for placing names on the waiting list. They were not placed in strict numerical order; instead, the chairman had discretion to include persons with "special skills."
. . .

The special admissions program operated with a separate committee, a majority of whom were members of minority groups. . . . On the 1973 application form, candidates were asked to indicate whether they wished to be considered as "economically and/or educationally disadvantaged" applicants; on the 1974 form the question was whether they wished to be considered as members of a "minority group," which the medical school apparently viewed as "Blacks," "Chicanos," "Asians," and "American Indians." . . . If these questions were answered affirmatively, the application was forwarded to the special admissions committee. No formal definition of "disadvantage" was ever produced, . . . but the chairman of the special committee screened each application to see whether it reflected economic or educational deprivation. Having passed this initial hurdle, the applications then were rated by the special committee in a fashion similar to that used by the general admissions committee, except that special candidates did not have to meet the 2.5 grade point average cut-off applied to regular applicants. About one-fifth of the total number of special applicants were invited for interviews in 1973 and 1974. Following each interview, the special committee assigned each special applicant a bench-mark score. The special committee then presented its top choices to the general admissions committee. The latter did not rate or compare the special candidates against the general applicants, . . . but could reject recommended special candidates for failure to meet course requirements or other specific deficiencies.
. . . The special committee continued to recommend special applicants until a number prescribed by faculty vote were admitted. While the overall class size was still 50, the prescribed number was eight; in 1973 and 1974, when the class size had doubled to 100, the prescribed number of special admissions also doubled, to 16. . . .

From the year of the increase in class size—1971—through 1974, the special program resulted in the admission of 21 black students, 30 Mexican-Americans, and 12 Asians, for a total of 63 minority students. Over the same period, the regular admissions program produced one black, six Mexican-Americans, and 12 Asians, for a total of 63 minority students. Over the same period, the regular admissions program produced one black, six Mexican-Americans, and 37 Asians, for a total of 44 minority students. Although disadvantaged whites applied to the special program in large numbers, see n. 5, supra, none received an offer of admission through that process. Indeed, in 1974, at least, the special committee explicitly considered only "disadvantaged" special applicants who were members of one of the designated minority groups. . . .

Allan Bakke is a white male who applied to the Davis Medical School in both 1973 and 1974. In both years Bakke's application was considered by the general admissions program, and he received an interview. His 1973 interview was with Dr. Theodore H. West, who considered Bakke "a very desirable applicant to [the] medical school." . . . Despite a strong benchmark score of 468 out of 500, Bakke was rejected. His application had come late in the year, and no applicants in the general admissions process with scores below 470 were accepted after Bakke's application was completed. . . . There were

---

[3] That is, applications were considered and acted upon as they were received, so that the process of filling the class took place over a period of months, with later applications being considered against those still on file from earlier in the year. . . .

four special admissions slots unfilled at that time, however, for which Bakke was not considered. . . . After his 1973 rejection, Bakke wrote to Dr. George H. Lowrey, Associate Dean and Chairman of the Admissions Committee, protesting that the special admissions program operated as a racial and ethnic quota. . . .

Bakke's 1974 application was completed early in the year. . . . His student interviewer gave him an overall rating of 94, finding him "friendly, well tempered, conscientious and delightful to speak with." . . . His faculty interviewer was, by coincidence, the same Dr. Lowrey to whom he had written in protest of the special admissions program. Dr. Lowrey found Bakke "rather limited in his approach" to the problems of the medical profession and found disturbing Bakke's "very definite opinions which were based more on his personal viewpoints than upon a study of the total problem." . . . Dr. Lowrey gave Bakke the lowest of his six ratings, an 86; his total was 549 out of 600. . . . Again, Bakke's application was rejected. In neither year did the chairman of the admissions committee, Dr. Lowrey, exercise his discretion to place Bakke on the waiting list. . . . In both years, applicants were admitted under the special program with grade point averages, MCAT scores, and benchmark scores significantly lower than Bakke's.[7]

After the second rejection, Bakke filed the instant suit in the Superior Court of California. He sought mandatory, injunctive, and declaratory relief compelling his admission to the Medical School. He alleged that the Medical School's special admissions program operated to exclude him from the school on the basis of his race, in violation of his rights under the Equal Protection Clause of the Fourteenth Amendment, Art. I, § 21 of the California Constitution, and § 601 of Title VI of the Civil Rights Act of 1964, 42 U.S.C. § 2000d. The University cross-complained for a declaration that its special admissions program was lawful. The trial court found that the special program operated as a racial quota, because minority applicants in the special program were rated only against one another . . . and 16 places in the class of 100 were reserved for them. . . . Declaring that the University could not take race into account in making admissions decisions, the trial court held the challenged program violative of the Federal Constitution, the state constitution and Title VI. The

[7] The following table compares Bakke's science grade point average, overall grade point average, and MCAT Scores with the average scores of regular admittees and of special admittees in both 1973 and 1974. . . .

Class Entering in 1973

| | | | | MCAT (Percentiles) | | |
	SGPA	OGPA	Verbal	Quanti-tative	Science	Gen. Infor.
Bakke	3.44	3.51	96	94	97	72
Average of Regular Admittees	3.51	3.49	81	76	83	69
Average of Special Admittees	2.62	2.88	46	24	35	33

Class Entering in 1974

| | | | | MCAT (Percentiles) | | |
	SGPA	OGPA	Verbal	Quanti-tative	Science	Gen. Infor.
Bakke	3.44	3.51	96	94	97	72
Average of Regular Admittees	3.36	3.29	69	67	82	72
Average of Special Admittees	2.42	2.62	34	30	37	18

Applicants admitted under the special program also had benchmark scores significantly lower than many students, including Bakke, rejected under the general admissions program, even though the special rating system apparently gave credit for overcoming "disadvantage." . . .

court refused to order Bakke's admission, however, holding that he had failed to carry his burden of proving that he would have been admitted but for the existence of the special program.

Bakke appealed from the portion of the trial court judgment denying him admission, and the University appealed from the decision that its special admissions program was unlawful and the order enjoining it from considering race in the processing of applications. The Supreme Court of California transferred the case directly from the trial court, "because of the importance of the issues involved." 18 Cal.3d 34, 39, 553 P.2d 1152, 1156 (1976). The California court accepted the findings of the trial court with respect to the University's program.[12] Because the special admissions program involved a racial classification, the supreme court held itself bound to apply strict scrutiny. . . . It then turned to the goals the University presented as justifying the special program. Although the court agreed that the goals of integrating the medical profession and increasing the number of physicians willing to serve members of minority groups were compelling state interest, . . . it concluded that the special admissions program was not the least intrusive means of achieving those goals. Without passing on the state constitutional or the federal statutory grounds cited in the trial court's judgment, the California court held that the Equal Protection Clause of the Fourteenth Amendment required that "no applicant may be rejected because of his race, in favor of another who is less qualified, as measured by standards applied without regard to race." . . .

Turning to Bakke's appeal, the court ruled that since Bakke had established that the University had discriminated against him on the basis of his race, the burden of proof shifted to the University to demonstrate that he would not have been admitted even in the absence of the special admissions program. . . . The court analogized Bakke's situation to that of a plaintiff under Title VII to the Civil Rights Act of 1964, 42 U.S.C. § 2000e–17, see, e.g., Franks v. Bowman Transportation Co., 424 U.S. 747, 772 (1976). . . . On this basis, the court initially ordered a remand for the purpose of determining whether, under the newly allocated burden of proof, Bakke would have been admitted to either the 1973 or the 1974 entering class in the absence of the special admissions program. . . . In its petition for rehearing below, however, the University conceded its inability to carry that burden.[14] . . . The California

---

[12] Indeed, the University did not challenge the finding that applicants who were not members of a minority group were excluded from consideration in the special admissions process. 18 Cal.3d, at 44, 553 P.2d, at 1159.

[14] Several amici suggest that Bakke lacks standing, arguing that he never showed that his injury—exclusion from the medical school—will be redressed by a favorable decision, and that the petitioner "fabricated" jurisdiction by conceding its inability to meet its burden of proof. Petitioner does not object to Bakke's standing, but inasmuch as this charge concerns our jurisdiction under Art. III, it must be considered and rejected. First, there appears to be no reason to question the petitioner's concession. It was not an attempt to stipulate to a conclusion of law or to disguise actual facts of record. Compare Swift & Co. v. Hocking Valley R. Co., 243 U.S. 281 (1917).

Second, even if Bakke had been unable to prove that he would have been admitted in the absence of the special program, it would not follow that he lacked standing. The constitutional element of standing is plaintiff's demonstration of any injury to himself that is likely to be redressed by favorable decision of his claim. Warth v. Seldin, 422 U.S. 490, 498 (1975). The trial court found such an injury, apart from failure to be admitted, in the University's decision not to permit Bakke to compete for all 100 places in the class, simply because of his race. . . . Hence the constitutional requirements of Art. III were met. The question of respondent's admission vel non is merely one of relief.

Nor is it fatal to Bakke's standing that he was not a "disadvantaged" applicant. Despite the program's purported emphasis on disadvantage, it was a minority enrollment program with a secondary disadvantage element. White disadvantaged students were never considered under the special program, and the University acknowledges that its goal in devising the program was to increase minority enrollment.

court thereupon amended its opinion to direct that the trial court enter judgment ordering Bakke's admission to the medical school. 18 Cal.3d, at 64, 553 P.2d, at 1172. That order was stayed pending review in this Court. We granted certiorari to consider the important constitutional issue.

II.

. . .

A.

At the outset we face the question whether a right of action for private parties exists under Title VI [of the Civil Rights Act of 1964]. . . .

We find it unnecessary to resolve this question in the instant case. The question of respondent's right to bring an action under Title VI was neither argued nor decided in either of the courts below, and this Court has been hesitant to review questions not addressed below. . . . We therefore do not address this difficult issue. Similarly, we need not pass upon petitioner's claim that private plaintiffs under Title VI must exhaust administrative remedies. We assume only for the purposes of this case that respondent has a right of action under Title VI. . . .[a]

B.

The language of § 601, like that of the Equal Protection Clause, is majestic in its sweep:

"No person in the United States shall, on the ground of race, color, or national origin, be excluded from participation in, be denied the benefits of, or be subjected to discrimination under any program or activity receiving Federal financial assistance."

The concept of "discrimination," like the phrase "equal protection of the laws," is susceptible to varying interpretations, for as Mr. Justice Holmes declared, "[a] word is not a crystal, transparent and unchanged, it is the skin of a living thought and may vary greatly in color and content according to the circumstances and the time in which it is used." Towne v. Eisner, 245 U.S. 418, 425 (1918). We must, therefore, seek whatever aid is available in determining the precise meaning of the statute before us. . . . Examination of the voluminous legislative history of Title VI reveals a congressional intent to halt federal funding of entities that violate a prohibition of racial discrimination similar to that of the Constitution. Although isolated statements of various legislators, taken out of context, can be marshalled in support of the proposition that § 601 enacted a purely color-blind scheme, without regard to the reach of the Equal Protection Clause, these comments must be read against the background of both the problem that Congress was addressing and the broader view of the statute that emerges from a full examination of the legislative debates.

. . . In view of the clear legislative intent, Title VI must be held to proscribe only those racial classifications that would violate the Equal Protection Clause or the Fifth Amendment.

[a] The question whether there is a private action for violations of Title VI was resolved, by implication, in Cannon v. University of Chicago, 441 U.S. 677 (1979). The Court held that Title IX of the Education Amendments of 1972 provided a private right of action. Title IX was patterned after Title VI of the 1964 Civil Rights Act. It used identical language, except that the word "sex" in Title IX replaced the words "race, color or national origin" in Title VI. Justice Stevens' opinion for the Court reasoned, in part, that Congress consciously modeled Title IX on Title VI, assuming that Title VI provided a private remedy. Justices White, Blackmun and Powell dissented.

III.

A.

Petitioner does not deny that decisions based on race or ethnic origin by faculties and administrations of state universities are reviewable under the Fourteenth Amendment. . . . For his part, respondent does not argue that all racial or ethnic classifications are per se invalid . . . The parties do disagree as to the level of judicial scrutiny to be applied to the special admissions program. Petitioner argues that the court below erred in applying strict scrutiny, as this inexact term has been applied in our cases. That level of review, petitioner asserts, should be reserved for classifications that disadvantage "discrete and insular minorities." See United States v. Carolene Products Co., 304 U.S. 144, 152 n. 4 (1938). Respondent, on the other hand, contends that the California court correctly rejected the notion that the degree of judicial scrutiny accorded a particular racial or ethnic classification hinges upon membership in a discrete and insular minority and duly recognized that the "rights established [by the Fourteenth Amendment] are personal rights." Shelley v. Kraemer, 334 U.S. 1, 22 (1948).

En route to this crucial battle over the scope of judicial review,[25] the parties fight a sharp preliminary action over the proper characterization of the special admissions program. Petitioner prefers to view it as establishing a "goal" of minority representation in the medical school. Respondent, echoing the courts below, labels it a racial quota.[26]

This semantic distinction is beside the point: the special admissions program is undeniably a classification based on race and ethnic background. To the extent that there existed a pool of at least minimally qualified minority applicants to fill the 16 special admissions seats, white applicants could compete only for 84 seats in the entering class, rather than the 100 open to minority applicants. Whether this limitation is described as a quota or a goal, it is a line drawn on the basis of race and ethnic status.[27]

---

[25] That issue has generated a considerable amount of scholarly controversy. See, e.g., Ely, The Constitutionality of Reverse Racial Discrimination, 41 U.Chi.L.Rev. 723 (1974); Greenawalt, Judicial Scrutiny of "Benign" Racial Preferences in Law School Admissions, 75 Colum.L.Rev. 559 (1975); Kaplan, Equal Justice in an Unequal World: Equality for the Negro, 61 Nw.U.L.Rev. 363 (1966); Karst & Horowitz, Affirmative Action and Equal Protection, 60 Va.L.Rev. 955 (1974); O'Neil, Racial Preference and Higher Education: The Larger Context, 60 Va.L.Rev. 925 (1974); Posner, The DeFunis Case and the Constitutionality of Preferential Treatment of Racial Minorities, 1974 Sup.Ct. Rev. 1; Redish, Preferential Law School Admissions and the Equal Protection Clause: An Analysis of the Competing Arguments, 22 U.C.L.A.L.Rev. 343 (1974); Sandalow, Racial Preferences in Higher Education: Political Responsibility and the Judicial Role, 42 U.Chi.L.Rev. 653 (1975); Sedler, Racial Preference, Reality and the Constitution: Bakke v. Regents of the University of California, 17 Santa Clara L.Rev. 329 (1977); Seeburger, A Heuristic Argument Against Preferential Admissions, 39 U.Pitt.L.Rev. 285 (1977).

[26] Petitioner defines "quota" as a requirement which must be met but can never be exceeded, regardless of the quality of the minority applicants. Petitioner declares that there is no "floor" under the total number of minority students admitted; completely unqualified students will not be admitted simply to meet a "quota." Neither is there a "ceiling," since an unlimited number could be admitted through the general admissions process. On this basis the special admissions program does not meet petitioner's definition of a quota.

The court below found—and petitioner does not deny—that white applicants could not compete for the 16 places reserved solely for the special admissions program. 18 Cal.3d, at 44, 553 P.2d, at 1159. Both courts below characterized this as a "quota" system.

[27] Moreover, the University's special admissions program involves a purposeful, acknowledged use of racial criteria. This is not a situation in which the classification on its face is racially neutral, but has a disproportionate racial impact. In that situation, plaintiff must establish an intent to discriminate. Village of Arlington Heights v. Metropolitan Housing Devel. Corp., 429 U.S. 252, 264–265 (1977); Washington v. Davis, 426 U.S. 229, 242 (1976); see Yick Wo v. Hopkins, 118 U.S. 356 (1886).

The guarantees of the Fourteenth Amendment extend to persons. Its language is explicit: "No state shall . . . deny to any person within its jurisdiction the equal protection of the laws." It is settled beyond question that the "rights created by the first section of the Fourteenth Amendment are, by its terms, guaranteed to the individual. They are personal rights," Shelley v. Kraemer, supra, at 22. . . . The guarantee of equal protection cannot mean one thing when applied to one individual and something else when applied to a person of another color. If both are not accorded the same protection, then it is not equal.

Nevertheless, petitioner argues that the court below erred in applying strict scrutiny to the special admissions programs because white males, such as respondent, are not a "discrete and insular minority" requiring extraordinary protection from the majoritarian political process. *Carolene Products Co.*, supra, at 152–153, n. 4. This rationale, however, has never been invoked in our decisions as a prerequisite to subjecting racial or ethnic distinctions to strict scrutiny. Nor has this Court held that discreteness and insularity constitute necessary preconditions to a holding that a particular classification is invidious.[28] See, e.g., Skinner v. Oklahoma, 316 U.S. 535, 541 (1942); Carrington v. Rash, 380 U.S. 89, 94–97 (1965). These characteristics may be relevant in deciding whether or not to add new types of classifications to the list of "suspect" categories or whether a particular classification survives close examination. See, e.g., Massachusetts Bd. of Retirement v. Murgia, 427 U.S. 307, 313 (1976) (age); San Antonio Indep. School Dist. v. Rodriguez, 411 U.S. 1, 28 (1973) (wealth); Graham v. Richardson, 403 U.S. 365, 372 (1971) (aliens). Racial and ethnic classifications, however, are subject to stringent examination without regard to these additional characteristics. We declared as much in the first cases explicitly to recognize racial distinctions as suspect:

> "Distinctions between citizens solely because of their ancestry are by their very nature odious to a free people whose institutions are founded upon the doctrine of equality." *Hirabayashi*, 320 U.S., at 100.

> ". . . [A]ll legal restrictions which curtail the rights of a single racial group are immediately suspect. That is not to say that all such restrictions are unconstitutional. It is to say that courts must subject them to the most rigid scrutiny." *Korematsu*, 323 U.S., at 216.

The Court has never questioned the validity of those pronouncements. Racial and ethnic distinctions of any sort are inherently suspect and thus call for the most exacting judicial examination.

B.

This perception of racial and ethnic distinctions is rooted in our Nation's constitutional and demographic history. The Court's initial view of the Fourteenth Amendment was that its "one pervading purpose" was "the freedom of the slave race, the security and firm establishment of that freedom, and the protection of the newly-made freeman and citizen from the oppressions of those who had formerly exercised dominion over him." Slaughter-House Cases, 16 Wall. 36, 71 (1873). The Equal Protection Clause, however, was "[v]irtually strangled in its infancy by post-civil-war judicial reactionism."[29] It was relegated to decades of relative desuetude while the Due Process Clause of the

---

[28] After Carolene Products, the first specific reference in our decisions to the elements of "discreteness and insularity" appears in Minersville School District v. Gobitis, 310 U.S. 586, 606 (1940) (Stone, J., dissenting). The next does not appear until 1970. Oregon v. Mitchell, 400 U.S. 112, 295 n. 14 (1970) (Stewart, J., concurring in part and dissenting in part). These elements have been relied upon in recognizing a suspect class in only one group of cases, those involving aliens. E.g., Graham v. Richardson, 403 U.S. 365, 372 (1971).

[29] Tussman & tenBroek, The Equal Protection of the Laws, 37 Calif.L.Rev. 341, 381 (1949).

Fourteenth Amendment, after a short germinal period, flourished as a corner-stone in the Court's defense of property and liberty of contract. See, e.g., Mugler v. Kansas, 123 U.S. 623, 661 (1887); Allgeyer v. Louisiana, 165 U.S. 578 (1897); Lochner v. New York, 198 U.S. 45 (1905). In that cause, the Fourteenth Amendment's "one pervading purpose" was displaced. See, e.g., Plessy v. Ferguson, 163 U.S. 537 (1896). It was only as the era of substantive due process came to a close, see, e.g., Nebbia v. New York, 291 U.S. 502 (1934); West Coast Hotel v. Parrish, 300 U.S. 379 (1937), that the Equal Protection Clause began to attain a genuine measure of vitality, see e.g., *Carolene Products,* supra; Skinner v. Oklahoma, supra.

By that time it was no longer possible to peg the guarantees of the Fourteenth Amendment to the struggle for equality of one racial minority. During the dormancy of the Equal Protection Clause, the United States had become a nation of minorities. Each had to struggle—and to some extent struggles still—to overcome the prejudices not of a monolithic majority, but of a "majority" composed of various minority groups of whom it was said—perhaps unfairly in many cases—that a shared characteristic was a willingness to disadvantage other groups. As the Nation filled with the stock of many lands, the reach of the Clause was gradually extended to all ethnic groups seeking protection from official discrimination. See Strauder v. West Virginia, 100 U.S. 303, 308 (1880) (Celtic Irishmen) (dictum); Yick Wo v. Hopkins, 118 U.S. 356 (1886) (Chinese); Truax v. Raich, 239 U.S. 33, 41 (1915) (Austrian resident aliens); *Korematsu,* supra (Japanese); Hernandez v. Texas, 347 U.S. 475 (1954) (Mexican-Americans). The guarantees of equal protection, said the Court in *Yick Wo,* "are universal in their application, to all persons within the territorial jurisdiction, without regard to any differences of race, of color, or of nationality; and the equal protection of the laws is a pledge of the protection of equal laws."

Although many of the Framers of the Fourteenth Amendment conceived of its primary function as bridging the vast distance between members of the Negro race and the white "majority," Slaughter-House Cases, supra, the Amendment itself was framed in universal terms, without reference to color, ethnic origin, or condition of prior servitude. . . .

Over the past 30 years, this Court has embarked upon the crucial mission of interpreting the Equal Protection Clause with the view of assuring to all persons "the protection of equal laws," *Yick Wo,* supra, at 369, in a Nation confronting a legacy of slavery and racial discrimination. See, e.g., Shelley v. Kraemer, 334 U.S. 1 (1948); Brown v. Board of Education, 347 U.S. 483 (1954); Hills v. Gautreaux, 425 U.S. 284 (1976). Because the landmark decisions in this area arose in response to the continued exclusion of Negroes from the mainstream of American society, they could be characterized as involving discrimination by the "majority" white race against the Negro minority. But they need not be read as depending upon that characterization for their results. It suffices to say that "[o]ver the years, this Court consistently repudiated '[d]istinctions between citizens solely because of their ancestry' as being 'odious to a free people whose institutions are founded upon the doctrine of equality.'" Loving v. Virginia, 388 U.S. 1, 11 (1967), quoting *Hirabayashi,* 320 U.S., at 100.

Petitioner urges us to adopt for the first time a more restrictive view of the Equal Protection Clause and hold that discrimination against members of the white "majority" cannot be suspect if its purpose can be characterized as "benign." [34] The clock of our liberties, however, cannot be turned back to

---

[34] In the view of Mr. Justice Brennan, Mr. Justice White, Mr. Justice Marshall, and Mr. Justice Blackmun, the pliable notion of "stigma" is the crucial element in analyzing racial classifications. . . . . The Equal Protection Clause is not framed in terms of "stigma." Certainly the word has no clearly defined constitutional meaning. It reflects a subjective judgment that is standardless. *All*

1868. Brown v. Board of Education, supra, at 492; accord, Loving v. Virginia, supra, at 9. It is far too late to argue that the guarantee of equal protection to all persons permits the recognition of special wards entitled to a degree of protection greater than that accorded others. "The Fourteenth Amendment is not directed solely against discrimination due to a 'two-class theory'—that is, based upon differences between 'white' and Negro." *Hernandez*, supra, at 478.

Once the artificial line of a "two-class theory" of the Fourteenth Amendment is put aside, the difficulties entailed in varying the level of judicial review according to a perceived "preferred" status of a particular racial or ethnic minority are intractable. The concepts of "majority" and "minority" necessarily reflect temporary arrangements and political judgments. As observed above, the white "majority" itself is composed of various minority groups, most of which can lay claim to a history of prior discrimination at the hands of the state and private individuals. Not all of these groups can receive preferential treatment and corresponding judicial tolerance of distinctions drawn in terms of race and nationality, for then the only "majority" left would be a new minority of White Anglo-Saxon Protestants. There is no principled basis for deciding which groups would merit "heightened judicial solicitude" and which would not.[36] Courts would be asked to evaluate the extent of the prejudice and consequent harm suffered by various minority groups. Those whose societal injury is thought to exceed some arbitrary level of tolerability then would be entitled to preferential classifications at the expense of individuals belonging to other groups. Those classifications would be free from exacting judicial scruti-

state-imposed classifications that rearrange burdens and benefits on the basis of race are likely to be viewed with deep resentment by the individuals burdened. The denial to innocent persons of equal rights and opportunities may outrage those so deprived and therefore may be perceived as invidious. These individuals are likely to find little comfort in the notion that the deprivation they are asked to endure is merely the price of membership in the dominant majority and that its imposition is inspired by the supposedly benign purpose of aiding others. One should not lightly dismiss the inherent unfairness of, and the perception of mistreatment that accompanies, a system of allocating benefits and privileges on the basis of skin color and ethnic origin. Moreover, Mr. Justice Brennan, Mr. Justice White, Mr. Justice Marshall, and Mr. Justice Blackmun offer no principle for deciding whether preferential classifications reflect a benign remedial purpose or a malevolent stigmatic classification, since they are willing in this case to accept mere *post hoc* declarations by an isolated state entity—a medical school faculty—unadorned by particularized findings of past discrimination, to establish such a remedial purpose.

[36] As I am in agreement with the view that race may be taken into account as a factor in an admissions program, I agree with my Brothers Brennan, White, Marshall, and Blackmun that the portion of the judgment that would proscribe all consideration of race must be reversed. See Part V, infra. But I disagree with much that is said in their opinion.

They would require as a justification for a program such as petitioner's, only two findings: (i) that there has been some form of discrimination against the preferred minority groups "by society at large," post, at 45 (it being conceded that petitioner had no history of discrimination), and (ii) that "there is reason to believe" that the disparate impact sought to be rectified by the program is the "product" of such discrimination:

"If it was reasonable to conclude—as we hold that it was—that the failure of Negroes to qualify for admission at Davis under regular procedures was due principally to the effects of past discrimination, then there is a reasonable likelihood that, but for pervasive racial discrimination, respondent would have failed to qualify for admission even in the absence of Davis's special admission program." . . .

The breadth of this hypothesis is unprecedented in our constitutional system. The first step is easily taken. No one denies the regrettable fact that there has been societal discrimination in this country against various racial and ethnic groups. The second step, however, involves a speculative leap: but for this discrimination by society at large, Bakke "would have failed to qualify for admission" because Negro applicants—nothing is said about Asians . . . —would have made better scores. Not one word in the record supports this conclusion, and the plurality offers no standard for courts to use in applying such a presumption of causation to other racial or ethnic classifications. This failure is a grave one, since if it may be concluded *on this record* that each of the minority groups preferred by the petitioner's special program is entitled to the benefit of the presumption, it would seem difficult to determine that any of the dozens of minority groups that have suffered "societal discrimination" cannot also claim it, in any area of social intercourse. See Part IV-B, infra.

ny. As these preferences began to have their desired effect, and the conse-quences of past discrimination were undone, new judicial rankings would be necessary. The kind of variable sociological and political analysis necessary to produce such rankings simply does not lie within the judicial competence—even if they otherwise were politically feasible and socially desirable.

Moreover, there are serious problems of justice connected with the idea of preference itself. First, it may not always be clear that a so-called preference is in fact benign. Courts may be asked to validate burdens imposed upon individual members of particular groups in order to advance the group's general interest. See United Jewish Organizations v. Carey, 430 U.S. 144, 172–173 (Brennan, J., concurring in part). Nothing in the Constitution supports the notion that individuals may be asked to suffer otherwise impermissible burdens in order to enhance the societal standing of their ethnic groups. Second, preferential programs may only reinforce common stereotypes holding that certain groups are unable to achieve success without special protection based on a factor having no relationship to individual worth. See DeFunis v. Odegaard, 416 U.S. 312, 343 (Douglas, J., dissenting). Third, there is a measure of inequity in forcing innocent persons in respondent's position to bear the burdens of redressing grievances not of their making.

By hitching the meaning of the Equal Protection Clause to these transitory considerations, we would be holding, as a constitutional principle, that judicial scrutiny of classifications touching on racial and ethnic background may vary with the ebb and flow of political forces. Disparate constitutional tolerance of such classifications well may serve to exacerbate racial and ethnic antagonisms rather than alleviate them. *United Jewish Organizations,* supra, at 173–174 (Brennan, J., concurring). Also, the mutability of a constitutional principle, based upon shifting political and social judgments, undermines the chances for consistent application of the Constitution from one generation to the next, a critical feature of its coherent interpretation. Pollock v. Farmers Loan & Trust Co., 157 U.S. 429, 650–651 (1895) (White, J., dissenting). In expounding the Constitution, the Court's role is to discern "principles sufficiently absolute to give them roots throughout the community and continuity over significant periods of time, and to lift them above the level of the pragmatic political judgments of a particular time and place." A. Cox, The Role of the Supreme Court in American Government 114 (1976).

If it is the individual who is entitled to judicial protection against classifica-tions based upon his racial or ethnic background because such distinctions impinge upon personal rights, rather than the individual only because of his membership in a particular group, then constitutional standards may be applied consistently. Political judgments regarding the necessity for the particular classification may be weighed in the constitutional balance, Korematsu v. United States, 323 U.S. 214 (1944), but the standard of justification will remain constant. This is as it should be, since those political judgments are the product of rough compromise struck by contending groups within the democratic process. When they touch upon an individual's race or ethnic background, he is entitled to a judicial determination that the burden he is asked to bear on that basis is precisely tailored to serve a compelling governmental interest. The Constitution guarantees that right to every person regardless of his background. Shelley v. Kraemer, 334 U.S. 1, 22 (1948); Missouri ex rel. Gaines v. Canada, 305 U.S. 337, 351 (1938).

C.

Petitioner contends that on several occasions this Court has approved preferential classifications without applying the most exacting scrutiny. Most of the cases upon which petitioner relies are drawn from three areas: school desegregation, employment discrimination, and sex discrimination. Each of the cases cited presented a situation materially different from the facts of this case.

The school desegregation cases are inapposite. Each involved remedies for clearly determined constitutional violations. E.g., Swann v. Charlotte-Mecklenburg Board of Education, 402 U.S. 1 (1971); McDaniel v. Barresi, 402 U.S. 39 (1971); Green v. County School Board, 391 U.S. 430 (1968). Racial classifications thus were designed as remedies for the vindication of constitutional entitlement. Moreover, the scope of the remedies was not permitted to exceed the extent of the violations. E.g., Dayton Board of Education v. Brinkman, 433 U.S. 406 (1977); Milliken v. Bradley, 418 U.S. 717 (1974); see Pasadena City Board of Education v. Spangler, 427 U.S. 424 (1976). See also Austin Indep. School Dist. v. United States, 429 U.S. 990, 991–995 (1976) (Powell, J., concurring). Here, there was no judicial determination of constitutional violation as a predicate for the formulation of a remedial classification.

The employment discrimination cases also do not advance petitioner's cause. For example, in Franks v. Bowman Transportation Co., 424 U.S. 747 (1975), we approved a retroactive award of seniority to a class of Negro truck drivers who had been the victims of discrimination—not just by society at large, but by the respondent in that case. While this relief imposed some burdens on other employees, it was held necessary " 'to make [the victims] whole for injuries suffered on account of unlawful employment discrimination.' " Id., at 771, quoting Albemarle Paper Co. v. Moody, 422 U.S. 405, 418 (1975). . . . But we have never approved preferential classifications in the absence of proven constitutional or statutory violations.

Nor is petitioner's view as to the applicable standard supported by the fact that gender-based classifications are not subjected to this level of scrutiny. E.g., Califano v. Webster, 430 U.S. 313, 316–317 (1977); e.g., Craig v. Boren, 429 U.S. 190, 211 n.* (1976) (Powell, J., concurring). Gender-based distinctions are less likely to create the analytical and practical problems present in preferential programs premised on racial or ethnic criteria. With respect to gender there are only two possible classifications. The incidence of the burdens imposed by preferential classifications is clear. There are no rival groups who can claim that they, too, are entitled to preferential treatment. Classwide questions as to the group suffering previous injury and groups which fairly can be burdened are relatively manageable for reviewing courts. See, e.g., Califano v. Goldfarb, 430 U.S. 199, 212–217 (1977); Weinberger v. Wiesenfeld, 420 U.S. 636, 645 (1975). The resolution of these same questions in the context of racial and ethnic preferences presents far more complex and intractable problems than gender-based classifications. More importantly, the perception of racial classifications as inherently odious stems from a lengthy and tragic history that gender-based classifications do not share. In sum, the Court has never viewed such classification as inherently suspect or as comparable to racial or ethnic classifications for the purpose of equal-protection analysis.

Petitioner also cites Lau v. Nichols, 414 U.S. 563 (1974), in support of the proposition that discrimination favoring racial or ethnic minorities has received judicial approval without the exacting inquiry ordinarily accorded "suspect" classifications. In *Lau,* we held that the failure of the San Francisco school system to provide remedial English instruction for some 1,800 students of oriental ancestry who spoke no English amounted to a violation of Title VI of the Civil Rights Act of 1964, 42 U.S.C. § 2000d, and the regulations promulgated thereunder. Those regulations required remedial instruction where inability to understand English excluded children of foreign ancestry from participation in educational programs. Because we found that the students in *Lau* were denied "a meaningful opportunity to participate in the educational program," ibid., we remanded for the fashioning of a remedial order.

Lau provides little support for petitioner's argument. The decision rested solely on the statute, which had been construed by the responsible administrative agency to reach educational practices "which have the effect of subjecting individuals to discrimination." We stated: "Under these state imposed standards there is no equality of treatment merely by providing students with the same facilities, textbooks, teachers and curriculum; for students who do not understand English are effectively foreclosed from any meaningful education." Moreover, the "preference" approved did not result in the denial of the relevant benefit—"meaningful participation in the educational program"—to anyone else. No other student was deprived by that preference of the ability to participate in San Francisco's school system, and the applicable regulations required similar assistance for all students who suffered similar linguistic deficiencies. Id., at 570–571 (Stewart, J., concurring).

In a similar vein,[42] petitioner contends that our recent decision in United Jewish Organizations v. Carey, 430 U.S. 144 (1977), indicates a willingness to approve racial classifications designed to benefit certain minorities, without denominating the classifications as "suspect." The State of New York had redrawn its reapportionment plan to meet objections of the Department of Justice under § 5 of the Voting Rights Act of 1965, 42 U.S.C. § 1973c. Specifically, voting districts were redrawn to enhance the electoral power of certain "nonwhite" voters found to have been the victims of unlawful "dilution" under the original reapportionment plan. *United Jewish Organizations,* like *Lau,* properly is viewed as a case in which the remedy for an administrative finding of discrimination encompassed measures to improve the previously disadvantaged group's ability to participate, without excluding individuals belonging to any other group from enjoyment of the relevant opportunity— meaningful participation in the electoral process.

In this case, unlike *Lau* and *United Jewish Organizations,* there has been no determination by the legislature or a responsible administrative agency that the University engaged in a discriminatory practice requiring remedial efforts. Moreover, the operation of petitioner's special admissions program is quite different from the remedial measures approved in those cases. It prefers the designated minority groups at the expense of other individuals who are totally foreclosed from competition for the 16 special admissions seats in every medical school class. Because of that foreclosure, some individuals are excluded from enjoyment of a state-provided benefit—admission to the medical school—they otherwise would receive. When a classification denies an individual opportunities or benefits enjoyed by others solely because of his race or ethnic background, it must be regarded as suspect. E.g., McLaurin v. Oklahoma State Regents, 339 U.S. 637, 641–642 (1950).

IV.

We have held that in "order to justify the use of a suspect classification, a State must show that its purpose or interest is both constitutionally permissible and substantial, and that its use of the classification is 'necessary . . . to the accomplishment' of its purpose or the safeguarding of its interest." In re Griffiths, 413 U.S. 717, 722–723 (1973) (footnotes omitted); Loving v. Virginia, 388 U.S. 1, 11 (1967); McLaughlin v. Florida, 379 U.S. 184, 196 (1964). The special admissions program purports to serve the purposes of: (i)

---

[42] Petitioner also cites our decision in Morton v. Mancari, 417 U.S. 535 (1974), for the proposition that the State may prefer members of traditionally disadvantaged groups. In *Mancari,* we approved a hiring preference for qualified Indians in the Bureau of Indian Affairs of the Department of the Interior (BIA). We observed in that case, however, that the legal status of BIA is *sui generis.* Id., at 554. Indeed, we found that the preference was not racial at all, but "an employment criterion reasonably designed to further the cause of Indian self-government and to make the BIA more responsive to groups [,] . . . whose lives are governed by the BIA in a unique fashion."

"reducing the historic deficit of traditionally disfavored minorities in medical schools and the medical profession;" (ii) countering the effects of societal discrimination; (iii) increasing the number of physicians who will practice in communities currently underserved; and (iv) obtaining the educational benefits that flow from an ethnically diverse student body. It is necessary to decide which, if any, of these purposes is substantial enough to support the use of a suspect classification.

A.

If petitioner's purpose is to assure within its student body some specified percentage of a particular group merely because of its race or ethnic origin, such a preferential purpose must be rejected not as insubstantial but as facially invalid. Preferring members of any one group for no reason other than race or ethnic origin is discrimination for its own sake. This the Constitution forbids. E.g., Loving v. Virginia, supra, at 11; McLaughlin v. Florida, supra, at 196; Brown v. Board of Education, 347 U.S. 483 (1954).

B.

The State certainly has a legitimate and substantial interest in ameliorating, or eliminating where feasible, the disabling effects of identified discrimination. The line of school desegregation cases, commencing with *Brown,* attests to the importance of this state goal and the commitment of the judiciary to affirm all lawful means towards its attainment. In the school cases, the States were required by court order to redress the wrongs worked by specific instances of racial discrimination. That goal was far more focused than the remedying of the effects of "societal discrimination," an amorphous concept of injury that may be ageless in its reach into the past.

We have never approved a classification that aids persons perceived as members of relatively victimized groups at the expense of other innocent individuals in the absence of judicial, legislative, or administrative findings of constitutional or statutory violations. See, e.g., Teamsters v. United States, 431 U.S. 324, 367–376 (1977); *United Jewish Organizations,* 430 U.S., at 155–156; South Carolina v. Katzenbach, 383 U.S. 308 (1966). After such findings have been made, the governmental interest in preferring members of the injured groups at the expense of others is substantial, since the legal rights of the victims must be vindicated. In such a case, the extent of the injury and the consequent remedy will have been judicially, legislatively, or administratively defined. Also, the remedial action usually remains subject to continuing oversight to assure that it will work the least harm possible to other innocent persons competing for the benefit. Without such findings of constitutional or statutory violations, it cannot be said that the government has any greater interest in helping one individual than in refraining from harming another. Thus, the government has no compelling justification for inflicting such harm.

Petitioner does not purport to have made, and is in no position to make, such findings. Its broad mission is education, not the formulation of any legislative policy or the adjudication of particular claims of illegality. For reasons similar to those stated in Part III of this opinion, isolated segments of our vast governmental structures are not competent to make those decisions, at least in the absence of legislative mandates and legislatively determined criteria. Cf. Hampton v. Mow Sun Wong, 426 U.S. 88 (1976). Compare n. 41, supra. Before relying upon these sorts of findings in establishing a racial classification, a governmental body must have the authority and capability to establish, in the record, that the classification is responsive to identified discrimination. See, e.g., Califano v. Webster, 430 U.S. 313, 316–321 (1977); Califano v. Goldfarb, 430 U.S. 199, 212–217 (1977). Lacking this capability, petitioner has not carried its burden of justification on this issue.

Hence, the purpose of helping certain groups whom the faculty of the Davis Medical School perceived as victims of "societal discrimination" does not justify a classification that imposes disadvantages upon persons like respondent, who bear no responsibility for whatever harm the beneficiaries of the special admissions program are thought to have suffered. To hold otherwise would be to convert a remedy heretofore reserved for violations of legal rights into a privilege that all institutions throughout the Nation could grant at their pleasure to whatever groups are perceived as victims of societal discrimination. That is a step we have never approved. Cf. Pasadena City Board of Education v. Spangler, 427 U.S. 424 (1976).

C.

Petitioner identifies, as another purpose of its program, improving the delivery of health care services to communities currently underserved. It may be assumed that in some situations a State's interest in facilitating the health care of its citizens is sufficiently compelling to support the use of a suspect classification. But there is virtually no evidence in the record indicating that petitioner's special admissions program is either needed or geared to promote that goal.
. . . .

Petitioner simply has not carried its burden of demonstrating that it must prefer members of particular ethnic groups over all other individuals in order to promote better health care delivery to deprived citizens. Indeed, petitioner has not shown that its preferential classification is likely to have any significant effect on the problem.

D.

The fourth goal asserted by petitioner is the attainment of a diverse student body. This clearly is a constitutionally permissible goal for an institution of higher education. Academic freedom, though not a specifically enumerated constitutional right, long has been viewed as a special concern of the First Amendment. The freedom of a university to make its own judgments as to education includes the selection of its student body. . . .

. . . The atmosphere of "speculation, experiment and creation"—so essential to the quality of higher education—is widely believed to be promoted by a diverse student body. . . . [I]t is not too much to say that the "nation's future depends upon leaders trained through wide exposure" to the ideas and mores of students as diverse as this Nation of many peoples.

Thus, in arguing that its universities must be accorded the right to select those students who will contribute the most to the "robust exchange of ideas," petitioner invokes a countervailing constitutional interest, that of the First Amendment. In this light, petitioner must be viewed as seeking to achieve a goal that is of paramount importance in the fulfillment of its mission.

It may be argued that there is greater force to these views at the undergraduate level than in a medical school where the training is centered primarily on professional competency. But even at the graduate level, our tradition and experience lend support to the view that the contribution of diversity is substantial. . . . Physicians serve a heterogeneous population. An otherwise qualified medical student with a particular background—whether it be ethnic, geographic, culturally advantaged or disadvantaged—may bring to a professional school of medicine experiences, outlooks and ideas that enrich the training of its student body and better equip its graduates to render with understanding their vital service to humanity.

Ethnic diversity, however, is only one element in a range of factors a university properly may consider in attaining the goal of a heterogeneous student body. Although a university must have wide discretion in making the sensitive judgments as to who should be admitted, constitutional limitations protecting individual rights may not be disregarded. Respondent urges—and the courts below have held—that petitioner's dual admissions program is a racial classification that impermissibly infringes his rights under the Fourteenth Amendment. As the interest of diversity is compelling in the context of a university's admissions program, the question remains whether the program's racial classification is necessary to promote this interest. In re Griffiths, 413 U.S. 717, at 721–722 (1973).

V.

A.

It may be assumed that the reservation of a specified number of seats in each class for individuals from the preferred ethnic groups would contribute to the attainment of considerable ethnic diversity in the student body. But petitioner's argument that this is the only effective means of serving the interest of diversity is seriously flawed. In a most fundamental sense the argument misconceives the nature of the state interest that would justify consideration of race or ethnic background. It is not an interest in simple ethnic diversity, in which a specified percentage of the student body is in effect guaranteed to be members of selected ethnic groups, with the remaining percentage an undifferentiated aggregation of students. The diversity that furthers a compelling state interest encompasses a far broader array of qualifications and characteristics of which racial or ethnic origin is but a single though important element. Petitioner's special admissions program, focused *solely* on ethnic diversity, would hinder rather than further attainment of genuine diversity.

Nor would the state interest in genuine diversity be served by expanding petitioner's two-track system into a multitrack program with a prescribed number of seats set aside for each identifiable category of applicants. Indeed, it is inconceivable that a university would thus pursue the logic of petitioner's two-track program to the illogical end of insulating each category of applicants with certain desired qualifications from competition with all other applicants.

The experience of other university admissions programs, which take race into account in achieving the educational diversity valued by the First Amendment, demonstrates that the assignment of a fixed number of places to a minority group is not a necessary means toward that end. An illuminating example is found in the Harvard College program:

"In recent years Harvard College has expanded the concept of diversity to include students from disadvantaged economic, racial and ethnic groups. Harvard College now recruits not only Californians or Louisianans but also blacks and Chicanos and other minority students.

. . .

"In practice, this new definition of diversity has meant that race has been a factor in some admission decisions. When the Committee on Admissions reviews the large middle group of applicants who are 'admissible' and deemed capable of doing good work in their courses, the race of an applicant may tip the balance in his favor just as geographic origin or a life spent on a farm may tip the balance in other candidates' cases. A farm boy from Idaho can bring something to Harvard College that a Bostonian cannot offer. Similarly, a black student can usually bring something that a white person cannot offer." . . .

. . .

"In Harvard college admissions the Committee has not set target-quotas for the number of blacks, or of musicians, football players, physicists or Californians to be admitted in a given year . . . .. But that awareness [of the necessity of including more than a token number of black students] does not mean that the Committee sets the minimum number of blacks or of people from west of the Mississippi who are to be admitted. It means only that in choosing among thousands of applicants who are not only 'admissible' academically but have other strong qualities, the Committee, with a number of criteria in mind, pays some attention to distribution among many types and categories of students." Brief for Columbia University, Harvard University, Stanford University, and the University of Pennsylvania, as *Amici Curiae,* App. 2, 3.

In such an admissions program, race or ethnic background may be deemed a "plus" in a particular applicant's file, yet it does not insulate the individual from comparison with all other candidates for the available seats. The file of a particular black applicant may be examined for his potential contribution to diversity without the factor of race being decisive when compared, for example, with that of an applicant identified as an Italian-American if the latter is thought to exhibit qualities more likely to promote beneficial educational pluralism. Such qualities could include exceptional personal talents, unique work or service experience, leadership potential, maturity, demonstrated compassion, a history of overcoming disadvantage, ability to communicate with the poor, or other qualifications deemed important. In short, an admissions program operated in this way is flexible enough to consider all pertinent elements of diversity in light of the particular qualifications of each applicant, and to place them on the same footing for consideration, although not necessarily according them the same weight. Indeed, the weight attributed to a particular quality may vary from year to year depending upon the "mix" both of the student body and the applicants for the incoming class.

This kind of program treats each applicant as an individual in the admissions process. The applicant who loses out on the last available seat to another candidate receiving a "plus" on the basis of ethnic background will not have been foreclosed from all consideration for that seat simply because he was not the right color or had the wrong surname. It would mean only that his combined qualifications, which may have included similar nonobjective factors, did not outweigh those of the other applicant. His qualifications would have been weighed fairly and competitively, and he would have no basis to complain of unequal treatment under the Fourteenth Amendment.

It has been suggested that an admissions program which considers race only as one factor is simply a subtle and more sophisticated—but no less effective—means of according racial preference than the Davis program. A facial intent to discriminate, however, is evident in petitioner's preference program and not denied in this case. No such facial infirmity exists in an admissions program where race or ethnic background is simply one element—to be weighed fairly against other elements—in the selection process. "A boundary line," as Mr. Justice Frankfurter remarked in another connection, "is none the worse for being narrow." McLeod v. Dilworth, 322 U.S. 327, 329 (1944). And a Court would not assume that a university, professing to employ a facially nondiscriminatory admissions policy, would operate it as a cover for the functional equivalent of a quota system. In short, good faith would be presumed in the absence of a showing to the contrary in the manner permitted by our cases. See, e.g., Arlington Heights v. Metropolitan Housing Development Corp., 429 U.S. 252 (1977); Washington v. Davis, 426 U.S. 229 (1976); Swain v. Alabama, 380 U.S. 202 (1965).

B.

In summary, it is evident that the Davis special admission program involves the use of an explicit racial classification never before countenanced by this Court. It tells applicants who are not Negro, Asian, or "Chicano" that they are totally excluded from a specific percentage of the seats in an entering class. No matter how strong their qualifications, quantitative and extracurricular, including their own potential for contribution to educational diversity, they are never afforded the chance to compete with applicants from the preferred groups for the special admission seats. At the same time, the preferred applicants have the opportunity to compete for every seat in the class.

The fatal flaw in petitioner's preferential program is its disregard of individual rights as guaranteed by the Fourteenth Amendment. Shelley v. Kraemer, 334 U.S. 1, 22 (1948). Such rights are not absolute. But when a State's distribution of benefits or imposition of burdens hinges on the color of a person's skin or ancestry, that individual is entitled to a demonstration that the challenged classification is necessary to promote a substantial state interest. Petitioner has failed to carry this burden. For this reason, that portion of the California court's judgment holding petitioner's special admissions program invalid under the Fourteenth Amendment must be affirmed.

C.

In enjoining petitioner from ever considering the race of any applicant, however, the courts below failed to recognize that the State has a substantial interest that legitimately may be served by a properly devised admissions program involving the competitive consideration of race and ethnic origin. For this reason, so much of the California court's judgment as enjoins petitioner from any consideration of the race of any applicant must be reversed.

VI.

With respect to respondent's entitlement to an injunction directing his admission to the Medical School, petitioner has conceded that it could not carry its burden of proving that, but for the existence of its unlawful special admissions program, respondent still would not have been admitted. Hence, respondent is entitled to the injunction, and that portion of the judgment must be affirmed.

. . . .

Opinion of Mr. Justice Brennan, Mr. Justice White, Mr. Justice Marshall, and Mr. Justice Blackmun, concurring in the judgment in part and dissenting.

The Court today, in reversing in part the judgment of the Supreme Court of California, affirms the constitutional power of Federal and State Government to act affirmatively to achieve equal opportunity for all. The difficulty of the issue presented—whether Government may use race-conscious programs to redress the continuing effects of past discrimination—and the mature consideration which each of our Brethren has brought to it have resulted in many opinions, no single one speaking for the Court. But this should not and must not mask the central meaning of today's opinions: Government may take race into account when it acts not to demean or insult any racial group but to remedy disadvantages cast on minorities by past racial prejudice, at least when appropriate findings have been made by judicial, legislative, or administrative bodies with competence to act in this area.

The Chief Justice and our Brothers Stewart, Rehnquist, and Stevens have concluded that Title VI of the Civil Rights Act of 1964, 78 Stat. 252, as amended, 42 U.S.C. § 2000d et seq. (1970 ed. and Supp. V), prohibits programs such as that at the Davis Medical School. On this statutory theory alone, they would hold that respondent Allan Bakke's rights have been violated and that he must, therefore, be admitted to the Medical School. Our Brother Powell, reaching the Constitution, concludes that, although race may be taken into account in university admissions, the particular special admissions program used by petitioner, which resulted in the exclusion of respondent Bakke, was not shown to be necessary to achieve petitioner's stated goals. Accordingly, these Members of the Court form a majority of five affirming the judgment of the Supreme Court of California insofar as it holds that respondent Bakke "is entitled to an order that he be admitted to the University." Bakke v. Regents of the University of California, 18 Cal.3d 34, 64, 132 Cal.Rptr. 680, 700, 553 P.2d 1152, 1172 (1976).

We agree with Mr. Justice Powell that, as applied to the case before us, Title VI goes no further in prohibiting the use of race than the Equal Protection Clause of the Fourteenth Amendment itself. We also agree that the effect of the California Supreme Court's affirmance of the judgment of the Superior Court of California would be to prohibit the University from establishing in the future affirmative action programs that take race into account. Since we conclude that the affirmative admissions program at the Davis Medical School is constitutional, we would reverse the judgment below in all respects. Mr. Justice Powell agrees that some uses of race in university admissions are permissible and, therefore, he joins with us to make five votes reversing the judgment below insofar as it prohibits the University from establishing race-conscious programs in the future.[1]

I.

Our Nation was founded on the principle that "all men are created equal." Yet candor requires acknowledgment that the Framers of our Constitution, to forge the Thirteen Colonies into one Nation, openly compromised this principle of equality with its antithesis: slavery. The consequences of this compromise are well known and have aptly been called our "American Dilemma." Still, it is well to recount how recent the time has been, if it has yet come, when the promise of our principles has flowered into the actuality of equal opportunity for all regardless of race or color.

The Fourteenth Amendment, the embodiment in the Constitution of our abiding belief in human equality, has been the law of our land for only slightly more than half its 200 years. And for half of that half, the Equal Protection Clause of the Amendment was largely moribund so that, as late as 1927, Mr. Justice Holmes could sum up the importance of that Clause by remarking that it was "the last resort of constitutional arguments." Buck v. Bell, 274 U.S. 200, 208 (1927). Worse than desuetude, the Clause was early turned against those whom it was intended to set free, condemning them to a "separate but equal" status before the law, a status always separate but seldom equal. Not until 1954—only 24 years ago—was this odious doctrine interred by our decision in Brown v. Board of Education, 347 U.S. 483 (1954) (*Brown I*), and its progeny, which proclaimed that separate schools and public facilities of all sorts were inherently unequal and forbidden under our Constitution. Even then inequality was not eliminated with "all deliberate speed." Brown v. Board of Education, 349 U.S. 294, 301 (1955). In 1968 and again in 1971, for example, we were forced to remind school boards of their obligation to eliminate racial discrimination root and branch. And a glance at our docket and at those of lower courts

---

[1] We also agree with Mr. Justice Powell that a plan like the "Harvard" plan . . . is constitutional under our approach, at least so long as the use of race to achieve an integrated student body is necessitated by the lingering effects of past discrimination.

will show that even today officially sanctioned discrimination is not a thing of the past.

Against this background, claims that law must be "colorblind" or that the datum of race is no longer relevant to public policy must be seen as aspiration rather than as description of reality. This is not to denigrate aspiration; for reality rebukes us that race has too often been used by those who would stigmatize and oppress minorities. Yet we cannot—and as we shall demonstrate, need not under our Constitution or Title VI, which merely extends the constraints of the Fourteenth Amendment to private parties who receive federal funds—let color blindness become myopia which masks the reality that many "created equal" have been treated within our lifetimes as inferior both by the law and by their fellow citizens.

II.

The threshold question we must decide is whether Title VI of the Civil Rights Act of 1964 bars recipients of federal funds from giving preferential consideration to disadvantaged members of racial minorities as part of a program designed to enable such individuals to surmount the obstacles imposed by racial discrimination. We join Parts I and V–C of our Brother Powell's opinion . . . .

In our view, Title VI prohibits only those uses of racial criteria that would violate the Fourteenth Amendment if employed by a State or its agencies; it does not bar the preferential treatment of racial minorities as a means of remedying past societal discrimination to the extent that such action is consistent with the Fourteenth Amendment. The legislative history of Title VI, administrative regulations interpreting the statute, subsequent congressional and executive action, and the prior decisions of this Court compel this conclusion. None of these sources lends support to the proposition that Congress intended to bar all race conscious efforts to extend the benefits of federally financed programs to minorities who have been historically excluded from the full benefits of American life.

. . .

We turn, therefore, to our analysis of the Equal Protection Clause of the Fourteenth Amendment.

III.

A.

The assertion of human equality is closely associated with the proposition that differences in color or creed, birth or status, are neither significant nor relevant to the way in which persons should be treated. Nonetheless, the position that such factors must be "[c]onstitutionally an irrelevance," Edwards v. California, 314 U.S. 160, 185 (1941) (Jackson, J., concurring), summed up by the shorthand phrase "[o]ur Constitution is color-blind," Plessy v. Ferguson, 163 U.S. 537, 559 (1896) (Harlan, J., dissenting), has never been adopted by this Court as the proper meaning of the Equal Protection Clause. Indeed, we have expressly rejected this proposition on a number of occasions.

Our cases have always implied that an "overriding statutory purpose," McLaughlin v. Florida, 379 U.S. 184, 192 (1964), could be found that would justify racial classifications. See, e.g., ibid.; Loving v. Virginia, 388 U.S. 1, 11 (1967); Korematsu v. United States, 323 U.S. 214, 216 (1944); Hirabayashi v. United States, 320 U.S. 81, 100–101 (1943). More recently, in McDaniel v. Barresi, 402 U.S. 39 (1971), this Court unanimously reversed the Georgia Supreme Court which had held that a desegregation plan voluntarily adopted by a local school board, which assigned students on the basis of race, was *per se* invalid because it was not colorblind. And in North Carolina State Board of Ed. v. Swann, 402 U.S. 43 (1971), we held, again unanimously, that a statute mandating colorblind school assignment plans could not stand "against the background of segregation," since such a limit on remedies would "render illusory the promise of *Brown* [*I,* supra]."

We conclude, therefore, that racial classifications are not *per se* invalid under the Fourteenth Amendment. Accordingly, we turn to the problem of articulating what our role should be in reviewing state action that expressly classifies by race.

B.

Respondent argues that racial classifications are always suspect and, consequently, that this Court should weigh the importance of the objectives served by Davis' special admissions program to see if they are compelling. In addition, he asserts that this Court must inquire whether, in its judgment, there are alternatives to racial classifications which would suit Davis' purposes. Petitioner, on the other hand, states that our proper role is simply to accept petitioner's determination that the racial classifications used by its program are reasonably related to what it tells us are its benign purposes. We reject petitioner's view, but, because our prior cases are in many respects inapposite to that before us now, we find it necessary to define with precision the meaning of that inexact term, "strict scrutiny."

Unquestionably we have held that a government practice or statute which restricts "fundamental rights" or which contains "suspect classifications" is to be subjected to "strict scrutiny" and can be justified only if it furthers a compelling government purpose and, even then, only if no less restrictive alternative is available. See, e.g., San Antonio Indep. School Dist. v. Rodriguez, 411 U.S. 1, 16–17 (1973); Dunn v. Blumstein, 405 U.S. 330 (1972). But no fundamental right is involved here. See *San Antonio,* supra, at 29–36. Nor do whites as a class have any of the "traditional indicia of suspectness: the class is not saddled with such disabilities, or subjected to such a history of purposeful unequal treatment, or relegated to such a position of political powerlessness as to command extraordinary protection from the majoritarian political process." Id., at 28; see United States v. Carolene Products Co., 304 U.S. 144, 152 n. 4 (1938).[31]

Moreover, if the University's representations are credited, this is not a case where racial classifications are "irrelevant and therefore prohibited." *Hirabayashi,* 320 U.S., at 100. Nor has anyone suggested that the University's purposes contravene the cardinal principle that racial classifications that stigmatize—because they are drawn on the presumption that one race is inferior to another or because they put the weight of government behind racial hatred and separatism—are invalid without more. . . .

On the other hand, the fact that this case does not fit neatly into our prior analytic framework for race cases does not mean that it should be analyzed by applying the very loose rational-basis standard of review that is the very least that is always applied in equal protection cases. " '[T]he mere recitation of a benign, compensatory purpose is not an automatic shield which protects against any inquiry into the actual purposes underlying a statutory scheme.' " Califano v. Webster, 430 U.S. 313, 317 (1977), quoting Weinberger v. Weisenfeld, 420 U.S. 636, 648 (1975). Instead, a number of considerations—developed in gender discrimination cases but which carry even more force when applied to racial classifications—lead us to conclude that racial classifications designed to

---

[31] Of course, the fact that whites constitute a political majority in our Nation does not necessarily mean that active judicial scrutiny of racial classifications that disadvantage whites is inappropriate. Cf. Castaneda v. Partida, 430 U.S. 482, 499–500 (1977); id., at 501 (Marshall, J., concurring).

further remedial purposes " 'must serve important governmental objectives and must be substantially related to achievement of those objectives.' " Califano v. Webster, supra, at 316, quoting Craig v. Boren, 429 U.S. 190, 197 (1976).[35]

First, race, like, "gender-based classifications too often [has] been inexcusably utilized to stereotype and stigmatize politically powerless segments of society." Kahn v. Shevin, 416 U.S. 351, 357 (1974) (dissenting opinion).

. . .

Second, race, like gender and illegitimacy, see Weber v. Aetna Cas. & Surety Co., 406 U.S. 164 (1972), is an immutable characteristic which its possessors are powerless to escape or set aside. . . .

. . .

In sum, because of the significant risk that racial classifications established for ostensibly benign purposes can be misused, causing effects not unlike those created by invidious classifications, it is inappropriate to inquire only whether there is any conceivable basis that might sustain such a classification. Instead, to justify such a classification an important and articulated purpose for its use must be shown. In addition, any statute must be stricken that stigmatizes any group or that singles out those least well represented in the political process to bear the brunt of a benign program. Thus our review under the Fourteenth Amendment should be strict—not " 'strict' in theory and fatal in fact," because it is stigma that causes fatality—but strict and searching nonetheless.

IV.

Davis' articulated purpose of remedying the effects of past societal discrimination is, under our cases, sufficiently important to justify the use of race-conscious admissions programs where there is a sound basis for concluding that minority underrepresentation is substantial and chronic, and that the handicap of past discrimination is impeding access of minorities to the medical school.

A.

At least since Green v. County School Board, 391 U.S. 430 (1968), it has been clear that a public body which has itself been adjudged to have engaged in racial discrimination cannot bring itself into compliance with the Equal Protection Clause simply by ending its unlawful acts and adopting a neutral stance. Three years later, Swann v. Charlotte-Mecklenburg Board of Ed., 402 U.S. 1 (1971), and its companion cases, Davis v. Board of School Comm'rs, 402 U.S.

---

[35] We disagree with our Brother Powell's suggestion . . . that the presence of "rival groups who can claim that they, too, are entitled to preferential treatment," . . . distinguishes the gender cases or is relevant to the question of scope of judicial review of race classifications. We are not asked to determine whether groups other than those favored by the Davis program should similarly be favored. All we are asked to do is to pronounce the constitutionality of what Davis has done.

But, were we asked to decide whether any given rival group—German-Americans for example—must constitutionally be accorded preferential treatment, we do have a "principled basis," . . . for deciding this question, one that is well-established in our cases: The Davis program expressly sets out four classes which receive preferred status. . . . The program clearly distinguishes whites, but one cannot reason from this to a conclusion that German-Americans, as a national group, are singled out for invidious treatment. And even if the Davis program had a differential impact on German-Americans, they would have no constitutional claim unless they could prove that Davis intended invidiously to discriminate against German-Americans. See Village of Arlington Heights v. Metropolitan Housing Corp., 429 U.S. 252, 264–265 (1977); Washington v. Davis, 426 U.S. 229, 238–241 (1976). If this could not be shown, then "the principle that calls for the closest scrutiny of distinctions in laws denying fundamental rights . . . is inapplicable," Katzenbach v. Morgan, 384 U.S. 641, 657 (1967), and the only question is whether it was rational for Davis to conclude that the groups it preferred had a greater claim to compensation than the groups it excluded. See ibid.; San Antonio Indep. School Dist. v. Rodriguez, 411 U.S. 1, 38–39 (1973) (applying *Katzenbach* test to state action intended to remove discrimination in educational opportunity). Thus, claims of rival groups, although they may create thorny political problems, create relatively simple problems for the courts.

33 (1971); McDaniel v. Barresi, supra; and North Carolina State Board of Ed. v. Swann, supra, reiterated that racially neutral remedies for past discrimination were inadequate where consequences of past discriminatory acts influence or control present decisions. See, e.g., *Charlotte-Mecklenburg,* supra, at 28. And the Court further held both that courts could enter desegregation orders which assigned students and faculty by reference to race, *Charlotte-Mecklenburg,* supra; *Davis,* supra; United States v. Montgomery County Board of Ed., 395 U.S. 225 (1969), and that local school boards could voluntarily adopt desegregation plans which made express reference to race if this was necessary to remedy the effects of past discrimination. McDaniel v. Barresi, supra. Moreover, we stated that school boards, even in the absence of a judicial finding of past discrimination, could voluntarily adopt plans which assigned students with the end of creating racial pluralism by establishing fixed ratios of black and white students in each school. *Charlotte-Mecklenburg,* supra, at 16. In each instance, the creation of unitary school systems, in which the effects of past discrimination had been "eliminated root and branch," *Green,* supra, at 438, was recognized as a compelling social goal justifying the overt use of race.

Finally, the conclusion that state educational institutions may constitutionally adopt admissions programs designed to avoid exclusion of historically disadvantaged minorities, even when such programs explicitly take race into account, finds direct support in our cases construing congressional legislation designed to overcome the present effects of past discrimination. Congress can and has outlawed actions which have a disproportionately adverse and unjustified impact upon members of racial minorities and has required or authorized race-conscious action to put individuals disadvantaged by such impact in the position they otherwise might have enjoyed. See Franks v. Bowman, supra; International Brotherhood of Teamsters v. United States, 431 U.S. 324 (1977). Such relief does not require as a predicate proof that recipients of preferential advancement have been individually discriminated against; it is enough that each recipient is within a general class of persons likely to have been the victims of discrimination. Nor is it an objection to such relief that preference for minorities will upset the settled expectations of nonminorities. See *Franks,* supra. In addition, we have held that Congress, to remove barriers to equal opportunity, can and has required employers to use test criteria that fairly reflect the qualifications of minority applicants vis-à-vis nonminority applicants, even if this means interpreting the qualifications of an applicant in light of his race. See Albemarle v. Moody, 422 U.S. 405, 435 (1975).

These cases cannot be distinguished simply by the presence of judicial findings of discrimination, for race-conscious remedies have been approved where such findings have not been made. McDaniel v. Barresi, supra; UJO, supra; see Califano v. Webster, supra; Schlesinger v. Ballard, supra; Kahn v. Shevin, supra. See also Katzenbach v. Morgan, 384 U.S. 641 (1967). Indeed, the requirement of a judicial determination of a constitutional or statutory violation as a predicate for race-conscious remedial actions would be self-defeating. Such a requirement would severely undermine efforts to achieve voluntary compliance with the requirements of law. And, our society and jurisprudence have always stressed the value of voluntary efforts to further the objectives of the law. Judicial intervention is a last resort to achieve cessation of illegal conduct or the remedying of its effects rather than a prerequisite to action.

Nor can our cases be distinguished on the ground that the entity using explicit racial classifications had itself violated § 1 of the Fourteenth Amendment or an antidiscrimination regulation, for again race-conscious remedies have been approved where this is not the case. See *UJO,* 430 U.S., at 157 (opinion of White, Blackmun, Rehnquist, and Stevens, JJ.); id., at 167 (opinion of

White, Rehnquist, and Stevens, JJ.); cf. Califano v. Webster, 430 U.S., at 317; Kahn v. Shevin, supra. Moreover, the presence or absence of past discrimination by universities or employers is largely irrelevant to resolving respondent's constitutional claims. The claims of those burdened by the race-conscious actions of a university or employer who has never been adjudged in violation of an antidiscrimination law are not any more or less entitled to deference than the claims of the burdened nonminority workers in Franks v. Bowman, 424 U.S. 747 (1976), in which the employer had violated Title VII, for in each case the employees are innocent of past discrimination. And, although it might be argued that, where an employer has violated an antidiscrimination law, the expectations of nonminority workers are themselves products of discrimination and hence "tainted," and therefore more easily upset, the same argument can be made with respect to respondent. If it was reasonable to conclude—as we hold that it was—that the failure of minorities to qualify for admission at Davis under regular procedures was due principally to the effects of past discrimination, then there is a reasonable likelihood that, but for pervasive racial discrimination, respondent would have failed to qualify for admission even in the absence of Davis' special admissions program.[41]

Thus, our cases under Title VII of the Civil Rights Act have held that, in order to achieve minority participation in previously segregated areas of public life, Congress may require or authorize preferential treatment for those likely disadvantaged by societal racial discrimination. Such legislation has been sustained even without a requirement of findings of intentional racial discrimination by those required or authorized to accord preferential treatment, or a case-by-case determination that those to be benefited suffered from racial discrimination. These decisions compel the conclusion that States also may adopt race-conscious programs designed to overcome substantial, chronic minority under-representation where there is reason to believe that the evil addressed is a product of past racial discrimination.[42]

[41] Our cases cannot be distinguished by suggesting, as our Brother Powell does, that in none of them was anyone deprived of "the relevant benefit." . . . Our school cases have deprived whites of the neighborhood school of their choice; our Title VII cases have deprived nondiscriminating employees of their settled seniority expectations; and *UJO* deprived the Hassidim of bloc voting strength. Each of these injuries was constitutionally cognizable as is respondent's here.

[42] We do not understand Mr. Justice Powell to disagree that providing a remedy for past racial prejudice can constitute a compelling purpose sufficient to meet strict scrutiny. . . . Yet, because petitioner is a university, he would not allow it to exercise such power in the absence of "judicial, legislative, or administrative findings of constitutional or statutory violations." . . . While we agree that reversal in this case would follow *a fortiori* had Davis been guilty of invidious racial discrimination or if a federal statute mandated that universities refrain from applying any admissions policy that had a disparate and unjustified racial impact, . . . we do not think it of constitutional significance that Davis has not been so adjudged.

Generally, the manner in which a State chooses to delegate governmental functions is for it to decide. Cf. Sweezy v. New Hampshire, 354 U.S. 234, 256 (1957) (Frankfurter, J., concurring). California, by constitutional provision, has chosen to place authority over the operation of the University of California in the Board of Regents. See Cal.Const. Art. IX, § 9(a) (1978). Control over the University is to be found not in the legislature, but rather in the Regents who have been vested with full legislative (including policymaking), administrative, and adjudicative powers by the citizens of California. . . . This is certainly a permissible choice, see *Sweezy,* supra, and we, unlike our Brother Powell, find nothing in the Equal Protection Clause that requires us to depart from established principle by limiting the scope of power the Regents may exercise more narrowly than the powers that may constitutionally be wielded by the Assembly.

Because the Regents can exercise plenary legislative and administrative power, it elevates form over substance to insist that Davis could not use race-conscious remedial programs until it had been adjudged in violation of the Constitution or an antidiscrimination statute. For, if the Equal Protection Clause required such a violation as a predicate, the Regents could simply have promulgated a regulation prohibiting disparate treatment not justified by the need to admit only qualified students, and could have declared Davis to have been in violation of such a regulation on the basis of the exclusionary effect of the admissions policy applied during the first two years of its operation. . . .

Title VII was enacted pursuant to Congress' power under the Commerce Clause and § 5 of the Fourteenth Amendment. To the extent that Congress acted under the Commerce Clause power, it was restricted in the use of race in governmental decisionmaking by the equal protection component of the Due Process Clause of the Fifth Amendment precisely to the same extent as are the States by § 1 of the Fourteenth Amendment. Therefore, to the extent that Title VII rests on the Commerce Clause power, our decisions such as *Franks* and *Teamsters,* supra, implicitly recognize that the affirmative use of race is consistent with the equal protection component of the Fifth Amendment and therefore of the Fourteenth Amendment. To the extent that Congress acted pursuant to § 5 of the Fourteenth Amendment, those cases impliedly recognize that Congress was empowered under that provision to accord preferential treatment to victims of past discrimination in order to overcome the effects of segregation, and we see no reason to conclude that the States cannot voluntarily accomplish under § 1 of the Fourteenth Amendment what Congress under § 5 of the Fourteenth Amendment validly may authorize or compel either the States or private persons to do. A contrary position would conflict with the traditional understanding recognizing the competence of the States to initiate measures consistent with federal policy in the absence of congressional pre-emption of the subject matter. Nothing whatever in the legislative history of either the Fourteenth Amendment or the Civil Rights Acts even remotely suggests that the States are foreclosed from furthering the fundamental purpose of equal opportunity to which the Amendment and those Acts are addressed. Indeed, voluntary initiatives by the States to achieve the national goal of equal opportunity have been recognized to be essential to its attainment. "To use the Fourteenth Amendment as a sword against such state power would stultify that Amendment." Railway Mail Assn. v. Corsi, 326 U.S. 88, 98 (Frankfurter, J., concurring). We therefore conclude that Davis' goal of admitting minority students disadvantaged by the effects of past discrimination is sufficiently important to justify use of race-conscious admissions criteria.

B.

Properly construed, therefore, our prior cases unequivocally show that a state government may adopt race-conscious programs if the purpose of such programs is to remove the disparate racial impact its actions might otherwise have and if there is reason to believe that the disparate impact is itself the product of past discrimination, whether its own or that of society at large. There is no question that Davis' program is valid under this test.

Certainly, on the basis of the undisputed factual submissions before this Court, Davis had a sound basis for believing that the problem of under-representation of minorities was substantial and chronic and that the problem was attributable to handicaps imposed on minority applicants by past and present racial discrimination. Until at least 1973, the practice of medicine in this country was, in fact, if not in law, largely the prerogative of whites. In 1950, for example, while Negroes comprised 10% of the total population, Negro physicians constituted only 2.2% of the total number of physicians. The overwhelming majority of these, moreover, were educated in two predominant-ly Negro medical schools, Howard and Meharry. By 1970, the gap between the proportion of Negroes in medicine and their proportion in the population had widened: The number of Negroes employed in medicine remained frozen at 2.2% while the Negro population had increased to 11.1%. The number of Negro admittees to predominantly white medical schools, moreover, had de-clined in absolute numbers during the years 1955 to 1964.

Moreover, Davis had very good reason to believe that the national pattern of underrepresentation of minorities in medicine would be perpetuated if it retained a single admissions standard. For example, the entering classes in 1968 and 1969, the years in which such a standard was used, included only one Chicano and two Negroes out of 100 admittees. Nor is there any relief from this pattern of underrepresentation in the statistics for the regular admissions program in later years.

Davis clearly could conclude that the serious and persistent underrepresentation of minorities in medicine depicted by these statistics is the result of handicaps under which minority applicants labor as a consequence of a background of deliberate, purposeful discrimination against minorities in education and in society generally, as well as in the medical profession. From the inception of our national life, Negroes have been subjected to unique legal disabilities impairing access to equal educational opportunity. . . .

. . . The generation of minority students applying to Davis Medical School since it opened in 1968—most of whom were born before or about the time *Brown I* was decided—clearly have been victims of this discrimination. Judicial decrees recognizing discrimination in public education in California testify to the fact of widespread discrimination suffered by California-born minority applicants; many minority group members living in California, moreover, were born and reared in school districts in southern States segregated by law. Since separation of school children by race "generates a feeling of inferiority as to their status in the community that may affect their hearts and minds in a way unlikely ever to be undone," *Brown I,* 347 U.S., at 494, the conclusion is inescapable that applicants to medical school must be few indeed who endured the effects of *de jure* segregation, the resistance to *Brown I,* or the equally debilitating pervasive private discrimination fostered by our long history of official discrimination, cf. Reitman v. Mulkey, supra, and yet come to the starting line with an education equal to whites.

. . .

C.

The second prong of our test—whether the Davis program stigmatizes any discrete group or individual and whether race is reasonably used in light of the program's objectives—is clearly satisfied by the Davis program.

It is not even claimed that Davis' program in any way operates to stigmatize or single out any discrete and insular, or even any identifiable, non-minority group. Nor will harm comparable to that imposed upon racial minorities by exclusion or separation on grounds of race be the likely result of the program. It does not, for example, establish an exclusive preserve for minority students apart from and exclusive of whites. Rather, its purpose is to overcome the effects of segregation by bringing the races together. True, whites are excluded from participation in the special admissions program, but this fact only operates to reduce the number of whites to be admitted in the regular admissions program in order to permit admission of a reasonable percentage—less than their proportion of the California population—of otherwise under-represented qualified minority applicants.[58]

---

[58] The constitutionality of the special admissions program is buttressed by its restriction to only 16% of the positions in the Medical School, a percentage less than that of the minority population in California and to those minority applicants deemed qualified for admission and deemed likely to contribute to the medical school and the medical profession. . . . This is consistent with the goal of putting minority applicants in the position they would have been in if not for the evil of racial discrimination. Accordingly, this case does not raise the question whether even a remedial use of race would be unconstitutional if it admitted unqualified minority applicants in preference to qualified applicants or admitted, as a result of preferential consideration, racial minorities in numbers significantly in excess of their proportional representation in the relevant population. Such programs might well be inadequately justified by the legitimate remedial objectives. Our allusion to the proportional percentage of minorities in the population of the State administering the program is not

Nor was Bakke in any sense stamped as inferior by the Medical School's rejection of him. Indeed, it is conceded by all that he satisfied those criteria regarded by the School as generally relevant to academic performance better than most of the minority members who were admitted. Moreover, there is absolutely no basis for concluding that Bakke's rejection as a result of Davis' use of racial preference will affect him throughout his life in the same way as the segregation of the Negro school children in *Brown I* would have affected them. Unlike discrimination against racial minorities, the use of racial preferences for remedial purposes does not inflict a pervasive injury upon individual whites in the sense that wherever they go or whatever they do there is a significant likelihood that they will be treated as second-class citizens because of their color. This distinction does not mean that the exclusion of a white resulting from the preferential use of race is not sufficiently serious to require justification; but it does mean that the injury inflicted by such a policy is not distinguishable from disadvantages caused by a wide range of government actions, none of which has ever been thought impermissible for that reason alone.

In addition, there is simply no evidence that the Davis program discriminates intentionally or unintentionally against any minority group which it purports to benefit. The program does not establish a quota in the invidious sense of a ceiling on the number of minority applicants to be admitted. Nor can the program reasonably be regarded as stigmatizing the program's beneficiaries or their race as inferior. The Davis program does not simply advance less qualified applicants; rather, it compensates applicants, whom it is uncontested are fully qualified to study medicine, for educational disadvantage which it was reasonable to conclude was a product of state-fostered discrimination. Once admitted, these students must satisfy the same degree requirements as regularly admitted students; they are taught by the same faculty in the same classes; and their performance is evaluated by the same standards by which regularly admitted students are judged. Under these circumstances, their performance and degrees must be regarded equally with the regularly admitted students with whom they compete for standing. Since minority graduates cannot justifiably be regarded as less well qualified than nonminority graduates by virtue of the special admissions program, there is no reasonable basis to conclude that minority graduates at schools using such programs would be stigmatized as inferior by the existence of such programs.

D.

We disagree with the lower courts' conclusion that the Davis program's use of race was unreasonable in light of its objectives. First, as petitioner argues, there are no practical means by which it could achieve its ends in the foreseeable future without the use of race-conscious measures. With respect to any factor (such as poverty or family educational background) that may be used as a substitute for race as an indicator of past discrimination, whites greatly outnumber racial minorities simply because whites make up a far larger percentage of the total population and therefore far outnumber minorities in absolute terms at every socio-economic level. For example, of a class of recent medical school applicants from families with less than $10,000 income, at least 71% were white. Of all 1970 families headed by a person *not* a high school graduate which included related children under 18, 80% were white and 20% were racial minorities. Moreover, while race is positively correlated with differences in GPA and MCAT scores, economic disadvantage is not. Thus, it appears that

intended to establish either that figure or that population universe as a constitutional benchmark. In this case, even respondent, as we understand him, does not argue that, if the special admissions program is otherwise constitutional, the allotment of 16 places in each entering class for special admittees is unconstitutionally high.

economically disadvantaged whites do not score less well than economically advantaged whites, while economically advantaged blacks score less well than do disadvantaged whites. These statistics graphically illustrate that the University's purpose to integrate its classes by compensating for past discrimination could not be achieved by a general preference for the economically disadvantaged or the children of parents of limited education unless such groups were to make up the entire class.

Second, the Davis admissions program does not simply equate minority status with disadvantage. Rather, Davis considers on an individual basis each applicant's personal history to determine whether he or she has likely been disadvantaged by racial discrimination. The record makes clear that only minority applicants likely to have been isolated from the mainstream of American life are considered in the special program; other minority applicants are eligible only through the regular admissions program. True, the procedure by which disadvantage is detected is informal, but we have never insisted that educators conduct their affairs through adjudicatory proceedings, and such insistence here is misplaced. A case-by-case inquiry into the extent to which each individual applicant has been affected, either directly or indirectly, by racial discrimination, would seem to be, as a practical matter, virtually impossible, despite the fact that there are excellent reasons for concluding that such effects generally exist. When individual measurement is impossible or extremely impractical, there is nothing to prevent a State from using categorical means to achieve its ends, at least where the category is closely related to the goal. . . . And it is clear from our cases that specific proof that a person has been victimized by discrimination is not a necessary predicate to offering him relief where the probability of victimization is great. . . .

E.

Finally, Davis' special admissions program cannot be said to violate the Constitution simply because it has set aside a predetermined number of places for qualified minority applicants rather than using minority status as a positive factor to be considered in evaluating the applications of disadvantaged minority applicants. For purposes of constitutional adjudication, there is no difference between the two approaches. In any admissions program which accords special consideration to disadvantaged racial minorities, a determination of the degree of preference to be given is unavoidable, and any given preference that results in the exclusion of a white candidate is no more or less constitutionally acceptable than a program such as that at Davis. Furthermore, the extent of the preference inevitably depends on how many minority applicants the particular school is seeking to admit in any particular year so long as the number of qualified minority applicants exceeds that number. There is no sensible, and certainly no constitutional, distinction between, for example, adding a set number of points to the admissions rating of disadvantaged minority applicants as an expression of the preference with the expectation that this will result in the admission of an approximately determined number of qualified minority applicants and setting a fixed number of places for such applicants as was done here.[63]

The "Harvard" program, . . . as those employing it readily concede, openly and successfully employs a racial criterion for the purpose of ensuring that some of the scarce places in institutions of higher education are allocated to disadvantaged minority students. That the Harvard approach does not also make public the extent of the preference and the precise workings of the system while the Davis program employs a specific, openly stated number, does not condemn the latter plan for purposes of Fourteenth Amendment adjudication.

---

[63] The excluded white applicant, despite Mr. Justice Powell's contention to the contrary . . . receives no more or less "individualized consideration" under our approach than under his.

It may be that the Harvard plan is more acceptable to the public than is the Davis "quota." If it is, any State, including California, is free to adopt it in preference to a less acceptable alternative, just as it is generally free, as far as the Constitution is concerned, to abjure granting any racial preferences in its admissions program. But there is no basis for preferring a particular preference program simply because in achieving the same goals that the Davis Medical School is pursuing, it proceeds in a manner that is not immediately apparent to the public.

IV.

Accordingly, we would reverse the judgment of the Supreme Court of California holding the Medical School's special admissions program unconstitutional and directing respondent's admission, as well as that portion of the judgment enjoining the Medical School from according any consideration to race in the admissions process.

Separate opinion of Mr. Justice White.

.   .   .

Mr. Justice Marshall.

I agree with the judgment of the Court only insofar as it permits a university to consider the race of an applicant in making admissions decisions. I do not agree that petitioner's admissions program violates the Constitution. For it must be remembered that, during most of the past 200 years, the Constitution as interpreted by this Court did not prohibit the most ingenious and pervasive forms of discrimination against the Negro. Now, when a State acts to remedy the effects of that legacy of discrimination, I cannot believe that this same Constitution stands as a barrier.

.   .   .

While I applaud the judgment of the Court that a university may consider race in its admissions process, it is more than a little ironic that, after several hundred years of class-based discrimination against Negroes, the Court is unwilling to hold that a class-based remedy for that discrimination is permissible. In declining to so hold, today's judgment ignores the fact that for several hundred years Negroes have been discriminated against, not as individuals, but rather solely because of the color of their skins. It is unnecessary in 20th century America to have individual Negroes demonstrate that they have been victims of racial discrimination; the racism of our society has been so pervasive that none, regardless of wealth or position, has managed to escape its impact. The experience of Negroes in America has been different in kind, not just in degree, from that of other ethnic groups. It is not merely the history of slavery alone but also that a whole people were marked as inferior by the law. And that mark has endured. The dream of America as the great melting pot has not been realized for the Negro; because of his skin color he never even made it into the pot.

These differences in the experience of the Negro make it difficult for me to accept that Negroes cannot be afforded greater protection under the Fourteenth Amendment where it is necessary to remedy the effects of past discrimination.

.   .   .   .

.   .   .

I fear that we have come full circle. After the Civil War our government started several "affirmative action" programs. This Court in the Civil Rights Cases and Plessy v. Ferguson destroyed the movement toward complete equality. For almost a century no action was taken, and this nonaction was with the tacit approval of the courts. Then we had Brown v. Board of Education and the Civil Rights Acts of Congress, followed by numerous affirmative action programs. *Now,* we have this Court again stepping in, this time to stop affirmative action programs of the type used by the University of California.

Mr. Justice Blackmun.

I participate fully, of course, in the opinion, . . . that bears the names of my Brothers Brennan, White, Marshall, and myself. I add only some general observations that hold particular significance for me, and then a few comments on equal protection.

.   .   .

I suspect that it would be impossible to arrange an affirmative action program in a racially neutral way and have it successful. To ask that this be so is to demand the impossible. In order to get beyond racism, we must first take account of race. There is no other way. And in order to treat some persons equally, we must treat them differently. We cannot—we dare not—let the Equal Protection Clause perpetrate racial supremacy.

.   .   .

Mr. Justice Stevens, with whom The Chief Justice, Mr. Justice Stewart, and Mr. Justice Rehnquist join, concurring in the judgment in part and dissenting in part.

.   .   .

III.

Section 601 of the Civil Rights Act of 1964 provides:

"No person in the United States shall, on the ground of race, color, or national origin, be excluded from participation in, be denied the benefits of, or be subjected to discrimination under any program or activity receiving Federal financial assistance."

The University, through its special admissions policy, excluded Bakke from participation in its program of medical education because of his race. The University also acknowledges that it was, and still is, receiving federal financial assistance. The plain language of the statute therefore requires affirmance of the judgment below. A different result cannot be justified unless that language misstates the actual intent of the Congress that enacted the statute or the statute is not enforceable in a private action. Neither conclusion is warranted.

.   .   .

The University's special admissions program violated Title VI of the Civil Rights Act of 1964 by excluding Bakke from the medical school because of his race. It is therefore our duty to affirm the judgment ordering Bakke admitted to the University.

Accordingly, I concur in the Court's judgment insofar as it affirms the judgment of the Supreme Court of California. To the extent that it purports to do anything else, I respectfully dissent.

FULLILOVE v. KLUTZNICK

448 U.S. 448, 100 S.Ct. 2758, 65 L.Ed.2d 902 (1980).

Mr. Chief Justice Burger announced the judgment of the Court and delivered an opinion in which Mr. Justice White and Mr. Justice Powell joined.

We granted certiorari to consider a facial constitutional challenge to a requirement in a congressional spending program that, absent an administrative waiver, 10% of the federal funds granted for local public works projects must be used by the state or local grantee to procure services or supplies from businesses owned and controlled by members of statutorily identified minority groups.   441 U.S. 960.

I.

In May 1977, Congress enacted the Public Works Employment Act of 1977, Pub.L. 95–28, 91 Stat. 116, which amended the Local Public Works Capital Development and Investment Act of 1976, Pub.L. 94–369, 90 Stat. 999. The 1977 amendments authorized an additional $4 billion appropriation for federal grants to be made by the Secretary of Commerce, acting through the Economic Development Administration (EDA), to state and local governmental entities for use in local public works projects. Among the changes made was the addition of the provision that has become the focus of this litigation. Section 103(f)(2) of the 1977 Act, referred to as the "minority business enterprise" or "MBE" provision, requires that:

"Except to the extent that the Secretary determines otherwise, no grant shall be made under this Act for any local public works project unless the applicant gives satisfactory assurance to the Secretary that at least 10 per centum of the amount of each grant shall be expended for minority business enterprises. For purposes of this paragraph, the term "minority business enterprise" means a business at least 50 per centum of which is owned by minority group members or, in case of a publicly owned business, at least 51 per centum of the stock of which is owned by minority group members. For the purposes of the preceding sentence, minority group members are citizens of the United States who are Negroes, Spanish-speaking, Orientals, Indians, Eskimos, and Aleuts."

. . . .

On November 30, 1977, petitioners filed a complaint in the United States District Court for the Southern District of New York seeking declaratory and injunctive relief to enjoin enforcement of the MBE provision. Named as defendants were the Secretary of Commerce, as the program administrator, and the State and City of New York, as actual and potential project grantees. Petitioners are several associations of construction contractors and subcontractors, and a firm engaged in heating, ventilation and air conditioning work. Their complaint alleged that they had sustained economic injury due to enforcement of the 10% MBE requirement and that the MBE provision on its face violated the Equal Protection Clause of the Fourteenth Amendment, the equal protection component of the Due Process Clause of the Fifth Amendment, and various statutory antidiscrimination provisions.

After a hearing held the day the complaint was filed, the District Court denied a requested temporary restraining order and scheduled the matter for an expedited hearing on the merits. On December 19, 1977, the District Court issued a memorandum opinion upholding the validity of the MBE program and denying the injunctive relief sought. Fullilove v. Kreps, 443 F.Supp. 253 (SDNY 1977).

The United States Court of Appeals for the Second Circuit affirmed, 584 F.2d 600 (CA2 1978), holding that "even under the most exacting standard of review the MBE provision passes constitutional muster." Id., at 603. Considered in the context of many years of governmental efforts to remedy past racial and ethnic discrimination, the court found it "difficult to imagine" any purpose for the program other than to remedy such discrimination. Id., at 605. In its view, a number of factors contributed to the legitimacy of the MBE provision, most significant of which was the narrowed focus and limited extent of the statutory and administrative program, in size, impact and duration, id., at 607–608; the court looked also to the holdings of other courts of appeals and district courts that the MBE program was constitutional, id., at 608–609. It expressly rejected petitioners' contention that the 10% MBE requirement violated the equal protection guarantees of the Constitution. 584 F.2d, at 609.

II.

A.

The MBE provision was enacted as part of the Public Works Employment Act of 1977, which made various amendments to Title I of the Local Public Works Capital Development and Investment Act of 1976. The 1976 Act was intended as a short-term measure to alleviate the problem of national unemployment and to stimulate the national economy by assisting state and local governments to build needed public facilities. . . .

. . .

The origin of the provision was an amendment to the House version of the 1977 Act, HR 11, offered on the floor of the House . . . by Representative Mitchell of Maryland. . . . [Mitchell's amendment was discussed and modified on the floor and then accepted by the House. In the Senate Senator Brooke offered on the floor a somewhat different version. He made a statement when offering it. The amendment was adopted by the Senate without debate. The Conference Committee adopted the House version of this Amendment with only a sentence of comment.]

. . .

The device of a 10% MBE participation requirement, subject to administrative waiver, was thought to be required to assure minority business participation; otherwise it was thought that repetition of the prior experience could be expected, with participation by minority business accounting for an inordinately small percentage of government contracting. The causes of this disparity were perceived as involving the longstanding existence and maintenance of barriers impairing access by minority enterprises to public contracting opportunities, or sometimes as involving more direct discrimination, but not as relating to lack—as Senator Brooke put it—"of capable and qualified minority enterprises who are ready and willing to work." In the words of its sponsor, the MBE provision was "designed to begin to redress this grievance that has been extant for so long."

. . .

III.

When we are required to pass on the constitutionality of an Act of Congress, we assume "the gravest and most delicate duty that this Court is called on to perform." Blodgett v. Holden, 275 U.S. 142, 148 (1927) (opinion of Holmes, J.). A program that employs racial or ethnic criteria, even in a remedial context, calls for close examination; yet we are bound to approach our task with appropriate deference to the Congress, a co-equal branch charged by the Constitution with the power to "provide for the . . . general Welfare of the United States" and "to enforce by appropriate legislation" the equal protection guarantees of the Fourteenth Amendment. Art. I, § 8, cl. 1; Amdt. 14, § 5. . . .

Here we pass, not on a choice made by a single judge or a school board but on a considered decision of the Congress and the President. However, in no sense does that render it immune from judicial scrutiny and it "is not to say we 'defer' to the judgment of the Congress . . . on a constitutional question," or that we would hesitate to invoke the Constitution should we determine that Congress has overstepped the bounds of its constitutional power. Columbia Broadcasting, supra, 412 U.S., at 103.

The clear objective of the MBE provision is disclosed by our necessarily extended review of its legislative and administrative background. The program was designed to ensure that, to the extent federal funds were granted under the Public Works Employment Act of 1977, grantees who elect to participate would not employ procurement practices that Congress had decided might result in perpetuation of the effects of prior discrimination which had impaired or foreclosed access by minority business to public contracting opportunities. The MBE program does not mandate the allocation of federal funds according to inflexible percentages solely based on race or ethnicity.

Our analysis proceeds in two steps. At the outset, we must inquire whether the *objectives* of this legislation are within the power of Congress. If so, we must go on to decide whether the limited use of racial and ethnic criteria, in the context presented, is a constitutionally permissible *means* for achieving the congressional objectives and does not violate the equal protection component of the Due Process Clause of the Fifth Amendment.

. . . .

B.

We now turn to the question whether, as a *means* to accomplish these plainly constitutional objectives, Congress may use racial and ethnic criteria, in this limited way, as a condition attached to a federal grant. We are mindful that "[i]n no matter should we pay more deference to the opinion of Congress than in its choice of instrumentalities to perform a function that is within its power," National Mutual Insurance Co. v. Tidewater Transfer Co., 337 U.S. 582, 603 (1949) (opinion of Jackson, J.). However, Congress may employ racial or ethnic classifications in exercising its Spending or other legislative Powers only if those classifications do not violate the equal protection component of the Due Process Clause of the Fifth Amendment. We recognize the need for careful judicial evaluation to assure that any congressional program that employs racial or ethnic criteria to accomplish the objective of remedying the present effects of past discrimination is narrowly tailored to the achievement of that goal.

Again, we stress the limited scope of our inquiry. Here we are not dealing with a remedial decree of a court but with the legislative authority of Congress. Furthermore, petitioners have challenged the constitutionality of the MBE provision on its face; they have not sought damages or other specific relief for injury allegedly flowing from specific applications of the program; nor have they attempted to show that as applied in identified situations the MBE provision violated the constitutional or statutory rights of any party to this case. In these circumstances, given a reasonable construction and in light of its projected administration, if we find the MBE program on its face to be free of constitutional defects, it must be upheld as within congressional power. . . .

. . . .

(1)

As a threshold matter, we reject the contention that in the remedial context the Congress must act in a wholly "color-blind" fashion. . . .

. . . .

Here we deal, as we noted earlier, not with the limited remedial powers of a federal court, for example, but with the broad remedial powers of Congress. It is fundamental that in no organ of government, state or federal, does there repose a more comprehensive remedial power than in the Congress, expressly charged by the Constitution with competence and authority to enforce equal protection guarantees. Congress not only may induce voluntary action to assure compliance with existing federal statutory or constitutional antidiscrimination provisions, but also, where Congress has authority to declare certain conduct unlawful, it may, as here, authorize and induce state action to avoid such conduct. Supra, at 22–28.

(2)

A more specific challenge to the MBE program is the charge that it impermissibly deprives nonminority businesses of access to at least some portion of the government contracting opportunities generated by the Act. It must be conceded that by its objective of remedying the historical impairment of access, the MBE provision can have the effect of awarding some contracts to MBE's which otherwise might be awarded to other businesses, who may themselves be innocent of any prior discriminatory actions. Failure of nonminority firms to receive certain contracts is, of course, an incidental consequence of the program, not part of its objective; similarly, past impairment of minority-firm access to public contracting opportunities may have been an incidental consequence of "business-as-usual" by public contracting agencies and among prime contractors.

It is not a constitutional defect in this program that it may disappoint the expectations of nonminority firms. When effectuating a limited and properly tailored remedy to cure the effects of prior discrimination, such "a sharing of the burden" by innocent parties is not impermissible. . . . The actual "burden" shouldered by nonminority firms is relatively light in this connection when we consider the scope of this public works program as compared with overall construction contracting opportunities.[72] Moreover, although we may assume that the complaining parties are innocent of any discriminatory conduct, it was within congressional power to act on the assumption that in the past some nonminority businesses may have reaped competitive benefit over the years from the virtual exclusion of minority firms from these contracting opportunities.

(3)

Another challenge to the validity of the MBE program is the assertion that it is underinclusive—that it limits its benefit to specified minority groups rather than extending its remedial objectives to all businesses whose access to government contracting is impaired by the effects of disadvantage or discrimination. Such an extension would, of course, be appropriate for Congress to provide; it is not a function for the courts.

Even in this context, the well-established concept that a legislature may take one step at a time to remedy only part of a broader problem is not without relevance. See Dandridge v. Williams, 397 U.S. 471 (1970); Williamson v. Lee Optical Co., 348 U.S. 483 (1955). We are not reviewing a federal program that seeks to confer a preferred status upon a nondisadvantaged minority or to give special assistance to only one of several groups established to be similarly disadvantaged minorities. Even in such a setting, the Congress is not without a certain authority. See, e.g., Personnel Administrator of Massachusetts v. Feeney, 442 U.S. 256 (1979); Califano v. Webster, 430 U.S. 313 (1977); Morton v. Mancari, 417 U.S. 535 (1974).

The Congress has not sought to give select minority groups a preferred standing in the construction industry, but has embarked on a remedial program to place them on a more equitable footing with respect to public contracting

---

[72] The Court of Appeals relied upon Department of Commerce statistics to calculate that the $4.2 billion in federal grants conditioned upon compliance with the MBE provision amounted to about 2.5% of the total of nearly $170 billion spent on construction in the United States during 1977. Thus, the 10% minimum minority business participation contemplated by this program would account for only 0.25% of the annual expenditure for construction work in the United States. Fullilove v. Kreps, 584 F.2d 600, 607 (CA2 1978).

opportunities. There has been no showing in this case that Congress has inadvertently effected an invidious discrimination by excluding from coverage an identifiable minority group that has been the victim of a degree of disadvantage and discrimination equal to or greater than that suffered by the groups encompassed by the MBE program. It is not inconceivable that on very special facts a case might be made to challenge the congressional decision to limit MBE eligibility to the particular minority groups identified in the Act. See Vance v. Bradley, 440 U.S. 93, 109–112 (1979); Oregon v. Mitchell, 400 U.S. 112, 240 (1970) (opinion of Brennan, White, and Marshall, JJ.). But on this record we find no basis to hold that Congress is without authority to undertake the kind of limited remedial effort represented by the MBE program. Congress, not the courts, has the heavy burden of dealing with a host of intractable economic and social problems.

(4)

It is also contended that the MBE program is overinclusive—that it bestows a benefit on businesses identified by racial or ethnic criteria which cannot be justified on the basis of competitive criteria or as a remedy for the present effects of identified prior discrimination. It is conceivable that a particular application of the program may have this effect; however, the peculiarities of specific applications are not before us in this case. We are not presented here with a challenge involving a specific award of a construction contract or the denial of a waiver request; such questions of specific application must await future cases.

This does not mean that the claim of overinclusiveness is entitled to no consideration in the present case. The history of governmental tolerance of practices using racial or ethnic criteria for the purpose or with the effect of imposing an invidious discrimination must alert us to the deleterious effects of even benign racial or ethnic classifications when they stray from narrow remedial justifications. Even in the context of a facial challenge such as is presented in this case, the MBE provision cannot pass muster unless, with due account for its administrative program, it provides a reasonable assurance that application of racial or ethnic criteria will be limited to accomplishing the remedial objectives of Congress and that misapplications of the program will be promptly and adequately remedied administratively.

It is significant that the administrative scheme provides for waiver and exemption. Two fundamental congressional assumptions underlie the MBE program: (1) that the present effects of past discrimination have impaired the competitive position of businesses owned and controlled by members of minority groups; and (2) that affirmative efforts to eliminate barriers to minority-firm access, and to evaluate bids with adjustment for the present effects of past discrimination, would assure that at least 10% of the federal funds granted under the Public Works Employment Act of 1977 would be accounted for by contracts with available, qualified, bona fide minority business enterprises. Each of these assumptions may be rebutted in the administrative process.

The administrative program contains measures to effectuate the congressional objective of assuring legitimate participation by disadvantaged MBE's. Administrative definition has tightened some less definite aspects of the statutory identification of the minority groups encompassed by the program.[73] There is

---

[73] The MBE provision, 42 U.S.C. § 6705(f)(2) (1976 ed. Supp. II), classifies as a minority business enterprise any "business at least 50 per centum of which is owned by minority group members or, in the case of a publicly owned business, at least 51 per centum of the stock of which is owned by minority group members." Minority group members are defined as "citizens of the United States who are Negroes, Spanish-speaking, Orientals, Indians, Eskimos and Aleuts." The administrative definitions are set out in the Appendix to this opinion, ¶ 3. These categories also are classified as minorities

administrative scrutiny to identify and eliminate from participation in the program MBE's who are not "bona-fide" within the regulations and guidelines; for example, spurious minority-front entities can be exposed. A significant aspect of this surveillance is the complaint procedure available for reporting "unjust participation by an enterprise or individuals in the MBE program." And even as to specific contract awards, waiver is available to avoid dealing with an MBE who is attempting to exploit the remedial aspects of the program by charging an unreasonable price, i.e., a price not attributable to the present effects of past discrimination. We must assume that Congress intended close scrutiny of false claims and prompt action on them.

Grantees are given the opportunity to demonstrate that their best efforts will not succeed or have not succeeded in achieving the statutory 10% target for minority firm participation within the limitations of the program's remedial objectives. In these circumstances a waiver or partial waiver is available once compliance has been demonstrated. A waiver may be sought and granted at any time during the contracting process, or even prior to letting contracts if the facts warrant.

Nor is the program defective because a waiver may be sought only by the grantee and not by prime contractors who may experience difficulty in fulfilling contract obligations to assure minority participation. It may be administratively cumbersome, but the wisdom of concentrating responsibility at the grantee level is not for us to evaluate; the purpose is to allow the Economic Development Administration to maintain close supervision of the operation of the MBE provision. The administrative complaint mechanism allows for grievances of prime contractors who assert that a grantee has failed to seek a waiver in an appropriate case. Finally, we note that where private parties, as opposed to governmental entities, transgress the limitations inherent in the MBE program, the possibility of constitutional violation is more removed. See United Steelworkers of America v. Weber, 443 U.S. 193, 200 (1979).

That the use of racial and ethnic criteria is premised on assumptions rebuttable in the administrative process gives reasonable assurance that application of the MBE program will be limited to accomplishing the remedial objectives contemplated by Congress and that misapplications of the racial and ethnic criteria can be remedied. In dealing with this facial challenge to the statute, doubts must be resolved in support of the congressional judgment that this limited program is a necessary step to effectuate the constitutional mandate for equality of economic opportunity. The MBE provision may be viewed as a pilot project, appropriately limited in extent and duration, and subject to reassessment and reevaluation by the Congress prior to any extension or re-enactment. Miscarriages of administration could have only a transitory economic impact on businesses not encompassed by the program, and would not be irremediable.

IV.

Congress, after due consideration, perceived a pressing need to move forward with new approaches in the continuing effort to achieve the goal of

in the regulations implementing the nondiscrimination requirements of the Railroad Revitalization and Regulatory Reform Act of 1976, 45 U.S.C. § 803, see 42 Fed.Reg. 4285, 4288 (1977), on which Congress relied as precedents for the MBE provision. See 123 Cong.Rec. S3910 (Mar. 10, 1977) (remarks of Sen. Brooke). The House Subcommittee on SBA Oversight and Minority Enterprise, whose activities played a significant part in the legislative history of the MBE provision, also recognized that these categories were included within the Federal Government's definition of "minority business enterprise." H.R.Rep. No. 94–468, pp. 20–21 (1975). The specific inclusion of these groups in the MBE provision demonstrates that Congress concluded they were victims of discrimination. Petitioners did not press any challenge to Congress' classification categories in the Court of Appeals; there is no reason for this Court to pass upon the issue at this time.

equality of economic opportunity. In this effort, Congress has necessary latitude to try new techniques such as the limited use of racial and ethnic criteria to accomplish remedial objectives; this is especially so in programs where voluntary cooperation with remedial measures is induced by placing conditions on federal expenditures. That the program may press the outer limits of congressional authority affords no basis for striking it down.

Petitioners have mounted a facial challenge to a program developed by the politically responsive branches of Government. For its part, the Congress must proceed only with programs narrowly tailored to achieve its objectives, subject to continuing evaluation and reassessment; administration of the programs must be vigilant and flexible; and, when such a program comes under judicial review, courts must be satisfied that the legislative objectives and projected administration give reasonable assurance that the program will function within constitutional limitations. . . .

Any preference based on racial or ethnic criteria must necessarily receive a most searching examination to make sure that it does not conflict with constitutional guarantees. This case is one which requires, and which has received, that kind of examination. This opinion does not adopt, either expressly or implicitly, the formulas of analysis articulated in such cases as University of California Regents v. Bakke, 438 U.S. 265 (1978). However, our analysis demonstrates that the MBE provision would survive judicial review under either "test" articulated in the several *Bakke* opinions. The MBE provision of the Public Works Employment Act of 1977 does not violate the Constitution.

Affirmed.

APPENDIX

1. The EDA guidelines, at 2–7, provide in relevant part:

"The primary obligation for carrying out the 10% MBE participation requirement rests with EDA Grantees. . . . The Grantee and those of its contractors which will make subcontracts or purchase substantial supplies from other firms (hereinafter referred to as 'prime contractors') must seek out all available *bona fide* MBE's and make every effort to use as many of them as possible on the project.

"An MBE is *bona fide* if the minority group ownership interests are real and continuing and not created solely to meet 10% MBE requirements. For example, the minority group owners or stockholders should possess control over management, interest in capital and interest in earnings commensurate with the percentage of ownership on which the claim of minority ownership status is based. . . .

"An MBE is available if the project is located in the market area of the MBE and the MBE can perform project services or supply project materials at the time they are needed. The relevant market area depends on the kind of services or supplies which are needed. . . . EDA will require that Grantees and prime contractors engage MBE's from as wide a market area as is economically feasible.

"An MBE is qualified if it can perform the services or supply the materials that are needed. Grantees and prime contractors will be expected to use MBE's with less experience than available nonminority enterprises and should expect to provide technical assistance to MBE's as needed. Inability to obtain bonding will ordinarily not disqualify an MBE. Grantees and prime contractors are expected to help MBE's obtain bonding, to include MBE's in any overall bond or to waive bonding where feasible. The Small Business Administration (SBA) is prepared to provide a 90% guarantee for the bond of any MBE participating in an LPW [local public works] project.

Lack of working capital will not ordinarily disqualify an MBE. SBA is prepared to provide working capital assistance to any MBE participating in an LPW project. Grantees and prime contractors are expected to assist MBE's in obtaining working capital through SBA or otherwise.

". . . [E]very Grantee should make sure that it knows the names, addresses and qualifications of all relevant MBE's which would include the project location in their market areas. . . . Grantees should also hold prebid conferences to which they invite interested contractors and representatives of . . . MBE support organizations.

"Arrangements have been made through the Office of Minority Business Enterprise . . . to provide assistance to Grantees and prime contractors in fulfilling the 10% MBE requirement. . . .

"Grantees and prime contractors should also be aware of other support which is available from the Small Business Administration. . . .

". . . [T]he Grantee must monitor the performance of its prime contractors to make sure that their commitments to expend funds for MBE's are being fulfilled. . . . Grantees should administer every project tightly. . . ."

2. The EDA guidelines, at 13–15, provide in relevant part:

"Although a provision for waiver is included under this section of the Act, EDA will only approve a waiver under exceptional circumstances. The Grantee must demonstrate that there are not sufficient, relevant, qualified minority business enterprises whose market areas include the project location to justify a waiver. The Grantee must detail in its waiver request the efforts the Grantee and potential contractors have exerted to locate and enlist MBE's. The request must indicate the specific MBE's which were contacted and the reason each MBE was not used. . . .

"Only the Grantee can request a waiver. . . . Such a waiver request would ordinarily be made after the initial bidding or negotiation procedures proved unsuccessful. . . .

"[A] Grantee situated in an area where the minority population is very small may apply for a waiver before requesting bids on its project or projects. . . .".

3. The EDA technical bulletin, at 1, provides the following definitions:

"(a) *Negro.* An individual of the black race of African origin.

"(b) *Spanish-Speaking.* An individual of a Spanish-speaking culture and origin or parentage.

"(c) *Oriental.* An individual of a culture, origin or parentage traceable to the areas south of the Soviet Union, east of Iran, inclusive of islands adjacent thereto, and out to the Pacific including but not limited to Indonesia, Indochina, Malaysia, Hawaii and the Philippines.

"(d) *Indian.* An individual having origins in any of the original people of North America and who is recognized as an Indian by either a tribe, tribal organization or a suitable authority in the community. (A suitable authority in the community may be: educational institutions, religious organizations, or state agencies.)

"(e) *Eskimo.* An individual having origins in any of the original peoples of Alaska."

"(f) *Aleut.* An individual having origins in any of the original peoples of the Aleutian Islands."

4. The EDA technical bulletin, at 19, provides in relevant part:

"Any person or organization with information indicating unjust participation by an enterprise or individuals in the MBE program or who believes that the MBE participation requirement is being improperly applied should contact the appropriate EDA grantee and provide a detailed statement of the basis for the complaint.

"Upon receipt of a complaint, the grantee should attempt to resolve the issues in dispute. In the event the grantee requires assistance in reaching a determination, the grantee should contact the Civil Rights Specialist in the appropriate Regional Office.

"If the complainant believes that the grantee has not satisfactorily resolved the issues raised in his complaint, he may personally contact the EDA Regional Office."

Mr. Justice Powell, concurring.

Although I would place greater emphasis than The Chief Justice on the need to articulate judicial standards of review in conventional terms, I view his opinion announcing the judgment as substantially in accord with my own views. Accordingly, I join that opinion and write separately to apply the analysis set forth by my opinion in University of California v. Bakke, 438 U.S. 265 (1978) (hereinafter *Bakke*).

The question in this case is whether Congress may enact the requirement in § 103(f)(2) of the Public Works Employment Act of 1977 (PWEA), that 10% of federal grants for local public work projects funded by the Act be set aside for minority business enterprises. Section 103(f)(2) employs a racial classification that is constitutionally prohibited unless it is a necessary means of advancing a compelling governmental interest. *Bakke* at 299, 305; see In re Griffiths, 413 U.S. 717, 721–722 (1973); Loving v. Virginia, 388 U.S. 1, 11 (1967); McLaughlin v. Florida, 379 U.S. 184, 196 (1964). For the reasons stated in my *Bakke* opinion, I consider adherence to this standard as important and consistent with precedent.

The Equal Protection Clause, and the equal protection component of the Due Process Clause of the Fifth Amendment, demand that any governmental distinction among groups must be justifiable. Different standards of review applied to different sorts of classifications simply illustrate the principle that some classifications are less likely to be legitimate than others. Racial classifications must be assessed under the most stringent level of review because immutable characteristics, which bear no relation to individual merit or need, are irrelevant to almost every governmental decision. See, e.g., Anderson v. Martin, 375 U.S. 399, 402–404 (1964). In this case, however, I believe that § 103(f)(2) is justified as a remedy that serves the compelling governmental interest in eradicating the continuing effects of past discrimination identified by Congress.

I.

Racial preference never can constitute a compelling state interest. " 'Distinctions between citizens solely because of their ancestry' [are] 'odious to a free people whose institutions are founded upon the doctrine of equality.' " Loving v. Virginia, 388 U.S., at 11, quoting Hirabayashi v. United States, 320 U.S. 81, 100 (1943). Thus, if the set-aside merely expresses a congressional desire to prefer one racial or ethnic group over another, § 103(f)(2) violates the equal protection component in the Due Process Clause of the Fifth Amendment. See Bolling v. Sharpe, 347 U.S. 497, 499 (1954).

The Government does have a legitimate interest in ameliorating the disabling effects of identified discrimination. *Bakke*, 438 U.S., at 307; see, e.g., Keyes v. School District No. 1, 413 U.S. 189, 236 (1973) (Powell, J., concurring in part and dissenting in part); McDaniel v. Barresi, 402 U.S. 39, 41 (1971); Board of Education v. Swann, 402 U.S. 43, 45–46 (1971); Green

v. County School Board, 391 U.S. 430, 437–438 (1968). The existence of illegal discrimination justifies the imposition of a remedy that will "make persons whole for injuries suffered on account of unlawful . . . discrimination." Albemarle Paper Co. v. Moody, 422 U.S. 405, 418 (1975). A critical inquiry, therefore, is whether § 103(f)(2) was enacted as a means of redressing such discrimination. But this Court has never approved race-conscious remedies absent judicial, administrative, or legislative findings of constitutional or statutory violations. *Bakke,* 438 U.S., at 307; see, e.g., Teamsters v. United States, 431 U.S. 324, 367–376 (1977); United Jewish Organizations v. Carey, 430 U.S. 144, 155–159 (1977) (opinion of White, J.); South Carolina v. Katzenbach, 383 U.S. 301, 308–315 (1966).

Because the distinction between permissible remedial action and impermissible racial preference rests on the existence of a constitutional or statutory violation, the legitimate interest in creating a race-conscious remedy is not compelling unless an appropriate governmental authority has found that such a violation has occurred. In other words, two requirements must be met. First, the governmental body that attempts to impose a race-conscious remedy must have the authority to act in response to identified discrimination. Cf. Hampton v. Mow Sun Wong, 426 U.S. 88, 103 (1976). Second, the governmental body must make findings that demonstrate the existence of illegal discrimination. In *Bakke,* the Regents failed both requirements. They were entrusted only with educational functions, and they made no findings of past discrimination. Thus, no compelling governmental interest was present to justify the use of a racial quota in medical school admissions. *Bakke,* 438 U.S., at 309–310.

Our past cases also establish that even if the government proffers a compelling interest to support reliance upon a suspect classification, the means selected must be narrowly drawn to fulfill the governmental purpose. In re Griffiths, 413 U.S., at 721–722. In *Bakke,* for example, the state university did have a compelling interest in the attainment of a diverse student body. But the method selected to achieve that end, the use of a fixed admissions quota, was not appropriate. The Regent's quota system eliminated some nonminority applicants from all consideration for a specified number of seats in the entering class, although it allowed minority applicants to compete for all available seats. 438 U.S., at 275–276. In contrast, an admissions program that recognizes race as a factor, but not the sole factor, in assessing an applicant's qualifications serves the University's interest in diversity while ensuring that each applicant receives fair and competitive consideration.

In reviewing the constitutionality of § 103(f)(2), we must decide: (i) whether Congress is competent to make findings of unlawful discrimination; (ii) if so, whether sufficient findings have been made to establish that unlawful discrimination has affected adversely minority business enterprises, and (iii) whether the 10% set-aside is a permissible means for redressing identifiable past discrimination. None of these questions may be answered without explicit recognition that we are reviewing an Act of Congress.

II.

The history of this Court's review of congressional action demonstrates beyond question that the National Legislature is competent to find constitutional and statutory violations. Unlike the Regents of the University of California, Congress properly may—and indeed must—address directly the problems of discrimination in our society. . . .

.   .   .

In addition, Congress has been given the unique constitutional power of legislating to enforce the provisions of the Thirteenth, Fourteenth, and Fifteenth Amendments. . . .

. . .

It is beyond question, therefore, that Congress has the authority to identify unlawful discriminatory practices, to prohibit those practices, and to prescribe remedies to eradicate their continuing effects. The next inquiry is whether Congress has made findings adequate to support its determination that minority contractors have suffered extensive discrimination.

III.

A.

The petitioners contend that the legislative history of § 103(f)(2) reflects no congressional finding of statutory or constitutional violations. Crucial to that contention is the assertion that a reviewing court may not look beyond the legislative history of the PWEA itself for evidence that Congress believed it was combatting invidious discrimination. But petitioners' theory would erect an artificial barrier to full understanding of the legislative process.

Congress is not an adjudicatory body called upon to resolve specific disputes between competing adversaries. Its constitutional role is to be representative rather than impartial, to make policy rather than to apply settled principles of law. The petitioners' contention that this Court should treat the debates on § 103(f)(2) as the complete "record" of congressional decisionmaking underlying that statute is essentially a plea that we treat Congress as if it were a lower federal court. But Congress is not expected to act as though it were duty bound to find facts and make conclusions of law. The creation of national rules for the governance of our society simply does not entail the same concept of recordmaking that is appropriate to a judicial or administrative proceeding. Congress has no responsibility to confine its vision to the facts and evidence adduced by particular parties. Instead, its special attribute as a legislative body lies in its broader mission to investigate and consider all facts and opinions that may be relevant to the resolution of an issue. One appropriate source is the information and expertise that Congress acquires in the consideration and enactment of earlier legislation. After Congress has legislated repeatedly in an area of national concern, its members gain experience that may reduce the need for fresh hearings or prolonged debate when Congress again considers action in that area.

Acceptance of petitioners' argument would force Congress to make specific factual findings with respect to each legislative action. Such a requirement would mark an unprecedented imposition of adjudicatory procedures upon a coordinate branch of Government. Neither the Constitution nor our democratic tradition warrants such a constraint on the legislative process. I therefore conclude that we are not confined in this case to an examination of the legislative history of § 103(f)(2) alone. Rather, we properly may examine the total contemporary record of congressional action dealing with the problems of racial discrimination against minority business enterprises.

B.

In my view, the legislative history of § 103(f)(2) demonstrates that Congress reasonably concluded that private and governmental discrimination had contributed to the negligible percentage of public contracts awarded minority contractors.[4] . . .

---

[4] I cannot accept the suggestion of the Court of Appeals that § 103(f)(2) must be viewed as serving a compelling state interest if the reviewing court can "perceive a basis" for legislative action. 588 F.2d 600, 604–605 (CA2 1978), quoting Katzenbach v. Morgan, 384 U.S., at 656. The "perceive a basis" standard refers to congressional authority to act, not to the distinct question whether that action violates the Due Process Clause of the Fifth Amendment.

In light of these legislative materials and the discussion of legislative history contained in The Chief Justice's opinion, I believe that a court must accept as established the conclusion that purposeful discrimination contributed significantly to the small percentage of federal contracting funds that minority business enterprises have received. Refusals to subcontract work to minority contractors may, depending upon the identity of the discriminating party, violate Title VI of the Civil Rights Act of 1964, 42 U.S.C. § 2000d, or 42 U.S.C. § 1981, or the Fourteenth Amendment. Although the discriminatory activities were not identified with the exactitude expected in judicial or administrative adjudication, it must be remembered that "Congress may paint with a much broader brush than may this Court. . . ." Oregon v. Mitchell, 400 U.S. 112, 284 (1970) (Stewart, J., concurring in part and dissenting in part).

IV.

Under this Court's established doctrine, a racial classification is suspect and subject to strict judicial scrutiny. As noted in Part I, the Government may employ such a classification only when necessary to accomplish a compelling governmental purpose. See *Bakke*, 438 U.S., at 305. The conclusion that Congress found a compelling governmental interest in redressing identified discrimination against minority contractors therefore leads to the inquiry whether use of a 10% set-aside is a constitutionally appropriate means of serving that interest. In the past, this "means" test has been virtually impossible to satisfy. Only two of this Court's modern cases have held the use of racial classifications to be constitutional. See Korematsu v. United States, 323 U.S. 214 (1944); Hirabayshi v. United States, 320 U.S. 81 (1943). Indeed, the failure of legislative action to survive strict scrutiny has lead some to wonder whether our review of racial classifications has been strict in theory, but fatal in fact. See Gunther, The Supreme Court, 1971 Term—Foreword: In Search of Evolving Doctrine on a Changing Court: A Model for a Newer Equal Protection, 86 Harv.L.Rev. 1, 8 (1972).

A.

Application of the "means" test necessarily demands an understanding of the type of congressional action at issue. This is not a case in which Congress has employed a racial classification solely as a means to confer a racial preference. Such a purpose plainly would be unconstitutional. Supra, at 2. Nor has Congress sought to employ a racially conscious means to further a nonracial goal. In such instances, a nonracial means should be available to further the legitimate governmental purpose. See *Bakke*, 438 U.S., at 310–311.

Enactment of the set-aside is designed to serve the compelling governmental interest in redressing racial discrimination. As this Court has recognized, the implementation of any affirmative remedy for redress of racial discrimination is likely to affect persons differently depending upon their race. See, e.g., Board of Education v. Swann, 402 U.S., at 45–46. Although federal courts may not order or approve remedies that exceed the scope of a constitutional violation, see Milliken v. Bradley, 433 U.S. 267, 280–281 (1977); Dayton v. Brinkman, 433 U.S. 406 (1977); Austin Independent School District v. United States, 429 U.S. 991 (1976) (Powell, J., concurring), this Court has not required remedial plans to be limited to the least restrictive means of implementation. We have recognized that the choice of remedies to redress racial discrimination is "a

---

In my view, a court should uphold a reasonable congressional finding of discrimination. A more stringent standard of review would impinge upon Congress' ability to address problems of discrimination; a standard requiring a court to "perceive a basis" is essentially meaningless in this context. Such a test might allow a court to justify legislative action even in the absence of affirmative evidence of congressional findings.

balancing process left, within appropriate constitutional or statutory limits, to the sound discretion of the trial court." Frank v. Bowman Transportation Co., 424 U.S., at 794 (1976) (Powell, J., concurring in part and dissenting in part).

I believe that the enforcement clauses of the Thirteenth and Fourteenth Amendments give Congress a similar measure of discretion to choose a suitable remedy for the redress of racial discrimination. . . .

. . .

I conclude, therefore, that the enforcement clauses of the Thirteenth and Fourteenth Amendments confer upon Congress the authority to select reasonable remedies to advance the compelling state interest in repairing the effects of discrimination. But that authority must be exercised in a manner that does not erode the guarantees of these Amendments. The Judicial Branch has the special responsibility to make a searching inquiry into the justification for employing a race-conscious remedy. Courts must be sensitive to the possibility that less intrusive means might serve the compelling state interest equally as well. I believe that Congress' choice of a remedy should be upheld, however, if the means selected are equitable and reasonably necessary to the redress of identified discrimination. Such a test allows the Congress to exercise necessary discretion but preserves the essential safeguard of judicial review of racial classifications.

B.

. . .

By the time Congress enacted § 103(f)(2) in 1977, it knew that other remedies had failed to ameliorate the effects of racial discrimination in the construction industry. . . .

The § 103(f)(2) set-aside is not a permanent part of federal contracting requirements. As soon as the PWEA program concludes, this set-aside program ends. The temporary nature of this remedy ensures that a race-conscious program will not last longer than the discriminatory effects it is designed to eliminate. It will be necessary for Congress to re-examine the need for a race-conscious remedy before it extends or re-enacts § 103(f)(2).

The percentage chosen for the set-aside is within the scope of congressional discretion. The Courts of Appeals have approved temporary hiring remedies insuring that the percentage of minority group workers in a business or governmental agency will be reasonably related to the percentage of minority group members in the relevant population. Boston Chapter NAACP v. Beecher, 504 F.2d, at 1027, Bridgeport Guard Inc. v. Bridgeport, 482 F.2d, at 1341; Carter v. Gallagher, 452 F.2d, at 331. Only 4% of contractors are members of minority groups, see Fullilove v. Kreps, 584 F.2d 600, 608 (CA2 1978), although minority group members constitute about 17% of the national population, see Contractors Association of Western Pennsylvania v. Kreps, 441 F.Supp. 936, 951 (WD Pa.1977), aff'd, 573 F.2d 811 (CA3 1978). The choice of a 10% set-aside thus falls roughly halfway between the present percentage of minority contractors and the percentage of minority group members in the Nation.

Although the set-aside is pegged at a reasonable figure, its effect might be unfair if it were applied rigidly in areas of the country where minority group members constitute a small percentage of the population. To meet this concern, Congress enacted a waiver provision into § 103(f)(2). The factors governing issuance of a waiver include the availability of qualified minority contractors in a particular geographic area, the size of the locale's minority population, and the efforts made to find minority contractors. Department of Commerce, Guidelines for 10% Minority Business Participation LPW Grants, App. 165a–167a. We have been told that 1261 waivers had been granted by September 9, 1979.

C.

A race-conscious remedy should not be approved without consideration of an additional crucial factor—the effect of the set-aside upon innocent third parties. See Teamsters v. United States, 431 U.S., at 374–375. In this case, the petitioners contend with some force that they have been asked to bear the burden of the set-aside even though they are innocent of wrongdoing. I do not believe, however, that their burden is so great that the set-aside must be disapproved. As noted above, Congress knew that minority contractors were receiving only 1% of federal contracts at the time the set-aside was enacted. The PWEA appropriated $4 billion for public work projects, of which it could be expected that approximately $400 million would go to minority contractors. The Court of Appeals calculated that the set-aside would reserve about .25% of all the funds expended yearly on construction work in the United States for approximately 4% of the Nation's contractors who are members of a minority group. 584 F.2d, at 607–608. The set-aside would have no effect on the ability of the remaining 96% of contractors to compete for 99.75% of construction funds. In my view the effect of the set-aside is limited and so widely dispersed that its use is consistent with fundamental fairness.

Consideration of these factors persuades me that the set-aside is a reasonably necessary means of furthering the compelling governmental interest in redressing the discrimination that affects minority contractors. Any marginal unfairness to innocent nonminority contractors is not sufficiently significant—or sufficiently identifiable—to outweigh the governmental interest served by § 103(f)(2). When Congress acts to remedy identified discrimination, it may exercise discretion in choosing a remedy that is reasonably necessary to accomplish its purpose. Whatever the exact breadth of that discretion, I believe that it encompasses the selection of the set-aside in this case.

V.

In the history of this Court and this country, few questions have been more divisive than those arising from governmental action taken on the basis of race. Indeed, our own decisions played no small part in the tragic legacy of government-sanctioned discrimination. See Plessy v. Ferguson, 163 U.S. 537 (1896); Dred Scott v. Sanford, 19 How. 393 (60 U.S.) (1857). At least since the decision in Brown v. Board of Education, 347 U.S. 483 (1954), the Court has been resolute in its dedication to the principle that the Constitution envisions a Nation where race is irrelevant. The time cannot come too soon when no governmental decision will be based upon immutable characteristics of pigmentation or origin. But in our quest to achieve a society free from racial classification, we cannot ignore the claims of those who still suffer from the effects of identifiable discrimination.

Distinguishing the rights of all citizens to be free from racial classifications from the rights of some citizens to be made whole is a perplexing, but necessary, judicial task. When we first confronted such an issue in *Bakke,* I concluded that the Regents of the University of California were not competent to make, and had not made, findings sufficient to uphold the use of the race-conscious remedy they adopted. As my opinion made clear, I believe that the use of racial classifications, which are fundamentally at odds with the ideals of a democratic society implicit in the Due Process and Equal Protection Clauses, cannot be imposed simply to serve transient social or political goals, however worthy they may be. But the issue here turns on the scope of congressional power, and Congress has been given a unique constitutional role in the enforcement of the post-Civil War Amendments. In this case, where Congress determined that minority contractors were victims of purposeful discrimination and where Congress chose a reasonably necessary means to effectuate its purpose, I find no constitutional reason to invalidate § 103(f)(2).

Mr. Justice Marshall, with whom Mr. Justice Brennan and Mr. Justice Blackmun join, concurring in the judgment.

My resolution of the constitutional issue in this case is governed by the separate opinion I coauthored in University of California Regents v. Bakke, 438 U.S. 265, 324–379 (1978). In my view, the 10% minority set-aside provision of the Public Works Employment Act of 1977 passes constitutional muster under the standard announced in that opinion.

I.

In *Bakke,* I joined my Brothers Brennan, White and Blackmun in articulating the view that "racial classifications are not per se invalid under [the Equal Protection Clause of] the Fourteenth Amendment." . . .

. . .

We concluded . . . that because a racial classification ostensibly designed for remedial purposes is susceptible to misuse, it may be justified only by showing "an important and articulated purpose for its use." Id., at 361. "In addition, any statute must be stricken that stigmatizes any group or that singles out those least well represented in the political process to bear the brunt of a benign program." In our view, then, the proper inquiry is whether racial classifications designed to further remedial purposes serve important governmental objectives and are substantially related to achievement of those objectives.

II.

Judged under this standard, the 10% minority set-aside provision at issue in this case is plainly constitutional. Indeed, the question is not even a close one.

. . .

In sum, it is clear to me that the racial classifications employed in the set-aside provision are substantially related to the achievement of the important and congressionally articulated goal of remedying the present effects of past racial discrimination. The provision, therefore, passes muster under the equal protection standard I adopted in *Bakke.*

III.

. . .

. . . Today, by upholding this race-conscious remedy, the Court accords Congress the authority necessary to undertake the task of moving our society toward a state of meaningful equality of opportunity, not an abstract version of equality in which the effects of past discrimination would be forever frozen into our social fabric. I applaud this result. Accordingly, I concur in the judgment of the Court.

Mr. Justice Stewart, with whom Mr. Justice Rehnquist joins, dissenting.

"Our Constitution is color-blind, and neither knows nor tolerates classes among citizens. . . . The law regards man as man, and takes no account of his surroundings or of his color. . . . " Those words were written by a Member of this Court 84 years ago. Plessy v. Ferguson, 163 U.S. 537, 559 (Harlan, J., dissenting). His colleagues disagreed with him, and held that a statute that required the separation of people on the basis of their race was constitutionally valid because it was a "reasonable" exercise of legislative power and had been "enacted in good faith for the promotion [of] the public good. . . ." Id., at 550.   Today, the Court upholds a statute that accords a preference to citizens who are "Negroes, Spanish-speaking, Orientals, Indians, Eskimos, and Aleuts," for much the same reasons.   I think today's decision is wrong for the same reason that Plessy v. Ferguson was wrong, and I respectfully dissent.

A.

The equal protection standard of the Constitution has one clear and central meaning—it absolutely prohibits invidious discrimination by government. . . . .

. . .

C.

The Fourteenth Amendment was adopted to ensure that every person must be treated equally by each State regardless of the color of his skin.   The Amendment promised to carry to its necessary conclusion a fundamental principle upon which this Nation had been founded—that the law would honor no preference based on lineage.   Tragically, the promise of 1868 was not immediately fulfilled, and decades passed before the States and the Federal Government were finally directed to eliminate detrimental classifications based on race. Today, the Court derails this achievement and places its imprimatur on the creation once again by government of privileges based on birth.

The Court, moreover, takes this drastic step without, in my opinion, seriously considering the ramifications of its decision.   Laws that operate on the basis of race require definitions of race.   Because of the Court's decision today, our statute books will once again have to contain laws that reflect the odious practice of delineating the qualities that make one person a Negro and make another white.   Moreover, racial discrimination, even "good faith" racial discrimination, is inevitably a two-edged sword.   "[P]referential programs may only reinforce common stereotypes holding that certain groups are unable to achieve success without special protection based on a factor having no relationship to individual worth."   University of California Regents v. Bakke, supra, 438 U.S., at 298 (opinion of Powell, J.).   Most importantly, by making race a relevant criterion once again in its own affairs, the Government implicitly teaches the public that the apportionment of rewards and penalties can legitimately be made according to race—rather than according to merit or ability— and that people can, and perhaps should, view themselves and others in terms of their racial characteristics.   Notions of "racial entitlement" will be fostered, and private discrimination will necessarily be encouraged.   See Hughes v. Superior Court, 339 U.S. 460, 463–464; T. Eastland & W. Bennett, Counting by Race 139–170 (1979); Van Alstyne, Rites of Passage: Race, the Supreme Court, and the Constitution, 46 U.Chi.L.Rev. 775 (1979).

There are those who think that we need a new Constitution, and their views may someday prevail.   But under the Constitution we have, one practice in which government may never engage is the practice of racism—not even "temporarily" and not even as an "experiment."

For these reasons, I would reverse the judgment of the Court of Appeals.

Mr. Justice Stevens dissenting.

The 10% set-aside contained in the Public Works Employment Act of 1977, 91 Stat. 116 ("the Act") creates monopoly privileges in a $400,000,000 market for a class of investors defined solely by racial characteristics.   The direct beneficiaries of these monopoly privileges are the relatively small number of persons within the racial classification who represent the entrepreneurial sub-class—those who have, or can borrow, working capital.

History teaches us that the costs associated with a sovereign's grant of exclusive privileges often encompass more than the high prices and shoddy workmanship that are familiar hand maidens of monopoly; they engender animosity and discontent as well. The economic consequences of using noble birth as a basis for classification in 18th century France, though disastrous, were nothing as compared with the terror that was engendered in the name of "egalite" and "fraternite." Grants of privileges on the basis of characteristics acquired at birth are far from an unmixed blessing.

Our historic aversion to titles of nobility is only one aspect of our commit-ment to the proposition that the sovereign has a fundamental duty to govern impartially. When government accords different treatment to different persons, there must be a reason for the difference. Because racial characteristics so seldom provide a relevant basis for disparate treatment, and because classifica-tions based on race are potentially so harmful to the entire body politic,[5] it is especially important that the reasons for any such classification be clearly identified and unquestionably legitimate.

The statutory definition of the preferred class includes "citizens of the United States who are Negroes, Spanish-speaking, Orientals, Indians, Eskimos, and Aleuts." All aliens and all nonmembers of the racial class are excluded. No economic, social, geographical or historical criteria are relevant for exclu-sion or inclusion. There is not one word in the remainder of the Act or in the legislative history that explains why any Congressman or Senator favored this particular definition over any other or that identifies the common characteristics that every member of the preferred class was believed to share. Nor does the Act or its history explain why 10% of the total appropriation was the proper amount to set aside for investors in each of the six racial subclasses.

Four different, though somewhat interrelated, justifications for the racial classification in this Act have been advanced: first, that the 10% set aside is a form of reparation for past injuries to the entire membership of the class; second, that it is an appropriate remedy for past discrimination against minority business enterprises that have been denied access to public contracts; third, that the members of the favored class have a special entitlement to "a piece of the action" when government is distributing benefits; and, fourth, that the program is an appropriate method of fostering greater minority participation in a

---

[5] Indeed the very attempt to define with precision a beneficiary's qualifying racial characteristics is repugnant to our constitutional ideals. The so-called guidelines developed by the Economic Develop-ment Administration, . . . are so general as to be fairly innocuous; as a consequence they are too vague to be useful. . . . If the National Government is to make a serious effort to define racial classes by criteria that can be administered objectively, it must study precedents such as the First Regulation to the Reichs Citizenship Law of November 14, 1935, translated in 4 Nazi Conspiracy and Aggression 1417–PS, pp. 8–9 (1946):

"On the basis of Article 3, Reichs Citizenship Law, of 15 Sept. 1935 (RGB1. I, page 146) the following is ordered:

. . .

"**Article 5**

"1. A Jew is anyone who descended from at least three grandparents who were racially full Jews. Article 2, par. 2, second sentence will apply.

"2. A Jew is also one who descended from two full Jewish parents, if: (a) he belonged to the Jewish religious community at the time this law was issued, or who joined the community later; (b) he was married to a Jewish person, at the time the law was issued, or married one subsequently; (c) he is the offspring from a marriage with a Jew, in the sense of Section 1, which was contracted after the Law for the protection of German blood and German honor became effective (RGB1. I, page 1146 of 15 Sept. 1935); (d) he is the offspring of an extramarital relationship, with a Jew, according to Section 1, and will be born out of wedlock after July 31, 1936."

competitive economy. Each of these asserted justifications merits separate scrutiny.

I.

Racial characteristics may serve to define a group of persons who have suffered a special wrong and who, therefore, are entitled to special reparations. . . .

. . . Racial classifications are simply too pernicious to permit any but the most exact connection between justification and classification. Quite obviously, the history of discrimination against black citizens in America cannot justify a grant of privileges to Eskimos or Indians.

Even if we assume that each of the six racial subclasses has suffered its own special injury at some time in our history, surely it does not necessarily follow that each of those subclasses suffered harm of identical magnitude. . . .

At best, the statutory preference is a somewhat perverse form of reparation for the members of the injured classes. For those who are the most disadvantaged within each class are the least likely to receive any benefit from the special privilege even though they are the persons most likely still to be suffering the consequences of the past wrong. A random distribution to a favored few is a poor form of compensation for an injury shared by many.

My principal objection to the reparation justification for this legislation, however, cuts more deeply than my concern about its inequitable character. We can never either erase or ignore the history that Mr. Justice Marshall has recounted. But if that history can justify such a random distribution of benefits on racial lines as that embodied in this statutory scheme, it will serve not merely as a basis for remedial legislation, but rather as a permanent source of justification for grants of special privileges. For if there is no duty to attempt either to measure the recovery by the wrong or to distribute that recovery within the injured class in an evenhanded way, our history will adequately support a legislative preference for almost any ethnic, religious, or racial group with the political strength to negotiate "a piece of the action" for its members.

Although I do not dispute the validity of the assumption that each of the subclasses identified in the Act has suffered a severe wrong at some time in the past, I cannot accept this slapdash statute as a legitimate method of providing classwide relief.

II.

The Act may also be viewed as a much narrower remedial measure—one designed to grant relief to the specific minority business enterprises that have been denied access to public contracts by discriminatory practices.

The legislative history of the Act does not tell us when, or how often, any minority business enterprise was denied such access. . . .

. . .

III.

The legislative history of the Act discloses that there is a group of legislators in Congress identified as the "Black Caucus" and that members of that group argued that if the Federal Government was going to provide $4,000,000,000 of new public contract business, their constituents were entitled to "a piece of the action."

. . .

In the short run our political processes might benefit from legislation that enhanced the ability of representatives of minority groups to disseminate patronage to their political backers. But in the long run any rule that authorized the award of public business on a racial basis would be just as objectionable as one that awarded such business on a purely partisan basis.

The legislators' interest in providing their constituents with favored access to benefits distributed by the Federal Government is, in my opinion, a plainly impermissible justification for this racial classification.

IV.

The interest in facilitating and encouraging the participation by minority business enterprises in the economy is unquestionably legitimate. Any barrier to such entry and growth—whether grounded in the law or in irrational prejudice—should be vigorously and thoroughly removed. Equality of economic and investment opportunity is a goal of no less importance than equality of employment opportunity. This statute, however, is not designed to remove any barriers to entry. Nor does its sparse legislative history detail any insuperable or even significant obstacles to entry into the competitive market.

. . .

The ultimate goal must be to eliminate entirely from governmental decisionmaking such irrelevant factors as a human being's race. The removal of barriers to access to political and economic processes serves that goal. But the creation of new barriers can only frustrate true progress. For as Mr. Justice Powell and Mr. Justice Douglas have perceptively observed, such protective barriers reinforce habitual ways of thinking in terms of classes instead of individuals. Preferences based on characteristics acquired at birth foster intolerance and antagonism against the entire membership of the favored classes. For this reason, I am firmly convinced that this "temporary measure" will disserve the goal of equal opportunity.

V.

A judge's opinion that a statute reflects a profoundly unwise policy determination is an insufficient reason for concluding that it is unconstitutional. . . .

Unlike Mr. Justice Stewart and Mr. Justice Rehnquist, however, I am not convinced that the Clause contains an absolute prohibition against any statutory classification based on race. I am nonetheless persuaded that it does impose a special obligation to scrutinize any governmental decisionmaking process that draws nationwide distinctions between citizens on the basis of their race and incidentally also discriminates against noncitizens in the preferred racial classes. For just as procedural safeguards are necessary to guarantee impartial decisionmaking in the judicial process, so can they play a vital part in preserving the impartial character of the legislative process.

In both its substantive and procedural aspects this Act is markedly different from the normal product of the legislative decisionmaking process. The very fact that Congress for the first time in the Nation's history has created a broad legislative classification for entitlement to benefits based solely on racial characteristics identifies a dramatic difference between this Act and the thousands of statutes that preceded it. This dramatic point of departure is not even mentioned in the statement of purpose of the Act or in the reports of either the House or the Senate Committee that processed the legislation and was not the subject of any testimony or inquiry in any legislative hearing on the bill that was enacted. It is true that there was a brief discussion on the floor of the House as well as in the Senate on two different days, but only a handful of legislators spoke and there was virtually no debate. This kind of perfunctory consideration of an unprecedented policy decision of profound constitutional importance to the Nation is comparable to the accidental malfunction of the legislative process that led to what I regarded as a totally unjustified discrimination in *Delaware Tribal Business Committee v. Weeks, supra*, 430 U.S., at 97.

Although it is traditional for judges to accord the same presumption of regularity to the legislative process no matter how obvious it may be that a busy Congress has acted precipitately, I see no reason why the character of their procedures may not be considered relevant to the decision whether the legislative product has caused a deprivation of liberty or property without due process of law. Whenever Congress creates a classification that would be subject to strict scrutiny under the Equal Protection Clause of the Fourteenth Amendment if it had been fashioned by a state legislature, it seems to me that judicial review should include a consideration of the procedural character of the decisionmaking process. . . .

In all events, rather than take the substantive position expressed in Mr. Justice Stewart's dissenting opinion, I would hold this statute unconstitutional on a narrower ground. It cannot fairly be characterized as a "narrowly tailored" racial classification because it simply raises too many serious questions that Congress failed to answer or even to address in a responsible way.[30] The risk that habitual attitudes toward classes of persons, rather than analysis of the relevant characteristics of the class, will serve as a basis for a legislative classification is present when benefits are distributed as well as when burdens are imposed. In the past, traditional attitudes too often provided the only explanation for discrimination against women, aliens, illegitimates, and black citizens. Today there is a danger that awareness of past injustice will lead to automatic acceptance of new classifications that are not in fact justified by attributes characteristic of the class as a whole.

When Congress creates a special preference, or a special disability, for a class of persons, it should identify the characteristic that justifies the special treatment. When the classification is defined in racial terms, I believe that such particular identification is imperative.

In this case, only two conceivable bases for differentiating the preferred classes from society as a whole have occurred to me: (1) that they were the victims of unfair treatment in the past and (2) that they are less able to compete in the future. Although the first of these factors would justify an appropriate remedy for past wrongs, for reasons that I have already stated, this statute is not such a remedial measure. The second factor is simply not true. Nothing in the record of this case, the legislative history of the Act, or experience that we may notice judicially provides any support for such a proposition. It is up to Congress to demonstrate that its unique statutory preference is justified by a relevant characteristic that is shared by the members of the preferred class. In my opinion, because it has failed to make that demonstration, it has also failed to discharge its duty to govern impartially embodied in the Fifth Amendment to the United States Constitution.

I respectfully dissent.[a]

---

[30] For example why were these six racial classifications, and no others, included in the preferred class? Why are aliens excluded from the preference although they are not otherwise ineligible for public contracts? What percentage of Oriental blood or what degree of Spanish-speaking skill is required for membership in the preferred class? How does the legacy of slavery and the history of discrimination against the descendants of its victims support a preference for Spanish-speaking citizens who may be directly competing with black citizens in some overpopulated communities? Why is a preference given only to owners of business enterprises and why is that preference unaccompanied by any requirement concerning the employment of disadvantaged persons? Is the preference limited to a subclass of persons who can prove that they are subject to a special disability caused by past discrimination, as the Court's opinion indicates? Or is every member of the racial class entitled to a preference as the statutory language seems plainly to indicate? Are businesses formed just to take advantage of the preference eligible?

[a] See Note, "Who is a Negro?" Revisited: Determining Individual Racial Status For Purposes of Affirmative Action, 35 U.Fla.L. 683 (1983).

SECTION 4.   PROTECTION OF PERSONAL LIBERTIES

A.   EQUAL PROTECTION AND RIGHTS SECURED BY OTHER CONSTITUTIONAL PROVISIONS

ZABLOCKI v. REDHAIL

434 U.S. 374, 98 S.Ct. 673, 54 L.Ed.2d 618 (1978).

Mr. Justice Marshall delivered the opinion of the Court.

At issue in this case is the constitutionality of a Wisconsin statute, Wis.Stat. §§ 245.10(1), (4), (5) (1973), which provides that members of a c rtain class of Wisconsin residents may not marry, within the State or elsewhere, without first obtaining a court order granting permission to marry. The class is defined by the statute to include any "Wisconsin resident having minor issue not in his custody and which he is under an obligation to support by any court order or judgment." The statute specifies that court permission cannot be granted unless the marriage applicant submits proof of compliance with the support obligation and, in addition, demonstrates that the children covered by the support order "are not then and are not likely thereafter to become public charges." No marriage license may lawfully be issued in Wisconsin to a person covered by the statute, except upon court order; any marriage entered into without compliance with § 245.10 is declared void; and persons acquiring marriage licenses in violation of the section are subject to criminal penalties.

After being denied a marriage license because of his failure to comply with § 245.10, appellee brought this class action under 42 U.S.C. § 1983, challenging the statute as violative of the Equal Protection and Due Process Clauses of the Fourteenth Amendment and seeking declaratory and injunctive relief. The United States District Court for the Eastern District of Wisconsin held the statute unconstitutional under the Equal Protection Clause and enjoined its enforcement. 418 F.Supp. 1061 (1976). We . . . affirm.

I.

Appellee Redhail is a Wisconsin resident who, under the terms of § 245.10, is unable to enter into a lawful marriage in Wisconsin or elsewhere so long as he maintains his Wisconsin residency. The facts, according to the stipulation filed by the parties in the District Court, are as follows. In January 1972, when appellee was a minor and a high school student, a paternity action was instituted against him in Milwaukee County Court, alleging that he was the father of a baby girl born out of wedlock on July 5, 1971. After he appeared and admitted that he was the child's father, the court entered an order on May 12, 1972, adjudging appellee the father and ordering him to pay $109 per month as support for the child until she reached 18 years of age. From May 1972 until August 1974, appellee was unemployed and indigent, and consequently was unable to make any support payments.

On September 27, 1974, appellee filed an application for a marriage license with appellant Zablocki, the County Clerk of Milwaukee County, and a few days later the application was denied on the sole ground that appellee had not obtained a court order granting him permission to marry, as required by § 245.10. Although appellee did not petition a state court thereafter, it is stipulated that he would not have been able to satisfy either of the statutory prerequisites for an order granting permission to marry. First, he had not satisfied his support obligations to his illegitimate child, and as of December 1974 there was an arrearage in excess of $3,700. Second, the child had been a public charge since her birth, receiving benefits under the Aid to Families with Dependent Children program. It is stipulated that the child's benefit payments were such that she would have been a public charge even if appellee had been current in his support payments.

On December 24, 1974, appellee filed his complaint in the District Court, on behalf of himself and the class of all Wisconsin residents who had been refused a marriage license pursuant to § 245.10(1) by one of the county clerks in Wisconsin. Zablocki was named as the defendant, individually and as representative of a class consisting of all county clerks in the State. The complaint alleged, among other things, that appellee and the woman he desired to marry were expecting a child in March 1975 and wished to be lawfully married before that time. The statute was attacked on the grounds that it deprived appellee, and the class he sought to represent of equal protection and due process rights secured by the First, Fifth, Ninth, and Fourteenth Amendments to the United States Constitution.

A three-judge court was convened . . ..

. . .

On the merits, the three-judge panel analyzed the challenged statute under the Equal Protection Clause and concluded that "strict scrutiny" was required because the classification created by the statute infringed upon a fundamental right, the right to marry. The court then proceeded to evaluate the interests advanced by the State to justify the statute, and, finding that the classification was not necessary for the achievement of those interests, the court held the statute invalid and enjoined the county clerks from enforcing it.

. . . We agree with the District Court that the statute violates the Equal Protection Clause.

II.

In evaluating §§ 245.10(1),(4),(5) under the Equal Protection Clause, "we must first determine what burden of justification the classification created thereby must meet, by looking to the nature of the classification and the individual interests affected." Memorial Hospital v. Maricopa County, 415 U.S. 250, 253 (1974). Since our past decisions make clear that the right to marry is of fundamental importance, and since the classification at issue here significantly interferes with the exercise of that right, we believe that "critical examination" of the state interests advanced in support of the classification is required. . . .

The leading decision of this Court on the right to marry is Loving v. Virginia, 388 U.S. 1 (1967). In that case, an interracial couple who had been convicted of violating Virginia's miscegenation laws challenged the statutory scheme on both equal protection and due process grounds. The Court's opinion could have rested solely on the ground that the statutes discriminated on the basis of race in violation of the Equal Protection Clause. But the Court went on to hold that the laws arbitrarily deprived the couple of a fundamental liberty protected by the Due Process Clause, the freedom to marry. The Court's language on the latter point bears repeating:

"The freedom to marry has long been recognized as one of the vital personal rights essential to the orderly pursuit of happiness by free men.

"Marriage is one of the 'basic civil rights of man,' fundamental to our very existence and survival." . . .

Although *Loving* arose in the context of racial discrimination, prior and subsequent decisions of this Court confirm that the right to marry is of fundamental importance for all individuals. . . .

More recent decisions have established that the right to marry is part of the fundamental "right of privacy" implicit in the Fourteenth Amendment's Due Process Clause.   In Griswold v. Connecticut, 381 U.S. 479 (1965), the Court observed:

> "We deal with a right of privacy older than the Bill of Rights—older than our political parties, older than our school system.   Marriage is a coming together for better or for worse, hopefully enduring, and intimate to the degree of being sacred.   It is an association that promotes a way of life, not causes; a harmony in living, not political faiths; a bilateral loyalty, not commercial or social projects.   Yet it is an association for as noble a purpose as any involved in our prior decisions."

.   .   .   .

Cases subsequent to *Griswold* and *Loving* have routinely categorized the decision to marry as among the personal decisions protected by the right of privacy.   .   .   .

It is not surprising that the decision to marry has been placed on the same level of importance as decisions relating to procreation, childbirth, child-rearing, and family relationships.   As the facts of this case illustrate, it would make little sense to recognize a right of privacy with respect to other matters of family life and not with respect to the decision to enter the relationship that is the foundation of the family in our society.   The woman whom appellee desired to marry had a fundamental right to seek an abortion of their expected child, see Roe v. Wade, supra, or to bring the child into life to suffer the myriad social, if not economic, disabilities that the status of illegitimacy brings, ... Surely, a decision to marry and raise the child in a traditional family setting must receive equivalent protection.   And, if appellee's right to procreate means anything at all, it must imply some right to enter the only relationship in which the State of Wisconsin allows sexual relations legally to take place.

By reaffirming the fundamental character of the right to marry, we do not mean to suggest that every state regulation which relates in any way to the incidents of or prerequisites for marriage must be subjected to rigorous scrutiny. To the contrary, reasonable regulations that do not significantly interfere with decisions to enter into the marital relationship may legitimately be imposed. See Califano v. Jobst, 434 U.S. 47, 1977.   The statutory classification at issue here, however, clearly does interfere directly and substantially with the right to marry.

Under the challenged statute, no Wisconsin resident in the affected class may marry in Wisconsin or elsewhere without a court order, and marriages contracted in violation of the statute are both void and punishable as criminal offenses. Some of those in the affected class, like appellee, will never be able to obtain the necessary court order, because they either lack the financial means to meet their support obligations or cannot prove that their children will not become public charges.   These persons are absolutely prevented from getting married. Many others, able in theory to satisfy the statute's requirements, will be sufficiently burdened by having to do so that they will in effect be coerced into foregoing their right to marry.   And even those who can be persuaded to meet the statute's requirements suffer a serious intrusion into their freedom of choice in an area in which we have held such freedom to be fundamental.

III.

When a statutory classification significantly interferes with the exercise of a fundamental right, it cannot be upheld unless it is supported by sufficiently important state interests and is closely tailored to effectuate only those interests. .   .   .   Appellant asserts that two interests are served by the challenged statute:

the permission-to-marry proceeding furnishes an opportunity to counsel the applicant as to the necessity of fulfilling his prior support obligations; and the welfare of the out-of-custody children is protected. We may accept for present purposes that these are legitimate and substantial interests, but, since the means selected by the State for achieving these interests unnecessarily impinge on the right to marry, the statute cannot be sustained.

There is evidence that the challenged statute, as originally introduced in the Wisconsin Legislature, was intended merely to establish a mechanism whereby persons with support obligations to children from prior marriages could be counselled before they entered into new marital relationships and incurred further support obligations. Court permission to marry was to be required, but apparently permission was automatically to be granted after counselling was completed. The statute actually enacted, however, does not expressly require or provide for any counselling whatsoever, nor for any automatic granting of permission to marry by the court, and thus it can hardly be justified as a means for ensuring counselling of the persons within its coverage. Even assuming that counselling does take place—a fact as to which there is no evidence in the record—this interest obviously cannot support the withholding of court permission to marry once counselling is completed.

With regard to safeguarding the welfare of the out-of-custody children, appellant's brief does not make clear the connection between the State's interest and the statute's requirements. At argument, appellant's counsel suggested that, since permission to marry cannot be granted unless the applicant shows that he has satisfied his court-determined support obligations to the prior children and that those children will not become public charges, the statute provides incentive for the applicant to make support payments to his children. . . . This "collection device" rationale cannot justify the statute's broad infringement on the right to marry.

First, with respect to individuals who are unable to meet the statutory requirements, the statute merely prevents the applicant from getting married, without delivering any money at all into the hands of the applicant's prior children. More importantly, regardless of the applicant's ability or willingness to meet the statutory requirements, the State already has numerous other means for exacting compliance with support obligations, means that are at least as effective as the instant statute's and yet do not impinge upon the right to marry. Under Wisconsin law, whether the children are from a prior marriage or were born out of wedlock, court-determined support obligations may be enforced directly via wage assignments, civil contempt proceedings, and criminal penalties. And, if the State believes that parents of children out of their custody should be responsible for ensuring that those children do not become public charges, this interest can be achieved by adjusting the criteria used for determining the amounts to be paid under their support orders.

There is also some suggestion that § 245.10 protects the ability of marriage applicants to meet support obligations to prior children by preventing the applicants from incurring new support obligations. But the challenged provisions of § 245.10 are grossly underinclusive with respect to this purpose, since they do not limit in any way new financial commitments by the applicant other than those arising out of the contemplated marriage. The statutory classification is substantially overinclusive as well: given the possibility that the new spouse will actually better the applicant's financial situation, by contributing income from a job or otherwise, the statute in many cases may prevent affected individuals from improving their ability to satisfy their prior support obligations. And, although it is true that the applicant will incur support obligations to any children born during the contemplated marriage, preventing the marriage may only result in the children being born out of wedlock, as in fact occurred in appellee's case. Since the support obligation is the same whether the child is born in or out of wedlock, the net result of preventing the marriage is simply more illegitimate children.

The statutory classification created by §§ 245.10(1), (4), (5) thus cannot be justified by the interests advanced in support of it. The judgment of the District Court is, accordingly, affirmed.

Mr. Chief Justice Burger, concurring.

I join Mr. Justice Marshall's opinion for the Court. . . .

Mr. Justice Stewart, concurring in the judgment.

I cannot join the opinion of the Court. To hold, as the Court does, that the Wisconsin statute violates the Equal Protection Clause seems to me to misconceive the meaning of that constitutional guarantee. The Equal Protection Clause deals not with substantive rights or freedoms but with invidiously discriminatory classifications. . . . The paradigm of its violation is, of course, classification by race. . . .

Like almost any law, the Wisconsin statute now before us affects some people and does not affect others. But to say that it thereby creates "classifications" in the equal protection sense strikes me as little short of fantasy. The problem in this case is not one of discriminatory classifications, but of unwarranted encroachment upon a constitutionally protected freedom. I think that the Wisconsin statute is unconstitutional because it exceeds the bounds of permissible state regulation of marriage, and invades the sphere of liberty protected by the Due Process Clause of the Fourteenth Amendment.

I.

I do not agree with the Court that there is a "right to marry" in the constitutional sense. That right, or more accurately, that privilege, is under our federal system peculiarly one to be defined and limited by state law. Sosna v. Iowa, 419 U.S. 393, 404. A State may not only "significantly interfere with decisions to enter into the marriage relationship," but may in many circumstances absolutely prohibit it. Surely, for example, a State may legitimately say that no one can marry his or her sibling, that no one can marry who is not at least 14 years old, that no one can marry without first passing an examination for venereal disease, or that no one can marry who has a living husband or wife. But, just as surely, in regulating the intimate human relationship of marriage, there is a limit beyond which a State may not constitutionally go.

The Constitution does not specifically mention freedom to marry, but it is settled that the "liberty" protected by the Due Process Clause of the Fourteenth Amendment embraces more than those freedoms expressly enumerated in the Bill of Rights. . . . And the decisions of this Court have made clear that freedom of personal choice in matters of marriage and family life is one of the liberties so protected. . . .

It is evident that the Wisconsin law now before us directly abridges that freedom. The question is whether the state interests that support the abridgment can overcome the substantive protections of the Constitution.
. . . .

If Wisconsin had said that no one could marry who had not paid all of the fines assessed against him for traffic violations, I suppose the constitutional invalidity of the law would be apparent. For while the state interest would certainly be legitimate, that interest would be both disproportionate and unrelated to the restriction of liberty imposed by the State. But the invalidity of the law before us is hardly so clear, because its restriction of liberty seems largely to be imposed only on those who have abused the same liberty in the past.

. . .

On several occasions this Court has held that a person's inability to pay money demanded by the State does not justify the total deprivation of a constitutionally protected liberty. . . .

The principle of those cases applies here as well. The Wisconsin law makes no allowance for the truly indigent. . . .

As directed against either the indigent or the delinquent parent, the law is substantially more rational if viewed as a means of assuring the financial viability of future marriages. In this context, it reflects a plausible judgment that those who have not fulfilled their financial obligations and have not kept their children off the welfare rolls in the past are likely to encounter similar difficulties in the future. But the State's legitimate concern with the financial soundness of prospective marriages must stop short of telling people they may not marry because they are too poor or because they might persist in their financial irresponsibility. The invasion of constitutionally protected liberty and the chance of erroneous prediction are simply too great. A legislative judgment so alien to our traditions and so offensive to our shared notions of fairness offends the Due Process Clause of the Fourteenth Amendment.

II.

In an opinion of the Court half a century ago, Mr. Justice Holmes described an equal protection claim as "the usual last resort of constitutional arguments." Buck v. Bell, 274 U.S. 200, 208. Today equal protection doctrine has become the Court's chief instrument for invalidating state laws. Yet, in a case like this one, the doctrine is no more than substantive due process by another name.

Although the Court purports to examine the bases for legislative classifications and to compare the treatment of legislatively defined groups, it actually erects substantive limitations on what States may do. Thus, the effect of the Court's decision in this case is not to require Wisconsin to draw its legislative classifications with greater precision or to afford similar treatment to similarly situated persons. Rather, the message of the Court's opinion is that Wisconsin may not use its control over marriage to achieve the objectives of the state statute. Such restrictions on basic governmental power are at the heart of substantive due process.

The Court is understandably reluctant to rely on substantive due process. See Roe v. Wade, 410 U.S., at 167–168 (concurring opinion). But to embrace the essence of that doctrine under the guise of equal protection serves no purpose but obfuscation. . . .

To conceal this appropriate inquiry invites mechanical or thoughtless application of misfocused doctrine. To bring it into the open forces a healthy and responsible recognition of the nature and purpose of the extreme power we wield when, in invalidating a state law in the name of the Constitution, we invalidate *pro tanto* the process of representative democracy in one of the Sovereign States of the Union.

Mr. Justice Powell, concurring in the judgment.

I concur in the judgment of the Court that Wisconsin's restrictions on the exclusive means of creating the marital bond, erected by Wis.Stat. §§ 245.10(1), (4), and (5) (1973), cannot meet applicable constitutional standards. I write separately because the majority's rationale sweeps too broadly in an area which traditionally has been subject to pervasive state regulation. . . .

I.

. . .

. . . Thus, *Loving* involved a denial of a "fundamental freedom" on a wholly unsupportable basis—the use of classifications "directly subversive of the principle of equality at the heart of the Fourteenth Amendment . . . ." It does not speak to the level of judicial scrutiny of, or governmental justification for, "supportable" restrictions on the "fundamental freedom" of individuals to marry or divorce.

In my view, analysis must start from the recognition of domestic relations as "an area that has long been regarded as a virtually exclusive province of the States." Sosna v. Iowa, 419 U.S. 393, 404 (1975). The marriage relation traditionally has been subject to regulation, initially by the ecclesiastical authorities, and later by the secular state. . . . State regulation has included bans on incest, bigamy, and homosexuality, as well as various preconditions to marriage, such as blood tests. Likewise, a showing of fault on the part of one of the partners traditionally has been a prerequisite to the dissolution of an unsuccessful union. A "compelling state purpose" inquiry would cast doubt on the network of restrictions that the States have fashioned to govern marriage and divorce.

II.

State power over domestic relations is not without constitutional limits. The Due Process Clause requires a showing of justification "when the government intrudes on choices concerning family living arrangements" in a manner which is contrary to deeply rooted traditions. . . .

. . . . .

. . . I do not agree with the suggestion in the Court's opinion that a State may never condition the right to marry on satisfaction of existing support obligations simply because the State has alternative methods of compelling such payments. To the extent this restriction applies to persons who are able to make the required support payments but simply wish to shirk their moral and legal obligation, the Constitution interposes no bar to this additional collection mechanism. The vice inheres not in the collection concept, but in the failure to make provision for those without the means to comply with child-support obligations. . . .

. . . .

The marriage applicant not only is required by the Wisconsin statute to submit proof of compliance with his support obligation, but also to demonstrate—in some unspecified way—that his children "are not then and are not likely thereafter to become public charges." . . . Apparently, no other jurisdiction has embraced this approach as a method of reducing the number of children on public assistance. Because the State has not established a justification for this unprecedented foreclosure of marriage to many of its citizens solely because of their indigency, I concur in the judgment of the Court.

Mr. Justice Stevens, concurring in the judgment.

. . . .

In sum, the public charge provision is either futile or perverse insofar as it applies to childless couples, couples who will have illegitimate children if they are forbidden to marry, couples whose economic status will be improved by marriage, and couples who are so poor that the marriage will have no impact on the welfare status of their children in any event. Even assuming that the right to marry may sometimes be denied on economic grounds, this clumsy and deliberate legislative discrimination between the rich and the poor is irrational in so many ways that it cannot withstand scrutiny under the Equal Protection Clause of the Fourteenth Amendment.

Mr. Justice Rehnquist, dissenting.

. . . I would view this legislative judgment in the light of the traditional presumption of validity. I think that under the Equal Protection Clause the statute need pass only the "rational basis test," Dandridge v. Williams, 397 U.S. 471, 485 (1970), and that under the Due Process Clause it need only be shown that it bears a rational relation to a constitutionally permissible objective. Williamson v. Lee Optical Co., 348 U.S. 483, 491 (1955); Ferguson v. Skrupa, 372 U.S. 726, 733 (1963) (Harlan, J., concurring). The statute so viewed is a permissible exercise of the State's power to regulate family life and to assure the support of minor children, despite its possible imprecision in the extreme cases envisioned in the concurring opinions.

. . .

DOES EQUAL PROTECTION ANALYSIS ADD ANYTHING?

For examples of other cases where the Court has applied equal protection analysis to cases controlled by other constitutional provisions, see Carey v. Brown, 447 U.S. 455 (1980) (first amendment), set out infra page 1170; Logan v. Zimmerman Brush Co., 455 U.S. 422 (1982) (procedural due process, set out supra page 650 and infra page 948. In any of these cases, do the analysis and result differ if equal protection standards are disregarded and the case is determined under the applicable constitutional provisions? For an extended argument that they do not, see Westin, *The Empty Idea of Equality,* 95 Harv.L.Rev. 537 (1982).

B. VOTING AND ELECTIONS

---

1. INTRODUCTION

THE CONSTITUTION AND THE FRANCHISE

(1) The Constitution of 1789. As originally adopted the Constitution left it to the states to determine who should have the right to vote in national as well as state elections. Art. II, § 1 provided for the selection of the President by electors appointed in each state "in such Manner as the Legislature thereof may direct"—a provision which has remained unchanged. Art. 1, § 2, cl. 1 provided that the persons voting for members of the House of Representatives "shall have the Qualifications requisite for Electors of the most numerous Branch of the State Legislature." Art. 1, § 3, cl. 1 provided that the members of the Senate should be chosen by the legislature of each state. It was not until the adoption of the seventeenth amendment in 1913 that it was provided that members of the Senate should be elected "by the people" of the respective states. That amendment also provided that the person voting for members of the Senate "shall have the qualifications requisite for electors of the most numerous branch of the State legislatures." Art. I, § 4, cl. 1 provided that the "Times, Places and Manner of holding Elections for Senators and Representatives shall be prescribed in each State by the Legislature thereof; but the Congress may at any time by Law make or alter such Regulations, except as to the Places of choosing Senators."

(2) **The Civil War Amendments.** Prior to the Civil War all but six states discriminated against Negroes in establishing qualifications to vote. Stephanson, *Race Distinctions in American Law* 285 (1910). The fourteenth amendment did not directly forbid discrimination in voting. Section 2 of the amendment did provide for a reduction in representation in the House of Representatives in proportion to the number of "male inhabitants" who were not permitted to vote. However, the fifteenth amendment was soon adopted providing that the "right of citizens of the United States to vote shall not be denied or abridged by the United States or by any State on account of race, color, or previous condition of servitude."

(3) **The Nineteenth, Twenty-Fourth, and Twenty-Sixth Amendments.** The Civil War amendments did not extend the franchise to all. Women were, of course, citizens but citizenship did not carry the right to vote. Minor v. Happersett, 88 U.S. (21 Wall.) 162 (1875). Only after a long campaign for women suffrage was the nineteenth amendment ratified in 1920 providing that the right of citizens to vote "shall not be denied or abridged by the United States or by any State on account of sex." In 1964 the twenty-fourth amendment was adopted providing that the right of any citizen to vote for the president, vice-president, or members of Congress "shall not be denied or abridged by the United States or any State by reason of failure to pay any poll tax or other tax." Finally the twenty-sixth amendment was adopted in 1971 providing that the right of any citizen eighteen years or older to vote "shall not be denied or abridged by the United States or by any State on account of age."

THE EQUAL PROTECTION CLAUSE AS THE SOURCE OF A RIGHT TO VOTE AND RUN FOR ELECTIVE OFFICE

In reading the cases in this section two general questions should be considered: (1) Does the court use the general language of the equal protection clause to establish a substantive right to vote and participate in elections which goes beyond the specific constitutional provisions summarized above? (2) Is there special constitutional justification for the Court to go beyond the express language of the Constitution to guarantee the broadest access to the political processes? Cf. Ely, *Democracy and Distrust* 117 (1980): "[U]nblocking stoppages in the democratic process is what judicial review ought preeminently to be about, and denial of the vote seems the quintessential stoppage."

The cases will be discussed in two groups: (1) Those relating to legislative districting; and (2) those relating to qualifications of voters.

2. LEGISLATIVE DISTRICTING

REYNOLDS v. SIMS

377 U.S. 533, 84 S.Ct. 1362, 12 L.Ed.2d 506 (1964).

Mr. Chief Justice Warren delivered the opinion of the Court.

Involved in these cases are an appeal and two cross-appeals from a decision of the Federal District Court for the Middle District of Alabama holding invalid, under the Equal Protection Clause of the Federal Constitution, the existing and two legislatively proposed plans for the apportionment of seats in the two houses of the Alabama Legislature, and ordering into effect a temporary reapportionment plan comprised of parts of the proposed but judicially disapproved measures.

. . . .

[Under the existing plan, in the Senate one county of 15,417 population had a Senate seat and another county of over 600,000 people also had only a single seat. In the House one county with a population of 13,462 had two seats while another of 314,301 had only three seats. The two proposed plans reduced these disparities somewhat but still had a House in which the population for a seat in one district was 5 times that of another district and a Senate still in the neighborhood of 59 to 1.]

Undeniably the Constitution of the United States protects the right of all qualified citizens to vote, in state as well as in federal elections. A consistent line of decisions by this Court in cases involving attempts to deny or restrict the right of suffrage has made this indelibly clear. It has been repeatedly recognized that all qualified voters have a constitutionally protected right to vote, Ex parte Yarbrough, 110 U.S. 651, and to have their votes counted, United States v. Mosley, 238 U.S. 383. In *Mosley* the Court stated that it is "as equally unquestionable that the right to have one's vote counted is as open to protection . . . as the right to put a ballot in a box." 238 U.S., at 386. The right to vote can neither be denied outright, . . . nor can it be destroyed by alteration of ballots, see United States v. Classic, 313 U.S. 299, 315, nor diluted by ballot-box stuffing. . . . As the Court stated in *Classic,* "Obviously included within the right to choose, secured by the Constitution, is the right of qualified voters within a state to cast their ballots and have them counted . . . ." 313 U.S., at 315. Racially based gerrymandering, Gomillion v. Lightfoot, 364 U.S. 339, and the conducting of white primaries, Nixon v. Herndon, 273 U.S. 536, Nixon v. Condon, 286 U.S. 73, Smith v. Allwright, 321 U.S. 649, Terry v. Adams, 345 U.S. 461, both of which result in denying to some citizens their right to vote, have been held to be constitutionally impermissible. And history has seen a continuing expansion of the scope of the right of suffrage in this country. The right to vote freely for the candidate of one's choice is of the essence of a democratic society, and any restrictions on that right strike at the heart of representative government. And the right of suffrage can be denied by a debasement or dilution of the weight of a citizen's vote just as effectively as by wholly prohibiting the free exercise of the franchise.

. . .

In Gray v. Sanders, 372 U.S. 368, we held that the Georgia county unit system, applicable in statewide primary elections, was unconstitutional since it resulted in a dilution of the weight of the votes of certain Georgia voters merely because of where they resided. . . .

In Wesberry v. Sanders, 376 U.S. 1, decided earlier this Term, we held that attacks on the constitutionality of congressional districting plans enacted by state legislatures do not present nonjusticiable questions and should not be dismissed generally for "want of equity." We determined that the constitutional test for the validity of congressional districting schemes was one of substantial equality of population among the various districts established by a state legislature for the election of members of the Federal House of Representatives.

. . .

Gray and *Wesberry* are of course not dispositive of or directly controlling on our decision in these cases involving state legislative apportionment controversies. Admittedly, those decisions, in which we held that, in statewide and in congressional elections, one person's vote must be counted equally with those of all other voters in a State, were based on different constitutional considerations and were addressed to rather distinct problems. But neither are they wholly inapposite. *Gray,* though not determinative here since involving the weighting of votes in statewide elections, established the basic principle of equality among voters within a State, and held that voters cannot be classified, constitutionally, on the basis of where they live, at least with respect to voting in statewide elections. And our decision in *Wesberry* was of course grounded on that language of the Constitution which prescribes that members of the Federal House of Representatives are to be chosen "by the People," while attacks on state legislative apportionment schemes, such as that involved in the instant cases, are principally based on the Equal Protection Clause of the Fourteenth Amendment. Nevertheless, *Wesberry* clearly established that the fundamental principle of representative government in this country is one of equal representation for equal numbers of people, without regard to race, sex, economic status, or place of residence within a State. Our problem, then, is to ascertain, in the instant cases, whether there are any constitutionally cognizable principles which would justify departures from the basic standard of equality among voters in the apportionment of seats in state legislatures.

III.

A predominant consideration in determining whether a State's legislative apportionment scheme constitutes an invidious discrimination violative of rights asserted under the Equal Protection Clause is that the rights allegedly impaired are individual and personal in nature. . . .

Legislators represent people, not trees or acres. Legislators are elected by voters, not farms or cities or economic interests. As long as ours is a representative form of government, and our legislatures are those instruments of government elected directly by and directly representative of the people, the right to elect legislators in a free and unimpaired fashion is a bedrock of our political system. It could hardly be gainsaid that a constitutional claim had been asserted by an allegation that certain otherwise qualified voters had been entirely prohibited from voting for members of their state legislature. And, if a State should provide that the votes of citizens in one part of the State should be given two times, or five times, or 10 times the weight of votes of citizens in another part of the State, it could hardly be contended that the right to vote of those residing in the disfavored areas had not been effectively diluted. It would appear extraordinary to suggest that a state could be constitutionally permitted to enact a law providing that certain of the state's voters could vote two, five, or 10 times for their legislative representatives, while voters living elsewhere could vote only once. And it is inconceivable that a state law to the effect that, in counting votes for legislators, the votes of citizens in one part of the State would be multiplied by two, five, or 10, while the votes of persons in another area would be counted only at face value, could be constitutionally sustainable. Of course, the effect of state legislative districting schemes which give the same number of representatives to unequal numbers of constituents is identical. Overweighting and overvaluation of the votes of those living here has the certain effect of dilution and undervaluation of the votes of those living there. The resulting discrimination against those individual voters living in disfavored areas is easily demonstrable mathematically. Their right to vote is simply not the same right to vote as that of those living in a favored part of the State. Two, five, or 10 of them must vote before the effect of their voting is equivalent to that of their favored neighbor. Weighting the votes of citizens differently, by any method or means, merely because of where they happen to reside, hardly seems justifiable. . . .

. . . Since the achieving of fair and effective representation for all citizens is concededly the basic aim of legislative apportionment, we conclude that the Equal Protection Clause guarantees the opportunity for equal participation by all voters in the election of state legislators. Diluting the weight of votes because of place of residence impairs basic constitutional rights under the Fourteenth Amendment just as much as invidious discriminations based upon factors such as race, Brown v. Board of Education, 347 U.S. 483, or economic status, Griffin v. People of State of Illinois, 351 U.S. 12, Douglas v. People of

State of California, 372 U.S. 353. Our constitutional system amply provides for the protection of minorities by means other than giving them majority control of state legislatures. And the democratic ideals of equality and majority rule, which have served this Nation so well in the past, are hardly of any less significance for the present and the future.

We are told that the matter of apportioning representation in a state legislature is a complex and many-faceted one. We are advised that States can rationally consider factors other than population in apportioning legislative representation. We are admonished not to restrict the power of the States to impose differing views as to political philosophy on their citizens. We are cautioned about the dangers of entering into political thickets and mathematical quagmires. Our answer is this: a denial of constitutionally protected rights demands judicial protection; our oath and our office require no less of us.

. . . Population is, of necessity, the starting point for consideration and the controlling criterion for judgment in legislative apportionment controversies. A citizen, a qualified voter, is no more nor no less so because he lives in the city or on the farm. This is the clear and strong command of our Constitution's Equal Protection Clause. This is an essential part of the concept of a government of laws and not men. This is at the heart of Lincoln's vision of "government of the people, by the people, [and] for the people." The Equal Protection Clause demands no less than substantially equal state legislative representation for all citizens, of all places as well as of all races.

IV.

We hold that, as a basic constitutional standard, the Equal Protection Clause requires that the seats in both houses of a bicameral state legislature must be apportioned on a population basis. Simply stated, an individual's right to vote for state legislators is unconstitutionally impaired when its weight is in a substantial fashion diluted when compared with votes of citizens living in other parts of the State. Since, under neither the existing apportionment provisions nor under either of the proposed plans was either of the houses of the Alabama Legislature apportioned on a population basis, the District Court correctly held that all three of these schemes were constitutionally invalid.

V.

. . .

The system of representation in the two Houses of the Federal Congress is one ingrained in our Constitution, as part of the law of the land. It is one conceived out of compromise and concession indispensable to the establishment of our federal republic. Arising from unique historical circumstances, it is based on the consideration that in establishing our type of federalism a group of formerly independent States bound themselves together under one national government. . . .

Political subdivisions of States—counties, cities, or whatever—never were and never have been considered as sovereign entities. Rather, they have been traditionally regarded as subordinate governmental instrumentalities created by the State to assist in the carrying out of state governmental functions. . . . The relationship of the States to the Federal Government could hardly be less analogous.

. . .

Since we find the so-called federal analogy inapposite to a consideration of the constitutional validity of state legislative apportionment schemes, we necessarily hold that the Equal Protection Clause requires both houses of a state legislature to be apportioned on a population basis. . . .

VI.

By holding that as a federal constitutional requisite both houses of a state legislature must be apportioned on a population basis, we mean that the Equal Protection Clause requires that a State make an honest and good faith effort to construct districts, in both houses of its legislature, as nearly of equal population as is practicable. We realize that it is a practical impossibility to arrange legislative districts so that each one has an identical number of residents, or citizens, or voters. Mathematical exactness or precision is hardly a workable constitutional requirement. . . .

. . . .

A State may legitimately desire to maintain the integrity of various political subdivisions, insofar as possible, and provide for compact districts of contiguous territory in designing a legislative apportionment scheme. Valid considerations may underlie such aims. Indiscriminate districting, without any regard for political subdivision or natural or historical boundary lines, may be little more than an open invitation to partisan gerrymandering. Single-member districts may be the rule in one State, while another State might desire to achieve some flexibility by creating multimember or floterial districts. Whatever the means of accomplishment, the overriding objective must be substantial equality of population among the various districts, so that the vote of any citizen is approximately equal in weight to that of any other citizen in the State. . . .

But neither history alone, nor economic or other sorts of group interests, are permissible factors in attempting to justify disparities from population-based representation. Citizens, not history or economic interests, cast votes. Considerations of area alone provide an insufficient justification for deviations from the equal-population principle. Again, people, not land or trees or pastures, vote. Modern developments and improvements in transportation and communications make rather hollow, in the mid-1960's, most claims that deviations from population-based representation can validly be based solely on geographical considerations. Arguments for allowing such deviations in order to insure effective representation for sparsely settled areas and to prevent legislative districts from becoming so large that the availability of access of citizens to their representatives is impaired are today, for the most part, unconvincing.

A consideration that appears to be of more substance in justifying some deviations from population-based representation in state legislatures is that of insuring some voice to political subdivisions, as political subdivisions. Several factors make more than insubstantial claims that a State can rationally consider according political subdivisions some independent representation in at least one body of the state legislature, as long as the basic standard of equality of population among districts is maintained. . . .

VIII.

That the Equal Protection Clause requires that both houses of a state legislature be apportioned on a population basis does not mean that States cannot adopt some reasonable plan for periodic revision of their apportionment schemes. Decennial reapportionment appears to be a rational approach to readjustment of legislative representation in order to take into account population shifts and growth. . . . In substance, we do not regard the Equal Protection Clause as requiring daily, monthly, annual or biennial reapportionment, so long as a State has reasonably conceived plan for periodic readjustment of legislative representation. . . .

. . . .

Affirmed and remanded.

[Justices Clark and Stewart concurred.   Justice Harlan filed a lengthy dissenting opinion.]

REYNOLDS AND THE FIRST ROUND OF REAPPORTIONMENT

(1) Along with *Reynolds* the Court decided cases involving five other states. One of those is worth special note.   In Colorado the voters in 1962 had defeated a proposed constitutional amendment which would have provided for apportionment of both houses of the legislature on a population basis and adopted another amendment which provided for a lower house based on population and an upper house based on a combination of population and other factors.   In Lucas v. Forty-Fourth General Assembly of Colorado, 377 U.S. 713 (1964), the Court held this plan invalid despite the fact that it had been adopted by a majority of the voters, saying: "An individual's constitutionally protected right to cast an equally weighted vote cannot be denied even by a vote of a majority of the State's electorate, if the apportionment scheme adopted by the voters fails to measure up to the requirements of the Equal Protection Clause."

(2) *Reynolds* touched off a nation-wide effort to reapportion legislatures in accordance with its standards based on the 1960 census.   In many states the political processes were incapable of achieving such a result and the federal courts found themselves faced with the duty of prescribing apportionment plans. Judicial doctrine developed rapidly towards the point that only mathematically equal districts would be approved—one-person, one-vote became a constitution-al standard—and various state limitations on the construction of legislative districts were invalidated as interfering with mathematical equality.   Little or no attention was paid in the cases to the realities of political representation. Legislators discovered that with the aid of computers mathematically equal districts could be created in ways which would favor incumbents or give undue representation in the legislatures to particular parties or interest groups.   For an elaborate and useful discussion of the background of *Reynolds* and its companion cases and of the litigation up to 1968, see Dixon, *Democratic Representation: Reapportionment in Law and Politics* (1968).   The literature on reapportionment during this period was enormous.   Aside from innumerable articles, there were, in addition to Dixon's, the following significant books:

Baker, *The Reapportionment Revolution* (1966); Cortner, *The Apportionment Cases* (1970); Lee, *One Man, One Vote: WMCA and the Struggle for Equal Representation* (1967); McKay, *The Law and Politics of Equal Representation* (1965); McKay, *Reapportionment Reappraisal: A Report on the One Man, One Vote Principle in Practice* (1968); Polsby (Ed.), *Reapportionment in the 1970s* (1971).

(3) The Court decided several more cases based on the reapportionments of the 1960s.   Since they are referred to in the more recent cases set out below, no attempt will be made here to cite or discuss them.

THE 1970 CENSUS AND THE SECOND ROUND OF REAPPORTIONMENT

The 1970 census set off a second round of reapportionment struggles in the legislatures and in the courts.   The legislatures faced the problem on the assumption that the Supreme Court would hold them very close to the goal of mathematical equality and would not inquire too deeply into the political and other consequences of apportionments meeting the numerical standard.   A mathematical standard could be easily quantified and measured.   To determine whether a particular apportionment scheme produced a fair representation of the various political groups or served to dilute the political power of particular minority groups was much more difficult.

The Supreme Court, perhaps better informed by the spate of literature and the presence of more sophisticated advocates, surprised many by shifting away from its almost exclusive reliance on equal numbers as the constitutional test when the 1970 cases began to come to it.

———

MAHAN v. HOWELL, 410 U.S. 315 (1973). A Virginia statute apportioned the House of Delegates so that the maximum percentage variation from the ideal was 16.4%—one district being 6.8% under the ideal and another 9.6% over. The minimum population percentage necessary to elect a majority of the House was 49.29%. The districts followed political jurisdictional lines of the counties and cities with the exception of Fairfax County which was divided into two five-member districts. In a suit brought to challenge this plan the district court held it violated constitutional standards and ordered its own plan into effect which reduced the maximum percentage variation to 10% but extended districts across subdivision lines in 12 instances. The Supreme Court reversed and reinstated the statutory plan. Justice Rehnquist, speaking for the Court, said that the strict standards applicable to congressional districting did not apply to state legislatures and stated the standard of review to be applied as follows:

"We are not prepared to say that the decision of the people of Virginia to grant the General Assembly the power to enact local legislation dealing with the political subdivisions is irrational. And if that be so, the decision of the General Assembly to provide representation to subdivisions *qua* subdivisions in order to implement that constitutional power is likewise valid when measured against the Equal Protection Clause of the Fourteenth Amendment. The inquiry then becomes whether it can reasonably be said that the state policy urged by Virginia to justify the divergences in the legislative reapportionment plan of the House is indeed furthered by the plan adopted by the legislature, and whether if so justified the divergences are also within tolerable limits. For a State's policy urged in justification of disparity in district population, however, rational, cannot constitutionally be permitted to emasculate the goal of substantial equality."

He applied this standard as follows:

"We hold that the legislature's plan for apportionment of the House of Delegates may reasonably be said to advance the rational state policy of respecting the boundaries of political subdivisions. The remaining inquiry is whether the population disparities among the districts which have resulted from the pursuit of this plan exceed constitutional limits. We conclude that they do not.

. . .

"Neither courts nor legislatures are furnished any specialized calipers which enable them to extract from the general language of the Equal Protection Clause of the Fourteenth Amendment the mathematical formula which establishes what range of percentage deviations are permissible, and what are not. The 16-odd percent maximum deviation which the District Court found to exist in the legislative plan for the reapportionment of the House is substantially less than the percentage deviations which have been found invalid in the previous decisions of this Court. While this percentage may well approach tolerable limits, we do not believe it exceeds them. Virginia has not sacrificed substantial equality to justifiable deviations."

Justices Brennan, Douglas, and Marshall, dissenting, stated their view of the constitutional standards to be applied:

"The holdings of our prior decisions can be restated in two unequivocal propositions. First the paramount goal of reapportionment must be the drawing of district lines so as to achieve precise equality in the population of each district. . . . The Constitution does not permit a State to relegate considerations of equality to secondary status and reserve as the primary goal of apportionment the service of some other state interest.

"Second, it is open to the State, in the event that it should fail to achieve the goal of population equality, to attempt to justify its failure by demonstrating that precise equality could not be achieved without jeopardizing some critical governmental interest. The Equal Protection Clause does not exalt the principle of equal representation to the point of nullifying every competing interest of the State. But we have held firmly to the view that variations in weight accorded each vote can be approved only where the State meets its burden of presenting cogent reasons in explanation of the variations, and even then only where the variations are small."

GAFFNEY v. CUMMINGS

412 U.S. 735, 93 S.Ct. 2321, 37 L.Ed.2d 298 (1973).

Mr. Justice White delivered the opinion of the Court.

The questions in this case are whether the population variations among the election districts provided by a reapportionment plan for the Connecticut General Assembly, proposed in 1971, made out a prima facie case of invidious discrimination under the Equal Protection Clause and whether an otherwise acceptable reapportionment plan is constitutionally vulnerable where its purpose is to provide districts that would achieve "political fairness" between the political parties.

I.

The reapportionment plan for the Connecticut General Assembly became law when published by the Secretary of the State in December 1971. Under the Connecticut Constitution, the state legislature is given the initial opportunity to reapportion itself in the months immediately following the completion of decennial census of the United States. Conn. Const., Art. III, § 6(b). In the present case, the legislature was unable to agree on a plan by the state constitutional deadline of April 1, 1971. The task was therefore transferred, as required by the constitution, to an eight-member bipartisan commission. Ibid. The Democratic and Republican Party leaders in the legislature each appointed four commissioners. The commission was given until July 1, 1971, to devise a reapportionment plan, id., § 6(c); but, although the commission approached agreement, it too was unable to adopt a plan within the deadline. Accordingly, as a final step in the constitutional process, a three-man bipartisan Board was constituted. Id., § 6(d). The Speaker of the House of Representatives, a Democrat, and the Republican Minority Leader of the House each chose a judge of the State Superior Court to be a Board member, and the two judges in turn designated a third Board member, who was a justice of the State Supreme Court. Id., § 6(d).

This Apportionment Board, using the census data available during the summer of 1971, and relying heavily on the legislative commission's tentative plans, filed a reapportionment plan on September 30, 1971, with one member dissenting.

. . . The Board's reapportionment plan provides for a Senate consisting of 36 senators elected from single-member districts. . . . The largest and smallest senatorial districts deviate by +0.88% and –0.93% respectively, making the total maximum deviation 1.81%.

The reapportionment plan proposed a House of 151 single-member districts. . . . The maximum deviation from the ideal is +3.93% and –3.9%. The maximum deviation between any two districts thus totals 7.83%.

. . . The Board also consciously and overtly adopted and followed a policy of "political fairness," which aimed at a rough scheme of proportional representation of the two major political parties. Senate and House districts were structured so that the composition of both Houses would reflect "as clearly as possible . . . the actual [statewide] plurality of vote on the House or Senate lines in a given election." [4] Rather than focus on party membership in the respective districts, the Board took into account the party voting results in the preceding three statewide elections, and, on that basis, created what was thought to be a proportionate number of Republican and Democratic legislative seats.

In November 1971, not long after the Board filed the reapportionment plan with the Secretary of the State, an action was brought in federal district court seeking declaratory and injunctive relief against implementation of the plan. . . .

. . .

II.

We think that appellees' showing of numerical deviations from population equality among the Senate and House districts in this case failed to make out a prima facie violation of the Equal Protection Clause of the Fourteenth Amendment, whether those deviations are considered alone or in combination with the additional fact that another plan could be conceived with lower deviations among the State's legislative districts. Put another way, the allegations and proof of population deviations among the districts fail in size and quality to amount to an invidious discrimination under the Fourteenth Amendment which would entitle appellees to relief absent some countervailing showing by the State.

. . .

As these pronouncements have been worked out in our cases, it has become apparent that the larger variations from substantial equality are too great to be justified by any state interest so far suggested. There were thus the enormous variations stricken down in the early cases beginning with Reynolds v. Sims, as well as the much smaller, but nevertheless unacceptable deviations, appearing in later cases such as Swann v. Adams, 385 U.S. 440 (1967); Kilgarlin v. Hill, 386 U.S. 120 (1967); and Whitcomb v. Chavis, 403 U.S. 124, 161–163 (1971). On the other hand, as Mahan v. Howell demonstrates, population deviations among districts may be sufficiently large to require justification but nonetheless be justifiable and legally sustainable. It is now time to recognize, in the context of the eminently reasonable approach of Reynolds v. Sims, that minor deviations from mathematical equality among state legislative districts are insufficient to make out a prima facie case of invidious discrimination under the Fourteenth Amendment so as to require justification by the State.

---

[4] Testimony of Judge George A. Saden, the Republican Board member. App. 264. According to Mr. James F. Collins, a staff member of the Board, the plan for the House resulted in approximately 70 safe Democratic seats, 55 to 60 safe Republican seats, with the balance characterized as probable or swing Democratic or Republican or "just plain swing," 341 F.Supp. 139, 147.

We doubt that *Reynolds* would mandate any other result if for no other reason than that the basic statistical materials which legislatures and courts usually have to work with are the results of the United States census taken at 10-year intervals and published as soon as possible after the beginning of each decade. These figures may be as accurate as such immense undertakings can be but they are inherently less than absolutely accurate. Those who know about such things recognize this fact, and, unless they are to be wholly ignored, it makes little sense to conclude from relatively minor "census population" variations among legislative districts that any person's vote is being substantially diluted. The "population" of a legislative district is just not that knowable to be used for such refined judgments.

What is more, it must be recognized that total population, even if absolutely accurate as to each district when taken, is nevertheless not a talismanic measure of the weight of a person's vote under a later adopted reapportionment plan. The United States census is more of an event than a process. It measures population at only a single instant in time. District populations are constantly changing, often at different rates in either direction, up or down. Substantial differentials in population growth rates are striking and well-known phenomena. So too, if it is the weight of a person's vote that matters, total population—even if stable and accurately taken—may not actually reflect that body of voters whose votes must be counted and weighed for the purposes of reapportionment, because "census persons" are not voters. . . .

. . . More fundamentally, *Reynolds* recognized that "the achieving of fair and effective representation for all citizens is . . . the basic aim of legislative apportionment", and it was for that reason that the decision insisted on substantial equality of populations among districts.

This is a vital and worthy goal, but surely its attainment does not in any commonsense way depend upon eliminating the insignificant population variations involved in this case. Fair and effective representation may be destroyed by gross population variations among districts, but it is apparent that such representation does not depend solely on mathematical equality among district populations. There are other relevant factors to be taken into account and other important interests that States may legitimately be mindful of. . . . An unrealistic overemphasis on raw population figures, a mere nose count in the districts, may submerge these other considerations and itself furnish a ready tool for ignoring factors that in day-to-day operation are important to an acceptable representation and apportionment arrangement.

Nor is the goal of fair and effective representation furthered by making the standards of reapportionment so difficult to satisfy that the reapportionment task is recurringly removed from legislative hands and performed by federal courts who themselves must make the political decisions necessary to formulate a plan or accept those made by reapportionment plaintiffs, who may have wholly different goals than those embodied in the official plan. . . . We doubt that the Fourteenth Amendment requires repeated displacement of otherwise appropriate state decisionmaking in the name of essentially minor deviations from perfect census-population equality that no one, with confidence can say will deprive any person of fair and effective representation in his state legislature.

That the Court was not deterred by the hazards of the political thicket when it undertook to adjudicate the reapportionment cases does not mean that it should become bogged down in a vast, intractable apportionment slough, particularly when there is little, if anything, to be accomplished by doing so.

. . .

. . . We have repeatedly recognized that state reapportionment is the task of local legislatures or of those organs of state government selected to perform it. Their work should not be invalidated under the Equal Protection Clause when only minor population variations among districts are proved. Here, the proof at trial demonstrated that the House districts under the State Apportionment Board's plan varied in population from one another by a *maximum* of only about 8% and that the average deviation from the ideal House district was only about 2%. The Senate districts had even less variations. On such a showing, we are quite sure that a prima facie case of invidious discrimination under the Fourteenth Amendment was not made.

III.

State legislative districts may be equal or substantially equal in population and still be vulnerable under the Fourteenth Amendment. A districting statute otherwise acceptable, may be invalid because it fences out a racial group so as to deprive them of their pre-existing municipal vote. Gomillion v. Lightfoot, 364 U.S. 339 (1960). A districting plan may create multimember districts perfectly acceptable under equal population standards, but invidiously discriminatory because they are employed "to minimize or cancel out the voting strength of racial or political elements of the voting population." Fortson v. Dorsey, 379 U.S. 433, 439 (1965). . . . We must, therefore, respond to appellees' claims in this case that even if acceptable populationwise, the Apportionment Board's plan was invidiously discriminatory because a "political fairness principle" was followed in making up the districts in both the House and Senate.

. . . Appellant insists that the spirit of "political fairness" underlying this plan is not only permissible, but a desirable consideration in laying out districts that otherwise satisfy the population standard of the reapportionment cases. Appellees, on the other hand, label the plan as nothing less than a gigantic political gerrymander, invidiously discriminatory under the Fourteenth Amendment.[18]

. . . The very essence of districting is to produce a different—a more "politically fair"—result than would be reached with elections at large, in which the winning party would take 100% of the legislative seats. Politics and political considerations are inseparable from districting and apportionment. . . . District lines are rarely neutral phenomena. They can well determine what district will be predominantly Democratic or predominantly Republican, or make a close race likely. Redistricting may pit incumbents against one another or make very difficult the election of the most experienced legislator. The reality is that districting inevitably has and is intended to have substantial political consequences.

It may be suggested that those who redistrict and reapportion should work with census, not political, data and achieve population equality without regard for political impact. But this politically mindless approach may produce, whether intended or not, the most grossly gerrymandered results; and, in any event, it is most unlikely that the political impact of such a plan would remain undiscovered by the time it was proposed or adopted, in which event the results would be both known and, if not changed, intended.

It is much more plausible to assume that those who redistrict and reapportion work with both political and census data. Within the limits of the population equality standards of the Equal Protection Clause, they seek, through compromise or otherwise, to achieve the political or other ends of the State, its

[18] Appellees also maintain that the shapes of the districts would not have been so "indecent" had the Board not attempted to "wiggle and joggle" boundary lines to ferret out pockets of each party's strength. That may well be true, although any plan that attempts to follow Connecticut's "oddly shaped" town lines . . . is bound to contain some irregularly shaped districts. But compactness or attractiveness has never been held to constitute an independent federal constitutional requirement for state legislative districts . . . .

constituents, and its office holders. What is done in so arranging for elections, or to achieve political ends or allocate political power, is not wholly exempt from judicial scrutiny under the Fourteenth Amendment. As we have indicated, for example, multimember districts may be vulnerable, if racial or political groups have been fenced out of the political process and their voting strength invidiously minimized. See White v. Regester, 412 U.S. 755; Whitcomb v. Chavis, supra. See also Gomillion v. Lightfoot, 364 U.S. 339 (1960). Beyond this, we have not ventured far or attempted the impossible task of extirpating politics from what are the essentially political processes of the sovereign States. Even more plainly, judicial interest should be at its lowest ebb when a State purports fairly to allocate political power to the parties in accordance with their voting strength and, within quite tolerable limits, succeeds in doing so. There is no doubt that there may be other reapportionment plans for Connecticut that would have different political consequences and that would also be constitutional. . . . But neither we nor the district courts have a constitutional warrant to invalidate a state plan, otherwise within tolerable population limits, because it undertakes, not to minimize or eliminate the political strength of any group or party, but to recognize it and, through districting, provide a rough sort of proportional representation in the legislative halls of the State.

Reversed.

[Justices Brennan, Douglas and Marshall dissented.]

KARCHER v. DAGGETT

462 U.S. 725, 103 S.Ct. 2653, 77 L.Ed.2d 133 (1983).

Justice Brennan delivered the opinion of the Court.

The question presented by this appeal is whether an apportionment plan for congressional districts satisfies Art. I, § 2 without need for further justification if the population of the largest district is less than one percent greater than the population of the smallest district. A three-judge District Court declared New Jersey's 1982 reapportionment plan unconstitutional on the authority of Kirkpatrick v. Preisler, 394 U.S. 526 (1969), and White v. Weiser, 412 U.S. 783 (1973), because the population deviations among districts, although small, were not the result of a good-faith effort to achieve population equality. We affirm.

I

. . . [T]he 200th Legislature returned to the problem of apportioning congressional districts when it convened in January, 1982, and it swiftly passed a bill . . . which created the apportionment plan at issue in this case. The bill was signed by the Governor on January 19, 1982, becoming P.L.1982, c. 1 (hereinafter Feldman Plan). A map of the resulting apportionment is appended infra.

Like every plan considered by the Legislature, the Feldman Plan contained 14 districts, with an average population per district (as determined by the 1980 census) of 526,059. Each district did not have the same population. On the average, each district differed from the "ideal" figure by 0.1384%, or about 726 people. The largest district, the Fourth District, which includes Trenton, had a population of 527,472, and the smallest, the Sixth District, embracing most of Middlesex County, a population of 523,798. The difference between them was 3,674 people, or 0.6984% of the average district. The populations of the other districts also varied. The Ninth District, including most of Bergen County, in the northeastern corner of the State, had a population of 527,349, while the population of the Third District, along the Atlantic shore, was only 524,825.

The Legislature had before it other plans with appreciably smaller population deviations between the largest and smallest districts. The one receiving the most attention in the District Court was designed by Dr. Ernest Reock, a political science professor at Rutgers University and Director of the Bureau of Government Research. A version of the Reock Plan introduced in the 200th Legislature by Assemblyman Hardwick had a maximum population difference of 2,375, or 0.4514% of the average figure.

Almost immediately after the Feldman Plan became law, a group of individuals with varying interests, including all incumbent Republican members of Congress from New Jersey, sought a declaration that the apportionment plan violated Article I, § 2 of the Constitution and an injunction against proceeding with the primary election for United States Representatives under the plan. A three-judge district court was convened pursuant to 28 U.S.C. § 2284(a). . . .

Shortly thereafter, the District Court issued an opinion and order declaring the Feldman Plan unconstitutional. . . .

II

Article I, § 2, establishes a "high standard of justice and common sense" for the apportionment of congressional districts: "equal representation for equal numbers of people." Wesberry v. Sanders, 376 U.S. 1, 18 (1964). Precise mathematical equality, however, may be impossible to achieve in an imperfect world; therefore the "equal representation" standard is enforced only to the extent of requiring that districts be apportioned to achieve population equality "as nearly as is practicable." . . .

Thus two basic questions shape litigation over population deviations in state legislation apportioning congressional districts. First, the court must consider whether the population differences among districts could have been reduced or eliminated altogether by a good-faith effort to draw districts of equal population. Parties challenging apportionment legislation must bear the burden of proof on this issue, and if they fail to show that the differences could have been avoided the apportionment scheme must be upheld. If, however, the plaintiffs can establish that the population differences were not the result of a good-faith effort to achieve equality, the State must bear the burden of proving that each significant variance between districts was necessary to achieve some legitimate goal. *Kirkpatrick,* 394 U.S., at 532; cf. Swann v. Adams, 385 U.S. 440, 443–444 (1967).

III

Appellants' principal argument in this case is addressed to the first question described above. They contend that the Feldman Plan should be regarded *per se* as the product of a good-faith effort to achieve population equality because the maximum population deviation among districts is smaller than the predictable undercount in available census data.

A

Kirkpatrick squarely rejected a nearly identical argument. "The whole thrust of the 'as nearly as practicable' approach is inconsistent with adoption of fixed numerical standards which excuse population variances without regard to the circumstances of each particular case." 394 U.S., at 530; see White v. Weiser, 412 U.S., at 790, n. 8, and 792–793. Adopting any standard other than population equality, using the best census data available, see 394 U.S., at 532, would subtly erode the Constitution's ideal of equal representation. If state legislators knew that a certain *de minimis* level of population differences were acceptable, they would doubtless strive to achieve that level rather than equality. Id., at 531. Furthermore, choosing a different standard would import a high degree of arbitrariness into the process of reviewing apportionment plans. Ibid. In this case, appellants argue that a maximum deviation of approximately 0.7% should be considered *de minimis*. If we accept that argument, how are we to regard deviations of 0.8%, 0.95%, 1%, or 1.1%?

Any standard, including absolute equality, involves a certain artificiality. As appellants point out, even the census data are not perfect, and the well-known restlessness of the American people means that population counts for particular localities are outdated long before they are completed. Yet problems with the data at hand apply equally to any population-based standard we could choose. As between two standards—equality or something-less-than equality—only the former reflects the aspirations of Art. I, § 2.

To accept the legitimacy of unjustified, though small population deviations in this case would mean to reject the basic premise of *Kirkpatrick* and *Wesberry*. We decline appellants' invitation to go that far. The unusual rigor of their standard has been noted several times. Because of that rigor, we have required that absolute population equality be the paramount objective of apportionment only in the case of congressional districts, for which the command of Art. I, § 2 as regards the national legislature outweighs the local interests that a State may deem relevant in apportioning districts for representatives to state and local legislatures, but we have not questioned the population equality standard for congressional districts. See, e.g., White v. Weiser, 412 U.S., at 793; White v. Regester, 412 U.S. 755, 763 (1973); Mahan v. Howell, 410 U.S. 315, 321–323 (1973). The principle of population equality for congressional districts has not proved unjust or socially or economically harmful in experience. Cf. Washington v. Dawson & Co., 264 U.S. 219, 237 (1924) (Brandeis, J., dissenting); B. Cardozo, The Nature of the Judicial Process 150 (1921). If anything, this standard should cause less difficulty now for state legislatures than it did when we adopted it in *Wesberry*. The rapid advances in computer technology and education during the last two decades make it relatively simple to draw contiguous districts of equal population and at the same time to further whatever secondary goals the State has. . . . We thus reaffirm that there are no *de minimis* population variations, which could practicably be avoided, but which nonetheless meet the standard of Art. I, § 2 without justification.[6]

. . .

[6] Justice White objects that "the rule of absolute equality is perfectly compatible with 'gerrymandering' of the worst sort," Wells v. Rockefeller, 394 U.S. 542, 551 (1969) (Harlan, J., dissenting). That may certainly be true to some extent: beyond requiring States to justify population deviations with explicit, precise reasons, which might be expected to have some inhibitory effect, *Kirkpatrick* does little to prevent what is known as gerrymandering. See generally Backstrom, Robins & Eller, Issues in Gerrymandering: An Exploratory Measure of Partisan Gerrymandering Applied to Minnesota, 62 Minn.L.Rev. 1121, 1144–1159 (1978); cf. 394 U.S., at 534, n. 4. *Kirkpatrick's* object, achieving population equality, is far less ambitious than what would be required to address gerrymandering on a constitutional level.

In any event, the additional claim that *Kirkpatrick* actually promotes gerrymandering (as opposed to merely failing to stop it) is completely empty. A federal principle of population equality does not prevent any State from taking steps to inhibit gerrymandering, so long as a good-faith effort is made to achieve population equality as well. See, e.g., Colo. Const. art. V, § 47 (guidelines as to compactness, contiguity, boundaries of political subdivisions, and communities of interest); Mass. Const. art. CI, § 1 (boundaries); N.Y.Elec. Law § 4–100(b) (McKinney 1978) (compactness and boundaries).

. . .

B

The sole difference between appellants' theory and the argument we rejected in *Kirkpatrick* is that appellants have proposed a *de minimis* line that gives the illusion of rationality and predictability: the "inevitable statistical imprecision of the census." They argue, "Where, as here, the deviation from ideal district size is less than the known imprecision of the census figures, that variation is the functional equivalent of zero." There are two problems with this approach. First, appellants concentrate on the extent to which the census systematically undercounts actual population—a figure which is not known precisely and which, even if it were known, would not be relevant to this case. Second, the mere existence of statistical imprecision does not make small deviations among districts the functional equivalent of equality.

. . .

The census may systematically undercount population, and the rate of undercounting may vary from place to place. Those facts, however, do not render meaningless the differences in population between congressional districts, as determined by uncorrected census counts. To the contrary, the census data provide the only reliable—albeit less than perfect—indication of the districts' "real" relative population levels. . . . Furthermore, because the census count represents the "best population data available," see *Kirkpatrick*, 394 U.S., at 528, it is the only basis for good-faith attempts to achieve population equality. Attempts to explain population deviations on the basis of flaws in census data must be supported with a precision not achieved here. See id., at 535.

C

Given that the census-based population deviations in the Feldman Plan reflect real differences among the districts, it is clear that they could have been avoided or significantly reduced with a good-faith effort to achieve population equality. For that reason alone, it would be inappropriate to accept the Feldman Plan as "functionally equivalent" to a plan with districts of equal population.

. . .

IV

By itself, the foregoing discussion does not establish that the Feldman Plan is unconstitutional. Rather, appellees' success in proving that the Feldman Plan was not the product of a good-faith effort to achieve population equality means only that the burden shifted to the State to prove that the population deviations in its plan were necessary to achieve some legitimate state objective. White v. Weiser demonstrates that we are willing to defer to state legislative policies, so long as they are consistent with constitutional norms, even if they require small differences in the population of congressional districts. See 412 U.S., at 795–797; cf. Upham v. Seamon, 456 U.S. 37 (1982); Connor v. Finch, 431 U.S. 407, 414–415 (1977). Any number of consistently applied legislative policies might justify some variance, including, for instance, making districts compact, respecting municipal boundaries, preserving the cores of prior districts, and avoiding contests between incumbent Representatives. As long as the criteria are nondiscriminatory, see Gomillion v. Lightfoot, 364 U.S. 339 (1961), these are all legitimate objectives that on a proper showing could justify minor population deviations. See, e.g., West Virginia Civil Liberties Union v. Rockefeller, 336 F.Supp. 395, 398–400 (SD W.Va.1972) (approving plan with 0.78% maximum deviation as justified by compactness provision in state constitution); cf. Reynolds v. Sims, 377 U.S. 533, 579 (1964); Burns v.

Richardson, 384 U.S. 73, 89, and n. 16 (1966). The State must, however, show with some specificity that a particular objective required the specific deviations in its plan, rather than simply relying on general assertions. The showing required to justify population deviations is flexible, depending on the size of the deviations, the importance of the State's interests, the consistency with which the plan as a whole reflects those interests, and the availability of alternatives that might substantially vindicate those interests yet approximate population equality more closely. By necessity, whether deviations are justified requires case-by-case attention to these factors.

. . .

The District Court properly found that appellants did not justify the population deviations in this case.

V

The District Court properly applied the two-part test of Kirkpatrick v. Preisler to New Jersey's 1982 apportionment of districts for the United States House of Representatives. It correctly held that the population deviations in the plan were not functionally equal as a matter of law, and it found that the plan was not a good-faith effort to achieve population equality using the best available census data. It also correctly rejected appellants' attempt to justify the population deviations as not supported by the evidence. The judgment of the District Court, therefore, is affirmed.

Justice Stevens, concurring.

As an alternate ground for affirmance, the appellees contended at oral argument that the bizarre configuration of New Jersey's congressional districts, is sufficient to demonstrate that the plan was not adopted in "good faith." This argument, as I understand it, is a claim that the district boundaries are unconstitutional because they are the product of political gerrymandering. Since my vote is decisive in this case, it seems appropriate to explain how this argument influences my analysis of the question that divides the Court. As I have previously pointed out, political gerrymandering is one species of "vote dilution" that is proscribed by the Equal Protection Clause. Because an adequate judicial analysis of a gerrymandering claim raises special problems, I shall comment at some length on the legal basis for a gerrymandering claim, the standards for judging such a claim, and their relevance to the present case.

I

Relying on Article I, § 2 of the Constitution, as interpreted in Wesberry v. Sanders, 376 U.S. 1 (1964), and subsequent cases, appellees successfully challenged the congressional districting plan adopted by the New Jersey Legislature. For the reasons stated in Justice Brennan's opinion for the Court, which I join, the doctrine of *stare decisis* requires that result. It can be demonstrated, however, that the holding in *Wesberry,* as well as our holding today, has firmer roots in the Constitution than those provided by Article I, § 2.

. . .

The Equal Protection Clause requires every State to govern impartially. When a State adopts rules governing its election machinery or defining electoral boundaries, those rules must serve the interests of the entire community. See Reynolds v. Sims, supra, 377 U.S., at 565–566. If they serve no purpose other than to favor one segment—whether racial, ethnic, religious, economic, or political—that may occupy a position of strength at a particular point in time, or to disadvantage a politically weak segment of the community, they violate the constitutional guarantee of equal protection.

There is only one Equal Protection Clause. Since the Clause does not make some groups of citizens more equal than others, see Zobel v. Williams, 457 U.S. 55, —— (1982) (Brennan, J., concurring), its protection against vote dilution cannot be confined to racial groups. As long as it proscribes gerrymandering against such groups, its proscription must provide comparable protection for other cognizable groups of voters as well. . . .

II

Like Justice White, I am convinced that judicial preoccupation with the goal of perfect population equality is an inadequate method of judging the constitutionality of an apportionment plan. I would not hold that an obvious gerrymander is wholly immune from attack simply because it comes closer to perfect population equality than every competing plan. On the other hand, I do not find any virtue in the proposal to relax the standard set forth in *Wesberry* and subsequent cases, and to ignore population disparities after some arbitrarily defined threshold has been crossed. . . .

. . . .

III

In this case it is not necessary to go beyond the reasoning in the Court's opinions in Wesberry v. Sanders, supra, 376 U.S. 1 (1964), Kirkpatrick v. Preisler, 394 U.S. 526 (1969), and White v. Weiser, 412 U.S. 783 (1973), to reach the correct result. None of the additional criteria that I have mentioned would cast any doubt on the propriety of the Court's holding in this case. Although I need not decide whether the plan's shortcomings regarding shape and compactness, subdivision boundaries, and neutral decisionmaking would establish a prima facie case, these factors certainly strengthen my conclusion that the New Jersey plan violates the Equal Protection Clause.

A glance at the map, shows district configurations well deserving the kind of descriptive adjectives—"uncouth" and "bizarre"—that have traditionally been used to describe acknowledged gerrymanders. I have not applied the mathematical measures of compactness to the New Jersey map, but I think it likely that the plan would not fare well. In addition, while disregarding geographical compactness, the redistricting scheme wantonly disregards county boundaries. For example, in the words of a commentator, "In a flight of cartographic fancy, the Legislature packed North Jersey Republicans into a new district many call 'the Swan.' Its long neck and twisted body stretch from the New York suburbs to the rural upper reaches of the Delaware River." That district, the Fifth, contains segments of at least seven counties. The same commentator described the Seventh District, comprised of parts of five counties, as tracing "a curving partisan path through industrial Elizabeth, liberal, academic Princeton and largely Jewish Marlboro in Monmouth County. The resulting monstrosity was called 'the Fishhook' by detractors." 40 Cong.Q. 1194–1195 (1982).

Such a map prompts an inquiry into the process that led to its adoption. The plan was sponsored by the leadership in the Democratic party, which controlled both houses of the State Legislature as well as the Governor's office, and was signed into law the day before the inauguration of a Republican Governor. The legislators never formally explained the guidelines used in formulating their plan or in selecting it over other available plans. Several of the rejected plans contained districts that were more nearly equal in population, more compact, and more consistent with subdivision boundaries, including one submitted by a recognized expert, Dr. Ernest Reock, Jr., whose impartiality and academic credentials were not challenged. The District Court found that the Reock plan "was rejected because it did not reflect the leadership's partisan concerns." 535 F.Supp., at 982. This conclusion, which arises naturally from the absence of persuasive justifications for the rejection of the Reock plan, is buttressed by a letter written to Dr. Reock by the Democratic Speaker of the New Jersey General Assembly. This letter frankly explained the importance to the Democrats of taking advantage of their opportunity to control redistricting after the 1980 census. The Speaker justified his own overt partisanship by describing the political considerations that had motivated the Republican majority in the adoption of district plans in New Jersey in the past—and in other states at the present. In sum, the record indicates that the decision-making process leading to adoption of the challenged plan was far from neutral. It was designed to increase the number of Democrats, and to decrease the number of Republicans, that New Jersey's voters would send to Congress in future years. Finally, the record does not show any legitimate justifications for the irregularities in the New Jersey plan, although concededly the case was tried on a different theory in the District Court.

Because I have not made a comparative study of other districting plans, and because the State has not had the opportunity to offer justifications specifically directed toward the additional concerns I have discussed, I cannot conclude with absolute certainty that the New Jersey plan was an unconstitutional partisan gerrymander. But I am in full agreement with the Court's holding that, because the plan embodies deviations from population equality that have not been justified by any neutral state objective, it cannot stand. Further, if population equality provides the only check on political gerrymandering, it would be virtually impossible to fashion a fair and effective remedy in a case like this. For if the shape of legislative districts is entirely unconstrained, the dominant majority could no doubt respond to an unfavorable judgment by providing an even more grotesque-appearing map that reflects acceptable numerical equality with even greater political inequality. If federal judges can prevent that consequence by taking a hard look at the shape of things to come in the remedy hearing, I believe they can also scrutinize the original map with sufficient care to determine whether distortions have any rational basis in neutral criteria. Otherwise, the promise of Baker v. Carr and Reynolds v. Sims—that judicially manageable standards can assure "full and effective participation by all citizens," 377 U.S., at 565—may never be fulfilled.

Justice White, with whom The Chief Justice, Justice Powell, and Justice Rehnquist join, dissenting.

. . .

I respectfully dissent from the Court's unreasonable insistence on an unattainable perfection in the equalizing of congressional districts. The Court's decision today is not compelled by Kirkpatrick v. Preisler, 394 U.S. 526 (1969) and White v. Weiser, 412 U.S. 783 (1973), and if the Court is convinced that our cases demand the result reached today, the time has arrived to reconsider these precedents. . . .

I

"The achieving of fair and effective representation for all citizens is concededly the basic aim of legislative apportionment." Reynolds v. Sims, 377 U.S. 533, 566 (1964). One must suspend credulity to believe that the Court's draconian response to a trifling 0.6984% maximum deviation promotes "fair and effective representation" for the people of New Jersey. The requirement that "as nearly as is practicable one man's vote in a congressional election is to be worth as much as another's," Wesberry v. Sanders, 376 U.S. 1, 7–8 (1964), must be understood in light of the malapportionment in the states at the time *Wesberry* was decided. The plaintiffs in *Wesberry* were voters in a congressional district (pop. 823,680) encompassing Atlanta that was three times larger than Georgia's smallest district (272,154) and more than double the size of an average district. Because the state had not reapportioned for 30 years, the Atlanta District possessing one-fifth of Georgia's population had only one-tenth of the Congressmen. Georgia was not atypical; congressional districts throughout the country had not been redrawn for decades and deviations of over 50% were the rule. These substantial differences in district size diminished, in a real sense, the representativeness of congressional elections. The Court's invalidation of these profoundly unequal districts should not be read as a demand for precise mathematical equality between the districts. Indeed, the Court sensibly observed that "it may not be possible [for the States] to draw Congressional districts with mathematical precision." Id., at 7–8. . . .

. . .

If today's decision simply produced an unjustified standard with little practical import, it would be bad enough. Unfortunately, I fear that the Court's insistence that "there are no *de minimis* population variations, which could practicably be avoided, but which nonetheless meet the standard of Art. I, § 2 without justification," invites further litigation of virtually every congressional redistricting plan in the nation. At least twelve states which have completed redistricting on the basis of the 1980 census have adopted plans with a higher deviation than that presented here, and four others have deviations quite similar to New Jersey's. Of course, under the Court's rationale, even Rhode Island's plan—whose two districts have a deviation of 0.02% or about 95 people—would be subject to constitutional attack.

In all such cases, state legislatures will be hard pressed to justify their preference for the selected plan. A good-faith effort to achieve population equality is not enough if the population variances are not "unavoidable." The court must consider whether the population differences could have been further "reduced or eliminated altogether." With the assistance of computers, there will generally be a plan with an even more minimal deviation from the mathematical ideal. Then, "the State must bear the burden of proving that each significant variance between districts was necessary to achieve some legitimate goal." As this case illustrates, literally any variance between districts will be considered "significant." The state's burden will not be easily met: "the State bears the burden of justifying the differences with particularity." When the state fails to sustain its burden, the result will generally be that a court must select an alternative plan. . . .

The only way a legislature or bipartisan commission can hope to avoid litigation will be to dismiss all other legitimate concerns and opt automatically for the districting plan with the smallest deviation. Yet no one can seriously contend that such an inflexible insistence upon mathematical exactness will serve to promote "fair and effective representation." The more likely result of today's extension of *Kirkpatrick* is to move closer to fulfilling Justice Fortas' prophecy that "a legislature might have to ignore the boundaries of common sense, running the congressional district line down the middle of the corridor of an apartment house or even dividing the residents of a single-family house between two districts." 394 U.S., at 538. Such sterile and mechanistic application only brings the principle of "one man, one vote" into disrepute.

II

One might expect the Court had strong reasons to force this Sisyphean task upon the states. Yet the Court offers no positive virtues that will follow from its decision. . . .

Instead the Court is purely defensive in support of its decision. . . .

. . .

Yet today the Court—with no mention of the contrary holdings in *Kirkpatrick*—opines: "Any number of consistently applied legislative policies might justify some variance, including for instance, making districts compact, respecting municipal boundaries, preserving the cores of prior districts, and avoiding contests between incumbent Representatives. I, of course, welcome the Court's overruling of these ill-considered holdings of *Kirkpatrick.* There should be no question but that state legislatures may account for political and geographic boundaries in order to preserve traditional subdivisions and achieve compact and contiguous districts. Justice Stevens recognizes that courts should "give greater weight to the importance of the State's interests and the consistency with which those interests are served than to the size of the deviations." Thus, a majority of the Court appears ready to apply this new standard "with a strong measure of deference to the legitimate concerns of the State." Post, (Powell, J., dissenting).

In order that legislatures have room to accommodate these legitimate noncensus factors, a range of *de minimis* population deviation, like that permitted in the legislative reapportionment cases, is required. The Court's insistence that every deviation, no matter how small, be justified with specificity discourages legislatures from considering these "legitimate" factors in making their plans, lest the justification be found wanting, the plan invalidated, and a judicially drawn substitute put in its place. Moreover, the requirement of precise mathematical equality continues to invite those who would bury their political opposition to employ equipopulous gerrymanders. A *de minimis* range would not preclude such gerrymanders but would at least force the political cartographer to justify his work on its own terms.

III

Our cases dealing with state legislative apportionment have taken a more sensible approach. We have recognized that certain small deviations do not, in themselves, ordinarily constitute a *prima facie* constitutional violation. Gaffney v. Cummings, 412 U.S. 735 (1973); White v. Regester, 412 U.S. 755 (1973). Moreover, we have upheld plans with reasonable variances that were necessary to account for political subdivisions, Mahan v. Howell, 410 U.S. 315 (1973), to preserve the voting strength of minority groups, and to insure political fairness, Gaffney v. Cummings, supra. . . .

Bringing together our legislative and congressional cases does not imply overlooking relevant differences between the two. States normally draw a larger number of legislative districts, which accordingly require a greater margin to account for geographical and political boundaries. "[C]ongressional districts are not so intertwined and freighted with strictly local interests as are state legislative districts." White v. Weiser, 412 U.S., at 793. Furthermore, because Congressional districts are generally much larger than state legislative districts, each percentage point of variation represents a commensurately greater number of people. But these are differences of degree. They suggest that the level at which courts should entertain challenges to districting plans, absent unusual circumstances, should be lower in the congressional cases, but not altogether nonexistent. Although I am not wedded to a precise figure, in light of the current range of population deviations, a 5% cutoff appears reasonable. I would not entertain judicial challenges, absent extraordinary circumstances, where the maximum deviation is less than 5%. Somewhat greater deviations, if rationally related to an important state interest, may also be permissible. Certainly, the maintaining of compact, contiguous districts, the respecting of political subdivisions, and efforts to assure political fairness, e.g., Gaffney v. Cummings, supra, constitute such interests.

I would not hold up New Jersey's plan as a model reflection of such interests. Nevertheless, the deviation involved here is *de minimis,* and, regardless of what other infirmities the plan may have, constitutional or otherwise, there is no violation of Art. I, § 2—the sole issue before us. It would, of course, be a different matter if appellees could demonstrate that New Jersey's plan invidiously discriminated against a racial or political group. See White v. Regester, 412 U.S. 755 (1973); Gaffney v. Cummings, supra, at 751–754; Whitcomb v. Chavis, 403 U.S. 124 (1971); Gomillion v. Lightfoot, 364 U.S. 339 (1960).

. . .

Justice Powell, dissenting.

I join Justice White's excellent dissenting opinion, and reaffirm my previously expressed doubt that "the Constitution—a vital and living charter after nearly two centuries because of the wise flexibility of its key provisions—could be read to require a rule of mathematical exactitude in legislative reapportionment." White v. Weiser, 412 U.S. 783, 798 (1973) (Powell, J., concurring). I write separately to express some additional thoughts on gerrymandering and its relation to apportionment factors that presumably were not thought relevant under Kirkpatrick v. Preisler, 394 U.S. 526 (1969).

. . .

II

The extraordinary map of the New Jersey congressional districts, prompts me to comment on the separate question of gerrymandering—"the deliberate and arbitrary distortion of district boundaries and populations for partisan or personal political purposes," *Kirkpatrick,* supra, at 538 (Fortas, J., concurring). I am in full agreement with Justice White's observation a decade ago that gerrymandering presents "a far greater potential threat to equality of representation" than a State's failure to achieve "precise adherence to admittedly inexact census figures." Id., at 555 (White, J., dissenting). I also believe that the injuries that result from gerrymandering may rise to constitutional dimensions. . . .

I therefore am prepared to entertain constitutional challenges to partisan gerrymandering that reaches the level of discrimination described by Justice Stevens.

In this case, one cannot rationally believe that the New Jersey Legislature considered factors other than the most partisan political goals and population equality. It hardly could be suggested, for example, that the contorted districts 3, 5, and 7 reflect any attempt to follow natural, historical, or local political boundaries. Nor do these district lines reflect any consideration of the likely effect on the quality of representation when the boundaries are so artificial that they are likely to confound the congressmen themselves. As Judge Gibbons stated eloquently in his dissent below:

> "The apportionment map produced by P.L.1982, c. 1 leaves me, as a citizen of New Jersey, disturbed. It creates several districts which are anything but compact, and at least one district which is contiguous only for yachtsmen. While municipal boundaries have been maintained, there has been little effort to create districts having a community of interests. In some districts, for example, different television and radio stations, different newspapers, and different transportation systems serve the northern and southern localities. Moreover the harshly partisan tone of Speaker Christopher Jackman's letter to Ernest C. Reock, Jr. is disedifying, to say the least. It is plain, as well, that partisanship produced artificial bulges or appendages of two districts so as to place the residences of Congressmen Smith and Courter

in districts where they would be running against incumbents." Daggett v. Kimmelman, 535 F.Supp. 978, 984 (NJ 1982).

This summary statement by Judge Gibbons, a resident of New Jersey, is powerful and persuasive support for a conclusion that the New Jersey Legislature's redistricting plan is an unconstitutional gerrymander. Because this precise issue was not addressed by the District Court, however, it need not be reached here. As to the issue of population equality, I dissent for the reasons set forth above and in Justice White's dissenting opinion.

––––––––

BROWN v. THOMSON, 462 U.S. 835 (1983). The Wyoming Constitution provides that its House of Representatives shall be apportioned according to population except that each county shall have at least one representative. In 1981 the apportionment statute provided for a scheme which gave a representative to Niobrara County even though its population was 60% below the mean. Overall the plan provided a maximum deviation of 89% and an average deviation of 16%. The statute also provided that if the allocation of a seat to Niobrara County was held invalid its population should be added to another county and the number of seats in the House reduced from 64 to 63. A suit was brought challenging this scheme. A majority of the Court in an opinion written by Justice Powell upheld the statute as applied to Niobrara County. The Court said that only its receiving a seat was challenged and hence it was not necessary to consider whether adherence to county boundaries justified the population deviations that exist throughout Wyoming districts. Looking only at the marginal effects of the grant to the one county, the Court found that "this case presents an unusually strong example of an apportionment plan the population variations of which are entirely the result of the consistent and nondiscriminatory application of a legitimate state policy." The Court found that Wyoming's interest in maintaining county representation in the legislature was not outweighed by the marginal impact giving a seat to Niobrara County had on representation in the entire House.

Justices O'Connor and Stevens, who had voted with the majority in Karcher v. Daggett, added a statement noting that the Court was deciding only the additional deviation caused by the allocation of a seat to Niobrara County and saying: "I have the gravest doubts that a statewide legislative plan with an 85% maximum deviation would survive constitutional scrutiny despite the presence of the State's strong interest in preserving county boundaries. I join the Court's opinion on the understanding that nothing in it suggests that this Court would uphold such a scheme."

Justices Brennan, White, Marshall, and Blackmun dissented.

––––––––

REYNOLDS AND LOCAL GOVERNMENTAL UNITS

In Hadley v. Junior College Dist., 397 U.S. 50 (1970), eight school districts had combined to form a junior college district governed by six trustees. The governing statute provided that if no school district had more than $33\frac{1}{3}\%$ of the population all trustees were elected at large; if a district had between $33\frac{1}{3}\%$ and 50% of the population it would elect two trustees with the rest elected at large from the remaining districts; if a district had between 50% and $66\frac{2}{3}\%$ it would elect three trustees; and if over $66\frac{2}{3}\%$ it would elect four. This scheme was challenged by residents of a school district having 60% of the population but permitted to elect only 50% of the trustees. The Court held this scheme invalid. Justice Black, speaking for the majority of the Court, said, in part: "[In Avery v. Midland County, 390 U.S. 474 (1968) we held that] a qualified voter in a local election also has a constitutional right to have his vote counted with substantially the same weight as that of any other voter in a case where the elected officials exercised 'general governmental powers over the entire geographic area served by the body.'

"Appellants in this case argue that the junior college trustees exercised general governmental powers over the entire district and that under *Avery* the State was thus required to apportion the trustees according to population on an equal basis, as far as practicable. Appellants argue that since the trustees can levy and collect taxes, issue bonds with certain restrictions, hire and fire teachers, make contracts, collect fees, supervise and discipline students, pass on petitions to annex school districts, acquire property by condemnation, and in general manage the operations of the junior college, their powers are equivalent, for apportionment purposes, to those exercised by the county commissioners in *Avery*. We feel that these powers, while not fully as broad as those of the Midland County Commissioners,[6] certainly show that the trustees perform important governmental functions within the districts, and we think these powers are general enough and have sufficient impact throughout the district to justify the conclusion that the principle which we applied in *Avery* should also be applied here. . . .

. . .

"When a court is asked to decide whether a State is required by the Constitution to give each qualified voter the same power in an election open to all, there is no discernible, valid reason why constitutional distinctions should be drawn on the basis of the purpose of the election. If one person's vote is given less weight through unequal apportionment, his right to equal voting participation is impaired just as much when he votes for a school board member as when he votes for a state legislator. . . .

"It has also been urged that we distinguish for apportionment purposes between elections for 'legislative' officials and those for 'administrative' officers. Such a suggestion would leave courts with an equally unmanageable principle since governmental activities 'cannot easily be classified in the neat categories favored by civics texts', *Avery*, supra, at 482, and it must also be rejected. We therefore hold today that as a general rule, whenever a state or local government decides to select persons by popular election to perform governmental functions, the Equal Protection Clause of the Fourteenth Amendment requires that each qualified voter must be given an equal opportunity to participate in that election, and when members of an elected body are chosen from separate districts, each district must be established on a basis that will insure, as far as is practicable, that equal numbers of voters can vote for proportionally equal numbers of officials. It is of course possible that there might be some case in which a State elects certain functionaries whose duties are so far removed from normal governmental activities and so disproportionately effect different groups that a popular election in compliance with *Reynolds*, supra, might not be required, but certainly we see nothing in the present case that indicates that the activities of these trustees fit in that category. Education has traditionally been a vital governmental function, and these trustees, whose election the State has opened to all qualified voters, are governmental officials in every relevant sense of that term. . . .

[6] The Midland County Commissioners established and maintained the county jail, appointed numerous county officials, made contracts, built roads and bridges, administered the county welfare system, performed duties in connection with elections, set the county tax rate, issued bonds, adopted the county budget, built and ran hospitals, airports, and libraries, fixed school district boundaries, established a housing authority, and determined the election districts for county commissioners. *Avery*, supra, at 476–477.

"Although the statutory scheme reflects to some extent a principle of equal voting power, it does so in a way that does not comport with constitutional requirements. This is so because the Act necessarily results in a systematic discrimination against voters in the more populous school districts. This discrimination occurs because whenever a large district's percentage of the total enumeration falls within a certain percentage range it is always allocated the number of trustees corresponding to the bottom of that range. . . . Such built-in discrimination against voters in large districts cannot be sustained as a sufficient compliance with the constitutional mandate that each person's vote count as much as another's, as far as practicable. Consequently Missouri cannot allocate the junior college trustees according to the statutory formula employed in this case. . . .

"In holding that the guarantee of equal voting strength for each voter applies in all elections of governmental officials, we do not feel that the States will be inhibited in finding ways to insure that legitimate political goals of representation are achieved. We have previously upheld against constitutional challenge an election scheme that required that candidates be residents of certain districts that did not contain equal numbers of people. Dusch v. Davis, 387 U.S. 112 (1967). Since all the officials in that case were elected at large, the right of each voter was given equal treatment.[a] We have also held that where a State chooses to select members of an official body by appointment rather than election, and that choice does not itself offend the Constitution, the fact that each official does not 'represent' the same number of people does not deny those people equal protection of the laws. Sailors v. Board of Education, 387 U.S. 105 (1967); cf. Fortson v. Morris, 385 U.S. 231 (1966).[b] And a State may, in certain cases, limit the right to vote to a particular group or class of people. As we said before, '[v]iable local governments may need many innovations, numerous combinations of old and new devices, great flexibility in municipal arrangements to meet changing urban conditions. We see nothing in the Constitution to prevent experimentation.' Sailors, supra, at 110–111. But once a State has decided to use the process of popular election and 'once the class of voters is chosen and their qualifications specified, we see no constitutional way by which equality of voting power may be evaded.' Gray v. Sanders, 372 U.S. 368, 381 (1963)."

In Lockport v. Citizens for Community Action, 430 U.S. 259 (1977), a New York law provided that a new county charter would go into effect only if approved in a referendum election by separate majorities of the voters who live in the cities within the county, and of those who live outside the cities. The Court held that this arrangement did not violate the equal protection clause in a case where there were many more voters in the cities than in the county outside

---

[a] See also Dallas County, Ala. v. Reese, 421 U.S. 477 (1975) in which the Court upheld a requirement that county commissioners be elected by countywide balloting but with a requirement that a member be elected from each of four districts having substantial population disparities. The Court said such a scheme could be overturned only on a showing that it "in fact operates impermissibly to dilute the voting strength of an identifiable element of the voting population."

[b] In Fortson the Court upheld a provision of the Constitution of Georgia that when no candidate for the office of Governor receives a majority of votes cast in the general election the Governor shall be elected by a majority of the members of the Georgia General Assembly from the two persons having the highest number of votes. The Court said: "There is no provision of the United States Constitution or any of its amendments which either expressly or impliedly dictates the method a State must use to select its Governor. A method which would be valid if initially employed is equally valid when employed as an alternative."

The Court relied on Fortson in Rodriguez v. Popular Democratic Party, 457 U.S. 1 (1982), sustaining a Puerto Rico statute permitting the political party of an incumbent legislator to appoint an interim replacement when the legislator vacates the position. The Court rejected an argument that the Constitution requires election of state legislators. The Constitution confers no "right to vote, per se," but a right to participate on an equal basis when elections are held.

the cities and where the charter was rejected because of its failure to secure a majority of the county voters. The city voters outnumbered the county voters and a majority of all the voters in the entire county voted in favor of the proposal. The Court noted that the interests of the city and the noncity voters were likely to be quite different with respect to the adoption of a new county charter, and concluded:

> "The provisions of New York law here in question no more than recognize the realities of these substantially differing electoral interests. Granting to these provisions the presumption of constitutionality to which every duly enacted state and federal law is entitled, we are unable to conclude that they violate the Equal Protection Clause of the Fourteenth Amendment."

In Salyer Land Co. v. Tulare Lake Basin Water Storage Dist., 410 U.S. 719 (1973), the defendant water storage district was organized under a California law which provided for elections for directors in which only the holders of title to land in the district were entitled to vote and in which each such voter was entitled to cast one vote for each $100 value of land and improvements in the district. 77 persons resided within the district. 189 persons owned land in amounts up to 80 acres each. Four large operators owned 85% of the land with one corporation owning enough to give it a majority of the board of directors. A landowner, a lessee, and a resident of the district brought suit in the federal court seeking declaratory and injunctive relief asserting that the restriction of voting to landowners and the weighting of votes according to valuation of land owned were unconstitutional. The trial court ruled for the defendant and the Supreme Court affirmed.

Justice Rehnquist, speaking for the Court, distinguished earlier cases invalidating restricting voting to landowners on the ground that those cases involved residents of units of local governments exercising general governmental power, whereas the district here "by reason of its special limited purpose and of the disproportionate effect of its activities on landowners as a group" is an exception to the rule of *Reynolds* and *Hadley.*

"The appellee district in this case, although vested with some typical governmental powers, has relatively limited authority. Its primary purpose, indeed the reason for its existence, is to provide for the acquisition, storage, and distribution of water for farming in the Tulare Lake Basin. It provides no other general public services such as schools, housing, transportation, utilities, roads or anything else of the type ordinarily financed by a municipal body. There are no towns, shops, hospitals or other facilities designed to improve the quality of life within the district boundaries and it does not have a fire department, police, buses, or trains.

"Not only does the district not exercise what might be thought of as 'normal governmental' authority, but its actions disproportionately affect landowners. All of the costs of district projects are assessed against land by assessors in proportion to the benefits received. Likewise, charges for services rendered are collectible from persons receiving their benefit in proportion to the services. When such persons are delinquent in payment, just as in the case of delinquency in payments of assessments, such charges become a lien on the land. Calif. Water Code §§ 47183, 46280. In short, there is no way that the economic burdens of district operations can fall on residents *qua* residents, and the operations of the districts primarily affect the land within their boundaries.

"Under these circumstances it is quite understandable that the statutory framework for election of directors of the appellee focuses on the land benefited, rather than on people as such."

With respect to the argument that weighting the vote according to assessed valuation constituted a denial of Equal Protection, he noted that the benefits and burdens to each landowner in the district are in proportion to the assessed value of the land. Thus, in a recent district project a small landowner who was given one vote was assessed $46 as his share of the cost while the large corporate farm which was given 37,825 votes was assessed $817,685 as its share. "We cannot say that the California legislative decision to permit voting in the same proportion is not rationally based."

Justices Douglas, Brennan and Marshall dissented.

In Ball v. James, 451 U.S. 355 (1981) the Court applied the *Salyer Land* case to uphold the system under which the Salt River Project Agricultural Improvement and Power District in Arizona elects its directors with voting limited to landowners and voting power apportioned according to the amount of land the voter owns. The Salt River District encompasses almost half the population of Arizona, including large parts of Phoenix and other cities. While all of its water is allocated according to land ownership, 25% of it goes for urban uses. The District generates and sells electric power, with 98% of its revenues coming from such sales. Despite these facts demonstrating that the District plays a major role in the lives of most Arizonians, Justice Stewart, writing for the majority, said:

> "[T]he District simply does not exercise the sort of governmental powers that invoke the strict demands of *Reynolds*. The District cannot impose ad valorem property taxes or sales taxes. It cannot enact any laws governing the conduct of citizens, nor does it administer such normal functions of government as the maintenance of streets, the operations of schools, or sanitation, health, or welfare services." He concluded that limiting the vote to landowners and making the weight of their vote dependent on the number of acres owned was valid because it bears "a reasonable relationship to its statutory objectives."

Justice Powell concurred in the Court's opinion, and added that in this case the public was adequately protected by the fact that the Arizona legislature could control the electoral composition of the District. Justices White, Brennan, Marshall, and Blackmun dissented.

THE EQUAL PROTECTION CLAUSE AND THE REQUIREMENT OF SUPER-MAJORITIES

In Gordon v. Lance, 403 U.S. 1 (1971), the Court had before it the question of the validity of a state constitutional provision requiring the approval of 60% of the voters in a referendum election before political subdivisions could incur bonded indebtedness or increase tax rates. The case resulted from a school election in which a bond issue and a tax increase received 51.5% of the vote but were declared defeated. In upholding the state constitutional provision, the Court said, in part:

> "Although West Virginia has not denied any group access to the ballot, it has indeed made it more difficult for some kinds of governmental actions to be taken. Certainly any departure from strict majority rule gives disproportionate power to the minority. But there is nothing in the language of the Constitution, our history or our cases that requires that a majority always prevail on every issue. . . .

> "The Federal Constitution itself provides that a simple majority vote is insufficient on some issues; the provisions on impeachment and ratification of treaties are but two examples. Moreover, the Bill of Rights removes

entire areas of legislation from the concept of majoritarian supremacy.
.   .   .
.   .   .

"We conclude that so long as such provisions do not discriminate against or authorize discrimination against any identifiable class they do not violate the Equal Protection Clause.   .   .   ."

3. QUALIFICATIONS OF VOTERS

HARPER v. VIRGINIA STATE BOARD OF ELECTIONS

383 U.S. 663, 86 S.Ct. 1079, 16 L.Ed.2d 169 (1966).

Mr. Justice Douglas delivered the opinion of the Court.[a]

These are suits by Virginia residents to have declared unconstitutional Virginia's poll tax. The three-judge District Court, feeling bound by our decision in Breedlove v. Suttles, 302 U.S. 277, dismissed the complaint. See 240 F.Supp. 270. The cases came here on appeal and we noted probable jurisdiction.   .   .   .

While the right to vote in federal elections is conferred by Art. I, § 2, of the Constitution   .   .   .   the right to vote in state elections is nowhere expressly mentioned. It is argued that the right to vote in state elections is implicit, particularly by reason of the First Amendment and that it may not constitutionally be conditioned upon the payment of a tax or fee.   .   .   .   We do not stop to canvass the relation between voting and political expression. For it is enough to say that once the franchise is granted to the electorate, lines may not be drawn which are inconsistent with the Equal Protection Clause of the Fourteenth Amendment. That is to say, the right of suffrage "is subject to the imposition of state standards which are not discriminatory and which do not contravene any restriction that Congress, acting pursuant to its constitutional powers, has imposed." Lassiter v. Northampton County Board of Elections, 360 U.S. 45, 51. We were speaking there of a state literacy test which we sustained, warning that the result would be different if a literacy test, fair on its face, were used to discriminate against a class. Id., at 53. But the *Lassiter* case does not govern the result here, because, unlike a poll tax, the "ability to read and write   .   .   .   has some relation to standards designed to promote intelligent use of the ballot." Id., at 51.

We conclude that a State violates the Equal Protection Clause of the Fourteenth Amendment whenever it makes the affluence of the voter or payment of any fee an electoral standard. Voter qualifications have no relation to wealth nor to paying or not paying this or any other tax. Our cases demonstrate that the Equal Protection Clause of the Fourteenth Amendment restrains the States from fixing voter qualifications which invidiously discriminate. Thus without questioning the power of a State to impose reasonable residence restrictions on the availability of the ballot (see Pope v. Williams, 193 U.S. 621), we held in Carrington v. Rash, 380 U.S. 89, that a State may not deny the opportunity to vote to a bona fide resident merely because he is a member of the armed services. "By forbidding a soldier ever to controvert the

---

[a] In the two decades 1934–1954, five states abolished the poll tax: Louisiana, Florida, Georgia, South Carolina and Tennessee. This voluntary action then stopped—probably because of feelings stirred by the 1954 *Brown* decision. As of 1963, payment of a poll tax was a prerequisite to voting in five states: Alabama, Arkansas, Mississippi, Texas and Virginia. Burke Marshall reported: "By now the tax is a negligible, bi-racial deterrent to voting." 27 Law & Contemp.Pr. 455, 464 (1962). In 1962 Congress proposed, and by 1964 the requisite number of states had ratified, the Twenty-fourth Amendment outlawing the "poll tax or other tax" as a condition for voting in federal elections.

presumption of non-residence, the Texas Constitution imposes an invidious discrimination in violation of the Fourteenth Amendment." Id., at 96. And see Louisiana v. United States, 380 U.S. 145. Previously we had said that neither homesite nor occupation "affords a permissible basis for distinguishing between qualified voters within the State." Gray v. Sanders, 372 U.S. 368, 380. We think the same must be true of requirements of wealth or affluence or payment of a fee.

Long ago in Yick Wo v. Hopkins, 118 U.S. 356, 370, the Court referred to "the political franchise of voting" as a "fundamental political right, because preservative of all rights." Recently in Reynolds v. Sims, 377 U.S. 533, 561–562, we said: "Undoubtedly, the right of suffrage is a fundamental matter in a free and democratic society. Especially since the right to exercise the franchise in a free and unimpaired manner is preservative of other basic civil and political rights, any alleged infringement of the right of citizens to vote must be carefully and meticulously scrutinized." . . .

It is argued that a State may exact fees from citizens for many different kinds of licenses; that if it can demand from all an equal fee for a driver's license, it can demand from all an equal poll tax for voting. But we must remember that the interest of the State, when it comes to voting, is limited to the power to fix qualifications. Wealth, like race, creed, or color, is not germane to one's ability to participate intelligently in the electoral process. Lines drawn on the basis of wealth or property, like those of race (Korematsu v. United States, 323 U.S. 214, 216), are traditionally disfavored. See Edwards v. People of State of California, 314 U.S. 160, 184–185 (Jackson, J., concurring); Griffin v. People of State of Illinois, 351 U.S. 12; Douglas v. People of State of California, 372 U.S. 353. To introduce wealth or payment of a fee as a measure of a voter's qualifications is to introduce a capricious or irrelevant factor. The degree of the discrimination is irrelevant. In this context—that is, as a condition of obtaining a ballot—the requirement of fee paying causes an "invidious" discrimination (Skinner v. State of Oklahoma, 316 U.S. 535, 541) that runs afoul of the Equal Protection Clause. Levy "by the poll," as stated in Breedlove v. Suttles, supra, 302 U.S. at 281, is an old familiar form of taxation; and we say nothing to impair its validity so long as it is not made a condition to the exercise of the franchise. Breedlove v. Suttles sanctioned its use as "a prerequisite of voting." Id., at 283. To that extent the *Breedlove* case is overruled.

We agree, of course, with Mr. Justice Holmes that the Due Process Clause of the Fourteenth Amendment "does not enact Mr. Herbert Spencer's Social Statics" (Lochner v. People of State of New York, 198 U.S. 45, 75). Likewise, the Equal Protection Clause is not shackled to the political theory of a particular era. In determining what lines are unconstitutionally discriminatory, we have never been confined to historic notions of equality, any more than we have restricted due process to a fixed catalogue of what was at a given time deemed to be the limits of fundamental rights. See Malloy v. Hogan, 378 U.S. 1, 5–6. Notions of what constitutes equal treatment for purposes of the Equal Protection Clause *do* change. This Court in 1896 held that laws providing for separate public facilities for white and Negro citizens did not deprive the latter of the equal protection and treatment that the Fourteenth Amendment commands. Plessy v. Ferguson, 163 U.S. 537. Seven of the eight Justices then sitting subscribed to the Court's opinion, thus joining in expressions of what constituted unequal and discriminatory treatment that sound strange to a contemporary ear. When, in 1954—more than a half-century later—we repudiated the "separate-but-equal" doctrine of *Plessy* as respects public education we stated: "In approaching this problem, we cannot turn the clock back to 1868 when the Amendment was adopted, or even to 1896 when Plessy v. Ferguson was written." Brown v. Board of Education, 347 U.S. 483, 492.

In a recent searching re-examination of the Equal Protection Clause, we held, as already noted, that "the opportunity for equal participation by all voters in the election of state legislators" is required. Reynolds v. Sims, supra, 377 U.S. at 566. We decline to qualify that principle by sustaining this poll tax. Our conclusion, like that in Reynolds v. Sims, is founded not on what we think governmental policy should be, but on what the Equal Protection Clause requires.

We have long been mindful that where fundamental rights and liberties are asserted under the Equal Protection Clause, classifications which might invade or restrain them must be closely scrutinized and carefully confined. See, e.g., Skinner v. State of Oklahoma, 316 U.S. 535, 541; Reynolds v. Sims, 377 U.S. 533, 561–562; Carrington v. Rash, supra; Baxstrom v. Herold, 383 U.S. 107; Cox v. State of Louisiana, 379 U.S. 536, 580–581 (Black, J., concurring).

Those principles apply here. For to repeat, wealth or fee paying has, in our view, no relation to voting qualifications; the right to vote is too precious, too fundamental to be so burdened or conditioned.

Reversed.

Mr. Justice Black, dissenting.

. . .   The Court   . . .   overrules *Breedlove* in part, but its opinion reveals that it does so not by using its limited power to interpret the original meaning of the Equal Protection Clause, but by giving that clause a new meaning which it believes represents a better governmental policy. From this action I dissent.

. . .

The Court's justification for consulting its own notions rather than following the original meaning of the Constitution, as I would, apparently is based on the belief of the majority of the Court that for this Court to be bound by the original meaning of the Constitution is an intolerable and debilitating evil; that our Constitution should not be "shackled to the political theory of a particular era," and that to save the country from the original Constitution the Court must have constant power to renew it and keep it abreast with this Court's more enlightening theories of what is best for our society. It seems to me that this is not only an attack on the great value of our Constitution itself but also on the concept of a written constitution which is to survive through the years as originally written unless changed through the amendment process which the Framers wisely provided. Moreover, when a "political theory" embodied in our Constitution becomes outdated, it seems to me that a majority of the nine members of this Court are not only without constitutional power but are far less qualified to choose a new constitutional political theory than the people of this country proceeding in the manner provided by Article V.

The people have not found it impossible to amend their Constitution to meet new conditions. The Equal Protection Clause itself is the product of the peoples' desire to use their constitutional power to amend the Constitution to meet new problems. . . .

Mr. Justice Harlan, whom Mr. Justice Stewart joins, dissenting.

The final demise of state poll taxes, already totally proscribed by the Twenty-Fourth Amendment with respect to federal elections and abolished by the States themselves in all but four States with respect to state elections, is perhaps in itself not of great moment. But the fact that the *coup de grace* has been administered by this Court instead of being left to the affected States or to the federal political process should be a matter of continuing concern to all interested in maintaining the proper role of this tribunal under our scheme of government.

. . .

DUNN v. BLUMSTEIN, 405 U.S. 330 (1972).　In holding invalid a statute imposing as a condition of voting residence in the state for one year and the county for three months prior to the election, the Court said:

A.

"Durational residence requirements completely bar from voting all residents not meeting the fixed durational standards.　By denying some citizens the right to vote, such laws deprive them of 'a fundamental political right, . . . preservative of all rights.'　Reynolds v. Sims, 377 U.S. 533, 562 (1964). There is no need to repeat now the labors undertaken in earlier cases to analyze this right to vote and to explain in detail the judicial role in reviewing state statutes which selectively distribute the franchise.　In decision after decision, this Court has made clear that a citizen has a constitutionally protected right to participate in elections on an equal basis with other citizens in the jurisdiction. See, e.g., Evans v. Cornman, 398 U.S. 419, 421–422 (1970); [a] Kramer v. Union Free School District No. 15, 395 U.S. 621, 626–628 (1969); [b] Cipriano v. City of Houma, 395 U.S. 701, 706 (1969); [c] Harper v. Virginia State Board of Elections, 383 U.S. 663, 667 (1966); Carrington v. Rash, 380 U.S. 89, 93–94 (1965); [d] Reynolds v. Sims, supra.　This 'equal right to vote,' Evans v. Cornman, supra, 398 U.S., at 426, is not absolute; the States have the power to impose voter qualifications, and to regulate access to the franchise in other ways. . . .　But, as a general matter, 'before that right [to vote] can be restricted, the purpose of the restriction and the assertedly overriding interests served by it must meet close constitutional scrutiny.'　Evans v. Cornman, 398 U.S. 419, 422 (1970);　see Bullock v. Carter, 405 U.S. 134 (1972). [e]

"Tennessee urges that this case is controlled by Drueding v. Devlin, 380 U.S. 125 (1965).　*Drueding* was a decision upholding Maryland's durational residence requirements.　The District Court tested those requirements by the equal protection standard applied to ordinary state regulations:　whether the exclusions are reasonably related to a permissible state interest.　234 F.Supp. 721, 724–725 (Md.1964).　We summarily affirmed *per curiam* without the benefit of argument.　But if it was not clear then, it is certainly clear now that a

[a] Persons living on the grounds of the National Institutes of Health, a federal reservation or enclave located within the boundaries of Maryland, were denied the right to vote in Maryland elections on the ground that they were not residents of Maryland.　The Court held the denial unconstitutional: "In nearly every election, federal, state, and local, for offices from the Presidency to the school board, and on the entire variety of ballot propositions, appellees have a stake equal to that of other Maryland residents.　As the District Court concluded, they are entitled under the Fourteenth Amendment to protect that stake by exercising the equal right to vote."

[b] A New York law provided that residents of school districts could vote in school district elections only if they (1) own or lease taxable real property in the district, or (2) are parents or have custody of children enrolled in the local public schools.　The Court noted that the statute was to be given "a close and exacting examination" because "statutes distributing the franchise constitute the foundation of our representative society."　The Court then held the statute unconstitutional because the state had not demonstrated a "compelling state interest" justifying the limitation on the franchise.

[c] A state provision giving only "property taxpayers" the right to vote in elections called to approve the issuance of revenue bonds by a municipal utility was held unconstitutional.　The Court found no basis for the limitation since "the benefits and burdens of the bond issue fall indiscriminately on the property owner and nonproperty owner alike."

[d] The Court held invalid a Texas constitutional provision prohibiting a member of the armed forces who moves his home to Texas from voting in any election so long as he is a member of the armed forces.

[e] A Texas law requiring candidates to pay large filing fees in order to have their names placed on the ballot in primary elections was held invalid.　The Court said:

"Because the Texas filing fee scheme has a real and appreciable impact on the exercise of the franchise, and because this impact is related to the resources of the voters supporting a particular candidate, we conclude, as in Harper, that the laws must be 'closely scrutinized' and found reasonably necessary to the accomplishment of legitimate state objectives in order to pass constitutional muster."

more exacting test is required for any statute which 'place[s] a condition on the exercise of the right to vote.' Bullock v. Carter, supra, 405 U.S. 134. This development in the law culminated in Kramer v. Union Free School District No. 15, supra, 395 U.S. 621 (1969). There we canvassed in detail the reasons for strict review of statutes distributing the franchise, id., at 626–630, noting *inter alia* that such statutes 'constitute the foundation of our representative society.' We concluded that if a challenged statute grants the right to vote to some citizens and denies the franchise to others, 'the Court must determine whether the exclusions are *necessary* to promote a *compelling* state interest.' Id., at 627 (emphasis added); Cipriano v. City of Houma, 395 U.S. 701, 704 (1969); City of Phoenix v. Kolodziejski, 399 U.S. 204, 205, 209 (1970).[f] Cf. Harper v. Virginia State Board of Elections, supra, 383 U.S., at 670. This is the test we apply here."

MARSTON v. LEWIS, 410 U.S. 679 (1973). Arizona required a voter to have resided in the state for 50 days prior to an election and also required registration at least 50 days prior. The Court held this requirement valid in the light of a state showing that it would be difficult to do the necessary paper work in any shorter period prior to the election, stating: "In the present case, we are confronted with a recent and amply justifiable legislative judgment that 50 days rather than 30 is necessary to promote the State's important interest in accurate voter lists. The Constitution is not so rigid that that determination and others like it may not stand." A dissent argued that the Court had fixed in *Dunn* the line of 30 days as that beyond which reliance on administrative convenience is extremely questionable and "we can avoid an unprincipled numbers game only if we insist that any deviations from the line we have drawn, after mature consideration, be justified by far more substantial evidence than that produced" in this case.

HILL v. STONE, 421 U.S. 289 (1975). Issuance of bonds to finance construction of a city library was defeated in a Fort Worth election. Residents brought this action in the federal court challenging the provision of Texas law limiting the right to vote in city bond issue elections to persons who have "rendered" or listed real, mixed, or personal property for taxation in the election district. Under the law mere listing of the property—not the payment of any tax—was the prerequisite to voting. The Court, by a vote of five to three, held the statute invalid under the Equal Protection Clause, stating, in part:

"The basic principle . . . is that as long as the election in question is not one of special interest, any classification restricting the franchise on grounds other than residence, age, and citizenship cannot stand unless the district or State can demonstrate that the classification serves a compelling state interest. See *Kramer,* supra, 395 U.S., at 626–627; *Cipriano,* supra, 395 U.S., at 704.

"The appellant's claim that the Ft. Worth election was one of special interest and thus outside the principles of the *Kramer* case runs afoul of our decision in City of Phoenix v. Kolodziejski, supra. In the *Phoenix* case, we expressly stated that a general obligation bond issue—even where the debt service will be paid entirely out of property taxes as in Ft. Worth—is a matter of general interest, and that the principles of *Kramer* apply to classifications limiting eligibility among registered voters.

[f] The Court held that a state could not restrict to real property taxpayers the vote in elections to approve the issuance of general obligation bonds.

"In making the alternative contentions that the 'rendering requirement' creates no real 'classification,' or that the classification created should be upheld as being reasonable, the appellant misconceives the rationale of *Kramer* and its successors. Appellant argues that since all property is required to be rendered for taxation, and since anyone can vote in a bond election if he renders any property, no matter how little, the Texas scheme does not discriminate on the basis of wealth or property. Our cases, however, have not held or intimated that only property-based classifications are suspect; in an election of general interest, restrictions on the franchise of any character must meet a stringent test of justification. The Texas scheme creates a classification based on rendering, and it in effect disfranchises those who have not rendered their property for taxation in the year of the bond election. Mere reasonableness will therefore not suffice to sustain the classification created in this case.

B.

"The appellant has sought to justify the State's rendering requirement solely on the ground that it extends some protection to property owners, who will bear the direct burden of retiring the city's bonded indebtedness. The *Phoenix* case, however, rejected this analysis of the 'direct' imposition of costs on property owners. Even under a system in which the responsibility of retiring the bonded indebtedness falls directly on property taxpayers, all members of the community share in the cost in various ways. Moreover, the construction of a library is not likely to be of special interest to a particular, well-defined portion of the electorate. . . .

"The appellee city officials argue that the rendering qualifications furthers another state interest: it encourages prospective voters to render their property and thereby helps enforce the State's tax laws. This argument is difficult to credit. The use of the franchise to compel compliance with other, independent state objectives is questionable in any context. . . .

"In sum, the Texas rendering requirement erects a classification that impermissibly disenfranchises persons otherwise qualified to vote, solely because they have not rendered some property for taxation. The *Phoenix* case establishes that Ft. Worth's election was not a 'special interest' election, and the state interests proffered by appellant and the city officials fall far short of meeting the 'compelling state interest' test consistently applied in *Kramer, Cipriano,* and *Phoenix.*"

NOTE

In Richardson v. Ramirez, 418 U.S. 24 (1974) the Court held valid California constitutional provisions and implementing statutes disenfranchising persons convicted of an "infamous crime." The Court said, in part:

"As we have seen, however, the exclusion of felons from the vote has an affirmative sanction in § 2 of the Fourteenth Amendment, a sanction which was not present in the case of the other restrictions on the franchise which were invalidated in the cases on which respondents rely. We hold that the understanding of those who adopted the Fourteenth Amendment, as reflected in the express language of § 2 and in the historical and judicial interpretation of the Amendment's applicability to state laws disenfranchising felons, is of controlling significance in distinguishing such laws from those other state limitations on the franchise which have been held invalid under the Equal Protection Clause by this Court."

THE FIRST AMENDMENT AS A LIMITATION ON STATE POWER TO FIX QUALIFICATIONS FOR VOTERS

The first amendment may also be a restriction on the power of states to set the qualifications of voters. In Kusper v. Pontikes, 414 U.S. 51 (1973), the Court held invalid a provision of the Illinois Election Code prohibiting a person from voting in the primary election of a political party if that person has voted in another party's primary within the preceding 23 months. The Court said: "There can no longer be any doubt that freedom to associate with others for the common advancement of political beliefs and ideas is a form of 'orderly group activity' protected by the First and Fourteenth Amendments. . . . The right to associate with the political party of one's choice is an integral part of this basic constitutional freedom. . . . To be sure, administration of the electoral process is a matter that the Constitution largely entrusts to the States. But, in exercising their powers of supervision over elections and in setting qualifications for voters, the States may not infringe upon basic constitutional protections." The Court went on to hold that the state had not shown that the restriction on voting in primary elections was closely related to a compelling state interest and hence it was invalid.

ACCESS TO THE BALLOT AND OTHER ELECTION LAWS

The states in addition to determining the qualifications for voters have extensively regulated the electoral process. Regulations relating to the following major areas exist: (1) Access of political parties and independent candidates to the ballot. (2) Political party nominating procedures. (3) Eligibility requirements for candidates. (4) Campaign regulations. See *Developments in the Law—Elections,* 88 Harv.L.Rev. 1111 (1975).

These laws have been attacked both as violations of equal protection and of the first amendment. For a discussion of the first amendment problems, see p. 1293, infra.

The following cases are among those relying principally on the equal protection clause.

BULLOCK v. CARTER, 405 U.S. 134 (1972). Texas imposed very high filing fees as a condition of becoming a candidate in a primary election. They were challenged by prospective candidates who asserted they were financially unable to pay the fees. The Court held the statute unconstitutional. In determining the standard of review to be applied, the Court said:

"The initial and direct impact of filing fees is felt by aspirants for office, rather than voters, and the Court has not heretofore attached such fundamental status to candidacy as to invoke a rigorous standard of review. However, the rights of voters and the rights of candidates do not lend themselves to neat separation; laws that affect candidates always have at least some theoretical, correlative effect on voters. Of course, not every limitation or incidental burden on the exercise of voting rights is subject to a stringent standard of review."

The Court then went on to note that the statute would exclude candidates without personal wealth or affluent backers. Not only would this limit the voters in their choice of candidates but also it would likely fall more heavily on the less affluent segments of society. Hence, because the scheme has a significant impact on the exercise of the franchise and because the impact is related to the resources of the voters, the Court concluded "that the laws must be 'closely scrutinized' and found reasonably necessary to the accomplishment of legitimate state objectives. . . ." The Court went on to hold that the state interests, including that of regulating the number of candidates on the ballot, did not justify the regulation.

———

LUBIN v. PANISH, 415 U.S. 709 (1974). California imposed modest filing fees for primary elections fixed at one to two percent of the annual salary for the office. A challenge made by a candidate who alleged that he could not afford to pay any filing fee was upheld by the Court. The Court concluded:

"The absence of any alternative means of gaining access to the ballot inevitably renders the California system exclusionary as to some aspirants. . . . [T]he payment of a fee is an absolute, not an alternative, condition, and failure to meet it is a disqualification from running for office. Thus, California has chosen to achieve the important and legitimate interest of maintaining the integrity of elections by means which can operate to exclude some potentially serious candidates from the ballot without providing them with any alternative means of coming before the voters. Selection of candidates solely on the basis of ability to pay a fixed fee without providing any alternative means is not reasonably necessary to the accomplishment of the State's legitimate election interests. Accordingly, we hold that in the absence of reasonable alternative means of ballot access, a State may not, consistent with constitutional standards, require from an indigent candidate filing fees he cannot pay."

———

CLEMENTS v. FASHING, 457 U.S. 957 (1982). A Texas statute provided that judges and other office holders could not cut short their existing terms of office in order to serve in the Texas legislature. A Justice of the Peace claimed that this statute violated the equal protection clause. The Court rejected the claim by a vote of 5 to 4 but without an opinion of the Court. The plurality, in an opinion by Justice Rehnquist, said that the statute "need only rest on a rational predicate in order to survive challenge under the Equal Protection Clause" and that it met this challenge. Justice Stevens concurring objected to the plurality opinion's discussion of levels of scrutiny. The Court also upheld the statute against a claim based on the first amendment.

C. TRAVEL AND INTERSTATE MIGRATION

———

SHAPIRO v. THOMPSON

394 U.S. 618, 89 S.Ct. 1322, 22 L.Ed.2d 600 (1969).

Mr. Justice Brennan delivered the opinion of the Court.

These three appeals were restored to the calendar for reargument. . . . Each is an appeal from a decision of a three-judge District Court holding unconstitutional a State or District of Columbia statutory provision which denies welfare assistance to residents of the State or District who have not resided within their jurisdictions for at least one year immediately preceding their applications for such assistance. We affirm the judgments of the District Courts in the three cases. . . .

II.

There is no dispute that the effect of the waiting-period requirement in each case is to create two classes of needy resident families indistinguishable from each other except that one is composed of residents who have resided a year or more, and the second of residents who have resided less than a year, in the jurisdiction. On the basis of this sole difference the first class is granted and the second class is denied welfare aid upon which may depend the ability of the families to obtain the very means to subsist—food, shelter, and other necessities of life. In each case, the District Court found that appellees met the test for residence in their jurisdictions, as well as all other eligibility requirements except the requirement of residence for a full year prior to their applications. On reargument, appellees' central contention is that the statutory prohibition of benefits to residents of less than a year creates a classification which constitutes an invidious discrimination denying them equal protection of the laws. We agree. The interests which appellants assert are promoted by the classification either may not constitutionally be promoted by government or are not compelling governmental interests.

III.

Primarily, appellants justify the waiting-period requirement as a protective device to preserve the fiscal integrity of state public assistance programs. It is asserted that people who require welfare assistance during their first year of residence in a State are likely to become continuing burdens on state welfare programs. Therefore, the argument runs, if such people can be deterred from entering the jurisdiction by denying them welfare benefits during the first year, state programs to assist long-time residents will not be impaired by a substantial influx of indigent newcomers.

There is weighty evidence that exclusion from the jurisdiction of the poor who need or may need relief was the specific objective of these provisions. . . .

We do not doubt that the one-year waiting period device is well suited to discourage the influx of poor families in need of assistance. An indigent who desires to migrate, resettle, find a new job, start a new life will doubtless hesitate if he knows that he must risk making the move without the possibility of falling back on state welfare assistance during his first year of residence, when his need may be most acute. But the purpose of inhibiting migration by needy persons into the State is constitutionally impermissible.

This Court long ago recognized that the nature of our Federal Union and our constitutional concepts of personal liberty unite to require that all citizens be free to travel throughout the length and breadth of our land uninhibited by statutes, rules or regulations which unreasonably burden or restrict this movement. . . .

We have no occasion to ascribe the source of this right to travel interstate to a particular constitutional provision. It suffices that, as Mr. Justice Stewart said for the Court in United States v. Guest, 383 U.S. 745, 757–758 (1966):

"The constitutional right to travel from one State to another . . . occupies a position fundamental to the concept of our Federal Union. It is a right that has been firmly established and repeatedly recognized.

"[The] right finds no explicit mention in the Constitution. The reason, it has been suggested, is that a right so elementary was conceived from the beginning to be a necessary concomitant of the stronger Union the Constitution created. In any event, freedom to travel throughout the United States has long been recognized as a basic right under the Constitution."

Thus, the purpose of deterring the in-migration of indigents cannot serve as justification for the classification created by the one-year waiting period, since that purpose is constitutionally impermissible. If a law has "no other purpose . . . than to chill the assertion of constitutional rights by penalizing those who choose to exercise them, then it [is] patently unconstitutional." United States v. Jackson, 390 U.S. 570, 581 (1968).

Alternatively, appellants argue that even if it is impermissible for a State to attempt to deter the entry of all indigents, the challenged classification may be justified as a permissible state attempt to discourage those indigents who would enter the State solely to obtain larger benefits. We observe first that none of the statutes before us is tailored to serve that objective. . . .

More fundamentally, a State may no more try to fence out those indigents who seek higher welfare benefits than it may try to fence out indigents generally. Implicit in any such distinction is the notion that indigents who enter a State with the hope of securing higher welfare benefits are somehow less deserving than indigents who do not take this consideration into account. But we do not perceive why a mother who is seeking to make a new life for herself and her children should be regarded as less deserving because she considers, among other factors, the level of a State's public assistance. Surely such a mother is no less deserving than a mother who moves into a particular State in order to take advantage of its better educational facilities.

Appellants argue further that the challenged classification may be sustained as an attempt to distinguish between new and old residents on the basis of the contribution they have made to the community through the payment of taxes. We have difficulty seeing how long-term residents who qualify for welfare are making a greater present contribution to the State in taxes than indigent residents who have recently arrived. If the argument is based on contributions made in the past by the long-term residents, there is some question, as a factual matter, whether this argument is applicable in Pennsylvania where the record suggests that some 40% of those denied public assistance because of the waiting period had lengthy prior residence in the State. But we need not rest on the particular facts of these cases. Appellants' reasoning would logically permit the State to bar new residents from schools, parks, and libraries or deprive them of police and fire protection. Indeed it would permit the State to apportion all benefits and services according to the past tax contributions of its citizens. The Equal Protection Clause prohibits such an apportionment of state services.[10]

We recognize that a State has a valid interest in preserving the fiscal integrity of its programs. It may legitimately attempt to limit its expenditures, whether for public assistance, public education, or any other program. But a State may not accomplish such a purpose by invidious distinctions between classes of its citizens. It could not, for example, reduce expenditures for education by barring indigent children from its schools. Similarly, in the cases before us, appellants must do more than show that denying welfare benefits to new residents saves money. The saving of welfare costs cannot be an independent ground for an invidious classification.

In sum, neither deterrence of indigents from migrating to the State nor limitation of welfare benefits to those regarded as contributing to the State is a constitutionally permissible state objective.

IV.

Appellants next advance as justification certain administrative and related governmental objectives allegedly served by the waiting-period requirement. They argue that the requirement (1) facilitates the planning of the welfare budget; (2) provides an objective test of residency; (3) minimizes the opportunity for recipients fraudulently to receive payments from more than one

---

[10] We are not dealing here with state insurance programs which may legitimately tie the amount of benefits to the individual's contributions.

jurisdiction; and (4) encourages early entry of new residents into the labor force.

At the outset, we reject appellants' argument that a mere showing of a rational relationship between the waiting period and these four admittedly permissible state objectives will suffice to justify the classification. . . . The waiting-period provision denies welfare benefits to otherwise eligible applicants solely because they have recently moved into the jurisdiction. But in moving from State to State or to the District of Columbia appellees were exercising a constitutional right, and any classification which serves to penalize the exercise of that right, unless shown to be necessary to promote a *compelling* governmental interest, is unconstitutional. . . .

The argument that the waiting-period requirement facilitates budget predictability is wholly unfounded. The records in all three cases are utterly devoid of evidence that either State or the District of Columbia in fact uses the one-year requirement as a means to predict the number of people who will require assistance in the budget year. . . .

The argument that the waiting period serves as an administratively efficient rule of thumb for determining residency similarly will not withstand scrutiny. The residence requirement and the one-year waiting-period requirement are distinct and independent prerequisites for assistance under these three statutes, and the facts relevant to the determination of each are directly examined by the welfare authorities. Before granting an application, the welfare authorities investigate the applicant's employment, housing, and family situation and in the course of the inquiry necessarily learn the facts upon which to determine whether the applicant is a resident.

Similarly, there is no need for a State to use the one-year waiting period as a safeguard against fraudulent receipt of benefits; for less drastic means are available, and are employed, to minimize that hazard. Of course, a State has a valid interest in preventing fraud by any applicant, whether a newcomer or a long-time resident. It is not denied however that the investigations now conducted entail inquiries into facts relevant to that subject. In addition, cooperation among state welfare departments is common. The District of Columbia, for example, provides interim assistance to its former residents who have moved to a State which has a waiting period. As a matter of course, District officials send a letter to the welfare authorities in the recipient's new community "to request the information needed to continue assistance." A like procedure would be an effective safeguard against the hazard of double payments. Since double payments can be prevented by a letter or a telephone call, it is unreasonable to accomplish this objective by the blunderbuss method of denying assistance to all indigent newcomers for an entire year.

Pennsylvania suggests that the one-year waiting period is justified as a means of encouraging new residents to join the labor force promptly. But this logic would also require a similar waiting period for long-term residents of the State. A state purpose to encourage employment provides no rational basis for imposing a one-year waiting-period restriction on new residents only.

We conclude therefore that appellants in these cases do not use and have no need to use the one-year requirement for the governmental purposes suggested. Thus, even under traditional equal protection tests a classification of welfare applicants according to whether they have lived in the State for one year would seem irrational and unconstitutional. But, of course, the traditional criteria do not apply in these cases. Since the classification here touches on the fundamental right of interstate movement, its constitutionality must be judged by the stricter standard of whether it promotes a *compelling* state interest. Under this standard, the waiting period requirement clearly violates the Equal Protection Clause.

V.

Connecticut and Pennsylvania argue, however, that the constitutional challenge to the waiting period requirements must fail because Congress expressly approved the imposition of the requirement by the States as part of the jointly funded AFDC program. . . .

But even if we were to assume, *arguendo,* that Congress did approve the imposition of a one-year waiting period, it is the responsive *state* legislation which infringes constitutional rights. By itself § 402(b) has absolutely no restrictive effect. It is therefore not that statute but only the state requirements which pose the constitutional question.

Finally, even if it could be argued that the constitutionality of § 402(b) is somehow at issue here, it follows from what we have said that the provision, insofar as it permits the one-year waiting-period requirement, would be unconstitutional. Congress may not authorize the States to violate the Equal Protection Clause. Perhaps Congress could induce wider state participation in school construction if it authorized the use of joint funds for the building of segregated schools. But could it seriously be contended that Congress would be constitutionally justified in such authorization by the need to secure state cooperation? Congress is without power to enlist state cooperation in a joint federal-state program by legislation which authorizes the States to violate the Equal Protection Clause. Katzenbach v. Morgan, 384 U.S. 641, 651 (1966).

VI.

The waiting-period requirement in the District of Columbia Code involved in No. 33 is also unconstitutional even though it was adopted by Congress as an exercise of federal power. In terms of federal power, the discrimination created by the one-year requirement violates the Due Process Clause of the Fifth Amendment. "[W]hile the Fifth Amendment contains no equal protection clause, it does forbid discrimination that is 'so unjustifiable as to be violative of due process.'" Schneider v. Rusk, 377 U.S. 163, 168 (1964); Bolling v. Sharpe, 347 U.S. 497 (1954). For the reasons we have stated in invalidating the Pennsylvania and Connecticut provisions, the District of Columbia provision is also invalid—the Due Process Clause of the Fifth Amendment forbids Congress from denying public assistance to poor persons otherwise eligible solely on the ground that they have not been residents of the District of Columbia for one year at the time their applications are filed.

Accordingly, the judgments in Nos. 9, 33, and 34 are

Affirmed.

Mr. Justice Stewart, concurring.

In joining the opinion of the Court, I add a word in response to the dissent of my Brother Harlan, who, I think, has quite misapprehended what the Court's opinion says.

The Court today does *not* "pick out particular human activities, characterize them as 'fundamental,' and give them added protection . . . ." To the contrary, the Court simply recognizes, as it must, an established constitutional right, and gives to that right no less protection than the Constitution itself demands. . . .

Mr. Chief Justice Warren, with whom Mr. Justice Black joins, dissenting.

In my opinion the issue before us can be simply stated: may Congress, acting under one of its enumerated powers, impose minimal nationwide residence requirements or authorize the States to do so? Since I believe that Congress does have this power and has constitutionally exercised it in these cases, I must dissent. . . .

Mr. Justice Harlan, dissenting. . . .

In upholding the equal protection argument, the Court has applied an equal protection doctrine of relatively recent vintage: the rule that statutory classifications which either are based upon certain "suspect" criteria or affect "fundamental rights" will be held to deny equal protection unless justified by a "compelling" governmental interest. . . .

The "compelling interest" doctrine, which today is articulated more explicitly than ever before, constitutes an increasingly significant exception to the long-established rule that a statute does not deny equal protection if it is rationally related to a legitimate governmental objective. The "compelling interest" doctrine has two branches. The branch which requires that classifications based upon "suspect" criteria be supported by a compelling interest apparently had its genesis in cases involving racial classifications, which have at least since Korematsu v. United States, 323 U.S. 214, 216 (1944), been regarded as inherently "suspect." The criterion of "wealth" apparently was added to the list of "suspects" as an alternative justification for the rationale in Harper v. Virginia Bd. of Elections, 383 U.S. 663, 668 (1966), in which Virginia's poll tax was struck down. The criterion of political allegiance may have been added in Williams v. Rhodes, 393 U.S. 23 (1968). Today the list apparently has been further enlarged to include classifications based upon recent interstate movement, and perhaps those based upon the exercise of *any* constitutional right, . . .

I think that this branch of the "compelling interest" doctrine is sound when applied to racial classifications, for historically the Equal Protection Clause was largely a product of the desire to eradicate legal distinctions founded upon race. However, I believe that the more recent extensions have been unwise. . . .

The second branch of the "compelling interest" principle is even more troublesome. For it has been held that a statutory classification is subject to the "compelling interest" test if the result of the classification may be to affect a "fundamental right," regardless of the basis of the classification. . . .

I think this branch of the "compelling interest" doctrine particularly unfortunate and unnecessary. It is unfortunate because it creates an exception which threatens to swallow the standard equal protection rule. Virtually every state statute affects important rights. This Court has repeatedly held, for example, that the traditional equal protection standard is applicable to statutory classifications affecting such fundamental matters as the right to pursue a particular occupation, the right to receive greater or smaller wages or to work more or less hours, and the right to inherit property. Rights such as these are in principle indistinguishable from those involved here, and to extend the "compelling interest" rule to all cases in which such rights are affected would go far toward making this Court a "super-legislature." This branch of the doctrine is also unnecessary. When the right affected is one assured by the federal Constitution, any infringement can be dealt with under the Due Process Clause. But when a statute affects only matters not mentioned in the federal Constitution and is not arbitrary or irrational, I must reiterate that I know of nothing which entitles this Court to pick out particular human activities, characterize them as "fundamental," and give them added protection under an unusually stringent equal protection test. . . .

DUNN v. BLUMSTEIN, 405 U.S. 330 (1972). In this case the Court upheld a challenge to a Tennessee law providing that in order to vote one must be a resident of the state for one year and of the county for three months prior to the date of the election. The Court, in an opinion by Justice Marshall, held that the residence requirement had to meet the *Shapiro* compelling state interest test because (1) it burdened the right to vote, and (2) it burdened the right to travel. The aspects of the case dealing with voting were considered supra, p. 873. As to the right to travel the Court responded to the argument of the state that durational residence requirements do not abridge the right to travel because they neither seek to deter travel nor actually do deter travel:

"This view represents a fundamental misunderstanding of the law. It is irrelevant whether disenfranchisement or denial of welfare is the more potent deterrent to travel. *Shapiro* did not rest upon a finding that denial of welfare actually deterred travel. Nor have other 'right to travel' cases in this Court always relied on the presence of actual deterrence. In *Shapiro* we explicitly stated that the compelling state interest test would be triggered by 'any classification which serves to *penalize* the exercise of that right [to travel] . . . .'

"Of course it is true that the two individual interests affected by Tennessee's durational residence requirements are affected in different ways. Travel is permitted, but only at a price; voting is prohibited. The right to travel is merely penalized, while the right to vote is absolutely denied. But these differences are irrelevant for present purposes. . . .

"The right to travel is 'an *unconditional* personal right,' a right whose exercise may not be conditioned. . . . Durational residence laws impermissibly condition and penalize the right to travel by imposing their prohibitions on only those persons who have recently exercised that right. In the present case, such laws force a person who wishes to travel and change residences to choose between travel and the basic right to vote. Cf. United States v. Jackson, 390 U.S. 570, 582–583. Absent a compelling state interest, a State may not burden the right to travel in this way."

The Court also restated the burden placed on the state to justify a statute which burdened the right to travel or the right to vote:

"It is not sufficient for the State to show that durational residence requirements further a very substantial state interest. In pursuing that important interest, the State cannot choose means which unnecessarily burden or restrict constitutionally protected activity. Statutes affecting constitutional rights must be drawn with 'precision,' . . . and must be 'tailored' to serve their legitimate objectives. Shapiro v. Thompson, supra, 394 U.S., at 631. And if there are other, reasonable ways to achieve those goals with a lesser burden on constitutionally protected activity, a State may not choose the way of greater interference. If it acts at all, it must choose 'less drastic means.' "

It then went on to hold that while the state had identified important and presumably "compelling" state interests—prevention of fraudulent voting and assuring knowledgeable voters—the durational residence requirement was not closely enough related to either of those interests.

Chief Justice Burger dissented. Justice Blackmun concurred in the result. Justices Powell and Rehnquist took no part in the decision.

MEMORIAL HOSPITAL v. MARICOPA COUNTY

415 U.S. 250, 94 S.Ct. 1076, 39 L.Ed.2d 306 (1974).

Mr. Justice Marshall delivered the opinion of the Court.

This case presents an appeal from a decision of the Arizona Supreme Court upholding an Arizona statute requiring a year's residence in a county as a condition to receiving nonemergency hospitalization or medical care at the

county's expense. The constitutional question presented is whether this durational residency requirement is repugnant to the Equal Protection Clause as
applied by this Court in Shapiro v. Thompson, 394 U.S. 618 (1969).

.   .   .

[Appellant, Henry Evaro, is an indigent suffering from a chronic asthmatic
and bronchial illness. Within a month after he moved from New Mexico to
Phoenix, Arizona, he suffered a severe respiratory attack. Pursuant to the
Arizona statute the county refused to provide non-emergency medical care to
Evaro. A suit was brought to determine whether the statute was constitutional
as applied. The Arizona Supreme Court ruled the statute valid. The Supreme
Court reversed that judgment.]

Appellees argue that the residency requirement before us is distinguishable
from those in *Shapiro,* while appellants urge that *Shapiro* is controlling. We
agree with appellants that Arizona's durational residency requirement for free
medical care must be justified by a compelling state interest and that such
interests being lacking, the requirement is unconstitutional.

III.

The right of interstate travel has repeatedly been recognized as a basic
constitutional freedom. Whatever its ultimate scope, however, the right to
travel was involved in only a limited sense in *Shapiro.* The Court was there
concerned only with the right to "[migrate], with intent to settle and abide" or,
as the Court put it, "to migrate, resettle, find a new job and start a new life."
Even a bona fide residence requirement would burden the right to travel, if
travel meant merely movement. But, in *Shapiro,* the Court explained that
"[t]he residence requirement and the one-year waiting-period requirement are
distinct and independent prerequisites" for assistance and only the latter was
held to be unconstitutional. 394 U.S., at 636. Later, in invalidating a
durational residency requirement for voter registration on the basis of *Shapiro,*
we cautioned that our decision was not intended to "cast doubt on the validity
of appropriately defined and uniformly applied bona fide residence requirements." Dunn v. Blumstein, 405 U.S. 330, 342 n. 13 (1972).

.   .   .

V.

Although any durational residence requirement impinges to some extent on
the right to travel, the Court in *Shapiro* did not declare such requirements to be
per se unconstitutional.   .   .   .

.   .   .

Thus, *Shapiro* and *Dunn* stand for the proposition that a classification which
"operates to *penalize* those persons .   .   . who have exercised their constitutional right of interstate migration," must be justified by a compelling state interest.
Oregon v. Mitchell, 400 U.S. 112, 238 (1971) (separate opinion of Brennan,
White, and Marshall, JJ.) (emphasis added.) Although any durational residency
requirement imposes a potential cost on migration, the Court, in *Shapiro,*
cautioned that some "waiting-periods .   .   . may not be penalties." 394 U.S.,
at 638 n. 21. In Dunn v. Blumstein, supra, the Court found that the denial of
the franchise, "a fundamental political right," Reynolds v. Sims, 377 U.S. 533,
562 (1964), was a penalty requiring application of the compelling state interest
test. In *Shapiro,* the Court found denial of the basic "necessities of life" to be a
penalty. Nonetheless, the Court has declined to strike down state statutes
requiring one year of residence as a condition to lower tuition at state
institutions of higher education.[12]

---

[12] See Vlandis v. Kline, 412 U.S. 441, 452–453 n. 9 (1973).

Whatever the ultimate parameters of the *Shapiro* penalty analysis, it is at least clear that medical care is as much "a basic necessity of life" to an indigent as welfare assistance. And, governmental privileges or benefits necessary to basic sustenance have often been viewed as being of greater constitutional significance than less essential forms of governmental entitlements. See, e.g., *Shapiro,* supra; Goldberg v. Kelly, 397 U.S. 254, 264 (1970); Sniadach v. Family Finance Corp., 395 U.S. 337, 340–342 (1969). It would be odd, indeed, to find that the State of Arizona was required to afford Evaro welfare assistance to keep him from discomfort of inadequate housing or the pangs of hunger but could deny him the medical care necessary to relieve him from the wheezing and gasping for breath that attend his illness.

.   .   .

Not unlike the admonition of the Bible that, "Ye shall have one manner of law, as well for the stranger as for one of your country." Leviticus, 24:22, the right of interstate travel must be seen as insuring new residents the same right to vital government benefits and privileges in the States to which they migrate as are enjoyed by other residents. The State of Arizona's durational residency requirement for free medical care penalizes indigents for exercising their right to migrate to and settle in that State. Accordingly, the classification created by the residency requirement, "unless shown to be necessary to promote a *compelling* [state] interest, is unconstitutional." *Shapiro,* supra, 394 U.S. at 634. (Emphasis original.)

VI.

We turn now to the question of whether the State has shown that its durational residence requirement is "legitimately defensible," in that it furthers a compelling state interest. A number of purposes are asserted to be served by the requirement and we must determine whether these satisfy the appellees' heavy burden of justification, and insure that the State, in pursuing its asserted objectives, has chosen means that do not necessarily burden constitutionally protected interests. NAACP v. Button, 371 U.S. 415, 438 (1963).

A.

.   .   .

The County thus attempts to sustain the requirement as a necessary means to insure the fiscal integrity of its free medical care program by discouraging an influx of indigents, particularly those entering the county for the sole purpose of obtaining the benefits of its hospital facilities.

First, a State may not protect the public fisc by drawing an invidious distinction between classes of its citizens, *Shapiro,* supra, 394 U.S., at 633, so appellees must do more than show that denying free medical care to new residents saves money.   .   .   .

Second, to the extent the purpose of the requirement is to inhibit the immigration of indigents generally, that goal is constitutionally impermissible. .   .   . Moreover, "a State may no more try to fence out those indigents who seek [better public medical facilities] than it may try to fence out indigents generally." *Shapiro,* supra, 394 U.S., at 631. An indigent who considers the quality of public hospital facilities in entering the State is no less deserving than one who moves into the State in order to take advantage of its better educational facilities. 394 U.S., at 631–632.

.   .   .

B.

The appellees also argue that the challenged statute serves some administrative objectives. They claim that the one-year waiting period is a convenient rule of thumb to determine bona fide residence. Besides not being factually defensible, this test is certainly overbroad to accomplish its avowed purpose. . . .

The appellees allege that the waiting period is a useful tool for preventing fraud. Certainly, a State has a valid interest in preventing fraud by any applicant for medical care, whether newcomer or old-time resident, *Shapiro*, 394 U.S., at 637, but the challenged provision is ill-suited to that purpose. . . .

Finally, appellees assert that the waiting period is necessary for budget predictability, but what was said in *Shapiro* is equally applicable to the case before us. . . .

VII.

The Arizona durational residency requirement for eligibility for non-emergency free medical care creates an "invidious classification" that impinges on the right of interstate travel by denying newcomers "basic necessities of life." Such a classification can only be sustained on a showing of a compelling state interest. Appellees have not met their heavy burden of justification, nor demonstrated that the State, in pursuing legitimate objectives, has chosen means which do not unnecessarily impinge on constitutionally protected interests. Accordingly, judgment of the Supreme Court of Arizona is reversed and the case remanded for further action not inconsistent with this opinion.

So ordered.

Reversed and remanded.

The Chief Justice and Mr. Justice Blackmun concur in the result.

Mr. Justice Douglas.

The legal and economic aspects of medical care are enormous; and I doubt if decisions under the Equal Protection Clause of the Fourteenth Amendment are equal to the task. So far as interstate travel *per se* is considered, I share the doubts of my Brother Rehnquist. The present case, however, turns for me on a different axis. . . .

. . .

The political processes rather than equal protection litigation are the ultimate solvent of the present problem. But in the setting of this case the invidious discrimination against the poor, Harper v. Virginia Board of Elections, 383 U.S. 663 (1966), not the right to travel interstate is in my view the critical issue.

Mr. Justice Rehnquist, dissenting.

. . .

The legal question in this case is simply whether the State of Arizona has acted arbitrarily in determining that access to local hospital facilities for non-emergency medical care should be denied to persons until they have established residency for one year. The impediment which this quite rational determination has placed on petitioner Evaro's "right to travel" is so remote as to be negligible: so far as the record indicates Evaro moved from New Mexico to Arizona three years ago and has remained ever since. The eligibility requirement has not the slightest resemblance to the actual barriers to the right of free ingress and egress protected by the Constitution, and struck down in cases such as *Crandall* and *Edwards*. And unlike *Shapiro* it does not involve an urgent need for the necessities of life or a benefit funded from current revenues to which the claimant may well have contributed. It is a substantial broadening of, and departure from, all of these holdings, all the more remarkable for the lack of explanation which accompanies the result. Since I can subscribe neither to the method nor the result, I dissent.

SOSNA v. IOWA

419 U.S. 393, 95 S.Ct. 553, 42 L.Ed.2d 532 (1975).

Mr. Justice Rehnquist delivered the opinion of the Court.

Appellant Carol Sosna married Michael Sosna on September 5, 1964, in Michigan. They lived together in New York between October 1967 and August 1971, after which date they separated but continued to live in New York. In August 1972, appellant moved to Iowa with her three children, and the following month she petitioned the District Court of Jackson County, Iowa, for a dissolution of her marriage. Michael Sosna, who had been personally served with notice of the action when he came to Iowa to visit his children, made a special appearance to contest the jurisdiction of the Iowa court. The Iowa court dismissed the petition for lack of jurisdiction, finding that Michael Sosna was not a resident of Iowa and appellant had not been a resident of the State of Iowa for one year preceding the filing of her petition. In so doing the Iowa court applied the provisions of Iowa Code § 598.6 requiring that the petitioner in such an action be "for the last year a resident of the state."

Instead of appealing this ruling to the Iowa appellate courts, appellant filed a complaint in the United States District Court for the Northern District of Iowa asserting that Iowa's durational residency requirement for invoking its divorce jurisdiction violated the United States Constitution. She sought both injunctive and declaratory relief against the appellees in this case, one of whom is the State of Iowa, and the other of whom is the judge of the District Court of Jackson County, Iowa, who had previously dismissed her petition.

A three-judge court, convened pursuant to 28 U.S.C. §§ 2281, 2284, held that the Iowa durational residency requirement was constitutional. 360 F.Supp. 1182 (N.D.Iowa 1973). We noted probable jurisdiction, 415 U.S. 911, and directed the parties to discuss "whether the United States District Court should have proceeded to the merits of the constitutional issue presented in light of Younger v. Harris, 401 U.S. 37 (1971) and related cases." For reasons stated in this opinion, we decide that this case is not moot, and hold that the Iowa durational residency requirement for divorce does not offend the United States Constitution. . . .

The durational residency requirement under attack in this case is a part of Iowa's comprehensive statutory regulation of domestic relations, an area that has long been regarded as a virtually exclusive province of the States. . . .

The imposition of a durational residency requirement for divorce is scarcely unique to Iowa, since 48 States impose such a requirement as a condition for maintaining an action for divorce. As might be expected, the periods vary among the States and range from six weeks to two years. The one-year period selected by Iowa is the most common length of time prescribed.

Appellant contends that the Iowa requirement of one year's residence is unconstitutional . . . because it establishes two classes of persons and discriminates against those who have recently exercised their right to travel to Iowa, thereby contravening the Court's holdings in Shapiro v. Thompson, 394 U.S. 618 (1969); Dunn v. Blumstein, 405 U.S. 330 (1972), and Memorial Hospital v. Maricopa County, 415 U.S. 250 (1974); . . .

State statutes imposing durational residency requirements were of course invalidated when imposed by States as a qualification for welfare payments,

Shapiro, supra, for voting, *Dunn,* supra, and for medical care, *Maricopa County,* supra. But none of those cases intimated that the States might never impose durational residency requirements, and such a proposition was in fact expressly disclaimed. What those cases had in common was that the durational residency requirements they struck down were justified on the basis of budgetary or record-keeping considerations which were held insufficient to outweigh the constitutional claims of the individuals. But Iowa's divorce residency require-ment is of a different stripe. Appellant was not irretrivably foreclosed from obtaining some part of what she sought, as was the case with the welfare recipients in *Shapiro,* the voters in *Dunn,* or the indigent patient in *Maricopa County.* She would eventually qualify for the same sort of adjudication which she demanded virtually upon her arrival in the State. Iowa's requirement delayed her access to the courts, but, by fulfilling it, a plaintiff could ultimately obtain the same opportunity for adjudication which she asserts ought to be hers at an earlier point in time.

Iowa's residency requirement may reasonably be justified on grounds other than purely budgetary considerations or administrative convenience. Cf. Kahn v. Shevin, 416 U.S. 351 (1974). A decree of divorce is not a matter in which the only interested parties are the State as a sort of "grantor," and a plaintiff such as appellant in the role of "grantee." Both spouses are obviously interested in the proceedings, since it will affect their marital status and very likely their property rights. Where a married couple has minor children, a decree of divorce would usually include provisions for their custody and support. With consequences of such moment riding on a divorce decree issued by its courts, Iowa may insist that one seeking to initiate such a proceeding have the modicum of attachment to the State required here.

Such a requirement additionally furthers the State's parallel interests in both avoiding officious intermeddling in matters in which another State has a paramount interest, and in minimizing the susceptibility of its own divorce decrees to collateral attack. A State such as Iowa may quite reasonably decide that it does not wish to become a divorce mill for unhappy spouses who have lived there as short a time as appellant had when she commenced her action in the state court after having long resided elsewhere. Until such time as Iowa is convinced that appellant intends to remain in the State, it lacks the "nexus between person and place of such permanence as to control the creation of legal relations and responsibilities of the utmost significance." Williams v. North Carolina, 325 U.S. 226, 229 (1945). Perhaps even more importantly, Iowa's interests extend beyond its borders and include the recognition of its divorce decrees by other States under the Full Faith and Credit Clause of the Constitu-tion, Art. IV, § 1. For that purpose, this Court has often stated that "judicial power to grant a divorce—jurisdiction, strictly speaking—is founded on domi-cil." *Williams,* supra; Andrews v. Andrews, 188 U.S. 14 (1903); Bell v. Bell, 181 U.S. 175 (1901). Where a divorce decree is entered after a finding of domicile in *ex parte* proceedings, this Court has held that the finding of domicile is not binding upon another State and may be disregarded in the face of "cogent evidence" to the contrary. *Williams,* supra, 325 U.S. at 236. For that reason, the State asked to enter such a decree is entitled to insist that the putative divorce plaintiff satisfy something more than the bare minimum of constitutional requirements before a divorce may be granted. The State's decision to exact a one-year residency requirement as a matter of policy is therefore buttressed by a quite permissible inference that this requirement not only effectuate state substantive policy but likewise provides a greater safeguard against successful collateral attack than would a requirement of bona fide residence alone. This is precisely the sort of determination that a State in the exercise of its domestic relations jurisdiction is entitled to make.

We therefore hold that the state interest in requiring that those who seek a divorce from its courts be genuinely attached to the State, as well as a desire to insulate divorce decrees from the likelihood of collateral attack, requires a different resolution of the constitutional issue presented than was the case in *Shapiro,* supra, *Dunn,* supra, and *Maricopa County,* supra.

. . .

[The Court also held that the statute did not violate due process by invoking a permanent and irrebuttable presumption of non-residence.]

Affirmed.

Mr. Justice White, dissenting.

. . .

Because I find that the case before the Court has become moot, I must respectfully dissent.

Mr. Justice Marshall, with whom Mr. Justice Brennan joins, dissenting.

The Court today departs sharply from the course we have followed in analyzing durational residency requirements since Shapiro v. Thompson, 394 U.S. 618 (1969). Because I think the principles set out in that case and its progeny compel reversal here, I respectfully dissent.

As we have made clear in *Shapiro* and subsequent cases, any classification that penalizes exercise of the constitutional right to travel is invalid unless it is justified by a compelling governmental interest. . . .

The Court's failure to address the instant case in these terms suggests a new distaste for the mode of analysis we have applied to this corner of equal protection law. In its stead, the Court has employed what appears to be an *ad hoc* balancing test, under which the State's putative interest in ensuring that its divorce plaintiffs establish some roots in Iowa is said to justify the one-year residency requirement. I am concerned not only about the disposition of this case, but also about the implications of the majority's analysis for other divorce statutes and for durational residency requirement cases in general.

. . .

McCARTHY v. PHILADELPHIA CIVIL SERVICE COMMISSION, 424 U.S. 645 (1976). Plaintiff's employment in the city fire department was terminated because he moved his permanent residence to another city in violation of a requirement that city employees be residents of the city. The state courts rejected his challenge to the validity of the regulation. On appeal the Supreme Court summarily affirmed, stating in its per curiam opinion:

"We have not, however, specifically addressed the contention made by appellant in this case that his constitutionally recognized right to travel interstate as defined in Shapiro v. Thompson, 394 U.S. 618; Dunn v. Blumstein, 405 U.S. 330, and Memorial Hospital v. Maricopa County, 415 U.S. 250, 94 S.Ct. 1076, is impaired. Each of those cases involved a statutory requirement of residence in the State for at least one year before becoming eligible either to vote, as in *Shapiro,* or to receive welfare benefits, as in *Dunn* and *Memorial Hospital.* Neither in those cases, nor in any others, have we questioned the validity of a condition placed upon municipal employment that a person be a resident *at the time* of his application. In this case appellant claims a constitutional right to be employed by the city of Philadelphia *while* he is living elsewhere. There is no support in our cases for such claim.

"We have previously differentiated between a requirement of continuing residency and a requirement of prior residency of a given duration. Thus in *Shapiro,* supra, 394 U.S. at 636, we stated '[t]he residence requirement and the one-year waiting-period requirement are distinct and independent prerequisites'.

And in *Memorial Hospital*, supra, 415 U.S. at 254–255, quoting *Dunn*, supra, 405 U.S. at 342 n. 13, the Court explained that *Shapiro* and *Dunn* did not question 'the validity of appropriately defined and uniformly applied bona fide residence requirements.'

"This case involves that kind of bona fide continuing residence requirement. The judgment of the Commonwealth Court of Pennsylvania is therefore affirmed."

———

JONES v. HELMS, 452 U.S. 412 (1981). A Georgia statute provided that parental abandonment of a child is a misdemeanor, but is a felony if the parent thereafter leaves the State. The lower federal court held the statute invalid because it infringed upon the right to travel, and the State's interests could be protected by less drastic means. On appeal, the Supreme Court unanimously reversed. Justice Stevens' opinion for the Court concluded that defendant's criminal conduct "necessarily qualified his right" to travel interstate. He noted, moreover, that this case did not involve, as did earlier "right to travel" cases, disparate treatment of residents and non-residents, or old and new residents. The question was the narrower one whether a state could enhance criminal punishment if the offender left the state after committing the crime. "Thus, although a simple penalty for leaving a State is plainly impermissible, if departure aggravates the consequences of conduct that is otherwise punishable, the State may treat the entire sequence of events, from the initial offense to departure from the State, as more serious than its separate components."

———

ZOBEL v. WILLIAMS

457 U.S. 55, 102 S.Ct. 2309, 72 L.Ed.2d 672 (1982).

Chief Justice Burger, delivered the opinion of the Court.

The question presented on this appeal is whether a statutory scheme by which a State distributes income derived from its natural resources to the adult citizens of the State in varying amounts, based on the length of each citizen's residence, violates the equal protection rights of newer state citizens. The Alaska Supreme Court sustained the constitutionality of the statute. . . .

We reverse.

I

The 1967 discovery of large oil reserves on state-owned land in the Prudhoe Bay area of Alaska resulted in a windfall to the State. The State, which had a total budget of $124 million in 1969, before the oil revenues began to flow into the state coffers, received $3.7 billion in petroleum revenues during the 1981 fiscal year. This income will continue, and most likely grow for some years in the future. Recognizing that its mineral reserves, although large, are finite and that the resulting income will not continue in perpetuity, the State took steps to assure that its current good fortune will bring long range benefits. To accomplish this Alaska in 1976 adopted a constitutional amendment establishing the Permanent Fund into which the State must deposit at least 25% of its mineral income each year. Alaska Const., Art. IX, § 15. The amendment prohibits the legislature from appropriating any of the principal of the fund but permits use of the fund's earnings for general governmental purposes.

In 1980, the legislature enacted a dividend program to distribute annually a portion of the Fund's earnings directly to the State's adult residents. Under the plan, each citizen 18 years of age or older receives one dividend unit for each year of residency subsequent to 1959, the first year of statehood. The statute fixed the value of each dividend unit at $50 for the 1979 fiscal year; a one-year resident thus would receive one unit, or $50, while a resident of Alaska since it became a State in 1959 would receive 21 units, or $1,050. The value of a dividend unit will vary each year depending on the income of the Permanent Fund and the amount of that income the State allocates for other purposes. The State now estimates that the 1985 fiscal year dividend will be nearly four times as large as that for 1979.

Appellants, residents of Alaska since 1978, brought this suit in 1980 challenging the dividend distribution plan as violative of their right to equal protection guarantees and their constitutional right to migrate to Alaska, to establish residency there and thereafter to enjoy the full rights of Alaska citizenship on the same terms as all other citizens of the State. . . .

II

The Alaska dividend distribution law is quite unlike the durational residency requirements we examined in Sosna v. Iowa, 419 U.S. 393 (1975); Memorial Hospital v. Maricopa County, 415 U.S. 250 (1974); Dunn v. Blumstein, 405 U.S. 330 (1972); and Shapiro v. Thompson, 394 U.S. 618 (1969). Those cases involved laws which required new residents to reside in the State a fixed minimum period to be eligible for certain benefits available on an equal basis to all other residents. The asserted purpose of the durational residency requirements was to assure that only persons who had established *bona fide* residence received rights and benefits provided for residents.

The Alaska statute does not impose any threshold waiting period on those seeking dividend benefits; persons with less than a full year of residency are entitled to share in the distribution. Alaska Stat. § 43.23.010. Nor does the statute purport to establish a test of the *bona fides* of state residence. Instead, the dividend statute creates fixed, permanent distinctions between an ever increasing number of perpetual classes of concededly *bona fide* residents, based on how long they have been in the State.

Appellants established residence in Alaska two years before the dividend law was passed. The distinction they complain of is not one which the State makes between those who arrived in Alaska after the enactment of the dividend distribution law and those who were residents prior to its enactment. Appellants instead challenge the distinctions made within the class of persons who were residents when the dividend scheme was enacted in 1980. The distinctions appellants attack include the preference given to persons who were residents when Alaska became a State in 1959 over all those who have arrived since then, as well as the distinctions made between all *bona fide* residents who settled in Alaska at different times during the 1959 to 1980 period.[5]

When a State distributes benefits unequally, the distinctions it makes are subject to scrutiny under the Equal Protection Clause of the Fourteenth Amendment. Generally, a law will survive that scrutiny if the distinction it makes rationally furthers a legitimate state purpose. Some particularly invidious distinctions are subject to more rigorous scrutiny. Appellants claim that the distinctions made by the Alaska law should be subjected to the higher level of scrutiny applied to the durational residency requirements in Shapiro v. Thompson, supra and Memorial Hospital v. Maricopa County, supra. The State, on the other hand, asserts that the law need only meet the minimum rationality test.

---

[5] . . .

The statute does not involve the kind of discrimination which the Privileges and Immunities Clause of Art. IV was designed to prevent. That Clause "was designed to insure to a citizen of State A who ventures into State B the same privileges which the citizens of State B enjoy." Toomer v. Witsell, 334 U.S. 385, 395 (1948). The Clause is thus not applicable to this case.

In any event, if the statutory scheme cannot pass even the minimal test proposed by the State, we need not decide whether any enhanced scrutiny is called for.

A

The State advanced and the Alaska Supreme Court accepted three purposes justifying the distinctions made by the dividend program: (a) creation of a financial incentive for individuals to establish and maintain residence in Alaska; (b) encouragement of prudent management of the Permanent Fund; and (c) apportionment of benefits in recognition of undefined "contributions of various kinds, both tangible and intangible, which residents have made during their years of residency."

As the Alaska Supreme Court apparently realized, the first two state objectives—creating a financial incentive for individuals to establish and maintain Alaska residence, and assuring prudent management of the Permanent Fund and the State's natural and mineral resources—are not rationally related to the distinctions Alaska seeks to make between newer residents and those who have been in the State since 1959. Assuming *Arguendo* that granting increased dividend benefits for each year of continued Alaska residence might give some residents an incentive to stay in the state in order to reap increased dividend benefits in the future, the State's interest is not in any way served by granting greater dividends to persons for their residency during the 21 years prior to the enactment.

Nor does the State's purpose of furthering the prudent management of the Permanent Fund and the state's resources support retrospective application of its plan to the date of statehood. On this score the state's contention is straightforward:

". . . If residents believed that twenty years from now they would be required to share permanent fund income on a per capita basis with the large population that Alaska will no doubt have by then, the temptation would be great to urge the legislature to provide immediately for the highest possible return on the investments of the permanent fund principal, which would require investments in riskier ventures."

The State similarly argues that equal per capita distribution would encourage rapacious development of natural resources. Even if we assume that the state interest is served by increasing the dividend for each year of residency beginning with the date of enactment, is it rationally served by granting greater dividends in varying amounts to those who resided in Alaska during the 21 years prior to enactment? We think not.

The last of the State's objectives—to reward citizens for past contributions—alone was relied upon by the Alaska Supreme Court to support the retrospective application of the law to 1959. However, that objective is not a legitimate state purpose. A similar "past contributions" argument was made and rejected in Shapiro v. Thompson, supra, 394 U.S., at 632–633: . . . Similarly, in Vlandis v. Kline, 412 U.S. 441 (1973), we noted that "apportion[ment] of tuition rates on the basis of old and new residency . . . would give rise to grave problems under the Equal Protection Clause of the Fourteenth Amendment."

If the States can make the amount of a cash dividend depend on length of residence, what would preclude varying university tuition on a sliding scale based on years of residence—or even limiting access to finite public facilities, eligibility for student loans, for civil service jobs, or for government contracts by length of domicile? Could States impose different taxes based on length of residence? Alaska's reasoning could open the door to state apportionment of other rights, benefits and services according to length of residency. It would permit the states to divide citizens into expanding numbers of permanent classes. Such a result would be clearly impermissible.

B

We need not consider whether the State could enact the dividend program prospectively only. . . .

III

. . .

We hold that the Alaska dividend distribution plan violates the guarantees of the Equal Protection Clause of the Fourteenth Amendment. Accordingly, the judgment of the Alaska Supreme Court is reversed and the case is remanded for further proceedings not inconsistent with this opinion.

Justice Brennan, with whom Justice Marshall, Justice Blackmun, and Justice Powell join, concurring.

I join the opinion of the Court, and agree with its conclusion that the retrospective aspects of Alaska's dividend-distribution law are not rationally related to a legitimate state purpose. I write separately only to emphasize that the pervasive discrimination embodied in the Alaska distribution scheme gives rise to constitutional concerns of somewhat larger proportions than may be evident on a cursory reading of the Court's opinion. In my view, these concerns might well preclude even the prospective operation of Alaska's scheme.

. . .

. . . In my view, it is difficult to escape from the recognition that underlying any scheme of classification on the basis of duration of residence, we shall almost invariably find the unstated premise that "some citizens are more equal than others." We rejected that premise and, I believe, implicitly rejected most forms of discrimination based upon length of residence, when we adopted the Equal Protection Clause.

Justice O'Connor, concurring in the judgment.

The Court strikes Alaska's distribution scheme, purporting to rely solely upon the Equal Protection Clause of the Fourteenth Amendment. The phrase "right to travel" appears only fleetingly in the Court's analysis, dismissed with an observation that "right to travel analysis refers to little more than a particular application of equal protection analysis." The Court's reluctance to rely explicitly on a right to travel is odd, because its holding depends on the assumption that Alaska's desire "to reward citizens for past contributions . . . is not a legitimate state purpose." Nothing in the Equal Protection Clause itself, however, declares this objective illegitimate. Instead, as a full reading of Shapiro v. Thompson, 394 U.S. 618 (1969) and Vlandis v. Kline, 412 U.S. 441 (1973), reveals, the Court has rejected this objective only when its implementation would abridge an interest in interstate travel or migration.

I respectfully suggest, therefore, that the Court misdirects its criticism when it labels Alaska's objective illegitimate. A desire to compensate citizens for their prior contributions is neither inherently invidious nor irrational. Under some circumstances, the objective may be wholly reasonable. . . .

Alaska's distribution plan distinguishes between long-term residents and recent arrivals. Stripped to its essentials, the plan denies non-Alaskans settling in the State the same privileges afforded longer-term residents. The Privileges and Immunities Clause of Article IV, which guarantees "[t]he Citizens of each State . . . all Privileges and Immunities of Citizens in the several States," addresses just this type of discrimination. Accordingly, I would measure Alaska's scheme against the principles implementing the Privileges and Immunities Clause. In addition to resolving the particular problems raised by Alaska's scheme, this analysis supplies a needed foundation for many of the "right to travel" claims discussed in the Court's prior opinions.

I

. . .

. . . Surely this scheme imposes one of the "disabilities of alienage" prohibited by Article IV's Privileges and Immunities Clause. See Paul v. Virginia, 8 Wall. 168, 180 (1869).

It could be argued that Alaska's scheme does not trigger the Privileges and Immunities Clause because it discriminates among classes of residents, rather than between residents and nonresidents. This argument, however, misinterprets the force of Alaska's distribution system. . . . Each group of citizens who migrated to Alaska in the past, or chooses to move there in the future, lives in the State on less favorable terms than those who arrived earlier. The circumstance that some of the disfavored citizens already live in Alaska does not negate the fact that "the citizen of State A who ventures into [Alaska]" to establish a home labors under a continuous disability.

If the Privileges and Immunities Clause applies to Alaska's distribution system, then our prior opinions describe the proper standard of review. . . .

Once the Court ascertains that discrimination burdens an "essential activity," it will test the constitutionality of the discrimination under a two-part test. First, there must be "something to indicate that non-citizens constitute a peculiar source of the evil at which the statute is aimed." Hicklin v. Orbeck, 437 U.S. 518, 525–526 (1978) (quoting Toomer v. Witsell, 334 U.S. 385, 398 (1948)). Second, the Court must find a "substantial relationship" between the evil and the discrimination practiced against the noncitizens.

Certainly the right infringed in this case is "fundamental." Alaska's statute burdens those nonresidents who choose to settle in the State. It is difficult to imagine a right more essential to the Nation as a whole than the right to establish residence in a new State. . . .

Alaska has not shown that its new residents are the "peculiar source" of any evil addressed by its disbursement scheme. . . .

Even if new residents were the peculiar source of these evils, Alaska has not chosen a cure that bears a "substantial relationship" to the malady. . . .

For these reasons, I conclude that Alaska's disbursement scheme violates Article IV's Privileges and Immunities Clause. I thus reach the same destination as the Court, but along a course that more precisely identifies the evils of the challenged statute.

. . .

Justice Rehnquist, dissenting.

Alaska's dividend distribution scheme represents one State's effort to apportion unique economic benefits among its citizens. Although the wealth received from the oil deposits of Prudhoe Bay may be quite unlike the economic resources enjoyed by most States, Alaska's distribution of that wealth is in substance no different from any other State's allocation of economic benefits. The distribution scheme being in the nature of economic regulation, I am at a loss to see the rationality behind the Court's invalidation of it as a denial of equal protection. This Court has long held that state economic regulations are presumptively valid, and violate the Fourteenth Amendment only in the rarest of circumstances: . . .

. . . [T]he illegitimacy of a State's recognizing the past contributions of its citizens has been established by the Court only in certain cases considering an infringement of the right to travel, and the majority itself rightly declines to apply the strict scrutiny analysis of those right-to-travel cases. The distribution scheme at issue in this case impedes no person's right to travel to and settle in Alaska; if anything, the prospect of receiving annual cash dividends would encourage immigration to Alaska. The State's third justification cannot, therefore, be dismissed simply by quoting language about its legitimacy from right-to-travel cases which have no relevance to the question before us.

. . . .

MARTINEZ v. BYNUM, 461 U.S. 321 (1983).   Texas law permits a school district to deny tuition-free admission to a minor who lives apart from a parent or guardian, if the minor's presence in the school district is for the primary purpose of attending public schools.   Reversing the decision of lower federal courts, the Supreme Court held that the statute was not unconstitutional on its face.   The durational residence cases permit "bona fide residence requirements."   In Vlandis v. Kline, 412 U.S. 441, 453–454 (1973), the Court had stated that a state's interest in preserving the right of residents to attend state universities on a preferential tuition basis permits a state to "establish such reasonable criteria for in-state status as to make virtually certain that students who are not, in fact, bona fide residents of the State, but who have come there solely for educational purposes, cannot take advantage of the in-state rates."   A school district would thus be justified in denying admission to all minor children whose parents did not satisfy traditional criteria of residency.   The Texas statute was not invalid because it went further and allowed enrollment by children whose parents were present in the district, without intent to remain indefinitely, or children who were present in the district for some purpose other than attending school.   Justice Marshall dissented.   (The full report in this case appears infra, p. 929.)

D.   WELFARE

WELFARE AS A FUNDAMENTAL RIGHT CALLING FOR STRICT SCRUTINY

A conscious attempt was made by lawyers involved in legal services programs to deal with what they regarded as inadequate welfare grants by persuading the Court to read a "right to life" into the equal protection clause that would guarantee an adequate minimum payment for every needy individual in society.   The story of this attempt is told in Krislov, *The OEO Lawyers Fail to Constitutionalize a Right to Welfare: A Study in the Uses and Limits of the Judicial Process*, 58 Minn.L.Rev. 211 (1973); Sparer, *The Right to Welfare* in *The Rights of Americans* 65 (N.Dorsen ed. 1971).

DANDRIDGE v. WILLIAMS

397 U.S. 471, 90 S.Ct. 1153, 25 L.Ed.2d 491 (1970).

[Maryland participated in the federal Aid to Families with Dependent Children program (AFDC), providing grants of a certain amount for each child but imposing an upper limit of $250 per month that any family could receive. The regulation was challenged in the federal district court by recipients having large families which received less aid per child than smaller families not affected by the maximum.   They contended that the state limit was contrary to the federal statute and that it discriminated against them merely because of the size of their families in violation of the equal protection clause.   The Court upheld the state limit, rejecting both the statutory and the constitutional claims. Portions of the opinions relating to the constitutional issues are printed below.]

Mr. Justice Stewart delivered the opinion of the Court.

. . .

II.

Although a State may adopt a maximum grant system in allocating its funds available for AFDC payments without violating the Act, it may not, of course, impose a regime of invidious discrimination in violation of the Equal Protection Clause of the Fourteenth Amendment. Maryland says that its maximum grant regulation is wholly free of any invidiously discriminatory purpose or effect, and that the regulation is rationally supportable on at least four entirely valid grounds. The regulation can be clearly justified, Maryland argues, in terms of legitimate state interests in encouraging gainful employment, in maintaining an equitable balance in economic status as between welfare families and those supported by a wage-earner, in providing incentives for family planning, and in allocating available public funds in such a way as fully to meet the needs of the largest possible number of families. The District Court, while apparently recognizing the validity of at least some of these state concerns, nonetheless held that the regulation "is invalid on its face for overreaching,"—that it violates the Equal Protection Clause "[b]ecause it cuts too broad a swath on an indiscriminate basis as applied to the entire group of AFDC eligibles to which it purports to apply, ..."

If this were a case involving government action claimed to violate the First Amendment guarantee of free speech, a finding of "overreaching" would be significant and might be crucial. For when otherwise valid governmental regulation sweeps so broadly as to impinge upon activity protected by the First Amendment, its very overbreadth may make it unconstitutional. See, e. g., Shelton v. Tucker, 364 U.S. 479. But the concept of "overreaching" has no place in this case. For here we deal with state regulation in the social and economic field, not affecting freedoms guaranteed by the Bill of Rights, and claimed to violate the Fourteenth Amendment only because the regulation results in some disparity in grants of welfare payments to the largest AFDC families.[16] For this Court to approve the invalidation of state economic or social regulation as "overreaching" would be far too reminiscent of an era when the Court thought the Fourteenth Amendment gave it power to strike down state laws "because they may be unwise, improvident, or out of harmony with a particular school of thought." Williamson v. Lee Optical of Oklahoma, Inc., 348 U.S. 483, 488. That era long ago passed into history. Ferguson v. Skrupa, 372 U.S. 726.

In the area of economics and social welfare, a State does not violate the Equal Protection Clause merely because the classifications made by its laws are imperfect. If the classification has some "reasonable basis," it does not offend the Constitution simply because the classification "is not made with mathematical nicety or because in practice it results in some inequality." Lindsley v. Natural Carbonic Gas Co., 220 U.S. 61, 78 . . . . . "A statutory discrimination will not be set aside if any state of facts reasonably may be conceived to justify it." McGowan v. Maryland, 366 U.S. 420, 426.

To be sure, the cases cited, and many others enunciating this fundamental standard under the Equal Protection Clause, have in the main involved state regulation of business or industry. The administration of public welfare assistance, by contrast, involves the most basic economic needs of impoverished

---

[16] Cf. Shapiro v. Thompson, 394 U.S. 618, where, by contrast, the Court found state interference with the constitutionally protected freedom of interstate travel.

human beings. We recognize the dramatically real factual difference between the cited cases and this one, but we can find no basis for applying a different constitutional standard.[17] . . . It is a standard that has consistently been applied to state legislation restricting the availability of employment opportunities. Goesaert v. Cleary, 335 U.S. 464; Kotch v. Board of River Port Pilot Comm'rs, 330 U.S. 552. . . . And it is a standard that is true to the principle that the Fourteenth Amendment gives the federal courts no power to impose upon the States their views of what constitutes wise economic or social policy.

Under this long-established meaning of the Equal Protection Clause, it is clear that the Maryland maximum grant regulation is constitutionally valid. We need not explore all the reasons that the State advances in justification of the regulation. It is enough that a solid foundation for the regulation can be found in the State's legitimate interest in encouraging employment and in avoiding discrimination between welfare families and the families of the working poor. By combining a limit on the recipient's grant with permission to retain money earned, without reduction in the amount of the grant, Maryland provides an incentive to seek gainful employment. And by keying the maximum family AFDC grants to the minimum wage a steadily employed head of a household receives, the State maintains some semblance of an equitable balance between families on welfare and those supported by an employed breadwinner.

It is true that in some AFDC families there may be no person who is employable. It is also true that with respect to AFDC families whose determined standard of need is below the regulatory maximum, and who therefore receive grants equal to the determined standard, the employment incentive is absent. But the Equal Protection Clause does not require that a State must choose between attacking every aspect of a problem or not attacking the problem at all. Lindsley v. Natural Carbonic Gas Co., 220 U.S. 61. It is enough that the State's action be rationally based and free from invidious discrimination. The regulation before us meets that test.

We do not decide today that the Maryland regulation is wise, that it best fulfills the relevant social and economic objectives that Maryland might ideally espouse, or that a more just and humane system could not be devised. Conflicting claims of morality and intelligence are raised by opponents and proponents of almost every measure, certainly including the one before us. But the intractable economic, social, and even philosophical problems presented by public welfare assistance programs are not the business of this Court. The Constitution may impose certain procedural safeguards upon systems of welfare administration, Goldberg v. Kelly, 397 U.S. 254. But the Constitution does not empower this Court to second-guess state officials charged with the difficult responsibility of allocating limited public welfare funds among the myriad of potential recipients.

The judgment is reversed.

[Justice Black, joined by Chief Justice Burger, and Justice Harlan filed concurring opinions. Justice Douglas dissented on the statutory issue.]

Mr. Justice Marshall, whom Mr. Justice Brennan joins, dissenting.

. . .

This classification process effected by the maximum grant regulation produces a basic denial of equal treatment. Persons who are concededly similarly situated (dependent children and their families), are not afforded equal, or even approximately equal, treatment under the maximum grant regulation. Subsis-

---

[17] It is important to note that there is no contention that the Maryland regulation is infected with a racially discriminatory purpose or effect such as to make it inherently suspect. Cf. McLaughlin v. Florida, 379 U.S. 184.

tence benefits are paid with respect to some needy dependent children; nothing is paid with respect to others. Some needy families receive full subsistence assistance as calculated by the State; the assistance paid to other families is grossly below their similarly calculated needs.

Yet, as a general principle, individuals should not be afforded different treatment by the State unless there is a relevant distinction between them and "a statutory discrimination must be based on differences that are reasonably related to the purposes of the Act in which it is found." Morey v. Doud, 354 U.S. 457, 465 (1957). See Gulf, Colorado & Santa Fe R. Co. v. Ellis, 165 U.S. 150, 155 (1897). Consequently, the State may not, in the provision of important services or the distribution of governmental payments, supply benefits to some individuals while denying them to others who are similarly situated. . . .

In the instant case, the only distinction between those children with respect to whom assistance is granted and those children who are denied such assistance is the size of the family into which the child permits himself to be born. The class of individuals with respect to whom payments are actually made (the first four or five eligible dependent children in a family), is grossly underinclusive in terms of the class that the AFDC program was designed to assist, namely, *all* needy dependent children. Such underinclusiveness manifests "a prima facie violation of the equal protection requirement of reasonable classification," compelling the State to come forward with a persuasive justification for the classification.

The Court never undertakes to inquire for such a justification; rather it avoids the task by focusing upon the abstract dichotomy between two different approaches to equal protection problems that have been utilized by this Court.

Under the so-called "traditional test," a classification is said to be permissible under the Equal Protection Clause unless it is "without any reasonable basis." Lindsley v. Natural Carbonic Gas Co., 220 U.S. 61, 78 (1911). On the other hand, if the classification affects a "fundamental right," then the state interest in perpetuating the classification must be "compelling" in order to be sustained. See, e.g., Shapiro v. Thompson, supra; . . . .

This case simply defies easy characterization in terms of one or the other of these "tests." The cases relied on by the Court, in which a "mere rationality" test was actually used, e.g., Williamson v. Lee Optical of Oklahoma, Inc., 348 U.S. 483 (1955), are most accurately described as involving the application of equal protection reasoning to the regulation of business interests. The extremes to which the Court has gone in dreaming up rational bases for state regulation in that area may in many instances be ascribed to a healthy revulsion from the Court's earlier excesses in using the Constitution to protect interests that have more than enough power to protect themselves in the legislative halls. This case, involving the literally vital interests of a powerless minority—poor families without breadwinners—is far removed from the area of business regulation, as the Court concedes. Why then is the standard used in those cases imposed here? We are told no more than that this case falls in "the area of economics and social welfare," with the implication that from there the answer is obvious.

In my view, equal protection analysis of this case is not appreciably advanced by the *a priori* definition of a "right," fundamental or otherwise. Rather, concentration must be placed upon the character of the classification in question, the relative importance to individuals in the class discriminated against of the governmental benefits that they do not receive, and the asserted state interests in support of the classification. . . .

It is the individual interests here at stake that, as the Court concedes, most clearly distinguish this case from the "business regulation" equal protection cases. AFDC support to needy dependent children provides the stuff that sustains those children's lives: food, clothing, shelter. And this Court has already recognized several times that when a benefit, even a "gratuitous" benefit, is necessary to sustain life, stricter constitutional standards, both procedural and substantive, are applied to the deprivation of that benefit.

. . .

In any event, it cannot suffice merely to invoke the spectre of the past and to recite from Lindsley v. Natural Carbonic Gas Co. and Williamson v. Lee Optical of Oklahoma, Inc. to decide the case. Appellees are not a gas company or an optical dispenser; they are needy dependent children and families who are discriminated against by the State. The basis of that discrimination—the classification of individuals into large and small families—is too arbitrary and too unconnected to the asserted rationale, the impact on those discriminated against—the denial of even a subsistence existence—too great, and the supposed interests served too contrived and attenuated to meet the requirements of the Constitution. In my view Maryland's maximum grant regulation is invalid under the Equal Protection Clause of the Fourteenth Amendment.

I would affirm the judgment of the District Court.

HARRIS v. McRAE

448 U.S. 297, 100 S.Ct. 2671, 65 L.Ed.2d 784 (1980).

Mr. Justice Stewart delivered the opinion of the Court.

This case presents statutory and constitutional questions concerning the public funding of abortions under Title XIX of the Social Security Act, commonly known as the "Medicaid" Act, and recent annual appropriations acts containing the so-called "Hyde Amendment." The statutory question is whether Title XIX requires a State that participates in the Medicaid program to fund the cost of medically necessary abortions for which federal reimbursement is unavailable under the Hyde Amendment. The constitutional question, which arises only if Title XIX imposes no such requirement, is whether the Hyde Amendment, by denying public funding for certain medically necessary abortions, contravenes the liberty or equal protection guarantees of the Due Process Clause of the Fifth Amendment, or either of the Religion Clauses of the First Amendment.

I.

. . .

Since September 1976, Congress has prohibited—either by an amendment to the annual appropriations bill for the Department of Health, Education, and Welfare or by a joint resolution—the use of any federal funds to reimburse the cost of abortions under the Medicaid program except under certain specified circumstances. This funding restriction is commonly known as the "Hyde Amendment," after its original congressional sponsor, Representative Hyde. The current version of the Hyde Amendment, applicable for fiscal year 1980, provides:

"[N]one of the funds provided by this joint resolution shall be used to perform abortions except where the life of the mother would be endangered if the fetus were carried to term; or except for such medical procedures necessary for the victims of rape or incest when such rape or incest has been reported promptly to a law enforcement agency or public health service." Pub.L. No. 96–123, § 109, 93 Stat. 926. See also Pub.L. No. 96–86, § 118, 93 Stat. 662.

. . .

After a lengthy trial, which inquired into the medical reasons for abortions and the diverse religious views on the subject, the District Court filed an opinion and entered a judgment invalidating all versions of the Hyde Amendment on constitutional grounds. . . .

The Secretary then applied to this Court for a stay of the judgment pending direct appeal of the District Court's decision. We denied the stay, but noted probable jurisdiction of this appeal.

II.

. . .

. . . [W]e conclude that Title XIX does not require a participating State to pay for those medically necessary abortions for which federal reimbursement is unavailable under the Hyde Amendment.[16]

III.

Having determined that Title XIX does not obligate a participating State to pay for those medically necessary abortions for which Congress has withheld federal funding, we must consider the constitutional validity of the Hyde Amendment. The appellees assert that the funding restrictions of the Hyde Amendment violate several rights secured by the Constitution—(1) the right of a woman, implicit in the Due Process Clause of the Fifth Amendment, to decide whether to terminate a pregnancy, (2) the prohibition under the Establishment Clause of the First Amendment against any "law respecting an establishment of religion," and (3) the right to freedom of religion protected by the Free Exercise Clause of the First Amendment. The appellees also contend that, quite apart from substantive constitutional rights, the Hyde Amendment violates the equal protection component of the Fifth Amendment.

It is well settled that, quite apart from the guarantee of equal protection, if a law "impinges upon a fundamental right explicitly or implicitly secured by the Constitution [it] is presumptively unconstitutional." Mobile v. Bolden, 446 U.S. 55, 76 (plurality opinion). Accordingly, before turning to the equal protection issue in this case, we examine whether the Hyde Amendment violates any substantive rights secured by the Constitution.

A.

We address first the appellees' argument that the Hyde Amendment, by restricting the availability of certain medically necessary abortions under Medicaid, impinges on the "liberty" protected by the Due Process Clause as recognized in Roe v. Wade, 410 U.S. 113, and its progeny.

In the *Wade* case, this Court held unconstitutional a Texas statute making it a crime to procure or attempt an abortion except on medical advice for the purpose of saving the mother's life. The constitutional underpinning of *Wade* was a recognition that the "liberty" protected by the Due Process Clause of the Fourteenth Amendment includes not only the freedoms explicitly mentioned in the Bill of Rights, but also a freedom of personal choice in certain matters of marriage and family life. This implicit constitutional liberty, the Court in *Wade* held, includes the freedom of a woman to decide whether to terminate a pregnancy.

But the Court in *Wade* also recognized that a State has legitimate interests during a pregnancy in both ensuring the health of the mother and protecting

---

[16] A participating State is free, if it so chooses, to include in its Medicaid plan those medically necessary abortions for which federal reimbursement is unavailable. See Beal v. Doe, supra, 432 U.S., at 447; Preterm, Inc. v. Dukekis, supra, 591 F.2d, at 134. We hold only that a State *need* not include such abortions in its Medicaid plan.

potential human life. These state interests, which were found to be "separate and distinct" and to "grow[ ] in substantiality as the woman approaches term," pose a conflict with a woman's untrammeled freedom of choice. . . .

In Maher v. Roe, 432 U.S. 464, the Court was presented with the question whether the scope of personal constitutional freedom recognized in Roe v. Wade included an entitlement to Medicaid payments for abortions that are not medically necessary. At issue in *Maher* was a Connecticut welfare regulation under which Medicaid recipients received payments for medical services incident to childbirth, but not for medical services incident to nontherapeutic abortions. The District Court held that the regulation violated the Equal Protection Clause of the Fourteenth Amendment because the unequal subsidization of childbirth and abortion impinged on the "fundamental right to abortion" recognized in *Wade* and its progeny.

It was the view of this Court that "the District Court misconceived the nature and scope of the fundamental right recognized in *Roe*." 432 U.S., at 471. The doctrine of Roe v. Wade, the Court held in *Maher*, "protects the woman from unduly burdensome interference with her freedom to decide whether to terminate her pregnancy," such as the severe criminal sanctions at issue in Roe v. Wade, supra, or the absolute requirement of spousal consent for an abortion challenged in Planned Parenthood of Central Missouri v. Danforth, 428 U.S. 52.

But the constitutional freedom recognized in *Wade* and its progeny, the *Maher* Court explained, did not prevent Connecticut from making "a value judgment favoring childbirth over abortion, and . . . implement[ing] that judgment by the allocation of public funds." As the Court elaborated:

"The Connecticut regulation before us is different in kind from the laws invalidated in our previous abortions decisions. The Connecticut regulation places no obstacles—absolute or otherwise—in the pregnant woman's path to an abortion. An indigent woman who desires an abortion suffers no disadvantage as a consequence of Connecticut's decision to fund childbirth; she continues as before to be dependent on private sources for the service she desires. The State may have made childbirth a more attractive alternative, thereby influencing the woman's decision, but it has imposed no restriction on access to abortions that was not already there. The indigency that may make it difficult—and in some cases, perhaps, impossible—for some women to have abortions is neither created nor in any way affected by the Connecticut regulation."

The Court in *Maher* noted that its description of the doctrine recognized in *Wade* and its progeny signaled "no retreat" from those decisions. In explaining why the constitutional principle recognized in *Wade* and later cases—protecting a woman's freedom of choice—did not translate into a constitutional obligation of Connecticut to subsidize abortions, the Court cited the "basic difference between direct state interference with a protected activity and state encouragement of an alternative activity consonant with legislative policy. Constitutional concerns are greatest when the State attempts to impose its will by force of law; the State's power to encourage actions deemed to be in the public interest is necessarily far broader." Thus, even though the Connecticut regulation favored childbirth over abortion by means of subsidization of one and not the other, the Court in *Maher* concluded that the regulation did not impinge on the constitutional freedom recognized in *Wade* because it imposed no governmental restriction on access to abortions.

The Hyde Amendment, like the Connecticut welfare regulation at issue in *Maher,* places no governmental obstacle in the path of a woman who chooses to terminate her pregnancy, but rather, by means of unequal subsidization of abortion and other medical services, encourages alternative activity deemed in the public interest. The present case does differ factually from *Maher* insofar as that case involved a failure to fund nontherapeutic abortions, whereas the Hyde Amendment withholds funding of certain medically necessary abortions. Accordingly, the appellees argue that because the Hyde Amendment affects a significant interest not present or asserted in *Maher*—the interest of a woman in protecting her health during pregnancy—and because that interest lies at the core of the personal constitutional freedom recognized in *Wade,* the present case is constitutionally different from *Maher.* It is the appellees' view that to the extent that the Hyde Amendment withholds funding for certain medically necessary abortions, it clearly impinges on the constitutional principle recognized in *Wade.*

It is evident that a woman's interest in protecting her health was an important theme in *Wade.* In concluding that the freedom of a woman to decide whether to terminate her pregnancy falls within the personal liberty protected by the Due Process Clause, the Court in *Wade* emphasized the fact that the woman's decision carries with it significant personal health implications—both physical and psychological. In fact, although the Court in *Wade* recognized that the state interest in protecting potential life becomes sufficiently compelling in the period after fetal viability to justify an absolute criminal prohibition of nontherapeutic abortions, the Court held that even after fetal viability a State may not prohibit abortions "necessary to preserve the life or health of the mother." Because even the compelling interest of the State in protecting potential life after fetal viability was held to be insufficient to outweigh a woman's decision to protect her life or health, it could be argued that the freedom of a woman to decide whether to terminate her pregnancy for health reasons does in fact lie at the core of the constitutional liberty identified in *Wade.*

But, regardless of whether the freedom of a woman to choose to terminate her pregnancy for health reasons lies at the core or the periphery of the due process liberty recognized in *Wade,* it simply does not follow that a woman's freedom of choice carries with it a constitutional entitlement to the financial resources to avail herself of the full range of protected choices. The reason why was explained in *Maher:* although government may not place obstacles in the path of a woman's exercise of her freedom of choice, it need not remove those not of its own creation. Indigency falls in the latter category. The financial constraints that restrict an indigent woman's ability to enjoy the full range of constitutionally protected freedom of choice are the product not of governmental restrictions on access to abortions, but rather of her indigency. Although Congress has opted to subsidize medically necessary services generally, but not certain medically necessary abortions, the fact remains that the Hyde Amendment leaves an indigent woman with at least the same range of choice in deciding whether to obtain a medically necessary abortion as she would have had if Congress had chosen to subsidize no health care costs at all. We are thus not persuaded that the Hyde Amendment impinges on the constitutionally protected freedom of choice recognized in *Wade.* [19]

[19] The appellees argue that the Hyde Amendment is unconstitutional because it "penalizes" the exercise of a woman's choice to terminate a pregnancy by abortion. See Memorial Hospital v. Maricopa County, 415 U.S. 250; Shapiro v. Thompson, 394 U.S. 618. This argument falls short of the mark. In *Maher,* the Court found only a "semantic difference" between the argument that Connecticut's refusal to subsidize nontherapeutic abortions "unduly interfere[d]" with the exercise of the constitutional liberty recognized in *Wade* and the argument that it "penalized" the exercise of that liberty. And, regardless of how the claim was characterized, the *Maher* Court rejected the argument that Connecticut's refusal to subsidize protected conduct, without more, impinged on the constitutional freedom of choice. This reasoning is equally applicable in the present case. A substantial constitutional question would arise if Congress had attempted to withhold all Medicaid benefits from an otherwise eligible candidate simply because that candidate had exercised her constitutionally protected freedom to terminate her pregnancy by abortion. This would be analogous to Sherbert v.

Although the liberty protected by the Due Process Clause affords protection against unwarranted government interference with freedom of choice in the context of certain personal decisions, it does not confer an entitlement to such funds as may be necessary to realize all the advantages of that freedom. To hold otherwise would mark a drastic change in our understanding of the Constitution. It cannot be that because government may not prohibit the use of contraceptives, Griswold v. Connecticut, 381 U.S. 479, or prevent parents from sending their child to a private school, Pierce v. Society of Sisters, 268 U.S. 510, government, therefore, has an affirmative constitutional obligation to ensure that all persons have the financial resources to obtain contraceptives or send their children to private schools. To translate the limitation on governmental power implicit in the Due Process Clause into an affirmative funding obligation would require Congress to subsidize the medically necessary abortion of an indigent woman even if Congress had not enacted a Medicaid program to subsidize other medically necessary services. Nothing in the Due Process Clause supports such an extraordinary result.[20] Whether freedom of choice that is constitutionally protected warrants federal subsidization is a question for Congress to answer, not a matter of constitutional entitlement. Accordingly, we conclude that the Hyde Amendment does not impinge on the due process liberty recognized in *Wade.*

B.

The appellees also argue that the Hyde Amendment contravenes rights secured by the Religion Clauses of the First Amendment. . . .

. . .

[The Court held that the Hyde Amendment did not contravene the establishment clause of the first amendment and that the parties lacked standing to raise a challenge under the free exercise clause.]

C.

It remains to be determined whether the Hyde Amendment violates the equal protection component of the Fifth Amendment. This challenge is premised on the fact that, although federal reimbursement is available under Medicaid for medically necessary services generally, the Hyde Amendment does not permit federal reimbursement of all medically necessary abortions. The District Court held, and the appellees argue here, that this selective subsidization violates the constitutional guarantee of equal protection.

The guarantee of equal protection under the Fifth Amendment is not a source of substantive rights or liberties,[25] but rather a right to be free from invidious discrimination in statutory classifications and other governmental

---

Verner, 374 U.S. 398, where this Court held that a State may not, consistent with the First and Fourteenth Amendments, withhold *all* unemployment compensation benefits from a claimant who would otherwise be eligible for such benefits but for the fact that she is unwilling to work one day per week on her Sabbath. But the Hyde Amendment, unlike the statute at issue in *Sherbert,* does not provide for such a broad disqualification from receipt of public benefits. Rather, the Hyde Amendment, like the Connecticut welfare provision at issue in *Maher,* represents simply a refusal to subsidize certain protected conduct. A refusal to fund protected activity, without more, cannot be equated with the imposition of a "penalty" on that activity.

[20] As this Court in *Maher* observed: "The Constitution imposes no obligation on the [Government] to pay the pregnancy-related medical expenses of indigent women, or indeed to pay any of the medical expenses of indigents."

[25] An exception to this statement is to be found in Reynolds v. Sims, 377 U.S. 533, and its progeny. Although the Constitution of the United States does not confer the right to vote in state elections, see Minor v. Happersett, 21 Wall. 162, 178, *Reynolds* held that if a State adopts an electoral system, the Equal Protection Clause of the Fourteenth Amendment confers upon a qualified voter a substantive right to participate in the electoral process equally with other qualified voters. See, e. g., Dunn v. Blumstein, 405 U.S. 330, 336.

activity. It is well-settled that where a statutory classification does not itself impinge on a right or liberty protected by the Constitution, the validity of classification must be sustained unless "the classification rests on grounds wholly irrelevant to the achievement of [any legitimate governmental] objective." McGowan v. Maryland, supra, 366 U.S., at 425. This presumption of constitutional validity, however, disappears if a statutory classification is predicated on criteria that are, in a constitutional sense, "suspect," the principal example of which is a classification based on race, e.g., Brown v. Board of Education, 347 U.S. 483.

1.

For the reasons stated above, we have already concluded that the Hyde Amendment violates no constitutionally protected substantive rights. We now conclude as well that it is not predicated on a constitutionally suspect classification. In reaching this conclusion, we again draw guidance from the Court's decision in Maher v. Roe. As to whether the Connecticut welfare regulation providing funds for childbirth but not for nontherapeutic abortions discriminated against a suspect class, the Court in *Maher* observed:

"An indigent woman desiring an abortion does not come within the limited category of disadvantaged classes so recognized by our cases. Nor does the fact that the impact of the regulation falls upon those who cannot pay lead to a different conclusion. In a sense, every denial of welfare to an indigent creates a wealth classification as compared to nonindigents who are able to pay for the desired goods or services. But this Court has never held that financial need alone identifies a suspect class for purposes of equal protection analysis." . . .

Thus, the Court in *Maher* found no basis for concluding that the Connecticut regulation was predicated on a suspect classification.

It is our view that the present case is indistinguishable from *Maher* in this respect. Here, as in *Maher,* the principal impact of the Hyde Amendment falls on the indigent. But that fact does not itself render the funding restriction constitutionally invalid, for this Court has held repeatedly that poverty, standing alone, is not a suspect classification. See, e.g., James v. Valtierra, 402 U.S. 137. That *Maher* involved the refusal to fund nontherapeutic abortions, whereas the present case involves the refusal to fund medically necessary abortions, has no bearing on the factors that render a classification "suspect" within the meaning of the constitutional guarantee of equal protection.

2.

The remaining question then is whether the Hyde Amendment is rationally related to a legitimate governmental objective. It is the Government's position that the Hyde Amendment bears a rational relationship to its legitimate interest in protecting the potential life of the fetus. We agree.

In *Wade,* the Court recognized that the State has "an important and legitimate interest in protecting the potentiality of human life." 410 U.S., at 162. That interest was found to exist throughout a pregnancy, "grow[ing] in substantiality as the woman approaches term." See also Beal v. Doe, 432 U.S. 438, 445–446. Moreover, in *Maher,* the Court held that Connecticut's decision to fund the costs associated with childbirth but not those associated with nontherapeutic abortions was a rational means of advancing the legitimate state interest in protecting potential life by encouraging childbirth. 432 U.S., at 478–479. See also Poelker v. Doe, 432 U.S. 519, 520–521.

It follows that the Hyde Amendment, by encouraging childbirth except in the most urgent circumstances, is rationally related to the legitimate governmental objective of protecting potential life. By subsidizing the medical expenses of indigent women who carry their pregnancies to term while not subsidizing the comparable expenses of women who undergo abortions (except those whose lives are threatened), Congress has established incentives that make childbirth a more attractive alternative than abortion for persons eligible for Medicaid. These incentives bear a direct relationship to the legitimate congressional interest in protecting potential life. Nor is it irrational that Congress has authorized federal reimbursement for medically necessary services generally, but not for certain medically necessary abortions. Abortion is inherently different from other medical procedures, because no other procedure involves the purposeful termination of a potential life.

After conducting an extensive evidentiary hearing into issues surrounding the public funding of abortions, the District Court concluded that "[t]he interests of . . . the federal government . . . in the fetus and in preserving it are not sufficient, weighed in the balance with the woman's threatened health, to justify withdrawing medical assistance unless the woman consents . . . to carry the fetus to term." In making an independent appraisal of the competing interests involved here, the District Court went beyond the judicial function. Such decisions are entrusted under the Constitution to Congress, not the courts. It is the role of the courts only to ensure that congressional decisions comport with the Constitution.

Where, as here, the Congress has neither invaded a substantive constitutional right or freedom, nor enacted legislation that purposefully operates to the detriment of a suspect class, the only requirement of equal protection is that congressional action be rationally related to a legitimate governmental interest. The Hyde Amendment satisfies that standard. It is not the mission of this Court or any other to decide whether the balance of competing interests reflected in the Hyde Amendment is wise social policy. If that were our mission, not every Justice who has subscribed to the judgment of the Court today could have done so. But we cannot, in the name of the Constitution, overturn duly enacted statutes simply "because they may be unwise, improvident, or out of harmony with a particular school of thought." Williamson v. Lee Optical Co., 348 U.S. 483, 488, quoted in Dandridge v. Williams, 397 U.S. 471, 484. Rather, "when an issue involves policy choices as sensitive as those implicated [here] . . ., the appropriate forum for their resolution in a democracy is the legislature." Maher v. Roe, supra, at 479.

IV.

For the reasons stated in this opinion, we hold that a State that participates in the Medicaid program is not obligated under Title XIX to continue to fund those medically necessary abortions for which federal reimbursement is unavailable under the Hyde Amendment. We further hold that the funding restrictions of the Hyde Amendment violate neither the Fifth Amendment nor the Establishment Clause of the First Amendment. It is also our view that the appellees lack standing to raise a challenge to the Hyde Amendment under the Free Exercise Clause of the First Amendment. Accordingly, the judgment of the District Court is reversed, and the case is remanded to that court for further proceedings consistent with this opinion.

It is so ordered.

Mr. Justice White, concurring.

I join the Court's opinion and judgment with these additional remarks.

. . . .

Roe v. Wade . . . dealt with the circumstances in which the governmental interest in potential life would justify official interference with the abortion choices of pregnant women. There is no such calculus involved here. The government does not seek to interfere with or to impose any coercive restraint on the choice of any woman to have an abortion. The woman's choice remains unfettered, the government is not attempting to use its interest in life to justify a coercive restraint, and hence in disbursing its Medicaid funds it is free to implement rationally what Roe v. Wade recognized to be its legitimate interest in a potential life by covering the medical costs of childbirth but denying funds for abortions. Neither Roe v. Wade nor any of the cases decided in its wake invalidates this legislative preference. .   .   .

.   .   .

Mr. Justice Brennan, with whom Mr. Justice Marshall and Mr. Justice Blackmun join, dissenting.

I agree entirely with my Brother Stevens that the State's interest in protecting the potential life of the fetus cannot justify the exclusion of financially and medically needy women from the benefits to which they would otherwise be entitled solely because the treatment that a doctor has concluded is medically necessary involves an abortion. I write separately to express my continuing disagreement with the Court's mischaracterization of the nature of the fundamental right recognized in Roe v. Wade, 410 U.S. 113 (1973), and its misconception of the manner in which that right is infringed by federal and state legislation withdrawing all funding for medically necessary abortions.

Roe v. Wade held that the constitutional right to personal privacy encompasses a woman's decision whether or not to terminate her pregnancy. *Roe* and its progeny established that the pregnant woman has a right to be free from state interference with her choice to have an abortion—a right which, at least prior to the end of the first trimester, absolutely prohibits any governmental regulation of that highly personal decision. The proposition for which these cases stand thus is not that the State is under an affirmative obligation to ensure access to abortions for all who may desire them; it is that the State must refrain from wielding its enormous power and influence in a manner that might burden the pregnant woman's freedom to choose whether to have an abortion. The Hyde Amendment's denial of public funds for medically necessary abortions plainly intrudes upon this constitutionally protected decision, for both by design and in effect it serves to coerce indigent pregnant women to bear children that they would otherwise elect not to have.[4]

When viewed in the context of the Medicaid program to which it is appended, it is obvious that the Hyde Amendment is nothing less than an attempt by Congress to circumvent the dictates of the Constitution and achieve indirectly what Roe v. Wade said it could not do directly. Under Title XIX of the Social Security Act, the Federal Government reimburses participating States for virtually all medically necessary services it provides to the categorically needy. The sole limitation of any significance is the Hyde Amendment's prohibition against the use of any federal funds to pay for the costs of abortions (except where the life of the mother would be endangered if the fetus were carried to term). As my Brother Stevens persuasively demonstrates, exclusion of medically necessary abortions from Medicaid coverage cannot be justified as a cost-saving device. Rather, the Hyde Amendment is a transparent attempt by the Legislative Branch to impose the political majority's judgment of the morally acceptable and socially desirable preference on a sensitive and intimate decision

---

[4] My focus throughout this opinion is upon the coercive impact of the congressional decision to fund one outcome of pregnancy—childbirth—while not funding the other—abortion. Because I believe this alone renders the Hyde Amendment unconstitutional, I do not dwell upon the other disparities that the Amendment produces in the treatment of rich and poor, pregnant and nonpregnant. I concur completely, however, in my Brother Stevens' discussion of those disparities.
.   .   .

that the Constitution entrusts to the individual. Worse yet, the Hyde Amendment does not foist that majoritarian viewpoint with equal measure upon everyone in our Nation, rich and poor alike; rather, it imposes that viewpoint only upon that segment of our society which, because of its position of political powerlessness, is least able to defend its privacy rights from the encroachments of state-mandated morality. The instant legislation thus calls for more exacting judicial review than in most other cases. "When elected leaders cower before public pressure, this Court, more than ever, must not shirk its duty to enforce the Constitution for the benefit of the poor and powerless." Beal v. Doe, 432 U.S. 438, 462 (1977) (Marshall, J., dissenting). Though it may not be this Court's mission "to decide whether the balance of competing interests reflected in the Hyde Amendment is wise social policy," it most assuredly is our responsibility to vindicate the pregnant woman's constitutional right to decide whether to bear children free from governmental intrusion.

Moreover, it is clear that the Hyde Amendment not only was designed to inhibit, but does in fact inhibit the woman's freedom to choose abortion over childbirth. "Pregnancy is unquestionably a condition requiring medical services. . . . Treatment for the condition may involve medical procedures for its termination, or medical procedures to bring the pregnancy to term, resulting in a live birth. '[A]bortion and childbirth, when stripped of the sensitive moral arguments surrounding the abortion controversy, are simply two alternative medical methods of dealing with pregnancy. . . .'" Beal v. Doe, supra, at 449 (Brennan, J., dissenting) (quoting Roe v. Norton, 408 F.Supp. 660, 663, n. 3 (Conn.1975)). In every pregnancy, one of these two courses of treatment is medically necessary, and the poverty-stricken woman depends on the Medicaid Act to pay for the expenses associated with that procedure. But under the Hyde Amendment, the Government will fund only those procedures incidental to childbirth. By thus injecting coercive financial incentives favoring childbirth into a decision that is constitutionally guaranteed to be free from governmental intrusion, the Hyde Amendment deprives the indigent woman of her freedom to choose abortion over maternity, thereby impinging on the due process liberty right recognized in Roe v. Wade.

The Court's contrary conclusion is premised on its belief that "[t]he financial constraints that restrict an indigent woman's ability to enjoy the full range of constitutionally protected freedom of choice are the product not of governmental restrictions on access to abortions, but rather of her indigency." Accurate as this statement may be, it reveals only half the picture. For what the Court fails to appreciate is that it is not simply the woman's indigency that interferes with her freedom of choice, but the combination of her own poverty and the government's unequal subsidization of abortion and childbirth.

A poor woman in the early stages of pregnancy confronts two alternatives: she may elect either to carry the fetus to term or to have an abortion. In the abstract, of course, this choice is hers alone, and the Court rightly observes that the Hyde Amendment "places no governmental obstacle in the path of a woman who chooses to terminate her pregnancy." But the reality of the situation is that the Hyde Amendment has effectively removed this choice from the indigent woman's hands. By funding all of the expenses associated with childbirth and none of the expenses incurred in terminating pregnancy, the government literally makes an offer that the indigent woman cannot afford to refuse. It matters not that in this instance the government has used the carrot rather than the stick. What is critical is the realization that as a practical matter, many poverty-stricken women will choose to carry their pregnancy to term simply because the government provides funds for the associated medical services, even though these same women would have chosen to have an abortion if the government had also paid for that option, or indeed if the government had stayed out of the picture altogether and had defrayed the costs of neither procedure.

The fundamental flaw in the Court's due process analysis, then, is its failure to acknowledge that the discriminatory distribution of the benefits of governmental largesse can discourage the exercise of fundamental liberties just as effectively as can an outright denial of those rights through criminal and regulatory sanctions. Implicit in the Court's reasoning is the notion that as long as the government is not obligated to provide its citizens with certain benefits or privileges, it may condition the grant of such benefits on the recipient's relinquishment of his constitutional rights.

It would belabor the obvious to expound at any great length on the illegitimacy of a state policy that interferes with the exercise of fundamental rights through the selective bestowal of governmental favors. It suffices to note that we have heretofore never hesitated to invalidate any scheme of granting or withholding financial benefits that incidentally or intentionally burdens one manner of exercising a constitutionally protected choice. . . .

The Medicaid program cannot be distinguished from these other statutory schemes that unconstitutionally burdened fundamental rights.[6] . . .

I respectfully dissent.

Mr. Justice Marshall, dissenting.

. . .

. . . The Court's decision today marks a retreat from Roe v. Wade and represents a cruel blow to the most powerless members of our society. I dissent.

. . .

I.

The record developed below reveals that the standards set forth in the Hyde Amendment exclude the majority of cases in which the medical profession would recommend abortion as medically necessary. Indeed, in States that have adopted a standard more restrictive than the "medically necessary" test of the Medicaid Act, the number of funded abortions has decreased by over 98%.

. . .

An optimistic estimate indicates that as many as 100 excess deaths may occur each year as a result of the Hyde Amendment. The record contains no estimate of the health damage that may occur to poor women, but it shows that it will be considerable.

II.

The Court resolves the equal protection issue in this case through a relentlessly formalistic catechism. Adhering to its "two-tiered" approach to equal protection, the Court first decides that so-called strict scrutiny is not required because the Hyde Amendment does not violate the Due Process Clause and is not predicated on a constitutionally suspect classification. . . .

---

[6] . . . [I]t is no answer to assert that no "penalty" is being imposed because the State is only refusing to pay for the specific costs of the protected activity rather than withholding other Medicaid benefits to which the recipient would be entitled or taking some other action more readily characterized as "punitive." Surely the government could not provide free transportation to the polling booths only for those citizens who vote for Democratic candidates, even though the failure to provide the same benefit to Republicans "represents simply a refusal to subsidize certain protected conduct," ibid, and does not involve the denial of any other governmental benefits. Whether the State withholds only the special costs of a disfavored option or penalizes the individual more broadly for the manner in which she exercises her choice, it cannot interfere with a constitutionally protected decision through the coercive use of governmental largesse.

I continue to believe that the rigid "two-tiered" approach is inappropriate and that the Constitution requires a more exacting standard of review than mere rationality in cases such as this one. Further, in my judgment the Hyde Amendment cannot pass constitutional muster even under the rational-basis standard of review.

A.

This case is perhaps the most dramatic illustration to date of the deficiencies in the Court's obsolete "two-tiered" approach to the Equal Protection Clause. See San Antonio School Dist. v. Rodriguez, 411 U.S. 1, 98–110 (1973) (Marshall, J., dissenting); Massachusetts v. Murgia, 427 U.S. 307, 318–321 (1976) (Marshall, J., dissenting); Maher v. Roe, supra, at 457–458 (Marshall, J., dissenting); Vance v. Bradley, 440 U.S. 93, 113–115 (1979) (Marshall, J., dissenting).[3] With all deference, I am unable to understand how the Court can afford the same level of scrutiny to the legislation involved here—whose cruel impact falls exclusively on indigent pregnant women—that it has given to legislation distinguishing opticians from ophthalmologists, or to other legislation that makes distinctions between economic interests more than able to protect themselves in the political process. . . . Heightened scrutiny of legislative classifications has always been designed to protect groups "saddled with such disabilities or subjected to such a history of purposeful unequal treatment, or relegated to such a position of political powerlessness as to command extraordinary protection from the majoritarian political process." San Antonio School District v. Rodriguez, supra, at 28 (1973).[4] And while it is now clear that traditional "strict scrutiny" is unavailable to protect the poor against classifications that disfavor them, Dandridge v. Williams, 397 U.S. 471 (1970), I do not believe that legislation that imposes a crushing burden on indigent women can be treated with the same deference given to legislation distinguishing among business interests.

B.

. . .

The class burdened by the Hyde Amendment consists of indigent women, a substantial proportion of whom are members of minority races. As I observed in *Maher,* nonwhite women obtain abortions at nearly double the rate of whites. . . . In my view, the fact that the burden of the Hyde Amendment falls exclusively on financially destitute women suggests "a special condition, which tends seriously to curtail the operation of those political processes ordinarily to be relied upon to protect minorities, and which may call for a correspondingly more searching judicial inquiry." United States v. Carolene Products, 304 U.S. 144, 152–153, n. 4 (1938). For this reason, I continue to believe that "a showing that state action has a devastating impact on the lives of minority racial groups must be relevant" for purposes of equal protection

---

[3] A number of individual Justices have expressed discomfort with the two-tiered approach, and I am pleased to observe that its hold on the law may be waning. See Craig v. Boren, 429 U.S. 190, 210–211, and n. * (1976) (Powell, J., concurring); id., at 211–212 (Stevens, J., concurring); post at 4-5, n. 4 (Stevens, J., dissenting). Further, the Court has adopted an "intermediate" level of scrutiny for a variety of classifications. See Trimble v. Gordon, 430 U.S. 762 (1977) (illegitimacy); Craig v. Boren, supra (sex discrimination); Foley v. Connelie, 435 U.S. 291 (1979) (alienage). Cf. University of California Regents v. Bakke, 438 U.S. 265, 324 (1978) (opinion of Brennan, White, Marshall, and Blackmun, JJ.) (affirmative action).

[4] For this reason the Court has on occasion suggested that classifications discriminating against the poor are subject to special scrutiny under the Fifth and Fourteenth Amendments. See McDonald v. Board of Election, 394 U.S. 802, 807 (1969); Harper v. Virginia Bd. of Elections, 383 U.S. 663, 668 (1966).

analysis. Jefferson v. Hackney, 406 U.S. 535, 575–576 (1972) (Marshall, J., dissenting).

As I explained in *Maher,* the asserted state interest in protecting potential life is insufficient to "outweigh the deprivation or serious discouragement of a vital constitutional right of especial importance to poor and minority women." 432 U.S., at 461. . . .

C.

Although I would abandon the strict-scrutiny/rational-basis dichotomy in equal protection analysis, it is by no means necessary to reject that traditional approach to conclude, as I do, that the Hyde Amendment is a denial of equal protection. My Brother Brennan has demonstrated that the Amendment is unconstitutional because it impermissibly infringes upon the individual's constitutional right to decide whether to terminate a pregnancy. And as my Brother Stevens demonstrates the Government's interest in protecting fetal life is not a legitimate one when it is in conflict with "the preservation of the life or health of the mother," Roe v. Wade, supra, at 165, and when the Government's effort to make serious health damage to the mother "a more attractive alternative than abortion" does not rationally promote the governmental interest in encouraging normal childbirth.

The Court treats this case as though it were controlled by *Maher.* To the contrary, this case is the mirror image of *Maher.* The result in *Maher* turned on the fact that the legislation there under consideration discouraged only nontherapeutic, or medically unnecessary, abortions. In the Court's view, denial of Medicaid funding for nontherapeutic abortions was not a denial of equal protection because Medicaid funds were available only for medically necessary procedures. Thus the plaintiffs were seeking benefits which were not available to others similarly situated. I continue to believe that *Maher* was wrongly decided. But it is apparent that while the plaintiffs in *Maher* were seeking a benefit not available to others similarly situated, respondents are protesting their exclusion from a benefit that is available to all others similarly situated. This, it need hardly be said, is a crucial difference for equal protection purposes.

. . .

III.

The consequences of today's opinion—consequences to which the Court seems oblivious—are not difficult to predict. Pregnant women denied the funding necessary to procure abortions will be restricted to two alternatives. First, they can carry the fetus to term—even though that route may result in severe injury or death to the mother, the fetus, or both. . . .

Ultimately, the result reached today may be traced to the Court's unwillingness to apply the constraints of the Constitution to decisions involving the expenditure of governmental funds. . . .

More than 35 years ago, Mr. Justice Jackson observed that the "task of translating the majestic generalities of the Bill of Rights . . . into concrete restraints on officials dealing with the problems of the twentieth century, is one to disturb self-confidence." West Virginia State Bd. of Educ. v. Barnette, 319 U.S. 624, 640 (1943). These constitutional principles, he observed for the Court, "grew in soil which also produced a philosophy that the individual['s] . . . liberty was attainable through mere absence of government restraints." Ibid. Those principles must be "transplant[ed] . . . to a soil in which the *laissez-faire* concept or principle of non-interference has withered at least as to economic affairs, and social advancements are increasingly sought through closer integration of society and through expanded and strengthened governmental controls." Id., at 640.

In this case, the Federal Government has taken upon itself the burden of financing practically all medically necessary expenditures. One category of medically necessary expenditure has been singled out for exclusion, and the sole basis for the exclusion is a premise repudiated for purposes of constitutional law in Roe v. Wade. The consequence is a devastating impact on the lives and health of poor women. I do not believe that a Constitution committed to the equal protection of the laws can tolerate this result. I dissent.

Mr. Justice Blackmun, dissenting.

I join the dissent of Mr. Justice Brennan and agree wholeheartedly with his and Mr. Justice Stevens' respective observations and descriptions of what the Court is doing in this latest round of "abortion cases." I need add only that I find what I said in dissent in Beal v. Doe, 432 U.S. 438, 462 (1977), and its two companion cases, Maher v. Roe, 432 U.S. 464 (1977), and Poelker v. Doe, 432 U.S. 519 (1977), continues for me to be equally pertinent and equally applicable in these Hyde Amendment cases. There is "condescension" in the Court's holding "that she may go elsewhere for her abortion"; this is "disingenuous and alarming"; the Government "punitively impresses upon a needy minority its own concepts of the socially desirable, the publicly acceptable, and the morally sound"; the "financial argument, of course, is specious"; there truly is "another world 'out there,' the existence of which the Court, I suspect, either chooses to ignore or fears to recognize"; the "cancer of poverty will continue to grow"; and "the lot of the poorest among us," once again, and still, is not to be bettered.

Mr. Justice Stevens, dissenting.

.   .   .

This case involves a special exclusion of women who, by definition, are confronted with a choice between two serious harms: serious health damage to themselves on the one hand and abortion on the other. The competing interests are the interest in maternal health and the interest in protecting potential human life. It is now part of our law that the pregnant woman's decision as to which of these conflicting interests shall prevail is entitled to constitutional protection.

.   .   .

.   .   . The Hyde amendments not only exclude financially and medically needy persons from the pool of benefits for a constitutionally insufficient reason; they also require the expenditure of millions and millions of dollars in order to thwart the exercise of a constitutional right, thereby effectively inflicting serious and long lasting harm on impoverished women who want and need abortions for valid medical reasons. In my judgment, these amendments constitute an unjustifiable, and indeed blatant, violation of the sovereign's duty to govern impartially.

I respectfully dissent.

E.   EDUCATION

SAN ANTONIO INDEPENDENT SCHOOL DIST. v. RODRIGUEZ

411 U.S. 1, 93 S.Ct. 1278, 36 L.Ed.2d 16 (1973).

Mr. Justice Powell delivered the opinion of the Court.

This suit attacking the Texas system of financing public education was initiated by Mexican-American parents whose children attend the elementary and secondary schools in the Edgewood Independent School District, an urban school district in San Antonio, Texas. They brought a class action on behalf of school children throughout the State who are members of minority groups or who are poor and reside in school districts having a low property tax base. Named as defendants were the State Board of Education, the Commissioner of Education, the State Attorney General, and the Bexar County (San Antonio) Board of Trustees. The complaint was filed in the summer of 1968 and a three-judge court was impaneled in January 1969. In December 1971 the panel rendered its judgment in a *per curiam* opinion holding the Texas school finance system unconstitutional under the Equal Protection Clause of the Fourteenth Amendment. . . . For the reasons stated in this opinion we reverse the decision of the District Court.

I.

. . .

[The Court described at length the Texas system of school financing. For present purposes it is enough to note that half of the total educational expenditures in Texas came from the Texas Minimum Foundation School Program. State revenues financed 80% of the Program, with the remaining 20% (known as the Local Fund Assignment) coming from the local districts under a formula designed to reflect each district's relative taxpaying ability. Each school district imposed a property tax to raise funds to satisfy its Local Fund Assignment and to provide the revenues needed above those received under the Foundation Program.]

The school district in which appellees reside, the Edgewood Independent School District, has been compared throughout this litigation with the Alamo Heights Independent School District. This comparison between the least and most affluent districts in the San Antonio area serves to illustrate the manner in which the dual system of finance operates and to indicate the extent to which substantial disparities exist despite the State's impressive progress in recent years. Edgewood is one of seven public school districts in the metropolitan area. Approximately 22,000 students are enrolled in its 25 elementary and secondary schools. The district is situated in the core-city sector of San Antonio in a residential neighborhood that has little commercial or industrial property. The residents are predominantly of Mexican-American descent: approximately 90% of the student population is Mexican-American and over 6% is Negro. The average assessed property value per pupil is $5,960—the lowest in the metropolitan area—and the median family income ($4,686) is also the lowest. At an equalized tax rate of $1.05 per $100 of assessed property—the highest in the metropolitan area—the district contributed $26 to the education of each child for the 1967–1968 school year above its Local Fund Assignment for the Minimum Foundation Program. The Foundation Program contributed $222 per pupil for a state-local total of $248. Federal funds added another $108 for a total of $356 per pupil.

Alamo Heights is the most affluent school district in San Antonio. Its six schools, housing approximately 5,000 students, are situated in a residential community quite unlike the Edgewood District. The school population is predominantly Anglo, having only 18% Mexican-Americans and less than 1% Negroes. The assessed property value per pupil exceeds $49,000 and the median family income is $8,001. In 1967–1968 the local tax rate of $.85 per $100 of valuation yielded $333 per pupil over and above its contribution to the Foundation Program. Coupled with the $225 provided from that Program, the district was able to supply $558 per student. Supplemented by a $36 per pupil grant from federal sources, Alamo Heights spent $594 per pupil.

. . . [1970–1971] figures also reveal the extent to which these two districts' allotments were funded from their own required contributions to the

Local Fund Assignment. Alamo Heights, because of its relative wealth, was required to contribute out of its local property tax collections approximately $100 per pupil, or about 20% of its Foundation grant. Edgewood, on the other hand, paid only $8.46 per pupil, which is about 2.4% of its grant. It does appear then that, at least as to these two districts, the Local Fund Assignment does reflect a rough approximation of the relative taxpaying potential of each.

Despite . . . recent increases, substantial interdistrict disparities in school expenditures found by the District Court to prevail in San Antonio and in varying degrees throughout the State still exist. And it was these disparities, largely attributable to differences in the amounts of money collected through local property taxation, that led the District Court to conclude that Texas' dual system of public school finance violated the Equal Protection Clause. . . .

Texas virtually concedes that its historically rooted dual system of financing education could not withstand the strict judicial scrutiny that this Court has found appropriate in reviewing legislative judgments that interfere with fundamental constitutional rights or that involve suspect classifications. If, as previous decisions have indicated, strict scrutiny means that the State's system is not entitled to the usual presumption of validity, that the State rather than the complainants must carry a "heavy burden of justification," that the State must demonstrate that its educational system has been structured with "precision" and is "tailored" narrowly to serve legitimate objectives and that it has selected the "least drastic means" for effectuating its objectives, the Texas financing system and its counterpart in virtually every other State will not pass muster. The State candidly admits that "[n]o one familiar with the Texas system would contend that it has yet achieved perfection." Apart from its concession that educational finance in Texas has "defects" and "imperfections," the State defends the system's rationality with vigor and disputes the District Court's finding that it lacks a "reasonable basis."

This, then, establishes the framework for our analysis. We must decide, first, whether the Texas system of financing public education operates to the disadvantage of some suspect class or impinges upon a fundamental right explicitly or implicitly protected by the Constitution, thereby requiring strict judicial scrutiny. If so, the judgment of the District Court should be affirmed. If not, the Texas scheme must still be examined to determine whether it rationally furthers some legitimate, articulated state purpose and therefore does not constitute an invidious discrimination in violation of the Equal Protection Clause of the Fourteenth Amendment.

II.

. . .

A.

The wealth discrimination discovered by the District Court in this case, and by several other courts that have recently struck down school financing laws in other States,[48] is quite unlike any of the forms of wealth discrimination heretofore reviewed by this Court. Rather than focusing on the unique features of the alleged discrimination, the courts in these cases have virtually assumed their findings of a suspect classification through a simplistic process of analysis: since, under the traditional systems of financing public schools, some poorer people receive less expensive educations than other more affluent people, these systems discriminate on the basis of wealth. This approach largely ignores the hard

---

[48] Serrano v. Priest, 96 Cal.Rptr. 601, 487 P.2d 1241, 5 Cal.3d 584 (1971); Van Dusartz v. Hatfield, 334 F.Supp. 870 (Minn.1971); Robinson v. Cahill, 118 N.J.Super. 223, 287 A.2d 187 (1972); Milliken v. Green, No. 54,809 (Mich.S.C., Jan. 1973).

threshold questions, including whether it makes a difference for purposes of consideration under the Constitution that the class of disadvantaged "poor" cannot be identified or defined in customary equal protection terms, and whether the relative—rather than absolute—nature of the asserted deprivation is of significant consequence. Before a State's laws and the justifications for the classifications they create are subjected to strict judicial scrutiny, we think these threshold considerations must be analyzed more closely than they were in the court below.

. . . .

However described, it is clear that appellees' suit asks this Court to extend its most exacting scrutiny to review a system that allegedly discriminates against a large, diverse, and amorphous class, unified only by the common factor of residence in districts that happen to have less taxable wealth than other districts. The system of alleged discrimination and the class it defines have none of the traditional indicia of suspectness: the class is not saddled with such disabilities, or subjected to such a history of purposeful unequal treatment, or relegated to such a position of political powerlessness as to command extraordinary protection from the majoritarian political process.

We thus conclude that the Texas system does not operate to the peculiar disadvantage of any suspect class. But in recognition of the fact that this Court has never heretofore held that wealth discrimination alone provides an adequate basis for invoking strict scrutiny, appellees have not relied solely on this contention. They also assert that the State's system impermissibly interferes with the exercise of a "fundamental" right and that accordingly the prior decisions of this Court require the application of the strict standard of judicial review. . . . It is this question—whether education is a fundamental right, in the sense that it is among the rights and liberties protected by the Constitution—which has so consumed the attention of courts and commentators in recent years.[68]

B.

In Brown v. Board of Education, 347 U.S. 483 (1954), a unanimous Court recognized that "education is perhaps the most important function of state and local governments." Id., at 493. What was said there in the context of racial discrimination has lost none of its vitality with the passage of time: . . .

Nothing this Court holds today in any way detracts from our historic dedication to public education. We are in complete agreement with the conclusion of the three-judge panel below that "the grave significance of education both to the individual and to our society" cannot be doubted. But the importance of a service performed by the State does not determine whether it must be regarded as fundamental for purposes of examination under the Equal Protection Clause. Mr. Justice Harlan, dissenting from the Court's application of strict scrutiny to a law impinging upon the right of interstate travel, admonished that "[v]irtually every state statute affects important rights." Shapiro v. Thompson, 394 U.S. 618, 655, 661 (1969). In his view, if the degree of judicial scrutiny of state legislation fluctuated depending on a majority's view of the importance of the interest affected, we would have gone "far toward making this Court a 'super-legislature.'" We would indeed then be assuming a

---

[68] See Serrano v. Priest, 96 Cal.Rptr. 601, 487 P.2d 1241, 5 Cal.3d 584 (1971); Van Dusartz v. Hatfield, 344 F.Supp. 870 (Minn.1971); Robinson v. Cahill, 118 N.J.Super. 223, 287 A.2d 187 (1972); J. Coons, W. Clune, and S. Sugarman, supra, n. 13, at 339–394; Goldstein, supra, n. 38, at 534–541; Vieira, Unequal Educational Expenditures: Some Minority Views on Serrano v. Priest, 37 Mo.L.Rev. 617, 618–624 (1972); Comment, Educational Financing, Equal Protection of the Laws, and the Supreme Court, 70 Mich.L.Rev. 1324, 1335–1342 (1972); Note, The Public School Financing Cases: Interdistrict Inequalities and Wealth Discrimination, 14 Ariz.L.Rev. 88, 120–124 (1972).

legislative role and one for which the Court lacks both authority and competence. But Mr. Justice Stewart's response in *Shapiro* to Mr. Justice Harlan's concern correctly articulates the limits of the fundamental rights rationale employed in the Court's equal protection decisions:

"The Court today does *not* 'pick out particular human activities, characterize them as "fundamental," and give them added protection. . . .' To the contrary, the Court simply recognizes, as it must, an established constitutional right, and gives to that right no less protection than the Constitution itself demands." 394 U.S., at 642. (Emphasis from original.)

. . .

. . . The right to interstate travel had long been recognized as a right of constitutional significance, and the Court's decision therefore did not require an *ad hoc* determination as to the social or economic importance of that right.

. . .

The lesson of these cases in addressing the question now before the Court is plain. It is not the province of this Court to create substantive constitutional rights in the name of guaranteeing equal protection of the laws. Thus the key to discovering whether education is "fundamental" is not to be found in comparisons of the relative societal significance of education as opposed to subsistence or housing. Nor is it to be found by weighing whether education is as important as the right to travel. Rather, the answer lies in assessing whether there is a right to education explicitly or implicitly guaranteed by the Constitution. Eisenstadt v. Baird, 405 U.S. 438 (1972);[73] Dunn v. Blumstein, 405 U.S. 330 (1972);[74] Police Department of the City of Chicago v. Mosley, 408 U.S. 92 (1972);[75] Skinner v. Oklahoma, 316 U.S. 535 (1942).[76]

Education, of course, is not among the rights afforded explicit protection under our Federal Constitution. Nor do we find any basis for saying it is implicitly so protected. . . .

We have carefully considered each of the arguments supportive of the District Court's finding that education is a fundamental right or liberty and have found those arguments unpersuasive. In one further respect we find this a particularly inappropriate case in which to subject state action to strict judicial scrutiny. The present case, in another basic sense, is significantly different from any of the cases in which the Court has applied strict scrutiny to state or federal legislation touching upon constitutionally protected rights. Each of our prior

---

[73] In *Eisenstadt,* the Court struck down a Massachusetts statute that prohibited the distribution of contraceptive devices, finding that the law failed "to satisfy even the more lenient equal protection standard." Id., at 447 n. 7. Nevertheless, in *dictum,* the Court recited the correct form of equal protection analysis: "if we were to conclude that the Massachusetts statute impinges upon fundamental freedoms under Griswold [v. Connecticut, 381 U.S. 479 (1965)], the statutory classification would have to be not merely *rationally related* to a valid public purpose but *necessary* to the achievement of a *compelling* state interest." Ibid. (emphasis from original).

[74] *Dunn* fully canvasses this Court's voting rights cases and explains that "this Court has made clear that a citizen has a *constitutionally protected right* to participate in elections on an equal basis with other citizens in the jurisdiction." Id., at 336 (emphasis supplied). The constitutional underpinnings of the right to equal treatment in the voting process can no longer be doubted even though, as the Court noted in Harper v. Virginia Bd. of Elections, 383 U.S. 663, 665 (1966), "the right to vote in state elections is nowhere expressly mentioned." . . .

[75] In *Mosley,* the Court struck down a Chicago antipicketing ordinance that exempted labor picketing from its prohibitions. The ordinance was held invalid under the Equal Protection Clause after subjecting it to careful scrutiny and finding that the ordinance was not narrowly drawn. The stricter standard of review was appropriately applied since the ordinance was one "affecting First Amendment interests." Id., at 101.

[76] *Skinner* applied the standard of close scrutiny to a state law permitting forced sterilization of "habitual criminals." Implicit in the Court's opinion is the recognition that the right of procreation is among the rights of personal privacy protected under the Constitution. See Roe v. Wade, 410 U.S. 113 (1973).

cases involved legislation which "deprived," "infringed," or "interfered" with the free exercise of some such fundamental personal right or liberty. See Skinner v. Oklahoma, supra, at 536; Shapiro v. Thompson, supra, at 634; Dunn v. Blumstein, supra, at 338–343. A critical distinction between those cases and the one now before us lies in what Texas is endeavoring to do with respect to education. . . . The Texas system of school finance . . . was implemented in an effort to *extend* public education and to improve its quality. Of course, every reform that benefits some more than others may be criticized for what it fails to accomplish. But we think it plain that, in substance, the thrust of the Texas system is affirmative and reformatory and, therefore, should be scrutinized under judicial principles sensitive to the nature of the State's efforts and to the rights reserved to the States under the Constitution.

C.

It should be clear, for the reasons stated above and in accord with the prior decisions of this Court, that this is not a case in which the challenged state action must be subjected to the searching judicial scrutiny reserved for laws that create suspect classifications or impinge upon constitutionally protected rights.

We need not rest our decision, however, solely on the inappropriateness of the strict scrutiny test. A century of Supreme Court adjudication under the Equal Protection Clause affirmatively supports the application of the traditional standard of review, which requires only that the State's system be shown to bear some rational relationship to legitimate state purposes. This case represents far more than a challenge to the manner in which Texas provides for the education of its children. We have here nothing less than a direct attack on the way in which Texas has chosen to raise and disburse state and local tax revenues. We are asked to condemn the State's judgment in conferring on political subdivisions the power to tax local property to supply revenues for local interests. In so doing, appellees would have the Court intrude in an area in which it has traditionally deferred to state legislatures. This Court has often admonished against such interferences with the State's fiscal policies under the Equal Protection Clause. . . .

Thus we stand on familiar ground when we continue to acknowledge that the Justices of this Court lack both the expertise and the familiarity with local problems so necessary to the making of wise decisions with respect to the raising and disposition of public revenues. . . .

In addition to matters of fiscal policy, this case also involves the most persistent and difficult questions of educational policy, another area in which this Court's lack of specialized knowledge and experience counsels against premature interference with the informed judgments made at the state and local levels. . . .

The foregoing considerations buttress our conclusion that Texas' system of public school finance is an inappropriate candidate for strict judicial scrutiny. These same considerations are relevant to the determination whether that system, with its conceded imperfections, nevertheless bears some rational relationship to a legitimate state purpose. It is to this question that we next turn our attention.

III.

. . . .

In sum, to the extent that the Texas system of school finance results in unequal expenditures between children who happen to reside in different districts, we cannot say that such disparities are the product of a system that is so irrational as to be invidiously discriminatory. Texas has acknowledged its shortcomings and has persistently endeavored—not without some success—to ameliorate the differences in levels of expenditures without sacrificing the benefits of local participation. The Texas plan is not the result of hurried, ill-conceived legislation. It certainly is not the product of purposeful discrimination against any group or class. On the contrary, it is rooted in decades of experience in Texas and elsewhere, and in major part is the product of responsible studies by qualified people. In giving substance to the presumption of validity to which the Texas system is entitled, Lindsey v. National Carbonic Gas Co., 220 U.S. 61, 78 (1911), it is important to remember that at every stage of its development it has constituted a "rough accommodation" of interests in an effort to arrive at practical and workable solutions. Metropolis Theatre Co. v. City of Chicago, 228 U.S. 69–70 (1913). One also must remember that the system here challenged is not peculiar to Texas or to any other State. In its essential characteristics the Texas plan for financing public education reflects what many educators for a half century have thought was an enlightened approach to a problem for which there is no perfect solution. We are unwilling to assume for ourselves a level of wisdom superior to that of legislators, scholars, and educational authorities in 49 States, especially where the alternatives proposed are only recently conceived and nowhere yet tested. The constitutional standard under the Equal Protection Clause is whether the challenged state action rationally furthers a legitimate state purpose or interest. McGinnis v. Royster, 410 U.S. 263, 270 (1973). We hold that the Texas plan abundantly satisfies this standard.

. . .

Reversed.

Mr. Justice Stewart, concurring.

. . .

Unlike other provisions of the Constitution, the Equal Protection Clause confers no substantive rights and creates no substantive liberties.[2] The function of the Equal Protection Clause, rather, is simply to measure the validity of *classifications* created by state laws.

There is hardly a law on the books that does not affect some people differently from others. But the basic concern of the Equal Protection Clause is with state legislation whose purpose or effect is to create discrete and objectively identifiable classes. And with respect to such legislation, it has long been settled that the Equal Protection Clause is offended only by laws that are invidiously discriminatory—only by classifications that are wholly arbitrary or capricious. . . .

. . .

Mr. Justice Brennan, dissenting.

Although I agree with my Brother White that the Texas statutory scheme is devoid of any rational basis, and for that reason is violative of the Equal Protection Clause, I also record my disagreement with the Court's rather distressing assertion that a right may be deemed "fundamental" for the purposes of equal protection analysis only if it is "explicitly or implicitly guaranteed by the Constitution." . . . As my Brother Marshall convincingly demonstrates, our prior cases stand for the proposition that "fundamentality" is, in large

---

[2] There is one notable exception to the above statement: It has been established in recent years that the Equal Protection Clause confers the substantive right to participate on an equal basis with other qualified voters whenever the State has adopted an electoral process for determining who will represent any segment of the State's population. See, e.g., Reynolds v. Sims, 377 U.S. 533; Kramer v. Union School District, 395 U.S. 621; Dunn v. Blumstein, 405 U.S. 330, 336. But there is no constitutional right to vote, as such. Minor v. Happersett, 88 U.S. 162. If there were such a right, both the Fifteenth Amendment and the Nineteenth Amendment would have been wholly unnecessary.

measure, a function of the right's importance in terms of the effectuation of those rights which are in fact constitutionally guaranteed. Thus, "[a]s the nexus between the specific constitutional guarantee and the nonconstitutional interest draws closer, the nonconstitutional interest becomes more fundamental and the degree of judicial scrutiny applied when the interest is infringed on a discriminatory basis must be adjusted accordingly." . . .

Here, there can be no doubt that education is inextricably linked to the right to participate in the electoral process and to the rights of free speech and association guaranteed by the First Amendment. . . . This being so, any classification affecting education must be subjected to strict judicial scrutiny, and since even the State concedes that the statutory scheme now before us cannot pass constitutional muster under this stricter standard of review, I can only conclude that the Texas school financing scheme is constitutionally invalid.

Mr. Justice White, with whom Mr. Justice Douglas and Mr. Justice Brennan join, dissenting.

. . .

The Equal Protection Clause permits discriminations between classes but requires that the classification bear some rational relationship to a permissible object sought to be attained by the statute. It is not enough that the Texas system before us seeks to achieve the valid, rational purpose of maximizing local initiative; the means chosen by the State must also be rationally related to the end sought to be achieved. . . .

Neither Texas nor the majority heeds this rule. If the State aims at maximizing local initiative and local choice, by permitting school districts to resort to the real property tax if they choose to do so, it utterly fails in achieving its purpose in districts with property tax bases so low that there is little if any opportunity for interested parents, rich or poor, to augment school district revenues. Requiring the State to establish only that unequal treatment is in furtherance of a permissible goal, without also requiring the State to show that the means chosen to effectuate that goal are rationally related to its achievement, makes equal protection analysis no more than an empty gesture. In my view, the parents and children in Edgewood, and in like districts, suffer from an invidious discrimination violative of the Equal Protection Clause.

. . .

Mr. Justice Marshall, with whom Mr. Justice Douglas concurs, dissenting.

. . .

II.

. . . [In the majority's view,] the Texas scheme must be tested by nothing more than that lenient standard of rationality which we have traditionally applied to discriminatory state action in the context of economic and commercial matters. . . . By so doing the Court avoids the telling task of searching for a substantial state interest which the Texas financing scheme, with its variations in taxable district property wealth, is necessary to further. I cannot accept such an emasculation of the Equal Protection Clause in the context of this case.

A.

To begin, I must once more voice my disagreement with the Court's rigidified approach to equal protection analysis. See Dandridge v. Williams, 397 U.S. 471, 519–521 (1970) (dissenting opinion); Richardson v. Belcher, 404 U.S. 78, 90 (1971) (dissenting opinion). The Court apparently seeks to establish today that equal protection cases fall into one of two neat categories which dictate the appropriate standard of review—strict scrutiny or mere rationality. But this Court's decisions in the field of equal protection defy such easy categorization. A principled reading of what this Court has done reveals that it has applied a spectrum of standards in reviewing discrimination allegedly violative of the Equal Protection Clause. This spectrum clearly comprehends variations in the degree of care with which the Court will scrutinize particular classifications, depending, I believe, on the constitutional and societal importance of the interest adversely affected and the recognized invidiousness of the basis upon which the particular classification is drawn. I find in fact that many of the Court's recent decisions embody the very sort of reasoned approach to equal protection analysis for which I previously argued—that is, an approach in which "concentration [is] placed upon the character of the classification in question, the relative importance to the individuals in the class discriminated against of the governmental benefits they do not receive, and the asserted state interests in support of the classification." Dandridge v. Williams, 397 U.S., at 520–521 (dissenting opinion).

I therefore cannot accept the majority's labored efforts to demonstrate that fundamental interests, which call for strict scrutiny of the challenged classification, encompass only established rights which we are somehow bound to recognize from the text of the Constitution itself. To be sure, some interests which the Court has deemed to be fundamental for purposes of equal protection analysis are themselves constitutionally protected rights. . . . But it will not do to suggest that the "answer" to whether an interest is fundamental for purposes of equal protection analysis is *always* determined by whether that interest "is a right . . . explicitly or implicitly guaranteed by the Constitution." . . .

. . .

The majority is, of course, correct when it suggests that the process of determining which interests are fundamental is a difficult one. But I do not think the problem is insurmountable. And I certainly do not accept the view that the process need necessarily degenerate into an unprincipled, subjective "picking-and-choosing" between various interests or that it must involve this Court in creating "substantive constitutional rights in the name of guaranteeing equal protection of the laws." . . . Although not all fundamental interests are constitutionally guaranteed, the determination of which interests are fundamental should be firmly rooted in the text of the Constitution. The task in every case should be to determine the extent to which constitutionally guaranteed rights are dependent on interests not mentioned in the Constitution. As the nexus between the specific constitutional guarantee and the nonconstitutional interest draws closer, the nonconstitutional interest becomes more fundamental and the degree of judicial scrutiny applied when the interest is infringed on a discriminatory basis must be adjusted accordingly. Thus, it cannot be denied that interests such as procreation, the exercise of the state franchise, and access to criminal appellate processes are not fully guaranteed to the citizen by our Constitution. But these interests have nonetheless been afforded special judicial consideration in the face of discrimination because they are, to some extent, interrelated with constitutional guarantees. Procreation is now understood to be important because of its interaction with the established constitutional right of privacy. The exercise of the state franchise is closely tied to basic civil and political rights inherent in the First Amendment. And access to criminal appellate processes enhances the integrity of the range of rights implicit in the Fourteenth Amendment guarantee of due process of law. Only if we closely protect the related interests from state discrimination do we ultimately ensure the integrity of the constitutional guarantee itself. This is the real lesson that must be taken from our previous decisions involving interests deemed to be fundamental.

. . .

In summary, it seems to me inescapably clear that this Court has consistently adjusted the care with which it will review state discrimination in light of the constitutional significance of the interests affected and the invidiousness of the particular classification. . . . The majority suggests, however, that a variable standard of review would give this Court the appearance of a "super-legislature." . . . I cannot agree. Such an approach seems to me a part of the guarantees of our Constitution and of the historic experiences with oppression of and discrimination against discrete, powerless minorities which underlie that Document. In truth, the Court itself will be open to the criticism raised by the majority so long as it continues on its present course of effectively selecting in private which cases will be afforded special consideration without acknowledging the true basis of its action.[67] . . .

. . .

As the Court points out, . . . no previous decision has deemed the presence of just a wealth classification to be sufficient basis to call forth "rigorous judicial scrutiny" of allegedly discriminatory state action. Compare, e.g., Harper v. Virginia Board of Elections, supra, with e.g., James v. Valtierra, 402 U.S. 137 (1971). That wealth classifications alone have not necessarily been considered to bear the same high degree of suspectness as have classifications based on, for instance, race or alienage may be explainable on a number of grounds. The "poor" may not be seen as politically powerless as certain discrete and insular minority groups. Personal poverty may entail much the same social stigma as historically attached to certain racial or ethnic groups. But personal poverty is not a permanent disability; its shackles may be escaped. Perhaps, most importantly, though, personal wealth may not necessarily share the general irrelevance as basis for legislative action that race or nationality is recognized to have. While the "poor" have frequently been a legally disadvantaged group, it cannot be ignored that social legislation must frequently take cognizance of the economic status of our citizens. Thus, we have generally gauged the invidiousness of wealth classifications with an awareness of the importance of the interests being affected and the relevance of personal wealth to those interests. See Harper v. Virginia Board of Elections, supra.

When evaluated with these considerations in mind, it seems to me that discrimination on the basis of group wealth in this case likewise calls for careful judicial scrutiny. . . .

. . .

PLYLER v. DOE

457 U.S. 202, 102 S.Ct. 2382, 72 L.Ed.2d 786 (1982).

Justice Brennan delivered the opinion of the Court.

The question presented by these cases is whether, consistent with the Equal Protection Clause of the Fourteenth Amendment, Texas may deny to undocumented school-age children the free public education that it provides to children who are citizens of the United States or legally admitted aliens.

[67] See generally Gunther, The Supreme Court, 1971 Term: Foreword, In Search of Evolving Doctrine on a Changing Court: A Model for a Newer Equal Protection, 86 Harv.L.Rev. 1 (1972).

I

Since the late nineteenth century, the United States has restricted immigration into this country. Unsanctioned entry into the United States is a crime, 8 U.S.C. § 1325, and those who have entered unlawfully are subject to deportation, 8 U.S.C. §§ 1251–1252. But despite the existence of these legal restrictions, a substantial number of persons have succeeded in unlawfully entering the United States, and now live within various States, including the State of Texas.

In May 1975, the Texas legislature revised its education laws to withhold from local school districts any state funds for the education of children who were not "legally admitted" into the United States. The 1975 revision also authorized local school districts to deny enrollment in their public schools to children not "legally admitted" to the country. Tex.Educ.Code Ann. § 21.031 (Vernon Cum.Supp.1981). These cases involve constitutional challenges to those provisions.

. . . .

II

The Fourteenth Amendment provides that "No State shall . . . deprive any person of life, liberty, or property, without due process of law; nor deny to *any person within its jurisdiction* the equal protection of the laws." Appellants argue at the outset that undocumented aliens, because of their immigration status, are not "persons within the jurisdiction" of the State of Texas, and that they therefore have no right to the equal protection of Texas law. We reject this argument. Whatever his status under the immigration laws, an alien is surely a "person" in any ordinary sense of that term. Aliens, even aliens whose presence in this country is unlawful, have long been recognized as "persons" guaranteed due process of law by the Fifth and Fourteenth Amendments. Shaughnessy v. Mezei, 345 U.S. 206, 212 (1953); Wong Wing v. United States, 163 U.S. 228, 238 (1896); Yick Wo v. Hopkins, 118 U.S. 356, 369 (1886). Indeed, we have clearly held that the Fifth Amendment protects aliens whose presence in this country is unlawful from invidious discrimination by the Federal Government. Mathews v. Diaz, 426 U.S. 67, 77 (1976).

. . . .

III

. . . . In applying the Equal Protection Clause to most forms of state action, we . . . seek only the assurance that the classification at issue bears some fair relationship to a legitimate public purpose.

But we would not be faithful to our obligations under the Fourteenth Amendment if we applied so deferential a standard to every classification. The Equal Protection Clause was intended as a restriction on state legislative action inconsistent with elemental constitutional premises. Thus we have treated as presumptively invidious those classifications that disadvantage a "suspect class," [14] or that impinge upon the exercise of a "fundamental right." [15] With

[14] Several formulations might explain our treatment of certain classifications as "suspect." Some classifications are more likely than others to reflect deep-seated prejudice rather than legislative rationality in pursuit of some legitimate objective. Legislation predicated on such prejudice is easily recognized as incompatible with the constitutional understanding that each person is to be judged individually and is entitled to equal justice under the law. Classifications treated as suspect tend to be irrelevant to any proper legislative goal. See McLaughlin v. Florida, 379 U.S. 184, 192 (1964); Hirabayashi v. United States, 320 U.S. 81, 100 (1943). Finally, certain groups, indeed largely the same groups, have historically been "relegated to such a position of political powerlessness as to command extraordinary protection from the majoritarian political process." San Antonio School District v. Rodriguez, 411 U.S. 1, 28 (1973); Graham v. Richardson, 403 U.S. 365, 372 (1971); see United States v. Carolene Products Co., 304 U.S. 144, 152–153, n. 4 (1938). The experience of our

respect to such classifications, it is appropriate to enforce the mandate of equal protection by requiring the State to demonstrate that its classification has been precisely tailored to serve a compelling governmental interest. In addition, we have recognized that certain forms of legislative classification, while not facially invidious, nonetheless give rise to recurring constitutional difficulties; in these limited circumstances we have sought the assurance that the classification reflects a reasoned judgment consistent with the ideal of equal protection by inquiring whether it may fairly be viewed as furthering a substantial interest of the State.[16] We turn to a consideration of the standard appropriate for the evaluation of § 21.031.

A

Sheer incapability or lax enforcement of the laws barring entry into this country, coupled with the failure to establish an effective bar to the employment of undocumented aliens, has resulted in the creation of a substantial "shadow population" of illegal migrants—numbering in the millions—within our borders. This situation raises the specter of a permanent caste of undocumented resident aliens, encouraged by some to remain here as a source of cheap labor, but nevertheless denied the benefits that our society makes available to citizens and lawful residents. The existence of such an underclass presents most difficult problems for a Nation that prides itself on adherence to principles of equality under law.[19]

The children who are plaintiffs in these cases are special members of this underclass. Persuasive arguments support the view that a State may withhold its beneficence from those whose very presence within the United States is the

Nation has shown that prejudice may manifest itself in the treatment of some groups. Our response to that experience is reflected in the Equal Protection Clause of the Fourteenth Amendment. Legislation imposing special disabilities upon groups disfavored by virtue of circumstances beyond their control suggests the kind of "class or caste" treatment that the Fourteenth Amendment was designed to abolish.

[15] In determining whether a class-based denial of a particular right is deserving of strict scrutiny under the Equal Protection Clause, we look to the Constitution to see if the right infringed has its source, explicitly or implicitly, therein. But we have also recognized the fundamentality of participation in state "elections on an equal basis with other citizens in the jurisdiction," Dunn v. Blumstein, supra, at 336, even though "the right to vote, *per se,* is not a constitutionally protected right." San Antonio School District, 411 U.S., at 35, n. 78. With respect to suffrage, we have explained the need for strict scrutiny as arising from the significance of the franchise as the guardian of all other rights. See Harper v. Virginia Bd. of Elections, 383 U.S. 663, 667 (1966); Reynolds v. Sims, 377 U.S. 533, 562 (1964); Yick Wo v. Hopkins, 118 U.S. 356, 370 (1886).

[16] See Craig v. Boren, 429 U.S. 190 (1976); Lalli v. Lalli, 439 U.S. 259 (1978). This technique of "intermediate" scrutiny permits us to evaluate the rationality of the legislative judgment with reference to well-settled constitutional principles. "In expounding the Constitution, the Court's role is to discern 'principles sufficiently absolute to give them roots throughout the community and continuity over significant periods of time, and to lift them above the level of the pragmatic political judgments of a particular time and place.'" University of California Regents v. Bakke, 438 U.S. 265, 299 (1978) (Opinion of Powell, J.), quoting A. Cox, The Role of the Supreme Court in American Government 114 (1976). Only when concerns sufficiently absolute and enduring can be clearly ascertained from the Constitution and our cases do we employ this standard to aid us in determining the rationality of the legislative choice.

[19] We reject the claim that "illegal aliens" are a "suspect class." No case in which we have attempted to define a suspect class, see e.g., n. 14 supra, has addressed the status of persons unlawfully in our country. Unlike most of the classifications that we have recognized as suspect, entry into this class, by virtue of entry into this country, is the product of voluntary action. Indeed, entry into the class is itself a crime. In addition, it could hardly be suggested that undocumented status is a "constitutional irrelevancy." With respect to the actions of the federal government, alienage classifications may be intimately related to the conduct of foreign policy, to the federal prerogative to control access to the United States, and to the plenary federal power to determine who has sufficiently manifested his allegiance to become a citizen of the Nation. No State may independently exercise a like power. But if the Federal Government has by uniform rule prescribed what it believes to be appropriate standards for the treatment of an alien subclass, the States may, of course, follow the federal direction. See De Canas v. Bica, 424 U.S. 351 (1976).

product of their own unlawful conduct.   These arguments do not apply with the same force to classifications imposing disabilities on the minor *children* of such illegal entrants.   At the least, those who elect to enter our territory by stealth and in violation of our law should be prepared to bear the consequences, including, but not limited to, deportation.   But the children of those illegal entrants are not comparably situated.   Their "parents have the ability to conform their conduct to societal norms," and presumably the ability to remove themselves from the State's jurisdiction; but the children who are plaintiffs in these cases "can affect neither their parents' conduct nor their own status." Trimble v. Gordon, 430 U.S. 762, 770 (1977).   Even if the State found it expedient to control the conduct of adults by acting against their children, legislation directing the onus of a parent's misconduct against his children does not comport with fundamental conceptions of justice.   . . .

Of course, undocumented status is not irrelevant to any proper legislative goal.   Nor is undocumented status an absolutely immutable characteristic since it is the product of conscious, indeed unlawful, action.   But § 21.031 is directed against children, and imposes its discriminatory burden on the basis of a legal characteristic over which children can have little control.   It is thus difficult to conceive of a rational justification for penalizing these children for their presence within the United States.   Yet that appears to be precisely the effect of § 21.031.

Public education is not a "right" granted to individuals by the Constitution. San Antonio School District, supra, at 35.   But neither is it merely some governmental "benefit" indistinguishable from other forms of social welfare legislation.   Both the importance of education in maintaining our basic institutions, and the lasting impact of its deprivation on the life of the child, mark the distinction.   The "American people have always regarded education and the acquisition of knowledge as matters of supreme importance."   Meyer v. Nebraska, 262 U.S. 390, 400 (1923).   We have recognized "the public school as a most vital civic institution for the preservation of a democratic system of government," Abington School District v. Schempp, 374 U.S. 203, 230 (1963) (Brennan, J., concurring), and as the primary vehicle for transmitting "the values on which our society rests."   Ambach v. Norwick, 441 U.S. 68, 76 (1979).   As noted early in our history, "some degree of education is necessary to prepare citizens to participate effectively and intelligently in our open political system if we are to preserve freedom and independence."   Wisconsin v. Yoder, 406 U.S. 205, 221 (1972).   And these historic "perceptions of the public schools as inculcating fundamental values necessary to the maintenance of a democratic political system have been confirmed by the observations of social scientists."   Ambach v. Norwick, supra, at 77.   In addition, education provides the basic tools by which individuals might lead economically productive lives to the benefit of us all.   In sum, education has a fundamental role in maintaining the fabric of our society.   We cannot ignore the significant social costs borne by our Nation when select groups are denied the means to absorb the values and skills upon which our social order rests.

In addition to the pivotal role of education in sustaining our political and cultural heritage, denial of education to some isolated group of children poses an affront to one of the goals of the Equal Protection Clause: the abolition of governmental barriers presenting unreasonable obstacles to advancement on the basis of individual merit.   Paradoxically, by depriving the children of any disfavored group of an education, we foreclose the means by which that group might raise the level of esteem in which it is held by the majority.   But more directly, "education prepares individuals to be self-reliant and self-sufficient participants in society."   Wisconsin v. Yoder, supra, at 221.   Illiteracy is an enduring disability.   The inability to read and write will handicap the individual deprived of a basic education each and every day of his life. The inestimable toll of that deprivation on the social, economic, intellectual and psychological well-being of the individual, and the obstacle it poses to individual achievement, makes it most difficult to reconcile the cost or the principle of a status-based denial of basic education with the framework of equality embodied in the Equal Protection Clause. What we said 28 years ago in Brown v. Board of Education, 347 U.S. 483 (1954), still holds true:

> ". . . In these days, it is doubtful that any child may reasonably be expected to succeed in life if he is denied the opportunity of an education. Such an opportunity, where the state has undertaken to provide it, is a right which must be made available to all on equal terms."

B

These well-settled principles allow us to determine the proper level of deference to be afforded § 21.031. Undocumented aliens cannot be treated as a suspect class because their presence in this country in violation of federal law is not a "constitutional irrelevancy." Nor is education a fundamental right; a State need not justify by compelling necessity every variation in the manner in which education is provided to its population. See San Antonio School Dist. v. Rodriguez, 411 U.S. 1, 28–39 (1973). But more is involved in this case than the abstract question whether § 21.031 discriminates against a suspect class, or whether education is a fundamental right. Section 21.031 imposes a lifetime hardship on a discrete class of children not accountable for their disabling status. The stigma of illiteracy will mark them for the rest of their lives. By denying these children a basic education, we deny them the ability to live within the structure of our civic institutions, and foreclose any realistic possibility that they will contribute in even the smallest way to the progress of our Nation. In determining the rationality of § 21.031, we may appropriately take into account its costs to the Nation and to the innocent children who are its victims. In light of these countervailing costs, the discrimination contained in § 21.031 can hardly be considered rational unless it furthers some substantial goal of the State.

IV

It is the State's principal argument, and apparently the view of the dissenting Justices, that the undocumented status of these children *vel non* establishes a sufficient rational basis for denying them benefits that a State might choose to afford other residents. The State notes that while other aliens are admitted "on an equality of legal privileges with all citizens under non-discriminatory laws," Takahashi v. Fish & Game Comm'n, 334 U.S. 410, 420 (1948), the asserted right of these children to an education can claim no implicit congressional imprimatur. Indeed, on the State's view, Congress' apparent disapproval of the presence of these children within the United States, and the evasion of the federal regulatory program that is the mark of undocumented status, provides authority for its decision to impose upon them special disabilities. Faced with an equal protection challenge respecting the treatment of aliens, we agree that the courts must be attentive to congressional policy; the exercise of congressional power might well affect the State's prerogatives to afford differential treatment to a particular class of aliens. But we are unable to find in the congressional immigration scheme any statement of policy that might weigh significantly in arriving at an equal protection balance concerning the State's authority to deprive these children of an education.

. . . .

To be sure, like all persons who have entered the United States unlawfully, these children are subject to deportation. 8 U.S.C. §§ 1251–1252. But there is no assurance that a child subject to deportation will ever be deported. An illegal entrant might be granted federal permission to continue to reside in this country, or even to become a citizen. See, e.g., 8 U.S.C. §§ 1252, 1253(h), 1254. In light of the discretionary federal power to grant relief from deportation, a State cannot realistically determine that any particular undocumented child will in fact be deported until after deportation proceedings have been completed. It would of course be most difficult for the State to justify a denial of education to a child enjoying an inchoate federal permission to remain.

We are reluctant to impute to Congress the intention to withhold from these children, for so long as they are present in this country through no fault of their own, access to a basic education. In other contexts, undocumented status, coupled with some articulable federal policy, might enhance State authority with respect to the treatment of undocumented aliens. But in the area of special constitutional sensitivity presented by this case, and in the absence of any contrary indication fairly discernible in the present legislative record, we perceive no national policy that supports the State in denying these children an elementary education. The State may borrow the federal classification. But to justify its use as a criterion for its own discriminatory policy, the State must demonstrate that the classification is reasonably adapted to *"the purposes for which the state desires to use it."* Oyama v. California, 332 U.S. 633, 664–665 (1948) (Murphy, J., concurring) (emphasis added). We therefore turn to the state objectives that are said to support § 21.031.

V

Appellants argue that the classification at issue furthers an interest in the "preservation of the state's limited resources for the education of its lawful residents." Of course, a concern for the preservation of resources standing alone can hardly justify the classification used in allocating those resources. Graham v. Richardson, supra, 403 U.S., at 374–375. The State must do more than justify its classification with a concise expression of an intention to discriminate. Examining Board v. Flores de Otero, 426 U.S. 572, 605 (1976). Apart from the asserted state prerogative to act against undocumented children solely on the basis of their undocumented status—an asserted prerogative that carries only minimal force in the circumstances of this case—we discern three colorable state interests that might support § 21.031.

First, appellants appear to suggest that the State may seek to protect the State from an influx of illegal immigrants. While a State might have an interest in mitigating the potentially harsh economic effects of sudden shifts in population, § 21.031 hardly offers an effective method of dealing with an urgent demographic or economic problem. There is no evidence in the record suggesting that illegal entrants impose any significant burden on the State's economy. To the contrary, the available evidence suggests that illegal aliens underutilize public services, while contributing their labor to the local economy and tax money to the State fisc. . . .

Second, while it is apparent that a state may "not . . . reduce expenditures for education by barring [some arbitrarily chosen class of] children from its schools," Shapiro v. Thompson, 394 U.S. 618, 633 (1969), appellants suggest that undocumented children are appropriately singled out for exclusion because of the special burdens they impose on the State's ability to provide high quality public education. But the record in no way supports the claim that exclusion of undocumented children is likely to improve the overall quality of education in the State. . . .

Finally, appellants suggest that undocumented children are appropriately singled out because their unlawful presence within the United States renders them less likely than other children to remain within the boundaries of the State, and to put their education to productive social or political use within the State. Even assuming that such an interest is legitimate, it is an interest that is most difficult to quantify. The State has no assurance that any child, citizen or not, will employ the education provided by the State within the confines of the State's borders. In any event, the record is clear that many of the undocumented children disabled by this classification will remain in this country indefinitely, and that some will become lawful residents or citizens of the United States. It is difficult to understand precisely what the State hopes to achieve by promoting the creation and perpetuation of a subclass of illiterates within our boundaries, surely adding to the problems and costs of unemployment, welfare, and crime. It is thus clear that whatever savings might be achieved by denying these children an education, they are wholly insubstantial in light of the costs involved to these children, the State, and the Nation.

VI

If the State is to deny a discrete group of innocent children the free public education that it offers to other children residing within its borders, that denial must be justified by a showing that it furthers some substantial state interest. No such showing was made here. Accordingly, the judgment of the Court of Appeals in each of these cases is

Affirmed.

Justice Marshall, concurring.

While I join the Court opinion, I do so without in any way retreating from my opinion in San Antonio School District v. Rodriguez, 411 U.S. 1, 70–133 (Marshall, J., dissenting). I continue to believe that an individual's interest in education is fundamental, and that this view is amply supported "by the unique status accorded public education by our society, and by the close relationship between education and some of our most basic constitutional values." Furthermore, I believe that the facts of these cases demonstrate the wisdom of rejecting a rigidified approach to equal protection analysis, and of employing an approach that allows for varying levels of scrutiny depending upon "the constitutional and societal importance of the interest adversely affected and the recognized invidiousness of the basis upon which the particular classification is drawn." . . .

Justice Blackmun, concurring.

I join the opinion and judgment of the Court.

Like Justice Powell, I believe that the children involved in this litigation "should not be left on the streets uneducated." I write separately, however, because in my view the nature of the interest at stake is crucial to the proper resolution of this case.

The "fundamental rights" aspect of the Court's equal protection analysis— the now-familiar concept that governmental classifications bearing on certain interests must be closely scrutinized—has been the subject of some controversy. . . .

. . .

I joined Justice Powell's opinion for the Court in *Rodriguez,* and I continue to believe that it provides the appropriate model for resolving most equal protection disputes. Classifications infringing substantive constitutional rights necessarily will be invalid, if not by force of the Equal Protection Clause, then through operation of other provisions of the Constitution. Conversely, classifications bearing on nonconstitutional interests—even those involving "the most basic economic needs of impoverished human beings," Dandridge v. Williams, 397 U.S. 471, 485 (1970)—generally are not subject to special treatment under the Equal Protection Clause, because they are not distinguishable in any relevant way from other regulations in "the area of economics and social welfare." Ibid.

With all this said, however, I believe the Court's experience has demonstrated that the *Rodriguez* formulation does not settle every issue of "fundamental rights" arising under the Equal Protection Clause. Only a pedant would insist that there are *no* meaningful distinctions among the multitude of social and political interests regulated by the States, and *Rodriguez* does not stand for quite so absolute a proposition. . . .

. . . .

In my view, when the State provides an education to some and denies it to others, it immediately and inevitably creates class distinctions of a type fundamentally inconsistent with . . . the Equal Protection Clause. Children denied an education are placed at a permanent and insurmountable competitive disadvantage, for an uneducated child is denied even the opportunity to achieve. And when those children are members of an identifiable group, that group— through the State's action—will have been converted into a discrete underclass. Other benefits provided by the State, such as housing and public assistance, are of course important; to an individual in immediate need, they may be more desirable than the right to be educated. But classifications involving the complete denial of education are in a sense unique, for they strike at the heart of equal protection values by involving the State in the creation of permanent class distinctions. Cf. *Rodriguez,* 411 U.S., at 115, n. 74 (Marshall, J., dissenting). In a sense, then, denial of an education is the analogue of denial of the right to vote: the former relegates the individual to second-class social status; the latter places him at a permanent political disadvantage.

This conclusion is fully consistent with *Rodriguez.* The Court there reserved judgment on the constitutionality of a state system that "occasioned an absolute denial of educational opportunities to any of its children," noting that "no charge fairly could be made that the system [at issue in *Rodriguez*] fails to provide each child with an opportunity to acquire . . . basic minimal skills." 411 U.S., at 37. . . .

. . . Whatever the State's power to classify deportable aliens, . . . and whatever the Federal Government's ability to draw more precise and more acceptable alienage classifications—the statute at issue here sweeps within it a substantial number of children who will in fact, and who may well be entitled to, remain in the United States. Given the extraordinary nature of the interest involved, this makes the classification here fatally imprecise. And, as the Court demonstrates, the Texas legislation is not otherwise supported by any substantial interests.

Because I believe that the Court's carefully worded analysis recognizes the importance of the equal protection and preemption interests I consider crucial, I join its opinion as well as its judgment.

Justice Powell, concurring.

I join the opinion of the Court, and write separately to emphasize the unique character of the case before us.

. . . .

Although the analogy is not perfect, our holding today does find support in decisions of this Court with respect to the status of illegitimates. In Weber v. Aetna Casualty & Surety Co., 406 U.S. 164, 175 (1972) we said: "visiting . . . condemnation on the head of an infant" for the misdeeds of the parents is illogical, unjust, and "contrary to the basic concept of our system that legal burdens should bear some relationship to individual responsibility or wrongdoing."

. . . .

In my view, the State's denial of education to these children bears no substantial relation to any substantial state interest. Both of the district courts found that an uncertain but significant percentage of illegal alien children will remain in Texas as residents and many eventually will become citizens. . . .

. . . [I]t hardly can be argued rationally that anyone benefits from the creation within our borders of a subclass of illiterate persons many of whom will remain in the State, adding to the problems and costs of both State and National Governments attendant upon unemployment, welfare and crime.

Chief Justice Burger, with whom Justice White, Justice Rehnquist, and Justice O'Connor join, dissenting.

Were it our business to set the Nation's social policy, I would agree without hesitation that it is senseless for an enlightened society to deprive any children— including illegal aliens—of an elementary education. I fully agree that it would be folly—and wrong—to tolerate creation of a segment of society made up of illiterate persons, many having a limited or no command of our language. However, the Constitution does not constitute us as "Platonic Guardians" nor does it vest in this Court the authority to strike down laws because they do not meet our standards of desirable social policy, "wisdom," or "common sense." See Tennessee Valley Authority v. Hill, 437 U.S. 153, 194–195 (1978). We trespass on the assigned function of the political branches under our structure of limited and separated powers when we assume a policymaking role as the Court does today.

The Court makes no attempt to disguise that it is acting to make up for Congress' lack of "effective leadership" in dealing with the serious national problems caused by the influx of uncountable millions of illegal aliens across our borders. The failure of enforcement of the immigration laws over more than a decade and the inherent difficulty and expense of sealing our vast borders have combined to create a grave socio-economic dilemma. It is a dilemma that has not yet even been fully assessed, let alone addressed. However, it is not the function of the judiciary to provide "effective leadership" simply because the political branches of government fail to do so.

The Court's holding today manifests the justly criticized judicial tendency to attempt speedy and wholesale formulation of "remedies" for the failures—or simply the laggard pace—of the political processes of our system of government. The Court employs, and in my view abuses, the Fourteenth Amendment in an effort to become an omnipotent and omniscient problem solver. That the motives for doing so are noble and compassionate does not alter the fact that the Court distorts our constitutional function to make amends for the defaults of others.

. . .

Once it is conceded—as the Court does—that illegal aliens are not a suspect class, and that education is not a fundamental right, our inquiry should focus on and be limited to whether the legislative classification at issue bears a rational relationship to a legitimate state purpose. Vance v. Bradley, 440 U.S. 93, 97 (1979); Dandridge v. Williams, 397 U.S. 471, 485–487 (1970).

. . .

Denying a free education to illegal alien children is not a choice I would make were I a legislator. Apart from compassionate considerations, the long-range costs of excluding any children from the public schools may well outweigh the costs of educating them. But that is not the issue; the fact that there are sound *policy* arguments against the Texas legislature's choice does not render that choice an unconstitutional one.

. . .

Congress, "vested by the Constitution with the responsibility of protecting our borders and legislating with respect to aliens," bears primary responsibility for addressing the problems occasioned by the millions of illegal aliens flooding across our southern border. Similarly, it is for Congress, and not this Court, to assess the "social costs borne by our Nation when select groups are denied the means to absorb the values and skills upon which our social order rests." While the "specter of a permanent caste" of illegal Mexican residents of the United States is indeed a disturbing one, it is but one segment of a larger problem, which is for the political branches to solve. I find it difficult to believe that Congress would long tolerate such a self-destructive result—that it would fail to deport these illegal alien families or to provide for the education of their children. Yet instead of allowing the political processes to run their course—albeit with some delay—the Court seeks to do Congress' job for it, compensating for congressional inaction. It is not unreasonable to think that this encourages the political branches to pass their problems to the judiciary.

The solution to this seemingly intractable problem is to defer to the political processes, unpalatable as that may be to some.

MARTINEZ v. BYNUM

461 U.S. 321, 103 S.Ct. 1838, 75 L.Ed.2d 879 (1983).

Justice Powell delivered the opinion of the Court.

This case involves a facial challenge to the constitutionality of the Texas residency requirement governing minors who wish to attend public free schools while living apart from their parents or guardians.

I

Roberto Morales was born in 1969 in McAllen, Texas, and is thus a United States citizen by birth. His parents are Mexican citizens who reside in Reynosa, Mexico. He left Reynosa in 1977 and returned to McAllen to live with his sister, petitioner Oralia Martinez, for the primary purpose of attending school in the McAllen Independent School District. Although Martinez is now Morales's custodian, she is not—and does not desire to become—his guardian. As a result, Morales is not entitled to tuition-free admission to the McAllen schools. Section 21.031(b) and (c) of the Texas Education Code would require the local school authorities to admit him if he or "his parent, guardian, or the person having lawful control of him" resided in the school district, Tex.Educ.Code Ann. § 21.031(b) and (c) (Supp.1982), but § 21.031(d) denies tuition-free admission for a minor who lives apart from a "parent, guardian, or other person having lawful control of him under an order of a court" if his presence in the school district is "for the primary purpose of attending the public free schools." Respondent McAllen Independent School District therefore denied Morales's application for admission in the fall of 1977.

In December 1977 Martinez, as next friend of Morales, and four other adult custodians of school-age children instituted the present action in the United States District Court for the Southern District of Texas against the Texas Commissioner of Education, the Texas Education Agency, four local school districts, and various local school officials in those districts. . . .

. . . .

Plaintiffs . . . seek only "a declaration that . . . § 21.031(d) is unconstitutional on its face," an injunction prohibiting defendants from denying the children admission to schools pursuant to § 21.031(d), restitution of certain tuition payments, costs, and attorney's fees. After a hearing on the merits, the District Court granted judgment for the defendants. Arredondo v. Brockette, 482 F.Supp. 212 (1979). The court concluded that § 21.031(d) was justified by the State's "legitimate interest in protecting and preserving the quality of its educational system and the right of its own bona fide residents to attend state schools on a preferred tuition basis." In an appeal by two plaintiffs, the United States Court of Appeals for the Fifth Circuit affirmed. 648 F.2d 425 (1981). In view of the importance of the issue, we granted Martinez's petition for certiorari. We now affirm.

II

This Court frequently has considered constitutional challenges to residence requirements. On several occasions the Court has invalidated requirements that condition receipt of a benefit on a minimum period of residence within a jurisdiction, but it always has been careful to distinguish such durational residence requirements from bona fide residence requirements. . . .

We specifically have approved bona fide residence requirements in the field of public education. The Connecticut statute before us in Vlandis v. Kline, 412 U.S. 441 (1973), for example, was unconstitutional becuase it created an irrebutable presumption of nonresidency for state university students whose legal addresses were outside of the State before they applied for admission. The statute violated the Due Process Clause because it in effect classified some bona fide state residents as nonresidents for tuition purposes. But we "fully recognize[d] that a State has a legitimate interest in protecting and preserving . . . the right of its own bona fide residents to attend [its colleges and universities] on a preferential tuition basis." This "legitimate interest" permits a "State [to] establish such reasonable criteria for in-state status as to make virtually certain that students who are not, in fact, bona fide residents of the State, but who have come there solely for educational purposes, cannot take advantage of the in-state rates." Last Term, in Plyler v. Doe, 457 U.S. 202 (1982), we reviewed an aspect of Tex.Educ.Code Ann. § 21.031—the statute at issue in this case. Although we invalidated the portion of the statute that excluded undocumented alien children from the public free schools, we recognized the school districts' right "to apply . . . established criteria for determining residence." . . .

A bona fide residence requirement, appropriately defined and uniformly applied, furthers the substantial state interest in assuring that services provided for its residents are enjoyed only by residents. Such a requirement with respect to attendance in public free schools does not violate the Equal Protection Clause of the Fourteenth Amendment. It does not burden or penalize the constitutional right of interstate travel, for any person is free to move to a State and to establish residence there. A bona fide residence requirement simply requires that the person *does* establish residence before demanding the services that are restricted to residents.

There is a further, independent justification for local residence requirements in the public-school context. . . . The provision of primary and secondary education, of course, is one of the most important functions of local government. Absent residence requirements, there can be little doubt that the proper planning and operation of the schools would suffer significantly. The State thus has a substantial interest in imposing bona fide residence requirements to maintain the quality of local public schools.

III

The central question we must decide here is whether § 21.031(d) is a bona fide residence requirement. Although the meaning may vary according to context, "residence" generally requires both physical presence and an intention to remain. . . . This classic two-part definition of residence has been recognized as a minimum standard in a wide range of contexts time and time again.

. . .

Section 21.031 is far more generous than this traditional standard. It compels a school district to permit a child such as Morales to attend school without paying tuition if he has a bona fide intention to remain in the school district indefinitely, for he then would have a reason for being there other than his desire to attend school: his intention to make his home in the district. Thus § 21.031 grants the benefits of residency to all who satisfy the traditional requirements. The statute goes further and extends these benefits to many children even if they (or their families) do not intend to remain in the district indefinitely. As long as the child is not living in the district for the sole purpose of attending school, he satisfies the statutory test. For example, if a person comes to Texas to work for a year, his children will be eligible for tuition-free admission to the public schools. Or if a child comes to Texas for six months for health reasons, he would qualify for tuition-free education. In short, § 21.031 grants the benefits of residency to everyone who satisfies the traditional residence definition and to some who legitimately could be classified as nonresidents. Since there is no indication that this extension of the traditional definition has any impermissible basis, we certainly cannot say that § 21.031(d) violates the Constitution.

IV

The Constitution permits a State to restrict eligibility for tuition-free education to its bona fide residents. We hold that § 21.031 is a bona fide residence requirement that satisfies constitutional standards. The judgment of the Court of Appeals accordingly is

Affirmed.

Justice Brennan, concurring.

I join the Court's opinion. I write separately, however, to stress that this case involves only a facial challenge to the constitutionality of the Texas statute. In upholding the statute, the Court does not pass on its validity as applied to children in a range of specific factual contexts. . . .

Justice Marshall, dissenting.

Shortly after petitioner Roberto Morales reached his eighth birthday, he left his parents' home in Reynosa, Mexico and returned to his birthplace, McAllen, Texas. He planned to make his home there with his married sister in order to attend school and learn English. Morales has resided with his sister in McAllen for the past five years and intends to remain with her until he has completed his schooling. The Texas statute grants free public education to every school-age child who resides in Texas except for one who lives apart from his parents or guardian for educational purposes. Accordingly, Morales has been refused free admission to the schools in the McAllen district.

The majority upholds the classification embodied in the Texas statute on the ground that it applies only to the class of children who are considered *non-residents*. The majority's approach reflects a misinterpretation of the Texas statute, a misunderstanding of the concept of residence, and a misapplication of this Court's past decisions concerning the constitutionality of residence requirements. In my view, the statutory classification, which deprives some children of an education because of their motive for residing in Texas, is not adequately justified by the asserted state interests. Because I would hold the statute unconstitutional on its face under the Equal Protection Clause, I respectfully dissent.

. . .

Chapter 12

DEFINING THE SCOPE OF "LIBERTY" AND "PROPERTY" PROTECTED BY THE DUE PROCESS CLAUSE—THE PROCEDURAL DUE PROCESS CASES

Introduction. In Chapter 9 we examined the question whether the due process clause was intended to provide more than a requirement of fair procedure. In Chapter 10 we examined at length the substantive interests that are protected under the due process clause. The purpose of this chapter is to return to the issue of procedure in order to pursue the general question whether the interests protected by a requirement of fair procedure are the same as those protected by commands of fairness in substance. No attempt is made in this chapter to present a complete picture of the constitutional requirements of fair procedure in criminal, civil, and administrative proceedings. Those requirements are discussed at length in separate courses.

Section 1 deals with the major intellectual question posed in a number of recent Supreme Court cases—whether there is, or ought to be, a difference in the interests protected by "substantive" and "procedural" due process. The question arises in two contexts. First, is every interest that is given substantive protection also accorded procedural protection? Does a determination that a particular interest is "liberty" or "property" that is substantively protected (in the sense that the state must establish some reason for imposing a burden on it) carry with it a correlative right to some kind of a hearing in which it can be determined whether the particular burden is justified? Second, does the requirement of fair procedure extend beyond those interests given substantive protection by the Constitution? When government extends protection to an interest it is not constitutionally required to recognize, is there a constitutionally imposed right to a hearing in which it can be determined that the particular burden on the interest is justified? For example, if a state provides for the payment of welfare to persons meeting certain criteria, may it also provide for the removal of individual recipients from the welfare rolls without some form of a hearing in which it can be determined whether the recipients meet the statutory criteria?

A second problem relates to the nature of the hearing required. To some degree decisions determining whether a hearing is required have been influenced by the timing and formality of the hearing contemplated. No attempt is made here to pursue this issue systematically, though a summary discussion is presented at the end of the cases in Section 1.

Section 2 presents the "irrebuttable presumption" cases that deal with the analytically separate question of the extent to which the due process clause limits the legislative power to classify by imposing a requirement of individualized hearings.

SECTION 1. WHAT CONSTITUTES A DEPRIVATION OF LIBERTY OR PROPERTY WHICH MANDATES THE PROVISION OF A HEARING?

BOARD OF REGENTS OF STATE COLLEGES v. ROTH

408 U.S. 564, 92 S.Ct. 2701, 33 L.Ed.2d 548 (1972).

Mr. Justice Stewart delivered the opinion of the Court.

In 1968 the respondent, David Roth, was hired for his first teaching job as assistant professor of political science at Wisconsin State University-Oshkosh. He was hired for a fixed term of one academic year. The notice of his faculty appointment specified that his employment would begin on September 1, 1968, and would end on June 30, 1969. The respondent completed that term. But he was informed that he would not be rehired for the next academic year.

The respondent had no tenure rights to continued employment. Under Wisconsin statutory law a state university teacher can acquire tenure as a "permanent" employee only after four years of year-to-year employment. Having acquired tenure, a teacher is entitled to continued employment "during efficiency and good behavior." A relatively new teacher without tenure, however, is under Wisconsin law entitled to nothing beyond his one-year appointment. There are no statutory or administrative standards defining eligibility for re-employment. State law thus clearly leaves the decision whether to rehire a nontenured teacher for another year to the unfettered discretion of University officials.

The procedural protection afforded a Wisconsin State University teacher before he is separated from the University corresponds to his job security. As a matter of statutory law, a tenured teacher cannot be "discharged except for cause upon written charges" and pursuant to certain procedures. A nontenured teacher, similarly, is protected to some extent *during* his one-year term. Rules promulgated by the Board of Regents provide that a nontenured teacher "dismissed" before the end of the year may have some opportunity for review of the "dismissal." But the Rules provide no real protection for a nontenured teacher who simply is not re-employed for the next year. He must be informed by February first "concerning retention or non-retention for the ensuing year." But "no reason for non-retention need be given. No review or appeal is provided in such case."

In conformance with these Rules, the President of Wisconsin State University-Oshkosh informed the respondent before February 1, 1969, that he would not be rehired for the 1969–1970 academic year. He gave the respondent no reason for the decision and no opportunity to challenge it at any sort of hearing.

The respondent then brought this action in a federal district court alleging that the decision not to rehire him for the next year infringed his Fourteenth Amendment rights. He attacked the decision both in substance and procedure. First, he alleged that the true reason for the decision was to punish him for certain statements critical of the University administration, and that it therefore violated his right to freedom of speech. Second, he alleged that the failure of University officials to give him notice of any reason for nonretention and an opportunity for a hearing violated his right to procedural due process of law.

The District Court granted summary judgment for the respondent on the procedural issue, ordering the University officials to provide him with reasons and a hearing. The Court of Appeals, with one judge dissenting, affirmed this partial summary judgment. We granted certiorari. The only question presented to us at this stage in the case is whether the respondent had a constitutional right to a statement of reasons and a hearing on the University's decision not to rehire him for another year. We hold that he did not.

I.

The requirements of procedural due process apply only to the deprivation of interests encompassed within the Fourteenth Amendment's protection of liberty and property. When protected interests are implicated the right to some kind of prior hearing is paramount. But the range of interests protected by procedural due process is not infinite.

. . .

"Liberty" and "property" are broad and majestic terms. They are among the "[g]reat [constitutional] concepts . . . purposely left to gather meaning from experience. . . . [T]hey relate to the whole domain of social and economic fact, and the statesmen who founded this Nation knew too well that only a stagnant society remains unchanged." National Ins. Co. v. Tidewater Co., 337 U.S. 582, 646 (Frankfurter, J., dissenting). For that reason the Court has fully and finally rejected the wooden distinction between "rights" and "privileges" that once seemed to govern the applicability of procedural due process rights. The Court has also made clear that the property interests protected by procedural due process extend well beyond actual ownership of real estate, chattels, or money. By the same token, the Court has required due process protection for deprivations of liberty beyond the sort of formal constraints imposed by the criminal process.

. . .

Yet, while the Court has eschewed rigid or formalistic limitations on the protection of procedural due process, it has at the same time observed certain boundaries. For the words "liberty" and "property" in the Due Process Clause of the Fourteenth Amendment must be given some meaning.

II.

. . .

There might be cases in which a State refused to re-employ a person under such circumstances that interests in liberty would be implicated. But this is not such a case.

The State, in declining to rehire the respondent, did not make any charge against him that might seriously damage his standing and associations in his community. It did not base the nonrenewal of his contract on a charge, for example, that he had been guilty of dishonesty, or immorality. Had it done so, this would be a different case. . . . In such a case, due process would accord an opportunity to refute the charge before University officials.[12] In the present case, however, there is no suggestion whatever that the respondent's interest in his "good name, reputation, honor or integrity" is at stake.

Similarly, there is no suggestion that the State, in declining to re-employ the respondent, imposed on him a stigma or other disability that foreclosed his freedom to take advantage of other employment opportunities. The State, for example, did not invoke any regulations to bar the respondent from all other public employment in State universities. Had it done so, this, again, would be a different case. . . .

To be sure, the respondent has alleged that the non-renewal of his contract was based on his exercise of his right to freedom of speech. But this allegation is not now before us. The District Court stayed proceedings on this issue, and

---

[12] The purpose of such notice and hearing is to provide the person an opportunity to clear his name. Once a person has cleared his name at a hearing, his employer, of course, may remain free to deny him future employment for other reasons.

the respondent has yet to prove that the decision not to rehire him was, in fact, based on his free speech activities.[14]

Hence, on the record before us, all that clearly appears is that the respondent was not rehired for one year at one University. It stretches the concept too far to suggest that a person is deprived of "liberty" when he simply is not rehired in one job but remains as free as before to seek another. Cafeteria Workers v. McElroy, supra, at 895–896.

III.

The Fourteenth Amendment's procedural protection of property is a safeguard of the security of interests that a person has already acquired in specific benefits. These interests—property interests—may take many forms.

.   .   .

Certain attributes of "property" interests protected by procedural due process emerge from these decisions. To have a property interest in a benefit, a person clearly must have more than an abstract need or desire for it. He must have more than a unilateral expectation of it. He must, instead, have a legitimate claim of entitlement to it. It is a purpose of the ancient institution of property to protect those claims upon which people rely in their daily lives, reliance that must not be arbitrarily undermined. It is a purpose of the constitutional right to a hearing to provide an opportunity for a person to vindicate those claims.

Property interests, of course, are not created by the Constitution. Rather, they are created and their dimensions are defined by existing rules or understandings that stem from an independent source such as state law—rules or understandings that secure certain benefits and that support claims of entitlement to those benefits. Thus the welfare recipients in Goldberg v. Kelly, supra, had a claim of entitlement to welfare payments that was grounded in the statute defining eligibility for them. The recipients had not yet shown that they were, in fact, within the statutory terms of eligibility. But we held that they had a right to a hearing at which they might attempt to do so.

Just as the welfare recipients' "property" interest in welfare payments was created and defined by statutory terms, so the respondent's "property" interest in employment at the Wisconsin State University-Oshkosh was created and defined by the terms of his appointment. Those terms secured his interest in employment up to June 30, 1969. But the important fact in this case is that they specifically provided that the respondent's employment was to terminate on June 30. They did not provide for contract renewal absent "sufficient cause." Indeed, they made no provision for renewal whatsoever.

Thus the terms of the respondent's appointment secured absolutely no interest in re-employment for the next year. They supported absolutely no

---

[14] .   .   .

When a State would directly impinge upon interests in free speech or free press, this Court has on occasion held that opportunity for a fair adversary hearing must precede the action, whether or not the speech or press interest is clearly protected under substantive First Amendment standards. Thus we have required fair notice and opportunity for an adversary hearing before an injunction is issued against the holding of rallies and public meetings. Carroll v. Princess Anne, 393 U.S. 175. Similarly, we have indicated the necessity of procedural safeguards before a State makes a large-scale seizure of a person's allegedly obscene books, magazines and so forth. A Quantity of Books v. Kansas, 378 U.S. 205; Marcus v. Search Warrant, 367 U.S. 717. See Freedman v. Maryland, 380 U.S. 51; Bantam Books v. Sullivan, 372 U.S. 58. See generally Monaghan, First Amendment "Due Process," 83 Harv. L.Rev. 518.

In the respondent's case, however, the State has not directly impinged upon interests in free speech or free press in any way comparable to a seizure of books or an injunction against meetings. Whatever may be a teacher's rights of free speech, the interest in holding a teaching job at a state university, *simpliciter,* is not itself a free speech interest.

possible claim of entitlement to re-employment. Nor, significantly, was there any state statute or University rule or policy that secured his interest in re-employment or that created any legitimate claim to it.[16] In these circumstances, the respondent surely had an abstract concern in being rehired, but he did not have a *property* interest sufficient to require the University authorities to give him a hearing when they declined to renew his contract of employment.

IV.

Our analysis of the respondent's constitutional rights in this case in no way indicates a view that an opportunity for a hearing or a statement of reasons for nonretention would, or would not, be appropriate or wise in public colleges and universities. For it is a written Constitution that we apply. Our role is confined to interpretation of that Constitution.

We must conclude that the summary judgment for the respondent should not have been granted, since the respondent has not shown that he was deprived of liberty or property protected by the Fourteenth Amendment. The judgment of the Court of Appeals, accordingly, is reversed and the case is remanded for further proceedings consistent with this opinion.

It is so ordered.

Mr. Justice Marshall, dissenting.

. . .

In my view, every citizen who applies for a government job is entitled to it unless the government can establish some reason for denying the employment. This is the "property" right that I believe is protected by the Fourteenth Amendment and that cannot be denied "without due process of law." And it is also liberty—liberty to work—which is the "very essence of the personal freedom and opportunity" secured by the Fourteenth Amendment.

. . .

It may be argued that to provide procedural due process to all public employees or prospective employees would place an intolerable burden on the machinery of government. Cf. Goldberg v. Kelly, supra. The short answer to that argument is that it is not burdensome to give reasons when reasons exist. Whenever an application for employment is denied, an employee is discharged, or a decision not to rehire an employee is made, there should be some reason for the decision. It can scarcely be argued that government would be crippled by a requirement that the reason be communicated to the person most directly affected by the government's action.

Where there are numerous applicants for jobs, it is likely that few will choose to demand reasons for not being hired. But, if the demand for reasons is exceptionally great, summary procedures can be devised that would provide fair and adequate information to all persons. As long as the government has a good reason for its actions it need not fear disclosure. It is only where the government acts improperly that procedural due process is truly burdensome. And that is precisely when it is most necessary. . . .[a]

---

[16] To be sure, the respondent does suggest that most teachers hired on a year-to-year basis by the Wisconsin State University-Oshkosh are, in fact, rehired. But the District Court has not found that there is anything approaching a "common law" of re-employment, see Perry v. Sindermann, post, at 602, so strong as to require University officials to give the respondent a statement of reasons and a hearing on their decision not to rehire him.

[a] Justices Douglas and Brennan also dissented. Justice Powell took no part in the decision.

In Perry v. Sindermann, 408 U.S. 593 (1972) a teacher's employment was terminated without notice of reasons or hearing after being employed by the college for four successive years under a series of one-year contracts. In his suit he alleged that the decision not to rehire him was based on his public criticism of policies of the college administration and thus infringed his right to free speech and that

BISHOP v. WOOD

426 U.S. 341, 96 S.Ct. 2074, 48 L.Ed.2d 684 (1976).

Mr. Justice Stevens delivered the opinion of the Court.

Acting on the recommendation of the Chief of Police, the City Manager of Marion, North Carolina, terminated petitioner's employment as a policeman without affording him a hearing to determine the sufficiency of the cause for his discharge. Petitioner brought suit contending that since a city ordinance classified him as a "permanent employee," he had a constitutional right to pretermination hearing. During pretrial discovery petitioner was advised that his dismissal was based on a failure to follow certain orders, poor attendance at police training classes, causing low morale, and conduct unsuited to an officer. Petitioner and several other police officers filed affidavits essentially denying the truth of these charges. The District Court granted defendants' motion for summary judgment. The Court of Appeals affirmed and we granted certiorari.

The questions for us to decide are (1) whether petitioner's employment status was a property interest protected by the Due Process Clause of the Fourteenth Amendment, and (2) assuming that the explanation for his discharge was false, whether that false explanation deprived him of an interest in liberty protected by that clause.

I.

Petitioner was employed by the city of Marion as a probationary policeman on June 9, 1969. After six months he became a permanent employee. He was dismissed on March 31, 1972. He claims that he had either an express or an implied right to continued employment.

A city ordinance provides that a permanent employee may be discharged if he fails to perform work up to the standard of his classification, or if he is negligent, inefficient or unfit to perform his duties. Petitioner first contends that even though the ordinance does not expressly so provide, it should be read to prohibit discharge for any other reason, and therefore to confer tenure on all permanent employees. In addition, he contends that his period of service, together with his "permanent" classification, gave him a sufficient expectancy of continued employment to constitute a protected property interest.

A property interest in employment can, of course, be created by ordinance, or by an implied contract. In either case, however, the sufficiency of the claim of entitlement must be decided by reference to state law. The North Carolina Supreme Court has held that an enforceable expectation of continued public employment in that State can exist only if the employer, by statute or contract, has actually granted some form of guarantee. Still v. Lance, 275 N.C. 254, 182 S.E.2d 403 (1971). Whether such a guarantee has been given can be determined only by an examination of the particular statute or ordinance in question.

the failure to give him notice and hearing violated procedural due process. The trial court granted summary judgment for the defendant college on the basis of affidavits denying that plaintiff's criticism was involved and asserting no need to provide a hearing. The Court held that this decision was in error for two reasons: (1) Plaintiff was entitled to a full hearing on his free speech claim because "a teacher's public criticism of his superiors on matters of public concern may be constitutionally protected and may, therefore, be an impermissible basis for termination of his employment." (2) Plaintiff was also entitled to a hearing on his allegation that he had in fact some form of tenure under the practices of the college. There "may be an unwritten 'common law' in a particular university that certain employees shall have the equivalent of tenure." Plaintiff was entitled to show whether that existed in this case and, if it did, he would be entitled to an order obligating college officials to give him a hearing.

See Simon, *Liberty and Property in the Supreme Court: A Defense of Roth and Perry,* 71 Calif.L. Rev. 146 (1983).

On its face the ordinance on which petitioner relies may fairly be read as conferring such a guarantee. However, such a reading is not the only possible interpretation; the ordinance may also be construed as granting no right to continued employment but merely conditioning an employee's removal on compliance with certain specified procedures.[8] We do not have any authoritative interpretation of this ordinance by a North Carolina state court. We do, however, have the opinion of the United States District Judge who, of course, sits in North Carolina and practiced law there for many years. Based on his understanding of state law, he concluded that petitioner "held his position at the will and pleasure of the city." This construction of North Carolina law was upheld by the Court of Appeals for the Fourth Circuit, albeit by an equally divided Court. In comparable circumstances, this Court has accepted the interpretation of state law in which the District Court and the Court of Appeals have concurred even if an examination of the state-law issue without such guidance might have justified a different conclusion.

In this case, as the District Court construed the ordinance, the City Manager's determination of the adequacy of the grounds for discharge is not subject to judicial review; the employee is merely given certain procedural rights which the District Court found not to have been violated in this case. The District Court's reading of the ordinance is tenable; it derives some support from a decision of the North Carolina Supreme Court, Still v. Lance, supra; and it was accepted by the Court of Appeals for the Fourth Circuit. These reasons are sufficient to foreclose our independent examination of the state law issue.

Under that view of the law, petitioner's discharge did not deprive him of a property interest protected by the Fourteenth Amendment.

II.

Petitioner's claim that he has been deprived of liberty has two components. He contends that the reasons given for his discharge are so serious as to constitute a stigma that may severely damage his reputation in the community; in addition, he claims that those reasons were false.

In our appraisal of petitioner's claim we must accept his version of the facts since the District Court granted summary judgment against him. His evidence established that he was a competent police officer; that he was respected by his peers; that he made more arrests than any other officer on the force; that although he had been criticized for engaging in high speed pursuits, he had promptly complied with such criticism; and that he had a reasonable explanation for his imperfect attendance at police training sessions. We must therefore assume that his discharge was a mistake and based on incorrect information.

In Board of Regents v. Roth, 408 U.S. 564, we recognized that the nonretention of an untenured college teacher might make him somewhat less attractive to other employers, but nevertheless concluded that it would stretch the concept too far "to suggest that a person is deprived of 'liberty' when he simply is not retained in one position but remains as free as before to seek another." This same conclusion applies to the discharge of a public employee whose position is terminable at the will of the employer when there is no public disclosure of the reasons for the discharge.

---

[8] This is not the construction which six Members of this Court placed on the federal regulations involved in Arnett v. Kennedy, 416 U.S. 134. In that case the Court concluded that because the employee could only be discharged for cause, he had a property interest which was entitled to constitutional protection. In this case, a holding that as a matter of state law the employee "held his position at the will and pleasure of the city" necessarily establishes that he had *no* property interest. The Court's evaluation of the federal regulations involved in *Arnett* sheds no light on the problem presented by this case.

In this case the asserted reasons for the City Manager's decision were communicated orally to the petitioner in private and also were stated in writing in answer to interrogatories after this litigation commenced. Since the former communication was not made public, it cannot properly form the basis for a claim that petitioner's interest in his "good name, reputation, honesty, or integrity" was thereby impaired. And since the latter communication was made in the course of a judicial proceeding which did not commence until after petitioner had suffered the injury for which he seeks redress, it surely cannot provide retroactive support for his claim. A contrary evaluation of either explanation would penalize forthright and truthful communication between employer and employee in the former instance, and between litigants in the latter.

Petitioner argues, however, that the reasons given for his discharge were false. Even so, the reasons stated to him in private had no different impact on his reputation than if they had been true. And the answers to his interrogatories, whether true or false, did not cause the discharge. The truth or falsity of the City Manager's statement determines whether or not his decision to discharge the petitioner was correct or prudent, but neither enhances nor diminishes petitioner's claim that his constitutionally protected interest in liberty has been impaired.[13] A contrary evaluation of his contention would enable every discharged employee to assert a constitutional claim merely by alleging that his former supervisor made a mistake.

The federal court is not the appropriate forum in which to review the multitude of personnel decisions that are made daily by public agencies.[14] We must accept the harsh fact that numerous individual mistakes are inevitable in the day-to-day administration of our affairs. The United States Constitution cannot feasibly be construed to require federal judicial review for every such error. In the absence of any claim that the public employer was motivated by a desire to curtail or to penalize the exercise of an employee's constitutionally protected rights, we must presume that official action was regular and, if erroneous, can best be corrected in other ways. The Due Process Clause of the Fourteenth Amendment is not a guarantee against incorrect or ill-advised personnel decisions.

The judgment is affirmed.

Mr. Justice Brennan, with whom Mr. Justice Marshall concurs, dissenting.

Petitioner was discharged as a policeman on the grounds of insubordination, "causing low morale," and "conduct unsuited to an officer." Ante, at 1. It is difficult to imagine a greater "badge of infamy" that could be imposed on one following petitioner's calling; in a profession in which prospective employees are invariably investigated, petitioner's job prospects will be severely constricted by the governmental action in this case. Although our case law would appear to

---

[13] Indeed, the impact on petitioner's constitutionally protected interest in liberty is no greater even if we assume that the City Manager deliberately lied. Such fact might conceivably provide the basis for a state law claim, the validity of which would be entirely unaffected by our analysis of the federal constitutional question.

[14] The cumulative impression created by the three dissenting opinions is that this holding represents a significant retreat from settled practice in the federal courts. The fact of the matter, however, is that the instances in which the federal judiciary has required a state agency to reinstate a discharged employee for failure to provide a pretermination hearing are extremely rare. The reason is clear. For unless we were to adopt Mr. Justice Brennan's remarkably innovative suggestion that we develop a federal common law of property rights, or his equally far reaching view that almost every discharge implicates a constitutionally protected liberty interest, the ultimate control of state personnel relationships is, and will remain, with the States; they may grant or withhold tenure at their unfettered discretion. In this case, whether we accept or reject the construction of the ordinance adopted by the two lower courts, the power to change or clarify that ordinance will remain in the hands of the City Council of the city of Marion.

require that petitioner thus be accorded an opportunity "to clear his name" of this calumny, see, e.g., Board of Regents v. Roth, 408 U.S. 564, 573 and n. 12 (1972); Arnett v. Kennedy, 416 U.S. 134, 157 (1974) (opinion of Rehnquist, J.), the Court condones this governmental action and holds that petitioner was deprived of no liberty interest thereby. . . .

I also fully concur in the dissenting opinions of Mr. Justice White and Mr. Justice Blackmun, which forcefully demonstrate the Court's error in holding that petitioner was not deprived of "property" without due process of law. I would only add that the strained reading of the local ordinance, which the Court deems to be "tenable," ante, at 6, cannot be dispositive of the existence *vel non* of petitioner's "property" interest. There is certainly a federal dimension to the definition of "property" in the Federal Constitution; cases such as Board of Regents v. Roth, supra, held merely that "property" interests encompass those to which a person has "a legitimate claim of entitlement," id., at 577, and *can* arise from "existing rules or understandings" that derive from "an independent source *such* as state law." Ibid. (emphasis supplied). But certainly, at least before a state law is definitively construed as not securing a "property" interest, the relevant inquiry is whether it was objectively reasonable for the employee to believe he could rely on continued employment. Cf. ibid. ("It is a purpose of the ancient institution of property to protect those claims upon which people rely in their daily lives, reliance that must not be arbitrarily determined.").[4] At a minimum, this would require in this case an analysis of the common practices utilized and the expectations generated by respondents, and the manner in which the local ordinance would reasonably be read by respondents' employees. These disputed issues of fact are not meet for resolution, as they were, on summary judgment, and would thus at a minimum require a remand for further factual development in the district court.

These observations do not, of course, suggest that a "federal court is . . . the appropriate forum in which to review the multitude of personnel decisions that are made daily by public agencies." Ante, at 8. However, the federal courts *are* the appropriate forum for ensuring that the constitutional mandates of due process are followed by those agencies of government making personnel decisions that pervasively influence the lives of those affected thereby; the fundamental premise of the Due Process Clause is that those procedural safeguards will help the government avoid the "harsh fact" of "incorrect or ill-advised personnel decisions." Ante, at 8. Petitioner seeks no more than that, and I believe that his "property" interest in continued employment and his "liberty" interest in his good name and reputation dictate that he be accorded procedural safeguards before those interests are deprived by arbitrary or capricious government action.

Mr. Justice White, with whom Mr. Justice Brennan, Mr. Justice Marshall, and Mr. Justice Blackmun join, dissenting.

I dissent because the decision of the majority rests upon a proposition which was squarely addressed and in my view correctly rejected by six Members of this Court in Arnett v. Kennedy, 416 U.S. 134 (1974). . . .

. . . The majority . . . concedes that the ordinance supplies the "grounds" for discharge and that the City Manager must determine them to be "adequate" before he may fire an employee. The majority's holding that

---

[4] By holding that States have "unfettered discretion" in defining "property" for purposes of the Due Process Clause of the Federal Constitution, see ante, at n. 10, the Court is, as my Brother White argues, effectively adopting the analysis rejected by a majority of the Court in Arnett v. Kennedy, 416 U.S. 134 (1974). More basically, the Court's approach is a resurrection of the discredited rights/privileges distinction, for a State may now avoid all due process safeguards attendant upon the loss of even the necessities of life, cf. Goldberg v. Kelly, 397 U.S. 254 (1970), merely by labeling them as not constituting "property." . . .

petitioner had no property interest in his job in spite of the unequivocal language in the city ordinance that he may be dismissed only for certain kinds of cause rests, then, on the fact that state law provides no *procedures* for assuring that the City Manager dismiss him only for cause. The right to his job apparently given by the first two sentences of the ordinance is thus redefined, according to the majority, by the procedures provided for in the third sentence and as redefined is infringed only if the procedures are not followed. . . .

. . . .

The views now expressed by the majority are thus squarely contrary to the views expressed by a majority of the Justices in *Arnett.*   As Mr. Justice Powell suggested in *Arnett,* they are also "incompatible with the principles laid down in *Roth* and *Sindermann.*"   416 U.S. at 166.   I would not so soon depart from these cases nor from the views expressed by a majority in *Arnett.*   The ordinance plainly grants petitioner a right to his job unless there is cause to fire him. Having granted him such a right it is the Federal Constitution,[3] not state law, which determines the process to be applied in connection with any state decision to deprive him of it.

Mr. Justice Blackmun, with whom Mr. Justice Brennan joins, dissenting.

I join Mr. Justice White's dissent for I agree that the Court appears to be adopting a legal principle which specifically was rejected by a majority of the Justices of this Court in Arnett v. Kennedy, 416 U.S. 134 (1974). . . . .[a]

VITEK v. JONES

445 U.S. 480, 100 S.Ct. 1254, 63 L.Ed.2d 552 (1980).

Mr. Justice White delivered the opinion of the Court, except as to Part IV–B.

The question in this case is whether the Due Process Clause of the Fourteenth Amendment entitles a prisoner convicted and incarcerated in the State of Nebraska to certain procedural protections, including notice, an adver-

---

[3] The majority intimates in n. 8 that the views of the three plurality Justices in Arnett v. Kennedy were rejected because the other six Justices disagreed on the question of how the federal *statute* involved in that case should be construed.   This is incorrect.   All Justices agreed on the meaning of the statute.   As the remarks of the six Justices quoted above indicate, it was the constitutional significance of the statute on which the six disagreed with the plurality.

Similarly, here, I do not disagree with the majority or the courts below on the meaning of the state law.   If I did, I might be inclined to defer to the judgments of the two lower courts.   The state law says that petitioner may be dismissed by the City Manager only for certain kinds of cause and then provides that he will receive notice and an explanation, but no hearing and no review.   I agree that as a matter of state law petitioner has no remedy no matter how arbitrarily or erroneously the City Manager has acted.   This is what the lower courts say the statute means.   I differ with those courts and the majority only with respect to the constitutional significance of an unambiguous state law.   A majority of the Justices in Arnett v. Kennedy, supra, stood on the proposition that the Constitution required procedures *not* required by state law when the state conditions dismissal on "cause."

[a] In *Arnett,* Justice Rehnquist, joined by Chief Justice Burger and Justice Stewart, had said that a statute could validly provide that a discharge shall be only for cause, and at the same time provide procedures for proving cause that were more limited than those mandated by due process.   He reasoned that when the very section of the statute which created the expectancy of job security also provided the procedures for enforcing that expectancy, the entitlement created went no further than the procedures provided.   The remainder of the Court disagreed.

Justice Stevens responded to the charge that Bishop v. Wood constituted an adoption of the Rehnquist position in footnote 8, supra.   Later, in Codd v. Velger, 429 U.S. 624 (1977) in an opinion joined by Justice Stewart, he made it clear that he viewed Bishop as resting on the conclusion that under the state law the plaintiff could be discharged at will and "a hearing would have been pointless because nothing plaintiff could prove would entitle him to keep his job."

sary hearing, and provision of counsel, before he is transferred involuntarily to a state mental hospital for treatment of a mental disease or defect.

I.

Neb.Rev.Stat. § 83–176(2) authorizes the Director of Correctional Services to designate any available, suitable and appropriate residence facility or institution as a place of confinement for any state prisoner and to transfer a prisoner from one place of confinement to another. Section 83–180(1), however, provides that when a designated physician or psychologist finds that a prisoner "suffers from a mental disease or defect" and "cannot be given proper treatment in that facility," the director may transfer him for examination, study and treatment to another institution within or without the Department of Corrections. Any prisoner so transferred to a mental hospital is to be returned to the Department if, prior to the expiration of his sentence, treatment is no longer necessary. Upon expiration of sentence, if the State desires to retain the prisoner in a mental hospital, civil commitment proceedings must be promptly commenced. Neb.Rev.Stat. § 83–180(3).

On May 31, 1974, Jones was convicted of robbery and sentenced to a term of three to nine years in state prison. He was transferred to the penitentiary hospital in January 1975. Two days later he was placed in solitary confinement, where he set his mattress on fire, burning himself severely. He was treated in the burn unit of a private hospital. Upon his release and based on findings required by § 83–180 that he was suffering from a mental illness or defect and could not receive proper treatment in the penal complex he was transferred to the security unit of the Lincoln Regional Center, a state mental hospital under the jurisdiction of the Department of Public Institutions.

Jones then intervened in this case, which was brought by other prisoners against the appropriate state officials (the State) challenging on procedural due process grounds the adequacy of the procedures by which the Nebraska statutes permit transfers from the prison complex to a mental hospital. . . . [after a trial] the District Court declared § 83–180 unconstitutional as applied to Jones, holding that transferring Jones to a mental hospital without adequate notice and opportunity for a hearing deprived him of liberty without due process of law contrary to the Fourteenth Amendment and that such transfers must be accompanied by adequate notice, an adversary hearing before an independent decisionmaker, a written statement by the factfinder of the evidence relied on and the reasons for the decision and the availability of appointed counsel for indigent prisoners. . . .

. . . The District Court then entered its judgment declaring § 83–180 unconstitutional as applied to Jones and permanently enjoining the State from transferring Jones to Lincoln Regional Center without following the procedures prescribed in its judgment.

. . . .

[Facts relating to a claim of mootness have been edited from this opinion. The Court rejected that claim in Part II of its opinion.]

III.

On the merits, the threshold question in this case is whether the involuntary transfer of a Nebraska state prisoner to a mental hospital implicates a liberty interest that is protected by the Due Process Clause. The District Court held that it did and offered two related reasons for its conclusion. The District Court first identified a liberty interest rooted in § 83–180(1), under which a prisoner could reasonably expect that he would not be transferred to a mental hospital without a finding that he was suffering from a mental illness for which he could not secure adequate treatment in the correctional facility. Second, the District Court was convinced that characterizing Jones as a mentally ill patient and transferring him to the Lincoln Regional Center had "some stigmatizing" consequences which, together with the mandatory behavior modification treatment to which Jones would be subject at the Lincoln Center, constituted a major change in the conditions of confinement amounting to a "grievous loss" that should not be imposed without the opportunity for notice and an adequate hearing. We agree with the District Court in both respects.

A.

We have repeatedly held that state statutes may create liberty interests that are entitled to the procedural protections of the Due Process Clause of the Fourteenth Amendment. There is no "constitutional or inherent right" to parole, Greenholtz v. Nebraska Penal Inmates, 442 U.S. 1, 7 (1979), but once a State grants a prisoner the conditional liberty properly dependent on the observance of special parole restrictions, due process protections attach to the decision to revoke parole. Morrissey v. Brewer, 408 U.S. 471 (1972). The same is true of the revocation of probation. Gagnon v. Scarpelli, 411 U.S. 778 (1973). . . .

. . .

We think the District Court properly understood and applied these decisions. Section 83–180(1) Neb.Rev.Stats. provides that if a designated physician finds that a prisoner "suffers from a mental disease or defect" that "cannot be given proper treatment" in prison, the Director of Correctional Services may transfer a prisoner to a mental hospital. The District Court also found that in practice prisoners are transferred to a mental hospital only if it is determined that they suffer from a mental disease or defect that cannot adequately be treated within the Penal Complex. This "objective expectation, firmly fixed in state law and official Penal Complex practice," that a prisoner would not be transferred unless he suffered from a mental disease or defect that could not be adequately treated in the prison, gave Jones a liberty interest that entitled him to the benefits of appropriate procedures in connection with determining the conditions that warranted his transfer to a mental hospital. Under our cases, this conclusion of the District Court is unexceptionable.

Appellants maintain that any state-created liberty interest that Jones had was completely satisfied once a physician or psychologist designated by the director made the findings required by § 83–180(1) and that Jones was not entitled to any procedural protections.[6] But if the State grants a prisoner a right or expectation that adverse action will not be taken against him except upon the occurrence of specified behavior, "the determination of whether such behavior has occurred becomes critical, and the minimum requirements of procedural process appropriate for the circumstances must be observed." Wolff v. McDonnell, 418 U.S., at 558. These minimum requirements being a matter of federal law, they are not diminished by the fact that the State may have specified its own procedures that it may deem adequate for determining the preconditions to adverse official action. . . . Nebraska's reliance on the opinion of a designated physician or psychologist for determining whether the conditions warranting a transfer exist neither removes the prisoner's interest from due process protection nor answers the question of what process is due under the Constitution.

[6.] A majority of the Justices rejected an identical position in Arnett v. Kennedy, 416 U.S. 134, 166–167 (opinion of Powell, J., joined by Blackmun, J.), 177–178 (opinion of White, J.), 210–211 (opinion of Marshall, J., joined by Douglas and Brennan, JJ.). . . .

B.

The District Court was also correct in holding that independently of § 83–180(1), the transfer of a prisoner from a prison to a mental hospital must be accompanied by appropriate procedural protections. The issue is whether after a conviction for robbery, Jones retained a residuum of liberty that would be infringed by a transfer to a mental hospital without complying with minimum requirements of due process.

We have recognized that for the ordinary citizen, commitment to a mental hospital produces "a massive curtailment of liberty," Humphrey v. Cady, 405 U.S. 504, 509 (1972), and in consequence "requires due process protection." Addington v. Texas, 441 U.S. 418, 425 (1979); O'Connor v. Donaldson, 422 U.S. 563, 580 (Burger, C.J., concurring). . . .

Were an ordinary citizen to be subjected involuntarily to these consequences, it is undeniable that protected liberty interests would be unconstitutionally infringed absent compliance with the procedures required by the Due Process Clause. We conclude that a convicted felon also is entitled to the benefit of procedures appropriate in the circumstances before he is found to have a mental disease and transferred to a mental hospital.

Undoubtedly a valid criminal conviction and prison sentence extinguish a defendant's right to freedom from confinement. Greenholtz v. Nebraska Penal Inmates, 442 U.S., at 7. Such a conviction and sentence sufficiently extinguish a defendant's liberty "to empower the state to confine him in any of its prisons." Meachum v. Fano, 427 U.S., at 224. It is also true that changes in the conditions of confinement having a substantial adverse impact on the prisoner are not alone sufficient to invoke the protections of the Due Process Clause "as long as the conditions or degree of confinement to which the prisoner is subjected is within the sentence imposed upon him." Montanye v. Haymes, 427 U.S., at 242.

Appellants maintain that the transfer of a prisoner to a mental hospital is within the range of confinement justified by imposition of a prison sentence, at least after certification by a qualified person that a prisoner suffers from a mental disease or defect. We cannot agree. None of our decisions holds that conviction for a crime entitles a State not only to confine the convicted person but also to determine that he has a mental illness and to subject him involuntarily to institutional care in a mental hospital. Such consequences visited on the prisoner are qualitatively different from the punishment characteristically suffered by a person convicted of crime. Our cases recognize as much and reflect an understanding that involuntary commitment to a mental hospital is not within the range of conditions of confinement to which a prison sentence subjects an individual. . . . . A criminal conviction and sentence of imprisonment extinguish an individual's right to freedom from confinement for the term of his sentence, but they do not authorize the State to classify him as mentally ill and to subject him to involuntary psychiatric treatment without affording him additional due process protections.

In light of the findings made by the District Court, Jones' involuntary transfer to the Lincoln Regional Center pursuant to § 83–180, for the purpose of psychiatric treatment, implicated a liberty interest protected by the Due Process Clause. Many of the restrictions on the prisoner's freedom of action at the Lincoln Regional Center by themselves might not constitute the deprivation of a liberty interest retained by a prisoner . . . . But here, the stigmatizing consequences of a transfer to a mental hospital for involuntary psychiatric treatment, coupled with the subjection of the prisoner to mandatory behavior modification as a treatment for mental illness constitute the kind of deprivations of liberty that require procedural protections.

[In Part IV of its opinion the Court concluded that a fairly elaborate hearing must be provided prisoners before they are transferred to mental hospitals. It affirmed the judgment of the district court except for its requirement that such prisoners were entitled to be represented by counsel in transfer hearings. Four justices voted to approve the requirement of counsel, but Justice Powell, whose vote was necessary for the judgment, disagreed on that point.]

Chief Justice Burger and Justices Blackmun, Rehnquist, and Stewart dissented on the ground that the case was moot and hence not properly before the Court.

HEWITT v. HELMS, 459 U.S. 460 (1983). After a prison riot, Helms was charged with participation and placed in administrative segregation. He was given some notice of the charges against him and a chance to reply but no in-person hearing was held. The Court, by a vote of 6 to 3, held that the due process clause gave no right to a hearing when such changes in custodial quarters were undertaken but that the state statutes and regulations here had created a protected liberty interest and hence a right to a hearing. By a vote of 5 to 4 the Court held that the informal hearing given here to the prisoner without a right to present his case personally to the reviewing official was sufficient.

OLIM v. WAKINEKONA, 461 U.S. 238 (1983). By a vote of 6 to 3 the Court held that the transfer of a prisoner from Hawaii to serve his time in a prison in California did not involve a liberty interest and hence require a hearing. The prisoner relied on Vitek v. Jones. The Court answered:

"We do not agree. Just as an inmate has no justifiable expectation that he will be incarcerated in any particular prison within a State, he has no justifiable expectation that he will be incarcerated in any particular State. Often, confinement in the inmate's home State will not be possible. . . . Overcrowding and the need to separate particular prisoners may necessitate interstate transfers. For any number of reasons, a State may lack prison facilities capable of providing appropriate correctional programs for all offenders.

. . . .

". . . Even when, as here, the transfer involves long distances and an ocean crossing, the confinement remains within constitutional limits. The difference between such a transfer and an intrastate or interstate transfer of shorter distance is a matter of degree, not of kind . . . .."

PARRATT v. TAYLOR, 451 U.S. 527 (1981). Respondent was an inmate of a Nebraska prison. He ordered certain hobby materials by mail valued at $23.50. They arrived at the prison but were lost and never delivered to respondent. He brought a suit for damages against prison officials in the federal district court under 42 U.S.C. § 1983. The district court entered summary judgment for the respondent and the Supreme Court reversed.

In an opinion by Justice Rehnquist, the Court first addressed the question whether negligent actions by state officials can be the basis for an action under § 1983 and concluded that they could. In a § 1983 action the two essential elements are: "(1) whether the conduct complained of was committed by a person acting under color of state law; and (2) whether this conduct deprived a person of rights, privileges, or immunities secured by the Constitution or laws of the United States." Here the action was under color of state law since it was action by state officials. The question then was whether respondent had been deprived of any right, privilege, or immunity secured by federal law.

The opinion then continued:

"Unquestionably, respondent's claim satisfies three prerequisites of a valid due process claim: the petitioners acted under color of state law; the hobby kit falls within the definition of property; and the alleged loss, even though negligently caused, amounted to a deprivation. Standing alone, however, these three elements do not establish a violation of the Fourteenth Amendment. Nothing in that Amendment protects against all deprivations of life, liberty, or property by the State. The Fourteenth Amendment protects only against deprivations 'without due process of law.' Our inquiry therefore must focus on whether the respondent has suffered a deprivation of property without due process of law. In particular, we must decide whether the tort remedies which the State of Nebraska provides as a means of redress for property deprivations satisfy the requirements of procedural due process.

"This Court has never directly addressed the question of what process is due a person when an employee of a State negligently takes his property. In some cases this Court has held that due process requires a predeprivation hearing before the State interferes with any liberty or property interest enjoyed by its citizens. In most of these cases, however, the deprivation of property was pursuant to some established state procedure and 'process' could be offered before any actual deprivation took place. . . . In all these cases, deprivations of property were authorized by an established state procedure and due process was held to require predeprivation notice and hearing in order to serve as a check on the possibility that a wrongful deprivation would occur.

"We have, however, recognized that postdeprivation remedies made available by the State can satisfy the Due Process Clause. In such cases, the normal predeprivation notice and opportunity to be heard is pretermitted if the State provides a postdeprivation remedy. . . . These cases recognize that either the necessity of quick action by the State or the impracticality of providing any meaningful predeprivation process can, when coupled with the availability of some meaningful means by which to assess the propriety of the State's action at some time after the initial taking, satisfy the requirements of procedural due process. . . .

"Our past cases mandate that some kind of hearing is required at some time before a State finally deprives a person of his property interests. The fundamental requirement of due process is the opportunity to be heard and it is an 'opportunity which must be granted at a meaningful time and in a meaningful manner.' However, as many of the above cases recognize, we have rejected the proposition that 'at a meaningful time and in a meaningful manner' *always* requires the State to provide a hearing prior to the initial deprivation of property. This rejection is based in part on the impracticability in some cases of providing any preseizure hearing under a state-authorized procedure, and the assumption that at some time a full and meaningful hearing will be available.

"The justifications which we have found sufficient to uphold takings of property without any predeprivation process are applicable to a situation such as the present one involving a tortious loss of a prisoner's property as a result of a random and unauthorized act by a state employee. In such a case, the loss is not a result of some established state procedure and the State cannot predict precisely when the loss will occur. It is difficult to conceive of how the State could provide a meaningful hearing before the deprivation takes place. The loss of property, although attributable to the State as action under 'color of law,' is in almost all cases beyond the control of the State. Indeed, in most cases it is not only impracticable, but impossible to provide a meaningful hearing before the deprivation. That does not mean, of course, that the State can take property without providing a meaningful post-deprivation hearing. The prior cases which have excused the prior-hearing requirement have rested in part on the availability of some meaningful opportunity subsequent to the initial taking for a determination of rights and liabilities.

. . .

"Application of the principles recited above to this case leads us to conclude the respondent has not alleged a violation of the Due Process Clause of the Fourteenth Amendment. Although he has been deprived of property under color of state law, the deprivation did not occur as a result of some established state procedure. Indeed, the deprivation occurred as a result of the unauthorized failure of agents of the State to follow established state procedure. There is no contention that the procedures themselves are inadequate nor is there any contention that it was practicable for the State to provide a predeprivation hearing. Moreover, the State of Nebraska has provided respondent with the means by which he can receive redress for the deprivation. The State provides a remedy to persons who believe they have suffered a tortious loss at the hands of the State. See Neb.Rev.Stat. § 81–8,209 et seq. (Reissue 1976). Through this tort claims procedure the state hears and pays claims of prisoners housed in its penal institutions. This procedure was in existence at the time of the loss here in question but respondent did not use it. It is argued that the State does not adequately protect the respondent's interests because it provides only for an action against the State as opposed to its individual employees, it contains no provisions for punitive damages, and there is no right to a trial by jury. Although the state remedies may not provide the respondent with all the relief which may have been available if he could have proceeded under § 1983, that does not mean that the state remedies are not adequate to satisfy the requirements of due process. The remedies provided could have fully compensated the respondent for the property loss he suffered, and we hold that they are sufficient to satisfy the requirements of due process.

"Our decision today is fully consistent with our prior cases. To accept respondent's argument that the conduct of the state officials in this case constituted a violation of the Fourteenth Amendment would almost necessarily result in turning every alleged injury which may have been inflicted by a state official acting under 'color of law' into a violation of the Fourteenth Amendment cognizable under § 1983. It is hard to perceive any logical stopping place to such a line of reasoning. Presumably, under this rationale any party who is involved in nothing more than an automobile accident with a state official could allege a constitutional violation under § 1983. Such reasoning 'would make the Fourteenth Amendment a font of tort law to be superimposed upon whatever systems may already be administered by the States.' Paul v. Davis, 424 U.S. 693, 701 (1976). We do not think that the drafters of the Fourteenth Amendment intended the Amendment to play such a role in our society."

Justice Stewart concurred in the opinion of the Court but added a separate opinion indicating his doubt that negligent acts of state officials causing property losses constituted a deprivation of property under the fourteenth amendment. Justices White and Blackmun joined the opinion but expressed reservations stated by Justice Blackmun. He indicated the Court's opinion did not apply to deprivations of life or liberty. He also said: "I also do not understand the Court to intimate that the sole content of the Due Process Clause is procedural regularity. I continue to believe that there are certain governmental actions that, even if undertaken with a full panoply of procedural protection, are, in and of themselves, antithetical to fundamental notions of due process." He also stated that he did not understand the Court to suggest that "the provision of 'postdeprivation remedies' within a state system would cure the unconstitutional nature of a state official's intentional act that deprives a person of property."

Justice Powell concurred in the result. He said he did not believe that negligent acts by state officials "constitute a deprivation of property within the meaning of the Fourteenth Amendment, regardless of whatever subsequent procedure a State may or may not provide." He found the Court's opinion "disturbing" in its failure to analyze the substantive content of due process. "The Due Process Clause imposes substantive limitations on state action, and under proper circumstances these limitations may extend to intentional and malicious deprivations of liberty and property, even where compensation is available under state law."

Justice Marshall indicated that he agreed with all of the majority opinion except its conclusion that the state remedies here were adequate. He said that a prisoner was entitled to be notified as to his rights under state law and that prison officials did not do this.

HUDSON v. PALMER, 104 S.Ct. 3194 (1984). The Court applied the principle of Parratt v. Taylor to a claim that prison officials intentionally destroyed a prisoner's property during a search. The Court said:

"While *Parratt* is necessarily limited by its facts to negligent deprivations of property, it is evident, as the Court of Appeals recognized, that its reasoning applies as well to intentional deprivations of property. The underlying rationale of *Parratt* is that when deprivations of property are effected through random and unauthorized conduct of a state employee, predeprivation procedures are simply 'impracticable' since the state cannot know when such deprivations will occur. We can discern no logical distinction between negligent and intentional deprivations of property insofar as the 'practicability' of affording predeprivation process is concerned. The State can no more anticipate and control in advance the random and unauthorized intentional conduct of its employees than it can anticipate similar negligent conduct. Arguably, intentional acts are even more difficult to anticipate because one bent on intentionally depriving a person of his property might well take affirmative steps to avoid signalling his intent.

"If negligent deprivations of property do not violate the Due Process Clause because predeprivation process is impracticable, it follows that intentional deprivations do not violate that Clause provided, of course, that adequate state postdeprivation remedies are available. Accordingly, we hold that an unauthorized intentional deprivation of property by a state employee does not constitute a violation of the procedural requirements of the Due Process Clause of the Fourteenth Amendment if a meaningful postdeprivation remedy for the loss is available. For intentional, as for negligent deprivations of property by state employees, the State's action is not complete until and unless it provides or refuses to provide a suitable postdeprivation remedy."

LOGAN v. ZIMMERMAN BRUSH CO., 455 U.S. 422 (1982). The Court held that when a state creates a remedy for a person charging discrimination on the basis of physical handicap, it creates a property interest which cannot be taken away without due procedures. The view that the claim is constitutionally protected, the Court said, "follows logically from the Court's more recent cases analyzing the nature of a property interest. The hallmark of property . . . is an individual entitlement grounded in state law which cannot be removed except 'for cause.' . . . Once that characteristic is found, the types of interest protected as 'property' are varied and, as often as not, intangible, relating 'to the whole domain of social and economic fact.'"

In *Logan* the deprivation took place because a state commission failed to take action within a defined length of time. The Court went on to hold that the fact that the statute creating the right also set up the procedures did not eliminate the constitutional problem. Minimum procedural requirements are a matter of federal not state law.

The Court also held that the ability of the complainant to get relief through an independent tort action was not sufficient. The Court said that *Parratt* was different because the loss there was a random and unauthorized act by a state employee not a result of some established state procedure. Here, on the other hand, the complainant was challenging an established state procedure which destroyed his entitlement without pro per procedural safeguards.

See generally Smolla, *The Displacement of Federal Due Process Claims by State Tort Remedies: Parratt v. Taylor and Logan v. Zimmerman Brush Company,* 1982 Un. of Ill.L.Rev. 831.

THE INTERRELATIONSHIPS OF SUBSTANTIVE AND PROCEDURAL DUE PROCESS

What is the relationship between the constitutional requirements of "fair substance" and "fair procedure"? In theory, the procedural requirement is conceptually distinct from any constitutional limit on the substance of government policy.

Hearings reinforce the rule of law by insuring official regularity and minimizing the scope for arbitrary decision-making. The procedural requirement may also serve, however, as a means for forcing the state to take more seriously than it might otherwise the substantive issues at stake. In Fuentes v. Shevin, 407 U.S. 67 (1972), the Court held invalid a state law which permitted summary seizure of property under a writ of replevin without prior notice or hearing to the possessor of the property. As part of its justification for requiring a prior hearing the Court said:

"The constitutional right to be heard is a basic aspect of the duty of government to follow a fair process of decisionmaking when it acts to deprive a person of his possessions. The purpose of this requirement is not only to ensure abstract fair play to the individual. Its purpose, more particularly, is to protect his use and possession of property from arbitrary encroachment—to minimize substantively unfair or mistaken deprivations of property, a danger that is especially great when the State seizes goods simply upon the application of and for the benefit of a private party. So viewed, the prohibition against the deprivation of property without due process of law reflects the high value, embedded in our constitutional and political history, that we place on a person's right to enjoy what is his, free of governmental interference. See Lynch v. Household Finance Corp., 405 U.S. 538.

"The requirement of notice and an opportunity to be heard raises no impenetrable barrier to the taking of a person's possessions. But the fair process of decisionmaking that it guarantees works, by itself, to protect against arbitrary deprivation of property. For when a person has an opportunity to speak up in his own defense, and when the State must listen to what he has to say, substantively unfair and simply mistaken deprivations of property interests can be prevented."

The problem of distinguishing substance and procedure is most complex where the state provides benefits it is not constitutionally compelled to provide. What are the procedural requirements, if any, when the state discharges an employee or terminates welfare benefits?   Three situations must be distinguished:

(1) The state in creating the benefit also creates standards to govern its termination. For example, a state provides that certain government employees can be discharged only for "good cause".   Even though the government is not obligated to provide the job, is it required by procedural due process to provide a fair hearing in applying its own standards to take a job away?

(2) The state in creating the benefit provides that it may be taken away at will. For example, a state provides that particular government employees may be fired in their superiors' discretion. The question now is whether the state may terminate a job in the unconstrained discretion of an administrative official? Is that question one of substantive due process? Or of procedural due process? If it is decided that the state can use standardless discretion to terminate the benefit, can there be any requirement of fair procedure? Or is the necessity for a hearing obviated in these situations because, as Justice Stevens observed in Codd v. Velger, 429 U.S. 624 (1977), "a hearing would [be] pointless because nothing plaintiff [can] prove [will] entitle him to keep his job"?

(3) The state creates the benefit, establishes standards to govern its termination, and provides the procedures to be used in determining whether the standards for termination have been met. If those procedures do not meet the minimum standards of fairness required by due process, will they be held invalid? In Arnett v. Kennedy, 416 U.S. 134 (1974) the Court had before it a federal statute which provided in one section that an individual employee "may be removed or suspended without pay only for such cause as will promote the efficiency of the service." Another portion of the same section provided that the employee could be removed through procedures which gave no right to an evidentiary hearing prior to termination. Justice Rehnquist, joined by Chief Justice Burger, and Justice Stewart argued that the employee's "right" to a job was necessarily subject to "the procedural limitations which Congress attached to it." However, Justices Powell, Blackmun, and White, concurring, asserted that the due process clause, not the statute, prescribed the hearing required. (They concluded that the hearing provided met due process standards.) Justices Marshall, Douglas, and Brennan dissented on the ground that the due process clause required an evidentiary hearing prior to termination. Thus six Justices agreed that once the state establishes standards for discharge of employees it must provide fair hearings. Can that be reconciled with the view that the state may avoid any hearing requirement when it authorizes standardless discretion for termination of employment?

SECTION 2. PROCEDURAL DUE PROCESS AND IRREBUTTABLE PRESUMPTIONS

Introduction. In Vance v. Bradley, 440 U.S. 93 (1979) the Court had before it a challenge under the equal protection clause to a statute requiring all foreign service officers to retire at age 60. In upholding the age classification the Court found it rational because Congress could reasonably believe that *many* employees at age 60 would be unfit to perform some of the tasks required of foreign service officers.

The cases in this section raise a potentially separate constitutional challenge to a classification such as that in *Bradley*. Congress could not reasonably believe that *all* employees were unfit at age 60. Can the due process clause then be read to require an individual hearing for each foreign service employee on the question of that employee's fitness? Or does the resolution of the equal protection issue limit the hearing right to the issue whether the employee has attained age 60?

Would the question be different if the statute read that all foreign service officers shall be subject to compulsory retirement when they become unfit to perform the relevant tasks and that it shall be conclusively presumed that any officer 60 years of age or older is unfit? Does casting the statute in that form give each employee who is retired at age 60 a due process right to a hearing on the issue of fitness?

VLANDIS v. KLINE

412 U.S. 441, 93 S.Ct. 2230, 37 L.Ed.2d 63 (1973).

[Connecticut required non-residents who enrolled in the state university system to pay tuition and other fees at higher rates than residents. It defined an unmarried student as a non-resident if his legal address for any part of the one-year period prior to his application for admission was outside of Connecticut. It defined a married student as a non-resident if his legal address at the time of application for admission was outside of Connecticut. It then provided that the status of a student as to residency established at the time of admission should be his status for his entire period of attendance.

Two students, one married and one unmarried, who were classified as non-residents at the time of application to the state university, but who later became residents of the state brought suit in the federal district court challenging the conclusive presumption of nonresidence as applied to force them to pay higher fees than other residents of the state. The district court ruled for the plaintiffs. The state appealed.]

Mr. Justice Stewart delivered the opinion of the Court.

.   .   .

Statutes creating permanent irrebuttable presumptions have long been disfavored under the Due Process Clause of the Fifth and Fourteenth Amendments.

.   .   .

The . . . case of Bell v. Burson, 402 U.S. 535 (1971), involved a Georgia statute which provided that if an uninsured motorist was involved in an accident and could not post security for the amount of damages claimed, his driver's license must be suspended without any hearing on the question of fault or responsibility. The Court held that since the State purported to be concerned with fault in suspending a driver's license, it could not, consistent with procedural due process, conclusively presume fault from the fact that the uninsured motorist was involved in an accident, and could not, therefore, suspend his driver's license without a hearing on that crucial factor.

Likewise, in Stanley v. Illinois, 405 U.S. 645 (1972), the Court struck down, as violative of the Due Process Clause, Illinois' irrebuttable statutory presumption that all unmarried fathers are unqualified to raise their children.   .   .   .

The same considerations obtain here. It may be that most applicants to Connecticut's university system who apply from outside the State or within a year of living out of State have no real intention of becoming Connecticut residents and will never do so. But it is clear that not all of the applicants from out of State inevitably fall in this category. Indeed, in the present case, both appellees possess many of the indicia of Connecticut residency, such as year-round Connecticut homes, Connecticut driver's licenses, car registrations, voter registrations, etc.; and both were found by the District Court to have become bona fide residents of Connecticut before the 1972 Spring semester. Yet, under the State's statutory scheme, neither was permitted any opportunity to demonstrate the bona fides of her Connecticut residency for tuition purposes, and neither will ever have such an opportunity in the future so long as she remains a student. . . .

In sum, since Connecticut purports to be concerned with residency in allocating the rates for tuition and fees at its university system, it is forbidden by the Due Process Clause to deny an individual the resident rates on the basis of a permanent and irrebuttable presumption of nonresidence, when that presumption is not necessarily or universally true in fact, and when the State has reasonable alternative means of making the crucial determination. Rather, standards of due process require that the State allow such an individual the opportunity to present evidence showing that he is a bona fide resident entitled to the in-state rates. Since § 126 precluded the appellees from ever rebutting the presumption that they were nonresidents of Connecticut, that statute operated to deprive them of a significant amount of their money without due process of law.

We are aware, of course, of the special problems involved in determining the bona fide residence of college students who come from out of State to attend that State's public university. Our holding today should in no wise be taken to mean that Connecticut must classify the students in its university system as residents, for purposes of tuition and fees, just because they go to school there. Nor should our decision be construed to deny a State the right to impose on a student, as one element in demonstrating bona fide residence, a reasonable durational residency requirement, which can be met while in student status. We fully recognize that a State has a legitimate interest in protecting and preserving the quality of its colleges and universities and the right of its own bona fide residents to attend such institutions on a preferential tuition basis.

We hold only that a permanent irrebuttable presumption of nonresidence— the means adopted by Connecticut to preserve that legitimate interest—is violative of the Due Process Clause, because it provides no opportunity for students who applied from out of State to demonstrate that they have become bona fide Connecticut residents. The State can establish such reasonable criteria for in-state status as to make virtually certain that students who are not, in fact, bona fide residents of the State, but who have come there solely for educational purposes, cannot take advantage of the in-state rates. . . .

Judgment affirmed.

Mr. Justice Marshall, with whom Mr. Justice Brennan joins, concurring.

I join the opinion of the Court except insofar as it suggests that a State may impose a one-year residency requirement as a prerequisite to qualifying for in-state tuition benefits. . . . That question is not presented by this case since here we deal with a permanent, irrebuttable presumption of nonresidency based on the fact that a student was a nonresident at the time he applied for admission to the state university system. . . .

Mr. Justice White, concurring in the judgment. . . .

Mr. Chief Justice Burger, with whom Mr. Justice Rehnquist joins, dissenting.

. . .

Mr. Justice Rehnquist, with whom The Chief Justice and Mr. Justice Douglas join, dissenting.

The Court's opinion relegates to the limbo of unconstitutionality a Connecticut law that requires higher tuition from those who come from out of State to attend its state universities than from those who come from within the State. The opinion accomplishes this result by a highly theoretical analysis that relies heavily on notions of substantive due process that have been authoritatively repudiated by subsequent decisions of the Court. Believing as I do that the Connecticut statutory scheme is a constitutionally permissible means of dealing with an increasingly acute problem facing state systems of higher education, I dissent. . . . .

CLEVELAND BOARD OF EDUCATION v. LaFLEUR

414 U.S. 632, 94 S.Ct. 791, 39 L.Ed.2d 52 (1974).

Mr. Justice Stewart delivered the opinion of the Court.

[LaFleur and Nelson brought suit challenging a school board rule requiring every pregnant teacher to take maternity leave without pay at least five months before the expected birth of her child, with application filed two weeks prior to date of departure. Despite their wish to finish the school year they were forced to take leave in March, their babies were born in late July and August. Cohen challenged the rule in another district requiring leave without pay four months prior to the expected birth with written notice six months prior to the date of expected birth. She was required to leave her job in December and her baby was born in May. The Court found the regulations unconstitutional.]

. . . .

II.

This Court has long recognized that freedom of personal choice in matters of marriage and family life is one of the liberties protected by the Due Process Clause of the Fourteenth Amendment. Roe v. Wade, 410 U.S. 113 (1973); Loving v. Virginia, 388 U.S. 1, 12 (1967); Griswold v. Connecticut, 381 U.S. 479 (1965); Pierce v. Society of Sisters, 268 U.S. 510 (1925); Meyer v. Nebraska, 262 U.S. 390 (1923). See also Prince v. Massachusetts, 321 U.S. 158 (1944); Skinner v. Oklahoma, 316 U.S. 535 (1942). As we noted in Eisenstadt v. Baird, 405 U.S. 438, 453 (1972), there is a right "to be free from unwarranted governmental intrusion into matters so fundamentally affecting a person as the decision whether to bear or beget a child."

By acting to penalize the pregnant teacher for deciding to bear a child, overly restrictive maternity leave regulations can constitute a heavy burden on the exercise of these protected freedoms. Because public school maternity leave rules directly affect "one of the basic civil rights of man," Skinner v. Oklahoma, supra, 316 U.S., at 541, the Due Process Clause of the Fourteenth Amendment requires that such rules must not needlessly, arbitrarily, or capriciously impinge upon this vital area of a teacher's constitutional liberty. The question before us in these cases is whether the interests advanced in support of the rules of the Cleveland and Chesterfield County School Boards can justify the particular procedures they have adopted.

The school boards in these cases have offered two essentially overlapping explanations for their mandatory maternity leave rules. First, they contend that the firm cut-off dates are necessary to maintain continuity of classroom instruction, since advance knowledge of when a pregnant teacher must leave facilitates the finding and hiring of a qualified substitute. Secondly, the school boards seek to justify their maternity rules by arguing that at least some teachers become physically incapable of adequately performing certain of their duties during the latter part of pregnancy. By keeping the pregnant teacher out of the classroom during these final months, the maternity leave rules are said to protect the health of the teacher and her unborn child, while at the same time assuring that students have a physically capable instructor in the classroom at all times.

It cannot be denied that continuity of instruction is a significant and legitimate educational goal. Regulations requiring pregnant teachers to provide early notice of their condition to school authorities undoubtedly facilitate administrative planning toward the important objective of continuity. . . .

Thus, while the advance notice provisions in the Cleveland and Chesterfield County rules are wholly rational and may well be necessary to serve the objective of continuity of instruction, the absolute requirements of termination at the end of the fourth or fifth month of pregnancy are not. Were continuity the only goal, cut-off dates much later during pregnancy would serve as well or better than the challenged rules, providing that ample advance notice requirements were retained. Indeed, continuity would seem just as well attained if the teacher herself were allowed to choose the date upon which to commence her leave, at least so long as the decision were required to be made and notice given of it well in advance of the date selected.

. . .

We thus conclude that the arbitrary cut-off dates embodied in the mandatory leave rules before us have no rational relationship to the valid state interest of preserving continuity of instruction as long as the teacher is required to give substantial advance notice of her condition, the choice of firm dates later in pregnancy would serve the boards' objectives just as well, while imposing a far lesser burden on the women's exercise of constitutionally protected freedom.

The question remains as to whether the fifth and sixth month cut-off dates can be justified on the other ground advanced by the school boards—the necessity of keeping physically unfit teachers out of the classroom. There can be no doubt that such an objective is perfectly legitimate, both on educational and safety grounds. And, despite the plethora of conflicting medical testimony in these cases, we can assume *arguendo* that at least some teachers become physically disabled from effectively performing their duties during the latter stages of pregnancy.

The mandatory termination provisions of the Cleveland and Chesterfield County rules surely operate to insulate the classroom from the presence of potentially incapacitated pregnant teachers. But the question is whether the rules sweep too broadly. See Shelton v. Tucker, 364 U.S. 479 (1961). That question must be answered in the affirmative, for the provisions amount to a conclusive presumption that every pregnant teacher who reaches the fifth or sixth month of pregnancy is physically incapable of continuing. There is no individualized determination by the teacher's doctor—or the school board's—as to any particular teacher's ability to continue at her job. The rules contain an irrebuttable presumption of physical incompetency, and that presumption applies even when the medical evidence as to an individual woman's physical status might be wholly to the contrary.

As the Court noted last Term in Vlandis v. Kline, 412 U.S. 441, 446 (1973), "permanent irrebuttable presumptions have long been disfavored under the Due Process Clause of the Fifth and Fourteenth Amendments." . . .

. . .

These principles control our decision in the cases before us. While the medical experts in these cases differed on many points, they unanimously agreed on one—the ability of any particular pregnant woman to continue at work past any fixed time in her pregnancy is very much an individual matter. Even assuming *arguendo* that there are some women who would be physically unable to work past the particular cut-off dates embodied in the challenged rules, it is evident that there are large numbers of teachers who are fully capable of continuing work for longer than the Cleveland and Chesterfield County regulations will allow. Thus, the conclusive presumption embodied in these rules, like that in *Vlandis,* is neither "necessarily nor universally true," and is violative of the Due Process Clause.

The school boards have argued that the mandatory termination dates serve the interest of administrative convenience, since there are many instances of teacher pregnancy, and the rules obviate the necessity for case-by-case determinations. Certainly, the boards have an interest in devising prompt and efficient procedures to achieve their legitimate objectives in this area. . . .

While it might be easier for the school boards to conclusively presume that all pregnant women are unfit to teach past the fourth or fifth month or even the first month, of pregnancy, administrative convenience alone is insufficient to make valid what otherwise is a violation of due process of law.[13] The Fourteenth Amendment requires the school boards to employ alternative administrative means, which do not so broadly infringe upon basic constitutional liberty, in support of their legitimate goals.

We conclude, therefore, that neither the necessity for continuity of instruction nor the state interest in keeping physically unfit teachers out of the classroom can justify the sweeping mandatory leave regulations that the Cleveland and Chesterfield County School Boards have adopted. While the regulations no doubt represent a good-faith attempt to achieve a laudable goal, they cannot pass muster under the Due Process Clause of the Fourteenth Amendment, because they employ irrebuttable presumptions that unduly penalize a female teacher for deciding to bear a child.

.   .   .

Mr. Justice Douglas concurs in the result.

Mr. Justice Powell (concurring in the result).

I concur in the Court's result, but I am unable to join its opinion. In my view these cases should not be decided on the ground that the mandatory maternity leave regulations impair any right to bear children or create an "irrebuttable presumption." It seems to me that equal protection analysis is the appropriate frame of reference. . . .

.   .   .

Mr. Justice Rehnquist, with whom The Chief Justice joins (dissenting).

The Court rests its invalidation of the school regulations involved in these cases on the Due Process Clause of the Fourteenth Amendment, rather than on any claim of sexual discrimination under the Equal Protection Clause of that Amendment. My Brother Stewart thereby enlists the Court in another quixotic engagement in his apparently unending war on irrebuttable presumptions. In this case we are told that although a regulation "requiring a termination of employment at some firm date during the last few weeks of pregnancy" (n. 13, opinion of the Court), might pass muster, the regulations here challenged requiring termination at the end of the fourth or fifth month of pregnancy violate due process of law. . . .

The lines drawn by the school boards in the city of Cleveland and Chesterfield County in these cases require pregnant teachers to take forced leave at a stage of their pregnancy when medical evidence seems to suggest that a majority

---

13. This is not to say that the only means for providing appropriate protection for the rights of pregnant teachers is an individualized determination in each case and in every circumstance. We are not dealing in these cases with maternity leave regulations requiring a termination of employment at some firm date during the last few weeks of pregnancy. We therefore have no occasion to decide whether such regulations might be justified by considerations not presented in these records—for example, widespread medical consensus about the "disabling" effect of pregnancy on a teacher's job performance during these latter days, or evidence showing that such firm cutoffs were the only reasonable method of avoiding the possibility of labor beginning while some teacher was in the classroom, or proof that adequate substitutes could not be procured without at least some minimal lead time and certainty as to the dates upon which their employment was to begin.

of them might well be able to continue teaching without any significant possibility of physical impairment. But so far as I am aware, the medical evidence also suggests that in some cases there may be physical impairment at the stage of pregnancy fastened on by the regulations in question, and that the probability of physical impairment increases as the pregnancy advances. If legislative bodies are to be permitted to draw a general line anywhere short of the delivery room, I can find no judicial standard of measurement which says the ones drawn here were invalid. I therefore dissent.[a]

WEINBERGER v. SALFI

422 U.S. 749, 95 S.Ct. 2457, 45 L.Ed.2d 522 (1975).

Mr. Justice Rehnquist delivered the opinion of the Court.

Appellants, the Department of Health, Education, and Welfare, its Secretary, the Social Security Administration and various of its officials, appeal from a decision of the United States District Court for the Northern District of California invalidating duration-of-relationship Social Security eligibility requirements for surviving wives and stepchildren of deceased wage earners. 373 F.Supp. 961 (1974). . . .

I.

Appellee Salfi married the deceased wage earner, Londo L. Salfi, on May 27, 1972. Despite his alleged apparent good health at the time of the marriage, he suffered a heart attack less than a month later, and died on November 21, 1972, less than six months after the marriage. Appellee filed applications for mother's insurance benefits for herself and child's insurance benefits for her daughter by a previous marriage, Doreen Kalnins. These applications were denied by the Social Security Administration, both initially and on reconsideration at the regional level, solely on the basis of the duration-of-relationship requirements of §§ 416(c)(5) and (e)(2), which define "widow" and "child." The definitions exclude surviving wives and stepchildren who had their respective relationships to a deceased wage earner for less than nine months prior to his death.

The named appellees then filed this action, ...

A three-judge District Court heard the case on cross-motions for summary judgment, and granted substantially all of the relief prayed for by appellees. . . . We noted probable jurisdiction of the Secretary's appeal from that judgment. . . .

III.

The District Court relied on congressional history for the proposition that the duration-of-relationship requirement was intended to prevent the use of sham marriages to secure Social Security payments. As such, concluded the court, "the requirement constitutes a presumption that marriages like Mrs. Salfi's, which did not precede the wage earner's death by at least nine months, were entered into for the purpose of securing Social Security benefits." The presumption was moreover, conclusive, because applicants were not afforded an opportunity to disprove the presence of the illicit purpose. The court held that under our decisions in Cleveland Board of Education v. LaFleur, 414 U.S. 632 (1974), Vlandis v. Kline, 412 U.S. 441 (1973), and Stanley v. Illinois, 405 U.S.

---

[a] In Turner v. Department of Employment, 423 U.S. 44 (1975), the Court invalidated a Utah law making pregnant women ineligible for unemployment benefits for a period extending from 12 weeks before the expected date of childbirth until a date six weeks after childbirth. The Court relied on the conclusive presumption analysis in the *Cleveland Board* case.

645 (1972), the requirement was unconstitutional, because it presumed a fact which was not necessarily or universally true.

. . .

We hold that these cases are not controlling on the issue before us now. Unlike the claims involved in *Stanley* and *LeFleur,* a noncontractual claim to receive funds from the public treasury enjoys no constitutionally protected status, Dandridge v. Williams, supra, though of course Congress may not invidiously discriminate among such claimants on the basis of a "bare congressional desire to harm a politically unpopular group," U.S. Dept. of Agriculture v. Moreno, 413 U.S. 528, 534 (1973), or on the basis of criteria which bear no rational relation to a legitimate legislative goal. Jimenez v. Weinberger, 417 U.S. 628, 636 (1974); U.S. Dept. of Agriculture v. Murry, 413 U.S. 508, 513–514 (1973). Unlike the statutory scheme in *Vlandis,* 412 U.S., at 449, the Social Security Act does not purport to speak in terms of the bona fides of the parties to a marriage, but then make plainly relevant evidence of such bona fides inadmissible. . . .

We think that the District Court's extension of the holdings of *Stanley, Vlandis* and *LaFleur* to the eligibility requirement in issue here would turn the doctrine of those cases into a virtual engine of destruction of countless legislative judgments which have heretofore been thought wholly consistent with the Fifth and Fourteenth Amendments to the Constitution. . . .

. . .

More recently, in Mourning v. Family Publications Service, Inc., 411 U.S. 356 (1973), the Court sustained the constitutionality of a regulation promulgated under the Truth in Lending Act which made the Act's disclosure provisions applicable whenever credit is offered to a consumer " 'for which either a finance charge is or may be imposed or which pursuant to an agreement, is or may be payable in more than four installments.' " Id., at 362. The regulation was challenged because it was said to conclusively presume that payments made under an agreement providing for more than four intallments necessarily included a finance charge, when in fact that might not be the case. The Court rejected the constitutional challenge in this language:

> "The rule was intended as a prophylactic measure; it does not presume that all creditors who are within its ambit assess finance charges, but rather, imposes a disclosure requirement on all members of a defined class in order to discourage evasion by a substantial portion of that class."

If the Fifth and Fourteenth Amendments permit this latitude to legislative decisions regulating the private sector of the economy, they surely allow no less latitude in prescribing the conditions upon which funds shall be dispensed from the public treasury. Dandridge v. Williams, supra. With these principles in mind, we turn to consider the statutory provisions which the District Court held invalid.

. . .

Under those standards, the question raised is not whether a statutory provision precisely filters out those, and only those, who are in the factual position which generated the congressional concern reflected in the statute. Such a rule would ban all prophylactic provisions, and would be directly contrary to our holding in *Mourning,* supra. Nor is the question whether the provision filters out a substantial part of the class which caused congressional concern, or whether it filters out more members of the class than nonmembers. The question is whether Congress, its concern having been reasonably aroused by the possibility of an abuse which it legitimately desired to avoid, could rationally have concluded both that a particular limitation or qualification would protect against its occurrence, and that the expense and other difficulties of individual determinations justified the inherent imprecision of a prophylactic rule. We conclude that the duration-of-relationship test meets this constitutional standard.

The danger of persons entering a marriage relationship not to enjoy its traditional benefits, but instead to enable one spouse to claim benefits upon the anticipated early death of the wage earner, has been recognized from the very beginning of the Social Security program. . . .

Undoubtedly the concerns reflected in this congressional material are legitimate, involving as they do the integrity of both the Social Security Trust Fund and the marriage relationship. It is also undoubtedly true that the duration-of-relationship requirement operates to lessen the likelihood of abuse through sham relationships entered in contemplation of imminent death. We also think that Congress could rationally have concluded that any imprecision from which it might suffer was justified by its ease and certainty of operation.

. . . .

While it is possible to debate the wisdom of excluding legitimate claimants in order to discourage sham relationships, and of relying on a rule which may not exclude some obviously sham arrangements, we think it clear that Congress could rationally choose to adopt such a course. . . .

The administrative difficulties of individual eligibility determinations are without doubt matters which Congress may consider when determining whether to rely on rules which sweep more broadly than the evils with which they seek to deal. In this sense, the duration-of-relationship requirement represents not merely a substantive policy determination that benefits should be awarded only on the basis of genuine marital relationships, but also a substantive policy determination that limited resources would not be well spent in making individual determinations. It is an expression of Congress' policy choice that the Social Security system, and its millions of beneficiaries, would be best served by a prophylactic rule which bars claims arising from the bulk of sham marriages which are actually entered, which discourages such marriages from ever taking place, and which is also objective and easily administered.

The Constitution does not preclude such policy choices as a price for conducting programs for the distribution of social insurance benefits. Cf. Geduldig v. Aiello, supra, at 496. Unlike criminal prosecutions, or the custody proceedings at issue in Stanley v. Illinois, such programs do not involve affirmative government action which seriously curtails important liberties cognizable under the Constitution. There is thus no basis for our requiring individualized determinations when Congress can rationally conclude not only that generalized rules are appropriate to its purposes and concerns, but also that the difficulties of individual determinations outweigh the marginal increments in the precise effectuation of congressional concern which they might be expected to produce.

The judgment of the District Court is

Reversed.

Mr. Justice Douglas, dissenting.

. . . .

On the merits, I believe that the main problem with these legislatively created presumptions is that they frequently invade the right to a jury trial. See Tot v. United States, 319 U.S. 463, 473 (1943) (concurring opinion). The present law was designed to bar payment of certain Social Security benefits when the purpose of the marriage was to obtain such benefits. Whether this was the aim of a particular marriage is a question of fact, to be decided by the jury in an appropriate case. I therefore would vacate and remand the case to give Mrs. Salfi the right to show that her marriage did not offend the statutory scheme, that it was not a sham.

Mr. Justice Brennan, with whom Mr. Justice Marshall joins, dissenting.

. . .

The merits of this case can be dealt with very briefly. For it is, I believe, apparent on the face of the Court's opinion that today's holding is flatly contrary to several recent decisions, specifically Vlandis v. Kline, 412 U.S. 441 (1973); U.S. Dept. of Agriculture v. Murry, 413 U.S. 508 (1973), and Jimenez v. Weinberger, 417 U.S. 628 (1974).

. . .

———

USERY v. TURNER ELKHORN MINING CO., 428 U.S. 1 (1976). Section 411(c)(3) of the Federal Coal Mine Health and Safety Act provides that a miner shown by X-ray or other clinical evidence to be afflicted with complicated pneumoconiosis is "irrebuttably presumed" to be totally disabled due to pneumoconiosis; if he has died, it is irrebuttably presumed that he was totally disabled by pneumoconiosis at the time of his death, and that his death was due to pneumoconiosis. In rejecting a challenge by coal mine operators to this provision the Court said:

". . . We think the District Court erred in equating this case with those in the mold of *Stanley* and *Vlandis.*

"As an operational matter, the effect of § 411(c)(3)'s 'irrebuttable presumption' of total disability is simply to establish entitlement in the case of a miner who is clinically diagnosable as extremely ill with pneumoconiosis arising out of coal mine employment. Indeed, the legislative history discloses that it was precisely this advanced and progressive stage of the disease that Congress sought most certainly to compensate. Were the Act phrased simply and directly to provide that operators were bound to provide benefits for all miners clinically demonstrating their affliction with complicated pneumoconiosis arising out of employment in the mines, we think it clear that there could be no due process objection to it. For, as we have already observed, destruction of earning capacity is not the sole legitimate basis for compulsory compensation of employees by their employers. New York Central R.R. Co. v. Bianc, 250 U.S. 596 (1919). We cannot say that it would be irrational for Congress to conclude that impairment of health alone warrants compensation. Since Congress can clearly draft a statute to accomplish precisely what it has accomplished through § 411(c)(3)'s presumption of disability, the argument is essentially that Congress has accomplished its result in an impermissible manner—by defining eligibility in terms of 'total disability' and erecting an 'irrebuttable presumption' of total disability upon a factual showing that does not necessarily satisfy the statutory definition of total disability. But in a statute such as this, regulating purely economic matters, we do not think that Congress' choice of statutory language can invalidate the enactment when its operation and effect are clearly permissible. Cf. Weinberger v. Salfi, 422 U.S. 749, 767–785 (1975); McDonald v. Bd. of Elections, 394 U.S. 802, 809 (1969); United States v. Carolene Products Co., 304 U.S. 144, 154 (1938)."

Chapter 13

APPLICATION OF THE POST CIVIL WAR AMENDMENTS TO PRIVATE CONDUCT: CONGRESSIONAL POWER TO ENFORCE THE AMENDMENTS

Introducpion. This chapter presents a mixture of issues that can best be described as those involved in the Civil Rights Cases with which this chapter begins. That 1883 decision took a narrow view of the reach of section 1 of the thirteenth amendment and section 1 of the fourteenth amendment in their application to private racial discrimination. The decision also adopted a correspondingly narrow view of Congressional power to enforce the amendments. After setting out the decision in the Civil Rights Cases in section 1, the remainder of this chapter explores the question whether its basic conceptions are still valid. Section 2, dealing with the "state action" concept, includes those cases concerning the application of constitutional limits of governmental action to private conduct. The subject of the rest of the chapter is Congressional power to enforce the Civil War Amendments, focusing particularly on the extent of the power to prohibit both private and state action that would be lawful in the absence of federal legislation. Section 3 presents a brief review of the surviving fragments of Reconstruction era legislation, and contemporary federal legislation protecting civil rights. Section 4 addresses the issue of Congressional power to prohibit private racial discrimination in enforcing the thirteenth amendment's prohibition of slavery and involuntary servitude. Section 5 focuses on Congressional power under the fourteenth amendment to prohibit private racial, and non-racial, discrimination. Section 6 broadens the focus beyond issues of private discrimination, examining the extent of Congressional power to prohibit state laws and practices that violate neither section 1 of the fourteenth amendment nor section 1 of the fifteenth amendment. This last section considers both the scope of Congressional power to provide broad remedies for conceded constitutional violations and, most controversial, to modify the substantive content of constitutional rights.

SECTION 1. EARLY INTERPRETATION

CIVIL RIGHTS CASES

109 U.S. 3, 3 S.Ct. 18, 27 L.Ed. 835 (1883).

Bradley, J. These cases are all founded on the first and second sections of the act of congress known as the "Civil Rights Act," passed March 1, 1875, entitled "An act to protect all citizens in their civil and legal rights." 18 Stat. 335. Two of the cases, those against Stanley and Nichols, are indictments for denying to persons of color the accommodations and privileges of an inn or hotel; two of them, those against Ryan and Singleton, are, one an information, the other an indictment, for denying to individuals the privileges and accommodations of a theater, the information against Ryan being for refusing a colored person a seat in the dress circle of Maguire's theater in San Francisco; and the indictment against Singleton being for denying to another person, whose color is not stated, the full enjoyment of the accommodations of the theater known as the Grand Opera House in New York, "said denial not being made for any reasons by law applicable to citizens of every race and color, and regardless of any previous condition of servitude." The case of Robinson and wife against the Memphis & Charleston Railroad Company was an action brought in the circuit court of the United States for the western district of Tennessee, to recover the penalty of $500 given by the second section of the act; and the *gravamen* was the refusal by the conductor of the railroad company to allow the wife to ride in the ladies' car, for the reason, as stated in one of the counts, that she was a person of African descent. The jury rendered a verdict for the defendants in this case upon the merits under a charge of the court, to which a bill of exceptions was taken by the plaintiffs. . . .

It is obvious that the primary and important question in all the cases is the constitutionality of the law; for if the law is unconstitutional none of the prosecutions can stand.

The sections of the law referred to provide as follows:

"Section 1. That all persons within the jurisdiction of the United States shall be entitled to the full and equal enjoyment of the accommodations, advantages, facilities, and privileges of inns, public conveyances on land or water, theaters, and other places of public amusement; subject only to the conditions and limitations established by law, and applicable alike to citizens of every race and color, regardless of any previous condition of servitude.

"Section 2. That any person who shall violate the foregoing section by denying to any citizen, except for reasons by law applicable to citizens of every race and color, and regardless of any previous condition of servitude, the full enjoyment of any of the accommodations, advantages, facilities, or privileges in said section enumerated, or by aiding or inciting such denial, shall, for every such offense, forfeit and pay the sum of $500 to the person aggrieved thereby, to be recovered in an action of debt, with full costs; and shall, also, for every such offense, be deemed guilty of a misdemeanor, and upon conviction thereof shall be fined not less than $500 nor more than $1,000, or shall be imprisoned not less than 30 days nor more than one year. . . ."

Has congress constitutional power to make such a law? Of course, no one will contend that the power to pass it was contained in the constitution before the adoption of the last three amendments. The power is sought, first, in the fourteenth amendment, and the views and arguments of distinguished senators, advanced while the law was under consideration, claiming authority to pass it by virtue of that amendment, are the principal arguments adduced in favor of the power. . . .

The first section of the fourteenth amendment,—which is the one relied on,—after declaring who shall be citizens of the United States, and of the several states, is prohibitory in its character, and prohibitory upon the states. It declares that "no state shall make or enforce any law which shall abridge the privileges or immunities of citizens of the United States; nor shall any state deprive any person of life, liberty, or property without due process of law; nor deny to any person within its jurisdiction the equal protection of the laws." It is state action of a particular character that is prohibited. Individual invasion of individual rights is not the subject-matter of the amendment. It has a deeper and broader scope. It nullifies and makes void all state legislation, and state action of every kind, which impairs the privileges and immunities of citizens of the United States, or which injures them in life, liberty, or property without due process of law, or which denies to any of them the equal protection of the laws. It not only does this, but, in order that the national will, thus declared, may not be a mere *brutum fulmen,* the last section of the amendment invests congress with power to enforce it by appropriate legislation. To enforce what? To enforce the prohibition. To adopt appropriate legislation for correcting the effects of such prohibited state laws and state acts, and thus to render them effectually null, void, and innocuous. This is the legislative power conferred upon congress, and this is the whole of it. It does not invest congress with power to legislate upon subjects which are within the domain of state legislation; but to provide modes of relief against state legislation, or state action, of the kind referred to. It does not authorize congress to create a code of municipal law for the regulation of private rights; but to provide modes of redress against the operation of state laws, and the action of state officers, executive or judicial, when these are subversive of the fundamental rights specified in the amendment. . . .

In this connection it is proper to state that civil rights, such as are guaranteed by the constitution against state aggression, cannot be impaired by the wrongful acts of individuals, unsupported by state authority in the shape of laws, customs, or judicial or executive proceedings. The wrongful act of an individual, unsupported by any such authority, is simply a private wrong, or a crime of that individual; an invasion of the rights of the injured party, it is true, whether they affect his person, his property, or his reputation; but if not sanctioned in some way by the state, or not done under state authority, his rights remain in full force, and may presumably be vindicated by resort to the laws of the state for redress. An individual cannot deprive a man of his right to vote, to hold property, to buy and to sell, to sue in the courts, or to be a witness or a juror; he may, by force or fraud, interfere with the enjoyment of the right in a particular case; he may commit an assault against the person, or commit murder, or use ruffian violence at the polls, or slander the good name of a fellow-citizen; but unless protected in these wrongful acts by some shield of state law or state authority, he cannot destroy or injure the right; he will only render himself amenable to satisfaction or punishment; and amenable therefor to the laws of the state where the wrongful acts are committed. . . .

Of course, these remarks do not apply to those cases in which congress is clothed with direct and plenary powers of legislation over the whole subject, accompanied with an express or implied denial of such power to the states, as in the regulation of commerce with foreign nations, among the several states, and with the Indian tribes, the coining of money, the establishment of post-offices and post-roads, the declaring of war, etc. In these cases congress has power to pass laws for regulating the subjects specified, in every detail and the conduct and transactions of individuals in respect thereof.

. . . .

. . . [T]he power of congress to adopt direct and primary, as distinguished from corrective, legislation on the subject in hand, is sought, in the second place, from the thirteenth amendment, which abolishes slavery. This amendment declares "that neither slavery, nor involuntary servitude, except as a punishment for crime, whereof the party shall have been duly convicted, shall exist within the United States, or any place subject to their jurisdiction;" and it gives congress power to enforce the amendment by appropriate legislation. . . .

It is true that slavery cannot exist without law any more than property in lands and goods can exist without law, and therefore the thirteenth amendment may be regarded as nullifying all state laws which establish or uphold slavery. But it has a reflex character also, establishing and decreeing universal civil and political freedom throughout the United States; and it is assumed that the power vested in congress to enforce the article by appropriate legislation, clothes congress with power to pass all laws necessary and proper for abolishing all badges and incidents of slavery in the United States; and upon this assumption it is claimed that this is sufficient authority for declaring by law that all persons shall have equal accommodations and privileges in all inns, public conveyances, and places of public amusement; the argument being that the denial of such equal accommodations and privileges is in itself a subjection to a species of servitude within the meaning of the amendment. . . .

It may be that by the black code, (as it was called), in the times when slavery prevailed, the proprietors of inns and public conveyances were forbidden to receive persons of the African race, because it might assist slaves to escape from the control of their masters. This was merely a means of preventing such escapes, and was no part of the servitude itself. A law of that kind could not have any such object now, however justly it might be deemed an invasion of the party's legal right as a citizen, and amenable to the prohibitions of the fourteenth amendment.

The long existence of African slavery in this country gave us very distinct notions of what it was, and what were its necessary incidents. Compulsory service of the slave for the benefit of the master, restraint of his movements except by the master's will, disability to hold property, to make contracts, to have a standing in court, to be a witness against a white person, and such like burdens and incapacities were the inseparable incidents of the institution. Severer punishments for crimes were imposed on the slave than on free persons guilty of the same offenses. Congress, as we have seen, by the civil rights bill of 1866, passed in view of the thirteenth amendment, before the fourteenth was adopted, undertook to wipe out these burdens and disabilities, the necessary incidents of slavery, constituting its substance and visible form; and to secure to all citizens of every race and color, and without regard to previous servitude, those fundamental rights which are the essence of civil freedom, namely, the same right to make and enforce contracts, to sue, be parties, give evidence, and to inherit, purchase, lease, sell, and convey property, as is enjoyed by white citizens. Whether this legislation was fully authorized by the thirteenth amendment alone, without the support which it afterwards received from the fourteenth amendment, after the adoption of which it was re-enacted with some additions, it is not necessary to inquire. It is referred to for the purpose of showing that at that time (in 1866) congress did not assume, under the authority given by the thirteenth amendment, to adjust what may be called the social rights of men and races in the community; but only to declare and vindicate those fundamental rights which appertain to the essence of citizenship, and the enjoyment or deprivation of which constitutes the essential distinction between freedom and slavery. . . .

The only question under the present head, therefore, is, whether the refusal to any persons of the accommodations of an inn, or a public conveyance, or a place of public amusement, by an individual, and without any sanction or support from any state law or regulation, does inflict upon such persons any manner of servitude, or form of slavery, as those terms are understood in this country? . . .

Now, conceding, for the sake of the argument, that the admission to an inn, a public conveyance, or a place of public amusement, on equal terms with all other citizens, is the right of every man and all classes of men, is it any more than one of those rights which the states by the Fourteenth Amendment are forbidden to deny to any person? And is the Constitution violated until the denial of the right has some State sanction or authority? Can the act of a mere individual, the owner of the inn, the public conveyance, or place of amusement, refusing the accommodation, be justly regarded as imposing any badge of slavery or servitude upon the applicant, or only as inflicting an ordinary civil injury, properly cognizable by the laws of the state, and presumably subject to redress by those laws until the contrary appears?

After giving to these questions all the consideration which their importance demands, we are forced to the conclusion that such an act of refusal has nothing to do with slavery or involuntary servitude, and that if it is violative of any right of the party, his redress is to be sought under the laws of the state; or, if those laws are adverse to his rights and do not protect him, his remedy will be found in the corrective legislation which congress has adopted, or may adopt, for counteracting the effect of state laws, or state action, prohibited by the four-teenth amendment. It would be running the slavery argument into the ground to make it apply to every act of discrimination which a person may see fit to make as to the guests he will entertain, or as to the people he will take into his coach or cab or car, or admit to his concert or theater, or deal with in other matters of intercourse or business. Innkeepers and public carriers, by the laws of all the states, so far as we are aware, are bound, to the extent of their facilities, to furnish proper accommodation to all unobjectionable persons who in good faith apply for them. If the laws themselves make any unjust discrimi-nation, amenable to the prohibitions of the fourteenth amendment, congress has full power to afford a remedy under that amendment and in accordance with it.

When a man has emerged from slavery, and by the aid of beneficent legislation has shaken off the inseparable concomitants of that state, there must be some stage in the progress of his elevation when he takes the rank of a mere citizen, and ceases to be the special favorite of the laws, and when his rights as a citizen, or a man, are to be protected in the ordinary modes by which other men's rights are protected. There were thousands of free colored people in this country before the abolition of slavery, enjoying all the essential rights of life, liberty, and property the same as white citizens; yet no one, at that time, thought that it was any invasion of their personal *status* as freemen because they were not admitted to all the privileges enjoyed by white citizens, or because they were subjected to discriminations in the enjoyment of accommodations in inns, public conveyances, and places of amusement. Mere discriminations on account of race or color were not regarded as badges of slavery. If, since that time, the enjoyment of equal rights in all these respects has become established by constitutional enactment, it is not by force of the thirteenth amendment, (which merely abolishes slavery,) but by force of the fourteenth and fifteenth amendments.

On the whole, we are of opinion that no countenance of authority for the passage of the law in question can be found in either the thirteenth or fourteenth amendment of the constitution; and no other ground of authority for its passage being suggested, it must necessarily be declared void, at least so far as its operation in the several states is concerned. . . .

Mr. Justice Harlan dissenting:

The opinion in these cases proceeds, it seems to me, upon grounds entirely too narrow and artificial. I cannot resist the conclusion that the substance and spirit of the recent Amendments of the Constitution have been sacrificed by a subtle and ingenious verbal criticism. "It is not the words of the law but the internal sense of it that makes the law; the letter of the law is the body; the sense and reason of the law is the soul." Constitutional provisions, adopted in the interest of liberty, and for the purpose of securing, through national legislation, if need be, rights inhering in a state of freedom, and belonging to American citizenship, have been so construed as to defeat the ends the people desired to accomplish, which they attempted to accomplish, and which they supposed they had accomplished by changes in their fundamental law. . . .

[In a long opinion Justice Harlan argued that both the 13th and 14th Amendments gave Congress power to legislate directly with reference to private individuals engaged in such quasi-public businesses as those involved in this case.]

My brethren say, that when a man has emerged from slavery, and by the aid of beneficent legislation has shaken off the inseparable concomitants of that state, there must be some stage in the progress of his elevation when he takes the rank of a mere citizen, and ceases to be the special favorite of the laws, and when his rights as a citizen, or a man, are to be protected in the ordinary modes by which other men's rights are protected. It is, I submit, scarcely just to say that the colored race has been the special favorite of the laws. The Statute of 1875, now adjudged to be unconstitutional, is for the benefit of citizens of every race and color. What the Nation, through Congress, has sought to accomplish in reference to that race, is—what had already been done in every State of the Union for the white race—to secure and protect rights belonging to them as freemen and citizens; nothing more. It was not deemed enough "to help the feeble up, but to support him after." The one underlying purpose of congressional legislation has been to enable the black race to take the rank of mere citizens. The difficulty has been to compel a recognition of the legal right of the black race to take the rank of citizens, and to secure the enjoyment of privileges belonging, under the law, to them as a component part of the people for whose welfare and happiness government is ordained. At every step, in this direction, the Nation has been confronted with class tyranny, which a contemporary English historian says is, of tyrannies, the most intolerable, "For it is ubiquitous in its operation, and weighs, perhaps, most heavily on those whose obscurity or distance would withdraw them from the notice of a single despot." Today, it is the colored race which is denied, by corporations and individuals wielding public authority, rights fundamental in their freedom and citizenship. At some future time, it may be that some other race will fall under the ban of race discrimination. If the constitutional Amendments be enforced, according to the intent with which, as I conceive, they were adopted, there cannot be in this Republic, any class of human beings in practical subjection to another class, with power in the latter to dole out to the former just such privileges as they may choose to grant. The supreme law of the land has decreed that no authority shall be exercised in this country upon the basis of discrimination, in respect of civil rights, against freemen and citizens because of their race, color or previous condition of servitude. To that decree—for the due enforcement of which, by appropriate legislation, Congress has been invested with express power—every one must bow, whatever may have been, or whatever now are, his individual views as to the wisdom or policy, either of the recent changes in the fundamental law, or of the legislation which has been enacted to give them effect.

For the reasons stated I feel constrained to withhold my assent to the opinion of the court.

THE RELATIONSHIP BETWEEN CONGRESSIONAL POWER TO ENFORCE THE CONSTITUTION AND SELF–ENFORCING PROVISIONS OF THE CONSTITUTION

While the ultimate issue in the Civil Rights Cases concerned the constitutional validity of a federal statute prohibiting private discrimination, the bulk of the opinion discusses the question whether private racial discrimination would violate the Constitution had there been no federal legislation. The case was a major decision concerning the application of the Constitution to private conduct only because the Court's rationale was that Congressional power to enforce the thirteenth and fourteenth amendments necessarily tracked the self-executing provisions of those amendments. The next section of this chapter will explore the extent to which the fourteenth amendment applies of its own force to private conduct. Sections 4 through 6 will return to the issue of Congressional power. It is appropriate at this point to entertain a preliminary inquiry whether the interpretations of section one of the thirteenth amendment and section one of the fourteenth amendment should mark the outer limits of Congress' power to "enforce" those amendments.

Consider the facts of one of the cases grouped for decision in the Civil Rights Cases—the owner of a private theatre enforcing a racially discriminatory policy in the selection of patrons. What are the consequences of judicial decision that section one of the fourteenth amendment requires preferring the rights of the excluded patrons to those of the owner? What are the consequences of a judicial decision that Congress has the power under section five of the fourteenth amendment to require the theatre owner to desist from racial discrimination in choice of patrons? Do those different consequences suggest that there should be differences in the reach of the self-enforcing provisions of section one and congressional power under section five? Can major differences in the reach of section one and Congressional power under section five be recognized without giving Congress limitless power no longer tied to any limitation that it be directed to "enforcing" the fourteenth amendment?

SECTION 2. APPLICATION OF THE CONSTITUTION TO PRIVATE CONDUCT

Introduction to the State Action Concept. With the exception of the thirteenth amendment the Constitution is a restraint on governmental action and does not provide one private citizen with rights against another. The Bill of Rights restrains the action of the federal government. The fourteenth amendment provides that "no state shall" deprive any person of due process or equal protection. The fifteenth amendment prohibits denial of voting rights "by the United States or by any State . . . ." The same verbal formula appears in the voting right protections of the nineteenth, twenty-fourth and twenty-sixth amendments.

A basic conception of the opinion in the Civil Rights Cases was that "civil rights, such as are guaranteed by the Constitution against state agression, cannot be impaired by the wrongful acts of individuals, unsupported by state authority in the shape of laws, customs, or judicial or executive proceedings." In a general sense, however, all private action is "supported by state authority" if the state has not chosen to make that private action illegal. It has proved to be extremely difficult to determine when state involvement with private action, beyond mere failure to prohibit it, brings into play the constitutional limitations on governmental action.

It has also proved to be difficult to organize the cases that involve the problem. Subsection A deals with the argument that constitutional limits apply because a private party is performing a function normally performed by government. Subsection B collects the cases where it is claimed that government has enforced the racially discriminatory decisions of private parties. Subsection C includes, quite simply, the rest of the cases where the argument has been made that government has "supported" the conduct of private parties by approving it, regulating it, or providing financial support to it.

From the end of World War II through 1968, all Supreme Court decisions that reached the question whether unconstitutional state action was present decided that it was. Since 1970, most Supreme Court decisions considering the same issue have not found unconstitutional state action. Part of the explanation may be found in significant changes in the Court's membership. (Compare Evans v. Newton, 382 U.S. 296 [1966], infra p. 969, with Evans v. Abney, 396 U.S. 435 [1970], infra p. 982; Amalgamated Food Employees Union v. Logan Val. Plaza, Inc., 391 U.S. 308 [1968], with Lloyd Corp. v. Tanner, 407 U.S. 551 [1972], both discussed infra p. 969.) Other explanations may stem from the fact that nearly all of the cases prior to 1968 dealt with racial discrimination. Since 1970, issues such as first amendment rights of access to private property and due process rights of fair procedure have been prominent. Is the extent of governmental action required to invoke constitutional protection less where racial discrimination is claimed than when other forms of discrimination, or other constitutional rights, are involved?

A related question concerns the impact of the growing body of federal legislation prohibiting private racial discrimination. (See sections 3, 4, 5 and 6 of this chapter.) The Civil Rights Act of 1964 prohibits private racial discrimination in places of public accommodation, employment, and activities—including private education—receiving Federal financial assistance. The 1968 Civil Rights Act prohibits racial discrimination in the private housing market, and provides criminal penalties for many forms of private racial violence. And, in 1968, the Court discovered that remaining fragments of the Civil Rights Act of 1866 reached broad areas of private racial discrimination. (See section 4 of this chapter.) There are few cases now where the issue whether federal law prohibits private racial discrimination will turn on whether sufficient indicia of state action are present to invoke the provisions of the fourteenth amendment. Does this suggest legitimate reasons for limiting state action doctrines, even as applied to racial discrimination?

A. PRIVATE PERFORMANCE OF "GOVERNMENT" FUNCTIONS

THE WHITE PRIMARY CASES

Despite the clear terms of the fifteenth amendment, for three-quarters of a century an effective means to block voting by Blacks was their exclusion from the Democratic Party in Southern States. Initially, it was argued that primary voting was beyond constitutional protection, even if state law mandated exclusion of Black voters from participation in the Democratic primaries. In Nixon v. Herndon, 273 U.S. 536 (1927), however, a Texas statute excluding Blacks from Democratic primaries was held to be unconstitutional as racial discrimination by the state. Texas' response was to repeal the offending statute, and to provide that a party's executive committee had the power to determine the party's membership. Exclusion of Blacks from the Democratic primary was again held unconstitutional on the ground that the new Texas statute had made the committee an agent of the state. Nixon v. Condon, 286 U.S. 73 (1932). When the Texas Democratic Party once again excluded Blacks from party membership, however, the exclusion survived constitutional attack on the ground that it was not state action, but the action of a private group. Grovey v. Townsend, 295 U.S. 45 (1935). Grovey v. Townsend was overruled in Smith v. Allwright, 321 U.S. 649 (1944), because "the place of the primary in the electoral scheme makes clear that state delegation to a party of the power to fix the qualifications of primary elections is delegation of a state function that may make the party's action the action of the state." That the Constitution prohibited exclusion of Blacks from participating in elections, whatever form the election took, was dramatized in Terry v. Adams, 345 U.S. 461 (1953), where Blacks were excluded from voting in a pre-primary straw vote of a Texas county political organization called the Jaybird Democratic Organization. Because winners in the Jaybird primary ran unopposed in the formal Democratic primaries, the Court decided that exclusion of Blacks from the Jaybird primary was a violation of the fifteenth amendment, despite the absence of formal state involvement in their exclusion.

STEELE v. LOUISVILLE AND NASHVILLE RAILROAD, 323 U.S. 192 (1944). The Brotherhood of Locomotive Firemen and Enginemen, under the terms of the Railway Labor Act, was exclusive bargaining representative for the railway firemen. Blacks who constituted a substantial minority of the labor force, were excluded from membership in the Brotherhood. As a result of negotiations an agreement was made in 1941 between the Railroad and the Brotherhood providing for restrictions on the hiring and promotion of Blacks with the ultimate aim of their exclusion from work as firemen. Steele, a Black fireman, brought suit against the Railroad and the Brotherhood based on the foregoing facts. The Supreme Court of Alabama affirmed the dismissal of the complaint. The United States Supreme Court, speaking through Chief Justice Stone, said:

"If, as the state court has held, the Act confers this power on the bargaining representative of a craft or class of employees without any commensurate statutory duty toward its members, constitutional questions arise. For the representative is clothed with power not unlike that of a legislature which is subject to constitutional limitations on its power to deny, restrict, destroy or discriminate against the rights of those for whom it legislates and which is also under an affirmative constitutional duty equally to protect those rights. . . .

"We think that the Railway Labor Act imposes upon the statutory representatives of a craft at least as exacting a duty to protect equally the interests of the members of the craft as the Constitution imposes upon a legislature to give equal protection to the interests of those for whom it legislates. Congress has seen fit to clothe the bargaining representative with powers comparable to those possessed by a legislative body both to create and restrict the rights of those whom it represents, . . . but it has also imposed on the representative a corresponding duty. . . .

"Reversed."

Justice Murphy, concurring, stated that the case presented "a grave constitutional issue that should be squarely faced." The Railway Labor Act must be construed to bar this discrimination: "Otherwise the Act would bear the stigma of unconstitutionality under the Fifth Amendment in this respect."

ACCESS TO COMPANY TOWNS AND SHOPPING CENTERS

Marsh v. Alabama, 326 U.S. 501 (1946), was one of two pre-1970 Supreme Court decisions, that presented the state action issue in some context other than racial discrimination. A member of Jehovah's Witnesses was prosecuted for trespass when she distributed religious literature on the streets of a company-owned town and refused to leave when ordered to do so. The town involved was described by the Court as being accessible to and freely used by the public in general with nothing to distinguish it from any other town except the fact that the title to the property belonged to a private corporation. In reversing the conviction the Court talked primarily about first amendment issues. It stated that had the corporation owned the segment of the state highway that paralleled the business street of the company town and operated that segment it would "have been the performance of a public function." The opinion then continued:

"We do not think it makes any significant constitutional difference as to the relationship between the rights of the owner and those of the public that here the State, instead of permitting the corporation to operate a highway, permitted it to use its property as a town, operate a 'business block' in the town and a street and sidewalk on that business block . . . .. Whether a corporation or a municipality owns or possesses the town the public in either case has an identical interest in the functioning of the community in such manner that the channels of communication remain free."

The other pre-1970 case not involving racial discrimination was Amalgamated Food Employees Union v. Logan Valley Plaza, Inc., 391 U.S. 308 (1968), which extended *Marsh* to require that picketers be given access to a large privately-owned shopping center. Justice Marshall's opinion for the majority concluded that there was no reason to draw a distinction between a privately owned business district surrounded by residential property under the same ownership, and one surrounded by property under other ownership. Justice Black, the author of the *Marsh* opinion but one of three dissenters in *Logan Valley*, argued that the company town in *Marsh* had all the attributes of a conventional municipality, but that the shopping center had only one—ownership of the business block. *Logan Valley* was criticized, but distinguished, in Lloyd Corp. v. Tanner, 407 U.S. 551 (1972), where anti-war leafletters were held not to have a constitutional right of access to a large privately-owned shopping center. The four Justices in the *Logan Valley* majority who were still on the Court dissented in *Lloyd*. In Hudgens v. NLRB, 424 U.S. 507 (1976), the Court concluded that *Lloyd* had overruled *Logan Valley* and that speakers had no constitutional right of access to large privately-owned shopping centers.

––––––––

EVANS v. NEWTON, 382 U.S. 296 (1966). In 1911, Senator Augustus O. Bacon executed a will devising land to the City of Macon, Georgia, for a park for Whites only. The city kept the park segregated for decades, but in some years prior to this suit permitted Blacks to use it on the ground that the city could not constitutionally maintain a segregated park. (See Pennsylvania v. Bd. of City Trusts, infra, p. 981.) This suit sought to remove the city as trustee. Black citizens of Macon intervened, asking the state court to refuse to appoint new private trustees. The trial court accepted the resignation of the city as trustee and appointed private trustees. The Supreme Court of Georgia affirmed. The United States Supreme Court reversed, holding that the park could not be maintained on a segregated basis, despite the city's resignation as trustee. Justice Douglas' opinion for the Court gave two reasons. First, his opinion read the record below as showing that the city remained "entwined in the management or control of the park." Second, the opinion stated:

"This conclusion [that the substitution of trustees did not transfer the park to the 'private sector'] is buttressed by the nature of the service rendered the community by a park. The service rendered even by a private park of this character is municipal in nature. It is open to every white person, there being no selective element other than race. Golf clubs, social centers, luncheon clubs, schools such as Tuskegee was at least in origin, and other like organizations in the private sector are often racially oriented. A park, on the other hand, is more like a fire department or police department that traditionally serves the community. Mass recreation through the use of parks is plainly in the public domain, Watson v. Memphis, 373 U.S. 526; and state courts that aid private parties to perform that public function on a segregated basis implicate the State in conduct proscribed by the Fourteenth Amendment. Like the streets of the company town in Marsh v. Alabama, supra, the elective process of Terry v. Adams, supra, and the transit system of Public Util. Comm'n v. Pollak, supra, the predominant character and purpose of this park are municipal."

Justice White concurred in the result. Justices Black, Harlan and Stewart dissented.

––––––––

FLAGG BROTHERS, INC. v. BROOKS

436 U.S. 149, 98 S.Ct. 1729, 56 L.Ed.2d 185 (1978).

Mr. Justice Rehnquist delivered the opinion of the Court.

The question presented by this litigation is whether a warehouseman's proposed sale of goods entrusted to him for storage, as permitted by New York Uniform Commercial Code § 7–210, is an action properly attributable to the State of New York. . . .

I.

According to her complaint, the allegations of which we must accept as true, respondent Shirley Brooks and her family were evicted from their apartment in Mount Vernon, N.Y., on June 13, 1973. The City Marshal arranged for Brooks' possessions to be stored by petitioner Flagg Brothers, Inc., in its warehouse. Respondent was informed of the cost of moving and storage, and she instructed the workmen to proceed, although she found the price too high. On August 25, 1973, after a series of disputes over the validity of the charges being claimed by petitioner, Flagg Brothers, Brooks received a letter demanding that her account be brought up to date within 10 days "or your furniture will be sold." . . . A series of subsequent letters from respondent and her attorneys produced no satisfaction.

Brooks thereupon initiated this class action in the District Court under 42 U.S.C. § 1983, seeking damages, an injunction against the threatened sale of her belongings, and the declaration that such a sale pursuant to § 7–210 would violate the Due Process and Equal Protection Clauses of the Fourteenth Amendment. . . . On July 7, 1975, the District Court, relying primarily on our decision in Jackson v. Metropolitan Edison Co., dismissed the complaint for failure to state a claim for relief under § 1983.

A divided panel of the Court of Appeals reversed. The majority noted that *Jackson* had suggested state action might be found in the exercise by a private party of "some power delegated to it by the State which is traditionally associated with sovereignty." . . . The majority found:

> "[B]y enacting § 7–210, New York not only delegated to the warehouseman a portion of its sovereign monopoly power over binding conflict resolution [citations omitted], but also let him, by selling stored goods, execute a lien and thus perform a function which has traditionally been that of the sheriff." . . .

II.

A claim upon which relief may be granted to respondents against Flagg Brothers under § 1983 must embody at least two elements. Respondents are first bound to show that they have been deprived of a right "secured by the Constitution and the laws" of the United States. They must secondly show that Flagg Brothers deprived them of this right acting "under color of any statute" of the State of New York. It is clear that these two elements denote two separate areas of inquiry. . . .

It must be noted that respondents have named no public officials as defendants in this action. The city marshal, who supervised their evictions, was dismissed from the case by the consent of all the parties. This total absence of overt official involvement plainly distinguishes this case from earlier decisions imposing procedural restrictions on creditors' remedies. . . . While as a factual matter any person with sufficient physical power may deprive a person of his property, only a State or a private person whose action "may fairly be treated as that of the State itself," . . . may deprive him of "an interest encompassed within the Fourteenth Amendment's protection," . . . Thus, the only issue presented by this case is whether Flagg Brothers' action may fairly be attributed to the State of New York. We conclude that it may not.

III.

Respondents' primary contention is that New York has delegated to Flagg Brothers a power "traditionally exclusively reserved to the State." *Jackson.* . . . They argue that the resolution of private disputes is a traditional function of civil government, and that the State in § 7–210 has delegated this function to Flagg Brothers. Respondents, however, have read too much into the language of our previous cases. While many functions have been traditionally performed by governments, very few have been "exclusively reserved to the State."

One such area has been elections. While the Constitution protects private rights of association and advocacy with regard to the election of public officials, our cases make it clear that the conduct of the elections themselves is an exclusively public function. This principle was established by a series of cases challenging the exclusion of blacks from participation in primary elections in Texas. Terry v. Adams, 345 U.S. 461 (1953); Smith v. Allwright, 321 U.S. 649 (1944); Nixon v. Condon, 286 U.S. 73 (1932). Although the rationale of these cases may be subject to some dispute, their scope is carefully defined. The doctrine does not reach to all forms of private political activity, but encompasses only state-regulated elections or elections conducted by organizations which in practice produce "the uncontested choice of public officials." . . .

A second line of cases under the public function doctrine originated with Marsh v. Alabama, 326 U.S. 501 (1946). Just as the Texas Democratic Party in *Smith* and the Jaybird Democratic Association in *Terry* effectively performed the entire public function of selecting public officials, so too the Gulf Shipbuilding Corp. performed all the necessary municipal functions in the town of Chickasaw, Ala., which it owned. . . .

These two branches of the public function doctrine have in common the feature of exclusivity.[8] Although the elections held by the Democratic Party and its affiliates were the only meaningful elections in Texas, and the streets owned by the Gulf Shipbuilding Corp. were the only streets in Chickasaw, the proposed sale by Flagg Brothers under § 7–210 is not the only means of resolving this purely private dispute. . . .

Whatever the particular remedies available under New York law, we do not consider a . . . detailed description of them necessary to our conclusion that the settlement of disputes between debtors and creditors is not traditionally an exclusive public function. . . . Our analysis requires no parsing of the difference between various commercial liens and other remedies to support the conclusion that this entire field of activity is outside the scope of *Terry* and *Marsh.* This is true whether these commercial rights and remedies are created by statute or decisional law. To rely upon the historical antecedents of a particular practice would result in the constitutional condemnation in one State of a remedy found perfectly permissible in another. . . .

---

[8] Respondents also contend that Evans v. Newton, 382 U.S. 296 (1966), establishes that the operation of a park for recreational purposes is an exclusively public function. We doubt that *Newton* intended to establish any such broad doctrine in the teeth of the experience of several American entrepreneurs who amassed great fortunes by operating parks for recreational purposes. We think *Newton* rests on a finding of ordinary state action under extraordinary circumstances. The Court's opinion emphasizes that the record showed "no change in the municipal maintenance and concern over this facility," id., at 301, after the transfer of title to private trustees. That transfer had not been shown to have eliminated the actual involvement of the city in the daily maintenance and care of the park.

Thus, even if we were inclined to extend the sovereign function doctrine outside of its present carefully confined bounds, the field of private commercial transactions would be a particularly inappropriate area into which to expand it. We conclude that our sovereign function cases do not support a finding of state action here.

Our holding today impairs in no way the precedental value of such cases as Norwood v. Harrison, 413 U.S. 455 (1973), or Gilmore v. City of Montgomery, 417 U.S. 556 (1974), which arose in the context of state and municipal programs which benefited private schools engaging in racially discriminatory admissions practices following judicial decrees desegregating public school systems. And we would be remiss if we did not note that there are a number of state and municipal functions not covered by our election cases nor governed by the reasoning of *Marsh* which have been administered with a greater degree of exclusivity by States and municipalities than has the function of so-called "dispute resolution." Among these are such functions as education, fire and police protection, and tax collection. We express no view as to the extent, if any, to which a city or State might be free to delegate to private parties the performance of such functions and thereby avoid the strictures of the Fourteenth Amendment. The mere recitation of these possible permutations and combinations of factual situations suffices to caution us that their resolution should abide the necessity of deciding them.

IV.

Respondents further urge that Flagg Brothers' proposed action is properly attributable to the State because the State has authorized and encouraged it in enacting § 7–210. Our cases state "that a State is responsible for the . . . act of a private party when the State, by its law, has compelled the act." . . . This Court, however, has never held that a State's mere acquiescence in a private action converts that action into that of the State. . . .

. . . .

Here, the State of New York has not compelled the sale of a bailor's goods, but has merely announced the circumstances under which its courts will not interfere with a private sale. Indeed, the crux of respondents' complaint is not that the State *has* acted, but that it has *refused* to act. This statutory refusal to act is no different in principle from an ordinary statute of limitations whereby the State declines to provide a remedy for private deprivations of property after the passage of a given period of time.

We conclude that the allegations of these complaints do not establish a violation of these respondents' Fourteenth Amendment rights by either respondent Flagg Brothers or by the State of New York. The District Court properly concluded that their complaints failed to state a claim for relief under 42 U.S.C. § 1983. The judgment of the Court of Appeals holding otherwise is

Reversed.

Mr. Justice Brennan took no part in the consideration or decision of this case.

Mr. Justice Stevens, with whom Mr. Justice White and Mr. Justice Marshall join, dissenting.

. . . In my judgment the Court's holding is fundamentally inconsistent with, if not foreclosed by, our prior decisions which have imposed procedural restrictions on the State's authorization of certain creditors' remedies. . . .

There is no question in this case but that respondents have a property interest in the possessions that the warehouseman proposes to sell. It is also clear that, whatever power of sale the warehouseman has, it does not derive from the consent of the respondents. The claimed power derives solely from the State, and specifically from § 7–210 of the New York Uniform Commercial Code. The question is whether a state statute which authorizes a private party to deprive a person of his property without his consent must meet the requirements of the Due Process Clause of the Fourteenth Amendment. This question must be answered in the affirmative unless the State has virtually unlimited power to transfer interests in private property without any procedural protections.

In determining that New York's statute cannot be scrutinized under the Due Process Clause, the Court reasons that the warehouseman's proposed sale is solely private action because the state statute *"permits* but does not compel" the sale, . . . (emphasis added), and because the warehouseman has not been delegated a power *"exclusively* reserved to the State," . . . (emphasis added). Under this approach a State could enact laws authorizing private citizens to use self-help in countless situations without any possibility of federal challenge. . . . [T]he distinctions between "permission" and "compulsion" on the one hand, and "exclusive" and "non-exclusive," on the other, cannot be determinative factors in state-action, analysis. . . . In this case, the State of New York, by enacting § 7–210 of the Uniform Commercial Code, has acted in the most effective and unambiguous way a State can act. This section specifically authorizes petitioner to sell respondents' possessions; it details the procedures that petitioner must follow; and it grants petitioner the power to convey good title to goods that are now owned by respondents to a third party.

While Members of this Court have suggested that statutory authorization alone may be sufficient to establish state action, it is not necessary to rely on those suggestions in this case because New York has authorized the warehouseman to perform what is clearly a state function. The test of what is a state function for purposes of the Due Process Clause has been variously phrased. Most frequently the issue is presented in terms of whether the State has delegated a function traditionally and historically associated with sovereignty. . . . In this Court, petitioners have attempted to argue that the nonconsensual transfer of property rights is not a traditional function of the sovereign. The overwhelming historical evidence is to the contrary, however, and the Court wisely does not adopt this position. Instead, the Court reasons that state action cannot be found because the State has not delegated to the warehouseman an *exclusive* sovereign function. This distinction, however, is not consistent with our prior decisions on state action [9] . . . .

. . . .

Whether termed "traditional," "exclusive," or "significant," the state power to order binding, nonconsensual resolution of a conflict between debtor and creditor is exactly the sort of power with which the Due Process Clause is concerned. And the State's delegation of that power to a private party is, accordingly, subject to due process scrutiny. . . .

It is important to emphasize that, contrary to the Court's apparent fears, this conclusion does not even remotely suggest that "all private deprivations of property [will] be converted into public acts whenever the State, for whatever reason, denies relief sought by the putative property owner." . . . The focus is not on the private deprivation but on the state authorization. "[W]hat is always vital to remember is that it is the *state's* conduct, whether action or inaction, not the *private* conduct, that gives rise to constitutional attack." H. Friendly, The Dartmouth College Case and The Public-Private Penumbra, p. 17

---

[9] The Court, for instance, attempts to distinguish Evans v. Newton, 382 U.S. 296. *Newton* concededly involved a function which is not exclusively sovereign—the operation of a park, but the Court claims that *Newton* actually rested on a determination that the City was still involved in the "daily maintenance and care of the park." Ante, n. 8. This stark attempt to rewrite the rationale of the *Newton* opinion is fully answered by Mr. Justice White's opinion in that case. . . .

(emphasis in original). The State's conduct in this case takes the concrete form of a statutory enactment, and it is that statute that may be challenged.

My analysis in this case thus assumes that petitioner's proposed sale will conform to the procedure specified by the state legislature and that respondents' challenge therefore will be to the constitutionality of that process. It is only what the State itself has enacted that they may ask the federal court to review in a § 1983 case. If there should be a deviation from the state statute—such as a failure to give the notice required by the state law—the defect could be remedied by a state court and there would be no occasion for § 1983 relief.
. . .

On the other hand, if there is compliance with the New York statute, the state legislative action which enabled the deprivation to take place must be subject to constitutional challenge in a federal court. Under this approach, the federal courts do not have jurisdiction to review every foreclosure proceeding in which the debtor claims that there has been a procedural defect constituting a denial of due process of law. Rather, the Federal District Court's jurisdiction under § 1983 is limited to challenges to the constitutionality of the state procedure itself . . . .

Finally, it is obviously true that the overwhelming majority of disputes in our society are resolved in the private sphere. But it is no longer possible, if it ever was, to believe that a sharp line can be drawn between private and public actions. The Court today holds that our examination of state delegations of power should be limited to those rare instances where the State has ceded one of its "exclusive" powers. As indicated, I believe that this limitation is neither logical nor practical. More troubling, this description of what is state action does not even attempt to reflect the concerns of the Due Process Clause, for the state action doctrine is, after all, merely one aspect of this broad constitutional protection.

In the broadest sense, we expect government "to provide a reasonable and fair framework of rules which facilitate commercial transactions. . . ." Mitchell v. W.T. Grant, : . . 416 U.S., at 624 (Powell, J., concurring). This "framework of rules" is premised on the assumption that the State will control nonconsensual deprivations of property and that the State's control will, in turn, be subject to the restrictions of the Due Process Clause. The power to order legally binding surrenders of property and the constitutional restrictions on that power are necessary correlatives in our system. In effect, today's decision allows the State to divorce these two elements by the simple expedient of transferring the implementation of its policy to private parties. Because the Fourteenth Amendment does not countenance such a division of power and responsibility, I respectfully dissent.

B. GOVERNMENTAL ENFORCEMENT OF "PRIVATE" DECISIONS

SHELLEY v. KRAEMER

334 U.S. 1, 68 S.Ct. 836, 92 L.Ed. 1161 (1948).

Mr. Chief Justice Vinson delivered the opinion of the Court.

These cases present for our consideration questions relating to the validity of court enforcement of private agreements, generally described as restrictive covenants, which have as their purpose the exclusion of persons of designated race or color from the ownership or occupancy of real property. Basic constitutional issues of obvious importance have been raised.

The first of these cases comes to this Court on certiorari to the Supreme Court of Missouri. On February 16, 1911, thirty out of a total of thirty-nine owners of property fronting both sides of Labadie Avenue between Taylor Avenue and Cora Avenue in the city of St. Louis, signed an agreement, which was subsequently recorded providing in part:

". . . the said property is hereby restricted to the use and occupancy for the term of Fifty (50) years from this date, so that it shall be a condition all the time and whether recited and referred to as [sic] not in subsequent conveyances and shall attach to the land, as a condition precedent to the sale of the same, that hereafter no part of said property or any portion thereof shall be, for said term of Fifty-years, occupied by any person not of the Caucasian race, it being intended hereby to restrict the use of said property for said period of time against the occupancy as owners or tenants of any portion of said property for resident or other purpose by people of the Negro or Mongolian Race."

The entire district described in the agreement included fifty-seven parcels of land. The thirty owners who signed the agreement held title to forty-seven parcels, including the particular parcel involved in this case. . . .

On August 11, 1945, pursuant to a contract of sale, petitioners Shelley, who are Negroes, for valuable consideration received from one Fitzgerald a warranty deed to the parcel in question. The trial court found that petitioners had no actual knowledge of the restrictive agreement at the time of the purchase.

On October 9, 1945, respondents, as owners of other property subject to the terms of the restrictive covenant, brought suit in the Circuit Court of the city of St. Louis praying that petitioners Shelley be restrained from taking possession of the property and that judgment be entered divesting title out of petitioners Shelley and revesting title in the immediate grantor or in such other person as the court should direct. The trial court denied the requested relief on the ground that the restrictive agreement, upon which respondents based their action, had never become final and complete . . . . .

The Supreme Court of Missouri sitting *en banc* reversed and directed the trial court to grant the relief for which respondents had prayed. That court held the agreement effective and concluded that enforcement of its provisions violated no rights guaranteed to petitioners by the Federal Constitution. At the time the court rendered its decision, petitioners were occupying the property in question.

The second of the cases under consideration comes to this Court from the Supreme Court of Michigan. The circumstances presented do not differ materially from the Missouri case. . . .

Petitioners have placed primary reliance on their contentions, first raised in the state courts, that judicial enforcement of the restrictive agreements in these cases has violated rights guaranteed to petitioners by the Fourteenth Amendment of the Federal Constitution and Acts of Congress passed pursuant to that Amendment. Specifically, petitioners urge that they have been denied the equal protection of the laws, deprived of property without due process of law, and have been denied privileges and immunities of citizens of the United States. We pass to a consideration of those issues.

I.

Whether the equal protection clause of the Fourteenth Amendment inhibits judicial enforcement by state courts of restrictive covenants based on race or color is a question which this Court has not heretofore been called upon to consider. . . .

. . . . .

It should be observed that these covenants do not seek to proscribe any particular use of the affected properties. Use of the properties for residential occupancy, as such, is not forbidden. The restrictions of these agreements, rather are directed toward a designated class of persons and seek to determine who may and who may not own or make use of the properties for residential purposes. The excluded class is defined wholly in terms of race or color; "simply that and nothing more."

It cannot be doubted that among the civil rights intended to be protected from discriminatory state action by the Fourteenth Amendment are the rights to acquire, enjoy, own and dispose of property. . . .

It is likewise clear that restrictions on the right of occupancy of the sort sought to be created by the private agreements in these cases could not be squared with the requirements of the Fourteenth Amendment if imposed by state statute or local ordinance. We do not understand respondents to urge the contrary. In the case of Buchanan v. Warley [245 U.S. 60] a unanimous Court declared unconstitutional the provisions of a city ordinance which denied to colored persons the right to occupy houses in blocks in which the greater number of houses were occupied by white persons, and imposed similar restrictions on white persons with respect to blocks in which the greater number of houses were occupied by colored persons. During the course of the opinion in that case, this Court stated: "The Fourteenth Amendment and these statutes enacted in furtherance of its purpose operate to qualify and entitle a colored man to acquire property without state legislation discriminating against him solely because of color."

In Harmon v. Tyler, 1927, 273 U.S. 668, a unanimous court, on the authority of Buchanan v. Warley, supra, declared invalid an ordinance which forbade any Negro to establish a home on any property in a white community or any white person to establish a home in a Negro community, "except on the written consent of a majority of the persons of the opposite race inhabiting such community or portion of the City to be affected."

But the present cases, unlike those just discussed, do not involve action by state legislatures or city councils. Here the particular patterns of discrimination and the areas in which the restrictions are to operate, are determined, in the first instance, by the terms of agreements among private individuals. Participation of the State consists in the enforcement of the restrictions so defined. The crucial issue with which we are here confronted is whether this distinction removes these cases from the operation of the prohibitory provisions of the Fourteenth Amendment.

Since the decision of this Court in the Civil Rights Cases, 1883, 109 U.S. 3, the principle has become firmly embedded in our constitutional law that the action inhibited by the first section of the Fourteenth Amendment is only such action as may fairly be said to be that of the States. That Amendment erects no shield against merely private conduct, however discriminatory or wrongful.

We conclude, therefore, that the restrictive agreements standing alone cannot be regarded as a violation of any rights guaranteed to petitioners by the Fourteenth Amendment. So long as the purposes of those agreements are effectuated by voluntary adherence to their terms, it would appear clear that there has been no action by the State and the provisions of the Amendment have not been violated. Cf. Corrigan v. Buckley, supra.

But here there was more. These are cases in which the purposes of the agreements were secured only by judicial enforcement by state courts of the restrictive terms of the agreements. The respondents urge that judicial enforcement of private agreements does not amount to state action; or, in any event, the participation of the State is so attenuated in character as not to amount to state action within the meaning of the Fourteenth Amendment. Finally, it is suggested, even if the States in these cases may be deemed to have acted in the constitutional sense, their action did not deprive petitioners of rights guaranteed by the Fourteenth Amendment. We move to a consideration of these matters.

II.

That the action of state courts and of judicial officers in their official capacities is to be regarded as action of the State within the meaning of the Fourteenth Amendment, is a proposition which has long been established by decisions of this Court. That principle was given expression in the earliest cases involving the construction of the terms of the Fourteenth Amendment. . . .

One of the earliest applications of the prohibitions contained in the Fourteenth Amendment to action of state judicial officials occurred in cases in which Negroes had been excluded from jury service in criminal prosecutions by reason of their race or color. These cases demonstrate, also, the early recognition by this Court that state action in violation of the Amendment's provisions is equally repugnant to the constitutional commands whether directed by state statute or taken by a judicial official in the absence of statute. . . .

The action of state courts in imposing penalties or depriving parties of other substantive rights without providing adequate notice and opportunity to defend, has, of course, long been regarded as a denial of the due process of law guaranteed by the Fourteenth Amendment. Brinkerhoff-Faris Trust & Savings Co. v. Hill, supra. Cf. Pennoyer v. Neff, 1878, 95 U.S. 714.

In numerous cases, this Court has reversed criminal convictions in state courts for failure of those courts to provide the essential ingredients of a fair hearing. . . .

But the examples of state judicial action which have been held by this Court to violate the Amendment's commands are not restricted to situations in which the judicial proceedings were found in some manner to be procedurally unfair. It has been recognized that the action of state courts in enforcing a substantive common-law rule formulated by those courts, may result in the denial of rights guaranteed by the Fourteenth Amendment, even though the judicial proceedings in such cases may have been in complete accord with the most rigorous conceptions of procedural due process. Thus in American Federation of Labor v. Swing, 1941, 312 U.S. 321, enforcement by state courts of the common-law policy of the State, which resulted in the restraining of peaceful picketing, was held to be state action of the sort prohibited by the Amendment's guaranties of freedom of discussion. . . .

The short of the matter is that from the time of the adoption of the Fourteenth Amendment until the present, it has been the consistent ruling of this Court that the action of the States to which the Amendment has reference, includes action of state courts and state judicial officials. Although, in construing the terms of the Fourteenth Amendment, differences have from time to time been expressed as to whether particular types of state action may be said to offend the Amendment's prohibitory provisions, it has never been suggested that state court action is immunized from the operation of those provisions simply because the act is that of the judicial branch of the state government.

III.

Against this background of judicial construction, extending over a period of some three-quarters of a century, we are called upon to consider whether enforcement by state courts of the restrictive agreements in these cases may be deemed to be the acts of those States; and, if so, whether that action has denied these petitioners the equal protection of the laws which the Amendment was intended to insure.

We have no doubt that there has been state action in these cases in the full and complete sense of the phrase. The undisputed facts disclose that petitioners were willing purchasers of properties upon which they desired to establish homes. The owners of the properties were willing sellers; and contracts of sale were accordingly consummated. It is clear that but for the active intervention of the state courts, supported by the full panoply of state power, petitioners would have been free to occupy the properties in question without restraint.

These are not cases, as has been suggested, in which the States have merely abstained from action, leaving private individuals free to impose such discriminations as they see fit. Rather, these are cases in which the States have made available to such individuals the full coercive power of government to deny to petitioners, on the grounds of race or color, the enjoyment of property rights in premises which petitioners are willing and financially able to acquire and which the grantors are willing to sell. The difference between judicial enforcement and nonenforcement of the restrictive covenants is the difference to petitioners between being denied rights of property available to other members of the community and being accorded full enjoyment of those rights on an equal footing.

The enforcement of the restrictive agreements by the state courts in these cases was directed pursuant to the common-law policy of the States as formulated by those courts in earlier decisions. In the Missouri case, enforcement of the covenant was directed in the first instance by the highest court of the State after the trial court had determined the agreement to be invalid for want of the requisite number of signatures. In the Michigan case, the order of enforcement by the trial court was affirmed by the highest state court. The judicial action in each case bears the clear and unmistakable imprimatur of the State. We have noted that previous decisions of this Court have established the proposition that judicial action is not immunized from the operation of the Fourteenth Amendment simply because it is taken pursuant to the state's common-law policy. Nor is the Amendment ineffective simply because the particular pattern of discrimination, which the State has enforced, was defined initially by the terms of a private agreement. State action, as that phrase is understood for the purposes of the Fourteenth Amendment, refers to exertions of state power in all forms. And when the effect of that action is to deny rights subject to the protection of the Fourteenth Amendment, it is the obligation of this Court to enforce the constitutional commands.

We hold that in granting judicial enforcement of the restrictive agreements in these cases, the States have denied petitioners the equal protection of the laws and that, therefore, the action of the state courts cannot stand. We have noted that freedom from discrimination by the States in the enjoyment of property rights was among the basic objectives sought to be effectuated by the framers of the Fourteenth Amendment. That such discrimination has occurred in these cases is clear. Because of the race or color of these petitioners they have been denied rights of ownership or occupancy enjoyed as a matter of course by other citizens of different race or color. . . .

Respondents urge, however, that since the state courts stand ready to enforce restrictive covenants excluding white persons from the ownership or occupancy of property covered by such agreements, enforcement of covenants excluding colored persons may not be deemed a denial of equal protection of the laws to the colored persons who are thereby affected. This contention does not bear scrutiny. The parties have directed our attention to no case in which a court, state or federal, has been called upon to enforce a covenant excluding members of the white majority from ownership or occupancy of real property on grounds of race or color. But there are more fundamental considerations. The rights created by the first section of the Fourteenth Amendment are, by its terms, guaranteed to the individual. The rights established are personal rights. It is, therefore, no answer to these petitioners to say that the courts may also be induced to deny white persons rights of ownership and occupancy on grounds of race or color. Equal protection of the laws is not achieved through indiscriminate imposition of inequalities. . . .

    . . .

For the reasons stated, the judgment of the Supreme Court of Missouri and the judgment of the Supreme Court of Michigan must be reversed.

Reversed.

Mr. Justice Reed, Mr. Justice Jackson, and Mr. Justice Rutledge took no part in the consideration or decision of these cases.

RESTRICTIVE COVENANTS

Restrictive covenants directed against minorities were used widely prior to the *Shelley* case, particularly in large cities in the North and West. These covenants were not only against Blacks but also Armenians, Jews, Mexicans, Syrians, Japanese, Chinese and American Indians. It has been estimated that 80% of the land in Chicago was restricted. *To Secure These Rights—The Report of the President's Committee on Civil Rights* 67–70 (1947).

The use of these covenants prior to *Shelley* contributed to the isolation of Blacks in congested and substandard housing. Partly as a result of limitations of Blacks' access to housing, they often were forced to pay higher rentals than Whites. Helfield & Groner, *Race Discrimination in Housing,* 57 Yale L.J. 426, 426–33 (1948). Would such evidence have been relevant to the *Shelley* decision? See Martin, *Segregation of Residences of Negroes,* 32 Mich.L.Rev. 721 (1934).[1]

BARROWS v. JACKSON, 346 U.S. 249 (1953). Plaintiff's predecessor and defendant, owners of real estate in the same neighborhood, entered into an agreement, recorded on the deeds and running against subsequent takers, that their property would be occupied only by Caucasians. Plaintiff sued defendant for damages alleging that, in violation of their agreement, defendant had sold his property without including the agreed restriction in the deed, and had permitted non-Caucasians to move in and occupy the premises. The California courts sustained a demurrer to the complaint on the authority of the *Shelley* case. Decisions in Missouri and Oklahoma had awarded damages in similar situations; the Supreme Court granted certiorari.

The United States Supreme Court affirmed California's denial of relief. Justice Minton, for the Court, wrote: "This Court will not permit or require California to coerce respondent to respond in damages for failure to observe a restrictive covenant that this Court would deny California the right to enforce in equity. . . ." The defendant, although a Caucasian, had standing to assert the constitutional question. In view of the demand for damages he had a real financial interest in the issue, and "it would be difficult if not impossible for the persons whose rights are asserted to present their grievance before any court."

---

[1] See also: Karst & Von Alstyne, *State Action,* 14 Stan.L.Rev. 3 (1961); Henkin, *Shelley v. Kraemer: Notes for a Revised Opinion,* 110 U.Pa.L.Rev. 473 (1962); *Effect of State Court Interpretation of a Contract,* 55 Mich.L.Rev. 871 (1957); *Police Enforcement of Private Discrimination,* 52 N.W. U.L.Rev. 774 (1958); *Criminal Penalties to Enforce Private Discrimination,* 57 Mich.L.Rev. 122 (1958); *Impact of Shelley v. Kraemer on the State Action Concept,* 44 Cal.L.Rev. 718 (1956).

Chief Justice Vinson dissented; Justices Reed and Jackson did not participate.

_____

PROSECUTION OF "SIT–IN" DEMONSTRATORS
IN THE 1960s

A significant phase of the civil rights struggle was the use of "sit-in"
demonstrations at Southern restaurants or lunch counters where Blacks were
segregated or refused service. Typically, Blacks would sit at a table or counter,
be asked to leave, and be arrested and convicted of trespass when they refused.
The Supreme Court reviewed the constitutionality of the convictions of literally
hundreds of sit-in demonstrators in the early sixties. While the convictions
were reversed, a majority of the Court never faced squarely the question
whether enforcement of a private property owner's discrimination was unconstitutional state action under Shelley v. Kraemer. In some cases, convictions were
reversed on the ground that the state trespass statute gave inadequate warning as
to whether it prohibited remaining on private property after being asked to
leave as well as unauthorized "entry." Bouie v. City of Columbia, 378 U.S.
347 (1964). Where convictions were reversed because of unconstitutional state
action, the grounds were narrow. E.g., Robinson v. Florida, 378 U.S. 153
(1964) (city ordinance required segregation although restaurant manager stated
that Blacks were excluded for business reasons); Griffin v. Maryland, 378 U.S.
130 (1964) (amusement park employee who asked Blacks to leave and arrested
them was also deputized as a sheriff).

The *Griffin* case is particularly interesting. The state argued that the
constitutional issues in the case were indistinguishable from those where the
trespass arrest had been made by a police officer not employed by the park.
The Court did not resolve the state's broad contention that no constitutional
violation followed from a police arrest and state conviction for trespass of a
person refusing to leave private property. The Court noted that Collins, the
park employee who asked the defendants to leave, wore a sheriff's badge and
"consistently identified himself as a deputy sheriff" when asking defendants to
leave and placing them under arrest. Collins had a contractual obligation to
enforce the park's policy. The case thus fell within the rule that a state (Collins)
could not undertake an obligation to enforce a private policy of racial discrimination. The three dissenters conceded that Collins was exercising state authority, but argued that "the involvement of the State is no different from what it
would have been had the arrests been made by a regular policeman dispatched
from police headquarters." Suppose Collins had not worn his badge nor
identified himself as a sheriff when he asked defendants to leave the amusement
park. When they refused, he called a regular policeman who arrived and made
the arrest. Can you think of a tenable theory that supports a conclusion that
there was unconstitutional state action on the facts in *Griffin,* but that there
would not be on the supposed facts?

The sit-in cases came to an end with the enactment of Title II of the Civil
Rights Act of 1964 which prohibited discrimination in places of public accommodation. (The Court held that the statute abated sit-in prosecutions that had
occurred prior to its enactment. Hamm v. City of Rock Hill, 379 U.S. 306
[1964].) In one of the last of the sit-in cases, five Justices did reach the broader
issue of the application of Shelley v. Kraemer to the sit-in situation. Bell v.
Maryland, 378 U.S. 226 (1964). Justice Douglas, joined by Justice Goldberg,
argued that *Shelley* should govern when trespass convictions were used to
enforce private discrimination that represented business preferences rather than
personal prejudices. (Justice Goldberg, joined by Chief Justice Warren and

Justice Douglas, also argued that access to public accommodations was a privilege of national citizenship). Justice Black's dissent, joined by Justices Harlan and White, argued that *Shelley* was inapplicable. A citizen who sought the law's protection of his property rights was not cast outside the law's protection because he called on law officers to enforce those rights. Shelley v. Kraemer was a case, according to Justice Black, where enforcement of a restrictive covenant operated to prohibit a willing seller from conveying to a Black purchaser and its principle did not apply to cases where the property owner was unwilling to permit occupation of his property by Blacks.

PENNSYLVANIA v. BOARD OF CITY TRUSTS

353 U.S. 230, 77 S.Ct. 806, 1 L.Ed.2d 792 (1957).

Per Curiam.

The motion to dismiss the appeal for want of jurisdiction is granted, 28 U.S.C. § 1257(2). Treating the papers whereon the appeal was taken as a petition for writ of certiorari, 28 U.S.C. § 2103, the petition is granted. 28 U.S.C. § 1257(3).

Stephen Girard, by a will probated in 1831, left a fund in trust for the erection, maintenance, and operation of a "college." The will provided that the college was to admit "as many poor white male orphans, between the ages of six and ten years, as the said income shall be adequate to maintain." The will named as trustee the City of Philadelphia. The provisions of the will were carried out by the State and City and the college was opened in 1848. Since 1869, by virtue of an act of the Pennsylvania Legislature, the trust has been administered and the college operated by the "Board of Directors of City Trusts of the City of Philadelphia." Pa.Laws 1869, No. 1258, p. 1276; Purdon's Pa. Stat.Ann., 1957, Tit. 53, § 16365.[a]

In February 1954, the petitioners Foust and Felder applied for admission to the college. They met all qualifications except that they were Negroes. For this reason the Board refused to admit them. They petitioned the Orphans' Court of Philadelphia County for an order directing the Board to admit them, alleging that their exclusion because of race violated the Fourteenth Amendment to the Constitution. The State of Pennsylvania and the City of Philadelphia joined in the suit also contending the Board's action violated the Fourteenth Amendment. The Orphans' Court rejected the constitutional contention and refused to order the applicants' admission. . . . This was affirmed by the Pennsylvania Supreme Court. 386 Pa. 548, 127 A.2d 287.

The Board which operates Girard College is an agency of the State of Pennsylvania. Therefore, even though the Board was acting as a trustee, its refusal to admit Foust and Felder to the college because they were Negroes was discrimination by the State. Such discrimination is forbidden by the Fourteenth Amendment. Brown v. Board of Education, 347 U.S. 483. Accordingly, the judgment of the Supreme Court of Pennsylvania is reversed and the cause is remanded for further proceedings not inconsistent with this opinion.

It is so ordered.

---

[a] The Board is composed of 15 persons, including the mayor, the president of the City Council and twelve other citizens appointed by the judges of the Court of Common Pleas of the County of Philadelphia. The treasurer of the city serves as treasurer of the board. Pursuant to the terms of the will the funds of the trust were held and invested by the city treasurer and an annual accounting made to the legislature. The expenses of operating the school were defrayed wholly from the trust fund. It appears that the Board of City Trusts took an active role in directing the administration of the School. See In re Girard's Estate, 386 Pa. 548, 127 A.2d 287 (1956).

STATE ENFORCEMENT OF CHARITABLE TRUSTS

After the decision in Pennsylvania v. Board of City Trusts, Pennsylvania courts substituted private trustees to effectuate Stephen Girard's "dominant purpose" to limit the College to White orphans. In re Girard College Trusteeship, 391 Pa. 434, 138 A.2d 844 (1958). The Supreme Court never reached the merits of the questions whether Girard College could be administered by private trustees and continue to exclude Blacks or whether the state court's substitution of trustees to permit continued exclusion of Blacks was itself unconstitutional state action. (The appeal was dismissed for lack of jurisdiction and certiorari was denied. 357 U.S. 570 [1958].) The grounds of decision in Evans v. Newton, supra p. 969, made it unnecessary to decide whether state enforcement of discriminatory testamentary trusts was in all cases unconstitutional state action.

Charitable trusts do not have identifiable beneficiaries and are enforced, at least nominally, by state officials. States will not enforce such trusts unless they serve worthy purposes. Finally, charitable trusts are exempt from taxation, and are free from otherwise applicable restrictions on indefinite accumulation of trust property. (The Girard trust grew from 2 to 98 million dollars.) Do these elements of state contact impose a constitutional obligation on all private trusts to avoid racial discrimination? See Clark, *Charitable Trusts, the Fourteenth Amendment and the Will of Stephen Girard*, 66 Yale L.J. 979 (1957). An additional issue presented in both the Girard trust litigation and Evans v. Newton was whether, under the doctrine of Shelley v. Kraemer, the action of a state court in replacing a government trustee with a private trustee, for the purpose of effectuating a testator's desire to discriminate, was in itself unconstitutional state action.

Lower federal courts have dealt with some of these issues in the context of educational testamentary trusts. The Court of Appeals for the Third Circuit held the state courts' substitution of private trustees in the *Girard College* case was unconstitutional state action. Pennsylvania v. Brown, 392 F.2d 120 (1968), cert. denied, 391 U.S. 921 (1968). Earlier, a United States District Court decided that the terms of an 1833 bequest limiting Tulane University to the education of Whites were no longer binding. Guillory v. Adm'r, Tulane Edu. Fund, 212 F.Supp. 674 (D.La.1962). Does the Supreme Court's decision in Evans v. Abney, which follows, cast doubt on the soundness of those lower court decisions?

EVANS v. ABNEY, 396 U.S. 435 (1970). After the decision in Evans v. Newton, the Supreme Court of Georgia ruled that Senator Bacon's intention to provide a park for whites only had become impossible to fulfill and that accordingly the trust had failed and the parkland and other trust property had reverted by operation of Georgia law to the heirs of the Senator. The Supreme Court upheld this action. Justice Black, writing for the Court, said, in part:

"When a city park is destroyed because the Constitution required it to be integrated, there is reason for everyone to be disheartened. We agree with petitioners that in such a case it is not enough to find that the state court's result was reached through the application of established principles of state law. . . . Here, however, the action of the Georgia Supreme Court declaring the Baconsfield trust terminated presents no violation of constitutionally protected rights, and any harshness that may have resulted from the State court's decision can be attributed solely to its intention to effectuate as nearly as possible the explicit terms of Senator Bacon's will.

"Petitioners first argue that the action of the Georgia court violates the United States Constitution in that it imposes a drastic 'penalty,' the 'forfeiture' of the park, merely because of the city's compliance with the constitutional mandate expressed by this Court in Evans v. Newton. Of course, Evans v. Newton did not speak to the problem of whether Baconsfield should or could continue to operate as a park; it held only that its continued operation as a park had to be without racial discrimination. But petitioners now want to extend that holding to forbid the Georgia courts from closing Baconsfield on the ground that such a closing would penalize the city and its citizens for complying with the Constitution. We think, however, that the will of Senator Bacon and Georgia law provide all the justification necessary for imposing such a 'penalty.' The construction of wills is essentially a state-law question . . . and in this case the Georgia Supreme Court, as we read its opinion, interpreted Senator Bacon's will as embodying a preference for termination of the park rather than its integration. Given this, the Georgia court had no alternative under its relevant trust laws, which are long standing and neutral with regard to race, but to end the Baconsfield trust and return the property to the Senator's heirs.

Justice Marshall took no part. Justices Brennan and Douglas dissented.

C. GOVERNMENT FINANCING, REGULATION AND AUTHORIZATION OF PRIVATE CONDUCT

---

1. PRIVATE ACTIVITY ON GOVERNMENT PROPERTY

BURTON v. WILMINGTON PARKING AUTHORITY

365 U.S. 715, 81 S.Ct. 856, 6 L.Ed.2d 45 (1961).

[The Eagle Coffee Shoppe, Inc. is a restaurant located within an offstreet automobile parking building in Wilmington, Delaware. The parking building is owned and operated by the Wilmington Parking Authority, an agency of the State of Delaware, and the restaurant is the Authority's lessee. Before it began actual construction of the facility, the Authority was advised by its retained experts that the anticipated revenue from the parking of cars and proceeds from sale of its bonds would not be sufficient to finance the construction costs of the facility. Moreover, the bonds were not expected to be marketable if payable solely out of parking revenues. To secure additional capital needed for its "debt-service" requirements, and thereby to make bond financing practicable, the Authority decided it was necessary to enter long-term leases with responsible tenants for commercial use of some of the space available in the projected "garage building." The public was invited to bid for these leases.

[In April 1957 such a private lease, for 20 years and renewable for another 10 years, was made with Eagle Coffee Shoppe, Inc., for use as a "restaurant, dining room, banquet hall, cocktail lounge and bar and for no other use and purpose." Other portions of the structure were leased to other tenants, including a bookstore, a retail jeweler, and a food store. Upon completion of the building, the Authority located at appropriate places thereon official signs indicating the public character of the building, and flew from mastheads on the roof both the state and national flags.

[In August 1958 Burton parked his car in the building and walked around to enter the restaurant by its front door on Ninth Street. He was refused service. He then filed this action seeking a declaratory judgment, alleging that he was refused service solely because he was a Negro. On motions for summary judgment the trial court ruled for Burton. The Delaware Supreme Court reversed on the ground that Eagle Coffee Shoppe was under no duty to serve because of a state statute providing: "No keeper of an inn, tavern, hotel, or restaurant, or other place of public entertainment or refreshment of travelers, guests, or customers shall be obliged, by law, to furnish entertainment or refreshment to persons whose reception or entertainment by him would be offensive to the major part of his customers and would injure his business. . . . ."]

Mr. Justice Clark delivered the opinion of the Court.

. . .

It is clear, as it always has been since the Civil Rights Cases (U.S.) supra, that "Individual invasion of individual rights is not the subject-matter of the amendment," at p. 11, and that private conduct abridging individual rights does no violence to the Equal Protection Clause unless to some significant extent the State in any of its manifestations has been found to have become involved in it. Because the virtue of the right to equal protection of the laws could lie only in the breadth of its application, its constitutional assurance was reserved in terms whose imprecision was necessary if the right were to be enjoyed in the variety of individual-state relationships which the Amendment was designed to embrace. For the same reason, to fashion and apply a precise formula for recognition of state responsibility under the Equal Protection Clause is an "impossible task" which "This Court has never attempted." Kotch v. River Port Pilot Comrs., 330 U.S. 552, 556. Only by sifting facts and weighing circumstances can the nonobvious involvement of the State in private conduct be attributed its true significance. . . .

Addition of all these activities, obligations and responsibilities of the Authority, the benefits mutually conferred, together with the obvious fact that the restaurant is operated as an integral part of a public building devoted to a public parking service, indicates that degree of state participation and involvement in discriminatory action which it was the design of the Fourteenth Amendment to condemn. It is irony amounting to grave injustice that in one part of a single building, erected and maintained with public funds by an agency of the State to serve a public purpose, all persons have equal rights, while in another portion, also serving the public, a Negro is a second-class citizen, offensive because of his race, without rights and unentitled to service, but at the same time fully enjoys equal access to nearby restaurants in wholly privately owned buildings. As the Chancellor pointed out, in its lease with Eagle the Authority could have affirmatively required Eagle to discharge the responsibilities under the Fourteenth Amendment imposed upon the private enterprise as a consequence of state participation. But no State may effectively abdicate its responsibilities by either ignoring them or by merely failing to discharge them whatever the motive may be. It is of no consolation to an individual denied the equal protection of the laws that it was done in good faith. Certainly the conclusions drawn in similar cases by the various Courts of Appeals do not depend upon such a distinction. By its inaction, the Authority, and through it the State, has not only made itself a party to the refusal of service, but has elected to place its power, property and prestige behind the admitted discrimination. The State has so far insinuated itself into a position of interdependence with Eagle that it must be recognized as a joint participant in the challenged activity, which, on that account, cannot be considered to have been so "purely private" as to fall without the scope of the Fourteenth Amendment.

Because readily applicable formulae may not be fashioned, the conclusions drawn from the facts and circumstances of this record are by no means declared as universal truths on the basis of which every state leasing agreement is to be tested. . . . Specifically defining the limits of our inquiry, what we hold today is that when a State leases public property in the manner and for the purpose shown to have been the case here, the proscriptions of the Fourteenth Amendment must be complied with by the lessee as certainly as though they were binding covenants written into the agreement itself.

The judgment of the Supreme Court of Delaware is reversed and the cause remanded for further proceedings consistent with this opinion.

[Justice Stewart concurred. Justices Frankfurter, Harlan, and Whittaker, dissented.]

REALITY v. APPEARANCE OF STATE ACTION

Consider the following hypothesis. In cases concerning racial discrimination, an important factor of decision is whether all of the circumstances create a public perception that the state approves the private discriminatory decision. Are appearances of state approval more important than an inquiry whether, appearances aside, racial discrimination can be traced to governmental decisions? The suggested hypothesis would support the results in the preceding cases of Pennsylvania v. Bd. of Trusts and Burton v. Wilmington Parking Authority. So long as the city ran the school, it appeared that the city and not the testator was making the choice to engage in a policy of racial discrimination. So long as the city operated the parking garage, it would appear that it approved racial discrimination by tenants in the parking structure. It can also be argued that the hypothesis explains the disparate results in the two cases concerning Senator Bacon's will—Evans v. Newton, supra p. 969, and Evans v. Abney, supra p. 982. The city had operated the park for so long as a segregated park that merely turning it over to a private trustee for continued segregated operation would not remove the appearance of a segregated city park. On the other hand, terminating the operation of the park because the city could no longer follow Senator Bacon's wish that it be segregated did not give the appearance that the city approved the testator's choice. (Consider the case of a private university refusing to accept a bequest because it *disapproves* conditions attached to it.)

Are you persuaded that *Abney* and *Newton* are both appropriately decided under the hypothesis suggested here? Do you think that the hypothesis is useful in marking the limits of state action doctrine? Is the hypothesis useful in explaining the disparate state-action and no-state-action conclusions in the cases that follow?

GILMORE v. MONTGOMERY, 417 U.S. 556 (1974). The case involved actions by a city in permitting the use of public park recreational facilities by private segregated school groups and any other non-school groups that allegedly discriminate in their membership on the basis of race. The Court held it invalid for the city to allocate use of park facilities to private segregated school groups where that action facilitated the avoidance of an outstanding school desegregation order. With respect to the use by other segregated groups the Court found the facts insufficiently developed to permit a ruling and sent the case back to the district court. In concluding its opinion the Court said:

"We close with this word of caution. It should be obvious that the exclusion of any person or group—all-Negro, all-oriental, or all-white—from public facilities infringes upon the freedom of the individual to associate as he chooses. Mr. Justice Douglas emphasized this in his dissent, joined by Mr. Justice Marshall, in *Moose Lodge.* He observed, 'The associational rights which our system honors permit all white, all black, all brown and all yellow clubs to be formed. They also permit all Catholic, all Jewish, or all agnostic clubs to be established. Government may not tell a man or woman who his or her associates must be. The individual can be as selective as he desires.' 407 U.S., at 179–180. The freedom to associate applies to the beliefs we share, and to those we consider reprehensible. It tends to produce the diversity of opinion that oils the machine of democratic government and insures peaceful, orderly change. Because its exercise is largely dependent on the right to own or use property, Healy v. James, 408 U.S. 169, 181–183 (1972), any denial of access to public facilities must withstand close scrutiny and be carefully circumscribed. Certainly, a person's mere membership in an organization which possesses a discriminatory admissions policy would not alone be ground for his exclusion from public facilities. Having said this, however, we must also be aware that the very exercise of the freedom to associate by some may serve to infringe that freedom for others. Invidious discrimination takes its own toll on the freedom to associate, and it is not subject to affirmative constitutional protection when it involves state action. Norwood v. Harrison, 413 U.S., at 470."

2. GOVERNMENT FINANCIAL ASSISTANCE TO PRIVATE ACTIVITIES

NORWOOD v. HARRISON, 413 U.S. 455 (1973). Mississippi had a statutory program under which textbooks were purchased by the state and lent to students in both public and private schools. A suit was brought challenging the application of this statute in lending textbooks to students attending schools with racially discriminatory admission policies. The Court held the statute invalid as applied to such schools. The Court said that it did not question the right of private citizens to operate such schools nor of parents to have their children attend them. It said that the question was rather whether the state may "provide tangible assistance to students attending private schools" which are racially discriminatory. On this question, the Court said:

"This Court has consistently affirmed decisions enjoining state tuition grants to students attending racially discriminatory private schools. A textbook lending program is not legally distinguishable from the forms of state assistance foreclosed by the prior cases. Free textbooks, like tuition grants directed to private school students, are a form of financial assistance inuring to the benefit of the private schools themselves. An inescapable educational cost for students in both public and private schools is the expense of providing all necessary learning materials. When, as here, that necessary expense is borne by the State, the economic consequence is to give aid to the enterprise; if the school engages in discriminatory practices the State by tangible aid in the form of textbooks thereby gives support to such discrimination. Racial discrimination in state-operated schools is barred by the Constitution and '[i]t is also axiomatic that a state may not induce, encourage or promote private persons to accomplish what it is constitutionally forbidden to accomplish.' Lee v. Macon County Bd. of Educ., 267 F.Supp. 458, 475–476 (M.D.Ala.1967).

"We do not suggest that a State violates its constitutional duty merely because it has provided *any* form of state service that benefits private schools said to be racially discriminatory. Textbooks are a basic educational tool and, like tuition grants, they are provided only in connection with schools; they are to be distinguished from generalized services government might provide to schools in common with others. Moreover, the textbooks provided to private school students by the State in this case are a form of assistance readily available from sources entirely independent of the State—unlike, for example, 'such necessities of life as electricity, water, and police and fire protection.' Moose Lodge No. 107 v. Irvis, 407 U.S. 163, 173 (1972). The State has neither an absolute nor operating monopoly on the procurement of school textbooks; anyone can purchase them on the open market.

"The District Court laid great stress on the absence of showing by appellants that 'any child enrolled in private school, if deprived of free textbooks, would withdraw from private school and subsequently enroll in the public schools.' 340 F.Supp., at 1013. We can accept this factual assertion; we cannot and do not know, on this record at least, whether state textbook assistance is the determinative factor in the enrollment of any students in any of the private schools in Mississippi. We do not agree with the District Court in its analysis of the legal consequences of this uncertainty, for the Constitution does not permit the State to aid discrimination even when there is no precise causal relationship between state financial aid to a private school and the continued well-being of that school. A State may not grant the type of tangible financial aid here involved if that aid has a significant tendency to facilitate, reinforce, and support private discrimination."

———

BLUM v. YARETSKY, 457 U.S. 991 (1982). A class of Medicaid patients brought suit claiming that private nursing homes violated their rights to procedural due process in transferring them to lower levels of care, or discharging them. The nursing homes receive reimbursement from the state for their services in caring for Medicaid patients. Decisions by the nursing home result in lower Medicaid benefits. The Court held that there was no state action that would trigger the Fourteenth Amendment's requirement of procedural due process. Justice Rehnquist's opinion for the Court said, in part:

"Respondents . . . argue that the State 'affirmatively commands' the summary discharge or transfer of Medicaid patients who are thought to be inappropriately placed in their nursing facilities. Were this characterization accurate, we would have a different question before us. However, our review of the statutes and regulations identified by respondents does not support respondents' characterization of them.

. . .

". . . [R]espondents' complaint is about nursing home decisions to discharge or transfer, not to admit, Medicaid patients. But we are not satisfied that the State is responsible for those decisions. . . . The regulations cited by respondents require [nursing homes] 'to make all efforts possible to transfer patients to the appropriate level of care or home as indicated by the patient's medical condition or needs' . . . The nursing homes are required to complete patient care assessment forms designed by the State and 'provide the receiving facility or provider with a current copy of same at the time of discharge to an alternate level of care facility or home.' . . .

"These regulations do not require the nursing homes to rely on the forms in making discharge or transfer decisions, nor do they demonstrate that the State is responsible for the decision to discharge or transfer particular patients. Those decisions ultimately turn on medical judgments made by private parties according to professional standards that are not established by the State. This case, therefore, is not unlike Polk County v. Dodson, 454 U.S. 312 (1981), in which the question was whether a public defender acts 'under color of' state law within the meaning of 42 U.S.C. § 1983 when representing an indigent defendant in a state criminal proceeding. Although the public defender was employed by the State and appointed by the State to represent the respondent, we concluded that '[t]his assignment entailed functions and obligations in no way dependent on state authority.' . . . The decisions made by the public defender in the course of representing his client were framed in accordance with professional canons of ethics, rather than dictated by any rule of conduct imposed by the State. The same is true of nursing home decisions to discharge or transfer particular patients because the care they are receiving is medically inappropriate."

Justices Brennan and Marshall dissented.

RENDELL–BAKER v. KOHN, 457 U.S. 830 (1982). Plaintiffs were discharged teachers, previously employed by a private school for maladjusted high school students. Most of the school's students had been referred to it by city and state agencies. Public funds account for 90 to 99% of the school's operating budget. Plaintiffs brought suit under 42 U.S.C. § 1983, claiming that their discharges were for constitutionally protected speech, in violation of the first amendment, and that they had been denied procedural due process. The Court held that the private school did not act under color of state law in dismissing the plaintiffs. Chief Justice Burger's opinion said, in part:

"The school . . . is not fundamentally different from many private corporations whose business depends primarily on contracts to build roads, bridges, dams, ships, or submarines for the government. Acts of such private contractors do not become acts of the government by reason of their significant or even total engagement in performing public contracts."

Justices Marshall and Brennan dissented.

3. Government Regulation of Private Activity

MOOSE LODGE v. IRVIS

407 U.S. 163, 92 S.Ct. 1965, 32 L.Ed.2d 627 (1972).

Mr. Justice Rehnquist delivered the opinion of the Court.

Appellee Irvis, a Negro . . . ., was refused service by appellant Moose Lodge, a local branch of the national fraternal organization located in Harrisburg, Pennsylvania. Appellee then brought this action under 42 U.S.C. § 1983 for injunctive relief in the United States District Court for the Middle District of Pennsylvania. He claimed that because the Pennsylvania liquor board had issued appellant Moose Lodge a private club license that authorized the sale of alcoholic beverages on its premises, the refusal of service to him was "state action" for the purposes of the Equal Protection Clause of the Fourteenth Amendment. He named both Moose Lodge and the Pennsylvania Liquor Authority as defendants, seeking injunctive relief that would have required the defendant liquor board to revoke Moose Lodge's license so long as it continued its discriminatory practices. Appellee sought no damages.

A three-judge district court, convened at appellee's request, upheld his contention on the merits, and entered a decree declaring invalid the liquor license issued to Moose Lodge "as long as it follows a policy of racial discrimination in its membership or operating policies or practices." Moose Lodge alone appealed from the decree, and we postponed decision as to jurisdiction until the hearing on the merits, 401 U.S. 992. Appellant urges in the alternative that we either vacate the judgment below because there is not presently a case or controversy between the parties, or that we reverse on the merits.

I.

The District Court in its opinion found that "a Caucasian member in good standing brought plaintiff, a Negro, to the Lodge's dining room and bar as his guest and requested service of food and beverages. The Lodge through its employees refused service to plaintiff solely because he is a Negro." It is undisputed that each local Moose Lodge is bound by the constitution and general by-laws of the Supreme Lodge, the latter of which contains a provision limiting membership in the lodges to white male Caucasians. The District Court in this connection found that "[t]he lodges accordingly maintain a policy and practice of restricting membership to the Caucasian race and permitting members to bring only Caucasian guests on lodge premises, particularly to the dining room and bar."

. . .

Any injury to appellee from the conduct of Moose Lodge stemmed not from the lodge's membership requirements, but from its policies with respect to the serving of guests of members. Appellee has standing to seek redress for injuries done to him, but may not seek redress for injuries done to others. . . . While this Court has held that in exceptional situations a concededly injured party may rely on the constitutional rights of a third party in obtaining relief, Barrows v. Jackson, 346 U.S. 249 (1953), in this case appellee was not injured by Moose Lodge's membership policy since he never sought to become a member. . . .

. . .

Because appellee had no standing to litigate a constitutional claim arising out of Moose Lodge's membership practices, the District Court erred in reaching that issue on the merits. But it did not err in reaching the constitutional claim of appellee that Moose Lodge's guest service practices under these circumstances violated the Fourteenth Amendment. Nothing in the positions taken by the parties since the entry of the District Court decree has mooted that claim, and we therefore turn to its disposition.

II.

Moose Lodge is a private club in the ordinary meaning of that term. It is a local chapter of a national fraternal organization having well defined requirements for membership. It conducts all of its activities in a building that is owned by it. It is not publicly funded. Only members and guests are permitted in any lodge of the order; one may become a guest only by invitation of a member or upon invitation of the house committee.

Appellee, while conceding the right of private clubs to choose members upon a discriminatory basis, asserts that the licensing of Moose Lodge to serve liquor by the Pennsylvania Liquor Control Board amounts to such State involvement with the club's activities as to make its discriminatory practices forbidden by the Equal Protection Clause of the Fourteenth Amendment. The relief sought and obtained by appellee in the District Court was an injunction forbidding the licensing by the liquor authority of Moose Lodge until it ceased its discriminatory practices. We conclude that Moose Lodge's refusal to serve food and beverages to a guest by reason of the fact that he was a Negro does not, under the circumstances here presented, violate the Fourteenth Amendment.

. . .

While the principle is easily stated, the question of whether particular discriminatory conduct is private, on the one hand, or amounts to "state action," on the other hand, frequently admits of no easy answer. . . .

Our cases make clear that the impetus for the forbidden discrimination need not originate with the State if it is state action that enforces privately originated discrimination.   Shelley v. Kraemer, supra.   .   .   .

The Court has never held, of course, that discrimination by an otherwise private entity would be violative of the Equal Protection Clause if the private entity receives any sort of benefit or service at all from the State, or if it is subject to state regulation in any degree whatever.   Since state-furnished services include such necessities of life as electricity, water, and police and fire protection, such a holding would utterly emasculate the distinction between private as distinguished from state conduct set forth in The Civil Rights Cases, supra, and adhered to in subsequent decisions.   Our holdings indicate that where the impetus for the discrimination is private, the State must have "significantly involved itself with invidious discriminations," Reitman v. Mulkey, 387 U.S. 369, 380 (1967), in order for the discriminatory action to fall within the ambit of the constitutional prohibition.

Our prior decisions dealing with discriminatory refusal of service in public eating places are significantly different factually from the case now before us. Peterson v. City of Greenville, 373 U.S. 244 (1963), dealt with trespass prosecution of persons who "sat in" at a restaurant to protest its refusal of service to Negroes.   There the Court held that although the ostensible initiative for the trespass prosecution came from the proprietor, the existence of a local ordinance requiring segregation of races in such places was tantamount to the State having "commanded a particular result," 373 U.S., at 248.   .   .   .

Here there is nothing approaching the symbiotic relationship between lessor and lessee that was present in *Burton,* where the private lessee obtained the benefit of locating in a building owned by the state created parking authority, and the parking authority was enabled to carry out its primary public purpose of furnishing parking space by advantageously leasing portions of the building constructed for that purpose to commercial lessees such as the owner of the Eagle Restaurant.   Unlike *Burton,* the Moose Lodge building is located on land owned by it, not by any public authority.   Far from apparently holding itself out as a place of public accommodation, Moose Lodge quite ostentatiously proclaims the fact that it is not open to the public at large.   Nor is it located and operated in such surroundings that although private in name, it discharges a function or performs a service that would otherwise in all likelihood be performed by the State.   In short, while Eagle was a public restaurant in a public building, Moose Lodge is a private social club in a private building.

With the exception hereafter noted, the Pennsylvania Liquor Control Board plays absolutely no part in establishing or enforcing the membership or guest policies of the club that it licenses to serve liquor.[3]   There is no suggestion in this record that the Pennsylvania law, either as written or as applied, discriminates against minority groups either in their right to apply for club licenses themselves or in their right to purchase and be served liquor in places of public accommodation.   The only effect that the state licensing of Moose Lodge to serve liquor can be said to have on the right of any other Pennsylvanian to buy or be served liquor on premises other than those of Moose Lodge is that for some purposes club licenses are counted in the maximum number of licenses which may be issued in a given municipality.   Basically each municipality has a quota of one retail license for each 1,500 inhabitants.   Licenses issued to hotels, municipal golf courses and airport restaurants are not counted in this quota, nor are club licenses until the maximum number of retail licenses is reached.

[3] Unlike the situation in Public Utilities Comm'n v. Pollak, 343 U.S. 451 (1952), where the regulatory agency had affirmatively approved the practice of the regulated entity after full investigation, the Pennsylvania Liquor Control Board has neither approved nor endorsed the racially discriminatory practices of Moose Lodge.

Beyond that point, neither additional retail licenses nor additional club licenses may be issued so long as the number of issued and outstanding retail licenses remains at or above the statutory maximum.

The District Court was at pains to point out in its opinion what it considered to be the "pervasive" nature of the regulation of private clubs by the Pennsylvania Liquor Control Board. . . .

However detailed this type of regulation may be in some particulars, it cannot be said to in any way foster or encourage racial discrimination. Nor can it be said to make the State in any realistic sense a partner or even a joint venturer in the club's enterprise. The limited effect of the prohibition against obtaining additional club licenses when the maximum number of retail licenses allotted to a municipality has been issued, when considered together with the availability of liquor from hotel, restaurant, and retail licensees falls far short of conferring upon club licensees a monopoly in the dispensing of liquor in any given municipality or in the State as a whole. We therefore hold that, with the exception hereafter noted, the operation of the regulatory scheme enforced by the Pennsylvania Liquor Control Board does not sufficiently implicate the State in the discriminatory guest policies of Moose Lodge so as to make the latter "state action" within the ambit of the Equal Protection Clause of the Fourteenth Amendment.

The District Court found that the regulations of the Liquor Control Board adopted pursuant to statute affirmatively require that "every club licensee shall adhere to all the provisions of its Constitution and By-Laws." Appellant argues that the purpose of this provision "is purely and simply and plainly the prevention of subterfuge," pointing out that the *bona fides* of a private club, as opposed to a place of public accommodation masquerading as a private club, is a matter with which the State Liquor Control Board may legitimately concern itself. Appellee concedes this to be the case, and expresses disagreement with the District Court on this point. There can be no doubt that the label "private club" can and has been used to evade both regulations of state and local liquor authorities, and statutes requiring places of public accommodation to serve all persons without regard to race, color, religion, or national origin. This Court in Daniel v. Paul, 395 U.S. 298 (1969), had occasion to address this issue in connection with the application of Title II of the Civil Rights Act of 1964, 78 Stat. 243, 42 U.S.C. § 2000a et seq.

. . .

Even though the Liquor Control Board regulation in question is neutral in its terms, the result of its application in a case where the constitution and by-laws of a club required racial discrimination would be to invoke the sanctions of the State to enforce a concededly discriminatory private rule. State action, for purposes of the Equal Protection Clause, may emanate from rulings of administrative and regulatory agencies as well as from legislative or judicial action. Robinson v. Florida, 378 U.S. 153, 156 (1964). Shelley v. Kraemer, 341 U.S. 1 (1948), makes it clear that the application of state sanctions to enforce such a rule would violate the Fourteenth Amendment. Although the record before us is not as clear as one would like, appellant has not persuaded us that the District Court should have denied any and all relief.

Appellee was entitled to a decree enjoining the enforcement of § 113.09 of the regulations promulgated by the Pennsylvania Liquor Control Board insofar as that regulation requires compliance by Moose Lodge with provisions of its constitution and by-laws containing racially discriminatory provisions. He was entitled to no more. The judgment of the District Court is reversed, and the cause remanded with instructions to enter a decree in conformity with this opinion.

Mr. Justice Douglas, with whom Mr. Justice Marshall joins, dissenting.

My view of the First Amendment and the related guarantees of the Bill of Rights is that they create a zone of privacy which precludes government from interfering with private clubs or groups. The associational rights which our system honors permits all white, all black, all brown, and all yellow clubs to be formed. They also permit all Catholic, all Jewish, or all agnostic clubs to be established. Government may not tell a man or woman who his or her associates must be. The individual can be as selective as he desires. So the fact that the Moose Lodge allows only Caucasians to join or come as guests is constitutionally irrelevant, as is the decision of the Black Muslims to admit to their services only members of their race.

The problem is different, however, where the public domain is concerned. I have indicated in Garner v. Louisiana, 368 U.S. 157, and Lombard v. Louisiana, 373 U.S. 267, that where restaurants or other facilities serving the public are concerned and licenses are obtained from the State for operating the business, the "public" may not be defined by the proprietor to include only people of his choice; nor may a State or municipal service be granted only to some. Evans v. Newton, 382 U.S. 296, 298–299.

Those cases are not precisely apposite, however, for a private club, by definition, is not in the public domain. And the fact that a private club gets some kind of permit from the State or municipality does not make it *ipso facto* a public enterprise or undertaking, any more than the grant to a householder of a permit to operate an incinerator puts the householder in the public domain. We must therefore examine whether there are special circumstances involved in the Pennsylvania scheme which differentiate the liquor license possessed by Moose Lodge from the incinerator permit.

. . . .

Were this regulation [enforcing the discriminatory membership clause] the only infirmity in Pennsylvania's licensing scheme, I would perhaps agree with the majority that the appropriate relief would be a decree enjoining its enforcement. But there is another flaw in the scheme not so easily cured. Liquor licenses in Pennsylvania, unlike driver's licenses, or marriage licenses, are not freely available to those who meet racially neutral qualifications. There is a complex quota system, which the majority accurately describes. What the majority neglects to say is that the Harrisburg quota, where Moose Lodge No. 107 is located, has been full for many years. No more club licenses may be issued in that city.

This state-enforced scarcity of licenses restricts the ability of blacks to obtain liquor, for liquor is commercially available *only* at private clubs for a significant portion of each week. Access by blacks to places that serve liquor is further limited by the fact that the state quota is filled. A group desiring to form a nondiscriminatory club which would serve blacks must purchase a license held by an existing club, which can exact a monopoly price for the transfer. The availability of such a license is speculative at best, however, for, as Moose Lodge itself concedes, without a liquor license a fraternal organization would be hard-pressed to survive.

Thus, the State of Pennsylvania is putting the weight of its liquor license, concededly a valued and important adjunct to a private club, behind racial discrimination. . . .

I would affirm the judgment below.

Mr. Justice Brennan, with whom Mr. Justice Marshall joins, dissenting.

When Moose Lodge obtained its liquor license, the State of Pennsylvania became an active participant in the operation of the Lodge bar. Liquor licensing laws are only incidentally revenue measures; they are primarily pervasive regulatory schemes under which the State dictates and continually supervises virtually every detail of the operation of the licensee's business. Very few, if any, other licensed businesses experience such complete state involvement. Yet the Court holds that that involvement does not constitute "state action" making the Lodge's refusal to serve a guest liquor solely because of his race a violation of the Fourteenth Amendment. The vital flaw in the Court's reasoning is its complete disregard of the fundamental value underlying the "state action" concept. . . .

Plainly, the State of Pennsylvania's liquor regulations intertwine the State with the operation of the Lodge bar in a "significant way [and] lend [the State's] authority to the sordid business of racial discrimination." . . .

This is thus a case requiring application of the principle that until today has governed our determinations of the existence of "state action": "Our prior decisions leave no doubt that the mere existence of efforts by the State, through legislation or otherwise, to authorize, encourage, or otherwise support racial discrimination in a particular facet of life constitutes illegal state involvement in those pertinent private acts of discrimination that subsequently occur." Adickes v. Kress & Co., 398 U.S., at 202 (separate opinion of Brennan, J.). . . .

I therefore dissent and would affirm the final decree entered by the District Court.

JACKSON v. METROPOLITAN EDISON CO.

419 U.S. 345, 95 S.Ct. 449, 42 L.Ed.2d 477 (1974).

[Plaintiff brought suit against defendant, a privately owned and operated utility corporation which holds a certificate of public convenience issued by the Pennsylvania Utilities Commission, seeking damages and injunctive relief under 42 U.S.C. § 1983 for termination of her electric service allegedly before she had been afforded notice, a hearing, and an opportunity to pay any amounts due. Plaintiff claimed that under state law she was entitled to reasonably continuous electric service and that respondent's termination for alleged nonpayment, permitted by a provision of its general tariff filed with the Commission, was state action depriving her of her property without due process of law. The Court of Appeals affirmed the District Court's dismissal of her complaint. The Supreme Court affirmed.]

Mr. Justice Rehnquist delivered the opinion of the Court.

. . . .

Here the action complained of was taken by a utility company which is privately owned and operated, but which in many particulars of its business is subject to extensive state regulation. The mere fact that a business is subject to state regulation does not by itself convert its action into that of the State for purposes of the Fourteenth Amendment. Moose Lodge No. 107 v. Irvis, supra, 407 U.S. at 176–177. Nor does the fact that the regulation is extensive and detailed, as in the case of most public utilities, do so. Public Utilities Comm'n v. Pollak, 343 U.S. 451, 462 (1952). It may well be that acts of a heavily regulated utility with at least something of a governmentally protected monopoly will more readily be found to be "state" acts than will the acts of an entity lacking these characteristics. But the inquiry must be whether there is a sufficiently close nexus between the State and the challenged action of the regulated entity so that the action of the latter may be fairly treated as that of the State itself. Moose Lodge No. 107, supra, at 176. The true nature of the State's involvement may not be immediately obvious, and detailed inquiry may be required in order to determine whether the test is met. Burton v. Wilmington Parking Authority, supra.

Petitioner advances a series of contentions which, in her view, lead to the conclusion that this case should fall on the *Burton* side of the line drawn in the *Civil Rights Cases,* supra, rather than on the *Moose Lodge* side of that line. We find none of them persuasive.

Petitioner first argues that "state action" is present because of the monopoly status allegedly conferred upon Metropolitan by the State of Pennsylvania. As a factual matter, it may well be doubted that the State ever granted or guaranteed Metropolitan a monopoly. But assuming that it had, this fact is not determinative in considering whether Metropolitan's termination of service to petitioner was "state action" for purposes of the Fourteenth Amendment. In *Pollak,* supra, where the Court dealt with the activities of the District of Columbia Transit Company, a congressionally established monopoly, we expressly disclaimed reliance on the monopoly status of the transit authority. Id., 343 U.S. at 462. Similarly, although certain monopoly aspects were presented in *Moose Lodge No. 107,* supra, we found that the Lodge's action was not subject to the provisions of the Fourteenth Amendment. In each of those cases, there was insufficient relationship between the challenged actions of the entities involved and their monopoly status. There is no indication of any greater connection here.

Petitioner next urges that state action is present because respondent provides an essential public service required to be supplied on a reasonably continuous basis by 66 Pa.Stat. § 1171, and hence performs a "public function." We have of course found state action present in the exercise by a private entity of powers traditionally exclusively reserved to the State. See, e.g., Nixon v. Condon, 286 U.S. 73 (1931) (election); Terry v. Adams, 345 U.S. 461 (1953) (election); Marsh v. Alabama, 326 U.S. 501 (1946) (company town); Evans v. Newton, 382 U.S. 296 (1966) (municipal park). If we were dealing with the exercise by Metropolitan of some power delegated to it by the State which is traditionally associated with sovereignty, such as eminent domain, our case would be quite a different one. But while the Pennsylvania statute imposes an obligation to furnish service on regulated utilities, it imposes no such obligation on the State. The Pennsylvania courts have rejected the contention that the furnishing of utility services is either a state function or a municipal duty. Girard Life Insurance Co. v. City of Philadelphia, 88 Pa. 393 (1879); Bailey v. Philadelphia, 184 Pa. 594, 39 A. 494 (1898).

Perhaps in recognition of the fact that the supplying of utility service is not traditionally the exclusive prerogative of the State, petitioner invites the expansion of the doctrine of this limited line of cases into a broad principle that all businesses "affected with the public interest" are state actors in all their actions.

We decline the invitation for reasons stated long ago in Nebbia v. New York, 291 U.S. 502 (1934), in the course of rejecting a substantive due process attack on state legislation: . . .

Doctors, optometrists, lawyers, Metropolitan, and *Nebbia's* upstate New York grocery selling a quart of milk are all in regulated businesses, providing arguably essential goods and services, "affected with a public interest." We do not believe that such a status converts their every action, absent more, into that of the State.

We also reject the notion that Metropolitan's termination is state action because the State "has specifically authorized and approved" the termination practice. In the instant case, Metropolitan filed with the Public Utilities Commission a general tariff—a provision of which states Metropolitan's right to terminate service for nonpayment. This provision has appeared in Metropolitan's previously filed tariffs for many years and has never been the subject of a hearing or other scrutiny by the Commission.[11] Although the Commission did hold hearings on portions of Metropolitan's general tariff relating to a general rate increase, it never even considered the reinsertion of this provision in the newly filed general tariff. The provision became effective 60 days after filing when not disapproved by the Commission.

As a threshold matter, it is less than clear under state law that Metropolitan was even required to file this provision as part of its tariff or that the Commission would have had the power to disapprove it. The District Court observed that the sole connection of the Commission with this regulation was Metropolitan's simple notice filing with the Commission and the lack of any Commission action to prohibit it.

The case most heavily relied on by petitioner is Public Utilities Comm'n v. Pollak, supra. There the Court dealt with the contention that Capital Transit's installation of a piped music system on its buses violated the First Amendment rights of the bus riders. It is not entirely clear whether the Court alternatively held that Capital Transit's action was action of the "State" for First Amendment purposes, or whether it merely assumed *arguendo* that it was and went on to resolve the First Amendment question adversely to the bus riders. In either event, the nature of the state involvement there was quite different than it is here. The District of Columbia Public Utilities Commission, on its own motion, commenced an investigation of the effects of the piped music, and after a full hearing concluded not only that Capital Transit's practices were "not inconsistent with public convenience, comfort, and safety," 81 P.U.R.(N.S.) 122, 126 (1950), but also that the practice "in fact through the creation of better will among passengers, . . . tends to improve the conditions under which the public rides." Id. Here, on the other hand, there was no such imprimatur placed on the practice of Metropolitan about which petitioner complains. The nature of governmental regulation of private utilities is such that a utility may frequently be required by the state regulatory scheme to obtain approval for practices a business regulated in less detail would be free to institute without any approval from a regulatory body. Approval by a state utility commission of such a request from a regulated utility, where the commission has not put its own weight on the side of the proposed practice by ordering it, does not transmute a practice initiated by the utility and approved by the commission into "state action." At most, the Commission's failure to overturn this practice amounted to no more than a determination that a Pennsylvania utility was authorized to employ such a practice if it so desired. Respondent's exercise of the choice allowed by state law where the initiative comes from it and not from the State, does not make its action in doing so "state action" for purposes of the Fourteenth Amendment.

We also find absent in the instant case the symbiotic relationship presented in Burton v. Wilmington Parking Authority, 365 U.S. 715 (1961). . . .

Metropolitan is a privately owned corporation, and it does not lease its facilities from the State of Pennsylvania. It alone is responsible for the provision of power to its customers. In common with all corporations of the State it pays taxes to the State, and it is subject to a form of extensive regulation by the State in a way that most other business enterprises are not. But this was likewise true of the appellant club in Moose Lodge No. 107 v. Irvis, . . .

All of petitioner's arguments taken together show no more than that Metropolitan was a heavily regulated private utility, enjoying at least a partial monopoly in the providing of electrical service within its territory, and that it elected to terminate service to petitioner in a manner which the Pennsylvania

---

[11] Petitioner does not contest the fact that Metropolitan had this right at common law. . . .

Public Utilities Commission found permissible under state law. Under our decision this is not sufficient to connect the State of Pennsylvania with respondent's action so as to make the latter's conduct attributable to the State for purposes of the Fourteenth Amendment.

We conclude that the State of Pennsylvania is not sufficiently connected with respondent's action in terminating petitioner's service so as to make respondent's conduct in so doing attributable to the State for purposes of the Fourteenth Amendment. We therefore have no occasion to decide whether petitioner's claim to continued service was "property" for purposes of that Amendment, or whether "due process of law" would require a State taking similar action to accord petitioner the procedural rights for which she contends. The judgment of the Court of Appeals for the Third Circuit is therefore

Affirmed.

Mr. Justice Douglas, dissenting.

I reach the opposite conclusion from that reached by the majority on the state action issue. . . .

Mr. Justice Brennan, dissenting.

I do not think that a controversy existed between petitioner and respondent entitling petitioner to be heard in this action. . . .

Mr. Justice Marshall, dissenting.

I agree with my Brother Brennan that this case is a very poor vehicle for resolving the difficult and important questions presented today. . . . Since the Court has disposed of the case by finding no state action, however, I think it appropriate to register my dissent on that point. . . .

. . .

The fact that the Metropolitan Edison Company supplies an essential public service that is in many communities supplied by the government weighs more heavily for me than for the majority. . . .

Private parties performing functions affecting the public interest can often make a persuasive claim to be free of the constitutional requirements applicable to governmental institutions because of the value of preserving a private sector in which the opportunity for individual choice is maximized. See Evans v. Newton, 382 U.S., at 298, H. Friendly, The Dartmouth College Case and the Private-Public Penumbra (1969). Maintaining the private status of parochial schools, cited by the majority, advances just this value. In the due process area, a similar value of diversity may often be furthered by allowing various private institutions the flexibility to select procedures that fit their particular needs. See Wahba v. New York University, 492 F.2d 96, 102 (2d Cir.), cert. denied, 419 U.S. 874 (1974). But it is hard to imagine any such interests that are furthered by protecting public utility companies from meeting the constitutional standards that would apply if the companies were state-owned. The values of pluralism and diversity are simply not relevant when the private company is the only electric company in town.

. . .

What is perhaps most troubling about the Court's opinion is that it would appear to apply to a broad range of claimed constitutional violations by the company. The Court has not adopted the notion, accepted elsewhere, that different standards should apply to state action analysis when different constitutional claims are presented. See Adickes v. S.H. Kress & Co., 398 U.S. 144, 190–191 (1970) (Brennan, J., concurring and dissenting); Grafton v. Brooklyn Law School, 478 F.2d 1137, 1142 (2d Cir.1973). Thus, the majority's analysis would seemingly apply as well to a company that refused to extend service to Negroes, welfare recipients, or any other group that the company preferred, for its own reasons, not to serve. I cannot believe that this Court would hold that the State's involvement with the utility company was not sufficient to impose upon the company an obligation to meet the constitutional mandate of nondiscrimination. Yet nothing in the analysis of the majority opinion suggests otherwise.

I dissent.

4. GOVERNMENT APPROVAL OF PRIVATE ACTIVITY

REITMAN v. MULKEY

387 U.S. 369, 87 S.Ct. 1627, 18 L.Ed.2d 830 (1967).

Mr. Justice White delivered the opinion of the Court.

The question here is whether Art. I, § 26 of the California Constitution denies "to any person . . . the equal protection of the laws" within the meaning of the Fourteenth Amendment of the Constitution of the United States. Section 26 of Art. I, an initiated measure submitted to the people as Proposition 14 in a statewide ballot in 1964, provides in part as follows:

"Neither the State nor any subdivision or agency thereof shall deny, limit or abridge, directly or indirectly, the right of any person, who is willing or desires to sell, lease or rent any part or all of his real property, to decline to sell, lease or rent such property to such person or persons as he, in his absolute discretion, chooses."

The real property covered by § 26 is limited to residential property and contains an exception for state-owned real estate.

. . . [T]he Mulkeys who are husband and wife and respondents here, sued under § 51 and § 52 of the California Civil Code alleging that petitioners had refused to rent them an apartment solely on account of their race. An injunction and damages were demanded. Petitioners moved for summary judgment on the ground that §§ 51 and 52, insofar as they were the basis for the Mulkeys' action, had been rendered null and void by the adoption of Proposition 14 after the filing of the complaint. The trial court granted the motion and respondents took the case to the California Supreme Court.

. . . [That court reversed, holding] that Art. I, § 26, was invalid as denying the equal protection of the laws guaranteed by the Fourteenth Amendment. 64 Cal.2d 529, 50 Cal.Rptr. 881, 413 P.2d 825. . . .

We affirm the judgment of the California Supreme Court. We first turn to the opinion of that court . . . ., which quite properly undertook to examine the constitutionality of § 26 in terms of its "immediate objective," its "ultimate effect" and its "historical context and the conditions existing prior to its enactment." Judgments such as these we have frequently undertaken ourselves. . . . But here the California Supreme Court has addressed itself to these matters and we should give careful consideration to its views because they concern the purpose, scope, and operative effect of a provision of the California Constitution.

First, the court considered whether § 26 was concerned at all with private discriminations in residential housing. This involved a review of past efforts by the California Legislature to regulate such discriminations. The Unruh Act, Civ.Code §§ 51-52, on which respondents based their cases, was passed in 1959. The Hawkins Act, formerly Health & Saf.Code §§ 35700-35741, followed and prohibited discriminations in publicly assisted housing. In 1961, the legislature enacted proscriptions against restrictive covenants. Finally, in 1963, came the Rumford Fair Housing Act, Health & Saf.Code §§ 35700-

35744, superseding the Hawkins Act and prohibiting racial discriminations in the sale or rental of any private dwelling containing more than four units. That act was enforceable by the State Fair Employment Practice Commission.

It was against this background that Proposition 14 was enacted. Its immediate design and intent, the California court said, was "to overturn state laws that bore on the right of private sellers and lessors to discriminate," the Unruh and Rumford Acts, and "to forestall future state action that might circumscribe this right." This aim was successfully achieved: the adoption of Proposition 14 "generally nullifies both the Rumford and Unruh Acts as they apply to the housing market," and establishes "a purported constitutional right to *privately* discriminate on grounds which admittedly would be unavailable under the Fourteenth Amendment *should state action* be involved."

Second, the court conceded that the State was permitted a neutral position with respect to private racial discriminations and that the State was not bound by the Federal Constitution to forbid them. But, because a significant state involvement in private discriminations could amount to unconstitutional state action, Burton v. Wilmington Parking Authority, 365 U.S. 715, the court deemed it necessary to determine whether Proposition 14 invalidly involved the State in racial discriminations in the housing market. Its conclusion was that it did.

To reach this result, the state court examined certain prior decisions in this Court in which discriminatory state action was identified. Based on these cases, . . . it concluded that a prohibited state involvement could be found "even where the state can be charged with only encouraging," rather than commanding discrimination. . . . To the California court "[t]he instant case presents an undeniably analogous situation" wherein the State had taken affirmative action designed to make private discriminations legally possible. Section 26 was said to have changed the situation from one in which discriminatory practices were restricted "to one wherein it is encouraged, within the meaning of the cited decisions"; § 26 was legislative action "which authorized private discrimination" and made the State "at least a partner in the instant act of discrimination . . . ." The court could "conceive of no other purpose for an application of section 26 aside from authorizing the perpetration of a purported private discrimination . . . ." The judgment of the California court was that § 26 unconstitutionally involves the State in racial discriminations and is therefore invalid under the Fourteenth Amendment.

There is no sound reason for rejecting this judgment. Petitioners contend that the California court has misconstrued the Fourteenth Amendment since the repeal of any statute prohibiting racial discrimination, which is constitutionally permissible, may be said to "authorize" and "encourage" discrimination because it makes legally permissible that which was formerly proscribed. But as we understand the California court, it did not posit a constitutional violation on the mere repeal of the Unruh and Rumford Acts. It did not read either our cases or the Fourteenth Amendment as establishing an automatic constitutional barrier to the repeal of an existing law prohibiting racial discriminations in housing; nor did the court rule that a State may never put in statutory form an existing policy of neutrality with respect to private discriminations. What the court below did was first to reject the notion that the State was required to have a statute prohibiting racial discriminations in housing. Second, it held the purpose and intent of § 26 was to authorize private racial discriminations in the housing market, to repeal the Unruh and Rumford Acts and to create a constitutional right to discriminate on racial grounds in the sale and leasing of real property. Hence, the court dealt with § 26 as though it expressly authorized and constitutionalized the private right to discriminate. Third, the court assessed the ultimate impact of § 26 in the California environment and concluded that the section would encourage and significantly involve the State in private racial discrimination contrary to the Fourteenth Amendment.

The California court could very reasonably conclude that § 26 would and did have wider impact than a mere repeal of existing statutes. Section 26 mentioned neither the Unruh nor Rumford Acts in so many words. Instead, it announced the constitutional right of any person to decline to sell or lease his real property to anyone to whom he did not desire to sell or lease. Unruh and Rumford were thereby *pro tanto* repealed. But the section struck more deeply and more widely. Private discriminations in housing were now not only free from Rumford and Unruh but they also enjoyed a far different status than was true before the passage of those statutes. The right to discriminate, including the right to discriminate on racial grounds, was now embodied in the State's basic charter, immune from legislative, executive, or judicial regulation at any level of the state government. Those practicing racial discriminations need no longer rely solely on their personal choice. They could now invoke express constitutional authority, free from censure or interference of any kind from official sources. All individuals, partnerships, corporations and other legal entities, as well as their agents and representatives, could now discriminate with respect to their residential real property, which is defined as any interest in real property of any kind or quality, "irrespective of how obtained or financed," and seemingly irrespective of the relationship of the State to such interests in real property. Only the State is excluded with respect to property owned by it.

. . . Here the California court, armed as it was with the knowledge of the facts and circumstances concerning the passage and potential impact of § 26, and familiar with the milieu in which that provision would operate, has determined that the provision would involve the State in private racial discriminations to an unconstitutional degree. We accept this holding of the California court.

The assessment of § 26 by the California court is similar to what this Court has done in appraising state statutes or other official actions in other contexts.

. . . .

None of these cases squarely controls the case we now have before us. But they do illustrate the range of situations in which discriminatory state action has been identified. They do exemplify the necessity for a court to assess the potential impact of official action in determining whether the State has significantly involved itself with invidious discriminations. Here we are dealing with a provision which does not just repeal an existing law forbidding private racial discriminations. Section 26 was intended to authorize, and does authorize, racial discrimination in the housing market. The right to discriminate is now one of the basic policies of the State. The California Supreme Court believes that the section will significantly encourage and involve the State in private discriminations. We have been presented with no persuasive considerations indicating that this judgment should be overturned.

Affirmed.

Mr. Justice Douglas, concurring.

While I join the opinion of the Court, I add a word to indicate the dimensions of our problem.

This is not a case as simple as the one where a man with a bicycle or a car or a stock certificate or even a log cabin asserts the right to sell it to whomsoever he pleases, excluding all others whether they be Negro, Chinese, Japanese, Russians, Catholics, Baptists, or those with blue eyes. We deal here with a problem in the realm of zoning, similar to the one we had in Shelley v. Kraemer, 334 U.S. 1, where we struck down restrictive covenants.

. . . .

Since the real estate brokerage business is one that can be and is state regulated and since it is state licensed, it must be dedicated, like the telephone companies and the carriers and the hotels and motels to the requirements of service to all without discrimination—a standard that in its modern setting is conditioned by the demands of the Equal Protection Clause of the Fourteenth Amendment.

. . . .

Mr. Justice Harlan, whom Mr. Justice Black, Mr. Justice Clark, and Mr. Justice Stewart join, dissenting.

I consider that this decision, which cuts deeply into state political processes, is supported neither by anything "found" by the Supreme Court of California nor by any of our past cases decided under the Fourteenth Amendment. In my view today's holding, salutary as its result may appear at first blush, may in the long run actually serve to handicap progress in the extremely difficult field of racial concerns. I must respectfully dissent. . . . .

. . . .

In the case at hand California, acting through the initiative and referendum, has decided to remain "neutral" in the realm of private discrimination affecting the sale or rental of private residential property; in such transactions private owners are now free to act in a discriminatory manner previously forbidden to them. In short, all that has happened is that California has effected a *pro tanto* repeal of its prior statutes forbidding private discrimination. This runs no more afoul of the Fourteenth Amendment than would have California's failure to pass any such antidiscrimination statutes in the first instance. The fact that such repeal was also accompanied by a constitutional prohibition against future enactment of such laws by the California Legislature cannot well be thought to affect, from a federal constitutional standpoint, the validity of what California has done. The Fourteenth Amendment does not reach such state constitutional action any more than it does a simple legislative repeal of legislation forbidding private discrimination.

. . . .

I.

The Court attempts to fit § 26 within the coverage of the Equal Protection Clause by characterizing it as in effect an affirmative call to residents of California to discriminate. The main difficulty with this viewpoint is that it depends upon a characterization of § 26 that cannot fairly be made. The provision is neutral on its face, and it is only by in effect asserting that this requirement of passive official neutrality is camouflage that the Court is able to reach its conclusion. In depicting the provision as tantamount to active state encouragement of discrimination the Court essentially relies on the fact that the California Supreme Court so concluded. It is said that the findings of the highest court of California as to the meaning and impact of the enactment are entitled to great weight. I agree, of course, that *findings of fact* by a state court should be given great weight, but this familiar proposition hardly aids the Court's holding in this case. . . .

. . . Put in another way, I cannot transform the California court's conclusion of law into a finding of fact that the State through the adoption of § 26 is actively promoting racial discrimination. It seems to me manifest that the state court decision rested entirely on what that court conceived to be the compulsion of the Fourteenth Amendment, not on any fact-finding by the state courts.

II.

There is no question that the adoption of § 26, repealing the former state antidiscrimination laws and prohibiting the enactment of such state laws in the future, constituted "state action" within the meaning of the Fourteenth Amendment. The only issue is whether this provision impermissibly deprives any person of equal protection of the laws. . . .

. . . .

A moment of thought will reveal the far-reaching possibilities of the Court's new doctrine, which I am sure the Court does not intend. Every act of private discrimination is either forbidden by state law or permitted by it. There can be little doubt that such permissiveness—whether by express constitutional or statutory provision, or implicit in the common law—to some extent "encourages" those who wish to discriminate to do so. Under this theory "state action" in the form of laws that do nothing more than passively permit private discrimination could be said to tinge *all* private discrimination with the taint of unconstitutional state encouragement.

. . . I believe the state action required to bring the Fourteenth Amendment into operation must be affirmative and purposeful, actively fostering discrimination. Only in such a case is ostensibly "private" action more properly labeled "official." I do not believe that the mere enactment of § 26, on the showing made here, falls within this class of cases.

III.

I think that this decision is not only constitutionally unsound, but in its practical potentialities short-sighted. Opponents of state antidiscrimination statutes are now in a position to argue that such legislation should be defeated because, if enacted, it may be unrepealable. More fundamentally, the doctrine underlying this decision may hamper, if not preclude, attempts to deal with the delicate and troublesome problems of race relations through the legislative process. . . .[a]

_____

PRECURSORS AND SUCCESSORS TO REITMAN v. MULKEY

The theory of Reitman v. Mulkey had been anticipated in two individual concurring opinions in significant state action cases. In Burton v. Wilmington Parking Auth., supra p. 983, Justice Stewart concurred because the Delaware Supreme Court had relied on a statute which authorized restaurant proprietors to refuse to serve persons whose presence would be offensive to a majority of customers. Justice Harlan's dissent in the same case conceded that if the Delaware court had construed the statute to authorize discriminatory classification based exclusively on race, he would "certainly agree" that the statute violated the Fourteenth Amendment. In Evans v. Newton, supra p. 969, Justice White's concurrence was premised on a Georgia statute which had been enacted in 1905, six years before Senator Bacon's will was executed. That statute explicitly authorized charitable trusts for public parks for the use of one race. While the statute did not compel trust settlors to discriminate, "if the validity of the racial condition in Senator Bacon's trust would have been in doubt but for the 1904 statute and if the statute removed such doubt only for racial restrictions, leaving the validity of nonracial restrictions still in question . . . .

a For discussion of the issues in Reitman v. Mulkey, see Black, *"State Action," Equal Protection, and California's Proposition 14,* 81 Harv.L.Rev. 69 (1967); Note, *The Unconstitutionality of Proposition 14,* 19 Stan.L.Rev. 232 (1966); Comments, 14 U.C.L.A.L.Rev. 1 (1966).

such a statute would depart from a policy of strict neutrality in matters of private discrimination.   . . . "

Is the disagreement between the majority and dissenting opinions in Reitman v. Mulkey applicable to those cases where a statute validating private conduct uses an express racial classification?   In Hunter v. Erickson, 393 U.S. 385 (1969), the Court held invalid a city charter provision which prevented the city council from implementing any ordinance dealing with racial, religious, or ancestral discrimination in housing without the approval of the majority of the city voters.   Justices Harlan and Stewart concurred, noting that since the challenged provision was discriminatory on its face, it bore a far heavier burden of justification than was required in *Reitman*.   Justice Black was the sole dissenter.

Justice Black, however, wrote the Court's opinion in James v. Valtierra, 402 U.S. 137 (1971), which upheld a provision of the California constitution requiring a referendum for publicly supported low-rent housing projects, because "California's entire history demonstrates the repeated use of referendums to give citizens a voice on questions of public policy."   Three Justices dissented, arguing that the challenged provision rested on the explicit suspect classification of poverty.   Without challenging the dissent's argument that explicit de jure classifications based on wealth were suspect, the Court concluded that the challenged provision could be invalidated only by extending the rationale of *Hunter* beyond cases where racial classifications were used, "and this we decline to do."

The Court relied on Hunter v. Erickson in Washington v. Seattle Sch. Dist. No. 1, 458 U.S. 457 (1982).   A voter initiative of the State of Washington was passed shortly after Seattle adopted a mandatory busing program to achieve desegregation.   The initiative's terms prohibited local school boards from requiring students to attend schools other than those nearest the students' homes.   The provision also barred seven methods of "indirect student assignment" by school boards, including the redefinition of attendance zones, pairing of schools, and the use of feeder schools.   The initiative permitted assignment of pupils to distant schools for purposes of special education, because of health or safety hazards, or physical barriers or obstacles between residence and school, or if the nearest school was overcrowded or lacked physical facilities.   Finally, the initiative expressly permitted busing for racial balance if ordered by a court of competent jurisdiction "adjudicating constitutional issues."   Holding the initiative unconstitutional, Justice Blackmun's opinion for the Court summarized the principle of Hunter v. Erickson as follows:

.   .   .   "As Justice Harlan noted while concurring in the Court's opinion in *Hunter,* laws structuring political institutions or allocating political power according to 'neutral principles'—such as the executive veto, or the typically burdensome requirements for amending state constitutions—are not subject to equal protection attack, though they may 'make it more difficult for minorities to achieve favorable legislation.' 393 U.S., at 394.   Because such laws make it more difficult for *every* group in the community to enact comparable laws, they 'provid[e] a just framework within which the diverse political groups in our society may fairly compete.' Id., at 393.   Thus, the political majority may generally restructure the political process to place obstacles in the path of everyone seeking to secure the benefits of governmental action.   But a different analysis is required when the State allocates governmental power non-neutrally, by explicitly using the *racial* nature of a decision to determine the decisionmaking process.   State action of this kind, the Court said, 'places *special* burdens on racial minorities within the governmental process,' id., at 391 (emphasis added), thereby 'making it *more* difficult for certain racial and religious minorities [than for other members of the community] to achieve legislation that is in their interest.' Id., at 395 (emphasis added) (Harlan, J., concurring).   Such a structuring of the political process, the Court said, was 'no more permissible than [is] denying [members of a racial minority] the vote, on an equal basis with others.' Id., at 391."

In this case, the initiative dealt only with desegregation of public schools, which "at bottom inures primarily to the benefit of the minority." And, by placing the power over desegregation at the state level, the initiative restructured the State's political process on the basis of a classification that differentiated between "racial matters and . . . other problems in the same area." Finally, the Court held that no inquiry was required into the question whether there was an "intent" to discriminate, under the doctrine of Washington v. Davis, 426 U.S. 229 (1976).   When "racially conscious" political decisionmaking "is singled out for peculiar and disadvantageous treatment, the government action plainly rests on distinctions based on race." Justice Powell, joined by Chief Justice Burger, Justice Rehnquist, and Justice O'Connor, dissented. Justice Powell argued that "racial minorities are not uniquely or comparatively burdened by the State's adoption of a policy that would be lawful if adopted by any School District in the State. . . .   The Constitution does not dictate to the States at what level of government decisions affecting the public schools must be taken."

Compare the decision in Crawford v. Los Angeles Board of Education, 458 U.S. 527 (1982).   California courts had required mandatory busing in the Los Angeles school district, interpreting the California Constitution to require alleviation of de facto, as well as de jure, school segregation.   An initiative amended the California Constitution to forbid California courts to order busing unless required by the United States Constitution.   The Court held that the initiative was constitutional. Justice Powell's opinion for the Court explained that the initiative employed no racial classification, and no discriminatory purpose had been shown.   "[T]he simple repeal or modification of desegregation or anti-discrimination laws, without more, never has been viewed as embodying a presumptively invalid racial classification." Justice Blackmun, concurring, argued that Washington v. Seattle Sch. Dist. No. 1 differed from *Crawford* because "the people of California—the same entity that put in place the State Constitution, and created the enforceable obligation to desegregate— have made the desegregation obligation judicially unenforceable." Justice Marshall dissented, stating: "I fail to see how a fundamental redefinition of the governmental decisionmaking structure with respect to the same racial issue can be unconstitutional when the State seeks to remove the authority from local school boards, yet constitutional when the State attempts to achieve the same result by limiting the power of its courts."

SECTION 3.   FEDERAL CIVIL RIGHTS LEGISLATION

―――

A. THE RECONSTRUCTION LEGACY

From 1866 to 1875 Congressional leaders attached great importance to national legislation in aid of civil rights.   State action which violated the new constitutional rights of freedmen could be resisted in court; but this means of vindicating constitutional guaranties depended on successful litigation by ex- slaves, and carried no sanction to deter unconstitutional action in those cases where private litigation could not succeed.   Hence Congress added the possibil- ity of federal criminal prosecution, directed not only against state officials but also against private individuals who interfered with the liberty of the new freedmen.

Only the following fragments remain.

REMAINING RECONSTRUCTION—ERA FEDERAL CIVIL RIGHTS STATUTES

1. Criminal Provisions:

18 U.S.C. § 241.[1] *"Conspiracy Against Rights of Citizens.* If two or more persons conspire to injure, oppress, threaten, or intimidate any citizen in the free exercise or enjoyment of any right or privilege secured to him by the Constitution or laws of the United States, or because of his having so exercised the same; or

"If two or more persons go in disguise on the highway, or on the premises of another, with intent to prevent or hinder his free exercise or enjoyment of any right or privilege so secured—

"They shall be fined not more than $10,000 or imprisoned not more than ten years, or both; and if death results, they shall be subject to imprisonment for any term of years or for life."

18 U.S.C. § 242.[2] *"Deprivation of Rights under Color of Law.* Whoever, under color of any law, statute, ordinance, regulation, or custom, willfully subjects any inhabitant of any State, Territory, or District to the deprivation of any rights, privileges, or immunities secured or protected by the Constitution or laws of the United States, or to different punishments, pains, or penalties, on account of such inhabitant being an alien, or by reason of his color, or race, than are prescribed for the punishment of citizens, shall be fined not more than $1,000 or imprisoned not more than one year, or both; and if death results shall be subject to imprisonment for any term of years or for life."

2. Civil Provisions:

42 U.S.C. § 1981.[3] *"Equal Rights under the Law.* All persons within the jurisdiction of the United States shall have the same right in every State and Territory to make and enforce contracts, to sue, be parties, give evidence, and to the full and equal benefit of all laws and proceedings for the security of persons and property as is enjoyed by white citizens, and shall be subject to like punishment, pains, penalties, taxes, licenses, and exactions of every kind, and to no other."

42 U.S.C. § 1982.[4] *"Property Rights of Citizens.* All citizens of the United States shall have the same right, in every State and Territory, as is enjoyed by white citizens thereof to inherit, purchase, lease, sell, hold, and convey real and personal property."

42 U.S.C. § 1983.[5] *"Civil Action for Deprivation of Rights.* Every person who, under color of any statute, ordinance, regulation, custom, or usage, of any State or Territory or the District of Columbia, subjects, or causes to be subjected, any citizen of the United States or other persons within the jurisdiction thereof to the deprivation of any rights, privileges or immunities secured by the Constitution and laws, shall be liable to the person injured in an action of law, suit in equity, or other proper proceedings for redress.   . . ."

---

[1] From § 6 of the 1870 Act.

[2] From § 2 of the 1866 Act, as amended by § 17 of the 1870 Act.

[3] From the 1866 and 1870 Acts.

[4] From the 1866 Act.

[5] From § 1 of the 1871 Act.

42 U.S.C. § 1985.[6] *"Conspiracy to Interfere with Civil Rights.* (1) [Conspiracies to prevent federal officers from performing duties] . . .. (2) [Obstructing justice] . . .. (3) If two or more persons in any State or Territory conspire or go in disguise on the highway or on the premises of another, for the purpose of depriving . . . any person or class of persons of the equal protection of the laws, or of equal privileges and immunities under the laws; or for the purpose of preventing or hindering the constituted authorities of any State or Territory from giving or securing to all persons within such State or Territory the equal protection of the laws . . . the party so injured or deprived may have an action for the recovery of damages, occasioned by such injury or deprivation, against any one or more of the conspirators."[7]

ENFORCING AND INTERPRETING THE CIVIL RIGHTS STATUTES

Sections 4 and 5 of this chapter will focus on issues of interpretation of these Reconstruction statutes that are relevant to issues of the scope of Congressional power to protect civil rights against the conduct of private individuals. These represent, however, only a fraction of the issues surrounding contemporary application of these statutes.

The civil rights acts were enforced vigorously during Reconstruction. In the peak year of 1873 there were 1271 prosecutions under their criminal provisions in Southern federal courts. Even before the decision in the Civil Rights Cases, the end of Reconstruction and the withdrawal of federal troops marked a significant change in enforcement. In 1878, there were 25 criminal cases. The change in national mood was reflected both in Congress and the Supreme Court. The last of the federal civil rights laws was enacted in 1875, and Congress retired from the scene for more than three quarters of a century. One year later the Court decided in United States v. Cruikshank, 92 U.S. 542 (1876), that an indictment against members of a lynch mob accused of killing two Blacks failed to state an offense under the 1870 Act. Other provisions of the civil rights acts were invalidated prior to the decision in the Civil Rights Cases. United States v. Reese, 92 U.S. 214 (1876), held provisions of the 1870 Act dealing with voting rights invalid because they were not limited to interference with voting on account of race, color or previous condition of servitude. United States v. Harris, 106 U.S. 629 (1883), invalidated the antilynching provisions of the 1871 Act, holding that Congress lacked power to punish private persons who removed Black prisoners from state custody and abused or killed them.

The decision in the Civil Rights Cases was followed by later decisions curtailing the power of the federal government to protect Blacks from private violence. For example, Hodges v. United States, 203 U.S. 1 (1906), held that Congress lacked power to protect Blacks from private violence that interfered with their employment. From 1909 to 1939, the criminal provisions of the federal civil rights acts lay dormant until Attorney General Frank Murphy established a Civil Rights Section in the Department of Justice.

One target of prosecution was unlawful violence against prisoners and arrestees. In those prosecutions under the predecessor of 18 U.S.C. § 242, two problems arose. First, it was contended that the lawless and unauthorized conduct of the police was not "under color of . . . law"; second, it was

-----

[6] From the 1871 Act.

[7] Other surviving sections from this period include 42 U.S.C. § 1986 (related to § 1985), the antipeonage legislation found in 18 U.S.C. § 1581 and 42 U.S.C. § 1994, and 28 U.S.C. § 1343 (the jurisdictional provision for deprivation of federal constitutional and civil rights).

claimed that the uncertain contours of constitutional rights rendered the criminal punishment of state officials for violating those rights unconstitutionally vague. Screws v. United States, 325 U.S. 91 (1945), held that state officials who wielded state power acted under color of law whether or not their conduct was illegal under state law. The problem of vagueness was addressed by requiring that the federal constitutional rights denied by the defendant be specifically defined by prior law or court decisions, and that the defendant be proved to have acted "wilfully" with specific intent to deprive the victim of those rights.

Vigorous enforcement of the criminal provisions of the remaining fragments of Reconstruction civil rights acts also led to rediscovery of their civil provisions. 42 U.S.C. § 1983 has become the primary vehicle for litigation requiring state officials to obey the commands of federal constitutional or statutory law. (See Chapter 3, pages 64–65.) Problems of interpretation have been numerous, particularly where the complaint under § 1983 seeks the award of damages. In Monroe v. Pape, 365 U.S. 167 (1961), the Court held that damages were available under § 1983 against police officers who engaged in an unlawful search and seizure. The Court adopted the definition of "color of law" from Screws v. United States, supra, but held the requirement of that case, that the defendant act "wilfully," inapplicable since § 1983 provided a civil remedy and was not a criminal statute. Thus, damages could be awarded although the constitutional right denied was not specifically defined and the defendant did not act with specific intent to deny that right.

The potential for damage awards against legislators who enacted laws later determined to be unconstitutional, judges who applied those laws, and state prosecutors who enforced them, has led to an elaborate body of judicially developed immunities from liability for damages under § 1983. A recent example of a controversial decision concerning the scope of the immunity from damage awards is Stump v. Sparkman, 435 U.S. 349 (1978), where a divided Court held that a judge was not liable for ordering the involuntary sterilization of a minor despite the "clear absence of all jurisdiction." In addition, individual defendants not entitled to absolute immunity have been allowed the defense that their action was taken in "good faith." In Wood v. Strickland, 420 U.S. 308 (1975), the Court divided 5–4 on the definition of good faith in a suit against school officials who expelled students without an adequate hearing. The potential for damage liability may also have resulted, in some cases, in a narrow definition of constitutional rights.

Section 1983 provides no basis for an action against state governments as such. Quern v. Jordan, 440 U.S. 332, 341 (1979). Monroe v. Pape, supra, had also held that local governments were not subject to suit under § 1983. That aspect of *Monroe* was overruled in Monell v. New York City Dept. of Social Services, 436 U.S. 658 (1978). Municipalities are not liable under *Monell*, however, on a respondeat superior theory for acts of their employees. Municipal liability for damages is limited to the denial of federal rights by "official policy." On the other hand, municipalities are not entitled to defend a 1983 action based on the good faith of their officials. Owen v. City of Independence, 445 U.S. 622 (1980).

B. CONTEMPORARY FEDERAL CIVIL RIGHTS LEGISLATION

The Civil Rights Acts of 1957 and 1960. The 1957 Act (71 Stat. 634) was the first to be adopted since Reconstruction. It established the Commission on Civil Rights and the Civil Rights Division in the Department of Justice. Its primary thrust was towards giving greater protection to voting rights by authorizing the Attorney General to bring suits for injunctions as well as criminal prosecutions. The primary focus of the 1960 (74 Stat. 86) act was also on voting, providing for the appointment of federal voting referees and federal registration to protect the right to vote where the courts found a pattern or practice of discrimination. It also added a provision penalizing obstruction of court orders, and others penalizing interstate transportation of explosives with the knowledge that they will be used to damage certain buildings. There was a penalty also for interstate travel to avoid state prosecution for damaging or destroying structures by fire or explosive.

The Civil Rights Act of 1964. The most comprehensive of contemporary federal civil rights laws is the Civil Rights Act of 1964 (78 Stat. 241). Title I on Voting Rights (42 U.S.C. § 1971), *inter alia,* limited the types of literacy tests that could be used as a qualification for voting in Federal elections. Title II on Discrimination in Places of Public Accommodation (42 U.S.C. § 2000a) sets forth elaborate provisions for injunctive relief against racial discrimination by hotels, restaurants, theatres and similar establishments. The scope and constitutional support for these provisions have already been examined in Chapter 4. Katzenbach v. McClung, 379 U.S. 294 (1964), page 214, supra.[1] Title III authorizes civil actions by the Attorney General against discrimination in public facilities; Title IV (*inter alia*) authorizes similar remedial action by the Attorney General against continued discrimination in public education (42 U.S.C. §§ 2000b–2000c). Title V added to the provisions governing the Commission on Civil Rights (42 U.S.C. § 1975a). Title VI prohibits "discrimination under any program or activity receiving Federal financial assistance" (42 U.S.C. § 2000d)—a provision of sweeping potential in view of the widespread dependence on federal spending.[2]

Title VII on Equal Employment Opportunity provided for an Equal Employment Opportunity Commission with power to institute proceedings for "conference, conciliation, and persuasion" that might eventually lead to a civil action by an aggrieved person; the Attorney General was given leave to intervene in a case that he certifies is of "general public importance". (42 U.S.C. § 2000e).[3]

The Voting Rights Act of 1965 (as amended and extended in 1970, 1975, and 1982). The confrontation at the bridge in Selma, Alabama crystallized support that led to the Voting Rights Act of 1965 (79 Stat. 437, 42 U.S.C. § 1973). The central theory of the Act was to move beyond the case-by-case litigation strategy of prior legislation, which had accomplished little in enforcing the command of the Fifteenth Amendment. The Act made special provision for "covered jurisdictions"—states or political subdivisions that on November 1, 1964, had used literacy tests as a qualification for voting, and where less than half of the voting-age residents voted in the 1964 presidential election. Literacy tests were suspended in covered jurisdictions and the Attorney General could appoint federal voting registrars. Any electoral changes in covered jurisdictions were made inoperative, unless precleared by the Attorney General, on a finding that the changes would not perpetuate voting discrimination. The preclearance procedures were extended by the 1970, 1975, and 1982 Acts, the 1982 Act extending them for an additional 25 years. The 1982 Act also provided for judicial challenges to existing voting legislation and voting laws of non-covered jurisdictions, that had the effect of denying voting rights to racial minorities. (As to the last-mentioned provision, see p. 771, supra.)

---

[1] The cases working out the details of coverage of Title II are summarized and references to further studies are given in 2 Dorsen, Bender, Nevborne & Law, *Political and Civil Rights in the United States,* 1023–1049 (4th ed. 1979).

[2] See Dunn, *Title VI, The Guidelines, and School Desegregation in the South,* 53 Va.L.Rev. 42 (1967); Emerson, Haber & Dorsen, supra, at 590–600, 716–719, 1125–1126.

[3] See Symposium, 7 B.C.Ind. & Com.L.R. 413 (1966); Note, *Title VII, Seniority Discrimination and the Incumbent Negro,* 80 Harv.L.Rev. 1260 (1967); Emerson, Haber & Dorsen, supra, at 906. See also: Ross (ed.), *Employment, Race and Poverty* (1967).

The only provision of the 1965 Act dealing with literacy tests beyond those in covered jurisdictions was § 4(e)—not part of the original bill, but introduced from the floor. New York excused from its literacy test for voting persons who had completed six grades of schooling in the English language. The effect of § 4(e) was to require New York to exempt also those who had successfully completed six grades in a school in Puerto Rico, even though the language of instruction was Spanish.

The 1965 provisions suspending literacy tests in covered jurisdictions, and § 4(e), were made obsolete in the 1970 Act. Congress suspended literacy tests for voting nationwide for a period of five years. The suspension was made permanent in the 1975 Act. The 1970 Act also contained a significant provision going beyond racial discrimination in voting, lowering the minimum age for voters in state and federal elections to 18. That provision was superceded by the twenty-sixth amendment in 1971.

The Civil Rights Act of April 11, 1968. The assassination of Dr. Martin Luther King on April 4, 1968, released emotions and pressures that speeded the enactment on April 11, 1968, of a further Civil Rights Act (P.L. 90–284; 90th Cong., H.R. 2516). The most controversial subject reached by the 1968 Act was racial discrimination in housing. But this is only one part (Title VIII) of a complex piece of legislation embracing ten Titles.

Title I establishes heavy criminal penalties for the use of force or threats to interfere with "federally protected activities" (18 U.S.C. § 245). These protected activities, in general, are those activities that have been blocked or deterred by racial discrimination. Title I, in addition, imposes criminal penalties directed at persons inciting or participating in riots (18 U.S.C. §§ 2101–2102).

Title VIII (Secs. 801–819) prohibits discrimination "because of race, color, religion or national origin" in sales or rentals of housing. If measures for "conference, conciliation and persuasion" fail to produce voluntary compliance (or if proceedings under a local fair housing law are not carried forward, and there is no substantially equivalent remedy in the state courts) an aggrieved person may bring a civil action in a United States district court to obtain an injunction or affirmative relief (Sec. 810(d)). The Act also authorizes the Attorney General to sue for injunctive relief in certain circumstances. One of these is "a pattern or practice of resistance to the full enjoyment of any of the rights granted by this title"; another is the denial to any "group of persons" of the rights granted by the title if this "denial raises an issue of general public importance" (Sec. 813.)

SECTION 4. FEDERAL POWER TO REGULATE PRIVATE CONDUCT UNDER THE THIRTEENTH AMENDMENT

Introduction. It will be recalled that the decision in the Civil Rights Cases conceded that Congressional power to enforce the thirteenth amendment extended to private racial discrimination that could be described as a badge of slavery. Its narrow construction of that concept, however, led to a narrow definition of Congressional power under the thirteenth amendment to regulate private racial discrimination. The cases discussed in this section, all decided since 1968, raise two questions. First, under the modern decisions, are there any forms of private racial discrimination that are *not* within Congressional power to prohibit? Second, to the extent that the thirteenth amendment empowers Congress to prohibit private *racial* discrimination, would the thirteenth amendment power sustain prohibition of similar *non-racial* discrimination, such as discrimination based on national origin, religion, gender, age or physical handicap?

JONES v. ALFRED H. MAYER CO.

392 U.S. 409, 88 S.Ct. 2186, 20 L.Ed.2d 1189 (1968).

Mr. Justice Stewart delivered the opinion of the Court.

In this case we are called upon to determine the scope and the constitutionality of an Act of Congress, 42 U.S.C. § 1982, which provides that:

"All citizens of the United States shall have the same right, in every State and Territory, as is enjoyed by white citizens thereof to inherit, purchase, lease, sell, hold, and convey real and personal property."

On September 2, 1965, the petitioners filed a complaint in the District Court for the Eastern District of Missouri, alleging that the respondents had refused to sell them a home in the Paddock Woods community of St. Louis County for the sole reason that petitioner Joseph Lee Jones is a Negro. Relying in part upon § 1982, the petitioners sought injunctive and other relief. The District Court sustained the respondents' motion to dismiss the complaint, and the Court of Appeals for the Eighth Circuit affirmed, concluding that § 1982 applies only to state action and does not reach private refusals to sell. We granted certiorari to consider the questions thus presented. For the reasons that follow, we reverse the judgment of the Court of Appeals. We hold that § 1982 bars *all* racial discrimination, private as well as public, in the sale or rental of property, and that the statute, thus construed, is a valid exercise of the power of Congress to enforce the Thirteenth Amendment.

I.

At the outset, it is important to make clear precisely what this case does *not* involve. Whatever else it may be, 42 U.S.C. § 1982 is not a comprehensive open housing law. In sharp contrast to the Fair Housing Title (Title VIII) of the Civil Rights Act of 1968, Pub.L. 90–284, 82 Stat. 73, the statute in this case deals only with racial discrimination and does not address itself to discrimination on grounds of religion or national origin. It does not deal specifically with discrimination in the provision of services or facilities in connection with the sale or rental of a dwelling. It does not prohibit advertising or other representations that indicate discriminatory preferences. It does not refer explicitly to discrimination in financing arrangements or in the provision of brokerage services. It does not empower a federal administrative agency to assist aggrieved parties. It makes no provision for intervention by the Attorney General. And, although it can be enforced by injunction, it contains no provision expressly authorizing a federal court to order the payment of damages.

Thus, although § 1982 contains none of the exemptions that Congress included in the Civil Rights Act of 1968, it would be a serious mistake to suppose that § 1982 in any way diminishes the significance of the law recently enacted by Congress. . . .

. . . .

III.

We begin with the language of the statute itself. In plain and unambiguous terms, § 1982 grants to all citizens, without regard to race or color, "the same right" to purchase and lease property "as is enjoyed by white citizens." As the Court of Appeals in this case evidently recognized, that right can be impaired as effectively by "those who place property on the market" as by the State itself. For, even if the State and its agents lend no support to those who wish to exclude persons from their communities on racial grounds, the fact remains that, whenever property "is placed on the market for whites only, whites have a right denied to Negroes." So long as a Negro citizen who wants to buy or rent a home can be turned away simply because he is not white, he cannot be said to enjoy "the *same* right . . . as is enjoyed by white citizens . . . to . . . purchase [and] lease . . . real and personal property." 42 U.S.C. § 1982. (Emphasis added.)

On its face, therefore, § 1982 appears to prohibit *all* discrimination against Negroes in the sale or rental of property—discrimination by private owners as well as discrimination by public authorities. Indeed, even the respondents seem to concede that, if § 1982 "means what it says"—to use the words of the respondents' brief—then it must encompass every racially motivated refusal to sell or rent and cannot be confined to officially sanctioned segregation in housing. Stressing what they consider to be the revolutionary implications of so literal a reading of § 1982, the respondents argue that Congress cannot possibly have intended any such result. Our examination of the relevant history, however, persuades us that Congress meant exactly what it said.

. . .

V.

The remaining question is whether Congress has power under the Constitution to do what § 1982 purports to do: to prohibit all racial discrimination, private and public, in the sale and rental of property. Our starting point is the Thirteenth Amendment, for it was pursuant to that constitutional provision that Congress originally enacted what is now § 1982. . . .

As its text reveals, the Thirteenth Amendment "is not a mere prohibition of State laws establishing or upholding slavery, but an absolute declaration that slavery or involuntary servitude shall not exist in any part of the United States." Civil Rights Cases, 109 U.S. 3, 20. It has never been doubted, therefore, "that the power vested in Congress to enforce the article by appropriate legislation," ibid., includes the power to enact laws "direct and primary, operating upon the acts of individuals, whether sanctioned by State legislation or not." Id., at 23.

Thus, the fact that § 1982 operates upon the unofficial acts of private individuals, whether or not sanctioned by state law, presents no constitutional problem. If Congress has power under the Thirteenth Amendment to eradicate conditions that prevent Negroes from buying and renting property because of their race or color, then no federal statute calculated to achieve that objective can be thought to exceed the constitutional power of Congress simply because it reaches beyond state action to regulate the conduct of private individuals. The constitutional question in this case, therefore, comes to this: Does the authority of Congress to enforce the Thirteenth Amendment "by appropriate legislation" include the power to eliminate all racial barriers to the acquisition of real and personal property? We think the answer to that question is plainly yes.

"By its own unaided force and effect," the Thirteenth Amendment "abolished slavery, and established universal freedom." Civil Rights Cases, 109 U.S. 3, 20. Whether or not the Amendment *itself* did any more than that—a question not involved in this case—it is at least clear that the Enabling Clause of that Amendment empowered Congress to do much more. For that clause clothed "Congress with power to pass *all laws necessary and proper for abolishing all badges and incidents of slavery in the United States.*" Ibid. (Emphasis added.)

. . .

. . . Surely Congress has the power under the Thirteenth Amendment rationally to determine what are the badges and the incidents of slavery, and the authority to translate that determination into effective legislation. Nor can we say that the determination Congress has made is an irrational one. For this Court recognized long ago that, whatever else they may have encompassed, the badges and incidents of slavery—its "burdens and disabilities"—included restraints upon "those fundamental rights which are the essence of civil freedom, namely, the same right . . . to inherit, purchase, lease, sell and convey property, as is enjoyed by white citizens." Civil Rights Cases, 109 U.S. 3, 22. Just as the Black Codes, enacted after the Civil War to restrict the free exercise of those rights, were substitutes for the slave system, so the exclusion of Negroes from white communities became a substitute for the Black Codes. And when racial discrimination herds men into ghettos and makes their ability to buy property turn on the color of their skin, then it too is a relic of slavery.

Negro citizens North and South, who saw in the Thirteenth Amendment a promise of freedom—freedom to "go and come at pleasure" and to "buy and sell when they please"—would be left with "a mere paper guarantee" if Congress were powerless to assure that a dollar in the hands of a Negro will purchase the same thing as a dollar in the hands of a white man. At the very least, the freedom that Congress is empowered to secure under the Thirteenth Amendment includes the freedom to buy whatever a white man can buy, the right to live wherever a white man can live. If Congress cannot say that being a free man means at least this much, then the Thirteenth Amendment made a promise the Nation cannot keep.

Representative Wilson of Iowa was the floor manager in the House for the Civil Rights Act of 1866. In urging that Congress had ample authority to pass the pending bill, he recalled the celebrated words of Chief Justice Marshall in McCulloch v. Maryland, 4 Wheat. 316, 421:

> "Let the end be legitimate, let it be within the scope of the constitution, and all means which are appropriate, which are plainly adapted to that end, which are not prohibited, but consist with the letter and spirit of the constitution, are constitutional."

"The end is legitimate," the Congressman said, "because it is defined by the Constitution itself. The end is the maintenance of freedom . . .. A man who enjoys the civil rights mentioned in this bill cannot be reduced to slavery. . . . This settles the appropriateness of this measure, and that settles its constitutionality."

We agree. The judgment is reversed.

[Mr. Justice Douglas filed a concurring opinion.]

Mr. Justice Harlan, whom Mr. Justice White joins, dissenting.

The decision in this case appears to me to be most ill-considered and ill-advised.

. . .

For reasons which follow, I believe that the Court's construction of § 1982 as applying to purely private action is almost surely wrong, and at the least is open to serious doubt. The issue of the constitutionality of § 1982, as construed by the Court, and of liability under the Fourteenth Amendment alone, also present formidable difficulties. Moreover, the political processes of our own era have, since the date of oral argument in this case, given birth to a civil rights statute embodying "fair housing" provisions which would at the end of this year make available to others, though apparently not to the petitioners themselves, the type of relief which the petitioners now seek. It seems to me that this latter factor so diminishes the public importance of this case that by far the wisest course would be for this Court to refrain from decision and to dismiss the writ as improvidently granted.

. . .

Like the Court, I began analysis of § 1982 by examining its language. . . . The Court finds it "plain and unambiguous" that this language forbids purely private as well as state-authorized discrimination. With all respect, I do not find it so. For me, there is an inherent ambiguity in the term "right," as used in § 1982. The "right" referred to may either be a right to equal status under the law, in which case the statute operates only against state-sanctioned discrimination, or it may be an "absolute" right enforceable against private individuals. To me, the words of the statute, taken alone, suggest the former interpretation, not the latter.[9]

. . .

In sum, the most which can be said with assurance about the intended impact of the 1866 Civil Rights Act upon purely private discrimination is that the Act probably was envisioned by most members of Congress as prohibiting official, community-sanctioned discrimination in the South, engaged in pursuant to local "customs" which in the recent time of slavery probably were embodied in laws or regulations. Acts done under the color of such "customs" were, of course, said by the Court in the Civil Rights Cases . . . to constitute "state action" prohibited by the Fourteenth Amendment. . . . Adoption of a "state action" construction of the Civil Rights Act would therefore have the additional merit of bringing its interpretation into line with that of the Fourteenth Amendment, which this Court has consistently held to reach only "state action." This seems especially desirable in light of the wide agreement that a major purpose of the Fourteenth Amendment, at least in the minds of its congressional proponents, was to assure that the rights conferred by the then recently enacted Civil Rights Act could not be taken away by a subsequent Congress.

. . .

OTHER INTERPRETATIONS OF RECONSTRUCTION–ERA CIVIL RIGHTS LEGISLATION PREMISED ON THE THIRTEENTH AMENDMENT

Since the decision in Jones v. Alfred H. Mayer Co., the Court has interpreted or re-interpreted a number of Reconstruction-era federal civil rights laws. Consider the implications of these decisions on the issue of the scope of Congressional enforcement power under § 2 of the thirteenth amendment.

(1) Application of 42 U.S.C. §§ 1981 and 1982 to conduct of private parties. In addition to § 1982, involved in Jones v. Alfred H. Mayer Co., another fragment of § 1 of the Civil Rights Act of 1866 is § 1981, providing that "all persons within the jurisdiction of the United States" have the same right "as is enjoyed by white citizens," to "make and enforce contracts." The Court has reaffirmed that the right to purchase property under § 1982 is a prohibition of private discrimination, and has extended that rationale to the right to make and enforce contracts under § 1981. Runyon v. McCrary, 427 U.S. 160 (1976). In Runyon, however, four Justices stated that §§ 1981 and 1982 were originally intended only to guarantee all citizens the legal capacity to purchase property or make contracts. Two of those four Justices, however,

---

[9] . . . In the Civil Rights Cases, 109 U.S. 3, 3 S.Ct. 18, the Court said of identical language in the predecessor statute to § 1982:

"[C]ivil rights, such as are guaranteed by the constitution against state aggression, cannot be impaired by the wrongful acts of individuals, unsupported by state authority . . ... The wrongful act of an individual, unsupported by any such authority, is simply a private wrong, or a crime of that individual; an invasion of the rights of the injured party, it is true . . .; but if not sanctioned in some way by the state, or not done under State authority, his rights remain in full force, and may presumably be vindicated by resort to the laws of the State for redress. An individual cannot deprive a man of his right . . . to hold property, to buy and sell . . .; he may, by force or fraud, interfere with the enjoyment of the right in a particular case; . . . but, unless protected in these wrongful acts by some shield of state law or state authority, he cannot destroy or injure the right . . .." 109 U.S., at 17.

concluded that it was inappropriate to overrule the decision of Jones v. Alfred H. Mayer Co. on that point. Justice Stevens summarized his reasons as follows:

> "The policy of the Nation as formulated by the Congress in recent years has moved constantly in the direction of eliminating racial segregation in all sectors of society. This Court has given a sympathetic and liberal construction to such legislation. For the Court now to overrule *Jones* would be a significant step backwards, with effects that would not have arisen from a correct decision in the first instance. Such a step would be so clearly contrary to my understanding of the *mores* of today that I think the Court is entirely correct in adhering to *Jones*."

(2) **Application of § 1982 to "property."** In Sullivan v. Little Hunting Park, 396 U.S. 229 (1969), the Court held that § 1982 applied to refusal by a residents' association, running a community swimming pool, to approve assignment of a membership share from a white owner to a black tenant. Since the tenant paid part of his monthly rental for assignment of the membership share, refusal to approve the membership transfer was an interference with his right to "lease" the house. In City of Memphis v. Greene, 451 U.S. 100 (1980), however, the Court concluded that closing a street through a white residential community did not give rise to a cause of action, under § 1982, for black residents of a nearby predominantly black neighborhood. Plaintiffs' injury was not an impairment of their "property interests."

(3) **Application of § 1981 to discrimination in private employment and admission to private schools.** McDonald v. Santa Fe Trail Transportation Co., 427 U.S. 273 (1976), confirmed earlier decisions that the equal right to "make and enforce contracts" affords a remedy against discrimination in private employment on the basis of race. Runyon v. McCrary, supra, held that § 1981 reaches a private schools' racial discrimination in admission.

(4) **Redress of private racial violence under 42 U.S.C. § 1985(3).** This statute provides an action for damages for private conspiracies "for the purpose of depriving * * * any person or class of persons of the equal protection of the laws, or of equal privileges and immunities under the laws." Collins v. Hardyman, 341 U.S. 651 (1951), had held that this provision was applicable only to conspiracies under color of state law. Griffin v. Breckenridge, 403 U.S. 88 (1971), overruled Collins v. Hardyman on this point, holding that § 1985(3) applied to conspiratorial private violence based on "racial, or perhaps otherwise class-based, invidious discriminatory animus." The *Collins* decision had reasoned that narrow construction of the statute was necessary to avoid constitutional problems. As applied to private racial violence, the perceived constitutional problems "simply do not exist" because "Congress was wholly within its powers under § 2 of the Thirteenth Amendment in creating a statutory cause of action for Negro citizens who have been the victims of conspiratorial, racially discriminatory private action aimed at depriving them of the basic rights that the law secures to all free men."

(5) **Application of §§ 1981 and 1982 to situations exempted from modern federal civil rights statutes.** The Court's expansive interpretation of §§ 1981 and 1982 has extended these fragments of the Civil Rights Act of 1866 to areas of private racial discrimination that are the subject of modern federal civil rights acts, such as housing, employment, and public accommodations. As the Court notes in its opinion in Jones v. Alfred H. Mayer Co., for example, the prohibition of housing discrimination in § 1982 "contains none of the exemptions that Congress included in the Civil Rights Act of 1968." Consider, particularly, the exemption for the "private club or other [private] establishment" in the public accommodation provisions of the Civil Rights Act of 1964. If an institution that meets the definition of a "private club" excludes racial minorities from its dining facilities, its conduct is not prohibited by the

1964 Act. Is that conduct also beyond the reach of § 1981? The Court has not yet squarely faced the question of how far exemptions in modern civil rights statutes should be read as an "implied repeal" of the unqualified provisions of §§ 1981 and 1982. In Sullivan v. Little Hunting Park, supra, the Court concluded that the defendant residents' association was not a "private club," since its membership was open to all residents of the geographic area without exclusiveness other than race. And, in Runyon v. McCrary, supra, the private club exemption of the 1964 Act, applicable only to discrimination in public accommodations, was irrelevant to discrimination in admission to a private school.

(6) **Application of § 1981 to "private" associational or contractual relationships.** The broad definition of the right to be free from discrimination in making "contracts" has raised the concern that § 1981 will be applied to a variety of "private associational relationships" where persons are excluded on the ground of race. In Runyon v. McCrary, supra, the argument was made that § 1981, as applied to a private school's admissions policy, would violate "constitutionally protected rights of free association and privacy, or a parent's right to direct the education of his children." The Court did not resolve the question whether § 1981 should be interpreted as inapplicable to certain "private" relationships. It rejected the argument on the ground that the rights of parents to send children to private schools, and the rights of parents and schools to determine the content of instruction, did not confer a right on private schools to operate "unfettered by reasonable government regulations". (The Court's opinion stated that the case did not present the question of the right of a private social organization to limit its membership on racial grounds.)

Justices White and Rehnquist, dissenting, suggested that future cases would involve the issue of private associational rights.

"Imaginative judicial construction of the word 'contract' is foreseeable; Thirteenth Amendment limitations on Congress' power to ban 'badges and incidents of slavery' may be discovered; the doctrine of the right to association may be bent to cover a specific situation. In any event, courts will be called upon to balance sensitive policy considerations against each other—which considerations have never been addressed by any Congress—all under the guise of 'construing' a statute. This is a task appropriate for the Legislature, not for the Judiciary."

Concurring, Justice Powell saw fewer difficulties in identifying contracts beyond the reach of § 1981 because they were "so personal as to have a discernible rule of exclusivity which is inoffensive to § 1981."

"§ 1981, as interpreted by our prior decisions, does reach certain acts that are 'private' in the sense that they involve no *state* action. But choices, including those involved in entering into a contract, that are 'private' in the sense that they are not part of a commercial relationship offered generally or widely, and that reflect the selectivity exercised by an individual entering into a personal relationship, certainly were not intended to be restricted by the 19th Century Civil Rights Acts"

For a discussion of the range of possible constitutional issues that might arise in the application of §§ 1981 and 1982 to "private" associations, see the majority and concurring opinions in Roberts v. United States Jaycees, 104 S.Ct. 3244 (1984) (upholding application of state statute to prohibit refusal of Jaycees to admit women to membership), infra page 1280.

(7) **Application of § 1981 to discrimination against white persons.** In McDonald v. Santa Fe Trail Transportation Co., supra, the Court rejected an argument that § 1981 was inapplicable to private racial discrimination against white persons. The court conceded that the rejected argument was supported

by a "mechanical reading" of the language granting all persons the same rights "as is enjoyed by white citizens." The legislative history of the 1866 act, however, showed that it was not intended solely for the protection of nonwhites.

> "Rather, the Act was meant, by its broad terms, to proscribe discrimination in the making or enforcement of contracts against, or in favor of, any race. Unlikely as it might have appeared in 1866 that white citizens would encounter substantial racial discrimination of the sort proscribed under the Act, the statutory structure and legislative history persuades us that the Thirty-Ninth Congress was intent upon establishing in the federal law a broader principle than would have been necessary simply to meet the particular and immediate plight of the newly freed Negro slaves."

In a footnote, the Court stated that its decision was not addressed to "an affirmative action program . . . whether judicially required or otherwise prompted."

SECTION 5. FEDERAL POWER TO REGULATE PRIVATE CONDUCT UNDER THE FOURTEENTH AMENDMENT

CIVIL RIGHTS LEGISLATION AND THE COMMERCE AND SPENDING POWERS

Whatever the scope of Congressional power under the thirteenth amendment to prohibit private racial discrimination, current decisions have not addressed the question of the reach of that power to other forms of discrimination. While the equal protection component of the fourteenth amendment has been extended beyond issues of racial discrimination, there are still unanswered questions about the reach of the fourteenth amendment enforcement power as applied to private conduct. It may be asked, however, whether it will ever be necessary to resolve those questions to sustain Congressional legislation prohibiting private discrimination. Modern civil rights laws have often been based upon Congress' power to regulate the economy and to control the conduct of federal grantees, and not upon the enforcement powers under the Reconstruction Amendments. The public accommodation provisions of the 1964 Civil Rights Act were based squarely upon the commerce power, for example, and were sustained by the Court in Heart of Atlanta Motel v. United States, supra p. 211, and Katzenbach v. McClung, supra p. 214, on that basis. In United Brotherhood of Carpenters v. Scott, 463 U.S. 825 (1983), the Court held that a private conspiracy to infringe first amendment rights, not motivated by racial bias, was not a violation of 42 U.S.C. § 1985(3). The four dissenters (Justice Blackmun, joined by Justices Brennan, Marshall and O'Connor) interpreted 1985(3) to provide a cause of action for private conspiracies to interfere with First Amendment rights. Both the majority and the dissent stated that if 1985(3) were interpreted to reach private interference with first amendment rights, Congress would have power to ban such conspiracies under the commerce clause. Under those decisions, can you think of any case where it would be necessary to determine the reach of Congress' power under section 5 of the fourteenth amendment in order to define Congress' power to regulate private conduct? Consider, particularly, those cases in Section 2 of this Chapter that have found insufficient state action to subject private conduct to the provisions of section one of the fourteenth amendment. Would any of those situations be beyond Congressional regulatory power under the commerce clause?

PRIVILEGES OF NATIONAL CITIZENSHIP

Curiously, one long established source of federal power to control private conduct stems from the concept of privileges of national citizenship recognized by the Slaughter-House Cases, supra p. 483. The curiosity is that the only express constitutional recognition of privileges of national citizenship is contained in section one of the fourteenth amendment. Nevertheless, the rationale of the Civil Rights Cases—that since section one of the fourteenth amendment prohibited only state action the enforcement power under section five did not extend to private conduct—was never held applicable to Congressional legislation which protected privileges of national citizenship from private interference. That is because the Slaughterhouse Cases defined privileges of national citizenship as those "which owe their existence to the Federal government, its National character, its Constitution, or its laws." Under that definition, privileges of national citizenship did not "owe their existence" to their inclusion in the fourteenth amendment, and Congressional power to protect them stemmed from implied federal power that was not limited to the enforcement power under the fourteenth amendment.

The decision in the Slaughterhouse Cases doomed much of the Reconstruction legislation by its narrow interpretation of the privileges and immunities clause. But, within that narrow interpretation, portions of those laws that were directed at purely private conduct were upheld as applied, and those provisions have survived. In this connection, the provisions of 18 U.S.C. § 241, penalizing private conspiracies to injure "any citizen in the free exercise or enjoyment of any right or privilege secured to him by the Constitution or laws of the United States," and of 42 U.S.C. § 1985(3), providing a civil action for private conspiracies to deny any person "equal privileges or immunities under the law," continue to be relevant.

A list of the privileges of national citizenship is contained in Justice Moody's opinion in Twining v. New Jersey, 211 U.S. 78, 97 (1908). Dicta or holdings in prosecutions under § 241 have identified these privileges of national citizenship, with concomitant federal power to protect them from private conduct. In United States v. Cruikshank, 92 U.S. 542 (1876), the Court held that the general rights of speech and assembly were not within the privileges of national citizenship, but announced in dicta that there was a federal right to assemble to petition Congress for a redress of grievances. Ex parte Yarbrough, 110 U.S. 651 (1884), added the right to vote in federal elections. (A more modern case, United States v. Classic, 313 U.S. 299 [1941], extended the right to primary elections for federal officers.) Logan v. United States, 144 U.S. 263 (1892), sustained prosecution of members of a lynch mob conspiring to injure a prisoner in custody of a United States Marshal. (Compare the decision nine years earlier, United States v. Harris, 106 U.S. 629 [1883], which declared unconstitutional a provision of the 1875 Act as applied to a lynch mob killing a state prisoner.) In re Quarles, 158 U.S. 532 (1895) decided that one right of federal citizenship was the right to inform federal officials of a violation of federal law.

In more recent cases, the "right to pass freely from State to State," which appeared first in Justice Moody's list of national privileges in *Twining*, has been prominent. One aspect of the decision in United States v. Guest, 383 U.S. 745 (1966), sustained an indictment under § 241 that alleged that defendants conspired to intimidate "Negro citizens of the United States" in their right to "travel freely to and from the State of Georgia." (That case grew out of the murder of Lemuel Penn, a nationally prominent incident involving Southern violence by Whites against Blacks, in 1964. Other aspects of the *Guest* decision will be discussed in the two notes that follow this one.) The Court concluded that not only did Congress have power under the commerce clause to protect free interstate travel, but that the right was one of those privileges protected by § 241. The *Guest* holding was reaffirmed in Griffin v. Breckenridge, 403 U.S. 88 (1971), which held that a private conspiracy to prevent persons from traveling interstate was actionable under § 1985(3).

Whether § 241 is applicable to other yet undefined privileges beyond those discussed in the preceding paragraphs is doubtful. The Court's opinion in *Guest* noted that criminal prosecution under § 241 was permissible for a conspiracy to interfere with interstate travel only because the right had been specifically defined in previous cases, and a specific intent by defendants to interfere with that right must be proved. (See Screws v. United States, discussed supra, p. 1006.) Justice Brennan, in his separate opinion, noted that § 241 was not "model legislation," and that relying on courts to "determine on a case-by-case basis whether the right purportedly threatened is a federal right . . . brings § 241 close to the danger line of being void for vagueness." 18 U.S.C. § 245, enacted two years later as part of the 1968 Civil Rights Act, is more specific. Among the private violence and intimidation made criminal by that statute are intended interferences with participation in programs, facilities or activities provided or administered by the United States, with federal employment, with service as a federal juror, and with participation in programs receiving federal financial assistance. Section 245 also punishes private interference with voting or campaigning in *any* election. The concept of privileges of national citizenship would sustain that statute as applied to federal elections. What theory sustains its application to elections for state and local offices? (See the note on *Private Interference With Fourteenth Amendment Rights* below, p. 1018.)

DENIAL OF FOURTEENTH AMENDMENT RIGHTS UNDER COLOR OF LAW OR CUSTOM

Even under the narrowest interpretation of the Civil Rights Cases, federal legislation can reach private conduct interfering with fourteenth amendment rights when that conduct contains sufficient indicia of state action to be prohibited by section one of the fourteenth amendment. Two important fragments of Reconstruction legislation explicitly reach denial of constitutional rights under color of law or "custom." Criminal penalties are provided by 18 U.S.C. § 242, and a civil action by 42 U.S.C. § 1983.

The two leading cases construing these statutes both involved allegations of unlawful police conduct. In Screws v. United States, 325 U.S. 91 (1945), the indictment under § 242 alleged that Screws, who held a grudge against his Black victim and had threatened to "get" him, had beaten him to death after arresting him and bringing him to the courthouse square where the jail was located. Monroe v. Pape, 365 U.S. 167 (1961), was a civil action under § 1983, alleging that the defendant police illegally invaded the plaintiff's home and searched it. In both cases, the Court rejected arguments that the police did not act "under color of law" if their conduct violated state law.

United States v. Price, 383 U.S. 787 (1966), for example, grew out of the widely publicized murder of three civil rights workers, Chaney, Goodman and Schwerner, outside Philadelphia, Mississippi in 1964. The indictment alleged a conspiracy between three law enforcement officials and fifteen private individuals to deprive the victims of their fourteenth amendment rights not to be "punished" without due process of law. The lower court had dismissed the indictments against the private defendants on the ground that they had not acted under color of law. The Court reversed and reinstated the indictments, holding that private parties jointly engaged with state officials in prohibited action are acting under color of law within the meaning of § 242. More recently, in Lugar v. Edmondson Oil Co., 457 U.S. 922 (1982), the same rationale was applied to a creditor using unconstitutional judicial procedures to collect a private debt, because he "acted in joint participation with state officials in seizure of the disputed property."

In United States v. Guest, supra, the indictment charged that defendants conspired to deprive Blacks of fourteenth amendment rights by, among other things, causing their arrest by false reports that they had committed criminal acts. The indictment was held to be a sufficient allegation of state involvement which could be proved by showing active connivance of state agents in making of the false reports "or other conduct amounting to official discrimination." (The opinion, although ambiguous, can be read to conclude by implication that there would be no state action if the proof merely showed that private individuals had made the false reports, without any involvement by public officials, and public officials had acted on those reports in good faith. The Court did state, however, that the case did not require, in order to sustain the indictment, any "determination of the threshold level that state action must attain in order to create rights under the Equal Protection Clause.")

Adickes v. Kress & Co., 398 U.S. 144 (1970), was a civil action under 42 U.S.C. § 1983 by a white woman who had been refused service in a lunch counter that she entered in the company of Blacks. Plaintiff claimed that the defendant had refused her service pursuant to a "custom of the community to segregate the races in public eating places." The majority of the Court interpreted the statute as requiring a showing of "state involvement" and "not simply a practice that reflects longstanding social habits, generally observed by the people in a locality." Hence, the plaintiff was required to show that custom "have the force of law by virtue of persistent practices of state officials." Justice Douglas, dissenting, asserted that it should be sufficient for plaintiff to show a custom in the sense of "the unwritten commitment, stronger than ordinances, statutes and regulations, by which men live and arrange their lives." Justice Brennan's dissent said it "means custom of the people of a State, not custom of state officials."

In Lugar v. Edmondson Oil Co., supra, the Court concluded that the breadth of the state action concept under the fourteenth amendment, and the reach of the "color of state law" clause in 42 U.S.C. § 1983, were identical. Certainly, the cases that conclude that a defendant acted under color of law are premised on the conclusion that there was fourteenth amendment state action, and these cases provide additional insight into the concept of state action. It should follow, too, that cases concluding that the defendant did not act under color of law represent a conclusion that there was no state action under the fourteenth amendment. Are some of the latter group of cases, however, more easily explained by pragmatic concerns with the growing burden of federal court actions under § 1983 for the tortious conduct of state officials? (See page 1006, supra.) Consider, for example, Polk County v. Dodson, 454 U.S. 312 (1981), where the court held that a publicly-employed public defender was not acting under color of state law in representing an indigent defendant in a state criminal proceeding. Does it follow from the fact that the public defender's actions are constrained by a professional code of ethics that they are not those of the state, within the meaning of the fourteenth amendment?

PRIVATE INTERFERENCE WITH FOURTEENTH AMENDMENT RIGHTS

It is time to return, once more, to a basic conception of the Civil Rights Cases. It will be recalled that the Court reasoned that, because section one of the fourteenth amendment prohibited only discrimination by the state, Congress lacked power under section five to prohibit private discrimination in public accommodations. Would that still be true? Could Congress have passed Title II of the 1964 Act (public accommodations), Title VII of the 1964 Act (employment), and Title VIII of the 1968 Act (housing), under its power to enforce the fourteenth amendment's guarantee of equal protection of the laws? (Note that all three statutes reach beyond racial discrimination, unlike the public accommodations law invalidated in the Civil Rights Cases.) While six Justices in United States v. Guest, supra, agreed to an important dictum that section five of the fourteenth amendment empowers Congress to enact laws punishing private interference with fourteenth amendment rights, the answers to the questions posed are still not clear.

To understand the ambiguity, it is necessary to analyze the *Guest* decision in some detail. The indictment alleged that the defendants, all private individuals, had conspired to deny Blacks the right to "equal utilization, without discrimination upon the basis of race" of state owned facilities. The district court had dismissed the indictment on the ground that the criminal provisions of § 241, which contain no requirement that defendants act under color of law, were limited to privileges of national citizenship and did not reach fourteenth amendment rights. In the *Price* case, supra, decided the same day, the Court had held that conspiracies under color of law to deprive victims of fourteenth amendment rights were punishable under § 241. In *Guest*, a majority of the Court concluded that a conspiracy to deny victims' fourteenth amendment rights could not be prosecuted under § 241 in the absence of proof of state action. (As indicated in the previous note, dismissal of the indictment was reversed on the ground that the indictment could be read to allege state action.)

Justice Brennan, Chief Justice Warren and Justice Douglas dissented from the Court's conclusion that all conspiracies to deprive persons of fourteenth amendment rights were beyond the reach of § 241 unless state involvement in the conspiracy was proved. Justice Brennan concluded that Congress had the power to enact § 241, if it were construed to reach private conspiracies to deny fourteenth amendment rights, and criticized the Court's opinion as casting doubt on that Congressional power. That, in turn, led three members of the majority (Justices Clark, Black and Fortas) to write separately, stressing that the majority had merely construed the statute, and had decided no questions concerning the scope of Congress' power to "punish private conspiracies that interfere with fourteenth amendment rights, such as the right to utilize public facilities." They concluded summarily that there was "no doubt" that Congress had that power. Justice Brennan then responded that a majority of the Court had expressed the view that Congress could control private conduct interfering with the exercise of fourteenth amendment rights.[1]

It should be emphasized that the portion of the indictment at issue in *Guest* alleged that the private defendants had conspired to deny their victims equal access to state facilities. The focus of the constitutional discussion in Justice Brennan's dissent and Justice Clark's separate opinion was the power to reach that conduct. Justice Brennan's rationale was that, in order to protect the

---

[1] Justice Brennan was required to discuss the constitutional question by his interpretation of § 241. As Justice Harlan remarked in his separate opinion, it was "extraordinary" that three members of the majority, who were not required to reach the constitutional question "cursorily pronounc[ed] themselves on the far-reaching constitutional questions deliberately not reached." An explanation is that President Johnson had, earlier in 1966, called for new legislation protecting civil rights workers and others exercising federal rights from violence and intimidation. The specific shape that legislation would take was delayed, awaiting the Court's decisions in the *Price* and *Guest* cases. A month after the decisions, the President submitted specific proposals. While those proposals died in a Senate filibuster, they were included in President Johnson's proposed 1967 civil rights bill and, with substantial amendments, were enacted as 18 U.S.C. § 245 in 1968.

constitutional right to equal utilization of state facilities, it was appropriate for Congress to punish private individuals who made it impossible for their victims to exercise those rights. (Contrast that with the position of the Civil Rights Cases that individuals who made it impossible for others to exercise their rights had not deprived them of those rights, and that Congress could not reach that individual conduct.)

The rationale of the six Justices in *Guest* can easily be expanded to other cases where private individuals effectively destroy or interfere with their victims' rights against the state. Specific provisions of 18 U.S.C. § 245, enacted in 1968, provide criminal penalties for individuals who deny others "because of . . . race, color, religion or national origin" their rights to attend public schools, participate in programs provided or administered by the state, or serve as jurors in state courts. The theory would probably also support federal power, that had been denied in United States v. Harris, 106 U.S. 629 (1883), to punish members of a lynch mob who took a prisoner from state custody.

Would the theory be broad enough to reach private conduct that was unrelated to any relationship between the victim and the state? Would it permit Congress to punish private discrimination by owners of restaurants and hotels, employers, and landlords? Those are questions beyond the scope of the *Guest* opinions, and there are no decisions squarely in point. To answer the questions, it is necessary to consider further the Court's contemporary treatment of the enforcement powers under the Civil War Amendments. The cases in the next section of this chapter are concerned with Congressional power under the fourteenth and fifteenth amendments to protect the franchise against contrary state laws. They thus do not involve directly the question of the extent of Congressional power to control private conduct. The theories that are advanced and discussed should be considered, however, for the additional light they might throw on the questions raised in this note.

SECTION 6. THE SCOPE OF CONGRESSIONAL POWER TO REDEFINE THE AMENDMENTS

A. "REMEDIAL" POWER

CITY OF ROME v. UNITED STATES

446 U.S. 156, 100 S.Ct. 1548, 64 L.Ed.2d 119 (1980).

Mr. Justice Marshall delivered the opinion of the Court.

At issue in this case is the constitutionality of the Voting Rights Act of 1965 and its applicability to electoral changes and annexations made by the city of Rome, Ga.

I.

This is a declaratory judgment action brought by appellant city of Rome, a municipality in northwestern Georgia, under the Voting Rights Act of 1965, 42 U.S.C. § 1971 et seq. (1976). In 1970 the city had a population of 30,759, the racial composition of which was 76.6% white and 23.4% Negro. The voting-age population in 1970 was 79.4% white and 20.6% Negro.

The governmental structure of the city is established by a charter enacted in 1918 by the General Assembly of Georgia. Before the amendments at issue in this case, Rome's city charter provided for a nine-member city commission and a five-member board of education to be elected concurrently on an at-large basis by a plurality of the vote. The city was divided into nine wards, with one city commissioner from each ward to be chosen in the citywide election. There was no residency requirement for board of education candidates.

In 1966, the General Assembly of Georgia passed several laws of local application that extensively amended the electoral provisions of the city's charter. These enactments altered the Rome electoral scheme in the following ways:

(1) the number of wards was reduced from nine to three;

(2) each of the nine commissioners would henceforth be elected at-large to one of three numbered posts established within each ward;

(3) each commissioner would be elected by majority rather than plurality vote, and if no candidate for a particular position received a majority, a run-off election would be held between the two candidates who had received the largest number of votes;

(4) the terms of the three commissioners from each ward would be staggered;

(5) the board of education was expanded from five to six members;

(6) each board member would be elected at-large, by majority vote, for one of two numbered posts created in each of the three wards, with runoff procedures identical to those applicable to city commission elections;

(7) board members would be required to reside in the wards from which they were elected;

(8) the terms of the two members from each ward would be staggered.

Section 5 of the Voting Rights Act of 1965 requires preclearance by the Attorney General or the United States District Court for the District of Columbia of any change in a "standard, practice, or procedure with respect to voting," 42 U.S.C. § 1973c (1976), made after November 1, 1964, by jurisdictions that fall within the coverage formula set forth in § 4(b) of the Act, 42 U.S.C. § 1973b(b) (1976). In 1965, the Attorney General designated Georgia a covered jurisdiction under the Act, 30 Fed.Reg. 9897, and the municipalities of that State must therefore comply with the preclearance procedure, United States v. Board of Commissioners of Sheffield, Alabama, 435 U.S. 110 (1978).

. . .   The Attorney General declined to preclear the provisions for majority vote, numbered posts, and staggered terms for city commission and board of education elections, as well as the residency requirement for board elections. He concluded that in a city such as Rome, in which the population is predominately white and racial bloc voting has been common, these electoral changes would deprive Negro voters of the opportunity to elect a candidate of their choice. . . .

. . .

The city and two of its officials then filed this action, seeking relief from the Act based on a variety of claims. A three-judge court, convened pursuant to 42 U.S.C. §§ 1973b(a) and 1973c (1976), rejected the city's arguments and granted summary judgment for the defendants. 472 F.Supp. 221 (D.C.1979). We noted probable jurisdiction, . . .   and now affirm.

. . .

A.

The appellants contend that the city may exempt itself from the coverage of the Act. To evaluate this argument, we must examine the provisions of the Act in some detail.

Section 5 of the Act requires that a covered jurisdiction that wishes to enact any "standard, practice, or procedure with respect to voting different from that in force or effect on November 1, 1964," must seek preclearance from the Attorney General or the United States District Court for the District of Columbia. 42 U.S.C. § 1973c (1976). Section 4(a) of the Act, 42 U.S.C. § 1973b(a) (1976), provides that the preclearance requirement of § 5 is applicable to "any State" that the Attorney General has determined qualifies under the coverage formula of § 4(b), 42 U.S.C. § 1973b(b) (1973), and to "any political subdivision with respect to which such determinations have been made as a separate unit." As we have noted, the city of Rome comes within the preclearance requirement because it is a political unit in a covered jurisdiction, the State of Georgia. United States v. Board of Commissioners of Sheffield, Alabama, 435 U.S. 110 (1978).

Section 4(a) also provides, however, a procedure for exemption from the Act. This so-called "bail out" provision allows a covered jurisdiction to escape the preclearance requirement of § 5 by bringing a declaratory judgment action before a three-judge panel of the United States District Court for the District of Columbia and proving that no "test or device" has been used in the jurisdiction "during the seventeen years preceding the filing of the action for the purpose or with the effect of denying or abridging the right to vote on account of race or color." The District Court refused to allow the city to "bail out" of the Act's coverage, holding that the political units of a covered jurisdiction cannot independently bring a § 4(a) bailout action. We agree.

. . . Under the plain language of the statute, it appears that any bailout action to exempt the city must be filed by, and seek to exempt all of, the State of Georgia.

III.

The appellants raise five issues of law in support of their contention that the Act may not properly be applied to the electoral changes and annexations disapproved by the Attorney General.

A.

The District Court found that the disapproved electoral changes and annexations had not been made for any discriminatory purpose, but did have a discriminatory effect. The appellants argue that § 5 of the Act may not be read as prohibiting voting practices that have only a discriminatory effect. The appellants do not dispute that the plain language of § 5 commands that the Attorney General may clear a practice only if it "does not have the purpose *and* will not have the effect of denying or abridging the right to vote on account of race or color." 42 U.S.C. § 1973c (1976) (emphasis added). By describing the elements of discriminatory purpose and effect in the conjunctive, Congress plainly intended that a voting practice not be precleared unless *both* discriminatory purpose and effect are absent. . . .

The appellants urge that we abandon this settled interpretation because in their view § 5, to the extent that it prohibits voting changes that have only a discriminatory effect, is unconstitutional. Because the statutory meaning and congressional intent are plain, however, we are required to reject the appellants' suggestion that we engage in a saving construction and avoid the constitutional issues they raise. . . . Instead we now turn to their constitutional contentions.

B.

Congress passed the Act under the authority accorded it by the Fifteenth Amendment. The appellants contend that the Act is unconstitutional because it exceeds Congress' power to enforce that Amendment. They claim that § 1 of the Amendment prohibits only purposeful racial discrimination in voting, and that in enforcing that provision pursuant to § 2, Congress may not prohibit voting practices lacking discriminatory intent even if they are discriminatory in effect. We hold that, even if § 1 of the Amendment prohibits only purposeful discrimination, the prior decisions of this Court foreclose any argument that Congress may not, pursuant to § 2, outlaw voting practices that are discriminatory in effect.

The appellants are asking us to do nothing less than overrule our decision in South Carolina v. Katzenbach, 383 U.S. 301 (1966), in which we upheld the constitutionality of the Act. The Court in that case observed that, after making an extensive investigation, Congress had determined that its earlier attempts to remedy the "insidious and pervasive evil" of racial discrimination in voting had failed because of "unremitting and ingenious defiance of the Constitution" in some parts of this country. Id., at 309. Case-by-case adjudication had proved too ponderous a method to remedy voting discrimination, and, when it had produced favorable results, affected jurisdictions often "merely switched to discriminatory devices not covered by the federal decrees." Id., at 314. In response to its determination that "sterner and more elaborate measures" were necessary, id., at 309, Congress adopted the Act, a "complex scheme of stringent remedies aimed at areas where voting discrimination has been most flagrant," id., at 315.

The Court then turned to the question whether the Fifteenth Amendment empowered Congress to impose the rigors of the Act upon the covered jurisdictions. The Court examined the interplay between the judicial remedy created by § 1 of the Amendment and the legislative authority conferred by § 2:

> "By adding this authorization [in § 2], the Framers indicated that Congress was to be chiefly responsible for implementing the rights created by § 1. 'It is the power of Congress which has been enlarged. Congress is authorized to *enforce* the prohibitions by appropriate legislation. Some legislation is contemplated to make the [Civil War] amendments fully effective.' Ex parte Virginia, 100 U.S. 339, 345. Accordingly, in addition to the courts, Congress has full remedial powers to effectuate the constitutional prohibition against racial discrimination in voting." Id., at 325–326 (emphasis in original).

Congress' authority under § 2 of the Fifteenth Amendment, we held, was no less broad than its authority under the Necessary and Proper Clause, see McCulloch v. Maryland, 4 Wheat. 316, 421 (1819). This authority, as applied by longstanding precedent to congressional enforcement of the Civil War Amendments, is defined in these terms:

> " 'Whatever legislation is appropriate, that is, adapted to carry out the objects the [Civil War] amendments have in view, whatever tends to enforce submission to the prohibitions they contain, and to secure to all persons the enjoyment of perfect equality of civil rights and the equal protection of the laws against State denial or invasion, if not prohibited, is brought within the domain of congressional power.' Ex parte Virginia, 100 U.S. [339,] 345–346." South Carolina v. Katzenbach, supra, at 327.

Applying this standard, the Court held that the coverage formula of § 4(b), the ban on the use of literacy tests and related devices, the requirement that new voting rules must be precleared and must lack both discriminatory purpose and effect, and the use of federal examiners were all appropriate methods for Congress to use to enforce the Fifteenth Amendment. Id., at 329–337.

The Court's treatment in South Carolina v. Katzenbach of the Act's ban on literacy tests demonstrates that, under the Fifteenth Amendment, Congress may prohibit voting practices that have only a discriminatory effect. The Court had earlier held in Lassiter v. Northampton County Board of Elections, 360 U.S. 45 (1959), that the use of a literacy test that was fair on its face and was not employed in a discriminatory fashion did not violate § 1 of the Fifteenth Amendment. In upholding the Act's *per se* ban on such tests in South Carolina v. Katzenbach, the Court found no reason to overrule *Lassiter.* Instead, the Court recognized that the prohibition was an appropriate method of enforcing the Fifteenth Amendment because for many years most of the covered jurisdictions had imposed such tests to effect voting discrimination and the continued use of even nondiscriminatory, fairly administered literacy tests would "freeze the effect" of past discrimination by allowing white illiterates to remain on the voting rolls while excluding illiterate Negroes. South Carolina v. Katzenbach, supra, 383 U.S., at 334. This holding makes clear that Congress may, under the authority of § 2 of the Fifteenth Amendment, prohibit state action that, though in itself not violative of § 1, perpetuates the effects of past discrimination.

Other decisions of this Court also recognize Congress' broad power to enforce the Civil War Amendments. In Katzenbach v. Morgan, 384 U.S. 641 (1966), the Court held that legislation enacted under authority of § 5 of the Fourteenth Amendment would be upheld so long as the Court could find that the enactment " 'is plainly adapted to [the] end' " of enforcing the Equal Protection Clause and "is not prohibited by but is consistent with 'the letter and spirit of the constitution,' " regardless of whether the practices outlawed by Congress in themselves violated the Equal Protection Clause. Id., at 651 (quoting McCulloch v. Maryland, supra, at 421). The Court stated that, "[c]orrectly viewed, § 5 is a positive grant of legislative power authorizing Congress to exercise its discretion in determining whether and what legislation is needed to secure the guarantees of the Fourteenth Amendment." Ibid. Four years later, in Oregon v. Mitchell, 400 U.S. 112 (1970), the Court unanimously upheld a provision of the Voting Rights Act Amendments of 1970, Pub.L. No. 91–285, 84 Stat. 315, imposing a five-year nationwide ban on literacy tests and similar requirements for registering to vote in state and federal elections. The Court concluded that Congress could rationally have determined that these provisions were appropriate methods of attacking the perpetuation of earlier, purposeful racial discrimination, regardless of whether the practices they prohibited were discriminatory only in effect. See id., at 132–133 (opinion of Black, J.); id., at 144–147 (opinion of Douglas, J.); id., at 216–217 (opinion of Harlan, J.); id., at 231–236 (opinion of Brennan, White, and Marshall, JJ.); id., at 282–284 (opinion of Stewart, J., joined by The Chief Justice and Blackmun, J.).

It is clear, then, that under § 2 of the Fifteenth Amendment Congress may prohibit practices that in and of themselves do not violate § 1 of the Amendment, so long as the prohibitions attacking racial discrimination in voting are "appropriate," as that term is defined in McCulloch v. Maryland and Ex parte Virginia. In the present case, we hold that the Act's ban on electoral changes that are discriminatory in effect is an appropriate method of promoting the purposes of the Fifteenth Amendment, even if it is assumed that § 1 of the Amendment prohibits only intentional discrimination in voting. Congress could rationally have concluded that, because electoral changes by jurisdictions with a demonstrable history of intentional racial discrimination in voting create the risk of purposeful discrimination, it was proper to prohibit changes that have a discriminatory impact. See South Carolina v. Katzenbach, supra, at 335; Oregon v. Mitchell, supra, at 216 (opinion of Harlan, J.). We find no reason, then, to disturb Congress' considered judgment that banning electoral changes that have a discriminatory impact is an effective method of preventing States from "'undo[ing] or defeat[ing] the rights recently won' by Negroes." Beer v. United States, 425 U.S. 130, 140 (1976) (quoting H.R.Rep. No. 91–397, 91st Cong. 1st Sess., 8 (1969)).

C.

The appellants next assert that, even if the Fifteenth Amendment authorized Congress to enact the Voting Rights Act, that legislation violates principles of federalism articulated in National League of Cities v. Usery, 426 U.S. 833 (1976). This contention necessarily supposes that *National League of Cities* signifies a retreat from our decision in South Carolina v. Katzenbach, supra, where we rejected the argument that the Act "exceed[s] the powers of Congress and encroach[es] on an area reserved to the States by the Constitution," 383 U.S., at 323, and determined that, "[a]s against the reserved powers of the States, Congress may use any rational means to effectuate the constitutional prohibition of racial discrimination in voting," id., at 324. To the contrary, we find no inconsistency between these decisions.

In *National League of Cities,* the Court held that federal legislation regulating minimum wages and hours could not constitutionally be extended to employees of state and local governments. The Court determined that the Commerce Clause did not provide Congress the authority to enact legislation "directly displac[ing] the States' freedom to structure integral operations in areas of traditional governmental functions," 426 U.S., at 852, which, it held, included employer-employee relationships in programs traditionally conducted by States, id., at 851–852.

The decision in *National League of Cities* was based solely on an assessment of congressional power under the Commerce Clause, and we explicitly reserved the question "whether different results might obtain if Congress seeks to affect integral operations of State governments by exercising authority granted it under other sections of the Constitution such as . . . § 5 of the Fourteenth Amendment." Id., at 852, n. 17. The answer to this question came four days later in Fitzpatrick v. Bitzer, 427 U.S. 445 (1976). That case presented the issue whether, in spite of the Eleventh Amendment, Congress had the authority to bring the States as employers within the coverage of Title VII of the Civil Rights Act of 1964, 42 U.S.C. § 2000e et seq., and to provide that successful plaintiffs could recover retroactive monetary relief. The Court held that this extension of Title VII was an appropriate method of enforcing the Fourteenth Amendment. . . .

We agree with the court below that *Fitzpatrick* stands for the proposition that principles of federalism that might otherwise be an obstacle to congressional authority are necessarily overridden by the power to enforce the Civil War Amendments "by appropriate legislation." Those Amendments were specifically designed as an expansion of federal power and an intrusion on state sovereignty. Applying this principle, we hold that Congress had the authority to regulate state and local voting through the provisions of the Voting Rights Act. *National League of Cities,* then, provides no reason to depart from our decision in South Carolina v. Katzenbach that "the Fifteenth Amendment supersedes contrary exertions of state power," 383 U.S., at 325, and that the Act is "an appropriate means for carrying out Congress' constitutional responsibilities," id., at 308.

D.

The appellants contend in the alternative that even if the Act and its preclearance requirement were appropriate means of enforcing the Fifteenth Amendment in 1965, they had outlived their usefulness by 1975, when Congress extended the Act for another seven years. We decline this invitation to overrule Congress' judgment that the 1975 extension was warranted.

. . .

It must not be forgotten that in 1965, 95 *years* after ratification of the Fifteenth Amendment extended the right to vote to all citizens regardless of race or color, Congress found that racial discrimination in voting was an "insidious and pervasive evil which had been perpetuated in certain parts of our country through unremitting and ingenious defiance of the Constitution." South Carolina v. Katzenbach, supra, at 309. In adopting the Voting Rights Act, Congress sought to remedy this century of obstruction by shifting "the advantage of time and inertia from the perpetrators of the evil to its victims." Id., at 328. Ten years later, Congress found that a seven-year extension of the Act was necessary to preserve the "limited and fragile" achievements of the Act and to promote further amelioration of voting discrimination. When viewed in this light, Congress' considered determination that at least another seven years of statutory remedies were necessary to counter the perpetuation of 95 years of pervasive voting discrimination is both unsurprising and unassailable. The extension of the Act, then, was plainly a constitutional method of enforcing the Fifteenth Amendment.

. . .

Mr. Justice Stevens, concurring.

Although I join the Court's opinion, the dissenting opinions prompt me to emphasize two points that are crucial to my analysis of the case; both concern the statewide nature of the remedy Congress authorized when it enacted the Voting Rights Act of 1965. The critical questions are: (1) whether, as a statutory matter, Congress has prescribed a statewide remedy that denies local political units within a covered State the right to "bail out" separately; and (2) if so, whether, as a constitutional matter, such statewide relief exceeds the enforcement powers of Congress. If, as I believe, Congress could properly impose a statewide remedy and in fact did so in the Voting Rights Act, then the fact that the city of Rome has been innocent of any wrongdoing for the last 17 years is irrevelant; indeed, we may assume that there has never been any racial discrimination practiced in the city of Rome. If racially discriminatory voting practices elsewhere in the State of Georgia were sufficiently pervasive to justify the statewide remedy Congress prescribed, that remedy may be applied to each and every political unit within the State, including the city of Rome.

I.

. . .

. . . The political subdivisions of a covered State, while subject to § 5's preclearance requirements, are not entitled to bail out in a piecemeal fashion; rather, they can only be relieved of their preclearance obligations if the entire State meets the conditions for a bailout.

. . .

II.

The second question is whether Congress has the power to prescribe a statewide remedy for discriminatory voting practices if it does not allow political units that can prove themselves innocent of discrimination to bail out of the statute's coverage. In Part III–B of its opinion, the Court explains why Congress, under the authority of § 2 of the Fifteenth Amendment, may prohibit voting practices that have a discriminatory effect in instances in which there is ample proof of a longstanding tradition of purposeful discrimination. I think it is equally clear that remedies for discriminatory practices that were widespread within a State may be applied to every governmental unit within the State even though some of those local units may have never engaged in purposeful discrimination themselves.[5] In short, Congress has the constitutional power to regulate voting practices in Rome, so long as it has the power to regulate such practices in the entire State of Georgia. Since there is no claim that the entire State is entitled to relief from the federal restrictions, Rome's separate claim must fail.

I therefore join the Court's opinion.

Mr. Justice Powell dissenting.

Two years ago this Court held that the term "State" in § 4(a) of the Voting Rights Act includes all political subdivisions that control election processes, and that those subdivisions are subject to the requirement in § 5 of the Act that federal authorities preclear changes in voting procedures. United States v. Board of Commissioners of Sheffield, Alabama, 435 U.S. 110 (1978) (*Sheffield*). Today the Court concludes that those subdivisions are within the term "State" when it comes to an action to "bail out" from the preclearance requirement. Because this decision not only conflicts with *Sheffield* but also raises grave questions as to the constitutionality of the Act, I dissent.

. . . .

III.

There is, however, more involved here than incorrect construction of the statute. The Court's interpretation of § 4(a) renders the Voting Rights Act unconstitutional as applied to the city of Rome. The preclearance requirement both intrudes on the prerogatives of state and local governments and abridges the voting rights of all citizens in States covered under the Act. Under § 2 of the Fifteenth Amendment, Congress may impose such constitutional deprivations only if it is acting to remedy violations of voting rights. See South Carolina v. Katzenbach, 383 U.S. 301, 327–328 (1966); Katzenbach v. Morgan, 384 U.S. 641, 667 (1966) (Harlan, J., dissenting). In view of the District Court finding that Rome has not denied or abridged the voting rights of blacks, the Fifteenth Amendment provides no authority for continuing those deprivations until the entire State of Georgia satisfies the bailout standards of § 4(a).

When this Court first sustained the Voting Rights Act of 1965, it conceded that the legislation was "an uncommon exercise of congressional power." South Carolina v. Katzenbach, supra, 383 U.S., at 334. The Court recognized that preclearance under the Act implicates serious federalism concerns. Id., at 324–327. As Mr. Justice Stevens noted in *Sheffield,* the statute's "encroachment on state sovereignty is significant and undeniable." 435 U.S., at 141 (dissenting opinion). That encroachment is especially troubling because it destroys local control of the means of self-government, one of the central values of our polity. Unless the federal structure provides some protection for a community's ordering of its own democratic procedures, the right of each community to determine its own course within the boundaries marked by the Constitution is at risk. Preclearance also operates at an individual level to diminish the voting

---

[5] The same principle applies to a court's exercise of its remedial powers. . . . The Court has recently applied this principle to school desegregation cases, holding that a systemwide remedy—as opposed to a remedy concentrating on specific instances of discrimination—may be justified by a prior history of pervasive, systemwide discrimination. Columbus Bd. of Educ. v. Penick, 443 U.S. 449; Dayton Bd. of Educ. v. Brinkman, 443 U.S. 526.

rights of residents of covered areas. Federal review of local voting practices reduces the influence that citizens have over policies directly affecting them, and strips locally elected officials of their autonomy to chart policy.

The Court in South Carolina v. Katzenbach, supra, did not lightly approve these intrusions on federalism and individual rights. It upheld the imposition of preclearance as a prophylactic measure based on the remedial power of Congress to enforce the Fifteenth Amendment. . . .

The Court in South Carolina v. Katzenbach emphasized, however, that a government subjected to preclearance could be relieved of federal oversight if voting discrimination in fact did not continue or materialize during the prescribed period. . . . As long as the bailout option is available, there is less cause for concern that the Voting Rights Act may overreach congressional powers by imposing preclearance on a nondiscriminating government. Without bailout, the problem of constitutional authority for preclearance becomes acute.

IV.

If there were reason to believe that today's decision would protect the voting rights of minorities in any way, perhaps this case could be viewed as one where the Court's ends justify dubious analytical means. But the District Court found, and no one denies, that for at least 17 years there has been no voting discrimination by the city of Rome. Despite this record, the Court today continues federal rule over the most local decisions made by this small city in Georgia. Such an outcome must vitiate the incentive for any local government in a State covered by the Act to meet diligently the Act's requirements. Neither the Framers of the Fifteenth Amendment nor the Congress that enacted the Voting Rights Act could have intended that result.

Mr. Justice Rehnquist, with whom Mr. Justice Stewart joins, dissenting.

We have only today held that the city of Mobile does not violate the Constitution by maintaining an at-large system of electing city officials unless voters can prove that system is a product of purposeful discrimination. City of Mobile v. Bolden, 446 U.S. 55 (1980). This result is reached even though the black residents of Mobile have demonstrated that racial "bloc" voting has prevented them from electing a black representative to the city government. The Court correctly concluded that a city has no obligation under the Constitution to structure its representative system in a manner that maximizes the black community's ability to elect a black representative. Yet in the instant case, the city of Rome is prevented from instituting precisely the type of structural changes which the Court says Mobile may maintain consistently with the Civil War Amendments, so long as their purpose be legitimate, because Congress has prohibited these changes under the Voting Rights Act as an exercise of its "enforcement" power conferred by those Amendments.

It is not necessary to hold that Congress is limited to merely providing a forum in which aggrieved plaintiffs may assert rights under the Civil War Amendments in order to disagree with the Court's decision permitting Congress to strait-jacket the city of Rome in this manner. Under § 5 of the Fourteenth Amendment and § 2 of the Fifteenth Amendment, Congress is granted only the power to "enforce" by "appropriate" legislation the limitations on state action embodied in those Amendments. While the presumption of constitutionality is due to any act of a coordinate branch of the Federal Government or of one of the States, it is this Court which is ultimately responsible for deciding challenges to the exercise of power by those entities. Marbury v. Madison, 5 U.S. (1 Cranch) 137 (1803); United States v. Nixon, 418 U.S. 683 (1974). Today's decision is nothing less than a total abdication of that authority, rather than an exercise of the deference due to a coordinate branch of the government.

. . .

II.

The Court holds today that the city of Rome can constitutionally be compelled to seek congressional approval for most of its governmental changes even though it has not engaged in any discrimination against blacks for at least 17 years. Moreover, the Court also holds that federal approval can be constitutionally denied even after the city has proven that the changes are not purposefully discriminatory. While I agree with Mr. Justice Powell's conclusion that requiring localities to *submit* to preclearance is a significant intrusion on local autonomy, it is an even greater intrusion on that autonomy to *deny* preclearance sought.

. . . Section 2 of the Fifteenth Amendment and § 5 of the Fourteenth provide that Congress shall have the power to "enforce" § 1 "by appropriate legislation." Congressional power to prohibit the electoral changes proposed by Rome is dependent upon the scope and nature of that power. There are three theories of congressional enforcement power relevant to this case. First, it is clear that if the proposed changes would violate the Constitution, Congress could certainly prohibit their implementation. It has never been seriously maintained, however, that Congress can do no more than the judiciary to enforce the Amendments' commands. Thus, if the electoral changes in issue do not violate the Constitution, as judicially interpreted, it must be determined whether Congress could nevertheless appropriately prohibit these changes under the other two theories of congressional power. Under the second theory, Congress can act remedially to enforce the judicially established substantive prohibitions of the Amendments. If not properly remedial, the exercise of this power could be sustained only if this Court accepts the premise of the third theory that Congress has the authority under its enforcement powers to determine, without more, that electoral changes with a disparate impact on race violate the Constitution, in which case Congress by a legislative Act could effectively amend the Constitution.

I think it is apparent that neither of the first two theories for sustaining the exercise of congressional power support this application of the Voting Rights Act. After our decision in *City of Mobile* there is little doubt that Rome has not engaged in *constitutionally* prohibited conduct. I also do not believe that prohibition of these changes can genuinely be characterized as a remedial exercise of congressional enforcement powers. Thus, the result of the Court's holding is that Congress effectively has the power to determine for itself that this conduct violates the Constitution. This result violates previously well-established distinctions between the Judicial Branch and the Legislative or Executive Branches of the Federal Government. See United States v. Nixon, 418 U.S. 683 (1974), Marbury v. Madison, (1 Cranch) 137 (1803).

A.

If the enforcement power is construed as a "remedial" grant of authority, it is this Court's duty to ensure that a challenged congressional act does no more than "enforce" the limitations on state power established in the Fourteenth and Fifteenth Amendments. Marbury v. Madison. The Court has not resolved the question of whether it is an appropriate exercise of remedial power for Congress to prohibit local governments from instituting structural changes in their government, which although not racially motivated, will have the effect of decreasing the ability of a black voting bloc to elect a black candidate.

. . . .

The precedent on which the Court relies simply does not support its remedial characterization. Neither Oregon v. Mitchell, 400 U.S. 112 (1970), nor South Carolina v. Katzenbach, supra, legitimize the use of an irrebuttable presumption that "vote diluting" changes are motivated by a discriminatory animus. The principal electoral practice in issue in those cases was the use of literacy tests. . . .

The presumption that the literacy tests were either being used to purposefully discriminate, or that the disparate effects of those tests were attributable to discrimination in state-administered education was not very wide of the mark.
. . .

The nationwide ban was also found necessary to effectively remedy past constitutional violations. . . .

Presumptive prohibition of vote diluting procedures is not similarly an "appropriate" means of exacting state compliance with the Civil War Amendments. First, these prohibitions are quite unlike the literacy ban, where the disparate effects were traceable to the discrimination of governmental bodies in education even if their present desire to use the tests was legitimate. Any disparate impact associated with the nondiscriminatory electoral changes in issue here results from bloc voting—private rather than governmental discrimination.
. . .

It is also clear that while most States still utilizing literacy tests may have been doing so to discriminate, a similar generalization could not be made about all government structures which have some disparate impact on black voting strength. . . .

Nor does the prohibition of all practices with a disparate impact enhance congressional prevention of purposeful discrimination. The changes in issues are not, like literacy tests, though fair on their face, subject to discriminatory application by local authorities. See Yick Wo v. Hopkins, 118 U.S. 356 (1886). They are either discriminatory from the outset or not.

Finally, the advantages supporting the imposition of a nationwide ban are simply not implicated in this case. No added administrative burdens are in issue since Congress has provided the mechanism for preclearance suits in any event, and the burden of proof for this issue is on the locality. And it is certain that the only constitutional wrong implicated—purposeful dilution—can be effectively remedied by prohibiting it where it occurs. For all these reasons, I do not think that the present case is controlled by the result in *Oregon*. By prohibiting all electoral changes with a disparate impact, Congress has attempted to prevent disparate impacts—not purposeful discrimination.

Congress unquestionably has the power to prohibit and remedy state action which intentionally deprives citizens of Fourteenth and Fifteenth Amendment rights. But unless these powers are to be wholly uncanalized, it cannot be appropriate remedial legislation for Congress to prohibit Rome from structuring its government in the manner as its population sees fit absent a finding or unrebutted presumption that Rome has, or is, intentionally discriminating against its black citizens. Rome has simply committed no constitutional violations, as this Court has defined them.

. . .

FULLILOVE v. KLUTZNICK

448 U.S. 448, 100 S.Ct. 2758, 65 L.Ed.2d 902 (1980).

[The report in this case appears supra at p. 815.]

B. "INTERPRETIVE" POWER

KATZENBACH v. MORGAN

384 U.S. 641, 86 S.Ct. 1717, 16 L.Ed.2d 828 (1966).

Mr. Justice Brennan delivered the opinion of the court.

These cases concern the constitutionality of § 4(e) of the Voting Rights Act of 1965. That law, in the respects pertinent in these cases, provides that no person who has successfully completed the sixth primary grade in a public school in, or a private school accredited by, the Commonwealth of Puerto Rico in which the language of instruction was other than English shall be denied the right to vote in any election because of his inability to read or write English. Appellees, registered voters in New York City, brought this suit to challenge the constitutionality of § 4(e) insofar as it *pro tanto* prohibits the enforcement of the election laws of New York requiring an ability to read and write English as a condition of voting. Under these laws many of the several hundred thousand New York City residents who have migrated there from the Commonwealth of Puerto Rico had previously been denied the right to vote, and appellees attack § 4(e) insofar as it would enable many of these citizens to vote. Pursuant to § 14(b) of the Voting Rights Act of 1965, appellees commenced this proceeding in the District Court for the District of Columbia seeking a declaration that § 4(e) is invalid and an injunction prohibiting appellants, the Attorney General of the United States and the New York City Board of Elections, from either enforcing or complying with § 4(e). A three-judge district court . . . granted the declaratory and injunctive relief appellees sought. . . . We reverse. We hold that, in the application challenged in these cases, § 4(e) is a proper exercise of the powers granted to Congress by § 5 of the Fourteenth Amendment and that by force of the Supremacy Clause, Article VI, the New York English literacy requirement cannot be enforced to the extent that it is inconsistent with § 4(e).

Under the distribution of powers effected by the Constitution, the States establish qualifications for voting for state officers, and the qualifications established by the States for voting for members of the most numerous branch of the state legislature also determine who may vote for United States Representatives and Senators, Art. I, § 2; Seventeenth Amendment; Ex parte Yarbrough, 110 U.S. 651, 663. But, of course, the States have no power to grant or withhold the franchise on conditions that are forbidden by the Fourteenth Amendment, or any other provision of the Constitution. Such exercises of state power are no more immune to the limitations of the Fourteenth Amendment than any other state action. The Equal Protection Clause itself has been held to forbid some state laws that restrict the right to vote.

The Attorney General of the State of New York argues that an exercise of congressional power under § 5 of the Fourteenth Amendment that prohibits the enforcement of a state law can only be sustained if the judicial branch determines that the state law is prohibited by the provisions of the Amendment that Congress sought to enforce . . . We disagree. Neither the language nor history of § 5 supports such a construction. . . . A construction of § 5 that would require a judicial determination that the enforcement of the state law precluded by Congress violated the Amendment, as a condition of sustaining the congressional enactment, would depreciate both congressional resourcefulness and congressional responsibility for implementing the Amendment. It would confine the legislative power in this context to the insignificant role of abrogating only those state laws that the judicial branch was prepared to adjudge unconstitutional, or of merely informing the judgment of the judiciary by particularizing the "majestic generalities" of § 1 of the Amendment. See Fay v. New York, 332 U.S. 261, 282–284.

Thus our task in this case is not to determine whether the New York English literacy requirement as applied to deny the right to vote to a person who successfully completed the sixth grade in a Puerto Rican school violates the Equal Protection Clause. Accordingly, our decision in Lassiter v. Northampton Election Bd., 360 U.S. 45, sustaining the North Carolina English literacy requirement as not in all circumstances prohibited by the first sections of the Fourteenth and Fifteenth Amendments is inapposite. . . . *Lassiter* did not present the question before us here: Without regard to whether the judiciary would find that the Equal Protection Clause itself nullifies New York's English literacy requirement as so applied, could Congress prohibit the enforcement of the state law by legislating under § 5 of the Fourteenth Amendment? In answering this question, our task is limited to determining whether such legislation is, as required by § 5, appropriate legislation to enforce the Equal Protection Clause.

By including § 5 the draftsmen sought to grant to Congress, by a specific provision applicable to the Fourteenth Amendment, the same broad powers expressed in the Necessary and Proper Clause, Art. I, § 8, cl. 18. The classic formulation of the reach of those two powers was established by Chief Justice Marshall in McCulloch v. Maryland, 4 Wheat. 316, 421.

"Let the end be legitimate, let it be within the scope of the constitution, and all means which are appropriate, which are plainly adapted to that end, which are not prohibited, but consist with the letter and spirit of the constitution, are constitutional."

. . .

We therefore proceed to the consideration whether § 4(e) is "appropriate legislation" to enforce the Equal Protection Clause, that is, under the McCulloch v. Maryland standard, whether § 4(e) may be regarded as an enactment to enforce the Equal Protection Clause, whether it is "plainly adapted to that end" and whether it is not prohibited by but is consistent with "the letter and spirit of the constitution." [10]

There can be no doubt that § 4(e) may be regarded as an enactment to enforce the Equal Protection Clause. Congress explicitly declared that it enacted § 4(e) "to secure the rights under the fourteenth amendment of persons educated in American-flag schools in which the predominant classroom language was other than English." The persons referred to include those who have migrated from the Commonwealth of Puerto Rico to New York and who have been denied the right to vote because of their inability to read and write English, and the Fourteenth Amendment rights referred to include those emanating from the Equal Protection Clause. More specifically, § 4(e) may be viewed as a measure to secure for the Puerto Rican community residing in New York nondiscriminatory treatment by government—both in the imposition of voting qualifications and the provision or administration of governmental services, such as public schools, public housing and law enforcement.

Section 4(e) may be readily seen as "plainly adapted" to furthering these aims of the Equal Protection Clause. The practical effect of § 4(e) is to

---

[10] Contrary to the suggestion of the dissent, § 5 does not grant Congress power to exercise discretion in the other direction and to enact "statutes so as in effect to dilute equal protection and due process decisions of this Court." We emphasize that Congress' power under § 5 is limited to adopting measures to enforce the guarantees of the Amendment: § 5 grants Congress no power to restrict, abrogate, or dilute these guarantees. Thus, for example, an enactment authorizing the States to establish racially segregated systems of education would not be—as required by § 5—a measure "to enforce" the Equal Protection Clause since that clause of its own force prohibits such state laws.

prohibit New York from denying the right to vote to large segments of its Puerto Rican community. Congress has thus prohibited the State from denying to that community the right that is "preservative of all rights." Yick Wo v. Hopkins, 118 U.S. 356, 370. This enhanced political power will be helpful in gaining nondiscriminatory treatment in public services for the entire Puerto Rican community. Section 4(e) thereby enables the Puerto Rican minority better to obtain "perfect equality of civil rights and the equal protection of the laws." It was well within congressional authority to say that this need of the Puerto Rican minority for the vote warranted federal intrusion upon any state interests served by the English literacy requirement. It was for Congress, as the branch that made this judgment, to assess and weigh the various conflicting considerations—the risk or pervasiveness of the discrimination in governmental services, the effectiveness of eliminating the state restriction on the right to vote as a means of dealing with the evil, the adequacy or availability of alternative remedies, and the nature and significance of the state interests that would be affected by the nullification of the English literacy requirement as applied to residents who have successfully completed the sixth grade in a Puerto Rican school. It is not for us to review the congressional resolution of these factors. It is enough that we be able to perceive a basis upon which the Congress might resolve the conflict as it did. There plainly was such a basis to support § 4(e) in the application in question in this case. Any contrary conclusion would require us to be blind to the realities familiar to the legislators.

The result is no different if we confine our inquiry to the question whether § 4(e) was merely legislation aimed at the elimination of an invidious discrimination in establishing voter qualifications. . . . Here again, it is enough that we perceive a basis upon which Congress might predicate a judgment that the application of New York's English literacy requirement to deny the right to vote to a person with a sixth grade education in Puerto Rican schools in which the language of instruction was other than English constituted an invidious discrimination in violation of the Equal Protection Clause.

There remains the question whether the congressional remedies adopted in § 4(e) constitute means which are not prohibited by, but are consistent "with the letter and spirit of the constitution." The only respect in which appellees contend that § 4(e) fails in this regard is that the section itself works an invidious discrimination in violation of the Fifth Amendment by prohibiting the enforcement of the English literacy requirement only for those educated in American-flag schools (schools located within United States jurisdiction) in which the language of instruction was other than English, and not for those educated in schools beyond the territorial limits of the United States in which the language of instruction was also other than English. This is not a complaint that Congress, in enacting § 4(e), has unconstitutionally denied or diluted anyone's right to vote but rather that Congress violated the Constitution by not extending the relief effected in § 4(e) to those educated in non-American-flag schools. . . .

Section 4(e) does not restrict or deny the franchise but in effect extends the franchise to persons who otherwise would be denied it by state law. Thus we need not decide whether a state literacy law conditioning the right to vote on achieving a certain level of education in an American-flag school (regardless of the language of instruction) discriminates invidiously against those educated in non-American-flag schools. We need only decide whether the challenged limitation on the relief effected in § 4(e) was permissible. In deciding that question, the principle that calls for the closest scrutiny of distinctions in laws *denying* fundamental rights, is inapplicable; for the distinction challenged by appellees is presented only as a limitation on a reform measure aimed at eliminating an existing barrier to the exercise of the franchise. Rather, in deciding the constitutional propriety of the limitations in such a reform measure we are guided by the familiar principles that a "statute is not invalid under the Constitution because it might have gone farther than it did," Roschen v. Ward, 279 U.S. 337, 339, that a legislature need not "strike at all evils at the same time," Semler v. Dental Examiners, 294 U.S. 608, 610, and that "reform may take one step at a time, addressing itself to the phase of the problem which seems most acute to the legislative mind," Williamson v. Lee Optical Co., 348 U.S. 483, 489.

Guided by these principles, we are satisfied that appellees' challenge to this limitation in § 4(e) is without merit. In the context of the case before us, the congressional choice to limit the relief effected in § 4(e) may, for example, reflect Congress' greater familiarity with the quality of instruction in American-flag schools, a recognition of the unique historic relationship between the Congress and the Commonwealth of Puerto Rico, an awareness of the Federal Government's acceptance of the desirability of the use of Spanish as the language of instruction in Commonwealth schools, and the fact that Congress has fostered policies encouraging migration from the Commonwealth to the States. We have no occasion to determine in this case whether such factors would justify a similar distinction embodied in a voting-qualification law that denied the franchise to persons educated in non-American-flag schools. We hold only that the limitation on relief effected in § 4(e) does not constitute a forbidden discrimination since these factors might well have been the basis for the decision of Congress to go "no farther than it did."

We therefore conclude that § 4(e), in the application challenged in this case, is appropriate legislation to enforce the Equal Protection Clause and that the judgment of the District Court must be and hereby is

Reversed.

Mr. Justice Douglas joins the Court's opinion except for the discussion of the question whether the congressional remedies adopted in § 4(e) constitute means which are not prohibited by, but are consistent with "the letter and spirit of the constitution." On that question, he reserves judgment until such time as it is presented by a member of the class against which that particular discrimination is directed.

Mr. Justice Harlan, whom Mr. Justice Stewart joins, dissenting.

Worthy as its purposes may be thought by many, I do not see how § 4(e) of the Voting Rights Act of 1965, 79 Stat. 439, 42 U.S.C. § 1973b(e) (1964 ed. Supp. I), can be sustained except at the sacrifice of fundamentals in the American constitutional system—the separation between the legislative and judicial function and the boundaries between federal and state political authority. . . . .

The pivotal question in this instance is what effect the added factor of a congressional enactment has on the straight equal protection argument dealt with above. The Court declares that since § 5 of the Fourteenth Amendment gives to the Congress power to "enforce" the prohibitions of the Amendment by "appropriate" legislation, the test for judicial review of any congressional determination in this area is simply one of rationality; that is, in effect, was Congress acting rationally in declaring that the New York statute is irrational? Although § 5 most certainly does give to the Congress wide powers in the field of devising remedial legislation to effectuate the Amendment's prohibition on arbitrary state action, Ex parte Virginia, 100 U.S. 339, I believe the Court has confused the issue of how much enforcement power Congress possesses under § 5 with the distinct issue of what questions are appropriate for congressional determination and what questions are essentially judicial in nature.

When recognized state violations of federal constitutional standards have occurred, Congress is of course empowered by § 5 to take appropriate remedial measures to redress and prevent the wrongs. See Strauder v. West Virginia, 100 U.S. 303, 310. But it is a judicial question whether the condition with which Congress has thus sought to deal is in truth an infringement of the Constitution, something that is the necessary prerequisite to bringing the § 5 power into play at all. . . .

. . . The question here is not whether the statute is appropriate remedial legislation to cure an established violation of a constitutional command, but whether there has in fact been an infringement of that constitutional command, that is, whether a particular state practice or, as here, a statute is so arbitrary or irrational as to offend the command of the Equal Protection Clause of the Fourteenth Amendment. That question is one for the judicial branch ultimately to determine. Were the rule otherwise, Congress would be able to qualify this Court's constitutional decisions under the Fourteenth and Fifteenth Amendments, let alone those under other provisions of the Constitution, by resorting to congressional power under the Necessary and Proper Clause. In view of this Court's holding in Lassiter, supra, that an English literacy test is a permissible exercise of state supervision over its franchise, I do not think it is open to Congress to limit the effect of that decision as it has undertaken to do by § 4(e). In effect the Court reads § 5 of the Fourteenth Amendment as giving Congress the power to define the *substantive* scope of the Amendment. If that indeed be the true reach of § 5, then I do not see why Congress should not be able as well to exercise its § 5 "discretion" by enacting statutes so as in effect to dilute equal protection and due process decisions of this Court. In all such cases there is room for reasonable men to differ as to whether or not a denial of equal protection or due process has occurred, and the final decision is one of judgment. Until today this judgment has always been one for the judiciary to resolve.

I do not mean to suggest in what has been said that a legislative judgment of the type incorporated in § 4(e) is without any force whatsoever. Decisions on questions of equal protection and due process are based not on abstract logic, but on empirical foundations. To the extent "legislative facts" are relevant to a judicial determination, Congress is well equipped to investigate them, and such determinations are of course entitled to due respect. . . .

But no such factual data provide a legislative record supporting § 4(e)[9] by way of showing that Spanish-speaking citizens are fully as capable of making informed decisions in a New York election as are English-speaking citizens. Nor was there any showing whatever to support the Court's alternative argument that § 4(e) should be viewed as but a remedial measure designed to cure or assure against unconstitutional discrimination of other varieties, e.g., in "public schools, public housing and law enforcement," to which Puerto Rican minorities might be subject in such communities as New York. There is simply no legislative record supporting such hypothesized discrimination of the sort we have hitherto insisted upon when congressional power is brought to bear on constitutionally reserved state concerns. See Heart of Atlanta Motel, supra; State of South Carolina v. Katzenbach, supra.

Thus, we have here not a matter of giving deference to a congressional estimate, based on its determination of legislative facts, bearing upon the validity *vel non* of a statute, but rather what can at most be called a legislative announcement that Congress believes a state law to entail an unconstitutional deprivation of equal protection. Although this kind of declaration is of course entitled to the most respectful consideration, coming as it does from a concur-

---

[9] There were no committee hearings or reports referring to this section, which was introduced from the floor during debate on the full Voting Rights Act. See 111 Cong.Rec. 11027, 15666, 16234.

rent branch and one that is knowledgeable in matters of popular political participation, I do not believe it lessens our responsibility to decide the fundamental issue of whether in fact the state enactment violates federal constitutional rights.

In assessing the deference we should give to this kind of congressional expression of policy, it is relevant that the judiciary has always given to congressional enactments a presumption of validity. . . . However, it is also a canon of judicial review that state statutes are given a similar presumption, ... Whichever way this case is decided, one statute will be rendered inoperative in whole or in part, and although it has been suggested that this Court should give somewhat more deference to Congress than to a state legislature,[10] such a simple weighing of presumptions is hardly a satisfying way of resolving a matter that touches the distribution of state and federal power in an area so sensitive as that of the regulation of the franchise. Rather it should be recognized that while the Fourteenth Amendment is a "brooding omnipresence" over all state legislation, the substantive matters which it touches are all within the primary legislative competence of the States. Federal authority, legislative no less than judicial, does not intrude unless there has been a denial by state action of Fourteenth Amendment limitations, in this instance a denial of equal protection. At least in the area of primary state concern a state statute that passes constitutional muster under the judicial standard of rationality should not be permitted to be set at naught by a mere contrary congressional pronouncement unsupported by a legislative record justifying that conclusion.

To deny the affectiveness of this congressional enactment is not of course to disparage Congress' exertion of authority in the field of civil rights; it is simply to recognize that the Legislative Branch like the other branches of federal authority is subject to the governmental boundaries set by the Constitution. To hold, on this record, that § 4(e) overrides the New York literacy requirement seems to me tantamount to allowing the Fourteenth Amendment to swallow the State's constitutionally ordained primary authority in this field. For if Congress by what, as here, amounts to mere *ipse dixit* can set that otherwise permissible requirement partially at naught I see no reason why it could not also substitute its judgment for that of the States in other fields of their exclusive primary competence as well.

I would affirm the judgments in each of these cases.

———

OREGON v. MITCHELL, 400 U.S. 112 (1970). The Court had before it the validity of the Voting Rights Act Amendments of 1970. It held unanimously that Congress had the power to bar the use of literacy tests for voting for a period of five years in all elections, state and national. It held with but one dissent that Congress had power to regulate residency requirements and provide for absentee balloting in national elections for presidential and vice-presidential electors. It held by a vote of 5 to 4 that Congress had power to establish a minimum age of 18 for voters in elections for national officers. It also held by a vote of 5 to 4 that Congress had no power to establish a minimum age of 18 for voters in state and local elections—a result later changed by the 26th amendment.

In the debate over the validity of the provision setting a minimum age of 18 for voters in state and local elections, several of the Justices addressed the question of the power of Congress to redefine the scope of the fourteenth amendment. Justice Black asserted that the Civil War amendments gave Congress enhanced power to deal with racial discrimination in voting. He

---

[10] See Thayer, The Origin and Scope of the American Doctrine of Constitutional Law, 7 Harv.L. Rev. 129, 154–155 (1893).

noted that the 18 year old vote provisions were not related to disenfranchisement by race. Then, he concluded:

"Since Congress has attempted to invade an area preserved to the States by the Constitution without a foundation for enforcing the Civil War amendments' ban on racial discrimination, I would hold that Congress has exceeded its powers in attempting to lower the voting age in state and local elections. On the other hand, where Congress legislates in a domain not exclusively reserved by the Constitution to the States, its enforcement power need not be tied so closely to the goal of eliminating discrimination on account of race."

Justice Stewart, joined by Chief Justice Burger and Justice Blackmun said:

"Although it was found necessary to amend the Constitution to confer a federal right to vote upon Negroes and upon females, the Government asserts that a federal right to vote can be conferred upon people between 18 and 21 years of age simply by this Act of Congress. Our decision in Katzenbach v. Morgan, 384 U.S. 641, it is said, established the power of Congress, under § 5 of the Fourteenth Amendment, to nullify state laws requiring voters to be 21 years of age or older if Congress could rationally have concluded that such laws are not supported by a 'compelling state interest.'

"In my view, neither the Morgan case, nor any other case upon which the Government relies, establishes such congressional power, even assuming that all those cases were rightly decided. . . .

"Katzenbach v. Morgan, supra, does not hold that Congress has the power to determine what are and what are not 'compelling state interests' for equal protection purposes. . . . The Court upheld the statute on two grounds: that Congress could conclude that enhancing the political power of the Puerto Rican community by conferring the right to vote was an appropriate means of remedying discriminatory treatment in public services; and that Congress could conclude that the New York statute was tainted by the impermissible purpose of denying the right to vote to Puerto Ricans, an undoubted invidious discrimination under the Equal Protection Clause. Both of these decisional grounds were far reaching. The Court's opinion made clear that Congress could impose on the States a remedy for the denial of equal protection that elaborated upon the direct command of the Constitution, and that it could override state laws on the ground that they were in fact used as instruments of invidious discrimination even though a court in an individual lawsuit might not have reached that factual conclusion.

"But it is necessary to go much further to sustain § 302. The state laws that it invalidates do not invidiously discriminate against any discrete and insular minority. Unlike the statute considered in Morgan, § 302 is valid only if Congress has the power not only to provide the means of eradicating situations that amount to a violation of the Equal Protection Clause, but also to determine as a matter of substantive constitutional law what situations fall within the ambit of the clause, and what state interests are "compelling." I concurred in Mr. Justice Harlan's dissent in Morgan. That case, as I now read it, gave congressional power under § 5 the furthest possible legitimate reach. Yet to sustain the constitutionality of § 302 would require an enormous extension of that decision's rationale. I cannot but conclude that § 302 was beyond the constitutional power of Congress to enact."

Justice Brennan, joined by Justices White and Marshall, took a broader view. Justice Douglas took a similar view in a separate opinion. Justice Brennan said, in part:

"As we have often indicated, questions of constitutional power frequently turn in the last analysis on questions of fact. This is particularly the case when an assertion of state power is challenged under the Equal Protection Clause of the Fourteenth Amendment. . . . . When a state legislative classification is subjected to judicial challenge as violating the Equal Protection Clause, it comes before the courts cloaked by the presumption that the legislature has, as it should, acted within constitutional limitations. Accordingly, "[a] statutory discrimination will not be set aside as the denial of equal protection of the laws if any state of facts reasonably may be conceived to justify it." Metropolitan Cas. Ins. Co. v. Brownell, 294 U.S. 580, 584 (1935).

"But, as we have consistently held, this limitation on judicial review of state legislative classifications is a limitation stemming, not from the Fourteenth Amendment itself, but from the nature of judicial review. . . . The nature of the judicial process makes it an inappropriate forum for the determination of complex factual questions of the kind so often involved in constitutional adjudication. Courts, therefore, will overturn a legislative determination of a factual question only if the legislature's finding is so clearly wrong that it may be characterized as 'arbitrary,' 'irrational,' or 'unreasonable.'

"Limitations stemming from the nature of the judicial process, however, have no application to Congress. . . . Should Congress . . . undertake an investigation in order to determine whether the factual basis necessary to support a state legislative discrimination actually exists, it need not stop once it determines that some reasonable men could believe the factual basis exists. Section 5 empowers Congress to make its own determination on the matter. . . . It should hardly be necessary to add that if the asserted factual basis necessary to support a given state discrimination does not exist, § 5 of the Fourteenth Amendment vests Congress with power to remove the discrimination by appropriate means. . . . The scope of our review in such matters has been established by a long line of consistent decisions.[31] . . .

"This scheme is consistent with our prior decisions in related areas. The core of dispute over the constitutionality of Title III of the 1970 Amendments is a conflict between state and federal legislative determinations of the factual issues upon which depends decision of a federal constitutional question—the legitimacy, under the Equal Protection Clause, of state discrimination against persons between the ages of 18 and 21. Our cases have repeatedly emphasized that, when state and federal claims come into conflict, the primacy of federal power requires that the federal finding of fact control. . . . The Supremacy Clause requires an identical result when the conflict is one of legislative, not judicial, findings.

. . . .

"In sum, Congress had ample evidence upon which it could have based the conclusion that exclusion of citizens 18 to 21 years of age from the franchise is wholly unnecessary to promote any legitimate interest the States may have in assuring intelligent and responsible voting. . . . If discrimination is unnecessary to promote any legitimate state interest, it is plainly unconstitutional under the Equal Protection Clause, and Congress has ample power to forbid it under § 5 of the Fourteenth Amendment. We would uphold § 302 of the 1970 Amendments as a legitimate exercise of congressional power."

---

[31] As we emphasized in Katzenbach v. Morgan, supra, "§ 5 does not grant Congress power to . . . enact 'statutes so as in effect to dilute equal protection and due process decisions of this Court.'" 384 U.S., at 651 n. 10. As indicated above, a decision of this Court striking down a state statute expresses, among other things, our conclusion that the legislative findings upon which the statute is based are so far wrong as to be unreasonable. Unless Congress were to unearth new evidence in its investigation, its identical findings on the identical issue would be no more reasonable than those of the state legislature.

THE VITALITY OF KATZENBACH v.
MORGAN AS PRECEDENT

In Oregon v. Mitchell, Justice Stewart's opinion characterized the portion of the Court's opinion in Katzenbach v. Morgan concerning Congressional power to interpret the fourteenth amendment as dicta. Whether or not that is the correct analysis, does the interpretive rationale of Katzenbach v. Morgan survive the decision in Oregon v. Mitchell? Five Justices did agree that Congressional power to enforce the fourteenth amendment did not authorize Congress to establish a minimum voting age of 18 in state elections. The absence of any opinion for the Court in Oregon v. Mitchell, however, complicates the question. Consider the following portion of Justice Rehnquist's dissent in City of Rome v. United States, which argues that Oregon v. Mitchell is an authoritative rejection of Katzenbach v. Morgan.

"[T]he theory that Congress was empowered to [interpret] the Fourteenth or Fifteenth Amendments . . . was rejected in the Civil Rights Cases, 109 U.S. 3 (1883). The Court emphasized that the power conferred was 'remedial' only. The Court reasoned that the structure of the Amendment made it clear that it did not 'authorize Congress to create a code of municipal law for the regulation of private rights; but to provide modes of redress against the operation of State laws, and the action of State officers . . ., when these are subversive of the fundamental right specified in the Amendment.' This interpretation is consonant with the legislative history surrounding the enactment of the Amendment.

"This construction has never been refuted by a majority of the Members of this Court. Support for this construction in current years has emerged in South Carolina v. Katzenbach, and Oregon v. Mitchell.[8] In South Carolina v. Katzenbach, the Court observed that Congress could not attack evils not comprehended by the Fifteenth Amendment. 383 U.S., at 326. In Oregon v. Mitchell, 400 U.S. 112 (1970), five Members of the Court were unwilling to conclude that Congress had the power to determine that establishing the age limitation for voting at 21 denied equal protection to those between the ages of 18 and 20.

"The opinion of Mr. Justice Stewart in that case, joined by Chief Justice Burger and Mr. Justice Blackmun, reaffirmed that Congress only has the power under the Fourteenth Amendment to 'provide the means of eradicating situations that amount to a violation of the Equal Protection Clause' but not to 'determine as a matter of substantive constitutional law that situations fall within the ambit of the clause.' Id., at 296. Mr. Justice Harlan, in a separate opinion, reiterated his belief that it is the duty of the Court, and not the Congress, to determine when States have exceeded constitutional limitations imposed upon their powers. Id., at 204–207. Cf. Oregon v. Hass, 420 U.S. 714 (1975); Cooper v. Aaron, 358 U.S. 1, 18 (1958). Mr. Justice Black also was unwilling

---

[8] Explicit support can also be derived from Mr. Justice Harlan's dissenting opinion, joined by Mr. Justice Stewart, in Katzenbach v. Morgan, 384 U.S. 641 (1966). Mr. Justice Harlan clarified the need for the remedial construction of congressional powers. It is also unnecessary, however, to read the majority opinion as establishing the Court's rejection of the remedial construction of the *Civil Rights Cases*. While Mr. Justice Brennan's majority opinion did contain language suggesting a rejection of the "remedial" construction of the enforcement powers, the opinion also advanced a remedial rationale which supports the determination reached by the Court. Compare the rationales forwarded at 384 U.S., at 654 with the statements, at 656. It would be particularly inappropriate to construe Katzenbach v. Morgan as a rejection of the remedial interpretation of congressional powers in view of this Court's subsequent decision in Oregon v. Mitchell, 400 U.S. 112 (1970).

to accept the broad construction of enforcement powers formulated in the opinion of Mr. Justice Brennan, joined by Justices White and Marshall.[9] "

CONGRESSIONAL EXPANSION OF DUE PROCESS AND EQUAL PROTECTION

It was suggested, at the beginning of section 5 of this chapter, that the wide scope of other Congressional powers may make it unnecessary to resolve the question whether the fourteenth amendment's enforcement powers are broad enough to support federal legislation forbidding private discrimination. It is appropriate now to ask whether that legislation could be supported on the ground that Congress can define the meaning of state action, or on the less contentious ground that the prohibition is an appropriate remedy for constitutional violations by the state.[1]

Ironically, the most troublesome issues of Congressional power to expand fourteenth amendment protections may concern federal legislation directed at states, rather than private individuals. That is because the one restriction defined by modern cases on the scope of the commerce power is that Congress may not impair the essential integrity of the states. On the other hand, the Court indicated in the *City of Rome* decision that the same limitation is inapplicable to Congressional enforcement of the Civil War Amendments.

EQUAL EMPLOYMENT OPPORTUNITY COMMISSION v. WYOMING

460 U.S. 226, 103 S.Ct. 1054, 75 L.Ed.2d 18 (1983).

[The report in this case appears supra, p. 416.]

MISSISSIPPI UNIVERSITY FOR WOMEN v. HOGAN

458 U.S. 718, 102 S.Ct. 3331, 73 L.Ed.2d 1090 (1982)

[The report in this case appears supra, p. 781.]

CONGRESSIONAL POWER TO DILUTE CONSTITUTIONAL RIGHTS

A major concern about conceding Congressional power to define due process and equal protection was expressed in Justice Harlan's dissent in Katzenbach v. Morgan. He stated that if Congress had the power to expand the substantive scope of the fourteenth amendment "I do not see why Congress should not be able as well to exercise its § 5 'discretion' by enacting statutes so as in effect to dilute equal protection and due process decisions of this Court." Consider Justice Brennan's contrary assertions in footnote 10 to his opinion for

---

[9] Since Mr. Justice Black found that congressional powers were more circumscribed when not acting to counter racial discrimination under the Fourteenth Amendment, he did not have to determine the precise nature of congressional powers when they were exercised in the field of racial relations. His analysis of the nationwide ban on literacy tests, also presented in Oregon v. Mitchell, however, is consistent with a remedial interpretation of those powers.

[1] See Leeds, *State Action Limitations on Courts and Congressional Power,* 60 No.Car.L.Rev. 747 (1982).

the Court in Katzenbach v. Morgan and footnote 31 to his opinion in Oregon v. Mitchell.[1] If Congressional power to expand due process and equal protection is based on Congress' asserted superior competence either to draw lines or to determine legislative facts, is it possible to maintain at the same time that Congress does not have equal competence to decide that a challenged state law is *constitutional?* Moreover, even if Justice Brennan is right that Congress can only expand constitutional rights, how will that theory be applied when Congress attempts to overrule a Supreme Court decision that adjusts competing constitutional rights?[2] Commentators who have approved the substantive results reached by Justice Brennan have questioned whether his theory opens the door to Congressional power to overrule unpopular constitutional decisions by ordinary legislation.[3]

It can be asked, finally, whether the possibility of Congressional veto of unpopular constitutional decisions of the Supreme Court can be avoided by a theory that limits the superior competence of Congress to defining the remedies which are appropriate for constitutional violations.[4] The obvious question arises whether Congress' power to expand judicially created remedies implies a concomitant power to restrict them. That issue has arisen in two contexts: Congressional attempts to permit the introduction of confessions in federal criminal prosecutions despite failure of federal law enforcement officials to comply with the requirements of Miranda v. Arizona, 384 U.S. 436 (1966); Congressional attempts to restrict the integration remedies employed by federal courts in school desegregation cases.[5]

Miranda's requirements that police give formal warnings concerning the right to remain silent and the right to counsel, and that they cease interrogation

[1] Justice Brennan made a similar assertion in his opinion for the Court in Shapiro v. Thompson, 394 U.S. 618 (1969), supra p. 706. Chief Justice Warren, joined by Justice Black, argued in dissent that Congress had approved state durational residency requirements of one year or less. Justice Brennan's opinion concluded that Congress had not done so, and if it had, "Congress may not authorize the States to violate the Equal Protection Clause." He cited footnote 10 of Katzenbach v. Morgan for the proposition.

[2] Justice White, who joined Justice Brennan's opinions in both Katzenbach v. Morgan and Oregon v. Mitchell, made this argument for Congressional power to define constitutional rights in Welsh v. United States, 398 U.S. 333 (1970), summarized, infra p. 1559. At issue was the claim that § 6(j) of the Selective Service Act was an establishment of religion. Section 6(j) defined religious training and belief, for purposes of the conscientious objector exemption from combat service, as "belief in a relation to a Supreme Being." The Court avoided the constitutional question whether the law would be invalid if it were limited to theistic religious beliefs by interpreting the statute to allow conscientious objector classification to those whose pacifist beliefs stemmed from sincere and deeply held non-theistic beliefs. Justice White dissented from the Court's construction of the statute, and argued that his narrower construction was not a violation of the Establishment Clause. He argued that the Congressional judgment should be accepted so long as the Court could "perceive a basis" for its resolution of a potential conflict between competing values of the free exercise and establishment clauses. He also asserted that his conclusion "involves no surrender of the Court's function as ultimate arbiter in disputes over interpretation of the Constitution," while citing Katzenbach v. Morgan as support. Chief Justice Burger and Justice Stewart, both of whom have denied any Congressional power to interpret the fourteenth amendment, joined Justice White's dissent. Note that the statute at issue was a federal statute, and the constitutional question thus involved solely the first amendment. Would Congress have more or less power to interpret the Bill of Rights as applied to federal laws than to interpret the Bill of Rights as incorporated into the fourteenth amendment and applied to state laws?

[3] See Burt, *Miranda and Title II: A Morganatic Marriage,* 1969 Sup.Ct.Rev. 81; Cox, *The Role of Congress in Constitutional Determinations,* 40 U.Cin.L.Rev. 199 (1971); Cohen, *Congressional Power to Interpret Due Process and Equal Protection,* 27 Stan.L.Rev. 603 (1975). Critics of the results have also stressed the potential for dilution of constitutional rights. Bickel, *The Voting Rights Cases,* 1966 Sup. Ct.Rev. 79, 85–101; Engdahl, *Constitutionality of the Voting Age Statute,* 39 Geo.Wash.L.Rev. 1 (1970).

[4] See Cohen, supra note 3, at 608–609.

[5] This legislation also raises the question of Congressional power to control the jurisdiction of federal courts. See Chapter 2, pp. 40–46, supra.

if a suspect asserts his right to remain silent, were justified as remedies to protect the suspect's privilege against self-incrimination. The Court expressly noted that "Congress and the States are free to develop their own safeguards for the privilege, so long as they are fully as effective. . . ." [6] The Congressional response, two years later, was a statute providing that in federal criminal trials, voluntary confessions were admissible in evidence.[7] Would a Congressional judgment that pre-*Miranda* law excluding involuntary confessions on a case-by-case basis was "fully effective" to protect against self-incrimination be controlling on the courts? [8]

The most controversial issue surrounding contemporary school integration cases has been the proper scope of the remedy for constitutional violations proved—including the propriety of "system-wide" remedies and court ordered school busing. President Nixon's 1972 proposals to limit federal court remedies in school integration cases were premised on the argument that the issue involved remedies and not rights.[9] In 1974, Congress enacted the Equal Education Opportunities and Transportation of Students Act. One provision forbids courts to order a plan requiring "transportation of a student to a school other than the school closest or next closest to his place of residence." Would that bind a federal court that otherwise would have concluded that busing was the only effective remedy for the defendants' constitutional violations? That issue will not need to be resolved, because another provision in the statute provides that it is "not intended to diminish the authority of the courts of the United States to enforce fully the fifth and fourteenth amendments. . . ." [10]

The proposed "Human Life Statute," introduced in both houses of Congress in 1981 (97th Cong., 1st Sess., H.R. 900 and S. 158), provided:

"The Congress finds that present-day scientific evidence indicates a significant likelihood that actual human life exists from conception.

"The Congress further finds that the fourteenth amendment to the Constitution of the United States was intended to protect all human beings.

"Upon the basis of these findings, and in the exercise of the powers of the Congress, including its power under section 5 of the fourteenth amendment to the Constitution of the United States, the Congress hereby declares that for the purpose of enforcing the obligation of the States under the fourteenth amendment not to deprive persons of life without due process of law, human life shall be deemed to exist from conception, without regard to race, sex, age, health, defect, or condition of dependency; and for this purpose 'person' shall include all human life as defined herein."

[6] 384 U.S. at 490. *Miranda* was decided the same day as Katzenbach v. Morgan.

[7] 18 U.S.C. § 3501. For extensive discussion of the enactment of this statute, its interpretation, and its constitutionality, see Burt, supra note 3.

[8] Apparently, the United States Department of Justice has followed a policy of not invoking 18 U.S.C. § 3501 to justify the admission of confessions in federal prosecutions, and no federal court has determined whether a "voluntary" confession to federal officers is admissible if *Miranda* requirements have not been met. One issue that arises in connection with statutes repealing or restricting judicial remedies is whether the remedy was itself required by the Constitution. See Chief Justice Burger's dissent in Bivens v. Six Unknown Agents, 403 U.S. 388, 411 (1971), urging Congress to enact legislation providing a "reasonable and effective" substitute for the rule excluding illegally seized evidence.

[9] Bork, *Constitutionality of the President's Busing Proposals* (1972).

[10] Consider the decision in North Carolina State Bd. of Ed. v. Swann, 402 U.S. 43 (1971), described, supra p. 680 which held unconstitutional a state statute forbidding any school assignment on the basis of race. Would a federal statute forbidding racial assignments as a "remedy" in federal school integration litigation fare any better?

If enacted, would this legislation have overruled the Supreme Court's decisions placing constitutional limits on state abortion laws? If so, would it be constitutional? [11]

FEDERALISM AND CONGRESSIONAL CONSENT TO UNCONSTITUTIONAL STATE LAWS

The examples and problems discussed in the previous note concern constitutional limits that bind Congress and the states alike. A number of constitutional limitations—the contract clause of Article I, Section 10, and the privileges and immunities clause of Article IV, Section 2, for example—apply only as limitations on the states. Other constitutional limitations that restrict both the national government and the states do so in different ways. Despite the "incorporation" of equal protection standards into the fifth amendment, Congress can adopt policies for the treatment of aliens that would be unconstitutional if contained in state legislation.[1] Limits on state territorial jurisdiction, such as the rules under the due process clause of the fourteenth amendment concerning the scope of in personam jurisdiction of state courts,[2] will not apply to a national government with nationwide territorial jurisdiction.

In one context, it is clear beyond dispute that Congress can "consent" to state laws that would otherwise violate a constitutional limit applicable to the states, but inapplicable to the national government. By ordinary legislation, Congress can validate state laws that would be unconstitutional unreasonable burdens on interstate commerce.[3] The traditional explanation for the power to consent has been two-fold: the limitation on state power is not express, but an implication from Congressional power to regulate interstate commerce; the limitation stems from an assumption that, if Congress is silent, it is presumed that Congress desired an unburdened interstate market.[4] Notice that those explanations are inapplicable to other constitutional limitations on state power that are express, and not merely implied from the existence of federal power. Justice Rutledge's opinion for the Court in Prudential Ins. Co. v. Benjamin, 328 U.S. 408 (1946) stated, however, that the conventional explanations "did not go to the heart of the matter," and do not explain the power of Congress to consent to state laws unreasonably burdening commerce.

Benjamin involved the McCarran-Ferguson Act of 1945, which provided that "silence on the part of the Congress shall not be construed to impose any barrier" to state regulation or taxation of insurance.[5] The Court held that the

---

[11] See Estreicher, *Congressional Power and Constitutional Rights: Reflections on Proposed "Human Life" Legislation,* 68 Va.L.Rev. 333 (1982).

[1] See Mathews v. Diaz, 426 U.S. 67 (1976), supra page 696; Hampton v. Mow Sun Wong, 426 U.S. 88 (1976); Plyler v. Doe, 457 U.S. 202 (1982), supra page 920.

[2] The Court described the inability of a state court to bind an absent defendant as stemming from the due process clause of the fourteenth amendment in Pennoyer v. Neff, 95 U.S. (5 Otto) 714, 733–734 (1878). Even before the adoption of the fourteenth amendment, however, the Court enforced limitations on state judicial jurisdiction without tying them to any particular clause of the constitution. See page 494, supra. Commerce clause limitations on state power have sometimes been concerned with the extraterritorial impact of state laws. See Baldwin v. G.A.F. Seelig, Inc., 294 U.S. 511 (1935), supra page 269; Edgar v. Mite Corp., 457 U.S. 624 (1982), supra page 314. As several cases in chapter 6 show, most recent cases limiting state power to tax interstate business have relied more on limits of territorial power imposed by the due process clause of the fourteenth amendment than on the limitations imposed by the commerce clause.

[3] These cases are discussed at pages 183–184, supra.

[4] See Dowling, *Interstate Commerce and State Power—Revised Version,* 47 Colum.L.Rev. 547 (1947).

[5] The Act was a response to the decision in United States v. South-Eastern Underwriters Ass'n, 322 U.S. 533 (1944), supra page 210.

Act validated discriminatory state taxes on out-of-state insurance companies that would otherwise violate the commerce clause. Justice Rutledge's opinion explained that:

"The power of Congress over commerce exercised without reference to coordinated action of the states is not restricted . . . by any limitation which forbids it to discriminate against interstate commerce and in favor of local trade. . . . This broad authority Congress may exercise alone [subject to constitutional limits on Congress' power], or in conjunction with coordinated action by the states, in which case limitations imposed for the preservation of their powers become inoperative and only those designed to forbid action altogether by any power or combination of powers in our governmental system remain effective. . . . Clear and gross must be the evil which would nullify such an exertion, one which could arise only by exceeding . . . limitation[s] imposed by a constitutional provision or provisions designed and intended to outlaw the action entirely from our constitutional framework." [6]

Does this mean that Congress can validate any state law, so long as Congress would have had the power to enact an identical or analogous law? For an argument along those lines, see W. Cohen, *Congressional Power to Validate Unconstitutional State Laws: A Forgotten Solution to an Old Enigma,* 35 Stan.L.Rev. 387 (1983).

[6] 328 U.S. at 434–436.

Part IV

CONSTITUTIONAL PROTECTION OF EXPRESSION AND CONSCIENCE

The first four chapters in this part provide a detailed look at issues of freedom of expression.[1] Chapter 14 examines the definition of constitutionally protected speech, and focuses on doctrine dealing with prohibition of expression because of its content. Chapter 15 deals with government restriction that purports to control the time, place, or manner of speaking rather than the content of expression. Chapter 16 concerns indirect government restrictions on expression and the definition of peripheral first amendment rights. (Specific topics include the control of communicative conduct, compelled affirmation and disclosure, denial of government employment because of an employee's speech or association, denial of other government benefits, and freedom of political association.) Chapter 17 pulls together cases concerning the printed and electronic media. That chapter examines whether the guarantee of freedom of the press imposes restrictions on government independent of, and in addition to those, imposed by the guarantee of freedom of speech. The protection of religious conscience and conduct is reserved for Chapter 18.

---

[1] For an excellent discussion applicable to many of the issues raised in Chapters 14–17, see Schauer, *Free Speech: A Philosophic Enquiry* (1982). The most recent comprehensive treatment is Nimmer, *A Treatise on the First Amendment* (1984).

Chapter 14

GOVERNMENTAL CONTROL OF THE CONTENT OF EXPRESSION

Introduction. This chapter focuses on the core problem in defining the contours of freedom of expression—the extent to which speech can be punished by government because of its content. Section 1 deals at length with speech advocating the violent overthrow of government. Section 2 is a deliberate digression, examining judicial techniques for avoiding decision whether speech can be controlled because of its content. This section examines the doctrine of prior restraint, and the doctrines of vagueness and overbreadth. Section 3 returns to the problem of content control, examining the Court's efforts to draw the distinction between protected and unprotected speech in four different contexts—defamation and privacy, obscenity, fighting words and offensive speech, and commercial speech.

SECTION 1. AN INTRODUCTION TO PROBLEMS OF CONTENT CONTROL OF SPEECH

A. HISTORICAL INTRODUCTION—THE STATUS OF FREE SPEECH UP TO THE 1920's

1. THE ENGLISH BACKGROUND

Freedom of thought and expression is taken so much as a matter of course in most western societies today that we are apt to forget how recently it has come to be accepted. As the distinguished English historian, J.B. Bury, emphasized in *A History of Freedom of Thought* (1913), "human societies (there are some brilliant exceptions) have been generally opposed to freedom of thought" and "it has taken centuries to persuade the most enlightened peoples that liberty to publish one's opinions and to discuss all questions is a good and not a bad thing" (Home University Library Ed., 1952, p. 2). This is due in part to the persistent inclination of men to cling to familiar and accepted opinion, and to dislike what is new, but other reasons are not difficult to discover.

Both the society and outlook of the Middle Ages were authoritarian; truth was divinely revealed and error was sin. Consequently to extirpate erroneous views was not only permissible but a high moral obligation and the unifying structure of the medieval Church provided the central authority for determining what was true and what was false. Thus the churchmen who in 1633 condemned Galileo to live the rest of his life in seclusion because he insisted that the earth was not the stationary center of the universe were only performing their duty as determined by the standards under which they had lived.[1]

Even after the impact of the Renaissance and Reformation, the rebirth of learning, and the development of nation-states, the modern concept of freedom of thought was slow to develop. Diversity replaced the unity of the Middle Ages and the invention of the printing press brought a new and previously unequalled medium of communication. But on the whole, the dissenters and reformers sought only to establish a new brand of truth (their own) and did not

---

[1] This incident is told in detail in De Santillana, *The Crime of Galileo* (1955).

recognize the value of general freedom of thought and speech as the means of arriving at truth.

The three centuries that elapsed between the appearance of the first book printed in England, by Caxton in 1476, and the Declaration of Independence in 1776 provide the immediate background of the American constitutional system, and the struggles of this period are particularly relevant in the area of freedom of thought and expression. They concerned two issues above all others, the separation of the English Church from that of Rome and the limitation of the prerogative of the Crown. Neither of these developments assured the freedom of the individual, but supplanted one religious establishment with another and made parliament supreme in areas that theretofore had been the province of the King. Dispute and domestic turmoil fomented discussion, as they always do, but the very limited freedom permitted to thought and speech is shown by the position of the press.

The invention of printing was almost as frightening to the mind of the fifteenth century as has been the discovery of atomic fission to the mind of the twentieth. The printing press, unless rigidly controlled, gave to dissident groups a powerful medium for "dangerous doctrine." No friend of the established order could view this situation with complacency at a time when religious truth, then an all-consuming subject, was deemed a matter of prior revelation and when political controversy was entering the crisis of the life-and-death struggle between King and Parliament. Three instruments for the legal control of discussion were used: (1) the concept of constructive treason; (2) the doctrine of seditious libel; and (3) the domination of the press through state monopoly and licensing.

The law of treason was based on the Statute 25 Edward III (1351), which defined the crime to include (1) compassing or imagining the King's death, (2) levying war against the King, or (3) adhering to his enemies. These three clauses, strictly construed, did not offer complete protection for the security of the monarch and of the state, or so it was believed. Hence there arose in the seventeenth century that judicial extension of the statute known as constructive treason. Compassing or imagining the King's death, like intending to wage war against him, being a mental state, could be proved only by overt acts. During the latter part of the seventeenth century the judges ruled that printed and sometimes spoken words could constitute overt acts. Thus John Twyn was convicted of treason and hanged, drawn, and quartered in 1664 for printing a book asserting that the King was accountable to the people who were entitled to revolt and take the government into their own hands.[2]

However, prosecutions for constructive treason were rare, only two printers being executed for the crime during the seventeenth century and one during the eighteenth.[3] A more effective method of suppression was available, the law of seditious libel, under which convictions ran into the hundreds. Conviction for this crime did not bring death but the penalties were often severe, including indefinite imprisonment and heavy fines. The law of seditious libel was developed in prosecutions before the Court of Star Chamber in the late sixteenth century, and when that body was abolished in 1641, the rules were taken over by the common law courts. The original theory of the offense was that the King was the fountainhead of justice and law whose acts were beyond popular criticism and that consequently it was wrong to censure him openly.[4] This doctrine was carried to such lengths that any reflection on the government in written or printed form might be held seditious libel. In 1704 Chief Justice

---

[2] This and similar cases are recounted in Siebert, *Freedom of the Press in England,* 1476–1776 (1952), p. 267.

[3] Siebert, op. cit., p. 365.

[4] Stephen, *History of Criminal Law in England* (1883) Vol. II, p. 299.

Holt declared: "If people should not be called to account for possessing the people with an ill opinion of the government, no government can subsist. For it is very necessary for all governments that the people should have a good opinion of it. And nothing can be worse to any government than to endeavour to procure animosities as to the management of it; this has always been looked upon as a crime, and no government can be safe without it." [5]

As the eighteenth century progressed juries became less inclined to bring in verdicts of guilty in seditious libel cases. The judges then took the position that truth was no defense and that the only issue to be submitted to the jury was whether or not the defendant had published the allegedly seditious statements. Whether or not the statements constituted a libel was a matter of law to be determined by the judge. This trend was strenuously opposed by the distinguished English barrister Thomas Erskine, among others, who contended that the jury should be asked to bring in a general verdict of guilty or not guilty and to determine the defendant's criminal intent as in other criminal cases. The final result of this struggle was the passage in 1792 of Fox's Libel Act which established Erskine's views and gave the jury the power to render a general verdict on the whole issue in a libel case rather than merely on the issue of publication.

The French revolution brought a flurry of seditious libel cases, including the prosecution of Thomas Paine in 1792 for the publication of his "Rights of Man", but these prosecutions and the enactment of Fox's Libel Act marked the end of seditious libel as an instrument for the suppression of free speech in England. [6]

The third method of controlling expression of opinion, and on the whole the most effective one, was the elaborate system of printing monopolies and licensing. The authority to regulate the printing press in England was claimed by the Crown as one of its prerogative rights until the supremacy of Parliament was established by the revolution of 1688. Beginning with Henry VIII (1509–1547) the press was held in check through royal proclamations, licenses, patents of monopoly, orders in Council, and Star Chamber decrees. The first English index of prohibited "heretical and blasphemous" books was created by royal proclamation in 1529 and a licensing system for all books was established in 1538 by a proclamation designed to stamp out "seditious opinions" as well as heretical views. Licensers were appointed and no book could lawfully be printed and distributed without their prior approval. The system was modified and extended by the charter granted the Stationers Company in 1557. Members of the Company were given extensive control over the press by the provision of the Charter prohibiting all printing within the realm except by members of the Company or by those having special license from the Crown. The Company enforced both its own licensing ordinances and those issued by the Crown; all member printers were required to obtain a license from the officers of the Company before printing any works and all presses were required to be registered with the Company.

The seventeenth century brought great changes to England in the form of the Puritan Revolution, the Commonwealth, and the triumph of Parliament through the revolution of 1688, but it did not bring freedom of the press, although eloquent voices, such as John Milton's,[7] were raised in its behalf. The

---

[5] Rex v. Tutchin, 14 *State Trials*, p. 1095, quoted in Siebert, op. cit., p. 271.

[6] The efforts of Thomas Erskine on behalf of liberalism in eighteenth century England, including his defense of Thomas Paine, are told in Lloyd Paul Stryker's biography of Erskine, *For the Defense* (1947).

[7] Milton had difficulties with the Stationers Company and the authorities over the publication of his pamphlets on divorce. He made his reply in Areopagitica (1644) which was a plea for the abolition of the licensing system. See Siebert, op. cit., p. 195. Milton's argument for freedom of the press cannot

licensing and other controls became less effective during this century, but the principal change was the shift in power from the Crown to Parliament. The objection of the Puritans to the control of the press was not so much to the control as to the fact that it was exercised by the King. With the fall of Charles I (1649) power passed to Parliament, and after the struggles of the Commonwealth (1649–1653), the Protectorate (1653–1659), and the Stuart restoration (1660–1689), the supremacy of Parliament was confirmed by the Revolution of 1688 and the Bill of Rights of 1689. However, that great document of English constitutional development did not contain any statement espousing general freedom of speech or the press. Its only provision on the subject merely stated: "That the freedom of speech and debates or proceedings in parliament ought not to be impeached or questioned in any court or place out of parliament". It was freedom of speech *in* Parliament, *not outside,* that was recognized.

The control of the press exercised by Parliament gradually relaxed during the century following the Bill of Rights. At the end of the seventeenth century the power of the Stationers Company was broken by the refusal of Parliament to continue its monopolies and special privileges. The methods of control then shifted from licensing to subsidization and taxation. The government resorted to subsidization in order to promote the opinion it desired; such literary figures as Defoe, Swift, Addison, Steele, and Fielding all engaged in political pamphleteering or journalism for which they were compensated in one form or another by the government or political leaders. In 1712, newspapers, pamphlets, advertisements, and paper were subjected to taxes which had the effect of suppressing many of the smaller ephemeral publications then sniping at the policies of the government. That this was the purpose of the taxes is suggested by the fact that books were exempted. These taxes were continued with varying degrees of effectiveness until the first half of the nineteenth century.

It was in the light of this background that Blackstone discussed freedom of thought and expression in his Commentaries, first published in 1765. It is important to note that he wrote at a time when licensing had been abandoned but the law of seditious libel was still in full vigor. His comments are as follows:

> "The liberty of the press is indeed essential to the nature of a free state; but this consists in laying no *previous* restraints upon publications, and not in freedom from censure for criminal matter when published. Every freeman has an undoubted right to lay what sentiments he pleases before the public: to forbid this, is to destroy the freedom of the press; but if he publishes what is improper, mischievous, or illegal, he must take the consequence of his own temerity. To subject the press to the restrictive power of a licenser, as was formerly done, both before and since the revolution, is to subject all freedom of sentiment to the prejudices of one man, and make him the arbitrary and infallible judge of all controverted points in learning, religion, and government. But to punish (as the law does at present) any dangerous or offensive writings, which, when published, shall on a fair and impartial trial be adjudged of a pernicious tendency, is necessary for the preservation of peace and good order, of government and religion, the only solid

be given here, but the following sentences deserve quotation: "Where there is much desire to learn, there of necessity will be much arguing, much writing, many opinions; for opinion in good men is but knowledge in the making. . . . And though all the winds of doctrine were let loose to play upon the earth, so Truth be in the field we do injuriously, by licensing and prohibiting, to misdoubt her strength. Let her and Falsehood grapple; whoever knew Truth put to the worse, in a free and open encounter? Her confuting is the best and surest suppressing. . . ." However, apparently Milton had reservations about complete freedom of expression, for he also said he would not tolerate "popery and open superstition."—Furthermore that "which is impious or evil absolutely either against faith or manners no law can possibly permit, that intends not to unlaw itself. . . ." *The Tradition of Freedom* (Mayer ed. 1957) pp. 26, 28, 29.

foundations of civil liberty. Thus the will of individuals is still left free; the abuse only of that free will is the object of legal punishment. Neither is any restraint hereby laid upon freedom of thought or inquiry: liberty of private sentiment is still left; the disseminating, or making public, of bad sentiments, destructive of the ends of society, is the crime which society corrects." (*Commentaries,* Book IV, pp. 151–152.) [8]

2. THE ADOPTION OF THE FIRST AMENDMENT AND THE CONTROVERSY OVER THE ALIEN AND SEDITION LAWS

(1) **The Original Intent.** Scholars have not been able to agree as to the purpose intended to be served by the first amendment. The basic question is whether it was intended as a charter of freedom or as no more than a determination that regulation of speech and press according to common law principles should be reserved to the states. The most recent scholarship supports the latter position. Leonard Levy concludes, for example, that the amendment was intended only as a restraint on Congress and not on the courts in enforcing the common law crime of seditious libel and "that the prohibition on Congress was motivated far less by a desire to give immunity to political expression than by a solicitude for states' rights and the federal principle. The primary purpose of the first amendment was to reserve to the states an exclusive authority, as far as legislation was concerned, in the field of speech and press." *Freedom of Press from Zenger v. Jefferson* lix (1966).[1] For a different view, see Brant, *The Bill of Rights* 223–236 (1965).

(2) **The Sedition Act.** The Sedition Act (part of a package known as the Alien and Sedition Laws), passed in 1798, made it a crime carrying imprisonment up to two years to write, utter, or publish "any false, scandalous and malicious writing . . . against the government of the United States, or either house of the congress . . . or the President . . . with intent to defame [them] . . . or to bring them . . . into contempt or disrepute; or to excite against them . . . the hatred of the good people of the United States, or to stir up sedition within the United States, or to excite any unlawful combinations therein, for opposing or resisting any law of the United States, or any act of the President of the United States, done in pursuance of any such law, or of the powers vested in him by the constitution of the United States, or to resist, oppose, or defeat any such law or act . . . .." The Act also provided that truth could be offered in defense and that the jury "shall have a right to determine the law and the fact, under the direction of the court, as in other cases." 1 Stat. 596 (1798).

The Sedition Act became the center of an enormous political controversy. Much attention was paid to the question whether it violated the first amendment. Levy contends that in this controversy there was a sudden breakthrough in libertarian thought with the Jeffersonian Republicans abandoning common law notions, arguing that free government required freedom of discussion, and asserting that only injurious conduct as manifested by deeds rather than words should be subjected to criminal punishment. *Freedom of the Press from Zenger to Jefferson* lxx–lxxix (1966).[2]

---

[8] For a general review of the English background of our Bill of Rights, see Brant, *The Bill of Rights,* 3–219 (1965). See also Chafee, *How Human Rights Got into the Constitution* (1952) and *Three Human Rights in the Constitution* (1956). For a convenient collection of the documentary sources, see Perry and Cooper, *Sources of our Liberties* (1959).

[1] Professor Levy in *Legacy of Suppression* (1960) reviews freedom of expression in early American history and concludes that in colonial America the people did not understand that freedom of thought means equal freedom for the other fellow, especially the one with hated ideas.

[2] More recently another author contends that the opposition to the Sedition Act was founded primarily on notions of states' rights rather than civil liberties with a primary motivation being the

The Sedition Act by its own terms was to be in force only until March 3, 1801. One of Jefferson's first acts as President was to pardon all persons convicted under the act. Jefferson's own view of the first amendment, however, seemed to be one of federalism rather than freedom—at least in his role as President subject to scurrilous attacks in opposition newspapers. In 1803 he wrote a letter to Governor McKean of Pennsylvania referring to the licentiousness and lying of the press and then asserting: "This is a dangerous state of things, and the press ought to be restored to its credibility if possible. The restraints provided by the laws of the states are sufficient for this if applied. And I have therefore long thought that a few prosecutions of the most prominent offenders would have a wholesome effect in restoring the integrity of the presses. Not a general prosecution, for that would look like persecution: but a selected one. The paper I now inclose appears to me to offer as good an instance in every respect to make an example of, as can be selected." [3]

In 1806 a common law prosecution of Connecticut editors for libel of President Jefferson and the Congress was brought in the federal courts. That avenue for controlling the press was eliminated by the Supreme Court on appeal from the conviction in that case—not because the prosecution violated the first amendment, but rather on the general proposition that federal courts had no common law criminal jurisdiction. United States v. Hudson and Goodwin, 11 U.S. (7 Cranch) 32 (1812). [4]

3. FREEDOM OF SPEECH AND PRESS IN THE NINETEENTH CENTURY

(1) **Introduction.** The Supreme Court did not begin to elaborate the protection accorded by the first amendment until the time of World War I. One should not draw from that fact the conclusion that there were no intrusions on freedom of speech and the press during this period of time. Developments in the states were unaffected by the first amendment. It was not until 1925 that the Court indicated that the fourteenth amendment had made the first applicable to the states. But there were episodes involving federal control, particularly of the press, that were not subjected to testing by the Supreme Court. [1]

(2) **Punishment for Contempt of Court.** Under the Judiciary Act of 1789 which authorized federal courts to punish "all contempts of authority in any cause or hearing" before them, federal courts early asserted the authority to punish newspapers and others who criticized court decisions. In one early case a federal district judge, James H. Peck, had one Lawless imprisoned and disbarred for publishing a criticism of a decision by Peck which was on appeal. Lawless had powerful political friends and as a result impeachment proceedings were brought against Judge Peck. Peck was acquitted but immediately thereafter Congress amended the statute to limit the contempt power to "misbehaviour of any person or persons in the presence of the said courts, or so near thereto as to obstruct the administration of justice." The story of this episode is told in Nye v. United States, 313 U.S. 33, 45 (1941). As a result of the change in the statute the federal courts for a long time did not assert the power to punish critics. (State courts, however, began increasingly to use contempt to punish

preservation of slavery. Berns, *Freedom of the Press and the Alien and Sedition Laws: A Reappraisal,* 1970 Sup.Ct.Rev. 109.

[3] The letter is set out in Levy, *Freedom of the Press from Zenger to Jefferson* 364 (1966). In a letter to Abigail Adams in 1805 he also said: "While we deny that Congress have a right to control the freedom of the press, we have ever asserted the right of the States, and their exclusive right, to do so." Id. at 366, 367.

[4] For the story of the case and Jefferson's somewhat belated disapproval of the prosecution, see Levy, *Jefferson and Civil Liberties—The Darker Side* 61 (1963).

[1] For an excellent brief general account of this period see Nelson, *Freedom of the Press from Hamilton to the Warren Court* xix–xxxvii (1967).

comments outside the court on the ground that they tended to interfere with the administration of justice.) In 1918 in Toledo Newspaper Co. v. United States, 247 U.S. 402 (1918), the Supreme Court interpreted the federal statute as not applying a geographical limitation on the contempt power of the federal courts and said that the test under the statute was "the character of the act done and its direct tendency to prevent and obstruct the discharge of judicial duty." The Court also rejected the claim that freedom of the press was violated when contempt was used to punish under this test. To state that proposition was to answer it, the Court said, "since it involves in its very statement the contention that the freedom of the press is the freedom to do wrong with impunity, and implies the right to frustrate and defeat the discharge of those governmental duties upon the performance of which the freedom of all, including that of the press, depends." By 1928 the judicial use of the contempt power to punish the press was widespread with most of the cases involving comments impugning the fairness, independence, or integrity of the judge.[2]

(3) **Control of Public Discussion of the Slavery Question.** Antislavery speech was regarded in the South as presenting a very real danger to the institution of slavery. While local dissenters were easily dealt with, the South also sought to exclude from the South any antislavery publications. In 1835 President Jackson asked Congress to enact a law prohibiting the circulation in the South through the mails "of incendiary publications intended to instigate the slaves to insurrection." Calhoun opposed this as a violation of freedom of the press, as being similar to the Sedition Act, but then he proposed a statute making it unlawful for a postmaster to receive and put into the mail any paper "touching the subject of slavery" and addressed to any person in a state which forbade by law the circulation of such materials. Neither of these bills passed but in practice postmasters in the South responded to local pressures and refused to deliver antislavery materials. By 1863 the Postmaster General was asserting the power—which was not challenged for a long time—to remove from the mails or prevent delivery of anti-Union writings or material considered to be obscene. This restraint on discussion of slavery carried over into Congress in which the House by a series of gag rules refused from 1836 to 1845 to entertain or to discuss any petition relating to slavery.[3]

(4) **The Civil War.** During the war there existed both a substantial amount of freedom by the press and a substantial amount of suppression by the military and the President. In one case President Lincoln went so far as to suppress newspapers and order trials of the publishers before military tribunals. For the documents in that case see Nelson, supra note 1, at 232–247. For a fuller account of the relationships between Lincoln and the press, see Randall, *Constitutional Problems Under Lincoln* 477–510 (1951).

(5) **Obscenity, and Control of the Mails.** In 1873 Congress passed the "Comstock law" providing for punishment of those who used the mails to transport obscene materials. State and federal prosecutions for obscenity reached new highs after the turn of the century.[4]

(6) **Civil and Criminal Libel under State Law.** Even if the Sedition Act controversy were viewed as excluding federal libel laws, states remained free of federal constitutional restraint. As late as 1922, the Supreme Court maintained

[2] For an account of the times, see Nelles & King, *Contempt by Publication in the United States,* 28 Colum.L.Rev. 401, 524 (1928).

[3] For a fuller treatment of these episodes, see Berns, *Freedom of the Press and the Alien and Sedition Laws: A Reappraisal,* 1970, Sup.Ct.Rev. 109, 142, 150; Nelson, *Freedom of the Press from Hamilton to the Warren Court* xxii-xxvi (1967).

[4] See generally on this period, Nelson, *Freedom of the Press from Hamilton to the Warren Court* xxviii-xxxii (1967). For an account of postal censorship see Deutsch, *The Freedom of the Press and of the Mails,* 36 Mich.L.Rev. 703 (1938).

that "neither the Fourteenth Amendment nor any other provision of the Constitution of the United States imposes upon the States any restrictions about 'freedom of speech' . . . ." Prudential Ins. Co. v. Cheek, 259 U.S. 530, 543 (1922). While decisional law established truth as a complete defense in civil libel cases, the press was subject to practically strict liability for statements that were innocently false. Criminal libel laws often provided only a qualified defense of truth. Prosecutions for criminal libel in the state courts increased sharply in the later 1800's and stayed high through World War I. In 1918, a law review author could still assert:

> "There is no such thing as an unlimited right to print whatever one may choose to print, regardless of its character and effect. Without law there can be no liberty, and freedom of the press does not mean irresponsibility for what is printed. All right-thinking men will join with Alexander Hamilton in his reprobation of 'the pestilential doctrine of an unchecked press,' and agree with him that ill-fated would be our country were this doctrine to prevail.

> "It is for the state to say what publications are harmful, what use of the press is permissible. It would be an act of tyranny under normal conditions to deprive a citizen of the right to own a gun, but it is essential to public safety to prevent him from using it to the injury of others. So it is with the printing press, an instrument not less dangerous than a shot gun. It is not tyrannous nor inconsistent with the freedom of the press that its owner should be held accountable for any improper use he may make of it." [5]

B. WORLD WAR I AND THE POST–WAR YEARS: PENALIZING THE ADVOCACY OF THE OVERTHROW OF GOVERNMENT BY FORCE OR VIOLENCE

THE CONCERN FOR RADICAL SPEECH IN THE FIRST QUARTER OF THE TWENTIETH CENTURY

In the early years, principal free speech and press disputes had involved the role of newspapers and periodicals—typically those of a different political persuasion than the party in power—in acting as critics of government. A rising concern with radicals began to surface at the turn of the century. Following President McKinley's assassination, the New York Criminal Anarchy law, which became a model for later state and federal legislation, made it a crime to belong to an organization that taught the doctrine that government should be overthrown by force or violence. The Immigration Act of 1903 provided that persons who believed in or advocated the overthrow of government by force and violence should be barred from entering the country, or deported if already here.

The fear of radicals was brought to a head, and fused with concern over enemy sympathizers, by the country's entry into the First World War.

In 1917 Congress passed the Espionage Act. This act made it a crime when the country was at war to "willfully make or convey false reports or false statements with intent to interfere" with the prosecution of the war or to promote the success of enemies, or willfully to "cause or attempt to cause insubordination, disloyalty, mutiny, or refusal of duty, in the military or naval forces of the United States, or willfully to "obstruct the recruiting or enlistment service of the United States . . . ." Another provision of the act forbade the mailing of any material in violation of the provisions of the act or "advocating or urging treason, insurrection, or forcible resistance to any law of

[5] Long, *The Freedom of the Press*, 5 Va.L.Rev. 225, 228, 229 (1918).

the United States . . . ." In 1918 the statute was amended to make criminal the utterance of language "intended to bring the form of government of the United States into contempt, scorn, contumely, or disrepute." This 1918 version of the Sedition Act was repealed in 1921. There were nearly 2,000 prosecutions under the 1917 and 1918 Acts, many publications were excluded from the mails, and a series of challenges under the first amendment came quickly to the Supreme Court.[1]

The antiradical sentiment of the war years became more intense after the war ended. The country was plagued by rumors of radical takeover of government. There was labor unrest, and the news featured incidents of riots and bombings. Radical leaders were prosecuted under state laws modeled after the 1902 New York Criminal Anarchy Law. Some of these cases, too, reached the Supreme Court and renewed the judicial debate concerning the meaning of free speech in the context of attempts to punish the advocates of radical doctrines.[2]

MASSES PUBLISHING CO. v. PATTEN, 244 F. 535 (S.D.N.Y.1917). The publisher of a revolutionary journal called "The Masses" brought suit to enjoin the postmaster of New York from refusing to accept the magazine in the mails. The postmaster argued that the magazine was nonmailable under the provision of the Espionage Act making nonmailable any publication that violated the other provisions of the Act. Part of the focus here was on the provisions of the Act penalizing the willful causing of disaffection in the military services and the willful obstruction of recruitment. On these points Judge Learned Hand construed the statute[3] as follows:

"The next phrase relied upon is that which forbids any one from willfully causing insubordination, disloyalty, mutiny, or refusal of duty in the military or naval forces of the United States. The defendant's position is that to arouse discontent and disaffection among the people with the prosecution of the war and with the draft tends to promote a mutinous and insubordinate temper among the troops. This, too, is true; men who become satisfied that they are engaged in an enterprise dictated by the unconscionable selfishness of the rich, and effectuated by a tyrannous disregard for the will of those who must suffer and die, will be more prone to insubordination than those who have faith in the cause and acquiesce in the means. Yet to interpret the word 'cause' so broadly would, as before, involve necessarily as a consequence the suppression of all hostile criticism, and of all opinion except what encouraged and supported the existing policies, or which fell within the range of temperate argument. It would contradict the normal assumption of democratic government that the suppression of hostile criticism does not turn upon the justice of its substance or the decency and propriety of its temper. Assuming that the power to repress such opinion may rest in Congress in the throes of a struggle for the very existence of the state, its exercise is so contrary to the use and wont of our people that only the clearest expression of such a power justifies the conclusion that it was intended.

"The defendant's position, therefore, in so far as it involves the suppression of the free utterance of abuse and criticism of the existing law, or of the policies of the war, is not, in my judgment, supported by the language of the statute. Yet there has always been a recognized limit to such expressions, incident indeed to the existence of any compulsive power of the state itself. One may

---

[1] See generally Chafee, *Freedom of Speech* (1920) for an account of the period.

[2] For a review of the cases from *Schenck* to *Whitney,* see Cover, *The Left, The Right and the First Amendment,* 40 Md.L.Rev. 349 (1981).

[3] Hand's grant of an injunction, based on that construction, was reversed by the Court of Appeals. 246 Fed. 24 (2d Cir.1917).

not counsel or advise others to violate the law as it stands. Words are not only the keys of persuasion, but the triggers of action, and those which have no purport but to counsel the violation of law cannot by any latitude of interpretation be a part of that public opinion which is the final source of government in a democratic state. The defendant asserts not only that the magazine indirectly through its propaganda leads to a disintegration of loyalty and a disobedience of law, but that in addition it counsels and advises resistance to existing law, especially to the draft. The consideration of this aspect of the case more properly arises under the third phrase of section 3, which forbids any willful obstruction of the recruiting or enlistment service of the United States, but, as the defendant urges that the magazine falls within each phrase, it is as well to take it up now. To counsel or advise a man to an act is to urge upon him either that it is his interest or his duty to do it. While, of course, this may be accomplished as well by indirection as expressly, since words carry the meaning that they impart, the definition is exhaustive, I think, and I shall use it. Political agitation, by the passions it arouses or the convictions it engenders, may in fact stimulate men to the violation of law. Detestation of existing policies is easily transformed into forcible resistance of the authority which puts them in execution, and it would be folly to disregard the causal relation between the two. Yet to assimilate agitation, legitimate as such, with direct incitement to violent resistance, is to disregard the tolerance of all methods of political agitation which in normal times is a safeguard of free government. The distinction is not a scholastic subterfuge, but a hard-bought acquisition in the fight for freedom, and the purpose to disregard it must be evident when the power exists. If one stops short of urging upon others that it is their duty or their interest to resist the law, it seems to me one should not be held to have attempted to cause its violation. If that be not the test, I can see no escape from the conclusion that under this section every political agitation which can be shown to be apt to create a seditious temper is illegal. I am confident that by such language Congress had no such revolutionary purpose in view.

"It seems to me, however, quite plain that none of the language and none of the cartoons in this paper can be thought directly to counsel or advise insubordination or mutiny, without a violation of their meaning quite beyond any tolerable understanding. I come, therefore, to the third phrase of the section, which forbids any one from willfully obstructing the recruiting or enlistment service of the United States. I am not prepared to assent to the plaintiff's position that this only refers to acts other than words, nor that the act thus defined must be shown to have been successful. One may obstruct without preventing, and the mere obstruction is an injury to the service; for it throws impediments in its way. Here again, however, since the question is of the expression of opinion, I construe the sentence, so far as it restrains public utterance, as I have construed the other two, and as therefore limited to the direct advocacy of resistance to the recruiting and enlistment service. If so, the inquiry is narrowed to the question whether any of the challenged matter may be said to advocate resistance to the draft, taking the meaning of the words with the utmost latitude which they can bear."

———————

SCHENCK v. UNITED STATES, 249 U.S. 47 (1919). Section 3 of Title I of the Espionage Act of 1917 established three offenses: "[1] Whoever, when the United States is at war, shall willfully make or convey false reports or false statements with intent to interfere with the operation or success of the military or naval forces of the United States or to promote the success of its enemies and [2] whoever, when the United States is at war, shall willfully cause or attempt to cause insubordination, disloyalty, mutiny, or refusal of duty, in the military or naval forces of the United States, or [3] shall willfully obstruct the recruiting or enlistment Service of the United States, to the injury of the service or of the United States, shall be punished by a fine of not more than $10,000 or imprisonment for not more than twenty years, or both."[1]   Section 4 of the same Title punished persons conspiring to violate Section 3, if any one of them did any act to effect the object of the conspiracy.   Schenck and the other defendants were indicted and convicted of a conspiracy to violate Section 3, by sending to drafted men, circulars calculated to cause insubordination in the armed services and to obstruct the recruiting and enlistment service of the United States.   The circulars asserted that conscription violated the idea of the Thirteenth Amendment and was despotism in the interest of Wall Street's chosen few.   Although the message "in form at least confined itself to peaceful measures," it urged the conscript not to "submit to intimidation" and denied the power of the government to send citizens abroad to shoot persons of other lands.   Defendant did not deny that the tendency of the circulars was to influence persons to obstruct the draft, but contended that any such tendency was protected by the First Amendment.

Justice Holmes' unanimous opinion for the Supreme Court contains the following statement:

"We admit that in many places and in ordinary times the defendants in saying all that was said in the circular would have been within their constitutional rights.   But the character of every act depends upon the circumstances in which it is done. . . .   The most stringent protection of free speech would not protect a man in falsely shouting fire in a theatre and causing a panic.   It does not even protect a man from an injunction against uttering words that may have all the effect of force. . . .   The question in every case is whether the words used are used in such circumstances and are of such a nature as to create a clear and present danger that they will bring about the substantive evils that Congress has a right to prevent.   It is a question of proximity and degree. When a nation is at war many things that might be said in time of peace are such a hindrance to its effort that their utterance will not be endured so long as men fight and that no Court could regard them as protected by any constitutional right.   It seems to be admitted that if an actual obstruction of the recruiting service were proved, liability for words that produced that effect might be enforced.   The statute of 1917 in § 4 punishes conspiracies to obstruct as well as actual obstruction.   If the act, (speaking, or circulating a paper,) its tendency and the intent with which it is done are the same, we perceive no ground for saying that success alone warrants making the act a crime. . . ."

The convictions were affirmed.[2]

ABRAMS v. UNITED STATES, 250 U.S. 616 (1919) involved the 1918 amendment to the Espionage Act.   Offenses under the Act included uttering, printing, writing, or publishing any disloyal, profane, scurrilous or abusive language or language intended to cause contempt, scorn, contumely or disrepute as regards the form of government of the United States;   any language intended

---

[1] 40 Stat. 219, which became 50 U.S.C. § 33, repealed June 25, 1948 when the present United States Code was enacted.   The numbers have been inserted to indicate the different clauses of the provision.

[2] One week later, on the authority of the Schenck decision, the Court sustained the conviction of a prominent socialist, Eugene V. Debs, under the same statute.   In the course of a general address on socialism and opposition to the war, Debs praised draft resisters and stated: "You need to know that you are fit for something better than slavery and cannon fodder."   Debs' 10 year sentence was affirmed because the jury could find that his remarks had a tendency to obstruct recruiting, and Debs had that intent.   Justice Holmes stated that, even if the tendency of the speech and Debs' intent were incidental to Debs' main point in his speech—opposition to the war—his speech was not "protected by reason of its being part of a general program and expressions of a general and conscientious belief." Debs v. United States, 249 U.S. 211, 215 (1919).

to incite resistance to the United States or promote the cause of its enemies; or any language urging curtailment of production of any things necessary to the prosecution of war with intent to hinder such prosecution. Abrams and his fellow defendants were indicted and convicted of conspiring to violate these provisions of the 1918 amendment, in that they printed and distributed some 5000 circulars in New York City on about August 22, 1918, which circulars were intended to bring the form of government of the United States into contempt; to encourage resistance to the United States in World War I; and to incite curtailment of war production. In the circulars, President Wilson was denounced as a hypocrite and a coward for sending troops into Russia to support the anti-Bolshevik forces; the workers of the world were urged to awake and put down the common enemy—capitalism; the general strike was advocated as the necessary reply to the "barbaric intervention" in Russia; and the toilers of America were to pledge themselves "to create so great a disturbance that the autocrats of America shall be compelled to keep their armies at home, and not be able to spare any for Russia."

The majority concluded that any question regarding the constitutionality of the Espionage Act as a whole had been disposed of by *Schenck* and related cases, leaving, as the major issue, the sufficiency of the evidence to sustain the guilty verdict. They held that it had been proved that the defendants published their circulars with intent to encourage resistance to the war with Germany and to incite curtailment of war production.[1]

Justice Holmes, joined by Justice Brandeis, wrote a dissenting opinion in which he concluded that the circulars did not show the requisite intent to provoke resistance to the war with Germany or to curtail production in order to cripple the war effort. The opinion concludes with the following paragraphs.

"In this case sentences of twenty years imprisonment have been imposed for the publishing of two leaflets that I believe the defendants had as much right to publish as the Government has to publish the Constitution of the United States now vainly invoked by them. Even if I am technically wrong and enough can be squeezed from these poor and puny anonymities to turn the color of legal litmus paper; I will add, even if what I think the necessary intent were shown; the most nominal punishment seems to me all that possibly could be inflicted, unless the defendants are to be made to suffer not for what the indictment alleges but for the creed that they avow—a creed that I believe to be the creed of ignorance and immaturity when honestly held, as I see no reason to doubt that it was held here, but which, although made the subject of examination at the trial, no one has a right even to consider in dealing with the charges before the Court.

"Persecution for the expression of opinions seems to me perfectly logical. If you have no doubt of your premises or your power and want a certain result with all your heart you naturally express your wishes in law and sweep away all opposition. To allow opposition by speech seems to indicate that you think the speech impotent, as when a man says that he has squared the circle, or that you do not care whole-heartedly for the result, or that you doubt either your power or your premises. But when men have realized that time has upset many fighting faiths, they may come to believe even more than they believe the very foundations of their own conduct that the ultimate good desired is better reached by free trade in ideas—that the best test of truth is the power of the thought to get itself accepted in the competition of the market, and that truth is the only ground upon which their wishes safely can be carried out. That at any rate is the theory of our Constitution. It is an experiment, as all life is an experiment. Every year if not every day we have to wager our salvation upon

---

[1] The majority found it unnecessary to review defendants' conviction on the count charging that the circulars were intended to bring the form of government of the United States into contempt.

some prophecy based upon imperfect knowledge. While that experiment is part of our system I think that we should be eternally vigilant against attempts to check the expression of opinions that we loathe and believe to be fraught with death, unless they so imminently threaten immediate interference with the lawful and pressing purposes of the law that an immediate check is required to save the country. I wholly disagree with the argument of the Government that the First Amendment left the common law as to seditious libel in force. History seems to me against the notion. I had conceived that the United States through many years had shown its repentance for the Sedition Act of 1798, by repaying fines that it imposed. Only the emergency that makes it immediately dangerous to leave the correction of evil counsels to time warrants making any exception to the sweeping command, 'Congress shall make no law . . . abridging the freedom of speech.' Of course I am speaking only of expressions of opinion and exhortations, which were all that were uttered here, but I regret that I cannot put into more impressive words my belief that in their conviction upon this indictment the defendants were deprived of their rights under the Constitution of the United States." [2]

HAND'S "ADVOCACY" TEST VS. HOLMES' "CLEAR AND PRESENT" TEST

Professor Corwin summarized the holdings of the *Schenck* and *Abrams* cases as follows:

> "To sum up, the following propositions seem to be established with respect to constitutional freedom of speech and press: first, Congress is not limited to forbidding words which are of a nature 'to create a clear and present danger' to national interest, but it may forbid words which are intended to endanger those interests if in the exercise of a fair legislative discretion it finds it 'necessary and proper' to do so; second, the intent of the accused in uttering the alleged forbidden words may be presumed from the reasonable consequences of such words, though the presumption is a rebuttable one; third, the court will not scrutinize on appeal the findings of juries in this class of cases more strictly than in other penal cases. In short, the cause of freedom of speech and press is largely in the custody of legislative majorities and of juries, which, so far as there is evidence to show, is just where the framers of the Constitution intended it to be." Corwin, *Freedom of Speech and Press Under the First Amendment: A Resume,* 30 Yale L.J. 48, 55 (1920), reprinted in 2 Selected Essays on Constitutional Law 1060, 1067 (1938).

In an excellent article—Gunther, *Learned Hand and the Origins of Modern First Amendment Doctrine: Some Fragments of History,* 27 Stanf.L.Rev. 719 (1975)—contemporary correspondence between Judge Hand and Justice Holmes is set forth making it clear that they had quite different points of view as to the appropriate limits on the punishment of radical speech. Holmes, in fact, started

---

[2] The *Abrams* case was the only one under the 1918 Act to reach the Supreme Court. That Act was repealed in 1921 (41 Stat. 1359), leaving the original 1917 Act to become what is now 18 U.S.C. § 2388. There have been intermittent prosecutions under the legislation. See Hartzel v. United States, 322 U.S. 680 (1944); United States v. Powell, 156 F.Supp. 526 (N.D.Cal.1957). The 1917 Act (by its original terms and as carried into 18 U.S.C. § 2388) applies only "when the United States is at war."

Related to the above legislation is a provision of the Universal Military Training and Service Act of 1948 which provides that one "who knowingly counsels, aids, or abets another to refuse or evade registration or service in the armed forces or any of the requirements of this title" is guilty of a crime. 50 U.S.C.App. § 462(a). Under this section, a dean of a college was convicted for telling a student who was refusing to register, "Do not let them coerce you into registering." Gara v. United States, 178 F.2d 38 (6th Cir.1949), affirmed by an equally divided vote, 340 U.S. 857 (1950).

with the observation that "free speech stands no differently than freedom from vaccination." In a letter to Professor Chafee in 1921 Hand summarized his objections to the Holmes approach as set forth in *Schenck* and *Abrams:*

> "I am not wholly in love with Holmesy's test and the reason is this. Once you admit that the matter is one of degree, while you may put it where it genuinely belongs, you so obviously make it a matter of administration, i.e., you give to Tomdickandharry, D.J., so much latitude that the jig is at once up. Besides their Ineffabilities, the Nine Elder Statesmen, have not shown themselves wholly immune from the 'herd instinct' and what seems 'immediate and direct' to-day may seem very remote next year even though the circumstances surrounding the utterance be unchanged. I own I should prefer a qualitative formula, hard, conventional, difficult to evade." Id. at 770.

The *Abrams* case suggested a somewhat different problem than *Schenck*. In *Schenck,* the statutory language prohibited conduct. *Abrams* involved a statute making criminal "language intended to incite resistance to the United States" and "language urging curtailment of production of any things necessary to the prosecution of war with intent to hinder such prosecution." In Gitlow v. New York, which is set out below, New York's statute penalized the advocacy of the "duty, necessity, or propriety" of overturning the government by force or violence.

GITLOW v. NEW YORK

268 U.S. 652, 45 S.Ct. 625, 69 L.Ed. 1138 (1925).

Mr. Justice Sanford delivered the opinion of the Court.

Benjamin Gitlow was indicted in the Supreme Court of New York, with three others, for the statutory crime of criminal anarchy. New York Penal Law, §§ 160, 161. He was separately tried, convicted, and sentenced to imprisonment. The judgment was affirmed by the Appellate Division and by the Court of Appeals.

The contention here is that the statute, by its terms and as applied in this case, is repugnant to the due process clause of the Fourteenth Amendment. Its material provisions are:

"Sec. 160. *Criminal Anarchy Defined.* Criminal anarchy is the doctrine that organized government should be overthrown by force or violence, or by assassination of the executive head or of any of the executive officials of government, or by any unlawful means. The advocacy of such doctrine either by word of mouth or writing is a felony.

"Sec. 161. *Advocacy of Criminal Anarchy.* Any person who:

"1. By word of mouth or writing advocates, advises or teaches the duty, necessity or propriety of overthrowing or overturning organized government by force or violence, or by assassination of the executive head or of any of the executive officials of government, or by any unlawful means; or,

"2. Prints, publishes, edits, issues or knowingly circulates, sells, distributes or publicly displays any book, paper, document, or written or printed matter in any form, containing or advocating, advising or teaching the doctrine that organized government should be overthrown by force, violence or any unlawful means, . . .

"Is guilty of a felony and punishable" by imprisonment or fine, or both.

The indictment was in two counts. The first charged that the defendant had advocated, advised and taught the duty, necessity and propriety of overthrowing and overturning organized government by force, violence and unlawful means, by certain writings therein set forth entitled "The Left Wing Manifesto"; the second that he had printed, published and knowingly circulated and distributed a certain paper called "The Revolutionary Age," containing the writings set forth in the first count advocating, advising and teaching the doctrine that organized government should be overthrown by force, violence and unlawful means.

The following facts were established on the trial by undisputed evidence and admissions: . . . It was admitted that the defendant signed a card subscribing to the Manifesto and Program of the Left Wing, which all applicants were required to sign before being admitted to membership; that he went to different parts of the State to speak to branches of the Socialist Party about the principles of the Left Wing and advocated their adoption; and that he was responsible for the Manifesto as it appeared, that "he knew of the publication, in a general way and he knew of its publication afterwards, and is responsible for circulation."

There was no evidence of any effect resulting from the publication and circulation of the Manifesto.

No witnesses were offered in behalf of the defendant.

. . .

The court, among other things, charged the jury, in substance, that they must determine what was the intent, purpose and fair meaning of the Manifesto; that its words must be taken in their ordinary meaning, as they would be understood by people whom it might reach; that a mere statement or analysis of social and economic facts and historical incidents, in the nature of an essay, accompanied by prophecy as to the future course of events, but with no teaching, advice or advocacy of action, would not constitute the advocacy, advice or teaching of a doctrine for the overthrow of government within the meaning of the statute; that a mere statement that unlawful acts might accomplish such a purpose would be insufficient, unless there was a teaching, advising and advocacy of employing such unlawful acts for the purpose of overthrowing government; and that if the jury had a reasonable doubt that the Manifesto did teach, advocate or advise the duty, necessity or propriety of using unlawful means for the overthrowing of organized government, the defendant was entitled to an acquittal.

The defendant's counsel submitted two requests to charge which embodied in substance the statement that to constitute criminal anarchy within the meaning of the statute it was necessary that the language used or published should advocate, teach or advise the duty, necessity or propriety of doing "some definite or immediate act or acts" of force, violence or unlawfulness directed toward the overthrowing of organized government. These were denied further than had been charged. Two other requests to charge embodied in substance the statement that to constitute guilt the language used or published must be "reasonably and ordinarily calculated to incite certain persons" to acts of force, violence or unlawfulness, with the object of overthrowing organized government. These were also denied. . . .

. . .

The sole contention here is, essentially, that as there was no evidence of any concrete result flowing from the publication of the Manifesto or of circumstances showing the likelihood of such result, the statute as construed and applied by the trial court penalizes the mere utterance, as such, of "doctrine" having no quality of incitement, without regard either to the circumstances of its utterance or to the likelihood of unlawful sequences; and that, as the exercise of the right of free expression with relation to government is only punishable "in circumstances involving likelihood of substantive evil," the statute contravenes the due process clause of the Fourteenth Amendment. . . .

The statute does not penalize the utterance or publication of abstract "doctrine" or academic discussion having no quality of incitement to any concrete action. It is not aimed against mere historical or philosophical essays. It does not restrain the advocacy of changes in the form of government by constitutional and lawful means. What it prohibits is language advocating, advising or teaching the overthrow of organized government by unlawful means. These words imply urging to action. . . .

The Manifesto, plainly, is neither the statement of abstract doctrine nor, as suggested by counsel, mere prediction that industrial disturbances and revolutionary mass strikes will result spontaneously in an inevitable process of evolution in the economic system. It advocates and urges in fervent language mass action which shall progressively foment industrial disturbances and through political mass strikes and revolutionary mass action overthrow and destroy organized parliamentary government. It concludes with a call to action in these words:

> "The proletariat revolution and the Communist reconstruction of society—*the struggle for these*—is now indispensable. . . . The Communist International calls the proletariat of the world to the final struggle!"

This is not the expression of philosophical abstraction, the mere prediction of future events; it is the language of direct incitement.

The means advocated for bringing about the destruction of organized parliamentary government, namely, mass industrial revolts usurping the functions of municipal government, political mass strikes directed against the parliamentary state, and revolutionary mass action for its final destruction, necessarily imply the use of force and violence, and in their essential nature are inherently unlawful in a constitutional government of law and order. That the jury were warranted in finding that the Manifesto advocated not merely the abstract doctrine of overthrowing organized government by force, violence and unlawful means, but action to that end, is clear.

For present purposes we may and do assume that freedom of speech and of the press—which are protected by the First Amendment from abridgment by Congress—are among the fundamental personal rights and "liberties" protected by the due process clause of the Fourteenth Amendment from impairment by the States. . . .

By enacting the present statute the State has determined, through its legislative body, that utterances advocating the overthrow of organized government by force, violence and unlawful means, are so inimical to the general welfare and involve such danger of substantive evil that they may be penalized in the exercise of its police power. That determination must be given great weight. . . . That utterances inciting to the overthrow of organized government by unlawful means, present a sufficient danger of substantive evil to bring their punishment within the range of legislative discretion, is clear. Such utterances, by their very nature, involve danger to the public peace and to the security of the State. They threaten breaches of the peace and ultimate revolution. And the immediate danger is none the less real and substantial, because the effect of a given utterance cannot be accurately foreseen. The State cannot reasonably be required to measure the danger from every such utterance in the nice balance of a jeweler's scale. A single revolutionary spark may kindle a fire that, smouldering for a time, may burst into a sweeping and destructive conflagration. It cannot be said that the State is acting arbitrarily or unreasonably when in the exercise of its judgment as to the measures necessary to protect the public peace and safety, it seeks to extinguish the spark without waiting until it has enkindled the flame or blazed into the conflagration. It cannot reasonably be required to defer the adoption of measures for its own peace and safety until the revolutionary utterances lead to actual disturbances of the public peace or imminent and immediate danger of its own destruction; but it may, in the exercise of its judgment, suppress the threatened danger in its incipiency. . . .

We cannot hold that the present statute is an arbitrary or unreasonable exercise of the police power of the State unwarrantably infringing the freedom of speech or press; and we must and do sustain its constitutionality.

This being so it may be applied to every utterance—not too trivial to be beneath the notice of the law—which is of such a character and used with such intent and purpose as to bring it within the prohibition of the statute. . . . In other words, when the legislative body has determined generally, in the constitutional exercise of its discretion, that utterances of a certain kind involve such danger of substantive evil that they may be punished, the question whether any specific utterance coming within the prohibited class is likely, in and of itself, to bring about the substantive evil, is not open to consideration. It is sufficient that the statute itself be constitutional and that the use of the language comes within its prohibition.

It is clear that the question in such cases is entirely different from that involved in those cases where the statute merely prohibits certain acts involving the danger of substantive evil, without any reference to language itself, and it is sought to apply its provisions to language used by the defendant for the purpose of bringing about the prohibited results. There, if it be contended that the statute cannot be applied to the language used by the defendant because of its protection by the freedom of speech or press, it must necessarily be found, as an original question, without any previous determination by the legislative body, whether the specific language used involved such likelihood of bringing about the substantive evil as to deprive it of the constitutional protection. In such cases it has been held that the general provisions of the statute may be constitutionally applied to the specific utterance of the defendant if its natural tendency and probable effect was to bring about the substantive evil which the legislative body might prevent. Schenck v. United States [249 U.S. 47, 51]; Debs v. United States [249 U.S. 211, 215, 216]. And the general statement in the Schenck Case, p. 52, that the "question in every case is whether the words used are used in such circumstances and are of such a nature as to create a clear and present danger that they will bring about the substantive evils,"—upon which great reliance is placed in the defendant's argument—was manifestly intended, as shown by the context, to apply only in cases of this class, and has no application to those like the present, where the legislative body itself has previously determined the danger of substantive evil arising from utterances of a specified character. . . .

And finding, for the reasons stated, that the statute is not in itself unconstitutional, and that it has not been applied in the present case in derogation of any constitutional right, the judgment of the Court of Appeals is

Affirmed.

Mr. Justice Holmes (dissenting). Mr. Justice Brandeis and I are of opinion that this judgment should be reversed. The general principle of free speech, it seems to me, must be taken to be included in the Fourteenth Amendment, in view of the scope that has been given to the word "liberty" as there used, although perhaps it may be accepted with a somewhat larger latitude of interpretation than is allowed to Congress by the sweeping language that governs or ought to govern the laws of the United States. If I am right then I think that the criterion sanctioned by the full Court in Schenck v. United States, 249 U.S. 47, 52, applies. . . . It is true that in my opinion this criterion was departed from in Abrams v. United States, 250 U.S. 616, but the convictions that I expressed in that case are too deep for it to be possible for me as yet to believe that it and Schaefer v. United States, 251 U.S. 466, have settled the law. If what I think the correct test is applied, it is manifest that there was no present danger of an attempt to overthrow the government by force on the part of the admittedly small minority who shared the defendant's views. It is said that this manifesto was more than a theory, that it was an incitement. Every idea is an incitement. It offers itself for belief and if believed it is acted on unless some other belief outweighs it or some failure of energy stifles the movement at its birth. The only difference between the expression of an opinion and an incitement in the narrower sense is the speaker's enthusiasm for the result. Eloquence may set fire to reason. But whatever may be thought of the redundant discourse before us it had no chance of starting a present conflagration. If in the long run the beliefs expressed in proletarian dictatorship are destined to be accepted by the dominant forces of the community, the only meaning of free speech is that they should be given their chance and have their way.

If the publication of this document had been laid as an attempt to induce an uprising against government at once and not at some indefinite time in the future it would have presented a different question. The object would have been one with which the law might deal, subject to the doubt whether there was any danger that the publication could produce any result, or in other words whether it was not futile and too remote from possible consequences. But the indictment alleges the publication and nothing more.

WHITNEY v. CALIFORNIA, 274 U.S. 357 (1927) arose under the California Criminal Syndicalism Act which defined "criminal syndicalism" as any doctrine advocating, teaching or abetting sabotage or other unlawful acts of violence as a means of accomplishing industrial or political change. It was made a crime for any person to organize, assist in organizing, or knowingly become a member of any organization or group of persons associated to advocate, teach or abet criminal syndicalism.

Miss Whitney was a socialist who in 1919 became a temporary member of the new Communist Labor Party and went as a delegate to a convention for organizing a California branch. There she supported a resolution which would have committed the organization to the use of peaceful and lawful methods of change, but this resolution lost and the convention adopted a program resembling Gitlow's Left Wing Manifesto. Miss Whitney was found guilty under the act in that she assisted in organizing and knowingly became a member of a group formed to advocate criminal syndicalism.

The United States Supreme Court sustained the conviction. The majority opinion made two principal points: (a) Whether or not Miss Whitney helped organize and became a member of the Communist Labor Party with knowledge of its program of criminal syndicalism was a question of fact upon which the verdict of the jury was conclusive. (b) The California act "may not be declared unconstitutional unless it is an arbitrary or unreasonable attempt to exercise the authority vested in the state in the public interest." Because of the danger to the public peace and security from an organization advocating violent and unlawful methods of change, the act could not be regarded as an unreasonable exercise of the police power, unwarrantably infringing any right of free speech and assembly.

Justice Brandeis, concurring in the decision, took this occasion to write a major dissenting opinion, joined by Justice Holmes. The clear and present danger doctrine was explained in passages including the following: "Fear of serious injury cannot alone justify suppression of free speech and assembly. Men feared witches and burnt women. It is the function of speech to free men from the bondage of irrational fears. To justify suppression of free speech there must be reasonable ground to fear that serious evil will result if free speech is practiced. There must be reasonable ground to believe that the danger apprehended is imminent. There must be reasonable ground to believe that the evil to be prevented is a serious one. Every denunciation of existing law tends in some measure to increase the probability that there will be a violation of it. Condonation of a breach enhances the probability. Expressions of approval add to the probability. Propagation of the criminal state of mind by teaching syndicalism increases it. Advocacy of law-breaking heightens it still further. But even advocacy of violation, however reprehensible morally, is not a justification for denying free speech where the advocacy falls short of incitement and there is nothing to indicate that the advocacy would be immediately acted on. The wide difference between advocacy and incitement, between preparation and attempt, between assembling and conspiracy, must be borne in mind. In order to support a finding of clear and present danger it must be shown either that immediate serious violence was to be expected or was advocated, or that the past conduct furnished reason to believe that such advocacy was then contemplated."

"Those who won our independence by revolution were not cowards. They did not fear political change. They did not exalt order at the cost of liberty. To courageous, self-reliant men, with confidence in the power of free and fearless reasoning applied through the processes of popular government, no danger flowing from speech can be deemed clear and present, unless the incidence of the evil apprehended is so imminent that it may befall before there is opportunity for full discussion. If there be time to expose through discussion the falsehood and fallacies, to avert the evil by the processes of education, the remedy to be applied is more speech, not enforced silence. Only an emergency can justify repression. Such must be the rule if authority is to be reconciled with freedom. Such, in my opinion, is the command of the Constitution. It is therefore always open to Americans to challenge a law abridging free speech and assembly by showing that there was no emergency justifying it.

"Moreover, even imminent danger cannot justify resort to prohibition of these functions essential to effective democracy, unless the evil apprehended is relatively serious. Prohibition of free speech and assembly is a measure so stringent that it would be inappropriate as the means for averting a relatively trivial harm to society. A police measure may be unconstitutional merely because the remedy, although effective as means of protection, is unduly harsh or oppressive. Thus, a State might, in the exercise of its police power, make any trespass upon the land of another a crime, regardless of the results or of the intent or purpose of the trespasser. It might, also, punish an attempt, a conspiracy, or an incitement to commit the trespass. But it is hardly conceivable that this Court would hold constitutional a statute which punished as a felony the mere voluntary assembly with a society formed to teach that pedestrians had the moral right to cross unenclosed, unposted, waste lands and to advocate their doing so, even if there was imminent danger that advocacy would lead to a trespass. The fact that speech is likely to result in some violence or in destruction of property is not enough to justify its suppression. There must be the probability of serious injury to the State. Among free men, the deterrents ordinarily to be applied to prevent crime are education and punishment for

violations of the law, not abridgment of the rights of free speech and assembly.
. . . ." a

THE BASIS OF THE BRANDEIS CONCURRENCE
IN THE WHITNEY CASE

Because Justice Brandeis' opinion in *Whitney* is both the most articulate and passionate defense of the clear and present danger test, it is often forgotten that he and Justice Holmes voted to affirm Anita Whitney's conviction. The reason for concurrence was explained as follows: "Whether in 1919, when Miss Whitney did the things complained of, there was in California such clear and present danger of serious evil, might have been made the important issue in the case. She might have required that the issue be determined either by the court or the jury. She claimed below that the statute as applied to her violated the federal Constitution; but she did not claim that it was void because there was no clear and present danger of serious evil, nor did she request that the existence of these conditions of a valid measure thus restricting the rights of free speech and assembly be passed upon by the court or a jury. On the other hand, there was evidence on which the court or jury might have found that such danger existed. I am unable to assent to the suggestion in the opinion of the court that assembling with a political party, formed to advocate the desirability of a proletarian revolution by mass action at some date necessarily far in the future, is not a right within the protection of the Fourteenth Amendment. In the present case, however, there was other testimony which tended to establish the existence of a conspiracy, on the part of members of the International Workers of the World, to commit present serious crimes, and likewise to show that such a conspiracy would be furthered by the activity of the society of which Miss Whitney was a member. Under these circumstances the judgment of the state court cannot be disturbed."

Note that the defendant was not charged with illegal advocacy, but was convicted for organizing and being a member of a group engaged in unlawful advocacy. Moreover, there was no evidence that she engaged personally in the unlawful advocacy. To the contrary, she had sponsored a competing resolution at the group's organizing meeting calling for peaceful and lawful change. Suppose the clear and present danger defense had been raised at the criminal trial, but it had been found, on sufficient evidence, that the party advocated present serious crimes, and that there was a clear and present danger that those crimes would be committed. Under the position of Justices Brandeis and Holmes, would the fact that defendant disagreed with the advocacy of criminal conduct and did not personally participate in that advocacy be the basis of a viable first amendment defense? Would it be sufficient for conviction that she remained as an active party member, knowing of its illegal advocacy?

DE JONGE v. OREGON, 299 U.S. 353 (1937). De Jonge was convicted on an indictment charging violation of the Oregon Criminal Syndicalism Law which defined "criminal syndicalism" as "the doctrine which advocates crime, physical violence, sabotage, or any unlawful acts or methods as a means of accomplishing or effecting industrial or political change or revolution." Among the offenses created were the teaching of criminal syndicalism, the printing or distribution of material advocating the doctrine, the organization of a society or

a The Whitney case and its background are discussed in Chafee, *Free Speech in the United States* (1941), pp. 343–354. Shortly after the Supreme Court's decision, Miss Whitney was pardoned by Governor Young of California, who in giving reasons for his action made reference to the opinion of Justice Brandeis.

group which advocates it, and presiding at or assisting in conducting a meeting of such an organization, society or group.

The indictment charged that the defendant had unlawfully presided at, and assisted in conducting "an assemblage of persons", to wit, the Communist Party, "which said assemblage of persons" did then and there unlawfully teach and advocate the doctrine of criminal syndicalism.

The evidence showed that De Jonge was a member of the Communist Party; that he presided over and otherwise participated in the public meeting held in Portland, Oregon, under the auspices of the Communist Party; that the meeting was held to protest against illegal raids on workers' halls and homes, and against the shooting of striking longshoremen by the Portland police; and at the meeting there were no unlawful acts done, nor any advocacy of criminal syndicalism. The Supreme Court of Oregon affirmed the conviction on the ground that in addition to the above evidence, there was evidence to show, as the indictment had charged, that the Communist Party at other times and places in Oregon, had taught and advocated criminal syndicalism.

Chief Justice Hughes, speaking for a unanimous Court, delivered an opinion containing the following paragraphs:

"Conviction upon a charge not made would be sheer denial of due process. It thus appears that, while defendant was a member of the Communist Party, he was not indicted for participating in its organization, or for joining it, or for soliciting members or for distributing its literature. He was not charged with teaching or advocating criminal syndicalism or sabotage or any unlawful acts, either at the meeting or elsewhere. He was accordingly deprived of the benefit of evidence as to the orderly and lawful conduct of the meeting and that it was not called or used for the advocacy of criminal syndicalism or sabotage or any unlawful action. His sole offense as charged, and for which he was convicted and sentenced to imprisonment for seven years, was that he had assisted in the conduct of a public meeting, albeit otherwise lawful, which was held under the auspices of the Communist Party. . . .

.   .   .

"Freedom of speech and of the press are fundamental rights which are safeguarded by the due process clause of the Fourteenth Amendment of the Federal Constitution. . . . The right of peaceable assembly is a right cognate to those of free speech and free press and is equally fundamental. As this Court said in United States v. Cruikshank, 92 U.S. 542, 552: 'The very idea of a government, republican in form, implies a right on the part of its citizens to meet peaceably for consultation in respect to public affairs and to petition for a redress of grievances.' The First Amendment of the Federal Constitution expressly guarantees that right against abridgement by Congress. But explicit mention there does not argue exclusion elsewhere. For the right is one that cannot be denied without violating those fundamental principles of liberty and justice which lie at the base of all civil and political institutions— principles which the Fourteenth Amendment embodies in the general terms of its due process clause. . . .

.   .   .

"It follows from these considerations that, consistently with the Federal Constitution, peaceable assembly for lawful discussion cannot be made a crime. The holding of meetings for peaceable political action cannot be proscribed. Those who assist in the conduct of such meetings cannot be branded as criminals on that score. The question, if the rights of free speech and peaceable assembly are to be preserved, is not as to the auspices under which the meeting is held but as to its purpose; not as to the relations of the speakers, but whether their utterances transcend the bounds of the freedom of speech which the Constitution protects. If the persons assembling have committed crimes elsewhere, if they have formed or are engaged in a conspiracy against the public peace and order they may be prosecuted for their conspiracy or other violation of valid laws. But it is a different matter when the State, instead of prosecuting them for such offenses, seizes upon mere participation in a peaceable assembly and a lawful public discussion as the basis for a criminal charge.

"We are not called upon to review the findings of the state court as to the objectives of the Communist Party. Notwithstanding those objectives, the defendant still enjoyed his personal right of free speech and to take part in a peaceable assembly having a lawful purpose, although called by that Party. The defendant was none the less entitled to discuss the public issues of the day and thus in a lawful manner, without incitement to violence or crime, to seek redress of alleged grievances. That was of the essence of his guaranteed personal liberty."

C. THE POST WORLD WAR II COLD WAR ERA: PROSECUTION OF COMMUNISTS UNDER THE SMITH ACT

THE SMITH ACT

During the years that followed the Second World War, anti-radical hysteria surpassed that of the Great Red Scare of the 1920's. The focus this time was the Russian threat, and the specific concern was espionage and subversion by the Communist Party of the United States. The output of both the national and state legislatures, passing laws dealing with loyalty and security, was enormous during this period. So too, were the number of cases, many decided by the United States Supreme Court. Many of those cases will be considered in Chapter 17. The cases that follow are only a small part of the story of the Supreme Court's treatment of anti-Communist legislation during the years of the cold war and after. They are, however, an important part since they continue the debate begun in *Schenck, Abrams, Gitlow* and *Whitney.*

The *Dennis* case, which follows, resulted from federal prosecution of the Communist Party's top national leaders. The *Yates* and *Scales* cases involved prosecutions of lower level Communist Party officials, that followed in the wake of the Court's affirmance of the convictions in *Dennis.* Ironically, the legislation under which the prosecutions were initiated had been enacted prior to the war. The Smith Act was passed in 1940 as a rider to other legislation and received little attention in or out of Congress until it was employed, after the war, as the vehicle for prosecution of Communist Party officials. The Smith Act was patterned on the New York Criminal Anarchy Act which had been sustained in *Gitlow v. New York.*

DENNIS v. UNITED STATES, 341 U.S. 494 (1951). Petitioners, leaders of the Communist Party, were prosecuted and convicted in a federal district court in New York of violating the Smith Act which provided:

"Sec. 2(a) It shall be unlawful for any person—

"(1) to knowingly or willfully advocate, abet, advise, or teach the duty, necessity, desirability, or propriety of overthrowing or destroying any government in the United States by force or violence, or by the assassination of any officer of any such government; . . .

"(3) to organize or help to organize any society, group, or assembly of persons who teach, advocate, or encourage the overthrow or destruction of any government in the United States by force or violence; or to be or become a member of, or affiliate with, any such society, group, or assembly of persons, knowing the purposes thereof. . . .

Sec. 3. It shall be unlawful for any person to attempt to commit, or to conspire to commit, any of the acts prohibited by the provisions of this title."

The indictment charged petitioners with conspiring (1) to organize as the Communist Party of the United States a group of persons who teach and advocate the overthrow of the Government of the United States by force and violence, and (2) to advocate and teach the duty and necessity of overthrowing the government of the United States by force and violence. After a protracted trial, the judge gave the jury instructions which included the following: "In further construction and interpretation of the statute I charge you that it is not the abstract doctrine of overthrowing or destroying organized government by unlawful means which is denounced by this law, but the teaching and advocacy of action for the accomplishment of that purpose, by language reasonably and ordinarily calculated to incite persons to such action. Accordingly, you cannot find the defendants or any of them guilty of the crime charged unless you are satisfied beyond a reasonable doubt that they conspired to organize a society, group and assembly of persons who teach and advocate the overthrow or destruction of the Government of the United States by force and violence and to advocate and teach the duty and necessity of overthrowing or destroying the Government of the United States by force and violence, with the intent that such teaching and advocacy be of a rule or principle of action and by language reasonably and ordinarily calculated to incite persons to such action, all with the intent to cause the overthrow or destruction of the Government of the United States by force and violence as speedily as circumstances would permit. . . .

"If you are satisfied that the evidence established beyond a reasonable doubt that the defendants, or any of them, are guilty of a violation of the statute, as I have interpreted it to you, I find as matter of law that there is sufficient danger of a substantive evil that the Congress has a right to prevent to justify the application of the statute under the First Amendment of the Constitution.

"This is a matter of law about which you have no concern. It is a finding on a matter of law which I deem essential to support my ruling that the case would be submitted to you to pass upon the guilt or innocence of the defendants. . . . ."

The convictions were affirmed by the Court of Appeals and the Supreme Court granted certiorari limited to the question of the constitutionality of the Smith Act as construed and applied. Several opinions were written, none of which obtained the approval of sufficient Justices to make it the opinion of the Court.

The opinion receiving the greatest assent was by Vinson, C.J., joined by Reed, Burton and Minton, JJ. "The obvious purpose of the statute," said the Chief Justice, "is to protect existing Government, not from change by peaceable, lawful and constitutional means, but from change by violence, revolution and terrorism. That it is within the *power* of the Congress to protect the Government of the United States from armed rebellion is a proposition which requires little discussion." Consequently the question before the Court was whether the *means* employed by Congress conflicted with the First and Fifth Amendments. Petitioners made several contentions in support of their argument that there was such conflict. It was contended that the statute unconstitutionally stifled free speech because it prohibited academic discussion of Marxism-Leninism, but the Chief Justice rejected this construction of the act saying: "It is directed at advocacy, not discussion. Thus, the trial judge properly charged the jury that they could not convict if they found that petitioners did 'no more than pursue peaceful studies and discussions or teaching and advocacy in the realm of ideas.' " But even with this construction, the statute limited speech and therefore, in the words of the Chief Justice, the case "squarely presented" the Court with the application of the "clear and present danger" test and required a decision as to "what that phrase imports." [a] "Obviously, the words cannot mean that before the Government may act, it must wait until the *putsch* is about to be executed, the plans have been laid and the signal is awaited. If Government is aware that a group aiming at its overthrow is attempting to indoctrinate its members and to commit them to a course whereby they will strike when the leaders feel the circumstances permit, action by the Government is required. The argument that there is no need for Government to concern itself, for Government is strong, it possesses ample power to put down a rebellion, it may defeat the revolution with ease needs no answer. For that is not the question. Certainly an attempt to overthrow the Government by force, even though doomed from the outset because of inadequate numbers of power of the revolutionists, is a sufficient evil for Congress to prevent. . . .

"The situation with which Justices Holmes and Brandeis were concerned in Gitlow was a comparatively isolated event, bearing little relation in their minds to any substantial threat to the safety of the community. . . . They were not confronted with any situation comparable to the instant one—the development of an apparatus designed and dedicated to the overthrow of the Government, in the context of world crisis after crisis.

"Chief Judge Learned Hand, writing for the majority below, interpreted the phrase as follows: 'In each case [courts] must ask whether the gravity of the "evil", discounted by its improbability, justifies such invasion of free speech as is necessary to avoid the danger.' 183 F.2d at 212. We adopt this statement of the rule. As articulated by Chief Judge Hand, it is as succinct and inclusive as any other we might devise at this time. It takes into consideration those factors which we deem relevant, and relates their significances. More we cannot expect from words.

"Likewise, we are in accord with the court below, which affirmed the trial court's finding that the requisite danger existed. The mere fact that from the period 1945 to 1948 petitioners' activities did not result in an attempt to overthrow the Government by force and violence is of course no answer to the fact that there was a group that was ready to make the attempt. The formation by petitioners of such a highly organized conspiracy, with rigidly disciplined members subject to call when the leaders, these petitioners, felt that the time had come for action, coupled with the inflammable nature of world conditions, similar uprisings in other countries, and the touch-and-go nature of our relations with countries with whom petitioners were in the very least ideologically attuned, convince us that their convictions were justified on this score. And this analysis disposes of the contention that a conspiracy to advocate, as distinguished from the advocacy itself, cannot be constitutionally restrained, because it comprises only the preparation. It is the existence of the conspiracy which creates the danger. . . . If the ingredients of the reaction are present, we cannot bind the Government to wait until the catalyst is added."

The Chief Justice also approved of the ruling below that withheld the issue of clear and present danger from the jury. "Bearing, as it does, the marks of a 'question of law', the issue is properly one for the judge to decide."

He concluded that the convictions should be affirmed.

Justice Frankfurter wrote an extensive concurring opinion in which he emphasized the importance of a careful examination of the conflicting interests

---

[a] The Chief Justice made it clear that he regarded the views of Holmes and Brandeis as having won the acceptance of the Court. "Although no case subsequent to *Whitney* and *Gitlow* has expressly overruled the majority opinions in those cases, there is little doubt that subsequent opinions have inclined toward the Holmes-Brandeis rationale."

of national security and free speech which the Court was required to assess in order to arrive at its decision. He believed that the prior decisions resolving conflicts between speech and competing interests, when viewed as a whole, expressed an attitude toward the judicial function and a standard of values which were decisive of the case. *"First.* Free speech cases are not an exception of the principle that we are not legislators, that direct policy-making is not our province. How best to reconcile competing interests is the business of legislatures, and the balance they strike is a judgment not to be displaced by ours, but to be respected unless outside the pale of fair judgment." . . . *Second.* A survey of the relevant decisions indicates that the results which we have reached are on the whole those that would ensue from careful weighing of conflicting interests." He emphasized that the clear and present danger test is no substitute for this careful weighing of values, and added: "It were far better that the phrase be abandoned than that it be sounded once more to hide from the believers in an absolute right of free speech the plain fact that the interest in speech, profoundly important as it is, is no more conclusive in judicial review than other attributes of democracy or than a determination of the peoples' representatives that a measure is necessary to assure the safety of government itself. *Third.* Not every type of speech occupies the same position on the scale of values. . . . The defendants have been convicted of conspiring to organize a party of persons who advocate the overthrow of the Government by force and violence. The jury has found that the object of the conspiracy is advocacy as 'a rule or principle of action,' 'by language reasonably and ordinarily calculated to incite persons to such action,' and with the intent to cause the overthrow 'as speedily as circumstances would permit.' On any scale of values which we have hitherto recognized speech of this sort ranks low."

Justice Jackson's concurring opinion contended that the clear and present danger test was inapplicable since the prosecution was for conspiracy and under circumstances greatly different from those in *Gitlow, Whitney,* and earlier cases. "I would save it, unmodified, for application as a 'rule of reason' in the kind of case for which it was devised. When the issue is criminality of a hot-headed speech on a street corner, or circulation of a few incendiary pamphlets, or parading by some zealots behind a red flag, or refusal of a handful of school children to salute our flag, it is not beyond the capacity of the judicial process to gather, comprehend, and weigh the necessary materials for decision whether it is a clear and present danger of substantive evil or a harmless letting off of steam. . . . If we must decide that this Act and its application are constitutional only if we are convinced that petitioner's conduct creates a 'clear and present danger' of violent overthrow, we must appraise imponderables, including international and national phenomena which baffle the best informed foreign offices and our most experienced politicians. . . . The judicial process simply is not adequate to a trial of such far-flung issues. The answers given would reflect our own political predilections and nothing more."

Justice Black's dissenting opinion emphasized that petitioners were not charged with an attempt to overthrow the Government, or with overt acts designed to overthrow the Government, or even with saying anything or writing anything designed to overthrow the Government. He argued that section 3 of the Smith Act was unconstitutional as a "virulent form of prior censorship of speech and press" in violation of the First Amendment. Justice Douglas also dissented, warning against the dangers of basing a prosecution for seditious conspiracy on speech alone. To make the criminality of the teaching of doctrine turn solely on the intent with which it is taught, made the offense similar to the old English crime of constructive treason. As to the clear and present danger rule, he observed: "There comes a time when even speech loses its constitutional immunity. Speech innocuous one year may at another time fan such destructive flames that it must be halted in the interests of the safety of the Republic. That is the meaning of the clear and present danger test. When conditions are so critical that there will be no time to avoid the evil that the speech threatens, it is time to call a halt. Otherwise, free speech which is the strength of the Nation will be the cause of its destruction. Yet free speech is the rule, not the exception. The restraint to be constitutional must be based on more than fear, on more than passionate opposition against the speech, on more than a revolted dislike for its contents. There must be some immediate injury to society that is likely if speech is allowed."

Justice Clark did not participate in the disposition of the case. The convictions were affirmed by a vote of six to two.

————

CLEAR AND PRESENT DANGER AS A TEST FOR THE VALIDITY OF LEGISLATION

It will be recalled that the Court in Gitlow v. New York rejected the clear and present danger test, noting that it had been used in Schenck v. United States only for the purpose of deciding when a defendant's speech violated a law that punished conduct. The *Gitlow* majority held that clear and present danger was an irrelevant concept when a law criminally punished certain categories of speech. Chief Justice Vinson's plurality opinion in Dennis v. United States conceded that the *Gitlow* rationale would make the clear and present danger test inapplicable to the Smith Act convictions reviewed by the Court, but he concluded that intervening Court opinions "have inclined toward the Holmes-Brandeis rationale." Accordingly, he interpreted that rationale as requiring an inquiry as to whether a clear and present danger justified application of the Smith Act to the particular facts. (The Court did not, however, review the sufficiency of the evidence to sustain the convictions, since that question had been removed from the case by the Court's limited grant of certiorari.)

Professor (now Justice) Linde argues that, although the decision was wrong in its result, the *Gitlow* court was right in rejecting clear and present danger as a test for determining the validity of laws that punish speech. Linde, *"Clear and Present Danger" Reexamined: Dissonance in the Brandenburg Concerto,* 22 Stan.L. Rev. 1163 (1970). He summarizes his position as follows: "The objective conditions under which the particular expression occurs . . .—whether stated as 'clear and present danger' or some other formula—can be a factor at the time when suppression of that particular occurrence is before a court. It cannot easily be an element in the constitutionality of the decision to make a law proscribing a kind of speech or publication in the future." Id. at 1175–1176. (Linde would reserve the clear and present danger test for cases, like *Schenck,* where the statute punished conduct and the defendant's speech was claimed to be a violation. He would invalidate the Smith Act under his standard for reviewing legislation directed against the communicative content of speech or press, arguing that the first amendment invalidates a law punishing speech if the proscribed content falls *under any circumstances* within the protection of the first amendment.)

————

YATES v. UNITED STATES

354 U.S. 298, 77 S.Ct. 1064, 1 L.Ed.2d 1356 (1957).

Mr. Justice Harlan delivered the opinion of the Court.

We brought these cases here to consider certain questions arising under the Smith Act which have not heretofore been passed upon by this Court, and otherwise to review the convictions of these petitioners for conspiracy to violate that Act.   Among other things, the convictions are claimed to rest upon an application of the Smith Act which is hostile to the principles upon which its constitutionality was upheld in Dennis v. United States, 341 U.S. 494.

These 14 petitioners stand convicted, after a jury trial in the United States District Court for the Southern District of California, upon a single count indictment charging them with conspiring (1) to advocate and teach the duty and necessity of overthrowing the Government of the United States by force and violence, and (2) to organize, as the Communist Party of the United States, a society of persons who so advocate and teach, all with the intent of causing the overthrow of the Government by force and violence as speedily as circumstances would permit.   . . .

Petitioners contend that the instructions to the jury were fatally defective in that the trial court refused to charge that, in order to convict, the jury must find that the advocacy which the defendants conspired to promote was of a kind calculated to "incite" persons to action for the forcible overthrow of the Government.   It is argued that advocacy of forcible overthrow as mere *abstract doctrine* is within the free speech protection of the First Amendment; that the Smith Act, consistently with that constitutional provision, must be taken as proscribing only the sort of advocacy which incites to illegal *action*; and that the trial court's charge, by permitting conviction for mere advocacy, unrelated to its tendency to produce forcible action, resulted in an unconstitutional application of the Smith Act.   The Government, which at the trial also requested the court to charge in terms of "incitement," now takes the position, however, that the true constitutional dividing line is not between inciting and abstract advocacy of forcible overthrow, but rather between advocacy as such, irrespective of its inciting qualities, and the mere discussion or exposition of violent overthrow as an abstract theory.   . . .

There can be no doubt from the record that in so instructing the jury the court regarded as immaterial, and intended to withdraw from the jury's consideration, any issue as to the character of the advocacy in terms of its capacity to stir listeners to forcible action.   . . .

We are thus faced with the question whether the Smith Act prohibits advocacy and teaching of forcible overthrow as an abstract principle, divorced from any effort to instigate action to that end, so long as such advocacy or teaching is engaged in with evil intent.   We hold that it does not.

The distinction between advocacy of abstract doctrine and advocacy directed at promoting unlawful action is one that has been consistently recognized in the opinions of this Court, beginning with Fox v. State of Washington, 236 U.S. 273; and Schenck v. United States, 249 U.S. 47.   This distinction was heavily underscored in Gitlow v. People of State of New York, 268 U.S. 652.   . . .

We need not, however, decide the issue before us in terms of constitutional compulsion, for our first duty is to construe this statute.   In doing so we should not assume that Congress chose to disregard a constitutional danger zone so clearly marked, or that it used the words "advocate" and "teach" in their ordinary dictionary meanings when they had already been construed as terms of art carrying a special and limited connotation.   . . .

In failing to distinguish between advocacy of forcible overthrow as an abstract doctrine and advocacy of action to that end, the District Court appears to have been led astray by the holding in *Dennis* that advocacy of violent action to be taken at some future time was enough.   It seems to have considered that, since "inciting" speech is usually thought of as something calculated to induce immediate action, and since *Dennis* held advocacy of action for future overthrow sufficient, this meant that advocacy, irrespective of its tendency to generate action, is punishable, provided only that it is uttered with a specific intent to accomplish overthrow. In other words, the District Court apparently thought that *Dennis* obliterated the traditional dividing line between advocacy of abstract doctrine and advocacy of action.

This misconceives the situation confronting the Court in *Dennis* and what was held there. Although the jury's verdict, interpreted in light of the trial court's instructions, did not justify the conclusion that the defendants' advocacy was directed at, or created any danger of, immediate overthrow, it did establish that the advocacy was aimed at building up a seditious group and maintaining it in readiness for action at a propitious time. . . . The essence of the *Dennis* holding was that indoctrination of a group in preparation for future violent action, as well as exhortation to immediate action, by advocacy found to be directed to "action for the accomplishment" of forcible overthrow, to violence as "a rule or principle of action," and employing "language of incitement," is not constitutionally protected when the group is of sufficient size and cohesiveness, is sufficiently oriented towards action, and other circumstances are such as reasonably to justify apprehension that action will occur. This is quite a different thing from the view of the District Court here that mere doctrinal justification of forcible overthrow, if engaged in with the intent to accomplish overthrow, is punishable *per se* under the Smith Act. That sort of advocacy, even though uttered with the hope that it may ultimately lead to violent revolution, is too remote from concrete action to be regarded as the kind of indoctrination preparatory to action which was condemned in *Dennis*. As one of the concurring opinions in *Dennis* put it: "Throughout our decisions there has recurred a distinction between the statement of an idea which may prompt its hearers to take unlawful action, and advocacy that such action be taken." There is nothing in *Dennis* which makes that historic distinction obsolete.

. . .

In light of the foregoing we are unable to regard the District Court's charge upon this aspect of the case as adequate. The jury was never told that the Smith Act does not denounce advocacy in the sense of preaching abstractly the forcible overthrow of the Government. We think that the trial court's statement that the proscribed advocacy must include the "urging," "necessity," and "duty" of forcible overthrow, and not merely its "desirability" and "propriety," may not be regarded as a sufficient substitute for charging that the Smith Act reaches only advocacy of action for the overthrow of government by force and violence. The essential distinction is that those to whom the advocacy is addressed must be urged to *do* something, now or in the future, rather than merely to *believe* in something. . . .

. . .

[The Court ordered an acquittal of five of the 14 petitioners,[a] finding "no adequate evidence in the record" to sustain their convictions on retrial.][b]

Mr. Justice Brennan and Mr. Justice Whittaker took no part in the consideration or decision of this case.

Mr. Justice Black, with whom Mr. Justice Douglas joins, concurring in part and dissenting in part.

I would reverse every one of these convictions and direct that all the defendants be acquitted. In my judgment the statutory provisions on which

---

[a] Upon remand of the *Yates* case, the lower court dismissed the indictments against the remaining defendants who had not been acquitted by the Supreme Court. This action was "reluctantly" requested by the Government because it could not . . . satisfy the evidentiary requirements laid down by the Supreme Court in its opinion reversing the conviction in this matter." New York Times, Dec. 3, 1957, p. 71.

[b] The types of evidence that led the Court to order the five acquitted, and not the remaining nine, are summarized in Scales v. United States, *infra*.

these prosecutions are based abridge freedom of speech, press and assembly in violation of the First Amendment to the United States Constitution. See my dissent and that of Mr. Justice Douglas in Dennis v. United States, 341 U.S. 494, 579, 581. Also see my opinion in American Communications Ass'n, C.I.O. v. Douds, 339 U.S. 382, 445. . . .

Mr. Justice Clark, dissenting.

The petitioners, principal organizers and leaders of the Communist Party in California, have been convicted for a conspiracy covering the period 1940 to 1951. They were engaged in this conspiracy with the defendants in Dennis v. United States, 1951, 341 U.S. 494. The *Dennis* defendants, named as co-conspirators but not indicted with the defendants here, were convicted in New York under the former conspiracy provisions of the Smith Act. They have served or are now serving prison terms as a result of their convictions. . . .

The conspiracy includes the same group of defendants as in the *Dennis* case though petitioners here occupied a lower echelon in the party hierarchy. They, nevertheless, served in the same army and were engaged in the same mission. The convictions here were based upon evidence closely paralleling that adduced in Dennis and in United States v. Flynn, 2 Cir., 1954, 216 F.2d 354, both of which resulted in convictions. This Court laid down in *Dennis* the principles governing such prosecutions and they were closely adhered to here, although the nature of the two cases did not permit identical handling.

I would affirm the convictions. . . .

SCALES v. UNITED STATES

367 U.S. 203, 81 S.Ct. 1469, 6 L.Ed.2d 782 (1961).

[Petitioner, Chairman of the North and South Carolina Districts of the Communist Party, was convicted of violating the membership clause of the Smith Act (18 U.S.C. § 2385), which made it a crime to become a member of an organization advocating the overthrow of the government by force or violence, knowing the purposes of such organization.[1] The trial court had instructed the jury that in order to convict it must find that (1) the Communist Party advocated the violent overthrow of the government, in the sense of present "advocacy of action" to accomplish that end as soon as circumstances were propitious; and (2) petitioner was an "active" member of the Party, and not merely "a nominal, passive, inactive, or purely technical" member with knowledge of the Party's illegal advocacy and a specific intent to bring about overthrow "as speedily as circumstances would permit." The Supreme Court affirmed the conviction.]

Mr. Justice Harlan delivered the opinion of the Court.

. . .

1. *Constitutional Challenge to the Membership Clause on Its Face.* . . .

Any thought that due process puts beyond the reach of the criminal law all individual associational relationships, unless accompanied by the commission of specific acts of criminality, is dispelled by familiar concepts of the law of

[1] Section 2385 (whose membership clause we place in italics) reads: . . .

"Whoever organizes or helps or attempts to organize any society, group, or assembly of persons who teach, advocate, or encourage the overthrow or destruction of any such government by force or violence; *or becomes or is a member of, or affiliates with, any such society, group, or assembly of persons, knowing the purposes thereof—*

"Shall be fined not more than $20,000 or imprisoned not more than twenty years, or both, and shall be ineligible for employment by the United States or any department or agency thereof, for the five years next following his conviction. . . . [Court's footnote.]

conspiracy and complicity. . . . In this instance it is an organization which engages in criminal activity, and we can perceive no reason why one who actively and knowingly works in the ranks of that organization, intending to contribute to the success of those specifically illegal activities, should be any more immune from prosecution than he to whom the organization has assigned the task of carrying out the substantive criminal act . . . . It must indeed be recognized that a person who merely becomes a member of an illegal organization, by that "act" alone need be doing nothing more than signifying his assent to its purposes and activities on one hand, and providing, on the other, only the sort of moral encouragement which comes from the knowledge that others believe in what the organization is doing. . . . [T]hese factors have weight and must be found to be overborne in a total constitutional assessment of the statute. We think, however, they are duly met when the statute is found to reach only "active" members having also a guilty knowledge and intent, and which therefore prevents a conviction on what otherwise might be regarded as merely an expression of sympathy with the alleged criminal enterprise, unaccompanied by any significant action in its support or any commitment to undertake such action. . . . It was settled in *Dennis* that the advocacy with which we are here concerned is not constitutionally protected speech, and it was further established that a combination to promote such advocacy, albeit under the aegis of what purports to be a political party, is not such association as is protected by the First Amendment. We can discern no reason why membership, when it constitutes a purposeful form of complicity in a group engaging in this same forbidden advocacy, should receive any greater degree of protection from the guarantees of that Amendment. . . .

   2. *Constitutional Challenge to the Statute as Applied: the Sufficiency of the Evidence.* . . .

   On this phase of the case petitioner's principal contention is that the evidence was insufficient to establish that the Communist Party was engaged in present advocacy of violent overthrow of the Government in the sense required by the Smith Act, that is, in "advocacy of action" for the accomplishment of such overthrow either immediately or as soon as circumstances proved propitious, and uttered in terms reasonably calculated to "incite" to such action. This contention rests largely on the proposition that the evidence on this aspect of the case does not differ materially from that which the Court in *Yates* stated was inadequate to establish that sort of Party advocacy there. . . .

   We agree with petitioner that the evidentiary question here is controlled in large part by *Yates*. The decision in *Yates* rested on the view (not articulated in the opinion, though perhaps it should have been) that the Smith Act offenses, involving as they do subtler elements than are present in most other crimes, call for strict standards in assessing the adequacy of the proof needed to make out a case of illegal advocacy. This premise is as applicable to prosecutions under the membership clause of the Smith Act, as it is to conspiracy prosecutions under that statute as we had in *Yates*.

   The impact of *Yates* with respect to this petitioner's evidentiary challenge is not limited, however, to that decision's requirement of strict standards of proof. *Yates* also articulates general criteria for the evaluation of evidence in determining whether this requirement is met. The *Yates* opinion, through its characterizations of large portions of the evidence which were either described in detail or referred to by reference to the record, indicates what type of evidence is needed to permit a jury to find that (a) there was "advocacy of action" and (b) the Party was responsible for such advocacy.

   First, *Yates* makes clear what type of evidence is not *in itself* sufficient to show illegal advocacy. This category includes evidence of the following: the teaching of Marxism-Leninism and the connected use of Marxist "classics" as textbooks; the official general resolutions and pronouncements of the Party at past conventions; dissemination of the Party's general literature, including the standard outlines on Marxism; the Party's history and organizational structure; the secrecy of meetings and the clandestine nature of the Party generally; statements by officials evidencing sympathy for and alliance with the U.S.S.R. It was the predominance of evidence of this type which led the Court to order the acquittal of several *Yates* defendants, with the comment that they had not themselves "made a single remark or been present when someone else made a remark which would tend to prove the charges against them." However, this kind of evidence, while insufficient in itself to sustain a conviction, is not irrelevant. Such evidence in the context of other evidence, may be of value in showing illegal advocacy.

Second, the *Yates* opinion also indicates what kind of evidence is sufficient. There the Court pointed to two series of events which justified the denial of directed acquittals as to nine of the *Yates* defendants. The Court noted that with respect to seven of the defendants, meetings in San Francisco . . . might be considered to be "the systematic teaching and advocacy of illegal action which is condemned by the statute." In those meetings, a small group of members were not only taught that violent revolution was inevitable, but they were also taught techniques for achieving that end. For example, the *Yates* record reveals that members were directed to be prepared to convert a general strike into a revolution and deal with Negroes so as to prepare them specifically for revolution. In addition to the San Francisco meetings, the Court referred to certain activities in the Los Angeles area "which might be considered to amount to 'advocacy of action'" and with which two *Yates* defendants were linked. . . . Thus, one member was "surreptitiously indoctrinated in methods . . . of moving 'masses of people in time of crisis'"; others were told to adopt such Russian pre-revolutionary techniques as the development of a special communication system through a newspaper similar to Pravda. Viewed together, these events described in *Yates* indicate at least two patterns of evidence sufficient to show illegal advocacy: (a) the teaching of forcible overthrow, accompanied by directions as to the type of illegal action which must be taken when the time for the revolution is reached; and (b) the teaching of forceful overthrow, accompanied by a contemporary, though legal, course of conduct clearly undertaken for the specific purpose of rendering effective the later illegal activity which is advocated.

Finally, *Yates* is also relevant here in indicating, at least by implication, the type and quantum of evidence necessary to attach liability for illegal advocacy to the Party. In discussing the Government's "conspiratorial-nexus theory" the Court found that the evidence there was insufficient because the incidents of illegal advocacy were infrequent, sporadic, and not fairly related to the period covered by the indictment. In addition, the Court indicated that the illegal advocacy was not sufficiently tied to officials who spoke for the Party as such.

Thus, in short, *Yates* imposes a strict standard of proof, and indicates the kind of evidence that is insufficient to show illegal advocacy under that standard, the kind of evidence that is sufficient, and what pattern of evidence is necessary to hold the Party responsible for such advocacy. With these criteria in mind, we now proceed to an examination of the evidence in this case.

[The Court's summary of the evidence is omitted.]

We conclude that this evidence sufficed to make a case for the jury on the issue of illegal Party advocacy. *Dennis* and *Yates* have definitely laid at rest any doubt but that present advocacy of *future* action for violent overthrow satisfies statutory and constitutional requirements equally with advocacy of *immediate* action to that end. Hence this record cannot be considered deficient because it contains no evidence of advocacy for immediate overthrow.

Since the evidence amply showed that Party leaders were continuously preaching during the indictment period the inevitability of eventual forcible overthrow, the first and basic question is a narrow one: whether the jury could permissibly infer that such preaching, in whole or in part, "was aimed at building up a seditious group and maintaining it in readiness for action at a propitious time . . . the kind of indoctrination preparatory to action which was condemned in *Dennis.*" On this score, we think that the jury, under instructions which fully satisfied the requirements of *Yates,* was entitled to infer from this systematic preaching . . . that "advocacy of action" was engaged in. . . .

Affirmed.

Mr. Justice Black, dissenting.

.   .   .

I think it is important to point out the manner in which this case re-emphasizes the freedom-destroying nature of the "balancing test" presently in use by the Court to justify its refusal to apply specific constitutional protections of the Bill of Rights. In some of the recent cases in which it has "balanced" away the protections of the First Amendment, the Court has suggested that it was justified in the application of this "test" because no direct abridgment of First Amendment freedoms was involved, the abridgment in each of these cases being, in the Court's opinion, nothing more than "an incident of the informed exercise of a valid governmental function." A possible implication of that suggestion was that if the Court were confronted with what it would call a direct abridgment of speech, it would not apply the "balancing test" but would enforce the protections of the First Amendment according to its own terms. This case causes me to doubt that such an implication is justified. Petitioner is being sent to jail for the express reason that he has associated with people who have entertained unlawful ideas and said unlawful things, and that of course is a *direct* abridgment of his freedoms of speech and assembly—under any definition that has ever been used for that term. Nevertheless, even as to this admittedly direct abridgment, the Court relies upon its prior decisions to the effect that the Government has power to abridge speech and assembly if its interest in doing so is sufficient to outweigh the interest in protecting these First Amendment freedoms. . . .

Mr. Justice Douglas, dissenting.

.   .   .

The case is not saved by showing that petitioner was an active member. None of the activity constitutes a crime. . . .

Not one single illegal act is charged to petitioner. That is why the essence of the crime covered by the indictment is merely belief—belief in the proletarian revolution, belief in Communist creed.

.   .   .

Mr. Justice Brennan with whom The Chief Justice and Mr. Justice Douglas join, dissenting.

[These Justices thought that in § 4(f) of the Internal Security Act Congress legislated immunity from prosecution under the membership clause of the Smith Act.] [a]

---

[a] Decided the same day as *Scales* was Noto v. United States, 367 U.S. 290 (1961), which involved another prosecution under the membership clause of the Smith Act. The conviction was reversed on the insufficiency of the evidence of illegal Communist Party advocacy (which must be proved in each case), rather than failure of proof of petitioner's personal criminal purpose, but regarding the latter element of the crime, the Court (per Harlan, J.) admonished: "This element of the membership crime, like its others, must be judged *strictissimi juris,* for otherwise there is a danger that one in sympathy

AFTERMATH OF THE YATES, SCALES AND NOTO CASES

Of 141 people indicted under the Smith Act, 29 served prison terms. These included the 11 defendants in *Dennis,* 17 defendants in two cases prior to *Yates* that the Court declined to review, and the single defendant in *Scales.* Emerson, *The System of Freedom of Expression* 124 (1970). The government had turned to membership clause prosecutions after *Yates,* because it concluded that it would be unable to satisfy the Court's requirement that each defendant be proved to have participated in advocacy of specific illegal acts. While the Court sustained the constitutionality of the membership clause in *Scales,* and also sustained the conviction, the *Scales* case marked the end of Smith Act prosecutions. Under the *Scales* and *Noto* cases, was the government required, in a membership clause case, to satisfy the same proof requirements imposed by *Yates?*

Consider, also, whether proof meeting the criteria imposed by the *Yates, Scales* and *Noto* cases would also sustain convictions under two older statutes contained in the federal criminal code, United States Code, Title 18:

§ 2383. Rebellion or Insurrection

Whoever incites, sets on foot, assists, or engages in any rebellion or insurrection against the authority of the United States or the laws thereof, or gives aid or comfort thereto, shall be fined not more than $10,000 or imprisoned not more than ten years, or both; and shall be incapable of holding any office under the United States.

§ 2384. Seditious Conspiracy

If two or more persons in any State or Territory, or in any place subject to the jurisdiction of the United States, conspire to overthrow, put down, or to destroy by force the Government of the United States, or to levy war against them, or to oppose by force the authority thereof, or by force to prevent, hinder, or delay the execution of any law of the United States, or by force to seize, take, or possess any property of the United States contrary to the authority thereof, they shall each be fined not more than $20,000 or imprisoned not more than twenty years, or both.

D. THE CURRENT STATUS OF THE CLEAR AND PRESENT DANGER TEST—THE "BRANDEN-BURG CONCERTO" [1]

BRANDENBURG v. OHIO

395 U.S. 444, 89 S.Ct. 1827, 23 L.Ed.2d 430 (1969).

Per Curiam.

The appellant, a leader of a Ku Klux Klan group, was convicted under the Ohio Criminal Syndicalism statute for "advocat[ing] . . . the duty, necessi-

with the legitimate aims of such an organization, but not specifically intending to accomplish them by resort to violence, might be punished for his adherence to lawful and constitutionally protected purposes, because of other and unprotected purposes which he does not necessarily share." This approach was taken in United States v. Spock, 416 F.2d 165 (1st Cir.1969), reversing the conviction of Dr. Spock and others for conspiracy to counsel, aid, and abet registrants to resist the draft. "When the alleged agreement is both bifarious [i.e. involving both legal and illegal conduct] and political within the shadow of the First Amendment, we hold that an individual's specific intent to adhere to the illegal portions may be shown in one of three ways:" by the defendant's unambiguous statements; by his subsequent commission of the very illegal act contemplated by the agreement; or by his subsequent legal act if clearly undertaken for the specific purpose of rendering effective the later illegal activity which is advocated. 416 F.2d at 173.

[1] Linde, supra, p. 1071.

ty, or propriety of crime, sabotage, violence, or unlawful methods of terrorism as a means of accomplishing industrial or political reform" and for "voluntarily assembl[ing] with any society, group, or assemblage of persons formed to teach or advocate the doctrines of criminal syndicalism."   Ohio Rev.Code Ann. § 2923.13.   He was fined $1,000 and sentenced to one to 10 years' imprisonment.   The appellant challenged the constitutionality of the criminal syndicalism statute under the First and Fourteenth Amendments to the United States Constitution, but the intermediate appellate court of Ohio affirmed his conviction without opinion.   The Supreme Court of Ohio dismissed his appeal, *sua sponte,* "for the reason that no substantial constitutional question exists herein." . . .   Appeal was taken to this Court, . . .   We reverse.

The record shows that a man, identified at trial as the appellant, telephoned an announcer-reporter on the staff of a Cincinnati television station and invited him to come to a Ku Klux Klan "rally" to be held at a farm in Hamilton County.   With the cooperation of the organizers, the reporter and a cameraman attended the meeting and filmed the events.   Portions of the films were later broadcast on the local station and on a national network.

The prosecution's case rested on the films and on testimony identifying the appellant as the person who communicated with the reporter and who spoke at the rally.   The State also introduced into evidence several articles appearing in the film, including a pistol, a rifle, a shotgun, ammunition, a Bible, and a red hood worn by the speaker in the films.

One film showed 12 hooded figures, some of whom carried firearms.   They were gathered around a large wooden cross, which they burned.   No one was present other than the participants and the newsmen who made the film.   Most of the words uttered during the scene were incomprehensible when the film was projected, but scattered phrases could be understood that were derogatory of Negroes and, in one instance, of Jews.[1]   Another scene on the same film showed the appellant, in Klan regalia, making a speech.   The speech, in full, was as follows:

"This is an organizers' meeting.   We have had quite a few members here today which are—we have hundreds, hundreds of members throughout the State of Ohio.   I can quote from a newspaper clipping from the Columbus, Ohio Dispatch, five weeks ago Sunday morning.   The Klan has more members in the State of Ohio than does any other organization.   We're not a revengent organization, but if our President, our Congress, our Supreme Court, continues to suppress the white, Caucasian race, it's possible that there might have to be some revengeance taken.

"We are marching on Congress July the Fourth, four hundred thousand strong.   From there we are dividing into two groups, one group to march on

---

[1] The significant portions that could be understood were:

"How far is the nigger going to—yeah."

"This is what we are going to do to the niggers."

"A dirty nigger."

"Send the Jews back to Israel."

"Let's give them back to the dark garden."

"Save America."

"Let's go back to constitutional betterment."

"Bury the niggers."

"We intend to do our part."

"Give us our state rights."

"Freedom for the whites."

"Nigger will have to fight for every inch he gets from now on."

St. Augustine, Florida, the other group to march into Mississippi. Thank you."

The second film showed six hooded figures one of whom, later identified as the appellant, repeated a speech very similar to that recorded on the first film. The reference to the possibility of "revengeance" was omitted, and one sentence was added: "Personally, I believe the nigger should be returned to Africa, the Jew returned to Israel." Though some of the figures in the films carried weapons, the speaker did not.

The Ohio Criminal Syndicalism Statute was enacted in 1919. From 1917 to 1920, identical or quite similar laws were adopted by 20 States and two territories. E. Dowell, A History of Criminal Syndicalism Legislation in the United States 21 (1939). In 1927, this Court sustained the constitutionality of California's Criminal Syndicalism Act, the text of which is quite similar to that of the laws of Ohio. Whitney v. California, 274 U.S. 357 (1927). The Court upheld the statute on the ground that, without more, "advocating" violent means to effect political and economic change involves such danger to the security of the State that the State may outlaw it. Cf. Fiske v. Kansas, 274 U.S. 380 (1927). But *Whitney* has been thoroughly discredited by later decisions. See Dennis v. United States, 341 U.S. 494, at 507 (1951). These later decisions have fashioned the principle that the constitutional guarantees of free speech and free press do not permit a State to forbid or proscribe advocacy of the use of force or of law violation except where such advocacy is directed to inciting or producing imminent lawless action and is likely to incite or produce such action.[2] As we said in Noto v. United States, 367 U.S. 290, 297–298 (1961), "the mere abstract teaching . . . of the moral propriety or even moral necessity for a resort to force and violence, is not the same as preparing a group for violent action and steeling it to such action." See also Herndon v. Lowry, 301 U.S. 242, 259–261 (1937); Bond v. Floyd, 385 U.S. 116, 134 (1966). A statute which fails to draw this distinction impermissibly intrudes upon the freedoms guaranteed by the First and Fourteenth Amendments. It sweeps within its condemnation speech which our Constitution has immunized from governmental control. Cf. Yates v. United States, 354 U.S. 298 (1957); De Jonge v. Oregon, 299 U.S. 353 (1937); Stromberg v. California, 283 U.S. 359 (1931). . . .

Measured by this test, Ohio's Criminal Syndicalism Act cannot be sustained. The Act punishes persons who "advocate or teach the duty necessity, or propriety" of violence "as a means of accomplishing industrial or political reform"; or who publish or circulate or display any book or paper containing such advocacy; or who "justify" the commission of violent acts "with intent to exemplify, spread or advocate the propriety of the doctrines of criminal syndicalism"; or who "voluntarily assemble" with a group formed "to teach or advocate the doctrines of criminal syndicalism." Neither the indictment nor the trial judge's instructions to the jury in any way refined the statute's bald definition of the crime in terms of mere advocacy not distinguished from incitement to imminent lawless action.[3]

---

[2] It was on the theory that the Smith Act, 54 Stat. 670, 18 U.S.C. § 2385, embodied such a principle and that it had been applied only in conformity with it that this Court sustained the Act's constitutionality. Dennis v. United States, 341 U.S. 494 (1951). That this was the basis for *Dennis* was emphasized in Yates v. United States, 354 U.S. 298, 320–324 (1957), in which the Court overturned convictions for advocacy of the forcible overthrow of the Government under the Smith Act, because the trial judge's instructions had allowed conviction for mere advocacy, unrelated to its tendency to produce forcible action.

[3] The first count of the indictment charged that appellant "did unlawfully by word of mouth advocate the necessity, or propriety of crime, violence, or unlawful methods of terrorism as a means of accomplishing political reform . . . ." The second count charged that appellant "did unlawfully voluntarily assemble with a group or assemblage of persons formed to advocate the doctrines of

Accordingly, we are here confronted with a statute which, by its own words and as applied, purports to punish mere advocacy and to forbid, on pain of criminal punishment, assembly with others merely to advocate the described type of action.[4] Such a statute falls within the condemnation of the First and Fourteenth Amendments. The contrary teaching of Whitney v. California, supra, cannot be supported, and that decision is therefore overruled.

Reversed.

Mr. Justice Black, concurring.

I agree with the views expressed by Mr. Justice Douglas in his concurring opinion in this case that the "clear and present danger" doctrine should have no place in the interpretation of the First Amendment. I join the Court's opinion, which, as I understand it, simply cites Dennis v. United States, 341 U.S. 494 (1951), but does not indicate any agreement on the Court's part with the "clear and present danger" doctrine on which *Dennis* purported to rely.

Mr. Justice Douglas, concurring.

While I join the opinion of the Court, I desire to enter a *caveat.*

. . . I see no place in the regime of the First Amendment for any "clear and present danger" test, whether strict and tight as some would make it, or free-wheeling as the Court in *Dennis* rephrased it.

When one reads the opinions closely and sees when and how the "clear and present danger" test has been applied, great misgivings are aroused. First, the threats were often loud but always puny and made serious only by judges so wedded to the *status quo* that critical analysis made them nervous. Second, the test was so twisted and perverted in *Dennis* as to make the trial of those teachers of Marxism an all-out political trial which was part and parcel of the cold war that has eroded substantial parts of the First Amendment. . . .

The line between what is permissible and not subject to control and what may be made impermissible and subject to regulation is the line between ideas and overt acts.

The example usually given by those who would punish speech is the case of one who falsely shouts fire in a crowded theatre.

This is, however, a classic case where speech is brigaded with action. They are indeed inseparable and a prosecution can be launched for the overt acts actually caused. Apart from rare instances of that kind, speech is, I think, immune from prosecution. Certainly there is no constitutional line between advocacy of abstract ideas as in *Yates* and advocacy of political action as in *Scales.* The quality of advocacy turns on the depth of the conviction; and government has no power to invade that sanctuary of belief and conscience.[a]

---

criminal syndicalism . . . ." The trial judge's charge merely followed the language of the indictment. No construction of the statute by the Ohio courts has brought it within constitutionally permissible limits. The Ohio Supreme Court has considered the statute in only one previous case, State v. Kassay, 126 Ohio St. 177, 184 N.E. 521 (1932), where the constitutionality of the statute was sustained.

[4] Statutes affecting the right of assembly, like those touching on freedom of speech, must observe the established distinctions between mere advocacy and incitement to imminent lawless action, for as Chief Justice Hughes wrote in De Jonge v. Oregon, supra, 299 U.S. at 364: "The right of peaceable assembly is a right cognate to those of free speech and free press and is equally fundamental." . . .

[a] For a review of the development of clear and present danger doctrine from prior to World War I through *Brandenburg,* see Rabban, *The Emergence of Modern First Amendment Doctrine,* 50 U.Chi.L. Rev. 1205 (1983).

THE CONSTITUTIONAL LAW IMPLICATIONS OF THE COURT'S SMITH ACT INTERPRETATION

Despite the fact that it is a *per curiam* decision [1] and despite possible arguments that much of the discussion of clear and present danger is dicta, *Brandenburg* has been read as an authoritative statement of the Court's position on the minimum protection afforded speech.[2] Subsequent cases have converted other aspects of the Court's construction of the Smith Act in the *Yates* and *Scales* cases into constitutional doctrine, further making the result in the *Dennis* case obsolete.

(1) **Specific Intent.** Even under the position taken by Justices Brandeis and Holmes, people could be punished for knowing membership in an organization advocating the commission of serious crimes, if there was a clear and present danger that those crimes would be committed. Justice Brandeis' *Whitney* concurrence did not require proof that the defendant participated in the advocacy or shared the organization's illegal purposes. Dicta in the *Scales* and *Noto* cases, however, required that there be proof, beyond defendant's knowledge of illegal advocacy by the organization, of the defendant's "active membership" and specific intent to accomplish the organization's illegal aims. Application of those requirements would have required the acquittal of the defendant in the *Whitney* case, even upon proof that her organization advocated specific criminal conduct and that there was a clear and present danger. Those requirements have, however, been converted from interpretations of the Smith Act to first amendment doctrine. The development occurred in a series of cases dealing with government requests for information, qualification for government employment and loyalty oaths; none of the cases involved criminal punishment.[3]

(2) **Deference to Legislative Judgment Concerning the Presence and Extent of Danger.** A major issue in the clear and present danger debate is whether courts should defer to legislative judgments concerning the danger posed by classes of speech or the defendant's speech. It will be recalled that, in *Gitlow,* the Court noted the New York legislature's implicit determination that *all* revolutionary speech was dangerous, and concluded "it must be given great weight." Justice Frankfurter's concurring opinion in *Dennis* argued that the case presented a clash of interests "[i]t is not for us to decide" since Congress had decided that the danger created by Communist Party speech justified its restriction. 341 U.S. at 550. Chief Justice Vinson's plurality opinion accepted clear and present danger as the appropriate standard, with the obligation of courts to examine whether there is a clear and present danger to justify application of the statute to the specific situation, and thus did not articulately refer to sustaining of legislative judgments. (The rejection of any requirement of imminence allowed the plurality to discover the requisite danger. The Court had, moreover, not granted certiorari to consider the sufficiency of the evidence, so the Court was not required to determine whether any particular Communist Party speech created danger.) Chief Justice Vinson's opinion can

---

[1] It is unusual that the Court's major expression of contemporary first amendment doctrine is contained in an unsigned opinion. The editors have been informed by a reliable source that the opinion had been written by Justice Fortas, who resigned prior to the Court's announcement of the decision. The same source states that the case was regarded as easy in its result, and very little attention was paid to what the opinion said.

[2] E.g., a state conviction for disorderly conduct based on an intemperate speech at a campus antiwar demonstration was reversed, on the authority of *Brandenburg,* in Hess v. Indiana, 414 U.S. 105 (1973). Specifically, the Court held that the *Brandenburg* criteria had not been met both because the defendant's speech did not advocate specific unlawful action, and there was insufficient evidence that his words were likely to produce imminent disorder.

[3] Elfbrandt v. Russell, 384 U.S. 11, 15–16 (1966); Keyishian v. Board of Regents, 385 U.S. 589, 606 (1967); Law Students Research Council v. Wadmond, 401 U.S. 154, 165 (1971). These cases appear, infra pp. 1352, 1350 and 1328.

be read as implicitly deferring to contemporary legislative and executive judgments concerning the danger to internal security presented by the Communist Party.

The Court discussed the issue of deference to legislative judgment in Landmark Communications, Inc. v. Virginia, 435 U.S. 829 (1978). The Court held unconstitutional a Virginia law punishing media disclosure of confidential investigations into judicial misconduct.[1] The Supreme Court of Virginia had relied on the clear and present danger standard to sustain the law. On this issue, Chief Justice Burger's opinion for the Court said, in part:

". . . We question the relevance of [the clear and present danger test] . . . here; moreover we cannot accept the mechanical application of the test which led that court to its conclusion. . . . Properly applied, the test requires a court to make its own inquiry into the imminence and magnitude of the danger said to flow from the particular utterance and then to balance the character of the evil, as well as its likelihood, against the need for free and unfettered expression. The possibility that other measures will serve the State's interests should also be weighed.

"Landmark argued in the Supreme Court of Virginia that 'before a state may punish expression, it must prove by "actual facts" the existence of a clear and present danger to the orderly administration of justice.' The court acknowledged that the record before it was devoid of such 'actual facts,' but went on to hold that such proof was not required when the legislature itself had made the requisite finding 'that a clear and present danger to the orderly administration of justice would be created by divulgence of the confidential proceedings of the Commission.' This legislative declaration coupled with the stipulated fact that Landmark published the disputed article was regarded by the court as sufficient to justify imposition of criminal sanctions.

"Deference to a legislative finding cannot limit judicial inquiry when First Amendment rights are at stake. In Pennekamp v. Florida, 328 U.S. 331, 335, Mr. Justice Reed observed that this Court is

'compelled to examine for [itself] the statements in issue and the circumstances under which they were made to see whether or not they do carry a threat of clear and present danger to the impartiality and good order of the courts or whether they are of a character which the principles of the First Amendment, as adopted by the Due Process Clause of the Fourteenth Amendment, protect.'

"Mr. Justice Brandeis was even more pointed in his concurrence in Whitney v. California, 274 U.S. 357, 378–379:

'[A legislative declaration] does not preclude enquiry into the question whether, at the time and under the circumstances, the conditions existed which are essential to validity under the Federal Constitution. . . . Whenever the fundamental rights of free speech are alleged to have been invaded, it must remain open to a defendant to present the issue whether there actually did exist at the time a clear danger; whether the danger, if any, was imminent; and whether the evil apprehended was one so substantial as to justify the stringent restriction interposed by the legislature.'

"A legislature appropriately inquires into and may declare the reasons impelling legislative action but the judicial function commands analysis of whether the specific conduct charged falls within the reach of the statute and if so whether the legislation is consonant with the Constitution. Were it otherwise, the scope of freedom of speech and of the press would be subject

---

[1] See infra, p. 1380.

to legislative definition and the function of the First Amendment as a check on legislative power would be nullified.

"It was thus incumbent upon the Supreme Court of Virginia to go behind the legislative determination and examine for itself 'the particular utterance here in question and the circumstances of [its] publication to determine to what extent the substantive evil of unfair administration of justice was a likely consequence, and whether the degree of likelihood was sufficient to justify [subsequent] punishment.'"

THE CLEAR AND PRESENT DANGER DEBATE—SOME GENERAL CONSIDERATIONS

The earlier debate, in an extensive literature, argued whether a tightly-drawn clear and present danger test was a *necessary* condition for protection of freedom of speech.[1] The Court's current adherence to it has muted that debate, and brought to the fore the question whether any version of the clear and present danger test is a *sufficient* condition for protection of freedom of speech.[2] Before turning to some of the arguments made in the debate, however, it is important to note that clear and present danger is not a doctrine for all first amendment seasons. In its focus on the danger of illegal conduct, at most its literal application is limited to those cases where the only societal interest asserted for restricting speech is that danger. As will be seen in Section 3 of this chapter, and in the following two chapters, whether or not clear and present danger is the appropriate test for speech urging violation of the law, it is not helpful in other problem areas.[3] Some general themes in the debate are, however, of broader application. Some of those themes are singled out for brief mention, below.

(1) **Political Speech Contrasted with Other Forms of Speech.** While the clear and present danger test is by its terms directed at any speech advocating the commission of a crime, all of the Supreme Court's cases have, in fact, involved some form of political speech—whether the general platform of a radical organization or a hot-tempered street-corner protest speech. A major criticism of the clear and present danger approach is that it permits stifling of radical political speech based on problematic assessments of public danger, while it over-protects dangerous speech in a non-political context.

The application of first amendment principles to criminal defendants who incite or solicit others, or agree among themselves to commit specific, serious

---

[1] The most articulate defense of the clear and present danger test is contained in Chafee, *Free Speech in the United States* (1941). For a contemporary defense, see Redish, *Advocacy of Unlawful Conduct and The First Amendment: In Defense of Clear and Present Danger,* 70 Calif.L.Rev. 1159 (1982).

[2] The earliest critical scholarly attack on the test as insufficiently protective of speech is Meiklejohn, *Free Speech and Its Relation to Self-Government* (1948).

[3] Prior to the *Dennis* case, the Court had employed the clear and present danger test in the context of a state contempt of court conviction of a newspaper and a labor leader for allegedly prejudicial statements concerning pending cases. Justice Black's opinion for the Court in Bridges v. California, 314 U.S. 252 (1941), held that these publications could not constitutionally constitute contempt in the absence of a clear and present danger to the administration of justice. Later cases involving contempt prosecutions for media criticism of judicial decisions have continued to reverse the convictions using the idiom of clear and present danger. Pennekamp v. Florida, 328 U.S. 331 (1946); Craig v. Harney, 331 U.S. 367 (1947); Wood v. Georgia, 370 U.S. 375 (1962). Those cases, however, can be read as imposing an absolute ban on contempt prosecution for media statements concerning pending cases, or criticism of judicial action. See Baltimore Radio Show, Inc. v. State, 193 Md. 300, 67 A.2d 497 (1949), cert. denied 338 U.S. 912 (1950).

Bridges, Pennekamp and *Craig* were prominent among the cases cited by Chief Justice Vinson in his opinion in the *Dennis* case for the proposition that the Court had "inclined toward the Holmes-Brandeis rationale." 341 U.S. at 507.

crimes in a non-political context has not been much explored.[4] Professor Chafee, the most ardent defender of Holmes' clear and present danger approach, argued that its source could be found in the general criminal law of attempt, which required that the defendant had made "dangerous progress toward the consummation" of the crime.[5] It will be recalled, however, that Holmes' opinions in *Schenck* and *Abrams* focused more on the speakers' "intent" than on their "dangerous progress." The requirement of progress toward consummation of the criminal conduct urged by speech seems not to be clearly reflected in criminal law doctrines of solicitation and conspiracy, which also focus primarily on issues of proof of the defendant's intent. The Model Penal Code, § 5.02, provides that a person is guilty of solicitation to commit a crime "if with the purpose of facilitating its commission he commands, encourages or requests another person to engage in specific conduct which would constitute such crime." No requirement that the person solicited is likely to commit the crime has been imposed. The crime of conspiracy, whether or not it requires the commission of an overt act as well as the agreement, has similarly not required a showing that the ultimate object of the conspiracy would occur.

The argument that clear and present danger affords too little protection in the arena of political speech was first put forward by Alexander Meiklejohn.[6] He argued that the principle of freedom of speech was rooted in principles of self-government, and that there should be absolute protection for the discussion of public issues, but considerably less protection for speech that did not discuss issues of public interest.[7] Critics of the Meiklejohn approach have questioned the ability to draw the distinction between political and other forms of speech, and have objected to the low level of protection afforded non-political speech under his theory.[8] Advocates of a political speech principle have disagreed with Meiklejohn's assessment of the level of protection to be afforded political speech [9] or with his conclusion that the first amendment was inapplicable to non-political speech.[10] It is, however, a useful inquiry to consider whether the pattern of the Court's decisions reflects a distinction between speech discussing public affairs and other kinds of communication.

(2) **Absolutes and Balances.** Justice Black was a consistent opponent of balancing competing interests as a technique of judicial adjudication. While his early opinions spoke of clear and present danger, he indicated in his *Dennis* dissent that he believed clear and present danger did not mark the outer boundaries of protected expression. For him, clear and present danger had become simply another technique for balancing competing interests. (Justice Frankfurter's *Dennis* concurrence, by contrast, criticized clear and present danger as too wooden a standard to permit the sensitive balancing of competing interests.) The position adopted by Justices Black and Douglas was that the first

---

[4] Compare, however, State v. Robertson, 293 Or. 402, 649 P.2d 569 (1982). The Oregon Supreme Court, in an opinion by Justice Linde, invalidated a statute making "criminal coercion" a crime. The challenged statute concerned compelling or inducing a person to do something he has a legal right not to do by making a threat to inflict specific harms, including exposing a secret. For extended comment on the decision, see Greenawalt, *Criminal Coercion and Freedom of Speech,* 78 Northwestern L.Rev. 1081 (1983).

[5] Chafee, supra note 1, at 47.

[6] Meiklejohn, supra note 2.

[7] Specifically, Meiklejohn argued that "freedom of speech" protected by the first amendment was non-abridgable, but that "liberty of speech" was protected only by the concept of due process and could be regulated for sufficient reasons. Id. at 37–39.

[8] E.g., Emerson, *The System of Freedom of Expression* 541 (1970); Chafee, *Book Review of Meiklejohn's Free Speech and its Relation to Self-Government,* 62 Harv.L.Rev. 891 (1949).

[9] Bork, *Neutral Principles and Some First Amendment Problems,* 47 Ind.L.J. 1 (1971).

[10] Be Vier, *The First Amendment and Political Speech: An Inquiry into the Substance and Limits of Principle,* 30 Stan.L.Rev. 299 (1978).

amendment forbids any government restriction on "speech" but permits the government to regulate "conduct." In their opinions in a number of cases, Justices Black and Harlan debated the question whether freedom of speech was absolutely protected [11] with Justice Black consistently maintaining that "the men who drafted our Bill of Rights did all the 'balancing' that was to be done in this field." [12]

Criticisms of both the balancers and the absolutists should be obvious. Given the intractable problem of assigning values to competing interests, it is claimed that balancing is not a process but simply a convenient method of rationalizing subjective conclusions. Moreover, it often has been employed with excessive deference to the interests that justify suppression of speech. Absolute protection, it is argued, over-protects intolerable speech, or requires sophistry in drawing speech-conduct distinctions, or both.[13] The clash of contentions about absolutism and balancing has abated in contemporary free speech cases, but some of the competing arguments may have re-appeared in a new form.

(3) **Ad Hoc and Definitional Balancing.** A major dispute in the debate surrounding clear and present danger was whether it was appropriate to focus on the danger of all revolutionary speech, or the danger of the defendant's particular speech in its context.[14] An analogous argument concerns the method for reconciling free speech values with competing governmental interests. Ad hoc balancing requires weighing the value of particular speech against the strength of competing interests in the particular case. Definitional balancing suggests that the competing interests should result not in ad hoc decisions but the framing of rules of general application.[15] For a "definitional balancer," the proper rule in a particular context may be one of absolute protection for speech, which may trigger at least part of the controversy between absolutism and balancing. Moreover, the distinction between ad hoc and definitional balancing

---

[11] E.g., Barenblatt v. United States, 360 U.S. 109 (1959); Konigsberg v. California, 366 U.S. 36 (1961); cf. Cohen v. California, 403 U.S. 15 (1971).

[12] 366 U.S. at 61.

[13] A sampling of the law review discussion includes Griswold, *Absolute is in the Dark—A Discussion of the Approach of the Supreme Court to Constitutional Questions,* 8 Utah L.Rev. 167 (1963); Frantz, *The First Amendment in the Balance,* 71 Yale L.J. 1424 (1962); Mendelson, *On the Meaning of the First Amendment: Absolutes in the Balance,* 50 Calif.L.Rev. 821 (1962); Frantz, *Is the First Amendment Law?—A Reply to Professor Mendelson,* 51 Calif.L.Rev. 729 (1963); Kalven, *Upon Re-reading Mr. Justice Black on the First Amendment,* 14 U.C.L.A.L.Rev. 428 (1967); Gunther, *In Search of Judicial Quality on a Changing Court: The Case of Justice Powell,* 24 Stanf.L.Rev. 1001 (1972); Powe, *Evolution to Absolutism: Justice Douglas and the First Amendment,* 74 Colum.L.Rev. 371 (1974).

It can be argued that Justice Black was forced to manipulate the boundaries separating expression and action. In Giboney v. Empire Storage and Ice Co., 336 U.S. 490 (1949), he wrote the opinion for a unanimous court sustaining a restraint of trade conviction of union picketers whose placards urged an ice distributor to stop selling ice to nonunion peddlers. His opinion stated that the placards were to effectuate an unlawful purpose, and the defendants had engaged in illegal conduct "carried out by means of language." In Cohen v. California, 403 U.S. 15 (1971), infra, p. 1214, the Court overturned a breach of the peace conviction of a person who wore a jacket in a courthouse bearing the words "Fuck the Draft." Justice Black joined Justice Blackmun's dissent, which stated that the defendant's "antic . . . was mainly conduct and little speech."

[14] See Linde, supra page 1071.

[15] The term "definitional balancing" first appears in Nimmer, *The Right to Speak from Times to Time: First Amendment Theory Applied to Libel and Misapplied to Privacy,* 56 Cal.L.Rev. 935 (1968), which still contains the most lucid description of the distinction between definitional and ad hoc balancing. Id. at 939–948. The most comprehensive treatment of freedom of expression issues which rejects both absolutism and ad hoc balancing is contained in Emerson, supra note 8. Another attempt to construct a general structure avoiding ad hoc balancing is contained in a series of articles by Professor C. Edwin Baker. They are cited in Shiffrin, *The First Amendment and Economic Regulation: Away from a General Theory of the First Amendment,* 78 Northwestern L.Rev. 1212, 1224 n. 83 (1983), and Baker's approach is both explained and criticized, id. at 1239–1251.

is itself slippery, since it turns on the level of generality at which a balance is struck or whether there is predictable content in a rule. The student should be alert, in the materials that follow, to the question whether particular free speech issues have been resolved by ad hoc or definitional balancing. A final question is whether the results reached, or the reasons given, represent a single, coherent theory of freedom of expression.

SECTION 2. INTERMEZZO: AN INTRODUCTION TO THE CONCEPTS OF VAGUENESS, OVERBREADTH AND PRIOR RESTRAINT

Introduction. Section 3 of this chapter will continue the inquiry begun in Section 1—exploring the societal interests that justify government control of the content of expression. This section involves judicial techniques that permit courts to reverse a defendant's conviction, or invalidate a statute, without deciding whether or not the content of expression or publication is constitutionally protected. The question to be asked is whether these techniques, as they are employed, respond to legitimate constitutional concerns or whether they are devices to avoid or postpone harder decisions concerning the limits of constitutionally protected speech. This section will not exhaust the study of vagueness, overbreadth and prior restraint. Decisions included in the remainder of this chapter, and the succeeding three chapters, are often based on these concepts.

A. VAGUENESS AND OVERBREADTH

HERNDON v. LOWRY, 301 U.S. 242 (1937). Herndon, who was Black, had gone to Alabama as a paid organizer for the Communist Party during the depression years of the 1930's. He enrolled at least five members and held some meetings. When he was arrested he had in his possession Communist literature, including a pamphlet urging self determination for Blacks and advocating strikes, boycotts and a revolutionary struggle for power. It did not appear that he had distributed the literature found in his possession nor that he had advocated anything other than relief for the needy. Herndon received a heavy sentence under a Georgia statute that had been aimed at slave insurrections in its earlier form, before the Civil War. (The statute would have permitted imposition of the death penalty in Herndon's case.) The statute defined "attempt to incite insurrection" as "any attempt, by persuasion or otherwise, to induce others to join in any combined resistance to the lawful authority of the State." Herndon appealed his conviction to the Georgia Supreme Court, arguing that the evidence was insufficient to sustain his conviction, because there was no proof that immediate serious violence was expected or advocated. The Georgia Supreme Court affirmed the conviction, ruling that such proof was unnecessary. A defendant did not have to intend that an insurrection should follow "instantly or at any given time, but it would be sufficient that he intended it to happen at any time, as a result of his influence, by those whom he sought to incite."

Herndon's major argument in the Supreme Court was that the insurrection statute as construed was unconstitutional, since no clear and present danger was required for conviction. The Court, however, reversed the conviction without overruling the holding of Gitlow v. New York, 268 U.S. 652 (1925), that a legislature could make revolutionary speech a crime without requiring proof of clear and present danger. The Court first analyzed the evidence, and concluded that Herndon had been convicted for merely talking about unemployment relief, since there was no proof he had distributed the single copies of the more inflammatory literature in his possession. Relying in part on De Jonge v.

Oregon, 299 U.S. 353 (1937) (Section 1, supra), the Court held on these facts that Herndon's conviction was an "unwarranted invasion of the right of freedom of speech." The Court's second ground of decision was that the insurrection statute was unconstitutional. Portions of Justice Roberts' discussion of that ground follow:

"The statute, as construed and applied in the appellant's trial, does not furnish a sufficiently ascertainable standard of guilt. . . .

". . . To be guilty under the law, as construed, a defendant need not advocate resort to force. He need not teach any particular doctrine to come within its purview. Indeed, he need not be active in the formation of a combination or group if he agitate for a change in the frame of government, however peaceful his own intent. If, by the exercise of prophesy, he can forecast that, as a result of a chain of causation, following his proposed action a group may arise at some future date which will resort to force, he is bound to make the prophesy and abstain, under pain of punishment, possibly of execution. Every person who attacks existing conditions, who agitates for a change in the form of government, must take the risk that if a jury should be of opinion he ought to have foreseen that his utterances might contribute in any measure to some future forcible resistance to the existing government he may be convicted of the offense of inciting insurrection. Proof that the accused in fact believed that his effort would cause a violent assault upon the state would not be necessary to conviction. It would be sufficient if the jury thought he reasonably might foretell that those he persuaded to join the party might, at some time in the indefinite future, resort to forcible resistance of government. The question thus proposed to a jury involves pure speculation as to future trends of thought and action. Within what time might one reasonably expect that an attempted organization of the Communist Party in the United States would result in violent action by that party? If a jury returned a special verdict saying twenty years or even fifty years, the verdict could not be shown to be wrong. The law, as thus construed, licenses the jury to create its own standard in each case.

. . .

. . .

"The statute as construed and applied, amounts merely to a dragnet which may enmesh any one who agitates for a change of government if a jury can be persuaded that he ought to have foreseen his words would have some effect in the future conduct of others. No reasonably ascertainable standard of guilt is prescribed. So vague and indeterminate are the boundaries thus set to the freedom of speech and assembly that the law necessarily violates the guarantees of liberty embodied in the Fourteenth Amendment." [a]

COATES v. CINCINNATI

402 U.S. 611, 91 S.Ct. 1686, 29 L.Ed.2d 214 (1971).

Mr. Justice Stewart delivered the opinion of the Court.

A Cincinnati, Ohio, ordinance makes it a criminal offense for "three or more persons to assemble . . . on any of the sidewalks . . . and there conduct themselves in a manner annoying to persons passing by . . . ." The issue before us is whether this ordinance is unconstitutional on its face.

The appellants were convicted of violating the ordinance, and the convictions were ultimately affirmed by a closely divided vote in the Supreme Court of Ohio, upholding the constitutional validity of the ordinance. 21 Ohio St.2d 66.

---

[a] For an interesting discussion of Herndon v. Lowry, see Chafee, *Free Speech in the United States* 388–398 (1941).

An appeal from that judgment was brought here . . .. The record brought before the reviewing courts tells us no more than that the appellant Coates was a student involved in a demonstration and the other appellants were pickets involved in a labor dispute. For throughout this litigation it has been the appellants' position that the ordinance on its face violates the First and Fourteenth Amendments of the Constitution. Cf. Times Film Corp. v. Chicago, 365 U.S. 43.

In rejecting this claim and affirming the convictions the Ohio Supreme Court did not give the ordinance any construction at variance with the apparent plain import of its language. . . .

We are thus relegated, at best, to the words of the ordinance itself. If three or more people meet together on a sidewalk or street corner, they must conduct themselves so as not to annoy any police officer or other person who should happen to pass by. In our opinion this ordinance is unconstitutionally vague because it subjects the exercise of the right of assembly to an unascertainable standard, and unconstitutionally broad because it authorizes the punishment of constitutionally protected conduct.

Conduct that annoys some people does not annoy others. Thus, the ordinance is vague not in the sense that it requires a person to conform his conduct to an imprecise but comprehensible normative standard, but rather in the sense that no standard of conduct is specified at all. As a result, "men of common intelligence must necessarily guess at its meaning." Connally v. General Construction Co., 269 U.S. 385, 391.

It is said that the ordinance is broad enough to encompass many types of conduct clearly within the city's constitutional power to prohibit. And so, indeed, it is. The city is free to prevent people from blocking sidewalks, obstructing traffic, littering streets, committing assaults, or engaging in countless other forms of anti-social conduct. It can do so through the enactment and enforcement of ordinances directed with reasonable specificity toward the conduct to be prohibited. Gregory v. Chicago, 394 U.S. 111, 118, 124–125 (Black, J., concurring). It cannot constitutionally do so through the enactment and enforcement of an ordinance whose violation may entirely depend upon whether or not a policeman is annoyed.

But the vice of the ordinance lies not alone in its violation of the due process standard of vagueness. The ordinance also violates the constitutional right of free assembly and association. Our decisions establish that mere public intolerance or animosity cannot be the basis for abridgment of these constitutional freedoms. . . . The First and Fourteenth Amendments do not permit a State to make criminal the exercise of the right of assembly simply because its exercise may be "annoying" to some people. If this were not the rule, the right of the people to gather in public places for social or political purposes would be continually subject to summary suspension through the good-faith enforcement of a prohibition against annoying conduct. And such a prohibition, in addition, contains an obvious invitation to discriminatory enforcement against those whose association together is "annoying" because their ideas, their lifestyle or their physical appearance is resented by the majority of their fellow citizens.

The ordinance before us makes a crime out of what under the Constitution cannot be a crime. It is aimed directly at activity protected by the Constitution. We need not lament that we do not have before us the details of the conduct found to be annoying. It is the ordinance on its face that sets the standard of conduct and warns against transgression. The details of the offense could no more serve to validate this ordinance than could the details of an offense charged under an ordinance suspending unconditionally the right of assembly and free speech.

The judgment is reversed.

Mr. Justice White, with whom The Chief Justice and Mr. Justice Blackmun join, dissenting.

The claim in this case, in part, is that the Cincinnati ordinance is so vague that it may not constitutionally be applied to any conduct. But the ordinance prohibits persons from assembling with others and "conduct[ing] themselves in a manner annoying to persons passing by . . . ." Cincinnati Code of Ordinances § 901–L6. Any man of average comprehension should know that some kinds of conduct, such as assault or blocking passage on the street, will annoy others and are clearly covered by the "annoying conduct" standard of the ordinance. It would be frivolous to say that these and many other kinds of conduct are not within the foreseeable reach of the law.

It is possible that a whole range of other acts, defined with unconstitutional imprecision, is forbidden by the ordinance. But as a general rule, when a criminal charge is based on conduct constitutionally subject to proscription and clearly forbidden by a statute, it is no defense that the law would be unconstitutionally vague if applied to other behavior. Such a statute is not vague on its face. It may be vague as applied in some circumstances, but ruling on such a challenge obviously requires knowledge of the conduct with which a defendant is charged. . . .

So . . . in United States v. National Dairy Prod. Corp., 372 U.S. 29 (1963), where we considered a statute forbidding sales of goods at "unreasonably" low prices to injure or eliminate a competitor, 15 U.S.C. § 13a, we thought the statute gave a seller adequate notice that sales below costs were illegal. The statute was therefore not facially vague, although it might be difficult to tell whether certain other kinds of conduct fell within this language. We said: "In determining the sufficiency of the notice a statute must of necessity be examined in the light of the conduct with which a defendant is charged." Id., at 33. See also United States v. Harriss, 347 U.S. 612 (1954). This approach is consistent with the host of cases holding that "one to whom application of a statute is constitutional will not be heard to attack the statute on the ground that impliedly it might also be taken as applying to other persons or other situations in which its application might be unconstitutional." United States v. Raines, 362 U.S. 17, 21 (1960), and cases there cited.

Our cases, however, including *National Dairy,* recognize a different approach where the statute at issue purports to regulate or proscribe rights of speech or press protected by the First Amendment. See United States v. Robel, 389 U.S. 258 (1967); Keyishian v. Board of Regents, 385 U.S. 589 (1967); Kunz v. New York, 340 U.S. 290 (1951). Although a statute may be neither vague, overbroad, nor otherwise invalid as applied to the conduct charged against a particular defendant, he is permitted to raise its vagueness or unconstitutional overbreadth as applied to others. And if the law is found deficient in one of these respects, it may not be applied to him either, until and unless a satisfactory limiting construction is placed on the statute. Dombrowski v. Pfister, 380 U.S. 479, 491–492 (1965). The statute, in effect, is stricken down on its face. This result is deemed justified since the otherwise continued existence of the statute in unnarrowed form would tend to suppress constitutionally protected rights. See United States v. National Dairy Prod. Corp., supra, at 36.

Even accepting the overbreadth doctrine with respect to statutes clearly reaching speech, the Cincinnati ordinance does not purport to bar or regulate speech as such. It prohibits persons from assembling and "conduct[ing]" themselves in a manner annoying to other persons. Even if the assembled defendants in this case were demonstrating and picketing, we have long recognized that picketing is not solely a communicative endeavor and has aspects which the State is entitled to regulate even though there is incidental impact on speech. In Cox v. Louisiana, 379 U.S. 559 (1965), the Court held valid on its face a statute forbidding picketing and parading near a courthouse. This was deemed a valid regulation of conduct rather than pure speech. The conduct reached by the statute was "subject to regulation even though [it was] intertwined with expression and association." Id., at 563. The Court then went on to consider the statute as applied to the facts of record.

In the case before us, I would deal with the Cincinnati ordinance as we would with the ordinary criminal statute. The ordinance clearly reaches certain conduct but may be illegally vague with respect to other conduct. The statute is not infirm on its face and since we have no information from this record as to what conduct was charged against these defendants, we are in no position to judge the statute as applied. That the ordinance may confer wide discretion in a wide range of circumstances is irrelevant when we may be dealing with conduct at its core.

I would therefore affirm the judgment of the Ohio court.

Mr. Justice Black.

. . .

[T]he First Amendment which forbids the State to abridge freedom of speech, would invalidate this city ordinance if it were used to punish the making of a political speech, even if that speech were to annoy other persons. In contrast, however, the ordinance could properly be applied to prohibit the gathering of persons in the mouths of alleys to annoy passersby by throwing rocks or by some other conduct not at all connected with speech. It is a matter of no little difficulty to determine when a law can be held void on its face and when such summary action is inappropriate. This difficulty has been aggravated in this case, because the record fails to show in what conduct these defendants had engaged to annoy other people. In my view, a record showing the facts surrounding the conviction is essential to adjudicate the important constitutional issues in this case. I would therefore, vacate the judgment and remand the case to the court below to give both parties an opportunity to supplement the record so that we may determine whether the conduct actually punished is the kind of conduct which it is within the power of the State to punish.

———

BROADRICK v. OKLAHOMA, 413 U.S. 601 (1973). An Oklahoma statute proscribed partisan political activity by state civil servants in substantially the same manner as the Hatch Act regulates federal employees. Plaintiffs, who had engaged in partisan political activities (including solicitation of money) among their co-workers, brought suit to enjoin enforcement of the statute. They conceded that the statute validly could prohibit the conduct they had engaged in but sought to have it declared unconstitutional because it forbade the wearing of political buttons and displaying bumper stickers—activity they had not engaged in. They argued that the statute was overbroad because buttons and stickers were protected expression.

Justice White, writing for the Court rejected this contention:

"[T]he Court has altered its traditional rules of standing to permit—in the First Amendment area—'attacks on overly broad statutes with no requirement that the person making the attack demonstrate that his own conduct could not be regulated by a statute drawn with the requisite specificity.' Dombrowski v. Pfister, 380 U.S. 479, 486 (1965). Litigants, therefore, are permitted to challenge a statute not because their own rights of free expression are violated, but because of a judicial prediction or assumption that the statute's very existence may cause others not before the court to refrain from constitutionally protected speech or expression.

"Such claims of facial overbreadth have been entertained in cases involving statutes which, by their terms, seek to regulate 'only spoken words.' Gooding v. Wilson, 405 U.S. 518, 520 (1972). . . . In such cases, it has been the judgment of this Court that the possible harm to society in permitting some unprotected speech to go unpunished is outweighed by the possibility that protected speech of others may be muted and perceived grievances left to fester because of the possible inhibitory effects of overly broad statutes. Overbreadth attacks have also been allowed where the Court thought rights of association were ensnared in statutes which, by their broad sweep, might result in burdening innocent associations. See Keyishian v. Board of Regents, 385 U.S. 589 (1967); United States v. Robel, 389 U.S. 258 (1967); Aptheker v. Secretary of State, 378 U.S. 500 (1964); Shelton v. Tucker, [364 U.S. 479 (1960)]. Facial overbreadth claims have also been entertained where statutes, by their terms, purport to regulate the time, place and manner of expressive or communicative conduct, see . . . Thornhill v. Alabama, 310 U.S. 88 (1940), and where such conduct has required official approval under laws that delegated standardless discretionary power to local functionaries, resulting in virtually unreviewable prior restraints on First Amendment rights. See Shuttlesworth v. Birmingham, 394 U.S. 147 (1969); Cox v. Louisiana, 379 U.S. 536, 553–558 (1965); Kunz v. New York, 340 U.S. 290 (1951); Lovell v. Griffin, 303 U.S. 444 (1938).

"The consequence of our departure from traditional rules of standing in the First Amendment area is that any enforcement of a statute thus placed at issue is totally forbidden until and unless a limiting construction or partial invalidation so narrows it as to remove the seeming threat or deterrence to constitutionally protected expression. Application of the overbreadth doctrine in this manner is, manifestly, strong medicine. It has been employed by the Court sparingly and only as a last resort. . . .

"It remains a 'matter of no little difficulty' to determine when a law may properly be held void on its face and when 'such summary action' is inappropriate. Coates v. Cincinnati, 402 U.S. 611, 617 (1971) (separate opinion of Black, J.). But the plain import of our cases is, at the very least, that facial overbreadth adjudication is an exception to our traditional rules of practice and that its function, a limited one at the outset, attenuates as the otherwise unprotected behavior that it forbids the State to sanction moves from 'pure speech' towards conduct and that conduct—even if expressive—falls within the scope of otherwise valid criminal laws that reflect legitimate state interests in maintaining comprehensive controls over harmful, constitutionally unprotected conduct. Although such laws, if too broadly worded, may deter protected speech to some unknown extent, there comes a point where that effect—at best a prediction—cannot, with confidence, justify invalidating a statute on its face and so prohibiting a State from enforcing the statute against conduct that is admittedly within its power to proscribe. Cf. Alderman v. United States, 394 U.S. 165, 174–175 (1969). To put the matter another way, particularly where conduct and not merely speech is involved, we believe that the overbreadth of a statute must not only be real, but substantial as well, judged in relation to the statute's plainly legitimate sweep. It is our view that § 818 is not substantially overbroad and that whatever overbreadth may exist should be cured through case-by-case analysis of the fact situations to which its sanctions, assertedly, may not be applied.[14] "

---

[14] My Brother Brennan asserts that in some sense a requirement of substantial overbreadth is already implicit in the doctrine. This is a welcome observation. It perhaps reduces our differences to our differing views of whether the Oklahoma statute is substantially overbroad. The dissent also insists that Coates v. City of Cincinnati, 402 U.S. 611 (1971), must be taken as overruled. But we are

Justice Douglas dissented on the ground that the whole statute violated the first amendment. Justice Brennan concluded a dissenting opinion joined by Justices Stewart and Marshall as follows:

"At this stage, it is obviously difficult to estimate the probable impact of today's decision. If the requirement of "substantial" overbreadth is construed to mean only that facial review is inappropriate where the likelihood of an impermissible application of the statute is too small to generate a "chilling effect" on protected speech or conduct, then the impact is likely to be small. On the other hand, if today's decision necessitates the drawing of artificial distinctions between protected speech and protected conduct, and if the "chill" on protected conduct is rarely, if ever, found sufficient to require the facial invalidation of an overbroad statute, then the effect could be very grave indeed. In my view, the principles set forth in Coates v. City of Cincinnati, are essential to the preservation and enforcement of the First Amendment guarantees. Since no subsequent development has persuaded me that the principles are ill-founded or that *Coates* was incorrectly decided, I would reverse the judgment of the District Court on the strength of that decision and hold the Oklahoma Merit Act unconstitutional on its face."

SUBSTANTIAL OVERBREADTH

"Substantial overbreadth" has sometimes been described in quantitative terms, by asking whether the constitutional application of the challenged statute "dwarfs its arguably impermissible applications." New York v. Ferber, 458 U.S. 747, 773 (1982). In Los Angeles v. Taxpayers for Vincent, 104 S.Ct. 2118 (1984), however, Justice Stevens' opinion for the Court said this about the concept of "substantial overbreadth":

"In the development of the overbreadth doctrine the Court has been sensitive to the risk that the doctrine itself might sweep so broadly that the exception to ordinary standing requirements would swallow the general rule. In order to decide whether the overbreadth exception is applicable in a particular case, we have weighed the likelihood that the statute's very existence will inhibit free expression. . . .

"The concept of 'substantial overbreadth' is not readily reduced to an exact definition. It is clear, however, that the mere fact that one can conceive of some impermissible applications of a statute is not sufficient to render it susceptible to an overbreadth challenge. On the contrary, the requirement of substantial overbreadth stems from the underlying justification for the overbreadth exception itself—the interest in preventing an invalid statute from inhibiting the speech of third parties who are not before the Court. . . . In short, there must be a realistic danger that the statute itself will significantly compromise recognized First Amendment protections of parties not before the Court for it to be facially challenged on overbreadth grounds. . . ."

For a general analysis and critique of overbreadth doctrine, see Redish, *The Warren Court, the Burger Court and the First Amendment Overbreadth Doctrine,* 78 Northwestern L.Rev. 1031 (1983).

---

unpersuaded that *Coates* stands as a barrier to a rule that would invalidate statutes for overbreadth only when the flaw is a substantial concern in the context of the statute as a whole. Our judgment is that the Oklahoma statute, when authoritative administrative constructions are accepted, is not invalid under such a rule.

SECRETARY OF STATE OF MARYLAND v. JOSEPH H. MUNSON CO., 104 S.Ct. 2839 (1984). A state statute prohibited charitable solicitation if more than 25% of the funds raised were used to pay fund-raising expenses. Plaintiff, a professional fund-raising organization, brought suit in a state court to enjoin enforcement of the statute. The Court concluded that the statute was unconstitutional on its face because it restricted fund-raising by organizations whose high costs were due to information dissemination, discussion and advocacy of public issues. Since it was conceded that a limitation on fund-raising expenditure could be applied to charities whose high expenses were not due to protected first amendment activities, it was argued that the statute was not substantially overbroad. The Court, in an opinion by Justice Blackmun, rejected the argument. This was not a case where the valid portion of the statute "covers a whole range of easily identifiable and constitutionally proscribable . . . . conduct." The Court said:

> "While there no doubt are organizations that have high fundraising costs not due to protected First Amendment activity and that, therefore, should not be heard to complain that their activities are prohibited, this statute cannot distinguish those organizations from charities that have high costs due to protected First Amendment activities. The flaw in the statute is not simply that it includes within its sweep some impermissible applications, but that in all its applications it operates on a fundamentally mistaken premise that high solicitation costs are an accurate measure of fraud. That the statute in some of its applications actually prevents the misdirection of funds from the organization's purported charitable goal is little more than fortuitous. It is equally likely that the statute will restrict First Amendment activity that results in high costs but is itself a part of the charity's goal or that is simply attributable to the fact that the charity's cause proves to be unpopular."

Justice Rehnquist, Chief Justice Burger, and Justices Powell and O'Connor, dissented. They argued that, given the extensive legitimate application of the statute to fundraising expenses not attributable to public education or advocacy, the overbreadth of the ordinance was not "substantial" in relationship to its "legitimate sweep."

FEDERAL COURT INJUNCTIONS AGAINST VAGUE AND OVERBROAD STATUTES

It is accurate to say that laws are judged for vagueness and overbreadth on their "face" only in the sense, as Justice Stewart points out in *Coates,* that it is unnecessary to know the details of the defendant's conduct, or to determine whether it was constitutionally protected. It is a mistake to conclude that statutes are judged for vagueness and overbreadth only with reference to their literal statutory language. A statute may appear to be vague and overbroad, but those problems may disappear if judicial construction clarifies its prohibitions and limits its potentially overbroad applications. A good example is the Smith Act, considered at length in Section 1 of this chapter. Were it not for the limiting constructions given the statute in the *Yates, Scales* and *Noto* cases, its literal application would require a conclusion that it is overbroad. State courts, too, can remove potential issues of vagueness and overbreadth by a limiting construction of the statute involved. Thus, in reviewing a case that originated in a state court, the issue before the Supreme Court is whether the statute, as construed by the state courts, is vague or overbroad. (Notice that in *Herndon* the vagueness problem stemmed, in part, from the state court's construction and, in *Coates,* the state court had not construed the statute beyond its plain language.)

The three cases in this section that sustained vagueness or overbreadth challenges overturned state criminal convictions. The other case, in which an overbreadth challenge failed, was a federal court suit to determine the validity of the state law. That does not, of course, suggest an invariable pattern of results.[1]   In any case in which issues of first amendment vagueness and overbreadth are raised there are difficult questions of degree—determining the degree of vagueness or overbreadth that will be fatal and deciding whether a party can raise the challenge that the statute is vague or overbroad as to other persons.   Those problems are, however, further complicated when the challenges are raised in a federal court suit to enjoin enforcement of the law as opposed to Supreme Court review of a state criminal conviction.   The first problem for the federal court is that it can only guess whether state courts would give an apparently vague or overbroad law a narrowing construction that would obviate the problem.   That can be particularly troublesome when the law sought to be enjoined is newly enacted and has never been construed in the state courts.   The second problem is to define standing to raise the challenges— obviously less of a problem where a defendant seeking Supreme Court review is attempting to overturn the very statutory provision under which he was convicted.   Allowing a defendant in a state criminal action to enjoin a pending prosecution can create inordinate delay in the state criminal process or create a mechanism by which state court decisions on federal issues are reviewed and "reversed" by lower federal courts and not by the Supreme Court.   On the other hand, permitting suit by any person who alleges a future intent to engage in behavior arguably within the statutory prohibition practically allows anyone to mount a vagueness or overbreadth challenge to a state law.   Allowing anyone alleging a subjective "chill" to ask a federal court to strike down a state law on the basis that there are some hypothetical uncertainties or applications to protected speech produces litigation with many of the undesirable features of advisory opinions.   The complex federal jurisdiction rules addressed to these problems were explored, in general terms, earlier in Chapter 3.   They will be examined here with reference to their impact on litigation of vagueness and overbreadth challenges.

(1) **Postponing Decision.**   A technique for addressing the possibility that state courts might narrow the statute's apparent vagueness or overbreadth is for the federal court to stay the action before it, allowing the parties to obtain an "authoritative" state court construction of the law.   (See Chapter 3, Section 2, Subsection C.)   In Baggett v. Bullitt, 377 U.S. 360 (1964), the Court invalidated, as impermissibly vague, a Washington loyalty oath for teachers requiring affirmation that the teacher was not a "subversive person."   In Dombrowski v. Pfister, 380 U.S. 479 (1965), a Louisiana law requiring registration of "subversive organizations" was invalidated for vagueness and overbreadth.   In both cases, the Court refused to postpone exercise of jurisdiction to allow state court interpretation.   Portions of Justice Brennan's opinion in *Dombrowski* can be read as suggesting that abstention to clarify state law is never appropriate when the law is challenged on vagueness and overbreadth grounds.   He emphasized that a major premise of vagueness and overbreadth doctrine was that such laws operated to chill constitutionally protected speech by those not "hardy enough to risk criminal prosecution."   He further pointed out that the abstention

---

[1] Concurring in Secretary of State of Maryland v. Joseph H. Munson Co., 104 S.Ct. 2839 (1984), Justice Stevens indicated that it was relevant to an overbreadth attack that the case before the Court came from a state court. "We need not construe the statute for ourselves; the state court has authoritatively done so. That construction greatly aids an informed analysis of the merits of the First Amendment overbreadth question. The State court's judgment that the illegitimate sweep of the statute is substantial in relationship to its legitimate applications surely merits serious consideration by this Court to the extent that the issue turns on a quantitative assessment of future applications of the statute."

process was time consuming and, in the intervening time, those affected remained subject to the statute's "chilling effect." Both opinions, however, also emphasized that the challenged laws presented a multitude of issues of interpretation that were not likely to be resolved in any single proceeding. More recently, the Court has held that abstention to allow state court interpretation is required where the uncertainty of a challenged statute concerns a single issue that can be resolved by state courts in a single proceeding. Babbitt v. United Farm Workers, 442 U.S. 289 (1979).

(2) **Dismissal.** Justice Brennan's discussion in *Dombrowski* of the "chilling effect" of vague and overbroad statutes upon parties not before the court also led lower federal courts to permit a proliferation of vagueness and overbreadth challenges to state criminal statutes. Younger v. Harris, 401 U.S. 37 (1971), substantially curbed that litigation. At issue in the case was the constitutional validity of the California criminal syndicalism law which had been upheld in Whitney v. California, 274 U.S. 357 (1927) (supra Section 1). Harris had been indicted under the act, and sued to enjoin his state prosecution. Other parties plaintiff were allowed to intervene—Progressive Labor Party members who alleged that Harris' prosecution inhibited them from advocacy of Party programs, and a college instructor who claimed he was uncertain whether he could teach about Marxism. The lower federal courts enjoined Harris' prosecution, holding the law unconstitutional. The Supreme Court reversed, concluding that the federal injunction suit should have been dismissed. The intervenors had not alleged a credible threat they would be prosecuted, and as to them there was no "live controversy." Allowing Harris to sue presented the opposite problem—undue interference with a pending state criminal proceeding. Harris could raise his constitutional defense in the pending prosecution. More broadly, Justice Black's opinion for the Court stated: "Procedures for testing the constitutionality of a statute 'on its face' in the manner apparently contemplated by *Dombrowski*, and for then enjoining all action to enforce the statute until the State can obtain court approval for a modified version, are fundamentally at odds with the function of federal courts in our constitutional plan." Among the difficulties, he listed the "speculative and amorphous nature of the required line-by-line analysis of detailed statutes [which] ordinarily results in a kind of case that is wholly unsatisfactory for deciding constitutional questions."

The seed of Younger v. Harris has grown into a luxuriant forest of rules. (See Chapter 3, Section 2, Subsection C.) Barring suit by persons actually prosecuted and those not threatened with prosecution has, however, left only a narrow corridor for bringing federal court actions to determine the constitutionality of state criminal laws. Suit for declaratory judgment of unconstitutionality (as opposed to an injunction) is permitted where the plaintiff shows a credible threat of prosecution, but has not been prosecuted. Steffel v. Thompson, 415 U.S. 452 (1974). Further, a temporary injunction against prosecution *pendente lite* may be issued on a sufficient showing of irreparable harm and likely success on the merits. Doran v. Salem Inn, Inc., 422 U.S. 922 (1975). If a temporary injunction is not entered, and state prosecution is begun before "proceedings of substance on the merits" have occurred in the federal declaratory judgment action, the federal action must be dismissed. Hicks v. Miranda, 422 U.S. 332 (1975). If a federal declaratory judgment of unconstitutionality is issued, it is an open question whether subsequent state prosecutions can then be enjoined by the federal court. (Justices White and Rehnquist expressed polar positions on that issue in concurring opinions in Hicks v. Miranda.) The question may be particularly perplexing if the statute is declared unconstitutional for vagueness and overbreadth, but there is a possibility that state court construction of the statute in the subsequent state prosecution might narrow the statute's interpretation. Shapiro, *State Courts and Federal Declaratory Judgments*, 80 N.W.U.L.Rev. 759 (1979).

An interesting situation occurs when the defendant has been prosecuted in a state court, and the conviction has become final. The defendant wishes to continue the conduct that resulted in conviction, and, without seeking to set aside the past conviction, asks a federal court to bar future prosecution. In that situation, a federal court may enjoin future state criminal prosecutions. Since the federal plaintiff is willing to let the past criminal conviction stand, there is no interference with state criminal actions and, in form, the federal trial court is not exercising quasi-appellate review of a state court decision. Wooley v. Maynard, 430 U.S. 705 (1977), infra, p. 1272; Carey v. Brown, 447 U.S. 455 (1980), infra, p. 1170. Neither *Wooley* nor *Carey* was decided on vagueness or overbreadth grounds. The implications of those cases, however, for vagueness and overbreadth challenges should be noted. The past state conviction gives some concreteness to the federal litigation. It is known what the defendant has done and intends to do in the future. The particular features of the statute at issue are defined by the previous conviction. And, most significant, a state court has had a prior opportunity to construe the statute and narrow its interpretation.

B. PRIOR RESTRAINT

Introduction. The historical introduction to this chapter referred to the English history of licensed presses and Blackstone's conclusion in 1765 that liberty of the press consisted in an absence of prior restraints upon publication, but imposed no limit on punishing the publisher after publication. (Section 1, Subsection A, 1.) As late as 1907, Justice Holmes, on first encountering the problem, repeated the Blackstone proposition that the Constitution forbade "all such *previous restraints* upon publication as have been practiced by other governments" but not "the subsequent punishment of such as may be deemed contrary to the public welfare."[1] It is now obvious that the Constitution does impose serious limits on the punishment of speech and publications. The prior restraint concept is not obsolete, however. A person, whose publication or speech is not constitutionally protected from punishment, under a properly drawn criminal statute, can still complain if it is inhibited by an unconstitutional prior restraint.

The traditional system of prior restraint was an administrative licensing mechanism, with the publisher forbidden to publish without prior approval of an executive official. The Court has upheld administrative licensing systems, where official permission in advance has been required for expressive activities conducted on public property. (The problems posed by requirements for parade permits are discussed in Chapter 15, beginning at page 1181.) The Court has sustained an administrative licensing system in only one context not involving use of public property. In Times Film Corp. v. City of Chicago, 365 U.S. 43 (1961), the Court concluded that a motion picture licensing ordinance was not invalid "on its face." The nation's existing motion picture licensing systems, however, did not survive the decision four years later in Freedman v. Maryland, 380 U.S. 51 (1965). The Court concluded that the motion picture licensing system under review was invalid because: (1) it did not require the administrative censor to seek judicial review if a permit was refused; (2) if the exhibitor sought judicial review, exhibition of the film was not permitted pending review; (3) there was no assurance of prompt judicial determination. The Court explained that there were important differences between judicial and administrative proceedings. "Unlike a prosecution for obscenity, a censorship

---

[1] Patterson v. Colorado, 205 U.S. 454, 462 (1907). It was not until 1919 that Holmes announced: "I wholly disagree with the argument . . . that the First Amendment left the common law as to seditious libel in force." Abrams v. United States, 250 U.S. 616, 630 (1919) (dissenting opinion).

proceeding puts the initial burden on the exhibitor or distributor. Because the censor's business is to censor, there inheres the danger that he may well be less responsive than a court—part of an independent branch of government—to the constitutionally protected interests in free expression." The Court also said that "only a judicial determination in an adversary proceeding ensures the necessary sensitivity to freedom of expression."

The two cases presented here do not involve administrative censorship but court injunctions. Near v. Minnesota, the Court's seminal decision on prior restraint, equated injunctions with administrative censorship. Vance v. Universal Amusement Co. also involves an injunction. Is an injunction any more "prior" than a criminal statute forbidding the same conduct?

NEAR v. MINNESOTA

283 U.S. 697, 51 S.Ct. 625, 75 L.Ed. 1357 (1931).

Mr. Chief Justice Hughes delivered the opinion of the Court.

Chapter 285 of the Session Laws of Minnesota for the year 1925 provides for the abatement, as a public nuisance, of a "malicious, scandalous and defamatory newspaper, magazine or other periodical." . . .

Under this statute . . . the county attorney of Hennepin county brought this action to enjoin the publication of what was described as a "malicious, scandalous and defamatory newspaper, magazine or other periodical," known as The Saturday Press, published by the defendants in the city of Minneapolis.
. . .

[T]he articles charged, in substance, that a Jewish gangster was in control of gambling, bootlegging, and racketeering in Minneapolis, and that law enforcing officers and agencies were not energetically performing their duties. . . . There is no question but that the articles made serious accusations against the public officers named and others in connection with the prevalence of crimes and the failure to expose and punish them. . . .

The court . . . found that the defendants through these publications did engage in the business of regularly and customarily producing, publishing and circulating a malicious, scandalous and defamatory newspaper, and that "the said publication under said name of The Saturday Press, or any other name, constitutes a public nuisance under the laws of the State." Judgment was thereupon entered adjudging that "the newspaper, magazine and periodical known as The Saturday Press," as a public nuisance, "be and is hereby abated." The judgment perpetually enjoined the defendants "from producing, editing, publishing, circulating, having in their possession, selling or giving away any publication whatsoever which is a malicious, scandalous or defamatory newspaper, as defined by law," and also "from further conducting said nuisance under the name and title of said The Saturday Press or any other name or title." [The judgment was affirmed by the State Supreme Court.]

This statute, for the suppression as a public nuisance of a newspaper or periodical, is unusual, if not unique, and raises questions of grave importance transcending the local interests involved in the particular action. It is no longer open to doubt that the liberty of the press and of speech is within the liberty safeguarded by the due process clause of the Fourteenth Amendment from invasion by state action. . . .

First. The statute is not aimed at the redress of individual or private wrongs. Remedies for libel remain available and unaffected. The statute, said the state court, "is not directed at threatened libel but at an existing business which, generally speaking, involves more than libel." It is aimed at the distribution of scandalous matter as "detrimental to public morals and to the general welfare," tending "to disturb the peace of the community" and "to provoke assaults and the commission of crime." . . .

Second. The statute is directed not simply at the circulation of scandalous and defamatory statements with regard to private citizens, but at the continued publication by newspapers and periodicals of charges against public officers of corruption, malfeasance in office, or serious neglect of duty. Such charges by their very nature create a public scandal. They are scandalous and defamatory within the meaning of the statute, which has its normal operation in relation to publications dealing prominently and chiefly with the alleged derelictions of public officers.

Third. The object of the statute is not punishment, in the ordinary sense, but suppression of the offending newspaper or periodical. The reason for the enactment, as the state court has said, is that prosecutions to enforce penal statutes for libel do not result in "efficient repression or suppression of the evils of scandal." . . .

This suppression is accomplished by enjoining publication, and that restraint is the object and effect of the statute.

Fourth. The statute not only operates to suppress the offending newspaper or periodical, but to put the publisher under an effective censorship. When a newspaper or periodical is found to be "malicious, scandalous and defamatory," and is suppressed as such, resumption of publication is punishable as a contempt of court by fine or imprisonment. Thus where a newspaper or periodical has been suppressed because of the circulation of charges against public officers of official misconduct, it would seem to be clear that the renewal of the publication of such charges would constitute a contempt, and that the judgment would lay a permanent restraint upon the publisher, to escape which he must satisfy the court as to the character of a new publication. Whether he would be permitted again to publish matter deemed to be derogatory to the same or other public officers would depend upon the court's ruling. . . .

If we cut through mere details of procedure, the operation and effect of the statute in substance is that public authorities may bring the owner or publisher of a newspaper or periodical before a judge upon a charge of conducting a business of publishing scandalous and defamatory matter—in particular that the matter consists of charges against public officers of official dereliction—and, unless the owner or publisher is able and disposed to bring competent evidence to satisfy the judge that the charges are true and are published with good motives and for justifiable ends, his newspaper or periodical is suppressed and further publication is made punishable as a contempt. This is of the essence of censorship.

The question is whether a statute authorizing such proceedings in restraint of publication is consistent with the conception of the liberty of the press as historically conceived and guaranteed. In determining the extent of the constitutional protection, it has been generally, if not universally, considered that it is the chief purpose of the guaranty to prevent previous restraints upon publication. . . .

The objection has . . . been made that the principle as to immunity from previous restraint is stated too broadly, if every such restraint is deemed to be prohibited. That is undoubtedly true; the protection even as to previous restraint is not absolutely unlimited. But the limitation has been recognized only in exceptional cases. "When a nation is at war many things that might be said in time of peace are such a hindrance to its effort that their utterance will not be endured so long as men fight and that no Court could regard them as protected by any constitutional right." Schenck v. United States, 249 U.S. 47,

52. No one would question but that a government might prevent actual obstruction to its recruiting service or the publication of the sailing dates of transports or the number and location of troops. On similar grounds, the primary requirements of decency may be enforced against obscene publications. The security of the community life may be protected against incitements to acts of violence and the overthrow by force of orderly government. . . . These limitations are not applicable here. Nor are we now concerned with questions as to the extent of authority to prevent publications in order to protect private rights according to the principles governing the exercise of the jurisdiction of courts of equity.

The exceptional nature of its limitations places in a strong light the general conception that liberty of the press, historically considered and taken up by the Federal Constitution, has meant, principally although not exclusively, immunity from previous restraints or censorship. . . .

The statute in question cannot be justified by reason of the fact that the publisher is permitted to show, before injunction issues, that the matter published is true and is published with good motives and for justifiable ends. . . .

For these reasons we hold the statute, so far as it authorized the proceedings in this action under clause (b) of section 1, to be an infringement of the liberty of the press guaranteed by the Fourteenth Amendment. We should add that this decision rests upon the operation and effect of the statute, without regard to the question of the truth of the charges contained in the particular periodical. The fact that the public officers named in this case, and those associated with the charges of official dereliction, may be deemed to be impeccable, cannot affect the conclusion that the statute imposes an unconstitutional restraint upon publication.

Judgment reversed.

Mr. Justice Butler (dissenting). . . .

. . .

The Court quotes Blackstone in support of its condemnation of the statute as imposing a previous restraint upon publication. But the *previous restraints* referred to by him subjected the press to the arbitrary will of an administrative officer. . . .

. . .

The Minnesota statute does not operate as a *previous* restraint on publication within the proper meaning of that phrase. It does not authorize administrative control in advance such as was formerly exercised by the licensers and censors, but prescribes a remedy to be enforced by a suit in equity. In this case there was previous publication made in the course of the business of regularly producing malicious, scandalous, and defamatory periodicals. The business and publications unquestionably constitute an abuse of the right of free press. The statute denounces the things done as a nuisance on the ground, as stated by the state supreme court, that they threaten morals, peace, and good order. There is no question of the power of the state to denounce such transgressions. The restraint authorized is only in respect of continuing to do what has been duly adjudged to constitute a nuisance. . . . It is fanciful to suggest similarity between the granting or enforcement of the decree authorized by this statute to prevent *further* publication of malicious, scandalous, and defamatory articles and the *previous restraint* upon the press by licensers as referred to by Blackstone and described in the history of the times to which he alludes.

. . .

The judgment should be affirmed.

Mr. Justice Van Devanter, Mr. Justice McReynolds, and Mr. Justice Sutherland concur in this opinion.

VANCE v. UNIVERSAL AMUSEMENT CO.

445 U.S. 308, 100 S.Ct. 1156, 63 L.Ed.2d 413 (1980).

Per Curiam.

The question presented in this unusual obscenity case is whether the United States Court of Appeals for the Fifth Circuit, 587 F.2d 159, correctly held a Texas public nuisance statute unconstitutional. The Court of Appeals read the Texas statute as authorizing a prior restraint of indefinite duration on the exhibition of motion pictures without a final judicial determination of obscenity and without any guarantee of prompt review of a preliminary finding of probable obscenity. Cf. Freedman v. Maryland, 380 U.S. 51 (1965); Southeastern Promotions, Ltd. v. Conrad, 420 U.S. 546 (1975). In this Court, Texas argues that such a restraint is no more serious than that imposed by its criminal statutes and that it is therefore . constitutional. We find Texas' argument unpersuasive and affirm the judgment of the Court of Appeals.

In 1973, appellee operated an indoor, adults-only motion picture theater. In October of that year, appellee's landlord gave notice that the theater's lease would be terminated. The notice stated that the County Attorney had informed the landlord that he intended to obtain an injunction to abate the theater as a public nuisance in order to prevent the future showing of allegedly obscene motion pictures. Appellee responded by filing suit in the United States District Court for the Northern District of Texas seeking an injunction and declaratory relief to forestall any action by the County Attorney . . . .

Art. 4667(a) [of the Texas Revised Civil Statutes], provides that certain habitual uses of premises shall constitute a public nuisance and shall be enjoined at the suit of either the State or any citizen. Among the prohibited uses is "the commercial manufacturing, commercial distribution, or commercial exhibition of obscene material."

. . . Recognizing that it is not unusual in nuisance litigation to prohibit future conduct on the basis of a finding of undesirable past or present conduct, the District Court read Near v. Minnesota, 283 U.S. 697 (1931), to require a special analysis when the prohibited future conduct may be protected by the First Amendment. The routine abatement procedure, which the District Court characterized as "the heavy hand of a public nuisance statute," was considered constitutionally deficient in the First Amendment context.

Specifically, the District Court noted that a general prohibition would operate as a prior restraint on unnamed motion pictures, and that even orders temporarily restraining the exhibition of specific films could be entered *ex parte.*[4] Moreover, such a temporary restraining order could be extended by a temporary injunction based on a showing of probable success on the merits and without a final determination of obscenity. The District Court concluded that the nuisance statutes, when coupled with the Texas Rules of Civil Procedure

---

[4] In dissent, Mr. Justice White incorrectly assumes that it is "undisputed that any injunction granted under Art. 4667(a) will be phrased in terms of the Miller v. California, 413 U.S. 15 (1973), definition of obscenity." This is by no means necessarily so. Under the Texas statutes a temporary injunction prohibiting the exhibition of specific named films could be entered on the basis of a showing of probability of success on the merits of the obscenity issue. Even if it were ultimately determined that the film is not obscene, the exhibitor could be punished for contempt of court for showing the film before the obscenity issue was finally resolved.

governing injunctions, operate as an invalid prior restraint on the exercise of First Amendment rights.

. . .

The Court of Appeals . . . en banc, . . . majority found the statute objectionable because it "would allow the issuance of an injunction against the future exhibition of unnamed films that depict particular acts enumerated in the state's obscenity statute," 587 F.2d 159, 168, and "lacks the procedural safeguards required under Freedman v. Maryland, 380 U.S. 51, ..." Id., at 169. The dissenters wrote that a pragmatic assessment of the statute's operation indicated that once the contemplated injunction was in effect, it would impose no greater a prior restraint than a criminal statute forbidding exhibition of materials deemed obscene under Miller v. California, 413 U.S. 15 (1973).

The Texas defendants appealed to this Court, and we noted probable jurisdiction. We limit our review to the two arguments advanced in appellants' brief: first, that an "obscenity injunction" under Art. 4667(a)(3) constitutes no greater a prior restraint than any criminal statute and, second, that the Court of Appeals erroneously held that no prior restraint of possible First Amendment materials is permissible.

I.

The Court of Appeals was quite correct in concluding both (a) that the regulation of a communicative activity such as the exhibition of motion pictures must adhere to more narrowly drawn procedures than is necessary for the abatement of an ordinary nuisance, and (b) that the burden of supporting an injunction against a future exhibition is even heavier than the burden of justifying the imposition of a criminal sanction for a past communication.

As the District Court and the Court of Appeals construed Art. 4667(a), when coupled with the Texas Rules of Civil Procedure, it authorizes prior restraints of indefinite duration on the exhibition of motion pictures that have not been finally adjudicated to be obscene.[14] Presumably, an exhibitor would be required to obey such an order pending review of its merits and would be subject to contempt proceedings even if the film is ultimately found to be nonobscene.[15] Such prior restraints would be more onerous and more objectionable than the threat of criminal sanctions after a film has been exhibited, since nonobscenity would be a defense to any criminal prosecution.

Nor does the fact that the temporary prior restraint is entered by a state trial judge rather than an administrative censor sufficiently distinguish this case from Freedman v. Maryland. . . . That a state trial judge might be thought more likely than an administrative censor to determine accurately that a work is obscene does not change the unconstitutional character of the restraint if erroneously entered.

Accordingly, we agree with the Court of Appeals' conclusion that the absence of any special safeguards governing the entry and review of orders restraining the exhibition of named or unnamed motion pictures, without regard to the context in which they are displayed, precludes the enforcement of these nuisance statutes against motion picture exhibitors.

---

[14] Those courts believed that a short-lived temporary restraining order could be issued on the basis of an *ex parte* showing, and that a temporary injunction of indefinite duration could be obtained on the basis of a showing of probable success on the merits.

We accept their construction of Texas law for purposes of decision. . . .

[15] Cf. Walker v. Birmingham, 388 U.S. 307, 317–321 (1967); United States v. United Mine Workers, 330 U.S. 258, 293 (1947).

II.

Contrary to the State's second argument, the Court of Appeals did not hold that there can never be a valid prior restraint on communicative activity. The Court of Appeals simply held that these Texas statutes were procedurally deficient and that they authorize prior restraints that are more onerous than is permissible under Freedman v. Maryland and Southeastern Promotions Ltd. v. Conrad.

Because we find no merit in the contentions advanced on behalf of appellants, the judgment is affirmed.

It is so ordered.

Mr. Chief Justice Burger, with whom Mr. Justice Powell joins, dissenting.

. . .

. . . The Court today assumes (1) that "a temporary injunction of indefinite duration" could be issued against a named motion picture "on the basis of a showing of probable success on the merits," and (2) that an exhibitor would be subject to criminal contempt proceedings for violating such an injunction even if the motion picture is ultimately adjudged nonobscene. If these assumptions are correct, the statute is obviously flawed. See Freedman v. Maryland, 380 U.S. 51 (1965). But there is ample reason to believe that the Court may be wrong in today's conjectures; indeed, there is a serious question as to whether the Texas statute even authorizes an injunction against a *named* film. . . . [O]nly by abstaining from decision can we know whether Texas law is as the Court today "forecasts" it to be. . . .[4]

Mr. Justice White, with whom Mr. Justice Rehnquist joins, dissenting.

. . .

The Court of Appeals . . . characterized Art. 4667(a) as a prior restraint on expression and invalidated it for this reason. I disagree. In my view, Art. 4667(a), standing alone, intrudes no more on First Amendment values than would a criminal statute barring exhibition of obscene films in terms that would be valid under our cases.

The Court of Appeals' analysis of Art. 4667(a), and that of this Court as well, glosses over what I take to be a crucial feature of that law. Before an exhibitor can be found to have violated an Art. 4667(a) injunction, there must be two quite separate judicial proceedings. First, the plaintiff must obtain temporary or permanent injunctive relief against the habitual use of the subject premises for the commercial exhibition of obscene motion pictures. Second, the exhibitor must be found in criminal or civil contempt for violating the terms of the injunction. When these separate proceedings are carefully distinguished, it becomes apparent that neither individually nor jointly do they impose an impermissible burden on the exercise of First Amendment freedoms.

. . . [I]t seems undisputed that any injunction granted under Art. 4667(a) will be phrased in terms of the Miller v. California, 413 U.S. 15 (1973), definition of obscenity. Hence an Art. 4667(a) injunction would not by its terms forbid the exhibition of any materials protected by the First Amendment and would impose no greater functional burden on First Amendment values than would an equivalent—and concededly valid—criminal statute. It simply declares to the exhibitor that the future showing of obscene motion

---

[4] Equally dubious is the Court's second assumption that an exhibitor could be punished for disobeying a temporary injunction even if the motion picture shown is ultimately found nonobscene. It is an open question whether Texas in these circumstances would apply a rule analogous to that invoked in Walker v. Birmingham, 388 U.S. 307 (1967), to bar a defendant from raising a First Amendment defense in an action for contempt.

pictures will be punishable. It is true that an Art. 4667(a) injunction is issued by a court of law while a criminal statute is imposed by a legislature. Yet this distinction seems irrelevant for First Amendment purposes.

Of course, an exhibitor who continues to show arguably obscene motion pictures after an Art. 4667(a) injunction has issued against him does run the risk of being held in contempt. The Court implies that this danger renders Art. 4667(a) unconstitutional because under Walker v. City of Birmingham, 388 U.S. 307, 317–321 (1967), an exhibitor could be held in contempt even if the film is ultimately found to be nonobscene. This conclusion is plainly wrong. As I have noted, and as the majority does not dispute, an Art. 4667(a) injunction, temporary injunction, or temporary restraining order will be phrased in terms of a constitutionally adequate definition of obscenity. Therefore, contrary to the Court's inference, the motion picture's nonobscenity would clearly defeat any contempt proceeding brought under Art. 4667(a), since if the film were not obscene, there would be no violation of the injunction.

There remains the question of whether the procedures employed at a contempt proceeding satisfy First Amendment requirements. I believe that they do. An exhibitor who shows a film arguably violative of the injunction would likely be tried for criminal contempt. At such a proceeding the exhibitor would have the constitutional rights of any criminal defendant. In particular, the State would bear the burden of proving beyond a reasonable doubt that the film which allegedly violated the injunction was obscene. Such procedures seem more than adequate to satisfy any procedural requirements that may exist with respect to criminal contempt proceedings in the First Amendment context.

The defendant might also be held in civil contempt if he refused to cease showing a specific motion picture proved to be obscene and contrary to the terms of the injunction. A civil contempt proceeding, unlike the original Art. 4667(a) injunction, could result in jailing or fining the exhibitor until he ceased showing a film that had been publicly determined to be obscene. But such procedures would fully satisfy the requirements of our cases. Under Texas law, no one may be held in civil contempt unless he has received notice, in the form of an order to show cause, and a hearing on the charge against him. The burden of bringing civil contempt charges is on the party seeking to suppress the exhibition; presumably, that party as plaintiff also bears the burden of showing noncompliance with the injunction, and in particular of proving that the exhibitor has shown obscene films. Since contempt proceedings are held before a court, a civil contempt order will not issue until there has been a final judicial determination that the defendant has exhibited and continues to exhibit obscene films. And even then the exhibitor could purge his contempt by ceasing to exhibit such films.

The Court of Appeals and the Court, therefore, too easily equate an injunction against the exhibition of unnamed, obscene films with a typical "prior restraint." The Art. 4667(a) injunction does, in a sense, "restrain" future speech by declaring punishable future exhibitions of obscene motion pictures. But in this weak sense of the term criminal obscenity statutes would also be considered "prior restraints." Prior restraints are distinct from, and more dangerous to free speech than, criminal statutes because, through caprice, mistake or purpose, the censor may forbid speech which is constitutionally protected, and because the speaker may be punished for disobeying the censor even though his speech was protected. Those dangers are entirely absent here. An injunction against the showing of unnamed obscene motion pictures does not and cannot bar the exhibitor from showing protected material, nor can the exhibitor be punished, through contempt proceedings, for showing such material. The Art. 4667(a) injunction, in short, does not impose a traditional prior restraint. On the contrary, it seems to me functionally indistinguishable from a criminal obscenity statute. Since an appropriately worded criminal statute is constitutionally valid, I believe that Art. 4667(a) is valid also.

.   .   .

INJUNCTIONS AND PRIOR RESTRAINT

In Pittsburgh Press Co. v. Pittsburgh Human Relations Comm'n, 413 U.S. 376, 389–390 (1973), the Court noted that not all injunctions against future publications were invalid prior restraints. "The special vice of a prior restraint is that communication will be suppressed, either directly or by inducing excessive caution in the speaker, before an adequate determination that it is protected by the First Amendment." The Court indicated that the challenged order—which required the newspaper to desist from segregating "help wanted" advertisements by gender—was not a prior restraint for two reasons: there was a continuing course of past conduct identical to that enjoined, making it unnecessary "to speculate as to the effect of publication"; the publication enjoined was clearly defined and not constitutionally protected.

In *Near* and *Vance,* does the constitutionality of the challenged injunction procedures depend on the question whether a contempt action for violation of the injunction would permit a defense that the alleged contempt was a constitutionally protected publication or exhibition? In Near v. Minnesota, Justice Butler's dissent made the point that in a contempt action the newspaper publisher would have available all defenses available in a criminal libel action. 283 U.S. at 730. Chief Justice Hughes opinion did not challenge that assertion. If one assumes that a criminal libel law is constitutional, and that only publications that constituted criminal libel could be punished as contempt, should an injunction against future libelous publications still be characterized as a prior restraint? In Vance v. Universal Amusement Co., does the issue whether the Texas statute authorizes prior restraints turn only on the narrow dispute between the Court and Justice White as to whether a temporary injunction could issue without proof that the enjoined film is obscene?

For recent discussion, see Blasi, *Toward a Theory of Prior Restraint: The Central Linkage,* 66 Minn.L.Rev. 11 (1981); Mayton, *Toward a Theory of First Amendment Process: Injunctions of Speech, Subsequent Punishment and the Costs of Prior Restraint Doctrine,* 67 Corn.L.Q. 245 (1982).

SECTION 3. SPEECH CONFLICTING WITH OTHER COMMUNITY VALUES: GOVERNMENT CONTROL OF THE CONTENT OF SPEECH

Introduction. Section 1 of this chapter examined the lengthy controversy concerning speech that advocates the commission of a crime, and speech advocating the violent overthrow of existing government. This section returns to the inquiry whether there are legitimate government interests that will justify punishing the speaker because of speech content. The four areas examined here—defamation and privacy, obscenity, fighting words and offensive speech, and commercial speech—have one thing in common. In the early 1940's, the Court stated categorically that they were outside the area of constitutional protection normally afforded by the first amendment. In Chaplinsky v. New Hampshire, 315 U.S. 568, 571–572 (1942), Justice Murphy's opinion for a unanimous court said:

"There are certain well-defined and narrowly limited classes of speech, the prevention and punishment of which has never been thought to raise any Constitutional problem. These include the lewd, and obscene, the profane, the libelous, and the insulting or 'fighting' words—those which by their very utterance inflict injury or tend to incite an immediate breach of the peace. It has been well observed that such utterances are no essential part of any exposition of ideas, and are of such slight social value as a step to truth that any benefit that may be derived from them is clearly outweighed by the social interest in order and morality."

Barely more than a month later, in Valentine v. Chrestensen, 316 U.S. 52 (1942), the Court added "purely commercial advertising" to the list of subjects outside the realm of first amendment protection.

Definitional problems to one side (and definitional problems have been particularly serious in the obscenity field), the approach of *Chaplinsky* and *Valentine* has not proved enduring. Within these areas of expression, the Court has imposed significant first amendment barriers to government control of the content of expression. At the same time, the Court has recognized legitimate governmental interests in these cases that permit some control of content. The most important question to be asked is whether the Court has drawn the lines that define constitutionally protected speech content in the right places. A second question is whether the first amendment law that has crystallized in each of these four categories is consistent with that in the other three.

A. PROTECTION OF INDIVIDUAL REPUTATION AND PRIVACY

BEAUHARNAIS v. ILLINOIS, 343 U.S. 250 (1952). An Illinois statute made criminal any publication which "portrays depravity, criminality, unchastity, or lack of virtue of a class of citizens, of any race, color, creed or religion which said publication . . . exposes the citizens of any race, color, creed or religion to contempt, derision, or obloquy or which is productive of breach of the peace or riots." Beauharnais was convicted under this statute for passing out leaflets in the form of a petition to the Mayor and City Council of Chicago "to halt the further encroachment, harassment and invasion of white people, their property, neighborhoods and persons, by the Negro." It also included a statement: "If persuasion and the need to prevent the white race from becoming mongrelized by the negro will not unite us, then the aggressions . . . rapes, robberies, knives, guns and marijuana of the negro, surely will." The Supreme Court upheld his conviction with four Justices dissenting. Justice Frankfurter, speaking for the Court, examined in detail the status of libel laws in the states and referred to earlier statements to the effect that punishment for libel presents no constitutional problem. He then said: . . . "[I]f an utterance directed at an individual may be the object of criminal sanctions, we cannot deny to a State power to punish the same utterance directed at a defined group, unless we can say this is a wilful and purposeless restriction unrelated to the peace and well-being of the State." After discussing problems in the cities he concluded that "we would deny experience to say that the Illinois legislature was without reason" in enacting the law.

At the end of his opinion he included the following paragraph: "Libelous utterances, not being within the area of constitutionally protected speech, it is unnecessary, either for us or for the State courts, to consider the issues behind the phrase 'clear and present danger.' Certainly no one would contend that obscene speech, for example, may be punished only upon a showing of such circumstances. Libel, as we have seen, is in the same class."

Justice Black, in dissent, complained that the Court was degrading first amendment freedoms to the "rational basis" level. He concluded as follows:

"To say that a legislative body can, with this Court's approval, make it a crime to petition for and publicly discuss proposed legislation seems as far-fetched to me as it would be to say that a valid law could be enacted to punish a candidate for President for telling the people his views. I think the First Amendment, with the Fourteenth, 'absolutely' forbids such laws without any 'ifs' or 'buts' or 'whereases.' Whatever the danger, if any, in such public discussions, it is a danger the Founders deemed outweighed by the danger incident to the stifling of thought and speech. The Court does not act on this view of the Founders. It calculates what it deems to be the danger of public discussion, holds the scales are tipped on the side of state suppression, and upholds state censorship. . . . If there be minority groups who hail this holding as their victory, they might consider the possible relevancy of this ancient remark: 'Another such victory and I am undone.' "

NEW YORK TIMES CO. v. SULLIVAN

376 U.S. 254, 84 S.Ct. 710, 11 L.Ed.2d 686 (1964).

Mr. Justice Brennan delivered the opinion of the Court.

We are required in this case to determine for the first time the extent to which the constitutional protections for speech and press limit a State's power to award damages in a libel action brought by a public official against critics of his official conduct.

Respondent L.B. Sullivan is one of the three elected Commissioners of the City of Montgomery, Alabama. He testified that he was "Commissioner of Public Affairs and the duties are supervision of the Police Department, Fire Department, Department of Cemetery and Department of Scales." He brought his civil libel action against the four individual petitioners, who are Negroes and Alabama clergymen, and against petitioner the New York Times Company, a New York corporation which publishes the New York Times, a daily newspaper. A jury in the Circuit Court of Montgomery County awarded him damages of $500,000, the full amount claimed, against all the petitioners, and the Supreme Court of Alabama affirmed. . . .

Respondent's complaint alleged that he had been libeled by statements in a full-page advertisement that was carried in the New York Times on March 29, 1960. Entitled "Heed Their Rising Voices," the advertisement [charged that peaceful demonstrations of Southern Negro students in behalf of their rights guaranteed by the Constitution] ". . . are being met by an unprecedented wave of terror by those who would deny and negate that document which the whole world looks upon as setting the pattern for modern freedom. . . ." Succeeding paragraphs purported to illustrate the "wave of terror" by describing certain alleged events. The text concluded with an appeal for funds for three purposes: support of the student movement, "the struggle for the right-to-vote," and the legal defense of Dr. Martin Luther King, Jr., leader of the movement, against a perjury indictment then pending in Montgomery. . . .

Of the 10 paragraphs of text in the advertisement, the third and a portion of the sixth were the basis of respondent's claim of libel. They read as follows:

Third paragraph:

"In Montgomery, Alabama, after students sang 'My Country, 'Tis of Thee' on the State Capitol steps, their leaders were expelled from school, and truckloads of police armed with shotguns and tear-gas ringed the Alabama State College Campus. When the entire student body protested to state authorities by refusing to re-register, their dining hall was padlocked in an attempt to starve them into submission."

Sixth paragraph:

"Again and again the Southern violators have answered Dr. King's peaceful protests with intimidation and violence. They have bombed his home almost killing his wife and child. They have assaulted his person. They have arrested him seven times—for 'speeding,' 'loitering' and similar 'offenses.' And now they have charged him with 'perjury'—a *felony* under which they could imprison him for *ten years.* . . . "

Although neither of these statements mentions respondent by name, he contended that the word "police" in the third paragraph referred to him as the Montgomery Commissioner who supervised the Police Department, so that he was being accused of "ringing" the campus with police. He further claimed that the paragraph would be read as imputing to the police, and hence to him, the padlocking of the dining hall in order to starve the students into submission. As to the sixth paragraph, he contended that since arrests are ordinarily made by the police, the statement "They have arrested [Dr. King] seven times" would be read as referring to him; he further contended that the "They" who did the arresting would be equated with the "They" who committed the other described acts and with the "Southern violators."

. . .

It is uncontroverted that some of the statements contained in the two paragraphs were not accurate descriptions of events which occurred in Montgomery. Although Negro students staged a demonstration on the State Capitol steps, they sang the National Anthem and not "My Country, 'Tis of Thee." Although nine students were expelled by the State Board of Education, this was not for leading the demonstration at the Capitol, but for demanding service at a lunch counter in the Montgomery County Courthouse on another day. Not the entire student body, but most of it, had protested the expulsion, not by refusing to register, but by boycotting classes on a single day; virtually all the students did register for the ensuing semester. The campus dining hall was not padlocked on any occasion, and the only students who may have been barred from eating there were the few who had neither signed a preregistration application nor requested temporary meal tickets. Although the police were deployed near the campus in large numbers on three occasions, they did not at any time "ring" the campus, and they were not called to the campus in connection with the demonstration on the State Capitol steps, as the third paragraph implied. Dr. King had not been arrested seven times, but only four; and although he claimed to have been assaulted some years earlier in connection with his arrest for loitering outside a courtroom, one of the officers who made the arrest denied that there was such an assault.

On the premise that the charges in the sixth paragraph could be read as referring to him, respondent was allowed to prove that he had not participated in the events described. Although Dr. King's home had in fact been bombed twice when his wife and child were there, both of these occasions antedated respondent's tenure as Commissioner, and the police were not only not implicated in the bombings, but had made every effort to apprehend those who were. Three of Dr. King's four arrests took place before respondent became Commissioner. Although Dr. King had in fact been indicted (he was subsequently acquitted) on two counts of perjury, each of which carried a possible five-year sentence, respondent had nothing to do with procuring the indictment.

Respondent made no effort to prove that he suffered actual pecuniary loss as a result of the alleged libel. One of his witnesses, a former employer, testified that if he had believed the statements, he doubted whether he "would want to be associated with anybody who would be a party to such things as are stated in that ad," and that he would not re-employ respondent if he believed "that he allowed the Police Department to do the things that the paper say he did." But neither this witness nor any of the others testified that he had actually believed the statements in their supposed reference to respondent. . . .

The trial judge submitted the case to the jury under instructions that the statements in the advertisement were "libelous per se" and were not privileged, so that petitioners might be held liable if the jury found that they had published the advertisement and that the statements were made "of and concerning" respondent. . . .

We reverse the judgment. We hold that the rule of law applied by the Alabama courts is constitutionally deficient for failure to provide the safeguards for freedom of speech and of the press that are required by the First and Fourteenth Amendments in a libel action brought by a public official against critics of his official conduct. We further hold that under the proper safeguards the evidence presented in this case is constitutionally insufficient to support the judgment for respondent. . . .

Under Alabama law as applied in this case, a publication is "libelous per se" if the words "tend to injure a person . . . in his reputation" or to "bring [him] into public contempt"; the trial court stated that the standard was met if the words are such as to "injure him in his public office, or impute misconduct to him in his office, or want of official integrity, or want of fidelity to a public trust . . . .." The jury must find that the words were published "of and concerning" the plaintiff, but where the plaintiff is a public official his place in the governmental hierarchy is sufficient evidence to support a finding that his reputation has been affected by statements that reflect upon the agency of which he is in charge. Once "libel per se" has been established, the defendant has no defense as to stated facts unless he can persuade the jury that they were true in all their particulars. . . . Unless he can discharge the burden of proving truth, general damages are presumed, and may be awarded without proof of pecuniary injury. . . .

The question before us is whether this rule of liability, as applied to an action brought by a public official against critics of his official conduct, abridges the freedom of speech and of the press that is guaranteed by the First and Fourteenth Amendments.

Respondent relies heavily, as did the Alabama courts, on statements of this Court to the effect that the Constitution does not protect libelous publications. Those statements do not foreclose our inquiry here. None of the cases sustained the use of libel laws to impose sanctions upon expression critical of the official conduct of public officials. . . . Like insurrection, contempt, advocacy of unlawful acts, breach of the peace, obscenity, solicitation of legal business, and the various other formulae for the repression of expression that have been challenged in this Court, libel can claim no talismanic immunity from constitutional limitations. It must be measured by standards that satisfy the First Amendment.

The general proposition that freedom of expression upon public questions is secured by the First Amendment has long been settled by our decisions. The constitutional safeguard, we have said, "was fashioned to assure unfettered interchange of ideas for the bringing about of political and social changes desired by the people." Roth v. United States, 354 U.S. 476, 484 . . . ..

Thus we consider this case against the background of a profound national commitment to the principle that debate on public issues should be uninhibited, robust, and wide-open, and that it may well include vehement, caustic, and sometimes unpleasantly sharp attacks on government and public officials. See Terminiello v. Chicago, 337 U.S. 1; De Jonge v. Oregon, 299 U.S. 353, 365. The present advertisement, as an expression of grievance and protest on one of the major public issues of our time, would seem clearly to qualify for the constitutional protection. The question is whether it forfeits that protection by the falsity of some of its factual statements and by its alleged defamation of respondent.

Authoritative interpretations of the First Amendment guarantees have consistently refused to recognize an exception for any test of truth, whether administered by judges, juries, or administrative officials—and especially not one that puts the burden of proving truth on the speaker. Cf. Speiser v. Randall, 357 U.S. 513, 525–526. The constitutional protection does not turn upon "the truth, popularity, or social utility of the ideas and beliefs which are offered." N.A.A.C.P. v. Button, 371 U.S. 415, 445. As Madison said, "Some degree of abuse is inseparable from the proper use of every thing; and in no instance is this more true than in that of the press." 4 Elliott's Debates on the Federal Constitution (1876), p. 571. . . .

Injury to official reputation affords no more warrant for repressing speech that would otherwise be free than does factual error. Where judicial officers are involved, this Court has held that concern for the dignity and reputation of the courts does not justify the punishment as criminal contempt of criticism of the judge or his decision. Bridges v. California, 314 U.S. 252. . . .

If neither factual error nor defamatory content suffices to remove the constitutional shield from criticism of official conduct, the combination of the two elements is no less inadequate. This is the lesson to be drawn from the great controversy over the Sedition Act of 1798, 1 Stat. 596, which first crystallized a national awareness of the central meaning of the First Amendment. See Levy, Legacy of Suppression (1960), at 258 et seq.; Smith, Freedom's Fetters (1956), at 426, 431 and *passim.* . . .

Although the Sedition Act was never tested in this Court, the attack upon its validity has carried the day in the court of history. . . . These views reflect a broad consensus that the Act, because of the restraint it imposed upon criticism of government and public officials, was inconsistent with the First Amendment.

. . .

What a State may not constitutionally bring about by means of a criminal statute is likewise beyond the reach of its civil law of libel. The fear of damage awards under a rule such as that invoked by the Alabama courts here may be markedly more inhibiting than the fear of prosecution under a criminal statute. . . . The judgment awarded in this case—without the need for any proof of actual pecuniary loss—was one thousand times greater than the maximum fine provided by the Alabama criminal statute, and one hundred times greater than that provided by the Sedition Act. And since there is no double-jeopardy limitation applicable to civil lawsuits, this is not the only judgment that may be awarded against petitioners for the same publication. Whether or not a newspaper can survive a succession of such judgments, the pall of fear and timidity imposed upon those who would give voice to public criticism is an atmosphere in which the First Amendment freedoms cannot survive. Plainly the Alabama law of civil libel is "a form of regulation that creates hazards to protected freedoms markedly greater than those that attend reliance upon the criminal law." Bantam Books, Inc. v. Sullivan, 372 U.S. 58, 70.

The state rule of law is not saved by its allowance of the defense of truth. . . . Allowance of the defense of truth, with the burden of proving it on the defendant, does not mean that only false speech will be deterred. . . . Under such a rule, would-be critics of official conduct may be deterred from voicing their criticism, even though it is believed to be true and even though it is in fact true, because of doubt whether it can be proved in court or fear of the expense of having to do so. They tend to make only statements which "steer far wider of the unlawful zone." Speiser v. Randall, supra, 357 U.S., at 526. The rule thus dampens the vigor and limits the variety of public debate. It is inconsistent with the First and Fourteenth Amendments.

The constitutional guarantees require, we think, a federal rule that prohibits a public official from recovering damages for a defamatory falsehood relating to his official conduct unless he proves that the statement was made with "actual malice"—that is, with knowledge that it was false or with reckless disregard of whether it was false or not. . . .

. . .

We think the evidence against the Times supports at most a finding of negligence in failing to discover the misstatements, and is constitutionally insufficient to show the recklessness that is required for a finding of actual malice. . . .

We also think the evidence was constitutionally defective in another respect: it was incapable of supporting the jury's finding that the allegedly libelous statements were made "of and concerning" respondent. Respondent relies on the words of the advertisement and the testimony of six witnesses to establish a connection between it and himself. . . .

Reversed and remanded.

Mr. Justice Black, with whom Mr. Justice Douglas joins (concurring).

I concur in reversing this half-million-dollar judgment against the New York Times and the four individual defendants. In reversing the Court holds that "the First and Fourteenth Amendments delimit a State's power to award damages for libel in an action brought by a public official against critics of his official conduct." I base my vote to reverse on the belief that the First and Fourteenth Amendments not merely "delimit" a State's power to award damages to "a public official against critics of his official conduct" but completely prohibit a State from exercising such a power. The Court goes on to hold that a State can subject such critics to damages if "actual malice" can be proved against them. "Malice," even as defined by the Court, is an elusive, abstract concept, hard to prove and hard to disprove. The requirement that malice be proved provides at best an evanescent protection for the right critically to discuss public affairs and certainly does not measure up to the sturdy safeguard embodied in the First Amendment. Unlike the Court, therefore, I vote to reverse exclusively on the ground that the Times and the individual defendants had an absolute, unconditional constitutional right to publish in the Times advertisement their criticisms of the Montgomery agencies and officials. . . .

Mr. Justice Goldberg, with whom Mr. Justice Douglas joins (concurring in the result).

. . .

In my view, the First and Fourteenth Amendments to the Constitution afford to the citizen and to the press an absolute, unconditional privilege to criticize official conduct despite the harm which may flow from excesses and abuses.

. . .

NEW YORK TIMES AND "THE CENTRAL MEANING OF THE FIRST AMENDMENT"

The relationship of *New York Times* to the old law of seditious libel and its potential importance for the future is explored in an excellent article. Kalven, *The New York Times Case: A note on "the Central Meaning of the First Amendment,"* 1964 Sup.Ct.Rev. 191, 209. Professor Kalven contended that freedom from prosecutions for seditious libel—freedom to criticize government—is essential to the existence of a free society. After careful examination he concluded that a major purpose of the opinion was to make it clear that the "central meaning" of the first amendment was that seditious libel cannot be sanctioned: "Although the total structure of the opinion is not without its difficulties, it seems to me to convey, however imperfectly, the following crucial syllogism: The central meaning of the Amendment is that seditious libel cannot be made the subject of government sanction. The Alabama rule on fair comment is closely akin to making seditious libel an offense. The Alabama rule therefore violated the central meaning of the Amendment."

GERTZ v. ROBERT WELCH, INC.

418 U.S. 323, 94 S.Ct. 2997, 41 L.Ed.2d 789 (1974).

Mr. Justice Powell delivered the opinion of the Court.

This Court has struggled for nearly a decade to define the proper accommodation between the law of defamation and the freedoms of speech and press protected by the First Amendment. With this decision we return to that effort. We granted certiorari to reconsider the extent of a publisher's constitutional privilege against liability for defamation of a private citizen. 410 U.S. 925 (1973).

I.

In 1968 a Chicago policeman named Nuccio shot and killed a youth named Nelson. The state authorities prosecuted Nuccio for the homicide and ultimately obtained a conviction for murder in the second degree. The Nelson family retained petitioner Elmer Gertz, a reputable attorney, to represent them in civil litigation against Nuccio.

Respondent publishes American Opinion, a monthly outlet for the views of the John Birch Society. Early in the 1960's the magazine began to warn of a nationwide conspiracy to discredit local law enforcement agencies and create in their stead a national police force capable of supporting a Communist dictatorship. As part of the continuing effort to alert the public to this assumed danger, the managing editor of American Opinion commissioned an article on the murder trial of Officer Nuccio. For this purpose he engaged a regular contributor to the magazine. In March of 1969 respondent published the resulting article under the title "FRAME–UP: Richard Nuccio And The War On Police." The article purports to demonstrate that the testimony against Nuccio at his criminal trial was false and that his prosecution was part of the Communist campaign against the police.

In his capacity as counsel for the Nelson family in the civil litigation, petitioner attended the coroner's inquest into the boy's death and initiated actions for damages, but he neither discussed Officer Nuccio with the press nor played any part in the criminal proceeding. Notwithstanding petitioner's remote connection with the prosecution of Nuccio, respondent's magazine portrayed him as an architect of the "frame-up." According to the article, the police file on petitioner took "a big, Irish cop to lift." The article stated that petitioner had been an official of the "Marxist League for Industrial Democracy, originally known as the Intercollegiate Socialist Society, which has advocated the violent seizure of our government." It labelled Gertz a "Leninist" and a "Communist-fronter." It also stated that Gertz had been an officer of the National Lawyers Guild, described as a Communist organization that "probably did more than any other outfit to plan the Communist attack on the Chicago police during the 1968 Democratic convention."

These statements contained serious inaccuracies. The implication that petitioner had a criminal record was false. Petitioner had been a member and officer of the National Lawyers Guild some 15 years earlier, but there was no evidence that he or that organization had taken any part in planning the 1968 demonstrations in Chicago. There was also no basis for the charge that petitioner was a "Leninist" or a "Communist-fronter." And he had never been a member of the "Marxist League for Industrial Democracy" or the "Intercollegiate Socialist Society."

The managing editor of American Opinion made no effort to verify or substantiate the charges against petitioner. Instead, he appended an editorial introduction stating that the author had "concluded extensive research into the Richard Nuccio case." And he included in the article a photograph of petitioner and wrote the caption that appeared under it: "Elmer Gertz of the Red Guild harasses Nuccio." Respondent placed the issue of American Opinion containing the article on sale at newsstands throughout the country and distributed reprints of the article on the streets of Chicago.

Petitioner filed a diversity action for libel in the United States District Court for the Northern District of Illinois. . . .

. . .

[T]he District Court concluded that the *New York Times* standard should govern this case even though petitioner was not a public official or public figure. . . .

Petitioner appealed to contest the applicability of the *New York Times* standard to this case. . . . The Court of Appeals . . . affirmed. . . . [W]e reverse . . . ..

II.

The principal issue in this case is whether a newspaper or broadcaster that publishes defamatory falsehoods about an individual who is neither a public official nor a public figure may claim a constitutional privilege against liability for the injury inflicted by those statements. The Court considered this question on the rather different set of facts presented in Rosenbloom v. Metromedia, Inc., 403 U.S. 29 (1971). Rosenbloom, a distributor of nudist magazines, was arrested for selling allegedly obscene material while making a delivery to a retail dealer. The police obtained a warrant and seized his entire inventory of 3,000 books and magazines. He sought and obtained an injunction prohibiting further police interference with his business. He then sued a local radio station for failing to note in two of its newscasts that the 3,000 items seized were only "reportedly" or "allegedly" obscene and for broadcasting references to "the smut literature racket" and to "girlie-book peddlers" in its coverage of the court proceeding for injunctive relief. He obtained a judgment against the radio station, but the Court of Appeals for the Third Circuit held the *New York Times* privilege applicable to the broadcast and reversed. 415 F.2d 892 (1969).

This Court affirmed the decision below, but no majority could agree on a controlling rationale. The eight Justices who participated in *Rosenbloom* announced their views in five separate opinions, none of which commanded more than three votes. The several statements not only reveal disagreement about the appropriate result in that case; they also reflect divergent traditions of thought about the general problem of reconciling the law of defamation with the First Amendment. One approach has been to extend the *New York Times* test to an expanding variety of situations. Another has been to vary the level of constitutional privilege for defamatory falsehood with the status of the person defamed. And a third view would grant to the press and broadcast media absolute immunity from liability for defamation. To place our holding in the proper context, we preface our discussion of this case with a review of the several *Rosenbloom* opinions and their antecedents.

In affirming the trial court's judgment in the instant case, the Court of Appeals relied on Mr. Justice Brennan's conclusion for the *Rosenbloom* plurality that "all discussion and communication involving matters of public or general concern" warrant the protection from liability for defamation accorded by the rule originally enunciated in New York Times Co. v. Sullivan, 376 U.S. 254 (1964) . . .[6]

Three years after *New York Times,* a majority of the Court agreed to extend the constitutional privilege to defamatory criticism of "public figures." This extension was announced in Curtis Publishing Co. v. Butts and its companion Associated Press v. Walker, 388 U.S. 130, 162 (1967). The first case involved the Saturday Evening Post's charge that Coach Wally Butts of the University of Georgia had conspired with Coach Bear Bryant of the University of Alabama to fix a football game between their respective schools. *Walker* involved an erroneous Associated Press account of Brigadier General Edwin Walker's participation in a University of Mississippi campus riot. Because Butts was paid by a private alumni association and Walker had retired from the Army, neither could be classified as a "public official" under *New York Times.* Although Mr. Justice Harlan announced the result in both cases, a majority of the Court agreed with Mr. Chief Justice Warren's conclusion that the *New York Times* test should apply to criticism of "public figures" as well as "public officials." The Court extended the constitutional privilege announced in that case to protect defamatory criticism of nonpublic officials who "are nevertheless intimately involved in the resolution of important public questions, or, by reason of their fame, shape events in areas of concern to society at large." Id., at 164.

In his opinion for the plurality in Rosenbloom v. Metromedia, Inc., 403 U.S. 29 (1971), Mr. Justice Brennan took the *New York Times* privilege one step further. He concluded that its protection should extend to defamatory false-hoods relating to private persons if the statements concerned matters of general or public interest. . . .

Two members of the Court concurred in the result in *Rosenbloom* but departed from the reasoning of the plurality. Mr. Justice Black restated his view, long shared by Mr. Justice Douglas, that the First Amendment cloaks the

---

[6] *New York Times* and later cases explicated the meaning of the new standard. In *New York Times* the Court held that under the circumstances the newspaper's failure to check the accuracy of the advertisement against news stories in its own files did not establish reckless disregard for the truth. 376 U.S. at 287–288. In St. Amant v. Thompson, 390 U.S. 727, 731 (1968), the Court equated reckless disregard of the truth with subjective awareness of probable falsity: "There must be sufficient evidence to permit the conclusion that the defendant in fact entertained serious doubts as to the truth of his publication." In Beckley Newspapers Corp. v. Hanks, 389 U.S. 81 (1967), the Court emphasized the distinction between the *New York Times* test of knowledge of falsity or reckless disregard of the truth and "actual malice" in the traditional sense of ill-will. Garrison v. Louisiana, 379 U.S. 64 (1964), made plain that the new standard applied to criminal libel laws as well as to civil actions and that it governed criticism directed at "anything which might touch on an official's fitness for office." Id., at 77. Finally, in Rosenblatt v. Baer, 383 U.S. 75, 85 (1966), the Court stated that "the 'public official' designation applies at the very least to those among the hierarchy of government employees who have, or appear to the public to have, substantial responsibility for or control over the conduct of governmental affairs."

In Time, Inc. v. Hill, 385 U.S. 374 (1967), the Court applied the New York Times standard to actions under an unusual state statute. The statute did not create a cause of action for libel. Rather, it provided a remedy for unwanted publicity. Although the law allowed recovery of damages for harm caused by exposure to public attention rather than by factual inaccuracies, it recognized truth as a complete defense. Thus, nondefamatory factual errors could render a publisher liable for something akin to invasion of privacy. The Court ruled that the defendant in such an action could invoke the New York Times privilege regardless of the fame or anonymity of the plaintiff. Speaking for the Court, Mr. Justice Brennan declared that this holding was not an extension of New York Times but rather a parallel line of reasoning applying that standard to this discrete context. . . .

news media with an absolute and indefeasible immunity from liability for defamation. Id., at 57. Mr. Justice White concurred on a narrower ground. Ibid. He concluded that "the First Amendment gives the press and the broadcast media a privilege to report and comment upon the official actions of public servants in full detail, with no requirement that the reputation or privacy of an individual involved in or affected by the official action be spared from public view." Id., at 62. He therefore declined to reach the broader questions addressed by the other Justices.

. . .

III.

We begin with the common ground. Under the First Amendment there is no such thing as a false idea. However pernicious an opinion may seem, we depend for its correction not on the conscience of judges and juries but on the competition of other ideas. But there is no constitutional value in false statements of fact. Neither the intentional lie nor the careless error materially advances society's interest in "uninhibited, robust, and wide-open" debate on public issues. New York Times Co. v. Sullivan, 376 U.S., at 270. . . .

Although the erroneous statement of fact is not worthy of constitutional protection, it is nevertheless inevitable in free debate. . . . And punishment of error runs the risk of inducing a cautious and restrictive exercise of the constitutionally guaranteed freedoms of speech and press. Our decisions recognize that a rule of strict liability that compels a publisher or broadcaster to guarantee the accuracy of his factual assertions may lead to intolerable self-censorship. Allowing the media to avoid liability only by proving the truth of all injurious statements does not accord adequate protection to First Amendment liberties. . . .

The need to avoid self-censorship by the news media is, however, not the only societal value at issue. If it were, this Court would have embraced long ago the view that publishers and broadcasters enjoy an unconditional and indefeasible immunity from liability for defamation. . . . Such a rule would indeed obviate the fear that the prospect of civil liability for injurious falsehood might dissuade a timorous press from the effective exercise of First Amendment freedoms. Yet absolute protection for the communications media requires a total sacrifice of the competing value served by the law of defamation.

The legitimate state interest underlying the law of libel is the compensation of individuals for the harm inflicted on them by defamatory falsehoods. We would not lightly require the State to abandon this purpose. . . .

. . .

The *New York Times* standard defines the level of constitutional protection appropriate to the context of defamation of a public person. Those who, by reason of the notoriety of their achievements or the vigor and success with which they seek the public's attention, are properly classed as public figures and those who hold governmental office may recover for injury to reputation only on clear and convincing proof that the defamatory falsehood was made with knowledge of its falsity or with reckless disregard for the truth. This standard administers an extremely powerful antidote to the inducement to media self-censorship of the common law rule of strict liability for libel and slander. And it exacts a correspondingly high price from the victims of defamatory falsehood. . . . For the reasons stated below, we conclude that the state interest in compensating injury to the reputation of private individuals requires that a different rule should obtain with respect to them.

. . .

[W]e have no difficulty in distinguishing among defamation plaintiffs. The first remedy of any victim of defamation is self-help—using available opportunities to contradict the lie or correct the error and thereby to minimize its adverse impact on reputation. Public officials and public figures usually enjoy significantly greater access to the channels of effective communication and hence have a more realistic opportunity to counteract false statements than private individuals normally enjoy. Private individuals are therefore more vulnerable to injury, and the state interest in protecting them is correspondingly greater.

More important than the likelihood that private individuals will lack effective opportunities for rebuttal, there is a compelling normative consideration underlying the distinction between public and private defamation plaintiffs. An individual who decides to seek governmental office must accept certain necessary consequences of that involvement in public affairs. He runs the risk of closer public scrutiny than might otherwise be the case. And society's interest in the officers of government is not strictly limited to the formal discharge of official duties. . . .

Those classed as public figures stand in a similar position. Hypothetically, it may be possible for someone to become a public figure through no purposeful action of his own, but the instances of truly involuntary public figures must be exceedingly rare. For the most part those who attain this status have assumed roles of especial prominence in the affairs of society. Some occupy positions of such persuasive power and influence that they are deemed public figures for all purposes. More commonly, those classed as public figures have thrust themselves to the forefront of particular public controversies in order to influence the resolution of the issues involved. In either event, they invite attention and comment.

Even if the foregoing generalities do not obtain in every instance, the communications media are entitled to act on the assumption that public officials and public figures have voluntarily exposed themselves to increased risk of injury from defamatory falsehoods concerning them. No such assumption is justified with respect to a private individual. He has not accepted public office nor assumed an "influential role in ordering society." Curtis Publishing Co. v. Butts, supra, 388 U.S., at 164 (Warren, C.J., concurring). He has relinquished no part of his interest in the protection of his own good name, and consequently he has a more compelling call on the courts for redress of injury inflicted by defamatory falsehood. Thus, private individuals are not only more vulnerable to injury than public officials and public figures; they are also more deserving of recovery.

For these reasons we conclude that the States should retain substantial latitude in their efforts to enforce a legal remedy for defamatory falsehood injurious to the reputation of a private individual. The extension of the *New York Times* test proposed by the *Rosenbloom* plurality would abridge this legitimate state interest to a degree that we find unacceptable. . . .

We hold that, so long as they do not impose liability without fault, the States may define for themselves the appropriate standard of liability for a publisher or broadcaster of defamatory falsehood injurious to a private individual. This approach provides a more equitable boundary between the competing concerns involved here. It recognizes the strength of the legitimate state interest in compensating private individuals for wrongful injury to reputation, yet shields the press and broadcast media from the rigors of strict liability for defamation. At least this conclusion obtains where, as here, the substance of the defamatory statement "makes substantial danger to reputation apparent." This phrase places in perspective the conclusion we announce today. Our inquiry would involve considerations somewhat different from those discussed above if a State purported to condition civil liability on a factual misstatement whose content did not warn a reasonably prudent editor or broadcaster of its defamatory potential. Cf. Time, Inc. v. Hill, 385 U.S. 374 (1967). Such a case is not now before us, and we intimate no view as to its proper resolution.

IV.

. . . For the reasons stated below, we hold that the States may not permit recovery of presumed or punitive damages, at least when liability is not based on a showing of knowledge of falsity or reckless disregard for the truth.

The common law of defamation is an oddity of tort law, for it allows recovery of purportedly compensatory damages without evidence of actual loss. Under the traditional rules pertaining to actions for libel, the existence of injury is presumed from the fact of publication. Juries may award substantial sums as compensation for supposed damage to reputation without any proof that such harm actually occurred. The largely uncontrolled discretion of juries to award damages where there is no loss unnecessarily compounds the potential of any system of liability for defamatory falsehood to inhibit the vigorous exercise of First Amendment freedoms. Additionally, the doctrine of presumed damages invites juries to punish unpopular opinion rather than to compensate individuals for injury sustained by the publication of a false fact. More to the point, the States have no substantial interest in securing for plaintiffs such as this petitioner gratuitous awards of money damages far in excess of any actual injury.

. . . It is necessary to restrict defamation plaintiffs who do not prove knowledge of falsity or reckless disregard for the truth to compensation for actual injury. We need not define "actual injury," as trial courts have wide experience in framing appropriate jury instructions in tort actions. Suffice it to say that actual injury is not limited to out-of-pocket loss. Indeed, the more customary types of actual harm inflicted by defamatory falsehood include impairment of reputation and standing in the community, personal humiliation, and mental anguish and suffering. Of course, juries must be limited by appropriate instructions, and all awards must be supported by competent evidence concerning the injury, although there need be no evidence which assigns an actual dollar value to the injury.

We also find no justification for allowing awards of punitive damages against publishers and broadcasters held liable under state-defined standards of liability for defamation. In most jurisdictions jury discretion over the amounts awarded is limited only by the gentle rule that they not be excessive. Consequently, juries assess punitive damages in wholly unpredictable amounts bearing no necessary relation to the actual harm caused. And they remain free to use their discretion selectively to punish expressions of unpopular views. Like the doctrine of presumed damages, jury discretion to award punitive damages unnecessarily exacerbates the danger of media self-censorship, but, unlike the former rule, punitive damages are wholly irrelevant to the state interest that justifies a negligence standard for private defamation actions. They are not compensation for injury. Instead, they are private fines levied by civil juries to punish reprehensible conduct and to deter its future occurrence. In short, the private defamation plaintiff who establishes liability under a less demanding standard than that stated by *New York Times* may recover only such damages as are sufficient to compensate him for actual injury.

V.

Notwithstanding our refusal to extend the *New York Times* privilege to defamation of private individuals, respondent contends that we should affirm the judgment below on the ground that petitioner is either a public official or a public figure. There is little basis for the former assertion. Several years prior to the present incident, petitioner had served briefly on housing committees appointed by the mayor of Chicago, but at the time of publication he had never held any remunerative governmental position. Respondent admits this but argues that petitioner's appearance at the coroner's inquest rendered him a "de facto public official." Our cases recognize no such concept. Respondent's suggestion would sweep all lawyers under the *New York Times* rule as officers of the court and distort the plain meaning of the "public official" category beyond all recognition. We decline to follow it.

Respondent's characterization of petitioner as a public figure raises a different question. That designation may rest on either of two alternative bases. In some instances an individual may achieve such pervasive fame or notoriety that he becomes a public figure for all purposes and in all contexts. More commonly, an individual voluntarily injects himself or is drawn into a particular public controversy and thereby becomes a public figure for a limited range of issues. In either case such persons assume special prominence in the resolution of public questions.

Petitioner has long been active in community and professional affairs. He has served as an officer of local civic groups and of various professional organizations, and he has published several books and articles on legal subjects. Although petitioner was consequently well-known in some circles, he had achieved no general fame or notoriety in the community. None of the prospective jurors called at the trial had ever heard of petitioner prior to this litigation, and respondent offered no proof that this response was atypical of the local population. We would not lightly assume that a citizen's participation in community and professional affairs rendered him a public figure for all purposes. Absent clear evidence of general fame or notoriety in the community, and pervasive involvement in the affairs of society, an individual should not be deemed a public personality for all aspects of his life. It is preferable to reduce the public figure question to a more meaningful context by looking to the nature and extent of an individual's participation in the particular controversy giving rise to the defamation.

In this context it is plain that petitioner was not a public figure. He played a minimal role at the coroner's inquest, and his participation related solely to his representation of a private client. He took no part in the criminal prosecution of Officer Nuccio. Moreover, he never discussed either the criminal or civil litigation with the press and was never quoted as having done so. He plainly did not thrust himself into the vortex of this public issue, nor did he engage the public's attention in an attempt to influence its outcome. We are persuaded that the trial court did not err in refusing to characterize petitioner as a public figure for the purpose of this litigation.

We therefore conclude that the *New York Times* standard is inapplicable to this case and that the trial court erred in entering judgment for respondent. Because the jury was allowed to impose liability without fault and was permitted to presume damages without proof of injury, a new trial is necessary. We reverse and remand for further proceedings in accord with this opinion.

It is so ordered.

Mr. Justice Blackmun, concurring.

I joined Mr. Justice Brennan's opinion for the plurality in Rosenbloom v. Metromedia, Inc., 403 U.S. 29 (1971). . . . If my vote were not needed to create a majority, I would adhere to my prior view. A definitive ruling, however, is paramount. . . .

. . . I join the opinion and the judgment of the Court.

Mr. Chief Justice Burger, dissenting.

The doctrines of the law of defamation have had a gradual evolution primarily in the state courts. In New York Times Co. v. Sullivan, 376 U.S. 254 (1964), and its progeny this Court entered this field.

. . . I would prefer to allow this area of law to continue to evolve as it has up to now with respect to private citizens rather than embark on a new doctrinal theory which has no jurisprudential ancestry. . . .

. . .

Mr. Justice Douglas, dissenting.

The Court describes this case as a return to the struggle of "defin[ing] the proper accommodation between the law of defamation and the freedoms of speech and press protected by the First Amendment." It is indeed a struggle, once described by Mr. Justice Black as "the same quagmire" in which the Court "is helplessly struggling in the field of obscenity." Curtis Publishing Co. v. Butts, 388 U.S. 130, 171 (concurring). I would suggest that the struggle is a quite hopeless one, for, in light of the command of the First Amendment, no "accommodation" of its freedoms can be "proper" except those made by the Framers themselves.

. . .

Mr. Justice Brennan, dissenting.

. . . I adhere to my view expressed in Rosenbloom v. Metromedia, Inc., supra, that we strike the proper accommodation between avoidance of media self-censorship and protection of individual reputations only when we require States to apply the New York Times Co. v. Sullivan, 376 U.S. 254 (1964), knowing-or-reckless-falsity standard in civil libel actions concerning media reports of the involvement of private individuals in events of public or general interest.

. . .

Mr. Justice White, dissenting.

For some 200 years—from the very founding of the Nation—the law of defamation and right of the ordinary citizen to recover for false publication injurious to his reputation have been almost exclusively the business of state courts and legislatures. . . .

But now, using that Amendment as the chosen instrument, the Court, in a few printed pages, has federalized major aspects of libel law by declaring unconstitutional in important respects the prevailing defamation law in all or most of the 50 States. That result is accomplished by requiring the plaintiff in each and every defamation action to prove not only the defendant's culpability beyond his act of publishing defamatory material but also actual damage to reputation resulting from the publication. Moreover, punitive damages may not be recovered by showing malice in the traditional sense of ill will; knowing falsehood or reckless disregard of the truth will now be required.

I assume these sweeping changes will be popular with the press, but this is not the road to salvation for a court of law. As I see it, there are wholly insufficient grounds for scuttling the libel laws of the States in such wholesale fashion, to say nothing of deprecating the reputation interest of ordinary citizens and rendering them powerless to protect themselves. I do not suggest that the decision is illegitimate or beyond the bounds of judicial review, but it is an ill-considered exercise of the power entrusted to this Court, particularly when the Court has not had the benefit of briefs and argument addressed to most of the major issues which the Court now decides. I respectfully dissent.

. . .

TIME, INC. v. FIRESTONE, 424 U.S. 448 (1976). Plaintiff sued Time, Inc., and recovered a $100,000 libel judgment based on an item appearing in Time that purported to describe the result of divorce litigation between plaintiff and her husband, Russell Firestone, the scion of one of America's wealthier industrial families. Time claimed that the *New York Times* standard applied because the plaintiff was a public figure and because the item in question constituted a report of a judicial proceeding. Justice Rehnquist, speaking for the Court, rejected both contentions:

". . . Respondent did not assume any role of especial prominence in the affairs of society, other than perhaps Palm Beach society, and she did not thrust herself to the forefront of any particular public controversy in order to influence the resolution of the issues involved in it.

"Petitioner contends that because the Firestone divorce was characterized by the Florida Supreme Court as a 'cause célèbre,' it must have been a public controversy and respondent must be considered a public figure. But in so doing petitioner seeks to equate 'public controversy' with all controversies of interest to the public. Were we to accept this reasoning, we would reinstate the doctrine advanced in the plurality opinion in Rosenbloom v. Metromedia, Inc., 403 U.S. 29 (1971), which concluded that the *New York Times* privilege should be extended to falsehoods defamatory of private persons whenever the statements concern matters of general or public interest. In *Gertz,* however, the Court repudiated this position, . . .

"Dissolution of a marriage through judicial proceedings is not the sort of 'public controversy' referred to in *Gertz,* even though the marital difficulties of extremely wealthy individuals may be of interest to some portion of the reading public. Nor did respondent freely choose to publicize issues as to the propriety of her married life. She was compelled to go to court by the State in order to obtain legal release from the bonds of matrimony. . . . Her actions, both in instituting the litigation and in its conduct, were quite different from those of General Walker in *Curtis Publishing Co.,* supra. She assumed no 'special prominence in the resolution of public questions.' *Gertz,* 418 U.S., at 351. We hold respondent was not a 'public figure' for the purpose of determining the constitutional protection afforded petitioner's report of the factual and legal basis for her divorce.

"For similar reasons we likewise reject petitioner's claim for automatic extension of the *New York Times* privilege to all reports of judicial proceedings. . . .

"The public interest in accurate reports of judicial proceedings is substantially protected by *Cox Broadcasting Co.,* 420 U.S. 469 (1975). As to inaccurate and defamatory reports of facts, matters deserving no First Amendment protection, see 418 U.S., at 340, we think *Gertz* provides an adequate safeguard for the constitutionally protected interests of the press and affords it a tolerable margin for error by requiring some type of fault."

Justice Brennan dissented on the court records ground. Justice Marshall dissented on the ground that the plaintiff was a public figure. Justice White also dissented.

———————

WOLSTON v. READER'S DIGEST ASSOCIATION, 443 U.S. 157 (1979). Plaintiff's name was included in a book's list of Soviet agents identified by official investigations in the United States and Canada. Wolston's aunt and uncle, Myra and Jack Sobel, pled guilty to federal charges of espionage in a widely-publicized case in the late 1950's. Wolston's conviction for contempt— for failure to appear before the federal grand jury investigating the suspected espionage ring involving the Sobels—was also widely covered in the media. In the 16 years between his conviction and the publication of the book, Wolston "succeeded for the most part in returning to . . . private life." The trial court held that Wolston was a public figure and granted summary judgment for the defendant. The conclusion that he was a "limited-purpose public figure" was premised on his involvement in a publicized procedure, and his failure to comply with the grand jury's subpoena which invited attention and comment. The Supreme Court reversed.

HUTCHINSON v. PROXMIRE, 443 U.S. 111 (1979). A scientist was awarded Senator Proxmire's "Golden Fleece" award for his federally funded research in aggressive animal behaviour. In his speech referring to "funding of this nonsense," the Senator said: "Dr. Hutchinson's studies should make the taxpayers as well as his monkeys grind their teeth. In fact, the good doctor has made a fortune from his monkeys and in the process made a monkey out of the American taxpayer." The trial court held that Hutchinson was a public figure, and granted the Senator summary judgment in Hutchinson's suit against him. The Supreme Court reversed. Hutchinson's successful applications for public funds and publications in professional journals did not give him a place of public prominence concerning broad questions of concern for public expenditures. The fact that some newspapers and wire services carried his response to the Golden Fleece award did not show that he was a person with access to the media, since his access was limited to responding to announcement of the "award."

The case is unique, among all defamation cases decided by the Supreme Court since *New York Times* in that it involved an individual, as opposed to a media, defendant. The Court stated that it "has never decided the question" whether the *New York Times* standard applies to an individual defendant. The question had not been raised in the case.

JURY INSTRUCTIONS, DIRECTED VERDICTS, SUMMARY JUDGMENTS, AND APPELLATE REVIEW

In granting summary judgment in the *Hutchinson* case, supra, the trial court had commented that, in cases involving public figures or public officials, summary judgment on the issue whether plaintiff had proved actual malice was the rule rather than the exception. On the other hand, the cases since Time, Inc. v. Firestone, supra, show that the Court is not disposed to review a jury's findings of defendant's fault and plaintiff's actual damage in cases not involving public figures. Thus, the only change mandated by *Gertz* in defamation cases not involving public officials or public figures may be a subtle shift in the jury instructions from those which had been given under traditional state defamation law.

In a footnote in his *Hutchinson* opinion, Chief Justice Burger, although he did not decide the question, expressed "some doubt about this so called 'rule' " of summary judgment. The *Hutchinson* footnote rested on the reasoning that the decision whether a statement was knowingly false, or made with reckless disregard of its falsity, depended on findings of fact concerning a state of mind. Bose Corp. v. Consumer's Union, 104 S.Ct. 1949 (1984), however, emphasized that, on appeal, findings that a statement was knowingly false or made with reckless disregard of its falsity must be independently examined by an appellate court to determine whether the record establishes actual malice with convincing clarity. Justice Stevens' opinion for the Court said that "the Court has regularly conducted an independent review of the record to be sure that the speech in question actually falls within the unprotected category within acceptably narrow limits in an effort to ensure that protected expression will not be inhibited. Providing triers of fact with a general description of the type of communication whose content is unworthy of protection has not, in and of itself, served sufficiently to narrow the category, nor served to eliminate the danger that decisions by triers of fact may inhibit the expression of protected ideas.''

COX BROADCASTING CORP. v. COHN

420 U.S. 469, 95 S.Ct. 1029, 43 L.Ed.2d 328 (1975).

Mr. Justice White delivered the opinion of the Court.

The issue before us in this case is whether, consistently with the First and Fourteenth Amendments a State may extend a cause of action for damages for invasion of privacy caused by the publication of the name of a deceased rape victim which was publicly revealed in connection with the prosecution of the crime.

I.

In August 1971, appellee's 17-year-old daughter was the victim of a rape and did not survive the incident. Six youths were soon indicted for murder and rape. Although there was substantial press coverage of the crime and of subsequent developments, the identity of the victim was not disclosed pending trial, perhaps because of Ga.Code Ann. § 26–9901 which makes it a misdemeanor to publish or broadcast the name or identity of a rape victim. In April 1972, some eight months later, the six defendants appeared in court. Five pled guilty to rape or attempted rape, the charge of murder having been dropped. The guilty pleas were accepted by the court, and the trial of the defendant pleading not guilty was set for a later date.

In the course of the proceedings that day, appellant Wassell, a reporter covering the incident for his employer, learned the name of the victim from an examination of the indictments which were made available for his inspection in the courtroom. That the name of the victim appears in the indictments and that the indictments were public records available for inspection are not disputed. Later that day, Wassell broadcast over the facilities of station WSB–TV, a television station owned by appellant Cox Broadcasting Corporation, a news report concerning the court proceedings. The report named the victim of the crime and was repeated the following day.

In May 1972, appellee brought an action for money damages against appellants, relying on § 26–9901 and claiming that his right to privacy had been invaded by the television broadcasts giving the name of his deceased daughter. Appellants admitted the broadcasts but claimed that they were privileged under both state law and the First and Fourteenth Amendments. The trial court, rejecting appellants' constitutional claims and holding that the Georgia statute gave a civil remedy to those injured by its violation, granted summary judgment to appellee as to liability, with the determination of damages to await trial by jury.

On appeal, the Georgia Supreme Court, [affirmed] . . . ..

We reverse . . .

. . . .

III.

Georgia stoutly defends both § 26–9901 and the State's common law privacy action challenged here. Her claims are not without force, for powerful arguments can be made, and have been made, that however it may be ultimately defined, there *is* a zone of privacy surrounding every individual, a zone within which the State may protect him from intrusion by the press, with all its attendant publicity. Indeed, the central thesis of the root article by Warren and Brandeis, The Right of Privacy, 4 Harv.L.Rev. 193, 196 (1890), was that the press was overstepping its prerogatives by publishing essentially private information and that there should be a remedy for the alleged abuses.

More compellingly, the century has experienced a strong tide running in favor of the so-called right of privacy. In 1967, we noted that "[i]t has been said that a 'right of privacy' has been recognized at common law in 30 States plus the District of Columbia and by statute in four States." Time, Inc. v. Hill, 385 U.S. 374, 383 n. 7 (1967). . . . Nor is it irrelevant here that the right of privacy is no recent arrival in the jurisprudence of Georgia, which has embraced the right in some form since 1905 when the Georgia Supreme Court decided the leading case of Pavesich v. New England Life Ins. Co., 122 Ga. 190, 50 S.E. 68 (1905).

These are impressive credentials for a right of privacy, but we should recognize that we do not have at issue here an action for the invasion of privacy involving the appropriation of one's name or photograph, a physical or other tangible intrusion into a private area, or a publication of otherwise private information that is also false although perhaps not defamatory. The version of the privacy tort now before us—termed in Georgia "the tort of public disclosure," 231 Ga., at 62, 200 S.E.2d, at 130—is that in which the plaintiff claims the right to be free from unwanted publicity about his private affairs, which, although wholly true, would be offensive to a person of ordinary sensibilities. Because the gravamen of the claimed injury is the publication of information, whether true or not, the dissemination of which is embarrassing or otherwise painful to an individual, it is here that claims of privacy most directly confront the constitutional freedoms of speech and press. The face-off is apparent, and the appellants urge upon us the broad holding that the press may not be made criminally or civilly liable for publishing information that is neither false nor misleading but absolutely accurate, however damaging it may be to reputation or individual sensibilities.

It is true that in defamation actions, where the protected interest is personal reputation, the prevailing view is that truth is a defense; and the message of New York Times v. Sullivan, 376 U.S. 254 (1964); Garrison v. Louisiana, 379 U.S. 64 (1964); Curtis Publishing Co. v. Butts, 388 U.S. 130 (1967), and like cases is that the defense of truth is constitutionally required where the subject of the publication is a public official or public figure. What is more, the defamed public official or public figure must prove not only that the publication is false but that it was knowingly so or was circulated with reckless disregard for its truth or falsity. Similarly, where the interest at issue is privacy rather than reputation and the right claimed is to be free from the publication of false or misleading information about one's affairs, the target of the publication must prove knowing or reckless falsehood where the materials published, although assertedly private, are "matters of public interest." Time, Inc. v. Hill, supra, 385 U.S., at 387–388.[19]

The Court has nevertheless carefully left open the question whether the First and Fourteenth Amendments require that truth be recognized as a defense in a

---

[19] In another "false light" invasion of privacy case before us this Term, Cantrell v. Forest City Publishing Co., 419 U.S. 245, 250–251 (1974), we observed that we had, in that case, "no occasion to consider whether a State may constitutionally apply a more relaxed standard of liability for a publisher or broadcaster of false statements injurious to a private individual under a false-light theory of invasion of privacy, or whether the constitutional standard announced in Time, Inc. v. Hill applies to all false-light cases. Cf. Gertz v. Robert Welch, Inc., 418 U.S. 323."

defamation action brought by a private person as distinguished from a public official or public figure. . . .

Those precedents, as well as other considerations, counsel similar caution here. In this sphere of collision between claims of privacy and those of the free press, the interests on both sides are plainly rooted in the traditions and significant concerns of our society. Rather than address the broader question whether truthful publications may ever be subjected to civil or criminal liability consistently with the First and Fourteenth Amendments, or to put it another way, whether the State may ever define and protect an area of privacy free from unwanted publicity in the press, it is appropriate to focus on the narrower interface between press and privacy that this case presents, namely, whether the State may impose sanctions on the accurate publication of the name of a rape victim obtained from public records—more specifically, from judicial records which are maintained in connection with a public prosecution and which themselves are open to public inspection. We are convinced that the State may not do so.

In the first place, in a society in which each individual has but limited time and resources with which to observe at first hand the operations of his government, he relies necessarily upon the press to bring to him in convenient form the facts of those operations. Great responsibility is accordingly placed upon the news media to report fully and accurately the proceedings of government, and official records and documents open to the public are the basic data of governmental operations. Without the information provided by the press most of us and many of our representatives would be unable to vote intelligently or to register opinions on the administration of government generally. With respect to judicial proceedings in particular, the function of the press serves to guarantee the fairness of trials and to bring to bear the beneficial effects of public scrutiny upon the administration of justice. See Sheppard v. Maxwell, 384 U.S. 333, 350 (1966).

. . .

The developing law surrounding the tort of invasion of privacy recognizes a privilege in the press to report the events of judicial proceedings. The Warren and Brandeis article, supra, noted that the proposed new right would be limited in the same manner as actions for libel and slander where such a publication was a privileged communication: "the right to privacy is not invaded by any publication made in a court of justice . . . and (at least in many jurisdictions) reports of any such proceedings would in some measure be accorded a like privilege."

. . .

Thus even the prevailing law of invasion of privacy generally recognizes that the interests in privacy fade when the information involved already appears on the public record. The conclusion is compelling when viewed in terms of the First and Fourteenth Amendments and in light of the public interest in a vigorous press. . . .

By placing the information in the public domain on official court records, the State must be presumed to have concluded that the public interest was thereby being served. Public records by their very nature are of interest to those concerned with the administration of government, and a public benefit is performed by the reporting of the true contents of the records by the media. The freedom of the press to publish that information appears to us to be of critical importance to our type of government in which the citizenry is the final judge of the proper conduct of public business. In preserving that form of government the First and Fourteenth Amendments command nothing less than that the States may not impose sanctions for the publication of truthful information contained in official court records open to public inspection.

We are reluctant to embark on a course that would make public records generally available to the media but forbid their publication if offensive to the sensibilities of the supposed reasonable man. Such a rule would make it very difficult for the press to inform their readers about the public business and yet stay within the law. The rule would invite timidity and self-censorship and very likely lead to the suppression of many items that would otherwise be published and that should be made available to the public. At the very least, the First and Fourteenth Amendments will not allow exposing the press to liability for truthfully publishing information released to the public in official court records. If there are privacy interests to be protected in judicial proceedings, the States must respond by means which avoid public documentation or other exposure of private information. Their political institutions must weigh the interests in privacy with the interests of the public to know and of the press to publish.[26] Once true information is disclosed in public court documents open to public inspection, the press cannot be sanctioned for publishing it. In this instance as in others reliance must rest upon the judgment of those who decide what to publish or broadcast. See Miami Herald Publishing Co. v. Tornillo, supra, 418 U.S., at 258.

Appellant Wassell based his televised report upon notes taken during the court proceedings and obtained the name of the victim from the indictments handed to him at his request during a recess in the hearing. Appellee has not contended that the name was obtained in an improper fashion or that it was not on an official court document open to public inspection. Under these circumstances, the protection of freedom of the press provided by the First and Fourteenth Amendments bars the State of Georgia from making appellants' broadcast the basis of civil liability.[27]

Reversed.

[The Chief Justice and Justice Douglas concurred in the judgment. Justice Rehnquist dissented on jurisdictional grounds.]

ZACCHINI v. SCRIPPS–HOWARD BROADCASTING CO., 433 U.S. 562 (1977). Hugo Zacchini was an entertainer, whose 15 second act consisted of being shot from a cannon into a net 200 feet away. A reporter for a local television station, attending the county fair where Zacchini was performing, was asked by Zacchini not to film his act. The reporter, however, returned the next day and videotaped the entire act. The tape, which ran 15 seconds, was shown on the 11:00 o'clock news that night. In the state trial court, Zacchini was awarded summary judgment in an action for appropriation of his "professional property." The Ohio Supreme Court reversed, relying on Time Inc. v. Hill, 385 U.S. 374 (1967), for the proposition that the television station had a privilege to report the act as a newsworthy event. The Supreme Court reversed. The Court's opinion, by Justice White, concluded that the *Hill* case was inapposite:

"Time, Inc. v. Hill, which was hotly contested and decided by a divided court, involved an entirely different tort than the 'right of publicity' recognized

------

[26] We mean to imply nothing about any constitutional questions which might arise from a state policy not allowing access by the public and press to various kinds of official records, such as records of juvenile-court proceedings.

[27] Appellants have contended that whether they derived the information in question from public records or instead through their own investigation, the First and Fourteenth Amendments bar any sanctions from being imposed by the State because of the publication. Because appellant has prevailed on more limited grounds, we need not address this broader challenge to the validity of § 26–9901 and of Georgia's right of action for public disclosure.

by the Ohio Supreme Court. As the opinion reveals in Time, Inc. v. Hill, the Court was steeped in the literature of privacy law and was aware of the developing distinctions and nuances in this branch of the law. . . . The Court was aware that it was adjudicating a 'false light' privacy case involving a matter of public interest, not a case involving 'intrusion,' 'appropriation' of a name or likeness for the purposes of trade, or 'private details' about a non-newsworthy person or event. It is also abundantly clear that Time, Inc. v. Hill did not involve a performer, a person with a name having commercial value, or any claim to a 'right of publicity.' This discrete kind of 'appropriation' case was plainly identified in the literature cited by the Court and had been adjudicated in the reported cases. . . .

"Wherever the line in particular situations is to be drawn between media reports that are protected and those that are not, we are quite sure that the First and Fourteenth Amendments do not immunize the media when they broadcast a performer's entire act without his consent. The Constitution no more prevents a State from requiring respondent to compensate petitioner for broadcasting his act on television than it would privilege respondent to film and broadcast a copyrighted dramatic work without liability to the copyright owner."

Justice Powell's dissent, joined by Justices Brennan and Marshall, emphasized that the case involved a 15 second clip that was part of a routine daily news program.

"In my view the First Amendment commands a different analytical starting point from the one selected by the Court. Rather than begin with a quantitative analysis of the performer's behavior—is this or is this not his entire act?—we should direct initial attention to the actions of the news media: what use did the station make of the film footage? When a film is used, as here, for a routine portion of a regular news program, I would hold that the First Amendment protects the station from a 'right of publicity' or 'appropriation' suit, absent a strong showing by the plaintiff that the news broadcast was a subterfuge or cover for private or commercial exploitation."

Justice Stevens, dissenting, would have remanded the case to the Ohio Supreme Court for clarification as to whether its decision denying liability rested on the constitutional ground.

B. CONTROL OF OBSCENITY

1. THE RATIONALE FOR PROHIBITING OBSCENITY

PARIS ADULT THEATRE I v. SLATON

413 U.S. 49, 93 S.Ct. 2628, 37 L.Ed.2d 446 (1973).

Mr. Chief Justice Burger delivered the opinion of the Court.

Petitioners are two Atlanta, Georgia, movie theatres and their owners and managers, operating in the style of "adult" theatres. On December 28, 1970, respondents, the local state district attorney and the solicitor for the local state trial court, filed civil complaints in that court alleging that petitioners were exhibiting to the public for paid admission two allegedly obscene films. . . . The two films in question, "Magic Mirror" and "It All Comes Out in the End," depict sexual conduct characterized by the Georgia Supreme Court as "hard core pornography" leaving "little to the imagination."

Respondents' complaints, made on behalf of the State of Georgia, demanded that the two films be declared obscene and that petitioners be enjoined from exhibiting the films.   . . .

On January 13, 1971, 15 days after the proceedings began, the films were produced by petitioners at a jury-waived trial.   Certain photographs, also produced at trial, were stipulated to portray the single entrance to both Paris Adult Theatre I and Paris Adult Theatre II as it appeared at the time of the complaints.   These photographs show a conventional, inoffensive theatre entrance, without any pictures, but with signs indicating that the theatres exhibit "Atlanta's Finest Mature Feature Films."   On the door itself is a sign saying: "Adult Theatre—You must be 21 and able to prove it.   If viewing the nude body offends you, Please Do Not Enter."

The two films were exhibited to the trial court.   The only other state evidence was testimony by criminal investigators that they had paid admission to see the films and that nothing on the outside of the theatre indicated the full nature of what was shown.   In particular, nothing indicated that the films depicted—as they did—scenes of simulated fellatio, cunnilingus, and group sex intercourse.   There was no evidence presented that minors had ever entered the theatres.   Nor was there evidence presented that petitioners had a systematic policy of barring minors, apart from posting signs at the entrance.   . . . [T]he trial judge dismissed respondents' complaints.   . . .

On appeal, the Georgia Supreme Court unanimously reversed.   228 Ga. 343, 185 S.E.2d 768.   It assumed that the adult theatres in question barred minors and gave a full warning to the general public of the nature of the films shown, but held that the films were without protection under the First Amendment.   . . .

I.

It should be clear from the outset that we do not undertake to tell the States what they must do, but rather to define the area in which they may chart their own course in dealing with obscene material.   . . .

. . .

II.

We categorically disapprove the theory, apparently adopted by the trial judge, that obscene, pornographic films acquire constitutional immunity from state regulation simply because they are exhibited for consenting adults only.

. . .

In particular, we hold that there are legitimate state interests at stake in stemming the tide of commercialized obscenity, even assuming it is feasible to enforce effective safeguards against exposure to juveniles and to the passerby. Rights and interests "other than those of the advocates are involved."   Breard v. Alexandria, 341 U.S. 622, 642 (1951).   These include the interest of the public in the quality of life and the total community environment, the tone of commerce in the great city centers, and, possibly, the public safety itself.   The Hill-Link Minority Report of the Commission on Obscenity and Pornography indicates that there is at least an arguable correlation between obscene material and crime.[8]   Quite apart from sex crimes, however, there remains one problem of large proportions aptly described by Professor Bickel:

"It concerns the tone of the society, the mode, or to use terms that have perhaps greater currency, the style and quality of life, now and in the future. A man may be entitled to read an obscene book in his room, or expose

[8] The Report of the Commission on Obscenity and Pornography 390–412 [Hill-Link Minority Report] (1970).   . . .

himself indecently there. . . . We should protect his privacy. But if he demands a right to obtain the books and pictures he wants in the market, and to foregather in public places—discreet, if you will, but accessible to all— with others who share his tastes, *then to grant him his right is to affect the world about the rest of us, and to impinge on other privacies.* Even supposing that each of us can, if he wishes, effectively avert the eye and stop the ear (which, in truth, we cannot), what is commonly read and seen and heard and done intrudes upon us all, want it or not." 22 The Public Interest 25, 25–26 (Winter 1971). (Emphasis added.)

As Chief Justice Warren stated there is a "right of the Nation and of the States to maintain a decent society. . . ." Jacobellis v. Ohio, 378 U.S. 184, 199 (1964) (Warren, C.J., dissenting). . . .

But, it is argued, there is no scientific data which conclusively demonstrates that exposure to obscene materials adversely affects men and women or their society. It is urged on behalf of the petitioner that, absent such a demonstration, any kind of state regulation is "impermissible." We reject this argument. It is not for us to resolve empirical uncertainties underlying state legislation, save in the exceptional case where that legislation plainly impinges upon rights protected by the Constitution itself. . . . Although there is no conclusive proof of a connection between antisocial behavior and obscene material, the legislature of Georgia could quite reasonably determine that such a connection does or might exist. . . .

From the beginning of civilized societies, legislators and judges have acted on various unprovable assumptions. Such assumptions underlie much lawful state regulation of commercial and business affairs. . . . On the basis of these assumptions both Congress and state legislatures have, for example, drastically restricted associational rights by adopting antitrust laws, and have strictly regulated public expression by issuers of and dealers in securities, profit sharing "coupons," and "trading stamps," commanding what they must and must not publish and announce. . . . Understandably, those who entertain an absolutist view of the First Amendment find it uncomfortable to explain why rights of association, speech, and press should be severely restrained in the marketplace of goods and money, but not in the marketplace of pornography.

. . .

If we accept the unprovable assumption that a complete education requires the reading of certain books . . . and the well nigh universal belief that good books, plays, and art lift the spirit, improve the mind, enrich the human personality and develop character, can we then say that a state legislature may not act on the corollary assumption that commerce in obscene books, or public exhibitions focused on obscene conduct, have a tendency to exert a corrupting and debasing impact leading to antisocial behavior? . . . The sum of experience, including that of the past two decades, affords an ample basis for legislatures to conclude that a sensitive, key relationship of human existence, central to family life, community welfare, and the development of human personality, can be debased and distorted by crass commercial exploitation of sex. Nothing in the Constitution prohibits a State from reaching such a conclusion and acting on it legislatively simply because there is no conclusive evidence or empirical data.

It is argued that individual "free will" must govern, even in activities beyond the protection of the First Amendment and other constitutional guarantees of privacy, and that government cannot legitimately impede an individual's desire to see or acquire obscene plays, movies, and books. We do indeed base our society on certain assumptions that people have the capacity for free choice. Most exercises of individual free choice—those in politics, religion and expression of ideas—are explicitly protected by the Constitution. Totally unlimited play for free will, however, is not allowed in ours or any other society. . . .

It is asserted, however, that standards for evaluating state commercial regulations are inapposite in the present context, as state regulation of access by consenting adults to obscene material violates the constitutionally protected right to privacy enjoyed by petitioners' customers. Even assuming that petitioners have vicarious standing to assert potential customers' rights, it is unavailing to compare a theatre, open to the public for a fee, with the private home of Stanley v. Georgia, 394 U.S. 557, 568 (1969), and the marital bedroom of Griswold v. Connecticut, 381 U.S. 479, 485–486 (1965). This Court, has, on numerous occasions, refused to hold that commercial ventures such as a motion-picture house are "private" for the purpose of civil rights litigation and civil rights statutes. See Sullivan v. Little Hunting Park, Inc., 396 U.S. 229, 236 (1969). . . .

. . .

It is also argued that the State has no legitimate interest in "control [of] the moral content of a person's thoughts," Stanley v. Georgia, supra, 394 U.S., at 565 (1969), and we need not quarrel with this. But we reject the claim that the State of Georgia is here attempting to control the minds or thoughts of those who patronize theatres. . . . Where communication of ideas, protected by the First Amendment, is not involved, nor the particular privacy of the home protected by *Stanley,* nor any of the other "areas or zones" of constitutionally protected privacy, the mere fact that, as a consequence, some human "utterances" or "thoughts" may be incidentally affected does not bar the State from acting to protect legitimate state interests. . . .

Finally, petitioners argue that conduct which directly involves "consenting adults" only has, for that sole reason, a special claim to constitutional protection. Our Constitution establishes a broad range of conditions on the exercise of power by the States, but for us to say that our Constitution incorporates the proposition that conduct involving consenting adults only is always beyond state regulation, is a step we are unable to take. Commercial exploitation of depictions, descriptions, or exhibitions of obscene conduct on commercial premises open to the adult public falls within a State's broad power to regulate commerce and protect the public environment. The issue in this context goes beyond whether someone, or even the majority, considers the conduct depicted as "wrong" or "sinful." The States have the power to make a morally neutral judgment that public exhibition of obscene material, or commerce in such material, has a tendency to injure the community as a whole, to endanger the public safety, or to jeopardize, in Mr. Chief Justice Warren's words, the States' "right . . . to maintain a decent society." Jacobellis v. Ohio, 378 U.S., at 199 (1964) (dissenting opinion).

To summarize, we have today reaffirmed the basic holding of United States v. Roth, supra, that obscene material has no protection under the First Amendment. . . .

Mr. Justice Brennan, with whom Mr. Justice Stewart and Mr. Justice Marshall join, dissenting.

. . . I am convinced that the approach initiated 16 years ago in Roth v. United States, 354 U.S. 476 (1957), and culminating in the Court's decision today, cannot bring stability to this area of the law without jeopardizing fundamental First Amendment values, and I have concluded that the time has come to make a significant departure from that approach. . . .

Our experience with the *Roth* approach has certainly taught us that the outright suppression of obscenity cannot be reconciled with the fundamental principles of the First and Fourteenth Amendments. For we have failed to formulate a standard that sharply distinguishes protected from unprotected speech. . . .

. . . .

The vagueness of the standards in the obscenity area produces a number of separate problems, and any improvement must rest on an understanding that the problems are to some extent distinct. . . .

The problems of fair notice and chilling protected speech are very grave standing alone. But it does not detract from their importance to recognize that a vague statute in this area creates a third, although admittedly more subtle, set of problems. These problems concern the institutional stress that inevitably results where the line separating protected from unprotected speech is excessively vague. In *Roth* we conceded that "there may be marginal cases in which it is difficult to determine the side of the line on which a particular fact situation falls . . . .." 354 U.S., at 491–492. Our subsequent experience demonstrates that almost every case is "marginal." And since the "margin" marks the point of separation between protected and unprotected speech, we are left with a system in which almost every obscenity case presents a constitutional question of exceptional difficulty. . . .

The severe problems arising from the lack of fair notice, from the chill on protected expression, and from the stress imposed on the state and federal judicial machinery persuade me that a significant change in direction is urgently required. . . .

. . . .

V.

Our experience since *Roth* requires us not only to abandon the effort to pick out obscene materials on a case-by-case basis, but also to reconsider a fundamental postulate of *Roth:* that there exists a definable class of sexually oriented expression that may be totally suppressed by the Federal and State Governments. Assuming that such a class of expression does in fact exist, I am forced to conclude that the concept of "obscenity" cannot be defined with sufficient specificity and clarity to provide fair notice to persons who create and distribute sexually oriented materials, to prevent substantial erosion of protected speech as a by-product of the attempt to suppress unprotected speech, and to avoid very costly institutional harms. Given these inevitable side-effects of state efforts to suppress what is assumed to be *unprotected* speech, we must scrutinize with care the state interest that is asserted to justify the suppression. For in the absence of some very substantial interest in suppressing such speech, we can hardly condone the ill-effects that seem to flow inevitably from the effort. . . .

The opinions in *Redrup* and *Stanley* reflected our emerging view that the state interests in protecting children and in protecting unconsenting adults may stand on a different footing from the other asserted state interests. It may well be, as one commentator has argued, that "exposure to [erotic material] is for some persons an intense emotional experience. A communication of this nature, imposed upon a person contrary to his wishes, has all the characteristics of a physical assault. . . . [And it] constitutes an invasion of his privacy . . . .." [24] But cf. Cohen v. California, 403 U.S. 15, 21–22 (1971). Similarly, if children are "not possessed of that full capacity for individual choice which is the presupposition of the First Amendment guarantees," Ginsberg v. New York, 390 U.S., at 649–650 (Stewart, J., concurring), then the State may have a substantial interest in precluding the flow of obscene materials even to consenting juveniles. . . .

. . . .

[24] T. Emerson, The System of Freedom of Expression 496 (1970).

In short, while I cannot say that the interests of the State—apart from the question of juveniles and unconsenting adults—are trivial or nonexistent, I am compelled to conclude that these interests cannot justify the substantial damage to constitutional rights and to this Nation's judicial machinery that inevitably results from state efforts to bar the distribution even of unprotected material to consenting adults. . . . Nothing in this approach precludes those governments from taking action to serve what may be strong and legitimate interests through regulation of the manner of distribution of sexually oriented material. . . . Since the Supreme Court of Georgia erroneously concluded that the State has power to suppress sexually oriented material even in the absence of distribution to juveniles or exposure to unconsenting adults, I would reverse that judgment and remand the case to that court for further proceedings not inconsistent with this opinion.

Mr. Justice Douglas, dissenting.

My Brother Brennan is to be commended for seeking a new path through the thicket which the Court entered when it undertook to sustain the constitutionality of obscenity laws and to place limits on their application. I have expressed on numerous occasions my disagreement with the basic decision that held that "obscenity" was not protected by the First Amendment. . . .

NEW YORK v. FERBER, 458 U.S. 747 (1982). A New York statute prohibits the distribution of materials depicting sexual performances by children under the age of 16. Ferber's conviction, for selling films of young boys masturbating, was reversed by the New York Court of Appeals, which reasoned that the statute violated the first amendment because it applied to materials that were not obscene. The Court reversed, holding that "child pornography" was a category of material outside the protection of the first amendment. Advertising and selling of child pornography could be prohibited to advance the state's interest in preventing sexual exploitation of children. The harm to the children portrayed is exacerbated by distribution of the materials, and closing the channels of commercial distribution is necessary to control initial production of the material. Permitting live performances and photographic reproductions of children engaged in sexual activity had value which is "exceedingly modest, if not *de minimus.*" The Court refused to apply overbreadth analysis and did not consider whether the statute could be applied outside "the hard core of child pornography." Concurring, Justice Brennan, joined by Justice Marshall, commented that, in his view, application of the statute to depictions with "serious literary, artistic, scientific or medical value" would violate the first amendment.

2. THE PROBLEM OF DEFINITION

MILLER v. CALIFORNIA

413 U.S. 15, 93 S.Ct. 2607, 37 L.Ed.2d 419 (1973).

Mr. Chief Justice Burger delivered the opinion of the Court.

This is one of a group of "obscenity-pornography" cases being reviewed by the Court in a re-examination of standards enunciated in earlier cases involving what Mr. Justice Harlan called "the intractable obscenity problem." Interstate Circuit, Inc. v. Dallas, 390 U.S. 676, 704 (1968) (concurring and dissenting).

Appellant conducted a mass mailing campaign to advertise the sale of illustrated books, euphemistically called "adult" material. After a jury trial, he was convicted of violating California Penal Code § 311.2(a), a misdemeanor, by knowingly distributing obscene matter,[1] and the Appellate Department, Superior Court of California, County of Orange, summarily affirmed the judgment without opinion. Appellant's conviction was specifically based on his conduct in causing five unsolicited advertising brochures to be sent through the mail in an envelope addressed to a restaurant in Newport Beach, California. The envelope was opened by the manager of the restaurant and his mother. They had not requested the brochures; they complained to the police.

The brochures advertise four books entitled "Intercourse," "Man-Woman," "Sex Orgies Illustrated," and "An Illustrated History of Pornography," and a film entitled "Marital Intercourse." While the brochures contain some descriptive printed material, primarily they consist of pictures and drawings very explicitly depicting men and women in groups of two or more engaging in a variety of sexual activities, with genitals often prominently displayed.

I.

This case involves the application of a State's criminal obscenity statute to a situation in which sexually explicit materials have been thrust by aggressive sales action upon unwilling recipients who had in no way indicated any desire to receive such materials. This Court has recognized that the States have a legitimate interest in prohibiting dissemination or exhibition of obscene material when the mode of dissemination carries with it a significant danger of offending the sensibilities of unwilling recipients or of exposure to juveniles. Stanley v. Georgia, 394 U.S. 557, 567 (1969). Ginsberg v. New York, 390 U.S. 629, 637–643 (1968). . . . It is in this context that we are called on to define the standards which must be used to identify obscene material that a State may regulate without infringing the First Amendment as applicable to the States through the Fourteenth Amendment.

. . . In Roth v. United States, 354 U.S. 476 (1957), the Court sustained a conviction under a federal statute punishing the mailing of "obscene, lewd, lascivious or filthy . . ." materials. The key to that holding was the Court's rejection of the claim that obscene materials were protected by the First Amendment. . . .

Nine years later in Memoirs v. Massachusetts, 383 U.S. 413 (1966), the Court veered sharply away from the *Roth* concept and, with only three Justices in the plurality opinion, articulated a new test of obscenity. The plurality held that under the *Roth* definition:

". . . as elaborated in subsequent cases, three elements must coalesce: it must be established that (a) the dominant theme of the material taken as a whole appeals to a prurient interest in sex; (b) the material is patently offensive because it affronts contemporary community standards relating to the description or representation of sexual matters; and (c) the material is utterly without redeeming social value." Id., 383 U.S., at 418.

---

[1] At the time of the commission of the alleged offense, which was prior to June 25, 1969, § 311 of the California Penal Code read in relevant part: . . .

"§ 311. Definitions

  "As used in this chapter:

    "(a) 'Obscene' means that to the average person, applying contemporary standards, the predominant appeal of the matter, taken as a whole, is to prurient interest, i.e., a shameful or morbid interest in nudity, sex, or excretion, which goes substantially beyond customary limits of candor in description or representation of such matters and is matter which is utterly without redeeming social importance. . . ."

The sharpness of the break with *Roth,* represented by the third element of the *Memoirs* test and emphasized by Justice White's dissent, id., 383 U.S., at 460–462, was further underscored when the *Memoirs* plurality went on to state:

> "The Supreme Judicial Court erred in holding that a book need not be 'unqualifiedly worthless before it can be deemed obscene.' A book cannot be proscribed unless it is found to be *utterly* without redeeming social value." (Emphasis in original.) 383 U.S., at 419.

While *Roth* presumed "obscenity" to be "utterly without redeeming social value," *Memoirs* required that to prove obscenity it must be affirmatively established that the material is *"utterly* without redeeming social value." Thus, even as they repeated the words of *Roth,* the *Memoirs* plurality produced a drastically altered test that called on the prosecution to prove a negative, i.e., that the material was *"utterly* without redeeming social value"—a burden virtually impossible to discharge under our criminal standards of proof. Such considerations caused Justice Harlan to wonder if the *"utterly* without redeeming social value" test had any meaning at all. See Memoirs v. Massachusetts, supra, 383 U.S., at 459 (1966) (Harlan, J., dissenting). . . .

Apart from the initial formulation in the *Roth* case, no majority of the Court has at any given time been able to agree on a standard to determine what constitutes obscene, pornographic material subject to regulation under the States' police power. See, e.g., Redrup v. New York, 386 U.S. 767, 770–771 (1967). We have seen "a variety of views among the members of the Court unmatched in any other course of constitutional adjudication [footnote omitted]." Interstate Circuit, Inc. v. Dallas, supra, 390 U.S., at 704–705 (1968) (Harlan, J., concurring and dissenting).[3] This is not remarkable, for in the area of freedom of speech and press the courts must always remain sensitive to any infringement on genuinely serious literary, artistic, political, or scientific expression. This is an area in which there are few eternal verities.

The case we now review was tried on the theory that the California Penal Code § 311 approximately incorporates the three-stage *Memoirs* test, supra. But now the *Memoirs* test has been abandoned as unworkable by its author[4] and no member of the Court today supports the *Memoirs* formulation.

II.

. . . State statutes designed to regulate obscene materials must be carefully limited. . . . As a result, we now confine the permissible scope of such regulation to works which depict or describe sexual conduct. That conduct must be specifically defined by the applicable state law, as written or authoritatively construed. A state offense must also be limited to works which, taken as a whole, appeal to the prurient interest in sex, which portray sexual conduct in a patently offensive way, and which, taken as a whole, do not have serious literary, artistic, political, or scientific value.

The basic guidelines for the trier of fact must be: (a) whether "the average person, applying contemporary community standards" would find that the work, taken as a whole, appeals to the prurient interest, (b) whether the work depicts

---

[3] In the absence of a majority view, this Court was compelled to embark on the practice of summarily reversing convictions for the dissemination of materials that at least five members of the Court, applying their separate tests, found to be protected by the First Amendment. Redrup v. New York, 386 U.S. 767 (1967). Thirty-one cases have been decided in this manner. Beyond the necessity of circumstances, however, no justification has ever been offered in support of the *Redrup* "policy." See Walker v. Ohio, 398 U.S. 434, 434–435 (dissenting opinions) (1970). The *Redrup* procedure has cast us in the role of an unreviewable board of censorship for the 50 States subjectively judging each piece of material brought before us.

[4] See the dissenting opinion of Mr. Justice Brennan in Paris Adult Theatre I v. Slaton, 413 U.S. 49, 73 (1973).

or describes, in a patently offensive way, sexual conduct specifically defined by the applicable state law, and (c) whether the work, taken as a whole, lacks serious literary, artistic, political, or scientific value. We do not adopt as a constitutional standard the *"utterly* without redeeming social value" test of Memoirs v. Massachusetts, 383 U.S., at 419 (1966); that concept has never commanded the adherence of more than three Justices at one time. If a state law that regulates obscene material is thus limited, as written or construed, the First Amendment values applicable to the States through the Fourteenth Amendment are adequately protected by the ultimate power of appellate courts to conduct an independent review of constitutional claims when necessary . . . .

We emphasize that it is not our function to propose regulatory schemes for the States. That must await their concrete legislative efforts. It is possible, however, to give a few plain examples of what a state statute could define for regulation under the second part (b) of the standard announced in this opinion, supra:

(a) Patently offensive representations or descriptions of ultimate sexual acts, normal or perverted, actual or simulated.

(b) Patently offensive representation or descriptions of masturbation, excretory functions, and lewd exhibition of the genitals.

Sex and nudity may not be exploited without limit by films or pictures exhibited or sold in places of public accommodation any more than live sex and nudity can be exhibited or sold without limit in such public places.[8] At a minimum, prurient, patently offensive depiction or description of sexual conduct must have serious literary, artistic, political, or scientific value to merit First Amendment protection. . . . For example, medical books for the education of physicians and related personnel necessarily use graphic illustrations and descriptions of human anatomy. In resolving the inevitably sensitive questions of fact and law, we must continue to rely on the jury system, accompanied by the safeguards that judges, rules of evidence, presumption of innocence and other protective features provide, as we do with rape, murder and a host of other offenses against society and its individual members.[9]

Mr. Justice Brennan . . . now maintains that no formulation of this Court, the Congress, or the States can adequately distinguish obscene material unprotected by the First Amendment from protected expression, Paris Adult Theatre I v. Slaton, 413 U.S. 49, 73 (1973) (Brennan, J., dissenting). Paradoxically, Mr. Justice Brennan indicates that suppression of unprotected obscene material is permissible to avoid exposure to unconsenting adults, as in this case, and to juveniles, although he gives no indication of how the division between protected and nonprotected materials may be drawn with greater precision for these purposes than for regulation of commercial exposure to consenting adults only. Nor does he indicate where in the Constitution he finds the authority to distinguish between a willing "adult" one month past the state law age of majority and a willing "juvenile" one month younger.

Under the holdings announced today, no one will be subject to prosecution for the sale or exposure of obscene materials unless these materials depict or describe patently offensive "hard core" sexual conduct specifically defined by the regulating state law, as written or construed. We are satisfied that these specific prerequisites will provide fair notice to a dealer in such materials that his public and commercial activities may bring prosecution. . . .

[8] Although we are not presented here with the problem of regulating lewd public conduct itself, the States have greater power to regulate nonverbal, physical conduct than to suppress depictions or descriptions of the same behavior. . . .

[9] The mere fact juries may reach different conclusions as to the same material does not mean that constitutional rights are abridged. . . .

It is certainly true that the absence, since *Roth,* of a single majority view of this Court as to proper standards for testing obscenity has placed a strain on both state and federal courts. But today, for the first time since *Roth* was decided in 1957, a majority of this Court has agreed on concrete guidelines to isolate "hard core" pornography from expression protected by the First Amendment. Now we may abandon the casual practice of Redrup v. New York, supra, and attempt to provide positive guidance to the federal and state courts alike. . . .

III.

Under a national Constitution, fundamental First Amendment limitations on the powers of the States do not vary from community to community, but this does not mean that there are, or should or can be, fixed, uniform national standards of precisely what appeals to the "prurient interest" or is "patently offensive." These are essentially questions of fact, and our nation is simply too big and too diverse for this Court to reasonably expect that such standards could be articulated for all 50 States in a single formulation, even assuming the prerequisite consensus exists. When triers of fact are asked to decide whether "the average person, applying contemporary community standards" would consider certain materials "prurient," it would be unrealistic to require that the answer be based on some abstract formulation. The adversary system, with lay jurors as the usual ultimate fact-finders in criminal prosecutions, has historically permitted triers-of-fact to draw on the standards of their community, guided always by limiting instructions on the law. To require a State to structure obscenity proceedings around evidence of a *national* "community standard" would be an exercise in futility. . . .

It is neither realistic nor constitutionally sound to read the First Amendment as requiring that the people of Maine or Mississippi accept public depiction of conduct found tolerable in Las Vegas, or New York City. . . . People in different States vary in their tastes and attitudes, and this diversity is not to be strangled by the absolutism of imposed uniformity. As the Court made clear in Mishkin v. New York, 383 U.S. 502, 508–509 (1966), the primary concern with requiring a jury to apply the standard of "the average person, applying contemporary community standards" is to be certain that, so far as material is not aimed at a deviant group, it will be judged by its impact on an average person, rather than a particularly susceptible or sensitive person—or indeed a totally insensitive one. We hold the requirement that the jury evaluate the materials with reference to "contemporary standards of the State of California" serves this protective purpose and is constitutionally adequate.

. . .

Mr. Justice Douglas, dissenting.

. . .

. . . I do not think we, the judges, were ever given the constitutional power to make definitions of obscenity. . . .

Mr. Justice Brennan, with whom Mr. Justice Stewart and Mr. Justice Marshall join, dissenting.

In my dissent in Paris Adult Theatre I v. Slaton, decided this date, I noted that I had no occasion to consider the extent of state power to regulate the distribution of sexually oriented material to juveniles or the offensive exposure of such material to unconsenting adults. In the case before us, petitioner was convicted of distributing obscene matter in violation of California Penal Code § 311.2, on the basis of evidence that he had caused to be mailed unsolicited brochures advertising various books and a movie. I need not now decide whether a statute might be drawn to impose, within the requirements of the

First Amendment, criminal penalties for the precise conduct at issue here. For it is clear that under my dissent in *Slaton,* the statute under which the prosecution was brought is unconstitutionally overbroad, and therefore invalid on its face.[a] . . .

JENKINS v. GEORGIA

418 U.S. 153, 94 S.Ct. 2750, 41 L.Ed.2d 642 (1974).

Mr. Justice Rehnquist delivered the opinion of the Court.

Appellant was convicted in Georgia of the crime of distributing obscene material. His conviction, in March 1972, was for showing the film "Carnal Knowledge" in a movie theater in Albany, Georgia. . . .

. . . We conclude here that the film "Carnal Knowledge" is not obscene under the constitutional standards announced in Miller v. California, 413 U.S. 15 (1973), and that the First and Fourteenth Amendments therefore require that the judgment of the Supreme Court of Georgia affirming appellant's conviction be reversed.

. . .

There is little to be found in the record about the film "Carnal Knowledge" other than the film itself. However, appellant has supplied a variety of information and critical commentary, the authenticity of which appellee does not dispute. The film appeared on many "Ten Best" lists for 1971, the year in which it was released. Many but not all of the reviews were favorable. We believe that the following passage from a review which appeared in the *Saturday Review* is a reasonably accurate description of the film:

"[It is basically a story] of two young college men, roommates and lifelong friends forever preoccupied with their sex lives. Both are first met as virgins. Nicholson is the more knowledgeable and attractive of the two; speaking colloquially, he is a burgeoning bastard. Art Garfunkel is his friend, the nice but troubled guy straight out of those early Feiffer cartoons, but *real.* He falls in love with the lovely Susan (Candice Bergen) and unknowingly shares her with his college buddy. As the 'safer' one of the two, he is selected by Susan for marriage.

"The time changes. Both men are in their thirties, pursuing successful careers in New York. Nicholson has been running through an average of a dozen women a year but has never managed to meet the right one, the one with the full bosom, the good legs, the properly rounded bottom. More than that, each and every one is a threat to his malehood and peace of mind, until at last, in a bar, he finds Ann-Margret, an aging bachelor girl with striking cleavage and, quite obviously, something of a past. 'Why don't we shack up?' she suggests. They do and a horrendous relationship ensues, complicated mainly by her paranoidal desire to marry. Meanwhile, what of Garfunkel? The sparks have gone out of his marriage, the sex has lost its savor, and Garfunkel tries once more. And later, even more foolishly, again."

Appellee contends essentially that under *Miller* the obscenity *vel non* of the film "Carnal Knowledge" was a question for the jury, and that the jury having resolved the question against appellant, and there being some evidence to

---

[a] In Kaplan v. California, 413 U.S. 115 (1973), decided the same day and by the same division of the Justices as the *Miller* case, the Court applied the *Miller* holding to books with no illustrations but "made up entirely of repetitive descriptions of physical, sexual conduct, 'clinically' explicit and offensive to the point of being nauseous".

support its findings, the judgment of conviction should be affirmed. We turn to the language of *Miller* to evaluate appellee's contention.

. . .

But all of this does not lead us to agree with the Supreme Court of Georgia's apparent conclusion that the jury's verdict against appellant virtually precluded all further appellate review of appellant's assertion that his exhibition of the film was protected by the First and Fourteenth Amendments. Even though questions of appeal to the "prurient interest" or of patent offensiveness are "essentially questions of fact," it would be a serious misreading of *Miller* to conclude that juries have unbridled discretion in determining what is "patently offensive." Not only did we there say that "the First Amendment values applicable to the States through the Fourteenth Amendment are adequately protected by the ultimate power of appellate courts to conduct an independent review of constitutional claims when necessary," 413 U.S., at 25, but we made it plain that under that holding "no one will be subject to prosecution for the sale or exposure of obscene materials unless these materials depict or describe patently offensive 'hard core' sexual conduct . . . ." Id.

We also took pains in *Miller* to "give a few plain examples of what a state statute could define for regulation under part (b) of the standard announced," that is, the requirement of patent offensiveness. Id. These examples included "representations or descriptions of ultimate sexual acts, normal or perverted, actual or simulated," and "representations or descriptions of masturbation, excretory functions, and lewd exhibition of the genitals." Ibid. While this did not purport to be an exhaustive catalog of what juries might find patently offensive, it was certainly intended to fix substantive constitutional limitations, deriving from the First Amendment, on the type of material subject to such a determination. It would be wholly at odds with this aspect of *Miller* to uphold an obscenity conviction based upon a defendant's depiction of a woman with a bare midriff, even though a properly charged jury unanimously agreed on a verdict of guilty.

Our own view of the film satisfies us that "Carnal Knowledge" could not be found under the *Miller* standards to depict sexual conduct in a patently offensive way. Nothing in the movie falls within either of the two examples given in *Miller* of material which may constitutionally be found to meet the "patently offensive" element of those standards, nor is there anything sufficiently similar to such material to justify similar treatment. While the subject matter of the picture is, in a broader sense, sex, and there are scenes in which sexual conduct including "ultimate sexual acts" is to be understood to be taking place, the camera does not focus on the bodies of the actors at such times. There is no exhibition whatever of the actors' genitals, lewd or otherwise, during these scenes. There are occasional scenes of nudity, but nudity alone is not enough to make material legally obscene under the *Miller* standards.

Appellant's showing of the film "Carnal Knowledge" is simply not the "public portrayal of hard core sexual conduct for its own sake, and for ensuing commercial gain" which we said was punishable in *Miller*. We hold that the film could not, as a matter of constitutional law, be found to depict sexual conduct in a patently offensive way, and that it is therefore not outside the protection of the First and Fourteenth Amendments because it is obscene. No other basis appearing in the record upon which the judgment of conviction can be sustained, we reverse the judgment of the Supreme Court of Georgia.

Reversed.

Mr. Justice Brennan, with whom Mr. Justice Stewart and Mr. Justice Marshall join, concurring in the result.

. . . Today's decision confirms my observation in Paris Adult Theatre I v. Slaton, 413 U.S. 49 (1973), that the Court's new formulation does not extricate us from the mire of case-by-case determinations of obscenity. . . .

. . .

[Justice Douglas also concurred in the reversal of the conviction.]

C. CONTROL OF "FIGHTING WORDS" AND OFFENSIVE SPEECH

CANTWELL v. CONNECTICUT, 310 U.S. 296 (1940). Cantwell, a member of the Jehovah's Witnesses, was engaged in proselyting in the streets of New Haven. He was convicted of a common law breach of the peace based on a showing that he stopped two men in the street, asked, and received, permission to play an anti-Catholic phonograph record. Both listeners were incensed by the contents of the record and were tempted to strike Cantwell unless he went away. On being told to be on his way he left their presence. The Court reversed his conviction. Justice Roberts, speaking for the Court, said, in part:

"The offense known as breach of the peace embraces a great variety of conduct destroying or menacing public order and tranquility. It includes not only violent acts but acts and words likely to produce violence in others. No one would have the hardihood to suggest that the principle of freedom of speech sanctions incitement to riot or that religious liberty connotes the privilege to exhort others to physical attack upon those belonging to another sect. When clear and present danger of riot, disorder, interference with traffic upon the public streets, or other immediate threat to public safety, peace, or order, appears, the power of the state to prevent or punish is obvious. Equally obvious is it that a state may not unduly suppress free communication of views, religious or other, under the guise of conserving desirable conditions. Here we have a situation analogous to a conviction under a statute sweeping in a great variety of conduct under a general and indefinite characterization, and leaving to the executive and judicial branches too wide a discretion in its application.

. . .

"We find in the instant case no assault or threatening of bodily harm, no truculent bearing, no intentional discourtesy, no personal abuse. On the contrary, we find only an effort to persuade a willing listener to buy a book or to contribute money in the interest of what Cantwell, however misguided others may think him, conceived to be true religion.

. . . .

"Although the contents of the record not unnaturally aroused animosity, we think that, in the absence of a statute narrowly drawn to define and punish specific conduct as constituting a clear and present danger to a substantial interest of the State, the petitioner's communication, considered in the light of the constitutional guarantees, raised no such clear and present menace to public peace and order as to render him liable to conviction of the common law offense in question."

CHAPLINSKY v. NEW HAMPSHIRE, 315 U.S. 568 (1942). Defendant, a Jehovah's Witness, got into an altercation on a public sidewalk with the City Marshal of Rochester, New Hampshire, and allegedly told the officer: "You are a God damned racketeer" and a "damned Fascist." Defendant was convicted under a statute forbidding a person to address "any offensive, derisive or annoying word to any other person who is lawfully in any street or other public place." The statute was construed by the state court to ban only "such words, as ordinary men know, are likely to cause a fight," thus to prohibit "the face-to-face words plainly likely to cause a breach of the peace by the address-ee." A unanimous Court sustained the conviction.

COHEN v. CALIFORNIA

403 U.S. 15, 91 S.Ct. 1780, 29 L.Ed.2d 284 (1971).

[Defendant was convicted of violating a California statute that prohibited "maliciously and willfully disturb[ing] the peace or quiet of any neighborhood or person" by "offensive conduct." In a Los Angeles courthouse corridor he had worn a jacket bearing the plainly visible words "Fuck the Draft." Women and children were present in the corridor. He testified that he wore the jacket as a means of informing the public of the depth of his feelings against the Vietnam war and the draft. In affirming, the California Court of Appeals held that "offensive conduct" means "behavior which has a tendency to provoke *others* to acts of violence or to in turn disturb the peace"; it was "certainly reasonably foreseeable" that defendant's conduct might cause others to commit an act of violence against defendant or attempt to forceably remove his jacket.]

Mr. Justice Harlan delivered the opinion of the Court.

.   .   .

[A]s it comes to us, this case cannot be said to fall within those relatively few categories of instances where prior decisions have established the power of government to deal more comprehensively with certain forms of individual expression simply upon a showing that such a form was employed. This is not, for example, an obscenity case. Whatever else may be necessary to give rise to the States' broader power to prohibit obscene expression, such expression must be, in some significant way, erotic. Roth v. United States, 354 U.S. 476 (1957). It cannot plausibly be maintained that this vulgar allusion to the Selective Service System would conjure up such psychic stimulation in anyone likely to be confronted with Cohen's crudely defaced jacket.

This Court has also held that the States are free to ban the simple use, without a demonstration of additional justifying circumstances, of so-called "fighting words," those personally abusive epithets which, when addressed to the ordinary citizen, are, as a matter of common knowledge, inherently likely to provoke violent reaction. Chaplinsky v. New Hampshire, 315 U.S. 568 (1942). While the four-letter word displayed by Cohen in relation to the draft is not uncommonly employed in a personally provocative fashion, in this instance it was clearly not "directed to the person of the hearer." Cantwell v. Connecticut, 310 U.S. 296, 309 (1940). No individual actually or likely to be present could reasonably have regarded the words on appellant's jacket as a direct personal insult. Nor do we have here an instance of the exercise of the State's police power to prevent a speaker from intentionally provoking a given group to hostile reaction. Cf. Feiner v. New York, 340 U.S. 315 (1951); Terminiello v. Chicago, 337 U.S. 1 (1949). There is . . . no showing that anyone who saw Cohen was in fact violently aroused or that appellant intended such a result.

Finally, in arguments before this Court much has been made of the claim that Cohen's distasteful mode of expression was thrust upon unwilling or unsuspecting viewers, and that the State might therefore legitimately act as it did in order to protect the sensitive from otherwise unavoidable exposure to appellant's crude form of protest. Of course, the mere presumed presence of unwitting listeners or viewers does not serve automatically to justify curtailing all speech capable of giving offense. . . . While this Court has recognized that government may properly act in many situations to prohibit intrusion into the privacy of the home of unwelcome views and ideas which cannot be totally banned from the public dialogue, e.g., Rowan v. Postmaster General, 397 U.S. 728 (1970), we have at the same time consistently stressed that "we are often 'captives' outside the sanctuary of the home and subject to objectionable speech." Id., at 738. The ability of government, consonant with the Constitution, to shut off discourse solely to protect others from hearing it is, in other words, dependent upon a showing that substantial privacy interests are being invaded in an essentially intolerable manner. Any broader view of this authority would effectively empower a majority to silence dissidents simply as a matter of personal predilections.

In this regard, persons confronted with Cohen's jacket were in a quite different posture than, say, those subjected to the raucous emissions of sound trucks blaring outside their residences. Those in the Los Angeles courthouse could effectively avoid further bombardment of their sensibilities simply by averting their eyes. And while it may be that one has a more substantial claim to a recognizable privacy interest when walking through a courthouse corridor than, for example, strolling through Central Park, surely it is nothing like the interest in being free from unwanted expression in the confines of one's own home. . . . Given the subtlety and complexity of the factors involved, if Cohen's "speech" was otherwise entitled to constitutional protection, we do not think the fact that some unwilling "listeners" in a public building may have been briefly exposed to it can serve to justify this breach of the peace conviction where, as here, there was no evidence that persons powerless to avoid appellant's conduct did in fact object to it, and where that portion of the statute upon which Cohen's conviction rests evinces no concern, either on its face or as construed by the California courts, with the special plight of the captive auditor, but, instead, indiscriminately sweeps within its prohibitions all "offensive conduct" that disturbs "any neighborhood or person."

Against this background, the issue flushed by this case stands out in bold relief. It is whether California can excise, as "offensive conduct," one particular scurrilous epithet from the public discourse, either upon the theory of the court below that its use is inherently likely to cause violent reaction or upon a more general assertion that the States, acting as guardians of public morality, may properly remove this offensive word from the public vocabulary.

The rationale of the California court is plainly untenable. . . . We have been shown no evidence that substantial numbers of citizens are standing ready to strike out physically at whoever may assault their sensibilities with execrations like that uttered by Cohen. . . .

Admittedly, it is not so obvious that the First and Fourteenth Amendments must be taken to disable the States from punishing public utterance of this unseemly expletive in order to maintain what they regard as a suitable level of discourse within the body politic. We think, however, that examination and reflection will reveal the shortcomings of a contrary viewpoint.

. . .

Against this perception of the constitutional policies involved, we discern certain more particularized considerations that peculiarly call for reversal of this conviction. First, the principle contended for by the State seems inherently boundless. How is one to distinguish this from any other offensive word? . . . For, while the particular four-letter word being litigated here is perhaps more distasteful than most others of its genre, it is nevertheless often true that one man's vulgarity is another's lyric. Indeed, we think it is largely because governmental officials cannot make principled distinctions in this area that the Constitution leaves matters of taste and style so largely to the individual.

Additionally, we cannot overlook the fact, because it is well illustrated by the episode involved here, that much linguistic expression serves a dual communicative function: it conveys not only ideas capable of relatively precise, detached explication, but otherwise inexpressible emotions as well. In fact, words are often chosen as much for their emotive as their cognitive force. . . .

Finally, and in the same vein, we cannot indulge the facile assumption that one can forbid particular words without also running a substantial risk of suppressing ideas in the process. Indeed, governments might soon seize upon the censorship of particular words as a convenient guise for banning the expression of unpopular views. . . .

It is, in sum, our judgment that, absent a more particularized and compelling reason for its actions, the State may not, consistently with the First and Fourteenth Amendments, make the simple public display here involved of this single four-letter expletive a criminal offense. . . .

Reversed.

Mr. Justice Blackmun, with whom The Chief Justice and Mr. Justice Black join.

I dissent. . . .

Cohen's absurd and immature antic, in my view, was mainly conduct and little speech. . . .

LEWIS v. NEW ORLEANS

415 U.S. 130, 94 S.Ct. 970, 39 L.Ed.2d 214 (1974).

Mr. Justice Brennan delivered the opinion of the Court.

Upon the Louisiana Supreme Court's reconsideration of this case in light of Gooding v. Wilson, 405 U.S. 518 (1972), pursuant to our remand, 408 U.S. 913 (1972), that court, three judges dissenting, again sustained appellant's conviction upon a charge of addressing spoken words to a New Orleans police officer in violation of New Orleans Ordinance 828 MCS, § 49–7.[1] We noted probable jurisdiction, and we reverse. We hold that § 49–7, as construed by the Louisiana Supreme Court, is overbroad in violation of the First and Fourteenth Amendments and is therefore facially invalid. Section 49–7 provides:

> "It shall be unlawful and a breach of the peace for any person wantonly to curse or revile or to use obscene or opprobrious language toward or with reference to any member of the city police while in the actual performance of his duty."

The Louisiana Supreme Court on remand did not refine or narrow these words, but took them as they stood: "The proscriptions are narrow and

----

[1] On January 3, 1970, appellant and her husband were in their pick-up truck following a police patrol car that was taking their young son to a police station after his arrest. An Officer Berner in another patrol car intercepted and stopped the truck. Berner left his car and according to his testimony, asked the husband for his driver's license. Words were exchanged between Berner and appellant and Berner arrested appellant on a charge of violating § 49–7. The parties' respective versions of the words exchanged were in sharp contradiction. Berner testified that appellant left the truck and "started yelling and screaming that I had her son or did something to her son and she wanted to know where he was . . . . She said, 'you god damn m. f. police—I am going to [the Superintendent of Police] about this.' " Appellant's husband testified that Berner's first words were "let me see your god damned license. I'll show you that you can't follow the police all over the streets; . . . After [appellant] got out and said, 'Officer I want to find out about my son.' He said 'you get in the car woman. Get your black ass in the god damned car or I will show you something.' " Appellant denied that she had used "any profanity toward the officer." The Municipal Judge credited Berner's testimony and disbelieved appellant and her husband.

specific—wantonly cursing, reviling, and using obscene or opprobrious language." Nonetheless, that court took the position that, as written, "it [§ 49–7]
is narrowed to 'fighting words' uttered to specific persons at a specific time.
. . ." But § 49–7 plainly has a broader sweep than the constitutional
definition of "fighting words" announced in Chaplinsky v. New Hampshire,
315 U.S. 568, 572 (1942), and reaffirmed in Gooding v. Wilson, supra, 405
U.S., at 522, namely, ". . . those [words] which by their very utterance
inflict injury or tend to incite an immediate breach of the peace." That the
Louisiana Supreme Court contemplated a broader reach of the ordinance is
evident from its emphasis upon the City's justification for regulation of "the
conduct of any person towards a member of the city police while in the actual
performance of his duty . . . . Permitting the cursing or reviling of or
using obscene or opprobrious words to a police officer while in the actual
performance of his duty would be unreasonable and basically incompatible with
the officer's activities and the place where such activities are performed." [2]

At least, the proscription of the use of "opprobrious language," embraces
words that do not "by their very utterance inflict injury or tend to incite an
immediate breach of the peace." That was our conclusion as to the word
"opprobrious" in the Georgia statute held unconstitutional in Gooding v.
Wilson, where we found that the common dictionary definition of that term
embraced words "conveying or intended to convey disgrace" and therefore that
the word was not limited to words which "by their very utterance inflict injury
or tend to invite an immediate breach of the peace." 405 U.S. at 525. The
same conclusion is compelled as to the reach of the term in § 49–7, for we find
nothing in the opinion of the Louisiana Supreme Court that makes any meaningful attempt to limit or properly define—as limited by Chaplinsky and Gooding —
"opprobrious," or indeed any other term in § 49–7. In that circumstance it is
immaterial whether the words appellant used might be punishable under a
properly limited statute. . . .

In sum, § 49–7 punishes only spoken words. It can therefore withstand
appellant's attack upon its facial constitutionality only if, as authoritatively
construed by the Louisiana Supreme Court, it is not susceptible of application to
speech, although vulgar or offensive, that is protected by the First and Fourteenth Amendments. Cohen v. California, 403 U.S. 15, 18–22 (1971); Terminiello v. Chicago, 337 U.S. 1, 4–5 (1949); Gooding v. Wilson, 405 U.S., at
520. Since § 49–7, as construed by the Louisiana Supreme Court, is susceptible
of application to protected speech, the section is constitutionally overbroad and
therefore is facially invalid.

The judgment of the Louisiana Supreme Court is reversed and the case is
remanded for further proceedings not inconsistent with this opinion.

Mr. Justice Powell, concurring in the result.

I previously concurred in the remand of this case, 408 U.S. 913 (1972), but
only for reconsideration in light of Chaplinsky v. New Hampshire, 315 U.S.
568 (1942). Pursuant to the remand order, we now have the Louisiana
Supreme Court's decision construing New Orleans Ordinance 828 M.C.S.
§ 49–7. I agree with the Court's conclusion today that the Louisiana Supreme
Court "did not refine or narrow these words [of the ordinance], but took them
as they stood." In conclusory language, that court construed the ordinance to
create a *per se* rule. Whenever "obscene or opprobrious language" is used
"toward or with reference to any member of the city police while in the actual

---

[2] We have no occasion in light of the result reached to address the conflict between this view and
that of the framers of the Model Penal Code that suggests that even "fighting words" as defined by
Chaplinsky should not be punished when addressed to a police officer trained to exercise a higher
degree of restraint than the average citizen. See Model Penal Code § 250.1, Comment 4 (Tent.Draft
No. 13, 1961).

performance of his duty," such language constitutes "fighting words" and hence a violation without regard to the facts and circumstances of a particular case. As so construed, the ordinance is facially overbroad.

Quite apart from the ambiguity inherent in the term "opprobrious," words may or may not be "fighting words," depending upon the circumstances of their utterance. It is unlikely, for example, that the words said to have been used here would have precipitated a physical confrontation between the middle-aged woman who spoke them and the police officer in whose presence they were uttered. The words may well have conveyed anger and frustration without provoking a violent reaction from the officer. Moreover, as noted in my previous concurrence, a properly trained officer may reasonably be expected to "exercise a higher degree of restraint" than the average citizen, and thus be less likely to respond belligerently to "fighting words." . . .

. . . .

. . . The present type of ordinance tends to be invoked only where there is no other valid basis for arresting an objectionable or suspicious person. The opportunity for abuse, especially where a statute has received a virtually open-ended interpretation, is self-evident.

I therefore concur in the result.

Mr. Justice Blackmun, with whom The Chief Justice and Mr. Justice Rehnquist join, dissenting. . . .

. . . The "overbreadth" and "vagueness" doctrines, as they are now being applied by the Court, quietly and steadily have worked their way into First Amendment parlance much as substantive due process did for the "old Court" of the 20's and 30's. These doctrines are being invoked indiscriminately without regard to the nature of the speech in question, the possible effect the statute or ordinance has upon such speech, the importance of the speech in relation to the exposition of ideas, or the purported or asserted community interest in preventing that speech. And it is no happenstance that in each case the facts are relegated to footnote status, conveniently distant and in a less disturbing focus. This is the compulsion of a doctrine that reduces our function to parsing words in the context of imaginary events. The result is that we are not merely applying constitutional limitations, as was intended by the Framers, and, indeed, as the history of our constitutional adjudication indicates, but are invalidating state statutes in wholesale lots because they "conceivably might apply to others who might utter other words." Gooding v. Wilson, supra, 405 U.S., at 535 (dissenting opinion).

. . . .

The speech uttered by Mrs. Lewis to the arresting officer "plainly" was profane, "plainly" it was insulting, and "plainly" it was fighting. It therefore is within the reach of the ordinance, as narrowed by Louisiana's highest court. The ordinance, moreover, poses no significant threat to protected speech. And it reflects a legitimate community interest in the harmonious administration of its laws. . . .

I see no alternative to our affirmance, and I therefore dissent.

FEDERAL COMMUNICATIONS COMMISSION v. PACIFICA FOUNDATION

438 U.S. 726, 98 S.Ct. 3026, 57 L.Ed.2d 1073 (1978).

Mr. Justice Stevens delivered the opinion of the Court (Parts I, II, III, and IV–C) and an opinion in which The Chief Justice and Mr. Justice Rehnquist joined (Parts IV–A and IV–B).

This case requires that we decide whether the Federal Communications Commission has any power to regulate a radio broadcast that is indecent but not obscene.

A satiric humorist named George Carlin recorded a 12-minute monologue entitled "Filthy Words" before a live audience in a California theater. He began by referring to his thoughts about "the words you couldn't say on the public, ah, airwaves, um, the ones you definitely wouldn't say, ever." He proceeded to list those words and repeat them over and over again in a variety of colloquialisms. The transcript of the recording . . . indicates frequent laughter from the audience.

At about 2 o'clock in the afternoon on Tuesday, October 30, 1973, a New York radio station owned by respondent, Pacifica Foundation, broadcast the "Filthy Words" monologue. A few weeks later a man, who stated that he had heard the broadcast while driving with his young son, wrote a letter complaining to the Commission. He stated that, although he could perhaps understand the "record's being sold for private use, I certainly cannot understand the broadcast of same over the air that, supposedly, you control."

The complaint was forwarded to the station for comment. In its response, Pacifica explained that the monologue had been played during a program about contemporary society's attitude toward language and that immediately before its broadcast listeners had been advised that it included "sensitive language which might be regarded as offensive to some." Pacifica characterized George Carlin as "a significant social satirist" who "like Twain and Sahl before him, examines the language of ordinary people. . . . Carlin is not mouthing obscenities, he is merely using words to satirize as harmless and essentially silly our attitudes towards those words." Pacifica stated that it was not aware of any other complaints about the broadcast.

On February 21, 1975, the Commission issued a Declaratory Order granting the complaint and holding that Pacifica "could have been the subject of administrative sanctions." The Commission did not impose formal sanctions, but it did state that the order would be "associated with the station's license file, and in the event that subsequent complaints are received, the Commission will then decide whether it should utilize any of the available sanctions it has been granted by Congress."

In its memorandum opinion the Commission stated that it intended to "clarify the standards which will be utilized in considering" the growing number of complaints about indecent speech on the airwaves. . . . Advancing several reasons for treating broadcast speech differently from other forms of expression, the Commission found a power to regulate indecent broadcasting in two statutes: 18 U.S.C. § 1464, which forbids the use of "any obscene, indecent, or profane language by means of radio communications," and 47 U.S.C. § 303(g), which requires the Commission to "encourage the larger and more effective use of radio in the public interest."

The Commission characterized the language used in the Carlin monologue as "patently offensive," though not necessarily obscene, and expressed the opinion that it should be regulated by principles analogous to those found in the law of nuisance where the "law generally speaks to *channeling* behavior more than actually prohibiting it. . . . [T]he concept of 'indecent' is intimately connected with the exposure of children to language that describes, in terms patently offensive as measured by contemporary community standards for the broadcast medium, sexual or excretory activities and organs, at times of the day when there is a reasonable risk that children may be in the audience." . . .

Applying these considerations to the language used in the monologue as broadcast by respondent, the Commission concluded that certain words depicted sexual and excretory activities in a patently offensive manner, noted that they "were broadcast at a time when children were undoubtedly in the audience (i.e., in the early afternoon)," and that the prerecorded language, with these offensive words "repeated over and over," was "deliberately broadcast." . . . In summary, the Commission stated: "We therefore hold that the language as broadcast was indecent and prohibited by 18 U.S.C. 1464."

After the order issued, the Commission was asked to clarify its opinion by ruling that the broadcast of indecent words as part of a live newscast would not be prohibited. The Commission issued another opinion in which it pointed out that it "never intended to place an absolute prohibition on the broadcast of this type of language, but rather sought to channel it to times of day when children most likely would not be exposed to it." The Commission noted that its "declaratory order was issued in a specific factual context," and declined to comment on various hypothetical situations presented by the petition. It relied on its "long standing policy of refusing to issue interpretive rulings or advisory opinions when the critical facts are not explicitly stated or there is a possibility that subsequent events will alter them." . . .

The United States Court of Appeals for the District of Columbia reversed, with each of the three judges on the panel writing separately. 556 F.2d 9. . . .

Having granted the Commission's petition for certiorari, . . . we must decide: (1) whether the scope of judicial review encompasses more than the Commission's determination that the monologue was indecent "as broadcast"; (2) whether the Commission's order was a form of censorship forbidden by § 326; (3) whether the broadcast was indecent within the meaning of § 1464; and (4) whether the order violates the First Amendment of the United States Constitution.

I.

The general statements in the Commission's memorandum opinion do not change the character of its order. Its action was an adjudication under 5 U.S.C. § 554(e); it did not purport to engage in formal rulemaking or in the promulgation of any regulations. . . . However appropriate it may be for an administrative agency to write broadly in an adjudicatory proceeding, federal courts have never been empowered to issue advisory opinions. See Herb v. Pitcairn, 324 U.S. 117, 126. Accordingly, the focus of our review must be on the Commission's determination that the Carlin monologue was indecent as broadcast.

II.

The relevant statutory questions are whether the Commission's action is forbidden "censorship" within the meaning of 47 U.S.C. § 326 and whether speech that concededly is not obscene may be restricted as "indecent" under the authority of 18 U.S.C. § 1464. The questions are not unrelated, for the two statutory provisions have a common origin. Nevertheless, we analyze them separately.

Section 29 of the Radio Act of 1927 provided:

"Nothing in this Act shall be understood or construed to give the licensing authority the power of censorship over the radio communications or signals transmitted by any radio station, and no regulation or condition shall be promulgated or fixed by the licensing authority which shall interfere with the right of free speech by means of radio communications. No person within the jurisdiction of the United States shall utter any obscene, indecent, or profane language by means of radio communication." 44 Stat. 1172–1173.

The prohibition against censorship unequivocally denies the Commission any power to edit proposed broadcasts in advance and to excise material considered inappropriate for the airwaves. The prohibition, however, has never been construed to deny the Commission the power to review the content of completed broadcasts in the performance of its regulatory duties.

. . .

Entirely apart from the fact that the subsequent review of program content is not the sort of censorship at which the statute was directed, its history makes it perfectly clear that it was not intended to limit the Commission's power to regulate the broadcast of obscene, indecent, or profane language. A single section of the 1927 Act is the source of both the anticensorship provision and the Commission's authority to impose sanctions for the broadcast of indecent or obscene language. Quite plainly, Congress intended to give meaning to both provisions. Respect for that intent requires that the censorship language be read as inapplicable to the prohibition on broadcasting obscene, indecent, or profane language.

. . .

III.

The only other statutory question presented by this case is whether the afternoon broadcast of the "Filthy Words" monologue was indecent within the meaning of § 1464. Even that question is narrowly confined by the arguments of the parties.

. . . Pacifica does not quarrel with the conclusion that this afternoon broadcast was patently offensive. Pacifica's claim that the broadcast was not indecent within the meaning of the statute rests entirely on the absence of prurient appeal.

The plain language of the statute does not support Pacifica's argument. The words "obscene, indecent, or profane" are written in the disjunctive, implying that each has a separate meaning. Prurient appeal is an element of the obscene, but the normal definition of "indecent" merely refers to nonconformance with accepted standards of morality.

IV.

Pacifica makes two constitutional attacks on the Commission's order. First, it argues that the Commission's construction of the statutory language broadly encompasses so much constitutionally protected speech that reversal is required even if Pacifica's broadcast of the "Filthy Words" monologue is not itself protected by the First Amendment. Second, Pacifica argues that inasmuch as the recording is not obscene, the Constitution forbids any abridgment of the right to broadcast it on the radio.

A.

The first argument fails because our review is limited to the question whether the Commission has the authority to proscribe this particular broadcast. As the Commission itself emphasized, its order was "issued in a specific factual context." . . . That approach is appropriate for courts as well as the Commission when regulation of indecency is at stake, for indecency is largely a function of context—it cannot be adequately judged in the abstract.

The approach is also consistent with Red Lion Broadcasting Co., Inc. v. FCC, 395 U.S. 367. In that case the Court rejected an argument that the Commission's regulations defining the fairness doctrine were so vague that they would inevitably abridge the broadcasters' freedom of speech. . . .

It is true that the Commission's order may lead some broadcasters to censor themselves. At most, however, the Commission's definition of indecency will deter only the broadcasting of patently offensive references to excretory and sexual organs and activities.[18] While some of these references may be protected, they surely lie at the periphery of First Amendment concern. Cf. Bates v. State Bar, 433 U.S. 350, 380–381. Young v. American Mini Theatres, Inc., 427 U.S. 50, 61. The danger dismissed so summarily in *Red Lion,* in contrast, was that broadcasters would respond to the vagueness of the regulations by refusing to present programs dealing with important social and political controversies. Invalidating any rule on the basis of its hypothetical application to situations not before the Court is "strong medicine" to be applied "sparingly and only as a last resort." Broadrick v. Oklahoma, 413 U.S. 601, 613. We decline to administer that medicine to preserve the vigor of patently offensive sexual and excretory speech.

B.

When the issue is narrowed to the facts of this case, the question is whether the First Amendment denies government any power to restrict the public broadcast of indecent language in any circumstances. For if the government has any such power, this was an appropriate occasion for its exercise.

The words of the Carlin monologue are unquestionably "speech" within the meaning of the First Amendment. It is equally clear that the Commission's objections to the broadcast were based in part on its content. The order must therefore fall if, as Pacifica argues, the First Amendment prohibits all governmental regulation that depends on the content of speech. Our past cases demonstrate, however, that no such absolute rule is mandated by the Constitution.

. . .

. . . [O]nly two Terms ago we refused to hold that a "statutory classification is unconstitutional because it is based on the content of communication protected by the First Amendment." Young v. American Mini Theatres, 427 U.S. 50, 52.

The question in this case is whether a broadcast of patently offensive words dealing with sex and excretion may be regulated because of its content. Obscene materials have been denied the protection of the First Amendment because their content is so offensive to contemporary moral standards. Roth v. United States, 354 U.S. 476. But the fact that society may find speech offensive is not a sufficient reason for suppressing it. Indeed, if it is the speaker's opinion that gives offense, that consequence is a reason for according it constitutional protection. For it is a central tenet of the First Amendment that the government must remain neutral in the marketplace of ideas. If there were any reason to believe that the Commission's characterization of the Carlin monologue as offensive could be traced to its political content—or even to the fact that it satirized contemporary attitudes about four letter words—First Amendment protection might be required. But that is simply not this case. These words offend for the same reasons that obscenity offends. Their place in the hierarchy of First Amendment values was aptly sketched by Mr. Justice Murphy when he said: "[s]uch utterances are no essential part of any exposition of ideas, and are of such slight social value as a step to truth that any benefit that may be derived

---

[18] A requirement that indecent language be avoided will have its primary effect on the form, rather than the content, of serious communication. There are few, if any, thoughts that cannot be expressed by the use of less offensive language.

from them is clearly outweighed by the social interest in order and morality."
Chaplinsky v. New Hampshire, 315 U.S. 568, 572.

Although these words ordinarily lack literary, political, or scientific value, they are not entirely outside the protection of the First Amendment. Some uses of even the most offensive words are unquestionably protected. . . . Indeed, we may assume, *arguendo,* that this monologue would be protected in other contexts. Nonetheless, the constitutional protection accorded to a communication containing such patently offensive sexual and excretory language need not be the same in every context. It is a characteristic of speech such as this that both its capacity to offend and its "social value," to use Mr. Justice Murphy's term, vary with the circumstances. Words that are commonplace in one setting are shocking in another. To paraphrase Mr. Justice Harlan, one occasion's lyric is another's vulgarity. Cf. Cohen v. California, 403 U.S. 15, 25.[25]

In this case it is undisputed that the content of Pacifica's broadcast was "vulgar," "offensive," and "shocking." Because content of that character is not entitled to absolute constitutional protection under all circumstances, we must consider its context in order to determine whether the Commission's action was constitutionally permissible.

C.

We have long recognized that each medium of expression presents special First Amendment problems. Joseph Burstyn, Inc. v. Wilson, 343 U.S. 495, 502–503. And of all forms of communication, it is broadcasting that has received the most limited First Amendment protection. Thus, although other speakers cannot be licensed except under laws that carefully define and narrow official discretion, a broadcaster may be deprived of his license and his forum if the Commission decides that such an action would serve "the public interest, convenience, and necessity." Similarly, although the First Amendment protects newspaper publishers from being required to print the replies of those whom they criticize, Miami Herald Publishing Co. v. Tornillo, 418 U.S. 241, it affords no such protection to broadcasters; on the contrary, they must give free time to the victims of their criticism. Red Lion Broadcasting Co., Inc. v. FCC, 395 U.S. 367.

The reasons for these distinctions are complex, but two have relevance to the present case. First, the broadcast media have established a uniquely pervasive presence in the lives of all Americans. Patently offensive, indecent material presented over the airwaves confronts the citizen, not only in public, but also in the privacy of the home, where the individual's right to be let alone plainly outweighs the First Amendment rights of an intruder. Rowan v. Post Office Department, 397 U.S. 728. Because the broadcast audience is constantly tuning in and out, prior warnings cannot completely protect the listener or viewer from unexpected program content. To say that one may avoid further

[25] The importance of context is illustrated by the *Cohen* case. That case arose when Paul Cohen entered a Los Angeles courthouse wearing a jacket emblazoned with the words "Fuck the Draft." After entering the courtroom, he took the jacket off and folded it. . . . So far as the evidence showed, no one in the courthouse was offended by his jacket. Nonetheless, when he left the courtroom, Cohen was arrested, convicted of disturbing the peace, and sentenced to 30 days in prison.

In holding that criminal sanctions could not be imposed on Cohen for his political statement in a public place, the Court rejected the argument that his speech would offend unwilling viewers; it noted that "there was no evidence that persons powerless to avoid [his] conduct did in fact object to it." . . . In contrast, in this case the Commission was responding to a listener's strenuous complaint, and Pacifica does not question its determination that this afternoon broadcast was likely to offend listeners. It should be noted that the Commission imposed a far more moderate penalty on Pacifica than the state court imposed on Cohen. Even the strongest civil penalty at the Commission's command does not include criminal prosecution. . . .

offense by turning off the radio when he hears indecent language is like saying that the remedy for an assault is to run away after the first blow. One may hang up on an indecent phone call, but that option does not give the caller a constitutional immunity or avoid a harm that has already taken place.[27]

Second, broadcasting is uniquely accessible to children, even those too young to read. Although Cohen's written message might have been incomprehensible to a first grader, Pacifica's broadcast could have enlarged a child's vocabulary in an instant. Other forms of offensive expression may be withheld from the young without restricting the expression at its source. Bookstores and motion picture theaters, for example, may be prohibited from making indecent material available to children. We held in Ginsberg v. New York, 390 U.S. 629, that the government's interest in the "well being of its youth" and in supporting "parents' claim to authority in their own household" justified the regulation of otherwise protected expression. . . . The ease with which children may obtain access to broadcast material, coupled with the concerns recognized in *Ginsberg,* amply justify special treatment of indecent broadcasting.

It is appropriate, in conclusion, to emphasize the narrowness of our holding. This case does not involve a two-way radio conversation between a cab driver and a dispatcher, or a telecast of an Elizabethan comedy. We have not decided that an occasional expletive in either setting would justify any sanction or, indeed, that this broadcast would justify a criminal prosecution. The Commission's decision rested entirely on a nuisance rationale under which context is all-important. The concept requires consideration of a host of variables. The time of day was emphasized by the Commission. The content of the program in which the language is used will also affect the composition of the audience, and differences between radio, television, and perhaps closed-circuit transmissions, may also be relevant. As Mr. Justice Sutherland wrote, a "nuisance may be merely a right thing in the wrong place—like a pig in the parlor instead of the barnyard." Euclid v. Ambler Realty Co., 272 U.S. 365, 388. We simply hold that when the Commission finds that a pig has entered the parlor, the exercise of its regulatory power does not depend on proof that the pig is obscene.

The judgment of the Court of Appeals is reversed.

Mr. Justice Powell, with whom Mr. Justice Blackmun joins, concurring.

.   .   .

I . . . agree with much that is said in Part IV of Mr. Justice Stevens' opinion, and with its conclusion that the Commission's holding in this case does not violate the First Amendment. Because I do not subscribe to all that is said in Part IV, however, I state my views separately.

I.

.   .   .

. . . [T]he language employed is, to most people, vulgar and offensive. It was chosen specifically for this quality, and it was repeated over and over as a sort of verbal shock treatment. The Commission did not err in characterizing the narrow category of language used here as "patently offensive" to most people regardless of age.

The issue, however, is whether the Commission may impose civil sanctions on a licensee radio station for broadcasting the monologue at two o'clock in the afternoon. The Commission's primary concern was to prevent the broadcast from reaching the ears of unsupervised children who were likely to be in the

[27] Outside the home, the balance between the offensive speaker and the unwilling audience may sometimes tip in favor of the speaker, requiring the offended listener to turn away. See Erznoznik v. Jacksonville, 422 U.S. 205 . . . .

audience at that hour. In essence, the Commission sought to "channel" the monologue to hours when the fewest unsupervised children would be exposed to it. . . . In my view, this consideration provides strong support for the Commission's holding.

. . . .

In most instances, the dissemination of this kind of speech to children may be limited without also limiting willing adults' access to it. Sellers of printed and recorded matter and exhibitors of motion pictures and live performances may be required to shut their doors to children, but such a requirement has no effect on adults' access. . . . The difficulty is that such a physical separation of the audience cannot be accomplished in the broadcast media. During most of the broadcast hours, both adults and unsupervised children are likely to be in the broadcast audience, and the broadcaster cannot reach willing adults without also reaching children. This, as the Court emphasizes, is one of the distinctions between the broadcast and other media to which we often have adverted as justifying a different treatment of the broadcast media for First Amendment purposes. . . . In my view, the Commission was entitled to give substantial weight to this difference in reaching its decision in this case.

A second difference, not without relevance, is that broadcasting—unlike most other forms of communication—comes directly into the home, the one place where people ordinarily have the right not to be assaulted by uninvited and offensive sights and sounds. . . . Although the First Amendment may require unwilling adults to absorb the first blow of offensive but protected speech when they are in public before they turn away, see, e.g., *Erznoznik*, 210–211, but cf. Rosenfeld v. New Jersey, 408 U.S. 901, 903–909 (1972) (Powell, J., dissenting), a different order of values obtains in the home. "That we are often 'captives' outside the sanctuary of the home and subject to objectionable speech and other sound does not mean we must be captives everywhere." Rowan v. Post Office Dept., supra, at 738. The Commission also was entitled to give this factor appropriate weight in the circumstances of the instant case. This is not to say, however, that the Commission has an unrestricted license to decide what speech, protected in other media, may be banned from the airwaves in order to protect unwilling adults from momentary exposure to it in their homes.[2] Making the sensitive judgments required in these cases is not easy. But this responsibility has been reposed initially in the Commission, and its judgment is entitled to respect.

It is argued that despite society's right to protect its children from this kind of speech, and despite everyone's interest in not being assaulted by offensive speech in the home, the Commission's holding in this case is impermissible because it prevents willing adults from listening to Carlin's monologue over the radio in the early afternoon hours. It is said that this ruling will have the effect of "reduc[ing] the adult population . . . to [hearing] only what is fit for children." Butler v. Michigan, 352 U.S. 380, 383 (1957). This argument is not without force. The Commission certainly should consider it as it develops standards in this area. But it is not sufficiently strong to leave the Commission powerless to act in circumstances such as those in this case.

The Commission's holding does not prevent willing adults from purchasing Carlin's record, from attending his performances, or, indeed, from reading the transcript reprinted as an appendix to the Court's opinion. On its face, it does not prevent respondent from broadcasting the monologue during late evening

---

[2] It is true that the radio listener quickly may tune out speech that is offensive to him. In addition, broadcasters may preface potentially offensive programs with warnings. But such warnings do not help the unsuspecting listener who tunes in at the middle of a program. In this respect, too, broadcasting appears to differ from books and records, which may carry warnings on their faces, and from motion pictures and live performances, which may carry warnings on their marquees.

hours when fewer children are likely to be in the audience, nor from broadcasting discussions of the contemporary use of language at any time during the day. The Commission's holding, and certainly the Court's holding today, does not speak to cases involving the isolated use of a potentially offensive word in the course of a radio broadcast, as distinguished from the verbal shock treatment administered by respondent here. In short, I agree that on the facts of this case, the Commission's order did not violate respondent's First Amendment rights.

II.

As the foregoing demonstrates, my views are generally in accord with what is said in Part IV(C) of Mr. Justice Stevens' opinion. . . . I therefore join that portion of his opinion. I do not join Part IV(B), however, because I do not subscribe to the theory that the Justices of this Court are free generally to decide on the basis of its content which speech protected by the First Amendment is most "valuable" and hence deserving of the most protection, and which is less "valuable" and hence deserving of less protection. . . . In my view, the result in this case does not turn on whether Carlin's monologue, viewed as a whole, or the words that comprise it, have more or less "value" than a candidate's campaign speech. This is a judgment for each person to make, not one for the judges to impose upon him.[4]

The result turns instead on the unique characteristics of the broadcast media, combined with society's right to protect its children from speech generally agreed to be inappropriate for their years, and with the interest of unwilling adults in not being assaulted by such offensive speech in their homes. Moreover, I doubt whether today's decision will prevent any adult who wishes to receive Carlin's message in Carlin's own words from doing so, and from making for himself a value judgment as to the merit of the message and words. . . .

Mr. Justice Brennan, with whom Mr. Justice Marshall joins, dissenting.

. . .

I.

. . .

A.

Without question, the privacy interests of an individual in his home are substantial and deserving of significant protection. In finding these interests sufficient to justify the content regulation of protected speech, however, the Court commits two errors. First, it misconceives the nature of the privacy interests involved where an individual voluntarily chooses to admit radio communications into his home. Second, it ignores the constitutionally protected interests of both those who wish to transmit and those who desire to receive broadcasts that many—including the FCC and this Court—might find offensive.

. . . I believe that an individual's actions in switching on and listening to communications transmitted over the public airways and directed to the public at-large do not implicate fundamental privacy interests, even when engaged in within the home. Instead, because the radio is undeniably a public medium,

---

[4] For much the same reason, I also do not join Part IV(A). I had not thought that the application *vel non* of overbreadth analysis should depend on the Court's judgment as to the value of the protected speech that might be deterred. . . . Except in the context of commercial speech, . . . it has not in the past. . . .

As Mr. Justice Stevens points out, however, . . . the Commission's order was limited to the facts of this case; "it did not purport to engage in formal rulemaking or in the promulgation of any regulations." In addition, since the Commission may be expected to proceed cautiously, as it has in the past, . . . I do not foresee an undue "chilling" effect on broadcasters' exercise of their rights. I agree, therefore, that respondent's overbreadth challenge is meritless.

these actions are more properly viewed as a decision to take part, if only as a listener, in an ongoing public discourse. . . .

. . . Where the individuals comprising the offended majority may freely choose to reject the material being offered, we have never found their privacy interests of such moment to warrant the suppression of speech on privacy grounds. . . .

B.

Most parents will undoubtedly find understandable as well as commendable the Court's sympathy with the FCC's desire to prevent offensive broadcasts from reaching the ears of unsupervised children. . . .

. . . As surprising as it may be to individual Members of this Court, some parents may actually find Mr. Carlin's unabashed attitude towards the seven "dirty words" healthy, and deem it desirable to expose their children to the manner in which Mr. Carlin defuses the taboo surrounding the words. Such parents may constitute a minority of the American public, but the absence of great numbers willing to exercise the right to raise their children in this fashion does not alter the right's nature or its existence. Only the Court's regrettable decision does that.

. . .

II.

. . .

My Brother Stevens also finds relevant to his First Amendment analysis the fact that "[a]dults who feel the need may purchase tapes and records or go to theatres and nightclubs to hear [the tabooed] words." . . . My Brother Powell agrees. . . . The opinions of my Brethren display both a sad insensitivity to the fact that these alternatives involve the expenditure of money, time, and effort that many of those wishing to hear Mr. Carlin's message may not be able to afford, and a naive innocence of the reality that in many cases, the medium may well be the message.

. . .

III.

It is quite evident that I find the Court's attempt to unstitch the warp and woof of First Amendment law in an effort to reshape its fabric to cover the patently wrong result the Court reaches in this case dangerous as well as lamentable. Yet there runs throughout the opinions of my Brothers Powell and Stevens another vein I find equally disturbing: a depressing inability to appreciate that in our land of cultural pluralism, there are many who think, act, and talk differently from the Members of this Court, and who do not share their fragile sensibilities. It is only an acute ethnocentric myopia that enables the Court to approve the censorship of communications solely because of the words they contain.

. . .

Today's decision will thus have its greatest impact on broadcasters desiring to reach, and listening audiences comprised of, persons who do not share the Court's view as to which words or expressions are acceptable and who, for a variety of reasons, including a conscious desire to flout majoritarian conventions, express themselves using words that may be regarded as offensive by those from different socio-economic backgrounds. In this context, the Court's decision may be seen for what, in the broader perspective, it really is: another of the dominant culture's inevitable efforts to force those groups who do not share its mores to conform to its way of thinking, acting, and speaking. . . .

. . .

Mr. Justice Stewart, with whom Mr. Justice Brennan, Mr. Justice White, and Mr. Justice Marshall join, dissenting.

. . .

. . . I think that "indecent" should properly be read as meaning no more than "obscene." Since the Carlin monologue concededly was not "obscene," I believe that the Commission lacked statutory authority to ban it. Under this construction of the statute, it is unnecessary to address the difficult and important issue of the Commission's constitutional power to prohibit speech that would be constitutionally protected outside the context of electronic broadcasting.

. . .

D. REGULATION OF COMMERCIAL ADVERTISING

VIRGINIA STATE BOARD OF PHARMACY v. VIRGINIA CITIZENS CONSUMER COUNCIL, INC.

425 U.S. 748, 96 S.Ct. 1817, 48 L.Ed.2d 346 (1976).

Mr. Justice Blackmun delivered the opinion of the Court.

The plaintiff-appellees in this case attack, as violative of the First and Fourteenth Amendments, that portion of § 54–524.35 of Va.Code Ann. (1974), which provides that a pharmacist licensed in Virginia is guilty of unprofessional conduct if he "(3) publishes, advertises or promotes, directly or indirectly, in any manner whatsoever, any amount, price, fee, premium, discount, rebate or credit terms . . . for any drugs which may be dispensed only by prescription." The three-judge District Court declared the quoted portion of the statute "void and of no effect," and enjoined the defendant-appellants, the Virginia State Board of Pharmacy and the individual members of that Board, from enforcing it. 373 F.Supp. 683 (E.D.Va.1974). We noted probable jurisdiction of the appeal.

I.

. . .

Inasmuch as only a licensed pharmacist may dispense prescription drugs in Virginia, § 54–524.48, advertising or other affirmative dissemination of prescription drug price information is effectively forbidden in the State. . . . The prohibition does not extend to nonprescription drugs, but neither is it confined to prescriptions that the pharmacist compounds himself. Indeed, about 95% of all prescriptions now are filled with dosage forms prepared by the pharmaceutical manufacturer.

II.

. . .

The present . . . attack on the statute is one made not by one directly subject to its prohibition, that is, a pharmacist, but by prescription drug consumers who claim that they would greatly benefit if the prohibition were lifted and advertising freely allowed. The plaintiffs are an individual Virginia resident who suffers from diseases that require her to take prescription drugs on a daily basis, and two nonprofit organizations. Their claim is that the First Amendment entitles the user of prescription drugs to receive information that pharmacists wish to communicate to them through advertising and other promotional means, concerning the prices of such drugs.

Certainly that information may be of value. Drug prices in Virginia, for both prescription and nonprescription items, strikingly vary from outlet to outlet even within the same locality. It is stipulated, for example, that in Richmond "the cost of 40 Achromycin tablets ranges from $2.59 to $6.00, a difference of 140% [*sic*]," and that in the Newport News-Hampton area the cost of tetracycline ranges from $1.20 to $9.00, a difference of 650%. . . .

III.

The question first arises whether, even assuming that First Amendment protection attaches to the flow of drug price information, it is a protection enjoyed by the appellees as recipients of the information, and not solely, if at all, by the advertisers themselves who seek to disseminate that information.

Freedom of speech presupposes a willing speaker. But where a speaker exists, as is the case here, the protection afforded is to the communication, to its source and to its recipients both. This is clear from the decided cases. In Lamont v. Postmaster General, 381 U.S. 301 (1965), the Court upheld the First Amendment rights of citizens to receive political publications sent from abroad. More recently, in Kleindienst v. Mandel, 408 U.S. 753, 762–763 (1972), we acknowledged that this Court has referred to a First Amendment right to "receive information and ideas," and that freedom of speech " 'necessarily protects the right to receive.' " And in Procunier v. Martinez, 416 U.S. 396, 408–409 (1974), where censorship of prison inmates' mail was under examination, we thought it unnecessary to assess the First Amendment rights of the inmates themselves, for it was reasoned that such censorship equally infringed the rights of noninmates to whom the correspondence was addressed. . . . If there is a right to advertise, there is a reciprocal right to receive the advertising, and it may be asserted by these appellees.

IV.

The appellants contend that the advertisement of prescription drug prices is outside the protection of the First Amendment because it is "commercial speech." There can be no question that in past decisions the Court has given some indication that commercial speech is unprotected. In Valentine v. Chrestensen, supra, the Court upheld a New York statute that prohibited the distribution of any "handbill, circular . . . or other advertising matter whatsoever in or upon any street." The Court concluded that, although the First Amendment would forbid the banning of all communication by handbill in the public thoroughfares, it imposed "no such restraint on government as respects purely commercial advertising." 316 U.S., at 54. Further support for a "commercial speech" exception to the First Amendment may perhaps be found in Breard v. Alexandria, 341 U.S. 622 (1951), where the Court upheld a conviction for violation of an ordinance prohibiting door-to-door solicitation of magazine subscriptions. The Court reasoned: "The selling . . . brings into the transaction a commercial feature," and it distinguished Martin v. Struthers, supra, where it had reversed a conviction for door-to-door distribution of leaflets publicizing a religious meeting, as a case involving "no element of the commercial." 341 U.S., at 642–643. Moreover, the Court several times has stressed that communications to which First Amendment protection was given were *not* "purely commercial." New York Times Co. v. Sullivan, 376 U.S. 254, 266 (1964); Thomas v. Collins, 323 U.S., at 533; Murdock v. Pennsylvania, 319 U.S. 105, 111 (1943); Jamison v. Texas, 318 U.S. 413, 417 (1943).

Since the decision in *Breard,* however, the Court has never *denied* protection on the ground that the speech in issue was "commercial speech." That simplistic approach, which by then had come under criticism or was regarded as of doubtful validity by members of the Court, was avoided in Pittsburgh Press Co. v. Pittsburgh Comm'n on Human Relations, 413 U.S. 376 (1973). . . .

Last Term, in Bigelow v. Virginia, 421 U.S. 809 (1975), the notion of unprotected "commercial speech" all but passed from the scene. . . .

Some fragment of hope for the continuing validity of a "commercial speech" exception arguably might have persisted because of the subject matter of the advertisement in *Bigelow*. We noted that in announcing the availability of legal abortions in New York, the advertisement "did more than simply propose a commercial transaction. It contained factual material of clear 'public interest.' " Id., at 822. . . .

Here, in contrast, the question whether there is a First Amendment exception for "commercial speech" is squarely before us. Our pharmacist does not wish to editorialize on any subject, cultural, philosophical, or political. He does not wish to report any particularly newsworthy fact, or to make generalized observations even about commercial matters. The "idea" he wishes to communicate is simply this: "I will sell you the X prescription drug at the Y price." Our question, then, is whether this communication is wholly outside the protection of the First Amendment.

V.

We begin with several propositions that already are settled or beyond serious dispute. It is clear, for example, that speech does not lose its First Amendment protection because money is spent to project it, as in a paid advertisement of one form or another. Buckley v. Valeo, 421 U.S. 1, 35–39 (1976); Pittsburgh Press Co. v. Pittsburgh Comm'n on Human Relations, 413 U.S., at 384; New York Times Co. v. Sullivan, 376 U.S., at 266. Speech likewise is protected even though it is carried in a form that is "sold" for profit, Smith v. California, 361 U.S. 147, 150 (1959) (books); Joseph Burstyn, Inc. v. Wilson, 343 U.S. 495, 501 (1952) (motion pictures); Murdock v. Pennsylvania, 319 U.S., at 111 (religious literature), and even though it may involve a solicitation to purchase or otherwise pay or contribute money. New York Times Co. v. Sullivan, supra; NAACP v. Button, 371 U.S. 415, 429 (1963); Jamison v. Texas, 318 U.S., at 417; Cantwell v. Connecticut, 310 U.S. 296, 306–307 (1940).

If there is a kind of commercial speech that lacks all First Amendment protection, therefore, it must be distinguished by its content. Yet the speech whose content deprives it of protection cannot simply be speech on a commercial subject. No one would contend that our pharmacist may be prevented from being heard on the subject of whether, in general, pharmaceutical prices should be regulated, or their advertisement forbidden. Nor can it be dispositive that a commercial advertisement is uneditorial, and merely reports a fact. Purely factual matter of public interest may claim protection. . . .

Our question is whether speech which does "no more than propose a commercial transaction," Pittsburgh Press Co. v. Pittsburgh Comm'n on Human Relations, 413 U.S., at 385, is so removed from any "exposition of ideas," Chaplinsky v. New Hampshire, 315 U.S. 568, 572 (1942), and from " 'truth, science, morality, and arts in general, in its diffusion of liberal sentiments on the administration of Government.' " Roth v. United States, 354 U.S. 476, 484 (1957), that it lacks all protection. Our answer is that it is not.

Focusing first on the individual parties to the transaction that is proposed in the commercial advertisement, we may assume that the advertiser's interest is a purely economic one. That hardly disqualifies him for protection under the First Amendment. . . .

As to the particular consumer's interest in the free flow of commercial information, that interest may be as keen, if not keener by far, than his interest in the day's most urgent political debate. Appellees' case in this respect is a convincing one. Those whom the suppression of prescription drug price information hits the hardest are the poor, the sick, and particularly the aged. A disproportionate amount of their income tends to be spent on prescription drugs; yet they are the least able to learn, by shopping from pharmacist to pharmacist, where their scarce dollars are best spent. When drug prices vary as strikingly as they do, information as to who is charging what becomes more than a convenience. It could mean the alleviation of physical pain or the enjoyment of basic necessities.

Generalizing, society also may have a strong interest in the free flow of commercial information. Even an individual advertisement, though entirely "commercial," may be of general public interest. . . . Obviously, not all commercial messages contain the same or even a very great public interest element. There are few to which such an element, however, could not be added. Our pharmacist, for example, could cast himself as a commentator on store-to-store disparities in drug prices, giving his own and those of a competitor as proof. We see little point in requiring him to do so, and little difference if he does not.

Moreover, there is another consideration that suggests that no line between publicly "interesting" or "important" commercial advertising and the opposite kind could ever be drawn. Advertising, however tasteless and excessive it sometimes may seem, is nonetheless dissemination of information as to who is producing and selling what product for what reason, and at what price. So long as we preserve a predominantly free enterprise economy, the allocation of our resources in large measure will be made through numerous private economic decisions. It is a matter of public interest that those decisions, in the aggregate, be intelligent and well informed. To this end, the free flow of commercial information is indispensable. . . . And if it is indispensable to the proper allocation of resources in a free enterprise system, it is also indispensable to the formation of intelligent opinions as to how that system ought to be regulated or altered. Therefore, even if the First Amendment were thought to be primarily an instrument to enlighten public decisionmaking in a democracy, we could not say that the free flow of information does not serve that goal.

Arrayed against these substantial individual and societal interests are a number of justifications for the advertising ban. These have to do principally with maintaining a high degree of professionalism on the part of licensed pharmacists. Indisputably, the State has a strong interest in maintaining that professionalism. . . .

Price advertising, it is argued, will place in jeopardy the pharmacist's expertise and, with it, the customer's health. It is claimed that the aggressive price competition that will result from unlimited advertising will make it impossible for the pharmacist to supply professional services in the compounding, handling, and dispensing of prescription drugs. . . . Price advertising, it is said, will reduce the pharmacist's status to that of a mere retailer.

The strength of these proffered justifications is greatly undermined by the fact that high professional standards, to a substantial extent, are guaranteed by the close regulation to which pharmacists in Virginia are subject. And this case concerns the retail sale by the pharmacist more than it does his professional standards. Surely, any pharmacist guilty of professional dereliction that actually endangers his customer will promptly lose his license. At the same time, we cannot discount the Board's justifications entirely. The Court regarded justifications of this type sufficient to sustain the advertising bans challenged on due process and equal protection grounds in Head v. New Mexico Board, supra; Williamson v. Lee Optical Co., supra; and Semler v. Dental Examiners, supra.

The challenge now made, however, is based on the First Amendment. This casts the Board's justifications in a different light.   . . .

It appears to be feared that if the pharmacist who wishes to provide low cost, and assertedly low quality services is permitted to advertise, he will be taken up on his offer by too many unwitting customers.   . . .

There is, of course, an alternative to this highly paternalistic approach. That alternative is to assume that this information is not in itself harmful, that people will perceive their own best interests if only they are well enough informed, and that the best means to that end is to open the channels of communication rather than to close them. If they are truly open, nothing prevents the "professional" pharmacist from marketing his own assertedly superior product, and contrasting it with that of the low-cost, high-volume prescription drug retailer. But the choice among these alternative approaches is not ours to make or the Virginia General Assembly's. It is precisely this kind of choice, between the dangers of suppressing information, and the dangers of its misuse if it is freely available, that the First Amendment makes for us. Virginia is free to require whatever professional standards it wishes of its pharmacists; it may subsidize them or protect them from competition in other ways. Cf. Parker v. Brown, 317 U.S. 341 (1943). But it may not do so by keeping the public in ignorance of the entirely lawful terms that competing pharmacists are offering. In this sense, the justifications Virginia has offered for suppressing the flow of prescription drug price information, far from persuading us that the flow is not protected by the First Amendment, have re-enforced our view that it is. We so hold.

VI.

In concluding that commercial speech, like other varieties, is protected, we of course do not hold that it can never be regulated in any way. Some forms of commercial speech regulation are surely permissible. We mention a few only to make clear that they are not before us and therefore are not foreclosed by this case.

There is no claim, for example, that the prohibition on prescription drug price advertising is a mere time, place, and manner restriction. We have often approved restrictions of that kind provided that they are justified without reference to the content of the regulated speech, that they serve a significant governmental interest, and that in so doing they leave open ample alternative channels for communication of the information.   . . .   Whatever may be the proper bounds of time, place, and manner restrictions on commercial speech, they are plainly exceeded by this Virginia statute, which singles out speech of a particular content and seeks to prevent its dissemination completely.

Nor is there any claim that prescription drug price advertisements are forbidden because they are false or misleading in any way. Untruthful speech, commercial or otherwise, has never been protected for its own sake. Gertz v. Robert Welch, Inc., 418 U.S. 323, 340 (1974); Konigsberg v. State Bar, 366 U.S. 36, 49 and n. 10 (1961). Obviously, much commercial speech is not provably false, or even wholly false, but only deceptive or misleading. We foresee no obstacle to a State's dealing effectively with this problem.[24]   The

---

[24] In concluding that commercial speech enjoys First Amendment protection, we have not held that it is wholly undifferentiable from other forms. There are commonsense differences between speech that does "no more than propose a commercial transaction" Pittsburgh Press Co. v. Pittsburgh Comm'n on Human Relations, 413 U.S., at 385, and other varieties. Even if the differences do not justify the conclusion that commercial speech is valueless, and thus subject to complete suppression by the State, they nonetheless suggest that a different degree of protection is necessary to insure that the flow of truthful and legitimate commercial information is unimpaired. The truth of commercial speech, for example, may be more easily verifiable by its disseminator than, let us say, news reporting or political commentary, in that ordinarily the advertiser seeks to disseminate information about a specific product or service that he himself provides and presumably knows more about than anyone

First Amendment, as we construe it today, does not prohibit the State from insuring that the stream of commercial information flows cleanly as well as freely. See, for example, Va.Code Ann. § 18.2–216 (1975).

Also, there is no claim that the transactions proposed in the forbidden advertisements are themselves illegal in any way. . . . Finally, the special problems of the electronic broadcast media are likewise not in this case. . . .

What is at issue is whether a State may completely suppress the dissemination of concededly truthful information about entirely lawful activity, fearful of that information's effect upon its disseminators and its recipients. Reserving other questions, we conclude that the answer to this one is in the negative.

The judgment of the District Court is affirmed.

It is so ordered.

Mr. Justice Stevens took no part in the consideration or decision of this case.

Mr. Chief Justice Burger, concurring.

.   .   .

Our decision today . . . deals largely with the State's power to prohibit pharmacists from advertising the retail price of *prepackaged* drugs. . . . [Q]uite different factors would govern were we faced with a law regulating or even prohibiting advertising by the traditional learned professions of medicine or law. . . .

.   .   .

Mr. Justice Stewart, concurring.

.   .   .

Today the Court ends the anomalous situation created by *Chrestensen* and holds that a communication which does no more than propose a commercial transaction is not "wholly outside the protection of the First Amendment." But since it is a cardinal principle of the First Amendment that "government has no power to restrict expression because of its message, its ideas, its subject matter, or its content," the Court's decision calls into immediate question the constitutional legitimacy of every state and federal law regulating false or deceptive advertising. I write separately to explain why I think today's decision does not preclude such governmental regulation. . . .

.   .   .

. . . Since the factual claims contained in commercial price or product advertisements relate to tangible goods or services, they may be tested empirically and corrected to reflect the truth without in any manner jeopardizing the free dissemination of thought. Indeed, the elimination of false and deceptive claims serves to promote the one facet of commercial price and product advertising that warrants First Amendment protection—its contribution to the flow of accurate and reliable information relevant to public and private decision-making.

else. Also, commercial speech may be more durable than other kinds. Since advertising is the sine qua non of commercial profits, there is little likelihood of its being chilled by proper regulation and foregone entirely.

Attributes such as these, the greater objectivity and hardiness of commercial speech, may make it less necessary to tolerate inaccurate statements for fear of silencing the speaker. Compare New York Times Co. v. Sullivan, 376 U.S. 254 (1964), with Dun & Bradstreet, Inc. v. Grove, 404 U.S. 898 (1971). They may also make it appropriate to require that a commercial message appear in such a form, or include such additional information, warnings and disclaimers, as are necessary to prevent its being deceptive. . . . They may also make inapplicable the prohibition against prior restraints.

.   .   .

Mr. Justice Rehnquist, dissenting.

The logical consequences of the Court's decision in this case, a decision which elevates commercial intercourse between a seller hawking his wares and a buyer seeking to strike a bargain to the same plane as has been previously reserved for the free marketplace of ideas, are far reaching indeed. Under the Court's opinion the way will be open not only for dissemination of price information but for active promotion of prescription drugs, liquor, cigarettes and other products the use of which it has previously been thought desirable to discourage. Now, however, such promotion is protected by the First Amendment so long as it is not misleading or does not promote an illegal product or enterprise. In coming to this conclusion, the Court has overruled a legislative determination that such advertising should not be allowed and has done so on behalf of a consumer group which is not directly disadvantaged by the statute in question. This effort to reach a result which the Court obviously considers desirable is a troublesome one, for two reasons. It extends standing to raise First Amendment claims beyond the previous decisions of this Court. It also extends the protection of that Amendment to purely commercial endeavors which its most vigorous champions on this Court had thought to be beyond its pale.

. . .

TIME, PLACE, AND MANNER REGULATION OF COMMERCIAL SPEECH

The dictum in Valentine v. Chrestensen that commercial speech was beyond first amendment protection was uttered in a context of what is considered to be a "time, place, and manner" regulation. Unlike the challenged statute in the *Virginia Board of Pharmacy* case, commercial messages were only denied one forum of distribution—distribution of leaflets to passersby on the streets. The question of the appropriate standards governing time, place, and manner restrictions on speech is postponed to Chapter 15. Much of the *Valentine* structure may have survived, however, in judging the validity of time, place, and manner restrictions on commercial speech. See Shiffrin, *The First Amendment and Economic Regulation: Away from a General Theory of the First Amendment,* 78 Northwestern L.Rev. 1212, 1276–1282 (1983).

ATTORNEY ADVERTISING

Chief Justice Burger's attempt, in his concurrence, to distinguish prohibitions on advertising by "traditional learned professions," proved to be unavailing. In Bates v. State Bar of Arizona, 433 U.S. 350 (1977), the Court held 5–4 that states could not prohibit lawyers from price advertising of "routine legal services." (Left open were questions concerning restrictions on the content of lawyer advertisements which would be appropriate to avoid misleading the public, given the lack of public sophistication concerning legal services.) The next year the Court turned to the issue of personal solicitation by lawyers in two cases in which the distinction between commercial and non-commercial speech proved to be crucial. In Ohralik v. Ohio State Bar Ass'n, 436 U.S. 447 (1978), the Court sustained discipline of an attorney soliciting contingent fee employment from accident victims. In re Primus, 436 U.S. 412 (1978), however, reversed disciplinary action against an ACLU lawyer who sent a letter to a woman who had been sterilized as a condition of receiving public assistance, offering legal assistance by the civil liberties organization. In distinguishing the two cases, the Court noted that Primus' letter came within the "generous zone of First Amendment protection reserved for associational freedom." The scope of the power to control "misleading" attorney advertising was at issue in In the Matter of R.M.J., 455 U.S. 191 (1982).

LINMARK ASSOCIATES v. TOWNSHIP OF WILLINGBORO, 431 U.S. 85 (1977). An ordinance prohibited posting of "For Sale" and "Sold" signs on real estate for the purpose of reducing "panic selling" by white homeowners in a racially integrated community. The Court, in an opinion by Justice Marshall, held that the ordinance violated the First Amendment.

". . . [T]he societal interest in "the free flow of commercial information," Virginia State Board of Pharmacy v. Virginia Citizens Consumer Council, Inc., 425 U.S., at 764, is in no way lessened by the fact that the subject of the commercial information here is realty rather than abortions or drugs.

"Respondents nevertheless argue that First Amendment concerns are less directly implicated by Willingboro's ordinance because it restricts only one method of communication. This distinction is not without significance to First Amendment analysis, since laws regulating the time, place or manner of speech stand on a different footing than laws prohibiting speech altogether. . . .

. . .

. . . [T]he Willingboro ordinance is not genuinely concerned with the place of the speech—front lawns—or the manner of the speech—signs. The township has not prohibited all lawn signs—or all lawn signs of a particular size or shape—in order to promote aesthetic values or any other value 'unrelated to the suppression of free expression,' United States v. O'Brien, 391 U.S. 367, 377 (1968). . . . Rather, Willingboro has proscribed particular types of signs based on their content because it fears their 'primary' effect—that they will cause those receiving the information to act upon it. That the proscription applies only to one mode of communication, therefore, does not transform this into a 'time, place, or manner' case. If the ordinance is to be sustained, it must be on the basis of the township's interest in regulating the content of the communication, and not on any interest in regulating the form.

. . .

"The record here demonstrates that respondents failed to establish that this ordinance is needed to assure that Willingboro remains an integrated community. . . .

"The constitutional defect in this ordinance, however, is far more basic. The Township Council here, like the Virginia Assembly in *Virginia Pharmacy Bd.,* acted to prevent its residents from obtaining certain information. That information, which pertains to sales activity in Willingboro, is of vital interest to Willingboro residents, since it may bear on one of the most important decisions they have a right to make: where to live and raise their families. The Council has sought to restrict the free flow of this data because it fears that otherwise, homeowners will make decisions inimical to what the Council views as the homeowners' self-interest and the corporate interest of the township: they will choose to leave town. The Council's concern, then, was not with any commercial aspect of 'For Sale' signs—with offerors communicating offers to offerees—but with the substance of the information communicated to Willingboro citizens. If dissemination of this information can be restricted, then every locality in the country can suppress any facts that reflect poorly on the locality, so long as a plausible claim can be made that disclosure would cause the recipients of the information to act 'irrationally.' . . ."

FRIEDMAN v. ROGERS, 440 U.S. 1 (1979). The Court upheld Texas' law prohibiting the practice of optometry under a trade name. Justice Powell's opinion for the Court conceded that a trade name may serve to convey information about the type, price and quality of optical services rendered. Since, however, Texas had experience with deceptive and misleading uses of optometrical trade names, and any information conveyed by the trade name could be conveyed by factual advertising directed to the kind and prices of services, there was no violation of the First Amendment.

"An optometrist may advertise the type of service he offers, the prices he charges, and whether he practices as a partner, associate, or employee with other optometrists. Rather than stifling commercial speech, § 5.13(d) ensures that information regarding optometrical services will be communicated more fully and accurately to consumers than it had been in the past when optometrists were allowed to convey the information through unstated and ambiguous associations with a trade name. In sum, Texas has done no more than require that commercial information about optometrical services 'appear in such a form . . . as [is] necessary to prevent its being deceptive.' "

Justice Blackmun, joined by Justice Marshall, in dissent, argued that the Court's decision sustained a law that prohibited "wholly truthful speech."

"The Court suggests that a State may prohibit 'misleading commercial speech' even though it is 'offset' by the publication of clarifying information. Corrected falsehood, however, is truth, and, absent some other regulatory justification, a State may not prohibit the dissemination of truthful commercial information. By disclosing his individual name along with his trade name, the commercial optometrist acts in the spirit of our First Amendment jurisprudence, where traditionally 'the remedy to be applied is more speech, not enforced silence.' "

––––––––

OVERBREADTH AND COMMERCIAL SPEECH

Justice Blackmun, for the Court, in Bates v. State Bar of Arizona, 433 U.S. 350, 379–381 (1977):

"In the usual case involving a restraint on speech, a showing that the challenged rule served unconstitutionally to suppress speech would end our analysis. In the First Amendment context, the Court has permitted attacks on overly broad statutes without requiring that the person making the attack demonstrate that in fact his specific conduct was protected. . . . Having shown that the disciplinary rule interferes with protected speech, appellants ordinarily could expect to benefit regardless of the nature of their acts.

"The First Amendment overbreadth doctrine, however, represents a departure from the traditional rule that a person may not challenge a statute on the ground that it might be applied unconstitutionally in circumstances other than those before the court. The reason for the special rule in First Amendment cases is apparent: an overbroad statute might serve to chill protected speech. First Amendment interests are fragile interests, and a person who contemplates protected activity might be discouraged by the *in terrorem* effect of the statute. Indeed, such a person might choose not to speak because of uncertainty whether his claim of privilege would prevail if challenged. The use of overbreadth analysis reflects the conclusion that the possible harm to society from allowing unprotected speech to go unpunished is outweighed by the possibility that protected speech will be muted.

"But the justification for the application of overbreadth analysis applies weakly, if at all, in the ordinary commercial context. As was acknowledged in Virginia Pharmacy Board v. Virginia Consumer Council, 425 U.S., at 771 n.

24, there are 'commonsense differences' between commercial speech and other varieties. Since advertising is linked to commercial well-being, it seems unlikely that such speech is particularly susceptible to being crushed by overbroad regulation. Moreover, concerns for uncertainty in determining the scope of protection are reduced; the advertiser seeks to disseminate information about a product or service that he provides, and presumably he can determine more readily than others whether his speech is truthful and protected. Ibid. Since overbreadth has been described by this Court as 'strong medicine,' which 'has been employed . . . sparingly and only as a last resort,' Broadrick v. Oklahoma, 413 U.S., at 613, we decline to apply it to professional advertising, a context where it is not necessary to further its intended objective.''

CENTRAL HUDSON GAS & ELECTRIC CORP. v. PUBLIC SERVICE COMMISSION

447 U.S. 557, 100 S.Ct. 2343, 65 L.Ed.2d 341 (1980).

Mr. Justice Powell delivered the opinion of the Court.

This case presents the question whether a regulation of the Public Service Commission of the State of New York violates the First and Fourteenth Amendments because it completely bans promotional advertising by an electrical utility.

I.

In December 1973, the Commission, appellee here, ordered electric utilities in New York State to cease all advertising that "promot[es] the use of electricity." The order was based on the Commission's finding that "the interconnected utility system in New York State does not have sufficient fuel stocks or sources of supply to continue furnishing all customer demands for the 1973–1974 winter."

Three years later, when the fuel shortage had eased, the Commission requested comments from the public on its proposal to continue the ban on promotional advertising. Central Hudson Gas & Electric Corporation, the appellant in this case, opposed the ban on First Amendment grounds. After reviewing the public comments, the Commission extended the prohibition in a Policy Statement issued on February 25, 1977.

The Policy Statement divided advertising expenses "into two broad categories: promotional—advertising intended to stimulate the purchase of utility services—and institutional and informational, a broad category inclusive of all advertising not clearly intended to promote sales." The Commission declared all promotional advertising contrary to the national policy of conserving energy. It acknowledged that the ban is not a perfect vehicle for conserving energy. For example, the Commission's order prohibits promotional advertising to develop consumption during periods when demand for electricity is low. By limiting growth in "off-peak" consumption, the ban limits the "beneficial side effects" of such growth in terms of more efficient use of existing power plants. And since oil dealers are not under the Commission's jurisdiction and thus remain free to advertise, it was recognized that the ban can achieve only "piecemeal conservationism." Still, the Commission adopted the restriction because it was deemed likely to "result in some dampening of unnecessary growth" in energy consumption.

The Commission's order explicitly permitted "informational" advertising designed to encourage "*shifts* of consumption" from peak demand times to periods of low electricity demand. Informational advertising would not seek to increase aggregate consumption, but would invite a leveling of demand throughout any given 24-hour period. The agency offered to review "specific proposals by the companies for specifically described [advertising] programs that meet these criteria."

. . .

Appellant challenged the order in state court, arguing that the Commission had restrained commercial speech in violation of the First and Fourteenth Amendments. The Commission's order was upheld by the trial court and at the intermediate appellate level. The New York Court of Appeals affirmed. . . . We noted probable jurisdiction, 444 U.S. 962 (1979), and now reverse.

II.

The Commission's order restricts only commercial speech, that is, expression related solely to the economic interests of the speaker and its audience. . . . In applying the First Amendment to this area, we have rejected the "highly paternalistic" view that government has complete power to suppress or regulate commercial speech. . . .

Nevertheless, our decisions have recognized "the 'commonsense' distinction between speech proposing a commercial transaction, which occurs in an area traditionally subject to government regulation and other varieties of speech." Ohralik v. Ohio State Bar Assn., 436 U.S. 447, 455–456 (1978); See Bates v. State Bar of Arizona, supra, at 381; see also Jackson & Jeffries, Commercial Speech: Economic Due Process and the First Amendment, 65 Va.L.Rev. 1, 38–39 (1979).[5] The Constitution therefore accords a lesser protection to commercial speech than to other constitutionally guaranteed expression. The protection available for particular commercial expression turns on the nature both of the expression and of the governmental interests served by its regulation.

. . .

If the communication is neither misleading nor related to unlawful activity, the government's power is more circumscribed. The State must assert a substantial interest to be achieved by restrictions on commercial speech. Moreover, the regulatory technique must be in proportion to that interest. The limitation on expression must be designed carefully to achieve the State's goal. Compliance with this requirement may be measured by two criteria. First, the restriction must directly advance the state interest involved; the regulation may not be sustained if it provides only ineffective or remote support for the

[5] In an opinion concurring in the judgment, Mr. Justice Stevens suggests that the Commission's order reaches beyond commercial speech to suppress expression that is entitled to the full protection of the First Amendment. We find no support for this claim in the record of this case. The Commission's Policy Statement excluded "institutional and informational" messages from the advertising ban, which was restricted to all advertising "clearly intended to promote sales." . . . Nevertheless, the concurring opinion of Mr. Justice Stevens views the Commission's order as suppressing more than commercial speech because it would outlaw, for example, advertising that promoted electricity consumption by touting the environmental benefits of such uses. Apparently the concurring opinion would accord full First Amendment protection to all promotional advertising that includes claims "relating to . . . questions frequently discussed and debated by our political leaders."

Although this approach responds to the serious issues surrounding our national energy policy as raised in this case, we think it would blur further the line the Court has sought to draw in commercial speech cases. It would grant broad constitutional protection to any advertising that links a product to a current public debate. But many, if not most, products may be tied to public concerns with the environment, energy, economic policy, or individual health and safety. We rule today in Consolidated Edison Co. v. Public Service Comm'n of New York, supra, that utilities enjoy the full panoply of First Amendment protections for their direct comments on public issues. There is no reason for providing similar constitutional protection when such statements are made only in the context of commercial transactions. . . .

government's purpose. Second, if the governmental interest could be served as well by a more limited restriction on commercial speech, the excessive restrictions cannot survive. . . .[8]

. . .

In commercial speech cases, then, a four-part analysis has developed. At the outset, we must determine whether the expression is protected by the First Amendment. For commercial speech to come within that provision, it at least must concern lawful activity and not be misleading. Next, we ask whether the asserted governmental interest is substantial. If both inquiries yield positive answers, we must determine whether the regulation directly advances the governmental interest asserted, and whether it is not more extensive than is necessary to serve that interest.

III.

We now apply this four-step analysis for commercial speech to the Commission's arguments in support of its ban on promotional advertising.

A.

The Commission does not claim that the expression at issue either is inaccurate or relates to unlawful activity. Yet the New York Court of Appeals questioned whether Central Hudson's advertising is protected commercial speech. Because appellant holds a monopoly over the sale of electricity in its service area, the state court suggested that the Commission's order restricts no commercial speech of any worth. The court stated that advertising in a "noncompetitive market" could not improve the decisionmaking of consumers. 47 N.Y.2d, at 110; 390 N.E.2d, at 757. The court saw no constitutional problem with barring commercial speech that it viewed as conveying little useful information.

This reasoning falls short of establishing that appellant's advertising is not commercial speech protected by the First Amendment. Monopoly over the supply of a product provides no protection from competition with substitutes for that product. Electric utilities compete with suppliers of fuel oil and natural gas in several markets, such as those for home heating and industrial power. . . .

B.

. . . The Commission argues, and the New York court agreed, that the State's interest in conserving energy is sufficient to support suppression of advertising designed to increase consumption of electricity. In view of our country's dependence on energy resources beyond our control, no one can doubt the importance of energy conservation. Plainly, therefore, the state interest asserted is substantial.

. . .

C.

Next, we focus on the relationship between the State's interests and the advertising ban. . . . There is an immediate connection between advertising and demand for electricity. Central Hudson would not contest the advertising ban unless it believed that promotion would increase its sales. Thus, we find a direct link between the state interest in conservation and the Commission's order.

---

[8] This analysis is not an application of the "overbreadth" doctrine. . . .

In this case, the Commission's prohibition acts directly against the promotional activities of Central Hudson, and to the extent the limitations are unnecessary to serve the State's interest, they are invalid.

D.

We come finally to the critical inquiry in this case: whether the Commission's complete suppression of speech ordinarily protected by the First Amendment is no more extensive than necessary to further the State's interest in energy conservation. The Commission's order reaches all promotional advertising, regardless of the impact of the touted service on overall energy use. But the energy conservation rationale, as important as it is, cannot justify suppressing information about electric devices or services that would cause no net increase in total energy use. In addition, no showing has been made that a more limited restriction on the content of promotional advertising would not serve adequately the State's interests.

Appellant insists that but for the ban, it would advertise products and services that use energy efficiently. These include the "heat pump," which both parties acknowledge to be a major improvement in electric heating, and the use of electric heat as a "back-up" to solar and other heat sources. Although the Commission has questioned the efficiency of electric heating before this Court, neither the Commission's Policy Statement nor its order denying rehearing made findings on this issue. In the absence of authoritative findings to the contrary, we must credit as within the realm of possibility the claim that electric heat can be an efficient alternative in some circumstances.

The Commission's order prevents appellant from promoting electric services that would reduce energy use by diverting demand from less efficient sources, or that would consume roughly the same amount of energy as do alternative sources. In neither situation would the utility's advertising endanger conservation or mislead the public. To the extent that the Commission's order suppresses speech that in no way impairs the State's interest in energy conservation, the Commission's order violates the First and Fourteenth Amendments and must be invalidated. See First National Bank of Boston v. Bellotti, supra.

The Commission also has not demonstrated that its interest in conservation cannot be protected adequately by more limited regulation of appellant's commercial expression. To further its policy of conservation, the Commission could attempt to restrict the format and content of Central Hudson's advertising. It might, for example, require that the advertisements include information about the relative efficiency and expense of the offered service, both under current conditions and for the foreseeable future. . . . In the absence of a showing that more limited speech regulation would be ineffective, we cannot approve the complete suppression of Central Hudson's advertising.

IV.

Our decision today in no way disparages the national interest in energy conservation. We accept without reservation the argument that conservation, as well as the development of alternate energy sources, is an imperative national goal. Administrative bodies empowered to regulate electric utilities have the authority—and indeed the duty—to take appropriate action to further this goal. When, however, such action involves the suppression of speech, the First and Fourteenth Amendments require that the restriction be no more extensive than is necessary to serve the state interest. In this case, the record before us fails to show that the total ban on promotional advertising meets this requirement.

Accordingly, the judgment of the New York Court of Appeals is reversed.

.   .   .

Mr. Justice Blackmun with whom Mr. Justice Brennan joins, concurring.

I agree with the Court that the Public Service Commission's ban on promotional advertising of electricity by public utilities is inconsistent with the First and Fourteenth Amendments. I concur only in the Court's judgment, however, because I believe the test now evolved and applied by the Court is not consistent with our prior cases and does not provide adequate protection for truthful, nonmisleading, noncoercive speech.

. . .

The Court recognizes that we have never held that commercial speech may be suppressed in order to further the State's interest in discouraging purchases of the underlying product that is advertised. Permissible restraints on commercial speech have been limited to measures designed to protect consumers from fraudulent, misleading, or coercive sales techniques. Those designed to deprive consumers of information about products or services that are legally offered for sale consistently have been invalidated.

I seriously doubt whether suppression of information concerning the availability and price of a legally offered product is ever a permissible way for the State to "dampen" demand for or use of the product. Even though "commercial" speech is involved, such a regulatory measure strikes at the heart of the First Amendment. This is because it is a covert attempt by the State to manipulate the choices of its citizens, not by persuasion or direct regulation, but by depriving the public of the information needed to make a free choice.

. . . .

. . .

It appears that the Court would permit the State to ban all direct advertising of air conditioning, assuming that a more limited restriction on such advertising would not effectively deter the public from cooling its homes. In my view, our cases do not support this type of suppression. If a governmental unit believes that use or over-use of air conditioning is a serious problem, it must attack that problem directly, by prohibiting air conditioning or regulating thermostat levels. Just as the Commonwealth of Virginia may promote professionalism of pharmacists directly, so too New York may *not* promote energy conservation "by keeping the public in ignorance." *Virginia Pharmacy Board,* 425 U.S., at 770.

Mr. Justice Stevens, with whom Mr. Justice Brennan joins, concurring.

Because "commercial speech" is afforded less constitutional protection than other forms of speech, it is important that the commercial speech concept not be defined too broadly lest speech deserving of greater constitutional protection be inadvertently suppressed. The issue in this case is whether New York's prohibition on the promotion of the use of electricity through advertising is a ban on nothing but commercial speech.

In my judgment one of the two definitions the Court uses in addressing that issue is too broad and the other may be somewhat too narrow. The Court first describes commercial speech as "expression related solely to the economic interests of the speaker and its audience." Although it is not entirely clear whether this definition uses the subject matter of the speech or the motivation of the speaker as the limiting factor, it seems clear to me that it encompasses speech that is entitled to the maximum protection afforded by the First Amendment. Neither a labor leader's exhortation to strike, nor an economist's dissertation on the money supply, should receive any lesser protection because the subject matter concerns only the economic interests of the audience. Nor should the economic motivation of a speaker qualify his constitutional protection; even Shakespeare may have been motivated by the prospect of pecuniary reward. Thus, the Court's first definition of commercial speech is unquestionably too broad.

The Court's second definition refers to "speech proposing a commercial transaction." A salesman's solicitation, a broker's offer, and a manufacturer's publication of a price list or the terms of his standard warranty would unquestionably fit within this concept. Presumably, the definition is intended to encompass advertising that advises possible buyers of the availability of specific products at specific prices and describes the advantages of purchasing such items. Perhaps it also extends to other communications that do little more than make the name of a product or a service more familiar to the general public. Whatever the precise contours of the concept, and perhaps it is too early to enunciate an exact formulation, I am persuaded that it should not include the entire range of communication that is embraced within the term "promotional advertising."

This case involves a governmental regulation that completely bans promotional advertising by an electric utility. This ban encompasses a great deal more than mere proposals to engage in certain kinds of commercial transactions. It prohibits all advocacy of the immediate or future use of electricity. It curtails expression by an informed and interested group of persons of their point of view on questions relating to the production and consumption of electrical energy—questions frequently discussed and debated by our political leaders. For example, an electric company's advocacy of the use of electric heat for environmental reasons, as opposed to wood-burning stoves, would seem to fall squarely within New York's promotional advertising ban and also within the bounds of maximum First Amendment protection. The breadth of the ban thus exceeds the boundaries of the commercial speech concept, however that concept may be defined.

The justification for the regulation is nothing more than the expressed fear that the audience may find the utility's message persuasive. Without the aid of any coercion, deception, or misinformation, truthful communication may persuade some citizens to consume more electricity than they otherwise would. I assume that such a consequence would be undesirable and that government may therefore prohibit and punish the unnecessary or excessive use of electricity. But if the perceived harm associated with greater electrical usage is not sufficiently serious to justify direct regulation, surely it does not constitute the kind of clear and present danger that can justify the suppression of speech.

. . .

In sum I concur in the result because I do not consider this to be a "commercial speech" case. Accordingly, I see no need to decide whether the Court's four-part analysis, adequately protects commercial speech—as properly defined—in the face of a blanket ban of the sort involved in this case.

Mr. Justice Rehnquist, dissenting.

. . .

The Court's analysis in my view is wrong in several respects. Initially, I disagree with the Court's conclusion that the speech of a state-created monopoly, which is the subject of a comprehensive regulatory scheme, is entitled to protection under the First Amendment. I also think that the Court errs here in failing to recognize that the state law is most accurately viewed as an economic regulation and that the speech involved (if it falls within the scope of the First Amendment at all) occupies a significantly more subordinate position in the hierarchy of First Amendment values than the Court gives it today. Finally, the Court in reaching its decision improperly substitutes its own judgment for that of the State in deciding how a proper ban on promotional advertising should be drafted. With regard to this latter point, the Court adopts as its final part of a four-part test a "no more extensive than necessary" analysis that will unduly impair a state legislature's ability to adopt legislation reasonably designed to promote interests that have always been rightly thought to be of great importance to the State.

I.

. . . When the source of the speech is a state-created monopoly such as this, traditional First Amendment concerns, if they come into play at all, certainly do not justify the broad interventionist role adopted by the Court today. . . .

. . .

. . . I . . . think New York's ban on such advertising falls within the scope of permissible state regulation of an economic activity by an entity that could not exist in corporate form, say nothing of enjoy monopoly status, were it not for the laws of New York.

II.

. . .

The Court's decision today fails to give due deference to this subordinate position of commercial speech. The Court in so doing returns to the bygone era of Lochner v. New York, 198 U.S. 45 (1905), in which it was common practice for this Court to strike down economic regulations adopted by a State based on the Court's own notions of the most appropriate means for the State to implement its considered policies.

. . . New York's order here is in my view more akin to an economic regulation to which virtually complete deference should be accorded by this Court.

I doubt there would be any question as to the constitutionality of New York's conservation effort if the Public Service Commission had chosen to raise the price of electricity, . . . to condition its sale on specified terms, . . . or to restrict its production, ... In terms of constitutional values, I think that such controls are virtually indistinguishable from the State's ban on promotional advertising.

An ostensible justification for striking down New York's ban on promotional advertising is that this Court "has previously rejected the 'highly paternalistic' view that government has complete power to suppress or regulate commercial speech. . . ." . . . .

The view apparently derives from the Court's frequent reference to the "marketplace of ideas," which was deemed analogous to the commercial market in which a *laissez faire* policy would lead to optimum economic decisionmaking under the guidance of the "invisible hand." See, e.g., Adam Smith, Wealth of Nations (1909). . . .

While it is true that an important objective of the First Amendment is to foster the free flow of information, identification of speech that falls within its protection is not aided by the methaphorical reference to a "marketplace of ideas." There is no reason for believing that the marketplace of ideas is free from market imperfections any more than there is to believe that the invisible hand will always lead to optimum economic decisions in the commercial market.

. . . I [do not] think there is any basis for concluding that individual citizens of the State will recognize the need for and act to promote energy conservation to the extent the government deems appropriate, if only the channels of communication are left open. Thus, even if I were to agree that commercial speech is entitled to some First Amendment protection, I would hold here that the State's decision to ban promotional advertising, in light of the substantial state interest at stake, is a constitutionally permissible exercise of its power to adopt regulations designed to promote the interests of its citizens.

. . .

III.

.   .   .

It is in my view inappropriate for the Court to invalidate the State's ban on commercial advertising here based on its speculation that in some cases the advertising may result in a net savings in electrical energy use, and in the cases in which it is clear a net energy savings would result from utility advertising the Public Service Commission would apply its ban so as to proscribe such advertising. Even assuming that the Court's speculation is correct, I do not think it follows that facial invalidation of the ban is the appropriate course. .   .   .

For the foregoing reasons, I would affirm the judgment of the New York Court of Appeals.

THE DEFINITION OF COMMERCIAL SPEECH

In Bolger v. Young's Drug Products, 463 U.S. 60 (1983), a manufacturer of prophylactics mailed "informational pamphlets" discussing the desirability and availability of prophylactics in general and the manufacturer's products in particular. The Court rejected an argument that the information pamphlets were not commercial speech because they linked a product to a public debate. (The Court, however, invalidated 39 U.S.C. § 3001(e)(2), which prohibits mailing of unsolicited contraceptive advertisements.)

Given the Court's concession in *Central Hudson* that commercial speech is afforded less protection, problems of definition can be important (as they were not in *Bolger*). Concurring in Metromedia, Inc. v. San Diego, 453 U.S. 490 (1981), Justice Brennan raised doubts that it is easy to determine whether a merchant's message "proposes a commercial transaction," particularly if a regulatory structure requires government officials, rather than courts, to draw the line in the first instance. As one example, he asked whether a city that banned "commercial" billboards could "decide that a United Automobile Workers billboard with the message 'Be a Patriot—do not buy Japanese-manufactured cars' is 'commercial' and therefore forbid it? What if the same sign is placed by Chrysler?"

Justice Powell's opinion in *Central Hudson* also defines commercial speech as that "related solely to the economic interests of the speaker and its audience." Is that the same as "speech proposing a commercial transaction"? Shiffrin, *The First Amendment and Economic Regulation: Away from a General Theory of the First Amendment*, 78 Northwestern L.Rev. 1212 (1983), criticizes both definitions. He concludes that the diversity of speech that is wholly or partly commercial requires a complex, eclectic approach to a multiplicity of problems. See, also, Barrett, *"The Uncharted Area"—Commercial Speech and the First Amendment*, 13 U.C. Davis L.Rev. 175 (1980).

Chapter 15

RESTRICTIONS ON TIME, PLACE, OR MANNER
OF EXPRESSION

Introduction. The title of this chapter signals an obvious shift in emphasis from controlling expression because of its content to restricting the time, place, or manner of expression. It is, however, a shift rather than a break in the analysis of freedom of speech. Time, place, or manner issues were prominent in some of the cases in the preceding chapter. Issues of speech content are often central to time, place, or manner restrictions. A repetitive question is whether any consistent principle can be formulated where government restrictions of expression blend considerations of time, place, or manner with considerations of content.

A new theme often presented in this chapter concerns the relevance of the distinction between public and private decision-making. The cases in the previous chapter presented clear clashes between claims of private, individual autonomy and attempted governmental prohibition. In some of the cases in this chapter the problem may be to define government and private decision-making—a variant of the "state action" problem previously discussed in Chapter 13. In many cases, the relationship between private and public decision-making becomes sufficiently complex that free speech principles based on a simple model of individual autonomy and government neutrality break down.

Section 1 of this chapter begins the examination of time, place, and manner rules with consideration of government policies that permit some speakers, but not others, to deliver their message at a particular time and place. Section 2 deals with regulation of the use of parks and streets for purposes of communication. Section 3 examines free speech rights on other public property, including, in subsection B, forums maintained by government primarily for expressive activities. Section 4 is concerned with restrictions on speech occurring on private property. Section 5 briefly deals with the special problem of restricting labor picketing.

SECTION 1. DISCRIMINATORY REGULATIONS

CAREY v. BROWN

447 U.S. 455, 100 S.Ct. 2286, 65 L.Ed.2d 263 (1980).

Mr. Justice Brennan delivered the opinion of the Court.

At issue in this case is the constitutionality under the First and Fourteenth Amendments of a state statute that bars all picketing of residences or dwellings, but exempts from its prohibition "the peaceful picketing of a place of employment involved in a labor dispute."

I.

On September 7, 1977, several of the appellees, all of whom are members of a civil rights organization entitled the Committee Against Racism, participated in a peaceful demonstration on the public sidewalk in front of the home of Michael Bilandic, then Mayor of Chicago, protesting his alleged failure to support the busing of school children to achieve racial integration. They were arrested and charged with Unlawful Residential Picketing in violation of Ill.Rev.Stat., ch. 38, § 21.1–2, which provides:

> "It is unlawful to picket before or about the residence or dwelling of any person, except when the residence or dwelling is used as a place of business. However, this Article does not apply to a person peacefully picketing his own residence or dwelling and does not prohibit the peaceful picketing of a place of employment involved in a labor dispute or the place of holding a meeting or assembly on premises commonly used to discuss subjects of general public interest."

Appellees pleaded guilty to the charge and were sentenced to periods of supervision ranging from 6 months to a year.

In April 1978, appellees commenced this lawsuit in the United States District Court for the Northern District of Illinois, seeking a declaratory judgment that the Illinois Residential Picketing Statute is unconstitutional on its face and as applied, and an injunction prohibiting appellants—various state, county, and city officials—from enforcing the statute. . . . The District Court, ruling on cross-motions for summary judgment, denied all relief. . . .

The Court of Appeals for the Seventh Circuit reversed. . . . Discerning "no principled basis" for distinguishing the Illinois statute from a similar picketing prohibition invalidated in Police Department of Chicago v. Mosley, 408 U.S. 92 (1972), the court . . . held that the statute, both on its face and as applied to appellees, violated the Equal Protection Clause of the Fourteenth Amendment. . . . We affirm.

II.

As the Court of Appeals observed, this is not the first instance in which this Court has had occasion to consider the constitutionality of an enactment selectively proscribing peaceful picketing on the basis of the placard's message. Police Department of Chicago v. Mosley, supra, arose out of a challenge to a Chicago ordinance that prohibited picketing in front of any school other than one "involved in a labor dispute." We held that the ordinance violated the Equal Protection Clause because it impermissibly distinguished between labor picketing and all other peaceful picketing without any showing that the latter was "clearly more disruptive" than the former. 408 U.S., at 100. Like the Court of Appeals, we find the Illinois Residential Picketing Statute at issue in the present case constitutionally indistinguishable from the ordinance invalidated in *Mosley.*

There can be no doubt that in prohibiting peaceful picketing on the public streets and sidewalks in residential neighborhoods, the Illinois statute regulates expressive conduct that falls within the First Amendment's preserve. . . . "Wherever the title of streets and parks may rest, they have immemorially been held in trust for the use of the public and, time out of mind, have been used for purposes of assembly, communicating thoughts between citizens, and discussing public questions." Hague v. CIO, 307 U.S. 496, 515 (1939) (opinion of Roberts, J.). "[S]treets, sidewalks, parks, and other similar public places are so historically associated with the exercise of First Amendment rights that access to them for the purpose of exercising such rights cannot constitutionally be denied broadly and absolutely." Hudgens v. NLRB, 424 U.S. 507, 515 (1976) (quoting Amalgamated Food Employees Union v. Logan Valley Plaza, 391 U.S. 308, 315 (1968)).

Nor can it be seriously disputed that in exempting from its general prohibition only the "peaceful picketing of a place of employment involved in a labor dispute," the Illinois statute discriminates between lawful and unlawful conduct based upon the content of the demonstrator's communication. On its face, the act accords preferential treatment to the expression of views on one particular subject; information about labor disputes may be freely disseminated, but discussion of all other issues is restricted. The permissibility of residential picketing under the Illinois statute is thus dependent solely on the nature of the message being conveyed.

In these critical respects, then, the Illinois statute is identical to the ordinance in *Mosley,* and it suffers from the same constitutional infirmities. When government regulation discriminates among speech-related activities in a public forum, the Equal Protection Clause mandates that the legislation be finely tailored to serve substantial state interests, and the justifications offered for any distinctions it draws must be carefully scrutinized. . . . As we explained in *Mosley,* "Chicago may not vindicate its interest in preventing disruption by the wholesale exclusion of picketing on all but one preferred subject. Given what Chicago tolerates from labor picketing, the excesses of some nonlabor picketing may not be controlled by a broad ordinance prohibiting both peaceful and violent picketing. Such excesses 'can be controlled by narrowly drawn statutes,' *Saia v. New York,* 334 U.S. at 562, focusing on the abuses and dealing evenhandedly with picketing regardless of subject matter." 408 U.S., at 101–102. Yet here, under the guise of preserving residential privacy, Illinois has flatly prohibited all nonlabor picketing even though it permits labor picketing that is equally likely to intrude on the tranquility of the home.

Moreover, it is the content of the speech that determines whether it is within or without the statute's blunt prohibition. What we said in *Mosley* has equal force in the present case:

"The central problem with Chicago's ordinance is that it describes permissible picketing in terms of its subject matter. . . .

"Necessarily, . . . under the Equal Protection Clause, not to mention the First Amendment itself, government may not grant the use of a forum to people whose views it finds acceptable, but deny use to those wishing to express less favored or more controversial views. And it may not select which issues are worth discussing or debating in public facilities. There is an 'equality of status in the field of ideas,' and government must afford all points of view an equal opportunity to be heard. Once a forum is opened up to assembly or speaking by some groups, government may not prohibit others from assembling or speaking on the basis of what they intend to say. Selective exclusions from a public forum may not be based on content alone, and may not be justified by reference to content alone." 408 U.S., at 95–96.

III.

Appellants nonetheless contend that this case is distinguishable from *Mosley.* They argue that the state interests here are especially compelling and particularly well-served by a statute that accords differential treatment to labor and nonlabor picketing. We explore in turn each of these interests, and the manner in which they are said to be furthered by this statute.

A.

Appellants explain that whereas the Chicago ordinance sought to prevent disruption of the schools, concededly a "substantial" and "legitimate" governmental concern, see id., at 99, 100, the Illinois statute was enacted to ensure privacy in the home, a right which appellants view as paramount in our constitutional scheme. For this reason, they contend that the same content-based distinctions held invalid in the *Mosley* context may be upheld in the present case.

We find it unnecessary, however, to consider whether the state's interest in residential privacy outranks its interest in quiet schools in the hierarchy of societal values. For even the most legitimate goal may not be advanced in a constitutionally impermissible manner. And though we might agree that certain state interests may be so compelling that where no adequate alternatives exist a content-based distinction—if narrowly drawn—would be a permissible way of furthering those objectives, this is not such a case.

First, the generalized classification which the statute draws suggests that Illinois itself has determined that residential privacy is not a transcendent objective: While broadly permitting all peaceful labor picketing notwithstanding the disturbances it would undoubtedly engender, the statute makes no attempt to distinguish among various sorts of nonlabor picketing on the basis of the harms they would inflict on the privacy interest. The apparent over- and underinclusiveness of the statute's restriction would seem largely to undermine appellants' claim that the prohibition of all nonlabor picketing can be justified by reference to the state's interest in maintaining domestic tranquility.

More fundamentally, the exclusion for labor picketing cannot be upheld as a means of protecting residential privacy for the simple reason that nothing in the content-based labor-nonlabor distinction has any bearing whatsoever on privacy. Appellants can point to nothing inherent in the nature of peaceful labor picketing that would make it any less disruptive of residential privacy than peaceful picketing on issues of broader social concern. Standing alone, then, the state's asserted interest in promoting the privacy of the home is not sufficient to save the statute.

B.

The second important objective advanced by appellants in support of the statute is the State's interest in providing special protection for labor protests. They maintain that federal and state law has long exhibited an unusual concern for such activities, and they contend that this solicitude may be furthered by a narrowly drawn exemption for labor picketing.

The central difficulty with this argument is that it forthrightly presupposes that labor picketing is more deserving of First Amendment protection than are public protests over other issues, particularly the important economic, social, and political subjects about which these appellees wish to demonstrate. We reject that proposition. Cf. T. Emerson, The System of Freedom of Expression 444–449 (suggesting that nonlabor picketing is more akin to pure expression than labor picketing and thus should be subject to fewer restrictions). . . . While the State's motivation in protecting the First Amendment rights of employees involved in labor disputes is commendable, that factor, without more, cannot justify the labor picketing exemption.

C.

Appellants' final contention is that the statute can be justified by some combination of the preceding objectives. This argument is fashioned on two different levels. In its elemental formulation, it posits simply that a distinction between labor and nonlabor picketing is uniquely suited to furthering the legislative judgment that residential privacy should be preserved to the greatest extent possible without also compromising the special protection owing to labor picketing. In short, the statute is viewed as a reasonable attempt to accommodate the competing rights of the homeowner to enjoy his privacy and the employee to demonstrate over labor disputes. But this attempt to justify the statute hinges on the validity of both of these goals, and we have already concluded that the latter—the desire to favor one form of speech over all others—is illegitimate.

The second and more complex formulation of appellants' position characterizes the statute as a carefully drafted attempt to prohibit that picketing which would impinge on residential privacy while permitting that picketing which would not. In essence, appellants assert that the exception for labor picketing does not contravene the State's interest in preserving residential tranquility because of the unique character of a residence that is a "place of employment." By "inviting" a worker into his home and converting that dwelling into a place of employment, the argument goes, the resident has diluted his entitlement to total privacy. In other words, he has "waived" his right to be free from picketing with respect to disputes arising out of the employment relationship, thereby justifying the statute's narrow labor exception at those locations.

The flaw in this argument is that it proves too little. Numerous types of peaceful picketing other than labor picketing would have but a negligible impact on privacy interests, and numerous other actions of a homeowner might constitute "nonresidential" uses of his property and would thus serve to vitiate the right to residential privacy. For example, the resident who prominently decorates his windows and front yard with posters promoting the qualifications of one candidate for political office might be said to "invite" a counter-demonstration from supporters of an opposing candidate. Similarly, a county chairman who uses his home to meet with his district captains and to discuss some controversial issue might well expect that those who are deeply concerned about the decision the chairman will ultimately reach would want to make their views known by demonstrating outside his home during the meeting. And, with particular regard to the facts of the instant case, it borders on the frivolous to suggest that a resident who invites a repairman into his home to fix his television set has "waived" his right to privacy with respect to a dispute between the repairman and the local union, but that the official who has voluntarily chosen to enter the public arena has not likewise "waived" his right to privacy with respect to a challenge to his views on significant issues of social and economic policy.

IV.

We therefore conclude that appellants have not successfully distinguished *Mosley.* We are not to be understood to imply, however, that residential picketing is beyond the reach of uniform and nondiscriminatory regulation. . . .

. . .

The judgment of the Court of Appeals is

Affirmed.

Mr. Justice Stewart, concurring.

The opinion of the Court in this case, as did the Court's opinion in Police Department of Chicago v. Mosley, 408 U.S. 92, invokes the Equal Protection Clause of the Fourteenth Amendment as the basis of decision. But what was actually at stake in *Mosley,* and is at stake here, is the basic meaning of the constitutional protection of free speech: . . .

It is upon this understanding that I join the opinion and judgment of the Court.

Mr. Justice Rehnquist, with whom The Chief Justice and Mr. Justice Blackmun join, dissenting.

. . . One who reads the opinion of the Court is probably left with the impression that Illinois has enacted a residential picketing statute which reads: "All residential picketing, except for labor picketing, is prohibited." . . . The complete language of the statute, set out accurately in the text of the

Court's opinion, reveals a legislative scheme quite different from that described by the Court in its narrative paraphrasing of the enactment.

The statute provides that residential picketing is prohibited, but goes on to exempt four categories of residences from this general ban. *First,* if the residence is used as a "place of business" *all* peaceful picketing is allowed. *Second,* if the residence is being used to "hold[ ] a meeting or assembly on premises commonly used to discuss subjects of general public interest" *all* peaceful picketing is allowed. *Third,* if the residence is also used as a "place of employment" which is involved in a labor dispute, labor-related picketing is allowed. *Finally,* the statute provides that a resident is entitled to picket his own home. Thus it is clear that information about labor disputes may *not* be "freely disseminated" since labor picketing is restricted to a narrow category of residences. And Illinois has *not* "flatly prohibited all nonlabor picketing" since it allows nonlabor picketing at residences used as a place of business, residences used as public meeting places, and at an individual's own residence.

. . . [T]he principal determinant of a person's right to picket a residence in Illinois is not content, as the Court suggests, but rather the character of the residence sought to be picketed. Content is relevant only in one of the categories established by the legislature.

The cases appropriate to the analysis therefore are those establishing the limits on a State's authority to impose time, place, and manner restrictions on speech activities. Under this rubric, even taking into account the limited content distinction made by the statute, Illinois has readily satisfied its constitutional obligation to draft statutes in conformity with First Amendment and equal protection principles. In fact the very statute which the Court today cavalierly invalidates has been hailed by commentators as "an excellent model" of legislation achieving a delicate balance among rights to privacy, free expression, and equal protection. See Kamin, Residential Picketing and the First Amendment, 61 Nw.U.L.Rev. 177, 207 (1966); Comment, 34 U.Chi.L.Rev. 106, 139 (1966). . . .

Here, where Illinois has drafted such a statute, avoiding an outright ban on all residential picketing, avoiding reliance on any vague or discretionary standards, and permitting categories of permissible picketing activity at residences where the State has determined the resident's own actions have substantially reduced his interest in privacy, the Court in response confronts the State with the Catch-22 that the less-restrictive categories are constitutionally infirm under principles of equal protection. Under the Court's approach today, the State would fare better by adopting *more* restrictive means, a judicial incentive I had thought this Court would hesitate to afford. Either that, or uniform restrictions will be found invalid under the First Amendment and categorical exceptions found invalid under the Equal Protection Clause, with the result that speech and only speech will be entitled to protection. This can only mean that the hymns of praise in prior opinions celebrating carefully drawn statutes are no more than sympathetic clucking, and in fact the State is damned if it does and damned if it doesn't.

. . .

I.

The Illinois statute in issue simply does not contravene the First Amendment.

. . .

. . . It is arguable that when a resident has voluntarily used his home for nonresidential uses in a way which reduces the resident's privacy interest, and the person seeking to picket the home has no alternative forum for effectively airing the grievance because it relates to this nonresidential use of the home, some form of residential picketing might be protected under the First Amendment. The courts which have found general prohibitions on residential picketing to be permissible under the First Amendment have considered the question more difficult under such circumstances. For example, in Walinsky v. Kennedy, 94 Misc.2d 121 (1977), the New York court enjoined all residential picketing but concluded that,

> "A more difficult question would be raised if the [resident's] office were in his home and there was no other suitable forum wherein he could be confronted or the picket's viewpoints could be heard." Id., at 132, n. 15.
> . . .

I would by no means say without more that the State would have to permit such residential picketing, but such circumstances would, as the courts have found, present the greatest potential for a complaint of overbreadth. The State in the present case has forestalled any such challenge, however, by exempting such groups from the ban on residential picketing. Whether *required* by the Constitution or not, such exemptions are the concern of this Court only if they *violate* the Constitution. . . .

II.

Even though the statute does not prohibit conduct which is protected, the statute must also survive the hurdle of the Equal Protection Clause of the Fourteenth Amendment. By choosing a less restrictive means approach and excluding pickets at residences used for nonresidential purposes from the general prohibition, the Court concludes the State has violated equal protection. I do not think this result can be sustained because the appellees have not been denied equal protection . . . .

. . . .

Despite the state interest in treating residences which are used for nonresidential purposes differently from residences which are not, the Court finds that the categories are improper because there is an element of content regulation in the statutory scheme. While content is clearly not the principal focus of the statutory categories, since content is only relevant in the one subcategory of "places of employment," the content restriction is quite clearly related to a legitimate state purpose. When an individual hires an employee to perform services in his home, it would not seem reasonable to conclude that the resident had so greatly compromised his residential status so as to permit picketing on any subject. The State may quite properly decide that the balance is better struck by the rule embodied in this statute which recognizes a more limited waiver of privacy interests by allowing only picketing relating to any labor dispute involving the resident *as employer* which has arisen out of the resident's choice of using his residence as a place of employment.

. . . .

———

EQUAL PROTECTION OR FIRST AMENDMENT?

Restrictions on speech or association may pose arguable issues of equal protection in at least two situations: where the state imposes burdens on some speakers or associators that it does not impose on others; and where the state imposes burdens on speech or association not placed on other forms of activity. Does it matter whether those issues are resolved as issues of equal protection or issues of freedom of speech and association? Does the equal protection clause impose restrictions on government action burdening or prohibiting speech that would not also be imposed by the first amendment? More particularly, is Justice Rehnquist correct, in his Carey v. Brown dissent, when he argues that if Illinois could enact a flat ban on all residential picketing, there is no first amendment issue if Illinois prohibits picketing of some residences and not others?

For discussions of these issues from somewhat differing points of view see Westin, *The Empty Idea of Equality,* 95 Harv.L.Rev. 537, 560–563 (1982); Barrett, *Judicial Supervision of Legislative Classification—A More Modest Role for Equal Protection,* 1976 B.Y.U.L.Rev. 89, 109–111; Karst, *Equality as a Central Principle in the First Amendment,* 43 U.Chi.L.Rev. 20 (1975); Stone, *Fora Americana: Speech in Public Places,* 1974 Sup.Ct.Rev. 233, 272.

SECTION 2.   THE TRADITIONAL PUBLIC FORUM: SPEECH ACTIVITIES IN STREETS AND PARKS

A.   THE CONSIDERATIONS JUSTIFYING DENIAL OF THE USE OF STREETS AND PARKS FOR SPEECH ACTIVITIES

SCHNEIDER v. NEW JERSEY (TOWN OF IRVINGTON), 308 U.S. 147 (1939). The Court had before it three cases involving city ordinances forbidding the distribution of handbills in the streets (and in one case in any public place). The cases involved convictions of persons distributing handbills giving notice of meetings on public issues in two cases and as an incident to labor picketing in the third. As to the question whether cities could forbid all distribution of handbills on public streets, the Court held they could not. The Court reversed the convictions in these three cases. Justice Roberts, speaking for the Court, said, in part:

"Municipal authorities, as trustees for the public, have the duty to keep their communities' streets open and available for movement of people and property, the primary purpose to which the streets are dedicated. So long as legislation to this end does not abridge the constitutional liberty of one rightfully upon the street to impart information through speech or the distribution of literature, it may lawfully regulate the conduct of those using the streets. For example, a person could not exercise this liberty by taking his stand in the middle of a crowded street, contrary to traffic regulations, and maintain his position to the stoppage of all traffic; a group of distributors could not insist upon a constitutional right to form a cordon across the street and to allow no pedestrian to pass who did not accept a tendered leaflet; nor does the guarantee of freedom of speech or of the press deprive a municipality of power to enact regulations against throwing literature broadcast in the streets. Prohibition of such conduct would not abridge the constitutional liberty since such activity bears no necessary relationship to the freedom to speak, write, print or distribute information or opinion.

.   .   .   .

"The motive of the legislation under attack in Numbers 13, 18 and 29 is held by the courts below to be the prevention of littering of the streets and, although the alleged offenders were not charged with themselves scattering paper in the streets, their convictions were sustained upon the theory that distribution by them encouraged or resulted in such littering. We are of opinion that the purpose to keep the streets clean and of good appearance is insufficient to justify an ordinance which prohibits a person rightfully on a public street from handing literature to one willing to receive it. Any burden imposed upon the city authorities in cleaning and caring for the streets as an indirect consequence of such distribution results from the constitutional protection of the freedom of speech and press. This constitutional protection does not deprive a city of all power to prevent street littering. There are obvious methods of preventing littering. Amongst these is the punishment of those who actually throw papers on the streets."

MINIMUM ACCESS v. EQUAL ACCESS TO THE PUBLIC FORUM

There are two famous quotations expressing polar positions. While sitting on the Massachusetts Supreme Judicial Court, Justice Holmes observed: "For the Legislature absolutely or conditionally to forbid public speaking in a highway or public park is no more an infringement of the rights of a member of the public than for the owner of a private house to forbid it in his house." Massachusetts v. Davis, 162 Mass. 510, 511 (1895), affirmed 167 U.S. 43, 47–48 (1897). Justice Roberts' plurality opinion in Hague v. C.I.O., 307 U.S. 496, 515–516 (1939) contains this often quoted dictum: "Wherever the title of streets and parks may rest, they have immemorially been held in trust for the use of the public and time out of mind, have been used for purposes of assembly, communicating thoughts between citizens, and discussing public questions. Such use of the streets and public places has, from ancient times, been a part of the privileges, immunities, rights, and liberties of citizens."

No Supreme Court decision has confronted the constitutionality of a municipality's decision to reserve its streets entirely for traffic and its parks as facilities for quiet rest and relaxation. In that context, the issue may be more theoretical than real. The cases before the Court have either involved time, place, or manner restrictions that did not totally preclude use of parks and streets for expression, or restrictions that denied equal access to the public facilities involved. Does resolution of the debate whether all parks and streets could be closed to expression affect the results in those cases? Does Justice Roberts' opinion in *Schneider* implicitly rest on accepting his dictum in *Hague*?

For discussion of these issues see Kalven, *The Concept of the Public Forum: Cox v. Louisiana*, 1965 Sup.Ct.Rev. 1; Stone, *Fora Americana: Speech in Public Places*, 1974 Sup.Ct.Rev. 233; Note, *The Public Forum: Minimum Access, Equal Access and the First Amendment*, 28 Stan.L.Rev. 117 (1975).

KOVACS v. COOPER, 336 U.S. 77 (1949). The Court upheld a prohibition against the use of "any device known as a sound truck, loud speaker, or sound amplifier . . . which emits therefrom loud and raucous noises and is attached to and upon any vehicle operated or standing upon" public streets or other public places. There was no opinion of the Court. The plurality opinion of Justice Reed (joined by Chief Justice Vinson and Justice Burton) construed the ordinance as prohibiting only those sound trucks that emitted "loud and raucous noises." As so construed, they found it valid. Their opinion concluded as follows:

"City streets are recognized as a normal place for the exchange of ideas by speech or paper. But this does not mean the freedom is beyond all control. We think it is a permissible exercise of legislative discretion to bar sound trucks with broadcasts of public interest, amplified to a loud and raucous volume, from the public ways of municipalities. On the business streets of cities like Trenton, with its more than 125,000 people, such distractions would be dangerous to traffic at all hours useful for the dissemination of information, and in the residential thoroughfares the quiet and tranquility so desirable for city dwellers would likewise be at the mercy of advocates of particular religious, social or political persuasions. We cannot believe that rights of free speech compel a municipality to allow such mechanical voice amplification on any of its streets.

". . . That more people may be more easily and cheaply reached by sound trucks, perhaps borrowed without cost from some zealous supporter, is not enough to call forth constitutional protection for what those charged with public welfare reasonably think is a nuisance when easy means of publicity are open. Section 4 of the ordinance bars sound trucks from broadcasting in a loud and raucous manner on the streets. There is no restriction upon the communication of ideas or discussion of issues by the human voice, by newspapers, by pamphlets, by dodgers. We think that the need for reasonable protection in the homes or business houses from the distracting noises of vehicles equipped with such sound amplifying devices justifies the ordinance."

Justices Frankfurter and Jackson construed the ordinance as prohibiting all use of sound trucks and argued that even so construed it was valid. Justices Black, Douglas, Rutledge, and Murphy dissented.

COX v. LOUISIANA (Cox I), 379 U.S. 536 (1965). The leader of a group of civil rights demonstrators was convicted for violation of a statute providing: "No person shall wilfully obstruct the free, convenient and normal use of any public sidewalk, street, highway, bridge, alley, road, or other passageway . . . by impeding, hindering, stifling, retarding or restraining traffic or passage thereon or therein." The record made it clear that the demonstrators obstructed the sidewalk. The Court reversed the conviction because the evidence showed that the statute had been construed to permit certain meetings and parades that obstruct traffic on seeking prior approval from local authorities. For a fuller presentation of the underlying facts see the report of another aspect of the case, infra p. 1185. On the question of restricting parades and demonstrations to prevent obstructions of traffic, the Court said:

". . . The rights of free speech and assembly, while fundamental in our democratic society, still do not mean that everyone with opinions or beliefs to express may address a group at any public place and at any time. The constitutional guarantee of liberty implies the existence of an organized society maintaining public order, without which liberty itself would be lost in the excesses of anarchy. The control of travel on the streets is a clear example of governmental responsibility to insure this necessary order. A restriction in that relation, designed to promote the public convenience in the interest of all, and not susceptible to abuses of discriminatory application, cannot be disregarded by the attempted exercise of some civil right which, in other circumstances, would be entitled to protection. One would not be justified in ignoring the familiar red light because this was thought to be a means of social protest. Nor could one, contrary to traffic regulations, insist upon a street meeting in the middle of Times Square at the rush hour as a form of freedom of speech or assembly. Governmental authorities have the duty and responsibility to keep their streets open and available for movement. A group of demonstrators could not insist upon the right to cordon off a street, or entrance to a public or private building, and allow no one to pass who did not agree to listen to their exhortations.
. . . .

"We emphatically reject the notion urged by appellant that the First and Fourteenth Amendments afford the same kind of freedom to those who would communicate ideas by conduct such as patrolling, marching, and picketing on streets and highways, as these amendments afford to those who communicate ideas by pure speech. . . .

"We have no occasion in this case to consider the constitutionality of the uniform, consistent, and nondiscriminatory application of a statute forbidding all access to streets and other public facilities for parades and meetings. Although the statute here involved on its face precludes all street assemblies and parades, it has not been so applied and enforced by the Baton Rouge authorities. City officials who testified for the State clearly indicated that certain meetings and parades are permitted in Baton Rouge, even though they have the effect of obstructing traffic, provided prior approval is obtained. . . ."

COX v. LOUISIANA (Cox II), 379 U.S. 559 (1965). A group of students had been arrested for picketing stores maintaining segregated lunch counters. The next day about 2,000 students marched to the courthouse to demonstrate in protest of segregation and the arrest and imprisonment of the picketers who were being held in the jail located on the upper floor of the courthouse building. The leader of the students was charged and convicted of violation of the following statute: "Whoever, with the intent of interfering with, obstructing, or impeding the administration of justice, or with the intent of influencing any judge, juror, witness, or court officer, in the discharge of his duty pickets or parades in or near a building housing a court of the State of Louisiana . . . shall be fined not more than five thousand dollars or imprisoned not more than one year, or both."

While the Supreme Court reversed his conviction, it held the statute valid on its face, saying: "This statute . . . is a precise, narrowly drawn regulatory statute which proscribes certain specific behavior. . . . It prohibits a particular type of conduct, namely, picketing and parading, in a few specified locations, in or near courthouses.

"There can be no question that a State has a legitimate interest in protecting its judicial system from the pressures which picketing near a courthouse might create. . . . A narrowly drawn statute such as the one under review is obviously a safeguard both necessary and appropriate to vindicate the State's interest in assuring justice under law.

"Nor does such a statute infringe upon the constitutionally protected rights of free speech and free assembly. The conduct which is the subject of this statute—picketing and parading—is subject to regulation even though intertwined with expression and association . . . .

"We hold that this statute on its face is a valid law dealing with conduct subject to regulation so as to vindicate important interests of society and that the fact that free speech is intermingled with such conduct does not bring it within constitutional protection."

UNITED STATES v. GRACE, 461 U.S. 171 (1983). The Court held invalid 40 U.S.C. § 13k insofar as it prohibited *all* picketing, display of signs, or distribution of literature on the public sidewalks surrounding the United States Supreme Court. The sidewalks were indistinguishable from all others in Washington, D.C., and were thus a traditional public forum. The absolute ban was not "narrowly tailored to serve a significant government interest." The government argued that the ban eliminated the appearance to the public that the Court was subject to influence by parades, picketing, or pressure groups. The Court responded that it doubted that it was more likely that the public would draw that inference "from a lone picketer carrying a sign on the sidewalks around the building than it would from a similar picket on the sidewalks across the street."

GRAYNED v. ROCKFORD, 408 U.S. 104 (1972). The Court had before it a conviction for violation of an anti-noise ordinance resulting from a demonstration in front of a high school. The ordinance read as follows: "[N]o person, while on public or private grounds adjacent to any building in which a school or any class thereof is in session, shall willfully make or assist in the making of any noise or diversion which disturbs or tends to disturb the peace or good order of such school session or class thereof. . . ." The Court, in an opinion by Justice Marshall, upheld the validity of the ordinance.

"We recognize that the ordinance prohibits some picketing that is neither violent nor physically obstructive. Noisy demonstrations that disrupt or are incompatible with normal school activities are obviously within the ordinance's reach. Such expressive conduct may be constitutionally protected at other places or other times, . . . but next to a school, while classes are in session, it may be prohibited. The antinoise ordinance imposes no such restriction on expressive activity before or after the school session, while the student/faculty "audience" enters and leaves the school.

". . . Rockford's modest restriction on some peaceful picketing represents a considered and specific legislative judgment that some kinds of expressive activity should be restricted at a particular time and place, here in order to protect the schools. Such a reasonable regulation is not inconsistent with the First and Fourteenth Amendments. The antinoise ordinance is not invalid on its face."

PARADE AND DEMONSTRATION PERMIT SYSTEMS

Despite traditional prior restraint law, systems requiring official permission in advance for parades and demonstrations have been upheld. In Cox v. New Hampshire, 312 U.S. 569 (1941), the Court sustained a licensing system for parades on public streets, designed to prevent traffic congestion and overlapping parades at the same time and place, and to give authorities notice in advance to afford opportunity for proper policing. A parade or demonstration permit ordinance is unconstitutional, however, if it allows the administrative official standardless discretion to deny permission, or if it authorizes denial on the basis of impermissible standards.[1] In Shuttlesworth v. Birmingham, 394 U.S. 147 (1969), for example, a parade ordinance was unconstitutional because it authorized denial of a permit if "the public welfare, peace, safety, health, decency, good order, morals, or convenience require that it be refused." A number of complex issues have arisen, however, with reference to the appropriate procedures for testing the constitutional validity of parade and demonstration permit ordinances and of individual decisions denying permits.

It is clear that if the ordinance is unconstitutional because it provides inadequate standards for granting or denial of permits, the defense is available in a prosecution for parading or demonstrating without a permit. The defendant need not have sought a permit, nor, if a permit were sought, have taken steps to review the official decision denying permission. The issue of the validity of the ordinance is open, too, whether or not permission could have

---

[1] A question that has not been considered by the Supreme Court is whether the permit applicant can be required to pay a portion of the municipality's costs for police and other municipal services occasioned by the parade or demonstration.

been denied under a properly drafted provision.[2]   The rationale has been that the unconstitutional ordinance is "void" and therefore it is appropriate to contest its validity without first seeking a permit under it.   Lovell v. Griffin, 303 U.S. 444 (1938).

Suppose, however, that the ordinance is valid but the licensing official denies permission for unconstitutional reasons.   Poulos v. New Hampshire, 345 U.S. 395 (1953), establishes that a state can require that the applicant seek review of the invalid denial of the permit under a valid ordinance.   *Poulos* reasoned that the rationale for requiring permission in advance for a parade or demonstration allowed the state to insist that the disappointed applicant not ignore the official denial of permission, and to require challenge through appropriate procedures before the parade or demonstration is held.   *Poulos* presents a real dilemma to the applicant unconstitutionally denied permission.[3]   The ordinance in *Poulos* required the applicant to seek judicial review of the denial and precluded him from holding his planned meeting pending those judicial proceedings.   Justice Reed's opinion in that case rejected the argument that judicial review would be so time-consuming as to make it impossible to hold the planned meeting, stating that while delay was "unfortunate," it was "a price citizens must pay for life in an orderly society."   In Freedman v. Maryland, 380 U.S. 51 (1965), however, a motion picture censorship ordinance was held unconstitutional because it did not require the licensing official to go to court after denying a license, and did not provide for prompt judicial review.   Southeastern Promotions v. Conrad, 420 U.S. 546 (1975), required the directors of a municipal auditorium to follow the *Freedman* procedures upon denial of permission to use the auditorium.   The Court has never considered whether *Freedman* requires that there be prompt judicial review or that licensing officials seek that review in denying parade and demonstration permits.

In Walker v. Birmingham, 388 U.S. 307 (1967), the Court reviewed the criminal contempt conviction of Black ministers who had been enjoined by a state court from holding a Good Friday march to protest racial discrimination. The Court's decision in Shuttlesworth v. Birmingham, supra, two years later made clear that the parade permit ordinance on which the injunction was based was unconstitutional, and that the clearly stated position of police commissioner Eugene "Bull" Conner, that no permit would be issued, rested on unconstitutional considerations.   Moreover, the grant of an *ex parte* injunction, without notice or opportunity to participate in the proceedings, probably also violated the first amendment.[4]   Alabama, however, was among the states following the rule that an injunction must be obeyed, even if erroneous, until it is set aside on appellate review.[5]   Accordingly, the Alabama Supreme Court refused to consid-

---

[2] In Kunz v. New York, 340 U.S. 290 (1951), for example, defendant's license application was denied because he had in the past ridiculed and denounced the religious beliefs of others, and there had been disorder.   His conviction for holding a public worship meeting on the streets without a permit was reversed because the ordinance lacked standards for permit denials.

[3] The dilemma is exacerbated if there is uncertainty concerning the constitutional validity of the underlying ordinance.   In Cox v. New Hampshire, 312 U.S. 569 (1941), the parade permit ordinance under which the defendants were convicted was silent about the standards for granting or denying permits.   The convictions were affirmed, however, because the New Hampshire Supreme Court interpreted the ordinance, on the defendants' appeal, to allow denial only upon considerations such as traffic congestion, overlapping parades, and risks of disorder.   In Shuttlesworth v. Birmingham, 394 U.S. 147 (1969), the Court reversed a conviction for parading without a license despite a similar limiting construction of the ordinance under which the defendants were convicted.   Given the language of the ordinance, and past administrative practice, it "would have taken extraordinary clairvoyance" for defendants to have foreseen, when they held their parade, the "remarkable job of plastic surgery" by the state court four years later.

[4] Carroll v. President and Comm'rs of Princess Anne, 393 U.S. 175 (1968).

[5] The rule is the same in the federal courts.   United States v. United Mine Workers, 330 U.S. 258 (1947).

er constitutional attacks on the injunction or the underlying parade ordinance. The Supreme Court affirmed, by a vote of five to four. Justice Stewart's opinion for the Court said that the "case would arise in quite a different constitutional posture if the petitioners, before disobeying the injunction, had challenged it in the Alabama Courts and had been met with delay or frustration of their constitutional claims." In United States v. Ryan, 402 U.S. 530, 533 n. 4 (1971) the Court said: "Our holding [in Walker v. Birmingham] that the claims there sought to be asserted were not open on review of petitioners' contempt convictions was based on the availability of review of those claims at an earlier stage."

B. THE HOSTILE AUDIENCE

FEINER v. NEW YORK

340 U.S. 315, 71 S.Ct. 303, 95 L.Ed. 295 (1951).

[Feiner was addressing an open-air meeting on a street corner in Syracuse, New York, when two police officers arrived to investigate. They found about seventy-five or eighty people, both black and white, filling the sidewalk and spreading out into the street. Petitioner, standing on a box on the sidewalk, was addressing the crowd through an amplifier in a "loud high-pitched voice." Although the purpose of his speech was to urge his listeners to attend a meeting later that night, he was making derogatory remarks concerning President Truman (calling him "a bum"), the Mayor of Syracuse (also labelling him "a bum") and the American Legion (characterizing it as "a Nazi Gestapo"). He also said: "The Negroes don't have equal rights; they should rise up in arms and fight for their rights." There was some pushing and shoving in the crowd but no disorder. After Feiner had been speaking about twenty minutes, a man said to the police officers, "If you don't get that son of a bitch off, I will go over and get him off there myself." In order to break up the crowd, the police then requested Feiner to stop speaking and, when he repeatedly refused to do so, arrested him. He was prosecuted and convicted of a misdemeanor under the New York disorderly conduct statute, charged with ignoring "reasonable police orders" given to control the crowd and to prevent a breach of the peace. He was sentenced to thirty days. On appeal the conviction was affirmed by the county court and the New York Court of Appeals.]

Mr. Chief Justice Vinson delivered the opinion of the Court.

. . . .

We are not faced here with blind condonation by a state court of arbitrary police action. Petitioner was accorded a full, fair trial. The trial judge heard testimony supporting and contradicting the judgment of the police officers that a clear danger of disorder was threatened. After weighing this contradictory evidence, the trial judge reached the conclusion that the police officers were justified in taking action to prevent a breach of the peace. The exercise of the police officers' proper discretionary power to prevent a breach of the peace was thus approved by the trial court and later by two courts on review. The courts below recognized petitioner's right to hold a street meeting at this locality, to make use of loud-speaking equipment in giving his speech, and to make derogatory remarks concerning public officials and the American Legion. They found that the officers in making the arrest were motivated solely by a proper concern for the preservation of order and protection of the general welfare, and that there was no evidence which could lend color to a claim that the acts of the police were a cover for suppression of petitioner's views and opinions. Petitioner was thus neither arrested nor convicted for the making or the content of his speech. Rather, it was the reaction which it actually engendered.

. . .

. . . It is one thing to say that the police cannot be used as an instrument for the suppression of unpopular views, and another to say that, when as here the speaker passes the bounds of argument or persuasion and undertakes incitement to riot, they are powerless to prevent a breach of the peace. Nor in this case can we condemn the considered judgment of three New York courts approving the means which the police, faced with a crisis, used in the exercise of their power and duty to preserve peace and order. The findings of the state courts as to the existing situation and the imminence of greater disorder coupled with petitioner's deliberate defiance of the police officers convince us that we should not reverse this conviction in the name of free speech.

Affirmed.

[Justices Frankfurter and Jackson concurred in separate opinions.]

Mr. Justice Black, dissenting.

The record before us convinces me that petitioner, a young college student, has been sentenced to the penitentiary for the unpopular views he expressed.

. . . . .

. . . The police of course have power to prevent breaches of the peace. But if, in the name of preserving order, they ever can interfere with a lawful public speaker, they first must make all reasonable efforts to protect him. Here the policemen did not even pretend to try to protect petitioner. According to the officers' testimony, the crowd was restless but there is no showing of any attempt to quiet it; pedestrians were forced to walk into the street, but there was no effort to clear a path on the sidewalk; one person threatened to assault petitioner but the officers did nothing to discourage this when even a word might have sufficed. Their duty was to protect petitioner's right to talk, even to the extent of arresting the man who threatened to interfere. Instead, they shirked that duty and acted only to suppress the right to speak.

. . .

Mr. Justice Douglas, with whom Mr. Justice Minton concurs, dissenting.

. . .

A speaker may not, of course, incite a riot any more than he may incite a breach of the peace by the use of "fighting words". See Chaplinsky v. New Hampshire, 315 U.S. 568. But this record shows no such extremes. It shows an unsympathetic audience and the threat of one man to haul the speaker from the stage. It is against that kind of threat that speakers need police protection. If they do not receive it and instead the police throw their weight on the side of those who would break up the meetings, the police become the new censors of speech. . . .

———

EDWARDS v. SOUTH CAROLINA, 372 U.S. 229 (1963). A group of Black students marched to the South Carolina State House grounds in Columbia for the purpose of expressing their protest against discriminatory actions of the citizens and the legislature. They were convicted of breach of the peace. The Court reversed, saying, in part:

"The circumstances in this case reflect an exercise of these basic constitutional rights in their most pristine and classic form. The petitioners felt aggrieved by laws of South Carolina which allegedly 'prohibited Negro privileges in this State.' They peaceably assembled at the site of the State Government and there peaceably expressed their grievances 'to the citizens of South Carolina, along with the Legislative Bodies of South Carolina.' Not until they were told by police officials that they must disperse on pain of arrest did they do more. Even then, they but sang patriotic and religious songs after one of their leaders had delivered a 'religious harangue.' There was no violence or threat of violence on their part, or on the part of any member of the crowd watching them. Police protection was 'ample.'

"This, therefore, was a far cry from the situation in *Feiner v. New York,* 340 U.S. 315, where two policemen were faced with a crowd which was 'pushing, shoving, and milling around,' . . ., where at least one member of the crowd 'threatened violence if the police did not act,' . . . where 'the crowd was pressing closer around petitioner and the officer,' id., at 318, and where 'the speaker passes the bounds of argument or persuasion and undertakes incitement to riot.' . . . And the record is barren of any evidence of 'fighting words.' See Chaplinsky v. New Hampshire, 315 U.S. 568.

". . .

"The Fourteenth Amendment does not permit a State to make criminal the peaceful expression of unpopular views. '[A] function of free speech under our system of government is to invite dispute. It may indeed best serve its high purpose when it induces a condition of unrest, creates dissatisfaction with conditions as they are, or even stirs people to anger. Speech is often provocative and challenging. It may strike at prejudices and preconceptions and have profound unsettling effects as it presses for acceptance of an idea. That is why freedom of speech, . . . is . . . protected against censorship or punishment, unless shown likely to produce a clear and present danger of a serious substantive evil that rises far above public inconvenience, annoyance, or unrest. . . . As in [Terminiello v. Chicago, 337 U.S. 1, 4–5], the courts of South Carolina have defined a criminal offense so as to permit conviction of the petitioners if their speech 'stirred people to anger, invited public dispute, or brought about a condition of unrest. A conviction resting on any of those grounds may not stand.' . . .'"

Justice Clark's dissent argued that, if there was a distinction between the gravity of the danger of disorder in *Feiner* and *Edwards,* the different historical background of the two cities involved and the difference in the numbers of demonstrators and audience showed a greater danger in *Edwards.*

COX v. LOUISIANA (COX I)

379 U.S. 536, 85 S.Ct. 453, 13 L.Ed.2d 471 (1965).

[On December 14, 1961, 23 students from Southern University, a Negro college, were arrested in downtown Baton Rouge for picketing stores that maintained segregated lunch counters. The next morning about 2000 students assembled at the old State Capitol Building; led by Cox, a Field Secretary of CORE, they marched to the courthouse where the 23 students were jailed. After discussion with Cox, police officers agreed (it was asserted) to permit a peaceful demonstration provided the demonstrators stayed across the street from the courthouse. The students lined up across the street, blocking the sidewalk but not the street, they sang songs and listened to a short speech by Cox in which he stated that the demonstration was a protest against the "illegal arrest" of the students. Cox urged his listeners to go eat and called attention to the stores that had segregated lunch counters. There was "muttering" and "grumbling" by the white onlookers. Deeming the appeal to the students to sit at the lunch counters to be "inflammatory," the Sheriff ordered the gathering to disperse and used tear gas to enforce his order. Cox was arrested the next day and charged with three statutory offenses: "disturbing the peace," "obstructing public passages," and "courthouse picketing." The Supreme Court reversed convictions on all three charges. Only the "disturbing the peace" conviction is considered here.]

Mr. Justice Goldberg delivered the opinion of the Court.

. . .

II. THE BREACH OF THE PEACE CONVICTION

Appellant was convicted of violating a Louisiana "disturbing the peace" statute . . . .

. . .   We hold that Louisiana may not constitutionally punish appellant under this statute for engaging in the type of conduct which this record reveals, and also that the statute as authoritatively interpreted by the Louisiana Supreme Court is unconstitutionally broad in scope.

. . .   Independent examination of the record . . .   shows no conduct which the State had a right to prohibit as a breach of the peace.

Appellant led a group of young college students who wished "to protest segregation" and discrimination against Negroes and the arrest of 23 fellow students. They assembled peaceably at the State Capitol building and marched to the courthouse where they sang, prayed and listened to a speech. A reading of the record reveals agreement on the part of the State's witnesses that Cox had the demonstration "very well controlled," and until the end of Cox's speech, the group was perfectly "orderly." Sheriff Clemmons testified that the crowd's activities were not "objectionable" before that time. They became objectionable, according to the Sheriff himself, when Cox, concluding his speech, urged the students to go uptown and sit in at lunch counters. The Sheriff testified that the sole aspect of the program to which he objected was "[t]he inflammatory manner in which he [Cox] addressed that crowd and told them to go on up town, go to four places on the protest list, sit down and if they don't feed you, sit there for one hour." Yet this part of Cox's speech obviously did not deprive the demonstration of its protected character under the Constitution as free speech and assembly. . . .

The State argues, however, that while the demonstrators started out to be orderly, the loud cheering and clapping by the students in response to the singing from the jail converted the peaceful assembly into a riotous one. The record, however, does not support this assertion. It is true that the students, in response to the singing of their fellows who were in custody, cheered and applauded. However, the meeting was an outdoor meeting and a key state witness testified that while the singing was loud, it was not disorderly. There is, moreover, no indication that the mood of the students was ever hostile, aggressive, or unfriendly. Our conclusion that the entire meeting from the beginning until its dispersal by tear gas was orderly and not riotous is confirmed by a film of the events taken by a television news photographer, which was offered in evidence as a state exhibit. We have viewed the film, and it reveals that the students, though they undoubtedly cheered and clapped, were well-behaved throughout. My Brother Black, concurring in this opinion . . . agrees "that the record does not show boisterous or violent conduct or indecent language on the part of the . . ." students. The singing and cheering do not seem to us to differ significantly from the constitutionally protected activity of the demonstrators in Edwards, who loudly sang "while stamping their feet and clapping their hands." Edwards v. South Carolina, supra, 372 U.S., at 233.

. . .

Finally, the State contends that the conviction should be sustained because of fear expressed by some of the state witnesses that "violence was about to erupt" because of the demonstration. It is virtually undisputed, however, that the students themselves were not violent and threatened no violence. The fear of violence seems to have been based upon the reaction of the group of white citizens looking on from across the street. . . . There is no indication, however, that any member of the white group threatened violence. And this small crowd estimated at between 100 and 300 was separated from the students by "seventy-five to eighty" armed policemen, including "every available shift of the City Police," the "Sheriff's Office in full complement," and "additional help from the State Police," along with a "fire truck and the Fire Department." As Inspector Trigg testified, they could have handled the crowd.

This situation, like that in Edwards, is "a far cry from the situation in Feiner v. New York, 340 U.S. 315." . . .

There is an additional reason why this conviction cannot be sustained. The statute at issue in this case, as authoritatively interpreted by the Louisiana Supreme Court, is unconstitutionally vague in its overly broad scope. . . .

For all these reasons we hold that appellant's freedoms of speech and assembly were denied by his conviction for disturbing the peace. The conviction on this charge cannot stand. . . .

[Justices Black, Clark, White, and Harlan concurred in the result.]

SECTION 3. THE NON–TRADITIONAL FORUM

A. SPEECH ACTIVITIES IN PUBLIC PROPERTY OTHER THAN PARKS AND STREETS

ADDERLEY v. FLORIDA

385 U.S. 39, 87 S.Ct. 242, 17 L.Ed.2d 149 (1966).

Mr. Justice Black delivered the opinion of the Court.

Petitioners . . . were convicted on a charge of "trespass with a malicious and mischievous intent" upon the premises of the county jail contrary to § 821.18 of the Florida statutes . . . . Petitioners, apparently all students of the Florida A. & M. University in Tallahassee, had gone from the school to the jail about a mile away, along with many other students, to "demonstrate" at the jail their protests because of arrests of other protesting students the day before, and perhaps to protest more generally against state and local policies and practices of racial segregation, including segregation of the jail. The county sheriff, legal custodian of the jail and jail grounds, tried to persuade the students to leave the jail grounds. When this did not work, he notified them that they must leave, that if they did not leave he would arrest them for trespassing, and that if they resisted he would charge them with that as well. Some of the students left but others, including petitioners, remained and they were arrested. On appeal the convictions were affirmed. . . .

Petitioners have insisted from the beginning of these cases that they are controlled and must be reversed because of our prior cases of Edwards v. South Carolina, 372 U.S. 229, and Cox v. Louisiana, 379 U.S. 536, 559. We cannot agree. . . .

In Edwards, the demonstrators went to the South Carolina State Capitol grounds to protest. In this case they went to the jail. Traditionally, state capitol grounds are open to the public. Jails, built for security purposes, are not. The demonstrators at the South Carolina Capitol went in through a public driveway and as they entered they were told by state officials there that they had a right as citizens to go through the State House grounds as long as they were peaceful. Here the demonstrators entered the jail grounds through a driveway used only for jail purposes and without warning to or permission from the sheriff. More importantly, South Carolina sought to prosecute its State Capitol demonstrators by charging them with the common-law crime of breach of the peace. The South Carolina breach-of-the-peace statute was . . . struck down as being so broad and all-embracing as to jeopardize speech, press, assembly and petition, ... And it was on this same ground of vagueness that in Cox v. Louisiana, supra, 379 U.S. at 551–552, 85 S.Ct. at 462–463, the Louisiana breach-of-the-peace law used to prosecute Cox was invalidated.

The Florida trespass statute under which these petitioners were charged cannot be challenged on this ground. It is aimed at conduct of one limited kind, that is for one person or persons to trespass upon the property of another with a malicious and mischievous intent. There is no lack of notice in this law, nothing to entrap or fool the unwary.

Petitioners seem to argue that the Florida trespass law is void for vagueness because it requires a trespass to be "with a malicious and mischievous intent . . . ." But these words do not broaden the scope of trespass so as to make it cover a multitude of types of conduct as does the common-law breach-of-the-peace charge. On the contrary, these words narrow the scope of the offense.
. . .

. . . [T]he jury was authorized to find that the State had proven every essential element of the crime, as it was defined by the state court. That interpretation is, of course, binding on us, leaving only the question of whether conviction of the state offense, thus defined, unconstitutionally deprives petitioners of their rights to freedom of speech, press, assembly or petition. We hold it does not. The sheriff, as jail custodian, had power, as the state courts have here held, to direct that this large crowd of people get off the grounds. There is not a shred of evidence in this record that this power was exercised, or that its exercise was sanctioned by the lower courts, because the sheriff objected to what was being sung or said by the demonstrators or because he disagreed with the objectives of their protest. The record reveals that he objected only to their presence on that part of the jail grounds reserved for jail uses. There is no evidence at all that on any other occasion had similarly large groups of the public been permitted to gather on this portion of the jail grounds for any purpose. Nothing in the Constitution of the United States prevents Florida from even-handed enforcement of its general trespass statute against those refusing to obey the sheriff's order to remove themselves from what amounted to the curtilage of the jailhouse. The State, no less than a private owner of property, has power to preserve the property under its control for the use to which it is lawfully dedicated. For this reason there is no merit to the petitioners' argument that they had a constitutional right to stay on the property, over the jail custodian's objections, because this "area chosen for the peaceful civil rights demonstration was not only 'reasonable' but also particularly appropriate . . . .' Such an argument has as its major unarticulated premise the assumption that people who want to propagandize protests or views have a constitutional right to do so whenever and however and wherever they please. That concept of constitutional law was vigorously and forthrightly rejected in two of the cases petitioners rely on, Cox v. Louisiana, supra, at 554–555 and 563–564. We reject it again. The United States Constitution does not forbid a State to control the use of its own property for its own lawful nondiscriminatory purpose.

These judgments are affirmed.

Mr. Justice Douglas, with whom The Chief Justice, Mr. Justice Brennan, and Mr. Justice Fortas concur, dissenting.

. . .

The jailhouse, like an executive mansion, a legislative chamber, a courthouse, or the statehouse itself (Edwards v. South Carolina, supra) is one of the seats of government whether it be the Tower of London, the Bastille, or a small county jail. And when it houses political prisoners or those whom many think are unjustly held, it is an obvious center for protest. . . .

There is no question that petitioners had as their purpose a protest against the arrest of Florida A. & M. students for trying to integrate public theatres. The sheriff's testimony indicates that he well understood the purpose of the rally. . . . There was no violence; no threats of violence; no attempted jail break; no storming of a prison; no plan or plot to do anything but protest.

. . .

We do violence to the First Amendment when we permit this "petition for redress of grievances" to be turned into a trespass action. . . .

. . .

There may be some public places which are so clearly committed to other purposes that their use for the airing of grievances is anomalous. There may be some instances in which assemblies and petitions for redress of grievances are not consistent with other necessary purposes of public property. A noisy meeting may be out of keeping with the serenity of the statehouse or the quiet of the courthouse. . . . But this is quite different than saying that all public places are off-limits to people with grievances. . . . And it is farther yet from saying that the "custodian" of the public property in his discretion can decide when public places shall be used for the communication of ideas, especially the constitutional right to assemble and petition for redress of grievances. . . .

. . .

TINKER v. DES MOINES SCHOOL DISTRICT

393 U.S. 503, 89 S.Ct. 733, 21 L.Ed.2d 731 (1969).

[In December, 1965, Petitioners, Des Moines high school and junior high students, wore black armbands to school to publicize their objections to United States operations in Vietnam. Anticipating such action, the school authorities had adopted a policy that any student wearing an armband to school would be requested to remove it, and if he refused he would be suspended until he returned without the armband. Petitioners refused to remove their armbands and were suspended. They sought a federal injunction restraining the school officials from disciplining them; the lower federal courts upheld the action of the school authorities on the ground that it was reasonable in order to prevent disturbance of school discipline.]

Mr. Justice Fortas delivered the opinion of the Court.

. . .

The District Court recognized that the wearing of an armband for the purpose of expressing certain views is the type of symbolic act that is within the Free Speech Clause of the First Amendment. See West Virginia v. Barnette, 319 U.S. 624 (1943); Stromberg v. California, 283 U.S. 359 (1931) . . . . As we shall discuss, the wearing of armbands in the circumstances of this case was entirely divorced from actually or potentially disruptive conduct by those participating in it. It was closely akin to "pure speech" which, we have repeatedly held, is entitled to comprehensive protection under the First Amendment. Cf. Cox v. Louisiana, 379 U.S. 536, 555 (1965); Adderley v. Florida, 385 U.S. 39 (1966).

First Amendment rights, applied in light of the special characteristics of the school environment, are available to teachers and students. It can hardly be argued that either students or teachers shed their constitutional rights to freedom of speech or expression at the schoolhouse gate. This has been the unmistakable holding of this Court for almost 50 years. In Meyer v. Nebraska, 262 U.S. 390 (1923), and Bartels v. Iowa, 262 U.S. 404 (1923), this Court, in opinions by Mr. Justice McReynolds, held that the Due Process Clause of the Fourteenth Amendment prevents States from forbidding the teaching of a foreign language to young students. Statutes to this effect, the Court held, unconstitutionally interfere with the liberty of teacher, student, and parent.[2]
. . . .

On the other hand, the Court has repeatedly emphasized the need for affirming the comprehensive authority of the States and of school authorities, consistent with fundamental constitutional safeguards, to prescribe and control conduct in the schools. See Epperson v. Arkansas, supra, 393 U.S. at 104; Meyer v. Nebraska, supra, 262 U.S. at 402. Our problem lies in the area where students in the exercise of First Amendment rights collide with the rules of the school authorities.

The problem presented by the present case does not relate to regulation of the length of skirts or the type of clothing, to hair style or deportment. . . . It does not concern aggressive, disruptive action or even group demonstrations. Our problem involves direct, primary First Amendment rights akin to "pure speech."

The school officials banned and sought to punish petitioners for a silent, passive, expression of opinion, unaccompanied by any disorder or disturbance on the part of petitioners. There is here no evidence whatever of petitioners' interference, actual or nascent, with the school's work or of collision with the rights of other students to be secure and to be let alone. . . .

The District Court concluded that the action of the school authorities was reasonable because it was based upon their fear of a disturbance from the wearing of the armbands. But, in our system, undifferentiated fear or apprehension of disturbance is not enough to overcome the right to freedom of expression. Any departure from absolute regimentation may cause trouble.
. . . .

In order for the State in the person of school officials to justify prohibition of a particular expression of opinion, it must be able to show that its action was caused by something more than a mere desire to avoid the discomfort and unpleasantness that always accompany an unpopular viewpoint. . . .

In the present case, the District Court made no such finding, and our independent examination of the record fails to yield evidence that the school authorities had reason to anticipate that the wearing of the armbands would substantially interfere with the work of the school or impinge upon the rights of other students. Even an official memorandum prepared after the suspension that listed the reasons for the ban on wearing the armbands made no reference to the anticipation of such disruption.

---

[2] Hamilton v. Regents of University of California, 293 U.S. 245 (1934) is sometimes cited for the broad proposition that the State may attach conditions to attendance at a state university that require individuals to violate their religious convictions. The case involved dismissal of members of a religious denomination from a land grant college for refusal to participate in military training. Narrowly viewed, the case turns upon the Court's conclusion that merely requiring a student to participate in school training in military "science" could not conflict with his constitutionally protected freedom of conscience. The decision cannot be taken as establishing that the State may impose and enforce any conditions that it chooses upon attendance at public institutions of learning, however violative they may be of fundamental constitutional guaranties. See, e.g., West Virginia v. Barnette, 319 U.S. 624 (1943). . . .

On the contrary, the action of the school authorities appears to have been based upon an urgent wish to avoid the controversy which might result from the expression, even by the silent symbol of armbands, of opposition to this Nation's part in the conflagration of Vietnam. . . .

It is also relevant that the school authorities did not purport to prohibit the wearing of all symbols of political or controversial significance. The record shows that students in some of the schools wore buttons relating to national political campaigns, and some even wore the Iron Cross, traditionally a symbol of Nazism. The order prohibiting the wearing of armbands did not extend to these. Instead, a particular symbol—black armbands worn to exhibit opposition to this Nation's involvement in Vietnam—was singled out for prohibition. Clearly, the prohibition of expression of one particular opinion, at least without evidence that it is necessary to avoid material and substantial interference with school work or discipline, is not constitutionally permissible. . . .

The principal use to which the schools are dedicated is to accommodate students during prescribed hours for the purpose of certain types of activities. Among those activities is personal intercommunication among the students. This is not only an inevitable part of the process of attending school, it is also an important part of the educational process. A student's rights therefore, do not embrace merely the classroom hours. When he is in the cafeteria, or on the playing field, or on the campus during the authorized hours, he may express his opinions, even on controversial subjects like the conflict in Vietnam, if he does so "[without] materially and substantially interfering with . . . appropriate discipline in the operation of the school" and without colliding with the rights of others. Burnside v. Byars, 363 F.2d at 749. But conduct by the student, in class or out of it, which for any reason—whether it stems from time, place, or type of behavior—materially disrupts classwork or involves substantial disorder or invasion of the rights of others is, of course, not immunized by the constitutional guaranty of freedom of speech. . . .

As we have discussed, the record does not demonstrate any facts which might reasonably have led school authorities to forecast substantial disruption of or material interference with school activities, and no disturbances or disorders on the school premises in fact occurred. These petitioners merely went about their ordained rounds in school. Their deviation consisted only in wearing on their sleeve a band of black cloth, not more than two inches wide. They wore it to exhibit their disapproval of the Vietnam hostilities and their advocacy of a truce, to make their views known, and by their example, to influence others to adopt them. They neither interrupted school activities nor sought to intrude in the school affairs or the lives of others. They caused discussion outside of the classrooms, but no interference with work and no disorder. In the circumstances, our Constitution does not permit officials of the State to deny their form of expression.

We express no opinion as to the form of relief which should be granted, this being a matter for the lower courts to determine. We reverse and remand for further proceedings consistent with this opinion.

Reversed and remanded.

Mr. Justice Stewart, concurring.

Although I agree with much of what is said in the Court's opinion, and with its judgment in this case, I cannot share the Court's uncritical assumption that, school discipline aside, the First Amendment rights of children are co-extensive with those of adults. . . .

Mr. Justice White, concurring.

While I join the Court's opinion, I deem it appropriate to note . . . that the Court continues to recognize a distinction between communicating by words and communicating by acts or conduct which sufficiently impinge on some valid state interest.   .   .   .

Mr. Justice Black, dissenting.

While the record does not show that any of these armband students shouted, used profane language or were violent in any manner, detailed testimony by some of them shows their armbands caused comments, warnings by other students, the poking of fun at them, and a warning by an older football player that other, nonprotesting students had better let them alone.   There is also evidence that the professor of mathematics had his lesson period practically "wrecked" chiefly by disputes with Mary Beth Tinker, who wore her armband for her "demonstration."   Even a casual reading of the record shows that this armband did divert students' minds from their regular lessons, and that talk, comments, etc., made John Tinker "self-conscious" in attending school with his armband.   While the absence of obscene or boisterous and loud disorder perhaps justifies the Court's statement that the few armband students did not actually "disrupt" the classwork, I think the record overwhelmingly shows that the armbands did exactly what the elected school officials and principals foresaw it would, that is, took the students' minds off their classwork and diverted them to thoughts about the highly emotional subject of the Vietnam war.   .   .   .

I deny   .   .   .   that it has been the "unmistakable holding of this Court for almost 50 years" that "students" and "teachers" take with them into the "schoolhouse gate" constitutional rights to "freedom of speech or expression." .   .   .   The truth is that a teacher of kindergarten, grammar school, or high school pupils no more carries into a school with him a complete right to freedom of speech and expression than an anti-Catholic or anti-Semitic carries with him a complete freedom of speech and religion into a Catholic church or Jewish synagogue.   Nor does a person carry with him into the United States Senate or House, or to the Supreme Court, or any other court, a complete constitutional right to go into those places contrary to their rules and speak his mind on any subject he pleases.   It is a myth to say that any person has a constitutional right to say what he pleases, where he pleases, and when he pleases.   .   .   .

Mr. Justice Harlan, dissenting.

.   .   .   .

GREER v. SPOCK, 424 U.S. 828 (1976).   Fort Dix Military Reservation is devoted to military training activities.   Civilian automobile and pedestrian traffic is permitted on roads and paths, although signs indicate vehicles are subject to search and civilians are occasionally stopped and asked the reason for their presence.   Military regulations prohibit demonstrations, picketing, political speeches and similar activity on the base.   They also forbid the distribution of papers, magazines, handbills, etc., which the commander finds constitute a clear danger to military loyalty, discipline, or morale.   These rules have been strictly enforced to prevent political campaign speeches.   However, civilian speakers have been invited to address military personnel on other subjects, visiting clergymen have been invited to conduct religious services, and theatrical and musical productions have been presented.

In 1972 Benjamin Spock and other People's Party candidates for public office sought permission to enter to distribute campaign literature and to hold a meeting to discuss election issues.   Permission was denied and they sued to enjoin the restrictions on political campaigning and the distribution of literature. A district court order issuing an injunction was reversed by the Court.

Justice Stewart, speaking for the Court, distinguished Flower v. United States, 407 U.S. 197 (1972) because it involved the right to distribute leaflets on a street in a military reservation that had been treated as a completely open street like the city streets.   He rejected the claim that that case stood for the proposition that whenever members of the public are permitted freely to visit a place owned or operated by the government that place becomes a "public forum" for first amendment purposes.   The state, like a private property owner, has the power to preserve property under its control for the use to which it is lawfully dedicated.   Hence, there was "no generalized constitutional right to make political speeches or distribute leaflets at Fort Dix" and the regulations were valid on their face.

HEFFRON v. INTERNATIONAL SOCIETY FOR KRISHNA CONSCIOUSNESS, INC., 452 U.S. 640 (1981).   The court upheld a rule that distribution of literature and solicitation of funds at the Minnesota State Fair could be conducted only at an assigned location within the fairgrounds.   The rule had been challenged by the society, espousing the views of the Krishna religion, because it forbade its members to walk about the grounds selling religious literature and soliciting funds.

Justice White's opinion concluded that the rule was a valid time, place and manner regulation: it was content-neutral, served a significant government interest in avoiding congestion and allowing orderly movement of crowds, and left open alternative means of expression in soliciting funds and distributing literature from a booth and orally propagating views anywhere on the grounds. Toward the end of his opinion, Justice White characterized the state fair as a "limited public forum."

Justices Brennan, Marshall, Blackmun, and Stevens concurred in the judgment of the Court insofar as it upheld the restriction of sale of literature and solicitation of funds to the fixed booth.   They dissented from the portion of the judgment limiting distribution of literature to the booth on the ground that the record did not show that such distribution would create additional disorder on the fairgrounds.   "The record is devoid of any evidence that the 125-acre fairgrounds could not accommodate peripatetic distributors of literature just as easily as it now accommodates peripatetic speechmakers and proselytizers."

UNITED STATES POSTAL SERVICE v. COUNCIL OF GREENBURGH CIVIC ASSOCIATIONS, 453 U.S. 114 (1981).   The Court upheld the validity of 28 U.S.C. § 1725, which prohibits the deposit of unstamped "mailable matter" in homeowners' letterboxes.   The Postal Service had threatened to enforce the statute to prevent the association from delivering messages by placing them in letterboxes of private homes.   Justice Rehnquist's opinion for the Court reasoned that it was not necessary to apply principles governing time, place and manner restrictions on the use of public forums (i.e., deciding whether the restriction was content-neutral, served a significant governmental interest, and left open adequate alternative channels of communication).   A letterbox in a private home was not "traditionally such a 'public forum'." Justice Brennan, concurring in the result, argued that a letterbox is a public forum, but that 28 U.S.C. § 1725 was a valid time, place and manner rule. Justice Marshall dissented, concluding that the statutory restriction burdened first amendment rights, and was not necessary for the efficiency of the postal service.   Justice White, concurring, and Justice Stevens, dissenting, both contended that cases involving denial of access to public property were not relevant. Justice White analyzed 28 U.S.C. § 1725 as no more than a requirement that a postage fee be paid for use of a portion of the postal system.   Justice Stevens argued that letterboxes were not government property, and the proper question was whether willing homeowners could be prevented from receiving communications.

PERRY EDUCATION ASSOCIATION v. PERRY LOCAL EDUCATORS' ASSOCIATION

460 U.S. 37, 103 S.Ct. 948, 74 L.Ed.2d 794 (1983).

Justice White delivered the opinion of the Court.

Perry Education Association is the duly elected exclusive bargaining representative for the teachers of the Metropolitan School District of Perry Township, Indiana. A collective bargaining agreement with the Board of Education provided that Perry Education Association, but no other union, would have access to the interschool mail system and teacher mailboxes in the Perry Township schools. The issue in this case is whether the denial of similar access to the Perry Local Educators' Association, a rival teacher group, violates the First and Fourteenth Amendments.

I

The Metropolitan School District of Perry Township, Indiana, operates a public school system of thirteen separate schools. Each school building contains a set of mailboxes for the teachers. Interschool delivery by school employees permits messages to be delivered rapidly to teachers in the district. The primary function of this internal mail system is to transmit official messages among the teachers and between the teachers and the school administration. In addition, teachers use the system to send personal messages and individual school building principals have allowed delivery of messages from various private organizations.

Prior to 1977, both the Perry Education Association (PEA) and the Perry Local Educators' Association (PLEA) represented teachers in the school district and apparently had equal access to the interschool mail system. In 1977, . . . PEA . . . was certified as the exclusive representative, as provided by Indiana law. . . .

. . . Following the election, PEA and the school district negotiated a labor contract in which the school board gave PEA "access to teachers' mailboxes in which to insert material" and the right to use the interschool mail delivery system to the extent that the school district incurred no extra expense by such use. The labor agreement . . . stipulate[d] that these access rights shall not be granted to any other "school employee organization" . . . .

The exclusive access policy applies only to use of the mailboxes and school mail system. PLEA is not prevented from using other school facilities to communicate with teachers. . . .

PLEA and two of its members filed this action under 42 U.S.C. § 1983 (1976) against PEA and individual members of the Perry Township School Board. Plaintiffs contended that PEA's preferential access to the internal mail system violates the First Amendment and the Equal Protection Clause of the Fourteenth Amendment. They sought injunctive and declaratory relief and damages. Upon cross-motions for summary judgment, the district court entered judgment for the defendants.

The Court of Appeals for the Seventh Circuit reversed. . . .

II

.   .   .   .

III

. . . . The existence of a right of access to public property and the standard by which limitations upon such a right must be evaluated differ depending on the character of the property at issue.

A

In places which by long tradition or by government fiat have been devoted to assembly and debate, the rights of the state to limit expressive activity are sharply circumscribed. At one end of the spectrum are streets and parks which "have immemorially been held in trust for the use of the public, and, time out of mind, have been used for purposes of assembly, communicating thoughts between citizens, and discussing public questions." Hague v. CIO, 307 U.S. 496, 515 (1939). In these quintessential public forums, the government may not prohibit all communicative activity. For the state to enforce a content-based exclusion it must show that its regulation is necessary to serve a compelling state interest and that it is narrowly drawn to achieve that end. Carey v. Brown, 447 U.S. 455, 461 (1980). The state may also enforce regulations of the time, place, and manner of expression which are content-neutral, are narrowly tailored to serve a significant government interest, and leave open ample alternative channels of communication. . . .

A second category consists of public property which the state has opened for use by the public as a place for expressive activity. The Constitution forbids a state to enforce certain exclusions from a forum generally open to the public even if it was not required to create the forum in the first place. Widmar v. Vincent, 454 U.S. 263 (1981) (university meeting facilities); City of Madison Joint School District v. Wisconsin Public Employment Relations Comm'n, 429 U.S. 167 (1976) (school board meeting); Southeastern Promotions, Ltd. v. Conrad, 420 U.S. 546 (1975) (municipal theater). Although a state is not required to indefinitely retain the open character of the facility, as long as it does so it is bound by the same standards as apply in a traditional public forum. Reasonable time, place and manner regulations are permissible, and a content-based prohibition must be narrowly drawn to effectuate a compelling state interest. Widmar v. Vincent, supra, 454 U.S., at 269–270.

Public property which is not by tradition or designation a forum for public communication is governed by different standards. We have recognized that the "First Amendment does not guarantee access to property simply because it is owned or controlled by the government." United States Postal Service v. Greenburgh Civic Ass'n, supra, 453 U.S., at 129. In addition to time, place, and manner regulations, the state may reserve the forum for its intended purposes, communicative or otherwise, as long as the regulation on speech is reasonable and not an effort to suppress expression merely because public officials oppose the speaker's view. Id., 453 U.S., at 131, n. 7. As we have stated on several occasions, "the State, no less than a private owner of property, has power to preserve the property under its control for the use to which it is lawfully dedicated." Id., 453 U.S., at 129; Greer v. Spock, 424 U.S. 828, 836, (1976); Adderley v. Florida, 385 U.S. 39, 48 (1966).

The school mail facilities at issue here fall within this third category. The Court of Appeals recognized that Perry School District's interschool mail system is not a traditional public forum: . . . On this point the parties agree. . . . The internal mail system, at least by policy, is not held open to the general public. It is instead PLEA's position that the school mail facilities have become a "limited public forum" from which it may not be excluded because of the periodic use of the system by private non-school connected groups, and

PLEA's own unrestricted access to the system prior to PEA's certification as exclusive representative.

Neither of these arguments is persuasive. The use of the internal school mail by groups not affiliated with the schools is no doubt a relevant consideration. If by policy or by practice the Perry School District has opened its mail system for indiscriminate use by the general public, then PLEA could justifiably argue a public forum has been created. This, however, is not the case. As the case comes before us, there is no indication in the record that the school mailboxes and interschool delivery system are open for use by the general public. Permission to use the system to communicate with teachers must be secured from the individual building principal. There is no court finding or evidence in the record which demonstrates that this permission has been granted as a matter of course to all who seek to distribute material. We can only conclude that the schools do allow some outside organizations such as the YMCA, Cub Scouts, and other civic and church organizations to use the facilities. This type of selective access does not transform government property into a public forum. In Greer v. Spock, supra, at 838, n. 10, the fact that other civilian speakers and entertainers had sometimes been invited to appear at Fort Dix did not convert the military base into a public forum. And in Lehman v. Shaker Heights, 418 U.S. 298 (1974) (Opinion of Blackmun, J.), a plurality of the Court concluded that a city transit system's rental of space in its vehicles for commercial advertising did not require it to accept partisan political advertising.

Moreover, even if we assume that by granting access to the Cub Scouts, YMCAs, and parochial schools, the school district has created a "limited" public forum, the constitutional right of access would in any event extend only to other entities of similar character. While the school mail facilities thus might be a forum generally open for use by the Girl Scouts, the local boys' club and other organizations that engage in activities of interest and educational relevance to students, they would not as a consequence be open to an organization such as PLEA, which is concerned with the terms and conditions of teacher employment.

PLEA also points to its ability to use the school mailboxes and delivery system on an equal footing with PEA prior to the collective bargaining agreement signed in 1978. Its argument appears to be that the access policy in effect at that time converted the school mail facilities into a limited public forum generally open for use by employee organizations, and that once this occurred, exclusions of employee organizations, thereafter must be judged by the constitutional standard applicable to public forums. The fallacy in the argument is that it is not the forum, but PLEA itself, which has changed. Prior to 1977, there was no exclusive representative for the Perry school district teachers. PEA and PLEA each represented its own members. Therefore the school district's policy of allowing both organizations to use the school mail facilities simply reflected the fact that both unions represented the teachers and had legitimate reasons for use of the system. PLEA's previous access was consistent with the school district's preservation of the facilities for school-related business, and did not constitute creation of a public forum in any broader sense.

. . . In the Court of Appeals' view, . . . the access policy adopted by the Perry Schools favors a particular viewpoint, that of the PEA, on labor relations, and consequently must be strictly scrutinized regardless of whether a public forum is involved. There is, however, no indication that the school board intended to discourage one viewpoint and advance another. We believe it is more accurate to characterize the access policy as based on the *status* of the respective unions rather than their views. Implicit in the concept of the nonpublic forum is the right to make distinctions in access on the basis of subject matter and speaker identity. These distinctions may be impermissible in a public forum but are inherent and inescapable in the process of limiting a nonpublic forum to activities compatible with the intended purpose of the property. The touchstone for evaluating these distinctions is whether they are reasonable in light of the purpose which the forum at issue serves.

B

The differential access provided PEA and PLEA is reasonable because it is wholly consistent with the district's legitimate interest in "preserv[ing] the property . . . for the use to which it is lawfully dedicated." *Postal Service,* supra, 453 U.S., at 129–130. Use of school mail facilities enables PEA to perform effectively its obligations as exclusive representative of *all* Perry Township teachers. Conversely, PLEA does not have any official responsibility in connection with the school district and need not be entitled to the same rights of access to school mailboxes. We observe that providing exclusive access to recognized bargaining representatives is a permissible labor practice in the public sector. . . . Moreover, exclusion of the rival union may reasonably be considered a means of insuring labor-peace within the schools. The policy "serves to prevent the District's schools from becoming a battlefield for inter-union squabbles."

. . .

Finally, the reasonableness of the limitations on PLEA's access to the school mail system is also supported by the substantial alternative channels that remain open for union-teacher communication to take place. These means range from bulletin boards to meeting facilities to the United States mail. During election periods, PLEA is assured of equal access to all modes of communication. There is no showing here that PLEA's ability to communicate with teachers is seriously impinged by the restricted access to the internal mail system. The variety and type of alternative modes of access present here compare favorably with those in other non-public forum cases where we have upheld restrictions on access. See, e.g., Greer v. Spock, 424 U.S. at 839 (servicemen free to attend political rallies off-base); Pell v. Procunier, 417 U.S. 817, 827–828 (1974) (prison inmates may communicate with media by mail and through visitors).

IV

The Court of Appeals also held that the differential access provided the rival unions constituted impermissible content discrimination in violation of the Equal Protection Clause of the Fourteenth Amendment. We have rejected this contention when cast as a First Amendment argument, and it fares no better in equal protection garb. . . .

The Seventh Circuit and PLEA rely on Police Department of Chicago v. Mosely, 408 U.S. 92 (1972) and Carey v. Brown, 447 U.S. 455 (1980). In *Mosely* and *Carey,* we struck down prohibitions on peaceful picketing in a public forum. . . . In both cases, we found the distinction between classes of speech violative of the Equal Protection Clause. The key to those decisions, however, was the presence of a public forum. In a public forum, by definition, all parties have a constitutional right of access and the state must demonstrate compelling reasons for restricting access to a single class of speakers, a single viewpoint, or a single subject.

When speakers and subjects are similarly situated, the state may not pick and choose. Conversely on government property that has not been made a public forum, not all speech is equally situated, and the state may draw distinctions which relate to the special purpose for which the property is used. As we have explained above, for a school mail facility, the difference in status between the exclusive bargaining representative and its rival is such a distinction.

V

The Court of Appeals invalidated the limited privileges PEA negotiated as the bargaining voice of the Perry Township teachers by misapplying our cases that have dealt with the rights of free expression on streets, parks and other fora generally open for assembly and debate. . . . The judgment of the Court of Appeals is

Reversed.

Justice Brennan, with whom Justice Marshall, Justice Powell, and Justice Stevens join, dissenting.

The Court today holds that an incumbent teachers' union may negotiate a collective bargaining agreement with a school board that grants the incumbent access to teachers' mailboxes and to the interschool mail system and denies such access to a rival union. Because the exclusive access provision in the collective bargaining agreement amounts to viewpoint discrimination that infringes the respondents' First Amendment rights and fails to advance any substantial state interest, I dissent.

I

. . . This case does not involve an "absolute access" claim. It involves an "equal access" claim. As such it does not turn on whether the internal school mail system is a "public forum." In focusing on the public forum issue, the Court disregards the First Amendment's central proscription against censorship, in the form of viewpoint discrimination, in any forum, public or nonpublic.

A

. . . Generally, the concept of content neutrality prohibits the government from choosing the subjects that are appropriate for public discussion. The content neutrality cases frequently refer to the prohibition against viewpoint discrimination and both concepts have their roots in the First Amendment's bar against censorship. But unlike the viewpoint discrimination concept, which is used to strike down government restrictions on speech by particular speakers, the content neutrality principle is invoked when the government has imposed restrictions on speech related to an entire subject area. The content neutrality principle can be seen as an outgrowth of the core First Amendment prohibition against viewpoint discrimination. See generally, Stone, Restrictions of Speech Because of its Content: The Peculiar Case of Subject-Matter Restrictions, 46 U.Chi.L.Rev. 81 (1978).

We have invoked the prohibition against content discrimination to invalidate government restrictions on access to public forums. See, e.g., Carey v. Brown, 447 U.S. 455 (1980); Grayned v. City of Rockford, 408 U.S. 104 (1972); Police Department of Chicago v. Mosley, 408 U.S. 92 (1972). We also have relied on this prohibition to strike down restrictions on access to a limited public forum. See, e.g., Widmar v. Vincent, 454 U.S. 263 (1981). Finally, we have applied the doctrine of content neutrality to government regulation of protected speech in cases in which no restriction of access to public property was involved. See, e.g., Consolidated Edison Company v. Public Service Commission, 447 U.S. 530 (1980); Erznoznik v. City of Jacksonville, 422 U.S. 205 (1975).

. . . .

Admittedly, this Court has not always required content neutrality in restrictions on access to government property. We upheld content-based exclusions in Lehman v. City of Shaker Heights, 418 U.S. 298 (1974), in Greer v. Spock,

424 U.S. 828 (1976), and in Jones v. North Carolina Prisoners' Union, 433 U.S. 119 (1977). All three cases involved an unusual forum, which was found to be nonpublic, and the speech was determined for a variety of reasons to be incompatible with the forum. These cases provide some support for the notion that the government is permitted to exclude certain subjects from discussion in nonpublic forums. They provide no support, however, for the notion that government, once it has opened up government property for discussion of specific subjects, may discriminate among viewpoints on those topics. Although *Greer, Lehman,* and *Jones* permitted content-based restrictions, none of the cases involved viewpoint discrimination. All of the restrictions were viewpoint-neutral. . . .

Once the government permits discussion of certain subject matter, it may not impose restrictions that discriminate among viewpoints on those subjects whether a nonpublic forum is involved or not. This prohibition is implicit in the *Mosley* line of cases, in Tinker v. Des Moines Independent Community School District, 393 U.S. 503 (1969), and in those cases in which we have approved content-based restrictions on access to government property that is not a public forum. We have never held that government may allow discussion of a subject and then discriminate among viewpoints on that particular topic, even if the government for certain reasons may entirely exclude discussion of the subject from the forum. In this context, the greater power does not include the lesser because for First Amendment purposes exercise of the lesser power is more threatening to core values. Viewpoint discrimination is censorship in its purest form and government regulation that discriminates among viewpoints threatens the continued vitality of "free speech."

B

. . . This case does not involve a claim of an absolute right of access to the forum to discuss any subject whatever. If it did, public forum analysis might be relevant. This case involves a claim of equal access to discuss a subject that the board has approved for discussion in the forum. In essence, the respondents are not asserting a right of access at all; they are asserting a right to be free from discrimination. The critical inquiry, therefore, is whether the board's grant of exclusive access to the petitioner amounts to prohibited viewpoint discrimination.

II

. . .

The Court responds to the allegation of viewpoint discrimination by suggesting that there is no indication that the board intended to discriminate and that the exclusive access policy is based on the parties' status rather than on their views. . . .

. . .

On a practical level, the only reason for the petitioner to seek an exclusive access policy is to deny its rivals access to an effective channel of communication. No other group is explicitly denied access to the mail system. In fact, as the Court points out, many other groups have been granted access to the system. Apparently, access is denied to the respondents because of the likelihood of their expressing points of view different from the petitioner's on a range of subjects. The very argument the petitioner advances in support of the policy, the need to preserve labor peace, also indicates that the access policy is not viewpoint-neutral.

In short, the exclusive access policy discriminates against the respondents based on their viewpoint. The board has agreed to amplify the speech of the petitioner, while repressing the speech of the respondents based on the respondents' point of view. This sort of discrimination amounts to censorship and infringes the First Amendment rights of the respondents. . . .[a]

. . .

LOS ANGELES v. TAXPAYERS FOR VINCENT

___ U.S. ___, 104 S.Ct. 2118, 80 L.Ed.2d 772 (1984).

Justice Stevens delivered the opinion of the Court.

Section 28.04 of the Los Angeles Municipal Code prohibits the posting of signs on public property. The question presented is whether that prohibition abridges appellees' freedom of speech within the meaning of the First Amendment.

In March 1979, Roland Vincent was a candidate for election to the Los Angeles City Council. A group of his supporters known as Taxpayers for Vincent ("Taxpayers") entered into a contract with a political sign service company known as Candidates Outdoor Graphics Service ("COGS") to fabricate and post signs with Vincent's name on them. COGS produced 15 × 44 inch cardboard signs and attached them to utility poles at various locations by draping them over cross-arms which support the poles and stapling the cardboard together at the bottom. The signs' message was: "Roland Vincent—City Council."

Acting under the authority of § 28.04 of the Municipal Code, employees of the City's Bureau of Street Maintenance routinely removed all posters attached to utility poles and similar objects covered by the ordinance, including the COGS signs. The weekly sign removal report covering the period March 1– March 7, 1979, indicated that among the 1,207 signs removed from public property during that week, 48 were identified as "Roland Vincent" signs. Most of the other signs identified in that report were apparently commercial in character.

On March 12, 1979, Taxpayers and COGS filed this action in the United States District Court for the Central District of California, naming the City, the Director of the Bureau of Street Maintenance, and members of the City Council as defendants. They sought an injunction against enforcement of the ordinance as well as compensatory and punitive damages. After engaging in discovery, the parties filed cross-motions for summary judgment on the issue of liability. The District Court entered findings of fact, concluded that the ordinance was constitutional, and granted the City's motion.

. . . .

In its conclusions of law the District Court characterized the esthetic and economic interests in improving the beauty of the City "by eliminating clutter and visual blight" as "legitimate and compelling." Those interests, together with the interest in protecting the safety of workmen who must scale utility poles and the interest in eliminating traffic hazards, adequately supported the sign prohibition as a reasonable regulation affecting the time, place, and manner of expression.

. . . [T]he Court of Appeals concluded that the City had not justified its total ban.

In its appeal to this Court the City challenges the Court of Appeals' holding that § 28.04 is unconstitutional on its face. Taxpayers and COGS defend that

---

[a] For a critique of the analytical distinctions applied between different kinds of public property, see Note, 35 Stan.L.Rev. 121 (1982).

holding and also contend that the ordinance is unconstitutional as applied to their posting of political campaign signs on the cross-arms of utility poles. There are two quite different ways in which a statute or ordinance may be considered invalid "on its face"—either because it is unconstitutional in every conceivable application, or because it seeks to prohibit such a broad range of protected conduct that it is unconstitutionally "overbroad." We shall analyze the "facial" challenges to the ordinance, and then address its specific application to appellees.

I

The seminal cases in which the Court held state legislation unconstitutional "on its face" did not involve any departure from the general rule that a litigant only has standing to vindicate his own constitutional rights. In Stromberg v. California, 283 U.S. 359 (1931) and Lovell v. Griffin, 303 U.S. 444 (1938), the statutes were unconstitutional as applied to the defendants' conduct, but they were also unconstitutional on their face because it was apparent that any attempt to enforce such legislation would create an unacceptable risk of the suppression of ideas. In cases of this character a holding of facial invalidity expresses the conclusion that the statute could never be applied in a valid manner. Such holdings invalidated entire statutes, but did not create any exception from the general rule that constitutional adjudication requires a review of the application of a statute to the conduct of the party before the Court.

. . .

. . . [O]n this record it appears that if the ordinance may be validly applied to COGS, it can be validly applied to most if not all of the signs of parties not before the Court. Appellees have simply failed to demonstrate a realistic danger that the ordinance will significantly compromise recognized First Amendment protections of individuals not before the Court. It would therefore be inappropriate in this case to entertain an overbreadth challenge to the ordinance.

. . . We therefore limit our analysis of the constitutionality of the ordinance to the concrete case before us, and now turn to the arguments that it is invalid as applied to the expressive activity of Taxpayers and COGS.

II

. . .

As *Stromberg* and *Lovell* demonstrate, there are some purported interests— such as a desire to suppress support for a minority party or an unpopular cause, or to exclude the expression of certain points of view from the marketplace of ideas—that are so plainly illegitimate that they would immediately invalidate the rule. The general principle that has emerged from this line of cases is that the First Amendment forbids the government from regulating speech in ways that favor some viewpoints or ideas at the expense of others. . . .

That general rule has no application to this case. For there is not even a hint of bias or censorship in the City's enactment or enforcement of this ordinance. There is no claim that the ordinance was designed to suppress certain ideas that the City finds distasteful or that it has been applied to appellees because of the views that they express. The text of the ordinance is neutral—indeed it is silent—concerning any speaker's point of view and the District Court's findings indicate that it has been applied to appellees and others in an evenhanded manner.

In United States v. O'Brien, 391 U.S. 367 (1968), the Court set forth the appropriate framework for reviewing a viewpoint neutral regulation of this kind:

"[A] government regulation is sufficiently justified if it is within the constitutional power of the Government; if it furthers an important or substantial governmental interest; if the governmental interest is unrelated to the suppression of free expression; and if the incidental restriction on alleged First Amendment freedoms is no greater than is essential to the furtherance of that interest." Id., at 377.

. . .

In this case, taxpayers and COGS do not dispute that it is within the constitutional power of the City to attempt to improve its appearance, or that this interest is basically unrelated to the suppression of ideas. Therefore the critical inquiries are whether that interest is sufficiently substantial to justify the effect of the ordinance on appellees' expression, and whether that effect is no greater than necessary to accomplish the City's purpose.

III

. . .

Metromedia, Inc. v. City of San Diego, 453 U.S. 490 (1981), dealt with San Diego's prohibition of certain forms of outdoor billboards. There the Court considered the city's interest in avoiding visual clutter, and seven Justices explicitly concluded that this interest was sufficient to justify a prohibition of billboards, see id., at 507–508, 510 (opinion of White, J., joined by Stewart, Marshall & Powell, JJ.); id., at 552 (Stevens, J., dissenting in part); id., at 559–561 (Burger, C. J., dissenting); id., at 570 (Rehnquist, J., dissenting). Justice White, writing for the plurality, expressly concluded that the city's esthetic interests were sufficiently substantial to provide an acceptable justification for a content neutral prohibition against the use of billboards; San Diego's interest in its appearance was undoubtedly a substantial governmental goal. Id., at 507–508.

We reaffirm the conclusion of the majority in *Metromedia.* The problem addressed by this ordinance—the visual assault on the citizens of Los Angeles presented by an accumulation of signs posted on public property—constitutes a significant substantive evil within the City's power to prohibit. . . .

IV

We turn to the question whether the scope of the restriction on appellees' expressive activity is substantially broader than necessary to protect the City's interest in eliminating visual clutter. The incidental restriction on expression which results from the City's attempt to accomplish such a purpose is considered justified as a reasonable regulation of the time, place, or manner of expression if it is narrowly tailored to serve that interest. . . . By banning these signs, the City did no more than eliminate the exact source of the evil it sought to remedy. The plurality wrote in *Metromedia:* "It is not speculative to recognize that billboards by their very nature, wherever located and however constructed, can be perceived as an 'esthetic harm.'" 453 U.S., at 510. The same is true of posted signs.

It is true that the esthetic interest in preventing the kind of litter that may result from the distribution of leaflets on the public streets and sidewalks cannot support a prophylactic prohibition against the citizens' exercise of that method of expressing his views. In Schneider v. State, 308 U.S. 147 (1939), the Court held that ordinances that absolutely prohibited handbilling on the streets were invalid. The Court explained that cities could adequately protect the esthetic interest in avoiding litter without abridging protected expression merely by penalizing those who actually litter. See id., at 162. Taxpayers contend that their interest in supporting Vincent's political campaign, which affords them a constitutional right to distribute brochures and leaflets on the public streets of Los Angeles, provides equal support for their asserted right to post temporary signs on objects adjacent to the streets and sidewalks. They argue that the mere fact that their temporary signs "add somewhat" to the city's visual clutter is entitled to no more weight than the temporary unsightliness of discarded handbills and the additional street cleaning burden that were insufficient to justify the ordinances reviewed in *Schneider.*

The rationale of *Schneider* is inapposite in the context of the instant case. There, individual citizens were actively exercising their right to communicate directly with potential recipients of their message. The conduct continued only while the speakers or distributors remained on the scene. In this case, appellees posted dozens of temporary signs throughout an area where they would remain unattended until removed. As the Court expressly noted in *Schneider,* the First Amendment does not "deprive a municipality of power to enact regulations against throwing literature broadcast in the streets. Prohibition of such conduct would not abridge the constitutional liberty since such activity bears no neces- sary relationship to the freedom to speak, write, print or distribute information or opinion." 308 U.S., at 160–161. In short, there is no constitutional impediment to "the punishment of those who actually throw paper on the streets." 308 U.S., at 162. A distributor of leaflets has no right simply to scatter his pamphlets in the air—or to toss large quantities of paper from the window of a tall building or a low flying airplane. Characterizing such an activity as a separate means of communication does not diminish the state's power to condemn it as a public nuisance. . . .

With respect to signs posted by appellees, . . . it is the tangible medium of expressing the message that has the adverse impact on the appearance of the landscape. In *Schneider,* an anti-littering statute could have addressed the substantive evil without prohibiting expressive activity, whereas application of the prophylactic rule actually employed gratuitously infringed upon the right of an individual to communicate directly with a willing listener. Here, the substantive evil—visual blight—is not merely a possible by-product of the activity, but is created by the medium of expression itself. In contrast to *Schneider,* therefore, the application of ordinance in this case responds precisely to the substantive problem which legitimately concerns the City. The ordinance curtails no more speech than is necessary to accomplish its purpose.

V

The Court of Appeals accepted the argument that a prohibition against the use of unattractive signs cannot be justified on esthetic grounds if it fails to apply to all equally unattractive signs wherever they might be located. A comparable argument was categorically rejected in *Metromedia.* In that case it was argued that the city could not simultaneously permit billboards to be used for on-site advertising and also justify the prohibition against offsite advertising on esthetic grounds, since both types of advertising were equally unattractive. The Court held, however, that the city could reasonably conclude that the esthetic interest was outweighed by the countervailing interest in one kind of advertising even though it was not outweighed by the other. So here, the validity of the esthetic interest in the elimination of signs on public property is not compromised by failing to extend the ban to private property. The private citizen's interest in controlling the use of his own property justifies the disparate treatment. Moreover, by not extending the ban to all locations, a significant opportunity to communicate by means of temporary signs is preserved, and private property owners' esthetic concerns will keep the posting of signs on their property within reasonable bounds. Even if some visual blight remains, a partial, content-neutral ban may nevertheless enhance the City's appearance.

Furthermore, there is no finding that in any area where appellees seek to place signs, there are already so many signs posted on adjacent private property that the elimination of appellees' signs would have an inconsequential effect on the esthetic values with which the City is concerned. There is simply no predicate in the findings of the District Court for the conclusion that the prohibition against the posting of appellees' signs fails to advance the City's esthetic interest.

VI

While the First Amendment does not guarantee the right to employ every conceivable method of communication at all times and in all places, Heffron v. International Society for Krishna Consciousness, 452 U.S. 640, 647 (1981), a restriction on expressive activity may be invalid if the remaining modes of communication are inadequate. See, e.g., United States v. Grace, 461 U.S. 171, 177 (1983); Heffron v. International Society for Krishna Consciousness, 452 U.S. 640, 654–655 (1981); Consolidated Edison Co. v. Public Serv. Comm'n, 447 U.S. 530, 535 (1980); Linmark Associates, Inc. v. Willingboro, 431 U.S. 85, 93 (1977). The Los Angeles ordinance does not affect any individual's freedom to exercise the right to speak and to distribute literature in the same place where the posting of signs on public property is prohibited. To the extent that the posting of signs on public property has advantages over these forms of expression, see, e.g., Talley v. California, 362 U.S. 60, 64–65 (1960), there is no reason to believe that these same advantages cannot be obtained through other means. To the contrary, the findings of the District Court indicate that there are ample alternative modes of communication in Los Angeles. Notwithstanding appellees' general assertions in their brief concerning the utility of political posters, nothing in the findings indicates that the posting of political posters on public property is a uniquely valuable or important mode of communication, or that appellees' ability to communicate effectively is threatened by ever-increasing restrictions on expression.

VII

Appellees suggest that the public property covered by the ordinance is either itself a "public forum" for First Amendment purposes, or at least should be treated in the same respect as the "public forum" in which the property is located. "Traditional public forum property occupies a special position in terms of First Amendment protection," United States v. Grace, 461 U.S. 171, 180 (1983), and appellees maintain that their sign-posting activities are entitled to this protection.

. . .

Appellees' reliance on the public forum doctrine is misplaced. They fail to demonstrate the existence of a traditional right of access respecting such items as utility poles for purposes of their communication comparable to that recognized for public streets and parks, and it is clear that "the First Amendment does not guarantee access to government property simply because it is owned or controlled by the government." United States Postal Service v. Greenburg Civic Ass'n, 453 U.S. 114, 129 (1981). Rather, the "existence of a right of access to public property and the standard by which limitations upon such a right must be evaluated differ depending on the character of the property at issue." Perry Education Ass'n v. Perry Local Educators' Ass'n, 460 U.S. 37, 44 (1983).

Lampposts can of course be used as signposts, but the mere fact that government property can be used as a vehicle for communication does not mean that the Constitution requires such uses to be permitted. Cf. United States Postal Service v. Greenburg Civic Ass'n, 453 U.S. 114, 131 (1981).[31] Public property which is not by tradition or designation a forum for public communication may be reserved by the state "for its intended purposes, communicative or otherwise, as long as the regulation on speech is reasonable and not an effort to suppress expression merely because public officials oppose the speaker's view." Perry Education Ass'n v. Perry Local Educators' Ass'n, 460 U.S. 37, 46 (1983). Given our analysis of the legitimate interest served by the ordinance, its viewpoint neutrality, and the availability of alternative channels of communication, the ordinance is certainly constitutional as applied to appellees under this standard.[32]

VIII

Finally, Taxpayers and COGS argue that Los Angeles could have written an ordinance that would have had a less severe effect on expressive activity such as theirs, by permitting the posting of any kind of sign at any time on some types of public property, or by making a variety of other more specific exceptions to the ordinance: for signs carrying certain types of messages (such as political campaign signs), for signs posted during specific time periods (perhaps during political campaigns), for particular locations (perhaps for areas already cluttered by an excessive number of signs on adjacent private property), or for signs meeting design specifications (such as size or color). Plausible public policy arguments might well be made in support of any such exception, but it by no means follows that it is therefore constitutionally mandated, . . . nor is it clear that some of the suggested exceptions would even be constitutionally permissible. For example, even though political speech is entitled to the fullest possible measure of constitutional protection, there are a host of other communications that command the same respect. An assertion that "Jesus Saves", that "Abortion is Murder", that every woman has the "Right to Choose", or that "Alcohol Kills", may have a claim to a constitutional exemption from the ordinance that is just as strong as "Robert Vincent—City Council." . . . To create an exception for appellees' political speech and not these other types of speech might create a risk of engaging in constitutionally forbidden content discrimination. See, e.g., Carey v. Brown, 447 U.S. 455 (1980); Police Department of Chicago v. Mosley, 408 U.S. 92 (1972). Moreover, the volume of permissible postings under such a mandated exemption might so limit the ordinance's effect as to defeat its aim of combatting visual blight.

Any constitutionally mandated exception to the City's total prohibition against temporary signs on public property would necessarily rest on a judicial determination that the City's traffic control and safety interests had little or no

---

[31] Any tangible property owned by the government could be used to communicate—bumper stickers may be placed on official automobiles—and yet appellees could not seriously claim the right to attach "Taxpayer for Vincent" bumper stickers to City-owned automobiles. At some point, the government's relationship to things under its dominion and control is virtually identical to a private owner's property interest in the same kinds of things, and in such circumstances, the State, "no less than a private owner of property, has power to preserve the property under its control for the use to which it is lawfully dedicated." Adderley v. Florida, 385 U.S. 39, 47 (1966).

[32] Just as it is not dispositive to label the posting of signs on public property as a discrete medium of expression, it is also of limited utility in the context of this case to focus on whether the tangible property itself should be deemed a public forum. Generally an analysis of whether property is a public forum provides a workable analytical tool. However, "the analytical line between a regulation of the 'time, place, and manner' in which First Amendment rights may be exercised in a traditional public forum, and the question of whether a particular piece of personal or real property owned or controlled by the government is in fact a 'public forum' may blur at the edges," United States Postal Service v. Greenburg Civic Ass'n, 453 U.S. 114, 132 (1981), and this is particularly true in cases falling between the paradigms of government property interests essentially mirroring analogous private interests and those clearly held in trust, either by tradition or recent convention, for the use of citizens at large.

applicability within the excepted category, and that the City's interests in esthetics are not sufficiently important to justify the prohibition in that category. But the findings of the District Court provide no basis for questioning the substantiality of the esthetic interest at stake, or for believing that a uniquely important form of communication has been abridged for the categories of expression engaged in by Taxpayers and COGS. Therefore, we accept the City's position that it may decide that the esthetic interest in avoiding "visual clutter" justifies a removal of signs creating or increasing that clutter. The findings of the District Court that COGS signs add to the problems addressed by the ordinance and, if permitted to remain, would encourage others to post additional signs, are sufficient to justify application of the ordinance to these appellees.

As recognized in *Metromedia,* if the city has a sufficient basis for believing that billboards are traffic hazards and are unattractive, "then obviously the most direct and perhaps the only effective approach to solving the problems they create is to prohibit them." 453 U.S., at 508. As is true of billboards, the esthetic interests that are implicated by temporary signs are presumptively at work in all parts of the city, including those where appellees posted their signs, and there is no basis in the record in this case upon which to rebut that presumption. These interests are both psychological and economic. The character of the environment affects the quality of life and the value of property in both residential and commercial areas. We hold that on this record these interests are sufficiently substantial to justify this content neutral, impartially administered prohibition against the posting of appellees' temporary signs on public property and that such an application of the ordinance does not create an unacceptable threat to the "profound national commitment to the principle that debate on public issues should be uninhibited, robust, and wide-open." New York Times Co. v. Sullivan, 376 U.S. 254, 270 (1963).

The judgment of the Court of Appeals is reversed and the case is remanded to that Court.

It is so ordered.

Justice Brennan, with whom Justice Marshall and Justice Blackmun join, dissenting.

The plurality opinion in Metromedia, Inc. v. San Diego, 453 U.S. 490 (1980), concluded that the City of San Diego could, consistently with the First Amendment, restrict the commercial use of billboards in order to "preserve and improve the appearance of the City." Id., at 493 (plurality opinion). Today, the Court sustains the constitutionality of Los Angeles' similarly motivated ban on the posting of political signs on public property. Because the Court's lenient approach towards the restriction of speech for reasons of aesthetics threatens seriously to undermine the protections of the First Amendment, I dissent.

. . .

My suggestion in *Metromedia* was that courts should exercise special care in addressing these questions when a purely aesthetic objective is asserted to justify a restriction of speech. Specifically, "before deferring to a city's judgment, a court must be convinced that the city is seriously and comprehensively address-ing aethestic concerns with respect to its environment." 453 U.S., at 531. I adhere to that view. Its correctness—premised largely on my concern that aesthetic interests are easy for a city to assert and difficult for a court to evaluate—is, for me, reaffirmed by this case.

The fundamental problem in this kind of case is that a purely aesthetic state interest offered to justify a restriction on speech—that is, a governmental objective justified solely in terms like "proscribing intrusive and unpleasant formats for expression,"—creates difficulties for a reviewing court in fulfilling its obligation to ensure that government regulation does not trespass upon protections secured by the First Amendment. The source of those difficulties is the unavoidable subjectivity of aesthetic judgments—the fact that "beauty is in the eye of the beholder." As a consequence of this subjectivity, laws defended on aesthetic grounds raise problems for judicial review that are not presented by laws defended on more objective grounds—such as national security, public health, or public safety. In practice, therefore, the inherent subjectivity of aesthetic judgments makes it all too easy for the government to fashion its justification for a law in a manner that impairs the ability of a reviewing court meaningfully to make the required inquiries.

Initially, a reviewing court faces substantial difficulties determining whether the actual objective is related to the suppression of speech. The asserted interest in aesthetics may be only a facade for content-based suppression.

. . .

For example, in evaluating the ordinance before us in this case, the City might be pursuing either of two objectives, motivated by two very different judgments. One objective might be the elimination of "visual clutter," attributable in whole or in part to signs posted on public property. The aesthetic judgment underlying this objective would be that the clutter created by these signs offends the community's desire for an orderly, visually pleasing environment. A second objective might simply be the elimination of the messages typically carried by the signs. In that case, the aesthetic judgment would be that the signs' messages are themselves displeasing. The first objective is lawful, of course, but the second is not. Yet the City might easily mask the second objective by asserting the first and declaring that signs constitute visual clutter. In short, we must avoid unquestioned acceptance of the City's bare declaration of an aesthetic objective lest we fail in our duty to prevent unlawful trespasses upon First Amendment protections.

. . .

Similarly, when a total ban is justified solely in terms of aesthetics, the means inquiry necessary to evaluate the constitutionality of the ban may be impeded by deliberate or unintended government manipulation. Governmental objectives that are purely aesthetic can usually be expressed in a virtually limitless variety of ways. Consequently, objectives can be tailored to fit whatever program the government devises to promote its general aesthetic interests. Once the government has identified a substantial aesthetic objective and has selected a preferred means of achieving its objective, it will be possible for the government to correct any mismatch between means and ends by redefining the ends to conform with the means.

In this case, for example, any of several objectives might be the City's actual substantial goal in banning temporary signs: (1) the elimination of all signs throughout the City, (2) the elimination of all signs in certain parts of the City, or (3) a reduction of the density of signs. Although a total ban on the posting of signs on public property would be the least restrictive means of achieving only the first objective, it would be a very effective means of achieving the other two as well. It is quite possible, therefore, that the City might select such a ban as the means by which to further its general interest in solving its sign problem, without explicitly considering which of the three specific objectives is really substantial. Then, having selected the total ban as its preferred means, the City would be strongly inclined to characterize the first objective as the substantial one. This might be done purposefully in order to conform the ban to the least-restrictive-means requirement, or it might be done inadvertently as a natural concomitant of considering means and ends together. But regardless of why it is done, a reviewing court will be confronted with a statement of substantiality the subjectivity of which makes it impossible to question on its face.

This possibility of interdependence between means and ends in the development of policies to promote aesthetics poses a major obstacle to judicial review of the availability of alternative means that are less restrictive of speech. Indeed, when a court reviews a restriction of speech imposed in order to promote an aesthetic objective, there is a significant possibility that the court will be able to do little more than pay lip service to the First Amendment inquiry into the availability of less restrictive alternatives. . . .

. . . .

The fact that there are difficulties inherent in judicial review of aesthetics-based restrictions of speech does not imply that government may not engage in such activities. As I have said, improvement and preservation of the aesthetic environment are often legitimate and important governmental functions. But because the implementation of these functions creates special dangers to our First Amendment freedoms, there is a need for more stringent judicial scrutiny than the Court seems willing to exercise.

In cases like this, where a total ban is imposed on a particularly valuable method of communication, a court should require the government to provide tangible proof of the legitimacy and substantiality of its aesthetic objective. Justifications for such restrictions articulated by the government should be critically examined to determine whether the government has committed itself to addressing the identified aesthetic problem.

In my view, such statements of aesthetic objectives should be accepted as substantial and unrelated to the suppression of speech only if the government demonstrates that it is pursuing an identified objective seriously and comprehensively and in ways that are unrelated to the restriction of speech. *Metromedia,* supra, 453 U.S., at 531 (Brennan, J., concurring in judgment). Without such a demonstration, I would invalidate the restriction as violative of the First Amendment. By requiring this type of showing, courts can ensure that governmental regulation of the aesthetic environment remains within the constraints established by the First Amendment. First, we would have a reasonably reliable indication that it is not the content or communicative aspect of speech that the government finds unaesthetic. Second, when a restriction of speech is part of a comprehensive and seriously pursued program to promote an aesthetic objective, we have a more reliable indication of the government's own assessment of the substantiality of its objective. And finally, when an aesthetic objective is pursued on more than one front, we have a better basis upon which to ascertain its precise nature and thereby determine whether the means selected are the least restrictive ones for achieving the objective.

This does not mean that a government must address all aesthetic problems at one time or that a government should hesitate to pursue aesthetic objectives. What it does mean, however, is that when such an objective is pursued, it may not be pursued solely at the expense of First Amendment freedoms, nor may it be pursued by arbitrarily discriminating against a form of speech that has the same aesthetic characteristics as other forms of speech that are also present in the community. See *Metromedia,* supra, at 531–534 (Brennan, J., concurring in judgment).

Accordingly, in order for Los Angeles to succeed in defending its total ban on the posting of signs, the City would have to demonstrate that it is pursuing its goal of eliminating visual clutter in a serious and comprehensive manner. Most importantly, the City would have to show that it is pursuing its goal through programs other than its ban on signs, that at least some of those programs address the visual clutter problem through means that do not entail the restriction of speech, and that the programs parallel the ban in their stringency, geographical scope, and aesthetic focus. In this case, however, as the Court of Appeals found, there is no indication that the City has addressed its visual clutter problem in any way other than by prohibiting the posting of signs—throughout the City and without regard to the density of their presence. Therefore, I would hold that the prohibition violates appellees' First Amendment rights.

In light of the extreme stringency of Los Angeles' ban—barring all signs from being posted—and its wide geographical scope—covering the entire City—it might be difficult for Los Angeles to make the type of showing I have suggested. Cf. *Metromedia,* supra, 453 U.S., at 533–534. A more limited approach to the visual clutter problem, however, might well pass constitutional muster. I have no doubt that signs posted on public property in certain areas—including, perhaps, parts of Los Angeles—could contribute to the type of eyesore that a city would genuinely have a substantial interest in eliminating. These areas might include parts of the City that are particularly pristine, reserved for certain uses, designated to reflect certain themes, or so blighted that broad gauged renovation is necessary. Presumably, in these types of areas, the City would also regulate the aesthetic environment in ways other than the banning of temporary signs. The City might zone such areas for a particular type of development or lack of development; it might actively create a particular type of environment; it might be especially vigilant in keeping the area clean; it might regulate the size and location of permanent signs; or it might reserve particular locations, such as kiosks, for the posting of temporary signs. Similarly, Los Angeles might be able to attack its visual clutter problem in more areas of the City by reducing the stringency of the ban, perhaps by regulating the density of temporary signs, and coupling that approach with additional measures designed to reduce other forms of visual clutter. There are a variety of ways that the aesthetic environment can be regulated, some restrictive of speech and others not, but it is only when aesthetic regulation is addressed in a comprehensive and focused manner that we can ensure that the goals pursued are substantial and that the manner in which they are pursued is no more restrictive of speech than is necessary.

In the absence of such a showing in this case, I believe that Los Angeles' total ban sweeps so broadly and trenches so completely on appellees' use of an important medium of political expression that it must be struck down as violative of the First Amendment.

I therefore dissent.[a]

B.   THE GOVERNMENT FORUM AND GOVERNMENT SUBSIDIES TO SPEECH

Introduction. In the previous cases in this chapter concerning use of public property as a forum, the property's primary use was for some purpose other than expression. This section raises the question of the government activity whose primary purpose is communication—whether it is as modest as a billboard or as imposing as a community-owned theatre. Specifically, if the government forum is opened to some third party expression, do the principles of the public forum cases, concerning equal access and content neutrality, apply? Is there need for some modification of those principles if the government itself is part of the communicative process or decides to subsidize, rather than restrict, a particular point of view?

----

[a] For a discussion of the cases, and a critique, see Goldberger, *Judicial Scrutiny in Public Forum Cases: Misplaced Trust in the Judgment of Public Officials,* 32 Buffalo L.Rev. 175 (1983).

THE GOVERNMENT AS SPEAKER

(1) The Role of Government Speech in Public Debate. No Supreme Court decision has interpreted the first amendment to require that government communications be neutral or present all sides of debate on controversial public issues, other than issues of religious doctrine. The Court's most relevant discussion was in Buckley v. Valeo, 424 U.S. 1, 92–93 (1976), where the Court rejected a first amendment challenge to provisions of the Federal Election Campaign Act of 1971 for public financing of presidential election campaigns. The Court's opinion stated:

> "Appellants next argue that 'by analogy' to the Religion Clauses of the First Amendment public financing of election campaigns, however meritorious, violates the First Amendment. We have of course held that the Religion Clauses—'Congress shall make no law respecting an establishment of religion, or prohibiting the free exercise thereof'—require Congress, and the States through the Fourteenth Amendment, to remain neutral in matters of religion. . . . The Government may not aid one religion to the detriment of others or impose a burden on one religion that is not imposed on others, and may not even aid all religions. . . . But the analogy is patently inapplicable to our issue here. Although 'Congress shall make no law . . . abridging the freedom of speech, or of the press,' Subtitle H is a congressional effort, not to abridge, restrict, or censor speech, but rather to use public money to facilitate and enlarge public discussion and participation in the electoral process, goals vital to a self-governing people. Thus, Subtitle H furthers, not abridges, pertinent First Amendment values.[127]"

(2) The Issue of Neutrality in Connection with the Government Forum. In the traditional public forum cases, involving communication in parks and streets, the constitutional requirement of government content neutrality was established in a context where government was playing no part in communication. Where the government operates a forum whose primary purpose is communication, government may play a variety of communicative roles—ranging from choosing the communication and communicators allowed to use the forum, to editor, to active speaker. Is it possible to reconcile a constitutional requirement of government content neutrality in the public forum with a conception of government as a partisan communicator? Consider Columbia Broadcasting System, Inc. v. Democratic Nat'l Committee, 412 U.S. 94 (1973), infra, p. 1399. The Court rejected statutory and constitutional claims that radio and television stations could not refuse to sell editorial advertising time. Justice Brennan's dissent, joined by Justice Marshall, concluded that the scheme of federal regulation of the electronic media constituted sufficient governmental action to require application of the first amendment to decisions made by owners of radio and television stations. He argued that the fact that the broadcast forum was designed specifically for communication made arguments for applying constitutional requirements of equal access to that forum even stronger than in the case of parks and streets, since a requirement of access "would in no sense divert that spectrum from its intended use." He conceded

---

[127] The historical bases of the Religion and Speech Clauses are markedly different. Intolerable persecutions throughout history led to the Framers' firm determination that religious worship—both in method and belief—must be strictly protected from government intervention. . . . But the central purpose of the Speech and Press Clauses was to assure a society in which "uninhibited, robust, and wide-open" public debate concerning matters of public interest would thrive, for only in such a society can a healthy representative democracy flourish. New York Times Co. v. Sullivan, 376 U.S. 254, 270 (1964). Legislation to enhance these First Amendment values is the rule, not the exception. Our statute books are replete with laws providing financial assistance to the exercise of free speech, such as aid to public broadcasting and other forms of educational media, 47 U.S.C. §§ 390–399, and preferential postal rates and antitrust exemptions for newspapers, 39 CFR § 132.2 (1975); 15 U.S.C. §§ 1801–1804.

that broadcasters have a first amendment interest in exercising "journalistic supervision," which would operate in "normal programming time," but concluded that the right of broadcasters to speak was less central to decisions that deal "only with the allocation of advertising time." Contrast Justice Douglas' assertion in his opinion concurring in the result in Lehman v. Shaker Heights, 418 U.S. 298, 306 (1974), that "[t]he First Amendment . . . draws no distinction between press privately owned, and press owned otherwise." (In the *C.B.S.* case, in polar contradiction to Justice Brennan, Justice Douglas argued that existing federal statutory requirements of broadcast impartiality and public access were unconstitutional.) Is it possible to reconcile an interpretation of the first amendment that overturns government requirements of neutrality for a privately owned communicative forum with another first amendment interpretation that imposes a constitutional requirement of neutrality for a similar governmentally owned forum? See Canby, *The First Amendment and the State as Editor: Implications for Public Broadcasting,* 52 Tex.L.Rev. 1123 (1974).

(3) **Public School Newspapers.** Newspapers or periodicals financed by public schools have been a frequent source of litigation. Some cases involve claims of access brought against student editors who have refused to accept advertisements or letters to the editor. Other cases have involved a clash between student editors and school officials, who have disciplined the student editors, withdrawn financial support from the publication, or imposed direct controls on publication content. Would it make sense to protect student editors from content controls imposed by school officials, while protecting student editors from access demands made by people not affiliated with the publication? See Cass, *First Amendment Access to Government Facilities,* 65 Va.L.Rev. 1287, 1350–1354 (1979), for a discussion of these problems, and citations to the lower court cases.

(4) **Other Issues of Government Speech.** Cases involving censorship of school newspapers by public school officials relate to the broader issue of government control of government speech. Does the first amendment preclude one level of government from restricting speech by subordinate government entities? Can a state legislature, for example, forbid the expenditure of funds by cities and counties to express their views on public issues?[1] A more pervasive issue is the extent to which government is entitled to control the content of speech by government officials and employees in the course of their employment. That issue has been most contentious in the context of academic freedom. To what extent can public school officials control the content of a teacher's classroom statements that are germane to the teacher's subject?[2] The issue has also arisen when school boards, or other governing boards of public

---

[1] In City of Boston v. Anderson, the Massachusetts Supreme Judicial Court had enjoined the city from expending public funds to support a referendum measure. Justice Brennan granted a stay of that injunction, concluding that there was a substantial constitutional question in light of First Nat'l Bank of Boston v. Bellotti, 435 U.S. 765 (1978), infra, p. 1357, which had overturned a Massachusetts law forbidding corporate expenditures on referendum issues. 439 U.S. 1389 (1978). While the Court denied a motion to vacate Justice Brennan's stay, 439 U.S. 951 (1978), it subsequently dismissed the city's appeal for want of a substantial federal question. 439 U.S. 1060 (1979). Three Justices dissented from dismissal of the appeal.

[2] The free speech rights of public school teachers seemed to be necessarily involved in Epperson v. Arkansas, 393 U.S. 97 (1968), infra, p. 1425, which struck down a state law forbidding teaching of evolution in public schools. The Court, however, characterized the free speech issue as a "thicket," and invalidated the law on the narrower ground that it violated the establishment clause. As noted, there is a constitutional requirement of neutrality on issues of religious doctrine, imposed by the establishment clause.

For differing views on the issue, compare Nahmod, *Controversy in the Classroom: The High School Teacher and Freedom of Expression,* 39 Geo.Wash.L.Rev. 1032 (1971) and Van Alstyne, *The Constitutional Rights of Teachers and Professors,* 1970 Duke L.J. 841, with Goldstein, *The Assessed Constitutional Right of Public School Teachers to Determine What They Teach,* 124 U.Pa.L.Rev. 1293 (1976).

libraries, have ordered librarians not to purchase, or to remove, particular books from the shelves.

For general discussion of the issues raised by government speech, see Shiffrin, *Government Speech,* 27 U.C.L.A.L.Rev. 565 (1980); Yudof, *When Government Speaks: Politics, Law and Government Expression in America* (1983), reviewed in Schauer, *Is Government Speech a Problem?*; 35 Stan.L.Rev. 373 (1983); Emerson, *The System of Freedom of Expression* 712–716 (1970).

BOARD OF EDUCATION v. PICO

457 U.S. 853, 102 S.Ct. 2799, 73 L.Ed.2d 435 (1982).

Justice Brennan announced the judgment of the Court, and delivered an opinion in which Justice Marshall and Justice Stevens joined, and in which Justice Blackmun joined except for Part II–A–(1).

The principal question presented is whether the First Amendment imposes limitations upon the exercise by a local school board of its discretion to remove library books from high school and junior high school libraries.

I

Petitioners are the Board of Education of the Island Trees Union Free School District No. 26, in New York, and [officers and members of the Board]. . . . Respondents . . . were students at the High School, and . . . a student at the Junior High School.

In September 1975 [3 officers and members of the Board] attended a conference sponsored by Parents of New York United (PONYU), a politically conservative organization of parents concerned about education legislation in the State of New York. At the conference these petitioners obtained lists of books described . . . as "objectionable," and . . . as "improper fare for school students." It was later determined that the High School library contained nine of the listed books, and that another listed book was in the Junior High School library. In February 1976, at a meeting with the superintendent of schools and the principals of the High School and Junior High School, the Board gave an "unofficial direction" that the listed books be removed from the library shelves and delivered to the Board's offices, so that Board members could read them. When this directive was carried out, it became publicized, and the Board issued a press release justifying its action. It characterized the removed books as "anti-American, anti-Christian, anti-Semitic, and just plain filthy," and concluded that "it is our duty, our moral obligation, to protect the children in our schools from this moral danger as surely as from physical and medical dangers."

A short time later, the Board appointed a "Book Review Committee," consisting of four Island Trees parents and four members of the Island Trees schools staff, to read the listed books and to recommend to the Board whether the books should be retained, taking into account the books' "educational suitability," "good taste," "relevance," and "appropriateness to age and grade level." In July, the Committee made its final report to the Board, recommending that five of the listed books be retained and that two others be removed from the school libraries. As for the remaining four books, the Committee could not agree on two, took no position on one, and recommended that the last book be made available to students only with parental approval. The Board substantially rejected the Committee's report later that month, deciding that only one book should be returned to the High School library without restriction, that another should be made available subject to parental approval, but that the remaining nine books should "be removed from elementary and secondary libraries and [from] use in the curriculum." The Board gave no reasons for rejecting the recommendations of the Committee that it had appointed.

Respondents reacted to the Board's decision by bringing the present action under 42 U.S.C. § 1983 in the United States District Court for the Eastern District of New York. They alleged that petitioners had

> "ordered the removal of the books from school libraries and proscribed their use in the curriculum because particular passages in the books offended their social, political and moral tastes and not because the books, taken as a whole, were lacking in educational value."

Respondents claimed that the Board's actions denied them their rights under the First Amendment. They asked the court for a declaration that the Board's actions were unconstitutional, and for preliminary and permanent injunctive relief ordering the Board to return the nine books to the school libraries and to refrain from interfering with the use of those books in the schools' curricula.

.   .   .   .

II

We emphasize at the outset the limited nature of the substantive question presented by the case before us. Our precedents have long recognized certain constitutional limits upon the power of the State to control even the curriculum and classroom. For example, Meyer v. Nebraska, 262 U.S. 390 (1923), struck down a state law that forbade the teaching of modern foreign languages in public and private schools, and Epperson v. Arkansas, 393 U.S. 97 (1968), declared unconstitutional a state law that prohibited the teaching of the Darwinian theory of evolution in any state-supported school. But the current action does not require us to re-enter this difficult terrain, which *Meyer* and *Epperson* traversed without apparent misgiving. For as this case is presented to us, it does not involve textbooks, or indeed any books that Island Trees students would be required to read. Respondents do not seek in this Court to impose limitations upon their school board's discretion to prescribe the curricula of the Island Trees schools. On the contrary, the only books at issue in this case are *library* books, books that by their nature are optional rather than required reading. Our adjudication of the present case thus does not intrude into the classroom, or into the compulsory courses taught there. Furthermore, even as to library books, the action before us does not involve the *acquisition* of books. Respondents have not sought to compel their school board to add to the school library shelves any books that students desire to read. Rather, the only action challenged in this case is the *removal* from school libraries of books originally placed there by the school authorities, or without objection from them.

The substantive question before us is still further constrained by the procedural posture of this case. Petitioners were granted summary judgment by the District Court. The Court of Appeals reversed that judgment, and remanded the action for a trial on the merits of respondents' claims. We can reverse the judgment of the Court of Appeals, and grant petitioners' request for reinstatement of the summary judgment in their favor, only if we determine that "there is no genuine issue as to any material fact," and that petitioners are "entitled to a judgment as a matter of law." Fed.Rule Civ.Proc. 56(c). In making our determination, any doubt as to the existence of a genuine issue of material fact must be resolved against petitioners as the moving party.   .   .   .

In sum, the issue before us in this case is a narrow one, both substantively and procedurally. It may best be restated as two distinct questions. First, Does the First Amendment impose *any* limitations upon the discretion of petitioners to remove library books from the Island Trees High School and Junior High School? Second, If so, do the affidavits and other evidentiary materials before the District Court, construed most favorably to respondents, raise a genuine issue of fact whether petitioners might have exceeded those limitations? If we answer either of these questions in the negative, then we must reverse the judgment of the Court of Appeals and reinstate the District Court's summary judgment for petitioners. If we answer both questions in the affirmative, then we must affirm the judgment below. We examine these questions in turn.

A

(1)

The Court has long recognized that local school boards have broad discretion in the management of school affairs. See, e.g., Meyer v. Nebraska, 262 U.S. 390, 402 (1923); Pierce v. Society of Sisters, 268 U.S. 510, 543 (1925). Epperson v. Arkansas, supra, 393 U.S. at 104, reaffirmed that, by and large, "public education in our Nation is committed to the control of state and local authorities," and that federal courts should not ordinarily "intervene in the resolution of conflicts which arise in the daily operation of school systems." Tinker v. Des Moines School Dist., 393 U.S. 503, 507 (1969), noted that we have "repeatedly emphasized   .   .   .   the comprehensive authority of the States and of school officials   .   .   .   to prescribe and control conduct in the schools." We have also acknowledged that public schools are vitally important "in the preparation of individuals for participation as citizens," and as vehicles for "inculcating fundamental values necessary to the maintenance of a democratic political system." Ambach v. Norwick, 441 U.S. 68, 76–77 (1979). We are therefore in full agreement with petitioners that local school boards must be permitted "to establish and apply their curriculum in such a way as to transmit community values," and that "there is a legitimate and substantial community interest in promoting respect for authority and traditional values be they social, moral, or political."

At the same time, however, we have necessarily recognized that the discretion of the States and local school boards in matters of education must be exercised in a manner that comports with the transcendent imperatives of the First Amendment. In West Virginia v. Barnette, 319 U.S. 624 (1943), we held that under the First Amendment a student in a public school could not be compelled to salute the flag. We reasoned that

> "Boards of Education   .   .   .   have, of course, important, delicate, and highly discretionary functions, but none that they may not perform within the limits of the Bill of Rights. That they are educating the young for citizenship is reason for scrupulous protection of Constitutional freedoms of the individual, if we are not to strangle the free mind at its source and teach youth to discount important principles of our government as mere platitudes." Id., at 637.

Later cases have consistently followed this rationale. Thus Epperson v. Arkansas, supra, invalidated a State's anti-evolution statute as violative of the Establishment Clause, and reaffirmed the duty of federal courts "to apply the First Amendment's mandate in our educational system where essential to safeguard the fundamental values of freedom of speech and inquiry." 393 U.S., at 104. And Tinker v. Des Moines School Dist., supra, held that a local school board had infringed the free speech rights of high school and junior high school students by suspending them from school for wearing black armbands in class as a protest against the Government's policy in Vietnam; we stated there that the "comprehensive authority   .   .   .   of school officials" must be exercised "consistent with fundamental constitutional safeguards." 393 U.S., at 507. In sum, students do not "shed their rights to freedom of speech or expression at the schoolhouse gate," id., at 506, and therefore local school boards must discharge their "important, delicate, and highly discretionary functions" within the limits and constraints of the First Amendment.

The nature of students' First Amendment rights in the context of this case requires further examination. West Virginia v. Barnette, supra, is instructive. There the Court held that students' liberty of conscience could not be infringed in the name of "national unity" or "patriotism." 319 U.S., at 640–641. . . . . Similarly, Tinker v. Des Moines School Dist., supra, held that students' rights to freedom of expression of their political views could not be abridged by reliance upon an "undifferentiated fear or apprehension of disturbance" arising from such expression. . . .

Of course, courts should not "intervene in the resolution of conflicts which arise in the daily operations of school systems" unless "basic constitutional values" are "directly and sharply implicate[d]" in those conflicts. Epperson v. Arkansas, 393 U.S., at 104. But we think that the First Amendment rights of students may be directly and sharply implicated by the removal of books from the shelves of a school library. Our precedents have focused "not only on the role of the First Amendment in fostering individual self-expression but also on its role in affording the public access to discussion, debate, and the dissemination of information and ideas." First National Bank of Boston v. Bellotti, 435 U.S. 765, 783 (1978). And we have recognized that "the State may not, consistently with the spirit of the First Amendment, contract the spectrum of available knowledge." Griswold v. Connecticut, 381 U.S. 479, 482 (1965). In keeping with this principle, we have held that in a variety of contexts "the Constitution protects the right to receive information and ideas." Stanley v. Georgia, 394 U.S. 557, 564 (1969); see Kleindienst v. Mandel, 408 U.S. 753, 762–763 (1972) (citing cases). This right is an inherent corollary of the rights of free speech and press that are explicitly guaranteed by the Constitution, in two senses. First, the right to receive ideas follows ineluctably from the *sender's* First Amendment right to send them: "The right of freedom of speech and press . . . embraces the right to distribute literature, . . . and necessarily protects the right to receive it." Martin v. Struthers, 318 U.S. 141, 143 (1943) (citation omitted). . . .

More importantly, the right to receive ideas is a necessary predicate to the *recipient's* meaningful exercise of his own rights of speech, press, and political freedom. Madison admonished us that

"A popular Government, without popular information, or the means of acquiring it, is but a Prologue to a Farce or a Tragedy; or, perhaps both. Knowledge will forever govern ignorance: And a people who mean to be their own Governors, must arm themselves with the power which knowledge gives." 9 Writings of James Madison 103 (G. Hunt ed. 1910). . . .

In sum, just as access to ideas makes it possible for citizens generally to exercise their rights of free speech and press in a meaningful manner, such access prepares students for active and effective participation in the pluralistic, often contentious society in which they will soon be adult members. Of course all First Amendment rights accorded to students must be construed "in light of the special characteristics of the school environment." Tinker v. Des Moines School Dist., supra, at 506. But the special characteristics of the school *library* make that environment especially appropriate for the recognition of the First Amendment rights of students.

A school library, no less than any other public library, is "a place dedicated to quiet, to knowledge, and to beauty." Brown v. Louisiana, 383 U.S. 131, 142 (1966) (Opinion of Fortas, J.). Keyishian v. Board of Regents, 385 U.S.

589 (1967), observed that "students must always remain free to inquire, to study and to evaluate, to gain new maturity and understanding." The school library is the principal locus of such freedom. . . . Petitioners emphasize the inculcative function of secondary education, and argue that they must be allowed *unfettered* discretion to "transmit community values" through the Island Trees schools. But that sweeping claim overlooks the unique role of the school library. It appears from the record that use of the Island Trees school libraries is completely voluntary on the part of students. Their selection of books from these libraries is entirely a matter of free choice; the libraries afford them an opportunity at self-education and individual enrichment that is wholly optional. Petitioners might well defend their claim of absolute discretion in matters of *curriculum* by reliance upon their duty to inculcate community values. But we think that petitioners' reliance upon that duty is misplaced where, as here, they attempt to extend their claim of absolute discretion beyond the compulsory environment of the classroom, into the school library and the regime of voluntary inquiry that there holds sway.

(2)

In rejecting petitioners' claim of absolute discretion to remove books from their school libraries, we do not deny that local school boards have a substantial legitimate role to play in the determination of school library content. We thus must turn to the question of the extent to which the First Amendment places limitations upon the discretion of petitioners to remove books from their libraries. . . .

Petitioners rightly possess significant discretion to determine the content of their school libraries. But that discretion may not be exercised in a narrowly partisan or political manner. If a Democratic school board, motivated by party affiliation, ordered the removal of all books written by or in favor of Republicans, few would doubt that the order violated the constitutional rights of the students denied access to those books. The same conclusion would surely apply if an all-white school board, motivated by racial animus, decided to remove all books authored by blacks or advocating racial equality and integration. Our Constitution does not permit the official suppression of *ideas.* Thus whether petitioners' removal of books from their school libraries denied respondents their First Amendment rights depends upon the motivation behind petitioners' action. If petitioners *intended* by their removal decision to deny respondents access to ideas with which petitioners disagreed, and if this intent was the decisive factor in petitioners' decision, then petitioners have exercised their discretion in violation of the Constitution. To permit such intentions to control official actions would be to encourage the precise sort of officially prescribed orthodoxy unequivocally condemned in *Barnette.* On the other hand, respondents implicitly concede that an unconstitutional motivation would *not* be demonstrated if it were shown that petitioners had decided to remove the books at issue because those books were pervasively vulgar. And again, respondents concede that if it were demonstrated that the removal decision was based solely upon the "educational suitability" of the books in question, then their removal would be "perfectly permissible." In other words, in respondents' view such motivations, if decisive of petitioners' actions, would not carry the danger of an official suppression of ideas, and thus would not violate respondents' First Amendment rights.

As noted earlier, nothing in our decision today affects in any way the discretion of a local school board to choose books to *add* to the libraries of their schools. Because we are concerned in this case with the suppression of ideas, our holding today affects only the discretion to *remove* books. In brief, we hold that local school boards may not remove books from school library shelves simply because they dislike the ideas contained in those books and seek by their removal to "prescribe what shall be orthodox in politics, nationalism, religion, or other matters of opinion." West Virginia v. Barnette, 319 U.S., at 642. Such purposes stand inescapably condemned by our precedents.

B

We now turn to the remaining question presented by this case: Do the evidentiary materials that were before the District Court, when construed most favorably to respondents, raise a genuine issue of material fact whether petitioners exceeded constitutional limitations in exercising their discretion to remove the books from the school libraries? We conclude that the materials do raise such a question, which forecloses summary judgment in favor of petitioners.

.   .   .

.   .   . The evidence plainly does not foreclose the possibility that petitioners' decision to remove the books rested decisively upon disagreement with constitutionally protected ideas in those books, or upon a desire on petitioners' part to impose upon the students of the Island Trees High School and Junior High School a political orthodoxy to which petitioners and their constituents adhered. Of course, some of the evidence before the District Court might lead a finder of fact to accept petitioners' claim that their removal decision was based upon constitutionally valid concerns. But that evidence at most creates a genuine issue of material fact on the critical question of the credibility of petitioners' justifications for their decision.   .   .   .

The mandate shall issue forthwith.

Affirmed.

Justice Blackmun, concurring in part and concurring in the judgment.

While I agree with much in today's plurality opinion, and while I accept the standard laid down by the plurality to guide proceedings on remand, I write separately because I have a somewhat different perspective on the nature of the First Amendment right involved.

I

To my mind, this case presents a particularly complex problem because it involves two competing principles of constitutional stature. On the one hand, .   .   . local education officials may attempt "to promote civic virtues," Ambach v. Norwick, 441 U.S., at 80, and to "awake[n] the child to cultural values." Brown v. Board of Education, 347 U.S. 483, 493 (1954).   .   .   . It therefore seems entirely appropriate that the State use "public schools [to] .   .   . inculcat[e] fundamental values necessary to the maintenance of a democratic political system." Ambach v. Norwick, 441 U.S., at 77.

On the other hand, as the plurality demonstrates, it is beyond dispute that schools and school boards must operate within the confines of the First Amendment.   .   .   .

.   .   .

In my view, .   .   . the principle involved here is both narrower and more basic than the "right to receive information" identified by the plurality. I do not suggest that the State has any affirmative obligation to provide students with information or ideas, something that may well be associated with a "right to receive." And I do not believe, as the plurality suggests, that the right at issue here is somehow associated with the peculiar nature of the school library if schools may be used to inculcate ideas, surely libraries may play a role in that process. Instead, I suggest that certain forms of state discrimination *between* ideas are improper. In particular, our precedents command the conclusion that the State may not act to deny access to an idea simply because state officials disapprove of that idea for partisan or political reasons.

. . .

II

In my view, we strike a proper balance here by holding that school officials may not remove books for the *purpose* of restricting access to the political ideas or social perspectives discussed in them, when that action is motivated simply by the officials' disapproval of the ideas involved. . . .

. . .

Because I believe that the plurality has derived a standard similar to the one compelled by my analysis, I join all but Part IIA(1) of the plurality opinion.

Justice White, concurring in the judgment.

The District Court found that the books were removed from the school library because the school board believed them "to be, in essence, vulgar". . . . Both Court of Appeals judges in the majority concluded, however, that there was a material issue of fact that precluded summary judgment sought by petitioners. The unresolved factual issue, as I understand it, is the reason or reasons underlying the school board's removal of the books. I am not inclined to disagree with the Court of Appeals on such a fact-bound issue and hence concur in the judgment of affirmance. Presumably this will result in a trial and the making of a full record and findings on the critical issues.

The Court seems compelled to go further and issue a dissertation on the extent to which the First Amendment limits the discretion of the school board to remove books from the school library. I see no necessity for doing so at this point. When findings of fact and conclusions of law are made by the District Court, that may end the case. If, for example, the District Court concludes after a trial that the books were removed for their vulgarity, there may be no appeal. In any event, if there is an appeal, if there is dissatisfaction with the subsequent Court of Appeals' judgment, and if certiorari is sought and granted, there will be time enough to address the First Amendment issues that may then be presented.

. . .

Chief Justice Burger, with whom Justice Powell, Justice Rehnquist, and Justice O'Connor join, dissenting.

. . .

It is true that where there is a willing distributor of materials, the government may not impose unreasonable obstacles to dissemination by the third party. . . . And where the speaker desires to express certain ideas, the government may not impose unreasonable restraints. . . . It does not follow, however, that a school board must affirmatively aid the speaker in its communication with the recipient. In short the plurality suggests today that if a writer has something to say, the government through its schools must be the courier. None of the cases cited by the plurality establish this broad-based proposition.

. . .

Whatever role the government might play as a conduit of information, schools in particular ought not be made a slavish courier of the material of third parties. The plurality pays homage to the ancient verity that in the administration of the public schools " 'there is a legitimate and substantial community interest in promoting respect for authority and traditional values be they social, moral, or political.' " If as we have held, schools may legitimately be used as vehicles for "inculcating fundamental values necessary to the maintenance of a democratic political system," Ambach v. Norwick, 441 U.S. 68, 77 (1979), school authorities must have broad discretion to fulfill that obligation. Presumably all activity within a primary or secondary school involves the conveyance of information and at least an implied approval of the worth of that information. How are "fundamental values" to be inculcated except by having school boards make content-based decisions about the appropriateness of retaining materials in the school library and curriculum. In order to fulfill its function, an elected school board *must* express its views on the subjects which are taught to its students. In doing so those elected officials express the views of their community; they may err, of course, and the voters may remove them. It is a startling erosion of the very idea of democratic government to have this Court arrogate to itself the power the plurality asserts today.

.   .   .

Justice Powell, dissenting.

.   .   .

I . . . view today's decision with genuine dismay. Whatever the final outcome of this suit and suits like it, the resolution of educational policy decisions through litigation, and the exposure of school board members to liability for such decisions, can be expected to corrode the school board's authority and effectiveness. . . .

.   .   .

Justice Rehnquist, with whom The Chief Justice and Justice Powell join, dissenting.

Addressing only those aspects of the constitutional question which must be decided to determine whether or not the District Court was correct in granting summary judgment, I conclude that it was. . . .

I

A

.   .   .

. . . Petitioners did not, for the reasons stated hereafter, run afoul of the First and Fourteenth Amendments by removing these particular books from the library in the manner in which they did. I would save for another day—feeling quite confident that that day will not arrive—the extreme examples posed in Justice Brennan's opinion.

B

Considerable light is shed on the correct resolution of the constitutional question in this case by examining the role played by petitioners. Had petitioners been the members of a town council, I suppose all would agree that, absent a good deal more than is present in this record, they could not have prohibited the sale of these books by private booksellers within the municipality. But we have also recognized that the government may act in other capacities than as sovereign, and when it does the First Amendment may speak with a different voice:

> "[I]t cannot be gainsaid that the State has interests as an employer in regulating the speech of its employees that differ significantly from those it possesses in connection with regulation of the speech of the citizenry in general. The problem in any case is to arrive at a balance between the interests of the teacher, as a citizen, in commenting upon matters of concern and the interests of the State, as an employer, in promoting the efficiency of the public services it performs through its employees." Pickering v. Board of Education, 391 U.S. 563, 568 (1968).

By the same token, expressive conduct which may not be prohibited by the State as sovereign may be proscribed by the State as property owner: "The State, no less than a private owner of property, has power to preserve the property under its control for the use to which it is lawfully dedicated." Adderley v. Florida, 385 U.S. 39, 47 (1967) (upholding state prohibition of expressive conduct on certain state property).

With these differentiated roles of government in mind, it is helpful to assess the role of government as educator, as compared with the role of government as sovereign. When it acts as an educator, at least at the elementary and secondary school level, the government is engaged in inculcating social values and knowledge in relatively impressionable young people. Obviously there are innumerable decisions to be made as to what courses should be taught, what books should be purchased, or what teachers should be employed. In every one of these areas the members of a school board will act on the basis of their own personal or moral values, will attempt to mirror those of the community, or will abdicate the making of such decisions to so-called "experts." . . . In the very course of administering the many-faceted operations of a school district, the mere decision to purchase some books will necessarily preclude the possibility of purchasing others. The decision to teach a particular subject may preclude the possibility of teaching another subject. A decision to replace a teacher because of ineffectiveness may by implication be seen as a disparagement of the subject matter taught. In each of these instances, however, the book or the exposure to the subject matter may be acquired elsewhere. The managers of the school district are not proscribing it as to the citizenry in general, but are simply determining that it will not be included in the curriculum or school library. In short, actions by the government as educator do not raise the same First Amendment concerns as actions by the government as sovereign.

II

Justice Brennan would hold that the First Amendment gives high school and junior high school students a "right to receive ideas" in the school. . . .

. . .

A

. . .

Despite Justice Brennan's suggestion to the contrary, this Court has never held that the First Amendment grants junior high school and high school students a right of access to certain information in school. . . .

. . . Our past decisions are . . . unlike this case where the removed books are readily available to students and non-students alike at the corner bookstore or the public library.

B

There are even greater reasons for rejecting Justice Brennan's analysis, however, than the significant fact that we have never adopted it in the past. "The importance of public schools in the preparation of individuals for participation as citizens, and in the preservation of the values on which our society rests, has long been recognized by our decisions." Ambach v. Norwick, 441 U.S. 68, 76 (1979). Public schools fulfill the vital role of teaching students the basic skills necessary to function in our society, and of "inculcating fundamental values necessary to the maintenance of a democratic political system." Id., at 77. The idea that such students have a right of access, *in the school,* to information other than that thought by their educators to be necessary is contrary to the very nature of an inculcative education.

Education consists of the selective presentation and explanation of ideas. The effective acquisition of knowledge depends upon an orderly exposure to relevant information. Nowhere is this more true than in elementary and secondary schools, where, unlike the broad-ranging inquiry available to university students, the courses taught are those thought most relevant to the young students' individual development. Of necessity, elementary and secondary educators must separate the relevant from the irrelevant, the appropriate from the inappropriate. Determining what information *not* to present to the students is often as important as identifying relevant material. This winnowing process necessarily leaves much information to be discovered by students at another time or in another place, and is fundamentally inconsistent with any constitutionally required eclecticism in public education.

· · ·

As already mentioned, elementary and secondary schools are inculcative in nature. The libraries of such schools serve as supplements to this inculcative role. Unlike university or public libraries, elementary and secondary school libraries are not designed for free-wheeling inquiry; they are tailored, as the public school curriculum is tailored, to the teaching of basic skills and ideas. Thus, Justice Brennan cannot rely upon the nature of school libraries to escape the fact that the First Amendment right to receive information simply has no application to the one public institution which, by its very nature, is a place for the selective conveyance of ideas.

After all else is said, however, the most obvious reason that petitioners' removal of the books did not violate respondents' right to receive information is the ready availability of the books elsewhere. Students are not denied books by their removal from a school library. The books may be borrowed from a public library, read at a university library, purchased at a bookstore, or loaned by a friend. The government as educator does not seek to reach beyond the confines of the school. Indeed, following the removal from the school library of the books at issue in this case, the local public library put all nine books on display for public inspection. Their contents were fully accessible to any inquisitive student.

C

Justice Brennan's own discomfort with the idea that students have a right to receive information from their elementary or secondary schools is demonstrated by the artificial limitations which he places upon the right—limitations which are supported neither by logic nor authority and which are inconsistent with the right itself. The attempt to confine the right to the library is one such limitation, the fallacies of which have already been demonstrated.

As a second limitation, Justice Brennan distinguishes the act of removing a previously acquired book from the act of refusing to acquire the book in the first place: . . . The failure of a library to acquire a book denies access to its contents just as effectively as does the removal of the book from the library's shelf. As a result of either action the book cannot be found in the "principal locus" of freedom discovered by Justice Brennan.

· · ·

The final limitation placed by Justice Brennan upon his newly discovered right is a motive requirement: the First Amendment is violated only "[i]f petitioners *intended* by their removal decision to deny respondents access to ideas with which petitioners disagreed." But bad motives and good motives alike deny access to the books removed. If Justice Brennan truly recognizes a constitutional right to receive information, it is difficult to see why the reason for the denial makes any difference. Of course Justice Brennan's view is that intent matters because the First Amendment does not tolerate an officially prescribed orthodoxy. But this reasoning mixes First Amendment apples and oranges. The right to receive information differs from the right to be free from an officially prescribed orthodoxy. Not every educational denial of access to information casts a pall of orthodoxy over the classroom.

It is difficult to tell from Justice Brennan's opinion just what motives he would consider constitutionally impermissible. I had thought that the First Amendment proscribes content-based restrictions on the market place of ideas. . . . Justice Brennan concludes, however, that a removal decision based solely upon the "educational suitability" of a book or upon its preceived vulgarity is " 'perfectly permissible.' " But such determinations are based as much on the content of the book as determinations that the book espouses pernicious political views.

Moreover, Justice Brennan's motive test is difficult to square with his distinction between acquisition and removal. If a school board's removal of books might be motivated by a desire to promote favored political or religious views, there is no reason that its acquisition policy might not also be so motivated. And yet the "pall of orthodoxy" cast by a carefully executed book-acquisition program apparently would not violate the First Amendment under Justice Brennan's view.

D

Intertwined as a basis for Justice Brennan's opinion, along with the "right to receive information," is the statement that "our Constitution does not permit the official suppression of *ideas.*" . . .

. . .

In the case before us the petitioners may in one sense be said to have "suppressed" the "ideas" of vulgarity and profanity, but that is hardly an apt description of what was done. They ordered the removal of books containing vulgarity and profanity, but they did not attempt to preclude discussion about the themes of the books or the books themselves. Such a decision, on respondents' version of the facts in this case, is sufficiently related to "educational suitability" to pass muster under the First Amendment.

E

. . .

. . . With respect to the education of children in elementary and secondary schools, the school board may properly determine in many cases that a particular book, a particular course, or even a particular area of knowledge is not educationally suitable for inclusion within the body of knowledge which the school seeks to impart. Without more, this is not a condemnation of the book or the course; it is only a determination akin to that referred to by the Court in Village of Euclid v. Ambler Realty Co., 272 U.S. 365, 388 (1926): "A nuisance may be merely a right thing in the wrong place—like a pig in the parlor instead of the barnyard."

III

Accepting as true respondents' assertion that petitioners acted on the basis of their own "personal values, morals, and tastes," I find the actions taken in this case hard to distinguish from the myriad choices made by school boards in the routine supervision of elementary and secondary schools. "Courts do not and cannot intervene in the resolution of conflicts which arise in the daily operation of school systems and which do not directly and sharply implicate basic constitutional values." Epperson v. Arkansas, 393 U.S., at 104. In this case respondents' rights of free speech and expression were not infringed, and by respondents' own admission no ideas were "suppressed." I would leave to another day the harder cases.

Justice O'Connor, dissenting.

. . .

———

FEDERAL COMMUNICATIONS COMMISSION v. LEAGUE OF WOMEN VOTERS

.—— U.S. ——, 104 S.Ct. 3106, 82 L.Ed.2d 278 (1984).

Justice Brennan delivered the opinion of the Court.

Moved to action by a widely felt need to sponsor independent sources of broadcast programming as an alternative to commercial broadcasting, Congress set out in 1967 to support and promote the development of noncommercial, educational broadcasting stations. A keystone of Congress' program was the Public Broadcasting Act of 1967, Pub.L. No. 90–129, 81 Stat. 365, 47 U.S.C. § 390 et seq., which established the Corporation for Public Broadcasting, a nonprofit corporation authorized to disburse federal funds to noncommercial television and radio stations in support of station operations and educational programming. Section 399 of that Act, as amended by the Public Broadcasting Amendments Act of 1981, Pub.L. No. 97–35, 95 Stat. 730, forbids any "noncommercial educational broadcasting station which receives a grant from the Corporation" to "engage in editorializing." 47 U.S.C. § 399. In this case, we are called upon to decide whether Congress, by imposing that restriction, has passed a "law . . . abridging the freedom of speech, or of the press" in violation of the First Amendment of the Constitution.

I

A

The history of noncommercial, educational broadcasting in the United States is as old as broadcasting itself. In its first efforts to regulate broadcasting, Congress made no special provision for noncommercial, educational broadcasting stations. Under the Radio Act of 1927 and the Communications Act of 1934, such stations were subject to the same licensing requirements as their commercial counterparts. . . .

. . .

Impetus for expanded federal involvement came in 1967 when the Carnegie Corporation sponsored a special commission to review the state of educational broadcasting. Finding that the prospects for an expanded public broadcasting system rested on "the vigor of its local stations," but that these stations were hobbled by chronic underfinancing, the Carnegie Commission called upon the Federal Government to supplement existing state, local, and private financing so that educational broadcasting could realize its full potential as a true alternative to commercial broadcasting. Carnegie Commission on Educational Television, Public Television: A Program for Action 33–34, 36–37 (1967). In fashioning a legislative proposal to carry out this vision, the Commission recommended the creation of a nonprofit, nongovernmental "Corporation for Public Television" to provide support for noncommercial broadcasting, including funding for new program production, local station operations, and the establishment of satellite interconnection facilities to permit nationwide distribution of educational programs to all local stations that wished to receive and use them. Id., at 37–38.

The Commission's report met with widespread approval and its proposals became the blueprint for the Public Broadcasting Act of 1967, which established the basic framework of the public broadcasting system of today. Titles I and III of the Act authorized over $38 million for continued HEW construction grants and for the study of instructional television. Title II created the Corporation for Public Broadcasting (CPB or Corporation), a nonprofit, private corporation governed by a 15-person, bipartisan board of directors appointed by the President with the advice and consent of the Senate. The Corporation was given power to fund "the production of educational television and radio programs for national or regional distribution," 47 U.S.C. § 396(g)(2)(B), to make grants to local broadcasting stations that would "aid in financing local educational . . . programming costs of such stations," § 396(g)(2)(C), and to assist in the establishment and development of national interconnection facilities. § 396(g)(2)(E). Aside from conferring these powers on the Corporation, Congress also adopted other measures designed both to ensure the autonomy of the Corporation and to protect the local stations from governmental interference and control. For example, all federal agencies, officers, and employees were prohibited from "exercis[ing] any direction, supervision or control" over the Corporation or local stations, § 398, and the Corporation itself was forbidden to "own or operate any television or radio broadcast station," § 396(g)(3), and was further required to "carry out its purposes and functions . . . in ways that will most effectively assure the maximum freedom . . . from interference with or control of program content" of the local stations. § 396(g)(1)(D).

B

Appellee Pacifica Foundation is a nonprofit corporation that owns and operates several noncommercial educational broadcasting stations in five major metropolitan areas. Its licensees have received and are presently receiving grants from the Corporation and are therefore prohibited from editorializing by the terms of § 399, as originally enacted and as recently amended. In April 1979, appellees brought this suit in the United States District Court for the Central District of California challenging the constitutionality of former § 399.

. . . .

The District Court granted summary judgment in favor of appellees, holding that § 399's ban on editorializing violated the First Amendment. . . . We . . . now affirm.

II

We begin by considering the appropriate standard of review. The District Court acknowledged that our decisions have generally applied a different First Amendment standard for broadcast regulation than in other areas, but after finding that no special characteristic of the broadcast media justified application of a less stringent standard in this case, it held that § 399 could survive constitutional scrutiny only if it served a "compelling" governmental interest.

. . . .

At first glance, of course, it would appear that the District Court applied the correct standard. Section 399 plainly operates to restrict the expression of editorial opinion on matters of public importance, and, as we have repeatedly explained, communication of this kind is entitled to the most exacting degree of First Amendment protection. . . . Were a similar ban on editorializing applied to newspapers and magazines, we would not hesitate to strike it down as violative of the First Amendment. E.g., Mills v. Alabama, 384 U.S. 214 (1966). But, as the Government correctly notes, because broadcast regulation involves unique considerations, our cases have not followed precisely the same approach that we have applied to other media and have never gone so far as to demand that such regulations serve "compelling" governmental interests. At the same time, we think the Government's argument loses sight of concerns that are important in this area and thus misapprehends the essential meaning of our prior decisions concerning the reach of Congress' authority to regulate broadcast communication.

The fundamental principles that guide our evaluation of broadcast regulation are by now well established. First, we have long recognized that Congress, acting pursuant to the Commerce Clause, has power to regulate the use of this scarce and valuable national resource. . . .

Second, Congress may, in the exercise of this power, seek to assure that the public receives through this medium a balanced presentation of information on issues of public importance that otherwise might not be addressed if control of the medium were left entirely in the hands of those who own and operate broadcasting stations. Although such governmental regulation has never been allowed with respect to the print media, Miami Herald Publishing Co. v. Tornillo, 418 U.S. 241 (1974), we have recognized that "differences in the characteristics of new media justify differences in the First Amendment standards applied to them." Red Lion Broadcasting Co. v. FCC, 395 U.S. 367, 386 (1969). The fundamental distinguishing characteristic of the new medium of broadcasting that, in our view, has required some adjustment in First Amendment analysis is that "[b]roadcasting frequencies are a scarce resource [that] must be portioned out among applicants." Columbia Broadcasting System, Inc. v. Democratic National Committee, 412 U.S. 94, 101 (1973). Thus, our cases have taught that, given spectrum scarcity, those who are granted a license to broadcast must serve in a sense as fiduciaries for the public by presenting "those views and voices which are representative of his community and which would otherwise, by necessity, be barred from the airwaves." Red Lion, supra, at 389. As we observed in that case, because "[i]t is the purpose of the First Amendment to preserve an uninhibited marketplace of ideas in which truth will ultimately prevail, . . . the right of the public to receive suitable access to social, political, esthetic, moral and other ideas and experiences [through the medium of broadcasting] is crucial here [and it] may not constitutionally be abridged either by the Congress or the FCC." Id., at 390.

Finally, although the government's interest in ensuring balanced coverage of public issues is plainly both important and substantial, we have, at the same time, made clear that broadcasters are engaged in a vital and independent form of communicative activity. As a result, the First Amendment must inform and give shape to the manner in which Congress exercises its regulatory power in this area. Unlike common carriers, broadcasters are "entitled under the First Amendment to exercise 'the widest journalistic freedom consistent with their public [duties].'" Columbia Broadcasting System, Inc. v. FCC, 453 U.S. 367, 395 (1981) (quoting Columbia Broadcasting System, Inc. v. Democratic National Committee, supra, at 110). . . . Indeed, if the public's interest in receiving a balanced presentation of views is to be fully served, we must necessarily rely in large part upon the editorial initiative and judgment of the broadcasters who bear the public trust. See Columbia Broadcasting System, Inc. v. Democratic National Committee, supra, at 124–127.

Our prior cases illustrate these principles. [13] . . .

---

[13] This Court's decision in FCC v. Pacifica Foundation, 438 U.S. 726 (1978), upholding an exercise of the Commission's authority to regulate broadcasts containing "indecent" language as applied to a particular afternoon broadcast of a George Carlin monologue, is consistent with the approach taken in our other broadcast cases. There, the Court focused on certain physical characteristics of broadcasting—specifically, that the medium's uniquely pervasive presence renders impossible any prior warning for those listeners who may be offended by indecent language, and, second, that the ease with which children may gain access to the medium, especially during daytime hours, creates a substantial risk

Thus, although the broadcasting industry plainly operates under restraints not imposed upon other media, the thrust of these restrictions has generally been to secure the public's First Amendment interest in receiving a balanced presentation of views on diverse matters of public concern. As a result of these restrictions, of course, the absolute freedom to advocate one's own positions without also presenting opposing viewpoints—a freedom enjoyed, for example, by newspaper publishers and soapbox orators—is denied to broadcasters. But, as our cases attest, these restrictions have been upheld only when we were satisfied that the restriction is narrowly tailored to further a substantial governmental interest. . . .

III

We turn now to consider whether the restraint imposed by § 399 satisfies the requirements established by our prior cases for permissible broadcast regulation. . . .

A

First, the restriction imposed by § 399 is specifically directed at a form of speech—namely, the expression of editorial opinion—that lies at the heart of First Amendment protection. . . .

The editorial has traditionally played precisely this role by informing and arousing the public, and by criticizing and cajoling those who hold government office in order to help launch new solutions to the problems of the time. Preserving the free expression of editorial opinion, therefore, is part and parcel of "our profound national commitment . . . that debate on public issues should be uninhibited, robust, and wide-open." New York Times v. Sullivan, 376 U.S. 254, 270 (1964). . . .

Second, the scope of § 399's ban is defined solely on the basis of the content of the suppressed speech. A wide variety of non-editorial speech "by licensees, their management or those speaking on their behalf," . . . is plainly not prohibited by § 399. Examples of such permissible forms of speech include daily announcements of the station's program schedule or over-the-air appeals for contributions from listeners. Consequently, in order to determine whether a particular statement by station management constitutes an "editorial" proscribed by § 399, enforcement authorities must necessarily examine the content of the message that is conveyed to determine whether the views expressed concern "controversial issues of public importance."

As Justice Stevens observed in Consolidated Edison Co. v. Public Service Commission, 447 U.S. 530 (1980), however, "[a] regulation of speech that is motivated by nothing more than a desire to curtail expression of a particular point of view on controversial issues of general interest is the purest example of a 'law . . . abridging the freedom of speech, or of the press.' A regulation that denies one group of persons the right to address a selected audience on 'controversial issues of public policy' is plainly such a regulation." Id., at 546 (concurring opinion); accord id., at 537–540 (majority opinion). Section 399 is just such a regulation, for it singles out noncommercial broadcasters and denies them the right to address their chosen audience on matters of public

that they may be exposed to such offensive expression without parental supervision. Id., at 748–749. The governmental interest in reduction of those risks through Commission regulation of the timing and character of such "indecent broadcasting" was thought sufficiently substantial to outweigh the broadcaster's First Amendment interest in controlling the presentation of its programming. Id., at 750. In this case, by contrast, we are faced not with indecent expression, but rather with expression that is at the core of First Amendment protections, and no claim is made by the Government that the expression of editorial opinion by noncommercial stations will create a substantial "nuisance" of the kind addressed in FCC v. Pacifica Foundation.

importance. Thus, in enacting § 399 Congress appears to have sought, in much the same way that the New York Public Service Commission had attempted through the regulation of utility company bill inserts struck down in *Consolidated Edison,* to limit discussion of controversial topics and thus to shape the agenda for public debate. Since, as we observed in *Consolidated Edison,* "[t]he First Amendment's hostility to content-based regulation extends not only to restrictions on particular viewpoints, but also to prohibition of an entire topic," id., at 537, we must be particularly wary in assessing § 399 to determine whether it reflects an impermissible attempt "to allow the government [to] control . . . the search for political truth." Id. at 538.

B

In seeking to defend the prohibition on editorializing imposed by § 399, the Government urges that the statute was aimed at preventing two principal threats to the overall success of the Public Broadcasting Act of 1967. According to this argument, the ban was necessary, first, to protect noncommercial educational broadcasting stations from being coerced, as a result of federal financing, into becoming vehicles for government propagandizing or the objects of governmental influence; and, second, to keep these stations from becoming convenient targets for capture by private interest groups wishing to express their own partisan viewpoints.[16] By seeking to safeguard the public's right to a balanced presentation of public issues through the prevention of either governmental or private bias, these objectives are, of course, broadly consistent with the goals identified in our earlier broadcast regulation cases. But, in sharp contrast to the restrictions upheld in *Red Lion* or in Columbia Broadcasting System, Inc. v. FCC, which left room for editorial discretion and simply required broadcast editors to grant others access to the microphone, § 399 directly prohibits the broadcaster from speaking out on public issues even in a balanced and fair manner. The Government insists, however, that the hazards posed in the "special" circumstances of noncommercial educational broadcasting are so great that § 399 is an indispensable means of preserving the public's First Amendment interests. We disagree.

(1)

When Congress first decided to provide financial support for the expansion and development of noncommercial educational stations, all concerned agreed that this step posed some risk that these traditionally independent stations might be pressured into becoming forums devoted solely to programming and views that were acceptable to the Federal government. That Congress was alert to these dangers cannot be doubted. It sought through the Public Broadcasting Act to fashion a system that would provide local stations with sufficient funds to

---

[16] The Government also contends that § 399 is intended to prevent the use of taxpayer monies to promote private views with which taxpayers may disagree. This argument is readily answered by our decision in Buckley v. Valeo, 424 U.S. 1, 90–93 (1976) (per curiam). As we explained in that case, virtually every congressional appropriation will to some extent involve a use of public money as to which some taxpayers may object. Id., at 91–92. Nevertheless, this does not mean that those taxpayers have a constitutionally protected right to enjoin such expenditures. Nor can this interest be invoked to justify a congressional decision to suppress speech. And, unlike Wooley v. Maynard, 430 U.S. 705 (1977), this is not a case in which an individual taxpayer is forced in his daily life to identify with particular views expressed by educational broadcasting stations. Even if this were a serious interest, it is belied by the under-inclusiveness of § 399. The Government concedes—indeed it insists—that all sorts of controversial speech are subsidized by the 1967 Act, and yet out of all of this potentially objectionable speech, only the expression of editorial opinion by local stations is selected for suppression. If angry taxpayers were really the central animating concern of Congress when it passed the 1967 Act, then § 399 does not go far enough in suppressing controversial speech in this medium. That the provision is so unrelated to this asserted purpose suggests that the Government's interest is not substantial. Cf. Buckley v. Valeo, supra, at 45; First National Bank of Boston v. Bellotti, supra, at 793.

foster their growth and development while preserving their tradition of autonomy and community-orientation. A cardinal objective of the Act was the establishment of a private corporation that would "facilitate the development of educational radio and television broadcasting and . . . afford maximum protection to such broadcasting from extraneous interference and control." 47 U.S.C. § 396(a)(6).

The intended role of § 399 in achieving these purposes, however, is not as clear. The provision finds no antecedent in the Carnegie Report, which generally provided the model for most other aspects of the Act. It was not part of the Administration's original legislative proposal. And it was not included in the original version of the Act passed by the Senate. The provision found its way into the Act only as a result of an amendment in the House. Indeed, it appears that, as the House Committee Report frankly admits, § 399 was added not because Congress thought it was essential to preserving the autonomy and vitality of local stations, but rather "out of an abundance of caution." H.R.Rep. No. 572, 90th Cong., 1st Sess. 20 (1967).

More importantly, an examination of both the overall legislative scheme established by the 1967 Act and the character of public broadcasting demonstrates that the interest asserted by the Government is not substantially advanced by § 399. First, to the extent that federal financial support creates a risk that stations will lose their independence through the bewitching power of governmental largesse, the elaborate structure established by the Public Broadcasting Act already operates to insulate local stations from governmental interference. Congress not only mandated that the new Corporation for Public Broadcasting would have a private, bi-partisan structure, see §§ 396(c)–(f), but also imposed a variety of important limitations on its powers. The Corporation was prohibited from owning or operating any station, § 396(g)(3), it was required to adhere strictly to a standard of "objectivity and balance" in disbursing federal funds to local stations, § 396(g)(1)(A), and it was prohibited from contributing to or otherwise supporting any candidate for office, § 396(f)(3).

The Act also established a second layer of protections which serve to protect the stations from governmental coercion and interference. Thus, in addition to requiring the Corporation to operate so as to "assure the maximum freedom [of local stations] from interference with or control of program content or other activities," § 396(g)(1)(D), the Act expressly forbids "any department, agency, officer, or employee of the United States [from] exercis[ing] any direction, supervision, or control over educational television or radio broadcasting, or over the Corporation or any of its grantees or contractors . . . .," § 398(a). Subsequent amendments to the Act have confirmed Congress' commitment to the principle that because local stations are the "bedrock of the system," their independence from governmental interference and control must be fully guaranteed. These amendments have provided long-term appropriations authority for public broadcasting, rather than allowing funding to depend upon yearly appropriations, see § 396(k)(1)(C), as amended, Pub.L. No. 97–35, title XII, § 1227, 95 Stat. 727 (1981); have strictly defined the percentage of appropriated funds that must be disbursed by the Corporation to local stations, § 396(k) (3)(A)–(B); and have defined objective criteria under which local television and radio stations receive basic grants from the Corporation to be used at the discretion of the station. §§ 396(k)(6)(A)–(B), 396(k)(7). The principal thrust of the amendments, therefore, has been to assure long-term appropriations for the Corporation and, more importantly, to insist that it pass specified portions of these funds directly through to local stations to give them greater autonomy in defining the uses to which those funds should be put. Thus, in sharp contrast to § 399, the unifying theme of these various statutory provisions is that they substantially reduce the risk of governmental interference with the editorial judgments of local stations without restricting those stations' ability to speak on matters of public concern.

Even if these statutory protections were thought insufficient to the task, however, suppressing the particular category of speech restricted by § 399 is simply not likely, given the character of the public broadcasting system, to reduce substantially the risk that the Federal Government will seek to influence or put pressure on local stations. An underlying supposition of the Government's argument in this regard is that individual noncommercial stations are likely to speak so forcefully on particular issues that Congress, the ultimate source of the stations' Federal funding, will be tempted to retaliate against these individual stations by restricting appropriations for all of public broadcasting. But, as the District Court recognized, the character of public broadcasting suggests that such a risk is speculative at best. There are literally hundreds of public radio and television stations in communities scattered throughout the United States and its territories, see CPB, 1983–84 Public Broadcasting Directory 20–50, 66–86 (Sept.1983). Given that central fact, it seems reasonable to infer that the editorial voices of these stations will prove to be as distinctive, varied, and idiosyncratic as the various communities they represent. More importantly, the editorial focus of any particular station can fairly be expected to focus largely on issues affecting only its community. Accordingly, absent some showing by the Government to the contrary, the risk that local editorializing will place all of public broadcasting in jeopardy is not sufficiently pressing to warrant § 399's broad suppression of speech.

Indeed, what is far more likely than local station editorials to pose the kinds of dangers hypothesized by the Government are the wide variety of programs addressing controversial issues produced, often with substantial CPB funding, for national distribution to local stations. Such programs truly have the potential to reach a large audience and, because of the critical commentary they contain, to have the kind of genuine national impact that might trigger a congressional response or kindle governmental resentment. The ban imposed by § 399, however, is plainly not directed at the potentially controversial content of such programs; it is, instead, leveled solely at the expression of editorial opinion by local station management, a form of expression that is far more likely to be aimed at a smaller local audience, to have less national impact, and to be confined to local issues. In contrast, the Act imposes no substantive restrictions, other than normal requirements of balance and fairness, on those who produce nationally distributed programs. Indeed, the Act is designed in part to encourage and sponsor the production of such programs and to allow each station to decide for itself whether to accept such programs for local broadcast.

Furthermore, the manifest imprecision of the ban imposed by § 399 reveals that its proscription is not sufficiently tailored to the harms it seeks to prevent to justify its substantial interference with broadcasters' speech. Section 399 includes within its grip a potentially infinite variety of speech, most of which would not be related in any way to governmental affairs, political candidacies or elections. Indeed, the breadth of editorial commentary is as wide as human imagination permits. But the Government never explains how, say, an editorial by local station management urging improvements in a town's parks or museums will so infuriate Congress or other Federal officials that the future of public broadcasting will be imperiled unless such editorials are suppressed. Nor is it explained how the suppression of editorials alone serves to reduce the risk of governmental retaliation and interference when it is clear that station management is fully able to broadcast controversial views so long as such views are not labelled as its own.

.   .   .

Finally, although the Government certainly has a substantial interest in ensuring that the audiences of noncommercial stations will not be led to think that the broadcaster's editorials reflect the official view of the government, this interest can be fully satisfied by less restrictive means that are readily available. To address this important concern, Congress could simply require public broadcasting stations to broadcast a disclaimer every time they editorialize which would state that the editorial represents only the view of the station's management and does not in any way represent the views of the Federal Government or any of the station's other sources of funding. Such a disclaimer—similar to those often used in commercial and noncommercial programming of a controversial nature—would effectively and directly communicate to the audience that the editorial reflected only the views of the station rather than those of the government. Furthermore, such disclaimers would have the virtue of clarifying the responses that might be made under the fairness doctrine by opponents of the station's position, since those opponents would know with certainty that they were responding only to the station's views and not in any sense to the government's position.

In sum, § 399's broad ban on all editorializing by every station that receives CPB funds far exceeds what is necessary to protect against the risk of governmental interference or to prevent the public from assuming that editorials by public broadcasting stations represent the official view of government. The regulation impermissibly sweeps within its prohibition a wide range of speech by wholly private stations on topics that do not take a directly partisan stand or that have nothing whatever to do with federal, state or local government.

(2)

Assuming that the Government's second asserted interest in preventing noncommercial stations from becoming a "privileged outlet for the political and ideological opinions of station owners and management," . . . is legitimate, the substantiality of this asserted interest is dubious. The patent over- and underinclusiveness of § 399's ban "undermines the likelihood of a genuine [governmental] interest" in preventing private groups from propagating their own views via public broadcasting. First National Bank of Boston v. Bellotti, supra, 435 U.S., at 793. . . .

In short, § 399 does not prevent the use of noncommercial stations for the presentation of partisan views on controversial matters; instead, it merely bars a station from specifically communicating such views on its own behalf or on behalf of its management. If the vigorous expression of controversial opinions is, as the Government assures us, affirmatively encouraged by the Act, and if local licensees are permitted under the Act to exercise editorial control over the selection of programs, controversial or otherwise, that are aired on their stations, then § 399 accomplishes only one thing—the suppression of editorial speech by station management. It does virtually nothing, however, to reduce the risk that public stations will serve solely as outlets for expression of narrow partisan views. . . .

Finally, the public's interest in preventing public broadcasting stations from becoming forums for lopsided presentations of narrow partisan positions is already secured by a variety of other regulatory means that intrude far less drastically upon the "journalistic freedom" of noncommercial broadcasters. . . . The requirements of the FCC's fairness doctrine, for instance, which apply to commercial and noncommercial stations alike, ensure that such editorializing would maintain a reasonably balanced and fair presentation of controversial issues. Thus even if the management of a noncommercial educational station were inclined to seek to further only its own partisan views when editorializing, it simply could not do so. Indeed, in considering the constitutionality of the FCC's fairness doctrine, the Court in *Red Lion* considered precisely the same justification invoked by the Government today in support of § 399: that without some requirement of fairness and balance, "station owners . . . would have unfettered power . . . to communicate only their own views on public issues . . . and to permit on the air only those with whom they agreed." 395 U.S., at 392. The solution to this problem offered by § 399, however, is precisely the opposite of the remedy prescribed by the FCC and endorsed by the Court in *Red Lion.* Rather than requiring noncommercial broadcasters who express editorial opinions on controversial subjects to permit *more speech* on such subjects to ensure that the public's First Amendment interest in receiving a balanced account of the issue is met, § 399 simply silences all editorial speech by such broadcasters. Since the breadth of § 399 extends so far beyond what is necessary to accomplish the goals identified by the Government, it fails to satisfy the First Amendment standards that we have applied in this area.

We therefore hold that even if some of the hazards at which § 399 was aimed are sufficiently substantial, the restriction is not crafted with sufficient precision to remedy those dangers that may exist to justify the significant abridgement of speech worked by the provision's broad ban on editorializing. The statute is not narrowly tailored to address any of the government's suggested goals. Moreover, the public's "paramount right" to be fully and broadly informed on matters of public importance through the medium of noncommercial educational broadcasting is not well served by the restriction, for its effect is plainly to diminish rather than augment "the volume and quality of coverage" of controversial issues. *Red Lion,* supra, at 393. Nor do we see any reason to deny noncommercial broadcasters the right to address matters of public concern on the basis of merely speculative fears of adverse public or governmental reactions to such speech.

IV

Although the Government did not present the argument in any form to the District Court, it now seeks belatedly to justify § 399 on the basis of Congress' Spending Power. Relying upon our recent decision in Regan v. Taxation With Representation, 461 U.S. 540 (1983), the Government argues that by prohibiting noncommercial educational stations that receive CPB grants from editorializing, Congress has, in the proper exercise of its Spending Power, simply determined that it "will not subsidize public broadcasting station editorials." In *Taxation With Representation,* the Court found that Congress could, in the exercise of its Spending Power, reasonably refuse to subsidize the lobbying activities of tax-exempt charitable organizations by prohibiting such organizations from using tax-deductible contributions to support their lobbying efforts. In so holding, however, we explained that such organizations remained free "to receive tax-deductible contributions to support non-lobbying activit[ies]." . . .

In this case, however, unlike the situation faced by the charitable organization in *Taxation With Representation,* a noncommercial educational station that receives only 1% of its overall income from CPB grants is barred absolutely from all editorializing. Therefore, in contrast to the appellee in *Taxation With Representation,* such a station is not able to segregate its activities according to the source of its funding. The station has no way of limiting the use of its Federal funds to all non-editorializing activities, and, more importantly, it is barred from using even wholly private funds to finance its editorial activity.

Of course, if Congress were to adopt a revised version of § 399 that permitted noncommercial educational broadcasting stations to establish "affiliate" organizations which could then use the station's facilities to editorialize with non-federal funds, such a statutory mechanism would plainly be valid under the reasoning of *Taxation With Representation.* Under such a statute, public broadcasting stations would be free, in the same way that the charitable organization in *Taxation With Representation* was free, to make known its views on matters of public importance through its non-federally funded, editorializing affiliate without losing federal grants for its non-editorializing broadcast activities. . . . But in the absence of such authority, we must reject the Government's contention that our decision in *Taxation With Representation* is controlling here.

V

In conclusion, we emphasize that our disposition of this case rests upon a narrow proposition. We do not hold that the Congress or the FCC are without power to regulate the content, timing, or character of speech by noncommercial educational broadcasting stations. Rather, we hold only that the specific interests sought to be advanced by § 399's ban on editorializing are either not sufficiently substantial or are not served in a sufficiently limited manner to justify the substantial abridgement of important journalistic freedoms which the First Amendment jealously protects. Accordingly, the judgment of the District Court is

Affirmed.

Justice Rehnquist, with whom The Chief Justice and Justice White join, dissenting.

All but three paragraphs of the Court's lengthy opinion in this case are devoted to the development of a scenario in which the government appears as the "Big Bad Wolf," and appellee Pacifica as "Little Red Riding Hood." In the Court's scenario the Big Bad Wolf cruelly forbids Little Red Riding Hood from taking to her grandmother some of the food that she is carrying in her basket. Only three paragraphs are used to delineate a truer picture of the litigants, wherein it appears that some of the food in the basket was given to Little Red Riding Hood by the Big Bad Wolf himself, and that the Big Bad Wolf had told Little Red Riding Hood in advance that if she accepted his food she would have to abide by his conditions. Congress in enacting § 399 of the Public Broadcasting Act, 47 U.S.C. (Supp. V) § 399, has simply determined that public funds shall not be used to subsidize noncommercial, educational broadcasting stations which engage in "editorializing" or which support or oppose any political candidate. I do not believe that anything in the First Amendment to the United States Constitution prevents Congress from choosing to spend public monies in that manner. Perhaps a more appropriate analogy than that of Little Red Riding Hood and the Big Bad Wolf is that of Faust and Mephistopheles; Pacifica, well aware of § 399's condition on its receipt of public money, nonetheless accepted the public money and now seeks to avoid the conditions which Congress legitimately has attached to receipt of that funding. . . .

The Court seems to believe that Congress actually subsidizes editorializing only if a station uses federal money specifically to cover the expenses that the Court believes can be isolated at editorializing expenses. But to me the Court's approach ignores economic reality. CPB's unrestricted grants are used for salaries, training, equipment, promotion, etc.—financial expenditures which benefit all aspects of a station's programming, including management's editorials. Given the impossibility of compartmentalizing programming expenses in any meaningful way, it seems clear to me that the only effective means for preventing the use of public monies to subsidize the airing of management's views is for Congress to ban a subsidized station from all on-the-air editorializing. Under the Court's view, if Congress decided to withhold a 100% subsidy from a station which editorializes, that decision would be constitutional under the principle affirmed in our *Taxation With Representation* decision. Surely on these facts, the distinction between the government's power to withhold a 100% subsidy, on the one hand and the 20–30% subsidy involved here, on the other hand, is simply trivialization.

This is not to say that the government may attach *any* condition to its largess; it is only to say that when the government is simply exercising its power to allocate its own public funds, we need only find that the condition imposed has a rational relationship to Congress' purpose in providing the subsidy and that it is not primarily "aimed at the suppression of dangerous ideas." Cammarano v. United States, 358 U.S. 498, 513 (1959), quoting Speiser v. Randall, 357 U.S. 513, 519 (1958). In this case Congress' prohibition is directly related to its purpose in providing subsidies for public broadcasting, and it is plainly rational for Congress to have determined that taxpayer monies should not be used to subsidize management's views or to pay for management's exercise of partisan politics. Indeed, it is entirely rational for Congress to have wished to avoid the appearance of government sponsorship of a particular view or a particular political candidate. Furthermore, Congress' prohibition is strictly neutral. In no sense can it be said that Congress has prohibited only editorial views of one particular ideological bent. Nor has it prevented public stations from airing programs, documentaries, interviews, etc. dealing with controversial subjects, so long as management itself does not expressly endorse a particular viewpoint. And Congress has not prevented station management from communicating its own views on those subjects through any medium other than subsidized public broadcasting. . . .

Justice White:

Believing that the editorializing and candidate endorsement proscription stand or fall together and being confident that Congress may condition use of its funds on abstaining from political endorsements, I join Justice Rehnquist's dissenting opinion.

Justice Stevens, dissenting.

The court jester who mocks the King must choose his words with great care. An artist is likely to paint a flattering portrait of his patron. The child who wants a new toy does not preface his request with a comment on how fat his mother is. Newspaper publishers have been known to listen to their advertising managers. Elected officials may remember how their elections were financed. By enacting the statutory provision that the Court invalidates today, a sophisticated group of legislators expressed a concern about the potential impact of government funds on pervasive and powerful organs of mass communication. One need not have heard the raucous voice of Adolph Hitler over Radio Berlin to appreciate the importance of that concern.

As Justice White correctly notes, the statutory prohibitions against editorializing and candidate endorsements rest on the same foundation. In my opinion that foundation is far stronger than merely "a rational basis" and it is not weakened by the fact that it is buttressed by other provisions that are also designed to avoid the insidious evils of government propaganda favoring particular points of view. The quality of the interest in maintaining government neutrality in the free market of ideas—of avoiding subtle forms of censorship and propaganda—outweigh the impact on expression that results from this statute. Indeed, by simply terminating or reducing funding, Congress could curtail much more expression with no risk whatever of a constitutional transgression. . . .

I

. . .

Neither the fact that the statute regulates only one kind of speech, nor the fact that editorial opinion has traditionally been an important kind of speech, is sufficient to identify the character or the significance of the statute's impact on speech. Three additional points are relevant. First, the statute does not prohibit Pacifica from expressing its opinion through any avenue except the radio stations for which it receives federal financial support. It eliminates the subsidized channel of communication as a forum for Pacifica itself, and thereby deprives Pacifica of an advantage it would otherwise have over other speakers, but it does not exclude Pacifica from the marketplace for ideas. Second, the statute does not curtail the expression of opinion by individual commentators who participate in Pacifica's programs. The only comment that is prohibited is a statement that Pacifica agrees or disagrees with the opinions that others may express on its programs. Third, and of greatest significance for me, the statutory restriction is completely neutral in its operation—it prohibits all editorials without any distinction being drawn concerning the subject matter or the point of view that might be expressed.

II

The statute does not violate the fundamental principle that the citizen's right to speak may not be conditioned upon the sovereign's agreement with what the speaker intends to say. On the contrary, the statute was enacted in order to protect that very principle—to avoid the risk that some speakers will be rewarded or penalized for saying things that appeal to—or are offensive to—the sovereign. The interests the statute is designed to protect are interests that underlie the First Amendment itself.

In my judgment the interest in keeping the Federal Government out of the propaganda arena is of overriding importance. That interest is of special importance in the field of electronic communication, not only because that medium is so powerful and persuasive, but also because it is the one form of communication that is licensed by the Federal Government. When the Government already has great potential power over the electronic media, it is surely legitimate to enact statutory safeguards to make sure that it does not cross the threshold that separates neutral regulation from the subsidy of partisan opinion.

. . . .

The magnitude of the present danger that the statute is designed to avoid is admittedly a matter about which reasonable judges may disagree. Moreover, I would agree that the risk would be greater if other statutory safeguards were removed. It remains true, however, that Congress has the power to prevent the use of public funds to subsidize the expression of partisan points of view, or to suppress the propagation of dissenting opinions. No matter how great or how small the immediate risk may be, there surely is more than a theoretical possibility that future grantees might be influenced by the ever present tie of the political purse strings, even if those strings are never actually pulled. . . .

III

The Court describes the scope of § 399's ban as being "defined solely on the basis of the content of the suppressed speech," and analogizes this case to the regulation of speech we condemned in Consolidated Edison Co. v. Public Serv. Comm'n, 447 U.S. 530 (1980). This description reveals how the Court manipulates labels without perceiving the critical differences behind the two cases.

In *Consolidated Edison* the class of speakers that was affected by New York's prohibition consisted of regulated public utilities that had been expressing their opinion on the issue of nuclear power by means of written statements inserted in their customers' monthly bills. Although the scope of the prohibition was phrased in general terms and applied to a selected group of speakers, it was obviously directed at spokesmen for a particular point of view. The justification for the restriction was phrased in terms of the potential offensiveness of the utilities' messages to their audiences. It was a classic case of a viewpoint-based prohibition.

In this case, however, although the regulation applies only to a defined class of noncommercial broadcast licensees, it is common ground that these licensees represent heterogenous points of view. There is simply no sensible basis for considering this regulation a viewpoint restriction—or to use the Court's favorite phrase, to condemn it as "content-based"—because it applies equally to station owners of all shades of opinion. Moreover, the justification for the prohibition is not based on the "offensiveness" of the messages in the sense that that term was used in *Consolidated Edison*. Here, it is true that taxpayers might find it offensive if their tax monies were being used to subsidize the expression of editorial opinion with which they disagree, but it is the fact of the subsidy—not just the expression of the opinion—that legitimates this justification. Furthermore, and of greater importance, the principal justification for this prohibition is the overriding interest in forestalling the creation of propaganda organs for the Government.

I respectfully dissent.

SECTION 4. SPEECH ON PRIVATE PREMISES

YOUNG v. AMERICAN MINI THEATRES, INC.

427 U.S. 50, 96 S.Ct. 2440, 49 L.Ed.2d 310 (1976).

Mr. Justice Stevens delivered the opinion of the Court.*

Zoning ordinances adopted by the city of Detroit differentiate between motion picture theaters which exhibit sexually explicit "adult" movies and those which do not. The principal question presented by this case is whether that statutory classification is unconstitutional because it is based on the content of communication protected by the First Amendment.

Effective November 2, 1972, Detroit adopted the ordinances challenged in this litigation. Instead of concentrating "adult" theaters in limited zones, these ordinances require that such theaters be dispersed. Specifically, an adult theater may not be located within 1,000 feet of any two other "regulated uses" or within 500 feet of a residential area. The term "regulated use" includes 10 different kinds of establishments in addition to adult theaters.

The classification of a theater as "adult" is expressly predicated on the character of the motion pictures which it exhibits. If the theater is used to present "material distinguished or characterized by an emphasis on matter depicting, describing or relating to 'Specified Sexual Activities' or 'Specified Anatomical Areas,'" it is an adult establishment.

The 1972 ordinances were amendments to an "Anti-Skid Row Ordinance" which had been adopted 10 years earlier. At that time the Detroit Common Council made a finding that some uses of property are especially injurious to a neighborhood when they are concentrated in limited areas. The decision to

---

* Part III of this opinion is joined only by The Chief Justice, Mr. Justice White and Mr. Justice Rehnquist.

add adult motion picture theaters and adult book stores to the list of businesses which, apart from a special waiver, could not be located within 1,000 feet of two other "regulated uses," was, in part, a response to the significant growth in the number of such establishments. In the opinion of urban planners and real estate experts who supported the ordinances, the location of several such businesses in the same neighborhood tends to attract an undesirable quantity and quality of transients, adversely affects property values, causes an increase in crime, especially prostitution, and encourages residents and businesses to move elsewhere.

Respondents are the operators of two adult motion picture theaters. One, the Nortown, was an established theater which began to exhibit adult films in March 1973. The other, the Pussy Cat, was a corner gas station which was converted into a "mini theater," but denied a certificate of occupancy because of its plan to exhibit adult films. Both theaters were located within 1,000 feet of two other regulated uses and the Pussy Cat was less than 500 feet from a residential area. The respondents brought two separate actions against appropriate city officials, seeking a declaratory judgment that the ordinances were unconstitutional and an injunction against their enforcement. Federal jurisdiction was properly invoked and the two cases were consolidated for decision.

The District Court granted defendants' motion for summary judgment. . . .

The Court of Appeals reversed. . . .

. . .

II.

Petitioners acknowledge that the ordinances prohibit theaters which are not licensed as "adult motion picture theaters" from exhibiting films which are protected by the First Amendment. Respondents argue that the ordinances are therefore invalid as prior restraints on free speech.

The ordinances are not challenged on the ground that they impose a limit on the total number of adult theaters which may operate in the city of Detroit. There is no claim that distributors or exhibitors of adult films are denied access to the market or, conversely, that the viewing public is unable to satisfy its appetite for sexually explicit fare. Viewed as an entity, the market for this commodity is essentially unrestrained.

It is true, however, that adult films may only be exhibited commercially in licensed theaters. But that is also true of all motion pictures. The city's general zoning laws require all motion picture theaters to satisfy certain locational as well as other requirements; we have no doubt that the municipality may control the location of theaters as well as the location of other commercial establishments, either by confining them to certain specified commercial zones or by requiring that they be dispersed throughout the city. The mere fact that the commercial exploitation of material protected by the First Amendment is subject to zoning and other licensing requirements is not a sufficient reason for invalidating these ordinances.

Putting to one side for the moment the fact that adult motion picture theaters must satisfy a locational restriction not applicable to other theaters, we are also persuaded that the 1,000-foot restriction does not, in itself, create an impermissible restraint on protected communication. The city's interest in planning and regulating the use of property for commercial purposes is clearly adequate to support that kind of restriction applicable to all theaters within the city limits. In short, apart from the fact that the ordinances treat adult theaters differently from other theaters and the fact that the classification is predicated on the content of material shown in the respective theaters, the regulation of the place where such films may be exhibited does not offend the First Amendment. We turn, therefore, to the question whether the classification is consistent with the Equal Protection Clause.

III.

A remark attributed to Voltaire characterizes our zealous adherence to the principle that the Government may not tell the citizen what he may or may not say. Referring to a suggestion that the violent overthrow of tyranny might be legitimate, he said: "I disapprove of what you say, but I will defend to the death your right to say it." The essence of that comment has been repeated time after time in our decisions invalidating attempts by the Government to impose selective controls upon the dissemination of ideas.

Thus, the use of streets and parks for the free expression of views on national affairs may not be conditioned upon the sovereign's agreement with what a speaker may intend to say. Nor may speech be curtailed because it invites dispute, creates dissatisfaction with conditions the way they are, or even stirs people to anger. The sovereign's agreement or disagreement with the content of what a speaker has to say may not affect the regulation of the time, place, or manner of presenting the speech.

If picketing in the vicinity of a school is to be allowed to express the point of view of labor, that means of expression in that place must be allowed for other points of view as well. . . .

[W]e learned long ago that broad statements of principle, no matter how correct in the context in which they are made are sometimes qualified by contrary decisions before the absolute limit of the stated principle is reached. When we review this Court's actual adjudications in the First Amendment area, we find this to have been the case with the stated principle that there may be no restriction whatever on expressive activity because of its content.

The question whether speech is, or is not, protected by the First Amendment often depends on the content of the speech. Thus, the line between permissible advocacy and impermissible incitation to crime or violence depends, not merely on the setting in which the speech occurs, but also on exactly what the speaker had to say. Similarly, it is the content of the utterance that determines whether it is a protected epithet or an unprotected "fighting comment." And in time of war "the publication of the sailing of transports or the number and regulation of troops may unquestionably be restrained," . . . although publication of news stories with a different content would be protected.

Even within the area of protected speech, a difference in content may require a different governmental response . . .

. . . .

More directly in point are opinions dealing with the question whether the First Amendment prohibits the state and federal governments from wholly suppressing sexually oriented materials on the basis of their "obscene character." In Ginsberg v. New York, 390 U.S. 629, the Court upheld a conviction for selling to a minor magazines which were concededly not "obscene" if shown to adults. Indeed, the Members of the Court who would accord the greatest protection to such materials have repeatedly indicated that the State could prohibit the distribution or exhibition of such materials to juveniles and consenting adults. Surely the First Amendment does not foreclose such a prohibition; yet it is equally clear that any such prohibition must rest squarely on an appraisal of the content of material otherwise within a constitutionally protected area.

Such a line may be drawn on the basis of content without violating the Government's paramount obligation of neutrality in its regulation of protected communication. For the regulation of the places where sexually explicit films may be exhibited is unaffected by whatever social, political, or philosophical message the film may be intended to communicate; whether the motion picture ridicules or characterizes one point of view or another, the effect of the ordinances is exactly the same.

Moreover, even though we recognize that the First Amendment will not tolerate the total suppression of erotic materials that have some arguably artistic value, it is manifest that society's interest in protecting this type of expression is of a wholly different, and lesser, magnitude than the interest in untrammeled political debate that inspired Voltaire's immortal comment. Whether political oratory or philosophical discussion moves us to applaud or to despise what is said, every schoolchild can understand why our duty to defend the right to speak remains the same. But few of us would march our sons and daughters off to war to preserve the citizen's right to see "Specified Sexual Activities" exhibited in the theaters of our choice. Even though the First Amendment protects communication in this area from total suppression, we hold that the State may legitimately use the content of these materials as the basis for placing them in a different classification from other motion pictures.

The remaining question is whether the line drawn by these ordinances is justified by the city's interest in preserving the character of its neighborhoods. On this question we agree with the views expressed by District Judges Kennedy and Gubow. The record discloses a factual basis for the Common Council's conclusion that this kind of restriction will have the desired effect. It is not our function to appraise the wisdom of its decision to require adult theaters to be separated rather than concentrated in the same areas. In either event, the city's interest in attempting to preserve the quality of urban life is one that must be accorded high respect. Moreover, the city must be allowed a reasonable opportunity to experiment with solutions to admittedly serious problems.

Since what is ultimately at stake is nothing more than a limitation on the place where adult films may be exhibited, even though the determination of whether a particular film fits that characterization turns on the nature of its content, we conclude that the city's interest in the present and future character of its neighborhoods adequately supports its classification of motion pictures. We hold that the zoning ordinances requiring that adult motion picture theaters not be located within 1,000 feet of two other regulated uses does not violate the Equal Protection Clause of the Fourteenth Amendment.

The judgment of the Court of Appeals is reversed.

Mr. Justice Powell, concurring in the judgment and portions of the opinion.

Although I agree with much of what is said in the plurality opinion, and concur in Parts I and II, my approach to the resolution of this case is sufficiently different to prompt me to write separately. I view the case as presenting an example of innovative land-use regulation, implicating First Amendment concerns only incidentally and to a limited extent. . . .

The Detroit zoning ordinance . . . affects expression only incidentally and in furtherance of governmental interests wholly unrelated to the regulation of expression. At least as applied to respondents, it does not offend the First Amendment. Although courts must be alert to the possibility of direct rather than incidental effect of zoning on expression, and especially to the possibility of pretextual use of the power to zone as a means of suppressing expression, it is clear that this is not such a case.

Mr. Justice Stewart, with whom Mr. Justice Brennan, Mr. Justice Marshall, and Mr. Justice Blackmun join, dissenting.

The Court today holds that the First and Fourteenth Amendments do not prevent the city of Detroit from using a system of prior restraints and criminal sanctions to enforce content-based restrictions on the geographic location of motion picture theaters that exhibit nonobscene but sexually oriented films. I dissent from this drastic departure from established principles of First Amendment law.

This case does not involve a simple zoning ordinance, or a content-neutral time, place and manner restriction, or a regulation of obscene expression or other speech that is entitled to less than the full protection of the First Amendment. The kind of expression at issue here is no doubt objectionable to some, but that fact does not diminish its protected status any more than did the particular content of the "offensive" expression in Erznoznik v. City of Jacksonville, 422 U.S. 205 (display of nudity on a drive-in movie screen); Lewis v. City of New Orleans, 415 U.S. 130 (utterance of vulgar epithet); Hess v. Indiana, 414 U.S. 105 (utterance of vulgar remark); Papish v. University of Missouri Curators, 410 U.S. 667 (indecent remarks in campus newspaper); Cohen v. California, 403 U.S. 15 (wearing of clothing inscribed with a vulgar remark); Brandenburg v. Ohio, 395 U.S. 444 (utterance of racial slurs); or Kingsley Pictures Corp. v. Regents, 360 U.S. 684 (alluring portrayal of adultery as proper behavior).

What this case does involve is the constitutional permissibility of selective interference with protected speech whose content is thought to produce distasteful effects. It is elementary that a prime function of the First Amendment is to guard against just such interference. By refusing to invalidate Detroit's ordinance the Court rides roughshod over cardinal principles of First Amendment law, which require that time, place and manner regulations that affect protected expression be content-neutral except in the limited context of a captive or juvenile audience. . . .

I can only interpret today's decision as an aberration. The Court is undoubtedly sympathetic, as am I, to the well-intentioned efforts of Detroit to "clean up" its streets and prevent the proliferation of "skid rows." But it is in those instances where protected speech grates most unpleasantly against the sensibilities that judicial vigilance must be at its height. . . .

The Court must never forget that the consequences of rigorously enforcing the guarantees of the First Amendment are frequently unpleasant. Much speech that seems to be of little or no value will enter the marketplace of ideas, threatening the quality of our social discourse and, more generally, the serenity of our lives. But that is the price to be paid for constitutional freedom.

Mr. Justice Blackmun, with whom Mr. Justice Brennan, Mr. Justice Stewart, and Mr. Justice Marshall join, dissenting.

I join Mr. Justice Stewart's dissent, and write separately to identify an independent ground on which for me, the challenged ordinance is unconstitutional. That ground is vagueness. . . .

————

SCHAD v. BOROUGH OF MOUNT EPHRAIM

452 U.S. 61, 101 S.Ct. 2176, 68 L.Ed.2d 671 (1981).

Justice White delivered the opinion of the Court.

In 1973, appellants began operating an adult bookstore in the commercial zone in the Borough of Mount Ephraim in Camden County, N.J. The store sold adult books, magazines and films. Amusement licenses shortly issued permitting the store to install coin-operated devices by virtue of which a customer could sit in a booth, insert a coin and watch an adult film. In 1976, the store introduced an additional coin-operated mechanism permitting the customer to watch a live dancer, usually nude, performing behind a glass panel. Complaints were soon filed against appellants charging that the bookstore's exhibition of live dancing violated § 99–15B of Mount Ephraim's zoning ordinance, which described the permitted uses in a commercial zone, in which the store was located, as follows:

"B.   Principal permitted uses on the land and in buildings.

"(1) Offices and banks; taverns; restaurants and luncheonettes for sit-down dinners only and with no drive-in facilities; automobile sales; retail stores, such as but not limited to food, wearing apparel, millinery, fabrics, hardware, lumber, jewelry, paint, wallpaper, appliances, flowers, gifts, books, stationery, pharmacy, liquors, cleaners, novelties, hobbies and toys; repair shops for shoes, jewels, clothes and appliances; barbershops and beauty salons; cleaners and laundries; pet stores; and nurseries.   Offices may, in addition, be permitted to a group of four (4) stores or more without additional parking, provided the offices do not exceed the equivalent of twenty percent (20%) of the gross floor area of the stores.

"(2) Motels."

Section 99–4 of the Borough's code provided that "[a]ll uses not expressly permitted in this chapter are prohibited."

Appellants were found guilty in the Municipal Court and fines were imposed.   Appeal was taken to the Camden County Court, where a trial *de novo* was held on the record made in the Municipal Court and appellants were again found guilty. . . .   The Supreme Court of New Jersey denied further review.

Appellants appealed to this Court.   Their principal claim is that the imposition of criminal penalties under an ordinance prohibiting all live entertainment, including nonobscene, nude dancing, violated their rights of free expression guaranteed by the First and Fourteenth Amendments of the United States Constitution.   We . . . set aside appellants' convictions.

I

As the Mount Ephraim code has been construed by the New Jersey courts . . . "live entertainment," including nude dancing, is "not a permitted use in any establishment" in the Borough of Mount Ephraim.   By excluding live entertainment throughout the Borough, the Mount Ephraim ordinance prohibits a wide range of expression that has long been held to be within the protections of the First and Fourteenth Amendments.   Entertainment, as well as political and ideological speech, is protected; motion pictures, programs broadcast by radio and television and live entertainment, such as musical and dramatic works, fall within the First Amendment guarantee. . . .   Nor may an entertainment program be prohibited solely because it displays the nude human figure. "[N]udity alone" does not place otherwise protected material outside the mantle of the First Amendment. . . .   Furthermore, as the state courts in this case recognized, nude dancing is not without its First Amendment protections from official regulation. . . .

Whatever First Amendment protection should be extended to nude dancing, live or on film, however, the Mount Ephraim ordinance prohibits all live entertainment in the Borough: no property in the Borough may be principally used for the commercial production of plays, concerts, musicals, dance or any other form of live entertainment.   Because appellants' claims are rooted in the First Amendment, they are entitled to rely on the impact of the ordinance on the expressive activities of others as well as their own.   "Because overbroad laws, like vague ones, deter privileged activit[ies], our cases firmly establish appellant's standing to raise an overbreadth challenge." Grayned v. City of Rockford, 408 U.S. 104, 114 (1972).

II

. . .

As an initial matter, this case is not controlled by Young v. American Mini Theatres, Inc., supra, the decision relied upon by the Camden County Court. Although the Court there stated that a zoning ordinance is not invalid merely because it regulates activity protected under the First Amendment, it emphasized that the challenged restriction on the location of adult movie theaters imposed a minimal burden on protected speech. 427 U.S., at 62. The restriction did not affect the number of adult movie theaters that could operate in the city; it merely dispersed them. The Court did not imply that a municipality could ban all adult theaters—much less all live entertainment or all nude dancing—from its commercial districts citywide. Moreover, it was emphasized in that case that the evidence presented to the Detroit Common Council indicated that the concentration of adult movie theaters in limited areas led to deterioration of surrounding neighborhoods, and it was concluded that the city had justified the incidental burden on First Amendment interests resulting from merely dispersing, but not excluding, adult theaters.

In this case, however, Mount Ephraim has not adequately justified its substantial restriction of protected activity. None of the justifications asserted in this Court was articulated by the state courts and none of them withstands scrutiny. First, the Borough contends that permitting live entertainment would conflict with its plan to create a commercial area that caters only to the "immediate needs" of its residents and that would enable them to purchase at local stores the few items they occasionally forgot to buy outside the Borough. No evidence was introduced below to support this assertion, and it is difficult to reconcile this characterization of the Borough's commercial zones with the provisions of the ordinance. Section 99–15A expressly states that the purpose of creating commercial zones was to provide areas for "local and *regional* commercial operations." (Emphasis added.) The range of permitted uses goes far beyond providing for the "immediate needs" of the residents. Motels, hardware stores, lumber stores, banks, offices, and car showrooms are permitted in commercial zones. The list of permitted "retail stores" is nonexclusive, and it includes such services as beauty salons, barber shops, cleaners, and restaurants. Virtually the only item or service that may not be sold in a commercial zone is entertainment, or at least live entertainment. The Borough's first justification is patently insufficient.

Second, Mount Ephraim contends that it may selectively exclude commercial live entertainment from the broad range of commercial uses permitted in the Borough for reasons normally associated with zoning in commercial districts, that is, to avoid the problems that may be associated with live entertainment, such as parking, trash, police protection, and medical facilities. The Borough has presented no evidence, and it is not immediately apparent as a matter of experience, that live entertainment poses problems of this nature more significant than those associated with various permitted uses; nor does it appear that the Borough's zoning authority has arrived at a defensible conclusion that unusual problems are presented by live entertainment. . . . We do not find it self-evident that a theater, for example, would create greater parking problems than would a restaurant. Even less apparent is what unique problems would be posed by exhibiting live nude dancing in connection with the sale of adult books and films, particularly since the bookstore is licensed to exhibit nude dancing on films. It may be that some forms of live entertainment would create problems that are not associated with the commercial uses presently permitted in

Mount Ephraim. Yet this ordinance is not narrowly drawn to respond to what might be the distinctive problems arising from certain types of live entertainment, and it is not clear that a more selective approach would fail to address those unique problems if any there are. The Borough has not established that its interests could not be met by restrictions that are less intrusive on protected forms of expression.

The Borough also suggests that § 99–15B is a reasonable "time, place and manner" restriction; yet it does not identify the municipal interests making it reasonable to exclude all commercial live entertainment but to allow a variety of other commercial uses in the Borough. . . . [T]he initial question in determining the validity of the exclusion as a time, place, and manner restriction is whether live entertainment is "basically incompatible with the normal activity [in the commercial zones.]" As discussed above, no evidence has been presented to establish that live entertainment is incompatible with the uses presently permitted by the Borough. Mount Ephraim asserts that it could have chosen to eliminate all commercial uses within its boundaries. Yet we must assess the exclusion of live entertainment in light of the commercial uses Mount Ephraim allows, not in light of what the Borough might have done.

To be reasonable, time, place, and manner restrictions not only must serve significant state interests but also must leave open adequate alternative channels of communication. . . . Here, the Borough totally excludes all live entertainment, including nonobscene nude dancing that is otherwise protected by the First Amendment. . . .

The Borough nevertheless contends that live entertainment in general and nude dancing in particular are amply available in close-by areas outside the limits of the Borough. Its position suggests the argument that if there were countywide zoning, it would be quite legal to allow live entertainment in only selected areas of the county and to exclude it from primarily residential communities, such as the Borough of Mount Ephraim. This may very well be true, but the Borough cannot avail itself of that argument in this case. There is no countywide zoning in Camden County, and Mount Ephraim is free under state law to impose its own zoning restrictions, within constitutional limits. Furthermore, there is no evidence in this record to support the proposition that the kind of entertainment appellants wish to provide is available in reasonably nearby areas. The courts below made no such findings; and at least in their absence, the ordinance excluding live entertainment from the commercial zone cannot constitutionally be applied to appellants so as to criminalize the activities for which they have been fined. "[O]ne is not to have the exercise of his liberty of expression in appropriate places abridged on the plea that it may be exercised in some other place." Schneider v. State, 308 U.S., at 163.

Accordingly, the convictions of these appellants are infirm and the judgment of the Appellate Division of the Superior Court of New Jersey is reversed and the case is remanded for further proceedings not inconsistent with this opinion.

So ordered.

Justice Blackmun, concurring.

I join the Court's opinion, but write separately to address two points that I believe are sources of some ambiguity in this still emerging area of the law.

First, I would emphasize that the presumption of validity that traditionally attends a local government's exercise of its zoning powers carries little, if any, weight where the zoning regulation trenches on rights of expression protected under the First Amendment. . . .

My other observation concerns the suggestion that a local community should be free to eliminate a particular form of expression so long as that form is available in areas reasonably nearby. In *Mini Theatres* the Court dealt with locational restrictions imposed by a political subdivision, the city of Detroit, that preserved reasonable access to the regulated form of expression within the boundaries of that same subdivision. It would be a substantial step beyond *Mini Theatres* to conclude that a town or county may legislatively prevent its citizens from engaging in or having access to forms of protected expression that are incompatible with its majority's conception of the "decent life" solely because these activities are sufficiently available in other locales. I do not read the Court's opinion to reach, nor would I endorse, that conclusion.

.   .   .

Justice Powell, with whom Justice Stewart joins, concurring.

I join the Court's opinion as I agree that Mount Ephraim has failed altogether to justify its broad restriction of protected expression. This is not to say, however, that some communities are not free—by a more carefully drawn ordinance—to regulate or ban all commercial public entertainment. In my opinion, such an ordinance could be appropriate and valid in a residential community where all commercial activity is excluded. Similarly, a residential community should be able to limit commercial establishments to essential "neighborhood" services permitted in a narrowly zoned area.

But the Borough of Mt. Ephraim failed to follow these paths. The ordinance before us was not carefully drawn and, as the Court points out, it is sufficiently overinclusive and underinclusive that any argument about the need to maintain the residential nature of this community fails as a justification.

Justice Stevens, concurring in the judgment.

The record in this case leaves so many relevant questions unanswered that the outcome, in my judgment, depends on the allocation of the burden of persuasion. If the case is viewed as a simple attempt by a small residential community to exclude the commercial exploitation of nude dancing from a "setting of tranquility," (Burger, C.J., dissenting), it would seem reasonable to require appellants to overcome the usual presumption that a municipality's zoning enactments are constitutionally valid.   .   .   .   On the other hand, if one starts, as the Court does, from the premise that "appellants' claims are rooted in the First Amendment," it would seem reasonable to require the Borough to overcome a presumption of invalidity.   .   .   .

Neither of these characterizations provides me with a satisfactory approach to this case. For appellants' business is located in a commercial zone, and the character of that zone is not unequivocally identified either by the text of the Borough's zoning ordinance or by the evidence in the record. And even though the foliage of the First Amendment may cast protective shadows over some forms of nude dancing, its roots were germinated by more serious concerns that are not necessarily implicated by a content-neutral zoning ordinance banning commercial exploitation of live entertainment. Cf. Young v. American Mini Theatres, Inc., 427 U.S. 50, 60–61.

One of the puzzling features of this case is that the character of the prohibition the Borough seeks to enforce is so hard to ascertain.   .   .   .

.   .   .

Without more information about this commercial enclave on Black Horse Pike, one cannot know whether the change in appellants' business in 1976 introduced cacophony into a tranquil setting or merely a new refrain in a local replica of Place Pigalle. If I were convinced that the former is the correct appraisal of this commercial zone, I would have no hesitation in agreeing with The Chief Justice that even if the live nude dancing is a form of expressive activity protected by the First Amendment, the Borough may prohibit it. But when the record is opaque, as this record is, I believe the Borough must shoulder the burden of demonstrating that appellants' introduction of live entertainment had an identifiable adverse impact on the neighborhood or on the Borough as a whole. It might be appropriate to presume that such an adverse impact would occur if the zoning plan itself were narrowly drawn to create categories of commercial uses that unambiguously differentiated this entertainment from permitted uses. However, this open-ended ordinance affords no basis for any such presumption.

The difficulty in this case is that we are left to speculate as to the Borough's reasons for proceeding against appellants' business, and as to the justification for the distinction the Borough has drawn between live and other forms of entertainment. While a municipality need not persuade a federal court that its zoning decisions are correct as a matter of policy, when First Amendment interests are implicated, it must at least be able to demonstrate that a uniform policy in fact exists and is applied in a content-neutral fashion. Presumably, municipalities may regulate expressive activity—even protected activity—pursuant to narrowly drawn content-neutral standards; however, they may not regulate protected activity when the only standard provided is the unbridled discretion of a municipal official. Compare Saia v. New York, 334 U.S. 558, with Kovacs v. Cooper, 336 U.S. 77. Because neither the text of the zoning ordinance nor the evidence in the record indicates that Mount Ephraim applied narrowly drawn content-neutral standards to the appellants' business, for me this case involves a criminal prosecution of appellants simply because one of their employees has engaged in expressive activity that has been assumed, *arguendo,* to be protected by the First Amendment. Accordingly, and without endorsing the overbreadth analysis employed by the Court, I concur in its judgment.

Chief Justice Burger, with whom Justice Rehnquist joins, dissenting.

. . . .

The Court depicts Mount Ephraim's ordinance as a ban on live entertainment. But, in terms, it does not mention any kind of entertainment. As applied, it operates as a ban on nude dancing in appellants' "adult" book store, and for that reason alone it is here. Thus, the issue *in the case that we have before us* is not whether Mount Ephraim may ban traditional live entertainment, but whether it may ban nude dancing, which is used as the "bait" to induce customers into the appellants' book store. When, and if, this ordinance is used to prevent a high school performance of "The Sound of Music," for example, the Court can deal with that problem.

An overconcern about draftsmanship and overbreadth should not be allowed to obscure the central question before us. It is clear that, in passing the ordinance challenged here, the citizens of the Borough of Mount Ephraim meant only to preserve the basic character of their community. It is just as clear that, by thrusting its live nude dancing shows on this community, the appellants alters and damages that community over its objections. As applied in this case, therefore, the ordinance speaks directly and unequivocally. It may be that, as applied in some other case, this ordinance would violate the First Amendment, but, since such a case is not before us, we should not decide it.

. . . .

CONSOLIDATED EDISON CO. v. PUBLIC SERVICE COMMISSION

447 U.S. 530, 100 S.Ct. 2326, 65 L.Ed.2d 319 (1980).

Mr. Justice Powell delivered the opinion of the Court.

The question in this case is whether the First Amendment, as incorporated by the Fourteenth Amendment, is violated by an order of the Public Service

Commission of the State of New York that prohibits the inclusion in monthly electric bills of inserts discussing controversial issues of public policy.

I.

The Consolidated Edison Company of New York, appellant in this case, placed written material entitled "Independence Is Still a Goal, and Nuclear Power Is Needed To Win The Battle" in its January 1976 billing envelope. The bill insert stated Consolidated Edison's views on "the benefits of nuclear power," saying that they "far outweigh any potential risk" and that nuclear power plants are safe, economical, and clean. The utility also contended that increased use of nuclear energy would further this country's independence from foreign energy sources.

In March 1976, the Natural Resources Defense Council, Inc. (NRDC) requested Consolidated Edison to enclose a rebuttal prepared by NRDC in its next billing envelope. When Consolidated Edison refused, NRDC asked the Public Service Commission of the State of New York to open Consolidated Edison's billing envelopes to contrasting views on controversial issues of public importance.

On February 17, 1977, the Commission, appellee here, denied NRDC's request, but prohibited "utilities from using bill inserts to discuss political matters, including the desirability of future development of nuclear power." The Commission explained its decision in a Statement of Policy on Advertising and Promotion Practices of Public Utilities issued on February 25, 1977. The Commission concluded that Consolidated Edison customers who receive bills containing inserts are a captive audience of diverse views who should not be subjected to the utility's beliefs. Accordingly, the Commission barred utility companies from including bill inserts that express "their opinions or viewpoints on controversial issues of public policy." The Commission did not, however, bar utilities from sending bill inserts discussing topics that are not "controversial issues of public policy." The Commission later denied petitions for rehearing filed by Consolidated Edison and other utilities.

Consolidated Edison sought review of the Commission's order in the New York state courts. . . . The Court of Appeals held that the order did not violate the Constitution because it was a valid time, place and manner regulation designed to protect the privacy of Consolidated Edison's customers. . . . We reverse.

II.

The restriction on bill inserts cannot be upheld on the ground that Consolidated Edison is not entitled to freedom of speech. In First National Bank of Boston v. Bellotti, 435 U.S. 765 (1978), we rejected the contention that a State may confine corporate speech to specified issues. . . .

. . . In the mailing that triggered the regulation at issue, Consolidated Edison advocated the use of nuclear power. The Commission has limited the means by which Consolidated Edison may participate in the public debate on this question and other controversial issues of national interest and importance. Thus, the Commission's prohibition of discussion of controversial issues strikes at the heart of the freedom to speak.

III.

The Commission's ban on bill inserts is not, of course invalid merely because it imposes a limitation upon speech. . . . We must consider whether the State can demonstrate that its regulation is constitutionally permissible. The Commission's arguments require us to consider three theories that might justify the state action. We must determine whether the prohibition is (i) a reasonable time, place, or manner restriction, (ii) a permissible subject-matter regulation, or (iii) a narrowly tailored means of serving a compelling state interest.

A.

This Court has recognized the validity of reasonable time, place, or manner regulations that serve a significant governmental interest and leave ample alternative channels for communication. . . .

A restriction that regulates only the time, place or manner of speech may be imposed so long as it is reasonable. But when regulation is based on the content of speech, governmental action must be scrutinized more carefully. . . . Therefore, a constitutionally permissible time, place, or manner restriction may not be based upon either the content or subject matter of speech.

The Commission does not pretend that its action is unrelated to the content or subject matter of bill inserts. Indeed, it has undertaken to suppress certain bill inserts precisely because they address controversial issues of public policy. The Commission allows inserts that present information to consumers on certain subjects, such as energy conservation measures, but it forbids the use of inserts that discuss public controversies. The Commission, with commendable candor, justifies its ban on the ground that consumers will benefit from receiving "useful" information, but not from the prohibited information. The Commission's own rationale demonstrates that its action cannot be upheld as a content-neutral time, place, or manner regulation.

B.

The Commission next argues that its order is acceptable because it applies to all discussion of nuclear power, whether pro or con, in bill inserts. The prohibition, the Commission contends, is related to subject matter rather than to the views of a particular speaker. Because the regulation does not favor either side of a political controversy, the Commission asserts that it does not unconstitutionally suppress freedom of speech.

The First Amendment's hostility to content-based regulation extends not only to restrictions on particular viewpoints, but also to prohibition of public discussion of an entire topic. . . .

. . .

C.

Where a government restricts the speech of a private person, the state action may be sustained only if the government can show that the regulation is a precisely drawn means of serving a compelling state interest. . . . The Commission argues finally that its prohibition is necessary (i) to avoid forcing Consolidated Edison's views on a captive audience, (ii) to allocate limited resources in the public interest, and (iii) to ensure that ratepayers do not subsidize the cost of the bill inserts.

The State Court of Appeals largely based its approval of the prohibition upon its conclusion that the bill inserts intruded upon individual privacy. The court stated that the Commission could act to protect the privacy of the utility's customers because they have no choice whether to receive the insert and the views expressed in the insert may inflame their sensibilities. . . . But the Court of Appeals erred in its assessment of the seriousness of the intrusion.

Even if a short exposure to Consolidated Edison's views may offend the sensibilities of some consumers, the ability of government "to shut off discourse solely to protect others from hearing it [is] dependent upon a showing that substantial privacy interests are being invaded in an essentially intolerable manner." Cohen v. California, 403 U.S., at 21. . . . Where a single speaker communicates to many listeners, the First Amendment does not permit the government to prohibit speech as intrusive unless the "captive" audience cannot avoid objectionable speech.

Passengers on public transportation, see Lehman v. Shaker Heights, 418 U.S., at 307–308 (Douglas, J., concurring in the judgment), or residents of a neighborhood disturbed by the raucous broadcasts from a passing soundtruck, cf. Kovacs v. Cooper, supra, may well be unable to escape an unwanted message. But customers who encounter an objectionable billing insert may "effectively avoid further bombardment of their sensibilities simply by averting their eyes." Cohen v. California, supra, at 21. See Spence v. Washington, 418 U.S. 405, 412 (1974) (per curiam). The customer of Consolidated Edison may escape exposure to objectionable material simply by transferring the bill insert from envelope to wastebasket.

The Commission contends that because a billing envelope can accommodate only a limited amount of information, political messages should not be allowed to take the place of inserts that promote energy conservation or safety, or that remind consumers of their legal rights. The Commission relies upon Red Lion Broadcasting v. Federal Communications Commission, 395 U.S. 367 (1969), in which the Court held that the regulation of radio and television broadcast frequencies permit the Federal Government to exercise unusual authority over speech. But billing envelopes differ from broadcast frequencies in two ways. First, a broadcaster communicates through use of a scarce, publicly owned resource. No person can broadcast without a license, whereas all persons are free to send correspondence to private homes through the mails. Thus, it cannot be said that billing envelopes are a limited resource comparable to the broadcast spectrum. Second, the Commission has not shown on the record before us that the presence of the bill inserts at issue would preclude the inclusion of other inserts that Consolidated Edison might be ordered lawfully to include in the billing envelope. Unlike radio or television stations broadcasting on a single frequency, multiple bill inserts will not result in a "cacophony of competing voices." Id., at 376.

Finally, the Commission urges that its prohibition would prevent ratepayers from subsidizing the costs of policy-oriented bill inserts. But the Commission did not base its order on an inability to allocate costs between the shareholders of Consolidated Edison and the ratepayers. Rather, the Commission stated "that using bill inserts to proclaim a utility's viewpoint on controversial issues (*even when the stockholder pays for it in full*) is tantamount to taking advantage of a captive audience. . . ." Accordingly, there is no basis on this record to assume that the Commission could not exclude the cost of these bill inserts from the utility's rate base.

IV.

The Commission's suppression of bill inserts that discuss controversial issues of public policy directly infringes the freedom of speech protected by the First and Fourteenth Amendments. The state action is neither a valid time, place, or manner restriction, nor a permissible subject-matter regulation, nor a narrowly drawn prohibition justified by a compelling state interest. Accordingly, the regulation is invalid. . . .

The decision of the New York Court of Appeals is reversed.

. . . .

Mr. Justice Stevens, concurring in the judgment.

Any student of history who has been reprimanded for talking about the World Series during a class discussion of the First Amendment knows that it is incorrect to state that a "time, place, or manner restriction may not be based upon either the content or subject matter of speech." And every lawyer who has read our Rules, or our cases upholding various restrictions on speech with specific reference to subject matter must recognize the hyperbole in the dictum, "But, above all else, the First Amendment means that Government has no power to restrict expression because of its message, its ideas, its subject matter or its content." Police Department v. Mosley, 408 U.S. 92, 95. Indeed, if that were the law, there would be no need for the Court's detailed rejection of the justifications put forward by the State for the restriction involved in this case.

There are, in fact, many situations in which the subject matter, or, indeed, even the point of view of the speaker, may provide a justification for a time, place and manner regulation. Perhaps the most obvious example is the regulation of oral argument in this Court; the appellant's lawyer precedes his adversary solely because he seeks reversal of a judgment. As is true of many other aspects of liberty, some forms of orderly regulation actually promote freedom more than would a state of total anarchy.

Instead of trying to justify our conclusion by reasoning from honeycombed premises, I prefer to identify the basis of decision in more simple terms. See Young v. American Mini Theatres, 427 U.S. 50, 65–66. A regulation of speech that is motivated by nothing more than a desire to curtail expression of a particular point of view on controversial issues of general interest is the purest example of a "law abridging the freedom of speech, or of the press." A regulation that denies one group of persons the right to address a selected audience on "controversial issues of public policy" is plainly such a regulation.

The only justification for the regulation relied on by the New York Court of Appeals is that the utilities' bill inserts may be "offensive" to some of their customers. But a communication may be offensive in two different ways. Independently of the message the speaker intends to convey, the form of his communication may be offensive—perhaps because it is too loud or too ugly in a particular setting. Other speeches, even though elegantly phrased in dulcet tones, are offensive simply because the listener disagrees with the speaker's message. The fact that the offensive form of some communication may subject it to appropriate regulation surely does not support the conclusion that the offensive character of an idea can justify an attempt to censor its expression. Since the Public Service Commission has candidly put forward this impermissible justification for its censorial regulation, it plainly violates the First Amendment.

Accordingly, I concur in the judgment of the Court.

Mr. Justice Blackmun, with whom Mr. Justice Rehnquist as to Parts I and II joins, dissenting.

. . . . I cannot agree with the Court that the New York Public Service Commission's ban on the utility bill insert somehow deprives the utility of its First and Fourteenth Amendment rights. Because of Consolidated Edison's monopoly status and its rate structure, the use of the insert amounts to an exaction from the utility's customers by way of forced aid for the utility's speech. And, contrary to the Court's suggestion, an allocation of the insert's cost between the utility's shareholders and the ratepayers would not eliminate this coerced subsidy.

I.

A public utility is a state-created monopoly. . . . Under the laws of New York and other States, a public utility cannot include in the rate base the costs of political advertising and lobbying. . . . These costs cannot be passed on to consumers because ratepayers derive no service-related benefits from political advertisements. The purpose of such advertising and lobbying is to benefit the utility's shareholders, and its cost must be deducted from profits otherwise available for the shareholders. . . .

II.

The Commission concluded, properly in my view, that use of the billing envelope to distribute management's pamphlets amounts to a forced subsidy of the utility's speech by the ratepayers. Consolidated Edison would counter this argument by pointing out that it is willing to allocate to shareholders the *additional* costs attributable to the inserts. . . .

I do not accept appellant's argument that preventing a "free ride" for the utility's message, is not a substantial, legitimate state concern. Even though the free ride may cost the ratepayers nothing additional by way of specific dollars, it still qualifies as forced support of the utility's speech. . . .

In suggesting that the State's interest in eliminating forced subsidization of the utility's speech can be achieved by allocating the expenses of the inserts to the utility's shareholders, the Court has glossed over the difficult allocation issue underlying this controversy. It is not clear to me from the Court's opinion whether it believes that charging the shareholders with the marginal costs associated with the inserts, that is, the costs of printing and putting them into the envelope, will satisfy the State's interest, or whether the Court is suggesting some division of the fixed costs of the mailing, that is, the postage, the envelope, the creation and maintenance of the mailing list, and any other overhead expense.

. . . The Commission's ban on bill inserts does not restrict the utility from using the shareholders' resources to finance communication of its viewpoints on any topic. Consolidated Edison is completely free to use the mails and any other medium of communication on the same basis as any other speaker. The order merely prevents the utility from relying on a forced subsidy from the ratepayers. This leads me to conclude that the State's attempt here to protect the ratepayers from unwillingly financing the utility's speech and to preserve the billing envelope for the sole benefit of the customers who pay for it does not infringe upon the First and Fourteenth Amendment rights of the utility.

. . . .

––––––––

VILLAGE OF SCHAUMBURG v. CITIZENS FOR A BETTER ENVIRONMENT

444 U.S. 620, 100 S.Ct. 826, 63 L.Ed.2d 73 (1980).

Mr. Justice White delivered the opinion of the Court.

The issue in this case is the validity under the First and Fourteenth Amendments of a municipal ordinance prohibiting the solicitation of contributions by charitable organizations that do not use at least 75 percent of their receipts for "charitable purposes," those purposes being defined to exclude solicitation expenses, salaries, overhead and other administrative expenses. The Court of Appeals held the ordinance unconstitutional. We affirm that judgment.

I.

The Village of Schaumburg (Village) is a suburban community located 25 miles northwest of Chicago, Ill. On March 12, 1974, the Village adopted "An Ordinance Regulating Soliciting by Charitable Organizations," . . . which regulates the activities of "peddlers and solicitors," Code § 22–1 et seq. (1974). Article III provides that "[e]very charitable organization, which solicits or intends to solicit contributions from persons in the village by door-to-door solicitation or the use of public streets and public ways, shall prior to such solicitation apply for a permit." . . . . Solicitation of contributions for charitable organizations without a permit is prohibited and is punishable by a fine of up to $500 for each offense. . . .

Section 22–20(g), which is the focus of the constitutional challenge involved in this case, requires that permit applications, among other things, contain "[s]atisfactory proof that at least seventy-five per cent of the proceeds of such solicitations will be used directly for the charitable purpose of the organization." In determining whether an organization satisfies the 75-percent requirement, the ordinance provides that:

"the following items shall not be deemed to be used for the charitable purposes of the organization, to wit:

"(1) Salaries or commissions paid to solicitors;

"(2) Administrative expenses of the organization, including, but not limited to, salaries, attorneys' fees, rents, telephone, advertising expenses, contributions to other organizations and persons, except as charitable contribution and related expenses incurred as administrative or overhead items."

. . . .

Respondent Citizens for a Better Environment (CBE) is an Illinois not-for-profit corporation organized for the purpose of promoting "the protection of the environment." CBE is registered with the Illinois Attorney General's Charitable Trust Division pursuant to Illinois law, and has been afforded tax-exempt status by the United States Internal Revenue Service, and gifts to it are deductible for federal income tax purposes. CBE requested permission to solicit contributions in the Village of Schaumburg, but the Village denied CBE a permit because CBE could not demonstrate that 75 percent of its receipts would be used for "charitable purposes" . . . .. CBE then sued the Village in the United States District Court for the Northern District of Illinois, charging that the 75-percent requirement of § 22–20(g) violated the First and Fourteenth Amendments. Declaratory and injunctive relief were sought.

In its amended complaint, CBE alleged that "[i]t was organized for the purpose, among others, of protecting, maintaining, and enhancing the quality of the Illinois environment." The complaint also alleged:

"[t]hat incident to its purpose, CBE employs 'canvassers' who are engaged in door-to-door activity in the Chicago metropolitan area, endeavoring to distribute literature on environmental topics and answer questions of an environmental nature when posed; solicit contributions to financially support the organization and its program; receive grievances and complaints of an environmental nature regarding which CBE may afford assistance in the evaluation and redress of these grievances and complaints."

. . . .

The District Court awarded summary judgment to CBE. . . .

The Court of Appeals for the Seventh Circuit affirmed. . . .

. . . .

II.

It is urged that the ordinance should be sustained because it deals only with solicitation and because any charity is free to propagate its views from door to door in the Village without a permit as long as it refrains from soliciting money.

But this represents a far too limited view of our prior cases relevant to canvassing and soliciting by religious and charitable organizations.

In Schneider v. State (Town of Irvington), 308 U.S. 147 (1939), a canvasser for a religious society, who passed out booklets from door to door and asked for contributions, was arrested and convicted under an ordinance which prohibited canvassing, soliciting or distribution of circulars from house to house without a permit, the issuance of which rested much in the discretion of public officials. The state courts construed the ordinance as aimed mainly at house-to-house canvassing and solicitation. This distinguished the case from Lovell v. Griffin, 303 U.S. 444 (1938), which had invalidated on its face and on First Amendment grounds an ordinance criminalizing the distribution of any handbill at any time or place without a permit. Because the canvasser's conduct "amounted to the solicitation and acceptance of money contributions without a permit" and because the ordinance was thought to be valid as a protection against fraudulent solicitations, the conviction was sustained. This Court disagreed, noting that the ordinance not only applied to religious canvassers but also to "one who wishes to present his views on political, social or economic questions," and holding that the city could not, in the name of preventing fraudulent appeals, subject door-to-door advocacy and the communication of views to the discretionary permit requirement. The Court pointed out that the ordinance was not limited to those "who canvass for profit," ibid., and reserved the question whether "commercial soliciting and canvassing" could be validly subjected to such controls.

Cantwell v. Connecticut, 310 U.S. 296 (1940), involved a state statute forbidding the solicitation of contributions of anything of value by religious, charitable or philanthropic causes without obtaining official approval. Three members of a religious group were convicted under the statute for selling books, distributing pamphlets and soliciting contributions or donations. Their convictions were affirmed in the state courts on the ground that they were soliciting funds and that the statute was valid as an attempt to protect the public from fraud. This Court set aside the convictions, holding that although "[a] general regulation, in the public interest, of solicitation, which does not involve any religious test and does not unreasonably obstruct or delay the collection of funds, is not open to any constitutional objection," to "condition the solicitation of aid for the perpetuation of religious views or systems upon a license, the grant of which rests in the exercise of a determination by state authority as to what is a religious cause," was considered to be an invalid prior restraint on the free exercise of religion. Although *Cantwell* turned on the free exercise clause, the Court has subsequently understood *Cantwell* to have implied that soliciting funds involves interests protected by the First Amendment's guarantee of freedom of speech. Virginia Pharmacy Board v. Virginia Consumer Council, 425 U.S. 748, 761 (1976); Bates v. State Bar of Arizona, 433 U.S. 350, 363 (1977).

. . . .

. . . . [I]n Jamison v. Texas, 318 U.S. 413 (1942), the Court, without dissent, . . . held that although purely commercial leaflets could be banned from the streets, a State could not "prohibit the distribution of handbills in the pursuit of a clearly religious activity merely because the handbills invite the purchase of books for the improved understanding of the religion or because the handbills seek in a lawful fashion to promote the raising of funds for religious purposes." The Court reaffirmed what it deemed to be an identical holding in *Schneider,* as well as the ruling in *Cantwell* that "a state might not prevent the collection of funds for a religious purpose by unreasonably obstructing or delaying their collection."

In the course of striking down a tax on the sale of religious literature, the majority opinion in Murdock v. Pennsylvania, 319 U.S. 105 (1943), reiterated the holding in *Jamison* that the distribution of handbills was not transformed into an unprotected commercial activity by the solicitation of funds. Recognizing that drawing the line between purely commercial ventures and protected distributions of written material was a difficult task, the Court went on to hold that the sale of religious literature by itinerant evangelists in the course of spreading their doctrine was not a commercial enterprise beyond the protection of the First Amendment.

On the same day, the Court invalidated a municipal ordinance that forbad the door-to-door distribution of handbills, circulars or other advertisements. None of the justifications for the general prohibition was deemed sufficient; the right of the individual resident to warn off such solicitors was deemed sufficient protection for the privacy of the citizen. Martin v. Struthers, 319 U.S. 141 (1943). On its facts, the case did not involve the solicitation of funds or the sale of literature.

. . . .

In 1951, Breard v. Alexandria, 341 U.S. 622, was decided. That case involved an ordinance making it criminal to enter premises without an invitation to sell goods, wares and merchandise. The ordinance was sustained as applied to door-to-door solicitation of magazine subscriptions. The Court held that the sale of literature introduced "a commercial feature," and that the householder's interest in privacy outweighed any rights of the publisher to distribute magazines by uninvited entry on private property. The Court's opinion, however, did not indicate that the solicitation of gifts or contributions by religious or charitable organizations should be deemed commercial activities, nor did the facts of *Breard* involve the sale of religious literature or similar materials. Martin v. Struthers, supra, was distinguished but not overruled.

Hynes v. Mayor of Oradell, 425 U.S. 610 (1976), dealt with a city ordinance requiring an identification permit for canvassing or soliciting from house to house for charitable or political purposes. Based on its review of prior cases, the Court held that soliciting and canvassing from door to door were subject to reasonable regulation so as to protect the citizen against crime and undue annoyance, but that the First Amendment required such controls to be drawn with "narrow specificity." Id., at 620. The ordinance was invalidated as unacceptably vague.

Prior authorities, therefore, clearly establish that charitable appeals for funds, on the street or door to door, involve a variety of speech interests—communication of information, the dissemination and propagation of views and ideas, and the advocacy of causes—that are within the protection of the First Amendment. Soliciting financial support is undoubtedly subject to reasonable regulation but the latter must be undertaken with due regard for the reality that solicitation is characteristically intertwined with informative and perhaps persuasive speech seeking support for particular causes or for particular views on economic, political or social issues, and for the reality that without solicitation the flow of such information and advocacy would likely cease. Canvassers in such contexts are necessarily more than solicitors for money. Furthermore, because charitable solicitation does more than inform private economic decisions and is not primarily concerned with providing information about the characteristics and costs of goods and services, it has not been dealt with in our cases as a variety of purely commercial speech.[7]

---

[7] To the extent that any of the Court's past decisions discussed in Part II hold or indicate that commercial speech is excluded from First Amendment protections, those decisions, to that extent, are no longer good law. Virginia Pharmacy Board v. Virginia Consumer Council, 425 U.S. 748, 758–759, 762 (1976). For the purposes of applying the overbreadth doctrine, however, it remains relevant to

III.

The issue before us, then, is not whether charitable solicitations in residential neighborhoods are within the protections of the First Amendment. It is clear that they are. . . .

The issue is whether the Village has exercised its power to regulate solicitation in such a manner as not unduly to intrude upon the rights of free speech. In pursuing this question we must first deal with the claim of the Village that summary judgment was improper because there was an unresolved factual dispute concerning the true character of CBE's organization. . . . The Village claims, however, that it should have had a chance to prove that the 75-percent requirement is valid as applied to CBE because CBE spends so much of its resources for the benefit of its employees that it may appropriately be deemed an organization, existing for private profit rather than for charitable purposes.

We agree with the Court of Appeals that CBE was entitled to its judgment of facial invalidity if the ordinance purported to prohibit canvassing by a substantial category of charities to which the 75-percent limitation could not be applied consistently with the First and Fourteenth Amendments, even if there was no demonstration that CBE itself was one of these organizations. Given a case or controversy, a litigant whose own activities are unprotected, may nevertheless challenge a statute by showing that it substantially abridges the First Amendment rights of other parties not before the court. . . . In these First Amendment contexts, the courts are inclined to disregard the normal rule against permitting one whose conduct may validly be prohibited to challenge the proscription as it applies to others because of the possibility that protected speech or associative activities may be inhibited by the overly broad reach of the statute.

. . . .

IV.

Although indicating that the 75-percent limitation might be enforceable against "the more traditional charitable organizations" or "where solicitors represent themselves as mere conduits for contributions," the Court of Appeals identified a class of charitable organizations as to which the 75-percent rule could not constitutionally be applied. These were the organizations whose primary purpose is not to provide money or services for the poor, the needy or other worthy objects of charity, but to gather and disseminate information about and advocate positions on matters of public concern. These organizations characteristically use paid solicitors who "necessarily combine" the solicitation of financial support with the "functions of information dissemination, discussion, and advocacy of public issues." These organizations also pay other employees to obtain and process the necessary information and to arrive at and announce in suitable form the organizations' preferred positions on the issues of interest to them. Organizations of this kind, although they might pay only reasonable salaries, would necessarily spend more than 25% of their budgets on salaries and administrative expenses and would be completely barred from solicitation in the Village.[9] The Court of Appeals concluded that such a prohibition was an unjustified infringement of the First and Fourteenth Amendments.

distinguish between commercial and noncommercial speech. Bates v. State Bar of Arizona, 433 U.S. 350, 381 (1977).

    [9] . . . Unlike the ordinance upheld in National Foundation v. Fort Worth, 415 F.2d 41 (CA5 1969), cert. denied, 396 U.S. 1040 (1970), the Village ordinance has no provision permitting an organization unable to comply with the 75-percent requirement to obtain a permit by demonstrating that its solicitation costs are nevertheless reasonable. . . .

We agree with the Court of Appeals that the 75-percent limitation is a direct and substantial limitation on protected activity that cannot be sustained unless it serves a sufficiently strong, subordinating interest that the Village is entitled to protect. We also agree that the Village's proffered justifications are inadequate and that the ordinance cannot survive scrutiny under the First Amendment.

. . .

Prevention of fraud is the Village's principal justification for prohibiting solicitation by charities that spend more than one-quarter of their receipts on salaries and administrative expenses. The submission is that any organization using more than 25% of its receipts on fundraising, salaries and overhead is not a charitable, but a commercial, for profit enterprise and that to permit it to represent itself as a charity is fraudulent. But, as the Court of Appeals recognized, this cannot be true of those organizations that are primarily engaged in research, advocacy or public education and that use their own paid staff to carry out these functions as well as to solicit financial support. . . .

The Village's legitimate interest in preventing fraud can be better served by measures less intrusive than a direct prohibition on solicitation. Fraudulent misrepresentations can be prohibited and the penal laws used to punish such conduct directly. . . . Efforts to promote disclosure of the finances of charitable organizations also may assist in preventing fraud by informing the public of the ways in which their contributions will be employed. Such measures may help make contribution decisions more informed, while leaving to individual choice the decision whether to contribute to organizations that spend large amounts on salaries and administrative expenses.

We also fail to perceive any substantial relationship between the 75-percent requirement and the protection of public safety or of residential privacy. . . .

. . . Other provisions of the ordinance, which are not challenged here, such as the provision permitting homeowners to bar solicitors from their property by posting signs reading "No Solicitors or Peddlers Invited," Code § 22–24, suggest the availability of less intrusive and more effective measures to protect privacy. . . .

We find no reason to disagree with the Court of Appeals' conclusion that § 22–20(g) is unconstitutionally overbroad. Its judgment is therefore affirmed.

It is so ordered.

Mr. Justice Rehnquist, dissenting.

The Court holds that Art. III of the Schaumburg Village Code is unconstitutional as applied to prohibit respondent Citizens for a Better Environment (CBE) from soliciting contributions door to door. If read in isolation, today's decision might be defensible. When combined with this Court's earlier pronouncements on the subject, however, today's decision relegates any local government interested in regulating door-to-door activities to the role of Sisyphus. . . .

The Court's neglect of its prior precedents in this regard is entirely understandable, since the earlier decisions striking down various regulations covering door-to-door activities turned upon factors not present in the instant case. A plurality of these decisions turned primarily, if not exclusively, upon the amount of discretion vested in municipal authorities to grant or deny permits on the basis of vague or even non-existent criteria. . . .

Another line of earlier cases involved the distribution of information, as opposed to requests for contributions. . . .

I believe that the Court overestimates the value, in a constitutional sense, of door-to-door solicitation for financial contributions and simultaneously underestimates the reasons why a village board might conclude that regulation of such activity was necessary. In Hynes v. Mayor of Oradell, supra, this Court referred with approval to Professor Zechariah Chafee's observation that "[o]f all the methods of spreading unpopular ideas, [house-to-house canvassing] seems the least entitled to extensive protection." Id., at 619, quoting Z. Chafee, Free Speech in the United States, 406 (1954). While such activity may be worthy of heightened protection when limited to the dissemination of information, see, e.g., Martin v. Struthers, supra, or when designed to propagate religious beliefs, see e.g., Cantwell v. Connecticut, supra, I believe that a simple request for money lies far from the core protections of the First Amendment as heretofore interpreted. In the case of such solicitation, the community's interest in ensuring that the collecting organization meet some objective financial criteria is indisputably valid. Regardless whether one labels noncharitable solicitation "fraudulent," nothing in the United States Constitution should prevent residents of a community from making the collective judgment that certain worthy charities may solicit door to door while at the same time insulating themselves against panhandlers, profiteers, and peddlers.

The central weakness of the Court's decision, I believe, is its failure to recognize, let alone confront, the two most important issues in this case: how does one define a "charitable" organization, and to which authority in our federal system is application of that definition confided? I would uphold Schaumburg's ordinance as applied to CBE because that ordinance, while perhaps too strict to suit some tastes, affects only door-to-door solicitation for financial contributions, leaves little or no discretion in the hands of municipal authorities to "censor" unpopular speech, and is rationally related to the community's collective desire to bestow its largess upon organizations that are truly "charitable." I therefore dissent.

———

SECRETARY OF STATE OF MARYLAND v. JOSEPH H. MUNSON CO., 104 S.Ct. 2839 (1984). The state charitable solicitation statute barred solicitation by charities whose fund-raising expenses exceeded 25% of the amount raised, but authorized waiver of the limitation where it "would effectively prevent the charitable organization from raising contributions." The Court conceded that *Schaumburg* left open the question whether the possibility of administrative waiver of percentage limitations on funds expended in charitable solicitation would remedy the constitutional deficiency in that ordinance. The Court concluded that the Maryland waiver provision would not. The waiver provision, as construed by the Maryland Court of Appeals, was limited to those organizations who could show financial necessity, and was not applicable to organizations whose high fund-raising costs were attributable to "information dissemination, discussion, and advocacy of public issues."

SECTION 5. LABOR PICKETING

———

INTERNATIONAL BROTHERHOOD OF TEAMSTERS v. VOGT, INC.

354 U.S. 284, 77 S.Ct. 1166, 1 L.Ed.2d 1347 (1957).

Mr. Justice Frankfurter delivered the opinion of the Court.

. . . Respondent owns and operates a gravel pit in Oconomowoc, Wisconsin, where it employs 15 to 20 men. Petitioner unions sought unsuccessfully to induce some of respondent's employees to join the unions and commenced to picket the entrance to respondent's place of business with signs reading, "The men on this job are not 100% affiliated with the A.F.L." "In consequence," drivers of several trucking companies refused to deliver and haul goods to and from respondent's plant, causing substantial damage to respondent. Respondent thereupon sought an injunction to restrain the picketing.

. . .

On appeal, the Wisconsin Supreme Court . . . canvassed the whole circumstances surrounding the picketing and held that "One would be credulous, indeed, to believe under the circumstances that the union had no thought of coercing the employer to interfere with its employees in their right to join or refuse to join the defendant union." Such picketing, the court held, was for "an unlawful purpose," since Wis.Stat. § 111.06(2)(b) made it an unfair labor practice for an employee individually or in concert with others to "coerce, intimidate or induce any employer to interfere with any of his employes in the enjoyment of their legal rights . . . or to engage in any practice with regard to his employes which would constitute an unfair labor practice if undertaken by him on his own initiative." Relying on Building Service Employees, etc. v. Gazzam, 339 U.S. 532, and Pappas v. Stacey, 151 Me. 36, 116 A.2d 497, the Wisconsin Supreme Court therefore affirmed the granting of the injunction on this different ground. 270 Wis. 321a, 74 N.W.2d 749.

We are asked to reverse the judgment of the Wisconsin Supreme Court,

. . . .

. . . .

[In 1940] the Court made sweeping pronouncements about the right to picket in holding unconstitutional a statute that had been applied to ban all picketing, with "no exceptions based upon either the number of persons engaged in the proscribed activity, the peaceful character of their demeanor, the nature of their dispute with an employer, or the restrained character and the accurateness of the terminology used in notifying the public of the facts of the dispute." Thornhill v. Alabama, 310 U.S. 88, 99. As the statute dealt at large with all picketing, so the Court broadly assimilated peaceful picketing in general to freedom of speech, and as such protected against abridgment by the Fourteenth Amendment.

These principles were applied by the Court in A.F.L. v. Swing, 312 U.S. 321, to hold unconstitutional an injunction against peaceful picketing, based on a State's common-law policy against picketing when there was no immediate dispute between employer and employee. On the same day, however, the Court upheld a generalized injunction against picketing where there had been violence because "it could justifiably be concluded that the momentum of fear generated by past violence would survive even though future picketing might be wholly peaceful." Milk Wagon Drivers Union v. Meadowmoor Dairies, 312 U.S. 287, 294.

Soon, however, the Court came to realize that the broad pronouncements, but not the specific holding, of *Thornhill* had to yield "to the impact of facts unforeseen," or at least not sufficiently appreciated. . . .

The implied reassessments of the broad language of the *Thornhill* case were finally generalized in a series of cases sustaining injunctions against peaceful picketing, even when arising in the course of a labor controversy, when such picketing was counter to valid state policy in a domain open to state regulation. The decisive reconsideration came in Giboney v. Empire Storage & Ice Co., 336 U.S. 490 [1949]. A union, seeking to organize peddlers, picketed a wholesale dealer to induce it to refrain from selling to nonunion peddlers. The state courts, finding that such an agreement would constitute a conspiracy in restraint of trade in violation of the state antitrust laws, enjoined the picketing. This Court affirmed unanimously.

"It is contended that the injunction against picketing adjacent to Empire's place of business is an unconstitutional abridgement of free speech because the picketers were attempting peacefully to publicize truthful facts about a labor dispute. . . . But the record here does not permit this publicizing to be treated in isolation. For according to the pleadings, the evidence, the findings, and the argument of the appellants, the sole immediate object of the publicizing adjacent to the premises of Empire, as well as the other activities of the appellants and their allies, was to compel Empire to agree to stop selling ice to nonunion peddlers. Thus all of appellants' activities . . . constituted a single and integrated course of conduct, which was in violation of Missouri's valid law. In this situation, the injunction did no more than enjoin an offense against Missouri law, a felony." Id., at 497–498. The Court therefore concluded that it was "clear that appellants were doing more than exercising a right of free speech or press. . . . They were exercising their economic power together with that of their allies to compel Empire to abide by union rather than by state regulation of trade." Id., at 503.

The following Term, the Court decided a group of cases applying and elaborating on the theory of *Giboney*. In Hughes v. Superior Court, 339 U.S. 460, the Court held that the Fourteenth Amendment did not bar use of the injunction to prohibit picketing of a place of business solely to secure compliance with a demand that its employees be hired in percentage to the racial origin of its customers. "We cannot construe the Due Process Clause as prohibiting California from securing respect for its policy against involuntary employment on racial lines by prohibiting systematic picketing that would subvert such policy." Id., at 466. The Court also found it immaterial that the state policy had been expressed by the judiciary rather than by the legislature.

On the same day, the Court decided International Brotherhood of Teamsters Union v. Hanke, 339 U.S. 470, holding that a State was not restrained by the Fourteenth Amendment from enjoining picketing of a business, conducted by the owner himself without employees, in order to secure compliance with a demand to become a union shop. . . .

A third case, Building Service Emp. Intern. Union v. Gazzam, 339 U.S. 532, was decided the same day. . . . The State, finding that the object of the picketing was in violation of its statutory policy against employer coercion of employees' choice of bargaining representative, enjoined picketing for such purpose. This Court affirmed, rejecting the argument that "the Swing case, supra, is controlling. . . ."

. . .

This series of cases, then, established a broad field in which a State, in enforcing some public policy, whether of its criminal or its civil law, and whether announced by its legislature or its courts, could constitutionally enjoin peaceful picketing aimed at preventing effectuation of that policy.

. . .

[T]he highest state court drew the inference from the facts that the picketing was to coerce the employer to put pressure on his employees to join the union, in violation of the declared policy of the State. . . . The cases discussed above all hold that, consistent with the Fourteenth Amendment, a State may enjoin such conduct.

Of course, the mere fact that there is "picketing" does not automatically justify its restraint without an investigation into its conduct and purposes. State courts, no more than state legislatures, can enact blanket prohibitions against picketing. . . . The series of cases following *Thornhill* and *Swing* demonstrate that the policy of Wisconsin enforced by the prohibition of this picketing is a valid one. In this case, the circumstances set forth in the opinion of the

Wisconsin Supreme Court afford a rational basis for the inference it drew concerning the purpose of the picketing.

Affirmed.

Mr. Justice Whittaker took no part in the consideration or decision of this case.

Mr. Justice Douglas, with whom The Chief Justice and Mr. Justice Black concur, dissenting.

The Court has now come full circle. In Thornhill v. Alabama, 310 U.S. 88, 102, we struck down a state ban on picketing on the ground that "the dissemination of information concerning the facts of a labor dispute must be regarded as within that area of free discussion that is guaranteed by the Constitution." Less than one year later, we held that the First Amendment protected organizational picketing on a factual record which cannot be distinguished from the one now before us. A.F.L. v. Swing, 312 U.S. 321. Of course, we have always recognized that picketing has aspects which make it more than speech. . . . That difference underlies our decision in Giboney v. Empire Storage & Ice Co., 336 U.S. 490. . . . Speech there was enjoined because it was an inseparable part of conduct which the State constitutionally could and did regulate.

But where, as here, there is no rioting, no mass picketing, no violence, no disorder, no fisticuffs, no coercion—indeed nothing but speech—the principles announced in *Thornhill* and *Swing* should give the advocacy of one side of a dispute First Amendment protection.

The retreat began when, in Teamsters Union v. Hanke, 339 U.S. 470, four members of the Court announced that all picketing could be prohibited if a state court decided that that picketing violated the State's public policy. The retreat became a rout in Plumbers Union v. Graham, 345 U.S. 192. It was only the "purpose" of the picketing which was relevant. The state court's characterization of the picketers' "purpose" had been made well-nigh conclusive. Considerations of the proximity of picketing to conduct which the State could control or prevent were abandoned, and no longer was it necessary for the state court's decree to be narrowly drawn to prescribe a specific evil.

Today, the Court signs the formal surrender. State courts and state legislatures cannot fashion blanket prohibitions on all picketing. But, for practical purposes, the situation now is as it was when Senn v. Tile Layers Union, 301 U.S. 468 was decided. State courts and state legislatures are free to decide whether to permit or suppress any particular picket line for any reason other than a blanket policy against all picketing. I would adhere to the principle announced in *Thornhill*. I would adhere to the result reached in *Swing*. I would return to the test enunciated in *Giboney*—that this form of expression can be regulated or prohibited only to the extent that it forms an essential part of a course of conduct which the State can regulate or prohibit. I would reverse the judgment below.[a]

---

[a] In American Radio Ass'n v. Mobile S.S. Ass'n, Inc., 419 U.S. 215 (1974) the Court relied upon *Vogt* to sustain a state court injunction against maritime union picketing of a foreign-flag ship to protest substandard wages paid the foreign crewmen. Justice Rehnquist's opinion concluded that the state court could prefer its interest in barring picketing by unions having no "primary dispute" with the employer to the union's interest in conveying its "Ship American" message through dockside picketing. Compare Madison Joint School Dist. No. 8 v. Wisconsin Employment Relations Comm'n, 429 U.S. 167 (1976). The Court held that a teacher could not be prohibited from speaking at a public meeting of the school board employing him because of a state rule prohibiting public employers from "bargaining" with individual members of a bargaining unit.

In N.L.R.B. v. Retail Store Employees Union, 447 U.S. 607 (1980), the Court upheld a Board order against picketing of a secondary employer. Concurring, Justice Stevens explained that the reason behind a constitutional distinction between picketing and distribution of handbills was that handbills "depend entirely on the persuasive force of the idea," while picketing "calls for an automatic response to a signal."

In International Longshoremen's Ass'n v. Allied International, Inc., 456 U.S. 212 (1982), the Court held that politically motivated refusal by a longshoremen's union to unload cargo from the Soviet Union was a secondary boycott prohibited by the National Labor Relations Act. The Court summarily rejected an argument based on the first amendment. If secondary picketing was not protected by the first amendment, "[i]t would seem even clearer that conduct designed not to communicate but to coerce merits still less consideration. . . ."

Chapter 16

PROTECTION OF PENUMBRAL FIRST AMENDMENT RIGHTS

Introduction. The constitutional protection of expression, belief and association extends to "peripheral" areas beyond individual freedom to utter or print. It should be emphasized that the term "peripheral" does not suggest lesser importance. The terms "penumbras" and "peripheral rights" first appeared in Griswold v. Connecticut, 381 U.S. 479 (1965). In demonstrating that the protection of the first amendment was not confined to the right to utter or print, Justice Douglas explained that "[w]ithout these peripheral rights the specific rights would be less secure."

Section 1 covers governmental power to regulate or prohibit expressive conduct. Section 2 deals with government compulsion requiring individuals to affirm a belief. Section 3 concerns freedom of association, including the right to associate, the right not to associate, and political association. Section 4 covers compelled disclosures of beliefs and associations. Section 5 is a comprehensive survey of the speech and association rights of government employees.

SECTION 1. SYMBOLIC SPEECH

UNITED STATES v. O'BRIEN

391 U.S. 367, 88 S.Ct. 1673, 20 L.Ed.2d 672 (1968).

Mr. Chief Justice Warren delivered the opinion of the Court.

[O'Brien burned his selective service registration certificate on the steps of the South Boston Courthouse in the presence of a sizable crowd. He was convicted for violation of a federal statute that made it a crime to knowingly destroy or mutilate the certificate.]

. . .

II.

O'Brien first argues that the [statute] is unconstitutional as applied to him because his act of burning his registration certificate was protected "symbolic speech" within the First Amendment. His argument is that the freedom of expression which the First Amendment guarantees includes all modes of "communication of ideas by conduct," and that his conduct is within this definition because he did it in "demonstration against the war and against the draft."

We cannot accept the view that an apparently limitless variety of conduct can be labelled "speech" whenever the person engaging in the conduct intends thereby to express an idea. However, even on the assumption that the alleged communicative element in O'Brien's conduct is sufficient to bring into play the First Amendment, it does not necessarily follow that the destruction of a registration certificate is constitutionally protected activity. This Court has held that when "speech" and "nonspeech" elements are combined in the same course of conduct, a sufficiently important governmental interest in regulating the nonspeech element can justify incidental limitations on First Amendment freedoms. To characterize the quality of the governmental interest which must appear, the Court has employed a variety of descriptive terms: compelling;

substantial; subordinating; paramount; cogent; strong. Whatever imprecision inheres in these terms, we think it clear that a government regulation is sufficiently justified if it is within the constitutional power of the Government; if it furthers an important or substantial governmental interest; if the governmental interest is unrelated to the suppression of free expression; and if the incidental restriction on alleged First Amendment freedom is no greater than is essential to the furtherance of that interest. We find that the [statute] meets all of these requirements, and consequently that O'Brien can be constitutionally convicted for violating it.

. . .

The many functions performed by Selective Service certificates establish beyond doubt that Congress has a legitimate and substantial interest in preventing their wanton and unrestrained destruction and assuring their continuing availability by punishing people who knowingly and wilfully destroy or mutilate them. . . .
     . . . The governmental interest and the scope of the [statute] are limited to preventing a harm to the smooth and efficient functioning of the Selective Service System. When O'Brien deliberately rendered unavailable his registration certificate, he wilfully frustrated this governmental interest. For this noncommunicative impact of his conduct, and nothing else, he was convicted.
     The case at bar is therefore unlike one where the alleged governmental interest in regulating conduct arises in some measure because the communication allegedly integral to the conduct is itself thought to be harmful. In Stromberg v. California, 283 U.S. 359 (1931), for example, this Court struck down a statutory phrase which punished people who expressed their "opposition to organized government" by displaying "any flag, badge, banner, or device." Since the statute there was aimed at suppressing communication it could not be sustained as a regulation of noncommunicative conduct. . . .
     In conclusion, we find that because of the Government's substantial interest in assuring the continuing availability of issued Selective Service certificates, because [the statute] is an appropriately narrow means of protecting this interest and condemns only the independent noncommunicative impact of conduct within its reach, and because the noncommunicative impact of O'Brien's act of burning his registration certificate frustrated the Government's interest, a sufficient governmental interest has been shown to justify O'Brien's conviction.

III.

O'Brien finally argues that the 1965 Amendment is unconstitutional as enacted because what he calls the "purpose" of Congress was "to suppress freedom of speech." We reject this argument because under settled principles the purpose of Congress, as O'Brien uses that term, is not a basis for declaring this legislation unconstitutional.
     It is a familiar principle of constitutional law that this Court will not strike down an otherwise constitutional statute on the basis of an alleged illicit legislative motive. . . .
     Inquiries into congressional motives or purposes are a hazardous matter. When the issue is simply the interpretation of legislation, the Court will look to statements by legislators for guidance as to the purpose of the legislature, because the benefit to sound decision-making in this circumstance is thought sufficient to risk the possibility of misreading Congress' purpose. It is entirely a different matter when we are asked to void a statute that is, under well-settled criteria, constitutional on its face, on the basis of what fewer than a handful of Congressmen said about it. What motivates one legislator to make a speech about a statute is not necessarily what motivates scores of others to enact it, and

the stakes are sufficiently high for us to eschew guesswork. We decline to void essentially on the ground that it is unwise legislation which Congress had the undoubted power to enact and which could be reenacted in its exact form if the same or another legislator made a "wiser" speech about it.

.   .   .

We think it not amiss, in passing, to comment upon O'Brien's legislative-purpose argument. There was little floor debate on this legislation in either House. Only Senator Thurmond commented on its substantive features in the Senate. . . . In the House debate only two Congressmen addressed themselves to the Amendment—Congressmen Rivers and Bray. . . . It is principally on the basis of the statements by these three Congressmen that O'Brien makes his congressional-"purpose" argument. We note that if we were to examine legislative purpose in the instant case, we would be obliged to consider not only these statements but also the more authoritative reports of the Senate and House Armed Services Committees. The portions of those reports explaining the purpose of the Amendment are reproduced in the Appendix in their entirety. While both reports make clear a concern with the "defiant" destruction of so-called "draft cards" and with "open" encouragement to others to destroy their cards, both reports also indicate that this concern stemmed from an apprehension that unrestrained destruction of cards would disrupt the smooth functioning of the Selective Service System.

IV.

.   .   . [T]he Court of Appeals should have affirmed the judgment of conviction entered by the District Court. . . .[a]

Mr. Justice Marshall took no part in the consideration or decision of these cases.

Mr. Justice Harlan, concurring.

The crux of the Court's opinion, which I join, is of course its general statement, that:

> "a government regulation is sufficiently justified if it is within the constitutional power of the Government; if it furthers an important or substantial governmental interest; if the governmental interest is unrelated to the suppression of free expression; and if the incidental restriction on alleged First Amendment freedoms is no greater than is essential to the furtherance of that interest."

I wish to make explicit my understanding that this passage does not foreclose consideration of First Amendment claims in those rare instances when an "incidental" restriction upon expression, imposed by a regulation which furthers an "important or substantial" governmental interest and satisfies the Court's other criteria, in practice has the effect of entirely preventing a "speaker" from reaching a significant audience with whom he could not otherwise lawfully communicate. This is not such a case, since O'Brien manifestly could have conveyed his message in many ways other than by burning his draft card.

Mr. Justice Douglas, dissenting.

[Justice Douglas' dissent was limited to the point that the case should be re-argued to consider the issue of the validity of peacetime conscription. Later, however, in his concurring opinion in Brandenburg v. Ohio, 395 U.S. 444, 455

---

[a] On the issue of legislative motivation in O'Brien, see Ely, *Legislative and Administrative Motivation in Constitutional Law*, 79 Yale L.J. 1205 (1970), and Brest, *Palmer v. Thompson: An Approach to the Problem of Unconstitutional Legislative Motive*, 1971 Sup.Ct.Rev. 95. Does the Court's treatment of the relevance of a legislative motivation to prohibit a form of expression require modification in light of the later decision in Washington v. Davis, 426 U.S. 229 (1976), supra p. 751.

(1969), he said: "O'Brien was not prosecuted for not having his draft card available when asked for by a federal agent. He was indicted, tried, and convicted for burning the card. And this Court's affirmance of that conviction was not, with all respect, consistent with the First Amendment."]

SPENCE v. WASHINGTON

418 U.S. 405, 94 S.Ct. 2727, 41 L.Ed.2d 842 (1974).

Per Curiam.

.   .   .

I.

On May 10, 1970, appellant, a college student, hung his United States flag from the window of his apartment on private property in Seattle, Washington. The flag was upside down, and attached to the front and back was a peace symbol (i.e., a circle enclosing a trident) made of removable black tape. The window was above the ground floor. The flag measured approximately three by five feet and was plainly visible to passersby. The peace symbol occupied roughly half of the surface of the flag.

Three Seattle police officers observed the flag and entered the apartment house. They were met at the main door by appellant, who said, "I suppose you are here about the flag. I didn't know there was anything wrong with it. I will take it down." Appellant permitted the officers to enter his apartment, where they seized the flag and arrested him. Appellant cooperated with the officers. There was no disruption or altercation.

Appellant was not charged under Washington's flag desecration statute. See Wash.Rev.Code § 9.86.030, as amended. Rather, the State relied on the so-called "improper use" statute, Wash.Rev.Code § 9.86.020. This statute provides, in pertinent part:

"No person shall, in any manner, for exhibition or display:

"(1) Place or cause to be placed any word, figure, mark, picture, design, drawing or advertisement of any nature upon any flag, standard, color, ensign or shield of the United States or of this state . . . or

"(2) Expose to public view any such flag, standard, color, ensign or shield upon which shall have been printed, painted or otherwise produced, or to which shall have been attached, appended, affixed or annexed any such word, figure, mark, picture, design, drawing, or advertisement . . .."   .   .   .

The State based its case on the flag itself and the testimony of the three arresting officers, who testified that they had observed the flag displayed from appellant's window and that on the flag was superimposed what they identified as a peace symbol. Appellant took the stand in his own defense. He testified that he put a peace symbol on the flag and displayed it to public view as a protest to the invasion of Cambodia and the killings at Kent State University, events which occurred a few days prior to his arrest. He said that his purpose was to associate the American flag with peace instead of war and violence:

"I felt there had been so much killing and that this was not what America stood for. I felt that the flag stood for America and I wanted people to know that I thought America stood for peace."

Appellant further testified that he chose to fashion the peace symbol from tape so that it could be removed without damaging the flag. The State made no effort to controvert any of appellant's testimony.

The trial court instructed the jury in essence that the mere act of displaying the flag with the peace symbol attached, if proven beyond a reasonable doubt, was sufficient to convict. There was no requirement of specific intent to do anything more than display the flag in that manner. The jury returned a verdict of guilty. The court sentenced appellant to 10 days in jail, suspended, and to a $75 fine. The Washington Court of Appeals reversed the conviction. 5 Wash. App. 752, 490 P.2d 1321 (1971). It held the improper use statute overbroad and invalid on its face under the First and Fourteenth Amendments. With one justice dissenting and two concurring in the result, the Washington Supreme Court reversed and reinstated the conviction. 81 Wash.2d 788, 506 P.2d 293 (1973).

II.

A number of factors are important in the instant case. First, this was a privately-owned flag. In a technical property sense it was not the property of any government. We have no doubt that the State or National Governments constitutionally may forbid anyone from mishandling in any manner a flag that is public property. But this is a different case. Second, appellant displayed his flag on private property. He engaged in no trespass or disorderly conduct. Nor is this a case that might be analyzed in terms of reasonable time, place or manner restraints on access to a public area. Third, the record is devoid of proof of any risk of breach of the peace. It was not appellant's purpose to incite violence or even stimulate a public demonstration. There is no evidence that any crowd gathered or that appellant made any effort to attract attention beyond hanging the flag out of his own window. Indeed, on the facts stipulated by the parties there is no evidence that anyone other than the three police officers observed the flag.

Fourth, the State concedes, as did the Washington Supreme Court, that appellant engaged in a form of communication. Although the stipulated facts fail to show that any member of the general public viewed the flag, the State's concession is inevitable on this record. The undisputed facts are that appellant "wanted people to know that I thought America stood for peace." To be sure, appellant did not choose to articulate his views through printed or spoken words. It is therefore necessary to determine whether his activity was sufficiently imbued with elements of communication to fall within the scope of the First and Fourteenth Amendments, for as the Court noted in United States v. O'Brien, 391 U.S. 367, 376 (1968), "[w]e cannot accept the view that an apparently limitless variety of conduct can be labeled 'speech' whenever the person engaging in the conduct intends thereby to express an idea." But the nature of appellant's activity, combined with the factual context and environment in which it was undertaken, lead to the conclusion that he engaged in a form of protected expression.

The Court for decades has recognized the communicative connotations of the use of flags. E.g., Stromberg v. California, 283 U.S. 359 (1931). In many of their uses flags are a form of symbolism comprising a "primitive but effective way of communicating ideas . . .," and "a short cut from mind to mind." Board of Education v. Barnette, 319 U.S. 624, 632 (1943). On this record there can be little doubt that appellant communicated through the use of symbols. The symbolism included not only the flag but also the superimposed peace symbol.

Moreover, the context in which a symbol is used for purposes of expression is important, for the context may give meaning to the symbol. See Tinker v. Des Moines School District, 393 U.S. 503 (1969). In *Tinker*, the wearing of black armbands in a school environment conveyed an unmistakable message about a contemporaneous issue of intense public concern—the Vietnam hostili-

ties. Id., at 505–514. In this case, appellant's activity was roughly simultane-
ous with and concededly triggered by the Cambodian incursion and the Kent
State tragedy, also issues of great public moment. Cf. Scheuer v. Rhodes, 416
U.S. 232 (1974). A flag bearing a peace symbol and displayed upside down by
a student today might be interpreted as nothing more than bizarre behavior, but
it would have been difficult for the great majority of citizens to miss the drift of
appellant's point at the time that he made it.

It may be noted, further, that this was not an act of mindless nihilism.
Rather, it was a pointed expression of anguish by appellant about the then
current domestic and foreign affairs of his government. An intent to convey a
particularized message was present, and in the surrounding circumstances the
likelihood was great that the message would be understood by those who
viewed it.

We are confronted then with a case of prosecution for the expression of an
idea through activity. Moreover, the activity occurred on private property,
rather than in an environment over which the State by necessity must have
certain supervisory powers unrelated to expression. . . . Accordingly, we
must examine with particular care the interests advanced by appellee to support
its prosecution. . . . The first interest at issue is prevention of breach of the
peace. In our view, the Washington Supreme Court correctly rejected this
notion. It is totally without support in the record.

We are also unable to affirm the judgment below on the ground that the
State may have desired to protect the sensibilities of passersby. "It is firmly
settled that under our Constitution the public expression of ideas may not be
prohibited merely because the ideas are themselves offensive to some of their
hearers." Street v. New York, supra, at 592. Moreover, appellant did not
impose his ideas upon a captive audience. Anyone who might have been
offended could easily have avoided the display. See Cohen v. California, 403
U.S. 15 (1971). Nor may appellant be punished for failing to show proper
respect for our national emblem. Street v. New York, supra, at 593; Board of
Education v. Barnette, supra.

We are brought, then, to the state court's thesis that Washington has an
interest in preserving the national flag as an unalloyed symbol of our country.
. . . Presumably, this interest might be seen as an effort to prevent the
appropriation of a revered national symbol by an individual, interest group, or
enterprise where there was a risk that association of the symbol with a particular
product or viewpoint might be taken erroneously as evidence of governmental
endorsement. Alternatively, it might be argued that the interest asserted by the
state court is based on the uniquely universal character of the national flag as a
symbol. For the great majority of us, the flag is a symbol of patriotism, of pride
in the history of our country. . . . . If it may be destroyed or permanently
disfigured, it could be argued that it will lose its capability of mirroring the
sentiments of all who view it.

But we need not decide in this case whether the interest advanced by the
court below is valid. We assume *arguendo* that it is. The statute is nonetheless
unconstitutional as applied to appellant's activity. There was no risk that
appellant's acts would mislead viewers into assuming that the Government
endorsed his viewpoint. To the contrary, he was plainly and peacefully
protesting the fact that it did not. Appellant was not charged under the
desecration statute, . . . nor did he permanently disfigure the flag or destroy
it. He displayed it as a flag of his country in a way closely analogous to the
manner in which flags have always been used to convey ideas. Moreover, his
message was direct, likely to be understood, and within the contours of the First
Amendment. Given the protected character of his expression and in light of
the fact that no interest the State may have in preserving the physical integrity of

a privately-owned flag was significantly impaired on these facts, the conviction must be invalidated.

The judgment is reversed.[a]

Mr. Justice Rehnquist, with whom The Chief Justice and Mr. Justice White join, dissenting.

. . . Although I agree with the Court that petitioner's activity was a form of communication, I do not agree that the First Amendment prohibits the State from restricting this activity in furtherance of other important interests. . . .

. . .

. . . What appellant here seeks is simply license to use the flag however he pleases, so long as the activity can be tied to a concept of speech, regardless of any state interest in having the flag used only for more limited purposes. I find no reasoning in the Court's opinion which convinces me that the Constitution requires such license to be given.

The fact that the State has a valid interest in preserving the character of the flag does not mean, of course, that it can employ all conceivable means to enforce it. It certainly could not require all citizens to own the flag or compel citizens to salute one. Board of Education v. Barnette, 319 U.S. 624 (1943). It presumably cannot punish criticism of the flag, or the principles for which it stands, any more than it could punish criticism of this country's policies or ideas. But the statute in this case demands no such allegiance. Its operation does not depend upon whether the flag is used for communicative or noncommunicative purposes; upon whether a particular message is deemed commercial or political; upon whether the use of the flag is respectful or contemptuous; or upon whether any particular segment of the State's citizenry might applaud or oppose the intended message. It simply withdraws a unique national symbol from the roster of materials that may be used as a background for communications. Since I do not believe the Constitution prohibits Washington from making that decision, I dissent.

CLARK v. COMMUNITY FOR CREATIVE NON–VIOLENCE

___ U.S. ___, 104 S.Ct. 3065, 82 L.Ed.2d 221 (1984).

Justice White delivered the opinion of the Court.

The issue in this case is whether a National Park Service regulation prohibiting camping in certain parks violates the First Amendment when applied to prohibit demonstrators from sleeping in Lafayette Park and the Mall in connection with a demonstration intended to call attention to the plight of the homeless. We hold that it does not and reverse the contrary judgment of the Court of Appeals.

I

The Interior Department, through the National Park Service, is charged with responsibility for the management and maintenance of the National Parks and is authorized to promulgate rules and regulations for the use of the parks in accordance with the purposes for which they were established. . . . The network of National Parks includes the National Memorial-core parks, Lafayette Park and the Mall, which are set in the heart of Washington, D.C., and which are unique resources that the Federal Government holds in trust for the American people. Lafayette Park is a roughly seven-acre square located across Pennsylvania Avenue from the White House. Although originally part of the

---

[a] Justices Blackmun and Douglas concurred in the result.

White House grounds, President Jefferson set it aside as a park for the use of residents and visitors. It "functions as a formal garden park of meticulous landscaping with flowers, trees, fountains, walks and benches." . . . The Mall is a stretch of land running westward from the Capitol to the Lincoln Memorial some two miles away. It includes the Washington Monument, a series of reflecting pools, trees, lawns, and other greenery. It is bordered by, *inter alia,* the Smithsonian Institution and the National Gallery of Art. Both the Park and the Mall were included in Major Pierre L'Enfant's original plan for the capitol. Both are visited by vast numbers of visitors from around the country, as well as by large numbers of residents of the Washington metropolitan area.

Under the regulations involved in this case, camping in National Parks is permitted only in campgrounds designated for that purpose. 36 CFR § 50.27(a). No such campgrounds have ever been designated in Lafayette Park or the Mall. Camping is defined as:

"the use of park land for living accommodation purposes such as sleeping activities, or making preparations to sleep (including the laying down of bedding for the purpose of sleeping), or storing personal belongings, or making any fire, or using any tents or . . . other structure . . . for sleeping or doing any digging or earth breaking or carrying on cooking activities." Ibid.

These activities, the regulation provides,

"constitute camping when it reasonably appears, in light of all the circumstances, that the participants, in conducting these activities, are in fact using the area as a living accommodation regardless of the intent of the participants or the nature of any other activities in which they may also be engaging." Ibid.

Demonstrations for the airing of views or grievances are permitted in the Memorial-core parks, but for the most part only by Park Service permits. 36 CFR § 50.19. Temporary structures may be erected for demonstration purposes but may not be used for camping. 36 CFR § 50.19(e)(8).

In 1982, the Park Service issued a renewable permit to respondent Community for Creative Non-Violence (CCNV) to conduct a wintertime demonstration in Lafayette Park and the Mall for the purpose of demonstrating the plight of the homeless. The permit authorized the erection of two symbolic tent cities: 20 tents in Lafayette Park that would accommodate 50 people and 40 tents in the Mall with a capacity of up to 100. The Park Service, however, relying on the above regulations, specifically denied CCNV's request that demonstrators be permitted to sleep in the symbolic tents.

CCNV and several individuals then filed an action to prevent the application of the anti-camping regulations to the proposed demonstration. . . . The District Court granted summary judgment in favor of the Park Service. The Court of Appeals, sitting en banc, reversed. . . . We . . . reverse.

II

We need not differ with the view of the Court of Appeals that overnight sleeping in connection with the demonstration is expressive conduct protected to some extent by the First Amendment. We assume for present purposes, but do not decide, that such is the case, cf. United States v. O'Brien, 391 U.S. 367, 376 (1968), but this assumption only begins the inquiry. Expression, whether oral or written or symbolized by conduct, is subject to reasonable time, place, and manner restrictions. We have often noted that restrictions of this kind are valid provided that they are justified without reference to the content of the regulated speech, that they are narrowly tailored to serve a significant governmental interest, and that they leave open ample alternative channels for communication of the information.

It is also true that a message may be delivered by conduct that is intended to be communicative and that, in context, would reasonably be understood by the viewer to be communicative. Spence v. Washington, 418 U.S. 405 (1974); Tinker v. Des Moines School District, 393 U.S. 503 (1969). Symbolic expression of this kind may be forbidden or regulated if the conduct itself may constitutionally be regulated, if the regulation is narrowly drawn to further a substantial governmental interest, and if the interest is unrelated to the suppression of free speech. United States v. O'Brien, supra.

The United States submits, as it did in the Court of Appeals, that the regulation forbidding sleeping is defensible either as a time, place, or manner restriction or as a regulation of symbolic conduct. We agree with that assessment. The permit that was issued authorized the demonstration but required compliance with 36 CFR § 50.19, which prohibits "camping" on park lands, that is, the use of park lands for living accommodations, such as sleeping, storing personal belongings, making fires, digging, or cooking. These provisions, including the ban on sleeping, are clearly limitations on the manner in which the demonstration could be carried out. That sleeping, like the symbolic tents themselves, may be expressive and part of the message delivered by the demonstration does not make the ban any less a limitation on the manner of demonstrating, for reasonable time, place, and manner regulations normally have the purpose and direct effect of limiting expression but are nevertheless valid. City Council v. Taxpayers for Vincent, supra; Heffron v. International Society for Krishna Consciousness, supra; Kovacs v. Cooper, 336 U.S. 77 (1949). Neither does the fact that sleeping, *arguendo,* may be expressive conduct, rather than oral or written expression, render the sleeping prohibition any less a time, place, or manner regulation. To the contrary, the Park Service neither attempts to ban sleeping generally nor to ban it everywhere in the Parks. It has established areas for camping and forbids it elsewhere, including Lafayette Park and the Mall. Considered as such, we have very little trouble concluding that the Park Service may prohibit overnight sleeping in the parks involved here.

The requirement that the regulation be content neutral is clearly satisfied. The courts below accepted that view, and it is not disputed here that the prohibition on camping, and on sleeping specifically, is content neutral and is not being applied because of disagreement with the message presented. Neither was the regulation faulted, nor could it be, on the ground that without overnight sleeping the plight of the homeless could not be communicated in other ways. The regulation otherwise left the demonstration intact, with its symbolic city, signs, and the presence of those who were willing to take their turns in a day-and-night vigil. Respondents do not suggest that there was, or is, any barrier to delivering to the media, or to the public by other means, the intended message concerning the plight of the homeless.

It is also apparent to us that the regulation narrowly focuses on the Government's substantial interest in maintaining the parks in the heart of our capitol in an attractive and intact condition, readily available to the millions of people who wish to see and enjoy them by their presence. To permit camping—using these areas as living accommodations—would be totally inimical to these purposes, as would be readily understood by those who have frequented the National Parks across the country and observed the unfortunate consequences of the activities of those who refuse to confine their camping to designated areas.

It is urged by respondents, and the Court of Appeals was of this view, that if the symbolic city of tents was to be permitted and if the demonstrators did not intend to cook, dig, or engage in aspects of camping other than sleeping, the incremental benefit to the parks could not justify the ban on sleeping, which was here an expressive activity said to enhance the message concerning the plight of the poor and homeless. We cannot agree. In the first place, we seriously doubt that the First Amendment requires the Park Service to permit a demonstration in Lafayette Park and the Mall involving a 24-hour vigil and the erection of tents to accommodate 150 people. Furthermore, although we have assumed for present purposes that the sleeping banned in this case would have an expressive element, it is evident that its major value to this demonstration would be facilitative. Without a permit to sleep, it would be difficult to get the poor and homeless to participate or to be present at all. This much is apparent from the permit application filed by respondents: "Without the incentive of sleeping space or a hot meal, the homeless would not come to the site." The sleeping ban, if enforced, would thus effectively limit the nature, extent, and duration of the demonstration and to that extent ease the pressure on the Parks.

Beyond this, however, it is evident from our cases that the validity of this regulation need not be judged solely by reference to the demonstration at hand. . . . Absent the prohibition on sleeping, there would be other groups who would demand permission to deliver an asserted message by camping in Lafayette Park. Some of them would surely have as credible a claim in this regard as does CCNV, and the denial of permits to still others would present difficult problems for the Park Service. With the prohibition, however, as is evident in the case before us, at least some around-the-clock demonstrations lasting for days on end will not materialize, others will be limited in size and duration, and the purposes of the regulation will thus be materially served. Perhaps these purposes would be more effectively and not so clumsily achieved by preventing tents and 24-hour vigils entirely in the core areas. But the Park Service's decision to permit non-sleeping demonstrations does not, in our view, impugn the camping prohibition as a valuable, but perhaps imperfect, protection to the parks. If the Government has a legitimate interest in ensuring that the National Parks are adequately protected, which we think it has, and if the parks would be more exposed to harm without the sleeping prohibition than with it, the ban is safe from invalidation under the First Amendment as a reasonable regulation on the manner in which a demonstration may be carried out. . . .

We have difficulty, therefore, in understanding why the prohibition against camping, with its ban on sleeping overnight, is not a reasonable time, place, and manner regulation that withstands constitutional scrutiny. Surely the regulation is not unconstitutional on its face. None of its provisions appears unrelated to the ends that it was designed to serve. Nor is it any less valid when applied to prevent camping in Memorial-core parks by those who wish to demonstrate and deliver a message to the public and the central government. Damage to the parks as well as their partial inaccessibility to other members of the public can as easily result from camping by demonstrators as by non-demonstrators. In neither case must the Government tolerate it. All those who would resort to the parks must abide by otherwise valid rules for their use, just as they must observe the traffic laws, sanitation regulations, and laws to preserve the public peace. This is no more than a reaffirmation that reasonable time, place, and manner restrictions on expression are constitutionally acceptable.

Contrary to the conclusion of the Court of Appeals, the foregoing analysis demonstrates that the Park Service regulation is sustainable under the four-factor standard of United States v. O'Brien, supra, for validating a regulation of expressive conduct, which, in the last analysis is little, if any, different from the standard applied to time, place, and manner restrictions.[8] No one contends that

---

[8] Reasonable time, place and manner restrictions are valid even though they directly limit oral or written expression. It would be odd to insist on a higher standard for limitations aimed at regulable

aside from its impact on speech a rule against camping or overnight sleeping in public parks is beyond the constitutional power of the Government to enforce. And for the reasons we have discussed above, there is a substantial government interest in conserving park property, an interest that is plainly served by, and requires for its implementation, measures such as the proscription of sleeping that are designed to limit the wear and tear on park properties. That interest is unrelated to suppression of expression.

We are unmoved by the Court of Appeals' view that the challenged regulation is unnecessary, and hence invalid, because there are less speech-restrictive alternatives that could have satisfied the government interest in preserving park lands. There is no gainsaying that preventing overnight sleeping will avoid a measure of actual or threatened damage to Lafayette Park and the Mall. The Court of Appeals' suggestions that the Park Service minimize the possible injury by reducing the size, duration, or frequency of demonstrations would still curtail the total allowable expression in which demonstrators could engage, whether by sleeping or otherwise, and these suggestions represent no more than a disagreement with the Park Service over how much protection the core parks require or how an acceptable level of preservation is to be attained. We do not believe, however, that either United States v. O'Brien or the time, place, and manner decisions assign to the judiciary the authority to replace the Park Service as the manager of the Nation's parks or endow the judiciary with the competence to judge how much protection of park lands is wise and how that level of conservation is to be attained.

Accordingly, the judgment of the Court of Appeals is

Reversed.

Chief Justice Burger, concurring.

I concur fully in the Court's opinion. . . .

The actions here claimed as speech entitled to the protections of the First Amendment simply are not speech; rather, they constitute conduct. . . .

Justice Marshall, with whom Justice Brennan joins, dissenting.

. . . .

II

Although sleep in the context of this case is symbolic speech protected by the First Amendment, it is nonetheless subject to reasonable time, place, and manner restrictions. I agree with the standard enunciated by the majority: "[R]estrictions of this kind are valid provided that they are justified without reference to the content of the regulated speech, that they are narrowly tailored to serve a significant governmental interest, and that they leave open ample alternative channels for communication of the information." I conclude, however, that the regulations at issue in this case, as applied to respondents, fail to satisfy this standard. . . .

In short, there are no substantial government interests advanced by the Government's regulations as supplied to respondents. All that the Court's decision advances are the prerogatives of a bureaucracy that over the years has shown an implacable hostility toward citizens' exercise of First Amendment rights.

conduct and having only an incidental impact on speech. Thus, if the time, place, and manner restriction on expressive sleeping, if that is what is involved in this case, sufficiently and narrowly serves a substantial enough governmental interest to escape First Amendment condemnation, it is untenable to invalidate it under *O'Brien* on the ground that the governmental interest is insufficient to warrant the intrusion on First Amendment concerns or that there is an inadequate nexus between the regulation and the interest sought to be served. . . .

III

The disposition of this case impels me to make two additional observations. First, in this case, as in some others involving time, place, and manner restrictions, the Court has dramatically lowered its scrutiny of governmental regulations once it has determined that such regulations are content neutral. The result has been the creation of a two-tiered approach to First Amendment cases: while regulations that turn on the content of the expression are subjected to a strict form of judicial review, regulations that are aimed at matters other than expression receive only a minimal level of scrutiny. The minimal scrutiny prong of this two-tiered approach has led to an unfortunate diminution of First Amendment protection. . . .

Second, the disposition of this case reveals a mistaken assumption regarding the motives and behavior of government officials who create and administer content-neutral regulations. The Court's salutary skepticism of governmental decisionmaking in First Amendment matters suddenly dissipates once it determines that a restriction is not content-based. The Court evidently assumes that the balance struck by officials is deserving of deference so long as it does not appear to be tainted by content discrimination. What the court fails to recognize is that public officials have strong incentives to overregulate even in the absence of an intent to censor particular views. This incentive stems from the fact that of the two groups whose interests officials must accommodate—on the one hand, the interests of the general public and on the other, the interests of those who seek to use a particular forum for First Amendment activity—the political power of the former is likely to be far greater than that of the latter.

. . . .

SECTION 2. COMPELLED AFFIRMATION OF BELIEF [1]

WEST VIRGINIA STATE BOARD OF EDUCATION v. BAR-NETTE, 319 U.S. 624 (1943). A resolution of the Board of Education made the flag salute a regular part of the school program and required all teachers and pupils to participate. Refusal to salute the flag was made "an act of insubordination" to "be dealt with accordingly," i.e., expulsion from school. A class action to restrain the enforcement of this regulation against Jehovah's Witnesses (who are conscientiously opposed to saluting the flag) was heard by a three-judge court. A restraining order issued; the Board of Education appealed.

Justice Jackson, in his opinion for the Court found the compulsory salute invalid on general first amendment grounds. Minersville School District v. Gobitis, 310 U.S. 586 (1940), which had sustained the validity of an identical requirement, was overruled. Justice Jackson noted that the flag salute in connection with the pledge is a form of utterance and that it requires "affirmation of a belief and an attitude of mind." His opinion included the following observations:

". . . It is now a commonplace that censorship or suppression of expression of opinion is tolerated by our Constitution only when the expression presents a clear and present danger of action of a kind the State is empowered to prevent and punish. It would seem that involuntary affirmation could be commanded only on even more immediate and urgent grounds than silence. But here the power of compulsion is invoked without any allegation that remaining passive during a flag salute ritual creates a clear and present danger that would justify an effort even to muffle expression. To sustain the compulso-

---

[1] See Graebler, *First Amendment Protection Against Compelled Expression and Association,* 23 Bost. Col.L.Rev. 995 (1982).

ry flag statute we are required to say that a Bill of Rights which guards the individual's right to speak his own mind, left it open to public authorities to compel him to utter what is not in his mind.

"Nor does the issue as we see it turn on one's possession of particular religious views or the sincerity with which they are held. While religion supplies appellees' motive for enduring the discomforts of making the issue in this case, many citizens who do not share these religious views hold such a compulsory rite to infringe constitutional liberty of the individual. It is not necessary to inquire whether non-conformist beliefs will exempt from the duty to salute unless we first find power to make the salute a legal duty.

"If there is any fixed star in our constitutional constellation, it is that no official, high or petty, can prescribe what shall be orthodox in politics, nationalism, religion, or other matters of opinion or force citizens to confess by word or act their faith therein. If there are any circumstances which permit an exception, they do not now occur to us."

———

WOOLEY v. MAYNARD, 430 U.S. 705 (1977).   George and Maxine Maynard were Jehovah's Witnesses, who had moral, religious and political objections to New Hampshire's license plate motto—"Live Free or Die." When they covered up the motto on their vehicle's license plates, Mr. Maynard was arrested and convicted under a law making it a misdemeanor to obscure the figures or letters on license plates. The federal district court enjoined the State from arresting or prosecuting the Maynards for covering the motto on the license plate. The United States Supreme Court affirmed.

Chief Justice Burger, in his opinion for the Court, decided that the case was controlled by West Virginia Board of Education v. Barnette.

"New Hampshire's statute in effect requires that appellees use their private property as a 'mobile billboard' for the State's ideological message—or suffer a penalty, as Maynard already has. As a condition to driving an automobile—a virtual necessity for most Americans—the Maynards must display 'Live Free or Die' to hundreds of people each day. The fact that most individuals agree with the thrust of New Hampshire's motto is not the test; most Americans also find the flag salute acceptable. The First Amendment protects the right of individuals to hold a point of view different from the majority and to refuse to foster, in the way New Hampshire commands, an idea they find morally objectionable.

"Identifying the Maynards' interests as implicating First Amendment protections does not end our inquiry however. We must also determine whether the State's countervailing interest is sufficiently compelling to justify requiring appellees to display the state motto on their license plates. The two interests advanced by the state are that display of the motto (1) facilitates the identification of passenger vehicles, and (2) promotes appreciation of history, individualism and state pride.

"The State first points out that only passenger vehicles, but not commercial, trailer, or other vehicles are required to display the state motto. Thus, the argument proceeds, officers of the law are more easily able to determine whether passenger vehicles are carrying the proper plates. . . . Even were we to credit the State's reasons and 'even though the governmental purpose be legitimate and substantial, that purpose cannot be pursued by means that broadly stifle fundamental personal liberties when the end can be more narrowly achieved. The breadth of legislative abridgment must be viewed in the light of less drastic means for achieving the same basic purpose.'

"The State's second claimed interest is not ideologically neutral. The State is seeking to communicate to others an official view as to proper 'appreciation of history, state pride, [and] individualism.' Of course, the State may legitimately pursue such interests in any number of ways. However, where the State's interest is to disseminate an ideology, no matter how acceptable to some, such interest cannot outweigh an individual's First Amendment right to avoid becoming the courier for such message."

Justice Rehnquist, joined by Justice Blackmun, in dissent, argued that the Maynards had not been forced to advocate any point of view.

"Since any implication that they affirm the motto can be so easily displaced, I cannot agree that the state statutory system for motor vehicle identification and tourist promotion may be invalidated under the fiction that appellees are unconstitutionally forced to affirm, or profess belief in, the state motto.

"The logic of the Court's opinion leads to startling, and I believe totally unacceptable, results. For example, the mottos 'In God We Trust' and 'E pluribus unum' appear on the coin and currency of the United States. I cannot imagine that the statutes, see 18 U.S.C. §§ 331 and 333, proscribing defacement of U.S. currency impinge upon the First Amendment rights of an atheist. The fact that an atheist carries and uses U.S. currency does not, in any meaningful sense, convey any affirmation of belief on his part in the motto 'In God We Trust.' "

PRUNEYARD SHOPPING CENTER v. ROBINS, 447 U.S. 74 (1980). A group of high school students sought to solicit support for petitions opposing a United Nations resolution against "Zionism." They were ordered by the owner of a large privately-owned shopping center to leave the premises, and brought suit to enjoin the owner from denying them access. The California Supreme Court interpreted the California Constitution to require the owner to allow use of its shopping center for speech and petitioning. The United States Supreme Court rejected an argument, based on the decision in Wooley v. Maynard, that private property owners were being required to participate in disseminating ideological messages they might oppose. It was unlikely that the owner would be identified with the messages of others, and any false identification could be easily disavowed. Concurring in the result, Justices Powell and White argued that there would be serious first amendment issues if speakers using the owner's premises expressed views strongly opposed by the owner.

SECTION 3. FREEDOM OF ASSOCIATION

A. THE RIGHT TO ASSOCIATE

NAACP v. ALABAMA

357 U.S. 449, 78 S.Ct. 1163, 2 L.Ed.2d 1488 (1958).

[The NAACP conducted activity in Alabama through unincorporated affiliates and considered itself exempt from the requirement that foreign corporations register with the Alabama Secretary of State before doing business in the State. In 1956 the State Attorney General brought suit in a state court to enjoin the Association from conducting further activities within the State. It was alleged, among other things, that the Association had recruited members, solicited contributions and opened a regional office in the State; also it had assisted Negro students seeking admission to the State University and had supported the Negro boycott of the bus lines in Montgomery to compel the seating of passengers without regard to race. The State's pre-trial motion for the production of a large number of the Association's records, including the names and addresses of all of its Alabama "members" and "agents," was granted. The Association produced a large portion of the records, but refused to supply the membership lists, and was fined for contempt.]

Mr. Justice Harlan, delivered the opinion of the Court.

. . .

Effective advocacy of both public and private points of view, particularly controversial ones, is undeniably enhanced by group association, ... It is beyond debate that freedom to engage in association for the advancement of beliefs and ideas is an inseparable aspect of the "liberty" assured by the Due Process Clause of the Fourteenth Amendment, which embraces freedom of speech. . . . Of course, it is immaterial whether the beliefs sought to be advanced by association pertain to political, economic, religious or cultural matters, and state action which may have the effect of curtailing the freedom to associate is subject to the closest scrutiny. . . .

We think that the production order, in the respects here drawn in question, must be regarded as entailing the likelihood of a substantial restraint upon the exercise by petitioner's members of their right to freedom of association. Petitioner has made an uncontroverted showing that on past occasions revelation of the identity of its rank-and-file members has exposed these members to economic reprisal, loss of employment, threat of physical coercion, and other manifestations of public hostility. Under these circumstances, we think it apparent that compelled disclosure of petitioner's Alabama membership is likely to affect adversely the ability of petitioner and its members to pursue their collective effort to foster beliefs which they admittedly have the right to advocate, in that it may induce members to withdraw from the Association and dissuade others from joining it because of fear of exposure of their beliefs shown through their associations and of the consequences of this exposure. . . .

We turn to the final question whether Alabama has demonstrated an interest in obtaining the disclosures it seeks from petitioner which is sufficient to justify the deterrent effect which we have concluded these disclosures may well have on the free exercise by petitioner's members of their constitutionally protected right of association. . . .

It is important to bear in mind that petitioner asserts no right to absolute immunity from state investigation, and no right to disregard Alabama's laws. As shown by its substantial compliance with the production order, petitioner does not deny Alabama's right to obtain from it such information as the State desires concerning the purposes of the Association and its activities within the State. Petitioner has not objected to divulging the identity of its members who are employed by or hold official positions with it. . . .

Whether there was "justification" in this instance turns solely on the substantiality of Alabama's interest in obtaining the membership lists. . . . Without intimating the slightest view upon the merits of these issues, we are unable to perceive that the disclosure of the names of petitioner's rank-and-file members has a substantial bearing on either of them. . . .

We hold that the immunity from state scrutiny of membership lists which the Association claims on behalf of its members is here so related to the right of the members to pursue their lawful private interest privately and to associate freely with others in so doing as to come within the protection of the Fourteenth Amendment. And we conclude that Alabama has fallen short of showing a controlling justification for the deterrent effect on the free enjoyment of the right to associate which disclosure of membership lists is likely to have. Accordingly, the judgment of civil contempt and the $100,000 fine which resulted from petitioner's refusal to comply with the production order in this respect must fall. . . .

SPEECH AND NON-SPEECH ASSOCIATION

NAACP v. Button, 371 U.S. 415 (1963), concerned application of Virginia statutes, forbidding solicitation of legal business, to the NAACP's activities in litigating public school desegregation cases. The Court concluded that NAACP litigation was expression. It was "not a technique of resolving private differences" but a "means of achieving the lawful objectives of equality of treatment by all government." It was thus "a form of political expression." The Court held that restrictions imposed on the NAACP's litigation activities violated the first amendment.

Button emphasized that the first amendment rights involved stemmed from "[r]esort to the courts to seek vindication of constitutional rights" rather than "avaricious use of the legal process for purely private gain." In Brotherhood of R.R. Trainmen v. Virginia, 377 U.S. 1 (1964), however, the Court considered application of the Virginia prohibition of solicitation of legal business to the group legal services plan of a labor union. The plan channeled workers' personal injury suits to a group of lawyers. The Court concluded that the union's activities fell "just as clearly within the protection of the First Amendment" as those involved in *Button,* and application of the statute violated the first amendment.[1]

NAACP v. Alabama had spoken of "association for the advancement of beliefs and ideas." NAACP v. Button stressed group activity seeking "through lawful means to achieve political ends." The *R.R. Trainmen* case, however, more broadly extended first amendment association rights to group activities "for the lawful purpose of helping and advising one another in asserting . . . rights." Does the first amendment's protection of freedom of association extend to all group activities of groups with political objectives? Does it extend to association for any purpose?

NAACP v. CLAIBORNE HARDWARE CO.

458 U.S. 886, 102 S.Ct. 3409, 73 L.Ed.2d 1215 (1982).

Justice Stevens delivered the opinion of the Court.

The term "concerted action" encompasses unlawful conspiracies and constitutionally protected assemblies. The "looseness and pliability" of legal doctrine applicable to concerted action led Justice Jackson to note that certain joint activities have a "chameleon-like" character. The boycott of white merchants in Claiborne County, Mississippi, that gave rise to this litigation had such a character; it included elements of criminality and elements of majesty. Evidence that fear of reprisals caused some black citizens to withhold their patronage from respondents' businesses convinced the Supreme Court of Mississippi that the entire boycott was unlawful and that each of the 92 petitioners was liable for all of its economic consequences. Evidence that persuasive rhetoric, determination to remedy past injustices, and a host of voluntary decisions by free citizens were the critical factors in the boycott's success presents us with the

---

[1] State restrictions on other labor union group legal services arrangements were held to violate the first amendment in United Mine Workers v. Illinois Bar Ass'n, 389 U.S. 217 (1967) and United Transp. Union v. State Bar of Michigan, 401 U.S. 576 (1971). For an argument that restrictions on the "unauthorized practice of law" also raise first amendment concerns, see Rhode, *Policing the Professional Monopoly: A Constitutional and Empirical Analysis of Unauthorized Practice Prohibitions,* 34 Stan.L.Rev. 1 (1981).

question whether the State Court's judgment is consistent with the Constitution of the United States.

I

[The boycott, begun in 1966, led to this state court action, filed in 1969 by several merchants, for damages and injunctive relief. Named as defendants were the NAACP, MAP (a Mississippi coalition implementing the federal "head start" program), Aaron Henry (President of the Mississippi NAACP), Charles Evers (Field Secretary for the Mississippi NAACP), and 144 individuals participating in the boycott. After a lengthy trial that concluded in 1976, the trial court found the defendants liable on three theories: the tort of malicious interference with plaintiffs' business, violation of a state statutory prohibition of secondary boycotts, and violation of the state antitrust statute. A broad permanent injunction was entered, and damages in excess of one and one quarter million dollars were awarded. The Mississippi Supreme Court upheld the imposition of liability only on the common law tort theory. Judgments against MAP and 37 individuals were reversed for insufficiency of proof, and the case was remanded to the trial court for recomputation of damages. The Supreme Court granted a petition for certiorari.]

II

This Court's jurisdiction to review the judgment of the Mississippi Supreme Court is, of course, limited to the federal questions necessarily decided by that court. We consider first whether petitioners' activities are protected in any respect by the Federal Constitution and, if they are, what effect such protection has on a lawsuit of this nature.

A

The boycott of white merchants at issue in this case took many forms. The boycott was launched at a meeting of a local branch of the NAACP attended by several hundred persons. Its acknowledged purpose was to secure compliance by both civic and business leaders with a lengthy list of demands for equality and racial justice. The boycott was supported by speeches and nonviolent picketing. Participants repeatedly encouraged others to join in its cause.

Each of these elements of the boycott is a form of speech or conduct that is ordinarily entitled to protection under the First and Fourteenth Amendments. The black citizens named as defendants in this action banded together and collectively expressed their dissatisfaction with a social structure that had denied them rights to equal treatment and respect. . . .

The right to associate does not lose all constitutional protection merely because some members of the group may have participated in conduct or advocated doctrine that itself is not protected. In De Jonge v. Oregon, 299 U.S. 353, the Court unanimously held that an individual could not be penalized simply for assisting in the conduct of an otherwise lawful meeting held under the auspices of the Communist Party, an organization that advocated "criminal syndicalism." . . .

Of course, the petitioners in this case did more than assemble peaceably and discuss among themselves their grievances against governmental and business policy. Other elements of the boycott, however, also involved activities ordinarily safeguarded by the First Amendment. In Thornhill v. Alabama, 310 U.S. 88, the Court held that peaceful picketing was entitled to constitutional protection, even though, in that case, the purpose of the picketing "was concededly to advise customers and prospective customers of the relationship existing between the employer and its employees and thereby to induce such customers not to patronize the employer." Id., at 99. . . . In Edwards v. South Carolina, 372 U.S. 229, we held that a peaceful march and demonstration was protected by the rights of free speech, free assembly, and freedom to petition for a redress of grievances.

Speech itself also was used to further the aims of the boycott. Nonparticipants repeatedly were urged to join the common cause, both through public address and through personal solicitation. These elements of the boycott involve speech in its most direct form. In addition, names of boycott violators were read aloud at meetings at the First Baptist Church and published in a local black newspaper. Petitioners admittedly sought to persuade others to join the boycott through social pressure and the "threat" of social ostracism. Speech does not lose its protected character, however, simply because it may embarrass others or coerce them into action. . . .

In Organization for a Better Austin v. Keefe, 402 U.S. 415, the Court considered the validity of a prior restraint on speech that invaded the "privacy" of the respondent. Petitioner, a racially integrated community organization, charged that respondent, a real estate broker, had engaged in tactics known as "blockbusting" or "panic peddling." Petitioner asked respondent to sign an agreement that he would not solicit property in their community. When he refused, petitioner distributed leaflets near respondent's home that were critical of his business practices. A state court enjoined petitioner from distributing the leaflets; an appellate court affirmed on the ground that the alleged activities were coercive and intimidating, rather than informative, and therefore not entitled to First Amendment protection. Id., at 418. This Court reversed. . . . In dissolving the prior restraint, the Court recognized that "offensive" and "coercive" speech was nevertheless protected by the First Amendment.

In sum, the boycott clearly involved constitutionally protected activity. . . . Through exercise of these First Amendment rights, petitioners sought to bring about political, social, and economic change. Through speech, assembly, and petition—rather than through riot or revolution—petitioners sought to change a social order that had consistently treated them as second-class citizens.

The presence of protected activity, however, does not end the relevant constitutional inquiry. Governmental regulation that has an incidental effect on First Amendment freedoms may be justified in certain narrowly defined instances. See United States v. O'Brien, 391 U.S. 367. A nonviolent and totally voluntary boycott may have a disruptive effect on local economic conditions. This Court has recognized the strong governmental interest in certain forms of economic regulation, even though such regulation may have an incidental effect on rights of speech and association. See Giboney v. Empire Storage, 336 U.S. 490; NLRB v. Retail Store Employees Union, 447 U.S. 607. The right of business entities to "associate" to suppress competition may be curtailed. National Soc. of Professional Engineers v. United States, 435 U.S. 679. Unfair trade practices may be restricted. Secondary boycotts and picketing by labor unions may be prohibited, as part of "Congress' striking of the delicate balance between union freedom of expression and the ability of neutral employers, employees, and consumers to remain free from coerced participation in industrial strife." NLRB v. Retail Store Employees Union, supra, at 617–618 (Blackmun, J., concurring). See International Longshoremen's Assoc. v. Allied International, ___ U.S. ___, ___.

While States have broad power to regulate economic activity, we do not find a comparable right to prohibit peaceful political activity such as that found in the boycott in this case. This Court has recognized that expression on public issues "has always rested on the highest rung of the hierarchy of First Amendment values." Carey v. Brown, 447 U.S. 455, 467. . . .

. . . .

It is not disputed that a major purpose of the boycott in this case was to influence governmental action. . . . Petitioners sought to vindicate rights of equality and of freedom that lie at the heart of the Fourteenth Amendment itself. The right of the States to regulate economic activity could not justify a complete prohibition against a nonviolent, politically-motivated boycott designed to force governmental and economic change and to effectuate rights guaranteed by the Constitution itself.

In upholding an injunction against the state supersedeas bonding requirement in this case, Judge Ainsworth of the Court of Appeals for the Fifth Circuit cogently stated:

"At the heart of the Chancery Court's opinion lies the belief that the mere organization of the boycott and every activity undertaken in support thereof could be subject to judicial prohibition under state law. This view accords insufficient weight to the First Amendment's protection of political speech and association. There is no suggestion that the NAACP, MAP or the individual defendants were in competition with the white businesses or that the boycott arose from parochial economic interests. On the contrary, the boycott grew out of a racial dispute with the white merchants and city government of Port Gibson and all of the picketing, speeches, and other communication associated with the boycott were directed to the elimination of racial discrimination in the town. This differentiates this case from a boycott organized for economic ends, for speech to protest racial discrimination is essential political speech lying at the core of the First Amendment." Henry v. First National Bank of Clarksdale, 595 F.2d 291, 303 (1979) (footnote omitted).

We hold that the nonviolent elements of petitioners' activities are entitled to the protection of the First Amendment.

B

The Mississippi Supreme Court did not sustain the chancellor's imposition of liability on a theory that state law prohibited a nonviolent, politically-motivated boycott. The fact that such activity is constitutionally protected, however, imposes a special obligation on this Court to examine critically the basis on which liability was imposed. In particular, we consider here the effect of our holding that much of petitioners' conduct was constitutionally protected on the ability of the State to impose liability for elements of the boycott that were not so protected.

The First Amendment does not protect violence. . . . Although the extent and significance of the violence in this case is vigorously disputed by the parties, there is no question that acts of violence occurred. No federal rule of law restricts a State from imposing tort liability for business losses that are caused by violence and by threats of violence. When such conduct occurs in the context of constitutionally protected activity, however, "precision of regulation" is demanded. NAACP v. Button, 371 U.S. 415, 438. Specifically, the presence of activity protected by the First Amendment imposes restraints on the grounds that may give rise to damage liability and on the persons who may be held accountable for those damages.

. . . .

. . . Civil liability may not be imposed merely because an individual belonged to a group, some members of which committed acts of violence. For liability to be imposed by reason of association alone, it is necessary to establish that the group itself possessed unlawful goals and that the individual held a specific intent to further those illegal aims. . . .

III

The chancellor awarded respondents damages for all business losses that were sustained during a seven year period beginning in 1966 and ending December 31, 1972. With the exception of Aaron Henry, all defendants were held jointly and severally liable for these losses. The chancellor's findings were consistent with his view that voluntary participation in the boycott was a sufficient basis on which to impose liability. The Mississippi Supreme Court properly rejected that theory; it nevertheless held that petitioners were liable for all damages "resulting from the boycott." In light of the principles set forth above, it is evident that such a damage award may not be sustained in this case.

. . .

IV

In litigation of this kind the stakes are high. Concerted action is a powerful weapon. History teaches that special dangers are associated with conspiratorial activity. And yet one of the foundations of our society is the right of individuals to combine with other persons in pursuit of a common goal by lawful means.

At times the difference between lawful and unlawful collective action may be identified easily by reference to its purpose. In this case, however, petitioners' ultimate objectives were unquestionably legitimate. The charge of illegality— like the claim of constitutional protection—derives from the means employed by the participants to achieve those goals. The use of speeches, marches, and threats of social ostracism cannot provide the basis for a damage award. But violent conduct is beyond the pale of constitutional protection.

The taint of violence colored the conduct of some of the petitioners. They, of course, may be held liable for the consequences of their violent deeds. The burden of demonstrating that it colored the entire collective effort, however, is not satisfied by evidence that violence occurred or even that violence contributed to the success of the boycott. A massive and prolonged effort to change the social, political, and economic structure of a local environment cannot be characterized as a violent conspiracy simply by reference to the ephemeral consequences of relatively few violent acts. Such a characterization must be supported by findings that adequately disclose the evidentiary basis for concluding that specific parties agreed to use unlawful means, that carefully identify the impact of such unlawful conduct, and that recognize the importance of avoiding the imposition of punishment for constitutionally protected activity. The burden of demonstrating that fear rather than protected conduct was the dominant force in the movement is heavy. A court must be wary of a claim that the true color of a forest is better revealed by reptiles hidden in the weeds than by the foliage of countless free-standing trees. The findings of the chancellor, framed largely in the light of two legal theories rejected by the Mississippi Supreme Court, are constitutionally insufficient to support the judgment that all petitioners are liable for all losses resulting from the boycott.

The judgment is reversed. The case is remanded for further proceedings not inconsistent with this opinion.

It is so ordered.

Justice Rehnquist concurs in the result.

Justice Marshall took no part in the consideration or decision of this case.

ROBERTS v. UNITED STATES JAYCEES

___ U.S. ___, 104 S.Ct. 3244, 82 L.Ed.2d 462 (1984).

Justice Brennan delivered the opinion of the Court.

This case requires us to address a conflict between a State's efforts to eliminate gender-based discrimination against its citizens and the constitutional freedom of association asserted by members of a private organization. In the decision under review, the Court of Appeals for the Eighth Circuit concluded that, by requiring the United States Jaycees to admit women as full voting members, the Minnesota Human Rights Act violates the First and Fourteenth Amendment rights of the organization's members. We . . . reverse.

I

A

The United States Jaycees (Jaycees), founded in 1920 as the Junior Chamber of Commerce, is a nonprofit membership corporation, incorporated in Missouri with national headquarters in Tulsa, Oklahoma. The objective of the Jaycees, as set out in its bylaws, is to pursue

"such educational and charitable purposes as will promote and foster the growth and development of young men's civic organizations in the United States, designed to inculcate in the individual membership of such organization a spirit of genuine Americanism and civic interest, and as a supplementary education institution to provide them with opportunity for personal development and achievement and an avenue for intelligent participation by young men in the affairs of their community, state and nation, and to develop true friendship and understanding among young men of all nations."

The organization's bylaws establish seven classes of membership, including individual or regular members, associate individual members, and local chapters. Regular membership is limited to young men between the ages of 18 and 35, while associate membership is available to individuals or groups ineligible for regular membership, principally women and older men. An associate member, whose dues are somewhat lower than those charged regular members, may not vote, hold local or national office, or participate in certain leadership training and awards programs. The bylaws define a local chapter as "any young men's organization of good repute existing in any community within the United States, organized for purposes similar to and consistent with those" of the national organization. The ultimate policymaking authority of the Jaycees rests with an annual national convention, consisting of delegates from each local chapter, with a national president and board of directors. At the time of trial in August 1981, the Jaycees had approximately 295,000 members in 7,400 local chapters affiliated with 51 state organizations. There were at that time about 11,915 associate members. The national organization's Executive Vice President estimated at trial that women associate members make up about two percent of the Jaycees' total membership.

New members are recruited to the Jaycees through the local chapters, although the state and national organizations are also actively involved in recruitment through a variety of promotional activities. A new regular member pays an initial fee followed by annual dues; in exchange, he is entitled to participate in all of the activities of the local, state, and national organizations. The national headquarters employs a staff to develop "program kits" for use by local chapters that are designed to enhance individual development, community development, and members' management skills. These materials include courses in public speaking and personal finances as well as community programs related to charity, sports, and public health. The national office also makes available to members a range of personal products, including travel accessories, casual wear, pins, awards, and other gifts. The programs, products, and other activities of the organization are all regularly featured in publications made available to the membership, including a magazine entitled "Future."

B

In 1974 and 1975, respectively, the Minneapolis and St. Paul chapters of the Jaycees began admitting women as regular members. Currently, the memberships and boards of directors of both chapters include a substantial proportion of women. As a result, the two chapters have been in violation of the national organization's bylaws for about 10 years. The national organization has imposed a number of sanctions on the Minneapolis and St. Paul chapters for violating the bylaws, including denying their members eligibility for state or national office or awards programs, and refusing to count their membership in computing votes at national conventions.

In December 1978, the president of the national organization advised both chapters that a motion to revoke their charters would be considered at a forthcoming meeting of the national board of directors in Tulsa. Shortly after receiving this notification, members of both chapters filed charges of discrimination with the Minnesota Department of Human Rights. The complaints alleged that the exclusion of women from full membership required by the national organization's bylaws violated the Minnesota Human Rights Act (Act), which provides in part:

"It is an unfair discriminatory practice:

"To deny any person the full and equal enjoyment of the goods, services, facilities, privileges, advantages, and accommodations of a place of public accommodation because of race, color, creed, religion, disability, national origin or sex." Minn.Stat. § 363.03, subd. 3 (1982).

The term "place of public accommodation" is defined in the Act as "a business, accommodation, refreshment, entertainment, recreation, or transportation facility of any kind, whether licensed or not, whose goods, services, facilities, privileges, advantages or accommodations are extended, offered, sold, or otherwise made available to the public." Id., § 363.01, subd. 18.

After an investigation, the Commissioner of the Minnesota Department of Human Rights found probable cause to believe that the sanctions imposed on the local chapters by the national organization violated the statute and ordered that an evidentiary hearing be held before a state hearing examiner. Before that hearing took place, however, the national organization brought suit against various state officials, appellants here, in the United States District Court for the District of Minnesota, seeking declaratory and injunctive relief to prevent enforcement of the Act. . . .

. . . The . . . District Court entered judgment in favor of the state officials. [A] divided Court of Appeals for the Eighth Circuit reversed. . . .

. . . .

II

Our decisions have referred to constitutionally protected "freedom of association" in two distinct senses. In one line of decisions, the Court has concluded that choices to enter into and maintain certain intimate human relationships must be secured against undue intrusion by the State because of the role of such relationships in safeguarding the individual freedom that is central to our constitutional scheme. In this respect, freedom of association receives protection as a fundamental element of personal liberty. In another set of decisions, the Court has recognized a right to associate for the purpose of engaging in those activities protected by the First Amendment—speech, assembly, petition for the redress of grievances, and the exercise of religion. The Constitution guarantees freedom of association of this kind as an indispensable means of preserving other individual liberties.

The intrinsic and instrumental features of constitutionally protected association may, of course, coincide. In particular, when the State interferes with individuals' selection of those with whom they wish to join in a common endeavor, freedom of association in both of its forms may be implicated. The Jaycees contend that this is such a case. Still, the nature and degree of constitutional protection afforded freedom of association may vary depending on the extent to which one or the other aspect of the constitutionally protected liberty is at stake in a given case. We therefore find it useful to consider separately the effect of applying the Minnesota statute to the Jaycees on what could be called its members' freedom of intimate association and their freedom of expressive association.

A

The Court has long recognized that, because the Bill of Rights is designed to secure individual liberty, it must afford the formation and preservation of certain kinds of highly personal relationships a substantial measure of sanctuary from unjustified interference by the State. E.g., Pierce v. Society of Sisters, 268 U.S. 510, 534–535 (1925); Meyer v. Nebraska, 262 U.S. 390, 399 (1923). Without precisely identifying every consideration that may underlie this type of constitutional protection, we have noted that certain kinds of personal bonds have played a critical role in the culture and traditions of the Nation by cultivating and transmitting shared ideals and beliefs; they thereby foster diversity and act as critical buffers between the individual and the power of the State. Moreover, the constitutional shelter afforded such relationships reflects the realization that individuals draw much of their emotional enrichment from close ties with others. Protecting these relationships from unwarranted state interference therefore safeguards the ability independently to define one's identity that is central to any concept of liberty.

The personal affiliations that exemplify these considerations, and that therefore suggest some relevant limitations on the relationships that might be entitled to this sort of constitutional protection, are those that attend the creation and sustenance of a family—marriage, e.g., Zablocki v. Redhail, [434 U.S. 374 (1978)]; childbirth, e.g., Carey v. Population Services Int'l, [431 U.S. 678 (1977)]; the raising and education of children, e.g., Smith v. Organization of Foster Families, [431 U.S. 816 (1977)]; and cohabitation with one's relatives, e.g., Moore v. City of East Cleveland, [431 U.S. 494 (1977)].

Family relationships, by their nature, involve deep attachments and commitments to the necessarily few other individuals with whom one shares not only a special community of thoughts, experiences, and beliefs but also distinctively personal aspects of one's life. Among other things, therefore, they are distinguished by such attributes as relative smallness, a high degree of selectivity in decisions to begin and maintain the affiliation, and seclusion from others in critical aspects of the relationship. As a general matter, only relationships with these sorts of qualities are likely to reflect the considerations that have led to an understanding of freedom of association as an intrinsic element of personal liberty. Conversely, an association lacking these qualities—such as a large business enterprise—seems remote from the concerns giving rise to this constitutional protection. Accordingly, the Constitution undoubtedly imposes constraints on the State's power to control the selection of one's spouse that would not apply to regulations affecting the choice of one's fellow employees.

Between these poles, of course, lies a broad range of human relationships that may make greater or lesser claims to constitutional protection from particular incursions by the State. Determining the limits of state authority over an individual's freedom to enter into a particular association therefore unavoidably entails a careful assessment of where that relationship's objective characteristics locate it on a spectrum from the most intimate to the most attenuated of personal attachments. See generally Runyon v. McCrary, 427 U.S. 160, 187–189 (1976) (Powell, J., concurring). We need not mark the potentially significant points on this terrain with any precision. We note only that factors that may be relevant include size, purpose, policies, selectivity, congeniality, and other characteristics that in a particular case may be pertinent. In this case, however, several features of the Jaycees clearly place the organization outside of the category of relationships worthy of this kind of constitutional protection.

The undisputed facts reveal that the local chapters of the Jaycees are large and basically unselective groups. At the time of the state administrative hearing, the Minneapolis chapter had approximately 430 members, while the St. Paul chapter had about 400. Apart from age and sex, neither the national organization nor the local chapters employs any criteria for judging applicants for membership, and new members are routinely recruited and admitted with no inquiry into their backgrounds. In fact, a local officer testified that he could recall no instance in which an applicant had been denied membership on any basis other than age or sex. Cf. Tillman v. Wheaton-Haven Recreational Ass'n, 410 U.S. 431, 438 (1973) (organization whose only selection criteria is race has "no plan or purpose of exclusiveness" that might make it a private club exempt from federal civil rights statute); Sullivan v. Little Hunting Park, Inc., 396 U.S. 229, 236 (1969) (same); Daniel v. Paul, 395 U.S. 298, 302 (1969) (same). Furthermore, despite their inability to vote, hold office, or receive certain awards, women affiliated with the Jaycees attend various meetings, participate in selected projects, and engage in many of the organization's social functions. Indeed, numerous non-members of both genders regularly participate in a substantial portion of activities central to the decision of many members to associate with one another, including many of the organization's various community programs, awards ceremonies, and recruitment meetings.

In short, the local chapters of the Jaycees are neither small nor selective. Moreover, much of the activity central to the formation and maintenance of the association involves the participation of strangers to that relationship. Accordingly, we conclude that the Jaycees chapters lack the distinctive characteristics that might afford constitutional protection to the decision of its members to exclude women. We turn therefore to consider the extent to which application of the Minnesota statute to compel the Jaycees to accept women infringes the group's freedom of expressive association.

B

An individual's freedom to speak, to worship, and to petition the Government for the redress of grievances could not be vigorously protected from interference by the State unless a correlative freedom to engage in group effort toward those ends were not also guaranteed. According protection to collective effort on behalf of shared goals is especially important in preserving political and cultural diversity and in shielding dissident expression from suppression by the majority. Consequently, we have long understood as implicit in the right to engage in activities protected by the First Amendment a corresponding right to associate with others in pursuit of a wide variety of political, social, economic, educational, religious, and cultural ends. See, e.g., NAACP v. Claiborne Hardware Co., 458 U.S. 886, 907–909, 932–933 (1982); Larson v. Valente, 456 U.S. 228, 244–246 (1982); In re Primus, 436 U.S. 412, 426 (1978);

Abood v. Detroit Board of Education, 431 U.S. 209, 231 (1977). In view of the various protected activities in which the Jaycees engage, that right is plainly implicated in this case.

Government actions that may unconstitutionally infringe upon this freedom can take a number of forms. Among other things, government may seek to impose penalties or withhold benefits from individuals because of their membership in a disfavored group, e.g., Healy v. James, 408 U.S. 169, 180–184 (1972); it may attempt to require disclosure of the fact of membership in a group seeking anonymity, e.g., Brown v. Socialist Workers '74 Campaign Committee, 459 U.S. 87, 91–92 (1982); and it may try to interfere with the internal organization or affairs of the group, e.g., Cousins v. Wigoda, 419 U.S. 477, 487–488 (1975). By requiring the Jaycees to admit women as full voting members, the Minnesota Act works an infringement of the last type. There can be no clearer example of an intrusion into the internal structure or affairs of an association than a regulation that forces the group to accept members it does not desire. Such a regulation may impair the ability of the original members to express only those views that brought them together. Freedom of association therefore plainly presupposes a freedom not to associate. See Abood v. Detroit Board of Education, supra, at 234–235.

The right to associate for expressive purposes is not, however, absolute. Infringements on that right may be justified by regulations adopted to serve compelling state interests, unrelated to the suppression of ideas, that cannot be achieved through means significantly less restrictive of associational freedoms. We are persuaded that Minnesota's compelling interest in eradicating discrimination against its female citizens justifies the impact that application of the statute to the Jaycees may have on the male members' associational freedoms.

On its face, the Minnesota Act does not aim at the suppression of speech, does not distinguish between prohibited and permitted activity on the basis of viewpoint, and does not license enforcement authorities to administer the statute on the basis of such constitutionally impermissible criteria. Nor do the Jaycees contend that the Act has been applied in this case for the purpose of hampering the organization's ability to express its views. Instead, as the Minnesota Supreme Court explained, the Act reflects the State's strong historical commitment to eliminating discrimination and assuring its citizens equal access to publicly available goods and services. That goal, which is unrelated to the suppression of expression, plainly serves compelling state interests of the highest order.

The Minnesota Human Rights Act at issue here is an example of public accommodations laws that were adopted by some States beginning a decade before enactment of their federal counterpart, the Civil Rights Act of 1875. Indeed, when this Court invalidated that federal statute in the Civil Rights Cases, 109 U.S. 3 (1883), it emphasized the fact that state laws imposed a variety of equal access obligations on public accommodations. Id., at 19, 25. In response to that decision, many more States, including Minnesota, adopted statutes prohibiting racial discrimination in public accommodations. These laws provided the primary means for protecting the civil rights of historically disadvantaged groups until the Federal Government reentered the field in 1957. Like many other States, Minnesota has progressively broadened the scope of its public accommodations law in the years since it was first enacted, both with respect to the number and type of covered facilities and with respect to the groups against whom discrimination is forbidden. In 1973, the Minnesota legislature added discrimination on the basis of sex to the types of conduct prohibited by the statute. Act of May 24, 1973, ch. 729, § 3, 1973 Minn.Laws 2158, 2164.

By prohibiting gender discrimination in places of public accommodation, the Minnesota Act protects the State's citizenry from a number of serious social and personal harms. In the context of reviewing state actions under the Equal Protection Clause, this Court has frequently noted that discrimination based on archaic and overbroad assumptions about the relative needs and capacities of the sexes forces individuals to labor under stereotypical notions that often bear no relationship to their actual abilities. It thereby both deprives persons of their individual dignity and denies society the benefits of wide participation in political, economic, and cultural life. These concerns are strongly implicated with respect to gender discrimination in the allocation of publicly available goods and services. . . .

In applying the Act to the Jaycees, the State has advanced those interests through the least restrictive means of achieving its ends. Indeed, the Jaycees have failed to demonstrate that the Act imposes any serious burdens on the male members' freedom of expressive association. . . . To be sure, as the Court of Appeals noted, a "not insubstantial part" of the Jaycees' activities constitutes protected expression on political, economic, cultural, and social affairs. . . . There is, however, no basis in the record for concluding that admission of women as full voting members will impede the organization's ability to engage in these protected activities or to disseminate its preferred views. The Act requires no change in the Jaycees' creed of promoting the interests of young men, and it imposes no restrictions on the organization's ability to exclude individuals with ideologies or philosophies different from those of its existing members. Cf. Democratic Party v. Wisconsin, 450 U.S., at 122 (recognizing the right of political parties to "protect themselves 'from intrusion by those with adverse political principles' "). Moreover, the Jaycees already invite women to share the group's views and philosophy and to participate in much of its training and community activities. Accordingly, any claim that admission of women as full voting members will impair a symbolic message conveyed by the very fact that women are not permitted to vote is attenuated at best. . . .

While acknowledging that "the specific content of most of the resolutions adopted over the years by the Jaycees has nothing to do with sex," . . . the Court of Appeals nonetheless entertained the hypothesis that women members might have a different view or agenda with respect to these matters so that, if they are allowed to vote, "some change in the Jaycees' philosophical cast can reasonably be expected," . . . Although such generalizations may or may not have a statistical basis in fact with respect to particular positions adopted by the Jaycees, we have repeatedly condemned legal decisionmaking that relies uncritically on such assumptions. In the absence of a showing far more substantial than that attempted by the Jaycees, we decline to indulge in the sexual stereotyping that underlies appellee's contention that, by allowing women to vote, application of the Minnesota Act will change the content or impact of the organization's speech.

In any event, even if enforcement of the Act causes some incidental abridgement of the Jaycees' protected speech, that effect is no greater than is necessary to accomplish the State's legitimate purposes. As we have explained, acts of invidious discrimination in the distribution of publicly available goods, services, and other advantages cause unique evils that government has a compelling interest to prevent—wholly apart from the point of view such conduct may transmit. Accordingly, like violence or other types of potentially expressive activities that produce special harms distinct from their communicative impact, such practices are entitled to no constitutional protection. . . .

III

We turn finally to appellee's contentions that the Minnesota Act, as interpreted by the State's highest court, is unconstitutionally vague and overbroad. . . . In deciding that the Act reaches the Jaycees, the Minnesota Supreme Court used a number of specific and objective criteria—regarding the organization's size, selectivity, commercial nature, and use of public facilities—typically employed in determining the applicability of state and federal anti-discrimination statutes to the membership policies of assertedly private clubs. National Organization for Women v. Little League Baseball, Inc., 127 N.J.Super. 522, 318 A.2d 33, aff'd mem., 67 N.J. 320, 338 A.2d 198 (1974). See generally NYU Survey 223–224, 250–252. The Court of Appeals seemingly acknowledged that the Minnesota court's construction of the Act by use of these familiar standards ensures that the reach of the statute is readily ascertainable. It nevertheless concluded that the Minnesota court introduced a constitutionally fatal element of uncertainty into the statute by suggesting that the Kiwanis Club might be sufficiently "private" to be outside the scope of the Act. . . .

The contrast between the Jaycees and the Kiwanis Club drawn by the Minnesota court . . . disposes of appellee's contention that the Act is unconstitutionally overbroad. . . . The state court's articulated willingness to adopt limiting constructions that would exclude private groups from the statute's reach, together with the commonly used and sufficiently precise standards it employed to determine that the Jaycees is not such a group, establish that the Act, as currently construed, does not create an unacceptable risk of application to a substantial amount of protected conduct.

IV

The judgment of the Court of Appeals is
Reversed.

Justice Rehnquist concurs in the judgment.

The Chief Justice and Justice Blackmun took no part in the decision of this case.

Justice O'Connor, concurring in part and concurring in the judgment.
. . . .

I part company with the Court over its First Amendment analysis in Part II–B of its opinion. I agree with the Court that application of the Minnesota law to the Jaycees does not contravene the First Amendment, but I reach that conclusion for reasons distinct from those offered by the Court. I believe the Court has adopted a test that unadvisedly casts doubt on the power of States to pursue the profoundly important goal of ensuring nondiscriminatory access to commercial opportunities in our society. At the same time, the Court has adopted an approach to the general problem presented by this case that accords insufficient protection to expressive associations and places inappropriate burdens on groups claiming the protection of the First Amendment.

I

The Court analyzes Minnesota's attempt to regulate the Jaycees' membership using a test that I find both over-protective of activities undeserving of constitutional shelter and under-protective of important First Amendment concerns. The Court declares that the Jaycees' right of association depends on the organization's making a "substantial" showing that the admission of unwelcome members "will change the message communicated by the group's speech." I am not sure what showing the Court thinks would satisfy its requirement of proof of a membership-message connection, but whatever it means, the focus on such a connection is objectionable.

Imposing such a requirement, especially in the context of the balancing-of-interests test articulated by the Court, raises the possibility that certain commercial associations, by engaging occasionally in certain kinds of expressive activities, might improperly gain protection for discrimination. The Court's focus raises other problems as well. How are we to analyze the First Amendment associational claims of an organization that invokes its right, settled by the Court in NAACP v. Alabama, 357 U.S. 449, 460–466 (1958), to protect the privacy of its membership? And would the Court's analysis of this case be different if, for example, the Jaycees membership had a steady history of opposing public issues thought (by the Court) to be favored by women? It might seem easy to conclude, in the latter case, that the admission of women to the Jaycees' ranks would affect the content of the organization's message, but I do not believe that should change the outcome of this case. Whether an association is or is not constitutionally protected in the selection of its membership should not depend on what the association says or why its members say it.

The Court's readiness to inquire into the connection between membership and message reveals a more fundamental flaw in its analysis. . . .

On the one hand, an association engaged exclusively in protected expression enjoys First Amendment protection of both the content of its message and the choice of its members. Protection of the message itself is judged by the same standards as protection of speech by an individual. Protection of the association's right to define its membership derives from the recognition that the formation of an expressive association is the creation of a voice, and the selection of members is the definition of that voice. . . . A ban on specific group voices on public affairs violates the most basic guarantee of the First Amendment—that citizens, not the government, control the content of public discussion.

On the other hand, there is only minimal constitutional protection of the freedom of *commercial* association. There are, of course, some constitutional protections of commercial speech—speech intended and used to promote a commercial transaction with the speaker. But the State is free to impose any rational regulation on the commercial transaction itself. The Constitution does not guarantee a right to choose employees, customers, suppliers, or those with whom one engages in simple commercial transactions, without restraint from the State. A shopkeeper has no constitutional right to deal only with persons of one sex.

. . . [A]n organization engaged in commercial activity enjoys only minimal constitutional protection of its recruitment, training, and solicitation activities. While the Court has acknowledged a First Amendment right to engage in non-deceptive commercial advertising, governmental regulation of the commercial recruitment of new members, stockholders, customers, or employees is valid if rationally related to the government's . . ..

Many associations cannot readily be described as purely expressive or purely commercial. No association is likely ever to be exclusively engaged in expressive activities, if only because it will collect dues from its members or purchase printing materials or rent lecture halls or serve coffee and cakes at its meetings. And innumerable commercial associations also engage in some incidental protected speech or advocacy. . . .

In my view, an association should be characterized as commercial, and therefore subject to rationally related state regulation of its membership and other associational activities, when, and only when, the association's activities are not predominantly of the type protected by the First Amendment. It is only when the association is predominantly engaged in protected expression that state regulation of its membership will necessarily affect, change, dilute, or silence one collective voice that would otherwise be heard. An association must choose its market. Once it enters the marketplace of commerce in any substantial degree it loses the complete control over its membership that it would otherwise enjoy if it confined its affairs to the marketplace of ideas.

Determining whether an association's activity is predominantly protected expression will often be difficult, if only because a broad range of activities can be expressive. . . . The purposes of an association, and the purposes of its members in adhering to it, are doubtless relevant in determining whether the association is primarily engaged in protected expression. Lawyering to advance social goals may be speech, NAACP v. Button, 371 U.S. 415, 429–430 (1963), but ordinary commercial law practice is not, see Hishon v. King and Spalding, 467 U.S. —— (1984). A group boycott or refusal to deal for political purposes may be speech, NAACP v. Claiborne Hardware Co., 458 U.S. 886, 912–915 (1982), though a similar boycott for purposes of maintaining a cartel is not. Even the training of outdoor survival skills or participation in community service might become expressive when the activity is intended to develop good morals, reverence, patriotism, and a desire for self-improvement.* . . .

. . . The proper approach to analysis of First Amendment claims of associational freedom is, therefore, to distinguish non-expressive from expressive associations and to recognize that the former lack the full constitutional protections possessed by the latter.

II

Minnesota's attempt to regulate the membership of the Jaycees chapters operating in that State presents a relatively easy case for application of the expressive-commercial dichotomy. . . .

. . . Notwithstanding its protected expressive activities, the Jaycees— otherwise known as the Junior Chamber of Commerce—is, first and foremost, an organization that, at both the national and local levels, promotes and practices the art of solicitation and management. The organization claims that the training it offers its members gives them an advantage in business, and business firms do indeed sometimes pay the dues of individual memberships for their employees. Jaycees members hone their solicitation and management skills, under the direction and supervision of the organization, primarily through their active recruitment of new members. "One of the major activities of the Jaycees is the sale of memberships in the organization. It encourages continuous recruitment of members with the expressed goal of increasing membership . . . . The Jaycees itself refers to its members as customers and membership as a product it is selling. More than 80 percent of the national officers' time is dedicated to recruitment, and more than half of the available achievement awards are in part conditioned on achievement in recruitment." The organization encourages record-breaking performance in selling memberships: the current records are 348 for most memberships sold in a year by one person, 134 for most sold in a month, and 1,586 for most sold in a lifetime.

Recruitment and selling are commercial activities, even when conducted for training rather than for profit. The "not insubstantial" volume of protected Jaycees activity found by the Court of Appeals is simply not enough to preclude state regulation of the Jaycees' commercial activities. The State of Minnesota has a legitimate interest in ensuring nondiscriminatory access to the commercial opportunity presented by membership in the Jaycees. The members of the Jaycees may not claim constitutional immunity from Minnesota's anti-discrimination law by seeking to exercise their First Amendment rights through this commercial organization.

. . . .

---

* See, e.g., Girl Scouts of the U.S.A., You Make the Difference (1980); W. Hillcourt, The Official Boy Scout Handbook (1979); P. Fussell, The Boy Scout Handbook and Other Observations 7–8 (1982) ("The Official Boy Scout Handbook, for all its focus on Axmanship, Backpacking, Cooking, First Aid, Flowers, Hiking, Map and Compass, Semaphore, Trees, and Weather, is another book about goodness. No home and certainly no government office, should be without a copy").

B. THE RIGHT NOT TO ASSOCIATE

ABOOD v. DETROIT BOARD OF EDUCATION

431 U.S. 209, 97 S.Ct. 1782, 52 L.Ed.2d 261 (1977).

Mr. Justice Stewart delivered the opinion of the Court.

The State of Michigan has enacted legislation authorizing a system for union representation of local governmental employees. A union and a local government employer are specifically permitted to agree to an "agency shop" arrangement, whereby every employee represented by a union—even though not a union member—must pay to the union, as a condition of employment, a service fee equal in amount to union dues. The issue before us is whether this arrangement violates the constitutional rights of government employees who object to public-sector unions as such or to various union activities financed by the compulsory service fees.

. . .

. . . Christine Warczak and a number of other named teachers filed a class action in a state court, naming as defendants the Board, the Union, and several Union officials. Their complaint, as amended, alleged that they were unwilling or had refused to pay dues and that they opposed collective bargaining in the public sector. . . . The complaint prayed that the agency-shop clause be declared invalid . . . under the United States Constitution as a deprivation of, *inter alia,* the plaintiffs' freedom of association protected by the First and Fourteenth Amendments, and for such further relief as might be deemed appropriate.

Upon the defendants' motion for summary judgment, the trial court dismissed the action for failure to state a claim upon which relief could be granted.

. . .

II.

A.

Consideration of the question whether an agency-shop provision in a collective-bargaining agreement covering governmental employees is, as such, constitutionally valid must begin with two cases in this Court that on their face go far toward resolving the issue. The cases are Railway Employes' Dept. v. Hanson, [351 U.S. 225] and Machinists v. Street, 367 U.S. 740.

In the *Hanson* case a group of railroad employees brought an action in a Nebraska court to enjoin enforcement of a union-shop agreement. The challenged clause was authorized, and indeed shielded from any attempt by a State to prohibit it, by the Railway Labor Act, 45 U.S.C. § 152 Eleventh. The trial court granted the relief requested. The Nebraska Supreme Court upheld the injunction on the ground that employees who disagreed with the objectives promoted by union expenditures were deprived of the freedom of association protected by the First Amendment. This Court agreed that "justiciable questions under the First and Fifth Amendments were presented," but reversed the judgment of the Nebraska Supreme Court on the merits. . . .

The record in *Hanson* contained no evidence that union dues were used to force ideological conformity or otherwise to impair the free expression of employees, and the Court noted that "[i]f 'assessments' are in fact imposed for purposes not germane to collective bargaining, a different problem would be presented." . . .

The Court faced a similar question several years later in the *Street* case, which also involved a challenge to the constitutionality of a union shop authorized by the Railway Labor Act. In *Street,* however, the record contained findings that the union treasury to which all employees were required to contribute had been used "to finance the campaigns of candidates for federal and state offices whom [the plaintiffs] opposed, and to promote the propagation of political and economic doctrines, concepts and ideologies with which [they] disagreed."

The Court . . . considered whether the Act could fairly be construed to avoid these constitutional issues. . . . The Court ruled, . . ., that the use of compulsory union dues for political purposes violated the Act itself. Nonetheless, it found that an injunction against enforcement of the union-shop agreement as such was impermissible under *Hanson,* and remanded the case to the Supreme Court of Georgia so that a more limited remedy could be devised.

To compel employees financially to support their collective-bargaining representative has an impact upon their First Amendment interests. An employee may very well have ideological objections to a wide variety of activities undertaken by the union in its role as exclusive representative. . . . But the judgment clearly made in *Hanson* and *Street* is that such interference as exists is constitutionally justified by the legislative assessment of the important contribution of the union shop to the system of labor relations established by Congress.

B.

. . .

While recognizing the apparent precedential weight of the *Hanson* and *Street* cases, the appellants advance two reasons why those decisions should not control decision of the present case. First, the appellants note that it is *government* employment that is involved here, thus directly implicating constitutional guarantees, in contrast to the private employment that was the subject of the *Hanson* and *Street* decisions. Second, the appellants say that in the public sector collective bargaining itself is inherently "political," and that to require them to give financial support to it is to require the "ideological conformity" that the Court expressly found absent in the *Hanson* case. We find neither argument persuasive.

. . .

C.

Because the Michigan Court of Appeals ruled that state law "sanctions the use of nonunion members' fees for purposes other than collective bargaining," and because the complaints allege that such expenditures were made, this case presents constitutional issues not decided in *Hanson* or *Street.* . . .[29]

Our decisions establish with unmistakable clarity that the freedom of an individual to associate for the purpose of advancing beliefs and ideas is protected by the First and Fourteenth Amendments. . . . Equally clear is the proposition that a government may not require an individual to relinquish rights guaranteed him by the First Amendment as a condition of public employment. E.g., Elrod v. Burns, 427 U.S. at 357–360 and cases cited; Perry v. Sindermann, 408 U.S. 593; Keyishian v. Board of Regents, 385 U.S. 589.

---

[29] In Lathrop v. Donohue, 367 U.S. 820, a companion case to *Street,* a lawyer sued for the refund of dues paid (under protest) to the integrated Wisconsin State Bar. The dues were required as a condition of practicing law in Wisconsin.

The only proposition about which a majority of the Court in *Lathrop* agreed was that the constitutional issues should be reached. However, due to the disparate views of those five Justices on the merits and the failure of the other four Members of the Court to discuss the constitutional questions, *Lathrop* does not provide a clear holding to guide us in adjudicating the constitutional questions here presented.

The appellants argue that they fall within the protection of these cases because they have been prohibited, not from actively associating, but rather from refusing to associate. They specifically argue that they may constitutionally prevent the Union's spending a part of their required service fees to contribute to political candidates and to express political views unrelated to its duties as exclusive bargaining representative. We have concluded that this argument is a meritorious one.

One of the principles underlying the Court's decision in Buckley v. Valeo, 424 U.S. 1, was that contributing to an organization for the purpose of spreading a political message is protected by the First Amendment. . . .

The fact that the appellants are compelled to make, rather than prohibited from making, contributions for political purposes works no less an infringement of their constitutional rights. For at the heart of the First Amendment is the notion that an individual should be free to believe as he will, and that in a free society one's beliefs should be shaped by his mind and his conscience rather than coerced by the State. . . .

These principles . . . are . . . applicable to the case at bar, and they thus prohibit the appellees from requiring any of the appellants to contribute to the support of an ideological cause he may oppose as a condition of holding a job as a public school teacher.

We do not hold that a union cannot constitutionally spend funds for the expression of political views, on behalf of political candidates, or toward the advancement of other ideological causes not germane to its duties as collective-bargaining representative. Rather, the Constitution requires only that such expenditures be financed from charges, dues, or assessments paid by employees who do not object to advancing those ideas and who are not coerced into doing so against their will by the threat of loss of governmental employment.

There will, of course, be difficult problems in drawing lines between collective-bargaining activities, for which contributions may be compelled, and ideological activities unrelated to collective bargaining, for which such compulsion is prohibited. . . . The allegations in the complaints are general ones, and the parties have neither briefed nor argued the question of what specific Union activities in the present context properly fall under the definition of collective bargaining. The lack of factual concreteness and adversary presentation to aid us in approaching the difficult line-drawing questions highlights the importance of avoiding unnecessary decision of constitutional questions. All that we decide is that the general allegations in the complaints, if proved, establish a cause of action under the First and Fourteenth Amendments.

III.

In determining what remedy will be appropriate if the appellants prove their allegations, the objective must be to devise a way of preventing compulsory subsidization of ideological activity by employees who object thereto without restricting the Union's ability to require every employee to contribute to the cost of collective-bargaining activities. . . .

. . . . [In Street] the Court sketched two possible remedies: First, "an injunction against expenditure for political causes opposed by each complaining employee of a sum, from those moneys to be spent by the union for political purposes, which is so much of the moneys exacted from him as is the proportion of the union's total expenditures made for such political activities to the union's total budget"; and second, restitution of a fraction of union dues paid equal to the fraction of total union expenditures that were made for political purposes opposed by the employee. . . .

The Court again considered the remedial question in *Railway Clerks v. Allen*, 373 U.S. 113. . . .

The Court in *Allen* described a "practical decree" that could properly be entered, providing for (1) the refund of a portion of the exacted funds in the proportion that union political expenditures bear to total union expenditures, and (2) the reduction of future exactions by the same proportion. . . .

Although *Street* and *Allen* were concerned with statutory rather than constitutional violations, that difference surely could not justify any lesser relief in this case. . . .

The Court of Appeals thus erred in holding that the plaintiffs are entitled to no relief if they can prove the allegations contained in their complaints, and in depriving them of an opportunity to establish their right to appropriate relief, such, for example, as the kind of remedies described in *Street* and *Allen*. . . .

. . .

[Concurring opinions by Justices Rehnquist and Stevens are omitted.]

Mr. Justice Powell, with whom The Chief Justice and Mr. Justice Blackmun join, concurring in the judgment.

. . .

The Court's extensive reliance on *Hanson* and *Street* requires it to rule that there is no constitutional distinction between what the government can require of its own employees and what it can permit private employers to do. To me the distinction is fundamental. . . .

. . .

. . . Under First Amendment principles that have become settled since *Hanson* and *Street* were decided, it is now clear, first, that *any* withholding of financial support for a public-sector union is within the protection of the First Amendment; and, second, that the State should bear the burden of proving that any union dues or fees that it requires of nonunion employees are needed to serve paramount governmental interests.

. . .

. . . I would adhere to established First Amendment principles and require the State to come forward and demonstrate, as to each union expenditure for which it would exact support from minority employees, that the compelled contribution is necessary to serve overriding governmental objectives. This placement of the burden of litigation, not the Court's, gives appropriate protection to First Amendment rights without sacrificing ends of government that may be deemed important.[a]

---

[a] Two cases involving employees who were not members of labor organizations, that were exclusive bargaining representatives for all employees, were decided in 1984. In Ellis v. Brotherhood of R.R. Airline and S.S. Clerks, 104 S.Ct. 1883 (1984), the Court interpreted the Railway Labor Act's union shop provisions to permit use of compulsory dues for union expenses including the costs of national union conventions and the union's monthly magazine. The Court held that, although these expenditures were for activities with "direct communicative content," there was no first amendment violation. "The very nature of the free-rider problem and the governmental interest in overcoming it require that a union have a certain degree of flexibility in its use of compelled funds."

Minnesota State Board for Community Colleges v. Knight, 104 S.Ct. 1058 (1984), involved a challenge to a state statute permitting exclusive bargaining representatives for state employees. As applied to faculty in the community college system, statewide and campus "meet and confer" sessions on a wide variety of governance issues were conducted only with faculty who were members of the bargaining representative. The Court conceded that nonmembers had an incentive to join, to have a voice in those sessions. But there was no first amendment violation, since that pressure was "no different from the pressure to join a majority party that persons in the minority always feel."

CONSOLIDATED EDISON CO. v. NEW YORK PUBLIC SERVICE COMMISSION

447 U.S. 530, 100 S.Ct. 2326, 65 L.Ed.2d 319 (1980).

[The report in this case appears, supra at p. 1244.]

C. POLITICAL ASSOCIATION

---

1. CHOOSING AND ELECTING CANDIDATES FOR PUBLIC OFFICE

POLITICAL ASSOCIATION AND SELECTION OF DELEGATES TO MAJOR NATIONAL PARTY CONVENTIONS

At one extreme, the activities of major political parties in candidate selection may be so influential in the election process that the activity will not be viewed as "private" political association at all. As the White Primary Cases demonstrate, a formally private political group that uniformly dictates the choice of the winning candidate performs a public function, and its freedom to bar participation in its election processes is limited by the fourteenth and fifteenth amendments. (See *supra,* p. 967). Even where political parties' candidate selection processes are not themselves "state action" for constitutional purposes, it is clear that a wide variety of state regulations of parties' delegate and candidate selection processes are justified as an indispensible part of regulation of elections.

Two cases raise the question whether there is a point where state legislation controlling the organization, delegate selection processes, and candidate selection processes, of political parties violates the rights of the party and its members to free political association. Both cases involved rules of the Democratic National Party concerning delegate selection for the Party's national convention. The Party's newly enacted rules, in both cases, conflicted with state law.

In Cousins v. Wigoda, 419 U.S. 477 (1975) the Court reviewed the decision of a state court that Illinois law governed seating of a state delegation at the 1972 Democratic National Convention. Illinois law was in conflict with party rules regarding, inter alia, inclusion of minorities, women, and young people, in the delegation. The Court decided that the Illinois law was unconstitutional. The Party's associational rights included the right to identify the people who comprised the Party and, subsidiary to that, the right to determine seating at the Convention. Illinois' interest in controlling electoral processes did not justify its insistence that the Convention seat the delegation chosen according to state law.

Primary elections, however, play an increasing role in the delegate selection process for major national party conventions. Democratic Party of United States v. La Follette, 450 U.S. 107 (1981), demonstrates that it is not easy to distinguish state interests in regulating primary elections and party interests in controlling delegate selection. Wisconsin's "open primary" law, enacted in 1903 and first applied to presidential primaries in 1906, allows voters to participate in any party's primary without regard to party affiliation and without public declaration of party preference. Delegates to party conventions are not chosen by the primary vote, but are bound to vote at national conventions in accord with the election results. In an action that was aimed at minimizing the cross-over voting in Wisconsin primaries, the National Democratic Party enacted a rule that participation in the delegate selection process for the 1980 Convention would be restricted to voters "who publicly declare their party preference." The Court held, 6–3, that Wisconsin could not compel the

National Party to seat a delegation bound, under state law, to vote for candidates according to the results of the open primary.

Justice Stewart's opinion for the Court conceded that Wisconsin could conduct an open primary. He said:

"The State has a substantial interest in the manner in which its elections are conducted, and the National Party has a substantial interest in the manner in which the delegates to its National Convention are selected. But these interests are not incompatible, and to the limited extent they clash in this case, both interests can be preserved. The National Party rules do not forbid Wisconsin from conducting an open primary. But if Wisconsin does open its primary, it cannot require that Wisconsin delegates to the National Party Convention vote there in accordance with the primary results, if to do so would violate Party rules. Since the Wisconsin Supreme Court has declared that the National Party cannot disqualify delegates who are bound to vote in accordance with the results of the Wisconsin open primary, its judgment is reversed."

Justice Powell's dissent (joined by Justices Blackmun and Rehnquist) characterized Wisconsin's law as directed to the conduct of the presidential preference primary, and only "indirectly" to the selection of delegates. Wisconsin's interest in open participation in primary elections, compared to the Party's minimal interest in requiring voters to formally identify with the Party before voting, justified that "indirect" infringement in requiring delegates to vote according to the primary results. Because national parties are not organized around the achievement of defined ideological goals, he noted that neither major party had ever sought to exclude participation by those with differing views. Justice Powell concluded:

"The history of state regulation of the major political parties suggests a continuing accommodation of the interests of the parties with those of the States and their citizens. In the process, 'the States have evolved comprehensive, and in many respects complex, election codes regulating in most substantial ways, with respect to both federal and state elections, the time, place, and manner of holding primary and general elections, the registration and qualifications of voters, and the selection and qualification of candidates.' Storer v. Brown, 415 U.S. 724, 730 (1974). Today, the Court departs from this process of accommodation. It does so, it seems to me, by upholding a First Amendment claim by one of the two major parties without any serious inquiry into the extent of the burden on associational freedoms and without due consideration of the countervailing state interests."

STORER v. BROWN

415 U.S. 724, 94 S.Ct. 1274, 39 L.Ed.2d 714 (1974).

Mr. Justice White delivered the opinion of the Court.

. . .

[Section 6830(d) of the California Election Code forbids ballot position to an independent candidate if he had a registered affiliation with a qualified political party at any time within one year prior to the immediately preceding primary election. A challenge brought by candidates who had been denied ballot status because of this provision was rejected by the district court and the Supreme Court affirmed.]

I.

We affirm the judgment of the District Court insofar as it refused relief to Storer and Frommhagen with respect to the 1972 general election. Both men were registered Democrats until early in 1972, Storer until January and Frommhagen until March of that year. This affiliation with a qualified political party within a year prior to the 1972 primary disqualified both men under § 6830(d); and in our view the State of California was not forbidden by the United States Constitution from enforcing that provision against these men.

In Williams v. Rhodes, 393 U.S. 23 (1968), the Court held that although the citizens of a State are free to associate with one of the two major political parties, to participate in the nomination of their chosen party's candidates for public office and then to cast their ballots in the general election, the State must also provide feasible means for other political parties and other candidates to appear on the general election ballot. . . .

In challenging § 6830(d), appellants rely on Williams v. Rhodes and assert that under this and subsequent cases dealing with exclusionary voting and candidate qualifications, e.g., Dunn v. Blumstein, 405 U.S. 330 (1972); Bullock v. Carter, 405 U.S. 134 (1972); Kramer v. Union Free School District No. 15, 395 U.S. 621 (1969), substantial burdens on the right to vote or to associate for political purposes are constitutionally suspect and invalid under the First and Fourteenth Amendments and under the Equal Protection Clause unless essential to serve a compelling state interest. These cases, however, do not necessarily condemn § 6830(d). It has never been suggested that the *Williams-Kramer-Dunn* rule automatically invalidates every substantial restriction on the right to vote or to associate. Nor could this be the case under our Constitution where the States are given the initial task of determining the qualifications of voters who will elect members of Congress. Art. I, § 2, cl. 1. Also Art. I, § 4, cl. 1, authorizes the States to prescribe "[t]he Times, Places and Manner of holding Elections for Senators and Representatives." Moreover, as a practical matter, there must be a substantial regulation of elections if they are to be fair and honest and if some sort of order, rather than chaos, is to accompany the democratic processes. In any event, the States have evolved comprehensive and in many respects complex election codes regulating in most substantial ways, with respect to both federal and state elections, the time, place, and manner of holding primary and general elections, the registration and qualifications of voters and the selection and qualification of candidates.

It is very unlikely that all or even a large portion of the state election laws would fail to pass muster under our cases; and the rule fashioned by the Court to pass on constitutional challenges to specific provisions of election laws provides no litmus-paper test for separating those restrictions that are valid from those that are invidious under the Equal Protection Clause. The rule is not self-executing and is no substitute for the hard judgments that must be made. Decision in this context, as in others, is very much a "matter of degree," Dunn v. Blumstein, supra, 405 U.S., at 348, very much a matter of "consider[ing] the facts and circumstances behind the law, the interests which the State claims to be protecting, and the interests of those who are disadvantaged by the classification." Williams v. Rhodes, supra, 393 U.S., at 30; Dunn v. Blumstein, supra, 405 U.S., at 335. What the result of this process will be in any specific case may be very difficult to predict with great assurance.

. . . .

Rosario v. Rockefeller, 410 U.S. 752 (1973), is more relevant to the problem before us. That case dealt with a provision that to vote in a party primary the voter must have registered as a party member 30 days prior to the previous general election, a date eight months prior to the presidential primary and 11 months prior to the non-presidential primary. Those failing to meet this deadline, with some exceptions, were barred from voting at either primary. We sustained the provision as "in no sense invidious or arbitrary," id., at 762, because it was "tied to [the] particularized legitimate purpose" of preventing interparty raiding, a matter which bore on "the integrity of the electoral process." Id., at 761–762.

Later the Court struck down similar Illinois provisions aimed at the same evil, where the deadline for changing party registration was 23 months prior to the primary date. Kusper v. Pontikes, 414 U.S. 51 (1973). . . .

. . .

Against this pattern of decision, we have no hesitation in sustaining § 6830(d). . . .

The requirement that the independent candidate not have been affiliated with a political party for a year before the primary is expressive of a general state policy aimed at maintaining the integrity of the various routes to the ballot. It involves no discrimination against independents. Indeed, the independent candidate must be clear of political party affiliations for a year before the primary; the party candidate must not have been registered with another party for a year before he files his declaration, which must be done not less than 83 and not more than 113 days prior to the primary. § 6490.

In Rosario v. Rockefeller, there was an 11-month waiting period for voters who wanted to change parties. Here, a person terminating his affiliation with a political party must wait at least 12 months before he can become a candidate in another party's primary or an independent candidate for public office. The State's interests recognized in *Rosario* are very similar to those that undergird the California waiting period; and the extent of the restriction is not significantly different. It is true that a California candidate who desires to run for office as an independent must anticipate his candidacy substantially in advance of his election campaign, but the required foresight is little more than the possible 11 months examined in *Rosario,* and its direct impact is on the candidate, and not voters. In any event, neither Storer nor Frommhagen is in position to complain that the waiting period is one year, for each of them was affiliated with a qualified party no more than six months prior to the primary. As applied to them, § 6830(d) is valid. . . .

Section 6830(d) . . . protects the direct primary process by refusing to recognize independent candidates who do not make early plans to leave a party and take the alternate course to the ballot. It works against independent candidacies prompted by short-range political goals, pique or personal quarrel. It is also a substantial barrier to a party fielding an "independent" candidate to capture and bleed off votes in the general election that might well go to another party.

A State need not take the course California has, but California apparently believes with the founding fathers that splintered parties and unrestrained factionalism may do significant damage to the fabric of government. See The Federalist, No. 10 (Madison). It appears obvious to us that the one-year disaffiliation provision furthers the State's interest in the stability of its political system. We also consider that interest not only permissible, but compelling and as outweighing the interest the candidate and his supporters may have in making a late rather than an early decision to seek independent ballot status. Nor do we have reason for concluding that the device California chose, § 6830(d), was not an essential part of its overall mechanism to achieve its acceptable goals. As we indicated in *Rosario,* the Constitution does not require the State to choose ineffectual means to achieve its aims. To conclude otherwise might sacrifice the political stability of the system of the State, with profound consequences for the entire citizenry, merely in the interest of particular candidates and their supporters having instantaneous access to the ballot.

We conclude that § 6830(d) is not unconstitutional, and Storer and Frommhagen were properly barred from the ballot as a result of its application.

. . .

. . .

Mr. Justice Brennan, with whom Mr. Justice Douglas and Mr. Justice Marshall concur, dissenting.

The Court's opinion in these cases, and that in American Party of Texas v. White, 415 U.S. 767 (1974), hold—correctly in my view—that the test of the validity of state legislation regulating candidate access to the ballot is whether we can conclude that the legislation, strictly scrutinized, is necessary to further compelling state interests. . . .

I have joined the Court's opinion in American Party of Texas v. White, supra, because I agree that, although the conditions for access to the general election ballot imposed by Texas law burden constitutionally protected rights, nevertheless those laws "are constitutionally valid measures, reasonably taken in pursuit of vital state objectives that cannot be served equally well in significantly less burdensome ways." I dissent, however, from the Court's holding in these cases . . .

. . . [I]n sustaining the validity of § 6830(d), the Court finds compelling the State's interests in preventing splintered parties and unrestricted factionalism and protecting the direct primary system.

But the identification of these compelling state interests, which I accept, does not end the inquiry. There remains the necessity of determining whether these vital state objectives "cannot be served equally well in significantly less burdensome ways." . . .

. . .

I have searched in vain for even the slightest evidence in the records of these cases of any effort on the part of the State to demonstrate the absence of reasonably less burdensome means of achieving its objectives. This crucial failure cannot be remedied by the Court's conjecture that other means "*might* sacrifice the political stability of the system of the State" (emphasis added).

. . .

Moreover, less drastic means—which would not require the State to give appellants "instantaneous access to the ballot"—seem plainly available to achieve California's objectives. First, requiring party disaffiliation 12 months before the primary elections is unreasonable on its face. There is no evidence that splintering and factionalism of political parties will result unless disaffiliation is effected that far in advance of the primaries. To the contrary, whatever threat may exist to party stability is more likely to surface only shortly before the primary, when the identities of the potential file of candidates and issues become known. See Williams v. Rhodes, supra, 393 U.S., at 33 (1968). Thus, the State's interests would be adequately served and the rights of the appellants less burdened if the date when disaffiliation must be effected were set significantly closer to the primaries. Second, the requirement of party disaffiliation could be limited to those independent candidates who actually run in a party primary. Section 6830(d) sweeps far too broadly in its application to potential independent candidates who though registered as affiliated with a recognized party, do not run for the party's nomination. Such an independent candidate plainly poses no threat of utilizing the party machinery to run in the primary, and then declaring independent candidacy, thereby splitting the party. . . .

———

ANDERSON v. CELEBREZZE, 460 U.S. 780 (1983). The Court held that an Ohio statute—requiring independent candidates for President to file statements of candidacy and nominating petitions in March in order to appear on the general election ballot in November—violated the first amendment. An early filing date burdens independent voters and candidates, because it excludes independent candidates who appeal to voters dissatisfied with the choices within the two major parties. Moreover, State restrictions on Presidential election processes, as contrasted to elections for statewide offices, have an impact beyond State borders implicating a "uniquely important national interest." Given modern communications, the early filing deadline did not substantially serve a goal of educating voters concerning candidate qualifications. The early filing requirement did not serve the goal of treating independent candidates equally with party primary candidates, who must declare their candidacy on the same date; the names of the eventual nominees of the major parties will appear on the Ohio general election ballot in November, even if the nominees had not qualified for the Ohio primary. The requirement was not justified, finally, by an interest in political stability; even if the State had an interest in preventing factionalism in the major parties, a political party cannot invoke State powers "to assure monolithic control over its own members and supporters." Justice Rehnquist, joined by Justices White, Powell, and O'Connor, dissented. The dissenters argued that this case was controlled by Storer v. Brown. The State's interest in the stability of the political system should allow denial of ballot access to unsuccessful party candidates who seek to refight party battles by forming an independent candidacy.

2. POLITICAL FUNDRAISING AND EXPENDITURES

BUCKLEY v. VALEO

424 U.S. 1, 96 S.Ct. 612, 46 L.Ed.2d 659 (1976).

Per Curiam.

These appeals present constitutional challenges to the key provisions of the Federal Election Campaign Act of 1971, . . . as amended in 1974. . . .

[A suit was brought in the district court in the District of Columbia pursuant to a special statutory review procedure. The plaintiffs included political candidates, contributors to candidates, party organizations, and other organizations; defendants were the relevant federal officials. A declaration of unconstitutionality and an injunction against enforcement were sought.]

I. CONTRIBUTION AND EXPENDITURE LIMITATIONS

The intricate statutory scheme adopted by Congress to regulate federal election campaigns includes restrictions on political contributions and expenditures that apply broadly to all phases of and all participants in the election process. The major contribution and expenditure limitations in the Act prohibit individuals from contributing more than $25,000 in a single year or more than $1,000 to any single candidate for an election campaign and from spending more than $1,000 a year "relative to a clearly identified candidate." Other provisions restrict a candidate's use of personal and family resources in his campaign and limit the overall amount that can be spent by a candidate in campaigning for federal office.

. . . .

A. General Principles

The Act's contribution and expenditure limitations operate in an area of the most fundamental First Amendment activities. Discussion of public issues and debate on the qualifications of candidates are integral to the operation of the system of government established by our Constitution. . . .

The First Amendment protects political association as well as political expression. . . .

It is with these principles in mind that we consider the primary contentions of the parties with respect to the Act's limitations upon the giving and spending of money in political campaigns. Those conflicting contentions could not more sharply define the basic issues before us. Appellees contend that what the Act regulates is conduct, and that its effect on speech and association is incidental at most. Appellants respond that contributions and expenditures are at the very core of political speech, and that the Act's limitations thus constitute restraints on First Amendment liberty that are both gross and direct.

. . .

We cannot share the view that the present Act's contribution and expenditure limitations are comparable to the restrictions on conduct upheld in *O'Brien*. The expenditure of money simply cannot be equated with such conduct as destruction of a draft card. Some forms of communication made possible by the giving and spending of money involve speech alone, some involve conduct primarily, and some involve a combination of the two. Yet this Court has never suggested that the dependence of a communication on the expenditure of money operates itself to introduce a nonspeech element or to reduce the exacting scrutiny required by the First Amendment. . . .

Nor can the Act's contribution and expenditure limitations be sustained, as some of the parties suggest, by reference to the constitutional principles reflected in such decisions as Cox v. Louisiana, supra, Adderley v. Florida, 385 U.S. 39 (1966), and Kovacs v. Cooper, 336 U.S. 77 (1949). . . . The critical difference between this case and those time, place and manner cases is that the present Act's contribution and expenditure limitations impose direct quantity restrictions on political communication and association by persons, groups, candidates and political parties in addition to any reasonable time, place, and manner regulations otherwise imposed.

A restriction on the amount of money a person or group can spend on political communication during a campaign necessarily reduces the quantity of expression by restricting the number of issues discussed, the depth of their exploration, and the size of the audience reached. This is because virtually every means of communicating ideas in today's mass society requires the expenditure of money. . . .

The expenditure limitations contained in the Act represent substantial rather than merely theoretical restraints on the quantity and diversity of political speech. The $1,000 ceiling on spending "relative to a clearly identified candidate," 18 U.S.C. § 608(e)(1), would appear to exclude all citizens and groups except candidates, political parties and the institutional press from any significant use of the most effective modes of communication. Although the Act's limitations on expenditures by campaign organizations and political parties provide substantially greater room for discussion and debate, they would have required restrictions in the scope of a number of past congressional and Presidential campaigns and would operate to constrain campaigning by candidates who raise sums in excess of the spending ceiling.

By contrast with a limitation upon expenditures for political expression, a limitation upon the amount that any one person or group may contribute to a candidate or political committee entails only a marginal restriction upon the contributor's ability to engage in free communication. A contribution serves as a general expression of support for the candidate and his views, but does not communicate the underlying basis for the support. . . . While contributions may result in political expression if spent by a candidate or an association to present views to the voters, the transformation of contributions into political debate involves speech by someone other than the contributor.

Given the important role of contributions in financing political campaigns, contribution restrictions could have a severe impact on political dialogue if the limitations prevented candidates and political committees from amassing the resources necessary for effective advocacy. There is no indication, however, that the contribution limitations imposed by the Act would have any dramatic adverse effect on the funding of campaigns and political associations. The overall effect of the Act's contribution ceilings is merely to require candidates and political committees to raise funds from a greater number of persons and to compel people who would otherwise contribute amounts greater than the statutory limits to expend such funds on direct political expression, rather than to reduce the total amount of money potentially available to promote political expression.

The Act's contribution and expenditure limitations also impinge on protected associational freedoms. Making a contribution, like joining a political party, serves to affiliate a person with a candidate. In addition, it enables like-minded persons to pool their resources in furtherance of common political goals. The Act's contribution ceilings thus limit one important means of associating with a candidate or committee, but leave the contributor free to become a member of any political association and to assist personally in the association's efforts on behalf of candidates. And the Act's contribution limitations permit associations and candidates to aggregate large sums of money to promote effective advocacy. By contrast, the Act's $1,000 limitation on independent expenditures "relative to a clearly identified candidate" precludes most associations from effectively amplifying the voice of their adherents, the original basis for the recognition of First Amendment protection of the freedom of association. . . .

In sum, although the Act's contribution and expenditure limitations both implicate fundamental First Amendment interests, its expenditure ceilings impose significantly more severe restrictions on protected freedoms of political expression and association than do its limitations on financial contributions.

B.   Contribution Limitations

1.   The $1,000 Limitation on Contributions by Individuals and Groups to Candidates and Authorized Campaign Committees . . .

(a)

As the general discussion in Subpart I–A, supra, indicated, the primary First Amendment problem raised by the Act's contribution limitations is their restriction of one aspect of the contributor's freedom of political association. . . .

The Act's $1,000 contribution limitation focuses precisely on the problem of large campaign contributions—the narrow aspect of political association where the actuality and potential for corruption have been identified—while leaving persons free to engage in independent political expression, to associate actively through volunteering their services, and to assist to a limited but nonetheless substantial extent in supporting candidates and committees with financial resources. Significantly, the Act's contribution limitations in themselves do not undermine to any material degree the potential for robust and effective discussion of candidates and campaign issues by individual citizens, associations, the institutional press, candidates, and political parties.

We find that, under the rigorous standard of review established by our prior decisions, the weighty interests served by restricting the size of financial contributions to political candidates are sufficient to justify the limited effect upon First Amendment freedoms caused by the $1,000 contribution ceiling.
. . .

(c)

Apart from these First Amendment concerns, appellants argue that the contribution limitations work such an invidious discrimination between incumbents and challengers that the statutory provisions must be declared unconstitutional on their face. In considering this contention, it is important at the outset to note that the Act applies the same limitations on contributions to all candidates regardless of their present occupations, ideological views, or party affiliations. Absent record evidence of invidious discrimination against challengers as a class, a court should generally be hesitant to invalidate legislation which on its face imposes evenhanded restrictions. . . .

. . .

The charge of discrimination against minor-party and independent candidates is more troubling, but the record provides no basis for concluding that the Act invidiously disadvantages such candidates. As noted above, the Act on its face treats all candidates equally with regard to contribution limitations. And the restriction would appear to benefit minor-party and independent candidates relative to their major-party opponents because major-party candidates receive far more money in large contributions. Although there is some force to appellants' response that minor-party candidates are primarily concerned with their ability to amass the resources necessary to reach the electorate rather than with their funding position relative to their major-party opponents, the record is virtually devoid of support for the claim that the $1,000 contribution limitation will have a serious effect on the initiation and scope of minor-party and independent candidacies. Moreover, any attempt to exclude minor parties and independents en masse from the Act's contribution limitations overlooks the fact that minor-party candidates may win elective office or have a substantial impact on the outcome of an election.

In view of these considerations, we conclude that the impact of the Act's $1,000 contribution limitation on major-party challengers and on minor-party candidates does not render the provision unconstitutional on its face.

[The Court also upheld the $5,000 limit on contributions by political committees, limitations on volunteers' incidental expenses, and the $25,000 limitation on total contributions during any calendar year.]

C. Expenditure Limitations

The Act's expenditure ceilings impose direct and substantial restraints on the quantity of political speech. . . . It is clear that a primary effect of these expenditure limitations is to restrict the quantity of campaign speech by individuals, groups, and candidates. The restrictions, while neutral as to the ideas expressed, limit political expression "at the core of our electoral process and of the First Amendment freedoms." Williams v. Rhodes, 393 U.S. 23, 32 (1968).

1. The $1,000 Limitation on Expenditures "Relative to a Clearly Identified Candidate"

. . .

[T]he constitutionality of § 608(e)(1) turns on whether the governmental interests advanced in its support satisfy the exacting scrutiny applicable to limitations on core First Amendment rights of political expression.

We find that the governmental interest in preventing corruption and the appearance of corruption is inadequate to justify § 608(e)(1)'s ceiling on independent expenditures. . . .

It is argued, however, that the ancillary governmental interest in equalizing the relative ability of individuals and groups to influence the outcome of elections serves to justify the limitation on express advocacy of the election or defeat of candidates imposed by § 608(e)(1)'s expenditure ceiling. But the concept that government may restrict the speech of some elements of our society in order to enhance the relative voice of others is wholly foreign to the First Amendment . . . The First Amendment's protection against governmental abridgement of free expression cannot properly be made to depend on a person's financial ability to engage in public discussion. . . .

For the reasons stated, we conclude that § 608(e)(1)'s independent expenditure limitation is unconstitutional under the First Amendment.

2. Limitation on Expenditures by Candidates from Personal or Family Resources . . .

The ceiling on personal expenditures by candidates on their own behalf, like the limitations on independent expenditures contained in § 608(e)(1), imposes a substantial restraint on the ability of persons to engage in protected First Amendment expression. . . .

The ancillary interest in equalizing the relative financial resources of candidates competing for elective office, therefore, provides the sole relevant rationale for Section 608(a)'s expenditure ceiling. That interest is clearly not sufficient to justify the provision's infringement of fundamental First Amendment rights. . . .

3. Limitations on Campaign Expenditures

Section 608(c) . . . places limitations on overall campaign expenditures by candidates seeking nomination for election and election to federal office. . . .

No governmental interest that has been suggested is sufficient to justify the restriction on the quantity of political expression imposed by § 608(c)'s campaign expenditure limitations. The major evil associated with rapidly increasing campaign expenditures is the danger of candidate dependence on large contributions. The interest in alleviating the corrupting influence of large contributions is served by the Act's contribution limitations and disclosure provisions rather than by § 608(c)'s campaign expenditure ceilings. . . .

The interest in equalizing the financial resources of candidates competing for federal office is no more convincing a justification for restricting the scope of federal election campaigns. . . .

The campaign expenditure ceilings appear to be designed primarily to serve the governmental interests in reducing the allegedly skyrocketing costs of political campaigns. . . . The First Amendment denies government the power to determine that spending to promote one's political views is wasteful, excessive, or unwise. In the free society ordained by our Constitution it is not the government but the people—individually as citizens and candidates and collectively as associations and political committees—who must retain control over the quantity and range of debate on public issues in a political campaign.

For these reasons we hold that § 608(c) is constitutionally invalid.

In sum, the provisions of the Act that impose a $1,000 limitation on contributions to a single candidate, § 608(b)(1), a $5,000 limitation on contributions by a political committee to a single candidate, § 608(b)(2), and a $25,000 limitation on total contributions by an individual during any calendar year, § 608(b)(3), are constitutionally valid. These limitations along with the disclosure provisions, constitute the Act's primary weapons against the reality or appearance of improper influence stemming from the dependence of candidates on large campaign contributions. The contribution ceilings thus serve the basic governmental interest in safeguarding the integrity of the electoral process without directly impinging upon the rights of individual citizens and candidates to engage in political debate and discussion. By contrast, the First Amendment requires the invalidation of the Act's independent expenditure ceiling, § 608(e)(1), its limitation on a candidate's expenditures from his own personal funds, § 608(a), and its ceilings on overall campaign expenditures, § 608(c). These provisions place substantial and direct restrictions on the ability of candidates, citizens, and associations to engage in protected political expression, restrictions that the First Amendment cannot tolerate.

[Chief Justice Burger and Justice Blackmun dissented from the ruling that the contribution limitations were valid. Justice Marshall dissented from the ruling that the section limiting campaign expenditures from the candidate's personal or family funds was unconstitutional. Justice White dissented from the ruling that the expenditure limitations were invalid.]

CONTRIBUTIONS TO BALLOT MEASURE CAMPAIGNS

The rationale of Buckley v. Valeo, sustaining contribution limitations to *candidates,* was inapplicable to contribution limits in connection with *ballot measures.* In Citizens Against Rent Control/Coalition For Fair Housing v. Berkeley, 454 U.S. 290 (1981), the Court invalidated a city ordinance limiting contributions to committees supporting or opposing ballot measures. The interest in preventing corruption of officials was inapplicable, and an interest in allowing voters to identify those speaking through ballot measure committees was served by disclosure requirements.

POLITICAL ACTION COMMITTEES

In California Medical Association v. Federal Election Commission, 453 U.S. 182 (1981), the Court upheld the $5000 political contribution limitation, as applied to a contribution by the association to its multi-candidate political action committee. The Court rejected the argument that, as applied, the restriction operated as a limit on expenditures rather than contributions. Only five Justices spoke to the merits, four dissenting on jurisdictional grounds. Four of the Justices reaching the merits stated that speech by proxy through an association's contributions to its political action committee was not "entitled to full First Amendment protection." The fifth Justice argued that the limitation should be tested by a "rigorous standard of review" but concluded that it was constitutional under that standard.

Common Cause v. Schmitt, 455 U.S. 129 (1982), did not authoritatively resolve the rationale applicable to the Presidential Election Campaign Fund Act provision limiting expenditures by unauthorized political committees supporting a presidential candidate to $1,000. The Court of Appeals had held the provision unconstitutional. The Supreme Court affirmed, but without opinion by an equally divided vote.

FIRST NATIONAL BANK OF BOSTON v. BELLOTTI

435 U.S. 765, 98 S.Ct. 1407, 55 L.Ed.2d 707 (1978).

Mr. Justice Powell delivered the opinion of the Court.

In sustaining a state criminal statute that forbids certain expenditures by banks and business corporations for the purpose of influencing the vote on referendum proposals, the Massachusetts Supreme Judicial Court held that the First Amendment rights of a corporation are limited to issues that materially affect its business, property, or assets. The court rejected appellants' claim that the statute abridges freedom of speech in violation of the First and Fourteenth Amendments. The issue presented in this context is one of first impression in this Court. We . . . reverse.

I.

The statute at issue, Massachusetts General Laws ch. 55, § 8, prohibits appellants, two national banking associations and three business corporations, from making contributions or expenditures "for the purpose of . . . influencing or affecting the vote on any question submitted to the voters, other than one materially affecting any of the property, business or assets of the corporation." The statute further specifies that "[n]o question submitted to the voters solely concerning the taxation of the income, property or transactions of individuals shall be deemed materially to affect the property, business or assets of the corporation." A corporation that violates § 8 may receive a maximum fine of $50,000; a corporate officer, director, or agent who violates the section may receive a maximum fine of $10,000 or imprisonment for up to one year, or both.

Appellants wanted to spend money to publicize their views on a proposed constitutional amendment that was to be submitted to the voters as a ballot question at a general election on November 2, 1976. The amendment would have permitted the legislature to impose a graduated tax on the income of individuals. After appellee, the Attorney General of Massachusetts, informed appellants that he intended to enforce § 8 against them, they brought this action seeking to have the statute declared unconstitutional. . . .

. . . .

II.

[The Court held that the case was not moot.]

III.

The court below framed the principal question in this case as whether and to what extent corporations have First Amendment rights. We believe that the court posed the wrong question. The Constitution often protects interests broader than those of the party seeking their vindication. The First Amendment, in particular, serves significant societal interests. The proper question therefore is not whether corporations "have" First Amendment rights and, if so, whether they are coextensive with those of natural persons. Instead, the question must be whether § 8 abridges expression that the First Amendment was meant to protect. We hold that it does.

A.

. . . .

The court below . . . held that corporate speech is protected by the First Amendment only when it pertains directly to the corporation's business interests. In deciding whether this novel and restrictive gloss on the First Amendment comports with the Constitution and the precedents of this Court, we need not survey the outer boundaries of the Amendment's protection of corporate speech, or address the abstract question whether corporations have the full measure of rights that individuals enjoy under the First Amendment. The question in this case, simply put, is whether the corporate identity of the speaker deprives this proposed speech of what otherwise would be its clear entitlement to protection. We turn now to that question.

B.

.　.　.

.　.　. [A]ppellee suggests that First Amendment rights generally have been afforded only to corporations engaged in the communications business or through which individuals express themselves, and the court below apparently accepted the "materially affecting" theory as the conceptual common denominator between appellee's position and the precedents of this Court. It is true that the "materially affecting" requirement would have been satisfied in the Court's decisions affording protection to the speech of media corporations and corporations otherwise in the business of communication or entertainment, and to the commercial speech of business corporations. In such cases, the speech would be connected to the corporation's business almost by definition. But the effect on the business of the corporation was not the governing rationale in any of these decisions. None of them mentions, let alone attributes significance to the fact, that the subject of the challenged communication materially affected the corporation's business.

The press cases emphasize the special and constitutionally recognized role of that institution in informing and educating the public, offering criticism, and providing a forum for discussion and debate. But the press does not have a monopoly on either the First Amendment or the ability to enlighten. Similarly, the Court's decisions involving corporations in the business of communication or entertainment are based not only on the role of the First Amendment in fostering individual self-expression but also on its role in affording the public access to discussion, debate, and the dissemination of information and ideas. Even decisions seemingly based exclusively on the individual's right to express himself acknowledge that the expression may contribute to society's edification.

Nor do our recent commercial speech cases lend support to appellee's business interest theory. They illustrate that the First Amendment goes beyond protection of the press and the self-expression of individuals to prohibit government from limiting the stock of information from which members of the public may draw. A commercial advertisement is constitutionally protected not so much because it pertains to the seller's business as because it furthers the societal interest in the "free flow of commercial information."

C.

.　.　.

Section 8 permits a corporation to communicate to the public its views on certain referendum subjects—those materially affecting its business—but not others. It also singles out one kind of ballot question—individual taxation—as a subject about which corporations may never make their ideas public. The legislature has drawn the line between permissible and impermissible speech according to whether there is a sufficient nexus, as defined by the legislature, between the issue presented to the voters and the business interests of the speaker.

In the realm of protected speech, the legislature is constitutionally disqualified from dictating the subjects about which persons may speak and the speakers who may address a public issue. If a legislature may direct business corporations to "stick to business," it also may limit other corporations—religious, charitable, or civic—to their respective "business" when addressing the public. Such power in government to channel the expression of views is unacceptable under the First Amendment. Especially where, as here, the legislature's suppression of speech suggests an attempt to give one side of a debatable public question an advantage in expressing its views to the people, the First Amendment is plainly offended. Yet the State contends that its action is necessitated by governmental interests of the highest order. We next consider these asserted interests.

IV.

. . .

. . . Appellee . . . advances two principal justifications for the prohibition of corporate speech. The first is the State's interest in sustaining the active role of the individual citizen in the electoral process and thereby preventing diminution of the citizen's confidence in government. The second is the interest in protecting the rights of shareholders whose views differ from those expressed by management on behalf of the corporation. However weighty these interests may be in the context of partisan candidate elections, they either are not implicated in this case or are not served at all, or in other than a random manner, by the prohibition in § 8.

A.

Preserving the integrity of the electoral process, preventing corruption, and "sustain[ing] the active, alert responsibility of the individual citizen in a democracy for the wise conduct of government" are interests of the highest importance. Preservation of the individual citizen's confidence in government is equally important.

Appellee advances a number of arguments in support of his view that these interests are endangered by corporate participation in discussion of a referendum issue. They hinge upon the assumption that such participation would exert an undue influence on the outcome of a referendum vote, and—in the end—destroy the confidence of the people in the democratic process and the integrity of government. According to appellee, corporations are wealthy and powerful and their views may drown out other points of view. If appellee's arguments were supported by record or legislative findings that corporate advocacy threatened imminently to undermine democratic processes, thereby denigrating rather than serving First Amendment interests, these arguments would merit our consideration. But there has been no showing that the relative voice of corporations has been overwhelming or even significant in influencing referenda in Massachusetts, or that there has been any threat to the confidence of the citizenry in government.

Nor are appellee's arguments inherently persuasive or supported by the precedents of this Court. Referenda are held on issues, not candidates for public office. The risk of corruption perceived in cases involving candidate elections, simply is not present in a popular vote on a public issue. To be sure, corporate advertising may influence the outcome of the vote; this would be its purpose. But the fact that advocacy may persuade the electorate is hardly a reason to suppress it . . . ..

B.

Finally, the appellee argues that § 8 protects corporate shareholders, an interest that is both legitimate and traditionally within the province of state law. The statute is said to serve this interest by preventing the use of corporate resources in furtherance of views with which some shareholders may disagree. This purpose is belied, however, by the provisions of the statute, which are both under- and over-inclusive.

The under-inclusiveness of the statute is self-evident. Corporate expenditures with respect to a referendum are prohibited, while corporate activity with respect to the passage or defeat of legislation is permitted, even though corporations may engage in lobbying more often than they take positions on ballot questions submitted to the voters. Nor does § 8 prohibit a corporation from expressing its views, by the expenditure of corporate funds, on any public issue until it becomes the subject of a referendum, though the displeasure of disapproving shareholders is unlikely to be any less.

The fact that a particular kind of ballot question has been singled out for special treatment undermines the likelihood of a genuine state interest in protecting shareholders. It suggests instead that the legislature may have been concerned with silencing corporations on a particular subject. Indeed, appellee has conceded that "the legislative and judicial history of the statute indicates . . . that the second crime was 'tailor-made' to prohibit corporate campaign contributions to oppose a graduated income tax amendment."

Nor is the fact that § 8 is limited to banks and business corporations without relevance. Excluded from its provisions and criminal sanctions are entities or organized groups in which numbers of persons may hold an interest or membership, and which often have resources comparable to those of large corporations. Minorities in such groups or entities may have interests with respect to institutional speech quite comparable to those of minority shareholders in a corporation. Thus the exclusion of Massachusetts business trusts, real estate investment trusts, labor unions, and other associations undermines the plausibility of the State's purported concern for the persons who happen to be shareholders in the banks and corporations covered by § 8.

The over-inclusiveness of the statute is demonstrated by the fact that § 8 would prohibit a corporation from supporting or opposing a referendum proposal even if its shareholders unanimously authorized the contribution or expenditure. Ultimately shareholders may decide, through the procedures of corporate democracy, whether their corporation should engage in debate on public issues.[34] Acting through their power to elect the board of directors or to insist upon protective provisions in the corporation's charter, shareholders normally are presumed competent to protect their own interests. In addition to intracorporate remedies, minority shareholders generally have access to the judicial remedy of a derivative suit to challenge corporate disbursements alleged to have been made for improper corporate purposes or merely to further the personal interests of management.

Assuming, *arguendo,* that protection of shareholders is a "compelling" interest under the circumstances of this case, we find "no substantially relevant correlation between the governmental interest asserted and the State's effort" to prohibit appellants from speaking.

---

[34] . . . *Street* and *Abood* are irrelevant to the question presented in this case. . . .

The critical distinction here is that no shareholder has been "compelled" to contribute anything. Apart from the fact, noted by the dissent, that compulsion by the State is wholly absent, the shareholder invests in a corporation of his own volition and is free to withdraw his investment at any time and for any reason. . . .

V.

Because that portion of § 8 challenged by appellants prohibits protected speech in a manner unjustified by a compelling state interest, it must be invalidated. The judgment of the Supreme Judicial Court is reversed.

[A concurring opinion by Chief Justice Burger is omitted. Portions of his opinion appear infra at p. 1357.]

Mr. Justice White, with whom Mr. Justice Brennan and Mr. Justice Marshall join, dissenting.

The Massachusetts statute challenged here forbids the use of corporate funds to publish views about referenda issues having no material effect on the business, property or assets of the corporation. . . . I do not suggest for a moment that the First Amendment requires a State to forbid such use of corporate funds, but I do strongly disagree that the First Amendment forbids state interference with managerial decisions of this kind.

By holding that Massachusetts may not prohibit corporate expenditures or contributions made in connection with referenda involving issues having no material connection with the corporate business, the Court not only invalidates a statute which has been on the books in one form or another for many years, but also casts considerable doubt upon the constitutionality of legislation passed by some 31 States restricting corporate political activity, as well as upon the Federal Corrupt Practices Act, 2 U.S.C. § 441(b). The Court's fundamental error is its failure to realize that the state regulatory interests in terms of which the alleged curtailment of First Amendment rights accomplished by the statute must be evaluated are themselves derived from the First Amendment. The question posed by this case, as approached by the Court, is whether the State has struck the best possible balance, i.e., the one which it would have chosen, between competing First Amendment interests. Although in my view the choice made by the State would survive even the most exacting scrutiny, perhaps a rational argument might be made to the contrary. What is inexplicable, is for the Court to substitute its judgment as to the proper balance for that of Massachusetts where the State has passed legislation reasonably designed to further First Amendment interests in the context of the political arena where the expertise of legislators is at its peak and that of judges is at its very lowest. Moreover, the result reached today in critical respects marks a drastic departure from the Court's prior decisions which have protected against governmental infringement the very First Amendment interests which the Court now deems inadequate to justify the Massachusetts statute.

I.

There is now little doubt that corporate communications come within the scope of the First Amendment. This, however, is merely the starting point of analysis, because an examination of the First Amendment values corporate expression furthers and the threat to the functioning of a free society it is capable of posing reveals that it is not fungible with communications emanating from individuals and is subject to restrictions which individual expression is not. Indeed, what some have considered to be the principal function of the First Amendment, the use of communication as a means of self-expression, self-realization and self-fulfillment, is not at all furthered by corporate speech.

. . .

. . .

I recognize that there may be certain communications undertaken by corporations which could not be restricted without impinging seriously upon the right to receive information. In the absence of advertising and similar promotional activities, for example, the ability of consumers to obtain information relating to products manufactured by corporations would be significantly impeded. There is also a need for employees, customers, and shareholders of corporations to be able to receive communications about matters relating to the functioning of corporations. Such communications are clearly desired by all investors and may well be viewed as an associational form of self-expression. Moreover, it is unlikely that such information would be disseminated by sources other than corporations. It is for such reasons that the Court has extended a certain degree of First Amendment protection to activities of this kind. None of these considerations, however, are implicated by a prohibition upon corporate expenditures relating to referenda concerning questions of general public concern having no connection with corporate business affairs.

. . .

. . . Massachusetts could permissibly conclude that not to impose limits upon the political activities of corporations would have placed it in a position of departing from neutrality and indirectly assisting the propagation of corporate views because of the advantages its laws give to the corporate acquisition of funds to finance such activities. Such expenditures may be viewed as seriously threatening the role of the First Amendment as a guarantor of a free marketplace of ideas. Ordinarily, the expenditure of funds to promote political causes may be assumed to bear some relation to the fervency with which they are held. Corporate political expression, however, is not only divorced from the convictions of individual corporate shareholders, but also, because of the ease with which corporations are permitted to accumulate capital, bears no relation to the conviction with which the ideas expressed are held by the communicator.

. . .

This Nation has for many years recognized the need for measures designed to prevent corporate domination of the political process. The Corrupt Practices Act, first enacted in 1907, has consistently barred corporate contributions in connection with federal elections. This Court has repeatedly recognized that one of the principal purposes of this prohibition is "to avoid the deleterious influences on federal elections resulting from the use of money by those who exercise control over large aggregations of capital." Although this Court has never adjudicated the constitutionality of the Act, there is no suggestion in its cases construing it, cited supra, that this purpose is in any sense illegitimate or deserving of other than the utmost respect; indeed, the thrust of its opinions, until today, has been to the contrary.

II.

There is an additional overriding interest related to the prevention of corporate domination which is substantially advanced by Massachusetts' restrictions upon corporate contributions: assuring that shareholders are not compelled to support and financially further beliefs with which they disagree where, as is the case here, the issue involved does not materially affect the business, property, or other affairs of the corporation. The State has not interfered with the prerogatives of corporate management to communicate about matters that have material impact on the business affairs entrusted to them, however much individual stockholders may disagree on economic or ideological grounds. Nor has the State forbidden management from formulating and circulating its views at its own expense or at the expense of others, even where the subject at issue is irrelevant to corporate business affairs. But Massachusetts *has* chosen to forbid corporate management from spending corporate funds in referenda elections absent some demonstrable effect of the issue on the economic life of the company. In short, corporate management may not use corporate monies to promote what does not further corporate affairs but in the last analysis are the purely personal views of the management, individually or as a group.

This is not only a policy which a State may adopt consistent with the First Amendment but one which protects the very freedoms that this Court has held to be guaranteed by the First Amendment. . . . Last Term, in Abood v. Detroit Board of Education, 431 U.S. 209 (1977), we confronted these constitutional questions and held that, a State may not, even indirectly, require an individual to contribute to the support of an ideological cause he may oppose as a condition of employment. . . .

Presumably, unlike the situations presented by *Street* and *Abood,* the use of funds invested by shareholders with opposing views by Massachusetts corporations in connection with referenda or elections would not constitute state action and, consequently, not violate the First Amendment. Until now, however, the States have always been free to adopt measures designed to further rights protected by the Constitution even when not compelled to do so. It could hardly be plausibly contended that just because Massachusetts' regulation of corporations is less extensive than Michigan's regulation of labor-management relations, Massachusetts may not constitutionally prohibit the very evil which Michigan may not constitutionally permit. Yet this is precisely what the Court today holds. . . .

The Court assumes that the interest in preventing the use of corporate resources in furtherance of views which are irrelevant to the corporate business and with which some shareholders may disagree is a compelling one, but concludes that the Massachusetts statute is nevertheless invalid because the State has failed to adopt the means best suited, in its opinion, for achieving this end. It proposes that the aggrieved shareholder assert his interest in preventing the expenditure of funds for nonbusiness causes he finds unconscionable through the channels provided by "corporate democracy" and purports to be mystified as to "why the dissenting shareholder's wishes are entitled to such greater solicitude in this context than in many others where equally important corporate decisions are made by management or by a predetermined percentage of the shareholders." It should be obvious that the alternative means upon the adequacy of which the majority is willing to predicate a constitutional adjudication is no more able to satisfy the State's interest than a ruling in *Street* and *Abood* leaving aggrieved employees to the remedies provided by union democracy would have satisfied the demands of the First Amendment. . . .

. . .

The necessity of prohibiting corporate political expenditures in order to prevent the use of corporate funds for purposes with which shareholders may disagree is not a unique perception of Massachusetts. This Court has repeatedly recognized that one of the purposes of the Corrupt Practices Act was to prevent the use of corporate or union funds for political purposes without the consent of the shareholders or union members and to protect minority interests from domination by corporate or union leadership. . . .

In my view, the interests in protecting a system of freedom of expression, set forth supra, are sufficient to justify any incremental curtailment in the volume of expression which the Massachusetts statute might produce. . . .

. . .

[A dissenting opinion by Justice Rehnquist is omitted.]

FEDERAL ELECTION COMMISSION v. NATIONAL RIGHT TO WORK COMMITTEE, 459 U.S. 197 (1982). The 1971 Federal Election Campaign Act of 1971 forbids corporations and labor unions from making contributions and expenditures in connection with federal elections. An exception permits these organizations to establish "separate segregated funds" for political purposes, subject to important restrictions. The restriction at issue in this case was a provision that a corporation without capital stock may solicit contributions to a fund it has established only from "members" of the corporation. The Court interpreted this provision to prohibit the Committee, a nonprofit corporation, from soliciting contributions to a fund to receive and make contributions on behalf of federal candidates. The Court concluded that its construction of the Act did not violate the First Amendment. Pointing to the long history of federal legislation forbidding corporation and union contributions to candidates for federal office, the Court accepted Congress' judgment that the prohibition prevented "both the actual corruption threatened by large financial contributions and the eroding of public confidence in the electoral process through the appearance of corruption." The statute could be applied to solicitation by "corporations and labor unions without great financial resources, as well as those more favorably situated" because the Court would not "second guess a legislative determination as to the need for prophylactic measures where corruption is the evil feared." In a footnote, the Court distinguished First National Bank of Boston v. Bellotti, as dealing with a prohibition of corporate contributions to a referendum measure rather than a candidate.

SECTION 4. COMPELLED DISCLOSURE OF BELIEFS AND ASSOCIATIONS

A. REGISTRATION AND REPORTING REQUIREMENTS

NAACP v. ALABAMA

357 U.S. 449, 78 S.Ct. 1163, 2 L.Ed.2d 1488 (1958).

[The report in this case appears, supra at p. 1273.]

NOTE

In New York ex rel. Bryant v. Zimmerman, 278 U.S. 63 (1928), the Court sustained a New York law, which required public registration of the membership lists of associations which demanded an oath as a condition of membership, as applied to a local chapter of the Ku Klux Klan. In his opinion in NAACP v. Alabama, Justice Harlan did not overrule that case, but distinguished it as "based on the particular character of the Klan's activities, involving acts of unlawful intimidation and violence, which the Court assumed was before the state legislature when it enacted the statute, and of which the Court itself took judicial notice."

ANTI–COMMUNIST LEGISLATION OF THE FIFTIES

(1) **Internal Security Act of 1950.** Deeming the Smith Act insufficient protection to national security against the Communist movement, Congress enacted the Internal Security Act of 1950, Title I of which had been developed as the Subversive Activities Control Act.[1] The Act was passed, over President Truman's veto, shortly after the outbreak of hostilities in Korea. It contains

---

[1] 64 Stat. 987 et seq., 50 U.S.C. § 781 et seq.

extensive legislative "findings" of "a world Communist movement . . . whose purpose it is, by treachery, deceit, infiltration . . . and any other means deemed necessary, to establish a Communist totalitarian dictatorship in the countries throughout the world through the medium of a world-wide Communist organization." "Communist organizations" (as defined)[2] were required to register with the Attorney General and file certain information, including lists of officers, members and contributors.[3] If a Communist organization failed to register as required, a Subversive Activities Control Board (SACB), upon petition of the Attorney General, was authorized to issue an order of enforcement. The Communist Party and affiliated organizations were not outlawed as such, but registration as a "Communist organization" or a registration order of the Board could result in important disabilities for the organization and its members. Mail and broadcasts by radio or television sent or sponsored by such an organization were required to carry an identification showing the origin; members might be barred from federal employment, work on defense contracts, the use of passports, and other privileges.

(2) **Communist Control Act of 1954.** In this legislation,[4] Congress found "that the Communist Party of the United States, although purportedly a political party, is in fact an instrumentality of a conspiracy to overthrow the Government of the United States." The findings concluded with the statement: "Therefore, the Communist Party should be outlawed." Although the Act was in response to a growing demand that Communist Party membership be made criminal, the legislation did not go that far. It declared that the Party, or any successor group with the same objectives, should "not be entitled to any of the rights, privileges, and immunities attendant upon legal bodies created under the jurisdiction of the United States or any political subdivision thereof. . . ." It provided further that whoever "knowingly and willfully becomes or remains a member" of the Party should be subject to the disabilities provided in the Internal Security Act of 1950 for a member of a "Communist-action" organization.[5] The Act then listed 13 types of evidence a jury "shall consider" in "determining membership or participation" in the Party, including: (a) the preparation of publications "in behalf of the objectives and purposes of the organization"; and (b) indication by word, action or any other way of "a willingness to carry out in any manner and to any degree the plans, designs, objectives, or purposes of the organization." See *Note, The Communist Control Act of 1954,* 64 Yale L.J. 712 (1955).

COMMUNIST PARTY v. SUBVERSIVE ACTIVITIES CONTROL BOARD, 367 U.S. 1 (1961). The Attorney General brought this proceeding under the Subversive Activities Control Act, seeking an order of the Board that the Communist Party register as a "Communist-Action organization" and file a registration statement pursuant to Section 7 of the Act. After a preliminary round of litigation, the Board issued the order which was affirmed by the Court of Appeals and taken to the Supreme Court by certiorari. The Court sustained the Act. On the question of First Amendment freedoms, the opinion contains the following paragraphs:

[2] "Communist organizations" were classified as "Communist action" and "Communist-front" organizations. An "action" organization was defined as one that is substantially directed or controlled by the foreign government or organization controlling "the world Communist movement" and that operates primarily to advance the objectives of that movement. A "front" organization is one that is substantially directed or controlled by an "action" organization and is primarily operated to aid an "action" organization, a Communist foreign government, or the world Communist movement.

[3] "Front" organizations were not required to list their members.

[4] 68 Stat. 775, 50 U.S.C. § 841 et seq.

[5] See footnote 2, supra.

"No doubt, a governmental regulation which requires registration as a condition upon the exercise of speech may in some circumstances affront the constitutional guarantee of free expression. . . .

"Similarly, we agree that compulsory disclosure of the names of an organization's members may in certain instances infringe constitutionally protected rights of association. . . . But to say this much is only to recognize one of the points of reference from which analysis must begin. . . .

"The present case differs from . . . NAACP [v. Alabama] . . . in the magnitude of the public interests which the registration and disclosure provisions are designed to protect and in the pertinence which registration and disclosure bear to the protection of those interests. Congress itself has expressed in § 2 of the Act both what those interests are and what, in its view, threatens them. On the basis of its detailed investigations Congress has found that there exists a world Communist movement, foreign-controlled, whose purpose it is by whatever means necessary to establish Communist totalitarian dictatorship in the countries throughout the world, and which has already succeeded in supplanting governments in other countries. . . . The purpose of the Subversive Activities Control Act is said to be to prevent the world-wide Communist conspiracy from accomplishing its purpose in this country.

"It is not for the courts to re-examine the validity of these legislative findings and reject them. . . .

"Certainly . . . secrecy of associations and organizations, even among groups concerned exclusively with political processes, may under some circumstances constitute a danger which legislatures do not lack constitutional power to curb. . . .

"Congress, when it enacted the Subversive Activities Control Act, did attempt to cope with precisely such a danger. In light of its legislative findings, based on voluminous evidence collected during years of investigation, we cannot say that that danger is chimerical, or that the registration requirement of § 7 is an ill-adjusted means of dealing with it. In saying this, we are not insensitive to the fact that the public opprobrium and obloquy which may attach to an individual listed with the Attorney General as a member of a Communist-action organization is no less considerable than that with which members of the National Association for the Advancement of Colored People were threatened in *NAACP* and *Bates*. . . . Where the mask of anonymity which an organization's members wear serves the double purpose of protecting them from popular prejudice and of enabling them to cover over a foreign-directed conspiracy, infiltrate into other groups, and enlist the support of persons who would not, if the truth were revealed, lend their support, see § 2(1), (6), (7), it would be a distortion of the First Amendment to hold that it prohibits Congress from removing the mask."

NOTE: THE SEQUEL

After the Supreme Court's 1961 decision in the Communist Party case, the Control Board's registration order became final and certain consequences resulted. One of these consequences followed from Section 6 of the Act which prohibited any member of a "Communist organization," with "knowledge or notice" that a registration order has become final, to make application for, to use, or attempt to use a passport. In Aptheker v. Secretary of State, 378 U.S. 500 (1964), this provision was held "unconstitutional on its face" because it "too broadly and indiscriminately" restricted the right to travel.

The Control Act, in Sections 8(a) and (c) and 13(a), also provides if an organization fails to comply with the Board's final registration order, a member of the organization may be ordered by the Board to register as such and file a registration statement. Such an order was before the Court in Albertson v. Subversive Activities Control Board, 382 U.S. 70 (1965) where the Communist Party members involved claimed the privilege against self-incrimination as a ground for refusing to comply with the order. The claim of privilege was sustained by the Supreme Court without dissent. In 1968 Congress amended the Act by repealing the provisions governing registration of Communist organizations and their members.

A federal statute required the post office department to detain and destroy unsealed mail from foreign countries determined to be "Communist political propaganda" unless the addressee returned a reply card indicating his desire to receive such piece of mail. This requirement was held invalid in Lamont v. Postmaster General, 381 U.S. 301 (1965) because it imposed an unconstitutional condition on the exercise of a First Amendment freedom.

The Subversive Activities Control Board, which had little to do for many years after the decisions discussed above, went out of existence in 1973 when no funds were appropriated to continue it.

BUCKLEY v. VALEO

424 U.S. 1, 96 S.Ct. 612, 46 L.Ed.2d 659 (1976).

Per Curiam.

These appeals present constitutional challenges to the key provisions of the Federal Election Campaign Act of 1971, . . . as amended in 1974. . . .

[A suit was brought against the relevant federal officials in the district court in the District of Columbia pursuant to a special statutory review procedure. The plaintiffs included political candidates, contributors to candidates, party organizations, and other organizations. A declaration of unconstitutionality and an injunction against enforcement were sought. Only the portion of the opinion relating to reporting and disclosure requirements is presented here.]

II.   REPORTING AND DISCLOSURE REQUIREMENTS

. . .

Each political committee is required to register with the Commission, § 433, and to keep detailed records of both contributions and expenditures, § 432(c), (d). These records are required to include the name and address of everyone making a contribution in excess of $10, along with the date and amount of the contribution. If a person's contributions aggregate more than $100, his occupation and principal place of business are also to be included. § 432(c)(d).

. . .

Each committee and each candidate also is required to file quarterly reports. § 434(a). The reports are to contain detailed financial information, including the full name, mailing address, occupation, and principal place of business of each person who has contributed over $100 in a calendar year, as well as the amount and date of the contributions. § 434(b). They are to be made available by the Commission "for public inspection and copying." § 438(a)(4). Every candidate for Federal office is required to designate a "principal campaign committee," which is to receive reports of contributions and expenditures made on the candidate's behalf from other political committees and to compile and file these reports, together with its own statements, with the Commission. § 432(f).

Every individual or group, other than a political committee or candidate, who makes "contributions" or "expenditures" of over $100 in a calendar year "other than by contribution to a political committee or a candidate" is required to file a statement with the Commission.　§ 434(e).　Any violation of these recordkeeping and reporting provisions is punishable by a fine of not more than $1,000 or a prison term of not more than a year, or both.　§ 441(a).

A.　General Principles

Unlike the overall limitations on contributions and expenditures, the disclosure requirements impose no ceiling on campaign-related activities.　But we have repeatedly found that compelled disclosure, in itself, can seriously infringe on privacy of association and belief guaranteed by the First Amendment. . . .

. . . .

The strict test established by NAACP v. Alabama is necessary because compelled disclosure has the potential for substantially infringing the exercise of First Amendment rights.　But we have acknowledged that there are governmental interests sufficiently important to outweigh the possibility of infringement, particularly when the "free functioning of our national institutions" is involved. Communist Party v. Subversive Activities Control Bd., 367 U.S. 1, 97 (1961).

The governmental interests sought to be vindicated by the disclosure requirements are of this magnitude.　They fall into three categories.　First, disclosure provides the electorate with information "as to where political campaign money comes from and how it is spent by the candidate" in order to aid the voters in evaluating those who seek federal office.　It allows voters to place each candidate in the political spectrum more precisely than is often possible solely on the basis of party labels and campaign speeches.　The sources of a candidate's financial support also alert the voter to the interests to which a candidate is most likely to be responsive and thus facilitates predictions of future performance in office.

Second, disclosure requirements deter actual corruption and avoid the appearance of corruption by exposing large contributions and expenditures to the light of publicity.　This exposure may discourage those who would use money for improper purposes either before or after the election.　A public armed with information about a candidate's most generous supporters is better able to detect any post-election special favors that may be given in return.　And, as we recognized in Burroughs v. United States, 290 U.S., at 548, Congress could reasonably conclude that full disclosure during an election campaign tends "to prevent the corrupt use of money to affect elections." . . .

Third, and not least significant, record-keeping, reporting and disclosure requirements are an essential means of gathering the data necessary to detect violations of the contribution limitations described above.

The disclosure requirements, as a general matter, directly serve substantial governmental interests.　In determining whether these interests are sufficient to justify the requirements we must look to the extent of the burden that they place on individual rights.

It is undoubtedly true that public disclosure of contributions to candidates and political parties will deter some individuals who otherwise might contribute. In some instances, disclosure may even expose contributors to harassment or retaliation.　These are not insignificant burdens on individual rights, and they must be weighed carefully against the interests which Congress has sought to promote by this legislation.　In this process, we note and agree with appellants' concession that disclosure requirements—certainly in most applications—appear to be the least restrictive means of curbing the evils of campaign ignorance and corruption that Congress found to exist.　Appellants argue, however, that the balance tips against disclosure when it is required of contributors to certain parties and candidates.　We turn now to this contention.

B.   Application to Minor Parties and Independents

Appellants contend that the Act's requirements are overbroad insofar as they apply to contributions to minor parties and independent candidates because the governmental interest in this information is minimal and the danger of significant infringement on First Amendment rights is greatly increased.

1.   Requisite Factual Showing

. . .

There could well be a case, similar to those before the Court in NAACP v. Alabama and *Bates,* where the threat to the exercise of First Amendment rights is so serious and the state interest furthered by disclosure so insubstantial that the Act's requirements cannot be constitutionally applied. But no appellant in this case has tendered record evidence of the sort proffered in NAACP v. Alabama. Instead, appellants primarily rely on "the clearly articulated fears of individuals, well experienced in the political process." At best they offer the testimony of several minor-party officials that one or two persons refused to make contributions because of the possibility of disclosure. On this record, the substantial public interest in disclosure identified by the legislative history of this Act outweighs the harm generally alleged.

2.   Blanket Exemption . . .

We recognize that unduly strict requirements of proof could impose a heavy burden, but it does not follow that a blanket exemption for minor parties is necessary. Minor parties must be allowed sufficient flexibility in the proof of injury to assure a fair consideration of their claim. The evidence offered need show only a reasonable probability that the compelled disclosure of a party's contributors' names will subject them to threats, harassment or reprisals from either Government officials or private parties. The proof may include, for example, specific evidence of past or present harassment of members due to their associational ties, or of harassment directed against the organization itself. A pattern of threats or specific manifestations of public hostility may be sufficient. New parties that have no history upon which to draw may be able to offer evidence of reprisals and threats directed against individuals or organizations holding similar views.

Where it exists the type of chill and harassment identified in NAACP v. Alabama can be shown. We cannot assume that courts will be insensitive to similar showings when made in future cases. We therefore conclude that a blanket exemption is not required.

C.   Section 434(e)

Section 434(e) requires "[e]very person (other than a political committee or candidate) who makes contributions or expenditures" aggregating over $100 in a calendar year "other than by contribution to a political committee or candidate" to file a statement with the Commission. Unlike the other disclosure provisions, this section does not seek the contribution list of any association. Instead, it requires direct disclosure of what an individual or group contributes or spends.

In considering this provision we must apply the same strict standard of scrutiny, for the right of associational privacy developed in NAACP v. Alabama derives from the rights of the organization's members to advocate their personal points of view in the most effective way. . . .

Unlike § 608(e)(1), § 434(e) as construed bears a sufficient relationship to a substantial governmental interest. As narrowed, § 434(e), like § 608(e)(1), does not reach all partisan discussion for it only requires disclosure of those expenditures that expressly advocate a particular election result. This might have been fatal if the only purpose of § 434(e) were to stem corruption or its appearance by closing a loophole in the general disclosure requirements. But the disclosure provisions, including § 434(e), serve another, informational interest, and even as construed § 434(e) increases the fund of information concerning those who support the candidates. It goes beyond the general disclosure requirements to shed the light of publicity on spending that is unambiguously campaign-related but would not otherwise be reported because it takes the form of independent expenditures or of contributions to an individual or group not itself required to report the names of its contributors. By the same token, it is not fatal that § 434(e) encompasses purely independent expenditures uncoordinated with a particular candidate or his agent. The corruption potential of these expenditures may be significantly different, but the informational interest can be as strong as it is in coordinated spending, for disclosure helps voters to define more of the candidates' constituencies.

Section 434(e), as we have construed it, does not contain the infirmities of the regulations before the Court in Talley v. California, 362 U.S. 60 (1960) and Thomas v. Collins, 323 U.S. 516 (1945). The ordinance found wanting in *Talley* forbade all distribution of handbills that did not contain the name of the printer, author, or manufacturer, and the name of the distributor. The city urged that the ordinance was aimed at identifying those responsible for fraud, false advertising, and libel, but the Court found that it was "in no manner so limited." 362 U.S., at 64. Here, as we have seen, the disclosure requirement is narrowly limited to those situations where the information sought has a substantial connection with the governmental interests sought to be advanced. *Thomas* held unconstitutional a prior restraint in the form of a registration requirement for labor organizers. The Court found the State's interest insufficient to justify the restrictive effect of the statute. The burden imposed by § 434(e) is no prior restraint, but a reasonable and minimally restrictive method of furthering First Amendment values by opening the basic processes of our federal election system to public view.

D. Thresholds

Appellants' third contention, based on alleged overbreadth, is that the monetary thresholds in the record-keeping and reporting provisions lack a substantial nexus with the claimed governmental interests, for the amounts involved are too low even to attract the attention of the candidate, much less have a corrupting influence. . . .

The $10 and $100 thresholds are indeed low. Contributors of relatively small amounts are likely to be especially sensitive to recording or disclosure of their political preferences. These strict requirements may well discourage participation by some citizens in the political process, a result that Congress hardly could have intended. . . . The line is necessarily a judgmental decision, best left in the context of this complex legislation to congressional discretion. We cannot say, on this bare record, that the limits designated are wholly without rationality.

. . .

[Chief Justice Burger dissented from the ruling upholding the "irrationally low ceilings of $10 and $100 for anonymous contributions." Justices White, Blackmun, and Rehnquist concurred in the Court's holding with reference to the reporting and disclosure requirements. Justice Stevens took no part in the decision.]

BROWN v. SOCIALIST WORKERS '74 CAMPAIGN COMMITTEE, 459 U.S. 87 (1982). Ohio requires candidates for political office to report campaign contributions and disbursements. The Court held that the first amendment prohibited enforcement of the disclosure requirements as to candidates of the Socialist Workers Party, which had been the object of harassment by government officials and private parties. Three dissenters (Justices O'Connor, Rehnquist and Stevens) argued that a stronger showing should be necessary to claim exemption from disclosure of campaign disbursements than from disclosure of campaign contributions. The purpose of requiring disclosure of expenditures was to prevent illegal expenditures. Disclosure that a person received expenditures from a minor unpopular party had less deterrent impact than disclosure that one had contributed to it.

B. LEGISLATIVE INVESTIGATIONS

Legislative investigation [1] was not born yesterday for, as one writer has aptly put it, "the history of Congressional investigations is in large part the history of American politics".[2] Almost from the very beginning of the government, Congress has from time to time investigated the operations of the executive branch, but it was not until the financial crisis of the post-Civil War period broke upon the country that the first great test of power arose. Jay Cooke's banking firm failed; it had been a depository of federal funds. In 1876 the House of Representatives authorized a select committee to investigate financial dealings between Cooke and a "real estate pool" on the ostensible theory that the government's interest as a creditor of Cooke's bank had been injured thereby. The committee subpoenaed the manager of the pool, Hallett Kilbourn, who refused to answer questions or produce documents, asserting that the House had no authority to investigate private business. After Kilbourn was cited for contempt and taken into custody,[3] he sued the Speaker of the House, the members of the investigating committee, and the Sergeant-at-Arms for false imprisonment.

Kilbourn won his case in the Supreme Court which held that the House had exceeded its powers. Kilbourn v. Thompson, 103 U.S. 168 (1881). In an opinion by Justice Miller, which from the standpoint of clarity is not one of his best, it is emphasized that the legislative power of investigation is subject to constitutional limitations that the Court will enforce. In language foreshadowing more recent criticism of legislative procedures, the Court asserted that "the investigation which the committee was directed to make was judicial . . . and could only be properly and successfully made by a court of justice." The House was engaged in "a fruitless investigation into the personal affairs of individuals", an investigation "that could result in no valid legislation on the subject" of the inquiry.[4]

The Court's opinion in *Kilbourn* gave scant recognition to the power of Congress to conduct investigations to obtain information for future legislation. However, in McGrain v. Daugherty, 273 U.S. 135 (1927) it was finally recognized that either House has the power "to compel a private individual to

---

[1] Writing on the loyalty investigations was voluminous. Carr, *The House Committee on Un-American Activities* (1952) is devoted to the federal scene. For discussions of activity in the states, see Gellhorn, (Ed.), *The States and Subversion* (1952); Barrett, *The Tenney Committee, Legislative Investigation of Subversive Activities in California* (1951); Chamberlain, *Loyalty and Legislative Action, A Survey of Activity by the New York State Legislature* (1951); Countryman, *Un-American Activities in the State of Washington* (1951).

[2] Taylor, *Grand Inquest, The Story of Congressional Investigations* (1955) p. 32. This book presents the historical background and the legal issues. Barth, *Government by Investigation* (1955) gives less attention to history and the judicial decisions.

[3] In Anderson v. Dunn, 19 U.S. (6 Wheat.) 204 (1821) the Court had sustained the implied power of either House to attach and punish a non-member for contempt of its authority.

[4] Justice Miller's correspondence shows that not even the sharp language of the Kilbourn opinion revealed the depth of his feeling on the subject. See Fairman, *Mr. Justice Miller* (1939), pp. 333–334.

appear before it or one of its committees and give testimony needed to enable it efficiently to exercise a legislative function belonging to it under the Constitution". The extent that this made inroads in the *Kilbourn* holding was indicated by Sinclair v. United States, 279 U.S. 263 (1929) where the Court affirmed the power of the Senate to carry on its investigation of fraudulent leases of government property. The president of the lessee corporation had refused to testify on the ground that the questions related to his private affairs and to matters cognizable only in the courts where they were pending. The Court rejected this argument, aided undoubtedly by the Senate's direction to the investigating committee to ascertain what, if any, additional legislation might be advisable. The Court sustained the Senate's power, in spite of the fact that the information sought might also have been useful in pending suits to recover the property. The Court did say, however, that the power "must be exerted with due regard for the right of witnesses" and "a witness rightfully may refuse to answer where the bounds of the power are exceeded or where the questions asked are not pertinent to the matter under inquiry."

WATKINS v. UNITED STATES, 354 U.S. 178 (1957). Watkins was prosecuted for refusing to answer questions when he was called as a witness before a Subcommittee of the Committee on Un-American Activities of the House of Representatives. He was candid about his own associations, but refused to say whether or not certain persons he knew were or had been members of the Communist Party. When refusing to answer the questions put to him, he claimed the protection of the First Amendment, not the Fifth. He was prosecuted and convicted of violating 2 U.S.C. § 192, which provides: "Every person who having been summoned as a witness by the authority of either House of Congress to give testimony or to produce papers upon any matter under inquiry before either House, or any joint committee established by a joint or concurrent resolution of the two Houses of Congress, or any committee of either House of Congress, wilfully makes default, or who, having appeared, *refuses to answer any question pertinent to the question under inquiry,* shall be deemed guilty of a misdemeanor", punishable by fine and imprisonment. (Emphasis added.)

The opinion of the Court was written by Chief Justice Warren. The Chief Justice first discussed the constitutional scope of the power of Congress to conduct investigations: that power is broad; it is inherent in the legislative process; it encompasses inquiries concerning the administration of existing laws as well as proposed or possibly needed statutes; it includes surveys of defects in our social, economic or political system for the purpose of enabling the Congress to remedy them. But broad as is this power of inquiry, it is not unlimited. There is no general authority to expose the private affairs of individuals. The public is entitled to be informed concerning the workings of its government; but there is no congressional power to expose for the sake of exposure.

Accommodation of the congressional need for particular information with the individual and personal interest in privacy is an arduous and delicate task for any court, the Chief Justice continued. It is not the function of a court to test the motives of the investigating committee members; consequently it must discharge its reviewing functions in other ways.

It is the responsibility of the Congress, in the first instance, to insure that compulsory process is used only in furtherance of a legislative purpose. That requires that the instructions to any investigating committee spell out that group's jurisdiction and purpose with sufficient particularity. Those instructions are embodied in the authorizing resolution. The resolution creating the Un-

American Activities Committee is as unspecific as can be imagined. The Committee is authorized to investigate from time to time the extent, character and diffusion within the United States of "un-American propaganda". An excessively broad charter, like that of this Committee, places the courts in an untenable position if they are to strike a balance between the public need for a particular interrogation and the right of citizens to carry on their affairs free from unnecessary governmental interference.

The function of the Court is also affected by the fact that defendant was prosecuted for refusal to answer "any question pertinent to the question under inquiry". Part of the standard of criminality, therefore, is the pertinency of the questions propounded to the witness. A witness faced with the choice of whether or not to answer questions is entitled to have knowledge of the subject to which the interrogation is deemed pertinent. Neither the authorizing resolution, the action of the full Committee authorizing the creation of the Subcommittee, nor by any statement of the Chairman at the time defendant refused to answer, did so.

The conviction was reversed with instructions that the indictment be dismissed.[a]

BARENBLATT v. UNITED STATES

360 U.S. 109, 79 S.Ct. 1081, 3 L.Ed.2d 1115 (1959).

Mr. Justice Harlan delivered the opinion of the Court.

Once more the Court is required to resolve the conflicting constitutional claims of congressional power and of an individual's right to resist its exercise. . . . The power of inquiry . . . is as penetrating and far-reaching as the potential power to enact and appropriate under the Constitution.

Broad as it is, the power is not, however, without limitations. Since Congress may only investigate into those areas in which it may potentially legislate or appropriate, it cannot inquire into matters which are within the exclusive province of one of the other branches of the Government. Lacking the judicial power given to the Judiciary, it cannot inquire into matters that are exclusively the concern of the Judiciary. Neither can it supplant the Executive in what exclusively belongs to the Executive. And the Congress, in common with all branches of the Government, must exercise its powers subject to the limitations placed by the Constitution on governmental action, more particularly in the context of this case the relevant limitations of the Bill of Rights.

. . .

In the setting of this framework of constitutional history, practice and legal precedents, we turn to the particularities of this case.

We here review petitioner's conviction under 2 U.S.C. § 192, for contempt of Congress, arising from his refusal to answer certain questions put to him by a Subcommittee of the House Committee on Un-American Activities during the course of an inquiry concerning alleged Communist infiltration into the field of education. . . .

Pursuant to a subpoena, and accompanied by counsel, petitioner on June 28, 1954, appeared as a witness before this congressional Subcommittee. After answering a few preliminary questions and testifying that he had been a graduate student and teaching fellow at the University of Michigan from 1947 to 1950 and an instructor in psychology at Vassar College from 1950 to shortly

-----

[a] For other cases, preceding *Barenblatt* see Sweezy v. New Hampshire, 354 U.S. 234 (1957); Uphaus v. Wyman, 360 U.S. 72 (1959).

before his appearance before the Subcommittee, petitioner objected generally to the right of the Subcommittee to inquire into his "political" and "religious" beliefs or any "other personal and private affairs" or "associational activities," upon grounds set forth in a previously prepared memorandum which he was allowed to file with the Subcommittee.

Thereafter petitioner specifically declined to answer each of the following five questions:

"Are you now a member of the Communist Party? [Count One.]

"Have you ever been a member of the Communist Party? [Count Two.]

"Now, you have stated that you knew Francis Crowley. Did you know Francis Crowley as a member of the Communist Party? [Count Three.]

"Were you ever a member of the Haldane Club of the Communist Party while at the University of Michigan? [Count Four.]

"Were you a member while a student of the University of Michigan Council of Arts, Sciences, and Professions?" [Count Five.]

In each instance the grounds of refusal were those set forth in the prepared statement. Petitioner expressly disclaimed reliance upon "the Fifth Amendment."

Following receipt of the Subcommittee's report of these occurrences the House duly certified the matter to the District of Columbia United States Attorney for contempt proceedings. An indictment in five Counts, each embracing one of petitioner's several refusals to answer, ensued. . . . [U]pon conviction under all Counts a general sentence of six months' imprisonment and a fine of $250 was imposed.

Since this sentence was less than the maximum punishment authorized by the statute for conviction under any one Count, the judgment below must be upheld if the conviction upon any of the Counts is sustainable. . . . As we conceive the ultimate issue in this case to be whether petitioner could properly be convicted of contempt for refusing to answer questions relating to his participation in or knowledge of alleged Communist Party activities at educational institutions in this country, we find it unnecessary to consider the validity of his conviction under the Third and Fifth Counts, the only ones involving questions which on their face do not directly relate to such participation or knowledge.
. . . .

The precise constitutional issue confronting us is whether the Subcommittee's inquiry into petitioner's past or present membership in the Communist Party transgressed the provisions of the First Amendment, which of course reach and limit congressional investigations. . . .

The Court's past cases establish sure guides to decision. Undeniably, the First Amendment in some circumstances protects an individual from being compelled to disclose his associational relationships. However, the protections of the First Amendment, unlike a proper claim of the privilege against self-incrimination under the Fifth Amendment, do not afford a witness the right to resist inquiry in all circumstances. Where First Amendment rights are asserted to bar governmental interrogation resolution of the issue always involves a balancing by the courts of the competing private and public interests at stake in the particular circumstances shown. . . .

The first question is whether this investigation was related to a valid legislative purpose, for Congress may not constitutionally require an individual to disclose his political relationships or other private affairs except in relation to such a purpose. . . .

That Congress has wide power to legislate in the field of Communist activity in this country, and to conduct appropriate investigations in aid thereof, is hardly debatable. The existence of such power has never been questioned by this Court, and it is sufficient to say, without particularization, that Congress has enacted or considered in this field a wide range of legislative measures, not a few of which have stemmed from recommendations of the very Committee whose actions have been drawn in question here. In the last analysis this power rests on the right of self-preservation, "the ultimate value of any society," Dennis v. United States, 341 U.S. 494, 509. Justification for its exercise in turn rests on the long and widely accepted view that the tenets of the Communist Party include the ultimate overthrow of the Government of the United States by force and violence, a view which has been given formal expression by the Congress.

. . .

We think that investigatory power in this domain is not to be denied Congress solely because the field of education is involved. . . . Indeed we do not understand petitioner here to suggest that Congress in no circumstances may inquire into Communist activity in the field of education. Rather, his position is in effect that this particular investigation was aimed not at the revolutionary aspects but at the theoretical classroom discussion of Communism.

In our opinion this position rests on a too constricted view of the nature of the investigatory process, and is not supported by a fair assessment of the record before us. An investigation of advocacy of or preparation for overthrow certainly embraces the right to identify a witness as a member of the Communist Party, . . ., and to inquire into the various manifestations of the Party's tenets. The strict requirements of a prosecution under the Smith Act, see Dennis v. United States, supra, and Yates v. United States, 354 U.S. 298, are not the measure of the permissible scope of a congressional investigation into "overthrow," for of necessity the investigatory process must proceed step by step. Nor can it fairly be concluded that this investigation was directed at controlling what is being taught at our universities rather than at overthrow. The statement of the Subcommittee Chairman at the opening of the investigation evinces no such intention, and so far as this record reveals nothing thereafter transpired which would justify our holding that the thrust of the investigation later changed. The record discloses considerable testimony concerning the foreign domination and revolutionary purposes and efforts of the Communist Party. That there was also testimony on the abstract philosophical level does not detract from the dominant theme of this investigation—Communist infiltration furthering the alleged ultimate purpose of overthrow. And certainly the conclusion would not be justified that the questioning of petitioner would have exceeded permissible bounds had he not shut off the Subcommittee at the threshold.

Nor can we accept the further contention that this investigation should not be deemed to have been in furtherance of a legislative purpose because the true objective of the Committee and of the Congress was purely "exposure." So long as Congress acts in pursuance of its constitutional power, the Judiciary lacks authority to intervene on the basis of the motives which spurred the exercise of that power. . . . Having scrutinized this record we cannot say that the unanimous panel of the Court of Appeals which first considered this case was wrong in concluding that "the primary purposes of the inquiry were in aid of legislative processes." 240 F.2d at page 881. . . .

Finally, the record is barren of other factors which in themselves might sometimes lead to the conclusion that the individual interests at stake were not subordinate to those of the state. There is no indication in this record that the Subcommittee was attempting to pillory witnesses. Nor did petitioner's appearance as a witness follow from indiscriminate dragnet procedures, lacking in probable cause for belief that he possessed information which might be helpful to the Subcommittee. And the relevancy of the questions put to him by the Subcommittee is not open to doubt.

We conclude that the balance between the individual and the governmental interests here at stake must be struck in favor of the latter, and that therefore the provisions of the First Amendment have not been offended. . . .

Mr. Justice Black, with whom The Chief Justice and Mr. Justice Douglas concur, dissenting.

. . .

I do not agree that laws directly abridging First Amendment freedoms can be justified by a congressional or judicial balancing process. . . .

. . .

But even assuming what I cannot assume, that some balancing is proper in this case, I feel that the Court after stating the test ignores it completely. At most it balances the right of the Government to preserve itself against Barenblatt's right to refrain from revealing Communist affiliations. Such a balance, however, mistakes the factors to be weighed. In the first place, it completely leaves out the real interest in Barenblatt's silence, the interest of the people as a whole in being able to join organizations, advocate causes and make political "mistakes" without later being subjected to governmental penalties for having dared to think for themselves. . . .

. . . Of course it has always been recognized that members of the Party who, either individually or in combination, commit acts in violation of valid laws can be prosecuted. But the Party as a whole and innocent members of it could not be attainted merely because it had some illegal aims and because some of its members were lawbreakers. . . .

Finally, I think Barenblatt's conviction violates the Constitution because the chief aim, purpose and practice of the House Un-American Activities Committee, as disclosed by its many reports, is to try witnesses and punish them because they are or have been Communists or because they refuse to admit or deny Communist affiliations. The punishment imposed is generally punishment by humiliation and public shame. There is nothing strange or novel about this kind of punishment. It is in fact one of the oldest forms of governmental punishment known to mankind; branding, the pillory, ostracism and subjection to public hatred being but a few examples of it. Nor is there anything strange about a court's reviewing the power of a congressional committee to inflict punishment. In 1880 this Court nullified the action of the House of Representatives in sentencing a witness to jail for failing to answer questions of a congressional committee. Kilbourn v. Thompson, 103 U.S. 168. The Court held that the Committee in its investigation of the Jay Cooke bankruptcy was seeking to exercise judicial power, and this, it emphatically said, no committee could do. It seems to me that the proof that the Un-American Activities Committee is here undertaking a purely judicial function is overwhelming, far stronger, in fact, than it was in the Jay Cooke investigation which, moreover, concerned only business transactions, not freedom of association. . . .

I would reverse this conviction.

Mr. Justice Brennan, dissenting.

I would reverse this conviction. It is sufficient that I state my complete agreement with my Brother Black that no purpose for the investigation of Barenblatt is revealed by the record except exposure purely for the sake of exposure. This is not a purpose to which Barenblatt's rights under the First Amendment can validly be subordinated. An investigation in which the processes of law-making and law-evaluating are submerged entirely in exposure of individual behavior—in adjudication, of a sort, through the exposure process—is outside the constitutional pale of congressional inquiry. . . .

GIBSON v. FLORIDA LEGISLATIVE INVESTIGATING COMMITTEE, 372 U.S. 539 (1963). A state legislative investigating committee ordered the president of the Miami branch of the NAACP to appear before the committee and bring with him records showing the identity of members of and contributors to the state and local NAACP. The reason advanced to support this demand was that the committee was interested in determining whether Communists had infiltrated the NAACP. There was no suggestion that the NAACP was a subversive organization or that its policies or activities were Communist-dominated or influenced. In holding that the president had a first amendment right to refuse to disclose whether persons identified as Communists were members of the NAACP the Court, by a vote of 5 to 4, held that the state had not established a sufficient foundation or nexus to justify the inquiry. It is, the Court held, "an essential prerequisite to the validity of an investigation which intrudes into the area of constitutionally protected rights of speech, press, association and petition that the State convincingly show a substantial relation between the information sought and a subject of overriding and compelling state interest." Referring to earlier cases the Court added:

"Thus, unlike the situation in *Barenblatt* . . . the Committee was not here seeking from the petitioner or the records of which he was custodian any information as to whether he, himself, or even other persons were members of the Communist Party, Communist front or affiliated organizations, or other allegedly subversive groups; instead, the entire thrust of the demands on the petitioner was that he disclose whether other persons were members of the NAACP, itself a concededly legitimate and nonsubversive organization. Compelling such an organization, engaged in the exercise of First and Fourteenth Amendment rights, to disclose its membership presents, under our cases, a question wholly different from compelling the Communist Party to disclose its own membership. Moreover, even to say, as in *Barenblatt*, . . . that it is permissible to inquire into the subject of Communist infiltration of educational or other organizations does not mean that it is permissible to demand or require from such other groups disclosure of their membership by inquiry into their records when such disclosure will seriously inhibit or impair the exercise of constitutional rights and has not itself been demonstrated to bear a crucial relation to a proper governmental interest or to be essential to fulfillment of a proper governmental purpose. The prior holdings that governmental interest in controlling subversion and the particular character of the Communist Party and its objectives outweigh the right of individual Communists to conceal party membership or affiliations by no means require the wholly different conclusion that other groups—concededly legitimate—automatically forfeit their rights to privacy of association simply because the general subject matter of the legislative inquiry is Communist subversion or infiltration. The fact that governmental interest was deemed compelling in *Barenblatt*, . . . and held to support the inquiries there made into membership in the Communist Party does not resolve the issues here, where the challenged questions go to membership in an admittedly lawful organization."

C. INFORMATION REQUESTS AS A CONDITION OF ISSUANCE OF A LICENSE TO PRACTICE A PROFESSION

Introduction. The three cases that follow involve questions about membership in subversive organizations on applications for admission to the bar. Do the varying results turn on the question whether answers to those questions, without further inquiry, would furnish a basis for denial of admission? (The question whether membership in certain organizations would be a constitutional basis for disqualification is addressed more directly in the cases in subsection B of the next section, dealing with loyalty programs. Notice, however, that the question is not absent from the Court's discussion here.

BAIRD v. ARIZONA, 401 U.S. 1 (1971). Sara Baird passed the Arizona Bar examination. In reply to one question on the bar admission questionnaire, she revealed all the organizations with which she had been associated since the age of 16, but she refused to answer another question, No. 27, which asked whether she had ever been a member of the Communist Party or any organization "that advocates overthrow of the United States Government by force or violence." Because of this refusal, she was denied admission to the Arizona Bar. The Bar Committee gave the following justification for insisting on an answer to question 27:

"Unless we are to conclude that one who truly and sincerely *believes* in the overthrow of the United States Government by force and violence is also qualified to practice law in our Arizona courts, then an answer to this question is indeed appropriate. The Committee again emphasizes that a mere answer of 'yes' would not lead to an automatic rejection of the application. It would lead to an investigation and interrogation *as to whether the applicant presently entertains the view* that a violent overthrow of the United States Government is something to be sought after. If the answer to this inquiry was 'yes' then indeed we would reject the application and recommend against admission." [Emphasis added by Justice Black.]

In the Supreme Court, Justice Black's plurality opinion (joined by Justices Douglas, Brennan, and Marshall) said:

". . . Sharp conflicts and close divisions have arisen in this Court concerning the power of States to refuse to permit applicants to practice law in cases where bar examiners have been suspicious about applicants' loyalties and their views on Communism and revolution. This has been an increasingly divisive and bitter issue for some years, especially since Senator Joseph McCarthy from Wisconsin stirred up anti-Communist feelings and fears by his 'investigations' in the early 1950's . . . ."

"The First Amendment's protection of association prohibits a State from excluding a person from a profession or punishing him solely because he is a member of a particular political organization or because he holds certain beliefs. United States v. Robel, 389 U.S. 258, 266 (1967); Keyishian v. Board of Regents, 385 U.S. 589, 607 (1967). Similarly, when a State attempts to make inquiries about a person's beliefs or associations, its power is limited by the First Amendment. Broad and sweeping state inquiries into these protected areas, as Arizona has engaged in here, discourage citizens from exercising rights protected by the Constitution. Shelton v. Tucker, 364 U.S. 479 (1960); Gibson v. Florida Legislative Investigation Committee, 372 U.S. 539 (1963); Cf. Speiser v. Randall, 357 U.S. 513 (1958).

"When a State seeks to inquire about an individual's beliefs and associations a heavy burden lies upon it to show that the inquiry is necessary to protect a legitimate state interest. Gibson v. Florida Legislative Investigation Committee, supra, 372 U.S. at 546. Of course Arizona has a legitimate interest in determining whether petitioner has the qualities of character and the professional competence requisite to the practice of law. But here petitioner has already supplied the committee with extensive personal and professional information to assist its determination. By her answers to questions other than No. 27 and her listing of former employers, law school professors, and other references, she has made available to the committee the information relevant to her fitness to practice law. And whatever justification may be offered, a State may not inquire about a man's views or associations solely for the purpose of withholding a right or benefit because of what he believes.

"Much has been written about the application of the First Amendment to cases where penalties have been imposed on people because of their beliefs. Some of what has been written is reconcilable with what we have said here and some of it is not. Without detailed reference to all prior cases, it is sufficient to say we hold that views and beliefs are immune from bar association inquisitions designed to lay a foundation for barring an applicant from the practice of law. Clearly Arizona has engaged in such questioning here."

Justice Stewart's concurrence said:

"The Court has held that under some circumstances simple inquiry into present or past Communist Party membership of an applicant for admission to the Bar is not as such unconstitutional. Konigsberg v. State Bar, 366 U.S. 36; In re Anastaplo, 366 U.S. 82.

"Question 27, however, goes further and asks applicants whether they have ever belonged to any organization 'that advocates overthrow of the United States Government by force or violence.' Our decisions have made clear that such inquiry must be confined to knowing membership to satisfy the First and Fourteenth Amendments. See, e.g., United States v. Robel, 389 U.S. 258, 265–266; Law Students Civil Rights Research Council v. Wadmond, 401 U.S. 154, 165. It follows from these decisions that mere membership in an organization can never, by itself, be sufficient ground for a State's imposition of civil disabilities or criminal punishment. Such membership can be quite different from knowing membership in an organization advocating the overthrow of the Government by force or violence, on the part of one sharing the specific intent to further the organization's illegal goals. See Scales v. United States, 367 U.S. 203, 228–230; Law Student Civil Rights Research Council v. Wadmond, supra.

"There is a further constitutional infirmity in Arizona's Question 27. The respondent State Bar is the agency entrusted with the administration of the standards for admission to practice law in Arizona. And the respondent's explanation of its purpose in asking the question makes clear that the question must be treated as an inquiry into political beliefs. For the respondent explicitly states that it would recommend denial of admission solely because of an applicant's beliefs that the respondent found objectionable. Cf. *Wadmond,* supra, at 162–163. Yet the First and Fourteenth Amendments bar a State from acting against any person merely because of his beliefs. E.g., West Virginia State Board of Education v. Barnette, 319 U.S. 624, 642; Cantwell v. Connecticut, 310 U.S. 296, 303–304. Cf. Carrington v. Rash, 380 U.S. 89, 94."

Justice Blackmun (joined by Burger, C.J., Harlan, J. and White, J.) filed a dissenting opinion making the following points:

The *Konigsberg* and *Anastaplo* cases have not been expressly overruled and they dictate a decision against Sara Baird.

The fact that Mrs. Baird answered the question calling for a list of her organization memberships since age 16, did not relieve her of the obligation to answer question 27; the two questions were not duplicative, because refusal to answer 27 would place on the Bar Committee the burden of determining which of the listed organizations, if any, was an arm of the Communist Party or advocated violent overthrow of the government.

Question 27 was directed "not at mere belief but at advocacy and at the call to violent action." As explained by the Bar Committee, an affirmative answer would lead to further inquiry as to Mrs. Baird's "expectation actively to support the objective of violent overthrow" and "if her membership is of a nominal character and she does not participate in the advocacy views, there would be no legal basis for refusing a recommendation for admission."

IN RE STOLAR, 401 U.S. 23 (1971).   Martin Stolar, a graduate of the University of Rochester and the New York University Law School, was admitted to the New York Bar in 1968 after giving satisfactory answers to questions regarding his organization memberships, his loyalty to the United States, and his belief in the principles underlying our form of government.   In 1969 he applied for admission to the Ohio Bar and made available to the Ohio authorities the information he had previously given to the New York Bar Committee.   However, he refused to answer the following questions on the Ohio Bar questionnaire:

"12(g).   State whether you have been, or presently are . . . a member of any organization which advocates the overthrow of the government of the United States by force . . ..

"13.   List the names and addresses of all clubs, societies or organizations of which you are or have been a member.

"7.   List the names and addresses of all clubs, societies or organizations of which you are or have become a member since registering as a law student."

Because of his refusal to answer these questions, Stolar was denied admission to the Ohio Bar.

In the Supreme Court, the Justices divided as they had done in the *Baird* case.   The opinion of Justice Black (joined by Douglas, Brennan, and Marshall, JJ.) contains the following statements:

"We deal first with Ohio's demands that petitioner Martin Stolar list all the organizations to which he has belonged since registering as a law student and those of which he has ever been a member . . . .   In our view requiring a Bar applicant to answer these questions is impermissible in light of the First Amendment, as was made clear in Shelton v. Tucker, 364 U.S. 479 (1960).   At issue in *Shelton* was an Arkansas statute that required every state teacher, as a condition of employment, to file an affidavit listing every organization to which he had belonged within the preceding five years.   The Court noted that this requirement impinged upon the teacher's right to freedom of association because it placed 'pressure upon a teacher to avoid any ties which might displease those who control his professional destiny . . . .'   Id., at 486. Similarly here, the listing of an organization considered by committee members to be controversial or 'subversive' is likely to cause delay and extensive interrogation or simply denial of admission to the Bar.   Respondent committee frankly suggests that the listing of an organization which it felt 'espoused illegal aims' would cause it to 'investigate further.'   Law students who know they must survive this screening process before practicing their profession are encouraged to protect their future by shunning unpopular or controversial organizations. Cf. Speiser v. Randall, 357 U.S. 513 (1958).

"The committee suggests its 'listing' question serves a legitimate interest because it needs to know whether an applicant has belonged to an organization which has 'espoused illegal aims' and whether the applicant himself has espoused such aims.   But the First Amendment prohibits Ohio from penalizing an applicant by denying him admission to the Bar solely because of his membership in an organization.   Baird v. State Bar of Arizona, supra; cf. United States v. Robel, 389 U.S. 258, 266 (1967); Keyishian v. Board of Regents, 385 U.S. 589, 607 (1967).   Nor may the State penalize petitioner solely because he personally, as the committee suggests, 'espouses illegal aims.'   See Cantwell v.

Connecticut, 310 U.S. 296, 303–304 (1940); Baird v. State Bar of Arizona, supra.

. . .

"We conclude also that Ohio may not require an applicant for admission to the Bar to state whether he has been or is a 'member of any organization which advocates the overthrow of the government of the United States by force.' As we noted above, the First Amendment prohibits Ohio from penalizing a man solely because he is a member of a particular organization. See also Baird v. State Bar of Arizona, supra. . . ."

Justice Stewart's complete concurring opinion is as follows:

"Ohio's questions 7 and 13 are plainly unconstitutional under Shelton v. Tucker, 364 U.S. 479. In addition, question 12(g) suffers from the same constitutional deficiency as does Arizona's question 27 in Baird v. State Bar of Arizona, 401 U.S. 1. For these reasons I agree that the judgment before us must be reversed."

Justice Blackmun dissented, joined by Burger, C.J., Harlan, J., and White, J. In the course of his opinion, he said:

". . . I may assume, for present purposes, that the general and broadly phrased list-your-organizations inquiries, that is, Questions 13 and 7, are improper and impermissible under the Court's holding, by another five-to-four vote, in Shelton v. Tucker, 364 U.S. 479 (1960), despite the presence of what seems to me to be a somewhat significant difference between nontenured school teachers and about-to-be-licensed attorneys. . . ."

Justice White filed a separate dissenting opinion covering both the *Baird* and *Stolar* cases. His view is stated in the opening paragraph:

"I am quite unable to join the opinions of the Court in these cases. It is my view that the Constitution does not require a State to admit to practice a lawyer who believes in violence and intends to implement that belief in his practice of law and advice to clients. I also believe that the State may ask applicants preliminary questions which will permit further investigation and reasoned, articulated judgment as to whether the applicant will or will not advise lawless conduct as a practicing lawyer. . . ."

LAW STUDENTS RESEARCH COUNCIL v. WADMOND

401 U.S. 154, 91 S.Ct. 720, 27 L.Ed.2d 749 (1971).

Mr. Justice Stewart delivered the opinion of the Court.

. . .

This case involves a broad attack, primarily on First Amendment vagueness and overbreadth grounds, upon this system for screening applicants for admission to the New York Bar. The appellants, plaintiffs in the trial court, are organizations and individuals claiming to represent a class of law students and law graduates similarly situated, seeking or planning to seek admission to practice law in New York. . . .

. . .

The three-judge District Court, although divided on other questions, was unanimous in finding no constitutional infirmity in New York's statutory requirement that applicants for admission to its Bar must possess "the character and general fitness requisite for an attorney and counsellor-at-law." We have no difficulty in affirming this holding. See Konigsberg v. State Bar, 366 U.S. 36, 40–41; Schware v. Board of Bar Examiners, 353 U.S. 232, 247 (Frankfurter, J., concurring). . . .

. . . New York has further standards of eligibility for admission to its Bar. . . . [B]efore he may be finally admitted to practice, an applicant must swear (or affirm) that he will support the Constitutions of the United States and of the State of New York. Reflecting these requirements, Rule 9406 of the New York Civil Practice Law and Rules directs the Committees on Character and Fitness not to certify an applicant for admission "unless he shall furnish satisfactory proof to the effect" that . . . he has complied with the applicable statutes and rules, and "believes in the form of the government of the United States and is loyal to such government."

The . . . constitutional attack is mounted against the requirement of belief "in the form of" and loyalty to the Government of the United States, and upon those parts of the questionnaires directed thereto.

We do not understand the appellants to question the constitutionality of the actual oath an applicant must take before admission to practice. In any event, there can be no doubt of its validity. It merely requires an applicant to swear or affirm that he will "support the constitution of the United States" as well as that of the State of New York. . . .

If all we had before us were the language of Rule 9406, which seems to require an applicant to furnish proof of his belief in the form of the Government of the United States and of his loyalty to the Government, this would be a different case. For the language of the Rule lends itself to a construction that could raise substantial constitutional questions, both as to the burden of proof permissible in such a context under the Due Process Clause of the Fourteenth Amendment, Speiser v. Randall, 357 U.S. 513, and as to the permissible scope of inquiry into an applicant's political beliefs under the First and Fourteenth Amendments, e.g., Baggett v. Bullitt, 377 U.S. 360; Barenblatt v. United States, 360 U.S. 109; . . . But this case comes before us in a significant and unusual posture: the appellees are the very state authorities entrusted with the definitive interpretation of the language of the Rule. We therefore accept their interpretation, however we might construe that language were it left for us to do so. . . . There are three key elements to this construction. First, the Rule places upon applicants no burden of proof. Second, "the form of the government of the United States" and the "government" refer solely to the Constitution, which is all that the oath mentions. Third, "belief" and "loyalty" mean no more than willingness to take the constitutional oath and ability to do so in good faith.

Accepting this construction, we find no constitutional invalidity in Rule 9406. There is "no showing of an intent to penalize political beliefs." Konigsberg v. State Bar, 366 U.S. 36, 54. At the most, the Rule as authoritatively interpreted by the appellees performs only the function of ascertaining that an applicant is not one who "swears to an oath *pro forma* while declaring or manifesting his disagreement with or indifference to the oath." Bond v. Floyd, 385 U.S. 116, 132.

As this case comes to us from the three-judge panel, the questionnaire applicants are asked to complete contains only two numbered questions reflecting the disputed provision of Rule 9406. They are as follows:

"26. (a) Have you ever organized or helped to organize or become a member of any organization or group of persons which, during the period of your membership or association, you knew was advocating or teaching that the government of the United States or any state or any political subdivision thereof should be overthrown or overturned by force, violence, or any unlawful means? If your answer is in the affirmative, state the facts below.

"(b) If your answer to (a) is in the affirmative, did you, during the period of such membership or association, have the specific intent to further the aims of such organization or group of persons to overthrow or overturn the government of the United States or any state or any political subdivision thereof by force, violence or any unlawful means?

"27. (a) Is there any reason why you cannot take and subscribe to an oath or affirmation that you will support the constitutions of the United States and of the State of New York? If there is, please explain.

"(b) Can you conscientiously, and do you, affirm that you are, without any mental reservation, loyal to and ready to support the Constitution of the United States?"

In dealing with these questions, we emphasize again that there has been no showing that any applicant for admission to the New York Bar has been denied admission either because of his answers to these or any similar questions, or because of his refusal to answer them. Necessarily, therefore, we must consider the validity of the questions only on their face, in light of Rule 9406 as construed by the agencies entrusted with its administration.

Question 26 is precisely tailored to conform to the relevant decisions of this Court. Our cases establish that inquiry into associations of the kind referred to is permissible under the limitations carefully observed here. We have held that knowing membership in an organization advocating the overthrow of the Government by force or violence, on the part of one sharing the specific intent to further the organization's illegal goals, may be made criminally punishable. Scales v. United States, 367 U.S. 203, 228–230. It is also well settled that Bar examiners may ask about Communist affiliations as a preliminary to further inquiry into the nature of the association and may exclude an applicant for refusal to answer. Konigsberg v. State Bar, 366 U.S. 36, 46–47. . . . Surely a State is constitutionally entitled to make such an inquiry of an applicant for admission to a profession dedicated to the peaceful and reasoned settlement of disputes between men, and between a man and his government. . . .

As to Question 27, there can hardly be doubt of its constitutional validity in light of our earlier discussion of Rule 9406 and the appellees' construction of that Rule. The question is simply supportive of the appellees' task of ascertaining the good faith with which an applicant can take the constitutional oath. Indeed, the "without any mental reservation" language of part (b) is the same phrase that appears in the oath required of all federal uniformed and civil service personnel. 5 U.S.C. § 3331 (Supp. V. 1970). . . .

Affirmed.

Mr. Justice Black, with whom Mr. Justice Douglas joins, dissenting.

. . .

In my view, the First Amendment absolutely prohibits a State from penalizing a man because of his beliefs. . . . Hence a State cannot require that an applicant's belief in our form of government be established before he can become a lawyer. . . .

I do not think that a State can, consistently with the First Amendment, exclude an applicant because he has belonged to organizations that advocate violent overthrow of the Government, even if his membership was "knowing" and he shared the organization's aims. . . .

. . . .

. . . . In *Baird* and *Stolar* five members of the Court agreed that questions asked by Bar admissions committees were invalid because they inquired about activities protected by the First Amendment. Why then is the same result not required here?

It may be argued, of course, that Question 26 is sufficiently specific under the majority's standard because parts (a) and (b) *taken together* do include a "specific intent" requirement. But the Court's holding permits the knowledge and specific intent elements of Question 26 to be split into two parts. This allows the State to force an applicant to supply information about his associations, which, even under the majority's rationale, are protected by the First Amendment.

But even if Questions 26(a) and 26(b) were combined into one question, this would not satisfy the standards set by the Court in United States v. Robel, 389 U.S. 258 (1967), and Brandenburg v. Ohio, 395 U.S. 444 (1969). . . .

For the foregoing reasons I respectfully dissent from the judgment of the Court.

Mr. Justice Marshall, whom Mr. Justice Brennan joins, dissenting.

. . .

Mr. Justice Harlan, concurring in [Wadmond], and dissenting in [Baird and Stolar].

. . .

While I hope that I am no less sensitive than others on the Court to First Amendment values, I must say that the pervasive supervision over state Bar admission procedures which is now asked of us would work a most extravagent expansion of the current "chilling effects" approach to First Amendment doctrine. Knowing something of the great importance which the New York Bar attaches to the independence of the individual lawyer, I have little doubt but that the candidates involved in *Wadmond* will promptly gain admission to the Bar if they straightforwardly answer the inquiries put to them without further ado. And I should be greatly surprised if the same were not true as to Mrs. Baird and Mr. Stolar in Arizona and Ohio. But if I am mistaken and it should develop that any of these candidates are excluded simply because of unorthodox or unpopular beliefs, it would then be time enough for this Court to intervene.

SECTION 5.   SPEECH AND ASSOCIATION RIGHTS OF GOVERNMENT EMPLOYEES

A.   CONDITIONING GOVERNMENT EMPLOYMENT ON SPEECH AND POLITICAL ACTIVITY

CONNICK v. MYERS

461 U.S. 138, 103 S.Ct. 1684, 75 L.Ed.2d 708 (1983).

Justice White delivered the opinion of the Court.

In Pickering v. Board of Education, 391 U.S. 563 (1968), we stated that a public employee does not relinquish First Amendment rights to comment on matters of public interest by virtue of government employment. We also recognized that the State's interests as an employer in regulating the speech of its employees "differ significantly from those it possesses in connection with regulation of the speech of the citizenry in general." . . . The problem, we thought, was arriving "at a balance between the interests of the [employee], as a citizen, in commenting upon matters of public concern and the interest of the State, as an employer, in promoting the efficiency of the public services it performs through its employees." . . . We return to this problem today and consider whether the First and Fourteenth Amendments prevent the discharge of a state employee for circulating a questionnaire concerning internal office affairs.

I

The respondent, Sheila Myers, was employed as an Assistant District Attorney in New Orleans for five and a half years. She served at the pleasure of petitioner Harry Connick, the District Attorney for Orleans Parish. During this period Myers competently performed her responsibilities of trying criminal cases.

In the early part of October, 1980, Myers was informed that she would be transferred to prosecute cases in a different section of the criminal court. Myers was strongly opposed to the proposed transfer and expressed her view to several of her supervisors, including Connick. Despite her objections, on October 6 Myers was notified that she was being transferred. Myers again spoke with Dennis Waldron, one of the first assistant district attorneys, expressing her reluctance to accept the transfer. A number of other office matters were discussed and Myers later testified that, in response to Waldron's suggestion that her concerns were not shared by others in the office, she informed him that she would do some research on the matter.

That night Myers prepared a questionnaire soliciting the views of her fellow staff members concerning office transfer policy, office morale, the need for a grievance committee, the level of confidence in supervisors, and whether employees felt pressured to work in political campaigns. Early the following morning, Myers typed and copied the questionnaire. She also met with Connick who urged her to accept the transfer. She said she would "consider" it. Connick then left the office. Myers then distributed the questionnaire to 15 assistant district attorneys. Shortly after noon, Dennis Waldron learned that Myers was distributing the survey. He immediately phoned Connick and informed him that Myers was creating a "mini-insurrection" within the office. Connick returned to the office and told Myers that she was being terminated because of her refusal to accept the transfer. She was also told that her distribution of the questionnaire was considered an act of insubordination. Connick particularly objected to the question which inquired whether employees "had confidence in and would rely on the word" of various superiors in the office, and to a question concerning pressure to work in political campaigns which he felt would be damaging if discovered by the press.

Myers filed suit under 42 U.S.C. § 1983, contending that her employment was wrongfully terminated because she had exercised her constitutionally-protected right of free speech. The District Court agreed, ordered Myers reinstated, and awarded backpay, damages, and attorney's fees. . . .

. . . [T]he United States Court of Appeals for the Fifth Circuit . . . affirmed on the basis of the District Court's opinion. . . .

II

For at least 15 years, it has been settled that a state cannot condition public employment on a basis that infringes the employee's constitutionally protected interest in freedom of expression. Keyishian v. Board of Regents, 385 U.S. 589, 605–606 (1967); Pickering v. Board of Education, 391 U.S. 563 (1968); Perry v. Sindermann, 408 U.S. 593, 597 (1972); Branti v. Finkel, 445 U.S. 507, 515–516 (1980). Our task, as we defined it in *Pickering,* is to seek "a balance between the interests of the [employee], as a citizen, in commenting upon matters of public concern and the interest of the State, as an employer, in promoting the efficiency of the public services it performs through its employees." . . . The District Court, and thus the Court of Appeals as well, misapplied our decision in *Pickering* and consequently, in our view, erred in striking the balance for respondent.

A

The District Court got off on the wrong foot in this case by initially finding that, "[t]aken as a whole, the issues presented in the questionnaire relate to the effective functioning of the District Attorney's Office and are matters of public importance and concern." . . . Connick contends at the outset that no balancing of interests is required in this case because Myer's questionnaire concerned only internal office matters and that such speech is not upon a matter of "public concern," as the term was used in *Pickering.* Although we do not agree that Myer's communication in this case was wholly without First Amendment protection, there is much force to Connick's submission. The repeated emphasis in *Pickering* on the right of a public employee "as a citizen, in commenting upon matters of public concern," was not accidental. This language, reiterated in all of *Pickering's* progeny, reflects both the historical evolvement of the rights of public employees, and the common sense realization that government offices could not function if every employment decision became a constitutional matter.

For most of this century, the unchallenged dogma was that a public employee had no right to object to conditions placed upon the terms of employment—including those which restricted the exercise of constitutional rights. The classic formulation of this position was Justice Holmes', who, when sitting on the Supreme Judicial Court of Massachusetts, observed: "A policeman may have a constitutional right to talk politics, but he has no constitutional right to be a policeman." McAuliffe v. Mayor of New Bedford, 155 Mass. 216, 220, 29 N.E. 517, 517 (1892). For many years, Holmes' epigram expressed this Court's law. Adler v. Board of Education, 342 U.S. 485 (1952); Garner v. Board of Public Works, 341 U.S. 716 (1951); United Public Workers v. Mitchell, 330 U.S. 75 (1947); United States v. Wurzbach, 280 U.S. 396 (1930); Ex Parte Curtis, 106 U.S. 371 (1882).

The Court cast new light on the matter in a series of cases arising from the widespread efforts in the 1950s and early 1960s to require public employees, particularly teachers, to swear oaths of loyalty to the state and reveal the groups with which they associated. In Wiemann v. Updegraff, 344 U.S. 183 (1952), the Court held that a State could not require its employees to establish their loyalty by extracting an oath denying past affiliation with Communists. In Cafeteria Workers v. McElroy, 367 U.S. 886 (1961), the Court recognized that the government could not deny employment because of previous membership in a particular party. See also Shelton v. Tucker, 364 U.S. 479, 490 (1960); Torasco v. Watkins, 367 U.S. 488 (1961); Cramp v. Board of Public Instruction, 368 U.S. 278 (1961). By the time Sherbert v. Verner, 374 U.S. 398 (1963), was decided, it was already "too late in the day to doubt that the liberties of religion and expression may be infringed by the denial of or placing of conditions upon a benefit or privilege." Id., at 404. It was therefore no surprise when in Keyishian v. Board of Regents, 385 U.S. 589 (1967), the Court invalidated New York statutes barring employment on the basis of membership in "subversive" organizations, observing that the theory that public employment which may be denied altogether may be subjected to any conditions, regardless of how unreasonable, had been uniformly rejected. Id., at 605–606.

In all of these cases, the precedents in which *Pickering* is rooted, the invalidated statutes and actions sought to suppress the rights of public employees to participate in public affairs. The issue was whether government employees could be prevented or "chilled" by the fear of discharge from joining political parties and other associations that certain public officials might find "subversive." . . .

Pickering v. Board of Education, supra, followed from this understanding of the First Amendment. In *Pickering,* the Court held impermissible under the First Amendment the dismissal of a high school teacher for openly criticizing the Board of Education on its allocation of school funds between athletics and education and its methods of informing taxpayers about the need for additional revenue. Pickering's subject was "a matter of legitimate public concern" upon which "free and open debate is vital to informed decision-making by the electorate." . . .

Our cases following *Pickering* also involved safeguarding speech on matters of public concern. The controversy in Perry v. Sindermann, 408 U.S. 593 (1972), arose from the failure to rehire a teacher in the state college system who had testified before committees of the Texas legislature and had become involved in public disagreement over whether the college should be elevated to four-year status—a change opposed by the Regents. In Mt. Healthy City Board of Ed. v. Doyle, 429 U.S. 274 (1977), a public school teacher was not rehired because, allegedly, he had relayed to a radio station the substance of a memorandum relating to teacher dress and appearance that the school principal had circulated to various teachers. The memorandum was apparently prompted by the view of some in the administration that there was a relationship between teacher appearance and public support for bond issues, and indeed, the radio station promptly announced the adoption of the dress code as a news item. Most recently, in Givhan v. Western Line Consolidated School District, 439 U.S. 410 (1979), we held that First Amendment protection applies when a public employee arranges to communicate privately with his employer rather than to express his views publicly. Although the subject-matter of Mrs. Givhan's statements were not the issue before the Court, it is clear that her statements concerning the school district's allegedly racially discriminatory policies involved a matter of public concern.

Pickering, its antecedents and progeny, lead us to conclude that if Myer's questionnaire cannot be fairly characterized as constituting speech on a matter of public concern, it is unnecessary for us to scrutinize the reasons for her discharge. When employee expression cannot be fairly considered as relating to any matter of political, social, or other concern to the community, government officials should enjoy wide latitude in managing their offices, without intrusive oversight by the judiciary in the name of the First Amendment. Perhaps the government employer's dismissal of the worker may not be fair, but ordinary dismissals from government service which violate no fixed tenure or applicable statute or regulation are not subject to judicial review even if the reasons for the dismissal are alleged to be mistaken or unreasonable. Board of Regents v. Roth, 408 U.S. 564 (1972); Perry v. Sindermann, 408 U.S. 593 (1972); Bishop v. Wood, 426 U.S. 341, 349–350 (1976).

We do not suggest, however, that Myers' speech, even if not touching upon a matter of public concern, is totally beyond the protection of the First Amendment. . . . For example, an employee's false criticism of his employer on grounds not of public concern may be cause for his discharge but would be entitled to the same protection in a libel action accorded an identical statement made by a man on the street. We hold only that when a public employee speaks not as a citizen upon matters of public concern, but instead as an employee upon matters only of personal interest, absent the most unusual circumstances, a federal court is not the appropriate forum in which to review the wisdom of a personnel decision taken by a public agency allegedly in reaction to the employee's behavior. Cf. Bishop v. Wood, 426 U.S. 341, 349–350 (1976). Our responsibility is to ensure that citizens are not deprived of fundamental rights by virtue of working for the government; this does not require a grant of immunity for employee grievances not afforded by the First Amendment to those who do not work for the state.

Whether an employee's speech addresses a matter of public concern must be determined by the content, form, and context of a given statement, as revealed by the whole record. In this case, with but one exception, the questions posed by Myers to her coworkers do not fall under the rubric of matters of "public concern." We view the questions pertaining to the confidence and trust that Myers' coworkers possess in various supervisors, the level of office morale, and the need for a grievance committee as mere extensions of Myers' dispute over her transfer to another section of the criminal court. Unlike the dissent, we do not believe these questions are of public import in evaluating the performance of the District Attorney as an elected official. Myers did not seek to inform the public that the District Attorney's office was not discharging its governmental responsibilities in the investigation and prosecution of criminal cases. Nor did Myers seek to bring to light actual or potential wrongdoing or breach of public trust on the part of Connick and others. Indeed, the questionnaire, if released to the public, would convey no information at all other than the fact that a single employee is upset with the status quo. While discipline and morale in the workplace are related to an agency's efficient performance of its duties, the focus of Myers' questions is not to evaluate the performance of the office but rather to gather ammunition for another round of controversy with her superiors. These questions reflect one employee's dissatisfaction with a transfer and an attempt to turn that displeasure into a cause célèbre.[8]

To presume that all matters which transpire within a government office are of public concern would mean that virtually every remark—and certainly every criticism directed at a public official—would plant the seed of a constitutional case. While as a matter of good judgment, public officials should be receptive to constructive criticism offered by their employees, the First Amendment does not require a public office to be run as a roundtable for employee complaints over internal office affairs.

One question in Myers' questionnaire, however, does touch upon a matter of public concern. Question 11 inquires if assistant district attorneys "ever feel pressured to work in political campaigns on behalf of office supported candidates." We have recently noted that official pressure upon employees to work for political candidates not of the worker's own choice constitutes a coercion of belief in violation of fundamental constitutional rights. Branti v. Finkel, 445 U.S. 507, 515–516 (1980); Elrod v. Burns, 427 U.S. 347 (1976). In addition, there is a demonstrated interest in this country that government service should depend upon meritorious performance rather than political service. CSC v. Letter Carriers, 413 U.S. 548 (1973); United Public Workers v. Mitchell, 330 U.S. 75 (1947). Given this history, we believe it apparent that the issue of whether assistant district attorneys are pressured to work in political campaigns is a matter of interest to the community upon which it is essential that public employees be able to speak out freely without fear of rataliatory dismissal.

B

Because one of the questions in Myers' survey touched upon a matter of public concern, and contributed to her discharge we must determine whether Connick was justified in discharging Myers. Here the District Court again

---

[8] This is not a case like *Givhan*, supra, where an employee speaks out as a citizen on a matter of general concern, not tied to a personal employment dispute, but arranges to do so privately. Mrs. Givhan's right to protest racial discrimination—a matter inherently of public concern—is not forfeited by her choice of a private forum. . . . Here, however, a questionnaire not otherwise of public concern does not attain that status because its subject matter could, in different circumstances, have been the topic of a communication to the public that might be of general interest. . . .

erred in imposing an unduly onerous burden on the state to justify Myers' discharge. The District Court viewed the issue of whether Myers' speech was upon a matter of "public concern" as a threshold inquiry, after which it became the government's burden to "clearly demonstrate" that the speech involved "substantially interfered" with official responsibilities. Yet *Pickering* unmistakably states, and respondent agrees, that the state's burden in justifying a particular discharge varies depending upon the nature of the employee's expression. Although such particularized balancing is difficult, the courts must reach the most appropriate possible balance of the competing interests.

C

The *Pickering* balance requires full consideration of the government's interest in the effective and efficient fulfillment of its responsibilities to the public. . . .

We agree with the District Court that there is no demonstration here that the questionnaire impeded Myers' ability to perform her responsibilities. The District Court was also correct to recognize that "it is important to the efficient and successful operation of the District Attorney's office for Assistants to maintain close working relationships with their superiors." . . . Connick's judgment, and apparently also that of his first assistant Dennis Waldron, who characterized Myers' actions as causing a "mini-insurrection", was that Myers' questionnaire was an act of insubordination which interfered with working relationships. When close working relationships are essential to fulfilling public responsibilities, a wide degree of deference to the employer's judgment is appropriate. Furthermore, we do not see the necessity for an employer to allow events to unfold to the extent that the disruption of the office and the destruction of working relationships is manifest before taking action. We caution that a stronger showing may be necessary if the employee's speech more substantially involved matters of public concern.

. . .

Also relevant is the manner, time, and place in which the questionnaire was distributed. As noted in Givhan v. Western Line Consolidated School Dist., supra, ... "Private expression . . . may in some situations bring additional factors to the *Pickering* calculus. When a government employee personally confronts his immediate superior, the employing agency's institutional efficiency may be threatened not only by the content of the employee's message but also by the manner, time, and place in which it is delivered." Here the questionnaire was prepared, and distributed at the office; the manner of distribution required not only Myers to leave her work but for others to do the same in order that the questionnaire be completed. Although some latitude in when official work is performed is to be allowed when professional employees are involved, and Myers did not violate announced office policy, the fact that Myers, unlike Pickering, exercised her rights to speech at the office supports Connick's fears that the functioning of his office was endangered.

Finally, the context in which the dispute arose is also significant. This is not a case where an employee, out of purely academic interest, circulated a questionnaire so as to obtain useful research. Myers acknowledges that it is no coincidence that the questionnaire followed upon the heels of the transfer notice. When employee speech concerning office policy arises from an employment dispute concerning the very application of that policy to the speaker, additional weight must be given to the supervisor's view that the employee has threatened the authority of the employer to run the office. Although we accept the District Court's factual finding that Myers' reluctance to accede to the transfer order was not a sufficient cause in itself for her dismissal, and thus does not constitute a sufficient defense under Mt. Healthy City Board of Ed. v.

Doyle, 429 U.S. 274 (1977), this does not render irrelevant the fact that the questionnaire emerged after a persistent dispute between Myers and Connick and his deputies over office transfer policy.

III

Myers' questionnaire touched upon matters of public concern in only a most limited sense; her survey, in our view, is most accurately characterized as an employee grievance concerning internal office policy. The limited First Amendment interest involved here does not require that Connick tolerate action which he reasonably believed would disrupt the office, undermine his authority, and destroy close working relationships. Myers' discharge therefore did not offend the First Amendment. We reiterate, however, the caveat we expressed in *Pickering,* . . .: "Because of the enormous variety of fact situations in which critical statements by . . . public employees may be thought by their superiors . . . to furnish grounds for dismissal, we do not deem it either appropriate or feasible to lay down a general standard against which all such statements may be judged."

Our holding today is grounded in our long-standing recognition that the First Amendment's primary aim is the full protection of speech upon issues of public concern, as well as the practical realities involved in the administration of a government office. Although today the balance is struck for the government, this is no defeat for the First Amendment. For it would indeed be a Pyrrhic victory for the great principles of free expression if the Amendment's safeguarding of a public employee's right, as a citizen, to participate in discussions concerning public affairs were confused with the attempt to constitutionalize the employee grievance that we see presented here. The judgment of the Court of Appeals is

Reversed.

Justice Brennan, with whom Justice Marshall, Justice Blackmun, and Justice Stevens join, dissenting.

. . . It is hornbook law . . . that speech about "the manner in which government is operated or should be operated" is an essential part of the communications necessary for self-governance the protection of which was a central purpose of the First Amendment. Mills v. Alabama, 384 U.S. 214, 218 (1966). Because the questionnaire addressed such matters and its distribution did not adversely affect the operations of the District Attorney's Office or interfere with Myers' working relationship with her fellow employees, I dissent.

I

. . .

The Court's decision today is flawed in three respects. First, the Court distorts the balancing analysis required under *Pickering* by suggesting that one factor, the context in which a statement is made, is to be weighed *twice*—first in determining whether an employee's speech addresses a matter of public concern and then in deciding whether the statement adversely affected the government's interest as an employer. Second, in concluding that the effect of respondent's personnel policies on employee morale and the work performance of the District Attorney's Office is not a matter of public concern, the Court impermissibly narrows the class of subjects on which public employees may speak out without fear of retaliatory dismissal. Third, the Court misapplies the *Pickering* balancing test in holding that Myers could constitutionally be dismissed for circulating a questionnaire addressed to at least one subject that *was* "a matter of interest to the community," in the absence of evidence that her conduct disrupted the efficient functioning of the District Attorney's Office.

II

. . .

The Court seeks to distinguish *Givhan* on the ground that speech protesting racial discrimination is "inherently of public concern." Ante, n. 8. In so doing, it suggests that there are two classes of speech of public concern: statements "of public import" because of their content, form and context, and statements that, by virtue of their subject matter, are "inherently of public concern." In my view, however, whether a particular statement by a public employee is addressed to a subject of public concern does not depend on where it was said or why. The First Amendment affords special protection to speech that may inform public debate about how our society is to be governed—regardless of whether it actually becomes the subject of a public controversy.

. . .

III

Although the Court finds most of Myers' questionnaire unrelated to matters of public interest, it does hold that one question—asking whether Assistants felt pressured to work in political campaigns on behalf of office-supported candidates—addressed a matter of public importance and concern. The Court also recognizes that this determination of public interest must weigh heavily in the balancing of competing interests required by *Pickering.* Having gone that far however, the Court misapplies the *Pickering* test and holds—against our previous authorities—that a public employer's mere apprehension that speech will be disruptive justifies suppression of that speech when all the objective evidence suggests that those fears are essentially unfounded.

. . .

Such extreme deference to the employer's judgment is not appropriate when public employees voice critical views concerning the operations of the agency for which they work. . . . In order to protect public employees' First Amendment right to voice critical views on issues of public importance, the courts must make their own appraisal of the effects of the speech in question.

. . .

IV

The Court's decision today inevitably will deter public employees from making critical statements about the manner in which government agencies are operated for fear that doing so will provoke their dismissal. As a result, the public will be deprived of valuable information with which to evaluate the performance of elected officials. Because protecting the dissemination of such information is an essential function of the First Amendment, I dissent.

UNITED STATES CIVIL SERVICE COMMISSION v. NATIONAL ASSOCIATION OF LETTER CARRIERS

413 U.S. 548, 93 S.Ct. 2880, 37 L.Ed.2d 796 (1973).

Mr. Justice White delivered the opinion of the Court.

[Section] 9(a) of the Hatch Act, now codified in 5 U.S.C. § 7324(a)(2), [prohibits] federal employees taking "an active part in political management or in political campaigns," . . . A divided three-judge court sitting in the District of Columbia had held the section unconstitutional. . . . We reverse the judgment of the District Court.

I.

The case began when the National Association of Letter Carriers, six individual federal employees and certain local Democratic and Republican political committees filed a complaint, asserting on behalf of themselves and all federal employees that 5 U.S.C. § 7324(a)(2) was unconstitutional on its face and seeking an injunction against its enforcement.

. . .

II.

As the District Court recognized, the constitutionality of the Hatch Act's ban on taking an active part in political management or political campaigns has been here before. This very prohibition was attacked in [United Public Workers v. Mitchell, 330 U.S. 75 (1947)] . . .

We unhesitatingly reaffirm the *Mitchell* holding that Congress had, and has, the power to prevent Mr. Poole and others like him from holding a party office, working at the polls, and acting as party paymaster for other party workers. An Act of Congress going no farther would in our view unquestionably be valid. So would it be if, in plain and understandable language, the statute forbade activities such as organizing a political party or club; actively participating in fund-raising activities for a partisan candidate or political party; becoming a partisan candidate for, or campaigning for, an elective public office; actively managing the campaign of a partisan candidate for public office; initiating or circulating a partisan nominating petition or soliciting votes for a partisan candidate for public office; or serving as a delegate, alternate or proxy to a political party convention. Our judgment is that neither the First Amendment nor any other provision of the Constitution invalidates a law barring this kind of partisan political conduct by federal employees. . . .

Until now, the judgment of Congress, the Executive and the country appears to have been that partisan political activities by federal employees must be limited if the Government is to operate effectively and fairly, elections are to play their proper part in representative government and employees themselves are to be sufficiently free from improper influences. E.g., 84 Cong.Rec. 9598, 9603; 86 Cong.Rec. 2360, 2621, 2864, 9376. The restrictions so far imposed on federal employees are not aimed at particular parties, groups or points of view, but apply equally to all partisan activities of the type described. They discriminate against no racial, ethnic or religious minorities. Nor do they seek to control political opinions or beliefs, or to interfere with or influence anyone's vote at the polls.

But as the Court held in Pickering v. Board of Education, 391 U.S. 563, 568 (1968), the government has an interest in regulating the conduct and "the speech of its employees that differ[s] significantly from those it possesses in connection with regulation of the speech of the citizenry in general. The problem in any case is to arrive at a balance between the interest of the [employee], as a citizen, in commenting upon matters of public concern and the interest of the [government], as an employer, in promoting the efficiency of the public services it performs through its employees." Although Congress is free to strike a different balance than it has, if it so chooses, we think the balance it has so far struck is sustainable by the obviously important interests sought to be served by the limitations on partisan political activities now contained in the Hatch Act.

. . .

. . . We agree with the basic holding of *Mitchell* that plainly identifiable acts of political management and political campaigning may constitutionally be prohibited on the part of federal employees. Until now this has been the judgment of the lower federal courts, and we do not understand the District Court in this case to have questioned the constitutionality of a law that was specifically limited to prohibiting the conduct in which Mr. Poole in the *Mitchell* case admittedly engaged.

III.

But however constitutional the proscription of identifiable partisan conduct in understandable language may be, the District Court's judgment was that § 7324(a)(2) was both unconstitutionally vague and fatally overbroad. Appellees make the same contentions here, but we cannot agree that the section is unconstitutional on its face for either reason. . . .

Judgment reversed.

Mr. Justice Douglas, with whom Mr. Justice Brennan and Mr. Justice Marshall concur, dissenting. . . .

BRANTI v. FINKEL

445 U.S. 507, 100 S.Ct. 1287, 63 L.Ed.2d 574 (1980).

Mr. Justice Stevens delivered the opinion of the Court.

The question presented is whether the First and Fourteenth Amendments to the Constitution protect an assistant public defender who is satisfactorily performing his job from discharge solely because of his political beliefs.

Respondents, Aaron Finkel and Alan Tabakman, commenced this action in the United States District Court for the Southern District of New York in order to preserve their positions as assistant public defenders in Rockland County, New York. . . .

. . .

Petitioner Branti's predecessor, a Republican, was appointed in 1972 by a Republican-dominated County Legislature. By 1977, control of the legislature had shifted to the Democrats and petitioner, also a Democrat, was appointed to replace the incumbent when his term expired. As soon as petitioner was formally appointed on January 3, 1978, he began executing termination notices for six of the nine assistants then in office. Respondents were among those who were to be terminated. With one possible exception, the nine who were to be appointed or retained were all Democrats and were all selected by Democratic legislators or Democratic town chairmen on a basis that had been determined by the Democratic caucus.

. . .

Having concluded that respondents had been discharged solely because of their political beliefs, the District Court held that those discharges [were not permissible]. . . .

. . .

. . . [T]he Second Circuit, . . . affirmed, ... We . . . affirm.

I.

In Elrod v. Burns [427 U.S. 347] the Court held that the newly elected Democratic sheriff of Cook County, Ill., had violated the constitutional rights of certain noncivil service employees by discharging them "because they did not support and were not members of the Democratic Party and had failed to obtain the sponsorship of one of its leaders." 427 U.S., at 351. That holding was supported by two separate opinions.

Writing for the plurality, Mr. Justice Brennan identified two separate but interrelated reasons supporting the conclusion that the discharges were prohibited by the First and Fourteenth Amendments. First, he analyzed the impact of a political patronage system[7] on freedom of belief and association. Noting that in order to retain their jobs, the sheriff's employees were required to pledge their allegiance to the Democratic party, work for or contribute to the party's candidates, or obtain a Democratic sponsor, he concluded that the inevitable tendency of such a system was to coerce employees into compromising their true beliefs.[8] . . .

Second, apart from the potential impact of patronage dismissals on the formation and expression of opinion, Mr. Justice Brennan also stated that the practice had the effect of imposing an unconstitutional condition on the receipt of a public benefit and therefore came within the rule of cases like Perry v. Sindermann, 408 U.S. 593. . . . that even an employee with no contractual right to retain his job cannot be dismissed for engaging in constitutionally protected speech . . . .

Mr. Justice Stewart's concurring opinion avoided comment on the first branch of Mr. Justice Brennan's analysis, but expressly relied on . . . Perry v. Sindermann . . . .

Petitioner argues that Elrod v. Burns should be read to prohibit only dismissals resulting from an employee's failure to capitulate to political coercion. Thus, he argues that, so long as an employee is not asked to change his political affiliation or to contribute to or work for the party's candidates, he may be dismissed with impunity—even though he would not have been dismissed if he had had the proper political sponsorship and even though the sole reason for dismissing him was to replace him with a person who did have such sponsorship. Such an interpretation would surely emasculate the principles set forth in *Elrod.* While it would perhaps eliminate the more blatant forms of coercion described in *Elrod,* it would not eliminate the coercion of belief that necessarily flows from the knowledge that one must have a sponsor in the dominant party in order to retain one's job. More importantly, petitioner's interpretation would require the Court to repudiate entirely the conclusion of both Mr. Justice Brennan and Mr. Justice Stewart that the First Amendment prohibits the dismissal of a public employee solely because of his private political beliefs.

In sum, there is no requirement that dismissed employees prove that they, or other employees, have been coerced into changing, either actually or ostensibly, their political allegiance. . . .

II.

Both opinions in *Elrod* recognize that party affiliation may be an acceptable requirement for some types of government employment. Thus, if an employ-

---

[7] Mr. Justice Brennan noted that many other practices are included within the definition of a patronage system, including placing supporters in government jobs not made available by political discharges, granting supporters lucrative government contracts, and giving favored wards improved public services. In that case, as in this, however, the only practice at issue was the dismissal of public employees for partisan reasons. . . . In light of the limited nature of the question presented, we have no occasion to address petitioner's argument that there is a compelling governmental interest in maintaining a political sponsorship system for filling vacancies in the public defender's office.

[8] . . .

Mr. Justice Brennan also indicated that a patronage system may affect freedom of belief more indirectly, by distorting the electoral process. Given the increasingly pervasive character of government employment, he concluded that the power to starve political opposition by commanding partisan support, financial and otherwise, may have a significant impact on the formation and expression of political beliefs.

ee's private political beliefs would interfere with the discharge of his public duties, his First Amendment rights may be required to yield to the State's vital interest in maintaining governmental effectiveness and efficiency. . . . In *Elrod,* it was clear that the duties of the employees—the chief deputy of the process division of the sheriff's office, a process server and another employee in that office, and a bailiff and security guard at the Juvenile Court of Cook County—were not of that character, . . .

As Mr. Justice Brennan noted in *Elrod,* it is not always easy to determine whether a position is one in which political affiliation is a legitimate factor to be considered. . . . Under some circumstances, a position may be appropriately considered political even though it is neither confidential nor policymaking in character. As one obvious example, if a State's election laws require that precincts be supervised by two election judges of different parties, a Republican judge could be legitimately discharged solely for changing his party registration. That conclusion would not depend on any finding that the job involved participation in policy decisions or access to confidential information. Rather, it would simply rest on the fact that party membership was essential to the discharge of the employee's governmental responsibilities.

It is equally clear that party affiliation is not necessarily relevant to every policymaking or confidential position. The coach of a state university's football team formulates policy, but no one could seriously claim that Republicans make better coaches than Democrats, or vice versa, no matter which party is in control of the state government. On the other hand, it is equally clear that the governor of a state may appropriately believe that the official duties of various assistants who help him write speeches, explain his views to the press, or communicate with the legislature cannot be performed effectively unless those persons share his political beliefs and party commitments. In sum, the ultimate inquiry is not whether the label "policymaker" or "confidential" fits a particular position; rather, the question is whether the hiring authority can demonstrate that party affiliation is an appropriate requirement for the effective performance of the public office involved.

Having thus framed the issue, it is manifest that the continued employment of an assistant public defender cannot properly be conditioned upon his allegiance to the political party in control of the county government. The primary, if not the only, responsibility of an assistant public defender is to represent individual citizens in controversy with the State.[13] . . .

Thus, whatever policymaking occurs in the public defender's office must relate to the needs of individual clients and not to any partisan political interests. Similarly, although an assistant is bound to obtain access to confidential information arising out of various attorney-client relationships, that information has no bearing whatsoever on partisan political concerns. Under these circumstances, it would undermine, rather than promote, the effective performance of an assistant public defender's office to make his tenure dependent on his allegiance to the dominant political party.

Accordingly, the entry of an injunction against termination of respondents' employment on purely political grounds was appropriate and the judgment of the Court of Appeals is

Affirmed.

Mr. Justice Stewart, dissenting.

I joined the judgment of the Court in Elrod v. Burns, 427 U.S. 347, because it is my view that, under the First and Fourteenth Amendments, "a nonpoli-

---

[13] This is in contrast to the broader public responsibilities of an official such as a prosecutor. We express no opinion as to whether the deputy of such an official could be dismissed on grounds of political party affiliation or loyalty. . . .

cymaking, nonconfidential government employee can[not] be discharged . . . from a job that he is satisfactorily performing upon the sole ground of his political beliefs." . . . That judgment in my opinion does not control the present case for the simple reason that the respondents here clearly are not "nonconfidential" employees.

. . . The analogy to a firm of lawyers in the private sector is a close one, and I can think of few occupational relationships more instinct with the necessity of mutual confidence and trust than that kind of professional association.

I believe that the petitioner, upon his appointment as Public Defender, was not constitutionally compelled to enter such a close professional and necessarily confidential association with the respondents if he did not wish to do so.*

Mr. Justice Powell with whom Mr. Justice Rehnquist joins, and with whom Mr. Justice Stewart joins as to Part I, dissenting.

The Court today continues the evisceration of patronage practices begun in Elrod v. Burns, 427 U.S. 347 (1976). With scarcely a glance at almost 200 years of American political tradition, the Court further limits the relevance of political affiliation to the selection and retention of public employees. Many public positions previously filled on the basis of membership in national political parties now must be staffed in accordance with a constitutionalized civil service standard that will affect the employment practices of federal, state, and local governments. Governmental hiring practices long thought to be a matter of legislative and executive discretion now will be subjected to judicial oversight. . . . I dissent.

I.

The Court contends that its holding is compelled by the First Amendment. In reaching this conclusion, the Court largely ignores the substantial governmental interests served by patronage. Patronage is a long-accepted practice that never has been eliminated totally by civil service laws and regulations. The flaw in the Court's opinion lies not only in its application of First Amendment principles, but also in its promulgation of a new, and substantially expanded, standard for determining which governmental employees may be retained or dismissed on the basis of political affiliation.[2]

. . .

The standard articulated by the Court is framed in vague and sweeping language certain to create vast uncertainty. . . .

. . .

. . . The Court's vague, overbroad decision may cast serious doubt on the propriety of dismissing United States Attorneys, as well as thousands of other policymaking employees at all levels of government, because of their membership in a national political party.[5]

. . .

II.

. . . The Court . . . relies upon the decisions in Perry v. Sindermann, 408 U.S. 593 (1972), and Keyishian v. Board of Regents, 385 U.S. 589 (1967). . . . But the propriety of patronage was neither questioned nor addressed in those cases.

---

* Contrary to repeated statements in the Court's opinion, the present case does not involve "private political beliefs," but public affiliation with a political party.

[2] The Court purports to limit the issue in this case to the dismissal of public employees. See ante, n. 7. . . .

[5] The Court notes that prosecutors hold "broader public responsibilities" than public defenders. Ante, n. 13. . . .

Both *Keyishian* and *Perry* involved faculty members who were dismissed from state educational institutions because of their political views. . . . In neither case did the State suggest that the governmental positions traditionally had been regarded as patronage positions. Thus, the Court correctly held that no substantial state interest justified the infringement of free speech. This case presents a question quite different from that in *Keyishian* and *Perry*.

. . .

III.

Patronage appointments help build stable political parties by offering rewards to persons who assume the tasks necessary to the continued functioning of political organizations. . . .

. . .

. . . The Court's opinion casts a shadow over this time-honored element of our system. It appears to recognize that the implementation of policy is a legitimate goal of the patronage system and that some, but not all, policymaking employees may be replaced on the basis of their political affiliation. But the Court does not recognize that the implementation of policy often depends upon the cooperation of public employees who do not hold policymaking posts. . . .

. . .

In sum, the effect of the Court's decision will be to decrease the accountability and denigrate the role of our national political parties. This decision comes at a time when an increasing number of observers question whether our national political parties can continue to operate effectively. . . . The decision to place certain governmental positions within a civil service system is a sensitive political judgment that should be left to the voters and to elected representatives of the people. But the Court's constitutional holding today displaces political responsibility with judicial fiat. In my view, the First Amendment does not incorporate a national civil service system. I would reverse the judgment of the Court of Appeals.

B. LOYALTY PROGRAMS

Introduction. Programs to insure the loyalty of government employees, or of private employees whose employment relates to a government interest (such as employees of defense contractors), have raised two types of issues:

(1) Does the standard used to limit employment violate the first amendment? (2) Do the procedures by which the standard is applied to particular cases violate the first amendment? These issues are typically dealt with together by the Court—in fact, most of the cases deal with problems of the procedures rather than with the validity of the standards. An attempt is made in the materials which follow to treat the issues separately in order to facilitate understanding.

Other constitutional provisions also are involved. The constitutional prohibition against bills of attainder is sometimes used by the Court as a means of avoiding first amendment issues and so is considered first. Problems of procedural due process and the privilege against self-incrimination arise in relation to the procedural issues and will be briefly noted there.

It is important, in analyzing the cases that follow, to note carefully *when* they were decided. The cases in the 1950s and 1960s—both those validating and those invalidating various aspects of public employee loyalty and security programs—were decided before: (a) the first amendment standard applicable to speech advocating overthrow of government in abstract terms was made more rigorous; [1] (b) it was established that the first amendment placed limits on discharge of public employees for constitutionally protected speech; [2] (c) it was established that tenured public employees are entitled to fair hearings in connection with their discharge. [3] Although all three of these issues were central to the controversy over loyalty programs for government employees, they were often not settled, and even not squarely faced, in that context.

The materials are divided as follows: (1) The application of the bill of attainder. (2) The first amendment and loyalty standards for employment. (3) Loyalty oaths. (4) The privilege against self-incrimination and procedural due process.

1. PROTECTION OF THE BILL OF ATTAINDER CLAUSES

THE EARLY CASES: CUMMINGS AND GARLAND

Regulations designed to keep disloyal persons out of public service go back to the post-Civil War period when state and federal legislation made use of the test oath as a means of keeping former supporters of the Confederate cause out of certain positions. A provision of the Constitution of Missouri of 1865 forbade any person to hold state office, to be a director or manager of a corporation, teacher in an educational institution, lawyer, or minister without first taking an oath that he had never, among other things, manifested his adherence to the cause of the Confederate States, on his desire for their triumph, or his sympathy with those engaged in carrying on rebellion against the United States. Violation of the provision was made a crime.

In Cummings v. Missouri, 71 U.S. (4 Wall.) 277 (1867) a Catholic priest was convicted and imprisoned for continuing to perform his religious duties without having taken the oath. The Court held, five to four, that the oath provision was unconstitutional as an *ex post facto* law because it imposed new punishment for past acts, and as a bill of attainder because it inflicted punishment without any judicial trial. Regarding the contention that the provision should be sustained as fixing reasonable qualifications for the pursuits and professions involved, the Court stated:

". . . There can be no connection between the fact that Mr. Cummings entered or left the State of Missouri to avoid enrollment or draft in the military service of the United States, and his fitness to teach the doctrines or administer the sacraments of his church; nor can a fact of this kind or the expression of words of sympathy, with some of the persons drawn into the Rebellion, constitute any evidence of the unfitness of the attorney or counselor to practice his profession; or of the professor to teach the ordinary branches of education; or of the want of business knowledge or business capacity in the manager of a corporation, or in any director or trustee. It is manifest upon the simple statement of many of the acts and of the professions and pursuits, that there is no such relation between them as to render a denial of the commission of the acts at all appropriate as a condition of allowing the exercise of the professions and pursuits. The oath could not, therefore, have been required as a means of ascertaining whether parties were qualified or not for their respective callings or the trusts with which they were charged. It was required in order to reach the person, not the calling. It was exacted, not from any notion that the several acts designated

---

[1] See Brandenburg v. Ohio, 395 U.S. 444 (1969), supra page 1078.

[2] See Pickering v. Board of Education, 391 U.S. 563 (1968), discussed in the Court's opinion in Connick v. Myers, supra page 1331.

[3] See Board of Regents v. Roth, 408 U.S. 564 (1972), supra page 933.

indicated unfitness for the callings, but because it was thought that the several acts deserved punishment, and that for many of them there was no way to inflict punishment except by depriving the parties who had committed them of some of the rights and privileges of the citizen."

In Ex parte Garland, 71 U.S. (4 Wall.) 333 (1867) the Court invalidated (again five to four) a Congressional statute requiring of all attorneys practicing in the federal courts an oath similar to that involved in the Cummings case.

In a dissenting opinion, applicable to both the *Cummings* and *Garland* cases, Mr. Justice Miller wrote: "I maintain that the purpose of the act of Congress was to require loyalty as a qualification of all who practice law in the national courts. The majority say that the purpose was to impose a punishment for past acts of disloyalty."

UNITED STATES v. LOVETT, 328 U.S. 303 (1946). In 1943, Representative Martin Dies, then Chairman of the House Committee on Un-American Activities, made a speech on the floor of the House, attacking 39 named government employees as "radical bureaucrats" and affiliates of "Communist front organizations." Among the persons named were the three respondents, Lovett, Watson, and Dodd. After debate, a subcommittee of the Appropriations Committee was authorized to investigate the charges. Hearings in secret executive session were held by the subcommittee which found respondents guilty of "subversive activity". As a result, an amendment was attached to the Urgent Deficiency Appropriations Bill of 1943 providing that no part of any appropriation "which is now, or which is hereafter made, available . . . shall be used, after November 15, 1943, to pay any part of the salary . . . of Goodwin B. Watson, William E. Dodd, Junior, and Robert Morss Lovett" unless prior to that date they should be reappointed with the advice and consent of the Senate. When respondents' pay ceased, they sued in the Court of Claims for compensation earned after November 15, 1943, and won. The Supreme Court unanimously affirmed, but divided six to two on the reasons.

Justice Black, speaking for the Court, held that the rider was unconstitutional as a bill of attainder, citing Cummings v. Missouri, 71 U.S. (4 Wall.) 277 (1867) and Ex parte Garland, 71 U.S. (4 Wall.) 333 (1867). These cases "stand for the proposition that legislative acts, no matter what their form, that apply either to named individuals or to easily ascertainable members of a group in such a way as to inflict punishment on them without a judicial trial are bills of attainder prohibited by the Constitution." The purpose of the rider "was not merely to cut off respondents' compensation through regular disbursing channels but permanently to bar them from governmental service. . . . The effect was to inflict punishment without the safeguards of a judicial trial and determined by no previous law or fixed rule."

Justice Frankfurter, joined by Justice Reed, although they concurred in the result, argued that the rider lacked "the essential declaration of guilt" and "the imposition of punishment in the sense appropriate for bills of attainder."

UNITED STATES v. BROWN

381 U.S. 437, 85 S.Ct. 1707, 14 L.Ed.2d 484 (1965).

Mr. Chief Justice Warren delivered the opinion of the Court.

In this case we review for the first time a conviction under § 504 of the Labor-Management Reporting and Disclosure Act of 1959, which makes it a crime for a member of the Communist Party to serve as an officer or (except in clerical or custodial positions) as an employee of a labor union. Section 504, the purpose of which is to protect the national economy by minimizing the danger of political strikes, was enacted to replace § 9(h) of the . . . . Taft-Hartley Act, which conditioned a union's access to the National Labor Relations Board upon the filing of affidavits by all of the union's officers attesting that they were not members of or affiliated with the Communist Party.

Respondent . . ., an open and avowed Communist, . . . was charged . . . with "knowingly and wilfully serv[ing] as a member of an executive board of a labor organization . . . while a member of the Communist Party, in wilful violation of Section 504." It was neither charged nor proven that respondent at any time advocated or suggested illegal activity by the union, or proposed a political strike. The jury found respondent guilty, and he was sentenced to six months' imprisonment. The Court of Appeals for the Ninth Circuit . . . reversed . . . holding that § 504 violates the First and Fifth Amendments to the Constitution.

Respondent urges—in addition to the grounds relied on by the court below—that the statute under which he was convicted is a bill of attainder, and therefore violates Art. I, § 9, of the Constitution. We agree . . . and affirm . . . on that basis. We therefore find it unnecessary to consider the First and Fifth Amendment arguments.

The provisions outlawing bills of attainder were adopted by the Constitutional Convention unanimously, and without debate. . . . A logical starting place for an inquiry into the meaning of the prohibition is its historical background. The bill of attainder, a parliamentary act sentencing to death one or more specific persons, was a device often resorted to in sixteenth, seventeenth and eighteenth century England for dealing with persons who had attempted, or threatened to attempt, to overthrow the government. . . . The "bill of pains and penalties" was identical to the bill of attainder, except that it prescribed a penalty short of death, e.g., banishment, deprivation of the right to vote, or exclusion of the designated party's sons from Parliament. . . .

. . . The best available evidence, the writings of the architects of our constitutional system, indicates that the Bill of Attainder Clause was intended not as a narrow, technical (and therefore soon to be outmoded) prohibition, but rather as an implementation of the separation of powers, a general safeguard against legislative exercise of the judicial function, or more simply—trial by legislature. . . .

[Discussion of the *Cummings, Garland* and *Lovett* cases is omitted.]

Under the line of cases just outlined, . . . § 504 plainly constitutes a bill of attainder. . . . The statute does not set forth a generally applicable rule decreeing that any person who commits certain acts or possesses certain characteristics (acts and characteristics which, in Congress' view, make them likely to initiate political strikes) shall not hold union office, and leave to courts and juries the job of deciding what persons have committed the specified acts or possess the specified characteristics. Instead, it designates in no uncertain terms the persons who possess the feared characteristics and therefore cannot hold union office without incurring criminal liability—members of the Communist Party. . . .

It is argued, however, that in § 504 Congress did no more than [enact] a general rule to the effect that persons possessing characteristics which make them likely to incite political strikes should not hold union office, and simply inserted in place of a list of those characteristics an alternative, shorthand criterion—membership in the Communist Party. Again, we cannot agree. The designation of Communists as those persons likely to cause political strikes is not the substitution of a semantically equivalent phrase; on the contrary, it rests

. . . . upon an empirical investigation by Congress of the acts, characteristics and propensities of Communist Party members. In a number of decisions, this Court has pointed out the fallacy of the suggestion that membership in the Communist Party, or any other political organization, can be regarded as an alternative, but equivalent, expression for a list of undesirable characteristics. . . . In utilizing the term "members of the Communist Party" to designate those persons who are likely to incite political strikes, it plainly is not the case that Congress has merely substituted a convenient shorthand term for a list of the characteristics it was trying to reach.

The Solicitor General argues that § 504 is not a bill of attainder because the prohibition it imposes does not constitute "punishment." In support of this conclusion, he urges that the statute was enacted for preventive rather than retributive reasons—that its aim is not to punish Communists for what they have done in the past, but rather to keep them from positions where they will in the future be able to bring about undesirable events. . . . It would be archaic to limit the definition of "punishment" to "retribution." Punishment serves several purposes; retributive, rehabilitative, deterrent—and preventive. One of the reasons society imprisons those convicted of crimes is to keep them from inflicting future harm, but that does not make imprisonment any the less punishment.

Historical considerations by no means compel restriction of the bill of attainder ban to instances of retribution. . . .

The Solicitor General urges us to distinguish *Lovett* on the ground that the statute struck down there "singled out three identified individuals." . . . We cannot agree that the fact that § 504 inflicts its deprivation upon the membership of the Communist Party rather than upon a list of named individuals takes it out of the category of bills of attainder.

. . . . .

Affirmed.

Mr. Justice White, with whom Mr. Justice Clark, Mr. Justice Harlan, and Mr. Justice Stewart join, dissenting. . . .

. . . . Congress is held to have violated the Bill of Attainder Clause here because, on the one hand, § 504 does not encompass the whole class of persons having characteristics that would make them likely to call political strikes and, on the other hand, § 504 does single out a particular group, members of the Communist Party, not all of whom possess such characteristics. Because of this combination of underinclusiveness and overinclusiveness the Court concludes that Communist Party members were singled out for punishment, thus rejecting the Government's contention that § 504 has solely a regulatory aim.

The Court's conclusion that a statute which is both underinclusive and overinclusive must be deemed to have been adopted with a punitive purpose assumes that legislatures normally deal with broad categories and attack all of an evil at a time. Or if partial measures are undertaken, a legislature singles out a particular group for regulation only because the group label is a "short hand phrase" for traits that are characteristic of the broader evil. But this Court has long recognized in equal protection cases that a legislature may prefer to deal with only part of an evil. See, e.g., Railway Express Agency, Inc. v. New York, 336 U.S. 106; . . . And it is equally true that a group may be singled out for regulation without any punitive purpose even when not all members of the group would be likely to engage in the feared conduct. "[I]f the class discriminated against is or reasonably might be considered to define those from whom the evil *mainly is to be feared,* it properly may be picked out." Patsone v. Commonwealth of Pennsylvania, 232 U.S., at 144. (Emphasis added.) That is, the focus of legislative attention may be the substantially greater likelihood that some members of the group would engage in the feared conduct compared to the likelihood that members of other groups would do so. . . . Admittedly the degree of specificity is a relevant factor—as when individuals are singled out by name—but because in many instances specificity of the degree here held impermissible may be wholly consistent with a regulatory, rather than a punitive purpose, the Court's *per se* approach cuts too broadly and invalidates legitimate legislative activity.[a]

. . .

2. PROTECTION OF THE FIRST AMENDMENT

Introduction. The cases in this and the next subsection obviously raise issues of allegedly subversive speech and association related to those presented at length in Chapter 15. The additional inquiry is whether there is a governmental interest in employee loyalty that justifies denial of employment for some speech or association that could not be punished criminally. The cases that follow should be considered with the cases in the next subsection, relating to loyalty oaths. Do they provide a direct answer to the question presented here?

FEDERAL LOYALTY SECURITY EXECUTIVE ORDERS

State and federal statutory restrictions on the employment by government of allegedly subversive or disloyal persons became common during the 1940s and 1950s. In 1947 President Truman issued an executive order applicable to all civilian employees of the federal government providing for removal of employees on grounds of disloyalty under the standard that, based "on all the evidence, reasonable grounds exist for belief that the person involved is disloyal to the Government of the United States." This order provided for certain procedural rights of notice and hearing. In 1953 President Eisenhower superseded the Truman program, issuing Executive Order No. 10450. That order made the head of each department and agency responsible for having "an effective program to insure that the employment and retention in employment of any civilian officer or employee within the department or agency is clearly consistent with the interests of the national security." Among the criteria listed in the order as relevant to the security determination was "Advocacy of use of force or violence to overthrow the government of the United States, or of the alteration of the form of government of the United States by unconstitutional means." In its original form the order also listed "Membership in, or affiliation or sympathetic association with, any . . . organization . . . which is totalitarian, Fascist, Communist, or subversive . . . or which seeks to alter the form of government of the United States by unconstitutional means." Under Order 10450 existing federal employees were given only limited procedural rights within the agency but no right to appeal the decision of the agency head. In 1956 the Supreme Court held that the statutory basis for the order did not

---

[a] Compare Speiser v. Randall, 357 U.S. 513 (1958), where persons otherwise entitled to a tax exemption refused to sign a form stating they did not advocate violent overthrow of government. Since denial of the tax exemption "penalized" speech, due process required that the government bear the burden of producing evidence and convincing a factfinder that a taxpayer engaged in the forbidden advocacy.

Compare, also, Nixon v. Administrator of Gen. Services, 433 U.S. 425 (1977), where the Court rejected a bill of attainder challenge to a statute that referred to President Nixon by name and imposed restrictions on the disposition of his papers not placed on other past Presidents. The Court concluded that President Nixon was a "legitimate class of one," supporting a "nonpunitive" purpose in safeguarding public access to the papers.

permit its application to dismissal of employees who do not occupy sensitive posts in government. Cole v. Young, 351 U.S. 536 (1956).

ADLER v. BOARD OF EDUCATION, 342 U.S. 485 (1952). A New York statute provided for the disqualification and removal of superintendents of schools, teachers, and employees in the public schools in any city or school district of the State who advocate the overthrow of the government by unlawful means or who are members of organizations which have a like purpose. The Court upheld the statute by a vote of 6 to 3 (Justice Frankfurter dissented on a procedural ground, Justices Black and Douglas on the merits). Justice Minton, writing for the Court, said that public school employees "have no right to work for the State in the school system on their own terms. . . . They may work for the school system upon the reasonable terms laid down by the proper authorities of New York. If they do not choose to work on such terms, they are at liberty to retain their beliefs and associations and go elsewhere. . . . In the employment of officials and teachers of the school system, the state may very properly inquire into the company they keep, and we know of no rule, constitutional or otherwise, that prevents the state, when determining the fitness and loyalty of such persons, from considering the organizations and persons with whom they associate."

KONIGSBERG v. STATE BAR OF CALIFORNIA, 366 U.S. 36 (1961). A California statute provided that no person could be certified to practice law "who advocates the overthrow of the Government of the United States or of this State by force, violence, or other unconstitutional means." In a hearing to determine his qualifications to be admitted Konigsberg refused to answer questions as to his present or past membership in the Communist Party. He was denied admission solely because of his refusal to answer such questions. This denial was upheld by the Court by a vote of 5 to 4. The Court said:

"As regards the questioning of public employees relative to Communist Party membership it has already been held that the interest in not subjecting speech and association to the deterrence of subsequent disclosure is outweighed by the State's interest in ascertaining the fitness of the employee for the post he holds, and hence that such questioning does not infringe constitutional protections. Beilan v. Board of Public Education, 357 U.S. 399; Garner v. Board of Public Works, 341 U.S. 716. With respect to this same question of Communist Party membership, we regard the State's interest in having lawyers who are devoted to the law in its broadest sense, including not only its substantive provisions, but also its procedures for orderly change, as clearly sufficient to outweigh the minimal effect upon free association occasioned by compulsory disclosure in the circumstances here presented."

KEYISHIAN v. BOARD OF REGENTS, 385 U.S. 589 (1967). The Court had before it again a challenge to the New York statute involved in *Adler*. The Court found major portions of the Act void for vagueness. It also departed from *Adler* and held unconstitutional the portion of the statute making membership in the Communist Party prima facie evidence of disqualification. The Court said that constitutional doctrine that had emerged since *Adler* had "rejected its major premise" that public employment "may be conditioned upon the surrender of constitutional rights which could not be abridged by direct government action." Moreover, mere knowing membership without a specific intent to further the unlawful aims of an organization was not a constitutionally adequate basis for exclusion from faculty positions.

———

UNITED STATES v. ROBEL, 389 U.S. 258 (1967).   The Subversive Activities Control Act of 1950, § 5(a)(1)(D) made it a crime for any member of a "Communist-action organization" [a] to engage "in any employment in any defense facility," if he had knowledge of a final order of the Subversive Activities Control Board requiring such organization to register.   This provision was challenged by appellee Robel who was employed as a machinist in a shipyard designated by the Secretary of Defense as a "defense facility" under the Act.   The Supreme Court held the provision unconstitutional in an opinion that concluded:

". . . The Government emphasizes that the purpose of § 5(a)(1)(D) is to reduce the threat of sabotage and espionage in the Nation's defense plants. The Government's interest in such a prophylactic measure is not insubstantial. But it cannot be doubted that the means chosen to implement that governmental purpose in this instance cuts deeply into the right of association. . . .

". . . That statute casts its net across a broad range of associational activities, indiscriminately trapping membership which can be constitutionally punished and membership which cannot be so proscribed.   It is made irrelevant to the statute's operation that an individual may be a passive or inactive member of a designated organization, that he may be unaware of the organization's unlawful aims, or that he may disagree with those unlawful aims.   It is also made irrelevant that an individual who is subject to the penalties of § 5(a)(1) (D) may occupy a nonsensitive position in a defense facility.   Thus, § 5(a)(1) (D) contains the fatal defect of overbreadth because it seeks to bar employment both for association which may be proscribed and for association which may not be proscribed consistently with First Amendment rights. . . ." [b]

———

3.   Loyalty Oaths

Introduction.   This subsection, and the next, focus on the procedures for determining employee loyalty.   A government agency that makes loyalty determinations concerning its employees can expend resources to investigate the background of prospective and present employees.   Many state and local agencies, reluctant to expend the resources necessary for investigation, implemented loyalty programs using two alternatives that raise their own constitutional problems.   The cases in this subsection concern required loyalty oaths for government employees.   The cases in the next subsection involve the problems of self-incrimination and procedural due process where the government employer relies on information obtained by compelling employees to reveal relevant information.

———

[a] The Act defined "communist-action organization" as: "any organization in the United States (other than a diplomatic representative or mission of a foreign government accredited as such by the Department of State) which (i) is substantially directed, dominated, or controlled by the foreign government or foreign organization controlling the world Communist movement . . . and (ii) operates primarily to advance the objectives of such world Communist movement . . .."

[b] See Gunther, *Reflections on Robel,* 20 Stan.L.Rev. 1140 (1968).

ELFBRANDT v. RUSSELL

384 U.S. 11, 86 S.Ct. 1238, 16 L.Ed.2d 321 (1966).

Mr. Justice Douglas delivered the opinion of the Court.

This case, which involves questions concerning the constitutionality of an Arizona Act requiring an oath from state employees, has been here before. We vacated the judgment of the Arizona Supreme Court which had sustained the oath and remanded the cause for reconsideration in light of Baggett v. Bullitt, 377 U.S. 360. On reconsideration the Supreme Court of Arizona reinstated the original judgment. The case is here on certiorari.

The oath reads in conventional fashion as follows:

"I, (type or print name) do solemnly swear (or affirm) that I will support the Constitution of the United States and the Constitution and laws of the state of Arizona; that I will bear true faith and allegiance to the same, and defend them against all enemies whatever, and that I will faithfully and impartially discharge the duties of the office of (name of office) according to the best of my ability, so help me God (or so I do affirm)."

The Legislature put a gloss on the oath by subjecting to a prosecution for perjury and for discharge from public office anyone who took the oath and who "knowingly and wilfully becomes or remains a member of the communist party of the United States or its successors or any of its subordinate organizations" or "any other organization" having for "one of its purposes" the overthrow of the government of Arizona or any of its political subdivisions where the employee had knowledge of the unlawful purpose. Petitioner, a teacher and a Quaker, decided she could not in good conscience take the oath, not knowing what it meant and not having any chance to get a hearing at which its precise scope and meaning could be determined. This suit for declaratory relief followed.

. . .

We recognized in Scales v. United States, 367 U.S. 203, 229, that "quasi-political parties or other groups . . . may embrace both legal and illegal aims." We noted that a "blanket prohibition of association with a group having both legal and illegal aims" would pose "a real danger that legitimate political expression or association would be impaired." The statute with which we dealt in *Scales* the so-called "membership clause" of the Smith Act was found not to suffer from this constitutional infirmity because as the Court construed it, the statute reached only "active" membership (id., at 222) with the "specific intent" of assisting in achieving the unlawful ends of the organization (id., at 229–230). The importance of this limiting construction from a constitutional standpoint was emphasized in Noto v. United States, 367 U.S. 290, 299–300, decided the same day. . . .

. . .

The oath and accompanying statutory gloss challenged here suffer from an identical constitutional infirmity. One who subscribes to this Arizona oath and who is, or thereafter becomes, a knowing member of an organization which has as "one of its purposes" the violent overthrow of the government, is subject to immediate discharge and criminal penalties. Nothing in the oath, the statutory gloss, or the construction of the oath and statutes given by the Arizona Supreme Court, purports to exclude association by one who does not subscribe to the organization's unlawful ends. Here as in Baggett v. Bullitt, supra, the "hazard of being prosecuted for knowing but guiltless behavior" (id., 377 U.S. at 373) is a reality. People often label as "communist" ideas which they oppose; and they make up our juries. "[P]rosecutors too are human." Cramp v. Board of Public Instruction, 368 U.S. 278, 287. Would a teacher be safe and secure in going to a Pugwash Conference? Would it be legal to join a seminar group predominantly Communist and therefore subject to control by those who are said to believe in the overthrow of the Government by force and violence? Juries might convict though the teacher did not subscribe to the wrongful aims of the organization. And there is apparently no machinery provided for getting clearance in advance.

Those who join an organization but do not share its unlawful purposes and who do not participate in its unlawful activities surely pose no threat, either as citizens or as public employees. . . .

. . . A law which applies to membership without the "specific intent" to further the illegal aims of the organization infringes unnecessarily on protected freedoms. It rests on the doctrine of "guilt by association" which has no place here. . . . Such a law cannot stand.

Reversed.

Mr. Justice White, with whom Mr. Justice Clark, Mr. Justice Harlan and Mr. Justice Stewart concur, dissenting.

According to unequivocal prior holdings of this Court, a state is entitled to condition public employment upon its employees abstaining from knowing membership in the Communist Party and other organizations advocating the violent overthrow of the government which employs them; the state is constitutionally authorized to inquire into such affiliations and it may discharge those who refuse to affirm or deny them. . . . The Court does not mention or purport to overrule these cases; nor does it expressly hold that a state must retain, even in its most sensitive positions, those who lend such support as knowing membership entails to those organizations, such as the Communist Party, whose purposes include the violent destruction of democratic government.

. . .

Even if Arizona may not take criminal action against its law enforcement officers or its teachers who become Communists knowing of the purposes of the Party, the Court's judgment overreaches itself in invalidating this Arizona statute. Whether or not Arizona may make knowing membership a crime, it need not retain the member as an employee and is entitled to insist that its employees disclaim, under oath, knowing membership in the designated organizations and to condition future employment upon future abstention from membership. . . .

———

COLE v. RICHARDSON, 405 U.S. 676 (1972). The Court held valid the following oath required of all public employees in Massachusetts:

"I do solemnly swear (or affirm) that I will uphold and defend the Constitution of the United States of America and the Constitution of the Commonwealth of Massachusetts and that I will oppose the overthrow of the government of the United States of America or of this Commonwealth by force, violence or by any illegal or unconstitutional method."

The Court summarized earlier oath cases as follows:

"We have made clear that neither federal nor state government may condition employment on taking oaths that impinge on rights guaranteed by the First and Fourteenth Amendments respectively, as for example those relating to political beliefs. . . . Nor may employment be conditioned on an oath that one has not engaged, or will not engage, in protected speech activities such as the following: criticizing institutions of government; discussing political doctrine that approves the overthrow of certain forms of government; and supporting candidates for political office. . . . Employment may not be conditioned on an oath denying past, or abjuring future, associational activities within constitutional protection; such protected activities include membership in organizations having illegal purposes unless one knows of the purpose and shares a specific intent to promote the illegal purpose. . . . And, finally, an oath may not be so vague that ' "men of common intelligence must necessarily guess at its meaning and differ as to its application, [because such an oath] violates the first essential of due process of law." ' Cramp v. Board of Public Instruction, 368 U.S., at 287. Concern for vagueness in the oath cases has been especially great because uncertainty as to an oath's meaning may deter individuals from engaging in constitutionally protected activity conceivably within the scope of the oath."

The Court concluded that the first clause of the oath here was valid. "Since there is no constitutionally protected right to overthrow a government by force, violence, or illegal or unconstitutional means, no constitutional right is infringed by an oath to abide by the constitutional system in the future." It construed the second clause of the oath as being redundant, imposing no obligation of positive action on oath takers, and so not void for vagueness.

4. THE PRIVILEGE AGAINST SELF-INCRIMINATION AND PROCEDURAL DUE PROCESS

THE PRIVILEGE AGAINST SELF–INCRIMINATION AND LOYALTY PROCEEDINGS

In a series of cases in the 1950s the Court held that a state could discharge an employee for claiming the privilege against self-incrimination and refusing to answer questions relevant to the employee's position. See, e.g., Beilan v. Board of Education, 357 U.S. 399 (1958); Lerner v. Casey, 357 U.S. 468 (1958). In Nelson v. County of Los Angeles, 362 U.S. 1 (1960), the Court went so far as to uphold the application of a California statute requiring discharge of any public employee who refused to answer any question relating to subversive activity put by the governing body of the employing agency or any state or federal legislative committee. In that case a county employee had refused to answer questions concerning such activity propounded by a federal investigating committee. In Cohen v. Hurley, 366 U.S. 117 (1961), the Court upheld the disbarment of a lawyer who had refused to provide information concerning "ambulance chasing" in an inquiry by the bar into his professional fitness.

In 1967, however in Spevack v. Klein, 385 U.S. 511, the Court overruled the *Cohen* case and held that the privilege against self-incrimination "should not be watered down by imposing the dishonor of disbarment and the deprivation of a livelihood as a price for asserting it." In Garrity v. New Jersey, 385 U.S. 493 (1967), the Court held that evidence obtained from policemen in an investigation after they had been warned that they would be discharged for refusal to answer could not be used against them in a criminal proceeding. And in Gardner v. Broderick, 392 U.S. 273 (1968), the Court held that a policeman could not be discharged for refusing to sign a waiver of immunity from prosecution, but suggested that given such an immunity he could be compelled to answer questions relevant to his employment. This last suggestion was elaborated on in the case that follows.

LEFKOWITZ v. TURLEY, 414 U.S. 70 (1973). New York statutes require public contracts to provide that if a contractor refused to waive immunity or to testify concerning state contracts, existing contracts may be canceled and that person disqualified from further transactions with the State for five years. Disqualification from contracting with public authorities was also required upon a person's failure to waive immunity or answer questions respecting state transactions. Two New York-licensed architects, when summoned to testify before a grand jury investigating various criminal charges, refused to sign waivers of immunity. Various contracting authorities were notified of their conduct and had their attention called to the applicable disqualification statutes. The architects brought an action challenging the statutes. The Court held the statutes unconstitutional. In an opinion by Justice White the Court said:

(1) The Fifth Amendment "not only protects the individual against being involuntarily called as a witness against himself in a criminal prosecution but also privileges him not to answer official questions put to him in any other proceeding, civil or criminal, formal or informal, where the answers might incriminate him in future criminal proceedings."

(2) This general rule applies even in cases such as this where the state is interrogating employees and contractors about their job performance. Hence the state may not discharge those who refuse to answer or to waive the privilege by waiving the immunity they would otherwise be entitled to and to use any incriminating answer obtained in subsequent criminal prosecutions.

(3) However, the state may compel such testimony if neither it nor its fruits are available for use in any criminal proceeding. Hence, "given adequate immunity, the State may plainly insist that employees either answer questions under oath about the performance of their job or suffer the loss of employment. By like token, the State may insist that the architects involved in this case either respond to relevant inquiries about the performance of their contracts or suffer cancellation of current relationships and disqualification from contracting with public agencies for an appropriate time in the future . . .. Hence, if answers are to be required in such circumstances States must offer to the witness whatever immunity is required to supplant the privilege and may not insist that the employee or contractor waive such immunity."

PROCEDURAL DUE PROCESS AND LOYALTY INQUIRIES

What kind of a hearing, if any, is required when a governmental employer refuses to employ or discharges a person because of beliefs and associations? Major controversies that arose during the 1950s and early 1960s concerned whether government employees suspected of disloyalty could be discharged with no hearing at all, or whether it was a violation of procedural due process to discharge an employee as disloyal on the basis of a hearing in which the decisionmaker relied on evidence not disclosed to the employee and not subject to cross-examination. In the context of loyalty discharges, the issue was never resolved in constitutional terms.[1] In Greene v. McElroy, 360 U.S. 474 (1959), the Court held that a hearing was required by statute in cases where a security clearance was revoked. In Cafeteria Workers v. McElroy, 367 U.S. 886 (1961), the Court held that a military commander could summarily revoke a security clearance that permitted a cook to work in a cafeteria on the premises of a government contractor. The Court has not re-examined these precedents in light of the more recent procedural due process cases set out supra, Chapter 12.

---

[1] In a number of cases, the discharged employee was ordered reinstated on the ground that applicable administrative regulations or statutes had not been followed. See, e.g., Peters v. Hobby, 349 U.S. 331 (1955); Service v. Dulles, 354 U.S. 363 (1957). In one case squarely raising the constitutional issue of the sufficiency of a hearing where the decisionmaker relied on secret evidence, a Court of Appeals decision that there was no constitutional violation was affirmed by an equally divided Court without opinion. Bailey v. Richardson, 341 U.S. 918 (1951).

Chapter 17

FREEDOM OF THE PRESS

Introduction. The materials pulled together in this chapter relate to the first amendment protections as applied to the print and electronic media. Many of the issues that have arisen in the three previous chapters are involved in these cases.

The introductory section considers the question whether freedom of the press is an independent constitutional constraint and examines the amenability of the press to general business regulation. Section 2 considers government action that restrains the press in its editorial judgments. Section 3 examines government restrictions on what the press can print—a context where the law of prior restraint is prominent. Section 4 deals with government demands for confidential press information. Section 5 turns to the converse situation, where the press is seeking access to confidential government information. Finally, section 6 introduces some of the special problems of regulation of the electronic media.

It has been suggested that the power of government to regulate the business of publishing is limited by the first amendment under three general principles. (1) The government may not impose special burdens on the press—at least where it appears that the purpose is to curb the press. (2) The government may not impose even nondiscriminatory burdens on the press where they are so heavy as to impair significantly the institutional viability of the press. (3) The government may not interfere with editorial control and judgment. Barrett, *Freedom of the Press, American Style,* in American Bar Association, *Legal Institutions Today: English and American Approaches Compared,* 214, 225–227 (H. Jones ed. 1977); DeVore & Nelson, *Commercial Speech and Paid Access to the Press,* 26 Hast. L.J. 745 (1975).

In examining the materials that follow the student should ask whether the cases support these limiting principles.

SECTION 1.   INTRODUCTION

A.   RELATIONSHIP BETWEEN THE SPEECH AND PRESS CLAUSES

The first amendment protects against "abridging the freedom of speech, or of the press." Does the latter phrase confer upon the press any freedom not otherwise conferred by the "freedom of speech" clause?

Justice Stewart argued in a speech that the free press clause does add to the protections accorded by the free speech clause. He said, in part:

"[T]he Free Press guarantee is, in essence, a *structural* provision of the Constitution. Most of the other provisions in the Bill of Rights protect specific liberties or specific rights of individuals: freedom of speech, freedom of worship, the right to counsel, the privilege against compulsory self-incrimination, to name a few. In contrast, the Free Press Clause extends protection to an institution. The publishing business is, in short, the only organized private business that is given explicit constitutional protection.

"This basic understanding is essential, I think, to avoid an elementary error of constitutional law. It is tempting to suggest that freedom of the

1356

press means only that newspaper publishers are guaranteed freedom of expression. They *are* guaranteed that freedom, to be sure, but so are we all, because of the Free Speech Clause. If the Free Press guarantee meant no more than freedom of expression, it would be a constitutional redundancy. Between 1776 and the drafting of our Constitution, many of the state constitutions contained clauses protecting freedom of the press while at the same time recognizing no general freedom of speech. By including both guarantees in the First Amendment, the Founders quite clearly recognized the distinction between the two.

"It is also a mistake to suppose that the only purpose of the constitutional guarantee of a free press is to insure that a newspaper will serve as a neutral forum for debate, a 'market place for ideas,' a kind of Hyde Park corner for the community. A related theory sees the press as a neutral conduit of information between the people and their elected leaders. These theories, in my view, again give insufficient weight to the institutional autonomy of the press that it was the purpose of the Constitution to guarantee." [1]

In a concurring opinion in a case concerned with other issues,[2] Chief Justice Burger expressed disagreement with Justice Stewart's position. He said:

"I perceive two fundamental difficulties with a narrow reading of the Press Clause. First, although certainty on this point is not possible, the history of the Clause does not suggest that the authors contemplated a 'special' or 'institutional' privilege. See Lange, The Speech and Press Clauses, 23 U.C.L.A.L.Rev. 77, 88–99 (1975). . . .

> . . .

"Those interpreting the Press Clause as extending protection only to, or creating a special role for, the 'institutional press' must either (a) assert such an intention on the part of the Framers for which no supporting evidence is available, (b) argue that events after 1791 somehow operated to 'constitutionalize' this interpretation, see Benzanson, The New Free Press Guarantee, 63 Va.L.Rev. 731, 788 (1977); or (c) candidly acknowledging the absence of historical support, suggest that the intent of the Framers is not important today. See Nimmer, Is Freedom of the Press a Redundancy: What Does It Add To Freedom of Speech?, 26 Hastings L.J. 639, 640–641 (1975).

"To conclude that the Framers did not intend to limit the freedom of the press to one select group is not necessarily to suggest that the Press Clause is redundant. The Speech Clause standing alone may be viewed as a protection of the liberty to express ideas and beliefs, while the Press Clause focuses specifically on the liberty to disseminate expression broadly and 'comprehends every sort of publication which affords a vehicle of information and opinion.' Yet there is no fundamental distinction between expression and dissemination. The liberty encompassed by the Press Clause, although complementary to and a natural extension of Speech Clause liberty, merited special mention simply because it had been more often the object of official restraints. . . .

> . . .

"The second fundamental difficulty with interpreting the Press Clause as conferring special status on a limited group is one of definition. The very task of including some entities within the 'institutional press' while excluding others, whether undertaken by legislature, court or administrative agency, is reminiscent of the abhorred licensing system of Tudor and Stuart England— a system the First Amendment was intended to ban from this country.

---

[1] *"Or of the Press,"* a speech given at Yale Law School, Nov. 2, 1974, as reprinted in 26 Hast.L.J. 631, 633–634 (1975).

[2] First Nat'l Bank of Boston v. Bellotti, 435 U.S. 765, 798–803 (1978).

Further, the officials undertaking that task would be required to distinguish the protected from the unprotected on the basis of such variables as content of expression, frequency or fervor of expression, or ownership of the technological means of dissemination. Yet nothing in this Court's opinions supports such a confining approach to the scope of Press Clause protection.

. . . .

. . . .

"Because the First Amendment was meant to guarantee freedom to express and communicate ideas, I can see no difference between the right of those who seek to disseminate ideas by way of a newspaper and those who give lectures or speeches and seek to enlarge the audience by publication and wide dissemination. . . . ."

B. REGULATION OF THE BUSINESS OF PUBLISHING

MINNEAPOLIS STAR AND TRIBUNE CO. v. MINNESOTA COMMISSIONER OF REVENUE

460 U.S. 575, 103 S.Ct. 1365, 75 L.Ed.2d 295 (1983).

Justice O'Connor delivered the opinion of the Court.

This case presents the question of a State's power to impose a special tax on the press and, by enacting exemptions, to limit its effect to only a few newspapers.

I

Since 1967, Minnesota has imposed a sales tax on most sales of goods for a price in excess of a nominal sum. . . . In general, the tax applies only to retail sales. . . . An exemption for industrial and agricultural users shields from the tax sales of components to be used in the production of goods that will themselves be sold at retail. . . . As part of this general system of taxation and in support of the sales tax, ... Minnesota also enacted a tax on the "privilege of using, storing or consuming in Minnesota tangible personal property." This use tax applies to any nonexempt tangible personal property unless the sales tax was paid on the sales price. . . . Like the classic use tax, this use tax protects the State's sales tax by eliminating the residents' incentive to travel to States with lower sales taxes to buy goods rather than buying them in Minnesota. . . .

The appellant, Minneapolis Star and Tribune Company "Star Tribune", is the publisher of a morning newspaper and an evening newspaper in Minneapolis. From 1967 until 1971, it enjoyed an exemption from the sales and use tax provided by Minnesota for periodic publications. 1967 Minn.Laws Sp.Sess. 2187, codified at Minn.Stat. § 297A.25(i). In 1971, however, while leaving the exemption from the sales tax in place, the legislature amended the scheme to impose a "use tax" on the cost of paper and ink products consumed in the production of a publication. Act of October 31, 1971, ch. 31, art. I, § 5, 1971 Minn.Laws Sp.Sess. 2561, 2565, codified with modifications at Minn.Stat. §§ 297A.14, 297A.25(i) (1982). Ink and paper used in publications became the only items subject to the use tax that were components of goods to be sold at retail. In 1974, the legislature again amended the statute, this time to exempt the first $100,000 worth of ink and paper consumed by a publication in any calendar year, in effect giving each publication an annual tax credit of $4,000. Act of May 24, 1973, ch. 650, art. XIII, § 1, 1973 Minn.Laws 1606, 1637, codified at Minn.Stat. § 297A.14 (1982). Publications remained exempt from the sales tax, § 2, 1973 Minn.Laws 1639.

After the enactment of the $100,000 exemption, 11 publishers, producing 14 of the 388 paid circulation newspapers in the State, incurred a tax liability in 1974. Star Tribune was one of the 11, and, of the $893,355 collected, it paid $608,634, or roughly two-thirds of the total revenue raised by the tax. . . . In 1975, 13 publishers, producing 16 out of 374 paid circulation papers, paid a tax. That year, Star Tribune again bore roughly two-thirds of the total receipts from the use tax on ink and paper. . . .

Star Tribune instituted this action to seek a refund of the use taxes it paid from January 1, 1974 to May 31, 1975. It challenged the imposition of the use tax on ink and paper used in publications as a violation of the guarantees of freedom of the press and equal protection in the First and Fourteenth Amendments. The Minnesota Supreme Court upheld the tax against the federal constitutional challenge. . . . We . . . reverse.

II

Star Tribune argues that we must strike this tax on the authority of Grosjean v. American Press Co., Inc., 297 U.S. 233 (1936). Although there are similarities between the two cases, we agree with the State that *Grosjean* is not controlling.

In *Grosjean,* the State of Louisiana imposed a license tax of 2% of the gross receipts from the sale of advertising on all newspapers with a weekly circulation above 20,000. Out of at least 124 publishers in the State, only 13 were subject to the tax. After noting that the tax was "single in kind" and that keying the tax to circulation curtailed the flow of information, id., at 250–251, this Court held the tax invalid as an abridgment of the freedom of the press. Both the brief and the argument of the publishers in this Court emphasized the events leading up to the tax and the contemporary political climate in Louisiana. . . . All but one of the large papers subject to the tax had "ganged up" on Senator Huey Long, and a circular distributed by Long and the governor to each member of the state legislature described "lying newspapers" as conducting "a vicious campaign" and the tax as "a tax on lying, 2c [*sic*] a lie." . . . Although the Court's opinion did not describe this history, it stated, "[The tax] is bad because, in the light of its history and of its present setting, it is seen to be a deliberate and calculated device in the guise of a tax to limit the circulation of information," 297 U.S., at 250, an explanation that suggests that the motivation of the legislature may have been significant.

Our subsequent cases have not been consistent in their reading of *Grosjean* on this point. Compare United States v. O'Brien, 391 U.S. 367, 384–385 (1968) (stating that legislative purpose was irrelevant in *Grosjean*) with Houchins v. KQED, Inc., 438 U.S. 1, 9–10 (1978) (plurality opinion) (suggesting that purpose was relevant in *Grosjean*); Pittsburgh Press Co. v. Pittsburgh Commission on Human Relations, 413 U.S. 376, 383 (1973) (same). Commentators have generally viewed *Grosjean* as dependent on the improper censorial goals of the legislature. See T. Emerson, The System of Freedom of Expression 419 (1970); L. Tribe, American Constitutional Law 592 n. 8, 724 n. 10 (1978). We think that the result in *Grosjean* may have been attributable in part to the perception on the part of the Court that the state imposed the tax with an intent to penalize a selected group of newspapers. In the case currently before us, however, there is no legislative history and no indication, apart from the structure of the tax itself, of any impermissible or censorial motive on the part of the legislature. We cannot resolve the case by simple citation to *Grosjean.* Instead, we must analyze the problem anew under the general principles of the First Amendment.

III

Clearly, the First Amendment does not prohibit all regulation of the press. It is beyond dispute that the States and the Federal Government can subject newspapers to generally applicable economic regulations without creating constitutional problems. See, e.g., Citizens Publishing Co. v. United States, 394 U.S. 131, 139 (1969) (antitrust laws); Lorain Journal Co. v. United States, 342 U.S. 143, 155–156 (1951) (same); Breard v. Alexandria, 341 U.S. 622 (1951) (prohibition of door-to-door solicitation); Oklahoma Press Publishing Co. v. Walling, 327 U.S. 186, 192–193 (1946) (Fair Labor Standards Act); Mabee v. White Plains Publishing Co., 327 U.S. 178 (1946) (same); Associated Press v. United States, 326 U.S. 1, 6–7, 19–20 (1945) (antitrust laws); Associated Press v. NLRB, 301 U.S. 103, 132–133 (1937) (NLRA); see also Branzburg v. Hayes, 408 U.S. 665 (1972) (enforcement of subpoenas). Minnesota, however, has not chosen to apply its general sales and use tax to newspapers. Instead, it has created a special tax that applies only to certain publications protected by the First Amendment. Although the State argues now that the tax on paper and ink is part of the general scheme of taxation, the use tax provision, quoted in note 2, supra, is facially discriminatory, singling out publications for treatment that is, to our knowledge, unique in Minnesota tax law.

Minnesota's treatment of publications differs from that of other enterprises in at least two important respects: it imposes a use tax that does not serve the function of protecting the sales tax, and it taxes an intermediate transaction rather than the ultimate retail sale. A use tax ordinarily serves to complement the sales tax by eliminating the incentive to make major purchases in States with lower sales taxes; it requires the resident who shops out-of-state to pay a use tax equal to the sales tax savings. . . . But the use tax on ink and paper serves no such complementary function; it applies to all uses, whether or not the taxpayer purchased the ink and paper in-state, and it applies to items exempt from the sales tax.

Further, the ordinary rule in Minnesota, as discussed above, is to tax only the ultimate, or retail, sale rather than the use of components like ink and paper. . . . Publishers, however, are taxed on their purchase of components, even though they will eventually sell their publications at retail.

By creating this special use tax, which, to our knowledge, is without parallel in the State's tax scheme, Minnesota has singled out the press for special treatment. We then must determine whether the First Amendment permits such special taxation. . . . The cases approving . . . economic regulation, . . . emphasized the general applicability of the challenged regulation to all businesses, e.g., Oklahoma Press Publishing Co. v. Walling, supra, 327 U.S., at 194; Mabee v. White Plains Publishing Co., supra, 327 U.S., at 184; Associated Press v. NLRB, supra, 301 U.S., at 132–133, suggesting that a regulation that singled out the press might place a heavier burden of justification on the State, and we now conclude that the special problems created by differential treatment do indeed impose such a burden.

. . . .

. . . A power to tax differentially, as opposed to a power to tax generally, gives a government a powerful weapon against the taxpayer selected. When the State imposes a generally applicable tax, there is little cause for concern. We need not fear that a government will destroy a selected group of taxpayers by burdensome taxation if it must impose the same burden on the rest of its constituency. See Railway Express Agency v. New York, 336 U.S. 106, 112–113 (1949) (Jackson, J., concurring). When the State singles out the press, though, the political constraints that prevent a legislature from passing crippling taxes of general applicability are weakened, and the threat of burdensome taxes becomes acute. That threat can operate as effectively as a censor to check critical comment by the press, undercutting the basic assumption of our political system that the press will often serve as an important restraint on government. . . .

. . .

IV

. . .

. . . Minnesota invites us to look beyond the form of the tax to its substance. The tax is, according to the State, merely a substitute for the sales tax, which, as a generally applicable tax, would be constitutional as applied to the press.[9] There are two fatal flaws in this reasoning. First, the State has offered no explanation of why it chose to use a substitute for the sales tax rather than the sales tax itself. The court below speculated that the State might have been concerned that collection of a tax on such small transactions would be impractical. . . . That suggestion is unpersuasive, for sales of other low-priced goods are not exempt. If the real goal of this tax is to duplicate the sales tax, it is difficult to see why the State did not achieve that goal by the obvious and effective expedient of applying the sales tax.

Further, even assuming that the legislature did have valid reasons for substituting another tax for the sales tax, we are not persuaded that this tax does serve as a substitute. The State asserts that this scheme actually *favors* the press over other businesses, because the same rate of tax is applied, but, for the press, the rate applies to the cost of components rather than to the sales price. We would be hesitant to fashion a rule that automatically allowed the State to single out the press for a different method of taxation as long as the effective burden was no different from that on other taxpayers or the burden on the press was lighter than that on other businesses. One reason for this reluctance is that the very selection of the press for special treatment threatens the press not only with the current *differential* treatment, but with the possibility of subsequent differentially *more burdensome* treatment. . . .

A second reason to avoid the proposed rule is that courts as institutions are poorly equipped to evaluate with precision the relative burdens of various methods of taxation. The complexities of factual economic proof always present a certain potential for error, and courts have little familiarity with the process of evaluating the relative economic burden of taxes. In sum, the possibility of error inherent in the proposed rule poses too great a threat to concerns at the heart of the First Amendment, and we cannot tolerate that possibility. Minnesota, therefore, has offered no adequate justification for the special treatment of newspapers.

V

Minnesota's ink and paper tax violates the First Amendment not only because it singles out the press, but also because it targets a small group of newspapers. The effect of the $100,000 exemption enacted in 1974 is that only a handful of publishers pay any tax at all, and even fewer pay any significant amount of tax. The State explains this exemption as part of a policy favoring an

---

[9] Star Tribune insists that the premise of the State's argument—that a generally applicable sales tax would be constitutional—is incorrect . . . We think that Breard v. Alexandria, 341 U.S. 622 (1951) . . . rebuts Star Tribune's argument. There, we upheld an ordinance prohibiting door-to-door solicitation, even though it applied to prevent the door-to-door sale of subscriptions to magazines, an activity covered by the First Amendment. Although Martin v. Struthers, 319 U.S. 141 (1943), had struck down a similar ordinance as applied to the distribution of free religious literature, the *Breard* Court explained that case as emphasizing that the information distributed was religious in nature and that the distribution was noncommercial. 341 U.S., at 642–643. . . .

"equitable" tax system, although there are no comparable exemptions for small enterprises outside the press. Again, there is no legislative history supporting the State's view of the purpose of the amendment. Whatever the motive of the legislature in this case, we think that recognizing a power in the State not only to single out the press but also to tailor the tax so that it singles out a few members of the press presents such a potential for abuse that no interest suggested by Minnesota can justify the scheme. It has asserted no interest other than its desire to have an "equitable" tax system. The current system, it explains, promotes equity because it places the burden on large publications that impose more social costs than do smaller publications and that are more likely to be able to bear the burden of the tax. Even if we were willing to accept the premise that large businesses are more profitable and therefore better able to bear the burden of the tax, the State's commitment to this "equity" is questionable, for the concern has not led the State to grant benefits to small businesses in general. And when the exemption selects such a narrowly defined group to bear the full burden of the tax, the tax begins to resemble more a penalty for a few of the largest newspapers than an attempt to favor struggling smaller enterprises.

VI

We need not and do not impugn the motives of the Minnesota legislature in passing the ink and paper tax. . . . Since Minnesota has offered no satisfactory justification for its tax on the use of ink and paper, the tax violates the First Amendment, and the judgment below is

Reversed.

Justice White, concurring in part and dissenting in part.

This case is not difficult. The exemption for the first $100,000 of paper and ink limits the burden of the Minnesota tax to only a few papers. This feature alone is sufficient reason to invalidate the Minnesota tax and reverse the judgment of the Minnesota Supreme Court. The Court recognizes that Minnesota's tax violates the First Amendment for this reason, and I subscribe to Part V of the Court's opinion and concur in the judgment.

. . .

There may be cases, I recognize, where the Court cannot confidently ascertain whether a differential method of taxation imposes a greater burden upon the press than a generally applicable tax. In these circumstances, I too may be unwilling to entrust freedom of the press to uncertain economic proof. But, as Justice Rehnquist clearly shows, this is not such a case. . . .

Justice Rehnquist, dissenting.

. . .

. . . We need no expert testimony from modern day Euclids or Einsteins to determine that the $1,224,747 paid in use taxes is significantly less burdensome than the $3,685,092 that could have been levied by a sales tax. *A fortiori,* the Minnesota taxing scheme which singles out newspapers for "differential treatment" has benefited, not burdened, the "freedom of speech, [and] of the press."

Ignoring these calculations, the Court concludes that "differential treatment" alone in Minnesota's sales and use tax scheme requires that the statutes be found "presumptively unconstitutional" and declared invalid "unless the State asserts a counterbalancing interest of compelling importance that it cannot achieve without differential taxation." The "differential treatment" standard that the Court has conjured up is unprecedented and unwarranted. . . .

. . .

The Court finds in very summary fashion that the exemption newspapers receive for the first $100,000 of ink and paper used also violates the First Amendment because the result is that only a few of the newspapers actually pay a use tax. I cannot agree. As explained by the Minnesota Supreme Court, the exemption is in effect a $4,000 credit which benefits all newspapers. . . . Minneapolis Star & Tribune was benefited to the amount of $16,000 in the two years in question; $4,000 each year for its morning paper and $4,000 each year for its evening paper. . . . Absent any improper motive on the part of the Minnesota legislature in drawing the limits of this exemption, it cannot be construed as violating the First Amendment. . . .

To collect from newspapers their fair share of taxes under the sales and use tax scheme and at the same time avoid abridging the freedoms of speech and press, the Court holds today that Minnesota must subject newspapers to millions of additional dollars in sales tax liability. Certainly this is a hollow victory for the newspapers and I seriously doubt the Court's conclusion that this result would have been intended by the "Framers of the First Amendment."

For the reasons set forth above, I would affirm the judgment of the Minnesota Supreme Court.

———

CALDER v. JONES, 104 S.Ct. 1482 (1984). The Court upheld the constitutionality of application of a state's "long arm" statute to provide jurisdiction over the reporter and editor of a magazine article in a civil suit for libel. (In a case decided the same day, Keeton v. Hustler Magazine, 104 S.Ct. 1473 (1984), the Court concluded that regular circulation of magazines in the forum state was sufficient to establish jurisdiction over the out-of-state publisher in a libel action.) The Court rejected an argument that the minimum contacts necessary to establish jurisdiction were affected by first amendment concerns. Justice Rehnquist said, for the Court: "The infusion of such considerations would needlessly complicate an already imprecise inquiry. . . . Moreover, the potential chill on protected First Amendment activity stemming from libel and defamation actions is already taken into account in the constitutional limitations on the substantive law governing such suits. . . . To reintroduce those concerns at the jurisdictional stage would be a form of double counting. We have already declined in other contexts to grant special procedural protections to defendants in libel and defamation actions in addition to the constitutional protections embodied in the substantive laws. See, e.g., Herbert v. Lando, 441 U.S. 153 (1979)."

SECTION 2. RESTRAINTS ON EDITORIAL JUDGMENT

———

PITTSBURGH PRESS CO. v. PITTSBURGH COMMISSION ON HUMAN RELATIONS

413 U.S. 376, 93 S.Ct. 2553, 37 L.Ed.2d 669 (1973).

Mr. Justice Powell delivered the opinion of the Court.

The Human Relations Ordinance of the City of Pittsburgh (the Ordinance) has been construed below by the courts of Pennsylvania as forbidding newspapers to carry "help-wanted" advertisements in sex-designated columns except where the employer or advertiser is free to make hiring or employment referral decisions on the basis of sex. We are called upon to decide whether the Ordinance as so construed violates the freedoms of speech, and of the press guaranteed by the First and Fourteenth Amendments. . . .

. . . . .

Respondents rely principally on the argument that this regulation is permissible because the speech is commercial speech unprotected by the First Amendment. The commercial speech doctrine is traceable to the brief opinion in Valentine v. Chrestensen, 316 U.S. 52 (1942). . . .

But Pittsburgh Press contends that *Chrestensen* is not applicable, as the focus in this case must be upon the exercise of editorial judgment by the newspaper as to where to place the advertisement rather than upon its commercial content. . . .

As for the present case, we are not persuaded that either the decision to accept a commercial advertisement which the advertiser directs to be placed in a sex-designated column or the actual placement there lifts the newspaper's actions from the category of commercial speech. By implication at least, an advertiser whose want-ad appears in the "Jobs—Male Interest" column is likely to discriminate against women in his hiring decisions. Nothing in a sex-designated column heading sufficiently disassociates the designation from the want-ads placed beneath it to make the placement severable for First Amendment purposes from the want-ads themselves. The combination, which conveys essentially the same message as an overtly discriminatory want-ad, is in practical effect an integrated commercial statement.

Pittsburgh Press goes on to argue that if this package of advertisement and placement is commercial speech, then commercial speech should be accorded a higher level of protection than *Chrestensen* and its progeny would suggest. Insisting that the exchange of information is as important in the commercial realm as in any other, the newspaper here would have us abrogate the distinction between commercial and other speech.

Whatever the merits of this contention may be in other contexts, it is unpersuasive in this case. Discrimination in employment is not only commercial activity, it is *illegal* commercial activity under the Ordinance. We have no doubt that a newspaper constitutionally could be forbidden to publish a want-ad proposing a sale of narcotics or soliciting prostitutes. Nor would the result be different if the nature of the transaction were indicated by placement under columns captioned "Narcotics for Sale" and "Prostitutes Wanted" rather than stated within the four corners of the advertisement. . . .

We emphasize that nothing in our holding allows government at any level to forbid Pittsburgh Press to publish and distribute advertisements commenting on the Ordinance, the enforcement practices of the Commission, or the propriety of sex preferences in employment. Nor, *a fortiori,* does our decision authorize any restriction whatever, whether of content or layout, on stories or commentary originated by Pittsburgh Press, its columnists, or its contributors. On the contrary, we reaffirm unequivocally the protection afforded to editorial judgment and to the free expression of views on these and other issues, however controversial. We hold only that the Commission's modified order, narrowly drawn to prohibit placement in sex-designated columns of advertisements for nonexempt job opportunities, does not infringe the First Amendment rights of Pittsburgh Press.

Affirmed.

Mr. Chief Justice Burger, dissenting.

Despite the Court's efforts to decide only the most narrow question presented in this case, the holding represents, for me, a disturbing enlargement of the "commercial speech" doctrine, Valentine v. Chrestensen, 316 U.S. 52 (1942), and a serious encroachment on the freedom of press guaranteed by the First Amendment. It also launches the courts on what I perceive to be a treacherous path of defining what layout and organizational decisions of newspapers are "sufficiently associated" with the "commercial" parts of the papers as to be constitutionally unprotected and therefore subject to governmental regulation. Assuming, *arguendo,* that the First Amendment permits the States to place restrictions on the content of commercial advertisements, I would not enlarge that power to reach the layout and organizational decisions of a newspaper.

. . .

Mr. Justice Douglas, dissenting.

. . .

Mr. Justice Stewart, with whom Mr. Justice Douglas joins, dissenting.

. . .

[W]hat the Court approves today is wholly different. It approves a government order dictating to a publisher in advance how he must arrange the layout of pages in his newspaper.

Nothing in Valentine v. Chrestensen, 316 U.S. 52 remotely supports the Court's decision. . . .

So far as I know, this is the first case in this or any other American court that permits a government agency to enter a composing room of a newspaper and dictate to the publisher the layout and makeup of the newspaper's pages. This is the first such case, but I fear it may not be the last. The camel's nose is in the tent. . . .

So long as Members of this Court view the First Amendment as no more than a set of "values" to be balanced against other "values," that Amendment will remain in grave jeopardy. . . .

Those who think the First Amendment can and should be subordinated to other socially desirable interests will hail today's decision. But I find it frightening. For I believe the constitutional guarantee of a free press is more than precatory. I believe it is a clear command that government must never be allowed to lay its heavy editorial hand on any newspaper in this country.

Mr. Justice Blackmun, dissenting.

I dissent substantially for the reasons stated by Mr. Justice Stewart in his opinion. . . .

———

MIAMI HERALD PUBLISHING CO. v. TORNILLO

418 U.S. 241, 94 S.Ct. 2831, 41 L.Ed.2d 730 (1974).

Mr. Chief Justice Burger delivered the opinion of the Court.

The issue in this case is whether a state statute granting a political candidate a right to equal space to reply to criticism and attacks on his record by a newspaper, violates the guarantees of a free press.

I.

In the fall of 1972, appellee, Executive Director of the Classroom Teachers Association, apparently a teachers' collective-bargaining agent, was a candidate for the Florida House of Representatives. On September 20, 1972, and again on September 29, 1972, appellant printed editorials critical of appellee's candidacy. In response to these editorials appellee demanded that appellant print verbatim his replies, defending the role of the Classroom Teachers Association and the organization's accomplishments for the citizens of Dade County. Appellant declined to print the appellee's replies, and appellee brought suit in Circuit Court, Dade County, seeking declaratory and injunctive relief and actual and punitive damages in excess of $5,000. The action was premised on Florida Statute § 104.38, a "right of reply" statute which provides that if a candidate for nomination or election is assailed regarding his personal character or official record by any newspaper, the candidate has the right to demand that the newspaper print, free of cost to the candidate, any reply the candidate may make to the newspaper's charges. The reply must appear in as conspicuous a place and in the same kind of type as the charges which prompted the reply, provided it does not take up more space than the charges. Failure to comply with the statute constitutes a first-degree misdemeanor.

Appellant sought a declaration that § 104.38 was unconstitutional. . . .

. . . [T]he Florida Supreme Court [held] that § 104.38 did not violate constitutional guarantees. . . .

III.

A.

. . .

Appellant contends the statute is void on its face because it purports to regulate the content of a newspaper in violation of the First Amendment. Alternatively it is urged that the statute is void for vagueness since no editor could know exactly what words would call the statute into operation. It is also contended that the statute fails to distinguish between critical comment which is and is not defamatory.

B.

The appellee and supporting advocates of an enforceable right of access to the press vigorously argue that government has an obligation to ensure that a wide variety of views reach the public.[8] The contentions of access proponents will be set out in some detail.[9] It is urged that at the time the First Amendment to the Constitution was enacted in 1791 as part of our Bill of Rights the press was broadly representative of the people it was serving. While many of the newspapers were intensely partisan and narrow in their views, the press collectively presented a broad range of opinions to readers. Entry into publishing was inexpensive; pamphlets and books provided meaningful alternatives to the organized press for the expression of unpopular ideas and often treated events and expressed views not covered by conventional newspapers. A true marketplace of ideas existed in which there was relatively easy access to the channels of communication.

Access advocates submit that although newspapers of the present are superficially similar to those of 1791 the press of today is in reality very different from that known in the early years of our national existence. In the past half century a communications revolution has seen the introduction of radio and television into our lives, the promise of a global community through the use of communications satellites, and the spectre of a "wired" nation by means of an expanding cable television network with two-way capabilities. The printed press, it is said, has not escaped the effects of this revolution. Newspapers have become big business and there are far fewer of them to serve a larger literate population. Chains of newspapers, national newspapers, national wire and news services, and one-newspaper towns, are the dominant features of a press that has become noncompetitive and enormously powerful and influential in its capacity to manipulate popular opinion and change the course of events. Major metropolitan newspapers have collaborated to establish news services national in scope. Such national news organizations provide syndicated "interpretative reporting"

---

[8] See generally Barron, Access to the Press—A New First Amendment Right, 80 Harv.L.Rev. 1641 (1967).

[9] For a good overview of the position of access advocates see Lange, The Role of the Access Doctrine in the Regulation of the Mass Media: A Critical Review and Assessment, 52 N.C.L.Rev. 1, 8–9 (1973) (hereinafter Lange).

as well as syndicated features and commentary, all of which can serve as part of the new school of "advocacy journalism."

The elimination of competing newspapers in most of our large cities, and the concentration of control of media that results from the only newspaper being owned by the same interests which own a television station and a radio station, are important components of this trend toward concentration of control of outlets to inform the public.

The result of these vast changes has been to place in a few hands the power to inform the American people and shape public opinion. Much of the editorial opinion and commentary that is printed is that of syndicated columnists distributed nationwide and, as a result, we are told, on national and world issues there tends to be a homogeneity of editorial opinion, commentary, and interpretative analysis. The abuses of bias and manipulative reportage are, likewise, said to be the result of the vast accumulations of unreviewable power in the modern media empires. In effect, it is claimed, the public has lost any ability to respond or to contribute in a meaningful way to the debate on issues. The monopoly of the means of communication allows for little or no critical analysis of the media except in professional journals of very limited readership. . . .

The obvious solution, which was available to dissidents at an earlier time when entry into publishing was relatively inexpensive, today would be to have additional newspapers. But the same economic factors which have caused the disappearance of vast numbers of metropolitan newspapers, have made entry into the marketplace of ideas served by the print media almost impossible. It is urged that the claim of newspapers to be "surrogates for the public" carries with it a concomitant fiduciary obligation to account for that stewardship. From this premise it is reasoned that the only effective way to insure fairness and accuracy and to provide for some accountability is for government to take affirmative action. The First Amendment interest of the public in being informed is said to be in peril because the "marketplace of ideas" is today a monopoly controlled by the owners of the market. . . .

IV.

However much validity may be found in these arguments, at each point the implementation of a remedy such as an enforceable right of access necessarily calls for some mechanism, either governmental or consensual. If it is governmental coercion, this at once brings about a confrontation with the express provisions of the First Amendment and the judicial gloss on that Amendment developed over the years.

. . .

Appellee's argument that the Florida statute does not amount to a restriction of appellant's right to speak because "the statute in question here has not prevented the *Miami Herald* from saying anything it wished" begs the core question. Compelling editors or publishers to publish that which " 'reason' tells them should not be published" is what is at issue in this case. The Florida statute operates as a command in the same sense as a statute or regulation forbidding appellant from publishing specified matter. . . . The Florida statute exacts a penalty on the basis of the content of a newspaper. The first phase of the penalty resulting from the compelled printing of a reply is exacted in terms of the cost in printing and composing time and materials and in taking up space that could be devoted to other material the newspaper may have preferred to print. It is correct, as appellee contends, that a newspaper is not subject to the finite technological limitations of time that confront a broadcaster but it is not correct to say that, as an economic reality, a newspaper can proceed to infinite expansion of its column space to accommodate the replies that a government agency determines or a statute commands the readers should have available.

Faced with the penalties that would accrue to any newspaper that published news or commentary arguably within the reach of the right of access statute, editors might well conclude that the safe course is to avoid controversy. Therefore, under the operation of the Florida statute, political and electoral coverage would be blunted or reduced. . . .

Even if a newspaper would face no additional costs to comply with a compulsory access law and would not be forced to forego publication of news or opinion by the inclusion of a reply, the Florida statute fails to clear the barriers of the First Amendment because of its intrusion into the function of editors. A newspaper is more than a passive receptacle or conduit for news, comment, and advertising. The choice of material to go into a newspaper, and the decisions made as to limitations on the size of the paper, and content, and treatment of public issues and public officials—whether fair or unfair—constitutes the exercise of editorial control and judgment. It has yet to be demonstrated how governmental regulation of this crucial process can be exercised consistent with First Amendment guarantees of a free press as they have evolved to this time. Accordingly, the judgment of the Supreme Court of Florida is reversed.

It is so ordered.

Mr. Justice Brennan, with whom Mr. Justice Rehnquist joins, concurring.

I join the Court's opinion which, as I understand it, addresses only "right of reply" statutes and implies no view upon the constitutionality of "retraction" statutes affording plaintiffs able to prove defamatory falsehoods a statutory action to require publication of a retraction. See generally Note, Vindication of the Reputation of a Public Official, 80 Harv.L.Rev. 1730, 1739–1747 (1967).

Mr. Justice White, concurring.

The Court today holds that the First Amendment bars a State from requiring a newspaper to print the reply of a candidate for public office whose personal character has been criticized by that newspaper's editorials. According to our accepted jurisprudence, the First Amendment erects a virtually insurmountable barrier between government and the print media so far as government tampering, in advance of publication, with news and editorial content is concerned.

. . . .

    .   .   .

SECTION 3. PROHIBITION OF PUBLICATION OF GOVERNMENT INFORMATION

NEW YORK TIMES CO. v. UNITED STATES

[The Cases of the Pentagon Papers.]

403 U.S. 713, 91 S.Ct. 2140, 29 L.Ed.2d 822 (1971).

Per Curiam.

We granted certiorari in these cases in which the United States seeks to enjoin the New York Times and the Washington Post from publishing the contents of a classified study entitled "History of U.S. Decision-Making Process on Viet Nam Policy." [commonly referred to as the "Pentagon Papers".]

"Any system of prior restraints of expression comes to this Court bearing a heavy presumption against its constitutional validity." Bantam Books, Inc. v. Sullivan, 372 U.S. 58, 70 (1963); see also Near v. Minnesota, 283 U.S. 697

(1931). The Government "thus carries a heavy burden of showing justification for the imposition of such a restraint." Organization for a Better Austin v. Keefe, 402 U.S. 415, 419 (1971). The District Court for the Southern District of New York in the *New York Times* case and the District Court for the District of Columbia and the Court of Appeals for the District of Columbia Circuit in the *Washington Post* case held that the Government had not met that burden. We agree.

The judgment of the Court of Appeals for the District of Columbia Circuit is therefore affirmed. The order of the Court of Appeals for the Second Circuit is reversed and the case is remanded with directions to enter a judgment affirming the judgment of the District Court for the Southern District of New York.

. . .

Mr. Justice Black, with whom Mr. Justice Douglas joins, concurring.

I adhere to the view that the Government's case against the Washington Post should have been dismissed and that the injunction against the New York Times should have been vacated without oral argument when the cases were first presented to this Court. I believe that every moment's continuance of the injunctions against these newspapers amounts to a flagrant, indefensible, and continuing violation of the First Amendment. Furthermore, after oral arguments, I agree completely that we must affirm the judgment of the Court of Appeals for the District of Columbia and reverse the judgment of the Court of Appeals for the Second Circuit for the reasons stated by my Brothers Douglas and Brennan. In my view it is unfortunate that some of my Brethren are apparently willing to hold that the publication of news may sometimes be enjoined. Such a holding would make a shambles of the First Amendment.

. . .

In my view, far from deserving condemnation for their courageous reporting, the New York Times, the Washington Post, and other newspapers should be commended for serving the purpose that the Founding Fathers saw so clearly. In revealing the workings of government that led to the Viet Nam war, the newspapers nobly did precisely that which the Founders hoped and trusted they would do. . . .

The Government argues in its brief that in spite of the First Amendment, "[t]he authority of the Executive Department to protect the nation against publication of information whose disclosure would endanger the national security stems from two interrelated sources: the constitutional power of the President over the conduct of foreign affairs and his authority as Commander-in-Chief." . . .

To find that the President has "inherent power" to halt the publication of news by resort to the courts would wipe out the First Amendment and destroy the fundamental liberty and security of the very people the Government hopes to make "secure." No one can read the history of the adoption of the First Amendment without being convinced beyond any doubt that it was injunctions like those sought here that Madison and his collaborators intended to outlaw in this Nation for all time. . . .

Mr. Justice Douglas, with whom Mr. Justice Black joins, concurring.

. . .

It should be noted at the outset that the First Amendment provides that "Congress shall make no law . . . abridging the freedom of speech or of the press." That leaves, in my view, no room for governmental restraint on the press.

There is, moreover, no statute barring the publication by the press of the material which the Times and Post seek to use. . . .

. . .

The stays in these cases that have been in effect for more than a week constitute a flouting of the principles of the First Amendment as interpreted in Near v. Minnesota.

Mr. Justice Brennan, concurring.

I.

I write separately in these cases only to emphasize what should be apparent: that our judgment in the present cases may not be taken to indicate the propriety, in the future, of issuing temporary stays and restraining orders to block the publication of material sought to be suppressed by the Government. So far as I can determine, never before has the United States sought to enjoin a newspaper from publishing information in its possession. . . .

II.

The error which has pervaded these cases from the outset was the granting of any injunctive relief whatsoever, interim or otherwise. The entire thrust of the Government's claim throughout these cases has been that publication of the material sought to be enjoined "could," or "might," or "may," prejudice the national interest in various ways. But the First Amendment tolerates absolutely no prior judicial restraints of the press predicated upon surmise or conjecture that untoward consequences may result.* Our cases, it is true, have indicated that there is a single, extremely narrow class of cases in which the First Amendment's ban on prior judicial restraint may be overridden. Our cases have thus far indicated that such cases may arise only when the Nation "is at war," Schenck v. United States, 249 U.S. 47, 52 (1919), during which times "no one would question but that a Government might prevent actual obstruction to its recruiting service or the publication of the sailing dates of transports or the number and location of troops." Near v. Minnesota, 283 U.S. 697, 716 (1931). Even if the present world situation were assumed to be tantamount to a time of war, or if the power of presently available armaments would justify even in peacetime the suppression of information that would set in motion a nuclear holocaust, in neither of these actions has the Government presented or even alleged that publication of items from or based upon the material at issue would cause the happening of an event of that nature. "The chief purpose of [the First Amendment's] guaranty [is] to prevent previous restraints upon publication." Near v. Minnesota, supra, at 713. Thus, only governmental allegation and proof that publication must inevitably, directly and immediately cause the occurrence of an event kindred to imperiling the safety of a transport already at sea can support even the issuance of an interim restraining order. In no event may mere conclusions be sufficient: for if the Executive Branch seeks judicial aid in preventing publication, it must inevitably submit the basis upon which that aid is sought to scrutiny by the judiciary. And therefore, every restraint issued in this case, whatever its form, has violated the First Amendment—and none the less so because that restraint was justified as necessary to afford the court an opportunity to examine the claim more thoroughly. Unless

---

* Freedman v. Maryland, 380 U.S. 51 (1965), and similar cases regarding temporary restraints of allegedly obscene materials are not in point. For those cases rest upon the proposition that "obscenity is not protected by the freedoms of speech and press." Roth v. United States, 354 U.S. 476, 481 (1957). Here there is no question but that the material sought to be suppressed is within the protection of the First Amendment; the only question is whether, notwithstanding that fact, its publication may be enjoined for a time because of the presence of an overwhelming national interest. Similarly, copyright cases have no pertinence here: the Government is not asserting an interest in the particular form of words chosen in the documents, but is seeking to suppress the ideas expressed therein. And the copyright laws, of course, protect only the form of expression and not the ideas expressed.

and until the Government has clearly made out its case, the First Amendment commands that no injunction may issue.

Mr. Justice Stewart, with whom Mr. Justice White joins, concurring.

In the governmental structure created by our Constitution, the Executive is endowed with enormous power in the two related areas of national defense and international relations. This power, largely unchecked by the Legislative and Judicial branches, has been pressed to the very hilt since the advent of the nuclear missile age. For better or for worse, the simple fact is that a President of the United States possesses vastly greater constitutional independence in these two vital areas of power than does, say, a prime minister of a country with a parliamentary form of government.

In the absence of the governmental checks and balances present in other areas of our national life, the only effective restraint upon executive policy and power in the areas of national defense and international affairs may lie in an enlightened citizenry—in an informed and critical public opinion which alone can here protect the values of democratic government. For this reason, it is perhaps here that a press that is alert, aware, and free most vitally serves the basic purpose of the First Amendment. For without an informed and free press there cannot be an enlightened people.

Yet it is elementary that the successful conduct of international diplomacy and the maintenance of an effective national defense require both confidentiality and secrecy. Other nations can hardly deal with this Nation in an atmosphere of mutual trust unless they can be assured that their confidences will be kept. And within our own executive departments, the development of considered and intelligent international policies would be impossible if those charged with their formulation could not communicate with each other freely, frankly, and in confidence. In the area of basic national defense the frequent need for absolute secrecy is, of course, self-evident.

I think there can be but one answer to this dilemma, if dilemma it be. The responsibility must be where the power is. If the Constitution gives the Executive a large degree of unshared power in the conduct of foreign affairs and the maintenance of our national defense, then under the Constitution the Executive must have the largely unshared duty to determine and preserve the degree of internal security necessary to exercise that power successfully. . . . [I]t is the constitutional duty of the Executive—as a matter of sovereign prerogative and not as a matter of law as the courts know law—through the promulgation and enforcement of executive regulations, to protect the confidentiality necessary to carry out its responsibilities in the fields of international relations and national defense.

This is not to say that Congress and the courts have no role to play. Undoubtedly Congress has the power to enact specific and appropriate criminal laws to protect government property and preserve government secrets. Congress has passed such laws, and several of them are of very colorable relevance to the apparent circumstances of these cases. And if a criminal prosecution is instituted, it will be the responsibility of the courts to decide the applicability of the criminal law under which the charge is brought. Moreover, if Congress should pass a specific law authorizing civil proceedings in this field, the courts would likewise have the duty to decide the constitutionality of such a law as well as its applicability to the facts proved.

But in the cases before us we are asked neither to construe specific regulations nor to apply specific laws. We are asked, instead, to perform a function that the Constitution gave to the Executive, not the Judiciary. We are asked, quite simply, to prevent the publication by two newspapers of material that the Executive Branch insists should not, in the national interest, be published. I am convinced that the Executive is correct with respect to some of the documents involved. But I cannot say that disclosure of any of them will surely result in direct, immediate, and irreparable damage to our Nation or its people. That being so, there can under the First Amendment be but one judicial resolution of the issues before us. I join the judgments of the Court.

Mr. Justice White, with whom Mr. Justice Stewart joins, concurring.

I concur in today's judgments, but only because of the concededly extraordinary protection against prior restraints enjoyed by the press under our constitutional system. I do not say that in no circumstances would the First Amendment permit an injunction against publishing information about government plans or operations. Nor, after examining the materials the Government characterizes as the most sensitive and destructive, can I deny that revelation of these documents will do substantial damage to public interests. Indeed, I am confident that their disclosure will have that result. But I nevertheless agree that the United States has not satisfied the very heavy burden which it must meet to warrant an injunction against publication in these cases, at least in the absence of express and appropriately limited congressional authorization for prior restraints in circumstances such as these.

The Government's position is simply stated: The responsibility of the Executive for the conduct of the foreign affairs and for the security of the Nation is so basic that the President is entitled to an injunction against publication of a newspaper story whenever he can convince a court that the information to be revealed threatens "grave and irreparable" injury to the public interest; and the injunction should issue whether or not the material to be published is classified, whether or not publication would be lawful under relevant criminal statutes enacted by Congress and regardless of the circumstances by which the newspaper came into possession of the information.

At least in the absence of legislation by Congress, based on its own investigations and findings, I am quite unable to agree that the inherent powers of the Executive and the courts reach so far as to authorize remedies having such sweeping potential for inhibiting publications by the press. . . .

What is more, terminating the ban on publication of the relatively few sensitive documents the Government now seeks to suppress does not mean that the law either requires or invites newspapers or others to publish them or that they will be immune from criminal action if they do. Prior restraints require an unusually heavy justification under the First Amendment; but failure by the Government to justify prior restraints does not measure its constitutional entitlement to a conviction for criminal publication. That the Government mistakenly chose to proceed by injunction does not mean that it could not successfully proceed in another way. . . .

The Criminal Code contains numerous provisions potentially relevant to these cases. . . .

It is thus clear that Congress has addressed itself to the problems of protecting the security of the country and the national defense from unauthorized disclosure of potentially damaging information. . . . It has not, however, authorized the injunctive remedy against threatened publication. It has apparently been satisfied to rely on criminal sanctions and their deterrent effect on the responsible as well as the irresponsible press. I am not, of course, saying that either of these newspapers has yet committed a crime or that either would commit a crime if they published all the material now in their possession. That matter must await resolution in the context of a criminal proceeding if one is instituted by the United States. In that event, the issue of guilt or innocence would be determined by procedures and standards quite different from those that have purported to govern these injunctive proceedings.

Mr. Justice Marshall, concurring.

. . .

In these cases there is no problem concerning the President's power to classify information as "secret" or "top secret." Congress has specifically recognized Presidential authority, which has been formally exercised in Executive Order 10501, to classify documents and information. See, e.g., 18 U.S.C. § 798; 50 U.S.C. § 783. Nor is there any issue here regarding the President's power as Chief Executive and Commander-in-Chief to protect national security by disciplining employees who disclose information and by taking precautions to prevent leaks.

The problem here is whether in this particular case the Executive Branch has authority to invoke the equity jurisdiction of the courts to protect what it believes to be the national interest. . . .

It would, however, be utterly inconsistent with the concept of separation of powers for this Court, to use its power of contempt to prevent behavior that Congress has specifically declined to prohibit. There would be a similar damage to the basic concept of these coequal branches of Government if when the Executive has adequate authority granted by Congress to protect "national security" it can choose instead to invoke the contempt power of a court to enjoin the threatened conduct. . . .

. . .

Mr. Chief Justice Burger, dissenting.

. . .

. . . [W]e have been forced to deal with litigation concerning rights of great magnitude without an adequate record, and surely without time for adequate treatment either in the prior proceedings or in this Court: . . . I agree generally with Mr. Justice Harlan and Mr. Justice Blackmun but I am not prepared to reach the merits. . . .

. . .

Mr. Justice Harlan, with whom The Chief Justice and Mr. Justice Blackmun join, dissenting.

With all respect, I consider that the Court has been almost irresponsibly feverish in dealing with these cases.

. . .

These are difficult questions of fact, of law, and of judgment; the potential consequences of erroneous decision are enormous. The time which has been available to us, to the lower courts, and to the parties has been wholly inadequate for giving these cases the kind of consideration they deserve. It is a reflection on the stability of the judicial process that these great issues—as important as any that have arisen during my time on the Court—should have been decided under the pressures engendered by the torrent of publicity that has attended these litigations from their inception.

Forced as I am to reach the merits of these cases, I dissent from the opinion and judgments of the Court. Within the severe limitations imposed by the time constraints under which I have been required to operate, I can only state my reasons in telescoped form, even though in different circumstances I would have felt constrained to deal with the cases in the fuller sweep indicated above.

. . .

It is plain to me that the scope of the judicial function in passing upon the activities of the Executive Branch of the Government in the field of foreign affairs is very narrowly restricted. This view is, I think, dictated by the concept of separation of powers upon which our constitutional system rests. . . .

I agree that, in performance of its duty to protect the values of the First Amendment against political pressures, the judiciary must review the initial Executive determination to the point of satisfying itself that the subject matter of the dispute does lie within the proper compass of the President's foreign relations power. Constitutional considerations forbid "a complete abandonment of judicial control." Cf. United States v. Reynolds, 345 U.S. 1, 8 (1953). Moreover, the judiciary may properly insist that the determination that disclosure of the subject matter would irreparably impair the national security be made by the head of the Executive Department concerned—here the Secretary of State or the Secretary of Defense—after actual personal consideration by that officer. . . .

But in my judgment the judiciary may not properly go beyond these two inquiries and redetermine for itself the probable impact of disclosure on the national security. . . .

Even if there is some room for the judiciary to override the executive determination, it is plain that the scope of review must be exceedingly narrow. I can see no indication in the opinions of either the District Court or the Court of Appeals in the *Post* litigation that the conclusions of the Executive were given even the deference owing to an administrative agency, much less that owing to a co-equal branch of the Government operating within the field of its constitutional prerogative. . . .

Pending further hearings in each case conducted under the appropriate ground rules, I would continue the restraints on publication. I cannot believe that the doctrine prohibiting prior restraints reaches to the point of preventing courts from maintaining the *status quo* long enough to act responsibly in matters of such national importance as those involved here.

Mr. Justice Blackmun.

I join Mr. Justice Harlan in his dissent. I also am in substantial accord with much that Mr. Justice White says, by way of admonition, in the latter part of his opinion.

. . .

I therefore would remand these cases to be developed expeditiously, of course, but on a schedule permitting the orderly presentation of evidence from both sides, with the use of discovery, if necessary, as authorized by the rules, and with the preparation of briefs, oral argument and court opinions of a quality better than has been seen to this point. In making this last statement, I criticize no lawyer or judge. I know from past personal experience the agony of time pressure in the preparation of litigation. But these cases and the issues involved and the courts, including this one, deserve better than has been produced thus far. . . .[a]

PROTECTION OF THE COURTS AGAINST CRITICISM

The early history of the use of the contempt power to punish the press for criticism of judges and judicial action was recounted in section 1 of Chapter 14. In 1941 the Court reinterpreted the federal statute restricting the use of contempt as preventing the federal courts from punishing for acts taken outside the geographical environs of the courthouse. Nye v. United States, 313 U.S. 33 (1941). Shortly thereafter the Court substantially eliminated the power of the state and federal courts to punish the press for publications alleged to interfere with judicial impartiality by holding that under the first amendment only publications that create an imminent and serious threat to the ability of the

------

[a] For the full background of the case see Shapiro, The Pentagon Papers and the Courts (1972).

court fairly to decide issues before it can be punished. Bridges v. California, 314 U.S. 252 (1941); Pennekamp v. Florida, 328 U.S. 331 (1946); Craig v. Harney, 331 U.S. 367 (1947).

NEBRASKA PRESS ASSOCIATION v. STUART

427 U.S. 539, 96 S.Ct. 2791, 49 L.Ed.2d 683 (1976).

Mr. Chief Justice Burger delivered the opinion of the Court.

The respondent State District Judge entered an order restraining the petitioners from publishing or broadcasting accounts of confessions or admissions made by the accused or facts "strongly implicative" of the accused in a widely reported murder of six persons. We granted certiorari to decide whether the entry of such an order on the showing made before the state court violated the constitutional guarantee of freedom of the press.

On the evening of October 18, 1975, local police found the six members of the Henry Kellie family murdered in their home in Sutherland, Neb., a town of about 850 people. Police released the description of a suspect, Erwin Charles Simants, to the reporters who had hastened to the scene of the crime. Simants was arrested and arraigned in Lincoln County Court the following morning, ending a tense night for this small rural community.

The crime immediately attracted widespread news coverage, by local, regional, and national newspapers, radio and television stations. Three days after the crime, the County Attorney and Simants' attorney joined in asking the County Court to enter a restrictive order relating to "matters that may or may not be publicly reported or disclosed to the public," because of the "mass coverage by news media" and the "reasonable likelihood of prejudicial news which would make difficult, if not impossible, the impaneling of an impartial jury and tend to prevent a fair trial." The County Court heard oral argument but took no evidence; no attorney for members of the press appeared at this stage. The County Court granted the prosecutor's motion for a restrictive order and entered it the next day, October 22. The order prohibited everyone in attendance from "releas[ing] or authoriz[ing] for public dissemination in any form or manner whatsoever any testimony given or evidence adduced"; . . .

. . .

The Nebraska Supreme Court . . . modified the District Court's order to accommodate the defendant's right to a fair trial and the petitioners' interest in reporting pretrial events. The order as modified prohibited reporting of only three matters: (a) the existence and nature of any confessions or admissions made by the defendant to law enforcement officers, (b) any confessions or admissions made to any third parties, except members of the press, and (c) other facts "strongly implicative" of the accused. . . .

. . .

III.

The problems presented by this case are almost as old as the Republic. Neither in the Constitution nor in contemporaneous writings do we find that the conflict between these two important rights was anticipated, yet it is inconceivable that the authors of the Constitution were unaware of the potential conflicts between the right to an unbiased jury and the guarantee of freedom of the press. . . .

. . .

The speed of communication and the pervasiveness of the modern news media have exacerbated these problems, however, as numerous appeals demonstrate. The trial of Bruno Hauptmann in a small New Jersey community for the abduction and murder of the Charles Lindbergh's infant child, probably was the most widely covered trial up to that time, and the nature of the coverage produced widespread public reaction. . . .

The excesses of press and radio and lack of responsibility of those in authority in the Hauptmann case and others of that era led to efforts to develop voluntary guidelines for courts, lawyers, press and broadcasters. See generally J. Lofton, Justice and the Press 117–130 (1966). The effort was renewed in 1965 when the American Bar Association embarked on a project to develop standards for all aspects of criminal justice, including guidelines to accommodate the right to a fair trial and the rights of a free press. See Powell, The Right to a Fair Trial, 51 ABA Journal 534 (1965). The resulting standards, approved by the Association in 1968, received support from most of the legal profession. American Bar Association, Standards for Criminal Justice, Fair Trial and Free Press (Approved Draft, 1968). . . .

In practice, of course, even the most ideal guidelines are subjected to powerful strains when a case such as Simants' arises, with reporters from many parts of the country on the scene. Reporters from distant places are unlikely to consider themselves bound by local standards. They report to editors outside the area covered by the guidelines, and their editors are likely to be guided only by their own standards. To contemplate how a state court can control acts of a newspaper or broadcaster outside its jurisdiction, even though the newspapers and broadcasts reach the very community from which jurors are to be selected, suggests something of the practical difficulties of managing such guidelines.

. . .

IV.

. . . .

In Sheppard v. Maxwell, 384 U.S. 333 (1966), the Court focused sharply on the impact of pretrial publicity and a trial court's duty to protect the defendant's constitutional right to a fair trial. With only Mr. Justice Black dissenting, and he without opinion, the Court ordered a new trial for the petitioner, even though the first trial had occurred 12 years before. Beyond doubt the press had shown no responsible concern for the constitutional guarantee of a fair trial; the community from which the jury was drawn had been inundated by publicity hostile to the defendant. But the trial judge "did not fulfill his duty to protect [the defendant] from the inherently prejudicial publicity which saturated the community and to control disruptive influences in the courtroom." Id., at 363. The Court noted that "unfair and prejudicial news comment on pending trials has become increasing prevalent," id., at 362, and issued a strong warning:

"Due process requires that the accused receive a trial by an impartial jury free from outside influences. Given the pervasiveness of modern communications and the difficulty of effacing prejudicial publicity from the minds of the jurors, *the trial courts must take strong measures to ensure that the balance is never weighed against the accused* . . . .. Of course, there is nothing that proscribes the press from reporting events that transpire in the courtroom. But where there is a reasonable likelihood that prejudicial news prior to trial will prevent a fair trial, the judge should *continue the case* until the threat abates, *or transfer it* to another county not so permeated with publicity. In addition, *sequestration of the jury* was something the judge should have raised sua sponte with counsel. If publicity during the proceedings threatens the fairness of the trial, a new trial should be ordered. But we must remember that reversals are but palliatives; the cure lies in those remedial measures that will prevent the prejudice at its inception. The courts must take such steps by rule and regulation that will protect their processes from prejudicial outside interferences. *Neither prosecutors, counsel for defense, the accused, witness-es, court staff nor enforcement officers coming under the jurisdiction of the court should be permitted to frustrate its function.* Collaboration between counsel and the press as to information affecting the fairness of a criminal trial is not only subject to regulation, but is highly censurable and worthy of disciplinary measures." Id., at 362–363 (emphasis added).

Because the trial court had failed to use even minimal efforts to insulate the trial and the jurors from the "deluge of publicity," id., at 357, the Court vacated the judgment of conviction and a new trial followed, in which the accused was acquitted.

Cases such as these are relatively rare, and we have held in other cases that trials have been fair in spite of widespread publicity. In Stroble v. California, 343 U.S. 181 (1952), for example, the Court affirmed a conviction and death sentence challenged on the ground that pretrial news accounts, including the prosecutor's release of the defendant's recorded confession, were allegedly so inflammatory as to amount to a denial of due process. The Court disapproved of the prosecutor's conduct, but noted that the publicity had receded some six weeks before trial, that the defendant had not moved for a change of venue, and that the confession had been found voluntary and admitted in evidence at trial. The Court also noted the thorough examination of jurors on *voir dire* and the careful review of the facts by the state courts, and held that petitioner had failed to demonstrate a denial of due process. See also Murphy v. Florida, 421 U.S. 794 (1975); Beck v. Washington, 369 U.S. 541 (1962).

Taken together, these cases demonstrate that pretrial publicity—even perva-sive, adverse publicity—does not inevitably lead to an unfair trial. The capacity of the jury eventually impaneled to decide the case fairly is influenced by the tone and extent of the publicity, which is in part, and often in large part, shaped by what attorneys, police, and other officials do to precipitate news coverage. The trial judge has a major responsibility. What the judge says about a case, in or out of the courtroom, is likely to appear in newspapers and broadcasts. More important, the measures a judge takes or fails to take to mitigate the effects of pretrial publicity—the measures described in *Sheppard*—may well determine whether the defendant receives a trial consistent with the require-ments of due process. That this responsibility has not always been properly discharged is apparent from the decisions just reviewed.

. . .

V.

The First Amendment provides that "Congress shall make no law . . . abridging the freedom . . . of the press," and it is "no longer open to doubt that the liberty of the press, and of speech, is within the liberty safeguarded by the due process clause of the Fourteenth Amendment from invasion by state action." Near v. Minnesota, 283 U.S. 697, 707 (1931). . . . The Court has interpreted these guarantees to afford special protection against orders that prohibit the publication or broadcast of particular informa-tion or commentary—orders that impose a "previous" or "prior" restraint on speech. None of our decided cases on prior restraint involved restrictive orders entered to protect a defendant's right to a fair and impartial jury, but the opinions on prior restraint have a common thread relevant to this case. . . .

. . .

A prior restraint, . . . has an immediate and irreversible sanction. If it can be said that a threat of criminal or civil sanctions after publication "chills" speech, prior restraint "freezes" it at least for the time.

. . .

VI.

We turn now to the record in this case to determine whether, as Learned Hand put it, "the gravity of the 'evil,' discounted by its improbability, justifies such invasion of free speech as is necessary to avoid the danger." Dennis v. United States, 183 F.2d 201, 212 (1950), aff'd, 341 U.S. 494 (1951); see also L. Hand, The Bill of Rights 58–61 (1958). To do so, we must examine the evidence before the trial judge when the order was entered to determine (a) the nature and extent of pretrial news coverage; (b) whether other measures would be likely to mitigate the effects of unrestrained pretrial publicity; (c) how effectively a restraining order would operate to prevent the threatened danger. The precise terms of the restraining order are also important. We must then consider whether the record supports the entry of a prior restraint on publication, one of the most extraordinary remedies known to our jurisprudence.

.   .   .

We have   .   .   .   examined this record to determine the probable efficacy of the measures short of prior restraint on the press and speech. There is no finding that alternative measures would not have protected Simants' rights, and the Nebraska Supreme Court did no more than imply that such measures might not be adequate. Moreover, the record is lacking in evidence to support such a finding.

.   .   .

To the extent that this order prohibited the reporting of evidence adduced at the open preliminary hearing, it plainly violated settled principles: "there is nothing that proscribes the press from reporting events that transpire in the courtroom." Sheppard v. Maxwell, supra, at 362–363.   .   .   .

The third prohibition of the order was defective in another respect as well. As part of a final order, entered after plenary review, this prohibition regarding "implicative" information is too vague and too broad to survive the scrutiny we have given to restraints on First Amendment rights.

.   .   .

Of necessity our holding is confined to the record before us. But our conclusion is not simply a result of assessing the adequacy of the showing made in this case; it results in part from the problems inherent in meeting the heavy burden of demonstrating, in advance of trial, that without prior restraint a fair trial will be denied. The practical problems of managing and enforcing restrictive orders will always be present. In this sense, the record now before us is illustrative rather than exceptional. It is significant that when this Court has reversed a state conviction because of prejudicial publicity, it has carefully noted that some course of action short of prior restraint would have made a critical difference.   .   .   .   However difficult it may be, we need not rule out the possibility of showing the kind of threat to fair trial rights that would possess the requisite degree of certainty to justify restraint. This Court has frequently denied that First Amendment rights are absolute and has consistently rejected the proposition that a prior restraint can never be employed. See New York Times v. United States, supra; Organization for a Better Austin v. Keefe, supra; Near v. Minnesota, supra.

.   .   .

Mr. Justice Brennan, with whom Mr. Justice Stewart and Mr. Justice Marshall concur, concurring in the judgment.

The question presented in this case is whether, consistently with the First Amendment, a court may enjoin the press, in advance of publication, from reporting or commenting on information acquired from public court proceedings, public court records, or other sources about pending judicial proceedings.

. . . . The right to a fair trial by a jury of one's peers is unquestionably one of the most precious and sacred safeguards enshrined in the Bill of Rights. I would hold, however, that resort to prior restraints on the freedom of the press is a constitutionally impermissible method for enforcing that right; judges have at their disposal a broad spectrum of devices for ensuring that fundamental fairness is accorded the accused without necessitating so drastic an incursion on the equally fundamental and salutary constitutional mandate that discussion of public affairs in a free society cannot depend on the preliminary grace of judicial censors. . . .

. . .

There is, beyond peradventure, a clear and substantial damage to freedom of the press whenever even a temporary restraint is imposed on reporting of material concerning the operations of the criminal justice system, an institution of such pervasive influence in our constitutional scheme. And the necessary impact of reporting even confessions can never be so direct, immediate and irreparable that I would give credence to any notion that prior restraints may be imposed on that rationale. It may be that such incriminating material would be of such slight news value or so inflammatory in particular cases that responsible organs of the media, in an exercise of self-restraint, would choose not to publicize that material, and not make the judicial task of safeguarding precious rights of criminal defendants more difficult. Voluntary codes such as the Nebraska Bar-Press Guidelines are a commendable acknowledgement by the media that constitutional prerogatives bring enormous responsibilities, and I would encourage continuation of such voluntary cooperative efforts between the bar and the media. However, the press may be arrogant, tyrannical, abusive, and sensationalist, just as it may be incisive, probing, and informative. But at least in the context of prior restraints on publication, the decision of what, when, and how to publish is for editors, not judges. . . . Every restrictive order imposed on the press in this case was accordingly an unconstitutional prior restraint on the freedom of the press, and I would therefore reverse the judgment of the Nebraska Supreme Court and remand for further proceedings not inconsistent with this opinion.

Mr. Justice White, concurring.

Technically there is no need to go farther than the Court does to dispose of this case, and I join the Court's opinion. I should add, however, that for the reasons which the Court itself canvasses there is grave doubt in my mind whether orders with respect to the press such as were entered in this case would ever be justifiable. It may be the better part of discretion, however, not to announce such a rule in the first case in which the issue has been squarely presented here. Perhaps we should go no farther than absolutely necessary until the federal courts, and ourselves, have been exposed to a broader spectrum of cases presenting similar issues. If the recurring result, however, in case after case is to be similar to our judgment today, we should at some point announce a more general rule and avoid the interminable litigation that our failure to do so would necessarily entail.

Mr. Justice Powell, concurring.

Although I join the opinion of the Court, in view of the importance of the case I write to emphasize the unique burden that rests upon the party, whether it be the state or a defendant, who undertakes to show the necessity for prior restraint on pretrial publicity.

In my judgment a prior restraint properly may issue only when it is shown to be necessary to prevent the dissemination of prejudicial publicity that otherwise poses a high likelihood of preventing, directly and irreparably, the impaneling of a jury meeting the Sixth Amendment requirement of impartiality. This requires a showing that (i) there is a clear threat to the fairness of trial, (ii) such a threat is posed by the actual publicity to be restrained, and (iii) no less restrictive alternatives are available. Notwithstanding such a showing, a restraint may not issue unless it also is shown that previous publicity or publicity from unrestrained sources will not render the restraint inefficacious. The threat to the fairness of the trial is to be evaluated in the context of Sixth Amendment law on impartiality, and any restraint must comply with the standards of specificity always required in the First Amendment context.

I believe these factors are sufficiently addressed in the Court's opinion to demonstrate beyond question that the prior restraint here was impermissible.

Mr. Justice Stevens, concurring in the judgment.

For the reasons eloquently stated by Mr. Justice Brennan, I agree that the judiciary is capable of protecting the defendant's right to a fair trial without enjoining the press from publishing information in the public domain, and that it may not do so. Whether the same absolute protection would apply no matter how shabby or illegal the means by which the information is obtained, no matter how serious an intrusion on privacy might be involved, no matter how demonstrably false the information might be, no matter how prejudicial it might be to the interests of innocent persons, and no matter how perverse the motivation for publishing it, is a question I would not answer without further argument. See Ashwander v. TVA, 297 U.S. 288, 346–347 (Brandeis, J., concurring). I do, however, subscribe to most of what Mr. Justice Brennan says and, if ever required to face the issue squarely, may well accept his ultimate conclusion.

COX BROADCASTING CORP. v. COHN

420 U.S. 469, 95 S.Ct. 1029, 43 L.Ed.2d 328 (1975).

[The report in this case appears, supra at p. 1122.]

LANDMARK COMMUNICATIONS, INC. v. VIRGINIA, 435 U.S. 829 (1978). A Virginia newspaper accurately reported that an inquiry was pending into the conduct of a judge before the State Commission supervising the judiciary. A Virginia statute provided that "all papers filed with and proceedings before the Commission, including the identification of the subject judge" were confidential. The newspaper was fined $500 for violation of a further provision that disclosure of confidential information concerning the Commission was a misdemeanor. The Supreme Court reversed the conviction.

Chief Justice Burger's opinion for the Court, said in part:

"The Commonwealth concedes that '[w]ithout question the First Amendment seeks to protect the freedom of the press to report and to criticize judicial conduct,' but it argues that such protection does not extend to the publication of information 'which by Constitutional mandate is to be confidential.' Our recent decision in Cox Broadcasting v. Cohn, is relied upon to support this interpretation of the scope of the freedom of speech and press guarantees. As we read *Cox*, it does not provide the answer to the question now confronting us. Our holding there was that a civil action against a television station for breach of privacy could not be maintained consistently with the First Amendment when the station had broadcast only information which was already in the public domain. . . . The broader question—whether the publication of truthful information withheld by law from the public domain is similarly privileged—was not reached and indeed was explicitly reserved in *Cox*. We need not address all the implications of that question here, but only whether in the circumstances of this case Landmark's publication is protected by the First Amendment.

. . .

"It can be assumed for purposes of decision that confidentiality of Commission proceedings serves legitimate state interests. The question, however, is whether these interests are sufficient to justify the encroachment on First Amendment guarantees which the imposition of criminal sanctions entails with respect to nonparticipants such as Landmark. The Commonwealth has offered little more than assertion and conjecture to support its claim that without criminal sanctions the objectives of the statutory scheme would be seriously undermined. While not dispositive, we note that more than 40 States having similar commissions have not found it necessary to enforce confidentiality by use of criminal sanctions against nonparticipants.

"Moreover, neither the Commonwealth's interest in protecting the reputation of its judges, nor in maintaining the institutional integrity of its courts is sufficient to justify the subsequent punishment of speech at issue here, even on the assumption that criminal sanctions do in fact enhance the guarantee of confidentiality. . . ."

In his brief concurrence, Justice Stewart said:

"Virginia has enacted a law making it a criminal offense for 'any person' to divulge confidential information about proceedings before its Judicial Inquiry and Review Commission. I cannot agree with the Court that this Virginia law violates the Constitution.

"There could hardly be a higher governmental interest than a State's interest in the quality of its judiciary. Virginia's derivative interest in maintaining the confidentiality of the proceedings of its Judicial Inquiry and Review Commission seems equally clear. Only such confidentiality, the State has determined, will protect upright judges from unjustified harm and at the same time insure the full and fearless airing in Commission proceedings of every complaint of judicial misconduct. I find nothing in the Constitution to prevent Virginia from punishing those who violate this confidentiality.

"But in this case Virginia has extended its law to punish a newspaper, and that it cannot constitutionally do. If the constitutional protection of a free press means anything, it means that government cannot take it upon itself to decide what a newspaper may and may not publish. Though government may deny access to information and punish its theft, government may not prohibit or punish the publication of that information once it falls into the hands of the press, unless the need for secrecy is manifestly overwhelming.*

"It is on this ground that I concur in the judgment of the Court."

SMITH v. DAILY MAIL PUBLISHING CO., 443 U.S. 97 (1979). Emphasizing that its holding was "narrow," the Court held unconstitutional a West Virginia law prohibiting newspaper publication of names of minors subject to juvenile court proceedings. Where no issue of prejudicial pretrial publicity nor of privacy was present, and where the information had been obtained lawfully by the newspaper, First Amendment rights prevailed over the State's interest in protecting juveniles. (The Court noted that only five states imposed criminal penalties on nonparties for publication of the juvenile's identity.) Even assuming that protection of the anonymity of juveniles served important state

---

* National defense is the most obvious justification for government restrictions on publication. Even then, distinctions must be drawn between prior restraints and subsequent penalties.

interests, the statute, moreover, failed to serve those interests since it was inapplicable to the electronic media.

SEATTLE TIMES CO. v. RHINEHART, 104 S.Ct. 2199 (1984). In a defamation action against the newspaper, plaintiff was required to disclose, in discovery, certain information. The state court trial judge entered a protective order forbidding the newspaper to use the disclosed information, which included the identity of donors to a religious group, for any purpose other than trial of the case. The Court held that the protective order did not offend the first amendment. An order prohibiting dissemination of discovered information before trial is not a classic prior restraint so long as it does not prevent a party from disseminating identical information obtained by independent means. Restraints placed on the use of information discovered, but not yet admitted into evidence, do not restrict a "traditionally public source of information." Thus, a protective order does not violate the first amendment if it is entered on a showing of good cause, is limited to the context of pretrial civil discovery, and does not restrict the dissemination of information gained from other sources.

SECTION 4. GOVERNMENT DEMANDS FOR CONFIDENTIAL PRESS INFORMATION

BRANZBURG v. HAYES

408 U.S. 665, 92 S.Ct. 2646, 33 L.Ed.2d 626 (1972).

Opinion of the Court by Mr. Justice White, announced by The Chief Justice.

[Branzburg was a Louisville Courier-Journal reporter who observed two persons synthesizing hashish from marihuana, a violation of local law. After making his observations the basis of a news article, he was called before a grand jury and refused to identify the persons involved. Pappas, a television-reporter-photographer, was sent to New Bedford, Massachusetts, to cover a Black Panther conference and gained entrance to the Panther headquarters. He was called before a grand jury investigating civil disorders and refused to testify as to anything he heard while within the Panther headquarters. Caldwell was a New York Times reporter assigned to cover the Black Panthers and other black militant groups. He wrote several articles and was called to testify and bring his records before a federal grand jury investigating possible threats and conspiracies to assassinate the President. He refused to appear. All three cases raised the issue whether requiring reporters to appear and testify before state or federal grand juries abridges the freedom of speech and press guaranteed by the First Amendment.]

Petitioners Branzburg and Pappas and respondent Caldwell press First Amendment claims that may be simply put: that to gather news it is often necessary to agree either not to identify the source of information published or to publish only part of the facts revealed, or both; that if the reporter is nevertheless forced to reveal these confidences to a grand jury, the source so identified and other confidential sources of other reporters will be measurably deterred from furnishing publishable information, all to the detriment of the free flow of information protected by the First Amendment. Although the newsmen in these cases do not claim an absolute privilege against official interrogation in all circumstances, they assert that the reporter should not be forced either to appear or to testify before a grand jury or at trial until and unless sufficient grounds are shown for believing that the reporter possesses information relevant to a crime the grand jury is investigating, that the information the reporter has is unavailable from other sources, and that the need for the information is sufficiently compelling to override the claimed invasion of First Amendment interests occasioned by the disclosure. . . .

We do not question the significance of free speech, press or assembly to the country's welfare. Nor is it suggested that news gathering does not qualify for First Amendment protection; without some protection for seeking out the news, freedom of the press could be eviscerated. But this case involves no intrusions upon speech or assembly, no prior restraint or restriction on what the press may publish, and no express or implied command that the press publish what it prefers to withhold. . . .

The sole issue before us is the obligation of reporters to respond to grand jury subpoenas as other citizens do and to answer questions relevant to an investigation into the commission of crime. . . .

Despite the fact that news gathering may be hampered, the press is regularly excluded from grand jury proceedings, our own conferences, the meetings of other official bodies gathered in executive session, and the meetings of private organizations. Newsmen have no constitutional right of access to the scenes of crime or disaster when the general public is excluded, and they may be prohibited from attending or publishing information about trials if such restrictions are necessary to assure a defendant a fair trial before an impartial tribunal. . . . Sheppard v. Maxwell, 384 U.S. 333 (1966) . . .

It is thus not surprising that the great weight of authority is that newsmen are not exempt from the normal duty of appearing before a grand jury and answering questions relevant to a criminal investigation. At common law, courts consistently refused to recognize the existence of any privilege authorizing a newsman to refuse to reveal confidential information to a grand jury. . . .

    . . .

A number of States have provided newsmen a statutory privilege of varying breadth, but the majority have not done so, and none has been provided by federal statute. Until now the only testimonial privilege for unofficial witnesses that is rooted in the Federal Constitution is the Fifth Amendment privilege against compelled self-incrimination. We are asked to create another by interpreting the First Amendment to grant newsmen a testimonial privilege that other citizens do not enjoy. This we decline to do. . . .

This conclusion itself involves no restraint on what newspapers may publish or on the type or quality of information reporters may seek to acquire, nor does it threaten the vast bulk of confidential relationships between reporters and their sources. Grand juries address themselves to the issues of whether crimes have been committed and who committed them. Only where news sources themselves are implicated in crime or possess information relevant to the grand jury's task need they or the reporter be concerned about grand jury subpoenas. Nothing before us indicates that a large number or percentage of *all* confidential news sources fall into either category and would in any way be deterred by our holding that the Constitution does not, as it never has, exempt the newsman from performing the citizen's normal duty of appearing and furnishing information relevant to the grand jury's task. . . .

The argument that the flow of news will be diminished by compelling reporters to aid the grand jury in a criminal investigation is not irrational, nor are the records before us silent on the matter. But we remain unclear how often and to what extent informers are actually deterred from furnishing information when newsmen are forced to testify before a grand jury. The available data indicates that some newsmen rely a great deal on confidential sources and that some informants are particularly sensitive to the threat of exposure and may be silenced if it is held by this Court that, ordinarily, newsmen must testify pursuant to subpoenas, but the evidence fails to demonstrate that there would be a significant constriction of the flow of news to the public if this Court reaffirms the prior common law and constitutional rule regarding the testimonial obligations of newsmen. Estimates of the inhibiting effect of such subpoenas on the willingness of informants to make disclosures to newsmen are widely divergent and to a great extent speculative. . . .

Accepting the fact, however, that an undetermined number of informants not themselves implicated in crime will nevertheless, for whatever reason, refuse to talk to newsmen if they fear identification by a reporter in an official investigation, we cannot accept the argument that the public interest in possible future news about crime from undisclosed, unverified sources must take precedence over the public interest in pursuing and prosecuting those crimes reported to the press by informants and in thus deterring the commission of such crimes in the future. . . .

It is said that currently press subpoenas have multiplied, that mutual distrust and tension between press and officialdom have increased, that reporting styles have changed, and that there is now more need for confidential sources, particularly where the press seeks news about minority cultural and political groups or dissident organizations suspicious of the law and public officials. These developments, even if true, are treacherous grounds for a far-reaching interpretation of the First Amendment fastening a nationwide rule on courts, grand juries, and prosecuting officials everywhere. . . .

The privilege claimed here is conditional, not absolute; given the suggested preliminary showings and compelling need, the reporter would be required to testify. Presumably, such a rule would reduce the instances in which reporters could be required to appear, but predicting in advance when and in what circumstances they could be compelled to do so would be difficult. . . .

We are unwilling to embark the judiciary on a long and difficult journey to such an uncertain destination. The administration of a constitutional newsman's privilege would present practical and conceptual difficulties of a high order. Sooner or later, it would be necessary to define those categories of newsmen who qualified for the privilege, a questionable procedure in light of the traditional doctrine that liberty of the press is the right of the lonely pamphleteer who uses carbon paper or a mimeograph just as much as of the large metropolitan publisher who utilizes the latest photocomposition methods. . . .

In each instance where a reporter is subpoenaed to testify, the courts would also be embroiled in preliminary factual and legal determinations with respect to whether the proper predicate had been laid for the reporters' appearance: Is there probable cause to believe a crime has been committed? Is it likely that the reporter has useful information gained in confidence? Could the grand jury obtain the information elsewhere? Is the official interest sufficient to outweigh the claimed privilege?

Thus, in the end, by considering whether enforcement of a particular law served a "compelling" governmental interest, the courts would be inextricably involved in distinguishing between the value of enforcing different criminal laws. By requiring testimony from a reporter in investigations involving some crimes but not in others, they would be making a value judgment which a legislature had declined to make, since in each case the criminal law involved would represent a considered legislative judgment, not constitutionally suspect, of what conduct is liable to criminal prosecution. The task of judges, like other officials outside the legislative branch is not to make the law but to uphold it in accordance with their oaths.

At the federal level, Congress has freedom to determine whether a statutory newsman's privilege is necessary and desirable and to fashion standards and rules as narrow or broad as deemed necessary to address the evil discerned and, equally important, to re-fashion those rules as experience from time to time may dictate. There is also merit in leaving state legislatures free, within First Amendment limits, to fashion their own standards in light of the conditions and problems with respect to the relations between law enforcement officials and press in their own areas. It goes without saying, of course, that we are powerless to erect any bar to state courts responding in their own way and construing their own constitutions so as to recognize a newsman's privilege, either qualified or absolute. . . .

Finally, as we have earlier indicated, news gathering is not without its First Amendment protections, and grand jury investigations if instituted or conducted other than in good faith, would pose wholly different issues for resolution under the First Amendment. Official harassment of the press undertaken not for purposes of law enforcement but to disrupt a reporter's relationship with his news sources would have no justification. Grand juries are subject to judicial control and subpoenas to motions to quash. We do not expect courts will forget that grand juries must operate within the limits of the First Amendment as well as the Fifth. . . .

[The Court ruled on the three cases as follows: (1) Caldwell had no constitutional privilege not to appear before the grand jury; (2) Branzburg was obligated to answer questions regarding the commission of crimes he had observed; and (3) in Pappas the decision of the Massachusetts Court was affirmed, holding that "petitioner must appear before the grand jury to answer the questions put to him, subject, of course, to the supervision of the presiding judge as to the propriety, purposes and scope of the grand jury inquiry and the pertinence of the probable testimony."]

Mr. Justice Powell, concurring in the opinion of the Court.

I add this brief statement to emphasize what seems to me to be the limited nature of the Court's holding. The Court does not hold that newsmen, subpoenaed to testify before a grand jury, are without constitutional rights with respect to the gathering of news or in safeguarding their sources. Certainly, we do not hold, as suggested in the dissenting opinion, that state and federal authorities are free to "annex" the news media as "an investigative arm of government." The solicitude repeatedly shown by this Court for First Amendment freedoms should be sufficient assurance against any such effort, even if one seriously believed that the media—properly free and untrammeled in the fullest sense of these terms—were not able to protect themselves.

As indicated in the concluding portion of the opinion, the Court states that no harassment of newsmen will be tolerated. If a newsman believes that the grand jury investigation is not being conducted in good faith he is not without remedy. Indeed, if the newsman is called upon to give information bearing only a remote and tenuous relationship to the subject of the investigation, or if he has some other reason to believe that his testimony implicates confidential source relationships without a legitimate need of law enforcement, he will have access to the Court on a motion to quash and an appropriate protective order may be entered. The asserted claim to privilege should be judged on its facts by the striking of a proper balance between freedom of the press and the obligation of all citizens to give relevant testimony with respect to criminal conduct. The balance of these vital constitutional and societal interests on a case-by-case basis accords with the tried and traditional way of adjudicating such questions.

In short, the courts will be available to newsmen under circumstances where legitimate First Amendment interests require protection.

Mr. Justice Douglas, dissenting.

.　.　.

It is my view that there is no "compelling need" that can be shown which qualifies the reporter's immunity from appearing or testifying before a grand jury, unless the reporter himself is implicated in a crime. His immunity in my view is therefore quite complete, for absent his involvement in a crime, the First Amendment protects him against an appearance before a grand jury and if he is involved in a crime, the Fifth Amendment stands as a barrier. Since in my view there is no area of inquiry not protected by a privilege, the reporter need not appear for the futile purpose of invoking one to each question. And, since in my view a newsman has an absolute right not to appear before a grand jury it follows for me that a journalist who voluntarily appears before that body may invoke his First Amendment privilege to specific questions. The basic issue is the extent to which the First Amendment . . . must yield to the Government's asserted need to know a reporter's unprinted information. . . .

.　.　.

Mr. Justice Stewart, with whom Mr. Justice Brennan and Mr. Justice Marshall join, dissenting.

The Court's crabbed view of the First Amendment reflects a disturbing insensitivity to the critical role of an independent press in our society. The question whether a reporter has a constitutional right to a confidential relationship with his source is of first impression here, but the principles which should guide our decision are as basic as any to be found in the Constitution. While Mr. Justice Powell's enigmatic concurring opinion gives some hope of a more flexible view in the future, the Court in these cases holds that a newsman has no First Amendment right to protect his sources when called before a grand jury. The Court thus invites state and federal authorities to undermine the historic independence of the press by attempting to annex the journalistic profession as an investigative arm of government. Not only will this decision impair performance of the press' constitutionally protected functions, but it will, I am convinced, in the long run, harm rather than help the administration of justice.
.　.　.

The reporter's constitutional right to a confidential relationship with his source stems from the broad societal interest in a full and free flow of information to the public. . . .

It is obvious that informants are necessary to the news-gathering process as we know it today. . . .

It is equally obvious that the promise of confidentiality may be a necessary prerequisite to a productive relationship between a newsman and his informants.
.　.　.

Finally, and most important, when governmental officials possess an unchecked power to compel newsmen to disclose information received in confidence, sources will clearly be deterred from giving information, and reporters will clearly be deterred from publishing it, because uncertainty about exercise of the power will lead to "self-censorship." . . .

The impairment of the flow of news cannot, of course, be proven with scientific precision, as the Court seems to demand. . . .

Posed against the First Amendment's protection of the newsman's confidential relationships in these cases is society's interest in the use of the grand jury to administer justice fairly and effectively. . . .

Yet the longstanding rule making every person's evidence available to the grand jury is not absolute. The rule has been limited by the Fifth Amendment, the Fourth Amendment, and the evidentiary privileges of the common law. . . .

Such an interest must surely be the First Amendment protection of a confidential relationship that I have discussed above. . . .

Accordingly, when a reporter is asked to appear before a grand jury and reveal confidences, I would hold that the government must (1) show that there is probable cause to believe that the newsman has information which is clearly relevant to a specific probable violation of law; (2) demonstrate that the information sought cannot be obtained by alternative means less destructive of First Amendment rights; and (3) demonstrate a compelling and overriding interest in the information.

This is not to say that a grand jury could not issue a subpoena until such a showing were made, and it is not to say that a newsman would be in any way privileged to ignore any subpoena that was issued. Obviously, before the government's burden to make such a showing were triggered, the reporter would have to move to quash the subpoena, asserting the basis on which he considered the particular relationship a confidential one. . . .

———

ZURCHER v. STANFORD DAILY, 436 U.S. 547 (1978). The Court held that the first and fourth amendments did not preclude issuance of a search warrant for search of a newsroom. On the first amendment issue, Justice White's opinion for the Court concluded that the first amendment did not immunize the media from search warrants issued on probable cause. Justice Powell, who supplied the controlling fifth vote, joined the Court's opinion but also wrote a concurring opinion, in which he asserted that "a warrant which would be sufficient to support the search of an apartment or automobile would [not necessarily] be reasonable in supporting the search of a newspaper office." He concluded that, while there was no justification for a separate procedure for searches of the press, first amendment values should be taken into account in making the "reasonableness" and "particularity" judgments under the fourth amendment.[1]

———

HERBERT v. LANDO, 441 U.S. 153 (1979). Herbert, a retired Army officer, brought a diversity suit in federal court, claiming that a CBS television documentary on Vietnamese war atrocities defamed him. In pretrial deposition, the program's producer was asked questions about his opinions with respect to the material gathered by him and about his conversations with editorial colleagues. The Court held that the First Amendment gave the producer no privilege to refuse to answer the questions. It was conceded that the libel plaintiff was a public figure who could not recover without proof of malice in the sense of knowing falsity or reckless disregard of the truth. New York Times Co. v. Sullivan, 376 U.S. 254 (1964); Curtis Pub. Co. v. Butts, 388 U.S. 130 (1967). Since that standard required plaintiff to prove the state of the defendant's mind, erecting a First Amendment privilege against disclosure of the editorial process "would constitute a substantial interference with the ability of a defamation plaintiff to establish the ingredients of malice as required by *New York Times.*" Justice White's opinion for the Court did, however, indicate that

———

[1] On October 13, 1980, the President signed P.L. 96–440, The Privacy Protection Act, which requires state and federal law enforcement officers to use subpoena procedures to obtain documents from persons engaged in the communications industry. Search warrants are permitted in exceptional circumstances, such as when it is believed that the desired documents would be destroyed.

editorial discussions may have some constitutional protection from "casual inquiry."

"There is no law that subjects the editorial process to private or official examination merely to satisfy curiosity or to serve some general end such as the public interest; and if there were, it would not survive constitutional scrutiny as the First Amendment is presently construed. No such problem exists here, however, where there is a specific claim of injury arising from a publication that is alleged to have been knowing or recklessly false."

Justices Brennan, Marshall and Stewart dissented in part.

SECTION 5. PRESS ACCESS TO GOVERNMENT INFORMATION

Barrett, *Freedom of the Press—American Style* in American Bar Association, *Legal Institutions Today; English and American Approaches Compared* 214, 238–239 (H. Jones ed. 1977): [a]

"The problem of access to public records and proceedings was not an issue when the first amendment became part of our Constitution. The common law accorded only a narrow right of access to public records, and habits of governmental secrecy were not challenged. Over the years political pressures to increase access were felt. At the state level the common law rule was gradually liberalized. By the 1940s the trend toward increasing openness was met by a counter-thrust toward secrecy, particularly at the federal level, resulting from the war and the tensions of the cold-war period. The rapid increase in the size of government dramatically increased the difficulties of securing information.

"Today substantial changes have been achieved through political processes. The Freedom of Information Act was enacted in 1966 after a decade of Congressional hearings. Most states have statutes extending varying degrees of access to public records and 'open meeting' laws. All of these statutes have substantial limitations and are not regarded, particularly by the press, as adequately insuring access to relevant governmental information. They are also proving complex, difficult to interpret and apply, and productive of expensive litigation whenever it is sought to challenge a refusal to provide requested information."

PRESS ACCESS DECISIONS PRIOR TO 1980

No Supreme Court decision, prior to 1980, sustained a press claim that the first amendment provided the press with a special right of access to information controlled by the government. The settled proposition, as explained by Justice Stewart for the Court in Pell v. Procunier, 417 U.S. 817 (1974), was that the "Constitution does not . . . require government to accord the press special access to information not shared by members of the public generally." In *Pell,* the Court sustained a California policy placing limits on interviews with individual prisoners. In Houchins v. KQED, 438 U.S. 1 (1978), the Court sustained a county jail policy limiting reporters' access to jail facilities. Both decisions were by a closely divided Court, with the dissenters arguing that a first amendment right of press access was necessary to allow the media to play its societal function in the discussion of public affairs.

In Gannett Co., Inc. v. DePasquale, 443 U.S. 368 (1979), the five-Justice majority rejected an alternative constitutional source of press access. In a murder case, pre-trial hearings to suppress evidence had been closed to the public and the press on motion of the criminal defendants. The Court held that the sixth amendment's guarantee of a public trial was only for the benefit of the accused, and did not give the public or the press any right of access to criminal trials. Significantly, one member of the majority, Justice Powell, wrote a concurrence arguing that there was a first amendment right of press access to criminal proceedings distinct from the general public's right of access.

RICHMOND NEWSPAPERS, INC. v. VIRGINIA

448 U.S. 555, 100 S.Ct. 2814, 65 L.Ed.2d 973 (1980).

Mr. Chief Justice Burger announced the judgment of the Court and delivered an opinion in which Mr. Justice White and Mr. Justice Stevens joined.

The narrow question presented in this case is whether the right of the public and press to attend criminal trials is guaranteed under the United States Constitution.

I.

In March 1976, one Stevenson was indicted for the murder of a hotel manager who had been found stabbed to death on December 2, 1975. Tried promptly in July 1976, Stevenson was convicted of second-degree murder in the Circuit Court of Hanover County, Va. The Virginia Supreme Court reversed the conviction in October 1977, holding that a bloodstained shirt purportedly belonging to Stevenson had been improperly admitted into evidence. . . .

Stevenson was retried in the same court. This second trial ended in a mistrial on May 30, 1978 when a juror asked to be excused after trial had begun and no alternate was available.

A third trial, which began in the same court on June 6, 1978, also ended in a mistrial. It appears that the mistrial may have been declared because a prospective juror had read about Stevenson's previous trials in a newspaper and had told other prospective jurors about the case before the retrial began.

Stevenson was tried in the same court for a fourth time beginning on September 11, 1978. Present in the courtroom when the case was called were appellants Wheeler and McCarthy, reporters for appellant Richmond Newspapers, Inc. Before the trial began, counsel for the defendant moved that it be closed to the public:

> "[T]here was this woman that was with the family of the deceased when we were here before. She had sat in the Courtroom. I would like to ask that everybody be excluded from the Courtroom because I don't want any information being shuffled back and forth when we have a recess as to what—who testified to what."

The trial judge, who had presided over two of the three previous trials, asked if the prosecution had any objection to clearing the courtroom. The prosecutor stated he had no objection and would leave it to the discretion of the court. Presumably referring to Virginia Code § 19.2-266, the trial judge then announced: "[T]he statute gives me that power specifically and the defendant has made the motion." He then ordered "that the Courtroom be kept clear of all parties except the witnesses when they testify." [2] The record does not show that any objections to the closure order were made by anyone present at the time, including appellants Wheeler and McCarthy.

Later that same day, however, appellants sought a hearing on a motion to vacate the closure order. The trial judge granted the request and scheduled a hearing to follow the close of the day's proceedings. When the hearing began, the court ruled that the hearing was to be treated as part of the trial; accordingly, he again ordered the reporters to leave the courtroom, and they complied.

. . .

. . . The court denied the motion to vacate and ordered the trial to continue the following morning "with the press and public excluded."

What transpired when the closed trial resumed the next day was disclosed in the following manner by an order of the court entered September 12, 1978:

"[I]n the absence of the jury, the defendant by counsel made a Motion that a mis-trial be declared, which motion was taken under advisement. At the conclusion of the Commonwealth's evidence, the attorney for the defendant moved the Court to strike the Commonwealth's evidence on grounds stated to the record, which Motion was sustained by the Court. And the jury having been excused, the Court doth find the accused NOT GUILTY of Murder, as charged in the Indictment, and he was allowed to depart." [3]

On September 27, 1978 the trial court granted appellants' motion to intervene *nunc pro tunc* in the *Stevenson* case. Appellants then petitioned the Virginia Supreme Court for writs of mandamus and prohibition and filed an appeal from the trial court's closure order. On July 9, 1979, the Virginia Supreme Court dismissed the mandamus and prohibition petitions and, finding no reversible error, denied the petition for appeal.

Appellants then sought review in this Court, . . .

The criminal trial which appellants sought to attend has long since ended, and there is thus some suggestion that the case is moot. . . . If the underlying dispute is "capable of repetition, yet evading review," Southern Pacific Terminal Co. v. ICC, 219 U.S. 498, 515 (1911), it is not moot.

Since the Virginia Supreme Court declined plenary review, it is reasonably foreseeable that other trials may be closed by other judges without any more showing of need than is presented on this record. More often than not, criminal trials will be of sufficiently short duration that a closure order "will evade review, or at least considered plenary review in this Court." *Nebraska Press,* supra, at 547. Accordingly, we turn to the merits.

II.

We begin consideration of this case by noting that the precise issue presented here has not previously been before this Court for decision. In Gannett Co., Inc. v. DePasquale, 443 U.S. 368 (1979), the Court was not required to decide whether a right of access to *trials,* as distinguished from hearings on *pre*trial motions, was constitutionally guaranteed. The Court held that the Sixth Amendment's guarantee to the accused of a public trial gave neither the public nor the press an enforceable right of access to a *pre*trial suppression hearing. One concurring opinion specifically emphasized that "a hearing on a motion before trial to suppress evidence is not a *trial. . . .*" 443 U.S., at 394

---

[2] Virginia Code § 19.2–266 provides in part:

"In the trial of all criminal cases, whether the same be felony or misdemeanor cases, the court may, in its discretion, exclude from the trial any persons whose presence would impair the conduct of a fair trial, provided that the right of the accused to a public trial shall not be violated."

[3] At oral argument, it was represented to the Court that tapes of the trial were available to the public as soon as the trial terminated.

(Burger, C.J., concurring).   Moreover, the Court did not decide whether the First and Fourteenth Amendments guarantee a right of the public to attend trials, id., at 392, and n. 24; nor did the dissenting opinion reach this issue. Id., at 447 (Blackmun, J., dissenting).

.   .   .

A.

The origins of the proceeding which has become the modern criminal trial in Anglo-American justice can be traced back beyond reliable historical records. We need not here review all details of its development, but a summary of that history is instructive. What is significant for present purposes is that throughout its evolution, the trial has been open to all who cared to observe.

.   .   .

B.

As we have shown, and as was shown in both the Court's opinion and the dissent in *Gannett,* supra, at 384, 386, n. 15; 418–425, the historical evidence demonstrates conclusively that at the time when our organic laws were adopted, criminal trials both here and in England had long been presumptively open. This is no quirk of history; rather, it has long been recognized as an indispensible attribute of an Anglo-American trial.   Both Hale in the 17th century and Blackstone in the 18th saw the importance of openness to the proper functioning of a trial; it gave assurance that the proceedings were conducted fairly to all concerned, and it discouraged perjury, the misconduct of participants, and decisions based on secret bias or partiality.   See, e.g., M. Hale, The History of the Common Law of England 343–345 (6th ed. 1820); 3 W. Blackstone, Commentaries *372–373. .   .   .

People in an open society do not demand infallibility from their institutions, but it is difficult for them to accept what they are prohibited from observing. When a criminal trial is conducted in the open, there is at least an opportunity both for understanding the system in general and its workings in a particular case: .   .   .

.   .   .

C.

From this unbroken, uncontradicted history, supported by reasons as valid today as in centuries past, we are bound to conclude that a presumption of openness inheres in the very nature of a criminal trial under our system of justice. .   .   .

Despite the history of criminal trials being presumptively open since long before the Constitution, the State presses its contention that neither the Constitution nor the Bill of Rights contains any provision which by its terms guarantees to the public the right to attend criminal trials. Standing alone, this is correct, but there remains the question whether, absent an explicit provision, the Constitution affords protection against exclusion of the public from criminal trials.

III.

A.

The First Amendment, in conjunction with the Fourteenth, prohibits governments from "abridging the freedom of speech, or of the press; or the right of the people peaceably to assemble, and to petition the Government for a redress of grievances."   These expressly guaranteed freedoms share a common core purpose of assuring freedom of communication on matters relating to the functioning of government. Plainly it would be difficult to single out any aspect of government of higher concern and importance to the people than the manner in which criminal trials are conducted; as we have shown, recognition of this pervades the centuries-old history of open trials and the opinions of this Court.

The Bill of Rights was enacted against the backdrop of the long history of trials being presumptively open. . . . In guaranteeing freedoms such as those of speech and press, the First Amendment can be read as protecting the right of everyone to attend trials so as to give meaning to those explicit guarantees. . . . Free speech carries with it some freedom to listen. "In a variety of contexts this Court has referred to a First Amendment right to 'receive information and ideas.' " Kleindienst v. Mandel, 408 U.S. 753, 762 (1972). What this means in the context of trials is that the First Amendment guarantees of speech and press, standing alone, prohibit government from summarily closing courtroom doors which had long been open to the public at the time that amendment was adopted. . . .

It is not crucial whether we describe this right to attend criminal trials to hear, see, and communicate observations concerning them as a "right of access," cf. *Gannett,* supra, at 397 (Powell, J., concurring); Saxbe v. Washington Post Co., 417 U.S. 843 (1974); Pell v. Procunier, 417 U.S. 817 (1974),[11] or a "right to gather information," for we have recognized that "without some protection for seeking out the news, freedom of the press could be eviscerated." Branzburg v. Hayes, 408 U.S. 665, 681 (1972). The explicit, guaranteed rights to speak and to publish concerning what takes place at a trial would lose much meaning if access to observe the trial could, as it was here, be foreclosed arbitrarily.

B.

The right of access to places traditionally open to the public, as criminal trials have long been, may be seen as assured by the amalgam of the First Amendment guarantees of speech and press; and their affinity to the right of assembly is not without relevance. From the outset, the right of assembly was regarded not only as an independent right but also as a catalyst to augment the free exercise of the other First Amendment rights with which it was deliberately linked by the draftsmen. . . . [A] trial courtroom . . . is a public place where the people generally—and representatives of the media—have a right to be present, and where their presence historically has been thought to enhance the integrity and quality of what takes place.

C.

The State argues that the Constitution nowhere spells out a guarantee for the right of the public to attend trials, and that accordingly no such right is protected. . . .

But arguments such as the State makes have not precluded recognition of important rights not enumerated. Notwithstanding the appropriate caution against reading into the Constitution rights not explicitly defined, the Court has acknowledged that certain unarticulated rights are implicit in enumerated guarantees. For example, the rights of association and of privacy, the right to be presumed innocent and the right to be judged by a standard of proof beyond a reasonable doubt in a criminal trial, as well as the right to travel, appear nowhere in the Constitution or Bill of Rights. Yet these important but unarticulated rights have nonetheless been found to share constitutional protection in common with explicit guarantees. . . .

---

[11] *Procunier* and *Saxbe,* supra, are distinguishable in the sense that they were concerned with penal institutions which, by definition, are not "open" or public places. . . .

We hold that the right to attend criminal trials [17] is implicit in the guarantees of the First Amendment; . . .

D.

Having concluded there was a guaranteed right of the public under the First and Fourteenth Amendments to attend the trial of Stevenson's case, we return to the closure order challenged by appellants. The Court in *Gannett,* supra, made clear that although the Sixth Amendment guarantees the accused a right to a public trial, it does not give a right to a private trial. 443 U.S., at 382. Despite the fact that this was the fourth trial of the accused, the trial judge made no findings to support closure; no inquiry was made as to whether alternative solutions would have met the need to ensure fairness; there was no recognition of any right under the Constitution for the public or press to attend the trial. In contrast to the pretrial proceeding dealt with in *Gannett,* supra, there exist in the context of the trial itself various tested alternatives to satisfy the constitutional demands of fairness. See, e.g., Nebraska Press Association v. Stuart, 427 U.S., at 563–565; Sheppard v. Maxwell, 384 U.S., at 357–362. There was no suggestion that any problems with witnesses could not have been dealt with by their exclusion from the courtroom or their sequestration during the trial. See Sheppard v. Maxwell, 384 U.S., at 359. Nor is there anything to indicate that sequestration of the jurors would not have guarded against their being subjected to any improper information. All of the alternatives admittedly present difficulties for trial courts, but none of the factors relied on here was beyond the realm of the manageable. Absent an overriding interest articulated in findings, the trial of a criminal case must be open to the public. Accordingly, the judgment under review is reversed.

Reversed.

Mr. Justice Powell took no part in the consideration or decision of this case.

Mr. Justice White, concurring.

This case would have been unnecessary had Gannett Co. v. DePasquale, 443 U.S. 368 (1979), construed the Sixth Amendment to forbid excluding the public from criminal proceedings except in narrowly defined circumstances. But the Court there rejected the submission of four of us to this effect, thus requiring that the First Amendment issue involved here be addressed. On this issue, I concur in the opinion of The Chief Justice.

Mr. Justice Stevens, concurring.

This is a watershed case. Until today the Court has accorded virtually absolute protection to the dissemination of information or ideas, but never before has it squarely held that the acquisition of newsworthy matter is entitled to any constitutional protection whatsoever. An additional word of emphasis is therefore appropriate.

Twice before, the Court has implied that any governmental restriction on access to information, no matter how severe and no matter how unjustified, would be constitutionally acceptable so long as it did not single out the press for special disabilities not applicable to the public at large. In a dissent joined by Mr. Justice Brennan and Mr. Justice Marshall in Saxbe v. Washington Post Co., 417 U.S. 843, 850, Mr. Justice Powell unequivocally rejected the conclusion "that *any* governmental restriction on press access to information, so long as it is not discriminatory, falls outside the purview of First Amendment concern." Id., at 857 (emphasis in original). And in Houchins v. KQED, Inc., 438 U.S. 1, 19–40, I explained at length why Mr. Justice Brennan, Mr. Justice Powell, and I were convinced that "[a]n official prison policy of concealing . . . knowl-

---

[17] Whether the public has a right to attend trials of civil cases is a question not raised by this case, but we note that historically both civil and criminal trials have been presumptively open.

edge from the public by arbitrarily cutting off the flow of information at its source abridges the freedom of speech and of the press protected by the First and Fourteenth Amendments to the Constitution." Id., at 38. Since Mr. Justice Marshall and Mr. Justice Blackmun were unable to participate in that case, a majority of the Court neither accepted nor rejected that conclusion or the contrary conclusion expressed in the prevailing opinions. Today, however, for the first time, the Court unequivocally holds that an arbitrary interference with access to important information is an abridgment of the freedoms of speech and of the press protected by the First Amendment.

It is somewhat ironic that the Court should find more reason to recognize a right of access today than it did in *Houchins*. For *Houchins* involved the plight of a segment of society least able to protect itself, an attack on a long-standing policy of concealment, and an absence of any legitimate justification for abridging public access to information about how government operates. In this case we are protecting the interests of the most powerful voices in the community, we are concerned with an almost unique exception to an established tradition of openness in the conduct of criminal trials, and it is likely that the closure order was motivated by the judge's desire to protect the individual defendant from the burden of a fourth criminal trial.[2]

In any event, for the reasons stated in Part II of my *Houchins* opinion, 438 U.S., at 30–38, as well as those stated by the Chief Justice today, I agree that the First Amendment protects the public and the press from abridgement of their rights of access to information about the operation of their government, including the Judicial Branch; given the total absence of any record justification for the closure order entered in this case, that order violated the First Amendment.

Mr. Justice Brennan, with whom Mr. Justice Marshall joins, concurring in the judgment.

Gannett Co. v. DePasquale, 443 U.S. 368 (1979), held that the Sixth Amendment right to a public trial was personal to the accused, conferring no right of access to pretrial proceedings that is separately enforceable by the public or the press. The instant case raises the question whether the First Amendment, of its own force and as applied to the States through the Fourteenth Amendment, secures the public an independent right of access to trial proceedings. Because I believe that the First Amendment—of itself and as applied to the States through the Fourteenth Amendment—secures such a public right of access, I agree with those of my Brethren who hold that, without more, agreement of the trial judge and the parties cannot constitutionally close a trial to the public.

I.

. . . . [T]he Court has not ruled out a public access component to the First Amendment in every circumstance. Read with care and in context, our decisions must therefore be understood as holding only that any privilege of access to governmental information is subject to a degree of restraint dictated by the nature of the information and countervailing interests in security or confidentiality. See *Houchins*, supra, at 8–9 (opinion of Burger, C.J.) (access to prisons); *Saxbe,* supra, at 849 (same); *Pell*, supra, at 831–832 (same); Estes v. Texas, 381 U.S. 532, 541–542 (1965) (television in courtroom); Zemel v. Rusk, 381 U.S. 1, 16–17 (1965) (validation of passport to unfriendly country).

---

[2] The absence of any articulated reason for the closure order is a sufficient basis for distinguishing this case from Gannett v. DePasquale, 443 U.S. 368. The decision today is in no way inconsistent with the perfectly unambiguous holding in *Gannett* that the rights guaranteed by the Sixth Amendment are rights that may be asserted by the accused rather than members of the general public.
. . . .

These cases neither comprehensively nor absolutely deny that public access to information may at times be implied by the First Amendment and the principles which animate it.

The Court's approach in right of access cases simply reflects the special nature of a claim of First Amendment right to gather information. Customarily, First Amendment guarantees are interposed to protect communication between speaker and listener. When so employed against prior restraints, free speech protections are almost insurmountable. . . . But the First Amendment embodies more than a commitment to free expression and communicative interchange for their own sakes; it has a *structural* role to play in securing and fostering our republican system of self-government. . . . Implicit in this structural role is . . . the antecedent assumption that valuable public debate—as well as other civic behavior—must be informed. The structural model links the First Amendment to that process of communication necessary for a democracy to survive, and thus entails solicitude not only for communication itself, but for the indispensable conditions of meaningful communication.

However, because "the stretch of this protection is theoretically endless," Brennan, supra, at 177, it must be invoked with discrimination and temperance. For so far as the participating citizen's need for information is concerned, "[t]here are few restrictions on action which could not be clothed by ingenious argument in the garb of decreased data flow." Zemel v. Rusk, supra, 381 U.S., at 16–17. An assertion of the prerogative to gather information must accordingly be assayed by considering the information sought and the opposing interests invaded.

This judicial task is as much a matter of sensitivity to practical necessities as it is of abstract reasoning. But at least two helpful principles may be sketched. First, the case for a right of access has special force when drawn from an enduring and vital tradition of public entree to particular proceedings or information. . . . Such a tradition commands respect in part because the Constitution carries the gloss of history. More importantly, a tradition of accessibility implies the favorable judgment of experience. Second, the value of access must be measured in specifics. Analysis is not advanced by rhetorical statements that all information bears upon public issues; what is crucial in individual cases is whether access to a particular government process is important in terms of that very process.

To resolve the case before us, therefore, we must consult historical and current practice with respect to open trials, and weigh the importance of public access to the trial process itself.

II.

. . .

Tradition, contemporaneous state practice, and this Court's own decisions manifest a common understanding that "[a] trial is a public event. What transpires in the court room is public property." Craig v. Harney, 331 U.S. 367, 374 (1947). . . .

III.

Publicity serves to advance several of the particular purposes of the trial (and, indeed, the judicial) process. Open trials play a fundamental role in furthering the efforts of our judicial system to assure the criminal defendant a fair and accurate adjudication of guilt or innocence. . . . But, as a feature of our governing system of justice, the trial process serves other, broadly political, interests, and public access advances these objectives as well. To that extent, trial access possesses specific structural significance.

. . . For a civilization founded upon principles of ordered liberty to survive and flourish, its members must share the conviction that they are governed equitably. . . .

Secrecy is profoundly inimical to this demonstrative purpose of the trial process. Open trials assure the public that procedural rights are respected, and that justice is afforded equally. Closed trials breed suspicion of prejudice and arbitrariness, which in turn spawns disrespect for law. Public access is essential, therefore, if trial adjudication is to achieve the objective of maintaining public confidence in the administration of justice. See Gannett, supra, at 428–429 (Blackmun, J., concurring and dissenting).

But the trial is more than a demonstrably just method of adjudicating disputes and protecting rights. It plays a pivotal role in the entire judicial process, and, by extension, in our form of government. Under our system, judges are not mere umpires, but, in their own sphere, lawmakers—a coordinate branch of *government*. While individual cases turn upon the controversies between parties, or involve particular prosecutions, court rulings impose official and practical consequences upon members of society at large. Moreover, judges bear responsibility for the vitally important task of construing and securing constitutional rights. Thus, so far as the trial is the mechanism for judicial factfinding, as well as the initial forum for legal decisionmaking, it is a genuine governmental proceeding.

. . . .

Finally, with some limitations, a trial aims at true and accurate factfinding. Of course, proper factfinding is to the benefit of criminal defendants and of the parties in civil proceedings. But other, comparably urgent, interests are also often at stake. A miscarriage of justice that imprisons an innocent accused also leaves a guilty party at large, a continuing threat to society. Also, mistakes of fact in civil litigation may inflict costs upon others than the plaintiff and defendant. Facilitation of the trial factfinding process, therefore, is of concern to the public as well as to the parties.

Publicizing trial proceedings aids accurate factfinding. . . .

Popular attendance at trials, in sum, substantially furthers the particular public purposes of that critical judicial proceeding.[22] In that sense, public access is an indispensable element of the trial process itself. Trial access, therefore, assumes structural importance in our "government of laws," Marbury v. Madison, 1 Cranch 137, 163 (1803).

IV.

As previously noted, resolution of First Amendment public access claims in individual cases must be strongly influenced by the weight of historical practice and by an assessment of the specific structural value of public access in the circumstances. With regard to the case at hand, our ingrained tradition of public trials and the importance of public access to the broader purposes of the trial process, tip the balance strongly toward the rule that trials be open. What countervailing interests might be sufficiently compelling to reverse this pre-

[22] In advancing these purposes, the availability of a trial transcript is no substitute for a public presence at the trial itself. As any experienced appellate judge can attest, the "cold" record is a very imperfect reproduction of events that transpire in the courtroom. Indeed, to the extent that publicity serves as a check upon trial officials, "[r]ecordation . . . would be found to operate rather as cloak[ ] than check[ ]; as cloak[ ] in reality, as check [ ] only in appearance." In re Oliver, supra, 333 U.S., at 271, quoting 1 Bentham, Rationale of Judicial Evidence 524 (1827); see Bentham, supra, at 577–578.

sumption of openness need not concern us now,[24] for the statute at stake here authorizes trial closures at the unfettered discretion of the judge and parties.[25] Accordingly, Va.Code 19.2–266 violates the First and Fourteenth Amendments, and the decision of the Virginia Supreme Court to the contrary should be reversed.

Mr. Justice Stewart, concurring in the judgment.

. . .

. . . [A] trial courtroom is a place where representatives of the press and of the public are not only free to be, but where their presence serves to assure the integrity of what goes on.

But this does not mean that the First Amendment right of members of the public and representatives of the press to attend civil and criminal trials is absolute. Just as a legislature may impose reasonable time, place and manner restrictions upon the exercise of First Amendment freedoms, so may a trial judge impose reasonable limitations upon the unrestricted occupation of a courtroom by representatives of the press and members of the public. Cf. Sheppard v. Maxwell, 384 U.S. 333. Much more than a city street, a trial courtroom must be a quiet and orderly place. Compare Kovacs v. Cooper, 336 U.S. 77 with Illinois v. Allen, 397 U.S. 337 and Estes v. Texas, 381 U.S. 532. Moreover, every courtroom has a finite physical capacity, and there may be occasions when not all who wish to attend a trial may do so.[3] And while there exist many alternative ways to satisfy the constitutional demands of a fair trial, those demands may also sometimes justify limitations upon the unrestricted presence of spectators in the courtroom.[5]

Since in the present case the trial judge appears to have given no recognition to the right of representatives of the press and members of the public to be present at the Virginia murder trial over which he was presiding, the judgment under review must be reversed.

It is upon the basis of these principles that I concur in the judgment.

Mr. Justice Blackmun, concurring in the judgment.

My opinion and vote in partial dissent last Term in Gannett Co. v. DePasquale, 443 U.S. 368, 406 (1979), compels my vote to reverse the judgment of the Supreme Court of Virginia.

. . .

II.

The Court's ultimate ruling in *Gannett,* with such clarification as is provided by the opinions in this case today, apparently is now to the effect that there is no *Sixth* Amendment right on the part of the public—or the press—to an open hearing on a motion to suppress. I, of course, continue to believe that *Gannett* was in error, both in its interpretation of the Sixth Amendment generally, and in its application to the suppression hearing, for I remain convinced that the right

[24] For example, national security concerns about confidentiality may sometimes warrant closures during sensitive portions of trial proceedings, such as testimony about state secrets. Cf. United States v. Nixon, 418 U.S. 683, 714–716 (1974).

[25] Significantly, closing a trial lacks even the justification for barring the door to pretrial hearings: the necessity of preventing dissemination of suppressible prejudicial evidence to the public before the jury pool has become, in a practical sense, finite and subject to sequestration.

[3] In such situations, representatives of the press must be assured access. Houchins v. KQED, Inc., 438 U.S. 1, 16 (concurring opinion).

[5] This is not to say that only constitutional considerations can justify such restrictions. The preservation of trade secrets, for example, might justify the exclusion of the public from at least some segments of a civil trial. And the sensibilities of a youthful prosecution witness, for example, might justify similar exclusion in a criminal trial for rape, so long as the defendant's Sixth Amendment right to a public trial were not impaired.

to a public trial is to be found where the Constitution explicitly placed it—in the Sixth Amendment.

The Court, however, has eschewed the Sixth Amendment route. The plurality turns to other possible constitutional sources and invokes a veritable potpourri of them—the speech clause of the First Amendment, the press clause, the assembly clause, the Ninth Amendment, and a cluster of penumbral guarantees recognized in past decisions. . . .

Having said all this, and with the Sixth Amendment set to one side in this case, I am driven to conclude, as a secondary position, that the First Amendment must provide some measure of protection for public access to the trial. . . .

I also would reverse, and I join the judgment of the Court.

Mr. Justice Rehnquist, dissenting.

. . .

For the reasons stated in my separate concurrence in Gannett Co., Inc. v. DePasquale, 443 U.S. 368, 403 (1979), I do not believe that either the First or Sixth Amendments, as made applicable to the States by the Fourteenth, require that a State's reasons for denying public access to a trial, where both the prosecuting attorney and the defendant have consented to an order of closure approved by the judge, are subject to any additional constitutional review at our hands. . . .

. . .

The issue here is not whether the "right" to freedom of the press conferred by the First Amendment to the Constitution overrides the defendant's "right" to a fair trial conferred by other amendments to the Constitution; it is instead whether any provision in the Constitution may fairly be read to prohibit what the trial judge in the Virginia state court system did in this case. Being unable to find any such prohibition in the First, Sixth, Ninth, or any other Amendments to the United States Constitution, or in the Constitution itself, I dissent.

PRESS ACCESS DECISIONS SINCE RICHMOND NEWSPAPERS, INC. v. VIRGINIA

In Globe Newspapers Co. v. Superior Court, 457 U.S. 596 (1982), Justice Brennan's opinion for the Court read the *Richmond Newspapers* case simply as establishing a right of access to criminal trials embodied in the first amendment. The Court held unconstitutional on its face a unique Massachusetts statute requiring exclusion of the press and public during testimony of the victim at trials for specified sexual offenses against persons under the age of 18. The Court conceded that the first amendment might not preclude restrictions on public and press access in individual cases based on "particularized determinations."

In Press-Enterprise Co. v. Superior Court, 104 S.Ct. 819 (1984), the Court held that a state court's decision closing the six weeks of *voir dire* examination of jurors in a criminal trial violated the Constitution. Chief Justice Burger's opinion for the Court stated that the "presumption of openness" of criminal trials "may be overcome only by an overriding interest based on findings that closure is essential to preserve higher values and is narrowly tailored to serve that interest."

SECTION 6. SPECIAL PROBLEMS OF THE ELECTRONIC MEDIA

COLUMBIA BROADCASTING SYSTEM, INC. v. DEMOCRATIC NATIONAL COMMITTEE

412 U.S. 94, 93 S.Ct. 2080, 36 L.Ed.2d 772 (1973).

Mr. Chief Justice Burger delivered the opinion of the Court (Parts I, II, and IV) together with an opinion (Part III) in which Mr. Justice Stewart and Mr. Justice Rehnquist joined.

We granted the writs of certiorari in these cases to consider whether a broadcast licensee's general policy of not selling advertising time to individuals or groups wishing to speak out on issues they consider important violates the Federal Communications Act of 1934, 47 U.S.C. § 151 et seq., or the First Amendment.

.   .   .

The complainants in these actions are the Democratic National Committee (DNC) and the Business Executives' Move for Vietnam Peace (BEM), a national organization of businessmen opposed to United States involvement in the Vietnam conflict.   In January 1970, BEM filed a complaint with the Commission charging that radio station WTOP in Washington, D.C., had refused to sell it time to broadcast a series of one-minute spot announcements expressing BEM views on Vietnam.   WTOP, in common with many but not all broadcasters, followed a policy of refusing to sell time for spot announcements to individuals and groups who wished to expound their views on controversial issues.   WTOP took the position that since it presented full and fair coverage of important public questions, including the Vietnam conflict, it was justified in refusing to accept editorial advertisements.   WTOP also submitted evidence showing that the station had aired the views of critics of our Vietnam policy on numerous occasions.   BEM challenged the fairness of WTOP's coverage of criticism of that policy, but it presented no evidence in support of that claim.

Four months later, in May 1970, the DNC filed with the Commission a request for a declaratory ruling:

"That under the First Amendment to the Constitution and the Communications Act, a broadcaster may not, as a general policy, refuse to sell time to responsible entities, such as DNC, for the solicitation of funds and for comment on public issues."

DNC claimed that it intended to purchase time from radio and television stations and from the national networks in order to present the views of the Democratic Party and to solicit funds.   Unlike BEM, DNC did not object to the policies of any particular broadcaster but claimed that its prior "experiences in this area make it clear that it will encounter considerable difficulty—if not total frustration of its efforts—in carrying out its plans in the event the Commission should decline to issue a ruling as requested."   DNC cited Red Lion Broadcasting Co. v. FCC, 395 U.S. 367 (1969), as establishing a limited constitutional right of access to the airwaves.

In two separate opinions, the Commission rejected respondents' claim that "responsible" individuals and groups have a right to purchase advertising time to comment on public issues without regard to whether the broadcaster has complied with the Fairness Doctrine.   .   .   .

.   .   .

A majority of the Court of Appeals reversed the Commission, ...

I.

Mr. Justice White's opinion for the Court in Red Lion Broadcasting Co. v. FCC, 395 U.S. 367 (1969), makes clear that the broadcast media pose unique and special problems not present in the traditional free speech case. Unlike other media, broadcasting is subject to an inherent physical limitation. Broadcast frequencies are a scarce resource; they must be portioned out among applicants. All who possess the financial resources and the desire to communicate by television or radio cannot be satisfactorily accommodated. The Court spoke to this reality when, in *Red Lion,* we said "it is idle to posit an unabridgeable First Amendment right to broadcast comparable to the right of every individual to speak, write, or publish." Id., at 388.

Because the broadcast media utilize a valuable and limited public resource, there is also present an unusual order of First Amendment values. *Red Lion* discussed at length the application of the First Amendment to the broadcast media. In analyzing the broadcasters' claim that the Fairness Doctrine and two of its component rules violated their freedom of expression, we held that "[n]o one has a First Amendment right to a license or to monopolize a radio frequency; to deny a station license because 'the public interest' requires it 'is not a denial of free speech.' " Id., at 389. Although the broadcaster is not without protection under the First Amendment, United States v. Paramount Pictures, Inc., 334 U.S. 131, 166 (1948), "[i]t is the right of the viewers and listeners, not the right of the broadcasters, which is paramount. . . . It is the right of the public to receive suitable access to social, political, esthetic, moral and other ideas and experiences which is crucial here. That right may not constitutionally be abridged either by Congress or by the FCC." *Red Lion,* supra, 395 U.S., at 390.

Balancing the various First Amendment interests involved in the broadcast media and determining what best serves the public's right to be informed is a task of a great delicacy and difficulty. The process must necessarily be undertaken within the framework of the regulatory scheme that has evolved over the course of the past half-century. For during that time, Congress and its chosen regulatory agency have established a delicately balanced system of regulation intended to serve the interests of all concerned. The problems of regulation are rendered more difficult because the broadcast industry is dynamic in terms of technological change; solutions adequate a decade ago are not necessarily so now, and those acceptable today may well be outmoded 10 years hence. . . . Thus, before confronting the specific legal issues in these cases, we turn to an examination of the legislative and administrative development of our broadcast system over the last half century.

II.

This Court has on numerous occasions recounted the origins of our modern system of broadcast regulation. See, e.g., *Red Lion,* supra, 395 U.S., at 375–386; National Broadcasting Co. v. United States, 319 U.S. 190, 210–217 (1943); . . . . .

The legislative history of the Radio Act of 1927, the model for our present statutory scheme, see FCC v. Pottsville Broadcasting Co., 309 U.S. 134, 137 (1940), reveals that in the area of discussion of public issues Congress chose to leave broad journalistic discretion with the licensee. Congress specifically dealt with—and firmly rejected—the argument that the broadcast facilities should be open on a nonselective basis to all persons wishing to talk about public issues. . . . Congress after prolonged consideration adopted § 3(h), which specifically provides that "a person engaged in radio broadcasting shall not, insofar as such person is so engaged, be deemed a common carrier."

Other provisions of the 1934 Act also evince a legislative desire to preserve values of private journalism under a regulatory scheme which would insure fulfillment of certain public obligations. Although the Commission was given the authority to issue renewable three-year licenses to broadcasters and to promulgate rules and regulations governing the use of those licenses, both consistent with the "public convenience, interest or necessity," § 326 of the Act specifically provides that:

"Nothing in this chapter shall be understood or construed to give the Commission the power of censorship over the radio communications or signals transmitted by any radio station, and no regulation or condition shall be promulgated or fixed by the Commission which shall interfere with the right of free speech by means of radio communication." 47 U.S.C. § 326.

From these provisions it seems clear that Congress intended to permit private broadcasting to develop with the widest journalistic freedom consistent with its public obligations. . . .

Subsequent developments in broadcast regulation illustrate how this regulatory scheme has evolved. Of particular importance, in light of Congress' flat refusal to impose a "common carrier" right of access for all persons wishing to speak out on public issues, is the Commission's "Fairness Doctrine," which evolved gradually over the years spanning federal regulation of the broadcast media. Formulated under the Commission's power to issue regulations consistent with the "public interest," the doctrine imposes two affirmative responsibilities on the broadcaster: coverage of issues of public importance must be adequate and must fairly reflect differing viewpoints. See *Red Lion,* supra, 395 U.S., at 377. In fulfilling its Fairness Doctrine obligations, the broadcaster must provide free time for the presentation of opposing views if a paid sponsor is unavailable, Cullman Broadcasting Co., 25 P & F Radio Reg. 895 (1963), and it must initiate programming on public issues if no one else seeks to do so. See John J. Dempsey, 6 P & F Radio Reg. 615 (1950); *Red Lion,* supra, 395 U.S., at 378. . . .

Thus, under the Fairness Doctrine broadcasters are responsible for providing the listening and viewing public with access to a balanced presentation of information on issues of public importance.[10] The basic principle underlying that responsibility is "the right of the public to be informed, rather than any right on the part of the government, any broadcast licensee or any individual member of the public to broadcast his own particular views on any matter. . . ." Report on Editorializing by Broadcast Licensees, 13 F.C.C. 1246, 1249 (1949). . . .

With this background in mind, we next proceed to consider whether a broadcaster's refusal to accept editorial advertisements is governmental action violative of the First Amendment.

III.

That "Congress shall make no law . . . abridging the freedom of speech, or of the press" is a restraint on government action, not that of private persons. Public Utilities Commission v. Pollak, 343 U.S. 451, 561 (1952).

---

[10] The Commission has also adopted various component regulations under the Fairness Doctrine, the most notable of which are the "personal attack" and "political editorializing" rules which we upheld in *Red Lion.* The "personal attack" rule provides that "when, during the presentation of views on a controversial issue of public importance, an attack is made on the honesty, character, integrity, or like personal qualities of an identified person," the licensee must notify the person attacked and give him an opportunity to respond. E.g., 47 CFR § 73.123. Similarly, the "political editorializing" rule provides that, when a licensee endorses a political candidate in an editorial, he must give other candidates or their spokesmen an opportunity to respond. E.g., Id., § 73.123.
. . . .

The Court has not previously considered whether the action of a broadcast licensee such as that challenged here is "governmental action" for purposes of the First Amendment. The holding under review thus presents a novel question, and one with far-reaching implications. See Jaffe, The Editorial Responsibility of the Broadcaster: Reflections on Fairness and Access, 85 Harv. L.Rev. 768, 782–787 (1972).

The Court of Appeals held that broadcasters are instrumentalities of the government for First Amendment purposes, relying on the thesis, familiar in other contexts, that broadcast licensees are granted use of part of the public domain and are regulated as "proxies" or "fiduciaries of the people." 450 F.2d, at 652. These characterizations are not without validity for some purposes, but they do not resolve the sensitive constitutional issues inherent in deciding whether a particular licensee action is subject to First Amendment restraints.

In dealing with the broadcast media, as in other contexts, the line between private conduct and governmental action cannot be defined by reference to any general formula unrelated to particular exercises of governmental authority.

. . . .

In deciding whether the First Amendment encompasses the conduct challenged here, it must be kept in mind that we are dealing with a vital part of our system of communication. The electronic media have swiftly become a major factor in the dissemination of ideas and information. More than 7,000 licensed broadcast stations undertake to perform this important function. To a large extent they share with the printed media the role of keeping people informed.

As we have seen, with the advent of radio a half century ago Congress was faced with a fundamental choice between total government ownership and control of the new medium—the choice of most other countries—or some other alternative. Long before the impact and potential of the medium was realized, Congress opted for a system of private broadcasters licensed and regulated by Government. The legislative history suggests that this choice was influenced not only by traditional attitudes toward private enterprise, but by a desire to maintain for licensees, so far as consistent with necessary regulation, a traditional journalistic role. The historic aversion to censorship led Congress to enact § 326 of the Act, which explicitly prohibits the Commission from interfering with the exercise of free speech over the broadcast frequencies. Congress pointedly refrained from divesting broadcasters of their control over the selection of voices; § 3(h) of the Act stands as a firm congressional statement that broadcast licensees are not to be treated as common carriers, obliged to accept whatever is tendered by members of the public. Both these provisions clearly manifest the intention of Congress to maintain a substantial measure of journalistic independence for the broadcast licensee.

The regulatory scheme evolved slowly, but very early the licensee's role developed in terms of a "public trustee" charged with the duty of fairly and impartially informing the public audience. In this structure the Commission acts in essence as an "overseer," but the initial and primary responsibility for fairness, balance and objectivity rests with the licensee. This role of the Government as an "overseer" and ultimate arbiter and guardian of the public interest and the role of the licensee as a journalistic "free agent" call for a delicate balancing of competing interests. The maintenance of this balance for more than 40 years has called on both the regulators and the licensees to walk a "tightrope" to preserve the First Amendment values written into the Radio Act and its successor, the Communications Act.

The tensions inherent in such a regulatory structure emerge more clearly when we compare a private newspaper with a broadcast licensee. The power of a privately owned newspaper to advance its own political, social, and economic views is bounded by only two factors: first, the acceptance of a sufficient number of readers—and hence advertisers—to assure financial success; and, second, the journalistic integrity of its editors and publishers. A broadcast licensee has a large measure of journalistic freedom but not as large as that exercised by a newspaper. A licensee must balance what it might prefer to do as a private entrepreneur with what it is required to do as a "public trustee." To perform its statutory duties, the Commission must oversee without censoring. . . .

The licensee's policy against accepting editorial advertising cannot be examined as an abstract proposition, but must be viewed in the context of its journalistic role. It does not help to press on us the idea that editorial ads are "like" commercial ads for the licensee's policy against editorial spot ads is expressly based on a journalistic judgment that 10 to 60 second spot announcements are ill suited to intelligible and intelligent treatment of public issues; the broadcaster has chosen to provide a balanced treatment of controversial questions in a more comprehensive form. Obviously the licensee's evaluation is based on its own journalistic judgment of priorities and newsworthiness.

Moreover, the Commission has not fostered the licensee policy challenged here; it has simply declined to command particular action because it fell within the area of journalistic discretion. The Commission explicitly emphasized that "there is of course no Commission policy thwarting the sale of time to comment on public issues." 25 F.C.C.2d, at 226. . . .

Thus, it cannot be said that the Government is a "partner" to the action of broadcast licensee complained of here, nor is it engaged in a "symbiotic relationship" with the licensee, profiting from the invidious discrimination of its proxy. Compare Moose Lodge No. 107 v. Irvis, 407 U.S. 163, 174–177 (1972), with Burton v. Wilmington Parking Authority, 365 U.S. 715, 723–724 (1961). The First Amendment does not reach acts of private parties in every instance where the Congress or the Commission has merely permitted or failed to prohibit such acts.

. . . .

Were we to read the First Amendment to spell out governmental action in the circumstances presented here, few licensee decisions on the content of broadcasts or the processes of editorial evaluation would escape constitutional scrutiny. In this sensitive area so sweeping a concept of governmental action would go far in practical effect to undermine nearly a half century of unmistakable congressional purpose to maintain—no matter how difficult the task— essentially private broadcast journalism held only broadly accountable to public interest standards. To do this Congress, and the Commission as its agent, must remain in a posture of flexibility to chart a workable "middle course" in its quest to preserve a balance between the essential public accountability and the desired private control of the media.

More profoundly, it would be anomalous for us to hold, in the name of promoting the constitutional guarantees of free expression, that the day-to-day editorial decisions of broadcast licensees are subject to the kind of restraints urged by respondents. To do so in the name of the First Amendment would be a contradiction. Journalistic discretion would in many ways be lost to the rigid limitations that the First Amendment imposes on government. Application of such standards to broadcast licensees would be antithetical to the very ideal of vigorous, challenging debate on issues of public interest. Every licensee is already held accountable for the totality of its performance of public interest obligations.

The concept of private, independent broadcast journalism, regulated by Government to assure protection of the public interest, has evolved slowly and cautiously over more than 40 years and has been nurtured by processes of adjudication. That concept of journalistic independence could not co-exist with a reading of the challenged conduct of the licensee as governmental action. Nor could it exist without administrative flexibility to meet changing needs and the swift technological developments. We therefore conclude that the policies complained of do not constitute governmental action violative of the First Amendment. . . .

IV.

There remains for consideration the question whether the "public interest" standard of the Communications Act requires broadcasters to accept editorial advertisements or, whether, assuming governmental action, broadcasters are required to do so by reason of the First Amendment. . . .

. . . .

The Commission was justified in concluding that the public interest in providing access to the marketplace of "ideas and experiences" would scarcely be served by a system so heavily weighted in favor of the financially affluent, or those with access to wealth. Cf. *Red Lion,* supra, 395 U.S., at 392, 89 S.Ct., at 1807. Even under a first-come-first-served system, proposed by the dissenting Commissioner in these cases, the views of the affluent could well prevail over those of others, since they would have it within their power to purchase time more frequently. Moreover, there is the substantial danger, as the Court of Appeals acknowledged, 450 F.2d, at 664, that the time allotted for editorial advertising could be monopolized by those of one political persuasion. . . .

. . . .

By minimizing the difficult problems involved in implementing . . . a right of access, the Court of Appeals failed to come to grips with another problem of critical importance to broadcast regulation and the First Amendment—the risk of an enlargement of government control over the content of broadcast discussion of public issues. . . . This risk is inherent in the Court of Appeals remand requiring regulations and procedures to sort out requests to be heard—a process involving the very editing that licensees now perform as to regular programming. . . .

Under a constitutionally commanded and Government supervised right-of-access system urged by respondents and mandated by the Court of Appeals, the Commission would be required to oversee far more of the day-to-day operations of broadcasters' conduct, deciding such questions as whether a particular individual or group has had sufficient opportunity to present its viewpoint and whether a particular viewpoint has already been sufficiently aired. Regimenting broadcasters is too radical a therapy for the ailment respondents complain of.

. . . Indeed, the likelihood of Government involvement is so great that it has been suggested that the accepted constitutional principles against control of speech content would need to be relaxed with respect to editorial advertisements.[20] To sacrifice First Amendment protections for so speculative a gain is not warranted, and it was well within the Commission's discretion to construe the Act so as to avoid such a result.[21] . . . .

. . . .

Conceivably at some future date Congress or the Commission—or the broadcasters—may devise some kind of limited right of access that is both practicable and desirable. Indeed, the Commission noted in these proceedings

---

[20] See Note, 85 Harv.L.Rev. 689, 697 (1973).

[21] DNC has urged in this Court that we at least recognize a right of our national parties to purchase airtime for the purpose of discussing public issues. We see no principled means under the First Amendment of favoring access by organized political parties over other groups and individuals.

that the advent of cable television will afford increased opportunities for the discussion of public issues. . . .

. . .

Reversed.

Mr. Justice Stewart, concurring.

While I join Parts I, II, and III of the Court's opinion, my views closely approach those expressed by Mr. Justice Douglas concurring in the judgment.

The First Amendment prohibits the Government from imposing controls upon the press. Private broadcasters are surely part of the press. United States v. Paramount Pictures, Inc., 334 U.S. 131, 166. Yet here the Court of Appeals held, and the dissenters today agree, that the First Amendment *requires* the Government to impose controls upon private broadcasters—in order to preserve First Amendment "values." The appellate court accomplished this strange convolution by the simple device of holding that private broadcasters *are* Government. This is a step along a path that could eventually lead to the proposition that private *newspapers* "are" Government. Freedom of the press would then be gone. In its place we would have such governmental controls upon the press as a majority of this Court at any particular moment might consider First Amendment "values" to require. It is a frightening specter.

. . .

I.

The First Amendment protects the press *from* governmental interference; it confers no analogous protection *on* the Government. To hold that broadcaster action is governmental action would thus simply strip broadcasters of their own First Amendment rights. They would be obligated to grant the demands of all citizens to be heard over the air, subject only to reasonable regulations as to "time, place and manner." . . . If, as the dissent today would have it, the proper analogy is to public forums—that is, if broadcasters are Government for First Amendment purposes—then broadcasters are inevitably drawn to the position of common carriers. For this is precisely the status of Government with respect to public forums—a status mandated by the First Amendment.

To hold that broadcaster action is governmental action would thus produce a result wholly inimical to the broadcasters' own First Amendment rights, and wholly at odds with the broadcasting system established by Congress and with our many decisions approving those legislative provisions. . . .

II.

Part IV of the Court's opinion, as I understand it, seems primarily to deal with the respondents' statutory argument—that the obligation of broadcasters to operate in the "public interest" supports the judgment of the Court of Appeals. Yet two of my concurring Brethren understand Part IV as a discussion of the First Amendment issue that would exist in these cases were the action of broadcasters to be equated with governmental action. So, according to my Brother Blackmun, "the governmental action issue does not affect the outcome of this case." . . .

I find this reasoning quite wrong and wholly disagree with it, for the simple reason that the First Amendment and the public interest standard of the statute are not coextensive . . . For example, the Fairness Doctrine is an aspect of the "public interest" regulation of broadcasters that would not be compelled or even permitted by the First Amendment itself if broadcasters were the Government.

If the "public interest" language of the statute were intended to enact the substance of the First Amendment, a discussion of whether broadcasters action is governmental action would indeed be superfluous. For anything that Government could not do because of the First Amendment, the broadcasters could not do under the statute. But this theory proves far too much, since it would make the statutory scheme, with its emphasis on broadcaster discretion and its proscription on interference with "the right of free speech by means of radio communication," a nullity. . . .

. . .

Mr. Justice White, concurring.

I join Parts I, II and IV of the Court's opinion and its judgment. I do not, however, concur in Part III of the opinion.

I do not suggest that the conduct of broadcasters must always, or even often, be considered that of a government for the purposes of the First Amendment. But it is at least arguable, and strongly so, that the Communications Act and the policies of the Commission, including the Fairness Doctrine, are here sufficiently implicated to require review of the Commission's orders under the First Amendment. . . .

In this context I am not ready to conclude, as the Court does in Part III, that the First Amendment may be put aside for lack of official action necessary to invoke its proscriptions. But, assuming *arguendo,* as the Court does in Part IV of its opinion, that Congress or the Commission is sufficiently involved in the denial of access to the broadcasting media to require review under the First Amendment, I would reverse the judgment of the Court of Appeals. Given the constitutionality of the Fairness Doctrine, and accepting Part IV of the Court's opinion, I have little difficulty in concluding that statutory and regulatory recognition of broadcaster freedom and discretion to make up their own programs and to choose their method of compliance with the Fairness Doctrine is consistent with the First Amendment.

Mr. Justice Blackmun, with whom Mr. Justice Powell joins, concurring.

In Part IV the Court determines "whether, assuming governmental action, broadcasters are required" to accept editorial advertisements "by reason of the First Amendment." The Court concludes that the Court of Appeals erred when it froze the "continuing search for means to achieve reasonable regulation compatible with the First Amendment rights of the public and the licensees" into "a constitutional holding." The Court's conclusion that the First Amendment does not compel the result reached by the Court of Appeals demonstrates that the governmental action issue does not affect the outcome of this case. I therefore refrain from deciding it.

Mr. Justice Douglas concurring in the judgment.

While I join the Court in reversing the judgment below, I do so for quite different reasons.

My conclusion is that the TV and radio stand in the same protected position under the First Amendment as do newspapers and magazines. The philosophy of the First Amendment requires that result, for the fear that Madison and Jefferson had of government intrusion is perhaps even more relevant to TV and radio than it is to newspapers and other like publications. . . .

Public broadcasting, of course, raises quite different problems from those tendered by the TV outlets involved in this litigation.

Congress has authorized the creation of the Corporation for Public Broadcasting, whose Board of Directors is appointed by the President by and with the advice and consent of the Senate. 47 U.S.C. § 396. A total of 223 television and 560 radio stations made up this nationwide public broadcasting system as of June 30, 1972. See 1972 Corporation for Public Broadcasting, Annual Report. It is a nonprofit organization and by the terms of § 396(b) is said not to be "an agency of establishment of the United States Government." Yet, since it is a creature of Congress whose management is in the hands of a Board named by the President and approved by the Senate, it is difficult to see why it is not a federal agency engaged in operating a "press" as that word is used in the First Amendment. If these cases involved that Corporation, we would have a situation comparable to that in which the United States owns and manages a prestigious newspaper like the New York Times, Washington Post, and Sacramento Bee. The government as owner and manager would not, as I see it, be free to pick and choose such news items as it desired. . . .

. . .

If a broadcast licensee is not engaged in governmental action for purposes of the First Amendment, I fail to see how constitutionally we can treat TV and the radio differently than we treat newspapers. . . .

The Court in National Broadcasting Co. v. United States, 319 U.S., 190, 226, said, "Unlike other modes of expression, radio inherently is not available to all. That is its unique characteristic, and that is why, unlike other modes of expression, it is subject to governmental regulation."

That uniqueness is due to engineering and technical problems. But the press in a realistic sense is likewise not available to all. Small or "underground" papers appear and disappear; and the weekly is an established institution. But the daily papers now established are unique in the sense that it would be virtually impossible for a competitor to enter the field due to the financial exigencies of this era. The result is that in practical terms the newspapers and magazines, like the TV and radio, are available only to a select few. Who at this time would have the folly to think he could combat the New York Times or Denver Post by building a new plant and becoming a competitor? . . .

But the prospect of putting Government in a position of control over publishers is to me an appalling one, even to the extent of the Fairness Doctrine. The struggle for liberty has been a struggle against Government. The essential scheme of our Constitution and Bill of Rights was to take Government off the backs of people. Separation of powers was one device. An independent judiciary was another device. The Bill of Rights was still another. And it is anathema to the First Amendment to allow Government any role of censorship over newspapers, magazines, books, art, music, TV, radio or any other aspect of the press. There is unhappiness in some circles at the impotence of Government. But if there is to be a change, let it come by constitutional amendment. The Commission has an important role to play in curbing monopolistic practices, in keeping channels free from interference, in opening up new channels as technology develops. But it has no power of censorship.

It is said, of course, that Government can control the broadcasters because their channels are in the public domain in the sense that they use the airspace that is the common heritage of all the people. But parks are also in the public domain. Yet people who speak there do not come under Government censorship. Lovell v. Griffin, 303 U.S. 444, 450–453; Hague v. CIO, 307 U.S. 496, 515–516. It is the tradition of Hyde Park, not the tradition of the censor, that is reflected in the First Amendment. TV and radio broadcasters are a vital part of the press; and since the First Amendment allows no Government control over it, I would leave this segment of the press to its devices.

Licenses are, of course, restricted in time and while, in my view, Congress has the power to make each license limited to a fixed term and nonrenewable, there is no power to deny renewals for editorial or ideological reasons. The reason is that the First Amendment gives no preference to one school of thought over others.

The Court in today's decision by endorsing the Fairness Doctrine sanctions a federal saddle on broadcast licensees that is agreeable to the traditions of nations that never have known freedom of press and that is tolerable in countries that do not have a written constitution containing prohibitions as absolute as those in the First Amendment. . . .

Mr. Justice Brennan, with whom Mr. Justice Marshall concurs, dissenting.

. . .

[W]e have explicitly recognized that, in light of the unique nature of the electronic media, the public have strong First Amendment interests in the reception of a full spectrum of views—presented in a vigorous and uninhibited manner—on controversial issues of public importance. And, as we have seen, it has traditionally been thought that the most effective way to insure this "uninhibited, robust, and wide-open" debate is by fostering a "free trade in ideas" by making our forums of communication readily available to all persons wishing to express their views. Although apparently conceding the legitimacy of these principles, the Court nevertheless upholds the absolute ban on editorial advertising because, in its view, the Commission's Fairness Doctrine, in and of itself, is sufficient to satisfy the First Amendment interests of the public. I cannot agree. . . . [T]he Fairness Doctrine does not in any sense require broadcasters to allow "nonbroadcaster" speakers to use the airwaves to express their own views on controversial issues of public importance. On the contrary, broadcasters may meet their fairness responsibilities through presentation of carefully edited news programs, panel discussions, interviews, and documentaries. As a result, broadcasters retain almost exclusive control over the selection of issues and viewpoints to be covered, the manner of presentation and, perhaps most important, who shall speak. Given this doctrinal framework, I can only conclude that the Fairness Doctrine, standing alone, is insufficient—in theory as well as in practice—to provide the kind of "uninhibited, robust, and wide-open" exchange of views to which the public is constitutionally entitled. . . .

Our legal system reflects a belief that truth is best illuminated by a collision of genuine advocates. Under the Fairness Doctrine, however, accompanied by an absolute ban on editorial advertising, the public is compelled to rely *exclusively* on the "journalistic discretion" of broadcasters, who serve in theory as surrogate spokesmen for all sides of all issues. . . .

. . .

. . . [T]he *absolute* ban on editorial advertising seems particularly offensive because, although broadcasters refuse to sell any airtime whatever to groups or individuals wishing to speak out on controversial issues of public importance, they make such airtime readily available to those "commercial" advertisers who seek to peddle their goods and services to the public. Thus, as the system now operates, any person wishing to market a particular brand of beer, soap, toothpaste, or deodorant has direct, personal, and instantaneous access to the electronic media. He can present his own message, in his own words, in any format he selects and at a time of his own choosing. Yet a similar individual seeking to discuss war, peace, pollution, or the suffering of the poor is denied this right to speak. Instead, he is compelled to rely on the beneficence of a corporate "trustee" appointed by the Government to argue his case for him.

It has been long recognized, however, that although access to public forums may be subjected to reasonable "time, place, and manner" regulations, "[s]elective exclusions from a public forum may not be based on *content* alone. . . ." Police Dept. of Chicago v. Mosley, supra, 408 U.S. at 96 (emphasis added). . . . Here, of course, the differential treatment accorded "commercial" and "controversial" speech clearly violates that principle. Moreover, and not without some irony, the favored treatment given "commercial" speech under the existing scheme clearly reverses traditional First Amendment priorities. For it has generally been understood that "commercial" speech enjoys *less* First Amendment protection than speech directed at the discussion of controversial issues of public importance. . . . ª

FEDERAL COMMUNICATIONS COMMISSION v. PACIFICA FOUNDATION

438 U.S. 726, 98 S.Ct. 3026, 57 L.Ed.2d 1073 (1978).

[The report in this case appears, supra at p. 1143.]

FEDERAL COMMUNICATIONS COMMISSION v. WNCN LISTENERS GUILD, 450 U.S. 582 (1981). The Court sustained an FCC Policy Statement that it would no longer, on station license renewal, consider a radio station's change of entertainment format. The Commission concluded that market forces rather than regulation would promote the greatest diversity in programming. Justice White's opinion for the Court concluded that the Policy Statement was not inconsistent with the Federal Communications Act. Speaking to a contention that the Policy Statement conflicted with the first amendment rights of listeners, the Court said:

"Red Lion Broadcasting Co. v. FCC, 395 U.S. 367, 390 (1969) . . . held that the Commission's 'fairness doctrine' was consistent with the public-interest standard of the Communications Act and did not violate the First Amendment, but rather enhanced First Amendment values by promoting 'the presentation of vigorous debate of controversial issues of importance and concern to the public.' Id., at 385. Although observing that the interests of the people as a whole were promoted by debate of public issues on the radio, we did not imply that the First Amendment grants individual listeners the right to have the Commission review the abandonment of their favorite entertainment programs. The Commission seeks to further the interests of the listening public as a whole by relying on market forces to promote diversity in radio entertainment formats and to satisfy the entertainment preferences of radio listeners.⁴⁶ This policy does not conflict with the First Amendment."

CBS, INC. v. FEDERAL COMMUNICATIONS COMMISSION, 453 U.S. 367 (1981). The Carter-Mondale Presidential Committee requested each of the three major networks to sell time for a 30-minute program during the December 4–7, 1979 period for a program in connection with President Carter's formal announcement of his candidacy. Each of the networks declined,

---

ª The literature on the subjects explored in the *CBS* case is enormous and complex. The following articles and their footnotes give access to much of that literature: Barrow, *The Fairness Doctrine: A Double Standard for Electronic and Print Media,* 26 Hast.L.J. 659 (1975); Bazelon, *FCC Regulation of the Telecommunications Press,* 1975 Duke L.J. 213; Robinson, *The FCC and the First Amendment: Observations on 40 Years of Radio and Television Regulation,* 52 Minn.L.Rev. 67 (1967).

For the official description of the government rules, see Federal Communication Commission, *Fairness Doctrine and Public Interest Standards—Fairness Report Regarding Handling of Public Issues,* 39 Fed.Reg. 26372 (July 18, 1974). See also Simmons, *Commercial Advertising and the Fairness Doctrine: The New F.C.C. Policy in Perspective,* 75 Colum.L.Rev. 1083 (1975).

⁴⁶ Respondents place particular emphasis on the role of foreign language programming in providing information to non-English-speaking citizens. However, the Policy Statement only applies to entertainment programming. It does not address the broadcaster's obligation to respond to community needs in the area of informational programming.

giving as a principal reason that it was too early to begin selling time for the 1980 Presidential campaign. The Carter-Mondale committee filed a complaint with the Federal Communications Commission charging that the networks had violated their statutory obligation (under 47 U.S.C. § 312(a)(7)) "to allow reasonable access to or to permit purchase of reasonable amounts of time for the use of a broadcasting station by a legally qualified candidate for Federal elective office on behalf of his candidacy." The Commission upheld the challenge. It held that under the statute it had the power to determine whether a campaign has begun and the statutory obligations have attached. It also held that the broadcasters must evaluate and respond to access requests on an individualized basis and offer reasons for denial which could be evaluated by the Commission. The Supreme Court, in an opinion by Chief Justice Burger, upheld the Commission in its determination as to the meaning of the statute and its application in this case. Responding to the argument by the network that as so construed the statute was in violation of the first amendment the Court said:

"A licensed broadcaster is 'granted the free and exclusive use of a limited and valuable part of the public domain; when he accepts that franchise it is burdened by enforceable public obligations.' Office of Communication of the United Church of Christ v. FCC, 359 F.2d 994, 1003 (1966). This Court has noted the limits on a broadcast license:

'A license permits broadcasting, but the licensee has no constitutional right to be the one who holds the license or to monopolize a . . . frequency to the exclusion of his fellow citizens. There is nothing in the First Amendment which prevents the Government from requiring a licensee to share his frequency with others . . . .' Red Lion Broadcasting Co. v. FCC, supra, 395 U.S., at 389.

. . .

". . . Section 312(a)(7) . . . makes a significant contribution to freedom of expression by enhancing the ability of candidates to present, and the public to receive, information necessary for the effective operation of the democratic process.

"Petitioners are correct that the Court has never approved a *general* right of access to the media. See, e.g., FCC v. Midwest Video Corp., 440 U.S. 689 (1979); Miami Herald Pub. Co. v. Tornillo, 418 U.S. 241 (1974); CBS, Inc. v. Democratic National Committee, supra. Nor do we do so today. Section 312(a)(7) creates a *limited* right to 'reasonable' access that pertains only to legally qualified federal candidates and may be invoked by them only for the purpose of advancing their candidacies once a campaign has commenced. The Commission has stated that, in enforcing the statute, it will 'provide leeway to broadcasters and not merely attempt *de novo* to determine the reasonableness of their judgments . . . .' 74 F.C.C.2d, at 672. If broadcasters have considered the relevant factors in good faith, the Commission will uphold their decisions. See 629 F.2d, at 25. Further, § 312(a)(7) does not impair the discretion of broadcasters to present their views on any issue or to carry any particular type of programming.

"Section 312(a)(7) represents an effort by Congress to assure that an important resource—the airwaves—will be used in the public interest. We hold that the statutory right of access, as defined by the Commission and applied in these cases, properly balances the First Amendment rights of federal candidates, the public, and broadcasters."

Justices White, Rehnquist, and Stevens dissented on the ground that the statute did not confer upon the Commission the power that it asserted in this case. They did not address the first amendment issue.

**FEDERAL COMMUNICATIONS COMMISSION v. LEAGUE
OF WOMEN VOTERS**

—— U.S. ——, 104 S.Ct. 3106, 82 L.Ed.2d 278 (1984).

[The report in this case appears supra at p. 1223.]

Chapter 18

RELIGION AND THE CONSTITUTION

Introduction. This chapter deals with the first amendment's prohibitions of laws "respecting an establishment of religion" and of laws "prohibiting the free exercise thereof." As Justice Rutledge stated in his dissenting opinion in Everson v. Board of Educ., 330 U.S. 1, 40 (1947): " 'establishment' and 'free exercise' were correlative and coextensive ideas, representing only different facets of the single great and fundamental freedom." A single ideal of government neutrality in matters of religion forbids both government aid to and government burdens on religious groups, religious activities, and individual religious beliefs.

Despite their common purpose, there has been an uneasy tension between applications of the free exercise and establishment clauses, caused by potential conflict between the two constitutional commands. Consider a common example. Suppose a state university permits a wide range of speakers on political or social issues to use a particular university facility without charge. If speakers engaged in religious conversion, worship, or advocacy are singled out and denied permission to speak, does this constitute discrimination against religion in violation of the free exercise clause? If religious speakers are permitted, is the state subsidizing religious worship in violation of the establishment clause? [1]

A question, then, that runs throughout this chapter is whether there is any single, reconciling interpretation of the establishment and free exercise clauses. A prominent attempt at reconciliation is Kurland, *Of Church and State and the Supreme Court*, 29 U.Chi.L.Rev. 1 (1961), *Selected Essays* 699 (1963). Professor Kurland's hypothesis is criticized in Pfeffer, *Religion-Blind Government*, 15 Stan.L. Rev. 389 (1963).

SECTION 1. THE ESTABLISHMENT CLAUSE

A. INTRODUCTION

The Court did not begin to elaborate the meaning of the establishment clause until the decision in Everson v. Board of Education in 1947—a case involving aid to students attending private religious schools. Between 1947 and 1963 the Court decided a series of cases involving the validity of various forms of religious exercises in the public school classrooms. In 1968 the Court returned to the theme of state aid to private religious education and has since elaborated on that theme in a number of cases.

Since establishment clause doctrine began with the *Everson* case it is presented in this introductory part. The following parts of this section will cover religion in the public schools, state financial aid to church-related schools, and other state practices beyond public or private education.

---

[1] Cf. Widmar v. Vincent, infra p. 1425.

EVERSON v. BOARD OF EDUCATION

330 U.S. 1, 67 S.Ct. 504, 91 L.Ed. 711 (1947).

Mr. Justice Black delivered the opinion of the Court.

A New Jersey statute authorizes its local school districts to make rules and contracts for the transportation of children to and from schools. The appellee, a township board of education, acting pursuant to this statute authorized reimbursement to parents of money expended by them for the bus transportation of their children on regular busses operated by the public transportation system. Part of this money was for the payment of transportation of some children in the community to Catholic parochial schools. These church schools give their students, in addition to secular education, regular religious instruction conforming to the religious tenets and modes of worship of the Catholic Faith. The superintendent of these schools is a Catholic priest.

The appellant, in his capacity as a district taxpayer, filed suit in a state court challenging the right of the Board to reimburse parents of parochial school students. . . . The New Jersey Court of Errors and Appeals [held] that neither the statute nor the resolution passed pursuant to it was in conflict with the State constitution or the provisions of the Federal Constitution in issue. . . .

The only contention here is that the state statute and the resolution, in so far as they authorized reimbursement to parents of children attending parochial schools, violate the Federal Constitution in these two respects, which to some extent, overlap. *First.* They authorize the State to take by taxation the private property of some and bestow it upon others, to be used for their own private purposes. This, it is alleged, violates the due process clause of the Fourteenth Amendment. *Second.* The statute and the resolution forced inhabitants to pay taxes to help support and maintain schools which are dedicated to, and which regularly teach, the Catholic Faith. This is alleged to be a use of state power to support church schools contrary to the prohibition of the First Amendment which the Fourteenth Amendment made applicable to the states.

First. . . . It is much too late to argue that legislation intended to facilitate the opportunity of children to get a secular education serves no public purpose. Cochran v. Louisiana State Board of Education, 281 U.S. 370. . . . The same thing is no less true of legislation to reimburse needy parents, or all parents, for payment of the fares of their children so that they can ride in public busses to and from schools rather than run the risk of traffic and other hazards incident to walking or "hitchhiking." . . .

Second. The New Jersey statute is challenged as a "law respecting an establishment of religion." The First Amendment, as made applicable to the states by the Fourteenth, . . . commands that a state "shall make no law respecting an establishment of religion, or prohibiting the free exercise thereof." . . . Whether this New Jersey law is one respecting the "establishment of religion" requires an understanding of the meaning of that language, particularly with respect to the imposition of taxes. Once again, therefore, it is not inappropriate briefly to review the background and environment of the period in which that constitutional language was fashioned and adopted.

A large proportion of the early settlers of this country came here from Europe to escape the bondage of laws which compelled them to support and attend government favored churches. . . .

These practices of the old world were transplanted to and began to thrive in the soil of the new America. The very charters granted by the English Crown to the individuals and companies designated to make the laws which would control the destinies of the colonials authorized these individuals and companies to erect religious establishments which all, whether believers or non-believers, would be required to support and attend. An exercise of authority was accompanied by a repetition of many of the old world practices and persecutions. . . .

These practices became so commonplace as to shock the freedom-loving colonials into a feeling of abhorrence. The imposition of taxes to pay ministers' salaries and to build and maintain churches and church property aroused their indignation. It was these feelings which found expression in the First Amendment. No one locality and no one group throughout the Colonies can rightly be given entire credit for having aroused the sentiment that culminated in adoption of the Bill of Rights' provisions embracing religious liberty. But Virginia, where the established church had achieved a dominant influence in political affairs and where many excesses attracted wide public attention, provided a great stimulus and able leadership for the movement. The people there, as elsewhere, reached the conviction that individual religious liberty could be achieved best under a government which was stripped of all power to tax, to support, or otherwise to assist any or all religions, or to interfere with the beliefs of any religious individual or group.

The movement toward this end reached its dramatic climax in Virginia in 1785–86 when the Virginia legislative body was about to renew Virginia's tax levy for the support of the established church. Thomas Jefferson and James Madison led the fight against this tax. Madison wrote his great Memorial and Remonstrance against the law. In it, he eloquently argued that a true religion did not need the support of law; that no person, either believer or non-believer, should be taxed to support a religious institution of any kind; that the best interest of a society required that the minds of men always be wholly free; and that cruel persecutions were the inevitable result of government-established religions. Madison's Remonstrance received strong support throughout Virginia, and the Assembly postponed consideration of the proposed tax measure until its next session. When the proposal came up for consideration at that session, it not only died in committee, but the Assembly enacted the famous "Virginia Bill for Religious Liberty" originally written by Thomas Jefferson. The preamble to that Bill stated among other things that

"Almighty God hath created the mind free; that all attempts to influence it by temporal punishments, or burthens, or by civil incapacitations, tend only to beget habits of hypocrisy and meanness, and are a departure from the plan of the Holy author of our religion who being Lord both of body and mind, yet chose not to propagate it by coercions on either . . .; that to compel a man to furnish contributions of money for the propagation of opinions which he disbelieves, is sinful and tyrannical; that even the forcing him to support this or that teacher of his own religious persuasion, is depriving him of the comfortable liberty of giving his contributions to the particular pastor, whose morals he would make his pattern. . . ."

And the statute itself enacted

"That no man shall be compelled to frequent or support any religious worship, place, or ministry whatsoever, nor shall be enforced, restrained, molested, or burthened, in his body or goods, nor shall otherwise suffer on account of his religious opinions or belief. . . ."

This Court has previously recognized that the provisions of the First Amendment, in the drafting and adoption of which Madison and Jefferson played such leading roles, had the same objective and were intended to provide the same protection against governmental intrusion on religious liberty as the Virginia

statute.[a]   .   .   .   Prior to the adoption of the Fourteenth Amendment, the First Amendment did not apply as a restraint against the states.   Most of them did soon provide similar constitutional protections for religious liberty.   But some states persisted for about half a century in imposing restraints upon the free exercise of religion and in discriminating against particular religious groups.
.   .   .

The meaning and scope of the First Amendment, preventing establishment of religion or prohibiting the free exercise thereof, in the light of its history and the evils it was designed forever to suppress, have been several times elaborated by the decisions of this Court prior to the application of the First Amendment to the states by the Fourteenth.   The broad meaning given the Amendment by these earlier cases has been accepted by this Court in its decisions concerning an individual's religious freedom rendered since the Fourteenth Amendment was interpreted to make the prohibitions of the First applicable to state action abridging religious freedom.   There is every reason to give the same application and broad interpretation to the "establishment of religion" clause.   .   .   .

The "establishment of religion" clause of the First Amendment means at least this: Neither a state nor the Federal Government can set up a church. Neither can pass laws which aid one religion, aid all religions, or prefer one religion over another.   Neither can force nor influence a person to go to or to remain away from church against his will or force him to profess a belief or disbelief in any religion.   No person can be punished for entertaining or professing religious beliefs or disbeliefs, for church attendance or nonattendance.   No tax in any amount, large or small, can be levied to support any religious activities or institutions, whatever they may be called, or whatever form they may adopt to teach or practice religion.   Neither a state nor the Federal Government can, openly or secretly, participate in the affairs of any religious organizations or groups and vice versa.   In the words of Jefferson, the clause against establishment of religion by law was intended to erect "a wall of separation between church and State."   Reynolds v. United States, supra, 98 U.S. at page 164.

We must consider the New Jersey statute in accordance with the foregoing limitations imposed by the First Amendment.   But we must not strike that state statute down if it is within the state's constitutional power even though it approaches the verge of that power.   .   .   .   New Jersey cannot consistently with the "establishment of religion" clause of the First Amendment contribute tax-raised funds to the support of an institution which teaches the tenets and faith of any church.   On the other hand, other language of the amendment commands that New Jersey cannot hamper its citizens in the free exercise of their own religion.   Consequently, it cannot exclude individual Catholics, Lutherans, Mohammedans, Baptists, Jews, Methodists, Non-believers, Presbyterians, or the members of any other faith, *because of their faith, or lack of it,* from receiving the benefits of public welfare legislation.   While we do not mean to intimate that a state could not provide transportation only to children attending public schools, we must be careful, in protecting the citizens of New Jersey against state-established churches, to be sure that we do not inadvertently prohibit New Jersey from extending its general state law benefits to all its citizens without regard to their religious belief.

Measured by these standards, we cannot say that the First Amendment prohibits New Jersey from spending tax-raised funds to pay the bus fares of

---

[a] For a very different reading of the historical record, see Howe, *Religion and the Free Society: The Constitutional Question, Selected Essays* 780 (1963).   Professor Howe, stressing that the Bill of Rights did not in its inception limit the states, argues that the prohibition on establishment was a "non-libertarian" limitation on national power.   Compare Pfeffer, *Church, State, and Freedom* 125–127 (1953).

parochial school pupils as a part of a general program under which it pays the fares of pupils attending public and other schools. It is undoubtedly true that children are helped to get to church schools. There is even a possibility that some of the children might not be sent to the church schools if the parents were compelled to pay their children's bus fares out of their own pockets when transportation to a public school would have been paid for by the State. The same possibility exists where the state requires a local transit company to provide reduced fares to school children including those attending parochial schools, or where a municipally owned transportation system undertakes to carry all school children free of charge. Moreover, state-paid policemen, detailed to protect children going to and from church schools from the very real hazards of traffic, would serve much the same purpose and accomplish much the same result as state provisions intended to guarantee free transportation of a kind which the state deems to be best for the school children's welfare. And parents might refuse to risk their children to the serious danger of traffic accidents going to and from parochial schools, the approaches to which were not protected by policemen. Similarly, parents might be reluctant to permit their children to attend schools which the state had cut off from such general government services as ordinary police and fire protection, connections for sewage disposal, public highways and sidewalks. Of course, cutting off church schools from these services, so separate and so indisputably marked off from the religious function, would make it far more difficult for the schools to operate. But such is obviously not the purpose of the First Amendment. That Amendment requires the state to be a neutral in its relations with groups of religious believers and non-believers; it does not require the state to be their adversary. State power is no more to be used so as to handicap religions, than it is to favor them.

This Court has said that parents may, in the discharge of their duty under state compulsory education laws, send their children to a religious rather than a public school if the school meets the secular educational requirements which the state has power to impose. See Pierce v. Society of Sisters, 268 U.S. 510. It appears that these parochial schools meet New Jersey's requirements. The State contributes no money to the schools. It does not support them. Its legislation, as applied, does no more than provide a general program to help parents get their children, regardless of their religion, safely and expeditiously to and from accredited schools.

. . .

The First Amendment has erected a wall between church and state. That wall must be kept high and impregnable. We could not approve the slightest breach. New Jersey has not breached it here.

Affirmed.

Mr. Justice Jackson [with whom Mr. Justice Frankfurter joined], dissenting.

. . .

. . . The Court's opinion marshals every argument in favor of state aid and puts the case in its most favorable light, but much of its reasoning confirms my conclusions that there are no good grounds upon which to support the present legislation. In fact, the undertones of the opinion, advocating complete and uncompromising separation of Church from State, seem utterly discordant with its conclusion yielding support to their commingling in educational matters. The case which irresistibly comes to mind as the most fitting precedent is that of Julia who, according to Byron's reports, "whispering 'I will ne'er consent,'— consented." . . .

Mr. Justice Rutledge, with whom Mr. Justice Frankfurter, Mr. Justice Jackson and Mr. Justice Burton, agree, dissenting.

. . .

Two great drives are constantly in motion to abridge, in the name of education, the complete division of religion and civil authority which our forefathers made. One is to introduce religious education and observances into the public schools. The other, to obtain public funds for the aid and support of various private religious schools. See Johnson, The Legal Status of Church-State Relationships in the United States (1934); Thayer, Religion in Public Education (1947); Note (1941) 50 Yale L.J. 917. In my opinion both avenues were closed by the Constitution. Neither should be opened by this Court. The matter is not one of quantity, to be measured by the amount of money expended. Now as in Madison's day it is one of principle, to keep separate the separate spheres as the First Amendment drew them; to prevent the first experiment upon our liberties; and to keep the question from becoming entangled in corrosive precedents. We should not be less strict to keep strong and untarnished the one side of the shield of religious freedom than we have been of the other.

The judgment should be reversed.

DENOMINATIONAL PREFERENCES

The Court was unanimous in *Everson* in the conclusion that the establishment clause forbids aid to all religions as well as aid to one religion. Still, in Larson v. Valente, 456 U.S. 228 (1982), the Court referred to the proposition that "one religious denomination cannot be officially preferred over another" as "the clearest command of the Establishment Clause." The Court invalidated a charitable contribution statute that exempted from its requirements religious organizations that solicit less than 50 percent of their funds from nonmembers. Justice White's dissent, joined by Justice Rehnquist, disagreed with the Court's conclusion that the distinction among religious organizations was a denominational preference, since it distinguished among religious organizations "on the source of their contributions, not on their brand of religion."

B. RELIGION IN PUBLIC SCHOOLS

ZORACH v. CLAUSON

343 U.S. 306, 72 S.Ct. 679, 96 L.Ed. 954 (1952).

Mr. Justice Douglas delivered the opinion of the Court.

New York City has a program which permits its public schools to release students during the school day so that they may leave the school buildings and school grounds and go to religious centers for religious instruction or devotional exercises. A student is released on written request of his parents. Those not released stay in the classrooms. The churches make weekly reports to the schools, sending a list of children who have been released from public school but who have not reported for religious instruction.

This "released time" program involves neither religious instruction in public school classrooms nor the expenditure of public funds. All costs, including the application blanks, are paid by the religious organizations. The case is therefore unlike McCollum v. Board of Education, 333 U.S. 203, which involved a "released time" program from Illinois. In that case the classrooms were turned over to religious instructors. We accordingly held that the program violated the First Amendment which (by reason of the Fourteenth Amendment) prohibits the states from establishing religion or prohibiting its free exercise.

Appellants, who are taxpayers and residents of New York City and whose children attend its public schools, challenge the present law, contending it is in essence not different from the one involved in the *McCollum* case. Their argument, stated elaborately in various ways, reduces itself to this: the weight and influence of the school is put behind a program for religious instruction; public school teachers police it, keeping tab on students who are released; the classroom activities come to a halt while the students who are released for religious instruction are on leave; the school is a crutch on which the churches are leaning for support in their religious training; without the cooperation of the schools this "released time" program, like the one in the *McCollum* case, would be futile and ineffective. The New York Court of Appeals sustained the law against this claim of unconstitutionality.

The briefs and arguments are replete with data bearing on the merits of this type of "released time" program. . . . Those matters are of no concern here, since our problem reduces itself to whether New York by this system has either prohibited the "free exercise" of religion or has made a law "respecting an establishment of religion" within the meaning of the First Amendment.

It takes obtuse reasoning to inject any issue of the "free exercise" of religion into the present case. No one is forced to go to the religious classroom and no religious exercise or instruction is brought to the classrooms of the public schools. A student need not take religious instruction. He is left to his own desires as to the manner or time of his religious devotions, if any.

There is a suggestion that the system involves the use of coercion to get public school students into religious classrooms. There is no evidence in the record before us that supports that conclusion.[6] The present record indeed tells us that the school authorities are neutral in this regard and do no more than release students whose parents so request. If in fact coercion were used, if it were established that any one or more teachers were using their office to persuade or force students to take the religious instruction, a wholly different case would be presented.[7] Hence we put aside that claim of coercion both as respects the "free exercise" of religion and "an establishment of religion" within the meaning of the First Amendment.

Moreover, apart from that claim of coercion, we do not see how New York by this type of "released time" program has made a law respecting an establishment of religion within the meaning of the First Amendment. . . . There cannot be the slightest doubt that the First Amendment reflects the philosophy that Church and State should be separated. And so far as interference with the "free exercise" of religion and an "establishment" of religion are concerned, the separation must be complete and unequivocal. The First Amendment within the scope of its coverage permits no exception; the prohibition is absolute. The First Amendment, however, does not say that in every and all respects there shall be a separation of Church and State. Rather, it

[6] Nor is there any indication that the public schools enforce attendance at religious schools by punishing absentees from the released time programs for truancy.

[7] Appellants contend that they should have been allowed to prove that the system is in fact administered in a coercive manner. The New York Court of Appeals declined to grant a trial on this issue, noting, *inter alia,* that appellants had not properly raised their claim in the manner required by state practice. 303 N.Y. 161, 174, 100 N.E.2d 463, 469. This independent state ground for decision precludes appellants from raising the issue of maladministration in this proceeding. . . .

The only allegation in the complaint that bears on the issue is that the operation of the program "has resulted and inevitably results in the exercise of pressure and coercion upon parents and children to secure attendance by the children for religious instruction." But this charge does not even implicate the school authorities. The New York Court of Appeals was therefore generous in labeling it a "conclusory" allegation. . . .

studiously defines the manner, the specific ways, in which there shall be no concert or union or dependency one on the other. That is the common sense of the matter. Otherwise the state and religion would be aliens to each other— hostile, suspicious, and even unfriendly. Churches could not be required to pay even property taxes. Municipalities would not be permitted to render police or fire protection to religious groups. Policemen who helped parishioners into their places of worship would violate the Constitution. Prayers in our legislative halls; the appeals to the Almighty in the messages of the Chief Executive; the proclamations making Thanksgiving Day a holiday; "so help me God" in our courtroom oath—these and all other references to the Almighty that run through our laws, our public rituals, our ceremonies would be flouting the First Amendment. A fastidious atheist or agnostic could even object to the supplication with which the Court opens each session: "God save the United States and this Honorable Court."

We would have to press the concept of separation of Church and State to these extremes to condemn the present law on constitutional grounds. The nullification of this law would have wide and profound effects. A Catholic student applies to his teacher for permission to leave the school during hours on a Holy Day of Obligation to attend a mass. A Jewish student asks his teacher for permission to be excused for Yom Kippur. A Protestant wants the afternoon off for a family baptismal ceremony. In each case the teacher requires parental consent in writing. In each case the teacher, in order to make sure the student is not a truant, goes further and requires a report from the priest, the rabbi, or the minister. The teacher in other words cooperates in a religious program to the extent of making it possible for her students to participate in it. Whether she does it occasionally for a few students, regularly for one, or pursuant to a systematized program designed to further the religious needs of all the students does not alter the character of the act.

We are a religious people whose institutions presuppose a Supreme Being. We guarantee the freedom to worship as one chooses. We make room for as wide a variety of beliefs and creeds as the spiritual needs of man deem necessary. We sponsor an attitude on the part of government that shows no partiality to any one group and that lets each flourish according to the zeal of its adherents and the appeal of its dogma. When the state encourages religious instruction or cooperates with religious authorities by adjusting the schedule of public events to sectarian needs, it follows the best of our traditions. For it then respects the religious nature of our people and accommodates the public service to their spiritual needs. To hold that it may not would be to find in the Constitution a requirement that the government show a callous indifference to religious groups. That would be preferring those who believe in no religion over those who do believe. Government may not finance religious groups nor undertake religious instruction nor blend secular and sectarian education nor use secular institutions to force one or some religion on any person. But we find no constitutional requirement which makes it necessary for government to be hostile to religion and to throw its weight against efforts to widen the effective scope of religious influence. The government must be neutral when it comes to competition between sects. It may not thrust any sect on any person. It may not make a religious observance compulsory. It may not coerce anyone to attend church, to observe a religious holiday, or to take religious instruction. But it can close its doors or suspend its operations as to those who want to repair to their religious sanctuary for worship or instruction. No more than that is undertaken here. . . .

In the *McCollum* case the classrooms were used for religious instruction and the force of the public school was used to promote that instruction. Here, as we have said, the public schools do no more than accommodate their schedules to a program of outside religious instruction. We follow the *McCollum* case. But we cannot expand it to cover the present released time program unless separation of Church and State means that public institutions can make no adjustments of their schedules to accommodate the religious needs of the people. We cannot read into the Bill of Rights such a philosophy of hostility to religion.

Affirmed.

Mr. Justice Black, dissenting.

. . .

In considering whether a state has entered this forbidden field the question is not whether it has entered too far but whether it has entered at all. New York is manipulating its compulsory education laws to help religious sects get pupils. This is not separation but combination of Church and State. . . .

Mr. Justice Frankfurter, dissenting.

By way of emphasizing my agreement with Mr. Justice Jackson's dissent, I add a few words. . . .

Of course a State may provide that the classes in its schools shall be dismissed, for any reason, or no reason, on fixed days, or for special occasions. The essence of this case is that the school system did not "close its doors" and did not "suspend its operations". . . .

The pith of the case is that formalized religious instruction is substituted for other school activity which those who do not participate in the released-time program are compelled to attend. The school system is very much in operation during this kind of released time. . . .

. . .

Mr. Justice Jackson, dissenting.

. . .

A number of Justices just short of a majority of the majority that promulgates today's passionate dialectics joined in answering them in McCollum v. Board of Education, 333 U.S. 203. The distinction attempted between that case and this is trivial, almost to the point of cynicism, magnifying its nonessential details and disparaging compulsion which was the underlying reason for invalidity. A reading of the Court's opinion in that case along with its opinion in this case will show such difference of overtones and undertones as to make clear that the *McCollum* case has passed like a storm in a teacup. The wall which the Court was professing to erect between Church and State has become even more warped and twisted than I expected. Today's judgment will be more interesting to students of psychology and of the judicial processes than to students of constitutional law.

ENGEL v. VITALE

370 U.S. 421, 82 S.Ct. 1261, 8 L.Ed.2d 601 (1962).

[The New York Board of Regents composed a "non-denominational" prayer: "Almighty God, we acknowledge our dependence upon Thee, and we beg Thy blessings upon us, our parents, our teachers and our country." A local board of education required that this prayer be recited daily by each class. A group of Unitarian, Ethical Culturist and agnostic parents claimed that this "religious activity" violated the establishment clause.]

Mr. Justice Black delivered the opinion of the Court.

. . . .

We think that by using its public school system to encourage recitation of the Regents' prayer, the State of New York has adopted a practice wholly inconsistent with the Establishment Clause. There can, of course, be no doubt that New York's program of daily classroom invocation of God's blessings as prescribed in the Regents' prayer is a religious activity. It is a solemn avowal of divine faith and application for the blessings of the Almighty. . . .

. . . [W]e think that the constitutional prohibition against laws respecting an establishment of religion must at least mean that in this country it is no part of the business of government to compose official prayers for any group of the American people to recite as a part of a religious program carried on by government.

It is a matter of history that this very practice of establishing governmentally composed prayers for religious services was one of the reasons which caused many of our early colonists to leave England and seek religious freedom in America. . . .

It is an unfortunate fact of history that when some of the very groups which had most strenuously opposed the established Church of England found themselves sufficiently in control of colonial governments in this country to write their own prayers into law, they passed laws making their own religion the official religion of their respective colonies. Indeed, as late as the time of the Revolutionary War, there were established churches in at least eight of the thirteen former colonies and established religions in at least four of the other five. But the successful Revolution against English political domination was shortly followed by intense opposition to the practice of establishing religion by law. . . .

By the time of the adoption of the Constitution, our history shows that there was a widespread awareness among many Americans of the dangers of a union of Church and State. . . . Our Founders were no more willing to let the content of their prayers and their privilege of praying whenever they pleased be influenced by the ballot box than they were to let these vital matters of personal conscience depend upon the succession of monarchs. The First Amendment was added to the Constitution to stand as a guarantee that neither the power nor the prestige of the Federal Government would be used to control, support or influence the kinds of prayer the American people can say—that the people's religions must not be subjected to the pressures of government for change each time a new political administration is elected to office. Under that Amendment's prohibition against governmental establishment of religion, as reinforced by the provisions of the Fourteenth Amendment, government in this country, be it state or federal, is without power to prescribe by law any particular form of prayer which is to be used as an official prayer in carrying on any program of governmentally sponsored religious activity.

There can be no doubt that New York's state prayer program officially establishes the religious beliefs embodied in the Regents' prayer. . . . Neither the fact that the prayer may be denominationally neutral, nor the fact that its observance on the part of the students is voluntary can serve to free it from the limitations of the Establishment Clause, as it might from the Free Exercise Clause, of the First Amendment, both of which are operative against the States by virtue of the Fourteenth Amendment. Although these two clauses may in certain instances overlap, they forbid two quite different kinds of governmental encroachment upon religious freedom. The Establishment Clause, unlike the Free Exercise Clause, does not depend upon any showing of direct governmental compulsion and is violated by the enactment of laws which establish an official religion whether those laws operate directly to coerce nonobserving individuals or not. This is not to say, of course, that laws officially prescribing a particular form of religious worship do not involve coercion of such individuals. When the power, prestige and financial support of government is placed behind a particular religious belief, the indirect coercive pressure upon religious minorities to conform to the prevailing officially approved religion is plain. But the purposes underlying the Establishment Clause go much further than that. Its first and most immediate purpose rested on the belief that a union of government and religion tends to destroy government and to degrade religion. . . .

It has been argued that to apply the Constitution in such a way as to prohibit state laws respecting an establishment of religious services in public schools is to indicate a hostility toward religion or toward prayer. Nothing, of course, could be more wrong. The history of man is inseparable from the history of religion. And perhaps it is not too much to say that since the beginning of that history many people have devoutly believed that "More things are wrought by prayer than this world dreams of." It was doubtless largely due to men who believed this that there grew up a sentiment that caused men to leave the cross-currents of officially established state religions and religious persecution in Europe and come to this country filled with the hope that they could find a place in which they could pray when they pleased to the God of their faith in the language they chose. . . . It is neither sacrilegious nor antireligious to say that each separate government in this country should stay out of the business of writing or sanctioning official prayers and leave that purely religious function to the people themselves and to those the people choose to look to for religious guidance.[21]

. . .

Reversed and remanded.

Mr. Justice Frankfurter took no part in the decision of this case.

Mr. Justice White took no part in the consideration or decision of this case.

Mr. Justice Douglas, concurring. . . . The point for decision is whether the Government can constitutionally finance a religious exercise. Our system at the federal and state levels is presently honeycombed with such financing.[1] Nevertheless, I think it is an unconstitutional undertaking whatever form it takes.

First, a word as to what this case does not involve.

---

[21] There is of course nothing in the decision reached here that is inconsistent with the fact that school children and others are officially encouraged to express love for our country by reciting historical documents such as the Declaration of Independence which contain references to the Deity or by singing officially espoused anthems which include the composer's professions of faith in a Supreme Being, or with the fact that there are many manifestations in our public life of belief in God. Such patriotic or ceremonial occasions bear no true resemblance to the unquestioned religious exercise that the State of New York has sponsored in this instance.

[1] "There are many 'aids' to religion in this country, at all levels of government. To mention but a few at the federal level, one might begin by observing that the very First Congress which wrote the First Amendment provided for chaplains in both Houses and in the armed services. There is compulsory chapel at the service academies, and religious services are held in federal hospitals and prisons. The President issues religious proclamations. The Bible is used for the administration of oaths. N.Y.A. and W.P.A. funds were available to parochial schools during the depression. Veterans receiving money under the 'G.I.' Bill of 1944 [38 U.S.C. § 1801 et seq.] could attend denominational schools, to which payments were made directly by the government. During World War II, federal money was contributed to denominational schools for the training of nurses. The benefits of the National School Lunch Act [42 U.S.C. § 1751 et seq.] are available to students in private as well as public schools. The Hospital Survey and Construction Act of 1946 [42 U.S.C. § 291 et seq.] specifically made money available to non-public hospitals. The slogan 'In God We Trust' is used by the Treasury Department, and Congress recently added God to the pledge of allegiance. There is Bible-reading in the schools of the District of Columbia, and religious instruction is given in the District's National Training School for Boys. Religious organizations are exempt from the federal income tax and are granted postal privileges. Up to defined limits—15 per cent of the adjusted gross income of individuals and 5 per cent of the net income of corporations—contributions to religious organizations are deductible for federal income tax purposes. There are no limits to the deductibility

Plainly, our Bill of Rights would not permit a State or the Federal Government to adopt an official prayer and penalize anyone who would not utter it. This, however, is not that case, for there is no element of compulsion or coercion in New York's regulation requiring that public schools be opened each day with the . . . [prayer in question].

. . .

At the same time I cannot say that to authorize this prayer is to establish a religion in the strictly historic meaning of those words. A religion is not established in the usual sense merely by letting those who choose to do so say the prayer that the public school teacher leads. Yet once government finances a religious exercise it inserts a divisive influence into our communities. . . .

. . .

My problem today would be uncomplicated but for Everson v. Board of Education, 330 U.S. 1, 17, which allowed taxpayers' money to be used to pay "the bus fares of parochial school pupils as a part of a general program under which" the fares of pupils attending public and other schools were also paid. The *Everson* case seems in retrospect to be out of line with the First Amendment. Its result is appealing, as it allows aid to be given to needy children. Yet by the same token, public funds could be used to satisfy other needs of children in parochial schools—lunches, books, and tuition being obvious examples. Mr. Justice Rutledge stated in dissent what I think is durable First Amendment philosophy. . . .

What New York does with this prayer is a break with that tradition. I therefore join the Court in reversing the judgment below.

Mr. Justice Stewart, dissenting. . . .

With all respect, I think the Court has misapplied a great constitutional principle. I cannot see how an "official religion" is established by letting those who want to say a prayer say it. On the contrary, I think that to deny the wish of these school children to join in reciting this prayer is to deny them the opportunity of sharing in the spiritual heritage of our Nation. . . .[a]

THE BIBLE READING CASES

In Abington School Dist. v. Schempp, 374 U.S. 203 (1963), the Court concluded that the practice of reading from the Bible at the beginning of the school day constituted an establishment of religion. Justice Clark's opinion for the Court included the following excerpts.

"The test may be stated as follows: what are the purpose and the primary effect of the enactment? If either is the advancement or inhibition of religion then the enactment exceeds the scope of legislative power as circumscribed by the Constitution. That is to say that to withstand the strictures of the Establishment Clause there must be a secular legislative purpose and a primary effect that neither advances nor inhibits religion. Everson v. Board of Education, supra, 330 U.S. 1; McGowan v. Maryland, supra, 366 U.S., at 442.

"The Free Exercise Clause, likewise considered many times here, withdraws from legislative power, state and federal, the exertion of any restraint on the free exercise of religion. Its purpose is to secure religious liberty in the

---

of gifts and bequests to religious institutions made under the federal gift and estate tax laws. This list of federal 'aids' could easily be expanded, and of course there is a long list in each state." Fellman, The Limits of Freedom (1959), pp. 40–41.

[a] The *Engle* case is discussed in Kurland, *The Regents' Prayer Case: "Full of Sound and Fury, Signifying . . ."*, 1962 Sup.Ct.Rev. 1. See also Brown, *Quis Custodiet Ipsos Custodes?—The School Prayer Cases*, 1963 Sup.Ct.Rev. 1.

individual by prohibiting any invasions thereof by civil authority. Hence it is necessary in a free exercise case for one to show the coercive effect of the enactment as it operates against him in the practice of his religion. The distinction between the two clauses is apparent—a violation of the Free Exercise Clause is predicated on coercion while the Establishment Clause violation need not be so attended.

"Applying the Establishment Clause principles to the cases at bar we find that the States are requiring the selection and reading at the opening of the school day of verses from the Holy Bible and the recitation of the Lord's Prayer by the students in unison. These exercises are prescribed as part of the curricular activities of students who are required by law to attend school. They are held in the school buildings under the supervision and with the participation of teachers employed in those schools. None of these factors, other than compulsory school attendance, was present in the program upheld in Zorach v. Clauson. . . .

. . . .

"The conclusion follows that . . . the laws require religious exercises and such exercises are being conducted in direct violation of the rights of the appellees and petitioners. Nor are these required exercises mitigated by the fact that individual students may absent themselves upon parental request, for that fact furnishes no defense to a claim of unconstitutionality under the Establishment Clause. . . . Further, it is no defense to urge that the religious practices here may be relatively minor encroachments on the First Amendment. The breach of neutrality that is today a trickling stream may all too soon become a raging torrent and, in the words of Madison, 'it is proper to take alarm at the first experiment on our liberties.' Memorial and Remonstrance Against Religious Assessments, quoted in *Everson,* supra, 330 U.S., at 65.

"It is insisted that unless these religious exercises are permitted a 'religion of secularism' is established in the schools. We agree of course that the State may not establish a 'religion of secularism' in the sense of affirmatively opposing or showing hostility to religion, thus 'preferring those who believe in no religion over those who do believe.' Zorach v. Clauson, supra, 343 U.S., at 314. We do not agree, however, that this decision in any sense has that effect. In addition, it might well be said that one's education is not complete without a study of comparative religion or the history of religion and its relationship to the advancement of civilization. It certainly may be said that the Bible is worthy of study for its literary and historic qualities. Nothing we have said here indicates that such study of the Bible or of religion, when presented objectively as part of a secular program of education, may not be effected consistently with the First Amendment. But the exercises here do not fall into those categories. They are religious exercises, required by the States in violation of the command of the First Amendment that the Government maintain strict neutrality, neither aiding nor opposing religion.

"Finally, we cannot accept that the concept of neutrality, which does not permit a State to require a religious exercise even with the consent of the majority of those affected, collides with the majority's right to free exercise of religion. While the Free Exercise Clause clearly prohibits the use of state action to deny the rights of free exercise to *anyone,* it has never meant that a majority could use the machinery of the State to practice its beliefs. . . ."

Justice Stewart was the lone dissenter. A portion of his opinion, follows:

"Our decisions make clear that there is no constitutional bar to the use of government property for religious purposes. On the contrary, this Court has consistently held that the discriminatory barring of religious groups from public property is itself a violation of First and Fourteenth Amendment guarantees.

Fowler v. Rhode Island, 345 U.S. 67; Niemotko v. Maryland, 340 U.S. 268. A different standard has been applied to public school property, because of the coercive effect which the use by religious sects of a compulsory school system would necessarily have upon the children involved. McCollum v. Board of Education, 333 U.S. 203. But insofar as the *McCollum* decision rests on the Establishment rather than the Free Exercise Clause, it is clear that its effect is limited to religious instruction—to government support of proselytizing activities of religious sects by throwing the weight of secular authority behind the dissemination of religious tenets.

"The dangers both to government and to religion inherent in official support of instruction in the tenets of various religious sects are absent in the present cases, which involve only a reading from the Bible unaccompanied by comments which might otherwise constitute instruction.   . . .

. . .

"To be specific, it seems to me clear that certain types of exercises would present situations in which no possibility of coercion on the part of secular officials could be claimed to exist. Thus, if such exercises were held either before or after the official school day, or if the school schedule were such that participation were merely one among a number of desirable alternatives, it could hardly be contended that the exercises did anything more than to provide an opportunity for the voluntary expression of religious belief. On the other hand, a law which provided for religious exercises during the school day and which contained no excusal provision would obviously be unconstitutionally coercive upon those who did not wish to participate. And even under a law containing an excusal provision, if the exercises were held during the school day, and no equally desirable alternative were provided by the school authorities, the likelihood that children might be under at least some psychological compulsion to participate would be great. In a case such as the latter, however, I think we would err if we *assumed* such coercion in the absence of any evidence." [a]

WIDMAR v. VINCENT, 454 U.S. 263 (1981). The Court sustained a freedom of speech challenge to a state university's policy of denying use of its facilities to student groups desiring to use them for religious worship and discussion. The Court rejected a contention that permitting use of the university forum for religious worship by student organizations would have violated the establishment clause. The Court concluded that benefits to religious groups would be "incidental" since a forum open to all speakers did not create an appearance of state approval. In a footnote at that point, the Court noted that university students are "young adults" and "less impressionable than younger students."

EPPERSON v. ARKANSAS, 393 U.S. 97 (1968). In 1928 Arkansas adopted a statute that made it unlawful for a teacher in any state-supported school or university "to teach the theory or doctrine that mankind ascended or descended from a lower order of animals," or "to adopt or use in any such institution a textbook that teaches" this theory. In 1965 the Little Rock school administration adopted a biology textbook which described the Darwinian Theory. Previous to this time the textbooks prescribed did not have such a section. A high school biology teacher brought an action in the Arkansas courts

---

[a] See Kauper, *Religion and the Constitution* (1964); Choper, *Religion in the Public Schools: A Proposed Constitutional Standard*, 47 Minn.L.Rev. 329 (1963); Schumb, *Church, State and the Public Schools*, 4 Santa Clara Law 54 (1963).

to have the statute declared invalid. The trial court held the statute invalid as restricting freedom to teach and freedom to learn in violation of the First Amendment principles of the Fourteenth Amendment. In a cryptic opinion the Supreme Court of Arkansas sustained the statute as "a valid exercise of the state's power to specify the curriculum in its public schools." The Arkansas court found it unnecessary to decide whether the statute prohibited any explanation of the Darwinian Theory as contrasted with a mere prohibition against teaching that the theory was true.

The argument, on appeal to the Supreme Court, was that the Arkansas law violated principles of academic freedom guaranteed by the first amendment's guarantee of freedom of speech. The argument was first premised on dicta in Shelton v. Tucker, 364 U.S. 479, 487 (1960)[1] and Keyishian v. Board of Regents, 385 U.S. 589, 603 (1967).[2] The second basis for the argument was the decision in Meyer v. Nebraska, 262 U.S. 390 (1923), which had invalidated a state law prohibiting private schools from teaching in foreign languages to pupils who had not completed the eighth grade.[3]

"For purposes of the present case," Justice Fortas wrote for the Court, "we need not re-enter the difficult terrain which the Court, in 1923, traversed without apparent misgivings. We need not take advantage of the broad premise which the Court's decision in *Meyer* furnishes, nor need we explore the implications of that decision in terms of the justiciability of the multitude of controversies that beset our campuses today. Today's problem is capable of resolution in the narrower terms of the First Amendment's prohibition of laws respecting an establishment of religion or prohibiting the free exercise thereof." Nor does "the State's undoubted right to prescribe the curriculum for its public schools . . . carry with it the right to prohibit on pain of criminal penalty, the teaching of a scientific theory or doctrine where that prohibition is based upon reasons that violate the First Amendment." There was no doubt that the Arkansas law had been adopted because of the fundamentalist belief of some citizens that the Book of Genesis must be the exclusive source of doctrine as to the origin of man. Therefore the law was "contrary to the mandate of the First, and in violation of the Fourteenth Amendment."

Black and Stewart, JJ., concurred on the ground that the statute was void for vagueness.

RELIGIOUS MOTIVATION AND THE ESTABLISHMENT CLAUSE

Justice Fortas avoided the issue whether the free speech clause of the first amendment requires some ideological neutrality in the public school curriculum[1] by turning to the "narrower terms" of the establishment clause. Granted that the establishment clause requires public school neutrality on issues of religious ideology, does the establishment issue turn on whether a public school's ideological position is religiously motivated?

On the issue of proof of religious motivation, contrast *Epperson* with Harris v. McRae, 448 U.S. 297 (1980), supra, p. 899, where the Court concluded that

[1] "The vigilant protection of constitutional freedoms is nowhere more vital than in the community of American schools."

[2] "[The First Amendment] does not tolerate laws that cast a pall of orthodoxy over the classroom."

[3] Justice McReynolds' opinion for the Court had said: "In order to submerge the individual and develop ideal citizens, Sparta assembled the males at seven into barracks and entrusted their subsequent education and training to official guardians. . . . [I]t hardly will be affirmed that any legislature could impose such restrictions upon the people of a state without doing violence to both letter and spirit of the Constitution." But, he pointed out that no "challenge [has] been made of the state's power to prescribe a curriculum for institutions which it supports." 262 U.S. at 402.

[1] See Board of Education v. Pico, supra, p. 1212.

the fact that restrictions on funding of abortions coincided with religious objections to abortion did not, "without more," prove a violation of the establishment clause. Would public school instruction which opposes birth control or abortion violate the establishment clause if those views coincided with the religious beliefs of the school board which directed the instruction? Would the answer be the same if the school board directed instruction that favored birth control or abortion?

C. FINANCIAL AID TO CHURCH–RELATED SCHOOLS

1. ELEMENTARY AND SECONDARY SCHOOLS

Introduction. Private elementary and secondary schools have a long tradition in this country. They serve, among other things, to lift from the state some of the financial burden involved in providing free public education. State assistance to private schools, or to parents sending their children to private schools, could be viewed simply as an alternative and less expensive means by which the state provides educational services. Establishment of religion problems arise, however, when the private schools involved are church-related and provide religious as well as secular education. These problems are made more severe by the fact that most private schools are not only church related but also related to a single church. It has been reported that in the early 1960s private schools enrolled about 11 percent of the national elementary and secondary school population—but that 90 percent of these children attended Catholic parochial schools, 5 percent Protestant and Jewish schools, and 5 percent secular private schools. Morgan, *The Establishment Clause and Sectarian Schools: A Final Installment?,* 1973 Sup.Ct.Rev. 57, 58.

In *Everson* the Court upheld the provision of transportation of students to religious schools. In Board of Educ. v. Allen, 392 U.S. 236 (1968), the Court by a vote of 6 to 3 upheld a New York law providing for the loaning of text books free of charge to students in all private schools, including church schools. The Court decided that the state statute was valid because "no funds or books are furnished to parochial schools, and the financial benefit is to parents and children, not to schools. Perhaps free books make it more likely that some children choose to attend a sectarian school, but that was true of the state-paid bus fares in *Everson* and does not alone demonstrate an unconstitutional degree of support for a religious institution."[1] Justice Black, who had written the *Everson* opinion, was one of the dissenters. He said: "[I]t is not difficult to distinguish books, which are the heart of any school, from bus fares, which provide a convenient and helpful general public transportation service."

WALZ v. TAX COMMISSION, 397 U.S. 664 (1970). The question presented was whether the New York State Tax Commission, acting pursuant to the New York Constitution and statutes, could exempt from taxation church property used solely for religious worship. The action was brought by an owner of real estate, who claimed the exemption violated the establishment clause of the Fourteenth Amendment. The New York Court gave summary judgment for the Tax Commission.

---

[1] Compare Norwood v. Harrison, 413 U.S. 455 (1973), where the Court held that it was a violation of the Fourteenth Amendment for the state to supply textbooks to pupils attending schools practicing racial discrimination. The Court noted that the establishment clause cases reflects a tension between that clause and the free exercise clause. Racial discrimination, unlike the free exercise of religion, has never been accorded affirmative constitutional protection. The free exercise clause accordingly "permits a greater degree of state assistance [to sectarian schools] than may be given to private schools which engage in discriminatory practices."

Burger, C.J., wrote the opinion of the Court which included the following statements:

"The course of constitutional neutrality in this area cannot be an absolutely straight line; rigidity could well defeat the basic purpose of these provisions, which is to insure that no religion be sponsored or favored, none commanded, and none inhibited. The general principle deducible from the First Amendment and all that has been said by the Court is this: that we will not tolerate either governmentally established religion or governmental interference with religion. . . .

. . .

". . . Yet an unbroken practice of according the exemption to churches, openly and by affirmative state action, not covertly or by state inaction, is not something to be lightly cast aside. . . .

"Nothing in this national attitude toward religious tolerance and two centuries of uninterrupted freedom from taxation has given the remotest sign of leading to an established church or religion and on the contrary it has operated affirmatively to help guarantee the free exercise of all forms of religious belief. Thus, it is hardly useful to suggest that tax exemption is but the 'foot in the door' or the 'nose of the camel in the tent' leading to an established church. If tax exemption can be seen as this first step toward 'establishment' of religion, as Mr. Justice Douglas fears, the second step has been long in coming. Any move which realistically 'establishes' a church or tends to do so can be dealt with 'while this Court sits.' "

Justices Brennan and Harlan concurred in separate opinions. Justice Douglas dissented.

LEMON v. KURTZMAN, 403 U.S. 602 (1971). A Rhode Island statute authorized the payment of a salary supplement up to 15% of current salary to teachers in nonpublic schools in which the per-pupil expenditure on secular education was less than the state average. The supplement went only to teachers in secular subjects who agreed not to teach religious subjects while receiving the supplement. A Pennsylvania statute authorized the reimbursement of nonpublic schools for their actual expenditures for teachers' salaries, textbooks, and instructional materials in the teaching of specified secular subjects. The Court held both statutes unconstitutional with only Justice White dissenting. Chief Justice Burger, speaking for the Court stated the tests to be: "First, the statute must have a secular legislative purpose; second, its principal or primary effect must be one that neither advances nor inhibits religion . . . .; finally, the statute must not foster 'an excessive government entanglement with religion.' " The Court said the statutes passed the first test, but that it was not necessary to decide whether they passed the second one because they fostered "an impermissible degree of entanglement." The opinion emphasized the political divisiveness of conflict on religious lines likely to result from attempts to expand or retract state aid of the kind involved here.

THE 1973 CASES

The Court decided five cases in 1973.[1] Only brief digests of three cases are given here. They and the issues presented by them are fully discussed in the 1977 case (Wolman v. Walter).

---

[1] See Morgan, *The Establishment Clause and Sectarian Schools: A Final Installment?*, 1973 Sup.Ct. Rev. 57.

(1) Committee for Public Education & Religious Liberty v. Nyquist, 413 U.S. 756 (1973). A New York law provided for three forms of assistance to nonpublic schools. Direct per-pupil money grants were made by the state to nonpublic schools serving a high concentration of low income families for the purpose of maintenance and repair of school facilities. Tuition reimbursements of $50 for each grade school child and $100 for each high school child were given to parents of children attending nonpublic schools whose annual income was less than $5,000. Tax credits ranging from $1,000 per child were given to those with an adjusted gross income of $9,000 or less to zero for those with an income of $25,000 or more. The Court held all three forms of assistance invalid as having the impermissible effect of advancing religion. The Court rejected the argument by the state that the purpose of the tuition grants was to promote the free exercise of religion by low-income parents, saying: "It is also true that a state law interfering with a parent's right to have his child educated in a sectarian school would run afoul of the Free Exercise Clause. But this Court repeatedly has recognized that tension inevitably exists between the Free Exercise and the Establishment Clauses, e.g., Everson v. Board of Education, supra; Walz v. Tax Commission, supra, and that it may often not be possible to promote the former without offending the latter. As a result of this tension, our cases require the State to maintain an attitude of 'neutrality,' neither 'advancing' nor 'inhibiting' religion. In its attempt to enhance the opportunities of the poor to choose between public and non-public education, the State has taken a step which can only be regarded as one 'advancing' religion."

Justice Rehnquist, joined by Chief Justice Burger and Justice White dissented from the invalidation of the tuition reimbursement and tax-credit features of the New York law. Justice White indicated that he would vote also to uphold the maintenance and repair grant.

(2) Sloan v. Lemon, 413 U.S. 825 (1973). The Court held invalid a Pennsylvania tuition grant statute similar to that in New York except that the grants were authorized to parents of children in nonpublic schools regardless of income level. The argument was made that since such grants would be valid as applied to non-sectarian schools it was a denial of equal protection of the laws to withhold them from parents sending children to sectarian schools. The Court rejected this argument: "The Equal Protection Clause has never been regarded as a bludgeon with which to compel a State to violate other provisions of the Constitution. Having held that tuition reimbursements for the benefit of sectarian schools violate the Establishment Clause, nothing in the Equal Protection Clause will suffice to revive that program."

(3) Levitt v. Committee for Public Education and Religious Liberty, 413 U.S. 472 (1973). The New York Legislature appropriated funds to reimburse nonpublic schools in the state for expenses of carrying out such state-mandated services as recordkeeping and examinations. Payment was an annual lump sum. Most of the mandated tests were traditional teacher-prepared tests. The Court held that these payments could not be made to parochial schools under the Establishment Clause because no attempt was made and no means were available to assure that internally prepared tests, which were "an integral part of the teaching process," were free of religious instruction and avoided inculcating students in the religious precepts of the sponsoring church.

WOLMAN v. WALTER

433 U.S. 229, 97 S.Ct. 2593, 53 L.Ed.2d 714 (1977).

Mr. Justice Blackmun delivered the opinion of the Court (Parts I, V, VI, VII, and VIII), together with an opinion (Parts II, III, and IV), in which The Chief Justice, Mr. Justice Stewart, and Mr. Justice Powell joined.

This is still another case presenting the recurrent issue of the limitations imposed by the Establishment Clause of the First Amendment, made applicable to the States by the Fourteenth Amendment, Meek v. Pittenger, 421 U.S. 349, 351 (1975) on state aid to pupils in church-related elementary and secondary schools. Appellants are citizens and taxpayers of Ohio. They challenge all but one of the provisions of Ohio Rev.Code § 3317.06 (Supp.1976) which authorize various forms of aid. . . . A three-judge court . . . held the statute constitutional in all respects.

I.

Section 3317.06 was enacted after this Court's May 1975 decision in Meek v. Pittenger, supra, and obviously is an attempt to conform to the teachings of that decision. . . . In broad outline, the statute authorizes the State to provide nonpublic school pupils with books, instructional materials and equipment, standardized testing and scoring, diagnostic services, therapeutic services, and field trip transportation.

The initial biennial appropriation by the Ohio Legislature for implementation of the statute was the sum of $88,800,000. Funds so appropriated are paid to the State's public school districts and are then expended by them. All disbursements made with respect to nonpublic schools have their equivalents in disbursements for public schools, and the amount expended per pupil in nonpublic schools may not exceed the amount expended per pupil in the public schools.

The parties stipulated that during the 1974–1975 school year there were 720 chartered nonpublic schools in Ohio. Of these, all but 29 were sectarian. More than 96% of the nonpublic enrollment attended sectarian schools, and more than 92% attended Catholic schools. It was also stipulated that, if they were called, officials of representative Catholic schools would testify that such schools operate under the general supervision of the bishop of their diocese; that most principals are members of a religious order within the Catholic Church; that a little less than one-third of the teachers are members of such religious orders; that "in all probability a majority of the teachers are members of the Catholic faith"; and that many of the rooms and hallways in these schools are decorated with a Christian symbol. All such schools teach the secular subjects required to meet the State's minimum standards. The state-mandated five-hour day is expanded to include, usually, one-half hour of religious instruction. Pupils who are not members of the Catholic faith are not required to attend religion classes or to participate in religious exercises or activities, and no teacher is required to teach religious doctrine as a part of the secular courses taught in the schools.

The parties also stipulated that nonpublic school officials, if called, would testify that none of the schools covered by the statute discriminate in the admission of pupils or in the hiring of teachers on the basis of race, creed, color, or national origin.

. . .

II.

The mode of analysis for Establishment Clause questions is defined by the three-part test that has emerged from the Court's decisions. In order to pass muster, a statute must have a secular legislative purpose, must have a principal or primary effect that neither advances nor inhibits religion, and must not foster an excessive government entanglement with religion.

In the present case we have no difficulty with the first prong of this three-part test. We are satisfied that the challenged statute reflects Ohio's legitimate interest in protecting the health of its youth and in providing a fertile educational environment for all the school children of the State. As is usual in our cases, the analytical difficulty has to do with the effect and entanglement criteria.

We have acknowledged before, and we do so again here, that the wall of separation that must be maintained between church and state "is a blurred, indistinct, and variable barrier depending on all the circumstances of a particular relationship." Nonetheless, the Court's numerous precedents "have become firmly rooted," and now provide substantial guidance. We therefore turn to the task of applying the rules derived from our decisions to the respective provisions of the statute at issue.

III. TEXTBOOKS

Section 3317.06 authorizes the expenditure of funds:

"(A) To purchase such secular textbooks as have been approved by the superintendent of public instruction for use in public schools in the state and to loan such textbooks to pupils attending nonpublic schools within the district or to their parents. Such loans shall be based upon individual requests submitted by such nonpublic school pupils or parents. Such requests shall be submitted to the local public school district in which the nonpublic school is located. Such individual requests for the loan of textbooks shall, for administrative convenience, be submitted by the nonpublic school pupil or his parent to the nonpublic school which shall prepare and submit collective summaries of the individual requests to the local public school district. As used in this section, 'textbook' means any book or book substitute which a pupil uses as a text or text substitute in a particular class or program in the school he regularly attends."

The parties' stipulations reflect operation of the textbook program in accord with the dictates of the statute. In addition, it was stipulated:

"The secular textbooks used in nonpublic schools will be the same as the textbooks used in the public schools of the state. Common suppliers will be used to supply books to both public and nonpublic school pupils.

"Textbooks, including book substitutes, provided under this Act shall be limited to books, reusable workbooks, or manuals, whether bound or in looseleaf form, intended for use as a principal source of study material for a given class or a group of students, a copy of which is expected to be available for the individual use of each pupil in such class or group."

This system for the loan of textbooks to individual students bears a striking resemblance to the systems approved in Board of Education v. Allen, 392 U.S. 236 (1968), and in Meek v. Pittenger. . . .

. . . [A]ppellants urge that we overrule *Allen* and *Meek.* This we decline to do. Accordingly, we conclude that § 3317.06(A) is constitutional.

IV. TESTING AND SCORING

Section 3317.06 authorizes expenditure of funds

"(J) To supply for use by pupils attending nonpublic schools within the district such standardized tests and scoring services as are in use in the public schools of the state."

These tests "are used to measure the progress of students in secular subjects." Nonpublic school personnel are not involved in either the drafting or scoring of the tests. The statute does not authorize any payment to nonpublic school personnel for the costs of administering the tests.

In Levitt v. Committee for Public Education, 413 U.S. 472 (1973), this Court invalidated a New York statutory scheme for reimbursement of church-sponsored schools for the expenses of teacher-prepared testing. The reasoning behind that decision was straightforward. The system was held unconstitutional because "no means are available, to assure that internally prepared tests are free of religious instruction."

There is no question that the State has a substantial and legitimate interest in insuring that its youth receive an adequate secular education. The State may require that schools that are utilized to fulfill the State's compulsory education requirement meet certain standards of instruction, and may examine both teachers and pupils to ensure that the State's legitimate interest is being fulfilled. Cf. Pierce v. Society of Sisters, 268 U.S. 510, 534 (1925). Under the section at issue, the State provides both the schools and the school district with the means of ensuring that the minimum standards are met. The nonpublic school does not control the content of the test or its result. This serves to prevent the use of the test as a part of religious teaching, and thus avoids that kind of direct aid to religion found present in *Levitt.* Similarly, the inability of the school to control the test eliminates the need for the supervision that gives rise to excessive entanglement. We therefore agree with the District Court's conclusion that § 3317.06(J) is constitutional.

V. DIAGNOSTIC SERVICES

Section 3317.06 authorizes expenditures of funds

"(D) To provide speech and hearing diagnostic services to pupils attending nonpublic schools within the district. Such service shall be provided in the nonpublic school attended by the pupil receiving the service.

. . .

"(F) To provide diagnostic psychological services to pupils attending nonpublic schools within the district. Such services shall be provided in the school attended by the pupil receiving the service."

It will be observed that these speech and hearing and psychological diagnostic services are to be provided within the nonpublic school. It is stipulated, however, that the personnel (with the exception of physicians) who perform the services are employees of the local board of education; that physicians may be hired on a contract basis; that the purpose of these services is to determine the pupil's deficiency or need of assistance; and that treatment of any defect so found would take place off the nonpublic school premises.

Appellants assert that the funding of these services is constitutionally impermissible. They argue that the speech and hearing staff might engage in unrestricted conversation with the pupil and, on occasion, might fail to separate religious instruction from secular responsibilities. They further assert that the communication between the psychological diagnostician and the pupil will provide an impermissible opportunity for the intrusion of religious influence.

The District Court found these dangers so insubstantial as not to render the statute unconstitutional. We agree. This Court's decisions contain a common thread to the effect that the provision of health services to all school children—public and nonpublic—does not have the primary effect of aiding religion. . . . Indeed, appellants recognize this fact in not challenging subsection (E) of the statute that authorizes publicly funded physician, nursing, dental, and optometric services in nonpublic schools. We perceive no basis for drawing a different conclusion with respect to diagnostic speech and hearing services and diagnostic psychological services.

In *Meek* the Court did hold unconstitutional a portion of a Pennsylvania statute at issue there that authorized certain auxiliary services—"remedial and accelerated instruction, guidance counseling and testing, speech and hearing services"—on nonpublic school premises. The Court noted that the teacher or guidance counselor might "fail on occasion to separate religious instruction and the advancement of religious beliefs from his secular educational responsibilities." The Court was of the view that the publicly employed teacher or guidance counselor might depart from religious neutrality because he was "performing important educational services in schools in which education is an integral part of the dominant sectarian mission and in which an atmosphere dedicated to the advancement of religious belief is constantly maintained." The statute was held unconstitutional on entanglement grounds, namely, that in order to insure that the auxiliary teachers and guidance counselors remained neutral, the State would have to engage in continuing surveillance on the school premises. Id., at 372. The Court in *Meek* explicitly stated, however, that the provision of diagnostic speech and hearing services by Pennsylvania seemed "to fall within that class of general welfare services for children that may be provided by the State regardless of the incidental benefit that accrues to church-related schools." The provision of such services was invalidated only because it was found unseverable from the unconstitutional portions of the statute.

The reason for considering diagnostic services to be different from teaching or counseling is readily apparent. First, diagnostic services, unlike teaching or counseling, have little or no educational content and are not closely associated with the educational mission of the nonpublic school. Accordingly, any pressure on the public diagnostician to allow the intrusion of sectarian views is greatly reduced. Second, the diagnostician has only limited contact with the child, and that contact involves chiefly the use of objective and professional testing methods to detect students in need of treatment. The nature of the relationship between the diagnostician and the pupil does not provide the same opportunity for the transmission of sectarian views as attends the relationship between teacher and student or that between counselor and student.

We conclude that providing diagnostic services on the nonpublic school premises will not create an impermissible risk of the fostering of ideological views. It follows that there is no need for excessive surveillance, and there will not be impermissible entanglement. We therefore hold that §§ 3317.06(D) and (F) are constitutional.

VI.   THERAPEUTIC SERVICES

Sections 3317.06(G), (H), (I), and (K) authorize expenditures of funds for certain therapeutic, guidance, and remedial services for students who have been identified as having a need for specialized attention. Personnel providing the services must be employees of the local board of education or under contract with the State Department of Health. The services are to be performed only in public schools, in public centers, or in mobile units located off the nonpublic school premises.   .   .   .

Appellants concede that the provision of remedial, therapeutic, and guidance services in public schools, public centers, or mobile units is constitutional if both public and nonpublic school students are served simultaneously. Their challenge is limited to the situation where a facility is used to service only nonpublic school students.   .   .   .

.   .   .

We recognize that, unlike the diagnostician, the therapist may establish a relationship with the pupil in which there might be opportunities to transmit ideological views. In *Meek* the Court acknowledged the danger that publicly employed personnel who provide services analogous to those at issue here might transmit religious instruction and advance religious beliefs in their activities. But   .   .   . the Court emphasized that this danger arose from the fact that the services were performed in the pervasively sectarian atmosphere of the church-related school. The danger existed there not because the public employee was likely deliberately to subvert his task to the service of religion, but rather because the pressures of the environment might alter his behavior from its normal course. So long as these types of services are offered at truly religiously neutral locations, the danger perceived in *Meek* does not arise.

The fact that a unit on a neutral site on occasion may serve only sectarian pupils does not provoke the same concerns that troubled the Court in *Meek*. The influence on a therapist's behavior that is exerted by the fact that he serves a sectarian pupil is qualitatively different from the influence of the pervasive atmosphere of a religious institution. The dangers perceived in *Meek* arose from the nature of the institution, not from the nature of the pupils.

Accordingly, we hold that providing therapeutic and remedial services at a neutral site off the premises of the nonpublic schools will not have the impermissible effect of advancing religion. Neither will there be any excessive entanglement arising from supervision of public employees to insure that they maintain a neutral stance. It can hardly be said that the supervision of public employees performing public functions on public property creates an excessive entanglement between church and state. Sections 3317.06(G), (H), (I), and (K) are constitutional.

VII. INSTRUCTIONAL MATERIALS AND EQUIPMENT

Sections 3317.06(B) and (C) authorize expenditures of funds for the purchase and loan to pupils or their parents upon individual request of instructional materials and instructional equipment of the kind in use in the public schools within the district and which is "incapable of diversion to religious use." Section 3717.06 also provides that the materials and equipment may be stored on the premises of a nonpublic school and that publicly hired personnel who administer the lending program may perform their services upon the nonpublic school premises when necessary "for efficient implementation of the lending program."

Although the exact nature of the material and equipment is not clearly revealed, the parties have stipulated: "It is expected that materials and equipment loaned to pupils or parents under the new law will be similar to such former materials and equipment except that to the extent that the law requires that materials and equipment capable of diversion to religious issues will not be supplied." Equipment provided under the predecessor statute included projectors, tape recorders, record players, maps and globes, science kits, weather forecasting charts, and the like. The District Court found the new statute, as now limited, constitutional because the Court could not distinguish the loan of material and equipment from the textbook provisions upheld in *Meek*.

In *Meek*, however, the Court considered the constitutional validity of a direct loan to nonpublic schools of instructional material and equipment, and, despite the apparent secular nature of the goods, held the loan impermissible. Mr. Justice Stewart, in writing for the Court, stated:

"The very purpose of many of those schools is to provide an integrated secular and religious education; the teaching process is, to a large extent, devoted to the inculcation of religious values and belief. Substantial aid to the educational function of such schools, accordingly, necessarily results in aid to the sectarian school enterprise as a whole. '[T]he secular education those schools provide goes hand in hand with the religious mission that is the only reason for the schools' existence. Within the institution, the two are inextricably intertwined.'"

Thus, even though the loan ostensibly was limited to neutral and secular instructional material and equipment, it inescapably had the primary effect of providing a direct and substantial advancement of the sectarian enterprise.

Appellees seek to avoid *Meek* by emphasizing that it involved a program of direct loans to nonpublic schools. In contrast, the material and equipment at issue under the Ohio statute are loaned to the pupil or his parent. In our view, however, it would exalt form over substance if this distinction were found to justify a result different from that in *Meek*. Before *Meek* was decided by this Court, Ohio authorized the loan of material and equipment directly to the nonpublic schools. Then, in light of *Meek*, the state legislature decided to channel the goods through the parents and pupils. Despite the technical change in legal bailee, the program in substance is the same as before: the equipment is substantially the same; it will receive the same use by the students; and it may still be stored and distributed on the nonpublic school premises. In view of the impossibility of separating the secular education function from the sectarian, the state aid inevitably flows in part in support of the religious role of the schools.

Indeed, this conclusion is compelled by the Court's prior consideration of an analogous issue in Committee for Public Education v. Nyquist, 413 U.S. 756 (1973). There the Court considered, among others, a tuition reimbursement program whereby New York gave low income parents who sent their children to nonpublic schools a direct and unrestricted cash grant of $50 to $100 per child (but no more than 50% of tuition actually paid). The State attempted to justify the program, as Ohio does here, on the basis that the aid flowed to the parents rather than to the church-related schools. The Court observed, however, that, unlike the bus program in Everson v. Board of Education, and the book program in *Allen*, there "has been no endeavor 'to guarantee the separation between secular and religious educational functions and to insure that State financial aid supports only the former.'" The Court thus found that the grant program served to establish religion. If a grant in cash to parents is impermissible, we fail to see how a grant in kind of goods furthering the religious enterprise can fare any better.[17] Accordingly, we hold §§ 3317.06(B) and (C) to be unconstitutional.[18]

---

[17] In many respects, *Nyquist* was a more difficult case than the present one. First, it was at least arguable in *Nyquist* that the tuition grant did not end up in the hands of the religious schools since the parent was free to spend the grant money as he chose. No similar argument could be made here since the parties have stipulated expressly that material and equipment must be used to supplement courses. Second, since the grant in *Nyquist* was limited to 50% of tuition, it was arguable that the grant should be seen as supporting only the secular part of the church-school enterprise. An argument of that kind also could not be made here, for *Meek* makes clear that the material and equipment are inextricably connected with the church-related school's religious function.

[18] There is, as there was in *Meek*, a tension between this result and Board of Education v. Allen, 392 U.S. 236 (1968). *Allen* was premised on the view that the educational content of textbooks is something that can be ascertained in advance and cannot be diverted to sectarian uses. In *Nyquist* the Court explained:

"In *Everson*, the Court found the bus fare program analogous to the provision of services such as police and fire protection, sewage disposal, highways, and sidewalks for parochial schools. Such services, provided in common to all citizens, are 'so separate and so indisputably marked off from the religious function,' that they may fairly be viewed as reflections of a neutral posture toward religious institutions. *Allen* is founded upon a similar principle. The Court there repeatedly emphasized that upon the record in that case there was no indication that textbooks would be provided for anything other than purely secular courses."

Board of Education v. Allen has remained law, and we now follow as a matter of *stare decisis* the principle that restriction of textbooks to those provided the public schools is sufficient to ensure that the books will not be used for religious purposes. In more recent cases, however, we have declined to extend that presumption of neutrality to other items in the lower school setting. It has been argued that the Court should extend *Allen* to cover all items similar to textbooks. When faced, however, with a choice between extension of the unique presumption created in *Allen* and continued adherence to the principles announced in our subsequent cases, we choose the latter course.

VIII. FIELD TRIPS

Section 3317.06 also authorizes expenditures of funds:

"(L) To provide such field trip transportation and services to nonpublic school students as are provided to public school students in the district. School districts may contract with commercial transportation companies for such transportation service if school district busses are unavailable."
. . .

The District Court, held this feature to be constitutionally indistinguishable from that with which the Court was concerned in Everson v. Board of Education. We do not agree. . . . [T]he bus fare program in *Everson* passed constitutional muster because the school did not determine how often the pupil traveled between home and school—every child must make one round trip every day—and because the travel was unrelated to any aspect of the curriculum.

The Ohio situation is in sharp contrast. First, the nonpublic school controls the timing of the trips and, within a certain range, their frequency and destinations. Thus, the schools, rather than the children, truly are the recipients of the service and, as this Court has recognized, this fact alone may be sufficient to invalidate the program as impermissible direct aid. Second, although a trip may be to a location that would be of interest to those in public schools, it is the individual teacher who makes a field trip meaningful. The experience begins with the study and discussion of the place to be visited; it continues on location with the teacher pointing out items of interest and stimulating the imagination; and it ends with a discussion of the experience. The field trips are an integral part of the educational experience, and where the teacher works within and for a sectarian institution, an unacceptable risk of fostering of religion is an inevitable byproduct. . . . Funding of field trips, therefore, must be treated as was the funding of maps and charts in Meek v. Pittenger, supra, the funding of buildings and tuition in Committee for Public Education v. Nyquist, supra, and the funding of teacher-prepared tests in Levitt v. Committee for Public Education; it must be declared an impermissible direct aid to sectarian education.

Moreover, the public school authorities will be unable adequately to insure secular use of the field trip funds without close supervision of the nonpublic teachers. This would create excessive entanglement. . . .

We hold § 3317.06(L) to be unconstitutional.

IX.

In summary, we hold constitutional those portions of the Ohio statute authorizing the State to provide nonpublic school pupils with books, standardized testing and scoring, diagnostic services, and therapeutic and remedial services. We hold unconstitutional those portions relating to instructional materials and equipment and field trip services.

The judgment of the District Court is therefore affirmed in part and reversed in part.

It is so ordered.

. . . Mr. Justice White and Mr. Justice Rehnquist concur in the judgment with respect to textbooks, testing, and scoring, and diagnostic and therapeutic services (Parts III, IV, V and VI of the opinion) and dissent from the judgment with respect to instructional materials and equipment and field trips (Parts VII and VIII of the opinion).

The Chief Justice dissents from Parts VII and VIII of the Court's opinion.

Mr. Justice Brennan, concurring and dissenting.

I join Parts I, VII, and VIII of the Court's opinion, and the reversal of the District Court's judgment insofar as that judgment upheld the constitutionality of §§ 3317.06(B), (C), and (L).

I dissent however from Parts II, III, and IV, (plurality opinion) and Parts V, and VI of the Court's opinion and the affirmance of the District Court's judgment insofar as it sustained the constitutionality of §§ 3317.06(A), (D), (F), (G), (H), (I), (J), and (K). The Court holds that Ohio has managed in these respects to fashion a statute that avoids an effect or entanglement condemned by the Establishment Clause. But "The [First] Amendment nullifies sophisticated as well as simple-minded . . ." attempts to avoid its prohibitions, and, in any event, ingenuity in draftsmanship cannot obscure the fact that this subsidy to sectarian schools amounts to $88,800,000 (less now the sums appropriated to finance §§ 3317.06(B) and (C) which today are invalidated) just for the initial biennium. The Court nowhere evaluates this factor in determining the compatibility of the statute with the Establishment Clause, as that Clause requires. Its evaluation, even after deduction of the amount appropriated to finance §§ 3317.06(B) and (C), compels in my view the conclusion that a divisive political potential of unusual magnitude inheres in the Ohio program. This suffices without more to require the conclusion that the Ohio statute in its entirety offends the First Amendment's prohibition against laws "respecting an establishment of religion."

Mr. Justice Marshall, concurring and dissenting.

I join Parts I, V, VII, and VIII of the Court's opinion. For the reasons stated below, however, I am unable to join the remainder of the Court's opinion or its judgment upholding the constitutionality of §§ 3317.06(A), (G), (H), (I), (J), and (K).

The Court upholds the textbook loan provision, § 3317.06(A), on the precedent of Board of Education v. Allen. It also recognizes, however, that there is "a tension" between *Allen* and the reasoning of the Court in Meek v. Pittenger. I would resolve that tension by overruling *Allen*. I am now convinced that *Allen* is largely responsible for reducing the "high and impregnable" wall between church and state erected by the First Amendment, to "a blurred, indistinct, and variable barrier," incapable of performing its vital functions of protecting both church and state.

In *Allen,* we upheld a textbook loan program on the assumption that the sectarian school's twin functions of religious instruction and secular education were separable. In *Meek,* we flatly rejected that assumption as a basis for allowing a State to loan secular teaching materials and equipment to such schools. . . . Thus, although *Meek* upheld a textbook loan program on the strength of *Allen,* it left the rationale of *Allen* undamaged only if there is a constitutionally significant difference between a loan of pedagogical materials directly to a sectarian school and a loan of those materials to students for use in sectarian schools. As the Court convincingly demonstrates there is no such difference.

. . .

It is, of course, unquestionable that textbooks are central to the educational process. Under the rationale of *Meek,* therefore they should not be provided by the State to sectarian schools because "[s]ubstantial aid to the educational function of such schools . . . necessarily results in aid to the sectarian school enterprise as a whole." It is also unquestionable that the cost of textbooks is certain to be substantial. Under the rationale of *Lemon,* therefore, they should not be provided because of the dangers of political "divisiveness on religious lines." I would, accordingly, overrule Board of Education v. Allen and hold unconstitutional § 3317.06(A).

By overruling *Allen,* we would free ourselves to draw a line between acceptable and unacceptable forms of aid that would be both capable of consistent application and responsive to the concerns discussed above. That line, I believe, should be placed between general welfare programs that serve children in sectarian schools because the schools happen to be a convenient place to reach the programs' target populations and programs of educational assistance. General welfare programs, in contrast to programs of educational assistance, do not provide "[s]ubstantial aid to the educational function" of schools, whether secular or sectarian, and therefore do not provide the kind of assistance to the religious mission of sectarian schools we found impermissible in *Meek.* Moreover, because general welfare programs do not assist the sectarian functions of denominational schools, there is no reason to expect that political disputes over the merits of those programs will divide the public along religious lines.

In addition to § 3317.06(A), which authorizes the textbook loan program, paragraphs (B), (C), and (L), held unconstitutional by the Court, clearly fall on the wrong side of the constitutional line I propose. Those paragraphs authorize, respectively, the loan of instructional materials and equipment and the provision of transportation for school field trips. There can be no contention that these programs provide anything other than educational assistance.

I also agree with the Court that the services authorized by paragraphs (D), (F) and (G) are constitutionally permissible. Those services are speech and hearing diagnosis, psychological diagnosis, and psychological and speech and hearing therapy. Like the medical, nursing, dental and optometric services authorized by paragraph (E) and not challenged by appellants, these services promote the children's health and well-being, and have only an indirect and remote impact on their educational progress.

The Court upholds paragraphs (H), (I), and (K), which it groups with paragraph (G), under the rubric of "therapeutic services." I cannot agree that the services authorized by these three paragraphs should be treated like the psychological services provided by paragraph (G). Paragraph (H) authorizes the provision of guidance and counseling services . . . that would directly support the educational programs of sectarian schools. It is, therefore, in violation of the First Amendment.

Paragraphs (I) and (K) provide remedial services and programs for disabled children . . . clearly intended to aid the sectarian schools to improve the performance of their students in the classroom. I would not treat them as if they were programs of physical or psychological therapy.

Finally, the Court upholds paragraph (J), which provides standardized tests and scoring services, on the ground that these tests are clearly nonideological and that the State has an interest in assuring that the education received by sectarian school students meets minimum standards. I do not question the legitimacy of this interest, and if Ohio required students to obtain specified scores on certain tests before being promoted or graduated, I would agree that it could administer those tests to sectarian school students to ensure that its standards were being met. The record indicates, however, only that the tests "are used to measure the progress of students in secular subjects." It contains no indication that the measurements are taken to assure compliance with state standards rather than for internal administrative purposes of the schools. To the extent that the testing is done to serve the purposes of the sectarian schools rather than the State, I would hold that its provision by the State violates the First Amendment.

Mr. Justice Powell, concurring in part and dissenting in part.

Our decisions in this troubling area draw lines that often must seem arbitrary. No doubt we could achieve greater analytical tidiness if we were to accept the broadest implications of the observation in Meek v. Pittenger, that "[s]ubstantial aid to the educational function of [sectarian] schools . . . necessarily results in aid to the sectarian enterprise as a whole." If we took that course, it would become impossible to sustain state aid of any kind—even if the aid is wholly secular in character and is supplied to the pupils rather than the institutions. *Meek* itself would have to be overruled, along with Board of Education v. Allen, and even perhaps Everson v. Board of Education. The persistent desire of a number of States to find proper means of helping sectarian education to survive would be doomed. This Court has not yet thought that such a harsh result is required by the Establishment Clause. Certainly few would consider it in the public interest. Parochial schools, quite apart from their sectarian purpose, have provided an educational alternative for millions of young Americans; they often afford wholesome competition with our public schools; and in some States they relieve substantially the tax burden incident to the operation of public schools. The State has, moreover, a legitimate interest in facilitating education of the highest quality for all children within its boundaries, whatever school their parents have chosen for them.

It is important to keep these issues in perspective. At this point in the 20th century we are quite far removed from the dangers that prompted the Framers to include the Establishment Clause in the Bill of Rights. The risk of significant religious or denominational control over our democratic processes—or even of deep political division along religious lines—is remote, and when viewed against the positive contributions of sectarian schools, any such risk seems entirely tolerable in light of the continuing oversight of this Court. Our decisions have sought to establish principles that preserve the cherished safeguard of the Establishment Clause without resort to blind absolutism. If this endeavor means a loss of some analytical tidiness, then that too is entirely tolerable. Most of the Court's decision today follows in this tradition, and I join Parts I through VI of its opinion.

With respect to Part VII, I concur only in the judgment. I am not persuaded, nor did *Meek* hold, that all loans of secular instructional material and equipment "inescapably [have] the primary effect of providing a direct and substantial advancement of the sectarian enterprise." If that were the case, then *Meek* surely would have overruled *Allen*. Instead the Court reaffirmed *Allen*, thereby necessarily holding that at least some such loans of materials helpful in the educational process are permissible—so long as the aid is incapable of diversion to religious uses, and so long as the materials are lent to the individual students or their parents and not to the sectarian institutions. Here the statute is expressly limited to materials incapable of diversion. Therefore the relevant question is whether the materials are such that they are "furnished for the use of *individual* students and at their request."

The Ohio statute includes some materials such as wall maps, charts and other classroom paraphernalia for which the concept of a loan to individuals is a transparent fiction. A loan of these items is indistinguishable from forbidden "direct aid" to the sectarian institution itself, whoever the technical bailee. Since the provision makes no attempt to separate these instructional materials from others meaningfully lent to individuals, I agree with the Court that it cannot be sustained under our precedents. But I would find no constitutional defect in a properly limited provision lending to the individuals themselves only appropriate instructional materials and equipment similar to that customarily used in public schools.

I dissent as to Part VIII, concerning field trip transportation. The Court writes as though the statute funded the salary of the teacher who takes the students on the outing. In fact only the bus and driver are provided for the limited purpose of physical movement between the school and the secular destination of the field trip. As I find this aid indistinguishable in principle from that upheld in *Everson,* I would sustain the District Court's judgment approving this part of the Ohio statute.

Mr. Justice Stevens, concurring in part and dissenting in part.

The distinction between the religious and secular is a fundamental one. To quote from Clarence Darrow's argument in the *Scopes* case:

"The realm of religion . . . is where knowledge leaves off, and where faith begins, and it never has needed the arm of the State for support, and wherever it has received it, it has harmed both the public and the religion that it would pretend to serve."

The line drawn by the Establishment Clause of the First Amendment must also have a fundamental character. It should not differentiate between direct and indirect subsidies, or between instructional materials like globes and maps on the one hand and instructional materials like textbooks on the other. For that reason, rather than the three-part test described in Part II of the Court's opinion, I would adhere to the test enunciated for the Court by Mr. Justice Black:

"No tax in any amount, large or small, can be levied to support any religious activities or institutions, whatever they may be called, or whatever form they may adopt to teach or practice religion." Everson v. Board of Education.

Under that test, a state subsidy of sectarian schools is invalid regardless of the form it takes. The financing of buildings, field trips, instructional materials, educational tests, and school books are all equally invalid. For all give aid to the school's educational mission, which at heart is religious. On the other hand, I am not prepared to exclude the possibility that some parts of the statute before us may be administered in a constitutional manner. The State can plainly provide public health services to children attending nonpublic schools. The diagnostic and therapeutic services described in Parts V and VI of the Court's opinion may fall into this category. Although I have some misgivings on this point, I am not prepared to hold this part of the statute invalid on its face.

This Court's efforts to improve on the *Everson* test have not proved successful. "Corrosive precedents" have left us without firm principles on which to decide these cases. As this case demonstrates, the States have been encouraged to search for new ways of achieving forbidden ends. What should be a "high and impregnable" wall between church and state, has been reduced to a "blurred, indistinct, and variable barrier." The result has been, as Clarence Darrow predicted, harm to "both the public and the religion that [this aid] would pretend to serve."

Accordingly, I dissent from Parts II, III and IV of the plurality's opinion.

COMMITTEE FOR PUBLIC EDUCATION AND RELIGIOUS LIBERTY v. REGAN, 444 U.S. 646 (1980). A 1974 New York statute provided public funds to private schools to reimburse costs of complying with state-mandated requirements, including the grading of state-prescribed examinations. The Court affirmed the decision of a federal district court, which had upheld the statute against attack under the Establishment Clause. The Court concluded that the controlling precedent was Wolman v. Walter, which had approved the supplying of standardized tests to private school pupils, and state scoring of those tests. That the New York law provided cash reimbursements to the schools for administering and grading the examinations was not controlling. "A contrary view would insist on drawing a constitutional distinction between paying the nonpublic school to do the grading and paying state employees or some independent service to perform that task. . . ." Justice Blackmun's dissent, joined by Justices Brennan and Marshall, insisted that just that distinction was mandated by the Court's decisions in Meek v. Pittenger, 421 U.S. 349 (1975) and Wolman v. Walter. Direct cash payments to sectarian schools created risks of furthering the schools' religious mission by subsidizing the educational mission as a whole, and of entanglement in administering the system of reimbursement. Justice Stevens also dissented.

MUELLER v. ALLEN

463 U.S. 388, 103 S.Ct. 3062, 77 L.Ed.2d 721 (1983).

Justice REHNQUIST delivered the opinion of the Court.

Minnesota allows taxpayers, in computing their state income tax, to deduct certain expenses incurred in providing for the education of their children. . . . The United States Court of Appeals for the Eighth Circuit held that the Establishment Clause of the First and Fourteenth Amendments was not offended by this arrangement. . . :

Minnesota, like every other state, provides its citizens with free elementary and secondary schooling. . . . It seems to be agreed that about 820,000 students attended this school system in the most recent school year. During the same year, approximately 91,000 elementary and secondary students attended some 500 privately supported schools located in Minnesota, and about 95% of these students attended schools considering themselves to be sectarian.

Minnesota, by a law originally enacted in 1955 and revised in 1976 and again in 1978, permits state taxpayers to claim a deduction from gross income for certain expenses incurred in educating their children. The deduction is limited to actual expenses incurred for the "tuition, textbooks and transportation" of dependents attending elementary or secondary schools. A deduction may not exceed $500 per dependent in grades K through six and $700 per dependent in grades seven through twelve. Minn.Stat. § 290.09.

Petitioners—certain Minnesota taxpayers—sued in the United States District Court for the District of Minnesota. . . .

. . .

. . . In this case we are asked to decide whether Minnesota's tax deduction bears greater resemblance to those types of assistance to parochial schools we have approved, or to those we have struck down. Petitioners place particular reliance on our decision in Committee for Public Education v. Nyquist, supra, where we held invalid a New York statute providing public funds for the maintenance and repair of the physical facilities of private schools and granting thinly disguised "tax benefits," actually amounting to tuition grants, to the parents of children attending private schools. . . .

The general nature of our inquiry in this area has been guided, since the decision in Lemon v. Kurtzman, 403 U.S. 602 (1971), by the "three-part" test laid down in that case:

> "First, the statute must have a secular legislative purpose; second, its principle or primary effect must be one that neither advances nor inhibits religion . . . ; finally, the statute must not foster 'an excessive government entanglement with religion.'" Id., at 612–613.

While this principle is well settled, our cases have also emphasized that it provides "no more than [a] helpful signpost" in dealing with Establishment

Clause challenges. Hunt v. McNair, supra, 413 U.S., at 741. With this *caveat* in mind, we turn to the specific challenges raised . . . under the *Lemon* framework.

Little time need be spent on the question of whether the Minnesota tax deduction has a secular purpose. Under our prior decisions, governmental assistance programs have consistently survived this inquiry even when they have run afoul of other aspects of the *Lemon* framework. . . . This reflects, at least in part, our reluctance to attribute unconstitutional motives to the states, particularly when a plausible secular purpose for the state's program may be discerned from the face of the statute.

A state's decision to defray the cost of educational expenses incurred by parents—regardless of the type of schools their children attend—evidences a purpose that is both secular and understandable. . . .

We turn therefore to the more difficult but related question whether the Minnesota statute has "the primary effect of advancing the sectarian aims of the non-public schools." . . . In concluding that it does not, we find several features of the Minnesota tax deduction particularly significant. First, an essential feature of Minnesota's arrangement is the fact that [it] is only one among many deductions—such as those for medical expenses, . . . and charitable contributions, . . .—available under the Minnesota tax laws. . . .

Other characteristics . . . argue equally strongly for the provision's constitutionality. Most importantly, the deduction is available for educational expenses incurred by *all* parents, including those whose children attend public schools and those whose children attend non-sectarian private schools or sectarian private schools. . . .

In this respect, as well as others, this case is vitally different from the scheme struck down in *Nyquist*. There, public assistance amounting to tuition grants, was provided only to parents of children in *nonpublic* schools. This fact had considerable bearing on our decision striking down the New York statute at issue; we explicitly distinguished both *Allen* and *Everson* on the grounds that "In both cases the class of beneficiaries included *all* schoolchildren, those in public as well as those in private schools." 413 U.S., at 782, n. 38 (emphasis in original). Moreover, we intimated that "public assistance (*e.g.,* scholarships) made available generally without regard to the sectarian-nonsectarian or public-nonpublic nature of the institution benefited," *ibid.,* might not offend the Establishment Clause. We think the tax deduction adopted by Minnesota is more similar to this latter type of program than it is to the arrangement struck down in *Nyquist*. . . .

We also agree with the Court of Appeals that, by channeling whatever assistance it may provide to parochial schools through individual parents, Minnesota has reduced the Establishment Clause objections to which its action is subject. It is true, of course, that financial assistance provided to parents ultimately has an economic effect comparable to that of aid given directly to the schools attended by their children. It is also true, however, that under Minnesota's arrangement public funds become available only as a result of numerous, private choices of individual parents of school-age children. . . . It is noteworthy that all but one of our recent cases invalidating state aid to parochial schools have involved the direct transmission of assistance from the state to the schools themselves. The exception, of course, was *Nyquist,* which, as discussed previously is distinguishable from this case on other grounds. . . .

. . . .

Petitioners argue that, notwithstanding the facial neutrality . . . ., in application the statute primarily benefits religious institutions. Petitioners rely, as they did below, on a statistical analysis of the type of persons claiming the tax deduction. They contend that most parents of public school children incur no tuition expenses, . . . and that other expenses deductible . . . are negligible in value; moreover, they claim that 96% of the children in private schools in 1978–1979 attended religiously-affiliated institutions. Because of all this, they reason, the bulk of deductions taken . . . will be claimed by parents of children in sectarian schools. Respondents reply that petitioners have failed to consider the impact of deductions for items such as transportation, summer school tuition, tuition paid by parents whose children attended schools outside the school districts in which they resided, rental or purchase costs for a variety of equipment, and tuition for certain types of instruction not ordinarily provided in public schools.

We need not consider these contentions in detail. We would be loath to adopt a rule grounding the constitutionality of a facially neutral law on annual reports reciting the extent to which various classes of private citizens claimed benefits under the law. Such an approach would scarcely provide the certainty that this field stands in need of, nor can we perceive principled standards by which such statistical evidence might be evaluated. Moreover, the fact that private persons fail in a particular year to claim the tax relief to which they are entitled—under a facially neutral statute—should be of little importance in determining the constitutionality of the statute permitting such relief.

Finally, private educational institutions, and parents paying for their children to attend these schools, make special contributions to the areas in which they operate. "Parochial schools, quite apart from their sectarian purpose, have provided an educational alternative for millions of young Americans; they often afford wholesome competition with our public schools; and in some States they relieve substantially the tax burden incident to the operation of public schools." *Wolman,* at 262, (Powell, J., concurring and dissenting). If parents of children in private schools choose to take especial advantage of the relief provided . . . ., it is no doubt due to the fact that they bear a particularly great financial burden in educating their children. More fundamentally, whatever unequal effect may be attributed to the statutory classification can fairly be regarded as a rough return for the benefits, discussed above, provided to the state and all taxpayers by parents sending their children to parochial schools. In the light of all this, we believe it wiser to decline to engage in the type of empirical inquiry into those persons benefited by state law which petitioners urge.

Thus, we hold that the Minnesota tax deduction for educational expenses satisfies the primary effect inquiry of our Establishment Clause cases.

Turning to the third part of the *Lemon* inquiry, we have no difficulty in concluding that the Minnesota statute does not "excessively entangle" the state in religion. . . .

For the foregoing reasons, the judgment of the Court of Appeals is

Affirmed.

Justice Marshall, with whom Justice Brennan, Justice Blackmun and Justice Stevens join, dissenting.

The Establishment Clause of the First Amendment prohibits a State from subsidizing religious education, whether it does so directly or indirectly. In my view, this principle of neutrality forbids not only the tax benefits struck down in Committee for Public Education v. Nyquist, 413 U.S. 756 (1973), but any tax benefit, including the tax deduction at issue here, which subsidizes tuition payments to sectarian schools. . . .

. . . .

The majority attempts to distinguish *Nyquist* by pointing to two differences between the Minnesota tuition-assistance program and the program struck down in *Nyquist*. Neither of these distinctions can withstand scrutiny.

.   .   .

That the Minnesota statute makes some small benefit available to all parents cannot alter the fact that the most substantial benefit provided by the statute is available only to those parents who send their children to schools that charge tuition. It is simply undeniable that the single largest expense that may be deducted under the Minnesota statute is tuition. The statute is little more than a subsidy of tuition masquerading as a subsidy of general educational expenses. The other deductible expenses are *de minimis* in comparison to tuition expenses.

.   .   .

The majority also asserts that the Minnesota statute is distinguishable from the statute struck down in *Nyquist* in another respect: the tax benefit available under Minnesota law is a "genuine tax deduction," whereas the New York law provided a benefit which, while nominally a deduction, also had features of a "tax credit." Under the Minnesota law, the amount of the tax benefit varies directly with the amount of the expenditure. Under the New York law, the amount of deduction was not dependent upon the amount actually paid for tuition but was a predetermined amount which depended on the tax bracket of each taxpayer. The deduction was designed to yield roughly the same amount of tax "forgiveness" for each taxpayer.

This is a distinction without a difference.   .   .   .

.   .   .

There can be little doubt that the State of Minnesota intended to provide, and has provided, "[s]ubstantial aid to the educational function of [church-related] schools," and that the tax deduction for tuition and other educational expenses "necessarily results in aid to the sectarian school enterprise as a whole." Meek v. Pittenger, 421 U.S., at 366. It is beside the point that the State may have legitimate secular reasons for providing such aid. In focusing upon the contributions made by church-related schools, the majority has lost sight of the issue before us in this case.   .   .   .

In my view, the lines drawn in *Nyquist* were drawn on a reasoned basis with appropriate regard for the principles of neutrality embodied by the Establishment Clause. I do not believe that the same can be said of the lines drawn by the majority today. For the first time, the Court has upheld financial support for religious schools without any reason at all to assume that the support will be restricted to the secular functions of those schools and will not be used to support religious instruction. This result is flatly at odds with the fundamental principle that a State may provide no financial support whatsoever to promote religion.   .   .   .

2.   HIGHER EDUCATION

TILTON v. RICHARDSON, 403 U.S. 672 (1971). The Higher Education Facilities Act of 1963 provided for federal grants to institutions of higher education for the construction of academic facilities. The Act provided that only facilities used for non-sectarian instruction would be financed and that the restriction to non-sectarian use would have to be observed for 20 years. The Court by a vote of 5 to 4, but without an opinion of the Court, sustained the application of the statute to grants made for buildings at four church-related colleges. The Court held invalid the portion of the Act that would have permitted religious uses of the buildings after 20 years.

HUNT v. McNAIR, 413 U.S. 734 (1973). South Carolina established an Educational Facilities Authority to assist through the issuance of revenue bonds higher educational institutions in constructing and financing buildings, facilities and site preparation, but not including any facility for sectarian instruction or religious worship. The Act was challenged here as applied to the issuance of bonds to finance the construction of dining hall facilities at a Baptist college. The Court upheld the statute, relying on Tilton v. Richardson. It said: "Aid normally may be thought to have a primary effect of advancing religion when it flows to an institution in which religion is so pervasive that a substantial portion of its functions are subsumed in the religious mission or when it funds a specifically religious activity in an otherwise substantially secular setting." In this case the Court relied on the fact that the college had no religious test for faculty or student body and that the Baptist percentage of the student body (60%) was about the same as the percentage of Baptists in the surrounding community.

ROEMER v. BOARD OF PUBLIC WORKS

426 U.S. 736, 96 S.Ct. 2337, 49 L.Ed.2d 179 (1976).

Mr. Justice Blackmun announced the judgment of the Court and delivered an opinion in which The Chief Justice and Mr. Justice Powell joined.

We are asked once again to police the constitutional boundary between church and state. Maryland, this time, is the alleged trespasser. It has enacted a statute which, as amended, provides for annual noncategorical grants to private colleges, among them religiously affiliated institutions, subject only to the restrictions that the funds not be used for "sectarian purposes." A three-judge District Court, by a divided vote, refused to enjoin the operation of the statute, 387 F.Supp. 1282 (Md.1974), and a direct appeal has been taken to this Court . . ..

Plaintiffs in this suit, appellants here, are four individual Maryland citizens and taxpayers. Their complaint sought a declaration of the statute's invalidity, an order enjoining payments under it to church-affiliated institutions, and a declaration that the State was entitled to recover from such institutions any amounts already disbursed. In addition to the responsible state officials, plaintiff-appellants joined as defendants the five institutions they claimed were constitutionally ineligible for this form of aid: Western Maryland College, College of Notre Dame, Mount Saint Mary's College, Saint Joseph College, and Loyola College. Of these, the last four are affiliated with the Roman Catholic Church; Western Maryland was a Methodist affiliate. The District Court ruled with respect to all five. Western Maryland, however, has since been dismissed as a defendant-appellee. We are concerned, therefore, only with the four Roman Catholic affiliates.

After carefully assessing the role that the Catholic Church plays in the lives of these institutions, a matter to which we return in greater detail below, and applying the three-part requirement of *Lemon I,* 403 U.S., at 612–613, that state aid such as this have a secular purpose, a primary effect other than the advancement of religion, and no tendency to entangle the State excessively in church affairs, the District Court ruled that the amended statute was constitutional and was not to be enjoined. . . .

II.

A system of government that makes itself felt as pervasively as ours could hardly be expected never to cross paths with the church. In fact, our State and Federal Governments impose certain burdens upon, and impart certain benefits to, virtually all our activities, and religious activity is not an exception. The Court has enforced a scrupulous neutrality by the State, as among religions, and also as between religious and other activities, but a hermetic separation of the two is an impossibility it has never required. It long has been established, for example, that the State may send a cleric, indeed even a clerical order, to perform a wholly secular task. In Bradfield v. Roberts, 175 U.S. 291 (1899), the Court upheld the extension of public aid to a corporation which, although composed entirely of members of a Roman Catholic sisterhood acting "under the auspices of said church," id., at 297, was limited by its corporate charter to the secular purpose of operating a charitable hospital.

And religious institutions need not be quarantined from public benefits that are neutrally available to all. The Court has permitted the State to supply transportation for children to and from church-related as well as public schools. Everson v. Board of Education, 330 U.S. 1 (1947). It has done the same with respect to secular textbooks loaned by the State on equal terms to students attending both public and church-related elementary schools. Board of Education v. Allen, 392 U.S. 236 (1968). Since it had not been shown in *Allen* that the secular textbooks would be put to other than secular purposes, the Court concluded that, as in *Everson,* the State was merely "extending the benefits of state laws to all citizens." Id., at 242. Just as *Bradfield* dispels any notion that a religious person can never be in the State's pay for a secular purpose,[13] *Everson* and *Allen* put to rest any argument that the State may never act in such a way that has the incidental effect of facilitating religious activity. The Court has not been blind to the fact that in aiding a religious institution to perform a secular task, the State frees the institution's resources to be put to sectarian ends.[14] If this were impermissible, however, a church could not be protected by the police and fire departments, or have its public sidewalk kept in repair. The Court never has held that religious activities must be discriminated against in this way.

Neutrality is what is required. The State must confine itself to secular objectives, and neither advance nor impede religious activity. Of course, that principle is more easily stated than applied. The Court has taken the view that a secular purpose and a facial neutrality may not be enough, if in fact the State is lending direct support to a religious activity. The State may not, for example, pay for what is actually a religious education, even though it purports to be paying for a secular one, and even though it makes its aid available to secular and religious institutions alike. The Court also has taken the view that the State's efforts to perform a secular task, and at the same time avoid aiding in the performance of a religious one, may not lead it into such an intimate relationship with religious authority that it appears either to be sponsoring or to be excessively interfering with that authority.[15] . . .

---

[13] It could scarcely be otherwise, or individuals would be discriminated against for their religion, and the Nation would have to abandon its accepted practice of allowing members of religious orders to serve in the Congress and in other public offices.

[14] See Hunt v. McNair, 413 U.S. 734, 743 (1973) ("the Court has not accepted the recurrent argument that all aid is forbidden because aid in one aspect of an institution frees it to spend its resources on religious ends"). . . .

[15] The importance of avoiding persistent and potentially frictional contact between governmental and religious authorities is such that it has been held to justify the *extension,* rather than the withholding, of certain benefits to religious organizations. The Court upheld the exemption of such organizations from property taxation partly on this ground. Walz v. Tax Commission, 397 U.S. 664, 674–675 (1970).

. . .

[The opinion next discussed in detail *Lemon I,* Tilton v. Richardson, Hunt v. McNair, *Nyquist, Levitt,* and Meek v. Pittenger.]

So the slate we write on is anything but clean. Instead, there is little room for further refinement of the principles governing public aid to church-affiliated private schools. Our purpose is not to unsettle those principles, so recently reaffirmed, see Meek v. Pittenger, supra, or to expand upon them substantially, but merely to insure that they are faithfully applied in this case.

III.

The first part of *Lemon I's* three-part test is not in issue; appellants do not challenge the District Court's finding that the purpose of Maryland's aid program is the secular one of supporting private higher education generally, as an economic alternative to a wholly public system. The focus of the debate is on the second and third parts, those concerning the primary effect of advancing religion, and excessive church-state entanglement. We consider them in the same order.

A.

While entanglement is essentially a procedural problem, the primary effect question is the substantive one of what private educational activities, by whatever procedure, may be supported by state funds. *Hunt* requires (1) that no state aid at all go to institutions that are so "pervasively sectarian" that secular activities cannot be separated from sectarian ones, and (2) that if secular activities *can* be separated out, they alone may be funded.

(1) The District Court's finding in this case was that the appellee colleges are not "pervasively sectarian." 387 F.Supp., at 1293. This conclusion it supported with a number of subsidiary findings concerning the role of religion on these campuses:

. . .

We cannot say that the foregoing findings as to the role of religion in particular aspects of the colleges are clearly erroneous. . . . The general picture that the District Court has painted of the appellee institutions is similar in almost all respects to that of the church-affiliated colleges considered in *Tilton* and *Hunt.* We find no constitutionally significant distinction between them, at least for purposes of the "pervasive sectarianism" test.

(2) Having found that the appellee institutions are not "so permeated by religion that the secular side cannot be separated from the sectarian," 387 F.Supp., at 1293, the District Court proceeded to the next question posed by *Hunt:* whether aid in fact was extended only to "the secular side." This requirement the court regarded as satisfied by the statutory prohibition against sectarian use, and by the administrative enforcement of that prohibition through the Council for Higher Education. We agree. . . . We must assume that the colleges, and the Council, will exercise their delegated control over use of the funds in compliance with the statutory, and therefore the constitutional, mandate. It is to be expected that they will give a wide berth to "specifically religious activity," and thus minimize constitutional questions. Should such questions arise, the courts will consider them. It has not been the Court's practice, in considering facial challenges to statutes of this kind, to strike them down in anticipation that particular applications may result in unconstitutional use of funds. See e.g., Hunt v. McNair, 413 U.S., at 744; Tilton v. Richardson, 403 U.S., at 682 (plurality opinion).

B.

If the foregoing answer to the "primary effect" question seems easy, it serves to make the "excessive entanglement" problem more difficult. The statute itself clearly denies the use of public funds for "sectarian purposes." It seeks to avert such use, however, through a process of annual interchange—proposal and approval, expenditure and review—between the colleges and the Council. In answering the question whether this will be an "excessively entangling" relationship, we must consider the several relevant factors identified in prior decisions:

(1) First is the character of the aided institutions. This has been fully described above. As the District Court found, the colleges perform "essentially secular educational functions," 387 F.Supp., at 1288, that are distinct and separable from religious activity. This finding, which is a prerequisite under the "pervasive sectarianism" test to any state aid at all, is also important for purposes of the entanglement test because it means that secular activities, for the most, can be taken at face value. There is no danger, or at least only a substantially reduced danger, that an ostensibly secular activity— the study of biology, the learning of a foreign language, an athletic event— will actually be infused with religious content or significance. The need for close surveillance of purportedly secular activities is correspondingly reduced.   .   .   .

(2) As for the form of aid, we have already noted that no particular use of state funds is before us in this case. The *process* by which aid is disbursed, and a use for it chosen, are before us. We address this as a matter of the "resulting relationship" of secular and religious authority.

(3) As noted, the funding process is an annual one.   .   .   .

We agree with the District Court that "excessive entanglement" does not necessarily result from the fact that the subsidy is an annual one. It is true that the Court favored the "one-time, single-purpose" construction grants in *Tilton* because they entailed "no continuing financial relationships or dependencies, no annual audits, and no government analysis of an institution's expenditures." 403 U.S., at 688 (plurality opinion). The present aid program cannot claim these aspects. But if the question is whether this case is more like *Lemon I* or more like *Tilton*—and surely that is the fundamental question before us—the answer must be that it is more like *Tilton*.

Tilton is distinguishable only by the form of aid.   .   .   .

While the form-of-aid distinctions of *Tilton* are thus of questionable importance, the character-of-institution distinctions of *Lemon I* are most impressive. To reiterate a few of the relevant points: the elementary and secondary schooling in *Lemon* came at an impressionable age; the aided schools were "under the general supervision" of the Roman Catholic diocese; each had a local Catholic parish that assumed "ultimate financial responsibility" for it; the principals of the schools were usually appointed by church authorities; religion "pervade[d] the school system"; teachers were specifically instructed by the "Handbook of School Regulations" that "[r]eligious formation is not confined to formal courses; nor is it restricted to a single subject area." 403 U.S. at 617–618. These things made impossible what is crucial to a nonentangling aid program: the ability of the State to identify and subsidize separate secular functions carried out at the school, without on-the-site inspections being necessary to prevent diversion of the funds to sectarian purposes. The District Court gave primary importance to this consideration, and we cannot say it erred.

(4) As for political divisiveness, the District Court recognized that the annual nature of the subsidy, along with its promise of an increasing demand for state funds as the colleges' dependency grew, aggravated the danger of "[p]olitical fragmentation . . . on religious lines." *Lemon I,* 403 U.S., at 623. Nonetheless, the District Court found that the program "does not create a substantial danger of political entanglement." 387 F.Supp., at 1291. Several reasons were given. As was stated in *Tilton,* the danger of political divisiveness is "substantially less" when the aided institution is not an elementary or secondary school, but a college, "whose student constituency is not local but diverse and widely dispersed." 403 U.S., at 688–689. Furthermore, political divisiveness is diminished by the fact that the aid is extended to private colleges generally, more than two thirds of which have no religious affiliation; this is in sharp contrast to *Nyquist,* for example, where 95% of the aided schools were Roman Catholic parochial schools. Finally, the substantial autonomy of the colleges was thought to mitigate political divisiveness, in that controversies surrounding the aid program are not likely to involve the Catholic Church itself, or even the religious character of the schools, but only their "fiscal responsibility and educational requirements." 387 F.Supp., at 1290–1291.

The District Court's reasoning seems to us entirely sound. . . .

There is no exact science in gauging the entanglement of church and state. The wording of the test, which speaks of *"excessive* entanglement," itself makes that clear. The relevant factors we have identified are to be considered "cumulatively" in judging the degree of entanglement. Tilton v. Richardson, 403 U.S., at 688. They may cut different ways, as certainly they do here. In reaching the conclusion that it did, the District Court gave dominant importance to the character of the aided institutions and to its finding that they are capable of separating secular and religious functions. For the reasons stated above, we cannot say that the emphasis was misplaced, or the finding erroneous.

The judgment of the District Court is affirmed.

It is so ordered.

Mr. Justice White, with whom Mr. Justice Rehnquist joins, concurring in the judgment.

While I join in the judgment of the Court, I am unable to concur in the plurality opinion substantially for the reasons set forth in my opinions in Lemon v. Kurtzman, 403 U.S. 602 (1971) (*Lemon I*), and Committee for Public Education v. Nyquist, 413 U.S. 756 (1973). I am no more reconciled now to *Lemon I* than I was when it was decided. See *Nyquist,* supra, at 820 (White, J. dissenting). The threefold test of *Lemon I* imposes unnecessary, and, as I believe today's plurality opinion demonstrates, superfluous tests for establishing "when the State's involvement with religion passes the peril point" for First Amendment purposes. Id., at 822.

"It is enough for me that the [State is] financing a separable secular function of overriding importance in order to sustain the legislation here challenged." *Lemon I,* supra, at 664 (opinion of White, J.). As long as there is a secular legislative purpose, and as long as the primary effect of the legislation is neither to advance nor inhibit religion, I see no reason—particularly in light of the "sparse language of the Establishment Clause," Committee for Public Education v. Nyquist, supra, at 820—to take the constitutional inquiry further. See *Lemon I,* supra, at 661 (opinion of White, J.); *Nyquist,* supra, at 813 (opinion of White, J.). However, since 1970, the Court has added a third element to the inquiry: whether there is "an excessive government entanglement with religion." Walz v. Tax Comm'n, 397 U.S. 664, 674. I have never understood the constitutional foundation for this added element; it is at once both insolubly paradoxical, see

Lemon I, supra, at 668, and—as the Court has conceded from the outset—a "blurred, indistinct and variable barrier." *Lemon I,* 403 U.S., at 614. It is not clear that the "weight and contours of entanglement as a separate constitutional criterion," *Nyquist,* supra, at 822, are any more settled now than when they first surfaced. Today's plurality opinion leaves the impression that the criterion really may not be "separate" at all. In affirming the District Court's conclusion that the legislation here does not create an "excessive entanglement" of church and state the plurality emphasizes with approval that "the District Court gave dominant importance to the character of the aided institutions and to its finding that they are capable of separating secular and religious functions." Yet these are the same factors upon which the plurality focus in concluding that the Maryland legislation satisfies the first part of the *Lemon I* test: that on the record the "appellee colleges are not 'pervasively sectarian,'" and that the aid at issue was capable of, and is in fact, extended only to "the secular side" of the appellee colleges' operations. It is unclear to me how the first and third parts of the *Lemon I* test are substantially different. The "excessive entanglement" test appears no less "curious and mystifying" than when it was first announced. *Lemon I,* supra, at 666.

I see no reason to indulge in the redundant exercise of evaluating the same facts and findings under a different label. No one in this case challenges the District Court's finding that the purpose of the legislation here is secular. And I do not disagree with the plurality that the primary effect of the aid program is not advancement of religion. That is enough in my view to sustain the aid programs against constitutional challenge, and I would say no more.

Mr. Justice Brennan, with whom Mr. Justice Marshall joins, dissenting.

I agree with Judge Bryan, dissenting from the judgment under review, that the Maryland Act *"in these instances* does in truth offend the Constitution by its provisions of funds, in that it exposes State money for use in advancing religion, no matter the vigilance to avoid it." 387 F.Supp., at 1298 (emphasis in original). Each of the institutions is a church-affiliated or church-related body. The subsidiary findings concerning the role of religion on each of the campuses, summarized by the plurality opinion, conclusively establish that fact. In that circumstance, I agree with Judge Bryan that "[o]f telling decisiveness here is the payment of the grants directly to the colleges unmarked in purpose. . . . Presently the Act is simply a blunderbuss discharge of public funds to a church-affiliated or church-related college." Id., at 1298–1299. In other words, the Act provides for payment of general subsidies to religious institutions from public funds and I have heretofore expressed my view that "[g]eneral subsidies of religious activities would, of course, constitute impermissible state involvement with religion." Walz v. Tax Commission, 397 U.S. 664, 690 (1970) (concurring opinion). This is because general subsidies "tend to promote that type of interdependence between religion and state which the First Amendment was designed to prevent." Abington School Dist. v. Schempp, 374 U.S. 203, 236 (1963) (Brennan, J., concurring). "What the Framers meant to foreclose, and what our decisions under the Establishment Clause have forbidden, are those involvements of religions with secular institutions which . . . serve the essentially religious activities of religious institutions." Id., at 294–295. . . .

The discrete interests of government and religion are mutually best served when each avoids too close a proximity to the other. . . .
. . .

Mr. Justice Stewart, dissenting.

In my view, the decisive differences between this case and Tilton v. Richardson, 403 U.S. 672, lie in the nature of the theology courses that are a compulsory part of the curriculum at each of the appellee institutions and the type of governmental assistance provided to these church-affiliated colleges. In *Tilton* the Court emphasized that the theology courses were taught as academic subjects. . . .

. . . Here, by contrast, the District Court was unable to find that the compulsory religion courses were taught as an academic discipline. . . .

In the light of these findings, I cannot agree with the Court's assertion that there is "no constitutionally significant distinction" between the colleges in *Tilton* and those in the present case. The findings in *Tilton* clearly established that the federal building construction grants benefited academic institutions that made no attempt to inculcate the religious beliefs of the affiliated church. In the present case, by contrast, the compulsory theology courses may be "devoted to deepening religious experiences in the particular faith rather than to teaching theology as an academic discipline." 387 F.Supp., at 1288. In view of this salient characteristic of the appellee institutions and the noncategorical grants provided to them by the State of Maryland, I agree with the conclusion of the dissenting member of the three-judge court that the challenged Act "*in these instances* does in truth offend the Constitution by its provisions of funds, in that it exposes State money for use in advancing religion, no matter the vigilance to avoid it." Id., at 1298 (emphasis in the original).

For the reasons stated, and those expressed by Mr. Justice Brennan and Mr. Justice Stevens, I dissent from the judgment and opinion of the Court.

Mr. Justice Stevens, dissenting.

My views are substantially those expressed by Mr. Justice Brennan. However, I would add emphasis to the pernicious tendency of a state subsidy to tempt religious schools to compromise their religious mission without wholly abandoning it. The disease of entanglement may infect a law discouraging wholesome religious activity as well as a law encouraging the propagation of a given faith.

D. OTHER GOVERNMENT PRACTICES

LYNCH v. DONNELLY

___ U.S. ___, 104 S.Ct. 1355, 79 L.Ed.2d 604 (1984).

The Chief Justice delivered the opinion of the Court.

We granted certiorari to decide whether the Establishment Clause of the First Amendment prohibits a municipality from including a crèche, or Nativity scene, in its annual Christmas display.

I

Each year, in cooperation with the downtown retail merchants' association, the City of Pawtucket, Rhode Island, erects a Christmas display as part of its observance of the Christmas holiday season. The display is situated in a park owned by a nonprofit organization and located in the heart of the shopping district. The display is essentially like those to be found in hundreds of towns or cities across the Nation—often on public grounds—during the Christmas season. The Pawtucket display comprises many of the figures and decorations traditionally associated with Christmas, including, among other things, a Santa Claus house, reindeer pulling Santa's sleigh, candy-striped poles, a Christmas tree, carolers, cutout figures representing such characters as a clown, an elephant, and a teddy bear, hundreds of colored lights, a larger banner that reads "SEASONS GREETINGS," and the crèche at issue here. All components of this display are owned by the City.

The crèche, which has been included in the display for 40 or more years, consists of the traditional figures, including the Infant Jesus, Mary and Joseph, angels, shepherds, kings, and animals, all ranging in height from 5" to 5'. In 1973, when the present crèche was acquired, it cost the City $1365; it now is valued at $200. The erection and dismantling of the crèche costs the City about $20 per year; nominal expenses are incurred in lighting the crèche. No money has been expended on its maintenance for the past 10 years.

Respondents, Pawtucket residents and individual members of the Rhode Island affiliate of the American Civil Liberties Union, and the affiliate itself, brought this action in the United States District Court for Rhode Island, challenging the City's inclusion of the crèche in the annual display. The District Court held that the City's inclusion of the crèche in the display violates the Establishment Clause, ..., which is binding on the states through the Fourteenth Amendment. . . . The City was permanently enjoined from including the crèche in the display.

A divided panel of the Court of Appeals for the First Circuit affirmed. . . . We . . . reverse.

II

A

This Court has explained that the purpose of the Establishment and Free Exercise Clauses of the First Amendment is

> "to prevent, as far as possible, the intrusion of either [the church or the state] into the precincts of the other." Lemon v. Kurtzman, 403 U.S. 602, 614 (1971).

At the same time, however, the Court has recognized that

> "total separation is not possible in an absolute sense. Some relationship between government and religious organizations is inevitable." Ibid.

In every Establishment Clause case, we must reconcile the inescapable tension between the objective of preventing unnecessary intrusion of either the church or the state upon the other, and the reality that, as the Court has so often noted, total separation of the two is not possible.

The Court has sometimes described the Religion Clauses as erecting a "wall" between church and state, see, e.g., Everson v. Board of Education, 330 U.S. 1, 18 (1947). . . . But the metaphor itself is not a wholly accurate description of the practical aspects of the relationship that in fact exists between church and state.

No significant segment of our society and no institution within it can exist in a vacuum or in total or absolute isolation from all the other parts, much less from government. "It has never been thought either possible or desirable to enforce a regime of total separation. . . . ." Committee for Public Education & Religious Liberty v. Nyquist, 413 U.S. 756, 760 (1973). Nor does the Constitution require complete separation of church and state; it affirmatively mandates accommodation, not merely tolerance, of all religions, and forbids hostility toward any. See, e.g., Zorach v. Clauson, 343 U.S. 306, 314, 315 (1952); McCollum v. Board of Education, 333 U.S. 203, 211 (1948). Anything less would require the "callous indifference" we have said was never intended by the Establishment Clause. Zorach, supra, 343 U.S., at 314. Indeed, we have observed, such hostility would bring us into "war with our national tradition as embodied in the First Amendment's guaranty of the free exercise of religion." McCollum, supra, 333 U.S., at 211–212.

B

The Court's interpretation of the Establishment Clause has comported with what history reveals was the contemporaneous understanding of its guarantees. A significant example of the contemporaneous understanding of that Clause is found in the events of the first week of the First Session of the First Congress in 1789. In the very week that Congress approved the Establishment Clause as part of the Bill of Rights for submission to the states, it enacted legislation providing for paid chaplains for the House and Senate. In Marsh v. Chambers, ___ U.S. ___ (1983), we noted that seventeen Members of that First Congress had been Delegates to the Constitutional Convention where freedom of speech, press and religion and antagonism toward an established church were subjects of frequent discussion. We saw no conflict with the Establishment Clause when Nebraska employed members of the clergy as official Legislative Chaplains to give opening prayers at sessions of the state legislature. Id., at ___.

The interpretation of the Establishment Clause by Congress in 1789 takes on special significance in light of the Court's emphasis that the First Congress

"was a Congress whose constitutional decisions have always been regarded, as they should be regarded, as of the greatest weight in the interpretation of that fundamental instrument," Myers v. United States, 272 U.S. 52, 174–175 (1926).

It is clear that neither the seventeen draftsmen of the Constitution who were Members of the First Congress, nor the Congress of 1789, saw any establishment problem in the employment of congressional Chaplains to offer daily prayers in the Congress, a practice that has continued for nearly two centuries. It would be difficult to identify a more striking example of the accommodation of religious belief intended by the Framers.

C

There is an unbroken history of official acknowledgment by all three branches of government of the role of religion in American life from at least 1789. . . .

Our history is replete with official references to the value and invocation of Divine guidance in deliberations and pronouncements of the Founding Fathers and contemporary leaders. Beginning in the early colonial period long before Independence, a day of Thanksgiving was celebrated as a religious holiday to give thanks for the bounties of Nature as gifts from God. President Washington and his successors proclaimed Thanksgiving, with all its religious overtones, a day of national celebration and Congress made it a National Holiday more than a century ago. Ch. 167, 16 Stat. 168 (1870). That holiday has not lost its theme of expressing thanks for Divine aid any more than has Christmas lost its religious significance.

Executive Orders and other official announcements of Presidents and of the Congress have proclaimed both Christmas and Thanksgiving National Holidays in religious terms. And, by Acts of Congress, it has long been the practice that federal employees are released from duties on these National Holidays, while being paid from the same public revenues that provide the compensation of the Chaplains of the Senate and the House and the military services. See J.Res. 5, 23 Stat. 516 (1885). Thus, it is clear that Government has long recognized—indeed it has subsidized—holidays with religious significance.

Other examples of reference to our religious heritage are found in the statutorily prescribed national motto "In God We Trust," 36 U.S.C. § 186, which Congress and the President mandated for our currency, see 31 U.S.C. § 324, and in the language "One nation under God," as part of the Pledge of

Allegiance to the American flag. That pledge is recited by thousands of public school children—and adults—every year.

Art galleries supported by public revenues display religious paintings of the 15th and 16th centuries, predominantly inspired by one religious faith. The National Gallery in Washington, maintained with Government support, for example, has long exhibited masterpieces with religious messages, notably the Last Supper, and paintings depicting the Birth of Christ, the Crucifixion, and the Resurrection, among many others with explicit Christian themes and messages. The very chamber in which oral arguments on this case were heard is decorated with a notable and permanent—not seasonal—symbol of religion: Moses with Ten Commandments. Congress has long provided chapels in the Capitol for religious worship and meditation.

There are countless other illustrations of the Government's acknowledgment of our religious heritage and governmental sponsorship of graphic manifestations of that heritage. Congress has directed the President to proclaim a National Day of Prayer each year "on which [day] the people of the United States may turn to God in prayer and meditation at churches, in groups, and as individuals." 36 U.S.C. § 169h. Our Presidents have repeatedly issued such Proclamations. Presidential Proclamations and messages have also issued to commemorate Jewish Heritage Week, Proclamation No. 4844, 46 Fed.Reg. 25,077 (1981), and the Jewish High Holy Days, 17 Weekly Comp.Pres.Doc. 1058 (Sept. 29, 1981). One cannot look at even this brief resume without finding that our history is pervaded by expressions of religious beliefs such as are found in *Zorach,* supra. Equally pervasive is the evidence of accommodation of all faiths and all forms of religious expression, and hostility toward none. . . .

III

This history may help explain why the Court consistently has declined to take a rigid, absolutist view of the Establishment Clause. . . . In our modern, complex society, whose traditions and constitutional underpinnings rest on and encourage diversity and pluralism in all areas, an absolutist approach in applying the Establishment Clause is simplistic and has been uniformly rejected by the Court.

Rather than mechanically invalidating all governmental conduct or statutes that confer benefits or give special recognition to religion in general or to one faith—as an absolutist approach would dictate—the Court has scrutinized challenged legislation or official conduct to determine whether, in reality, it establishes a religion or religious faith, or tends to do so. . . .

In each case, the inquiry calls for line drawing; no fixed, *per se* rule can be framed. . . .

In the line-drawing process we have often found it useful to inquire whether the challenged law or conduct has a secular purpose, whether its principal or primary effect is to advance or inhibit religion, and whether it creates an excessive entanglement of government with religion. *Lemon,* supra. But, we have repeatedly emphasized our unwillingness to be confined to any single test or criterion in this sensitive area. See e.g. Tilton v. Richardson, 403 U.S. 672, 677–678 (1971); *Nyquist,* supra, 413 U.S., at 773. In two cases, the Court did not even apply the *Lemon* "test." We did not, for example, consider that analysis relevant in *Marsh,* supra. Nor did we find *Lemon* useful in Larson v. Valente, 456 U.S. 228 (1982), where there was substantial evidence of overt discrimination against a particular church.

In this case, the focus of our inquiry must be on the crèche in the context of the Christmas season. See, e.g., Stone v. Graham, 449 U.S. 39 (1980) (*per curiam*); Abington School District v. Schempp, supra. In *Stone,* for example, we invalidated a state statute requiring the posting of a copy of the Ten Commandments on public classroom walls. But the Court carefully pointed out that the Commandments were posted purely as a religious admonition, not "integrated into the school curriculum, where the Bible may constitutionally be used in an appropriate study of history, civilization, ethics, comparative religion, or the like." 449 U.S., at 42. Similarly, in *Abington,* although the Court struck down the practices in two States requiring daily Bible readings in public schools, it specifically noted that nothing in the Court's holding was intended to "indicat[e] that such study of the Bible or of religion, when presented objectively as part of a secular program of education, may not be effected consistently with the First Amendment." 374 U.S., at 225. Focus exclusively on the religious component of any activity would inevitably lead to its invalidation under the Establishment Clause.

The Court has invalidated legislation or governmental action on the ground that a secular purpose was lacking, but only when it has concluded there was no question that the statute or activity was motivated wholly by religious considerations. See, e.g., Stone v. Graham, supra, 449 U.S., at 41; Epperson v. Arkansas, 393 U.S. 97, 107–109 (1968); Abington School District v. Schempp, supra, 374 U.S., at 223–224; Engel v. Vitale, 370 U.S. 421, 424–425 (1962). Even where the benefits to religion were substantial, as in *Everson,* supra; Board of Education v. Allen, 392 U.S. 236 (1968), *Walz,* supra, and *Tilton,* supra, we saw a secular purpose and no conflict with the Establishment Clause. Cf. Larkin v. Grendel's Den, 459 U.S. 116 (1982).

The District Court inferred from the religious nature of the crèche that the City has no secular purpose for the display. In so doing, it rejected the City's claim that its reasons for including the crèche are essentially the same as its reasons for sponsoring the display as a whole. The District Court plainly erred by focusing almost exclusively on the crèche. When viewed in the proper context of the Christmas Holiday season, it is apparent that, on this record, there is insufficient evidence to establish that the inclusion of the crèche is a purposeful or surreptitious effort to express some kind of subtle governmental advocacy of a particular religious message. In a pluralistic society a variety of motives and purposes are implicated. The City, like the Congresses and Presidents, however, has principally taken note of a significant historical religious event long celebrated in the Western World. The crèche in the display depicts the historical origins of this traditional event long recognized as a National Holiday. . . .

The narrow question is whether there is a secular purpose for Pawtucket's display of the crèche. The display is sponsored by the City to celebrate the Holiday and to depict the origins of that Holiday. These are legitimate secular purposes. The District Court's inference, drawn from the religious nature of the crèche, that the City has no secular purpose was, on this record, clearly erroneous.

The District Court found that the primary effect of including the crèche is to confer a substantial and impermissible benefit on religion in general and on the Christian faith in particular. Comparisons of the relative benefits to religion of different forms of governmental support are elusive and difficult to make. But to conclude that the primary effect of including the crèche is to advance religion in violation of the Establishment Clause would require that we view it as more beneficial to and more an endorsement of religion, for example, than expenditure of large sums of public money for textbooks supplied throughout the country to students attending church-sponsored schools, Board of Education v. Allen, supra; expenditure of public funds for transportation of students to church-sponsored schools, Everson v. Board of Education, supra; federal grants for college buildings of church-sponsored institutions of higher education combining secular and religious education, *Tilton,* supra; noncategorical grants to church-sponsored colleges and universities, Roemer v. Board of Public Works, 426 U.S. 736 (1976); and the tax exemptions for church properties sanctioned in *Walz,* supra. It would also require that we view it as more of an endorsement of religion than the Sunday Closing Laws upheld in McGowan v. Maryland, 366 U.S. 420 (1961); the release time program for religious training in *Zorach,* supra; and the legislative prayers upheld in *Marsh,* supra.

We are unable to discern a greater aid to religion deriving from inclusion of the crèche than from these benefits and endorsements previously held not violative of the Establishment Clause. . . .

. . .

. . . Here, whatever benefit to one faith or religion or to all religions, is indirect, remote and incidental; display of the crèche is no more an advancement or endorsement of religion than the Congressional and Executive recognition of the origins of the Holiday itself as "Christ's Mass," or the exhibition of literally hundreds of religious paintings in governmentally supported museums.

The District Court found that there had been no administrative entanglement between religion and state resulting from the City's ownership and use of the crèche. But it went on to hold that some political divisiveness was engendered by this litigation. Coupled with its finding of an impermissible sectarian purpose and effect, this persuaded the court that there was "excessive entanglement." The Court of Appeals expressly declined to accept the District Court's finding that inclusion of the crèche has caused political divisiveness along religious lines, and noted that this Court has never held that political divisiveness alone was sufficient to invalidate government conduct.

Entanglement is a question of kind and degree. In this case, however, there is no reason to disturb the District Court's finding on the absence of administrative entanglement. There is no evidence of contact with church authorities concerning the content or design of the exhibit prior to or since Pawtucket's purchase of the crèche. No expenditures for maintenance of the crèche have been necessary; and since the City owns the creche, now valued at $200, the tangible material it contributes is *de minimis.* In many respects the display requires far less ongoing, day-to-day interaction between church and state than religious paintings in public galleries. There is nothing here, of course, like the "comprehensive, discriminating, and continuing state surveillance" or the "enduring entanglement" present in *Lemon,* supra, 403 U.S., at 619–622.

The Court of Appeals correctly observed that this Court has not held that political divisiveness alone can serve to invalidate otherwise permissible conduct. And we decline to so hold today. This case does not involve a direct subsidy to church-sponsored schools or colleges, or other religious institutions, and hence no inquiry into potential political divisiveness is even called for, . . . In any event, apart from this litigation there is no evidence of political friction or divisiveness over the crèche in the 40-year history of Pawtucket's Christmas celebration. The District Court stated that the inclusion of the crèche for the 40 years has been "marked by no apparent dissension" and that the display has had a "calm history." Curiously, it went on to hold that the political divisiveness engendered by this lawsuit was evidence of excessive entanglement. A litigant cannot, by the very act of commencing a lawsuit, however, create the appearance of divisiveness and then exploit it as evidence of entanglement.

We are satisfied that the City has a secular purpose for including the crèche, that the City has not impermissibly advanced religion, and that including the crèche does not create excessive entanglement between religion and government.

IV

Justice Brennan describes the crèche as a "re-creation of an event that lies at the heart of Christian faith." The crèche, like a painting, is passive; admittedly it is a reminder of the origins of Christmas. . . .

. . . To forbid the use of this one passive symbol—the crèche—at the very time people are taking note of the season with Christmas hymns and carols in public schools and other public places, and while the Congress and Legislatures open sessions with prayers by paid chaplains would be a stilted overreaction contrary to our history and to our holdings. If the presence of the crèche in this display violates the Establishment Clause, a host of other forms of taking official note of Christmas, and of our religious heritage, are equally offensive to the Constitution.

. . . .

VI

We hold that, notwithstanding the religious significance of the crèche, the City of Pawtucket has not violated the Establishment Clause of the First Amendment. Accordingly, the judgment of the Court of Appeals is reversed.

It is so ordered.

Justice O'Connor, concurring.

I concur in the opinion of the Court. I write separately to suggest a clarification of our Establishment Clause doctrine. The suggested approach leads to the same result in this case as that taken by the Court, and the Court's opinion, as I read it, is consistent with my analysis.

I

The Establishment Clause prohibits government from making adherence to a religion relevant in any way to a person's standing in the political community. Government can run afoul of that prohibition in two principal ways. One is excessive entanglement with religious institutions, which may interfere with the independence of the institutions, give the institutions access to government or governmental powers not fully shared by nonadherents of the religion, and foster the creation of political constituencies defined along religious lines. E.g., Larkin v. Grendel's Den, 459 U.S. 116 (1982). The second and more direct infringement is government endorsement or disapproval of religion. Endorsement sends a message to nonadherents that they are outsiders, not full members of the political community, and an accompanying message to adherents that they are insiders, favored members of the political community. Disapproval sends the opposite message. See generally Abington School District v. Schempp, 374 U.S. 203 (1963).

Our prior cases have used the three-part test articulated in Lemon v. Kurtzman, 403 U.S. 602, 612–613 (1970), as a guide to detecting these two forms of unconstitutional government action. It has never been entirely clear, however, how the three parts of the test relate to the principles enshrined in the Establishment Clause. Focusing on institutional entanglement and on endorsement or disapproval of religion clarifies the *Lemon* test as an analytical device.

. . . .

III

The central issue in this case is whether Pawtucket has endorsed Christianity by its display of the crèche. To answer that question, we must examine both what Pawtucket intended to communicate in displaying the crèche and what message the City's display actually conveyed. The purpose and effect prongs of the *Lemon* test represent these two aspects of the meaning of the City's action.

The meaning of a statement to its audience depends both on the intention of the speaker and on the "objective" meaning of the statement in the community. . . .

The purpose prong of the *Lemon* test asks whether government's actual purpose is to endorse or disapprove of religion. The effect prong asks whether, irrespective of government's actual purpose, the practice under review in fact conveys a message of endorsement or disapproval. An affirmative answer to either question should render the challenged practice invalid.

A

The purpose prong of the *Lemon* test requires that a government activity have a secular purpose. That requirement is not satisfied, however, by the mere existence of some secular purpose, however dominated by religious purposes. . . . The proper inquiry under the purpose prong of *Lemon,* I submit, is whether the government intends to convey a message of endorsement or disapproval of religion. . . . I would find that Pawtucket did not intend to convey any message of endorsement of Christianity or disapproval of nonChristian religions. The evident purpose of including the crèche in the larger display was not promotion of the religious content of the crèche but celebration of the public holiday through its traditional symbols. Celebration of public holidays, which have cultural significance even if they also have religious aspects, is a legitimate secular purpose.

. . .

B

Focusing on the evil of government endorsement or disapproval of religion makes clear that the effect prong of the *Lemon* test is properly interpreted not to require invalidation of a government practice merely because it in fact causes, even as a primary effect, advancement or inhibition of religion. . . . What is crucial is that a government practice not have the effect of communicating a message of government endorsement or disapproval of religion. It is only practices having that effect, whether intentionally or unintentionally, that make religion relevant, in reality or public perception, to status in the political community.

Pawtucket's display of its crèche, I believe, does not communicate a message that the government intends to endorse the Christian beliefs represented by the crèche. Although the religious and indeed sectarian significance of the crèche, as the district court found, is not neutralized by the setting, the overall holiday setting changes what viewers may fairly understand to be the purpose of the display—as a typical museum setting, though not neutralizing the religious content of a religious painting, negates any message of endorsement of that content. . . .

. . .

Justice Brennan, with whom Justice Marshall, Justice Blackmun and Justice Stevens join, dissenting.

. . . The Court's decision implicitly leaves open questions concerning the constitutionality of the public display on public property of a crèche standing alone, or the public display of other distinctively religious symbols such as a cross. Despite the narrow contours of the Court's opinion, our precedents in my view compel the holding that Pawtucket's inclusion of a life-sized display depicting the biblical description of the birth of Christ as part of its annual Christmas celebration is unconstitutional. Nothing in the history of such practices or the setting in which the City's crèche is presented obscures or diminishes the plain fact that Pawtucket's action amounts to an impermissible governmental endorsement of a particular faith.

I

Last Term, I expressed the hope that the Court's decision in Marsh v. Chambers, ___ U.S. ___ (1983), would prove to be only a single, aberrant departure from our settled method of analyzing Establishment Clause cases. Id., at ___ (Brennan, J., dissenting). That the Court today returns to the settled analysis of our prior cases gratifies that hope. At the same time, the Court's less than vigorous application of the *Lemon* test suggests that its commitment to those standards may only be superficial. . . .

.   .   .

In sum, considering the District Court's careful findings of fact under the three-part analysis called for by our prior cases, I have no difficulty concluding that Pawtucket's display of the crèche is unconstitutional.

B

The Court advances two principal arguments to support its conclusion that the Pawtucket crèche satisfies the *Lemon* test. Neither is persuasive.

First. The Court, by focusing on the holiday "context" in which the nativity scene appeared, seeks to explain away the clear religious import of the crèche and the findings of the District Court that most observers understood the crèche as both a symbol of Christian beliefs and a symbol of the City's support for those beliefs. . . .

.   .   .

.   .   . [E]ven in the context of Pawtucket's seasonal celebration, the crèche retains a specifically Christian religious meaning. I refuse to accept the notion implicit in today's decision that non-Christians would find that the religious content of the crèche is eliminated by the fact that it appears as part of the City's otherwise secular celebration of the Christmas holiday. The nativity scene is clearly distinct in its purpose and effect from the rest of the Hodgson Park display for the simple reason that it is the only one rooted in a biblical account of Christ's birth. It is the chief symbol of the characteristically Christian belief that a divine Savior was brought into the world and that the purpose of this miraculous birth was to illuminate a path toward salvation and redemption. For Christians, that path is exclusive, precious and holy. But for those who do not share these beliefs, the symbolic re-enactment of the birth of a divine being who has been miraculously incarnated as a man stands as a dramatic reminder of their differences with Christian faith. . . . To be so excluded on religious grounds by one's elected government is an insult and an injury that, until today, could not be countenanced by the Establishment Clause.

Second. The Court also attempts to justify the crèche by entertaining a beguilingly simple, yet faulty syllogism. The Court begins by noting that government may recognize Christmas day as a public holiday; the Court then asserts that the crèche is nothing more than a traditional element of Christmas celebrations; and it concludes that the inclusion of a crèche as part of a government's annual Christmas celebration is constitutionally permissible.

.   .   .

When government decides to recognize Christmas day as a public holiday, it does no more than accommodate the calendar of public activities to the plain fact that many Americans will expect on that day to spend time visiting with their families, attending religious services, and perhaps enjoying some respite from pre-holiday activities. The Free Exercise Clause, of course, does not necessarily compel the government to provide this accommodation, but neither is the Establishment Clause offended by such a step. Cf. Zorach v. Clauson, 343 U.S. 306 (1952). Because it is clear that the celebration of Christmas has both secular and sectarian elements, it may well be that by taking note of the holiday, the government is simply seeking to serve the same kinds of wholly secular goals—for instance, promoting goodwill and a common day of rest—that were found to justify Sunday Closing laws in *McGowan*. If public officials go further and participate in the *secular* celebration of Christmas—by, for example, decorating public places with such secular images as wreaths, garlands or Santa Claus figures—they move closer to the limits of their constitutional power but nevertheless remain within the boundaries set by the Establishment Clause. But when those officials participate in or appear to endorse the distinctively religious elements of this otherwise secular event, they encroach upon First Amendment freedoms. For it is at that point that the government brings to the forefront the theological content of the holiday, and places the prestige, power and financial support of a civil authority in the service of a particular faith.

II

Although the Court's relaxed application of the *Lemon* test to Pawtucket's crèche is regrettable, it is at least understandable and properly limited to the particular facts of this case. The Court's opinion, however, also sounds a broader and more troubling theme. Invoking the celebration of Thanksgiving as a public holiday, the legend "In God We Trust" on our coins, and the proclamation "God save the United States and this Honorable Court" at the opening of judicial sessions, the Court asserts, without explanation, that Pawtucket's inclusion of a crèche in its annual Christmas display poses no more of a threat to Establishment Clause values than these other official "acknowledgments" of religion.

Intuition tells us that some official "acknowledgment" is inevitable in a religious society if government is not to adopt a stilted indifference to the religious life of the people. . . . It is equally true, however, that if government is to remain scrupulously neutral in matters of religious conscience as our Constitution requires, then it must avoid those overly broad acknowledgments of religious practices that may imply governmental favoritism toward one set of religious beliefs. This does not mean, of course, that public officials may not take account, when necessary, of the separate existence and significance of the religious institutions and practices in the society they govern. Should government choose to incorporate some arguably religious element into its public ceremonies, that acknowledgment must be impartial; it must not tend to promote one faith or handicap another; and it should not sponsor religion generally over non-religion. . . .

. . . . .

. . . Inclusion of the crèche is not necessary to accommodate individual religious expression. This is plainly not a case in which individual residents of Pawtucket have claimed the right to place a crèche as part of a wholly private display on public land. . . . Nor is the inclusion of the crèche necessary to serve wholly secular goals; it is clear that the City's secular purposes of celebrating the Christmas holiday and promoting retail commerce can be fully served without the crèche. . . . And the crèche, because of its unique association with Christianity, is clearly more sectarian than those references to God that we accept in ceremonial phrases or in other contexts that assure neutrality. The religious works on display at the National Gallery, Presidential references to God during an Inaugural Address, or the national motto present no risk of establishing religion. To be sure, our understanding of these expressions may begin in contemplation of some religious element, but it does not end there. Their message is dominantly secular. In contrast, the message of the crèche begins and ends with reverence for a particular image of the divine.

By insisting that such a distinctively sectarian message is merely an unobjectionable part of our "religious heritage," the Court takes a long step backwards to the days when Justice Brewer could arrogantly declare for the Court that "this is a Christian nation." Church of Holy Trinity v. United States, 143 U.S. 457, 471 (1892). Those days, I had thought, were forever put behind us by the Court's decision in Engel v. Vitale, supra, in which we rejected a similar argument advanced by the State of New York that its Regent's Prayer was simply an acceptable part of our "spiritual heritage." Id., 370 U.S., at 425.

III

The American historical experience concerning the public celebration of Christmas, if carefully examined, provides no support for the Court's decision.
. . .

Indeed, the Court's approach suggests a fundamental misapprehension of the proper uses of history in constitutional interpretation. Certainly, our decisions reflect the fact that an awareness of historical practice often can provide a useful guide in interpreting the abstract language of the Establishment Clause. . . . Attention to the details of history should not blind us to the cardinal purposes of the Establishment Clause, nor limit our central inquiry in these cases—whether the challenged practices "threaten those consequences which the Framers deeply feared." Abington School Dist. v. Schempp, supra, 374 U.S., at 236 (Brennan, J., concurring). In recognition of this fact, the Court has, until today, consistently limited its historical inquiry to the particular practice under review.

. . . Thus, in Marsh v. Chambers, after marshalling the historical evidence which indicated that the First Congress had authorized the appointment of paid chaplains for its own proceedings only three days before it reached agreement on the final wording of the Bill of Rights, the Court concluded on the basis of this "unique history" that the modern-day practice of opening legislative sessions with prayer was constitutional. . . .

Although invoking these decisions in support of its result, the Court wholly fails to discuss the history of the public celebration of Christmas or the use of publicly-displayed nativity scenes. . . .

. . .

I dissent.

Justice Blackmun, with whom Justice Stevens joins, dissenting.

. . .

SECTION 2. THE FREE EXERCISE OF RELIGION

A. BELIEF, EXPRESSION AND CONDUCT

Introduction. Many of the cases covered in the preceding chapters on freedom of speech involved religious expression. The early cases, summarized below, limited the free exercise clause to the protection of religious belief and expression. If the Court had continued to adhere to that view, would the free exercise clause have had any significance independent of the free speech clause? On the other hand, if the free exercise clause does, in proper circumstances, protect freedom of conduct compelled by religious belief, is there any point in continuing to distinguish religious belief and expression from religious conduct? Those are the questions addressed in this subsection. The next subsection will examine the dimensions of the free-exercise clause as applied to religiously-motivated conduct.

THE MORMON POLYGAMY CASES

In 1879, the Court affirmed a conviction under a federal statute making polygamy a crime in federal territories, including Utah. Reynolds v. United States, 98 U.S. 145 (1879). The trial judge had refused to submit to the jury the defendant's defense that Mormon doctrine, to which he adhered, did not simply permit plural marriage, but required it "when circumstances would admit" under pain of "damnation in the life to come." The Court also rejected that defense, saying that the first amendment furnished no defense in any case where a statute of general application punished conduct compelled by religious belief. "Laws are made for the government of actions, and while they cannot interfere with mere religious belief and opinions, they may with practices." Chief Justice Waite's opinion offered, as examples, belief in human sacrifice, and a widow's religious belief that it was her duty to burn herself on the funeral pyre of her dead husband.

A case over ten years later suggests that moral abhorrence of polygamous marriage may have played a major role in the decision. In Davis v. Beason, 133 U.S. 333 (1890), the Court sustained an Idaho territorial statute requiring voters to take an oath that they were not members of organizations which teach, advise, counsel or encourage the crime of bigamy. Justice Field's opinion treated the issue as resolved by the *Reynolds* case, despite the fact that the oath was aimed at advocacy. He pointed out that polygamy was a crime in all "civilized and Christian countries." Moreover, to call advocacy of polygamy "a tenet of religion is to offend the common sense of mankind." Justice Field reasoned that if polygamy can be made a crime, then teaching, advising and counseling polygamy were "proper subjects of punishment, as aiding and abetting crime are in all other cases.   .   .   . Crime is not the less odious because sanctioned by what any particular sect may designate as religion."

THE FLAG SALUTE CASES

In Minersville School Dist. v. Gobitis, 310 U.S. 586 (1940), the Court sustained the school district's requirement that pupils participate in the flag salute, which had been challenged by parents and children with religious objection to the exercise. Justice Frankfurter's opinion for the Court viewed the issue as involving constitutional protection for conduct compelled by religious belief. He concluded that conscientious scruples could not relieve an individual of the legal obligation to obey a law of general obligation not aimed at restricting religious belief. Three years later, the case was overruled. West Virginia Bd. of Educ. v. Barnette, 319 U.S. 624 (1943). Justice Jackson's opinion stated that the major error in *Gobitis* had been to characterize the issue as involving the free exercise clause's protection for religiously motivated conduct. The problem instead was the protection of the free speech clause as applied to government's compulsion that an individual profess a belief. In analyzing that issue, it was irrelevant whether objection to the flag salute stemmed from religious belief. (The free speech analysis, of the *Barnette* case and the Court's later decision in Wooley v. Maynard, 430 U.S. 705 (1977), is summarized, supra, at pp. 1271–1273.)

CANTWELL v. CONNECTICUT, 310 U.S. 296 (1940).   The Court held invalid a state statute regulating solicitation for religious or charitable causes as applied to a member of Jehovah's Witnesses.   The opinion included the following paragraph:

"We hold that the statute, as construed and applied to the appellants, deprives them of their liberty without due process of law in contravention of the Fourteenth Amendment. . . . The constitutional inhibition of legislation on the subject of religion has a double aspect.   On the one hand, it forestalls compulsion by law of the acceptance of any creed or the practice of any form of worship.   Freedom of conscience and freedom to adhere to such religious organization or form of worship as the individual may choose cannot be restricted by law.   On the other hand, it safeguards the free exercise of the chosen form of religion.   Thus the Amendment embraces two concepts,— freedom to believe and freedom to act.   The first is absolute but, in the nature of things, the second cannot be.   Conduct remains subject to regulation for the protection of society.   The freedom to act must have appropriate definition to preserve the enforcement of that protection.   In every case the power to regulate must be so exercised as not, in attaining a permissible end, unduly to infringe the protected freedom.   No one would contest the proposition that a State may not, by statute, wholly deny the right to preach or to disseminate religious views.   Plainly such a previous and absolute restraint would violate the terms of the guarantee.   It is equally clear that a State may by general and non-discriminatory legislation regulate the times, the places, and the manner of soliciting upon its streets, and of holding meetings thereon; and may in other respects safeguard the peace, good order and comfort of the community, without unconstitutionally invading the liberties protected by the Fourteenth Amendment.   The appellants are right in their insistence that the Act in question is not such a regulation.   If a certificate is procured, solicitation is permitted without restraint but, in the absence of a certificate, solicitation is altogether prohibited." [a]

McDANIEL v. PATY

435 U.S. 618, 98 S.Ct. 1322, 55 L.Ed.2d 593 (1978).

Mr. Chief Justice Burger announced the judgment of the Court and delivered an opinion in which Mr. Justice Powell, Mr. Justice Rehnquist, and Mr. Justice Stevens joined.

The question presented by this appeal is whether a Tennessee statute barring "Ministers of the Gospel, or priest[s] of any denomination whatever" from serving as delegates to the State's limited constitutional convention deprived appellant McDaniel, an ordained minister, of the right to the free exercise of religion guaranteed by the First Amendment and made applicable to the States by the Fourteenth Amendment.   The First Amendment forbids all laws "prohibiting the free exercise" of religion.

I.

In its first constitution, in 1796, Tennessee disqualified ministers from serving as legislators.[1]   That disqualifying provision has continued unchanged since its adoption; it is now Art. 9, § 1 of the State Constitution.   The state

---

[a] The *Cantwell* case was decided only two weeks before the *Gobitis* case, supra.

[1] "Whereas Ministers of the Gospel are by their profession, dedicated to God and the care of Souls, and ought not to be diverted from the great duties of their functions; therefore, no Ministers of the Gospel, or priest of any denomination whatever, shall be eligible to a seat in either House of the Legislature." Tenn.Const. of 1796, Art. VIII, § 1.

legislature applied this provision to candidates for delegate to the State's 1977 limited constitutional convention when it enacted ch. 848, § 4 of the 1976 Tenn.Pub.Acts: "Any citizen of the state who can qualify for membership in the House of Representatives of the General Assembly may become a candidate for delegate to the convention. . . ."

McDaniel, an ordained minister of a Baptist Church in Chattanooga, Tenn., filed as a candidate for delegate to the constitutional convention. An opposing candidate, appellee Selma Cash Paty, sued in the Chancery Court for a declaratory judgment that McDaniel was disqualified to serve as a delegate and for a judgment striking his name from the ballot. Chancellor Franks of the Chancery Court held that § 4 of ch. 848 violated the First and Fourteenth Amendments to the Federal Constitution and declared McDaniel eligible for the office of delegate. Accordingly, McDaniel's name remained on the ballot and in the ensuing election he was elected by a vote almost equal to that of three opposing candidates.

After the election, the Tennessee Supreme Court reversed the Chancery Court, holding that the disqualification of clergy imposed no burden upon "religious belief" and restricted "religious action . . . [only] in the law making process of government—where religious action is absolutely prohibited by the establishment clause . . . ." The state interest in preventing the establishment of religion and in avoiding the divisiveness and tendency to channel political activity along religious lines, resulting from clergy participation in political affairs, were deemed by that court sufficiently weighty to justify the disqualification, notwithstanding the guarantee of the Free Exercise Clause.

We noted probable jurisdiction.

[The Court reviewed the history of exclusion of clergy from public office.]

Today Tennessee remains the only State excluding ministers from certain public offices.

The essence of this aspect of our national history is that in all but a few States the selection or rejection of clergymen for public office soon came to be viewed as something safely left to the good sense and desires of the people.

B.

. . .

. . . [T]he right to the free exercise of religion unquestionably encompasses the right to preach, proselyte, and perform other similar religious functions, or, in other words, to be a minister of the type McDaniel was found to be. Tennessee also acknowledges the right of its adult citizens generally to seek and hold office as legislators or delegates to the state constitutional convention. Yet under the clergy-disqualification provision, McDaniel cannot exercise both rights simultaneously because the State has conditioned the exercise of one on the surrender of the other. . . .

If the Tennessee disqualification provision were viewed as depriving the clergy of a civil right solely because of their religious beliefs, our inquiry would be at an end. The Free Exercise Clause categorically forbids government from regulating, prohibiting or rewarding religious beliefs as such. In Torcaso v. Watkins, 367 U.S. 488 (1961), the Court reviewed the Maryland constitutional requirement that all holders of "any office of profit or trust in this State" declare their belief in the existence of God. In striking down the Maryland requirement, the Court did not evaluate the interests assertedly justifying it but rather held that it violated freedom of religious belief.

In our view, however, *Torcaso* does not govern. By its terms, the Tennessee disqualification operates against McDaniel because of his *status* as a "minister" or "priest." The meaning of those words is, of course, a question of state law.

And although the question has not been examined extensively in state law sources, such authority as is available indicates that ministerial status is defined in terms of conduct and activity rather than in terms of belief. Because the Tennessee disqualification is directed primarily at status, acts and conduct it is unlike the requirement in *Torcaso,* which focused on *belief.* Hence, the Free Exercise Clause's absolute prohibition of infringements on the "freedom to believe" is inapposite here.

This does not mean, of course, that the disqualification escapes judicial scrutiny or that McDaniel's activity does not enjoy significant First Amendment protection. The Court recently declared in Wisconsin v. Yoder, 406 U.S. 205 at 215 (1972):

> "The essence of all that has been said and written on the subject is that only those interests of the highest order and those not otherwise served can overbalance legitimate claims to the free exercise of religion."

Tennessee asserts that its interest in preventing the establishment of a state religion is consistent with the Establishment Clause and thus of the highest order. . . . Tennessee has failed to demonstrate that its views of the dangers of clergy participation in the political process have not lost whatever validity they may once have enjoyed. The essence of the rationale underlying the Tennessee restriction on ministers is that if elected to public office they will necessarily exercise their powers and influence to promote the interests of one sect or thwart the interests of another, thus pitting one against the others, contrary to the antiestablishment principle with its command of neutrality. However widely that view may have been held in the 18th century by many, including enlightened statesmen of that day, the American experience provides no persuasive support for the fear that clergymen in public office will be less careful of antiestablishment interests or less faithful to their oaths of civil office than their unordained counterparts.

We hold that § 4 of ch. 848 violates McDaniel's First Amendment right to the free exercise of his religion made applicable to the States by the Fourteenth Amendment. Accordingly, the judgment of the Tennessee Supreme Court is reversed and the case is remanded to that court for further proceedings not inconsistent with this opinion.

Reversed and remanded.

Mr. Justice Blackmun took no part in the consideration or decision of this case.

Mr. Justice Brennan, with whom Mr. Justice Marshall joins, concurring in the judgment.

I would hold that § 4 of the legislative call to the Tennessee constitutional convention, to the extent that it incorporates Art. 9, § 1, of the Tennessee Constitution, violates both the Free Exercise and Establishment Clauses of the First Amendment as applied to the States through the Fourteenth Amendment. I therefore concur in the reversal of the judgment of the Tennessee Supreme Court.

I.

. . .

The characterization of the exclusion as one burdening appellant's "career or calling" and not religious belief cannot withstand analysis. Clearly freedom of belief protected by the Free Exercise Clause embraces freedom to profess or practice that belief, even including doing so to earn a livelihood. One's religious belief surely does not cease to enjoy the protection of the First Amendment when held with such depth of sincerity as to impel one to join the ministry.

Whether or not the provision discriminates among religions . . . , it establishes a religious classification—involvement in protected religious activity—governing the eligibility for office which I believe is absolutely prohibited. The provision imposes a unique disability upon those who exhibit a defined level of intensity of involvement in protected religious activity. Such a classification as much imposes a test for office based on religious conviction as one based on denominational preference. A law which limits political participation to those who eschew prayer, public worship, or the ministry as much establishes a religious test as one which disqualifies Catholics, or Jews, or Protestants. . . .

. . .

The plurality recognizes that *Torcaso* held "categorically prohibit[ed]," a provision disqualifying from political office on the basis of religious belief, but draws what I respectfully suggest is a sophistic distinction between that holding and Tennessee's disqualification provision. The purpose of the Tennessee provision is not to regulate activities associated with a ministry, such as dangerous snake-handling or human sacrifice, which the State validly could prohibit, but to bar from political office persons regarded as deeply committed to religious participation because of that participation—participation itself not regarded as harmful by the State and which therefore must be conceded to be protected. . . .

II.

. . .

The State's goal of preventing sectarian bickering and strife may not be accomplished by regulating religious speech and political association. The Establishment Clause does not license government to treat religion and those who teach or practice it, simply by virtue of their status as such, as subversive of American ideals and therefore subject to unique disabilities. . . .

Mr. Justice Stewart, concurring in the judgment.

Like Mr. Justice Brennan, I believe that Torcaso v. Watkins, 367 U.S. 488, controls this case. . . .

Mr. Justice White, concurring in the judgment.

While I share the view of my Brothers that Tennessee's disqualification of ministers from serving as delegates to the State's constitutional convention is constitutionally impermissible, I disagree as to the basis for this invalidity. Rather than relying on the Free Exercise Clause, as do the other Members of the Court, I would hold ch. 848, § 4 of the 1976 Tenn.Pub. Acts unconstitutional under the Equal Protection Clause of the Fourteenth Amendment.

The plurality states that § 4 "has encroached upon McDaniel's right to the free exercise of religion," but fails to explain in what way McDaniel has been deterred in the observance of his religious beliefs. Certainly he has not felt compelled to abandon the ministry as a result of the challenged statute, nor has he been required to disavow any of his religious beliefs. Because I am not persuaded that the Tennessee statute in any way interferes with McDaniel's ability to exercise his religion as he desires, I would not rest the decision on the Free Exercise Clause but instead would turn to McDaniel's argument that the statute denies him equal protection of the laws.

. . .

B. REGULATION OF CONDUCT COMPELLED BY RELIGIOUS BELIEF

Introduction. As the opinions in McDaniel v. Paty, supra, demonstrate, the Court has abandoned its earlier, simple proposition that the free exercise clause protects only religious belief and expression. The cases that have dealt with the application of the free exercise clause to conduct compelled by religious belief have, however, raised three new, and difficult, problems. First is the necessity to resolve the obvious tension with the establishment clause if the free exercise clause is interpreted to require government to make an exception for those with religious objections to a law but not for those with other forms of objection. Second, if religious scruples provide a constitutional defense to government obligations in some cases, but not others, how is the judiciary to evaluate the competing demands of God and Caesar? Do the Court's decisions provide guidance beyond their precise facts? Third, if religious beliefs are given a special status distinct from other ideological views, how is one to distinguish religious belief from other forms of belief?

THE SUNDAY CLOSING DECISIONS

For a number of years a serious question had existed regarding the constitutionality of statutes in various states requiring a large number of businesses to remain closed on Sunday while exempting from this requirement certain kinds of businesses such as the sale of drugs or gasoline, the furnishing of amusement and the sale of refreshments at or near places of amusement. On May 29, 1961, the Supreme Court decided four cases involving the application of such statutes in Maryland, Pennsylvania, and Massachusetts. In two of the cases, McGowan v. Maryland, 366 U.S. 420 (1961), arising in Maryland, and Two Guys from Harrison-Allentown v. McGinley, 366 U.S. 582 (1961), arising in Pennsylvania, the parties complaining of the legislation proved only the economic injury resulting from being compelled to close their business on Sunday and did not show that because of religious convictions they also closed their business on another day of the week. The other two cases, Braunfeld v. Brown, 366 U.S. 599 (1961), also from Pennsylvania, and Gallagher v. Crown Kosher Super Market, 366 U.S. 617 (1961) from Massachusetts, involved Orthodox Jews who complained that because the tenets of their religion prevented them from doing business on Saturday, Sunday closing subjected them to a special burden not imposed on persons of other faiths. These cases as a group raised issues of equal protection of the laws, religious liberty and establishment of religion.

In the *McGowan* case, the Court held that Sunday closing laws did not violate the establishment clause. The Court reviewed the history of Sunday closing laws and concluded: "In the light of the evolution of our Sunday closing Laws through the centuries, and of their more or less recent emphasis upon secular considerations, it is not difficult to discern that as presently written and administered, most of them, at least, are of a secular rather than of a religious character, and that presently they bear no relationship to establishment of religion as those words are used in the Constitution of the United States. . . . To say that the States cannot prescribe Sunday as a day of rest for these [secular] purposes solely because centuries ago such laws had their genesis in religion would give a constitutional interpretation of hostility to the public welfare rather than one of mere separation of church and state." Similar disposition was made of the *Two Guys* case.

In the *Braunfeld* case, the appellants were Orthodox Jewish merchants in Philadelphia who engaged in the retail sale of clothing and home furnishings. They alleged that Sunday closing would impair their ability to earn a livelihood and would render at least one of them unable to continue his business thereby resulting in a loss of capital; they contended that the Sunday closing legislation prohibited the free exercise of their religion because they would lose substantial business to their non-Sabbatarian competitors if they continued their Sabbath observance and if they did not they would be forced to give up a basic tenet of their religious faith. Similar contentions were made in the *Crown Kosher* case which involved a super market in Springfield, Massachusetts. In these cases the Chief Justice wrote the leading opinion but spoke only for himself and Justices Black, Clark, and Whittaker; Justices Frankfurter and Harlan concurred separately and Justices Brennan, Stewart, and Douglas dissented.

In his *Braunfeld* opinion the Chief Justice emphasized the distinction between freedom to believe and worship, on the one hand, and freedom to act, on the other. After referring to Reynolds v. United States, 98 U.S. 145 and West Virginia State Board of Education v. Barnette, 319 U.S. 624 (the flag salute case), he continued:

"Thus, in Reynolds v. United States, this Court upheld the polygamy conviction of a member of the Mormon faith despite the fact that an accepted doctrine of his church then imposed upon its male members the *duty* to practice polygamy. And, in Prince v. Commonwealth of Massachusetts, 321 U.S. 158, this Court upheld a statute making it a crime for a girl under eighteen years of age to sell any newspapers, periodicals or merchandise in public places despite the fact that a child of the Jehovah's Witnesses faith believed that it was her religious *duty* to perform this work.

"It is to be noted that, in the two cases just mentioned, the religious practices themselves conflicted with the public interest. In such cases, to make accommodation between the religious action and an exercise of state authority is a particularly delicate task, id., 321 U.S. at page 165, because resolution in favor of the State results in the choice to the individual of either abandoning his religious principle or facing criminal prosecution.

"But, again, this is not the case before us because the statute at bar does not make unlawful any religious practices of appellants; the Sunday law simply regulates a secular activity and, as applied to appellants, operates so as to make the practice of their religious beliefs more expensive. Furthermore, the law's effect does not inconvenience all members of the Orthodox Jewish faith but only those who believe it necessary to work on Sunday. And even these are not faced with as serious a choice as forsaking their religious practices or subjecting themselves to criminal prosecution. Fully recognizing that the alternatives open to appellants and others similarly situated— retaining their present occupations and incurring economic disadvantage or engaging in some other commercial activity which does not call for either Saturday or Sunday labor—may well result in some financial sacrifice in order to observe their religious beliefs, still the option is wholly different than when the legislation attempts to make a religious practice itself unlawful.

"To strike down, without the most critical scrutiny, legislation which imposes only an indirect burden on the exercise of religion, i.e., legislation which does not make unlawful the religious practice itself, would radically restrict the operating latitude of the legislature. Statutes which tax income and limit the amount which may be deducted for religious contributions impose an indirect economic burden on the observance of the religion of the citizen whose religion requires him to donate a greater amount to his church; statutes which require the courts to be closed on Saturday and Sunday impose a similar indirect burden on the observance of the religion of the trial lawyer whose religion requires him to rest on a weekday. The list of legislation of this nature is nearly limitless."

Appellants contended that their religious practice could be protected while the secular purposes of the state were achieved if the legislation excepted from its Sunday closing ban those persons who, because of their religious convictions, observed a day of rest other than Sunday. To this the Chief Justice replied:

"A number of States provide such an exemption, and this may well be the wiser solution to the problem. But our concern is not with the wisdom of legislation but with its constitutional limitation. Thus, reason and experience teach that to permit the exemption might well undermine the State's goal of providing a day that, as best possible, eliminates the atmosphere of commercial noise and activity. Although not dispositive of the issue, enforcement problems would be more difficult since there would be two or more days to police rather than one and it would be more difficult to observe whether violations were occurring.

"Additional problems might also be presented by a regulation of this sort. To allow only people who rest on a day other than Sunday to keep their businesses open on that day might well provide these people with an economic advantage over their competitors who must remain closed on that day; this might cause the Sunday-observers to complain that their religions are being discriminated against. With this competitive advantage existing, there could well be the temptation for some, in order to keep their businesses open on Sunday, to assert that they have religious convictions which compel them to close their businesses on what had formerly been their least profitable day. This might make necessary a state-conducted inquiry into the sincerity of the individual's religious beliefs, a practice which a State might believe would itself run afoul of the spirit of constitutionally protected religious guarantees. Finally, in order to keep the disruption of the day at a minimum, exempted employers would probably have to hire employees who themselves qualified for the exemption because of their own religious beliefs, a practice which a State might feel to be opposed to its general policy prohibiting religious discrimination in hiring. For all of these reasons, we cannot say that the Pennsylvania statute before us is invalid, either on its face or as applied."

Justices Brennan and Stewart dissented in *Braunfeld* and *Crown Kosher* on the ground that the Pennsylvania and Massachusetts statutes, as applied to Orthodox Jewish persons who for conscientious reasons did no business on Saturday, unconstitutionally interfered with the free exercise of their religion. In his *Braunfeld* opinion Justice Brennan said:

"What, then, is the compelling state interest which impels the Commonwealth of Pennsylvania to impede appellants' freedom of worship? . . . It is not even the interest in seeing that everyone rests one day a week, for appellants' religion requires that they take such a rest. It is the mere convenience of having everyone rest on the same day. It is to defend this interest that the Court holds that a State need not follow the alternative route of granting an exemption for those who in good faith observe a day of rest other than Sunday.

. . .

"In fine, the Court, in my view, has exalted administrative convenience to a constitutional level high enough to justify making one religion economically disadvantageous. . . ."

SHERBERT v. VERNER

374 U.S. 398, 83 S.Ct. 1790, 10 L.Ed.2d 965 (1963).

Mr. Justice Brennan delivered the opinion of the Court.

Appellant, a member of the Seventh-day Adventist Church was discharged by her South Carolina employer because she would not work on Saturday, the Sabbath Day of her faith. When she was unable to obtain other employment because from conscientious scruples she would not take Saturday work, she filed a claim for unemployment compensation benefits under the South Carolina Unemployment Compensation Act. . . . The appellee Employment Security Commission, in administrative proceedings under the statute, found that appellant's restriction upon her availability for Saturday work brought her within the provision disqualifying for benefits insured workers who fail, without good cause, to accept "suitable work when offered . . . by the employment office or the employer . . . ." The Commission's finding was sustained . . . by the South Carolina Supreme Court, ...[4] . . . .

II.

We turn first to the question whether the disqualification for benefits imposes any burden on the free exercise of appellant's religion. We think it is clear that it does. In a sense the consequences of such a disqualification to religious principles and practices may be only an indirect result of welfare legislation within the State's general competence to enact; it is true that no criminal sanctions directly compel appellant to work a six-day week. But this is only the beginning, not the end, of our inquiry. For "[i]f the purpose or effect of a law is to impede the observance of one or all religions or is to discriminate invidiously between religions, that law is constitutionally invalid even though the burden may be characterized as being only indirect." Braunfeld v. Brown [366 U.S.] at 607. Here not only is it apparent that appellant's declared ineligibility for benefits derives solely from the practice of her religion, but the pressure upon her to forego that practice is unmistakable. The ruling forces her to choose between following the precepts of her religion and forfeiting benefits, on the one hand, and abandoning one of the precepts of her religion in order to accept work, on the other hand. Governmental imposition of such a choice puts the same kind of burden upon the free exercise of religion as would a fine imposed against appellant for her Saturday worship.

Nor may the South Carolina court's construction of the statute be saved from constitutional infirmity on the ground that unemployment compensation benefits are not appellant's "right" but merely a "privilege." It is too late in the day to

---

[4] It has been suggested that appellant is not within the class entitled to benefits under the South Carolina statute because her unemployment did not result from discharge or layoff due to lack of work. It is true that unavailability for work for some personal reasons not having to do with matters of conscience or religion has been held to be a basis of disqualification for benefits. But appellant claims that the Free Exercise Clause prevents the State from basing the denial of benefits upon the "personal reason" she gives for not working on Saturday. Where the consequence of disqualification so directly affects First Amendment rights, surely we should not conclude that every "personal reason" is a basis for disqualification in the absence of explicit language to that effect in the statute or decisions of the South Carolina Supreme Court. Nothing we have found in the statute or in the cited decisions, and certainly nothing in the South Carolina Court's opinion in this case so construes the statute. Indeed, the contrary seems to have been that court's basic assumption, for if the eligibility provisions were thus limited, it would have been unnecessary for the court to have decided appellant's constitutional challenge to the application of the statute under the Free Exercise Clause.

Likewise, the decision of the State Supreme Court does not rest upon a finding that appellant was disqualified for benefits because she had been "discharged for misconduct"—by reason of her Saturday absences—within the meaning of § 68–114(2). That ground was not adopted by the South Carolina Supreme Court, and the appellees do not urge in this Court that the disqualification rests upon that ground.

doubt that the liberties of religion and expression may be infringed by the denial of or placing of conditions upon a benefit or privilege. . . . [T]o condition the availability of benefits upon this appellant's willingness to violate a cardinal principle of her religious faith effectively penalizes the free exercise of her constitutional liberties.

Significantly South Carolina expressly saves the Sunday worshipper from having to make the kind of choice which we here hold infringes the Sabbatarian's religious liberty. When in times of "national emergency" the textile plants are authorized by the State Commission of Labor to operate on Sunday, "no employee shall be required to work on Sunday . . . who is conscientiously opposed to Sunday work . . .." The unconstitutionality of the disqualification of the Sabbatarian is thus compounded by the religious discrimination which South Carolina's general statutory scheme necessarily effects.

III.

We must next consider whether some compelling state interest enforced in the eligibility provisions of the South Carolina statute justifies the substantial infringement of appellant's First Amendment right. It is basic that no showing merely of a rational relationship to some colorable state interest would suffice; in this highly sensitive constitutional area, "[o]nly the gravest abuses, endangering paramount interests, give occasion for permissible limitation," Thomas v. Collins, 323 U.S. 516, 530. No such abuse or danger has been advanced in the present case. The appellees suggest no more than a possibility that the filing of fraudulent claims by unscrupulous claimants feigning religious objections to Saturday work might not only dilute the unemployment compensation fund but also hinder the scheduling by employers of necessary Saturday work. But that possibility is not apposite here because no such objection appears to have been made before the South Carolina Supreme Court, and we are unwilling to assess the importance of an asserted state interest without the views of the state court. Nor, if the contention had been made below, would the record appear to sustain it; there is no proof whatever to warrant such fears of malingering or deceit as those which the respondents now advance. Even if consideration of such evidence is not foreclosed by the prohibition against judicial inquiry into the truth or falsity of religious beliefs, United States v. Ballard, 322 U.S. 78—a question as to which we intimate no view since it is not before us—it is highly doubtful whether such evidence would be sufficient to warrant a substantial infringement of religious liberties. For even if the possibility of spurious claims did threaten to dilute the fund and disrupt the scheduling of work, it would plainly be incumbent upon the appellees to demonstrate that no alternative forms of regulation would combat such abuses without infringing First Amendment rights.

In these respects, then, the state interest asserted in the present case is wholly dissimilar to the interests which were found to justify the less direct burden upon religious practices in Braunfeld v. Brown, supra. The Court recognized that the Sunday closing law which that decision sustained undoubtedly served "to make the practice of [the Orthodox Jewish merchants'] . . . religious beliefs more expensive," 366 U.S., at 605. But the statute was nevertheless saved by a countervailing factor which finds no equivalent in the instant case—a strong state interest in providing one uniform day of rest for all workers. That secular objective could be achieved, the Court found, only by declaring Sunday to be that day of rest. Requiring exemptions for Sabbatarians, while theoretically possible, appeared to present an administrative problem of such magnitude, or to afford the exempted class so great a competitive advantage, that such a requirement would have rendered the entire statutory scheme unworkable. In the present case no such justifications underlie the determination of the state court that appellant's religion makes her ineligible to receive benefits.

IV.

In holding as we do, plainly we are not fostering the "establishment" of the Seventh-day Adventist religion in South Carolina, for the extension of unemployment benefits to Sabbatarians in common with Sunday worshippers reflects nothing more than the governmental obligation of neutrality in the face of religious differences, and does not represent that involvement of religious with secular institutions which it is the object of the Establishment Clause to forestall. See School District of Abington Township v. Schempp, ante, p. 203. Nor does the recognition of the appellant's right to unemployment benefits under the state statute serve to abridge any other person's religious liberties. Nor do we, by our decision today, declare the existence of a constitutional right to unemployment benefits on the part of all persons whose religious convictions are the cause of their unemployment. This is not a case in which an employee's religious convictions serve to make him a nonproductive member of society. Finally, nothing we say today constrains the States to adopt any particular form or scheme of unemployment compensation. Our holding today is only that South Carolina may not constitutionally apply the eligibility provisions so as to constrain a worker to abandon his religious convictions respecting the day of rest. . . .

. . . .

The judgment of the South Carolina Supreme Court is reversed and the case is remanded for further proceedings not inconsistent with this opinion.

Mr. Justice Stewart, concurring in the result.

. . . This case represents a double-barreled dilemma, which in all candor I think the Court's opinion has not succeeded in papering over. The dilemma ought to be resolved.

. . . .

. . . [T]he Establishment Clause as construed by this Court not only *permits* but affirmatively *requires* South Carolina equally to deny the appellant's claim for unemployment compensation when her refusal to work on Saturdays is based upon her religious creed. . . . In the words of the Court in Engel v. Vitale, 370 U.S., at 431, . . . the Establishment Clause forbids the "financial support of government" to be "placed behind a particular religious belief."

To require South Carolina to so administer its laws as to pay public money to the appellant under the circumstances of this case is thus clearly to require the State to violate the Establishment Clause as construed by this Court. This poses no problem for me, because I think the Court's mechanistic concept of the Establishment Clause is historically unsound and constitutionally wrong. . . .

. . . With all respect, I think it is the Court's duty to face up to the dilemma posed by the conflict between the Free Exercise Clause of the Constitution and the Establishment Clause as interpreted by the Court. It is a duty, I submit, which we owe to the people, the States, and the Nation, and a duty which we owe to ourselves. . . .

My second difference with the Court's opinion is that I cannot agree that today's decision can stand consistently with Braunfeld v. Brown, supra. The Court says that there was a "less direct burden upon religious practices" in that case than in this. With all respect, I think the Court is mistaken, simply as a matter of fact. The *Braunfeld* case involved a state *criminal* statute. . . .

The impact upon the appellant's religious freedom in the present case is considerably less onerous. We deal here not with a criminal statute, but with the particularized administration of South Carolina's Unemployment Compensation Act. Even upon the unlikely assumption that the appellant could not find suitable non-Saturday employment, the appellant at the worst would be denied a maximum of 22 weeks of compensation payments. I agree with the Court that the possibility of that denial is enough to infringe upon the appellant's constitutional right to the free exercise of her religion. But it is clear to me that in order to reach this conclusion the Court must explicitly reject the reasoning of Braunfeld v. Brown. I think the *Braunfeld* case was wrongly decided and should be overruled, and accordingly I concur in the result reached by the Court in the case before us.

[A concurring opinion by Douglas, J., is omitted.]

Mr. Justice Harlan, whom Mr. Justice White joins, dissenting.

Today's decision is disturbing both in its rejection of existing precedent and in its implications for the future. The significance of the decision can best be understood after an examination of the state law applied in this case.

South Carolina's Unemployment Compensation Law was enacted in 1936 in response to the grave social and economic problems that arose during the depression of that period. . . . Thus the purpose of the legislature was to tide people over, and to avoid social and economic chaos, during periods when *work was unavailable.* . . .

The South Carolina Supreme Court has uniformly applied this law in conformity with its clearly expressed purpose. It has consistently held that one is not "available for work" if his unemployment has resulted not from the inability of industry to provide a job but rather from personal circumstances, no matter how compelling. The reference to "involuntary unemployment" in the legislative statement of policy, whatever a sociologist, philosopher, or theologian might say, has been interpreted not to embrace such personal circumstances. . . . Thus in no proper sense can it be said that the State discriminated against the appellant on the basis of her religious beliefs or that she was denied benefits *because* she was a Seventh-day Adventist. She was denied benefits just as any other claimant would be denied benefits who was not "available for work" for personal reasons.[1]

. . . What the Court is holding is that if the State chooses to condition unemployment compensation on the applicant's availability for work, it is constitutionally compelled to *carve out an exception*—and to provide benefits—for those whose unavailability is due to their religious convictions.[2] Such a holding has particular significance in two respects.

First, despite the Court's protestations to the contrary, the decision necessarily overrules Braunfeld v. Brown, 366 U.S. 599, which held that it did not

---

[1] I am completely at a loss to understand note 4 of the Court's opinion. Certainly the Court is not basing today's decision on the unsupported supposition that *some* day, the South Carolina Supreme Court may conclude that there is *some personal* reason for unemployment that may not disqualify a claimant for relief. In any event, I submit it is perfectly clear that South Carolina would not compensate persons who became unemployed for *any* personal reason, as distinguished from layoffs or lack of work, since the State Supreme Court's decisions make it plain that such persons would not be regarded as "available for work" within the manifest meaning of the eligibility requirements. Nor can I understand what this Court means when it says that "if the eligibility provisions were thus limited, it would have been unnecessary for the [South Carolina] court to have decided appellant's constitutional challenge . . . .."

[2] The Court does suggest, in a rather startling disclaimer, that its holding is limited in applicability to those whose religious convictions do not make them "nonproductive" members of society, noting that most of the Seventh-day Adventists in the Spartanburg area are employed. But surely this disclaimer cannot be taken seriously, for the Court cannot mean that the case would have come out differently if none of the Seventh-day Adventists in Spartanburg had been gainfully employed, or if the appellant's religion had prevented her from working on Tuesdays instead of Saturdays. Nor can the Court be suggesting that it will make a value judgment in each case as to whether a particular individual's religious convictions prevent him from being "productive." I can think of no more inappropriate function for this Court to perform.

offend the "Free Exercise" Clause of the Constitution for a State to forbid a Sabbatarian to do business on Sunday. The secular purpose of the statute before us today is even clearer than that involved in *Braunfeld.* . . .

Second, the implications of the present decision are far more troublesome than its apparently narrow dimensions would indicate at first glance. The meaning of today's holding, as already noted, is that the State must furnish unemployment benefits to one who is unavailable for work if the unavailability stems from the exercise of religious convictions. The State, in other words, must *single out* for financial assistance those whose behavior is religiously motivated, even though it denies such assistance to others whose identical behavior (in this case, inability to work on Saturdays) is not religiously motivated.

It has been suggested that such singling out of religious conduct for special treatment may violate the constitutional limitations on state action. See Kurland, Of Church and State and The Supreme Court, 29 U. of Chi.L.Rev. 1; cf. Cammarano v. United States, 358 U.S. 498, 515 (concurring opinion). My own view, however, is that at least under the circumstances of this case it would be a permissible accommodation of religion for the State, if it *chose* to do so, to create an exception to its eligibility requirements for persons like the appellant. The constitutional obligation of "neutrality" . . . is not so narrow a channel that the slightest deviation from an absolutely straight course leads to condemnation. There are too many instances in which no such course can be charted, too many areas in which the pervasive activities of the State justify some special provision for religion to prevent it from being submerged by an all-embracing secularism. . . .

. . . Those situations in which the Constitution may require special treatment on account of religion are, in my view, few and far between, and this view is amply supported by the course of constitutional litigation in this area. . . . Such compulsion in the present case is particularly inappropriate in light of the indirect, remote, and insubstantial effect of the decision below on the exercise of appellant's religion and in light of the direct financial assistance to religion that today's decision requires. . . .

For these reasons I respectfully dissent from the opinion and judgment of the Court.

THOMAS v. REVIEW BOARD OF THE INDIANA EMPLOYMENT SECURITY DIVISION, 450 U.S. 707 (1981). Thomas, a Jehovah's Witness, quit his job because of religious opposition to participating in the production of armaments, when his employer transferred him to a department making turrets for military tanks. He was denied unemployment compensation. The Indiana Supreme Court upheld the denial, because the unemployment compensation statute denied compensation to employees "who quit work voluntarily for personal reasons" that were not objectively job-related. Relying on Sherbert v. Verner, the Supreme Court reversed. It was not a relevant distinction that Thomas had quit religiously objectionable work while Sherbert was fired for refusing work. The record contained no evidence that the number of people who refuse work because of religious beliefs was so large that honoring their claims for compensation would create widespread unemployment. Nor was there evidence that honoring such claims would cause prospective employers to make detailed inquiry into applicants' religious beliefs.

The sole dissenter, Justice Rehnquist, argued that Sherbert v. Verner should be overruled. He argued that the Court was inconsistent in requiring monetary aid to religion in free exercise cases such as *Sherbert* and *Thomas,* while prohibiting aid to religion in establishment clause cases where government had not thrown the weight of secular authority behind dissemination of religious tenets. In a footnote, he argued that *Sherbert* was, in any event, distinguishable from *Thomas* because the Indiana statute had been construed to make *every* personal subjective reason for refusing employment a basis for disqualification.

WHEN IS OBJECTION TO WAR RELIGIOUSLY CONSCIENTIOUS? THE SEEGER AND WELSH CASES

Prior to its amendment in 1967, § 6(j) of the Military Service Act exempted from combat training and service anyone "who by reason of religious training and belief, is conscientiously opposed to participation in war in any form. Religious training and belief in this connection means an individual's belief in a relation to a Supreme Being involving duties superior to those arising from any human relation, but does not include essentially political, sociological or philosophical views or a merely personal moral Code." In two decisions the Court construed this language without reaching the First Amendment objections to it.

In three cases decided as United States v. Seeger, 380 U.S. 163 (1965), a unanimous Court (per Clark, J.) sustained the conscientious objection of three draftees. The Government contended that they did not have the requisite belief in a Supreme Being. "We have concluded" said the Court, "that Congress, in using the expression 'Supreme Being' rather than the designation 'God', was merely clarifying the meaning of religious training and belief so as to embrace all religions and to exclude political, sociological, or philosophical views. We believe that under this construction, the test of belief 'in a relation to a Supreme Being' is whether a given belief that is sincere and meaningful occupies a place in the life of its possessor parallel to that filled by the orthodox belief in God of one who clearly qualifies for the exemption. Where such beliefs have parallel positions in the lives of their respective holders we cannot say that one is 'in a relation to a Supreme Being' and the other is not."

In Welsh v. United States, 398 U.S. 333 (1970), conscientious objections were sustained in a situation quite similar to that in *Seeger,* which the Government attempted to distinguish on the ground that Welsh had been more explicit than Seeger in refusing to categorize his views as religious. In rejecting this distinction, Black, J. (joined by Douglas, Brennan and Marshall, JJ.), said: "We certainly do not think that § 6(j)'s exclusion of those persons with 'essentially political, sociological, or philosophical views or a merely personal moral code' should be read to exclude those who hold strong beliefs about our domestic and foreign affairs or even those whose conscientious objection to participation in all wars is founded to a substantial extent upon considerations of public policy. The two groups of registrants that obviously do fall within these exclusions from the exemption are those whose beliefs are not deeply held and those whose objection to war does not rest at all upon moral, ethical, or religious principle but instead rests solely upon considerations of policy, pragmatism, or expediency. In applying § 6(j)'s exclusion of those whose views are 'essentially political, sociological, or philosophical' or of those who have a 'merely personal moral code,' it should be remembered that these exclusions are definitional and do not therefore restrict the category of persons who are conscientious objectors by 'religious training and belief.'"

Harlan, J., concurred in the result on constitutional grounds, disagreeing with the Court's statutory interpretation and acknowledging that he had "made a mistake" in *Seeger.* He now read § 6(j) as "limiting this draft exemption to those opposed to war in general because of theistic beliefs." However, he concluded that it would violate the establishment clause for Congress to "draw a line between theistic or nontheistic religious beliefs on the one hand and secular beliefs on the other."

White, J. (joined by Burger, C.J., and Stewart, J.) dissented with the conclusion: "Whether or not *Seeger* accurately reflected the intent of Congress . . . ., I cannot join today's construction of § 6(j) extending draft exemption to those who disclaim religious objections to war and whose views about war represent a purely personal code arising not from religious training and belief as the statute requires but from readings in philosophy, history, and sociology." And if the establishment clause issue were reached, he would not find the "religious training and belief" requirement unconstitutional.[a]

GILLETTE v. UNITED STATES, 401 U.S. 437 (1971).   The provision of § 6(j) of the Military Selective Service Act restricting the exemption to those "conscientiously opposed to participation in war in any form" was challenged in two cases by persons whose objections were limited to the Viet Nam war rather than war in general.   Gillette defended a prosecution for failure to report for induction on the ground that he viewed the Viet Nam war as "unjust" and that based on "a humanist approach to religion" his personal decision not to serve in an unjust war was guided by fundamental principles of conscience and deeply held views about the purpose and obligation of human existence.   Negre sought judicial review of the failure of the Army to discharge him as a conscientious objector after he received orders to Viet Nam.   In line with religious counseling and numerous religious texts, Negre, a devout Catholic, believed that it was his duty as a faithful Catholic to discriminate between "just" and "unjust" wars and to foreswear participation in the latter.   Both claims were denied below and the Supreme Court affirmed.

Justice Marshall, speaking for the Court, first addressed the argument that the special statutory status accorded to conscientious objection to all war, but not objection to a particular war, constitutes an establishment of religion because it accords benefits to adherents of some religions but not those of other religions. "The question of governmental neutrality is not concluded by the observation that § 6(j) on its face makes no discrimination between religions, for the Establishment Clause forbids subtle departures from neutrality, 'religious gerrymanders,' as well as obvious abuses."   In this case, however, no discrimination was shown since the statute served "a number of valid purposes having nothing to do with a design to foster or favor any sect, religion, or cluster of religions." He then said:

"Naturally the considerations just mentioned are affirmative in character, going to support the existence of an exemption rather than its restriction specifically to persons who object to all war.   The point is that these affirmative purposes are neutral in the sense of the Establishment Clause.   Quite apart from the question whether the Free Exercise Clause might require some sort of exemption, it is hardly impermissible for Congress to attempt to accommodate free exercise values, in line with 'our happy tradition' of 'avoiding unnecessary clashes with the dictates of conscience.'   .   .   .   In the draft area for 30 years the exempting provision has focused on individual conscientious belief, not on sectarian affiliation.   The relevant individual belief is simply objection to all war, not adherence to any extraneous theological viewpoint.   And while the objection must have roots in conscience and personality that are 'religious' in nature, this requirement has never been construed to elevate conventional piety or religiosity of any kind above the imperatives of a personal faith.

[a] See Freeman, *The Misguided Search for the Constitutional Definition of Religion*, 71 George.L. Rev. 1519 (1983).

"In this state of affairs it is impossible to say that § 6(j) intrudes upon 'voluntarism' in religious life, . . . or that the congressional purpose in enacting § 6(j) is to promote or foster those religious organizations that traditionally have taught the duty to abstain from participation in any war. A claimant, seeking judicial protection for his own conscientious beliefs, would be hard put to argue that § 6(j) encourages membership in putatively 'favored' religious organizations, for the painful dilemma of the sincere conscientious objector arises precisely because he feels himself bound in conscience not to compromise his beliefs or affiliations."

Justice Marshall then added that not only are the affirmative purposes behind the exemption neutral and secular "but also that valid neutral reasons exist for limiting the exemption to objectors to all war, and that the section therefore cannot be said to reflect a religious preference." He referred to the government's need for manpower, the difficulty of applying an exemption for claims related to particular wars in a fair and consistent manner, and the danger that such an exemption might open the doors to a general theory of selective disobedience to law and jeopardize the binding quality of democratic decisions. He concluded: "Of course we do not suggest that Congress would have acted irrationally or unreasonably had it decided to exempt those who object to particular wars. Our analysis of the policies of § 6(j) is undertaken in order to determine the existence *vel non* of a neutral, secular justification for the lines Congress has drawn. We find that justifying reasons exist and therefore hold that the Establishment Clause is not violated."

Next he rejected a claim based on the free exercise clause, saying:

"[O]ur holding that § 6(j) comports with the Establishment Clause does not automatically settle the present issue. For despite a general harmony of purpose between the two religious clauses of the First Amendment, the Free Exercise Clause no doubt has a reach of its own. Abington School District v. Schempp, 374 U.S. 203, 222–223 (1963).

"Nonetheless, our analysis of § 6(j) for Establishment Clause purposes has revealed governmental interests of a kind and weight sufficient to justify under the Free Exercise Clause the impact of the conscription laws on those who object to particular wars. . . . The conscription laws, applied to such persons as to others, are not designed to interfere with any religious ritual or practice, and do not work a penalty against any theological position. The incidental burdens felt by persons in petitioners' position are strictly justified by substantial governmental interests that relate directly to the very impacts questioned. And more broadly, of course, there is the Government's interest in procuring the manpower necessary for military purposes, pursuant to the constitutional grant of power to Congress to raise and support armies. Art. I, § 8."

Justice Black concurred in the judgment and Justice Douglas dissented.

WISCONSIN v. YODER

406 U.S. 205, 92 S.Ct. 1526, 32 L.Ed.2d 15 (1972).

[Respondents Yoder, Yutzy and Miller were members of the Amish religious sect and residents of Wisconsin where it was required that children attend school until the age of 16. Because of their religion's tenets, they refused to send their children (ages 14 and 15) to school after completing the eighth grade. They believe that by sending their children to high school they would not only expose themselves to possible censure of their church community, but also endanger their own salvation and that of their children. It was agreed that respondents' religious beliefs were sincere. Those beliefs required members of the community to make their living by farming or closely related activities. High school, and higher education generally, was objected to because the values taught were in marked contrast with Amish values and way of life. Respondents were convicted of violating the Wisconsin compulsory attendance law; the Supreme Court of Wisconsin reversed the conviction, sustaining respondents' claim under the free exercise clause of the first amendment.]

Mr. Chief Justice Burger delivered the opinion of the Court.

.   .   .

The essence of all that has been said and written on the subject is that only those interests of the highest order and those not otherwise served can overbalance legitimate claims to the free exercise of religion. We can accept it as settled, therefore, that however strong the State's interest in universal compulsory education, it is by no means absolute to the exclusion or subordination of all other interests.   .   .   .

We come then to the quality of the claims of the respondents concerning the alleged encroachment of Wisconsin's compulsory school attendance statute on their rights and the rights of their children to the free exercise of the religious beliefs they and their forebears have adhered to for almost three centuries. In evaluating those claims we must be careful to determine whether the Amish religious faith and their mode of life are, as they claim, inseparable and interdependent. A way of life, however virtuous and admirable, may not be interposed as a barrier to reasonable state regulation of education if it is based on purely secular considerations; to have the protection of the Religion Clauses, the claims must be rooted in religious belief. Although a determination of what is a "religious" belief or practice entitled to constitutional protection may present a most delicate question, the very concept of ordered liberty precludes allowing every person to make his own standards on matters of conduct in which society as a whole has important interests. Thus, if the Amish asserted their claims because of their subjective evaluation and rejection of the contemporary secular values accepted by the majority, much as Thoreau rejected the social values of his time and isolated himself at Walden Pond, their claim would not rest on a religious basis. Thoreau's choice was philosophical and personal rather than religious, and such belief does not rise to the demands of the Religion Clause.

Giving no weight to such secular considerations, however, we see that the record in this case abundantly supports the claim that the traditional way of life of the Amish is not merely a matter of personal preference, but one of deep religious conviction, shared by an organized group, and intimately related to daily living. That the Old Order Amish daily life and religious practice stems from their faith is shown by the fact that it is in response to their literal interpretation of the Biblical injunction from the Epistle of Paul to the Romans, "Be not conformed to this world   .   .   .." This command is fundamental to the Amish faith. Moreover, for the Old Order Amish, religion is not simply a matter of theocratic belief. As the expert witnesses explained, the Old Order Amish religion pervades and determines virtually their entire way of life, regulating it with the detail of the Talmudic diet through the strictly enforced rules of the church community.   .   .   .

So long as compulsory education laws were confined to eight grades of elementary basic education imparted in a nearby rural schoolhouse, with a large proportion of students of the Amish faith, the Old Order Amish had little basis to fear that school attendance would expose their children to the worldly influence they reject. But modern compulsory secondary education in rural areas is now largely carried on in a consolidated school, often remote from the student's home and alien to his daily home life.   .   .   .   The conclusion is inescapable that secondary schooling, by exposing Amish children to worldly influences in terms of attitudes, goals and values contrary to beliefs, and by substantially interfering with the religious development of the Amish child and his integration into the way of life of the Amish faith community at the crucial adolescent state of development, contravenes the basic religious tenets and practice of the Amish faith, both as to the parent and the child. . . .

In sum, the unchallenged testimony of acknowledged experts in education and religious history, almost 300 years of consistent practice, and strong evidence of a sustained faith pervading and regulating respondents' entire mode of life support the claim that enforcement of the State's requirement of compulsory formal education after the eighth grade would gravely endanger if not destroy the free exercise of respondents' religious beliefs.

.   .   .   .

The State advances two primary arguments in support of its system of compulsory education. It notes, as Thomas Jefferson pointed out early in our history, that some degree of education is necessary to prepare citizens to participate effectively and intelligently in our open political system if we are to preserve freedom and independence. Further, education prepares individuals to be self-reliant and self-sufficient participants in society. We accept these propositions.

However, the evidence adduced by the Amish in this case is persuasively to the effect that an additional one or two years of formal high school for Amish children in place of their long established program of informal vocational education would do little to serve those interests. Respondents' experts testified at trial, without challenge, that the value of all education must be assessed in terms of its capacity to prepare the child for life. It is one thing to say that compulsory education for a year or two beyond the eighth grade may be necessary when its goal is the preparation of the child for life in modern society as the majority live, but it is quite another if the goal of education be viewed as the preparation of the child for life in the separated agrarian community that is the keystone of the Amish faith. See Meyer v. Nebraska, 262 U.S., at 400.

.   .   .   .

Whatever their idiosyncrasies as seen by the majority, this record strongly shows that the Amish community has been a highly successful social unit within our society even if apart from the conventional "mainstream." Its members are productive and very law-abiding members of society; they reject public welfare in any of its usual modern forms. The Congress itself recognized their self-sufficiency by authorizing exemption of such groups as the Amish from the obligation to pay social security taxes.

It is neither fair nor correct to suggest that the Amish are opposed to education beyond the eighth grade level. What this record shows is that they are opposed to conventional formal education of the type provided by a certified high school because it comes at the child's crucial adolescent period of religious development. . . .

The State, however, supports its interest in providing an additional one or two years of compulsory high school education to Amish children because of the possibility that some such children will choose to leave the Amish community, and that if this occurs they will be ill-equipped for life. The State argues that if Amish children leave their church they should not be in the position of making their way in the world without the education available in the one or two additional years the State requires. However, on this record, that argument is highly speculative. There is no specific evidence of the loss of Amish adherents by attrition, nor is there any showing that upon leaving the Amish community Amish children, with their practical agricultural training and habits of industry and self-reliance would become burdens on society because of educational shortcomings. . . .

In these terms, Wisconsin's interest in compelling the school attendance of Amish children to age 16 emerges as somewhat less substantial than requiring such attendance for children generally. For, while agricultural employment is not totally outside the legitimate concerns of the child labor laws, employment of children under parental guidance and on the family farm from age 14 to age 16 is an ancient tradition which lies at the periphery of the objectives of such laws. There is no intimation that the Amish employment of their children on family farms is in any way deleterious to their health or that Amish parents exploit children at tender years. Any such inference would be contrary to the record before us. Moreover, employment of Amish children on the family farm does not present the undesirable economic aspects of eliminating jobs which might otherwise be held by adults. . . .

Contrary to the suggestion of the dissenting opinion of Mr. Justice Douglas, our holding today in no degree depends on the assertion of the religious interest of the child as contrasted with that of the parents. It is the parents who are subject to prosecution here for failing to cause their children to attend school, and it is their right of free exercise, not that of their children, that must determine Wisconsin's power to impose criminal penalties on the parent. . . .

Our holding in no way determines the proper resolution of possible competing interests of parents, children, and the State in an appropriate state court proceeding in which the power of the State is asserted on the theory that Amish parents are preventing their minor children from attending high school despite their expressed desires to the contrary. Recognition of the claim of the State in such a proceeding would, of course, call into question traditional concepts of parental control over the religious upbringing and education of their minor children recognized in this Court's past decisions. It is clear that such an intrusion by a State into family decisions in the area of religious training would give rise to grave questions of religious freedom comparable to those raised here and those presented in Pierce v. Society of Sisters. On this record we neither reach nor decide those issues. . . .

For the reasons stated we hold, with the Supreme Court of Wisconsin, that the First and Fourteenth Amendments prevent the State from compelling respondents to cause their children to attend formal high school to age 16. Our disposition of this case, however, in no way alters our recognition of the obvious fact that courts are not school boards or legislatures, and are ill-equipped to determine the "necessity" of discrete aspects of a State's program of compulsory education. . . .

Nothing we hold is intended to undermine the general applicability of the State's compulsory school attendance statutes or to limit the power of the State to promulgate reasonable standards that, while not impairing the free exercise of religion, provide for continuing agricultural vocational education under parental and church guidance by the Old Order Amish or others similarly situated. The States have had a long history of amicable and effective relationships with church-sponsored schools, and there is no basis for assuming that, in this related context, reasonable standards cannot be established concerning the content of the continuing vocational education of Amish children under parental guidance, provided always that state regulations are not inconsistent with what we have said in this opinion.

Affirmed.

Mr. Justice Powell and Mr. Justice Rehnquist took no part in the consideration or decision of this case.

Mr. Justice Stewart, with whom Mr. Justice Brennan joins, concurring.

. . .

This case in no way involves any questions regarding the right of the children of Amish parents to attend public high schools, or any other institutions of learning, if they wish to do so. As the Court points out, there is no suggestion whatever in the record that the religious beliefs of the children here concerned differ in any way from those of their parents. . . .

Mr. Justice White, with whom Mr. Justice Brennan and Mr. Justice Stewart, join, concurring.

Cases such as this one inevitably call for a delicate balancing of important but conflicting interests. I join the opinion and judgment of the Court because I cannot say that the State's interest in requiring two more years of compulsory education in the ninth and tenth grades outweighs the importance of the concededly sincere Amish religious practice to the survival of that sect.

. . .

I join the Court because the sincerity of the Amish religious policy here is uncontested, because the potential adverse impact of the state requirement is great and because the State's valid interest in education has already been largely satisfied by the eight years the children have already spent in school.

Mr. Justice Douglas, dissenting in part.

I agree with the Court that the religious scruples of the Amish are opposed to the education of their children beyond the grade schools, yet I disagree with the Court's conclusion that the matter is within the dispensation of parents alone. The Court's analysis assumes that the only interests at stake in the case are those of the Amish parents on the one hand, and those of the State on the other. The difficulty with this approach is that, despite the Court's claim, the parents are seeking to vindicate not only their own free exercise claims, but also those of their high-school-age children.

. . .

. . . Frieda Yoder has in fact testified that her own religious views are opposed to high-school education. I therefore join the judgment of the Court as to respondent Jonas Yoder. But Frieda Yoder's views may not be those of Vernon Yutzy or Barbara Miller. I must dissent, therefore, as to respondents Adin Yutzy and Wallace Miller as their motion to dismiss also raised the question of their children's religious liberty.

This issue has never been squarely presented before today. Our opinions are full of talk about the power of the parents over the child's education. See Pierce v. Society of Sisters, 268 U.S. 510; Meyer v. Nebraska, 262 U.S. 390. And we have in the past analyzed similar conflicts between parent and State with little regard for the views of the child. See Prince v. Massachusetts, 321 U.S. 158. Recent cases, however, have clearly held that the children themselves have constitutionally protectible interests. . . .

. . .

The views of the two children in question were not canvassed by the Wisconsin courts. The matter should be explicitly reserved so that new hearings can be held on remand of the case. . . .

. . .

UNITED STATES v. LEE, 455 U.S. 252 (1982). A self-employed farmer and carpenter was a member of the Old Order Amish, and employed several other Amish to work on his farm and in his carpentry shop. The Social Security Act exempts members, "of a recognized religious sect . . . conscientiously opposed to acceptance of the benefits of any private or public insurance" for death, disability, old-age or retirement, from payment of social security *self-employment* taxes if those persons waive benefits. 26 U.S.C. § 1402(g). The exemption does not extend, however, to taxes imposed on employees or employers. Distinguishing Wisconsin v. Yoder, the Court concluded that there was no violation of the free exercise clause in requiring appellee to withhold social security taxes from his employees' wages and pay the employer's share of social security taxes. The Court accepted the contention that Amish beliefs opposed both payment of social security taxes and acceptance of benefits, and that there was a conflict between Amish faith and the obligations of the statute. The obligation to pay social security taxes was not, however, different from the obligation to pay any tax, despite the fact that, theoretically, social security taxes were segregated to pay benefits. Thus, any infringement on religious liberty was "essential to accomplish an overriding governmental interest." Chief Justice Burger's opinion concluded that: "[t]he tax system could not function if denominations were allowed to challenge the tax system because tax payments were spent in a manner that violates their religious belief." Concurring, Justice Stevens doubted that the result was consistent with the Court's announced test that religious duty must prevail over enforcement of a valid general law unless enforcement of the law is "essential" to accomplishment of an "overriding" government interest. Justice Stevens also expressed doubt that the Court's holding was consistent with Wisconsin v. Yoder. He concurred in the result because, in his view, "it is the objector who must shoulder the burden of demonstrating that there is a unique reason for allowing him a special exemption."

BOB JONES UNIVERSITY v. UNITED STATES, 461 U.S. 574 (1983). The Court held that private schools that practiced racial discrimination were not "charitable," and thus not entitled to tax exemption under § 501(c)(3) of the Internal Revenue Code of 1954. It was contended that denial of tax exemption violated the free exercise clause, as applied to schools that engage in racial discrimination on the basis of sincerely held religious beliefs. The Court responded that the governmental interest in eradicating racial discrimination in education was compelling, and "substantially outweighs whatever burden denial of tax benefits places on petitioners' exercise of their religious beliefs." In a footnote, the Court emphasized that its decision dealt with schools and not churches or other purely religious organizations, since the governmental interest involved was elimination of racial discrimination in education.

APPENDIX

THE UNITED STATES SUPREME COURT

A CHART

1789–1985 *

The following chart is designed to provide a means of identifying the composition of the Court at any specified date, and thereby to help the student follow the relationship between changes in the personnel and doctrines of the Court.

If the student is concerned with a decision bearing a date which approximates a change in the Court's personnel it will be necessary to consult the footnotes. These notes show, following the dates of birth and death, political affiliation, and home state at the time of appointment, each justice's dates of commission and termination of service. Of course, members do not always participate in decisions rendered during their term of service; the fact of participation must be independently verified. Large X's indicate vacancies.

The information reflected in the chart and footnotes has been gathered primarily from the Dictionary of American Biography,[1] Warren, The Supreme Court in United States History[2] and for dates of commission and termination of service, the Senate Manual, and the Official Reports of the Supreme Court.

* This chart was originally prepared by Paul Gay, and has been updated by the editors.
[1] New York, Scribner, 1928–37. 20 v. Supplement one, 1944; Supplement two, 1959.
[2] Boston, Little Brown, 1922. 3 v.

Washington 1789–1797	Adams 1797–01	Jefferson 1801–1809	Madison 1809–1817

Jay [1] 1789– –1795	[2] Ellsworth [10] 1796–1800	Marshall [13] 1801–	

| Rutledge [2] | Johnson [7] | Paterson [8] 1793–   –1806 | Livingston [15] 1806– |

| Cushing [3] 1789–   –1810 | Story [17] 1811– |

| Wilson [4] 1789–   –1798 | Washington [11] 1798– |

| Blair [5] 1789–   –1796 | Chase [9] 1796–   –1811 | Duvall [18] 1811– |

| Iredell [6] 1790–   –1799 | Moore [12] 1799–   –1804 | Johnson [14] 1804– |

| Todd [16] 1807– |

1. John Jay, 1745–1829. Fed., N. Y. 9–26–1789 to 6–29–1795.

2. John Rutledge, 1739–1800. Fed., S. C. 9–26–1789 to 3–5–1791. Comm. C.J. 7–1–1795 (recess appoint.) pres. August term 1795, rejected by Senate 12–15–1795.

3. William Cushing, 1732–1810. Fed., Mass. 9–27–1789 to 9–13–1810.

4. James Wilson, 1742–1798. Fed., Pa. 9–29–1789 to 8–21–1798.

5. John Blair, 1732–1800. Fed., Va. 9–30–1789 to 1–27–1796.

6. James Iredell, 1751–1799. Fed., N. C. 2–10–1790 to 10–20–1799.

7. Thomas Johnson, 1732–1819. Fed., Md. 11–7–1791 to 2–1–1793.

8. William Paterson, 1745–1806. Fed., N. J. 3–4–1793 to 9–9–1806.

9. Samuel Chase, 1741–1811. Fed., Md. 1–27–1796 to 6–19–1811.

10. Oliver Ellsworth, 1745–1807. Fed., Conn. 3–4–1796 to 12–15–1800.

11. Bushrod Washington, 1762–1829. Fed., Va. 12–20–1798 to 11–26–1829.

12. Alfred Moore, 1755–1810. Fed., N. C. 12–10–1799 to 1–26–1804.

13. John Marshall, 1755–1835. Fed., Va. 1–31–1801 to 7–6–1835.

14. William Johnson, 1771–1834. Rep., S. C. 3–26–1804 to 8–4–1834.

15. [Henry] Brockholst Livingston, 1757–1823. Rep., N. Y. 11–10–1806 to 3–18–1823.

16. Thomas Todd, 1765–1826. Rep., Ky. 3–3–1807 to 2–7–1826.
    Post created by Congress by Act February 24, 1807.

17. Joseph Story, 1779–1845. Rep., Mass. 11–18–1811 to 9–10–1845.

18. Gabriel Duval[1], 1752–1844. Rep., Md. 11–18–1811 to 1–14–1835.

Monroe 1817–1825	J. Q. Adams 1825–29	Jackson 1829–1837	Van Buren 1837–41	Harrison 3/4–4/4 Tyler 1841–45

Marshall			Taney [24]	
		–1835	1836–	

Livingston	Thompson [19]			
–1823	1823–		–1843	X N [29]

Story

Washington	Baldwin [22]			
–1829	1830–		–1844	X

Duvall		Barbour [25]		Daniel [28]
	–1835	1836–	–1841	1841–

Johnson		Wayne [23]		
	–1834	1835–		

Todd	Trim-ble [20] '26–8	McLean [21]		
–1826		1829–		

			Catron [26] 1837–	

			McKinley [27] 1837–	

19. Smith Thompson, 1768–1843. Rep., N. Y. 12–9–1823 to 12–18–1843.

20. Robert Trimble, 1777–1828. Rep., Ky. 5–9–1826 to 8–25–1828.

21. John McLean, 1785–1861. Dem./Rep., Ohio 3–7–1829 to 4–4–1861.

22. Henry Baldwin, 1780–1844. Dem., Pa. 1–6–1830 to 4–21–1844.

23. James Moore Wayne, 1790–1867. Dem., Ga. 1–9–1835 to 7–5–1867.

24. Roger Brooke Taney, 1777–1864. Dem., Md. 3–15–1836 to 10–12–1864.

25. Philip Pendleton Barbour, 1783–1841. Dem., Va. 3–15–1836 to 2–25–1841.

26. John Catron, ca. (1778–86) 1865. Dem., Tenn. 3–8–1837 to 5–30–1865.
    Post created by Congress by Act of March 3, 1837 and abolished by Congress by Act of July 23, 1866.

27. John McKinley, 1780–1852. Dem., Ky./Ala. 9–25–1837 to 7–19–1852.
    Post created by Congress by Act of March 3, 1837.

28. Peter Vivian Daniel, 1784–1860. Dem., Va. 3–3–1841 to 5–31–1860.

Polk 1845–49	Taylor 1849–50 Fillmore 1850–53	Pierce 1853–57	Buchanan 1857–61	Lincoln 1861– 4/15/65	Johnson 1865–69	Grant 1869–
Taney				–1864	**Chase** [39] 1864–	–1873
Nelson[29]						–1872
S **Woodbury** [30] 1845– –1851	**Curtis** [32] 1851– –1857		**Clifford** [34] 1858–			
X **Grier** [31] 1846–						**S** [40] –1870 1870–
Daniel			–1860 X **Miller** [36] 1862–			
Wayne					–1867 X **B** [41] 1870–	
McLean				**Swayne** [35] –1861 1862–		
Catron				–1865 * X		
McKinley –1852 X **Campbell** [33] 1853–		–1861 X **Davis** [37] 1862–				
				Field [38] 1863–		

29. Samuel Nelson, 1792–1873. Dem., N. Y. 2–13–1845 to 11–28–1872.

30. Levi Woodbury, 1789–1851. Dem., N. H. 9–20–1845 to 9–4–1851.

31. Robert Cooper Grier, 1794–1870. Dem., Pa. 8–4–1846 to 1–31–1870.

32. Benjamin Robbins Curtis, 1809–1874. Whig, Mass. 12–20–1851 to 9–30–1857.

33. John Archibald Campbell, 1811–1889. Dem., Ala. 3–22–1853 to 4–30–1861.

34. Nathan Clifford, 1803–1881. Dem., Me. 1–12–1858 to 7–25–1881.

35. Noah Haynes Swayne, 1804–1884. Rep., Ohio 1–24–1862 to 1–24–1881.

36. Samuel Freeman Miller, 1816–1890. Rep., Iowa 7–16–1862 to 10–13–1890.

37. David Davis, 1815–1886. Rep./Dem., Ill. 12–8–1862 to 3–4–1877.

38. Stephen Johnson Field, 1816–1899. Dem., Cal. 3–10–1863 to 12–1–1897.
    Post created by Congress by Act of March 3, 1863.

39. Salmon Portland Chase, 1808–1873. Rep., Ohio 12–6–1864 to 5–7–1873.

40. William Strong, 1808–1895. Dem./Rep., Pa. 2–18–1870 to 12–14–1880.

41. Joseph P. Bradley, 1813–1892. Whig/Rep., N. J. 3–21–1870 to 1–22–1892.

* Post abolished by Congress by Act of July 23, 1866.

Grant –1877	Hayes 1877–81	Garfield 3/4–9/19 Arthur 1881–85	Cleveland 1885–89	Harrison 1889–93	Cleveland 1893–97	McKinley 1897– 9/14/1901
Waite [43] 1874–			–1888	Fuller [50] 1888–		
Hunt [42] 1872–		–1882 Blatchford [48] 1882–		–1893	White [55] 1894–	
Clifford –1881	Gray [47] 1881–					
Strong –1880	Woods [45] 1880–		–1887 Lamar [49] 1888–	–1893 Jackson [54] 1893–5	Peckham [56] 1895–	
Miller				–1890 Brown [52] 1890–		
Bradley				–1892 Shiras [53] 1892–		
Swayne –1881	Matthews [46] 1881–		–1889 Brewer [51] 1889–			
Davis –1877	Harlan [44] 1877–					
Field					–1897 McKenna [57] 1898–	

42. Ward Hunt, 1810–1886. Rep., N. Y. 12–11–1872 to 1–27–1882.
43. Morrison Remick Waite, 1816–1888. Rep., Ohio 1–21–1874 to 3–23–1888.
44. John Marshall Harlan, 1833–1911. Rep., Ky. 11–29–1877 to 10–14–1911.
45. William Burnham Woods, 1824–1887. Rep., Ga. 12–21–1880 to 5–14–1887.
46. [Thomas] Stanley Matthews, 1824–1889. Rep., Ohio 5–12–1881 to 3–22–1889.
47. Horace Gray, 1828–1902. Rep., Mass. 12–20–1881 to 9–15–1902.
48. Samuel Blatchford, 1820–1893. Rep., N. Y. 3–22–1882 to 7–7–1893.
49. Lucius Quintus Cincinnatus Lamar, 1825–1893. Dem., Miss. 1–16–1888 to 1–23–1893.
50. Melville Weston Fuller, 1833–1910. Dem., Ill. 7–20–1888 to 7–4–1910.
51. David Josiah Brewer, 1837–1910. Rep., Kan. 12–18–1889 to 3–28–1910.
52. Henry Billings Brown, 1836–1913. Rep., Mich. 12–29–1890 to 5–28–1906.
53. George Shiras, 1832–1924. Rep., Pa. 7–26–1892 to 2–23–1903.
54. Howell Edmunds Jackson, 1832–1895. Whig/Dem., Tenn. 2–18–1893 to 8–8–1895.
55. Edward Douglass White, 1845–1921. Dem., La. Asso. Just. 2–19–1894 to 12–18–1910; C.J. 12–12–1910 to 5–19–1921.
56. Rufus Wheeler Peckham, 1838–1909, Dem., N. Y. 12–9–1895 to 10–24–1909.
57. Joseph McKenna, 1843–1926. Rep., Cal. 1–21–1898 to 1–5–1925.

T. Roosevelt 1901–1909	Taft 1909–13	Wilson 1913–1921	Harding 1921–8/2/23	Coolidge 1923–1929
Fuller —1910	White[55] 1910—		—1921 Taft[69] 1921–1930	
White —1910	Van Devanter[63] 1910—			
Gray —1902 Holmes[58] 1902—				
Peckham —1909	Lurton[61] 1909— —1914	McReynolds[66] 1914—		
Brown —1906 Moody[60] 1906–1910	Lamar[64] 1910— —1916	Brandeis[67] 1916—		
Shiras —1903 Day[59] 1903—			—1922 Butler[71] 1922—	
Brewer —1910	Hughes[62] 1910— —1916	Clarke[68] 1916— —1922	Sutherland[70] 1922—	
Harlan —1911	Pitney[65] 1912—	—1922 Sanford[72] 1923—		
McKenna —1925				Stone[73] 1925—

55. Edward Douglass White, 1845–1921. Dem., La. Asso. Just. 2–19–1894 to 12–18–1910; C. J. 12–12–1910 to 5–19–1921.

58. Oliver Wendell Holmes, 1841–1935. Rep., Mass. 12–4–1902 to 1–12–1932.

59. William Rufus Day, 1849–1923. Rep., Ohio 2–23–1903 to 11–13–1922.

60. William Henry Moody, 1853–1917. Rep., Mass. 12–12–1906 to 11–20–1910.

61. Horace Harmon Lurton, 1844–1914. Dem., Tenn. 12–20–1909 to 7–12–1914.

62. Charles Evans Hughes, 1862–1948. Rep., N. Y. Asso. Just. 5–2–1910 to 6–10–1916; C. J. 2–13–1930 to 6–30–1941.

63. Willis Van Devanter, 1859–1941. Rep., Wyo. 12–16–1910 to 6–2–1937.

64. Joseph Rucker Lamar, 1857–1916. Dem., Ga. 12–17–1910 to 1–2–1916.

65. Mahlon Pitney, 1858–1924. Rep., N. J. 3–13–1912 to 12–31–1922.

66. James Clark McReynolds, 1862–1946. Dem., Tenn. 8–29–1914 to 1–31–1941.

67. Louis Dembitz Brandeis, 1856–1941. Dem., Mass. 6–1–1916 to 2–13–1939.

68. John Hessin Clarke, 1857–1945. Dem., Ohio 7–24–1916 to 9–18–1922.

69. William Howard Taft, 1857–1930. Rep., Conn. 6–30–1921 to 2–3–1930.

70. George Sutherland, 1862–1942. Rep., Utah 9–5–1922 to 1–17–1938.

71. Pierce Butler, 1866–1939. Dem., Minn. 12–21–1922 to 11–16–1939.

72. Edward Terry Sanford, 1865–1930. Rep., Tenn. 1–29–1923 to 3–8–1930.

73. Harlan Fiske Stone, 1872–1946. Rep., N. Y. Asso. Just. 2–5–1925 to 7–2–1941; C. J. 7–3–1941 to 4–22–1946.

Hoover 1929–33	F. D. Roosevelt 1933–4/12/1945	Truman 1945–1953

T. '30 | **Hughes** [62] 1930– | –1941 | **Stone** [73] 1941– –1946 | **Vinson** [85] 1946– –1953

Van Devanter –1937 | **Black** [76] 1937–

Holmes –1932 | **Cardozo** [75] 1932– –1938 | **Frankfurter** [78] 1939–

McReynolds –1941 | **B.** [81] '41–2 | **Rutledge** [83] 1943– –1949 | **Minton** [87] 1949–

Brandeis –1939 | **Douglas** [79] 1939–

Butler –1939 | **Murphy** [80] 1940– –1949 | **Clark** [86] 1949–

Sutherland –1938 | **Reed** [77] 1938–

S. '30 | **Roberts** [74] 1930– –1945 | **Burton** [84] 1945–

Stone (To C. J.) –1941 | **Jackson** [82] 1941–

62. Charles Evans Hughes, 1862–1948. Rep., N. Y. Asso. Just. 5–2–1910 to 6–10–1916; C. J. 2–13–1930 to 6–30–1941.
73. Harlan Fiske Stone, 1872–1946. Rep., N. Y. Asso. Just. 2–5–1925 to 7–2–1941; C. J. 7–3–1941 to 4–22–1946.
74. Owen Josephus Roberts, 1875–1955. Rep., Pa. 5–20–1930 to 7–31–1945.
75. Benjamin Nathan Cardozo, 1870–1938. Dem., N. Y. 3–2–1932 to 7–9–1938.
76. Hugo Lafayette Black, 1886–1971. Dem., Ala. 8–18–1937 to 9–17–1971.
77. Stanley Forman Reed, 1884–1980. Dem., Ky. 1–27–1938 to 2–25–1957.
78. Felix Frankfurter, 1882–1965. Ind., Mass. 1–20–1939 to 8–28–1962.
79. William Orville Douglas, 1898–1980. Dem., Conn. 4–15–1939 to 11–12–1975.
80. Frank Murphy, 1890–1949. Dem., Mich. 1–18–1940 to 7–19–1949.
81. James Francis Byrnes, 1879–1972. Dem., S. C. 6–25–1941 to 10–3–1942.
82. Robert Houghwout Jackson, 1892–1954. Dem., N. Y. 7–11–1941 to 10–9–1954.
83. Wiley Blount Rutledge, 1894–1949. Dem., Iowa 2–11–1943 to 9–10–1949.
84. Harold Hitz Burton, 1888–1964. Rep., Ohio 9–22–1945 to 10–13–1958.
85. Frederick Moore Vinson, 1890–1953. Dem., Ky. 6–21–1946 to 9–8–1953.
86. Thomas Campbell Clark, 1899–1977. Dem., Texas 8–19–1949 to 6–12–1967.
87. Sherman Minton, 1890–1965. Dem., Ind. 10–5–1949 to 10–15–1956.

[D1784]

Eisenhower 1953–1961	Kennedy 1961–1963	Johnson 1963–1969

Warren [88]
1953–

Black

Frankfurter		**Goldberg** [94]		**Fortas** [95]
	–1962	1962–	–1965	1965–

Minton	**Brennan** [90]
–1956	1956–*

Douglas

Clark		**Marshall** [96]
	–1967	1967–*

Reed	**Whittaker** [91]	**White** [93]
–1957	1957– –1962	1962–*

Burton	**Stewart** [92]
–1958	1958–

J	**Harlan** [89]
'54	1954–

88. Earl Warren, 1891–1974. Rep., Cal. 10–2–1953 to 6–23–1969.
89. John Marshall Harlan, 1899–1971. Rep., N. Y. 3–17–1955 to 9–23–1971.
90. William Joseph Brennan, 1906–. Dem., N. J. 10–15–1956 to –.
91. Charles Evans Whittaker, 1901–1973. Rep., Mo. 3–19–1957 to 4–1–1962.
92. Potter Stewart, 1915–. Rep., Ohio 10–13–1958 to 7–7–1981.
93. Byron R. White, 1917–. Dem., Colo. 4–16–1962 to –.
94. Arthur Joseph Goldberg, 1908–. Dem., Ill. 10–1–1962 to 7–26–65.
95. Abe Fortas, 1910–1982. Dem., Tenn. 10–4–1965 to 5–15–1969.
96. Thurgood Marshall, 1908–. Dem., N. Y. 10–2–1967 to –.

[D1783]

Nixon 1969–1974	Ford 1974–1977	Carter 1977–1981	Reagan 1981–*

Warren –1969	**Burger** [97] 1969–*		
Black –1971	**Powell** [99] 1971–*		
Fortas –1969	**Blackmun** [98] 1970–*		
Brennan			
Douglas –1975	**Stevens** [101] 1975–*		
Marshall			
White			
Stewart		–1981	**O'Connor** [102] 1981–*
Harlan –1971	**Rehnquist** [100] 1971–*		

97. Warren Earl Burger, 1907–. Rep., Va. 6–23–1969 to –.
98. Harry Andrew Blackmun, 1908–. Rep., Minn. 5–14–1970 to –.
99. Lewis Franklin Powell, Jr., 1907–. Rep., Va. 12–9–1971 to –.
100. William Hubbs Rehnquist, 1924–. Rep., Ariz. 12–15–1971 to –.
101. John Paul Stevens, 1920–. Rep., Ill. 12–19–1975 to –.
102. Sandra Day O'Connor, 1930–. Rep., Ariz., 9–25–1981 to –.
* This table represents the composition of the Court to January 20, 1985.

[D1788]

*

INDEX

References are to Pages

ABORTION
Advertising abortions, 1155.
Governmental financing of, 899.
Hyde Amendment, 899.
State regulation of, 585–617.

ABSTENTION, 79–80

ACADEMIC FREEDOM
See Education; Freedom of Association; Religion.

ACADEMIC TENURE, 933, 936

ADMINISTRATIVE REMEDIES
Exhaustion of, 80.

ADVISORY OPINIONS, 87

AFFIRMATIVE ACTION, 766–835

AGE
Classifications based on, 416, 744, 950, 1036.

AIRPLANES
Flight over land as taking, 564.
Property taxes, 369.

ALIENS
Admission to practice law, 693.
Deportation, 495.
   Legislative veto, 451.
Discrimination against, as suspect classification, 690.
Equal protection of the laws, 690–699.
Federal regulation of, 244, 495, 497, 691, 696.
Government employment, 692.
Illegal aliens,
   Right to public education, 920.
Public schools, right to teach in, 693.
Right to work, 692.
State regulation of, 690–699.
Welfare benefits, 690, 696.

AMENDMENTS TO CONSTITUTION
Adoption as judicial questions, 133, 147.
Amendment process, 144, 148.
Bill of Rights, 17–19, 479–483.
Civil War Amendments (13th, 14th, 15th),
   Early interpretations, 483, 960.
   History, 19, 483, 960.
Equal Rights Amendment proposed, 744.
Proposal of, 144.
Ratification, 146.

APPEAL
By state as double jeopardy, 499.
Counsel on, 519, 625.
Discretionary dismissal of, 63.
Filing fees, 625.
Review by, 44, 48, 56, 58.

**APPORTIONMENT, STATE OR LOCAL TAX-
   ES,** 343, 369–371, 372–387

APPORTIONMENT OF VOTERS
   See also Equal Protection; Franchise; Voting.
Congressional districts, 855.
Local government units, 764, 865–869, 1020.
Racial considerations, 764, 1020.
State legislative districts, 133, 764, 844–869.

ARREST
Law governing, 518.

ARTICLES OF CONFEDERATION, 15

ASSEMBLY
See Freedom of Expression.

ASSOCIATION
See Freedom of Association.

ATTORNEYS
Canon of Ethics and First Amendment, 1275.
Enjoining speech of to protect fair trial, 1375.
Regulation of legal profession and first amendment, 1275.

BAIL
Right to under Eighth Amendment, 519.

BANK OF THE UNITED STATES
Constitutionality, 159.
History, 158.
State power to tax, 164.

BANKING
State regulation of, 308.

BIBLE READING IN PUBLIC SCHOOLS
See Religion.

BILL OF ATTAINDER, 477, 544, 1345, 1346
See also Loyalty Tests.

BILL OF RIGHTS
Adoption, reasons for, 17–19, 477, 1050.
Applicability to states, 19, 479, 498–516, 1061.
Colonial charters, 17.
Debates in constitutional convention, 18–19.
Early application of, 477–483, 498–508, 1050–1052.
English background, 17, 1046.
Fourteenth Amendment as incorporation, 498–519, 1061.
Madison's role, 18, 19.
Virginia, 17.

BILLBOARDS
Regulation of, 1200.

BOYCOTT
Of white merchants, 1275.

BRANDEIS BRIEF, 528

BUSING
Integration of schools, to achieve, 673, 680, 684.

CARRIERS, MOTOR
Gross receipts tax, 349.
Net income tax, 351.
State regulation of, 248, 251, 255, 257, 268.

CENSORSHIP
See Freedom of Expression.

CERTIORARI
Review by, 44, 48, 50–59, 65.
Rule of four to grant, 59.

CHARITABLE TRUSTS
Discrimination by, 969, 981, 982.

CHILD LABOR
Commerce power regulation, 190, 204.
Taxing power regulation, 191–192.

CITIZENSHIP
See also Naturalization.
Acquisition, 496–497.
Deprivation, 497.
Privileges of state citizenship, 483, 494, 499, 508.
Residence, distinguished from, 346.

CIVIL RIGHTS ACTS
1866, 20–21, 64, 1004, 1009, 1012–1015.
1870, 65, 1004.
1871, 66, 1004.
1875, 66, 960.
1957, 1006.
1960, 1006.
1964, 211, 214, 1007, 1018.
1965, 1007, 1020.
1968, 1008, 1009.
1970, 1007, 1036.

CIVIL WAR AMENDMENTS
Adoption of, 19, 483.

"CLEAR AND PRESENT DANGER" DOCTRINE
See Freedom of Expression.

COMMERCE
National regulation,
  Admiralty power, 245.
  Agricultural adjustment, 197, 208.
  Child labor, 190, 191–192, 204.
  Coal mining, 195.
  Current of commerce cases, 192.
  Depression and New Deal, 192.
  Early developments, 158–208.
  Fair Labor Standards Act, 204.
  Firearms, 223.
  ICC regulations, origin, 184.
  Insurance, 210.
  Interstate shipment, 181, 190, 204.
  Interstate travel, 214, 216.
  Labor conditions, 190, 193, 195, 201, 203, 204.
  Loan sharks, 217.
  Manufacturing, 183, 186, 201.
  Marshall's view of national power, 159–176.
  Monopolies, 186, 187.
  Navigable waters, 181, 246.
  NLRB jurisdiction, 201, 203.
  NRA program, 193.
  Organized crime, 216.
  Political limits on national power, 221.
  Racial discrimination, 211, 214.
  Railroad rates, 187, 190.
  Railroad safety, 187, 250.
  Roads and canals, 166.
  Taxation as regulation of, 192–193, 223, 340, 341.
  Tenth Amendment as limit, 207, 407, 409.
  Twenty-first amendment as limit, 327.
State regulation,
  Business,
    Conducted by state, 295, 300, 302, 318.
    Entry into state, 308, 314.
  Concurrent vs. exclusive power theories, 168–184, 247.
  Dams on navigable streams, 175.
  Discriminatory burdens, 254, 257, 270, 286.
  Early developments, 158, 168, 175, 176, 178, 181–184.
  Electrical energy, 292.
  Environmental protection legislation, 286, 331.
  Fishing and hunting, 289.
  Foreign corporation, qualification of, 182.
  Gas, 282.
  Highways, 248, 251, 255, 257, 268.
  Insurance companies, 210.
  Interstate travel, 315.
  Licensing power, 248, 250, 283.
  Liquor control, 183, 323–330.
  Marshall's view of state power, 168, 175.
  Milk containers, regulation of, 277.
  Milk regulation, 269, 270, 277, 283.
  Motor carriers, 248, 251, 255, 257.

COMMERCE—Cont'd
National consent to, 178, 183.
Natural resources, 281, 289, 292, 293, 295, 302.
Original package doctrine, 362–364.
Packaging of fruits and vegetables, 274, 281.
Pilot regulations, 178.
Preemption by federal action, 330–344.
Quarantine measures, 268, 269, 289.
Railroad rate regulations, 187, 190.
Railroad safety or convenience, 250, 253.
Ships, 331.
State as market participant, 295, 300, 302, 318.
Timber, regulation of, 302.
Train limits, 253.
Trucks, 251, 255, 257.
Twenty-first Amendment, 323–330.
Underground water, 293.
State taxation, 182, 340–390.
See also Income Taxes, Net, State or Local; Privilege Taxes, State or Local; Sales Taxes, State or Local; Taxes, State or Local.

COMMUNISTS
See Freedom of Association; Freedom of Expression.

COMPACTS, INTERSTATE
Boundary disputes, 434.
Multistate Tax Compact, 372, 434.
Scope and use, 433–434.

CONGRESS
See also Separation of Powers.
Control over Supreme Court jurisdiction, 43–47.
Power to exclude or expel members, 135.
Power to redefine scope of Civil War Amendments, 1020–1044.

CONGRESSIONAL INVESTIGATIONS
See Governmetal Investigations.

CONSTITUTION
Amendments, 9–15.
Ratification, 16.
Text, 2–15.

CONSTITUTIONAL CONVENTION
Bill of Rights, 17–19.
Council of Revision, 23–24.
Proceedings on national power, 150–157.
Virginia plan, 150.

CONSTITUTIONALITY
Judicial notice of underlying facts, 522, 528, 533.
Presumption of,
Bill of Rights, 541.
Economic regulations, 520–543.

CONTRACT CLAUSE
Compared with due process, 543, 550.
Emergencies, as affected by, 543.
Eminent domain, as affected by, 546.

CONTRACT CLAUSE—Cont'd
Executed contracts, as covered, 477, 544.
Federal government not limited, 542.
Grants by states, application to, 477.
Historical background, 543, 550.
Mortgage moratoria, application to, 543, 550.
Obligation of, 550.
Police power, bargaining away, 551.
Private contracts, as affected by, 545, 550, 556, 559.
Remedies, applicability to, 543.
Standard of review, 543, 550, 556.
Tax exemptions, applicability of, 546.

CORPORATIONS, FOREIGN
Discrimination against, by states, 182, 347.
Special taxes on, 347.
State power to exclude, 479.
Taxation, by state, 347.

COUNSEL, RIGHT OF ACCUSED TO
See also Attorneys.
On appeal, 625.
Sixth Amendment and the states, 508, 516, 518.

CRUEL AND UNUSUAL PUNISHMENT
Eighth Amendment as applied to states, 519.

DECLARATORY JUDGMENT
Constitutional litigation, 65, 90, 123.
Contrasted with injunction, 123.

DEFAMATION
See Freedom of Expression; Freedom of the Press.

DEMONSTRATIONS
See Freedom of Expression.

DEPORTATION
Legislative veto, 451.

DISCRIMINATION
See also Equal Protection; State Action.
Affirmative action, 776–835.
Aliens, against, 690–698, 920.
Benign classifications, 776–835.
Charitable trusts, 969, 981, 982, 1028.
Discriminatory advertising and First Amendment, 1363.
Education, 666–689, 763, 781, 786, 911–931, 981, 986, 1012.
Fair housing legislation, constitutionality, 988, 997, 1008, 1009.
Franchise, 764, 772, 843–877, 882, 967, 1031, 1036.
Gender, 708–744, 761, 776–785.
Housing,
Civil Rights Act of 1866, pp. 1004, 1009.
Civil Rights Act of 1968, pp. 1008, 1009.
Restrictive covenants, 974, 979.
Jury selection, 773.
Labor unions, 968.
Legitimacy, based on, 699–708.

DISCRIMINATION—Cont'd

Miscegenation statutes, 653.

National legislation against, see Civil Rights Acts.

Private clubs, 988, 985, 1280.

Public accommodations, 211, 214, 960, 980, 985, 988.

Purpose, relevance of discriminatory impact, 751–775.

Race, based on, 629, 653–689, 751, 758, 763, 764, 768, 772, 773, 815, 1046.

Railroads, 630.

Segregation, 663–689, 763, 786.

Sex, based on, 708–744, 761, 776–785, 1280.

"Sit-in" demonstrations, 980.

Speech, discrimination against, 1170, 1176.

Standard of review, 692, 699, 709, 713, 744, 786, 815.

State taxation discriminating against interstate commerce, 324, 340, 342, 344–349.

Statistical demonstration of, 713, 751, 773, 911.

Suspect classifications,
  Age, 744, 950.
  Alienage, 690–699, 920.
  Legitimacy, 699–708.
  Nationality, 690.
  Race, 629, 653–689, 751, 758, 763, 764, 768, 772, 773, 815, 1046.
  Sex, 708–744, 761, 776–785, 1280.
  Wealth, 625, 648, 750, 836, 876, 877, 883, 895–900.

DOUBLE JEOPARDY, 499, 518

DUE PROCESS OF LAW

Abortion, regulation of, 585–617, 879.

Compelling state interest, standard of review, 589, 619, 836, 877–895, 911, 1294.

Compulsory process, 519.

Confrontation of witnesses, 519.

Contract clause compared, 543, 550.

Counsel, right to, 519, 625.

Cruel and unusual punishment, 519.

Discriminatory regulations, as forbidding, 632, 669, 676, 773.

Early interpretations of, 481, 491, 494, 495, 498–516, 520–535.

Economic regulations,
  General business, 520–542.
  History of application to, 520–523.
  Labor laws, 523–529, 532, 535.
  Liberty of contract, 523–532, 539–540.
  Price regulation, 521, 522, 529, 530, 535.
  Retroactive legislation, 540, 544.
  Standard of review, 640–652, 896.
  State courts, application to, 542.

Eminent domain, 518, 546, 577.

Fair jury, 508, 516.

Fair trial, 495, 502, 508, 518, 519, 535, 1375, 1389, 1398.

Family life and personal autonomy, 577–617, 879.

Fundamental principles of government, 494, 495, 578.

DUE PROCESS OF LAW—Cont'd

Impairment of property values, 518, 559–577.

Jurisdiction, notice and hearing in civil cases, 495, 932–949, 1354–1355.

Jury trial, 508–517, 1375.

Origin in Magna Carta, 17, 481, 520.

Privacy, 577–617, 899.

Procedural restrictions and substantive property interests, 949.

Property regulations, 518, 520–542, 559–577, 933–940.

Reasonable doubt standard, 517.

Retroactive judicial decisions, 35.

Retroactive legislation, 540, 544.

Self-incrimination as, 502, 518.

State institutions, rights of persons detained, 623.

Taxation, state or local, 182, 342–344, 373–390.

EDUCATION

See also Religion.

Books, exclusion from school library, 1212.

Curricular freedom,
  Language studies, 577.
  Teaching of evolution, 1425.

Discrimination, 663–690, 763, 781, 786, 911, 920, 929, 981, 986, 1012, 1482.

Financing of, 911, 920.

Illegal aliens, 929.

Parental rights, 577, 579, 1012, 1413, 1429, 1477, 1481.

Private schools protected, 577, 985, 986, 1012, 1477, 1481.

Procedural rights of teachers, 933, 936.

School newspapers, control over, 1211.

Schools, picketing near, 1180.

Segregated schools, 663–690, 765, 981, 986, 1012.

Student rights,
  Compulsory flag salute, 1271, 1463.
  Wearing of armbands, 1189.

Tenure, 933, 936.

ELECTIONS

See also Apportionment of Voters; Franchise; Voting.

Apportionment of state legislatures, 133, 844–869.

Candidates, qualifications of, 876, 877.

Congressional districting, 855.

Districting of local government units, 865–869.

Districting of state legislatures, 133, 844–855, 865.
  Approval of plan by voters, relevance of, 849.
  Multi-member districts, 764, 854, 1020.

Extraordinary majorities, requirement of, 869.

Federal Election Commission, 464.

Filing fees, 876.

Government employees, restrictions on political activity, 1091, 1331–1343.

Judicial supervision of, 849, 851, 967.

Pay while voting, 542.

ELECTIONS—Cont'd
Political campaign restrictions, 1293–1310.
  Contribution limitations, 1298, 1303, 1310.
  Expenditure limitations, 1298, 1304, 1310.
Public financing, 1210.
Qualifications of voters, federal power over, 870–874, 967.
Racial considerations in districting, 764, 771, 1020.
Referendum, requirement of, 869, 1001.
Residence requirements, durational, 873, 874, 882.
White primary, 967.

ELEVENTH AMENDMENT
In general, 66–78.
Bars federal injunction against pendent state law claims, 66.
Power of Congress to confer jurisdiction, 76–78.
Suits against cities and counties, 75.

EMERGENCIES
As justifying regulations, 544.

EMINENT DOMAIN
Contract clause, as limited by, 546.
Just compensation, 577.
Public use, 571.
Taking, what constitutes, 559–576.

ENCLAVES OF FEDERALLY–OWNED LAND
Federal control, extent of, 240.
Residents of, right to vote in state and local elections, 873.
State law, applicability of, 240.

ENVIRONMENT
State protection legislation, 286, 331, 571.

EQUAL PROTECTION
  See also Discrimination; Education; Elections; Franchise.
Affirmative action, 776–835.
Aliens, as entitled to, 690–699, 920.
Applicability to federal government, 632, 669, 696, 711.
Apportionment of voters,
  Local governments, 764, 865–869.
  Racial considerations, 764, 1020.
  State legislatures,
    Approval of plan by voters, relevance of, 849.
    Federal analogy, 849.
    Multi-member districts, 764, 854, 1020.
Benign classifications, 776–835.
Compelling state interest standard of review, 578, 637, 653, 657, 709, 744, 786, 792, 815, 836, 872, 873, 876, 877, 882, 883, 895, 911, 920, 1170, 1294.
Congressional districting, 895.
Degrees of harm, 635, 638.
Early interpretation, 483, 629–632, 663, 843, 960, 967, 1003.
Economic regulations, 635–652, 896.
  Standard of review, 635–652, 896.

EQUAL PROTECTION—Cont'd
First Amendment, overlap with, 1170, 1176.
Intermediate standard of review, 692, 696, 699, 700, 713, 725, 733, 806, 908, 918.
Power of Congress to redefine scope, 1020–1044.
Purpose, need to show, 751–776.
Qualification of voters, 870–877.
Referendum, requirement of, 869, 1001.
Sex as basis for classification, 708–744, 761, 776, 779, 780, 781, 1280.
Speech, discrimination against, 1170, 1176.
Suspect classifications, 653–835.
  Age, 744, 950.
  Alienage, 690–696.
  Nationality, 690.
  Race, 653–690, 751, 758, 763, 764, 772, 773, 786, 815.
  Sex, 708–744, 761, 776, 779, 780, 781, 1280.
    Draft registration, 733.
    Statutory rape statute, 725.
  Wealth, 625, 648, 750, 836, 876, 877, 883, 895–911, 1294.
Taxation, state or local, 346–348.
Theory of, 640–652, 629–635.

EQUAL RIGHTS AMENDMENT
Ratification of, 146, 744.
Text, 744.

EQUALITY
See Discrimination; Equal Protection; Segregation.

ESTABLISHMENT CLAUSE
See Religion.

EX POST FACTO LAWS, 477, 544

EXECUTIVE AGREEMENTS
See Foreign Affairs; Military Power.

EXECUTIVE POWER
Secrecy, 468, 472, 474.

EXPORTS
  See also Imports.
Gross receipts tax on terminal railroad, 364.

FACTS
Judicial notice of, 522, 528, 534, 585.
Supreme Court review of state findings of, 1183, 1184, 1185.

FAIR LABOR STANDARDS ACT
As applied to state employees, 408.
Federal power to enact, 204.
Wages and hours provisions, validity of, 204.

FAIR PROCEDURE
In civil cases, 495, 1354–1355.

FEDERAL COURTS
Decision of issues of state law, 48–50, 66, 79.
Jurisdiction, 43–144.
Obligation of Congress to create, 36–37.
Three-judge courts, 65.

FEDERAL ELECTION COMMISSION
Appointment of members, 464.

FIFTEENTH AMENDMENT, 19–22, 764, 967
History of, 19–22.

FIRST AMENDMENT
See also Freedom of Association; Freedom of Expression; Freedom of the Press; Religion.
Alien and Sedition Laws, relation to, 1050, 1110, 1111.
Applicability to states, 1050, 1051, 1059, 1110.
"Balancing" test, 1085, 1086.
Central meaning of, 1111.
"Chilling" effect, 1078–1097.
Early history, 1050–1052.
English background, 1046–1050.
Privacy, as protecting, 585, 601, 1012, 1122.
Time, place, and manner regulations, 1170.
World War I cases, 1053–1067.

FOREIGN AFFAIRS
Executive agreements,
    Court-martial jurisdiction, 238.
    Roosevelt-Litvinov agreement, 236, 237, 444.
    Treaty power distinguished, 238, 444.
National power,
    Constitutional provisions, 230.
    Extra-constitutional sources, 231.
Treaties,
    Effect on state power, 234.
    Executive agreements distinguished, 238, 244.
    Inconsistent congressional legislation, 234.
    Supremacy over state law, 237, 238.
    United Nations relations, 239.

FOREIGN COMMERCE
See Commerce.

FOREIGN RELATIONS
See Foreign Affairs.

FOURTEENTH AMENDMENT
See also Due Process of Law; Equal Protection; Privileges and Immunities; State Action.
Early interpretations, 483–495, 663, 843, 960, 961.
Freedom of economic enterprise, early developments, 520–542.
History, 19–22, 520–542.
Incorporation of Bill of Rights, 498–519.
Liberty as protected by, 522–535, 932–950.
Power of Congress to redefine its scope, 1020–1044.

FOURTEENTH AMENDMENT—Cont'd
Privileges and immunities clause, 483, 494, 498, 502, 507, 1016.
Special reference to Negro, 483, 629, 657.
Validity of adoption, 22.

FOURTH AMENDMENT, 518

FRANCHISE
See also Apportionment of Voters; Elections; Equal Protection; Freedom of Association; Voting.
Age qualifications, 843, 1036.
Armed services, members of, 873.
Candidates, qualifications of, 873, 876.
Extraordinary majority, requirement of, 869.
Fifteenth Amendment, as affecting, 486, 766, 843, 967.
Government employees, political activity of, 1091, 1331–1355.
History of restrictions on, 843.
Literacy tests, 870, 1023, 1031, 1036.
Poll taxes, 843, 870.
Property qualifications, 868, 870, 873.
Racial classifications in districting, 764, 1020.
Racial discrimination in voting, 843, 870, 967.
Residence requirements, 873, 874, 882.
Residents of federal enclaves, 873.
Wealth discrimination in voting, 870.
White primary, 967.

FREEDOM OF ASSOCIATION
Anti-Communist legislation,
    Communist Control Act, 1311, 1312, 1313.
    Internal Security Act, 1311.
As limit on power to regulate private conduct under Fourteenth Amendment, 985, 988, 1012, 1275.
Boycott, as protected, 1275.
Constitutional right recognized, 985, 988, 1065, 1074, 1078, 1273–1288.
Demonstrations,
    Boycott, 1275.
    Supreme Court grounds, 1180.
Expressive association, 1280.
Freedom of assembly, 1005, 1179–1189, 1192.
Intimate association, 1280.
Right not to associate, 1289–1293.
Subversive Activities Control Board, 1311, 1312, 1313.
    Ku Klux Klan, 1078.
Subversive associations, 1074, 1078, 1273, 1319, 1320, 1324–1331, 1344–1359.
    Registration, 1312, 1313.
    Smith Act prosecutions, 1067–1078, 1082.
Teachers, 1320, 1350.
Zoning regulations, 621, 1200, 1235, 1239.

FREEDOM OF EXPRESSION
See also Freedom of Association; Freedom of the Press; Religion.

FREEDOM OF EXPRESSION—Cont'd
Billboards, regulation of, 1200.
Books, excluded from school library, 1212.
Boycott, 1275.
Chilling effect, 1088, 1091, 1093–1097,
    1107, 1112.
Clear and present danger concept,
    Advocacy vs. incitement, 1054–1059,
        1062–1087.
    Dangerous tendency test, 1056, 1059,
        1063, 1067.
    Origin, 1055–1059.
    Rejected by Taft court as constitutional
        doctrine, 1059.
    Restated by Brandeis and Holmes, 1063.
    Vinson Court's views, 1067.
    Warren Court's views, 1071, 1074, 1078.
Commercial speech, 1153–1169.
Compelled disclosure of beliefs and as-
    sociations, 1244, 1273–1275, 1318–
    1324.
    Governmental investigations, 1311–1324.
    Registration and reporting require-
        ments, 1311–1317.
Compelled speech, 1244, 1271–1273.
Conspiracy and solicitation, 1078, 1084.
Contempt, 1051, 1098, 1101, 1182, 1368,
    1374, 1375.
Courthouse picketing, 1180.
Criminal syndicalism, 1053–1065, 1078.
Demonstrations,
    Breach of the peace offenses, 1184,
        1185.
    Courthouse, 1180.
    Jail house grounds, 1187.
    State house grounds, 1180.
    Streets, 1177–1184.
Door-to-door solicitation, 1249, 1255.
English background, 1046–1050.
"Fighting words", 1138, 1139, 1141.
Government, criticism of, 1050, 1052, 1106–
    1111.
Government employment, limitations on,
    1331–1355.
    Bill of Attainder, 1345–1349.
    Loyalty procedures, 1354, 1355.
    Loyalty standards, 1349–1354.
    Oaths, loyalty, 1351–1354.
    Political activity, 1331–1334.
Government forum, 1209–1235.
Governmental action, 1223, 1280, 1399.
Handbill distribution, 1177, 1178, 1192,
    1193, 1244.
Home letter boxes, use of, 1193.
Hostile audience, 1138, 1179, 1183–1187.
Interschool mail system, access to, 1194.
Libel, 1106–1125.
        See also Freedom of the Press.
    Group libel, 1106.
Littering, noise, traffic interference, 1177–
    1178.
Mail distribution, 1193, 1194.
Obscenity, 1126–1138, 1143.
    Community standards, 1131, 1136.
    Minors' protection, 1131, 1135, 1136,
        1143.
    Procedures for controlling, 1098–1105.

FREEDOM OF EXPRESSION—Cont'd
Offensive language, 1138, 1139, 1141,
    1143.
Pentagon Papers Case, 1368.
Permit systems, 1181–1183.
Picketing, 968, 1170, 1180, 1255–1259.
    Labor picketing, 1170, 1255.
    Private property, 1170.
    Public property, 1180.
Political campaigning,
    Contribution limitations, 1293, 1310.
    Expenditure limitations, 1298, 1304,
        1310.
    Government employees, 1091, 1331,
        1338, 1340.
Political party patronage, 1338, 1340.
Prior restraint, 1097–1105.
    Broadcast restrictions, 1143, 1223, 1399.
    Electronic media, 1143, 1223, 1399.
    Injunctions, 1051, 1098, 1101, 1105,
        1181–1183.
Public forum concept, 1194, 1200, 1209–
    1235.
School newspapers, 1211.
Seditious libel, 1050, 1107, 1111.
Signs on public property, regulation of,
    1200.
Slavery, discussion of, 1052.
Solicitation of contributions, 1249, 1255.
Sound amplification, 1178.
State fair grounds, 1193.
Subversive speech, 1053–1077.
Symbolic speech,
    Armbands, 1189, 1263.
    Camping in park, 1266.
    Draft card burning, 1260.
    Flag display, 1263.
Theaters, zoning of, 1235.
Time, place, and manner restrictions, 1170–
    1259.
    Permit requirements, 1181–1183.
    Private property, 1235–1255.
    Streets and parks, 1177–1183.
        Other public property, 1187–1209.
Unwilling audience, 1244, 1249.
Vagueness and overbreadth, 1087–1105,
    1126, 1161, 1239.
World War I espionage cases, 1053–1059.

FREEDOM OF RELIGION
See Religion.

FREEDOM OF SPEECH
See Freedom of Expression; Freedom of
    the Press.

FREEDOM OF THE PRESS
    See also Freedom of Expression.
Access to press as required, 1365, 1382,
    1387, 1399.
Access by press to governmental informa-
    tion, 1388–1398.
    Freedom of Information Act, 1388.
    Judicial proceedings, 1388, 1389, 1398.
    Open meeting laws, 1388.
    Prisons, 1388.
    Reporter's privilege, 1382, 1387.

FREEDOM OF THE PRESS—Cont'd
Sunshine laws, 1388.
As independent guaranty, 1358.
Broadcasting, 1143, 1223, 1399.
Commercial advertising, 1106, 1153–1169.
    False advertising, 1153–1160, 1162.
    Illegal products, 1363.
Courts,
    Criticism of, 1051, 1374.
    Fair trial, 1375, 1389, 1398.
    Records of, 1051.
Defamation, 1106–1125.
    Negligence standard, 1112.
    New York Times standard, 1107, 1112.
    Non-media defendants, 1121.
    Public figures, 1112, 1120, 1121.
    Right of privacy distinguished, 1122.
Definition of the press, 1382.
Disclosure of editorial process, 1387.
Editorial control and judgment protected,
    1210, 1223, 1363, 1365, 1388.
Electronic media contrasted with print me-
    dia, 1143, 1223, 1365, 1409.
Fair trial, free press, 1375, 1388, 1389,
    1398.
Federal Communications Commission reg-
    ulations, 1143, 1223, 1399, 1409, 1411.
General business regulations, 1358, 1363.
Government as publisher or broadcaster,
    1210, 1223, 1399.
Government demands for information,
    1382–1387.
Governmental action and broadcasting,
    1399.
Informants, protection of by journalists,
    1382.
Institutional viability protected, 1363.
Newsgathering as protected, 1382, 1388,
    1389, 1398.
Obscenity, see Freedom of Expression.
Prior restraint,
    Press and jury trials, 1374.
    See also Freedom of Expression.
Privacy, right of, 1122, 1382.
Professions, advertising by, 1153, 1159.
    Law and medicine, 1159.
Publishing, regulation of business of, 1358,
    1363, 1365.
School newspapers, 1211.
Search of newsroom, 1387.
Taxation, 1358.

FREEDOM TO TRAVEL, 315, 490, 877–894,
    1016

GENDER DISCRIMINATION
See Discrimination; Sex Discrimination.

GOVERNMENT EMPLOYEES
Right to notice and hearing before dis-
    charge, 933, 937, 950, 1331.

GOVERNMENT PROCUREMENT
Sales and use taxes, 391.
State licensing of contractors, 404.

GOVERNMENTAL INVESTIGATIONS
Grand jury investigation, 1382.
Legislative investigations,
    Early cases, 1318.
    Legislative power, 1319–1324.
Legislator's immunity, 475.

**GROSS RECEIPTS TAXES, STATE OR LO-
CAL,** 341, 344, 349, 360

GUARANTY CLAUSE, 134

HOURS OF WORK, 204, 523, 528, 535

HOUSING, FAIR
Civil Rights Act of 1866,
    Modern application, 1009.
Fair housing legislation, constitutionality
    of, 988, 997, 1009.

ILLEGITIMACY
See Legitimacy.

IMMIGRATION
See Naturalization.

IMPORTS
Definition of, 362.
Original package doctrine, 362–364.
State taxation of, 362–366.
Twenty-First Amendment and imports of
    alcohol, 324, 346.

INCOME TAXES, NET, STATE OR LOCAL
Apportionment, 346–347, 372–387.
Exclusively interstate business, 349.
Federal statute limiting, 372.
Gross receipts taxes distinguished, 341–
    342.
Income from property outside state, 343,
    373, 378.
Income from solicitation, 372.
Privileges and immunities clause, 346.
Trucking company, 349.

INDIGENT PERSONS
Abortion, access to, 585, 602, 899.
Access to bankruptcy court, 626.
Court fees in divorce actions, 626.
Free transcripts on appeal, 625.
Housing, access to, 758.
Right of access to courts, 625–628.
Right to counsel, 625.
Right to education, 911, 920, 929.
Voting, 870, 876, 877.
Welfare, right to, 624, 883, 895–911.

**INHERENT LIMITATIONS ON LEGISLATIVE
POWER,** 477, 494, 495

INJUNCTIONS
Anti-injunction statute, 82, 84.
Constitutional litigation, 82–87, 90.
Criminal proceedings, restraint of, 82–87.
Exhausting state judicial remedies, 81.
Exhaustion of administrative remedies, 80.
Federal statute, constitutionality of, 75.

INJUNCTIONS—Cont'd
First Amendment limitations, 1051, 1098, 1101, 1105.
Pending state judicial proceedings, 82–87.
State rate regulations, 81.
State statutes,
    Enforcement of,
        Discretion of federal court to refuse, 79.
        Three-judge court, 65.
State tax collections, 81.

INSURANCE
Federal regulation, 210.
State regulation, 210.

INTERGOVERNMENTAL IMMUNITY
    See also Intergovernmental Relationships.
In general, 391–435.

INTERGOVERNMENTAL RELATIONSHIPS
Compacts, 433.
Fair Labor Standards Act and state employees, 408.
Regulation,
    Federal regulation of state activity, 407–432.
    State regulation of federal activity, 404–432.
State railroad, 407, 416.
Taxation,
    Federal taxation of state activities, 398–404.
    State taxation of federal activities, 391–398.
Voting by residents of enclaves, 873.

INTERNAL IMPROVEMENTS
Johnson's letter to Monroe, 168.
Madison's veto, 167.
Monroe's veto, 167.

INTERNATIONAL AGREEMENTS
See Foreign Affairs.

INTERSTATE AND FOREIGN COMMERCE
See Commerce.

INTERSTATE COMMERCE
See Commerce.

INTIMIDATION
Federal legislation against, with reference to civil rights or federal activities, 1008.

INTOXICATING BEVERAGES
Federal power to regulate and Twenty-First Amendment, 328.
State regulation of,
    In general, 176, 183, 323, 324, 327.
    Under Twenty-First Amendment, 323, 324, 327.
State taxation of under Twenty-First Amendment, 324, 346.

JUDICIAL NOTICE
Brandeis brief, 528.
Of underlying facts, 522, 528, 534, 585.

JUDICIAL REVIEW
Abstention, 79.
Acts of president, 33.
Case and controversy, 87–144, 454.
Disputes within the executive branch, 469–470.
Effect of declaration of unconstitutionality, 35–36.
Establishment of, 23.
Jurisdictional basis, 43–63.
Legitimacy of, 23–36.
Lincoln's views, 33.
Of rationality of legislation, 629–636.
Political questions, 88, 144, 455.
Purpose of legislation, 640.
Raising constitutional issues, 89–90.
Ripeness and concreteness, 121–132.
Theory of, 24–35.

JUDICIARY ACT OF 1789
Section 25, 43–44.

JURISDICTION
Federal courts,
    Advisory opinion, 87–89.
    Moot cases, 115–120.
Notice and hearing in civil cases, 495, 945, 1331.
Supreme Court,
    Adequate non-federal ground, 48–56.
    Appeal or certiorari, 56.
    Appellate, 44–48, 56–63.
    Congressional control over, 36–42.

JURORS
Discrimination in selection,
    Race, 629, 773.

JURY TRIAL
Abolition by states, 500, 508, 516.
Misdemeanors, required in, 508.
Petty offenses, 511.
Press reporting, impact on, 1375.
Twelve jurors not required, 516.
Unanimous jury not required, 516.

JUST COMPENSATION, 577

LABOR RELATIONS
Regulation of and due process, 523–529, 532, 535.

LABOR UNIONS
Discrimination, 968.
Federal regulation of, 201, 535.
State regulation of, 528, 535.

LAISSEZ FAIRE ECONOMICS
Due process as element of, 527.

LEGISLATIVE INVESTIGATIONS
See Governmental Investigations.

LEGISLATIVE VETO, 451

LEGITIMACY
Classifications based on, 699–708.

LIBEL
See Freedom of Expression; Freedom of the Press.

LIBERTY
See also Liberty of Contract.
Deprivation of and fair procedure, 932–950.
Fourteenth Amendment and substantive restrictions, 577–628, 877–895, 949.

LIBERTY OF CONTRACT, 522–532, 535

LIMITATIONS, STATUTE OF
Retroactive changes, 544.

LIQUOR
See Intoxicating Beverages.

LOYALTY TESTS
Bar examination questionnaires, 1324–1331, 1350.
Oaths,
    Civil War test oaths, 1345.
    Labor union official's liability, 1346, 1351.
    Public officials, 1345, 1346, 1349, 1352, 1353.

MADISON
Bill of Rights drafting, 18, 19.
On Council of Revision, 23.

MAGNA CARTA
In general, 17, 481.
Relation to Bill of Rights, 17, 481, 520.

MANDAMUS
Federal officers, 24.

MANUFACTURING
As commerce, 183, 186.
Gross income taxes, 344.
Net income taxes, 373, 378.

MARRIAGE
State power to regulate, 580, 586, 653, 836.

MASS MEDIA
See Freedom of the Press.

MILITARY POWER
Congressional rent control, 232.
First Amendment limitations, 1192.
Japanese curfew and evacuation cases, 659.
Presidential power, 230, 231, 447.
    Blockade, 447.
    Steel Seizure Case, 437.
Vietnam controversy, 449, 450.
War-making power, 230–234, 449–451.

MILK
Containers, regulation of, 277.
Prices, regulation of, 269, 530.

MILK—Cont'd
Imitation milk, regulation of, 532.
State, regulation of, 269, 270, 277, 283, 530.

MINIMUM WAGES
See also Wages and Hours.
As due process, 528, 532, 535.

MISCEGENATION
State power to forbid, 653.

MISSOURI COMPROMISE, 483

MONETARY POWER
Gold clause legislation, 242.

MONOPOLIES
As violation of Fourteenth Amendment, 483.

MOOTNESS, 115–120

MORTGAGE MORATORIA
Contract clause, applicability to, 543, 554.

NATIONAL CITIZENSHIP
Privileges of, 483, 494, 502, 507, 1017.

NATIONALITY
As suspect classification, 690.

NATURALIZATION
National power, 244, 691, 696.

NEGRO
See Discrimination; Equal Protection; Franchise; Segregation; State Action.

NET INCOME TAXES
See Income Taxes, Net, State or Local.

NEW DEAL LEGISLATION, 192, 195

NINTH AMENDMENT, 581, 587

NOTICE AND HEARING
As a prerequisite to liberty deprivations, 932–950.
As a prerequisite to loss of job, 933, 937, 950.
As a prerequisite to property deprivations, 934, 941, 945, 948.
Distinguishing substance and procedure, 949.
Early cases, 495.
Irrebuttable presumptions and requirement of individualized hearings, 950–959.
Loyalty inquiries, 1331–1355.
Prior hearing, 945, 993.

OBSCENITY
See Freedom of Expression.

ONE–PERSON, ONE–VOTE
See Apportionment of Voters; Elections; Equal Protection.

ORIGINAL PACKAGE DOCTRINE, 362

PENDENT STATE LAW CLAIMS
Barred by eleventh amendment, 66.

PENTAGON PAPERS CASE, 1368
See also Freedom of Expression.

PENUMBRA DOCTRINE
As source of federal regulatory power, 220.

PERSON
Alien, as within meaning of Fourteenth Amendment, 690, 692, 696, 920.
Corporation as, within meaning of Fourteenth Amendment, 1521.
Fetus, 589.
Within meaning of Fourteenth Amendment, 589, 690, 692, 696, 920.

PERSONAL LIBERTIES
As compared with property interests, 534, 949.

PETITION OF RIGHT
Relation to Bill of Rights, 17.

PICKETING
See Freedom of Expression.

POLICE
See also Arrest.
Beating prisoner as federal crime, 1017.

POLICE POWER
Definition of, 522, 523.

POLITICAL QUESTIONS
Court review of, 132–144, 455.

PREEMPTION
Interstate commerce, 330–339.

PRESIDENT
See Separation of Powers.

PRESS
See Freedom of the Press.

PRESUMPTIONS IRREBUTTABLE, 950–959

PRICES, REGULATION OF
As due process, 521, 522, 529, 530.

PRISONERS
Right to notice and hearing before changes in custody, 941, 954.

PRIVACY
Abortion, 585–617, 899.
Constitutional basis of right,
First Amendment, 579, 587, 1280.
Fourteenth Amendment, 587, 617, 836.
Fourth Amendment, 579, 587.
Ninth Amendment, 581, 587.
Contraceptives, ban on, 578, 584, 597.
Family relationships, 577, 585, 596, 597, 599, 601, 602, 616, 617, 836, 899, 1014.

PRIVACY—Cont'd
First Amendment protections, 579, 587, 1014, 1280.
Homes, 580, 617.
Marriage, 580, 596, 653, 836.
Press invasion, 1122, 1143, 1382.
Private clubs, right to, 988, 993, 1014, 1411.
Private schools, 577, 578, 1012, 1477.
Theater, 1126.

PRIVATE CLUBS
Discrimination by, 988, 993, 1014, 1280, 1411.

PRIVILEGE AGAINST SELF-INCRIMINATION
See Self-Incrimination, Privilege Against.

PRIVILEGE TAXES, STATE OR LOCAL, 343, 349, 360

PRIVILEGES AND IMMUNITIES
Article IV (Interstate privileges), 346, 478, 479, 494.
Fourteenth Amendment and privileges and citizenship, 483, 494, 498, 502, 507, 508, 1017.
National citizenship, character and privileges of, 483, 494, 498, 502, 1016.
State citizenship, 317–323, 477–479, 494.

PROPERTY POWER
National power, 240.

PROPERTY RIGHTS
As compared with personal liberties, 534, 949.
Negligence of official as basis for action, 945.
Procedural protections for substantive interests, 949.

PROPERTY TAXES, STATE OR LOCAL, 182, 343, 348, 366

PUBLIC EMPLOYEES
See also Loyalty Tests.
Political freedom, 1091, 1331–1355.

PUBLIC INTEREST, BUSINESSES AFFECTED WITH
See Prices, Regulation of; Rates, Regulation of.

PUBLIC SCHOOLS
See Education; Religion.

PUBLIC TRIAL, 519

PUBLIC USE, 540

PUBLIC UTILITIES
Rate regulation, 521, 522.
State action by, 993.

RACE
See Discrimination; Equal Protection;
    Franchise; Segregation: State Action.

RAILROADS
National regulation of, 187–190.
Property taxes, 343, 348.
Rate regulation, 187, 190.
Safety regulations, 180, 248, 253.
Taxation of rolling stock, 343.

RATES, REGULATION OF, 187, 190, 521,
    522

**RATIONAL BASIS STANDARD FOR JUDI-
    CIAL REVIEW,** 535, 538, 635–652, 896

RELIGION
See also Freedom of Expression.
Aid to church schools, 1427–1451.
    Auxiliary services, 1429.
    Buildings, 1444, 1445.
    Grants to, 1428, 1429, 1440, 1445.
    Higher education distinguished, 1445.
    Instructional materials, provision of,
        1429.
    Tax credits, 1427, 1441.
    Teachers' compensation, 1428.
    Textbooks, 1427, 1429.
    Transportation, 1413, 1429.
    Tuition grants, 1429.
Aid to churches,
    Sunday closing laws, 1467.
    Tax exemptions, 1427, 1482.
Conduct regulation and religious beliefs,
    Flag salute, 1462.
    Polygamy, 1462.
    Solicitation, 1463.
    Sunday closing, 1467.
    Work, on day of rest, 1470, 1474.
Creche, display of on public property, 1451.
Denominational preferences, 1417.
Establishment, 1412–1461, 1467.
Federal support of, 1422, 1444.
Free exercise, 1461–1482.
Freedom of nonconformity,
    Compulsory flag salute, 1462.
    Compulsory military service, 1475, 1476.
    Compulsory school attendance, 1477,
        1481.
    Right to religious schools, 577, 1477.
    Sabbatarians' right to unemployment
        benefits, 1470, 1474.
    Sunday closing, 1467.
Government aid to, 1413, 1427–1450.
Legislature, minister serving in, 1463.
Religion in public schools,
    Bible reading, 1423.
    Evolution and creation, teaching of,
        1425.
    Prayers, 1420.
    Released time, 1417.
Religious motivation and the establishment
    clause, 1426, 1451.

RELIGION—Cont'd
Role in American life, 1453.
Secular purpose, 1455.
Standard for judicial review of restrictions
    on, 1463, 1477, 1454.

REPLEVIN
Prior hearing, requirement of, 949.

REPUBLICAN FORM OF GOVERNMENT
Guaranty of, 137.

RESIDENCE
Amount of benefits determined by length
    of residence, 890.
Durational requirements,
    Divorce, 887.
    Welfare, 690, 696, 877, 883.
Required for public education, 895, 929.

RESTRICTIVE COVENANTS
Enforcement of, as state action, 974, 979.
Suit for damages as enforcement, 979.

**RETROACTIVITY OF CONSTITUTIONAL
    DECISIONS,** 36

RIOTS
Federal legislation against, 1008.

ROOSEVELT COURT PLAN, 200

SALES TAXES, STATE OR LOCAL
Federal government contractors, 391.
Imports, 176.
Interstate sales, 176, 387.

SCHOOLS
See Education; Religion; Segregation.

SEGREGATION
Attendance zones, creation to achieve inte-
    gration, 673, 685, 689.
Busing to achieve integration of schools,
    673, 680, 685.
Courtrooms, 671.
Creation of new school districts to avoid
    integration, 685.
Interdistrict remedies, 685, 689.
Public accommodations, 211, 214, 671, 960,
    970, 983, 988, 985.
Public transportation, 663, 671.
Racial balances or quotas, 673, 680, 684,
    763, 787.
Schools, 663–689, 981, 986, 1012, 1482.
Social science materials, 670.
Teachers, 673.

**SELF–INCRIMINATION,   PRIVILEGE
    AGAINST**
As aspect of fair trial, 502, 518.
As fundamental right, 498, 502, 518.
Comment on failure to testify, 502.
Loyalty proceedings, 1354, 1355.

SEPARATION OF POWERS
Appointment of officers of the United States, 464.
Article III courts, 36–42.
Bicameralism, 457.
Congressional control of jurisdictions of Article III courts, 36–42.
Congressional immunities, 475.
Domestic affairs, 436–443.
Executive immunities, 468–475.
Executive immunity from Congressional inquiry, 468.
Executive privilege and the courts, 468.
Impeachment, 467.
Independence of the Judiciary, 36–42.
International agreements, 230, 234, 237, 238, 444.
Legislative veto, 451.
Pentagon Papers case, 1368.
Presentment clause, 456.
Seizure of industry by President, 437.
Speech or Debate Clause, 475.
Theory of, 436.
War, conduct or declaration of, 447–451.
War and foreign relations, 447–451.

SEVERANCE TAX
Validity, 354.

SEX DISCRIMINATION
See also Discrimination; Equal Protection.
In general, 708–744, 761, 776, 779, 780, 781, 1280.
Equal Rights Amendment, proposed, 744.

"SIT–IN" DEMONSTRATIONS, 980, 1018, 1185

SLAVERY
Badges of slavery, 960, 1009.
Involuntary servitude, 483, 1009.
Missouri Compromise, validity of, 483.
Property concept, 483, 484–487.
Sanctioned in Constitution, 19.
Thirteenth Amendment, 19, 484, 1009.
Thirteenth Amendment as basis for federal regulation of private conduct, 960, 1009.

SOCIAL SCIENCE RESEARCH
Use in segregation cases, 670.

SOUND AMPLIFICATION
See Freedom of Expression.

SOVEREIGN IMMUNITY
Cities, counties, school districts, 65.
Power of Congress to confer jurisdiction, 76–78.
Suit against federal officer, 65.
Suit against state in federal court, 66–78.
Suit against state officer in federal court, stripping doctrine, 69–70, 75, 76.

SPEECH OR DEBATE CLAUSE, 475

SPENDING POWER
Agricultural adjustment, 195.
Civil rights legislation, 1003.
Financing election campaigns, 229, 1210.
Impact of federal grants to states, 204.
Social security, 226–229.

STANDING
In general, 90–115.
Citizen, 106–115.
Constitutional dimension, 106–115.
Doctor re impact of statute on patients, 104.
Economic injury not required, 100.
First Amendment cases, 1087–1096, 1141, 1181–1183, 1239.
Organizations as representatives of particular community interests, 94–98.
Ripeness and concreteness, 121–132.
Taxpayers, 106–115.
Third party rights, 103.
To challenge legality of military action, 449, 450.
Void on face doctrine in First Amendment cases, 1087–1096, 1141, 1181–1183.

STATE ACTION
In general, 961–1044.
Acts of public officials, 974, 980, 981, 982, 1017.
As basis for federal regulatory power, 960, 1003–1008, 1017.
Broadcasters, 1223, 1399.
California referendum, 997.
Charitable trusts, 986.
Company towns, 968.
Constitutional limitations on anti-discrimination legislation, 997, 1001.
Custom as, 1018.
Enforcement of private arrangements, 974–1003.
Judges, 974.
Private clubs, discrimination by, liquor license, effect of, 988, 1280.
Private housing, 974, 979, 1009.
Private sale by bailee, 970.
Private store in public building, 983.
Private violence, 1005, 1017.
Prosecution of "sit-in" demonstrators, 980.
Public accommodations, 960, 968, 980, 985, 988, 1012, 1018.
Public utilities, 993.
Restrictive covenants, 949–979.
Shopping centers, 968.
Television network, 1399.
Thirteenth Amendment, not required under, 1008–1015.

STATE COURTS
Decisions based on state constitutional grounds, review of, 56.
Resistance to Supreme Court orders, 47.
Review of decision by United States Supreme Court,
Adequate non-federal ground, 48.
Ambiguous grounds of decision, 51.
Case and controversy doctrine in, 119.

STATE INSTITUTIONS
Rights of persons detained in, 623.

STEAMSHIP COMPANY
Property, taxation of, 366.
Safety regulations by state, 331.

STEVEDORING
Gross receipts tax, 360.

SUBVERSIVE SPEECH
See Freedom of Expression.

SUPERSESSION
See Preemption.

SUPREMACY CLAUSE
See Intergovernmental Immunity; Intergovernmental Relationships; Preemption.

SUPREME COURT
Caseload, 57, 58.
Conference, 58.
Congressional control over jurisdiction, 36–42.
Control of own caseload, 56–63.
Findings of fact by state courts, review of, 1183, 1184, 1185.
Jurisdiction, 43–63.
Law clerks, 58.
Picketing of, 1180.
Proposals for changes in jurisdiction, 57.
Review of federal court decisions, 63.
Review of state court decisions,
   Ambiguous grounds of decision, 51–56.
   Independent state ground, 48–56.
Rule of four to grant certiorari, 59.
Summary dispositions, precedential weight of, 60–63.

SYMBOLIC SPEECH
See Freedom of Expression.

TAKING
Of property without just compensation, 559–577.

TAXATION
Intergovernmental,
   Early development, 398.
   Privately owned federal instrumentalities, 159.
   Salaries of governmental officials, 399–401.
   Sales and use taxes, 391.
   State business activities, 398.
   United State property, 391.
Liquor and Twenty-First Amendment, 324, 346.
Of the press, 1358.
State travel, 398.

TAXES, STATE OR LOCAL, 340–390, 391

TAXPAYERS' SUITS, 106

TEACHERS
See Discrimination; Education; Segregation.

TENTH AMENDMENT
As limitation of federal commerce power, 207, 407, 409, 426.
State immunity from federal regulation, 407, 409.

THIRTEENTH AMENDMENT
Adoption of, 19, 484, 485.
Property servitudes, as applicable to, 483.
State action not required, 1008–1015.

TRADE SECRET
Property in, 572.
Protected by taking clause, 572.

TRANSPORTATION
Federal regulation of, 178, 182, 187, 190.
State regulation of, 248–268, 331.
State taxation of, 348, 349, 366.

TRAVEL, RIGHT TO
See Freedom to Travel.

TREATIES
See Foreign Affairs.

TRUSTS
Discrimination in, 969, 981, 982.

TWENTY–FIRST AMENDMENT
   See also Intoxicating Beverages.
Gender discrimination, 709.
Gross receipts tax on imports of liquor, 346.
Liquor regulation, 327–330.
Liquor taxation, 324–327, 346.
State regulation of commerce, 327–330.
State taxation of commerce, 324–327, 346.

UNCONSTITUTIONALITY
Effect of declaration of, 35.
Retroactive effect of declaration of, 35, 36.

UNITED NATIONS
See Foreign Affairs.

USE TAX, STATE OR LOCAL
Collection of, 387.
Compensating for sales tax, 343.

VAGUENESS
   See also Freedom of Expression.
Civil rights enforcement, 1006.
Criminal cases, 1006, 1087, 1088, 1094.
First Amendment cases, 1087–1097, 1141, 1161, 1181, 1185, 1187, 1239.

VOTING
   See also Apportionment of Voters; Elections; Equal Protection; Franchise.
Voting Rights Act of 1965, 1007.
Voting Rights Amendments of 1970, 1007.

WAGES AND HOURS
Wages and hour regulations and due process, 528–529, 532, 533, 535.

WAR CRIMES
See Military Power.

WAR POWER
As source of federal regulatory authority, 230–234.
Separation of powers, 447–451.

WATER
Underground, regulation of, 293.

WEALTH
As suspect classification, 624–628, 648, 750, 836, 873, 874, 883, 895–910.

WELFARE BENEFITS
Aliens, 690, 696, 920.
Classifications in administration, 690, 877, 883, 929.
Right to under due process, 617, 896, 899.

ZONING
Due process restrictions, 559, 576.
First Amendment limitations, 1235.
Racial, 974, 979.

†